ENCYCLOPÆDIA Britannica

2005 BOOK OF THE YEAR®

ENCYCLOPÆDIA Britannica®

Encyclopædia Britannica, Inc. Chicago • London • New Delhi • Paris • Seoul • Sydney • Taipei • Tokyo

ENCYCLOPÆDIA

Britannica

2005 BOOK OF THE YEAR®

Library of Congress Catalog Card Number: 38-12082
International Standard Book Number: 1-59339-246-X
International Standard Serial Number: 0068-1156

Britannica.com may be accessed on the Internet at http://www.britannica.com.

(*Trademark Reg. U.S. Pat. Off.*) *Printed in U.S.A.*

Foreword

The stakes in 2004 were high for many—for the U.S. administration of Pres. George W. Bush in restoring order and preparing for elections in Iraq; for President Bush in his reelection campaign; for Greece in triumphantly bringing the modern-day Olympics home to Athens, the birthplace of the Games; for same-sex couples who sought to marry; for scientists exploring the solar system, particularly Mars; for workers facing the prospect of having their jobs "offshored"; and for prisoners of war seeking the human rights guaranteed them under the Geneva Conventions. To feature these major topics of the year, the Britannica editors selected all of these subjects for coverage in Special Reports.

Health issues once again captured centre stage, with worries over a resurgence of polio in Africa, a craze among dieters for curbing carbohydrates, and concern among American seniors over selecting appropriate prescription-drug discount cards. Many wondered about the state of the electricity grid after the 2003 blackout in the U.S., while others marveled at the medical and scientific inventions created with nanotechnology. In greater numbers consumers were ordering energy-efficient hybrid cars, scooping up graphic novels, and subscribing to the new darling of the airwaves—satellite radio. Reports on the astounding discovery of the remains of a new hominin (hominid) that existed only 18,000 years ago underscored the fact that much remained unknown about humans' prehistory, including the possible interactions of humans with Neanderthals. Ten countries joined the European Union, but they would still have to meet a number of criteria to join the euro zone. On December 26 a horrific Indian Ocean tsunami claimed hundreds of thousands of lives in Asia and triggered what might become the largest humanitarian relief effort in history. Sidebars are devoted to these topics.

Hurricanes punished the U.S. and the Caribbean, and typhoons slammed into Asia. A number of high-profile deaths occurred, including those of former U.S. president Ronald Reagan, musician Ray Charles, Palestinian leader Yasir Arafat, actor and activist Christopher Reeve, writer Susan Sontag, Swiss-born psychiatrist Elisabeth Kübler-Ross, and culinary queen Julia Child.

It was not a completely gloomy year, however. After 86 years Major League Baseball's Boston Red Sox captured its first World Series; American swimmer Michael Phelps won eight medals at the Olympics, tying the record for medals at a single Olympiad; the privately funded SpaceShipOne reached space twice within a two-week period, winning the $10 million Ansari X Prize and proving the notion that space travel might one day be a routine endeavour; and stunning new architectural and civil engineering projects brightened the landscape, including the Seattle (Wash.) Public Library and the Millau (France) viaduct over the Tarn Gorge, the highest bridge in the world. There were royal weddings in Brunei, Denmark, and Spain; and spectacular photos were taken of the planet Saturn's rings. Turn the pages with me to recapture those moments and events that had a lasting impact on us.

Karen Sparks, Editor

Contents 2005

DATES OF 2004

PEOPLE OF 2004

EVENTS OF 2004

THE WORLD IN 2004

SPECIAL REPORTS

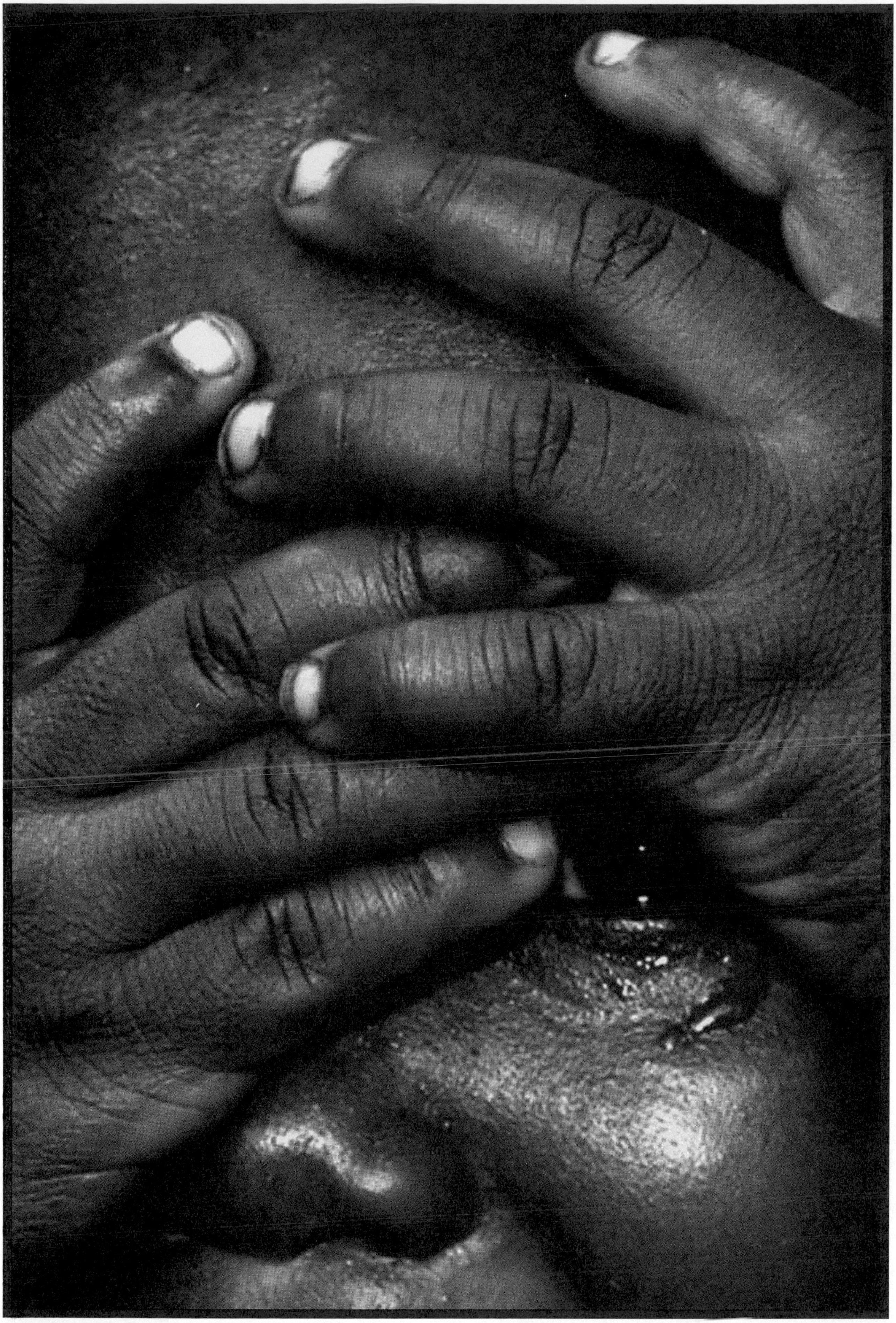

Dates of 2004

A NOAA satellite image shows Hurricane Jeanne centred east-southeast of Vero Beach, Fla., in midafternoon, September 25.

January

It turns out we were all wrong, probably, in my judgment.

David Kay, former U.S. chief weapons inspector in Iraq, in testimony to the U.S. Senate Armed Services Committee, January 28

1 Haitian Pres. Jean-Bertrand Aristide leads a smaller-than-planned observance of the bicentennial of Haiti's independence from France; rebellions against Aristide's rule force curtailment of the celebrations.

•

Pakistan's electoral college ratifies Pervez Musharraf's presidency, allowing him to remain in office into 2007; opposition parties boycott the election.

•

A law pardoning those who were punished for violating Switzerland's neutrality laws by assisting victims of Nazi Germany goes into effect in Switzerland.

•

In the annual college football postseason Rose Bowl, the top-ranked University of Southern California defeats the University of Michigan 28–14. (*See* January 4.)

2 British Airways cancels a flight scheduled from London to Washington, D.C.; it is the seventh international flight to the U.S. in less than a week halted because of security concerns.

•

The seven countries of the South Asian Association for Regional Co-operation agree to a framework for a free-trade zone; the following day the leaders of those countries arrive in Islamabad, Pak., for a formal meeting of the organization.

•

Eritrea rejects the appointment of Canadian diplomat Lloyd Axworthy to mediate its border dispute with Ethiopia, which refuses to accept a border designated by an international commission under the terms of a peace agreement.

3 NASA's robotic rover Spirit arrives on Mars; the following day it begins transmitting photographs.

•

The National Society of Film Critics chooses *American Splendor* as the best film of 2003.

4 Mikhail Saakashvili, who drove Eduard Shevardnadze from power, is overwhelmingly elected president of Georgia; he takes office on January 25.

•

Afghanistan's *Loya Jirga* (assembly) agrees to a new constitution; the document is signed by Pres. Hamid Karzai and enters into force on January 26.

•

Louisiana State University defeats the University of Oklahoma 21–14 in college football's annual Sugar Bowl to win the Bowl Championship Series trophy; LSU shares the unofficial national championship with the University of Southern California. (See January 1.) (Photo left.)

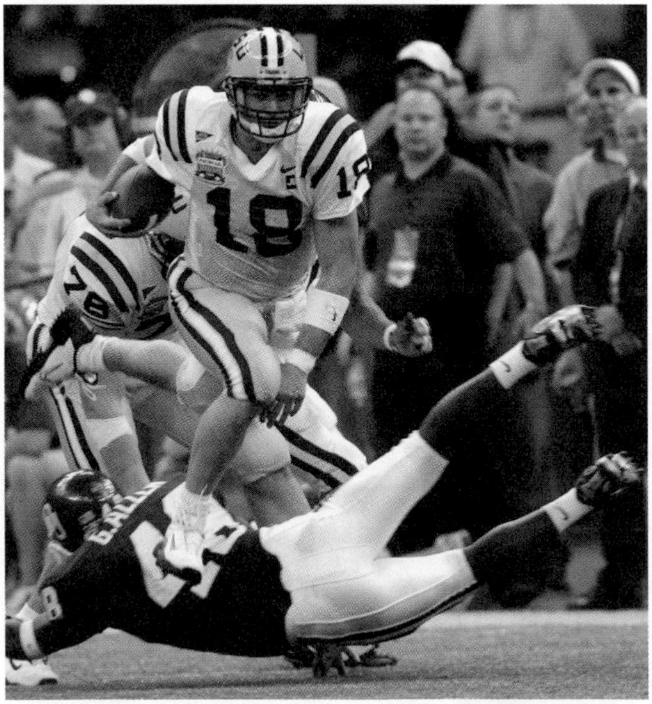

AP/Wide World Photos

5 The U.S. begins a program of fingerprinting and photographing all passengers from certain countries arriving at a major airport or ship port in the U.S.

•

China announces a decision to kill all palm civets being held in Guangdong province in an effort to head off another outbreak of SARS (severe acute respiratory syndrome), which has been diagnosed in one person in 2004.

6 A design called "Reflecting Absence," featuring a grove of trees and deep reflecting pools in the footprints of the Twin Towers, is chosen as the memorial to the victims of the Sept. 11, 2001, terrorist attacks that destroyed the World Trade Center in New York City.

•

An Iranian government official declares that Iran and Egypt have decided to restore diplomatic relations, which were broken off in 1979 because of Egypt's agreement to the Camp David Accords and its role in hosting Iran's exiled shah.

•

Hitter Paul Molitor and pitcher Dennis Eckersley are elected to the National Baseball Hall of Fame.

7 The government of The Sudan signs an agreement with the Sudan People's Liberation Army to split both oil and non-oil revenues equally throughout the six years of the planned interim government; this has been the most important issue standing in the way of peace.

•

Greek Prime Minister Konstantinos Simitis surprises observers by announcing plans to hold a parliamentary election on March 7 and to resign the day following the balloting.

•

A cyclone with winds reaching 298 km/h (185 mph) nearly destroys Alofi, the capital of Niue, a Pacific island state.

8 A U.S. Army helicopter is shot down near Fallujah, Iraq, leaving nine soldiers dead, less than a week after another U.S. helicopter was shot down in the same region.

•

The American blue jeans manufacturer Levi Strauss & Co. closes its last two sewing plants in the U.S., in San Antonio, Texas; the company's presence in the U.S. is now reduced to headquarters, design, sales, and distribution.

•

The sale of the urban clothing brand Phat Fashions, founded by hip-hop impresario Russell Simmons, to the Kellwood Co., a large traditional clothing producer, is announced.

9 The U.S. names captured Iraqi leader Saddam Hussein a prisoner of war, which means that he must be treated in accordance with the terms of the Geneva Conventions.

•

The U.S. government lowers the terror alert level to yellow, or elevated; it had been at orange, or high, since Dec. 21, 2003.

•

Libya agrees to pay $1 million to the heirs of each of the 170 victims of a French airliner that was shot down over the Ténéré desert in the central Sahara in 1989.

10 Six members of South Korea's National Assembly and Son Kil Seung, chairman of the troubled business conglomerate SK Group, are arrested in an investigation into a bribery and corruption scandal.

11 Israel begins building a concrete barrier around Jerusalem, walling it off from Palestinian suburbs.

•

In Iran the Guardian Council disqualifies half the candidates for election to the Majlis (legislature), including about one-third of the sitting members of the assembly; elections are scheduled for February 20.

•

New York Film Critics awards are presented; *The Lord of the Rings: The Return of the King* wins top honours.

12 Scientists from Brookhaven National Laboratory describe an experiment that they believe produced a predicted dense, puddinglike state of subatomic matter called a colour glass condensate in which gluons briefly merge.

•

It is reported that some 6,000 chickens on a farm in Yamaguchi prefecture in Japan have died of the highly contagious H5 strain of avian flu.

•

In the field of children's literature, the Newbery Medal is awarded to Kate DiCamillo for *The Tale of Despereaux: Being the Story of a Mouse, a Princess, Some Soup, and a Spool of Thread,* and Mordicai Gerstein wins the Caldecott Medal for his picture book *The Man Who Walked Between the Towers*.

•

The new Cunard cruise liner *Queen Mary 2,* the biggest cruise ship in every dimension that has ever been floated, departs Southampton, Eng., on its maiden voyage.

13 The Constitutional Court of Italy invalidates a law that protected top officials in the government from prosecution while they held office; the law had primarily protected Prime Minister Silvio Berlusconi from having to stand trial on charges of bribery.

•

The U.S. Securities and Exchange Commission reports that it has found numerous instances of mutual funds' illegally paying off brokers to steer unwitting investors in their direction.

•

At the Summit of the Americas in Monterrey, Mex., Haitian Pres. Jean-Bertrand Aristide announces plans to hold legislative elections within six months; the terms of most members of the parliament had expired the previous day.

14 The U.S. conglomerate J.P. Morgan Chase & Co. agrees to acquire Bank One Corp., a consumer bank, creating a company close in size to Citigroup Inc., the country's largest bank.

•

France's National Assembly approves a plan to change the status of French Polynesia from "overseas territory" to "overseas country," a status that grants the entity greater autonomy.

•

The UN announces that Libya has ratified the Nuclear Test-Ban Treaty; the country has also agreed to join the Chemical Weapons Convention.

•

In a speech at NASA headquarters in Washington, D.C., U.S. Pres. George W. Bush calls for a program to return to the Moon by 2020 and build a base there from which astronauts would travel to Mars.

•

Officials from the Russian Ministry of Culture announce that the two Rodin bronzes that were stolen from a Volgograd museum three years ago, *The Kiss* and *Jealousy,* have been recovered.

15 In a response to a suicide bombing that killed four Israelis the previous day, Israel seals off the Gaza Strip.

•

NASA's rover Spirit makes its first foray from its landing platform on Mars as planned, rolling down a ramp and forward about 3 m (10 ft).

•

Germany's federal office of statistics reveals that the country's economy shrank by 0.1% in 2003, its worst year since 1993.

16 NASA decides to cancel a planned maintenance mission to the Hubble Space Telescope, upsetting scientists and the public, who lament that astronomy's best resource will be allowed to deteriorate into uselessness.

•

Taiwanese Pres. Chen Shui-bian changes the terms of a referendum scheduled for March 20; instead of asking whether China should renounce the use of force against Taiwan, it will ask if Taiwan should strengthen its defensive capabilities and whether negotiations should take place between Taiwan and China.

•

The government of Myanmar (Burma) claims to have released from detention 26 members of the opposition National League for Democracy; it is unclear whether they are among the people arrested in May 2003 with Aung San Suu Kyi.

17 Pakistani Pres. Pervez Musharraf makes his first address before the parliament since he seized power in 1999; though he is heckled throughout, he maintains that it is necessary for the country to fight religious extremism and to attempt to negotiate peace with India.

•

Three men are executed in Lebanon; it is the first time in five years that capital punishment has been carried out in the country.

18 A truck bomb explodes at the main gate of the headquarters of the U.S. occupation in Baghdad, Iraq, killing at least 31 people, mostly Iraqi civilians, and wounding at least 120 others.

•

Conrad M. Black agrees to sell his controlling stake in Hollinger International, which publishes a number of prominent newspapers, to British entrepreneurs David and Frederick Barclay; the board of directors, which believes Black has misappropriated $200 million, opposes the move.

•

The 26th annual Dakar Rally finishes; the winners are French driver Stéphane Peterhansel (a previous motorcycle division winner), in a Mitsubishi Pajero, Spanish driver Nani Roma, on a KTM LC4 660 motorcycle, and Russian driver Vladimir Chagin, in a Kamaz 4911 truck.

19 The Communist Party of China publishes a massive plan in the *People's Daily* to improve workplace safety in China; almost 15,000 people died in industrial accidents in China in 2003.

•

Ten of thousands of people march peacefully through Baghdad, Iraq, in support of Shi'ite cleric Ayatollah Ali al-Sistani's demands that the interim government for Iraq be chosen by direct election rather than by the caucuses planned by the U.S. (Photo above.)

AP/Wide World Photos

•

U.S. and British weapons experts return to Libya to begin the dismantling of illegal weapons under the supervision of the International Atomic Energy Agency.

•

Members of the Episcopalian Church in the U.S. who opposed the consecration of openly gay Bishop V. Gene Robinson meet in Plano, Texas, to form the Network of Anglican Communion Dioceses and Parishes, a conservative movement within the American Anglican Council.

20 U.S. Pres. George W. Bush delivers his third state of the union address; he stresses that the U.S. is still vulnerable to terrorism and condemns the idea of gay marriage.

•

China's National Bureau of Statistics reports that the country's economy grew an astonishing 9.1% in 2003.

•

The estate of Joan Kroc, widow of McDonald's Corp. head Ray Kroc, announces a gift to the Salvation Army of approximately $1.5 billion, which is to be used to build and maintain community centres in the U.S.

21 The European Commission releases a report saying that the European Union has lost momentum in reaching its goal of creating a single market from its 15 members' economies and is likely to miss deadlines it set for itself.

•

Some 20,000 people march in Port-au-Prince in support of Haitian Pres. Jean-Bertrand Aristide; those demanding his ouster are driven away with tear gas.

•

Norway's Crown Prince Haakon and his wife, Crown Princess Mette-Marit, become the parents of a daughter, Princess Ingrid Alexandra, who, as a result of a 1990 constitutional amendment, is the first female in line to inherit the throne in six centuries.

22 In honour of the Chinese New Year, as well as of its partnership with the Oriental Pearl Tower in Shanghai, the Eiffel Tower in Paris is lit with red light and begins hosting a series of Chinese cultural events; this is the Year of the Monkey.

•

Chea Vichea, a prominent member of Cambodia's opposition Sam Rainsy Party, is shot to death in Phnom Penh; the party has refused to join in a coalition with the Cambodian People's Party, which does not hold enough legislative seats to rule alone.

23 The infrared camera of the European Space Agency's Mars Express orbiter confirms the presence of water ice at the south pole of Mars; also, the NASA rover Spirit sends signals that suggest it may be broken, though not fatally.

•

Thailand reports its first cases of avian flu in humans; the news causes alarm in the World Health Organization, which says the scale of the avian flu outbreak throughout Asia is unprecedented and could presage a human pandemic.

•

David Kay resigns as chief weapons inspector for the U.S. Central Intelligence Agency; in subsequent interviews he indicates that Iraq's weapons programs had been in a great state of disarray, with scientists proposing and getting funding for imaginary systems. (*See* January 28.)

24 Italian Prime Minister Silvio Berlusconi celebrates the 10th anniversary of his political party, Forza Italia.

•

Winning films at the Sundance Film Festival awards ceremony in Park City, Utah, include *DiG!*, *Primer*, *Born into Brothels*, and *Maria Full of Grace*.

25 NASA's second Mars rover, Opportunity, successfully lands on the opposite side of the planet from Spirit and begins sending back images.

•

At the Golden Globe Awards in Beverly Hills, Calif., best picture honours go to *The Lord of the Rings: The Return of the King* and *Lost in Translation;* best director goes to Peter Jackson for *The Lord of the Rings: The Return of the King;* and the screenplay award goes to Sofia Coppola for *Lost in Translation.*

•

Costa Rica agrees to join the Central American Free Trade Agreement a month after having withdrawn from negotiations with the countries that agreed to the pact with the U.S.—El Salvador, Guatemala, Honduras, and Nicaragua.

26 In Thoroughbred horse racing's 2003 Eclipse Awards, Mineshaft is named Horse of the Year.

•

Celebrity interviewer Barbara Walters announces that she is leaving the television newsmagazine *20/20* after 25 years on the show.

27 UN Secretary-General Kofi Annan announces that the organization will send a team to Iraq to help negotiate the means of transferring power from the U.S. to an Iraqi government as soon as its security can be guaranteed.

•

Mark Haddon wins the 2003 Whitbread Book of the Year Award, given for books published in the U.K., for his young-adult murder mystery *The Curious Incident of the Dog in the Night-Time*.

•

The multimedia presentation "Salvador Dalí and Mass Culture" opens at the Caixa-Forum in Barcelona, Spain, as the beginning of a planned yearlong celebration of the centennial of Dalí's birth.

28 Former chief weapons inspector in Iraq David Kay testifies before the U.S. Senate Armed Services Committee that he has concluded that Iraq did not possess stockpiles of chemical or biological weapons before the U.S.-led invasion, nor was it close to nuclear capability. (*See* January 23.)

•

A judge on Great Britain's Royal Courts of Justice rules that Prime Minister Tony Blair's government did not deliberately mislead the public over the threat represented by Iraq prior to the U.S.-led invasion and that the BBC had been wrong to suggest otherwise in a May 2003 broadcast; BBC chairman Gavyn Davies immediately resigns.

29 A prisoner swap between Israel and the Lebanese militia group Hezbollah takes place in Cologne, Ger., after which Israel releases hundreds of Palestinian prisoners.

•

Somalian warlords sign an agreement in Nairobi, Kenya, to establish a national parliament in Somalia as a start toward creating a national government; Somalia has been without a government since 1991.

•

Lieut. Charlotte Atkinson takes over command of HMS *Brecon,* becoming the first woman to command an operational warship in the history of the British Royal Navy.

•

It is announced that a woman in Gujarat, India, has given birth to her own twin grandchildren; she was acting as a surrogate for her daughter, who has no uterus.

30 Former French prime minister Alain Juppé is convicted of corruption in a ghost payrolling and graft scheme; Juppé, who is head of the centre-right Union for a Popular Movement party, is barred from public office for 10 years.

•

At a news conference, scientists say the Mars rover Opportunity appears to have found evidence of iron oxide, which strongly suggests the possibility that water was present at one time.

31 British Airways and Air France cancel five flights to the U.S. over security fears rather than acquiesce to U.S. suggestions of putting armed air marshals on the flights.

•

Abdul Qadeer Khan, known as the "father of the Islamic bomb," is removed as special adviser to Pakistan's prime minister in the ongoing investigation of links between Pakistan's nuclear program and those of other countries, including Libya, Iran, and North Korea that have initiated programs in contravention of international agreements. (*See* February 5.)

•

Belgian Justine Henin-Hardenne defeats her countrywoman Kim Clijsters to win the Australian Open tennis tournament in her third major tennis tournament victory; the following day Roger Federer of Switzerland defeats Marat Safin of Russia to win the men's title.

•

Quarterback John Elway, running back Barry Sanders, tackle Bob Brown, and defensive end Carl Eller are elected to the Pro Football Hall of Fame.

February

The Constitution cannot be drowned in the blood of the Haitian people. For that reason, tonight I am resigning in order to avoid a bloodbath.

Jean-Bertrand Aristide, in his letter of resignation as president of Haiti dated February 28

1 Suicide bombers attack the offices of the two main Kurdish political parties in Irbil, Iraq, killing at least 101 people.

•

In Mina, Saudi Arabia, at least 251 people are trampled to death in a stampede during the ritual stoning of the devil, a part of the annual hajj.

•

In Houston, Texas, the New England Patriots squeak by the Carolina Panthers 32–29 to win Super Bowl XXXVIII; the football game is upstaged somewhat by a moment in the halftime show when singer Justin Timberlake rips away part of the costume of performer Janet Jackson, revealing her right breast. (Photo right.)

2 Israeli Prime Minister Ariel Sharon astonishes observers by announcing plans to evacuate nearly all Jewish settlements in the Gaza Strip.

•

The leader of the Islamic Iran Participation Front, the main reformist political party in Iran, announces that the party will boycott the legislative elections scheduled for later in the month on the grounds that the elections will not be legal. (*See* February 20.)

•

In the wake of a scandal involving unauthorized currency trading as well as other financial missteps, Frank Cicutto resigns as CEO of National Australia Bank Ltd., the country's biggest banking company.

3 The U.S. and North Korea reach an agreement to resume six-party talks about North Korea's illegal nuclear weapons program; the talks had been stalemated since the first round in August 2003. (*See* February 28.)

•

The International Crisis Group reports the emergence of a new militant Islamic group, the Mujahidin Kompak, in Indonesia; the new group is said to have splintered from Jemaah Islamiyah, an al-Qaeda affiliate.

•

The U.S. Senate shuts down its three office buildings after powdered ricin, a lethal poison, is discovered in the office of Senate Majority Leader Bill Frist.

•

A passenger train for the first time arrives in the northern port city of Darwin in Australia three days after it left the southern port city of Adelaide; the train, called the Ghan, traveled on newly built tracks from Alice Springs to Darwin and was the first to cross the north–south expanse of the country.

•

French yachtsman Francis Joyon breaks the record for a solo trip around the world, completing the journey in just under 73 days; the previous record was 93 days.

4 Following a bitterly divisive debate, the supreme court of Massachusetts rules that the terms of the state constitution will not be satisfied by permitting "civil unions" for same-sex partners; instead, full matrimony must be made available to same-sex as well as heterosexual couples. (*See* February 12.)

© Win McNamee/Reuters/Corbis

Angola's minister of the interior announces that the government is seeking a knowledgeable mediator to assist in the ongoing crisis with the breakaway exclave of Cabinda, separated from the rest of Angola by part of the Democratic Republic of the Congo.

•

The U.S. National Academy of Sciences releases a report saying that the technology to produce hydrogen-fueled cars, a goal promoted by U.S. Pres. George W. Bush, is decades away from being useful enough for mass production.

•

Sotheby's auction house announces that the Forbes family has sold its collection of Fabergé objets d'art—including the Imperial Easter eggs commissioned by Tsar Alexander III as gifts for his wife—to Viktor Vekselberg, a Russian oil businessman.

5 Latvia's Parliament passes a law requiring that at least 60% of public-school classes be taught in Latvian; there are widespread protests because about one-third of the country's population is Russian.

•

Pakistani Pres. Pervez Musharraf grants a full pardon to Abdul Qadeer Khan. (*See* January 31.)

•

Israeli Prime Minister Ariel Sharon is questioned by police in a bribery scandal that is taking centre stage in Israel; in January a developer was indicted on charges of having bribed the prime minister through his son to gain approval of a project.

6 A bomb explodes on a crowded subway train in downtown Moscow, killing at least 41 people and injuring some 130 others; authorities blame a suicide bomber.

•

The Licey Tigers of the Dominican Republic clinch the championship of the baseball Caribbean Series; it is the Dominican Republic's 15th title in the four-nation tournament and the 9th for Licey.

•

The destruction of 12,000 chickens is ordered in Delaware after a strain of avian flu is detected there.

7 Pres. Chandrika Kumaratunga of Sri Lanka dissolves Parliament and sets elections for April 2, three years early; the president has long been at odds with Prime Minister Ranil Wickremesinghe.

•

A team of electoral experts from the UN arrives in Baghdad, Iraq, to assess whether it will be possible to hold direct elections for the interim government to which the U.S. plans to hand over power on June 30.

8 At the Grammy Awards in Los Angeles, the top winner is Beyoncé, who wins five awards; the award for record of the year is won by Coldplay's "Clocks"; for album of the year, *Speakerboxxx/The Love Below* by OutKast; for song of the year, Luther Vandross's "Dance with My Father"; and for best new artist, Evanescence.

•

American Chad Hedrick unexpectedly wins the world all-around speed-skating championship in Hamar, Nor.; Renate Groenewold of The Netherlands captures the women's title.

9 On the Indonesian island of Bali, a panel of judges finds Suranto Abdul Ghoni guilty of having helped plan the attacks and create the bombs that killed 202 people in Bali nightclubs in October 2002 and sentences him to life in prison.

•

King Abdullah of Jordan and Pres. Bashar al-Assad of Syria unveil a plaque at the Yarmuk River in northern Jordan to mark the beginning of the building of a hydroelectric dam that will provide water to Jordan and electric power to Syria.

•

Outside Montevideo, Uruguay, work begins to raise the World War II German warship *Admiral Graf Spee* from the mouth of the Río de la Plata, where it was scuttled after a battle in 1939.

10 A car bomb explodes outside the police station in Iskandariya, Iraq, killing at least 54 people standing in line to apply for jobs; the following day a similar attack kills some 47 job applicants in Baghdad.

•

France's National Assembly, the lower house of its legislature, approves by an overwhelming majority a ban on the wearing or display of religious symbols, such as Muslim head scarves or Jewish yarmulkes, in public schools.

•

Darbydale's All Rise Pouchcove, a black Newfoundland, wins Best in Show at the Westminster Kennel Club Dog Show.

11 Israel makes two raids in the Gaza Strip, an action that leads to major gun battles that leave 15 Palestinians dead.

•

Comcast Corp., the biggest cable television company in the U.S., makes a hostile takeover bid for the entertainment giant Walt Disney Co.; Disney rejects the deal on February 16.

12 Two scientists at Seoul (S.Kor.) National University, Woo Suk Hwang and Shin Yong Moon, report that they have cloned human embryos and extracted stem cells from them in order to advance medical research.

•

In response to a request from Mayor Gavin Newsom, the county clerk of San Francisco begins issuing marriage licenses to same-sex couples, and more than 50 such couples exchange vows; the first to be wed are Phyllis Lyon and Del Martin, a lesbian couple who have been living together for more than 50 years. (*See* February 4 and 20.)

•

Four people, including the personal trainer of baseball star Barry Bonds, are indicted on charges of having provided steroids and other illegal performance-enhancing substances to professional athletes.

•

A contingent of 33 Armenian troops joins NATO-led peacekeeping forces in the Serbian province of Kosovo; it is the first time that Armenia has contributed troops to a military mission outside the country.

13 Greek Cypriot Pres. Tassos Papadopoulos and Turkish Cypriot leader Rauf Denktash agree to a plan created by UN Secretary-General Kofi Annan that would lead to the reunification of Cyprus before May 1, when Cyprus is scheduled to become a member of the European Union. (*See* April 1.)

•

Blizzards, among the worst in decades, sink ships in the Aegean Sea and paralyze Istanbul under 35 cm (14 in) of snow and Athens under as much as 50 cm (20 in).

•

South Korea's legislature approves a plan to send 3,000 troops to support U.S. peacekeeping efforts in Iraq beginning at the end of March.

•

The U.S. Department of Commerce releases a report showing that in 2003 the country's trade deficit reached a record $489.4 billion, by far the highest it has ever been.

14 Guerrilla fighters attack the police station in Fallujah, Iraq, killing at least 23 Iraqi police officers and freeing about 87 prisoners.

•

Tunisia defeats Morocco 2–1 to capture its first association football (soccer) African Cup of Nations championship.

•

Four staff members of Afghanistan's agency to clear the country of land mines are set upon and killed in an ambush that is part of an ongoing campaign to destabilize the government.

15 It is reported that Turkey has seized 219 companies belonging to the powerful Uzan family, whom the government accuses of massive bank fraud; members of the family, in hiding in the U.S., respond that the government is pursuing a political vendetta against them.

•

In Daytona Beach, Fla., three years after the death of his father in the same race, Dale Earnhardt, Jr., wins the Daytona 500; it is his first victory in NASCAR's premier race.

16 A new program of national service gets under way in Malaysia at 44 camps around the country, attended by some 85,000 high-school graduates chosen at random to participate in a three-month program that includes physical training, community service, and classes on nation building.

•

Israel's Knesset (legislature) approves $22 million in new spending on housing, the vast majority of which is to support Israeli settlements in the West Bank.

17 Just under the wire, Cingular Wireless undercuts Vodafone's bid to acquire AT&T Wireless and wins the takeover contest; the merger will make Cingular the biggest cellular telephone provider in the U.S.

•

A UN report is released describing a burgeoning AIDS crisis in Eastern Europe; the countries with the fastest rate of increase are Estonia, Russia, and Ukraine.

18 Russia suspends all gas supplies to Belarus as well as to countries that receive gas through the Beltransgaz pipeline, in response to Belarus's refusal either to pay more for the gas or to allow the Russian gas monopoly Gazprom a controlling stake in the pipeline.

•

In an unusually outspoken statement, the International Committee of the Red Cross denounces the barrier that Israel is building in the West Bank as being extremely damaging to the Palestinian people living in the area and as thus against international law regarding the treatment of people in occupied territory.

•

Pres. Azali Assoumani ceremonially opens the University of the Comoros in Moroni, the capital; it is the first university in the country.

19 Swaziland's prime minister declares a state of national emergency, citing the combination of drought, poverty, and the high incidence of HIV/AIDS.

•

At a conference in Marina del Rey, Calif., French astrophysicists describe findings from a European X-ray satellite, the XMM-Newton, of large star clusters that seem to behave in a way that is at odds with prevailing theories about the composition of the universe.

•

Simon Wiesenthal, who devoted most of his life to finding and bringing to justice former Nazi war criminals, is awarded an honorary knighthood by Queen Elizabeth II of the United Kingdom.

20 Parliamentary elections are held in Iran; the turnout is low, and hard-liners win 156 of the 290 seats, a major victory in an election boycotted by reformists. (*See* February 2.)

•

A judge on San Francisco's Superior Court declines to enter an injunction prohibiting the issuance of marriage licenses to same-sex couples, saying that he is unconvinced that the weddings are causing damage; some 3,000 same-sex couples have already been issued licenses. (*See* February 12 and 24.)

•

Mexico and the U.S. sign an agreement related to security at the border between the two countries; one provision requires the U.S. to return intercepted illegal immigrants to their homes rather than simply across the Mexican border.

•

U.S. scientists report on evidence from the Hubble Space Telescope that indicates that the strength of dark energy, or antigravity, remains more or less constant over time, which suggests that the universe will neither be ripped apart nor collapse but rather will gently expire.

21 Members of the rebel Lord's Resistance Army attack a refugee camp in northern Uganda, leaving more than 190 people dead.

•

Pres. Vaira Vike-Freiberga of Latvia appoints as prime minister Indulis Emsis of the Greens and Farmers Union to replace Einars Repse, who lost his position when he jettisoned a member of his coalition; Emsis is the first member of a Green party to become prime minister of a European country.

•

Israel announces that it will dismantle eight kilometres (five miles) of the barrier it is building so that two Palestinian villages in the West Bank will no longer be completely sealed off.

22 ***Insurgents opposed to the regime of Haitian Pres. Jean-Bertrand Aristide seize control of Cap-Haïtien, Haiti's second biggest city. (See February 28.) (Photo right.)***

•

The Iraqi Governing Council allows that it is unable to negotiate an agreement on the role of the U.S. military under a future Iraqi government, though the plan to return sovereignty to Iraq requires that such an agreement be reached prior to the selection of an interim government.

•

In London, *Jerry Springer—the Opera* wins four Laurence Olivier Awards: best actor in a musical (David Bedella), best sound design, best performance in a supporting role in a musical (the chorus), and best new musical.

Parties are held throughout New York City as friends and family gather to watch the final episode of *Sex and the City,* a cable television show that became a cultural phenomenon during its six-year run.

23 Ralph Nader announces that he will run independently as a candidate for president of the United States; he ran on the Green Party ticket in 2000.

Hearings before the International Court of Justice begin on the legality of the barrier that Israel is building to seal itself off from the West Bank.

KorAm Bank, the sixth largest bank in South Korea, announces that it will be sold to Citigroup Inc., the world's biggest financial concern; KorAm thus becomes the first bank in South Korea to be owned by a foreign bank.

Volunteers begin a three-day polio vaccination drive in nine African countries in an attempt to stop the spread of polio from the regions in Nigeria where religious leaders have banned vaccination, falsely claiming that it causes infertility in girls.

24 U.S. Pres. George W. Bush openly declares that he believes the U.S. Constitution should be amended in order to prohibit same-sex marriage. (*See* February 20.)

Russian Pres. Vladimir Putin suddenly fires Prime Minister Mikhail M. Kasyanov—as well as the rest of the cabinet—without naming a successor.

25 Director Mel Gibson's much-hyped and very controversial movie *The Passion of the Christ* opens in theatres across North America.

The Zayed International Prize for the Environment, the richest such award in the world, is given in Dubai to the BBC for its coverage of environmental issues; the prize, named for the president of the United Arab Emirates, was first awarded to former U.S. president Jimmy Carter in 2001.

AP/Wide World Photos

26 Macedonian Pres. Boris Trajkovski is killed in an airplane crash in Bosnia and Herzegovina while on his way to attend a conference in the Bosnian city of Mostar.

Iraq's Grand Ayatollah Ali al-Sistani releases a statement demanding that elections be held in Iraq before the end of the year and that the interim government that will be installed on June 30 devote itself to arranging for the election of a legitimate government within a few months.

A Delaware state judge denies Conrad Black the right to sell his controlling stake in the newspaper publisher Hollinger International, Inc., to David and Frederick Barclay, ruling that the right to dispose of the company's assets belongs to its board of directors instead.

Russian Pres. Vladimir Putin formally opens the final link of the transcontinental highway, running 10,000 km (6,000 mi) from Moscow to Vladivostok; the last segment completed connects Chita and Khabarovsk in the Far East.

27 The UN Security Council approves a peacekeeping force of some 6,000 members to be sent to Côte d'Ivoire.

In Caracas, Venez., protesters seeking the removal of Pres. Hugo Chávez fight with government troops; at least two people are killed.

Shoko Asahara, head of the AUM Shinrikyo cult—which in 1995 carried out an attack using sarin nerve gas on subway trains in Tokyo that killed 12 people and injured more than 5,000—is found guilty on 13 counts, including the killing of 15 other people, and is sentenced to death by a court in the Japanese capital.

28 Haitian Pres. Jean-Bertrand Aristide yields to internal and external pressure and signs a letter of resignation; the following day, escorted by U.S. military personnel, he boards a jet that takes him to the Central African Republic. (*See* February 22.)

At a summit meeting in Sirte, Libya, the African Union agrees to form a multinational peacekeeping force.

The Iraqi Governing Council misses an agreed-upon deadline for producing an interim constitution for the country, but its members continue working on the document and produce it only one day late.

The second round of six-way talks between the U.S., Russia, China, Japan, and North and South Korea ends with no conclusions being reached, but this round is said to have been more productive than the first, and another round is contemplated. (*See* February 3.)

29 Academy Awards are won by, among others, *The Lord of the Rings: The Return of the King* (which wins 11 awards) and its director, Peter Jackson, as well as actors Sean Penn, Charlize Theron, Tim Robbins, and Renée Zellweger.

At St. Justin Church in Pittsburgh, Pa., the Slippery Rock University of Pennsylvania's orchestra premieres *In Memoriam: A Requiem for Mr. Rogers,* a piece composed by Luke Mayernik in memory of children's television star Fred Rogers, who died in February 2003.

March

March 11 now has its place in the history of infamy.

Spanish Prime Minister José María Aznar,
on the terrorist train bombings in Madrid, March 11

1 Rebels pour into Port-au-Prince, the capital of Haiti; the previous day Boniface Alexandre was sworn in as interim head of government. (*See* February 28 and March 2 and 8.)

•

Russian Pres. Vladimir Putin confounds commentators when he names a low-profile man of wide competency, Mikhail Fradkov, the new prime minister.

2 Explosions in the Iraqi cities of Baghdad and Karbala kill some 170 Shi'ite Iraqis celebrating the last day of Ashura, on which Shi'ites commemorate the martyrdom of Husayn, grandson of the Prophet Muhammad, in Karbala.

•

Three people attack a procession of Shi'ites observing Ashura in Quetta, Pak., causing the death of at least 43 people; fighting then breaks out between Shi'ites and Sunnites.

•

Rebel leader Guy Philippe declares that he is in charge of Haiti; rebel forces begin destroying artwork from a museum designed to honour Haiti's bicentennial in 2004.

•

The European Space Agency's *Rosetta* spacecraft is launched from Kourou, French Guiana; *Rosetta* is meant to reach Comet 67P/Churyumov-Gerasimenko in 2014; there it will conduct investigations about the comet's chemistry and geology from orbit and by means of a small lander sent to its surface.

3 A new government with former Yugoslav president Vojislav Kostunica as prime minister is approved by Serbia's parliament.

•

Multnomah county in Oregon (including the city of Portland) begins issuing marriage licenses to same-sex couples.

•

The board of Walt Disney Co. votes Michael Eisner out as chairman, although he retains his post as CEO.

4 The U.S. government lifts the ban on U.S. citizens' traveling to Libya; the ban had been in effect since 1981.

•

The National Book Critics Circle Awards are won by Paul Hendrickson, for *Sons of Mississippi: A Story of Race and Its Legacy,* Edward P. Jones, for *The Known World,* William Taubman, for *Khrushchev: The Man and His Era,* Susan Stewart, for *Columbarium,* and Rebecca Solnit, for *River of Shadows;* the Ivan Sandrof Lifetime Achievement Award goes to Studs Terkel.

5 Lifestyle entrepreneur Martha Stewart is found guilty on all four counts of obstructing justice and making false statements in relation to her sale of ImClone stock just before the stock's price plummeted in reaction to bad news about ImClone's cancer-treatment drug. (*See* March 15.)

•

France reportedly has completed an inspection of some 32,190 km (20,000 mi) of railroad in reaction to letters sent to the government claiming that bombs had been planted along the country's rail network.

•

Science magazine publishes a report by scientists saying that a group of fossils discovered in 2002 has been classified as a new, very early hominid species, *Ardipithecus kadabba,* dating to 5.5 million years ago.

6 Twelve Russian scientists whose research station was destroyed when the ice shelf on which it was located began breaking up are rescued from an ice floe in the Arctic Ocean; the station had been built in April 2003 to study climate change.

7 Tropical Cyclone Gafilo makes landfall on Madagascar; over the next three days, it leaves at least 74 people dead and 200,000 homeless.

•

Parliamentary elections in Greece result in a victory for the conservative New Democracy Party, which ousts the socialist PASOK from power; Konstantinos Karamanlis is sworn in as prime minister on March 10.

•

In the Austrian province of Carinthia, the Freedom Party, led by ultranationalist Jörg Haider, wins the most seats in the provincial legislature.

•

Gene V. Robinson takes the crozier in a ceremony in Concord, N.H., to become the first openly gay Episcopalian bishop.

8 After much last-minute politicking, 25 members of the Iraqi Governing Council or their representatives ceremonially sign the interim Iraqi constitution; immediately afterward the Shi'ite members of the council say they intend to amend it.

Boniface Alexandre is ceremonially installed as interim president of Haiti as a council set up under a Caribbean Community plan interviews candidates for interim prime minister; on March 9 Gérard Latortue, a businessman who has lived outside Haiti since 1988, is selected. (*See* March 1.)

9 In a courtroom in Manassas, Va., John A. Muhammad, who terrified the Washington, D.C., area in October 2002 with a series of sniper killings, is sentenced to death.

Five British citizens who were held for two years at the U.S. Guantánamo Bay military base in Cuba arrive back in Great Britain after having been released into government custody; by the following day, all have been freed without charge.

French yachtsman Jean-Luc Van den Heede breaks the world record for sailing around the world westbound, arriving in Oessant, France, after 122 days 14 hours 3 minutes 49 seconds at sea.

10 The Internet providers America Online, Earthlink, Yahoo!, and Microsoft announce that they have filed the first lawsuits under the federal antispam law in an attempt to shut down the largest disseminators of unwanted e-mail solicitations, or spam.

The U.S. House of Representatives passes a measure, popularly known as the Cheeseburger Bill, that bans lawsuits against producers and sellers of food and soft drinks based on obesity claims.

Authorities in Zimbabwe say that they are holding 64 men who were traveling on a charter plane seized three days earlier in Harare because they have been found to be mercenaries planning to overthrow the government of Equatorial Guinea.

The European Parliament adopts a number of laws that will make it easier for a citizen of any European Union country to settle in another EU country.

11 Bombs explode on trains in three railway stations in Madrid, killing 191 people and wounding more than 1,400 during the morning rush hour; most of the damage occurs at the huge Atocha station; the government initially blames the Basque terrorist organization ETA. (*See* March 13.)

The Supreme Court of the state of California orders San Francisco to stop issuing marriage licenses to same-sex couples, pending review of lawsuits filed with regard to the practice.

12 South Korea's National Assembly, for the first time in its history, votes to impeach the president and suspends his powers; Pres. Roh Moo Hyun is accused of illegal campaigning. (*See* May 14.)

Greece requests that NATO assist in providing security for the Olympic Games in Athens in August.

Bowling against Sri Lanka, Australian cricketer Shane Warne becomes only the second person ever to have bowled 500 Test wickets; Warne only recently completed a 12-month suspension for taking a banned diuretic. (*See* March 16.)

13 In response to a motion of censure by the International Atomic Energy Agency, Iran suspends international inspection of its nuclear facilities, suggesting that inspections might again be permitted beginning in late April.

Unrest caused by Kurdish demonstrations for increased rights spreads through cities in northeastern Syria; some 25 people are killed over two days.

Spain reveals that a videotape has surfaced in which al-Qaeda claims responsibility for the train bombings in Madrid. (*See* March 11 and 19.)

The Indian team plays its first cricket match against Pakistan in Pakistan for the first time in 15 years; on March 24 India wins the one-day series 3–2.

As part of a series of farewell concerts leading to his retirement in 2005, famed Italian tenor Luciano Pavarotti sings the role of Cavaradossi in **Tosca,** ***his last appearance in an opera at New York City's Metropolitan Opera House. (Photo right.)***

14 In Spain's parliamentary elections, the opposition Socialist Workers' Party unexpectedly defeats the ruling centre-right Popular Party.

Russian Pres. Vladimir Putin wins reelection by a landslide, to the surprise of no one.

China's National People's Congress adopts constitutional amendments that protect human rights and guard private property.

15 After soldiers refuse to allow Georgian Pres. Mikhail Saakashvili to enter Ajaria, a mostly Muslim region that seeks to secede from Georgia, Saakashvili orders a blockade of the province; the blockade is lifted three days later, however.

Researchers describe the discovery of a planetoid in the far reaches of the solar system with an aphelion (maximum distance from the Sun) of 135 billion km (84 billion mi); the body, not much smaller than Pluto, is tentatively named Sedna.

The Rock and Roll Hall of Fame in Cleveland, Ohio, inducts the performers Jackson Browne, George Harrison, Prince, and Bob Seger, the bands The Dells, Traffic, and ZZ Top, and *Rolling Stone* magazine founder and publisher Jann Wenner.

Martha Stewart resigns her posts as director and chief creative officer of Martha Stewart Living Omnimedia. (*See* March 5.)

AP/Wide World Photos

16 Lithuania's Constitutional Court begins impeachment hearings against Pres. Rolandas Paksas, who is accused of abusing his powers in multiple ways.

•

Mitch Seavey of Seward, Alaska, wins Alaska's annual Iditarod Trail Sled Dog Race, arriving in Nome 9 days 12 hours 20 minutes 22 seconds after departing from Anchorage.

•

In a match against Australia in Kandy, Sri Lanka, Muttiah Muralitharan becomes only the third bowler in Test history to have taken 500 wickets; he completes the feat in far fewer matches than had either Courtney Walsh or Shane Warne, who previously reached the 500-wicket mark. (*See* March 12.)

17 An enormous explosion destroys the Mount Lebanon Hotel in Baghdad, Iraq, killing at least 27 people and wounding more than 40.

•

The worst violence since 1999 breaks out in several places in the UN-administered enclave of Kosovo in Serbia and Montenegro; 22 people are killed, and NATO sends in reinforcements.

•

Charles A. McCoy, Jr., is arrested in Las Vegas, Nev., in connection with a series of random shootings on Interstate 270 in Ohio that have unnerved residents and drivers since spring 2003.

•

George F.R. Ellis, a South African theoretical cosmologist, is named the winner of the Templeton Prize for Progress Toward Research or Discoveries About Spiritual Realities.

18 The Pan-African Parliament, planned to have representatives from all 53 members of the African Union, is inaugurated in Addis Ababa, Eth.

•

The U.S. files the first-ever case against China with the World Trade Organization, accusing China of unfair taxes against imported semiconductors.

•

U.S. Secretary of State Colin Powell announces that Pakistan will be designated a major non-NATO ally of the U.S.; the new status will enable Pakistan to buy advanced weaponry from the U.S.

•

An asteroid some 30 m (100 ft) in diameter passes within 42,640 km (26,500 mi) of the Earth, the closest encounter between an asteroid and the planet ever recorded, though scientists believe closer encounters occur without being noticed.

19 Three Moroccans and two Indians are charged in Spain with responsibility for the train bombing in Madrid; several other people have been arrested but not yet charged in connection with the attack. (*See* March 13.)

•

Taiwanese Pres. Chen Shui-bian and Vice Pres. Annette Lu are shot and slightly wounded while riding in a campaign motorcade in Tainan.

•

India tests a medium-range nuclear-capable missile with a range of 200 km (125 mi), enough to reach Pakistan; 10 days earlier Pakistan had tested a Shaheen 2 missile, which could deliver a nuclear warhead into India.

20 Taiwan's Central Election Commission declares that Pres. Chen Shui-bian is the winner of the presidential election by a razor-thin margin; his opponent, Lien Chan, calls for a recount.

•

Brig. Gen. Mark Kinnon announces charges against six soldiers in connection with reported abuse of Iraqi prisoners being held in Abu Ghraib prison, notorious for torture under the regime of Saddam Hussein; 11 others have been suspended from duty.

21 Antonio Saca, of the ruling rightist, pro-U.S. ARENA party, wins El Salvador's presidential election.

•

In parliamentary elections in Malaysia, the moderate coalition of Prime Minister Abdullah Badawi easily wins the majority of seats.

•

Kenenisa Bekele of Ethiopia wins the world cross country championship in Brussels, finishing the 12-km course in 35 minutes 52 seconds and becoming the first person ever to have won both the long- and short-course titles three consecutive times.

22 Israeli military forces target and kill Sheikh Ahmed Yassin, the paraplegic founder and head of the militant Palestinian organization Hamas, in the Gaza Strip.

•

Grand Ayatollah Ali al-Sistani makes public a letter he delivered to UN envoy Lakhdar Brahimi warning that he will not cooperate with the UN in any way if the UN endorses the recently signed interim constitution; Shi'ites, the majority in Iraq, object to provisions that would increase the powers of minorities, in particular Sunnites and Kurds.

•

The UN's humanitarian coordinator for The Sudan says that ethnic cleansing is taking place in the Darfur region, with the complicity of the government, and that since hostilities began in February, it has become the biggest humanitarian crisis in the world.

•

Iraqi-born architect Zaha Hadid is named the winner of the 2004 Pritzker Architecture Prize.

23 The Palestinian organization Hamas chooses the firebrand Abdel Aziz Rantisi as its new leader.

•

In parliamentary elections in Antigua and Barbuda, the opposition United Progressive Party wins 12 of the 17 seats, and Baldwin Spencer is sworn in as prime minister the following day.

•

David Hempleman-Adams reaches an altitude of 12,800 m (42,000 ft) in an open-basket hot-air balloon over Greeley, Colo., setting a new record for gas and hot-air balloons; the previous record, 11,737 m (38,507 ft), was set in 1999.

•

NASA scientists report that data from the Mars rover Opportunity indicate that there were once shallow salty seas on Mars; investigators believe the rover is exploring on the shore of one such sea.

24 A railway worker in France discovers a bomb buried under the rail line that runs between Paris and Basel, Switz.; this is the second bomb found since the obscure group AZF starting making threats.

•

The European Commission approves a decision by the EU's competition commissioner, Mario Monti, that Microsoft must pay a fine of €497 million, offer a version of Windows that is not bundled with MediaPlayer

© Yannis Behrakis/Reuters/Corbis

audiovisual software, and reveal software codes to competitors.

•

The World Trade Organization rules in a suit brought by Antigua and Barbuda that the U.S. ban on cross-border gambling on the Internet violates international trade agreements.

25 British Prime Minister Tony Blair makes an official visit to Libyan leader Muammar al Qaddafi, signaling the end of Libya's long international isolation.

•

An antigovernment protest in Abidjan, Côte d'Ivoire, is met by harsh measures, and some 25 people are killed in the worst outbreak of violence since the peace accord was implemented in January 2003.

•

The Olympic torch is ceremonially lit in Olympia, Greece; for the next 78 days, it will be carried around the world before arriving in Athens for the Olympic Games. (Photo above.)

26 As many as 16 people, including a television cameraman, die in gun battles in Fallujah, Iraq.

•

Protests against the certification of Pres. Chen Shui-bian as the winner of the election in Taiwan turn violent, and China warns that it will not tolerate deterioration of the situation.

•

A court in Moscow bans activities on the part of Jehovah's Witnesses in the city on the basis of, among other things, the charge of sowing religious discord.

27 On the last day of the world figure-skating championships, in Dortmund, Ger., Shizuka Arakawa of Japan wins the gold medal in the ladies' competition; earlier Yevgeny Plushchenko of Russia had won in the men's program for the second consecutive year.

•

France wins the round-robin Rugby Union Six Nations without a single defeat.

•

Pleasantly Perfect, winner of the Breeder's Cup Classic in 2003, outruns favourite Medaglia d'Oro to win the Dubai World Cup, the richest horse race in the world.

28 Attacks take place on several military posts and broadcast facilities in Kinshasa, the capital of the Democratic Republic of the Congo; the actions of the attackers are believed to be an attempted coup.

•

In Baghdad, Iraq, U.S. authorities shut down *Al-Hawza,* a popular extremist Shi'ite newspaper, accusing it of inciting violence; thousands of Iraqis take to the streets in protest.

•

A hurricane makes landfall in South America, causing extensive damage in Brazil's southern Santa Catarina state and killing at least two people; this is the first time on record that a hurricane has formed in the South Atlantic Ocean, so no name for it was immediately available.

•

New Zealand launches a Maori television station, in which at least half of the programming will be in the Maori language.

29 In a ceremony in Washington, D.C., U.S. Pres. George W. Bush welcomes seven countries—Bulgaria, Estonia, Latvia, Lithuania, Romania, Slovakia, and Slovenia—as members of NATO; a later ceremony will be held in Brussels.

•

Suicide bombers in Tashkent, Uzbekistan, kill at least 19 people; the following day government forces kill at least five people identified as terrorists in the village of Yalangach.

•

The state legislature of Massachusetts approves an amendment to the state constitution to ban same-sex marriage but permit civil union; it must be passed in another legislative session and in a public referendum to become law.

•

A ban on smoking in any place of work, including restaurants and pubs, goes into effect in Ireland.

•

The storied Liechtenstein Museum, containing one of the world's richest private collections of art, reopens in Vienna.

30 Two days after the ruling party in France was trounced in regional elections, Pres. Jacques Chirac accepts the resignation of Prime Minister Pierre Raffarin but then immediately reappoints him.

•

Solomon D. Trujillo steps down as CEO of Orange, the wireless branch of France Telecom and the biggest wireless carrier in France and Great Britain.

31 In Fallujah, Iraq, four American men working for a private security company are ambushed and killed; within minutes a large mob forms, burning the cars and then, with apparent jubilation, mutilating the corpses.

•

An international donors' conference in Berlin pledges $4.4 billion in donations and low-cost loans to help Afghanistan rebuild in the next year, with $8.2 billion in pledges over the next three years.

•

The International Court of Justice rules that the rights of 51 Mexican citizens sentenced to death in the U.S. were violated and orders U.S. courts to review the sentences.

•

The U.S. Navy's Roosevelt Roads Naval Station outside Ceiba, P.R., closes; the navy had maintained the base on the island since 1940, and it was an important factor in the local economy.

April

You can't create one nation out of two. You can allow them to begin living together by treating them as equals, allowing trust to grow between them.

Turkish Cypriot leader Rauf Denktash, after the failure of a referendum on a UN unification plan for Cyprus, April 24

1 No agreement is reached after three days of negotiations between representatives of Greece, Greek Cyprus, Turkey, Turkish Cyprus, and the UN on a plan created by UN Secretary-General Kofi Annan for the unification of Cyprus; nonetheless, the plan will be presented in a referendum to the people of Cyprus. (*See* February 13 and April 24.)

•

Some 50,000 people march in protest against King Gyanendra's policies in Kathmandu, Nepal, demanding the return of democratic policies.

•

The KTX high-speed train begins service in South Korea between Seoul and Taegu, with service to be extended to Pusan; the train travels at 298 km/h (185 mph) and is expected to halve the travel time to Pusan.

2 In parliamentary elections in Sri Lanka, Pres. Chandrika Kumaratunga's party, the People's Alliance, wins the highest number of seats, though not enough to form a government on its own. (*See* April 6.)

•

The UN director for relief in The Sudan tells the UN Security Council that ethnic cleansing is taking place in the Darfur region, near the border with Chad, against black Muslim Africans, with the tolerance of the Sudanese government.

•

The U.S. Department of Homeland Security announces that as of September 30, travelers to the U.S. from 27 industrialized countries must be photographed and fingerprinted on arrival.

3 As Spanish authorities get ready to raid an apartment building in Madrid where four suspects in the train bombings of March 11 are said to be, the suspects set off an explosion and blow themselves up.

•

The winner of the Grand National steeplechase horse race in Great Britain is 12-year-old Amberleigh House, ridden by Graham Lee and trained by Donald "Ginger" McCain, trainer of three-time winner Red Rum.

4 In the Iraqi cities of Baghdad, Najaf, Kufa, and Amara, thousands of supporters of the anti-American Shi'ite cleric Moktada al-Sadr—many of them members of his militia, the Mahdi Army—rise up, and eight U.S. soldiers are killed; the previous day, the insurgents had marched in Baghdad as a show of strength.

•

In Formula 1 auto racing, Ferrari's driver Michael Schumacher is the winner of the inaugural Bahrain Grand Prix.

5 The Canadian government orders the slaughter of 19 million chickens, turkeys, and ducks, approximately 80% of British Columbia's poultry, in a desperate attempt to contain an outbreak of avian flu.

•

In New York City the winners of the 2004 Pulitzer Prizes are announced; journalistic awards go to, among others, the *Los Angeles Times,* which wins five awards; winners in arts and letters include Edward P. Jones in fiction and Doug Wright in drama.

•

The National Collegiate Athletic Association (NCAA) championship in men's basketball is won by the University of Connecticut (UConn), which defeats Georgia Tech 82–73; the following day UConn defeats the University of Tennessee 70–61 for its third consecutive women's NCAA title.

•

Elected to the Naismith Memorial Basketball Hall of Fame are players Clyde Drexler, Lynette Woodard, Maurice Stokes, and Drazen Dalipagic, coach Bill Sharman, and owner Jerry Colangelo.

•

American adventurer Steve Fossett breaks the around-the-world sailing record, traveling 35,020 km (21,760 mi) in a 38-m (125-ft) catamaran with a 12-member crew in 58 days 9 hours; the previous record, set by Bruno Peyron in 2002, was 64 days 8 hours.

6 Lithuanian Pres. Rolandas Paksas is removed from office

AP/Wide World Photos

after he is impeached; he is the first European leader to be so removed.

•

Mahinda Rajapakse is sworn in as prime minister of Sri Lanka, at the head of a minority government. (*See* April 2.)

•

Canada wins its eighth consecutive world championship in women's ice hockey, defeating the U.S. 2–0 in Halifax, N.S. (Photo right.)

7 Afghani Pres. Hamid Karzai orders Afghan National Army troops to the northern province of Faryab in order to retake the area from a militia loyal to the Uzbek warlord Abdul Rashid Dostum.

•

Mounir el-Motassadeq, the only person convicted for the terrorist attacks of Sept. 11, 2001 (his conviction was overturned), is released in Hamburg, Ger., pending a new trial.

8 Three Japanese civilians—two aid workers and a journalist—are kidnapped in Iraq, and their captors threaten to execute them unless Japan withdraws its 550 troops from Iraq; the hostages are released unharmed on April 15.

•

The government of The Sudan and two rebel groups in the Darfur region agree to a 45-day cease-fire to allow relief groups into the region.

•

Abdelaziz Bouteflika is reelected president of Algeria in a landslide.

9 L. Paul Bremer III, the U.S. administrator in Iraq, orders a cease-fire in Fallujah.

•

As 25,000 people demonstrate against the rule of King Gyanendra, more than a thousand people are arrested in Kathmandu, Nepal, for defying a ban on public gatherings.

•

Some 10,000 people demonstrate in downtown Yerevan, Armenia, to demand the resignation of Pres. Robert Kocharian.

•

Science magazine publishes an article in which French researchers posit that a burial of a person together with a wildcat dating to 7500 BC in Cyprus suggests that domestication of the cat began some 9,500 years ago, 5,000 years earlier than previously thought.

10 In Taipei, Taiwan, a large demonstration demanding an investigation into the presidential election turns violent, and skirmishes with riot police go on for an hour after sunset.

•

Mud slides near Machu Picchu in Peru strand some 1,500 tourists, 11 of whom cannot be found.

11 In his annual Easter mass, Pope John Paul II prays for peace in Africa and the Middle East and enjoins the people of the world to unite against terrorism.

•

As Iraqi intermediaries seek a negotiated solution with insurgents, U.S. troops stand down outside three cities in Iraq that have fallen to the insurgents.

•

Crowd favourite Phil Mickelson wins the Masters golf tournament in Augusta, Ga., his first victory in a major tournament.

12 Canada begins its biggest seal hunt in 50 years, with a quota of 350,000 baby harp seals; the hunting of seals was ended 25 years ago because of popular revulsion over the killing of the baby seals, but this year's hunt includes new guidelines meant to minimize cruelty.

•

Brian Lara of the West Indies becomes the first person ever to hold the record for the highest Test score in cricket twice when his 400 not out against England in Antigua surpasses the 380 Australia's Matthew Hayden scored against Zimbabwe in October 2003.

•

The 2004 Avery Fisher Prize for outstanding achievement in music is awarded to the Emerson String Quartet.

13 Turkish Cypriot Prime Minister Mehmet Ali Talat crosses the border into Greek Cyprus to campaign in favour of the UN unification plan.

•

San Francisco Giants slugger Barry Bonds hits his 661st career home run in San Francisco against the Milwaukee Brewers, passing Willie Mays to become third on the roster for most career home runs in Major League Baseball.

14 U.S. Pres. George W. Bush startles world opinion when, in a joint statement with Israeli Prime Minister Ariel Sharon, he fully accepts the withdrawal of settlements from Gaza and the maintenance of settlements in the West Bank and agrees that Palestinians do not have a right to return to their former home.

•

France-Albert René retires as president of Seychelles,

and his vice president, James Michel, is sworn in as president; René had been head of state in Seychelles since he seized power in 1977.

•

Bartholomew I, ecumenical patriarch of the Eastern Orthodox Church, formally accepts the apology offered by Pope John Paul II in 2001 for the sacking of Constantinople by Crusader armies in 1204.

15 The U.S. agrees to a proposal put forward by UN envoy Lakhdar Brahimi that the U.S.-appointed Iraqi Governing Council be supplanted by a transitional government named by the UN on June 30, the date the U.S. chose for the transfer of sovereignty to Iraq.

•

Legislative elections in South Korea place the legislature in the hands of liberals for the first time in 43 years and implicitly rebuke the National Assembly for its impeachment of Pres. Roh Moo Hyun; on the following day the Constitutional Court announces that impeachment proceedings will go forward anyway.

•

The Finnish Technology Award Foundation names Tim Berners-Lee, inventor of the World Wide Web, the winner of its inaugural Millennium Technology Prize, which carries an award of €1 million (about $1.2 million).

•

At 508 m (1,667 ft), the Taipei 101 skyscraper in Taiwan is declared the tallest building in the world.

16 José Luis Rodríguez Zapatero receives a majority vote in the lower house of parliament and the following day is sworn in as prime minister of Spain.

•

India wins its first cricket Test series outside India since 1993 by defeating Pakistan 2–1; the event is also remarkable because it marks India's first tour to Pakistan in 15 years and because political tensions between the two countries were not carried over onto the pitch or into the grandstands.

17 Abdel Aziz Rantisi, the newly named head of the Palestinian militant organization Hamas, is killed by an Israeli helicopter strike on his car in Gaza City.

•

Ernst Welteke resigns as president of Germany's Bundesbank.

18 New Spanish Prime Minister José Luis Rodríguez Zapatero orders all Spanish troops in Iraq to return home.

•

Ivan Gasparovic is elected president of Slovakia.

•

In his first London Marathon, Evans Rutto of Kenya wins with a time of 2 hr 6 min 18 sec; the fastest woman there is Margaret Okayo of Kenya, also in her first London Marathon, with a time of 2 hours 22 minutes 35 seconds.

•

World auto rally champion Petter Solberg of Norway wins the Rally of New Zealand.

19 King Abdullah of Jordan cancels a planned visit with U.S. Pres. George W. Bush in response to Bush's approval of Israeli Prime Minister Ariel Sharon's policy toward Palestine.

•

North Korean leader Kim Jong Il arrives in Beijing for a secret visit to discuss the international crisis surrounding North Korea's nuclear arms program.

•

The 108th Boston Marathon is won by Timothy Cherigat of Kenya with a time of 2 hr 10 min 37 sec; Catherine Ndereba of Kenya is the women's winner for the third time, with a time of 2 hours 24 minutes 27 seconds.

20 A circuit court judge in Oregon orders Multnomah county to stop issuing marriage licenses to same-sex couples but rules that the 3,000 licenses issued so far are to be treated as valid.

•

The telecommunications company WorldCom emerges from bankruptcy under the name MCI.

•

Gravity Probe B is launched into a polar orbit from a rocket at Vandenberg Air Force Base, California; in a yearlong mission the spacecraft will test predictions of Einstein's general theory of relativity about the way gravity affects space and time.

21 Car bombs go off outside three police stations and a police academy in Basra, Iraq, killing 50 people, many of them schoolchildren.

•

A suicide car bomb is detonated outside a police station in Riyadh, Saudi Arabia; 4 people are killed and 148 are injured.

•

The prison sentences of four Kurdish members of the Turkish parliament who had been convicted in 1994 of being connected with an illegal Kurdish political party are upheld in a retrial in Turkey; EU officials immediately condemn the outcome.

22 A huge explosion rocks the city of Ryongchong, N. Kor., when three railcars carrying ammonium nitrate and fuel oil collide; there are 154 known dead, 1,300 injuries, and 8,000 people left homeless.

•

Photographs of flag-draped coffins of U.S. soldiers killed in the war in Iraq are published on the Web site* Memory Hole*; the publication of such photos is in contravention of U.S. policy, and the Pentagon responds quickly, sternly, and negatively. (Photo right.)

•

China's government reports that at least two people have been hospitalized with possible SARS (severe acute respiratory syndrome) and five others who had been in contact with one of them have been hospitalized with fever.

23 In an outbreak of violence among the Muslim population of southern Thailand, some 50 buildings, including more than a dozen schools, are set on fire; there are two fatalities.

•

U.S. Pres. George W. Bush authorizes the establishment of a U.S. diplomatic post in Libya and relaxes sanctions against that country.

•

Nepal becomes the 147th member of the World Trade Organization.

24 In separate referenda on UN Secretary-General Kofi Annan's plan for the reunification of Cyprus, Turkish Cypriots vote for reunification and Greek Cypriots vote against it, so the plan does not pass and only Greek Cyprus will be permitted to join the EU. (*See* April 1.)

USAF/www.thememoryhole.org/Reuters/Corbis

•

The Manzanar National Historic Site, a museum describing the internment of Japanese Americans during World War II, opens in Manzanar, Calif., the site of one of the camps where people of Japanese ethnicity were held.

•

In Los Angeles heavyweight boxer Vitali Klitschko of Ukraine is ruled the winner over Corrie Sanders of South Africa when the match is stopped in the eighth round; Klitschko thereby assumes the World Boxing Conference heavyweight title that was vacated by Lennox Lewis of the U.K.

25 The Social Democrat candidate, Heinz Fischer, is elected to the presidency of Austria.

•

Hundreds of thousands of activists demonstrate in Washington, D.C., in support of abortion rights, which many feel are in danger of being curtailed by administration policies in the U.S.

•

Driving for Ferrari, Michael Schumacher wins the San Marino Grand Prix for his fourth consecutive win in Formula 1 auto racing.

•

In Gävle, Swed., in the world curling championships, Sweden defeats Germany 7–6 to win the men's championship; in the women's game Canada defeats Norway to win its eighth straight championship.

26 Libyan leader Muammar al-Qaddafi makes his first visit to Europe in 15 years; European Commission Pres. Romano Prodi meets him upon his arrival in Brussels.

•

The U.S.-appointed Iraqi Governing Council reveals the new flag it has chosen for the country; the flag, which triggers considerable opposition, is not adopted by the Iraqi authorities.

•

China rules that Hong Kong may not vote directly for its president in the election scheduled for 2007 and that legislative voting by the general public may not be expanded in the election of 2008.

•

In Shanghai at a meeting of the UN Economic and Social Commission for Asia and the Pacific, 23 countries sign the Asian Highway Agreement, which commits them to planning and building a highway that will run from Tokyo to Istanbul.

•

Desmond Cardinal Connell, who has been criticized for his handling of accusations of sexual abuse on the part of Irish clergy, is replaced as archbishop of Dublin by Diarmuid Martin.

•

The Boeing Co. announces that it has received its largest order ever—50 new 7E7 Dreamliner jets for All Nippon Airways.

27 Morocco rejects the idea of sovereignty for Western Sahara, which it annexed in 1975; UN Secretary-General Kofi Annan has committed himself to trying to resolve the international dispute over the area.

•

A bomb goes off in a neighbourhood of foreign embassies in Damascus, Syria, and a gun battle ensues.

28 Photographs of Iraqi prisoners being tortured and sexually humiliated by U.S. military personnel in the Abu Ghraib prison outside Baghdad are broadcast on the CBS television show *60 Minutes II*.

•

The UN Security Council approves a resolution calling on all member countries to take steps to prevent chemical, biological, and nuclear weapons from being available to "non-state actors," or terror groups.

•

In a runoff presidential election, centre-left candidate Branko Crvenkovski is elected president of Macedonia.

•

Tipped off ahead of time, authorities in southern Thailand are ready for an attack by Muslim insurgents and kill 107 of them; 5 members of the Thai military and police forces are killed.

•

The final Oldsmobile to be produced, an Alero, rolls off a General Motors assembly line in Lansing, Mich.; the first mass-produced Oldsmobile, the Curved Dash, debuted in 1901.

29 The U.S. Senate agrees to extend a ban on taxing access to the Internet until 2007.

•

Google announces that it will conduct its stock offering in the form of an auction intended to make it easy for individual buyers to invest.

30 The UN Security Council approves a multinational peacekeeping mission to be sent to Haiti to replace the U.S.-led force; the UN force, to be led by Brazil, is to arrive on June 1 and stay for a minimum of six months.

•

As outrage over the broadcast photos of Iraqi prisoner abuse at Abu Ghraib prison outside Baghdad is expressed worldwide, U.S. Pres. George W. Bush publicly declares his disgust at the treatment of the prisoners.

•

Carlos Slim Helú, believed to be the wealthiest man in Latin America, steps down as chairman of Teléfonos de Mexico, handing the reins to his son, Carlos Slim Domit.

May

> *I was always certain that if I ever found myself in the position I am today, I would follow my inner voice. Today, that voice tells me that I must humbly decline this post.*

Indian National Congress party president Sonia Gandhi, turning down the post of prime minister of India, May 18

1 In a ceremony in Dublin, Irish Prime Minister Bertie Ahern, president of the European Union, formally welcomes 10 new members into the union.

•

Terrorist gunmen attack several locations in Yanbu, Saudi Arabia, killing five workers from the U.S., Great Britain, and Australia in an engineering office.

•

In the 130th running of the Kentucky Derby, the undefeated Smarty Jones wins by 2¾ lengths.

2 Martín Torrijos, the son of former dictator Omar Torrijos, is elected president of Panama.

•

The unpopular and scandal-plagued Leszek Miller resigns as prime minister of Poland and is replaced by Marek Belka.

•

Militias of the Christian Tarok people raid the largely Muslim Hausa-Fulani town of Yelwa in Nigeria's Plateau state and kill some 630 people; the raid is allegedly in retribution for an earlier Muslim raid on Christian communities. (*See* May 12.)

•

Israeli Prime Minister Ariel Sharon's Likud Party rejects his plan to withdraw from the Gaza Strip.

3 Air France merges with the Dutch airline KLM to form the largest airline in the world in terms of sales; in terms of passenger traffic, Air France–KLM ranks third, behind American Airlines and United Airlines.

•

Taliban ambushes kill at least 10 Afghani police and military personnel near Kandahar.

•

U.S. Attorney General John Ashcroft dedicates a federal building in Oklahoma City, Okla., that replaces the one that was destroyed by a terrorist bombing in 1995.

•

A new character is officially added to Morse Code, designed by the International Telecommunication Union: @, which is to be rendered by • – – • – •.

4 Rodrigo Rato, former Spanish minister of finance, is named head of the International Monetary Fund to replace Horst Köhler. (*See* May 23.)

•

Taiwan's parliament passes a law requiring official documents to be written horizontally and from left to right in order to conform to international standards; works of art and literature may still use the right-to-left or top-to-bottom format.

5 U.S. Pres. George W. Bush appears before an Arab-speaking audience on al-Arabiyah television to denounce the abuse of Iraqi prisoners by American guards at Abu Ghraib prison in Iraq.

•

A two-week protest march by some 10,000 Maori activists against plans to put coastal areas under national ownership concludes in Wellington, N.Z.; the Maori say that by custom and treaty the coastal areas belong to them.

•

Picasso's *Boy with a Pipe,* from his short-lived Rose Period, sells to an anonymous bidder at a Sotheby's auction for more than $104 million, eclipsing by more than $20 million the 1990 record price for a painting sold at auction.

6 Turkish Prime Minister Recep Tayyip Erdogan arrives in Greece for talks with Greek Prime Minister Konstantinos Karamanlis; it is the first time in 16 years that a Turkish prime minister has visited Greece.

•

Ajarian separatist leader Aslan Abashidze flees Ajaria for Russia, and the locals celebrate as the mostly Muslim republic on the Black Sea coast is returned to Georgian control.

•

Five Bulgarian nurses and a Palestinian doctor are convicted of having injected hundreds of children with HIV-infected blood products to start an AIDS epidemic in Libya, and they are sentenced to death; Western doctors believe that an outbreak in that hospital predated the arrival of the condemned personnel.

Seven former executives of Mitsubishi Motors are arrested in Japan, accused of having falsified reports of defects in wheel hubs on trucks in order to avoid a recall; the defect caused a number of accidents, one of them fatal.

7 A bomb kills at least 14 people, including the head cleric, at a Shiʿite mosque attached to a school in Karachi, Pak.

Surya Bahadur Thapa resigns as prime minister of Nepal after weeks of demonstrations against the royalist rule of the country; Thapa had been installed as prime minister at the behest of the king.

8 To the surprise of observers, Iran's Guardian Council approves a bill—passed by the outgoing reformist Majlis (legislature)—forbidding the use of torture in interrogation; three similar bills had previously been rejected by the council.

In a match against Zimbabwe in Harare, Sri Lankan cricketer Muttiah Muralitharan bowls his 520th Test wicket, breaking the record set by Courtney Walsh three years earlier.

9 A bomb explodes in a stadium in Grozny, the capital of the Russian republic of Chechnya, killing the republic's president, Akhmad Kadyrov, and at least 13 others.

Construction on the first tunnel to be built under the Bosporus begins in Istanbul; it is expected to be completed in 2008.

In Prague, Canada defeats Sweden to win the gold medal in the ice hockey world championship tournament.

10 Pres. Gloria Macapagal Arroyo is the winner in a very close presidential election in the Philippines.

Carlos Gomes, Jr., is sworn in as prime minister of Guinea-Bissau at the head of the country's first government since a coup eight months earlier.

11 An Islamist Web site posts a video showing the decapitation of American civilian Nicholas Berg by a man believed to be Abu Musab al-Zarqawi.

U.S. Pres. George W. Bush imposes economic sanctions against Syria, saying it has done nothing to stop or contain terrorism.

12 Muslim mobs attack Christians in Kano, Nigeria, in revenge for the massacre in Yelwa and kill at least 30 people. (*See* May 2 and May 18.)

13 Election results in India reveal an unforeseen defeat for the ruling Bharatiya Janata Party; Atal Bihari Vajpayee resigns as prime minister.

Pres. Sam Nujoma of Namibia and Pres. Levy Mwanawasa of Zambia officially dedicate a highway and bridge across the Zambezi River connecting the two countries; the projects are part of the Trans-Caprivi Highway, which provides an Atlantic port link to landlocked countries of southern Africa.

South Africa grants asylum to deposed Haitian president Jean-Bertrand Aristide.

AP/Wide World Photos

14 South Korea's Constitutional Court dismisses impeachment charges against Pres. Roh Moo Hyun and restores his presidential powers. (*See* March 12.)

Crown Prince Frederik of Denmark marries Australian Mary Elizabeth Donaldson. (Photo above.)

Metropolitan Laurus, head of the body known as the Russian Orthodox Church Outside of Russia, meets with Patriarch Aleksey II of the Russian Orthodox Church in Moscow in the first trip to Russia by a leader of the sect, which broke from the Russian church after the 1917 revolution.

Piers Morgan resigns as editor of the *Daily Mirror* in London after an investigation concluded that photographs published by the paper on May 1 that purported to show British soldiers abusing Iraqi prisoners had been staged.

15 Smarty Jones, the Kentucky Derby winner, wins the Preakness Stakes by 11 ½ lengths, the biggest margin of victory in the history of the race.

South Africa is chosen to host the 2010 World Cup association football (soccer) championship tournament.

16 Voters in the Dominican Republic, which is in the throes of an economic crisis, elect the opposition candidate, former president Leonel Fernández Reyna.

China, led by Lin Dan, defeats Denmark for the Thomas Cup world team badminton championship in Jakarta, Indon.; the previous day, in women's badminton, China beat South Korea for the Uber Cup.

17 A suicide attack at a U.S. checkpoint in Baghdad, Iraq, kills at least seven people, among them Ezzedine Salim, president of the Iraqi Governing Council under the rotation system.

An official of the Iraqi National Congress, a group headed by Ahmad Chalabi that had been favoured by the U.S. Department of

Defense, says that the U.S. has decided to halt payments to the group for gathering intelligence after sovereignty is transferred to an interim government at the end of June. (*See* May 20.)

•

In compliance with a ruling by the state's Supreme Judicial Court, Massachusetts begins issuing marriage licenses to same-sex couples; it is the first U.S. state to permit same-sex couples to marry legally.

•

The Civilian Space eXploration Team successfully launches a rocket with a payload into space, where it remains for several minutes before falling back to Earth; the rocket, called the GoFast rocket, is the first privately built rocket to achieve this milestone.

•

The International Commission on Stratigraphy officially gives the name Ediacaran to the geologic period between 600 million and 542 million years ago; often previously called the Vendian, the Ediacaran immediately precedes the Cambrian Period and is the first new division to be added to the geologic time scale in 120 years.

•

Appa Sherpa breaks his own record, set last year, by successfully climbing Mt. Everest for the 14th time. (*See* May 21.)

18 Sonia Gandhi stuns her fellow citizens when she unexpectedly declines the post of prime minister of India.

•

Avery Fisher career grants are awarded to violinist Tai Murray, cellist Clancy Newman, bassoonist Peter Kolbay, and harpist Bridget Kibbey.

•

Nigerian Pres. Olusegun Obasanjo declares a state of emergency in Plateau state in central Nigeria because of the violence between Christians and Muslims; the move suspends civil government there, and Obasanjo installs a retired general as administrator. (*See* May 12.)

19 Manmohan Singh, who is credited with having salvaged India's economy as minister of finance in the early 1990s, is named prime minister.

•

The Spanish association football (soccer) club Valencia CF defeats Olympique de Marseille from France to win the UEFA Cup in Göteborg, Swed.

•

Movie theatres in Iran bow to pressure from religious hard-liners and cancel showings of an immensely popular satiric film, *The Lizard,* about a thief who disguises himself as a mullah and finds the many benefits of his new life.

•

The RSPCA's National Animal Valor Award goes to Lulu the kangaroo, which saved its owner's life in September 2003 by summoning help after he was felled by a tree branch in Australia's Victoria state; Lulu is the first marsupial to win the award.

20 In presidential elections in Malawi, Bingu wa Mutharika wins with some 36% of the vote; though his four opponents claim that the election was unfair, Mutharika is sworn in on May 24.

•

U.S. and Iraqi forces raid the headquarters of Iraqi Governing Council member and erstwhile U.S. favourite Ahmad Chalabi; he is accused of having passed U.S. intelligence secrets to Iran.

21 Russia signs a trade agreement with the European Union, which promises support for Russia's membership in the World Trade Organization; in return, Russia agrees to ratify the Kyoto environmental treaty.

•

Pemba Dorje Sherpa sets a new speed record for ascending Mt. Everest, reaching the summit in 8 hours 10 minutes; the previous record, set in May 2003 by Lakpa Gelu Sherpa, was 10 hours 46 minutes. (*See* May 17.)

22 The members of the Commonwealth of Nations agree to end the suspension of Pakistan, which had been barred from the organization since 1999, when Pres. Pervez Musharraf took power in a coup.

•

The Arab League summit meeting, postponed from March, opens in Tunis, Tun.; Libyan leader Muammar al-Qaddafi walks out in disagreement with the entire agenda.

•

Japanese Prime Minister Junichiro Koizumi visits North Korea, promising medical aid and supplies of rice and returning to his country with five of the children who were born to Japanese citizens kidnapped by North Korea in the 1970s.

•

Spain enjoys the gala wedding of Crown Prince Felipe and the television journalist Letizia Ortiz.

•

At the Cannes film festival, American director Michael Moore's film *Fahrenheit 9/11* wins the Palme d'Or; the Grand Prix goes to South Korean director Park Chan Wook's *Oldboy.*

•

In the annual trination Super 12 Rugby Union championship, Australia's Brumbies defeat New Zealand's Crusaders 47–38 to take the crown.

23 Horst Köhler is elected president of Germany. (*See* May 4.)

•

In the deadliest incident in several months in the disputed Kashmir region between India and Pakistan, a bus carrying Indian soldiers and their families from the summer to the winter capital hits a land mine; at least 28 passengers are killed.

•

A section of the roof of the new terminal at the Charles de Gaulle International Airport in Paris collapses, killing four people.

•

The new Central Library, designed by Rem Koolhaas's architectural firm, opens in Seattle, Wash. (Photo right.)

24 The U.S. and Great Britain introduce a draft resolution to the UN Security Council for the transfer of authority to an interim government in Iraq.

•

U.S. Pres. George W. Bush makes a speech laying out his goals for the United States in Iraq: to relinquish authority on June 30, to remain in the country to provide security and help build infrastructure, to encourage international assistance, and to work toward a national election.

25 Catastrophic flooding and mud slides caused by three days of rain and complicated by deforestation continue in the Dominican Republic and Haiti, and the death toll rises to nearly 2,000.

•

The governor of Kano state in northern Nigeria agrees,

© Kevin P. Casey/Corbis

after an eight-month ban, to allow the World Health Organization to vaccinate children against polio.

A fire that broke out the previous day in a warehouse in London is extinguished, but not before much of the valuable collection of contemporary art owned by Charles Saatchi has been destroyed.

MTV Networks announces plans to start a cable channel aimed specifically at gay viewers; the channel, to be called Logo, is expected to begin broadcasting in February 2005.

26 A far-reaching peace agreement is signed in Naivasha, Kenya, between the government of The Sudan and Christian and animist rebels from the southern region that will end 21 years of civil war in the area; the UN, however, warns of a crisis in the Darfur region of western Sudan.

It is reported that residents of Singapore are permitted for the first time since 1992 to purchase and use chewing gum; citizens must register, however, for permission to acquire gum.

27 Iraqi leaders succeed in brokering a truce between the militia of Moktada al-Sadr and U.S. forces in Najaf.

Riots over the rising cost of living, in particular the price of fuel, break out in and around Beirut, Lebanon; five people are killed by police in a suburb.

Pope John Paul II appoints Bernard Cardinal Law, who resigned from the archdiocese of Boston because of his mishandling of sexual-abuse charges against priests in his jurisdiction, to head a major basilica in Rome.

28 To the surprise of many observers, a member of the Iraqi Governing Council, Ayad Allawi, is named prime minister of the incoming interim government of Iraq.

Thousands of opponents of Venezuelan Pres. Hugo Chávez go to voting centres in an effort to verify enough signatures to make a recall petition valid.

The U.S., Costa Rica, El Salvador, Guatemala, Honduras, and Nicaragua formally sign the Central American Free Trade Agreement.

A court in Chile revokes the immunity from prosecution that former dictator Augusto Pinochet has enjoyed since 2002, as doubt has been cast on claims that Pinochet is too frail to withstand the stress of a trial.

The last link of the span of the Millau bridge in France is completed; soaring 270 m (885 ft) over the Tarn River, it is the tallest bridge in the world.

29 Four armed militants enter and take control of a luxury residential complex housing mostly Western oil company executives in Khobar, Saudi Arabia; the following day Saudi armed forces storm the complex, freeing most of the residents (though 22 had been killed by the militants) but failing to apprehend three of the terrorists.

The Kurdistan Workers Party in Turkey announces that as of June 1 its five-year cease-fire will come to an end.

The long-awaited World War II Memorial, located between the Reflecting Pool and the Washington Monument in Washington, D.C., is dedicated; tens of thousands of people attend the ceremony.

30 Mufti Nizammudin Shamzai, a prominent pro-Taliban Sunni cleric in Pakistan, is assassinated in Karachi, which prompts a rampage on the part of his supporters.

Luca Cordero di Montezemolo is named to replace Umberto Agnelli, who died two days earlier, as chairman of the Italian automobile company Fiat; Giuseppe Morchio promptly resigns as CEO of the company.

The 88th Indianapolis 500 auto race is won by Buddy Rice, the first American to do so since 1998.

Call Me Ishmael, an English-language opera based on the Herman Melville novel *Moby Dick,* with lyrics from the novel, premieres in Amsterdam; music and libretto are by Gary Goldschneider.

31 A bomb in a Shi'ite mosque in Karachi, Pak., kills some 20 people and injures nearly 40 others.

The governing party of Singapore ratifies the appointment of Lee Hsien Loong as the next prime minister; Lee, the son of Lee Kuan Yew, who held the post from 1959 to 1990, will take office in July when Goh Chok Tong steps down in his favour.

June

Dear Free People: Our dear Iraq is now at a setback, but it is a very temporary setback, and we will rise up after that like mountains, standing up very firm.

Iraqi interim Prime Minister Ayad Allawi, on accepting sovereignty documents from outgoing CPA head L. Paul Bremer III, June 28

1 An interim government of 33 ministers is named in Iraq; after naming Ghazi al-Yawar president of the interim government, the Iraqi Governing Council dissolves itself.

•

The U.S. military forces begin turning over control of a reeling Haiti to UN peacekeeping forces.

•

Mel Karmazin resigns as president and chief operating officer of the media conglomerate Viacom Inc.

2 Five aid workers with Doctors Without Borders are ambushed and killed in northwestern Afghanistan; a Taliban spokesman claims responsibility.

•

King Gyanendra of Nepal reappoints Sher Bahadur Deuba prime minister.

3 George Tenet resigns as U.S. director of central intelligence.

•

Venezuela's National Electoral Council says that petitions for a recall of Pres. Hugo Chávez are valid, which means that a recall referendum must be held.

•

The day after rebel military commanders seized control of the city of Bukavu, protesters storm UN facilities in towns throughout the country, angry that UN peacekeepers had failed to prevent Bukavu from falling into the hands of the rebels.

•

In San Francisco, former Ukrainian prime minister Pavlo Lazarenko is convicted of extortion and money laundering; he faces murder charges in Ukraine.

•

In the Scripps National Spelling Bee, David Tidmarsh of South Bend, Ind., spells *autochthonous* correctly to win the contest.

4 A bomb explodes in an outdoor market in Samara, Russia, killing at least nine people and injuring dozens.

•

Authorities in Kano, Nigeria, cancel an annual parade held to celebrate the birth of the founder of the Quadiriyah Sufi sect of Islam because of recent violence against Christians by Muslims in the city.

•

U.S. Pres. George W. Bush meets with Pope John Paul II at the Vatican.

5 Former U.S. president Ronald W. Reagan dies at the age of 93, 10 years after having been diagnosed with Alzheimer disease.

•

The 225th Derby (now the Vodafone Derby) at Epsom Downs in Surrey, Eng., is won by North Light, ridden by Kieren Fallon.

•

Birdstone squashes Smarty Jones's bid to win Thoroughbred racing's Triple Crown by overtaking the favourite 100 yd from the finish line and winning the Belmont Stakes by one length.

•

Anastasiya Myskina of Russia defeats her countrywoman Yelena Dementyeva to win the French Open tennis title; the following day Gaston Gaudio of Argentina defeats Guillermo Coria, also of Argentina, in the finals to win the men's title.

6 ***World leaders gather on the Normandy coast of France to commemorate the 60th anniversary of the D-Day invasion; for the first time, leaders of both Germany and Russia take part in the observances. (Photo right.)***

•

Israeli Prime Minister Ariel Sharon wins limited approval to prepare for withdrawal from Gaza and, to a lesser degree, from the West Bank, though not approval for actual withdrawal of any settlements.

•

The 58th annual Tony Awards are presented in New York City; winners include the plays *I Am My Own Wife*, *Avenue Q*, *Henry IV*, and *Assassins* and the actors Jefferson Mays, Phylicia Rashad, Hugh Jackman, and Idina Menzel.

7 Former Rwandan president Pasteur Bizimungu is sentenced to 15 years in prison for having embezzled money and fomented ethnic strife.

•

The Japan Arts Association awards the Praemium Imperiale to Georg Baselitz of Germany for painting, Abbas Kiarostami of Iran for film, Bruce Nauman of the U.S. for sculpture, Oscar Niemeyer of Brazil for architecture, and Krzysztof Penderecki of Poland for music.

•

The Tampa Bay Lightning defeats the Calgary Flames to win the Stanley Cup, the National Hockey League championship; the score of the final game is 2–1.

•

The Council of Fashion Designers of America awards Menswear Designer of the Year to rap impresario Sean ("P. Diddy") Combs for his Sean John line of clothing.

8 The planet Venus transits the face of the Sun for the first time since 1882.

•

The UN Security Council approves a U.S. and British resolution to transfer authority to an interim government in Iraq but continue to provide security as part of a multinational force.

•

Emir Sheikh Hamad ibn Khalifah al-Thani approves Qatar's first constitution, which will permit elections to an advisory body when the new basic law takes effect in 2005.

•

Mathematician Louis de Branges de Bourcia of Purdue University, West Lafayette, Ind., claims to have proved the Riemann hypothesis regarding the distribution of prime numbers; the hypothesis, put forth in 1859, seems to be true but has resisted proof.

9 At the Group of Eight summit meeting in Sea Island, Ga., U.S. Pres. George W. Bush meets Ghazi Ajil al-Yawar, the new Iraqi interim president.

•

An appeals court in Turkey releases from prison four former members of the Grand National Assembly, who had spent 10 years behind bars for belonging to an illegal Kurdish party; laws seeking to repress Kurdish national and cultural expression have been repealed over the past few years.

10 The journal *Nature* publishes a report by the European Project for Ice Coring in Antarctica, which has extracted an ice core providing a climate record of the past 740,000 years; initial analysis suggests that Earth is a little less than halfway through its present interglacial warm period, which has lasted 12,000 years.

11 Pres. Joseph Kabila of the Democratic Republic of the Congo reports that his government has successfully averted a coup attempt by members of his own bodyguard.

•

Polish Pres. Aleksander Kwasniewski again nominates Marek Belka to the post of prime minister, in spite of Belka's earlier rejection by the Sejm (parliament). (*See* June 24.)

•

Pakistan reports that three days of fighting in South Waziristan, a mountainous tribal area near the Afghanistan border that government forces have attacked in an effort to root out Islamist militants affiliated with al-Qaeda, have left at least 53 people dead, with casualties on both sides.

•

A report commissioned by Republika Srpska in Bosnia and Herzegovina for the first time admits that the government of the republic had responsibility for the 1995 massacre of some 7,000 Muslims in Srebrenica.

•

The Prince of Asturias Award for Letters goes to Claudio Magris, an Italian novelist and essayist.

12 In a referendum in Ireland, voters choose to end a constitutional provision that confers Irish citizenship on any baby born in Ireland regardless of how recently the parents may have arrived.

•

In the U.S. Commonwealth of the Northern Marianas Islands, the commemoration of the 60th anniversary of the World War II Battle of Saipan and Tinian includes an exhibit of panels narrating the experiences of Chamorro and Carolinian people in World War II, showing for the first time the islanders' perspective on the battle.

13 A suicide car bomb in Baghdad, Iraq, apparently targeting a police patrol, kills at least 12 Iraqis, among them 4 policemen; also, for the second day in a row, an Iraqi ministry official is killed.

•

A truck bomb rams a convoy of foreign power-plant workers in Baghdad, Iraq, killing at least 13 people, while two other bombings elsewhere kill 8 more people.

•

Annika Sörenstam of Sweden wins the Ladies Professional Golf Association championship for the second consecutive year, defeating Ahn Shi Hyun of South Korea.

14 Maoist rebels attack two police trucks in Nepal, killing 21 policemen.

•

The pro-independence Oscar Temaru is elected president of French Polynesia.

AP/Wide World Photos

•

The Aventis Prize for popular science writing goes to American travel writer Bill Bryson for *A Short History of Nearly Everything.*

•

Denmark's Tom Kristensen, driving with Japanese driver Seiji Ara for #5 Audi Sport Japan Team Goh, wins the Le Mans 24-hour endurance race for the sixth time, equaling the record of Belgian driver Jacky Ickx.

15 Afghani Pres. Hamid Karzai and U.S. Pres. George W. Bush appear together at a press conference in Washington, D.C., where Bush declares Afghanistan a success in the war on terrorism and reaffirms U.S. commitment to democracy in Afghanistan.

•

The Detroit Pistons defeat the Los Angeles Lakers 100–87 to win the National Basketball Association championship; Chauncey Billups of the Pistons is named Most Valuable Player of the finals.

16 Scientists report that two separate teams have succeeded in teleporting atoms—that is, transferring the physical characteristics, in the form of information, of an atom to another atom and thereby making it a replica of the original atom.

•

Iranian Pres. Mohammad Khatami says that if the International Atomic Energy Agency passes a resolution criticizing Iran for lack of cooperation, Iran will no longer feel morally bound not to resume uranium enrichment, a precursor to the development of a nuclear weapons program.

•

The trial of Mikhail Khodorkovsky, former chairman of Yukos Oil and the wealthiest man in Russia, on charges of fraud and tax evasion gets under way in Moscow.

•

More than 1,000 people gather in Dublin to reenact the actions described in James Joyce's novel *Ulysses* in celebration of the centenary of Bloomsday, named for the novel's main character, Leopold Bloom.

17 A car bomb explodes outside an Iraqi army recruiting station in Baghdad, killing at least 32 Iraqis waiting to enlist and wounding well over 100.

•

In a case that has riveted and appalled Belgium since the mid-1990s, Marc Dutroux, a convicted pedophile, is found guilty of having kidnapped and repeatedly raped six girls and of having murdered an accomplice and two of the girls; his ex-wife is convicted of the murder of two of the other girls.

•

Scientists describe the findings of the Stardust spacecraft mission to Comet Wild 2 at a NASA news conference: to their astonishment, the surface of the comet's nucleus features numerous craterlike depressions, mesas and canyons, and jets of dust and gas spewing into space.

•

The annual International IMPAC Dublin Literary Award goes to *This Blinding Absence of Light;* the prize will be split between the Moroccan author, Tahar Ben Jelloun, and his translator, Linda Coverdale.

18 Leaders of the 25 members of the European Union approve a constitution for the organization that has been four years in the making; it must now be ratified by each member country.

•

The kidnapped American Paul M. Johnson is beheaded by his captors in Saudi Arabia; within hours Abdelaziz al-Muqrin, the leader of the group that claimed responsibility for this as well as other attacks on foreign workers in Saudi Arabia, is killed by Saudi security forces.

•

Japan, for the first time, approves the use of Japanese troops in a multinational peacekeeping and rebuilding force approved by the UN to work in Iraq after sovereignty is handed over to the interim Iraqi government.

19 Sudanese Pres. Omar Hassan Ahmad al-Bashir orders the complete disarming of all illegal militias, including the Janjaweed, who have been attacking black Africans in Darfur.

•

U.S. forces conduct an air strike on houses in Fallujah, Iraq, killing at least 17 people; accounts differ as to whether the targeted houses contained insurgents or civilians.

20 Algeria's official news agency reports that an offensive on the part of Algerian forces has taken out the leadership of the Salafist Group for Preaching and Combat, believed to be the biggest and best-organized Islamic terrorist group in North Africa.

•

South African golfer Retief Goosen wins the U.S. Open golf tournament by two strokes.

21 Iran seizes three British Royal Navy boats in the Shatt al-Arab, a waterway that forms part of the border between Iraq and Iran and gives access to the Persian Gulf, and arrests the eight sailors aboard the boats.

•

A private spacecraft, dubbed* SpaceShipOne, *carrying a civilian test pilot, Michael W. Melvill, is carried aloft by a specially designed aircraft,* White Knight, *released and flown on a suborbital mission to the outer edge of Earth's atmosphere, and then piloted back to Earth. (Photo right.)

•

Under investigation for corruption, John G. Rowland announces his resignation as governor of Connecticut.

•

In Barcelona, Spain, the UN High Commissioner for Refugees' 50th annual Nansen Refugee Award, for people or organizations that work on behalf of refugees, is presented to the Russian Memorial Human Rights Centre.

22 Kim Sun Il, a South Korean interpreter who had been kidnapped five days earlier near Fallujah, Iraq, is beheaded by his captors when South Korea fails to comply with their demand that it cancel a planned deployment of troops to Iraq.

•

The UN High Commissioner for Refugees opens an office in the Darfur region of The Sudan; the agency's offices in Chad are operating eight camps for refugees from the region.

•

It is reported that a large militia from the Russian republic of Chechnya conducted an overnight raid into Nazran and two other towns in the neighbouring republic of Ingushetia, killing at least 75 people and escaping with a cache of weapons.

23 At the beginning of the third round of six-

© Mike Blake/Reuters/Corbis

party talks on North Korea's nuclear program in Beijing, the U.S. proposes to North Korea a program of aid and security guarantees in return for a phasing out of its nuclear weapons development program.

•

Luis Moreno-Ocampo, the chief prosecutor of the International Criminal Court, announces that the court is opening its first investigation, into possible war crimes in the Democratic Republic of the Congo.

•

NASA scientists report that data from the *Cassini* spacecraft have confirmed that Saturn's strangely behaving farthest moon, Phoebe, is an object, possibly a comet, captured from the Kuiper belt on the outskirts of the solar system.

24 A series of apparently coordinated attacks in five cities in Iraq leaves dead at least 100 people, both Iraqis and Americans.

•

A bomb explodes on a crowded bus in Istanbul, killing 4 people and seriously injuring some 15 more; authorities believe the bomb went off prematurely while being transported to its true target.

•

Poland's Sejm (parliament) approves Marek Belka as prime minister. (*See* June 11.)

25 The UN takes military command of peacekeeping troops in Haiti, though authority was officially transferred weeks ago.

•

The Norwegian government invokes emergency laws to end an eight-day strike by oil and gas workers over pensions and job security after employers threatened a lockout that would have shut down the entire industry; the strike has contributed to escalating oil prices worldwide.

26 Pakistani Prime Minister Zafarullah Khan Jamali announces his resignation; in a move seen as orchestrated by Pres. Pervez Musharraf, Chaudry Shujaat Hussain is to be his interim replacement.

•

A bus carrying women election registration workers in Jalalabad, Afg., is blown up and two of the women killed, with 11 wounded; the bomb seems to have been set off by the driver.

27 Runoff presidential elections in Serbia result in victory for Boris Tadic, the former minister of defense for Serbia and Montenegro, over Tomislav Nikolic; Tadic is the leader of the Democratic Party and had the support of the federal government.

•

The Japanese-born dance duo Eiko and Koma are awarded the Samuel H. Scripps American Dance Festival Award, honouring lifetime achievement in contemporary dance.

28 In an unannounced low-key, secret ceremony, U.S. administrator L. Paul Bremer III dissolves the Coalition Provisional Authority, hands over power to the interim Iraqi government two days early, and flies out of the country; shortly afterward the members of the interim government are sworn in.

•

The U.S. Supreme Court rules that those deemed "enemy combatants," both in the U.S. and at Guantánamo Bay in Cuba, must be given the right to challenge the legality of their detention before a judge or other neutral party.

•

The U.S. restores direct diplomatic relations with Libya and opens a liaison office in Tripoli.

•

Parliamentary elections in Canada prove not to be as close as anticipated; Prime Minister Paul Martin emerges with a plurality but not a majority.

29 The interim government of Iraq announces that on June 30 it will take legal, though not physical, custody of ousted dictator Saddam Hussein as well as 11 of his top associates and will file charges against them.

•

South Korea's National Assembly approves the appointment of Lee Hai Chan as prime minister, replacing Goh Kun, who resigned in May.

•

The U.S. Army announces plans to activate the Individual Ready Reserve, consisting of people who were honorably discharged from the service before completing eight years of active duty.

•

A 24-hour subway strike begins at 6:30 PM in London on all 12 lines, leaving three million riders without service.

•

A Singapore Airlines Airbus A340-500 airliner lands in Newark, N.J., more than 18 hours after it took off in Singapore, ending the longest nonstop commercial flight ever made.

•

William F. Buckley formally relinquishes control of *National Review,* the influential conservative political journal that he founded in 1955.

30 New U.S. rules go into effect that drastically limit the frequency with which U.S. citizens may visit relatives in Cuba and restrict the amount of goods that can be remitted to relatives.

•

Israel's Supreme Court orders that a portion of the barrier being built to wall Israel off from the West Bank be rerouted in order to reduce the harm imposed on Palestinians living in the West Bank who have been cut off from their farmland by the barrier.

July

> *I'm sorry to disappoint science fiction fans, but if information is preserved, there is no possibility of using black holes to travel to other universes.*

cosmologist Stephen Hawking, addressing the
17th International Conference of General Relativity and Gravitation in Dublin, July 21

1 The presidency of the European Union rotates from Ireland's prime minister, Bertie Ahern, to the prime minister of The Netherlands, Jan Peter Balkenende.

•

The International Ship and Port Facility Security Code, intended to help safeguard the world's ports from terrorism, comes into force.

•

Hundreds of thousands of people demonstrate in Hong Kong, demanding greater democracy from the government of China.

•

Sir Peter Davis resigns as chairman of J Sainsbury, the oldest supermarket chain in Great Britain, as a result of a dispute over a large bonus granted to him in spite of the poor financial performance of the company.

•

The Motion Picture Association of America chooses Dan Glickman, a former secretary of agriculture and a former representative in Congress, to replace Jack Valenti as president of the organization.

•

To the astonishment of prognosticators, the Colombian club Once Caldas defeats the defending champions Boca Juniors of Argentina to win the South American association football (soccer) Libertadores Cup.

2 Outbreaks of violence leave 22 people dead in several incidents in Kashmir.

•

A rocket attack is launched against two hotels in Baghdad that housed foreign workers and journalists; three Iraqi security guards are injured.

•

After the resignation of Vladimir Spidla as prime minister of the Czech Republic, Pres. Vaclav Klaus names Stanislav Gross to the position.

•

The Cassini spacecraft returns its first close-up (from about 322,000 km [200,000 mi] away) pictures of Saturn's giant moon Titan; analysis of the photos throws into doubt many assumptions about the nature of the satellite.

3 Pres. Omar Hassan Ahmad al-Bashir of The Sudan pledges to UN Secretary-General Kofi Annan that his government will take steps to disarm the Arab Janjaweed militia and any other militias that have been attacking black Africans in the Darfur region and will send government troops to protect the displaced.

•

Russian tennis player Mariya Sharapova defeats defending champion Serena Williams of the U.S. to take the All-England (Wimbledon) women's tennis championship; the following day Roger Federer of Switzerland wins the men's title for the second consecutive year when he defeats American Andy Roddick.

4 The cornerstone of Freedom Tower is ceremonially laid at the site of the former World Trade Center in New York City; the tower is expected to be completed in 2008.

•

The team from Greece defeats the heavily favoured team from Portugal to win the UEFA association football (soccer) European Championship in Lisbon. (Photo left.)

•

In golf, American Meg Mallon wins the U.S. Women's

© Mike Finn-Kelcey/Reuters/Corbis

Open tournament in South Hadley, Mass.; Stephen Ames defeats Steve Lowery by two strokes to win the Western Open in Lemont, Ill.; and in Straffan, Ire., South African Retief Goosen wins the European Open.

5 Indonesia's first-ever direct presidential election results in no candidate's receiving a majority of votes; the top two vote getters, Susilo Bambang Yudhoyono and Pres. Megawati Sukarnoputri, will contest a runoff election. (*See* September 20.)

•

José Manuel Durão Barroso resigns as prime minister of Portugal in preparation for assuming the presidency of the European Commission.

•

An official of the African Union announces that the organization is preparing to send hundreds of troops to protect unarmed observers in the troubled Darfur region of The Sudan.

6 Iraqi Prime Minister Ayad Allawi signs a law giving him the power to declare emergency martial law anywhere in the country.

•

During the African Union summit in Addis Ababa, Eth., Pres. Teodoro Obiang Nguema Mbasogo of Equatorial Guinea and Pres. Omar Bongo of Gabon agree to conduct joint explorations for oil in Corisco Bay while UN mediators decide on the border dispute in the bay.

•

The archdiocese of Portland, Ore., files for bankruptcy protection in the face of growing claims from victims of sexual abuse at the hands of priests; it is the first Roman Catholic diocese in the U.S. to take this step.

7 The Parliament of the World's Religions meets for the fourth time since 1893, in Barcelona, Spain.

•

Charges relating to the collapse of the energy company Enron Corp. are brought against Kenneth Lay, its former chairman and CEO.

•

The painting *Young Woman Seated at the Virginals,* believed for decades to be a probable fake but recently determined to be a genuine painting by Dutch master Johannes Vermeer, is sold at auction by Sotheby's for $30 million.

8 Heinz Fischer becomes president of Austria two days after the death of his predecessor, Thomas Klestil.

9 It is reported that the number of military deaths in the U.S.-led coalition in Iraq since the invasion began in March 2003 has passed 1,000.

•

The International Court of Justice rules that most of the barrier that Israel is building to wall itself off from the West Bank violates international law because it is built on Palestinian land; it also rules that Palestinians on whose land the wall is built must be compensated.

•

In a general cabinet shake-up, Atef Ebeid resigns as prime minister of Egypt, and Pres. Hosni Mubarak chooses Ahmed Nazif to replace him.

•

In a U.S. federal court, the dominant diamond company De Beers agrees to plead guilty to charges of price fixing; the admission is expected to allow De Beers to reenter the U.S. market, from which it had departed almost 50 years ago.

•

Paul Klebnikov, the editor in chief of *Forbes Russia,* a Russian edition of the American business magazine, and an investigative journalist who had written extensively on the business climate in Russia, is shot and killed outside the magazine's offices.

10 The World Health Organization's first progress report on the so-called 3 by 5 program, intended to deliver antiretroviral treatment to three million people infected with HIV by the end of 2005, estimates that 440,000 persons worldwide are receiving treatment, about 60,000 behind target, though the organization believes it can still achieve its overall goal.

11 Boris Tadic takes office as the first president in two years of the republic of Serbia in Serbia and Montenegro.

•

The 15th International AIDS Conference opens in Bangkok, with speeches by Thai Prime Minister Thaksin Shinawatra and UN Secretary-General Kofi Annan.

12 In Serbia and Montenegro the legislature in Montenegro adopts a flag, national anthem, and statehood day.

•

Minutes before the trial is to start, the major securities company Morgan Stanley agrees to settle a sex-discrimination suit for $54 million.

13 A bomb explodes as the motorcade of Sergey Abramov, acting president of the separatist Russian republic of Chechnya, passes in Grozny.

•

Rustam Kasimjanov of Uzbekistan wins two tie-breaking matches against Michael Adams of England to win the FIDE world chess championship in Tripoli, Libya; almost all the world's top players boycotted or were banned from taking part in the tournament, however.

14 In response to threats by Iraqi insurgents that they will behead a Filipino hostage unless Philippine troops are withdrawn from Iraq earlier than planned, the Philippines begins pulling out its 51 troops.

•

A suicide car bombing at the gates of the U.S.-occupied zone in Baghdad, Iraq, kills at least 10 people, while elsewhere the governor of the province of Nineveh is assassinated.

•

Afghani Pres. Hamid Karzai issues a decree ordering severe punishments for those who fail to cooperate with the UN disarmament program or retain allegiance to private militias rather than Afghanistan's official armed forces.

•

Swedish director Ingmar Bergman announces his retirement from the theatre; his last production, for the Royal Dramatic Theatre in Sweden, was in 2002.

•

The Spanish flamenco guitarist Paco de Lucía wins the Prince of Asturias Award for the Arts.

15 Hun Sen is formally approved as Cambodia's prime minister by the National Assembly almost a year after legislative elections that gave no party a majority.

•

Officials of the World Food Programme say that the

organization has an agreement with Libya that will allow it to transport food through Libya to Sudanese refugees in the Darfur area and Chad.

•

Collapsed and disgraced energy giant Enron wins approval to emerge from bankruptcy protection as a much smaller collection of assets to be known as Primsa Energy International.

•

James F. Parker surprises industry observers by resigning as CEO of the extremely successful Southwest Airlines; he is replaced by Gary C. Kelly.

16 Amid increasing lawlessness in the Gaza Strip, Palestinian militants briefly kidnap and hold four French aid workers and two Palestinian security officials, including the chief of police; the following day the Palestinian National Security Council declares a state of emergency in Gaza.

•

In the wake of the disappearance of two computer storage devices containing classified information as well as several other security and safety lapses, all work at the Los Alamos, N.M., nuclear research facility is halted pending a thorough security review.

•

Legendary chess great Bobby Fischer is arrested in Tokyo for trying to travel on an expired passport; he has been in exile from the U.S. since his indictment on charges of violating sanctions against Yugoslavia for playing a chess match there in 1992.

•

Lifestyle entrepreneur Martha Stewart is sentenced to five months in prison and five months of house arrest, the minimum possible; she remains free pending her appeal of her conviction.

Kristine A. Strom

•

In downtown Chicago the long-awaited Millennium Park, featuring gardens, theatres, and public sculpture, has its grand opening. (Photo above.)

17 Palestinian Prime Minister Ahmad Qurei submits his resignation, but Palestinian leader Yasir Arafat refuses to accept it.

18 In a referendum in Bolivia, voters approve Pres. Carlos Mesa Gisbert's plan for development of the country's hydrocarbon reserves, which includes leaving them in the hands of foreign energy companies.

•

Iraqi Prime Minister Ayad Allawi approves a U.S. air strike against insurgents in Fallujah and reopens *Al-Hawza;* the newspaper—affiliated with rebel cleric Moktada al-Sadr—had been shut down by U.S. administrators in March.

•

Three American men—Jack Idema, Brent Bennett, and Edward Caraballo—appear in court on charges of running a private jail and acting as vigilantes in Afghanistan; the men claim to be working for the U.S. and Afghani governments, but officials of both governments deny it.

•

The relatively unknown American golfer Todd Hamilton wins the British Open tournament in Troon, Scot., defeating Ernie Els of South Africa in a four-hole play-off.

•

In the Nagoya Basho in Japan, Asashoryu defeats Kaio to win his fourth consecutive Emperor's Cup in sumo.

19 Russian Pres. Vladimir Putin dismisses Gen. Anatoly Kvashnin, chief of the general staff of armed services, and three top officials in charge of security in the Caucasus.

•

Officials of the Aredor mining company in Guinea confirm that a good-quality 182-carat diamond, four times the size of the Hope diamond, has been found.

•

India's Supreme Court rules that the $325 million compensation for the catastrophic gas leak at a Union Carbide plant in Bhopal in 1984 that killed at least 5,000 people should be paid directly to the victims rather than continue being held by the government.

•

The European Commission approves the proposed merger of the recorded-music arms of the Sony Corp. and Bertelsmann, to be called Sony BMG.

20 The UN General Assembly passes a resolution calling on Israel to obey the World Court ruling requiring it to remove the barrier being built on the West Bank.

•

Greece agrees to allow U.S. Special Forces soldiers to carry arms under NATO auspices at the Olympic Games in Athens in August.

21 The cosmologist Stephen Hawking concedes at a conference in Dublin that he lost a bet he made with the physicist John Preskill in 1997 regarding his assertion that information about matter that disappears into a black hole is destroyed when the black hole evaporates, which violates the laws of quantum physics; Hawking says he has since concluded that information can escape from a black hole.

•

A lesbian couple who married in Ontario on June 18, 2003, files for divorce; Canada's Divorce Act, however, does not take into account same-sex marriages, which are legal in several provinces.

22 After a 19-month investigation, the congressional 9/11 Commission, headed by Thomas Kean, releases its final report; it finds that the terrorist attacks on Sept. 11, 2001, "should not have come as a surprise" and that a thorough overhaul of U.S. intelligence services should be undertaken.

•

In response to the kidnapping in Iraq of three Kenyans, the government of Kenya orders all Kenyans in Iraq to leave that country.

•

A court in Germany acquits Deutsche Bank CEO Josef Ackermann and five other defendants of betraying stockholders by granting excessive bonuses to the management of the communications conglomerate Mannesmann; the court does not look kindly on the bonuses, however.

•

A merger is announced between the U.S. beer company Adolph Coors and Canada's largest brewer, Molson.

23 Celebrations including dancers, high divers, and fireworks mark the reopening of the Stari Most, the 16th-century bridge at Mostar, Bosnia and Herzegovina; rebuilding of the bridge, which had been blown up in 1993 during the civil war, made use of much the same materials and methods used by its original Ottoman Turkish builders.

•

Slavs riot in Struga, Macedonia, over a redrawing of municipal boundaries that many see as gerrymandering that will increase the power of ethnic Albanians.

•

In China 52 people are convicted of organized trafficking in babies; some are sentenced to death and others to prison.

24 A group that identifies itself as the European branch of al-Qaeda says that both Italy and Australia can expect to be attacked if they do not end their military presence in Iraq.

25 Spain's Banco Santander Central Hispano reaches an agreement to buy Great Britain's Abbey National Bank; the combined entity will be the eighth biggest bank in the world.

•

American Lance Armstrong becomes the first person to win the Tour de France six times as he coasts to his sixth consecutive victory in the bicycle race 6 min 19 sec ahead of German Andreas Klöden.

•

In an exciting game, Brazil defeats Argentina in a penalty shoot-out in Lima, Peru, to win the Copa América in association football (soccer) for the seventh time.

•

The National Baseball Hall of Fame in Cooperstown, N.Y., inducts pitcher Dennis Eckersley and hitter Paul Molitor; broadcaster Lon Simmons and sportswriter Murray Chass are honoured for their contributions to baseball.

26 In Iraq a kidnapped Egyptian diplomat is freed, two Jordanian truck drivers are kidnapped, an official of the Ministry of the Interior and two of his bodyguards are killed, two Iraqi cleaning women with British employers are killed, and three Iraqis are killed by a car bomb outside an American base.

•

Guatemalan Pres. Oscar Berger orders 1,600 soldiers into action in an attempt to combat violent crime in Guatemala City.

•

AltaVista, Lycos, Yahoo!, and Google search engines are disrupted by the latest version of the MyDoom computer worm, which queries search engines to identify valid e-mail addresses.

27 Spain announces that a joint Spanish-Moroccan peacekeeping mission will be sent to Haiti; it is the first-ever joint mission between the two countries, which have frequently been at odds.

•

In the Chilean embassy in San José, Costa Rica, a Costa Rican guard takes 10 people hostage; after hours of negotiation, police storm the embassy and find that the hostage taker has killed four people, including himself.

•

Four French citizens who have been held for more than two years at the U.S. military base in Guantánamo Bay, Cuba, are released to France, which detains them under antiterrorism laws.

28 A suicide bombing in a public square near a police station kills at least 70 people in Ba'qubah, Iraq, while fighting in south-central Iraq between insurgents and Iraqi and foreign forces leave some 42 people dead.

•

The operational director of Doctors Without Borders announces that it is withdrawing from Afghanistan, where it has provided assistance for 24 years, because of the failure of the government to prosecute those who killed five of the organization's staffers in June and because of fears for the safety of its remaining workers.

•

China opens its first Arctic research station, the Yellow River Station, on Spitsbergen in Norway.

29 Democratic Party delegates, meeting at their national convention in Boston, nominate John Kerry, senator from Massachusetts, and John Edwards, senator from North Carolina, as the party's candidates for U.S. president and vice president, respectively.

•

The U.S. Internal Revenue Service releases figures showing that personal income in the U.S. shrank for two consecutive years (2001 and 2002) for the first time since World War II, falling a total of 9.2% over the two years.

30 The UN Security Council passes a resolution demanding that The Sudan show progress in disarming and bringing to justice Arab militias in the Darfur region within 30 days or face punitive measures.

•

During a World Trade Organization meeting in Geneva that is part of the Doha Round, the U.S. and other wealthy nations agree to cut some of their farm subsidies by 20%.

•

In spite of a U.S. Supreme Court ruling that military detainees at Guantánamo Bay, Cuba, do have the right to file petitions challenging their detention, the Department of Justice rules that the detainees do not have the right to speak to their lawyers.

31 The government of Iran confirms that it has resumed building centrifuges for the purpose of enriching uranium in view of the failure of France, Germany, and the U.K. to resolve questions about Iranian compliance with the International Atomic Energy Agency.

August

These have been unforgettable dream Games. These Games were held in peace and brotherhood. These were the Games where it became increasingly difficult to cheat and where clean athletes were better protected.

IOC president Jacques Rogge
at the closing ceremonies of the XXVIII Olympiad in Athens, August 29

1 The World Trade Organization agrees that its new framework for global trade rules will include the elimination of farm subsidies in rich countries, including the U.S.

•

In Iraq, bombs explode near four Christian churches in Baghdad and one in Mosul, all during Sunday services; at least 12 people are killed.

•

U.S. government officials announce that several financial institutions in and around New York City and Washington, D.C., have been found to be in imminent danger of terrorist attack; news later emerges that the information was originally received several years previously.

•

The Warsaw Rising Museum, commemorating the 63-day rebellion against the Nazis in which 200,000 died in the summer of 1944, opens in the Polish capital. (Photo right.)

•

Karen Stupples of England defeats Rachel Teske of Australia and emerges the winner of the British Women's Open golf tournament.

2 The government of Colombia offers to create a safe haven for two rival right-wing paramilitary groups if they declare a cease-fire and begin to disarm.

3 Voters in the U.S. state of Missouri approve an amendment to the state constitution that permits only a marriage between a man and a woman to be legally recognized.

•

NASA launches the space probe Messenger, which is scheduled to enter orbit around Mercury in 2011 and spend a year collecting data.

•

U.S. Pres. George W. Bush signs a free-trade agreement with Australia.

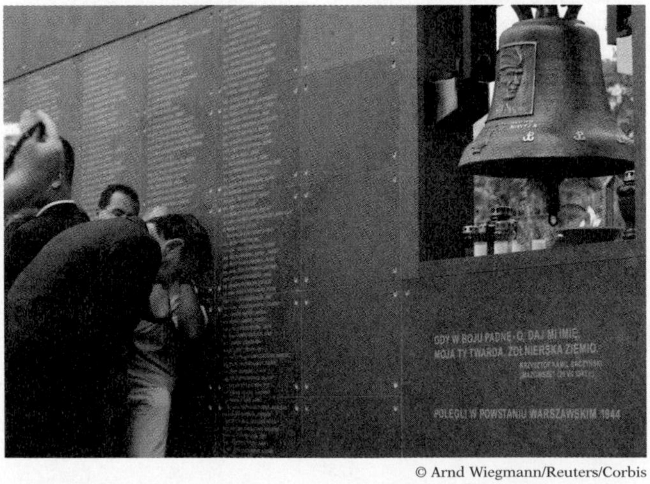

© Arnd Wiegmann/Reuters/Corbis

4 The African Union agrees to broaden its peacekeeping mission in the Darfur region of The Sudan, while tens of thousands of people in Khartoum demonstrate against the United Nations, which has threatened to take action if the ethnic cleansing does not stop.

•

Swarms of locusts, which have been devastating large areas of North Africa and West Africa, inundate Nouakchott, the capital of Mauritania. (*See* August 10.)

•

Over the objections of Spain, the inhabitants of Gibraltar celebrate 300 years of British ownership of the peninsula.

5 Israel pulls back its troops in northern Gaza and says that it will open the border checkpoint between Gaza and Egypt, where some 2,000 Palestinians have been stranded since Israel closed the crossing in mid-July.

•

The World Trade Organization issues a preliminary ruling that subsidies paid by the European Union to assist its sugar producers violate trade rules.

•

Peruvian Pres. Alejandro Toledo formally inaugurates a 731-km (462-mi) gas pipeline that links the gas field at Camisea to Lima, the capital.

6 After two days of battle in Najaf, Iraq, against forces loyal to rebel cleric Moktada al-Sadr, U.S. military spokesmen report that some 300 Iraqis have been killed.

•

An appeals court in Indonesia overturns the convictions of four of the five people found guilty of war crimes in the violence that led to the death of some 1,500 people after East Timor elected to become independent; the sentence of the fifth person is reduced.

•

The U.S. signs an agreement with Denmark and the home-rule government of Greenland to upgrade the early-warning radar system at the base at Thule, near the North Pole; the U.S. intends Thule to be part of its missile-shield plan.

•

It is reported that poachers have reduced the last known population of northern white rhinoceroses in the wild by about half, leaving no more than 22 of them in Garamba National Park in the Democratic Republic of the Congo.

7 Violent anti-Japanese protests erupt outside Worker's Stadium in Beijing after Japan defeats China 3–1 there to win the Asian Cup title in association football (soccer).

•

Windsong's Legacy, driven by Trond Smedshammer, wins the Hambletonian, the first contest in harness racing's trotting Triple Crown.

•

Iraqi Prime Minister Ayad Allawi orders the television network al-Jazeera to close its Baghdad bureau for at least a month, saying the network's coverage of kidnappings and executions has encouraged the terrorists.

•

In South Africa the New National Party, the successor to the apartheid-era ruling National Party, announces that it will dissolve itself and merge with the now-ruling African National Congress.

8 A magistrate in Iraq orders the arrest of former American protégé Ahmad Chalabi on charges of counterfeiting.

•

The Pro Football Hall of Fame in Canton, Ohio, inducts offensive tackle Bob Brown, defensive end Carl Eller, quarterback John Elway, and running back Barry Sanders.

•

A birder on Martha's Vineyard, Mass., spots what proves to be a red-footed falcon; native to Eastern Europe and West Africa, the bird has never before been seen in the Western Hemisphere.

9 The power-sharing cabinet of Côte d'Ivoire meets for the first time since opposition ministers walked out in late March, but the country remains divided in half by civil strife.

•

The bankrupt Italian dairy conglomerate Parmalat files suit against the Italian branch of Deutsche Bank, seeking to recover money it paid back to the bank on credit lines.

•

The Velebit Speleological Society announces that what is believed to be the world's deepest vertical drop has been found in a cave in the Velebit mountain range in Croatia; the drop has been measured at 516 m (1,693 ft).

10 The U.S. Department of Homeland Security announces plans to give border patrol agents power—without judicial oversight—to deport illegal aliens arriving over the borders with Mexico and Canada.

•

Election officials in Afghanistan approve a total of 18 candidates to contest the presidential election scheduled for October 9.

•

Mauritania's minister of defense makes a radio broadcast saying that during the previous week the government foiled a coup attempt by renegade soldiers.

•

Chad and Niger ask for international aid in fighting the locust infestation that threatens the area with food shortages. (*See* August 4.)

11 South Korean Prime Minister Lee Hai Chan announces that the government has chosen the Yeongi-Kongju region of South Ch'ungch'ong province as the location for the new administrative capital of the country; construction is planned to begin in 2007, with completion set for 2030. (*See* October 21.)

•

Macedonia's legislature approves a redrawing of municipal boundaries to increase the power of the Albanian minority in the country, as required by the 2001 peace agreement.

•

Residents of Pitcairn Island, a British dependency in the Pacific Ocean, are ordered to surrender their firearms by September 7; authorities are fearful that the upcoming trial of seven men on sex-crime charges could lead to violence.

•

The head of Brazil's anti-AIDS program announces that the government plans to distribute three billion free condoms annually in order to decrease the transmission of HIV/AIDS.

12 A tentative accord is reached for Mitsubishi Tokyo Financial Group, the second biggest bank in Japan, to acquire UFJ Holdings; the combined company would be the largest bank in the world.

•

Lee Hsien Loong is sworn in as the new prime minister of Singapore.

•

Gov. James E. McGreevey of New Jersey announces that he is a practicing homosexual and that he will resign from office.

•

The Vatican shuts down the Roman Catholic seminary of Sankt Pölten, Austria; in recent months the seminary had been revealed to have become a hotbed of forbidden sexual activity.

•

California's Supreme Court rules that the 4,000 same-sex marriages that took place in San Francisco in February and March are legally invalid.

•

Two bombs explode in Spain, one in downtown Santander and one at a beach in Gijón; coupled with two other bombs four days earlier, this marks the first incidence of violence by the Basque separatist group ETA (Euskadi Ta Askatasuna) since the spring.

•

Ted Kooser of Nebraska is named U.S. poet laureate.

13 Opening ceremonies for the Olympic Games thrill 75,000 spectators in Athens.

•

A refugee camp in Burundi housing ethnic Tutsi who fled from the Democratic Republic of the Congo is attacked by a Burundian Hutu militia, who kill nearly 200 of the refugees.

•

Hurricane Charley, with 233-km/hr (145-mph) winds, makes landfall in western Florida and the Punta Gorda–Port Charlotte area is devastated; a powerful typhoon makes landfall in China, leaving 115 people dead.

14 The Iraqi interim government declares that truce talks with forces loyal to rebel cleric Moktada al-Sadr have failed.

•

Government officials in Afghanistan say that battles have broken out in Herat province as its forces have invaded in an attempt to dislodge the governor and warlord Ismail Khan; 21 people have died in the fighting.

•

At a ceremony in Namibia, a German government official for the first time offers a formal apology for the massacre of some 65,000 Herero in quelling a rebellion against German rule in 1904 and describes the events as genocide.

•

At the Olympic Games in Athens, American swimmer Michael Phelps breaks his own world record in the 400-m individual medley with a time of 4 min 8.26 sec.

15 The referendum to recall Pres. Hugo Chávez in Venezuela fails; Chávez wins the right to remain in office by a wide margin in a vote that international observers certify as free and fair.

•

In rowing at the Olympic Games in Athens, both the U.S. men's and women's eights break the 2,000-m-race records.

•

Vijay Singh defeats Justin Leonard and Chris DiMarco in a three-hole play-off to win his second Professional Golfers' Association of America championship; Jane Park, age 17, wins the U.S. women's amateur golf championship.

•

Michael Schumacher wins the Hungarian Grand Prix Formula 1 auto race, a record seventh consecutive victory on the Grand Prix circuit.

16 U.S. Pres. George W. Bush announces plans to realign the deployment of U.S. troops around the world; some 70,000 troops currently stationed in Europe and Asia are expected to be moved.

•

Leonel Fernández is sworn in as president of the Dominican Republic for the second time.

•

Prince Hans-Adam II of Liechtenstein transfers day-to-day responsibility for government to his son, Crown Prince Alois, although Hans-Adam does not intend to abdicate.

•

Longtime judge and official Kalkot Mataskelekele is elected president of Vanuatu.

•

NASA scientists report that the Cassini spacecraft has discovered two previously unseen moons orbiting Saturn, bringing the total number known to 33.

17 Delegates from the national conference in Baghdad, Iraq, are turned away from Najaf by Moktada al-Sadr; they had gone to ask him to join the political process.

•

India's Supreme Court orders the reopening of 2,472 cases arising from the violence between Hindus and Muslims in Gujarat state in 2002; half the cases had been dismissed, and half had resulted in acquittals.

•

Serbia's legislature replaces its coat of arms and national anthem, which were those of Yugoslavia, with the ones it used before 1918, when it was an independent kingdom.

18 Iraq's national conference succeeds in choosing an interim national congress.

•

Maoist rebels in Nepal declare a blockade on all roads leading to Kathmandu.

•

Paul Hamm becomes the first American gymnast ever to take the Olympic gold medal in the men's all-around competition; the U.S. women's relay swim team sets a new record in the 4 × 200-m freestyle event.

19 After an unexpectedly low-priced IPO, shares of Google skyrocket on the first day of trading, making it the third richest IPO in Nasdaq history.

•

Alaska's Interagency Coordinating Center reports that wildfires have exceeded a record that has stood since 1957 for acreage destroyed; so far more than two million hectares (five million acres) have been burned, and more than 100 wildfires are still burning.

20 Mongolia's Great Hural (legislature) elects Tsakhiagiyn Elbegdorj prime minister.

•

A Chinese health official reports to a World Health Organization conference in Beijing that the strain of avian influenza that killed 23 people in Asia has been found in pigs at several farms; pigs are believed to have been the source of influenza pandemics such as the Spanish flu in 1918–19.

21 Several bombs explode at a rally for the opposition Awami League Party in Dhaka, Bangladesh; at least 19 people are killed, and the following day violence spreads to other cities.

•

At the Olympics, Belarusian runner Yuliya Nesterenko wins the gold medal in the women's 100-m sprint; the American men's swim team sets a new world record in the 4 × 100-m medley relay.

22 In Nairobi, Kenya, where peace negotiations among the warring factions in Somalia have been taking place, the Transitional Federal Assembly, Somalia's new provisional legislature, is sworn in.

•

Thieves steal *The Scream* and *Madonna,* Edvard Munch's best-known paintings, from the wall of the Munch Museum in Oslo in front of startled viewers.

•

The 45th Edward MacDowell Medal for outstanding contribution to the arts is awarded to video artist Nam June Paik at the MacDowell Colony in Peterborough, N.H.

23 Israel announces plans to expand its West Bank settlements in the Jerusalem area.

•

Controversial new rules governing who is eligible for overtime pay go into effect in the U.S.

Panama recalls its ambassador to Cuba; at issue is the treatment of four anti-Castro Cubans in prison in Panama, who Cuba fears will be pardoned.

•

The National Underground Railroad Freedom Center, a museum and learning centre, is ceremonially opened in Cincinnati, Ohio.

24 Within three minutes, two passenger planes that departed the same airfield in Moscow explode and crash, killing 90 people; the incidents are later discovered to have been the work of Chechen terrorists.

•

Police in Nairobi, Kenya, turn back Masai demonstrators attempting to march to the British High Commission to protest white ownership of land that was taken from their people during the colonial era.

•

Maoist insurgents in Nepal announce that they are lifting their blockade of Kathmandu.

25 Wealthy businessman Ferenc Gyurcsany is named to replace Peter Medgyessy as prime minister of Hungary.

•

Interim Prime Minister Chaudry Shujaat Hussain of Pakistan resigns in favour of Shaukat Aziz, who takes office three days later.

•

Sir Mark Thatcher, the son of former British prime minister Margaret Thatcher, is arrested in South Africa on suspicion of having provided financial support for a plot to overthrow the government of Equatorial Guinea in March.

•

Meeting in Tripoli, Libya, Italian Prime Minister Silvio Berlusconi and Libyan leader Muammar Qaddafi agree on measures to stop the flow of illegal immigrants from Africa through Libya.

AP/Wide World Photos

26 Hours after returning to Iraq after medical treatments abroad, Grand Ayatollah Ali al-Sistani proposes an agreement to end the fighting in Najaf; it is accepted by the interim Iraqi government and rebel cleric Moktada al-Sadr.

•

The Chiron Corp., a California-based company that manufactures influenza vaccines in a plant in Liverpool, Eng., and supplies about half of the vaccine used in the U.S., announces that it has detected contamination in its new supply; Chiron says the problem will delay delivery of flu vaccine.

27 It is reported that Enzo Baldoni, an Italian journalist working for *Diario della Settimana* who was kidnapped in Iraq while traveling to Najaf, has been beheaded by his captors.

•

Members of the Mahdi Army, loyal to rebel cleric Moktada al-Sadr, abandon the Imam Ali Shrine in Najaf to the control of Grand Ayatollah Ali al-Sistani.

•

An icon known as* Our Lady of Kazan, *first seen in the city of Kazan, Tatarstan, is returned to Aleksey II, patriarch of the Russian Orthodox Church; the icon disappeared from Russia about 1917 and had hung in the private chapel of the Roman Catholic pope since the 1970s. (Photo above.)

28 The day after a large anti-American demonstration against his proposed visit, U.S. Secretary of State Colin Powell cancels plans to attend the closing ceremonies of the Olympic Games in Athens.

•

Argentina wins the men's association football (soccer) championship at the Olympic Games as well as a gold in men's basketball, defeating Italy 84–69.

29 A car bomb explodes at the offices of an American contractor in Kabul, Afg., that provides security guards and training for the Afghan police force; at least seven people are killed.

•

The Games of the XXVIII Olympiad close in Athens.

•

The Pabao Little League team from Willemstad, Curaçao, Netherlands Antilles, becomes the first team from the Caribbean to win the Little League World Series when it defeats the Conejo Valley Little League team from Thousand Oaks, Calif., 5–2.

30 The UN-imposed deadline for The Sudan to begin credibly disarming the Arab Janjawid militia in the Darfur region passes without significant progress.

31 A suicide bomber blows herself up outside a subway station in Moscow, killing at least 9 people and injuring 50; responsibility is claimed by a Chechen group.

•

Cambodia joins the World Trade Organization.

•

The UN Convention on the International Trade in Endangered Species of Wild Fauna and Flora bans exports of caviar from countries bordering the Caspian Sea, as the countries have not complied with a 2001 agreement to protect sturgeon stocks.

September

We are dealing with the direct intervention of international terror against Russia, with total and full-scale war. . . . In these conditions, we simply cannot, we should not, live as carelessly as before.

Russian Pres. Vladimir Putin on September 4, addressing the country after viewing the carnage at Middle School No. 1 in Beslan, North Ossetia

1 At the Republican national convention in New York City, U.S. Pres. George W. Bush and Vice Pres. Richard Cheney are nominated as the party's candidates in the upcoming presidential election in November.

•

On the first day of school at Middle School No. 1, serving students from ages 6 to 16 in Beslan, North Ossetia, Russia, some 30 terrorists invade the school and take all 1,200 people inside hostage, rigging the building with explosives.

•

Millions of Sikhs, including Prime Minister Manmohan Singh, gather in their holy city of Amritsar in northern India to celebrate the 400th anniversary of their scripture, the Adi Granth.

•

Martin Torrijos is sworn in as president of Panama shortly after his predecessor, Mireya Moscoso, pardoned four Cuban exiles accused of plotting to assassinate Cuban Pres. Fidel Castro, which led both Cuba and Venezuela to break diplomatic relations with Panama.

2 On the first day of the new school year in France, the controversial ban on the wearing of religious symbols in school, including head scarves by Muslim girls, goes into effect, although two French reporters have been kidnapped in Iraq and their captors threaten to behead them if the ban is not repealed.

•

Junichiro Koizumi becomes the first sitting Japanese prime minister to travel to see the Kuril Islands—known in Japan as the Northern Territories and owned by Russia—since the end of World War II.

•

Malaysia's High Court overturns the conviction of former deputy prime minister Anwar Ibrahim on sodomy charges, and he is released from custody.

•

The judges in the UN war crimes tribunal trying former Yugoslav president Slobodan Milosevic revoke his right to conduct his own defense, imposing on him the two British lawyers who had been his assigned advisers heretofore.

3 In Middle School No. 1 in Beslan, North Ossetia, Russia, two explosions lead to a gun battle that ends the hostage siege; at least 330 people, mostly students, teachers, and parents, are killed.

•

Lebanon's parliament passes an amendment to the constitution extending the term of the president by three years, a move dictated by Syria but opposed by all segments of society in Lebanon.

4 In the worst of several attacks in Iraq, a car bomb kills at least 17 people, 14 of them policemen, outside a police academy in Kirkuk.

•

The huge and slow-moving Hurricane Frances makes landfall in Florida, working its way across the state over the next two days.

5 Two earthquakes with magnitudes of 6.9 and 7.3 shake sparsely populated areas of western Japan; the following day a strong typhoon hits Japan.

•

The inaugural Rally of Japan automobile race, in Tokachi, Hokkaido, is won by reigning world champion Norwegian Petter Solberg driving a Subaru.

6 Former U.S. president Bill Clinton undergoes a quadruple coronary artery bypass operation.

•

Vijay Singh of Fiji surpasses Tiger Woods to become the top golfer in the World Golf Ranking with his win in the Deutsche Bank championship.

7 NASA officials report that Hurricane Frances caused major damage to several Kennedy Space Center buildings at Cape Canaveral, Florida, in particular the hangar in which space shuttles are prepared for flight.

•

Hurricane Ivan lays waste to Grenada, leaving half the population homeless, destroying the cocoa and nutmeg crops, and killing at least 39 people.

© Reuters TV/Reuters/Corbis

8 Families of victims of the Washington-area sniper attacks in 2002 win a large settlement with the manufacturer and dealer of the gun used in the attacks; it is the third time (all in the past few months) that a gun dealer has paid for allowing a gun to fall into the hands of a criminal and the first time that a manufacturer has paid for such negligence.

•

NASA's Genesis space capsule, which spent more than two years collecting samples of the solar wind, returns to Earth as scheduled, but its parachutes fail to deploy and it crashes into the ground at Dugway Proving Ground, Utah. (Photo above.)

9 Costa Rica withdraws from the U.S.-led coalition for Iraq after a court ruling that such inclusion violates a constitutional prohibition against military action not authorized by the UN.

•

Al-Muhtadee Billah Bolkiah, crown prince of Brunei, marries Sarah Salleh, the 17-year-old daughter of a Bruneian and a European, in an opulent ceremony in Bandar Seri Begawan.

•

A car bomb explodes outside the Australian embassy in Jakarta, Indon.; at least nine people, all Indonesian, are killed.

•

U.S. Secretary of State Colin Powell says that he has concluded that genocide has taken place and may continue to take place in the Darfur region of The Sudan; it is the first time that a member of the administration in the U.S. has applied the term in this situation.

10 Hurricane Ivan reaches Jamaica, roaring along the southern coast during the night and next morning and leaving at least 15 people dead; though Kingston is hit hard, a change of course by the storm spares the island a direct hit.

•

The embattled CEO of Walt Disney Co., Michael Eisner, announces that he will retire at the end of his contract, in September 2006.

11 A helicopter carrying a religious delegation headed by Patriarch Petros VII of Alexandria, Egypt, head of the Greek Orthodox Church in Africa, from Athens to the monastery of Mt. Athos in Greece crashes shortly before its scheduled landing, killing all 12 on board.

•

In an unusually bold move, Afghanistan's interim government removes longstanding warlord Ismail Khan as governor of Herat.

•

Svetlana Kuznetsova of Russia defeats her countrywoman Yelena Dementyeva to win the U.S. Open tennis championship; the following day Roger Federer of Switzerland defeats Lleyton Hewitt of Australia to win the men's tournament and become the first man to win three Grand Slam titles in a single year since 1988.

12 A series of mortar attacks and suicide bombings throughout Baghdad, Iraq, leave at least 25 people dead in the city, with some 34 others being killed elsewhere in the country.

•

US Airways files for bankruptcy protection for the second time; it previously filed in August 2002.

•

Rubens Barrichello of Brazil wins the Italian Grand Prix; his Ferrari teammate Michael Schumacher of Germany comes in second.

13 Russian Pres. Vladimir Putin demands enormous changes to the country's political system, including an end to the popular election of governors and the placement of congressional elections on national party slates rather than district lists.

•

The 1994 ban on the private ownership of military-style assault weapons in the U.S. is allowed to lapse without a vote in Congress.

•

A consortium with Sony Corp. of America at its head and including the cable company Comcast reaches an agreement to buy the movie studio Metro-Goldwyn-Mayer, shortly before it was to have been sold to Time Warner.

•

U.S. Secretary of the Interior Gale Norton signs documents turning the Great Sand Dunes National Monument in the Sangre de Cristo Mountains in Colorado into the Great Sand Dunes National Park, with increased acreage and resources.

•

In Ontario province the first divorce of a same-sex couple is granted.

14 A suicide car bomb kills at least 47 people outside a police station in Baghdad, Iraq, many of them waiting to apply for jobs; 12 other people, 11 of them Iraqi police, are killed in an ambush in Ba'qubah.

•

Canada defeats Finland 3–2 to win the ice hockey World Cup in Toronto.

15 Hurricane Ivan achieves category 4 strength and makes landfall on the Gulf Coast of the U.S., and Alabama, Florida, Louisiana, and Mississippi declare states of emergency; by the end of the following day, at least 23 people have lost their lives.

•

Iceland's Foreign Minister Halldór Ásgrímsson and Prime Minister Davíd Oddsson exchange jobs.

16 Peace talks between leaders of the Protestant and Roman Catholic factions in Northern Ireland open in Leeds Castle in England with an eye toward reviving the power-sharing government.

•

South Africa announces that it has opened full diplomatic relations with Western Sahara, which is nominally under Moroccan administration.

•

Karen Kain, who was the prima ballerina of the National Ballet of Canada before her retirement in 1997, is named chairman of the Canada Council for the Arts.

17 In Mexico City, Mexican Pres. Vicente Fox and Japanese Prime Minister Junichiro Koizumi sign a free-trade agreement.

•

Argentine Pres. Néstor Kirchner surprises analysts by sacking Alfonso Prat-Gay as head of the country's central bank, replacing him with Martín Redrado, and making other personnel changes as well.

18 Flooding caused by Tropical Storm Jeanne leaves at least 1,500 people dead in Haiti, most of them in and around Gonaïves.

•

The International Atomic Energy Agency adopts a resolution calling on Iran to stop enriching uranium; the following day Iran announces its refusal to do so.

•

In the worst of several attacks around the country, a suicide car bomb kills 19 people when it explodes within a group of people looking for work with the Iraqi National Guard in Kirkuk.

•

Bernard Hopkins defeats Oscar de la Hoya by knockout in the ninth round to retain the undisputed world middleweight boxing championship in Las Vegas, Nev.

•

Miss Alabama, Deidre Downs, wins the title of Miss America in Atlantic City, N.J.; on October 20 ABC TV announces that it will no longer broadcast the Miss America Pageant, which imperils the survival of the annual gala.

19 Chinese Pres. Hu Jintao succeeds Jiang Zemin as head of the country's military and in an unusually orderly transition thereby becomes leader of the country in fact as well as name.

AP/Wide World Photos

•

After cutting a swathe of destruction through the Caribbean, the remnants of Hurricane Ivan cause flooding in southern Pennsylvania that leaves six people dead.

•

At the IAAF World Athletics Final in Monte-Carlo, the Athletes of the Year are distance runner Kenenisa Bekele of Ethiopia and pole-vaulter Yelena Isinbayeva of Russia. (Photo above.)

•

In golf's Ryder Cup competition, Europe defeats the U.S. with a record-breaking 18.5–9.5 margin of victory.

•

The Emmy Awards are presented in Los Angeles; winners include the television shows *Arrested Development* and *The Sopranos,* the miniseries *Angels in America,* and the actors Kelsey Grammer, James Spader, Sarah Jessica Parker, Allison Janney, David Hyde Pierce, Michael Imperioli, Cynthia Nixon, and Drea de Matteo.

20 Susilo Bambang Yudhoyono handily defeats Megawati Sukarnoputri in runoff presidential elections in Indonesia.

•

U.S. Pres. George W. Bush ends all economic sanctions against Libya, and two days later the European Union follows suit.

•

The first criminal trial resulting from the meltdown of Enron Corp. opens in Houston, Texas.

•

A new Pendolino tilting train makes the trip from London to Manchester, Eng., in a record one hour and 53 minutes, 15 minutes faster than the previous record.

21 U.S. Pres. George W. Bush addresses the UN General Assembly, pushing for the advancement of democracy to counter terrorism and defending the war in Iraq as doing the UN's work, though the war was not sanctioned by the UN.

•

The National Museum of the American Indian opens on the National Mall in Washington, D.C.

•

In New York City, the Dance Theater of Harlem announces that it is laying off all its dancers through the end of its fiscal year in June 2005.

22 The U.S. Securities and Exchange Commission opens an investigation into the activities of the mortgage backer Fannie Mae.

•

Interstate Bakeries, maker of Hostess products and Wonder bread, files for bankruptcy protection.

•

It is reported that China has for the first time set out fuel-economy rules for automobiles in an attempt to lessen its dependence on foreign supplies of oil.

23 A racketeering case against the tobacco industry in the U.S. begins, with attorneys for the U.S. government declaring that for 50 years the industry hid what it knew about the link between cancer and smoking.

•

Olusegun Obasanjo, president of Nigeria and head of the African Union, says that the AU intends to send some 4,000 peacekeeping troops to the Darfur region of The Sudan early in October in response to a UN Security Council resolution.

•

The Oxford Dictionary of National Biography, 60 volumes with nearly 55,000 subjects and the first complete reworking of Great Britain's famous *DNB* since its original publication in 1885–1900, is released to the public.

24 Porter Goss, a former U.S. representative from Florida, becomes director of the Central Intelligence Agency two days after his confirmation in the post by the U.S. Senate.

•

State regulators in California approve a plan to reduce vehicle emissions of greenhouse gases greatly over the next 11 years; California is by far the biggest automobile market in the United States.

25 Hurricane Jeanne makes landfall in Florida; this is the fourth hurricane to hit the state since August.

•

In Iraq an ambush kills seven men applying for jobs with the Iraqi National Guard in Baghdad, and the U.S. conducts an air strike in Fallujah.

•

The Port Adelaide Power wins its first Australian Football League championship, defeating the defending Brisbane Lions 17.11 (113)–10.13 (73).

26 In a victory for the anti-immigration Swiss People's Party, voters in Switzerland reject a proposal that would have made it easier for Swiss-born children of immigrants to acquire Swiss passports and another that would have given passports automatically to third-generation immigrants in Switzerland.

•

A major revision of Turkey's penal code is passed by the parliament; the changes are intended to enhance Turkey's prospects of becoming a member of the European Union.

•

The winners of the 2004 Albert Lasker Medical Research Awards are announced; they are Elwood V. Jensen, Pierre Chambon, and Ronald M. Evans for their work uncovering molecular mechanisms by which hormones exert their effects on cells; Charles D. Kelman (who is the first to receive the award posthumously) for developing the standard in cataract and other eye surgery; and Matthew S. Meselson for his discoveries about DNA and for his efforts to eliminate chemical and biological weapons.

•

Amjad Hussain Farooqi—the man who is believed to have been behind the two assassination attempts against Pakistani Pres. Pervez Musharraf and is also thought to have been involved in the killing of American reporter Daniel Pearl—is killed by Pakistani law enforcement.

•

In Formula 1 auto racing, Rubens Barrichello of Brazil, driving for Ferrari, wins the inaugural Grand Prix of China race.

27 Hundreds of UN peacekeepers are sent to flood-ravaged Gonaïves, Haiti, to try to restore order so food can be distributed; some 300,000 people were left homeless by the flooding.

•

The mortgage backer Fannie Mae agrees after negotiations with its federal regulator to reform its accounting and management practices, which have made the company appear to be in better shape than it is and have made top executives wealthy.

•

Plácido Domingo announces that James Conlon will become music director of the Los Angeles Opera in summer 2006, replacing Kent Nagano.

•

Sir Richard Branson announces plans to form a company called Virgin Galactic that will sell suborbital rocket rides beginning in 2007.

•

The television network NBC announces that Conan O'Brien, host of *Late Night,* will succeed Jay Leno as the host of *The Tonight Show* in 2009.

28 In Cuzco, Peru, 20 foreign tourists who were kidnapped by coca growers who want the government to end coca-eradication efforts are freed by Peruvian authorities.

•

Health officials in Thailand report on a possible case of human-to-human transmission of A (H5N1) avian influenza; a woman who died of the disease had had no known contact with birds but visited her daughter, who worked with chickens, in the hospital when the daughter was dying of the disease.

•

A magnitude-6 earthquake takes place in rural Parkfield, Calif., which sits on the San Andreas Fault; the last earthquake there was in 1966.

29 A U.S. federal judge rules that a section of the USA PATRIOT Act that permits the government to order an Internet service provider to turn over personal information about subscribers and not notify anyone that it has received the order is in violation of the Constitution.

•

In Yemen two men are sentenced to death for the attack on the USS *Cole* in 2000, and four others are sentenced to a maximum of 10 years in prison.

•

Hungary's legislature elects Ferenc Gyurcsany prime minister.

•

In New Zealand the trial of seven men from Pitcairn Island on numerous sex-abuse charges begins; the defendants make up nearly half the adult male population of Pitcairn.

•

Bud Selig, commissioner of Major League Baseball, announces that the Montreal Expos team will move to Washington, D.C., next season; Washington has been without a baseball team since 1971.

•

The Cendant Corp., owner of Avis car rental and Days Inn motels, agrees to buy Orbitz, the online travel service that was created by a consortium of airlines in 2000.

•

The dumbbell-shaped asteroid Toutatis passes within 1.5 million km (1 million mi) of Earth; it is the largest known asteroid—about five kilometres (three miles) long—to have come close to the planet since astronomers developed the means to track them accurately.

30 Israeli security forces move into a refugee camp in northern Gaza; in the ensuing battle at least 28 Palestinians and 3 Israelis are killed; it is the highest death toll in two years.

•

At a celebration for the opening of a new sewage plant in Baghdad, Iraq, two car bombs kill at least 41 Iraqis, the vast majority of them children gathered to receive candy from U.S. soldiers.

•

With Russia's endorsement of the Kyoto Protocol on global warming, it becomes possible for the agreement to take effect.

•

The pharmaceutical company Merck withdraws its extremely popular prescription pain and arthritis medicine Vioxx from the worldwide market after having found in testing for a further use that it increases the risk of heart attack and stroke.

•

Jazz at Lincoln Center in New York City announces the induction of the first 14 people into the Ertegun Jazz Hall of Fame, which will open to the public on October 21; they include Louis Armstrong, Bix Beiderbecke, Miles Davis, and Charlie Parker.

October

Indonesia will be a democratic country, open, modern, pluralistic, and tolerant.

Indonesian Pres. Susilo Bambang Yudhoyono, at his inauguration, October 20

1 ***Some 5,000 U.S. and Iraqi troops begin a major battle to retake the Iraqi city of Samarra' from insurgent forces; they regain control of the city on October 3. (Photo right.)***

•

A bomb explodes in a Shi'ite mosque in Sialkot, Pak., as worshippers attend the Friday sermon; at least 23 people are killed.

•

The World Health Organization announces a campaign to immunize more than 80 million children in 23 countries in Africa against polio, its largest such project to date.

•

Seattle Mariners slugger Ichiro Suzuki sets a new record for the number of hits in a single baseball season with his 258th hit; the previous record was set by George Sisler of the St. Louis Browns in 1920.

2 Three bombs explode in the town of Dimapur in the Indian state of Nagaland, killing 26 people, while bombs and gunfire in attacks by separatists in Assam state leave 19 people dead.

•

Violence continues for a third straight day in Port-au-Prince, Haiti; the death toll so far is seven.

3 Parliamentary elections in Slovenia lead to a surprising victory for the opposition Slovenian Democratic Party.

•

Pope John Paul II beatifies five people, among them Charles, the last emperor of Austria-Hungary, whose reign coincided with the end of World War I and concluded with the dissolution of the kingdom.

4 Two car bombs in downtown Baghdad and one in Mosul leave at least 26 people dead in Iraq.

•

Cambodia's lower house of parliament ratifies an agreement made in 2003 with the United Nations to form a tribunal to try Khmer Rouge figures for atrocities committed during the late 1970s; this was considered the last major obstacle to the formation of a tribunal.

•

The Nobel Prize for Physiology or Medicine is awarded to Americans Richard Axel and Linda B. Buck for their work in unraveling the workings of the human olfactory system.

•

The private rocket ship SpaceShipOne achieves an altitude of 112.17 km (about 70 mi) and safely returns to Earth in the Mojave Desert in California, thus exceeding 100 km twice within a week and winning the $10 million Ansari X Prize.

5 In Stockholm the Nobel Prize for Physics is awarded to three Americans—David J. Gross, H. David Politzer, and Frank Wilczek—for their work in investigating the strong force, which binds quarks in the atomic nucleus; their discoveries led to the theory of quantum chromodynamics.

•

U.S. health officials announce that British authorities have suspended the license of the Liverpool laboratory of Chiron Corp.

because of contamination discovered in August; the lab manufactures about half of the American supply of vaccine against influenza.

•

Niger produces its first gold bar, from a mine in a goldfield discovered some 15 years earlier, in a ceremony attended by Pres. Tandja Mamadou; it is expected that the mine will produce 5,000 oz of gold annually for the next six years.

6 The Nobel Prize for Chemistry is awarded to two Israelis, Aaron Ciechanover and Avram Hershko, and American Irwin Rose for their discovery of the chemical process by which cells mark proteins for degradation.

•

The European Commission rules that Turkey has met the criteria for talks to begin about Turkey's becoming a member of the EU.

•

Syndicated radio personality Howard Stern announces that he has signed a deal to begin working in January 2006 for Sirius Satellite Radio, a pay-based satellite service that is not regulated by the U.S. Federal Communications Commission.

7 King Norodom Sihanouk abdicates the throne of Cambodia, citing ill health and asking that a council be formed to select the next king.

•

At a rally of Sunni Muslims in Multan, Pak., two bombs go off, killing at least 39 people.

•

Three resorts popular with Israeli tourists in the southeastern Sinai Peninsula in Egypt are destroyed by bombs, and at least 33 people are left dead.

•

The Nobel Prize for Literature is awarded to Elfriede Jelinek of Austria.

•

Italian Prime Minister Silvio Berlusconi visits Tripoli, Libya, to join Libyan leader Muammar al-Qaddafi in opening an oil pipeline between the countries and to discuss with him the curbing of illegal immigration of Africans through Libya to Italy.

•

The quadrennial Bishops' Council of the Russian Orthodox Church announces plans for bilateral talks aimed at unifying the Russian Orthodox Church and the Russian Orthodox Church Outside of Russia, based in the U.S.

8 The Nobel Peace Prize is awarded to Kenyan environmentalist Wangari Maathai; the committee cites her work combining science with social engagement and politics.

•

News organizations receive a video showing the beheading of British engineer Kenneth Bigley, who had been kidnapped in Iraq the previous month; he is the first British hostage to be executed in Iraq.

•

Miguel Angel Rodríguez resigns as secretary-general of the Organization of American States (OAS) after being accused of having accepted bribes when he was president (1998–2002) of Costa Rica. (*See* October 21.)

•

The Council on Tall Buildings and Urban Habitat formally certifies the skyscraper Taipei 101, in Taiwan, as the tallest building in the world; it is 56 m (184 ft) taller than Petronas Towers, in Kuala Lumpur, Malaysia, previously the tallest building. (*See* April 15.)

9 Afghanistan's presidential election takes place peacefully; it is expected to be several weeks before the votes are tallied. Hamid Karzai is officially declared to be the winner on November 3.

•

In parliamentary elections in Australia, Prime Minister John Howard's Liberal Party wins decisively.

•

With his win in two straight heats of the Kentucky Futurity, Windsong's Legacy becomes the first horse to win the Trotting Triple Crown since 1972.

10 A suicide bomber kills himself and at least three others outside a Shi'ite mosque in Lahore, Pak.

•

Meeting in Kenya, Somalia's transitional parliament elects Abdullahi Yusuf Ahmed the interim president of the war-torn country; he takes office on October 14.

11 Members of rebel Shi'ite cleric Moktada al-Sadr's Mahdi Army begin surrendering their weapons, in accordance with an agreement made between the group and the Iraqi government and U.S. military commanders in Baghdad, Iraq.

•

The European Union lifts sanctions, including an arms embargo, against Libya.

•

Paul Biya is reelected president of Cameroon in elections that are viewed as flawed but credible.

•

The Nobel Memorial Prize in Economic Sciences goes to Norwegian Finn Kydland and American Edward Prescott.

12 For the first time, the Romanian government admits that Romania took part in the Holocaust during World War II and concedes that some 240,000 Jews died at that time in Romania.

•

In Japan authorities find nine people in two separate vehicles who have committed suicide together; it is believed that the participants met each other and planned their deaths in chat rooms on the Web.

•

The U.S. Federal Communications Commission fines 169 Fox television channels a total of $1.18 million for having aired an episode of *Married by America* that the commission felt was too sexually suggestive.

13 Daiei, the Japanese discount supermarket and retailing chain, agrees to accept a government bailout; Daiei epitomizes the troubles Japanese banks have had with bad loans.

•

The Seattle Storm defeats the Connecticut Sun 74–60 to win the Women's National Basketball Association championship, in Seattle, Wash., two games to one.

•

The official beginning of the National Hockey League season passes without any games' being played; a lockout of the players' union by the owners has continued for almost a month.

14 A throne council in Cambodia chooses Norodom Sihamoni, a son of King Norodom Sihanouk, to succeed his father as king.

•

In Beijing, Russian Pres. Vladimir Putin and Chinese Pres. Hu Jintao sign an agreement demarcating the 4,345-km (2,700-mi) border between Russia and China for the first time.

•

Astronauts Leroy Chiao of the U.S. and Salizhan Sharipov of Russia, escorted by Yury Shargin, blast off from the Baikonur Cosmodrone in Kazakhstan; Chiao and Sharipov will replace American Mike Fincke and Russian Gennady Padalka as the crew of the International Space Station.

15 Muslims around the world begin observations of the holy month of Ramadan.

•

The High Court in Harare, Zimb., acquits political opposition leader Morgan Tsvangirai of treason charges.

16 Israeli military forces complete a redeployment from built-up areas of the Gaza Strip to hills overlooking the major refugee camps.

•

Bombs explode in five Christian churches in Baghdad, Iraq, causing damage but no casualties.

•

The Royal Institute of British Architects announces that the Stirling Prize for 2004 goes to Norman Foster for the London skyscraper 30 St. Mary Axe.

•

Italian cyclist Paolo Bettini, after a 28th place showing in the Tour of Lombardy, becomes the only person ever to win the World Cup of cycling three times despite not having won a single race.

17 In a blatantly manipulated referendum in Belarus, an amendment to the constitution allowing the president to seek an unlimited number of terms in office is passed, and in legislative elections supporters of Pres. Alyaksandr Lukashenka win every seat.

•

The first UN peacekeepers from China ever deployed in the Western Hemisphere arrive in Haiti; Haitian interim prime minister Gérard Latortue publicly accuses deposed president Jean-Bertrand Aristide of orchestrating the violence in Haiti from his exile in South Africa.

•

Russia opens its largest military base outside its own territory, in Tajikistan; some 5,000 soldiers and an air force unit will be stationed there.

•

French driver Sébastien Loeb clinches the world rally championship with two races to go when he comes in second at the Rally of Corsica, behind Markko Märtin of Estonia.

18 A roadside explosion kills five people, one of them an election official, in an election commission jeep in southeastern Afghanistan.

•

The notorious bandit Veerappan, thought to have killed more than 100 people, is killed in a shootout with police in India.

•

The Lambeth Commission, convened by Rowan Williams, archbishop of Canterbury, issues a report calling on the Episcopal Church USA to refrain from ordaining gay clergy and blessing gay unions and to express regret for the difficulties taking these actions has caused within the Anglican Communion.

•

By tying with Peter Leko of Hungary in a chess match in Brissago, Switz., Vladimir Kramnik of Russia retains the classic world chess champion title and the right to play the winner of the Fédération Internationale des Échecs match scheduled for January 2005; chess authorities are trying to reunify the world chess championship.

19 Myanmar (Burma) announces that Soe Win has replaced Khin Nyunt as prime minister.

•

Opposition leader Anatoly V. Lebedko is arrested and beaten on the second night of demonstrations against official, but widely disbelieved, election results in Belarus.

•

Margaret Hassan, the British-Iraqi head of the relief organization CARE International and a 30-year resident of Iraq, is kidnapped in Baghdad.

•

The Man Booker Prize for Fiction goes to British writer Alan Hollinghurst for his novel *The Line of Beauty.*

•

Scientists and European heads of state gather in Geneva to celebrate the 50th anniversary of the establishment of CERN, the European Organization for Nuclear Research.

20 Susilo Bambang Yudhoyono is inaugurated as Indonesia's first directly elected president.

•

Rafiq al-Hariri resigns as prime minister of Lebanon; the following day the pro-Syrian Omar Karami is named to replace him.

•

A record 10th typhoon for the season hits Japan, leaving at least 77 dead in addition to the more than 102 people killed by the previous 9 typhoons; Japan's storm records go back to 1551.

21 South Korea's constitutional court rules that the plan to move the country's capital is illegal; either a national referendum or an amendment to the constitution would be required in order to make the move. (*See* August 11.)

•

Authorities in Costa Rica arrest Rafael Angel Calderón on charges of having accepted bribes during his presidency (1990–94) of the country. (*See* October 8.)

•

The Court of Arbitration for Sport rules that American Paul Hamm retains his Olympic gold medal in the men's all-around gymnastics competition in spite of the fact that judges had wrongly deducted a tenth of a point from the score of South Korean competitor Yang Tae Young.

•

Trump Hotels and Casino Resorts, Inc., announces that it has reached a preliminary debt-restructuring agreement that may make it possible for the company to avoid having to file for bankruptcy.

22 A gargantuan mosque opens in the village of Kipchak, the birthplace of Turkmenistan's Pres. Saparmurat Niyazov; in part a monument to Niyazov, the structure features inscriptions from his writings as well as from the Qu'ran.

•

Avianca Airlines, the national carrier of Colombia, reaches a settlement with the U.S. Department of Justice, which believes that the airline knowingly allowed itself to be used to transport cocaine and heroin; a monitoring agency selected by U.S. authorities will henceforth be allowed to inspect cargo loaded onto U.S.-bound planes.

23 Legislative elections in the UN-administered area of Kosovo in Serbia and Montenegro are boycotted by Serbs, who fear participating will aid ethnic Albanians in making the area independent.

Insurgents dressed as police officers ambush and kill some 50 newly trained members of the Iraqi National Guard.

In Rio Grande, P.R., Sweden wins the 2004 women's world amateur team championship in golf.

24 The U.S. government acknowledges that some 380 tons of explosives disappeared from a facility called al-Qaqaa in Iraq some time after the 2003 U.S.-led invasion.

Israel's cabinet approves a formula for the financial compensation of Israeli settlers to be removed from the Gaza Strip under Prime Minister Ariel Sharon's plan.

25 International Steel Group Inc., the biggest U.S. steel manufacturer, announces a complex transaction in which it will be acquired by a Dutch company controlled by Lakshmi Mittal to form a new company, Mittal Steel Co. NV, which will be the largest steel concern in the world.

Jeffrey W. Greenberg resigns as chairman and CEO of Marsh & McLennan Co., the world's biggest insurance broker, in the wake of a suit brought by New York Attorney General Eliot Spitzer for false dealing.

The Seibu Lions defeat the Chunichi Dragons 7–2 in the decisive game seven to win the Japan Series baseball championship.

The seventh annual Mark Twain Prize for American Humor is presented to Lorne Michaels, the creator and producer of the television show *Saturday Night Live,* in a ceremony at the John F. Kennedy Center for the Performing Arts in Washington, D.C.

In France, Pink TV, a gay and lesbian cable- and satellite-television channel, begins broadcasting.

26 The Cassini spacecraft passes within 1,172 km (728 mi) of Saturn's largest moon, Titan, and returns close-up pictures and radar data to Earth.

Officials in Thailand reveal that at least 78 people of the more than 1,300 arrested during a ruthlessly suppressed demonstration in heavily Muslim Narathiwat province died of suffocation while being transported in trucks to a military barracks.

In a crucial vote, the Israeli Knesset (legislature) approves Prime Minister Ariel Sharon's proposal to remove all Israeli settlements from the Gaza Strip

27 The Federation Council, the upper house of Russia's legislature, votes to ratify the Kyoto Protocol, a treaty to limit greenhouse-gas emissions, five days after the State Duma, the lower house, approved it.

The Boston Red Sox defeat the St. Louis Cardinals 3–0 in St. Louis, Mo., in the fourth game of the World Series to sweep the Major League Baseball championship; it is the first World Series championship win for the Sox since 1918.

With a ceremonial reenactment and other displays, New York City celebrates the centennial of its subway.

28 The defection of a coalition partner causes the government of Latvia to collapse; Prime Minister Indulis Emsis resigns.

The journal *Nature* publishes a report revealing the astonishing discovery on the Indonesian island of Flores of what appears to be a population of miniaturized hominids, named *Homo floresiensis,* approximately a metre (3.3 ft) in height, who lived there as recently as 18,000 years ago.

Palestinian officials announce that Yasir Arafat will be flown to Paris the following day to be hospitalized; the nature and severity of his illness is unclear.

29 ***Norodom Sihamoni is crowned king of Cambodia in a traditional Buddhist ceremony that includes a bathing in nine jars of holy water. (Photo right.)***

The leaders of the countries of the European Union ceremonially sign the new EU constitution.

The television network al-Jazeera broadcasts a videotape of al-Qaeda leader Osama bin Laden addressing the U.S. to warn against interference in Muslim affairs; it is the first videotape from bin Laden since Sept. 10, 2003.

On Pitcairn Island sentences ranging from community service to six years in prison are pronounced for six men convicted of various sexual assaults over a period of 40 years; the sentences, issued by judges from New Zealand, are suspended pending an appeal of jurisdiction. (*See* September 29.)

30 One car bomb kills eight U.S. Marines near Abu Ghraib prison, outside Baghdad, Iraq, and another kills seven people outside the Baghdad offices of the television network al-Arabiyah.

Portions of a four-year study commissioned by the Arctic Council are made public; it says that climate warming in the Arctic is driven by greenhouse-gas emissions and is accelerating.

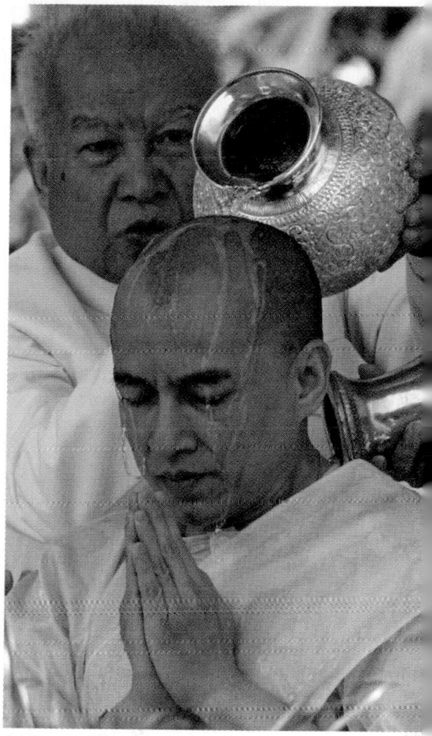

© Adrees Latif/Reuters/Corbis

31 Tabaré Vázquez of the Socialist Party wins the presidential election in Uruguay.

A highly contentious presidential election in Ukraine, with 24 candidates, results in the need for a runoff between Viktor Yushchenko and Viktor Yanukovych.

After two days of fighting in Henan province in China between ethnic Han and Muslim Hui, martial law is declared; the fighting, which was touched off by a traffic accident, has resulted in some 150 deaths.

November

I feel awful, it's horrible. First it was euphoria, and now the people are yelling in the streets. . . . You see, they have let this genie out of the bottle.

Oleksandra Ruzhel, a member of Ukrainian presidential candidate Viktor Yanukovich's staff, on the Supreme Court's ruling delaying the election results, November 25

1 In separate incidents in Baghdad, Iraq, the deputy governor of Baghdad province is assassinated, and four foreign workers are kidnapped.

•

King Bhumibol Adulyadej of Thailand summons Prime Minister Thaksin Shinawatra to tell him to exercise leniency in his dealings with rebellious Muslims; the king intervenes with the government only in rare moments of crisis, this one triggered by the suffocation of 78 Muslims in military custody a few days previously.

•

Japan introduces a redesigned currency for the first time in 20 years in an attempt to thwart forgery, which has increased greatly with the advent of increasingly sophisticated computer and printing technology.

2 In a close presidential election in the U.S., Pres. George W. Bush wins with 51% of the popular vote and 286 electoral votes, against challenger John Kerry's 48% and 251 electoral votes, though the results are not known until the following day.

•

Dutch filmmaker Theo van Gogh is murdered in Amsterdam by a Muslim extremist, apparently provoked by a short television film van Gogh made that painted Muslims as misogynists. (*See* November 13.)

•

Pres. Sheikh Zayid ibn Sultan Al Nahyan of the United Arab Emirates dies; the following day his son, Sheikh Khalifah ibn Zayid Al Nahyan, is chosen to replace him in the presidency.

3 Hungary announces that it will withdraw its troops from Iraq by March 2005.

•

A fire that broke out in the Liuhuanggou coalfield in China's Sinkiang region in 1874 is extinguished by firefighters; it is believed that 1.8 million tons of coal were consumed annually by the fire.

4 Russian Pres. Vladimir Putin signs the country's ratification of the Kyoto Protocol governing greenhouse-gas emissions; 90 days after the documents are submitted to the UN, the treaty will go into effect. (*See* October 27.)

•

After a yearlong cease-fire, the government of Côte d'Ivoire conducts bombing raids against two rebel strongholds, in violation of a UN-sponsored truce.

•

The U.S. announces that it will recognize Macedonia's formal name as the Republic of Macedonia.

5 The chief of Chile's army, Gen. Juan Emilio Cheyre, declares publicly that the army accepts collective and institutional responsibility for the human rights violations that occurred during the 1974–90 dictatorship of Augusto Pinochet Ugarte.

•

A court in the Canadian province of Saskatchewan rules that laws banning same-sex marriage are unconstitutional; five provinces and one territory in Canada had already made the same ruling in the past several months.

•

Voters on the Caribbean island of Saba express their preference to break away from the Netherlands Antilles to become a direct dependency of The Netherlands.

6 Four car bombs and three attacks on police stations in Samarra', Iraq, leave some 40 people dead.

•

On the third day of government attacks against rebel-held areas, eight French peacekeepers are killed and 23 wounded in the town of Bouaké, Côte d'Ivoire.

•

Australian Rachael Grinham wins the women's British Open squash championship for the second consecutive year, and Australian David Palmer takes the men's title, also for the second straight year.

7 U.S. troops begin an expected siege of Fallujah, Iraq, by seizing control of two bridges and a hospital.

•

A referendum to rescind the autonomy granted to ethnic Albanians in Macedonia fails because of low voter turnout; the government had urged a boycott of the referendum.

•

British runner Paula Radcliffe is the fastest woman at the New York Marathon, with a time of 2 hr 23 min 10 sec; the winner of the race is Hendrik Ramaala of South Africa, with a time of 2 hr 9 min 28 sec.

8 An assault force of 6,500 U.S. troops and 2,000 Iraqi soldiers enters Fallujah, Iraq, over a railroad embankment at the north end of the city.

•

The International Rescue Committee becomes the third aid organization, after Doctors Without Borders and CARE International, to cease operations in Iraq because of the danger to aid workers in the country.

•

A U.S. federal judge ruling that military commissions convened to try war detainees at Guantánamo Bay, Cuba, are unconstitutional immediately ends the first trial before such a tribunal.

•

It is announced at the International Supercomputer Conference in Pittsburgh, Pa., that IBM's prototype Blue Gene/L has surpassed Japan's NEC Earth Simulator as the fastest computer in the world.

•

The ice hockey Hall of Fame in Toronto inducts defensemen Ray Bourque, Paul Coffey, and Larry Murphy and manager Cliff Fletcher.

9 The Supreme Court of Belgium rules that the Vlaams Blok party has violated antiracism laws and is thus not a legal political party; the party, very popular in Flanders, campaigns against immigration and in favour of Flemish independence.

•

The U.S. Supreme Court rules that immigrants may not be deported for driving under the influence of alcohol, even if injury is caused; a number of people have already been deported because the government has been defining such conduct as a "crime of violence."

•

Tim McGraw and Kenny Chesney each win two Country Music Association Awards, McGraw for song of the year and single of the year for "Live like You Were Dying" and Chesney for entertainer of the year and album of the year for *When the Sun Goes Down*.

10 U.S. Pres. George W. Bush nominates Alberto Gonzales to replace John Ashcroft as attorney general; Ashcroft had announced his resignation the previous day, declaring that the U.S. was now safe from terror and crime.

•

Swaziland's High Court convenes for the first time since all its members resigned in November 2002 in protest against the refusal of the monarchy to recognize a ruling; King Mswati III has agreed to abide by the court's rulings henceforth.

11 After days of conflicting reports on his condition, Palestinian Authority Pres. Yasir Arafat dies in a hospital in Paris; hours later Mahmoud Abbas—also known by his nom de guerre, Abu Mazen—is chosen to succeed him as head of the Palestine Liberation Organization.

•

Minnesota Twins pitcher Johan Santana is unanimously chosen winner of Major League Baseball's American League Cy Young Award.

12 ***In a highly publicized five-month trial in California, fertilizer salesman Scott Peterson is found guilty of having murdered his wife, Laci, and their unborn child in 2002. (Photo below.)***

•

Dutch authorities raid what they believe to be a terrorist training camp for the Kurdistan Workers' Party, a separatist group in Turkey, in the southern Netherlands town of Liempde.

13 Violence grows in the Iraqi cities of Al-Ramadi and Mosul as U.S. and Iraqi forces fight their way into the last insurgent-held area of Fallujah; the takeover of Fallujah is completed the following day.

•

A mosque in Limburg province in The Netherlands is burned down; it is the 20th incident in which either a mosque or a church has been set on fire since the murder of filmmaker Theo van Gogh. (*See* November 2.)

14 D.C. United wins its fourth Major League Soccer title in nine years with a 3–2 victory over the Kansas City Wizards in the MLS Cup game.

•

R&B artist Usher wins four awards and hip-hop duo OutKast wins three at the American Music Awards in Los Angeles.

HE'S GUILTY

FRIDAY November 12, 2004 San Mateo County Times PM EDITION

sanmateocountytimes.com The Peninsula's Hometown Newspaper 50 cents

Verdict: Scott killed Laci

☐ First-degree murder ☐ Could be executed ☐ 5-month trial ends

THE PLAYERS

LACI PETERSON Murder victim

AMBER FREY Scott's mistress

MARK GERAGOS Defense attorney

SCOTT PETERSON Defendant

RICK DISTASO Prosecutor

ALFRED DELUCCHI Judge

SCOTT PETERSON, the defendant, and Mark Geragos, the lead defense attorney, with attorney Pat Harris (right) listen to jury instructions from Judge Alfred Delucchi last week.

By Jason Dearen
STAFF WRITER

REDWOOD CITY

SCOTT PETERSON, a fertilizer salesman catapulted to international notoriety when his wife, Laci, disappeared two years ago on Christmas Eve, today was convicted of murdering her and their unborn son.

After 6½ days of tumultuous deliberations, the six men and six women of the jury unanimously announced a first-degree conviction in the death of Laci and a second-degree murder conviction in the death of the unborn child the couple intended to name Conner.

As the clerk read the verdicts, Laci's family let out a collective and audible gasp and began to hug tightly. Tears immediately flowed.

Please see VERDICT, News 8

INSIDE: What's next for Peterson, and the trial's Top 10 highlights. News 8

Cheers erupt outside court

By T.S. Mills-Faraudo, Christine Morente and Malaika Fraley
STAFF WRITER

REDWOOD CITY — Cheers erupted outside the Redwood City Hall of Justice today as hundreds of spectators reacted to news that the jury convicted Scott Peterson of murdering his wife and unborn son.

People began arriving in droves when the news broke at 11:30 a.m. that a verdict had been reached in the case. The crowd heard the verdict live from the audio feeds in the media tents that lined the courthouse after speculating for over an hour on what would

Please see CHEERS, News 8

15 Colin Powell announces his resignation as U.S. secretary of state; the following day Pres. George W. Bush nominates Condoleezza Rice, his national security adviser, to replace Powell.

•

In negotiations with France, Great Britain, and Germany, Iran agrees to freeze its uranium-enrichment program while negotiations continue over inducements.

•

The UN Security Council imposes an immediate arms embargo on Côte d'Ivoire, with further sanctions to come into force on December 15 if the cease-fire agreement has not been restored by that time.

•

Major League Baseball's National League names Barry Bonds Most Valuable Player for a record fourth consecutive year.

16 Al-Jazeera television network reports having received a videotape that appears to depict the execution in Iraq of kidnapped CARE International Iraq director Margaret Hassan.

•

The unmanned NASA scramjet X-43A reaches approximately Mach 9.6, a new speed record, in a test flight over the Pacific Ocean.

•

Major League Baseball's American League Most Valuable Player award for the 2004 season is awarded to Vladimir Guerrero of the Anaheim Angels.

17 The retailers Kmart and Sears announce a merger in which Kmart will buy Sears and become Sears Holdings, the third largest retailing entity in the United States.

•

The U.S. National Medal of Arts is awarded to Ray Bradbury, Carlisle Floyd, Frederick Hart, Anthony Hecht, John Ruthven, Vincent Scully, Twyla Tharp, and the Andrew W. Mellon Foundation.

•

The National Book Awards are presented to Lily Tuck, Kevin Boyle, Jean Valentine, and Pete Hautman; young-adult book author Judy Blume is given the Medal for Distinguished Contribution to American Letters.

•

Archaeologist Albert Goodyear reports that his investigation of flint tools found in Allendale county, S.C., have led him to conclude that humans occupied the site some 50,000 years ago; it has been generally believed that humans first reached the Americas only about 12,000 years ago.

18 The European Parliament approves a new European Commission several weeks after the incoming commission's president, José Manuel Barroso, was forced to withdraw a proposed team because the Parliament objected to Barroso's choice of justice commissioner.

•

In Chile a law comes into effect that for the first time permits divorce; Malta and the Philippines are the only countries where divorce is still illegal.

•

Google announces the inauguration of a search service, called Google Scholar, specifically for scientists and academic researchers.

•

The presidential library of former president Bill Clinton opens in Little Rock, Ark.

19 During a meeting of the UN Security Council in Nairobi, Kenya—only the fourth time the body has met outside UN headquarters in New York City—the government of The Sudan and the Sudan People's Liberation Movement/Army pledge to reach a peace agreement before the end of the year.

•

Speaking before the UN Security Council meeting in Nairobi, Kenya, the newly installed Somali president, Abdullahi Yusuf Ahmed, requests an international peacekeeping force for his country; the Security Council declines on the grounds that there is as yet no peace to keep.

•

UN Secretary-General Kofi Annan announces that he is sending an investigative team immediately to look into allegations of sexual abuse of women and children by UN peacekeeping troops in the Democratic Republic of the Congo.

•

Thousands of protesters march in the streets of Santiago, Chile, as the Asia-Pacific Economic Cooperation (APEC) conference holds its annual meeting in the city for the first time.

•

Science magazine publishes a report by paleontologists who have discovered near Barcelona, Spain, fossils of a species named *Pierolapithecus catalaunicus* that date to 13 million years ago and might be the last common ancestor of humans and all great apes living today.

20 In fighting between government forces and Maoist rebels in Pandon, Nepal, at least 26 people are killed.

•

NASA, in conjunction with the space programs of Italy and Great Britain, successfully launches Swift, a satellite observatory that will find and record enigmatic cosmic explosions known as gamma-ray bursts, which may signal the birth of black holes or the collision of neutron stars.

•

New York City's Museum of Modern Art ceremonially reopens in its redesigned and expanded gallery after two years of construction. (Photo right.)

21 Ukraine holds its runoff presidential election between Viktor Yanukovich and Viktor Yushchenko; the following day Yanukovich declares victory, international observers release a preliminary report finding the elections undemocratic, and supporters of Yushchenko fill Independence Square in Kiev, believing their candidate to have won.

•

The Paris Club of creditor countries agrees to cancel 80% of the debt that Iraq owes to its members.

•

The Toronto Argonauts defeat the British Columbia Lions 27–19 in Ottawa to capture the 92nd Canadian Football League Grey Cup.

22 In accordance with its agreement with Germany, France, and the U.K., Iran suspends its uranium-enrichment operations.

•

Sheikh Muhammad Amin al-Faidhi, a prominent Sunni cleric, is killed in Mosul, Iraq, and the bodies of four Iraqi soldiers are found.

23 U.S., Iraqi, and British forces begin a major offensive in the area south of Baghdad, Iraq, that has become known as the "triangle of death."

•

Wal-Mart Stores in China issues a statement saying it

Fred R. Conrad/The New York Times NYT45

would respect a request from employees to form a union, in accordance with the law in China; Wal-Mart had always opposed unionization throughout its stores.

•

Dan Rather announces that he will retire as anchor and managing editor of the *CBS Evening News* television show in March 2005.

24 The government of Ukraine declares Viktor Yanukovich the winner of the presidential election, in spite of international reports of fraud and growing demonstrations by supporters of Viktor Yushchenko.

•

Pakistani Prime Minister Shaukat Aziz travels to India to continue peace talks with Indian Prime Minister Manmohan Singh; it is the first time in 13 years that a Pakistani prime minister has gone to India.

25 Ukraine's Supreme Court rules that the results of the presidential election cannot be made final until the allegations of electoral fraud and intimidation have been investigated; crowds of supporters of opposition candidate Viktor Yushchenko have filled Kiev's Independence Square since the election.

•

India's Supreme Court rules that the Taj Mahal should be reopened to night viewing for five nights around the time of each full moon; night viewing had been banned since 1984, when Sikh militancy caused fears of attack.

26 Marwan Barghouti, who has been frequently mentioned as a possible candidate for president of the Palestinian Authority (although he is serving five life sentences in prison in Israel), agrees not to run and puts his support behind Mahmoud Abbas.

•

Dozens of defendants are convicted of having planned to overthrow the government of Equatorial Guinea in March and are sentenced to long prison terms.

27 Ukraine's Supreme Council meets in a special session and declares the results of the presidential election invalid; the body cannot overturn an election, however.

•

In Vatican City, Pope John Paul II ceremonially delivers to Ecumenical Patriarch Bartholomew I of the Eastern Orthodox Church relics of St. John Chrysostom and St. Gregory of Nazianzus; the relics had been removed from Constantinople many centuries earlier. (*See* August 27.)

•

The famed and opulent Apollo Gallery in the Louvre Museum in Paris reopens after a massive three-year restoration project.

•

Sumo wrestling grand champion Asashoryu becomes the first person in 18 years to win five tournaments in a single year when his defeat of Chiyotaikai at the Kyushu Basho brings him his ninth Emperor's Cup.

28 Nicolas Sarkozy is elected leader of the Gaullist Union for a Popular Movement Party, the dominant political party in France.

•

King Abdullah of Jordan rescinds the title of crown prince from his half brother, Hamza ibn Hussein.

29 Meeting in Vientiane, Laos, the members of the Association of Southeast Asian Nations and China sign an agreement to create the largest free-trade zone in the world.

•

Pres. Ricardo Lagos Escobar of Chile announces that the government will give a lifetime stipend to compensate the victims of torture during the dictatorship of Augusto Pinochet Ugarte.

•

Edwy Plenel resigns as editor in chief of *Le Monde,* France's leading newspaper.

•

Popular African American radio and television host Tavis Smiley quits his daily talk show on National Public Radio.

30 A general strike over government economic policy brings Italy to a halt as tens of thousands of protesters march in cities throughout the country.

•

A report commissioned by Secretary-General Kofi Annan recommends a number of changes to the UN, most notably an expansion of the Security Council to 24 members from its current 15.

•

Tom Ridge announces his resignation as U.S. secretary of homeland security.

•

Kweisi Mfume surprises observers by announcing his resignation as president of the NAACP (National Association for the Advancement of Colored People).

•

U.S. Pres. George W. Bush makes his first official visit to Canada.

•

After an astonishing 74-game winning streak, Ken Jennings finally loses on the television game show *Jeopardy!* after having won more than $2 million.

December

> *All the planet is vibrating.*

Enzo Boschi, director of Italy's National Geophysics Institute, describing the earthquake that unleashed the Indian Ocean tsunami, December 26

1 Rallies are held in cities throughout South Asia in observance of World AIDS Day; HIV/AIDS is a growing problem in the region.

•

The U.S. government announces plans to increase the number of troops in Iraq by about 12,000 to a total of 150,000 in the next several weeks; the extra manpower is intended to provide security for the national election scheduled for Jan. 30, 2005.

•

The second John W. Kluge Prize in the Human Sciences, established by the U.S. Library of Congress to honour lifetime achievement, is awarded to American intellectual historian Jaroslav Pelikan and French philosopher Paul Ricoeur.

2 The European Union officially takes over peacekeeping duties in Bosnia and Herzegovina from NATO.

3 Ukraine's Supreme Court rules that the presidential runoff election on November 21 was fraudulent and overturns the results; a new runoff is to be held no later than December 26.

•

Tommy G. Thompson steps down as U.S. secretary of health and human services.

•

In the enclave of Kosovo in Serbia and Montenegro, the legislature chooses former ethnic Albanian guerrilla leader Ramush Haradinaj to be prime minister, though he is being investigated by the UN war crimes tribunal.

•

In a number of attacks in both Baghdad and Mosul in Iraq, mostly against police stations, 27 Iraqi police and civilians are killed.

4 In the runoff presidential election in Niger, Pres. Tandja Mamadou wins reelection.

•

A suicide car bomb destroys a police station in Baghdad, Iraq, while another one hits a convoy of Kurdish soldiers in Mosul; at least 25 Iraqis are killed in the two attacks.

•

Miss Peru, María Julia Mantilla García, wins the Miss World beauty pageant, which takes place on Hainan Island, China.

5 In municipal elections across Bolivia, Indian and peasant reform parties win most races against traditional party candidates.

•

An attack on a busload of Iraqi contractors working for U.S. forces in Tikrit, Iraq, brings the death toll for the past three days to 80.

•

The annual Kennedy Center Honors are presented in Washington, D.C., to Warren Beatty, Ossie Davis, Ruby Dee, Sir Elton John, Dame Joan Sutherland, and John Williams.

•

Carlos Moya leads Spain's tennis team to victory over the U.S. and to the Davis Cup title in Seville, Spain.

6 Five men attack the U.S. consulate in Jiddah, Saudi Arabia, and a three-hour gun battle ensues in which four of the attackers and five consulate employees are killed; the attackers are believed to be members of al-Qaeda.

•

The Basque separatist organization Euskadi Ta Askatasuna explodes seven small bombs, one in each of seven cities, in Spain; because ETA phoned in warnings, however, there are no serious casualties.

•

Britain's Turner Prize is presented to installation artist Jeremy Deller, who wins on the strength of his film *Memory Bucket: A Film About Texas.*

7 Hamid Karzai is sworn in as president of Afghanistan.

•

John Kufuor wins a second term as president of Ghana.

•

IBM announces that it has reached a deal to sell its personal computer business to Lenovo, the biggest PC maker in China; the computers will continue to be made in the U.S., however.

•

Chinese Pres. Hu Jintao tells German Chancellor Gerhard Schröder that he will support Germany's bid to gain a permanent seat on the UN Security Council.

•

The La Scala opera house in Milan has a gala reopening after having been closed since Dec. 31, 2001, for renovation; it opens with the opera that first opened the theatre in 1778, Antonio Salieri's *Europa riconosciuta.*

8 In Cuzco, Peru, representatives of 12 countries sign an agreement to create the South American Community of Nations.

•

U.S. Secretary of Defense Donald Rumsfeld holds a question-and-answer session in Kuwait with soldiers headed for Iraq and is apparently surprised to be asked about the shortage of armour for vehicles used in the conflict.

•

During an appearance in a nightclub in Columbus, Ohio, a man leaps onto the stage and shoots to death the heavy-metal guitar player "Dimebag" Darrell Abbott and three others.

9 The House of Assembly, Zimbabwe's legislature, approves a law that will ban foreign-based and foreign-supported organizations, including churches, that promote greater human rights in the country.

•

New Zealand's Parliament passes a law that gives same-sex partners the same civil rights enjoyed by married couples.

•

The crew aboard the International Space Station is asked to cut back on food until the arrival of the next supply ship, scheduled for December 25; keeping adequate supplies on the station has become more difficult after the grounding of the U.S. space shuttle fleet.

•

The Right Livelihood Awards are presented in Stockholm to Indian religious figures Swami Agnivesh and Asghar Ali Engineer for their work promoting harmony between communities; Memorial, a Russian human rights organization; Bianca Jagger, a Nicaraguan human rights and environmental activist; and Raúl Montenegro, an Argentine scientist and environmentalist.

10 After a trial that dragged on for four years, a panel of judges in a criminal court in Milan acquits Italian Prime Minister Silvio Berlusconi of three corruption charges and dismisses a fourth charge.

•

A bomb goes off in a crowded outdoor market in Quetta, Pak., killing at least 10 people; Baluchistan nationalists are believed to be responsible.

•

Japan adopts a new military plan that focuses more on defense against China and North Korea and less on defense against Russia.

11 Tests by doctors in Vienna confirm that opposition Ukrainian presidential candidate Viktor Yushchenko was poisoned with dioxin.

•

Legislative elections in Taiwan give a slim majority to the Nationalist Party and its allies, which downplay the issue of Taiwan's independence from mainland China.

•

The 2004 Heisman Trophy for college football is awarded to University of Southern California quarterback Matt Leinart.

•

The German-Turkish film *Gegen die Wand* is named the best picture at the European Film Awards in Barcelona, Spain.

12 The presidential election in Romania is unexpectedly won by the opposition candidate, Traian Basescu.

•

Under pressure from the U.S. and the European Union, China agrees to impose tariffs on some of its textile exports.

•

Having again announced his candidacy on December 1, Marwan Barghouti bows out of the race for president of the Palestinian Authority for the second time.

•

A bomb explodes in a busy public market in General Santos, Phil., killing at least 15 people.

•

At the 46th Wrangler National Finals Rodeo in Las Vegas, Nev., Trevor Brazile wins his third consecutive all-around title.

13 A judge in Chile rules that Augusto Pinochet Ugarte is mentally fit to stand trial for human rights abuses committed during his 1974–90 dictatorship and orders him placed under house arrest; the order is immediately appealed.

•

Representatives of Iran, France, Germany, the U.K., and the European Union begin a new round of negotiations in Brussels to resolve the impasse over Iran's nuclear policy.

•

The day after two Sudanese employees of the charity Save the Children are killed in the Darfur region of The Sudan, the UN suspends relief operations in the area.

•

Sean O'Keefe announces his resignation as head of NASA.

•

After a long struggle, the business database company Oracle acquires the business software company PeopleSoft in a hostile takeover.

14 ***In France the Millau Viaduct, at 270 m (886 ft) the world's highest bridge and at 2,460 m (8,071 ft) the world's longest all-span cable-stayed bridge, is dedicated by President Jacques Chirac. (Photo below.)***

© Eric Cabanis/AFP/Getty Images

•

The U.S. Department of Commerce reports that the U.S. reached an all-time record trade deficit of $55.5 billion in October, breaking the record set in June.

•

The European Commission grants France and Germany another year to lower their deficits to the required 3% benchmark.

•

Google announces an agreement with several major research libraries to digitize and make available through its regular online search service the contents of millions of books that are no longer under copyright.

•

The U.S. Presidential Medal of Freedom is awarded to Gen. Tommy R. Franks, the commander of the U.S.-led forces that invaded Iraq in 2003; L. Paul Bremer III, the U.S. administrator of occupied Iraq; and George Tenet, former director of central intelligence.

15 The U.S. Securities and Exchange Commission, finding the mortgage broker Fannie Mae to be in violation of accounting rules, orders it to restate its earnings for the past four years.

•

In an attempt to prevent the auction of its prize oil-producing unit, the Russian energy company Yukos files for bankruptcy protection in Houston, Texas, where it says it has some assets.

•

Cellular phone companies Sprint and Nextel Communications announce plans to merge to create the third biggest carrier in the U.S.

•

The first full flight test since 2002 of the U.S. missile defense system fails when the interceptor missile shuts down just before its planned launch against an in-flight simulated ICBM; the previous test also failed.

•

Researchers report the existence of a species of macaque previously unknown to science—a stocky, brown-haired, short-tailed primate living in Arunachal Pradesh state, India, that they have named *Macaca munzala*.

16 An audiotape from Osama bin Laden is posted on a Web site; he excoriates the rulers of Saudi Arabia for their association with the U.S. and praises the attackers of the U.S. embassy in Jiddah.

•

A bomb explodes outside a major Shi'ite shrine in Karbala', Iraq, killing at least 9 people and injuring 40, among them an aide to Ayatollah Ali al-Sistani; the aide may have been the target.

•

In an enormous child sex-abuse scandal that has been rocking Portugal, Carlos Silvino, who is charged with 634 offenses, including child rape and procuring, and is the first defendant to go on trial, pleads guilty.

17 Armando Guebuza of the ruling Frelimo party is declared the winner of the presidential election that took place in Mozambique December 1–2.

•

The drug company Pfizer says that a national trial has shown that large doses of Celebrex triple the risk of heart attack and stroke; three days later Pfizer announces that it will cease all advertising for its popular prescription pain medication, although the company apparently does not intend to withdraw it from the market.

•

Turkish Prime Minister Recip Tayyip Erdogan accepts the invitation, made on December 16, to engage in accession talks with the European Union starting in October 2005.

18 A two-week international conference on global warming in Buenos Aires, Arg., concludes with an agreement to hold an informal workshop in 2005 to discuss the matter; the U.S. is accused of foot dragging and preventing a more substantive agreement.

•

Representatives of the African Union say that The Sudan has begun withdrawing government troops from the Darfur region hours before a deadline the union imposed to repair leaks in the cease-fire, but an incident the following day prompts the AU to declare that the government did not meet the deadline.

19 A previously unknown company, the Baikal Finans Group, which registered a last-minute bid, wins the auction for the huge oil-producing unit of Yukos, the Russian energy company, after well-known entities either withdraw or fail to bid.

•

Car bombs go off in the Iraqi cities of Najaf and Karbala', killing at least 61 people between them, and three election workers in Baghdad are pulled from their cars and executed.

20 A Gulf Cooperation Council meeting in Manama, Bahrain, is notable for the absence of Saudi Arabia's Crown Prince Abdullah; he is said to be upset over a recent free-trade agreement between Bahrain and the U.S.

•

The U.S. government agrees to settle a case brought by Jewish survivors of World War II from Hungary seeking compensation for valuables that were looted from them by Nazis and then appropriated by U.S. forces in 1945 before they could be returned to their rightful owners.

•

In Zürich, Switz., Brazilian Ronaldinho (who plays for Barcelona, Spain) and Birgit Prinz of Germany are named FIFA World Player and FIFA Women's World Player of the Year in association football (soccer).

•

The Repertory Theatre in Birmingham, Eng., cancels a production of *Behzti*, a play that depicts sexual abuse and murder within a Sikh temple, after hundreds of Sikh demonstrators protest strenuously, causing the theatre to fear for the safety of theatregoers and those involved in the production.

21 British Prime Minister Tony Blair makes an unexpected visit to Baghdad, Iraq, where he meets with interim Iraqi prime minister Ayad Allawi and meets with British troops in Basra.

•

An explosion in a mess tent in an American military base in Mosul, Iraq, at lunchtime kills at least 24 people, among them 14 U.S. soldiers and 4 American contractors.

•

UN peacekeeping troops begin moving into the North Kivu region of the Democratic Republic of the Congo, hoping to create a buffer zone between government and rebel forces.

•

Astronomers announce that NASA's Galaxy Evolution Explorer satellite has found some three dozen massive, recently formed galaxies that may resemble our own Milky Way Galaxy in its youth.

•

The Washington Post Co. announces its purchase from

Microsoft of the pioneering online magazine *Slate*.

22 The World Health Organization (WHO) announces that blood tests performed on poultry workers in Japan have uncovered at least one case, and probably five, of asymptomatic infections in people of the frequently fatal A(H5N1) strain of avian influenza (bird flu).

•

It is revealed that Contrack International Inc., which had been selected to do road and bridge reconstruction in Iraq, has canceled its contract, citing the difficult security situation and problems with supplies that made it almost impossible to operate.

•

Saudi Arabia withdraws its ambassador from Libya and expels the Libyan ambassador in Riyadh, believing it has found evidence that Libya plotted to assassinate Crown Prince Abdullah.

•

Scientists say that Martian volcanoes photographed by the European Space Agency spacecraft Mars Express show signs of geologically recent eruptions, which leads to speculation that they may still be active.

23 The U.S. dollar reaches a record low against the euro and declines against other major currencies; the dollar has fallen about 7% since early November.

•

Palestinian municipal elections are held for the first time since 1976; Hamas candidates do well.

•

Afghani Pres. Hamid Karzai announces his new cabinet; unlike the body of warlords he chose as interim president, this cabinet is composed largely of technocrats.

24 U.S. Secretary of Defense Donald Rumsfeld makes a Christmas Eve visit to U.S. soldiers in Iraq.

•

A tanker truck loaded with butane gas and wired with explosives and apparently headed for the Jordanian embassy in Baghdad, Iraq, explodes, destroying a house and killing nine people.

25 In St. Peter's Square in Vatican City, Pope John Paul II delivers Christmas greetings in 62 languages to the crowds and prays for peace.

•

Ukraine's Constitutional Court approves a series of changes in the electoral law.

26 A magnitude-9.0 earthquake under the Indian Ocean unleashes a powerful tsunami that kills hundreds of thousands of people in more than 10 countries and destroys coastlines in Indonesia, Sri Lanka, Thailand, Malaysia, Maldives, and India.

•

In the repeat runoff presidential election in Ukraine, opposition candidate Viktor Yushchenko wins a convincing victory.

•

Legislative elections are held in Uzbekistan that international observers say offer the voters no serious choice, because opposition groups were barred from the ballot.

27 Israel releases 159 Palestinian prisoners in a move that Palestinian leaders say they welcome, although they still call for more substantive progress.

•

A large explosion occurs in Baghdad outside the headquarters of the biggest Shi'ite political party in Iraq; 9 people are killed and 67 injured, but the party leader, Abdul Aziz al-Hakim, is unhurt.

AP/Wide World Photos

28 Several attacks in the region north of Baghdad, Iraq, kill at least 23 Iraqi police and national guard members.

•

Following a hand recount, the pro-commonwealth candidate, Aníbal Acevedo-Vilá, is certified as the winner of the November 2 election for governor of Puerto Rico.

29 The U.S. partially lifts its ban on the importation of cattle from Canada, in place since May 2003, when a cow in Alberta was found to have mad-cow disease.

•

An agreement to stop people from immigrating to one country to seek asylum in another goes into effect, closing all border points between Canada and the U.S. to refugees.

30 Senegal signs a peace agreement with separatist rebels in the Casamance region.

•

The legislature of the Basque country surprises observers by approving a plan that says the region has the right to secede from Spain.

•

Democrat Christine Gregoire is certified as the winner of the November 2 election for governor of the U.S. state of Washington; the original results showed Republican Dino Rossi as the winner, and a machine recount confirmed him as the winner by a much smaller margin, but a hand recount gave the race to Gregoire.

•

Ethiopia announces that the 1,700-year-old Obelisk of Axum, taken by Italian forces after Italy conquered Ethiopia in 1937, will be returned in 2005.

•

Fireworks ignited by a patron at a nightclub in Buenos Aires, Arg., set the club on fire; 188 people are killed and 700 injured.

31 ***Promises of aid for the victims of the Indian Ocean tsunami pour in, and the U.S. raises its pledge 10-fold to $350 million. In the photo above a woman in India hails the arrival of an aid helicopter.***

•

A peace accord is signed in Nairobi, Kenya, between the government of The Sudan and representatives of rebel groups in the south of the country.

•

Following his loss in contentious elections, Viktor Yanukovich resigns as prime minister of Ukraine.

Disasters

Listed here are major disasters that occurred in 2004. The list includes NATURAL and nonmilitary MECHANICAL disasters that claimed more than 15 lives and/or resulted in significant damage to PROPERTY.

Aviation

January 3, Red Sea, off the coast of Ra's Nasrani (Sharm el-Sheikh), Egypt. An Egyptian charter plane, a Boeing 737 carrying mostly French tourists from a popular resort in Egypt to Paris, crashes in the ocean; all 148 on board are killed.

January 13, Tashkent, Uzbekistan. A domestic airliner crashes in heavy fog on its approach; it is feared that all 37 aboard, including the top UN official for the country, have been killed.

February 10, al-Shariqah, U.A.E. An Iranian passenger plane crashes on its approach to the airport; 44 of the 46 passengers are killed.

May 14, Near Manaus, Braz. A turboprop domestic airliner crashes in thick jungle after suspending landing procedures to allow a plane transporting people to a hospital to precede it; all 33 aboard are lost.

June 8, Off Libreville, Gabon. A small commercial airplane crashes into the sea shortly after taking off; 19 people are killed, and 11 survive.

June 29, Near Yengema, Sierra Leone. A helicopter carrying UN peacekeepers on a routine trip crashes into a hillside, killing all 24 on board; the cause is under investigation.

August 5, Western Siberia, Russia. An Mi-8 helicopter carrying workers surveying for forest fires crashes, reportedly after developing engine trouble; all 15 aboard are killed.

August 21, Northern Venezuela. A military plane carrying civilians as well as military personnel from a base on Orchila Island to Maracay crashes into a mountainside; all 25 aboard are killed.

November 21, Baotou, Inner Mongolia, China. A China Eastern Airlines commuter plane bursts into flames shortly after takeoff and falls into a frozen lake; all 53 people aboard and 2 on the ground are killed.

November 30, Solo, Indon. A Lion Air MD-82 passenger plane skids off a runway and breaks in two after landing in heavy rain, and at least 25 of the 146 aboard are killed.

December 10, Near El Junquito, Venez. An airplane belonging to the National Guard and bound for an air base in Caracas crashes into a mountain, killing all 16 personnel, some of them high-ranking officers.

Fires and Explosions

January 19, Skikda, Alg. An explosion at a liquefied natural gas plant kills 30 and injures 74; this is the worst disaster in three decades in what had been an extremely safe industry.

January 23, Srirangam, Tamil Nadu, India. A fire, probably caused by an electrical short circuit, breaks out at a thatched-roof wedding pavilion, killing at least 45 people, including the groom, and injuring about 50, including the bride.

February 6, Moscow. An explosion on a subway train causes an intense fire, with smoke filling the tunnel; at least 22 people die.

February 15, China. In Jilin a fire breaks out in a four-story mall that contains shops, a dance hall, and public baths, and at least 53 people die; another fire in a temple in the city of Haining kills 39.

February 26, Chita, Siberia, Russia. An explosion evidently caused by a gas leak takes place in a small cafe, killing at least 17 people and injuring an equal number.

March 16, Arkhangelsk, Russia. An explosion, possibly caused by vandals removing fittings from gas valves, destroys an apartment building, killing 58 people, many of them buried in the rubble.

May 2, Azizabad, Afg. A welding accident leads to the explosion of a fuel tank on a truck, which causes another fuel truck to explode in a bazaar; at least 45 people lose their lives, and 28 are wounded.

May 17, San Pedro Sula, Honduras. A late-night fire, caused by a short circuit, possibly in an air conditioner, breaks out at an extremely overcrowded prison, leaving more than 100 inmates dead.

June 10, Pingxiang, Jiangxi province, China. An explosion in a fireworks factory leaves an 80-sq-m (860-sq-ft) crater; 16 women working in the factory die.

July 16, Kumbakonam, Tamil Nadu, India. A fire destroys the Lord Krishna School, killing at least 90 children; the private school had a thatched roof and lacked fire escapes.

July 30, Ath, Belg. In Belgium's worst industrial disaster since 1967, a gas pipeline in an industrial park explodes, engulfing two factories, killing at least 18 people, and injuring more than 100; some of the dead are firefighters who were summoned to the scene by construction workers who said they had accidentally pierced the gas line.

August 1, Asunción, Paraguay. An intense fire, possibly triggered by a gas leak, breaks out in a supermarket, and at least 464 people are incinerated; it appears that after the fire broke out, emergency exits were locked to prevent theft.

September 16, Near Lagos, Nigeria. People attempting to steal oil from a state-owned pipeline cause an explosion and fire that kill some 50 people.

November 9, Kyzyl, Tuva republic, Russia. A fire in a hostel kills at least 25 people; it is thought that it may have been caused by an illegal attempt at a power connection in the bitter cold, as the power had been cut off because of nonpayment.

December 21, Sanki-Ilado, Nigeria. As thieves who damaged an oil pipeline to steal from it run from police, the pipeline explodes, and more than 20 people are killed.

December 26, Mulhouse, France. A gas leak leads to an explosion that destroys a five-story apartment building; 17 of the residents are killed, and 15 are injured.

December 30, Buenos Aires, Arg. In an overcrowded nightclub, its emergency exits reportedly locked to bar people from sneaking in, an audience member sets off a flare, igniting the ceiling; in the ensuing inferno at least 188 people die, and more than 700 are injured.

Marine

January 9, Adriatic Sea. A high-speed inflatable boat carrying people attempting to emigrate illegally from Albania to Italy founders in a storm; 21 people die, many of exposure, and 11 are rescued.

January 16, Off the Canary Islands. A boat carrying migrants from Morocco capsizes, and at least 16 of the passengers drown.

January 19, North Sea, off Bjoroey Island, Norway. A freighter capsizes in shallow water only about 200 m (218 yd) from shore; 18 crew members perish.

January 24, Caribbean Sea. A boat carrying would-be migrants from the Dominican Republic to Puerto Rico capsizes; 20 of the passengers are missing, and 3 are rescued.

January 31, Democratic Republic of the Congo. A ferry traveling the Congo River from Lukolela to Mbandaka catches fire and is quickly engulfed in flames; some 200 of the approximately 500 passengers are feared dead.

February 1, Lake Albert, Democratic Republic of the Congo. An overloaded boat capsizes, and it is feared that at least 45 people have perished.

February 13, The Bosporus, Turkey. In the worst of several maritime accidents occasioned by an unusual and severe blizzard, a coal freighter sinks in the Black Sea just outside the strait; all 21 crew members are lost.

February 28, Off the coast of Chincoteague Island, Virginia. A Norwegian tanker carrying industrial ethanol suffers an explosion and sinks, leaving 3 people dead and 18 missing.

March 7, Off the coast of Madagascar. A ferry at sea in a cyclone sinks, drowning 111 of 113 aboard; the total death toll from the cyclone jumps to 154.

March 18, Maldives. A ferry traveling between islands capsizes; though 99 people are rescued, at least 18 people drown, and more than 50 are declared missing.

March 18, Indonesia. A ferry, many of the passengers of which were traveling to attend a wedding, founders as it travels between the remote islands of Salibabu and Kabaruang; at least 23 people are lost.

Late March, Arabian Sea. A boat attempting to reach Yemen from Somalia capsizes; the crew survives, but the passengers, believed to be some 100 Somalis, are said to be lost.

April 15, Lake Tanganyika. An overcrowded ferry sinks in the Democratic Republic of the Congo; at least 43 people are reported dead, and 10 are missing.

April 15, Off the coast of Malta. A boat believed to be carrying some 100 migrants goes down in rough seas; none are believed to have survived.

April 30, Off the coast of Ca Mau, Vietnam. A fishing boat carrying students on a holiday tour capsizes, leaving at least 39 of the 150 aboard dead.

May 23, Meghna River, Bangladesh. A double-decker ferry, the *MV Lighting Sun,* sinks during a storm; 74 of the passengers drown, and a slightly larger number are rescued or swim to shore; a number of other boats sink during the same storm.

July 15, India. A boat capsizes in a river running high from monsoon rains, drowning at least 25 people.

August 7, Mediterranean Sea. A container ship rescues more than 70 would-be migrants from a drifting boat from North Africa trying to reach Sicily; some 28 of the refugees had died during the previous nine days.

August 10, Off the coast of Nagua, Dom.Rep. Fisherman find some 33 of the approximately 80 people who left the country in a boat headed for Puerto Rico; the others died during two weeks adrift at sea after the boat's motor failed.

October 4, Off the coast of Tunisia. A boat carrying illegal immigrants from Morocco and Tunisia splits in two and sinks off the coast of Tunisia shortly after departure in an attempt to reach Italy; at least 22 are drowned, and another 42 are missing.

October 10, Lake Kivu, Democratic Republic of the Congo. In separate incidents two large overloaded canoes bound for Goma overturn in windy weather; at least 41 on one canoe and at least 27 on the second canoe lose their lives, and at least 50 people are missing.

November 17, Off the coast of the Dominican Republic. A boat attempting to carry refugees from the Dominican Republic to Puerto Rico capsizes; at least 8 people die, and 15 are missing.

November 30, Near Zakhu, Iraq. A large flat-bottomed boat crowded with Kurdish migrant workers trying to reach Turkey overturns in the Tigris River, and at least 40 passengers drown.

Mining and Construction

February 2, Konya, Turkey. An 11-story apartment building collapses, killing 89 people; poor construction is blamed for the catastrophe.

February 9, Shanxi province, China. Explosions set to seal off an abandoned coal mine kill 29 workers.

February 11, Liupanshui, Guizhou province, China. A gas explosion in a coal mine kills 24 miners; 15 others escape.

February 20, Jamadoa, Jharkhand state, India. Water seeping into a coal mine from a nearby stream floods the mine, trapping 50 miners.

February 23, Jixi, Heilongjiang province, China. At least 24 workers are killed in a coal mine explosion, with 13 more trapped underground.

April 10, Osinniki, Kemerovo *oblast,* Russia. A methane explosion in a coal mine kills 47 miners in Russia's worst mining accident since 1997.

June 14, Santa Cruz province, Arg. A fire in Argentina's only coal mine, near the border with Chile, leaves seven miners dead and seven missing.

July 19, Ukraine. An explosion at the Krasnolimanskaya coal mine leaves at least 31 workers dead and 5 missing.

August 2, Tehri, Uttaranchal state, India. A tunnel being built as part of a controversial hydroelectric dam project caves in, most likely because of floods; 29 of the workers in the tunnel are killed.

October 20, Xinmi, Henan province, China. A gas explosion in the Daping coal mine kills 148 of the more than 400 miners working there at the time.

November 11, Liangwa, Henan province, China. The Xinsheng coal mine suffers an explosion that results in the death of 29 workers.

November 20, Shahe, Hebei province, China. An electrical cable starts a fire in an iron ore mine that leaves at least 61 people dead.

November 28, Shaanxi province, China. In one of China's worst coal-mining accidents in recent years, 166 miners perish in an explosion in the Chenjishan coal mine.

December 5, Near Karaganda, Kazakhstan. An explosion in the Shakhtinskaya coal mine kills 23 miners.

December 9, Near Yangquan, Shanxi province, China. A gas explosion at the Dazian Sanking coal mine kills 28 miners and 5 rescuers.

Natural

January 2, Northern India. Officials in India report that a cold snap in the past two weeks has killed more than 200 people, most of them elderly or homeless.

February 6, Papua, Indon. An earthquake measuring 6.9 in magnitude kills at least 23 people and injures hundreds of others; another, stronger quake the next day raises the death toll to 31.

February 14, Moscow. The glass roof of an indoor water park collapses under the weight of snow, killing at least 26 people and injuring well over 100.

February 14, Northern Pakistan. Two earthquakes leave some 24 people dead.

February 24, Northern Morocco. A magnitude-6.5 earthquake with its epicentre 160 km (100 mi) off Morocco in the Mediterranean Sea collapses buildings and kills at least 628 people.

March 7, Madagascar. Cyclone Gafilo leaves hundreds of thousands of people homeless and a death toll in the vicinity of 200, with another 160 unaccounted for.

March 14, Near Almaty, Kazakhstan. A landslide in a village destroys an apartment building and leaves at least 28 people dead.

March 26, Sulawesi Selatan, Indon. Landslides cause some 5,000 people to flee; 2 people are killed, and 31 are missing and presumed dead.

April 5, Piedras Negras, Mex. Heavy rains cause the Escondido River to overflow, which leads to flash floods that leave at least 34 people dead and 70 missing.

April 14, Northern Bangladesh. Tornadoes destroy thousands of flimsily built homes and leave at least 66 people dead.

Mid-April, East Africa. Flooding caused by torrential rains leaves at least 16 people dead in Kenya and drowns at least 30 people in Djibouti.

April 23, Sumatra, Indon. A mud slide engulfs a bus, smothering at least 37 people and injuring another 14.

April 25, Budalyk, Kyrgyzstan. Landslides destroy several homes and leave at least 33 people dead.

Early May, Northern Bangladesh. A prolonged heat wave leads to the death of at least 17 people.

May 19, Catanduanes province, Phil. A typhoon destroys several villages and leaves 19 people dead.

May 24, Haiti and Dominican Republic. Catastrophic flooding and mud slides caused by heavy rains coupled with deforestation bring a death toll of at least 1,950, with several hundred people missing.

May 28, Northern and central Iran. A magnitude-6.2 earthquake causes serious damage in some 80 villages and kills at least 35 people.

June–August, South Asia. An unusually bad monsoon season leaves 1,972 people dead in the region from drowning, landslides, electrocution, and waterborne diseases; the hardest-hit country is Bangladesh.

June 26, Cerro Musun, Nic. Mud slides caused by heavy rains take a heavy toll on villages around the mountain, leaving at least 16 people dead and 24 missing.

June 29, Philippines. Typhoon Mindulle makes landfall on Luzon, leaving 31 people dead, before proceeding to Taiwan, where on July 1 it kills another 15 people.

Early July, China. Heavy rains lead to flooding and landslides in the southern and central regions of the country; nearly 400 people die as a result.

July 2, Agri province, Turkey. An earthquake collapses village houses, leaving 18 people dead.

July 5, Taiwan. The worst flooding in a quarter century kills at least 21 people, with a further 14 missing.

July 5, India. A landslide sweeps away a section of highway in the Himalayas, taking with it a busload of pilgrims on their way to the shrine at Badrinath; 18 people die, and 2,500 are left stranded.

The Deadliest Tsunami

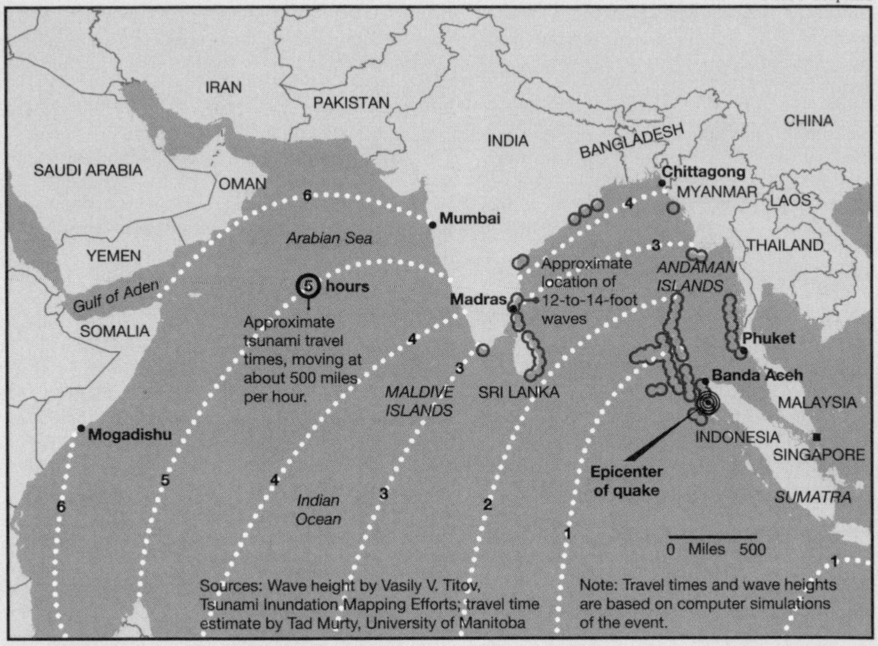

The location of the earthquake and reach of the tsunami caused it to impact a large number of populated areas, leading to a huge death toll. The areas marked in red, indicating where waves at least 12 to 14 feet in height occurred, suffered the greatest devastation.

On Dec. 26, 2004, at 7:59 AM local time, an undersea earthquake with a magnitude of 9.0 struck off the coast of the Indonesian island of Sumatra. (*See* EARTH SCIENCES: *Geophysics.*) Over the next seven hours, a tsunami—a series of immense ocean waves— triggered by the quake reached out across the Indian Ocean, devastating coastal areas as far away as East Africa. (*See* MAP.) Some locations reported that the waves had even reached a height of 9 m (30 ft) or more when they hit the shoreline. At least 225,000 people were killed across a dozen countries, with Indonesia, Sri Lanka, India, Maldives, and Thailand sustaining massive damage. Indonesian officials estimated that the death toll there could exceed 200,000, particularly in northern Sumatra's Aceh province. Tens of thousands were reported dead or missing in Sri Lanka and India, a large number of them from the Indian Andaman and Nicobar islands. The low-lying island nation of Maldives reported more than a hundred casualties and economic damage that could exceed the country's gross domestic product. Several thousand non-Asian tourists vacationing in the region also were reported dead or missing. The lack of food, clean water, and medical treatment—combined with the Herculean task faced by relief workers trying to get supplies into some remote areas where roads had been destroyed or civil war raged—increased the likelihood that the casualty list would continue to grow. Long-term environmental damage was almost as unimaginable as the loss of life, with tourist resorts, villages, farmland, and fishing grounds demolished or inundated with debris, bodies, and plant-killing salt water.

Late July, Peru. Officials declare a state of emergency as unusually cold weather in the Andes Mountains leaves at least 46 children dead and takes a heavy toll on livestock.

August 12, Zhejiang province, China. Typhoon Rananim makes landfall and proceeds inland, leaving a path of destruction and killing at least 164 people; it is the most powerful typhoon to hit China in seven years.

August 12, Adamawa state, Nigeria. Flash floods caused by days of heavy rain drown at least 23 people as they sleep.

August 13, Southwestern Florida. Hurricane Charley roars into Charlotte Harbor and across the state, devastating Punta Gorda and Port Charlotte and leaving 27 people dead.

August 24, Taiwan. Typhoon Aere hits the northern part of the island, leaving at least 24 people dead; it goes on to claim five lives in the Philippines.

September 7–17, Caribbean. Hurricane Ivan devastates Grenada, killing 39 people and destroying its two main crops, then kills at least 18 in Jamaica, and finally strengthens to hit the Gulf Coast of the U.S., leaving some 52 people dead in several states.

September 8, Southwestern China. Catastrophic flooding after a week of torrential storms leaves at least 177 people dead; by mid-month, at the end of the three-month rainy season, the official death toll is 1,029.

September 18, Haiti. Tropical Storm Jeanne makes landfall in the area of Gonaïves, already devastated by flooding in May; the death toll from the resultant flooding is more than 3,000.

September 21, Uttar Pradesh state, India. After heavy rains fall for more than 24 hours, flash flooding sweeps away homes, leading to the death of at least 44 people.

October 9, Assam state, India. After a week of heavy rains, flash flooding sweeps down hills, inundating dozens of villages and leaving more than 100 dead; flooding has also killed at least 44 people in Bangladesh and Nepal.

October 20, Japan. Typhoon Tokage, an unusually large storm—and the 10th to hit the country in 2004, a record—causes the death of at least 83 people.

October 23, Niigata prefecture, Japan. A series of earthquakes, the strongest measured at magnitude 6.8, kill at least 37 people; thousands are injured.

November 12, Alor, Indon. A magnitude-6.0 earthquake kills at least 21 people and leaves some 8,000 homeless.

November 29, Philippines. Typhoon Winnie brings flooding and landslides, with a death toll of at least 412.

December 2, Philippines. Rescue efforts addressing the effects of Typhoon Winnie have hardly begun when the country is hit by the even stronger Typhoon Nanmadol; more than 1,000 people are dead or missing.

December 2, Guizhou province, China. A mountain landslide destroys dozens of houses, killing 32 people.

December 26, Indian Ocean. A magnitude-9.0 underwater earthquake off Sumatra triggers a tremendous tsunami. (*See* Sidebar.)

Railroad

February 18, Neyshabur, Iran. A freight train carrying gasoline, fertilizer, and sulfur products somehow begins moving on its own, picks up speed going downhill, and derails, causing an explosion that kills at least 195 people.

February 27, West Bengal, India. An express train crashes into a truck at an unmanned rail crossing; the 30 dead are passengers on the truck traveling to a wedding.

March 22, Republic of the Congo. A car decouples from a train bound from Pointe-Noire to Brazzaville and falls into a ravine, killing some 30 people, mostly stowaways.

April 22, Ryongchon, N.Kor. Two freight trains, one reportedly carrying gasoline and the other liquefied petroleum gas, collide; the resultant explosion kills some 160 people and destroys more than 8,000 homes.

June 16, India. After monsoon rains leave boulders on the train tracks, a train bound for Mumbai (Bombay) strikes the rocks and derails, killing at least 20 people and injuring 100 others.

July 22, Near Pamukova, Turkey. A train running from Istanbul to Ankara derails, killing 37 people; although the high-speed service had only recently been inaugurated, the trains ran on old tracks.

August 11, Turkey. Two passenger trains crash head-on after one of them runs through a stop signal some 30 km (50 mi) east of Istanbul; at least 27 people are killed.

December 14, Punjab state, India. An express train and a local train crash head-on, killing at least 31 people and injuring 50.

Traffic

January 7, Near Aligarh, India. A bus takes a wrong turn in dense fog and drives into a canal; 20 people lose their lives.

January 8, Near Bhakkar, Pak. An overcrowded bus suffers a broken front axle and falls into a canal, causing the death of at least 56 passengers.

February 22, Near Fortaleza, Braz. A bus leaves the road and enters the waters impounded by Cipo dam; at least 40 people are believed to have drowned.

February 27, Uttaranchal state, India. A bus plunges into a gorge, leaving at least 23 people, including the driver, dead.

March 19, Finland. On an icy road a bus collides with a tractor-trailer, and 25 people, many of them teenagers, are killed, mostly crushed by huge rolls of paper from the truck's cargo.

March 26, Near Addis Ababa, Eth. An overcrowded bus falls into a gorge, killing 37 passengers.

April 2, Jammu and Kashmir state, India. An overcrowded bus falls into a ravine, killing 34 passengers and injuring 35.

April 4, Serbia and Montenegro. A bus carrying Bulgarian students to a resort on the Adriatic coast falls off a mountain road into a river after blowing a tire; nine students are killed, and three are missing.

April 5, Guizhou province, China. Two minibuses collide and fall into a valley; 27 passengers die, and 4 are injured.

April 5, Near Gonabad, Iran. A truck collides with a passenger bus, killing at least 30 people.

April 29, Bogotá, Colom. A backhoe falls down a hillside onto a highway, crushing a school bus and killing at least 21 children and 2 adults.

May 22, Near Itanagar, Arunachal Pradesh, India. The driver of a bus carrying 70 passengers loses control; the bus goes off the road into a deep gorge, killing at least 40 people.

May 24, Mihailesti, Rom. An overturned truck carrying ammonia explodes as firefighters are working to extinguish the fire after the traffic accident; eight firefighters, two journalists, the truck driver, and eight people in cars nearby are killed.

June 7, Bihar state, India. A bus carrying a wedding party skids into the river while crossing a low bridge over the rain-swollen Baghmati River; at least 19 people are drowned.

June 7, Near Abbotabad, Pak. A passenger truck loses control at a sharp bend in the road and falls into a ravine, causing the death of at least 38 people.

June 16, Near Islamabad, Pak. A tractor-trailer rear-ends a crowded bus on a bridge, knocking it into a dry riverbed and leaving more than 40 people dead.

June 16, Near Xinyu, Jiangxi province, China. A bus carrying pilgrims on their way to a temple swerves to avoid another vehicle and slides into a lake, killing 21 people.

June 17, Near Chongqing, China. A truck carrying electrical workers slams into a roadside rail, killing 16 of the approximately 30 workers.

June 21, Central Bolivia. A bus carrying tin miners goes over a cliff, killing at least 38 people.

June 24, Southeastern Iran. A fuel truck plows into six buses at a roadblock, exploding and engulfing another fuel truck in the fire; at least 90 die in the conflagration.

July 19, West Bengal state, India. The driver of a bus loses control, and the bus falls into a canal; at least 37 people are killed.

August 14, Near Carolina, El Salvador. A bus carrying members of a church group through a mountainous region goes into a ravine; at least 35 of the passengers are killed.

August 18, Southeastern Iran. A collision between a truck and a bus leaves at least 15 people dead.

September 4, Chongqing, China. A bus is swept off a bridge and is carried away by a flooding river; it is feared that some 30 passengers have drowned.

September 13, Near Kusma, Nepal. A bus carrying at least 50 people, some of them tourists, falls into a river; at least 16 people are killed.

September 16, Chittagong, Bangladesh. A bus carrying a party returning from a wedding collides with a truck; at least 22 people are killed, and 30 are critically injured.

October 9, Near Memphis, Tenn. A tour bus traveling from Chicago to Mississippi goes off the road and overturns; 15 of the 31 people aboard are killed, and the rest are injured.

October 14, Near Fushe Arrez, Alb. A bus carrying teenagers home to Kosovo in Serbia and Montenegro after a school trip collides with a car and is knocked off a bridge; at least 15 of the students and the driver of the car are killed.

November 7, Near Minya, Egypt. A bus carrying Egyptian pilgrims back from Mecca, Saudi Arabia, collides with a truck attempting to pass a car; there are 33 fatalities.

November 11, Near Maurilandia, Braz. The driver of a truck carrying cooking-gas canisters veers into oncoming traffic, causing a head-on collision with a bus carrying 20 workers, of whom 19 are killed.

December 19, Peru. A passenger bus goes off a bridge in heavy rain; 49 passengers are killed.

December 25, Near Jhelum, Pak. A passenger bus goes off the road and falls into a ravine; 18 people are killed and 39 injured.

December 27, Colombia. Two buses carrying holiday revelers collide, leaving at least 17 dead.

Miscellaneous

January 3, Gonder region, Eth. It is learned that a week earlier the roof of an 800-year-old stone church collapsed, killing at least 15 people; because of the remote location, the news took a week to reach the outside.

February 1, Mina, Saudi Arabia. At least 251 people are trampled to death in a stampede during the ritual stoning of the devil during the hajj; this is by far the highest death toll at the event since 1997.

February 5, China. During the Lantern Festival 37 people are crushed to death near a footbridge in a park in a suburb of Beijing when an accidental fall sets off a chain reaction.

February 5, Morecambe Bay, England. Twenty illegal Chinese immigrants drown in the incoming tide while harvesting cockles; it is believed they were being exploited by a human trafficking gang.

April 12, Lucknow, India. At a public birthday party that was to conclude with the distribution of free saris, 22 women are trampled to death in a stampede for the saris.

Late April–early June, Eastern Kenya. Over a period of six weeks, some 80 people die of food poisoning from eating food made from corn (maize) that had become contaminated with aflatoxin, a mold.

May 5, Zhengzhou, Henan province, China. Storage shelves packed with tons of garlic collapse, burying some 34 workers, at least 15 of whom succumb.

Mid-May–early June, Hyderabad, Pak. About three weeks after polluted water from a lake discharged into the Indus River, some 30 people have died from drinking the contaminated water.

May 27, Hubei province, China. A cofferdam collapses on the Dalongtan reservoir, causing flooding that sweeps away a minibus and drowns 12 children, their teacher, their driver, and 4 underwater construction workers.

Mid-June, Shiraz, Iran. It is reported that over the past week at least 17 people have died, and 20 more are in critical condition, from having drunk a toxic home-brewed alcoholic beverage that possibly contained methanol.

December 28, Mumbai (Bombay). Indian authorities report that illegal liquor sold in a suburb the previous weekend has killed at least 37 people, with nearly 100 still hospitalized and victims still appearing.

People of 2004

On September 2 an infant who has been released by the Chechen terrorists who seized a school in Beslan, North Ossetia, Russia, is carried to safety by a Russian special forces officer.

Nobel Prizes

Laureates in 2004 included a Kenyan ENVIRONMENTALIST, an Austrian writer, business-cycle analysts, and scientists who investigated the strong nuclear FORCE, the sense of SMELL, and PROTEIN destruction in cells.

PRIZE FOR PEACE

The 2004 Nobel Prize for Peace was awarded to Wangari Maathai, a Kenyan environmentalist and advocate for women's rights. The first African woman to receive the prize, she was best known as the founder and leader of the Green Belt Movement, which among other things had been responsible for the planting of more than 30 million trees in Kenya and elsewhere in Africa. Maathai and her movement were also involved in a number of other activities, economic and political as well as environmental, and in announcing the prize, the Norwegian Nobel Committee observed, "She has taken a holistic approach to sustainable development that embraces democracy, human rights and women's rights in particular." Acknowledging that the committee was, in effect, broadening the scope of the prize, its chairman noted that "with this award, we have expanded the term 'peace' to encompass environmental questions. . . .Peace on earth depends on our ability to secure our living environment."

Wangari Muta Maathai was born on April 1, 1940, in Nyeri, Kenya. She received a bachelor's degree in the biological sciences from Mount St. Scholastica College (now Benedictine College) in Atchison, Kan., in 1964 and a master's degree in biology from the University of Pittsburgh, Pa., in 1966. Returning to Kenya, she then studied at the University of Nairobi, where she received a doctorate in veterinary medicine in 1971. She was the first woman in East Africa to earn a doctoral degree, and in 1976 she became chair of the university's department of veterinary anatomy. That same year she joined the National Council of Women of Kenya, and she was chair of the group from 1981 to 1987. In 1977, as a way both of conserving the land and of empowering the women, she established the Green Belt Movement and embarked on the program of recruiting women to plant trees in areas that had been deforested. Over time the movement came to include programs in civic and environmental education, advocacy and networking, the training of workers in other African countries, and the development of life skills for women. It also conducted "safaris," or exchange visits, as a way of sharing cultures and of participating in activities and projects that furthered conservation.

An outspoken critic of government corruption and of such policies as land-grabbing, the taking of public lands by officials and their cronies for exploitation, Maathai often ran afoul of the regime of Daniel arap Moi in the 1970s and '80s. She was sometimes physically attacked, and at one point she was jailed. She also became known as an advocate for the cancellation of the debts of poor African nations. With the election of a reform government in 2002, she won a seat in Kenya's parliament and was subsequently appointed assistant minister for the environment, natural resources, and wildlife. Her writings included the book *The Green Belt Movement: Sharing the Approach and the Experience* (1988).

(ROBERT RAUCH)

Wangari Maathai

PRIZE FOR ECONOMICS

The Nobel Memorial Prize in Economic Sciences was awarded in 2004 to Finn E. Kydland of Norway and American Edward C. Prescott "for their contributions to dynamic macroeconomics: the time consistency of economic policy and the driving forces behind business cycles." Kydland and Prescott, working separately and together, influenced the monetary and fiscal policies of governments and laid the basis for the increased independence of many central banks, notably those in the U.K., Sweden, and New Zealand.

Kydland and Prescott were honoured for their joint contributions to two closely connected but distinct areas of macroeconomic research. The first related to the formulation of economic policy to deal with fluctuations in output and employment. From the 1930s until the early 1970s, macroeconomic analysis was dominated by the theories of British economist John Maynard Keynes. Keynesian analysis posits that short-term output and unemployment fluctuations result from variations in total demand and that recessions result from a lack of demand, not least because of consumer and business pessimism. The perceived solution was for economic policy makers to reduce unemployment permanently by allowing high rates of inflation. By the late 1960s the methodology of Keynesian models was being criticized, and by the late 1970s Keynesian analysis was proving inadequate to explain "stagflation"—simultaneous high rates of inflation and unemployment—which occurred in the 1970s in combination with a world slowdown in output and large rises in oil prices that were linked to supply rather than to demand.

In their seminal article "Rules Rather than Discretion: The Inconsistency of Optimal Plans" (1977), Kydland and Prescott demonstrated how a declared commitment to a low inflation rate by policy makers might create expectations of low inflation and unemployment rates. If this monetary policy is then changed and interest rates are reduced—for example, to take political advantage of the prosperity generated by increased inflation or to give a short-term boost to employment—the policy maker's (and thus the government's) credibility will be lost and conditions worsened by the "discretionary" policy.

In their joint article "Time to Build and Aggregate Fluctuations" (1982), Kydland and Prescott established the microeconomic foundation for business cycle analyses. Business cycles had previously been thought to be led by variations in aggregate demand. The two economists, however, demonstrated that technology changes or supply shocks, such as oil price hikes, could be reflected in investment and relative price movements and thereby create short-term fluctuations around the long-term economic growth path.

Kydland was born in December 1943 in Ålgård, near Stavanger, Nor., and was educated at the Norwegian School of Economics and Business Administration (NHH; B.S., 1968) and Carnegie

Elfriede Jelinek

Mellon University, Pittsburgh, Pa. (Ph.D., 1973), where Prescott advised on his doctorate. Kydland was an assistant professor of economics at NHH (1973–78) and taught at Carnegie Mellon (1978–2004) before being named Henley Professor of Economics at the University of California, Santa Barbara, in July 2004. He was also an adjunct professor at NHH and a consultant research associate to the Federal Reserve banks of Dallas, Texas, and Cleveland, Ohio. Kydland's teaching and research interests included business cycles, monetary and fiscal policy, and labour economics. He was a fellow of the Econometric Society from 1992.

Prescott was born Dec. 26, 1940, in Glens Falls, N.Y. He studied mathematics at Swarthmore (Pa.) College (B.A., 1962), operations research at Case Western Reserve University, Cleveland (M.S., 1963), and economics at Carnegie Mellon (Ph.D., 1967). He was a lecturer (1966–67) and assistant professor (1967–71) of economics at the University of Pennsylvania and then assistant professor (1971–72), associate professor (1972–75), and professor (1975–80) at Carnegie Mellon. After teaching at the University of Minnesota (1980–98 and 1999–2003), he moved to Arizona State University, where he held the W.P. Carey Chair from 2003. From 1980 he was an adviser to the Federal Reserve Bank of Minneapolis, Minn. Prescott was a fellow of the Brookings Institution, the Guggenheim Foundation, the Econometric Society (from 1980), and the American Academy of Arts and Sciences. He was a coeditor of *Economic Theory* and a former president (1992–95) of the Society of Economic Dynamics and Control. He also held associate editorships with the *Journal of Econometrics* (1976–82), the *International Economic Review* (1980–1990), and the *Journal of Economic Theory* (1990–92). Prescott's extensive writings covered such wide-ranging topics as business cycles, economic development, general equilibrium theory, and finance.

(JANET H. CLARK)

PRIZE FOR LITERATURE

Austrian writer and polemical feminist Elfriede Jelinek was awarded the 2004 Nobel Prize for Literature, the 10th woman to be honoured since the creation of the prize. Though known primarily to German-speaking readers, Jelinek gained international notoriety with the French-language film version of her semiautobiographical novel of sexual repression and perversity entitled *Die Klavierspielerin* (1983; *The Piano Teacher,* 1988). It was adapted for the screen in 2001 as *La Pianiste* (*The Piano Teacher*), directed by Michael Haneke. One of the most provocative and controversial writers of her generation, Jelinek was cited by the Swedish Academy "for her musical flow of voices and counter-voices in novels and plays that with extraordinary linguistic zeal reveal the absurdity of society's clichés and their subjugating power."

Jelinek, the only child of a Viennese mother of Romanian-German extraction and a Catholic and a Czechoslovak-Jewish father, was born on Oct. 20, 1946, in Mürzzuschlag, Styria province, Austria. She received her education in Vienna, where her combination of academic studies with a rigorous program of musical training at the Vienna Conservatory contributed in part to her emotional breakdown at the age of 17. It was during her recovery that Jelinek turned to writing as a form of self-expression and introspection. After attending the University of Vienna, she made her literary debut with the publication in 1967 of *Lisas Schatten,* a collection of poems, and followed that in 1970 with her first published novel, *wir sind lockvögel baby!*

Influenced by the tenets of social criticism espoused by precursors such as Karl Kraus, Ödön von Horváth, and Elias Canetti, as well as the avant-garde Vienna Group, which included H.C. Artmann and Konrad Bayer, Jelinek rejected the conventions of traditional literary technique in favour of linguistic and thematic experimentation. Using language and the structural interplay of class consciousness as a means to explore the social and cultural parameters of dependency and authority, Jelinek earned critical recognition with the publication in 1972 of her novel *Michael: Ein Jugendbuch für die Infantilgesellschaft* and emerged as a significant voice in Postmodern Austrian fiction with the publication of *Die Liebhaberinnen* (1975; *Women as Lovers,* 1994), a satiric novel of entrapment and the victimization of women within a dehumanizing and patriarchal society. She further enhanced her reputation with the staging of her first major play, *Was geschah, nachdem Nora ihren Mann verlassen hatte oder Stützen der Gesellschaften* (1980; *What Happened After Nora Left Her Husband; or, Pillars of Society,* 1994), written as a sequel to Henrik Ibsen's *A Doll's House.*

She was awarded the Georg Büchner Prize in 1998 as well as the Else Lasker-Schüler Prize and the Stig Dagerman Prize, in 2003 and 2004, respectively. Jelinek defined herself as an advocate for the weak and defenseless and remained defiant in her opposition to the exclusion and exploitation of women, as she illustrated in plays such as *Clara S.: musikalische Tragödie* (1984; *Clara S.,* 1997), *Krankheit oder moderne Frauen* (1987), *Ein Sportstück* (1998), and *Das Lebewohl* (2000), as well as in notable works of fiction that included *Die Ausgesperrten* (1980; *Wonderful, Wonderful Times,* 1990), *Oh Wildnis, oh Schutz vor ihr* (1985), *Lust* (1989; translated into English in 1992 under the same title), *Die Kinder der Toten* (1995), and *Gier: Ein Unterhaltungsroman* (2000).

Though acclaimed for her depiction of gender relations, female sexuality, and the manipulation of popular culture, she was chastised for elements in her work deemed pornographic and overtly sensational. Jelinek was an outspoken critic of oppression and violence, anti-Semitism, and racism. From 1974 to 1991 she was a member of the Austrian Communist Party, and throughout her career she encoded within her writing an ideological agenda for systemic change. For Jelinek, literature was both confessional and combative, serving as a form of social commentary and political engagement in order to cleanse and to liberate. (STEVEN R. SERAFIN)

PRIZE FOR CHEMISTRY

Three scientists who discovered an ingenious mechanism by which the cells of most living organisms cull unwanted proteins were awarded the 2004 Nobel Prize for Chemistry. The mechanism involved a process for tagging the unwanted proteins and then destroying them within structures in the cell that function as microscopic garbage disposals. Sharing the prize equally were two Israelis, Aaron J. Ciechanover and Avram Hershko of the Technion–Israel Institute of Technology, Haifa, and an American, Irwin Rose of the University of California, Irvine. Much of their prizewinning research was done in the late 1970s and early 1980s, when the three scientists worked together at the Fox Chase Cancer Center, Philadelphia.

Ciechanover was born Oct. 1, 1947, in Haifa. He received an M.D. from Hebrew University–Hadassah Medical School, Jerusalem, in 1974, and in 1981 he received a D.Sc. from the Technion, where he was a graduate student of Hershko's. Ciechanover held a variety of academic positions at the Technion beginning in 1977, and in 2002 he became a distinguished research professor. Hershko was born Dec. 31, 1937, in Karcag, Hung., and studied at the Hebrew University–Hadassah Medical School, where he received an M.D. in 1965 and a Ph.D. in 1969. He joined the faculty of the Technion in 1972 and became a distinguished professor in 1998. Rose was born July 16, 1926, in Brooklyn, N.Y., and received a Ph.D. in biochemistry from the University of Chicago in 1952. He served (1954–63) on the faculty at Yale University School of Medicine and was a senior member (1963–95) of the Fox Chase Cancer Center. In 1997 he joined the department of physiology and biophysics at the University of California, Irvine.

Proteins are very complex molecules built from individual amino acids that are linked together in chains. The typical human cell contains some 100,000 different proteins. Some are enzymes, which speed up biochemical reactions. Others include hormones, which serve a signaling function, and antibodies, which the immune system uses to fight disease. Proteins also serve as construction materials that give the cell its structure. Before the work of Ciechanover, Hershko, and Rose, a large amount of research had already been focused on understanding how cells make proteins, namely, the way cells use chemically coded instructions in DNA to link amino acids into highly precise sequences. Indeed, five Nobel Prizes had been awarded for such work.

Through their research in the 1970s and early 1980s, Ciechanover, Hershko, and Rose discovered a process that involves a series of carefully orchestrated steps by which cells degrade, or destroy, the proteins that no longer serve any useful purpose. In the first step, a tag attaches to the protein targeted for destruction. The tag is a molecule called ubiquitin (from the Latin *ubique,* meaning "everywhere," because it occurs in so many different cells and organisms). Once attached to the fated protein, ubiquitin accompanies it to a proteasome—essentially a sack of powerful enzymes that chop the protein into its component amino acids. (The typical human cell contains about 30,000 proteasomes.) The outer membrane of the proteasome admits only proteins carrying a ubiquitin molecule. The ubiquitin molecule detaches before entering the proteasome, and cells—forever thrifty—reuse it to tag yet another protein for destruction.

Ciechanover, Hershko, and Rose demonstrated that ubiquitin-mediated protein degradation also plays a key role in a kind of a cellular quality-control program—ubiquitin and proteasomes cull about one in every three new proteins manufactured by cells, apparently because of manufacturing defects. The three scientists also showed that ubiquitin-mediated protein degradation helps control a number of other critical biochemical processes. These include cell division, the repair of defects in DNA, and gene transcription, the process in which genes use their coded instructions to manufacture a protein.

Diseases result when the protein-degradation system does not work normally. For example, in cystic fibrosis, a hereditary disease, the protein-degradation system corrals and destroys a protein needed by the lungs and certain other organs to function normally. As a result, thick mucus accumulates inside the organs, impairing their function and increasing the risk of serious infections. Faulty protein degradation also helps explain the link between infection with human papillomavirus and

AP/Wide World Photos

Frank Wilczek

© Phil Klein/Reuters/Corbis

David J. Gross

an increased risk of cervical cancer. This type of infection causes the destruction of a protein needed by the cells to repair errors in DNA and thereby permits the accumulation of mutations that can lead to the development of cancer. By understanding the ubiquitin-mediated system of protein degradation, researchers hoped eventually to develop drugs against these and other similar diseases.

(MICHAEL WOODS)

PRIZE FOR PHYSICS

Three American researchers shared the 2004 Nobel Prize for Physics for discoveries about the force that binds together quarks—the smallest building blocks of matter—and holds together the nucleus of the atom. The recipients of the award were David J. Gross of the Kavli Institute for Theoretical Physics at the University of California, Santa Barbara; H. David Politzer of the California Institute of Technology (Caltech); and Frank Wilczek of the Massachusetts Institute of Technology (MIT).

Gross was born Feb. 19, 1941, in Washington, D.C. He received a Ph.D. in physics from the University of California, Berkeley, in 1966. In 1969 he joined the faculty at Princeton University, where he served until 1997, when he became the director of the Kavli Institute. Politzer, born Aug. 31, 1949, in New York City, received a Ph.D. in physics from Harvard University in 1974. He joined the faculty at Caltech in 1975. Wilczek, born May 15, 1951, was also born in New York City. As a graduate student, Wilczek studied under Gross, and he received a Ph.D. in physics from Princeton University in 1974. Wilczek served on the faculty at Princeton University from 1974 to 1981, and he was a professor at the Institute for Advanced Study, Princeton, N.J., from 1989 until 2000, when he moved to MIT.

The prizewinning work of the three scientists arose from physics experiments conducted in the early 1970s with particle accelerators, or "atom smashers," to study quarks and the force that acts on them. This force, called the strong force, or colour force, is one of the four fundamental forces in nature. The other three are the weak force, which is involved in the radioactive decay of certain chemical elements; the electromagnetic force, responsible for phenomena such as magnetism and friction; and gravitation, the attractive force between all particles having mass.

The two most familiar forces are the electromagnetic force and gravitation. Although they differ in strength, both become weaker with distance. Gross, Politzer, and Wilczek discovered that the force that governs the interaction between quarks worked in a way that seemed to defy logic. It appeared that quarks were so tightly bound together that they could not be separated as individual particles but that the closer quarks approached one another, the weaker the strong force became. When quarks were brought very close together, the force was so weak that the quarks acted almost as if they were free particles not bound together by any force. When the distance between two quarks increased, the force became greater—an effect analogous to the stretching of a rubber band. In 1973 Gross, Politzer, and Wilczek expressed this odd behaviour, known as "asymptotic freedom," within a mathematical framework. Their work led to a completely new physical theory, quantum chromodynamics (QCD), to describe the strong force. The theory was subsequently validated in many particle-physics experiments.

Quantum chromodynamics put the finishing touches on the Standard Model of particle physics, which describes the fundamental particles in nature and how they interact with one another through the strong force, the electromagnetic force, and the weak force (but not gravitation). "Perhaps the most tantalizing effect of QCD asymptotic freedom is that it opens up the possibility of a unified description of Nature's forces," said the Royal Swedish Academy of Sciences, which awarded the physics prize. "Thanks to their discovery, David Gross, David Politzer, and Frank Wilczek have brought physics one step closer to fulfilling a grand dream . . . a theory of everything." Such a theory, often called a grand unified theory, would describe all four fundamental forces in a single mathematical framework. It would describe all objects in the universe and how they interact with one another, applying to everything from the tiniest particles crammed together inside the nucleus of atoms to the biggest celestial objects separated by billions of kilometres.

(MICHAEL WOODS)

PRIZE FOR PHYSIOLOGY OR MEDICINE

Two American scientists who conducted pioneering research on the sense of smell were awarded the 2004 Nobel Prize for Physiology or Medicine. The two researchers discovered a family of genes that form smell, or olfactory, receptors. They also identified the way in which the receptors allow humans to recognize and remember some 10,000 odours. Sharing the prize equally were Richard Axel of the Howard Hughes Medical Institute at Columbia University, New York City, and Linda B. Buck of the Fred Hutchinson Cancer Research Center, Seattle, Wash.

Richard Axel

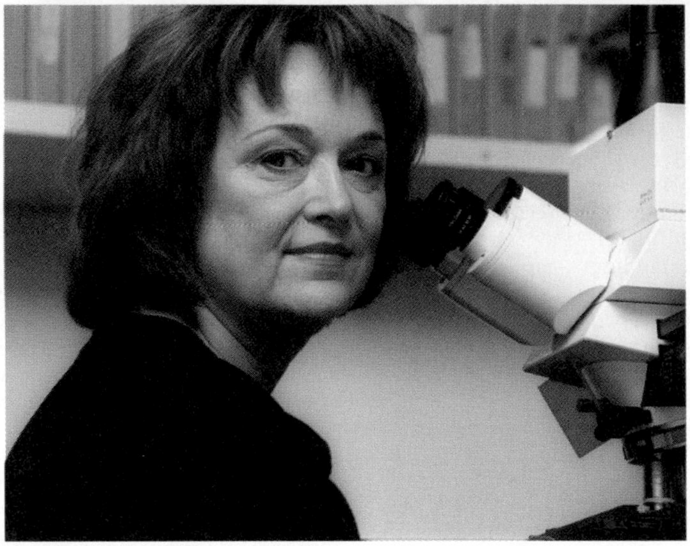

Linda Buck

Axel was born July 2, 1946, in New York City. He received an M.D. from Johns Hopkins University School of Medicine, Baltimore, Md., in 1970. He joined the Howard Hughes Medical Institute as an investigator in 1984. Buck, born Jan. 29, 1947, in Seattle, received a Ph.D. in immunology in 1980 from the University of Texas Southwestern Medical Center. The two first worked together in the early 1980s at Columbia University, where Axel was a professor and Buck was his postdoctoral student. Buck held various positions at the Howard Hughes Medical Institute and at Harvard Medical School from 1984 until 2002, when she joined the Fred Hutchinson Cancer Institute.

In 1991 Axel and Buck jointly published a landmark scientific paper, based on research they had conducted with laboratory rats, that contained the first description of a family of approximately 1,000 types of olfactory receptors. Olfactory receptors are proteins responsible for detecting the odorant molecules that waft through the air and for generating the signals that the brain interprets as smells. The proteins, called G-proteins, were known to play a role in other kinds of cell signaling. The scientific paper also described the family of 1,000 genes that encode, or produce, olfactory receptors. Axel and Buck showed that every olfactory receptor cell expresses (turns on) only one of the odorant-receptor genes. By recording electric signals from single olfactory receptor cells, Buck and Axel showed that each type of receptor could react to several related odorous substances.

Olfactory receptors are located in cells clustered within a small area in the back of the nasal cavity and are embedded in the surface of nerve cells. Odorant molecules from flowers, perfumes, food, and other sources drift through the air and enter the nose. There they attach to and activate corresponding types of olfactory receptors, which send electric signals to the brain. Nerves link the receptor cells directly to the olfactory bulb, the main region of the brain involved in the sense of smell. Nerve signals from the olfactory receptors indicate that an odour is present in the environment. Buck and Axel showed that each receptor cell has only one type of odour receptor, which is specialized to recognize a few odours. Olfactory receptor cells specializing in the same type of odours are linked to the same areas of the brain. Most odours consist of several different kinds of odorant molecules. The brain combines information from several types of receptors in specific patterns, which are experienced as distinct odours.

Although their initial research was on laboratory rats, Axel and Buck later determined that most of the details they uncovered about the sense of smell are virtually identical in rats, humans, and other animals. The work of Axel and Buck also helped boost scientific interest in the possible existence of human pheromones, odorant molecules known to trigger sexual activity and certain other behaviour in many animals. One difference they discovered was that humans have only about 350 types of working olfactory receptors, about one-third the number in rats. Nevertheless, the genes that encode olfactory receptors in humans still account for about 3% of all human genes. Scientists were astounded at the sheer number of the types of olfactory receptors needed for the sense of smell. (The human eye can distinguish an enormous number of variations in colour with only three types of receptors—blue, green, and red.) Some odour receptor genes in humans were probably lost during evolution because the sense of smell became less important than the other senses for human survival. In other animals, however, the sense of smell remains critical for survival. Many newborn animals use the sense of smell to locate the mother's teats and begin nursing. Smells also help adult animals locate food and alert them to enemies and other threats. (MICHAEL WOODS)

Biographies

The SUBJECTS of these biographies are the people who in the editors' opinions captured the IMAGINATION of the world in 2004—the most INTERESTING and/or IMPORTANT PERSONALITIES of the year.

Allawi, Ayad

On June 28, 2004, the U.S.-led Coalition Provisional Authority officially transferred sovereignty in Iraq to the newly chosen Iraqi leadership. To the surprise of many, Ayad Allawi, a secular Shi'ite and former member of the Arab Ba'th Socialist Party, was named prime minister of the interim government. He was to hold office until general elections, scheduled for January 2005, could be held. As prime minister, Allawi adopted a policy of trying to reconcile with Ba'thists who had not been involved in criminal acts during former president Saddam Hussein's regime. Allawi held out the prospect of pardon for all rebels—Shi'ite or Sunni—willing to lay down their arms, though he remained tough on insurgents and supported the U.S. assault on the city of Fallujah.

Allawi was born in Baghdad on May 31, 1944, into a middle-class family. His father was a physician; his mother came from a well-known Lebanese family. He joined the Ba'thists in 1961 and became active in the Iraqi National Students' Union while studying at the College of Medicine in Baghdad. In 1972 he was sent to England to pursue advanced medical studies and to head the Ba'th National Students' Union there. He received a degree in neurology (1982), but he never practiced medicine, preferring politics.

In 1976 Allawi broke with the Ba'th Party and reportedly established ties with the British intelligence service MI6. Two years later he and his wife survived a brutal assassination attempt, presumably perpetrated by Saddam's secret police. He recovered but sustained serious scars and thereafter walked with a limp. In 1979 he began organizing a political group composed of disaffected Ba'thists, which by 1991 had metamorphosed into the Iraqi National Accord (INA), a party in opposition to Saddam.

The Gulf War of 1990–91 opened new horizons for Allawi. Seeking Saddam's overthrow, the U.S. began to look for Iraqi exiles with ties inside Iraq and by 1992 had established contact with him. He was favoured by the CIA and some other agencies as a counterweight to Ahmad al-Chalabi, then a more prominent Iraqi exile opposition leader. During the 1990s the INA was responsible for attacks inside Iraq aimed at destabilizing Saddam's regime, including a failed CIA-sponsored coup in 1996. After the United States-led invasion of Iraq in early 2003, Allawi was chosen as one of the 25 members of the U.S.-backed provisional governing council.

Allawi was not known for his charismatic personality; rather he was a reserved man who avoided confrontation. His Ba'thist training, however, had made him a behind-the-scenes operator and a political survivor, and his INA was expected to mount a strong campaign in the general elections. (LOUAY BAHRY)

Arbour, Louise

© Denis Balibouse/Reuters/Corbis

When Louise Arbour became UN high commissioner for human rights in June 2004, she had already had a distinguished career. She replaced Sérgio Vieira de Mello, who was killed in August 2003 when the UN headquarters in Baghdad, Iraq, was bombed. Prior to Arbour's appointment to the UN, she was a justice of the Supreme Court of Canada from 1999 to 2004. Earlier, she had served (1996–99) as the chief prosecutor of war crimes before the International Criminal Tribunals for Rwanda and for the Former Yugoslavia in The Hague. During this time she indicted former Yugoslav leader Slobodan Milosevic and others for crimes against humanity. In 1995 Arbour was appointed head of a commission of inquiry into events at the Prison for Women in Kingston, Ont., and delivered a scathing report on the condition and treatment of women prisoners. In 1990 she became the first Francophone to be appointed to the Court of Appeal for Ontario.

Louise Berenice Arbour was born on Feb. 10, 1947, in Montreal to owners of a hotel chain. After obtaining a degree in civil law at the University of Montreal in 1970 and being admitted to the Quebec bar in 1971, she served for two years as a law clerk for Justice Louis-Philippe Pigeon of the Supreme Court of Canada. During this time, while also completing graduate studies at the University of Ottawa, she met her partner, Larry Taman; she learned English from him, and he learned French from her.

In 1977 Arbour was admitted to the Ontario bar, and throughout the 1970s and '80s, she held a variety of positions. She taught at Osgoode Hall Law School in Toronto, where she eventually became an associate dean. Arbour conducted research for the Law Reform Commission of Canada and served as vice president of the Canadian Civil Liberties Association. She was also involved in a number of controversial legal issues, including campaigning for prisoners' voting rights and challenging what was known as the "rape-shield" law. Arbour successfully argued that the law might lead to the conviction of innocent men.

Arbour received many awards and medals, including the Franklin Delano Roosevelt Four Freedoms Medal (Freedom from Fear) from the Franklin and Eleanor Roosevelt Institute (2000), the Lord Reading Law Society's Human Rights Award (2000), and the EID-UL-ADHA Award from the Association of Progressive Muslims of Ontario (2001). She also received an honorary fellowship from the American College of Trial Lawyers, the Médaille de la Faculté de droit de l'Université de Montréal, and was inducted into the International Hall of Fame at the International Women's Forum, both in 2003.

Throughout her career Arbour sought to liberate both the oppressed and their oppressors by creating a safe climate for diversity and dissent. (ELIZABETH RHETT WOODS)

Arcand, Denys

In 2004 the career of French Canadian filmmaker Denys Arcand reached climatic heights as his 2003 film *Les Invasions barbares* (*The Barbarian Invasions*) collected major award after major award. The film, written and directed by Arcand, follows the final days of Rémy, a history professor, womanizer, and devout leftist

© Robert Galbraith/Reuters/Corbis

Canadian filmmaker Denys Arcand

who is dying of cancer in a Montreal hospital. His banker son, ex-wife, and friends old and new gather to comfort Rémy in his final days and reflect on the vagaries of life.

The accolades for *The Barbarian Invasions* began in 2003 at the Cannes Festival, where Arcand received the top honours for his screenplay and Marie-Josée Croze was hailed as best actress for her performance as an addict who provides the pain-wracked Rémy with heroin. The film was also named best Canadian film at the 2003 Toronto International Film Festival. The momentum carried into 2004 as Arcand was named a Commander of the Order of Arts and Letters—the highest cultural honour in France. On February 21 in Paris *The Barbarian Invasions* received three César Awards for original screenplay, director, and best film. The next day at the Jutra Awards in Montreal, Arcand again received awards for screenplay, direction, and best film. The following weekend in Los Angeles, Arcand's film won the Academy Award for best foreign-language film.

Arcand was born on June 25, 1941, in Deschambault, Que. He was raised in a devout Catholic home and educated by Jesuits before entering the University of Montreal, where he studied history and made his first film. A job at the National Film Board (NFB) followed graduation. There he began making documentaries, most notably films about the early history of Quebec. Arcand had been an outspoken leftist since he was a young man, and in 1970 he made *On est au coton* (*Cotton Mill, Treadmill*), an exposé of the textile industry that was so controversial that it was banned by the NFB. He soon moved into feature films, beginning with *La Maudite Galette* (*Dirty Money*) in 1972. He directed the film *Le Crime d'Ovide Plouffe* (*Murder in the Family*) in 1984 and the television miniseries based on it that followed the next year, and in 1986 he made his first big splash on the international film scene with *Le Déclin de l'empire américain* (*The Decline of the American Empire*). The movie, which was nominated for an Academy Award for best foreign-language film, was centred on a gourmet dinner with a group of intellectuals—the same friends featured in *The Barbarian Invasions* and starring many of the same actors. Arcand scored another international hit with *Jésus de Montréal* (1989; *Jesus of Montreal*). Although Arcand's films were sometimes criticized for an excess of sentimentality, they all embodied his intellectual curiosity and passion for politics, art, and life.

(JAMES HENNELLY)

Badawi, Datuk Seri Abdullah Ahmad

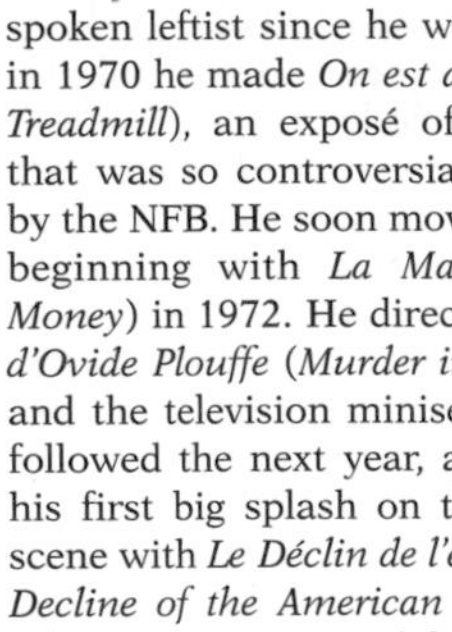

© Bazuki Muhammad/Reuters/Corbis

Five months after he took office as prime minister of Malaysia, Datuk Seri Abdullah Ahmad Badawi received a surprisingly strong personal mandate in general elections held on March 21, 2004. The gains made by his party, the United Malays National Organization, demonstrated widespread support for Abdullah in the ethnically and religiously diverse country, despite his having been handpicked for the premiership by his predecessor, Mahathir bin Mohamad. Abdullah vowed to attack poverty and to eliminate the cronyism that had been a byword of Mahathir's long tenure. Two high-profile arrests in February suggested that Abdullah would make good his anticorruption pledge. When Abdullah announced his cabinet appointments after the elections, however, critics expressed disappointment; the group included several scandal-tainted holdovers from the previous administration. In September the Malaysian High Court's unanticipated release of Anwar Ibrahim, the former deputy prime minister who had been imprisoned on questionable charges since 1998, resolved one of the most troubling of legacies of the Mahathir era and brought new accolades for Abdullah's housecleaning efforts.

Moving with quiet authority on the international stage, in January Abdullah initiated a rapprochement with neighbouring Singapore, seeking to end decades of territorial bickering. Responding in February to U.S. Pres. George W. Bush's charge that Malaysia was trafficking in nuclear secrets, Abdullah questioned the evidence for the claim but also called for a police investigation of his son's alleged involvement in the matter. In May Abdullah urged the world powers to renew efforts to end the Israeli-Palestinian conflict, and he criticized President Bush for sanctioning Israel's apparent abandonment of the "road map for peace" that had been endorsed by the UN Security Council in 2003. In June Abdullah called for the formation of an East Asian economic community, modeled on the European Union, to give Asian nations greater clout in world affairs.

Abdullah was born on Nov. 26, 1939, in Kampung Perlis on the island of Penang, then part of the British Straits Settlements colony. In 1964 he graduated with a B.A. (with honours) in Islamic studies from the University of Malaya. He then joined the Malayan civil service. He served on the National Operation Council, which exercised executive power during a nationwide state of emergency (1969–70). In 1971 he moved to the Ministry of Culture, Youth, and Sports. He resigned from the civil service in 1978 and campaigned successfully for election to the federal parliament. Also in 1978 he received his first administrative appointment in the Federal Territory Ministry. Under Mahathir, Abdullah served as minister in the Prime Minister's Department (1981–84), as well as minister of education (1984–86) and defense (1986–87). In 1991 he was appointed minister of foreign affairs, a position he held until 1999, when Mahathir named him deputy prime minister and minister of home affairs. On Oct. 31, 2003, Abdullah became Malaysia's fifth prime minister.

(JANET MOREDOCK)

Bailey, Jerry

Al Messerschmidt/WireImage.com

Winning jockey Jerry Bailey

When the 2003 Thoroughbred racing Eclipse Awards were handed out on Jan. 26, 2004, Jerry Bailey was proclaimed the outstanding jockey in North America for an unprecedented seventh time (1995–97 and 2000–03); in 1997 he had been the first jockey to win three consecutive Eclipse Awards. Bailey had recorded more victories in the prestigious Breeders' Cup World Thoroughbred Championships (13) than any other rider in the 20-year history of the competition and had led the nation's riders in total purse earnings seven times, including a record $23,354,960 in 2003. Although he might not be as universally recognized as such legendary jockeys as Johnny Longden, Eddie Arcaro, Willie Shoemaker, and Bill Hartack, the intensely competitive Bailey remained at the top of his game after a 30-year career, and his dominance of Thoroughbred racing over the previous decade had earned him a historical place in their company.

Jerry Dale Bailey was born Aug. 29, 1957, in Dallas, Texas, the son of a prominent dentist who dabbled in racing as a horse owner. He had ambitions to participate in team sports, but his diminutive stature (1.65 m [5 ft 5 in] tall) eventually led him to the racetrack to pursue a career as a jockey. He began his professional riding career at New Mexico's Sunland Park, where, in November 1974 at age 17, he won the very first race in which he rode, astride a horse named Fetch. Bailey enjoyed considerable success around the country prior to establishing his presence as a rising star on the New York state circuit in 1982. He solidified his national stature with victories astride Hansel in the 1991 Preakness and Belmont Stakes, won his first Kentucky Derby in 1993 with Sea Hero, and was inducted into the National Racing Hall of Fame two years later. Bailey won his second Kentucky Derby riding Grindstone in 1996, added another Preakness win in 2000 with Red Bullet, and captured the 2003 Belmont on Empire Maker. In July 1996 he guided Cigar, a two-time Horse of the Year, to a 16th consecutive victory, equaling the modern era record set by 1948 Triple Crown champion Citation. On May 6, 2001, at Aqueduct Racetrack in New York, Bailey recorded his milestone 5,000th career win, and later that year he became the first rider to reach $20 million in purse earnings for a single season.

In recent years Bailey had established personal limits on the number of horses he rode

based on criteria that emphasized quality rather than quantity. In 2004 he ranked second on the all-time jockey earnings list (with $270,473,779) and 15th on the all-time win list (with 5,667 career victories), but the sport's preeminent "thinking man's rider" was likely to rise on both lists before his career was over.
(JOHN G. BROKOPP)

Bement, Arden

The head of the National Science Foundation (NSF) for most of 2004 was Arden Bement, a metallurgical engineer and science administrator whose career included successful stints in academia, government, and private industry. Bement became acting director of the NSF on February 22 after the previous director, Rita R. Colwell, stepped down on 10 days' notice, and on November 24 he became director. Colleagues praised Bement's ability to work with the various components of scientific bureaucracies and to get them to work together harmoniously.

Following his confirmation as director of the NSF, Bement announced that he was stepping down as director of the National Institute of Standards and Technology (NIST), a position he had assumed in 2001. Under Bement's leadership, NIST had taken a more active role in national security, spurred on by concerns following the Sept. 11, 2001, attacks on the World Trade Center and the Pentagon. In addition to conducting a major investigation into the collapse of the World Trade Center towers and researching new methods of cyber security to protect the nation's utilities from computer attacks, NIST took a leading role in work toward developing new biometric technologies, such as fingerprint scanners and metal detectors.

Arden Lee Bement, Jr., was born on May 22, 1932, in Pittsburgh, Pa. As a young man, Bement had no plans to attend college until his supervisor at a Colorado molybdenum mill offered him a challenge: if Bement could complete a semester of college, the supervisor would pay him $75. Bement took the bet and never looked back. He attended the Colorado School of Mines, where he earned an Engineer of Metallurgy degree. He went on to earn a master's degree in metallurgical engineering at the University of Idaho and a doctorate in metallurgical engineering from the University of Michigan.

His early career in private industry included positions as a researcher at the General Electric Co. and manager of the metallurgy research department at Battelle Northwest Laboratories (Richland, Wash.; now Pacific Northwest Laboratories) before he joined the faculty at the Massachusetts Institute of Technology in 1970. In 1976 he accepted his first government position, serving as the director of the Office of Materials Science at the Defense Advanced Research Projects Agency in the U.S. Department of Defense. In 1979 he became deputy undersecretary of defense for research and engineering. A year later he returned to private industry, joining TRW Inc. to serve as its vice president of technical resources and of science and technology. In 1992 Bement began his second stint in academia at Purdue University, West Lafayette, Ind., where his positions included the David A. Ross Distinguished Professor of Nuclear Engineering and head of the nuclear engineering department. In October 2001, U.S. Pres. George W. Bush nominated Bement for the top job at NIST. In relatively short order, Bement was confirmed by the Senate in November, and he was sworn in on December 7. Bement, a member of the U.S. National Academy of Engineering, had served from 1999 to 2001 as the chairman of the NIST Advanced Technology Program advisory committee.
(ANTHONY G. CRAINE)

Beyoncé

The first solo album of singing star Beyoncé, *Dangerously in Love*, debuted to rave reviews; after two songs from the album reached number one on Billboard's Hot 100, the CD itself hit the top of Billboard's album chart in 2004. The success of the album at the 2004 Grammy Awards, where it won five prizes, including that for best contemporary R&B album, cemented her new celebrity status and marked her arrival as a genuine adult superstar. The album, heavily produced with booming beats, vocal overdubs, and lengthy interjections by Jay-Z and other male rappers, featured songs written mostly by Beyoncé herself; if her lyrics were usually about hot young lust ("Tonight I'll be your naughty girl"), her sweet little-girl voice lent them a safe air of innocence for her teenage female following.

Beyoncé Giselle Knowles was born on Sept. 4, 1981, in Houston, Texas. She and three other youngsters formed the singing-rapping girl group Destiny's Child when she was nine years old. Her father, Matthew Knowles, managed the group. At first, fame eluded Destiny's Child. In 1992 the group lost on the *Star Search* television talent show, and three years later it was dropped from a recording contract before an album had been released. The group, which now included Beyoncé's cousin Kelly Rowland, nonetheless had a local following, and Matthew was determined to make them a success, even selling the family home in 1996 to support the girls. In 1997 Destiny's Child's fortunes reversed with a Columbia recording contract and then an eponymous debut album that yielded three hit singles. Though Destiny's Child's second CD, *The Writing's on the Wall* (1999), sold eight million copies, two of the quartet's singers decided their destiny was elsewhere. By the time of the release of their third album, *Survivor* (2001), Destiny's Child had become a trio.

Singing sensation Beyoncé

© Bruno Bebert/Pool/Reuters/Corbis

Beyoncé was clearly the group's star and increasingly took a leading role in the group, writing hit songs such as "Bootylicious." By this time, however, Destiny's Child could no longer contain the ambitions of its members, all of whom sought solo projects. In 2001, the year she became the first African American woman to be named ASCAP's Pop Songwriter of the Year, Beyoncé began her acting career in MTV's *Carmen: A Hip Hopera.* Her role as Foxxy Cleopatra in *Austin Powers in Goldmember* (2002) made her a film star and led to a part in *The Fighting Temptations* (2003). With the 2003 release of *Dangerously in Love,* Beyoncé shed her last name. She was already a Pepsi-Cola spokesperson by the time of her 2004 Grammy triumphs. Meanwhile, her second solo album, *Beyoncé Live at Wembley,* released on DVD with multimedia components, climbed the hit charts, and she secured a part as a pop singer in Blake Edwards's prequel to *The Pink Panther* (set for a 2005 release). Despite her solo success, Beyoncé reunited with the other members of Destiny's Child to record *Destiny Fulfilled* (2004). (JOHN LITWEILER)

Brady, Tom

Tom Brady, the quarterback of the New England Patriots, would probably not be rated the best passer in the National Football League (NFL). He certainly was not the most mobile quarterback in the league, and he did not have the strongest arm. In 2004, however, Brady showed that he was the best NFL quarterback in one very important category—winning. The Patriots ended the 2003–04 season with a 15-game winning streak that was capped off with a 32–29 victory over the Carolina Panthers in Super Bowl XXXVIII on Feb. 1, 2004. Brady, who completed 32 of 48 pass attempts for 354 yd and three touchdowns, was named the Super Bowl Most Valuable Player (MVP) for the second time in his career.

Brady and the Patriots continued their winning ways in the 2004–05 season, collecting victories in their first six games. Their streak of 21 consecutive wins, which was ended by the Pittsburgh Steelers on Oct. 31, 2004, shattered the previous record of 18 games set by the 1972–73 Miami Dolphins. The Patriots also set a NFL record for consecutive regular-season victories with a total of 18. Although one player could not take credit for such a long winning streak, the professionalism and determination of the Patriots seemed to be perfectly reflected in their young quarterback. Thomas Edward Patrick Brady, Jr., was born on Aug. 3, 1977, in San Mateo, Calif. The 2-m (6-ft 4-in)-tall signal caller enjoyed a solid career at the University of Michigan, where he developed a reputation as an intelligent and determined player but one who lacked any exceptional physical skills. Selected by the Patriots in the sixth round of the 2000 NFL draft, Brady worked hard in his rookie season to master the offensive playbook, to bulk up physically, and to improve his strength and technique. When the Patriots star quarterback, Drew Bledsoe, went down with an injury in the second game of the 2001 season, Brady was named the new starter, an opportunity that he seized. His play was not spectacular, but he was steady, making the simple plays and minimizing his mistakes. The team seemed to gain confidence from his cool-headed leadership and went on to post an 11–3 record. The momentum carried on through the play-offs, where Brady won his first Super Bowl MVP as the team scored a dramatic upset over the St. Louis Rams in Super Bowl XXXVI. In the following seasons, Brady built his reputation as a smart quarterback who consistently made plays that would win games. During his first three seasons as the starting quarterback, the Patriots became one of the NFL's elite teams, posting a 40–12 record. (JAMES HENNELLY)

Brahimi, Lakhdar

On Jan. 1, 2004, diplomat Lakhdar Brahimi celebrated his 70th birthday and was named special adviser to UN Secretary-General Kofi Annan. Brahimi's primary duties involved conflict prevention and resolution, areas that would take him to the world's toughest and most dangerous places. It was a path that he had trod before at the UN; Brahimi had headed missions to South Africa and Haiti. He also led the reconstruction effort in Afghanistan for the UN, following the U.S.-led mission that toppled the Taliban regime there in late 2001. When the focus of U.S. antiterrorism efforts was diverted from Afghanistan to Iraq, Brahimi was also diverted to Iraq. In May 2004 he arrived in Iraq to aid in the effort to restore independence, which hinged on the country's first democratic elections, scheduled for early 2005. Keeping in mind Iraq's ethnic and religious diversity, Brahimi helped build a transitional government, forming a National Assembly of 100 members and overseeing the June implementation of the Coalition Provisional Authority and the selection of Ayad Allawi (*q.v.*) as interim Iraqi prime minister. Concerned about the country's continuing instability, Brahimi left Iraq before the transfer of power at the end of June; he implied that the U.S. invasion in 2002 might have caused more problems than it had solved.

Brahimi was born on Jan. 1, 1934, in Algeria, which at the time was under the rule of France. He was educated in both countries, and he participated in Algeria's struggle for independence from France in the late 1950s and early '60s as a diplomatic representative of the National Liberation Front (FLN) in Southeast Asia. Continuing in his role as foreign ambassador through the 1970s, he represented independent Algeria within Egypt,

© Lucas Schifres/Corbis

UN envoy Lakhdar Brahimi

The Sudan, the United Kingdom, and the Arab League. He served in the Algerian government as presidential adviser (1982–84) and then served as under-secretary-general (1984–91) of the League of the Arab States before returning to the Algerian government as foreign minister (1991–93).

Brahimi joined the UN in 1992, when he attended the Earth Summit. He first represented the UN in Afghanistan in 1997–99. He was lauded for his report in 2000 that was critical of UN inaction in Rwanda in 1994 and in Srebrenica, Bosnia and Herzegovina, in 1995, the sites of horrific massacres. In 2002, while he was working in Afghanistan, he was honoured by Harvard University Law School with its annual Great Negotiator Award. (TOM MICHAEL)

Brin, Sergey, and Page, Larry

On Aug. 19, 2004, Sergey Brin and Larry Page went from being promising computer science graduate students to multibillionaire technology mavens when Google, Inc., the online search engine company they had founded in 1998, issued its much-anticipated initial public offering (IPO). By creating the easy-to-use hypertext search engine Google, one of the most successful applications in the history of the Internet, Brin and Page had provided World Wide Web browsing at its simplest to millions of ordinary computer users and had added a new verb, *to google*, to the English language.

Sergey Brin was born in the Soviet Union in 1973 and moved with his family from Moscow to the United States in 1979. After receiving degrees (1993) in computer science and mathematics at the University of Maryland, he entered Stanford University's graduate program. Lawrence Page was born in 1972 in East Lansing, Mich., where his father was a computer science professor. He received a computer engineering degree from the University of Michigan. In early 1995 Brin was assigned to show a new Stanford graduate student—Page—around campus, and by year's end the duo had joined forces.

Brin and Page were intrigued with the idea of enhancing the ability to extract meaning from the mass of data accumulating on the Internet. They began working from Page's dormitory room to devise a new type of search technology, which they dubbed BackRub. The key was to leverage Web users' own ranking abilities by tracking each Web site's "backing links"—that is, the number of other pages linked to them. Most search engines simply returned a list of Web sites ranked by how often a search phrase appeared on them. Brin and Page incorporated into the search function the number of links each Web site had—i.e., a Web site with thousands of links would logically be more valuable than one with just a few links, and the search engine thus would place the heavily linked site higher on a list of possibilities. Further, a link from a heavily linked Web site would be a more valuable "vote" than one from a more obscure Web site. Meanwhile, the partners established an idealistic 10-point corporate philosophy that included "Focus on the user and all else will follow," "Fast is better than slow," and "You can make money without doing evil."

Google founders Larry Page (left) and Sergey Brin

© Kim Kulish/Corbis

In mid-1998 Brin and Page began receiving outside financing (one of their first investors was a cofounder of Sun Microsystems, Inc.). They ultimately raised about $1 million from investors, family, and friends and set up shop in Menlo Park, Calif., under the name Google, which was derived from a misspelling of Page's original planned name, googol (a mathematical term for the number one followed by 100 zeroes). By mid-1999, when Google received a $25 million round of venture capital funding, it was processing 500,000 queries per day. Activity exploded when Google became the client search engine for one of the Web's most popular sites, Yahoo!, and by 2004 users were "googling" 200 million times a day (roughly 138,000 queries per minute). The IPO, which netted more than $3.8 billion apiece for Brin and Page, cemented Google's amazing transformation from dorm room hobby to multibillion-dollar technology powerhouse. (CHRISTOPHER O'LEARY)

Brown, Dan

The phenomenal success of Dan Brown's *The Da Vinci Code* (2003) showed no signs of slowing in 2004 as the thriller remained a fixture on best-seller lists around the world and even inspired its own genre. With more than 7.5 million copies sold and editions available in some 40 languages, *The Da Vinci Code* was one of the fastest-selling books of all time. Intense interest in the novel resulted in a spate of *Code*-related books and sparked sales of Brown's earlier works; in 2004 all four of his novels appeared simultaneously on the *New York Times* best-seller lists. *The Da Vinci Code*'s immense popularity lay in Brown's intricate weaving of art history, Christianity's origins, and arcane theories into a spellbinding thriller. It was his second novel to feature Robert Langdon, a Harvard professor of symbology, and it followed Langdon's attempts to solve the murder of the Louvre's curator. As the investigation deepens, Langdon encounters mysterious organizations (Opus Dei and the Priory of Sion), discusses the hidden messages in Leonardo da Vinci's art, raises the possibility that Jesus Christ married Mary Magdalene and fathered a child, and discovers the Holy Grail. *The Da Vinci Code* proved controversial, and many theologians and art scholars dismissed Brown's notions. Readers, however, were riveted by the novel's furious pace and thought-provoking ideas.

Brown was born on June 22, 1964, in Exeter, N.H. He attended Phillips Exeter Academy, a prep school where his father was a math teacher, and in 1986 graduated from Amherst (Mass.) College. He then moved to California to pursue a career as a songwriter. Although he had little success in the music industry, in 1990 he wrote his first book, *187 Men to Avoid,* a dating survival guide for women; it was published in 1995. In 1993 Brown joined the faculty at Exeter as an English and creative-writing teacher. Several years later the U.S. Secret Service visited the school to interview a student who had written an e-mail in which he joked about killing the president. The incident sparked Brown's interest in covert intelligence agencies, which formed the basis of his first novel, *Digital Fortress* (1998). Well researched and centred on secret organizations and code breaking, the novel became a model for Brown's later works.

In his next novel, *Angels & Demons* (2000), Brown introduced Langdon. The fast-paced thriller followed Langdon's attempts to protect the Vatican from the Illuminati, a secret society formed during the Renaissance that opposed the Roman Catholic Church. Although the novel received positive reviews, it failed to catch on with readers. After his third novel, *Deception Point* (2001), Brown returned to Langdon with *The Da Vinci Code.* An immediate success—it debuted atop the *New York Times* best-seller list—it was optioned for a movie in 2003. In 2004 Brown was at work on his third Langdon novel, which focused on the secret history of Washington, D.C.

(AMY TIKKANEN)

Burnett, Mark

Proving once again his mastery of reality-television programming, American TV producer Mark Burnett, the creative force behind the blockbuster hit *Survivor,* scored another smash hit in 2004 with *The Apprentice.* The show, which was nominated for four Emmy Awards, revolved around 16 ambitious candidates competing for a full-time job with billionaire real-estate developer Donald Trump (*q.v.*). *The Apprentice* tapped the same reservoir of voyeurism and vicarious vengefulness in viewers that Burnett had already mined so successfully with his first hit reality series, *Survivor* (2000), which was still rated among the top 10 shows at the completion of its eighth season. In addition, *Survivor* spawned a multitude of dating games and competitions based on contestants doing everything from making home improvements to eating creepy crawlies. Preferring the term *unscripted drama* to *reality show,* Burnett also produced *The Casino* (2004), a behind-the-scenes look at the revamped Golden Nugget hotel and casino in Las Vegas, Nev. Less-successful projects included the documentary-style show *The Restaurant* (2003–04), which chronicled the turbulent life of a Manhattan eatery, *Combat Missions* (2002), and a competition for would-be astronauts that was abandoned at the planning stage. Scheduled to debut in 2005 were *The Contender,* which would follow a select group of young boxers as they competed against one another, and the tentatively titled *Rock Star,* a search for a new lead singer for the band INXS.

© Frank Trapper/Corbis

Reality-TV pioneer Mark Burnett

James Mark Burnett was born on July 17, 1960, into a working-class family in Myland, Essex, Eng. After completing missions in the Falkland Islands/Islas Malvinas and Northern Ireland with the British Parachute Regiment, he moved to Los Angeles, where he worked as a nanny for two years before becoming a T-shirt salesman on nearby Venice Beach, an experience he later described as his "first foray" into American entrepreneurship. Seeking to combine his desire for wealth with his taste for high adventure, in the early 1990s Burnett conceived the Eco-Challenge, an international extreme-sports competition. First broadcast in 1995, the *Eco-Challenge* television series featured mixed-sex teams in arduous multisport competitions emphasizing esprit de corps (a team was disqualified if one member dropped out) and environmental consciousness (competitors were required to carry away all waste). In addition to offering the gorgeous presentation of the dramatic race settings, each series laid bare the sufferings of competitors under harsh conditions and the inevitable friction between team members, an approach that would later prove magnetizing in *Survivor.* In 2000 *Eco-Challenge: Morocco* won a Sports Emmy and a Banff Rockie Award.

Burnett also published a number of books—*Survivor: The Ultimate Game* (2000), *Survivor II: The Field Guide* (2001), and the autobiographical *Dare to Succeed: How to Survive and Thrive in the Game of Life* (2001).

(JANET MOREDOCK)

Bush, George W.

On Nov. 2, 2004, George W. Bush was elected to a second term as president of the United States. He received 51% of the popular vote, to 48% for Democratic candidate Massachusetts Sen. John Kerry (*q.v.*); the vote in the electoral college was 286–251. Those who said that the threat of terrorism was the nation's most serious problem overwhelmingly backed Bush. Suburbs and rural areas of the country's interior, including parts of the Midwest, the South, and the Plains and Mountain states, provided him with solid support.

The defining event of Bush's first term had been the terrorist attacks of Sept. 11, 2001, in New York City and Washington, D.C. The president came to be seen by a majority of Americans as a decisive leader, and making this the foundation of his reelection campaign, Bush ran as a war president. Charges against the administration—for example, that it had diverted resources from the struggle against terrorism to an unjustified war in Iraq—proved ineffective with a slim majority of voters, many of whom saw the administration's aggressive, unilateral foreign policy as the best protection against terrorism.

President Bush also touted a number of domestic policies that resonated with many voters. Perhaps foremost among these were large tax cuts, which the administration justified as

© Jason Reed/Reuters/Corbis

Reelected Pres. George W. Bush

a response to the recession that occurred early in the Bush presidency. The stimulus created by these cuts was hailed as a success, despite a sluggish economic recovery, lagging job growth, and record budget deficits. Policies such as the loosening of business and environmental regulations appealed to many mainstream conservatives, and the president's support for a constitutional amendment that would ban same-sex marriages attracted the religious right.

Bush performed poorly in the first of three debates against Kerry, and polls showed that barely half of all Americans approved of his performance as president. As a result, Republicans turned the campaign from a referendum on the Bush presidency into a vote on Kerry's record, and character charges largely replaced the serious discussion of issues. The attacks on Kerry's military record, allegations of "flip-flopping," and questions about his ability to lead the nation in a time of terrorists threats were instrumental in helping Bush win reelection.

George Walker Bush was born on July 6, 1946, in New Haven, Conn. He had degrees from Yale University (B.A., 1968) and Harvard Business School (M.B.A., 1975). After working in the oil industry in Texas, he was an adviser in the successful 1988 presidential campaign of his father, George H.W. Bush, and then a managing partner (1989–94) of a group that owned the Texas Rangers baseball team. In 1994 he was elected governor of Texas; he was reelected in 1998. In 2000, after prolonged political and legal disputes over the results in Florida, he was narrowly elected the 43rd president of the U.S. with a vote of 271–266 in the electoral college, although his Democratic opponent, Vice Pres. Al Gore, had a margin of 0.51% in the popular vote. After the 2004 election Bush made a large number of cabinet changes—which included replacing Secretary of State Colin Powell and Attorney General John Ashcroft—and he immediately began to promote the permanent extension of earlier tax cuts and the partial privatization of social security, both major elements of his second-term agenda. (ROBERT RAUCH)

Byatt, A.S.

The year 2004 showed British author A.S. Byatt at the apex of her career as an author, literary critic, and academic. She received critical praise for *Little Black Book of Stories* (2004), a collection of five Gothic tales that tackled such tough issues as aging and death. In discussing her subject matter, Byatt said that she wanted to look at old age "while I'm still physically fit enough to look at it objectively." She added, "I know that my work is better than it has ever been." Robust sales of her books, continuing accolades from critics, and ever-increasing speaking engagements bore out her own assessment of her career.

Antonia Susan Drabble was born on Aug. 24, 1936, in Sheffield, Eng. Her father was a judge, and her half sister and literary rival Margaret Drabble also achieved fame as a British novelist. Byatt graduated with first-class honours in English from Newnham College, Cambridge, where she remained an honorary fellow, and undertook graduate studies at Bryn Mawr (Pa.) College and Somerville College, Oxford. She then embarked on a successful career as a lecturer and published her first novel, *The Shadow of the Sun* (1964). Four more titles followed before her rise to international acclaim came in 1990 with *Possession: A Romance.* The novel garnered that year's Booker Prize, among other awards, and was later adapted into a film starring Gwyneth Paltrow. Byatt's next work was *Angels and Insects: Two Novellas* (1992). The first of the novellas was also adapted for the screen. Later publications included the novels *Babel Tower* (1996) and *The Biographer's Tale* (2000), along with collections of short stories and many works of nonfiction, mostly literary criticism. In 1999 Byatt was made a dame.

Byatt was hailed by John F. Baker in *Publishers Weekly* as "somewhat of a pillar in the English intellectual establishment" with a "compendious" mind. Her many passions—such as history, fairy tales, and literary criticism—surfaced constantly in her writing. Her page-turning plots unfolded in a lush and exuberant writing style, captivating critics and the reading public alike. At the heart of her work was a search for what connects literature and life: she confessed that she was excited by "literature as a complicated, huge, interrelating pattern." Her own output was similar; she deftly rendered sketches from academia and Postmodern debate interwoven with credible characters and stories of authentic depth and detail.

Byatt offered that for her next book she would cover the years 1880 to 1918 in a lengthy novel that was completely different from her previous work. (SIOBHAN DOWD)

Calatrava, Santiago

On Jan. 22, 2004, Spanish architect, engineer, and sculptor Santiago Calatrava revealed his spectacular plans for a new Port Authority Trans-Hudson (PATH) terminal, to be located on the site of the former World Trade Center in New York City. From ground level Calatrava's structure was to be a soaring glass-and-steel winged oval, capable of opening to admit fresh air. Below ground, the construction would exhibit clean, uninterrupted lines and light-soaked space and would connect commuter and New York City subway trains and provide underground pedestrian walkways to many nearby buildings.

The PATH Terminal was only one of several Calatrava projects that took centre stage in 2004. Another was his renovation and integration of the components of the Athens sports complex (built mostly in 1982), site of the 2004 Olympics, which included—among other structures—a breathtaking new roof for the main stadium. He also designed a new roof for the Velodrome, a kinetic "wave" sculpture, and a number of parks, plazas, and other public spaces for the complex, giving it a unified look.

Santiago Calatrava Valls was born on July 28, 1951, in the town of Benimamet, near Valencia, Spain. In addition to regular school, he attended the Valencia School of Arts and Crafts. At age 13 he went to Paris as an exchange student, and he later studied in Switzerland. He attended the Valencia School of Architecture from 1969 to 1974, and in 1979 he earned a Ph.D. in civil engineering from the Federal Institute of Technology in Zürich, Switz. This combination of architectural training and engineering was strengthened still more by his innate creativity and his sensitivity to the natural environment. Four years after earning his doctorate, he won his first competition—for the design and construction of a railway station in Zürich.

He also designed railway stations in Belgium, France, Portugal, and Spain and an airport terminal in Bilbao, Spain. These buildings—together with a host of bridges built in such cities as Barcelona, Spain; Venice; Buenos Aires, Arg.; Hoofddorp, Neth.; and Orléans, France—were especially pleasing projects for Calatrava, who saw stations and bridges as "two of the more active generators of cities." His public buildings included the Quadracci Pavilion of the Milwaukee (Wis.) Art Museum, an opera house in Tenerife, Canary Islands, and several structures (including an opera house, an arboretum, and a planetarium) for the City of Arts and Sciences in Valencia. Calatrava's intense interest in the use of zoomorphic forms in architecture was especially apparent in the design of Turning Torso, his unique apartment tower in Malmö, Swed. Its sculptural shape suggested a twisted spinal

Architect Santiago Calatrava (front)

© Ramin Talaie/Corbis

column. The asymmetrical, curvilinear shapes characteristic of his bridges and building entrances suggested not only wave action but the human eye and eyebrow. Calatrava was also recognized as a sculptor, and his work was exhibited at the Museum of Modern Art, New York City, and in London, Florence, Athens, and Dallas, Texas. (KATHLEEN KUIPER)

de Hoop Scheffer, Jaap

With NATO struggling to overcome a fractious membership divided over the wars in Afghanistan and Iraq, it chose Jaap de Hoop Scheffer, a career civil servant turned politician, to serve as its 11th secretary-general, beginning on Jan. 1, 2004. He was the third Dutchman to lead the 26-member alliance, succeeding Great Britain's George Robertson. The new secretary-general was regarded by his peers as a pragmatist rather than an ideologue. In his previous job as foreign minister, he had supported the U.S.-led invasion of Iraq in 2003 but without contributing Dutch troops, a move that displayed solidarity with the United States without alienating France and Germany.

Jakob Gijsbert de Hoop Scheffer was born in Amsterdam on April 3, 1948. He graduated with a degree in law from Leiden University (1974), having written his thesis on the U.S. military presence in Europe following World War II. He performed his obligatory military service with the Royal Netherlands Air Force from 1974 to 1976 and was discharged as a reserve officer.

De Hoop Scheffer in addition to Dutch was fluent in English, French, and German. He honed his diplomatic skills in the foreign service. From 1976 to 1978 he worked at the Dutch embassy in Accra, Ghana; he then served with The Netherlands' permanent delegation to NATO in Brussels until 1980. Subsequently, he headed the private offices of four successive Dutch ministers of foreign affairs until 1986.

He became involved in politics in 1979, joining the left-liberal D66 party (Democrats 1966, the year of its foundation), but he quit because it opposed cruise-missile deployment in Europe. In June 1986 de Hoop Scheffer sought public office as a candidate for the right-of-centre Christian Democratic Alliance (CDA) and was elected to the House of Representatives of the States General. He became the party's spokesman on foreign policy as well as refugee policy and European justice matters. He chaired the Permanent Committee on Development Cooperation from 1989 until 1994.

Between 1997 and 2001 he was leader of the CDA during its time in opposition. A power struggle within the party in 2001 prompted his resignation as parliamentary leader. Following elections in May 2002, however, the CDA led a coalition government, and de Hoop Scheffer was named foreign minister by Prime Minister Jan Peter Balkenende. He was reappointed to that position following elections in January 2003. (PETER SARACINO)

Edwards, John

Although he had won a primary contest in only one state, John Edwards, a first-term senator from North Carolina, held the second largest number of delegates by the time he withdrew from the race for the Democratic presidential nomination in March 2004. Further, he had gained a reputation as an effective campaigner, and in July, Massachusetts Sen. John Kerry (*q.v.*) chose Edwards as his vice presidential running mate. It was the first time since 1960 that two U.S. senators had appeared together on the national ticket of either of the major parties. Despite an energetic campaign, however, Kerry and Edwards lost to their Republican opponents in the election on Nov. 2, 2004.

Vice presidential hopeful John Edwards

Johnny Reid Edwards was born on June 10, 1953, in Seneca, S.C., but the family later moved to Robbins, N.C., where the boy grew up and attended public schools. He was the son of working-class parents and the first member of his family to go to college. After receiving a B.S. degree in textile management from North Carolina State University in 1974, he earned a J.D. degree from the University of North Carolina at Chapel Hill in 1977. By the mid-1980s he was working as a trial lawyer, specializing in personal-injury cases that involved medical malpractice and product liability, and he was extraordinarily successful, with awards for clients that set records in the state.

In 1998, in his first attempt to gain public office, Edwards ran successfully for the U.S. Senate. Although only a freshman, he was chosen by his fellow senators to depose witnesses and to deliver arguments in the impeachment trial of Pres. Bill Clinton. Edwards later worked with Senators Edward Kennedy, Democrat of Massachusetts, and John McCain, Republican of Arizona, to pass a patients' bill of rights that would guarantee access to medical services, but the measure, which was opposed by the administration of Pres. George W. Bush, did not make it past the House of Representatives. As a member of the Senate Select Committee on Intelligence, Edwards gained knowledge of foreign affairs.

In January 2003 Edwards announced that he would seek the Democratic nomination for the presidency. His campaign was characterized by the populist theme of "two Americas," which emphasized the wide disparities between haves and have-nots in such matters as education and health insurance. Contrary to some candidates' support for free trade, he advocated policies aimed at protecting American jobs. At the same time, he expressed a decidedly positive outlook, and he was noted for refraining from criticism of the other Democratic candidates. After his withdrawal from the contest, he actively supported front-runner Kerry, and as the candidate for vice president, Edwards was joined in the campaign by his wife, Elizabeth, also a lawyer. (ROBERT RAUCH)

Farmer, Paul

By 2004 anthropologist, epidemiologist, and public-health administrator Paul Farmer had spent more than two decades and more than 4.8 million km (3 million mi) in the air shuttling between Boston—where he served as an attending physician in infectious diseases and chief of the division of Social Medicine and Health Inequalities at the Brigham and Women's Hospital—and Cange, Haiti. In Haiti he demonstrated, almost single-handedly, that multidrug-resistant tuberculosis (MDR TB) could be treated cost-effectively among the poor in a country with few resources and had determined that the progression of MDR TB could be halted only if the poor were given adequate resources as well as medication.

Paul Edward Farmer was born in 1959 in North Adams, Mass. His father moved the family often. While living in Birmingham, Ala., the family purchased a bus for family vacations, but the vehicle became their permanent home for five years after they moved to Brooksville, Fla. He won a full scholarship to Duke University, Durham, N.C., from which he graduated (1982) summa cum laude. In 1990 Farmer earned both an M.D. and a Ph.D. in anthropology from Harvard University.

He was still a student when he began touring North Carolina tobacco plantations, where Haitians toiled in severe circumstances. After graduating from Duke, he visited the Krome detention center in Miami, Fla., and began protesting U.S. immigration policies that returned Haitian refugees home but welcomed Cuban refugees. In 1983 Farmer helped establish a community-based health project in Cange, and four year later he cofounded Partners in Health (PIH) to support clinics, schools, and training programs for medical outreach workers in impoverished countries. His work in Haiti led to the thesis of his 1992 book *AIDS and Accusation.* The following year Farmer was awarded a MacArthur Foundation fellowship and donated the prize money to PIH for the formation of the Institute for Health and Social Justice.

In 1994 Farmer adopted a community-based model, akin to the one in Haiti, for treating disease and securing residents' access to health care in Carabayllo, a Peruvian shantytown. Two years later PIH and its Peruvian partner, Socios en Salud, developed a successful scheme for treating drug-resistant TB patients. In 1999 the World Heath Organization appointed Farmer and PIH worker Jim Yong Kim to launch international MDR TB treatment programs and establish effective antibiotic delivery. Following a $44.7 million grant from the Bill & Melinda Gates Foundation to PIH and Harvard Medical School to fund MDR TB research, Farmer established individualized drug-therapy programs for patients in Haiti, Peru, and Russia.

Farmer, who also served as professor of medical anthropology at Harvard Medical School, published numerous books and was the winner of the 2003 Heinz Award for the Human Condition. A biography of Farmer, *Mountains Beyond Mountains* by Tracy Kidder, appeared in 2003. (KAREN J. SPARKS)

Fisher, Allison

Continuing to rack up impressive victories on the Women's Professional Billiards Association (WPBA) tour in 2004 was England's Allison Fisher. The woman known as the "Duchess of Doom" for her deadly consistent shot making and no-nonsense style of play won a high-profile showdown with her fiercest rivals in November. In the single-elimination Ladies Challenge of Champions, held at the Mohegan Sun Casino in Uncasville, Conn., Fisher met Karen Corr of Northern Ireland in the semifinals. Despite having traded the WPBA's number one ranking with Corr during the past several years, Fisher seemed to have little trouble earning a win in straight sets. In the finals she then met American Jeannette Lee, who had defeated Fisher to clinch the 2003 Challenge. This time Fisher took advantage of some early mistakes by Lee and never looked back, coasting to another straight-sets victory and the winner-take-all purse of $25,000. Her performance at the Challenge of Champions followed a string of first-place showings at other WPBA events during the year, including the Delta Classic in Robinsonville, Miss., in February; the San Diego (Calif.) Classic in March; and the Midwest Classic in East Peoria, Ill., in June. By the end of 2004, Fisher had amassed a record 48 WPBA tour titles and regained the number one position. She was also the all-time leading purse winner on the tour and owned the record for consecutive tournament wins (eight in 1996–97). These achievements led many observers to deem Fisher the best female pocket billiards player in history.

Fisher was born on Feb. 24, 1968, in Cheshunt, Eng., near London. At the age of seven, she developed an interest in snooker after she saw the billiards game played on television. By her early teens she had joined a league and begun practicing under the guidance of coach Frank Callan. She won a national title at age 15 and in 1985 won the first of her seven individual world professional snooker championships.

Relocating to the U.S. in 1995, Fisher joined the WPBA tour and quickly became one of its marquee attractions. She placed ninth in her first tournament but won two of the next three, and by the following year she was virtually unstoppable. From September 1996 to June 2001, Fisher held the first-place spot in the WPBA's player rankings—an unprecedented stay at the top—and she was named *Billiard's Digest* and *Billiards Magazine*'s Player of the Year five consecutive times during that span.

Although Corr overtook Fisher in the WPBA rankings in 2001, Fisher bounced back with strong 2002 and 2003 seasons to reclaim the number one position. Aside from her demanding tournament schedule, Fisher made many exhibition appearances and also kept busy as a pool instructor at the school she cofounded, Allison's World Champion Academy, in Charlotte, N.C. (SHERMAN HOLLAR)

Fujishima, Akira, and Honda, Kenichi

Japanese scientists Akira Fujishima and Kenichi Honda were named winners of the 2004 Japan Prize, an international award given annually to individuals who have made outstanding contributions to science and technology. The award cited Fujishima and Honda's pioneering research on photochemical catalysis and its application for the environment. Working together in the late 1960s and early '70s, when Fujishima was completing his Ph.D. course work under Honda's supervision, the two found that a relatively inexpensive and widely available material, titanium dioxide, acts as a photocatalyst—a substance that facilitates a chemical reaction when it is exposed to sunlight. In their experiments titanium dioxide exposed to light caused water to decompose, producing hydrogen and oxygen. This discovery, which gained worldwide attention as the "Honda-Fujishima effect" after it was reported in a 1972 issue of the journal *Nature*, opened up new and diverse paths of research. By the early 21st century, photocatalyst technology was being developed for a variety of products, including self-cleaning coatings for tile, streetlight covers, and automobile mirrors. There was also hope that photocatalysts could be used to break down pollutants such as harmful fossil fuel by-products and remove them from the environment.

Akira Fujishima was born on March 10, 1942, in Tokyo. He earned a bachelor's degree in engineering from Yokohama National University in 1966 and a Ph.D. in chemistry from the University of Tokyo in 1971. He taught (1971–75) at Kanagawa University, was a postdoctoral fellow (1976–77) at the University of Texas at Austin, and then was named associate professor at the University of Tokyo in 1978. He became full professor at the university in 1986 and was given emeritus status in 2003. That same year he was appointed chairman of the Kanagawa Academy of Science and Technology. Fujishima also served as president of the Electrochemical Society of Japan and was an advisory member of the Japanese Photochemistry Association. He was the author of nearly 600 research papers.

Kenichi Honda was born on Aug. 23, 1925, in Tokyo. After receiving a bachelor's degree in engineering from the University of Tokyo in 1949, he studied at the University of Paris (Ph.D., 1957) and at the University of Tokyo (Ph.D., 1961). He accepted a position as lecturer (1965) at the University of Tokyo and went on to earn full professorship by 1975. From 1983 to 1989 Honda served as professor at Kyoto University; he then joined the faculty of Tokyo Polytechnic University, where he was eventually named dean of the faculty of arts in 1994 and president of the university in 1996. He was an honorary member of a number of scientific societies, including the Chemical Society of Japan and the Japanese Photochemistry Association. In 1997 he received one of Japan's highest honours, the designation as a "Person of Cultural Merit." (SHERMAN HOLLAR)

Fukui, Toshihiko

Toshihiko Fukui, governor of the Bank of Japan (BOJ), marked the completion of a full year on the job in March 2004 with all signs pointing toward a solid economic recovery for Japan following years of recession. During the preceding 12 months, the Nikkei-225 Stock Average had risen 47%—its best annual performance in 31 years—and during the final quarter of 2003, the Japanese economy had posted a robust 6.4% annualized gain, the best quarterly performance in more than a decade. Employment numbers were also up; export rates were growing; and the Japanese yen was trading at its highest level in four years. Much of the credit for the long-awaited turnaround went to Fukui, who had risked implementing a series of unorthodox monetary policies in order to combat the lingering malaise. His success had prompted some observers to dub him "the Alan Greenspan of Japan." In its praise of the BOJ chief, *The Economist* magazine simply declared Fukui "the world's best central banker."

Fukui was born on Sept. 7, 1935, in Osaka, Japan. He earned a law degree from the University of Tokyo in 1958 and upon graduation embarked on a long career with the BOJ. Over the next 40 years, he was appointed to a succession of increasingly responsible positions, including general manager of the Takamatsu branch in 1980, director-general of the banking department in 1986 and of the Policy Planning Office in 1989, and deputy governor of the central bank in 1994.

As BOJ deputy governor, Fukui was widely viewed as the successor-in-waiting to the governor, Yasuo Matsushita, but in 1998 both men resigned their posts to take responsibility for a scandal involving a senior BOJ official. The official had been arrested for leaking market-sensitive information to financial institutions in exchange for lavish gifts. Fukui subsequently accepted the chairmanship of the Fujitsu Research Institute, a private think tank. In 2001 he was named vice-chairperson of Keizai Doyukai (the Japan Association of Corporate Executives). Prime Minister Junichiro Koizumi selected Fukui to replace retiring Masaru Hayami as BOJ governor in March 2003.

Koizumi's appointment of a career bureaucrat like Fukui was derided by some critics who thought that the post should go to someone with more of a reformist image. Fukui proved quickly, however, that he was more than open to reform, implementing a number of radical policies and taking an approach that one economist described as "activist and interventionist." One of Fukui's more unorthodox policies involved "monetary easing"—in effect, flooding the markets with cash in part through increased stock buys from commercial banks. The move had its intended effect, greatly slowing the deflationary pressures that had been blamed for much of Japan's economic malaise. Fukui was pleased with the positive signs but remained cautious in his outlook, warning that it would take more time before the economy had fully recovered.

(SHERMAN HOLLAR)

Gaiman, Neil

In the eight years since the conclusion of his groundbreaking *Sandman* series for DC Comics, Neil Gaiman had established himself as a successful novelist, an outspoken activist for authors' legal rights, and a creator of children's tales in the fantastic and macabre tradition of the Brothers Grimm. In 2004 he concluded his best-selling series *1602* for Marvel Comics. The story reinterpreted classic Marvel superheroes and marked Gaiman's first foray into the superhero genre since his run on the critically acclaimed but legally troubled *Miracleman* in the early 1990s. Fittingly, the proceeds from *1602,* one of the year's best-selling comics, were used to free *Miracleman* from the copyright issues that had entangled it since 1998.

Gaiman was born on Nov. 10, 1960, in Porchester, Eng. He grew up in Sussex and attended Whitgift School in Croydon. Upon graduating, he freelanced as a journalist before earning his first author credit for a paperback biography of the pop music group Duran Duran in 1984. While the subject matter was certainly not indicative of his later work, its success was, and the first printing sold out in a matter of days. It was around this time that he met artist Dave McKean, and the two collaborated on the graphic novel *Violent Cases* (1987). The work established them as rising stars in the comic world, and soon the two were noticed by publishers on both sides of the Atlantic. They submitted story and art treatments to DC Comics, and the result was *Black Orchid* (1988), a three-part miniseries that helped establish the atmosphere for the DC renaissance of the late 1980s. Along with Alan Moore's work on *Watchmen* (1987) and *Swamp Thing* (1983–87) and Frank Miller's gritty interpretation of Batman in *The Dark Knight Returns* (1986), the success of *Black Orchid* showed that a market existed for dark, mature stories written for an adult audience. This became even clearer with the launch of *Sandman* in 1989.

Sandman was a completely new kind of comic. While McKean stayed on as cover artist for the entire run of the series, a rotating series of interior artists helped flavour each individual story arc. In addition, the stories were unlike any previously seen in mainstream comics. The protagonist was Morpheus, the manifestation of the ability of sentient beings to dream. Like many other pantheons, the Endless, Morpheus's siblings, were godlike beings with human foibles and drives. A typical story was so littered with literary allusions and historical references that Internet fan sites soon began offering detailed annotations of individual issues. By the time the series ended in 1996, *Sandman* had captured an enviable list of awards and was DC's top-selling title. Gaiman also topped best-seller lists with his novels *Good Omens* (with Terry Pratchett, 1990), *Neverwhere* (1996), *Stardust* (1999), and *American Gods* (2001) and with his children's book *Coraline* (2002). In 2003 he revisited the *Sandman* characters in *Endless Nights,* an anthology that had the distinction of being the first graphic novel to earn a place on the *New York Times* best-seller list for hardcover fiction.

(MICHAEL RAY)

Gibson, Mel

Temporarily setting aside his career as one of the world's best-known action heroes, American-born Australian actor, director, and producer Mel Gibson fulfilled a personal mission by bringing to the screen *The Passion of the Christ,* one of the most popular motion pictures of 2004. At its opening on Ash Wednesday (February 25), the film took in $23.6 million, the sixth highest opening-day total in motion picture history. By midsummer *The Passion* ranked among the 10 top-grossing films of all time. Based primarily on the biblical Gospels and with a dialogue in Aramaic and Latin (with English subtitles), Gibson's pet project stirred controversy long before it arrived in theatres. Religious groups and editorialists assailed the film as anti-Semitic, and many were appalled by its violence and skeptical of its historical accuracy. Some critics praised Gibson's storytelling and artistic vision, however, and the film did find some support among Jews. Gibson denied the charges of anti-Semitism, saying the film was intended "to inspire, not offend." Adding to the furor was a report in December 2003 that Pope John Paul II had endorsed the film, which was closely followed by the Vatican's denial that the pope had expressed an opinion about it.

Mel Columcille Gerard Gibson was born on Jan. 3, 1956, in Peekskill, N.Y. His father, a railroad worker, later became known for his contentious writings on religion. His mother was an Australian opera singer. The family moved to Australia when Gibson was 12 years old. From 1974 to 1977 he studied at the National Institute of Dramatic Art in Sydney. He landed the leading roles in the futuristic action film *Mad Max* (1979) and in the romance *Tim* (1979), with the latter earning Gibson the Australian Film Institute's award for best actor. He won the award again in 1981 for his performance in the war drama *Gallipoli. Mad Max 2* (1981), released in the United States as *The Road Warrior* (1982), brought Gibson international stardom. He established himself as a top box-office draw in *Mad Max Beyond Thunderdome* (1985) and the action-packed *Lethal Weapon* series, as well as more serious fare, including *The Year of Living Dangerously* (1982), *Hamlet* (1990), and *Signs* (2002). Gibson also starred in a string of romantic comedies. In 1993 he made his directorial debut with *The Man Without a Face.* He next directed the epic *Braveheart* (1995), in which he also starred as the Scottish national hero Sir William Wallace. The film won five Academy Awards, including best picture and best director. A Harris Poll ranked Gibson among the five most popular movie stars in the United States every year since 1993, the year the poll began, and in 2004 the American business magazine *Forbes* named him the most powerful celebrity in the world.

(JANET MOREDOCK)

Goss, Porter J.

On Aug. 10, 2004, Porter Goss, an eight-term Republican congressman from Florida and House Intelligence Committee chairman, was tapped to replace George Tenet as director of central intelligence. The top CIA post had become a lightning rod for criticism, and Tenet was perceived as a liability for the administration of Pres. George W. Bush. In June Tenet abruptly announced that he was retiring, and Bush moved to plug the power vacuum. Goss's appointment came at a critical juncture for the CIA, which was under fire for having failed to crack the Sept. 11, 2001, terrorist plot and was taking the blame for the overselling of the likelihood that Saddam Hussein possessed weapons of mass destruction, the main rationale for the U.S.-led invasion of Iraq in March 2003. More generally the agency was facing pressure to revamp its intelligence-gathering capabilities and improve interagency cooperation in the face of likely terrorist threats. Bush billed Goss as a "force for positive change," and his friends praised him as a seasoned, pragmatic lawmaker. Many Democrats, however, criticized the appointment as having most to do with Florida's being a swing state in the upcoming elections and complaining of Goss's partisanship and cozy relationship with the Bush administration. Critics also noted that the 9/11 Commission Report in June 2004 had reproved not only U.S. intelligence agencies but also congressional oversight of them.

Porter Johnston Goss was born on Nov. 26, 1938, in Waterbury, Conn. He was educated at the Hotchkiss School, Lakeville, Conn., and Yale University, where he earned a B.A. in classics and Greek in 1960. Goss trained as a military intelligence officer before joining the CIA in 1962. Owing to his being fluent in Spanish, his first posting was to Miami, Fla., at the height of the Cuban Missile Crisis. "I had some very interesting moments in the Florida Straits," he divulged recently, but he was otherwise reticent about his intelligence activities. It was known that he undertook clandestine assignments in Haiti, the Dominican Republic, Mexico, and Europe. His field career was cut short, however, when he was stricken with a debilitating bacteriological infection in 1970. He subsequently moved to Sanibel Island, off Florida's Gulf coast, to recuperate, and in 1972 he quit the CIA.

Goss cofounded a local newspaper and became Sanibel's first mayor in 1974. His opposition to commercial development on the island persuaded the then governor (Democrat Bob Graham, who was later Goss's opposite number on the Senate Intelligence Committee) to appoint him to the Lee County Board of Commissioners in 1983. This post was the springboard for his successful 1988 congressional run. In the House, besides overseeing intelligence matters, Goss served on the Rules Committee and the Select Committee for Homeland Security.

Arriving at CIA headquarters in Langley, Va., Goss pledged to give field agents greater license to gather intelligence aggressively. His tenure got off to a rocky start, however, when it emerged that his pick for CIA third in command had previously been forced to quit the agency for shoplifting. Several high-ranking CIA officials also resigned during a shake-up of the organization by Goss. (STEPHEN J. PHILLIPS)

Guy, Buddy

In early 2004 Buddy Guy's *Blues Singer* won the 2004 Grammy Award for best traditional blues album as well as the W.C. Handy Blues Award for album of the year. The news in 2003 that Guy, guitarist and owner of the Chicago nightclub Buddy Guy's Legends, had released his 24th album was hardly unusual. The noteworthy feature of *Blues Singer,* however, was that for the first time in his life the king of electric Chicago blues had created a classic acoustic album. On *Blues Singer* Guy's rich, raspy voice heavy with experience and backed by such musical greats as B.B. King and Eric Clapton—wraps around the mostly spare and lonely sound associated with hard times in the Mississippi Delta.

Kevin Mazur/WireImage.com

Blues legend Buddy Guy

The Delta sound was certainly not alien to Guy. He was born George Guy on July 30, 1936, in the hamlet of Lettsworth, La. As a boy listening to the radio, he yearned for a guitar. He made his own at age 13 and, inspired by the music of classic bluesmen such as John Lee Hooker, taught himself to play. Guy moved as a young man to Baton Rouge, where he started to play in the clubs, and in 1957 he went on to Chicago, the northern capital of the blues. There he was discovered by blues legend Muddy Waters, who helped him find his first steady job—at the well-known 708 Club, where he met other legendary masters of the blues, including King and bassist-arranger Willie Dixon. Guy was signed briefly to Cobra Records and (in 1960–67) to the famous Chess label, for which he recorded several early hits, including "Leave My Girl Alone," "Let Me Love You, Baby," "Stone Crazy," and "No Lie." He also worked as a sideman for Howlin' Wolf, Little Walter, Koko Taylor, and others.

Although he continued to make recordings in the 1970s and '80s, performing often with blues harmonica player Junior Wells, Guy fell victim to the growing popularity of rock music. It was not until younger white musicians, among them Clapton, Stevie Ray Vaughn, Keith Richards, and Jeff Beck, acknowledged a heavy debt to Guy and other bluesmen that his fortunes again began to rise. In the 1990s he accepted four Grammy Awards: three times winning for best contemporary blues album—*Damn Right, I've Got the Blues* (1991), *Feels like Rain* (1993), *Slippin' In* (1995)—and once (with Bonnie Raitt, King, and others) for best rock instrumental performance, on the track "SRV Shuffle" from *A Tribute to Stevie Ray Vaughan* (1996). Between 1982 and 2002 Guy received 19 W.C. Handy Awards, and the three he won for *Blues Singer*—for best album, best acoustic blues album, and contemporary blues male artist—showed that he had found yet another way to display his unique musical gift. In late 2004 it was announced that Guy would be inducted into the Rock and Roll Hall of Fame the following year. (KATHLEEN KUIPER)

Harper, Stephen

Stephen Harper—spokesman for the Conservative Party (CP), the combined opposition to the Liberal government of Prime Minister Paul Martin—confirmed his position as an important new figure on the Canadian political scene following the general election on June 28, 2004. Harper's party won 99 of the 308 seats in the House of Commons. As a result, the Liberals were forced to head a minority government.

Harper's task was not an easy one. His home base was the Reform Party, later called the Canadian Alliance, a group founded to express a distinctive role for the Western provinces in the Canadian federation. Although the party put forward ideas of democratic reform, such as an elected rather than an appointed Senate, its views on social issues were often to the right of mainstream Canadian opinion. In addition, Harper's party was partnered on the right with the historic Progressive Conservative Party (PCP), with which it merged in late 2003 to form the CP. The PCP, with countrywide roots, contained many shades of opinion, from the liberal views of the "Red Tories" to fiscal conservatives advocating a more restricted role for government. Harper was elected leader of the new grouping in March 2004, only three months before voters went to the polls in the general election.

Harper attempted to define a moderate stance for the new party. He advocated that tax relief, a balanced budget, and transparency should be the hallmarks of a responsible Canadian government. He believed that publicly funded health care should be maintained and improved, the federal government should help to make higher education more accessible, and cities should be assisted in the expensive task of providing streets and public services.

© Shaun Best/Reuters/Corbis

Canada's Conservative leader Stephen Harper

Harper advocated the strengthening of the Canadian military from its present level of 65,000 to 80,000. He felt that participation in peacekeeping or peace-enforcing roles should be determined by the national interest and governed by careful rules of engagement and that it was important that Canada build up combat-trained forces for a variety of assignments. On the vital question of relations with the United States, Harper's party promised support for farmers and lumbermen in trade disputes. On global issues he believed that Canada should stand "shoulder to shoulder" with its powerful neighbour when interests coincided but that its ally should be met "eyeball to eyeball" when they did not.

Stephen Joseph Harper was born on April 30, 1959, in Toronto but moved at an early age to Calgary, Alta. After graduating from the University of Calgary (B.A., 1985; M.A., 1991), he directed his career toward politics and public-policy analysis. Harper was a member of Parliament in the early 1990s for the Reform Party and later headed a public advocacy group. In 2002 he defeated Stockwell Day for leadership of the Canadian Alliance.

(DAVID M.L. FARR)

Henin-Hardenne, Justine

At the 2004 Australian Open, Belgian tennis player Justine Henin-Hardenne defeated her countrywoman Kim Clijsters to win her third Grand Slam title in the span of four major events. With the victory Henin-Hardenne, who had also captured the 2003 French and U.S. Open titles, stood in a rare class as one of only nine women to have held three Grand Slam singles titles simultaneously. Although relatively small (1.6 m [5 ft 5 in] tall) for an athlete, the gutsy Belgian applied tenacity and a majestic backhand to establish herself as one of the finest woman tennis players in the world.

In April 2004, however, Henin-Hardenne was diagnosed with cytomegalovirus, a viral condition that causes extreme fatigue. It kept her out of the game for six weeks leading up to the French Open, and she lost in the second round at Roland Garros, becoming the first top-seeded woman at the tournament to lose before the third round. She did not compete again until 10 weeks later in August at the Olympic Games in Athens. Remarkably, she rescued herself from 1–5 down in the final set of her semifinal against French Open victor Anastasiya Myskina of Russia and then took the gold medal over Amélie Mauresmo of France. Henin-Hardenne seemed like herself again but not for long. At the U.S. Open two weeks later, she was ousted in the fourth round by Russian Nadya Petrova—the first time since 1980 that a number one seed had been beaten before the semifinals in that tournament. Soon after, the Belgian champion announced that she would not compete for the remainder of the year.

Born Justine Henin on June 1, 1982, in Liège, she set high standards as a junior competitor, taking the Junior Orange Bowl international tennis championship crown in Miami, Fla., in 1996 and winning the French Open junior championships the following year. She turned professional on Jan. 1, 1999, at age 16 and finished 2000 among the top 50 players in the world. She concluded 2001 at number seven and 2002 at number five. During the 2003 season, Henin-Hardenne, who had married Pierre-Yves Hardenne the previous year, captured two major championships, ousting Clijsters in the finals of both the French and U.S. Opens; her victory at Roland Garros marked her first Grand Slam title. Moreover, she was victorious in 75 of 86 matches, winning 8 tournaments altogether and reaching the semifinals or better in 16 of the 20 events she entered. Her supreme consistency and determination enabled Henin-Hardenne to finish the year as the top-ranked woman in the game. She seemed certain to resume her winning ways in 2005, as long as her health allowed her to perform prodigiously again. (STEVE FLINK)

Belgian tennis ace Justine Henin-Hardenne

© Tim de Waele/Corbis; right: Action Images/WireImage.com

Henry, Thierry

In mid-2004 Thierry Henry clinched the 2003–04 Golden Shoe as Europe's leading association football (soccer) goal scorer (with 30) and helped the English Football Association (FA) club Arsenal to another Premier League championship. If anyone deserved credit for turning Henry into one of the finest players in the world, it was Arsenal manager Arsene Wenger, who was responsible for transforming the young Frenchman from an average winger into a formidable striker. Henry was honoured as European Footballer of the Year for 2002 and 2003 and finished runner-up as Fédération Internationale de Football Association (FIFA) World Player of the Year in 2003 and 2004.

French footballer Thierry Henry

Thierry Daniel Henry was born in the Paris suburb of Châtillon on Aug. 17, 1977, of French West Indian stock, and his childhood was spent in low-income housing in Les Ulis, south of Paris. After gaining a place in the national technical centre in Clairefontaine, he joined FC (football club) Versailles in 1992, and, after attracting other club scouts, he was snapped up by Monaco in 1995. Although Henry played as a striker until he was 17, he switched to left wing for Monaco. Monaco won the 1997 French championship, and Henry's game improved noticeably. Midway through the 1998–99 season, a contract mix-up almost sent him to Real Madrid; instead, he was traded to Juventus in Turin, Italy, for £9 million (about $14.9 million). Two weeks before his 22nd birthday, he was on the move again in a £10.5 million (about $17 million) deal to join Wenger at Arsenal.

Wenger shifted Henry to striker, giving him more responsibility at the cutting edge of the attack, and the Frenchman soon revealed his true ability. With a deceivingly casual approach, the 1.88-m (6-ft 2-in), 85-kg (187-lb) Henry could glide like a fleet-footed gazelle past opposing players, initiate and finish moves, score goals either with a light touch from short range or fiercely from long distances, and contribute his share of headed goals. In all first-team matches for Arsenal, he reached 151 goals by the end of 2003–04, and the club achieved two league titles (2002, 2004) and two FA Cup trophies (2002, 2003), as well as finishing as runner-up in the 2000 Union des Associations Européennes de Football Cup final.

Henry's international honours when playing for France were equally impressive. In 1996 he was a member of the European under-18 championship team, and two years later he collected a FIFA World Cup title. In 2000 France added the European championship, and in 2003 Henry had a triple success when he scored the winning goal for France in the FIFA Confederations Cup and was awarded both the Golden Ball (as player of the tournament) and the Golden Shoe (as top scorer).

First selected to play for his country on Oct. 11, 1997, against South Africa, by the end of the 2004 European championship, Henry had scored 27 goals in 63 full international games. (JACK ROLLIN)

Hersh, Seymour

In 2004 the world was as stunned by the torture of Iraqi inmates by American soldiers at the Abu Ghraib prison as it had been by the massacre of the villagers of My Lai by U.S. troops during the Vietnam War. Both horrifying stories were broken by investigative journalist Seymour Hersh, who for some 35 years had exposed misconduct at the loftiest reaches of the U.S. government and in the darkest corners of U.S. involvement abroad.

Seymour Myron Hersh was born in Chicago on April 8, 1937. He was the son of Polish and Lithuanian immigrants whose deep belief in American democracy had long informed his idealistic muckraking. After graduating from the University of Chicago (1958) and dropping out of law school, he landed at the City News Bureau of Chicago. Following military service, Hersh cofounded a suburban newspaper, then worked for United Press International and the Associated Press before a brief stint in 1967 as press secretary for presidential candidate Eugene McCarthy. In 1969, acting on a tip, Hersh interviewed U.S. Army Lieut. William L. Calley, who recounted the killing in March 1968 of hundreds of South Vietnamese civilians by troops under his command. Hersh's syndicated account helped end U.S. involvement in the Vietnam War and provided the basis for his Pulitzer Prize-winning book *My Lai 4* (1970).

Joining the staff of the *New York Times* in 1972, Hersh did groundbreaking reporting on the Watergate Scandal, though most of the credit for that story went to Carl Bernstein and Hersh's longtime rival Bob Woodward (*q.v.*). Nonetheless, Hersh's investigation led him to write *The Price of Power: Kissinger in the Nixon White House* (1983), a damning portrait of Henry Kissinger that won the National Book Critics Circle Award. Among the subjects of Hersh's seven other books were the Soviet downing of a Korean Air Lines plane, Israel's acquisition of nuclear arms, and a much-criticized behind-the-scenes portrayal of Pres. John F. Kennedy.

In 1993 Hersh became a regular contributor to *The New Yorker* magazine, for which he wrote a series of articles on the war on terrorism and U.S. involvement in Iraq. Those articles—later collected in *Chain of Command: The Road from 9/11 to Abu Ghraib* (2004)—

culminated in Hersh's earthshaking exposé of prisoner abuse at Abu Ghraib, which he traced beyond the soldiers involved to policy formulated at the highest levels of the administration of Pres. George W. Bush. Hersh characterized Bush's prosecution of the war as the product of misguided neoconservative idealism. Having built his career on earning the trust of sources (usually unnamed) in the government, the military, and the intelligence community, Hersh described his mission as holding public officials "to the highest possible standard of decency and of honesty."

(JEFF WALLENFELDT)

Hopkins, Bernard

When Bernard Hopkins's hand was raised in victory following his ninth-round knockout of Oscar de la Hoya on Sept. 18, 2004, in Las Vegas, Nev., it was a climax in the 39-year-old Hopkins's inspirational journey from the penitentiary to the top of the boxing world. The win was also his 19th successful defense of the middleweight title, a division record. Thanks to his career-long commitment to physical conditioning and mastery of virtually every aspect of his craft, Hopkins—with a professional career record of 45 wins (32 by knockout), 2 losses by decision, and 1 draw—was able to compete at the highest level at an age when most boxers are retired.

Hopkins was born in Philadelphia on Jan. 15, 1965, and became involved in street crime as a teenager. At the age of 17, he was convicted of armed robbery and sentenced to prison, where he took up boxing. He served 56 months, and after his release on parole in 1988, he maintained a clean record.

Hopkins had his first professional bout on Oct. 11, 1988, in Atlantic City, N.J., but he was unable to earn a living as a full-time boxer and supplemented his income by washing pots and pans in the kitchen of a Philadelphia hotel. Later he worked at an auto transmission repair shop owned by his trainer, Bouie Fisher. Hopkins won the vacant International Boxing Federation (IBF) middleweight title by knocking out Segundo Mercado in the seventh round on April 29, 1995, in Landover, Md., but even with this victory behind him, he struggled to find meaningful bouts.

Although highly respected for his formidable skills and dedication, Hopkins continued to toil in relative anonymity until 2001, when he entered a tournament organized by promoter Don King to unify the middleweight title. In the first bout of the series, on April 14 in New York City, Hopkins retained the IBF title and won the World Boxing Council (WBC) version with a 12-round decision over Keith Holmes. In his second bout, on September 29 at New York City's Madison Square Garden, Hopkins stopped the previously undefeated Félix Trinidad in the 12th round in a major upset to retain the IBF and WBC belts and win the World Boxing Association title. Hopkins thus became the first unified middleweight champion since Marvin Hagler lost the title in 1987. This achievement earned Hopkins Fighter of the Year honours for 2001 from both the Boxing Writers Association of America and *Ring* magazine. Following four

© Christopher Farina/Corbis

Middleweight boxing champion Bernard Hopkins

more defenses of the unified title, Hopkins earned a career-high purse of approximately $10 million for knocking out de la Hoya.

Considered an iconoclastic figure within the boxing industry, Hopkins feuded with promoters throughout much of his career, frequently battling in court just as fiercely as he did inside the ring. An outspoken advocate of reform, he also testified in 1999 before the National Association of Attorneys General Boxing Task Force about corruption and various other problems within the sport.

(NIGEL COLLINS)

Howard, Michael

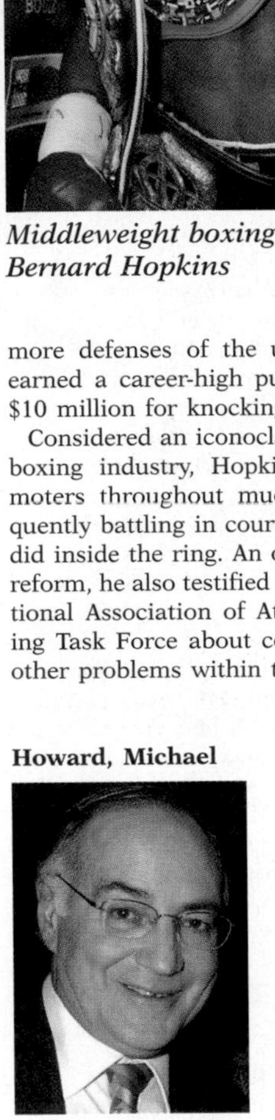

In 2004 Michael Howard, leader of the United Kingdom's Conservative Party (CP) since November 2003, had an immense task on his hands. The Tories had suffered two crushing defeats in successive general elections, and despite growing dissatisfaction among the electorate with Prime Minister Tony Blair, the CP showed few signs of recovery.

Howard was born in Gorseinon, South Wales, on July 7, 1941. His father, Bernat Hecht, was a Jewish Romanian-born shopkeeper who had emigrated in 1939 and changed his name to Bernard Howard. (Other members of the family remained behind, including Howard's grandmother, who later died in a Nazi concentration camp.) After graduating from Peterhouse, Cambridge, Howard became a barrister. His ambition, however, was always to become a politician, and he fought unsuccessfully for a seat in the House of Commons in the 1966 and 1970 general elections. In 1983 he was elected MP for the south coast seat of Folkestone and Hythe.

In 1985 Howard joined Prime Minister Margaret Thatcher's government as a junior minister at the Department of Trade and Industry. He won respect for overseeing the deregulation (known as the Big Bang) of London's financial district; in 1987 he was promoted to minister for local government. This position brought him to national prominence when he introduced legislation to abandon Britain's traditional form of local taxation, the property-based "rates" system, and replace it with a poll tax, or "community charge," in which every adult not on welfare benefits was to be charged the same amount for local services. Although Howard succeeded in securing the passage of the bill, the poll tax was immensely unpopular. It contributed to Thatcher's downfall in 1990, and one of the first decisions taken by John Major, her successor as prime minister, was to scrap the poll tax and revert to a property-based system of local taxation. Howard, however, survived the storm and in 1990 joined the cabinet as employment secretary. In 1993 he was promoted to home secretary, a position in which he gained a reputation as a right-winger. He introduced stricter policies on both immigration and prisons.

Following the Labour Party victory in 1997, Howard stood for the Tory leadership, but he was eliminated in the first round, following the remark by one of his former Home Office colleagues that he had "something of the night" about him, alluding to his demeanour and to the fact that his ancestry, like Dracula's, was Romanian. He did not stand when the vacancy arose in 2001, but the new CP leader, Iain Duncan Smith, failed to improve the party's fortunes. When Conservative MPs voted to eject Duncan Smith in October 2003, Howard, then the party's shadow chancellor, was the only candidate to replace him and was elected unopposed. Howard's repeated criticisms of Blair (and, implicitly, U.S. Pres. George W. Bush) for having issued false information ahead of the U.S.-led war in Iraq, made him unpopular in Washington. Early in his leadership, he suffered the embarrassment for a Conservative of being told that he would not be invited to Washington to meet President Bush.

(PETER KELLNER)

Hwang Woo Suk and Moon Shin Yong

In February 2004 two researchers from Seoul (S.Kor.) National University announced that they had successfully cloned human embryos. Hwang Woo Suk, a specialist in veterinary medicine, and Moon Shin Yong, an obstetrician, harvested eggs from donors and developed cloned embryos. One of the embryos yielded stem cells—undifferentiated cells capable of developing into specific cell types. Scientists believed that stem cells might one day be used to treat illnesses resulting from damaged cells, including juvenile diabetes, Parkinson disease, and Alzheimer disease.

The announcement set off a new round of debates regarding the ethics of human cloning. Hwang and Moon voiced strong opposition to reproductive cloning and insisted that their research was conducted solely for the purpose of therapeutic cloning—that is,

Alan Davidson/WireImage.com

for fighting disease. Opponents were not appeased. Some believed that the development opened the door to reproductive cloning. Many others continued to oppose stem-cell research of any kind on religious grounds.

Human cells had been cloned before, but the resulting fragile embryos died quickly. Hwang and Moon credited the success of their research to several factors. One was the large number of eggs they had available: 242. They were obtained from 16 female volunteer donors who underwent a rigorous screening process to ensure that they understood the implications of their participation. Another factor was the way in which material was extracted from the eggs. Whereas past researchers had used suction, Hwang and Moon used a squeezing technique, which helped reduce damage to the eggs.

Hwang was born Dec. 15, 1953, in Buyeo, S.Kor. He studied at the College of Veterinary Medicine at Seoul National University, receiving a B.S. (1977) in veterinary medicine and an M.S. (1979) and a Ph.D. (1982) in theriogenology, the study of animal reproduction. In 1984 he joined the faculty of Hokkaido University, Sapporo, Japan, as a visiting fellow, and from 1986 he was a faculty member at Seoul National University.

Moon was born April 1, 1948, in Kongju, Korea (now in South Korea). He studied in the College of Medicine at Seoul National University (B.S., 1974; M.S., 1977; Ph.D., 1987). He joined the faculty of the College of Medicine of the university in 1983 and was named director of the university's Institute of Reproductive Medicine and Population in 1999. He also studied at the Jones Institute for Reproductive Medicine in Norfolk, Va., in the mid-1980s.

Hwang, who received South Korea's top scientist prize in April 2004, had earned a name for himself by developing methods for cloning cows and pigs. In 2002, having decided to begin work on human cloning, he approached Moon, who had done extensive work with in vitro fertilization. (ANTHONY G. CRAINE)

Hytner, Nicholas

When *Stuff Happens*—David Hare's dissection of the Second Persian Gulf War, with U.S. Pres. George W. Bush, members of his administration, and British Prime Minister Tony Blair as the main characters—opened at the National Theatre (NT) in September 2004, it was only the latest in a string of diverse, innovative productions that Nicholas Hytner had brought to London audiences since assuming the theatre's artistic directorship in 2003. Beginning with shows ranging from William Shakespeare's *Henry V* with a black king to *Jerry Springer—the Opera,* complete with an assortment of sordid character types associated with its namesake's television program, and going on to such shows as *Mourning Becomes Electra, Democracy,* and a six-hour, two-play adaptation of the three young-adult books in Philip Pullman's (*q.v.*) *His Dark Materials* series—in addition to introducing new policies that guaranteed low-priced tickets for two-thirds of the seats in one of the NT theatres—he reinvigorated London's theatre scene and attracted new audiences to the complex on the South Bank of the River Thames.

Nicholas Robert Hytner was born on May 7, 1956, in Didsbury, a suburb of Manchester, Eng., and was educated at Trinity Hall, Cambridge. He had first exhibited his interest in theatre when he performed in grammar-school productions, and at Cambridge he directed plays by Bertolt Brecht and became involved with the Cambridge Footlights Revue. After Cambridge he assisted in productions at English National Opera and worked in provincial theatres. Among those theatres was the Royal Exchange Theatre in Manchester, where from 1985 to 1989 he served as associate director. In 1989 Hytner began his association with the NT (then the Royal National Theatre), directing his first blockbuster hit, the Vietnam War-era musical *Miss Saigon.* From 1990 to 1997 he was associate director at the RNT, and during that time productions he directed included *The Madness of George III* (1991), whose film version, *The Madness of King George* (1994), marked Hytner's film directorial debut, and a hugely successful revival of *Carousel* (1992), whose subsequent Broadway run garnered five Tony Awards—a best director award for Hytner among them.

Hytner also directed productions for television and for such companies as the Royal Shakespeare Company and English National Opera, and he counted *The Crucible* (1996) and *The Object of My Affection* (1998) among his film credits. Back in London in 1999, he directed the RNT's *The Lady in the Van,* and in 2000 he was named Cameron Mackintosh Visiting Professor of Contemporary Theatre at the University of Oxford. (BARBARA WHITNEY)

English theatre director Nicholas Hytner

© Robbie Jack/Corbis

Kanehara, Hitomi, and Wataya, Risa

In early 2004 two young female novelists—Risa Wataya and Hitomi Kanehara—shared Japan's most prestigious literary award, the Akutagawa Prize for promising new authors, and created a media sensation in Japan with works that captured the perspectives of a generation coming of age in Japan's postbubble economy. Both Wataya's *Keritai senaka* (roughly translated in English as "The Back I Want to Kick") and Kanehara's *Hebi ni piasu* ("Snakes and Earrings") focused on youths in a contemporary Japan undergoing sweeping social change. Both works were "radical depictions of our time," said Ryu Murakami, a past Akutagawa Prize winner and a member of the 2004 awards committee.

Wataya, the youngest-ever recipient of the award, was born on Feb. 1, 1984, in Kyoto, Japan. She debuted as an author at age 17 with *Install* (2001), for which she won the 2001 Bungei literary prize. The novel depicted a troubled high-school girl's experience with the erotic world of adults through Internet chat rooms. A film version was scheduled for release in early 2005. In *Keritai senaka* Wataya, a junior at Waseda University in Tokyo, vividly portrayed the self-consciousness and alienation that a girl in her first year of high school experiences. The teen struggles to relate to her peers and develops a love-hate relationship with a loner male classmate. The novel sold more than one million copies in March alone, which made it the best-selling Akutagawa Prize-winning novel since Ryu Murakami's *Almost Transparent Blue* (1977), which dealt with youthful drug addiction.

Kanehara was born on Aug. 8, 1983, in Tokyo. She temporarily stopped going to elementary school and, as a teenager, attempted suicide by cutting her wrists. She later attended writing seminars taught by her father, a university professor and translator of children's books. Kanehara eventually dropped out of high school but kept writing. She made her literary debut with *Hebi ni paisu,* which described a 19-year-old girl's obsession with body alteration. The explicit novel painted a bleak picture of the isolated alcoholic teen's underground life as she adds painful tattoos to her back and pierces her tongue. Kanehara incorporated the vocabulary of the Tokyo streets into her prose and used powerful, precise language to describe the heroine's peculiar sex-and-violence-filled behaviour. The novel won the 2003 Subaru literary award in Japan and sold more than a half million copies. Her second novel, *Ash Baby,* appeared in 2004.

The March 2004 issue of the quarterly literary magazine *Bungei shinju* featured both novels and sold more than 1.1 million copies, breaking its previous sales record. Nevertheless, the awarding of the Akutagawa Prize to these two young women was the subject of much debate in Japan. Many critics hailed the depictions of troubled youth in a changing social milieu, but others saw the award as an effort to boost sales by selecting attractive young writers who explored shocking themes at a time when the book industry was struggling. (KIMIYO NAKA-MICHAELI)

Karamanlis, Kostas
Ending 11 years of centre-left rule, Konstantinos ("Kostas") Karamanlis in 2004 became the youngest prime minister in recent Greek history. In the process, he defeated the scion of another famous Greek political family, former foreign minister Georgios Papandreou, whose father and grandfather had both been prime ministers.

Karamanlis was born in Athens on Sept. 14, 1956. He was the nephew of Konstantinos Karamanlis (1907–98), who, as government minister, prime minister, and president, shaped Greek politics for nearly half a century. The young Karamanlis started his political activities in New Democracy (ND), the party his uncle had founded after the restoration of democracy in Greece in 1974. Although Karamanlis held high positions within the party's youth and student organizations between 1974 and 1979, his political career remained unremarkable during most of the 1970s and '80s as he focused first on his studies (law, economics, and international relations in universities in Greece and the U.S.) and then on his professions as an educator and lawyer.

Karamanlis's political career really took off only after he entered the parliament in June 1989. In 1993 he became a member of the ND central committee and political council. At the fourth ND congress in March 1997, Karamanlis was elected party president at the age of only 40 years, winning against several high-profile candidates, including the incumbent

© Grigoris Siamidis/Reuters/Corbis

Greek Prime Minister Kostas Karamanlis

ND leader, Miltiadis Evert, and Georgios Souflias, a leader of the party's liberal wing.

In April 2000 Karamanlis narrowly lost the parliamentary elections to then prime minister Kostas Simitis and his Panhellenic Socialist Movement (PASOK), but the ND was successful in all other elections after Karamanlis took over as party leader. Remarkably, Karamanlis managed to forge relative unity in a party that was traditionally riddled by factionalism between its more traditionalist-conservative and liberal wings, and he managed to persuade several politicians who had quit the party to return, including Souflias and former Athens mayor Dimitrios Avramopoulos.

On March 7, 2004, the ND roundly defeated PASOK. Karamanlis was sworn in as prime minister, and on March 22 the new parliament voted confidence in him and his government. With less than five months to go until the start of the Athens Olympic Games, Karamanlis also took over the Ministry of Culture, which had overall responsibility for athletics and therefore for overseeing the preparations for the Games.

As prime minister, Karamanlis would have to initiate political and economic reform while at the same time trying to limit the social costs. A rather cautious approach in his first six months in office gave the public an impression of a politician who was hesitant to take tough and possibly controversial positions. (STEFAN KRAUSE)

Kerry, John
In the election held on Nov. 2, 2004, Democratic candidate John Kerry, senator from Massachusetts, lost his bid for the U.S. presidency to Republican incumbent George W. Bush (*q.v.*). Kerry won 48% of the popular vote, compared with 51% for Bush, with the vote in the electoral college 251 to 286. Kerry found support principally among voters who disapproved of the U.S. led-Iraq war and among those who said that domestic matters such as the economy and health care were the nation's most serious problems. He fared well in cities, in the Northeast, and on the West Coast. Although most observers agreed that he had outperformed Bush in their debates, much of Kerry's support was thought to be based on anti-Bush sentiment.

John Forbes Kerry was born on Dec. 11, 1943, at Fitzsimons Army Hospital, in what is now Aurora, Colo., but grew up mostly in Massachusetts and Washington, D.C. After graduating from Yale University in 1966 with a B.A. degree in political science, he enlisted in the U.S. Navy and volunteered for service in Vietnam. During his second tour of duty, he commanded a river patrol boat, and he was decorated with Silver and Bronze stars and received three Purple Hearts. Following his discharge in 1970, he was active in the antiwar movement and in 1971 testified against the war before the Senate Foreign Relations Committee. The following year he ran unsuccessfully for a Massachusetts congressional seat. Graduating from Boston College Law School in 1976, he worked as an assistant district attorney and then in private practice. In 1982 he was elected lieutenant governor of Massachusetts, and in 1984 he won election to the first of four terms to the U.S. Senate. In the Senate he conducted a number of high-profile investigations, including a probe of the Iran-Contra Affair. He was a member of the Foreign Relations Committee and, as chairman of the Senate Select Committee on POW-MIA Affairs, worked with Republican Sen. John McCain of Arizona to account for missing U.S. servicemen in Vietnam.

© Jim Bourg/Reuters/Corbis

Democratic presidential contender John Kerry

In 1995 Kerry married his second wife, Teresa Heinz (the widow of Republican Sen. John Heinz), who, having changed her party affiliation, actively campaigned for her husband.

Kerry formally entered the race for the Democratic nomination in September 2003. He won early victories in January 2004 in Iowa and New Hampshire and by March had claimed enough delegates to guarantee the nomination. In July he chose John Edwards (*q.v.*), senator from North Carolina and his main primary opponent, as his vice presidential running mate. From the beginning Kerry emphasized his military experience, but a group of Vietnam veterans with Republican ties accused him of misrepresenting his record. He also campaigned on a number of domestic issues, particularly criticizing the Bush administration for job losses and for large tax cuts for high-income Americans. As the campaign progressed, Kerry became increasingly critical of the president's handling of the war in Iraq, but Republicans accused him of "flip-flopping" on this and other issues, a charge that stuck with many voters. Kerry retained his Senate seat, with four years remaining in the current term.
(ROBERT RAUCH)

Klochkova, Yana
At the 2004 Olympic Games in Athens, swimmer Yana Klochkova staked her claim as one

of the most dominant and versatile athletes in the history of her sport. The 22-year-old Ukrainian notched victories in both the 200-m and 400-m individual medleys, matching her performance four years earlier in Sydney, Australia. Klochkova thus completed a historic "double double," becoming only the third swimmer—and the first woman—to have won consecutive pairs of Olympic gold medals in the same events. Another measure of her dominance was the fact that since the Sydney Games she had lost only one individual medley race in major international competition. By the end of 2004, her career medal tally stood at 4 Olympic golds, 1 Olympic silver, 4 world championship titles, and 10 European championship gold medals.

Klochkova was born into a sports-oriented family on Aug. 7, 1982, in the Crimean capital, Simferopol, U.S.S.R. (now in Ukraine). Her parents had both participated in track and field, and Klochkova, who began swimming at the age of seven, showed tremendous athletic promise. By her mid-teens she was competing internationally, and in early 1998, at age 15, she took silver in the 400-m individual medley at the world championships. At the European championships the following year, she won both individual medleys in addition to placing third in the 400-m freestyle event.

It was at the Sydney Games, however, that Klochkova fully emerged as an international star and began to be referred to as the "medley queen." The 1.82-m (6-ft)-tall teenager immediately took command at those Games, breaking a world record in the 400-m medley on the opening night of the swimming competition with a time of 4 min 33.59 sec. She followed up with an Olympic record 2 min 10.68 sec in the 200-m medley, but she had to settle for silver behind American Brooke Bennett in the 800-m freestyle, with a time of 8 min 22.66 sec. In the aftermath of the Games, she was voted Ukraine's Athlete of the Year in a poll of that country's sports media.

AP/Wide World Photos

Ukrainian swimmer Yana Klochkova

Despite entering the Athens Olympics as the reigning world champion in the medleys, Klochkova faced stiff challenges in both events. In the 200-m final, she won with a time of 2 min 11.14 sec, besting American Amanda Beard by less than six-tenths of a second. In an equally thrilling 400-m final, Klochkova and American Kaitlin Sandeno entered the last turn in a dead heat. The Ukrainian prevailed, however, beating Sandeno by just a hand's length to take the gold in 4 min 34.83 sec. Klochkova received a literal hero's welcome upon her return home, as Ukrainian Pres. Leonid Kuchma awarded the accomplished young swimmer the title Hero of Ukraine—the nation's highest honour. Another honour came her way in December when *Swimming World* magazine named Klochkova its female World Swimmer of the Year.

(SHERMAN HOLLAR)

Kobia, Samuel

It did not take long after the Rev. Samuel Kobia became general secretary of the World Council of Churches (WCC) in January 2004 for the Kenyan Methodist minister to show his willingness to confront injustices in his native country and continent. At a news conference in Nairobi in April, he said that Christians had failed to address genocide when it took place in Rwanda a decade earlier. He also denounced the increasing incidence of rape of children in much of Africa, calling it "an abomination to the sanctity of life, open disgrace to God and the human community."

Kobia was born on March 20, 1947, in Miathene, Meru, Kenya. He earned degrees in theology from St. Paul's United Theological College in Limuru, Kenya; the Christian Theological Seminary in Indianapolis, Ind.; and Fairfax University in Baton Rouge, La. He also received a diploma in urban ministry from McCormick Theological Seminary in Chicago and a master's degree in city planning from the Massachusetts Institute of Technology.

Kobia served as the WCC's executive secretary for urban rural mission from 1978 to 1987, when he became director of church development activities with the National Council of Churches of Kenya. Three years later he became general secretary of that organization. In 1993 he became executive director of the WCC's Unit III—Justice, Peace and Creation. He directed the global ecumenical organization's Cluster on Issues and Themes from 1999 to 2002 and served as director and special representative for Africa in 2003. In August 2003 he was elected general secretary of the World Council, which had 342 Protestant and Orthodox member churches from more than 120 countries.

Kobia met with 16 leaders of six African American denominations in Washington, D.C., in March 2004 and challenged them to address such issues as the spread of HIV/AIDS and the role of the United States as the only remaining superpower. "As an African," he said, "I can understand the anger that so many ordinary people feel at the arrogance [of the U.S. administration]." In May he met with UN Secretary-General Kofi Annan in New York City, when they discussed the situation in Iraq, the Israeli-Palestinian conflict, and the role of religion in political affairs. At an ecumenical gathering in Berlin in July, he called for interreligious dialogue to combat the "blatant misuse of religion in the mobilization of war" and negative caricatures of Muslims. A day after the U.S. presidential election in November, Kobia released a letter on behalf of the WCC chiding some U.S. churches for having presented God in partisan terms during the campaign. "The harsh claims that make most of the headlines, that invoked the judgement of a partisan God, have provoked deep concern around the world," he wrote.

(DARRELL J. TURNER)

Kolakowski, Leszek

On Nov. 5, 2003, Polish philosopher and historian of philosophy Leszek Kolakowski was awarded the first John W. Kluge Prize for Lifetime Achievement in the Humanities and Social Sciences. The Kluge Prize, awarded by the U.S. Library of Congress, was intended to cover disciplines in the humanities not included in the Nobel Prizes. In 2003 it carried an award of $1 million.

Kolakowski was born on Oct. 23, 1927, in Radom, Pol. He was educated privately and in the underground school system during the German occupation of Poland. He studied philosophy at the University of Lodz (M.A., 1950) and the University of Warsaw (Ph.D., 1953). He taught at the University of Warsaw from 1950 to 1968. Kolakowski began his scholarly career as an orthodox Marxist. He was a member of the communist youth organization and joined the Polish United Workers' Party (PUWP; the communist party) in 1945, but when he was sent to Moscow for a course for promising intellectuals, he began to become disenchanted with the Soviet Marxist system. He became a part of the movement for democratization that led to the Polish workers' uprising of 1956. His revisionist critique of Stalin, "What Is Socialism?," was officially banned in Poland but was widely circulated nonetheless. His 1959 essay "The Priest and the Jester," in which Kolakowski explored the roles of dogmatism and skepticism in intellectual history, brought him to national prominence in Poland. In the 1950s and '60s, he published a series of books on the history of Western philosophy and a study of religious consciousness and institutional religion, at the same time attempting to define a humanistic Marxism; the latter resulted in *Kultura i fetysze* (1967; *Towards a Marxist Humanism,* 1970).

A speech of Kolakowski's on the 10th anniversary of the 1956 uprising led to his expulsion from the PUWP in 1966. In 1968 he was dismissed from his professorship and soon afterward left Poland. He was elected in 1970 to a senior research fellowship at All Souls College, Oxford, where he remained until his retirement in 1995.

Kolakowski eventually abandoned Marxism, which he described as "the greatest fantasy of our century." In his most influential work, *Głowne nurtu marksizmu* (1976; *Main Currents of Marxism: Its Rise, Growth and Dissolution.* 1978), he described the principal currents of Marxist thought and chronicled the origins, rise, and decline of Marxist communism. As an adviser and supporter of the Solidarity trade union, which challenged the communist regime in Poland, Kolakowski played a practical as well as theoretical part in the collapse of the Soviet empire in the 1980s. Kolakowski wrote much on religion and the spiritual basis of culture and was the author of three plays and three volumes of stories. He was the recipient of the German Booksellers Peace Prize (1977), the Erasmus Prize (1980), a MacArthur fellowship (1983), and the Jefferson Award of the National Endowment for the Humanities (1986). (MARTIN L. WHITE)

Kooser, Ted

The announcement in August 2004 that Midwesterner Ted Kooser would be the next U.S. poet laureate consultant in poetry to the Library of Congress was widely applauded. Kooser, who assumed the post in October, was the first poet from the Great Plains to be so honoured. In addition to arranging readings and writing poems for presidential inaugurations and other affairs of state, Kooser was expected, like recent poets laureate, to try to broaden the visibility of poetry in a nation not particularly known for cherishing it. The title of his upcoming book for 2005—*The Poetry Home Repair Manual: Practical Advice for Beginning Poets*—hinted, perhaps, at what his sphere of influence might be.

Theodore Kooser was born in Ames, Iowa, on April 25, 1939. He attended Iowa State University (B.S., 1962) and the University of Nebraska (M.A. in English, 1968) and briefly taught high-school English before settling into an insurance career. He rose to the position of vice president of Lincoln Benefit Life Insurance Co. and retired in 1998. In 1970 he also began to teach creative writing part time at the University of Nebraska at Lincoln. He published his first volume of poetry, *Official Entry Blank,* in 1969 and followed with nine more books, including *Braided Creek: A Conversation in Poetry* (with his good friend Jim Harrison) in 2003 and *Delights and Shadows* in 2004. Kooser won numerous local and national honours, including two National Endowment for the Arts (NEA) fellowships, the Pushcart Prize, and the Stanley Kunitz Prize.

Kooser's poems were short and mostly concerned the land and people in the region around his farm in Garland, northwest of Lincoln, an area jocularly called the "Bohemian Alps" owing to the large number of Czech immigrants who had settled there. His most common poetic technique was an extended metaphor in which he selected a specific image and enriched it in surprising ways. Critics had compared Kooser to, among others, Wendell Berry of Kentucky as a poet of place, Robert Frost for his sympathy with and ability to depict homespun America, Philip Larkin for his passion of discovery, Anton Chekhov for his tender wisdom, and Edgar Lee Masters and Edward Arlington Robinson for the cumulative effect of his work over time. Critic Dana Gioia, now the head of the NEA, was quoted as saying that "Kooser has written more perfect poems than any poet of his generation." In one of his best-known poems, "Selecting a Reader" from *Sure Signs* (1980), Kooser writes with his typical wry, understated humour in imagining a reader inspecting his work: "She will take out her glasses, and there/in the bookstore, she will thumb/over my poems, then put the book back/up on its shelf. She will say to herself/'For that kind of money, I can get my raincoat cleaned.' And she will." (CHARLES TRUMBULL)

Krauss, Alison

Bluegrass fiddler Alison Krauss, who appeared at the 2004 Academy Award ceremonies wearing a $2 million pair of diamond-encrusted stiletto heels to sing songs from the film *Cold Mountain,* was clearly not a traditional bluegrass musician. A champion fiddler, silver-voiced soprano, and leader of the masterful bluegrass quintet Union Station, Krauss had a musical career filled with anomalies. She recorded on Rounder, a folk-music-oriented independent label of the kind that hardly expected huge sales, yet Krauss had five gold, platinum, and double-platinum CDs. In 2004 the million-selling *Alison Krauss + Union Station Live* was awarded the Grammy for best bluegrass album; "Cluck Old Hen," the band's showcase for her fiddle, won best country instrumental; and her duet with pop artist James Taylor, "How's the World Treating You," was named best country collaboration with vocals. With these three trophies Krauss became the female recording artist who had won more Grammys than any other: a total of 17, one more than the previous top diva, Aretha Franklin.

Bluegrass music's Alison Krauss

Krauss was born on July 23, 1971, in Champaign, Ill., where she began studying violin at the age of five. She proved to be a bluegrass prodigy—a flamboyant fiddler, she won contest after contest, led a band when she was 10, won the Illinois State Fiddling Championship two years later, and signed a recording contract when she was just 14. In 1990 she won her first Grammy for her third album, *I've Got That Old Feeling.* Krauss's first Union Station group included her older brother Viktor, who went on to become Lyle Lovett's bassist, and almost from the beginning the group became a favourite of bluegrass fans. As Union Station evolved and changed, Krauss's singing became a primary element in its success; her voice recalled the young Dolly Parton, and she began treating folk, gospel, standard country, and pop songs to the unamplified bluegrass style. Her videos were appearing on television, and the ensemble was already the leading bluegrass act by 1995. That was the year of their breakthrough CD, a "best of" compilation, *Now That I've Found You,* which wound up among *Billboard* magazine's top 10 pop albums and included her hit single "When You Say Nothing at All." Each of her successive albums became a best seller as well.

As Union Station added songs of the Beatles, the Allman Brothers, Todd Rundgren, and other rock performers to its repertoire, murmurs of disapproval were heard from hardcore bluegrass lovers. Krauss further distanced herself from bluegrass purity by appearing with stars as disparate as Parton, Phish, Sting, the Chieftains, Bad Company, and Yo-Yo Ma. Still she was determined to expand her range. While her work in the Coen brothers' 2000 film *O Brother, Where Art Thou?* and the ensuing Down from the Mountain Tour pleased some purists, Krauss could not ignore the criticism. "If we were really selling out," she countered, "our lives would be a lot different." (JOHN LITWEILER)

Lang Lang

By 2004 Chinese-born pianist Lang Lang had firmly established himself as one of the most promising young musical talents on the international scene. Only 22 years of age, he had already performed with many of the leading American orchestras and conductors and had played in major concert halls across Europe, North America, and Asia. Frequently praised for his superb technical skill, Lang Lang was also known as an intense and charismatic performer—and one who clearly had an eye toward mass appeal. He made well-publicized television appearances on *Good Morning America* and *The Tonight Show with Jay Leno.* His self-titled debut CD, recorded live in recital at the Tanglewood Music Center in Lenox, Mass., was released in 2001 and quickly leaped to number four on *Billboard's* classical music charts. Follow-up CDs enjoyed similar success and included *Lang Lang Live at the Proms* (2002) and *Lang Lang Live at Carnegie Hall* (2004).

Lang Lang was born in Shenyang, China, in 1982. He began taking piano lessons at the age of three and gave his first public recital two years later. In 1991 he entered the Central Music Conservatory in Beijing. He soon began to attract wide attention as a musical prodigy. At the age of 13, he won first prize at the Tchaikovsky International Young Musicians' Competition in Japan and also appeared at the Beijing Concert Hall, where he performed the complete Chopin *Études.* The following year he was featured as a soloist at the China National Symphony's inaugural concert, with Pres. Jiang Zemin in attendance.

Leaving China for the U.S. in 1997, Lang Lang enrolled at the Curtis Institute of Music, Philadelphia, where he had been offered a scholarship. For the next five years, he studied under noted pianist Gary Graffman, president of the Curtis Institute. Lang Lang's pace of development was astonishing. He made his American debut with the Baltimore (Md.) Symphony Orchestra in 1998. In August 1999, in Highland Park, Ill., at the Ravinia Festival's "Gala of the Century," Lang Lang stepped in

Linda Matlow/Pix Int'l/WireImage.com

Chinese-born pianist Lang Lang

at the last moment for an ailing André Watts and earned rave reviews for his performance of Tchaikovsky's First Piano Concerto with the Chicago Symphony Orchestra. He became famous virtually overnight. He went on to sell out Carnegie Hall in an April 2001 concert with the Baltimore Symphony that the *New York Times* described as "stunning." Later that year Lang Lang made a triumphant return tour to China with the Philadelphia Orchestra, during which he played for an audience of 8,000 at Beijing's Great Hall of the People.

In July 2002 the Schleswig-Holstein Festival awarded Lang its first-ever Leonard Bernstein Award for distinguished musical talent. He again toured China in August 2003, and at the close of the 2003–04 season, he became the first Chinese pianist ever to perform with the Berlin Philharmonic. Lang Lang's hectic touring schedule and the slick marketing campaign that was created for him began to alarm some critics, however, who worried that in such a commercialized atmosphere the young pianist risked becoming more of a showman than a serious artist. Nevertheless, Lang showed no signs of slowing his pace, launching an ambitious coast-to-coast recital tour of the U.S. in late 2004 and recording works by Rachmaninov and Paganini for a new CD scheduled for release in 2005. (SHERMAN HOLLAR)

Latham, Mark

The opposition Labor Party (ALP) emerged from the October 2004 election in Australia weaker than it had entered it, as Labor's outspoken leader, Mark Latham, was routed by the conservative coalition led by Prime Minister John Howard on his way to a fourth term. In a tough campaign Howard battered Latham on what he described as his weak economic credentials, warning that as prime minister Latham would allow interest rates to rise. In an attempt to learn from one of the worst Labor defeats in history, Latham responded by bolstering his party's economic credentials with new appointments to his shadow ministry. Latham, who focused his campaign on education and health care reform, enjoyed a high rate of support in the spring, but throughout the summer his standing in opinion polls fluctuated. In what became a pivotal issue, he adopted a hard-line stance against Australia's involvement in the U.S.-led war in Iraq, pledging to remove Australian troops from the conflict, which even prompted a rejoinder from U.S. Pres. George W. Bush.

Latham was born on Feb. 28, 1961, in Sydney. He graduated with a degree in economics from the University of Sydney in 1982. Entering politics, he worked in the office of former ALP prime minister Gough Whitlam. In 1987 Latham was elected to the city council in the Sydney suburb of Liverpool, and he became mayor there in 1991. He later sought federal office and in 1994 was elected to represent Werriwa in the House of Representatives; it was the former seat (1952–78) of his mentor, Whitlam. When the ALP went into opposition following the 1996 elections, Latham became shadow minister of education with a seat on the front bench, but he resigned from his position after disagreements with opposition leader Kim Beazley during the 1998 elections. After Simon Crean replaced Beazley following the 2001 elections, Latham was brought back to the front bench, this time as shadow minister for economic ownership. In 2003 Crean rewarded him with the posts of shadow treasurer and manager of opposition business. Later that year, when Crean lost the confidence of his party and resigned, he threw his support to Latham. At age 42 Latham was confirmed by his party in December 2003 to become the youngest ALP leader in 100 years. Latham was sometimes criticized as having a brash, divisive demeanour, which others saw as the strength of individualism. The author of several books on policy, he looked to develop a new strategy for the ALP in order to deal with the challenges facing the party and his leadership. (TOM MICHAEL)

Lee Hsien Loong

On Aug. 12, 2004, Lee Hsien Loong formally assumed office as the new prime minister of Singapore, replacing the outgoing Goh Chok Tong in a ceremony that marked the culmination of a lengthy succession process. When Goh had come into office 14 years earlier, Lee—the eldest son of Singapore's longtime leader and first prime minister, Lee Kuan Yew—had immediately been tapped to serve as deputy prime minister and from that time had been recognized as Goh's designated successor. With the 52-year-old Lee finally ascending to the prime ministership, his family's influence over the country seemed as potent as ever. His 80-year-old father, who had run Singapore with an iron hand from 1959 to 1990, was appointed to the newly created cabinet post of "minister mentor." In addition, Lee's wife, Ho Ching, served as executive director of the government-run investment firm Temasek Holdings, which owned stakes in some of Singapore's largest companies. While observers expected Lee to retain tight control over the prosperous city-state, he appeared sensitive to the desire among many Singaporeans for a more open society. In his inaugural address Lee vowed to bring new faces into the government. He also promised to permit greater freedoms in a country where rigid social policies and limits on political expression were strictly enforced.

Lee was born in Singapore on Feb. 10, 1952. He distinguished himself academically as a young man, studying mathematics and graduating with a first-class degree from the University of Cambridge before earning a master's degree in public administration from Harvard University's Kennedy School of Government. He then became an officer in the Singaporean military, eventually rising to the rank of brigadier general.

Lee's political career began when he joined his father's party, the ruling People's Action Party, in 1984. Two years later he was elected to the party's Central Executive Committee. In the early 1990s, while serving as deputy prime minister, Lee was treated for lymphoma. The cancer ultimately went into remission, and he made a vigorous return to political life, even taking on the added responsibilities of finance minister and central bank chairman.

Despite the promises included in Lee's inaugural address, few changes had been made by year's end. The new cabinet, although it included for the first time two women ministers of state, was made up primarily of appointees who had been reassigned from other ministry posts. Revised guidelines on free speech were announced shortly after Lee was sworn in, but while certain restrictions were eased—licenses for indoor political meetings were no longer required, for example—many remained intact. (SHERMAN HOLLAR)

Liu Xiang

On Aug. 27, 2004, Chinese track athlete Liu Xiang won the 110-m hurdles at the Olympic Games in Athens, equaling the world record of 12.91 sec. The ecstatic Liu at once fulfilled the great promise he had shown in setting a world junior record two years earlier and raised the hopes of his compatriots for a repeat victory at the 2008 Games in Beijing. Liu said that his performance, which brought China its first men's Olympic gold medal in track and field, "changes the opinion that Asian countries don't get good results in sprint races. I want to prove to all the world that Asians can run very fast." In his comments Liu gave voice to his country's cultural stereotype, which, judging from editorial comments in Chinese newspapers, he was not alone in believing. "I am a Chinese," he said, "and considering the physiology of the Chinese people, it is something unbelievable." Liu improved his personal best of 13.06 sec, set earlier in the year, and became just the sixth man to have dipped under 13.00 sec. He finished the season with 4 of the year's 10 fastest clockings. Reaching 17 finals in the 60-m indoor hurdles and the 110-m hurdles, he lost just 2, both to American Allen Johnson. Liu, at 1.89 m (6 ft 2 in) and 85 kg (187 kg), was taller

© Bazuki Muhammad/Reuters/Corbis

© Gary Hershorn/Reuters/Corbis

Hurdler Liu Xiang of China

than most sprint hurdlers, and he showed spectacular athleticism in constraining his naturally long stride to the three-step pattern necessary for avoiding the alternation of lead legs in hurdling.

Liu was born on July 13, 1983, in Shanghai, the only child of a truck driver and a housewife. He was selected in the fourth grade to attend a junior sports school and won the national high-jump title for boys his age in his first year of competition. At age 15 he met hurdle coach Sun Haiping, who persuaded him to switch events. Although Sun described his pupil's technique as "terrible" in the beginning, Liu debuted internationally at the world junior championships in 2000 and finished fourth in the 110-m hurdles. He then won the event at the 2001 World University Games and in 2002 set world junior records indoors in the 60-m hurdles (7.55 sec) and outdoors in the 110-m hurdles (13.12 sec). In 2003 he raised his hopes for Athens, earning bronze medals at the indoor and outdoor world championships and the vote of Chinese sports journalists as his country's Male Athlete of the Year.

Liu, a 21-year-old student at East China Normal University at the time of his Athens victory, became the object of a bidding war between commercial sponsors. The Chinese Track and Field Association restricted him to four such deals. (SIEG LINDSTROM)

Maal, Baaba

One of the leading names in popular music in his native Senegal, singer and instrumentalist Baaba Maal raised his profile with a critically acclaimed North American tour in 2004. The 34-date tour featured acoustic arrangements of his extensive catalog and took his unique blend of traditional African rhythms and modern Western influences to venues not traditionally associated with the world music scene. Maal also used the exposure to bring attention to the spread of HIV/AIDS in Africa and to address the dangers of hunger and poverty in his homeland.

Maal was born on Nov. 12, 1953, in Podor, Senegal. Although his family was not of the griot, or musician, class, he spent his childhood surrounded by music. He frequently joined his father, the muezzin at the local mosque, for the daily call to prayer—an exercise that led to the development of a resonant voice that needed little or no amplification. From his mother Maal learned the folk songs of the Tukulor people and the "women's music" of the *yela,* a $\frac{3}{4}$ beat derived from the rhythms produced while pounding grain. After completing his secondary education, he was offered a scholarship to the École des Beaux Arts in Dakar. He was accompanied by Mansour Seck, a griot and a longtime friend and musical mentor, and the two joined Asly Fouta, a 70-piece orchestra that toured West Africa in a celebration of Tukulor culture. The pair left the group in 1977, and in 1982 Maal was offered a scholarship to complete his studies at the Paris Conservatory. Seck again followed him, and the two recorded their debut album, *Djam leelii,* in Brussels later that year. Maal returned to Podor after the death of his mother in 1984 and formed the nine-piece group Daande Lenol ("The Voice of the People") the following year. Over the next few years, the group released a series of cassettes for the local market, and their popularity grew. Daande Lenol did not shy away from social or political topics, however, and it was not long before authorities in Mauritania banned their recordings.

A series of fruitful collaborations increased Maal's popularity in Europe. He performed with British singer Peter Gabriel on the sound track of *The Last Temptation of Christ* (1988) and became a frequent presence at Gabriel's Real World studios in Bath, Eng. Maal signed with world music label Mango Records and released *Baayo* in 1991. He followed with the disco-influenced *Lam toro* (1992) and the pop-tinged *Firin' in Fouta* (1994), for which he received a Grammy nomination for best world music album. While 1998's *Nomad Soul* continued in the Afropop vein, it was evident that Maal was drifting back toward his Tukulor roots. His 2001 release, *Missing You (Mi yeewnii),* was a stripped-down acoustic masterpiece that utilized the ambient sounds of the African environment as a background track. In July 2003 he was named a youth emissary by the UN Development Programme in recognition of his social works and his growing world popularity. (MICHAEL RAY)

Senegalese musician Baaba Maal

Jon Furniss/WireImage.com

Mandelson, Peter

In 2004 Peter Benjamin Mandelson, one of the United Kingdom's most talented but controversial politicians, took over one of the European Union's most important jobs when he was appointed Britain's member of the EU Commission and given the EU trade portfolio. One of his main responsibilities in this post would be to represent the EU at the World Trade Organization. The appointment was a remarkable comeback for a man who had twice had to resign from Prime Minister Tony Blair's government over allegations of wrongdoing.

Mandelson was born in London on Oct. 21, 1953. The grandson of Herbert Morrison, deputy prime minister during the Labour government of 1945–51, Mandelson was interested in politics from childhood. A brief flirtation with communism ended while he was a student at St. Catherine's College, Oxford, and he became a member of the Labour Party. After receiving his degree in philosophy, politics, and economics, he joined the staff of the Trades Union Congress. In 1979, by then a committed Labour Party moderate, he was elected to Lambeth borough council in South London, but he resigned in 1982, disillusioned with the borough's left-wing leadership.

That same year he became a producer of a weekly television political program, *Weekend World,* a vantage point that sharpened his view of Labour's defects and the party's need to modernize its policies and appeal. In 1985 Mandelson was appointed Labour's director of communications by Labour Party leader Neil Kinnock. He promoted Kinnock's modernization agenda and ensured high media profiles for some of Labour's rising stars, then in their 30s, such as Blair and Gordon Brown.

In 1992 Mandelson was elected Labour MP for Hartlepool, a coastal town in northeastern England. In 1997, following Labour's return to government and Blair's election as prime minister, Mandelson became a middle-ranking minister. One of his responsibilities was to oversee the early stages of the building of the controversial and, eventually, ill-fated Millennium Dome at Greenwich, southeast London. A year later he was promoted to the cabinet as trade and industry secretary. In December 1998 he resigned following the disclosure that he had borrowed money from a fellow minister to buy a house and had not officially declared the fact. By October 1999, however, Blair felt that Mandelson had paid an adequate price for his mistake and returned him to the cabinet as Northern Ireland secretary. This lasted until January 2001, when he was compelled to resign again, this time over allegations that he had acted improperly over the

© Toby Melville/Reuters/Corbis

issuing of U.K. passports to two wealthy Indian businessmen.

A subsequent inquiry exonerated Mandelson, but he accepted that he was unlikely to be given a third chance to join Blair's cabinet. Nevertheless, he remained a close ally of Blair's, especially in arguing that Britain should work more closely with the rest of the EU member countries. Blair's decision to appoint him as the U.K.'s EU commissioner in July 2004 was a logical way of both pursuing a pro-European strategy and bringing Mandelson's troubled domestic political career to a civilized end. In September he resigned from Parliament to move to Brussels and start his new job. (PETER KELLNER)

McDonald, Audra

In 2004 soprano Audra McDonald, best known as the luminous golden-voiced star of the American musical theatre, was rewarded with a Tony Award (her fourth) for best performance by a featured actress for her portrayal of Ruth Younger in the drama *A Raisin in the Sun.* In the dozen years since she had gained

AP/Wide World Photos

Singer and actress Audra McDonald

international attention for her first Tony-winning role—the fecund Carrie Snow in British director Nicholas Hytner's (*q.v.*) Lincoln Center Theatre revival of *Carousel,* McDonald had fashioned a barrier-busting career. Her credits encompassed not only the mainstream musical theatre but also an eclectic program of concerts and recordings, straight dramatic roles in contemporary plays and (with the 2003 Broadway staging of *Henry IV*) Shakespeare, singing and nonsinging roles in made-for-TV movies, and appearances on prime- time television.

By her own admission, Audra Ann McDonald, who was born on July 3, 1970, in Berlin and grew up in Fresno, Calif., had always been a drama queen. "I'm completely overly dramatic and completely hypersensitive to everything," she declared, only half-jokingly. During her childhood, music was everywhere—her parents were pianists and singers, and five of her aunts toured the West Coast as the singing McDonald Sisters in the 1970s—and by the age of nine, McDonald was performing big and small parts at the local dinner theatre. By the time she was playing musical leads in high school, her eyes were on New York City. It was the continuation of her vocal training at the Juilliard School that took McDonald to New York City and eventually brought her to the attention of Hytner. Her supporting-role Tony for *Carousel* was followed by similar accolades for *Ragtime* (1998) and *Master Class* (1996). Perhaps equally impressive were her 2004 season sold-out solo recitals at Carnegie Hall and with the New York Philharmonic, in which McDonald's rare versatility was on display in songs ranging from cabaret standards to Kurt Weill's "Seven Deadly Sins" cycle to art songs by young composers Adam Guettel (*The Light in the Piazza*) and Michael John LaChiusa (*Marie Christine,* a musical retelling of *Medea* written especially for McDonald).

Whatever her successes as an actress, it was likely that audiences would continue to dote on McDonald's lustrous lyric soprano, which she controlled to exquisite effect whether in a buoyant or a mournful mode. McDonald considered singing a form of acting.

Her future plans included singing the role of Kitty Oppenheimer, wife of the director of the Manhattan Project, in avant-garde composer John Adams's upcoming opera *Dr. Atomic,* about the making of the A-bomb. Many wondered if there was anything performers could do on the legitimate stage that McDonald could not do. Grand opera, perhaps? Not likely. On her work schedule for 2006 was a production of Francis Poulenc's *La Voix humaine* at the Houston (Texas) Grand Opera. (JIM O'QUINN)

McGraw, Phil

By 2004 talk-show host, author, and psychologist-educator Phil McGraw had secured his place as "America's therapist" with the success of the nationally syndicated *Dr. Phil,* which debuted in 2002 and showcased McGraw's talent for dispensing real solutions to real problems in his characteristically blunt but clearly caring manner.

Phillip C. McGraw was born on Sept. 1, 1950, in Vinita, Okla. He attended the University of Tulsa, Okla., on a football scholarship but turned his attention to psychology after an injury cut short his future on the gridiron. McGraw earned his master's degree and Ph.D. from the University of North Texas and, like his father, launched a career as a psychologist. After graduation he joined his father and another partner to form a company that operated self-motivation and life-skills seminars throughout the country. Soon after establishing his own practice, McGraw realized that he did not have the patience for the subtleties and ambiguous time frames of traditional talk therapy; he closed the practice and began conducting corporate consultant work.

In 1989 he and a lawyer friend launched Courtroom Sciences, Inc. (CSI), a firm that provided mock trial, jury selection, and mediation services to lawyers. CSI attained a national reputation after successfully guiding to victory the defense lawyers of the famed *Exxon Valdez* oil-spill trial. In 1996, when television talk-show queen Oprah Winfrey was sued for defamation by disgruntled Texas cattlemen, her defense team sought out CSI's assistance. McGraw and company coached Winfrey and her defense team, who eventually emerged victorious. In gratitude, Winfrey invited McGraw to appear on her show; her audiences were so taken with his down-home charm and what they perceived as his razor-sharp psychological analyses that he soon became a regular fixture on Winfrey's show. McGraw was featured on Winfrey's "Change Your Life" segments before graduating to weekly appearances as the main attraction on her wildly popular "Tuesdays with Dr. Phil."

In 2002 "Tell It like It Is Phil" (Winfrey's sobriquet) became the host of *Dr. Phil,* which was nominated for two Daytime Emmy Awards in its first season. McGraw—who eschewed psychobabble and touchy-feely approaches—continued to remind his viewers that what he was providing was education, not "eight-minute cures" or true psychotherapy. His books *Life Strategies* (1999), *Relationship Rescue* (2000), and *Self Matters* (2001) were all best sellers. *The Ultimate Weight Solution* and *The Ultimate Weight Solution Food Guide* appeared in 2003, and though some questioned the ability and authority of a trained psychologist to provide viable dietary guidelines, these criticisms did little to dilute his popularity among his millions of adoring fans. His latest book was *Family First* (2004). (SHANDA SILER)

Minogue, Kylie

In February 2004 pop sensation Kylie Minogue won her first Grammy, for best dance recording, with "Come into My World." For American audiences it was indeed an invitation into her world, which was already well known to fans in Europe and Australia, where her success and endurance arguably eclipsed that of fellow superstar Madonna. *Longevity* was not a word generally associated with the often-fickle pop music scene, but Kylie—as her legions of fans called her—had filled an impressive 17-year span with 40 hit singles and 40 million albums sold, and she remained a sex symbol at age 36, which some considered old for female celebrities who relied mainly on sex appeal. Though a native Australian, Minogue was also adopted by Britain, where in April 2004 she was calculated as the most-played female singer on British radio; that fall she became the new spokesperson for British Airways.

Kylie Ann Minogue was born in Melbourne, Vic., on May 28, 1968, and had some success as a child actress (like her younger sister, Dannii). Minogue first came to fame in the popular soap opera *Neighbours* in Australia and Great Britain in 1985–88. She left television for a singing career, making her recording debut in 1988 with the album *Kylie,* as part of the London hit factory Stock, Aitken & Waterman, and her first number one single, "I Should Be So Lucky." Her cover of Little Eva's "Locomotion" broke into the American Top 10, where she would not reappear for another 14 years.

With media savvy and a strong work ethic, the diminutive (1.5-m [5-ft]-tall) Minogue saw her career skyrocket in Europe. Her music was lauded as "the pristine embodiment of pop—simple, undemanding, unthreatening fun," and her stage shows became big draws. A natural in front of the camera, with a diva's

AP/Wide World Photos

Australian pop diva Kylie Minogue

sense of fashion, she became a darling of the tabloids, which spilled untold amounts of ink praising her rear end. Minogue parlayed her sexy image and much-admired derrière into further publicity—she dated rock stars, endorsed perfumes and automobiles, sold millions of calendars as a sexy pinup, and promoted her own line of underwear, called Love Kylie.

Minogue left Stock, Aitken & Waterman, and her musical career slumped in the second half of the '90s as she assumed a punky look and recorded with "indie" rockers. She returned to her saucy pop roots in 2000, donning hot pants in the video for her comeback single, "Spinning Around," from the album *Light Years.* Led by the blockbuster "Can't Get You out of My Head," her comeback even returned her to U.S. shores, where the album *Fever* (2001) reached the Top 3 in 2002, outselling all of her previous albums there combined. Her renewed popularity continued with the release of *Body Language* (2003).

(TOM MICHAEL)

Mosley, Walter

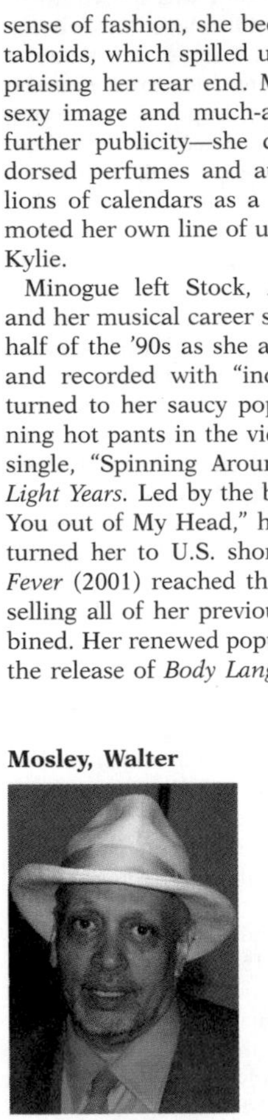

© Nancy Kaszerman/ZUMA/Corbis

The year 2004 offered a golden opportunity for Walter Mosley to showcase his talents as both a popular novelist and a progressive voice on social issues. In January he published *The Man in My Basement.* Through the bizarre exchanges between the two main characters, Mosley reflected on the dark side of human nature while he explored themes of injustice and manipulation. In July Mosley brought back his best-known fictional character, Ezekiel ("Easy") Porterhouse Rawlins, in *Little Scarlet,* his highly anticipated ninth entry in the Easy Rawlins mystery series.

Walter Ellis Mosley was born on Jan. 12, 1952, in Los Angeles and grew up in the Watts neighbourhood, where violent race riots raged in 1965. His father, a school custodian, had moved to California to escape Jim Crow-era Louisiana, while his mother was from a family of Polish-Jewish immigrants who had witnessed segregation and racial atrocities in Eastern Europe. Mosley later attributed his strong feelings about injustice in the world to his parents' experiences. After graduating from Johnson (Vt.) State College (B.A., 1977), he moved to New York City, where he worked for more than 10 years as a computer programmer. He also wrote stories and attended the writing program at the City College of New York.

His first published novel, *Devil in a Blue Dress* (1990), introduced Rawlins, an African American amateur detective living in the jazz scene of 1940s Los Angeles. Mosley helped adapt the book for the big screen in 1995; actor Denzel Washington played the role of Rawlins. During his presidential campaign in 1992, Bill Clinton proclaimed Mosley one of his favourite writers. This endorsement immediately tripled Mosley's sales and elevated his reputation among the general reading public. Other Easy Rawlins mysteries such as *Black Betty* (1994) and *A Little Yellow Dog* (1996) went straight to the *New York Times* best-sellers list. *RL's Dream* (1995), based on the legendary bluesman Robert Johnson, won the 1996 Black Caucus of the American Library Association Literary Award. Mosley introduced Socrates Fortlow, an ex-convict who moves from the Deep South to South Central Los Angeles immediately after the 1992 riots, in *Always Outnumbered, Always Outgunned* (1998), which he adapted for HBO television. Fortlow reappeared in *Walkin' the Dog* (1999). After publishing two science-fiction works, *Blue Light* (1998) and *Futureland* (2001), Mosley introduced Fearless Jones in the mystery novels *Fearless Jones* (2001) and *Fear Itself* (2003).

Mosley became (1996) the first artist in residence for New York University's Institute of African American Affairs, which served as the catalyst for an ongoing forum of black intellectuals and artists, and was coeditor of the forum's collection of essays, *Black Genius: African American Solutions to African American Problems* (1999). He also started a publishing training institute at the City College of Harlem.

He temporarily set aside fiction to explore his political conscience with the nonfiction *Workin' on the Chain Gang: Shaking Off the Dead Hand of History* (2000) and *What Next: A Memoir Toward World Peace* (2003). Mosley's two new novels in 2004, however, showed that he was not about to abandon his many fans.

(SARA WOOD)

Murthy, Narayana

Narayana Murthy, chairman and chief mentor of Indian software giant Infosys Technologies Ltd., had plenty to celebrate in 2004. In April he announced that the Bangalore-based company had posted $1.06 billion in total annual revenues, an astonishing 33% increase in revenues over the previous fiscal year. The company's growth was all the more remarkable because it came in the midst of a global downturn in the information technology industry. Infosys thus became the only publicly traded IT company in India to have reached the $1 billion milestone. Murthy, who had led the transformation of Infosys from a small software services firm into a global operation with such clients as Visa, Reebok, Boeing Co., and Cisco Systems, hailed his company's achievement in a statement and described surpassing $1 billion in revenues as "the beginning of a new journey."

Murthy was born on Aug. 20, 1946, in Kolar, Karnataka state, India. He earned his bachelor's degree in electrical engineering from the University of Mysore in 1967 and his master's degree in technology from the Indian Institute of Technology, Kanpur, in 1969. During the 1970s he worked in Paris, where, among other projects, he helped design an operating system for handling air cargo at Charles de Gaulle Airport. Returning to India, he accepted a position with a computer systems company in Pune, but eventually he decided to launch his own company. He cofounded Infosys with six fellow computer professionals in 1981.

The company grew slowly until the early 1990s, when the Indian government's decisive move toward economic liberalization and deregulation contributed to dramatic growth in the country's high-technology and computer sectors. Murthy aggressively expanded his company's services and client base, negotiating deals with many overseas businesses to provide them with consulting, systems integration, software development, and product engineering services. By 1999 Infosys had joined Nasdaq, becoming the first Indian company to be listed on an American stock exchange. The following year *Asiaweek* included Murthy in its Power 50, the magazine's annual list of the most powerful people in the region. In addition, *Business Week* named him one of its "Stars of Asia" for three consecutive years (1998–2000), and he was *Fortune* magazine's 2003 Asian Businessman of the Year.

Such phenomenal success was not without controversy, however. In early 2004 a political debate that erupted in the U.S. over job losses caused by offshoring, the outsourcing of work overseas, was of serious concern to Infosys, which derived more than two-thirds of its revenue from American corporations. Murthy responded that it was "normal" that concerns over job losses would be voiced, and while he indicated that he thought outsourcing was "here to stay," he made efforts to assuage some of the anger by announcing that Infosys would establish a consulting unit in the U.S. that would employ 500 workers. The controversy in the end appeared not to have significantly dented Infosys's business. On top of its

2004 performance, Murthy's company was forecasting a revenue increase of 25% for fiscal year 2005. (SHERMAN HOLLAR)

OutKast

Rap duo OutKast, which helped put Atlanta, Ga., on the hip-hop map in the 1990s, topped the charts in fall 2003 with the double album *Speakerboxxx /The Love Below,* which won three top Grammy Awards in 2004: album of the year, best rap album, and best urban/alternative performance for the boisterous "Hey Ya!"

In the 1990s OutKast released a series of albums, each of which outdid its predecessor in sales and plaudits from the critics. Their music was regarded as the best exemplar of the often profane style of hip-hop that had emerged in southern cities and had thus become known as "Dirty South." Their crossover masterpiece *Stankonia* placed at or near the top of most critics' "best of" lists in 2000. OutKast's Andre 3000 and Big Boi in effect became solo artists together with *Speakerboxxx/ The Love Below,* on which each took the lead on one disc. In the process OutKast both renewed its mastery of "old school" rap, largely on the Big Boi-dominated *Speakerboxxx,* and

OutKast: Big Boi (left) and Andre 3000

continued its assault on the boundaries of hip-hop, primarily on *The Love Below,* on which Andre 3000 sang as much as he rapped and included a healthy dose of funk in the mix.

Andre Benjamin (b. May 27, 1975, Atlanta) and Antwan Patton (b. Feb. 1, 1975, Savannah, Ga.) joined forces at a performing arts high school in Atlanta. Discovering their mutual admiration for hip-hop and the funk musicians that became their stylistic touchstones (Parliament-Funkadelic, Sly and the Family Stone, and Prince), they formed a rap group, 2 Shades Deep. Recording in a basement studio under the guidance of the Organized Noize production team, Andre and Antwan, now known individually as Dre and Big Boi, respectively, and collectively as OutKast, had a breakthrough hit single with "Player's Ball" in 1993. Soon after honour student Big Boi graduated (Dre had already left school to concentrate on music), the duo's first album, *Southernplayalisticadillacmuzik* (1994), went platinum. Featuring the hit "Elevators (Me and You)," OutKast's second album, *ATLiens* (1996), sold 1.5 million copies. Their third effort, the double-platinum *Aquemini* (1998), employed more live instruments and earned a Grammy nomination for the single "Rosa Parks."

As OutKast deepened the sophistication of its frequently life-affirming lyrics and broadened its musical eclecticism, it never lost its unique sense of humour. The group's image also became a signature, especially the increasingly flamboyant wardrobe of Dre (renamed Andre 3000), and their theatricality and stylish music videos became OutKast hallmarks. Propelled by "B.O.B" ("Bombs over Baghdad"), *Stankonia* shot up the charts and earned Grammy Awards for best rap album and best performance by a rap duo/group for the heartfelt "Ms. Jackson." The separate nature of *Speakerboxxx/The Love Below* and the relocation of Andre 3000 to Los Angeles to pursue film acting, fueled rumours that the group might be ready to call it quits, but the end of the year found the duo preparing to collaborate on a film sound-track album.

(JEFF WALLENFELDT)

Penn, Sean

Although Sean Penn had been nominated for an Academy Award three times before, it was not until 2004, when he wanted to demonstrate his pride in *Mystic River,* that he actually attended the awards ceremony. His performance in that film—in the role of the grief-stricken father of a murdered young woman—had earned him a best actor nomination, and before the evening was over, the former "bad boy" was declared the winner. The audience greeted that announcement with a standing ovation.

Sean Justin Penn was born on Aug. 17, 1960, in Santa Monica, Calif. The son of show business parents, he chose to forgo college and instead joined the Los Angeles Repertory Theatre. After a few television appearances, including his debut on *Barnaby Jones,* he moved to New York City in 1980. Well-received performances in the Off-Broadway *Heartlands* and the film *Taps* (both 1981) paved the way for Penn's fame-making role as a surfer dude in *Fast Times at Ridgemont High* (1982). He followed with a variety of roles that showcased his intensity and versatility—including a teenage delinquent in *Bad Boys* (1983), a punk rocker/burglar in *Crackers* (1984), a World War II Marine about to ship out in the romantic *Racing with the Moon* (1984), and a spy selling U.S. government secrets to the KGB in *The Falcon and the Snowman* (1985)—garnering favourable notices from critics even when the vehicle he per-

Oscar winner Sean Penn

formed in was not as well liked. Penn's career took a downturn, however, during his relationship with pop star Madonna, whom he married in 1985. There were frequent confrontations with paparazzi, a number of them combative, and Penn spent a month in jail in 1987. The marriage ended in 1989—but not before the couple had costarred in *Shanghai Surprise* (1986), which was almost universally panned.

Penn's subsequent movies did better, however, and he also branched out, writing and directing *Indian Runner* (1991), directing *The Crossing Guard* (1995), and even announcing that he was giving up acting to concentrate on directing. Nevertheless, he was soon a busier actor than before, adding a number of his finest films to his list of credits. Penn earned his first Oscar nomination for *Dead Man Walking* (1995); costarred opposite his second wife—Robin Wright Penn—in *She's So Lovely* (1997), for which he was named best actor at the Cannes Festival; gained a second Oscar nomination for *Sweet and Lowdown* (1999) and a third for *I Am Sam* (2001); and won best actor honours at the Venice Film Festival for *21 Grams* (2003). He also added another impressive directorial effort, *The Pledge* (2001). Penn was an active opponent of the war in Iraq, making trips to Baghdad and publishing reports on these trips, and included among his upcoming films were two that would reflect his political interests: *The Assassination of Richard Nixon,* based on an actual attempt on the president's life, and *The Interpreter,* a political thriller involving the UN.

(BARBARA WHITNEY)

Perry, Grayson

Having achieved celebrity status by winning the 2003 Turner Prize, one of the art world's premier honours, British potter Grayson Perry in 2004 mounted a solo exhibition at the Tate St. Ives in Cornwall and saw *I Want to Be an Artist* (1996), the first of his vases to be sold at auction, fetch £36,000 (about $66,000), more than twice the presale estimate. The Turner Prize frequently generated controversy, and Perry's award was widely perceived as a continuation of this trend, though perhaps for different reasons from those in the past. Perry was the first potter to win the prize, and the fact that he dressed openly as a transvestite, with his doll-like alter ego, Claire, making frequent appearances (often accompanied by his wife and daughter), added to the controversy. Furthermore, the colourful surfaces of Perry's classically shaped vases served as a seductive camouflage for inscribed images and messages that were distinctly at odds with their decorative medium. Domestic violence, child abuse, pedophilia, and cultural stereotypes were some of the troubling themes that the artist habitually explored in these inscriptions. Perry acknowledged his exploitation of the decorative appeal of his pots, describing them as a "guerrilla tactic" or "stealth tactic," under the cover of which "a polemic or an ideology" waited to be discovered.

Perry was born into a working-class family in Chelmsford, Essex, Eng., on March 24, 1960. His interest in ceramics was kindled during childhood, and by the age of 13 he had confided his transvestism to his diary. He studied at the Braintree College of Further Education in Essex and at Portsmouth Polytechnic in Hampshire, but it was not until the early 1980s, when he was living in a squat in London's Camden Town, that he returned to the serious study of ceramics by way of evening art classes. At the time, he was appearing in performance pieces and art films and nursing his own aspirations as a filmmaker. He disliked the compromising and collaborating that he felt went hand-in-hand with filmmaking, however, and when in 1984 the first solo exhibition of his ceramic works—all created in his evening classes—sold well, he made pottery his main art form, though he continued to work in other media. From the 1990s Perry also worked in embroidery, creating such pieces as *Mother of All Battles* (1996), a woman's folk costume stitched with ethnic symbols and images of weapons and killings, and *Claire's Coming Out Dress* (2000). In 2004 Great Britain's Channel 4 commissioned him to make a television documentary about transvestism. Perry was also the author of a novel, *Cycle of Violence* (1992).

(JANET MOREDOCK)

Phelps, Michael

At the 2004 Olympics in Athens, as he won a record eight swimming medals, American Michael Phelps showed why many considered him the world's dominant swimmer. Entering the Games amid high expectations and intense media scrutiny, Phelps remained focused enough to capture six gold medals (200-m and 400-m individual medley, 100-m and 200-m butterfly, 4 × 200-m freestyle relay, and 4 × 100-m medley relay) and two bronze (200-m freestyle and 4 × 100-m freestyle relay) while setting five Olympic or world records. His four individual swimming gold medals tied a record set by American Mark Spitz in 1972. Phelps also made news out of the pool when he gave up his spot on the medley-relay team to Ian Crocker, who had not yet earned a gold in Athens. Because Phelps had swum in the preliminary heats, he was awarded a gold medal when the U.S. won the event.

Phelps was born on June 30, 1985, in Baltimore, Md., and was reared in a family of swimmers. At age seven he joined the North Baltimore Aquatic Club, a prestigious swim club, and in 1996 he signed with a trainer and coach, Bob Bowman, who played an influential role in Phelps's later success. In 2000 Phelps finished fifth in the 200-m butterfly at the Olympic Games in Sydney, Australia. At the 2001 U.S. spring nationals, after posting 1 min 54.92 sec in the 200-m butterfly, he became, at age 15, the youngest world-record holder in men's swimming. He improved on his time to win his first international title later that year at the world championships in Fukuoka, Japan. After turning professional and earning the Swimmer of the Year title from USA Swimming in 2001, Phelps was a standout at the 2002 Pan Pacific championships as he claimed five medals, including three gold (200-m and 400-m individual medley and 4 × 100-m medley relay).

In 2003 Phelps established his supremacy in the pool with a string of record-setting performances. At the U.S. spring nationals, he became the first male swimmer to claim titles in three different strokes at a single national championship, and he later broke an unprecedented five individual world records at the world championships in Barcelona, Spain. Phelps, noted for having an intense training regime, also captured five titles at the U.S. summer nationals—the most won by a male swimmer at a single championship; he repeated the feat at the 2004 spring nationals. Phelps finished 2003 ranked first in the world in the 200-m butterfly and the 200-m and 400-m individual medley, and he received the Sullivan Award and his second U.S. Swimmer of the Year honour. Shortly after the Athens Games, Phelps announced that he was already training for the 2008 Olympics in Beijing, where many believed he would challenge Spitz's record of seven Olympic gold medals at a single Games.

(AMY TIKKANEN)

Plushchenko, Yevgeny

Even though Yevgeny Plushchenko was performing with an injured knee and was facing a number of strong opponents, he dominated the three programs of the 2004 world ice-skating championships and won his third title—his second consecutive—with a dazzling free skate marred only by a fall caused by his skate blade's encounter with a sequin on the ice. Before that, however, he had thrilled the audience and earned high marks from the judges, including four perfect 6.0s, with a program that included two quadruple jumps—one of them as part of his trademark quad toe loop–triple toe loop–double loop combination—and the first triple Axel–half loop–triple flip combination landed cleanly in competition, as well as complex straight-line footwork.

Yevgeny Viktorovich Plushchenko was born on Nov. 3, 1982, in Solnechny, Khabarovsk *kray*, U.S.S.R., and moved with his family to Volgograd when he was a young boy. He began skating at the age of four after family friends gave him a pair of skates they no longer wanted. It soon became apparent that Plushchenko had a real talent for skating, and he progressed rapidly. In 1993, however, the

AP/Wide World Photos

Figure-skating champ Yevgeny Plushchenko

skating school where he was training closed because, as an aftereffect of the dissolution of the Soviet Union in 1991, the government could no longer support it. His mother took him to St. Petersburg, where he began working with skating coach Aleksey Mishin at the St. Petersburg Figure Skating School. He was already able to perform the triple jumps roughly, and by the time he was 12, he had perfected them. At 14 he landed a quad for the first time. He also added the difficult Biellmann spin to his repertoire of moves, one of the few men to perform it. Plushchenko began competing in 1996 and within a year had won the world junior championships. He then moved into the senior ranks, taking a silver medal at the European championships and a bronze at worlds in 1998 and the silver at worlds the following year. In 2000 he could manage only fourth place at worlds, but he came back in 2001 to win his first world championship gold. Plushchenko took silver at the 2002 Winter Olympics, but injuries kept him out of worlds. Later that year, however, at the Cup of Russia competition, he entered the record books once again—this time with the first quad toe–triple toe–triple loop combination landed cleanly in competition—and in 2003 he regained his world championship title.

Plushchenko had entered the 2004 world championships with a number one ranking, and he maintained that position as the 2004–05 season began. In October he commemorated his 10 years of working with Mishin by performing in an exhibition program in St. Petersburg. He dedicated his performances to the victims of the terrorist attack on a school in Beslan, and a portion of the show's proceeds was channeled to the victims' families.

(BARBARA WHITNEY)

Prince

The resurgence in 2004 of the multitalented American recording artist known once again simply as Prince was a surprise not because he was back—he had never really gone away—but because he reemerged in such a big way. Sales of his recordings had dipped deeply at the end of the 1990s, and his name had literally disappeared (replaced by an unpronounceable glyph—his choice), but in 2004 Prince was a phenomenon again, riding high on his induction into the Rock and Roll Hall of Fame and the success of his best-selling, critically acclaimed album *Musicology.*

Prince Rogers Nelson was born in Minneapolis, Minn., on June 7, 1958, and named after the Prince Rogers Trio, a jazz combo led by his father. Following his parents' divorce, Prince lived intermittently with both, but he was eventually adopted by the family of a schoolboy bandmate. Prince mastered several instruments and while still a teenager signed a recording contract with Warner Brothers. He wrote and produced his own often-suggestive songs and arrived at a contagious mix of soul, rock, pop, and funk driven by his virtuoso guitar playing and impassioned (frequently falsetto) vocals. Performing live, Prince was magnetic and risqué as he led his band, the Revolution, through carefully choreographed funk workouts. After a series of releases, including *Dirty Mind* (1980) and *Controversy* (1981), Prince had a huge hit in 1982

Kevin Mazur/WireImage.com

Rock and Roll Hall of Famer Prince

with the double album *1999* (featuring "Little Red Corvette"). The sound track for *Purple Rain* (1984), the semiautobiographical film starring Prince, was an even bigger smash, partly on the wings of the singles "When Doves Cry" and "I Would Die 4 U." In the process, Prince joined Michael Jackson not only in breaking the colour barrier for African Americans on MTV but also in dominating (along with Madonna) popular music in the 1980s and early '90s.

Although the hits continued—including the masterful *Sign o' the Times* (1987) and several songs written for other artists—Prince became increasingly frustrated with his contract with Warner Brothers, which owned his master recordings. In protest he changed his name in 1993 to a symbol (becoming the Artist Formerly Known as Prince) and began writing "slave" on his face for performances. Only after he was formally released from the contract in 1999 did he become Prince again; after putting out his final album for Warner Brothers in 1996, he began releasing music on his own label, New Power Generation, to mixed reviews and lacklustre sales. Prince's return to the limelight began with two dynamic live appearances—a duet with singer Beyoncé (*q.v.*) at the 2004 Grammy Awards and a pair of incendiary performances at the Hall of Fame induction ceremonies (including a much-remarked-upon guitar solo during the all-star jam on "While My Guitar Gently Weeps"). It culminated with his Musicology tour, which included his new back-to-basics album in the ticket price. (JEFF WALLENFELDT)

Pullman, Philip

The year 2004 saw Philip Pullman's best-selling fantasy trilogy, *His Dark Materials,* adapted to the stage in an ambitious, sold-out production in London's National Theatre. In addition, a major film version of the trilogy was promised from the makers of *The Lord of the Rings,* and playwright Tom Stoppard was hired to produce the script. Meanwhile, Pullman's new novel for children, *The Scarecrow and the Servant* (2004), was published to acclaim, and he continued work on a prequel to his blockbuster fantasy, tentatively entitled *The Book of Dust.* The *New York Times* reported that *His Dark Materials* had sold more than seven million copies in Britain and the United States and had been translated into 37 languages, making Pullman one of the best-known writers for children in the world.

Philip Nicholas Pullman was born on Oct. 19, 1946, in Norwich, Eng. The son of a Royal Air Force officer, he moved many times as a child, settling for some years in Rhodesia (now Zimbabwe). In his own words, he "started telling stories as soon as I knew what stories were." On the long journeys dictated by his father's various postings, he regaled his younger brother with his fantasy tales. After his father died in a plane crash, young Philip was sent back to England to live with his grandparents. Following his mother's remarriage, Pullman moved to Australia briefly before the family settled in Harlech, Wales. After reading English at the University of Oxford, Pullman remained resident in Oxford, working as a teacher.

One of his first publications was the 1978 adult novel *Galatea;* it was followed in the 1980s and '90s by many titles for children and young adults. Pullman's Sally Lockhart detective stories, set in Victorian London, were published between 1985 and 1994. *His Dark Materials* appeared between 1995 and 2000. *Northern Lights* (1996; U.S. title, *The Golden Compass*), the first volume of that trilogy, won the 1996 Carnegie Medal, and *The Amber Spyglass,* the third volume, won the Whitbread Prize. Pullman was dubbed a worthy successor to J.R.R. Tolkien, author of *The Lord of the Rings,* and C.S. Lewis, who wrote the Narnia chronicles. All three writers were inspired by living in Oxford and by legends and landscapes of "the north." Unlike Lewis, Pullman eschewed religious parable, instead embracing in his work a humanistic morality. His vivid page-turning saga grappled with fundamental questions of life and death while the action flowed between several possible worlds. References were drawn from a vast repository, with elements of mythology, history, and string theory, while characters included witches, angels, armoured bears, and, perhaps most thought-provoking, demons (animals, representing the spirit, that faithfully accompany their owner from the cradle to the grave). When a fan recently asked Pullman what sort of demon he would like to have, he replied "a magpie or a jackdaw . . . one of those birds that steal bright things." (SIOBHAN DOWD)

Qaddafi, Muammar al-

In 2004 Libyan leader Muammar al-Qaddafi continued to oversee dramatic change in his country. A decade's worth of efforts to improve relations with the West culminated with the U.S.'s lifting most of its sanctions against Libya and restoring diplomatic relations. This came one year after the UN had ended its own sanctions and after Qaddafi had announced that Libya was abandoning its weapons of mass destruction (WMD) program. He also seemed prepared to reverse his radical socialist approach to his country's economy, as he allowed Prime Minister Shokri Ghanem to explore reforms that included privatization and economic regulations.

Qaddafi was born near Surt in 1942. After graduating from the University of Libya (1963) and the Libyan military academy (1965), he rose to the rank of captain and in 1969 led a coup that deposed King Idris I. A governing body, the Revolutionary Command Council, was established with Qaddafi as its chairman. His shrewd handling of Libya's immense oil reserves—he played a major role in the fourfold increase in the price of oil in the early 1970s—brought him international attention. He later nationalized petroleum operations and most sectors of the economy as part of a brand of Islamic socialism that he promoted from 1974. Qaddafi's system, which he outlined in *The Green Book* (2 vol; 1976, 1980), was a "third way" between Western capitalism and Soviet communism, calling for a centralized and planned economy. He also introduced a unique form of popular participation in public affairs while retaining all the levers of power.

Starting in the 1970s, Qaddafi made additional headlines with his foreign policy. A strong proponent of Arab nationalism, he tried unsuccessfully to merge Libya with other Arab countries. He was vocal in his opposition to Israel, rejecting all negotiations with that country, and he supported the Palestine Liberation Organization. His government also became well known for assisting and funding terrorist groups worldwide and was implicated in several coup attempts in Africa. Libya's links with terrorism in the 1980s brought severe trade sanctions and diplomatic isolation as well as military strikes. Following the 1986 bombing of a Berlin disco, in which a U.S. serviceman was killed, the U.S. attacked Tripoli and Banghazi in Libya, nearly killing Qaddafi. His government's involvement in the downing of passenger jets over Lockerbie, Scot. (1988), and Niger (1989) led to further sanctions by the U.S. and the UN.

By the early 1990s Qaddafi was signaling that he was prepared for some rapprochement. In 1999 he handed over two Libyan intelligence agents who were implicated in the Lockerbie crash, a move that resulted in the suspension of UN sanctions. The UN officially lifted sanctions in 2003, when Libya agreed to financial settlements in the Lockerbie and Niger plane crashes. That year the U.S. entered into negotiations with the U.K. and Libya that resulted in Qaddafi's agreement in December 2003 to halt WMD production.

(EDITOR)

Rahman, A.R.

Although it opened on Broadway in April 2004 to scathing reviews, the musical *Bombay Dreams* was a commercial hit and exposed North American audiences to A.R. Rahman, India's hottest composer. Rahman's score for *Bombay Dreams,* a lush electronic fusion of East and West, was seen as a possible drawing card for a new generation of musical theatre fans. The show was produced by the reigning "old guard" of musicals, Andrew Lloyd Webber, who had handpicked Rahman for the job, hoping to inject an international flavour into the art form and perhaps draw new audiences.

Rahman was born A.S. Dileep Kumar on Jan. 6, 1966, in Madras (now Chennai), India. His father, R.K. Sekhar, was a prominent Tamil musician who composed scores for the Malayalam film industry. Rahman began studying piano at the age of four. The boy's interests lay in electronics and computers, but his father's serendipitous purchase of a synthesizer allowed him to pursue his passion and to learn to love music at the same time. Sekhar died when Rahman was 9 years old, and by age 11 the boy was playing piano professionally to help support his family. He dropped out of school, but his professional experience led to a scholarship to study at Trinity College, Oxford, where he received a degree in Western classical music.

In 1988 his entire family converted to Islam following a sister's recovery from a serious illness, and he then took the name Allah Rakha Rahman. He grew bored with playing in bands and eventually turned his talents toward creating advertising jingles. He wrote more than 300 jingles and would later say that the experience taught him discipline because jingle writing required delivery of a powerful message or mood in a short time. In 1991, while at a ceremony to receive an award for his work on a coffee advertisement, Rahman met Bollywood film director Mani Ratnam, who persuaded him to write for the big screen. Their first project was *Roja,* which resulted in Rahman's first film sound-track hit. More than 100 movie scores followed, including the music for *Lagaan* (2001), the first Bollywood film nominated for an Academy Award. Rahman's albums sold more than 100 million copies.

Lloyd Webber heard some of Rahman's sound tracks and asked the composer if he would be interested in writing a stage musical. Working with lyricist Don Black, Rahman composed the score for *Bombay Dreams,* a colourful satire of Bollywood films, and the show opened in London's West End in 2002 without much fanfare. Rahman was already well known among London's large Indian population, however, and ticket sales were strong, which prompted the launch of the Broadway version of the show in 2004. At year's end Rahman was working on his second stage project, a musical version of *The Lord of the Rings* that was scheduled to premiere in London in 2005.

(ANTHONY G. CRAINE)

Rai, Aishwarya

In 2004 actress Aishwarya Rai, whom American film star Julia Roberts described as "the most beautiful woman in the world," was at the forefront of a revolution in Indian cinema. Rai, whose onscreen talent and mesmerizing blue-green eyes had inspired more than 17,000 worshipful Web sites, starred in *Bride and Prejudice,* a music- and dance-filled Bollywood adaptation of Jane Austen's *Pride and Prejudice* that was directed by Gurinder Chadha, director of the 2002 hit *Bend It like Beckham.* As Lalita Bakshi, the Indian equivalent of the strong-willed Elizabeth Bennett of Austen's novel, Rai brought her star power and radiant beauty to her first major English-language film.

Rai was born on Nov. 1, 1973, in Mangalore, Karnataka state, India. She was raised in a traditional South Indian home and was pursuing an education in architecture when her life took a dramatic turn in 1994. That year she was crowned Miss World, a title that put her on the fast track of the modeling business. She landed lucrative jobs with PepsiCo and *Vogue* magazine, and in 2003 she signed on as a spokesmodel for L'Oréal Paris. Her acting career began in earnest with acclaimed performances in *Iruvar* (1997; *The Duo*) and . . . *Aur pyaar ho gaya* (1997; based on the 1994 movie *Only You*), both films that broke from the simplistic structure typical of Bollywood films at the time and helped to push Rai to the forefront of the "New Bollywood." For decades the Indian film industry, based in Mumbai (Bombay) and commonly referred to as Bollywood, had produced a large number of very predictable and clichéd feature films that were enjoyed almost exclusively by South Asians. Changes in Bollywood in regard to financing and production, however, had seen the industry move to improve the artistic quality of its product and to expand its audience beyond South Asia.

Rai established herself as the new "queen of Bollywood" with her moving performance as the jilted lover Paro in *Devdas* (2002), one of the most acclaimed and popular films to ever come out of Bollywood and the first to be screened at the Cannes Festival. She followed with a critically acclaimed performance in *Chokher Bali* (2003; *Choker Bali: A Passion Play*), a tense drama based on the novel by Rabindranath Tagore. That same year she became the first Indian actress to serve as a jury member at the Cannes Festival. In early 2004 Rai was introduced to American audiences as a featured performer in a touring stage show of Indian actors. Later, even before the October release of the much-anticipated *Bride and Prejudice,* she began preparing to film two more English-language films—*Chaos,* with French director Coline Serreau and Rai's first major Hollywood costar, Oscar-winning actress Meryl Streep, and *Singularity,* directed by Roland Joffé and costarring Brendan Fraser—as well as several more back home in Bollywood.

(JAMES HENNELLY)

Indian film star Aishwarya Rai

Rehman, Shabana

Pakistani-born Norwegian performer Shabana Rehman was no stranger to controversy; being a Muslim woman and a stand-up comic in itself might be cause for some controversy, but she really stirred things up in April 2004 when she physically lifted a mullah. At a public discussion with Mullah Krekar, the former leader of the militant fundamentalist group Ansar al-Islam and now a resident of Norway, Rehman asked if the Muslim cleric would participate in a test to see if he had really become adapted to liberal Norwegian society. He agreed, and Rehman proceeded to wrap her arms around the mullah's thighs and lift him into the air. While many laughed at the test, the stunned Krekar expressed his humiliation and outrage and made a hasty exit. The news of the incident filled the Norwegian papers and soon made its way throughout the globe.

Rehman remained unapologetic, as tweaking mullahs and drawing the ire of the Muslim establishment had been routine since she started doing stand-up in 1999. Her act began with her arriving on stage wearing a burka, the long concealing robes worn by fundamentalist Muslim women. After a few jokes about her attire (she suggested it was excellent for "scaring away children"), Rehman discarded the burka to reveal a red cocktail dress. She continued to jab at what she perceived as the backwardness of conservative Muslims and the regrettable tolerance of these practices by moderates. She also had much to say about the Norwegians and their shortcomings in dealing with the nation's growing immigrant population. Her show was entitled "Skiing Across Greenland," a reference to a legendary feat by Norwegian hero Fridtjof Nansen as well as a pun on "Greenland," which was the name of an immigrant section of Oslo.

In 2003 she posed nude on the cover of a national magazine, her body painted like the Norwegian flag. It was an act that annoyed some members of both the Muslim and Norwegian communities. For Rehman, however, the meaning of the photo was apparent. "I wanted to make it clear that even as a Muslim woman I am free to dispose of my body as I wish. I also wanted to demonstrate to Norwegians that you can be Scandinavian even if you were born in the Punjab."

Rehman was born in 1976 in Karachi, Pak., and a year later her family relocated to Oslo. She attended university, where she studied ethics and media. In addition to her comedy act, she regularly appeared on Norwegian television and wrote a column for the liberal newspaper *Dagbladet* in Oslo. Despite the fact that they were sometimes the subjects of her jokes, her parents and seven siblings remained supportive of Rehman's comedy career.

(JAMES HENNELLY)

Ruscha, Ed

By 2004 Ed Ruscha, widely celebrated for his deadpan take on American pop culture, was regarded as one of the most important American artists of the 20th century. His works provided a new way of looking at and thinking about the American landscape and connecting the verbal with the visual; his vision was often referred to as photographic in that he saw the landscape and depicted what he saw, as if viewed through a camera lens. In 2004 his first retrospective of drawings and works on paper, "Cotton Puffs, Q-tips®, Smoke and Mirrors: The Drawings of Ed Ruscha," premiered at the Whitney Museum of American Art, New York City. The exhibition brought together an array of seminal painter, photographer, printmaker, and filmmaker Ruscha's works on paper using uncommon materials from chocolate to juice to gunpowder.

Edward Joseph Ruscha was born on Dec. 16, 1937, in Omaha, Neb., and was raised in Oklahoma City. In 1956, at the age of 19, he drove to Los Angeles, where he studied painting, photography, and graphic arts at Chouinard Art Institute (now CalArts). He worked as a commercial artist doing sign painting, typography, and layout, and then he applied those techniques and visual tendencies to his artworks. Between 1963 and 1978 Ruscha systematically photographed southern California's built environments—including vacant parking lots, swimming pools, gasoline stations, and nightspots—which he made into wordless artist's books, such as *Every Building on the Sunset Strip*. This art form became a staple of Conceptualism, and his 16 books were widely influential among younger generations of artists, while they also provided further insight into how he applied his unique perspective to his paintings and drawings. Ruscha also made two short films, *Premium* (1969–70) and *Miracle* (1975), and in 1978 he collaborated with Lawrence Weiner on *Hard Light*, a film in book format.

Ruscha first became widely known in the 1960s, with paintings that featured dramatic, diagonal compositions depicting roadside architecture and signs, along with his paintings and drawings that reflected the visual and emotive power of single words. His signature works of dark humour included *The Los Angeles County Museum of Art on Fire*, 1965–68, a painting depicting the institution in flames; *Actual Size*, 1962, a bright painting of a flying can of Spam beneath the logo; and *Large Trademark with Eight Spotlights*, 1962, a dramatic representation of the Twentieth Century-Fox logo. Ruscha's work called attention to consumerism's role in art and culture, with a witty, dark humour less apparent in the Pop Art of his contemporaries. His recent works included paintings and prints of Hollywood crossroads and anagrams and puns painted over snow-capped mountains.

Since 1963, when he first exhibited with the groundbreaking Ferus Gallery in Los Angeles, Ruscha's work had been presented in solo exhibitions at important art museums around the world, and in 2004 a catalogue raisonné of his paintings from 1958 to 1970 was published. In 2005 Ruscha was to represent the U.S. at the Venice Biennale. (ALI J. SUBOTNICK)

Russo, Patricia F.

In 2004 Patricia Russo, CEO of telecommunications firm Lucent Technologies, accomplished what few had expected. One of the most widely held stocks in the late 1990s, Lucent had seen its share price plummet to less than $1 per share by 2002. As business dried up and layoffs and financial losses persisted, the chances of Lucent's recovery seemed slim. It was a bold move, then, for the firm to appoint former Lucent insider Russo as its new CEO in January 2002. Bolder still was Russo's promise to return the company to profitability before the end of 2003, but she kept her word, met that goal, and led Lucent through four profitable quarters in fiscal year 2004.

Patricia Fiorello Russo was born June 12, 1952, in Trenton, N.J. Among her six siblings were twin brothers with disabilities, and Russo said that growing up with them had helped her learn the lessons of caring for others. She was active in sports and captained the cheerleading squad before graduating from Lawrence High School in 1969. In 1973 she earned a bachelor's degree in political science and history from Georgetown University, Washington, D.C., and moved directly to IBM for an eight-year career in sales and marketing. While with IBM, Russo developed a customer-oriented perspective that would influence her future management style.

Joining AT&T in 1981, Russo spent the next decade in marketing, human resources, operations, and strategic planning. She completed Harvard University's rigorous Advanced Management Program in 1989, and three years later AT&T chose her to restructure its faltering Business Communications Systems division as its president. Russo's turnaround permitted AT&T to spin off the division as Avaya, Inc. She moved to Lucent in time for its $3 billion initial public offering in 1996, serving as executive vice president for corporate operations (1997–99) and vice president and CEO of Lucent's core business, the service provider networks group (1999–2000). Russo left in 2000 and became president and chief operating officer of Eastman Kodak in April 2001—only to return in 2002 as Lucent's president and CEO. She was elevated to chairman and CEO in February 2003.

Russo led Lucent on a course of modest but steady growth that emphasized service and customer contact, although the year's profits came largely through slashes in spending, and cuts to retiree benefits and reductions in research-and-development budgets spurred protests. Russo's focus on service was expected to build strong customer ties, but critics feared that Lucent, left to fill gaps in its product lineup by selling competitors' hardware, risked losing its edge in new product development. Even so, the firm chalked up several important contracts in 2004, and the future—for Lucent and Russo—looked bright.

(SARAH FORBES ORWIG)

Saakashvili, Mikhail

The year 2004 was an eventful one for Mikhail Saakashvili. Having rapidly emerged in late 2003 as Georgia's leading politician and played a large role in easing longtime Pres. Eduard Shevardnadze from office in November, Saakashvili won the ballot to replace him with over 96% of the vote on Jan. 4, 2004, and was inaugurated as president three weeks later. Saakashvili immediately plunged into the work of finding solutions for Georgia's manifold problems by appointing a new slate of government officials and attacking endemic corruption. Most important, however, he threw himself into the job of keeping the country together in the face of secessionist movements in Georgia's ethnic republics of Abkhazia, Ajaria, and South Ossetia. He was aided in his quests by his obvious popularity, his youth and vigour, and his international profile.

Saakashvili was born in Tbilisi, Georgia, U.S.S.R., on Dec. 21, 1967. He graduated from the law faculty of Kiev (Ukraine) University's Institute of International Relations and continued graduate studies in France, Italy, and The Netherlands and at Columbia University, New York City. From 1993 to 1995 he worked for a New York law firm. Saakashvili returned to Georgia in 1995 at the invitation of Zurab Zhvania, then chairman of the Union of Citizens of Georgia (SMK), and was elected to Parliament in November 1995 on the SMK ticket. From 1995 to 1998 he served as chairman of Parliament's Committee on Legal Affairs and lobbied unsuccessfully for faster and more comprehensive reforms. In August 1998 he was elected head of the SMK faction in Parliament. In October 2000 Saakashvili was appointed justice minister and set about reforming the legal system and improving prison conditions. Fueling the reputation for populism he had acquired as a parliamentarian, he also solicited popular support for his crackdown on perceived high-level corruption. In August 2001 Saakashvili came into direct opposition with Shevardnadze and resigned unexpectedly after a mysterious burglary at his home. He was reelected to Parliament in a by-election, and in November he declared his open opposition to Shevardnadze and founded the National Movement. He was subsequently elected chairman of Tbilisi's city council. In that post he raised pensions, donated school textbooks, and personally helped repair dilapidated residential buildings.

When the incumbent leadership announced on Nov. 3, 2003, that the pro-Shevardnadze For a New Georgia bloc was set to win the previous day's parliamentary election, Saakashvili, together with Zhvania and Parliament speaker Nino Burdjanadze, launched protests in Tbilisi and other cities against the perceived falsification of the vote, calling for Shevardnadze's resignation. On November 22 Saakashvili and a group of supporters forced their way unopposed into the Parliament building. Shevardnadze fled the building, and he formally announced his resignation the following day. (ELIZABETH FULLER)

Saca González, Elías Antonio

On June 1, 2004, Elías Antonio Saca González, best known as the popular sportscaster Tony Saca, became El Salvador's president. He was born on March 9, 1965, in Usulután, El Salvador, and was the grandson of Palestinian Catholics who moved to El Salvador from Bethlehem early in the 20th century. His family had prospered as merchants and cotton dealers, but when his parents' cotton mill in Usulután failed, they moved to San Salvador. While still in school, Saca got jobs at several radio stations and worked alongside experienced sportscaster Mauricio Saade Torres. In 1982 Saca started the *Only Sports* program on the Sonora radio chain, and he later became a TV sportscaster on Channel 4, where he was sports director for more than a decade. His coverage of association football (soccer) games earned him widespread visibility.

Saca entered the University of El Salvador in 1984 but never completed his journalism degree, focusing instead on his professional career. After helping in 1987 to form the Radio América chain, in 1993 he left Channel 4 and Radio América to launch the SAMIX chain of radio stations with his wife. Saca won numerous awards in the radio and television industry, and the success of SAMIX led to leadership posts on professional and civic boards and committees. He served (1997–2001) as president of the Salvadoran Association of Radio Broadcasters and chaired the Freedom of Expression Committee of the International Radio Association. In 2001 he became president of the National Association of Private Enterprise (ANEP). A survey that same year revealed that Saca was the third most popular personality in the country, trailing only San Salvador Mayor Héctor Silva Argüello and Pres. Francisco Flores Pérez.

In 1989 Saca affiliated himself with the right-wing National Republican Alliance (ARENA), and as head of ANEP he supported Flores's pro-U.S. policies and the decision to adopt the U.S. dollar as El Salvador's national currency. Although strongly committed to a market economy, Saca expressed sympathy for labour, which led Flores to name him to head a commission that brought a small increase in the minimum wage. ARENA, which faced strong opposition from the Farabundo Martí Front for National Liberation (FMLN) in the 2004 presidential election, turned to Saca as a candidate whose popularity was more important than his ideological stance. Despite his lack of political experience, he united the party and campaigned effectively against FMLN candidate Schafik Jorge Hándal, a former guerrilla commander. While appealing to labour with promises not to privatize the country's social security and health care systems, Saca made anticommunism a major issue and warned that an FMLN victory would destroy El Salvador's good relations with the U.S. After a bitter campaign, Saca triumphed on March 21, winning 57.7% of the votes against Hándal's 35.6%. In his inaugural address Saca promised to "forget the past without hate or rancour" and to put the social agenda as his top priority.

(RALPH LEE WOODWARD, JR.)

Schilling, Curt

While the Boston Red Sox and their memorable play-off run were the story of Major League Baseball in 2004, the story within the story was Boston pitcher Curt Schilling's eventful (and painful) experience during the postseason. Playing despite a serious ankle injury, Schilling helped the Sox rally from a three games-to-none deficit to their bitter rivals, the New York Yankees, to win the American League Championship Series (ALCS) and then sweep the St. Louis Cardinals in the World Series, ending the Red Sox 86-year world championship drought.

Traded from the Arizona Diamondbacks to the Red Sox before the 2004 season started, Schilling arrived in Boston with a reputation as a winner who could help end the drought that had become an obsession for many New England baseball fans. Through the regular season he pitched brilliantly, amassing 21 wins and a 3.26 earned run average. He pitched well in his start against the Anaheim Angels in the division series, but during that game he tore the sheath surrounding the tendon in his ankle. Despite the injury, Schilling was scheduled to start game one of the ALCS in Yankee Stadium, and before the game he boasted that he looked forward to "making 55,000 people from New York shut up." Schilling, however—clearly bothered by his injured ankle—lasted only three innings, giving up six runs, and the Red Sox lost the game. For his next start he underwent a surgical procedure that stabilized the tendon by placing three sutures through the skin. The procedure was painful and only temporary (the sutures were removed after he pitched), but it allowed the burly right-hander a shot at redemption in game six in Yankee Stadium. With blood from the sutures soaking through his sock, he pitched seven innings and surrendered only one run as the Red Sox tied the ALCS. He underwent the procedure once more to win the second game of the World Series. Schilling's courage in fighting through the pain seemed to underscore the determination of the Red Sox finally to put to rest years of disappointment and heartache for their loyal fans.

Curtis Montague Schilling was born on Nov. 14, 1966, in Anchorage, Alaska, and in 1988

Jim Rogash/WireImage.com

Boston Red Sox hero Curt Schilling

he made his major league debut with the Baltimore Orioles. In addition to the Red Sox and the Orioles, he also pitched for the Houston Astros (1991), the Philadelphia Phillies (1992–2000), and the Diamondbacks (2000–03). He came to prominence as a starting pitcher with the Phillies in 1993, when he helped that team win the National League pennant. In 2001 he teamed with left-hander Randy Johnson to form the most imposing pitching duo in baseball. That year the Diamondbacks upset the Yankees in the World Series, with Schilling and Johnson sharing Most Valuable Player honours. (JAMES HENNELLY)

Singh, Manmohan

Manmohan Singh, who had been credited with saving India from economic collapse during his tenure as finance minister (1991–96), was appointed India's 14th prime minister on May 22, 2004; he was the first Sikh to hold the post. As prime minister Singh, one of India's most experienced policy makers and a highly regarded economist, repeatedly emphasized India's credentials as a multicultural, multiethnic, multilingual, pluralistic, and secular democracy. He stressed the need for increased economic growth, upward of 7% annually, and for India to be a more open economy and to live in peace with its neighbours.

Singh was born on Sept. 26, 1932, in the village of Gah, Punjab province, British India (now in Pakistan), but after the 1947 partition he and his family migrated to India. After completing (1948) his undergraduate degree at Panjab University, Chandigarh, and serving a brief stint in teaching, he attended the University of Cambridge on scholarship and earned (1957) a first-class-honours degree in economics. Singh collected a doctorate (1962) in economics from Nuffield College, Oxford.

Singh served on the faculties of Panjab University and the prestigious Delhi School of Economics, where his colleagues included Nobel economist Amartya Sen and international trade theorist Jagdish Bhagwati. From 1987 to 1990 Singh was secretary-general of the South Commission in Geneva.

His career in government began in 1971, when he joined the government of India as economic adviser in the Ministry of Commerce and Industry. In 1972 he was chief economic adviser in the Ministry of Finance. Among the many governmental positions that Singh held were secretary in the Ministry of Finance, deputy chairman of the Planning Commission, governor of the Reserve Bank of India, adviser to the prime minister, and chairman of the University Grants Commission.

In what was to become the turning point in the economic history of independent India, Singh spent five years as the country's finance minister, ushering in a comprehensive policy of economic reforms that became recognized worldwide. His book *India's Export Trends and Prospects for Self-Sustained Growth* (1964) was an early critique of India's inward-oriented trade policy and provided the direction for trade liberalization during his tenure as finance minister.

Singh, who had never won a popular election (he was appointed to all of his posts), had been a member, at the invitation of the Congress Party, of India's Rajya Sabha (upper house of Parliament) since 1991. There he was leader of the opposition from 1998 until the Congress Party won the general election in 2004. His appointment as prime minister came after Singh, one of the "cleanest" politicians in the country, was recommended by party leader Sonia Gandhi for the post.

The most prominent among Singh's awards and honours included the Padma Vibhushan (1987), India's second highest civilian honour; the Jawaharlal Nehru Birth Centenary Award of the Indian Science Congress (1995); the Asia Money Award for Finance Minister of the Year (1993 and 1994); and the Euro Money Award for Finance Minister of the Year (1993). (SANJAYA BARU)

Sistani, Ali al-

In 2004 the leading power in war-torn Iraq may not have been anyone in the U.S. military or on the Iraqi Governing Council but the country's leading Shi'ite cleric, Grand Ayatollah Ali al-Sistani. At age 74 the reclusive Islamic leader, who liked to give the impression that he did not mix religion with politics, proved to be a major player in the planning for Iraq's first democratic government in the run-up to elections set for early 2005. Living in Najaf, Sistani was the spiritual leader of the Shi'ite majority in Iraq, but he also commanded the respect of Sunni Arabs and Kurds. His support for free elections in Iraq, underscored by his decree in the autumn that Iraqis register to vote, was thought to have more weight than a fleet of U.S. or UN diplomatic envoys or even the interim government of Prime Minister Ayad Allawi (*q.v.*). Deftly working through operatives while retaining his aura as a religious leader not involved in politics, Sistani had a known interest in seeing a Shi'ite majority emerge from the 2005 elections. His strong and moderating influence among the Iraqi populace as a whole had earned him the respect of U.S. diplomats and Iraqi leaders, who silently submitted to many of his wishes.

With many challenges from outside in 2004, Sistani also faced challenges from within. In August he traveled to Britain to undergo heart surgery, leaving Najaf in the control of Muqtada al-Sadr, a young militant cleric who waged a fierce guerrilla battle against U.S. and Iraqi forces. The heart operation a success, Sistani returned triumphantly to Najaf to conclude the military operation as well, dramatically reining in Sadr and brokering a peace.

Sistani, born in northeastern Iran in 1930, was a studious child of the Qur'an. In his early 20s he left Iran to continue his studies in Iraq, becoming a disciple of Grand Ayatollah Abul Qassim al-Khoei in Najaf. Known for his intelligence and charisma, Sistani rose quickly through the clerical ranks, and unlike a fellow cleric in Najaf—Ruhollah Khomeini, who ruled (1979–89) in Iran—Sistani eschewed militancy for a "quietist" philosophy. Shortly after Khoei's death in 1992, Sistani achieved *marja,* the highest rank of Shi'ite clerics. An Islamic conservative who retained Iranian citizenship, Sistani was devoted to ensuring power for a Shi'ite majority in his adopted country, which had put forth a Sunni majority for three centuries. (TOM MICHAEL)

Spitzer, Eliot

In 2004 Eliot Spitzer, the crusading New York state attorney general, continued to venture where few others dared to tread with his investigation of suspected malfeasance in the upper echelons of the American financial industry. After earlier probes had led to reforms in the banking industry, in 2004 he took on mutual-fund companies and insurance brokerages, where he also found questionable business practices. In the fall of 2003, Spitzer first began his study of improper trading within mutual-fund companies, citing several firms for illegal after-hours trades. His investigations yielded their largest settlement in May 2004 when CEO Richard Strong and the Wisconsin-based company he founded, Strong

© Chip East/Reuters/Corbis

New York Attorney General Eliot Spitzer

Capital Management, agreed to pay $60 million and $80 million, respectively, in addition to other penalties for unacceptable methods such as market timing, or short-term and rapid trades. While some industry watchers dismissed Spitzer's high-profile accusations as grandstanding, they nonetheless closely monitored his activities to see where he would strike next. Others heralded his investigations as aggressive attempts to clean up an industry beset by corporate scandals.

Just days after the Strong settlement, Spitzer filed a civil lawsuit against Richard Grasso, former chairman of the New York Stock Exchange (NYSE), claiming that Grasso had misled the NYSE about the specifics of his extraordinary compensation in salary. A few weeks later Spitzer served subpoenas to the nation's leading insurance companies in pursuit of insurance brokers who he claimed were profiting at the expense of the corporate employees they were hired to serve. Other issues Spitzer pursued through his office in 2004 were labour rights and consumer protections against such abuses as improper billings, fraudulent advertising, and identity theft. He also sought to punish corporate polluters and reform the lax government regulators of such polluters.

Spitzer was born on June 10, 1959, into a well-to-do household in the Riverdale section of the Bronx, N.Y. He was educated at Princeton University (B.A., 1981) and Harvard Law School (J.D., 1984), where he was an editor of the *Harvard Law Review.* After graduation he served as a clerk to a judge and an associate at a law firm before leaving to become assistant district attorney (1986–92) in Manhattan, where he prosecuted notorious mobsters. He made a run for New York attorney general in 1994 that was unsuccessful, but on his second attempt, in 1998, he won narrowly. He was reelected in 2002 after his yearlong headline-grabbing investigation of wrongdoing at investment banks—most notably at Merrill Lynch, the world's largest brokerage company—led to huge cash settlements and new rules on greater segregation between the research and investment divisions of a bank. In December 2004 Spitzer made a public announcement regarding his future political plans, confirming what many observers had long suspected—that he would run for New York state governor after the conclusion of his term as attorney general in 2006.

(TOM MICHAEL)

Stewart, Jon

With more and more people getting their news from late-night television comedy shows, Jon Stewart proved in 2004 that although he might not yet be the U.S.'s most trusted news source, he definitely was one of its funniest. As host of Comedy Central's *The Daily Show with Jon Stewart,* a newscast parody that spoofed newsmakers and those who reported the news, Stewart and a madcap team of correspondents recapped the day's events and nonevents, offering satiric commentary on politics and pop culture. The show, which also featured a celebrity interview, covered topics ranging from the Iraqi conflict (upgraded from "Mess O'Potamia" to "Giant Mess O'Potamia") to a man who constructed a UFO welcome centre on his front lawn. Stewart, who joined the program in 1999 and also served as a writer, earned particular praise for his self-deprecating and acerbic humour. After signing a four-year contract extension in March 2004, he led the show's coverage of the presidential election, dubbed "Indecision 2004," to critical acclaim and saw the publication later in the year of *The Daily Show with Jon Stewart Presents America (the Book): A Citizen's Guide to Democracy Inaction,* which he co-wrote.

Emmy Award winner Jon Stewart

AP/Wide World Photos

Jonathan Stewart Leibowitz was born on Nov. 28, 1962, in New York City and graduated (1984) from the College of William and Mary in Williamsburg, Va. He then held a series of odd jobs, including puppeteer, before pursuing a career in comedy. In the late 1980s he began performing stand-up under the name Jon Stewart and quickly became popular on the club circuit. By the early 1990s he was appearing regularly on television, and after hosting the MTV series *You Wrote It, You Watch It* (1992), he was given his own program, *The Jon Stewart Show.* Featuring celebrity interviews and comedy sketches, it debuted in 1993 but lasted only two years despite having received positive reviews. Stewart continued to appear on various shows and from 1996 to 1998 was a frequent guest on the HBO series *The Larry Sanders Show.* Stewart, who made his big-screen debut in the 1994 film *Mixed Nuts,* also appeared in a number of films, including *Half Baked* (1998), *The Faculty* (1998), and *Big Daddy* (1999).

Stewart did not return to the host's chair until January 1999, when he replaced Craig Kilborn on *The Daily Show.* With Stewart as anchor, the show increased its viewership dramatically. During the 2000 presidential campaign, its satiric and comprehensive "Indecision 2000" coverage— *The Daily Show* correspondents reported from the caucuses and national conventions—became so popular that on election night its viewership rivaled that of some serious news programs. In 2000 the show earned a Peabody Award, and at the 2003 Emmys *The Daily Show* won for best series and best writing in the variety, music, or comedy category.

(AMY TIKKANEN)

Tani, Ryoko

Japanese judo queen Ryoko Tani claimed her second straight Olympic gold medal at the 2004 Games in Athens, becoming the first woman *judoka* to have won two Olympic titles. Using her fabulous inside leg technique to defeat Frederique Jossinet of France in the final, Tani proved herself one of the world's exceptional judo masters, underscoring a celebrated career that included six consecutive world championships in the 48-kg class. Her hunt for the gold in Athens meant a professional triumph for the 28-year-old Tani. One month before the Games, she had suffered a foot injury that prevented her from training

© Issei Kato/Reuters/Corbis

Japanese Olympic judoka *Ryoko Tani*

for three weeks. She also achieved her personal goal of bringing home a gold medal under her married name. Athens was the first world stage for Tani, formerly known as Tamura, since she married Japanese professional baseball player (and fellow Olympian) Yoshitomo Tani in 2003.

Tani was born on Sept. 6, 1975, in Fukuoka and began attending a dojo at age eight, following her older brother. Within four months she was using her newly learned throw technique to beat large boys at a competition held at a local Shinto shrine. At age 14 she took third in the Kyushu women's tournament in the 48-kg class, and in 1988 she placed first in the competition. In July of the same year, she was third in the national women's tournament, and five months later she achieved her first major victory by defeating the renowned Karen Briggs of England in the Fukuoka international women's judo tournament.

Tani studied literature at Teikyo University in Tokyo, and for a time she attended Nippon Sport Science University's graduate program, majoring in physical education, but her judo accomplishments from age 16 encouraged her to keep pursuing her career and entering larger international arenas. In 1990 she captured the first of 13 consecutive titles at the Fukuoka international. Three years later she won her first world championship and received the fourth *dan,* the highest rank an active judo player could obtain. After appearing as a finalist in her first Olympic Games in Barcelona, Spain, in 1992, Tani went four years and 84 matches without a loss until she was defeated by Kye Sun Hi of North Korea at the 1996 Olympics in Atlanta, Ga., and had to settle for another silver. Four years later at the Games in Sydney, Australia, however, Tani succeeded in bringing home her dream-come-true gold.

Tani, widely known in Japan as "Yawara-chan" (a name that was derived from a *manga* character), won numerous awards. She was honoured by Japanese Prime Minister Junichiro Koizumi in 2002 and by Emperor Akihito in 2003. She was also an immensely popular celebrity in Japan, and her wedding, which reportedly cost some $3 million, was televised throughout the country.

(KIMIYO NAKA-MICHAELI)

Theron, Charlize

Throughout Charlize Theron's acting career, the one attribute that was sure to be mentioned was her beauty. She managed to put at least a temporary stop to that, however, when—in completely inhabiting the character of real-life serial killer Aileen Wuornos in the 2003 motion picture *Monster*—she was almost unrecognizable, thanks partly to a nearly 14-kg (30-lb) weight gain, stringy hair, and a dental prosthesis. For her performance, in which she brought out Wuornos's humanity in addition to her troubled, brutal side, Theron was awarded

© Lucy Nicholson/Reuters/Corbis

South African actress Charlize Theron

the 2004 Academy Award for best actress, the first South African to be so honoured.

Theron was born on Aug. 7, 1975, in Benoni, S.Af., and grew up on a farm near that town. Her home life was stormy, and at age 13, wanting to continue ballet studies she had begun when she was 6, she began attending a boarding school that specialized in the arts. During a visit home when she was 15, however, she was witness to her mother's shooting and killing her father in self-defense after being attacked by him while he was drunk. Soon after that, Theron learned that her mother had entered her in a modeling contest some months earlier and that she had been awarded a contract in Italy. She moved to Milan at age 16, studied dance in addition to modeling, and two years later, in New York City on assignment and at the end of her contract, stayed there, continued modeling, and began studying at the Joffrey Ballet's school. A knee injury ended her chances of a career in dance, however, and she attempted, unsuccessfully, to pursue acting jobs. Theron's mother then persuaded her to move to Hollywood, but she was having no luck there either until—in true Hollywood-legend style—an agent noticed her when she made a loud scene because a bank would not cash a check from a New York modeling job. She began getting some small parts, one of which—in *2 Days in the Valley* (1996)—gained her favourable notice and paved the way for her first lead, in *The Devil's Advocate* (1997). That film showcased her acting ability and versatility and led to further substantial roles, notably in *Mighty Joe Young* (1998), *Celebrity* (1998), *The Cider House Rules* (1999), and *The Italian Job* (2003).

Following *Monster* Theron was seen in the 2004 films *The Life and Death of Peter Sellers* and *Head in the Clouds* and filmed *Aeon Flux*, due to be released in 2005. Future projects were to include *Class Action*, also scheduled to be seen in 2005, and *The Italian Job II* and *The Ice at the Bottom of the World*, both planned for a 2006 release. In addition, in August 2004 it was announced that Theron had signed a three-year contract to star in advertisements as the face of the Christian Dior perfume J'adore.

(BARBARA WHITNEY)

Trump, Donald

A master of the lucrative business deal and of unabashed self-promotion, real-estate baron Donald Trump scored a media coup in 2004 when he starred in the hit reality-TV show *The Apprentice*, which in its first season soared to the top of the ratings and attracted more than 40 million viewers in its two-hour finale. During the daunting boardroom scenes at the end of each weekly program, Trump crushed the aspirations of one candidate by exclaiming "You're fired!," which soon became a popular national catchphrase. The tables were turned on Trump, however, when his publicly traded company Trump Hotels & Casino Resorts, Inc., filed for Chapter 11 bankruptcy and he was forced to relinquish his role as CEO. He also lost his majority stake in the company.

Donald John Trump was born on June 14, 1946, in Queens, N.Y. At an early age he showed an interest in his father's successful real-estate business and often accompanied him on inspections to construction sites. Boisterous and assertive as a youth, Trump was enrolled in a New York military academy, where he excelled under the disciplinary environment and exhibited his leadership skills. He attended Fordham University, Bronx, N.Y., for a short time before enrolling at the University of Pennsylvania's Wharton School of Finance, where, according to a friend, "Donald always used to talk about changing the Manhattan skyline." After graduating from Wharton in 1968, Trump returned to New York to work with his father at the Trump Organization. After just five years, Trump's business deals had helped to raise the organization's assets by 500%.

Although his father influenced his career, Trump's ultimate hero was real-estate mogul William Zeckendorf, who built highly extravagant residences for the wealthy and after whom the young developer patterned his own negotiations. Trump's first major independent deal, despite his father's initial apprehension, was the purchase of the unsuccessful Commodore Hotel in 1975; reopened as the Grand Hyatt in 1980, it was worth an estimated $300 million in just seven years. "The Donald" expanded his empire to include the fabulous Trump Tower and Trump Parc in Manhattan, the Trump Plaza, and more than 25,000 rental and co-op apartment units in New York City. The Trump name was also associated with golf courses and casino-hotels, such as the Trump Taj Mahal in Atlantic City, N.J. In 2002 his plans were approved to construct the luxurious Trump International Hotel & Tower in Chicago, which upon completion would stand as the city's fourth tallest building.

Despite his recent financial difficulties and two well-publicized divorces, by 2004 Trump had accrued a net worth estimated by *Forbes* business magazine to be $2.5 billion. In June 2004 Trump began hosting a 90-second radio commentary program called *Trumped!*, and in the fall he launched his own line of men's clothing and introduced his second board game called Trump, the Game. His newest book was titled *Think like a Billionaire* (2004).

(BARBARA A. SCHREIBER)

Warren, Rick

The phenomenal influence of a book titled *The Purpose-Driven Life* won its author, Rick Warren, a reputation in 2004 as perhaps the most influential pastor in the U.S. Within two years of its publication in 2002, the book had sold some 16 million copies and spurred 40-day studies in more than 20,000 congregations representing 80 denominations. Warren's own congregation, Saddleback Church in Lake Forest, Calif., numbered more than 15,000 members and conducted Sunday services at 6 times and 10 locations on its 49-ha (120-ac) campus.

Warren, a fourth-generation Southern Baptist pastor, was born in 1954 in San Jose, Calif., and grew up in Ukiah. He earned a Bachelor of Arts degree from California Baptist College, a Master of Divinity from Southwestern Baptist Theological Seminary in Fort Worth, Texas, and a Doctor of Ministry from Fuller Theological Seminary in Pasadena, Calif. Turning down an offer to become pastor of a 5,000-member church in Texas during his last year in seminary, he, his wife, Kay, and their baby daughter arrived in California's Saddleback Valley in January 1980 to plant a church.

On Easter Sunday 1980, Saddleback Church held its first public service, with 205 people, most of whom had never been churchgoers. The congregation subsequently started 34 daughter churches and sent nearly 5,000 members on mission projects around the world. It had some 175 full-time paid staff members and 13 pastors, all of whom had seminary degrees.

Warren's 1995 book, *The Purpose-Driven Church*, won him renown by focusing on worship, evangelism, fellowship, discipleship, and ministry. It was translated into 21 languages and used in more than 120 countries by over 320,000 pastors who adapted its principles to their cultural and denominational settings. *Christianity Today* magazine said in 2002 that Warren's model took five elements that had been emphasized separately by various authors and movements "and systematically integrate[d] them into the life of the church." *The Purpose-Driven Life* encouraged individuals to ask, "What am I here for?" and told them that they were planned for God's pleasure, formed for God's family, created to become like Christ, shaped for serving God, and made for a mission. In addition to churches, the message won an appreciative audience in the White House of George W. Bush, corporate suites, and prisons.

In 2003 Warren stopped taking his $110,000 annual salary from Saddleback and returned the money the church had paid him for the previous 23 years. He pledged to donate 90% of his book royalties to the church and the three foundations he had created with his wife to promote evangelism and to fight poverty, illiteracy, and disease. A substance-abuse treatment program called Celebrate Recovery that Warren pioneered at Saddleback was adopted by a California prison in 2004.

(DARRELL J. TURNER)

Westwood, Vivienne

On April 1, 2004, a retrospective devoted to the creations of Vivienne Westwood opened at the Victoria and Albert Museum in London. "Vivienne Westwood: 34 Years in Fashion" was the largest exhibition the museum had ever dedicated to a British designer. Westwood was best known, however, for her association with Malcolm McLaren, the manager of the Sex Pistols, the 1970s punk-rock band that captivated hordes of disaffected British youths with its anger-laced politically subversive anthems.

Vivienne Isabel Swire was born on April 8, 1941, in Glossop, Derbyshire, Eng. She was a schoolteacher before she married in 1962 and had her first child. A self-taught designer, in 1965 Westwood met and moved in with McLaren when he was an 18-year-old painting student, and they pursued a career in fashion together. Initially, they operated Let It Rock, a stall selling secondhand 1950s vintage clothing, along with McLaren's rock-and-roll record collection. "He took me by the hand and made me more stylish," claimed Westwood of the charismatic McLaren, who fathered her second child and encouraged her to style her hair into an avant-garde spiked, peroxided crop. She produced clothing designs based on his provocative ideas, and their customized T-shirts—ripped and emblazoned with shocking antiestablishment slogans and graphics—rubberwear, and bondage trousers—black pants featuring straps inspired by sadomasochistic costume—flew out of the London shop of which the couple became proprietors in 1971. Their boutique—variously named Too Fast to Live, Too Young to Die; Sex; and finally Seditionaries—was a youth fashion mecca. Their erotically charged fashion image enraged Britain's right-wing press, however. Soon after Westwood and McLaren staged Pirates, their first commercial ready-to-wear collection, in 1981, they ended their personal relationship. They remained professional partners for an additional five years, but Westwood soon established her identity as a leading independent designer. Her "mini-crini" design—a thigh-grazing crinoline produced in both cotton and tweed that debuted as part of her spring-summer 1985 collection—marked a turning point. For the next two decades she created collections that took inspiration from classical sources, notably the paintings of Jean-Honoré Fragonard, François Boucher, and Thomas Gainsborough, as well as historical British dress, including the 19th-century bustle, which Westwood incorporated under tartan miniskirts and knitwear dresses. Though Westwood's later collections (in collaboration with her second husband, Andreas Kronthaler) were no longer consistently at fashion's cutting edge, her accomplishments were recognized in 1992 when she was made OBE. A year later she was appointed professor of fashion at the Hochschule der Künste, Berlin.

Independently, Westwood built her own eponymous mini fashion empire, operating boutiques in London and Hong Kong and producing two menswear and three women's wear collections annually as well as bridal clothes, shoes, hosiery, eyewear, scarves, ties, knitwear, cosmetics, and two perfumes, Boudoir and Libertine.

(BRONWYN COSGRAVE)

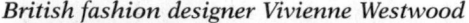

British fashion designer Vivienne Westwood

Witten, Edward

Edward Witten, a theoretical physicist who had a hand in many of the important developments in string theory from the mid-1980s onward, was named by *Time* magazine as one of the world's 100 most influential people of 2004. String theory is an attempt to link quantum mechanics and general relativity, which would thereby lead to a "theory of everything" applicable to all physical forces and forms of matter. According to string theory, matter at a fundamental level consists of vibrating one-dimensional elements (called strings), not point-like particles.

Witten was born Aug. 26, 1951 in Baltimore, Md. He intended to become a journalist and attended Brandeis University, Waltham, Mass., where he received a B.A. in history in 1971. He went on to Princeton University and earned an M.A. (1974) and Ph.D. (1976) in physics. He held a fellowship at Harvard University (1976–77) and was a junior fellow in the Harvard Society of Fellows (1977–80). He joined the faculty at Princeton University in 1980 and was a professor of physics there until 1987, when he assumed a professorship at the Institute for Advanced Study, Princeton, N.J. From 1997 he was the Charles Simonyi Professor of Physics there.

Witten's early work in physics was in electromagnetics. As the study of string theory gained importance in the early 1980s, he turned his attention to that field and was soon considered its leading mind. In the 1990s he proposed a theory, called M-theory, that unified five different string theories (called superstring theories) and a theory for 11-dimensional supergravity. This unification moved scientists a giant step toward a theory of everything and became known as the "second revolution in superstring theory." Colleagues such as physicist Nathan Seiberg were quoted as saying that Witten was leading the scientific community to all of its major breakthroughs in superstring theory. Seiberg and others credited Witten with having unsurpassed skills in mathematics as well as physics, which made him uniquely qualified to blaze new trails in his field.

Witten received numerous honours and awards, most notably the Fields Medal, the top prize in mathematics, which he was given at the International Congress of Mathematicians in Kyoto, Japan, in 1990. He held a

MacArthur Foundation fellowship in 1982 and in 1985 received the Einstein Medal of the Einstein Society and the Dirac Medal of the International Center for Theoretical Physics. He was elected to the National Academy of Sciences in 1988.

(ANTHONY G. CRAINE)

Woodward, Bob

The reporter became the story when *Plan of Attack,* the latest book from legendary *Washington Post* journalist Bob Woodward, was leaked to the Associated Press three days ahead of its scheduled release date in April 2004. The book, which included interviews with Washington political insiders and provided a behind-the-scenes look at the administration of U.S. Pres. George W. Bush (*q.v.*) in the 16 months leading up to the war in Iraq, immediately shot to number one on the Amazon.com sales list. Within weeks it reached the top of the *New York Times* best-seller list, becoming Woodward's 10th book to achieve that feat.

Robert Upshur Woodward was born on March 26, 1943, in Geneva, Ill. He grew up in Wheaton, a suburb of Chicago, where his father was a prominent jurist. It was thought that he would follow his father into the legal profession when he enrolled at Yale University on a naval ROTC scholarship. After receiving his B.A. in history and English literature in 1965, Woodward began a five-year tour of duty as a communications officer. Upon his return, he was accepted (1970) at Harvard Law School. He chose not to pursue a law degree; instead, he petitioned the editors of the *Washington Post* for an unpaid two-week internship. While none of the stories he submitted was printed, the editors saw potential in the aspiring reporter and referred him to the *Montgomery County Sentinel,* a weekly paper in suburban Maryland. Within a year Woodward had polished his skills enough that the *Post* was willing to give him another chance. He had been covering the police beat for nine months when a call came in about a burglary at the Democratic National Committee headquarters at the Watergate complex. Working with fellow *Post* reporter Carl Bernstein, Woodward eventually connected the break-in to the highest levels of the administration of U.S. Pres. Richard Nixon. For Woodward and Bernstein's reporting, the *Post* was awarded the 1973 Pulitzer Prize for public service. The names Woodward and Bernstein became virtually synonymous with investigative journalism, and their book, *All the President's Men* (1974), topped the best-seller list. The 1976 film version of the book, with Woodward portrayed by Robert Redford, was also a great success.

Woodward continued his work at the *Post* and was named assistant managing editor in 1979. In the following years, however, he became better known for his books than for his newspaper reporting. Exposés on personalities as varied as comedian John Belushi and former U.S. vice president Dan Quayle drew both admiration and criticism, with reviewers praising his ability to unearth volumes of information while disparaging his tendency to dwell on sordidness. His recent material, however, focused on hard news and the power and politics of Washington. He led a team that earned another Pulitzer for the *Post* in 2002 for the paper's coverage of the repercussions of the Sept. 11, 2001, terrorist attacks in the U.S.

(MICHAEL RAY)

Zagajewski, Adam

In 2004 Polish poet, fiction writer, and essayist Adam Zagajewski—already the recipient of several notable literary honours, including the Swedish PEN's Kurt Tucholsky Prize, the Tomas Tranströmer Prize (Västerås, Swed.), and the Prix de la Liberté (France)—added the Neustadt International Prize for Literature, which is awarded every other year by the University of Oklahoma and the journal *World Literature Today.* Zagajewski's writings were grounded in the turbulent history of his homeland and concerned with the quandary of the modern intellectual. They interwove the historical and political with the more spiritual aspects of life. "Zagajewski may be looking at Eastern Europe, but his gaze wraps itself around the whole globe," wrote *The Threepenny Review.*

Zagajewski was born on June 21, 1945, in Lwow, Pol. (now Lviv, Ukraine), a city where his family had resided for many centuries. Shortly after his birth, Lwow was incorporated into the Soviet Union, and his family was forcibly repatriated to Poland. As a romantic poet in whose world view memory and nostalgia were key elements, Zagajewski never let go of his sense of loss of historical roots. His family moved to Silesia and then later to Krakow, where Zagajewski graduated from the Jagiellonian University. His first collections of poetry, *Komunikat* (1972; "Communiqué") and *Sklepy mięsne* (1975; "Meat Shops"), came out of the Polish "New Wave" movement, which sought to expose the falseness of official communist propaganda. Zagajewski was a major figure in the Solidarity movement of the 1980s, and his volume *List: Oda do wielości* (1982; "Letter: An Ode to Multiplicity") contained poems reacting to the imposition of martial law in Poland. His first novel, *Ciepło, zimno* (1975; "Warm and Cold"), was about a young intellectual who, tormented by self-doubts and unable to accept unambiguous principles, became a servant of the police state. Zagajewski left Poland for Paris in 1982, and there his work grew more lyrical and more personal. In his memoir *W cudzym pięknie* (1998; *Another Beauty,* 2000), he wrote of his growing conviction that "a poem, essay, or story must grow from an emotion, an observation, a joy, a sorrow that is my own, and not my nation's." His second novel, *Cienka kreska* (1983; "The Thin Line"), explored the spiritual dilemma of the contemporary artist who is caught between the splendour and the triviality of everyday experience.

Zagajewski was coeditor of the Paris-based Polish-language *Literary Review,* although he recently had moved his primary residence from France back to Krakow, where he completed a new essay collection, *Obrona żarliwości* (2002; *A Defense of Ardor,* 2004).

(ANNA POPLAWSKA)

Zapatero, José Luis Rodríguez

Socialist leader José Luis Rodríguez Zapatero was sworn in as Spanish prime minister on April 17, 2004. Six weeks earlier almost no one except Zapatero himself had believed that he could win the elections on March 14. All this changed following the March 11 al-Qaeda attacks in Madrid and the perceived inept response of the Popular Party (PP) government. For some the Socialists' surprise electoral victory confirmed that Zapatero had *baraka* ("a charmed life").

Zapatero, the son of a lawyer, was born on Aug. 4, 1960, in the northern Spanish city of Valladolid and was reared in neighbouring León. Academically gifted, he was given a teaching job in the university's law faculty immediately after graduating in 1982. His heart, however, lay in politics and the Socialist Party (PSOE), which he had joined in 1979. By 1988 he was general secretary of the party's conflictive León provincial federation, and he already had two years' experience as the youngest member of the national parliament, representing León. He soon established a reputation as a capable, hardworking deputy, but he held no public office in the Socialist governments. Despite being party spokesman on public administrations, Zapatero remained virtually unknown outside the parliament during the PP's first government (1996–2000) and even after the Socialists' second successive electoral defeat in March 2000.

At the PSOE national congress in July 2000, however, he defeated three other candidates to become party general secretary. Echoing the British Labour Party's Third Way and the German Social Democratic Party's New Centre, Zapatero's ill-defined New Way promised to modernize both the party and its policies. He offered a new, younger face with a modern-sounding agenda that revolved around economic efficiency, women's rights, democratic participation, laicism, and "constructive" opposition to the PP government.

His election as PSOE leader and de facto candidate for the prime ministership made little impact on the voters. The party had been confident that it would capitalize on Spaniards' intense opposition to the war in Iraq, but the PSOE did worse than expected in the local and regional elections in May 2003. Five months later a corruption scandal robbed the Socialists of their star prize, the Madrid regional government, which went to the PP after repeat elections. Only the PP's lacklustre campaign suggested that things would be different in March 2004. Then came the terrorist attacks on March 11, and three days later the Socialists were swept to power.

Zapatero appointed a cabinet that combined established and emerging figures, half of whom were women. Within six months he had withdrawn the Spanish troops serving with the U.S.-led coalition in Iraq, moved on the always difficult regional issue, and introduced several parliamentary measures. After the U.S. elections in November, he also sought to mend damaged relations with Washington. Charges that Zapatero was more about style than content appeared to be unfounded.

(JUSTIN BYRNE)

Obituaries

In 2004 the world LOST many leaders, pathfinders, NEWSMAKERS, heroes, CULTURAL ICONS, and ROGUES. The pages below RECAPTURE the lives and ACCOMPLISHMENTS of those we REMEMBER best.

Abbas, Abu (MUHAMMAD ABBAS), Palestinian guerrilla leader (b. 1948/49?, near Haifa?, Palestine/Israel?—d. March 8/9, 2004, near Baghdad, Iraq), was best known as the mastermind behind the 1985 hijacking of the Italian cruise ship *Achille Lauro,* during which a wheelchair-bound American Jewish man, Leon Klinghoffer, was shot and pushed into the sea; this act brought worldwide condemnation, and Abbas was sentenced in absentia to life in prison in Italy. Abbas grew up in a Palestinian refugee camp in Syria and, under the nom de guerre Abu Abbas, became a rising star in Ahmad Jibril's Popular Front for the Liberation of Palestine–General Command, which was known for its daring, ruthless, and frequently disastrous attacks on Israel. In the mid-1970s Abbas founded his own faction, the Palestine Liberation Front. The *Achille Lauro* hijacking was reportedly a botched attempt to infiltrate Israel from the sea by four people under Abbas's command. With his public acceptance of the Oslo peace agreements, he was permitted in 1996 to return to Gaza, where he apologized for the hijacking and for Klinghoffer's murder. Abbas was captured in Baghdad by American troops in April 2003 and died while in U.S. military custody.

Abelson, Philip Hauge, American scientist, editor, and administrator (b. April 27, 1913, Tacoma, Wash.—d. Aug. 1, 2004, Bethesda, Md.), rose to prominence for his research on uranium and for his co-discovery (with American physicist Edwin McMillan) of neptunium. In the 1940s Abelson devised a process for isolating uranium isotopes that aided in the development of the atomic bomb. He also helped establish the feasibility of building nuclear submarines. Abelson was formally trained in physics and chemistry, but in his career of more than 60 years, he also blazed trails in biology, geology, engineering, and biochemistry. He was among the first scientists to recognize the potential of the bacterium *Escherichia coli* for use in genetic engineering, and his discovery that amino acids in fossils could survive millions of years influenced studies in biochemistry and paleontology. When elected to the National Academy of Sciences in 1959, Abelson was eligible for work he did in any of seven scientific disciplines; he chose to be inducted as a geologist. In 1962 he was named editor of *Science,* the principal publication of the American Association for the Advancement of Science (AAAS). He held the position more than 20 years and subsequently served as contributing editor until the late 1990s. As editor, Abelson wrote more than 500 editorials on subjects ranging from medicine to energy, and he often expressed his strong opinions and engaged other scientists in heated debate. Abelson served as acting executive director (1974, 1975, 1984) of the AAAS and as president (1971–78) of the Carnegie Institution of Washington, D.C. In 1987 he was awarded the National Medal of Science.

Abramovitz, Max, American architect (b. May 23, 1908, Chicago, Ill.—d. Sept. 12, 2004, Pound Ridge, N.Y.), partnered with Wallace K. Harrison to influence the development of modernist architecture and helped shape the Manhattan skyline with his designs for a number of midtown buildings. He collaborated on such high-profile projects as the United Nations complex in New York City and the Central Intelligence Agency headquarters in Langley, Va., but he was best known for his work on Philharmonic Hall (later Avery Fisher Hall) at Lincoln Center, New York City.

Adair, Red (PAUL NEAL ADAIR), American firefighter (b. June 18, 1915, Houston, Texas—d. Aug. 7, 2004, Houston), demonstrated remarkable daring and creativity in fighting oil blowouts and fires. He took his first job in the oil industry in 1938 and served during World War II with the 139th Bomb Disposal Squad in Japan. After returning to Houston, he began working as an oil-field firefighter, and in 1959 he started the Red Adair Co. His reputation as an exceptionally talented firefighter was established in 1962 when his team extinguished the "Devil's Cigarette Lighter," a gas fire that had been raging in the desert of Algeria for six months. This daring feat was reenacted in the film *Hellfighters* (1968), in which John Wayne portrayed Adair. His teams were credited with fighting more than 2,000 fires in his career, including the Bay Marchand blaze off the coast of Louisiana in 1970, the IXTOC blowout in the Gulf of Mexico in 1979, and the 1988 Piper Alpha disaster in the North Sea. In 1991 Adair was asked to help cap the oil fires set by Iraqi troops fleeing Kuwait during the Persian Gulf War. Although it was thought that controlling these fires would take years to accomplish, Adair's team capped 117 wells and aided other teams in completing the job in eight months. Adair retired from firefighting in 1994.

Adams, Eddie (EDWARD THOMAS ADAMS), American photojournalist (b. June 12, 1933, New Kensington, Pa.—d. Sept. 19, 2004, New York, N.Y.), won hundreds of awards during his 45-year career and counted 13 wars among the events he covered but was most renowned for the Pulitzer Prize-winning photograph he took in 1968 at the moment a South Vietnamese general shot a Viet Cong prisoner to death on the streets of Saigon. More important to him, however, was the fact that his series of photos of Vietnamese refugees who had sailed to Thailand only to have Thai marines tow their small boat back out to sea helped persuade the administration of Pres. Jimmy Carter to accept nearly 200,000 boat people in the U.S.

Agnelli, Umberto, Italian business executive (b. Nov. 1, 1934, Lausanne, Switz.—d. May 27, 2004, Turin, Italy), saved the Fiat automobile company from financial ruin by slashing its $3.5 billion debt in half after he succeeded his brother Giovanni as corporate chairman when the latter died in January 2003. Agnelli implemented a number of cost-cutting measures, injected new financing, boosted sales with the creation of several new Fiat models, and prevented General Motors from buying out the company. These actions were instrumental in preserving the Agnelli family dynasty, which had controlled Fiat for more than a century. Outside the automobile business, Agnelli earned (1959) a law degree from the University of Turin and served (1976–79) as a Christian Democrat senator. He became chairman of the Juventus association football (soccer) team at age 22 and was the team's honorary chairman at the time of his death.

Aiken, Joan Delano, British author (b. Sept. 4, 1924, Rye, Sussex, Eng.—d. Jan. 4, 2004, Petsworth, West Sussex, Eng.), wrote fantasy, adventure, horror, and suspense tales for both juvenile and adult readers. Aiken, the daughter of the American writer Conrad Aiken, was educated at home as a child and grew up with a love of literature. She was perhaps best known for *The Wolves of Willoughby Chase* (1962), an adventure story that follows the fortunes of two girls unwittingly left in the grip of evil caretakers. It was the first of Aiken's more than 60 short-story collections and novels for young people.

Anand, Mulk Raj, Indian author (b. Dec. 12, 1905, Peshawar, India [now in Pakistan]—d. Sept. 28, 2004, Pune, India), was a founder of the English-language novel in India, best known for his works that focused on the injustices of India's caste system, especially the exploitation of the poor. Anand studied at the University of the Punjab, Lahore (now in Pakistan), the University of Cambridge, and University College, London, where he received (1929) a doctorate in English philosophy. He wrote several books on South Asian culture, including *Persian Painting* (1930) and *The Hindu View of Art* (1933), before his first novel, *Untouchable,* was published in 1935. This fictional recounting of a day in the life of a young lavatory cleaner attracted international attention with its realistic portrayal of poverty and its use of colloquial expressions. Anand continued to chronicle the oppressed in such novels as *Coolie* (1936), *Two Leaves and a Bud* (1937), and *The Big Heart* (1945; rev. ed. 1980). Other major works included a trilogy—*The Village* (1939), *Across the Black Waters* (1940), and *The Sword and the Sickle* (1942)—and four volumes of a projected seven-book autobiographical novel, *Seven Ages of Man.* In *Conversations in Bloomsbury* (1981), he recounted his discussions with such leading literary figures as Aldous Huxley, E.M. Forster, and Virginia Woolf. Anand, who founded the influential art quarterly *Marg* in 1946, was also noted for his short stories and critical essays.

Anand, Vijay ("GOLDIE"), Indian film director, writer, and actor (b. Jan. 22, 1934, Gurdaspur, Punjab, India—d. Feb. 23, 2004, Mumbai [Bombay], India), was the visionary director of some of Bollywood's most respected movies and the younger brother of the legendary actor Dev Anand. He learned the craft while working with his older brother Chetan, and the three brothers collaborated under the auspices of the film company Navketan. Anand's work on the script of the 1954 Bollywood film *Taxi Driver* led to his first directing job, on *Nau do gyarah* (*Nine Plus Two Makes Eleven;* 1957). Of the dozens of successful Bollywood films with which he was involved, the most acclaimed was *Guide* (1965), which won several Filmfare Awards.

Anderson, Carl (CARLTON EARL ANDERSON), American actor and singer (b. Feb. 27, 1945, Lynchburg, Va.—d. Feb. 23, 2004, Los Angeles, Calif.), took over the role of Judas in *Jesus Christ Superstar* on Broadway in 1971 when Ben Vereen became ill, alternated with Vereen for several months, and went on to fill that role in the film version (1973) as well as in tours of the show in 1992 and 2002. Anderson's other notable roles were in the film *The Color Purple* (1985) and the Broadway musical *Play On!* (1997).

Arafat, Yasir (MUHAMMAD 'ABD AL-RA'UF AL-QUDWAH AL-HUSAYNI), Palestinian leader (b. Aug. 24?, 1929, Cairo, Egypt?—d. Nov. 11, 2004, Paris, France), was credited with creating the Palestinian nationalist movement, but he never wholly cut his ties to terrorism and failed in the goal of establishing an independent state. By the age of 17, he was smuggling arms to Palestinians fighting nascent Israel. In 1947 he began studies at Cairo University; although his education was interrupted by the Arab-Israeli War of 1948–49, he graduated with a degree in civil engineering in 1956. He served in the Egyptian army in the Suez War (1956) and subsequently worked in Kuwait. In the late 1950s, with others, he founded the organization Fatah, which by 1969 had gained dominance within the Palestine Liberation Organization (PLO). Arafat became chairman of the PLO, which was headquartered in Jordan until it came to pose a threat to the government and was driven out in 1971. Arafat fled to Lebanon, and in 1974 he addressed the UN to demand the establishment of a Palestinian state. When in 1982 the Israelis expelled the PLO from Lebanon, Arafat moved his headquarters to Tunisia, although attacks against Israel continued. In 1988 Arafat accepted a UN resolution calling for recognition of Israel, and he formally renounced terrorism. Talks between the Palestinians and the Israelis culminated in 1993 in the Oslo Accords, which provided for mutual recognition and a transition to Palestinian self-rule in the West Bank and in Gaza. The following year Arafat shared the Nobel Prize for Peace with two Israelis, Prime Minister Yitzhak Rabin and Foreign Minister Shimon Peres. Arafat returned to Palestinian soil, and in 1996 he was elected president of the provisional Palestinian Authority, but his administration was charged with being dictatorial and corrupt. By 2000 further talks had led to an agreement that included the transfer of some 95% of the West Bank and all of Gaza to the Palestinians and to divided control of Jerusalem, an offer Arafat eventually rejected. After a second *intifadah* (uprising) began in September 2000, and with Arafat unable or unwilling to control militants within the Palestinian movement, the Israelis confined him to his compound in Ram Allah, where he remained until he was taken to Paris for medical treatment in the month before his death.

Arosemena Monroy, Carlos Julio, Ecuadorean politician (b. Aug. 24, 1919, Guayaquil, Ecuador—d. March 5, 2004, Guayaquil), was installed as president of Ecuador after the military overthrew Pres. José María Velasco Ibarra in 1961. Arosemena, who rose from the post of vice president, was among the most dynamic and controversial presidents in the country's history. During his tumultuous 20-month term in office, he promoted reformist causes, such as low-cost housing, progressive income taxes, and yearly bonuses for workers. His support of Fidel Castro's revolution in Cuba caused an ongoing conflict with Congress and the military. After surviving two attempts by Congress to impeach him, owing to erratic behaviour, Arosemena was finally overthrown by a military coup in 1963, reportedly after a particularly embarrassing drunken incident at a public function; he was exiled to Panama. Arosemena eventually returned to Ecuadoran politics and formed the Nationalist Revolutionary Party; he was elected several times to Congress.

Astley, Thea Beatrice May, Australian writer and teacher (b. Aug. 25, 1925, Brisbane, Queen., Australia—d. Aug. 17, 2004, New South Wales, Australia), used satire to examine the lives of repressed and isolated people, especially those living in small towns. Considered one of Australia's leading writers, she was praised for her caustic wit, keen observations, and lyrical prose. Astley, who graduated (1947) from the University of Queensland, began teaching in 1944 and often worked in remote locations, which provided material for her work. From 1968 to 1980 she also was on the faculty at Macquarie University in Sydney. In her first novel, *Girl with a Monkey* (1958), Astley chronicled a schoolteacher's last day in a small town as she leaves a violent boyfriend. The parochialism and brutality of insular communities figured prominently in many of her novels, including *A Descant for Gossips* (1960) and *An Item from the Late News* (1982). She also frequently explored themes of self-delusion and human folly, and her novels often reached violent conclusions. In *The Acolyte* (1972) an egocentric musician destroys those around him, while *Beachmasters* (1985) chronicled the failed attempt by Pacific Islanders to free themselves from foreign rule. The mistreatment of Aboriginals was addressed in *A Kindness Cup* (1974) and *It's Raining in Mango* (1987). Astley's other notable works included *The Well Dressed Explorer* (1962), *The Slow Natives* (1965), and *Drylands* (1999). The recipient of numerous honours, Astley was a four-time winner of the Miles Franklin Award, Australia's highest literary prize.

Auerbach, Ellen (ELLEN ROSENBERG; "PIT"), German-born avant-garde photographer (b. May 20, 1906, Karlsruhe, Ger.—d. July 31, 2004, New York, N.Y.), created innovative experimental advertising images and portraits, particularly during the Weimar Republic (1919–33). Auerbach studied in Berlin with Walter Peterhans of the Bauhaus design school. When Peterhans relocated to Dessau, Auerbach and fellow student Grete Stern took over his Berlin studio, opening a commercial photography studio that they called ringl + pit after their respective nicknames. The studio's work, influenced by Constructivism and Surrealism, was widely exhibited, and in 1933 ringl + pit won first prize at an international exhibition in Brussels. That same year, however, with the rise of the Nazi Party in Germany, both women fled the country. Auerbach and her husband eventually settled in the U.S., where she became a citizen in 1942. Although she never again knew such professional success, the work of ringl + pit was rediscovered in the late 1980s, and a major retrospective was staged at the Akademie der Künste in Berlin in 1998.

Avedon, Richard, American photographer (b. May 15, 1923, New York, N.Y.—d. Oct. 1, 2004, San Antonio, Texas), gained renown as

© Allen Ginsberg/Corbis

Fashion photographer Richard Avedon

the revolutionary fashion photographer who placed his models in candid and dramatic yet casual situations instead of the rigid, formal poses that had been the norm and in the process introduced the concept of the supermodel. The character portrayed by Fred Astaire in the film *Funny Face* (1957)—a fashion photographer who transforms a bookstore assistant (Audrey Hepburn) into a top model—was in fact modeled on Avedon. He later also became celebrated for his stark black-and-white portraits, which he took by having his subjects face straight forward in front of a white background, with no props or distractions. Although Avedon had earlier shown an interest in taking pictures, it was not until he served in the photography division of the U.S. Merchant Marine (1942–44) that he abandoned plans to be a poet. His career in fashion photography began first with work for a department store and progressed to stints at *Harper's Bazaar* (1945–65) and *Vogue* (on staff 1966–70 but associated with the magazine until 1990), as well as work for advertising accounts. Avedon also put together a number of documentary projects, often employing his stark portrait style to record the lives of ordinary people as, for example, for the "In the American West" museum exhibition. His work was featured in numerous other exhibitions and retrospectives and in several books. In 1992 Avedon became the first staff photographer for *The New Yorker* magazine, where his portraits appeared regularly. He died while on assignment for that publication.

Axelrod, Julius, American neuroscientist and pharmacologist (b. May 30, 1912, New York, N.Y.—d. Dec. 29, 2004, Rockville, Md.), discovered biochemical processes that play a crucial role in the mechanisms by which chemicals called neurotransmitters carry nerve impulses between cells in the nervous system. In particular, he identified an enzyme that neutralizes the neurotransmitter noradrenaline (norepinephrine) after it is no longer needed to transmit a nerve impulse. For this work Axelrod shared the Nobel Prize for Physiology or Medicine in 1970 with British biophysicist Sir Bernard Katz and Swedish physiologist Ulf von Euler. Axelrod's research helped lead to the development of selective serotonin reuptake inhibitors, a class of antidepressant medications that includes Prozac. Axelrod received an M.S. (1941) in chemistry from New York University and a Ph.D. (1955) in pharmacology from George Washington University, Washington, D.C. From 1949 to 1955 he was a chemist at the National Heart Institute, Bethesda, Md., and from 1955 to 1984 he was the chief of the pharmacology section of the National Institute of Mental Health, Bethesda.

Axton, Estelle Stewart, American music publisher (b. Sept. 11, 1918, Middleton, Tenn.—d. Feb. 24, 2004, Memphis, Tenn.), founded with her brother, Jim Stewart, Stax Records, a soul music label from Memphis that was second in influence only to Motown Records. Spurred into the business by witnessing the success of the company that launched the career of local legend Elvis Presley, she soon came to represent such artists as Otis Redding, Isaac Hayes, Wilson Pickett, the Staple Singers, Sam and Dave, and Booker T. and the MG's, which was the label's house band. By the time the company closed in 1975, she had already left and helped found Fretone Records.

Barnes, Peter, British playwright and screenwriter (b. Jan. 10, 1931, London, Eng.—d. July 1, 2004, London), was an imaginative, thoroughly unorthodox—and often underappreciated—writer best known for the satiric play *The Ruling Class* (1968), which he adapted for a 1972 film starring Peter O'Toole. Barnes combined unconventional dramatic sensibilities and extravagant wit with an appreciation of earlier playwrights who included Frank Wedekind, Ben Jonson, and Georges Feydeau. Barnes's many other works included the Oliver Award-winning play *Red Noses* (1985) and the Oscar-nominated screenplay for *Enchanted April* (1992).

Barrymore, John Drew, American actor (b. June 4, 1932, Beverly Hills, Calif.—d. Nov. 29, 2004, Los Angeles, Calif.), was a fourth-generation member of one of the most famous American theatrical families—and the father of actress Drew Barrymore—but lifestyle and substance-abuse difficulties prevented him from attaining the success he might have enjoyed. He appeared on the stage, in such films as *The Sundowners* (1950) and *While the City Sleeps* (1956), and then in some television series, but in later years he became reclusive.

Batata (PAULINO SALGADO VALDEZ), Colombian master drummer, singer, and composer (b. 1929, San Basilio de Palenque, Colom.—d. Jan. 24, 2004, Bogotá, Colom.), was the leading figure in Afro-Colombian music. Batata hailed from a city in Colombia founded by escaped slaves, and his music thus reflected a strong West African influence. He toured for two decades with singer Totó la Momposina. Batata's story was told in the documentary film *Sons of Benkos* (2000), and his only solo album, *Radio Bakongo,* was released in 2003.

Beene, Geoffrey, American fashion designer (b. Aug. 30, 1927, Haynesville, La.—d. Sept. 28, 2004, New York, N.Y.), revolutionized the American fashion industry with minimalist designs that incorporated a variety of materials and emphasized comfort over couture. He spent three years studying medicine at Tulane University, New Orleans, but dropped out with the intention of enrolling at the University of Southern California. Instead, he found a job in the display department of upscale retailer I. Magnin. Having decided on a career in fashion, Beene enrolled (1947) in New York's Traphagen School of Fashion and continued his studies in Paris. Beene returned to New York in 1951 and established his portfolio with a number of Seventh Avenue designers. He landed a full-time position with Teal Traina in 1954 and remained at that studio until he launched his own company in 1963. His collections were noted for flattering the human form. He described his approach as having "respect for the body, respect for the fabric, and respect for a woman's desires." Beene drew widespread praise for his 1967 design of Lynda Bird Johnson's wedding dress, and his spring collection that year was generally regarded as his finest. In 1974 he launched a line of inexpensive sportswear that he dubbed Beene Bag, and two years later he became the first American designer to open a show in Milan. His work earned him induction into the Fashion Hall of Fame, eight Coty Fashion Critics Awards, and a 1998 lifetime achievement award from the Council of Fashion Designers of America.

Bemer, Robert William, American computer programmer (b. Feb. 8, 1920, Sault Ste.

Marie, Mich.—d. June 22, 2004, Possum Kingdom Lake, Texas), was instrumental in helping to develop ASCII (American Standard Code for Information Interchange), a system that, upon becoming operational in 1963, greatly facilitated the exchange of data between various makes of computers. Bemer's contribution—as part of the committee that set the standard—was centred on the formation of an "escape sequence" in character codes that would permit the information system to break out of one alphabet and enter another; as a result, extra-ASCII alphabets were created for Greek, Arabic, and languages using the Cyrillic script, among numerous others. In addition, his escape system served as the basis for such technologies as cursor movement, laser printers, video games, and computer-generated films. Bemer was working for IBM when he served on the committee that adopted ASCII. He also served as an adviser in the development in 1959 of another computer programming language—COBOL (Common Business Oriented Language), a standard desired by the U.S. government—and was credited with implementing the FORTRANSIT programming system. Besides working for IBM (1955–62), Bemer was employed by Sperry Rand (1962–65), General Electric (1965–70), and Honeywell Information Systems (1970–82) before forming his own software company, for which he served as president from 1982 until his death.

Benveniste, Jacques, French immunologist (b. March 12, 1935, Paris, France—d. Oct. 4, 2004, Paris), was responsible for numerous advances in allergy medicine and immunology, gaining prominence as part of the research team that isolated platelet-activating factor (an important blood-clotting protein), but his brilliant career was diminished in later years by his controversial ideas on homeopathy, a form of alternative medical treatment based on the belief that a substance that causes certain symptoms can relieve those symptoms when administered in doses minute enough to stimulate the immune system but not produce side effects. Perhaps the most controversial aspect of Benveniste's work was his hypothesis (first published in the journal *Nature* in 1988) that when dissolved in water, a substance acts like a template, altering the electromagnetic properties of the water. In subsequent dilutions these properties would be transferred to newly added water, the water would thus retain a "memory" of the substance dissolved in the initial solution.

Bergström, Sune Karl, Swedish biochemist (b. Jan. 10, 1916, Stockholm, Swed.—d. Aug. 15, 2004, Stockholm), laid the groundwork for chemical research on prostaglandins, an important group of natural hormonelike substances that affect blood pressure, body temperature, allergic reactions, and other physiological functions. In the late 1950s he was the first to isolate prostaglandins (specifically PGE and PGF) and to determine their chemical composition. For their work on prostaglandins Bergström, Swedish biochemist Bengt I. Samuelsson (a student of Bergström's), and British pharmacologist John Robert Vane (*q.v.*) were jointly awarded the 1982 Nobel Prize for Physiology or Medicine. Bergström received doctoral degrees (1944) in medicine and biochemistry from the Karolinska Institute, Stockholm. After holding research fellowships in London, New York, and Basel, Switz., he returned to Sweden in 1947 as professor of physiological chemistry at the University of Lund. He spent more than 20 years (1958–80) as professor of chemistry at the Karolinska Institute, where he also served as dean (1963–66) of the medical faculty and as the institute's rector (1969–77). Bergström was chairman of the Nobel Foundation (1975–87) and of the World Health Organization's Global Advisory Committee on Medical Research (1977–82).

Bernhard, Prince (Bernhard Leopold Frederik Everhard Julius Coert Karel Godfried Pieter, prince of The Netherlands, prince of Lippe-Biesterfeld), German-born Dutch royal (b. June 29, 1911, Jena, Ger.—d. Dec. 1, 2004, Utrecht, Neth.), was the husband of one Dutch queen, Juliana (*q.v.*),

Prince Bernhard and Princess (later Queen) Juliana in 1937

and the father of another, Beatrix. Bernhard gained international respect as a Dutch patriot (especially during World War II) and as the founding president (1961–77) of the World Wildlife Fund, despite initial Dutch reservations regarding his German heritage, a youthful reputation for fast cars and reckless habits, and accusations in 1976 that he had accepted bribes from American aircraft manufacturer Lockheed Corp. Bernhard was born into a German royal family and was educated in Germany and Switzerland. In 1936, while working for a German chemical company in Paris, he met Juliana; they were married on Jan. 7, 1937.

Bernstein, Elmer, American film composer (b. April 4, 1922, New York, N.Y.—d. Aug. 18, 2004, Ojai, Calif.), created the scores for more than 200 motion pictures during a career that spanned half a century and produced some of Hollywood's most memorable film music, fashioning its style to reflect the mood and action of its film; his scores were often widely acknowledged as more notable than the movies themselves. Although he garnered 14 Academy Award nominations—including those for the scores of *The Man with the Golden Arm* (1955), *The Magnificent Seven* (1960), *To Kill a Mockingbird* (1962), *Trading Places* (1983), and *Far from Heaven* (2002)—he won only once, for *Thoroughly Modern Millie* (1967), considered one of his lesser efforts. Bernstein was headed for a career as a concert pianist, but during his World War II army service, he composed scores for military radio broadcasts. In 1950 he began writing music for films, and in 1952, with his score for *Sudden Fear,* he demonstrated the drama and originality that would distinguish his works. Although his support for left-wing causes hindered his career somewhat during the early 1950s, Bernstein continued to get work, and in the mid-'50s he established his reputation with the groundbreaking jazz-infused score for *The Man with the Golden Arm* and proved his versatility with the stirring music for *The Ten Commandments* (1956). Later notable scores included those for *Sweet Smell of Success* (1957), *Some Came Running* (1958), *Walk on the Wild Side* (1962), *Animal House* (1978), *Airplane!* (1980), *Ghostbusters* (1984), and *My Left Foot* (1989), and he also composed works for symphony orchestras and scores for television programs and the documentary *The Making of the President 1960* (1963).

Berry, (William) Jan, American singer and songwriter (b. April 3, 1941, Los Angeles, Calif.—d. March 26, 2004, Los Angeles), composed songs that reflected the free-spirited surfing and hot-rod culture of California during the 1960s and was the creative force behind the pop music duo Jan & Dean. Berry and partner Dean Torrence reached the height of their success in 1963–64 after releasing their first number one hit song, "Surf City" (1963), which was co-written by Berry's friend Brian Wilson of the Beach Boys. Other notable hit songs included "The Little Old Lady from Pasadena," "Sidewalk Surfin'," and "Dead Man's Curve." Jan & Dean's successful partnership ended in 1966 when Berry slammed his Corvette Stingray into a parked truck at a speed of 145 km/h (90 mph) on a Beverly Hills street. Although he suffered partial paralysis and brain damage from the accident, Berry pursued his music career well into the 1990s; his solo album *Second Wave* was released in 1997.

Journalist and author Pierre Berton

Zuma Press

Berton, Pierre, Canadian print and broadcast journalist (b. July 12, 1920, Whitehorse, Yukon Territory—Nov. 30, 2004, Toronto, Ont.), wrote popular works on national history, such as *Klondike* (1958), which chronicled the gold rush; *The National Dream* (1970), a story about the Canadian Pacific Railway; and *The Invasion of Canada* (1980), which recounted the War of 1812. Though widely known as a television host, Berton was also a regular columnist for Canadian newspapers and magazines, the author of some 50 books, and managing editor of *Maclean's* magazine in the 1950s. In his writings he advocated Canadian nationalism and liberalism.

Blankers-Koen, Fanny (FRANCINA ELSJE BLANKERS-KOEN; "THE FLYING HOUSEWIFE"), Dutch athlete (b. April 26, 1918, near Baarn, Neth.—d. Jan. 25, 2004, Amsterdam, Neth.), confounded her critics and captured gold in the 100-m and 200-m sprints, the 80-m hurdles, and the 4 × 100-m relay at the 1948 Olympic Games in London; at the time of her death, she was still the only woman to have won four track-and-field gold medals at a single Olympics. (Americans Jesse Owens and Carl Lewis won four track gold medals in 1936 and 1984, respectively.) Fanny Koen first competed for The Netherlands at the 1936 Olympics in Berlin, and in the 1940s she set world records in the 100-yd dash, the 80-m hurdles, the high jump, and the long jump. She married her coach, former Olympic triple jumper John Blankers, in 1940. By the time the next Olympics were held in 1948, she was 30 years old, had survived several years of deprivation under the Nazi occupation of The Netherlands, and often trained only twice a week for two hours with her two children in tow. Since women were permitted to compete in only three individual events at the 1948 Games, Blankers-Koen's choice of the two sprints and the hurdles barred her from the high and long jumps, in which she had held the world records since 1943. She was undefeated in 11 races (including heats and semifinals) in eight days and won all four gold medals; it later came out that she had been pregnant at the time. At the 1952 Olympics in Helsinki, Fin., she was ill and had to drop out of the hurdles, which were won by her Australian rival Shirley Strickland de la Hunty (*q.v.*). Blankers-Koen set world records 16 times in eight different events, including the pentathlon in 1951, won five European titles between 1946 and 1950, and won Dutch national championship titles. In 1999 International Association of Athletics Federations named her the greatest female athlete of the 20th century.

Olympic athlete Fanny Blankers-Koen

© KPA/Zuma/Corbis

Boorstin, Daniel Joseph, American social historian (b. Oct. 1, 1914, Atlanta, Ga.—d. Feb. 28, 2004, Washington, D.C.), recounted in his writings the importance of ordinary objects that shape a person's daily life and warned that modern methods of communication were—in an effort to gain the interest of readers or viewers—creating illusions rather than disseminating knowledge. Boorstin majored in English history and literature at Harvard University (B.A., 1934). He obtained a Rhodes scholarship to Balliol College, Oxford, where he took first-class degrees in history (1936) and civil law (1937). Boorstin was admitted to the bar at the Inner Temple in London before returning to the U.S., where he taught history at Harvard and Radcliffe College while he earned his law degree (1940) at Yale University. He was admitted to the Massachusetts bar in 1942 and practiced law while teaching history at Swarthmore College. In 1944 Boorstin joined the history faculty at the University of Chicago, where he remained until 1969. Boorstin was briefly a member of the Communist Party during the late 1930s but became increasingly conservative in his political views over time; in 1953 he presented the House Un-American Activities Committee with the names of other communists. He became increasingly conservative and was a severe critic of the radicals of the 1960s. Among Boorstin's principal writings were *The Lost World of Thomas Jefferson* (1948); *The Genius of American Politics* (1953); *The Image, or What Happened to the American Dream* (1962; published in paperback as *The Image: A Guide to Pseudo-Events in America*), in which he analyzed the influence of the media on American culture; and his especially popular trilogy on the social history of the United States, *The Americans,* comprising *The Colonial Experience* (1958), *The National Experience* (1965), and *The Democratic Experience* (1973), which received the Pulitzer Prize for history in 1974. His later works included *The Discoverers* (1983), *The Creators* (1992), and *The Seekers* (1998), a trilogy about geographic, creative, and intellectual discovery. In 1969 he became director of the National Museum of History and Technology at the Smithsonian Institution, now known as the American History Museum. Despite some liberal opposition, Boorstin was appointed librarian of Congress in 1975; in this post he attempted to make the institution more accessible to the public by ordering the large bronze doors to be kept open, installing a picnic area on the terrace, and organizing concerts and cultural events. He also served (1983–88) on the Encyclopædia Britannica board of editors.

AP/Wide World Photos

Brando, Marlon, American actor (b. April 3, 1924, Omaha, Neb.—d. July 1, 2004, Los Angeles, Calif.), brought a revolutionary new attitude to film acting in the 1950s—finding small details that added dimension to and insight into his characters and employing a raw, visceral, spontaneous, and naturalistic delivery instead of the deliberate, controlled style that most actors usually employed—and became an icon for generations of Method actors. Although his early performances led many people to consider him the finest actor of the 20th century, much of his later work was erratic and disappointed his audience. After his expulsion from a military school during his senior year, Brando moved (1943) to New York City. There he studied acting at the Dramatic Workshop of the New School for Social Research. He made his Broadway debut in *I Remember Mama* (1944). Three years and several shows later, Brando burst into Broadway stardom with his sensually brutal portrayal of Stanley Kowalski in *A Streetcar*

Named Desire. He made his motion picture debut in 1950 in *The Men*, and in 1951 he returned to the character of Kowalski for the film version of *Streetcar*, garnering his first Academy Award nomination. He was nominated again for *Viva Zapata!* (1952) and *Julius Caesar* (1953) and played one of his most famous roles, the leader of a motorcycle gang in *The Wild One* (1953), before winning his first best-actor Oscar for the role that many considered his finest performance—as Terry Malloy, an ex-boxer who lost his chance to be a contender when he threw a fight but later finds the inner strength to testify about union corruption on the docks, in *On the Waterfront* (1954). Brando followed with a string of uneven efforts, including *Guys and Dolls* (1955), *Sayonara* (1957), for which he received another Oscar nomination, and *One-Eyed Jacks* (1961), which he also directed, before returning to form, and another Oscar win, in *The Godfather* (1972). Although he refused that award in protest against Hollywood's treatment of Native Americans, he was nominated again in 1974 for his intense performance in the sexually explicit *L'ultimo tango a Parigi* (1972; *Last Tango in Paris*). Among Brando's few films over the next several years were *Superman* (1978), *Apocalypse Now* (1979), *A Dry White Season* (1989), for which he was nominated for a best-supporting-actor Oscar, *The Freshman* (1990), in which he spoofed his *Godfather* character, and *Don Juan DeMarco* (1995), considered the most popular of his last films. Brando published an autobiography, *Songs My Mother Taught Me*, in 1994.

Screen legend Marlon Brando as Stanley Kowalski

Branigan, Laura, American pop singer (b. July 3, 1957, Brewster, N.Y.—d. Aug. 26, 2004, East Quogue, N.Y.), enjoyed a string of hits in the 1980s, most notably "Gloria" in 1982. The song spent 36 weeks on the pop charts. Later she scored hits with "Solitaire," "Self Control," and "How Am I Supposed to Live Without You?" She acted occasionally in films and on television, and in 2002 she starred in *Love, Janis*, a musical about Janis Joplin.

Pop star Laura Branigan

Brizola, Leonel de Moura, Brazilian politician (b. Jan. 22, 1922, Carazinho, Braz.—d. June 21, 2004, Rio de Janeiro, Braz.), was a left-wing leader who sparked a fiercely loyal following when he attempted to thwart the military coup that overthrew Pres. João Goulart in 1964; as a result, both men were exiled to Uruguay. At age 25 Brizola began his political career when he represented the Brazilian Labour Party in the state legislature. Seven years later he served as federal deputy in Congress, and at age 36 he became the youngest state governor in Brazilian history when he was elected to the office in Rio Grande do Sul. Soon after he returned from exile in 1979, Brizola founded the Democratic Labour Party and served as its president. Although his campaigns for the presidency in 1989 and 1994 were unsuccessful, Brizola was elected state governor of Rio de Janeiro twice (1982–86; 1990–94).

Broca, Philippe de (PHILIPPE-CLAUDE-ALEX DE BROCA DE FERRUSSAC), French film director (b. March 15, 1933, Paris, France—d. Nov. 26, 2004, Neuilly-sur-Seine, France), achieved international success in the 1960s with his irreverent comedies, including the espionage spoof *L'Homme de Rio* (1964; *That Man from Rio*) and the antiwar satire *Le Roi de couer* (1966; *The King of Hearts*). A former assistant to New Wave directors François Truffaut and Claude Chabrol, Broca made some 40 movies, most of which he wrote or co-wrote. His last film, *Vipère au poing* (*Viper in the Fist*), was released just weeks before his death.

Brown, Herbert (HERBERT BROVARNIK), British-born American chemist (b. May 22, 1912, London, Eng.—d. Dec. 19, 2004, Lafayette, Ind.), did extensive research into the chemical element boron and advanced the field of organic chemistry with the development of a class of chemicals called organoboranes—compounds of boron, carbon, and hydrogen. Organoboranes proved to be extremely useful in synthesizing carbon compounds, both for laboratory research and for industrial purposes, including the production of pharmaceutical and agricultural chemicals. He was awarded the Nobel Prize for Chemistry in 1979 together with German chemist Georg Wittig. Brown received both a B.S. (1936) and a Ph.D. (1938) in chemistry from the University of Chicago. He taught there and at Wayne University (now Wayne State) in Detroit, but he spent most of his academic career as a professor (1947–78) at Purdue University, West Lafayette, Ind. He was elected to the National Academy of Sciences in 1957 and was awarded the U.S. National Medal of Science in 1969.

Brown, (Elizabeth) Iona, British violinist and conductor (b. Jan. 7, 1941, Salisbury, Wiltshire, Eng.—d. June 5, 2004, Salisbury), directed (1974–80) London's Academy of St. Martin in the Fields chamber orchestra during the time that it became one of the most recorded in the world. Born into a family of musicians (her three siblings all performed professionally), she established herself as a soloist and conductor before assuming directing roles at St. Martin and later in Oslo, Los Angeles, and Birmingham, Eng. She was appointed OBE in 1986.

Brown, Roosevelt, American football player (b. Oct. 20, 1932, Charlottesville, Va.—d. June 9, 2004, Columbus, N.J.), manned the left-tackle position on the offensive line for the New York Giants and was instrumental in helping the team win one National Football League title and six division titles. Brown was drafted out of Morgan State College (now Morgan State University), Baltimore, Md., in 1953 and during his 13-year playing career (1956–63) with the Giants was named to eight All-Pro teams. He was enshrined in the Pro Football Hall of Fame in 1975. Brown went on to coach and scout for the Giants after his playing career ended.

Bruce, Robert Arthur, American cardiologist (b. Nov. 20, 1916, Boston, Mass.—d. Feb. 12, 2004, Seattle, Wash.), invented the treadmill cardiac stress test used to diagnose heart disease. Considered the founder of exercise cardiology, he created the Bruce Protocol in the early 1960s, monitoring the heart signals of a patient on a treadmill set at successive stages of difficulty.

Bucher, Lloyd Mark, ("PETE"), U.S. naval officer (b. Sept. 1, 1927, Pocatello, Idaho—d. Jan. 28, 2004, Poway, Calif.), commanded the American intelligence ship USS *Pueblo* until its capture by the North Korean navy. The *Pueblo* was patrolling off the coast of North Korea on Jan. 23, 1968, engaging in surveillance, when it was surrounded and fired upon by North Korean ships. Wounded in the attack along with 10 others (including one who died of his injuries), Bucher surrendered the *Pueblo* without having fired a shot in defense. He and his 82 surviving crew members spent 11 months in captivity, experiencing torture and deprivation. After Bucher's release, a board of naval officials recommended his court-martial for having given up his ship without resisting, but Navy Secretary John H. Chafee rejected the recommendation. The surviving crew members were finally awarded POW medals by the U.S. government more than 20 years later.

Bullock, Alan Louis Charles, British historian (b. Dec. 13, 1914, Trowbridge, Wiltshire, Eng.—d. Feb. 2, 2004, Oxford, Eng.), was founding master of St. Catherine's College, Oxford, and the author of major historical studies and biographies, notably *Hitler: A Study in Tyranny* (1952), *Hitler and Stalin: Parallel Lives* (1991), and the three-volume *The Life and Times of Ernest Bevin* (1960, 1967, and 1983). His other principal historical works included *The Humanist Tradition in the West* (1985). Bullock was educated at Bradford Grammar School and Wadham College, Oxford, and took first-class degrees in both classical greats (1936) and modern history (1938). After working for the BBC during World War II, he took up a fellowship at New College, Oxford, where he taught modern history and served as dean. He became known to the general public by appearing on the BBC radio program *The Brains Trust.* In 1952 Bullock became head of the St. Catherine's Society (for students unable to afford residence at a college), and he was instrumental in its transformation into St. Catherine's College in 1962. He was master of St. Catherine's until 1980 and served as vice-chancellor of the university from 1969 to 1973. Outside Oxford, he served as chairman of the National Advisory Committee on the Training and Supply of Teachers (1963–65), the School's Council (1966–69), the Committee of Inquiry into Reading and the Use of English (1972–74), and the Committee of Inquiry on Industrial Democracy (1976–77). He was a founding member of the Social Democratic Party (later the Liberal Democratic Party). He was knighted in 1972 and was made a life peer, as Baron Bullock of Leafield, in 1976.

Burchfield, R(obert) W(illiam), New Zealand-born British scholar and lexicographer (b. Jan. 27, 1923, Wanganui, N.Z.—d. July 5, 2004, Abingdon, Oxfordshire, Eng.), ushered into print the four-volume *Supplement to the Oxford English Dictionary* (1972–86); he was personally responsible for adding words and phrases of non-British origin as well as controversial vulgarisms to the OED. Burchfield moved to England in 1949 as a Rhodes scholar at the University of Oxford and held several teaching posts there. He was named editor of the *Supplement* in 1957 and was chief editor of Oxford English Dictionaries from 1971 to 1984. A noted workaholic, he also wrote and edited a number of books on language, including *The New Fowler's Modern English Usage,* 3rd ed. (1996). Burchfield was made CBE in 1975.

Butler, Richard Girnt, American white supremacist (b. Feb. 23, 1918, near Denver, Colo.—d. Sept. 8, 2004, Hayden, Idaho), founded (1973) the Aryan Nations group and served as leader of its world headquarters, an 8-ha (20-ac) compound in Idaho. The group was bankrupted in 2000 and had to sell its property, however, after the Southern Poverty Law Center won a judgment of $6.3 million in a civil lawsuit it had filed on behalf of two Native Americans whom the compound's guards had assaulted in 1998.

Cahill, Joe (JOSEPH CAHILL), Irish paramilitary organization leader (b. May 19, 1920, Belfast, Ire.—d. July 23, 2004, Belfast, N.Ire.), dedicated his life to the cause of ending British rule in Northern Ireland and reuniting Ireland; in 1969 he helped to establish the Provisional Irish Republican Army, the paramilitary wing of the IRA. Cahill became active with the IRA in his late teens. In 1942 he and five other IRA members were arrested and sentenced to hang for the shooting of a police officer during an effort to mark the anniversary of the Easter Rising. Just days before his execution date, Cahill's sentence was reduced to life imprisonment. After his release from prison in 1949, he resumed his often-violent involvement with the IRA. After the founding of the "Provos," he served as commander, and in 1973 he was arrested for smuggling weapons into Ireland from Libya. In 1998 Cahill supported the Good Friday Agreement and other peacemaking efforts of the nationalist political party Sinn Fein. He was an honourary vice president of Sinn Fein.

Caminiti, Kenneth Gene, American baseball player (b. April 21, 1963, Hanford, Calif.—d. Oct. 10, 2004, New York, N.Y.), won the National League's Most Valuable Player (MVP) award in 1996 as a member of the San Diego Padres. In 2002 he told *Sports Illustrated* magazine that he had used steroids during his MVP season and warned that Major League Baseball was facing an epidemic of steroid use. Caminiti's 15-year career included stints with four teams and three invitations to the All-Star Game as a third baseman.

Cantalupo, Jim (JAMES RICHARD CANTALUPO), American businessman (b. Nov. 14, 1943, Oak Park, Ill.—d. April 19, 2004, Orlando, Fla.), established the McDonald's Corp. as an international presence and revived the slumping fast-food giant during his second term as the company's CEO. A graduate of the University of Illinois, he started his career as a CPA for the accounting firm Arthur Young (later Ernst & Young). While Cantalupo was there, one of his clients was the McDonald's Corp, which soon hired him away; he took over as the firm's controller in 1974. Cantalupo quickly advanced through the corporate ranks, with appointments as vice president (1975), senior vice president (1981), chief of operations for the northeastern U.S. (1985), and president of McDonald's International (1987). Under his leadership the number of restaurants abroad increased enormously, and he opened the first McDonald's locations in Russia and China. His performance earned him the title of president and CEO in 1991. Cantalupo guided the company through a period of rapid expansion until his retirement in 2001. His departure coincided with a dip in company revenues, a wave of restaurant closures, and increased scrutiny of the negative health aspects of fast food. Cantalupo later was called out of retirement, and he rejoined McDonald's as chairman and CEO on Jan. 1, 2003. Over the next 16 months, his innovations, including the introduction of healthier menu items, resulted in a major increase in the company's stock price.

Cartier-Bresson, Henri, French photographer (b. Aug. 22, 1908, Chanteloup, France—d. Aug. 3, 2004, Céreste, France), was a master of street photography, capturing enduring images of spontaneous though impeccably composed and timed glimpses—waiting for what he called "the decisive moment"—both of everyday life and of many of the 20th century's most important historical events and people. With his artistic photojournalism he set a standard for excellence that served as an inspiration and a challenge to those who followed. Cartier-Bresson rejected the idea of going into the family textile business and studied art instead before switching to photography. In the early 1930s he began using a small Leica to shoot black-and-white photos in natural light. He preferred to be unobtrusive, blending into the cultures he was preparing to photograph and often camouflaging parts of his camera. He was meticulous in his framing of shots, and he would not allow his pictures to be cropped. In 1932 he took one of the most famous of his iconic photos—that of a man whose leap above a puddle near a Paris train station is echoed by posters behind him. Cartier-Bresson traveled extensively, and photos taken on his trips were published in a number of magazines. In 1933 in Madrid he had the first of his numerous exhibitions; shows in Mexico City and New York City followed soon thereafter. Cartier-Bresson also worked in film. In addition to making his own documentaries, he assisted Jean Renoir on such motion pictures as *Une partie de campagne* (1936; *A Day in the Country*) and *La Règle du jeu* (1939; *The Rules of the Game,* 1950).

© Alain Nogues/Corbis Sygma

Master photographer Henri Cartier-Bresson

During his army service in World War II, Cartier-Bresson was taken prisoner by the Germans. He escaped on his third attempt, joined the Resistance, and helped document the German occupation and retreat and the return home of French prisoners and deportees. In 1947 Cartier-Bresson helped found the Magnum Photos cooperative agency. He remained affiliated with Magnum until 1966, when he largely gave up photography and turned to drawing. Cartier-Bresson and his photographs were the subjects of a number of books, of which the most notable was *Images à la sauvette* (1952; *The Decisive Moment*).

Casey, Albert Vincent, American businessman (b. Feb. 28, 1920, Boston, Mass.—d. July 10, 2004, Dallas, Texas), led American Airlines through the first years of deregulation and later oversaw the dismantling of failed savings and loan institutions. After eight years as president of the Times Mirror Co. in Los Angeles, Casey became president and chairman of the board of American Airlines in 1974. The company had prospered under the Civil Aeronautics Board, which regulated routes and fares, but was having increasing financial difficulties that were exacerbated by deregulation. Casey moved the headquarters of American Airlines from New York City to Fort Worth, Texas, in 1979 and returned the airline to profitability. He retired as president in 1980 and as chairman in 1985. In 1991 he was appointed president and CEO of the Resolution Trust Corp., which was created by Congress to sell the assets of failed savings and loan associations after a rash of failures; he held that position until 1993.

Cave, Hugh Barnett, American pulp-fiction author (b. July 11, 1910, Chester, Eng.—d. June 27, 2004, Vero Beach, Fla.), entertained and astonished readers with engaging stories covering a wide range of genres, including science fiction, westerns, romances, detective yarns, adventures, supernatural and horror tales, and, during World War II, even military nonfiction. Cave's lifelong writing career began at age 15, when his first short story, "Retribution," was published in the *Boston Globe*. He was best known for his bizarre plots, which appeared in pulp magazines such as *Horror Stories, Spicy Adventure, Thrilling Mystery, Weird Tales,* and *Strange Tales,* for which he wrote his famous New England vampire story "Murgunstrumm." Cave continued to write stories well into his 90s; his shudder-pulp voodoo novel *The Mountains of Madness* was published shortly before his death.

Chang, Iris Shun-Ru, American historian (b. March 28, 1968, Princeton, N.J.—d. Nov. 9, 2004, Los Gatos, Calif.), documented, in the best-selling book *The Rape of Nanking: The Forgotten Holocaust of World War II* (1997), the mass atrocities of murder and rape committed by the Japanese military while destroying the Chinese city during the Nanking Massacre of 1937–38. Her books *Thread of the Silkworm* (1995) and *The Chinese in America* (2003) examined Chinese American history. Her death was an apparent suicide.

© Handout/Reuters/Corbis

Charles, Pierre, Dominican politician (b. June 30, 1954, Grand Bay, Dominica—d. Jan. 6, 2004, Roseau, Dominica), was selected by Dominica Labour Party leaders to become prime minister of the country after the death of Roosevelt Douglas in 2000. A onetime schoolteacher, Charles was elected to the parliament in 1985 after having denounced the 1983 U.S. invasion of Grenada. As prime minister he implemented a series of austerity measures that elicited labour strikes but also prompted the IMF in December 2003 to approve a special three-year credit to be used to combat poverty.

Charles, Ray (RAY CHARLES ROBINSON; "THE GENIUS"), American musician (b. Sept. 23, 1930, Albany, Ga.—d. June 10, 2004, Beverly Hills, Calif.), sang with a rough voice, original style, and raw passion that made him one of the most popular and influential performers of the 20th century. He treated ballads and pop with original blues and gospel-music inflections, introducing the "soul music" style that influenced singers from early rock musicians to 21st-century pop divas; he also became a country music innovator by singing Nashville laments accompanied by string sections and his own bluesy piano. Born into dire poverty, Charles was raised by his mother and had completely lost his eyesight by the age of seven. By then he had already begun playing piano; he learned to read music by braille at Florida's state school for the blind in St. Augustine. In his teens he toured as a pianist in blues bands, and by 1950 he was singing blues in a Nat King Cole-like manner. His original style emerged in the later 1950s as he led an outstanding small band, including saxophonists David ("Fathead") Newman and Hank Crawford, and made rhythm-and-blues hits (including "Talking About You" and "Lonely Avenue") from thinly disguised gospel songs. "What'd I Say?" (1959), his first million-seller, and "Hit the Road, Jack" (1961), a number one hit, both featured the Raelettes, his female vocal quartet. His ventures with a string-orchestra setting yielded hits in "Georgia on My Mind" (number one, 1960) and a superior country song, "I Can't Stop Loving You" (1962); he also began leading a big jazz band and played both piano and alto saxophone on instrumental albums. His personal life was often stormy: he fathered 11 or 12 children, and he endured an almost 20-year heroin addiction before ending it in 1965. His repertoire of pop songs, including Broadway tunes and "America the Beautiful," expanded over the years as he became an American favourite through extensive touring, television appearances, and films (including *The Blues Brothers*); altogether he won 12 Grammy Awards. His autobiography, *Brother Ray,* appeared in 1978.

Paul Warner/WireImage.com

Music original Ray Charles

Charles, (William) John ("THE GENTLE GIANT"), Welsh association football (soccer) player (b. Dec. 27, 1931, Cwmdu, Wales—d. Feb. 21, 2004, Wakefield, West Yorkshire, Eng.), was hailed as the best footballer ever to come out of Wales, which he represented 38 times in international matches, including Wales's only World Cup appearance in 1958; he was also the first British footballer to achieve success in Italy. At age 16 Charles signed with Leeds United, for which he played both centre-half and centre-forward. In 1953–54 he scored 42 goals, and two years later he helped Leeds win promotion to the First Division, where he scored 38 goals in 40 games that season. In 1957 the Italian team Juventus paid Leeds a then-record £65,000 (about $181,500) transfer fee to acquire him. During his five years (1957–62) with Juventus, the team won three Serie A championships and two Italian Cups, while Charles scored 93 goals in 155 matches, was named Italy's Player of the Year his first season, and was twice a finalist for European Player of the Year. He returned briefly to Leeds United in 1962, played for Rome (1962–63) and Cardiff City (1963–66), and then managed Hereford United (1966–71). The massive 1.88-m (6-ft 2-in) Charles was dubbed *Il buon gigante* ("The Gentle Giant") by his rabid Italian fans for his unusual agility and his mild temperament even when provoked—in his 18-year career he was never cautioned or sent off. Charles was made CBE in 2001.

Chase, Merrill Wallace, American immunologist (b. Sept. 17, 1905, Providence, R.I.—d. Jan. 5, 2004, New York, N.Y.), discovered the importance of white blood cells in the human immune system. Previous to his work, the scientific community believed that humoral immunity, which involves antibodies, constituted the body's only defense against disease. In the early 1940s, however, Chase found that he could not transfer immunity to tuberculosis from one guinea pig to another by using antibodies in blood serum. When he transferred white blood cells, he successfully immunized the animal and thus identified the second branch of the immune system, cell-mediated immunity. He was elected to the National Academy of Sciences in 1975.

Chern, Shiing-shen, Chinese American mathematician (b. Oct. 26, 1911, Jiaxing, Zhejiang province, China—d. Dec. 3, 2004, Tianjin, China), advanced the field of differential geometry with new insights into the curvature of objects. His study of the "characteristic classes" of surfaces had resonance in such disparate fields as physics and computer graphics. Chern was educated in China, Germany, and France and taught in China and the U.S. In 1981 he cofounded the Mathematical Sciences Research Institute at the University of California, Berkeley, where a chair was later endowed in his name. In 1985 he established the Institute for Mathematics at Nankai University, his alma mater in Tianjin. In part through his efforts, by the century's end differential geometry, a field that had languished in the early 20th century, had been elevated to a major discipline in mathematics.

Child, Julia Carolyn McWilliams, American chef, television personality, and author (b. Aug. 15, 1912, Pasadena, Calif.—d. Aug. 13,

TV chef Julia Child

2004, Montecito, Calif.), brought the art of French cookery to a vast number of Americans through her books and, especially, her programs on public television. With an outsize personality to match her towering 1.9-m (6-ft 2-in) frame and hearty voice, she endeared herself to her audience, demystifying the creation of French cuisine, unpretentiously letting any difficulties or mistakes show, and signing off with a jaunty "Bon appetit!" Child was educated at Smith College, Northampton, Mass., and worked at a few inconsequential jobs before joining the Office of Strategic Services during World War II and being sent to Ceylon (now Sri Lanka). After the war she married Paul Child, whom she had met in Ceylon, and because of his work for the United States Information Agency, they lived first in Washington, D.C., and then in Paris. Desiring to improve her cooking skills, she attended the well-known Cordon Bleu cooking school. In 1951 Child and two French friends, Simone Beck and Louisette Bertholle, founded their own school, L'École des Trois Gourmandes, and set about to write a cookbook for the American market. They continued to work on it as the Childs moved to various postings and finally settled in Cambridge, Mass., and in 1961 the first volume of *Mastering the Art of French Cooking* was published, to instant acclaim. A promotional appearance on television led to an offer to host a cooking series on Boston's public television station, and *The French Chef* began in 1962 and went on to comprise 206 episodes, shown all over the U.S. She won a Peabody Award in 1965 and an Emmy Award in 1966. Shows that followed included *Julia Child and Company* (1978), *Dinner at Julia's* (premiered 1983), and *Baking with Julia* (1996). In addition to the second volume of *Mastering the Art of French Cooking* (1970), later books included *The Way to Cook* (1989) and *Cooking with Master Chefs* (1993). In 2000 the French government awarded Child the Legion of Honour, and in 2003 she was given the Presidential Medal of Freedom. A portion of her kitchen and some of her kitchen implements were put on display at the Smithsonian Institution in Washington, D.C.

Chodorov, Jerome, American playwright (b. Aug. 10, 1911, New York, N.Y.—d. Sept. 12, Nyack, N.Y.), authored more than a dozen successful Broadway plays, most notably the comedy *My Sister Eileen* (1940) and its musical adaptation *Wonderful Town* (1953). Chodorov, who was blacklisted in the 1950s as a member of the Communist Party, saw his prospects in Hollywood vanish overnight. He continued to have mixed success on Broadway throughout the 1960s and '70s.

Clough, Brian Howard, British association football (soccer) player and manager (b. March 21, 1935, Middlesbrough, Yorkshire, Eng.—d. Sept. 20, 2004, Derby, Eng.), was a brilliant and charismatic but abrasive and egocentric club manager who twice transformed a Second Division football club into the Premier League champion. After scoring 251 goals in 274 games as a player with Middlesbrough (1952–61) and Sunderland (1961–64)—and failing to score in two matches for England (1959)—Clough suffered a career-ending injury and turned to managing Hartlepools in the Fourth Division. In 1967 he joined Derby County, pushing that club to the Second Division title (1969) and the League title (1972). At Nottingham Forest (1975–93), he guided that club from the bottom half of the Second Division to promotion to the First Division (1977), the league championship (1978), four League Cups (1978–79, 1989–90), and two European Cups (1979–80). Unfortunately, he never again had such success, and when he retired at the end of the 1993 season, Nottingham was relegated back to the Second Division. Clough was named Manager of the Year in 1978 and was made OBE in 1991.

Coleman, Cy (SEYMOUR KAUFMAN), American jazz pianist and composer (b. June 14, 1929, New York, N.Y.—d. Nov. 18, 2004, New York City), was at first a classical pianist but then turned to jazz and began partnering with lyricists to write songs. Many of them became popular standards, as did songs from his numerous Broadway musicals and motion picture scores. Coleman, a musical prodigy, began classical piano lessons at age four and made his Carnegie Hall debut at age seven. He was educated at New York's High School of Music and Art and at the New York College of Music and began playing popular music and jazz at cocktail lounges, nightclubs, and parties. Coleman soon began teaming with lyricists; most notable among these was Carolyn Leigh, with whom he had a long and productive, though stormy, relationship. Among their hits were "Witchcraft" (1955), "The Best Is Yet to Come" (1959), "Hey, Look Me Over" from their score for the Broadway musical *Wildcat* (1960), and "I've Got Your Number" and "Real Live Girl" from their score for *Little Me* (1962). Coleman then collaborated with Dorothy Fields on *Sweet Charity* (1964), which yielded three popular songs—"Hey, Big Spender," "If My Friends Could See Me Now," and "The Rhythm of Life"—and on *Seesaw* (1973). *I Love My Wife*, written with Michael Stewart. followed in 1977, and in 1978 came Coleman's first Tony Award-winning score, for *On the Twentieth Century*, with book and lyrics by Betty Comden and Adolph Green. Coleman also won Tonys for *City of Angels* (1980) and *The Will Rogers Follies* (1981). Later stage musicals included *Welcome to the Club* (1989) and *The Life* (1997). Coleman also produced television specials and composed scores for films.

Cooke, Alistair (ALFRED COOKE), British-born American broadcaster and journalist (b. Nov. 20, 1908, Salford, Greater Manchester, Eng.—d. March 30, 2004, New York, N.Y.), charmed and enlightened radio and television audiences on both sides of the Atlantic for more than five decades. His quarter-hour *Letter from America* (originally called *American Letter*) on BBC—broadcast from March 1946 to February 2004 and totaling 2,869 shows—took his personal observations to more than 50 countries and became the longest-running radio program in the world; meanwhile, as a remarkably erudite TV host on the arts magazine show *Omnibus* from 1952 to 1961 and PBS's *Masterpiece Theatre* from 1971 to 1992, he became a familiar presence in many American homes. While a student at Jesus College, Cambridge, Cooke edited a literary magazine, became active in theatre, and (on his 22nd birthday) changed his first name from Alfred to the more sophisticated Alistair. He earned a bachelor's degree summa cum laude (1930) and an education diploma (1931) and was awarded a fellowship for studies in the U.S., which took place at Yale University and Harvard University. Travels throughout the country during

those years ignited Cooke's interest in the American scene, and following brief stints as a Hollywood screenwriter, a BBC film critic in London, and the London correspondent for NBC, he returned (1937) to the U.S., settled in New York City, and became (1941) an American citizen. Besides continuing his BBC broadcasts, including the first of his *Letter from America* programs, he worked as a freelance writer for a number of British publications and in the mid-1940s began what would become 26 years of service as a correspondent for *The Manchester Guardian* (now *The Guardian*). Texts of many *Letter from America* programs were published in such collections as *One Man's America* (1952) and *Talk About America* (1968). Cooke's observations were also put forth in the 13-part BBC-produced NBC series *America: A Personal History of the United States* and in the best-selling book based on it, *Alistair Cooke's America* (1973). Other of his books included *Six Men* (1977), *Masterpieces* (1981), and *America Observed* (1988). Among Cooke's honours were Peabody Awards in 1951, 1972, and 1982 for outstanding contributions in radio broadcasting and television and an honorary knighthood in 1973.

Cooper, (Leroy) Gordon, Jr., American astronaut (b. March 6, 1927, Shawnee, Okla.—d. Oct. 4, 2004, Ventura, Calif.), made history

AP/Wide World Photos

Mercury astronaut Gordon Cooper

as one of the most enduring names in the U.S. space program. Cooper was one of seven pilots chosen for the Mercury series of one-man spacecraft, and he was the youngest member of the first generation of American manned spaceflight. Before NASA selected him from more than 100 candidates in April 1959, Cooper earned a B.S. in aeronautical engineering (1956) from the Air Force Institute of Technology, Wright-Patterson Air Force Base, Ohio, and served as a test pilot at Edwards Air Force Base, California. Cooper, whose nickname "Gordo" was immortalized in the book (1979) and film (1983) *The Right Stuff*, spent four years watching his fellow astronauts reach for the stars before his turn came on May 15, 1963. Piloting the capsule Faith 7 on the final Mercury mission, he set a U.S. record by completing 22 orbits of the Earth and remaining in space for 34 hours and 20 minutes. When the capsule's automatic landing system failed on reentry, Cooper manually guided it to within eight kilometres (five miles) of his U.S. Navy recovery ship. He made history again on Aug. 21, 1965, when he commanded the Gemini 5 mission and became the first person to reach orbit twice. Although equipment problems caused them to fall one hour shy of that mission's eight-day target, Cooper and fellow astronaut Charles Conrad were successful in conducting a series of experiments and exercises that paved the way for the Apollo program. At the time of his retirement from the air force in 1970, Cooper had amassed more than 225 hours in space and had served as backup commander for the Gemini 12 and Apollo 10 missions. His memoir, *Leap of Faith: An Astronaut's Journey into the Unknown* (2000), caused a stir with claims of UFO contact and government cover-ups.

Copper, Bob (ROBERT JAMES COPPER), British traditional folk singer and folklorist (b. Jan. 6, 1915, Rottingdean, East Sussex, Eng.—d. March 29, 2004, Brighton, East Sussex, Eng.), was considered by many to be the patriarch of traditional English folk music. Having inherited a 200-year tradition of family singing from his father, grandfather, and uncle, Copper began performing in public with his family at an early age. The family later came to the attention of the BBC, which arranged a live radio broadcast in 1950 and engaged Copper to collect folk music and regional dialects. He wrote books to accompany several Copper Family records, notably *A Song for Every Season: A Hundred Years of a Sussex Farming Family* (1971) and *Songs and Southern Breezes* (1973). He also wrote several volumes detailing rural life, including *Early to Rise: A Sussex Boyhood* (1976). By the time they recorded *Coppersongs 3* (1998), the Copper Family had grown to include Bob, his two children, and all six grandchildren.

Cornell, Don (LUIGI FRANCISCO VARLARO), American singer (b. April 21, 1919, Bronx, N.Y.—d. Feb. 23, 2004, Aventura, Fla.), recorded a series of hit ballads in the 1950s and early '60s and sold more than 50 million records during his career. Cornell, a baritone, joined bandleader Sammy Kaye's orchestra at the age of 23 and scored one of his early major hits in 1950 with his rendition of "It Isn't Fair." Soon afterward, Cornell struck out on his own, and he crooned his way to stardom with "I'll Walk Alone," "Hold My Hand," and "Love Is a Many-Splendored Thing." Even into his 80s he was a regular on the supper-club circuit.

Counsilman, Doc (JAMES EDWARD COUNSILMAN), American coach (b. Dec. 28, 1920, Birmingham, Ala.—d. Jan. 4, 2004, Bloomington, Ind.), was widely recognized as one of the greatest coaches in the history of swimming and its leading innovator. He guided the 1964 and 1976 U.S. men's Olympic teams to a combined 21 gold medals and the Indiana University men's team to 6 National Collegiate Athletic Association championships (1968–73) and 20 consecutive Big Ten titles (1961–80); among the swimmers he coached was Mark Spitz. Noted for his scientific approach to the sport, Counsilman introduced the pace clock and pool lane markers and was an authority on stroke technique; his *The Science of Swimming* (1968) continued to be essential. In 1979, at age 58, Counsilman became the then-oldest person to have swum across the English Channel. He was inducted into the International Swimming Hall of Fame in 1976.

Cox, Archibald, American lawyer (b. May 17, 1912, Plainfield, N.J.—d. May 29, 2004, Brooksville, Maine), spent many years in government and teaching positions before serving for five months in 1973 as special prosecutor during the Watergate scandal until Pres. Richard M. Nixon ordered his firing—in what came to be known as the Saturday Night Massacre and which helped lead to Nixon's resignation the following year—when he insisted that audiotapes of conversations and phone calls in the Oval Office be turned over to the investigators. Cox later returned to teaching, served as chairman of Common Cause (1980–92), and wrote a number of books.

Crick, Francis Harry Compton, British biologist (b. June 8, 1916, Northampton, Eng.—d. July 28, 2004, San Diego, Calif.), together with American biologist James D. Watson, in 1953 made what was widely considered the most momentous discovery in modern biology: the double-helix structure of large molecules of DNA. Crick and Watson were endeavouring to understand the molecular nature of genetic material when they discovered DNA's structure. They quickly determined how the double-helix structure gives DNA unique properties for retaining and replicating the genetic information of living things. For their discoveries Crick and Watson, along with New Zealand-born British biophysicist Maurice Wilkins (*q.v.*), were awarded the Nobel Prize for Physiology or Medicine in 1962. Crick went on to play a major role in advancing knowledge in the field of molecular biology. Among other accomplishments, he showed how the sequence of molecular subunits along a strand of DNA in a cell carries information designating the structure of proteins needed for the cell's life functions. In the late 1970s Crick turned away from molecular biology in order to study problems in neurobiology, in particular the biological basis for consciousness. *The Astonishing Hypothesis: The Scientific Search for the Soul* (1994) presented his view that all manifestations of the soul can essentially be reduced to the activity of the brain. Crick

© Bettmann/Corbis

studied physics at University College, London (B.Sc., 1937). During World War II he served as a physicist under the British Admiralty, but after the war he decided to pursue studies in biology. He joined the University of Cambridge's Strangeways Research Laboratory in 1947, and in 1949 he transferred to the Medical Research Council Unit at the university's Cavendish Laboratories. Crick received his doctorate from Cambridge in 1954. In 1977 he left Britain for the Salk Institute in San Diego, where he held the position of distinguished professor and served (1994–95) as president. Crick was made (1959) a fellow of the Royal Society for his work on DNA, proteins, and viruses; he received the Order of Merit in 1991. *What Mad Pursuit: A Personal View of Scientific Discovery* was published in 1988.

Cullman, Joseph Frederick, III, American executive (b. April 9, 1912, New York, N.Y.—d. April 30, 2004, New York City), oversaw the growth of Philip Morris, Inc., into one of the world's largest corporations. In his 21 years (1957–78) as top executive of the tobacco company, he diversified its holdings, acquiring assets such as Miller Brewing Co. and Seven-Up Co., and revamped the Marlboro brand, which became the world's most popular cigarette. He was also a vocal opponent of antismoking regulations.

Cunningham, Agnes ("SIS"), American folk-song composer (b. Feb. 19, 1909, Watongo, Okla.—d. June 27, 2004, New Paltz, N.Y.), cofounded in 1962 the small but inspirational folk-song journal *Broadside* with her husband, Gordon Friesen. Although its circulation never topped four figures, the journal proved instrumental in promoting folk music that delivered strong leftist political messages during the 1960s; among the more than 1,000 songs published in the journal were Bob Dylan's "Blowin' in the Wind" and Pete Seeger's "Waist Deep in the Big Muddy." An accomplished guitar and accordion player, Cunningham joined Woody Guthrie and Seeger in the 1940s to form the groundbreaking urban folk music group the Almanac Singers; *Dear Mr. President* (c. 1942) was among the group's notable albums. In 1999 *Red Dust and Broadsides,* a joint autobiography written by Cunningham and her husband, was published.

Dalton, Katharina Dorothea Kuipers, British gynecologist (b. Nov. 11, 1916, London, Eng.—d. Sept. 17, 2004, Poole, Dorset, Eng.), identified the symptoms suffered by women before and during their menstrual cycles as those of an actual physical disorder, which she called premenstrual syndrome, or PMS. Dalton noticed that the migraines she normally suffered every month prior to menstruation disappeared during her first pregnancy and that premenstrual symptoms endured by many of her patients disappeared during their pregnancies. She undertook an intensive research program with endocrinologist Raymond Greene; in the early 1950s the pair published their results. Dalton found that test doses of natural progesterone administered to herself and her patients brought swift relief from PMS symptoms. She established (1957) the world's first PMS clinic in London, which she ran for 40 years, and authored more than 100 papers on PMS.

Dangerfield, Rodney (JACOB COHEN), American comedian (b. Nov. 22, 1921, Babylon, N.Y.—d. Oct. 5, 2004, Los Angeles, Calif.), immortalized the line "I don't get no respect" as part of his stand-up comedy act. His perpetually agitated look and hilariously self-deprecating one-liners landed him regular appearances on *The Tonight Show,* and a guest spot on *Saturday Night Live* led to a scene-stealing role in the film *Caddyshack* (1980). Dangerfield enjoyed commercial success in such films as *Easy Money* (1983), *Back to School* (1986), and the animated *Rover Dangerfield* (1991), and he received the Lifetime Creative Achievement Award from the American Comedy Awards in 1994.

© Archive Photos/Getty Images

Disrespected comic Rodney Dangerfield

Danziger, Paula, American children's author (b. Aug. 18, 1944, Washington, D.C.—d. July 8, 2004, New York, N.Y.), wrote more than 30 books, notably the popular Amber Brown series, that presented serious issues with humour and honesty. Danziger was also well known for her warm and flamboyant personal style. Her first book, *The Cat Ate My Gymsuit* (1974), was an immediate success that became a classic of young readers' literature. The Amber Brown series (actually two series, one aimed at middle-school readers and one for younger children) began with *Amber Brown Is Not a Crayon* (1993). Her books, all of which remained in print, won numerous awards.

Dash, Samuel, American lawyer (b. Feb. 27, 1925, Camden, N.J.—d. May 29, 2004, Washington, D.C.), had a more than 50-year-long career, including about 40 years as a professor at Georgetown University Law Center, Washington, D.C., but attained national renown as chief counsel for what was known as the Senate Watergate Committee; his probe into the secret audiotaping system in the White House's Oval Office forced the release of the tapes' contents and led to the 1974 resignation of Pres. Richard M. Nixon. Dash was in the public eye again in the 1990s when he served for four years as ethics adviser to independent counsel Kenneth Starr in the Whitewater investigation but resigned when it became apparent to him that Starr was not impartial but instead was advocating the impeachment of Pres. Bill Clinton.

Davis, (Roquel) Billy, American songwriter and advertising executive (b. July 11, 1932, Detroit, Mich.—d. Sept. 2, 2004, New Rochelle, N.Y.), collaborated with Gwen Gordy and her brother Berry Gordy, Jr., in the 1950s on Jackie Wilson's hits "Reet Petite" and "Lonely Teardrops." In 1958 he cofounded Anna Records, which later evolved into Motown Records. In 1961 Davis moved to Chess Records, where he produced the 1965 hit "Rescue Me." He joined the advertising agency McCann Erickson in 1968 and wrote the hugely popular song "I'd Like to Teach the World to Sing," which was based on his jingle featured in a Coca-Cola advertisement.

Davis, Skeeter (MARY FRANCES PENICK), American country music singer (b. Dec. 30, 1931, Dry Ridge, Ky.—d. Sept. 19, 2004, Nashville, Tenn.), began performing on the *Grand Ole Opry* radio program in 1959 and remained a regular for more than 40 years. Her best-known hit, "The End of the World," climbed high on the pop charts in 1963.

Debreu, Gerard, French-born American economist (b. July 4, 1921, Calais, France—d. Dec. 31, 2004, Paris, France), won the Nobel Memorial Prize in Economic Sciences in 1983 for his examination of how prices affect the balance, or equilibrium, of supply and demand. Debreu's use of mathematical modeling in economics was somewhat uncommon and proved influential in the field. The strength and breadth of his mathematical research bolstered his economic theories, and this strict discipline was evident in his classic monograph *Theory of Value: An Axiomatic Analysis of Economic Equilibrium* (1959). After the Allied landings in June 1944, Debreu interrupted his study of economics at the University of Paris (Ph.D., 1946) to join the army and fight to free France from German occupation. Immigrating to the United States, he joined the Cowles Commission for Research in Economics in 1950; he transferred with that group in 1955 when it moved from Chicago to Yale University. In 1960 he relocated to California to conduct research at Stanford University, before joining the staff of the University of California, Berkeley, in 1962 as a professor of economics and mathematics. The 1983 Nobel honour arrived during his long tenure at Berkeley, from which he retired in 1991. Debreu became a U.S. citizen in 1975.

Dee, Frances, American actress (b. Nov. 26, 1907, Los Angeles, Calif.—d. March 6, 2004,

AP/Wide World Photos

Norwalk, Conn.), was a movie star of the 1930s and '40s who was known for her serene beauty, which was showcased in such films as *An American Tragedy* (1931), *Little Women* (1933), *Of Human Bondage* (1934), and the cult classic *I Walked with a Zombie* (1943). She was married to actor Joel McCrea for 57 years, until his death in 1990, and the couple became two of California's wealthiest landowners.

Dellinger, David, American peace activist (b. Aug. 22, 1915, Wakefield, Mass.—d. May 25, 2004, Montpelier, Vt.), embraced pacifism and civil disobedience for much of his life, being imprisoned twice in the early 1940s for refusing to be drafted and in the 1960s becoming a leader in the anti-Vietnam War movement. He helped organize the 1967 march on and encirclement of the Pentagon that Norman Mailer's book *Armies of the Night* (1968) recounted, and in 1969 he became one of the Chicago Seven defendants tried for criminal conspiracy and incitement to riot following the antiwar demonstrations that took place during the 1968 Democratic national convention. Though Dellinger and four other defendants were found guilty of the incitement charges, the convictions were overturned on appeal.

AP/Wide World Photos

Derrida, Jacques (JACKIE DERRIDA), French philosopher (b. July 15, 1930, El Biar, Alg.—d. Oct. 8, 2004, Paris, France), played a leading role in popularizing the controversial method of reading philosophical texts known as deconstruction. Considered by its opponents a subversive instrument of relativism and nihilism, deconstruction was seen by its adherents as a tool for uncovering, by close reading, hidden blind spots and contradictions (*aporia*) in the texts that could serve as the starting point for going beyond conventional readings. Derrida adopted the notion from German philosopher Martin Heidegger's concept of *Destruktion.* He attempted to apply a radical deconstruction to the works of philosophers Friedrich Nietzsche, Edmund Husserl, Emmanuel Levinas, Heidegger, linguist Ferdinand de Saussure, anthropologist Claude Lévi-Strauss, psychologist Sigmund Freud, and others. Derrida argued that Western philosophy was characterized by a "metaphysics of presence" (privileging of being over appearance) and "logocentrism" (the idea that meanings exist independently of the language used to express them); that Western thought had wrongly privileged speech over writing, treating writing as a mere "supplement"; that what he called "différance" (a term combining the meanings of "difference" and "deferral") was a requirement of all writing; that there was "no escaping from the text," by which he meant that the meaning of a sentence could be given only in other sentences

© Julio Donoso/Corbis Sygma

Controversial philosopher Jacques Derrida

but which had been used as a basis for charges of relativism against him. In the United States, deconstruction was largely associated with literary and cultural criticism, in part because of Derrida's collaboration with critics Paul de Man and J. Hillis Miller at Yale University. Derrida went to school in Algeria, where he faced discrimination because of his Jewishness. He attended the Lycée Louis-le-Grand in Paris for two years before being admitted to the École Normale Supériure in Paris, where he studied under Michel Foucault and Louis Althusser and received his teaching license in 1956. He taught at a lycée in Le Mans, at the Sorbonne (from which he received his doctorate in 1980), and at the École Normale before becoming director of studies at the École des Hautes Études en Sciences Sociales, Paris, in 1984. In 1992 the awarding of an honorary doctorate by the University of Cambridge provoked great opposition and criticism of Derrida by British academics, who maintained that his reputation was due to personal style rather than philosophical accomplishment and that his obscure mode of expression, which included puns and neologisms, was designed to hide philosophical shallowness. Derrida's first publication was a French translation of and introduction to Husserl's *Origins of Geometry* (*Die Frage nach dem Ursprung der Geometrie als intentional-historisches Problem,* 1939). He came to international prominence with three books published in 1967, *De la grammatologie* (*Of Grammatology,* 1976), *La Voix et la phénomène* (*Speech and Phenomena,* 1973), and *L'Écriture et la différance* (*Writing and Difference,* 1978). His later writings departed somewhat, tending rather to be concerned with questions of ethics and politics.

Devonshire, Andrew Robert Buxton Cavendish, 11th duke of, British landowner (b. Jan. 2, 1920, London, Eng.—d. May 3, 2004, Chatsworth House, Derbyshire, Eng.), set an example to other British aristocrats when he paid off crushing inheritance taxes and rescued Chatsworth, his family's vast Derbyshire estate, by putting the 297-room 16th-century house into trust and generating profits through paying visitors and other income-producing measures. The younger son of the 10th duke of Devonshire, he unexpectedly came in line for the title on the death of his older brother, William (a brother-in-law of future U.S. president John F. Kennedy), in 1944. After his father's death in November 1950, the new duke and his wife, the former Deborah Freeman-Mitford (youngest of the six celebrated Mitford sisters), devised varied schemes for paying the inheritance tax (which totaled some $20 million). They donated the family's 16th-century Hardwick House to the nation; sold valuable paintings, thousands of hectares of farmland, and other assets; and turned Chatsworth into a working farm and a popular tourist destination. The duke, who was estimated to be richer than the queen, also was patron to numerous charities, raised Thoroughbred racehorses, and served (1960–64) in Prime Minister Harold Macmillan's cabinet. He was granted a knighthood in 1996.

Di Palma, Carlo, Italian cinematographer (b. April 17, 1925, Rome, Italy—d. July 9, 2004, Rome), created masterful illusions of lighting and colour in order to portray an altered sense of reality in his films. He first gained international recognition for his work as director of photography on Michelangelo Antonioni's experimental films *Il deserto rosso* (1964; *The Red Desert*) and *Blow-Up* (1966). For several years Di Palma focused on Italian comedies, and he made his directorial debut with *Teresa la ladre* (1972; *Teresa the Thief*). Di Palma enjoyed even greater success during the 1980s and '90s when he collaborated with American filmmaker Woody Allen on 11 films, including *Hannah and Her Sisters* (1986),

© Brian Hamill/Getty Images

Cinematographer Carlo Di Palma

Shadows and Fog (1992), and *Deconstructing Harry* (1997).

Distel, Sacha (ALEXANDRE DISTEL), French musician and entertainer (b. Jan. 29, 1933, Paris, France—d. July 22, 2004, Le Rayol-Canadel-sur-Mer, France), established himself as the best jazz guitarist in France by the time he reached his early 20s; his debonair appearance and suave voice also made him popular in the U.S., where he performed alongside such jazz greats as Miles Davis and Dizzy Gillespie. Distel's singing career took off in 1958 with his smash single "Scoubidou." This was followed by a string of hits, including the French versions of Stevie Wonder's "You Are the Sunshine of My Life" (1967) and Burt Bacharach's "Raindrops Keep Falling on My Head" (1970), the song that cemented his fame in the U.K. Distel also hosted several television series and appeared in numerous films; he made his theatrical debut in 2000 in the musical *Chicago.* Distel was awarded the Legion of Honour in 1997.

Djerrkura, Gatjil, Australian Aboriginal leader (b. June 30, 1949, Yirrkala Mission, East Arnhem Land, N.Terr., Australia—d. May 26, 2004, Nhulunbuy, East Arnhem Land), was hereditary leader in the Yolngu Wangurri clan. He devoted his life to the economic, social, and political advancement of Australia's indigenous people and to reconciliation with the federal government, notably as chairman (1996–99) of the Aboriginal and Torres Strait Islander Commission (ATSIC). Djerrkura was one of the first Aboriginals to attend the South Australian Institute of Technology. His success as the head (1986–96) of the Yirrkala Business Enterprises and as chairman (1990–96) of the ATSIC Commercial Development Corp. brought him national attention. Djerrkura's other posts included chairman of the Batchelor Institute of Indigenous Tertiary Education, chairman of the board of the Indigenous Land Corp., and delegate to the 1998 Australian Constitutional Convention. He was awarded a Medal in the Order of Australia in 1984.

Dodd, Sir Coxsone (CLEMENT SEYMOUR DODD), Jamaican record producer and entrepreneur (b. Jan. 26, 1932, Kingston, Jam.—d. May 4, 2004, Kingston), was one of the pioneers of modern Jamaican popular music and played a pivotal role in the development of ska, a blend of Caribbean and jazz rhythms, as well as in the emergence of reggae. Though Dodd grew up in Kingston, it was while working as a cane cutter in the U.S. South that he was exposed to both outdoor dance parties and rhythm and blues. Returning to Jamaica, he became one of the originators of the huge portable sound systems that became a sensation on the island in the 1950s, providing a movable feast of mostly American rhythm-and-blues records. An outstanding cricket player, Dodd was nicknamed Coxsone after a well-known English cricketer from the 1940s, and Dodd's famous sound system was christened Sir Coxsone's Downbeat. Dodd was at the centre of the creation of Jamaica's native ska, whose prime movers included groups such as the Skatalites, the house band at Studio One, the legendary recording studio Dodd established (1963) in Jamaica. As ska progressed toward reggae in the 1960s, Dodd introduced the world to reggae king Bob Marley (a singer with the Wailers), Toots and the Maytals, and later (1970s) Dennis Brown, Burning Spear, and Sugar Minott; in the process, rhythm tracks were developed that became essential elements of Jamaican music. From the 1980s Dodd divided his time between Kingston and New York City, where he operated a record shop. In 1991 Dodd was the recipient of Jamaica's third highest honour, the Order of Distinction.

Dumas, Charles Everett, American athlete (b. Feb. 12, 1937, Tulsa, Okla.—d. Jan. 5, 2004, Inglewood, Calif.), was the first high jumper to clear seven feet and months after accomplishing the feat won a gold medal in the event at the 1956 Olympics in Melbourne, Australia. Knee injuries ended his career in 1964.

Duncan, (Otis) Dudley, American sociologist (b. Dec. 2, 1921, Nocona, Texas—d. Nov. 16, 2004, Santa Barbara, Calif.), showed that education was more influential than social status in determining future success. He was an early leader in the field of quantitative sociology, borrowing statistical models from biology to use in sociology. Duncan was a professor at the Universities of Chicago, Michigan, Arizona, and California, Santa Barbara. Notable among his books were *The American Occupational Structure* (1967) and *Notes on Social Measurement* (1984).

Ebb, Fred, American lyricist (b. April 8, 1928?, New York, N.Y.—d. Sept. 11, 2004, New York City), collaborated with composer John Kander for more than 40 years, and together they created enduring music for a number of classic Broadway shows. Kander and Ebb became legendary not only for such Tony Award-winning shows as *Cabaret* (1966), *Woman of the Year* (1981), and *Kiss of the Spider Woman* (1993)—as well as *Chicago* (1975), whose 2002 film version won a best-picture Oscar—but also for their title song from the film *New York, New York* (1977), which became an anthem for its namesake city. Kander and Ebb teamed up in the early 1960s and soon had written their first hit song, "My Coloring Book." Their first Broadway musical, *Flora, the Red Menace* (1965), marked the first of their many collaborations with Liza Minnelli and, though the show was not a great success, the team's willingness to take chances with edgy subjects led to the hugely popular *Cabaret* the following year. Other projects with Minnelli included the film version of *Cabaret* (1972), the Emmy Award-winning television special *Liza with a Z* (1972), the Broadway show *The Act* (1977), and the film *New York, New York.*

Emerson, Gloria, American journalist (b. May 19, 1929, New York, N.Y.—d. Aug. 3, 2004, New York City), covered the Vietnam War for the *New York Times,* reporting on the impact of the war on the lives of both the Vietnamese people and American soldiers. In 1978 her book about the war, *Winners and Losers* (1976), won the National Book Award. She reported on conflicts throughout the world, including those in Northern Ireland, Palestine, and Nigeria.

Faget, Maxime Allan, American aerospace engineer (b. Aug. 26, 1921, Stann Creek, British Honduras [now Belize]—d. Oct. 9, 2004, Houston, Texas), led the design of the blunt-ended Mercury space capsule that allowed for safe reentry into Earth's atmosphere. He was a leading scientist in the Gemini and Apollo space programs, and his principles were also adopted by the Soviets for their Soyuz program. Faget also contributed to the development of the space shuttle.

Fassie, Brenda, South African pop singer (b. Nov. 3, 1964, Cape Town, S.Af.—d. May 9, 2004, Johannesburg, S.Af.), delighted audiences with her uplifting music and inspiring lyrics, through which she often provided a voice for underprivileged South Africans. Her songs were especially poignant during the period under apartheid, notably "Black President," which was dedicated to Nelson Mandela, who was in prison at the time. Fassie, who sang in English, Xhosa, Sotho, and Zulu, formed the group Brenda and the Big Dudes and rocketed to fame in 1983 with the song "Weekend Special." Although she struggled with a drug problem throughout most of her career, she continued to record a string of best-selling albums, including *Memeza* (1998). Because of her fiery temper and controversial lifestyle, Fassie was dubbed the "black Madonna of the townships" in reference to the American pop idol Madonna.

Favors, Malachi Maghostut, American jazz bassist (b. Aug. 22, 1927, Lexington, Miss.—d. Jan. 30, 2004, Chicago, Ill.), was devoted to a rich, pure, unamplified sound as he played swinging accompaniments and dense, extended solos; he painted his face in ceremo-

Jazz innovator Malachi Favors

nial designs and wore traditional costumes from Africa when he performed. For 38 years, from 1966, he played in the Art Ensemble (later, Art Ensemble of Chicago), a flamboyant, innovative free-jazz group that joined blues, bop, abstraction, African and classical music, and colourful percussion; his earthy bass lines were the unifying element in the Art Ensemble's explorations; he also recorded with such free-jazz masters as Muhal Richard Abrams, Archie Shepp, and the Ritual Trio and led his own groups.

Fischer, O(tto) W(ilhelm), German film actor (b. April 1, 1915, Klosterneuburg, Austria-Hungary [now in Austria]—d. Feb. 1, 2004, Lugano, Switz.), played the lead in dozens of light romantic comedies and historical pieces, becoming one of the highest-paid actors in German-language film in the 1950s; his popularity was at its highest from the early 1940s to the mid-1960s.

Fitzsimmons, (Lowell) Cotton, American basketball coach (b. Oct. 7, 1931, Hannibal, Mo.—d. July 24, 2004, Phoenix, Ariz.), guided teams to the National Basketball Association play-offs 12 times and was twice named NBA Coach of the Year (1979 and 1989). Fitzsimmons began his coaching career in 1958 at Moberly (Mo.) Junior College and moved to Kansas State University in 1967. His NBA career began in 1970 with the Phoenix Suns. He then coached the Atlanta Hawks (1972–76), leading them to the play-offs in his first season with them. After a single season with the Buffalo Braves (1977–78), he served as head coach of the Kansas City Kings (1978–84), leading them to the play-offs four times. Two more play-off appearances came with the San Antonio Spurs (1984–86), after which Fitzsimmons for the second time was head coach of the Phoenix Suns (1988–92), taking them to the play-offs four times. He also coached the Suns in 1996, leading them to the play-offs that year.

Foot, Paul Mackintosh, British investigative journalist and writer (b. Nov. 8, 1937, Haifa, Palestine [now in Israel]—d. July 18, 2004, Stansted, Essex, Eng.), was known and respected for his integrity, his unswerving loyalty to his socialist ideals, and his tireless investigative work on behalf of the powerless. Foot was born into a prominent family (his uncle Michael Foot was the Labour Party leader during 1980–83) and began working for the *Daily Record* shortly after graduation from University College, Oxford. He contributed to the satiric magazine *Private Eye* and to such newspapers as *The Guardian* and the *Socialist Worker* (of which he was editor in 1974–75). His most famous association, however, was with the *Daily Mirror,* for which he contributed an investigative column for 14 years (1979–93). He wrote a number of books, among them *Who Killed Hanratty?* (1971), *Why You Should Be a Socialist* (1977), and *Articles of Resistance* (2000).

Frame, Janet Paterson (JANET PATERSON FRAME CLUTHA), New Zealand writer (b. Aug. 28, 1924, Dunedin, N.Z.—d. Jan. 29, 2004, Dunedin), created a unique body of work that presents perhaps the most recognized voice of New Zealand outside her native country. Although her early life was marked by poverty, illness, and the horrific deaths by drowning of two sisters, she developed an acute appreciation of language and literature. Intensely shy, Frame had a difficult adolescence and early adulthood, and she entered a psychiatric hospital in 1947. During the following eight years, she voraciously read literary classics. She was subject to frequent electroshock therapy and—but for a discovery that she had won a literary prize for *The Lagoon* (1951), her first book of stories—might have undergone a lobotomy (which severs the nerve fibres to the front of the brain). When she was released to the care of the writer Frank Sargeson, she struggled to readjust to life outside the hospital and to continue writing. *Owls Do Cry* (1957), her first novel, was followed by a number of other novels, including *Faces in the Water* (1961), *The Edge of the Alphabet* (1962), and *Scented Gardens for the Blind* (1963), in which she examined meaning in the lives of those on the margins of society from the perspective of one who knew. In addition to a volume of poetry, a children's book, and several more novels and collections of stories, Frame wrote three volumes of autobiography, *To the Is-Land* (1982), *An Angel at My Table* (1984), and *The Envoy from Mirror City* (1985), all of which were tapped for the widely popular movie of her life, *An Angel at My Table* (1990), by New Zealand director Jane Campion. In 1990 Frame was made a Member of the Order of New Zealand, the country's highest civil honour. In 2003 she received one of the inaugural Prime Minister's Awards for Literary Achievement, along with poet Hone Tuwhare and historian Michael King (*q.v.*).

Fujita, Den, Japanese businessman (b. 1926, Osaka, Japan—d. April 21, 2004, Tokyo, Japan), was the charismatic founder of McDonald's Japan, which opened in 1971 and became the largest among all food industries in Japan after only a decade in operation. Fujita adopted Western business practices and a hands-on management style; he made surprise visits to "Golden Arches" restaurants and charmed patrons and employees with his easygoing nature. His empire of more than 3,000 outlets began to crumble, however, when other fast-food chains made their appearance and customers worried that beef might be tainted by mad cow disease. Fujita, who was chairman of his family trading company, Fujita & Co., also introduced the first Toys "Я" Us stores in Japan. When Fujita's attempt to diversify the menu failed to revitalize the hamburger business, McDonald's brought in its own handpicked executives to turn the company around. Fujita stepped down as chief executive of the McDonald's Japanese operation in 2003.

Furtado, Celso Monteiro, Brazilian economist (b. July 26, 1920, Pombal, Braz.—d. Nov. 20, 2004, Rio de Janeiro, Braz.), played a leading role in forming Latin American economic policies during the 20th century, in part through his influential book *Formação econômica do Brasil* (1959; *The Economic Growth of Brazil,* 1963). Furtado joined the Brazilian government in 1958 and was named the minister of planning in 1963, but a military coup in 1964 forced him to flee to Paris. Furtado returned in the 1980s and served as minister of culture (1986–88).

Gades, Antonio (ANTONIO ESTEVE RÓDENAS), Spanish dancer and choreographer (b. Nov. 14, 1936, Elda, Spain—d. July 20, 2004, Madrid, Spain), popularized flamenco and other Spanish dances with his elegant performances and powerful choreography. He was trained by the great dancer Pilar López—who chose the name Gades as more suitable for him—and worked with her company for nearly a decade before forming his own, Ballet Antonio Gades. He also was the first director (1978–80) of the National Ballet of Spain. Some of Gades's best work was captured on film, notably in a number of collaborations with Spanish filmmaker Carlos Saura, including *Bodas de sangre* (1981; *Blood Wedding*), *Carmen* (1983), and *El amor brujo* (1986).

Garland, Hank (WALTER LOUIS GARLAND), American musician (b. Nov. 11, 1930, Cowpens, S.C.—d. Dec. 27, 2004, Orange Park, Fla.), was a legendary country, jazz, and rock guitarist, best known for his studio work with such performers as Elvis Presley, Roy Orbison, the Everly Brothers, and Patsy Cline. Garland, nicknamed "Sugarfoot" for his first hit, "Sugarfoot Rag" (1949), was seriously injured in a 1961 car accident that effectively ended his career.

Geyelin, Philip, American journalist and editor (b. Feb. 27, 1923, Devon, Pa.—d. Jan. 9, 2004, Washington, D.C.), gradually shifted the editorials in the *Washington Post* to an anti-Vietnam War stance from the pro-government position of Russ Wiggins, his predecessor as editor of the editorial page. During Geyelin's tenure of overseeing the editorial page (1968–79), the newspaper also gained renown for its coverage of the Watergate Scandal. After military service in World War II, he worked for the Associated Press and *The Wall Street Journal* before joining the *Washington Post* in 1967. Geyelin received the Pulitzer Prize for editorial writing in 1970.

Ghiaurov, Nicolai, (NIKOLAY GEORGIEV GYAUROV), Bulgarian opera singer (b. Sept. 13, 1929, Velingrad, Bulg.—d. June 2, 2004, Modena, Italy), enraptured audiences worldwide with his commanding onstage presence and his tremendous bass voice. Considered one of the 20th century's greatest bass vocalists, Ghiaurov was perhaps best known for his portrayal of Mephistopheles in Gounod's *Faust,* singing the role in several languages before audiences in Italy, Russia, the U.S., France, and Spain. Other notable roles included the title characters in Mozart's *Don Giovanni* and Mussorgsky's *Boris Godunov,*

Philip II in Verdi's *Don Carlos,* Don Basilio in Rossini's *The Barber of Seville,* and Cervantes's antihero in Massenet's *Don Quichotte.*

Gold, Thomas, Austrian-born astronomer (b. May 22, 1920, Vienna, Austria—d. June 22, 2004, Ithaca, N.Y.), originated bold, unconventional theories in cosmology and other areas of science. Together with Hermann Bondi and Fred Hoyle, he formulated the steady-state theory of the universe, which holds that the universe exists without beginning or end and that, though the universe is expanding, it remains essentially constant because of a continual creation of matter throughout space. The steady-state theory gained many adherents following its introduction in 1948, but later astronomical observations provided strong evidence that the universe began at an initial event (the "big bang"). Among the confirmed or widely accepted scientific theories for which Gold became known were that pulsars are extremely dense bodies (neutron stars) that are rotating rapidly, that structures of the human inner ear function as amplifiers in distinguishing frequencies of sound, that the surface of the Moon is covered by a fine powder of pulverized rock, and that the stream of charged particles continually emitted by the Sun interacts with the Earth's magnetic field to form a shock wave. One of his most recent—and controversial—theories was that petroleum, natural gas, and coal are formed from hydrocarbon material that slowly rises from within the Earth, where it was trapped during the Earth's formation. In *The Deep Hot Biosphere* (1999), Gold proposed that this material supports primitive thermophilic (heat-loving) bacteria living in rock pores deep inside the Earth's crust. Gold studied at Trinity College, Cambridge (B.A., 1942; M.Sc., 1946); he eventually received his doctorate from Cambridge in 1969. During World War II he helped develop radar for the British Admiralty. In 1956 he left the staff of the Royal Greenwich Observatory to take a position as a professor of astronomy at Harvard University. In 1959 he became a professor of astronomy at Cornell University, Ithaca, where he served as the director (1959–81) of the university's Center for Radiophysics and Space Research. He retired in 1987. Gold was a fellow of the Royal Society and a member of the National Academy of Sciences.

Goldsmith, Jerry (JERRALD KING GOLDSMITH), American composer (b. Feb. 10, 1929, Los Angeles, Calif.—d. July 21, 2004, Beverly Hills, Calif.), demonstrated his versatility and originality in more than 300 scores for movies and television programs, often experimenting with unusual techniques, such as having horn players remove the mouthpieces from their instruments, to create a specific effect. Notable among his film scores were those for *Planet of the Apes* (1968), *Chinatown* (1974), *The Omen* (1976), for which he won an Academy Award, *Total Recall* (1990), and *L.A. Confidential* (1997). TV credits ranged from *Studio One* in the late 1940s to *Gunsmoke, Perry Mason,* and *The Twilight Zone* in the '50s, *Dr. Kildare, Ben Casey,* and *The Man from U.N.C.L.E.* in the '60s, *The Waltons* in the '70s, *Star Trek: The Next Generation* in the '80s, and *Star Trek: Voyager* in the '90s, as well as the fanfare for the Oscar telecasts (from 1998).

Goldsmith, Olivia (RANDY GOLDFIELD), American novelist (b. 1949, New York, N.Y.—d. Jan. 15, 2004, New York City), used her own bitter divorce experience as the basis of her best-known work, *The First Wives Club* (1992), in which three women whose wealthy husbands divorce them in order to acquire young trophy wives get their revenge; a popular film version was released in 1996. She had earlier had a successful business career, becoming one of the first women to gain a partnership at the Booz Allen Hamilton consulting firm, and she also wrote children's books under the name Justine Rendal, which she had taken after her divorce. Goldsmith died as a result of a heart attack she suffered after being given anesthesia for cosmetic surgery.

Goldstine, Herman Heine, American mathematician and computer scientist (b. Sept. 13, 1913, Chicago, Ill.—d. June 16, 2004, Bryn Mawr, Pa.), helped build the first modern computers and was instrumental in developing the military's famous ENIAC (Electronic Numerical Integrator and Calculator) in 1945. As a staff member of the Institute for Advanced Study, Princeton, N.J., he assisted John von Neumann in introducing the EDVAC (Electronic Discrete Variable Automatic Computer) in 1952. During the late 1950s Goldstine joined the staff of IBM, where he eventually served as director of scientific development for data processing; in the late 1960s he became a scientific consultant to the research director and was made an IBM fellow. Goldstine authored one of the earliest textbooks on the history of computers, *The Computer from Pascal to von Neumann* (1972).

Golub, Leon, American painter (b. Jan. 21, 1922, Chicago, Ill.—d. Aug. 8, 2004, New York, N.Y.), expressed his strong opposition to the Vietnam War through his series of paintings entitled *Napalm, Vietnam,* and *Assassins.* His monumental paintings typically depicted acts of brutality, revealing truths about both the attackers and the victims. He was married to the noted painter Nancy Spero.

Grau, Enrique, Colombian artist (b. Dec. 18, 1920, Panama City, Pan.—d. April 1, 2004, Bogotá, Colom.), depicted Afro-Colombian and Indian figures in a style that helped define contemporary art in Colombia. He trained at the Art Students League in New York City and studied advanced techniques in Italy before returning to Colombia in 1943. Along with Fernando Botero and Alejandro Obregón, Grau helped establish Colombian art in the international market. Although he initially made his name as a painter, in later years he expanded his portfolio to include sculpture. He bequeathed more than 1,300 works to his hometown of Cartegena to establish a museum. For this and other contributions to the city, Grau was honoured with the title Hijo Predilecto ("Favourite Son") of the city.

Gray, Spalding, American writer, monologuist, and actor (b. June 5, 1941, Barrington, R.I.—found dead March 7, 2004, New York, N.Y.), was a master storyteller who used his own life experiences for a series of monologues, including his most famous, *Swimming to Cambodia* (1984; filmed 1987), as well as such others as *Monster in a Box* (1990; filmed 1992) and *Gray's Anatomy* (1993; filmed 1996). He also appeared in more than 30 movies, including *The Killing Fields* (1984), *Beaches* (1988), and *Beyond Rangoon* (1995), and on Broadway in *Our Town* (1988) and *Gore Vidal's The Best Man* (2000). Gray, who had been troubled by depression for several years, had been missing since January 10 and was thought to have taken his own life.

© Time Life Pictures/DMI/Time Life Pictures/Getty Images

Actor and storyteller Spalding Gray

Gruau, René (RENATO ZAVAGLI RICCIARDELLI DELLE CAMMINATE), Italian-born graphic designer and illustrator (b. Feb. 4, 1909, Rimini, Italy—d. March 31, 2004, Rome, Italy), created stylish graphics and elegant, sophisticated ads for high-fashion houses and magazines. With his works that suggested an inspired melding of Japanese drawing and Toulouse-Lautrec posters, Gruau, who was self-taught, formed a bridge between the celebrated French poster tradition and modern advertising. His clients included couturiers such as Christian Dior, Givenchy, and Pierre Balmain, Vichy water, the Moulin Rouge nightclub, Air France, and Cinzano.

Gunn, Thom(son) William, British-born American poet and critic (b. Aug. 29, 1929, Gravesend, Kent, Eng.—d. April 25, 2004, San Francisco, Calif.), presented a singular voice in a writing career that stretched from the undergraduate work *Fighting Terms* (1954) to *Boss Cupid* (2000). Though both his style and subject matter underwent considerable change over the course of his writing life, Gunn never lost his appreciation for the traditional poetic forms he early mastered and transformed with his modernity. After completing two years of military service, Gunn attended Trinity College, Cambridge (B.A., 1953). While there he met American Mike Kitay, who became his lifelong partner. Gunn moved to California in 1954, taught at Stanford University, and published his second volume of poetry, which included one of his best-known poems, "On the Move," a celebration of the tough motorcycle culture. Gunn moved permanently to San Francisco in 1960 and became a part of the drugs-and-free-love culture prevalent there. He produced several volumes during the '60s—*My Sad Captains* (1961), *Misanthropos* (1965), *Positives* (1966, with photographs by his younger brother, Ander Gunn), and *Touch* (1967)—as well as editing a volume of Fulke Greville's poetry and sharing a volume, *Selected Poems* (1962), with future British poet laureate Ted Hughes. Gunn's evident pleasure in his life showed itself in his growing flexibility as a poet and his increasing openness about his lifestyle. Among his later volumes of poetry were *Moly* (1971), *Jack Straw's Castle* (1975), and *The Man with Night Sweats* (1992), an unflinching portrait of the AIDS epidemic in San Francisco. He also wrote two volumes of occasional essays and criticism, *The Occasions of Poetry* (1982) and *Shelf Life* (1993).

Hagen, Uta Thyra, German-born American actress and teacher (b. June 12, 1919, Göttingen, Ger.—d. Jan. 14, 2004, New York, N.Y.), thrilled theatre audiences with her talent and versatility and also became a widely respected acting teacher and writer. She counted three Tony Awards among her numerous honours, one of them for her creation of the role of the acid-tongued Martha in Edward Albee's *Who's Afraid of Virginia Woolf?*, the portrayal that many considered her most memorable. Hagen's family moved to the U.S. when she was seven. After studying for a short time at the Royal Academy of Dramatic Art in London and then at the University of Wisconsin, she made her professional debut when she was 18 in Eva Le Gallienne's production of *Hamlet.* Hagen made her Broadway debut in 1938 as Nina in *The Seagull,* a production that starred Alfred Lunt and Lynn Fontanne. That same year Hagen performed opposite José Ferrer in *The Latitude of Love.* Hagen and Ferrer were later married, and over the 10 years of their marriage, they acted together in several productions. In 1947 Hagen appeared in *The Whole World Over* along with Herbert Berghof, whom she married in 1951. The two founded and began teaching at the Herbert Berghof Studio (known as the HB Studio) in New York City's Greenwich Village; it became one of the city's best performing arts schools. In 1948 Hagen starred as Blanche DuBois in the road company production of *A Streetcar Named Desire* and then took over the role on Broadway, and in 1950 she appeared in the role for which she won her first Tony, Georgie in Clifford Odets's *The Country Girl.* Hagen was blacklisted in the 1950s but made her stage comeback in *Who's Afraid of Virginia Woolf?* (1962). She also traveled with that play to London—winning the Drama Critics Award. In 1999 Hagen was honoured with her third Tony Award, this one for lifetime achievement.

Uta Hagen in The Country Girl

Hägg, Gunder, Swedish middle-distance runner (b. Dec. 31, 1918, Sörbygden, Swed.—d. Nov. 27, Malmö, Swed.), set 15 world records during his career, 10 of which were registered during a three-month period in 1942. "Gunder the Wonder" was the first athlete to run the 5,000 m in under 14 minutes (in 1942) and the last runner to hold a world record of more than 4 minutes in the mile; his record of 4 min 1.4 sec in the latter distance stood from 1945 until 1954, when Britain's Roger Bannister broke the 4-minute barrier.

Hailey, Arthur, British-born writer (b. April 5, 1920, Luton, Bedfordshire, Eng.—d. Nov. 24, 2004, Lyford Cay, New Providence Island, Bahamas), helped launch the disaster-movie genre when his novel *Airport* (1968) was made into a motion picture in 1970. Hailey's meticulously researched 11 books—among them *Hotel* (1965; filmed 1967, filmed for television 1983, and adapted as a TV series 1983–88), *Wheels* (1971; filmed as a TV miniseries 1978), *Strong Medicine* (1984; filmed for TV 1986), and *The Moneychangers* (1975; TV miniseries 1976)—were published in 40 countries in 38 languages and sold more than 170 million copies. His 1956 screenplay *Flight into Danger* eventually became the inspiration for the disaster-film spoof *Airplane!* (1980).

Hamburger, Philip, American writer (b. July 2, 1914, Wheeling. W.Va.—d. April 23, 2004, New York, N.Y.), worked under all five editors of *The New Yorker* magazine beginning in 1939. Hamburger, who was a reporter-at-large, wrote about all manner of subjects and people in pieces that included U.S. city portraits, coverage of the political realm, presidential and other profiles, and reflections on New York itself (as Our Man Stanley in Talk of the Town). He produced several compilations of his *New Yorker* writings, notably *Friends Talking in the Night: Sixty Years of Writing for The New Yorker* (1999) and *Matters of State* (2000).

Hampshire, Sir Stuart Newton, British philosopher (b. Oct. 1, 1914, Healing, Lincolnshire, Eng.—d. June 13, 2004, Oxford, Eng.), brought aesthetics, politics, and psychology to bear on the philosophy of mind. Hampshire was educated at Repton School and Balliol College, Oxford. He took a first-class degree in Greats in 1936, after which he was elected to a fellowship at All Souls College, Oxford, where he encountered John Langshaw Austin, A.J. Ayer, and Isaiah Berlin. After serving in army intelligence during World War II, Hampshire was a lecturer (1947–50) at University College, London (UCL), where Ayer was head of the philosophy department. Hampshire returned to Oxford, taking up fellowships at New College (1950–55) and All Souls (1955–60). He was Grote Professor of Philosophy of Mind and Logic at UCL (1960–63) before moving to Princeton University, where he became chairman of the philosophy department in 1963. At Princeton he was credited with helping prevent violence during anti-Vietnam War demonstrations. He moved back to England as warden (1970–84) of Wadham College, Oxford, but he finished his academic career at Stanford University (1984–91). Among Hampshire's major books, *Spinoza* (1951) was still considered the best short introduction to that philosopher; *Thought and Action* (1959), which shows the influence of Spinoza, develops an intentionalist philosophy of mind; *Two Theories of Morality* (1977) contrasts the ethical theories of Spinoza and Aristotle and anticipates what came to be called communitarianism; and *Justice Is Conflict* (1999) argues that moral conflict is inevitable and that the best that can be done is to develop social institutions to fairly mediate that conflict. In addition to philosophy, Hampshire wrote widely on subjects in literature and art. He was knighted in 1979.

Hansen, Joseph, American mystery writer and gay rights activist (b. July 19, 1923, Aberdeen, S.D.—d. Nov. 24, 2004, Laguna Beach, Calif.), featured as his protagonist a homosexual detective, considered to be one of the first such characters in the genre. The fictional Dave Brandstetter appeared in a dozen hard-boiled detective novels, from *Fadeout* (1970) to *A Country of Old Men* (1991). Hansen also taught writing at the university level. Hansen, who also wrote under the pen names James Colton and Rose Brock, published some 40 books, a few of them volumes of poetry.

Hanson of Edgerton, James Edward Hanson, Baron, British business magnate (b. Jan. 20, 1922, Huddersfield, Yorkshire, Eng.—d. Nov. 1, 2004, Newbury, Berkshire, Eng.), cofounded, with his partner Gordon White (later Lord White of Hull), Hanson PLC and, through a succession of aggressive business takeover deals throughout Britain and the United States, built it into one of the U.K.'s biggest conglomerates. Hanson's billion-dollar empire earned him the nickname "Lord Moneybags." He was knighted under Labour Prime Minister Harold Wilson in 1976, and he was granted a life peerage in 1983, during the Conservative prime ministership of Margaret Thatcher, of whom he was a loyal supporter.

Hargis, Billy James, American evangelist (b. Aug. 3, 1925, Texarkana, Texas—d. Nov. 27, 2004, Tulsa, Okla.), founded the Christian Crusade, an international ministry with a special interest in battling communism. He built a powerful media empire, reaching millions through television, radio, books, and pamphlets. In 1970 he founded the American Christian Crusade College in Tulsa. His ministry slowly crumbled, however, after the Christian Crusade lost its tax-exempt status in the 1960s and he was accused of sexual misconduct at his college in the mid-1970s.

Hazare, Vijay, Indian cricketer (b. March 11, 1915, Sangli, Maharashtra, British India—d. Dec. 18, 2004, Baroda, Gujarat, India), was one of India's finest batsmen in the years just after World War II. A solid right-handed batsman and medium-pace bowler, he played in 30 Test matches (14 as captain) between 1946 and 1953, scoring 2,192 runs (average 47.65) and seven centuries, including two in one Test against Don Bradman's formidable national side in Adelaide, Australia, in 1947–48. Hazare made 18,740 runs (average 58.38) in first-class cricket, with a personal high of 316 not out in 1939–40 and a world-record 577-run partnership with Gul Mohammad in 1946–47.

Heatley, Norman George, British biochemist (b. Jan. 10, 1911, Woodbridge, Suffolk, Eng.—d. Jan. 5, 2004, Oxford, Eng.), devised a way to isolate penicillin from its substrate and measure its activity and was instrumental in proving the efficacy of the antibiotic and creating the means to mass-produce it. Heatley was a member of a team of scientists at the University of Oxford that included Ernst Chain and was headed by Howard Florey when in 1939 the team began looking into Sir Alexander Fleming's 1928 discovery of penicillin. Heatley, a resourceful inventor, found the assay method to measure the activity of penicillin, discovered the conditions under which the antibiotic is stable, and devised a multistage technique to extract and purify penicillin. In 1940 the team produced enough penicillin to test it on mice, and the following year, after Heatley had invented a method to produce sufficient quantities of the substance, the first human test was conducted. Heatley was appointed OBE in 1978, and in 1990 Oxford awarded him its first honorary doctorate in medicine.

Hecht, Anthony Evan, American poet (b. Jan. 16, 1923, New York, N.Y.—d. Oct. 20, 2004, Washington, D.C.), served as consultant in poetry to the Library of Congress (poet laureate) from 1982 to 1984. A formalist poet, he mastered a wide range of poetic forms and was noted for both the elegance and the intelligence of his work. The subject matter of his poems often touched on his experiences as an infantryman during World War II and expressed his despair over human cruelty. After the war he attended Kenyon College, Gambier, Ohio, where he came under the influence of John Crowe Ransom, a leader of the New Critic movement, who persuaded him to pursue a career in teaching. Hecht's first book of poems, *A Summoning of Stones* (1954), was well received, but it was his second collection, *The Hard Hours* (1967), that showed him at his best. The book, which contained "Dover Bitch," a celebrated parody of Matthew Arnold's "Dover Beach," received the Pulitzer Prize in 1968. He pioneered a form of light verse called double dactyls that gained popularity in the 1960s and led to his collaborated work *Jiggery-Pokery: A Compendium of Double Dactyls* (1967). He was awarded the Tanning Prize in 1997 for a career of artistic accomplishment in poetry.

Hench, John, American designer (b. June 29, 1908, Cedar Rapids, Iowa—d. Feb. 5, 2004, Burbank, Calif.), was closely associated with the Disney brand, designing theme parks, providing sketches for motion pictures (he won an Academy Award for his special effects for the film *20,000 Leagues Under the Sea* [1954]), and serving as the official portrait artist for Mickey Mouse. Hench joined Walt Disney Studio in 1939 as a story artist, contributed to notable Disney films, and supervised the design of Disneyland in California, Walt Disney World and Epcot Center in Florida, and Tokyo Disneyland. He also worked on Disney's opening and closing ceremonies for the 1960 Olympic Games in Los Angeles and the 1964 World's Fair in New York City. Hench published *Designing Disney* in 2003.

Hickey, James Aloysius Cardinal, American Roman Catholic prelate (b. Oct. 11, 1920, Midland, Mich.—d. Oct. 24, 2004, Washington, D.C.), held to conservative theological policies while serving (1980–2000) as archbishop of Washington, D.C. During his tenure Hickey also took activist roles in support of gun control and nuclear disarmament and in opposition to right-wing military groups in Central America. He was respected for his openness in dealing with incidents of sexual abuse by priests. Hickey was elevated to the College of Cardinals in 1988 but was a nonvoting member following his retirement in 2000.

James Cardinal Hickey

© Cynthia Johnson/Time Life Pictures/Getty Images

Hill-Norton, Peter John (BARON HILL-NORTON OF SOUTH NUTFIELD), British naval officer (b. Feb. 8, 1915, Germiston, S.Af.—d. May 16, 2004, Studland, Dorset, Eng.), rose through the military ranks to become chief of defense staff (Britain's most senior serving officer) with the title admiral of the fleet in April 1971. Hill-Norton joined the Royal Navy as a cadet at age 13. By 1962 he had received his rear admiral's flag as assistant chief of naval staff. He was promoted to vice admiral in 1965 and second sea lord in 1967. A strict disciplinarian, Hill-Norton abolished the Royal Navy's traditional daily nip of rum in 1970. From 1974 to 1977 he was chairman of NATO's military committee. Granted a life peerage in 1979, he became an active member of the House of Lords.

Hinton, William Howard, American agronomist (b. Feb. 2, 1919, Chicago, Ill.—d. May 15, 2004, Concord, Mass.), authored *Fanshen: A Documentary of Revolution in a Chinese Village* (1966) and *Shenfan: The Continuing Revolution in a Chinese Village* (1983), two studies that chronicled the impact of the Maoist revolution on a peasant village. Hinton spent six years in China documenting the turning over of the landlords' land to the peasants as dictated by Mao Zedong's communist revolution. When Hinton returned to the U.S., however, his notes were confiscated; though he eventually retrieved them after five years, the publication of his book was delayed another eight years when he was suspected of treason during the Joseph McCarthy era.

Hirsch, Crazylegs (ELROY LEON HIRSCH), American athlete and sports administrator (b. June 17, 1923, Wausau, Wis.—d. Jan. 28, 2004, Madison, Wis.), became one of professional football's leading receivers, known for his big-play receptions, as a member of the Los Angeles Rams (1949–57) of the National Football League (NFL). In 1942 Hirsch played halfback on the University of Wisconsin's football team and earned the nickname "Crazylegs" for an unorthodox running style that made him difficult to tackle. The following year he enlisted in the Marines and began officer training at the University of Michigan. There he became the school's only athlete to letter in four sports in the same year (football, basketball, baseball, and track). After World War II, Hirsch began playing professional football with the Chicago Rockets (1946–48) of the All-America Football Conference and endured several injury-plagued seasons before joining the Rams in 1949. Moved to the split end position, he became an integral part of the team's formidable offense, which relied heavily on the forward pass. In the 1951 season he led the league in catches (66) and touchdown receptions (17) and set an NFL record for receiving yards (1,495). His play helped the Rams win a national championship that year. Hirsch's immense popularity led to appearances in several movies, including the autobiographical *Crazylegs* (1953). In 1957 he retired from professional football with 387 career receptions, 7,029 receiving yards, and 60 touchdowns. He later served as athletic director (1969–87) at the University of Wisconsin and helped turn around the school's struggling sports program. Hirsch was inducted into the Pro Football Hall of Fame in 1968.

Holm, Eleanor (ELEANOR HOLM-JARRETT; ELEANOR HOLM WHALEN), American athlete and entertainer (b. Dec. 6, 1913, Brooklyn, N.Y.—d. Jan. 31, 2004, Miami, Fla.), made international headlines after being dismissed from the U.S. Olympic swimming team for drinking and breaking curfew during the voyage to the 1936 Berlin Games. Although the incident ended her swimming career, which included a gold medal in the 100-m backstroke at the 1932 Olympics in Los Angeles and 21 national titles, the publicity surrounding it paved the way to her success as an entertainer.

© Bettmann/Corbis

Scandalous swimmer Eleanor Holm

Hookes, David William, Australian cricketer (b. May 3, 1955, Adelaide, Australia—d. Jan. 19, 2004, Melbourne, Australia), played 23 Test matches for Australia between 1977 and 1986; in 41 innings he scored 1,306 runs at an average of 34.36, with one century. In his Test debut, at the Centenary Test against England at Melbourne in 1977, he scored 56, including five successive fours in a single over. Hookes played for two years in Kerry Packer's unofficial World Series Cricket before returning to the Australia national side in 1980. After retiring from first-class cricket in 1992 with 12,671 runs (average 43.99), he was a radio and television cricket commentator and served as coach of the Victoria state side. He was killed in a fight outside a Melbourne pub.

Hounsfield, Sir Godfrey Newbold, British electrical engineer (b. Aug. 28, 1919, Newark, Nottinghamshire, Eng.—d. Aug. 12, 2004, Kingston upon Thames, Surrey, Eng.), invented the CT (computed tomography) scanner, also known as the CAT (computerized axial tomography) scanner, a medical imaging device that revolutionized medical diagnosis. For the development of this imaging technique, Hounsfield received the 1979 Nobel Prize for Physiology or Medicine, which he shared with South African-born American physicist Allan M. Cormack, who had independently described a similar technique. After receiving a diploma from the Faraday House Electrical Engineering College, London, Hounsfield joined (1951) the research staff of Electric and Musical Industries (later EMI Ltd.). He led the EMI design team that built the first all-transistor computer in Great Britain (1958–59). In the late 1960s Hounsfield conceived the idea of a device that could show internal structure with more detail than was possible with conventional X-ray techniques. In a typical CT scanner, a series of X-ray exposures—produced by a beam of X-rays that sweeps across the body—is analyzed by a computer to create a detailed cross-sectional image of the body. After a period of development at EMI, the CT scanner was introduced in 1972. In addition to the Nobel Prize, Hounsfield received the Albert Lasker Medical Research Award (1975) and other awards. He was knighted in 1981.

Hughes, Emlyn Walter, British association football (soccer) player (b. Aug. 28, 1947, Barrow-in-Furness, Lancashire, Eng.—d. Nov. 9, 2004, Sheffield, Eng.), was one of England's finest footballers of the 1970s; during 12 years (1967–79) with Liverpool, the exuberant left-half known as "Crazy Horse" led that club to the Football Association Cup (1974), four league championships (1973, 1976–77, 1979), two Union des Associations Européennes de Football Cups (1973, 1976), and two European Cups (1977–78). He was named Player of the Year in 1977. In 1979 he transferred to Wolverhampton, which he took to the League Cup title the next season. Hughes also played 62 international matches for England, 23 as captain. After retiring he went into broadcasting, notably on the BBC television quiz show *A Question of Sport*. He was made OBE in 1980.

© Evening Standard/Getty Images

Footballer Emlyn Hughes

Hyland, Frances, Canadian actress (b. April 25, 1927, Shaunavon, Sask.—d. July 11, 2004, Toronto, Ont.), concentrated mostly on stage work, starring in and directing productions at the Stratford and Shaw festivals in Ontario in addition to performing in numerous theatres across Canada and occasionally on Broadway and in London during her 50-year career. She also made a few film and television appearances, notably in the TV series *Road to Avonlea* (1990). Hyland was made an Officer of the Order of Canada in 1971.

Iverson, Kenneth Eugene, Canadian-born mathematician and computer scientist (b. Dec. 17, 1920, Camrose, Alta.—d. Oct. 19, 2004, Toronto, Ont.), pioneered a very compact high-level computer programming language called APL (the initials of his book *A Programming Language* [1962]). The language made efficient use of the slow communication speeds of the computer terminals of that time, and APL enjoyed an enthusiastic following. Iverson taught mathematics at Harvard University from 1955 to 1960 and then served on the staff of the research division of IBM from 1960 to 1980.

Jacquet, (Jean Baptiste) Illinois, American musician and bandleader (b. Oct. 31, 1922, Broussard, La.—d. July 22, 2004, New York, N.Y.), thrilled Jazz at the Philharmonic (JATP) audiences by playing tenor saxophone solos full of riffs, honking tones, and screaming high-register notes; his soulful blues playing and crowd-pleasing "freak" sounds were a major influence on rhythm-and-blues saxophonists. His two choruses on Lionel Hampton's recording of "Flying Home" (1942) constituted one of the most imitated solos of the decade. Though Jacquet was most noted for his big tone and aggressive, extroverted antics, he also had a sweetly melodic way of playing ballads and a care for solo form that made him a lasting influence on jazz saxophonists. Jacquet grew up in Houston, Texas, and played in Southwestern bands; he then moved to Los Angeles after he graduated from high school. Pianist Nat King Cole introduced him to Hampton, whose band he joined in 1941; Jacquet also played in the bands of Cab Calloway (1943–44) and Count Basie (1945–46). Meanwhile, in 1944 he appeared in the historic short film *Jammin' the Blues* (1944) and early JATP concerts, both produced by Norman Granz; from 1946 to 1957 then he joined the JATP troupe for annual tours of the U.S. and, eventually, around the world. Jacquet's own playing originated in swing stylists Lester Young and Herschel Evans, but he used bebop musicians in his own groups, which recorded hits such as "Black Velvet" and "Robbins Nest." In the 1960s he startled listeners by playing jazz on the bassoon as well as the tenor. Jacquet, the subject of the 1991 documentary film *Texas Tenor: The Illinois Jacquet Story,* led a successful Basie-styled big band from 1983 until six days before his death.

James, Rick (JAMES AMBROSE JOHNSON), American musician and singer (b. Feb. 1, 1948, Buffalo, N.Y.—d. Aug. 6, 2004, Los Angeles, Calif.), was the creator of such classic funk hits as "Super Freak" and "Give It to Me." He released his debut album, *Come and Get It,* in 1978. The long-haired, leather-clad James was known for his sexually explicit lyrics, unforgettable beats, and a wild offstage lifestyle that led to his long bout with drug addiction.

James, Sidney Lorraine, American journalist (b. Aug. 6, 1906, St. Louis, Mo.—d. March 11, 2004, Alameda, Calif.), succeeded in establishing *Sports Illustrated* as a viable magazine despite initial doubts from industry observers. James, who was founding editor of the magazine (1954), served as managing editor (1954–60) and publisher (1960–65); in the late 1960s he became a vice president of Time, Inc. As chairman of the National Public Affairs Center for Television, he was also responsible for public television's coverage of the U.S. Senate Watergate hearings.

Jennings, Sir Robert Yewdall, British lawyer and jurist (b. Oct. 19, 1913, Idle, West Yorkshire, Eng.—d. Aug. 4, 2004, Cambridge, Eng.), served as Whewell Professor of International Law at the University of Cambridge (1955–82) and as a judge on the International Court of Justice (1982–95, president 1991–94) at The Hague. Although Jennings was not a prolific writer, the edition of *Oppenheim's International Law* (1992) that he co-wrote with Sir Arthur Watts was considered a classic in the field. Jennings was knighted in 1982.

Johnson, Samuel Curtis, American business executive (b. March 2, 1928, Racine, Wis.—d. May 22, 2004, Racine), served for more than 30 years, until 2000, as head of S.C. Johnson & Son, a company founded by his great-grandfather in 1886. Under his guidance the company, known for its Johnson Wax, enlarged its range of products to include such items as bug sprays and air fresheners and was transformed into four separate businesses. The environmentally conscious Johnson ended the company's use of chlorofluorocarbons three years before the U.S. government prohibition of them.

Jones, Elvin Ray, American musician (b. Sept. 9, 1927, Pontiac, Mich.—d. May 18, 2004, Englewood, N.J.), began a revolution in jazz drumming with his powerful playing in the John Coltrane Quartet during 1960–65 and then had a long career of leading combos, including the popular Elvin Jones Jazz Machine. Jones was from an outstanding musical family—his brother Hank was a top bop pianist, and his brother Thad was a distinguished cornetist-composer-bandleader. Jones grew up in Detroit, where he began playing in his teens; after performing in a U.S. Army band (1946–49), he played in the house band at a Detroit nightclub. His 1956 move to New York City launched him into national prominence, and he worked and recorded with Sonny Rollins, Miles Davis, and other major figures. The passion of Coltrane's tenor saxophone improvisations ignited Jones's equally passionate rhythmic explorations. Using an unusually resonant drum kit and blessed with a remarkably free sense of swing, he created rich textures and dense polyrhythms in interplay with Coltrane's intense explorations of harmonic extremes; though piano and bass were present, many of the group's performances were effectively tenor sax–drums duets. Jones's liberated accenting inspired later drummers to abandon their instruments' traditional timekeeping role altogether. After leaving Coltrane, Jones on his own became a top jazz-club and festival attraction by leading a series of small groups, featuring noted veteran saxophonists such as Sonny Fortune and Frank Foster and introducing new jazz stars, including trumpeter Nicholas Payton and saxophonist Ravi Coltrane.

AP/Wide World Photos

Jazz drummer Elvin Jones

Jones, E(uine) Fay, American architect (b. Jan. 31, 1921, Pine Bluff, Ark.—d. Aug. 30, 2004, Fayetteville, Ark.), designed Thorncrown Chapel in Eureka Springs, Ark., which the American Institute of Architects rated among the five best American buildings of the 20th century. Fay studied under Frank Lloyd Wright and embraced Wright's theories of organic architecture. In the many houses and chapels that he designed, Jones relied on natural materials such as stone and wood.

Jordan, James J., Jr., American advertiser (b. Aug. 3, 1930, Germantown, Pa.—d. Feb. 4, 2004, Virgin Islands), wrote popular advertising slogans that became indelibly identified with the services or products for which they were created, such as Delta Airlines ("Delta is ready when you are"); Wisk laundry detergent ("Ring around the collar"); Quaker oatmeal ("It's the right thing to do"); Schaefer beer ("Schaefer is the one beer to have when you're having more than one"); and Tareyton cigarettes ("Us Tareyton smokers would rather fight than switch"). He worked at various New York City ad agencies from the 1950s and came to head his own agency in 1978.

Juliana, Princess (JULIANA LOUISE EMMA MARIE WILHELMINA, PRINCESS OF ORANGE-NASSAU), Dutch former monarch (b. April 30, 1909, Noordeinde Palace, The Hague, Neth.—d. March 20, 2004, Soestdijk Palace, Baarn, Neth.), reigned over The Netherlands for 32 years (1948–80) during a time that included the rebuilding of the country after World War II and the dismantling of the Dutch colonial empire. She was the only child of Queen Wilhelmina and Prince Hendrik. Juliana married Prince Bernhard of Lippe-Biesterfeld (*q.v.*) on Jan. 7, 1936. When Germany invaded The Netherlands in May 1940, the royal family left the country. Juliana soon took refuge in Ottawa, Ont., with her daughters, Beatrix (born in 1938) and Irene (born in 1939). Her husband joined them in 1941, and a third daughter, Margriet, was born in Canada in 1943. Maria Christina, their fourth daughter and last child, was born (1947) virtually blind as the result of German measles her mother had contracted during pregnancy. Juliana assumed the throne on Sept. 4, 1948, when Queen Wilhelmina abdicated in her favour. Juliana's first major act as queen was the transfer of sovereignty to Indonesia in 1949. She was a much-loved figure, particularly after she and Bernhard donned boots and helped with disaster relief in 1953 when a flood killed more than 1,800 people and tens of thousands of cattle and destroyed thousands of homes in the southwestern Netherlands. She was also appreciated for her down-to-earth, relaxed style. Only three times was Juliana's reign rocked by a major scandal: in 1956, when she was forced to give up her association with Greet Hofmans, a faith healer she had befriended in the hope of curing Christina's worsening eye problems; in 1966, when Beatrix married the German diplomat Claus von Amsburg, reawakening anti-German sensitivities still fresh from World War II; and in 1976, when Bernhard was accused of accepting bribes from the American aircraft manufacturer Lockheed and was forced to relinquish his military rank and all of his official public offices. Nevertheless, through it all Juliana remained popular with the Dutch and throughout Europe. She was awarded the United Nations Peace Medal in 1974. In 1980 Juliana followed her mother's example and abdicated the throne in favour of her eldest daughter, who became Queen Beatrix on April 30 of that year. After stepping down, the former queen and her husband lived quietly.

Justice, Donald Rodney, American poet (b. Aug. 12, 1925, Miami, Fla.—d. Aug. 6, 2004,

AP/Wide World Photos

Iowa City, Iowa), was admired for his mastery of a wide range of poetic forms as well as his keen sense of poetic invention and his emotional depth. He was one of the first great poets to emerge from the Writers Workshop at the University of Iowa, which he attended in the 1950s. Justice's first published collection of poems, *The Summer Anniversaries* (1960), included the heralded poem "On the Death of Friends in Childhood." The book received the Lamont Award from the Academy of American Poets. In 1979 Justice published *Selected Poems,* which won the Pulitzer Prize (1980) and contained one of his best-known works, "Ode to a Dressmaker's Dummy." He won the Bollingen Prize for Poetry in 1991. He taught at Syracuse (N.Y.) University, the University of Iowa, the University of California, Irvine, Princeton University, and the University of Florida. He also influenced such young poets as Mark Strand and Rita Dove and the novelist John Irving. The final volume of his *Collected Poems* was published posthumously.

Karaca, Cem, Turkish rock musician (b. April 5, 1945, Istanbul, Turkey—d. Feb. 8, 2004, Istanbul), blended traditional Anatolian music with progressive rock and leftist political themes to become Turkey's biggest pop star in the late 1960s and early '70s. He had a forceful bass voice, with which he fronted several bands, releasing a steady supply of records. Political turmoil in Turkey led Karaca to move to West Germany in the late 1970s. The Turkish military government ordered him to return to face charges related to his politics and stripped him of his citizenship when he refused. Karaca returned to Turkey in 1987, and his citizenship was eventually restored by the civilian government; his later music explored less-controversial themes.

Kase, Toshikazu, Japanese diplomat (b. Jan. 12, 1903, Chiba, Japan—d. May 21, 2004, Kamakura, Japan), in 1955 became Japan's first ambassador to the United Nations. A career diplomat, he was on the embassy staff in Washington D.C., at the time of the attack on Pearl Harbor in 1941 and was a member of the Japanese delegation that formally surrendered to the United States aboard the USS *Missouri* four years later. He played a key role in rebuilding Japanese-American relations after World War II.

Kaye, M(ary) M(argaret), British writer and illustrator (b. Aug. 21, 1908, Simla, India—d. Jan. 29, 2004, Lavenham, Suffolk, Eng.), captured life in India and Afghanistan during the Raj in her immensely popular novel *The Far Pavilions* (1978). The daughter of a British civil servant working in India, Kaye spent her early childhood there. She was sent to boarding school in England at age 10. After graduating from art school in England, she found work as an illustrator and soon began to write. She married a British army officer in 1945. Before achieving worldwide success with *The Far Pavilions*—which became a television miniseries in 1984—she wrote a number of children's books (as Mollie Kaye), several detective novels set in the various regions of the world to which her husband had been posted, and other historical novels. She also wrote three volumes of autobiography, *The Sun in the Morning* (1990), *Golden Afternoon* (1997), and *Enchanted Evening* (1999).

Keel, Howard (HAROLD CLIFFORD LEEK), American actor-singer (b. April 13, 1919, Gillespie, Ill.—d. Nov. 7, 2004, Palm Desert, Calif.), had a booming baritone voice that, combined with his good looks, gained him the lead roles in a succession of Hollywood musicals in the early 1950s opposite the leading musical ingenues of the day. In later life he attracted a new audience when he spent some 10 years in the cast (portraying Clayton Farlow) of the hugely popular television series *Dallas.* Keel began his career in show business as a singing waiter, and while working for Douglas Aircraft during World War II, he served as a roving entertainer at the company's plants. He received his big break when he was hired to step into the roles of Billy Bigelow in *Carousel* and Curly in *Oklahoma!* to replace the Broadway stars and then in 1947 originated the latter role in the London production. Keel made his film debut in *Annie Get Your Gun* (1950) and followed up with such classic musicals as *Show Boat* (1951), *Kiss Me Kate* (1953), *Seven Brides for Seven Brothers,* his favourite (1954), and *Kismet* (1955).

Keeshan, Bob (ROBERT JAMES KEESHAN), American television performer (b. June 27, 1927, Lynbrook, Long Island, N.Y.—d. Jan. 23,

Bob Keeshan, aka Captain Kangaroo

2004, Windsor, Vt.), entertained millions of children with his television portrayal of Captain Kangaroo. The walrus-mustached Captain—with such friends as Mr. Green Jeans, Bunny Rabbit, Dancing Bear, and Mr. Moose—brought education disguised as entertainment to his audiences and endeared himself to generations of young viewers. When Keeshan was a senior in high school, he landed a job as a page at NBC in New York City. After high school he served in the Marines, and in 1946 he returned to New York and to his job at NBC and also attended Fordham University. His desk at NBC was next to Buffalo Bob Smith's office, and Keeshan soon was helping Buffalo Bob with a Saturday morning children's radio show. The next year, when Buffalo Bob starred in an afternoon show, he featured a puppet—Howdy Doody—and Keeshan was invited to join the cast. On Jan. 3, 1948, he debuted as Clarabell the Clown on what later became *The Howdy Doody Show,* and by 1950 the show had moved to television and was a big hit. Keeshan's next stint was as Corny the Clown on ABC's *Time for Fun,* and he then performed on that network's *Tinker's Workshop. Captain Kangaroo*—given that name because in the show's early years Keeshan wore an oversize coat with large pockets reminiscent of kangaroo pouches—began on Oct. 3, 1955, played on CBS until late 1984, and eventually was seen for six more years on public television. It won six Emmy Awards and three Peabody Awards. Keeshan also wrote several books and involved himself in a number of civic causes, especially those concerning children.

Kelley, John Adelbert, American marathoner (b. Sept. 6, 1907, West Medford, Mass.—d. Oct. 6, 2004, South Yarmouth, Mass.), ran the Boston Marathon a record 61 times. He ran his first Boston Marathon in 1928, won it in 1935 and 1945, and finished 18 times in the top 10. He was the first road runner inducted into the National Track and Field Hall of Fame and was named Runner of the Century by *Runner's World* magazine.

Kelly, Margaret, Irish-born French dancer and choreographer (b. June 24, 1910, Dublin, Ire.—d. Sept. 11, 2004, Paris, France), was a professional chorus-line dancer by the time she was 14 and in 1932 formed what became the Bluebell Girls cabaret dance troupe. For more than half a century, she led the troupe, which not only entertained Parisians but also toured internationally, dazzling its audiences with energetic high-kicking routines. By the time she retired in 1986, Kelly had trained some 14,000 dancers. She was made OBE in 1996.

Kelly, Molly (MOLLY CRAIG), Australian Aboriginal icon (b. c. 1917, Jigalong, W.Aus., Australia—d. Jan. 13, 2004, Jigalong), walked, with her younger sister and a cousin, some 1,600 km (1,000 mi) home from the settlement she had been taken to as a young teenager; her journey inspired the 2002 movie *Rabbit-Proof Fence.* From 1905 to 1971, Australia followed a policy of attempting to assimilate mixed-race Aboriginals into white society by removing mixed-race children from Aboriginal families. Kelly was taken, with her sister and cousin, in 1931. Knowing that her home was along the fence built to barricade rabbits from farmland that ran the length of Australia, she took the two younger girls and fled the settlement, arriving home nine weeks later. One of Kelly's two daughters, who was taken from her under the same policy, wrote the book *Follow the Rabbit-Proof Fence* (1996) about her mother's experience.

Kelman, Charles, American ophthalmic surgeon (b. May 23, 1930, Brooklyn, N.Y.—d. June 1, 2004, Boca Raton, Fla.), was given the

2004 Albert Lasker Award for Clinical Medical Research posthumously for having revolutionized the surgical removal of cataracts; he turned a 10-day hospital stay into an outpatient procedure and dramatically reduced surgical complications.

Kente, Gibson ("BRA GIB"), South African playwright (b. July 23, 1932, East London, S.Af.—d. Nov. 7, 2004, Soweto, S.Af.), introduced musical theatre to the impoverished townships of South Africa. Considered the founding father of black township theatre, he was responsible for helping to launch the careers of other South African entertainers such as Brenda Fassie (*q.v.*). Through his plays Kente connected with local audiences not only by entertaining them with laughter, music, and dance but also by dealing with social issues such as crime, poverty, and apartheid. In 2003 Kente publicly announced that he was HIV-positive, a brave act that earned him praise from political leader Nelson Mandela.

Kessel, Barney, American jazz musician (b. Oct. 17, 1923, Muskogee, Okla.—d. May 6, 2004, San Diego, Calif.), was a pioneer electric guitarist in 1940s swing and bebop bands and the noted short film *Jammin' the Blues* (1944); he brought his sparkling lyric style to tours with Jazz at the Philharmonic and the Oscar Peterson Trio and starred as leader or sideman on many albums during the 1950s peak of "cool" West Coast jazz. The frequent winner of *Down Beat* and *Playboy* magazine jazz polls, Kessel also became an unusually versatile Hollywood studio musician, playing on film sound tracks and recording with pop stars from Doris Day to Elvis Presley and the Beach Boys; in the 1970s and '80s, he joined Herb Ellis and Charlie Byrd on concert tours as the Great Guitars.

Keys, Ancel, American physiologist (b. Jan. 26, 1904, Colorado Springs, Colo.—d. Nov. 20, 2004, Minneapolis, Minn.), created the ready-to-eat portable meals known as K rations that were used by American soldiers during World War II. After the war Keys's research on starvation shaped relief efforts in Europe. The University of Minnesota professor also conducted landmark research on the causes of heart disease and promoted the Mediterranean diet, which emphasized fruits, vegetables, and olive oil.

Khan, Vilayat Hussain, Indian sitar player and composer (b. Aug. 8, 1928, Gouripur, East Bengal, India [now in Bangladesh]—d. March 13, 2004, Mumbai [Bombay], India), developed a style of playing known as *gayaki ang* ("vocal style"), in which the sitar is used to mimic the sound of the human voice, and advanced the art of improvisation with his knack for finding the interesting patterns and unusual twists in the ragas he played. Khan was born into a long-standing family of classical musicians, and gave his first public performance at the age of 6. Besides touring and performing internationally, he composed and recorded music for motion pictures, notably the Merchant Ivory film *The Guru* (1969).

Khoo Teck Puat, Singaporean financier and hotelier (b. Jan. 13, 1917, Singapore—d. Feb. 21, 2004, Singapore), was the richest person in Singapore, with an estimated fortune of $2.6 billion; *Forbes* magazine ranked Khoo as the 137th richest person in the world in 2003. His 13.5% stake in the British-based Standard Chartered Bank made him the bank's largest single shareholder and was considered Khoo's most valuable asset at the time of his death. One of the founders of Malayan Banking (now known as Maybank), Khoo went on to serve briefly (1964–65) as a Malaysian senator before Singapore declared its independence. He subsequently acquired a string of hotels that included the Goodwood Park Hotel—considered a national landmark in Singapore. In later life Khoo was well known for his philanthropy.

Kiley, Dan (DANIEL URBAN KILEY), American landscape architect (b. Sept. 2, 1912, Boston, Mass.—d. Feb. 21, 2004, Charlotte, Vt.), helped design the iconic Gateway Arch in St. Louis, Mo., with Eero Saarinen. Though inspired by the pioneering work of Frederick Law Olmsted, Kiley ventured into modernism, collaborating with some of the foremost architects of the second half of the 20th century.

Killingsworth, Edward Abel, American architect (b. Nov. 4, 1917, Taft, Calif.—d. July 6, 2004, Long Beach, Calif.), designed elegant modernist houses in southern California and luxury hotels in Hawaii, Indonesia, and South Korea. Shortly after forming (1953) the architectural firm of Killingsworth, Brady & Smith, Killingsworth began designing low-cost homes on small-sized lots, among them the stunning Opdahl House, which was built in Long Beach in 1958. John Entenza, editor of *Arts and Architecture* magazine, chose Killingsworth to participate in the Case Study Houses project to design modern cost-effective houses. He designed six houses, four of which were constructed, the best-known being Case Study House No. 25, the Eddie Frank house, which was built in 1962. This project brought Killingsworth's work to the attention of Hilton Hotels, and he designed the Kahala Hilton (now the Kahala Mandarin Oriental), which opened in Honolulu in 1964.

King, Alan (IRWIN ALAN KNIBERG), American comedian (b. Dec. 26, 1927, New York, N.Y.—d. May 9, 2004, New York City), was renowned for his satiric monologues delivered in an agitated manner. He began his comedic career performing in nightclubs and bars but later refined his act, making it more personal, and gained popularity for his hilarious critique of suburban life in the 1950s. He appeared numerous times on television and was also an author, an actor, and a Broadway producer.

King, Michael, New Zealand historian and biographer (b. Dec. 15, 1945, Wellington, N.Z.—d. March 30, 2004, near Maramarua, N.Z.), wrote accessible scholarly works on New Zealand history and culture, both Maori and Pakeha (white), and contributed greatly to intercultural understanding; his greatest commercial success came with the best-selling *Penguin History of New Zealand* (2003). King learned the Maori language and began his career writing studies of aspects of Maori culture and biographies of important Maori figures, and he later expanded his scope to include the history and culture of white New Zealand. He wrote, singly or in collaboration, more than 30 well-received books. His many awards included an OBE in 1988 and in 2003—along with novelist Janet Frame (*q.v.*) and Maori poet Hone Tuwhare—the inaugural Prime Minister's Awards for Literary Achievement. King was killed in a car accident.

Kirkpatrick, Clayton, American journalist (b. Jan. 8, 1915, Waterman, Ill.—d. June 19, 2004, Glen Ellyn, Ill.), had a more than 40-year career in journalism most notable for his tenure as editor of the *Chicago Tribune* from 1969 to 1979. Under his guidance the newspaper was transformed from a publication with a decidedly Republican slant into a less-partisan and more influential paper.

Kleiber, Carlos, German-born conductor (b. July 3, 1930, Berlin, Ger.—d. July 13, 2004, Slovenia), was widely regarded as one of the most important opera and symphony concert conductors of the latter half of the 20th century—despite a strictly controlled repertory, infrequent public performances, capricious behaviour, and a limited number of commercial recordings. Although Kleiber could be demanding and difficult (he often walked out on rehearsals or canceled performances at the last minute), his passionate interpretations and distinctive conducting style earned acclaim and made him much sought after. He was the son of the legendary Austrian conductor Erich Kleiber and was born in Germany while his father was general music director of the Berlin State Opera. In 1935 the family moved to Argentina, where Kleiber studied music and made his conducting debut in 1952.

Klestil, Thomas, Austrian diplomat and politician (b. Nov. 4, 1932, Vienna, Austria—d. July 6, 2004, Vienna), worked to earn international respect for Austria, serving as an ambassador, as foreign minister, and, finally, as president from 1992. Klestil began his career in the Foreign Ministry in 1962. After serving as Austrian ambassador to the UN (1978–82) and to the U.S. (1982–87), he returned home to head the Foreign Ministry. After Klestil succeeded Kurt Waldheim as president, he devoted his energies to rehabilitating Austria's image, which had suffered because of its apparent tolerance of Waldheim's Nazi past. Klestil was reelected in 1998. He faced a political crisis in 2000 when the ruling conservative People's Party formed a coalition with the right-wing Freedom Party and the country was ostracized by the member-states

AP/Wide World Photos

of the European Union, which it had joined in 1995. The diplomatic sanctions were lifted after about seven months. Klestil died in office two days before the end of his second term.

Klinger, Georgette (GEORGETTE ECKSTEIN), Czech-born American skin-care innovator (b. 1915, Brno, Czechoslovakia [now in the Czech Republic]—d. Jan. 9, 2004, New York, N.Y.), revolutionized the field of cosmetics and skin care by developing products and techniques to treat the skin rather than simply cover it with makeup. She opened her first salon in Czechoslovakia in 1938 but was forced to flee the country when the Nazi rule began. Klinger opened another salon in New York City in 1941, and she eventually came to have stores nationwide. Under her influence the industry came to recognize the individual characteristics of different skin types and to see the value of facials, herbal treatments (many of which Klinger herself had developed while a child suffering from acne), and nutrition to the health of skin. Her salons were a precursor of the multibillion-dollar spa industry.

Koenig, Pierre, American architect (b. Oct. 17, 1925, San Francisco, Calif.—d. April 4, 2004, Los Angeles, Calif.), advanced the Modernist school of architecture in southern California. His low-cost steel-and-glass dwellings were designed to bring the efficiency of the Modernist aesthetic to middle-class suburbia. His Case Study House Number 22, built in 1960 in the Hollywood Hills overlooking downtown Los Angeles, became one of the most photographed private residences in the world. While he received ample critical acclaim, the environmentally friendly designs never found widespread acceptance with the middle-class audience that Koenig sought. He spent 40 years at the University of Southern California, initially as a design instructor and later as the coordinator of the school's Natural Forces Laboratory.

König, Franz Cardinal, Austrian Roman Catholic archbishop (b. Aug. 3, 1905, Rabenstein an der Pielach, Austria-Hungary [now in Austria]—d. March 13, 2004, Vienna, Austria), as archbishop of Vienna (1956–85), worked tirelessly to create ties with countries in the Soviet bloc. Consecrated cardinal by Pope John XXIII in 1958, König, who was known for his ecumenism and liberalism, sought reconciliation with other Christian churches throughout the world and became one of the most influential members of the College of Cardinals. He was a major participant in the Second Vatican Council (1962–65), pushing for greater engagement with the modern world, and was president (1965–80) of the Vatican Secretariat for Non-Believers. König was a papal candidate in 1963 and 1978 and was instrumental in the election (1978) of John Paul II, the first non-Italian pope in more than four centuries.

Ku Sang, South Korean poet (b. Sept. 16, 1919, Seoul, S.Kor.—d. May 11, 2004, Seoul), first gained acclaim for his book *Choto-ui shi* (1956; *Wastelands of Fire* [1998]), which examined the suffering caused by the Korean War. The two 100-poem cycles *Pat ilgi* and *Christopher ui gang* (1967 and 1978, respectively; published in English in the single volume *River and Fields: a Korean Century* [1991]) were regarded as his best work, embodying the lightness and spiritual warmth for which he was known.

Kübler-Ross, Elisabeth, Swiss-born American psychiatrist and author (b. July 8, 1926, Zürich, Switz.—d. Aug. 24, 2004, Scottsdale, Ariz.), was a pioneer in the study of death and dying whose work helped revolutionize the care of the terminally ill and helped change attitudes toward pain control and death itself. She was especially known for having identified five stages of grief experienced by the dying: denial, anger, bargaining, depression, and acceptance. Kübler-Ross, one of identical triplets whose survival was at first doubtful, knew at a young age that she wanted to be a doctor and defied her father's plans for her to be his secretary in the business he managed. Instead, she worked at a variety of jobs and, when World War II ended, did volunteer relief work in Poland before studying at the University of Zürich, from which she received her medical degree in 1957. She moved to the U.S. the following year and was disturbed to discover the medical community's tendency to refuse to acknowledge the reality of death to terminally ill patients and therefore to deny those patients the help they needed for dealing with it. In the early 1960s, as a teaching fellow at the University of Colorado's medical school, Kübler-Ross began to try to enlighten her students on the subject, and while working in Chicago, she held seminars in which the terminally ill were interviewed and allowed to express themselves. It was from these interviews that she developed her description of the five stages, which she set forth in her best-selling *On Death and Dying* (1969). Gradually, the medical profession adopted new methods of treating patients at the end of life. In the 1970s, however, Kübler-Ross became enamoured of more eccentric views—out-of-body experiences, spirit guides, and psychic channeling, for example—that diminished her reputation in the eyes of many people. Kübler-Ross wrote more than 20 books, including her autobiography, *The Wheel of Life: A Memoir of Living and Dying* (1997), and *On Grief and Grieving,* due to be published in 2005.

Kucher, Karol Kennedy, American ice skater (b. 1931/32, Shelton, Wash.—d. June 25, 2004, Seattle, Wash.), was—along with her brother, Peter—one of the "Kennedy Kids," the figure-skating pairs team who won five consecutive national championships (1948–52), became the first Americans to win the world pairs championship (1950), and captured an Olympic silver medal (1952). They were inducted into the U.S. Figure Skating Hall of Fame in 1991.

Kuron, Jacek Jan, Polish dissident (b. March 3, 1934, Lvov, Pol. [now Lviv, Ukraine]—d. June 17, 2004, Warsaw, Pol.), was the intellectual leader of the Solidarity labour union movement in Poland in the 1980s; he negotiated the end of the communist regime there and served as a crucial adviser to Lech Walesa, Solidarity's chairman and president of Poland (1990–95). Beginning in the 1960s, Kuron organized both student and union protests against the authoritarian Polish government and was imprisoned three times as a result. After a democratic government was formed in 1989, he served as labour minister (1989–90 and 1992–93).

Lacy, Steve (STEVEN NORMAN LACKRITZ), American musician and composer (b. July 23, 1934, New York, N.Y.—d. June 4, 2004, Boston, Mass.), helped introduce a neglected instrument, the soprano saxophone, into modern jazz in the mid-1950s, creating simple, lyric melodies with an individualistic concept of solo form and giving the traditionally high, piping horn a personal warmth and range of expression. While many modal and free-jazz saxophonists followed in his footsteps, Lacy remained one of the rare soprano saxophonists to concentrate exclusively on that instrument. He played with top Dixieland and swing musicians in his teens before forming an original modern style as a member of Cecil Taylor's radical quartet (1955–57). For many years Lacy played Thelonious Monk's idiosyncratic repertoire almost exclusively; as his style evolved, he began playing in the new free-jazz idiom with a unique melodic simplicity, as showcased in his 1967–68 tours of Europe and South America. After settling in Europe in 1969, he alternated between Monk's repertoire, his original free-jazz songs, and themeless, free improvisation, often in solo saxophone concerts. Lacy led a series of small groups that usually included his wife, singer-cellist-violinist Irene Aebi; he created musical settings of texts by Lao Tzu, Herman Melville, Robert Creeley, Bengali poet Taslima Nasrin, and others, and he collaborated with dancers and visual artists. In four decades of reunions with trombonist Roswell Rudd and, in duets and combos, with pianist Mal Waldron, he progressed from melodic Monk variations to the most extreme abstraction. Lacy recorded more than 200 albums, a feat matched by few other jazz musicians. He received a MacArthur Foundation fellowship in 1992. Ten years later he moved back to the U.S. to teach at the New England Conservatory of Music in Boston.

Laforet (Díaz), Carmen, Catalan writer (b. Sept. 6, 1921, Barcelona, Spain—d. Feb. 28, 2004, Madrid, Spain), helped to revitalize Spanish literature by introducing modernism and the existential voice in her first and best-known novel, *Nada* (1945; "Nothingness"; Eng. trans., *Nada,* 1958). A direct and unaffected

AP/Wide World Photos

portrait of a demoralized and sordid post-Civil War Barcelona as seen through the eyes of a young woman, *Nada* became a classic of modern Spanish literature and has remained in print.

Lanin, (Nathaniel) Lester, American bandleader (b. Aug. 26, 1907, Philadelphia, Pa.—d. Oct. 27, 2004, New York, N.Y.), provided the music for several decades' worth of high-society parties and balls with his tasteful mix of music types, including his debutante ball standard "Pink Petal Waltz." He had as many as 12 bands on the road at times during his more than 70-year career, and they played for over 30,000 events. Lanin's businessman's bounce—a fast two-beat dance tempo—also was heard on some three dozen record albums.

LaRue, Frederick Cheney, American businessman and political figure (b. Oct. 11, 1928, Athens, Texas—d. July 24, 2004, Biloxi, Miss.), served as an aide to Pres. Richard M. Nixon and was a prominent figure in the cover-up of the Watergate break-in during the reelection campaign in 1972. Although he was the "bagman" who delivered the payoff money to the burglars to encourage their silence and served 136 days in prison after pleading guilty to obstruction of justice, he was rumoured to be "Deep Throat"—the insider who helped reporters Bob Woodward and Carl Bernstein in their investigation of the story for the *Washington Post*—an allegation he denied.

Lasky, Melvin Jonah, American editor (b. Jan. 15, 1920, New York, N.Y.—d. May 19, 2004, Berlin, Ger.), gained a reputation as an ardent soldier in the cultural Cold War while editor of the magazine *Encounter* from 1958 to 1990. The liberal and devoutly anticommunist magazine initially flourished under Lasky's editorship, attracting leading thinkers and writers, such as Bertrand Russell, Arthur Koestler, and Vladimir Nabokov, but its prestige plummeted after 1967 when it was revealed that the magazine received financial support from the CIA.

Lauder, Estée (JOSEPHINE ESTHER MENTZER), American businesswoman (b. July 1, 1906?, Queens, N.Y.—d. April 24, 2004, New York, N.Y.), founded the international cosmetics empire that bears her name. Her business acumen was apparent at an early age. Her uncle, John Schotz, was a chemist who brewed beauty concoctions in a converted stable behind the family home. While still a teenager, she helped promote his Super-Rich All-Purpose Cream to women in her neighbourhood. These early experiences influenced her hands-on approach to both marketing and product development. She initially sold her products through beauty salons, and her emphasis on quality was apparent from the beginning. The highest-quality materials were used for both her beauty products and the packaging that contained them. In 1946, with the assistance of her husband, Joseph, she founded the Estée Lauder Co. Although the company initially had only four products and $400 a week in revenues, by 1958 yearly sales were approaching $1 million. Much of this success was due to Lauder's personal touch and persistence. By targeting high-end retailers such as Saks Fifth Avenue and Bloomingdale's, Lauder made her brand synonymous with style and class. Her trademark "gift with purchase" became a standard for beauty-product marketing, and her allergy-tested Clinique line (introduced in 1968) added an air of science to the fragrance counter. Other lines included Aramis for men (introduced in 1964), Prescriptives (1979), and Origins (1990). By the time the company went public in 1995, its estimated worth was over $2 billion.

Cosmetics empress Estée Lauder

Lawrence, Jerome, American playwright and director (b. July 14, 1915, Cleveland, Ohio—d. Feb. 29, 2004, Malibu, Calif.), had a writing partnership with Robert E. Lee for about half a century, during which they created 39 plays, a dozen of which were produced on Broadway. Among their best-known works were *Inherit the Wind* (1955; filmed 1960), *Auntie Mame* (1956; filmed 1958; adapted into the musical *Mame,* 1966; filmed 1974), *The Night Thoreau Spent in Jail* (1970), and *First Monday in October* (1978; filmed 1981).

Lee-Potter, Lynda (LYNDA HIGGINSON), British journalist (b. May 2, 1935, Leigh, Lancashire, Eng.—d. Oct. 20, 2004, Stoborough, Dorset, Eng.), was admired for her sharp wit, notorious for her derisive criticism of celebrities and other notable persons, and controversial for her attacks on such social targets as single mothers and political correctness, particularly in her weekly column for the *Daily Mail* newspaper from 1972. With her working-class background, the "First Lady of Fleet Street" was attuned to the mind-set of her readers, and she possessed a unique talent for putting their thoughts into words. Lee-Potter's book *Class Act: How to Beat the British Class System* was published in 2000.

Leigh, Janet (JEANETTE HELEN MORRISON), American actress (b. July 6, 1927, Merced, Calif.—d. Oct. 3, 2004, Beverly Hills, Calif.), had a half-century-long career that comprised some 60 motion pictures as well as television appearances, but it was for one role in particular that she was most remembered, Marion Crane in Alfred Hitchcock's *Psycho* (1960). In that film she suffered one of filmdom's most memorable and shocking screen deaths—a 45-second shower stabbing attack that was astonishing not only for its impact but also for the fact that the star was killed before the movie was half over. Leigh's career began in the style of a classic Hollywood legend; film star Norma Shearer saw her photograph at the ski resort where Leigh's father worked and recommended her to an agent. Her debut was in *The Romance of Rosy Ridge* (1947), in which she was the ingenue lead. Other such roles that followed included Meg in *Little Women* (1949) and the title character in *My Sister Eileen* (1955). Leigh's 1951 marriage to actor Tony Curtis was seen by fans as a perfect Hollywood love story. The couple divorced, however, in 1962. While married, they costarred in a few lesser-quality movies, but during those years Leigh also made her best films, *Touch of Evil* (1958), *Psycho,* and *The Manchurian Candidate* (1962). Later films included *Bye Bye Birdie* (1963), *Harper* (1966), *The Fog* (1980), and *Halloween H20: 20 Years Later* (1998), in the latter two of which she performed with her daughter Jamie Lee Curtis. Leigh also made appearances in television series and wrote two novels, *House of Destiny* (1995) and *The Dream Factory* (2002).

Psycho *actress Janet Leigh*

Lenart, Jozef, Czechoslovak politician (b. April 3, 1923, Liptovska Porubka, Czechoslovakia [now in Slovakia]—d. Feb. 11, 2004, Prague, Czech Rep.), through a studied ambiguity that permitted him to be seen as all things to all people, remained at the pinnacle of the communist political system in Czechoslovakia for more than two decades. He became first secretary of Czechoslovakia's Communist Party in 1962 and prime minister of Czechoslovakia in 1963, positions he retained as reforms accelerated toward the Prague Spring in 1968. He was dismissed as prime minister in April of that year, but he remained on the Czechoslovak Communist Party's presidium and was first secretary of the Slovak Communist Party from 1970 until the year before the collapse of the communist system in 1989. In 1995 Lenart was indicted for treason in connection with his role in the Soviet suppression of the Prague Spring. He was acquitted in 2002, but his role in those events remained unelucidated.

Leônidas (LEÔNIDAS DA SILVA), Brazilian association football (soccer) player (b. Sept. 6, 1913, Rio de Janeiro, Braz.—d. Jan. 24, 2004, São Paulo, Braz.), was Brazil's first football hero and the high scorer at the 1938 World Cup finals with eight goals, including four against Poland in a round-of-16 match in which he played barefoot when his shoes came off in the mud. He was unexpectedly left out for the team's semifinal match against Italy, which Brazil duly lost, but he scored twice in Brazil's 4–2 victory over Sweden for third place. Known as the "Diamante Negro" ("Black Diamond"), the mixed-race Leônidas was a quick and agile centre-forward and a master of the flamboyant bicycle kick, which he was often credited with having invented. As a professional he helped win the Rio state championship for Vasco da Gama (1934), Botafogo (1935), and Flamengo (1939). After serving an eight-month prison sentence for having forged a certificate to avoid military service, he transferred to São Paulo and helped that team win its state title five times in seven years. He retired in 1951 and later became one of Brazil's best-known radio sports commentators.

Lerner, Alexander Yakob (ALEKSANDR YAKOVLEVICH LERNER), Soviet mathematician (b. Sept. 7, 1913, Vinnytsya, Ukraine—d. April 5, 2004, Rehovot, Israel), was a pioneer in cybernetics—the study of control and communication applied to humans, animals, electronic devices, and organizations. He was the author of scores of scientific papers and a dozen books, notably *Nachala kibernetiki* (1967; *Fundamentals of Cybernetics,* 1972), which remained a standard comparison of electronic and biological control systems. As one of the first "refuseniks" who sought permission to emigrate and move to Israel, Lerner was fired (1971) from his post as head of the U.S.S.R. Academy of Sciences' department of large systems control theory and spent 17 years seeking an exit visa. After finally being allowed to leave the U.S.S.R. in January 1988, he joined the mathematics faculty at the Weizmann Institute of Science in Rehovot, where he worked on the development of an artificial heart.

Levin, (Henry) Bernard, British journalist (b. Aug. 19, 1928, London, Eng.—d. Aug. 7, 2004, London), applied his acerbic wit for almost 40 years as a political columnist and entertainment critic for such newspapers as *The Spectator, The Guardian,* the *Daily Mail,* and, especially, *The Times,* where he was chief columnist from 1971 to 1997. In 1962 he made his television debut as a commentator on the BBC satire *That Was the Week That Was.* Levin was an unsparing critic of MPs on both sides of the aisle and was credited with having coined the term "nanny state" to describe the increasing role of government in personal affairs. He was appointed CBE in 1990.

Lewis, Edward B., American geneticist (b. May 20, 1918, Wilkes-Barre, Pa.—d. July 21, 2004, Pasadena, Calif.), discovered how certain genes control early development in embryos. For this work Lewis was awarded the 1995 Nobel Prize for Physiology or Medicine jointly with two other geneticists, Christiane Nüsslein-Volhard and Eric F. Wieschaus, whose independent research had complemented Lewis's studies. While on the faculty of the California Institute of Technology, Lewis studied the chromosomes of fruit flies for many years. He identified a group of genes that control development of the flies' body segments and found that the linear arrangement of the genes on the chromosome corresponds to the order of the body segments they control. He also discovered that the operation of these genes is turned on and off by a gene cluster that serves as a master control switch. Molecular biologists later determined that genes analogous to those identified by Lewis in fruit flies are present in most vertebrates (including humans) and that these genes control embryonic development in strikingly similar ways. In the mid-1950s Lewis conducted a landmark study on the effect of radiation as a source of cancer. His results challenged the U.S. government's position that there existed a level of radiation, called the threshold dose, below which a person could be safely exposed without cancer's being induced. Among the many honours Lewis accrued during his long career was election to the National Academy of Sciences (1968) and to the American Philosophical Society (1990). He also became (1989) a foreign member of the Royal Society and was awarded (1990) the National Medal of Science.

Lewitzky, Bella, American dancer and choreographer (b. Jan. 13, 1916, Los Angeles, Calif.—d. July 16, 2004, Pasadena, Calif.), began her performing career with Lester Horton's company before forming (1966) the Bella Lewitzky Dance Company in Los Angeles, which she danced with until 1978 and directed until she disbanded it in 1997. Besides being an influential modern dance figure who worked to establish modern dance as a prominent art form in California and pushed for government support for the arts, she also was a champion of artistic freedom; in 1990 she mounted a successful legal challenge against the National Endowment for the Arts after it instituted a requirement that grant recipients sign an antiobscenity pledge.

López Portillo, José, Mexican politician (b. June 16, 1920, Mexico City, Mex.—d. Feb. 17,

AP/Wide World Photos

Mexican president José López Portillo

2004, Mexico City), served as president of Mexico from 1976 to 1982; although he presided over a spectacular oil boom, inefficiency and corruption in his government brought the country to the brink of economic collapse, and he spent much of his later life in self-imposed exile in Europe. López Portillo attended the National Autonomous University of Mexico, where one of his classmates and close friends was future president Luís Echeverría Álvarez. After graduation, López Portillo briefly practiced law and then returned to the university as a professor of law, political science, and public administration. He eventually joined Mexico's ruling Institutional Revolutionary Party (PRI) and held a number of government posts before Echeverría took office and appointed him minister of finance in 1973. Although the inflation rate and unemployment rose under the Echeverría administration, López Portillo was credited with modernizing tax-collection procedures, pursuing tax evaders, and reducing public spending. Before leaving the presidency, Echeverría designated López Portillo as his successor. An energetic and charismatic man whose wide-ranging interests included writing, painting, boxing, and javelin throwing, López Portillo initially enjoyed widespread popularity as president. He succeeded in bringing about several important political reforms, most notably an increase in the size of the federal Chamber of Deputies to 400 members, with a minimum of 100 seats reserved for opposition parties. This measure was designed to permit more minority participation in Mexican politics, which had been dominated by the PRI since 1929. López Portillo also benefited from the discovery of huge petroleum reserves in Veracruz and Tabasco states. He launched an ambitious program to exploit these reserves, rapidly expanding the country's oil exports. Much of the resulting wealth was squandered, however. The government borrowed heavily abroad against future oil revenues, and billions of dollars were lost to rampant government corruption. When world oil prices collapsed in 1981, Mexico was left with a huge foreign debt, and López Portillo left office in disgrace a year later. To escape withering criticism at home, he immediately fled to Europe, but he eventually returned to settle in Mexico in the late 1990s as his health deteriorated.

Manchester, William Raymond, American historian (b. April 1, 1922, Attleboro, Mass.—d. June 1, 2004, Middletown, Conn.), penned three popular volumes about Pres. John F. Kennedy. Manchester was a friend and confidant of the president and in 1962 published *Portrait of a President: John F. Kennedy in Profile,* an account of Kennedy's first year in office. Two years later Jacqueline Kennedy commissioned him to write a book about the president's assassination, but she then sought to block the publication of *The Death of a President* (1967) over concerns that it revealed private family matters. The public quarrel was resolved when Manchester removed several passages. His third book on President Kennedy, *One Brief Shining Moment* (1983), looked fondly back on the era of "Camelot." In Baltimore, Md., Manchester served as foreign correspondent for the *Evening Sun* before pursuing historical writing. His books *The Arms of Krupp, 1587–1968* (1968), which examined the powerful German family, and *American Caesar, Douglas MacArthur, 1880–1964* (1978) were immensely popular. *Goodbye, Darkness* (1980), which recounted his personal experiences in the Pacific during World War II, was widely praised for its gripping depiction of combat. Manchester was able to complete only two volumes of *The Last Lion* (1983 and 1988), his biographical trilogy of Winston Churchill.

Mara, Ratu Sir Kamisese (RATU SIR KAMISESE KAPAIWAI TUIMACILAI MARA), Fijian politician (b. May 6, 1920, Lomaloma, Vanua Balavu Island, Lau Archipelago, Fiji—d. April 18, 2004, Suva, Fiji), was the founding father of modern Fiji as the country's first prime minister, from 1970 to 1992 (except for a few months in 1987); he later served as vice president (1992–93) and president (1994–2000). Mara, who was born into a noble family, studied medicine at the University of Otago in Dunedin, N.Z., and modern history at Wadham College, Oxford. After graduation he returned to Fiji and entered politics, succeeding his father as paramount chief of the Lau Archipelago and rising to join (1959) the executive council. As Fiji sought independence from Great Britain in the 1960s, Mara founded (1964) the multiracial Alliance Party and consolidated his power. He led Fiji to independence in 1970. By 1971 he had marshalled together a South Pacific Forum (later the Pacific Islands Forum) and had become recognized as the region's leading statesman. At home he expanded both tourism and the sugar industry. A coup in 2000 led to his retirement.

Markandaya, Kamala (KAMALA PURNAIYA TAYLOR), Indian-born novelist (b. 1924, Chimakurti, Mysore, India—d. May 16, 2004, London, Eng.), pioneered in examining the issues facing postcolonial Indians as one of the first Indian novelists to write for an English-language audience. Though her characters were ordinary people, she conveyed through them acutely felt stories—told quietly and skillfully—of human endurance in a changing world. Taylor was born into a Brahman family and studied history at the University of Madras. From 1940 to 1947 she wrote short fiction and worked as a journalist. She left India for London in 1948 and made her home there, marrying an Englishman. She returned often to India, however, and her works retained their authenticity. *Nectar in a Sieve* (1954), the first of her 10 novels to be published, presented the realities of life for a suffering but resolute woman in rural India. It was an immediate best seller in the U.S., and many regarded it as the book that introduced Americans to life in India. Of her later novels, *A Handful of Rice* (1966) and *The Nowhere Man* (1972) were often included in the curriculum of literature courses across the U.S. Her final novel, *Pleasure City* (1982; U.S. title *Shalimar*), told in her trademark lyrical but realistic style, was somewhat overshadowed by the publication one year earlier of Salman Rushdie's allegorical novel *Midnight's Children,* which signaled a change in the taste of the reading public.

Markova, Dame Alicia (LILIAN ALICIA MARKS), British ballet dancer (b. Dec. 1, 1910, London, Eng.—d. Dec. 2, 2004, Bath, Eng.), was the first true British prima ballerina and one of the finest dancers of the 20th century and as such helped establish a ballet tradition in her country. Although she danced a wide range of roles, her light, ethereal quality lent itself especially to the role with which she was most closely associated, the title character in *Giselle.* Markova began studying dance to correct weak legs and feet, and by the time she was 10 she was earning money dancing in pantomimes. At 14 she joined Sergey Diaghilev's Ballets Russes, with which she remained until Diaghilev's death in 1929. Markova and Anton Dolin—her partner for most of her career—founded the Markova-Dolin Ballet (1935–37, re-formed in 1945), which eventually (1969) became the London Festival Ballet and later (1989) the English National Ballet. They danced with other companies, notably the Ballet Russe de Monte-Carlo and Ballet Theatre (later American Ballet Theatre) in New York City. After Markova ceased dancing (1963), she taught, staged ballets, and served as director of the Metropolitan Opera Ballet in New York City (until 1969). Markova was made CBE in 1958 and DBE in 1963.

Martin, Agnes Bernice, American painter (b. March 22, 1912, Macklin, Sask.—d. Dec. 16, 2004, Taos, N.M.), developed a spare, meticulously drawn, and meditative style that made her one of the giants of 20th-century Abstract Expressionism. In 1931, already interested in art, she moved to the United States for teacher training. While in New York City, where she attended (1941–42) Columbia University, she began to paint portraits and landscapes and to work seriously as an artist. Martin moved to Albuquerque, N.M., in 1946 and became a U.S. citizen in 1950. She moved often in the next several years, earning an M.A. in New York, living in Taos, teaching in Oregon, and in 1957 returning to New York. There she had her first one-woman gallery show (1958), and—in association with artists such as Barnett Newman, Lenore Tawney, and Ellsworth Kelly—she began painting the gridlike abstractions that drew attention to her. In 1967 she abruptly left New York and the art world, beginning to paint again only in 1974. Thereafter, she lived in New Mexico and, until the last months of her life, painted her characteristic six-foot-square (in her later years, five-foot-square) canvases with light-soaked, quiet, endlessly absorbing abstractions.

Martin, Bill, Jr. (WILLIAM IVAN MARTIN, JR.), American author (b. March 20, 1916, Hiawatha, Kan.—d. Aug. 11, 2004, Commerce, Texas), wrote more than 300 children's books in his career. Though not an avid reader as a child, Martin was inspired to encourage youngsters to read. His first book, *The Little Squeegy Bug,* was illustrated by his brother Bernard and appeared in 1948. His best books, such as *Brown Bear, Brown Bear, What Do You See?* (1967) and *Chicka, Chicka, Boom, Boom* (1989), contained an adventurous spirit and rhythmic wordplay.

Máspoli, Roque Gastón, Uruguayan association football (soccer) player (b. Oct. 12, 1917, Montevideo, Uruguay—d. Feb. 22, 2004, Montevideo), was a national sports hero in Uruguay for his role as the national team's goalkeeper in the 1950 World Cup finals, in which Uruguay upset Brazil, the heavily favoured host country, 2–1 in the decisive final match to win its second World Cup trophy. As goalkeeper (1940–55) for the renowned Peñarol football club, Máspoli helped that team win five league championships. He later coached Peñarol to three more league titles, the 1966 Libertadores Cup, and the 1966 Intercontinental Cup over European champion Real Madrid. Máspoli was coach of the national side in the early 1980s and guided Uruguay to victory in the Copa de Oro, a competition of all former World Cup winners, in 1980.

Maynard Smith, John, British evolutionary biologist (b. Jan. 6, 1920, London, Eng.—d. April 19, 2004, Lewes, East Sussex, Eng.), was renowned for explaining evolutionary strategies, especially the origin of sex, by means of the mathematical theory of games. Maynard Smith graduated (1941) from Trinity College, Cambridge, with an engineering degree. Having been rejected for World War II military service because of poor eyesight, he worked on military aircraft design (1942–47). Thereafter, he went to University College, London (UCL), to study zoology with geneticist J.B.S. Haldane, a fellow Marxist and member of the Communist Party who became his mentor. After earning his doctorate in 1951, Maynard Smith remained at UCL as a lecturer. He quit the Communist Party following the Soviet invasion of Hungary in 1956. In 1965 he left UCL to become the founding dean of the School of Biological Sciences at Sussex University, where he remained until his retirement in 1985. Among his major books were *The Theory of Evolution* (1958), *The Evolution of Sex* (1978), *Evolution and the Theory of Games* (1982), *The Major Transitions in Evolution* (with Hungarian biochemist Eors Szathmary, 1995), and *Animal Signals* (2003). Maynard Smith was a recipient of Sweden's Crafoord Prize in 1999 and the Kyoto Prize in 2001.

McCain, Harrison, Canadian entrepreneur (b. Nov. 3, 1927, Florenceville, N.B.—d. March 18, 2004, Boston, Mass.), launched (1956) McCain Foods Ltd. (with his brother Wallace), which grew steadily under his leadership to become the world's leading supplier of frozen, oven-ready French fries. McCain's driving force behind the business catapulted it from a rural 30-person operation headquartered in his hometown in the late 1950s to a $6.4 billion enterprise that employed approximately 18,000 people and operated 55 facilities worldwide in 2003. Nicknamed the "king of the frozen French fry," McCain was recognized by *Forbes* magazine in its 2004 list of billionaires.

McCambridge, (Carlotta) Mercedes (Agnes), American actress (b. March 17, 1916, Joliet, Ill.—d. March 2, 2004, La Jolla, Calif.), had a long career in radio, film, and television and on the stage during which she especially excelled in roles calling for strong women. She won a best supporting actress Academy Award for her film debut in *All the King's Men* (1949) and went on to prominent roles in such films as *Johnny Guitar* (1954), *Giant* (1956), *Touch of Evil* (1958), and *Suddenly Last Summer* (1959). She was never seen, however, in what was perhaps her best-known film role—the demon voice of the possessed child in *The Exorcist* (1973). In the early 1990s McCambridge took over the role of the stern grandmother in Neil Simon's *Lost in Yonkers*, and by the time she left the play, she had performed it 560 times on Broadway and on the road.

McClelland, Jack (JOHN GORDON MCCLELLAND), Canadian book publisher (b. July 30, 1922, Toronto, Ont.—d. June 14, 2004, Toronto), invigorated the world of Canadian literature with his passionate support of writers and with his wild publicity stunts to promote their books. Such exhibitions included dressing in a toga and riding down Toronto's busiest streets in a chariot and riding the city's streetcars wearing a "coat of many authors"—a jacket imprinted with book covers of works he had published. Even though his publishing company, McClelland & Stewart, struggled financially, McClelland was known to place his authors' careers ahead of his own profit. Through his perseverance McClelland brought attention to the works of such famous Canadian writers as Margaret Atwood, Pierre Berton (*q.v.*), Leonard Cohen, Margaret Laurence, Alice Munro, and Mordecai Richler.

McGraw, Tug (FRANK EDWIN MCGRAW, JR.), American baseball player (b. Aug. 30, 1944, Martinez, Calif.—d. Jan. 5, 2004, Nashville, Tenn.), was a relief pitching hero for the New York Mets and Philadelphia Phillies professional baseball teams. Though a failure as a starter, McGraw learned to pitch a screwball and then became a reliever in 1969, the year that the "Miracle Mets" won their first world championship; four years later his late-season pitching and his slogan "You gotta believe!" inspired the Mets' rise from last place in August to the National League pennant. During 1975–84 he pitched for the Phillies as they made it to the play-offs for six seasons, including two National League championships; his finest season was 1980, when he pitched in 57 games with an extraordinary 1.46 earned run average and clinched Philadelphia's World Series victory by striking out the last batter of the last game.

McGrory, Mary, American journalist (b. Aug. 22, 1918, Boston, Mass.—d. April 21, 2004, Washington, D.C.), broke ground as a female newspaper political columnist and enjoyed a more-than-50-year career. Her gift for lucid yet poetic writing combined with her love of the art of reporting won her the respect and affection of her colleagues and several generations of newspaper readers. McGrory, who throughout her career took pride in her Boston Irish heritage, began her journalism career as a book reviewer at the *Boston Herald,* moving to the *Washington Star* in 1947. She was promoted to reporter in 1954 and did her first extended reporting on the hearings in which the army accused Sen. Joseph McCarthy of interfering with military operations in his search for communists. In 1960 her column went into national syndication, and in 1975 she won a Pulitzer Prize for her reporting of the Watergate hearings. She moved to the *Washington Post* in 1981 after the *Star* went out of business. An eloquent liberal voice, McGrory made the infamous "enemies list" of Pres. Richard M. Nixon. She continued writing a column for the *Post* until early 2003, when a stroke curtailed her career.

© Gjon Mili/Time Life Pictures/Getty Images

Political columnist Mary McGrory

McWhirter, Norris Dewar, British publisher (b. Aug. 12, 1925, London, Eng.—d. April 19, 2004, Kington Langley, Wiltshire, Eng.), cofounded, along with his twin brother, Ross, *The Guinness Book of Records* (later *Guinness World Records*). The statistical tome, which was first published in 1955, surveyed achievements both heroic and absurd and remained one of the world's best-selling books. Norris McWhirter parlayed notable athletic success as a youth into a career as a sportswriter before cofounding, also with his brother, a business selling sporting facts to newspapers. In 1954 the pair persuaded the Guinness Brewery to finance a book of facts to settle bar bets, and in 1972 they began appearing on the television show *Record Breakers.* The brothers were also conservative political activists, and Ross was murdered in 1975 by Irish Republican Army terrorists. Norris continued to edit the *Book of Records* and several related volumes until 1986 and served as an advisory editor until 1996. He was made CBE in 1980.

Meader, (Abbott) Vaughn, American comedian (b. March 20, 1936, Waterville, Maine—d. Oct. 29, 2004, Auburn, Maine), became famous by means of his impersonation of Pres. John F. Kennedy on his satiric album *The First Family* (1962), which sold some 7.5 million copies and in 1963 won a Grammy Award. His career was halted by Kennedy's assassination later that year, however, and he struggled with substance-abuse troubles for many years before finding a new life as a bluegrass musician.

Merrill, Robert (MOISHE MILLER), American opera singer (b. June 4, 1917, Brooklyn, N.Y.—d. Oct. 23, 2004, New Rochelle, N.Y.), employed his powerful, precise baritone voice for some 31 seasons (1945–75) at New York City's Metropolitan Opera, where he was especially noted for his performances in the operas of Giuseppe Verdi. Besides being hailed for filling such roles as Germont in *La traviata* and the title role in *Rigoletto,* however, he also was renowned for his rendition of "The Star-Spangled Banner," which for many years from 1969 was a season-opening tradition at baseball's Yankee Stadium. Merrill was honoured with the National Medal of Arts in 1993.

Messerer, Sulamith Mikhaylovna, Russian-born ballet dancer and teacher (b. Aug. 27, 1908, Moscow, Russia—d. June 3, 2004, London, Eng.), devoted her life to the Bolshoi Ballet as a student, prima ballerina, teacher, choreographer, and artistic ambassador until she defected to the West (1980); she then settled in London, where she remained a guest teacher with the Royal Ballet School. A vibrant and athletic dancer, Messerer joined the Bolshoi Ballet School in 1920. She abruptly moved up from the corps de ballet in 1926 when she substituted for an injured soloist, and within three years she was one of the Bolshoi's leading dancers. In the 1930s she was allowed to travel outside the Soviet Union with her brother and frequent partner, Asaf (who also became a teacher), and in the early 1960s she was sent to Tokyo to found the first ballet school in Japan. Messerer was awarded the Stalin Prize in 1946 and was declared a

AP/Wide World Photos

People's Artist of the Russian S.F.S.R. in 1962. In 2000 Messerer was made OBE.

Meyer, Russ, American filmmaker (b. March 21, 1922, Oakland, Calif.—d. Sept. 18, 2004, Los Angeles, Calif.), brought exuberant sexuality into the Hollywood mainstream with films such as *Faster Pussycat! Kill! Kill!* (1966) and *Beyond the Valley of the Dolls* (1970). He transcended the "sexploitation" label by introducing humorous dialogue, genuine craftsmanship, and an unmistakable sense of style to that genre. In recognition of his work, the Museum of Modern Art in New York City added 4 of his 26 films to its permanent collection.

Miller, Ann (JOHNNIE LUCILLE ANN COLLIER), American dancer and actress (b. April 12, 1919?, Chireno, Texas—d. Jan. 22, 2004, Los Angeles, Calif.), had a powerful machine-gun tap-dancing style—she claimed a speed of

MGM/The Kobal Collection

Tap-dancing actress Ann Miller

500 taps a minute—that, accompanied by her effervescent personality, dazzled movie audiences of the 1940s and '50s and in the late 1970s and early '80s made her a star of the musical stage. Although she never achieved top-ranked movie stardom, her performance with Mickey Rooney in the vaudeville-style *Sugar Babies* on Broadway from 1979 to 1982 and then on tour brought her the celebrity status she had long sought. When she was a small child, Miller suffered from rickets and was given dancing lessons to straighten her legs. She began her career before she was a teenager, dancing on the vaudeville stage and in clubs, and made her film debut in *New Faces of 1937*. She went on to roles in *Stage Door* (1937), *You Can't Take It with You* (1938), and a series of low-budget movies that gained her the nickname "queen of the B's." Her luck changed, however, when Cyd Charisse broke her leg and was unable to appear in *Easter Parade*, and Miller was chosen to replace her. This led to important roles in several films, including the classic *On the Town* (1949), *Kiss Me Kate* (1953), and *Deep in My Heart* (1954). With the waning in popularity of the movie musical in the 1950s, Miller concentrated more on performing in nightclubs and on television, and in 1969 she was a hit on Broadway when she took over the title role in *Mame*. In 1972 her flamboyant style was put to good use when she appeared in a TV commercial that featured a splashy production number with Miller dancing on a huge soup can. In her final motion picture role, she portrayed an eccentric landlady in David Lynch's *Mulholland Dr.* (2001).

Miller, Keith Ross, Australian cricketer (b. Nov. 28, 1919, Sunshine, Vic., Australia—d. Oct. 11, 2004, near Melbourne, Australia), was one of the best all-rounders of the 20th century and a key member of Don Bradman's Australian team that was unbeaten on its 1948 tour of England. A glamourous middle-order right-hand batsman and right-arm fast bowler, he scored 181 runs for Victoria on his first-class debut. Miller served as a fighter pilot during World War II, and in 1945 he made 2 centuries in the unofficial Victory Tests and 185 centuries for the Dominions versus England. He made his Test debut against New Zealand in 1946 and batted his first Test century (141 not out) in the fourth Test at Adelaide in the 1946–47 series against England. Though hampered by back trouble on the 1948 England tour, Miller took seven wickets in the first Test at Nottingham and scored more than a thousand runs for the tour. He retired from Test cricket in 1956 after having played in 55 matches and scored 2,958 runs (for an average of 36.97), with seven centuries and a high score of 147. As a bowler he took 170 wickets (average 22.97), taking 5 wickets in a match seven times and 10 wickets in a match once. Miller also took 38 catches, fielding primarily in the slips. In domestic cricket he played 18 matches for Victoria and 50 for New South Wales, where he served as captain. Miller was made MBE in 1956. He became a journalist after his retirement from the game.

Miłosz, Czesław, Polish-born poet, essayist, critic, and translator (b. June 30, 1911, Šateiniai, Lithuania, Russian Empire [now in Lithuania]—d. Aug. 14, 2004, Kraków, Pol.), as a witness to World War II and the subsequent Soviet takeover of Eastern Europe, crafted emotional and provocative works that examined inhumanity, displacement, and loss. Considered one of the major poets of the 20th century, he was awarded the Nobel Prize for Literature in 1980. Miłosz received a law degree (1934) from Stefan Batory University in Wilno, Pol. (now Vilnius, Lithuania). A member of the Catastrophist group of poets, he

© Sophie Bassouls/Corbis Sygma

Man of letters Czesław Miłosz

foreshadowed World War II in his first book of verse, *Poemat o czasie zastygłym* (1933; "Poem of Frozen Time"). Following Germany's invasion of Poland in 1939, Miłosz moved to Warsaw and became active in the resistance. The poems he wrote during the occupation were collected in *Ocalenie* (1945; "Rescue"). After the war he served as a diplomat for Poland's communist government before defecting in 1951. He eventually settled in the U.S., where he taught (1960–80) at the University of California, Berkeley. He became a U.S. citizen in 1970. Although Miłosz was primarily a poet, perhaps his best-known work was *Zniewolony umysł* (1953; *The Captive Mind*, 1953), a collection of essays in which he described the life of intellectuals under communist rule. His other writings included scholarly texts, novels, and the autobiography *Rodzinna Europa* (1959; *Native Realm*, 1968). He also translated a number of works into Polish. Regarded as a national hero by many Poles, Miłosz returned to Poland in the early 1990s following the fall of communism.

Mitchelson, Marvin Morris, American lawyer (b. May 7, 1928, Detroit, Mich.—d. Sept. 18, 2004, Beverly Hills, Calif.), established the concept of palimony—the right of a long-time, but unmarried, live-in partner to sue for alimony—in the 1976 California Supreme Court case *Marvin* v. *Marvin*. Mitchelson won fame as a divorce lawyer to the stars, but his Hollywood lifestyle drew the attention of the Internal Revenue Service. He was disbarred and sentenced to two years in prison for tax fraud in 1993, but in 2000 he successfully petitioned the authorities to regain his license to practice.

© Paul Harris/Getty Images

Mitrokhin, Vasily Nikitich, Soviet intelligence archivist (b. March 3, 1922, Yurasovo,

Russian S.F.S.R. [now in Russia]—d. Jan. 23, 2004, London, Eng.), spent 12 years meticulously transcribing and concealing KGB documents that he later delivered to the British intelligence agency MI6, exposing secrets from 1917 to 1984. Mitrokhin began working for the KGB's predecessor organization in 1948. In 1956 he was transferred to the service's archives, becoming chief archivist in 1972. At that time he began keeping detailed records of all the archives (hidden in containers buried at his home); he continued until his retirement in 1984. After the dissolution of the Soviet Union, he walked into the British embassy in Riga, Latvia, with a sample of his cache, and shortly MI6 operatives extracted his trove of documents and him and his family. His work became public knowledge with the publication of *The Mitrokhin Archive* (1999), which he co-wrote with Christopher Andrew.

Moorer, Thomas Hinman, U.S. Navy admiral (b. Feb. 9, 1912, Mount Willing, Ala.—d. Feb. 5, 2004, Bethesda, Md.), was chief of naval operations (1967–70) and chairman of the Joint Chiefs of Staff (1970–74) during the Vietnam War. A naval aviator in World War II stationed at Pearl Harbor, Moorer rose through the ranks of the U.S. Navy to command the Pacific Fleet from 1964. In the 1960s he advocated attacking targets in North Vietnam to dissuade insurgencies in South Vietnam and Laos.

Moraes, Dom (DOMINIC FRANCIS MORAES), Indian writer (b. July 19, 1938, Bombay [now Mumbai], India—d. June 2, 2004, Mumbai), produced poetry and prose that revealed his ambiguity about his place in the world. English was his only language. The son of the first Indian editor of *The Times of India,* Moraes traveled widely in his youth and settled for a time in England. He was at age 19 the youngest winner of England's Hawthornden Prize for the best work of imaginative literature—for *A Beginning* (1958)—and was at the time of his death still the award's only non-British recipient. He considered himself a poet, but he was perhaps better known for *My Son's Father* (1968) and other memoirs.

Morgan, (George) Frederick, American man of letters (b. April 25, 1922, New York, N.Y.—d. Feb. 20, 2004, New York City), founded in 1947 *The Hudson Review,* a quarterly that published some of the finest writers and poets of the second half of the 20th century. The journal, which he edited for 55 years, had an influence far greater than its sparse circulation, and it adhered to no prescribed academic or political allegiances. A mainstay on the New York literary scene, Morgan became known for his own poetry late in life.

Morris, Norval, New Zealand-born American criminologist (b. Oct. 1, 1923, Auckland, N.Z.—d. Feb. 21, 2004, Chicago, Ill.), spent 55 years in academe—40 of them at the University of Chicago, where he served as founding director of the Center for Studies in Criminal Justice, dean of the law school, and professor of law and criminology. During his career he wrote numerous books and articles and through them built an international reputation as an expert on criminal justice systems and the shortcomings of prison systems.

Moten, Etta (ETTA MOTEN BARNETT), American actress and singer (b. Nov. 5, 1901, Weimar, Texas—d. Jan. 2, 2004, Chicago, Ill.), was best remembered for her powerful singing performances in two 1933 films—*Gold Diggers of 1933,* with her emotional rendition of "Remember My Forgotten Man," and *Flying Down to Rio,* with her joyous "Carioca"—and for becoming (1934) the first African American woman to perform at the White House. She was also a pioneer in dubbing the singing voices of nonsinging film stars. Moten took over the role of Bess in a Broadway revival of *Porgy and Bess* in 1942 and remained in it, on Broadway and on the road, until 1945. In later years she represented the U.S. at ceremonies in Africa and was active in civic organizations.

Munif, 'Abd al-Rahman, Arab writer and economist (b. 1933, Amman, Transjordan [now in Jordan]—d. Jan. 24, 2004, Damascus, Syria), wrote with intelligence and passion some of the greatest Arab novels of the 20th century. Born of a Saudi father and an Iraqi mother, he became an Arab nationalist—secular and socialist—after the declaration of Israel's statehood in 1948. In 1963, for his opposition to the Saudi royal family, he was stripped of his Saudi citizenship. He worked as an economist in the oil industry until the late 1970s, when he began to focus on his writing. He moved to Damascus in the 1980s. He was best known for his *Cities of Salt* quintet, three volumes of which were published in English: *Mudun al-milh* (1984; *Cities of Salt,* 1987), *Al-ukhdud* (*The Trench,* 1991), and *Taqasim al-layl wa al-nahar* (*Variations on Night and Day,* 1993). Also translated into English was his *Sirat madinah* (1994; *Story of a City: A Childhood in Amman,* 1996).

Murphy, John Cullen, American illustrator (b. May 3, 1919, New York, N.Y.—d. July 2, 2004, Greenwich, Conn.), drew the finely detailed comic strip *Prince Valiant* from 1970 until March 2004. He began studying art at the age of nine and in his teens came under the tutelage of Norman Rockwell, who was a neighbour. Murphy sold his first illustration when he was 17 and his first magazine cover before he was 20. After service during World War II, he worked as an illustrator for magazines, including *Collier's* and *Esquire.* In 1949 Murphy began drawing the comic strip *Big Ben Bolt,* about a young boxer, which lasted for 25 years. Hal Foster, who created *Prince Valiant,* hired Murphy to do the drawing on the strip in 1970 and turned the strip over to him in 1979.

Murray, Len (LIONEL MURRAY, BARON MURRAY OF EPPING FOREST), British trade unionist (b. Aug. 2, 1922, Hadley, Shropshire, Eng.—d. May 20, 2004, London, Eng.), was the enormously powerful assistant general secretary (1969–73) and general secretary (1973–84) of the Trades Union Congress (TUC). During his tenure as TUC leader, he enjoyed a close relationship with the Labour government of Prime Minister Harold Wilson, but after 1979 Murray was powerless to curb the growing public antagonism toward the TUC and the antiunion policies of Tory Prime Minister Margaret Thatcher. He was made a life peer in 1985.

Mydans, Carl Mayer, American photojournalist (b. May 20, 1907, Boston, Mass.—d. Aug. 16, 2004, Larchmont, N.Y.), was celebrated for his war photography for *Life* magazine, which he joined in 1936. He first gained notice for his photos of farm families during the Depression. During World War II he and his wife (a *Life* reporter) were captured by the Japanese and held for almost two years. After their release (1943), he covered the war in Europe with George Silk (*q.v.*) and others. Mydan's best-known photo was of Gen. Douglas MacArthur returning to the Philippines in 1945.

Nachman, Jerry (JEROME A. NACHMAN), American journalist (b. Feb. 24, 1946, Brooklyn, N.Y.—d. Jan. 19/20, 2004, Hoboken, N.J.), became well known for his street-smart bluntness and humour during the course of his career in television news. He worked for CBS (1971–81) and NBC (1981–87) before serving (1989–92) as editor in chief of the *New York Post.* In 2002 Nachman was made a vice president of MSNBC and the host of *Nachman,* a news talk show on that channel. He received a Peabody Award and an Edward R. Murrow Award and was nominated for an Emmy Award.

Nahyan, Sheikh Zayid ibn Sultan Al, U.A.E. political leader (b. c. 1918, British protectorate of Abu Dhabi—d. Nov. 2, 2004), as the chief architect and first president (1971–2004) of the United Arab Emirates, was responsible for modernizing the country and helped to make it one of the wealthiest in the world. The youngest son of Sheikh Sultan ibn Zayid Al Nahyan (ruler of the emirate of Abu Dhabi from 1922 to 1926), Zayid entered public life in 1946 as ruler's representative (governor) in Abu Dhabi's Eastern Province, and he soon became known for his progressive views and skillful diplomacy. In 1966 he deposed his brother to become emir of Abu Dhabi. After the U.K. announced that it was withdrawing from the region, Zayid played a major role in persuading other emirates to join in a federation, and in 1971 the emirs elected him president. Using the country's immense oil revenues, he transformed the U.A.E. from tribal fiefs into a modern nation and leading financial centre. He oversaw the construction of hospitals and schools and expanded government services to include free health care and education. Zayid also pushed

© Central Press/Getty Images

for greater equality for women. In foreign policy he improved relations with the West and promoted unity within the Arab world. He was also a noted philanthropist and conservationist. Widely admired at home and abroad, Zayid was reelected president six times.

Nakamura, Kiharu (KAZUKO NAKAMURA), Japanese geisha (b. 1913, Tokyo, Japan—d. Jan. 5, 2004, Queens, N.Y.), was one of the last authentic participants in the Japanese art of the geisha. Her affluent parents were shocked when she rejected a traditional future that would have included an arranged marriage and instead chose to learn the arts of entertaining, conversing, and dancing. By the age of 15, Nakamura had become a *hangyoku*, the first level of the geisha. She was the first geisha to learn English, and as such she was much sought after by Western guests, including Babe Ruth, Charlie Chaplin, and Jean Cocteau. In 1956 Nakamura moved to New York City. Her best-selling autobiography, *Edokko geisha ichidaiki* (1983; "The Memoirs of a Tokyo-born Geisha"), decried the post-World War II image of the geisha as little more than that of a prostitute.

Newton, Helmut (HELMUT NEUSTÄDTER), German-born fashion photographer (b. Oct. 31, 1920, Berlin, Ger.—d. Jan. 23, 2004, Los Angeles, Calif.), revolutionized his field by introducing the element of danger and the transgressive with his sexy, fetishistic photographs. Each shot implied a story behind it, usually ambiguous, sometimes violent, and always sexually charged, while his models—chiefly tall, cool, blonde women—were often clad in little or nothing but stiletto heels. Newton, who was born into a wealthy Jewish family in the often decadent Weimar Republic, fled Nazi Germany with his parents in 1938. The 18-year-old chose to seek his fortune in Singapore, but he was interned as an enemy alien and sent to Australia. He served in the Australian army from 1940 to 1945 and settled in Sydney after the war. In 1948 he married Australian model and actress June Brunell, who became his collaborator and colleague. In 1956 the Newtons moved to London, and a year later they moved to Paris, where he found work with high-fashion magazines such as *Vogue, Elle,* and *Marie-Claire.* By the 1970s he had gained an international reputation. Although some critics denounced Newton's work as near pornography, his popularity did not diminish as he aged, and his provocative photographs were in demand up until the time of his death in a car accident.

Nicolson, Nigel, British biographer, publisher, and politician (b. Jan. 19, 1917, London, Eng.—d. Sept. 23, 2004, Sissinghurst, Kent, Eng.), created a furor in 1973 with *Portrait of a Marriage,* a frank and—to many—shocking analysis of the unorthodox 50-year marriage of his parents, writer-gardener Vita Sackville-West and diplomat Sir Harold Nicolson, in which he examined their close relationship as well as their numerous homosexual affairs. The Oxford-educated Nicolson was a founding director of the publishing house Weidenfeld & Nicolson, a Conservative Party MP (1952–59), and the author of several other works, including a biography of Virginia Woolf, a military history of Earl Alexander of Tunis, and the Whitbread Award-winning biography *Mary Curzon* (1977). He also edited a six-volume edition (1975–80) of Woolf's letters; *Vita and Harold* (1992), a collection of his parents' letters to each other; and three volumes of his father's diaries and letters. After leaving Weidenfeld & Nicolson in 1992, he wrote columns for *The Spectator* and the *Sunday Telegraph.* Nicolson was appointed MBE in 1945 and elevated to OBE in 2000.

Nikolayev, Andriyan Grigoryevich, Soviet cosmonaut (b. Sept. 5, 1929, Shorshely, Chuvashia, U.S.S.R [now in Russia]—d. July 3, 2004, Cheboksary, Chuvashia, Russia), was one of the Soviet Union's pioneers in space; he set endurance records in orbit in 1962 and 1970. Nikolayev initially worked in forestry, but when he was drafted into the military in 1950, he was trained as a pilot. His interest, aptitude, and reputation for being coolheaded under pressure led to his being chosen in 1959 as one of the first 20 people to be trained as cosmonauts and in the following year to be trained for the first Soviet manned spaceflights. The Soviet Union took a decisive lead in the space race with the U.S. when Vostok 3, carrying Nikolayev, blasted off on Aug. 11, 1962, followed by Pavel Popovich in Vostok 4 on the following day. The two spacecraft traveled in parallel orbits, close enough at times for the cosmonauts to make visual contact, and pictures of Nikolayev were beamed back to Earth, the first televised pictures from space. After 96 hours and 64 orbits (the previous record had been a little over 25 hours and 17 orbits), Nikolayev's spacecraft safely returned to Earth. Nikolayev and Popovich were lionized as national heroes for the next few years, which included Nikolayev's very public marriage (1963–82) to Valentina Tereshkova, the first woman in space. In 1970 Nikolayev set a new endurance record in space, with Vitaly Sevastyanov on Soyuz 9, spending almost 18 days in orbit in a mission to learn the effects of prolonged spaceflight.

Nitze, Paul Henry, American military strategist (b. Jan. 16, 1907, Amherst, Mass.—d. Oct. 19, 2004, Washington, D.C.), played a vital role in shaping U.S. nuclear-arms strategy during the Cold War era. In 1950 he was appointed head of policy planning at the Department of State and wrote the famous NSC-68 document that described Soviet aspirations of world domination and called for a massive defense buildup. NSC-68 became the basis for U.S. policy regarding the Soviet Union for much of the Cold War. During the administrations of Presidents John F. Kennedy and Lyndon B. Johnson, Nitze served in high-level Department of Defense positions and expanded the U.S. military presence in Europe. He was disappointed when he was not given a key position in the administration of Pres. Jimmy Carter and became a vocal critic of Carter's arms-control efforts. Under Pres. Ronald Reagan (*q.v.*), Nitze served as the chief nuclear-arms negotiator. In a 1982 meeting in Geneva, with his Soviet counterpart Yuly Kvitsinsky, Nitze negotiated a treaty to eliminate intermediate-range nuclear missiles. The events of the negotiation were dramatized in the Broadway play *A Walk in the Woods.* While neither nation accepted the proposed treaty, it established a framework for future arms-control agreements. In 1985 Nitze was awarded the Presidential Medal of Freedom, the highest U.S. civilian honour.

Nougaro, Claude, French chanson singer and songwriter (b. Sept. 9, 1929, Toulouse, France—d. March 4, 2004, Paris, France), combined an interest in the traditional French chanson with an affection for American jazz and Brazilian and African music over the course of some 50 years and 20 albums. These non-European influences, together with Nougaro's Toulousian accent, made him a favourite with Parisians and around the world. Many of his songs were recorded by other singers, including Edith Piaf. Nougaro's hits included "Toulouse," "Cécile ma fille," and "Bidonville."

O'Donnell, May, American dancer and choreographer (b. 1906, Sacramento, Calif.—d. Feb. 1, 2004, New York, N.Y.), performed with the Martha Graham and José Limón dance companies, creating a number of notable roles, including the Pioneer Woman in Graham's *Appalachian Spring* (1944). She also taught dance all over the U.S., had a choreographic career that spanned more than half a century, and founded two dance companies—the San Francisco Dance Theater (1939), with her husband, composer Ray Green, and the May O'Donnell Dance Company in New York City (1949).

Oliphant, Betty (NANCY ELIZABETH OLIPHANT), British-born Canadian dance educator (b. Aug. 5, 1918, London, Eng.—d. July 12, 2004, St. Catherines, Ont.), became a ballet dancer in London and, after moving to Canada in 1947, opened her own school in Toronto. She became ballet mistress of the National Ballet of Canada in 1951 and from 1969 to 1975 served as associate artistic director of the company. In addition, in 1959 Oliphant and company founder Celia Franca founded the National Ballet School, which Oliphant directed until 1989; the school's theatre had been named in her honour the preceding year. Her autobiography, *Miss O: My Life in Dance,* was published in 1996.

Omar, Dullah (ABDULLAH MOHAMED OMAR), South African human rights lawyer and politician (b. May 26, 1934, Observatory, S.Af.—d. March 13, 2004, Cape Town, S.Af.), was an antiapartheid activist who became minister of

© Bettmann/Corbis

justice (1994–99) in Pres. Nelson Mandela's postapartheid administration. During his tenure Omar was responsible for dismantling the legal structure of apartheid, setting up the Truth and Reconciliation Commission, and overhauling the judiciary. Omar set up his own law practice in 1960 because, owing to his racial classification as "Coloured," he could not get a position in an established firm. He defended victims of apartheid in political trials and affiliated himself with the banned Pan-Africanist Congress, the Unity Movement, and, from 1983, the United Democratic Front. His passport was revoked; he was frequently arrested; and his movements were restricted by the government. After the end of apartheid, however, Omar joined the new government. In 1999 he was given the transportation portfolio under Mandela's successor, Pres. Thabo Mbeki.

Onley, Toni (NORMAN ANTONY ONLEY), Canadian painter (b. Nov. 20, 1928, Douglas, Isle of Man—d. Feb. 29, 2004, Maple Ridge, B.C.), was internationally known for his evocative Impressionist paintings of western and northern Canada and was famous for his 1983 threat to burn his entire inventory in an ultimately successful fight against Revenue Canada. Onley, who loved to fly his plane into the backcountry to paint, died when his float plane plunged into the Fraser River 48 km (30 mi) east of Vancouver while he was practicing takeoffs and landings.

Orbach, Jerry (JEROME BERNARD ORBACH), American actor and singer (b. Oct. 20, 1935, Bronx, N.Y.—d. Dec. 28, 2004, New York, N.Y.), made his mark in the theatre world as a Broadway song-and-dance man—originating such roles as El Gallo in the Off-Broadway *The Fantasticks* (1960), Paul Berthalet in *Carnival* (1961, his Broadway debut), Chuck Baxter in *Promises, Promises* (1968; Tony Award, 1969), Billy Flynn in *Chicago* (1975), and Julian Marsh in *42nd Street* (1980)—but later became better known to the American television-viewing public as Detective Lennie Briscoe in 12 seasons of *Law & Order* and to movie audiences as the father in *Dirty Dancing* (1987). At the time of his death, Orbach was filming episodes of a new spin-off series, *Law & Order: Trial by Jury.*

© Lisa O'Connor/ZUMA/Corbis

Osmond, Humphry Fortescue, British psychiatrist (b. July 1, 1917, Surrey, Eng.—d. Feb. 6, 2004, Appleton, Wis.), introduced writer Aldous Huxley to hallucinogenic drugs, commenting, "To fathom Hell or soar angelic, just take a pinch of psychedelic." Huxley famously described the incident in his book *The Doors of Perception* (1954). Working primarily in North America, Osmond examined schizophrenia and pioneered drug studies that advocated the use of LSD to treat mental problems. His research was greatly curtailed in the 1960s following the countercultural abuses of hallucinogenics.

Paar, Jack Harold, American humorist (b. May 1, 1918, Canton, Ohio—d. Jan. 27, 2004, Greenwich, Conn.), defined the format for late-night television during his years (1957–62) as host of *The Tonight Show* (eventually *The Jack Paar Show*), adopting a simple set made up of sofa and desk and introducing the use of an opening monologue and friendly banter with the announcer. With his wit, urbanity, and conversational skills—punctuated with his signature "I kid you not," which became a popular catchphrase—he engaged his guests, many of whom got their boost to stardom on his show, in intelligent, entertaining chats and set the standard for TV talk shows. Paar quit school when he was 16 and went to work first as a radio announcer and later as a comic and disc jockey on a series of radio stations. He entered the army in 1942 and spent the remainder of World War II as a disc jockey and entertainer, delighting his audience of enlisted men by skewering authority figures, especially military officers. After the war Paar performed on radio as a vacation replacement for Jack Benny and Arthur Godfrey, had a few short-lived shows, and had small parts in a few movies, and in 1954 he began an 11-month stint as host of the *CBS Morning Show.* Despite the fact that none of his shows had lasted long, he was chosen to replace Steve Allen as host of *The Tonight Show.* He caught the public's attention immediately and held it not only with fascinating guests and features—he went to Cuba to interview Fidel Castro, and he showed film clips that gave Americans their first glimpse of the Beatles—but also with unpredictable behaviour. The emotional Paar even quit the show abruptly once during a broadcast in 1960 when an NBC censor cut a humorous story because it contained the term *W.C.,* for "water closet," but he returned a few weeks later, beginning his opening statements with a simple "As I was saying. . . ." After leaving the show, he served as host of a weekly TV show until 1965. Paar wrote four books, including *I Kid You Not* (1960; with John Reddy) and *Three on a Toothbrush* (1965).

Talk-show host Jack Paar with photos of some of his famous guests

© AFP/Getty Images

Pake, George Edward, American physicist (b. April 1, 1924, Jeffersonville, Ohio—d. March 4, 2004, Tucson, Ariz.), assembled (1970) a team of crack scientists and engineers for the Xerox Corp. at the newly established Palo Alto Research Center in California and oversaw its explorations into the emerging field of computer science. Under his leadership, which fostered collegiality, a number of inventions were created, including the laser printer, office networking, the graphical user interface, and a desktop computer called the Xerox Star. Such companies as Apple Computer and Microsoft later capitalized on these inventions and took them to the commercial market. While earning a Ph.D. (1948) in physics from Harvard University, Pake conducted pathbreaking work that led to the development of magnetic resonance imaging (MRI). In 1987 Pake was awarded the National Medal of Science.

Palmer, Bruce, Canadian bass guitarist (b. Sept. 9, 1946, Liverpool, N.S.—d. Oct. 1, 2004, Belleville, Ont.), was a founding member of the influential folk-rock band Buffalo Springfield. The group, which also included Palmer's good friend Neil Young, lasted for only two years (1966–68) but produced three acclaimed albums and one hit, "For What It's Worth" (1967). Palmer's bass lines strengthened the group's rock edge, and his habit of performing with his back to the crowd lent him an air of eccentricity.

Pantani, Marco ("IL PIRATA" ["THE PIRATE"]), Italian cyclist (b. Jan. 13, 1970, Cesenatico, Italy—d. Feb. 14, 2004, Rimini, Italy), won both the Tour de France, cycling's premier road race, and the Tour of Italy (Giro d'Italia) in 1998; he was the first Italian to win the Tour de France since Felice Gimondi in 1965. His accomplishments, however, were overshadowed by injuries, chronic depression, and unproven accusations of drug use. The lean 1.7-m (5-ft 7-in) Pantani was known as much for his trademark shaved head, prominent ears, and bandana as he was for his attacking climbing style on mountain stages. He turned professional in 1992, and in 1994 he won two stages in the Giro, finishing second overall. He suffered serious injuries in crashes in 1995 and again in 1997. In 1999 he won four stages of the Giro and held an overall lead when he was expelled from the race just before the final stage after a blood test showed a high hematocrit level (an indication of possible use of the blood-boosting hormone erythropoietin). Pantani was found dead in a hotel room; tests later determined that he had died of an accidental cocaine overdose.

Pantridge, Frank (JAMES FRANCIS PANTRIDGE), Irish-born cardiologist (b. Oct. 3, 1916, Hillsborough, Ire. [now N.Ire.]—d. Dec. 26, 2004), developed (1965) the first portable heart defibrillator, a life-saving device for providing rapid emergency treatment to heart-attack victims. Defibrillators, which are used to apply an electric shock to the chest to overcome ventricular fibrillation, a typically fatal irregular rhythm of the heart that often follows a heart attack, were previously available only in hospitals. He was made CBE in 1978.

Paredes, Carlos, Portuguese guitarist and composer (b. Feb. 16, 1925, Coimbra, Port.—d. July 23, 2004, Lisbon, Port.), mastered the distinctive round-shaped Portuguese guitar, a 12-string mandolin-like instrument usually associated with the national style of music known as fado. Though he often performed alone, Paredes composed songs for the legendary *fadista* Amália Rodrigues and was known for his collaborations with other musicians, including bassist Charlie Haden and the Kronos Quartet.

Partridge, Frances Catherine Marshall, British biographer and diarist (b. March 15, 1900, London, Eng.—d. Feb. 5, 2004, London), documented her experiences on the edge of the Bloomsbury group; beginning in her late 70s she published two volumes of autobiography and six diaries. She was married (from 1933 until his death in 1960) to Ralph Partridge, the "hopelessly heterosexual" man with whom the noted biographer Lytton Strachey had been in love. When Frances Marshall met her future husband, he was married to the artist Dora Carrington, who was, in turn, in love with Strachey and who committed suicide upon Strachey's death in 1932.

Paschke, Ed (EDWARD FRANCIS PASCHKE, JR.), American artist (b. June 22, 1939, Chicago, Ill.—d. Nov. 25, 2004, Chicago), created outlandish works of Pop Art, breaking through with the Chicago Imagists (a figurative movement) of the 1960s. Paschke studied at the School of the Art Institute of Chicago and taught for 27 years at Northwestern University, Evanston, Ill. Connecting the line between Andy Warhol, who was a major influence, and Jeff Koons, Paschke rendered images from popular culture in garish fluorescent colours and the staticky lines of electronic video.

Passmore, John Arthur, Australian philosopher (b. Sept. 9, 1914, Manly, N.S.W., Australia—d. July 25, 2004, Canberra, Australia), was a leading figure in the field of applied philosophy, in which philosophical research is applied to practical matters, such as medical ethics and the environment. He wrote a score of books, and his best-known work, *A Hundred Years of Philosophy* (1957), was a significant contribution to the study of the history of philosophy. Passmore studied at the University of Sydney on a scholarship and taught there, at the University of Otago, Dunedin, N.Z. (1950–55), and at the Australian National University (1955–79), as well as serving as a visiting scholar at universities in Britain and North America.

Peel, John (JOHN ROBERT PARKER RAVENSCROFT), British disc jockey (b. Aug. 30, 1939, Heswall, Cheshire, Eng.—d. Oct. 25, 2004, Cuzco, Peru), fueled the independent music scene in Britain by debuting such performers as David Bowie, Joy Division, and the Smiths. After a brief stint with the pirate station Radio London, he joined BBC Radio 1 in 1967. Peel was one of the only BBC disc jockeys to be afforded complete creative control over his playlists, and bands flooded his mailbox with demo tapes and clamoured to be featured on his legendary "Peel Sessions" live sets. He was made OBE in 1998 and was a perennial choice as *NME* magazine's favourite DJ of the year.

Petros VII (PETROS PAPAPETROU), Greek Orthodox cleric (b. Sept. 3, 1949, Sichari, British Cyprus—d. Sept. 11, 2004, while flying over the Aegean Sea), viewed his position as the Greek Orthodox patriarch of Africa as an opportunity to strengthen and spread the message of Greek Orthodoxy throughout that continent and to promote Christian-Muslim dialogue. He arrived in Alexandria, Egypt, in the 1970s to serve as a deacon to Patriarch Nicolaos VI. Returning to Athens, Petros studied to become a priest; after he was ordained in 1978, he returned to Egypt to serve as patriarchal vicar of Cairo. Two years later he was appointed vicar general of Johannesburg, S.Af. He later assumed posts in Ghana, Cameroon, and the archdiocese encompassing Kenya, Tanzania, and Uganda before his appointment as patriarch of Alexandria and Africa in 1997.

Peynaud, Émile, French wine expert (b. 1912, Madiran, France—d. July 18, 2004, Talence, France), revolutionized winemaking by clarifying for traditional producers (particularly in his native Bordeaux) the scientific processes—from the timing of harvests to better hygiene in the cellars to temperature control in fermentation—that would produce richer, more flavourful wines. An approachable, plain-spoken man, Peynaud had worked with wine from age 14, eventually earning a doctorate in the subject and becoming a professor of enology at the University of Bordeaux. He was the author of several authoritative books on the subject.

Pickering, William Hayward, New Zealand-born American engineer and physicist (b. Dec. 24, 1910, Wellington, N.Z—d. March 15, 2004, La Cañada Flintridge, Calif.), was one of the pioneering figures of the American space program; as director of the Pasadena, Calif.-based Jet Propulsion Laboratory (JPL) from 1954 to 1976, he oversaw the team that developed Explorer 1, the first American orbiting satellite, and headed NASA's unmanned lunar- and planetary-exploration programs. In 1940, after studying at the California Institute of Technology, where he earned bachelor's and master's degrees in electrical engineering and a Ph.D. in physics, Pickering joined the institute's staff. Working under American physicist Robert A. Millikan, he developed cosmic-radiation-detection gear for high-altitude balloon flights. Following the outbreak of World War II, Pickering began work for JPL, serving as manager of the Corporal rocket project, which brought about important early advances in rocket guidance and communication techniques. He also led in the development of the Sergeant solid-fuel missile. He was named chief of JPL's guided-missile electronics division in 1951 and assumed directorship of the entire laboratory three years later. After the Soviet Union stunned the world with its launch of Sputnik 1 in October 1957, Pickering and his staff rushed to finish construction of Explorer 1. The satellite, which was successfully launched on Jan. 31, 1958, was lifted into orbit by a rocket developed by noted German engineer Wernher von Braun and was equipped with instruments developed by American radiation physicist James Van Allen. The three scientists—Pickering, Braun, and Van Allen—were afterward celebrated as national heroes. Pickering went on to supervise numerous other important space-exploration projects, including the Ranger spacecraft flights in 1964–65 that tested the suitability of the Moon's surface for a manned landing, the Mariner flights that surveyed Venus in 1962 and Mars in 1964–65, and the two Viking missions to the surface of Mars in 1976. After stepping down as director of JPL, he served for two years as director of the research institute of the University of Petroleum and Minerals in Saudi Arabia. He then returned to Pasadena to establish a private consulting practice. Among the many honours bestowed on him were the National Medal of Science in 1975 and an honorary knighthood by Queen Elizabeth II in 1976. He was also appointed to the Order of New Zealand, the country's highest honour, in 2003.

Pietri, Pedro, Puerto Rican poet and playwright (b. March 21, 1944, Ponce, P.R.—d. March 3, 2004, in flight from Mexico to New York, N.Y.), inspired young Puerto Ricans living in New York City, called Nuyoricans, by composing poetry that instilled pride in their culture and heritage. His poems often reflected strong political views and denounced the political and social oppression of Nuyoricans in American society. In 1973 he helped to establish the Nuyorican Poets Café, where young Nuyoricans were able to recite their own poetry, and in that same year he published *Puerto Rican Obituary,* his most well-known epic poem.

Pintasilgo, Maria de Lourdes Ruivo da Silva, Portuguese civil servant (b. Jan. 18, 1930, Abrantes, Port.—d. July 10, 2004, Lisbon, Port.), was the first woman prime minister of Portugal (1979–80) and only the second female prime minister of a European nation. While in office she reformed social security and improved labour legislation, education, and health care. A stout defender of women's rights, Pintasilgo trained and worked as a chemical and industrial engineer during the 1950s and eventually rose to project director of Companhia União Fabril, one of Portugal's largest monopolies. She served (1975–79) as Portugal's ambassador to UNESCO, became the first woman to run (1986) for president of Portugal, and was a member of the European Parliament (1987–89) on the Socialist Party's list. Pintasilgo also authored books on such varied subjects as economics, religion, and feminism.

Poe, Fernando, Jr. (RONALD ALLAN KELLEY POE), Filipino actor and politician (b. Aug. 20, 1939, San Carlos City, Phil.—d. Dec. 13, 2004, Manila, Phil.), starred in nearly 300 films in his 46-year career as the Philippines' premier action star and earned the nickname "Da King" for his portrayal of rugged underdog heroes. Despite his lack of political experience, he emerged as the main opposition candidate in the 2004 presidential elections, but he lost to incumbent Gloria Macapagal Arroyo by 3.5% of the popular vote.

Pople, Sir John Anthony, British mathematical chemist (b. Oct. 31, 1925, Burnham-on-Sea, Somerset, Eng.—d. March 15, 2004, Chicago, Ill.), won the Nobel Prize for Chemistry in 1998 for his development of computational methods for modeling chemical reactions; he shared the award with Austrian-born American physical chemist Walter Kohn. In particular, Pople wrote what became the standard research tool for physical chemists, the computer program Gaussian, which enabled researchers to calculate, rather than measure, the shape and properties of molecules on the basis of quantum theory. Gaussian proved to be particularly useful in the search for new pharmaceuticals. Pople earned a doctorate (1951) from the University of Cambridge, where he remained as a fellow at Trinity College (1951–58) and a lecturer in mathematics (1954–58) until he left in 1958 to head the basic physics division at the National Physical Laboratory in Teddington, Eng. In 1964 he moved to the United States, where he taught at the Carnegie Institute of Technology (later Carnegie Mellon University), Pittsburgh, Pa. (1964–93), and at Northwestern University, Evanston, Ill. (1993–2004). Although Pople never took a chemistry course and was initially turned down for membership in the American Chemical Society, he was awarded the Wolf Prize in Chemistry in 1992. He remained a British citizen and was knighted in 2003.

Potter, Maureen (MARIA PHILOMENA POTTER), Irish actress (b. 1925, Fairview, near Dublin, Ire.—d. April 7, 2004, Dublin), was a popular entertainer for some seven decades and was particularly well regarded for her physically demanding comic roles. As a child she was an Irish dancing champion and excelled in comedy and pantomime, notably at the Gaiety Theatre in Dublin. Potter appeared with traveling troupes, in music halls and cabarets, on Irish television, and in films. Later in life she took on roles in more serious stage productions, including plays by Sean O'Casey and Samuel Beckett.

Quine, Robert, American guitarist (b. Dec. 30, 1942, Akron, Ohio—d. found dead May 31, 2004, New York, N.Y.), was a distinctive stylist best remembered for his contribution as a member of the protopunk band the Voidoids (led by Richard Hell), particularly on *Blank Generation,* and for his work on albums by Lou Reed. Quine was older and more technically proficient than most punk musicians, and he was much influenced by the Velvet Underground (his bootlegged tapes of their concerts were commercially released in 2003), Ritchie Valens, and Hank Marvin. Quine also recorded with Marianne Faithfull, Tom Waits, and Matthew Sweet. Despondent over the death of his wife in 2003, Quine took his own life.

Rakosi, Carl (CALLMAN RAWLEY), American poet and psychotherapist (b. Nov. 6, 1903, Berlin, Ger.—d. June 24, 2004, San Francisco, Calif.), with George Oppen, Louis Zukovsky, and Charles Reznikoff formed a poetic movement known as Objectivism. (The movement placed emphasis on viewing poems as objects that could be considered and analyzed in terms of mechanical features.) Rakosi changed his name to Callman Rawley in 1926, keeping his original name as his pen name. After 1939 he became a social worker and psychotherapist, and, though he wrote much in his field, he ceased writing poetry. In 1967, a year before his retirement, he was lured back to poetry, however, and before his death he published eight highly acclaimed volumes, the last, *The Old Poet's Tale,* in 1999.

Raksin, David, American film composer (b. Aug. 4, 1912, Philadelphia, Pa.—d. Aug. 9, 2004, Los Angeles, Calif.), created the music for some 400 motion pictures and television series, the most notable of which was the haunting score for the film *Laura* (1944), which subsequently was recorded more than 400 times. Other scores included those for the films *Forever Amber* (1947), *The Bad and the Beautiful* (1952), and *Separate Tables* (1958), and themes for TV series included *Wagon Train* (1957) and *Ben Casey* (1961). Raksin also composed concert works and music for ballets and stage shows, served as president of the Composers and Lyricists Guild of America, and taught at the University of Southern California.

Ramanna, Raja, Indian nuclear physicist (b. Jan. 28, 1925, Tumkur, India—d. Sept. 24, 2004, Mumbai [Bombay], India), played a key role in the development of India's nuclear weapons program. As director (1972–78, 1981–83) of the Bhabha Atomic Research Centre, India's top nuclear research facility, Ramanna oversaw the country's first nuclear weapons test in 1974. He also headed India's atomic energy commission (1984–87) and served as secretary of defense (1990–92). In addition to his work and advocacy in developing nuclear arms, Ramanna held offices in a number of Indian professional societies, including the Indian Academy of Sciences, the Indian Institute of Science, and the National Institute of Advanced Studies.

Ramone, Johnny (JOHN CUMMINGS), American rock musician (b. Oct. 8, 1948, Long Island, N.Y.—d. Sept. 15, 2004, Los Angeles, Calif.), cofounded the legendary punk band the Ramones in 1974 His guitar work on songs such as "Blitzkrieg Bop," "Judy Is a Punk," and "I Wanna Be Sedated" helped

Punk rocker Johnny Ramone

define the New York punk sound, and the band's appearance in director Roger Corman's *Rock 'n' Roll High School* (1979) spawned waves of imitators in leather jackets and ripped jeans. The Ramones performed in more than 2,000 shows between 1974 and 1997, and in 2002 they were inducted into the Rock and Roll Hall of Fame in Cleveland, Ohio.

Randall, Tony (LEONARD ROSENBERG), American actor (b. Feb. 26, 1920, Tulsa, Okla.—d. May 17, 2004, New York, N.Y.), was most closely identified with the character Felix Unger, the fastidious fussbudget he portrayed opposite Jack Klugman's sloppy Oscar Madison on the TV series *The Odd Couple* (1970–75); he won an Emmy Award for the last season of the show. Randall studied speech and drama at Northwestern University, Evanston, Ill., for a year and then moved to New York City, where he studied acting at the Neighborhood Playhouse School of the Theatre and began working in radio. He made his stage debut in *A Circle of Chalk* in 1941 before being drafted into the army. After being discharged in 1946, Randall returned to radio work, toured in *The Barretts of Wimpole Street*, and appeared on Broadway in *Antony and Cleopatra*, *To Tell the Truth*, and *Caesar and Cleopatra*. In 1952 he attracted major notice with his role as schoolteacher Harvey Weskit in the TV series *Mr. Peepers*, which ran until 1955. Onstage he appeared in *Oh, Men! Oh, Women!* (1954), and in 1957 he began his Hollywood career with the film version of that play. Roles in three Rock Hudson–Doris Day films—*Pillow Talk* (1959), *Lover Come Back* (1961), and *Send Me No Flowers* (1964)—solidified both his stardom and his signature persona. He played seven roles in his next movie, *7 Faces of Dr. Lao* (1964). On TV, Randall also starred in *The Tony Randall Show* (1976–78) and *Love, Sidney* (1981–83). Among his later stage roles was the one he considered his all-time favourite, a love-struck diplomat in *M. Butterfly* (1989). In 1991 Randall founded the National Actors Theatre in New York City—funding it partly with $1 million of his own money—with the aim of bringing the classics to the public at affordable prices. Randall also served as national chairman of the Myasthenia Gravis Foundation for some 30 years.

Comic actor Tony Randall and friend in Fluffy

© Bettmann/Corbis

Rao, P(amulaparti) V(enkata) Narasimha, Indian politician (b. June 28, 1921, Karimnagar, Andhra Pradesh, India—d. Dec. 23, 2004, New Delhi, India), as leader of the Congress (I) Party and prime minister (1991–96), saved India from bankruptcy, moving it away from its semisocialistic economic program; Rao's shift toward market capitalism encouraged domestic growth and foreign investment but incurred higher deficits and inflation. Many analysts traced India's robust economy at the turn of the 21st century to the foundation of his reforms. His tenure, however, was also marked by a rise in sectarian violence, with ongoing clashes between Muslims and Hindus. Rao served the state of Andhra Pradesh as a legislator (1957–77) and chief minister (1971–73). He backed Prime Minister Indira Gandhi in her creation of a new wing of the Congress Party in 1969 and was elected to the Lok Sabha (lower house of Parliament) in 1977. Rao held several cabinet posts and twice served as foreign minister (1980–84, 1988–89). He became prime minister after the assassination of Prime Minister Rajiv Gandhi in May 1991. After his party was roundly defeated in the 1996 elections, Rao resigned amid allegations of corruption and bribery. Shortly after leaving office, he was convicted on charges of corruption and bribery, but his conviction was later overturned. A formidable scholar, Rao was the author of many literary translations, a book of fiction, and poetry.

Reed, Leonard, American tap dancer (b. Jan. 7, 1907, Lightning Creek, Okla.—d. April 5, 2004, Covina, Calif.), gained his greatest fame as one of the inventors—along with his partner, Willie Bryant—of the flashy routine known as the Shim Sham Shimmy, which they created as the finale for their renowned 1920s dance act. He later produced shows on Broadway and at the Cotton Club in New York City's Harlem, wrote songs, was a bandleader and a comedian, produced for record companies, and for some 20 years served as the master of ceremonies at the Apollo Theater in Harlem. Reed was honoured with a lifetime achievement award from the American Music Awards in 2000.

Reeve, Christopher, American actor (b. Sept. 25, 1952, New York, N.Y.—d. Oct. 10, 2004, Mount Kisco, N.Y.), was first known to the moviegoing public as the title character in *Superman* (1978) and went on to star in three sequels as well as a number of other films. After a fall from a horse during an equestrian competition in 1995 broke his neck and left him a quadriplegic, however, he took on a new, even more heroic role—that of activist for medical research, including the search for a cure for spinal-cord injuries. Reeve grew up in Princeton, N.J., where he performed in school plays and was involved with the local professional theatre. While receiving his education at Cornell University, Ithaca, N.Y., and the Juilliard School, New York City, he also worked at theatres in Europe and for two years was a cast member of the soap opera *Love of Life*. Reeve appeared on Broadway with Katharine Hepburn in *A Matter of Gravity* in 1976 and made his film debut in *Gray Lady Down* (1978). Then came *Superman* and superstardom. Not wanting to be associated with only that role, Reeve did more stage work and also appeared in films that ranged from romance (*Somewhere in Time* [1980]) to mystery-thriller (*Deathtrap* [1982]) to period piece

© Hulton Archive/Getty Images

"Superman" Christopher Reeve

(continued on page 132)

Reagan, Ronald Wilson

40th president (1981–89) of the United States (b. Feb. 6, 1911, Tampico, Ill.—d. June 5, 2004, Los Angeles, Calif.), was a Hollywood actor who became one of the most popular presidents of the 20th century—the winner of two landslide victories in the elections of 1980 and 1984 and the leader of a conservative revival in American politics. Called "the Great Communicator" for his remarkable skill as an orator and for his effective use of television to promote his agenda, Reagan succeeded in attracting supporters beyond the traditional base of the Republican Party. The oldest person ever elected to the White House, he was nevertheless noted for his youthful optimism and jaunty personality. In his two terms as president, he oversaw an economic recovery, albeit one that coincided with record budget deficits. In foreign affairs he sought a more assertive role for the U.S., and his policies, which included the largest peacetime military buildup in American history, were credited by some with having helped to end the Cold War.

Pres. Ronald Reagan; (below) as George Gipp in Knute Rockne—All American

"Dutch" Reagan, the son of a ne'er-do-well shoe salesman, spent most of his childhood in Dixon, Ill., and attended nearby Eureka College. After graduating (1932) with a bachelor's degree in economics and sociology, he worked as a sportscaster for radio stations in Davenport and Des Moines, Iowa. On a trip to California to cover the Chicago Cubs baseball team at its spring training camp in 1937, Reagan landed a screen test with Warner Brothers and soon thereafter signed a long-term contract with the movie studio.

Over the next quarter of a century, Reagan appeared in more than 50 films, most notably *Knute Rockne—All American* (1940), in which his role as George Gipp earned him the lifelong nickname "the Gipper," *Kings Row* (1942), and *The Hasty Heart* (1949). He was twice president (1947–52, 1959–60) of the Screen Actors Guild, in which position he cooperated with efforts to combat alleged communist influences in the motion picture industry. He was divorced from his first wife, actress Jane Wyman, in 1948 and four years later married actress Nancy Davis. Reagan was hired as a public-relations spokesman for the General Electric Co. and served (1954–62) as host of its TV program, *General Electric Theater.* He made his only appearance as a villain in his last film, *The Killers* (1964), and spent one season (1965–66) as the host of TV's *Death Valley Days* before giving up Hollywood for politics.

Once a liberal Democrat, Reagan gradually changed his political affiliation to conservative Republican. He became a fund-raiser for conservative groups and in 1964 was active in the presidential campaign of Sen. Barry Goldwater. Reagan's television address entitled "A Time for Choosing" raised a million dollars for Goldwater and marked an impressive debut for the neophyte politician on the national political stage. Reagan was elected governor of California in 1966 and was reelected in 1970, but during his two terms he was only moderately successful in carrying out his conservative programs.

After having nearly taken the Republican presidential nomination away from Pres. Gerald Ford in 1976, Reagan swept to victory over Pres. Jimmy Carter four years later, in part by making inroads among such longtime Democratic constituencies as blue-collar workers, white southerners, and Roman Catholics. Shortly after taking office, Reagan was shot in an assassination attempt but, though seriously wounded, made a quick and complete recovery. In 1981 Congress approved much of his "supply-side" economic program, which relied on drastic cuts in personal income taxes and domestic spending. A recession (1982–84) was followed by several years of economic growth, and while the inflation rate dropped significantly, the national debt doubled by 1986 and nearly tripled by the time he left office.

A fervent anticommunist, Reagan adopted an early hard-line stance against the Soviet Union, which he famously denounced as an "evil empire." In 1983 he proposed construction of the Strategic Defense Initiative as a means of defending the U.S. from potential Soviet nuclear attacks. That same year he also authorized a military invasion of Grenada, ostensibly to prevent the island nation from becoming a Soviet outpost. During Reagan's second term, however, he embraced negotiations with Mikhail Gorbachev in response to signals of glasnost under the new Soviet leader. The two met several times, ultimately signing a historic nuclear disarmament pact in December 1987.

Although Reagan had been reelected by an overwhelming margin over challenger Walter Mondale in 1984, his image and governing authority were weakened for a time by revelations stemming from the Iran-Contra Affair. In eight hours of videotaped testimony about a secret plot to sell American weapons to Iran and divert the money illegally to Nicaraguan rebels, Reagan repeatedly swore, "I don't recall." The scandal, however, did not permanently damage the popularity of the president, whose uncanny ability to deflect criticism prompted some to describe him as "Teflon-coated." At the time he left office, he held the highest approval ratings (68%) of any retiring president in the history of modern-day polling. In 1994 Reagan disclosed publicly that he had been diagnosed with Alzheimer disease. Aged 93 at his death, he was the nation's longest-surviving president.

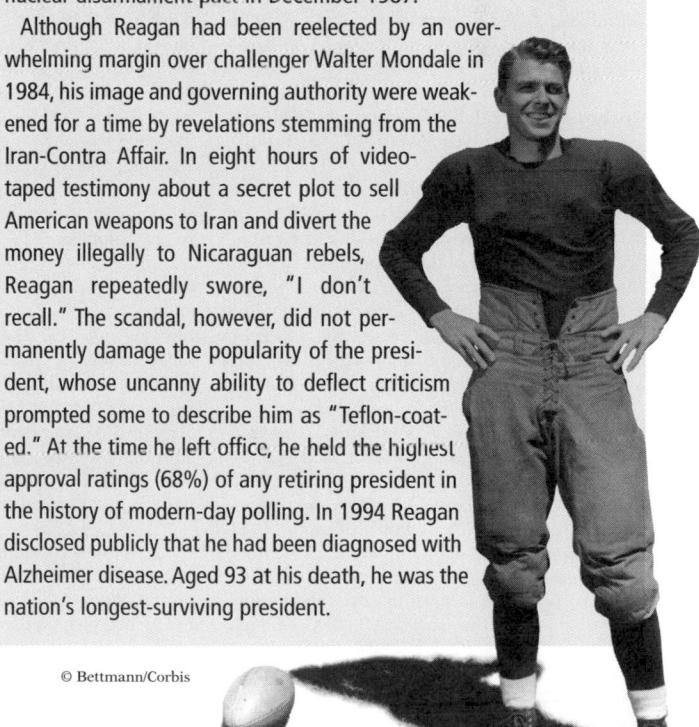

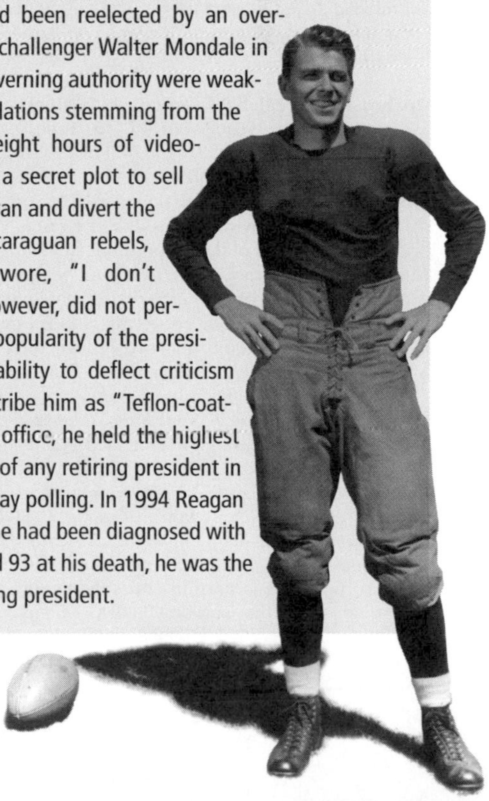

(continued from page 130)
(*The Bostonians* [1984] and *The Remains of the Day* [1993]) to farce (*Switching Channels* [1988] and *Noises Off* [1992]). Following his accident, Reeve, who had already been a political activist, became an advocate for the disabled while he worked to improve his own condition, and in 1999 he established the Christopher Reeve Paralysis Foundation to help fund research projects. He also remained involved in television work, with the starring role in a 1998 update of *Rear Window* and the direction of *The Brooke Ellison Story* (2004) among his credits.

Riedel, Claus Josef, Czech-born glassmaker (b. Feb. 19, 1925, Polaun, Czech. [now in the Czech Republic]—d. March 17, 2004, Genoa, Italy), designed several lines of quality glassware precisely for their ability to enhance the taste of the liquid—typically wine—they held. Riedel, who took control of his family's glassware company in 1957, concerned himself with the physics of liquid-delivery systems: a glass's capacity, the thickness of its walls and its rim, and its shape. In addition to their elegant, wine-specific shapes, Riedel's glasses were admired for the extraordinarily long decay of the bell-like sound they made when tapped. The largest Riedel glass—a 1958 Burgundy Grand Cru—held a record 1,110 ml (37 oz).

Ripley, Alexandra (ALEXANDRA BRAID), American writer (b. Jan. 8, 1934, Charleston, S.C.—d. Jan. 10, 2004, Richmond, Va.), wrote *Scarlett* (1991), the officially sanctioned sequel to *Gone with the Wind* (1936), after having established her career with a number of best-selling historical novels set in the South, including *Charleston* (1981), *On Leaving Charleston* (1984), and *New Orleans Legacy* (1987). Although *Scarlett* was panned by critics, it nevertheless became a best seller and was eventually translated into more than a dozen languages. In 1994 CBS paid more than $8 million (then a record) for the rights to shoot a miniseries based on Ripley's book, and it was aired later that year.

Roche, James Michael, American businessman (b. Dec. 16, 1906, Elgin, Ill.—d. June 6, 2004, Belleair, Fla.), served (1967–71) as chairman and chief executive officer of General Motors. He joined GM as a statistician in 1927 and slowly worked his way up through the ranks, becoming president of the corporation in 1965. After devastating race riots in 1968, he improved relations with the city of Detroit and made GM the first major corporation to have an African American on its board of directors by hiring the Rev. Leon Sullivan in 1971.

Rockefeller, Laurance Spelman, American philanthropist, venture capitalist, and conservationist (b. May 26, 1910, New York, N.Y.—d. July 11, 2004, New York City), as a member of one of the richest families in the U.S., used his business acumen to fund start-up companies, greatly augmenting his wealth, and promoted conservation, notably by donating land to the National Park Service.

Philanthropist Laurance Rockefeller

Rockefeller inherited a seat on the New York Stock Exchange in 1937; the following year he provided financial backing to World War I pilot Eddie Rickenbacker to found Eastern Airlines. Rockefeller later provided seed money to Intel Corp. and Apple Computer, Inc. In 1942 he made his first land donation, providing the acreage that became Tallman Mountain State Park in New York; his most recent donation was in 2001 and greatly expanded Wyoming's Grand Teton National Park. His work as a mediator in the 1960s made possible the creation of Redwood National Park in California. He was awarded the Congressional Gold Medal in 1991, at which time he was described as a "hidden national treasure."

Rouch, Jean-Pierre, French documentary filmmaker and ethnologist (b. May 31, 1917, Paris, France—d. Feb. 18, 2004, northern Niger), pioneered the cinéma vérité style and techniques, notably the use of the hand-held camera. Rouch first went to Africa as a civil engineer in 1941; what he saw there inspired him to take up both ethnology and cinematography. He made more than 100 films, the most respected of which included *Au pays des mages noirs* (1947), *Les Maîtres fous* (1955), *Moi, un noir* (1958), and *Chronique d'un été* (*Chronicle of a Summer,* 1961). Rouch was in Niger attending a film festival of his work when he died in a car accident.

Ryan, Claude, Canadian politician and journalist (b. Jan. 26, 1925, Montreal, Que.—d. Feb. 9, 2004, Montreal), led the Liberal Party in Quebec province from 1978 to 1982; a committed federalist, he helped defeat a referendum in 1980 on the proposed secession of the French-speaking province from Canada. Ryan served in the Ministry of Education for two years before joining *Le Devoir,* an influential Montreal-based newspaper, as editor in 1964. He eventually became the newspaper's publisher as well as a noted columnist before campaigning successfully for the Liberal leadership in 1978. From 1985 until his retirement in 1994, Ryan held a series of posts in the provincial cabinet of Robert Bourassa, his successor as Liberal Party leader.

Sabanci, Sakip, Turkish businessman and philanthropist (b. April 7, 1933, Akcakaya, Kayseri, Turkey—d. April 10, 2004, Istanbul, Turkey), was regarded as the wealthiest man in Turkey. Known affectionately as "Sakip Aga" (a title of respect), he had the appeal of a populist despite heading one of the top 100 family-owned businesses in the world. Sabanci's conglomerate, Sabanci Holding, acquired interests in banking, automobiles, food and tobacco, tourism, and chemicals, while his philanthropic umbrella group, Vaska, managed more than 100 charitable organizations in Turkey. Sabanci University's Sakip Sabanci Museum, which opened in 2002 in his historic former home in Istanbul, housed his magnificent collection of paintings and Ottoman calligraphy.

Sagan, Françoise (FRANÇOISE QUOIREZ), French novelist and dramatist (b. June 21, 1935, Cajarc, France—d. Sept. 24, 2004, Honfleur, France), created an international sensation as a teenager with the publication of her first novel, *Bonjour tristesse* (1954), a precocious story of amorality, seduction, and infidelity that she wrote in only a few weeks after having failed her exams at the Sorbonne. The novel's rebelliousness and cynicism, as well as its frank discussion of adolescent sex, defined a generation of disillusioned French youth. An international best seller translated into some 20 languages, it was also adapted into a movie (1958). Sagan wrote more than 30 other novels, including *Un Certain Sourire* (1956; *A Certain Smile,* 1956), *Dans un mois, dans un an* (1957; *Those Without Shadows,*

French icon and author Françoise Sagan

1957), and *Aimez-vous Brahms?* (1959; filmed as *Goodbye Again*, 1961), although none matched the success of *Bonjour tristesse*. Written in a spare, classical style, her novels typically focused on the adulterous relationships and hedonism of the idle rich. She also wrote short stories, film scripts, nonfiction, and plays. An iconic figure in France, Sagan made headlines with her glamorous lifestyle—highlighted by a love of gambling and driving fast cars—which she celebrated in some of her fiction and which often attracted more attention than her later works.

Salinger, Pierre Emil George, American journalist and political figure (b. June 14, 1925, San Francisco, Calif.—d. Oct. 16, 2004, Cavaillon, France), served as press secretary (1961–64) to Presidents John F. Kennedy and Lyndon B. Johnson; he later was a Paris-based international correspondent for ABC News (1978–93). He damaged his credibility, however, when he espoused extreme conspiracy theories concerning the explosion of Pan Am Flight 103 over Lockerbie, Scot., in 1988 and the crash of TWA Flight 800 off Long Island, N.Y., in 1996.

Sampson, Anthony Terrell Seward, British journalist and author (b. Aug. 3, 1926, Billingham-on-Tees, Durham, Eng.—d. Dec. 18, 2004, Wardour, Wiltshire, Eng.), scrutinized political power and influence, especially in the U.K. and South Africa, and highlighted human rights issues in his many works. He contributed to several newspapers, including *The Observer* and *The Independent*, and wrote more than 20 books, most notably *Anatomy of Britain* (1962), a seminal study of the British establishment, and *Mandela* (1999), an authorized biography of Nelson Mandela. From 1951 to 1955 Sampson was the editor of the black South African magazine *Drum*.

Sanford, Isabel, American actress (b. Aug. 29, 1917, New York, N.Y.—d. July 9, 2004, Los Angeles, Calif.), was best known for her role as Louise ("Weezy") Jefferson in the long-running (1975–85) situation comedy *The Jeffersons*. Sanford's acting debut was in the American Negro Theater's 1946 production of *On Strivers Row*, and her first movie role was as Tillie in *Guess Who's Coming to Dinner* (1967). She caught the eye of television producer Norman Lear, who in 1971 cast her in the recurring role of Louise Jefferson in the groundbreaking series *All in the Family*. She continued in the role in the spin-off series *The Jeffersons*, for which she won the Emmy Award for best performance by an actress in a comedy series in 1981; she was the first black actress to win the award.

Sangster, Robert, British businessman and Thoroughbred racehorse owner (b. May 23, 1936, Liverpool, Eng.—d. April 7, 2004, London, Eng.), as chief financier of Coolmore Stud, was one of Europe's most successful racehorse breeders and owners for more than 25 years. Horses racing in Coolmore's distinctive white, emerald green, and royal blue silks won more than two dozen European Classic races, including the Epsom and Irish derbies, the English and Irish 2,000 Guineas races, the Prix du Jockey-Club (French Derby), and the Prix de l'Arc de Triomphe, and Sangster was named Britain's champion owner five times between 1977 and 1984. He initially bankrolled his bloodstock and racing horse purchases with the income from Vernons Pools, the sports betting company founded by his father, but he sold Vernons in 1988 for some £90 million (about $150 million).

Scanlon of Davyhulme, Hugh Parr Scanlon, Baron, British trade-union leader (b. Oct. 26, 1913, Melbourne, Australia—d. Jan. 27, 2004, Broadstairs, Kent, Eng.), tenaciously and unswervingly upheld trade-union principles and workers' rights and influenced public policy in Great Britain during the late 1960s and the 1970s. Scanlon joined the Amalgamated Engineering Union while still a teenager and became a shop steward in 1935, rising to the presidency of the union in 1968. A convinced socialist, he changed the political orientation of the union and browbeat employers and the government to adhere to union demands. He accepted a life peerage in 1979 but continued to support the trade-union movement from Parliament's House of Lords.

Scavullo, Francesco, American photographer (b. Jan. 16, 1921, Staten Island, N.Y.—d. Jan. 6, 2004, New York, N.Y.), developed the concept of the magazine "cover girl," which celebrated the beauty of women and focused on sexuality and glamour, over the course of a half-century career, more than 30 years of which were spent shooting "Cosmo girl" covers for *Cosmopolitan* magazine. As an assistant to several world-famous photographers at *Vogue*, Scavullo developed techniques that would make him one of the most in-demand portrait photographers of his time; he used cloth filters or reflective surfaces with his light source to blur imperfections. Among his subjects were Farrah Fawcett, Elizabeth Taylor, Grace Kelly, Kim Basinger, and Madonna, as well as Brooke Shields in a famous and controversial photo as a child.

Schart Hyman, Trina, American illustrator (b. April 8, 1939, Philadelphia, Pa.—d. Nov. 19, 2004, Lebanon, N.H.), illustrated more than 150 children's books, including Caldecott Medal winner *St. George and the Dragon* (1984; written by Margaret Hodges). During the 1970s she developed a reputation as a talented and versatile illustrator for *Cricket*, a children's magazine. Later she provided art for tales by such noted writers as Hans Christian Andersen, Mark Twain, and John Updike (*A Child's Calendar*, 1999). She also wrote several children's books.

Schoening, Peter K., American mountaineer (b. July 30, 1927, Seattle, Wash.—d. Sept. 22, 2004, Kenmore, Wash.), single-handedly averted the loss in 1953 of an entire expedition on K2, the world's second highest peak. After his climbing team experienced a chain-reaction series of falls, Schoening displayed almost superhuman strength by anchoring the entire group and pulling four of the five to safety. His feat came to be referred to as "the Belay" (a commonly used mountaineering term referring to the securing of an object or person by rope). Schoening was part of the 1966 team that made the first ascent of Mt. Vinson, the tallest peak in Antarctica, and he went on to summit the highest mountains on five continents.

Schott, Marge (MARGARET UNNEWEHR), American sports executive (b. Aug. 18, 1928, Cincinnati, Ohio—d. March 2, 2004, Cincinnati), became notorious for making outrageous and offensive public statements about blacks, homosexuals, and Asians, among others, while serving (1984–99) as the owner of the Cincinnati Reds major league baseball team. Schott, a wealthy widow, purchased a limited partnership in the team in 1981, bought controlling interest in the Reds in December 1984, and officially became the team's president and chief executive officer the following year. Though the Reds won the World Series in 1990, the team's victory was overshadowed by Schott's inflammatory off-the-field remarks, which led ultimately to fines and to her suspension for the 1993 season. She famously declared that Adolf Hitler "was good in the beginning, but went too far," a statement that was instrumental in her suspension from 1996 to 1999, when she was forced to sell her controlling interest. Nonetheless, Schott donated millions of dollars to local schools, museums, and cultural institutions.

AP/Wide World Photos

Flamboyant baseball owner Marge Schott

Schwartz, Julius ("JULIE"), American comic-book and science-fiction editor (b. June 19, 1915, New York, N.Y.—Feb. 8, 2004, Mineola, N.Y.), reenergized the comic-book industry in

AP/Wide World Photos

the late 1950s and '60s by reviving the wartime superhero genre at DC Comics. Schwartz ushered in the "Silver Age" of comics with such classics as the Flash, Green Lantern, Batman, and the Justice League of America. Prior to joining DC comics, he was an editor and literary agent for major science-fiction writers.

Scott, the Most Rev. Edward Walter ("TED"), Canadian cleric (b. April 30, 1919, Edmonton, Alta.—d. June 21, 2004, near Parry Sound, Ont.), supported such causes as abortion rights, same-sex marriage, and the ordination of women priests as the liberal archbishop and leader (1971–86) of the Anglican Church of Canada. He also defended social justice and spoke out passionately against apartheid in South Africa. Scott was ordained in 1940 and was named bishop of Kootenay in 1966. Five years later he became the youngest primate of the Anglican Church of Canada, and from 1975 to 1983 he served as moderator of the central committee of the World Council of Churches. He was elected president of the Canadian Council of Churches in 1985. Scott was dubbed the "Pink Primate" and "Red Ted" by those who disapproved of his activism. In 1988 he was the recipient of the Pearson Peace Medal, given by the United Nations Association in Canada. Scott was killed in an auto accident.

Sein Lwin, U, Burmese brigadier general (b. 1922?—d. April 9, 2004, Yangon [Rangoon], Myanmar), was president of Burma (now Myanmar) for 17 days in 1988, but he was better known as the "Butcher of Rangoon," the brutal cohort of U Ne Win (Burma's military dictator from 1962 to 1988) and the man responsible for the ruthless suppression of dissent, notably antigovernment protests in 1962 in which scores of university students were slaughtered. Sein Lwin was named chairman of the Burmese Socialist Program Party and president in July 1988 after Ne Win stepped down amid massive pro-democracy violence. The new president ordered the army to quash the protests, but he was compelled to resign in August after a number of demonstrators, possibly as many as 3,000, had been killed.

Selby, Hubert, Jr. ("CUBBY"), American writer (b. July 23, 1928, Brooklyn, N.Y.—d. April 26, 2004, Los Angeles, Calif.), showcased the dark underside of American urban life in his debut novel, *Last Exit to Brooklyn* (1964). Selby lacked formal training as a writer, but his unstructured style and coarse language helped to accurately convey the bleak, violent world he observed as a youth. After the U.S. entered World War II, he dropped out of school to follow his father into the merchant marine. Although he was only 15 at the time, he was able to persuade recruiters to allow him to join. While at sea in 1947, Selby contracted tuberculosis and was told that he had less than a year to live. An experimental drug treatment and the removal of 10 ribs saved his life, but more than a year of recuperation left him with an addiction to painkillers that took decades to overcome. A childhood friend encouraged him to use writing as an outlet, and in 1961 Selby's short story *Tralala* was published in *The Provincetown Review.* The story was a brutal examination of the life of a waterfront prostitute, and it drew condemnation from a number of circles. When Selby included it with five other stories in his novel *Last Exit to Brooklyn,* it was the target of obscenity charges on both sides of the Atlantic. His stark, unforgiving view of the world was equally apparent in later works, such as *The Room* (1971), *The Demon* (1976), and *Requiem for a Dream* (1978). His output slowed in later years, but he returned to prominence when he co-wrote the screenplay for Darren Aronofsky's film adaptation *Requiem for a Dream* (2000).

Seregni, Líber, Uruguayan general and politician (b. Dec. 13, 1916, Montevideo, Uruguay—d. July 31, 2004, Montevideo), was a cofounder and the first president of Frente Amplio (FA), a leftist political party formed in 1971 to break the hegemony of Uruguay's two controlling political parties, the Colorados and the Blancos (Reds and Whites). Seregni was commander of the army when he resigned in 1968 in protest against the government's handling of a guerrilla problem. Shortly after the military seized control of the government in 1973, Seregni was imprisoned, and he remained a political prisoner for the next 11 years. He made two unsuccessful runs (1971 and 1989) for the presidency.

Seybold, John Warren, American printing innovator and electronic publishing pioneer (b. March 8, 1916, Newburgh, Ind.—d. March 14, 2004, Haverford, Pa.), revolutionized the publishing industry by computerizing typesetting techniques with the development of a software program that enabled publishers to create, edit, and format text for commercial printing on computers. In 1963 he founded Rocappi, Inc. (Research on Computer Applications in the Printing and Publishing Industries), the world's first company to offer commercial-quality computerized typesetting services; in 1971 he and his son Jonathan established an authoritative newsletter for the electronic and desktop-publishing industries called the *Seybold Report.*

Shadbolt, Maurice Francis Richard, New Zealand author (b. June 4, 1932, Auckland, N.Z.—d. Oct. 10, 2004, Taumarunui, N.Z.), was celebrated for historical novels about his native country. His trilogy on the Maori wars of the 19th century—*Season of the Jew* (1986), *Monday's Warriors* (1990), and *The House of Strife* (1993)—was widely regarded as his best work. Shadbolt attended Auckland University College and initially worked as a journalist and as a documentary film director and scriptwriter. His early short stories, which often focused on the clash between modern New Zealand and its traditional culture, were collected in *The New Zealanders* (1959) and *Summer Fires and Winter Country* (1963). Shadbolt's novels set in contemporary New Zealand included *Among the Cinders* (1965), *This Summer's Dolphin* (1969), *Strangers and Journeys* (1972), and *A Touch of Clay* (1974). In 1980 he turned to historical fiction with *The Lovelock Version,* a chronicle of a pioneer family. Shadbolt was a frequent contributor to magazines that included *National Geographic.* His other nonfiction work included *The Shell Guide to New Zealand* (1968) and *One of Ben's* (1993), an autobiography. Shadbolt's works garnered numerous literary awards, including New Zealand Book of the Year four times; in 1989 he was made CBE.

Shamir, Moshe, Israeli novelist and politician (b. Sept. 15, 1921, Zefat, British Palestine—d. Aug. 20, 2004, Rishon LeZiyyon, Israel), championed the socialist ideals of kibbutz life in his novels; in the 1960s he launched a political career as a member of the conservative Likud Party, but after the 1979 peace treaty with Egypt was negotiated, he quit to form a more right-wing party. An active member of the underground during the Israeli war of independence, he created the movement's newsletter, *Ba-mahaneh,* a publication that would become the official magazine of the Israeli army. The author of more than 50 novels and plays, as well as short stories and essays, Shamir received the Israel Prize for Literature in 1998.

Sharp, Mitchell William, Canadian politician and economist (b. May 11, 1911, Winnipeg, Man.—d. March 19, 2004, Ottawa, Ont.), served as an influential adviser to Prime Ministers Lester B. Pearson and Pierre Trudeau. In 1963 Sharp was elected to Parliament for Elington, and soon afterward Pearson appointed him minister of trade and commerce; in 1965 he became minister of finance. As minister of external affairs under Trudeau (1968–74), Sharp was instrumental in forging successful diplomatic relations with China; he retired in 1978. Sharp returned to politics in 1993 as a personal adviser to Prime Minister Jean Chrétien for the yearly salary of Can$1; he resigned the day before Chrétien left office.

Shaw, Artie (ARTHUR JACOB ARSHAWSKY), American clarinetist and bandleader (b. May 23, 1910, New York, N.Y.—d. Dec. 30, 2004, Newbury Park, Calif.), played soaring melodic solos and created many of the Swing era's most popular records, yet he remained ambivalent about playing music all his life. A "compulsive perfectionist," as he called himself, he led a series of big bands, some of which were expanded to include string sections, before disbanding each, usually after a short time. He was among the first white bandleaders to hire black musicians; those he hired included singer Billie Holiday and trumpeters "Hot Lips" Page and Roy Eldridge. Shaw's airy rendition of "Begin the Beguine" (1938) was the first in a series of big band hits that, for a time, eclipsed those of clarinetist and rival Benny Goodman. At the peak of his fame in 1939, Shaw abandoned music to live in Mexico. Returning to the U.S. in 1940, he formed a band that played new favourites, such as "Frenesi" and his classic version of "Stardust," and that included his band-within-a-band, the Gramercy Five,

AP/Wide World Photos

Swing era virtuoso Artie Shaw

which recorded the hit "Summit Ridge Drive." Shaw led a U.S. Navy band in the Pacific war zone during 1943–44. He then formed various ensembles, from big dance bands to a classical-music-oriented unit to small combos, before he retired from playing altogether in 1954. Shaw, who had a mercurial personality, was harshly critical of himself and of the music business. He was married eight times—actresses Lana Turner and Ava Gardner were his most famous wives—and he was a farmer, a theatre producer, and an author of autobiography (*The Trouble with Cinderella* [1952]) and fiction (including the collection of stories *I Love You, I Hate You, Drop Dead!* [1965]). In the mid-1980s he was persuaded to conduct an Artie Shaw revival band for a time, but he did not play his clarinet again.

Shearer, Hugh Lawson, Jamaican trade unionist and politician (b. May 18, 1923, Martha Brae, Jam.—d. July 5, 2004, Kingston, Jam.), served as independent Jamaica's third prime minister (1967–72) and thereafter was a trade union president. In 1941 Shearer joined the Bustamante Industrial Trade Union, Jamaica's main labour organization, and became a protégé of Sir Alexander Bustamante, founder of the Jamaica Labour Party. Shearer's political career prospered as he also rose through the ranks of the union. He became prime minister upon the death in office of Sir Donald Sangster, and under Shearer Jamaica enjoyed a period of strong economic growth and a great increase in the number of schools. In 1977 Shearer became president of the Bustamante Industrial Trade Union. From 1980 to 1989 he served as Jamaica's foreign minister, and in 1994 he became the first president of the Jamaica Confederation of Trade Unions.

Shemer, Naomi Sapir, Israeli composer (b. 1930, Kibbutz Kinneret, Palestine—d. June 26, 2004, Tel Aviv, Israel), wrote inspiring Hebrew-language songs that embodied the land, the people, and the culture of Israel; "Yerushalayim shel zahav" ("Jerusalem of Gold"), which she composed for the Israeli Song Festival in early 1967, became almost an unofficial national anthem after the Six-Day War later that year. Shemer also devised popular children's songs, theatrical musicals, and Hebrew translations of foreign poetry, notably an adaptation of Walt Whitman's "O Captain! My Captain!" that she composed in 1995 in honour of Prime Minister Yitzhak Rabin after he was assassinated. Shemer was awarded the Israel Prize in 1983. After her funeral, which was attended by Prime Minister Ariel Sharon and other government ministers, it was announced that an Israeli stamp would be issued in her honour.

Shipman, Harold Frederick, British physician and serial killer (b. Jan. 14, 1946, Nottingham, Eng.—d. Jan. 13, 2004, Wakefield, West Yorkshire, Eng.), was given the sobriquet "Dr. Death" after it became known that he had killed at least 215 of his patients over a 23-year period. Shipman began working as a general practitioner in Todmorden, Lancashire, in 1974 but was soon discovered to be addicted to the painkiller pethidine. After treatment he resumed practice in the Manchester suburb of Hyde in 1977, and he opened his own private practice there in 1993. It was not until he forged the will of one of his victims in 1998 that he was caught; in 2000 he was convicted of having murdered 15 patients by injecting them with lethal doses of painkillers and was given 15 life sentences. An official inquiry concluded in 2002 that he had killed between 215 and 260 of his patients. He was found hanged from the bars of his cell window in the Wakefield prison.

Sik, Ota, Czech economist (b. Sept. 11, 1919, Plzen, Czech.—d. Aug. 22, 2004, Sankt Gallen, Switz.), laid the economic groundwork for the reforms of the Prague Spring of 1968. By proposing a "third way" between free-market capitalism and a Soviet-style planned economy, he sought to bring "socialism with a human face" to the Czechoslovak government. In April 1968 he was named vice-premier and economics minister, but he was out of the country when the Warsaw Pact troops arrived in August. After the Soviet crackdown he spent the next two decades in exile in Switzerland. Sik briefly returned to public life when, in the wake of the Velvet Revolution of 1989, he was appointed to Pres. Vaclav Havel's board of economic advisers.

Silk, George, New Zealand-born American photographer (b. Nov. 17, 1916, Levin, N.Z.—d. Oct. 23, 2004, Norwalk, Conn.), worked for *Life* magazine from 1943 until 1972. He at first was a combat photographer and was one of the first to photograph Nagasaki, Japan, after the atomic bomb was dropped on it in 1945, but he later turned to sports photography and pioneered the adaptation of a racetrack photo-finish camera for use in capturing shots of athletes in motion.

Sisco, Joseph John, American diplomat (b. Oct. 31, 1919, Chicago, Ill.—d. Nov. 23, 2004, Chevy Chase, Md.), shaped American foreign policy in the Middle East as the chief mediator for that region from 1968 to 1976. Widely regarded as Secretary of State Henry Kissinger's top aide, Sisco used his influence to contain a number of conflicts, most notably when he prevented the military leadership of Greece from responding to the Turkish invasion of Cyprus in 1974.

Smith, Jeff (JEFFREY L. SMITH), American television personality (b. Jan. 22, 1939, Tacoma, Wash.—d. July 7, 2004, Seattle, Wash.), hosted the extremely popular TV cooking show *The Frugal Gourmet* on PBS from 1983 until accusations of sexual misconduct derailed his career in 1997. Smith was ordained a minister in the United Methodist Church in 1965 and became a chaplain at the University of Puget Sound in Tacoma, where he taught a course on food. In 1972 he opened and ran the Chaplain's Pantry, which served as a restaurant and store and offered cooking classes; he sold it in 1983. His television career began in 1973 with a local TV show called *Cooking Fish Creatively;* this program became *The Frugal Gourmet,* which in 1983 was picked up by the Chicago PBS station. Smith delighted viewers with his low-key, humorous, and educational approach, and his recipes were collected in more than 10 well-received cookbooks.

Snodgress, Carrie (CAROLINE SNODGRESS), American actress (b. Oct. 27, 1946, Barrington, Ill.—d. April 1, 2004, Los Angeles, Calif.), gained acclaim, an Academy Award nomination, and two Golden Globe Awards for her portrayal of a put-upon homemaker in the film

Life photographers George Silk (right) and Carl Mydans (q.v.)

Diary of a Mad Housewife (1970) but then abandoned her performing career for several years to live with rock star Neil Young and care for their son. She later starred in *Pale Rider* (1985) and had roles in such movies as *The Fury* (1978), *Blue Sky* (1994), and *Wild Things* (1998) and in several television series.

Sokolof, Philip, American businessman (b. Dec. 14, 1921, Omaha, Neb.—d. April 15, 2004, Omaha), launched a personal mission to combat high cholesterol. He had already amassed a small fortune as a construction supplies manufacturer when, in 1965, a near-fatal heart attack alerted him to the importance of a healthy diet. Over almost two decades, Sokolof spent an estimated $15 million on campaigns to raise cholesterol awareness. In 1985 he formed the National Heart Savers Association, an organization that successfully lobbied Congress to pass legislation requiring nutritional labels on food. He also raised his own profile by taking out a series of ads in national newspapers criticizing the major fast-food chains.

Sontag, Susan (SUSAN ROSENBLATT), American essayist, critic, and novelist (b. Jan. 16, 1933, New York, N.Y.—d. Dec. 28, 2004, New York City), was a leading intellectual in the U.S., best known for her provocative essays on modern culture. Sontag, who graduated from high school at age 15, attended the University of Chicago (B.A., 1951) and Harvard University, where she studied English literature (M.A., 1954) and philosophy (M.A., 1955). Her reputation was established in 1964 with "Notes on 'Camp,'" a seminal essay that examined certain sensibilities toward popular culture, especially within the gay community. Philosophical discussions of film, music, art, and other facets of modern culture became a major focus of Sontag's essays, and her most notable works included *Against Interpretation, and Other Essays* (1966), *On Photography* (1977; winner of the National Book Critics Circle Award), *Illness as Metaphor* (1977), and *AIDS and Its Metaphors* (1988). She also wrote reviews, screenplays, and fictional works, including the historical novels *The Volcano Lover* (1992), which centred on the love affair between Lord Nelson and Lady Hamilton, and *In America* (2000; winner of the National Book Award), based on the life of Polish American actress Helena Modjeska. Sontag, who described herself as a "zealot of seriousness," was also active in politics and a champion of numerous human rights causes.

American intellectual Susan Sontag

Sorsa, (Taisto) Kalevi, Finnish politician (b. Dec. 21, 1930, Keuruu, Fin.—d. Jan. 16, 2004, Helsinki, Fin.), served as Finland's prime minister four times (1972–75, 1977–79, 1982–83, 1983–87), holding the position longer than any other person, and was to a great extent the architect of the welfare state in Finland. A leading light in Finland's Social Democratic Party as well as Europe's Socialist International, he was known for his idealism and his talent for building a consensus.

Souzay, Gérard (GÉRARD MARCEL TISSERAND), French concert and opera singer (b. Dec. 8, 1918, Angers, France—d. Aug. 17, 2004, Antibes, France), performed in concerts and recitals around the world for more than three decades and made hundreds of recordings; he was best known for his sensitive interpretation of French and German art songs. Souzay, who was possessed of a supple but not large baritone voice, studied at the Paris Conservatoire and gave his first recital in 1945. His first venture into opera, however, was not until 1960; his most successful role was that of Golaud in Claude Debussy's *Pelléas et Mélisande.*

Sprouse, Stephen, American fashion designer and artist (b. Sept. 12, 1953, Ohio—d. March 4, 2004, New York, N.Y.), made a splash on the fashion scene in the early 1980s with creations that sported Day-Glo colours, mirrored sequins, and Velcro attachments, and his designs commanded high prices in vintage stores even after he lost financial backing for his business. He was 14 years old when he began sketching for designer Bill Blass, and in the 1980s Sprouse worked with Andy Warhol on a collection inspired by Warhol's "Camouflage" series of paintings. Sprouse reemerged in the 1990s, but it was his 2001–02 graffiti-motif clothing (for Target) and handbags (for Louis Vuitton) that fueled his reputation as a design pioneer. Sprouse also clothed a former neighbour—Debbie Harry of the rock group Blondie.

St. John, Sir Harold Bernard, Barbadian politician (b. Aug. 16, 1931, Christ Church, Barbados—d. Feb. 29, 2004, Bridgetown, Barbados), served as prime minister of Barbados in 1985–86 and was the longtime leading light of the ruling Barbados Labour Party. Trained as a lawyer, he entered politics in the late 1950s, while Barbados was still a British colony. Following independence St. John served in several posts, helping to develop the tourist industry and attempting to better integrate the regional Caribbean economy.

Stark, Ray, American film producer (b. Oct. 3, 1915, New York, N.Y.—d. Jan. 17, 2004, West Hollywood, Calif.), was the power behind more than 125 movies and was considered one of the most successful of Hollywood's independent producers. He was especially noted for his working relationships with Barbra Streisand—whose career he launched with his stage (1964) and film (1968) versions of *Funny Girl,* in which Streisand starred in the role of comedienne Fanny Brice, Stark's mother-in-law—and Neil Simon, 11 of whose scripts Stark produced. Films he produced included *The Sunshine Boys* (1975), *The Goodbye Girl* (1977), and *Steel Magnolias* (1989). The Academy of Motion Picture Arts and Sciences honoured Stark with its Irving G. Thalberg Award in 1980.

Stoller, Ezra, American photographer (b. May 16, 1915, Chicago, Ill.—d. Oct. 29, 2004, Williamstown, Mass.), captured the beauty of modern architecture through his black-and-white photography. Trained as an architect, Stoller would spend several days exploring the spaces and shadows of a building before taking any pictures. Architects revered his work, and he photographed buildings designed by such noted ones as Frank Lloyd Wright, Eero Saarinen, and Louis Kahn. *Modern Architecture: Photographs by Ezra Stoller,* a monograph of his work, was published in 1990.

Straus, Roger Williams, Jr., American publisher (b. Jan. 3, 1917, New York, N.Y.—d. May 25, 2004, New York City), founded the New York-based publishing house Farrar, Straus & Co. in 1946; it became Farrar, Straus & Giroux in 1964. Under his leadership the firm built a reputation for literary excellence, publishing the works of such notable writers as T.S. Eliot, Flannery O'Connor, and Isaac Bashevis Singer. He sold the firm in 1994 but remained largely in control.

Strickland de la Hunty, Shirley Barbara, Australian athlete (b. July 18, 1925, Guildford, Australia—d. Feb. 17, 2004, Perth, Australia), was her country's most successful track-and-field athlete, with seven Olympic medals (three gold, one silver, and three bronze); she was also the first female athlete to win a medal in three consecutive Olympics (1948, 1952, and 1956) and, by winning the 80-m hurdles in both 1952 and 1956, became the first woman to defend an Olympic title successfully. At the 1948 Olympics in London, Strickland finished third in the 100-m sprint and the 80-m hurdles and was a member of the silver-medal-winning 4 × 100-m relay team. She was ruled fourth in the 200-m final, though a photograph of the finish later showed that she should have been awarded the bronze. In all four events the Dutch champion Fanny Blankers-Koen (*q.v.*) was the gold medalist. Strickland married geologist Laurence de la Hunty in 1950 and arrived in Helsinki, Fin., for the 1952 Games determined to avenge her earlier losses. She captured another bronze in the 100-m sprint and a gold (in world-record time) in the 80-m hurdles; her longtime rival Blankers-Koen was ill and dropped out. Strickland de la Hunty gave birth to the first of her four children in 1953 and immediately returned to competition. In

1955, at age 30, she set a world record in the 100 m at the World University Games in Warsaw, and the next year she won both the 80-m hurdles and the 4 × 100-m relay at the Melbourne Olympics, the first to be held in her homeland. She failed to qualify for the 1960 Olympics and won her last title at the Australian national championships in 1962. Strickland de la Hunty received a degree in physics from the University of Western Australia in 1946, and after retiring from athletics she taught university-level physics and mathematics and coached track. At the 2000 Games in Sydney, she was one of Australia's fabled "Golden Girls" who carried the Olympic torch in the opening ceremony.

Suraiya (SURAIYA JAMAL SHEIKH), Indian actress and singer (b. 1929, Lahore, India [now in Pakistan]—d. Jan. 31, 2004, Mumbai [Bombay], India), captivated Bollywood movie audiences in the 1940s and early 1950s with her beauty and her melodious singing voice; she was one of the few Indian film actors to do her own singing and often worked as a playback singer, recording songs to be dubbed into other actresses' performances. After making her debut at age 12 in *Taj Mahal* (1941), Suraiya appeared in scores of films, including at least 25 between 1946 and 1950, and at her peak was one of Bollywood's highest-paid stars. She costarred several times with Hindu matinee idol Dev Anand, but their offscreen romance ended unhappily in 1951 when her Muslim family refused to allow her to marry him. She made only a few films after 1952 and retired in 1963 at age 34.

Suzuki, Zenko, Japanese politician (b. Jan. 11, 1911, Yamada, Japan—d. July 19, 2004, Tokyo, Japan), served as prime minister of Japan from 1980 to 1982, when he suddenly announced that he would not run in the upcoming elections. Beginning in 1947, Suzuki was elected to the Diet (parliament) 13 times, holding several cabinet posts, and he was chosen a record 10 times to head the executive council of the Liberal Democratic Party. Nonetheless, he was regarded as sufficiently anonymous that observers were surprised when he was chosen for the top post. His tenure was noted for bringing Japan closer to the U.S. but also for a foreign policy misstep in relations with China.

Sweeney, Charles William, American pilot (b. Dec. 27, 1919, Lowell, Mass.—d. July 16, 2004, Boston, Mass.), flew the plane that dropped the atomic bomb on Nagasaki, Japan, at the end of World War II. Sweeney joined the U.S. Army Air Forces in 1941. In September 1944 he became a member of the group that was secretly training for the atomic bombing mission. He had been promoted to major by the time of the mission, and he flew a plane that accompanied the *Enola Gay* to Hiroshima to drop measuring instruments behind the bomb. On Aug. 9, 1945, he piloted the borrowed B-29 Superfortress bomber *Bockscar,* which had a malfunctioning fuel pump. Finding the initial target, Kokura, obscured by clouds, Sweeney flew on to Nagasaki and dropped "Fat Man," a plutonium bomb more powerful than the one dropped on Hiroshima; some 70,000 people were killed and nearly half the city destroyed. Japan surrendered six days later.

Sweezy, Paul Marlor, American economist (b. April 10, 1910, New York, N.Y.—d. Feb. 28, 2004, Larchmont, N.Y.), was one of the leading Marxist intellectuals of the second half of the 20th century, notably as publisher of *Monthly Review,* a journal he cofounded in 1949. Trained at Harvard University and the London School of Economics, Sweezy charted an independent path through the tangle of the political left during the Cold War, wielding significant influence on the counterculture philosophy of the 1960s. His best-known work on economics was *Monopoly Capital* (1966), cowritten with Paul A. Baran.

Taras, John, American choreographer and ballet master (b. April 18, 1919, New York, N.Y.—d. April 2, 2004, New York City), gained international renown not only for creating imaginative ballets but also for staging and rehearsing the works of other notable choreographers for numerous dance companies. One of his longest relationships was with choreographer George Balanchine and New York City Ballet (NYCB); both in Taras's work with that company and in his stagings of Balanchine ballets for major companies elsewhere, he was noted for his faithful adherence to Balanchine's neoclassical style. Taras began his dancing career with a Ukrainian folk dance group when he was 9 years old, and when he was 16 he began ballet studies in New York City. After performing stints with Catherine Littlefield's Philadelphia Ballet and NYCB precursors, he was (1942–46) a member of Ballet Theatre (later American Ballet Theatre [ABT]). There he not only danced and served as ballet master but in 1945 choreographed his first major ballet, *Graziana.* In 1946 Taras choreographed *Camille* for the Original Ballet Russe, and in 1948 he created one of his most enduring works, *Design with Strings,* for the Metropolitan Ballet of London. Also in 1948 he became choreographer and ballet master for the Grand Ballet du Marquis de Cuevas in Paris, an association that lasted, with breaks for work with other companies, until 1959. Notable among his ballets for the de Cuevas company was *Piège de lumière* (1952). Besides serving as ballet master for the Paris Opéra Ballet (1969–70) and as artistic director of West Berlin's Deutsche Oper (1971–72), Taras was affiliated with NYCB from 1959 until Balanchine's death in 1983, serving as ballet master and Balanchine's assistant. He choreographed such ballets as *Ebony Concerto* (1960), *Arcade* (1963), which featured Suzanne Farrell's first solo role, and *Souvenir de Florence* (1981) for NYCB and an acclaimed version of *Firebird* for Dance Theatre of Harlem (1982). In 1984 Taras was named associate director of ABT, a position he held until 1990.

Taylor, June, American choreographer (b. Dec. 14, 1917, Chicago, Ill.—d. May 17, 2004, Miami, Fla.), began dancing professionally when she was 12, had her career ended by tuberculosis at age 20, and thereupon became a choreographer. Her June Taylor Dancers attained success in nightclubs and then in 1948 began being seen on television, first on Ed Sullivan's *Toast of the Town* and on *Cavalcade of Stars* but then, most notably, on *The Jackie Gleason Show* (1952–59 and 1962–70), which opened each week with Taylor's high-kicking dancers and brought the chorus line before the TV audience. In 1978 Taylor came out of retirement to take charge of the Miami Dolphins football team's cheerleaders and turned them into a dance unit, which she directed until 1990.

Taylor, Theodore Brewster, American nuclear physicist and weapons designer (b. July 11, 1925, Mexico City, Mex.—d. Oct. 28, 2004, Silver Spring, Md.), devised the most powerful fission explosives in the U.S. arsenal as well as the smallest and lightest (the 23-kg [51-lb] Davy Crockett in 1961) and in 1965 was the recipient of the Ernest Orlando Lawrence Award for the development, use, or control of nuclear energy, awarded by the U.S. Atomic Energy Agency (now the U.S. Department of Energy). He worried about the dangers of small nuclear weapons of the type he had created falling into the wrong hands, however, and became deeply concerned about his country's readiness to use nuclear weapons. In the last years of his life, he wrote and lectured passionately against U.S. nuclear policy.

Tcherina, Ludmila (MONIKA [MONIQUE] AVENIROVNA TCHEMERZINA), French ballet dancer, actress, artist, and writer (b. Oct. 10,

French ballerina Ludmila Tcherina

1924, Paris, France—d. March 21, 2004, Paris), was known almost as much for her beauty and flair as for her talent as a performer. Besides premiering roles for top choreographers, including Serge Lifar and Maurice Béjart, she appeared in films—notably *The Red Shoes* (1948) and *The Tales of Hoffmann* (1951)—as well as on television and the stage, wrote novels and a screenplay, and created works of art.

Tebaldi, Renata, Italian soprano (b. Feb. 1, 1922, Pesaro, Italy—d. Dec. 19, 2004, San Marino), was one of the foremost opera singers of the post-World War II period. With a rich and powerful voice, over which she exercised great control, she was especially identified with works by Giuseppe Verdi, Giacomo Puccini, and other Italian composers. Tebaldi studied at conservatories in Pesaro and Parma, and her stage debut took place in 1944 in Rovigo. In 1946 conductor Arturo Toscanini invited her to sing in the concert marking the reopening of Milan's La Scala, and from 1949 to 1954 she was a member of its company. She also had a long association with the Metropolitan Opera in New York City, where between 1955 and 1973 she sang 270 performances. After her retirement from the opera stage in 1973, she gave recitals, the last at La Scala in 1976. Among her roles were Puccini's *Tosca* and Mimi in *La Bohème,* Verdi's *Aida* and Desdemona in *Otello,* and Madeleine in Umberto Giordano's *Andrea Chénier.* Her many esteemed recordings included one of a live performance (1958) of Verdi's *La forza del destino,* in which she sang the role of Leonora. A highly publicized rivalry with Maria Callas was fueled by partisan fans and the press.

Thanom Kittikachorn, Thai military strongman (b. Aug. 11, 1911, Tak, Siam [now Thailand]—d. June 16, 2004, Bangkok, Thai.), as the ruler (1963–73) of Thailand, was one of the staunchest allies of the United States in Southeast Asia until he was overthrown in a student-led uprising. Thanom joined the army in 1931 and rose to the rank of field marshal. In 1957 he participated in a military coup that gained control of the Thai government; he became prime minister in 1963 (having served briefly in that role in 1958). Although he claimed to embrace democracy, overseeing the creation of a new constitution in 1968 and holding elections in 1969 (which he easily won), his government quickly suppressed any dissent. During the Vietnam War, Thanom, concerned about communist insurgents in his own country, sent troops to fight the Viet Cong and allowed U.S. bombing missions to use Thai air bases. In 1971 he dissolved the parliament, suspended the constitution, and formed a military junta led by himself, his son, Col. Narong Kittikachorn, and his son's father-in-law, Field Marshal Praphas Charusathien. The "Three Tyrants," as they became known, gained a reputation for corruption and ruthlessness. The violent suppression of student protests in October 1973 led to the collapse of the military government as well as to Thanom's exile. He was allowed to return to Thailand in 1976. In his later years he campaigned in defense of his actions as prime minister and asserted his belief in democracy.

Thelwell, Norman, British cartoonist (b. May 3, 1923, Birkenhead, Cheshire, Eng.—d. Feb. 7, 2004, Romsey, Hampshire, Eng.), drew some 1,500 cartoons for the satiric magazine *Punch* and was best known for his drawings of a small girl and her rotund pony. Thelwell began his professional career while in the army during World War II. He contributed cartoons to many publications, including *London Opinion, News Review, News Chronicle,* and *Sunday Dispatch,* in addition to his contributions to *Punch,* which included 60 full-colour covers. He also produced 32 books, starting with *Angels on Horseback and Elsewhere* (1957) and including *The Effluent Society* (1971) and *Some Damn Fool's Signed the Rubens Again* (1982); Thelwell was also known as a talented landscape artist and a dedicated conservationist.

Thomas, Frank, American animator (b. Sept. 5, 1912, Santa Monica, Calif.—d. Sept. 8, 2004, Flintridge, Calif.), created some of the most memorable moments in animated film history, most notably the spaghetti dinner scene in Walt Disney's *The Lady and the Tramp* (1955). One of Disney's core circle of master animators—a group that Disney referred to as his "Nine Old Men"—Thomas drew praise for his ability to convey emotion through his characters without straying into excessive sentimentality.

Thorn, George Widmer, American physician (b. Jan. 15, 1906, Buffalo, N.Y.—d. June 26, 2004, Beverly, Mass.), did groundbreaking work in the treatment of Addison disease and kidney failure. As physician in chief (1942–72) at Peter Bent Brigham Hospital (now Brigham and Women's Hospital) in Boston, Thorn developed an early test for Addison disease and began the use of cortisone to treat it, a major advance over then-prevalent treatment methods. He was instrumental in acquiring the first kidney dialysis machine for the U.S., and he assembled the team that performed the first successful human organ transplant, a kidney transplant between identical twins, in 1954. He played a vital role in the creation and development of the Howard Hughes Medical Institute, serving as director of medical research (1955–81), president (1981–84), and chairman (1984–90). Thorn held academic positions at several universities and was a founding editor of the medical textbook *Harrison's Principles of Internal Medicine.* The George W. Thorn Center for Endocrine Disorders was established in 1986 at Brigham and Women's Hospital.

Thulin, Ingrid, Swedish film actress (b. Jan. 27, 1926, Sollefteå, Swed.—d. Jan. 7, 2004, Stockholm, Swed.), was regarded as one of Sweden's best actresses, finding particular success in her work with director Ingmar Bergman. Thulin studied ballet and theatre and made her screen debut in 1948. Her breakthrough came in Bergman's *Smultronstället* (*Wild Strawberries;* 1957), and she shared the Cannes Film Festival's best actress award with her costars for her performance in his *Nära livet* (1958; U.S. title, *Brink of Life*). Especially noteworthy among Thulin's more than 60 films were *Ansiktet* (1958; U.S. title, *The Magician*), *Nattvardsgästerna* (*Winter Light;* 1963), *Tystnaden* (*The Silence;* 1963), and *Viskningar och rop* (*Cries and Whispers;* 1972).

Toland, John Willard, American historian (b. June 29, 1912, La Crosse, Wis.—d. Jan. 4, 2004, Danbury, Conn.), wrote several best-selling historical books about World War II. After having served in the Army Air Corps during that war, Toland became a freelance journalist. His first nonfiction book, *Ships in the Sky* (1957), was about dirigibles. More notable were *The Rising Sun: The Decline and Fall of the Japanese Empire, 1936–1945* (1970), written from the Japanese point of view and the recipient of the 1971 Pulitzer Prize for general nonfiction; *Adolf Hitler* (1976), widely held to be one of the most comprehensive biographies of the German leader; and *Infamy: Pearl Harbor and Its Aftermath* (1982), in which Toland claimed that U.S. Pres. Franklin D. Roosevelt knew about the planned attack on Pearl Harbor in advance but allowed it to take place to provide a reason for the U.S. to enter the war. Toland's memoir, *Captured by History,* was published in 1997.

Trajkovski, Boris, Macedonian politician (b. June 25, 1956, Strumica, Yugos. [now in Macedonia]—d. Feb. 26, 2004, near Stolac, Bosnia and Herzegovina), served as president of Macedonia from 1999. Trajkovski trained as a lawyer and a lay Methodist preacher in a country largely divided between Eastern Orthodox Christians and Muslims. He was credited with having averted civil war between ethnic Macedonians and minority Albanians in 2001. He sought international help and brokered compromise between the warring factions in spite of the relative lack of power of Macedonia's presidency; he also championed his country's integration into Europe. He was killed in a plane crash on his way to an international conference.

Troy, Doris (DORIS HIGGENSEN), American soul singer (b. Jan. 6, 1937, New York, N.Y.—d. Feb. 16, 2004, Las Vegas, Nev.), found great popularity in Britain, where she resettled in 1969, recording backing vocals with the Rolling Stones, Pink Floyd, and George Harrison. She first came to fame in New York City behind the strength of her song "Just One Look" (1963). The musical *Mama, I Want to Sing* (1983) was based on her life story.

Ustinov, Sir Peter Alexander, British entertainer, writer, and humanitarian (b. April 16, 1921, London, Eng.—d. March 28, 2004, Genolier, Switz.), enjoyed a versatile career that spanned more than 60 years, during which he excelled in numerous areas of the arts while gaining renown—especially by means of lectures and one-man shows—as a witty raconteur. In addition to achieving success as a film, stage, and television actor, playwright, film director, screenwriter, and novelist, he served as an unpaid goodwill ambassador for UNICEF

Peter Ustinov as Hercule Poirot

for some 35 years. While still in his teens, Ustinov wrote and appeared in revues, acted in plays and films, and wrote his first produced play, *House of Regrets.* He continued playwriting during his World War II military service, and after the war he returned to acting. Ustinov's role in *Quo Vadis?* (1951) gained him international acclaim and his first Academy Award nomination. He later won two best supporting actor Oscars, for *Spartacus* (1960) and *Topkapi* (1964). Other notable early films were *Hotel Sahara* (1951), *We're No Angels* (1955), *The Sundowners* (1960), and *Billy Budd* (1962), on which Ustinov served as coadapter, director, and producer as well as filling the role of Captain Vere. He was a memorable Hercule Poirot in several filmed versions of the Agatha Christie novels featuring the Belgian detective, including *Death on the Nile* (1978), *Evil Under the Sun* (1982), and *Appointment with Death* (1988). Ustinov won Emmy Awards for his performances in the television productions *The Life of Samuel Johnson* (1958), *Barefoot in Athens* (1966), and *A Storm in Summer* (1970) and earned a 1959 Grammy for his narration of Sergey Prokofiev's *Peter and the Wolf.* He enjoyed success as a playwright with such hits as *The Love of Four Colonels* (1951), *Romanoff and Juliet* (1956; filmed 1961, directed by Ustinov), *The Unknown Soldier and His Wife* (1967), and *Beethoven's 10th* (1983). His storytelling skills were demonstrated in several books, including the short-story collection *Add a Dash of Pity* (1959), the novels *The Loser* (1960) and *Krumnagel* (1971), the historical study *My Russia* (1983), and the autobiographical *Dear Me* (1977), *Ustinov at Large* (1991), and *Ustinov Still at Large* (1993). Ustinov was made CBE in 1975 and was knighted in 1990.

Valderrama, Juanito (JUAN VALDERRAMA BLANCA), Spanish singer-songwriter (b. May 24, 1916, Torredelcampo, Spain—d. April 12, 2004, Espartinas, Spain), won critical acclaim from the mid-1930s as a performer of flamenco and from the 1950s achieved towering success recording a popular song form known as *copla.* Simultaneously viewed both as the court performer of dictator Francisco Franco and as Spain's first protest singer, the Andalusian native was best known for his song "El Emigrante" (1949), which became part of the national consciousness. A skilled impresario, Valderrama led a touring company that included his second wife, flamenco singer Dolores Abril.

Valentine, Alfred Lewis ("ALF"), Jamaican cricketer (b. April 29, 1930, Spanish Town, near Kingston, Jam.—d. May 11, 2004, Orlando, Fla.), along with his spin-bowling partner Sonny Ramadhin, spearheaded the attack in the West Indies' 1950 tour of England, inspiring a calypso song containing the line, "With those little pals of mine, Ramadhin and Valentine." Valentine became interested in cricket at St. Catherine's School in Spanish Town. His coach in local club cricket, former English bowler Jack Mercer, took an interest in the young left-arm slow spin bowler, encouraging him to spin the ball as much as possible and recommending him to the Jamaican cricket authorities. The West Indies team had an abundance of batting at the time but lacked quality bowling, so, despite having played in only two first-class matches, Valentine was selected for the 1950 England tour. He won his place in the Test side by taking 13 wickets for 67 runs in a tour match against Lancashire. In the Test series he took 33 wickets (still a West Indies record for a four-Test series) at an average of 20.42, and in all first-class matches he took 123 wickets at an average of 17.94. The West Indies not only won its first Test match in England but also won the series 3–1, causing great excitement both in the Caribbean and among the large population of West Indian immigrants in England. In 1954, at age 23, Valentine became the youngest bowler, and the first West Indian, to take 100 Test wickets. He played for the West Indies until 1962 (taking 139 wickets in 36 matches at an average of 30.32) and played for Jamaica until 1965, compiling first-class figures of 475 wickets in 125 matches at an average of 26.21. After retiring from first-class cricket, he played in the English Birmingham League. Valentine retired to Florida in 1978.

Van Andel, Jay, American entrepreneur (b. June 3, 1924, Grand Rapids, Mich.—d. Dec. 7, 2004, Ada, Mich.), cofounded Amway, a direct-sales company that generated billion-dollar revenues around the world. He founded Amway (short for American Way) with his childhood friend Richard DeVos in 1959. The company originally sold vitamins and quickly expanded its business into soaps and other household products. Amway's large sales force was particularly known for converting customers into salespeople.

Van Duyn, Mona, American poet (b. May 9, 1921, Waterloo, Iowa—d. Dec. 2, 2004, University City, Mo.), wrote about ordinary middle-class suburban life with clarity and humour. She used the rigour of formal technique to examine moments of domesticity in an unpretentious manner. After graduating from Iowa State Teachers College (now the University of Northern Iowa) and the University of Iowa, she began teaching. She founded the periodical *Perspective: A Quarterly of Literature and the Arts* in 1947, together with her husband, Jarvis A. Thurston, a fellow academic. Her first book of poetry, *Valentines to the Wide World,* was published in 1959. Her third book of verse, *To See, to Take* (1970), captured the National Book Award. In 1991 she won the Pulitzer Prize for poetry for *Near Changes,* and the following year she was selected as U.S. poet laureate, the first woman to be named to the post. Van Duyn taught at the University of Iowa, the University of Louisville, Ky., and Washington University, St. Louis, Mo. *Selected Poems,* which appeared in 2002, was a survey of her career.

Vane, Sir John Robert, British pharmacologist (b. March 29, 1927, Tardebigg, Worcestershire, Eng.—d. Nov. 19, 2004, Farnborough, Kent, Eng.), conducted pioneering research in the study of hormonelike substances in the body called prostaglandins; he shared the 1982 Nobel Prize for Physiology or Medicine with Swedish biochemists Sune K. Bergström (*q.v.*) and Bengt I. Samuelsson. Vane discovered in 1971 that the beneficial effects of aspirin, which include the reduction of fever, pain, inflammation, and blood-clot formation, were the result of aspirin's property of blocking the formation of prostaglandins and related substances. His research led to the discovery of prostacyclin, a prostaglandin derivative that is important for the health of blood vessels, and to the development of ACE (angiotensin-converting enzyme) inhibitors, widely used in the treatment of high blood pressure. Vane received a doctorate (1953) in pharmacology from St. Catherine's College, Oxford. He joined (1955) the faculty of the Institute of Basic Medical Sciences, London, and later became the director (1973) of research and development at the Wellcome Foundation. He was also the founding director (1986) of the William Harvey Research Institute, London, which specialized in cardiovascular research. Vane was knighted in 1984.

Viscardi, Henry, Jr., American activist (b. May 10, 1912, New York, N.Y.—d. April 13, 2004, Roslyn, N.Y.), campaigned for the inclusion of the physically handicapped in the workforce. Born with legs that terminated at mid-thigh, he used personal experience to help establish a rehabilitation program for disabled veterans at Walter Reed Army Hospital, Washington, D.C., during World War II. His efforts attracted the attention of Eleanor Roosevelt, and at her urging Viscardi founded Abilities, Inc., in 1952. In 1991 the organization, created as an employment agency for the disabled, merged with two other groups to create the National Center for Disability Services.

Vonk, Hans, Dutch conductor (b. June 18, 1942?, Amsterdam, Neth.—d. Aug. 29, 2004, Amsterdam), excelled in the works of Romantic composers; he was much respected for his musicianship and for his many fine recordings. His first professional appointment was as conductor for the Dutch Ballet in 1966, and he became assistant conductor at Amsterdam's Concertgebouw in 1969. Vonk served as conductor of the Netherlands Radio Philharmonic (1973–79) and chief conductor of the Netherlands Opera (1976–85) and of the Residentie Orchestra in The Hague (1980–91), while making guest appearances throughout the world. Outside The Netherlands, he was associate conductor of London's Royal Philharmonic in 1976–79. He was appointed director of both the Staatskapelle and the Staatsoper of Dresden (then in East Germany) in 1985 and took over the Radio Symphony Orchestra of Cologne, Ger., in 1991. Vonk was chief conductor of the St. Louis (Mo.) Symphony Orchestra from 1996 until a degenerative nerve disease forced him to retire in 2002.

Waller, Charlie (CHARLES OTIS WALLER), American bluegrass vocalist, guitarist, and songwriter (b. Jan. 19, 1935, Joinerville, Texas—d. Aug. 18, 2004, Gordonsville, Va.), was a founding member (1957) of the Country Gentlemen, a group that began the "new grass revival," modernizing and taking bluegrass music to wider audiences, especially on college campuses and at urban nightclubs.

Ward, Rodger, American race car driver (b. Jan. 10, 1921, Beloit, Kan.—d. July 5, 2004, Anaheim, Calif.), won the Indianapolis 500 twice and was a racing star in the late 1950s and early '60s. Ward started racing midgets in 1946. In 1951 he won the AAA stock car championship and raced at Indianapolis for the first time. In the Indianapolis 500 of 1955, however, Ward's car broke an axle, triggering a multicar crash in which the driver Bill Vukovich was killed. Ward considered quitting, but in 1959 he joined car owner Bob Wilke and mechanic A.J. Watson to form the team Leader Card Racing, and later that year he won his first Indy as well as the United States Auto Club (USAC) national championship. In 1962 he again won both the Indianapolis 500 and the USAC championship. Ward retired from racing in 1966 and was inducted into the International Motorsports Hall of Fame in 1992.

Watanabe, Yoko, Japanese opera singer (b. July 12, 1953, Fukuoka, Japan—d. July 15, 2004, Milan, Italy), made her professional debut on the opera stage in 1978 and over the next 22 years became renowned for the intensity of her portrayals of the major heroines, most notably Cio-Cio-San in Puccini's *Madama Butterfly.* By the time she retired in 2000, she had starred at the world's top four opera houses—La Scala in Milan, the Vienna State Opera, the Royal Opera House at Covent Garden in London, and the Metropolitan Opera in New York City—the first Japanese soprano to do so.

Wheeler, (John) Harvey, American political scientist and writer (b. Oct. 17, 1918, Waco, Texas—d. Sept. 6, 2004, Carpinteria, Calif.), was the author of numerous nonfiction political science books but was best known for the work of fiction he co-wrote with Eugene Burdick, *Fail-Safe* (1962), which—with its theme of accidental nuclear attack—struck a chord with a nervous public upon its release at a time of heightened Cold War tensions. *Fail-Safe* was filmed in 1964 and was dramatized live on television in 2000.

Whipple, Fred Lawrence, American astronomer (b. Nov. 5, 1906, Red Oak, Iowa—d. Aug. 30, 2004, Cambridge, Mass.), was an expert on meteors, meteorites, and comets. In 1950 he hypothesized that a comet has a nucleus that is made up of a mixture of dust and frozen water, ammonia, methane, and carbon dioxide and that some of the frozen material is vaporized by solar energy as the comet passes through the inner solar system. This idea, which became known as the dirty-snowball theory, was confirmed in 1986 by close-up space-probe images of Halley's Comet and was an important contribution to the understanding of the solar system. In the 1950s, at the beginning of the space age, he helped develop a satellite-tracking network. Whipple received a Ph.D. (1931) in astronomy from the University of California, Berkeley. He joined (1931) the staff at Harvard College Observatory and was a professor (1950–77) of astronomy at Harvard University. He also served as director of the Smithsonian Astrophysical Observatory, Cambridge, from 1955 until 1973, when he helped complete a merger between the two observatories. He received a gold medal (1983) from the Royal Astronomical Society. Whipple discovered six comets, all of which bear his name.

White, Reggie (REGINALD HOWARD WHITE),

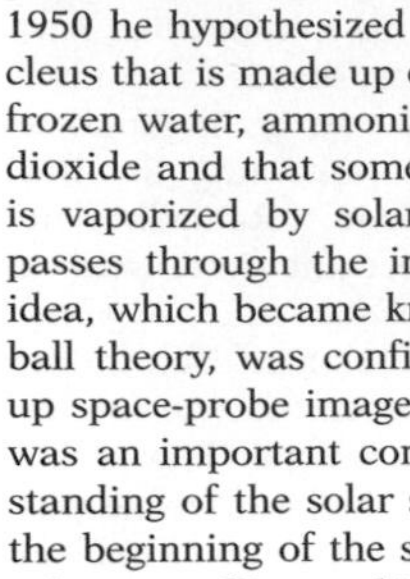

American professional football player (b. Dec. 19, 1961, Chattanooga, Tenn.—d. Dec. 26, 2004, Huntersville, N.C.), was considered one of the best defensive linemen in the history of the National Football League. During a 15-year career, which included stints with the Philadelphia Eagles (1985–92) and the Green Bay Packers (1993–98), a franchise he helped lead to a Super Bowl title in 1997, White set a record for career sacks (198) and was selected to the Pro Bowl an unprecedented 13 consecutive times (1986–98). An ordained minister, he was known as the "Minister of Defense."

Wilkins, Maurice Hugh Frederick, New Zealand-born British biophysicist (b. Dec. 15, 1916, Pongaroa, N.Z.—d. Oct. 5, 2004, London, Eng.), used X-ray crystallography to investigate the DNA molecule and thereby contributed to the discovery of DNA's structure by James Watson and Francis Crick (*q.v.*), with whom he shared the 1962 Nobel Prize for Physiology or Medicine. Wilkins's role in unraveling the structure of DNA was less well known than that of the more celebrated Watson and Crick; at his lab at King's College, London, in the early 1950s, Wilkins (with his colleague Rosalind Franklin) used the then-

© Loomis Dean/Time Life Pictures/Getty Images

Biophysicist Maurice Wilkins

new technique of X-ray crystallography to study the chemical bonds and atomic orientation of the DNA molecule. Meanwhile, Watson and Crick were trying to elucidate the molecule's structure by building models in their laboratory at the University of Cambridge. Franklin's and Wilkins's findings helped the Cambridge duo determine the correct model for the physical structure of DNA. In 1953 the findings of Wilkins and Franklin were published in the same issue of the journal *Nature* as those of Watson and Crick, but the latter two scientists received most of the world's attention. (Franklin died in 1958, before the Nobel Prize was awarded.) Wilkins studied at St. John's College, Cambridge, and the University of Birmingham and worked on the Manhattan Project during World War II. After the war he switched to studying biological systems and became an ardent voice for nuclear disarmament, helping to establish the British Society for Social Responsibility in Science in 1969. Wilkins was made CBE in 1963. His autobiography, *The Third Man of the Double Helix* (2003), offered a reflective account of the atmosphere surrounding the DNA studies of 50 years earlier.

Winfield, Paul Edward, American actor (b.

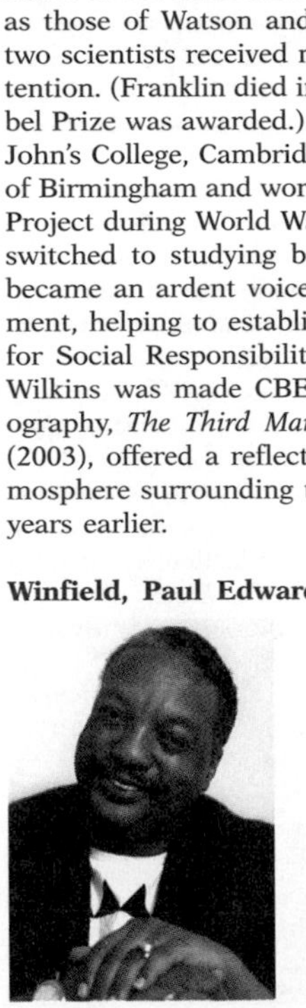

May 22, 1941, Los Angeles, Calif.—d. March 7, 2004, Los Angeles), had such a versatility as a performer that he was equally convincing in such varied roles as Diahann Carroll's boyfriend in the sitcom *Julia* (1968), a sharecropper struggling to take care of his family in *Sounder* (1972), baseball player Roy Campanella in the TV film *It's Good to Be Alive* (1974), and the Rev. Martin Luther King, Jr., in the TV miniseries *King* (1978). His

centre: Allen Kee/WireImage.com;
bottom: AP/Wide World Photos

performance as a federal judge in a guest appearance on the TV series *Picket Fences* won him an Emmy Award in 1995.

Winter, Fred (FREDERICK THOMAS WINTER), British steeplechase (jump) jockey and trainer (b. Sept. 20, 1926, Andover, Hampshire, Eng.—d. April 5, 2004, Swindon, Wiltshire, Eng.), was the National Hunt champion jockey four times in an 18-year riding career (1947–64) and then champion trainer eight times between 1965 and 1987, when he was forced to retire after suffering a massive stroke. His many victories included the Grand National (twice as a jockey and twice as a trainer), the Cheltenham Gold Cup (twice as a jockey and once as a trainer), and the Champion Hurdle (three times as a jockey and four as a trainer); at the time of his death, he was the only man to have won all three major races in both roles. Winter was made CBE in 1963.

Woodbridge, George Charles, American cartoonist and illustrator (b. Oct. 3, 1930, Flushing, Queens, N.Y.—d. Jan. 20, 2004, Staten Island, N.Y.), had his beautifully detailed cross-hatched pen-and-ink drawings—caricatures and satiric works—featured in nearly every issue of *Mad* magazine for almost 50 years and also created fine, carefully researched drawings for military history books. Considered his most famous effort for *Mad* was his work illustrating the chaotic, nonsensical sport described in "43-Man Squamish," which appeared in 1965.

Wray, (Vina) Fay, Canadian-born actress (b. Sept. 15, 1907, near Cardston, Alta.—d. Aug. 8, 2004, New York, N.Y.), appeared in more than 90 motion pictures, including a number of silent films, and acted opposite some of Hollywood's most notable male stars, but it was for her performance as the love object of a giant gorilla in *King Kong* (1933) that she

Big-screen screamer Fay Wray in King Kong

was best remembered. Given the role partially because she was a good screamer, she showcased that talent especially in the film's famous Empire State Building scene, in which she was placed on a high ledge of the building while Kong struggled against fighter planes and finally succumbed to their attack. Wray made her film debut in *Gasoline Love* in 1923 and in 1928 had her first significant role in Erich von Stroheim's *The Wedding March,* the film she considered her best. A number of horror movies followed, and it was in those that she gained her reputation for having the best scream. Following *King Kong* and several more horror films, Wray appeared in a few British films in an attempt to change her image but soon returned to the U.S. and performed on the stage and on radio; acted in a few more films, including *Treasure of the Golden Condor* and *Small Town Girl* (both 1953); and starred in the television series *The Pride of the Family* (1953–55). Wray also wrote some plays that were staged in regional theatres, and in 1989 her autobiography, *On the Other Hand,* was published—its title a tribute to the giant model of Kong's hand in which she did her most famous acting.

Yardley, George Harry, American basketball player (b. Nov. 23, 1928, Hollywood, Calif.—d. Aug. 12, 2004, Newport Beach, Calif.), was the first player in the National Basketball Association (NBA) to score over 2,000 points in one season. This feat was accomplished while he was a member of the Detroit Pistons during the 1957–58 season. The sharp-shooting forward enjoyed a seven-year career in the NBA (1953–60) and was elected into the Basketball Hall of Fame in 1996.

Yassin, Sheikh Ahmed, Palestinian Islamist leader (b. mid-1930s?, Tor, Palestine [now in Israel]—d. March 22, 2004, Gaza City, Israel), cofounded and provided spiritual inspiration for the militant Palestinian organization Hamas. Yassin grew up in Palestinian refugee camps in Gaza, then part of Egypt. A boyhood sporting accident injured his spine and left him crippled. He became affiliated with the Muslim Brotherhood as a young man, eventually becoming leader of the local chapter in Gaza, from which he extended his influence to the West Bank branch of the organization. With the founding of a centre that provided social services to Palestinians, his more religiously oriented organization was seen by Israel as less threatening than the Palestine Liberation Organization. With the start of the 1987 *intifadah,* however, Yassin helped found Hamas, which undertook suicide bombings and other terrorist attacks against Israel and Palestinians who cooperated with Israel. Yassin was imprisoned in 1989 but was released in a prisoner exchange in 1997. When the second *intifadah* began in 2000, Yassin's stature increased still further. He was killed in a targeted Israeli strike.

Yokoyama, Mitsuteru, Japanese *manga* artist (b. June 18, 1934, Kobe, Japan—d. April 15, 2004, Tokyo, Japan), created the characters Tetsujin 28 (known as Gigantor in the United States) and Giant Robo. Basing his designs on the American bombers that flew over his childhood home, Yokoyama almost single-handedly created the giant robot or "mech" school of *manga.* His Tetsujin 28 Go series was notable as one of the earliest examples of Japanese animation to be rebroadcast in the U.S. While he was best known for his animated work, Yokoyama's critical masterpiece was his massive 60-volume adaptation of the Chinese classic *Romance of the Three Kingdoms.*

Yuro, Timi (ROSEMARIE TIMOTEA AURRO), American pop singer (b. Aug. 4, 1940, Chicago, Ill.—d. March 30, 2004, Las Vegas, Nev.), bridged musical genres with her husky, soulful voice. Her signature vocal style was influenced by early exposure to African American blues and gospel singers such as Dinah Washington. Though she was signed to Liberty Records in 1959, her career took two years to take off; she wowed label executives and the public alike with her version of Roy Hamilton's R&B hit "Hurt." Later hits included "What's a Matter Baby," produced by Phil Spector, and "The Love of a Boy," written by Burt Bacharach and Hal David. Her 1963 album *Make the World Go Away* was one of the first appearances of songs by a then-unknown country talent named Willie Nelson.

Zimmerman, Joseph James, Jr., American inventor (b. 1912, Milwaukee, Wis.—d. March 31, 2004, Brookfield, Wis.), in 1948 developed, with George Danner, the first telephone answering machine. His Electronic Secretary sold more than 6,000 units before General Telephone Corp. (later GTE) purchased the patent for the device in 1957. While AT&T initially stated that answering machines would be harmful to existing telephone lines, "Baby Bell" companies would later help popularize the systems with their customers. In later years Zimmerman improved on his earlier design, created a telephone auto-dialer system, and patented a magnetic heart monitor.

Zvobgo, Eddison, Zimbabwean politician (b. Oct. 2, 1935, near Fort Victoria, Southern Rhodesia [now Masvingo, Zimb.]—d. Aug. 22, 2004, Harare, Zimb.), was one of the founding fathers of independent Zimbabwe. In 1960, after helping to found the pro-independence National Democratic Party, Zvobgo began studies in the U.S., returning home after the founding (1963) of the Zimbabwe African National Union (ZANU). He was jailed (1964) by the white regime, and after his release (1971) he returned to the U.S., where he earned a Ph.D. from Harvard University and became a criminal law professor. In 1978 he joined Robert Mugabe in exile in Mozambique, and in 1979 Zvobgo acted as ZANU spokesman in the independence negotiations in London. From the time of independence, he represented Masvingo in Parliament, and he served in Mugabe's cabinet from 1980 until 2000. Though he was instrumental in making constitutional changes that increased the power of the president in 1987, Zvobgo later became critical of Mugabe's increasingly autocratic rule.

Events of 2004

Artists symbolizing ancient Greece perform at the opening ceremony of the Athens Olympic Games, August 13.

Agriculture and Food Supplies

Food EMERGENCIES caused by violence, drought, PESTS, and disease were major concerns during the year. BIRD FLU and BSE remained, while a NEW THREAT to American crops arrived.

WORLD MARKETS

World agricultural markets in 2004 reflected crop supplies in 2003 and 2004. Early 2004 prices were strong because 2003 global crop production was low. The 2003–04 world grain production was 1,847,000,000 metric tons, with oilseed production at 336,730,000 metric tons. Larger 2004 production resulted in lower crop prices in the fall. Global grain production in the 2004–05 crop year rose to 2,005,240,000 metric tons, and oilseed production was 390,540,000 metric tons. Between spring and fall oilseed prices halved and grain prices fell roughly one-third.

Food Emergencies. Chronic hunger continued to afflict 850 million people, and several countries faced food crises. North Korea again required external food assistance. Several African states had difficulties owing to political discord or insurgencies. In Zimbabwe, for example, the government's land-reform program contributed to declining farm output, and in northern Uganda fighting caused farmers to abandon crops and flee to refugee camps. A food crisis accompanied the ethnic and political violence in the Darfur region of The Sudan. Rainfall was sparse and infrequent, so crops suffered. Lack of support by the Sudanese government hindered international relief efforts and left millions in jeopardy. The World Food Programme was able to feed 1.3 million Sudanese in September but reached only 1.1 million in October because many people remained in areas inaccessible to relief efforts. Expectations were for continued need by 1.45 million refugees in 2005 and by perhaps 2.8 million Darfuri villagers under threat of starvation until the 2005 crops could be harvested. Ethiopia tried to combat chronic hunger created by earlier civil strife and drought by relocating farmers from the highlands to more productive areas.

Locusts. Just as a several-year-long drought in western Africa seemed to be ending with the welcome arrival of seasonal rains, a new danger appeared in the form of swarms of locusts, the worst in the area in 15 years. Having risen in North Africa as early as late 2003, billions of locusts swept westward in July and August 2004 across the Sahel and into Chad, northern Nigeria, Mali, Mauritania, and Senegal, even invading the Canary Islands by the end of November. Mauritania, the country worst hit, reported that about half its cereal crop had been lost. The UN Food and Agriculture Organization (FAO) estimated in September that 2.5 million rural households could suffer food shortages, and the agency asked for $100 million in international aid to combat the infestation. Locusts swarmed in the eastern Mediterranean region in November as well, but countries such as Egypt, Israel, and Cyprus were better equipped than the West African states to combat the insects, and crop losses there were relatively small.

Agricultural Subsidies. Agricultural subsidies distort agricultural production and international trade. In 2003 the European Union spent $121 billion to support agriculture, about 25% of the value of gross farm income; the United States spent $39 billion (20%); and Japan, South Korea, Norway, and Switzerland all paid subsidies that represented well over half of farm income. Such subsidies hurt farmers in less-developed countries (LDCs) and other places with lower-level farm subsidies.

World Trade Organization (WTO) rulings in 2004 were expected to affect global farm-subsidy programs as well as the outcome of current trade negotiations. The anger of LDCs at U.S. support for cotton farmers had been one reason for the collapse of world trade talks in 2003. In April, in a mixed ruling on a complaint filed by Brazil against U.S. cotton subsidies, the WTO supported the use by the U.S. of direct, decoupled payments and some export credit-guarantee programs but found other guarantees and safety-net price-support programs to be in violation of WTO rules. Since the U.S. supported grains and oilseeds with similar programs, it was feared that the WTO ruling might affect those commodities as well. Another flash point, EU support to sugar producers, was found to violate WTO rules because the subsidies exceeded allowable limits. Excess European sugar would lower world prices and put more efficient producers at a disadvantage.

World Trade Organization Negotiations. In August negotiators in the Doha Development Round of WTO talks reached a framework agreement that rejuvenated the talks to liberalize global agricultural markets that had collapsed in 2003. Under the framework, countries pledged to eliminate export subsidies, lower domestic subsidies, expand market access, and impose discipline on state trading and export-credit programs. Developed nations agreed to cut farm subsidies by 20% in the year following an agreement—a promise that could turn out to be less generous than

Richard Graulich/Palm Beach Post/Zuma Press

On September 6 grapefruit float through a flooded orchard near Fort Pierce in east-central Florida. Four hurricanes in 2004 threatened not only the state's annual citrus crop but also the long-term health of the trees.

The Craze for Curbing Carbs

Despite lingering concerns about the effectiveness and possible health risks of low-carbohydrate diets, almost 12% of Americans—some 34 million persons—were thought to be on carb-restrictive diets in 2004, a number great enough to send shockwaves through the food industry. The phenomenon was not limited to the U.S., birthplace of the Atkins Diet and its low-carb progeny diets such as the South Beach Diet, the Zone Diet, and Protein Power. In the U.K. an estimated 3.8 million persons were counting carbs in 2003, and *Dr. Atkins' New Diet Revolution* ousted perennial local favourite Harry Potter from the top of a British best-seller list.

The low-carb regimens turned upside down the conventional wisdom for losing weight. The regimens promised dieters that they could eat their way to leanness by loading up on protein-rich foods such as meat, cheese, and eggs while spurning carb-laden fare such as bread, pasta, and—during the diet's initial stages, at least—most fruits and vegetables.

The medical establishment remained skeptical, but a study published in the May 18 issue of *Annals of Internal Medicine* offered supporting evidence, finding that over a six-month period, low-carb dieters shed an average of 5.5 kg (12 lb) more than those following conventional low-fat diets. A second study in the same issue, however, showed that after a full year, the weight-loss results for the two diets tended to even out. Moreover, concerns remained about both the long-term health effects of consuming large amounts of animal fat and protein and the nutritional deficiencies related to restricting carbohydrate intake.

Such caveats, however, did not dent the insatiable consumer demand for everything low-carb. Industry observer LowCarbiz predicted that the low-carb economy in the U.S. would swell to $25 billion in 2004, up from $15 billion in 2003; and 95% of Europe's food manufacturers cited low-carb dieting as a major market force. In April, riding the demand created by carb-conscious consumers, leading American meat processor Tyson Foods posted a $47 million increase in quarterly earnings over the previous year. The change in eating habits sent Kraft Foods and other food manufacturers scrambling to reformulate recipes and roll out low-carb products. Restaurant chain T.G.I. Friday's served up Atkins-friendly menu items, and fast-food vendor Burger King introduced "hold-the-bun" burgers.

On the flip side, pasta maker New World Pasta filed for bankruptcy, citing the toll from consumers' low-carb fixation, and erstwhile corporate high-flyer Krispy Kreme Doughnuts also implicated the diet trend in its financial woes. Battling slumping sales, the bread and potato industries mounted marketing counteroffensives, promoting the nutritional benefits of their products. Panera Bread and Subway hedged their bets and cooked up low-carb variants of their own. Although there were signs that the craze might be fading, low-carb dieting—whether fad or permanent fixture—was a commercial force no one could currently afford to ignore. (STEPHEN J. PHILLIPS)

it appeared, because the cuts would be measured from the maximum allowed farm subsidy, not from actual subsidy outlays. Tariffs would be substantially reduced by all but the poorest nations, and LDCs would be given longer to reduce tariffs and could have special rules and safeguards for sensitive commodities. The Doha round deadline of Jan. 1, 2005, however, clearly would not be met.

Regional Trade Agreements. The United States signed regional free-trade accords with Central American countries and with Australia. In the Central American case, trade in horticultural products was liberalized and trade in sugar was expanded somewhat. Beef, dairy, and sugar were sensitive products in Australian-U.S. trade. Under the agreement between those two countries, scheduled to enter into force on Jan. 1, 2005, U.S. beef duties were to be phased out over 18 years; for dairy products the U.S. would not change its above-quota tariff, but the quota was expanded slightly. Australian access to the U.S. sugar market was unchanged.

Livestock Diseases. Outbreaks of livestock disease disrupted global livestock trade again in 2004. Avian influenza outbreaks were reported in January and February in Cambodia, China, Japan, South Korea, Laos, Thailand, and Vietnam, and there were some cases in which the disease had infected humans. Millions of birds were destroyed, and poultry trade originating in areas with the disease was halted. Cases of avian influenza were found in some U.S. states in February, but most foreign importers banned only imports originating from those regions reporting diseased birds. New outbreaks occurred during the summer in China, Thailand, and Vietnam; by year's end more than 30 human deaths from bird flu had been reported.

After one cow in Washington state was diagnosed with bovine spongiform encephalopathy (BSE, or mad cow disease) in late December 2003, most countries banned imports of U.S. cattle and beef. During 2004 the ban affected global meat markets as importing countries shifted purchases to other beef exporters, such as Australia, or increased purchases of other meats, especially pork. U.S. pork exports rose sharply. Once it had been determined that no other American cattle had BSE, the U.S. sought to restart its beef exports. Shipments to Mexico resumed, but trade with other major beef-importing nations remained banned until late in 2004, when framework agreements for the resumption of U.S. beef exports to Japan, South Korea, and Taiwan were adopted. One stumbling block was testing rules; Japan, for example, tested every bovine slaughtered. The U.S. argued that BSE had never been detected in animals younger than 30 months and that testing every animal was costly and did not increase safety. The two sides compromised by agreeing that testing animals under 20 months old was not necessary. Under the shadow of the discovery of animals with BSE in 2003, Canada's border with the U.S. remained closed to live cattle, beef from cattle over 30 months of age, and beef containing bone or specified risk material. Limited imports from Canada were due to resume in March 2005.

Soybean Rust. In November Asian soybean rust *(Phakopsora pachyrhizi)*, a fungal disease that can devastate crop yields, was identified in nine southern U.S. states; Argentina reported it in December. Other major soybean exporters in South America had soybean rust, but the U.S. had theretofore been rust-free. It was believed that the rust spores had been blown to the U.S. from South America by hurricanes.

Genetically Modified Food. Genetically modified (GM) crops and foods continued to be resisted in many countries, especially in Europe. In May a six-year moratorium on imports of genetically modified corn (maize) into Europe ended, but cultivation of GM crops in Europe still faced obstacles. British studies concluded that GM maize, sugar beets, and rapeseed did not threaten the environment and were safe, but the European Union had so far not approved their cultivation. Monsanto Co. put on hold plans to sell GM wheat for production in the United States because of fears that the output could not be sold in Europe or Japan. In Brazil (the second largest producer of soybeans, after the U.S.) legislation that would allow the growing of GM soybeans passed the Senate and was being considered by the lower house. China was considering permitting production of GM rice in order to reduce pesticide use.

(PHILIP L. PAARLBERG)

FISHERIES

Figures published in 2004 by the UN Food and Agriculture Organization (FAO) indicated that in 2002, the latest year for which figures were available, the total production for the world's capture fisheries increased slightly, by 0.35%, from the 2001 figure of 92,862,-087 metric tons to a total of 93,190,654 metric tons. Marine capture fisheries recorded a 0.34% increase of 288,492 metric tons over the 2001 figure to 84,452,487 metric tons, while freshwater capture fisheries recorded a 0.46% increase of 40,075 metric tons to 8,738,167 metric tons.

The overall world fish catch during 2002 totaled 132,989,225 metric tons, up 2.3 million metric tons over 2001. Aquaculture production accounted for almost all of the increase, with a total production in 2002 of 39,789,571 metric tons, compared with 37,789,095 metric tons in 2001.

China continued as the world's leading fishing nation, although its total output for 2002 remained almost static at 16,553,144 metric tons. Peru (again in second place) and Chile (in sixth) recorded significant increases in their catch during 2002, with 8.91% and 11.11% increases, respectively. The U.S. retained third position in the list of top producing nations, but Indonesia overtook Japan in fourth with a 5.15% increase as the total Japanese catch continued its decade-long decline. Russia, which had recorded a year-on-year decline in total catch since 1996, registered a further 12.26% decrease to 3,232,295 metric tons.

Among the leading fish species caught during 2002, number one by far was the anchoveta (Peruvian anchovy), which is fished commercially off the Pacific coast of South America and is subject to huge variations in the numbers of fish reaching maturity each year. The latest figures showed that the quantity of anchoveta caught during 2002 increased by 25.66% over the previous year to 9,702,614 metric tons and was the main explanation for the increases in total catch recorded by Peru and Chile.

The Alaska pollock catch dropped by 18.44% to 2,654,854 metric tons. It was announced during 2004 that following a three-year assessment process, the Bering Sea/Aleutian Islands pollock fishery had been awarded certification to the Marine Stewardship Council's standards for sustainable fisheries. This was regarded as a visible acknowledgement of the growing awareness of the need to manage commercial fisheries in a responsible and sustainable way. Other species that recorded a significant reduction in landings included Chilean jack mackerel (43.36%), which dropped from third to seventh in the list of leading species caught, blue whiting (13.72%), and chub mackerel (23.26%). Skipjack tuna moved up to third position in 2002 from sixth the previous year as a result of a 10.64% increase, while capelin rose from ninth to fourth, courtesy of a 14.84% boost.

(MARTIN J. GILL)

Production Trends for the Top 10 Catching Nations, 1993–2002 (in metric tons)

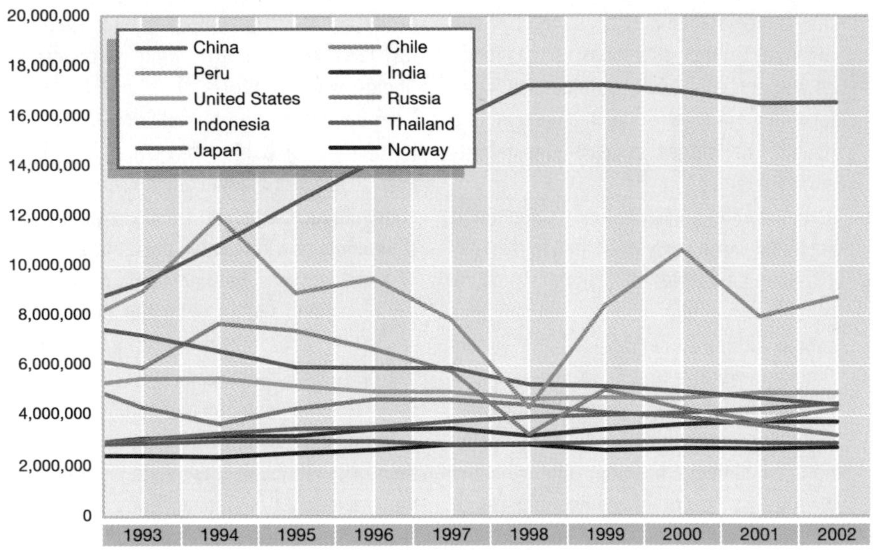

Catch Trends for the Top Five Caught Fish Species, 1993–2002 (in metric tons)

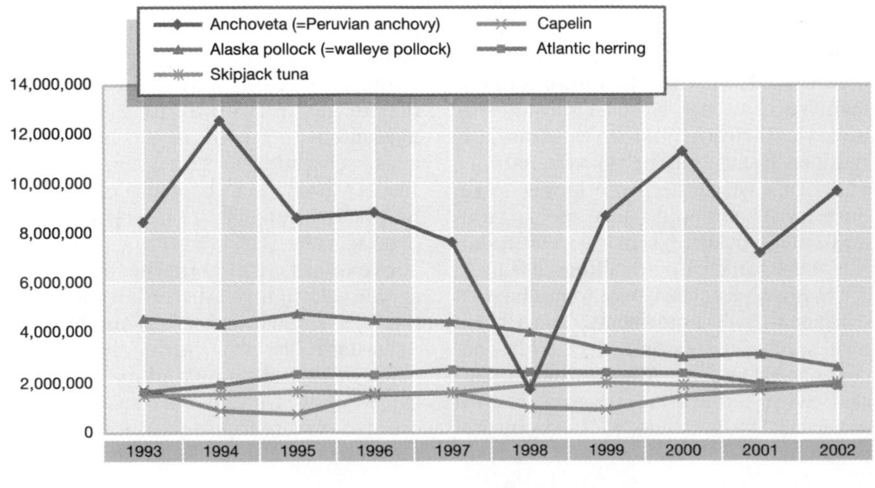

Anthropology and Archaeology

Genetic studies of CHIMPANZEES showed their close relationship to humans, and a genetic change in JAW MUSCLES was linked to human evolution. The remains of MINIATURE HOMINIDS in Indonesia were a surprising find. Discoveries pushed back the date of the earliest practice of ancient ANDEAN RELIGION and the earliest use of JEWELRY.

ANTHROPOLOGY

Key developments in 2004 in the area of physical anthropology focused on genetic comparisons between humans and their closest living relative—the chimpanzee (*Pan troglodytes*). These comparisons were made possible by the release of a rough draft of the whole-genome sequence of the chimpanzee by sequencing centres at Washington University, St. Louis, Mo., and the Massachusetts Institute of Technology/Broad Institute. In addition, the Japanese-led International Chimpanzee Chromosome 22 Consortium published a high-quality DNA sequence of 33.3 million bases of chromosome 22 in the chimpanzee and compared the sequence with its human counterpart, chromosome 21. The comparison documented nearly 68,000 insertions (gains) or deletions (losses) between the two sequences, and it revealed that 1.44% of the two sequences differed because of single-base substitutions (a value comparable to earlier estimates of 1.24% for the average genomic nucleotide difference between humans and chimpanzees). Among the significant differences between the two chromosomes are various genes that are associated with embryonic development, early brain development, heart development, cell-cycle progression, the peripheral nervous system, collagen formation, and the immune response against various pathogens.

Preliminary results from the effort by Celera Genomics to sequence most of the chimpanzee exons (DNA sequences that are translated into proteins) showed that the proteins involved in amino-acid metabolism were highly selected in human evolution, whereas those correlated with neural development surprisingly were not. The Celera findings, coupled with whole-genome sequence comparisons that yielded evidence for the possible rapid evolution of genes involved in host defense, reinforced the dictum in evolutionary biology that diet and pathogens are the dominant selective forces in the evolution of the vast majority of species, including humans and chimpanzees.

In other studies documenting human-chimpanzee genomic differences, humans were found to have more recombination hotspots (DNA sites prone to breaking and being joined with other DNA), more extensive methylation (especially in brain tissue), and a greater rate of gene loss among olfactory receptor genes. Brain gene-expression profiles between humans and chimpanzees utilizing probes to about 10,000 human genes revealed that approximately 10% of the genes studied differed in their expression in at least one region of the brain. A majority of these genes were more highly expressed (more active) in human than in chimpanzee brains, and, contrary to expectation, no major change in expression pattern occurred in Broca's area, a part of the brain functionally correlated with the evolutionary acquisition of spoken language in humans. Another study concentrated on the gene-expression profiles of the anterior cingulate cortex from human, chimpanzee, gorilla, and macaque samples. This region of the brain had been associated with human grammar and with vocal calls in nonhuman primates. The study concluded that the chimpanzee gene-expression profile was more like the profile of humans than that of the gorilla and thereby provided another piece of evidence that chimpanzees are the primates most closely related to humans. The chimpanzee lineage showed

The skull at left was among the remains of an adult hominin (hominid) that were found in Indonesia and assigned to a new species, **Homo floresiensis.** *At right is a skull of an adult modern* **Homo sapiens.**

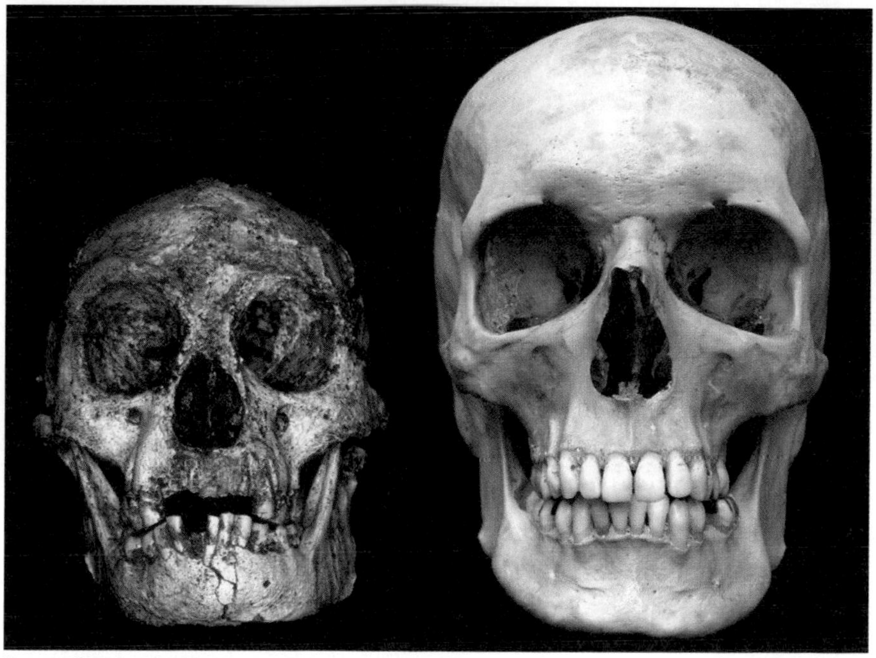

European Pressphoto Agency

as much regulatory gene evolution in the anterior cingulate cortex as the human lineage; however, humans exhibited some up-regulated (increased) expression of genes related to aerobic metabolism and neural functions, which suggests that increased neuron activity required increased supplies of energy.

A team of scientists at the University of Pennsylvania found the first molecular difference between human and nonhuman primates that is potentially related to an anatomical difference of major evolutionary significance. The discovery concerned a mutation dated to have occurred approximately 2.4 million years ago in a gene for muscle protein. The gene, *MYH 16*, encodes the myosin heavy chain, an important protein component of muscle fibre subunits called sarcomeres. The mutation resulted in marked reductions in the size of individual muscle fibres and in entire masticatory muscles such as the *temporalis*, whose function is to close the jaws. The mutant gene arose from the deletion of two nucleotides, causing a premature "stop" codon, which in turn prevents the synthesis of a normal MYH 16 protein. All monkeys and apes sequenced for this locus had an intact normal copy of the *MYH 16* gene and a relatively large amount of MYH 16 protein in their jaw muscles. All persons tested from six geographically diverse human populations possessed only the mutant form of the *MYH 16* gene. The authors speculated that the appearance of the smaller jaw muscles in *Homo erectus/Homo ergaster* by 1.8 million–2 million years ago might have removed an evolutionary constraint on the development of a larger brain. Thus, a small change in a craniofacial muscle gene more than 2 million years ago may have ultimately been responsible for the increased cranial capacity that characterized later hominin (hominid) evolution.

On October 28 Australian and Indonesian scientists published a report of one of the most stunningly unexpected finds in the history of paleoanthropology: the skeleton of a Late Pleistocene female adult hominin that they assigned to a new species of the genus *Homo*. The fragile partial skeleton was recovered from a limestone cave called Liang Bua on Flores Island in eastern Indonesia. Associated deposits contained stone artifacts, Komodo dragon remains, and the remains of a dwarf species of *Stegodon* (an extinct elephant). Chronometric dating indicated that the skeleton, together with a premolar of an individual from an older deposit, represented a hominin population that existed from before 38,000 years ago until at least 18,000 years ago. The skeleton (designated as LB1) included a fairly complete skull (*see* photograph on page 147), right leg, and left innominate (pelvic) bone. The new species to which the scientists assigned LB1 and the premolar was *Homo floresiensis*. With an estimated stature of 106 cm (about 3.5 ft) and a chimpanzee-sized cranial capacity of 380 cc (23 cu in), LB1 lay outside the range of any other specimen previously placed in the genus *Homo*. Although these primitive features were reminiscent of australopithecine traits, the facial, dental, and postcranial anatomy exhibited derived features that supported its assignment to the genus *Homo*. Phylogenetically, it was hypothesized that *H. floresiensis* was descended from a *H. erectus* population that became isolated on Flores Island more than 800,000 years ago (as indicated by the presence of ancient stone tools and faunal remains reported in 1998). Thus, LB1 was claimed to be an example of island-endemic dwarfism. The Flores hominins underscored the fact that following the dispersal of *Homo* out of Africa, much greater morphological variation arose in the genus than had previously been documented.

(STEPHEN L. ZEGURA)

These shell beads, part of a collection excavated from a cave in southern Africa and dated to 73,000 BC, pushed back the date of earliest known jewelry making by some 30,000 years.

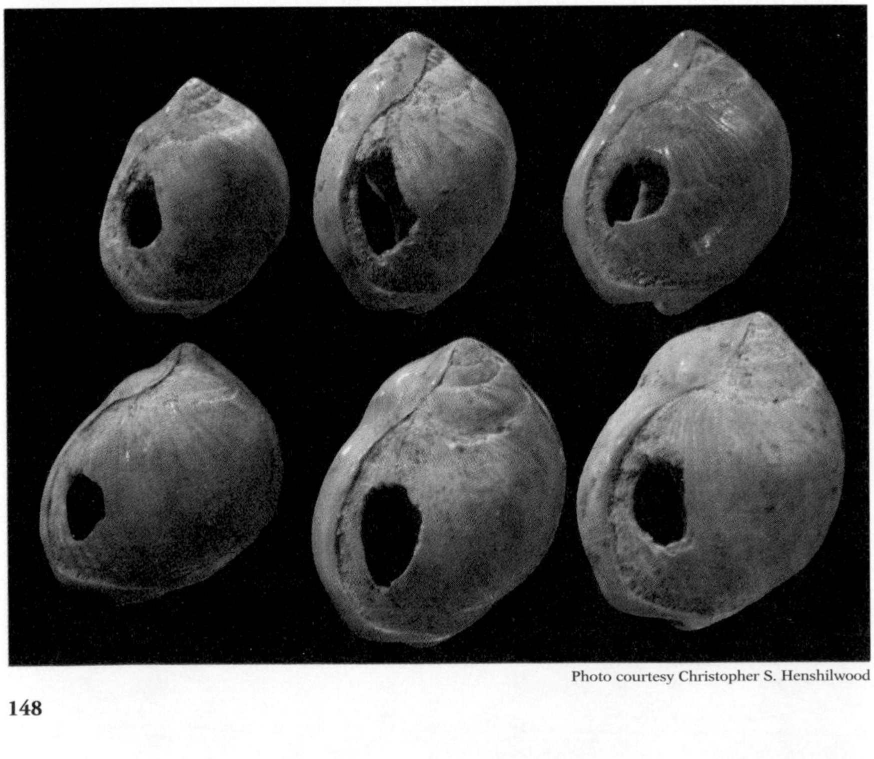

Photo courtesy Christopher S. Henshilwood

ARCHAEOLOGY

Eastern Hemisphere. The year 2004 witnessed many exciting discoveries throughout the Old World.

The war in Iraq continued to take an extraordinary toll on archaeological sites in the cradle of civilization. Despite the adoption in 2003 of UN Security Council Resolution 1483, which banned the trade in looted Iraqi antiquities, a lawless environment and weak border controls fomented the continued plundering of archaeological sites. Particularly hard hit were numerous 5,000-year-old Sumerian city-states—among them Umma, Isin, Adab, Zabalam, and Shuruppak—in the southern Iraqi province of Dhi Qar. Further destruction of sites was a direct result of the war, such as the installation of a U.S. military base atop the remains of the ancient city of Babylon. The collapse of substantial portions of the Babylonian temples of Nabu and Ninmah, which dated to the 6th century BC, was attributed to war-related helicopter activity.

Excavations at Blombos Cave, on the southern tip of Africa, yielded a collection of 41 shell beads that were dated to about 75,000 years ago, 30,000 years before the previous earliest known ex-

Neanderthals—the Latest News

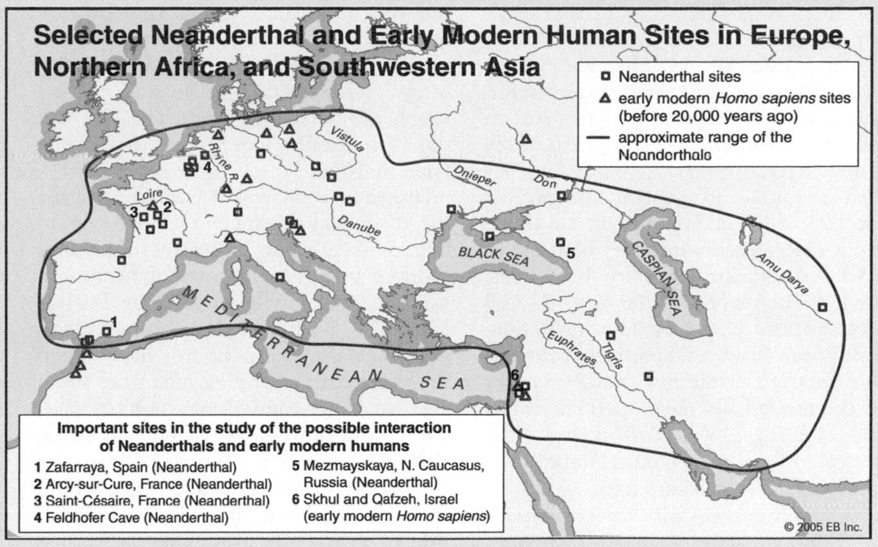

In the nearly 150 years since Neanderthal (or Neandertal) fossil remains were first discovered in Germany, dozens of whole and partial skeletons of this hominid type have been recovered. Though many questions about their behaviour, ecology, and biology remained unanswered in 2004, researchers in a variety of fields uncovered clues to help understand the relationship and possible interaction between Neanderthals and modern *Homo sapiens.*

Neanderthals flourished from roughly 200,000 to 30,000 years ago; the Neanderthals known as "classic Neanderthals" appeared after about 100,000 years ago. Fossil remains of Neanderthals are found from Atlantic Europe to Central Asia. (*See* Map.) In physical characteristics, the Neanderthals closely resembled modern *H. sapiens.* Neanderthals had a brain that was as large as that of most modern human populations, and their bodies, while heavy-boned and robust, differed only in degree, not in kind, from the bodies of modern humans. Nonetheless, there is considerable disagreement about the taxonomic relationship between Neanderthals and modern *H. sapiens.* Recent tests of sequences of mitochondrial DNA recovered from several Neanderthal fossil specimens show that they are quite different from that of any known modern human population. Some researchers argue that this difference justifies assigning Neanderthals to a separate species (*H. neanderthalensis*), but others believe that they should be considered a subspecies of *H. sapiens.*

Many geneticists interpret the distributions of certain genetic markers among living human populations as evidence that their ancestors dispersed rapidly out of Africa sometime in the past 100,000 years. Most geneticists believe that invading modern humans either wiped out the Neanderthals or quickly absorbed them within their own populations and that Neanderthals contributed little or nothing to the modern human genome. Archaeological and fossil evidence shows, however, that some Neanderthals survived in places such as the Iberian Peninsula and the Caucasus Mountains until as late as 30,000 years ago, more than 10,000 years after modern humans are believed to have first entered Eurasia. Archaeological evidence also reveals that the Neanderthals were capable of behaviour more sophisticated than formerly believed— behaviour that might have helped them resist the expansion of *H. sapiens* into the areas where Neanderthals lived. Most Neanderthal fossils are associated with distinctive forms of flaked stone tools that are identified with Middle Paleolithic technologies. Using these simple tools, Neanderthals probably hunted large game animals, including deer, wild horse, and wild cattle. A chemical analysis of the fossilized bones of Neanderthals suggests that Neanderthals were largely, if not exclusively, carnivorous. The Middle Paleolithic was followed by Upper Paleolithic culture in most of Eurasia after 45,000 years ago. Archaeologists for many years considered the Upper Paleolithic—whose artifacts include complex multipart tools, personal ornaments, and representational art—to be the product of modern *H. sapiens* exclusively. At two sites in France, however, Neanderthal fossils were found to be associated with early Upper Paleolithic artifacts, including ornaments and tools of bone and antler. Some researchers subsequently argued that these Upper Paleolithic Neanderthals were simply imitating the more sophisticated cultures of the modern human groups they had begun to encounter. The Aurignacian, a widespread early Upper Paleolithic culture, is often cited as the source of many innovations. Recently, researchers learned that some associations that had been made between anatomically modern skeletons and Aurignacian artifacts were based on an erroneous reconstruction of geologic stratigraphy, opening up the question of who gave rise to Aurignacian culture. Some archaeologists have suggested it was late Neanderthals who produced the Aurignacian and that Neanderthals, therefore, underwent rapid behavioral development independently of groups of *H. sapiens* living at that time. Research continues in an effort to clarify the cultural and genetic relationships between Neanderthals and coexisting modern humans.

(STEVE KUHN)

amples of jewelry. According to Christopher S. Henshilwood of the University of Bergen, Nor., the beads, made of shells from a pea-size gastropod (*Nassarius kraussianus*, native to South African tidal waters), might have been strung together and worn as either necklaces or bracelets. Traces of red ochre that were found on several beads indicated that either the beads or the surfaces against which they were worn might have been coated with iron-oxide pigment.

In Egypt a Polish team excavating a site not far from the Roman Theatre at

Alexandria unearthed 13 lecture halls thought to have been part of that city's 5th-century AD university—the oldest in the world. Each of the halls, which were identical in size, contained several semicircular rows of stepped benches and an elevated seat at the centre, presumably for a lecturer.

Archaeologists excavating the prehistoric cave site of Klisoura in southern Greece discovered what they believed to be the oldest known clay fireplaces. Dated to between 34,000 and 23,000 years ago, the clay hearths represented a midpoint in the transition from the stone hearths used by earlier peoples and the more fully developed clay kilns discovered at Dolni Vestonice in the Czech Republic, which dated to between 28,000 and 26,000 years ago.

A 3,700-year-old Minoan settlement was found at Miletus in southwestern Turkey, further attesting to the mercantile expansion of a people once thought to have ventured little beyond their Cretan homeland. According to Wolf-Dietrich Niemeier of the German Archaeological Institute in Athens, the Anatolian colony, which was located on the Menderes River, might have been established to export copper, gold, and silver back to Crete. Niemeier and his team uncovered the remains of a courtyard surrounded by storage facilities and what were thought to be cult buildings as well as thousands of pottery and fresco fragments. In Israel archaeologists carrying out rescue excavations in preparation for the installation of a new sewer pipe in southern Jerusalem came upon a pool that had served as a principal reservoir in the city some 2,000 years ago. According to the Israel Antiquities Authority, the Pool of Siloam was fed by the nearby Gihon Spring.

In Italy an Etruscan road thought to have once linked Pisa, on the Tyrrhenian coast, with the Adriatic port of Spina, three days' travel away, was unearthed at Capannori, near Lucca. According to archaeologist Michelangelo Zecchini, who found the site during rescue excavations, the 6th-century BC byway had seen significant chariot traffic, evident in the pronounced ruts still visible in the road.

The first Viking burial ground to be found in Britain came to light at Cumwhitton, Cumbria, in northwestern England. The 10th-century cemetery—found with the aid of a metal detector—contained the graves of four men and two women buried with an extraordinary array of weapons, jewelry, fire-making equipment, and horse trappings. Prior to this discovery Viking remains had been found at Ingleby, east of Cumwhitton, but the bodies had been cremated, not buried. The Vikings, who traded with and raided much of Europe between the 9th and the 12th century, conquered the British Isles in 1013.

The year 2004 was a banner year for the discovery of ancient Chinese technological advances. Distinctive spiral grooves found on a suite of ornamental jade rings included in elite burials from the Spring and Autumn Period (770–476 BC) appear to have been incised with a complex machine, some 300 years earlier than such devices were thought to have existed, according to Peter J. Lu, a Harvard University graduate student. The jade rings, which vary in size from that of a quarter to that of a bracelet, bear what is known as an Archimedean spiral (although they predate the birth of Archimedes by several centuries), which almost certainly could have been made only by using a machine that linked rotational and linear motion. What was purported to be the earliest known blast blower used to smelt bronze was found in a tomb at Turpan in the Xinjiang Uygur Autonomous Region, China, according to Lu Enguo of Xinjiang's archaeological research institute. The bronze blowpipe was made during the Warring States period (475–221 BC). Thirty-one tombs, which dated from a period between the late Neolithic Period and the early Bronze Age and contained a wealth of pottery, stone tools, and jade ware, were found in Fujian province, in eastern China. The 4,000-year-old burials, each of which measures about 2 × 0.5 m (6 × 1.6 ft), were a chance find, their location having been exposed when recent drought conditions dried up the Dongzhang Reservoir in Fuqing. A well-preserved 5,000-year-old kiln—complete with kiln chamber, workshop, fireplace, and ash pit—was found during the excavation of a pair of prehistoric village sites at Puchengdian in Henan province. In addition to the kiln, archaeologists recovered numerous artifacts of bronze, stone, bone, shell, and ceramic made between the Neolithic Period and the Song dynasty (960–1279 AD), and they also uncovered building foundations from the Xia dynasty (c. 2205–c. 1766 BC). What was thought to be an imperial tomb group of the Western Zhou dynasty (1046–771 BC) was unearthed at the Zhougong Temple site in northwestern Shaanxi province. According to Lei Xingshan of Beijing University, 12 multichambered tombs had been excavated along with seven chariot pits.

In Tirunelveli district, Tamil Nadu state, on the southern tip of India, archaeologists uncovered six prehistoric burial urns, or *mudhumakkal thaazhi* (meaning "large pots for the old" in the local Tamil language). The urns, dated to around 2,800 years ago, measured up to 172 cm (68 in) high and 170 cm in diameter. Some contained smaller earthen pots—quite possibly to hold food offerings—in addition to skeletal remains. It was the second such cache of early burial urns unearthed in the area in recent months.

(ANGELA M.H. SCHUSTER)

Western Hemisphere. In 2004 archaeologists reached widespread agreement that the first settlement of the Americas took place almost 20,000 years ago, though exactly when remained controversial. Many experts believed that the first Paleo-Indians traveled south along the coasts of present-day Alaska and British Columbia, moved inland, and then spread rapidly through North America.

Canadian archaeologists recently unearthed the earliest stone spear points ever found in Quebec. Claude Chapdelaine and his colleagues discovered the points, estimated to be between 12,000 and 12,500 years old, on a terrace overlooking Spider Lake in the Lake Mégantic region. The broken artifacts had carefully fluted (thinned) bases and resembled the Folsom-style projectile points known to have been made by Paleo-Indian peoples to the south. The discovery extended the history of human habitation of Quebec back more than 2,000 years.

The impending construction of a telecommunications tower on Tenderfoot Mountain above Gunnison, in southwestern Colorado, led archaeologist Mark Stiger to examine the top of the 2,600-m (8,500-ft) mesa for archaeological sites. Initially he found Folsom points of Paleo-Indian origin. In later surveys he identified at least 15 sites and recovered more than 50 complete or partial spearheads. In 2003 he unearthed a series of rocks and boulders set in a circle. Inside the ring lay Folsom points and some chunks of wall mud. Believing the find to have been a rudimentary house of timber, brush, and clay built between 12,000 and 13,000 years ago, he theorized it was a winter house used over a period of time by an otherwise nomadic Folsom group. This discovery extended the

The carved stone panel, discovered at Cancuen, Guat., contains a well-preserved image of a royal Mayan ceremony from the 8th century AD.

known range of Folsom people, who were traditionally associated with the Great Plains, to the western slopes of the Rocky Mountains.

High-technology science of the 21st century continued to make important contributions to American archaeology. A multidisciplinary team of archaeologists, botanists, and soil scientists used tests for strontium, a trace element, to determine the origin of corn (maize) cobs found in Chaco Canyon, a major centre of Ancestral Pueblo culture in present-day New Mexico. By comparing the strontium content of the cobs with that of soil samples they obtained from adjoining regions, the team found that the cobs came from corn grown in soil more than 80 km (50 mi) away. This finding suggested that at least some of the corn consumed in the canyon was obtained through trade, an important survival strategy in an environment with unpredictable rainfall and frequent droughts. With more analyses, the corn research might show the extent to which the Ancestral Pueblo communities at Chaco Canyon depended on outsiders.

Mound A is the largest of seven Mississippian mounds overlooking the Tennessee River within Shiloh National Military Park, Tennessee. The mound was probably built about 1,000 years ago. In excavating Mound A, archaeologists David Anderson and John Cornelison found that it was constructed in at least five stages, with each successive stage built upon previous construction. When the mound was about half its present size, the builders used red, gray, yellow, and dark brown clays to produce a "tiger-striped" layer. The clays must have come from elsewhere, and their source had yet to be identified. The base of the mound lay about 2.4 m (8 ft) below ground level; the early builders built up a surrounding plaza, perhaps to enhance the appearance of the then-incomplete monument.

Fort Sidney Johnston (1864) was the centrepiece of the Confederate defense works at Mobile, Ala. The site of the fort was uncovered by archaeologists working ahead of railroad construction in the area. Although the location of the fort was shown on historic maps, many details of the fort's structure were unknown. Excavations revealed a large brick wall that was part of an ammunition magazine or shelter and a massive floor of wooden planks preserved in the moist soil.

In the Mayan lowlands of Central America, an important carved stone panel was found in a royal ball court during excavations of one of the most extensive ancient Mayan palaces ever discovered, at Cancuen, Guat. The ornate panel, weighing 91 metric tons (100 short tons), depicts Taj Chan Ank, a ruler of the 8th century AD. He wears a turtle headdress and a jaguar skin as he presides over a ceremony accompanied by two local rulers. Another marker from the same court shows the ruler playing ball against a visiting allied dignitary.

Mayan rule presented a minefield of factional disputes, and every lord—however unimportant—had to be politically adept to survive. A reanalysis of a hieroglyphic stela from Moral-Reforma, a small Mayan capital in present-day Tabasco state, Mexico, showed how a local ruler changed sides. An inscription on the stela depicts lord Hawk Skull being crowned in AD 662, in the presence of Yuknoom the Great, ruler of the great city of Calakmul, which lay a great distance away. Thirty years later he was crowned again, this time in a ritual supervised by Lord Kan Bahlam, ruler of the city of Palenque, a strong rival to Calakmul. Moral-Reforma lay amid rich agricultural lands, which made it a rich prize for ambitious leaders eager to control food sources. In many cases Mayan rulers conquered neighbouring lands, but they also used diplomacy to dominate weaker neighbours, which seemed to have been the case with Moral-Reforma.

Agriculture was an important topic of study for Mayan archaeology. A team of archaeologists headed by T. Patrick Culbert of the University of Arizona located more than 70 new archaeological sites in northern Guatemala's Petén rain forest. The researchers also investigated whether the dense Mayan farming population of AD 550 to 850 used the area's seasonal wetlands, known as *bajos*, during the dry season to increase agricultural productivity. Since *bajos* covered 40% of the land area, it seemed likely that they were placed under cultivation at a time when the population grew rapidly.

The discovery of a 4,000-year-old gourd fragment from a cemetery in the Norte Chico region, some 190 km (120 mi) north of Lima, Peru, pushed back the date of the earliest known practice of ancient Andean religion 1,000 years. The incised and painted fragment, radiocarbon dated to about 2250 BC, depicts a fanged creature with splayed feet. Its left arm ends in a snake's head, and its right arm holds a staff. Andean art experts believed the figure to be the earliest image of the Staff God, a seminal deity of Peru's Formative Period (1000–200 BC). The Staff God continued to be important in Andean belief for many centuries after that time, and it figured prominently in the divine pantheon of the highland Wari and Tiwanaku states (AD 600–1000). (BRIAN FAGAN)

Architecture and Civil Engineering

Major buildings with UNUSUAL SHAPES were completed in Europe and elsewhere, the WORLD WAR II MEMORIAL opened on the Mall in Washington, D.C., and Zaha Hadid became the FIRST WOMAN awarded the Pritzker Prize.

ARCHITECTURE

If there was a theme in world architecture in 2004, it was excitement about new supertall buildings. Many of these skyscrapers took surprising new shapes, including cigar shapes and the shape of slivers of broken glass. "Hold On to Your Hats: Tall Buildings Are Coming to London," was the title of one article in a British architectural magazine. Probably the most notable skyscraper of the year was the long-anticipated 30 St Mary Axe, which opened in London in May. Designed by architect Sir Norman Foster, the round 40–story tower looked so much like an upended pickle that the public nicknamed it the "gherkin." The building was an example of two worldwide trends. The first was the movement toward so-called green architecture, in which buildings were designed to reduce the use of energy for heating, lighting, and cooling and thereby contribute less to global warming. The other trend was the creation of more pleasant environments for office workers by providing natural daylight and a variety of informal places for meeting and socializing.

Several other towers were planned for sites in Britain, including the London Bridge Tower proposed by Italian architect Renzo Piano. A high-rise in the shape of a tapering prism that Piano called "the shard," it would be mostly office space, with a hotel at the top, and at 310 m (1,016 ft) would be the tallest building in Europe. Torre Agbar, a corporate headquarters, opened during the summer in Barcelona, Spain. The structure, designed by French architect Jean Nouvel, was cigar-shaped and rose to a height of 144 m (474 ft).

East Asia was home to most of the tallest buildings that had been contracted in recent years, and it was expected to gain many more, most notably the Jinling Tower in Nanjing, China. The building was to twist 90° as it rose to a height of 320 m (1,050 ft). In Shanghai, however, a law was proposed that would limit future building heights to 18 stories.

In New York City, Spanish architect Santiago Calatrava (*see* BIOGRAPHIES) proposed an innovative 255-m (835-ft) tower of residences called Townhouses in the Sky that would contain only 12 apartments. Each apartment would be a four-story glass cube, and the cubes would be stacked to form the tower. Controversy swirled around the 541-m (1,776-ft) Freedom Tower, which was planned for the site of the former World Trade Center (WTC) as part of the master plan by Polish-born American architect Daniel Libeskind. The proposed design was an awkward-looking compromise between Libeskind's ideas and those of architect David Childs, of the firm Skidmore, Owings & Merrill. Childs had been hired by a private developer who held the right to build on the site. Also in New York City, the Skyscraper Museum moved into new quarters in Manhattan and presented an exhibit of the high-rise designs of Frank Lloyd Wright.

The main atrium of New York City's Museum of Modern Art, newly renovated by Japanese architect Yoshio Taniguchi, holds American artist Barnett Newman's **Broken Obelisk** *(1969).*

© Mandel Ngan/AFP/Getty Images

Awards. The most prestigious architecture award in the world, the Pritzker Prize for lifetime achievement, went to a woman for the first time in its 26 years of existence. Zaha Hadid, 54, an Iraqi-born architect who practiced out of London, won for a daring body of work that became influential among architects even before much of it had been built. Among her completed works were the Center for Contemporary Art in Cincinnati, Ohio, a fire station for the Vitra Furniture Co. in Germany, a car park and tramway in France, and a ski jump in Austria. Many other of her buildings were in design, including the Price Tower Arts Center in Bartles-

The national World War II Memorial, designed by Friedrich St. Florian, opened on the Mall in Washington, D.C., on April 29, 2004. This view shows the Pacific Pavilion flanked by some of the memorial's 56 pillars.

ville, Okla., a BMW plant in Germany, a train station in Naples, and the National Center of Contemporary Arts in Rome. Hadid was known for her brilliant drawings, in which she represented buildings as a free flow of shapes and spaces, that used few right angles or conventional motifs.

Rem Koolhaas of The Netherlands won the 2004 Gold Medal of the Royal Institute of British Architects, and Frei Otto of Germany won the 2005 Gold Medal (because of a change in schedule, both awards were announced in the same year). Brazilian architect Oscar Niemeyer, 96, received Japan's $135,000 Premium Imperiale. Calatrava received the 2005 Gold Medal of the American Institute of Architects. Both an engineer and an architect, Calatrava was known for soaring white birdlike or cathedral-like structures. The AIA presented its 25-Year Award, given to an American building that had proved its worth over time, to the East Building of the National Gallery of Art in Washington, D.C., by I.M. Pei. The AIA also named 16 American buildings for its Honor Awards. Among the more notable were the Seaside Interfaith Chapel in Florida, by Merrill and Pastor; the Center of Gravity Foundation Hall, a Zen meditation centre in New Mexico, by Predock Frane; the Salt Lake City, Utah, Public Library by Moshe Safdie; and State Street Village, Chicago, a student residence by Murphy/Jahn.

The Aga Khan Award for distinguished architecture in the Muslim world, awarded every three years, was presented to seven works. They ranged from the Petronas Towers in Malaysia, two of the tallest buildings in the world, to Sandbag Shelters Prototypes, an experimental system of earth construction for housing that was intended to be built cheaply by the residents of poor countries.

Buildings of the Year. The year 2004 proved to be an exceptional one for remarkable buildings around the world. Many made playful use of new technologies that permitted architects to make shapes that had not been seen before. Also noteworthy was the extent to which architecture had become an international activity, with prominent buildings in one country often designed by an architect from another.

Among the most widely noted new structures built in the United States were the national World War II Memorial, designed by Friedrich St. Florian, with an outdoor plaza and pool shaped by traditional curved colonnades on the Mall in Washington, D.C.; the Central Library in Seattle, Wash., by Rem Koolhaas, a widely praised building that looked, wrote one reviewer, "like a pile of books wrapped in taut netting"; the Campus Center at the Illinois Institute of Technology in Chicago, also by Koolhaas, a student activities centre squeezed under an overhead rail line; a renovation and addition to the Museum of Modern Art, New York City, by Japanese architect Yoshio Taniguchi; the Nasher Sculpture Center, a skylit pavilion and walled garden for the display of a collection of modern sculpture in Denver, Colo., by Piano; the Stata Center at Massachusetts Institute of Technology, in Cambridge, a science research and teaching facility by Frank Gehry, whose design was free-form and humorous and gave parts of the building the appearance of colliding or collapsing; and the Genzyme Center, also in Cambridge, by the German firm Behnisch, Behnisch & Partner. The world headquarters of a drug company, the latter building was considered to be the best example in the U.S. of "green" design. The 12-story building was also admired for its indoor gardens and terraces spilling down the sides of a skylit atrium.

Among noted structures elsewhere were a building for the new independent Parliament in Scotland, a boldly sculpted Modernist building designed by the late Spanish architect Enric Miralles; the Forum Building in Barcelona, a vast exhibition and meeting hall on a waterfront site, by Herzog and de Meuron of Switzerland; Padre Pio Pilgrimage Church in Italy, also by Piano, able to accommodate 7,200 people in an interior space spanned by bold stone arches; Jubilee Church in Rome by American Richard Meier, a complex of white walls that curved like shells; Kunsthaus Graz in Graz, Austria, by Peter Cook and Colin Fournier of Britain, an art museum that was described by one magazine as "a whopper of a big, bright, blue bubble with a shiny, scaly, acrylic glass skin" and was an example of what was being called "blob architecture"—buildings in free curvy shapes that were made possible through computer design; Sharp Centre for Design, Ontario College of Art and Design in Toronto, by the British Will Alsop, an amazing two-story box of galleries that seemed to float on thin stilts in the air above older buildings; Selfridges department store in Birmingham, Eng., by a firm called Future Systems, another "blob" with an undulating shape, covered with a skin of 15,000 aluminum disks resembling sequins; and Auditorio de Tenerife, an opera house in the Canary Islands, Spain, designed by Calatrava in a free white shape that reminded some of a bird skeleton, others of a seashell. Calatrava also designed much of the architecture for the Athens Olympic Games, including the architecture for the huge main stadium.

Exhibitions and Competitions. More than 5,000 persons entered a competition to choose a design for a memorial to those who died in the terrorist attacks of Sept. 11, 2001. It was the largest design competition that had ever been held. The winner was a young New York architect, Michael Arad. The winning proposal, which he named "Reflecting Absence," called for two recessed pools on the location of the footprints of the WTC Twin Towers. Also in New York, Santa Monica, Calif., architect Thom Mayne of the firm Morphosis won a competition to design an Olympic Village in Queens, to be built should the city succeed in hosting the 2012 Olympic Games.

The Venice Architectural Biennale, directed by architectural historian Kurt W. Foster, presented a controversial display of what Foster called a new architectural era, one that was represented by organic forms and compound curves shaped by the computer. Not all visitors agreed. "A desert of trendy, pretentious, vacuous, computer-aided form-making," sniffed *Architectural Review*.

Preservation. There was rising concern over threats of demolition or alteration of classic buildings of the Modernist era of the 20th century. Private houses by notable architects such as Richard Neutra and Rudolf Schindler were torn down in California. In New York City, Two Columbus Circle, originally a museum by Edward Durrell Stone, continued to be a source of controversy arising from the attempt by the Museum of Arts and Design to resurface its exterior. The Mostar Bridge, a World Heritage Site in Bosnia and Herzegovina, reopened after a meticulous reconstruction. Originally built in 1566, it was destroyed in 1993 during a civil war. In Venice the famed La Fenice Opera House, rebuilt after a 1996 fire, was reopened.

Controversies. Many American architects were concerned about the effect that increased security measures—required after the attacks on U.S. embassies and the WTC—were having on design quality. Of particular concern were new embassies, which, instead of being designed as examples of an open, welcoming democratic society, were increasingly being sited in isolated suburban locations and designed as secure fortresses. Instead of the previous policy of designing embassies to respond to local culture and climate, the U.S. Department of State created a standard design intended to be employed everywhere, with little modification.

Deaths. Fay Jones, 83 (*see* OBITUARIES), died in August 2004. He was a winner of the Gold Medal of the American Institute of Architects and designer of the Thorncrown Chapel in Arkansas, which the AIA in 1991 had voted the best American building of the 1980s. Once a student of Frank Lloyd Wright, Jones liked to work with modest natural materials such as stone and wood. Edward Larrabee Barnes, who died in November, was a leading member of a generation of architects who studied under Walter Gropius at Harvard in the 1940s. Barnes was known for crisp, geometric modern buildings, such as his Haystack Mountain School of Craft in Maine. Pierre Koenig, 78 (*see* OBITUARIES), died in April. He was a designer of classic Modernist houses in southern California. Josef Kleihues, 71, and J. Irwin Miller, 95, both died in August. Kleihues was an architect influential in the rebuilding of Berlin, and Miller, among other achievements, sponsored dozens of buildings by notable architects in his hometown of Columbus, Ind.

(ROBERT CAMPBELL)

Daytime and nighttime views of the Kunsthaus Graz reveal its distinctive design, created by London architects Peter Cook and Colin Fournier. The building, located in a historic area of Graz, Austria, contains two large exhibition rooms for multidisciplinary art; the grid of lights on the outside of the building can be used to produce video-like displays.

Kunsthaus Graz/Zepp-Cam. 2004/Graz, Austria

Notable Civil Engineering Projects (in work or completed, 2004)

Name	Location		Year of completion	Notes
Airports		**Terminal area (sq m)**		
Suvarnabhumi ("Golden Land")	near Bangkok, Thai.	563,000	2006	To replace Don Muang Airport, Southeast Asia's busiest airport
Barajas International Airport (new Terminal 4)	northeast of Madrid, Spain	470,000	2005	New terminal in leading airport for Europe–Latin America flights
Changi international (new Terminal 3)	eastern Singapore	430,000	2006	New terminal in Asia's 4th largest airport
Pearson International (new Terminal 1)	Toronto, Ont.	340,000	2004	Opened April 6; new terminal at Canada's busiest airport
Baiyun ("White Cloud") Int'l (replacement)	near Guangzhou (Canton), China	305,000	2004	Opened August 5; main hub airport of south China (excl. Hong Kong)
Ben-Gurion Int'l (new Terminal 3)	southeast of Tel Aviv, Israel	223,000	2004	Opened Nov. 2; new international terminal at Middle East's busiest airport
Central Japan International	artificial island off Nagoya, Japan	220,000	2005	To be Japan's 3rd largest airport
Dallas/Fort Worth Int'l (new Terminal D)	Irving, Texas	195,000	2005	New international terminal
Heathrow (new Terminal 5)	southwest of London, Eng.	70,000	2008	Biggest construction project in the U.K. from 2002
Bridges		**Length (main span; m)**		
Hangzhou Bay	near Jiaxing, China–near Cixi, China	2,600	2009	To be world's longest (35.6 km) transoceanic bridge/causeway; begun 2003
I-95 (Woodrow Wilson #2)	Alexandria, Va.–Md. suburbs of D.C.	1,829[1]	2006	2 bascule spans forming higher inverted V shape for ships; begun 2000
Nancha (1 bridge of 2-section Runyang)	Zhenjiang, China (across the Yangtze)	1,490	2005	To be world's 3rd longest (and China's first major) suspension bridge
Sutong	Nantong, China (100 km from Yangtze mouth)	1,088	2008	To be world's longest cable-stayed bridge
Stonecutters	Tsing Yi–Sha Tin, Hong Kong, China	1,018	2008	To be world's 2nd longest cable-stayed bridge; *see* Sutong
Tacoma Narrows (#3)	the Narrows of Puget Sound, Tacoma, Wash.	853	2008	Built over collapsed TN #1; longest U.S. suspension bridge since 1964
Rion–Antirion	near Patrai, Greece (across Gulf of Corinth)	560	2004	Opened Aug. 8; 2nd longest all-span cable-stayed (2,252 m); *see* Millau
(New) Cooper River	Charleston, S.C.–Mt. Pleasant, S.C.	471	2005	To be longest cable-stayed bridge in North America
Millau Viaduct	Tarn Gorge, west of Millau, France	342	2004	Opened Dec. 14; world's highest (270 m) bridge and longest all-span cable-stayed (2,460 m) bridge
Shibanpe	Chongqing, China (across the Yangtze)	330	2005	To be world's longest prestressed-concrete box girder bridge
Buildings		**Height (m)**		
Burj ("Tower") Dubai	Dubai, United Arab Emirates	805	2008	To be world's tallest building
Freedom Tower	New York, N.Y.	"1,776 ft" (541 m)	2008	Cornerstone laid July 4; to be tallest building in North America
Taipei 101 (Taipei Financial Center)	Taipei, Taiwan	508	2003	Declared world's tallest building April 15, 2004; opened in stages from Nov. 2003
Shanghai World Financial Center	Shanghai, China	492	2007	Begun 1997, resumed 2003; to be world's 2nd tallest building (in 2007)
Union Square Phase 7	Hong Kong, China	474	2007	Begun 2002; to be world's 3rd tallest (in 2007); 16-building complex
Federation Tower A	Moscow, Russia	340	2007	To be tallest building in Europe
Eureka Tower	Melbourne, Australia	300	2005	To be Australia's 2nd tallest building and world's 2nd tallest residential
Dams and Hydrologic Projects		**Crest length (m)**		
Three Gorges (3rd of 3 phases)	west of Yichang, China	1,983	2009	To create world's largest reservoir (620 km long) beginning 2003 + 1/9th of nat'l total generated power
Sardar Sarovar (Narmada) Project	Narmada River, Madhya Pradesh, India	1,210	2007	Largest dam of controversial 30-dam project; drinking water for Gujarat
Bakun Dam	Balui River, Sarawak, Borneo, Malaysia	740	2007	To be largest dam in Southeast Asia; hydroelectricity to all of Borneo
Caruachi (3rd of 5-dam Lower Caroní Development scheme)	Caroní River, northern Bolívar, Venez.	360	2003–06	Hydroelectric generation began Feb. 28, 2003
Belo Monte	Xingú River, Pará, Braz.	?	2008	To be 3rd largest dam in the world in terms of electricity output
Tucuruí (upgrade)	Tocantins River, eastern Pará, Braz.	?	2005	Generating capacity to be doubled; 1st Brazilian Amazon dam (1984)
Project Moses (flood-protection plan)	Venice, Italy	–	2010	79 submerged gates in 3 lagoon openings will rise in flood conditions
Highways		**Length (km)**		
Golden Quadrilateral superhighway	Mumbai–Chennai–Kolkata–Delhi, India	5,846	2005	Upgrade to 4 lanes; to link India's 4 largest metropolitan areas
Trans-Siberian highway (final stage)	Khabarovsk–Chita, Russia	2,165	2004	Opened Feb. 26; last link in 10,000-km Moscow–Vladivostok highway
Highway 1	Kabul–Kandahar–Herat, Afg.	1,048	2005	Final, 566-km Kandahar–Herat section to open Sept. 2005
Egnatia Motorway	Igoumenitsa–Kipi, Greece	680	2006	First Greek highway at int'l standards; 76 tunnels, 1,650 bridges
Croatian Motorway	Zagreb–Split, Croatia	380	2005	Mountainous terrain with unstable slopes, caves, and unexploded ordnance
Land Reclamation		**Area (sq km)**		
The Palms ("Jumeirah, Jebel Ali" and *Deira* islands)	in Persian Gulf, off Dubai, U.A.E.	"c. 20 and 40 sq km" and *c. 80 sq km*	2006–09	Date-palm-tree-shaped islands ("two 17 fronds + trunk" and *one 41 fronds + trunk)*; ultraexclusive
Railways (Heavy)		**Length (km)**		
Trans-Kazakhstan	Dostyq (Druzhba), Kazakh.–Gorgan, Iran	3,943	2008	China to Europe link, bypassing Russia + Uzbek.; 3,083 km in Kazakh.
Qinghai–Tibet	China: Golmud, Qinghai–Lhasa, Tibet	1,142	2007	World's highest railway (5,072 m at summit); 86% above 4,000 m
Xi'an–Nanjing	China: Xi'an, Shaanxi–Nanjing, Jiangsu	1,129	2007	For economic growth in interior; 954-km Xi'an Hefei section finished 2003
Ferronorte (extension to Rondonópolis)	Alto Araguaia–Rondonópolis, Braz.	270	2007	For soybean/cereal exports from Mato Grosso (Braz. interior)
Bothnia Line (Botniabanan)	Nyland–Umeå, Swed.	190	2010	Along north Swedish coast; difficult terrain with 25 km of tunnels
Railways (High Speed)		**Length (km)**		
Spanish high speed (second line)	Madrid, Spain, to France (via Barcelona)	719	2009	To reach Barcelona in 2007?; Madrid–Lleida corridor opened Oct. 11, 2003
Korea Train Express (KTX)	Seoul–Pusan, S.Kor.	412	2008	Will connect largest and 2nd largest cities; to Taegu as of April 1, 2004
Taiwan high speed	Hsi-chih–Tso-ying, Taiwan	345	2005	Links Taiwan's 2 largest cities (Taipei and Kao-hsiung) along west coast
Eastern France high speed	eastern outskirts of Paris–near Metz, Fr.	300	2007	106-km extension to Strasbourg in planning stage
Italian high speed (second line)	Rome–Naples, Italy	205	2005	Entire N–S (Turin–Naples) high-speed routes (844 km) completed 2009?
Channel Tunnel Rail Link	near Folkestone–central London, Eng.	109	2007	74-km section (Folkestone–north Kent) opened Sept. 16, 2003
Subways/Metros/Light Rails		**Length (km)**		
Shanghai Metro	Shanghai, China	99.9	2005–06	Length of 4 lines under construction in late 2004
Barcelona Metro (Line 9)	airport–northeast Barcelona, Spain	47.0	2008	Connections to other metro lines and future high-speed rail
Guangzhou (Canton) Metro (line 3)	Guangzhou, China (north-south line)	36.1	2006	15-line system planned; 83 km in 4 lines under construction in 2004
Shenzhen Metro (phase 1; lines 1 and 4)	Shenzhen, China (adjacent to Hong Kong)	21.8	2004	Phase 1 of both lines began operation Dec. 28
Delhi Metro (Line 1)	Delhi, India	21.3	2004	Opened March 31; 30.2 km of lines 2 and 3 to open in 2005
Copenhagen Metro (last extension)	Copenhagen, Den.	21.0	2007	Connects city centre to airport
Bangkok Blue Line	north-south line in central Bangkok, Thai.	20.0	2004	Opened to the public July 3; Thailand's first underground system
Hiawatha Light Rail	Downtown Minneapolis–Bloomington, Minn.	19.3	2004	Opened December 4
Las Vegas Monorail	Las Vegas, Nev. (east side of L.V. Strip)	6.1	2004	Opened July 14, temp. closure Sept. 8–Dec. 23; 5-km extension by 2007?
Tunnels		**Length (m)**		
Apennine Range tunnels (9)	Bologna–Florence, Italy (high-speed railway)	73,400	2008	Longest tunnel (Vaglia, 18.6 km); tunnels to cover 93% of railway
Lötschberg #2	Frutigen–Raron, Switz.	34,577	2007	To be world's 3rd longest rail tunnel; France–Italy link
Guadarrama	50 km north-northwest of Madrid, Spain	28,377	2007	To be world's 4th longest rail tunnel; Valladolid high-speed link
Södra Länken ("Southern Link")	part of Stockholm, Swed., ring road	16,600	2004	Opened Oct. 24; complex of underground interchanges
Hsüeh-shan ("Snow Mountain")	near Taipei, Taiwan	12,900	2005	Breakthrough Sept. 16, 2004; world's 4th longest road tunnel
East and West tunnels of A86 ring road	western outskirts of Paris, Fr.	10,000/7,500	2007	Two tunnels under Versailles and nearby protected woodlands

1 m=3.28 ft; 1 km=0.62 mi; 1 ha=2.47 ac

[1]Length of each span.

Art and Art Exhibitions

Works of art inspired by the GOTHIC or the GROTESQUE, drawings on PAPER by young artists, art inspired by the U.S. presidential ELECTION, and DISTURBING images of abuse at ABU GHRAIB prison in Iraq exemplified the art world during 2004.

ART

The year 2004 in art was marked by a continued trend toward globalism; contemporary artists and art lovers traveled around the world to biennials in Shanghai; New York City; Pittsburgh, Pa.; Seville, Spain; Liverpool, Eng.; and San Sebastián, Spain, among other cities. Drawings were big on the contemporary gallery circuit, which featured an abundance of shows devoted to works on paper by young and emerging artists. Another trend was the tendency toward the gothic or grotesque. Young artists such as Sue de Beer, Olaf Breuning, David Altmejd, Cameron Jamie, and Aïda Ruilova represented the "Modern Gothic," as coined by the *Village Voice* newspaper critic Jerry Saltz, and the group exhibition "Scream: 10 Artists × 10 Writers × 10 Scary Movies" was presented at New York City's Anton Kern Gallery and the Moore Space in Miami, Fla. In New York City, in keeping with the wanderlust of contemporary art, Austrian Franz West installed his large candy-coloured sculptures in Lincoln Center, and Italian Rudolf Stingel spread a floral carpet in Grand Central Station. Still, one of the most talked-about exhibitions was a single-channel video presented in a New York City gallery; in the video the artist, Andrea Fraser, is seen having sex with a collector who paid nearly $20,000 to participate in the piece, which consisted of the sexual act and one edition of the DVD.

One of the most anticipated events of the year in art was the reopening on November 20 of the Museum of Modern Art (MoMA) in New York City, after three years at a temporary exhibition space in Queens. Designed by architect Yoshio Taniguchi, the new museum—at 58,530 sq m (630,000 sq ft)—was almost twice the size of the former facility and included a new six-story exhibition space. The reopening coincided with the 75th anniversary of the institution and included historic exhibitions of drawings from 1880 to the present and a photography show covering the 1890s to the 1950s, as well as a project by Mark Dion and an exhibition of photographs by German artist Michael Wesely. To help finance the new billion-dollar building and raise funds for acquisitions, MoMA sold nine Modernist masterpieces at Christie's New York. Works sold included Giorgio de Chirico's *The Great Metaphysician* (1917), which fetched $7,175,500, and a major Jackson Pollock drip painting, *Number 12, 1949,* which went for $11,655,500, along with works by Marc Chagall, Jean Dubuffet, Fernand Léger, René Magritte, and Pablo Picasso. While MoMA was undergoing renovation, the institution lent over 200 works from its permanent collection to Neue Nationalgalerie for "MoMA in Berlin." MoMA also shared its holdings with another New York City museum, El Museo del Barrio, for the exhibit "MoMA at El Museo: Latin American and Caribbean Art from the Collection of the Museum of Modern Art" (*see* photograph on page 158), and the Mori Art Museum in Tokyo presented "Modern Means: Continuity and Change in Art, 1880 to the Present," which showcased 300 items, ranging from painting and sculpture to electronic media art.

The art market proved its unfaltering vitality with the record-breaking sale of Picasso's *Boy with a Pipe* (1905) for $93 million ($104.1 million, including the auction house's 12% premium). In the contemporary market one of the most talked-about sales was Maurizio Cattelan's *The Ballad of Trotsky* (1996), a stuffed horse hanging in a leather sling from the ceiling, which sold for $2,080,000, well above its estimated selling price of $800,000. Cattelan was also responsible for one of the year's biggest art scandals. In May the Nicola Trussardi Foundation installed his *Untitled* sculpture, which consisted of mannequins of three young boys (*see* photograph on page 159), each hanging by a noose from the branch of a tree in Milan's historic Piazza XXIV Maggio. After less than 48 hours on view,

Rudolf Stingel made art news in 2004 with his covering of New York City's Grand Central Station with floral-patterned wall-to-wall nylon carpeting.

Plan B, by Rudolf Stingel, 2004; produced by Art Production Fund
Photo Tom Powel; courtesy Paula Cooper Gallery, New York

Courtesy of Friedrich Petzel Gallery, New York

Artist Andrea Fraser's untitled 60-minute DVD, in which she and her client are filmed having sex, was shown during 2004 at New York City's Friedrich Petzel Gallery.

the sculpture was attacked by an angry Milanese resident, who climbed the tree, cut down two of the mannequins, and then fell out of the tree, sustaining a broken arm. Authorities removed the remaining mannequin and revoked the permits necessary to keep the sculpture on view. Opinions were divided between those in favour of free expression and supportive of Cattelan's capacity to incite debate and those who were opposed to what they deemed a violent and shocking work.

The 35th edition of Art Basel, the world's biggest art fair, confirmed the strength of the market even further with consistent sales of works by contemporary artists as well as Old Masters and blue-chip artists. Richard Prince's seminal 1983 work *Spiritual America,* the artist's copy of photographer Gary Gross's controversial photo of a nude 10-year-old Brooke Shields posing seductively in a bath, reportedly sold for $1 million. The annual Baloise Art Prize (25,000 Swiss francs [about $20,000] per recipient) was awarded to Aleksandra Mir and Tino Sehgal. Other worldwide fairs continued to draw strong crowds and bring in steady sales, including the Armory Show in New York City (Contemporary), the Art Show in New York City (Old Masters, Modern, and Contemporary), the European Fine Art Fair in Maastricht, Neth. (Old Masters and Modern), ARCO in Madrid (Modern and Contemporary), and the Frieze Art Fair in London (Contemporary).

The heated U.S. presidential campaigns of Republican Pres. George W. Bush and Democratic challenger John Kerry led the left-leaning art world to support Kerry and the Democratic Party with benefits, exhibitions, and other events. The newly created political action group Downtown for Democracy (D4D) held a silent auction on June 29, and a larger auction of 170 works by contemporary artists, organized by two pro-Democratic groups, America Coming Together and Arts PAC, took place the same evening at Phillips, de Pury & Co. in New York City. D4D also organized a benefit street fair in September, which featured a fake-tattoo booth, Pop Art posters, and other politically minded presentations by artists and musicians. An exhibition curated by writer Neville Wakefield and artist Adam McEwen, "Power, Corruption and Lies" at New York City's Roth Horowitz gallery, included politically themed works by Philip Guston, Christopher Wool, Andy Warhol, and Richard Hamilton, among others. In addition, several top artists donated works to a benefit auction to support a new campaign to protect individual civil rights from attack under the USA PATRIOT Act and other antiterrorist laws. For the exhibition "Experimental Party DisInformation Center" at New York City's LUXE Gallery, artists and activists presented a multimedia installation under the auspices of the fictional U.S. Department of Art & Technology, timed for the Republican national convention. The magazine *Artforum* joined the bandwagon with its September issue, which featured special projects by contemporary artists reacting to the elections and the current political climate.

The winner of the annual Turner Prize (awarded to a British artist under 50 years of age for an outstanding exhibition of his or her work in the previous 12 months) was filmmaker and performance director Jeremy Deller, who won for his film *Memory Bucket,* which explored Crawford, Texas, the hometown of President Bush, and the 1993 siege of the Branch Davidians in nearby Waco. Potter Grayson Perry (*see* BIOGRAPHIES) won the 2003 Turner. The Guggenheim's Hugo Boss Prize 2004 went to Thai installation and action artist Rirkrit Tiravanija. Other nominees included British conceptualist Simon Starling, the Dutch filmmaking team Jeroen de Rijke and Willem de Rooij, German painter Franz Ackermann, Brazilian sculptor Rivane Neuenschwander, and Chinese filmmaker Yang Fudong.

In other news, a devastating fire swept through the Momart art warehouse in London in May, destroying nearly 300 original artworks with a value close to £60 million (about $106 million). Losses included some 100 contemporary works from the celebrated collection of British advertising magnate Charles Saatchi, including several iconic works by Young British Artists, such as *Hell,* a 2.6-sq-m (28-sq-ft) tableau of a Nazi concentration camp by Jake and Dinos Chapman, and Tracey Emin's embroidered tent, *Everyone I Have Ever Slept With 1963–1995.*

(ALI J. SUBOTNICK)

ART EXHIBITIONS

Spanning generations and drawing connections between young emerging artists and established artists was a frequent format for the large-scale international exhibitions that were held in 2004. The Whitney Biennial in New York City included works created by a cross-generational list of artists, ranging from videos by pioneering performance artist Marina Abramovic to an allover sound-and-video installation by assume vivid astro focus (Eli Sudbrack), to drawings and watercolours from veteran artist Raymond Pettibon (the 2004 recipient of the Whitney's $100,000 Bucksbaum Award for a gifted visual artist), and to a wall drawing of the history of rock and roll by young Los Angeles-based Dave Muller; the intergenerational mix provided a comprehensive look at current art making and its influences and sources, including popular culture, art history, and social and political history. The Carnegie International, which was held in Pittsburgh, Pa., presented small in-depth surveys of works by three established figures: R. Crumb, Mangelos (Dimitrije Basicevic [1921–87]), and Lee Bontecou; in addition, smaller clusters of works by other artists were grouped by theme or formal aspects. Curator Laura Hoptman organized the exhibition to show how art could be used as a meaningful vehicle to confront the unanswerable questions such as death and the meaning of life and faith and the existence of God. In Europe the fifth edition of Manifesta, the international biennial of European artists, presented in San Sebastián, Spain, included more than 50 artists, some exhibiting their work publicly for the first time, along with a handful of historical works by artists such as Belgian Marcel Broodthaers (1924–76), Ukrainian Boris Mikhailov, and Dutchman Bas Jan Ader. The exhibition had an overall theme of memory and social engagement and was presented in five venues in the area. The 2004 Site Santa Fe (N.M.) Biennial, "Disparities and Deformations: Our Grotesque," curated by Robert Storr, explored the grotesque tradition in art by showcasing the works of more than 50 contemporary artists such as John Currin, Kara Walker, Louise Bourgeois, Crumb, Jörg Immendorff, and John Waters. Each of these large-scale international shows, which centred on specific themes and contexts, moved away from previous attempts to focus solely on new discoveries and virgin artists, choosing instead to establish connections between the young and the old.

Minimalism was reconsidered in several large exhibitions. The Museum of Contemporary Art, Los Angeles, presented "A Minimal Future? Art as Object, 1958–1968," a historic exhibition of American Minimalism. The show included seminal works by the founding fathers of the movement, including Carl Andre, Dan Flavin (1933–96), Donald Judd (1928–94), and Sol LeWitt. At the Solomon R. Guggenheim Museum in New York City, "Singular Forms (Sometimes Repeated): Art from 1951 to the Present" included many works from the museum's permanent collection, ranging from Robert Rauschenberg's *White Painting [seven panel]* (1951) to Damien Hirst's *Armageddon* (2002), a painting composed of resin-covered dead flies. "Beyond Geometry: Experiments in Form, 1940s–70s," at the Los Angeles County Museum of Art, featured a selection of international artists' works dating back to 1945. In London the Tate Modern presented a survey of work by Judd that featured about 40 of the artist's "specific objects" produced from 1961 to 1993. The National Gallery of Art in Washington, D.C., weighed in on the Minimalism trend with a Flavin retrospective; it included 44 of his works and drawings and was the first comprehensive retrospective of the American artist.

One of the works featured at the joint exhibit of the Museum of Modern Art and El Museo del Barrio in New York City from March through July was a 1943 gouache, The Jungle, *by Wilfredo Lam.*

© AFP/Getty Images

Several other thematic shows brought an inspired look at art and its relation to society. The Getty Center in Los Angeles organized a curious exhibition entitled "The Business of Art: Evidence from the Art Market," which provided a documentary look at the maneuverings of the art business over the last 400 years. Drawn from the Getty's research library, the show spanned the 16th through the 20th century and included letters, inventories, diaries, auction manuals, and press clippings. In Philadelphia "The Big Nothing" went on view at the Institute of Contemporary Art; the exhibit featured works that had something to do with nothing and nothingness and included almost 60 artists, including Maurizio Cattelan, Roe Ethridge, Yves Klein (1928–62), William Pope.L, and Andy Warhol (1928–87). Skateboarding, graffiti, and urban life were the organizing principle for the exhibition "Beautiful Losers: Contemporary Art and Street Culture" at the Contemporary Arts Center in Cincinnati, Ohio.

Several important monographic exhibitions provided in-depth examinations of the work of one artist. "Roth Time: A Dieter Roth Retrospective" at the MoMA QNS and P.S.1 Contemporary Art Center, Queens, N.Y., was the first comprehensive survey of the German-born artist (1930–98) in the U.S. since 1984 and included 375 works made over five decades. In his first American museum exhibition, held at the Institute of Contemporary Art, Boston,

Photo by: Attilio Maranzano
Courtesy: Fondazione Nicola Trussardi, Milano

Maurizio Cattelan's untitled multimedia work showing life-size mannequins of three children hanging from tree limbs in Milan's Piazza XXIV Maggio shocked and incensed residents in May.

young German artist Kai Althoff presented 15 years' worth of work, including drawings, video, watercolours, installations, and music and texts, treating adolescence, German history, and religion. At the Whitney Museum of American Art, New York City, "Cotton Puffs, Q-tips®, Smoke and Mirrors" gathered over 200 works on paper by Ed Ruscha (*see* BIOGRAPHIES) for the first large survey of the Los Angeles-based artist's iconic signs and text images, which mixed graphic design and puns with media and materials. Ruscha's seminal photo series of gas stations, parking lots, and swimming pools, along with snapshots taken on his first European trip, were presented in a complimentary show. The Whitney also mounted a 15-year survey of influential Cuban exile Ana Mendieta's (1948–85) groundbreaking sculptures and documentation of her performances exploring the female body.

Prints and drawings were the focus of several significant exhibitions, including the first major print retrospective of 81-year-old Richard Hamilton at the Yale Center for British Art, New Haven, Conn., which featured over 150 works by the British Pop Art pioneer. For "Chuck Close Prints: Process and Collaboration" at the Metropolitan Museum of Art in New York City, more than 100 images—ranging from the artist's first (1972) mezzotint to *Emma,* a 113-colour Japanese-style wood print made in 2002—provided a broad view of the influential American painter's working process. In anticipation of the February 2005 installation in New York City's Central Park of *The Gates* by Christo and Jeanne-Claude, the museum also presented a show of 50 preparatory drawings and collages, 60 photographs, and 10 maps and technical diagrams detailing the controversial project. In Los Angeles, "Visions of Grandeur: Drawing in the Baroque Age" at the J. Paul Getty Museum featured works drawn from the museum's permanent collection by Gianlorenzo Bernini, Pietro da Cortona, Claude Lorrain, Nicholas Poussin, and Peter Paul Rubens.

Other shows of artistic historical interest included "A Beautiful and Gracious Manner: The Art of Parmigianino" at the Frick Collection in New York City, where 50 drawings and 5 small-scale paintings were displayed. "American Attitude: Whistler and His Followers" at the Detroit Institute of Arts featured 13 paintings by James McNeill Whistler (1834–1903) and 50 works by John Singer Sargent (1856–1925), William Merritt Chase (1849–1916), Thomas Wilmer Dewing (1851–1938), and other artists. The Jewish Museum presented the first major exhibition of Amedeo Modigliani (1884–1920) in New York City in more than 50 years and featured more than 100 works by the legendary bohemian. The show paid special attention to his heritage as an Italian Sephardic Jew. The Museum Tinguely in Basel, Switz., premiered a major retrospective of Kurt Schwitters (1887–1948). The centrepiece of the exhibition was a walk-in reconstruction of the artist's *Merzbau,* which he began building in 1923 and which was destroyed in 1943 during World War II. Meanwhile, the Kunstmuseum Basel presented "Schwitters Arp," an exhibition of nearly 140 collages, reliefs, sculptures, and assemblages by Schwitters and Hans Arp (1887–1966). The two modern artists had begun their artistic exchange of ideas when they performed together at Dada events in 1922 and collaborated on both driftwood reliefs and a novel in 1923.

(ALI J. SUBOTNICK)

PHOTOGRAPHY

The political and emotional power of the image was never more evident than in 2004. On a number of occasions, public concern over the conduct and consequences of the U.S.-led war and occupation of Iraq and the changes that digital photography and communications media had brought worked together to deprive the U.S. military of the control it had traditionally enjoyed over wartime photographs, and some of the more shocking aspects of military life were publicized as never before.

In April images of the flag-draped coffins of American war dead loaded in the holds of cargo planes bound for the U.S. were published on Internet sites and the front pages of newspapers around the world, apparently in contravention of Pentagon policies that dated back to the First Gulf War in 1991. The photos ignited discussion of political censorship and the public's right to know. Even more shocking to the public were images of sexual humiliation and torture being inflicted on Iraqi detainees by U.S. soldiers at the Abu Ghraib military prison in Iraq, first published by *The New Yorker* magazine in May. If previous wars had been documented exclusively by photojournalists working for or authorized by the military, almost every soldier abroad now carried a personal digital camera. Images could be exchanged rapidly and sent home by e-mail or cell phone. Writing in the *New York Times,* author Susan Sontag (*see* OBITUARIES) saw that the very nature of photography had changed; pictures such as those taken at Abu Ghraib were now "less objects to be saved than messages to be disseminated." Because of a photograph's seemingly unimpeachable truth—what Sontag called the "insuperable power" of photographs to determine our collective memory—she found it likely that the images of the U.S. preemptive war in Iraq that would remain in people's minds were likely to be these photographs of Americans torturing Iraqis at Abu Ghraib. In the same vein, Michael Moore's quasi-documentary film *Fahrenheit 9/11,* which scrutinized the photo opportunities manipulated by media managers and "spin doctors," also focused public attention on the power of photo images to mold public perceptions.

Two dramatic blockbuster shows mounted by the International Center of Photography in 2004 included "Only Skin Deep: Changing Visions of the

American Self" and "Between Past and Future: New Photography and Video from China." Together these exhibitions sketched a new direction in contemporary photography, one that was hinted at in the 2002 Documenta—that is, a political engagement by artists and photographers with issues of personal and cultural identity in the rapidly changing "mediascape" of contemporary global culture.

Larry Fink's show at the Powerhouse Gallery in New York City, "The Forbidden Pictures: A Political Tableau," began in June and came down the week after the Republican Party held its national convention in that city. Representing many high-profile political figures in compromising and scandalous situations, Fink's work was yet another example of the ubiquity of political satire during the U.S. presidential election year. Another Fink show, "Social Graces: Vintage Photographs," was on view at Edwynn Houk Gallery, New York City.

The major historical exhibition of the year was held at the San Francisco Museum of Modern Art (SFMOMA). "Diane Arbus: Revelations" showcased her unmatched capacity for getting close to and showing the intrinsic humanity in each of her subjects. The show was to visit the Metropolitan Museum of Art, New York City, in 2005. "Street Credibility: Photographs from the 1940s to the 1970s," on view at the Museum of Contemporary Art, Los Angeles, placed Arbus's work in a rich historical and cultural context. The exhibit, which featured 100 Arbus photographs from the 1940s to the '70s, examined the period of time when the notion of photography's unflinching truth and the boundaries between documentary and fine art first began to fall under question. The work of Larry Clark, Robert Frank, Lee Friedlander, and Garry Winogrand was included, as was a selection of work by Arbus's predecessors, including Lisette Model and August Sander. In the spring photo auctions, Arbus's *Identical Twins (Cathleen and Colleen), Roselle, N.J., 1967* set an artist record at auction, selling for $478,400. The second highest price ever achieved for an Arbus photograph was $198,400 for the 1966 print of *A Young Man in Curlers at Home on West 20th Street.*

Photography from the 1970s made a definite comeback. Representing this trend were the New York City group shows "Six from the Seventies: The Last Years of Modern Photography," at Howard Greenberg Gallery, and "Seventies Color Photography," at Marianne Boesky Gallery. The work of such artists as Richard Misrach, Joel Sternfeld, and William Eggleston—all of whom also had solos shows in 2004—was featured at the Boesky Gallery.

The J. Paul Getty Museum, Los Angeles © Eggleston Artistic Trust, Gift of Caldecot Chubb

American photographer William Eggleston was in the news throughout 2004; in the spring his dye-transfer print **Greenwood, Mississippi (Red Ceiling)** *sold for $217,440, an auction record for the artist.*

The first exhibition of colour photography at the Museum of Modern Art, New York City, was an Eggleston show in 1976. Though the exhibit was first designated "the most hated of the year," it was later seen as a pivotal moment in the history of photography. In 2004 Eggleston's "Los Alamos" was presented at SFMOMA in a show organized first by the Museum Ludwig in Cologne, Ger. This historical exhibition featured photographs taken in the photographer's hometown of Memphis, Tenn., as well as the work he produced on a road trip through New Mexico in 1973, specifically exploring the town of Los Alamos, the site where the atom bomb was developed in the early 1940s. The 88 prints in the exhibition displayed Eggleston's keen eye, his ability to link disparate subjects through the coherency of his vision, and the intensity of his saturated colour palette. In the final tribute room of Eggleston's "Los Alamos" show was a large print by Alec Soth entitled *Sleeping by the Mississippi,* one of the prints that resulted from Soth's own journey down the Mississippi in 1999. Earlier in 2004 Soth had made his debut at the 2004 Whitney Biennial and held his first exhibition in New York City (*Sleeping by the Mississippi*), at Yossi Milo Gallery. As a sign of the increasing interest in Eggleston, the print *Greenwood, Mississippi (Red Ceiling)* sold for $217,440 at Phillips de Pury and Luxembourg in the spring, marking a new auction record for the artist. Though Eggleston was primarily recognized for his pioneering work in colour photography, Cheim & Read Gallery, New York City, offered an Eggleston show called "Precolor: The Black and White Pictures," which, seen together with the other exhibitions on view, provided a full spectrum of the artist's accomplishments.

Other notable shows by artists who first gained public notice for their work in the 1970s were Misrach's "On the Beach," at PaceWildenstein Gallery, New York City, and Sternfeld's "American Prospects and Before," at Luhring Augustine Gallery, New York City. Meanwhile, Sternfeld's *On This Site: Landscape in Memoriam (1993–96),* a set of 53 colour prints depicting various crime scenes, sold for $153,100.

In other news Magnum Photos launched *M,* a magazine devoted to contemporary photojournalism. The premier issue, "Unlikely Encounters," featured photographers Susan Meiselas, Chien-Chi Chang, Martin Parr, Bruce Davidson, and Inge Morath, among others. Several important photographers died during the year, including Eddie Adams, Ellen Auerbach, Richard Avedon, Henri Cartier-Bresson, Carl Mydans, Helmut Newton, George Silk, and Ezra Stoller. (*See* OBITUARIES.)

(MARLA CAPLAN)

Computers and Information Systems

Concerns about Internet SECURITY and e-mail SPAM were at the top of the news in the COMPUTER INDUSTRY in 2004, but E-COMMERCE expanded, especially with the boom in DOWNLOADABLE online music and personal music players.

Computer Security and Crime. Internet users in 2004 faced numerous threats to computer security because of the ongoing emergence of new versions of malicious Internet software known as viruses and worms and because of security flaws in commercial computer software. According to the Internet Security Threat Report published by Symantec Corp., in the first half of 2004 there was a sharp increase in malicious Internet software aimed at computers using Microsoft Corp.'s Windows operating system (OS), and the number of newly discovered software security flaws in Windows-based applications rose in the first half of 2004 after having declined in the second half of 2003. Microsoft recommended that Windows XP users upgrade to the latest version of the software, called Service Pack 2, which it said added security features and removed applications that potentially were security risks. Service Pack 2 itself, however, also required some security patches.

After his arrest in Germany in May, Sven Jaschan, an 18-year-old German student, confessed to having created two harmful Internet worms, Netsky and Sasser. His creations took advantage of security flaws in Microsoft software, and one software-security company said that the worms had been responsible for up to 70% of the Internet computer-worm infections in the first half of 2004. In May alone the Sasser worm disrupted hundreds of thousands of computers.

Some of the threats posed to computer security were illustrated in June when a flaw in Microsoft's Internet Explorer Web browser was exploited by hackers on the Internet to install spyware on users' computers. (Spyware is a program that can surreptitiously divulge private information, including lists of Web sites visited and keyboarded passwords and credit-card numbers, to unknown parties via the Internet.) The attack that exploited the flaw in the browser was headed off by blocking a Web server in Russia that was playing a major role in the attack. Microsoft did not offer a corrective software patch for the security hole until late July. The incident indicated that hackers could find security holes in software faster than software developers could plug them.

In addition to attacks from worms and spyware, Internet users were hit with a surge of unsolicited commercial e-mail (spam). With spam out of control and clogging e-mail in-boxes everywhere, the U.S. government passed a law to outlaw it. The law, called the CAN-SPAM Act, went into effect in January 2004, but it did little to dampen the volume of spam. By August spam represented about 65% of all e-mail, up from 58% when the law was passed, according to Symantec. Taking their own initiative, some Internet companies—including Microsoft, online marketer Amazon.com, Internet portal Yahoo!, and Internet service providers America Online (AOL) and EarthLink—sued groups they considered to be major producers of spam. Another widespread problem for Internet users was e-mail with fraudulent requests for information (a practice known as phishing, as in "fishing" for information). About 17 times as many such attacks were reported in July 2004 as in December 2003, according to the Anti-Phishing Working Group, an industry association that focused on the problem.

The U.S. government said in August that more than 150 people had been arrested for Internet-related crimes that involved spam, phishing, or corporate espionage that resulted in the theft of about $215 million. In one case a software engineer working for AOL was arrested after he sold about 92 million AOL customer screen names to an outsider for more than $100,000. The man who purchased the names later sent spam to the AOL customers. In another case a Texas man arrested for using phishing techniques received an unusually severe sentence of 46

Computer viruses and other problems continued to affect productivity in 2004. Here a group of Japanese businessmen avail themselves of a Shinto purification ceremony for their laptops in January at Tokyo's Kanda Myojin shrine.

months in jail. He had created e-mails that appeared to be from either AOL or online-payment firm PayPal in order to trick consumers into revealing their credit-card numbers. The e-mails told them that their accounts had lapsed and could be restored only if they submitted their credit-card numbers and passwords.

The U.S. government also passed a new identity-theft law to help curb online fraud. The law added two years to the prison sentences of those convicted of using stolen credit-card numbers or other personal information to commit a crime and five years to the sentences of those who used such data for terrorist offenses. For four years identity theft had been the most frequent consumer complaint received by the U.S. Federal Trade Commission (FTC), and Internet-related fraud accounted for more than half of all consumer-fraud complaints. The FTC also brought suit against a number of software firms that were alleged to have infected computers with software that delivered unwanted pop-up advertising and then to have tried to persuade owners of the computers to pay $30 each to fix the problem. The suit sought an end to the practice, as well as the payment of restitution to those affected. The U.S. Congress was considering legislation that would increase penalties for the use of such software, but there was concern in the software industry that the legislation was overly broad and might impede legitimate efforts to use the Internet for remotely updating computer application software and security programs.

Other varieties of illegal computer-related activity also received the attention of law-enforcement officials. In April law-enforcement officials seized more than 200 computers in the U.S., Europe, and Asia with the aim of breaking up an online distribution network for $50 million of pirated music, motion pictures, and software. According to the industry trade group Business Software Alliance, the value of pirated software worldwide was estimated at nearly $29 billion in 2003, or about 60% of the value of legally purchased desktop software that year.

The federal E-rate program, which subsidized the cost of connecting financially needy schools to the Internet, came under fire after allegations of fraud or waste were disclosed in hearings in the U.S. Congress. The program, paid for by telephone-company customers, financed the wiring of schools for Internet access, beginning in 1998; by mid-2004 about $8.1 billion had been spent. In a controversial decision, the U.S. Federal Communications Commission (FCC) suspended funding for the effort. The move was estimated to have delayed the disbursement of about $1 billion in government grants in 2004.

Frank Quattrone, a former investment banker who made tens of millions of dollars during the Internet-stock boom, was sentenced to 18 months in prison and two years' probation and fined $90,000 for having obstructed government investigations of technology stock offerings. The case against him was based largely on an e-mail from December 2000 in which he urged company employees to "clean up" their files during ongoing government investigations.

Economic News. It was a difficult year for those seeking employment in high-tech jobs. Hiring in the United States was modest at best as companies waited for evidence of a turnaround in the slowed national economy. A report funded by the Ford Foundation in early 2004 showed that about 403,300 jobs in information technology (IT) had been lost in the United States over the previous three years and indicated that the outlook for American workers remained unfavourable. Another report said that American technology companies—including those in computers, electronics, telecommunications, and e-commerce—had eliminated more than 118,000 jobs in the first three quarters of 2004.

Offshoring, the controversial practice of outsourcing jobs to countries where wages were lower, continued to be a top labour issue. There were varying estimates of how many IT jobs had been lost in the U.S.; some labour groups claimed that as many as 160,000 IT jobs had been sent to other countries over a three-year period. Defenders of the offshoring of IT jobs said that it would reduce the labour costs of technology companies and boost their competitiveness in the marketplace. (*See* ECONOMIC AFFAIRS: *Special Report.*)

Microsoft underscored the unsettled nature of the technology economy when it said that it planned to cut costs by nearly $1 billion in the 2004–05 fiscal year, and it predicted that the number of Windows-based personal computers (PCs) in use around the world would grow by 60%, to one billion machines, by 2010. Analysts said that the cutbacks were being made because Microsoft had continued to invest in new projects during the slowdown in the technology industry, which meant that in recent years corporate expenses had risen faster than revenues.

Comdex, one of the key conventions of the computer industry during the Internet boom, canceled its 2004 show for lack of attendees and exhibitors. During the boom years the Las Vegas, Nev.–based show had attracted more than 200,000 visitors a year. Though an effort was made in 2003 to revitalize Comdex by reorienting the convention toward the corporate market and away from consumers, former exhibitors had already begun to shift the focus of their efforts to the Consumer Electronics Show, which was also held in Las Vegas.

E-Commerce. In 2004 online advertising more than recovered from the slowdown that followed the dot-com boom year of 2000. Internet advertising revenue was a record $2.37 billion in the second quarter of 2004, up 43% from the previous year, and it even exceeded the levels of revenue reached during the boom. Leading the surge was a near doubling in advertising tied to Internet search engines. Some analysts suggested that the growth of online advertising did not represent the independent emergence of a new advertising medium so much as it represented the diversion of existing direct-mail advertising revenue to the Web.

Internet shopping also was on the rise. A survey by the Pew Internet and American Life Project in Washington, D.C., showed that 65% of Internet users were online shoppers. In 2000, 47% of Internet users had shopped online. Amazon.com and eBay began selling inexpensive used books in such large numbers that the book industry began to wonder whether new book sales were being harmed. Particularly disturbing to the publishers was the fact that sales of used books did not generate royalties for the publishers or the writers and that the used editions were being marketed alongside new ones. Some surveys showed that used books were making up a slightly larger percentage of total book sales than before.

Online fantasy sports leagues were increasingly seen as an advertising-supported business. Participants in the leagues put together sports teams of their choice to compete in imaginary games. In hopes of attracting new subscribers and retaining existing ones, AOL introduced a service in which anyone could play for free rather than having to pay to play, as required by several earlier Internet fantasy sports leagues.

Google Inc., the brainchild of two former Stanford University graduate students, Sergey Brin and Lawrence Page (*see* BIOGRAPHIES), became the envy of many e-commerce businesses in 2004 because its superior search-engine technology made it into the equivalent of an Internet portal site—a starting point for Web surfers. With 200 million searches a day, it had a popularity in its chosen niche that was unparalleled, although Microsoft promised to catch up in the search-engine business. Google also set the pace for change in free Web e-mail. It announced plans for a free e-mail service called Gmail that offered an unprecedented one gigabyte (one billion bytes) of free e-mail storage space but also presented the users of the service with advertisements based on keywords Google found in their messages. A preliminary version was made available to the public in April. Microsoft's Hotmail and Yahoo! quickly responded to the announcement by greatly increasing the amount of storage space they provided with their free e-mail services. In December Google announced that it was working with several major libraries to begin making their holdings freely available on the Internet.

Companies. Changes in accounting practices forced changes in the way that many computer companies paid their employees. Stock options, a favourite method of compensating workers in addition to their salaries, had not been included on income statements, and the omission tended to boost reported corporate profits. In early 2004, however, the Financial Accounting Standards Board voted to include options in income statements, arguing that their inclusion provided investors with a more accurate picture of a company's financial condition. The ruling set off a firestorm of protest by technology firms. A bill seeking to overturn the FASB ruling was introduced in the U.S. Congress, but as of the end of 2004 the fate of the bill was unclear.

Google's initial public offering on August 19 was viewed as a major Wall Street event, and it raised $1.66 billion for the company and some of its shareholders. Google executives and bankers, fearing the offering might not be as successful as they had originally hoped, lowered the initial stock price to $85 a share from a planned range of $108–$135. The stock was well received by the market, however, and by year's end it had more than doubled its initial offering price. The stock offering also made news because of the unusual way it was handled. Shares were sold in a public auction intended to put the average investor on an equal footing with the professionals of the financial industry.

Advanced Micro Devices (AMD), Inc., expanded its operations in China with plans for a $100-million investment in testing and manufacturing facilities. China had gained favour with American technology companies because it offered relatively low costs for labour and electricity, two of the major expenses in manufacturing.

Intel Corp., facing stiff competition from AMD, introduced a microprocessor for large corporation servers and for high-end desktop workstations. It could process 64 bits of data at once and was backward compatible with the existing 32-bit computing standard. AMD had made a similar move a year earlier.

At Computer Associates International, Inc., the world's fourth largest software firm, former executives disclosed in guilty pleas that there had been a conspiracy to backdate company contracts, which thus enabled the firm to match Wall Street profit predictions. A company restatement of 2000 and 2001 financial results reflected improper booking of $2.2 billion in revenue. Former executives also pleaded guilty to having conspired to lie to prosecutors and to the company's own lawyers about their business practices. In a settlement with government investigators, Computer Associates agreed to pay $225 million in restitution to shareholders who had incurred financial losses because of the fraudulent practices.

IBM Corp. partially settled a class-action lawsuit over its pension plan by agreeing to pay $320 million to current and former employees. If the courts were to find that a new IBM pension plan was illegally discriminatory, IBM's liability under the settlement was limited to an additional $1.4 billion.

German firm Infineon Technologies AG pleaded guilty in the U.S. to having fixed prices of memory chips for three years and agreed to pay a $160 million fine. U.S. prosecutors said Infineon was one of several companies in a worldwide cartel that cooperated in fixing prices for dynamic random access memory chips (DRAMs).

Microsoft, which generated $1 billion a month in extra cash and already had large amounts of cash on hand, had been under pressure to share its wealth with stockholders. In July it announced a one-time dividend of $3 a share, or $32 billion, which was a substantial portion of the more than $50 billion in cash reserves that the company had at the time. The move was seen by some observers as an acknowledgment that Microsoft shares had become a blue-chip stock, bought for dependability as an investment, rather than a hot stock, bought for an anticipated sharp increase in price. Microsoft also settled most of the consumer class-action suits that were still pending against it. The civil suits, which revolved around Microsoft's alleged use of monopoly power to set prices for consumer software, had continued long after the U.S. settled its antitrust suit with the company. The largest settlement was $1.1 billion in a California suit. Separately, a federal appeals court upheld the 2002 settlement of the U.S. government's antitrust case against Microsoft. In another matter Microsoft agreed to pay Sun Microsystems $1.95 billion to settle a lawsuit brought by Sun over antitrust and patent claims.

Mergers and Acquisitions. Acquisition activity was dominated by the long-running effort of Oracle to mount an unfriendly takeover of PeopleSoft and by PeopleSoft's determination to fight it. The battle ended in December, when the two companies reached an agreement under which Oracle would acquire PeopleSoft for $10.3 billion. Oracle appeared to have the advantage after it defeated a federal antitrust lawsuit that had sought to block the takeover as anticompetitive. The takeover battle was unusual, both because the participants were important software firms and because unfriendly takeovers were rare in the technology field, since they often backfired when the acquired firm's brightest employees fled the company.

The struggle, which had begun with Oracle's initial bid for PeopleSoft in 2003, created turmoil in the market for Enterprise Resource Planning (ERP) software—software that corporations used to record and share corporatewide information about accounting, finance, inventory, and human resources. Some competitors said that their business was being hurt because the market uncertainty over the Oracle-PeopleSoft takeover battle was causing customers to defer purchases until a winner became apparent.

The U.S. Department of Justice (DOJ) opposed the acquisition on antitrust grounds and sued to stop the deal, which had fluctuated in value over many months as Oracle changed its bid price. The government said that the deal would reduce competition and cause an increase in ERP software prices, and government lawyers at the ensuing antitrust trial insisted that Oracle and PeopleSoft were the only companies other than SAP AG, a German software company, that competed for the largest enterprise customers. Oracle insisted, however, that competition would not be hurt by its acquisition of PeopleSoft because it had other ERP competitors, even though the total number of competitors was declining owing to industry consolidation. Oracle won the case when a federal judge ruled that the acquisition would not give Oracle enough market power to impede competition.

During the course of the year, the Oracle-PeopleSoft battle took a number of twists. PeopleSoft sought to show that it was moving ahead with its own business by announcing a technology partnership with IBM that would involve a minimum investment of $1 billion by the two firms over five years. Soon afterward PeopleSoft's CEO, Craig Conway, was fired over what the board of directors of the company called a loss of confidence in his leadership. Some analysts said that the move indicated that PeopleSoft might be willing to begin merger talks with Oracle. Meanwhile, the battle shifted to a state court in Delaware, where Oracle sought to eliminate antitakeover measures put in place by PeopleSoft. One such measure was designed to raise the acquisition cost in the event of a takeover by greatly increasing the number of shares of PeopleSoft stock.

Symantec announced that it would purchase Veritas Software Corp., a data storage and management firm, in a stock transaction valued at about $13.5 billion. The deal was expected to produce the world's fourth largest software firm.

IBM, which once dominated the personal computer business, said it would sell its PC business to China-based Lenovo for $1.75 billion worth of cash, stock, and debt. The sale underscored the fact that personal computers had become a commodity business with relatively low profit margins.

Juniper Networks, Inc., a manufacturer of network gear, agreed to buy NetScreen Technologies, Inc., one of the leading firms in computer security, for about $4 billion in stock. Analysts said that the large amount paid reflected heightened concerns about corporate and home computer security.

Orbitz, Inc., an online travel business started in 2000 by five American airlines, was acquired for $1.25 billion in cash by Cendant Corp., a travel and real-estate firm that also owned rental car and hotel companies. The move came at a time when some airlines were offering lower fares for flights booked online instead of through a travel agent in an attempt to save on booking costs.

Computer-chip designer ARM Holdings PLC paid more than $910 million in cash and stock to acquire Artisan Components, Inc., a designer of chip components. The deal was described as one likely to improve computer-system-on-a-chip design efforts.

AOL paid $435 million in cash to acquire Advertising.com, Inc., a firm that helped companies advertise on the Internet and measure the results of those marketing campaigns. In addition, Time Warner ended a two-year federal investigation by agreeing to pay the U.S. government $510 million to settle criminal and civil charges that its America Online business improperly inflated revenue figures. AOL also laid off about 750 employees in a cost-cutting and business-repositioning move; the layoffs followed two years in which the number of subscribers to its Internet access service had declined by about four million.

Personal computer maker Gateway, Inc., bought privately owned eMachines, Inc., a low-cost PC manufacturer, for $289.5 million. The deal was seen as a way to remake Gateway, which had reported a long string of quarterly financial losses, by making it the third largest PC firm in the U.S. market and strengthening its low-end PC product line. The CEO of eMachines became the CEO of Gateway, which also reorganized, laying off thousands of employees and closing its retail stores.

The eBay Inc. online marketplace company bought a 25% ownership of craigslist, an unorthodox community-oriented online business that sold employment advertising to for-profit businesses but allowed free listings for housing, garage sales, professional services, and dating. The craigslist Web site had listings for 60 cities. Terms of the deal were not disclosed.

Lucent Technologies, a large provider of telecommunications equipment, whose return to profitability had been led by its CEO Patricia Russo (*see* BIOGRAPHIES), continued to form partnerships with computer networking firms to add newer technologies such as Internet Protocol transmission and Ethernet networking. The firm had been hurt by the telecommunications industry's move toward Voice over Internet Protocol (VoIP), which had reduced demand for Lucent's traditional communications gear.

Governmental Issues. The FCC made a tentative finding that VoIP phone calls, also known as Internet telephone service, should be subject to government wiretapping in cases involving suspected criminal or terrorist activity. Though VoIP calls would therefore be subject to the same wiretapping regulations as conventional telephone lines, it appeared by year's end that the FCC would demand less overall regulation of VoIP than of traditional phones. It remained unclear what the cost to VoIP service providers might be to comply with the wiretapping requirement, since there were technology hurdles that might be difficult and expensive to overcome.

Microsoft appeared to have lost its fight over a European Union antitrust ruling against the company that carried a $665.4 million fine. In March the European Commission had ruled that Microsoft was guilty of using the dominance of its Windows OS to improve its position in new markets, including that of network server computers. In an appeal to an EU court, Microsoft argued that the antitrust ruling would hurt customers, create market confusion, and damage Microsoft by forcing it to share proprietary information with competitors. In December Microsoft lost its appeal. The court ruled that the company must pay the fine and comply with the penalties imposed by the European Commission, which included a requirement that Microsoft offer computer manufacturers a version of Windows without its media player, software that played music and video files. Microsoft could still appeal the ruling to the European Court of Justice, but it was unclear whether it would do so. The court rejected Microsoft's request to delay the penalties pending any appeal.

The European Commission also filed complaints against France, The Netherlands, Sweden, and Finland for allegedly favouring Intel in government computer-purchasing contracts. According to the complaint, the contracts required that the computers contain Intel computer chips or the equivalent, and Intel rival AMD complained about the practice. Separately, the commission reopened an antitrust investigation of Intel that two years earlier had produced no evidence of anticompetitive actions. The status of the new antitrust investigation remained unclear.

The U.S. Supreme Court upheld a lower-court decision to block the Child Online Protection Act, an antipornography law that would have set fines of up to $50,000 for making it easy for children to obtain Internet material deemed harmful to minors. The law would have required adults to register or to use access codes in order to be able to see such material. In a 5–4 decision, the Supreme Court said that the 1998 law was an unconstitutional limit on free speech. The case was returned to a lower court for trial, however, to give the government another opportunity to prove that the law was not unconstitutional.

A federal court ruled that e-mail messages could be intercepted without violating U.S. antiwiretapping laws, provided the messages were stored briefly on the computer of an Internet service provider while they were being processed. The ruling effectively outlined a legal loophole that made it permissible for the government or other groups to read supposedly private e-mail messages without first obtaining a court order. The DOJ said that the ruling created an undesirable gap in Internet-related wiretapping laws and asked an appeals court to review the decision.

The Internet. Sales of personal music players were bound up in the battle for supremacy in online music purchases. Apple Computer, Inc., found itself embroiled in a dispute with RealNetworks, Inc., which decided to provide consumers with software for converting downloadable songs from a RealNetworks music service into a format that could be played on Apple's highly successful iPod. The move followed an unsuccessful effort by RealNetworks to license the iPod music format. The apparent motive was to lure customers away from Apple's iTunes online music service, since the iPod could play music only in a format used by iTunes or in the widely available MP3 format. RealNetworks insisted that it was within its rights, but Apple accused the firm of unethical behaviour.

The battle underscored the growing competition in the online music market, which some analysts estimated would generate $270 million in sales in 2004, more than double 2003 sales. In April Apple said its iTunes service had sold more than 70 million songs at 99 cents each during its first year, although that fell somewhat short of the 100 million songs the company had projected it would sell in that period. It surpassed the 100-million-song mark three months later. Apple faced a growing field of online music competitors, including Microsoft's MSN Music, RealNetwork's Rhapsody, Yahoo!'s Musicmatch, Roxio's Napster, and Sony's Connect. Yahoo!, a late entry to the market, had paid $160 million for the Musicmatch online music business.

Some surveys showed that more than 20 million people in the U.S. continued to download free music from the Internet in apparent violation of copyright laws. The music industry's trade association, the Recording Industry Association of America, continued to

Nanotechnology—Small Is Beautiful

The popular media were abuzz in 2004 with a new term, *nanotechnology,* which refers to the manufacture of materials and devices at an extremely small scale. The prefix *nano* derives from the Greek *nanos,* meaning "dwarf." A nanometre is one-billionth of a metre, and nanotechnology is generally considered to be the realm of objects having a dimension of 100 nanometres or less. (The thickness of a human hair is about 80,000 nanometres, and a strand of DNA is 2.5 nanometres wide.) At this scale, particles or thin films of some materials have chemical and physical properties much different from those the material has in bulk. The idea of working at this superminiature level was suggested by American physicist Richard Feynman as early as 1959, and the term *nanotechnology* was introduced by researcher Norio Taniguchi in Japan in the 1970s. Nanotechnology holds promise for significant advances in a wide variety of applications, from devices that clean the Earth's atmosphere to new means of conquering disease and the aging process.

An example of nanoscale devices already at work are the carbon nanotubes, discovered by Sumio Iijima in Japan in 1991, in use in "jumbotron" lamps installed in many sports stadiums. Other practical applications of nanoscale technology include materials used in computer disk drives, automotive sensors, tires, land-mine detectors, and solid-state compasses. The technology is used in the manufacture of dressings for burns and wounds, water filtration, catalytic converters, and sunscreens.

Some of the most exciting nanoscale technology has no practical application as yet. Such technology includes the self-assembling "nano-elevators" reported by developers at the University of California, Los Angeles, in 2004, in which two interlocking molecules (imagine a three-pin plug set in a three-hole socket) can be made to pop in and out. It is expected that within the next few years, nanotechnological solar cells in roof tiles will provide an economical way to increase the generation of electricity by solar power and thereby reduce pollution from conventional electric-power plants. Even more exciting prospects are the implantation of nanoscale devices into the human body—to deliver and control drugs or to identify cancer cells—and environmental applications, such as sensors to detect chemicals and toxins in the air. The U.S. government has provided hefty funding for developing nanotechnology for use against terrorism. One potential application would be the use of carbon nanotubes to sense minuscule amounts of nerve agents in the air and—applying nanoscale devices on a megascale basis—to incorporate the sensors as part of a national system to monitor the atmosphere over the U.S. continuously for the presence of biological pathogens or dangerous chemicals.

As with any new technology, nanotechnology has characteristics that are frightening to some, and creepy little machines have already infiltrated science-fiction writing—for example, the body-altering "nanoprobes" used by *Star Trek*'s Borg or the malevolent self-replicating "nanobots" in Michael Crichton's 2002 novel *Prey.* Perhaps a more realistic worry—as suggested in some toxicology reports over the past few years—is that nanoparticles could prove harmful to living creatures. Nevertheless, nanotechnology is expected to become a $1 trillion industry by 2015.

(ALAN STEWART)

file copyright-infringement lawsuits against consumers whose computers were found to be sharing copyrighted music. The music was typically downloaded by means of online file-sharing services by which a computer user essentially opened a window into his or her computer and allowed other participants in the service to copy the music files. Although the participants could use false names, their computers could be identified by their IP addresses, which in turn could be traced to individual file sharers through their Internet service providers.

One major effort of the music and motion picture industries had been to stop the Internet file-sharing networks that consumers used to download copyrighted music. The U.S. Supreme Court, however, rebuffed the music and movie industries when it declined to review a lower-court ruling that Internet peer-to-peer networks (which linked individual consumer PCs) were not legally liable if their users exchanged copyrighted music and movies. The 2003 lower-court decision the Supreme Court let stand also said that the music and motion picture industries could not rely on subpoenas alone to force Internet service providers to disclose the names of customers who allegedly shared copyrighted files; a court review would be required first.

The U.S. Congress considered aiding the music industry in its fight against file-sharing networks. The Senate introduced a bill, called the Inducing Infringement of Copyrights Act, that would make a person who induced another to violate copyright law legally liable for the violation. The legislation would, in effect, ban the peer-to-peer networks, but some analysts feared that it also could adversely affect some consumer electronics products, such as MP3-music players, that could potentially be used in violation of copyright.

The success of online music sales piqued Hollywood's interest in online movie rentals. The distribution of online movies was being handled through authorized movie-download services that permitted viewing a rental for a limited period of time. The services generally offered a relatively small selection of titles, but some permitted rental of an unlimited number of the available films for a flat monthly fee. The process of downloading feature films was slow and could take hours. TiVo, the maker of a digital video recorder that copied television programming onto a computer hard disk, planned an alternative service that would enable consumers to download movies and music from the Internet for a fee.

High-speed, or broadband, service for Internet access continued to grow. By some estimates it was being used by slightly more than one-half of U.S. residential users who had some type of Internet access, up from slightly less than 40% one year earlier. Broadband service was offered both by telephone companies, typically through a digital subscriber line (DSL), and by cable TV firms. The number of broadband subscribers worldwide was expected to more than triple between the beginning of 2004 and the end of 2008. In the long run, wireless Internet service and satellite Internet service also were expected to contribute to the spread of broadband. A handful of U.S. cities, including Philadelphia, expressed interest in providing broadband service to their citizens through wireless technology.

Computer Games. The U.S. Army continued to use PC games as a recruiting tool. Two years after the launch of *America's Army,* a series of free realistic combat games for the PC, there were more than four million registered online players. The army said prospective recruits who played the game before contacting a recruiter were more likely to enlist than those who had not played. A commercial version of *Full Spectrum Warrior,* a game commissioned by the U.S. Army, focused on military strategy in street combat.

The long-awaited PC game *Doom 3,* a follow-up to the original game that a decade earlier had helped create the category of violent video games called first-person shooter, debuted to mixed reviews. It was visually impressive and required the capabilities of a high-end personal computer to generate its special effects, but many players found the game to be lacking in game-play innovation.

Online gaming, long a staple of the PC market and growing among users of game consoles from Sony and Microsoft, remained a relatively small part of the computer-game business. The business continued to promote online play in the belief that participation would increase as the use of high-speed Internet connections grew and that online game playing would generate additional revenue through subscriptions or advertising.

The convergence of movies and computer games continued, and production costs rose as games were developed with detail-laden imagery, special effects, elaborate musical soundtracks, and the voices of well-known actors. Game-production costs were more than triple those of the late 1990s, and for some new titles marketing expenses sharply increased the total cost. There was concern in the industry that game-development costs would rise even more sharply once Sony, Microsoft, and Nintendo introduced new game consoles within one to two years. New versions of the Microsoft Xbox and Sony PlayStation 2, in particular, were expected to have increased computing power that would require more sophisticated game software. Some software firms predicted game-development costs could double or triple, which in turn might force some companies to exit the game business.

Nintendo introduced a dual-screen version of its Game Boy for the holiday selling season, and Sony promised to introduce its PlayStation Portable in early 2005. Nintendo had long controlled the handheld gaming market with devices that were limited to game play; since 1989 it had sold about 170 million Game Boy units. Sony said that it would market a different type of

© Spencer Platt/Getty Images

The eagerly awaited video game Doom 3 *made it onto the market in 2004. The violent "first-person-shooter" game won kudos for its technology but got mixed reviews from seasoned gamers.*

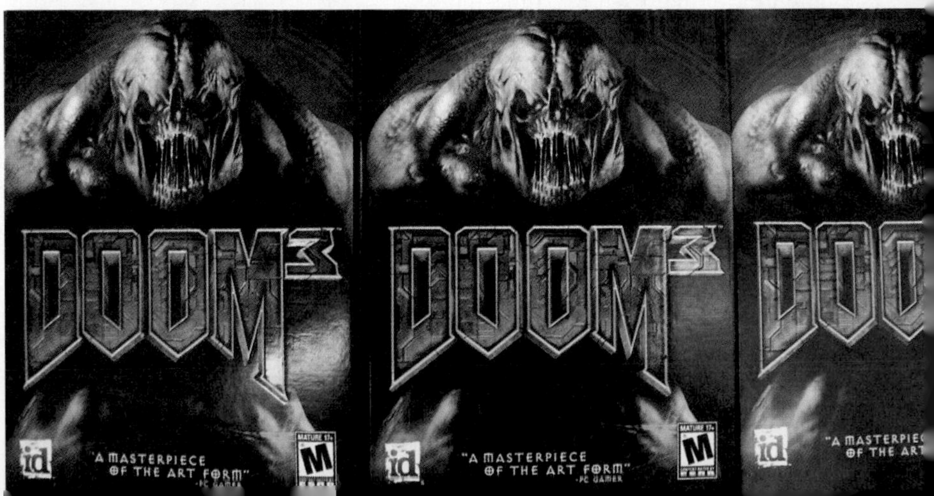

handheld game player, which would also play digital music and video.

In a nod to the employment potential of the computer-game industry, a number of universities began offering game-related studies. Rensselaer Polytechnic Institute, Troy, N.Y., reported that its students would be able to minor in video-game studies. The University of Southern California formed a partnership with Electronic Arts, the largest game firm, to create a degree program in video-game design. Other universities that offered video-game-related classes included Princeton and Carnegie Mellon, Pittsburgh, Pa.

New Technology. Technology contributed to a shift in PC sales toward laptops. According to analysts, consumer enthusiasm for laptops was driven by their increasing computing power (which nearly matched that of desktops), a desire for portability, and the growing availability of built-in Wi-Fi wireless Internet capability for going online. Laptop Wi-Fi could be used with Wi-Fi connections available in many coffee shops, airports, hotels, and other public places either for free or for a monthly fee, and many people had a wireless network at home so that several desktop or laptop computers could share a high-speed Internet connection. From mid-2003 to mid-2004, about 51% of the revenue from U.S. retail sales of computers was from laptops, surpassing sales revenue from desktop PCs for the first time. Desktop PCs, which typically cost less than laptops, continued to lead with 64% in retail unit sales.

While Wi-Fi use grew steadily, some companies that tried to market the service had a difficult time. One such company, a joint venture of Intel, AT&T, and IBM called Cometa Networks, closed for lack of funding after having faced stiff competition from similar Wi-Fi companies and from the increasing popularity of free Wi-Fi service.

Intel announced that it was investing in a longer-range wireless Internet technology called WiMax, which could reach several kilometres, compared with only a few hundred metres for most Wi-Fi installations. WiMax held the promise of connecting hundreds or thousands of widely separated computers to the Internet through a single centralized antenna.

Intel shifted its PC microprocessor production to a new design that included more than one processor on a chip. The shift was made because raising the clock speed (measured in gigahertz) of single-processor chips generated too much heat inside a PC. Because this thermal barrier limited future improvements, Intel abandoned some existing chip-development projects and focused on the new dual-processor technology, in which the two processors shared the PC's workload.

Floppy-disk drives continued their slow decline as PC manufacturers increasingly left them out of basic configurations. Although the drives remained available as an add-on option for PCs, many consumers were turning to writable CDs or flash-memory devices as better ways to make data portable. The standard floppy disk, almost unchanged for a decade, stored up to 1.44 MB, whereas CDs stored up to about 700 MB. Various models of finger-sized flash-memory devices, called flash drives, which were designed to be attached to the USB port of a computer, had storage capacities ranging from 32 MB to 2 gigabytes (2,000 MB). Sales of flash drives were reported to have tripled since 2003.

Linux, an open-source operating system, received increased attention as a result of efforts to make it a stronger competitor to the Windows OS. (With open-source software the underlying programming, or source code, was shared among independent developers; this practice contrasted with the traditional approach used by software companies of closely guarding source code.) The Free Standards Group, a nonprofit trade organization, promoted a new version of the Linux OS called Linux Standard Base 2.0. The group hoped to re-create a worldwide standard for the OS. Since the release of the original version of Linux in 1991, the operating system had mutated into several different commercial versions, which diluted its influence as an alternative to Windows. Several companies backed the new standard, including IBM, Intel, AMD, Dell Computer Corp., and Hewlett-Packard Co. (HP). Microsoft acknowledged that Linux was a serious competitor when it told the Securities and Exchange Commission that open-source software was putting increasing pressure on all parts of its business.

Microsoft delayed some of the technological improvements that it had promised with Longhorn, the code name for its long-awaited upgrade of the Windows XP operating system. The company had diverted much of its resources to the improvement of the security features of the existing Windows XP after a number of vulnerabilities were highlighted, analysts said. The introduction of the final version of Longhorn was rescheduled for 2006.

The U.S government made use of development contracts to spur technological advancement among several suppliers of high-speed scientific computers called supercomputers. The machines were used for research in scientific fields, including weather, astronomy, and biotechnology, as well as in classified government defense operations. The company that developed the fastest supercomputer was expected to have the best chance of selling its product to American scientists, who believed that they were falling behind Japanese researchers who were using the world's fastest supercomputer—the Earth Simulator, built by Japanese firm NEC. The Earth Simulator had a speed of 35.86 trillion calculations per second, but by year's end an annual industry review had ranked IBM's BlueGene/L as the fastest supercomputer in the world, with 70.72 trillion calculations per second.

At the small end of the computing spectrum, sales of hand-held personal digital assistants (PDAs) continued to fall because of competition from smartphones, cell phones that possessed sufficient computer power to allow them to provide PDA features, such as calendars and contact lists, and to function as digital cameras and MP3 music players. As a result, Sony dropped out of the American and European PDA markets, although it continued to offer PDAs in Japan.

Apple, which had become a relatively small competitor in the market for personal computers, introduced an unusual new iMac in which the computer processor and other components fit within a compartment behind a flat-panel monitor. To maintain its lead in the music-player market, Apple cut prices for the iPod and unveiled new models. Inside their pocket-sized cases, iPods held tiny hard drives that packed as much as 60 gigabytes of storage.

Several other companies entered the market with small hard-drive-based music players, among them HP and Dell. Microsoft tried to broaden the functions of such devices with a device called the Portable Media Center, which could play music, recorded TV programs, and videos, as well as display photographs. Apple responded with iPod Photo, which, in addition to playing music, could store thousands of digital photos and display them on the screen of a conventional TV set. (STEVE ALEXANDER)

Earth Sciences

A satellite radar mapping technique called InSAR was revolutionizing the study of DEFORMATIONS of the Earth's crust, and a newly discovered IMPACT crater on the ocean floor near Australia was linked to a major mass EXTINCTION. Scenarios concerning ABRUPT climate change were a hot topic, and measurements of global SEA LEVEL indicated that it was RISING.

GEOLOGY AND GEOCHEMISTRY

In August 2004 thousands of geologists from all over the world shared recent developments in Earth science at the quadrennial International Geological Congress (the 32nd) in Florence. The themes of the congress were the renaissance of geology and the application of geology to mitigate natural risks and preserve cultural heritage. Among the points made in the message from the organizers of the congress were that societies face complex problems and the geologic sciences must play a key role in finding solutions for them and that geologists must communicate both with the public to build awareness of the role of geology and with governments to ensure the long-term sustainability of the Earth for human habitation.

Among the many symposia on environmental geology were presentations that demonstrated how geology affects human health. People breathe in and drink substances that have been incorporated into the atmosphere and water from rocks and soils. Health can suffer from either an excess or a deficiency of some of these substances, including iodine, fluorine, arsenic, dust, radon gas, and asbestos. In recent years, for example, the litigation arising from the lung problems caused by just one of the substances—asbestos—has led to huge financial losses for the companies that mined it or manufactured asbestos products. Growing recognition of the significance of such health-related issues was manifested by the launching of a new organization to deal with them: the International Medical Geology Association.

Enrico Bonatti of the Institute of Marine Science of the Italian National Research Council in Venice delivered one of seven plenary lectures, "The Internal Breathing of the Earth." He described the relationships between volatile materials in the mantle, plate tectonics, and the Earth's climate with many complex geologic illustrations. One example bearing on current concerns about global warming was the enhancement of volcanism about 100 million years ago through deep-Earth thermal effects. This episode increased the amount of carbon dioxide in the atmosphere, which could have caused the unusually hot climate, the existence of which scientists had deduced from an analysis of the oxygen isotopes found in deep-sea sediments of that age.

The potential for volcanoes to influence long-term global climatic changes by the emission of carbon dioxide had been discussed for many years, but it was in 1986 that geologists learned of the devastating short-term effects of volcanic carbon-dioxide emission. Volcanic carbon dioxide escaped from solution in the waters deep within Lake Nyos, which occupies an old volcanic crater in Cameroon, and killed 1,800 people by asphyxiation. In 2004 Michel Halbwachs of the Université de Savoie, France, and coauthors reported the results of their continuing studies on the causes and mechanisms of such events, which are called limnic eruptions. The seepage of carbon dioxide into the lake is less than one-tenth the flow of carbon dioxide into the air in the volcanic area of Mammoth Mountain in California, for example, but the deep, stagnant layers of water in Lake Nyos trap the gas under pressure. A large volume of the gas can suddenly bubble to the surface and spread over the surrounding area. The scientists reported on mitigation procedures they had developed in which a vertical plastic pipe carried deep CO_2-rich water up toward the surface. The degassing of the CO_2 from the water as it rose created a self-sustaining flow of water through the pipe.

The Geological Society of America's presidential address by Clark Burchfiel of the Massachusetts Institute of Technology discussed how GPS (Global Positioning System) data from parts of India and China were forcing field geologists to look in new ways at crustal structures and geologic processes. International cooperative studies with Chinese geologists through the previous decade or so had been directed toward sorting out the complex geologic rearrangements arising from the collision of the Indian landmass with that of Asia. The mapping of enormous and intricate fault systems by field geologists had begun to be complemented in dramatic fashion by GPS-derived information giving the direction and rate of motion of many individual points across the vast terrane.

Reports by Matthew Pritchard and Mark Simons of Princeton University and the California Institute of Technology and Alessandro Ferretti of Tele-Rilevamento, Milan, and colleagues from Italy and the U.S. demonstrated how measurements from satellite radar instruments, which complement GPS studies, had revolutionized tectonic studies of topographic maps and deformations of large and small areas of the crust. Applications included the study of volcanoes, active faults, landslides, oil fields, and glaciers. The technique that was used, called InSAR, involved successive imaging of a given area using synthetic aperture radar (SAR). The images were then superposed to generate interferograms, revealing changes in elevation that had occurred during the time between measurements.

Pritchard and Simons summarized the InSAR results gathered over 11 years from the central subduction arc of South America, a region along the Pacific coast containing about 900 volcanic structures. They studied the deformation within four circular volcanic structures having diameters of 40–60 km (25–37 mi). The deformation within each structure was greatest at the centre, with a displacement of 10–20 cm

(4–8 in), and decreased symmetrically from the centre. Of the four structures (none of which was an actively erupting volcano), two structures were associated with the inflation of large stratovolcanoes and one was associated with the sinking of a large volcanic caldera. The scientists calculated that these deformations could be explained by the injection or withdrawal, respectively, of magma at a depth 8–13 km (5–8 mi) below the surface. The connection between fairly frequent short-lived pulses of magma movement at depth and surface eruptions remained uncertain. Monitoring deformations through the use of InSAR was expected to become a critical tool for understanding volcanic hazards, elucidating the processes at depth that lead to an eruption.

Ferretti and colleagues modified the InSAR technique, improving its precision sufficiently to measure surface motions with an accuracy of better than one millimetre per year (0.04 in per year). Using this technique to reveal complex patterns of surface motions in the San Francisco Bay area, they found that the San Andreas strike-slip fault was accommodating 40 mm per year of relative motion and the Hayward fault was slipping by about 5 mm per year. Throughout the area the rate of tectonic uplift was generally less than one millimetre per year, with some local regions of more rapid uplift. Areas of unconsolidated sediment and fill flanking the bay exhibited the highest rates of change, with a subsidence of about two centimetres per year. Superimposed on the slow tectonic uplift of the East Bay Hills area of 0.4 mm per year were deep-seated creeping landslides in the Berkeley Hills moving downhill at an average speed of 27–38 mm per year, accelerating during wet months and ceasing during summer months.

(PETER J. WYLLIE)

In this map of western South America, each colour band corresponds to a five-centimetre movement of the Earth's crust for 1992–2003, as determined with InSAR, a mapping technique. Earthquakes caused the large coastal areas of deformation. The inset detail shows active deformation of four volcanic areas.

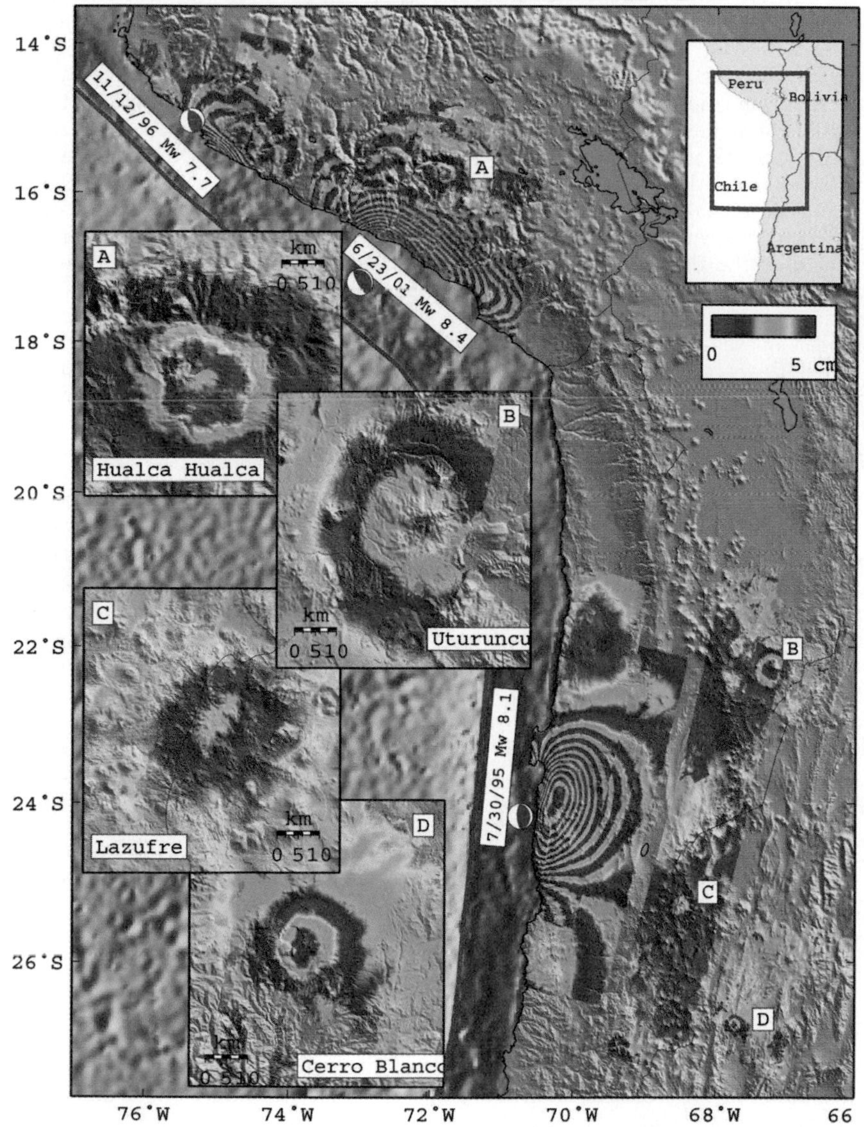

Figure provided by Matt Pritchard (Princeton University) and Mark Simons (California Institute of Technology)

GEOPHYSICS

On December 26 an undersea earthquake with an epicentre west of the northern end of Sumatra in Indonesia had a moment magnitude of 9.0, the largest since the 9.2-magnitude Alaska earthquake in 1964. A portion of the ocean floor shifted upward along more than 1,000 km (600 mi) of the fault that lies between the Burma and Indian tectonic plates. The movement displaced an enormous volume of seawater and created a tsunami—a series of long-period ocean waves. A tsunami can travel a great distance at speeds as fast as 800 km/hr (500 mph), but as the waves reach a shoreline, their speed is reduced and they build in height. As an example, Sri Lanka, though located approximately 1,200 km (750 mi) from the fault, was struck some two hours later by waves that were reported to have reached a height of 9 m (30 feet). With deadly and devastating force, the Indian Ocean tsunami overran the coastal areas of many countries, from Malaysia in Southeast Asia to Tanzania in East Africa. The greatest loss of life occurred in Banda Aceh and other coastal cities in northern Sumatra. (*See* DISASTERS: Sidebar.)

In January 2004 a group of seismologists from Princeton University published a new 3-D tomographic model of the Earth's interior. They produced the model by processing seismic waves, in much the same manner that images of a fetus within the womb are made by processing earthquake-generated ultrasound waves. Using an innovative algorithm to process the seismic-wave data, the seismologists were able to reveal the existence of cylindrical plumes of material that extend from the core-mantle boundary, some 2,900 km (1,800 mi) beneath the surface of the Earth, to "hot spots" of volcanic activity at the Earth's surface. (The volcanic

Courtesy NASA/JPL-Caltech

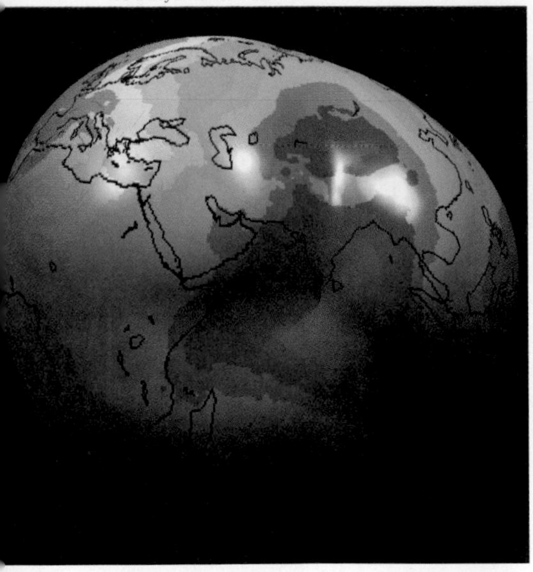

The image depicts in an exaggerated manner irregularities in the Earth's gravity field as determined by an earth-science satellite mission called GRACE. A low point in the field occurs below the Indian Ocean near India.

activity of hot spots is generally unrelated to the volcanic activity that occurs at tectonic plate boundaries.) The material in the plumes was thought to be slowly rising through the mantle and to be hundreds of degrees warmer than its surroundings, remaining solid until it is within a few kilometres of the surface. Not all the plumes in the model originate at the core-mantle boundary. The plume associated with the Icelandic hot spot, for example, begins at a depth of only about 700 km (430 mi).

A new crystalline structure for the mineral $MgSiO_3$ was discovered during the year by a group of Japanese researchers. This mineral is the predominant component of the Earth's lower mantle. The researchers found that when the common form of $MgSiO_3$, called perovskite, is subjected to extreme pressure and temperature (specifically, 125 gigapascals and 2,230 °C), its crystalline structure changes into a denser form called the post-perovskite phase. Conditions necessary for the formation of the post-perovskite phase exist in the mantle at and below a depth of 2,700 km (1,700 mi). The presence of this phase deep within the mantle may explain many of the enigmatic seismological properties of that region. For example, the reflection of seismic waves from what appears to be a structure above the core-mantle boundary may be caused by the difference in density between the post-perovskite phase and perovskite, and the fact that the elastic properties of the post-perovskite phase are anisotropic (vary with direction) may be the reason the velocity of seismic waves in the lower mantle depends on the waves' polarization.

In 2002 two identical satellites were launched into orbit for an earth science mission called GRACE, operated through a partnership between NASA and the German Aerospace Centre. The satellites orbited the Earth at an altitude of about 500 km (300 mi) and provided data for measuring the Earth's gravitational field. In 2004 scientists published the first results from the GRACE mission, presenting a global map of gravity anomalies with a spatial resolution about 10 times greater than that of previous maps. The gravity anomalies are largely caused by variations in the density of materials from place to place within the Earth, and they give clues to understanding the creeping convective motion of material within the Earth's mantle. Some gravity anomalies vary with time, and the scientists reported a strong seasonal variation in South America. This variation appeared to be related to the flow of groundwater in the Amazon basin, and the new observations would help hydrologists merge models of well-studied local systems of water flow into a continental-scale model.

In mid-2004 scientists reported the discovery of an impact crater in the shallow waters off the northwestern coast of Australia. The geologic feature, known as the Bedout High, is overlain by a layer of sediment about three kilometers (two miles) deep and was first identified as a potential impact site from an analysis of data from a marine seismological experiment. The scientists used a combination of geologic, geochemical, and geophysical observations to confirm the identity of the crater and to link it with the mass extinction that occurred between the Permian and Triassic geologic periods about 250 million years ago. Although this extinction event was less well known than the one that included the demise of the dinosaurs between the Cretaceous and Tertiary periods, it was the more severe of the two—about 90% of all marine species and 70% of land vertebrate species became extinct. The scientists pointed out that a massive amount of volcanic activity in Siberia produced large flows of basalt at about the time the Bedout High impact crater was formed, and they speculated that there might be a connection between the two events.

(KEITH KOPER)

METEOROLOGY AND CLIMATE

In 2004 abrupt climate change was a topic widely discussed in news reports and was the subject of a popular disaster movie. A number of scientists believed there was reason to be concerned that within a matter of decades a warming of the climate in the Arctic could lead to cooler climates in Europe and parts of North America. In theory, an increase in Arctic air temperature would lead to greater rainfall and to the melting of ice in the Arctic, which in turn would increase the flow of fresh water into the northern Atlantic Ocean in the area south of Greenland. Fresh water being more buoyant than salt water, it would interfere with the surface ocean currents of the oceanic circulation system known as the Atlantic conveyor belt, which transports warm water northward from the tropics. Without this warm water, the climates of Europe and parts of North America would become colder, and precipitation patterns would change in various parts of the world.

Although evidence existed that the northern Atlantic Ocean was becoming significantly less salty, scientists did not know how great the change in salinity would have to be in order to trigger a major shift in climate. A number of scientists were skeptical that abrupt climate change was a near-term threat. David Battisti of the University of Washington noted that at the rate at which the salinity was decreasing, it would take 200 years or more to slow the circulation of the Atlantic conveyor belt. In addition, warming of the upper layers of the ocean might substantially offset the loss of buoyancy and moderate the effects associated with a decrease in salinity. A recent report from the U.S. Climate Change Science Program suggested that recent changes in the distribution of fresh and saline ocean waters were occurring in ways that might be linked to global warming.

Various studies involving the measurement of global sea level indicated that it was rising. The rise was believed to be caused by the thermal expansion of the oceans (which would correspond to recent warming trends) and by the melting of continental ice, such as gla-

NASA's Earth Observatory

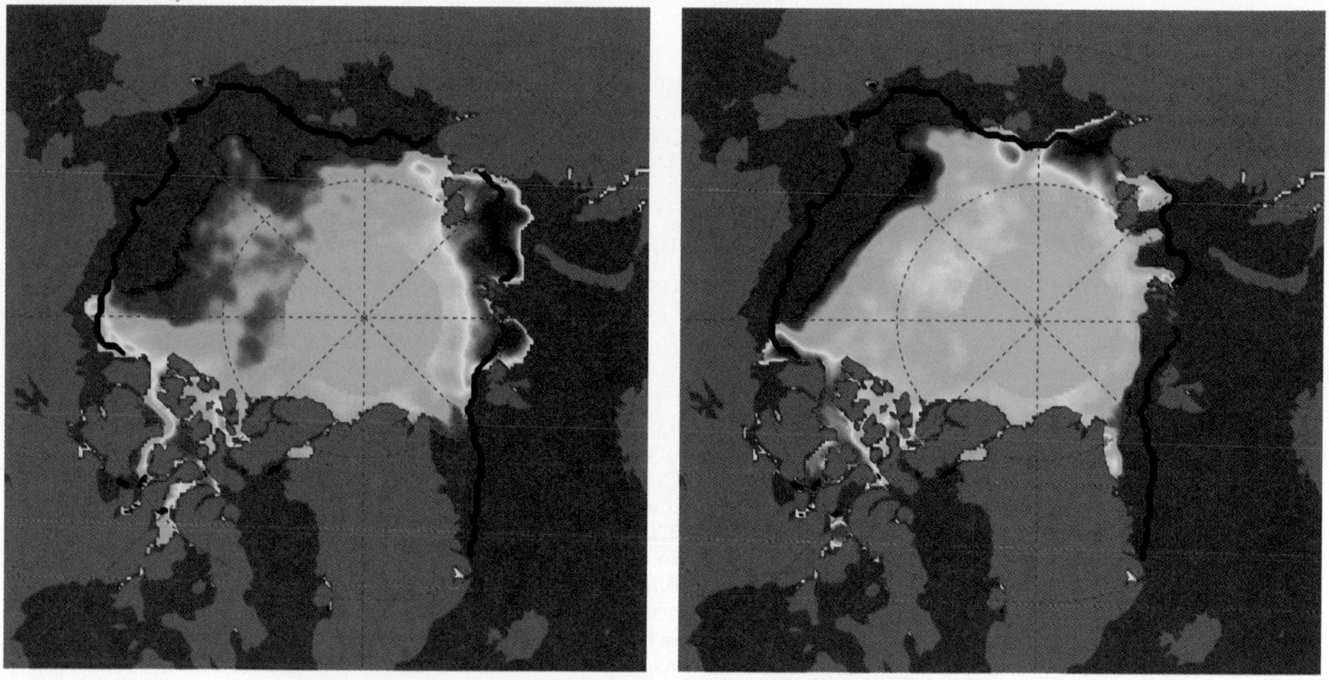

The extent of Arctic sea ice is shown for September 2003 (left) and for September 2004 (right). The thick black line is the median edge of the ice cap for 1979–2000 and indicates a decline in sea-ice cover. Colour is used to show the variation in ice concentration from the mean, with the greatest increase in dark red and the greatest decrease in dark blue. (The green circular area around the North Pole is excluded.)

ciers, with a subsequent increase of the volume of the oceans. Researchers Peter Wadhams of the University of Cambridge and Walter Munk of the Scripps Institution of Oceanography, La Jolla, Calif., determined that the warming of the oceans was causing a rise in sea level of about 0.5 mm (1 mm = about 0.4 in) per year and that glacial melting contributed about another 0.6 mm per year—resulting in a total rate of 1.1 mm per year. Other researchers calculated higher rates. For example, John A. Church and colleagues of CSIRO Marine Research, Hobart, Tas., Australia, found a global increase of 1.8 mm per year for the period 1950 to 2000. Scientists in the U.S. Climate Change Science Program found a similar overall rate of increase (1.5 to 2 mm per year) and noted that their research provided evidence suggesting that the melting of polar ice sheets could play an important role in rising sea levels.

Additional research conducted as part of the U.S. Climate Change Science Program used satellite data to show that the portion of the Arctic Ocean covered by perennial sea ice had declined by about 9% per decade since 1978 and that the decline could have large-scale consequences on climate. No direct evidence was found that greenhouse gases were responsible for the melting of sea ice or for a reduction of snow cover in the Arctic, but some evidence showed that the natural weather pattern known as the North Atlantic Oscillation/Northern Annular Mode might have contributed to the overall decrease in Arctic sea ice. Weather patterns that changed from year to year were a major cause of variability in snow and ice coverage. For example, a pattern of cold weather that persisted in central and eastern North America during the summer resulted in the lingering of ice on the waters of Hudson Bay through the end of August for the first time since 1994. An Arctic Climate Impact Assessment study issued in November 2004 concluded that the Arctic "is now experiencing some of the most rapid and severe climate change on earth" and indicated that climate change was expected to accelerate over the next 100 years.

In September 2004 the United States released the first draft of its plan to monitor the Earth as part of the U.S. Integrated Earth Observation System, a component of the Global Earth Observation System involving nearly 50 countries. The draft plan, produced through the collaborative effort of 18 federal agencies under the auspices of the National Science and Technology Council, focused on nine areas of study with potential benefit to society, including weather forecasting and the prediction and mitigation of climate variability and change. The plan was to be incorporated within a larger intergovernmental document to be presented at the third global Earth Observation Summit in Brussels in February 2005.

A large portion of the annual rainfall across the southwestern United States and northwestern Mexico occurs during thunderstorms generated by a seasonal shift of wind patterns between June and the end of September. Improved forecasts of this summer monsoon were seen as an important goal for meteorologists to help predict drought in these water-scarce areas. The field phase of the North American Monsoon Experiment began in June 2004. For nearly four months, scientists from the United States, Mexico, and several Central American countries collaborated in collecting extensive atmospheric, oceanic, and land-surface observations in northwestern Mexico, the southwestern United States, and adjacent oceanic areas. Scientists hoped to use the data to explore improvements in global models of weather and climate, potentially resulting in better forecasts of summer precipitation months to seasons in advance.

(DOUGLAS LE COMTE)

Economic Affairs

In 2004 the world economy grew at a FASTER pace, but worries over terrorism, the high price of oil, the OUTSOURCING of jobs, and the U.S. trade and current-account DEFICITS led to a DECLINING dollar and weakened some industries.

The IMF-projected acceleration in world GDP to 5% from 3.9% in 2003 made growth in 2004 the fastest in three decades. The expansion in trade and output was unexpected. It was led by the U.S. and Japan, with only lacklustre recovery in the euro zone. The U.S. demand was fueled by investment and consumption at the expense of growing fiscal and current-account deficits, which in turn led to an apparently relentless decline in the value of the dollar. This created concerns at home and abroad. In contrast, expansion in Japan and the euro zone was export driven.

While the global economy remained heavily dependent on the U.S., the economic emphasis was shifting to Asia, where much faster growth was being fueled by domestic and external demand. In this regard China's role was paramount. Its remarkable economic performance was helped by its membership in the World Trade Organization (WTO) and was underpinning growth in neighbouring countries, including Japan. With exports and imports rising at around 35%, China's demand pushed up the prices of many commodities, particularly oil, which had global repercussions on producers and user countries. The increased economic power of China gave it new confidence and outspokenness that surprised many observers. In November China's central bank responded to growing pressure for a revaluation of its currency to help curb the soaring U.S. trade deficit, proffering advice to the U.S. and criticism of U.S. policies.

For the third consecutive year, global inflows of foreign direct investment (FDI) fell. The 17.6% decline to $560 billion in 2003 was accounted for by the 28% decrease to developed countries ($384 billion), with flows to the U.S. dropping 45% to $40 billion. FDI in less-developed countries (LDCs) rose 9%, with increases to Africa, Asia, and the Pacific. China overtook the U.S. to become the world's largest recipient of FDI. Competition to attract investment continued to be strong, and 82 countries made 220 regulatory changes to make their countries more favourable destinations, while some resumed privatization programs.

Fundamental changes in the pattern of investment continued. Transnational corporations from LDCs increased their share of FDI stock to $859 billion following a rise of 8% in 2003. In all regions there was a shift in the composition of FDI away from the primary sector and manufacturing. The services sector accounted for two-thirds of all FDI inflows and some 60% of FDI stock, compared with one-quarter in the 1970s and less than half in 1990. While services were growing increasingly important, many were not tradable and had to be produced when and where they were consumed. The increasing availability of information and communications, however, was enabling more services to be produced in one location and consumed in another. This was creating a growing trend toward offshoring and outsourcing. (*See* Special Report.)

NATIONAL ECONOMIC POLICIES

The IMF projected a 3.6% rise in GDP in the advanced countries following a 2.1% increase in 2003.

United States. The IMF projected growth in 2004 of 4.3%, compared with the 3% achieved in 2003. The early part of the year was marked by strong expansion, with first-quarter output rising 4.5% (annualized rate). In the second quarter, the quarter-on-quarter rate decelerated sharply to an annualized rate of 3.3%. A drop in consumer confidence was prompted by increased oil prices and slower-than-expected employment growth; spending on durable goods, particularly motor vehicles, suffered most. In the second half, growth accelerated, with third-quarter output rising at an annualized 4.4%, helped by a recovery in personal consumption to an annual growth rate of 4% against 1.6% in the second quarter.

During the year the fall in the value of the dollar and the rising cost of oil were causes for concern, but the economy demonstrated a resilience that surprised many observers. It was better able to absorb increased oil costs than it had been at the time of previous oil shocks (1973, 1979, and 1991). In 2004 corporate profits and business investment remained strong, and while interest-rate rises had removed some of the stimulus to business activity, monetary policy was still supportive. The fears of deflation that were prevalent at the end of 2003 ironically gave way to apprehension in the first half of the year that inflation would resurface. This prompted the U.S. Federal Reserve (Fed) to reassure financial markets that it was prepared to intervene. In the second half of the year, more aggressive prices pushed the consumer price index (CPI) to end 2004 up 3.3% on December 2003, although the core rate (excluding food and energy) rose only 2.2%. There was limited pressure from wages, which in December were rising at 2.7% above year-earlier levels. While job creation was weak in the first half of the year, the number of hours worked increased by an annualized 4.1% in the third quarter, and the unemployment rate, at 5.4% in December, was well down on the year before (5.7%).

As in 2003, public finances were a cause of domestic and international concern. The federal deficit for the year was $422 billion, or 3.6% of GDP. Spending increases under Pres. George W. Bush had escalated to an annual average 5.1% from 1.5% and 1.9% under former presidents Bill Clinton and George H.W. Bush, respectively. To maintain the government's borrowing ability, in November the president signed into law an $800 billion increase in the U.S. government's debt limit to $8.18 trillion; this brought the amount by which the limit had been raised to 25% since he took office in 2001. This allayed international fears that the U.S. would default on its debt. At the same time, Fed Chairman Alan Greenspan was warning that the country's burgeoning current-account deficit was "increasingly less tenable." His comments on November 19 in an address to finance ministers and central bank governors in Frankfurt, Ger., ahead of the Group of 20 (G-20) meeting in Berlin had the effect of sending the dollar into further decline.

United Kingdom. For most of 2004 the economy remained surprisingly resilient, and output was projected to expand at an above-trend rate of 3.4%, although the outcome was likely to be closer to 3%. Output in the second quarter rose at an annual rate of 3.7%, the fastest in four years. The third quarter saw a marked slowdown. Several industries experienced decline, and overall output contracted by 1.4% following a 1.2% increase in the second quarter. Service-sector activity moderated, and retail spending grew more slowly.

Much of the impetus came from private consumption that was being supported by continued income growth and rising housing wealth. Consumer spending had outpaced GDP growth for the previous eight years. A continuing boom in the housing market, where prices had been rising at around 20% annually for five years, low unemployment, and an economy running at close to capacity generated fears of overheating. By the second half of the year, interest-rate increases were dampening the housing market, and in November the number of mortgage approvals fell to 77,000 in the steepest drop since 1995. House prices fell marginally in October and December, and annual house price inflation in 2004 eased to 12.7% from 15% in 2003. Jobs in the private sector declined slightly during the year, while public-sector employment continued to increase. Although the unemployment rate reached a new low at 4.6%, the number of unemployed claimants rose slightly in September and October, while total employment at 28.4 million was at its highest since records began in 1984. At the same time, employment in manufacturing fell to a record low of 3.35 million.

Nevertheless, the manufacturing industry spearheaded growth in e-commerce, which more than doubled to £40 billion (£1 = about $1.79 at year-end 2003) in 2003, compared with 2002. Manufacturers' sales almost trebled to £15 billion as many required their customers to order online to keep costs down. Research showed that the larger the company was, the more it used the Internet. Nearly a third of spending by businesses with more than 1,000 employees was online, compared with 14% by companies with fewer than 10 employees. While consumers increased their online shopping by 78% in 2003, their share of online spending fell to 29%. The U.K. had the largest e-commerce economy in Europe.

Japan. The strong economic recovery in 2003 continued to gather momentum in early 2004, and output was projected to increase by 4.4% following a 2.5% rise in 2003. In the first quarter, output rose sharply to an annualized rate of 6.3%, but it fell in the second quarter to 1.3%, largely because of the drawing down of inventories and a decline in public final demand. Recovery continued to falter, with third-quarter annual growth in real GDP slowing to 0.3%, although in nominal terms the rate accelerated and even in real terms the year-on-year figures showed real GDP was still growing at 3.9%. Output for the year was likely to rise by nearer to 4%. The increased cost of oil imports on which Japan was heavily dependent was not helping the recovery. Japan was the world's third largest oil consumer, after the U.S. and China, but led the world in energy efficiency. A second fact hindering recovery was the slowdown in China, which had become Japan's largest trading partner.

There were signs that after nine years of deflation, prices had stabilized and would begin to rise, bringing to an end the malaise that had eroded corporate profits and increased the real cost of the debt burden on borrowers. In November the CPI was up 0.8% on a year earlier, although it was still half a percentage point down over the year. Restructuring of the labour market continued, and labour was becoming more flexible. Many companies were no longer able to offer employees the traditional job for life, and more people were moving between jobs. Given the need to supplement family incomes and to insure against redundancy, female participation in the workforce was increasing. Because of the changes being made, unit labour costs declined, productivity was rising, and wage costs were lower. At the same time, the job-offers-to-applicants ratio rose to a 10-year high, and the unemployment rate in November fell to 4.5%, its lowest level since January 1999.

Table I. Real Gross Domestic Products of Selected Developed Countries
% annual change

Country	2000	2001	2002	2003	2004[1]
United States	3.7	0.8	1.9	3.0	4.3
Japan	2.8	0.4	–0.3	2.5	4.4
Germany	2.9	0.8	0.1	–0.1	2.0
France	4.2	2.1	1.1	0.5	2.6
Italy	3.0	1.8	0.4	0.3	1.4
United Kingdom	3.9	2.3	1.8	2.2	3.4
Canada	5.2	1.8	3.4	2.0	2.9
All developed countries	3.9	1.2	1.6	2.1	3.6
Seven major countries above	3.5	1.0	1.2	2.2	3.7
European Union	3.7	1.8	1.2	1.1	2.6

[1]Estimated.
Note: Seasonally adjusted at annual rates.
Source: *IMF World Economic Outlook*, September 2004.

Table II. Standardized Unemployment Rates in Selected Developed Countries
% of total labour force

Country	2000	2001	2002	2003	2004[1]
United States	4.0	4.8	5.8	6.0	5.5
Japan	4.7	5.0	5.4	5.3	4.8
Germany	7.3	7.4	8.2	9.1	9.2
France	9.4	8.7	9.0	9.7	9.8
Italy	10.7	9.6	9.1	8.8	8.1
United Kingdom	5.5	5.1	5.2	5.0	4.7
Canada	6.8	7.2	7.6	7.6	7.2
All developed countries	5.9	6.2	6.7	6.9	6.6
Seven major countries above	5.7	5.9	6.5	6.7	6.4
Euro zone[2]	8.4	8.0	8.4	8.8	8.8

[1]Projected. [2]Austria, Belgium, France, Germany, Greece, Ireland, Italy, Luxembourg, The Netherlands, Norway, Portugal, and Spain.
Source: OECD, *Economic Outlook*, November 2004.

Euro Zone. As in 2003, the euro zone as a whole lagged the performance of Japan, the U.K., and the U.S. The economy recovered strongly in the first half of the year, and output was projected to increase 2.2%, compared with a 0.5% expansion in 2003. The promising start gave way to a dismal performance in the second half, and output growth for the year was unlikely to reach 2% in the wake of three years of below-trend growth. Factors contributing to the deterioration included the increased cost of oil imports and the weaker global conditions. International competitiveness was eroded by the appreciation of the euro. In general, the area remained dependent on external demand. In the first half of the year, a surge in exports pushed up industrial output, particularly in Germany, Italy, The Netherlands, and Spain, and in September industrial production was running at 2.9% above year-earlier levels. The rate of consumer price inflation showed signs of accelerating and for much of the year was running at slightly above the European Central Bank's 2% ceiling. Higher oil costs and indirect tax increases were largely responsible, but given the high level of unemployment—which in November stood at 8.9%, unchanged over a year earlier—there was no fear of a wage-price spiral.

The composition and pace of growth varied widely across the region. In Germany, the euro zone's largest country, output was projected to increase by 2% following a 0.1% decline in 2003, but it was unlikely to exceed 1.5%. The surge in exports in the first half of the year had spearheaded the euro-zone recovery but moderated in the second half because of the fall in global demand, the stronger euro, and higher oil prices. Domestic demand during the year remained weak. Investment spending fell 2.5% year on year in the second quarter—the 14th consecutive decline. Despite household incomes' being boosted by lower taxes, in the first half of 2004, consumer spending remained flat, and retail sales were down 1.5% in the third quarter. Rigidities in the labour market kept the level of unemployment high and intractable, and at 10.7% in October, it was up on a year before (10.5%) and did little to boost consumer confidence. In France economic growth was more broad-based, and output was increasing at double the rate in Germany. France, however, also suffered high unemployment, which in November stood at 9.9%, unchanged from a year earlier. Rapid expansion in France in the first half of the year was fueled by strong domestic demand, with household and government spending and investment all contributing, but output faltered in the second half.

The Countries in Transition. Nearly all countries participated in the acceleration in output to 6.1% in 2004 from 5.6% in 2003. In the first half of the year, significant moves were made toward closer integration within Europe. On May 1 eight countries of Central and Eastern Europe (Czech Republic, Estonia, Hungary, Latvia, Lithuania, Poland, Slovakia, and Slovenia) joined the European Union, together with Cyprus and Malta. This subjected them to much tighter fiscal discipline to meet the requirements of the EU Stability and Growth Pact. (*See* WORLD AFFAIRS: *European Union:* Sidebar.) In June, Estonia, Lithuania, and Slovenia joined the European exchange-rate mechanism in a move toward adoption of the euro. Entry for the others was delayed so that they could reduce their budget deficits and inflation rates. The initial effects of accession were mixed. It contributed to acceleration in inflation to 4.5% (from 2.9% in 2003) but improved investment potential and export opportunities.

As it had since 2000, output increased fastest in the Commonwealth of Independent States, where growth was underpinned by high commodity prices. The highest projected growth rates were for Armenia (7%), Azerbaijan (9.1%), Kazakhstan (9%), and Tajikistan (10%). Ukraine, where output was projected to increase by 12.5%, was expected to be the star performer before the uncertainty that followed the elections. (*See* WORLD AFFAIRS: *Ukraine.*) In Russia output was expected to decelerate slightly to 6.9%. In most of the southeastern European countries, output gains were made and GDP was projected to increase 5% from 4.4% in 2003, with Albania (6.2%) and Romania (5.8%) outperforming, while Macedonia lagged behind the trend (2.5%) because of a lack of investment. In nearly all countries of the region, inflation rates rose, and the median rate was projected to increase from 4.8% to 6.3%. Notable exceptions were Romania, Serbia and Montenegro, and Belarus, where there were sharp drops in double-digit rates.

Less-Developed Countries. The IMF projected acceleration in output in the LDCs to 6.6% in 2004 from 6.1% in 2003, which was the fastest growth rate in a decade. While some industrialized countries provided strong markets, it was the dynamic performance of the large LDCs, particularly China and India, that boosted LDCs as a whole. Regional disparities remained, but these were less than in recent years. Latin America had been the laggard in 2003, but in 2004 that region's output increased faster than at any other time since 1997.

Led by China, LDCs in Asia continued to spearhead growth. East Asian economies grew by 8.4% in the first half of the year, though the rate for the year was expected to slow to 7.3%. China was the world's most dynamic economy in 2004, expanding by 9.5% in the first half of the year. Despite the imposition of "macroeconomic controls" to rein in growth and prevent overheating, growth over the year was 9.5%, while the rate of inflation accelerated, reaching a seven-year high of 4.4% in May. The economies of Taiwan and Hong Kong were also buoyant. Investment

On the day before the European Union enlargement ceremony in Dublin, a worker checks the flag of the EU and those of its member countries and of 10 more countries that would formally join the EU at the ceremony on May 1.

© Ian Waldie/Getty Images

provided strong stimulus, and although the flow into China slowed, it was still running 20–30% above year-earlier levels. Imports mainly of raw materials spiraled to more than 20% and outpaced exports. Increased domestic demand in all three economies contributed to GDP growth. Because of weaker domestic demand and the higher cost of oil, the South Korean economy performed less well as the year progressed.

After three years of stagnation, output in Latin America staged an impressive recovery and was expected to increase by 4.6%. Nearly all countries performed better. Brazil resumed robust growth of 4%, following a 0.2% decline in 2003. Fears that Mexico (up 4%) would lose market share to China abated as exports rose strongly and large European and American firms made new investments. Recovery in Argentina (7%) continued, helped by high commodity prices. The major oil exporters (Colombia, Ecuador, Mexico, and Venezuela) benefited from higher prices, while the damage to oil importers was largely offset by increased prices of agricultural products (in Argentina, Brazil, and Uruguay) and metals (Chile, Jamaica, and Peru). Lower interest rates enabled many countries to reschedule their debt.

In the Middle East growth slowed from 6% to a projected 5.1%. Risks associated with the conflict in Iraq and fears of terrorist attacks on oil infrastructures in the region deterred investors. There was little scope for oil production to increase as it had in 2003. Nevertheless, incomes in the oil-exporting countries were rising, and domestic demand was thus increasing. In the Mashreq countries (Egypt, Jordan, Lebanon, and Syria), exports strengthened, helped in Egypt by a depreciation of the Egyptian pound, which in turn exacerbated the inflation rate.

Output in Africa rose 4.5%, the fastest since 1996. Lagging behind the trend was South Africa, which accounted for half the GDP of sub-Saharan Africa but only 11% of the population. While the 40% appreciation of the South African rand since 2002 had helped reduce inflation, it slowed export growth and stimulated imports. Elsewhere the oil-importing countries suffered from increased costs, but many countries benefited from both increased oil production (Angola, Chad, and Equatorial Guinea) and an end to the drought (Malawi and Rwanda). In several countries—notably Burundi, the Central African Republic, and Madagascar—greater political stability increased investor and consumer confidence. In Zimbabwe the steep economic decline continued, with output down (−5.2%) for the sixth consecutive year and consumer prices up by 350%. GDP growth in Nigeria slowed from 10.7% to 4% as the oil production gains in 2003 leveled off.

Table III. Changes in Output in Less-Developed Countries
% annual change in real gross domestic product

Area	2000	2001	2002	2003	2004[1]
All less-developed countries	5.9	4.0	4.8	6.1	6.6
Regional groups					
Africa	2.9	4.0	3.5	4.3	4.5
Asia	6.7	5.5	6.6	7.7	7.6
Middle East	5.5	3.6	4.3	6.0	5.1
Western Hemisphere	3.9	0.5	–0.1	1.8	4.6
Central and Eastern Europe	4.9	0.2	4.4	4.5	5.5
Commonwealth of Independent States	9.1	6.4	5.4	7.8	8.0

[1]Projected.
Source: *IMF World Economic Outlook*, September 2004.

Table IV. Changes in Consumer Prices in Less-Developed Countries
% change from preceding year

Area	2000	2001	2002	2003	2004[1]
All less-developed countries	7.3	6.8	6.0	6.1	6.0
Regional groups					
Africa	13.1	12.0	9.7	10.3	8.4
Asia	1.9	2.7	2.1	2.6	4.5
Middle East	8.5	7.1	7.5	8.0	9.2
Western Hemisphere	6.7	6.0	9.0	10.6	6.5

[1]Projected.
Source: *IMF World Economic Outlook*, September 2004.

INTERNATIONAL TRADE AND PAYMENTS

The increase in the volume of world trade in goods and services was expected to exceed the projected 8.8% in 2004, which was the third consecutive year of strong recovery. This followed an expansion of 5.1% in 2003 and reflected the high level of industrial output and investment activity. China accounted for more than 20% of the increase in merchandise trade, as its trading role was enhanced by WTO membership and its share of world exports doubled from 2.9% to 5.8% between 2000 and 2004. China's demand for minerals and oil bolstered the volume of its imports, which rose by a third over the year, and stimulated world commodity prices. For the eighth time in nine years, the export volume growth of LDCs (10.8%) exceeded that of the advanced economies (8.1%). In dollar values world exports were projected to rise 17.4% to $10,806,000,000,000. Services accounted for about 80% of the total and grew by 14.2%.

Current-account imbalances in the world economy became the largest in modern history. The overall current account of the balance of payments in the advanced economies remained in deficit for the sixth straight year. The total surplus rose from $247 billion to $266 billion. The U.S. deficit again exceeded the total surplus and at $631 billion had increased from the year before ($531 billion) to 5.4% of GDP. Its size provoked much international comment and speculation. When Fed Chairman Greenspan criticized this deficit as unsustainable, the downward pressure on the already-depreciating dollar increased. The growth in the deficit occurred in spite of the increase in exports aided by the weaker dollar. This was outpaced by the higher cost of oil, which added at least $10 billion a month to the widening deficit, as well as the rise in imports to meet the unexpectedly strong demand. The U.S. had a large and growing bilateral trade deficit with China that was a periodic cause of friction. This was at the expense of China's large trade deficit with other LDCs from which it imported the intermediate and primary goods to produce the finished goods it exported to the U.S.

The largest deficits were in the Anglo-Saxon countries, with that in the U.K. rising to $43 billion (from $33 billion) but only 2% of GDP, while in Australia, at $32 billion, it reached 5.9% of GDP. The euro zone surplus nearly tripled to

Workers assemble parts at an electronics factory in Panyu, Guangdong province, China. China's export trade was booming, and its share of world exports had doubled to almost 6% in the past four years.

$72 billion because of the surge in Germany's surplus from $53 billion to $119 billion, while in Japan the surplus reached $159 billion (from $136 billion). The surplus of the four Asian newly industrialized countries (Hong Kong, Singapore, South Korea, and Taiwan) was unchanged from 2003 at $85 billion.

After many years in deficit, the LDCs were in surplus for the fifth straight year. The surplus rose strongly to $201 billion from $149 billion in 2003, boosted by a near doubling of the Middle East surplus to $104 billion. The less-developed Asian countries' surplus fell from $86 billion to $69 billion as a result of the upsurge in imports. The aggregate positions of the LDC regions obscured the weakness of the more than 50 individual countries that had deficits in excess of 5% of GDP. Most of these were in Africa and Latin America. Indebtedness of all LDC regions except Africa and Latin America increased slightly, raising the total to $2,763,000,000,000.

Interest Rates. Early in 2004 the developed countries expected that falling inflation rates (or even deflation) and historically low interest rates would continue to be the norm. This changed as the U.S. economy exhibited growing strength and increasing employment rates. The extent and speed of tightening was the only question. The Fed made its first move to tighten the loose U.S. monetary policy on June 30 with a quarter-point rise. Four more quarter-point hikes brought the rate to 2.25% by year's end. In the euro zone Germany's hopes of interest-rate reductions were dashed by the expected rise in the U.S., as well as by an acceleration in the zone's inflation rate. The U.K. rate rose moderately and finished 2004 at 4.75%, up by 0.75% over the year. In Japan the authorities kept their commitment to a zero-rate policy. Tightening had taken place earlier than in the U.S. in Switzerland and New Zealand, while in Australia rates were already higher in 2003 and remained unchanged in 2004 because inflationary pressures were building.

Exchange Rates. The increase in the size of the U.S. public and current-account deficits led to the continued depreciation of the U.S. dollar, which was the main determinant of 2004 exchange-rate movements worldwide. In the industrialized countries nearly all currencies appreciated against the dollar on trade-weighted terms over the year. The Australian dollar fell marginally and was an exception. Among the major LDCs only the Chinese currency (renminbi) depreciated. Because it was pegged to the dollar, the renminbi fell 10.7% in both local currency and dollar terms between Dec. 31, 2003, and Dec. 31, 2004. In most other countries the local currencies appreciated mainly because of improved oil and other commodity prices or because of increased confidence in their economies.

Among the industrialized countries, the extent to which the euro rose against the dollar surprised many observers. Given the relative weakness of the euro-zone economy and the expectation that its interest rates would hold steady while those in the U.S. rose, there was no rational explanation. While the exchange rate rose nearly 8% over the year, its trade-weighted value had increased only 6.2%. Against British sterling the euro weakened in the first half of the year, after which it strengthened, with sterling back to €1.41. Intervention by the authorities in Japan to support the yen meant that its rise was negligible in trade-weighted terms and appreciated less than 5% in currency units. Of significance, however, was the trade-weighted rise of 10% in the Canadian dollar.

The perceived undervaluation of the renminbi provoked criticism from industrialized countries that believed that China should change its fixed exchange-rate policy, under which the renminbi was fixed to the dollar. In November the deputy governor of the People's Bank of China made it clear that China would not be rushed into revaluation. Toward year's end, however, rumours that China might move some of its reserves out of dollars caused panic in currency markets. As of September 2004, China's central bank held $174.4 billion in U.S. Treasury Bonds and was the second largest foreign holder, after Japan. Fears persisted that China and other Asian central banks, which had bought huge amounts of dollars to curb the appreciation of their own currencies, might dump U.S. assets to avoid large losses as the dollar fell. (IEIS)

STOCK MARKETS

Confidence in equities returned in 2004. As the year began, investors seemed to base their longer-term strategies on the generally positive outlook for the corporate sector. Improved global growth prospects, corporate financial strength, and rising stock prices buoyed investors' confidence so well that the MSCI World index, which had gained 32% in 2003, gained a further 3% in just the first eight weeks of 2004. Thereafter, equities tended to trade within a narrow price range, caught between geopolitical uncertainty, oil-price hikes, and rising official interest rates on the one hand and robust corporate performance on the other.

Markets were shaken by the terrorist attacks in Madrid on March 11 and entertained niggling worries about the possible effect of rising official interest rates on consumer spending in countries undergoing a housing boom, such as the U.K., Spain, and Ireland. Major stock markets weakened in late March and again in late May and mid-August. Equity investors turned more risk-averse in the second and third quarters of 2004 on concerns about the real strength of the global economic recovery. More immediately behind these reversals, though, were corporate profit warnings and weaker-than-expected macroeconomic data. By the end of August, the Standard & Poor's index of 500 large-company stocks (S&P 500) was 3% lower than at the end of June, and similarly, the Dow Jones Euro STOXX index of 50 European blue-chip equities and the Tokyo Stock Price Index (TOPIX) of large-company stocks were down 3% and 4%, respectively. Warnings of lower-than-expected profits by technology firms such as Cisco Systems, Hewlett Packard, Nokia, and Intel hit particularly hard. Oil prices rose steadily from the end of June, peaking in October at more than $55 a barrel. Investors seemed less concerned about the potential for inflation, however, than the possible dampening effect on aggregate demand and corporate profits.

After mid-August, major equity markets climbed back to earlier levels and then rose a little, or at least held steady. World stock markets rose sharply on the decisive result of the U.S. presidential election on November 2. (*See* WORLD AFFAIRS: *United States:* Special Report.) The widely followed Dow Jones Industrial Average (DJIA) immediately gained as much as 150 points, or 1.5%, before drifting lower and then rose to peak at 10,854.54 on December 28. After the election the *Financial Times* Stock Exchange index of 100 stocks (FTSE 100) closed at 4718.5, the highest level since June 2002, before continuing its climb to the year's high (4820.10) on December 30. As of December 1 the Morgan Stanley Capital International (MSCI) World index was up 10%; it finished the year at a 12-month high of 1170.74, a 13% gain on the year. (*See* TABLE V.) (IEIS)

Table V. Selected Major World Stock Market Indexes[1]

Country and Index	2004 range[2] High	2004 range[2] Low	Year-end close	Percent change from 12/31/2003
Argentina, Merval	1390	840	1375	28
Australia, Sydney All Ordinaries	4057	3275	4053	23
Belgium, Brussels BEL20	2950	2271	2933	31
Brazil, Bovespa	26,196	17,604	26,196	18
Canada, Toronto Composite	9287	8124	9247	12
China, Shanghai A	1864	1322	1330	–15
Denmark, KFX	287	249	287	18
Finland, HEX General	7362	5229	6228	3
France, Paris CAC 40	3844	3485	3821	7
Germany, Frankfurt Xetra DAX	4262	3647	4256	7
Hong Kong, Hang Seng	14,266	10,968	14,230	13
Hungary, Bux	14,775	9465	14,743	57
India, Sensex (BSE-30)	6603	4505	6603	13
Indonesia, Jakarta Composite	1004	668	1000	45
Ireland, ISEQ Overall	6212	4973	6198	26
Italy, S&P/MIB	30,904	26,198	30,903	15
Japan, Nikkei Average	12,164	10,365	11,489	8
Mexico, IPC	13,032	8818	12,918	47
Netherlands, The, AEX	365	311	348	3
Pakistan, KSE-100	6218	4474	6218	39
Philippines, Manila Composite	1852	1388	1823	26
Poland, Wig	26,636	21,299	26,636	28
Russia, RTS	782	518	614	8
Singapore, Straits Times	2066	1700	2066	17
South Africa, Johannesburg All Share	12,676	9748	12,657	22
South Korea, Composite Index	936	720	896	10
Spain, Madrid Stock Exchange	960	804	959	19
Switzerland, SMI	5934	5310	5693	4
Taiwan, Weighted Price	7034	5317	6140	4
Thailand, Bangkok SET	794	582	668	–13
United Kingdom, FTSE 100	4820	4287	4814	8
United States, Dow Jones Industrials	10,855	9750	10,783	3
United States, Nasdaq Composite	2178	1752	2175	9
United States, NYSE Composite	7254	6217	7250	12
United States, Russell 2000	655	517	652	17
United States, S&P 500	1214	1063	1212	9
World, MS Capital International	1171	997	1171	13

[1]Index numbers are rounded. [2]Based on daily closing price.
Sources: *Financial Times, Wall Street Journal.*

United States. The American public's preoccupation with the presidential election, a sometimes murky economic outlook, and continuing unrest abroad resulted in investors' spending much of 2004 waiting for uncertainties to resolve. As a result, stocks traded in a narrow range for much of the year until November, when the reelection of Pres. George W. Bush sparked a sustained year-end rally in the markets. The S&P 500, a broad gauge of the overall market, ended the year up 8.99%. The Nasdaq (National Association of Securities Dealers automated quotations) composite index gained 8.59%, but the more narrowly focused DJIA climbed only 3.15% in value. (*See* GRAPH.)

The year began on a relatively bullish note, but the Federal Reserve (Fed) set a different tone on January 28 when it announced that after three years of aggressively low interest rates, the risk of inflation was becoming substantial enough to make higher rates desirable in the future. In the months that followed, the Fed's rate-setting Federal Open Market Committee (FOMC) made good on its promise by raising its short-term interest-rate target 0.25% a total of five times. While this left the key federal funds rate at 2.25% (still lower than it had been in four decades), companies that had become accustomed to even lower borrowing costs suffered nonetheless, and their shares reflected this.

Fear of looming higher interest rates dominated investor behaviour in 2004. By February the market had adopted a pattern of perversely rewarding signs of economic weakness in the hope that it would delay the inevitable rate increase, while news that would traditionally have been considered positive was shunned as giving the Fed a reason to move with greater speed. Hedge funds (and other speculative investors), which eschew traditional long-term investment strategies in order to capture short-term trading advantages, fed into this contrarian activity. Once limited to a handful of secretive investment firms, the hedge fund industry had grown to encompass about 8,000 hedge funds controlling more than $900 billion in assets and accounting for fully half of all stock trading volume. On the whole, the retail investors who drove stock prices higher in the late 1990s remained largely absent, driven away by the losses that followed the market boom.

(continued on page 180)

Offshoring

by Christopher O'Leary

By 2004 offshoring—the practice of companies outsourcing operations overseas, usually to less- developed countries (LDCs) with the intention of reducing costs—had already become one of the major economic controversies of the decade. While the ultimate impact of offshoring had yet to be measured, surveys estimated that in 2004 some 14 million Americans, 10% of the nation's workforce, held positions that were susceptible to being outsourced.

Offshoring jobs and infrastructure to countries with more lax regulations and far lower standards of living was nothing new. Many manufacturing jobs, for example, were exported from the U.S. to nations such as China during the 1960s and '70s. What had changed, however, was the nature of the work being exported. With the advent of Internet-based communications technology and improved education in many LDCs, increasing numbers of highly skilled jobs in such areas as information technology (IT) and financial management were heading overseas each year.

The practice had its proponents, who claimed that offshoring's impact was being overstated and that employers, able to use offshoring to reduce overhead costs, were then able to free up capital for new investment and thus create new jobs. Some advocates of this argument included the president of the U.S. Chamber of Commerce, Thomas Donohue, and Federal Reserve Chairman Alan Greenspan. Detractors, however, claimed that the practice had greatly hurt the working class in the United States and could decimate the American middle class.

Unsurprisingly, the issue became a battleground in the 2004 presidential election. Sen. John Kerry, the Democratic Party's candidate, denounced CEOs whose companies engaged in outsourcing as traitorous "Benedict Arnolds." He introduced a bill that would require call-centre employees to disclose their physical locations to consumers and proposed a plan to eliminate all tax breaks to American companies that export jobs. Kerry's proposals had parallels at the state legislative level; as analysts estimated that at least 13 bills that would ban some form of offshore outsourcing had been introduced in states, including New Jersey, Michigan, and Indiana. Pres. George W. Bush, while a far-less-severe critic of offshoring than his opponent, also felt political pressure to slow its pace. In January the president signed an appropriations bill that contained an amendment forbidding some government divisions to use foreign companies when outsourcing work.

Actual data about offshoring's impact on the U.S. economy was preliminary and at times contradictory. In 2004 general estimates were that 250,000–300,000 jobs were leaving the U.S. annually, while some surveys found that about 240,000 technology jobs had gone offshore since January 2001 and about 830,000 general service-sector jobs would have gone overseas by the end of 2005. Some studies were quite grim in their future predictions; Forrester Research Inc. estimated that 3.4 million service-sector jobs (which included most IT positions) would leave the U.S. by 2015. Although outsourcing was not as far advanced in Europe, especially in non-English-speaking countries, Forrester reported that spending on offshoring by European businesses was expected to increase from €82 billion (almost $100 billion) in 2002 to some €129 billion (about $156 billion) in 2008.

A report released in June by the U.S. Department of Labor downplayed offshoring's effects, stating that in the first quarter of 2004 offshoring represented only 2.5% of the total U.S. job losses posted in that period. Critics said that the report understated the impact of offshoring because the study's results came from asking companies if their layoffs were due to offshoring—something many executives would not care to disclose publicly. The same month, a joint survey by Roland Berger Strategy Consultants and the UN Conference on Trade and Development revealed that more than 40% of the European companies canvassed planned to offshore jobs, primarily to save money.

New Frontiers. Perhaps the most contentious area of offshoring was in IT, which had been one of the best-paying and fastest-growing job sectors in the U.S. during the previous 20 years. Ironically, massive IT job transfers overseas were possible only because of the advances made by the technology industry in the past decade. Technology consultants estimated that 10% of American computer service and software jobs would have moved offshore by the end of 2004, while other surveys predicted that up to 25% of all IT jobs in Western countries would relocate offshore by 2010.

In the past, companies had focused their outsourcing efforts mainly on transplanting low-skilled jobs, including customer-service call centres. More recently, companies were tapping the growing pool of university-trained technology graduates in countries that included India, the Philippines, and Malaysia for such tasks as software engineering, computer chip design, and code writing. For example, General Electric Corp. offshored about 70% of its technology

needs; Motorola was increasing the staff in its technology research operations in Beijing, while Intel was doing the same in Russia. Aetna planned to cut up to 10% of its IT staff while likely increasing outsourcing agreements with Indian companies such as Infosys Technologies Ltd. Even Infosys CEO Narayana Murthy (*see* BIOGRAPHIES) was compelled to address the issue.

A major factor driving IT offshoring was the vast disparity between highly paid U.S. tech workers and their counterparts in LDCs. Analysts estimated that the average Indian information technology worker earned roughly $10 per hour, 13% of his or her American counterpart's salary.

Similar factors were spurring offshoring's growth in the financial services industry, ranging from banking to insurance to securities trading. Within the past year, financial institutions in North America and Europe had increased offshoring to an average of 1,500 positions per firm, a massive increase from the 300-positions-per-firm average estimated in 2003. Surveys calculated that 80% of the world's largest financial institutions—those companies with market capitalizations of $10 billion or greater—currently had offshore operations or agreements. Among the top financial institutions with offshore operations were GE Capital, which had roughly 15,000 employees in India; HSBC, with 8,000 employees scattered around the Pacific Rim; and Citigroup, with 3,200 employees located in India, according to estimates from research firm Celent Communications.

Some observers predicted that by 2010 more than 20% of the financial industry's global cost base, approximately $400 billion, would have been outsourced to LDCs. Analysts estimated that about 2.3 million jobs in the banking and securities industries were at risk for offshoring in the next six years and predicted that in the same period about 30% of the banking industry's operations and technology spending

would shift to offshore locations. Again, the wage disparity between Western nations and LDCs was enormous. In 2003 the average Indian financial service industry employee with an MBA earned roughly 14% of his or her American equivalent's wages. Analysts estimated that the financial and insurance industries had saved $11.6 billion in the past four years via offshoring.

Is Offshoring Inevitable? Given offshoring's potential to generate massive savings, it seemed unlikely that the practice would fade any time soon. Offshoring's future was not entirely assured, however, and not every business was enamoured of the practice. Companies such as Capital One and Lehman Brothers had canceled outsourcing contracts with Indian firms, citing poor employee training, inadequate support levels, and security concerns, among other reasons. Furthermore, if more and more job losses could be attributed to offshoring practices, pressure would certainly increase for politicians to enact antioffshoring legislation.

As the standard of living improved in countries to which Western firms had exported jobs, however, that improvement in turn could diminish the savings companies gained. For example, India's daily wages were expected to rise by more than 150% by 2007, and in 2004 Indian call-centre companies were already facing high attrition rates and were being forced to raise wages and improve employee conditions. While these rising costs had made rival countries such as China (where English was mandatory in all schools) and West African nations such as Ghana more attractive offshoring prospects, American and European companies also were finding that the farther down the economic-development scale they went, the greater the potential for cultural conflicts, government corruption, and employee inefficiency.

Thus, in 2004 the practice of offshoring stood at a crossroads—it could become a primary method of doing business in the U.S. and could radically reshape the American labour market, or it could simply be a limited cost cutting trend that at some point would stop making economic sense. The years ahead would determine which scenario would prove true.

Christopher O'Leary is Assistant Managing Editor of Investment Dealers Digest.

(continued from page 177)

Hedge fund speculation played a role in an unprecedented rally in the oil market, but strong demand from a recovering global economy and supply disruptions in several nations ranging from Iraq to Russia (where government pressure shut down leading oil producer Yukos) were more substantial factors. On October 25 the benchmark contract for light sweet crude touched an all-time high of $55.67 a barrel. While oil prices eventually receded, businesses and consumers alike still suffered under the increased burden of buying fuel.

In 2003 tax cuts and low interest rates had created a catalyst for explosive economic growth. As the stimulating effects of these policies waned in 2004, however, economic expansion slowed to a more subdued but sustainable pace. The labour market remained a controversial topic throughout the year, and inflation, led by rising fuel and commodity prices, became a threat to continued economic expansion—and investor sentiment—as the year wore on.

All 10 broad stock sectors classified by Dow Jones extended their 2003 rallies in 2004, though some showed only narrow gains. Energy stocks, an obvious beneficiary of the oil boom, ended the year up 29.94% as activity increased in segments of the oil and gas industry, from the giant producers to small companies prospecting for fresh sources of supply. China's hunger for steel and other basic materials for its own economic expansion supported a 10.62% gain for commodities producers. The telecommunications sector was another of the year's winners, climbing 14.88% as investors finally overcame their reluctance to add traditional telephone stocks to their already wireless-rich portfolios. On the other hand, demand waned for technology shares, the darlings of 2003, leaving the sector up only 1.37%. Health care stocks also struggled to rise 3.21%, pulled lower by regulatory concerns and the looming expiration of key drug patents.

Within narrower segments of the market, mining companies logged the highest returns of any industry for the second year in a row, up 97.15%, followed by consumer electronics makers, which gained 73.82%. The high price of fuel translated into strong performance for oil-field-equipment stocks, as well as second-tier petroleum producers and, significantly, shares in coal-mining companies. Still, 9 of the market's 83 industrial groups—a diverse array of companies ranging from the long-suffering airlines and semiconductor manufacturers to automobile makers—lost ground in 2004.

Some of the market's largest companies struggled during the year as investors shifted their focus from traditional blue-chip stocks to more obscure names with growth potential. The Dow Jones industrials languished, while the Russell 2000 index, stuffed with small-capitalization (small-cap) growth companies, surged 17% to 651.57. The April 8 revision of the DJIA components also cooled interest in the three companies dropped from the venerable index (AT&T, Eastman Kodak, and International Paper) while fueling short-term demand for their replacements (American International Group, Pfizer, and Verizon Communications) from index fund managers and retail investors alike. (For Change in Share Price of Selected U.S. Blue-Chip Stocks, *see* TABLE VI.)

The market-timing scandal of 2003 expanded beyond a few mutual fund companies to challenge several of the foundations of the securities industry. The Securities and Exchange Commission (SEC) followed the lead of New York Attorney General Eliot Spitzer (*see* BIOGRAPHIES) by taking a more active interest in any transaction that presented financial companies with opportunities to act against the public interest. As a result, directed brokerage and other "soft dollar" practices (in which brokerage firms and mutual fund companies trade noncash compensation for preferential service or product placement) were banned. The mutual fund companies were fined more than $2 billion for various infractions, setting in motion the collapse or transformation of such venerable firms as Invesco, Pilgrim Baxter (now Liberty Ridge Capital), and Putnam Investments. Even the secretive hedge funds that initially made the controversial trades were forced to register with the SEC and abide by new rules. Meanwhile, Spitzer and the SEC turned their attention to a similar array of practices at insurance companies, uncovering a host of apparent abuses.

Although the fund families that filled the headlines suffered in the eyes of investors, the mutual fund industry overall managed to expand. Total assets under management edged up 3.6% to $7.94 trillion as of November 30, led higher by $167 billion in net inflows to stock funds and $327 billion going into sophisticated hybrid funds, which combine stock and bond investments.

Mutual funds investing primarily in large-cap stocks gained only 3.78% in 2004, substantially lagging their performance in the previous year. Funds concentrating on smaller companies delivered slightly better returns, up an average of 5.27%. The biggest U.S. stock fund by assets, the Vanguard Group's 500 Index Fund, gained 10.7% in value, while the next-largest fund, the Fidelity Group's Magellan Fund, returned 7.5%.

Closing Prices of Selected U.S. Stock Market Indexes, 2004

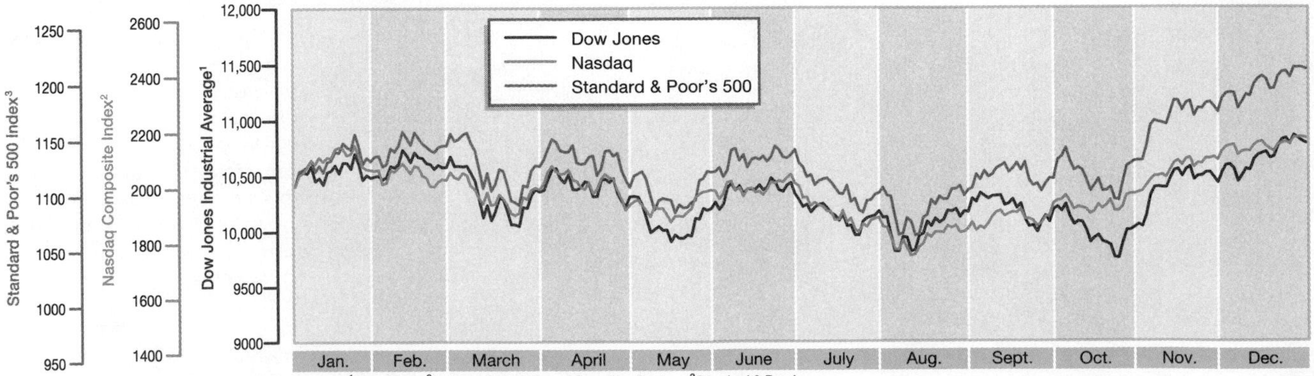

Sources: [1]Dow Jones, [2]National Association of Securities Dealers, [3]Standard & Poor's.

Table VI. Change in Share Price of Selected U.S. Blue-Chip Stocks[1] (in U.S. dollars)

Company	Starting price January 2004	Closing price year-end 2004	Percent change
General Electric Co.	30.98	36.50	17.82
ExxonMobil Corp.	41.00	51.26	25.02
Microsoft Corp.	27.37	26.72	–2.37
Citigroup, Inc.	48.54	48.18	–0.74
Wal-Mart Stores, Inc.	53.05	52.82	–0.43
Pfizer, Inc.	35.33	26.89	–23.89
Johnson & Johnson	51.66	63.42	22.76
American International Group, Inc.	66.28	65.67	–0.92
International Business Machines Corp.	92.68	98.58	6.37
Intel Corp.	32.05	23.39	–27.02
Procter & Gamble Co.[2]	49.50	55.08	11.27
J.P. Morgan Chase & Co.	36.73	39.01	6.21
Altria Group, Inc.	54.42	61.10	12.27
Verizon Communications, Inc.	35.08	40.51	15.48
Coca-Cola Co.	50.75	41.64	–17.95
Home Depot, Inc.	35.49	42.74	20.43
SBC Communications, Inc.	26.07	25.77	–1.15
American Express Co.	48.23	56.37	16.88
Merck & Co., Inc.	46.20	32.14	–30.43
3M Co.	85.03	82.07	–3.48

[1]In order of market capitalization as of Dec. 31, 2004. [2]Price adjusted for a two-for-one stock split in 2004.

An average of 1.46 billion shares changed hands every day on the New York Stock Exchange (NYSE)—a significant increase from 2003. In dollar terms, trading activity increased dramatically to $46.1 billion a day, up 20% from 2003 as retail investors cautiously returned to the market and hedge funds stepped up their activity. The number of stocks listed on the exchange held steady at 3,612 as new listings only slightly outnumbered companies being acquired or otherwise leaving the market. Market breadth for the year was decidedly mixed, with 2,358 issues ending higher, 1,235 losing ground, and 19 closing unchanged. Lucent Technologies, under CEO Patricia Russo (*see* BIOGRAPHIES), remained the most commonly traded stock, followed by Nortel Networks and General Electric.

A total of 30 of the 1,366 NYSE memberships, or "seats," changed hands in 2004, but the price of these once-exclusive commodities plunged 33% as the year progressed. On December 14 a seat brought $1,030,000, a level not seen since 1995. The generally wary tone on the exchange was echoed by an increase in short interest, by which investors bet that stocks will fall in price. Short positions on the NYSE rose 6% over the previous year to 7,715,766,807 shares. Likewise, margin borrowing, a sign of confidence, went back on the rise, pushing aggregate margin debt on the exchange to $196 billion (nearly a three-year high) by November.

Average daily volume of stocks traded on the Nasdaq stock market climbed to 1.8 billion shares, largely owing to the increased adoption of third-party electronic trading networks, and average daily dollar volume rose to $34.6 billion. Sirius Satellite Radio became the most heavily traded stock on the market, but computer-oriented shares such as Microsoft, Cisco Systems, and Intel maintained respectable trading volumes. A total of 170 companies started trading on the Nasdaq in 2004, almost triple the number of initial public offerings (IPOs) completed in 2003. The most noteworthy of these debuts, Web search engine company Google, was the largest Internet offering ever, raising $1.7 billion. Although the company, founded by Sergey Brin and Lawrence Page (*see* BIOGRAPHIES), created some confusion by bypassing Wall Street underwriters to auction off shares directly to investors, the deal still sparked renewed interest in the once-desolate IPO market. Despite the increase in new listings, the number of companies trading on the Nasdaq fell to 3,358 from 3,725 as market regulators continued to prune from the list companies that no longer met size or other requirements.

The American Stock Exchange (Amex) was the home of 1,273 issues, including a growing number of exchange-traded funds (ETFs) and other derivative investment vehicles. On average, 66 million shares a day were traded; once again, the most active security traded on the exchange continued to be the ETF equivalent of the Nasdaq 100 index.

Headlines were filled with the hunt for conflicts of interest within the securities industry on an institutional level, but on a more mundane level investors found fewer grounds for dispute in their relationships with stockbrokers and other financial advisers. The number of arbitration cases that were filed with the National Association of Securities Dealers, the market's supervisory organization, fell 8% to 7,575.

Negative factors for the bond market were numerous. Caught between rising interest rates, the threat of resurgent inflation, and a substantially weaker dollar, sophisticated investors fled from Treasury securities into higher-yielding corporate paper or the currency advantages of euro-denominated bonds.

Investors overseas became less eager to fund the massive U.S. current-account and trade deficits, both of which climbed to record levels owing to a ballooning $2.4 trillion federal budget and continued consumer demand for cheap imports. Fading foreign capital flows into dollar-denominated Treasury bonds weakened demand for the U.S. currency, pushing the dollar to four- and five-year lows against the Japanese yen and the euro, respectively. The unfavourable exchange rate in turn depressed the effective returns on Treasury bonds in terms of foreign currencies, creating a vicious circle that punished both bonds and the dollar.

Nonetheless, continued interest in Treasury paper, considered the safest investment in the world, allowed both prices and effective yields to end the year almost unchanged in dollar terms. The yield on the benchmark 10-year Treasury note ended the year at 4.22%, slightly below 2003 levels. The Lehman Aggregate bond index, which includes corporate, mortgage, and government agency securities as well as Treasury debt, ended the year up only 4.3%, only marginally above the return investors would have received from simply holding long-term government bonds. Investors looking for more substantial rewards flooded into corporate bonds, which are more speculative than securities backed by the U.S. government but offer higher interest rates. Even in the riskiest areas of the market, demand for corporate debt regardless of credit rating narrowed the gap (or spread) between high-yield junk and investment-grade bonds to a six-year low of three percentage points.

The weakness in the Treasury market was also felt in bond-oriented mutual fund holdings, but sophisticated managers still managed to eke out decent investment returns. Long-term government bond funds tracked by Morningstar gained 7.3% in 2004, but their short-term equivalents saw only a 0.93% increase in value. By contrast, bond funds with an international focus surged 8.91%. (BETH KOBLINER)

Canada. Booming commodity prices and a robust domestic economy propelled the Canadian stock market, the world's seventh largest, to its second consecutive year of positive performance. A strong Canadian dollar, however, made it difficult for manufacturing companies to export their products and left their shares from flat to lower.

As a broad measure of all stocks traded on the Toronto Stock Exchange (TSE), the S&P/TSX Composite index climbed 12.48%. The S&P/TSX 60, a basket of the exchange's biggest stocks, advanced 11.60%. Most sectors ended the year in positive territory, but returns were mixed. Winners were led by oil and gas shares, up 29%, and the continued rebound of information technology (IT) stocks, up 23%. Sectors in disfavour included health care companies, industrial manufacturers, and the gold group, which lists the majority of the world's bullion-mining concerns.

Telecommunications equipment maker Nortel Networks, by far the most widely held company on the exchange, lost 25% of its value, ending the year at Can$4.16 (Can$1 = about U.S.$0.84 at year-end 2004). Other actively traded TSE stocks included industrial conglomerate Bombardier as well as Wheaton River Minerals, which made headlines on December 23 by agreeing to merge with fellow gold miner Goldcorp.

Average daily trading reached a new record level of 242.7 million shares, up 9.9% from the previous year, while the dollar value of these trades jumped to Can$3.3 billion per day, reflecting both increased volume and higher share prices. A total of 1,421 companies were listed on the exchange at year's end, reflecting 115 IPOs.

The Canadian dollar continued to appreciate in value, reaching a 12-year high as its U.S. counterpart declined. Global demand for gold, oil, and Canada's other commodity products helped the economy grow at a surprising pace in the first half of 2004, but the strong currency and high fuel prices tempered the expansion by summer. The Bank of Canada maintained an activist stance toward interest-rate policy, lowering its official overnight-rate target three times (in January, March, and April) before raising it twice (in September and October), each by 0.25%. The rate ended the year at 2.50%.

In November the national Investment Dealers Association fined three brokerage firms a total of Can$25 million for abetting trades similar to those that drew the wrath of regulators onto the U.S. securities industry. Only about 200,000 new Canadian mutual fund accounts were opened in 2004, but total assets in such funds surged an estimated 13.3% to a new record level. (BETH KOBLINER)

Western Europe. Economic recovery in the euro zone remained sluggish, and the terrorist bombings in Madrid on March 11 further undermined business and investor confidence, adding to markets' fragility. In the aftermath, European markets were down by between 1% and 2% in early trading, following a 1.6% drop in the DJIA. Madrid's Ibex 35 lost 1.5%. Share prices also fell in Tokyo, Hong Kong, and Singapore, as well as in Sydney, Australia, and Seoul, S.Kor. Investors' risk aversion became more marked in continental Europe with the drop in share prices and spike in volatilities that followed the attacks. Later in the year the impact of the U.S. dollar's weakness on European exports caused concern.

Nevertheless, relatively high market valuations allowed companies to strengthen their balance sheets and reengage in mergers and acquisitions. Earnings had recovered substantially from 2001–02 lows, and listed companies' profits were ahead of forecasts in 2003, rising almost 100% year on year in the euro area. European stock markets closed the third quarter down 0.4% in local currency terms.

Investors tended to focus on finding European companies with exposure to China. Formal enlargement of the EU from 15 to 25 countries in May added only 5% to the region's GDP and had limited impact on the long-term growth prospects for corporate earnings.

From January to midyear, investors judged European equities fairly valued, but a brief rally at the end of the second quarter ended in July when corporate results disappointed. The IT and consumer sectors were especially weak, and the IT sector was afflicted by doubts over the strength of the pickup in technology spending. The big markets of the U.K., France, and Germany were lacklustre. During the year, the S&P Europe index of 350 stocks rose by less than 9%, with the French CAC 40 and the German Xetra DAX up 7.4% and 7.3%, respectively (all in euro terms), and the FTSE 100 up 7.5% in sterling terms. Many smaller European markets did far better. (*See* TABLE V.)

Other Countries. Investment growth turned upward in most regions during the year. Before a brief sell-off in late January, equity prices in emerging markets outperformed most other markets. Improved fundamentals and high levels of liquidity supported investor confidence. Although overall performance of emerging markets was strong, from the end of the first quarter through late May, major emerging stock markets fell sharply, following the pattern of the major stock markets of the advanced economies and indicating substantial correlation between markets. The downturn was driven in part by uncertainty about the impact of oil-price rises, as well as the effects on emerging economies of weaker-than-expected recovery in the major economies.

Asian markets, which had performed strongly in 2003, were weaker in 2004. In the first half of the year, investors worried about possible overheating in the Chinese economy, the impact of high oil prices, and the direction of U.S. official interest rates. From mid-April the equity market sell-off was by far the sharpest in Japan and other Asian markets. The Japanese markets were particularly volatile in May. Although in the first quarter the strength of Japan's recovery exceeded expectations, the announcement on May 13 of lower-than-expected machinery orders prompted a 2% drop in the Nikkei 225 index. In the third quarter the Nikkei lost 9.6% when a disappointing second-quarter GDP result was published. By the end of July, the TOPIX was up 3.8%, and the index ended the year up 13% in dollar terms (10.2% in yen terms). The Nikkei ended July up 0.7% and ended the year up 10.7% in dollar terms (7.6% in yen terms). India's Sensex and Hong Kong's Hang Seng index each rose more than 13%, while China's previously strong Shanghai and Shenzhen composite indexes plunged 15.2% and 16.5%, respectively.

The strong performance of Latin America in the third quarter took many investors by surprise. The MSCI Latin America index jumped 17% in dollar terms over the third quarter, with a range of 4% for Mexico to 28% for Argentina. Brazil rose 17%. The rally led to a return for the MSCI Latin Amer-

Pedestrians pass a stock market sign board in Tokyo on May 10. Japan's Nikkei stock index was down by 210.49 points at the time of the photo and was especially volatile in May, but it finished the year up 7.6% in yen terms.

AP/Wide World Photos

ica index of 39.8% over 12 months and of 38.7% for the S&P Latin America 40 (in dollar terms). The region easily outperforming developed stock markets and the Asia-Pacific region.

Commodities. Prices trended up over the year, boosted by demand for raw materials from China. After more than a decade of relatively low prices for their goods, minerals and metals producers enjoyed an outstandingly good year. On December 1 the Reuters-CRB index, a basket of 17 commodity futures tracked by investors, hit a 23-year high.

Oil took centre stage. Speculation by noncommercial traders—including institutional investors and hedge funds—was blamed for much of the increase in price during 2004. As most other markets began to lose steam through the year, traders turned their attention to commodities in general—and oil in particular. Speculative activity rose sharply in expectation of higher prices. By late November, U.S. crude prices were still around $49 a barrel, although $6 down from late October's record, as the highest OPEC production in 25 years rebuilt stocks in consuming countries.

In late November, as the dollar fell to a record low against the euro, gold reached $450 a troy ounce for the first time since June 1988. Global gold equity indexes moved less strongly, on fears that the rally was not sustainable. Consumer demand for gold in the second quarter of 2004 rose 25% in dollar terms as gold reclaimed safe-haven status and a weaker dollar made dollar-denominated gold cheaper for holders of other currencies, especially the euro.

Even coffee, after four years of prices so depressed that many growers abandoned the crop, made a substantial, if still fragile, recovery. The price rose from an average of 48 cents a pound in 2002 to an average of 60.8 cents a pound in March 2004.

The *Economist* Commodity Price All Items Dollar index ended 2004 up 1.8%. According to the index, food was down 2.9%, with metals (21.1%), oil (34.1%), and gold (6.5%) up. (IEIS)

BUSINESS OVERVIEW

For the U.S. economy 2004 was a year with two faces. At times the economy seemed to have shed the last traces of the past recession, yet it also seemed to be bogged down throughout the year; the annual growth rate of gross domestic product fell to 3.5% by late 2004 after having been on a 5% pace earlier in the year. Job losses waned and waxed with each month, and many sectors contended with serious price hikes. The health of the economy became a central issue of the U.S. presidential campaign as Pres. George W. Bush pointed to indicators of economic recovery while his Democratic challenger, Sen. John Kerry, cited continued layoffs as a sign that the economy was still fragile. Each candidate had plenty of evidence to bolster his case. (*See* WORLD AFFAIRS: *United States:* Special Report.) The outsourcing of jobs to less-developed countries was also a significant economic issue in the campaign, and the number of jobs being outsourced from the United States continued to increase during the year. (*See* Special Report.)

Although price inflation hit sectors that ranged from steel production to titanium mining, no industry was more defined by high prices in 2004 than the energy industry. Producers of oil and gas, coal-mining concerns, and other energy companies benefited from skyrocketing prices. Crude-oil prices rose above $55 per barrel in late October, the highest price posted since the New York Mercantile Exchange began trading oil in 1983. Oil prices, historically adjusted, remained below their all-time highs of the early 1980s; nevertheless, they translated into pain for consumers. Gasoline prices in the U.S., for example, remained above $2 per gallon for most of 2004. The price hikes had a number of causes, including low producer inventories and unstable global conditions. Energy traders said that fears about global conditions at times created a $10-per-barrel risk premium in oil-futures trading. Even OPEC, which for decades had been able to control oil prices, proved powerless to manage prices in 2004. Few analysts expected any halt to the rise of oil prices in the short term. Demand was being driven by China's growing thirst for oil, which at 5.5 million bbl a day was second only to that of the U.S., and supply remained tight; in 2004 spare oil-pumping capacity, which was about one million barrels per day, was no greater than what it was in 1973, but the demand for oil had risen by 44% since then.

Despite being flooded with cash, few oil companies were pushing to find new drilling opportunities. The six global oil "supermajors," including ExxonMobil and TotalFina Elf, were expected to gain $138 billion in cash flow in 2004, up 28% from 2003, but at the same time, the capital spending by these companies was expected to rise only 8%. Top oil companies concentrated instead on selling off poorly performing assets and buying back shares. Some analysts predicted an increase in exploration activity in 2005, since energy firms gained a tax break in October 2004 for the domestic production of oil and gas, but many analysts expected most new activity to come from low-risk efforts to boost production at existing sites.

Not all top oil producers flourished in 2004, however. Notably, Royal Dutch/Shell Group revealed that it had been greatly overstating its oil and gas reserves, and in January it reduced its proven reserves by 22%—by nearly four billion barrels, which was worth about $400 million. The subsequent shock to its stock value, along with lawsuits and government probes, caused Shell's board to oust its chairman, Sir Philip Watts, and the company's head of exploration and production, Walter van de Vijver. After he was sacked, van de Vijver claimed that he had been warning Shell officials since 2001 that reserve levels were being inflated. Buoyed by increased revenues from price hikes as the year went on, Shell managed to control the crisis and in August settled with the U.K.'s Financial Services Authority and the U.S. Securities and Exchange Commission without admitting or denying its responsibility for the overbooking.

Other top oil companies were not so lucky. Yukos, which was Russia's largest oil producer and accounted for 2% of global oil production, spent 2004 in a desperate fight for its life. Following the jailing of Yukos founder Mikhail Khodorkovsky for fraud and tax evasion in October 2003, the Russian government claimed that Yukos owed back taxes that at times were estimated to be in the $28 billion range. Yukos maintained that it could not make those payments. In December the Russian government sold off the company's major production facilities to the previously unknown BaikalFinansGroup, and it was expected to continue to dismember the company in 2005. In what appeared to be a last bid to avoid destruction, Yukos filed for bankruptcy protection in a Texas court, though Yukos's argument that its Houston-based banking accounts qualified it as having a presence in the U.S. and thus having protection under U.S. laws was immediately challenged. Despite this turmoil, Western oil companies increased their involvement in Russia. In September ConocoPhillips paid nearly $2 billion for the government's stake in Lukoil, which was Russia's second largest oil producer.

Electric utilities had disparate results, since many utilities had to contend with the high production costs caused by soaring oil prices and a doubling of the price of coal. Some companies, having cleaned up their balance sheets and sold off underperforming units, greatly outperformed analyst expectations. TXU Corp., for example, posted a 69% increase in net income in the third quarter of 2004 compared with the same period in 2003. Profits fell, however, for a number of other utilities, including Northeast Utilities, Duquesne Light Holdings, Ameren, and Xcel Energy. (*See* Sidebar.)

The airline industry was defined by bankruptcies, labour battles, and rising costs, as it had been since 2001. Rising costs in particular were a serious problem for many airlines, crippling the slight recoveries some carriers had enjoyed early in 2004. Airlines typically needed oil prices to be no more than $33 per barrel to break even, so it was a serious blow when prices soared to the $40–$50-per-barrel range for most of the year.

Few domestic carriers ended 2004 in good shape. United Airlines remained under bankruptcy protection, having failed to win federal loan guarantees; US Airways filed for bankruptcy for the second time in two years in September, and it indicated that unless it won major labour concessions, it would have to start to liquidate its assets in early 2005. Even discount airlines were not immune, as ATA Airlines filed for bankruptcy in October. Delta Airlines, which unlike most of its competitors had fairly easily weathered the economic storm following the terrorist attacks of Sept. 11, 2001, flirted with bankruptcy throughout the year. It entered into desperate negotiations with its unions to stave off collapse and planned to lay off 12% of its workforce. Delta had posted losses of $5.6 billion since 2001 and had piled up more than $20 billion in debt. Were Delta to file for bankruptcy, about 42% of the American air-carrier industry would be under court protection.

Aircraft producers were in no better shape. The Boeing Co. still trailed its European rival Airbus in the construction of commercial jets and spent much of the year embroiled in scandal as a former top U.S. Air Force weapons buyer, Darleen Druyun—who later became a Boeing executive—admitted that she had favoured Boeing in rewarding air force contracts and that Boeing would not have won some bids without her influence. Boeing rivals such as Lockheed Martin Corp. called for further investigations into past Boeing deals, and analysts predicted that Boeing would ultimately have to pay substantial fines and possibly face strong third-party monitoring.

Domestic carmakers had a tumultuous year, the result of sporadic sales hindered by rising gasoline prices and overproduction, estimated at 14 million vehicles. As of September, total year-to-date American auto sales were down 5.6% compared with 2003. Car sales were down 2.4% from previous-year totals, although light-truck sales were up 12.4%. The Big Three American carmakers continued to lag behind their foreign competitors in terms of profitability. Toyota Motor Corp., for example, earned about 10 times as much per vehicle as General Motors Corp. (GM), while Ford Motor Co. and DaimlerChrysler posted losses per vehicle because of aggressive discounting. The Big Three were giving up to $5,000 in discounts per car, while their Japanese rivals were providing only up to one-half that figure.

Another growing problem for American carmakers was the increased burden of their massive pension and employee medical programs. GM, which covered the health care costs of 1.1 million current and former employees and could face $68 billion in retirement health care costs over the next few decades, had annual health care spending of $5.1 billion in 2004, compared with $3 billion in 1996. Ford's obligations rose to an average of $12,443 per worker, compared with an inflation-adjusted figure of $2,300 per employee in 1970. Health care costs for Japanese carmakers were nowhere near as high.

Ford, under the leadership of Bill Ford Jr. (Henry Ford's great-grandson), moved away from volume-oriented to value-oriented business strategies, and it saw a combination of dwindling market share and increasing revenues. Ford's American market share as of September was 11.7%, less than Toyota's 14.5% share and down from Ford's 25.4% market share a decade before. Although its market share had dwindled, Ford rebounded financially. The company posted $537 million in earnings for the third quarter of 2004,

Mikhail Khodorkovsky, former head of the Yukos oil company and once one of Russia's richest people, finds himself behind bars in a Moscow court in August under investigation by the Russian Tax Ministry.

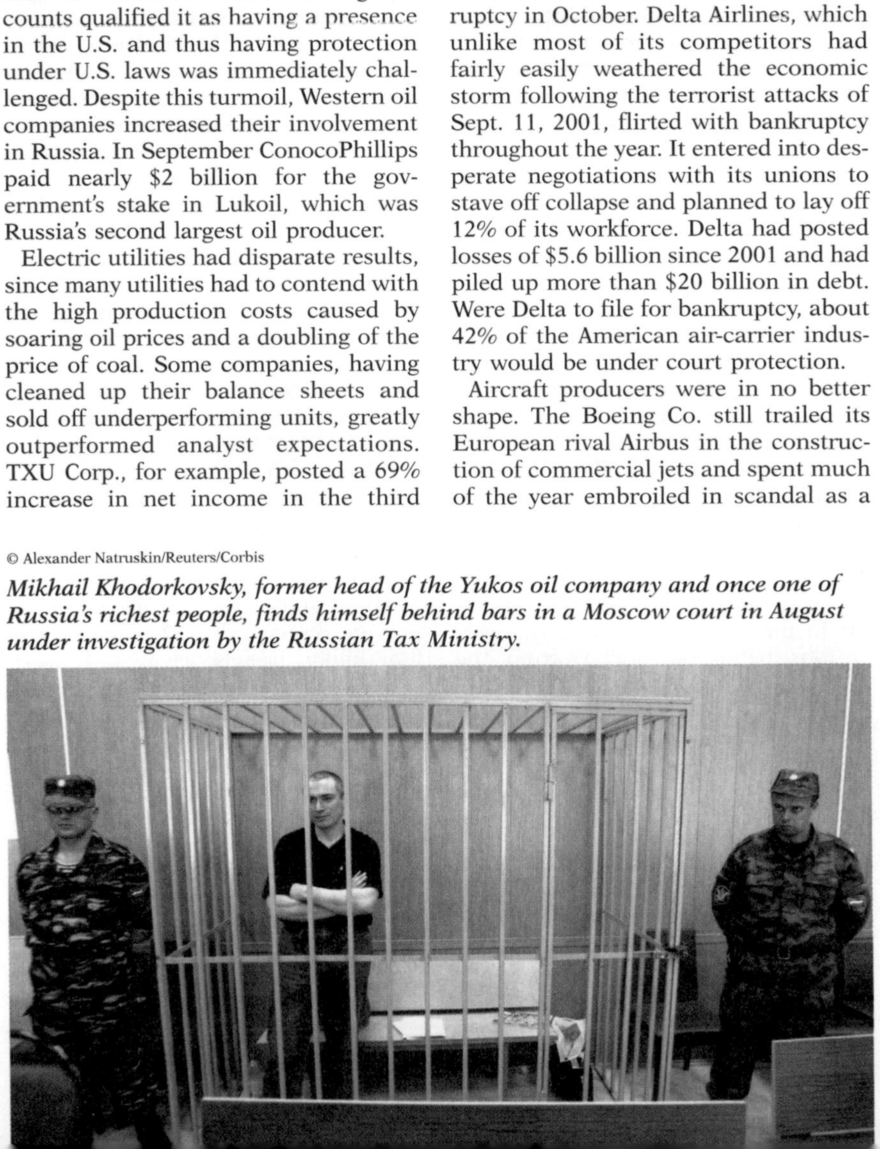

compared with $242 million in the same period in 2003. Ford also took steps to shore up its troubled European operations by slashing jobs at its underperforming Jaguar unit.

GM remained the world's largest carmaker, but it had a troubled year. Its third-quarter earnings fell short of analysts' expectations—$440 million, compared with $448 million in the third quarter of 2003. Worse, a large part of these earnings came from GM's lending operations, since its automotive operations lost $130 million, one of its worst performances in a decade. GM also suffered from declines in its European businesses (posting a $236 million loss in the third quarter alone). To reduce expenses, GM slashed 12,000 jobs in Europe and mandated that its global units standardize parts and design cars so that they could be sold in any country with few alterations—a break from GM's long tradition of giving overseas units a fair degree of autonomy. GM also tried to push into new markets such as China, where it planned to spend up to $3 billion by 2007 to beef up production, particularly of luxury cars. Analysts estimated that China could provide 20% of the Cadillac customer base by 2010.

DaimlerChrysler had a successful year. It hammered out an agreement with the United Auto Workers in which the union agreed to a two-tier pay scale and some outsourcing, and DaimlerChrysler posted a $1.21 billion profit for the third quarter of 2004. Analysts said that there were promising signs for the carmaker's future growth—for one thing, its upcoming product line was the freshest of the Big Three, since it was expected that 88% of its volume would be replaced by 2008, compared with 66% for Ford and GM. Yet the corporation did not escape controversy. In April DaimlerChrysler chose not to bail out troubled Mitsubishi Motors, of which it was the largest shareholder. It was a blow to CEO Jürgen Schrempp, who had been a strong advocate of increasing DaimlerChrysler's ownership of global competitors such as Mitsubishi and Hyundai.

Japanese carmakers put in stronger performances on the whole than their American counterparts but faced their own share of troubles. Mitsubishi was left reeling after DaimlerChrysler declined to extend it cash, and it devised a restructuring plan that would entail cutting more than 10,000 jobs. Honda's net income cratered owing to slumping sales in North America. Other Japanese carmakers had a sunnier year, none more so than Toyota. Toyota cemented its position as the world's second largest carmaker, and it was the most profitable; the company reported $2.5 billion in net income for the second quarter of 2004, more than the profits of GM and Ford combined. Toyota benefited from an increase in sales worldwide (Asian sales alone shot up 65% over 2003), and it was set on achieving a 15% global market share by the end of the decade, up from its current 10% position.

By contrast, many European carmakers had an indifferent-to-down year, and some undertook major renovations to improve their businesses. Volkswagen, which saw its net profit fall 65% in the third quarter, planned to further increase its Chinese operations, and it hired Wolfgang Bernhard, a former top official at Chrysler, to revive its depressed auto business. Volkswagen was the largest foreign carmaker in China and was planning to open a $240 million factory there to step up production.

The Alarming State of the U.S. Electricity Grid

The massive power blackout of Aug. 14, 2003, which affected the midwestern and northeastern United States and parts of Canada, highlighted the precarious condition of the U.S. electricity grid, but a full year after the blackout, only recommendations but no new regulations or major changes to the grid's infrastructure had been made. The U.S. electricity grid, which was described by former U.S. energy secretary Bill Richardson after the 2003 blackout as a "third-world electrical grid," was widely considered to be overburdened and in serious need of new infrastructure. For many years it had suffered sporadic failures, ranging from major blackouts to the minor brownouts that had become commonplace during summer months, especially in the West. Furthermore, during the previous 10 years the demand for electric power in the United States had grown at the same time that the nature of delivering electrical power had radically changed as policies for the deregulation of the electric power industry were implemented. With deregulation, independent suppliers began delivering most of the electric power to utility companies and, for economic reasons, could contract to deliver the electric power from distant locations. Thus, a utility that owned a segment of the electricity grid often served more as a conduit for transmitting electric power between third parties than as a supplier of electric power to its own customers.

Much of the infrastructure for transmitting electric power in the United States was built in the 1960s and early '70s, and few significant improvements had been made since. Estimates of the cost to upgrade the grid lay between $50 billion and $100 billion. Individual utility companies had little incentive to make large-scale investments to improve their segments of the grid for several reasons, including a confusing mix of government regulations and deregulation policies for the utilities and the patchwork nature of the grid that resulted from its being owned by a host of competing regional utilities. Government regulations mandated a cap on the rate of return for many utilities and on the amount they could charge consumers, which thereby limited—in the utilities' view—their ability to recoup costs for any major structural improvements they might make. In addition, the organizations that oversaw the electricity grid, such as the utility industry's North American Electric Reliability Council (NERC) and the government's Federal Energy Regulatory Commission (FERC), had little power to enforce their own recommendations.

A joint U.S. and Canadian task force established to examine the causes of the August 2003 blackout issued a report in April 2004 that called for such reforms as making reliability standards mandatory (thereby giving FERC greater power to enforce the standards), increasing the role of regional reliability councils, and improving the data collection and cooperation of various regional utilities. Despite the favourable attention these recommendations received, various energy bills concerning electric power languished in subcommittees of the House of Representatives. Lacking any federal legislation for energy-related reform in 2004, the U.S. electricity grid was left in essentially the same condition it was in at the time of the 2003 blackout.

(CHRISTOPHER O'LEARY)

China was a major factor in the battering of the American textile sector, and American textile companies were bracing for an event that could shatter the domestic industry. On Jan. 1, 2005, a 40-year-old system of quotas on Chinese-made clothing was to end, and many expected Chinese manufacturers to flood the U.S. with inexpensive apparel. The World Trade Organization estimated that once the quotas ended, Chinese apparel would account for 50% of American textile imports, up from roughly 16% in 2004. Saying that the import wave could cost hundreds of thousands of jobs, American textile makers ferociously lobbied the Bush administration for renewed protections.

Many textile makers engaged in desperate pricing strategies to push up sagging revenues. Levi Strauss & Co., for example, launched a new line of jeans, the price of which was half that of its core lines. Levi Strauss had shuttered all its American operations and had cut more than 75% of its staff. Other humbled former giants in the American textile industry had chosen to be acquired by private investment groups. Galey & Lord Inc. filed for bankruptcy for a second time as part of its acquisition by buyout firm Patriarch Partners. Cone Mills and Guilford Mills undertook similar moves.

The American steel industry, which had come close to collapse just a few years earlier, was in the midst of a rebirth. Solid years were posted by the new top steelmakers, including U.S. Steel Corp., which returned to profitability in the first quarter and kept going strong throughout the year. The greatest transformation came in October, however, when International Steel Group (ISG), which had gone public in December 2003, was sold to the Mittal family. The family, which was from India and had interests in steel mills in 14 countries, planned to merge ISG with the steel companies it already owned—Ispat International and LNM Group—to form the world's largest steel company.

Steelmakers around the globe benefited from a tide of rising steel prices that lifted every boat in the harbour. The price of domestic hot-rolled steel was $650 a ton late in the summer of 2004, compared with $260 a ton the year before. Behind this price wave was one key factor—China, whose insatiable demand for steel (about double the annual production of steel in the U.S.) was so great that some producers revived long-shuttered steel mills to meet production needs. A series of strikes at several North American mines also affected prices.

A worker cuts slabs of steel at an International Steel Group plant in Cleveland, Ohio, in July. ISG was sold to an international group in October, a major development in the growing globalization of the steel industry.

AP/Wide World Photos

As the ISG merger demonstrated, however, American steelmakers might soon have to decide whether to go global. Competition was increasing. Luxembourg's Arcelor bought a stake in a major Brazilian crude-steel producer, CST, and planned to transfer much of its production from Europe to Brazil in order to cut costs, a move that would transform Brazil into a top steel-producing nation. China both boosted steel prices and presented a growing threat to American steelmakers. China's top steelmaker, Shanghai Baosteel Corp., was rapidly expanding its production capability and, unlike its American competitors, did not have to deal with pension-related costs. In addition, it was backed by generous government support.

The price of aluminum rose through the year, hitting a nine-year high in 2004, and inflated prices were expected to be the norm for the next two years, with estimates for 2005 of about $1,730 per metric ton. The American annual rate of production as of September was 2.5 million metric tons, down 7.7% from the 2003 annual rate of 2.7 million metric tons. Top producers such as Alcan pursued ambitious plans to expand market share. Alcan, which had purchased Pechiney in late 2003, planned to spin off its rolled-products assets to resolve antitrust issues with regulators. The newly formed company, called Novelis, would become the world's largest producer of aluminum rolled products.

Long-term high prices were reached in almost every metals sector, from platinum (which hit a 24-year high) to titanium (up 100% over 2003) to silver (which reached a 17-year high). The price of gold had risen 50% in the past two years and hit $458 per troy ounce, a 16-year high, late in the year. For much of the year, the price remained above the $400 mark, a psychologically important achievement that spurred investors' belief that gold's price run would extend for some time. (There were signs late in the year, however, that metal prices had peaked.)

The allure of high gold prices led to ambitious maneuvering in the gold-mining sector. Russia's top metal company, Norilsk Nickel, in March purchased a 20% stake in Gold Fields, a major South African mining company, and became its largest shareholder. A tentative merger agreement between Gold Fields and Canada's Iamgold (which had failed to buy Wheaton River Minerals) was challenged by Harmony Gold Mining, which in October launched a hostile takeover bid for Gold Fields. Norilsk supported the hostile bid against the wishes of other Gold Fields shareholders. If the Harmony–Gold Fields merger succeeded, it would create the largest gold producer in the world, knocking leader Newmont Mining into second place.

The paper-and-timber industry slowly recovered from the malaise of the past few years. The weak U.S. dollar helped a number of American paper companies to achieve better cost structures for exports, while Canadian paper manufacturers, which exported 80% of Canada's paper shipments to the U.S., improved their profitability. Many storied paper companies, however, spent the year looking for ways to cut their ties to traditional paper manufacturing. Boise Cascade Corp. sold off its paper- and timber-manufacturing assets to private-equity investment firm Madison Dearborn in July and decided to concentrate on its Office Max office-supplies retail chain, which it had purchased in 2003. Louisiana Pacific Corp. also sold off its remaining timber assets.

Many chemical companies scrambled to compete with the largest American chemical maker, Dow Chemical Co., which had slashed its workforce by 7% in 2003 and had embarked on a campaign of aggressive cost cutting. Lyondell Chemical Co.'s $2.3 billion acquisition of Millennium Chemicals Inc., which created the third largest publicly held chemical company in North America, was completed in response to Dow's growing threat. DuPont Co. planned to cut about 6% of its workforce by the end of the year—in response, it said, to the rise in natural gas prices and its desire to push into faster-growing markets, such as South America and Asia. Also in 2004, U.S. and European prosecutors stepped up investigations into alleged price-fixing by top chemical companies.

At long last the hotel sector appeared to have recovered from the post-9/11 collapse of the travel industry. Top American hotel operator Marriott International Inc. posted third-quarter profits that showed a 45% increase compared with the same period in 2003 as its room rates increased faster than occupancy for the first time since 9/11. Revenue per available room, the primary measure of fiscal health for the industry, rose by 8.3% for North American hotels in the third quarter, and international customers at American hotels rose by 21%—a sign that tourism and business travel had resumed its normal pace.

A number of hoteliers, including Choice Hotels, Starwood Hotels & Resorts, and InterContinental Hotels Group, planned new boutique chains that offered relatively cheap rooms ($100 or less a night) with improved amenities—a sort of "business-class" hotel. These new boutique hotels were meant to trump rivals such as Hilton Hotels and Best Western in the bid for the business traveler's dollar, as many market players believed the hotel industry might be oversaturated and highly competitive in the next few years. It was expected that about 100,000 new rooms would be built in 2005, up from 75,000 in 2004.

Other industries remained embroiled in scandals and political battles. Tobacco manufacturers underwent yet another round of lawsuits and investigations, years after a $250 billion manufacturer settlement with U.S. state governments. This time the federal government led the charge. In September the case brought by the Department of Justice opened against Philip Morris, R.J. Reynolds, and Brown & Williamson. The case alleged that the companies, by colluding to downplay and hide smoking risks, had violated the Racketeer Influenced and Corrupt Organizations (RICO) Act, a statute that heretofore had usually been applied against organized crime. The federal government sought to have the companies return about $280 billion in profits. Besieged by such cases and losing market share to importers and to discount cigarette manufacturers (whose market share had risen since 1977 from 2% to 12%), top cigarette manufacturers considered accepting the once unthinkable—Food and Drug Administration (FDA) jurisdiction over tobacco products. Tobacco manufacturers sought a compromise; they would accept government regulation (which would include such changes as reduced marketing, greater disclosure of health hazards, and limits on tar and nicotine content) in exchange for the end of 60-year-old production quotas that had kept domestic crop prices high. The tobacco industry achieved an enormous victory, however, when lawmakers stripped out the FDA regulation requirements during negotiations to draft the final $10.1 billion quota buyout bill (which had been attached to a massive corporate tax-cutting bill). The bill, which was signed into law by President Bush in October, provided roughly $9.6 billion in compensation to tobacco growers in exchange for the end, after the 2004 growing season, of the federal programs regulating tobacco production.

The insurance industry was roiled when New York Attorney General Eliot Spitzer (*see* BIOGRAPHIES) began probes into fraud and bid rigging in the insurance industry. In particular, he investigated allegations that Marsh & McLennan, the world's biggest insurance broker, had received payments from insurance companies in exchange for sending client business to insurers and that the firm had concocted false bids. In October Spitzer announced that he was suing Marsh in civil court and that two executives at insurer American International Group had pleaded guilty to bid rigging.

The pharmaceuticals industry also bore the brunt of political attacks throughout 2004. Drug pricing was a critical issue during the presidential campaign, with Democratic candidate Kerry excoriating large drug companies for high prices. American demand for cheaper Canadian drugs at times led to shortages in Canada, and some Canadian drug sellers began importing drugs from countries with even tighter price controls, such as Australia, to meet demand. Nevertheless, in trade negotiations during the summer, the U.S. sought increased protections against foreign generic-drug manufacturers.

Brand-name drugmakers relied on the strategy of having a few "blockbuster" drugs generate the lion's share of their revenues and of creating variations of such drugs in order to replace market share when the initial drug went generic. By relying on a core of therapeutic drugs for revenues, however, drugmakers were increasingly at risk when a particular cash-cow drug encountered controversy. The company that presented the most notable example of this situation in 2004 was Merck, which had to pull its successful painkiller Vioxx from store shelves after it acknowledged that the drug had a host of dangerous side effects, including an increased risk of heart attacks and strokes. Merck had spent tens of millions of dollars to advertise Vioxx, which had racked up sales of $2.5 billion in 2003, roughly 11% of Merck's total revenues. Analysts speculated that Merck, deprived of its Vioxx revenues and faced with many consumer lawsuits, could be the target of a hostile takeover or could be forced into a defensive merger.

Merger activity in the pharmaceuticals industry was heavy. French drugmaker Sanofi-Synthelabo won a $65 billion takeover bid for its French-German rival, Aventis, to create the world's third largest drug company. The merger, which was encouraged by the French government, might benefit from the success of a new drug created by Aventis that combatted both obesity and smoking. Bayer bought the over-the-counter-drug business of Swiss conglomerate Roche to create the world's largest nonprescription drugmaker.

Some generic drug manufacturers decided to join forces with their former competitors. The second largest generic manufacturer, Mylan Laboratories, took steps to acquire King Pharmaceuticals in a $4 billion deal that would enable Mylan to break into the branded-drug business. In a variation on the theme, branded-drug manufacturer GlaxoSmithKline signed deals with generic manufacturers to produce authorized generic versions of its former patent-protected drugs, such as Paxil.

(CHRISTOPHER O'LEARY)

Education

Gender equality, childhood OBESITY, the role of RELIGION and PATRIOTISM in schools, voucher programs, HIGH DROPOUT RATES, rising TEXTBOOK COSTS, the integration of 10 new European Union member states in the existing EU EDUCATIONAL SYSTEM, and the expansion of EXTENSION UNIVERSITIES were some of the key concerns of educators in 2004.

PRIMARY AND SECONDARY EDUCATION

By 2004, 52 of the 128 countries for which statistics were available had reached the goal to ensure that by 2005 the proportion of girls attending school would be the same as that of boys. A total of 164 governments at the 2000 World Education Forum in Dakar, Senegal, had endorsed the UNESCO initiative "Gender and Education for All: The Leap to Equality." Though the 76 remaining countries would miss the 2005 deadline, 22 of them were still on track to achieve parity at both the elementary- and secondary-school levels by 2015. There were 54 countries—many in sub-Saharan Africa and East Asia—that would not likely reach parity by 2015.

Though the United States achieved a record enrollment of 74.6 million students, encompassing nursery school through college, Pres. George W. Bush's nationwide education program, "No Child Left Behind," completed its third year of operation with a mixture of successes and problems. Many schools improved student scores on reading and mathematics tests, and tutoring services were being provided for thousands of students who had performed poorly on tests. On the downside, the same achievement goal was set for all students, despite differences between them in ability, family background, and home language; subjects other than reading and mathematics were increasingly neglected; only 2% of students from schools with low test scores took advantage of the opportunity to move to higher-scoring schools; and more than 20 states denounced the program for being inadequately funded by the federal government.

Alarmed by a rapid increase in childhood obesity, schools in various nations took steps to improve students' eating and exercise habits. In recent years the rise in students' consumption of junk foods (foods high in sugar and fat and low in nutritional value) had been accompanied by a decline in physical activity. As a result, more youths grew seriously overweight. A survey of 30,000 students in 15 industrialized countries revealed that the United States had a higher rate of teenage obesity than did the other 14 nations. Nearly 15% of 15-year-old Americans were obese, an increase from 5% in 1970. In addition, 31% of girls and 28% of boys were moderately overweight. This rise in obesity was paralleled by increased childhood diabetes, high blood pressure, and sleep apnea. Other nations that ranked high in adolescent obesity were Greece, Portugal, Israel, Ireland, and Denmark. A study in Japan showed that the proportion of overweight sixth-grade boys rose from 6.7% in 1977 to 11.7% in 2002.

Attempts to curb obesity included banning the sale of unhealthful foods at schools (e.g., sodas, candy, and potato chips), improving the quality of school lunches, teaching wholesome nutritional practices, and advocating more individual physical activities. The most controversial of these was the effort to eliminate the sale of carbonated drinks. School districts had often awarded contracts to soda distributors to sell soft drinks at schools in exchange for a share of the profits. Consequently, school officials often were unwilling to prohibit the sale of sodas at schools. For example, four Alabama high schools that had received $190,000 in a single year from soda sales would lose those funds if vending machines were outlawed. The problem was serious in other countries as well. In China between 1993 and 2004, the Coca-Cola Co. donated $4.2 million to charity projects, including college scholarships for rural students and

Arkansas Gov. Mike Huckabee hoists a Little Rock fifth-grader onto his back to illustrate the amount of weight he had recently lost and the dangers of obesity in children, as reported in a recent statewide study. Childhood obesity was of growing concern throughout the U.S. as well as in Japan and other countries.

AP/Wide World Photos

© Jean-Paul Pelissier/Reuters/Corbis

In January in Marseille, a Mediterranean city with a large North African population, a group of Muslim women hold up the French flag to protest an imminent government ban on the wearing in schools of overtly religious symbols such as Islamic women's head scarves.

funds for building 52 primary schools and more than 100 libraries.

Controversies over religion and patriotism in schools continued in France, Italy, India, Japan, and the U.S. In both France and Italy, growing numbers of non-Christian residents challenged the continuation of Christian traditions in public schools. In France school authorities objected to female Islamic students' wearing head scarves, and the authorities claimed that such apparel represented a religious statement in secular public schools. Islamic leaders, representing France's five million Muslims, responded by charging that Catholic students were allowed to wear crosses. The National Assembly voted to ban Islamic head scarves, Jewish yarmulkes, large Christian crosses, and some other religious symbols in public schools. In 2003 an Islamic activist in Italy filed a lawsuit over the legality of the display of a Christian cross in the school that his two sons attended. When a judge ordered the crucifix removed, the matter became the focus of nationwide debate in Italy's secular but culturally Catholic society; a 1923 law still required public schools to exhibit a cross.

In India the defeat in May of the ruling Hindu nationalist Bharatiya Janata Party (BJP) by the United Progressive Alliance coalition led to the appointment of a panel of historians that was assigned to remove the pervasive discussion of Hindu culture, traditions, and values (such as using astrology to predict earthquakes and other natural disasters) that had been a part of secondary-school textbooks since 1998, when the BJP came to power.

Japanese officials in March ordered the punishment of teachers who failed to stand during secondary-school graduation ceremonies for the singing of the anthem "Kimigayo" ("His Majesty's Reign"), which in 1999 had been declared by law to be the Japanese national anthem. The order was issued after some 200 teachers refused to stand and sing "Kimigayo" because they felt that the anthem and the national flag were too closely linked to Japan's traditional imperial system and militarist past. The teachers contended that the ruling unfairly restricted their constitutional freedom of thought and conscience.

In the U.S. the question of whether the phrase "under God" could remain legally in the Pledge of Allegiance went unanswered. An atheist challenged before the U.S. Supreme Court the addition of that phrase, which Congress had added to the oath after the word *nation* in 1954, despite protests that it violated the principle of keeping religion out of public schooling. He claimed that his daughter's rights were being violated by her school's requirement that she include the "under God" portion of the oath. The court rejected the father's challenge, but only on the procedural grounds that he was not qualified to represent his daughter's welfare.

The popularity of school-voucher programs in the U.S. increased as more students were awarded private or public funds to pay their way at a school of their choice, including private schools sponsored by religious orders. Whereas there was little or no opposition to privately funded vouchers, publicly financed voucher programs often led to impassioned controversy; critics charged that such plans violated the nation's traditional separation of church and state. Proponents of financing vouchers with tax money won support for their cause in early 2004 when the Republican-controlled Congress approved a voucher plan for the District of Columbia. In addition, President Bush asked Congress to provide $50 million for a national pilot program that would allow children to attend private and religious schools at federal taxpayers' expense.

As a step toward universal schooling in India, a three-and-a-half-year, $3.5 billion project aimed to reduce by at least nine million the number of children who were out of school, to narrow gender and social gaps, and to improve the quality of education. The ultimate goal of India's effort was to ensure that all children aged 6 to 14 had eight years of education. Though the number of out-of-school children had already been reduced from 39 million to 25 million between 1999 and 2003, India still accounted for one-fourth of the world's 104 million children not in school.

Pupils' dropping out of school at an early age was cited as a factor contributing to nations' lagging behind in social and economic progress. The Mexican government reported that 300,000 children annually dropped out of school after the sixth grade. As a result, by age 14 the average Mexican student was no longer in school. Nearly one-third of 12th-year South Australian students left school without earning a graduation certificate, a fact that prompted educational planners to wonder if the certificate requirements were too strongly oriented toward university studies and thereby neglected skills useful in the nation's basic workforce. In India and Pakistan 50% of children dropped out of school before completing the fifth grade; enrollment for girls in Pakistan declined from 61% in primary school to 33% in middle school and to 20% in secondary school. Pressure on schools to earn high test-score results was cited as an important cause of dropouts in both the U.K. and the U.S. Observers suggested that a portion of the estimated 100,000 students who annually left British schools were "push-outs," those whose poor test scores led school officials to either neglect or harass them until they dropped out. In Boston nearly 25% of high-school students departed without a diploma, and in North Carolina 20% of ninth graders left school poorly equipped to find satisfying employment in an increasingly high-tech economy.

In Canada a lack of consistent upkeep was blamed for the crumbling of school buildings in Ontario that would require $4.2 billion for repair or replacement. Rioting students in Kenya continued to burn and demolish dozens of secondary schools, and authorities were unable to quell the rampage. The students' stated reasons for their behaviour ranged from claims of unfair disciplinary and testing practices to poor-quality meals. The tradition in Kenya's church-sponsored and public schools of assigning political appointees rather than professional educators as school principals was cited as one cause of the disorder.

By 2004 at least 32 U.S. states had adopted aggressive antiharassment policies meant to prevent bullying and to provide intervention when it occurred. Studies showed that bullying, which tended to reach its peak in middle school and continue into high school, could not only make life miserable for the students being tormented but also drive some victims of harassment to retaliate in violent ways, such as by shooting schoolmates. The National Education Association estimated that 160,000 children missed school each day for fear of being tormented.

A survey of 8,000 British teenagers showed that formal sex-education classes led by students resulted in more constructive attitudes toward sexual behaviour than did classes led by teachers. For example, students who had participated in peer-led sessions knew more about how to protect themselves against sexually transmitted infections than did those who had been instructed by teachers. The research supported an earlier study's conclusion that sex education was too often taught by embarrassed teachers.

HIGHER EDUCATION

Plans were set by the European Union's member states to include in their higher-education system the 10 additional nations that joined the Union in May—Cyprus, Czech Republic, Estonia, Hungary, Latvia, Lithuania, Malta, Poland, Slovakia, and Slovenia. The EU's higher-education goal for 2010 was to have students move freely within a "single education market" composed of all 25 member states, pursuing courses that were compatible and degrees that were matched across Europe. By 2005 bachelor's and master's programs would be introduced throughout the EU and a uniform credit-point system established for university teaching. Implementation of the plan would first require that the 10 new members restructure their university policies and administrative practices.

A study of education in advanced industrial nations predicted that the 17.3 million people in the U.S. enrolled in college in 2000 would increase 13% to 19.6 million by 2015. Such growth would fail to match the rate of increase in a variety of other developed countries, however, such as Canada, South Korea, and Sweden, which aggressively prepared students academically to succeed in college and helped pay college expenses. According to the study, the ability of the United States to compete in higher-education enrollments had been undermined by excessive high-school dropout rates, low college participation among low-income and minority students, and state budget cuts that increased the college costs students were obliged to bear.

The number of ethnic-minority students attending college in the U.S. more than doubled during 1981–2001 from 2 million to 4.3 million, setting a trend that continued into 2004. During those two decades, the enrollment of blacks grew by 56% to 1.7 million, Hispanic enrollment tripled to 1.5 million, and Asian American attendance tripled to 1 million. The rate of increase of minority women in college was greater than that of men. By the early 21st century, 40% of African Americans and 34% of Hispanics were enrolled, compared with 46% of whites.

Publishers of college textbooks in the U.S. were accused of exploiting students by issuing expensive new editions about every three years and including unnecessary materials such as CD-ROMs and study guides in order to boost prices. As a result, the cost of textbooks rose 35% during 1999–2004. A survey of universities in California and Oregon revealed that the cost of an average new textbook was $103, or 58% more than a used text. Thus, the typical student would pay $900 for books during 2004.

As more Asians looked for schools outside the U.S. and Europe for advanced education, Singapore officials unveiled a plan to make their city-state a major higher-education centre by tripling the number of foreign students enrolled to 150,000 by 2012. An estimated 22,000 new jobs would come from local and foreign institutions over the next 10 years. American universities that already had campuses in Singapore were the University of Chicago, Johns Hopkins, the Massachusetts Institute of Technology, and Stanford. France's business school INSEAD and the Technische Universiteit Eindhoven of The Netherlands also offered study programs there.

China intended to increase the number of government-funded students studying abroad from 2,700 annually to 5,000 by 2007. Candidates from 12 relatively poor regions in western China would be given special opportunities to study overseas. Among the 38,000 doctoral students who would graduate in China during 2004–06, many would be sent abroad to prestigious foreign universities for specialized training.

A survey comparing the proportions of males and females in Australian universities showed that the enrollment of men had fallen to an all-time low of 43% and that women surpassed men in academic performance. Observers suggested that such results meant that women no longer needed the special preference in funding that had been provided under a 1990 regulation designed to aid six groups that were considered disadvantaged—women, indigenous students, students from rural and isolated areas, those from low-income backgrounds, individuals with disabilities, and those from non-English-speaking backgrounds.

July marked the first anniversary of the founding of Venezuela's Bolivarian University, established by the country's president, Hugo Chávez Frías, to furnish more higher-education opportunities for the poor. During 2004 the university enrolled 10,000 students on five campuses distributed across the country. Though the nation's other 24 public universities depended heavily on standardized-test scores for student admittance, Bolivarian University's applicants were judged only on their goals and their disadvantaged social status. The Bolivarian mission emphasized social activism in three major fields of endeavour—journalism, environmental management, and local-development management.

In an effort to maintain high academic quality in colleges, officials in Russia and South Africa closed a variety of institutions that failed to meet government standards. The Russian Education Ministry revoked the accreditation of 9 institutions and limited the licenses of 7 others during a campaign to assess the quality of instruction in the nation's 1,000 higher-learning institutions, which in recent times had spawned about 2,000 affiliates and branches. South Africa's Council for Higher Education stripped accreditation from 10 of the country's 28 master-of-business-administration programs because they met less than 15% of the council's minimum standards.

(R. MURRAY THOMAS)

The Environment

RUSSIA ratified the Kyoto Protocol, and **EU** rules for labeling products from **GENETICALLY MODIFIED** crops came into force. The effects of **GLOBAL WARMING** on the range of species were seen as increasing **EXTINCTION** risks, and a survey of the world's **RAREST** ape brought its world population to 50.

INTERNATIONAL ACTIVITIES

At a meeting held in Cheju, S.Kor., in late March 2004, environment ministers from about 90 countries discussed such topics as deoxygenation of oceans and lakes, waste management in small island states, and dust storms. Klaus Töpfer, UN Environment Programme (UNEP) executive director, informed the ministers about oceanic "dead zones" up to 70,000 sq km (27,000 sq mi) in extent. In these areas the overgrowth and decomposition of microscopic marine organisms feeding on excess nitrogen from fertilizers, waste, and vehicle and industrial emissions had depleted the water of the oxygen needed by fish to survive. He also spoke of the success of countries bordering the Rhine River in reducing by 37% the amount of nitrogen entering the North Sea.

The Rotterdam Convention on trade in dangerous chemicals came into force in February, requiring exporters of any of 27 designated substances to obtain prior informed consent from the importing country before making shipment. The substances included a number of pesticides and several forms of asbestos. An additional 14 substances were added in September.

The Zayid International Prize for the Environment, established in honour of Sheikh Zayid ibn Sultan Al Nahyan (president of the United Arab Emirates; *see* OBITUARIES), was presented on February 24 in Dubai at the end of the four-day Dubai International Conference on Atmospheric Pollution. Winners in three categories were chosen. The prize of $500,000 for global leadership went to the BBC. Godwin Obasi, Mustafa Tolba, and Bert Bolin shared the prize of $300,000 for scientific and technological achievement. Obasi was a former secretary-general of the World Meteorological Organization; Tolba was a former executive director of UNEP; and Bolin was a former chairman of the Intergovernmental Panel on Climate Change (IPCC). The prize of $200,000 for action leading to positive change in society was awarded jointly to Badria al-Awadhi, founder of the Kuwait Environment Protection Society, and Jamal Safi, founder of the Environmental Protection and Research Institute in Gaza.

On April 19, at a ceremony in San Francisco, the 2004 Goldman Environmental Prize was awarded to eight recipients. Margie Eugene-Richard (U.S.) campaigned against pollution from a Shell Chemical plant in Norco, La.; Rudolf N. Amenga-Etego (Ghana) was successful in obtaining a suspension of a water-privatization project that would have impeded access to clean drinking water; Rashida Bee and Champa Devi Shukla (India) led the fight to hold Dow Chemical accountable for the 1984 Union Carbide gas leak in Bhopal, India; Libia R. Grueso (Colombia) secured territorial rights over more than 2.4 million ha (1 ha = about 2.5 ac) for Afro-Colombian communities; Manana Kochladze (Georgia) won concessions to protect villagers and the environment from any damage caused by the construction in Georgia of the world's largest oil pipeline; and Demetrio do Amaral de Carvalho (East Timor) championed the issues of sustainable development and environmental protection in East Timor.

The Blue Planet Prize was awarded in June to two recipients. Susan Solomon of the National Oceanic and Atmospheric Administration in Washington, D.C., was honoured for her work in the 1980s that showed the role of cold stratospheric clouds above Antarctica in accelerating the destruction of stratospheric ozone by chlorofluorocar-

Workers clean up an oil spill of more than 20,000 bbl of crude petroleum from an abandoned Shell Petroleum Development Co. well in Bayelsa state in southern Nigeria. The well was closed in 1977 and leaked for years before the June 2004 spill.

bons. Gro Harlem Brundtland was honoured for building international cooperation on environmental issues. Her work as chair of the UN World Commission on Environment and Development helped lead to the UN Conference on Environment and Development (the Earth Summit) in 1992. Each winner received ¥50 million (about $460,000) from the Asahi Glass Foundation.

NATIONAL DEVELOPMENTS

European Union. On November 1, a Greek lawyer, Stavros Dimas, became the EU environment commissioner and left his former position as employment commissioner of the EU.

On Oct. 29, 2003, the European Commission had tabled draft legislation to overhaul the regulation of chemicals. The regulations for the registration, evaluation, and authorization of chemicals (REACH) required chemical manufacturers and importers to register all chemicals that they proposed to market in quantities exceeding one metric ton (about 2,205 lb). The most hazardous substances would be authorized for use only if the manufacturer convinced the regulating authority that they would be used safely for specified purposes. Three years after the regulations came into force, companies would have to register carcinogenic substances, mutagenic substances, and reprotoxic substances (substances detrimental to reproduction) that were handled in amounts exceeding one metric ton and other substances in a quantity of more than 1,000 metric tons. Quantities of 100–1,000 metric tons would have to be registered after six years; quantities of 1–100 metric tons, after 11 years.

Following publication of the draft, concerns remained that the Commission had not adequately assessed the economic effect of the scheme, especially its effect on international trade. Animal-welfare groups feared that REACH would mean a sharp increase in animal testing. In March 2004 the Asia-Pacific Economic Cooperation organization, representing key EU trading partners—including the U.S., Canada, Mexico, Australia, Japan, China, Indonesia, South Korea, and Malaysia—described the draft as "overly expansive, burdensome, and costly." In April the French chemical industry calculated that implementation would cost France €28 billion (about $35 billion) over 10 years, a much higher figure than the Commission assessment of €5.2 billion (about $6.4 billion) over 11 years for the 15 member states. Arguments broke out again following the announcement of the findings of a study presented to the European Parliament's industry committee on August 31. The study found that the controls would reduce GDP by 2.9%, cost the chemical industry €3.3 trillion (about $4.1 trillion) over 20 years, and reduce the output of the industry by 25%.

On Feb. 26, 2004, the European Parliament and the Council of Ministers agreed to end the production and use of 13 persistent organic pollutants: aldrin, chlordane, dieldrin, endrin, heptachlor, hexachlorobenzene, mirex, toxaphene, PCBs, DDT, chlordecone, hexabromobiphenyl, and lindane.

Canada. In May the government announced a 10-year program to cost Can$400 million (about $290 million) for cleaning up a site at Sydney, N.S., contaminated with 700,000 metric tons of chemicals from wastes discharged into the nearby river. The residue included 45,000 metric tons of PCBs, polycyclic aromatic hydrocarbons, arsenic, lead, and dioxins, and at least 30 sewer pipes continued to discharge material. The Sydney Steel Co. had occupied the 33-ha (82-ac) site for 90 years.

Denmark. In a ruling published on Dec. 17, 2003, Denmark's Science Ministry dismissed criticisms that the Danish Committee on Scientific Dishonesty had made of environmentalist Bjørn Lomborg. In his book *The Skeptical Environmentalist,* Lomborg was critical of views widely held by environmentalists. The ministry found that the committee had presented no evidence for the allegations it had made of bias and unscientific methodology in his book, had failed to give Lomborg an opportunity to defend himself, and had based its judgments on media reports rather than an independent assessment of the book. In January a group of senior Dutch scientists published the result of their examination of the Danish criticism, finding that only a few minor accusations against Lomborg were valid. In June 2004 Lomborg resigned from his post as director of Denmark's Environmental Assessment Institute to return to the University of Århus, Den., as an associate professor.

North Korea. *DPR Korea: State of the Environment 2003,* the first-ever assessment of the environment in North Korea, was published in Pyongyang in August. Written by the country's national coordinating council for the environment, comprising officials from 20 government and academic agencies, together with the UN Development Programme (UNDP) and UNEP, the report covered the state of forests, water, air, land, and biodiversity. It found that forests, which currently covered 74% of the country, were declining in area and deteriorating in quality owing to timber production, firewood production, fires, insect pests associated with drought, and deforestation to provide farmland. Large amounts of untreated wastewater and sewage were being discharged into rivers, with adverse health effects. Air quality was deteriorating, especially in industrial and urban areas. Energy consumption was expected to double over 30 years, and this made it important to develop technologies for clean coal combustion, exhaust-gas purification, energy efficiency, and renewable energy. Soil quality was also deteriorating, due to deforestation, droughts, floods, and acidification owing to overuse of chemicals. Ri Jung Sik, secretary-general of the national coordinating council, and UNEP Executive Director Töpfer signed a framework agreement on joint activities to address these issues.

United States. In July the attorneys general of California, Connecticut, Iowa, New Jersey, New York, Rhode Island, Vermont, Wisconsin, and New York City sued the five companies that were the greatest carbon-dioxide emitters in the U.S. for creating a public nuisance. The five companies—the American Electric Power Co., the Tennessee Valley Authority, the Southern Co., Cinergy Corp., and Xcel Energy—together produced 10% of all U.S. carbon dioxide emissions. The suit called on each company to reduce its emissions by 3% a year for 10 years, a target the plaintiffs maintained could be achieved without large increases in energy prices by making generating plants more efficient, promoting energy conservation, and using wind power and solar power.

In December new federal rules were issued that relaxed environmental reviews of the management of U.S. national forests.

ENVIRONMENTAL ISSUES

Climate Change. The ninth Conference of the Parties to the Framework Convention on Climate Change was held in Milan on Dec. 1–12, 2003. Prior to the opening of the conference, the executive secretary of the convention, Joke

Hybrid Cars Hit the Road

Hybrid cars began grabbing headlines in 2004, especially after movie stars were seen arriving at the Academy Awards in these environmentally friendly vehicles. With worries over air pollution and with gasoline prices topping $2 a gallon, the public imagination has seized on hybrid cars as a high-tech, high-fashion solution.

The state of California provided the major commercial impetus in the U.S. for the development of electric (battery), electric-gasoline (hybrid), and fuel-cell vehicles. In 1990 the California Air Resources Board mandated a schedule for sales of light-duty vehicles in the state in order to reduce air pollution. The first modern hybrid cars, the Toyota Prius and the Honda Insight, went on sale in Japan in 1997 and 1999, respectively, and in the U.S. in very limited numbers in 2000. Greater numbers—although still fewer than 50,000 in the U.S. (compared with some 17 million gasoline vehicles sold each year)—became available with the 2004 model year. Sales took off, with dealers reporting waiting lists of from six months to a year. American manufacturers countered in the summer and fall of 2004. Ford introduced the Escape, the world's first hybrid sport utility vehicle; General Motors offered hybrid versions of its Chevrolet Silverado and GMC Sierra trucks; and DaimlerChrysler came up with a hybrid version of its Dodge Ram truck.

© John Hillery/Reuters/Corbis

Toyota's Prius 2004 is a hybrid car that uses an electric-drive motor with a 1.5-litre four-cylinder gasoline engine.

Hybrids typically use nickel–metal-hydride (NiMH) batteries to provide power for an electric motor that shares duties with a small gasoline motor. Either or both motors may be operating, according to driving conditions. When the car is idling at a stop, going downhill, or cruising at low speeds, the gasoline motor is shut off. (Unlike conventional gasoline vehicles, hybrids get better mileage in the city than on the highway.) Under full-throttle acceleration, when climbing hills, or while cruising at high speeds, the two engines operate in tandem by means of a sophisticated electronic transmission. When decelerating or braking, the force used to slow the car is harnessed to charge the battery.

Although non-internal-combustion automobile engines were not mass-produced for decades, many alternatives were tried over the years. Throughout the late 19th century, electric, steam, and gasoline vehicles competed fender-to-fender in the marketplace. There were 1,684 steam, 1,575 electric, and 963 gasoline vehicles manufactured in the U.S. in 1900. Electric vehicles lost out to gas-driven cars because of disadvantages in the weight and range of their storage batteries and, especially, owing to their cost. In 1912 the gasoline-powered Ford Model T, for example, sold for $550, while a typical electric vehicle cost three times as much. The earliest production-model hybrid, the Woods gasoline-electric of 1916, sold for even more—$2,650. Today's hybrid vehicles suffer from a similar cost disadvantage because of their extra motor and batteries. With an eye to market share, hybrid automakers have so far underwritten their costs in an effort to keep prices in the $20,000 range and competitive with standard cars. They are gambling that mileage figures in the range of 50–60 mpg (4–5 litres per 100 km), the clean and quiet operation, and the stylishness of the new vehicles will continue to attract buyers even as manufacturer and government price subsidies begin to be lifted.

(WILLIAM L. HOSCH)

Waller-Hunter, said that 119 countries had ratified the Kyoto Protocol and that many less-developed countries were already working to reduce their greenhouse-gas emissions even though they were not required to do so.

On Dec. 12, 2003, European Union heads of government approved a communiqué expressing concern over the economic costs of limiting greenhouse-gas emissions. It was projected that more than half of the member states would miss their emissions targets set by the protocol for 2008–12. For example, it was projected that by 2010 the EU countries as a whole would have reduced emissions by only 0.5% of their 1990 levels rather than by the target 8%.

On January 27 Spanish Energy Minister José Folgado indicated that his government was unhappy with its greenhouse-gas limitation under the Kyoto Protocol. A ministry spokesperson later explained that Folgado was simply reiterating statements made by Energy Commissioner Loyola de Palacio questioning the potential costs of the Kyoto agreement.

In February, Finnish Industry Minister Mauri Pekkarinen said that unless the Kyoto Protocol came into force soon, Finland should campaign within the EU for a renegotiation of national targets for limiting greenhouse gases. At an EU ministerial meeting in Brussels on March 2, Italian Environment Minister Altero Matteoli attempted to force from the meeting a declaration that any action on cutting emissions should depend on Russian ratification of the Kyoto Protocol. Spain and, to a lesser extent, Finland supported the Italian position.

On April 14 the Russian Interfax news agency reported Andrey Illarionov, economic adviser to Pres. Vladimir Putin, as having said that the Kyoto Protocol would stifle economic growth by progressively decreasing permitted carbon emissions, and on

Forest fires on the island of Sumatra, Indonesia, affected air quality over areas of Southeast Asia. The skyline of Malaysia's capital, Kuala Lumpur, was obscured by the smoke, as seen in the photograph on the right taken June 23, 2004. The photograph on the left was taken about two weeks earlier.

May 18 the Russian Academy of Sciences advised against ratification of the protocol. Following a meeting with EU leaders on May 21 at which the EU agreed to Russia's joining the World Trade Organization (WTO), however, President Putin said Russia would speed its progress toward ratification and that his government supported the Kyoto Protocol. After the lower and upper houses of parliament approved ratification in October, President Putin signed the ratification document on November 5.

Ozone Layer. A meeting of the parties to the Montreal Protocol, held in Nairobi, Kenya, broke down on Nov. 14, 2003, when the U.S. warned that it might overrule the treaty if its demand to continue using methyl bromide pesticide was not met. Industrialized countries were required to cease using methyl bromide by 2005 except for specified exemptions. A UN panel had supported the exemption of one-third of the amount requested by the U.S. for continued use, but the U.S. demanded more. The EU then proposed that all national exemptions be capped at 30% of their baseline methyl bromide consumption.

On April 14 the Polish government decided to ban immediately the use of chlorofluorocarbons (CFCs) in freezers and air-conditioning systems. The use of CFCs as aerosol propellants would only be phased out, because their discontinuance might involve changing pharmaceutical laws. The withdrawal of metered-dose inhalers using CFCs, however, was commenced immediately and was to be completed by the end of 2005.

On June 22, at a conference in Brussels on "green" refrigerants supported by UNEP and Greenpeace, Coca-Cola, McDonald's, and Unilever announced that they would phase out their use of hydrofluorocarbon (HFC) refrigerants. Together, these companies operated 12 million coolers and freezers. They planned to replace HFCs with other hydrocarbon gases, carbon dioxide, Stirling motors, and thermoacoustic refrigeration. Unilever said its equipment should be free of HFCs within 10 years; the others were less specific. Coca-Cola had first declared its intention of phasing out HFCs in 2000.

Air Pollution. The European Environment Agency announced in October that smog levels in 2003 were the highest in nearly 10 years, and it attributed the elevated levels to unusually hot, sunny weather. Between April and August the public advisory threshold for ozone levels was exceeded at least once in 23 out of the 31 countries monitored. Breaches lasted an average 3.5 hours. The threshold for issuing a public warning was exceeded four times in the first eight months of the year. After this threshold value was reduced by 30% in September, it was exceeded in 15 countries before the end of the year.

In June smoke from forest fires on the Indonesian Island of Sumatra disrupted flights from the airport at the city of Pekanbaru and affected many cities in Malaysia. The haze over Kuala Lumpur was said to be the worst since 1997–98.

Marine Pollution. Members of the International Maritime Organization (IMO) agreed in February on the terms of a convention aimed at improving the management of ballast water on ships in order to prevent the inadvertent transport of living organisms to new environments where they often became invasive. Equipment to treat ballast water would have to be fitted to all newly built ships by 2009 and to all ships by 2016. The convention would come into force 12 months after it had been ratified by 30 countries that together represented 35% of the world's merchant shipping tonnage. At a meeting in London in late March, the IMO Marine Environment Committee provisionally agreed to give the Baltic Sea special status to afford it greater environmental protection.

In August, at the Offshore Northern Seas conference in Stavanger, Nor., UNEP issued a report prepared by its Global International Waters Assessment division warning of threats to the Barents Sea, currently one of Europe's cleanest seas. The report said that cod and haddock stocks were being overexploited and that although current levels of radioactivity were low, the area around Murmansk, Russia, held more radioactive waste than anywhere else in the world and long-term strategies were needed for its safe management. The gravest risk, however, came from the development of Russian offshore oil and gas deposits, which would increase sixfold the amount of traffic passing through the sea by 2020. Apart from the risk of spills, the increase in traffic posed a risk of accidentally introducing alien species in ballast water.

Persistent Organic Pollutants. The three-month countdown to the implementation of the Stockholm Convention on Persistent Organic Pollutants began on February 17 when France became the

50th country to have ratified the agreement, and the convention came into force on May 17. The first phase covered aldrin, dieldrin, chlordane, DDT, dioxins, endrin, furans, heptachlor, hexachlorobenzene, PCBs, and toxaphene.

Disagreement was anticipated over the risks from brominated flame retardants such as hexabromocyclododecane (HBCD) and decabromodiphenyl ether (decaBDE) that might be included in the second phase. These substances entered the environment during manufacture processes and use and could accumulate in human and animal tissues. HBCD was recognized as being toxic, but there was some doubt over decaBDE. Tens of thousands of metric tons of both substances were being manufactured every year.

Pesticides. In September the UN Food and Agriculture Organization (FAO) warned that large amounts of toxic chemical waste from obsolete pesticides were being stored at unmanaged sites in a number of countries, particularly in Poland, Ukraine, Macedonia, Moldova, China, Algeria, Cameroon, Eritrea, and Senegal. The FAO program to destroy the stockpiles was due to expire at the end of 2004 and could be extended only if donor countries provided funding. Mark Davis, head of the FAO program dealing with the problem, said that as little as $1 million would allow work to continue.

Genetically Modified Foods. Results from a British three-year field-scale evaluation of genetically modified (GM) crops were published in October 2003 in the *Philosophical Transactions of the Royal Society B.* The study, the biggest ecological experiment ever attempted, was conducted on 200 plots at about 60 sites. It compared conventional varieties and herbicide-tolerant GM varieties of oilseed rape (canola), sugar beet, and corn (maize). The study found that weed suppression was more efficient on GM rape and beet sites, with a consequent decrease in invertebrate animals. An increase in populations of certain soil organisms (collembola) in GM rape and beet and in conventional corn was due to an increase in weed biomass during early stages of crop growth and the subsequent killing of the weeds, supplying abundant food for microorganisms that eat decaying matter. GM corn led to an increase in weeds and more invertebrate life. Investigators believed this was due to the fact that the herbicide used for corn was atrazine. GM corn could not improve on the weed control achieved by atrazine, which was especially effective but would soon be banned. Much less herbicide was used on the GM crops, and in some cases farmers used no herbicide at all on them. The evaluation produced no evidence for any new environmental damage resulting from GM technology. The effects that were detected were no different from what would be expected from the introduction of a new, more effective herbicide.

EU rules on the traceability and labeling of GM products came into force on April 18. They required that food containing more than 0.9% GM ingredients be clearly labeled as such, with a 0.5% limit for ingredients awaiting final safety approval. Food was to be traced from its source of production to its point of sale, and manufacturers and packagers were to test food for traces of GM ingredients. In late January the European Commission approved commercial production of Bt-11, a GM pest-resistant corn developed by Syngenta AG, and on May 19 the Commission authorized its marketing. This action marked the end of the EU's six-year unofficial moratorium on GM products. The authorization would last 10 years and apply to canned food grown mainly in the U.S. In September, for the first time, the EU approved a GM variety for planting: MON810 corn developed by Monsanto Co. to resist the European corn borer. Spain and France had approved it in 1998, and it had been grown in Spain. Under EU law a seed approved in one member country was automatically approved in all the others. Ending the moratorium allowed the European Commission to approve this corn throughout the EU.

On March 2 voters in Mendocino county, Calif., voted to ban the planting of GM crops. Trinity county, Calif., introduced a similar ban on August 3, and opponents of GM technology were campaigning for bans in several other parts of the U.S. (MICHAEL ALLABY)

WILDLIFE CONSERVATION

A study published in January 2004 of the distribution of 1,103 native species of plants, mammals, birds, reptiles, amphibians, and invertebrates in six highly biodiverse regions projected that climate change related to global warming through 2050 would place 15–37% of the studied species at risk of extinction. The study used computer models to simulate how the ranges occupied by the species were expected to shift in response to changes in climate. The models showed that the effects of global warming on climate posed a major extinction threat and that it would be particularly devastating when the ability of a species to move to new areas to survive was limited by a loss of habitat.

In February attention was focused on chimpanzees, the species of great ape that most closely resembles humans

The black rhinoceros, shown here on a game farm in Malelane, S.Af., is critically endangered. In 2004 CITES (the Convention on International Trade in Endangered Species of Wild Fauna and Flora) granted Namibia and South Africa requests they made for permission to allow trophy hunting of the animal, with a quota of five animals annually for each.

genetically and provides a link to our evolutionary history. An action plan by conservation groups highlighted that only about 150,000 chimpanzees remained of the one million–two million at the beginning of the 20th century. The dramatic reduction in number was caused by habitat destruction, disease (including human infectious diseases), the bushmeat trade, and the capture of young chimpanzees as pets. All four subspecies of the chimpanzee were categorized as endangered on the World Conservation Union's Red List of Threatened Species.

The status of the saiga antelope continued to be a serious cause for concern. The Red List status of the Mongolian saiga, *Saiga tatarica mongolica*, was expected to be officially changed from vulnerable to endangered, following the reassignment in 2002 of *S. tatarica tatarica*, of Kazakhstan and the Republic of Kalmykia, Russia, from a status of lower risk to critically endangered. Populations of both species fell dramatically because of heavy poaching.

In April 2004, for the first time in more than 50 years, a newborn western gorilla (*Gorilla gorilla gorilla*) was seen in the Lefini Reserve, Republic of the Congo. Its mother, a 16-year-old orphan of the bushmeat trade, was released into the Lefini Reserve in January 2003 along with two other females and two males (one of which was the father of the baby). The group of five adult gorillas was the first group to be released as part of a long-term program to reintroduce the species to the reserve.

Brazil announced in June the creation of two national forests and two extractive reserves (areas protected by law in which the sustainable extraction of natural resources was permitted). The four newly protected areas were in the states of Paraná (Piraí do Sul National Forest, 125 ha [1 ha = about 2.5 ac]), Paraíba (Restinga de Cabedelo, 103 ha), Maranhão (Cururupu Extractive Reserve, 185,000 ha), and Amazonas (Capanã Grande Extractive Reserve, 304,000 ha). Capanã Grande was an area identified in the Amazon Region Protected Areas program, a 10-year program of WWF Brazil to protect 50,000,000 ha.

A survey in September of the world's rarest ape, the eastern black-crested gibbon, *Nomascus nasutus*, counted 37 individuals in the Ngo Khe-Phong Nam forest in Cao Bang province, Vietnam, near the Chinese border. The eastern black-crested gibbon was critically endangered and known to exist at only one other location, a site in China with 13 individuals. The survey increased the total known population of the ape by one-third and included five infants, an indication that the population was increasing. Three new groups were located, which brought the total number of groups in Cao Bang province to eight. The gibbons, referred to locally as Cao Vit, lived on isolated limestone mountain peaks. They were rarely seen by the local people but were renowned for their beautiful calls at dawn.

Uroplatus phantasticus, *the fantastic leaf-tailed gecko, is named for the shape of its body, which provides camouflage among leaves in the rainforests of Madagascar. Exportation of the animal to other countries as a pet has led to a decline of its population in the wild.*

In October the 13th meeting of the Conference of the Parties to the Convention on International Trade in Endangered Species of Wild Fauna and Flora (CITES) agreed upon a number of decisions to strengthen wildlife management, combat illegal trafficking, and update the trade rules for plant and animal species. Ramin (a tree that produces high-value timber) and agarwood (a tree that produces agar oil) were placed on the convention's Appendix II, which imposed trade controls, to help national officials manage stocks and tackle illegal trade. The great white shark and the humphead wrasse were also added to Appendix II and could therefore be traded only under permit. The Irrawaddy dolphin was transferred from Appendix II to Appendix I, which forbade all commercial trade. The conference agreed to a plan to regulate elephant ivory in domestic markets in an effort to prevent the markets from serving as outlets for poached ivory. A request by Namibia for an annual quota for ivory from its elephant population was not accepted, but the country received permission to continue the sale of ivory carvings under strict controls. Namibia and South Africa were allowed to open up trophy hunting of the black rhinoceros, with an annual quota of five animals each, and Swaziland was allowed to export some of its white rhinoceroses and, under strict controls, to open up hunting of the animal. To facilitate trophy hunting of the Namibian population of the Nile crocodile, it was transferred from Appendix I to Appendix II, as was the Cuban population of the American crocodile to facilitate the supply of eggs and hatchlings to ranching operations. More protection was given to 5 species of Asian turtles and tortoises and 11 species of the leaf-tailed geckos of Madagascar by listing them on Appendix II. Trade rules were strengthened for a number of medicinal plants, including hoodia (used in diet pills), cistanche (a natural tonic), and the Chinese yew tree (which had some cancer-fighting properties).

Investigations in the Eastern Arc mountains in Tanzania showed that gold was being mined illegally in several areas that were of global importance for biodiversity conservation. The mining was causing water pollution harmful to many birds, amphibians, aquatic invertebrates, and other animals that inhabited the mountain streams and forests in the area. Despite efforts by the Tanzanian government to curb the illegal activity, small clandestine groups working at night continued prospecting in the smaller streams and swampy areas within protected areas, especially the Amani Nature Reserve.

(MARTIN FISHER)

Fashions

Celebrity dressing FADED from centre stage of the fashion scene in 2004, and PRACTICAL clothes, especially JEANS, became the new byword; ELECTRIC BLUE was declared the hot colour FOR EVERYTHING from evening gowns to accessories.

After several years of the sartorial opulence that led up to and followed the turn of the new millennium, fashion in 2004 shifted away from overt luxury toward more practical dressing, and the change seemed to be a direct response to the uncertain times—the war in Iraq, skyrocketing oil prices, and a slew of hurricanes—that were dampening retail sales.

The Gucci Group made fashion-industry headlines. Opulent long dresses of electric blue and emerald green adorned with smoke gray sequins dominated Gucci's autumn-winter collection—produced for the year's most anticipated runway presentation—the final offering created by Tom Ford, the company's charismatic 42-year-old creative director. In November 2003 Ford had announced that he would resign as creative director of Gucci and Yves Saint Laurent (YSL) Rive Gauche and that his boss, Domenico De Sole, Gucci president and CEO, would also leave; the two had failed to renegotiate their contracts with the company's French owner, luxury-goods conglomerate Pinault Printemps-Redoute. Ford's last collection for YSL's ready-to-wear line, Rive Gauche—for which Ford had assumed design control in 1999—was composed of rich jewel-toned satins. Both collections, however, seemed best suited to the lifestyle of top Hollywood actresses, such as Nicole Kidman, Demi Moore, and Charlize Theron. (*See* BIOGRAPHIES.) When his tenure at Gucci ended, Ford decamped to Los Angeles, where he pursued his dream of writing and directing a feature film. *Tom Ford,* a coffee-table tribute tome—complete with contributions from Anna Wintour and Graydon Carter, the editors of *Vogue* and *Vanity Fair*, respectively—was published by Rizzoli International Publications. At Gucci former senior design directors Alessandra Facchinetti, John Ray, and Frida Giannini assumed Ford's previous responsibilities as creative directors of women's wear, menswear, and accessories, respectively. Promoted to Ford's position as YSL Rive Gauche creative director was Stefano Pilati, a 38-year-old Milanese designer, who had served as design director of the brand for four years. Previously Pilati had a two-year stint designing Prada's Miu Miu collection.

© Patrick Hertzog/Getty Images

Tom Ford's electric blue evening gown, which premiered at his last collection for Gucci, typifies one of the year's hottest trends in colour.

Despite the plethora of satin, sequins, gold, leather, marabou, and fur seen at Gucci and most other autumn-winter fashion runways, practical clothes seemed most sought after by women. Denim jeans manufactured by a number of American cult labels—such as Juicy, Seven for All Mankind, Rogan, Hudson, Habitual, and Paper Denim & Cloth—emerged as the year's most coveted wardrobe item. British fashion designer Matthew Williamson produced a high-priced line of jeans for Levi, and the waist-hugging denim trousers and skirts Phoebe Philo designed for Chloé were favoured by fashion critics. In the Gap's popular "How Do You Wear It?" instructional autumn-winter advertising campaign, Sarah Jessica Parker—who in June received the Fashion Icon award from the Council of Fashion Designers of America—displayed the versatility of the label's affordable denim trousers produced in traditional styles and a more directional cropped look inspired by those created by Costume National, Valentino, and Burberry. In American *Vogue*'s April issue, Kate Moss was called the "girl of the moment" and pictured in jeans, black-leather knee-high boots, and vintage fur. In the London magazine *ES Fashion,* elegant jewelry designer Nathalie Hambro claimed jeans to be her most reliable wardrobe element. "Jeans of different lengths, colours, and styles [are] a basic for dressing high or dressing low," she said.

Stilettos emerged as key accessories in high-fashion spring-summer collections—notably Michael Kors's Perspex and black-leather open-toe sandals and Gucci's strappy silk-ribbon evening shoes. In addition, less-expensive ballet slippers proved to be overwhelmingly popular, especially those produced by Louis Vuitton and Carolina Herrera. London's leading high-street chain, TOPSHOP, sold out of gold and silver ballet flats in summer. Meanwhile, writer, director, and Marc Jacobs muse Sofia Coppola—nominated by *Vanity Fair* as one of the best-dressed women of 2004 and winner of the Academy Award for best original screenplay for *Lost in Translation*—crossed the red carpet at the Golden Globe awards in January in black Marc Jacobs ballet slippers.

High-fashion magazines promoted lavish accessories, such as Louis Vuitton's gold leather-trimmed $4,000 Trianon handbag and a Bottega Veneta "knot" bag—a clutch made from expensive material such as crocodile, python, and crystal. According to *Vogue*'s September issue, precious jewelry replaced handbags as the key accessory to own. New jewelry collections abounded, and Liz Goldwyn—the 26-year-old granddaughter of 1930s Hollywood film mogul Sam Goldwyn—launched her own line. Diane von Furstenberg and Rio de Janeiro fine jeweler H. Stern introduced a collection in October called Diane von Furstenberg by H. Stern; the 18-karat-gold 50-piece collection displayed semiprecious stones, precious stones, and pavé diamonds.

This ensemble by Marc Jacobs uses staples, such as tank tops, to pull together a look favoured by young women.

© Mark Mainz/Getty Images

A number of fashion designers cornered the affordable-fashion sector. With the intention of reaching a larger customer base, Oscar de la Renta, the former couturier of Balmain, launched O Oscar, a line of reasonably priced clothes based on his ready-to-wear designs. "It's the well rounded wardrobe," explained Tommy Hilfiger of H, his collection composed of $250 blazers and $150 pants, sold at Macy's and Bloomingdale's. "It can be worn by someone like Iman who is chic and refined or a mom who picks up her children at school and then meets her husband for dinner at a nice restaurant." In the spring Karl Lagerfeld produced Cinq à Sept, a luxurious evening-wear line produced by Chanel in association with five couture adornment specialists the company had acquired in 2002, including an embroidery house (Lesage) and a custom shoemaker (Massaro); Lagerfeld also collaborated with the high-street chain H&M and produced a capsule collection of autumn-winter street fashion.

Harper's Bazaar used the words *staples* and *easy pieces* to describe the style of reliable, timeless clothes popular among women, including trench coats produced in variations by Burberry, Donna Karan, and Derek Lam; versatile knitwear separates; and tank tops and conservative skirt suits inspired by the boxy cut pioneered by Coco Chanel and adapted by a cross section of designers that included young labels such as Proenza Schouler and Luella Bartley as well as established names such as Jacobs and Oscar de la Renta.

During 2004 Prada produced what the press considered to be two of the year's most directional shows—for summer the style was a 1950s-inspired look based on a seaside theme with wraparound skirts featuring Mediterranean designs and ombre cardigans, and the winter look featured jewel-embellished satin coats and skirts. On July 16 Miuccia Prada arrived in Los Angeles to open Prada's first Epicenter, a $35 million high-tech retail space that was designed by Dutch architects Rem Koolhaas and Ole Scheeren. At 2,230 sq m (24,000 sq ft), the store was the largest designer shop on Rodeo Drive, the retail mecca of Beverly Hills. Though Prada announced a

© Charles Platiau/Reuters/Corbis

Michael Kors's handbag is one of several designer bags that were "must haves" in 2004.

33% increase in profits and remained intent on floating the company on the stock market, *European Business* magazine claimed that the company's earnings were inflated and that Prada was operating on a margin of 2.7%. In November Prada and German fashion designer Jil Sander parted ways for the second time. Sander had sold her label to Prada in 1999 and then served as chair before stepping down in 2000, apparently after disagreements with Prada's chief executive, Patrizio Bertelli. In May 2003 Sander returned to Prada in an effort to resurrect her minimalist concept. By mid-2004, however, the brand had lost $22 million, following a net loss of $36.7 million in 2003, and Prada failed to renew Sander's contract. Armani was operating on a 20% margin, and the company opened a Shanghai boutique and announced plans for an additional 30 shops in China by 2008. Hermès, which for autumn-winter 2004 successfully relaunched its ready-to-wear men's and women's fashion labels with Jean-Paul Gaultier as design director, had a 27% operating margin, and LVMH Moët Hennessy Louis Vuitton posted a 32% margin.

Economic analysts—assessing Donatella Versace's decision to go public on July 29 with the news that she had checked into a rehabilitation centre to seek treatment for cocaine addiction—claimed that the announcement would not harm the pursuit by investment banks Crédit Suisse First Boston and Lazard to sell a minority stake in the Milan fashion empire to an outside investor, given the brand image. Italian designer Roberto Cavalli emerged as the favourite among women who would otherwise wear Versace—notably celebrities Beyoncé (*see* BIOGRAPHIES),

This creation by Roberto Cavalli is emblematic of his opulent and sexy designs.

Alessandra Benedetti/WireImage.com

Jennifer Lopez, and Lucy Liu. Cavalli produced feather- and crystal-encrusted evening dresses reminiscent of those made for Cher in the 1970s by Hollywood costume designer Bob Mackie. Cavalli classified his opulent look as "especially sexy," but he also worried that sometimes it would be "too much." His designs were also embraced by socialites such as Jade Jagger, Elle Macpherson, and *Vanity Fair* magazine fashion director Elizabeth Saltzman, who were all photographed wearing Cavalli gowns at the annual June Serpentine Gallery party, London's premiere summer social event.

Another standout was French vintage evening wear produced in Paris by the late Tunisian-born designer Loris Azzaro; during the 1970s he dressed actresses Marisa Berenson, Liza Minnelli, and Raquel Welch in long, sinuous jersey and satin gowns frequently embellished at the neckline with sequins or crystals. At the 76th Academy Awards ceremony, actress Diane Lane appeared in a long white crystal-studded vintage Azzaro gown, and her profile enhanced the launch of a 35-piece collection produced by Vanessa Seward, the company's new Argentine designer, who had previously worked for Chanel and YSL Rive Gauche.

Fashion's focus on celebrity dressing dimmed as 2004 drew to a close. Some celebrities seemed weary of the media's preoccupation with their images rather than with their talent. On a *Vogue* magazine photo shoot, actress Kirsten Dunst refused to be overtly styled or to wear a Prada dress proposed by a fashion editor. "I'm a young girl; I don't wear gowns. I want to look as much like myself as I can," she said. Though fashion magazines featured celebrities such as Julia Roberts, Nicole Kidman, Halle Berry, and Scarlett Johansson on their covers through most of the year, Wintour claimed that reality TV had cheapened fame's currency. Instead of placing an actress on the front cover of the magazine's most important issue (September), Wintour featured nine fashion models. Inside the magazine was a cross section of 20 working women, including an attorney, a real-estate broker, a grade-school teacher, and a violinist who selected clothes from the autumn-winter runways and explained how they merged with their lifestyles. "I think we're already fed up with the pseudo fashion parades that take place at countless award shows and remieres," Wintour claimed in her editor's letter in the September *Vogue,* which totaled 832 pages and was its largest edition ever produced.

Fashion designers looked beyond Hollywood for inspiration. The muse for the Jacobs autumn-winter collection and advertising campaign was New York sculptor Rachel Feinstein, famed for her experimental work, her mostly vintage wardrobe, and the portraits painted by her husband, John Currin. On the championship tennis circuit, Serena Williams attracted attention in the experimental corseted, flounced, fringed, and tasseled tennis dresses she produced in collaboration with Nike, her sponsor. Upon the invitation of the choreographer Dimitris Papaioannou, creative director of the opening and closing ceremonies of the 2004 Athens Olympic Games, the Greek London-based designer Sofia Kokosalaki dressed the 8,000 dancers and performers who appeared. British fashion designer Vivienne Westwood (*see* BIOGRAPHIES) had a huge retrospective of her work at the Victoria and Albert Museum in London. Indian actress Aishwarya Rai (*see* BIOGRAPHIES), who had signed a lucrative deal with *Vogue* magazine, also began appearing as the spokesmodel for L'Oréal Paris. Giorgio Armani saved Milan's Olimpia basketball team from folding by investing $3.7 million dollars in the club, which was renamed Armani Jeans Milano.

During the year the fashion industry lost several notable figures, including designers Geoffrey Beene and Stephen Sprouse, fashion photographers Richard Avedon and Francesco Scavullo, and cosmetics entrepreneur Estée Lauder. (*See* OBITUARIES.)

(BRONWYN COSGRAVE)

Vintage Loris Azzaro gowns were a favourite among celebrities in 2004.

Jesse Grant/WireImage.com

Health and Disease

FLU VACCINE was in short supply in the U.S. and BIRD FLU emerged in Asia as a deadly threat to humans. The pain drug VIOXX was pulled from the market and related drugs were scrutinized. Korean scientists reported the cloning of HUMAN EMBRYOS from which they extracted stem cells.

More than 17,000 delegates gathered in Bangkok on July 11–16, 2004, for the 15th International AIDS Conference, the theme of which was "Access for All." The biennial event had evolved from a strictly scientific conference into a forum that covered all facets of the HIV/AIDS pandemic and was attended by persons who represented a large variety of voices, experiences, and concerns.

On the eve of the conference, the Joint United Nations Programme on HIV/AIDS (UNAIDS) released its *2004 Report on the Global AIDS Epidemic,* which painted a very grim picture. The report indicated that in 2003 more people had contracted HIV—close to 5 million—and more people had died from AIDS—nearly 3 million—than in any other single year since the deadly virus emerged. Nowhere was the picture bleaker than in sub-Saharan Africa, home to 25 million of the estimated 38 million people infected with HIV worldwide.

The report sounded an alarm over the rapid rise of HIV in Eastern Europe and Asia. China, Vietnam, Indonesia, and Russia were experiencing the steepest increases in HIV infections, while India had the largest number of infected people outside South Africa. UNAIDS Executive Director Peter Piot compared the epidemic in Asia in 2004 to the situation in southern Africa 15 years earlier.

Globally women made up almost half of the number of adults who were living with HIV/AIDS, and the number of infected women had increased in every region of the world. Moreover, women were physically more susceptible to HIV infection than men, and gender-based violence in many countries exacerbated their vulnerability. A widely discussed topic at the Bangkok conference was the development of microbicides—in the form of gels, creams, or other substances—that could be applied vaginally to reduce the risk of the transmission of HIV and other sexually transmitted infections. The promise of microbicides was that they would offer women a prevention method that they could control.

UNAIDS described the 3 by 5 Initiative of the World Health Organization (WHO) as one of the most ambitious health projects that had ever been conceived. Launched on World AIDS Day (December 1) in 2003, the 3 by 5 Initiative was established to provide antiretroviral drug treatment to three million people in less-developed countries by the end of 2005. A six-month progress report on the initiative indicated that 40,000 people had started therapy by mid-2004; the target had been 100,000. Not all efforts had fallen short of their goals, however. Notable progress had been made in many countries in building health care infrastructures with the capacity to support HIV/AIDS treatment; about 15,000 health care workers had been trained to deliver and monitor antiretroviral therapy, and nearly 5,000 sites were providing HIV testing and counseling.

Another positive development was the reduction in cost of antiretroviral drugs in less-developed countries to about $150 per person annually. New generic formulations that combined three drugs in a single pill were found to be as effective as expensive patented drugs used by patients in developed countries but at only about two-fifths the cost.

Volunteer health workers meet for training at the Arulagam Hospice, Tamil Nadu state, India. They help treat minor health problems in addition to providing care to persons with HIV/AIDS.

© Sukree Sukplang/Reuters/Corbis

Livestock officials on a farm in Thailand collect sacks of dead chickens. The officials wear protective clothing to shield themselves from the avian (bird) flu, which caused health and economic damage in Asia.

Avian Flu. Beginning in late December 2003, an epidemic of avian (bird) flu, a deadly disease of birds caused by type A influenza viruses, devastated poultry populations in most of Southeast Asia. The outbreaks led to the slaughter of more than 100 million fowl.

In late January 2004 the first cases of human infection with the avian flu strain known as A(H5N1) were reported in Vietnam and Thailand. By the end of October, 44 human cases and 32 deaths had been confirmed in the two countries. That humans could catch bird flu had been demonstrated in Hong Kong in 1997, when 18 people were infected with A(H5N1) and 6 died. In fact, several avian flu strains were known to have "jumped the species barrier" and infected humans. The human cases of the disease in Vietnam and Thailand were acquired through either direct or indirect contact with infected poultry. In late September, however, a 26-year-old woman who lived in a suburb of Bangkok might have contracted the illness directly from her daughter. While staying with her aunt in a rural village, the 11-year-old girl had become ill with H5N1 flu after she helped dispose of sick chickens. The mother tended her severely ill daughter until the daughter died. Several days later the mother came down with the flu, and she died shortly thereafter. WHO called this a possible case of human-to-human transmission.

Although a relatively small number of humans had been infected, the death rate was extraordinarily high—72%. Public health officials were duly alarmed. There was considerable evidence that in the nearly seven years since the Hong Kong outbreak, H5N1 had grown more virulent. It had also acquired the ability to replicate in mammals—most notably in pigs. Because pigs are susceptible to both avian and human influenza viruses, flu experts believed that they might serve as "mixing vessels" in which the H5N1 virus could swap genetic material with a human type A influenza virus; a virulent new strain that could be readily transmitted from human to human and to which humans would have no immunity might then emerge. There was little doubt that such a scenario could set off a pandemic on the scale of the deadliest influenza outbreak the world had ever seen, the 1918 "Spanish flu." (Ominously, American and British influenza researchers—who had been studying preserved lung tissue from people who succumbed to the 1918 flu—reported in February that it was likely that the influenza, responsible for 20 million to 40 million deaths worldwide, started as a form of bird flu. Their studies suggested that minute changes in a single amino acid in an avian flu virus might have allowed it to infect humans.)

In mid-November WHO convened a meeting of international vaccine manufacturers and national health officials to address the need for sufficient quantities of vaccine to protect people around the world against H5N1. Klaus Stöhr, WHO's senior influenza expert, said that it was "not a question of if, but of when" a pandemic would occur. The U.S. government did not wait for the November meeting to take steps to prepare for a flu pandemic; in September it contracted with a vaccine manufacturer to prepare and store two million doses of an H5N1 vaccine.

Flu-Shot Shortage. In the midst of the alarm over a possible avian flu outbreak, people around the world were taking the imminent 2004–05 flu season very seriously, and unprecedented numbers sought flu-vaccination shots, the best protection available. In the United States, however, 50 million doses of flu vaccine—about half the intended U.S. supply—were never delivered. The government had contracted with only two manufacturers for its supply. (In contrast, the U.K. obtained its supply of influenza vaccine from five manufacturers and was not caught short, nor were shortages a problem in Europe.) One supplier of American vaccine, Chiron Corp., discovered in August that some of the flu vaccine produced in its manufacturing plant in Liverpool, Eng., was contaminated by bacteria. Although the company claimed that the problem was "limited in scope to a few batches," in early October the British Medicines and Healthcare Products Regulatory Agency suspended Chiron's license. This action effectively prevented the company from releasing any of its influenza vaccine. The other supplier, Aventis Pasteur, delivered about 58 million doses. The U.S. Centers for Disease Control and Prevention (CDC) issued guidelines for rationing the sharply reduced supply of influenza vaccine. Priority groups included children aged 6 months–23 months, adults 65 and older, people with chronic medical conditions, pregnant women, residents of nursing homes and long-term-care facilities, children on continuous aspirin therapy, health care workers involved in direct patient care, and people in close contact with children younger than six months.

In addition to the Aventis Pasteur flu shots, there were about three million doses of FluMist, a live influenza virus nasal spray, which was an immunization option for healthy individuals aged 5–49. The government had also stockpiled enough antiviral medication to treat more than seven million people infected with the flu. In early December the Department of Health and Human Services purchased 1.2 million doses of flu vaccine from U.K.-based pharmaceutical company GlaxoSmithKline (GSK). Because the vaccine had not undergone U.S. Food and Drug Administration (FDA) approval, it would have investigational new drug status, and recipients would be required to sign an informed-consent form.

Researchers tested the possibility of stretching the flu vaccine supply by injecting a small amount into skin (rather than muscle). They found that a dose as small as one-fifth of a standard flu shot was as effective as or more effective than a full dose in healthy adults younger than 60. An advantage of injecting vaccine directly into the skin was that the skin contains abundant dendritic cells, white blood cells that are capable of triggering a strong immune response. Health officials did not recommend that shots be given in this way until the method had been more extensively tested and technical challenges and regulatory hurdles had been overcome.

Other Infectious Diseases. The West Nile virus (WNV) season in the U.S. in 2004 was mild compared with that of 2003, when 9,862 human cases and 264 deaths were reported to the CDC. In 2004 there were 2,448 confirmed human cases of WNV and 87 deaths in 41 states; 36% of infections were severe and involved inflammation of the brain (encephalitis) or the membrane that surrounds the brain or spinal cord (meningitis). (WNV is most often transmitted by mosquitoes that have fed on birds that harboured the virus.) Since the first WNV outbreak in the U.S., which occurred in 1999 and was confined to the New York City area, annual outbreaks had pushed steadily westward. Before 2004 California had experienced only a few human cases; in 2004, however, the state reported 760 cases—almost twice as many as any other state. Washington remained free of WNV, and Oregon experienced only three human cases.

In 2004 deaths from tuberculosis (TB) increased for the first time in more than 40 years. One reason was the rise of drug-resistant strains of *Mycobacterium tuberculosis*, the causative organism. A WHO survey found that of an estimated 300,000 new cases of drug-resistant TB in 2004, nearly 80% were caused by superstrains—that is, strains resistant to at least three of the four drugs commonly used to treat active TB. Another reason for the increase in TB deaths was that 12 million people worldwide were coinfected with TB and HIV. The synergistic effects of HIV and *M. tuberculosis* are especially lethal. TB had become the leading killer of people with AIDS. It was responsible for one-third of the deaths in that group.

SARS (severe acute respiratory syndrome), the deadly new infectious disease that took the world by surprise in 2003, when it infected almost 8,000 people and killed about 800, fortunately did not reemerge in epidemic fashion in 2004. SARS did, however, infect a handful of people in Beijing and in Anhui province in China. The outbreak was traced to two workers at the National Institute of Virology in Beijing, where experiments on the SARS virus had taken place but biosafety practices reportedly were lax. The workers spread the infection to at least nine people outside the lab, including one lab worker's mother, who died. Chinese authorities acted swiftly—they closed the Beijing lab, traced the contacts of those known to be infected, quarantined more than 500 persons, and screened travelers at airports and railroad stations—and there were no additional cases.

Cardiovascular Disease. Statins, a family of drugs also known as HMG-CoA reductase inhibitors, were much in the news in 2004. Statins lower low-density lipoprotein cholesterol (LDL-C) and can reduce the risk of a heart attack or stroke by as much as 40%. The U.S. National Cholesterol Education Program (NCEP) issued new cholesterol guidelines based on the findings of five clinical trials that had involved more than 50,000 people and had been completed since 2001, when the NCEP's guidelines were last revised.

One of the key new recommendations for people at high risk of heart attack was that statins be used to achieve an extreme lowering of LDL-C levels, to under 70 mg/dl (milligrams per decilitre) of blood. The guidelines increased the number of people in the U.S. who met the criteria for statin therapy to 36 million—more than three times the number who took the drugs in 2004. Globally, there was an even bigger gap. Though it was estimated that more than 200 million people would benefit, only 25 million were receiving statin therapy.

In July pharmacies in the U.K. began to sell the statin drug simvastatin (Zocor) in a low (10-mg) dosage without a doctor's prescription to people at moderate risk of heart disease—a group that was estimated to include 5 million–10 million people. The decision to make simvastatin available over the counter was based on the consensus of experts that the benefits outweighed the risks. In general, the drugs were considered extremely safe—much safer, in fact, than aspirin, which millions of people took on a daily basis to prevent heart attacks.

Cancer. The question whether men should have an annual blood test that measures prostate-specific antigen (PSA), a protein produced by the prostate gland, had long been controversial. Generally, the higher a man's PSA level was, the more likely it was that he had prostate cancer, and the test was widely used to screen men over age 50 for prostate cancer. The majority of tumours discovered by PSA tests were harmless, however, so it remained unclear whether the chief reason for PSA screening—to catch tumours early—outweighed the risk of complications from unnecessary treatment. Moreover, there remained no way to distinguish between cancers that could be safely left alone and those that would kill.

The findings of two studies shed new light on the limitations of PSA screening. A National Cancer Institute (NCI)-sponsored study of men with low or normal PSA levels (four nanograms of PSA per millilitre of blood or less) found, through biopsies, that 15% of them had prostate tumours, of which 15% were high-grade and aggressive. In other words, standard PSA screening would have missed a significant number of potentially deadly tumours.

In a study of men who had been treated for prostate cancer, those whose PSA levels rose more than two points in the year prior to their cancer diagnosis had a higher risk of dying from aggressive tumours within seven years, even after they underwent radical surgery. The investigators calculated that the *change* in a man's PSA level in the year before diagnosis was 10 times more predictive of deadly prostate tumours than the level per se.

Dieting. Twin epidemics of obesity and diabetes were intimately linked and threatened to reduce both the quality and the length of life for people around the world. Although the guru of low-carbohydrate diets, Robert Atkins, died in 2003, the craze he started for high-protein, high-fat, low-carb eating endured. A few studies published during

In Sight: A World Without Polio

Reinvigorated immunization efforts to eradicate poliomyelitis (polio) from the world led a UNICEF official in Nigeria, where an outbreak had left more than 700 children paralyzed in 2004, to express confidence that polio had "no hiding place anymore." The immunization program had its beginnings in 1988, when the World Health Organization (WHO), buoyed by the success of the global smallpox eradication campaign (which had been completed a decade earlier), determined that it was technically feasible to purge the world of a second ancient scourge. In partnership with UNICEF, Rotary International, and the U.S. Centers for Disease Control and Prevention, WHO launched the largest public-health campaign ever undertaken, the Global Polio Eradication Initiative (GPEI).

Polio, a highly communicable viral disease that mainly affects young children, can invade the nervous system and cause irreversible paralysis in a matter of hours. Although only one infection in 200 leads to paralysis, all who are infected shed poliovirus in their feces, which allows the disease to spread rapidly, especially among persons who live in crowded conditions with poor sanitation. About 80% of the children in a given region must be fully immunized against polio in order to stop the chain of person-to-person transmission. The GPEI's strategy was straightforward: vaccinate every child under age five with three or four doses of oral polio vaccine (OPV) administered several weeks apart in the 125 countries where polio still crippled an estimated 350,000 youngsters a year.

© Raj Patidar/Reuters/Corbis

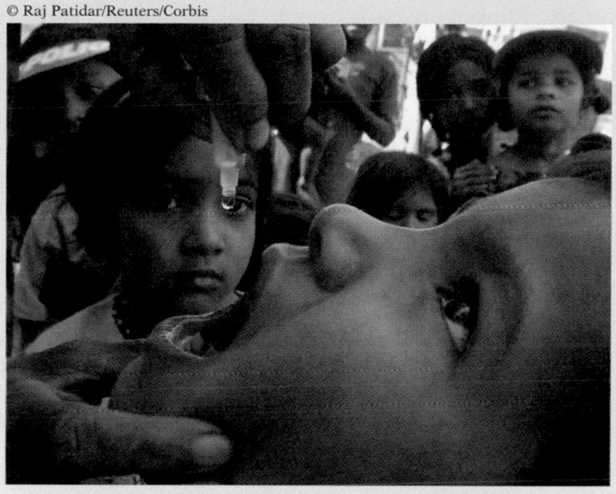

A child in Bhopal, India, receives a drop of polio vaccine. Since 1988 at least two billion children have been immunized as part of a global effort to eradicate the disease.

In 2001 there were fewer than 400 cases of paralytic polio in the world, and the end of the crippling disease seemed tantalizingly close. A 2002 polio epidemic in India increased the number of cases to 1,900, but public-health workers drove the number of cases worldwide down to fewer than 800 in 2003. Sixteen years and more than $3.1 billion after the program began, at least two billion children had been protected against polio, and the GPEI partners believed that "the world had an unprecedented opportunity to finish the job [of eradicating polio] in 2004." That optimism belied the fact that a scenario was unfolding in Africa that threatened to undo years of progress that had been so painstakingly achieved. In the northern Nigerian state of Kano, Muslim leaders were not allowing children to receive OPV because, they contended, the vaccine contained hormones that would sterilize Muslim girls. (Some also believed the vaccine would infect recipients with HIV.) In August 2003 the state governor suspended the immunization program. Predictably, as immunization levels plummeted, northern Nigeria became the epicentre of a polio outbreak that ultimately spread to 12 previously polio-free countries in western and central Africa.

Pressure on Kano's leaders to have the suspension lifted was applied by international public health officials, the Organization of the Islamic Conference, and Nigeria's most powerful sultan. Kano's governor relented when tests of OPV conducted in independent laboratories demonstrated its purity. Polio immunization of the state's four million children under age five resumed in late July (with vaccine that was produced in Indonesia, a Muslim country). In October and November tens of thousands of volunteers overcame many difficulties to administer drops of OPV into the mouths of nearly 80 million children in 23 African countries. Despite the devastating 11-month setback, at the end of 2004 the GPEI partners stood ready to finish in one year the formidable job of ending polio forever.

(ELLEN BERNSTEIN)

the year found that, in the short term, people lost more weight faster on restricted-carbohydrate eating plans than on low-fat diets, but at one year the difference in weight loss with the two diets was minimal. No studies had demonstrated that weight lost the low-carb way would be maintained, and the long-term health effects were unknown. (*See* AGRICULTURE: Sidebar.)

Pharmaceuticals. One of the biggest medical news stories of the year was the withdrawal from the market of the arthritis drug rofecoxib (Vioxx) in late September. Available by prescription since 1999, Vioxx had been used by more than 80 million people worldwide, and at the time the manufacturer, Merck & Co., decided to take it off the market, the drug was being used by almost two million people for relief from the symptoms of arthritis, acute pain, and menstrual pain. The decision followed the discovery that people who took the drug for more than 18 months had twice the risk of heart attack and stroke than those who took a placebo.

A week after the withdrawal of Vioxx, a paper published online by the British medical journal *The Lancet* reviewed 18 trials of rofecoxib that had included more than 25,000 patients and found that a significant risk of heart attack in patients who took the drug was evident by the end of 2000. An accompanying editorial by *Lancet*'s editor lambasted Merck and the FDA for having "acted out of ruthless, short-sighted, and irresponsible self-interest" in not having recalled Vioxx years earlier.

Following the recall, David Graham, a senior drug reviewer in the FDA's Office of Drug Safety, testified before the Senate Finance Committee that the regulatory agency was "incapable of protecting

America." Referring to the increased cardiovascular risks with Vioxx, he said, "We are faced with what may be the single greatest drug-safety catastrophe in this country or the history of the world." In his invective against the FDA, he cited five other drugs that he believed should not be on the market. They were valdecoxib; sibutramine hydrochloride monohydrate (Meridia), a diet drug associated with serious cardiovascular problems and sometimes death; salmeterol xinafoate (Serevent), an asthma medication that had caused life-threatening asthma episodes and deaths; rosuvastatin calcium (Crestor), a cholesterol-lowering agent linked to acute kidney failure and to a serious muscle-weakening disease; and isotretinoin (Accutane), an acne drug that had caused severe birth defects.

Revelation of the heart-attack risk associated with rofecoxib prompted further scrutiny of other drugs in its class, cyclooxygenase-2 (COX-2) inhibitors. This class of drugs became rapidly popular when first introduced in the late 1990s because the drugs appeared to cause fewer adverse gastrointestinal effects than traditional nonsteroidal anti-inflammatory drugs (NSAIDs)—aspirin, ibuprofen, and naproxen. There was little evidence, though, that COX-2 inhibitors (which are also NSAIDs) offered superior relief of pain or inflammation. Of the two other COX-2 inhibitors on the market, celecoxib (Celebrex) and valdecoxib (Bextra), valdecoxib had been shown to increase heart-attack risk in patients who had undergone coronary-artery bypass surgery. In mid-December a large NCI trial that was investigating the potential of celecoxib to prevent colon cancer was discontinued when data revealed a 2.5-fold increased risk of cardiovascular events for participants taking celecoxib (200 mg twice daily) compared with those who were taking a placebo. Less than a week later, a study of the potential of celecoxib and the over-the-counter NSAID naproxen (Aleve) to prevent Alzheimer disease found that people taking naproxen had a significantly increased risk of stroke and heart attack; no increased risk was evident for people taking celecoxib. In light of the new evidence, the FDA advised caution concerning the use of COX-2 inhibitors, naproxen, and other NSAIDs pending further review of data that were continuing to be collected.

The Vioxx withdrawal raised important questions about the role of direct-to-consumer advertising in creating "blockbuster" drugs. Merck had spent at least $100 million annually to promote Vioxx to consumers, which paid off in $2.5 billion in sales in 2003. In late December the manufacturer of Celebrex and Bextra, Pfizer Inc., agreed to sell Bextra with a warning label and to pull all consumer-aimed ads for Celebrex. Sales of the two drugs had totaled more than $2.5 billion in 2003. Critics of direct-to-consumer advertising emphasized that consumers were being bombarded by ads for costly newer drugs, for which the long-term effects were unknown.

The pharmaceutical industry was at the centre of another drug-safety controversy, which concerned the manufacturers of selective serotonin reuptake inhibitors (SSRIs), a widely used class of antidepressants. The manufacturers had failed to disclose the results of clinical trials that found that the drugs lacked effectiveness in children and teenagers and that they were associated with an increased risk of suicidal thoughts and acts. In June, New York Attorney General Eliot Spitzer (*see* BIOGRAPHIES) sued one of the manufacturers, U.K.-based GSK, for having committed fraud by withholding the results of four of five studies on the use of the SSRI paroxetine (Paxil) in children and adolescents. A settlement was reached in August under which GSK agreed to disclose all information on clinical studies of Paxil to the public on its Web site. GSK also made plans to post all of its clinical trial data for its other marketed medicines on the Internet.

The first part of the reforms made to Medicare took effect in June, when drug discount cards became available. The cards were an interim measure meant to offer relief to seniors (as well as to some people with disabilities) from high prescription-drug prices until the full prescription-drug benefits took effect in 2006. But confusion reigned as seniors were faced with more than 70 different cards from which to choose. An analysis carried out by the House of Representatives Government Reform Committee revealed that "the prices available with the new Medicare discount drug cards [were] far higher than the prices available in Canada and no lower than the prices available to individuals who [did] not have the cards." (*See* SOCIAL PROTECTION: Sidebar.)

Ironically, the Medicare Web site that allowed beneficiaries to compare drug prices may have driven more people to have their prescriptions filled in Canada. Indeed, well over one million Americans were buying their prescription drugs from Canada, where the same drug often cost 25% to 80% less than in the United States. Despite the huge traffic in cross-border prescription-drug sales, the FDA maintained its opposition to the importation of foreign drugs on safety grounds.

Stem Cells. Early in the year, Hwang Woo Suk and Moon Shin Yong (*see* BIOGRAPHIES) at Seoul National University reported that through a complex process of cloning called nuclear transfer, they had created human embryos, from which they had then extracted stem cells. The cells were capable of developing into virtually any tissue type or organ, and the stem-cell line they created could be grown in a laboratory culture indefinitely. The South Koreans published a detailed report of their work in the journal *Science.* They stated that their intention was solely to advance understanding of human diseases and provide the foundation for novel therapies. Upon learning of the achievement by the South Koreans, Leon R. Kass, chairman of the U.S. President's Council on Bioethics, said, "The age of human cloning has apparently arrived: today, cloned blastocysts for research, tomorrow cloned blastocysts for babymaking." He went on to call for Congress to enact a law that would ban all human cloning.

In March, Boston scientists reported that they had derived 17 new human embryonic stem-cell lines from 286 frozen human embryos produced by in vitro fertilization. Their goal was to facilitate the "understanding of the mechanisms by which differentiation of embryonic stem cells may be controlled to produce cell types for drug development and for transplantation in the treatment of disease." They were making the newly created stem-cell lines available to researchers, but because of regulations that had been imposed by U.S. Pres. George W. Bush in August 2001, none of the lines could be used for federally funded research.

Although the president had not budged on his position, in the November election California voters decisively approved Proposition 71, the Stem Cell Research and Cures Initiative, a $3 billion bond measure to fund stem-cell research. The passage of "Prop 71" was expected to make California a global leader in the pioneering field of stem-cell research.

(ELLEN BERNSTEIN)

Law, Crime, and Law Enforcement

U.S. conduct in combating terrorism and prosecuting the war in IRAQ topped the list of LEGAL issues in 2004. TERRORISTS struck back in SPAIN, RUSSIA, and elsewhere.

INTERNATIONAL LAW

The Coalition Provisional Authority (CPA) of Iraq handed over power to an interim Iraqi government on June 30, 2004. Sovereignty of the new government was not absolute, however. The U.S. retained control over a number of governmental functions, most notably national security and the prison system. It also retained control over the custody of former Iraqi Pres. Saddam Hussein. No U.S. troops were withdrawn from Iraq in conjunction with the transition, and many U.S. administrators from the CPA moved into advisory positions in the new government.

The U.S. treatment of prisoners in Iraq, particularly in Abu Ghraib prison, received considerable attention. Many prisoners were subjected to various forms of physically and psychologically abusive treatment. They were kept naked for days at a time, photographed in that state, and forced to pose in sexually explicit positions. They were also deprived of sleep and threatened with electric shock or with attacks by military dogs. This treatment violated international humanitarian law, specifically the Geneva Conventions, which prohibited the humiliating or degrading treatment of prisoners of war. (*See* MILITARY AFFAIRS: Special Report.) According to investigators from the International Committee of the Red Cross, some of the abuses could be classified as torture and therefore violate not only the Geneva Conventions but also the International Covenant on Civil and Political Rights, the Convention Against Torture, and the Universal Declaration of Human Rights. Soldiers accused of having perpetrated the abuses were arraigned in U.S. military courts, and by the end of 2004 several of the soldiers had been given jail sentences.

The Iraqi Special Tribunal, a court established specifically for prosecuting Saddam Hussein and his former officials, also received much attention. Unlike many other war-crimes courts, the tribunal was not an independent international judiciary; it was located in Iraq, it comprised Iraqi judges, and it relied on Iraqi law. In addition, the United States had a substantial role in the formation and operation of the tribunal; it was established by the U.S.-appointed Iraqi Governing Council and financed by the U.S. government, with U.S. personnel engaged in sifting through the evidence to be presented in the case and largely responsible for prosecuting Saddam and other defendants. Saddam was arraigned by the tribunal, and in July he appeared before it for the first time. He faced charges of genocide, war crimes, and crimes against humanity. Saddam and his lawyers challenged the legitimacy of the court and the ability of Saddam to receive a fair trial in Iraq. Human rights groups also challenged the court's legitimacy, arguing that an international court would be more appropriate to issue judgment in the case.

The two main cases brought before the International Court of Justice (ICJ) were *Romania* v. *Ukraine,* which concerned the establishment of a maritime boundary between the two states, and *Benin* v. *Niger,* a border dispute. Upon a request from the UN General Assembly, the court agreed to make an advisory ruling on the security barrier that Israel was building in occupied Palestinian territory to seal off the West Bank. In July the ICJ issued a 14–1 opinion (a U.S. judge dissented) that asserted that it had jurisdiction to issue an opinion and that the barrier violated international humanitarian and human rights law. Subsequently, the UN General Assembly passed a resolution that accepted the advisory opinion of the court, demanded that Israel comply with the legal obligations outlined in the opinion, and requested that the UN assess damages associated with the construction of the barrier.

When the International Criminal Court (ICC) entered into force in 2002, the U.S. successfully lobbied the UN Security Council to pass a resolution that exempted from prosecution U.S. participants in UN-authorized missions. The U.S. successfully renewed the exemption once, but in 2004 it became clear that the exemption would not be renewed a second time. The U.S. continued to work to shield itself from the reach of the ICC by pressuring other countries to sign bilateral immunity agreements under which each country promised not to turn over to the ICC any U.S. nationals or employees who worked for the U.S. government or military. As of December 1, more than 90 countries had signed such agreements.

In 2004 attacks by the Arab militia known as the Janjawid resulted in mass killings, rapes, looting, and starvation in the Darfur region of The Sudan, but

(continued on page 208)

On July 1, deposed Iraqi president Saddam Hussein reacts to a reading of the charges that he and other defendants will face later in an Iraqi court.

The Legal Debate over Same-Sex Marriages

by Andrew Koppelman

Same-sex marriage came to the United States in 2004. The Massachusetts Supreme Court decided in November 2003 that the denial of marriage licenses to same-sex couples violated the state constitution and gave the state six months to comply with its order. The state consequently started issuing the licenses on May 17, 2004.

The question of whether couples of the same sex should be allowed to marry has roiled American politics since a 1993 Hawaii Supreme Court decision seemed to indicate that that state would shortly have to recognize such marriages. Americans, however, have consistently opposed same-sex marriage by wide margins. In 1996 Congress enacted the federal Defense of Marriage Act, which declared that no same-sex marriage would be recognized for federal purposes, such as filing joint tax returns, the award of Social Security survivor's benefits, or medical insurance for the families of federal employees. The act also indicated (in a restatement of existing law) that no state (or other U.S. territory) was required to recognize marriages from another state when it had strong public policies to the contrary. To date, 43 states have enacted laws declaring that they will not recognize same-sex marriages from other states.

The Hawaii court decision was overruled by a state constitutional amendment in 1998, but other states moved toward recognition of same-sex couples. In 1999 the Vermont Supreme Court declared that same-sex couples were entitled under the state constitution to the same legal rights as married heterosexual couples, and the legislature shortly thereafter enacted a law creating the status of "civil unions," with

all the rights of marriage but not the name. In 2003 California enacted a similar statute, calling the relationships "domestic partnerships." Officials in some smaller jurisdictions, notably San Francisco, joined the controversy in mid-2004 by issuing marriage licenses in defiance of local prohibitions. All of these were soon held to be invalid.

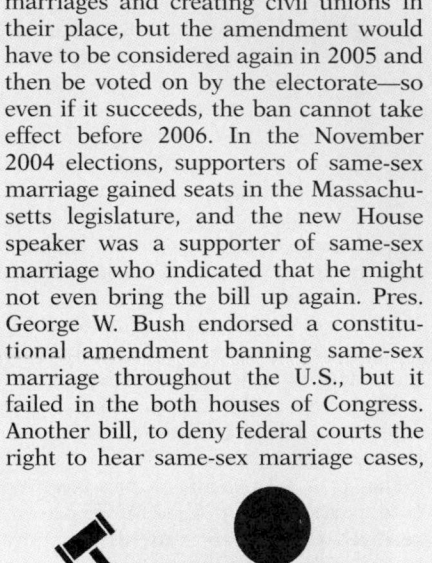

The Massachusetts decision was not the first legal recognition of same-sex marriage. The Netherlands (in April 2001), Belgium (June 2003), and Canada (July 2003) had already recognized such unions. Like the earlier Hawaii court decision, however, the Massachusetts ruling provoked a negative response in the U.S. The Massachusetts legislature narrowly passed a state constitutional amendment banning same-sex marriages and creating civil unions in their place, but the amendment would have to be considered again in 2005 and then be voted on by the electorate—so even if it succeeds, the ban cannot take effect before 2006. In the November 2004 elections, supporters of same-sex marriage gained seats in the Massachusetts legislature, and the new House speaker was a supporter of same-sex marriage who indicated that he might not even bring the bill up again. Pres. George W. Bush endorsed a constitutional amendment banning same-sex marriage throughout the U.S., but it failed in the both houses of Congress. Another bill, to deny federal courts the right to hear same-sex marriage cases,

passed the House of Representatives but got no farther.

A Two-Pronged Debate. Part of the complexity of the issue is that the debate over same-sex marriage is really two different debates. The first is a normative debate about what relationships to value or even to sanctify. The second is a debate about administration—that is, which relationships ought to have legal consequences.

The normative debate, which contains religious dimensions for many people, concerns what relationships are intrinsically valuable. The key question is one about objective moral reality: are same-sex relationships as such morally equal to heterosexual relationships, or do heterosexual relationships partake of a good that homosexual relationships cannot possibly share?

On this issue Americans are divided, with different groups adhering to very different moral visions. According to the anti-same-sex-marriage vision, sex can be morally worthy precisely and only because of its place in procreation. Even the marriages of infertile heterosexual couples take their meaning from the fact that they form a union of the procreative kind. From this perspective the movement for same-sex marriage is a misguided attempt to deny fundamental moral distinctions. According to the other moral vision, sex is valuable, either in itself or because it draws people toward friendship of a singular degree and kind. This bringing together of persons has intrinsic worth, whether or not it leads to childbearing or child rearing. On this account, sexuality is linked to the flourishing of the next generation only to the extent that it is one of a number of factors that can bond adults together into stable familial units in which children are likely to thrive. From this perspective it is the devaluation of same-sex intimacy that is immoral, because it reflects arbitrary and irrational discrimination.

The administrative debate concerns what relationships between persons ought to be given legal recognition. Here the issue is more mundane: how should resources be allocated and unfair disruption of people's lives be prevented? Households, of whatever kind, and relationships of dependency exist, and members of those households have wants and needs if some unprovided-for contingency arises, such as the illness or death of one member. Financial issues such as inheritance rights and employer benefits for dependents of employees, also come into play.

Are "Civil Unions" the Answer? Because the moral and the administrative questions are distinct, many jurisdictions besides Vermont and California have opted to grant same-sex couples some or all of the rights of married couples without the honorific of "marriage." Denmark, Sweden, Norway, Finland, Iceland, and New Zealand have legalized partnerships that are nearly identical to marriage, while more limited rights and responsibilities are available to same-sex couples in France, Germany, Austria, Hungary, South Africa, and Portugal, as well as in parts of Australia, Spain, and Switzerland. The U.S. constitutional amendment failed in part because it was so broadly worded that it seemed to some to prohibit civil unions as well as same-sex marriages.

Civil unions, however, are also controversial. Many conservatives believe that same-sex relationships are morally wrong and should not be given any recognition at all by the state, while gay rights advocates object that withholding the name of "marriage" implies an inferior status. Finally, gay men and lesbians are not unanimous in support of same-sex marriage. Some gay rights proponents contend that their movement should focus instead on AIDS prevention, HIV and health care, antigay violence, immigration, employment discrimination, and the military's exclusion of gay service members.

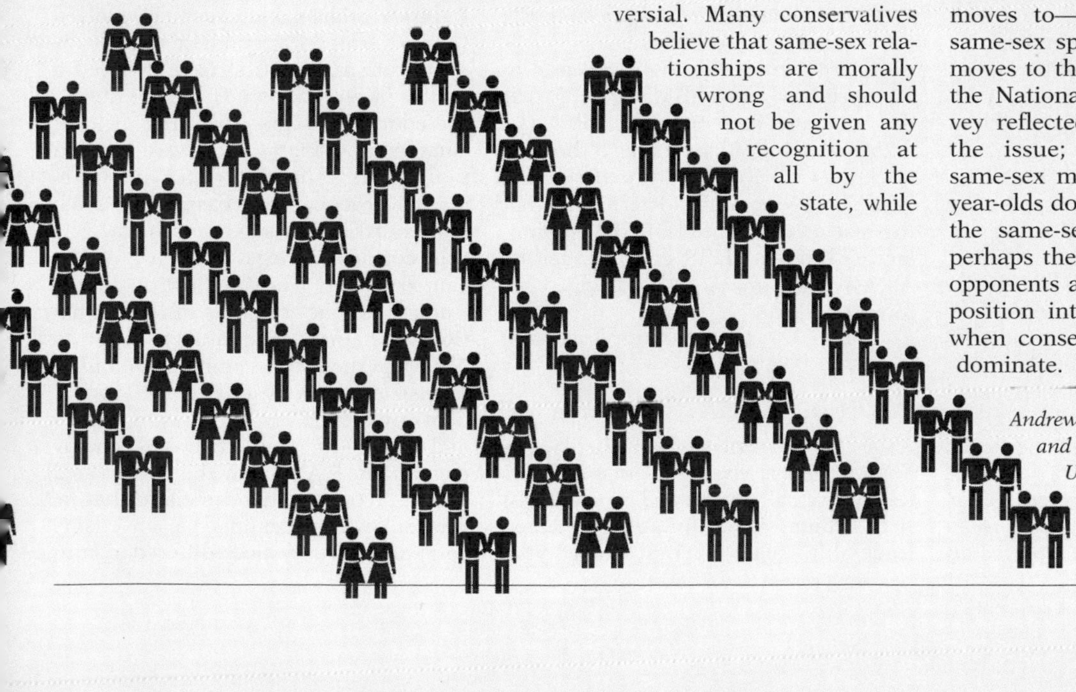

Many legal scholars have developed defensible arguments that same-sex marriage should be protected under the federal constitution, under either the guarantee of equal protection of the laws or the fundamental right to marry. It seems unlikely, however, that the U.S. Supreme Court will adopt these arguments in the near future. In *Lawrence* v. *Texas*, a 2003 decision that struck down laws criminalizing homosexual sex, the Court made clear that it was not about to touch the marriage question. Even if the court is inclined to support same-sex marriage—which is far from clear—it appears to grasp that any such decision would almost certainly be overruled by a constitutional amendment.

Future Prospects. Same-sex marriage is likely to remain part of the American scene for a long time, but it is not likely to spread very widely any time soon. Massachusetts law cannot change until 2006, and even if the state court is overruled, it is not clear that marriages already in existence will not continue. Other states are beginning to sort out what effect Massachusetts marriages will have elsewhere. It is unclear what will happen if the validity of a same-sex marriage comes into question when a Massachusetts resident is visiting—or moves to—another state, or when a same-sex spouse from another country moves to the U.S. Meanwhile, a poll by the National Annenberg Election Survey reflected a generational divide on the issue; most Americans oppose same-sex marriage, but most 18-to-29-year-olds do not. The long-term goals of the same-sex-marriage movement are perhaps the most powerful reason why opponents are so eager to cement their position into the law now—at a time when conservative political forces still dominate.

Andrew Koppelman is Professor of Law and Political Science at Northwestern University, Chicago, Ill., and the author of The Gay Rights Question in Contemporary American Law.

(continued from page 205)
the international community was slow to act. The question of whether the violence legally constituted genocide brought international law to the forefront of the crisis, because as a signatory of international genocide treaties the government of The Sudan was obligated to act to prevent genocide within its borders.

Headlining the work of the International Criminal Tribunal for the Former Yugoslavia (ICTY) in 2004 was the trial of former Yugoslav president Slobodan Milosevic. Milosevic, who served as his own defense counsel, planned to rest his defense on the contention that the court was illegitimate and had no jurisdiction over him. The progress of the defense portion of the trial was delayed repeatedly because of his poor health, which doctors said was aggravated by the stress of defending himself. Worried about the delays, the court appointed defense counsel for Milosevic in September. The new lawyers appealed the decision, on Milosevic's behalf, and as of November the appeal was pending. The lawyers later asked the court to remove them from the case, stating that they were unable to defend Milosevic because of his refusal to cooperate with them. In mid-2004 the appeals chamber of the ICTY overturned the convictions of Radislav Krstic and Tihomir Blaskic on some charges and reduced their sentences. Both men had been high-ranking military officials and had been convicted of genocide-related activities. Several key figures in the Yugoslav wars, including Bosnian Serbs Radovan Karadzic and Ratko Mladic, remained at large.

The Special Court for Sierra Leone was a tribunal backed by the UN that operated in that West African state with the cooperation of the government. Its mandate was to try rebel military commanders who had been charged with killings, rapes, enslavement of children as soldiers, and mutilation committed during Sierra Leone's 10-year civil war. The leader of the rebel group, Foday Sankoh, had died of natural causes in UN custody in 2003, but the remaining rebel leaders in custody were brought to trial in June. Former Liberian president Charles Taylor, who had been indicted by the court in 2003 for having supported and funded the rebels, appealed the indictment on grounds that a court in one country had no jurisdiction over the leader of another. In May the appeals panel of the court rejected his argument, stating that the special court did have jurisdiction because it was an international tribunal. Taylor was in exile in Nigeria, which refused to turn him over for prosecution. In a related case, Liberian human rights groups called for the creation of an international tribunal for atrocities committed in Liberia's 14-year civil war. If such a court was established, Taylor would likely face indictment there as well.

In October the Cambodian legislature voted to establish a UN-assisted tribunal, similar to the one in Sierra Leone, to punish the top leaders of the Khmer Rouge, the group that had led Cambodia from 1975 to 1979 and was responsible for the death of more than 1.5 million Cambodians. In April several groups in Côte d'Ivoire requested UN assistance in establishing a tribunal to investigate ongoing human rights violations allegedly committed by government security forces since 2000. A UN-assisted court was operating in East Timor (Timor-Leste), but concern with potential damage to relationships with Indonesia led officials in East Timor to reject calls for an independent international tribunal to try Indonesian troops responsible for violence during East Timor's 1999 movement for independence.

In The Netherlands, Sebastien Nzapali, an army officer under Mobutu Sese Seko, former president of Zaire (now the Democratic Republic of the Congo), was sentenced to 30 months in prison for having tortured people in his country in 1995 and 1996. Nzapali had been living in The Netherlands since 1998 seeking political asylum, but he had not been granted refugee status. He was arrested in 2003 after three Congolese nationals filed charges against him. His conviction came under a Dutch law, the 1988 Implementation Act to the UN Convention Against Torture.

Roma (Gypsies) brought a case in Switzerland against IBM, alleging that the company had provided the Nazis with technology that enabled them to track and kill Roma in the 1930s and '40s. The Swiss courts determined that the case could proceed. In 2001 a similar case brought in U.S. courts under the Alien Tort Claims Act was dropped before being heard.

(VICTORIA C. WILLIAMS)

COURT DECISIONS

The 2003–04 term of the United States Supreme Court was distinguished by its relatively small docket and by Chief Justice William H. Rehnquist's reduced leadership role. During his 18-year tenure as chief justice, Rehnquist had overseen the development of a solidly conservative institution and the membership of the court had not changed for a decade. With an ideological majority at his side, Rehnquist had been able to assert the authority of the judiciary while he exercised a doctrine of judicial restraint, advanced an agenda of states' rights in federalism-oriented cases, and attempted to restore the degree of legitimacy that the institution had lost in the 2000 case of *Bush* v. *Gore*.

The cases in 2004 that involved seemingly political questions fell into two basic categories—those that concerned conventional matters in districting systems and political speech and cases that involved what had become known simply as the "war on terrorism." In the first category the court upheld congressional-redistricting plans in Pennsylvania that had exhibited a Republican bias in elections. The plan, drawn by the Republican majority in the state legislature, had the effect of displacing Democratic incumbents. Although the court had previously rejected districting plans on the basis of racial gerrymandering, the plurality for the case of *Vieth* v. *Jubelirer* insisted that cases concerning partisan gerrymandering should not be entitled to legal standing in federal courts because the courts lacked a uniform standard for judging and resolving them. Regarding political speech, the court decided in *McConnell* v. *Federal Election Commission* that the McCain-Feingold ban on soft money (virtually unlimited and unregulated contributions to political parties) and various restrictions on election-period advertising were constitutionally permissible. The cases of *Rasul* v. *Bush* and *Hamdi* v. *Rumsfeld* addressed issues that involved U.S. governmental conduct in the war on terrorism. The first case involved a matter of jurisdiction. By a vote of 6–3, the court ruled that detainees held at Guantánamo Bay, Cuba, were entitled to file writs of habeas corpus and to request a review of their cases in U.S. federal courts, because Guantánamo Bay was considered legal territory of the United States. The implication of the ruling was that hundreds of foreign national detainees had a legal right to challenge their imprisonment. *Hamdi* v. *Rumsfeld* challenged the U.S. president's presumed broad power to declare and detain American citizens as "enemy combatants." Although the court ruled 6–3 in favour of Hamdi's claim that he was unlawfully detained as an enemy combatant, the justices differed significantly on the precise reasons why that should be the case. For Chief Justice Rehnquist and Justices Stephen Breyer, Anthony Kennedy, and Sandra Day O'Connor, it was an entitlement to rebut the government before an impartial tribunal; for Justices David Souter and Ruth Bader Ginsburg, it was the absence of congressional authorization.

In the related field of criminal law, the court decided six noteworthy cases. Three dealt with police conduct in general and with self-incrimination in particular. In *Hiibel* v. *Sixth Judicial District Court of Nevada,* the court rejected Fourth and Fifth Amendment claims and ruled 5–4 that criminal suspects must identify themselves to police. In *Missouri* v. *Seibert* the court rejected a practice of interrogating suspects twice—once before and once after they had been informed of their Miranda rights—as a method of obtaining a confession. In the related case of *United States* v. *Patane,* the court was considerably less supportive of Miranda rights, and it ruled that physical evidence that police obtained on the basis of information provided by a criminal suspect who had not been read his rights was legally admissible in a court of law. In the case of *Crawford* v. *Washington,* Scalia wrote for the court that the confrontation clause of the Sixth Amendment guarantees defendants the right to confront their accusers, and in this case the court declared unconstitutional the practice of prosecutors' introducing the testimony of absent witnesses without offering the defense the opportunity to engage in cross-examination. In *Blakely* v. *Washington* the court barred judges from imposing sentences in excess of the state maximum, but it allowed juries to do so as long as the facts of the case were deemed to have merit "beyond a reasonable doubt." Finally, in the case of *Schriro* v. *Summerlin,* a divided court refused to apply retroactively a 2002 decision that invalidated the death penalty in cases in five states. Among the consequences of the ruling was that approximately 100 detainees would be returned to death row.

In the realm of civil liberties and civil rights, the court decided a number of disparately related yet important cases. Regarding discrimination, in *Tennessee* v. *Lane* the court upheld the right of disabled citizens to sue states if the states violated the Americans with Disabilities Act. The case involved a courthouse that had been inaccessible to persons with diminished ambulatory abilities. In *Pennsylvania State Police* v. *Suders,* the court developed guidelines for assessing allegations of sexual harassment. The baseline for its analysis was that employers would be liable for maintaining a workplace environment that would compel a reasonable person to resign. With procedures in place an employer could claim protection if an employee failed to use them, but if the harassment alleged corresponded to direct disciplinary action, then that blanket of protection would disappear.

In *Locke* v. *Davey* the court addressed the perennial issue of church-state relations as they pertained to educational opportunities. Under the establishment clause of the First Amendment, the court had increasingly accommodated a closer relationship between religious and governmental institutions, but in the present case the court was asked to answer whether the free-exercise clause requires religious schools to be included in various state "school-choice" programs. The court ruled 7–2 that it does not—that state subsidies for secular college education do not have to be paired with or necessarily include an obligation to fund divinity students. Finally, in what clearly ranked as the highest-profile case of the year, the court addressed the "under God" provision in the Pledge of Allegiance. Two years earlier the 9th Circuit Court of Appeals had drawn considerable attention—and heat—for having ruled that the phrase "under God" amounted to a state-led demonstration of religious devotion and therefore compromised the wall of separation dividing church and state. The decision of the U.S. Supreme Court in the case of *Elk Grove Unified School District* v. *Newdow* was much less dramatic; indeed, it scarcely addressed the matter of religious establishment or free exercise. O'Connor and Rehnquist did argue that "under God" was a political rather than a purely religious statement, given that in 1954, when the phrase was adopted, the United States was confronting the "godless communism" of the Soviet Union. The majority, however, simply asserted that the ruling of the lower court should be overturned because the petitioner, Michael Newdow, lacked legal standing. Newdow had brought the suit on behalf of his minor child, but Newdow and the child's mother, who possessed primary legal custody, were in conflict over the child's educational and religious upbringing. The court stated that Newdow therefore could not assert the exclusive legal right to bring suit on behalf of the child, and the decision of the lower court was overturned with surprisingly little fanfare.

(BRIAN SMENTKOWSKI)

CRIME

Terrorism. On March 11, 2004, on the eve of the Spanish national election, multiple bomb blasts killed at least 200 rail commuters and injured more than 1,500 in Madrid. Though immediate blame for the blasts was placed on the Basque separatist group Euskadi Ta Askatasuna (ETA), subsequent investigations revealed that the attack was perpetrated by a group that was part of a complex European-wide network of radical Muslims with links to Osama bin Laden and his al-Qaeda movement.

On September 1 in Beslan, in Russia's North Ossetian Republic, a local school was attacked by 32 armed Chechen militants, who seized more than 1,100 hostages, including pupils (aged 7 to 17), parents, relatives, and teachers, who had gathered to celebrate the opening day of the new school year. The siege ended abruptly 54 hours later when explosive devices carried by the militants blew up prematurely and Russian security forces stormed the building. More than 340 people were killed, including at least 150 children, and more than 500 persons were injured, with many others missing. (*See* photograph on page 210.) Responsibility for the atrocity was claimed by Riyadus-Salikhin, a Chechen liberation group led by notorious rebel warlord Shamil Basayev. That same group also claimed responsibility for suicide-bombing attacks on two Russian passenger jets, which had crashed within minutes of one another on August 24; 89 persons were killed. In the wake of these attacks, the Russian government, led by Pres. Vladimir Putin, introduced new and sweeping antiterrorism laws in the parliament and sought international support for a UN Security Council resolution to expand the definition of banned terrorist organizations to include liberation groups such as the Chechens and the Palestinians.

In its annual review of patterns of global terrorism, released in June, the U.S. Department of State (DOS) reported that during 2003 there were 208 acts of international terrorism. A total of 625 persons were killed in these attacks, and 3,646 were injured, a sharp increase from the 2,013 persons who had been wounded the previous year. The report noted that most of the attacks occurring in Iraq during 2003 did not meet the "long-standing U.S. definition of international terrorism because they were directed at combatants, that is, U.S. and coalition forces on duty."

In Iraq there was a significant increase during 2004 in the number of noncombatants, including foreign-aid workers and journalists, who were taken hostage. Though some of these hostages were released others, including American construction engineers and a British colleague, were decapitated by their captors.

In September Pakistani Pres. Pervez Musharraf announced the elimination of Amjad Hussain Farooqui, Pakistan's leading al-Qaeda figure and most-wanted terrorist. Farooqui, the alleged mastermind behind a number of terrorist attacks, including two recent attempts to assassinate Musharraf and the 2002 beheading in Pakistan of *The Wall Street Journal* reporter Daniel Pearl, was killed by security forces during a raid in Nawabshah, a city in southern Pakistan.

The scene in the school gymnasium in Beslan, North Ossetia, on September 4, the day after the bloody end of the hostage-seizure crisis between Chechen rebels and Russian special forces troops. More than 340 people were killed in the bomb blasts.

© Denis Marinin/Reuters/Corbis

Drug, Human, and Weapons Trafficking. In March U.S. Pres. George W. Bush sent to Congress his annual report, which listed the names of 23 major illicit-drug-producing and drug-transit countries, including Afghanistan, Myanmar (Burma), China, Colombia, India, Mexico, Pakistan, and Vietnam. President Bush also expressed concern over heroin and methamphetamine trafficking linked to North Korea. In September DOS officials informed Congress that poppy cultivation in Afghanistan, the world's leading supplier of illicit opium, morphine, and heroin, was anticipated to rise by 40% during the year. In 2003 the narcotics trade had reportedly generated $2.3 billion in income for Afghanistan, which produced three-quarters of the world's heroin, including 90% of the heroin trafficked to Europe.

In May a report by Amnesty International alleged that up to 2,000 women, many of them underage girls, had in recent years been forced into sexual slavery in the southeastern European province of Kosovo. The growth in sex trafficking and prostitution rackets had taken place since NATO-led peacekeepers occupied the province in 1999. Military personnel from a number of countries were reportedly involved in the rackets, with women being traded for up to $3,500 and kept in appalling conditions by their "owners."

Muhammad al-Baradi'i, who was the head of the International Atomic Energy Agency (IAEA), warned that a nuclear black market of "fantastic cleverness" was supplying countries that were seeking to develop illicit nuclear weapons. The IAEA confirmed that Libya and Iran had made extensive use of connections to top Pakistani scientists, including 'Abd-al Qadir Khan, the leader of that nation's nuclear weapons program. In February Khan, hitherto a national hero for having developed the "Islamic bomb," made a public confession of wrongdoing while issuing a plea for clemency. Granting the plea, President Musharraf insisted there was no official involvement in Khan's activities, which were motivated by personal greed. Commentators remained skeptical, however, noting that Pakistan's nuclear program was supposed to be under close military control.

Murder and Other Violence. Preliminary figures released in June from the FBI's Uniform Crime Reporting Program indicated that despite an increase of 1.3% in murder over the previous year, violent crime in the U.S. declined 3.2% in 2003 compared with 2002, and property crimes in 2003 remained relatively unchanged from the 2002 figure.

In July the British Home Office reported that the crime rate in England and Wales fell by a further 5% during 2003 to produce the longest sustained drop since 1898.

Gun-control advocates expressed dismay in the U.S. when a 10-year federal ban on some types of assault weapons expired in September. The ban, imposed in the wake of a number of multiple slayings at schools and other places by persons armed with military-style weaponry, was credited with a dramatic decline in the use of these guns by criminals.

In the first case of cannibalism in Germany since the 1920s, Armin Meiwes, a former soldier, was convicted of manslaughter in January for having killed and eaten his male lover. Meiwes—who had used Internet chat rooms to solicit his allegedly willing victim, Bernd-Jürgen Brandes—was sentenced to be imprisoned for eight years and five months. Fears that the widely publicized case might spawn copycat killings were realized in October when Berlin police found the dismembered body of Joe Ritzkowsky in a refrigerator. Ralf Meyer confessed to having killed and butchered his lover; cannibalism was not an offense under German law.

White-Collar Crime, Corruption, and Fraud. Federal regulators in the U.S. achieved a number of high-profile successes in their ongoing efforts to prosecute and punish individuals believed responsible for some of the most notorious corporate excesses of the late 1990s. Former Enron chairman and CEO Kenneth Lay was indicted in July on 11 counts, including securities and wire fraud and bank fraud. If convicted, Lay, who continued to profess his innocence, faced a maximum sentence of 175 years in prison and huge fines. Earlier, federal prosecutors had also charged Bernard Ebbers, the former CEO of WorldCom, with conspiracy, securities fraud, and filing false statements in connection with that company's $11 billion accounting scandal, which led to the largest bankruptcy in U.S. history. Scott Sullivan, former CFO of WorldCom, pleaded guilty to the same criminal charges and agreed to testify against Ebbers in exchange for possible leniency in his sentencing. In October Martha Stewart, one of the best-known businesswomen in the U.S., began a five-month prison sentence after her conviction in March on charges of conspiracy, making false statements, and obstruction of justice. New York Attorney General Eliot Spitzer (*see* BIOGRAPHIES), who had successfully prosecuted a number of Wall Street firms, took aim at the insurance industry in October. Europe also had its fair share of corporate crimes, including the Mannesmann case (*see* WORLD AFFAIRS: *Germany*) and the Parmalat probe (*see* WORLD AFFAIRS: *Italy*).

Law Enforcement. The dramatic shift in FBI priorities after Sept. 11, 2001, was revealed in a report released in April by Inspector General Glenn A. Fine of the U.S. Department of Justice. With a major focus on antiterrorism efforts, FBI investigations targeting drug trafficking, organized crime, and white-collar crime were greatly reduced. The largest cuts occurred in the FBI's investigations involving Mexican drug organizations, primarily in the U.S Southwest. Other federal agencies, including the Drug Enforcement Administration, had taken up some of these responsibilities.

In a separate report in July, most of which was classified as secret, Fine drew attention to the significant management challenges facing the FBI in translating all the terrorist-related material it received from wiretaps and other sources of intelligence. The FBI's electronic surveillance collection alone, in languages primarily related to counterterrorism activities—Arabic, Farsi, Urdu, and Pashto—increased by 45% in 2003 compared with 2001. The FBI indicated that nearly 24% of its ongoing Foreign Intelligence Surveillance Act (FISA) intercepts were not being monitored, while more than 120,000 hours of potentially valuable terrorism-related recordings remained untranslated.

On July 22 the final report of the bipartisan National Commission on Terrorist Attacks upon the United States (the *9/11 Commission Report*) was released. The report pointed to numbers of missed "operational opportunities" to discover the plot by al-Qaeda to launch its 9/11 attack and identified weaknesses in the approach taken by law enforcement, including the FBI, to counter the terrorist threat from Islamic extremists. The FBI's approach to investigations was said to be case specific, decentralized, and geared toward prosecution. Effective counterterrorism strategies were hampered by limited resources, training, and information sharing. The commission recommended a number of measures, including the establishment of a National Counterterrorism Center, within the executive office of the U.S. president, to coordinate planning and give direction to counterterrorism efforts. The commission also recommended the appointment of a new national intelligence director with two main jobs: to oversee national intelligence centres and to coordinate the agencies that contributed to the national intelligence program. In December President Bush signed into law an intelligence-reform bill that would organize the 15 separate intelligence agencies under the command of a national intelligence director.

Widespread public protests concerning the state of crime and the lack of personal security were reported in a number of Latin American countries during the year. Hundreds of thousands of citizens marched in the streets of Buenos Aires, Arg., in April following the murder of a kidnapped student. In Mexico a study found that 96% of crimes between 1996 and 2003 went unpunished, while in Brazil reportedly only about 8% of some 50,000 murders committed annually were being prosecuted successfully. Critics suggested that a major part of the problem was the lack of public confidence in the police, many of whom were involved in serious crimes such as kidnapping and drug trafficking.

In the United Kingdom sweeping changes were announced in January in the handling of cases involving mothers who were suspected of having killed their babies. British Attorney General Lord Goldsmith said that 258 cases would be reviewed involving a parent who had been convicted within the past 10 years of murder, manslaughter, or infanticide of a child under two years of age. The announcement came after British courts questioned a number of the convictions in which uncertainty existed among experts about the cause of sudden infant deaths.

Macedonian authorities charged a number of police officers with murder and issued a warrant in May for the arrest of former minister of the interior Ljube Boskovski after a lengthy investigation into the March 2002 deaths of seven young men (six from Pakistan and one from India) who had been shot dead in a remote spot shortly after they entered Macedonia from Bulgaria. Though the police claimed that the victims were terrorists, the investigation found that the seven men were illegal immigrants who had been en route to Greece to find work. They were killed in cold blood apparently in an effort to impress U.S. officials of Macedonia's credentials as a loyal ally in the war on terror.

(DUNCAN CHAPPELL)

DEATH PENALTY

Some small gains were registered in 2004 in the drive to eliminate the death penalty. Two more countries—Samoa and Bhutan—abolished the death penalty for all crimes, and, thus, for the first time totally abolitionist countries outnumbered those that retained the death penalty for ordinary crimes. Abolition of the death penalty was among a number of proposals submitted to the Mexican legislature by Pres. Vicente Fox. Kyrgyzstan extended for another year its moratorium on executions; Kazakhstan gave teeth to its December 2003 moratorium by replacing a number of death sentences with life imprisonments in January 2004; and Tajikistan adopted a similar ban in November. After commuting the death sentences of 44 soldiers who had been condemned for their role in a failed 1997 coup, Zambian Pres. Levy Mwanawasa insisted that he would not sign a death warrant for as long as he remained in office. In Malawi 79 death sentences were commuted. A national debate on whether the death penalty should be abolished was initiated in Nigeria. The U.S. Supreme Court announced that it would consider the legality of executing people who were under the age of 18 at the time of their crime; the court's decision was expected in early 2005.

The first execution in Afghanistan since the fall of the Taliban occurred in April 2004, two and a half years after the establishment of the interim government. Dhananjoy Chatterjee, convicted of the rape and murder of a 14-year-old girl, became the first person to be executed in India since 1995, and in Indonesia capital punishment was used for the first time in three years. A five-year de facto moratorium on the death penalty in Lebanon also came to an end when three men were executed in January. The U.S. state of Maryland reinstituted the death penalty after a six-year hiatus. Nationwide there were 59 executions in 2004.

(STUART MACDONALD)

Libraries and Museums

Libraries and museums coped with the THEFT of precious manuscripts and works of ART (*The Scream*) but celebrated the OPENING of the new Central Library in Seattle, Wash., and the Smithsonian's National Museum of the American Indian; MoMA also RETURNED to its renovated home in New York City.

LIBRARIES

During 2004 forces that affected nations and individuals buffeted libraries around the world: war, terrorism, limited resources, protest movements, legal issues, technology, crime, and disasters. In an effort to help restore and preserve American cultural treasures, develop online catalogs, and train Iraqi library professionals, grant funding was secured by the University of California, Berkeley and Los Angeles; Harvard University; Cornell University, Ithaca, N.Y.; and Simmons College, Boston. Iraq's war-ravaged libraries received international assistance. British publishers, universities, and businesses collected 10 tons of books and journals for delivery to Iraqi academic libraries in Baghdad and Mosul. The National Library of Iran donated books, computers, and furniture to Afghan libraries that had languished during the Taliban regime.

In January a group of Hindu activists calling themselves the Shambhaji Brigade destroyed some 30,000 rare manuscripts at the Bhandarkar Oriental Research Institute in Pune, India. The library of the Islamia Higher Secondary School, a leader in efforts to modernize Islam, lost to arson in July some 30,000 Islamic texts, including one of the oldest known Qu'rans. A Tamil library in Jaffna, Sri Lanka, that burned in 1981 during the war between the Tamils and the majority Sinhalese reopened after 23 years. As many as 100,000 volumes had been destroyed in the arson; they were replaced by some 40,000 donated volumes. Officials in Great Britain and Canada branded firebombings of Jewish libraries "racist acts." A Montreal Jewish school lost almost its entire collection in an April attack. Two such attacks in Britain resulted in the destruction of priceless Torah scrolls.

U.S. Pres. George W. Bush urged the extension of the USA PATRIOT Act during his state of the union address. Some months later a legislative attempt to amend the act to prohibit searches of library records failed by a narrow margin. Interestingly, legislators on both the far left and the far right supported the amendment.

Old-fashioned crime also had its effects. The curator in chief of manuscripts at the French Bibliothèque Nationale was arrested for the theft of Hebrew religious texts from the 13th–15th centuries. As many as 100 manuscripts might have been taken, and the investigation was continuing. The theft over a decade of some 3,200 rare volumes from the Royal Danish Library led to the jailing of four people in June. The stolen materials were valued at $48.4 million, and only 1,556 volumes were recovered. A staff member of the library at the University of Texas at San Antonio was indicted for the theft of some $200,000 between 1997 and 2003. The money came from fines collected for overdue and lost books and videos. The library worker faced two felony counts, and each was punishable with a sentence of 5 to 99 years. In Toronto police arrested a 55-year-old library worker for the 1969 shooting of a Chicago police officer. Joseph Pannell had jumped bail, fled to Canada, and lived there for 35 years under an assumed name.

Natural disasters took their toll. A valuable sheet-music collection sustained water damage in February as firefighters fought to control a fire in St. Petersburg's Aleksandr Blok Library. In Weimar, Ger., a catastrophic fire in September in the Duchess Anna Amalia Library destroyed some 25,000 volumes and damaged 40,000 others. About 6,000 volumes, including a 1534 Martin Luther Bible, were saved. At North Carolina Central University, about two-thirds of the library's 567,000 volumes were threatened by mold. Library users and staff who had asthma and allergies were warned to avoid the area and not use the materials. Florida Orchestra officials scrambled to move their sheet-music collection to higher ground as Hurricane Charley threatened the Tampa area in August.

Protests forced Egypt's Bibliotheca Alexandrina to remove a display of an Arabic edition of the *Protocols of the Elders of Zion*, a notorious early 20th-century forgery. Rock-throwing student protesters caused Dominican Republic Pres. Hippolito Mejía Domínguez to flee the dedication of a new library. Employees of the Ghana Library Board (GLB) went on a nationwide strike to protest salary structures and working conditions. The GLB called on the government to close all public libraries if it could not resolve the situation. Despite the fears of some, the San Francisco Public Library moved ahead with plans to use microchips to keep track of library materials. Those who opposed the plan believed the devices would permit the tracking of city residents and collection of personal information. The library sought to find some $300,000 in its budget to begin the program. The Vatican Library embarked on a similar scheme, but the microchips would not be used for circulation; the pope is the only person allowed to remove materials from the library.

There was some positive news for libraries during the year. A stunning new $165 million Central Library designed by acclaimed Dutch architect Rem Koolhaas opened in Seattle, Wash., and 28,000 library patrons entered the building on its first day of operation. *Newsweek* magazine described the building as "eye popping," "wired to the max," and yet "book-centric." The *New York Times* critic described the library as the most exciting new building he had reviewed in 30 years of writing about architecture. A new National Library of Singapore, expected to open in 2005, received a $33.4 million donation, one-third of the building's cost,

© Gordon Schmidt/Reuters/Corbis

Smoke pours from the Duchess Anna Amalia Library in Weimar, Ger., during a disastrous fire on September 3. Some 25,000 volumes were destroyed and 40,000 others damaged, but a rare Martin Luther Bible was saved.

from the Lee Foundation. In administrative news, John Tsebe was appointed the first black director of the National Library of South Africa, and Singaporean R. Ramachandran became the first Asian librarian to be appointed Secretary General of the International Federation of Library Associations and Institutions. In December the Internet search engine Google announced that it had reached agreements with several major libraries to scan their collections and make the digital files searchable on the Web. (THOMAS M. GAUGHAN)

MUSEUMS

The year 2004 ended with the successful reopening in November of the Museum of Modern Art (MoMA), which housed the world's preeminent collection of modern and contemporary art, following a four-year closure for an $858 million reconstruction. During the interim MoMA had used an exhibition space it created in a former factory in Queens. Expansion in the museum sector was worldwide, with many building projects coming to fruition despite some negative financial circumstances.

The two global museum chains—the State Hermitage Museum in St. Petersburg and the Solomon R. Guggenheim Foundation in New York City—had contrasting fortunes. The Hermitage expanded its international presence, adding to its London branch with a new outpost in Amsterdam and announcing plans to create a Hermitage Hiroshima in Japan and a Hermitage Kazan in Tatarstan to take its collections to an ever-wider audience. The Guggenheim's project to open a museum in Taichung, Taiwan, stalled over funding issues, however, and Guggenheim Rio was blocked by a court order following a challenge by the political opponents of the mayor of Rio de Janeiro.

The opening in 1997 of the Frank Gehry-designed Guggenheim Bilbao marked the beginning of the museum sector's infatuation with big-name architects. In 2004 this love affair was as passionate as ever. Gehry's MARTa Herford, a museum of art and craft in Herford, Ger., opened to the public, and he announced proposals for a Museum of Biodiversity in Panama. Washington's Smithsonian Institution appointed high-profile British architect Norman Foster to enclose the courtyard of the American Art Museum and the National Portrait Gallery to create a 2,600-sq-m (28,000-sq-ft) glass atrium. In New York City the Whitney Museum of American Art announced Renzo Piano as the new architect behind its expansion plans. This new appointment established the Italian as the leading American museum architect—in 2004 he was working on museum projects in Atlanta, Ga.; Chicago; Cambridge, Mass.; and Los Angeles. The Smithsonian's National Museum of the American Indian opened in September, 15 years after the U.S. Congress approved its construction. Native Americans were involved in every element of the museum's creation; the architect, the director, one-third of the museum staff, and major patrons were of Indian descent. The grounds surrounding its curvaceous limestone building were landscaped to recall the Native American plant environment before European contact.

The boom continued to be international in scale. From the new Rubin Museum of Art in Manhattan, showcasing Himalayan culture, to the opening of Taiwan's Bunker Museum of Contemporary Art, sited in an island military fortification, the variety of museums and collections on exhibit increased worldwide. The prince of Liechtenstein's art treasures were rehoused in a new museum in Vienna. Italy established the Museo Fotografia Contemporanea, its first museum of contemporary photography, in Milan. In London the Royal Academy of Arts put its collection of British art on display for the first time in a restored suite of rooms.

Matt Dunn/The New York Times

Navajo ethnobotanist Donna House, who created the landscaping for the site, poses in front of the National Museum of the American Indian on the National Mall in Washington, D.C. Originally approved by Congress in 1989, the museum opened to the public on September 21.

The homecoming of the Olympic Games to their birthplace in Athens was an opportunity for the city's museums to highlight Greece's ancient heritage. Although an extensive program of exhibitions was launched in Athens and worldwide (under the banner of the Cultural Olympiad), the city suffered some setbacks. The National Archaeological Museum was not renovated in time for the Games; the upper floors remained closed, and work on the proposed New Acropolis Museum stalled. London's British Museum continued to refuse the return of the Elgin Marbles, carvings that originally had been housed in the Athenian Parthenon. Athens wanted to make the Marbles the centrepiece of its cultural celebrations.

Beijing declared that it would build 20 new museums in time for the Olympic Games in Beijing in 2008. The year 2004 saw a surge of interest in the country's antiquity, with exhibitions of Chinese art traveling to venues ranging from the Musée Guimet in Paris to the Field Museum in Chicago. A number of museums used commemorative dates to frame their exhibition programs. The National Gallery of Ireland marked 150 years with a special-events schedule, and the Jewish Museum in New York City celebrated its centenary with a major Modigliani show. The anniversaries of the birth of Salvador Dalí and the death of Frida Kahlo were celebrated with shows in the Catalonia region of Spain and Mexico City, respectively. The biggest exhibition festival, however, was not related to an anniversary. For "Rubens 2004" more than 10 cities worldwide staged exhibitions of the Baroque master's art.

A fire at a Momart storage facility in London brought attention to the risks museums took when using private companies to store and transport art. The most high-profile losses were contemporary works owned by British collector Charles Saatchi. Nevertheless, the theft in August of two Edvard Munch masterpieces, *The Scream* and *Madonna,* from Oslo's Munch Museum showed that works were not always secure in the institutions themselves. Such worries did not stop the Sudanese National Museum of Khartoum from lending its treasures for display in the British Museum. Following the humanitarian disaster in the Darfur region of The Sudan, the British Museum dropped the admission fee and asked the public to instead donate to charities working in the Darfur area. In October Chicago's Terra Museum of American Art closed its doors after some 24 years in operation.

Iraqi conservators continued to work to restore Baghdad's National Museum following the looting that took place in the aftermath of the U.S.-led war there the previous year. Although the museum stayed closed in 2004, the majority of the 14,000 works looted were returned and the international museum community offered valuable support. Italy, for example, donated laboratory equipment to the conservators. Copenhagen's United Exhibits Group announced its intention to stage a worldwide tour of Iraqi treasures in 2005, with the support of the Iraqi Governing Council. During the year the West also made moves to establish cultural diplomacy with Iran. The British Council organized the first show of British art in the Islamic Republic, and the Oriental Institute at the University of Chicago returned a set of 300 small ancient clay tablets to Iran.

(SAM PHILLIPS)

Life Sciences

Researchers studied BROOD PARASITISM in birds and AGGRESSION and THERMOREGULATION in insects. A skull exam of *ARCHAEOPTERYX* suggested the animal was able to fly. Research into the role of microRNAs in GENE EXPRESSION made significant progress, and interest grew in the use of BIOPLASTICS. Scientists determined the GROWTH RATE of *Tyrannosaurus rex* and continued making exciting fossil finds in China.

ZOOLOGY

During 2004 advances in zoological research of birds and insects increased scientists' understanding of the complexity of biological systems involving brood parasitism, aggression, and thermoregulation. Studies of fish and bats revealed information about the role that ecology and single phenotypic traits (observable properties) could play in the evolutionary divergence that might lead to the formation of species. Through an examination of the fossilized skull of *Archaeopteryx*, insights were gained into the way flight evolved in the earliest birds. In the field of conservation, two endangered West Indian insectivorous mammals were found to represent the only remaining species of an evolutionary divergence that occurred during the Cretaceous Period. DNA analyses played a prominent role in much of this work.

Brown-headed cowbirds (*Molothrus ater*) lay their eggs in the nests of birds of different species—a behaviour that is called brood parasitism. The unsuspecting foster parents raise the baby cowbirds as their own. Offspring of some brood parasite species kill host young to ensure for themselves greater resources from attending parents. Likewise, it might appear to be in the baby cowbird's best interests for survival to kill the host birds' offspring, but baby cowbirds seldom do so. Rebecca M. Kilner and Joah R. Madden of the University of Cambridge and Mark E. Hauber of the University of Auckland, N.Z., studied this behaviour with an experiment in which single cowbird eggs were placed in each of 20 nests of the Eastern phoebe (*Sayornis phoebe*). Once a cowbird egg hatched, the researchers removed the remaining eggs from the nest. In 10 of the nests, they left the cowbird as the only bird in the nest. In the other 10 nests, the researchers introduced two newly hatched phoebes. Therefore, adult phoebes in 10 of the nests were left with a single baby bird (a cowbird) to tend, and in the other 10 nests, the parents were left with three baby birds. Using body weight as a measure of how effectively the baby cowbirds acquired food, the investigators found that cowbirds with two nest mates gained weight more rapidly than cowbirds alone in a nest. By filming the birds in their nests, the researchers discovered that parent birds with three baby birds brought food about 2½ times more often than those in nests with a single bird. A cowbird in a nest with two phoebes typically took more than half the food the parents brought, so it fared better than the lone cowbirds even though the lone cowbirds got all of the food that was brought to their nests. The study demonstrated that a cowbird's apparent altruism toward baby birds of other species is simply a strategy to get more food.

Female honeybees (*Apis mellifera*) regulate the temperature of their hives, maintaining it close to 35 °C (95 °F) by fanning their wings for cooling in hot weather and huddling to generate heat from their bodies in cold weather. Honeybees operate as a single superorganism to regulate the temperature inside a hive as the outside temperature rises or falls. Julia C. Jones and colleagues of the University of Sydney, Australia, combined behaviour observations and DNA analyses to demonstrate that the temperature in a hive is more stable and better controlled when the bees are the offspring produced by the mating of the queen with a number of drones rather than with only a single drone. The researchers conducted experiments on pairs of hives having an equal number of bees. One hive had worker bees of mixed genetic parentage (offspring of a single queen and multiple drones), whereas the

Among the chicks in this nest of an Eastern phoebe, the largest gape belongs to a brown-headed cowbird chick, a brood parasite.

other housed bees of uniform genetic heritage (offspring of a single queen and a single drone). Worker bees in both hives ultimately maintained an average temperature of 35 °C. In the hive with bees of a mixed genetic makeup, the temperature remained relatively constant, regardless of the outside temperature. In contrast, the temperature in the hive with bees of uniform genetic makeup varied greatly and took longer to regulate than in the genetically diverse hive. The researchers then used DNA tests to confirm the existence of a relationship between genetics and the behaviour of bees of a genetically mixed hive. The tests showed that all the bees that started fanning at a given temperature were more likely to have the same father than those that began fanning at some other temperature. These results suggested that the threshold temperature at which an individual bee begins participating in thermostatic regulation in the hive is genetically based. The bees in a genetically diverse hive are able to keep the temperature more stable because they respond to a broader range of temperatures, some bees beginning the cooling or warming process sooner than others.

Markus Knaden and Rüdiger Wehner of the University of Zürich, Switz., studied aggression in Saharan desert ants (*Cataglyphis fortis*), which become combative upon encountering ants from colonies other than their own. Desert ants will travel more than 100 m (1 m = 3.3 ft) to gather resources, and as the ant moves away from its nest, its level of aggression decreases. The greater belligerence of the ants in the vicinity of their nest might serve a protective role in guarding the nest of a colony, but the way in which the ants determine their proximity to the nest was unknown. The researchers trained ants to visit a feeding area 20 m from their homes, a distance at which the ants have reduced aggressiveness toward other ants. Ants from four different colonies were captured at the feeding area and then were marked with coloured dots for identification and transported to a distant site. Upon being released at the distant site, the ants immediately began crawling toward their respective nests. Some ants were allowed to travel 20 m toward their nest; others were allowed to travel only a quarter that distance. The investigators then captured the ants again and took them to a laboratory to test their level of aggression. Each ant was paired in a box with an ant from a different colony, and their behaviour was videotaped. Ants that had traveled the 20 m toward their nest were significantly more likely to attack than those that had traveled only the shorter distance. The experiment suggested that the aggressiveness of the Saharan desert ant is based on its perception of the proximity to its home and that the ant does not use sight, smell, or landmarks in determining its location. Instead, some yet-to-be-understood internal means of navigation allows the Saharan desert ant to know how far it has traveled from home.

Tigga Kingston of Boston University and Stephen J. Rossiter of Queen Mary, University of London, showed that the echolocation used by three distinct sizes (morphs) of large-eared hoseshoe bats (*Rhinolophus philippinenesis*) of Indonesia is accomplished at the same basic frequency of sound but with harmonically distinctive echolocation calls. The different harmonics allow each morph to use echolocation to detect its own suitable prey. The researchers suggested that natural selection for prey-related shifts in echolocation harmonics can lead to related shifts in the sounds used for communication within morphs during mating. These shifts would enhance evolutionary divergence by means of assortative mating (selective mating between individuals in a population) and subsequent reproductive isolation. The investigators showed through DNA analyses that the three morphs have indeed become genetically diverse, while remaining sympatric (occupying the same geographic area).

Studies with three-spined sticklebacks (*Gasterosteus aculeatus*) by Jeffrey S. McKinnon of the University of Wisconsin at Whitewater and colleagues provided further evidence that evolutionary divergence and reproductive isolation can be caused by only one or a few ecologically significant traits. Sticklebacks make up a species complex that includes two ecotypes—stream-dwelling populations and anadromous populations (populations that live in the ocean and migrate to fresh water to breed). Both types are found across the Northern Hemisphere and are found together, but typically only minor genetic exchange occurs between them. The researchers collected samples of both ecotypes from a variety of locations and maintained them in the laboratory. Anadromous sticklebacks typically grow to a larger size than stream-dwelling sticklebacks, but the investigators controlled the growth of the fish to produce females with a range of body sizes in both types. During experiments the primary factor influencing mating compatibility between females and normal-sized males was similarity in body size, although similar-sized pairs of the same ecotype were slightly more compatible reproductively than similar-sized pairs of different ecotypes. Colour patterns and genetic similarities were not significant factors.

Archaeopteryx, which lived in the Late Jurassic Period, is the epitome of a transitional form on an evolutionary continuum: it possesses teeth characteristic of a reptile but also has feathers, which are characteristic of birds. Although a number of fossils of *Archaeopteryx* have been discovered and studied, the question remained whether the animal was able to fly. Patricio Domínguez Alonso and colleagues of Complutensian University, Madrid, examined *Archaeopteryx* fossils with computed tomography, a technique for obtaining cross-sectional images of a solid object by scanning it with X-rays. The investigators found unequivocal evidence of an enlarged forebrain and of optic and auditory systems typical of animals adapted for flight.

Only two species of insectivorous mammals are extant in the West Indies. Both are extremely rare and endangered. One, *Solenodon cubanus*, is found in Cuba and the other, *S. paradoxus*, is found on Hispaniola. Alfred L. Roca, Gila Kahila Bar-Gal, and William J. Murphy of the Laboratory of Genomic Diversity, Frederick, Md., and colleagues used DNA gene sequencing to determine that the solenodons diverged from the insectivores, such as shrews, moles, and hedgehogs, during the Cretaceous Period 76 million years ago and that the two species diverged from each other around the time Cuba and Hispaniola split into separate islands, 25 million years ago. The continued existence of both species was being threatened by a variety of human-caused environmental changes, including deforestation and the introduction of predatory species such as dogs, cats, and mongooses. From the perspective of conservation, the findings accentuated the significance of the two species, since they represent a complete phylogenetic lineage that predates the appearance of many present-day orders of mammals. (J. WHITFIELD GIBBONS)

BOTANY

Research into microRNAs—short strands of RNA that regulate gene expression—made significant progress in

Arabidopsis thaliana *is widely used in genetics research, including studies of microDNA. One strain has been genetically engineered to be sensitive to nitrogen dioxide gas to help in the detection of land mines.*

2004. Hundreds of different kinds of microRNAs were believed to exist in every species of plant and animal, but the function of only a few had been understood. Researchers found that the microRNA called miR164 played a vital role in the development of flowers, leaves, and stems of *Arabidopsis thaliana,* a plant commonly used in genetics studies. The researchers created one mutant strain that produced excess miR164 and another that was not affected by it. In both mutant strains the leaves and flowers developed abnormally; in the strain that made excess miR164, the organs tended to fuse together, and in the strains that did not respond to it, the wrong number of petals or other organs formed.

Another type of microRNA was found to act as part of a gene-switching mechanism dating back 400 million years to the very first land-based plants. Plant biologists at the University of California, Davis, found that the microRNA controlled a gene family called class III HD-Zip, which is required for the development of stems and leaves. The microRNA behaved in the same way in all the major groups of land plants that were studied. It was also the first microRNA shown to regulate genes in nonflowering plants such as mosses.

Scientists at the John Innes Centre and Institute of Food Research in Norwich, Eng., reported the discovery of a gene that offered the hope of breeding food crops that have both an increased resistance to disease and properties that promote human health. The gene, HQT, was identified in tomato plants and produces chlorogenic acid (CGA), which functions as an antioxidant—that is, a substance that inhibits chemical reactions involving reactive forms of oxygen. By increasing the activity of HQT in tomato plants, the scientists raised the levels of CGA in tomato fruits, helping to protect them from bacterial disease. The antioxidant had also been shown to be beneficial in humans, especially in protecting against age-related disease.

One way a plant controls the sprouting of branches, which affects the overall shape of the plant, was traced to a gene called MAX3. Researchers reported that *Arabidopsis* plants that bear an unusually high number of side shoots tended to have mutations in this gene. Auxin and cytokine hormones were already known to influence branching, but they also were known to have a wide range of other developmental effects. It was hoped that disruption of the MAX3 gene could be used to modify branching without these additional effects. Such modification could potentially offer benefits in plant breeding, including improvements in the appearance of ornamental plants and a reduction in branching in trees grown for timber.

Progress in genetic modification produced some fascinating new plants. Aresa Biodetection, a Danish biotechnology company, developed a genetically modified variety of *A. thaliana* that could help detect land mines. Buried land mines typically emit a small amount of nitrogen dioxide gas, and the plant was modified so that within a few weeks' exposure of the roots to the gas, the leaves of the plant would change colour from green to red. The researchers manipulated the natural anthocyanin pigments in the plant leaves by first turning off the genes that produce the red version of the pigment and then inserting a gene that turns on the pigment-making apparatus when nitrogen dioxide is present.

A previously unknown form of natural protection from disease was discovered in cocoa leaves. Biologists had been baffled by the vast variety of fungal species that live inside plant leaves and had assumed that many of the fungi were parasites. Scientists studying cocoa trees, however, found that some of the fungi inside the leaves of the cocoa tree are beneficial to the tree. The research involved growing cocoa seedlings under conditions that kept some of the leaves free from fungi and then introducing a fungal disease known as Phytophthora. Leaves devoid of fungi were three times as likely to die from the disease as the leaves that contained the fungi, and they lost twice as much leaf tissue. This finding could lead to an inexpensive and environmentally friendly way to protect cocoa trees and many other crops from the ravages of microbial diseases.

Worrying indications were found of the effects on plants of the increasing levels of carbon dioxide (CO_2) in the atmosphere and how this in turn could have an impact on global climate. A team of botanists discovered that large fast-growing trees in a pristine part of the Amazon rainforest had been increasingly dominating their slower-growing neighbours over the past 20 years. The fast-growing trees might have gained the upper hand over other trees by being able to absorb more CO_2 to support photosynthesis and hence growth. This phenomenon could potentially reinforce the threat of increased CO_2 emissions on the global climate because the demise of the slower-growing trees might lead to a drop in the amount of CO_2 that the rainforest removes from the atmosphere. In comparison with fast-growing trees, slower-growing trees tend to absorb more carbon dioxide from the atmosphere because they have denser wood and a higher carbon content. The entire Amazon rainforest absorbed around 600 million metric tons of the gas per year (around 8% to 10% of that emitted in air pollution) and thereby helped hold in check its greenhouse effect on rising global temperatures.

The rising level of CO_2 was decreasing the rate of photorespiration in plants. Photorespiration is a process in which plants turn sugars produced during photosynthesis back into carbon dioxide and water. The process had long baffled plant scientists because it uses up about 25% of the energy that a plant captures during photosynthesis. As photorespiration rates decreased, some biologists sought through genetic engineering to eliminate photorespiration altogether in crop plants to make them more productive. A team of University of California, Davis, researchers led by Arnold Bloom warned against such efforts, however, because they had determined that photorespiration enables plants to absorb nitrates from the soil and convert them into chemical compounds the plants need for their growth. Inhibiting photorespiration eventually starves the plant of nitrogen, weakening the plant. "This explains why many plants are unable to sustain rapid growth when there is a significant increase in atmospheric carbon dioxide," said Professor Bloom. "As we anticipate a doubling of atmospheric carbon dioxide associated with global climate change by the end of this century, our results suggest that it would not be wise to decrease photorespiration in crop plants."

Scientists also found that changes in the amount of CO_2 in the atmosphere played a vital role in plant evolution. Between 340 million and 380 million years ago, when the amount of the gas in the atmosphere plunged, the size of plant leaves increased 25-fold, on average. Examination of two fossil species revealed that the average number of leaf pores, called stomata, on each leaf increased eight times over the same period. "This all suggests that the crash in carbon dioxide triggered the evolution of leaves," said Colin Osborne at Sheffield (Eng.) University. When plants first appeared on land, the atmosphere was so rich in CO_2 they hardly needed leaves, but when the level of CO_2 plunged, the plants were left "suffocating" and evolved bigger leaves to absorb more of the gas. (PAUL SIMONS)

MOLECULAR BIOLOGY AND GENETICS

The Brave New World of Bioplastics. Plastics are polymers—assemblies of like chemical subunits, which are called monomers, linked in the form of a chain. The properties of a plastic, like those of other polymers, are defined by the monomers it contains and by the number of links and cross-links in its structure. Cross-linking of the monomers increases a polymer's rigidity and thermal stability. As their name suggests, plastics can readily be molded into various shapes. Plastics such as polystyrene (polymerized styrene $[CH_2{=}CH(C_6H_5)]$), polyethylene (polymerized ethylene $[CH_2{=}CH_2]$), or polypropylene (polymerized propylene $[CH_2{=}CH(CH_3)]$) are molded into a wide variety of everyday and specialized products—eating utensils, coffee cups, synthetic fabrics, park benches, automobile parts, and surgical implants, to name but a few.

The past 100 years have seen an explosion in the development and use of plastics, and their utility and importance have become so great that it is difficult to imagine modern life without them. Virtually all plastics are derived from petroleum, through chemical extraction and synthesis. Because petroleum-based plastics are generally not biodegradable, plastic refuse is very durable, and disposing of it can become a problem. Despite efforts to encourage and support recycling, landfills are becoming filled with plastic refuse, which also accumulates in the environment. An additional problem with petroleum-based plastics is that sources of petroleum are being used up; conservative sources estimate that at current rates of consumption, all known sources of petroleum on Earth will have been depleted before the turn of the next century. How can quality of life, with its dependence on plastics, be maintained in the long term, given that petroleum is a nonrenewable resource and that petroleum-derived plastic waste degrades the environment? The answer might be bioplastics.

Bioplastics are polymers of monomers that are either derived from or synthesized by microbes such as bacteria or by genetically modified plants. As is the case with petroleum-based plastics, the physical properties of bioplastics differ according to both their monomer composition and their macromolecular structure. Unlike traditional plastics, bioplastics are obtained from renewable resources, and, best of all, they are biodegradable.

The first known bioplastic, poly(3-hydroxybutyrate), or PHB, was discovered in 1926 by the French researcher Maurice Lemoigne from his work with a bacterium called *Bacillus megaterium*. Unfortunately, the significance of the discovery was overlooked for many decades, in large part because petroleum was inexpensive and abundant. The petroleum crisis of the mid-1970s brought renewed interest in finding alternatives to petroleum-based products. The rise of molecular

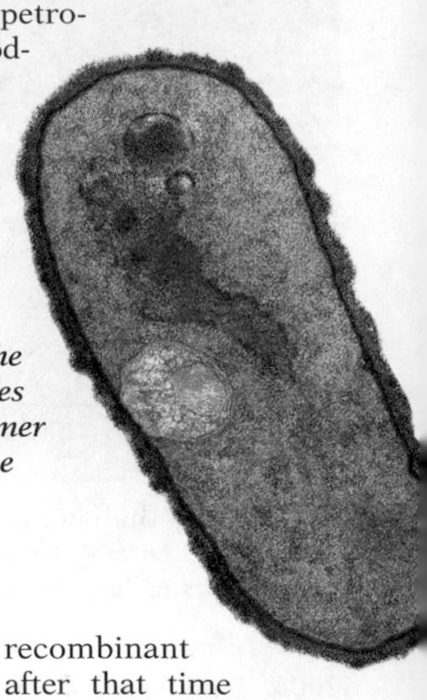

In this colourized micrograph of the Bacillus megaterium, *the bright red bodies contain a polymer produced by the bacterium.*

Mediscan

genetics and recombinant biotechnology after that time further spurred research, so that by late 2004 the structure, method of production, and application for numerous types of bioplastics had become established. Bioplastics that were either in use or under study included PHB and PHA [poly(3-hydroxyalkanoate)], both of which are synthesized within specialized microbes, and polylactic acid (PLA), which is polymerized from lactic acid monomers produced by microbial fermentation of plant-derived sugars and starches. Recent technological advances further improved the strength and thermal stability of bioplastics by permitting the incorporation of strong plant fibres. Although the commercial manufacture of bioplastics initially had low yields and was expensive, improvements in metabolic and genetic engineering produced microbial and plant strains that significantly improved yields and production capabilities while reducing overall costs.

Bioplastics production was still insignificant in terms of the total world production of plastics in 2004, but Toyota Motor Corp. was using bioplastics (primarily for interiors) in some new vehicles, and Sony Corp. was using bioplastics in the casing of Walkman portable stereos. Technical improvements in the production of bioplastics and their application, together with an increase in oil prices and environmental awareness, were sure to expand the market share of bioplastics in the years to come.

Advances in Personalized Medicine. Personalized medicine continued to develop as an area of study in which biomedical researchers and health-care providers explored the genetic differences between individuals and investigated how to take these differences into account in order to provide health care tailored to each individual. One of the toughest challenges in providing proper medical care arises from the fact that a disease can affect different people in different ways. In two patients with the same disease, there can be large variations in the symptoms, severity, and progression of the disease, as well as in how well each patient responds to a specific form of treatment. Some of the variations have behavioral causes, such as whether the patient smokes, exercises regularly, or eats a healthy diet. Other variations however, appear to be intrinsic to the individual, and are likely genetic in origin.

Relevant genetic differences between patients can include mutations that alter the structure of proteins that are targetted by a specific drug, rendering the patient either more or less susceptible to treatment by the drug. Genetic differences might also have an effect on the expression levels of numerous non-target genes and proteins in the cell and thereby produce cellular environments with either a heightened or a muted sensitivity to a given drug. For example, there could be genetic differences that alter the efficiency with which the drug enters the cell or the efficiency with which the drug is metabolized and thereby either activated or inactivated.

Many of the studies that were being conducted simply searched for correlations between patient outcome and specific mutations or expression profiles. (An expression profile for a cell or tissue does not identify mutations but rather describes the levels at which many different genes are expressed.) Understanding the mechanisms that lead to specific patient outcomes might be the ultimate goal, but the identification of correlations between outcome and mutations or expression profiles could itself be a powerful advance. For example, a recent collaborative study led by researchers from Massachusetts demonstrated that patients with lung cancer whose tumour cells carried specific mutations in their epidermal growth-factor receptor (EGFR) gene were more likely to respond to therapy with the drug gefitinib (Iressa), an EGFR kinase inhibitor, than were patients whose tumours did not carry the mutations. Another study, led by researchers from Oregon, involved expression profiling of the so-called GABAergic-system genes in patients with neuroblastoma. The expression profiles that the researchers obtained improved their ability to predict patient outcome beyond what was achieved with other prognostic indicators.

Many diseases remained poorly understood, and identifying which genetic markers were relevant and identifying their influence on the severity of a disease and the disease's response to treatment could be determined only empirically. New studies that monitored large numbers of patient markers and compared this information with the treatment and outcome of certain diseases offered both physicians and patients a new tool to help them make the often difficult choices between different types of treatment. Sets of markers that were associated with the occurrence of breast cancer, cardiovascular disease, and other diseases were becoming better defined, and markers that indicated a patient's response to certain diseases and specific treatments were also becoming more apparent. Additional examples included markers that helped in predicting a patient's susceptibility to atherosclerosis and markers that were linked to how well a patient with prostate cancer responded to treatment with selenium.

As simple correlations, these data enabled physicians to begin making choices among potential treatments for certain diseases. Already patients with specific forms of cancer, including breast cancer, prostate cancer, and lung cancer, have benefitted from the first forays of the medical profession into the world of personalized medicine. Perhaps more important, investigations into the mechanistic reasons different genetic or expression profiles in patients have different outcomes might enable the development of improved forms of treatment.

(JUDITH L. FRIDOVICH-KEIL)

PALEONTOLOGY

The year 2004 in paleontology began with a press conference in February sponsored by the U.S. National Science Foundation at which the discovery of two dinosaurs from Antarctica was announced. One dinosaur was a small Late Cretaceous theropod (a bipedal flesh-eating dinosaur); the other, an Early Jurassic sauropod (a plant-eating dinosaur with a long neck and tail). The theropod was collected on Ross Island, off the Antarctic Peninsula. The primitive sauropod was retrieved on Mt. Kirkpatrick near the site that in 1991 yielded *Cryolophosaurus,* the first theropod discovered in Antarctica. Mt. Kirkpatrick is only about 600 km (370 mi) from the South Pole.

A combination of recent advances in techniques for measuring annual growth rings in fossil bones and for estimating the body mass that would be supported by dinosaur bones of different sizes was used to calculate growth curves for *Tyrannosaurus rex* and three other theropods closely related to it. The study showed that *T. rex* reached skeletal maturity in about 20 years and lived for as long as 28 years. All four dinosaurs experienced a comparable period of rapid growth during adolescence, but the growth rate of *T. rex*—an average of 2.1 kg (4.6 lb) per day over four years—was several times faster than that of the other dinosaurs.

A remarkable pterosaur specimen recently found in the Early Cretaceous Santana Formation of Brazil has the tooth of a spinosaurid theropod dinosaur embedded in one of the cervical vertebrae—an indication that spinosaurs might have been capable of catching flying prey. New views of the internal features of skulls of pterosaurs and fossil early bird skulls made possible by computed tomography scans helped in interpreting how these animals flew. A paper describing the large size of a pterosaur inner ear indicated that pterosaurs had well-developed balance organs, which would have given them agility during flight. A new study of the brain case of *Archaeopteryx* suggested that its brain was similar to that of modern birds. (*See* LIFE SCIENCES: *Zoology.*)

The 125-million-year-old (Early Cretaceous) Yixian Formation of Liaoning province, China—a feature known for its well-preserved specimens of feathered dinosaurs and birds—continued to be a source of notable discoveries. A cluster of 34 juvenile specimens of the ornithischian dinosaur *Psittacosaurus* was unearthed together with a single adult, which indicated that psittacosaurs provided parental care to their offspring. An amazing specimen showing an embryo of a pterosaur inside an egg was found, evidence that pterosaurs, like dinosaurs, were egg layers. Another discovery was a feathered dinosaur—a troodontid—with its head tucked under a forearm. The fos-

Mick Ellison

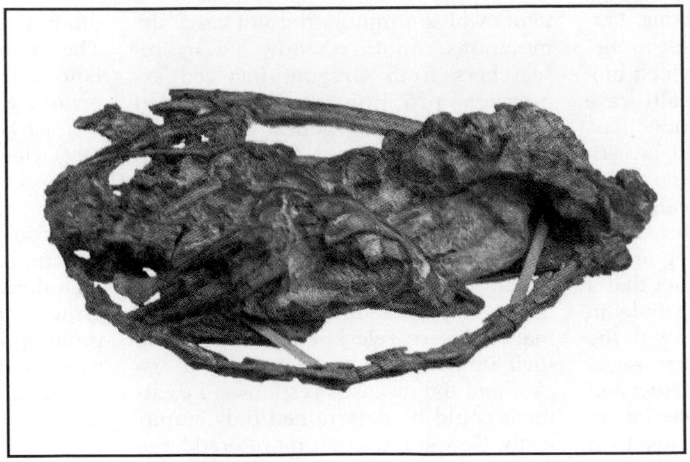

Mick Ellison

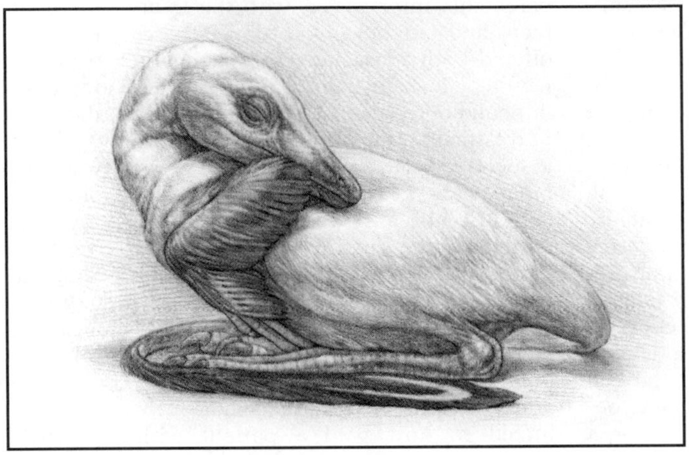

Paleontologists in China uncovered the first-ever fossil of a sleeping dinosaur (top), a troodontid, which exhibits a birdlike repose, as shown above in an artist's reconstruction.

sil, called *Mei long* (Chinese for "soundly sleeping dragon"), was 130 million years old and the earliest known specimen to exhibit such markedly birdlike behaviour. Yet another discovery from the region was *Sinodelphys,* which, with an age of 125 million years, was 50 million years older than the next oldest known marsupial. The oldest known placental mammals were also from the Yixian Formation, which suggested that both groups might have originated in Asia in the early part of the Cretaceous. In a related story published in 2004, Chinese paleontologists expressed concern that the treasure trove of magnificent fossils in the Liaoning deposits was being rapidly depleted by the illegal collection and sale of specimens. They claimed that weak laws together with a failure to enforce them were to blame for the situation, and they were working to help establish the governmental reforms necessary to stop the illegal trade of Chinese fossils.

Other dinosaurs from China that were described included a number of specimens found in Mongolia: *Pinacosaurus* from the Late Cretaceous and a duckbilled dinosaur from the Early Cretaceous. A comparison of the *Pinacosaurus* specimens showed how the dinosaur grew and changed as it aged. The duckbill was the oldest known specimen from Asia; it raised the possibility that duckbilled dinosaurs might have originated there before spreading to other parts of Laurasia (the land mass that became Asia, Europe, and North America). Deposits dated to 55 million years ago (Early Eocene) of the Hengyang Basin in China recently yielded the oldest known euprimate, *Teilhardina.* Euprimates are animals with modern primate features.

A find in northwestern China of a new crocodylomorph from the Middle Jurassic was identified as a sphenosuchian (a class of small, slender land-dwelling animals) that had several features typical of living alligators and crocodiles. It was speculated that this animal was the closest relative of the living crocodilians.

A recent study of Neanderthal tooth enamel concluded that Neanderthals grew up and reached maturity much faster than *Homo sapiens* individuals. The authors suggested that this finding strongly supported the idea that *H. neanderthalensis* was a separate species rather than a subspecies of *H. sapiens.* (*See* ANTHROPOLOGY AND ARCHAEOLOGY Sidebar.)

A fossil lower jaw found in Belgium represented the first known Late Devonian tetrapod from Western Europe. The jaw was very similar to that of *Ichthyostega,* from the Late Devonian of Greenland, and confirmed a link between Greenland and Europe.

Newly discovered well-preserved soft-bodied fossils of deuterostomes from the Lower Cambrian Chengjiang deposits near Kunming in southwestern China represented a new group of echinoderms (a group of marine animals). Named vetulocystids, these deuterostomes were a diverse superphylum that included the chordates, hemichordates, and echinoderms. The find shed some light on the origin of the echinoderms.

A fossilized specimen of the newly described arthropod *Marrella splendens* from the 505-million-year-old (Cambrian) Burgess Shale of British Columbia showed the organism in the act of molting. Before 2004 the existence of molting in early arthropods had been only inferred from what was known about their living relatives. In other news related to arthropods, a fragmentary fossil found in Scotland's Old Red Sandstone deposits (396 million to 407 million years old) was called the world's oldest known true insect. The specimen had features common to winged insects, which suggested that the origin of wings might have occurred earlier than previously believed.

A study dealing with the regeneration of arms in crinoids indicated that they suffered nonlethal attacks by predators. The analysis of Paleozoic crinoids showed an increase in the incidence of arm regeneration during the Silurian and the Devonian. The authors referred to the increase in the diversity of shell-crushing predators and the antipredatory morphologies crinoids and other prey species developed in response as the Middle Paleozoic Marine Revolution.

Newly discovered soft-bodied fossils from Spaniard's Bay in eastern Newfoundland showed a greater level of preservation than previously described Ediacaran (Late Precambrian) fossils. The fossils were classified as rangeomorphs, a group that dominated what is called the Mistaken Point assemblage, which lived from 575 million to 560 million years ago. The study indicated that the rangeomorphs were not ancestral to any organisms known to have existed since the beginning of the Cambrian. (WILLIAM R. HAMMER)

Literature

Feminist Elfriede Jelinek won the NOBEL Prize. Collections of SHORT STORIES and essays fared well in many countries, as did HISTORICAL novels. Fantasy and the cosmos flavoured SCANDINAVIAN fiction. Arab IMMIGRANT authors in Europe and Israel found their voices. Japanese readers were surprised when stories from the YOUTH CULTURE won top prizes.

ENGLISH

United Kingdom. If any single theme shaped British fiction in the year 2004, it was the impact of political forces on the everyday lives of individuals. With the war in Iraq dominating the year's news headlines, this was perhaps not surprising. The Orange Prize for Fiction short list was a case in point. Of the six books nominated for the women-only prize, four were set against a backdrop of war or political strife. While all of these were set in the past, they invited comparisons to contemporary events. American Shirley Hazzard's *The Great Fire* (winner of the National Book Award for Fiction in 2003) told the story of an English officer witnessing the cultural and social convulsions of China and Japan in the aftermath of World War II. *Ice Road* by South African-born London-based author Gillian Slovo was set in Russia during Joseph Stalin's purges and the siege of Leningrad. Another Orange Prize contender was *Purple Hibiscus* (2003), a debut novel by Nigerian author Chimamanda Ngozi Adichie, which depicted a 15-year-old Nigerian girl responding to changes in the texture of her personal life after a military coup shook the foundations of her country. The prizewinner was Andrea Levy for her novel *Small Island,* which explored the problems of Jamaican migration into London in the aftermath of World War II. Themes of racism, war, and empire ran through Levy's story of Gilbert Joseph, a Caribbean man who had fought Adolf Hitler with the British Royal Air Force but was made to feel unwelcome in postwar London now that he was out of uniform.

Even children's fiction revealed Britain's preoccupation with war. The winner of the Whitbread Children's Book Award, David Almond's *The Fire-Eaters,* was a novel about Bobby Burns, a young boy whose world was fraught with uncertainty during the Cuban missile crisis. War likewise figured in three of the eight books competing for the Guardian Children's Fiction award. In Meg Rosoff's debut novel, *How I Live Now,* which won the award, war rips through the 21st-century British countryside, exposing the characters to unspeakable horrors. Another contender, Berkshire-based writer Leslie Wilson's *Last Train from Kummersdorf,* was a complex and morally ambivalent tale about a boy and a girl trying to survive in the ruins of Nazi Germany at the end of World War II. The most widely reviewed novel on the list was well-known children's writer Michael Morpurgo's *Private Peaceful,* which introduced children to the waking nightmare of World War I. Morpurgo used the novel to draw attention to the need to pardon those teenagers who had eagerly signed up for that war without knowing the horrors that awaited them and who were subsequently executed for trying to desert. He stated, "The New Zealanders have pardoned their executed soldiers. So can we. A nation that refuses to deal with its shame cannot be called civilised."

Nigerian author Chimamanda Ngozi Adichie's first novel, **Purple Hibiscus,** *was nominated for the Orange Prize.*

A study of the Stasi in former communist East Germany won the £30,000 (about $55,000) Samuel Johnson Prize, the U.K.'s most important prize for nonfiction. Australian Anna Funder spent several years interviewing both the victims and the former operatives of East Germany's secret police to write *Stasiland: True Stories from Behind the Berlin Wall* (2003), described by one reviewer as "brilliant and necessary." The chair of the Samuel Johnson Prize judges, Michael Wood, said that the book was "a highly original close-up of what happens to people in the corrosive atmosphere of a totalitarian state. An intimate portrait of survivors caught between their desire to forget and the need to remember."

The political and social climate of 1980s London created the backdrop for the 2004 Man Booker Prize-winning novel, *The Line of Beauty.* Alan Hollinghurst's fifth novel bitterly satirized what one commentator called "the excessive greed and furious social climbing of Thatcherite Britain." Its protagonist Nick Guest is initially taken in by the artificial glamour of the Fedden family, with its private recitals and the Guardi painting above the mantelpiece. His love affair with the upwardly mobile Tory family ends in disgrace and disillusionment, however: "In the remorseless glare of the news, . . . the flat looked even more tawdry and pretentious. He was puzzled to think he had spent so much time in it so happily and conceitedly. The pelmets and mirrors, the spotlights and blinds, seemed rich in criticism. It was what you did if you had millions but no particular taste:

© Colin McPherson/Corbis

Alan Hollinghurst's satiric novel **The Line of Beauty** *won the 2004 Man Booker Prize.*

you made your private space like a swanky hotel; just as such hotels flattered their customers by being vulgar simulacra of lavish private homes. A year ago it had at least the glamour of newness." *The Line of Beauty* faced stiff competition for the Man Booker from David Mitchell's *Cloud Atlas,* a best seller and favourite with the bookmakers that interwove the stories of six characters inhabiting disparate times and spaces, including a 19th-century adventurer in the Pacific and a cloned slave bred to work in an underground fast-food eatery in a dystopian 22nd-century Korea. Each narrative was conveyed in a different stylistic genre, from science fiction to picaresque. Mitchell's eccentric morphing of the English language made for some wildly original prose, but it was the novel's overarching message that captured many critics' praise. A reviewer for *The Daily Telegraph* described it as "a grand fictional treatise about the will to power—whether corporate or tribal, personal or consumer." Another worthy contender was Londoner Gerard Woodward's *I'll Go to Bed at Noon,* which charted the course of a dysfunctional family of alcoholics in the years preceding the Thatcherite revolution.

By curious coincidence, several novelists created fictional homages to the fin de siècle novelist Henry James. In *The Line of Beauty,* Hollinghurst's protagonist is writing a Ph.D. thesis on James, with whom he is fascinated. Another contender for the Man Booker, *The Master* by Irish author Colm Tóibín, provided a prodigiously researched fictional portrait of James, tracing his life from January 1895, the month that his historical drama *Guy Domville* flopped on the London stage, to a family reunion in 1899. The time frame allowed Tóibín to examine the paranoia that presided over the late 1890s, the era in which Oscar Wilde was tried for homosexuality, and to imagine the effect it had on James, whose own sexuality was ambiguous and thwarted. The opening scene of Tóibín's novel resurfaced later in another form with the publication of David Lodge's strikingly authentic yet fictional account of Henry James, *Author, Author.* Lodge depicted James's humiliating five-year campaign to win success writing for the British stage, contrasting it with the career of his successful friend George Du Maurier, the *Punch* magazine cartoonist and author of *Trilby* (1894). The result was a deft examination of the compulsions, jealousies, and failures that often accompany the life of a writer. Earlier, Emma Tennant had produced *Felony* (2002), a novel that unraveled the story behind James's creation of *The Aspern Papers* (1888). A fifth novel inspired by James was Toby Litt's *Ghost Story,* which was a contemporary reworking of James's eerie masterpiece *The Turn of the Screw* (1898).

Virginia Woolf was another author who attracted press coverage in 2004, when the last of six essays originally published in *Good Housekeeping* magazine in 1931 was found by an enterprising publisher in the archives of the University of Sussex. The sketch of an eccentric London gossip called Mrs. Crowe was published along with the other five essays by Woolf in a volume titled *The London Scene.*

Novels appealing to both children and adults continued to dominate the market. Mark Haddon's *The Curious Incident of the Dog in the Night-Time* (2003), a mystery novel whose protagonist is a young boy with Asperger syndrome, sold almost one million copies. It also won the 2003 Whitbread Book of the Year Award and was voted both Children's Book of the Year and winner of the Literary Fiction Award at the British Book Awards. In a joint statement, the Whitbread judges said, "It has been claimed of many recent books that they could be read equally by adolescents or by adults. We felt that this was a rare and genuine example of a book which would sit equally well on the shelves of any bedroom." J.K. Rowling's Harry Potter books likewise continued to sell in the millions to both children and adults, bringing her estimated earnings of £1.37 billion (about $2.49 billion). In August Rowling announced unexpectedly that she planned to add an eighth book to the series; she had previously vowed to write only seven Potter adventures.

Christian readers critical of the benign image of witchcraft in Rowling's books found a riveting alternative in the works of G.P. Taylor, a policeman turned vicar. His popular children's novel *Shadowmancer* (2002) was followed by its much-lauded sequel *Wormwood.* Taylor's Gothic tales of 18th-century Britain are interlaced with Christian imagery, inviting comparisons to writers J.R.R. Tolkien and C.S. Lewis. *Wormwood,* set in London, is replete with evil sorcerers, angel warriors, and an ancient leather-bound book that contains the secrets of the universe. Taylor's books rivaled Rowling's series on the best-seller lists.

(continued on page 224)

AP/Wide World Photos

The award-winning novel by Mark Haddon, **The Curious Incident of the Dog in the Night-Time,** *appealed to young readers and adults alike.*

WORLD LITERARY PRIZES 2004

All prizes are annual and were awarded in 2004 unless otherwise stated. Currency equivalents as of July 1, 2004, were as follows: €1 = $1.219; £1 = $1.819; Can$1 = $0.750; ¥1 = $0.009; SKr 1 = $0.133; and DKr 1 = $0.164.

Nobel Prize for Literature

Awarded since 1901; included in the behest of Alfred Nobel, who specified a prize for those who "shall have produced in the field of literature the most outstanding work in an ideal direction." The prizewinners are selected in October by the Swedish Academy and receive the award on December 10 in Stockholm. Prize: a gold medal and an award that varies from year to year; in 2004 the award was SKr 10,000,000.
Elfriede Jelinek (Austria)

International IMPAC Dublin Literary Award

First awarded in 1996, this is the largest international literary prize; it is open to books written in any language. The award is a joint initiative of Dublin City Council, the Municipal Government of Dublin City, and the productivity-improvement company IMPAC. It is administered by Dublin City Public Libraries. Prize: €100,000, of which 25% goes to the translator if the book was not written in English, and a Waterford crystal trophy. The awards are given at Dublin Castle in May or June.
This Blinding Absence of Light by Tahar Ben Jalloun (Morocco); translated from the French by Linda Coverdale

Neustadt International Prize for Literature

Established in 1969 and awarded biennially by the University of Oklahoma and World Literature Today. Novelists, poets, and dramatists are equally eligible. Prize: $50,000, a replica of an eagle feather cast in silver, and a certificate.
Adam Zagajewski (Poland), awarded in 2004

Commonwealth Writers Prize

Established in 1987 by the Commonwealth Foundation. In 2003 there was one award of £10,000 for the best book submitted and an award of £3,000 for the best first book. In each of the four regions of the Commonwealth, two prizes of £1,000 are awarded: one for the best book and one for the best first book.

Best Book	*A Distant Shore* by Caryl Phillips
Best First Book	*The Curious Incident of the Dog in the Night-Time* by Mark Haddon
Regional winners—Best Book	
Africa	*The Good Doctor* by Damon Galgut (South Africa)
Caribbean & Canada	*Deafening* by Frances Itani (Canada)
Eurasia	*A Distant Shore* by Caryl Phillips (U.K.)
Southeast Asia & South Pacific	*The Hamilton Case* by Michelle de Kretser (Australia)

Booker Prize

Established in 1969, sponsored by Booker McConnell Ltd. and, beginning in 2002, the Man Group; administered by the National Book League in the U.K. Awarded to the best full-length novel written by a citizen of the Commonwealth or the Republic of Ireland and published in the U.K. during the 12 months ended September 30. Prize: £50,000.
The Line of Beauty by Alan Hollinghurst

Whitbread Book of the Year

Established in 1971. The winners of the Whitbread Book Awards for Poetry, Biography, Novel, and First Novel as well as the Whitbread Children's Book of the Year each receive £5,000, and the winner of the Whitbread Book of the Year prize receives an additional £25,000. Winners are announced in January of the year following the award.
The Curious Incident of the Dog in the Night-Time by Mark Haddon (2003 award)

Orange Prize for Fiction

Established in 1996. Awarded to a work of published fiction written by a woman in English and published in the U.K. during the 12 months ended March 31. Prize: £30,000.
Small Island by Andrea Levy (U.K.)

PEN/Faulkner Award

The PEN/Faulkner Foundation each year recognizes the best published works of fiction by contemporary American writers. Named for William Faulkner, the PEN/Faulkner Award was founded by writers in 1980 to honour their peers and is now the largest juried award for fiction in the U.S. Prize: $15,000.
The Early Stories by John Updike

Pulitzer Prizes in Letters and Drama

Begun in 1917, awarded by Columbia University, New York City, on the recommendation of the Pulitzer Prize Board for books published in the previous year. Five categories in Letters are honoured: Fiction, Biography, and General Non-Fiction (authors of works in these categories must be American citizens); History (the subject must be American history); and Poetry (for original verse by an American author). The Drama prize is for "a distinguished play by an American author, preferably original in its source and dealing with American life." Prize: $10,000 in each category.

Fiction	*The Known World* by Edward P. Jones
Biography	*Khrushchev: The Man and His Era* by William Taubman
Poetry	*Walking to Martha's Vineyard* by Franz Wright
History	*A Nation Under Our Feet* by Steven Hahn
General Non-Fiction	*Gulag: A History* by Anne Applebaum
Drama	*I Am My Own Wife* by Doug Wright

National Book Awards

Awarded since 1950 by the National Book Foundation, a consortium of American publishing groups. Categories have varied, beginning with 3—Fiction, Nonfiction, and Poetry swelling to 22 awards in 1983, and returning to 4 (the initial 3 plus Young People's Literature) in 2001. Prize: $10,000 and a bronze statue.

Fiction	*Madeleine Is Sleeping* by Sarah Shun-lien Bynum
Nonfiction	*Arc of Justice: A Saga of Race, Civil Rights, and Murder in the Jazz Age* by Kevin Boyle
Poetry	*Shoah Train* by William Heyen

Frost Medal

Awarded annually since 1930 by the Poetry Society of America for distinguished lifetime service to American poetry.
Richard Howard

Governor General's Literary Awards

Canada's premier literary awards. Prizes are given in 14 categories altogether: Fiction, Poetry, Drama, Translation, Nonfiction, and Children's Literature (Text and Illustration), each in English and French. Established in 1937. Prize: Can$15,000.

Fiction (English)	*A Complicated Kindness* by Miriam Toews
Fiction (French)	*Le Cercle parfait* by Pascale Quiviger
Poetry (English)	*Short Journey Upriver Toward Ōishida* by Roo Borson
Poetry (French)	*Les Jours à vif* by André Brochu

Griffin Poetry Prize

Established in 2001 and administered by the Griffin Trust for Excellence in Poetry, the award honours first-edition books of poetry published during the preceding year. Prize: Can$40,000 each for the two awards.

Canadian Award	*Loop* by Anne Simpson
International Award	*The Strange Hours Travelers Keep* by August Kleinzahler (U.S.)

Büchner Prize

Georg-Büchner-Preis. Awarded for a body of literary work in the German language. First awarded in 1923; now administered by the German Academy for Language and Literature. Prize: €40,000.
Wilhelm Genazino (Germany)

Hooft Prize

P.C. Hooftprijs. The Dutch national prize for literature, established in 1947. Prize: €60,000.
Cees Nooteboom for prose

Nordic Council Literary Prize

Established in 1961. Selections are made by a 10-member jury from among original works first published in Danish, Norwegian, or Swedish during the past two years or other Nordic languages (Finnish, Faroese, Sami, etc.) during the past four years. Prize: DKr 350,000.
Juoksuhaudantie ("The Trench Road") by Kari Hotakainen (Finland)

Prix Goncourt

Prix de l'Académie Goncourt. First awarded in 1903 from the estate of French literary figure Edmond Huot de Goncourt, to memorialize him and his brother, Jules. Prize: €10.
Le Soleil des Scorta by Laurent Gaudé

Prix Femina

Established in 1904. The awards for works "of imagination" are announced by an all-women jury in the categories of French fiction, fiction in translation, and nonfiction. Announced in November together with the Prix Médicis. Prize: Not stated (earlier the award was F 5,000 [about $690]).

French Fiction	*Une Vie française* by Jean-Paul Dubois

Cervantes Prize for Hispanic Literature

Premio Cervantes. Established in 1976 and awarded for a body of work in the Spanish language. Announced in December and awarded the following April. Prize: €90,151.
Raphael Sánchez Ferlosio (Spain)

Planeta Prize

Premio Planeta de Novela. Established in 1951 by the Planeta Publishing House for the best unpublished, original novel in Spanish. Awarded in Barcelona in October. Prize: €600,000 and publication by Planeta.
Un milagro en equilibrio by Lucía Etxebarría

Camões Prize

Premio Luis da Camões da Literatura. Established in 1988 by the governments of Portugal and Brazil to honour a "representatative" author writing in the Portuguese language. Prize: $100,000.
Agustina Bessa-Luis (Portugal)

Russian Booker Prize

Awarded since 1992, the Russian Booker Prize has sometimes carried the names of various sponsors—e.g., Smirnoff in 1997–2001. In 2004 it was underwritten by the Open Russia Charitable Organization and called the Booker/Open Russia Literary Prize. Awards: $15,000 for the winner; $1,000 for each finalist.
Volteryantsy i Volteryanki ("Voltaireans Male and Female") by Vasily Aksyonov

Naguib Mahfouz Medal for Literature

Established in 1996 and awarded for the best contemporary novel published in Arabic. The winning work is translated into English and published in Cairo, London, and New York. Prize: $1,000 and a silver medal.
Al-Mahbubat ("The Loved Ones") by Alia Mamdouh (Iraq)

Jun'ichirō Tanizaki Prize

Tanizaki Jun'ichirō Shō. Established in 1965 to honour the memory of novelist Jun'ichirō Tanizaki. Awarded annually to a Japanese author for an exemplary literary work. Prize: ¥1,000,000 and a trophy.
Horie Toshiyuki for *Yukinuma to sono shūhen* ("Yukinuma and Its Environs")

Ryūnosuke Akutagawa Prize

Akutagawa Ryūnosuke Shō. Established in 1935 and now sponsored by the Association for the Promotion of Japanese Literature, the prize is awarded in January and June for the best serious work of fiction by a promising new Japanese writer published in a magazine or journal. Prize: ¥1,000,000 and a commemorative gift.
"Keritai senaka" ("Kick Me") by Wataya Risa (130th prize, second half of 2003)
"Kaigo nyūmon" ("Guide for the Care of the Elderly") by Mobu Norio (131st prize, first half of 2004)

Mao Dun Literary Award

Established in 1981 to honour contemporary Chinese novels and named after novelist Shen Yanbing (1896–1981), whose nom de plume was Mao Dun; awarded every five years. Latest awards were announced on Oct. 12, 2000 (the same day as the Nobel Prize for Literature).
Jueze ("Hard Choice") by Zhang Ping
Chang hen ge (2000; "Song of Everlasting Sorrow") by Wang Anyi
Chen'ai luo ding (1999; "When Dust Settles") by Ah Lai
Nanfang you jiamu ("Fine Tree Possessed in the Southland") and *Buye zhi hou* ("Delightful Marquis to Break Drowsiness"), from *Charen sanbuqu* ("Trilogy of Tea Men") by Wang Xufeng

(continued from page 222)

In the nonfiction category, Lynne Truss's *Eats, Shoots & Leaves* (2003), appropriately subtitled *The Zero Tolerance Approach to Punctuation,* became a runaway best seller, with over 500,000 copies in print in the U.K. alone. Responding to an age of "ignorance and indifference," and sloppy usage on the Internet, Truss made an entertaining case for the proper use of commas, semicolons, and apostrophes. "For any true stickler, . . . the sight of the plural word 'Book's' with an apostrophe in it will trigger a ghastly private emotional process similar to the stages of bereavement, though greatly accelerated."

Well-known American travel writer Bill Bryson, a resident of Britain, won the 2004 Aventis Prize for his first astonishing foray into popular science writing. *A Short History of Nearly Everything* (2003) attempted to comprehend everything from the big bang to the rise of human civilization, tackling subjects as diverse as geology, chemistry, paleontology, climatology, astronomy, and particle physics along the way. Reviewers commended Bryson for breathing life into his topics by including chats with living experts and humorous vignettes about some of history's more eccentric scientists. Human interest also enlivened dry science in Andrew Brown's book *In the Beginning Was the Worm* (2003). Brown's study of the struggle to sequence the genome of a common microscopic worm was short-listed for the Aventis Prize.

Top food writer Nigel Slater successfully switched genres when he turned his hand to autobiography in *Toast: The Story of a Boy's Hunger* (2003). Slater's method of retrieving episodes of his bleak childhood and motherless adolescence through memories of food led one critic to name him the "Proust of the Nesquik Era." For a *New York Times* reviewer, Slater summoned up "Nick Hornby, Martin Amis, and Philip Larkin all at the same time." *Toast* was voted Biography of the Year at the British Book Awards. Veteran author A.S. Byatt (*see* BIOGRAPHIES) explored aging and death in *Little Black Book of Stories,* a collection of five Gothic tales.

On the poetry front, playwright Harold Pinter received the prestigious Wilfred Owen award for poetry for his volume *War* (2003), a collection of eight poems and one speech critical of the war in Iraq. Pinter's poem "God Bless America" was widely quoted in the press but vilified by the American right. "Here they go again/ The Yanks in their armoured parade/ Chanting their ballads of joy/ As they gallop across the big world/ Praising America's God./ The gutters are clogged with the dead." Less controversy was stirred when Scottish poet and musician Don Paterson won the 2003 Whitbread Poetry Award, worth £10,000 (about $18,000), as well as the 2003 T.S. Eliot Prize for poetry, worth £5,000 (about $9,000). (Both prizes were awarded in 2004.) The poems in *Landing Light* (2003) were described by a reviewer in *The Guardian* newspaper as "examinations of becoming, of the processes of life," even when they deal with everyday themes such as ice-skating or waking up with one's child. Meanwhile, Scottish poet Kathleen Jamie won the £10,000 Forward Poetry Prize for *The Tree House,* a volume of poetry filled with "lichen-crusted bedrock," alder trees, copulating frogs, and "brittle waves." "What's most in need of re-negotiation and repair," Jamie explained, ". . . is our relationship with the natural world. We're learning, or re-learning, that this is the only world, it's not an anteroom or preparation for something 'better.' Neither is it an infinite 'resource.' " The book's epigraph was from Friedrich Hölderlin. The world may, or may not, be ending its lyric phase, but despite everything, "it is beautiful to unfold our souls and our short lives."

(CAROL PEAKER)

© Colin McPherson/Corbis

Literary editor Lynne Truss had a best seller with a book about punctuation, **Eats, Shoots & Leaves.**

United States. A survey sponsored by the National Endowment for the Arts appeared in the summer of 2004 and warned of a decline in literary reading among Americans. Nonetheless, some of the best American writers wrote on, making the year, and the fall season in particular, a good one for American letters, regardless of the size of the audience.

Philip Roth, a writer who had from time to time worried out loud about the small number of serious American readers, thundered onto the best-seller list with *The Plot Against America,* a powerful work of alternative history. Though critic Frank Rich declared in the *New York Times* that the subgenre was "low-rent," it served nevertheless as a marvelous vehicle for Roth's depiction of paranoia lost. In the novel isolationist and Nazi sympathizer Charles Lindbergh defeats Franklin Roosevelt in the 1940 presidential race, striking fear in the hearts of the family of young Philip and most other American Jews.

The prolific writer Joyce Carol Oates produced two books of fiction, a collection of short stories titled *I Am No One You Know* and the massive multigenerational novel *The Falls,* which moved along with the power of the rough white-water rapids leading to the great cataract at Niagara. Reading the best of Oates was something like trying to navigate the rushing Niagara River of her novel at that point when "at first you think that your actions are propelling your little boat along at such speed; then you realize that the speed, the propulsion, has nothing to do with you. It is something happening to you."

Other works by veteran novelists met with more mixed responses. Russell Banks's *The Darling,* about a modern radical woman in Africa, and T.C. Boyle's *The Inner Circle,* his version of the story of controversial sex researcher Alfred Kinsey, were hobbled at the outset by murderous reviews by *New York Times* critic Michiko Kakutani. *True North,* Jim Harrison's new novel, a generational tale set in Michigan, did not make much headway either. *The Dew Breaker,* Edwidge Danticat's novel in stories about Haitian émigrés, seemed to find a devoted audience. Craig Nova's novel about crime and justice in Vermont—*Cruisers*—deserved a larger audience than it found, as did *Project X,* Jim Shepard's linguistically daring version of a Columbine High School-like massacre. Francisco Goldman's *The Divine Husband,* his attempt to write the great

(Central) American novel, did not rise to that standard. Madison Smartt Bell completed his Haitian trilogy with the publication of *The Stone That the Builder Refused.*

Powerful battle scenes and the measured steadiness of men approaching mortal combat made up the pages of Donald Pfarrer's magnificent *The Fearless Man,* his novel about the Vietnam War, as in the sequence in which a gunnery officer leads a small group of riflemen toward the hidden enemy: "First stop, Ambush Alley. Cross it. Don't even think about using it. Then a stream to worry about. Then around, not over, two hills . . . and back into the jungle at the bottom. Choose a place and set in. Set up the gun. Post a watch to cover the place where the river and the trail cross. Go to sleep. Listen to the maniacs in the brain as you slide into slumber."

Just as persuasive was the annealing prose in Marilynne Robinson's long-awaited second novel, *Gilead,* the story of several generations of itinerant Midwestern American preachers: "I don't write the way I speak. I'm afraid you would think I didn't know any better. I don't write the way I do for the pulpit, either, insofar as I can help it. That would be ridiculous, in the circumstances. I do try to write the way I think. But of course that all changes as soon as I put it into words. And the more it does seem to be my thinking, the more pulpitish it sounds, which I guess is inevitable. I will resist that inflection, nevertheless." Robinson certainly resisted it, creating a marvelous skein of pure American plain-style prose.

Also quite convincing and wonderfully entertaining was Percival Everett's *American Desert,* a satire on everything from born-again religious groups to academia and the military. A little more strident (and less effective) was another novel that Everett published during the year, this one coauthored with James Kincaid, *A History of the African-American People [Proposed] by Strom Thurmond.* Christopher Buckley had readers look at the Middle East through a cracked lens in his successful satire *Florence of Arabia.*

Nicholas Delbanco went to some major American cultural figures, Henry Ford and Harvey Firestone among them, to populate the Michigan landscape in *The Vagabonds.* Maria Flook remained in her native New England in the romantic mystery *Lux.* Octogenarian Louis Auchincloss kept his eye on New York City's upper crust in *East Side Story,* his 60th book. Samantha Gillison brought out her second novel, *The King of America,* a book based on the life of the late Michael Rockefeller and set mostly along the coast of New Guinea, where Rockefeller was last seen. Andrew Sean Greer's second novel, *The Confessions of Max Tivoli,* won much critical praise.

The once immensely popular novelist Herman Wouk, 89, brought out his first novel in 10 years, *A Hole in Texas,* an entertaining spoof about a particle physicist on the job in Texas and the workings of Capitol Hill in Washington, D.C. Another best-selling writer, John Grisham, weighed in with *The Last Juror,* which was less effective than his other legal thrillers. *The Tarnished Eye,* Judith Guest's novel about a family massacred in northern Michigan, showed off her best talents. A best-seller-list phenomenon was the jointly authored *The Rule of Four* by first-time writers Ian Caldwell and Dustin Thomason.

A few impressive first novels made the bookstore shelves, if not the best-seller lists. Among them were *Loving Che* by Ana Menéndez, *Country of Origin* by Don Lee, *The Rope Eater* by Ben Jones, *Symptomatic* by Danzy Senna, *The Pink Institution* by Selah Saterstrom, and *Ask Me Anything* by Francesca Delbanco (the daughter of novelist Nicholas Delbanco).

A number of elder statesmen published short-story collections, notably Ray Bradbury (*The Cat's Pajamas*), John Barth (*The Book of Ten Nights and a Night*), E.L. Doctorow (*Sweet Land Stories*), and Gilbert Sorrentino (*The Moon in Its Flight*). Wendell Berry released *That Distant Land,* his collected stories. Joy Williams focused on themes of illness and decay in *Honored Guest.* Virginia writer John Rolfe Gardiner signed in with *The Magellan House Stories. Los Angeles Times* award winner David Means did not disappoint his growing audience with *The Secret Goldfish,* his third collection. Naturalist and essayist Barry Lopez stirred up some aesthetic controversy with his polemical collection *Resistance.* Brooklyn, N.Y., writer Jonathan Lethem showed off his gift for the short-story form with *Men and Cartoons.* Nominated for the National Book Award, Joan Silber's *Ideas of Heaven* drew new critical attention for this New England-based writer. Bret Anthony Johnston made an impressive debut with the stories in *Corpus Christi.* Among reprints to notice were *Echo Tree: The Collected Short Fiction of Henry Dumas* (2003). *The Collected Stories of Truman Capote* came out along with a volume of his letters (*Too Brief a Treat,* edited by Gerald Clarke).

American poets continued to write powerfully in the lyric mode about perennial subjects. In *Danger on Peaks* Gary Snyder brought nature into the reader's inner vision: "Hammering a dent out of a bucket/ a woodpecker answers from the woods." *The Clerk's Tale,* Spencer Reece's debut work, focused on the world in which he made his living—haberdashery:

> I am thirty-three and working in an expensive clothier,
>
> selling suits to men I call "Sir."
>
> These men are muscled, groomed and cropped—
>
> with wives and families that grow exponentially.
>
> Mostly I talk of rep ties and bow ties,
>
> of full-Windsor knots and half-Windsor knots,
>
> of tattersall, French cuff, and English spread collars.

A number of poets issued volumes of collected verse. Santa Cruz poet Robert Sward delivered *The Collected Poems of Robert Sward, 1957–2004,* which focused on the comedy of love and the spiritual: "They say there is a monk on the Santa Cruz Mountains,/ his white

Brooklyn, N.Y.-based author Jonathan Lethem's short-story collection,* Men and Cartoons, *attracted attention in 2004.

robes floating, three hundred feet beneath the sky." *Collected Poems* came from Donald Justice (*see* OBITUARIES), Jean Valentine issued *Door in the Mountain,* William Matthews released *Search Party: Collected Poems of William Matthews,* Rodney Jones offered *Kingdom of the Instant,* and Thomas Lux published *The Cradle Place.* Barry Spacks released *Regarding Women* and *The Hope of the Air,* and Richard Howard produced *Inner Voices: Selected Poems, 1963–2003.* Robert Pinsky, with Maggie Dietz, edited *An Invitation to Poetry,* another volume (with a DVD) in the Favorite Poem Project, which he began when he was U.S. poet laureate. Nebraskan Ted Kooser (*see* BIOGRAPHIES) was named poet laureate for 2004–05, and he published a new book of poetry during the year.

Standing out among various works of nonfiction was Luis Alberto Urrea's *The Devil's Highway,* a burning account of illegal Mexican immigrants attempting to cross the desert into Arizona. Octogenarian novelist and essayist Mary Lee Settle presented a travel book about Spain, *Spanish Recognitions: The Roads to the Present.* Richard Rhodes delivered a well-received biography in *John James Audubon: The Making of an American.* Mary V. Dearborn contributed *Mistress of Modernism: The Life of Peggy Guggenheim.* Architecture critic Ada Louise Huxtable entered a brief but pithy biographical volume, *Frank Lloyd Wright,* in the Penguin Lives series.

Among literary biographies Barry Silesky's *John Gardner: Literary Outlaw* was a useful contribution, as were Philip McFarland's *Hawthorne in Concord,* Jeffrey Meyers's *Somerset Maugham,* Christopher Sawyer-Lauçanno's *E.E. Cummings,* Eileen Warburton's *John Fowles,* and Joan Reardon's *Poet of the Appetites: The Lives and Loves of M.F.K. Fisher.* Evelyn C. White signed in with *Alice Walker: A Life.*

During the past decade a deluge of memoirs had been published. Those worth taking seriously during the year included Kathryn Harrison's *The Mother Knot* and *In My Father's Footsteps* by Sebastian Matthews, son of poet William Matthews. Another memoir with a father at the centre of the action was Nick Flynn's *Another Bullshit Night in Suck City.*

A wonderfully invigorating polemical tone inhabited scholar-critic Mark Edmunson's latest book, *Why Read?:* "Literature and truth? The humanities and truth? Come now. What could be more ridiculous? What could be more superannuated than that?" *Will in the World,* Stephen Greenblatt's book on "How Shakespeare Became Shakespeare," moved toward the discerning public's best-seller lists. Another nonfiction volume with more than academic appeal was science-fiction writer Ursula K. LeGuin's *The Wave in the Mind: Talks and Essays on the Writer, the Reader, and the Imagination.* Another eminently accessible book for the general public was essayist Phillip Lopate's *Waterfront: A Journey Around Manhattan.*

Among interesting historical studies, the year saw the publication of Walter A. McDougall's *Freedom Just Around the Corner: A New American History 1585–1828,* Shirley Christian's *Before Lewis and Clark,* David Hackett Fischer's *Washington's Crossing,* and Thomas Parrish's *The Submarine.* The late Edward W. Said's political columns about the Middle East turmoil appeared under the title *From Oslo to Iraq and the Road Map.* In *The Open Space of Democracy,* Terry Tempest Williams created a lyrical polemic about politics and the environment. Novelist Rick Bass, who had written often on environmental questions, produced *Caribou Rising: Defending the Porcupine Herd, Gwich-'in Culture, and the Arctic National Wildlife Refuge.* One of the most interesting cultural studies of 2004 was Alan Trachtenberg's *Shades of Hiawatha: Staging Indians, Making Americans, 1880–1930.*

The 2004 Pulitzer Prizes were awarded to works that appeared in 2003. The fiction prize went to Edward P. Jones for his novel *The Known World,* the poetry prize to Franz Wright for *Walking to Martha's Vineyard,* the biography prize to William Taubman for *Khrushchev: The Man and His Era,* and the Pulitzer for general nonfiction to Anne Applebaum for *Gulag: A History.* At the PEN/Faulkner Award ceremonies in May, John Updike won the top prize for *The Early Stories, 1953–1975* (2003). Luís Alberto Urrea won the Lannan Foundation Literary Award for Nonfiction. Later in 2004 the PEN/Malamud Award for excellence in short fiction went to Richard Bausch and Nell Freudenberger.

The National Book Award for Fiction went to Lily Tuck's *The News from Paraguay,* a novel set in 19th-century Paraguay about the relationship between a young Irishwoman and the dictator Francisco Solano López. In the nonfiction category Kevin Boyle's *Arc of Justice: A Saga of Race, Civil Rights, and Murder in the Jazz Era,* the story of a black family's fight to live in a predominately white Detroit neighbourhood during the 1920s, captured the award.

John Updike was the recipient of the 2004 PEN/Faulkner Award for **The Early Stories, 1953–1975**

Among the deaths during the year were those of fiction writers William Herrick and Ronald Sukenick. In addition to Justice, a number of poets died, including Thom Gunn, Anthony Hecht, Carl Rakosi, and Mona Van Duyn. Cultural historian Daniel Boorstin, historian Iris Chang, mystery writer Joseph Hansen, writer Hubert Selby, Jr., children's author Paula Danziger, and critic and novelist Susan Sontag also left the literary scene. (*See* OBITUARIES.)

(ALAN CHEUSE)

Canada. The search for a home, refuge, person, or object was a common theme in Canadian literature in 2004. In *Claire's Head,* Catherine Bush depicted a woman who did not allow her migraine headaches to prevent her from looking for her sister; in *Cat's Pilgrimage,* Marilyn Bowering's young heroine and her father sought refuge in a utopian community; in Bill Gaston's

Sointula, a mother kayaked along the British Columbia coastline on a quest for her son; and in Kate Pullinger's *A Little Stranger,* a daughter searched for the alcoholic, homeless mother she could not forget. A Muslim woman in Shauna Singh Baldwin's *The Tiger Claw* searched for her Jewish lover in Nazi Germany, while Harold Eustache, in *Shuswap Journey,* based his tale of a father looking for his abducted daughter on a traditional legend. More unusual was the severed arm sought in the bowels of Mumbai (Bombay) by Anosh Irani's protagonist in *The Cripple and His Talismans.* The pursuit of truth informed Des Kennedy's *Flame of Separation,* in which a teacher reexamined his life, and the quest for redemption in the eye of a hurricane preoccupied the narrator of Paul Quarrington's *Galveston.*

The experiences of newcomers to Canada were explored in Esi Edugyan's *The Second Life of Samuel Tyne,* about a Ghanaian struggling to make sense of life in Alberta, and in Wayson Choy's *All That Matters,* the continuing saga of the Chen family in Vancouver, while someone desperate to be an immigrant was the subject of *The Stowaway,* Robert Hough's fact-based novel. In Merilyn Simonds's *The Holding,* a Scottish pioneer spoke across the years through her diary to the modern-day woman reading it.

Other novels included Anne Cameron's *Dahlia Cassidy,* a satiric view of a small British Columbian town; Miriam Toews's gentler depiction of the denizens of a small Mennonite town in *A Complicated Kindness;* Trevor Cole's tour de force *Norman Bray in the Performance of His Life;* and Colin McAdam's *Some Great Thing,* in which the paths of two powerful men intersect with unexpected consequences.

There were also Douglas Coupland's strange coupling of extremes in *Eleanor Rigby;* Monica Kidd's *The Momentum of Red,* in which a father and daughter struggle together to end his domination of her life; Richard B. Wright's amalgam of mistress, misery, and murder in *Adultery;* and poet Don Coles's first novel, *Doctor Bloom's Story,* about the ethical dilemma faced by a creative-writing teacher regarding a student.

One way or another, many short-story collections, such as Ramona Dearing's *So Beautiful,* were about the people one gets stuck with—not only family but roommates, teachers, spouses, and fellow passengers. Alice Munro's *Runaway* scouted the depths of ordinary lives; George Bowering's *Standing on Richards* was a wealth of stories in all their various disguises; Bonnie Dunlop's *The Beauty Box* plucked tales of bittersweet midnights and regrets; and Mavis Gallant's *Montreal Stories* addressed the consequences of returning home.

David Bezmozgis's *Natasha and Other Stories* was a rich mixture of the minutiae of Jewish domestic life; Kelly Cooper's *Eyehill* was a sequence of linked stories centred on a prairie town; and Yashin Blake's tales in *Nowhere Fast* reflected the structure and improvisation of contemporary jazz.

Surrealism was the mode of Carrie Snyder's *Hair Hat,* in which 11 lives are affected by this weird headgear, and it also flavoured Annabel Lyon's three novellas in *The Best Thing for You,* painfully accurate portraits of parents bedeviled by their offspring.

Poets saw the glass both half-full and half-empty. Some of life's bleaker aspects were explored by Patrick Lane in *Go Leaving Strange;* Eve Joseph in her volume of ghazals on physical and spiritual loss and death, *The Startled Heart;* George Fetherling in his memorial to his father, *Singer: An Elegy;* and Sue Goyette in *Undone,* meditations edged with dark longings. In counterbalance were Mari-Lou Rowley's *Viral Suite,* exuberant excursions into bodily sensations and intimate acts; Roo Borson's meticulously rendered interior landscapes, in *Short Journey Upriver Toward Ōishida;* and bill bisset's innocent insights and irrepressible humour in *narrativ engima/rumours uv hurricane.* Tom Walmsley's sex-sodden *Honeymoon in Berlin* was an eclectic collection of verbal riffs; Jan Zwicky's *Robinson's Crossing* engaged the nature of history; Tim Bowling's *The Memory Orchard* plucked images from the past like apples, or guitars; while Wayde Compton's *Performance Bond* fused verbal excursions of hip-hop and jazz into urban renewal.

(ELIZABETH RHETT WOODS)

Other Literature in English. Important works in English representing a variety of genres by authors young and old, emerging and established, highlighted the literary offerings for 2004 from sub-Saharan Africa, New Zealand, and Australia. Outstanding new releases from Africa included Chimamanda Ngozi Adichie's *Purple Hibiscus,* in which the protagonist, Kambili, struggles with the abuse, hypocrisy, and deep pathology of her father and the Roman Catholic Church in a narrative informed by political and ideological issues. The acclaimed South African playwright, poet, journalist, painter, and author Zakes Mda brought out his latest novel, *The Whale Caller,* which was lauded for its deft characterizations and vivid atmosphere—"a poignant love story of outsiders, whales and dreams." Mda's 39-year-old countryman Troy Blacklaws, who resided in Frankfurt, Ger., drew praise for *Karoo Boy,* his breakthrough novel, which takes place in the Karoo outback and centres on the relationship between the protagonist, Douglas, and Moses, an old Xhosa man, as the two plan to travel together to Cape Town. Distinguished Somali author Naruddin Farah brought out his latest

***Canadian short-story writer Mavis Gallant, who lives in Paris, returned home with her collection* Montreal Stories.**

novel, *Links,* which, in Dantean fashion, exposes life in his native country's capital, Mogadishu, "the city of death." Veteran writers and Nobel laureates J.M. Coetzee and Nadine Gordimer had end-of-the-year releases in 2003 that spawned great interest and were predictably short-listed for numerous national and international literary awards in 2004. Coetzee's *Elizabeth Costello* marked somewhat of a departure for the author in that it combined essayistic narrative with a fictional framework. Gordimer brought out *Loot, and Other Stories,* her 12th collection. André Brink pleased his longtime readers with the publication of *Before I Forget,* in which the protagonist, a 78-year-old writer who fears he has lost his talent as an author, reflects on his life by recalling his numerous love affairs.

In New Zealand, Booker Prize winner Keri Hulme broke her silence of over a decade with the publication of *Stonefish,* a collection of short stories and verse. The winners of the Montana New Zealand Book Awards 2004 included Annamarie Jagose's novel *Slow Water* (winner of the Deutz Medal for Fiction) and Anne Kennedy's verse collection *Sing-song* (winner in the poetry category). Named one of the runners-up for the award in fiction was *The Scornful Moon,* which marked the return of renowned author Maurice Gee. Also of note was the latest release by C.K. Stead entitled *Mansfield,* a fictional portrait of New Zealand-born literary great Katherine Mansfield. Australia welcomed the latest verse collection by John Kinsella, *Peripheral Light: Selected and New Poems,* which was hailed by American critic Harold Bloom, who wrote in his introduction, "We are poised before the onset of what I prophesy will be a major art."

Sadly, 2004 marked the passing of Thea Astley, one of Australia's most celebrated novelists, and of New Zealand authors Janet Frame and Maurice Shadbolt and historian Michael King. (*See* OBITUARIES.)

(DAVID DRAPER CLARK)

GERMANIC

German. The German-speaking literary world was caught completely off guard by the October 2004 announcement that the Nobel Prize for Literature would be awarded to Austrian writer Elfriede Jelinek (*see* NOBEL PRIZES), a prominent critic of contemporary Austria. In poems, plays, novels, screenplays, and radio plays, Jelinek addressed sexual inequality, relationships in which power was a factor, and political oppression. She was as surprised as anyone by the award, which the great Austrian novelist and playwright Thomas Bernhard (1931–89) had not received. The Georg Büchner Prize, the most important German prize for lifetime literary achievement, went to writer Wilhelm Genazino, whose work addressed the understated comedy of the everyday life of ordinary figures in a West German milieu. The Ingeborg Bachmann Prize for the best emerging author in the German language went to 35-year-old East German writer Uwe Tellkamp for a linguistically and thematically ambitious novel in progress that was framed around a streetcar ride through Dresden.

East German author Irina Liebmann published her best novel to date, the semiautobiographical *Die freien Frauen,* which told the story of Elisabeth Schlosser, a melancholy middle-aged woman living alone in the centre of Berlin and dealing with the various problems of aging—sadness, regret, physical ailments, concern for her depressed son, the complete transformation of the urban environment around her, and the end of all dreams for a socialist utopia. In the end Schlosser, who, like Liebmann, was born in Moscow in 1943, makes a journey of discovery to Poland.

In his novel **Don Juan,** *veteran author Peter Handke retold the story of the legendary lover, ostensibly in Don Juan's own words.*

© Jerry Bauer

Syrian-born writer Rafik Schami, who moved to Germany in 1971, published a major German-language novel, *Die dunkle Seite der Liebe,* a massive exploration of the Arab world in general and the city of Damascus in particular; the work was full of various crisscrossing stories and figures. Schami's novel clearly demonstrated what had been increasingly evident for many years—that the German-speaking literary world was no longer just the preserve of ethnic Germans, Austrians, and Swiss and that the German language was also being used by a host of multiethnic and multicultural citizens of Germany, Austria, and Switzerland, some of whom wrote at a very high level.

Novelist Martin Walser published *Der Augenblick der Liebe,* which dealt on one level with the fictional German hobbyist historian Gottlieb Zürn—who had appeared in Walser's novels *Das Schwanenhaus* (1980) and *Jagd* (1988)—and on another level with the life of the real historical figure Julien Offray de La Mettrie, a French Enlightenment philosopher whose life Zürn chronicles in a lecture. The first level relates a love affair between the elderly Zürn and a young graduate student in the United States; the second level explores La Mettrie's materialist philosophy and attempt to free humans from feelings of guilt, an attempt that Walser might see as a parallel to his own highly publicized criticisms of German feelings of historical guilt. Just as Walser had been the subject of heated debate in the German literary world in the last decade, so too was Zürn the subject of heated debate in the novel.

Peter Handke's novel *Don Juan (erzählt von ihm selbst)* was a retelling of the story of the legendary lover, as told by Don Juan to the cook at a monastery where he has sought refuge. The story, which relates Don Juan's erotic travels through Europe and Asia, also deals with the protagonist's sorrow over the loss of his wife and only son. It is this loss that becomes the inspiration for Don Juan's erotic quest.

Burkhard Spinnen's short-story collection *Der Reservetorwart* contained stories about ordinary German people trying to preserve their self-constructed normality. The protagonist of the short story for which the collection was named is a second-string goalie who manages to injure himself when he actually gets the chance to play a game and thereby maintains the unobtrusiveness of his own existence. Most of the other protagonists of Spinnen's stories are German losers trying to preserve their fragile illusions. Patrick Roth's short-story collection *Starlite Terrace* told the stories of four residents of an apartment complex in Los Angeles; the narrator, like Roth himself, is a German living in Los Angeles. Roth's stories, full of high drama, made ample references to Hollywood and film history. Ulrike Draesner's short-story collection *Hot Dogs* dealt with contemporary sexuality and relationships from a female perspective; the protagonist of the main story is a German woman who, unbeknownst to her male German lovers, illegally sells their sperm for a high price in the United States.

Sven Regener's novel *Neue Vahr Süd,* named after a neighbourhood in Bremen, was a prequel to his highly successful 2001 novel *Herr Lehmann; Neue Vahr Süd* told the story of the protagonist's early years in Bremen before moving to Berlin in the 1980s. Austrian writer Thomas Stangl released his first novel, *Der einzige Ort,* which told the story of a journey to the legendary Malian city of Timbuktu.

(STEPHEN BROCKMANN)

Netherlandic. Hella S. Haasse received the Prijs der Nederlandse Letteren for 2004. The most important literary prize of the Dutch-language area was awarded every three years, alternately by the Dutch and Belgian heads of state. In this case the prize was given to recognize the artistic and human qualities of Haasse's more than 70 titles, which had "so worthily and emphatically placed Dutch literature upon the international stage."

The Libris Literatuur Prijs was awarded to Arthur Japin for his novel *Een schitterend gebrek,* which told the story of Lucia, Giacomo Casanova's first lover, whom Casanova mentioned in his memoirs as one of the few people whom he had wronged. Published in 2003, Japin's novel was reprinted three times in quick succession. Arnon Grunberg's novel *De asielzoeker* (2003), a study in the difficulties of contemporary human existence, netted him the AKO Literatuur Prijs for 2004—his second—as well as the F. Bordewijk-prijs.

The year 2004 saw the publication of *De nieuwe Bijbelvertaling,* commissioned by an ecumenical collective of religious denominations and Dutch and Flemish Bible societies. The work of hundreds of translators, readers, and supervisors, the process of translation had spanned more than a decade. The simultaneous publication in various editions (some 200,000 copies) was a

Arnon Grunberg's novel De asielzoeker *won him two top Dutch literary prizes in 2004.*

literary as well as religious event, as this new translation of the Bible unleashed a public discussion of proper methods and goals of translation. Many of the readers invited to comment as the translation progressed were (nonconfessional) members of the intelligentsia; comparisons to the 17th-century States translation were inevitable in light of commonly held notions of the influence of the older translation on Dutch literary language. The translation was made available on the Internet, both in written form and in sound files.

The importance of translation in Dutch literary life was underscored by the P.C. Hooftprijs awarded to Cees Nooteboom. The jury praised Nooteboom's prose for its "literary eloquence, scope, and originality," among the best produced in The Netherlands in the last 50 years. Nooteboom's reputation abroad—his work had been translated into 20 languages—contributed to his recognition in the Low Countries.

(JOLANDA VANDERWAL TAYLOR)

Danish. In 2004 Danish writers found an eager audience for their works of fantasy and imagination. Prolific veteran Klaus Rifbjerg combined autobiography, invention, sense, and nonsense in *Alea: En tilfældighedsroman* (2003). In *Mojácar,* Rifbjerg and Swedish photographer Georg Oddner portrayed Rifbjerg's Spanish summer home. Maria Grønlykke, a newcomer to the literary scene, described everyday life and the extraordinary characters that inhabited the island Fyn, where she made her home, in her short-story collections *Fisketyven* (2003) and *En lille sang om Stella.* In *København,* Katrine Marie Guldager sketched a cosmopolitan metropolis, questioned the loss of shared values, and explored the implications of individual responsibility. Jens Christian Grøndahl depicted Denmark and the Danish people through the eyes of a young Romanian, Elena, in *Piazza Bucarest.* In *Thorsten Madsens ego,* Mathilde Walter Clark described a competitive businessman in a world gone awry. With her novel *Hengivelsen,* poet Pia Tafdrup explored a new genre and traced the course of one-sided love. Julia Butschkow, an alumna of Denmark's Forfatterskolen, also explored the limits of the genre in her single-sentence novel *Lunatia,* a horrific tale of childhood incest. In *Musikken og kødet,* Vibeke Marx used a single event, a concert, as the setting for stories of love and musical artistry.

Danish novelists also explored different settings and time frames in their works. Kim Michael Alberg delved into Thailand's drug trade and crime and punishment in his suspense story *Smilenes land.* Bjarne Reuter's *Løgnhalsen fra Umbrien* traced the steps of a 14th-century Florentine charmer, Giuseppe Emanuele Pagamino, and his search for an elixir. In *Hvalens øje,* Arthur Krasilnikoff described Faroese Astur's coming-of-age in the midst of dangers and dilemmas. In *Når himlen falder ned,* historian Birgitte Jørkov created a female protagonist, Elne, who thrives as a merchant in the masculine milieu of 15th-century Elsinore.

Birgitte Berntsen's novel about Hans Christian Andersen (*Fremmed af verden*), Jette Kaarsbøl's depiction of literary critic Georg Brandes and his friends (*Den lukkede bog*), and Bodil Wamberg's account of Louise Rasmussen's rise from the working class to the elite (*Grevinden—et portræt af Grevinde Danner*) showed the abiding appeal of biographical and historical novels. In *Atlas over huller i verden,* Ursula Andkjær Olsen offered a potpourri of verses and enigmatic poems. F.P. Jac's *En græssende glæde til dit ydre* was a heartfelt tribute to the seasons. In *Timebog,* Suzanne Brøgger and artist Barbara Wilson created an 18-page treasure trove of lyrical and visual art.

During September and October, the city of Århus hosted the International Book Festival 2004. Three authors—

Dorrit Willumsen, Kirsten Thorup, and Guldager—shared nomination for festival sponsor BG Bank's Annual Literature Prize; Thorup was selected as the winner. Book Forum's Debutant Prize (2003) went to Grønlykke for *Fisketyven.* Jette Kaarsbøl won both the Danish Library Association Readers' Prize and the Golden Laurels Booksellers' Award. Celebrated poet-novelist Per Højholt died in October.

(LANAE HJORTSVANG ISAACSON)

Norwegian. Existential questioning characterized Norwegian literature in 2004. Hanne Ørstavik was awarded the Brage Prize for *Presten,* which followed a chaplain pondering how to comprehend the truth and communicate it to others. Fulfilling the expectations raised by his debut novel, Karl Ove Knausgård's epic *En tid for alt*—a reflection on good and evil among angels and humanity in biblical and modern times—was nominated for the 2005 Nordic Council Literature Prize. Ingvar Ambjørnsen, who received the 2004 Anders Jahre Prize for cultural contribution, won acclaim for *Innocentia Park,* a novel about the midlife crisis of a wealthy proprietor who, finding no meaning in life, retreats to a neighbourhood park. The protagonists of Jonny Halberg's *Gå til fjellet,* nominated for the Brage Prize, and *Doppler,* by the popular Erlend Loe, similarly retreat to nature.

The psychological mystery novels *Turneren,* by the established Knut Faldbakken, and *Det er natt,* Ole Asbjørn Ness's debut, addressed repressed yearnings and resentments. Nikolaj Frobenius's *Teori og praksis* and Espen Haavardsholm's *Gutten på passbildet,* which both incorporated autobiography into narratives about traumatic adolescence, were well received.

The time-honoured poet Stein Mehren was nominated for the 2005 Nordic Council Literature Prize for *Imperiet lukker seg,* which was acclaimed for the author's strong sense of aesthetics and philosophical concerns. Dramatist Arne Lygre was awarded the Brage Short Story Prize for *Tid inne,* about individuals' struggles to bond. *Oscar Wildes heis,* a collection of stories portraying adolescent vulnerability, was related in the distinctive voice of novelist Lars Saabye Christensen.

Acclaimed youth literature author Harald Rosenløw Eeg was awarded the Brage Prize for Youth Literature for *Yatzy,* a novel portraying a foster child's struggles. Princess Märtha Louise's *Hvorfor de kongelige ikke har krone på hodet,* illustrated by Svein Nyhus, was a fairy tale about a royal Norwegian family of immigrants. Tor Bomann-Larsen's portrayal of the royal family in *Folket: Haakon & Maud II,* which questioned the paternity of deceased King Olav, was awarded the Brage Prize for Nonfiction. Ingar Sletten Kolloen's *Hamsun: erobreren* completed his two-volume work on Nobel Prize-winning novelist Knut Hamsun's life. Jørgen Haugan's biography of Hamsun, *Solgudens fall: Knut Hamsun—en litterær biografi,* and Atle Næss's biography of painter Edvard Munch, *Munch: en biografi,* were also highly praised. (ANNE G. SABO)

Swedish. Experiments in prose and poetry form and travels in space and time were the highlights of Swedish literature in 2004. Attempts to open readers' minds to crossover sensations of technique and nature, history and the future, were frequent.

Lotta Lotass ventured into the space age in *Tredje flykthastigheten,* where her sharp and clear fragmentary style and sharp contrasts of rural poverty and high technology were employed to paint the fate of Soviet cosmonaut Yury Gagarin. Mikael Niemi returned to the bookshops after his 2000 best seller *Populärmusik från Vittula* (*Popular Music from Vittula,* 2003) with *Svålhålet,* a science-fiction-inspired short-story collection. Lars Jacobson used the same inspiration and genre in his horror-provoking *Berättelser om djur och andra.* In his poetry collection *Apolloprojektet,* Malte Persson made fragments of the optimism of the space project mix with everyday life in the form of a lyrical collage. In *Någon gång regn i Ngorongoro,* Tuija Nieminen Kristofersson juxtaposed the human life span and the vastness of geologic eons in a dizzy, lyrical time odyssey. Debut author Susanne Holmgren used contrasts between the perspectives of the human visitor and the grand Arctic wildlife in her prose poem *Arktica.*

Several authors used history to explore the fates of well-known people. Kjell Espmark highlighted a dramatic moment in Bela Bartok's flight from Nazism in *Béla Bartók mot Tredje Riket.* Per Odensten wrote from the viewpoint of Emily Dickinson in *Vänterskans flykt.* Per Olov Enquist's *Boken om Blanche och Marie* speculated about a friendship between two-time Nobel Prize winner Marie Sklodowska Curie and Blanche Wittman, the so-called queen of the hysterics and neuropathologist Jean-Martin Charcot's star patient at Paris's Salpêtière asylum. Christina Bergil retold Sigmund Freud's famous case of the Wolf Man in *Sju vita vargar i ett träd,* while Sara Stridsberg's first novel, *Happy Sally,* drew a parallel between Sally Bauer, the late Swedish swimmer of the English Channel, and a modern challenger. Journalist Bengt Ohlsson's first novel, *Gregorius,* the winner of the 2004 August Prize for fiction, took up a secondary character in Hjalmar Söderberg's 1905 classic *Doktor Glas,* changed the viewpoint, and gave a full-size portrait of the Reverend Gregorius.

Top-quality poetical works in 2004 included Tomas Tranströmer's new collection, *Den stora gåtan,* which was short-listed for the August Prize for poetry. (IMMI LUNDIN)

FRENCH

France. Despite the record number of first-time authors published in 2004 in France (of the fall season's nearly 700 titles, 121 were first novels), most attention was focused on established writers. Among these was J.-M.-G. Le Clézio, whose *L'Africain* told of the author's first meeting with his father at the age of eight in 1948 Nigeria. Interspersed with his father's photos of Africa, Le Clézio's text probed the role that paternal absence had played in the author's numerous novels. A similar revelation arose in prizewinning author Jean Rouaud's *L'Invention de l'auteur,* an inquiry into what in Rouaud's life had inspired him to become a writer. Among the many factors, Rouaud singled out the absence of his father, who had died suddenly one Christmas when the author was 11 years old. Rouaud explains his autobiographical novels as attempts to regain the father he desperately misses.

The most troubling account of a father-son relationship, however, was that described in well-known journalist Franz-Olivier Giesbert's autobiographical *L'Américain.* Giesbert's father, an American suffering from survivor's guilt after his participation in the bloody Normandy invasion of 1945, had taken his self-loathing out on his wife and children throughout the author's childhood and adolescence. Strangely, however gruesome the scenes of their violent, abusive relationship become, Giesbert never condemns the father he once hated, as the passage of time has given way to understanding and regret.

Three best-selling novels fictionalized the sufferings of real historical women. In *Les Jours fragiles,* Philippe Besson novelized the life of Isabelle, sister of the 19th-century poet Arthur Rimbaud, her intense shame at her brother's scandalous life of poetry, homosexuality, and debauchery, and her attempt to bring him back on his deathbed to a relationship with God. Michèle Desbordes told in *La Robe bleue* the well-known story of Camille Claudel, the 19th–20th-century sculptor driven to insanity by her tumultuous love affair with the sculptor Auguste Rodin. Though many French works have been devoted to Claudel, Desbordes broke new ground by portraying Claudel's inner monologue during her long institutionalization, with all her pain, fantasies, and longings. In a similar vein, Claude Pujade-Renaud's *Chers disparus* novelized the feelings of five historical women—not famous for themselves but rather married to famous writers—who had devoted their lives to their husbands and their husbands' art only to find themselves purposeless once widowed.

The theme of emotional wounds also ran through Patrick Lapeyre's *L'Homme-sœur,* the story of Cooper, a man unable to live or love because of his perverse, debilitating, and reciprocated passion for his sister Louise. In this novel, in which Cooper waits for his sister to return after having long avoided her brother, the reader is put in the uncomfortable position of hoping against better judgment that Louise will return to her brother's side, if only to end his suffering. Similarly, Laurent Mauvignier's *Seuls* recounted the story of Tony, a man in love with a female friend but unable to admit his feelings. When this woman enters a relationship with another man, Tony quickly slides into a frenetic jealousy that destroys his life as his family and friends stand helplessly by.

Three of the best-received of the year's novels were sequels. First, Ahmadou Kourouma's posthumously published, unfinished *Quand on refuse on dit non* resumed the story of Birahima, who in Kourouma's 2000 work *Allah n'est pas obligé* had been a child soldier in the vicious wars in Liberia and Sierra Leone and who, now older and a little wiser, is involved in the bloodbaths of Pres. Laurent Gbagbo's Côte d'Ivoire. Daniel Picouly published *La Treizième Mort du chevalier,* a sequel to his 1999 romp through Revolutionary France, *L'Enfant léopard,* in which an attempt to save Marie Antoinette's life had involved a black-and-white-spotted child, the son of a French noblewoman and an African. In his sequel Picouly told the tale of a black nobleman, Saint-Georges, who may possibly have been the father of the "leopard child," whose mother now may have been Marie Antoinette herself. Finally, Philippe Delerm's *Enregistrements pirates* was a follow-up to his internationally acclaimed 1997 work *La Première Gorgée de bière et autres plaisirs minuscules,* a description of the small joys of everyday existence to which few people pay attention. In his new work Delerm turned his gaze outward, capturing and slowing down small scenes from life—a woman walking her dog, people on the subway—extracting the moments' juice and distilling their uniqueness.

Sequels, such as Daniel Picouly's historical novel La Treizième Mort du chevalier, *were popular in France in 2004.*

Jean-Paul Dubois won the Prix Femina for his novel *Une vie française,* a saga that, through one man's family, tells the story of the French baby-boom generation, from its 1960s idealism to its 1990s embrace of capitalism. Marie Nimier won the Prix Médicis for *La Reine du silence,* an autobiofiction recounting the author's relationship with her absent father, a famous right-wing writer who died when she was five years old. The Prix Renaudot went to *Suite française,* a work about occupied France's miseries written 63 years earlier by Irène Némirovsky, when she was in hiding before she was sent to her death in Auschwitz, and published only now. The Prix Goncourt went to Laurent Gaudé's *Le Soleil des Scorta,* a family saga taking place between 1870 and 1980 in a poor village in southern Italy. The Scorta family, founded in a rape, lives under the village's disapproval but passes down from generation to generation a lust for life under the Italian sun.

(VINCENT AURORA)

Canada. The year 2004 in French Canadian literature was a varied one. Politics impinged on the book world, as usual, with the popularity of retired Lieut. Gen. Roméo Dallaire's 2003 memoir about his role in the events in Rwanda during the genocide. His book, entitled *J'ai serré la main du diable* (*Shake Hands with the Devil: The Failure of Humanity in Rwanda,* 2003), sparked debate about Canada's role as a peacekeeping nation. Dallaire won the Governor General's Award for English-language nonfiction for his memoir. Equally popular was Janette Bertrand's *Ma vie en trois actes,* an autobiography. The doyenne of women's liberation in French Canada, Bertrand served as something of a barometer when it came to popular perceptions of women's issues.

A new publisher began making waves in 2004: Mémoire d'Encrier, piloted by Rodney Saint-Éloi. This publisher issued books mostly about Haiti, such as *Nul n'est une île,* a collection of stories designed to raise money for that island nation, which had so often suffered from natural and man-made disasters. Two years after the death of Émile Ollivier, another pillar of the Haitian literary community in French Canada, his novel *La Brûlerie* was published.

Nelly Arcan continued to enjoy the fruits of scandal with her confessional novel *Folle,* which followed on the heels of her earlier phenomenon, *Putain* (2001). Both books played on the narrow difference between real life and fiction and kept fascinated readers wondering if the scandalous events Ms. Arcan related could actually be true.

On a more literary note, several novels stood out. A new young voice arrived with Nadine Bismuth, whose *Scrapbook* was set in a university environment. Readers in their 20s and 30s, a group often neglected in publishing, found their lives reflected in this novel. Jean Barbe weighed in with *Comment devenir un monstre,* a novel set in an anonymous country during a time of war. Barbe had already distinguished himself as a journalist and television personality before turning to novel writing.

Two stalwarts of the French Canadian novel returned. Readers could renew their love affair with Yves Beauchemin, with his book *Charles le Téméraire,* and with Michel Tremblay, with his work of fiction *Le Cahier rouge.*

(DAVID HOMEL)

ITALIAN

One of the main events in the 2004 Italian literary scene was the publication of Umberto Eco's novel *La misteriosa fiamma della regina Loana,* which appeared in bookstores, perhaps not coincidentally, on Bloomsday (June 16, which in 2004 was the 100th anniversary of the day in the life of Leopold Bloom described in James Joyce's *Ulysses*). Yambo, the protagonist, tries to recover his lost memory through the exploration of his childhood home. Old stamps, toys, vinyl records, and, in particular, comic strips are the scattered pieces with which he tries to reconstruct his life. Eco used these documents (some of which are reproduced in the novel) to give voice to the story of an entire generation caught between Fascist propaganda and World War II. The result was an encyclopaedic novel that combined different styles and registers and explored the links between visual expression and the written word.

Ugo Riccarelli received the Strega Prize for *Il dolore perfetto,* a novel that revisited a century and a half of Italian history through the stories of two families who embody, respectively, idealism and practicality. These two seemingly irreconcilable tendencies are brought together by the marriage of two of their offspring, Cafiero and Annina. The novel is framed by Annina's last moments as she admires the "wondrous spectacle" of her life as it separates from her. The Campiello Prize was awarded to Paola Mastrocola, who in *Una barca nel bosco* described the struggle of a sensitive and genial boy, with a passion for Latin and poetry, in the depressing environment of a northern Italian high school.

Carmine Abate continued his exploration of the consequences and meanings of emigration in *La festa del ritorno.* The life of the young protagonist is punctuated by the return visits of his father from France, to which the family's financial situation and the Calabria region's scarcity of employment forced him to move. Presented as an effort to promote dialogue and reconciliation between "those who stay and those who go," the book offered an intriguing linguistic mélange resulting from the insertion of italicized foreign words and of entire sentences in Arbëreshë (the language spoken by the Albanian Italian community to which both Abate and his protagonists belong).

Detective stories dominated the scene once again. Following the example of Andrea Camilleri with his creation of Inspector Montalbano, several authors recently had organized their novels around a central character who each time is called to solve a different mystery. This was the case with Marco Vichi, author of *Il nuovo venuto: un'indagine del commissario Bordelli,* and Giuseppe Pederiali, who in *Camilla e i vizi apparenti* narrated another investigation impeccably conducted by female inspector Camilla Cagliostri. Camilleri himself offered another glimpse of the personality of his hero in *La prima indagine di Montalbano,* a portrait of Montalbano as a young detective, able to solve his first mystery thanks to his passion for Jorge Luis Borges. More ambitious—and rich with references to the recent past—was Giuseppe Genna's *Grande madre rossa,* which opens with the explosion of the Palazzo di Giustizia in Milan. The novel follows Inspector Guido Lopez, the protagonist of three of Genna's earlier novels, as he works to rescue the Palazzo's mysterious and precious archives.

At age 90 Mario Luzi confirmed his pivotal role in Italian poetry with the publication of a new collection, *Dottrina dell'estremo principiante,* the title of which epitomized the author's notion of poetry as endless searching, continuous renewal, and bearer of civic values. In consideration of Luzi's achievements, Italian Pres. Carlo Azeglio Ciampi appointed him a member of the Senate for life.

Academic life was dominated by the 700th anniversary of Petrarch's (Francesco Petrarca's) birth, which inspired conferences in many Italian and foreign cities, from Barcelona, Spain, to Kolkata (Calcutta). Marco Santagata's edition of the *Canzoniere* was republished for this occasion. The publishing house Adelphi continued in its effort to promote the works of Anna Maria Ortese, one of the greatest Italian writers of the 20th century. In *La lente scura,* a reprinted collection of her articles on various Italian and foreign cities (including Moscow and Paris), the author's view is one filtered through a particular attitude, the melancholic "dark lens" to which the title alludes, that provides unconventional insights into the cities she visited.

Several important intellectual figures died during the year, including literary critic Cesare Garboli (1928–2004), who was famous for his translations of Shakespeare and Molière, and Giovanni Raboni (1932–2004), an accomplished poet and translator of Marcel Proust's *À la recherche du temps perdu.* A renowned international correspondent and expert on Asia, Tiziano Terzani (1938–2004) meditated on the cancer that caused his death in *Un altro giro di giostra: viaggio nel bene e nel male del nostro tempo.* Begun as a search for the best therapy, the book became an intense meditation on "the disease that affects us all: mortality."

(LAURA BENEDETTI)

SPANISH

Spain. The fourth year of the 21st century brought a greater visibility of women to the literary field in Spain. Olga Merino described the immigration of Andalusian workers to Barcelona after the Spanish Civil War in her novel *Espuelas de papel.* In *Viajes con mi padre* (2003), Luisa Castro told a universal story, beautiful and moving, funny, magical and real, about a woman living between her mother's pragmatic world and her father's kind and amusing world. Her mother attempts to escape secular poverty, and her father is a sailor with little ambition.

Lucía Etxebarría was awarded the Planeta Prize for her novel *Un milagro en equilibrio,* written in the form of a letter from a young mother addressing her newborn daughter so that the child can get to know her better when she grows up. The Alfaguara Prize went to the Colombian Laura Restrepo's *Delirio,* a novel about madness and love.

Arturo Pérez-Reverte's latest novel, *Cabo Trafalgar,* described the defeat of the Spanish-French navy in 1805. The book portrayed the politicians as being responsible for the disaster, sending thousands of men to a sure death. The novel had abundant onomatopoeia and deliberate anachronisms. José María Merino published *Cuentos de los días raros,* a collection of 15 short stories about those weird days that evince the fascination or the uneasiness of the unexpected and show what can lie behind everyday images. Through the remembrance of smells and colours, José Manuel Caballero Bonald invited readers to go through the childhood and

© Jerry Bauer

Spanish novelist Javier Marías published **Baile y sueño,** *the second part of his* **Tu rostro mañana** *trilogy, in 2004.*

apprenticeship of a poet in *Tiempo de guerras perdidas. Baile y sueño,* the second book of the trilogy *Tu rostro mañana* by Javier Marías, continues the story of Jaime or Jacobo or Jacques Deza that was started in *Fiebre y lanza.* Deza's "gift" is to know what people will do in the future.

Lorenzo Silva was awarded the Primavera Prize for his novel *Carta blanca,* a book that told the story of a man whose life elapses parallel to the convoluted events in Spain during the 1920s and '30s. The National Prize for Narrative went to Juan Manuel de Prada for his novel *La vida invisible,* which had won the Primavera Prize in 2003. The book described the life of a writer who travels to Chicago in the wake of the terrorist attacks of Sept. 11, 2001. His life changes drastically when he learns about Fanny, a pin-up girl from the 1950s who had suddenly disappeared, and after he meets Elena, a woman who has gone mad following a heartbreak.

Chantal Maillard, a Belgian poet who lived in Málaga, received the National Prize for Poetry for her book *Matar a Platón.* The Cervantes Prize, considered the top Spanish-language literary prize, was awarded to Rafael Sánchez Ferlosio for an outstanding career as a novelist and essayist who always showed a critical attitude toward social issues.

(VERÓNICA ESTEBAN)

Latin America. The year 2004 saw the arrival of the ninth volume of *Historia crítica de la literatura argentina,* an important critical work directed by Noé Jitrik. The history was to consist of a total of 12 volumes. Volume 9, titled *El oficio se afirma,* was edited by Sylvia Saítta and collected essays dedicated to the 1930s and to prominent authors, including Jorge Luis Borges, Adolfo Bioy Casares, Julio Cortázar, Leopoldo Marechal, and Ernesto Sábato. Five other volumes had appeared earlier. Also in Argentina, Gloria da Cunha edited *La narrativa histórica de escritoras latinoamericanas,* a book of essays about 19th-century women authors.

Chilean writer Antonio Skármeta published a lyrical book of memories titled *Neruda por Skármeta,* about his friend and countryman Pablo Neruda, to celebrate the centennial of the poet's birth. Argentine David Viñas delivered a book of essays titled *Crisis de la ciudad señorial,* in which he developed a sociological study of Gregorio de Laferrère's dramatic work in relation to the zenith and the decadence of Buenos Aires's oligarchy.

The Alfaguara Prize was awarded unanimously to Colombian Laura Restrepo for her novel *Delirio,* which was enthusiastically praised by jury member José Saramago. It was a familiar saga, seen through the eyes of three generations of wealthy landowners. Restrepo analyzed the past to try to explain the present—that is, the insanity of Agustina, the protagonist, who is a victim of drug trafficking and of the violence that penetrates her own family. The novel transformed this into a metaphor of Colombia's national problems. The Planeta Prize went to Argentine Martin Caparrós for his novel *Valfierno.* Valfierno was the name of the man who masterminded the theft of the *Mona Lisa* in 1911 from the Louvre and was able to hang on to it for two years. Casa de las Américas awarded its Extraordinary Prize for essays on women's studies to Colombian Carmiña Navia Velasco for her work *Guerras y paz en Colombia: las mujeres escriben.*

An Argentine who resided in France, Juan José Saer, shared the Unión Latina de Literaturas Romances Prize with Romanian Virgil Tanase.

Prolific Colombian writer Fernando Vallejo, winner of the 2003 Rómulo Gallegos Prize, published *Mi hermano el alcalde,* in which he retold the vicissitudes of his brother, the mayor of Támesis, a lost town in the mountains of Colombia. Political and personal memoirs were, as always, intertwined in Vallejo's writing; he also combined humour with horror and tenderness with satire. Ending a 10-year silence, Gabriel García Márquez returned in 2004 with the short novel *Memoria de mis putas tristes,* the story of an old man who wants to have his last sexual experiences with an adolescent, who falls incurably in love with him.

Anagrama published Chilean author Roberto Bolaño's vast posthumous novel that bore the enigmatic title *2666.* In the novel four European professors dedicate their lives to finding facts about an almost unknown German author. Their search takes them to the fictional Mexican city of Santa Teresa (a faithful representation of Ciudad Juárez) and thereby gives the narrator the opportunity to treat violence and Latin American corruption. Another work by Bolaño, *Entre paréntesis,* was a compilation of articles and lectures published between 1998 and 2003. The

Laura Restrepo's Alfaguara Prize-winning novel **Delirio** *was seen as a metaphor for her native Colombia's national problems.*

© Jerry Bauer

title, "Between Brackets," referred to the spare time the author had between writing his novels.

Uruguayan Eduardo Galeano published a book of short stories with the title *Bocas del tiempo,* written, he said, to rescue the greatness of small things. Carlos María Domínguez, an Argentine living in Uruguay, had tremendous success with *La casa de papel,* a short novel of intrigue that was, at the same time, a tribute to bibliophiles and to storytellers such as Joseph Conrad, Borges, Juan Carlos Onetti, and García Márquez. Domínguez displayed his obsession with the eastern shore of the Río de la Plata as well as with books—those other rivers without borders.

Andrés Neuman, an Argentine living in Spain, published his third novel, *Una vez Argentina,* which was a finalist for the Herralde Prize. The novel was an effort to retrieve the time and space lost by Neuman's family who emigrated to Argentina and by his own peregrinations. Neuman used a poetic language that emphasized the contrast between the Castilian of Spain and the Río de la Plata dialect. *Jardines de Kensington* by Rodrigo Fresán, another Argentine who resided in Spain, was a delirious novel about childhood and the human condition.

Two authors, Chilean Luis Sepúlveda and Uruguayan Mario Delgado Aparaín, worked together on a singular book with the parodic title *Los peores cuentos de los hermanos Grim.* These Grim(m) brothers are Abel and Caín, two gaucho minstrels who travel through Patagonia and Uruguay playing the guitar, singing, drinking, and running afoul of the police. The novel took the form of an epistolary between two odd characters who research the life of the *payadores* (gaucho minstrels), coming to conflicting conclusions that deconstruct the myths of *rioplatense* literature. Their correspondence is introduced by a fictional professor named José Sarajevo, who also writes the conclusion.

(LEDA SCHIAVO)

PORTUGUESE

Portugal. Portuguese literature suffered a grievous loss in 2004 with the death in Lisbon on July 2 of Sophia de Mello Breyner Andresen, one of the greatest poets in the language. She was a prolific author and left a large body of work in print. By combining sharp observation with imagery inspired by the philosophy and culture of ancient Greece, she created a world of her own that lived on through the magic of words.

It was often said that Portugal is a country of poets. That could well be true, considering the growing success of Gastão Cruz. Cruz was awarded the 2004 Great Prize for Poetry by the Association of Portuguese Writers for his 2002 collection *Rua de Portugal,* and in 2004 he added another work, *Repercussão.* The qualities of verbal discipline that distinguished de Mello Breyner's work were found in Cruz's as well. His poems recalled the dead and the living in memories of place and time.

Among good works of fiction, the biggest success was the novel *Equador* by Miguel Sousa Tavares, a journalist and media star. This was his first novel, and it was an eminently readable piece of work. It dealt with the problems of a governor sent to an equatorial island country (part of the Portuguese empire) to persuade the planters to abolish slavery. Their unwillingness to comply generates a conflict between the governor and the settlers and leads to a personal drama and a tragic ending. José Saramago, the 1998 Nobel Prize winner, produced another fascinating novel and fine political allegory, *Ensaio sobre a lucidez,* which showed the attitudes of the electorate in a democratic society. The voters, fed up with politicians and their promises, have given them a blank vote en masse. Shaken to its foundations, the government tries to save the system by resorting to violence and thus snuffs out the spirit of free society. The story was impressively terrifying and contained dire warnings for the present.

The 2004 Great Prize for Fiction by the Association of Portuguese Writers was won by Mafalda Ivo Cruz for her novel *Vermelho.* It was a lively narrative, full of youthful zest for life. The Camões Prize, the highest to be awarded in the Portuguese language for an author with a full body of published work, went to Agustina Bessa Luís, a prolific novelist and a subtle chronicler of family life. (L.S. REBELO)

Brazil. Chico Buarque's novel *Budapeste* (2003) emerged as a best seller in Brazil in 2004. The tale traced the romantic affairs of José Costa, a ghostwriter, who found himself "lost in love" in Hungary while en route to Istanbul. *Fragmentos da grande guerra,* Leandro Fortes's first novel, mixed fact and fiction in a narration of the bloody Paraguayan War (1864/65–70) presented through an army general's address to the Brazilian emperor's Senate in 1869. Fortes's work seemed inspired by both Euclides da Cunha's epic *Os sertões,* an early 20th-century narration of another Brazilian rebellion, and the contemporary international scene of tragic conflict and genocide.

The complete collection of the poems of Francisco Alvim, *Poemas (1968–2000),* brought together all of his previously published works. Alvim might be considered a latter-day Brazilian Modernist poet, in the tradition of Oswald de Andrade or Carlos Drummond de Andrade, owing to his focus on the colloquial language of Brazil in his poems.

Poet and literary critic Antônio Carlos Secchin was admitted to the Brazilian Academy of Letters, which awarded its 2003 Essay Prize to Élio Gaspari for the first three volumes of his multivolume study of the Brazilian military dictatorship (1964–85). *A ditadura encurralada* (2004), the fourth volume, dealt with the years 1974–77. The Pan American Health Organization awarded its 2003 Champion of Health in the Americas prize to Maurício de Sousa, known as the Brazilian Walt Disney. Sousa's comic-book character Mônica, a seven-year-old girl, and her "gang" were the featured characters in the organization's Vaccination Week in the Americas campaign.

Rachel de Queiroz, the first lady of Brazilian letters and the first woman to be elected to the Brazilian Academy of Letters, died in late 2003. *O quinze* (1930), her first novel, established the modern tradition of the Northeastern novel of the drought as well as defined the role of the strong woman character in modern Brazilian fiction. During her lifetime she published many other novels and folklore of her native Ceará. Dramatist Pedro Bloch, whose *Mãos de Eurídice* and *Dona Xepa* became two of the most widely performed Brazilian theatre pieces, died in February 2004.

(IRWIN STERN)

RUSSIAN

Although not an epochal year, 2004 in Russian literature saw several new trends, the most important of which was a return to plot-based narrative fiction. After several years dominated by nonfiction or fiction in which the narrative element was either parodied or concealed, virtually all of the year's most noted books were novels in the traditional sense. The most important of these was probably Lyudmila Petrushevskaya's *Nomer odin, ili v sadakh inykh vozmozhnostey* ("Number One, or in the Gardens of Other Possibilities"), which was nominated for both the Russian Booker and Andrey Bely prizes. Petrushevskaya, one of Russia's most highly regarded playwrights and prose writers of the second half of the 20th century, first came to public attention in the 1970s and '80s with her dark, dense naturalism that at times bordered on the surreal; she then turned to folklore and the fantastic for her plots. In her new novel the two lines converge, although with the addition of elements from the thriller genre and from the realm of computer games. *Nomer odin* described the mysterious, archaic encounter of a Russian ethnographer with a remote Siberian tribe, including his own death and rebirth in another body. Petrushevskaya depicted the contemporary world as one in which primitive instincts and Stone Age passions have been reawakened, in which cultural strata that have taken centuries of civilization to construct are being destroyed.

With his most recent two novels, Vladimir Sorokin, whose stylistic games and scandalous storytelling gained him a wide audience in the 1990s, struck out in a new direction. His latest, *Put Bro* ("Bro's Path"), was filled with gnostic themes and read like a saga of the "chosen few" who, possessing cosmic knowledge, must resist the rest of humanity.

Among other prose works, special mention was due Aleksandr Kabakov's new novel, *Vsyo popravimo* ("All Fixed"), which described an intellectual's attempts to adapt to changing conditions in the period stretching from the 1950s to the '90s; Nikolay Kononov's *Nezhny teatr* ("Tender Theatre"), which explored themes already established in his earlier works: agonizing love for the father, an estranged relationship to the world of things, and sexual initiation and its consequences; Vasily Aksyonov's new historical novel *Volteryantsy i Volteryanki* ("Voltaireans Male and Female"), which captured the 2004 Booker–Open Russian literary prize and displayed greater artistry than others of his more recent novels (one of which, the three-volume *Moskovskaya saga* ["Moscow Saga"], was made into a television miniseries in 2004); the late Georgy Vladimov's major autobiographical work *Dolog put' do Tippereri* ("A Long Way to Tipperary"), the first part of which was published in the journal *Znameni*; Yevgeny Grishkovets's *Rubashka* ("The Shirt"), a brief, lively novel about one day in the life of a provincial architect on a visit to Moscow; and Igor Gelbakh's *Uteryanny Blyum* "Bloom Lost"), a finely crafted, elegant work that takes place in an imagined Russia at the beginning of the 20th century.

Perhaps the most important publication of the year in poetry was Oleg Yuryev's *Izbrannye stikhi i khori* ("Selected Poems and Choruses"). Yuryev, a major poet who first became prominent in the 1980s, was the founder and leader of the poetic group the Cloakroom ("Kamera Khraneniya"), whose members included Olga Martynova, Sergey Volf, Igor Bulatovsky, and others. Two years earlier, with the establishment of a Web site <www.newkamera.de>, the group had renewed its public activity, publishing the work both of its members and of other contemporary poets. The Cloakroom also published its first *Vremennik* ("Chronicle"), an anthology of works selected from the Web site, during the year.

There were also significant new books of poetry during the year from Mikhail Gendelev, Yelizaveta Mnatsakanova, Yelena Shvarts, Lev Losev, Yelena Fanaylova, Mariya Stepanova, Nikolay Baytov, and Yevgeny Myakyshev.

As always, literary prizes served to reflect, at least in part, Russia's literary life. A happy, although unexpected, event was the awarding of Triumph—the Russian prize for excellence in arts and literature—rarely given to poets, to Shvarts, which confirmed her unique place in contemporary Russian poetry. The Andrey Bely Prizes went to Moscow poet-critic Mikhail Aizenberg, prose writer Margarita Meklina, and eminent philologist, linguist, and giant of Russian academic life Vladimir N. Toporov. Viktor Pelevin was awarded the National Best-Seller Prize for his rather mediocre novel *DPP.* Boris Strugatsky, the venerable science fiction writer, had to be content with being one of the three finalists for the Apollon Grigoryev Prize, which ultimately went to Yury Arabov. Besides the already-mentioned works by Petrushevskaya, Aksyonov, and Grishkovets, the short list for the Russian Booker Prize included Oleg Zayonchkovsky's *Sergeyev i gorodok* ("Sergeyev and the Town"), Anatoly Kurchatkin's *Solntse siyalo* ("The Sun Shone"), Marta Petrova's *Valtorna Shilklopera* ("Shilkloper's Horn"), and Aleksey Slapovsky's *Kachestvo zhizni* ("Quality of Life").

Finally, the year saw the appearance in Moscow of a new upscale literary magazine, *Novy ochevidets* ("The New Observer"), and the transfer of many of the operations of the Moscow poetry publisher OGI to St. Petersburg. This included the opening of a café-club, Platforma, and an ambitious publishing program that promised a lively encounter between the traditionally counterposed poetic cultures of Moscow and St. Petersburg. (VALERY SHUBINSKY)

JEWISH

Hebrew. A.B. Yehoshua, the prolific, ever-changing author, published in 2004 a new novel, *Sheliḥuto shel ha-memume al ma'shabe enosh* ("The Mission of the Human Resource Man"), but the moralist tale failed to repeat his previous literary achievements. New books by other veteran writers did not reflect any major changes in their style. Such were Aharon Appelfeld's *Periḥa pir'it* ("Wild Blossoming"), Yoram Kaniuk's *Haberlina'ee ha'aharon* ("Der letzte Berliner"), and Dan Tsalḳah's *Sefer ha-alef-bet* ("Tsalka's ABC"), which won the 2004 Sapir Prize. The nature of the Israeli home, real and metaphoric, was illuminated in the novels of Eshkol Nevo (*Arba'ah batim ve-ga'agua;* "Osmosis") and Meron Ḥ. Izaḳson (*ha-Dirah bi-Shelomoh ha-melekh;* "The Flat on King Solomon Street"). Among the many writers who published their first novels or first collection of stories, a handful stood out: Alon Hilu with *Mot ha-nazir* ("Death of a Monk"), Efrat Danon and

Veteran Israeli author A.B. Yehoshua brought out a new novel in 2004, Sheliḥuto shel ha-memume al ma'shabe enosh *("The Mission of the Human Resource Man").*

her *Dag ba-beten* ("Bellyfish"), Tamar Gelbetz's *At bi-tekufah tovah* ("You're Doing Fine"), and Shlomo Shilton's *Ratsim kemo meshuga 'im* ("Running Like Mad").

In poetry 2004 was the year of the veterans. Natan Zach penned a witty, moving collection, *ha-Zamir kevar lo gar po yoter* ("The Nightingale No Longer Lives Here"); Ori Bernstein collected his poems in *Shirim 1962–2002* ("Poems 1962–2002"); and Mosheh Ben-Sha'ul published a selection from his previous books as *Kol levadai mivḥar shirim, 1954–2003* ("Selected Poems 1954–2003"). Other collections by veteran poets were Aharon Almog's *Im tir'u sukka a'fa* ("When You See a Sukka Flying") and Aryeh Sivan's *Hozer halila* ("Recurrence"). The younger generation was represented by Admiel Kosman's *Arba 'im shire ahavah* (2003; "Forty Love Poems") and Orit Gidali's *'Eśrim ne'arot le-ḳane* ("Twenty Girls to Envy Me").

The novel of Sayed Kashua (*Va-yehi boḳer;* "Let It Be Morning") and the poems of Salman Matsalḥah (*Eḥad mi-kan;* "In Place"), both Arab Israelis writing in Hebrew, posed intriguing questions regarding the scope and nature of Hebrew literature.

Most scholarly works were dedicated to modern Hebrew poetry. Hannan Hever studied aesthetics and politics in Uri Zvi Greenberg's poetry (*Moledet hamavet yafa;* "Beautiful Motherland of Death"); Hillel Barzel examined prophetic expressionism in the poems of Greenberg, Isaak Lamdan, and Matityahu Shoham (*Shirat Erets-Yiśrael;* "A History of Hebrew Poetry, vol. VI"); and Itzhak Bakon contributed another study of Haim Nahman Bialik's poems (*Tsofeh hayiti be-enav shel olam;* "I Watch Through the Eye of the World").

(AVRAHAM BALABAN)

Yiddish. Among the most interesting books in Yiddish in 2004 was *Lomir hern gute psures: brokhes un kloles* ("Let's Hear Only Good News: Yiddish Blessings and Curses") by Hebrew University of Jerusalem lexicographer Yosef Guri. This was an illustrated dictionary of 200 blessings and 450 curses, the first attempt to assemble and describe this genre of folklore in which each original Yiddish expression was accompanied by its equivalent in English, Hebrew, and Russian.

Three authors penned noteworthy novels. New York City editor Boris Sandler published a grim historical novel, *Ven der golem hot farmakht di oygn* ("When the Golem Shut His Eyes"), based on archival sources and historical documentation. The author wove an arresting narrative set against a background of the turbulent events of the 1903 pogrom in Kishinev, Russia (now Chisinau, Moldova), that claimed several thousand victims. One of the leading post-World War II poets and dramatists, Mikhal Felzenboym, penned the compelling *Shabesdike shvebelekh* ("Sabbath Matches"), drawing his readers into a many-layered mystical world of wonders. Ikhil Shraybman's illustrated novel *Zibn yor un zibn khadoshim* ("Seven Years and Seven Months") was an affectionate reminiscence about Lithuanian cities and shtetls composed in an opulent Yiddish that was both artistic and populist, with an irony that called to mind the phrase "laughter through tears."

The posthumous bilingual Hebrew and Yiddish anthology *Ksavi Avrom Lebensart* ("The Writings of Avrom Lebensart") reflected the author's personal concerns about social injustice and the abyss between the haves and the have-nots. His story "The Ruminator" was an amusing description of an observer of the social scene. With an acute ear for colloquial turns of phrase, Lebensart described spouses' attitudes toward their deceased husbands in the drama "Widows." Tsvi-Hirsh Smoliakov accomplished a tour de force in exemplifying and rescuing Lithuanian-Yiddish vocabulary and idiomatic expressions in his tripartite collection of stories *A yunger tsiter* ("A Young Shiver"). Simkhe Simkhovitsh offered his readers a collection of probing essays focusing on his postwar writer, poet, and artist colleagues—especially Canadians—in *Nokh dem blut-mabul* ("After the Torrent of Blood"). A special issue of the journal *Yerusholaymer almanakh* was dedicated to one of the most respected contemporary Yiddish poets, the survivor of Stalinist persecution Josef Kerler (1918–2000).

(THOMAS E. BIRD)

TURKISH

Turkey's publishing world experienced an annus mirabilis in 2004; a book of essays, *İçimizde bir yer* ("A Place Inside Us"), by major figure Ahmet Altan, had three unprecedented printings—250,000, 300,000, and 450,000—totaling an unheard-of one million copies in a country where 200,000 copies were considered impressive even for a half-century stalwart such as Yashar Kemal or a runaway international sensation such as Orhan Pamuk. Many authors and publishers, long dismayed over huge sales of cheap pirated editions, rejoiced that a new era might be dawning, thanks to the low price of the Altan book, which enabled it to become an all-time best seller and to preempt piracy.

Pamuk's stature grew outside Turkey owing to *Snow,* the English-language version (translated from the Turkish by Maureen Freely) of his novel *Kar* (a best seller in 2003 that had generated a lukewarm critical reception in Turkey). *Snow* won kudos, including favourable reviews by Canadian novelist Margaret Atwood and critic Richard Eder in the *New York Times.* Young novelist Elif Shafak attracted wide attention in Turkey with her *Araf* ("Between Paradise and Hell") and abroad with its English original entitled *The Saint of Incipient Insanities,* a novel about Turks and other foreigners striving to come to terms with life in the U.S.

Fiction writers held sway—Oya Baydar with her *Erguvan kapısı* ("Judas-tree Gate"), a succès d'estime about love and ideology in Istanbul from Byzantine times to the present day; Ayşe Kulin, whose *Gece sesleri* ("Night Voices") topped the best-seller lists for months; Vedat Türkali with his *Kayıp romanlar* ("Lost Novels"), about the aftermath of political exile; the late Orhan Kemal with his *Cemile* (reissued 52 years after its initial publication); Şebnem İyigüzel with her *Çöplük* ("Dumping Ground"), a metaphor for the modern world; the versatile former cabinet minister Yılmaz Karakoyunlu with his *Yorgun mayıs kısrakları* ("Tired Mares of May"); and the unique stylist Latife Tekin with her *Unutma bahçesi* ("Garden of Oblivion").

Prominent poet Fazıl Hüsnü Dağlarca turned 90 and was feted. Criticism and poetry had an unusually dim year.

Notable collections of essays included *Yazmasam olmazdı* ("I Could Not Help but Write") by Özdemir İnce, *İnferno* by İlhan Berk, and *Zamansız yazılar* ("Timeless-Untimely—Pieces") by Füsun Akatlı, the last two reprints from 1994.

(TALAT SAIT HALMAN)

PERSIAN

What the output of the year 2004 may have lacked in memorable accomplishments, it more than made up for it by renewed efforts to publish the recent work of authors in all the Persian-speaking countries. *Bagh-i bisyar dirakht* ("Orchard of Countless Trees") was the first post-Soviet-era anthology of Persian poetry and featured works by 189 poets from Uzbekistan, Tajikistan, Afghanistan, and Iran. In Tajikistan a few literary works rolled off newly installed presses, both in Cyrillic and Perso-Arabic scripts, and at least one new self-instructional textbook was published to teach Persian-speaking Central Asians to read and write their language in the ancestral script.

In Iran old and established writers reentered the field of literary production. Veteran fiction writer Ismāʿīl Faṣīḥ published *ʿIshq va marg* ("Love and War"), notable for its autobiographical details. Poet Aḥmad-Riẓā Aḥmadī released *Hamah-yi ān sālhā* (1992; "All Those Years"), his most avant-garde collection of poetry in a few decades. Īraj Pizishkzād's *Khānavādah-ʾi Nīk'akhtar* (2001; "The Nikakhtar Family") was yet another hilarious satire on cross-border misunderstandings between Iranians at home and as expatriates. It was rivaled by *Majnūn-i Laylī* (2003), a new satiric work in the form of an epistolary novel, by Ibrāhīm Nabavī, a religiously inclined journalist.

Works by women writers continued to gain momentum both in Iran and among expatriate Iranians. Parīnūsh Ṣanīʿī's *Sahm-i man* (2002; "My Lot") and Shuhrah Vakīlī's *Shab-i arusi-yi man* ("My Wedding Night") won popular acclaim and ranked among the best-selling works of fiction. While the first was a vaguely philosophical work, the story in the second was impressive in its concrete handling of a perennial theme that continued to rattle modern Iranian society: patriarchy's obsession with female virginity.

A stylistically sophisticated work, Zūyā Pīrzād's new novel *ʿAdat mī'kunīm* ("We'll Grow Accustomed") showcased her usual attention to detail. The U.S.-based expatriate playwright and fiction writer ʿIzzat Gūshahgīr published in Sweden *An zan, an utaq-i kuchak, va ʿishq* ("The Woman, The Room, and Love"), which treated women's quest for unencumbered love.

(AHMAD KARIMI-HAKKAK)

ARABIC

The principal concern in Arabic literature in 2004 was the problematic relationship between writers and the state. Egyptian writers in particular were worried about the power granted to al-Azhar, the Cairo-based international Islamic cultural academy, which monitored creative writing in Muslim countries for any slight to Islam. Though the only legal restrictions pertained to unlicensed Islamic religious books, the true extent of al-Azhar's power was uncertain. At the top of al-Azhar's list of objectionable books was Nawāl Saʿdāwī's *Suqūṭ al-imām* (1987; *The Fall of the Imam,* 2002). The action came on the heels of a controversy after the writer Ṣun ʿAllāh Ibrāhīm had rejected the Egyptian Ministry of Culture's Arab novel award at presentation ceremonies on Oct. 22, 2003. As reasons for refusing the award, Ibrahim cited the failed foreign policy of the Arab regimes and his government's lack of credibility. Ahmed Bouzfour of Morocco made a similar statement in January 2004, when he turned down his country's book prize for 2002. His gesture was in reaction to the poor literacy rate in Morocco, as reflected in the small number of copies in print of his prizewinning book and the even smaller number distributed and sold.

Possibly in order to avoid confrontation with their respective governments, some Arab writers were shifting their attention to safe topics such as memories of childhood and youth—stories with or without symbolic significance. In his collection of short stories *Nīrān ṣadīqah* ("Friendly Fires"), ʿAlāʾ al-Aswānī decried the loose conduct of men and women he had met. Muḥammad Yūsuf Quʿayd retraced a trip to Upper Egypt in his novel *Qiṭār al-ṣaʿīd* ("Upper Egypt Train"), in which he portrayed the tribulations of a journalist confronting the tight-knit society of the region.

Much was being done through experimentation with the Arabic language itself, particularly by Jamāl al-Ghīṭānī, who crowned his semiautobiographical series *Dafātir al-tadwīn* (2003; "Notebooks") with a fourth volume, *Nawāfidh al-nawāfidh* ("Windows on Windows"). As he looked at the world through various windows that restricted his scope, he provided the reader with innovative images expressed in curt, quick phrases.

In this turbulent year, two groups of writers remained bound by their people's suffering and tribulations. The Iraqi writers living in exile reflected on the difficulties that resulted from the invasion of their country and on their state of loss far from their homeland. The literary magazine *Mashāref* had dedicated a 2003 issue to their reactions to the war and life in exile. Palestinian writers continued to be bound up with the political and humanitarian issues befalling their people. In interviews with Egyptian author Ahdaf Soueif, writers living in the West Bank and Israel explained their inability to detach themselves from the conflict and the daily aggravations of life under occupation. As writers, they were torn between delving into personal topics and addressing the concerns of their people and their cause, wondering whether there was "room to write outside the situation." Their inability to distance themselves from the events of the Palestinian tragedy as a whole was explained by Mourid Barghouti: "The moment of contact between the event and your soul, that's where literature is born." Their unique situation turned some Palestinian writers to the genre of the essay—or "fragments" as they called it—a form that satisfied their need for an immediate response to events.

A new generation of Dutch Maghribi writers was gradually carving a niche for itself, replicating to a certain extent the trajectory of the pioneer North African writers of the second half of the 20th century in France. Like their predecessors, these writers were infusing European literature with Arabic culture and achieving a harmonious blend of the two. Many were inspired by the magic of the well-known *Arabian Nights.* In 2004 the young Moroccan Dutch writer Hafid Bouazza received a Belgian prize for his book *Paravion* ("Paravion" [a proper name]). This largely autobiographical novel related the story of his family's immigration to The Netherlands.

The Moroccan-born Dutch novelist Hafid Bouazza was prominent among the Maghribi authors who were blending Arabic and European cultures in their work.

Though the bulk of Francophone literature continued to emanate from Maghribi writers living in the Maghrib or in Europe, some works written in French trickled in occasionally from the Mashriq (the countries between and including Egypt and Iraq). The Syrian writer Marām al-Miṣrī related the sorrows and joys of a housewife in her collection of poetry *Doux leurre* ("Sweet Delusion").

On a sad note, the Arab world lost poet Fadwá Ṭūqān, who died in December 2003. ʿAbd al-Raḥmān Munīf, a prolific writer and the author of the famous quintet *Mudun al-milḥ* (1984–89; *Cities of Salt,* 1987–93), passed away in January 2004. (*See* OBITUARIES.) Egyptian poet and literary critic ʿAbd al-ʿAzīz Sharaf died in the summer.

(AIDA A. BAMIA)

CHINESE

In Chinese literature 2004 would be remembered as a harvest year because of two exceptional novels, both published by Spring Breeze, a small publishing house in Shenyang, a northern provincial capital. The first, *Shou huo* ("Enjoyment"), was written by Yan Lianke, one of China's premier novelists. Yan's visibility as an author had grown steadily since the early 1990s, owing to his robust portrayal of the desperation of rural life and his sharp criticism of social reality.

In *Shou huo* Yan communicated his deep skepticism of what was promoted in China as modernization. The novel vividly portrayed a mountain hamlet called Shou Huo Zhuang ("Village of Enjoyment"), where most residents are disabled and live a life so isolated from the outside world that the village does not even appear on official maps. In the mid-1950s, however, Shou Huo Zhuang is overrun by the socialist revolutionary wave from outside and is placed under the jurisdiction of the county government. Meanwhile, the disabled join the *gongshe,* a kind of paragovernmental agricultural-production organization. After suffering greatly from the socialist revolution, in the 1990s the villagers eagerly embrace market-economy reforms and support a harebrained county government project: to buy the mummified corpse of Lenin and put it on display to attract tourists from far and wide. Predictably, this leads to more suffering for the villagers. In the final part of the novel, the disabled decide to bid farewell to the world of those who are not handicapped. They cut off their official relationships with the government and return to their separate, nonnormal, and poor—but safer—former life. The top county official, despairing over the failure of his pet project, moves to the village after having purposefully disabled himself by using his official car to crush his foot. Yan Lianke's fertile imagination and strong writing style had rarely been equaled in Chinese fiction published in the previous 20 years.

The other novel of note during the year was Ge Fei's *Ren mian tao hua* (a quotation from a Tang dynasty poem, the original meaning of which is "girl's face and peach blossom"). Ge was one of the leading experimental writers in the late 1980s and was later a professor of literature in Beijing. *Ren mian tao hua,* which took more than 10 years to complete, showcased an exquisite narrative style that kept readers in suspense until the very end of the story. The book carefully illuminates the spiritual path, as well as the imagined experiences, of the heroine, Xiumi, a dreamy country girl, and concentrates on the grand dream of establishing a completely fair and moral society in modern China. This ideal inspires all the leading characters in the novel—a crazy retired official, an old bandit leader, a returned student from Japan, and, of course, Xiumi—to give all they have for it, even their lives. With evident sympathy the author vividly displayed the indomitable spirit of those pursuing their dream, although he described in detail what serious disasters such dream seeking could bring to the people and their land.

(WANG XIAOMING)

Judges for Japan's Akutagawa Prize surprised the public by honouring very young authors in 2004; Hitomi Kanehara won for her story, "Hebi ni piasu" ("Snakes and Earrings").

Ko Sasaki

JAPANESE

The most significant event in Japanese literature of 2004 came at the beginning of the year. In January the Akutagawa Prize, awarded semiannually to the most promising new Japanese writers of fiction, went to two young women, Hitomi Kanehara, 20, and Risa Wataya, 19 (*see* BIOGRAPHIES), who broke the record for the youngest winners. The previous record was shared by Shintaro Ishihara, Kenzaburo Ōe, Kenji Maruyama, and Keiichirō Hirano, all of whom won the prize at 23. Rui, the heroine of Kanehara's story "Hebi ni piasu" ("Snakes and Earrings"), first published in the November 2003 issue of *Subaru,* tries hard to define her pseudo-eternal living space by reconstructing her body. She enlarges a pierced hole in her tongue so that it splits like that of a snake's and has a *kirin* (a unicorn-like creature) and a dragon tattooed on her back so that they face the society from which she is estranged as well as link her to the society of the underground. In contrast to Kanehara's story, Wataya's "Keritai senaka" ("The Back I Want to Kick"), which first appeared in the autumn 2003 issue of *Bungei,* pictured the rather ordinary life of high-school students. Hatsu, the heroine, at first dislikes her classmate Ninagawa, a boy who is keen on a famous female model whom he can meet only through TV or magazines, but she soon starts feeling sympathy for this harmless young boy. Wataya's story sold more than a million copies, including some 10,000 copies electronically via cell phones. Both stories were also published on their own as novels. The support young readers gave Kanehara and Wataya was a boon to Japanese publishers, whose sales had been falling for seven consecutive years.

In the second half of the year, the Akutagawa Prize was given to Norio Mobu's "Kaigo nyūmon" ("Introduction to Caregiving") from the June 2004 issue of *Bungakukai.* The story involved an angry young rocker who shows love for his grandmother who is ill with dementia amid Japan's crumbling welfare system.

Graphic Novels: *Not* Just Comic Books

Long a fixture on the fringes of American popular culture, the graphic novel seemed poised to enter the literary mainstream once again in 2004. The year saw the film adaptation of Harvey Pekar's *American Splendor* nominated for an Academy Award, the final issues of both Dave Sim's 6,000-page magnum opus *Cerebus* and Jeff Smith's influential *Bone,* and the long-awaited debut of Alan Moore's *Lost Girls.* With collected volumes of *Sandman* by Neil Gaiman (*see* BIOGRAPHIES) and Japanese *manga* titles becoming a common sight on public library shelves and film versions of landmark books such as *Sin City, Watchmen,* and *Batman: Year One* in production, the graphic novel had reached levels of respectability and marketability that transcended the disparaging label "comic book."

While the graphic novel format had a long tradition in Europe (albums collecting Belgian artist Hergé's Tintin stories appeared as early as the 1930s) and Japan (with *manga* publications aimed at every age and interest), it struggled to take hold in the United States. One reason for this was the creation of the Comics Code Authority in 1954. The Authority, created by the comics industry to police itself, had a chilling effect on creativity. Publishers dared run only the tamest of stories; sales plummeted; and a once-thriving medium was soon seen as disposable entertainment for children. By the late 1980s, however, most major publishers had dropped the code's certification stamp from their books, and, not coincidentally, a flood of creativity had followed.

The other difficulty faced by the medium is the necessarily vague answer to the question "What is a graphic novel?" Most loosely defined, it is an illustrated story that stands alone or as part of a limited series (a distinction that sets it apart from monthly comic books or serials). The book frequently cited as the first modern graphic novel, Will Eisner's *A Contract with God* (1978), is actually a collection of four semiautobiographical novellas. Art Spiegelman's *Maus* (1986) is perhaps the most critically acclaimed graphic novel, and yet it is not a novel at all but a work of nonfiction that uses animal characters to depict the horrors of the Holocaust. The conflict in the Balkans produced notable works that could most accurately be called illustrated journalism. Joe Kubert's *Fax from Sarajevo* (1996) and Joe Sacco's *Safe Area Gorazde* (2000) stretched the boundaries of the medium by offering uniquely personal accounts of life in a modern war zone. Eisner has suggested the term *sequential art* to more accurately describe this evolving genre, but it appears that, however inaccurate it may be, the current label will stick.

AP/Wide World Photos

Will Eisner (1917–2005) worked as a cartoonist for almost 70 years. His A Contract with God *(1978) is considered the first modern graphic novel.*

With the advent of direct marketing to bookstores and specialty shops (thus bypassing the Comics Code and the newsstand comics vendors), publishers are far more open to the graphic novel format than they were in the past. The continued interest in groundbreaking titles such as Moore's *Watchmen* (1987), Frank Miller's *Batman: The Dark Knight Returns* (1986), and Gaiman's *Black Orchid* (1988) has opened the door for the next generation of graphic novelists. Craig Thompson's *Good-bye, Chunky Rice* (1999), Chris Ware's *Jimmy Corrigan: The Smartest Kid on Earth* (2000), and Marjane Satrapi's *Persepolis* (2003) eschew the superheroic to focus on human stories of friendship, hope, and despair. Critical acclaim has led to increased sales and a more prominent place in the retail landscape. Although graphic novels still account for less than one percent of the book trade in the United States, they represent one of the fastest-growing markets, with over $120 million in sales in 2003. (MICHAEL RAY)

Haruki Murakami's new novel *Afutādāku* ("Afterdark") appeared in September and commemorated the 25 years since his debut. Murakami portrayed the darkness and dreams of Japan's night scene, and the story bore a close resemblance to his 1993 story "Nemuri" ("Sleep"). Banana Yoshimoto published a new fantasy in July, *Hatsukoi* ("High and Dry"), in which a 14-year-old girl first falls in love.

Japan's major literary critics Takaaki Yoshimoto (Banana's father) and Kōjin Karatani left important works in 2004. In "Sensō to heiwa" ("War and Peace"), Yoshimoto wrote about the dispatch of Japan's Self Defense Force to Iraq, which, he made clear, never reflected the wishes of the nation. Karatani completed his collection of works, which were especially valued for his clear and keen eye to the modernization of Japan from the standpoint of literature.

The Yomiuri Prize for Literature went to Yōko Ogawa's *Hakase no aishita sūshiki* ("The Numerical Formula That the Doctor Loved"), which also won several new Japanese booksellers' awards. The Junichirō Tanizaki Prize for fiction was awarded to Toshiyuki Horie's *Yukinuma to sono shūhen* ("Snow Swamp and Its Surroundings"). Among the best-selling books of the year were Ryū Murakami's *Jūsansai no harō wāku* ("Job Guidance for 13-year-olds"), in which the author suggested that jobs be based not on one's education but rather on one's interests. Two popular fiction writers, Tsutomu Mizukami and Megumu Sagisawa, died in 2004. (YOSHIHIKO KAZAMARU)

Media and Publishing

The FCC imposed hefty INDECENCY fines. AIR AMERICA was launched as a liberal radio network, and LIFE magazine was revived as a weekly. Big-name PERSONALITIES departed from TV news. The use of digital video recorders grew, and more newspapers launched TABLOID-format editions.

TELEVISION

Organization and Regulation. Singer Janet Jackson drew large fines from the U.S. Federal Communications Commission for her performance in the 2004 Super Bowl halftime show, in which she, through the assistance of her singing partner, Justin Timberlake, exposed most of one of her breasts. The FCC imposed a $550,000 fine on CBS for the Super Bowl flashing incident, a levy the network contested on the grounds that it had no advance knowledge of the singer's plans regarding the costume. Although the move appeared to many observers to have been intentional, Timberlake claimed the exposure was the result of a "wardrobe malfunction." The incident cast a veil of caution over TV for the rest of the year. When the ABC network scheduled an airing of an uncensored version of Steven Spielberg's Oscar-winning World War II film *Saving Private Ryan* on Veterans Day, more than 60 affiliates declined to carry it, including those in Boston, Atlanta, Ga., Detroit, and Dallas, Texas. They did not want to take the risk of being fined for indecency for the occasional occurrences of obscene language in the movie. In that same month, ABC took heat for a sexually suggestive promotion that ran in advance of a *Monday Night Football* telecast and showed Nicollette Sheridan, star of the ABC series *Desperate Housewives,* wearing only a towel and attempting to seduce Philadelphia Eagles star Terrell Owens into not playing in that night's game. In response to thousands of viewer complaints, the FCC considered whether to impose fines. In November Viacom, Inc., parent company of CBS, agreed to pay the FCC a $3.5 million fine that regulators had imposed for indecent TV and radio programming apart from the Jackson incident.

A television crew for al-Sharqiya, Iraq's first privately owned satellite channel, films a reality-TV show called **Labour and Materials,** *which features the rebuilding of war-damaged houses.*

© Wathiq Khuzaie/Getty Images

Comcast Corp., the leading American cable operator, attempted to acquire Disney, parent of ABC, as a programming-content wing, but the $54 billion bid that the Philadelphia-based company made for Disney was rebuffed. NBC worked to make a coherent single entity out of its takeover of Vivendi Universal, which was completed in May. The new company, NBC Universal, established single sales, marketing, and publicity departments over all of its television networks: NBC, MSNBC, CNBC, Telemundo, and Bravo as well as former Universal companies USA Network, Sci Fi Channel, and Trio. The synergy worked during the telecast of the Olympic Games from Athens; the Games were shown across many NBC Universal networks, which gave viewers multiple options for coverage.

Reelection campaign advertisements for Pres. George W. Bush on American TV made reference to the Olympics, and International Olympic Committee officials objected on the grounds that it was a political use of the name. The ads, which highlighted the Olympic participation of Iraq and Afghanistan as "two more free nations," aired on MSNBC, CNBC, and other NBC cable networks during the broadcast of the Athens Olympics.

Australian-born American Rupert Murdoch planned to move the headquarters of News Corp. to New York. In the second quarter net profit rose 7.8%, mainly from TV ($351 million), cable ($154 million), and newspaper ($144 million) affiliates. Brazil's antitrust regulator CADE (Administrative Council of Economic Defense) imposed conditions on the acquisition of Hughes Electronics by News Corp., which gave News Corp. a monopoly of satellite TV markets in Latin America.

Britain's biggest commercial free-to-air TV broadcaster ITV PLC became the majority shareholder of breakfast-TV producer GMTV after acquiring another 25% of its stock. ITV was formed by the merger of Granada and Carlton, each of which owned 25% of GMTV. The German cartel office opposed cable-TV operator Kabel Deutschland's takeover plans of three regional cable-network operators, Ish (Cologne), Iesy (Frankfurt), and Kabel Baden-Württemberg (Heidelberg). Pursuant to the German Takeover Act, Viacom (owner of MTV Networks Europe) published in June its intention to acquire 75.8% of Viva Media AG. In November TDC, a leading telecommunications company in Denmark, acquired Swedish broadband company Song Networks Holding AB, which was to be renamed TDC Song.

Galaxy Satellite Broadcasting's Jim Blomfield resigned in August amid rumours of international satellite operator Intelsat's pullout from the joint venture with Hong Kong's Television Broadcasts Ltd. Lenovo Group Ltd., China's leading personal computer maker, formed a multimedia venture with Sun Media Investment Holdings

Ltd., the private-investment firm of popular TV program host (and company chairman) Yang Lan and her husband, Bruno Wu Zheng. TV Tokyo traded on the Tokyo Stock Exchange with an initial public offering of 3.79 million shares. Tokyo Regional Taxation Bureau ordered Nippon Television Network to pay ¥90 million (about $850,000) in additional taxes and penalties for having failed to declare taxable income over a three-year period ended March 31, 2003.

Australia's media ownership bill was not dealt with by Parliament "due to a backlog of bills in the Senate upper house." Communications Minister Darryl Williams had reintroduced the bill in November 2003 and had argued that the growth of the sector was being limited by an outmoded regulatory framework.

Dan MacMedan/ContourPhotos.com

(From left) Nicollette Sheridan, Eva Longoria, Marcia Cross, Teri Hatcher, and Felicity Huffman star in Desperate Housewives, *ABC's surprise big hit of the fall 2004 TV season.*

Programming. The most popular show in American television programming at the end of the 2003–04 TV season in May was the CBS crime drama *CSI: Crime Scene Investigation,* and it retained that rank in the first months of the next season. Emmy Awards went to HBO's *The Sopranos,* a first-time winner for outstanding dramatic series, and to the first-year Fox show *Arrested Development,* the winner for outstanding comedy. The big fall hit was ABC's *Desperate Housewives,* a campy soap opera about lithe and licentious women on a comfy suburban block. The series rapidly became one of TV's top-three shows in all key demographic groups. Such a rapid ascent was surprising for any TV series in the cable-and-Internet era, but it was especially surprising for a scripted series. *Desperate Housewives* brought new hope to near-desperate writers, agents, and actors; all of the instant ratings successes in recent years had come from so-called reality series, and this led to a kind of panic in Hollywood's creative community. NBC could not parlay its Olympics success into fall-season ratings. The massive hit sitcom *Friends* retired in May, and after the first couple of months of the 2004–05 TV season, the network was losing ground in the most valuable viewer demographic (18–49-year-old adults) for the first time in a decade. The network was hurt when *The Apprentice,* the surprise early-year reality hit that featured real-estate developer Donald Trump (*see* BIOGRAPHIES) as he led would-be acolytes through business challenges, did not fare as well in its fall edition.

Two lions of network television news retired in 2004. Don Hewitt stepped down as executive producer of CBS's venerable *60 Minutes,* the pioneering newsmagazine he founded in 1968, and NBC News anchor Tom Brokaw gave up his anchor chair, yielding to Brian Williams. With the announcement by CBS News anchor Dan Rather that he would retire in 2005, only ABC's Peter Jennings remained of the longtime big-three TV-network anchors. Also retiring in 2004 was respected TV journalist Bill Moyers. Because of the rise of cable news and the shrinking of the audience for network news, it was widely believed that the next generation of news anchors would cast much shorter shadows. Rather had found himself in the eye of a political firestorm because of a story he reported during the 2004 presidential campaign. His report, for the spinoff program *60 Minutes Wednesday,* alleged that President Bush's National Guard service in the early 1970s had been spotty, at best. The story, however, was based on alleged National Guard documents that CBS was forced to admit had not been properly authenticated. A panel was appointed by CBS to investigate the blunder.

The commercial arm of the BBC partnered with digital broadcaster Japan MediArk Co., and on December 1 they launched BBC Japan, an entertainment channel that ran programming specifically developed for the Japanese audience. In Great Britain the BBC announced that its digital terrestrial TV service Freeview was reaching four million homes with integrated digital TV (iDTV). The BBC, BSkyB, and Crown Castle International made up the Freeview consortium. In April BBC news reporters began attending two-hour seminars on impartial journalism following criticisms by the Hutton Report on the coverage of the death of scientist David Kelly. BBC World, the BBC's 24-hour international news and information channel, won Best News Channel in the seventh HOT BIRD TV awards. The awards were held in Venice on October 2 and were broadcast by Eutelsat, one of the world's largest satellite operators.

With guidance from fertility expert Allen Pacey of the University of Sheffield, Eng., the BBC televised a sperm race as part of the educational *Lab Rats* series on BBC Three. The race between the sperm of scientist Mike Leahy and comedian Zeron Gibson took place in glass capillary tubes and was shown by means of a microscope connected to a big screen. (Gibson's won.) *Vee-TV,* Britain's Channel 4 program for the deaf, decided to exclude offensive signs characterizing homosexuals, ethnic groups, and racial minorities from its sign language. Britain's Office of Fair Trading branded as illegal the collective sale of TV media rights for horse racing at 49 racecourses to a joint venture of Arena Leisure, BSkyB, and Channel 4 called Attheraces. English premier league association football (soccer) was broadcast by BSkyB, but in agreement with European competition regulators, it sublicensed rights for several games. Sportech launched ahead of Euro 2004 Littlewoods Bet Direct, the only fixed-odds betting service available 24 hours a day and seven days a week within ITV's interactive menu. Meanwhile, the Ligue de Football Professionnel of France launched the auction of broadcasting rights to its top matches over the following three years. Fierce competition erupted between rights holder Canal Plus and Television Par Satellite, the digital TV platform of Television Francaise 1 SA and M6-Metropole TV. Shows on Iraqi TV's al-Sharqiya channel were becoming popular. One program, *Ration Card,* randomly drew the national ration-card number of an Iraqi citizen. Producers then showed up on the winner's doorstep and handed over $1,000.

Mexico's Grupo Televisa SA changed the name of its global unit to Televisa Estudios and added licensing and merchandising services for video and DVD products. Colombia's Caracol network signed a five-year distribution contract with DirecTV, which also started to beam Puerto Rican programming from WAPA America as part of its Para Todos service on September 1.

Among other TV-related stories worldwide, a six-episode Thai TV show called *Nok Hunt* was staged by new budget airline Nok Air to choose 10 flight attendants from among 20 applicants who underwent several tests. A New Delhi woman set fire to herself because her husband and three children were glued to the India-Pakistan cricket series on TV. In Manitoba a 20-year-old was jailed for having hurled a bagful of vomit and feces inside a Winnipeg bus, similar to an episode on the MTV show *Jackass.* German news service Deutsche Welle celebrated its 10th year online with reports in the *Star Trek*-based Klingon language (created by linguist Marc Okrand).

Technology. Television technology marched forward aggressively in 2004 as high-definition television (HDTV) and various services for time-shifting programs made a push toward the mainstream. "Consumers will have more flexibility over what they watch and when they watch it," said Phillip Swann, president of TVPredictions.com. Swann pegged growing usage of HDTV, digital video recorders (DVRs) such as TiVo, and on-demand video service as the year's most important TV trends.

Although HDTV remained a prohibitively expensive proposition for most consumers, prices for the necessary equipment began to decline significantly in 2004, and the number of high-definition programs that were being offered grew. The telecasting of sports was a key factor in driving the growth, experts said. For example, Cox Cable in San Diego, Calif., saw its "take rate" for high-definition services jump 40% after San Diego Padres baseball games began to be offered in the new, more vivid format.

The use of DVRs, long predicted as the wave of TV's future, finally began to climb in 2004, largely because cable-TV operators began to offer them packaged inside their cable boxes. This arrangement was simpler than TiVo's, which typically required users to purchase and install a separate audio-video appliance. Independent industry analysts predicted that the number of DVR-equipped homes would explode from 7 million at the end of 2004 to some 30 million, or close to one-third of American households, within four years. Also popular were new video-on-demand cable-TV services, which allowed a user to call up an episode of HBO's *The Sopranos,* for example, from an on-screen menu and watch it immediately rather than wait for the show to appear on the regular HBO schedule. The two technologies together were forcing networks and advertising agencies to rethink the traditional 30-second TV advertisement.

On the basis of its tracking of DVR usage by its 800,000 customers, TiVo revealed that the most-watched Olympic moment was gymnast Paul Hamm's high-bar performance. The most-replayed Super Bowl moment was Jackson's "wardrobe malfunction." In October Nielsen Media Research, the company that provided the Nielsen ratings, began culling data on DVR use from 5,000–10,000 TiVo households that had agreed to participate. TiVo faced off against operators that provided cable and satellite services with DVR functions. Hollywood studios and the U.S. National Football League blocked TiVo from allowing its subscribers to transfer recorded shows to other devices, but TiVo and Netflix agreed to develop a service for customers to rent videos by downloading them through TiVo.

Microsoft Corp. unveiled MSN TV2, made by Thomson for RCA, which offered a subscription package that included MSN, NBC, Discovery Channel, and Fox Sports. At the same time, Microsoft introduced the new Windows XP Media Center software, which made it possible for a PC to function as a photo album, jukebox, DVD player, TV receiver, and DVR.

In August Toshiba introduced Qosmio, the first laptop integrated with audio and video features, DVD drive, TV tuner with a no-waiting TV mode, enhanced speakers, and near-TV-quality display. The Samsung MM-A700 cellphone used MobiTV technology to function as a TV. It could show news updates, sports clips, weather forecasts, music videos, and cartoons from 14 cable stations of streaming video provided by the Sprint network. Samsung also launched HDTV with a picture-enhancing feature called DNIe (digital natural image engine). Ahead of the holidays Dell released its first plasma-screen TV. It had released its first LCD (liquid-crystal display) TV in December 2003. Sharp, Japan's top maker of LCD panels, announced its latest product, a 114-cm (45-in) LCD TV, to keep up with demands for 102-cm (40-in) or larger flat TVs. Earlier, it had introduced the world's first wireless flat-panel TV, the Aquos LC-15L1U-S, with a 38-cm (15-in) display screen and built-in battery.

Patients in 32 British hospitals complained about TV sets in their rooms having no "off" switch. Even when they refused to subscribe, the TVs blared ads for the service and messages from hospital authorities. Television service, installed by private firm Patientline, cost patients $5.75 per day.

RADIO

Air America, a new liberal radio network intended to counter the prevailing right-wing themes of American talk radio, signed on in March 2004 with comic Al Franken as its marquee host. Also cohosting a show was comedian and actress Janeane Garofalo. Despite the abundance of news in an election year, the network had startup woes. It quickly lost its Chicago outlet, piled up debt, and within the first three months underwent a corporate restructuring. By year's end, however, Air America had more than 40 outlets, including some owned by the giant Clear Channel conglomerate, and it was proving popular with young-adult listeners. Much like Howard Stern's show, Franken's show was also turned into a regular telecast, on cable TV's Sundance Channel.

Meanwhile, Stern, the popular New York-based talk host, was preparing to abandon over-the-air radio for the new medium of satellite radio. (*See* Sidebar.) Fed up with what he considered to be harassment in the form of fines from an FCC that was newly vigilant about what it termed indecency, Stern opted to sign with Sirius Satellite Radio, one of two competitors in the emerging satellite arena. With a contract said to be valued at $500 million and scheduled to start in 2006, Stern brought new credibility to a medium that had struggled to attract listeners.

Also helping satellite was the arrival of Bob Edwards, the longtime host of NPR's flagship *Morning Edition* broadcast. Edwards began hosting an eponymous interview show on XM Satellite Radio in October, five months after NPR pushed him out of the hosting chair. NPR's demotion of Edwards, less than a year shy of his 25th anniversary as host, proved wildly unpopular with listeners, who logged more than 30,000 protests, according to the public-radio programming service. NPR management said the move was undertaken to inject new life into the morning broadcast but later admitted that they had badly mishandled the departure. Nonetheless, at year's end the levels of listener donations to local NPR stations did not seem to be showing any long-term effects of the Edwards affair, according to company officials. NPR continued to gain listeners, a popularity boom that many analysts interpreted as

New Frontiers in Radio

At a promotional event in November 2004, flanked by his usual assemblage of strippers and adoring fans, Howard Stern helped bring the public's attention to satellite radio, an uncensored and still new outlet for radio programming. (Unlike regular, or terrestrial, radio, which is broadcast from Earth-based antennas, the digitally encoded signals for satellite radio are transmitted from Earth-orbiting satellites and have a very wide coverage.) Stopping traffic around Manhattan's Union Square, the preeminent shock jock in the United States gave away satellite-radio receivers and announced that his newly chosen venue "will be the dominant medium in the future because there's no government interference. It's the beginning." Advocates of satellite radio hoped so. American listeners had been slow to subscribe to either of the two competing satellite-radio services—XM and Sirius—since they debuted in 2001 and 2002, respectively. A spate of high-profile signings in 2004, however, topped by on-air talent Stern and Sirius's new chief executive, Mel Karmazin, the former chief of Viacom (and Stern's former corporate boss), had many analysts labeling 2004 as the pivotal year for the still-unprofitable satellite-radio genre.

Tim Soter/WireImage.com

Radio shock jock Howard Stern and his crew promote Sirius Satellite Radio in November 2004 in New York City.

XM Satellite Radio, based in Washington, D.C., had already set up a show for the popular duo Opie and Anthony, who had been fired from commercial radio after they broadcast what they alleged to be a couple having sex in a Roman Catholic cathedral, and one for Bob Edwards, the longtime NPR *Morning Edition* host who had been relieved of his hosting duties for reasons NPR never fully articulated. In October Sirius Satellite Radio, based in New York City, signed the bawdy Stern, who claimed to be fed up with years of close monitoring by the newly vigilant U.S. Federal Communications Commission and with its fines. Sirius publicists called the Stern signing "the most important deal in radio history." That statement might have been hyperbole, but the deal was certainly one of the most expensive in radio history. The announced cost of producing the Stern show, including compensation, stock, and other considerations, was $100 million annually for five years beginning January 2006, after the expiration of Stern's contract with over-the-air Infinity Broadcasting.

"Satellite radio became a business today," said Stern in *USA Today*. "When radio's biggest star voluntarily takes himself off terrestrial radio and an empire, you know it's the real deal. I'm saying to the medium, I'm saying to the industry, I'm saying to my fellow broadcasters, 'We do have a choice.'" An article in *The Wall Street Journal* said, "If he [Stern] makes good on his promise to lure other high-profile personalities to satellite, terrestrial radio eventually could find itself falling behind satellite in ratings and buzz, just as broadcast television is struggling with cable." The publicity value of Stern, one of American radio's biggest stars, proved instantly beneficial to Sirius. It had been the laggard in satellite radio, with just 600,000 people willing to pay its $12.95 monthly subscription rate. That audience was much smaller than Stern's estimated terrestrial-radio audience of 12 million, and it was some 2 million fewer than had signed up for rival XM, at $9.99 a month. After Stern's announcement and aggressive promoting of his future employer, Sirius subscriptions quickly climbed past the 700,000 mark.

Fans of satellite radio praised its crisp, clear sound. They also liked its abundance of programming choices, especially in comparison with the increasingly homogenized offerings of terrestrial radio. Local terrestrial radio also found itself under fire from growth in access to the Internet, which made terrestrial stations that broadcast over the Internet available worldwide. Satellite radio, nevertheless, claimed advantages of convenience and variety over Earth-based options. For example, devotees of the alternative-country format, typified by such artists as Lyle Lovett and Robert Earl Keen, would have had a hard time finding such music on regular radio, but the satellite services devoted space on their dozens of channels to almost every genre, from sports to talk to very specific musical interests—most commercial-free. Still, the fledgling satellite-radio business faced significant hurdles to growth. Not only did it have to persuade people to pay for something that they had always received free, but it required them to buy a new, stand-alone piece of equipment—a satellite-radio receiver. Both XM and Sirius worked with automakers to offer such receivers as options in new cars.

Except for some traffic and weather, satellite-radio channels were transmitted nationally rather than locally and therefore reduced the feelings of regional affinity that terrestrial radio could still inspire. Although most radio analysts were bullish on the Stern hiring, several expressed concern that Stern's devotees might not follow him to a pay service, which would leave the shock jock a marginalized figure and find Sirius losing more money than before.

(STEVE JOHNSON)

an audience reaction to the increasing homogenization of commercial radio. Its share of radio listeners had grown fivefold in two decades, to more that 5% of the total radio audience in the U.S. A record $236 million bequest in 2003 from Joan Kroc, widow of McDonald's founder Ray Kroc, had the radio service planning to hire many new reporters, including some to fill in news beats it considered to be inadequately covered, such as the media.

In commercial radio a second successive year of little to no advertising growth had the big broadcasters scrambling for solutions. The big two, Clear Channel and Infinity, decided to trim the number of commercials aired per hour in an attempt to make the time more valuable and reduce listener ad fatigue. Both Clear Channel

Communications and the Viacom conglomerate, which owned Infinity, made moves to boost their influence in the growing Hispanic radio market. Viacom bought 10% of the Spanish Broadcasting System, and Clear Channel announced plans to convert 20 to 25 of its stations to Hispanic formats.

Radio Arman ("Radio Hope"), Afghanistan's first privately owned independent FM radio station, was begun in 2003 by the Mohseni brothers Saad, Zaid, and Jahed. In 2004 it was broadcasting 24 hours a day, seven days a week, a mix of talk shows, traffic updates, and music—Indian, Western, Arabic, and Afghani. A hit with young Afghans, the disc jockeys were aged 19 to 25, and half of them were women. In September Radio Arman launched a talent search for new Afghan superstars. Four winners recorded CDs for promotion on the air.

Established by the British in 1954, Radio Uganda celebrated its golden jubilee in September. For a time Radio Uganda had been overshadowed by newer FM stations in Kampala, and high-powered shortwave transmitters at the station eventually fell into disuse. Using satellite links, Radio Uganda later came to reach the whole country. Developments in radio programming facilitated the promotion of Uganda's amnesty program, particularly on Mega FM, the most popular station in northern Uganda. Its well-known program *Dwogpaco* ("Come Back Home") featured ex-LRA (Lord's Resistance Army) members asking their fellow combatants to surrender. The show was conducted in the language of the Acholi, the largest ethnic group in the area. The show was also broadcast on Radio Juba in The Sudan, where many LRA members were still based. During the launching of the Radio Uganda Listeners Association on the occasion of Radio Uganda's golden jubilee, the minister of state for information, James Nsaba Buturo, announced the merger of Radio Uganda and Uganda Television.

Imprisoned murderer Jiri Kajinek was paid to star in an advertising campaign by Czech pop station Kiss Radio. Some 500 billboards showed 43-year-old Kajinek wearing headphones under the slogan "Radio for life." Kajinek had become a local legend when he escaped from a maximum-security prison and evaded recapture for more than a month.

(RAMONA MONETTE SARGAN FLORES; STEVE JOHNSON)

NEWSPAPERS

Newspapers in 2004 were rocked by scandals that dented the industry's credibility as executives came to grips with a blasé advertising recovery. The pressure on profitability combined with ongoing structural changes in the advertising and readership markets made for a challenging climate in a year otherwise expected to be economically better than the previous three years, which were marked by recession. Newspaper managements responded with format changes and new young-adult products.

The restoration of credibility rose to the top of the newspaper-industry agenda after a series of high-profile cases involving alleged corporate malfeasance and inflation of circulation numbers. Conrad Black, chairman of global media giant Hollinger Inc., and other top corporate executives were investigated by regulatory agencies over alleged fraud, misstatements to shareholders, and improper diversion of funds as part of transactions. One regulator accused Black and former *Chicago Sun-Times* publisher David Radler of having abused a public company and treated it as their "personal piggy bank."

As investigations continued throughout 2004, Hollinger sold Telegraph Group Ltd., which published London's highest circulated quality newspaper, *The Daily Telegraph,* to David and Frederick Barclay, owners of *The Scotsman* newspaper and of London's Ritz Hotel. The U.K. purchase came after a ferocious public-bidding war for the group. Later in the year Hollinger sold the *Jerusalem Post* to Canada-based CanWest and an Israeli media group.

Meanwhile, investigations by new management at Hollinger revealed that circulation at the *Chicago Sun-Times* had been overstated, and tens of millions of dollars had to be reimbursed to advertisers whose rates were based on the audited circulation numbers. Similar investigations in the United States found Tribune properties in New York, *Newsday* and *Hoy,* as well as Belo Corp.'s *Dallas* (Texas) *Morning News* to have had similar inflated circulations over varying periods of time. Similar advertiser reimbursements were implemented. The U.S. Audit Bureau of Circulations (ABC) promised tighter auditing standards in the future and censured the offending newspapers by excluding them later in the year from a crucial industry-circulation report for advertisers.

In the U.S. there was a nearly 1% decline in circulation. Declines were sharply higher in urban markets, where publishers such as the *Washington Post* and the *Miami* (Fla.) *Herald* indicated a willingness to experiment with shorter stories, more graphics, and quick-read sections in response to circulation declines. A Deutsche Bank report, though, suggested that new ABC rules allowing newspapers to more easily count deeply discounted circulation was masking the fact that nondiscounted circulation had dropped closer to 5% over the previous two years.

The year 2004 was projected to be the end of a three-year advertising slump for newspapers. Publishers looked to the pattern of the previous global recession in 1990–91 and also counted on the Athens Olympic Games and the U.S. elections as further impetus for advertising growth. Newspapers got the growth, but at only half the percentage that had been forecast. In the U.S. the decade-long decline of traditional mass-merchandise retailers that relied on advertising and the rise of discounters such as Wal-Mart that did not rely on advertising impacted recovery expectations. By year's end major retailers Kmart and Sears had announced a corporate merger. Leading analysts such as Goldman Sachs and Merrill Lynch predicted that the mediocre advertising performance of all media industries, notably newspapers, would continue through 2005.

Another major impact on newspaper revenues was the ongoing shift of employment advertising from print to online. While 69% of major American newspapers had developed Web-only classified advertising options by 2004, the rise of national-employment Web

AP/Wide World Photos

Spanish-language newspapers such as Hoy, *being read here by a newspaper-stand vendor in Los Angeles, experienced an increase in circulation in the United States in 2004.*

sites in countries worldwide continued to take market share away from newspapers. A report by Borrell Associates in the U.S. indicated that all of the market-share shift of employment advertising to online since 2000 had come from newspapers. Fighting back, newspapers around the globe continued to create local online classified advertising options, while one-time print competitors banded together to aggregate classifieds to fend off national online competitors such as Monster.com. With most quality newspapers heavily reliant on classified advertising in their profit models, the tepid global job growth combined with content shifts to the Internet caused newspaper revenues to stagnate.

Paper manufacturers, having faced a decline in demand for newspaper pages since 2001, were able to increase newsprint prices sharply in 2004, despite the fact that no major increase in newsprint consumption was seen in most parts of the world, with the exception of Asia. In recent years publishers had become accustomed to the lowest inflation-adjusted newsprint prices in modern newspaper history.

After experiencing weak retail and classified-advertising sales, circulation erosion, and higher newsprint costs, many publishers were forced to cut staffing, notably in editorial departments that had been largely spared during the recent recession. Other content cutbacks could be seen in traditional newspaper features such as the comics, theatre listings, obituaries, and other sections—some of which publishers migrated to their Web sites.

Leading global financial newspapers such as *The Wall Street Journal* and the *Financial Times*, reliant on the weak business-to-business advertising sector, continued to report weak earnings.

Despite credibility issues and economic strains, pockets of innovation remained at newspapers. While a change in format had been implemented by newspapers worldwide in the past decade, the launch in London of tabloid editions alongside broadsheet editions of *The Times* and *The Independent* in late 2003 sparked a wave of similar moves throughout Europe in 2004. Both London newspapers eventually dropped their broadsheet editions in 2004 as more than 70% of the market began daily choosing the tabloid. *Gazet van Antwerpen* in Belgium and *Blick* in Switzerland also began publishing in dual formats, only to drop their historic broadsheets. Other newspapers to launch a tabloid version were *De Standaard* in Belgium, the *Irish Independent* in Ireland, *Die Welt* in Germany, *The Scotsman, Dagens Nyheter* in Sweden, and *Het Parool* in The Netherlands. The *New Straits Times* in Malaysia became the first major Asian quality broadsheet to launch a tabloid edition. Format change results varied widely, with some newspapers reporting short-term increases in circulation, notably among women and young adults. Though newspaper executives advocated that broadsheet advertising prices remain the same in tabloid format, advertisers fought for pricing based on space measurement—again, with varying results from market to market.

In South Africa the success of the two-year-old down-market *Daily Sun* continued to put pressure on the country's 17 other daily newspapers, mostly positioned as middle- and upper-market products. In a country of nearly 47 million people dominated by an economically ascendant black population, only 1.1 million daily newspapers had been sold daily prior to the *Daily Sun*'s launch. By 2004 the newspaper's daily circulation had surpassed 400,000 copies, 75% of which represented "aspiring blacks" who had never before read a newspaper. Modeled after Britain's *Sun*, minus the topless pictures of women, South Africa's *Daily Sun* stood in contrast to the Nigerian-owned up-market broadsheet *ThisDay*, which closed after only one year of publication.

A microcosm of an increasingly integrated Europe came with the continued growth of *Fakt*, a picture-oriented popular daily launched in Poland in 2003 by German publisher Axel Springer. Within months of its launch, *Fakt* surpassed *Gazeta Wyborcza* to become Poland's highest-selling daily newspaper, with more than 500,000 copies purchased daily. The significance of a German publisher's having success in another European country might portend other cross-border ventures by Axel Springer and other publishers in the quickly evolving European Union.

New newspapers aimed at young-adult urban-commuting markets continued to grow in influence. The success of *Metro* and *20 Minutes* in Europe—free commuter newspapers that attracted young adults and women more than their paid daily newspaper counterparts did—spawned similar ventures throughout North America, South America, and Asia. Traditional publishers such as Associated Newspapers in England, De Telegraaf in The Netherlands, Tribune and Belo in the United States, and Quebecor in Canada all managed urban newspapers, mostly free. In the U.S. Gannett continued to launch weekly young-adult-oriented tabloids in its regional markets.

Publishers experimented with newspapers in nonnative languages. While Spanish-language newspapers continued their rise in the U.S., new Chinese-language newspapers appeared in Asia where pockets of Chinese speakers lived. An Argentine newspaper, *La Razon*, was published in languages in various parts of the world, including China, as part of an effort to attract business to its native country.

Convergence was an oft-used term in newspaper companies during the year. Leading companies such as Tribune, New York Times, CanWest, Media General, and Belo explored ways to sell local multimedia advertising packages that included newspapers, online subscriptions, television programming, outdoor billboards, and other options. As U.S. lawmakers balked at regulatory attempts to liberalize local cross-media ownership, Australia appeared on the brink of loosening such regulations—which would have the potential to open the door for newspaper publishers to explore more commercial options.

Aside from the Hollinger divestitures, 2004 was not known as a year for major sales of newspaper companies. The biggest move might have come when News Corp. shareholders voted to move the $48 billion media empire founded on the backs of Australian newspapers from Australia to the U.S. The move, approved by 90% of News Corp. shareholders, was designed to attract institutional investors.

(EARL J. WILKINSON)

MAGAZINES

Both the U.S. and worldwide magazine industries bounced back in 2004 after three years of little or no growth. U.S. advertising revenue for September increased for the fifth consecutive month and topped the previous September by more than 17%. Ad revenue for the first nine months of 2004 was 10% higher than for the first nine months of 2003.

Internet advertising, which included online magazines, was expected to reach $10 billion in 2004, which would mark a 34% increase over 2003 and would top the record 2000 intake.

An annual guide to new magazine launches—published by Samir Husni, a professor at the University of Mississippi—reported that the 949 new titles in 2003 represented the most new introductions since 1998. Nearly 800 new launches through the first 10 months of 2004 indicated that 2004 start-ups might equal that figure.

The year, however, also saw a troubling trend with the outsourcing of magazine design and content development to foreign firms. *Folio* magazine reported in June that firms in India and the Philippines had contracted with a number of small-circulation American magazines to do various aspects of their production work. Copy editors and graphic designers were among the employees cited as most at risk of losing their jobs to overseas competitors. (*See* ECONOMIC AFFAIRS: Special Report.)

For the second time, Time Inc. revived its historic *Life* magazine, which was launched on October 1 in over 70 daily newspapers. Time called *Life* a "newspaper-distributed magazine" and

Life *magazine, revived by Time Inc. as a weekly, was launched with this issue dated Oct. 1, 2004.*

not a "supplement" like its competitors *Parade* and *USA Weekend*. *Life* would be published weekly with Friday issues of newspapers. *Folio* described the new *Life* as a "breezy lifestyle magazine for relatively upscale urban consumers." The original *Life* had debuted in 1936, and it ran weekly until 1972. The company revived it as a monthly from 1978 to 2000.

The Committee to Protect Journalists honoured journalists from four countries with International Press Freedom Awards at a New York City dinner on November 23. The organization gave a posthumous award to Paul Klebnikov, the editor of *Forbes Russia*, who was shot by an assassin on July 9 in Moscow. Klebnikov, an American of Russian descent, had joined *Forbes* in 1989 and had risen to senior editor before leaving the U.S.-based magazine to become editor of *Forbes Russia* in April 2004. In May the magazine attracted significant attention when it published a list of Russia's wealthiest people, including 33 Moscow billionaires. Klebnikov became the 15th journalist to have been murdered in Russia since 2000.

The Russian-language edition of *Cosmopolitan* appeared in the *Guinness Book of World Records* as the glossy magazine with the highest monthly circulation in Europe. It reached a record-breaking circulation of 610,000 with its March 2004 issue. British *Glamour* magazine placed second in Europe with a monthly circulation of 580,000, and French-language *Marie Claire* was third with 380,000 copies. *Cosmopolitan* was the first glossy magazine to be published in post-Soviet Russia.

The widely respected *World Press Review*, which published news and commentary from around the world for 30 years, released its last issue in April 2004. Sustained by the Stanley Foundation throughout its life, the 50,000-circulation magazine had never been profitable, and the foundation finally withdrew its support. Publisher Teri Schure, however, purchased the magazine's name and Web site (<www.worldpress.org>) and continued to publish it as an online magazine. In October 2004 Dow Jones & Co. announced that beginning in December its unprofitable Hong Kong-based *Far Eastern Economic Review* would cease publication as a newsweekly and instead would appear as a monthly opinion journal.

Revenues and circulation for *Martha Stewart Living* and its parent company, Martha Stewart Living Omnimedia, continued to reel from the legal woes of founder, former chairwoman, and CEO Martha Stewart. Circulation for the magazine fell from 2.4 million to 1.9 million between June 2003 and June 2004. The company's revenues (through the first nine months of 2004) also fell about 25%. In March, Stewart was convicted of having lied to government investigators about why she sold nearly 4,000 shares of ImClone Systems stock. She was sentenced in July to five months in prison and began serving the term in a West Virginia prison on October 8.

In November 2003 a Manhattan judge had ruled that there was no winner in the ugly court battle between entertainer Rosie O'Donnell and Gruner + Jahr USA, saying neither side would collect any damages. The publishers had sued O'Donnell for $100 million, alleging breach of contract for having walked away in mid-September 2002 from the magazine *Rosie*. She countersued for $125 million, saying that Gruner + Jahr broke its contract with her by cutting her out of key editorial decisions. The former *McCall's* magazine had begun publishing as *Rosie* in April 2001 and folded with the December 2002 issue. (DAVID E. SUMNER)

BOOK PUBLISHING

United States. In a year that saw a heightened national focus on writers, books, and publishing, many in the industry watched with disquiet a continuing softness in book sales in 2004. The Association of American Publishers (AAP) domestic book-publishing sales report noted that, as of September (the most recent month for which figures were available), total trade sales were up only 1.2%, totaling $8,302,700.

This continued a trend of underwhelming book sales in the U.S. The Book Industry Study Group's (BISG's) *Book Industry Trends 2004* projected total consumer expenditures of all book sales in 2004 of $38.9 billion, a rise of 2.9%. As had been the case for several years, however, that growth was projected to be realized on a minuscule rise in unit sales. For 2004 that was an uptick of 1.2%, following an estimated unit decline of 1% in 2003. R.R. Bowker, publisher of *Books in Print*, projected that U.S. title output in 2003 increased 19%—to 175,000 new titles and editions—the highest total ever recorded.

Much of the national awareness of publishing in 2004 among both consumers and the media was a direct result of the bruising U.S. presidential campaign. The fractious partisan debates regarding both the policies and the personalities of the candidates helped to secure many nonfiction books prominent spots in off-the-book-page media coverage and on best-seller lists. From the entire range of the political spectrum, titles emerged for their moment of face-out celebrity on bookstore shelves, often serving as the leads of news reports. From the right, with titles such as *Unfit for Command,* and from the left, with titles such as *New York Times* columnist Maureen Dowd's *Bushworld,* book releases piqued the interest of a public invested in the George W. Bush–John Kerry contest, and sales surged.

Underscoring this, the AAP reported that as of September there had been a 7.6% rise in publishers' gross sales of adult hardcover books, with a 10.2% rise in unit sales. Beyond the activity of recent hardcover releases, however, the picture was less sanguine. AAP figures showed that domestic book-publishing sales of adult paperbacks—a staple of consumer publishers—had grown only 1.8%. While any reports regarding children's books were likely to pale compared with 2003—which saw the publication of the phenomenally successful *Harry Potter and the Order of the Phoenix*—sales of children's and young-adult hardcover books were down 27.4%. Interestingly, and perhaps not surprisingly in a year in which "moral values" played such a prominent role in national debates, the AAP figures showed that the sales of religious books had grown 23.6%.

Entering the crucially important holiday period, the major chain book retailers reported very small increases in same-store sales, and both chain and independent booksellers were keeping their fingers crossed that early signs of an economic recovery would help fuel strong fourth-quarter book sales. According to the U.S. Census Bureau, as of September (the most recent figures available), year-to-date bookstore sales were up only 0.5% over 2003. For independents one of the bright spots of 2004 was the release of a report from Ipsos BookTrends that showed that in 2003 independent bookstores did well on a unit basis, with demand outpacing the overall trade-book industry. The independent/small-chain bookstore channel's market position reached a five-year share high of 16%, which was posted against a backdrop of a steady hold in overall consumer demand for general trade books compared with 2002 (the most recent figures available). Americans bought close to the same number of books in 2003—1,176,000,000—as they did in 2002—1,177,000,000. In 2003 independent bookstores secured 18% of total spending for trade books, up from 16% in 2002. Overall spending on books dropped about 2% in 2003—to $11 billion from $11.3 billion in 2002—according to Ipsos figures.

In a year of strong political interest, one issue found particular resonance. Opposition to the controversial Sec. 215 of the USA PATRIOT Act—which gave the FBI greatly expanded authority to search business records, including the records of bookstores and libraries—resulted in the collection in bookstores and libraries of almost 200,000 signatures on petitions calling for Congress "to restore readers' privacy rights." The petition drive was spearheaded by the American Booksellers Association, the American Library Association, the Association of American Publishers, and PEN American Center. (DAN CULLEN)

International. Confusion as to the desirability of resale price maintenance (RPM) in the newly enlarged European Union continued to hold sway in the book-publishing industry in 2004. The existing RPM exemption was due to expire at the end of December.

Publishing bodies in the U.K. continued to attempt to shut down book-piracy operations in India. In January one of India's biggest operations was closed down in Meerut, and 24,000 counterfeit volumes were confiscated; in April, Mumbai's (Bombay's) largest supplier of pirated books was arrested, and 15,000 titles were seized. Despite the fact that one in five books was counterfeit, prosecution had been unsuccessful.

Much of the book-publishing industry continued to be beset with falling sales and profitability. In August 2004, however, the Amsterdam-based multinational publisher Wolters Kluwer increased its share price after having implemented cost-cutting procedures, reduced its debt, and improved its corporate structures. Its much-improved cash-flow situation produced a resurgence of takeover activity.

At the end of November 2003, the Bundeskartellamt, the German antitrust body, finally approved the purchase of trade publisher Heyne by Bertelsmann subsidiary Random House Deutschland, subject to the sale of certain paperback interests to Sweden's Bonnier Group.

In January 2004, despite its previous opposition to Lagardère Group's attempt to take over Editis (the former Vivendi Universal Publishing), independent French publisher La Martinière announced its intention to take over its ally, Le Seuil, and thereby formed the third largest publishing house in France. This proposal in turn stirred up opposition from other independent publishers distributed by Le Seuil; they were fearful that the merged company would become overly focused on profitability.

In late February five bids were tabled for a majority stake in Dutch book and newspaper publisher PCM, which also owned Belgium's largest book publisher, Standaard Uitgeverij. An offer from Apax Partners to purchase a 52.5% stake was accepted. On March 1 Monaco-based Éditions du Rocher bought (for an undisclosed sum) French literary publisher Le Serpent à Plumes, with 400 titles on its backlist, from Éditions du Forum. That same day Ebury Press, part of Random House, acquired (for an undisclosed price) the 200 titles published by C.W. Daniel.

In November 2003 Taylor & Francis had acquired the Dekker Group of the U.S. for $138.6 million, as well as Swets & Zeitlinger Publishers for €16.75 million (€1 = about $1.24); Taylor & Francis continued to pursue its expansionary path, merging with business publisher Informa in May to create T&F Informa. In the all-share deal, T&F shareholders received 17 shares in the new company for every 10 existing T&F shares they held.

In April a bid worth £940 million (£1 = about $1.80) was tabled for the whole of WH Smith (including Hodder Headline) by venture group Permira. In August, however, WH Smith agreed to sell subsidiary Hodder Headline to Lagardère for £210 million in cash and an additional £13 million to shore up the pension fund.

In May, Wolters Kluwer sold 80% of its Dutch subsidiary ten Hagen & Stam (for an undisclosed sum in cash and shares) to legal and governmental publisher Sdu Uitgevers, a subsidiary of Sdu. Also in May, Lagardère put 60% of French publisher Editis up for sale, and this was acquired by Wendel Investissement for €660 million, thereby creating the second largest publishing group in France. (PETER CURWEN)

Military Affairs

U.S.-led operations in IRAQ and Afghanistan dominated MILITARY NEWS in 2004, but other conflicts in the Middle East, Africa, Asia, and Latin America also made headlines. Meanwhile, NATO expanded again, and European troops increased their PEACEKEEPING activities.

IRAQ

In 2004 the tactics of the year-old war in Iraq devolved into a classic guerrilla campaign fought with all its attendant misery. Although the forces of the U.S.-led coalition launched successful offensives in many cities, its troops continued to die steadily in small numbers as the result of hit-and-run attacks by Iraqi and foreign insurgents. Progress on the battlefield was marred by a series of widely publicized incidents that undercut support for the U.S.-led war at home and abroad. The first was the publication in April of appalling images of Iraqi prisoners being abused by U.S. troops at Abu Ghraib prison. (*See* Special Report.) Several U.S. soldiers were jailed for their part in the incidents, and Brig. Gen. Janis Karpinski, the officer in charge of the prison, was suspended. Prisoner abuse scandals also rocked the British, Danish, and Polish contingents in Iraq.

International support for the war shrank, and coalition partners Spain (1,300 troops), Honduras (370), Hungary (300), and the Philippines (51) withdrew their forces. Poland said that it would pull its 2,500 troops out after the January 2005 Iraqi elections. Australia, however, announced that it would add to the 850 troops it had already committed to Iraq. Successive attempts to uncover deposed Iraqi president Saddam Hussein's alleged stockpiles of weapons of mass destruction (WMD) yielded no conclusive evidence that any such weapons existed, and this failure also undermined international support for the war.

In April U.S. forces laid siege to the city of Fallujah in search of the perpetrators of the gruesome killings of four American civilian contractors. The operation failed, and U.S. troops eventually handed the city back to resistance forces. The siege of Fallujah and reports that hundreds of civilians had been killed sparked uprisings across the country. U.S. troops returned to Fallujah in November, however, and engaged in some of the most intense urban warfare they had experienced since the Vietnam War. The price for the U.S. was 51 dead and about 400 wounded in more than eight days of fighting. Some 1,200 Iraqi insurgents were killed, but there were no reliable estimates of civilian casualties.

By year's end the American military presence in Iraq had grown to nearly 150,000, the highest level since the invasion in 2003; the number of U.S. military dead had surpassed 1,300, and the U.K. had suffered 74 military deaths. The British medical journal *The Lancet* reported that the number of civilian deaths in Iraq could exceed 100,000, a figure far larger than estimates of 14,000–27,000 made by other agencies. (*See also* WORLD AFFAIRS: *Iraq:* Special Report).

WMD, ARMS CONTROL, AND DISARMAMENT

The foreign ministers of 42 countries issued a statement calling the entry into force of the 1996 Comprehensive Test Ban Treaty "more urgent today than ever before"; however, by 2004, 12 of the 44 states required for ratification of the treaty—including China, India, Iran, Israel, North Korea, Pakistan, and the United States—had not yet done so. Mohamed ElBaradei, director-general of the International Atomic Energy Agency (IAEA), said that he was certain that North Korea had processed enough spent nuclear fuel to make four to six nuclear bombs. Russian Pres. Vladimir Putin announced that his country was developing a new generation of nuclear-armed missiles. The U.S. Congress eliminated funding that Pres. George W. Bush had requested for research to develop a new generation of small nuclear weapons.

The charred bodies of foreign contract workers hang from a bridge over the Euphrates River in the city of Fallujah, west of Baghdad, as Iraqis chant anti-American slogans on March 31. The two workers, along with two others, had been killed when their SUVs were attacked.

AP/Wide World Photos

Following renunciation of its WMD programs in 2003, Libya ratified the Comprehensive Test-Ban Treaty. Libya also submitted initial declarations to the Organization for the Prohibition of Chemical Weapons (OPCW) and the IAEA. OPCW inspectors verified the destruction of Libya's stockpile of unfilled chemical weapons munitions, and IAEA inspectors were granted broader access to Libyan nuclear facilities. On April 28 the UN Security Council passed Resolution 1540, which called on all states to prevent terrorist groups and other nonstate actors from acquiring WMD and their means of delivery. India and Pakistan agreed in June to notify each other at least 24 hours in advance of missile test launches.

OTHER CONFLICTS

Russia. More than 330 people—nearly half of them children—died in September during the siege of a school in the town of Beslan in Russia's North Ossetian Republic. The siege was widely blamed on separatist Chechen rebels, and there was much public criticism that the death toll was unnecessarily high because Russian special forces troops had bungled the rescue. The attack in Beslan followed the midair destruction of two Russian civilian airliners in August that was blamed on Chechen women suicide-bombers. Akhmad Kadyrov, Chechnya's pro-Russian president, was killed in a massive bomb blast in Grozny in May.

Europe. The European Union began its largest-ever peacekeeping operation by taking command of forces in Bosnia and Herzegovina. The first of 7,000 EU Force (EUFOR) troops from more than 30 countries (including non-EU states Canada, Switzerland, and Turkey) began deploying across the country to maintain the nine-year-old peace agreement that had previously been supervised by NATO. Several hundred British, Italian, and U.S. troops were sent to reinforce the 17,500-strong German-led NATO Kosovo Force (KFOR) after rioting broke out between ethnic Albanians and Serbs. With 19 killed and hundreds injured, it was the worst violence Kosovo had seen since 1999.

Latin America and the Caribbean. Following formal peace talks with the Colombian government in November, 450 paramilitary fighters from the right-wing United Self-Defense Forces of Colombia (AUC) were demobilized. All 15,000 of the AUC's members were due to be disarmed by 2006, which would allow the government to concentrate on defeating the Marxist-led insurgency. The UN Stabilization Mission in Haiti (MINUSTAH) arrived in February after dozens of people were killed in violent demonstrations and Pres. Jean-Bertrand Aristide was forced to flee. MINUSTAH included troops from 20 countries and was led by 1,200 Brazilians, the largest contingent that country had ever contributed to a UN mission. It replaced a U.S.-led multinational force that had arrived after Aristide fled.

AP/Wide World Photos

British soldiers come under attack in Basra, Iraq, on March 22. Iraqis protesting the lack of jobs and the Israeli assassination of Hamas founder Sheikh Ahmed Yassin threw Molotov cocktails at the soldiers.

Middle East. Israel credited construction of the first quarter of a 720-km (450-mi) security barrier separating it from much of the occupied West Bank with having dramatically lowered the number of Palestinian suicide bombings in 2004. Israeli forces mounted major operations in Gaza in which dozens of Palestinians were killed and hundreds wounded. Israel said the actions were mounted in response to Palestinian militants who fired mortar shells and rockets at Jewish settlements as well as firing on Israeli army convoys. Government troops in Yemen battled supporters of dissident cleric Hussein al-Houthi in the north of the country; estimates of the dead ranged from 80 to more than 600. Al-Houthi was reportedly killed in September.

South and Central Asia. Three years after the U.S.-led coalition invaded Afghanistan, the search for Osama bin Laden and Taliban leader Mullah Mohammed Omar continued to prove fruitless. With about 18,000 troops (16,500 of them U.S.), the coalition launched offensives around the country to eliminate remnants of the former Taliban regime and al-Qaeda extremists. Foreign-aid workers and local government officials were subject to numerous attacks and kidnappings around the country, however. A Franco-German-led unit called Eurocorps took over command of NATO's International Security Assistance Force (ISAF) in Afghanistan. Fielding about 6,500 troops, ISAF concentrated its efforts on providing security in the capital, Kabul, but also sent provincial reconstruction teams to conduct humanitarian and development work in other parts of the country.

About 25,000 Pakistani troops searched the mountainous border region near Afghanistan for foreign militants and Pakistani supporters of al-Qaeda. (*See* WORLD AFFAIRS: *Pakistan:* map.) The offensive sparked a backlash from local tribesmen and religious groups, however, and dozens of soldiers and hundreds of militants were reported killed.

India began withdrawing 40,000 of the half million troops it had stationed in Jammu and Kashmir, where it had been battling Islamic independence groups since 1989. Despite objections from Pakistan, India completed a 550-km (330-mi) electrified fence along the Line of Control separating Indian-controlled Jammu and Kashmir from Pakistan. Nepalese Maoist rebels staged a weeklong blockade of Kathmandu that stopped supplies from reaching the city.

Southeast Asia. Indonesia extended martial law in its troubled province of Aceh. The government said that it had killed 2,000 rebels of the separatist Free Aceh Movement since it began offensives in the province in 2003. Violent clashes between security forces and Islamist militants in the south of Thailand left hundreds of people dead and led to the establishment of martial law in the largely Muslim region. U.S. combat troops, ships, and aircraft were central to the tsunami relief efforts in the Indian Ocean area in late December, and their rapid deployment for humanitarian goals helped improve foreign perceptions of U.S. global military might and operational efficiency.

Africa. Simmering tensions in Africa's Great Lakes region were reignited when Congolese rebels, allegedly backed by Rwanda, seized a town in the eastern Democratic Republic of the Congo

(continued on page 252)

POWs and the Global War on Terrorism

by Peter Saracino

The conduct of the parties in the global war on terrorism declared by the United States and the war in Iraq stirred up great controversy in 2004. The applicability of the accepted rules of war to these conflicts came under special scrutiny. Once the invasion of Afghanistan began in October 2001, the administration of Pres. George W. Bush declared that captured members of the al-Qaeda terrorist organization were "unlawful combatants" who had no right to protection under international law. Furthermore, such persons could be held indefinitely without formal charges under powers that Congress granted the president to fight terrorism. The administration also said it would apply the Geneva Conventions to soldiers of Afghanistan's deposed Taliban regime but would not grant them status as prisoners of war (POWs; combatants who surrendered or were unable to fight owing to illness or wounds and were captured by their enemy). Since that time, more than 600 persons captured in Afghanistan and elsewhere had been detained in a U.S. military facility at Guantánamo Bay, Cuba. The detainees included nationals of more than 30 countries, including the U.K., France, and Australia.

In March 2003 the U.S. led an invasion of Iraq to depose dictator Saddam Hussein. By the time President Bush declared an end to major combat operations in May 2003, coalition forces were holding more than 7,000 Iraqi POWs. Their fate and that of combatants captured since then became a global issue after photographs of U.S. soldiers abusing prisoners in Abu Ghraib prison near Baghdad were published starting in April 2004. During the furor that ensued, more evidence came to light that prisoners held by the U.S. in various locations had been beaten, sexually assaulted, deprived of sleep and medical attention, frightened by dogs, and subjected to other forms of intimidation, humiliation, and abuse. These acts were part of interrogations, supposedly to get prisoners to reveal useful information about terrorist activities. The existence of "ghost detainees"—so called because their identities and locations were being kept secret, potentially in contravention of international law—was also reported.

Andres Leighton/Associated Press

The Law of Prisoners. Warfare has always contained an element of lawlessness, and POWs are among the most vulnerable of its victims. In ancient times it was common for POWs to be killed, tortured, or enslaved. By the 17th century, POWs had come to be regarded as prisoners of the detaining state and not the property of individual captors. It was not until 1899, with the signing of the First Hague Convention, however, that the international community agreed to codify rules for safeguarding POWs against neglect and mistreatment. Though these rules were strengthened somewhat in the Second Hague Convention of 1907, they still proved to be inadequate protection for POWs during World War I. Despite numerous reports of POWs' having been abused, little effort was made after 1918 to punish those responsible.

The Third Geneva Convention was drafted in 1929 specifically to address issues surrounding the treatment of POWs. (The First Geneva Convention [1864] dealt with the care of wounded soldiers; a second convention covered warfare at sea.) The 1929 convention made it illegal to torture POWs and stated that a prisoner was required to provide only his or her name, date of birth, rank, and service number (if applicable). Prisoners also had to be supplied food sufficient to keep them in good health, adequate clothing, and medical care, and they were to be protected against violence, degrading or humiliating treatment, and public curiosity. The convention also called for POWs to be released and repatriated without delay once hostilities had ended. Another important measure to ensure humane treatment of prisoners, visits by the International Committee of the Red Cross, was stipulated under the convention, and the detaining government was enjoined to follow the ICRC's advice.

The Third Geneva Convention was in force during World War II. Because Japan and the Soviet Union had not signed it, however, both states declared that they were not required to treat POWs according to its rules. This led to widespread abuses and retaliation by Nazi Germany against Soviet prisoners under its control. After the war many German and Japanese officers were tried and convicted for the maltreatment and murder of POWs.

The Third Geneva Convention was revised in 1949, and a fourth section was added to protect civilians. The entire set is currently referred to as the "Geneva Conventions of 1949" or, more commonly, the "Geneva Conventions." Together these form the basis of modern international humanitarian law (also known as the laws of war), and 192 countries—including Afghanistan, Iraq, and the U.S.—are parties to them. In 1977 two protocols were added to the Geneva Conventions that significantly altered the criteria of eligibility for POW status, but Afghanistan, Iraq, and the U.S. were not signatories.

The Geneva Conventions. The Geneva Conventions divide all persons in an armed conflict into two categories: combatants and civilians. Combatants are authorized to fight in accordance with the laws of war on behalf of a party to the conflict. Civilians are not authorized to fight but are protected from deliberate targeting by combatants as

In this undated photo—one of the iconic images of 2004 from Abu Ghraib prison—an Iraqi prisoner is shown hooded and handcuffed to a railing.

long as they do not take up arms. Under the Geneva Conventions, parties to an armed conflict have the right to capture and intern enemy combatants as well as civilians who pose a danger to the security of the state. Enemy combatants are not presumed to be guilty of any crime; rather, they are detained to remove them as a threat on the battlefield. The detaining power has the right to punish enemy soldiers and civilians for crimes committed prior to their capture as well as during captivity, but only after a fair trial in accordance with applicable international law. The Geneva Conventions stipulate that POWs should be tried in a military court unless the existing laws of the detaining power permit trials of its own military personnel in a civil court for the same offense. POWs have the right to defense by a qualified advocate or counsel of his or her own choice, to the calling of witnesses, and, if he or she deems it necessary, to the services of a competent interpreter. For example, former Panamanian leader Gen. Manuel Noriega was given a 30-year prison term for drug trafficking and other crimes even though he was a POW captured during the U.S. invasion of Panama in 1989. According to the ICRC, all detainees taken in war are protected by the Geneva Conventions, and violations of the accords may constitute either war crimes or crimes against humanity.

To be considered POWs under the Geneva Conventions, detainees must fall under one of these categories:

1. Members of the regular armed forces of a party to the conflict or of militias or volunteer corps forming part of such armed forces
2. Members of other militias or other volunteer corps, including those of organized resistance movements, as long as they: (a) are part of an identifiable command structure; (b) have fixed distinctive insignia recognizable at a distance; (c) carry their arms openly; (d) conduct their operations in accordance with the laws of war
3. Members of regular armed forces who profess allegiance to a government or an authority not recognized by the detaining power
4. Inhabitants of a nonoccupied territory who have spontaneously taken up arms to resist an invading force, provided that they carry arms openly and respect the laws of war.

The Geneva Conventions state that should any doubt arise as to whether detainees fit these categories, they "shall enjoy the protection of the present convention" until "their status has been determined by a competent tribunal." Also, precedents can be set that expand or reinforce definitions. During the Korean War the U.S. and its allies treated Chinese detainees as POWs even though the People's Republic of China was not yet recognized diplomatically. Also, Viet Cong guerrillas captured by the U.S. during the Vietnam War were given POW status despite the fact that they often wore civilian clothing with no insignia and did not carry their arms openly.

New Interpretations. In June 2004 the U.S. Supreme Court ruled that terrorism suspects, including the prisoners held at Guantánamo Bay, have a right to question their detention in U.S. courts. The military began establishing tribunals in July to determine the status of suspects accused of being unlawful combatants; however, the suspects were permitted only military representatives and not their own personal civilian lawyers. In September it was reported that the U.S. Army was revising its basic interrogation manual to bring it more in line with accepted international standards. Judge James Robertson ruled in November that President Bush had overstepped his constitutional bounds and improperly skirted the Geneva Conventions in establishing military commissions to try detainees at Guantánamo as war criminals. The High Court in the United Kingdom ruled in December that British troops anywhere in the world could be tried under the Human Rights Act for abusing prisoners in their custody. Danish Defense Minister Søren Gade recalled several army officers serving in Iraq following investigations into the abuse of prisoners. Allegations of abuses by Polish troops were also being investigated.

Peter Saracino is a freelance defense journalist.

(continued from page 249)
(DRC). Rwandan troops were said to have entered the DRC, attacked villages, and forced thousands of civilians to flee.

Nine French peacekeepers and dozens of civilians were killed in Côte d'Ivoire after an 18-month cease-fire broke down. France had approximately 5,000 troops stationed in the West African country, and they, along with 6,000 UN peacekeepers, monitored a buffer zone between the rebel-held north and the loyalist south. Following the clashes, more than 9,000 Westerners were forced to flee the country.

Sudanese government forces moved to suppress a rebel uprising in the western region of Darfur and displaced at least 100,000 civilians in the process. The UN reported that pro-government Arab militias, called Janjawid, were systematically killing non-Arab villagers. By September, U.S. Secretary of State Colin Powell had applied the term *genocide* to the situation amid reports that more than 70,000 people had been killed in Darfur and 1,500,000 others made refugees, with as many as 200,000 seeking safety in neighbouring Chad. Earlier in the year, the Sudanese government had concluded a peace deal with non-Muslim rebels in the south of the country, ending a civil war that had begun in 1983 and cost nearly 2,000,000 lives.

MILITARY TECHNOLOGY

Many of the coalition casualties in Iraq resulted from the insurgents' using remotely detonated improvised explosives, so the U.S. Army rushed into service robotic devices called unmanned ground vehicles. One type, the Omni-Directional Inspection System (ODIS), replaced the traditional method of inspecting the underside of a vehicle with a hand-held mirror. The 18-kg (40-lb), 10-cm (4-in) ODIS allowed troops to conduct vehicle inspections from more than 100 m (330 ft) away. A joint U.S.-Israeli program tested the Mobile Tactical High Energy Laser by successfully shooting down seven mortar rounds in flight, the first time a laser weapon had demonstrated this capability.

The U.S. Navy commissioned the first of a new class of nuclear-powered fast-attack submarines in October. The USS *Virginia* cost $2.2 billion to build and was billed as the most advanced submarine in the world. The *Virginia*-class submarine was the first in the U.S. fleet designed to operate in littoral waters and to support special forces operations. It was also equipped with interchangeable multimission modules, which allowed it to conduct various types of warfare. China launched the first of a new class of ballistic-missile submarines. The Type 094 would provide China with its first truly intercontinental nuclear-missile-delivery capability. The Swedish navy began testing what it believed to be the stealthiest ship in the world. The Visby corvette, designed and built by shipbuilder Kockums, had a highly camouflaged hull comprising a PVC core with a carbon fibre and vinyl laminate. The material combined high strength and rigidity with low weight and was difficult to detect with radar or magnetic sensors.

The U.S. Air Force declared operational its new Counter Satellite Communications System, which was designed to jam enemy satellite communications. The ground-based system used electromagnetic energy to disrupt transmissions without permanently damaging or destroying enemy satellites. Proponents of the system said that it would help U.S. forces control space without creating debris that could threaten friendly satellites or manned spacecraft. For the first time, an unmanned combat aircraft delivered a precision-guided bomb on target without human assistance. The U.S.'s developmental X-45A successfully dropped an inert Global Positioning System-guided bomb from 10,500 m (35,000 ft), striking within a few centimetres of the truck it had been preprogrammed to hit. A human operator 125 km (80 mi) away authorized the bombing but did not participate directly in it.

The first six Ground-Based Interceptor missiles of the U.S. Ballistic Missile Defense System were installed in their underground silos at Ft. Greely, Alaska. The system was to have been declared operational by the end of 2004 but with a "limited capability" to destroy ballistic missiles targeted at the U.S.; however, following the failure of a test launch in December, the announcement was deferred until 2005.

MILITARY AND SOCIETY

In the biggest expansion of the alliance since its creation in 1949, NATO welcomed seven former communist countries as members. The addition of Bulgaria, Estonia, Latvia, Lithuania, Romania, Slovakia, and Slovenia raised membership to a total of 26 states. Defense ministers from the EU states agreed to create a rapid-reaction force that could be deployed on short notice to hot spots around the world. The total force would comprise about 18,000 troops, with each country contributing units of up to 2,000. In a change to long-standing policy, the government of the United Kingdom announced that Commonwealth citizens serving in sensitive military posts would have to take British citizenship in order to keep their jobs.

Germany announced that it would close 105 military bases as part of a major plan to modernize the military and save up to €200 million ($250 million). The armed forces were to be reduced from 285,000 personnel to 250,000, and the civilian staff was to be cut as well. The Czech government abolished conscription and thereby created a fully professional force of 35,000 men and women and brought to an end the 136-year-old tradition of compulsory military service first introduced in 1868 by the Austro-Hungarian monarchy.

India and Russia signed their largest military contract since the collapse of the Soviet Union. The $1.6 billion deal included the refurbishment and transfer of the mothballed aircraft carrier *Admiral Gorshkov* as well as its outfitting with MiG-29K combat aircraft and helicopters. The carrier was due to be handed over to India in 2008.

Reportedly, in the first nine months of 2004, more than 900 Russian service members died, the majority from causes other than combat. Russia's defense minister admitted that over 500 personnel had died while off duty, about 25% of them by committing suicide. HIV/AIDS had infected one in four soldiers in the South African National Defence Force, and the country's ability to contribute troops to UN peacekeeping missions was severely handicapped. A program to provide infected soldiers and their families with free antiretroviral drugs began in February.

On a trial basis the Israel Defense Force revived the venerable Camel Corps, which had been disbanded in the 1970s, to patrol the desert border with Egypt. It was determined that mounted camel patrols were the best means to thwart smugglers taking drugs, prostitutes, and weapons into Israel.

In August the Bush administration announced the biggest change in the basing of U.S. forces overseas since the end of the Cold War. Once fully implemented, the plan would establish new foreign bases but also transfer up to 70,000 troops and 100,000 family members back to the United States.

(PETER SARACINO)

Performing Arts

In a year of POLITICS and MILITARY actions, the performing arts showed RESILIENCE and innovation: music featured NEW and OLD works alike; dance remembered BALANCHINE and ASHTON; theatre homed in on CURRENT events; and in the movie houses BIOPICS made a strong comeback.

MUSIC

Classical Music. One of the hallmarks of Western classical music is its sheer resilience, its ability to renew and refresh itself as an art form even as its core repertoire continues to speak—over years, decades, and centuries—to the soul and intellect of humankind. This resilience is manifest in many ways, many of which were illustrated in the year 2004 in classical music.

In the spring, while scholars were preparing the art exhibit *Botticelli and Filippino: Grace and Passion in 15th Century Florentine Painting* in Florence, a music specialist from the University of Toronto noticed that the notes on a scroll in Filippino Lippi's painting *Madonna and Child with Singing Angels* corresponded to an actual Renaissance song. When that song was transcribed and performed at Florence's Palazzo Strozzi at the start of the exhibit, it marked the first time that "Fortuna desperata" had been heard in 500 years. In January, Ottorino Respighi's opera *Marie Victoire,* which was written before World War I, received its world premiere at the Rome Opera House. When it was presented in October in Essen, Ger., Felix Mendelssohn's comic opera *The Uncle from Boston* was heard for the first time since the composer created it in 1823, at age 14. A four-minute work for organ, *Voluntary on Tallis's Lamentations,* written by Benjamin Britten in 1940, debuted at the London Proms; and a 40-second piece by Edward Elgar, *Smoking Cantata,* received its world premiere in a broadcast by the BBC Radio 4 program *Today.* These pieces had been discovered in various European archives in recent years. Other works that had been seemingly lost to the world were similarly recovered, including a wedding cantata by Johann Sebastian Bach, which had been missing for 80 years, and the manuscript of Sergey Rachmaninoff's *Symphony No. 2,* which had disappeared shortly after the composer wrote it in 1908.

Even as older pieces were being reborn, new works were being heard for the first time. Following the success of his first opera, *Dead Man Walking,* in 2000, composer Jake Heggie unveiled his next, *The End of the Affair,* at the Houston (Texas) Grand Opera in March. Other operas receiving premieres included Ishmael Wallace's *The Stranger,* Grigori Frid's *The Diary of Anne Frank,* and William Bolcom's *A Wedding;* the last made its debut as part of the commemorations of the 50th anniversary season of the Lyric Opera of Chicago. Fittingly, given the subject, in Jon Gibson's opera *Violet Fire,* based on the life of magnetism-and-electricity mastermind Nikola Tesla, performers were wired with microphones and the energy waves from their bodies were picked up and telecast onto an onstage video screen during the debut in February.

Anna Christy and Patrick Miller star in the premiere of William Bolcom's opera A Wedding, *from the 1978 Robert Altman movie of the same name.*

AP/Wide World Photos

New instrumental works were also presented for the first time, among them Elliott Carter's *Dialogues* (which the composer described as "a conversation between the soloist and the orchestra"), George Walker's *Sinfonia No. 3,* and Sir Harrison Birtwistle's *Night's Black Bird.* Even as these and other new works were appearing, announcements were being made about works that loomed tantalizingly on the horizon. British composer John Tavener, whose pieces traditionally drew heavily from his Russian Orthodox faith, told the media that in 2005 he would premiere a new choral work based on the 99 names for God in Islam. The first complete performance of Karlheinz Stockhausen's 29-hour-long *Licht* operatic cycle was scheduled to be presented in 2008 in a €10 million (about $13.3 million) production.

In a unique attempt to keep new pieces in the repertoire, conductor Sir Simon Rattle announced that he would be the patron of the Encore project, in which works that had recently received their premieres but had since gone unperformed would be revisited by London's Royal Philharmonic Orchestra over the next four years. Not content only to reinvigorate newer works, Rattle offered a singular slant on one of the warhorses of the classical repertoire, Igor Stravinsky's 1913 watershed work *Le Sacre du printemps,* by adding surrealistic visuals to his performance of the piece at the Berlin Film Festival in February. The English National Opera announced that it had commissioned the Asian Dub Foundation, a group of pop-electronica artists, to write an opera about Libyan leader Muammar al-Qaddafi, which would debut in 2006. Meanwhile, in Halberstadt, Ger., an intrepid group of musicians added two notes to their performance of John Cage's *Organ²*/ASLSP (ASLSP being an abbreviation of Cage's instruction that performance of the piece be "as slow as possible"), which was scheduled to continue on a semiannual basis for the next 639 years (in the next installment, in March 2006, two notes were to be subtracted).

Various musical milestones were also marked and celebrated in 2004. In March Italian tenor Luciano Pavarotti, arguably the most famous classical music artist of his generation, gave his final performance on the operatic stage in a production of Giacomo Puccini's *Tosca* at New York City's Metropolitan Opera. At the end of that performance, Pavarotti's 379th with the company, the sold-out audience gave him an 11-minute standing ovation. In February the Met's general manager, Joseph Volpe, announced his retirement from the company that he had led for 40 years; his successor, record executive Peter Gelb, was named later in the year. Without relinquishing his post as the Met's music director, conductor James Levine raised his baton at a concert in October as the first U.S.-born music director of the Boston Symphony Orchestra. On December 7 Milan's newly renovated La Scala had a gala reopening with a production of Antonio Salieri's *Europa riconosciuta,* which had not been performed since it was commissioned for the opera house's original opening in 1778.

The London Symphony Orchestra celebrated its 100th season, while Chicago enjoyed two 100-year commemorations—of Orchestra Hall, the home of the Chicago Symphony Orchestra, and of the Ravinia Festival, for which the New York Philharmonic gave a special performance. The original members of the Guarneri String Quartet reunited for a tour that marked the ensemble's 40th anniversary. Conductor Gerard Schwarz was honoured for his 20th anniversary with the Seattle (Wash.) Symphony Orchestra, and Kent Nagano was offered accolades for his 25th year at the helm of the Berkeley (Calif.) Symphony Orchestra. Seiji Ozawa, for 29 years, until 2002, the director of the Boston Symphony Orchestra, returned from his post at the Vienna State Opera to the Tanglewood Festival in Massachusetts to take part in a performance marking the 10th anniversary of the concert hall that was named for him.

Gustav Mahler figured prominently in the classical music categories at the year's Grammy Awards. Recordings of his *Symphony No. 3* won separate Grammys for best classical album (by Michael Tilson Thomas and the San Francisco Symphony) and best orchestral performance (by Pierre Boulez and the Vienna Philharmonic). At the same ceremony, iconic American pianist Van Cliburn was honoured with an award for lifetime achievement. New Tonalist composer Paul Moravec's *Tempest Fantasy*—based on William Shakespeare's *The Tempest*—won the Pulitzer Prize for music, while film composer John Williams and diva Joan Sutherland were among the recipients of the year's Kennedy Center Honors presented by Pres. George W. Bush and first lady Laura Bush at the White House in December. Czech mezzo-soprano Magdalena Kozena was named artist of the year at the 27th annual Gramophone Awards in London in October. The young Chinese piano sensation Lang Lang (*see* BIOGRAPHIES) was named a UNICEF goodwill ambassador in May.

Other milestones of a sadder sort occurred as well. The world of film and musicals lost Oscar-winning composer Jerry Goldsmith in July, Elmer Bernstein and David Raksin in August, and lyricist Fred Ebb in September; among conductors, Iona Brown died in June, Carlos Kleiber passed in July, and Hans Vonk was taken by Lou Gehrig's disease in August; Italian soprano Renata Tebaldi died in December; French baritone Gérard Souzay died in August, and American baritone Robert Merrill succumbed in October (a loss for the world of baseball as well as opera, as Merrill sang the national anthem on opening day at Yankee Stadium every year); Indian sitar player and composer Vilayat Hussein Khan died in March; and the Israeli composer Naomi Sapir Shemer, who wrote inspirational and art songs, died in June. (*See* OBITUARIES.)

The year was not without other moments that ranged from the eccentric and frivolous to the downright comic. Bugs Bunny turned up on a video screen at a concert in August to "conduct" the Cleveland (Ohio) Orchestra in a program that included such classical favourites as *What's Opera, Doc?* and *The Rabbit of Seville.* The concert, dubbed *Bugs Bunny on Broadway,* drew the largest audience of the orchestra's summer season. String players of the Bonn (Ger.) Beethoven Orchestra were not kidding, however, when they sued the orchestra in March. The musicians maintained that the string players had more notes to play than their counterparts on other instruments and that they therefore deserved a pay raise. There was, as usual, the yearly controversy at the Bayreuth Festival in Bavaria. This time it involved a dispute between Christoph Schlingensief, who was directing a production of Richard Wagner's *Parsifal,* which was booed by the opening-night audience, and his leading tenor, Endrik Wottrich. The former charged that the latter was a racist because he allegedly objected to having black singers in the cast; Wottrich responded by calling Schlingensief a "Nazi." Diva Elisabeth Schwarzkopf went both of them one better (or worse), however, by admitting that she *had been* a member of the Nazi Party during the Hitler era. In her memoirs, *Les Autres Soirs,* published in July, Schwarzkopf wrote that she joined the party in the 1930s as "a strictly administrative gesture."

A documentary that debuted in September speculated that Wolfgang Amadeus Mozart, the legendarily foul-mouthed and uncouth musical genius, might have suffered from Tourette syndrome, an inherited neurological disorder that can cause involuntary grunting and other vocal tics as well as a compulsion to utter obscenities. Scientists in Salzburg, Austria, began the process of unearthing the bodies of Mozart's father, maternal grandmother, and niece to glean DNA samples that might prove that a skull at the city's International Mozarteum Foundation was that of the composer himself.

Great Britain, however, was the stage for the year's most celebrated musical flap. In March American soprano Deborah Voigt was dropped from a production of Richard Strauss's *Ariadne auf Naxos* because her girth was deemed too substantial to fit into one of the costumes. Wags weighed in with all manner of bad jokes, but the incident also raised serious artistic questions, such as whether operatic heroines necessarily had to be fashion-model svelte.

Their foibles notwithstanding, the music makers of 2004 outdid themselves with the music they made. The year included a wealth of recordings that brought new life to a wide range of works. Nagano led 200 performers in an incisive recording of Leonard Bernstein's stylistically sprawling *Mass* (Harmonia Mundi), while Ozawa offered elegant readings of Olivier Messiaen's *Turangalila Symphony* and *Vingt regards sur l'Enfant-Jésus* (RCA).

Nikolaus Harnoncourt revealed new aspects of the young Mozart's budding genius in his set of the composer's *Mozart: Early Symphonies* (Deutsche Harmonia Mundi), and violinist Nigel Kennedy displayed his impassioned virtuosity on *Vivaldi II* (EMI). Two recordings released by RCA provided new insights into two of the greatest masters. A new addition to the label's re-Discovered series featured recordings that the 19-year-old Itzhak Perlman had made for his debut record in 1965. The recordings, which were shelved at the time, were finally released in 2004. They documented the intensity and abandon of the young violinist at the start of his illustrious career. The fabled voice of tenor Enrico Caruso finally received the orchestral accompaniment it was originally denied on gramophone recordings, owing to technological limitations in the early 20th century. On *Caruso: amor ti vieta: Great Opera Arias,* the original recordings with piano accompaniment were augmented by a modern orchestra, and 21st-century listeners were thereby allowed to hear Caruso as his contemporaries had in the concert halls of his day. These recordings, like so much else that came to life—or back to life—in 2004, captured the timelessness not only of the music itself but also of those who served it. (HARRY SUMRALL)

Jazz. The deaths of Ray Charles, Malachi Favors, Elvin Jones, and Steve Lacy left the jazz world reeling in 2004. (*See* OBITUARIES.) The most popular of jazz artists, usually accompanied by large and small bands of top musicians, Charles soloed on piano and organ in instrumental albums, more famed as the most distinctive of singers, he crossed pop-music borders with rare swinging freedom and originality. The losses of the other three men were felt especially keenly because they were crucial figures in the evolution of the jazz avant-garde in the 1960s and '70s. The passionate drummer Jones, the lyric soprano saxophone explorer Lacy, and the uniquely sensitive yet potent bassist Favors offered shattering innovations that exerted major influences on the jazz idiom.

Despite obviously failing health, Jones, whose polyrhythms had ignited a revolution in jazz percussion, insisted on leading groups in clubs and concerts almost to the end of his life. Lacy, who taught at the New England Conservatory of Music, Boston, while suffering from cancer, performed settings of poems by Beat Generation poets in 2004, when he also debuted his Monksieland band. Monksieland was an experimental quintet in which Lacy, trumpeter Dave Douglas, trombonist Roswell Rudd, bassist Jean-Jacques Avenel, and drummer John Betsch interpreted Thelonious Monk songs in a new Dixieland-influenced collective-improvisational manner.

© 2004 Jack Vartoogian/FrontRowPhotos

Bassist Henry Grimes performs at New York City's Vision Festival in May as he continues with the remarkable resurrection of his career after a 35-year disappearance.

The loss of Favors, the senior musician among these three, might have been most painful. He was the heartbeat of the Art Ensemble of Chicago, which had stayed together for more than three decades. The 1999 death of trumpeter Lester Bowie was devastating to the Art Ensemble; three original members—Favors, saxophonist Roscoe Mitchell, and drummer Famoudou Don Moye—persisted, and in 2003 saxophonist Joseph Jarman returned. It was Favors, however, who was essential to their singular, shared perceptions of musical form, line, and colour; after bassist Jaribu Shahid replaced him, the group added trumpeter Corey Wilkes and percussionist Baba Sissoko and struggled to forge a new Art Ensemble style.

This new Art Ensemble of Chicago toured Europe and played at Iridium, the Broadway nightclub where Cecil Taylor presented his Orchestra Humaine in March. It was a rare appearance for this fiery big band, which improvised wildly on suites of Taylor themes; the occasion was the pianist-leader's 75th birthday. Henry Grimes, an important bassist of the 1960s who had emerged from decades of self-imposed obscurity in 2003, advanced his second jazz career with European tours and appearances at New York's Vision Festival. At the same festival, the Revolutionary Ensemble ended its 27-year retirement; this pioneering violin-bass-drums trio also debuted a CD, *And Now . . .* (Pi), and had its rarest album, *The Psyche* (Mutable Music), reissued in 2004.

Among other highlights, nearly two million people flocked to the 25th Montreal Jazz Festival, which concluded with a performance by Cirque de Soliel. Trumpeter Wynton Marsalis led the Lincoln Center Jazz Orchestra at the grand opening of Jazz at Lincoln Center, possibly the grandest jazz spa of all. Located on New York City's Columbus Circle, it included a main hall with more than 1,000 seats, a smaller theatre with 420–500 seats, and a nightclub named Dizzy's Club Coca-Cola, where the Dizzy Gillespie Festival was held in the autumn. Two nights before the opening, PBS broadcast its *Live from Lincoln Center* television show from the new building. Meanwhile, trumpeter Jon Faddis, who had led the now-defunct Carnegie Hall Jazz Band, was named director of the Chicago Jazz Ensemble, based at that city's Columbia College. The Chicago Jazz Philharmonic, a project with some 55 players, played compositions by yet another trumpeter-leader, Orbert Davis, in its premiere performance at the Chicago Jazz Festival.

The Chicago festival also introduced American audiences to Ten Part Invention, drummer John Pochee's all-star 10-piece Australian band, which featured compositions by noted saxophonist Sandy Evans. A 10-piece all-star British jazz band led by another drummer, Charlie Watts of the Rolling Stones, offered the album *Watts at Scott's.* Meanwhile, in reaction to the U.S.-led Iraq war and the administration of Pres. George W. Bush, Charlie Haden unveiled his new Liberation Music Orchestra, with scores by Carla Bley; "We play for peace," stated Haden, who had led previous LMOs during the Vietnam War and the First Gulf War. Colourist composer Maria Schneider bypassed the ongoing crisis in the recording industry by selling her orchestra album *Concert in the Garden* only on the Internet; she was the most prominent of the jazz artists signed to ArtistShare.com.

Two important essay collections, *Jazz in Search of Itself* by Larry Kart and *Living with Jazz* by Dan Morgenstern, were published in 2004. Among other new recordings were pianist Marilyn

Crispell's *Storyteller* and singer Diana Krall's *The Girl in the Other Room*, with songs composed by herself and husband Elvis Costello. Quite the most extraordinary of the year's recording projects was *Holy Ghost*, a heavy box of 10 CDs culled from private and broadcast recordings from 1962–70 by the tragic revolutionary tenor saxophonist Albert Ayler. The box included a book of commentary, reproductions of posters from the period, writings by Ayler, and a pressed flower.

The Kabell Years: 1971–1979 collected valuable solo trumpet and ensemble works by Wadada Leo Smith. *All Music* by Warne Marsh, *All-Star Swing Sessions* by Bud Freeman, and a boxed set, *The Complete Roy Eldridge Verve Studio Sessions*, were some of the year's other outstanding reissues. The jazz world in 2004 also mourned the loss of clarinetist Artie Shaw, tenor saxophonist Illinois Jacquet, and guitarist Barney Kessel. (*See* OBITUARIES.) Other deaths during the year were those of violinist-guitarist Claude Williams and drummer Walter Perkins. (JOHN LITWEILER)

Popular. *International.* The year 2004 was brimming with music from the arid wasteland of the Sahara in North Africa. The most intriguing release came from Tinariwen, a band from northern Mali that had learned to play while exiled in the refugee camps of Libya at a time when the Tuareg people were in armed revolt against the Malian government. Tinariwen claimed that at least one member of the band had gone into battle with a guitar on one shoulder and an AK-47 on the other. With the war over, the group returned home and became global stars. Their much-praised album *Amassakoul* was based on slinky, bluesy guitar riffs with an Arabic edge, along with a dash of reggae, chanting vocals, and even a demonstration of Malian toasting and rap. Onstage they wore long desert robes, and for one of their more memorable concerts during the year, they were joined onstage in London by Taj Mahal, the veteran American blues guitarist, for a rousing display of the links between African styles and the blues.

It was also a good year for artists from Algeria. Rachid Taha argued that there were also links between North African styles and rock, and his album *Tekitoi* mixed North African influences with an attack worthy of the punk era. The standout track "Rock el Casbah" was a reworking of the Clash song "Rock the Casbah"; this time the wailing desert flutes were mixed with guitar riffs. Khaled, one of the best-selling artists across the Arabic-speaking world, took a very different approach with his album *Ya-Rayi*. In the past he had mixed *rai*, an Arabic pop music, with anything from hip-hop to funk and reggae, but in his new album he produced a lighter set, influenced by his early days in Algeria; Khaled incorporated the oud (a stringed instrument) and his own work on mandolin and accordion, along with an Egyptian string section.

The Tuareg band Tinariwen from northern Mali played in concerts on world stages in 2004 and released an acclaimed second album, Amassakoul.

© Eric Mullet

Egyptian musicians—famous across North Africa—were much in demand. Youssou N'Dour of Senegal produced a highly experimental album, *Egypt*, in which he moved away from the local *mbalax* dance styles and pop ballads to record music in praise of Islam and to explore the musical links between Senegal and Egypt. The result was an album of swirling Egyptian strings, drums, and flutes that was matched against his distinctive, powerful vocals.

There was more such experimental fusion work from Latin America, where two of the best new albums came from female Mexican singers who incorporated influences from north of the border. Mexican American Lhasa de Sela (known simply as Lhasa) released *The Living Road*, an unusual, compelling set of songs that made use of anything from Mexican dance themes to European balladry. Lhasa made her home in Quebec and sang in Spanish, French, and English. Lila Downs, another singer and songwriter of both Mexican and American parentage, produced *Una Sangre*, which mixed Mexican influences with jazz and American folk-blues and included a remarkably fresh reworking of the well-worn favourite "La Bamba."

From Europe there was more interesting fusion work from Spanish singer Amparo Sánchez, leader of the band Amparanoia. Her album *Rebeldia con alegria* mixed Cuban rhythms with songs by her friend Manu Chao and cheerful political anthems. If the sassy Sánchez shook up Spanish music, then the veteran Enzo Avitabile did the same for Italy. His latest venture involved a percussion section bashing away at enormous wine barrels—a tradition that dated back to medieval times. The sound was extraordinary, and on his album *Save the World* he persuaded African musicians, including Khaled, to participate.

In Great Britain the much-praised teenage soul star Joss Stone topped the album charts with *Mind Body and Soul*, but at the prestigious Mercury Music Prize awards, she was beaten by Glaswegian guitar band Franz Ferdinand. The Kinks' songwriter Ray Davies was shot by a mugger in New Orleans but recovered to give a series of rousing concerts celebrating the 40th anniversary of the Kinks' song "You Really Got Me"—which again became a best seller. Australian pop singer Kylie Minogue (*see* BIOGRAPHIES), who was also a favourite in Britain, won her first Grammy, for best dance recording, with "Come into My World."

Among the deaths during the year were those of Colombian drummer Batata, Jamaican record producer and entrepreneur Coxsone Dodd, and French singer Claude Nougaro. (*See* OBITUARIES.) (ROBIN DENSELOW)

United States. In the U.S., urban acts OutKast (*see* BIOGRAPHIES) and Alicia Keys began 2004 atop the pop charts, but Janet Jackson's "wardrobe malfunction" at the Super Bowl halftime show on February 1 soon overshadowed all things musical. During a nationally televised dual performance, Justin Timberlake popped off a portion of Jackson's corset, exposing most of her breast and igniting a controversy that generated a half million complaints to the Federal Communications Commission (FCC). The FCC fined CBS $550,000, and Viacom Inc., the owner of CBS, protested the fine.

The Grammy Awards took place one week after the Super Bowl, and the show aired with a five-minute delay (to prevent another televised mishap). Jackson's planned appearance was scrapped owing to the controversy, but Timberlake was allowed to appear (he won two awards). The night's big winner was singer Beyoncé (*see* BIOGRAPHIES), who notched five Grammys. OutKast's double CD *Speakerboxxx/The Love Below* won album of the year in a further underscoring of hip-hop's place in the American mainstream. Beyoncé and OutKast also won multiple awards at the *Billboard*/AURN R&B/Hip-Hop Awards in August, though R. Kelly's seven trophies topped their totals. At September's Latin Grammy Awards, Spain's Alejandro Sanz won four awards, including best album honours for *No es lo mismo*.

Genre lines blurred in several instances in 2004. Smokie Norful, Vickie Winans, CeCe Winans, and other gospel artists found their way onto *Billboard*'s mainstream R&B chart, and hip-hop artist Kanye West released an explicitly Christian single, "Jesus Walks," that reached *Billboard*'s all-genre Top 20. More blurring occurred when St. Louis, Mo.-based rapper Nelly recruited country superstar Tim McGraw for vocal assistance on "Over and Over," a track from Nelly's *Suit* album. With his appearance on "Over and Over," McGraw became the first country artist to appear on *Billboard*'s Hot R&B/Hip-Hop Singles chart.

McGraw's *Live like You Were Dying* album sold 766,000 copies during its first week, and his "Live like You Were Dying" single topped *Billboard*'s country chart for seven weeks. Other major country-music stories included the revival of country sales, with a double-digit increase over 2003; Gretchen Wilson's *Here for the Party*, which recorded the largest first-week sales (227,000) for a debut album in country history; and Kenny Chesney's top entertainer and album prizes at the Country Music Association Awards in November.

Pop singer Gwen Stefani performs at the MTV Europe Music Awards in Rome. In 2004 she released her first solo album, Love.Angel.Music.Baby.

© Frank Micelotta/Getty Images

With a November presidential election that pitted incumbent Pres. George W. Bush against Democratic challenger John Kerry, numerous music figures involved themselves in politics. Hip-hop magnate Sean ("P. Diddy") Combs's Citizen Change group sought to register urban youth to vote through its "Vote or Die!" campaign. Rock icon Bruce Springsteen made several campaign appearances with Kerry and was among the artists who embarked on a "Vote for Change" tour in October. Eminem used the Internet to release the anti-Bush single "Mosh."

Satellite radio continued to surge forward as competitors Sirius and XM reeled in subscribers to their multichannel services. At year's end XM had more than 2.5 million users. (*See* MEDIA AND PUBLISHING: *Radio*: Sidebar.) Another trend favoured cellular phone "ringtones"; people paid several dollars to download a song that would play when triggered by an incoming phone call. In November *Billboard* initiated a ringtone chart, topped first by Usher and Alicia Keys's "My Boo."

In February industry mogul Clive Davis took over as chairman and CEO of BMG North America. In July the Federal Trade Commission approved a merger between BMG Entertainment and Sony Music Entertainment. With the merger 80% of recorded music was owned by four companies, and the newly created Sony BMG became the second largest music company in the world (behind Universal Music Group).

The year ended with major acts—including Eminem, vocal group Destiny's Child, pop artist Gwen Stefani, Southern hip-hop force Lil Jon & the East Side Boyz, rapper Snoop Dogg, and Irish band U2—releasing albums and competing for holiday sales. Among the inductees into the Rock and Roll Hall of Fame were the late George Harrison, Jackson Browne, and Prince (*see* BIOGRAPHIES), who also had critical and commercial success with his album *Musicology*.

Musicians who died during the year included soul icon Ray Charles, country singer Skeeter Davis, Ramones guitarist Johnny Ramone (John Cummings), session guitar legend Hank Garland, and Jan and Dean member Jan Berry. (*See* OBITUARIES.) (PETER COOPER)

DANCE

North America. During 2004, especially in the early months, the rich legacy of Russian émigré George Balanchine was celebrated in North America to commemorate the 100th anniversary of his birth. The later months of the year were devoted to marking the centenary of the birth of another great choreographer, Sir Frederick Ashton.

The most extensive Balanchine celebration occurred in New York City, where "Mr. B." had made his home and established his New York City Ballet. NYCB's winter season, "Heritage," stressed the roots of the choreographer's work, and its spring season, "Vision," stressed his new ballets. One work, *Shambards,* by NYCB resident choreographer Christopher Wheeldon and set to the music of James MacMillan, was fairly substantive and remarkable. The others included two inconclusive works by NYCB ballet master in chief Peter Martins—*Chichester Psalms,* featuring music by Leonard Bernstein, and *Eros Piano,* set to music by John Adams—and *Musagète* by Russian choreographer Boris Eifman, a sprawling and, some thought, "tasteless" creation ostensibly based on Balanchine's life and career. In addition, there were several Balanchine exhibitions, notably those at the New York Public Library for the Performing Arts, the Harvard Theater Collection, and the San Francisco Performing Arts Library & Museum. Screenings of the choreographer's work on film and video also became celebrative events, including one at the Museum of Television & Radio in New York City. DVD releases included two discs featuring Balanchine's work with the "Dance in America" series, offered by Nonesuch, and a two-part biographical study from Kultur.

By midyear the Lincoln Center Festival in New York City had begun its two-week celebration of Ashton, British ballet's guiding genius and founder of the Royal Ballet. The Royal Ballet and the Birmingham (Eng.) Royal Ballet performed an all-Ashton repertory alongside the Joffrey Ballet of Chicago and Japan's K-Ballet Company. Notable among the festival's offerings were a revival by the Birmingham company of Ashton's 1940 *Dante Sonata,* which addressed the cataclysm of World War II, and the Royal Ballet's new production of the choreographer's incomparable 1948 *Cinderella.* In April 2004 PBS broadcast American Ballet Theatre's (ABT's) successful 2002 revival of *The Dream,* Ashton's moving ballet based on Shakespeare's *A Midsummer Night's Dream* and set to the music of Felix Mendelssohn.

In addition to a specially planned mixed bill of Balanchine ballets, one highlight of ABT's eight-week season at the Metropolitan Opera House in New York City was a new production of *Raymonda.* The three-act 1898 work, which was first performed in St. Petersburg and choreographed by Marius Petipa, was reduced to two acts and co-produced with the Finnish National Ballet. Among the several casts leading ABT's performances of this French- and Hungarian-styled ballet set to the music of Aleksandr Glazunov were some of the troupe's most gifted young dancers: David Hallberg and Michele Wiles as the main couple, and Herman Cornejo and Marcelo Gomes alternating as the ballet's "exotic" intruder. The troupe's now-annual fall season in New York City at the City Center included once-familiar stagings of works by Michel Fokine and a new work by Trey McIntyre.

Beyond offering ballets by Balanchine and Ashton, American companies amplified their repertoires with new creations from contemporary choreographers. Two of the more ambitious undertakings were a new and wholly original version of Léo Delibes's *Sylvia* for the San Francisco Ballet by modern-dance creator Mark Morris; the production was met with much critical acclaim. In a similar vein, as part of its own 40th anniversary celebrations, the Pennsylvania Ballet presented a new staging of Tchaikovsky's broadly popular *Swan Lake.* Wheeldon reworked and reduced most of the standard and traditional staging of the classic work into a scheme that moved the action into the milieu of a 19th-century French ballet studio; reactions were somewhat mixed. The Houston (Texas) Ballet, under the fairly new direction of Australian-born Stanton Welch, presented the director's multiact *Tales of Texas* and later featured "Women@Art," a bill focusing on ballets by female choreographers.

The Cincinnati (Ohio) Ballet opened its fall season with a continuation of its successful 2003 programming that celebrated the legacy of the Ballet Russe de Monte Carlo. The Cincinnati troupe presented Léonide Massine's staging of Beethoven's *Seventh Symphony,* which had not been seen since the performances given decades earlier by Ballet Russe de Monte Carlo. Pacific Northwest Ballet spent the better part of its year saying farewell to its longtime artistic directors team Kent Stowell and Francia Russell, as well as screening candidates to replace the couple as head of the ballet troupe and its affiliate school.

Andrea Mohin/The New York Times

American Ballet Theatre presents a spectacular reworking of Marius Petipa's classic 1898 ballet Raymonda.

Miami (Fla.) City Ballet added to its repertoire not only Balanchine's setting of Ravel's *La Valse* but also Paul Taylor's *Piazzolla Caldera.* The Paul Taylor Dance Company marked its 50th anniversary with an official kickoff season at the American Dance Festival (Durham, N.C.) and a 50-state tour as it worked toward climaxing the celebration of its founder's golden milestone. Earlier in the year the troupe had given the premiere of Taylor's newest creation, *Dante Variations,* set to music by Gyorgy Ligeti.

Experimentalist choreographer John Jasperse gave American Dance Festival his *California,* a formalist work that was motivated by the political situation in California that led to Arnold Schwarzenegger's becoming governor. Merce Cunningham Dance Company presented the work of its founder-choreographer widely. The company also helped kick off the Fall for Dance Festival, an inaugural presentation of City Center, for which all seats were priced at $10. Thirty companies (five per night for six nights) participated in the event, which was meant to revive a one-time tradition of free dance concerts in the city's Central Park during the late summer. Participants included both established troupes (the Martha Graham Dance Company) and more recent newcomers (David Neumann).

Mikhail Baryshnikov, a ballet superstar turned modern-dance and experimental-dance advocate, took time off from his solo tour to recover from injury. By summer, however, he was back touring, with a prominent appearance at the

Lincoln Center Festival in *Forbidden Christmas, or the Doctor and the Patient,* Rezo Gabriadze's enchanting dance-theatre production, complete with spoken text. Touring stints included the Royal Danish Ballet at the Kennedy Center and the Hamburg (Ger.) Ballet performing *Nijinsky* by John Neumeier (on the West and East coasts). The Bolshoi Ballet, more or less displaced owing to the refurbishment of its august home in Moscow, toured the U.S. and Mexico with three standard-fare Soviet-ballet-styled classics—*Raymonda, Giselle,* and *Don Quixote*—as well as a more modern treatment of *Romeo and Juliet.*

Institution building was strong in New York City. ABT announced the opening of a company-affiliated academy named the Jacqueline Kennedy Onassis School, and the Alvin Ailey American Dance Theater, which was in the process of building its own multistory headquarters and school, received a $1 million gift from the Oprah Winfrey Foundation to support a similarly named scholarship program for a select number of the school's most talented students.

Choreographer Twyla Tharp kept her long-running Billy Joel-inspired *Movin' Out* in the news by presenting as part of its evolving cast of notable performers the stellar Desmond Richardson, a onetime dancer with the Alvin Ailey company. The late Broadway and ballet legend choreographer Jerome Robbins had his works presented by a number of companies, and dance critic Deborah Jowitt published *Jerome Robbins: His Life, His Theater, His Dance.*

The National Ballet of Canada (NBC) had as one of its major events a grand send-off for Rex Harrington, its much-beloved leading male dancer, who had celebrated his 20th anniversary with the company during the year. After dancing his final performance in the title role of John Cranko's *Onegin* (set to Tchaikovsky music) in Ottawa, Harrington gave his final NBC performance in Toronto, as "A Man" in director James Kudelka's version of Vivaldi's *The Four Seasons.* Two different premiere stagings of Sergey Prokofiev's *Cinderella* took place during the year, one with NBC by Kudelka and another in Calgary by Jean Grand-Maitre for Alberta Ballet. Val Caniparoli's *A Cinderella Story,* set to the tunes of Richard Rodgers and evoking a 1950s atmosphere, entered the repertoire of the Royal Winnipeg Ballet, which also toured during the year with Mark Godden's *Dracula* (music by Gustav Mahler) and *The Magic Flute* (set to Mozart). Director John Alleyne gave his company, Ballet British Columbia, a new staging of the perennially popular *Carmina Burana* in April, set to the music of Carl Orff. The *butoh*-based Kokoro Dance company produced the Vancouver International Dance Festival in the spring. Montreal's 21st annual "Gala des Étoiles," with its strong basis in virtuoso ballet dancing, showcased performers ranging from those with the Madrid-based Nuevo Ballet Espagnol to Canadian modern-dance-based soloist Margie Gillis.

Deaths included those of tap-dancing actress Ann Miller; dancer-choreographers June Taylor, May O'Donnell, John Taras, and Bella Lewitzky; tap artist Leonard Reed; and teacher Betty Oliphant. (*See* OBITUARIES.) Other losses included those of dancers Homer Avila, Carlos Orta, and Larry White, dancer-ballet master Basil Thompson, dancer-choreographer Zachary Solov, choreographer Genia Melikova, and ballet company founder Josephine Schwarz. (ROBERT GRESKOVIC)

Europe. The year 2004 saw not only the centenaries of the birth of two of the greatest choreographers of the 20th century, George Balanchine and Sir Frederick Ashton, but also the 75th anniversary of the death of Sergey Diaghilev. The anniversaries were celebrated across Europe, with some important revivals of ballets not seen for many years.

Ashton was remembered as the founding choreographer of the oldest ballet companies in Britain, the Royal Ballet and the Rambert Dance Company. The Rambert troupe made a new version (choreographed by Ian Spink) of Ashton's first work, *A Tragedy of Fashion,* which was shown in a program that also included Ashton's *Five Brahms Waltzes in the Manner of Isadora Duncan.* The Royal Ballet's major contribution was a revival of *Sylvia,* made for Margot Fonteyn in 1952 but not seen in its full three-act version for nearly 40 years; the company also revived *A Wedding Bouquet* after a long absence and published a commemorative book of photographs. The Birmingham Royal Ballet showed Ashton's *Enigma Variations* and *The Two Pigeons* both at home and during a short New York season. The Bolshoi Ballet danced *La Fille mal gardée* in Moscow, and the Dutch National Ballet featured *The Dream* and *Cinderella.*

The Royal Ballet also programmed a bill of four works associated with Diaghilev, including Michel Fokine's *Le Spectre de la rose,* which the company had not performed since it moved to the Royal Opera House in 1946. The young Ivan Putrov had a particular success in the title role.

Also in London, the English National Ballet revived Derek Deane's "in the round" production of *Swan Lake* at the Royal Albert Hall, with Polina Semionova, a 19-year-old Russian ballerina from the Staatsoper Ballet in Berlin, making a spectacular debut as Odette/Odile on opening night. Sylvie Guillem appeared with George Piper Dances (more familiarly known as the Ballet Boyz) in a program of choreography by Russell Maliphant, which included *Broken Fall,* the big hit he had made for these dancers in 2003. William Tuckett premiered his version of Igor

From left, Tamara Rojo, Johan Kobborg, Alina Cojocaru, and Zenaida Yanowsky perform in the Royal Ballet's revival of Sir Frederick Ashton's 1937 **A Wedding Bouquet.**

Linda Rich/Dance Picture Library

Stravinsky's *The Soldier's Tale,* starring Adam Cooper, Zenaida Yanowsky, and Matthew Hart. The Royal New Zealand Ballet appeared in London and on tour with Christopher Hampson's production of *Romeo and Juliet,* which successfully translated the action to the mid-20th century, and the Bolshoi Ballet had a summer season at the Royal Opera House—the first London appearance of the full company for several years. San Francisco Ballet, which in recent years had become a London favourite, also made a welcome return.

The big success story from the rest of the country was the revitalization of Scottish Ballet under its new director, Ashley Page. Several well-constructed programs attracted much praise from both critics and audiences, though Page's new *Nutcracker* had a more mixed reception. Northern Ballet Theatre showed a triple bill for the first time in five years, including the world premiere of *Dividing Silence* by young choreographer Cathy Marston, previously known mainly for her studio pieces made for the Royal Ballet. Later in the year NBT gave its first performances of director David Nixon's *Dangerous Liaisons,* originally given by BalletMet in the U.S.

The Paris Opéra Ballet (POB) began the year with an all-Balanchine program and moved on to a series of full-length classics. The Royal Ballet's Alina Cojocaru made an acclaimed company debut in *Giselle,* and POB appointed two new stars of its own; Marie-Agnès Gillot and Mathieu Ganio were both promoted to the rank of étoile. Ganio, the son of two former POB dancers, was elevated at the exceptionally early age of 20. In September the company joined with the Royal Ballet to produce a gala celebrating the 100th anniversary of the signing of the historic Franco-British Entente Cordiale. The Paris troupe's announcement of its new season program was met with some dismay from a section of the audience, who saw it as moving away from the company's classical tradition to a more contemporary pattern.

Other European companies celebrated still more anniversaries. For Maurice Béjart, director of Béjart Ballet Lausanne (Switz.), it was 50 years since he first established a company of his own; and the Hamburg Ballet marked John Neumeier's completion of 30 years as director by presenting 16 of his works, culminating in a Jubilee Gala. The annual gala of the Bavarian State Ballet in Munich, Ger., honoured Balanchine. In Düsseldorf, Ger., the Ballet of the Deutsche Oper am Rhein premiered director Youri Vamos's new view of a classic, *Coppélia am Montmartre,* while the Stuttgart (Ger.) Ballet devoted a whole program to new work that included *Lachrymae,* a piece choreographed by Douglas Lee, the company's British principal dancer, and set to music by Benjamin Britten. A later bill, entitled Stravinsky Inspires, featured the world premiere of a work by Kevin O'Day. William Forsythe's Frankfurt (Ger.) Ballet gave its last performances. It was announced that Forsythe would lead a new company to be based in Dresden as well as in Frankfurt in early 2005.

The Danish Royal Ballet began preparations for its 2005 festival, marking the 200th anniversary of the birth of its own great choreographer, August Bournonville. His works were introduced gradually into the repertory during the year, including the rarely seen *Abdallah.* Neumeier made a new pas de deux, *A Wedding Gift,* to celebrate the marriage of the crown prince of Denmark; it was danced by Kenneth and Marie-Pierre Greve, both principal dancers of the company. The major premiere of the year was *Anna Karenina,* choreographed by Aleksey Ratmansky, who had danced with the Danish company before he took up the directorship of the Bolshoi Ballet. Greve and Caroline Cavallo shared the title role.

Ratmansky became director of the Bolshoi Ballet on January 1. The company visited Paris in that month and London in July, but only Paris saw Ratmansky's *The Bright Stream,* a reworking of a ballet from the Soviet era, with music by Dmitry Shostakovich. In London the company showed its "modern" *Romeo and Juliet,* directed by Declan Donnellan and with choreography by the young Moldovan Radu Poclitaru. Although popular with audiences, it was panned by most of the critics but had fine performances by both Mariya Aleksandrova and Anastasiya Meskova, who shared the role of Juliet. The Marinsky Ballet of St. Petersburg honoured Balanchine with performances of his *Jewels,* a triple bill of his ballets, and two exhibitions about his life and work. The company also gave its first performances of three works by Forsythe: *The Vertiginous Thrill of Exactitude, Steptext,* and *In the Middle, Somewhat Elevated.* Darya Pavlenko, much admired in recent tours to the West, was promoted to principal dancer.

A biennial competition for choreographers, offering valuable prizes, was held for the first time, at the Place in London. The nearly 200 entries, from all over the world, were reduced to a short list of 20 and then to five finalists, and the Place Prize of £25,000 (about $45,000) was won by Rafael Bonachela, associate choreographer of the Rambert Dance Company. Those passing from the dance scene during the year included Bolshoi prima ballerina and teacher Sulamith Messerer, Spanish dancer Antonio Gades, French dancer Ludmila Tcherina, and Margaret Kelly, founder of the famous Bluebell Girls chorus line. (*See* OBITUARIES.) (JANE SIMPSON)

THEATRE

Great Britain and Ireland. There was no escaping the war in Iraq, as the global political situation seeped into the British theatre to an almost unprecedented degree in 2004. Not since the protest plays of the 1960s and '70s had the stage been so tuned in to its own times.

Dominating all was David Hare's *Stuff Happens* at the National Theatre. The lead-up to the U.S.-led offensive in Iraq was rivetingly shown as a series of power games and office bartering between all the major participants, with Colin Powell, played by visiting African American actor Joe Morton, holding centre stage as a man of conscience and propriety.

After viewing the production, UN weapons inspector Hans Blix marveled at the way such a complicated process had been condensed into three hours of electrifying theatre. Hare said that nothing in the narrative was "knowingly untrue" and that the scenes of direct address quoted the actual people involved verbatim.

The portraits of U.S. Pres. George W. Bush, British Prime Minister Tony Blair, U.S. Vice Pres. Dick Cheney, U.S. National Security Advisor Condoleezza Rice, and U.S. Defense Secretary Donald Rumsfeld were remarkably rounded, even restrained, and the actors veered only slightly toward cartoonish impersonation. Particularly brilliant were Alex Jennings as Bush and Dermot Crowley, who portrayed Rumsfeld. The production, by Nicholas Hytner (*see* BIOGRAPHIES), showed how the decisions followed each other with dire inevitability.

Elsewhere, Tim Robbins brought his far more simplistic *Embedded,* a satire about the journalists embedded with the U.S. military during the Second Persian Gulf War, to the Riverside Studios in Hammersmith, while the Tricycle Theatre in Kilburn staged an unashamedly partisan documentary about the detainees at Guantánamo Bay, *Guantánamo: "Honour Bound to Defend Freedom"* (these two shows passed each other crossing the Atlantic); and Justin Butcher's crassly enjoyable *The Madness of George Dubya* transferred from a London fringe theatre to the West End.

Greek tragedy was reanimated by the events, with two great plays about flawed war heroes—Sophocles' little-known *Trachiniae* in a stunning new version by Martin Crimp called *Cruel and Tender* at the Young Vic, directed by Luc Bondy; and Euripides' *Iphigenia at Aulis*, directed in Don Taylor's translation by Katie Mitchell at the National—proving, perhaps, that time and distance were needed to focus the immediate human dramas more effectively.

With the arrival at the Donmar Warehouse of an astounding and powerful new interpretation of Euripides' *Hecuba* by Frank McGuinness, Clare Higgins reinforced her claim to membership in the front rank of actors. London audiences felt the full force of the pain, suffering, and anguish of war, aspects that had been only touched on in *Stuff Happens. Hecuba,* with its tit-for-tat atrocities committed on children, evoked the other real-life nightmare scenario of the year—the terrorist storming of a school in Beslan, Russia, in September. When such things happen, they alter forever the way one looks at the world, and theatre is similarly transformed.

One of the year's most striking productions, *Wolf,* visited Sadler's Wells from Belgium; directed by Alain Platel, the show used a graffiti-strewn shopping mall as a backdrop for a cast of characters on the fringes of society, including a contortionist, an aerialist, and two deaf performers. Featured were Mozart's arias, performed by three leading soloists and the Klangforum Orchestra from Vienna, along with 19 musicians, 10 dancers, 3 singers, and 14 dogs.

Opening the big musical season in the autumn was Andrew Lloyd Webber's *The Woman in White* at the Palace. Though Lloyd Webber owned the Palace, it had been host for 18 years to Cameron Mackintosh's production of *Les Miserables,* which moved around the corner to the Queen's on Shaftesbury Avenue.

Lloyd Webber's collaborators were playwright Charlotte (*Humble Boy*) Jones, Broadway lyricist David (*City of Angels*) Zippel, director Trevor Nunn, and designer William Dudley. The show, based on Wilkie Collins's ghostly Victorian novel, was a thrilling return to the full-blown romanticism of Lloyd Webber's *The Phantom of the Opera.* The original Phantom, Michael Crawford, returned to London as the villainous, enormously fat Count Fosco. The designs were state-of-the-art video projections, the content absorbing, and the performances superb. Maria Friedman portrayed spinsterish heroine Marian Halcombe, and Martin Crewes starred as Walter Hartwright, the pivotal art teacher who unravels the mystery in pursuit of his beloved Laura (Jill Paice). Meanwhile, Lloyd Webber's *Bombay Dreams,* by composer A.R. Rahman (*see* BIOGRAPHIES), transferred to Broadway.

The jury remained out for the prospects of long-term success for *The Producers* at the Theatre Royal, Drury Lane. Removed from its natural Broadway environment, Mel Brooks's delirious mayhem and Susan Stroman's vibrant knockout production seemed destined to struggle to create the big-city buzz of the original show. In addition, Richard Dreyfuss and Lee Evans as the hapless con men did not have the same shyster authenticity as Nathan Lane and Matthew Broderick.

The third big musical was the spectacular collaboration between Disney and Mackintosh on *Mary Poppins* at the Prince Edward Theatre. Richard Eyre's production re-created the original stories by P. L. Travers and was scripted by Julian (*Gosford Park*) Fellowes; several jaunty new songs were added to the film score by George Stiles and Anthony Drewe. Laura Michelle Kelly was a high-flying Mary, and Gavin Lee her not-too-Dick Van Dyke-ish Bert. Meanwhile, *Mamma Mia!* celebrated its fifth anniversary by moving from the Prince Edward into the splendidly refurbished Prince of Wales Theatre.

Elsewhere in the West End, Lee Evans warmed up for *The Producers* by playing opposite Michael Gambon in a short season of Samuel Beckett's *Endgame* at the Albery. This theatre was occupied at year's end by the Royal Shakespeare Company (RSC) with its transfers from Stratford-upon-Avon of *Macbeth* (Greg Hicks and Sian Thomas as Macbeth and Lady Macbeth), *Hamlet* (featuring a crowd-pleasing, energetic Toby Stephens), and *King Lear* (starring a subdued Corin Redgrave). The Albery also hosted Diana Rigg in Tennessee Williams's *Suddenly Last Summer* and an imaginative all-Indian *Twelfth Night,* relocated to India; Illyria was indeed another country.

Christian Slater led a powerful revival of Ken Kesey's *One Flew over the Cuckoo's Nest* from the Edinburgh Festival fringe into the Gielgud. Nunn began the year by directing his wife, Imogen Stubbs, as Gertrude in an acclaimed *Hamlet* at the Old Vic (newcomer Ben Wishaw seemed like a young high schooler fretting over exam results). Nunn also directed Stubbs's first play, *We Happy Few,* which was presented at the Gielgud. The meandering tale of an all-women theatre company

Michael Crawford stars as Count Fosco and Maria Friedman as Marian Halcombe in Andrew Lloyd Webber's new musical, **The Woman in White,** *directed by Trevor Nunn at London's Palace Theatre.*

AP/Wide World Photos

traveling around the country during World War II did not survive long.

Other, more regrettable, flops included *Calico,* a fascinating play by Michael Hastings about James Joyce's daughter, stunningly played by newcomer Romola Garai, and the transfer from the Almeida Theatre of Edward Albee's *The Goat, or Who Is Sylvia?,* starring Jonathan Pryce as the troubled architect and his real-life partner, Kate Fahy, as the wife supplanted in his affections by a goat. The Almeida returned to Shaftesbury Avenue with its subversive, nerve-jangling version of the Danish film *Festen;* Jane Asher's ice-cool matriarch presided over a family feast during which skeletons of child abuse come tumbling out of the cupboard.

After months, if not years, of press launches, press conferences, parties, and hoopla, American actor Kevin Spacey finally moved into the Old Vic as artistic director and opened with a new play, *Cloaca,* that unpromisingly translated as "sewer." An older New York vintage, the writing team of George S. Kaufman and Howard Teichmann, bubbled up at the Garrick Theatre with their 1953 comedy *The Solid Gold Cadillac,* starring Roy Hudd and Patricia Routledge.

The West End, though, had no real answer to the continued ascendancy of Hytner's National. Not just the Hare play but also Alan Bennett's *The History Boys* generated huge public interest and coverage in the media. The Bennett show (not really a play) was a loosely arranged satiric school pageant—a sequel, really, to his first big West End success, *Forty Years On*—which questioned the educational system's obsession with examination results and considered the vocational aspect of teaching allied to the slightly tricky area of sexual attraction of pupil for master.

The third big National blockbuster was Nicholas Wright's adaptation of *His Dark Materials,* a trilogy by Philip Pullman (*see* BIOGRAPHIES), into two three-hour dramas that swept across the huge Olivier stage like a tidal wave, establishing the work as the next big global children's phenomenon after Harry Potter and *Lord of the Rings.* Hytner thus completed a "new work" hattrick as a director—Pullman, Bennett, and Hare—that overshadowed even multitasking Nunn.

The National also presented immensely successful productions of *Measure for Measure,* directed by Simon McBurney; *A Funny Thing Happened on the Way to the Forum,* directed by Edward Hall (though Desmond Barrit's lascivious slave Pseudolus was less hard-hitting than his imposing Dick Cheney in *Stuff Happens*); and a gorgeous Marivaux comedy, *The False Servant,* translated by Crimp and directed by Jonathan Kent, that featured Charlotte Rampling as a sexually besieged countess.

The RSC at Stratford-upon-Avon claimed record attendances for its season of tragedies, and artistic director Michael Boyd announced that an overall deficit of £2.8 million (about $5.1 million) had been reduced, in his first year in charge, to just under £500,000 (about $900,000). Despite a successful season of Spanish Golden Age drama in the Swan, the company's passion seemed slightly manufactured.

There were signs of revival in Liverpool, where the declining Everyman and Playhouse theatres were placed under one management. Highlights were Corin Redgrave as Archie Rice in John Osborne's *The Entertainer* and Sheila Hancock leading the Everyman's 40th birthday celebrations in Bill MacIllwraith's 1966 black comedy *The Anniversary.* The Salisbury Playhouse remained an essential venue, with a revelatory revival of N.C. Hunter's *Waters of the Moon* (1951).

The resurgent Bristol Old Vic and the lively Theatre Royal at Northampton both offered new stage versions of John Milton's *Paradise Lost,* an extraordinary coincidence of programming that did full justice, in different ways, to the greatest dramatic poem in the language outside Shakespeare. Michael Grandage, artistic director of the Sheffield Theatres (Crucible and Lyceum), stepped down after five successful years but continued to be in charge of the Donmar Warehouse. In Sheffield he bowed out with Friedrich Schiller's *Don Carlos,* starring Sir Derek Jacobi. At the Donmar, Grandage directed a stunning new version by Sir Tom Stoppard of Pirandello's *Henry IV,* with Ian McDiarmid giving one of the great performances of the year as the fantasy-bound monarch.

International cooperation was the name of the game at the West Yorkshire Playhouse in Leeds, where a cast of Catalan and British actors (five of each) performed an imaginatively powerful version of George Orwell's *Homage to Catalonia.* The Catalan actors came from Calixto Bieito's Theatre Romea in Barcelona, Spain. The controversial but brilliant "bad boy" Bieito directed a disappointing version of Fernando de Rojas's Spanish classic *Celestina* for the Birmingham Repertory Theatre at the Edinburgh Festival. Edinburgh international highlights were Olivier Py's 12-hour production of Paul Claudel's *Le Soulier de satin* and Peter Zadek's roller-coaster *Peer Gynt* from the Berliner Ensemble.

In Ireland the Abbey Theatre in Dublin celebrated its centenary with a yearlong program of old favourites and new plays, although the theatre itself was in turmoil over the resignation of its director, Ben Barnes. The Dublin Theatre

Nicholas Wright's adaptation of Philip Pullman's trilogy His Dark Materials, *starring Anna Maxwell Martin (centre) as Lyra Belacqua, was a soaring success at the National Theatre in London.*

Festival had an unusually rich program, bolstered by the Abbey's centenary but also boasting Conor McPherson's fine new play, *Shining City,* in a co-production by the Royal Court and the Gate Theatre, and a *Twelfth Night* directed by Declan Donnellan for a Russian cast drawn from Moscow's various ensembles. (MICHAEL COVENEY)

U.S. and Canada. The real-world drama of a divisive U.S. presidential election made happenings on American stages seem rather tepid in 2004, despite the theatre's willingness to delve into many of the same hot-button topics that were being debated in the U.S. Perhaps the difference was that such subjects as the sex-abuse scandals of the Roman Catholic Church, the human rights of incarcerated prisoners of war, and the acceptance of gay relationships, which had been frequently served up in the media as polarizing sound bites, were treated more often in the theatre as complex, multidimensional issues with individual human repercussions.

Such was the case with the debut in November of *Doubt* by *Moonstruck* scribe John Patrick Shanley. Set in the 1960s at a Bronx (N.Y.) Catholic school, where a stern nun grows suspicious of a priest who seems to be taking too much interest in a young male student, *Doubt* broached its sensational subject on a human scale and in a spirit of poetic restraint. The sensitive production, directed by Doug Hughes and mounted by the Manhattan Theatre Club (MTC), was illuminated by the flawless performances of Cherry Jones as the buttoned-up nun and Brían F. O'Byrne (winner of the season's best featured actor Tony Award for Bryony Lavery's *Frozen*) as the extroverted priest. The church's troubles got a more objective treatment in Michael Murphy's well-received courtroom docudrama *Sin (A Cardinal Deposed),* produced by New York's New Group, directed by Carl Forsman, and featuring veteran actor John Cullum as the beleaguered Bernard Cardinal Law of the archdiocese of Boston.

Another docudrama, *Guantanamo: Honor Bound to Defend Freedom,* first seen at London's Tricycle Theatre and imported to New York by the Culture Project, was one of several 2004 stage works that aimed to expose the human cost of the "war on terrorism." Other politically charged works included the LAByrinth Theater Company's production of Brett C. Leonard's *Guinea Pig Solo,* a drama starring John Ortiz as a disturbed veteran of the war in Iraq struggling to stay afloat in New York.

Tim Robbins's *Embedded,* which transferred to New York's Public Theater from the film star's Los Angeles home company, the Actor's Gang, was an unabashedly leftist agitprop comedy attacking U.S. policy on the war in Iraq. The pseudonymous playwright Jane Martin's over-the-top satire *Laura's Bush* posited that the first lady was blinking a Morse Code cry for help in her public appearances—it turned out that her husband had been replaced by a captured body double of former Iraqi leader Saddam Hussein.

Avenue Q *was the surprise winner of the Tony Award for best musical. The producers planned to take the show to a commercial run in Las Vegas, Nev.*

© Jeff Christensen/Reuters/Corbis

A lighthearted note was also struck by perhaps the year's most successful play, *Avenue Q,* a quirky musical comedy that embraced such real-world issues as racism and sex with the earnest glee—and the human-and-puppet format—of television's *Sesame Street.* Created by book writer Jeff Whitty and songwriters Robert Lopez and Jeff Marx, *Avenue Q* was a downtown sensation when it opened in March 2003 as a co-production of the New Group and the Vineyard Theatre. In short order it moved to Broadway, where it not only found an enthusiastic audience but also bested the odds-on favourite, the blockbuster musical *Wicked,* to win the Tony Award for best musical. *Avenue Q*'s producers then startled the Broadway establishment by announcing that rather than going on national tour, the show would commit to an open-ended commercial run in Las Vegas, Nev.

It was, in fact, a year of many firsts for Broadway theatre. Phylicia Rashad, who played the matriarch in a popular revival of Lorraine Hansberry's groundbreaking drama *A Raisin in the Sun,* became the first African American woman to win a Tony for best actress in a play; she appeared opposite Audra McDonald (*see* BIOGRAPHIES), whose portrayal of Ruth Younger earned the soprano her fourth Tony for best performance by a featured actress in a play. Doug Wright's idiosyncratic play *I Am My Own Wife* also earned a place in the record books after becoming the first one-person play to win a Tony for best play. The drama cataloged Wright's obsession with Charlotte von Mahlsdorf, an East German transvestite, and introduced a captivating young actor, Jefferson Mays.

Several important new works by major playwrights appeared during the year. Donald Margulies's first play since his Pulitzer Prize-winning *Dinner with Friends*—the father-son drama *Brooklyn Boy*—was co-produced by Manhattan Theatre Club and California's South Coast Repertory. The prolific Craig Lucas offered an ambitious time-leaping comedy-drama, *Singing Forest,* which contrasted refined 1930s Vienna with contemporary vapid, overcommercialized society; the Intiman Theatre of Seattle's production drew fascinated response, despite the play's three-and-a-half-hour length. Another Lucas play, *Small Tragedy,* a backstage affair about a troubled production of *Oedipus Rex,* quickly came and went at New York's Playwrights Horizons but earned an Obie Award for best American play. Edward Albee raised eyebrows and expectations by attaching a new first act to his famous 1959 play *The Zoo Story* and by giving the expanded version, which debuted at Connecticut's Hartford Stage, the title *Peter and Jerry.*

There were some important flops as well. Stephen Sondheim's legendary early work *The Frogs,* a spoof of the ancient Greek play by Aristophanes, was freely adapted by comic actor Nathan Lane for a production at Lincoln Center Theater, but not even Lane's exuberance in the leading role could keep the new version afloat. A Broadway revival of *After the Fall,* a 1964 confessional drama by Arthur Miller (whose new play, *Finishing the Picture,* made a minimal impression at Chicago's Goodman Theatre), received a glum response, although newcomer Carla Gugino acquitted herself admirably in the role based on Marilyn Monroe. *Drowning Crow,* a rambling riff on *The Seagull* by up-and-coming playwright Regina Taylor, tried to bring a hip-hop sensibility to Anton Chekhov, but it proved an ill-conceived adventure for MTC.

In Canada two of the American theatre's most exportable musical comedy hits proved anything but in Toronto. A seemingly sure-fire production of *The Producers,* Mel Brooks's film-derived extravaganza, closed prematurely in July, and *Hairspray,* based on John Waters's campy movie, met the same fate in November. Observers speculated that this might signal the end of Toronto as a long-run hub for American shows.

The most-praised Canadian productions of the year were mounted by the venerable Shaw Festival in Niagara-on-the-Lake, Ont. An uncut six-hour staging of George Bernard Shaw's *Man and Superman* by director Neil Munro drew superlatives, as did an inventive environmental staging of the Adam Guettel musical *Floyd Collins,* in which director Eda Holmes surrounded the audience with action. One-person shows were prominent on Canadian stages, with especially strong performances in Toronto by Daniel MacIvor, whose confessional *Cul-de-sac* ran at Buddies in Bad Times Theatre, and Rick Miller, who incorporated video in his irreverent *Bigger than Jesus* at the Factory Theatre. Big hits of the year in Toronto also included a CanStage production of the Alberta Hunter musical *Cookin' at the Cookery,* with Jackie Richardson impersonating the legendary jazz singer.

The Canadian troupe Cirque du Soleil opened a fourth show in Las Vegas and took its acrobatics to the high seas in a deal with Celebrity Cruises. Cirque also planned to establish permanent shows in Tokyo, London, and New York.

Theatre figures who passed away in 2004 included the Broadway composer Fred Ebb, actor and producer Tony Randall, playwright Jerome Lawrence, actor and teacher Uta Hagen, and performance artist Spalding Gray. (*See* OBITUARIES.) (JIM O'QUINN)

MOTION PICTURES

United States. With Hollywood production reflecting the taste of the dominant teenage and preteen audience, it was no surprise that one of the runaway movie successes of 2004 was *Harry Potter and the Prisoner of Azkaban,* with Alfonso Cuarón taking over the series as director. Another predictable success, Sam Raimi's *Spider-Man 2,* improved on the original with a rich, intelligent script by Alvin Sargent.

Walt Disney Pictures/Zuma Press

Pixar Studios' computer-animated film The Incredibles, *which features a family of superheroes forced to live as regular people to avoid lawsuits, was a hit with both children and adults.*

American cinema evinced a rare overt political commitment in the aftermath of the 2003 invasion of Iraq. Michael Moore's *Fahrenheit 9/11* was a commercial success as well as a source of infinite debate and denial. Other documentary filmmakers who took up the attack were Joseph Mealey and Michael Shoob (*Bush's Brain*), Nickolas Perry and Harry Thomason (*The Hunting of the President*), Robert Greenwald (*Uncovered: The War on Iraq* and the Orwellesque *Outfoxed: Rupert Murdoch's War on Journalism*), and Alison Maclean and Tobias Perse (*Persons of Interest,* about the rounding up of innocent U.S. citizens in the post-9/11 panic). Actor Tim Robbins made a digital adaptation of his stage play *Embedded/Live,* a ferocious attack on the handling of the Iraq war. In turn, *Fahrenheit 9/11* stirred opposition, with attacks on Moore's investigative methods in Michael Wilson's *Michael Moore Hates America,* Kevin Knoblock's *Celsius 41.11: The Temperature at Which the Brain ... Begins to Die,* and Alan Peterson's *Fahrenhype 9/11.* In the same genre, Morgan Spurlock's *Super Size Me* was a documentary dealing with obese Americans and the fast-food industry that helps make them that way.

Biopics proliferated. Martin Scorsese's *The Aviator* recounted the early career of Howard Hughes as film producer and aviator. Cole Porter was chronicled in Irwin Winkler's *De-Lovely,* sex researcher Alfred Kinsey in Bill Condon's *Kinsey,* Ray Charles in Taylor Hackford's *Ray,* singer Bobby Darin in Kevin Spacey's U.K.-German co-production *Beyond the Sea,* and Bobby Jones in Rowdy Herrington's *Bobby Jones, Stroke of Genius.* Among U.S.-U.K. co-productions, Stephen Hopkins's *The Life and Death of Peter Sellers,* which featured 2004 best actress Oscar winner Charlize Theron (*see* BIOGRAPHIES) as Britt Ekland, recalled the comedian's talents for giving public pleasure and private pain, while Marc Forster's *Finding Neverland* considered how the strange psychology of the British playwright James Barrie (played by Johnny Depp) led to the creation of *Peter Pan.* Oliver Stone's European-made *Alexander,* meticulous in its historical reconstruction, was notably less successful at the box office than Wolfgang Petersen's more conventional sword-and-sandals epic *Troy.* Mel Gibson's (*see* BIOGRAPHIES) *The Passion of the Christ,* dogged by controversy and charges of anti-Semitism, concentrated unsparingly on the reality of the cruelty and humiliation inflicted on Christ. Niels Mueller's *The Assassination of Richard Nixon,* starring Sean Penn (*see* BIOGRAPHIES), used a real event as the background to a fictional narrative.

Among established Hollywood directors, Clint Eastwood in *Million Dollar Baby* fashioned a dark, contemplative film about an elderly trainer who dedicates his efforts to a woman boxer. Spike Lee's *She Hate Me* was a topical story of a man who is ruined after he blows the whistle on corporate corruption and finds a new career as a personal fertilization service for lesbian couples; the same director's made-for-TV *Sucker Free City* was a more familiar Lee study of the urban subculture as experienced by three youngsters from varied backgrounds. Michael Mann's *Collateral* recounted how a hit man (Tom Cruise) forces a taxi driver (Jamie Foxx) to ferry him on his lethal rounds. In *The Terminal* Steven Spielberg created a timely comic fable about an immigrant who is prevented by political events from either entering the U.S. or returning home and thus must make his home at a New York airport. Joel Schumacher's film captured the theatricality of Andrew Lloyd Webber's stage musical *The Phantom of the Opera.*

Among the best work of newer directors, Nicole Kassell's *The Woodsman* was a compassionate story of a man (sensitively played by Kevin Bacon) battling to resist his pedophilic inclinations. John Curran's *We Don't Live Here Anymore* was a mature, intelligent, nonjudgmental picture of two adulterous couples in a university environment, from stories by the late Andre Dubus. *Sideways,* a film by Alexander Payne, was a coming-of-middle-age drama about successes and failures.

Although most of the year's remakes—for example, the Coen brothers' *The Ladykillers,* Frank Oz's *The Stepford Wives,* Charles Shyer's *Alfie,* and John Moore's *Flight of the Phoenix*—seemed at best superfluous, Jonathan Demme's *The Manchurian Candidate* updated and even improved upon its 1962 original. Steven Soderbergh's *Ocean's Twelve* was a highly entertaining lightweight crime caper, a sequel in no way inferior to its two predecessors, the 1960 *Ocean's Eleven* and its 2001 remake. The same could be said about the endearing animated film *Shrek 2* as well as *Meet the Fockers,* a sequel to *Meet the Parents* (2000), both of which were 2004 box-office blockbusters.

Sophisticated digital techniques continued to boost animation production and were used with increasing suppleness in works such as Brad Bird's witty *The Incredibles* and Stephen Hillenburg's *The SpongeBob SquarePants Movie,* developed from his TV cartoon series. Robert Zemeckis's *The Polar Express* employed computer graphic embodiments of live actors.

Promising year-end additions to cinema marquees included *Hotel Rwanda,* featuring an outstanding lead performance by Don Cheadle, and *Lemony Snicket's A Series of Unfortunate Events,* the motion-picture premiere of this author's darkly humorous tales written ostensibly for children.

British Isles. Veteran filmmakers offered the year's outstanding works. Mike Leigh's *Vera Drake,* a 1950s story of a good woman whose samaritan assistance with abortions brings disaster on her family, won the Golden Lion of the Venice Film Festival. Ken Loach's *Ae Fond Kiss,* scripted by Paul Laverty, was a gritty portrayal of the Romeo and Juliet romance between a Glasgow-born Muslim and a Catholic schoolteacher.

The British taste for social drama was in evidence in Kenneth Glenaan's *Yasmin,* a sometimes awkward but timely and sincere illustration of the backlash to 9/11 as suffered by innocent Muslims living and working in provincial Britain. From Wales, Amma Asante's *A Way of Life* was a bold and challenging portrait of a single mother totally beaten down by society yet provoking no easy sympathy.

Gurinder Chadha's *Bride and Prejudice* was only distantly inspired by the social and amorous threads of Jane Austen's novel in its sprightly mix of Bollywood and Western sitcom for a character-based tale of cultural clash; it starred Bollywood cinema siren Aishwarya Rai (*see* BIOGRAPHIES) in her first major English-language film. A predictable commercial success was the episodic sequel to *Bridget Jones's Diary* (2001), Beeban Kidron's *Bridget Jones: The Edge of Reason.* Michael Winterbottom challenged censors worldwide with his digitally shot *9 Songs,* in which a young couple alternates visits to rock concerts with sexual encounters, filmed explicitly.

The Irish-British *King Arthur,* directed by Antoine Fuqua from a script by David Franzoni, was a serious attempt to re-create the true history of mid-5th-century Britain, at the end of the Roman occupation. Also from Ireland, Pete Travis's *Omagh,* co-written for TV by Paul Greengrass, the maker of *Bloody Sunday,* was an unsparing re-creation of the events of the Omagh bombing outrage.

Lions Gate/The Kobal Collection/Connor, Frank

Terry George's searing multinational production Hotel Rwanda *starred Don Cheadle in the true-life story of a hotel manager who sheltered hundreds of Tutsi from rampaging Hutu during the 1994 genocide in Rwanda.*

Canada and Australia. One of the best films from Canada in a lean year was writer-director G.B.Yates's *Seven Times Lucky,* an effective grifter thriller enriched with strong character development. French-Canadian director Denys Arcand (*see* BIOGRAPHIES) continued to receive kudos for his 2003 blockbuster *Les Invasions barbares* (*The Barbarian Invasions*). In Australia the veteran Paul Cox's *Human Touch* feelingly told the story of the relationship that evolves between a 30-ish singer and the elderly photographer for whom she poses, while Cate Shortland's debut feature, *Somersault,* was a gripping road movie chronicling an adolescent girl's nascent sexual compulsions.

Western Europe. Among French films that attracted international attention were Patrice Leconte's *Confidences trop intimes* (*Intimate Strangers*), in which a distraught woman mistakes a gentle tax man for a psychiatrist; Agnès Jaoui's *Comme une image* (*Look at Me*), a perfectly observed portrayal of an egocentric writer and the overweight daughter who yearns vainly for his approval; and *La Demoiselle d'honneur,* Claude Chabrol's appreciative adaptation of Ruth Rendell's novel *The Bridesmaid.* Wide success was enjoyed by Christophe Barratier's *Les Choristes,* a remake of Jean Dreville's 1945 *La Cage aux rossignols,* about an inspirational teacher who creates a choir in a small-town boarding school for difficult children. Jean-Pierre Jeunet directed Audrey Tautou, the star of his 2001 success *Amélie,* in an adaptation of Sébastien Japrisot's World War I novel *Un Long Dimanche de fiançailles* (*A Very Long Engagement*).

Of Italy's senior directors, Pupi Avati, with *La rivincita di Natale* (*Christmas Rematch*), provided a sequel to his 1986 *Regalo di Natale,* with the same dubious group of gamblers meeting for an evening that turns into a game of revenge. Gianni Amelio's moving *Le chiavi di casa* (*The House Keys*) was based on Giuseppe Pontiggia's autobiographical account of coming to terms with his severely handicapped son. Young director Paolo Sorrentino's *Le conseguenze dell'amore* (*The Consequences of Love*) portrayed an obsessive with a mechanical

INTERNATIONAL FILM AWARDS 2004

Golden Globes, awarded in Beverly Hills, California, in January 2004

Best motion picture drama	*The Lord of the Rings: The Return of the King* (U.S./New Zealand; director, Peter Jackson)
Best musical or comedy	*Lost in Translation* (U.S./Japan; director, Sofia Coppola)
Best director	Peter Jackson (*The Lord of the Rings: The Return of the King,* U.S./ New Zealand)
Best actress, drama	Charlize Theron (*Monster,* U.S./Germany)
Best actor, drama	Sean Penn (*Mystic River,* U.S./Australia)
Best actress, musical or comedy	Diane Keaton (*Something's Gotta Give,* U.S.)
Best actor, musical or comedy	Bill Murray (*Lost in Translation,* U.S./Japan)
Best foreign-language film	*Osama* (Afghanistan/Netherlands/Japan; director, Siddiq Barmak)

Sundance Film Festival, awarded in Park City, Utah, in January 2004

Grand Jury Prize, dramatic film	*Primer* (U.S.; director, Shane Carruth)
Grand Jury Prize, documentary	*DiG!* (U.S.; director, Ondi Timoner)
Audience Award, dramatic film	*Maria Full of Grace* (U.S./ Colombia; director, Joshua Marston)
Audience Award, documentary	*Born into Brothels* (India; directors, Zana Briski and Ross Kauffman)
Best director, dramatic film	Debra Granik (*Down to the Bone,* U.S.)
Best director, documentary	Morgan Spurlock (*Super Size Me,* U.S.)
Special Jury Prize, dramatic film	*Brother to Brother* (U.S.; director, Rodney Evans); *Down to the Bone* (U.S.; lead actress, Vera Farmiga)
Special Jury Prize, documentary	*Farmingville* (U.S.; directors, Carlos Sandoval and Catherine Tambini)

Berlin International Film Festival, awarded in February 2004

Golden Bear	*Gegen die Wand* (Germany/Turkey; director, Fatih Akin)
Silver Bear, Grand Jury Prize	*El abrazo partido (Lost Embrace)* (Argentina/France/ Italy/Spain; director, Daniel Burman)
Best director	Kim Ki Duk (*Samaria,* South Korea)
Best actress	Catalina Sandino Moreno (*Maria Full of Grace,* U.S./ Colombia); Charlize Theron (*Monster,* U.S./ Germany)
Best actor	Daniel Hendler (*El abrazo partido* [*Lost Embrace*], Argentina/France/Italy/Spain)

Césars (France), awarded in February 2004

Best film	*Les Invasions barbares (The Barbarian Invasions)* (Canada/France; director, Denys Arcand)
Best director	Denys Arcand (*Les Invasions barbares* [*The Barbarian Invasions*], Canada/France)
Best actress	Sylvie Testud (*Stupeur et tremblements,* France/Japan)
Best actor	Omar Sharif (*Monsieur Ibrahim et les fleurs du Coran,* France)
Most promising actor	Grégori Derangère (*Bon voyage,* France)
Most promising actress	Julie Depardieu (*La Petite Lili* [*Little Lili*], France/Canada)

British Academy of Film and Television Arts, awarded in London in February 2004

Best film	*The Lord of the Rings: The Return of the King* (U.S./New Zealand; director, Peter Jackson)
Best director	Peter Weir (*Master and Commander: The Far Side of the World,* U.S.)
Best actress	Scarlett Johansson (*Lost in Translation,* U.S./Japan)
Best actor	Bill Murray (*Lost in Translation,* U.S./Japan)
Best supporting actress	Renée Zellweger (*Cold Mountain,* U.S.)
Best supporting actor	Bill Nighy (*Love Actually,* U.K./U.S.)
Best foreign-language film	*In This World* (U.K.; director, Michael Winterbottom)

Academy of Motion Picture Arts and Sciences (Oscars, U.S.), awarded in Los Angeles in March 2004

Best film	*The Lord of the Rings: The Return of the King* (U.S./New Zealand; director, Peter Jackson)
Best director	Peter Jackson (*The Lord of the Rings: The Return of the King,* U.S./New Zealand)
Best actress	Charlize Theron (*Monster,* U.S./Germany)
Best actor	Sean Penn (*Mystic River,* U.S.)
Best supporting actress	Renée Zellweger (*Cold Mountain,* U.S.)
Best supporting actor	Tim Robbins (*Mystic River,* U.S.)
Best foreign-language film	*Les Invasions barbares* (*The Barbarian Invasions*) (Canada/France; director, Denys Arcand)

Cannes Film Festival, France, awarded in May 2004

Palme d'Or	*Fahrenheit 9/11* (U.S.; director, Michael Moore)
Grand Jury Prize	*Oldboy* (*Old Boy*) (South Korea; director, Park Chan Wook)
Special Jury Prize	Irma P. Hall (actress in *The Ladykillers,* U.S.); *Sud pralad* (*Tropical Malady*) (Thailand/France/Germany/Italy; director, Apichatpong Weerasethakul)
Best director	Tony Gatlif (*Exils,* France)
Best actress	Maggie Cheung (*Clean,* Canada/France/U.K.)
Best actor	Yuya Yagira (*Dare mo shiranai* [*Nobody Knows*], Japan)
Caméra d'Or	*Mon trésor* (France/Israel; director, Keren Yedaya)

Locarno International Film Festival, Switzerland, awarded in August 2004

Golden Leopard	*Private* (Italy; director, Saverio Costanzo)
Silver Leopard	*En garde* (Germany; director, Ayse Polat)
Special Jury Prize	*Tony Takitani* (Japan; director, Jun Ichikawa)
Best actress	Maria Kwiatkowski (*En garde,* Germany); Pinar Erinein (*En garde,* Germany)
Best actor	Mohammad Bakri (*Private,* Italy)

Montreal World Film Festival, awarded in September 2004

Best film (Grand Prix of the Americas)	*The Syrian Bride* (France/Germany/Israel; director, Eran Riklis)
Best actress	Karin Viard (*Le Rôle de sa vie,* France)
Best actor	Christopher Walken (*Around the Bend,* U.S.); Wei Fan (*Kan che ren de qi yue,* China)
Best director	Carlos Saura (*El séptimo día* [*The Seventh Day*], Spain)
Grand Prix of the Jury	*Around the Bend* (U.S.; director, Jordan Roberts); *Kan che ren de qi yue* (China; director, Zhanjun An)
Best screenplay	*Le Rôle de sa vie* (France; writers, Jérôme Beaujour, Roger Bohbot, François Favrat, and Julie Lopes-Curval)
International cinema press award	*The Syrian Bride* (France/Germany/Israel; director, Eran Riklis)

Toronto International Film Festival, awarded in September 2004

Best Canadian feature film	*It's All Gone Pete Tong* (director, Michael Dowse)
Best Canadian feature film—Special Jury Citation	*ScaredSacred* (director, Velcrow Ripper)
Best Canadian first feature	*La Peau blanche* (director, Daniel Roby)
Best Canadian short film	*Man Feel Pain* (director, Dylan Akio Smith)
International Federation of Film Critics Prize	*In My Father's Den* (New Zealand/U.K.; director, Brad McGann)
People's Choice Award	*Hotel Rwanda* (Canada/U.K./Italy/South Africa; director, Terry George)

Venice Film Festival, awarded in September 2004

Golden Lion	*Vera Drake* (U.K./France/New Zealand; director, Mike Leigh)
Jury Grand Prize, Silver Lion	*Mar adentro* (Spain/France/Italy; director, Alejandro Amenábar)
Best director	Kim Ki Duk (*Bin-jip,* South Korea)
Volpi Cup, best actress	Imelda Staunton (*Vera Drake,* U.K./France/New Zealand)
Volpi Cup, best actor	Javier Bardem (*Mar adentro,* Spain/France/Italy)
Marcello Mastroianni Prize for new actor or actress	Marco Luisi, Tommaso Ramenghi (*Lavorare con lentezza,* Italy)
Luigi de Laurentiis Award for best first film	*Le Grand Voyage* (France/Morocco; director, Ismaël Ferroukhi)

Chicago International Film Festival, awarded in October 2004

Best feature film	*Kontroll* (*Control*) (Hungary; director, Nimrod Antal)
Special Jury Prize	*Lakposhtha ham parvaz mikonand* (*Turtles Can Fly*) (Iran/Iraq; director, Bahman Ghobadi)
New Directors Silver Hugo	Minh Nguyen Vo (*Mua len trau* [*The Buffalo Boy*], Vietnam/Belgium/France)
International Federation of Film Critics Prize	*Medurat Hashevet* (Israel; director, Joseph Cedar)

San Sebastián International Film Festival, Spain, awarded in September 2004

Best film	*Lakposhtha ham parvaz mikonand* (*Turtles Can Fly*) (Iran/Iraq; director, Bahman Ghobadi)
Special Jury Prize	*San zimske noci* (Serbia and Montenegro; director, Goran Paskaljevic)
Best director	Xu Jinglei (*Yi geng mo sheng nu ren de lai xin* [*A Letter from an Unknown Woman*], China)
Best actress	Connie Nielsen (*Brødre* [Brothers], Denmark)
Best actor	Ulrich Thomsen (*Brødre* [Brothers], Denmark)
Best photography	Marcel Zyskind (*9 Songs,* U.K.)
New Directors Prize	Lucile Hadzihalilovic (*Innocence,* Belgium/France)
International Critics Award	*Bombon—El Perro* (Argentina/Spain; director, Carlos Sorin)

Vancouver International Film Festival, awarded in October 2004

Federal Express Award (most popular Canadian film)	*What Remains of Us* (directors, Hugo Latulippe and François Prévost); *Being Caribou* (directors, Leanne Allison and Diana Wilson)
AGF People's Choice Award	*Machuca* (Chile/Spain/U.K.; director, Andrés Wood)
National Film Board Award (documentary feature)	*In the Realms of the Unreal* (U.S.; director, Jessica Yu)
Citytv Western Canadian Feature Film Award	*Seven Times Lucky* (director, Gary Yates)
Keystone Award (best Western Canadian short film)	*Riverburn* (director, Jennifer Calvert)
Dragons and Tigers Award for Young East Asian Cinema	*The Soup, One Morning* (Japan; director, Takahashi Izumi)

European Film Awards, awarded in December 2004

Best European film of the year	*Gegen die Wand* (Germany/Turkey; director, Fatih Akin)
Best actress	Imelda Staunton (*Vera Drake,* U.K./France/New Zealand)
Best actor	Javier Bardem (*Mar adentro,* Spain/France/Italy)

(DAVID ROBINSON)

regime of weekly drug dosing, watching a desirable woman in a hotel lobby, and, more perilously, carrying money for the Mafia. Saverio Costanzo's *Private,* though shot in Italy, convincingly evoked the nightmare of a Palestinian home taken over by Israeli soldiers.

In six episodes and 11⅓ hours, German director Edgar Reitz's *Heimat 3—Chronik einer Zeitenwende* continued the saga of the fictional Simon family begun in 1984 and continued in a further series in 1992. Winner of the Berlin Festival Golden Bear, Fatih Akin's *Gegen die Wand* (*Head-On*) related the adventures of two bedeviled immigrant Turks caught up in a marriage of convenience but ultimately falling in love. Achim von Borries's *Was nützt die Liebe in Gedanken* (*Love in Thoughts*), based on a true-life event of the late 1920s when five upper-class students shared an amorous weekend that ended with a bungled suicide pact, caught the atmosphere of Germany on the eve of Nazism. Volker Schlöndorff's *Der neunte Tag* (*The Ninth Day*) offered a classically styled story of the confrontations between a young Gestapo officer and a Catholic priest in 1942. Oliver Hirschbiegel's *Der Untergang* (*The Downfall: Hitler and the End of the Third Reich*) starred Bruno Ganz as the fallen dictator. Wim Wenders sought American-European reconciliation with *Land of Plenty,* recounting the reunion of a terrorist-hunting Vietnam veteran with his Christian niece who has lived in Palestine.

Spanish veteran Carlos Saura's *El séptimo día* (*The Seventh Day*) chronicled a real-life rural massacre that resulted from a family feud in 1990. Pedro Almodóvar's *La mala educación* (*Bad Education*) was a complex melodrama of homosexuality, transvestism, and sexual peccadilloes in the Roman Catholic Church. Gracia Querejeta's *Héctor* described the vicissitudes of the life of a 16-year-old boy sent to live with his aunt's family after the death of his mother.

In Portugal the 95-year-old Manoel de Oliveira filmed José Régio's play *O Quinto Império—ontem como hoje,* discovering parallels between the imperialistic and anti-Muslim adventures of the 16th-century King Sebastian and today's new forms of imperialism.

In a generally unremarkable year in Scandinavia, Finnish-Swedish director Åke Lindman's *Framom främsta linjen* (*Beyond Enemy Lines*) mixed fiction and actuality in the story of one regiment in the Russo-Finnish War of Continuation of 1941–44. Richard Hobert's low-budget period film *Tre solar* (*Three Suns*) from Sweden was an engaging story of a woman's journeys through the troubled world of the era of the Crusades. From Denmark, director Nikolaj Arcel's *Kongekabale* (*King's Game*) was a strong political drama about parliamentary corruption.

Eastern Europe. Russian filmmakers showed a new inclination to reexamine the Soviet and wartime eras. Dmitry Meskhiyev's *Svoi* (*Us*) was a drama of escape from invading German troops in 1941. Marina Razbezhkina's *Vremya zhatvy* (*Harvest Time*) recalled the privations—and also the simple pleasures—of life on a collective farm in 1950. Aleksandr Veledinsky's *Russkoye* was based on the autobiographical writings of Eduard Limonov, the maverick teenage hooligan poet of the 1950s, today an eccentric political activist. More modern themes were treated in Valery Todorovsky's *Moy svodny brat Frankenshteyn* (*My Step Brother Frankenstein*), an impressive melodrama on the effect on a family of the return of a young veteran from the Chechen campaign wounded in body and mind.

From Serbia and Montenegro, Goran Paskaljević's *San zimske noći* (*Midwinter Night's Dream*), an intimate story of a veteran who befriends an autistic girl and her mother, served as a mirror for postconflict Serbia. Less satisfying was Emir Kusturica's self-imitating *Život je čudo* (*Life Is a Miracle*), a rambunctiously comic portrayal of the denizens of a small provincial town at the outbreak of war in Bosnia and Herzegovina. Hungary enjoyed a major international success with Nimród Antal's *Kontroll* (2003), a wholly original, offbeat drama set in Budapest among the city's unpopular ticket inspectors. István Szabó's *Being Julia* was an elegant English-language adaptation of W. Somerset Maugham's novel *Theatre,* about a stage star who falls in love with a man much younger than herself. Greek master Theo Angelopoulos seemed to repeat himself in the lifeless *Trilogia I: to livadi pou dakryzei* (*Trilogy I: The Weeping Meadow*), about immigrants returning home from Odessa after the Russian Revolution.

Middle East. The prolific cinema of Iran extended its range from its familiar reflective and poetic style, with unexpected works such as Dariush Mehrjui's boisterous family comedy *Mehman-e maman* (*Mama's Guest*), Ahmad Reza Darvish's action drama about the Iran-Iraq War and its aftermath, *Duel,* and Mohammad Shirvani's *Nahf* (*Navel*), a stylish modern story of four men and a woman rooming together in Tehran. Gifted Kurdish director Bahman Ghobadi feelingly treated the plight of orphaned children in a refugee camp on the Iraqi-Turkish border just before the 2003 invasion of Iraq in *Lakposhtha hām parvaz mikonand* (*Turtles Can Fly*).

Afghanistan enjoyed international success with one of its rare film productions, Atiq Rahimi's *Khakestar-o-khak* (*Earth and Ashes*), scripted by Iranian Kambuzia Partovi and relating a minimal anecdote of an old man and his grandson, on a difficult journey to the boy's father to break the news of the death of his family.

Egypt offered two highly politicized films. Veteran Youssef Chahine's *Alexandrie . . . New York* was an autobiographical recollection of student days in a California drama school and an angry but sincere indictment of American cultural values and political dominance. Yousry Nasrallah's four-and-a-half-hour *Bab el shams* (*The Gate of the Sun*) was a passionate protest against the plight of Palestine.

Israel's major international success of the year was Eran Riklis's *ha-Kala ha-Surit* (*The Syrian Bride*), a generous, civilized commentary on political folly and inhumanity through the story of a young woman from an Israeli-occupied territory whose marriage to a Syrian will prevent her from ever returning to Israel to be reunited with her family.

India. While the Bollywood commercial cinema extended its range to include melodramas on contemporary subjects such as terrorism (Farah Khan's *Main hoon na*) and an Indian-Pakistani Romeo and Juliet story (Yash Chopra's *Veer-Zaara*), Shyam Benegal made *Bose: The Forgotten Hero,* the biography of a militant Bengali freedom fighter and contemporary of Gandhi. On another level, Buddhadeb Dasgupta's *Swapner din* (*Chased by Dreams*) took as its central character a young man who tours with a mobile film projector and a repertory of government propaganda films, interweaving an often uncomfortable reality and his dream life.

East and Southeast Asia. Among films that stood out from Japan's familiar genre productions, Hirokazu Koreda's *Dare mo shiranai* (*Nobody Knows*) was inspired by a real incident in 1988 when four children, abandoned by their mother, lived alone and unheeded for six months. Jun Ichikawa brought a dry, elegant, appropriate stylization to

China Film Group Corporation/The Kobal Collection/Bai Xiao Yan

Zhang Ziyi starred in the beautiful and thrilling martial arts romance Shi mian mai fu *(*House of Flying Daggers*).*

Tony Takitani, his adaptation of Haruki Murakami's short story about a solitary and emotionless illustrator who briefly finds love and, after his wife's death, tries to recapture the emotion with her double. Mamoru Hoshi filmed Koki Mitani's adaptation of his own play *Warai no daigaku* (*University of Laughs*) about a young playwright whose confrontations with wartime censorship, in the shape of a mirthless bureaucrat, prove creative to his play. Among the burgeoning productions of animated features, Katsuhiro Ōtomo's *Steamboy* deserved mention for its surprising setting—Victorian England and the Great Exhibition of 1851, during which a Manchester lad called Ray battles to wrest powerful new technology from the wrong hands.

The range and freedom of films from China continued to expand, particularly in co-productions with Hong Kong, such as Wong Kar Wai's *2046,* dedicated to the premise that the clock cannot be turned back. Beginning in the year 2046 (the date for Hong Kong's final integration with China), the action moves back 80 years, to hotel room 2046, where a womanizing writer has a series of erotic encounters. Zhang Yimou's *Shi mian mai fu* (*House of Flying Daggers*) was rated as one of the fastest and most deft martial arts films, with a high romantic denouement to its tragic period story. China's recent past was treated in Lu Yue's *The Foliage,* a delicate and frank story of the lives of young people sent to the country during the Cultural Revolution, and Liu Hao's *Hao da yi dui yang* (*Two Great Sheep*), a wryly satiric tale of a simple peasant's problems when he is honoured with the responsibility of caring for a pair of costly foreign sheep.

Malaysia's most costly and ambitious production ever, Saw Teong Hin's romantic epic *Puteri gunung ledang* (*A Legendary Love*) related a story of conflict between love and duty.

Africa. From Morocco, Mohamed Asli's *À Casablanca les anges ne volent pas* (*In Casablanca Angels Don't Fly*), a co-production with Italy, offered a comic but touching story of three men from rural Morocco exploited as workers in a busy Casablanca café. Ismaël Ferroukhi's *Le Grand Voyage* was an attractive road movie about an elderly man who obliges his unwilling Parisian-born son to drive him to Mecca. Algerian Nadir Moknèche's *Viva Laldjérie* was a vivacious story of a former cabaret dancer and her attractive daughter resisting the encroachment of fundamentalism.

Film production resumed in Angola with Maria João Ganga's account of an orphan child on the loose in the war-devastated capital of Luanda in 1991, *Na cidade vazia* (*Hollow City*), and Zézé Gamboa's *O herói* (*The Hero*), about the rehabilitation of a mutilated veteran of the 30-year war and his rediscovery of his son in Luanda. The 81-year-old Senegalese master Ousmane Sembene made one of his finest films in *Moolaadé,* the story of a group of women who rise up in protest against age-old rituals of female genital mutilation. In South Africa the memory of apartheid occupied Ian Gabriel's drama *Forgiveness* and Zola Maseko's *Drum,* about a sports journalist who begins to cover politics in the 1950s.

Latin America. From Argentina, in co-production with Chile and Peru, Walter Salles's *Diarios de motocicleta* (*The Motorcycle Diaries*) was a richly atmospheric account of the 23-year-old Che Guevara's discovery of his political conscience in the course of a 1952 motorcycle tour of Latin America. Ana Poliak's *Parapalos* (*Pin Boy*) examined the lives of society's least privileged through the life of a lad working at setting up the pins in a bowling alley. An Uruguayan-Argentine-German co-production, *Whisky,* directed by Juan Pablo Rebella and Pablo Stoll, was a gentle deadpan comedy of character that recalled the best of the Finnish master Aki Kaurismäki. From Chile, Andrés Wood's *Machuca* (*Revenge*) used the story of an educational experiment in integrating boys from different social classes as a metaphor for the failure of Chile's brief socialist democracy under Salvador Allende. Jonathan Jakubowicz's Venezuelan production *Secuestro express* (*Kidnap Express*) depicted the kind of kidnapping now epidemic in Latin America. From Peru, Josué Méndez's *Días de Santiago* (*Days of Santiago*) was an intense study of the problems of a young war veteran who is readjusting to civil life in the Lima slums, while Fabrizio Aguilar's *Paloma de papel* (*Paper Dove*) was a classically constructed story of an 11-year-old peasant caught up in the civil war. Sergio Cabrera's *Perder es cuestión de método* (*The Art of Losing*) was a drama that exposed Colombia's wide-ranging institutional corruption. (DAVID ROBINSON)

Nontheatrical Films. *My Architect: A Son's Journey,* a 2003 release, traced the search of Nathaniel Kahn to know his father, renowned architect Louis I. Kahn. Nathaniel, the director, neatly combined interview sequences with narration and used music deftly to underscore mood swings in the famed architect's life. The film was nominated for an Academy Award, was chosen as best-directed documentary by the Directors Guild, and took top honours at the Chicago International Film Festival, the High Falls Film Festival (Rochester, N.Y.), and other events. In *Coral Reef Adventure* (2003), Greg MacGillivray documented the endangerment of the world's coral reefs. The 45-minute film warned that a rise in ocean temperature of 2 °C (3.6 °F), coupled with continued commercial fishing, could deplete the ecologically sensitive reefs. It won a 2004 CINE Masters Series Award and the Grand Prix at the 2004 U.S. International Film and Video Festival.

From Inspiration to Innovation, a fast-paced film from the Finnish production company Avset Oy, documented how the use of innovative technology keeps Finland's industry competitive worldwide. Its effort won the grand prize at the 2004 WorldMediaFestival in Hamburg, Ger., as well as high honours at the Houston (Texas) WorldFest in April and Finland's Media & Message Festival in August. *Mellem os* (2003; *Between Us*) won a Student Academy Award and other international prizes for Danish student Laurits Munch-Petersen, whose film showed all the polish of a professional production. (THOMAS W. HOPE)

Physical Sciences

Experimenters used IONS in the teleportation of QUANTUM STATES, and scientists synthesized two new SUPERHEAVY chemical elements, a new type of FULLERENE called C_{50}, and a COMPLEX molecule formed by three interlinked rings. Spacecraft at MARS and SATURN provided a wealth of information, and SpaceShipOne claimed the Ansari X PRIZE.

CHEMISTRY

Nuclear Chemistry. The periodic table of the elements once contained only 92 naturally occurring elements, from hydrogen (the lightest building block of matter, with atomic number 1) to uranium (the heaviest, with atomic number 92). To this group, scientists have added many artificially created elements beginning with neptunium in 1940. These elements are very heavy and are produced in nuclear reactions that combine the nuclei of lighter elements. Atoms of many of the new elements exist only very briefly before decaying into other atoms. By 2003 the periodic table contained 114 elements.

In 2004 scientists in the United States and Russia announced the synthesis of two new superheavy elements, elements 113 and 115. Their interim names pending the confirmation of their discovery were ununtrium (113) and ununpentium (115), names derived from scientific Latin indicating their atomic numbers. Scientists of the Lawrence Livermore National Laboratory, Livermore, Calif., and the Joint Institute for Nuclear Research, Dubna, Russia, announced the result. At a particle accelerator in Dubna, they had smashed calcium atoms (atomic number 20) into americium atoms (atomic number 95) to produce an atom with an atomic number of 115, which then decayed into an atom with an atomic number of 113.

Both new elements had very short half-lives. It took just a fraction of a second for ununpentium to decay to ununtrium, which itself survived for a second before decaying. Researchers said that the discovery strengthened expectations concerning the existence of an "island of stability," an area at the outer reaches of the periodic table and theorized to contain superheavy elements with a longer half-life, possibly long enough for commercial or industrial applications.

Carbon Chemistry. Fullerenes are hollow cagelike structures of carbon atoms that debuted in 1985 with the discovery of C_{60}, or buckminsterfullerene. Since then, scientists had made a variety of fullerenes, including cylindrical structures termed carbon nanotubes. Synthesis of certain highly sought smaller fullerenes, however, remained elusive.

In 2004 Xie Su Yuan and associates of the State Key Laboratory for Physical Chemistry of Solid Surfaces, Xiamen, China, reported the synthesis of one such fullerene, C_{50}, which they described as the "little sister" of C_{60}. Like C_{60}, it has a ball-like shape, but it is surrounded by a ring of 10 chlorine atoms. The synthesis of C_{50} involved introducing carbon tetrachloride, the source of the chlorine atoms, into the fabrication process that was typically used to make fullerenes.

Predictions suggested that fullerenes smaller than C_{60} might have unusual electronic, magnetic, and mechanical properties because of the high curvature of their surface. The process developed by the researchers produced relatively large amounts of C_{50}, which enabled them to begin studying its properties. The researchers believed the process could be used to make stable forms of other small fullerenes that they hoped to study.

Topological Chemistry. Beginning in the 1960s, chemists synthesized a variety of elegantly shaped molecules that resembled knots, interlinked rings, or other structures. Two independent research groups took this work, referred to as topological chemistry, to a striking new level of complexity. In one project Kelly S. Chichak and his colleagues at the University of California, Los Angeles, reported the synthesis of a molecular Borromean ring—three rings linked together in such a way that cutting one link also releases the other two. (The Borromean ring was named for the Borromeo family, which used it as its family crest in 15th-century Tuscany; the rings also symbolized a giant's heart in Nordic mythology and the holy trinity in Christianity.) Synthesis of the Borromean ring was a tour de force, since closing one molecular ring through another so the rings were linked together like segments of a chain was in itself a notable accomplishment. In another research project Leyong Wang and associates at Johannes Gutenberg University, Mainz, Ger., reported synthesis of two molecules, each of which contained four molecular rings that were mutually interlinked. Far from being mere gimmicks, scientists stated that such structures might eventually have application

The photograph on the left shows a strand of hair on which a microscopic polymer structure made by a technique called MAP has been created, leaving the surface of the hair intact. The photograph on the right provides a close-up view.

Christopher N. LaFratta

in nanomachines and other forms of nanotechnology.

Physical Chemistry. The trend toward ever-smaller portable digital music players, cell phones, and other electronic devices sparked concern whether a molecular size barrier existed that would limit further miniaturization of digital memory devices and other electronics components that used thin layers of ferroelectric materials. Such materials show an electric polarization that can be quickly switched from one state to another—from a "1" to a "0," for instance—in ways that make them ideal for digital applications. Scientists believed there might be a critical thickness below which the materials would lose their ferroelectric properties. Dillon D. Fong and colleagues of Argonne National Laboratory near Chicago reported the first experimental evidence that ferroelectric materials remain ferroelectric down to a thickness of 1.2 billionth of a metre and would therefore not impose a limit to miniaturization in ultrasmall electronic devices.

The innermost structure of metals, ceramics, and other materials is important because it largely determines the strength, conductivity, and other key properties of the material. In metals, for example, the smaller the average grain size in the microstructure is, the greater is the strength of the metal. Chemists and materials scientists used powerful X-ray diffraction devices to investigate the three-dimensional microstructure of materials. In a major advance in efforts to characterize the microstructure of materials, Søren Schmidt and associates of Risø National Laboratory in Roskilde, Den., added a fourth dimension—time—to those studies. They developed a modification to the three-dimensional X-ray diffraction microscope at the European Synchrotron Radiation Facility in Grenoble, France, producing a four-dimensional microscope. They used the microscope to watch the formation of crystals in a sample of aluminum as it was put under stress and deformed. The initial findings challenged the widely accepted idea that new grains in the crystalline structure of a metal grow in a smooth spherical fashion. Scientists planned to use the microscope to study the underlying mechanisms of solidification, precipitation, and other phenomena that affect the properties of a wide range of materials.

Astrochemistry. Phosphorus is central to life. It forms the backbone of DNA and RNA molecules, is part of the adenosine triphosphate (ATP) molecules that serve as an energy source for life processes, and forms cell membranes and other structures, yet phosphorus is much rarer than the other chemical elements that were needed for life to emerge on the primordial Earth. For every phosphorus atom in the oceans, there are 974 million carbon atoms, 633 million nitrogen atoms, 49 million hydrogen atoms, and 25 million oxygen atoms. In addition, the most common phosphorus-bearing terrestrial mineral, apatite, releases only minute amounts of phosphorus when mixed with water.

So where did terrestrial life get its phosphorus? At the 228th national American Chemical Society meeting in Philadelphia, Matthew A. Pasek of the University of Arizona reported a possible solution to the long-standing mystery: meteorites. Meteorites bear several phosphorus-containing minerals, the most important of which is the iron-nickel phosphide called schreibersite. Pasek and colleagues showed that schreibersite mixed with water at room temperature yields several phosphorus compounds. Among them was P_2O_7, a compound similar to the phosphate in ATP.

Previous experiments had formed P_2O_7, but only at high temperature and other extreme conditions. Researchers said the identification of meteorites as rich sources of phosphate that could be readily released into water solution allowed some informed speculation on the origin of life on Earth. On the basis of this finding, life on Earth probably originated near a freshwater source where a meteorite had recently fallen, and the meteorite was probably an iron meteorite, which has up to 100 times as much schreibersite as other types of meteorites.

Applied Chemistry. Scientists reported the first use of multiphoton absorption photopolymerization (MAP) to build intricate three-dimensional nanostructures that might become the basis for microscopic machines and electronic devices. A research group headed by John T. Fourkas of Boston College reported the development of an acrylate resin that made it possible to fabricate microstructures on a biological material without damage. The resin, similar to Plexiglas, was hardened at the focal point of a laser beam that was directed over the resin in a three-dimensional scanning pattern to build up structures that were 1,000 times smaller than the diameter of a human hair. Unhardened resin was then washed away. In a dramatic demonstration of the size of the features that could be produced, Fourkas fabricated various structures on the surface of a human hair, including microscopic three-dimensional letters spelling the word "hair." Fourkas envisioned eventually using MAP to build sensors, drug-delivery systems, and other structures directly on skin, blood vessels, and even inside living cells. He emphasized that such applications of MAP would require much additional research. The current research, however, brought them closer to reality. (MICHAEL WOODS)

PHYSICS

Particle Physics. In 2004 experimenters at the University of Tokyo's Super-Kamiokande Laboratory expanded and quantified the results of their investigation of the neutrino for which they were awarded the Nobel Prize for Physics in 2002. Neutrinos, which are the most elusive of stable fundamental particles, exist as three types: muon-neutrinos, tau-neutrinos, and electron-neutrinos. Super-Kamiokande experiments in the 1990s were the first to suggest an oscillation between muon-neutrinos and tau-neutrinos—that is, a conversion of one type of neutrino to another. This phenomenon implied that neutrinos had mass (albeit a very small mass), contrary to the prevailing view that neutrinos were massless particles. According to theory, the probability that a muon-neutrino would change into the tau type and vice versa depended on its energy, the distance it had traveled, and the relative masses of the two neutrino types. New data showed a sinusoidal variation in the number of muon-neutrinos detected, which confirmed the theory and enabled the relative masses of the two neutrino types to be calculated.

Another fundamental particle that gave physicists headaches was the muon. The generally accepted theory of fundamental particles, called the Standard Model, very precisely predicted the value of a property of these particles called the magnetic moment. Physicists at the Brookhaven National Laboratory, Upton, N.Y., conducted an experiment to make exact measurements of the magnetic moment of negatively charged muons and announced results that flouted the predicted value.

On the other hand, physicists were able to refine the precision of other predictions that the Standard Model was able to make. The predictions involved calculations using parameters, such as particle masses, whose values constrain other parts of the model. The DØ collaboration, formed by physicists from 19 countries working with the Tevatron proton-antiproton collider at Fermi National Accelerator Laboratory (Fermilab), near Chicago, measured the mass of the top quark to a greatly improved precision of around 2%. Among the benefits anticipated with this greater precision were improved predictions concerning characteristics of the yet-to-be-observed Higgs boson, the particle postulated to account for the fact that fundamental particles have mass.

Condensed-Matter Physics. Experiments that involved cooling a few thousand gas atoms to a temperature closely approaching absolute zero (0 K, −273.15 °C, or −459.67 °F) were being pursued in a number of laboratories. When a cooled gas consists of atoms with zero or integral intrinsic spin (atoms classified as bosons), the result is a state of matter known as a Bose-Einstein condensate. Rather than existing as independent particles, the bosons become one "superparticle" described by a single set of quantum state functions. When the cooled gas consists of atoms with an intrinsic spin of 1/2, 3/2, 5/2, and so on (atoms classified as fermions), the atoms cannot fall to the same condensed state, as described by the Pauli exclusion principle. Instead, they tidily fill up all available states starting from the lowest energy. Physicists were studying such fermionic condensates in an attempt to observe a phenomenon called Cooper pairing. Cooper pairing of electrons (which are fermions) in some solids and liquids at low temperatures produces superconductivity (the complete lack of electrical resistance) and superfluidity (the lack of viscosity). In the case of fermionic condensates, physicists believed that a similar phenomenon should be possible in which pairs of atoms would strongly interact, forming a Cooper pair that would have the properties of a boson. The production and study of fermionic condensates exhibiting Cooper pairing was expected to help unravel the theory underlying superconductivity and superfluidity, and many laboratories were involved in the race to develop such condensates.

Early in 2004 Rudolf Grimm and colleagues of the University of Innsbruck, Austria, reported producing fermionic condensates that had very low viscosity. This property was necessary but not sufficient evidence that the production of Cooper pairing had been achieved. At JILA (formerly the Joint Institute for Laboratory Astrophysics), Boulder, Colo., Deborah Jin and co-workers also worked with a fermionic condensate. In an earlier experiment they had used a magnetic field to bind potassium atoms into loose molecule-like associations that could then form a Bose-Einstein condensate. In a new experiment they adjusted the magnetic field to prevent the molecular associations but still observed a pairing of atoms that formed a condensate. Although the group did not yet claim that Cooper pairing was taking place, it was clear that one or another laboratory would shortly obtain conclusive evidence for the production of Cooper pairing in this new form of matter.

Quantum Physics. The phenomenon of quantum teleportation was quickly changing from being an exotic by-product of quantum theory to becoming a practical application in computing and information transfer. Teleportation concerns the instantaneous transfer of information from one place to another. It circumvents the restriction on exceeding the speed of light (a restriction imposed by relativity theory) by making use of the phenomenon called entanglement. If two quantum systems are prepared together, so that their states are "entangled," then separated to an arbitrarily large distance, measurement of the state of one system will instantaneously define the state of the second system. The state is said to represent a qubit, or quantum bit, of information.

Two scientific teams using different systems achieved teleportation of the quantum states of ions (electrically charged atoms). Previous experiments had demonstrated teleportation only with the quantum states of beams of light. The ion-teleportation experiments consisted essentially of preparing the initial quantum state of one particle and then teleporting that state to a second particle at the push of a button. Mark Riebe and co-workers at the Institute for Experimental Physics, University of Innsbruck, used three calcium ions trapped together at an ultrahigh vacuum. One ion constituted the source, and the second served essentially as carrier of information to the third, the receiver. Murray Barrett and his colleagues at the National Institute of Standards and Technology, Boulder, Colo., produced similar results with beryllium ions, using a different form of trap and a different experimental layout. Although there are many types of particles that might function as the basis of practical devices for storing and transporting qubits, including photons and atoms, trapped ions, or quantum dots, tiny isolated clumps of semiconductor atoms with nanometer dimensions, it was generally agreed that the ion-trap setup used in these experiments was one of the most promising candidates.

Meanwhile, advances continued to be made in experiments on teleportation of light. Rupert Ursin and co-workers at the Institute for Experimental Physics, University of Vienna, described teleportation of photons over a distance of 600 m (about 2,000 ft) and Zhao Zhi and co-workers at the University of Science and Technology of China demonstrated five-photon entangled states, an important step on the road to the development of quantum communication. Other experimenters were considering the transfer of quantum information via the interaction of matter and light. Physicist Boris Blinov and colleagues in the department of physics at the University of Michigan succeeded in observing entanglement between a trapped ion and an optical photon.

On the other hand, Irinel Chiorescu and colleagues at Delft (Neth.) University of Technology coupled a two-state system—made up of three in-line Josephson junctions—to a superconducting quantum interference device (SQUID) on the same semiconductor segment. The SQUID served as a detector for the quantum states, and entangled states could be generated and controlled. The experiment pointed the way to the possible use of solid-state quantum devices for controlling and manipulating quantum information. Such experiments were made possible by advances in a number of fields, from precision laser spectroscopy to techniques involving ultralow temperature and ultrahigh vacuum. In the midst of this experimental ferment, it was not yet clear which path might eventually lead to the building of large-scale quantum computers, overcoming the inherent restrictions of electronic devices.

Experimental techniques in microscopy reached a level of sophistication that made it possible to study the spin of a single electron a short distance below the surface of a solid. Dan Rugar and co-workers at the IBM Almaden Research Center, San Jose, Calif., combined the techniques of magnetic resonance imaging and atomic force microscopy to create a technique called magnetic resonance force microscopy (MRFM). The researchers mounted a micromagnetic probe on a tiny cantilever a short distance above the surface of the material being studied. The probe generated a magnetic-field gradient so large that the interaction between the probe's magnetic field and that of a single electron produced a measurable mechanical force on the probe. The new technique not only dramatically increased the resolution of magnetic resonance imaging but also held promise for helping make use of atomic spin for qubits in information storage.

Anton Zeilinger and co-workers at the Institute for Experimental Phases of the University of Vienna carried out an experiment concerning the transition between the quantum and classical realms of physics. It demonstrated the fallacy of the common tendency to separate qualitatively the quantum behaviour of extremely small particles, such as electrons, from the classical behaviour of everyday objects, such as billiard balls. Using relatively large cagelike carbon C_{70} molecules, Zeilinger's group observed a smooth transition between quantum and classical behaviour. They heated the molecules and sent them through a series of gratings onto a detector, in a rerun of the seminal two-slit experiment that showed the quantum nature of fundamental particles such as electrons. At low temperatures the molecules formed an interference pattern at the detector—a manifestation of quantum behaviour. As the temperature of the molecules was increased, however, there was a swift but smooth transition to behaviour like that of classical objects.

This experiment demonstrated that the division between the quantum and classical realms is not a function of the size of the particle but most likely a function of the interaction of the particle with the outside world (in this case the emission of radiation by the heated molecules). (DAVID G.C. JONES)

ASTRONOMY

Solar System. Two NASA spacecraft, the Mars rovers Spirit and Opportunity, touched down on the red planet in early 2004. Spirit landed in a crater called Gusev, which in area was about the size of the state of Connecticut. Opportunity landed on the opposite side of the planet, in a crater on the Martian equatorial plain called the Meridiani Planum. The mission of each rover

D. Kiselman, et al. (Institute for Solar Physics), Royal Swedish Academy of Sciences

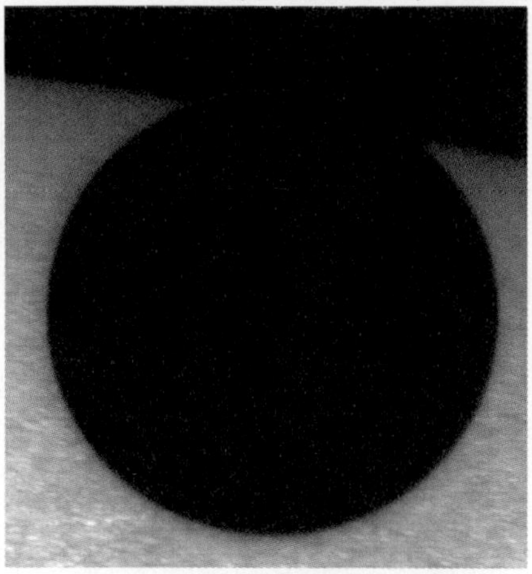

In a rare event, Venus passes directly in front of the Sun on June 8. While Venus crosses in front of the edge of the face of the Sun, sunlight refracted by the atmosphere of Venus outlines the upper edge of the planet.

was to study the chemical and physical composition of the surface at various locations in order to help determine whether water had ever existed on the planet and to search for other signs that the planet might have supported some form of life. Using an alpha-particle spectrometer, Spirit revealed that the chemical composition of the soil in the area where it had landed was similar to that found previously by Mars landers at other sites. This finding suggested that winds on Mars widely dispersed the dusty material found on its surface. Opportunity uncovered evidence that the rocks in the crater where it landed had been deposited in salty water at least 5 cm (2 in) deep that had been flowing at 10–50 cm per second.

On June 30, following a seven-year, 3.5-billion-km (2.2-billion-mi) journey, the Cassini spacecraft arrived at Saturn, and it became the first spacecraft to enter into orbit around the planet. Cassini's mission, slated to last four years, was to study not only the planet but also its elaborate ring system and its moons. It carried a probe, called Huygens, that was scheduled to be released December 25 and land on Saturn's giant moon Titan three weeks later. The first images of the ring system obtained by Cassini in orbit around Saturn were more detailed than any that had been obtained by previous spacecraft. Among the features they showed were wave patterns thought to be caused by the gravitation of Saturn's moons. The rings appeared to be composed primarily of water ice mixed with dust that was similar in composition to the material detected on the moon Phoebe. While making its one close approach to Phoebe, Cassini revealed that the surface of the moon was heavily cratered. The cratering supported the idea that some of Saturn's smaller moons might have been formed from material that was ejected from Phoebe in a collision with a passing comet or asteroid. As Cassini passed within 339,000 km (211,000 mi) of Titan, onboard infrared detectors provided detailed images of its methane clouds. The appearance of the clouds was seen to change significantly over a period of only a few hours.

On March 15 Michael E. Brown of the California Institute of Technology and collaborators Chad Trujillo of the Gemini Observatory, on Mauna Kea, Hawaii, and David Rabinowitz of Yale University announced the discovery of the most distant object of the solar system that had ever been observed, at a distance of 13 billion km (8.1 billion mi). Its discoverers named the new object Sedna, after the Inuit goddess said to live in a cave at the bottom of the Arctic Ocean. The new object was about three-quarters the size of Pluto and somewhat larger than the planetoid (planetlike object) Quaoar, which was discovered by the same group in 2002. Sedna was found to have a highly elliptical orbit, which took it from 76 times the Earth–Sun distance to about 900 times that distance and back in a period of 10,000 years. Observations of Sedna quickly raised a number of puzzling questions. Astronomers had thought that all objects in the outer solar system would be icy and therefore white or gray in appearance, but Sedna was almost as red as Mars. Its extremely elliptical orbit resembled the orbits of objects thought to exist in the Oort cloud, a distant cloud of icy objects that had been postulated by Dutch astronomer Jan Oort more than a half century before to account for the origin of comets. Sedna, however, was observed at a distance 10 times closer than the predicted inner edge of the Oort cloud. The proposal that Sedna had been kicked toward the inner solar system by the gravitation of a passing star was just one of several ideas that was being explored to account for its orbit.

For many Earth-bound skywatchers, the astronomical event of the year was the transit of Venus on June 8, a rare event in which the planet was seen to pass directly between Earth and the

Sun. During the transit Venus was visible for six hours as a small dark disk that crossed the bright disk of the Sun. The previous transit of Venus had occurred on Dec. 6, 1882. The next Venus transit would occur in only eight years, but the one following it would be more than a century later, in 2117. The transits of Venus were once of great importance to astronomers because careful timings of the events permitted the calculation of the distance between Earth and the Sun.

Stars. Over the past decade, more than 135 exoplanets (planets outside the solar system) had been detected in orbit around a wide variety of stars. Almost all of the planets had a mass in the range of 100 to 1,000 times that of Earth, and all of them were probably gas giants, such as Jupiter and Saturn. The presence of a planet in orbit around a star had usually been determined by studying variations in the speed of the star as it moved through space. In 2004, for the first time, a group of astronomers, using a network of 10-cm (4-in)-diameter telescopes at the Astrophysical Institute of the Canary Islands, Spain, discovered a Jupiter-sized planet in orbit around a star by detecting a periodic decrease in the brightness of the star as the planet passed in front of it.

Small rocky planets, such as Earth, were believed to have at most a mass about 10 times that of Earth. Exoplanets with a mass in that range had been found, but they were in orbit around millisecond pulsars, an unlikely habitat for life. In 2004 three separate groups announced that they had detected exoplanets with a mass ranging from 14 to 40 times the mass of Earth. These planets, therefore, would likely be icy giant planets, such as Uranus and Neptune. Studies by George Rieke and collaborators from the University of Arizona, using NASA's Spitzer Infrared Space Telescope, in Earth orbit, found that of 266 young stars they had studied, 71 were surrounded by a disk of dusty debris. The observation suggested that there might exist many stars with small rocky planets. Other astronomers using the Spitzer Space Telescope detected a gap in the ring system surrounding the young star CoKu Tau 4, which suggested that there was a Jupiter-like planet in orbit around the star. Finally, a group of astronomers who used the advanced adaptive optics system on the European Southern Observatory's Very Large Telescope in Chile might have obtained the first near-infrared image of an exoplanet. The Jupiter-sized object orbited a relatively young nearby brown dwarf star of very low mass, called 2M1207. The various studies of exoplanets gave an indication that exoplanets were ubiquitous, and they gave further impetus for the search for Earth-like exoplanets in the Milky Way Galaxy.

Galaxies and Cosmology. Over the previous six years, a consistent picture of the origin and evolution of the universe had emerged from two kinds of observational evidence. Visible-light observations of Type Ia supernovae—exploding stars that all had roughly the same intrinsic luminosities—indicated that the galaxies in which they were found were moving away from one another at ever-increasing speeds. This observation implied that the rate of expansion of the universe was increasing with time. Detailed independent observations of minute fluctuations in the microwave background radiation left from the Big Bang provided confirmation of the accelerating expansion rate. Taken together, these observations also indicated that only 5% of the universe consisted of normal atomic matter, 70% consisted of dark energy, and roughly 25% consisted of an unknown cool dark matter. In 2004 observations made with three of NASA's Great Observatories—the Hubble Space Telescope, the Chandra X-Ray Observatory, and the Spitzer Infrared Space Telescope—helped confirm and clarify these findings. Using the Chandra Observatory, Andrew Fabian and collaborators from the University of Cambridge made detailed observations of distant clusters of galaxies that were 1 billion–8 billion light-years from Earth. The hot gases that filled the space between the member galaxies of the cluster emitted a prodigious amount of X-rays. By analyzing the X-ray spectra of 26 such clusters, the team concluded that they contained dark energy and matter in agreement with the earlier—and completely independent—studies.

On March 9 NASA reported the first results from a study of an image obtained from the Hubble Space Telescope that showed objects in the universe more distant than had been seen before. The image required a total exposure of one million seconds (11.6 days) and was made by using both the Hubble's Advanced Camera for Surveys and the Near Infrared Camera and Multi-Object Spectrometer. Called the Hubble Ultra Deep Field, the image contained an estimated 10,000 galaxies that lay in a small patch of the sky that extended only one-tenth the angular diameter of the moon. The galaxies were estimated to have been formed only 400 million–800 million years after the Big Bang. The infrared, visible, microwave, and X-ray observations indicated that the age of the universe was about 13.7 billion years, give or take some 200 million years.

(KENNETH BRECHER)

Earth Perihelion and Aphelion, 2005	
Jan. 2	Perihelion, approx. 01:00[1]
July 5	Aphelion, approx. 05:00[1]
Equinoxes and Solstices, 2005	
March 20	Vernal equinox, 12:33[1]
June 21	Summer solstice, 06:46[1]
Sept. 22	Autumnal equinox, 22:23[1]
Dec. 21	Winter solstice, 18:35[1]
Eclipses, 2005	
April 8	Sun, annular-total (begins 17:51[1]), visible along a path beginning southeast of New Zealand; extending through the southern Pacific Ocean, the eastern Pacific Ocean, Panama; ending in northern South America; with a partial phase visible in New Zealand, most of the southern Pacific Ocean, southern North America, and most of South America (except the eastern and southern parts).
April 24	Moon, penumbral (begins 7:50[1]), the beginning visible in North America, South America, most of Antarctica, most of the Pacific Ocean (except the western part), eastern Australia; the end visible in western North America, most of Antarctica, the Pacific Ocean, western Asia, Australia, the southeastern Indian Ocean.
Oct. 3	Sun, annular (begins 7:35[1]), visible along a path beginning in the northern Atlantic Ocean; extending through Spain, northern Africa, eastern Africa; ending in the Indian Ocean; with a partial phase visible in most of the northern Atlantic Ocean, Europe, Africa, southwestern Asia, southern Asia, and most of the Indian Ocean.
Oct. 17	Moon, partial umbral (begins 11:34[1]), visible in most of North America (except the eastern part), the Pacific Ocean, Australia, most of Asia (except the western part).

[1] Universal time.
Source: *The Astronomical Almanac for the Year 2005* (2004).

SPACE EXPLORATION

The era of privately funded human space travel arrived in 2004 with successful suborbital flights to the edge of space to claim the $10 million Ansari X Prize. Earlier in the year, the United States had announced plans to return humans to the Moon, to press onward

(continued on page 276)

The Mystique of Mars

by Dave Dooling

On Aug. 27, 2003, thousands of people lined up at telescopes to glimpse Mars during its closest approach to Earth in more than 60,000 years (at a distance of 56 million km [35 million mi]). Even though more highly detailed images were readily available from robotic spacecraft, why did people want a firsthand view? Simple: Mars attracts. Of all the planets, it is the most similar to Earth in many ways. It has a transparent atmosphere (though thin and consisting largely of carbon dioxide), a day that is only 37 minutes longer than that of Earth, and even an ice cap that waxes and wanes with the seasons. Most important of all, Mars might harbour life.

Fascination with Mars took off with a simple mistranslation. Among the surface features reported in 1877 by Italian astronomer Giovanni Schiaparelli were *canali*. By that term he meant *channels* (which can be of natural origin), but the translation to English was *canals*, which implied that the features had been built artificially. No oceans or other bodies of water were visible, so it became all too easy to conjure images of a dying Martian civilization engaged in immense irrigation projects to delay inevitable desertification.

American astronomer Percival Lowell picked up on this fanciful thinking, and in his observations he saw exquisitely fine structures that he associated with canals. He then helped popularize them in his writings, including *Mars* (1895) and *Mars as the Abode of Life* (1908). Other astronomers were unable to reproduce Lowell's observations, however, and later studies of the planet eventually dispelled the notion of canals. (A possible explanation for Lowell's observations is that he was seeing, with striking clarity, the blood vessels in the retina of his eye; Lowell masked the secondary mirror of his telescope to such an extent to dim the brightness of Mars that he might have, in effect, turned the telescope into an ophthalmoscope.)

In the 1960s and '70s, the robot surrogates of the Space Age brought Mars closer to its human observers. NASA's Mariner 4, the first spacecraft to fly by Mars (July 1965), sent back pictures of a bleak, cratered world. The Mariner 6 and 7 flyby missions (July and August 1969) reaffirmed this view. When Mariner 9 went into Martian orbit (November 1971), a planet wide dust storm was at its height, but as the dust settled, the improved imaging devices on the probe revealed dazzling geologic features, from towering extinct volcanoes to gaping dry valleys.

Mars 3, launched by the U.S.S.R., was the first Mars lander (Dec. 2, 1971), but it went silent after only 20 seconds on the surface. The Viking 1 and 2 landers, NASA spacecraft designed to detect life on Mars, touched down successfully (July 20 and Sept. 3, 1976). Over the next few years, onboard labs did not detect life as it is known on Earth, but they did reveal some unusual chemistry in the surface material they analyzed. The inconclusive results stirred controversy for many years.

In the mid-1990s the public was showered anew with images of Mars. These images were provided by the Mars Global Surveyor, which went into orbit around Mars (September 1997), and the Sojourner rover, which landed on and traveled over its surface (July 4, 1997). Also in 1996 NASA scientists announced what they believed to be signs of life inside a meteorite named ALH84001, which had been discovered in near-pristine condition in Antarctica. The composition of the meteorite showed that it was from Mars (as are some 1% of all known meteorites). Microscopic examinations had revealed structures that the NASA scientists took to be minute bacteria, but some other scientists judged the structures to be the result of nonbiological chemical processes. Most scientists agreed, though, that ALH84001 contained carbonates that were formed by water-based processes on Mars.

Exploration of Mars suffered a setback with the back-to-back failures of the Mars Climate Orbiter (launched 1998) and the Mars

Polar Lander (1999) and its Deep Space 2 surface-penetration probes. (About a third of all space missions sent to Mars have failed.) After a thorough reassessment, NASA pressed on successfully with the Mars Odyssey orbiter and the twin Mars Exploration Rovers, Spirit (landed Jan. 3, 2004) and Opportunity (Jan. 25, 2004). Europe had success with the Mars Express orbiter (2003), but lost its Beagle 2 lander (2003).

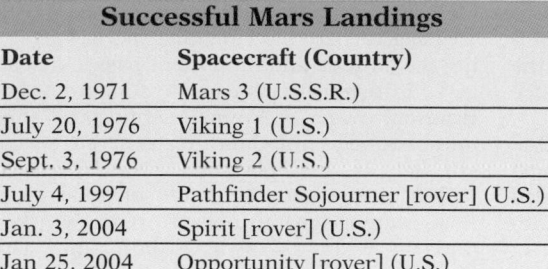

Successful Mars Landings

Date	Spacecraft (Country)
Dec. 2, 1971	Mars 3 (U.S.S.R.)
July 20, 1976	Viking 1 (U.S.)
Sept. 3, 1976	Viking 2 (U.S.)
July 4, 1997	Pathfinder Sojourner [rover] (U.S.)
Jan. 3, 2004	Spirit [rover] (U.S.)
Jan 25, 2004	Opportunity [rover] (U.S.)

A common finding for all of these missions was evidence that Mars once had plentiful water. The Mars Odyssey orbiter and the Mars Express orbiter sent back to Earth thousands of images revealing outflow channels and valley networks that apparently had been formed by flowing water. Among the discoveries of Spirit and Opportunity, which were equipped with tools to assay chemicals in rocks, were the mineral jarosite (which is typically formed in acidic lakes or hot springs), rock indentations called vugs (which are typically formed when crystals dissolve from rocks), and spherules (which are sometimes formed by minerals emerging from porous rock). Images of the Martian surface taken by cameras on Opportunity showed types of sand banding called festooning and crossbedding, which led American scientists to announce that the landing site might once have been the shore of a salty sea. Data from the Mars Global Surveyor indicated that the sea would have been as large as the Great Lakes or the Baltic Sea. A separate finding by the Mars Express orbiter was the existence of traces of methane in the Martian atmosphere. Because the methane would normally have become oxidized within a few hundred years, scientists believed it undergoes replenishment, with the mostly likely sources being volcanoes or living organisms.

Future robotic missions include the Mars Reconnaissance Orbiter (a U.S. spacecraft to arrive at Mars in 2006) for high-resolution imagery of potential landing sites and the Mars Science Laboratory (U.S., 2009) to roam the planet for a full Martian year. For the decade following, the United States and France plan missions that would return to Earth with samples from the surface of Mars, but sending humans to explore the planet has become the long-term goal.

Even as it was reaching the Moon, NASA sketched plans for human expeditions to Mars. In September 1969 a presidential task group envisioned expeditions with two separate ships under nuclear propulsion, each carrying six astronauts. The first landings were to come as early as 1982, but no funding was forthcoming. Indeed, the U.S. pulled back from plans to explore Mars and canceled the Apollo program as well, ending exploration of the Moon. Several false starts followed, most notably the high-priced proposals of the "90-Day Study" commissioned by Pres. George H.W. Bush in 1989. The loss of space shuttle *Columbia* on Feb. 1, 2003, seemed to serve as a turning point in returning to plans for the human exploration of Mars. In the wake of the tragedy, the administration of Pres. George W. Bush moved to retire the shuttle program around 2010 and to discontinue U.S. participation aboard the International Space Station at that time. NASA was directed instead to start planning exploration programs that would take humans back to the Moon by 2020, setting the stage for going onward to Mars. A new Crew Exploration Vehicle would be designed to carry humans to space starting in 2014. A wide range of technologies would need to be developed, including nuclear rockets, which had been abandoned in the 1970s, and advanced radiation shielding to protect astronauts living for years in space.

"Mankind is drawn to the heavens for the same reason we were once drawn into unknown lands and across the open sea," President Bush said at the Jan. 14, 2004, White House ceremony announcing the new direction in the U.S. space program. "We choose to explore space because doing so improves our lives and lifts our national spirit. So let us continue the journey."

Dave Dooling is the Education and Public Outreach Officer at the National Solar Observatory, Sacramento Peak, New Mexico, and he is coauthor of the book Engineering Tomorrow.

Photograph of Mars: NASA/JPL/Malin Space Science Systems;
Photograph of rover: NASA/Goddard Space Flight Center; Photo illustration: Christine McCabe

(continued from page 273)
to Mars in the coming decades, and to retire the aging space shuttle and withdraw from most activities aboard the International Space Station (ISS) once the station had been completed.

Manned Spaceflight. SpaceShipOne (SS1) captured headlines as it claimed the Ansari X Prize. The prize, founded by American space visionary Peter Diamandis, was modeled after the Orteig Prize, which helped spur Charles Lindbergh's nonstop solo transatlantic flight in 1927. The purpose of the Ansari X Prize was to open human space flight to commercial ventures for travel, tourism, and commerce. To win, a spacecraft had to carry at least one person (but be capable of flying three) to the edge of space (an altitude of 100 km [62 mi]), return safely to Earth, and then repeat the trip within two weeks.

Several groups lined up to compete for the prize, but early on, the Mojave Aerospace Ventures team, led by the American aviation pioneer Burt Rutan (builder of the world-circling *Voyager* aircraft) and backed by American Microsoft billionaire Paul Allen, was the odds-on favourite. Rutan designed SS1, based in Mojave, Calif., as a lightweight three-person craft to be carried by an aircraft called *White Knight* to an altitude of 14 km (8.7 mi) and then released so that it could be pushed into space by its own hybrid rocket. After two earlier supersonic flights, SS1 became the first private spacecraft when it flew 124 m (407 ft) beyond the 100-km boundary on June 21 in a demonstration flight. Although minor difficulties were encountered, the flight proved the basic design of the spacecraft. The attempt for the Ansari X Prize by SS1 began on September 29 with a flight to 103 km (64 mi), and it was completed on October 4 with a flight to 112 km (69.6 mi). For 2006 a second competition, the X Prize Cup, was planned with the goal of decreasing turnaround time and increasing the altitude and number of passengers. British entrepeneur Sir Richard Branson, owner of Virgin Atlantic airlines, teamed with Rutan to form Virgin Galactic and plan space tourism with a five-passenger version of SS1. Real-estate magnate Robert T. Bigelow took the wraps off plans to build inflatable space stations and offered a $50 million America's Space Prize for establishing a reliable manned orbital transport service. Legislation to regulate the new space-tourism industry was introduced in the U.S. Congress but stalled over discussions concerning crew and passenger safety requirements that would have had the effect of stifling the new business.

Efforts by NASA to resume space shuttle flights continued slowly, and the date for the next mission slipped to mid-2005. The immediate cause of the 2003 *Columbia* accident was the detachment of foam insulation from a support on the external tank; the foam then smashed through critically important heat-shield tiles on the leading edge of the left wing. To prevent a repetition of the accident, NASA replaced the insulation with electrical heaters at the point where the detachment occurred on the *Columbia*. Preparations for resuming space shuttle flights were slowed after the Kennedy Space Center was damaged by three hurricanes in August and September.

In the aftermath of the loss of *Columbia,* NASA restricted future shuttle missions, including those supporting the ISS. It also canceled service missions to the Hubble Space Telescope, which prompted an outcry by the international astronomy community. NASA relented and in June announced plans to develop a robotic spacecraft that would be able to service the telescope, including the installation of new cameras and replacement gyroscopes. The robot would use a Canadian-made Special Purpose Dexterous Manipulator, a remotely controlled arm that was originally developed for the ISS. A service mission scheduled for 2007 would keep the Hubble operating until the launch of the James Webb Space Telescope, planned for 2011. Meanwhile, the ISS crew was reduced to two persons, the number for which the Russian Soyuz-TMA and Progress-M spacecraft could carry supplies. The next Chinese manned space flight, Shenzhou 6, was expected in 2005.

Space Probes. Scrutiny of Mars intensified with the successful landings of two U.S.-built surface rovers, Spirit and Opportunity, on January 3 and January 25, respectively. Within a few days of landing, each rover had begun exploring the Martian surface. Each was designed for a nominal 90-day mission but functioned so well that operations were extended several times. As 2004 neared a close, NASA planned to continue operating the two landers until they failed to respond to commands from Earth. By October, Spirit had traveled more than 3.6 km (2.2 mi) and Opportunity more than 1.6 km (1 mi). Through January, the European Space Agency (ESA) tried in vain to establish contact with its Beagle 2 lander, sent to the surface on Dec. 25, 2003, from the Mars Express orbiter. An investigation into the loss of the lander revealed a number of management shortfalls that might have led to its failure. Meanwhile, the orbiter started returning a series of striking images of the Martian surface after settling into orbit on January 28. Data from onboard instruments indicated the presence of trace quantities of methane over an area containing water ice. This finding was taken as a possible sign of microbial life on Mars. (*See* Special Report.) Japan's attempt to put its Nozomi ("Hope") Mars probe into orbit on Dec. 9, 2003, failed, and the craft ended up in an orbit around the Sun.

ESA launched its first lunar probe, Small Missions for Advanced Research and Technology (SMART)-1, on Sept. 27, 2003. The 370-kg (82-lb) probe had a xenon-ion engine that generated only 7 g (0.2 oz) of thrust, but it was sufficient to nudge SMART-1 from its first stop (the L1 libration point between Earth and Sun) into lunar orbit, planned around November 15. Once

Human Spaceflight Launches and Returns, 2004

Country	Flight	Crew[1]	Dates[2]	Mission/payload
Russia	Soyuz TMA-4 (up)	Gennady Padalka Mike Fincke André Kuipers	April 19	transport of replacement crew to ISS
Russia	Soyuz TMA-3 (down)	Aleksandr Kaleri Michael Foale André Kuipers	April 30	return of departing ISS crew to Earth
U.S.	SS1-1	Mike Melvill	June 21	Ansari X Prize demonstration flight
U.S.	SS1-2	Mike Melvill	September 29	first Ansari X Prize flight
U.S.	SS1-3	Brian Binnie	October 4	second Ansari X Prize flight
Russia	Soyuz TMA-5 (up)	Salizhan Sharipov Leroy Chiao Yury Shargin	October 13	transport of replacement crew to ISS
Russia	Soyuz TMA-4 (down)	Gennady Padalka Mike Fincke Yury Shargin	October 24	return of departing ISS crew to Earth

[1] For Soyuz flights, commander is listed first.
[2] Soyuz launch or return date for ISS missions.

there, SMART-1 was to scan the Moon for signs of water in polar craters and to map terrain and minerals.

Saturn received its first permanent visitor from Earth—the Cassini-Huygens spacecraft—on June 30, after a nearly seven-year journey. The Cassini orbiter, developed by the United States, would spend four years studying Saturn and its moons. During this time it was scheduled to make numerous flybys of the moons, including a series of 44 flybys of Titan. The orbiter's Huygens probe, developed by ESA to study Titan, was released December 25 and was to parachute through Titan's methane atmosphere for a landing on its surface on Jan. 14, 2005—the first attempted landing on any celestial body beyond Mars. Huygens was expected to provide data on the atmospheric structure of Titan and could possibly return some images from the surface.

The first attempt since the early 1970s to bring to Earth materials collected from outer space ended as a near-total failure when the Genesis spacecraft crashed into the Utah desert on September 8. The spacecraft had been launched on Aug. 8, 2001, and spent 884 days orbiting the Sun with ultrapure sample plates exposed to collect a few micrograms (less than a millionth of an ounce) of the particles that make up the solar wind. The intent was to determine directly the composition of the Sun in order to provide more certain results than those obtained by means of spectral data from telescopic observations. Genesis was to have been recovered by helicopter as it parachuted to Earth. The parachutes did not deploy, apparently because, as investigations later suggested, drawings for the craft's gravity sensors were reversed. Despite damage to the sample capsule, the Genesis science team said it could salvage some specimens.

ESA launched its Rosetta craft on a 10-year mission to obtain sample materials from Comet 67P/Churyumov-Gerasimenko. The expectation was that, like the Rosetta Stone, the craft would help decode ancient history—in this case, the history of the solar system. The 654-million-km (406-million-mi) cruise was to involve three gravity-assisted flybys of Earth and one of Mars before arriving at the comet in 2014. Rosetta would then deploy a 100-kg (220-lb) probe, Philae, that would use two harpoons to anchor itself to the surface of the comet. Data would be collected by an alpha-particle spectrometer and a set of six panoramic cameras, and a drill would be used to extract samples for chemical analysis. Messenger, the second-ever mission to Mercury, was launched by the U.S. on August 3. (The first mission, in 1974–75, was a flyby of Mercury by Mariner 10.) To alter the trajectory of Messenger in preparation for insertion in orbit around Mercury in 2011, the spacecraft was to fly past Earth once, Venus twice, and Mercury three times.

NASA/JPL/University of Colorado

The composition of Saturn's rings is not uniform, as seen in this ultraviolet image obtained by the Cassini spacecraft when it entered into orbit around Saturn on June 30. Ringlets shown in turquoise have a greater content of frozen water than those shown in red.

Unmanned Satellites. Gravity Probe B (GP-B) was launched April 20 into polar orbit. It carried four gyroscopes of ultraprecision 4-cm (1.6-in) polished quartz spheres spinning in liquid helium. Measurements during its one-year mission were to test Einstein's general theory of relativity. Specifically, they would prove or disprove the frame dragging effect—a very subtle phenomenon in which the rotation of a body (in this case, Earth) slowly drags the space-time continuum with it.

China launched two space-physics satellites into Earth orbit: Double Star 1, launched into an equatorial orbit on Dec. 29, 2003, and Double Star 2, launched into polar orbit on July 25, 2004. The two satellites carried identical instruments made by Chinese and European scientists to measure the density, speed, mass, and electrical charge of plasmas and neutral gases in space. Aura, the latest in the NASA series of Earth observation satellites, was launched July 15 into polar orbit. Aura carried instruments to measure the chemical makeup and activity in Earth's stratosphere and troposphere, including concentration levels of ozone and of gases that destroy ozone. Swift, a satellite designed to swing into the proper orientation to catch the first few seconds of gamma-ray bursts, was launched on November 20.

Launch Vehicles. The privately funded SpaceX Falcon launch vehicle moved closer to operational status with the placement of the first flight unit on the launch pad at Vandenberg Air Force Base, California, for a launch planned in 2005. The Falcon was to be able to place into orbit a 680-kg (1,500-lb) payload for about $6 million, saving half the cost of using other launch vehicles, in part by using a recoverable first stage. SpaceX planned to develop a larger Falcon V vehicle to compete with the Delta family of launchers.

The Delta IV heavy-lift launch vehicle was launched for the first time on December 21. It had a 4.6-m (15-ft) core rocket and two identical boosters, each powered by RS-68 liquid hydrogen engines derived from the space shuttle main engine. The last Atlas 2 rocket was launched on August 31. Atlas started as an intercontinental ballistic missile and, like other missiles, was drafted into use as a space launcher in the 1950s. The Atlas 2 rocket retained the missile's basic design.

(DAVE DOOLING)

Religion

In 2004 ISLAMIC LEADERS condemned violence by groups professing allegiance to that faith; disagreements over blessing SAME-SEX RELATIONSHIPS continued to divide the ANGLICAN Communion and other Christian groups; and a MOTION PICTURE and a NOVEL stirred religious controversy.

War and Sectarian Violence. Suicide bombers killed more than 140 people in attacks on Shi'ite Muslim shrines in the Iraqi cities of Karbala' and Basra in March on Ashura, a holy day marking the anniversary of a 7th-century battle in which the grandson of the prophet Muhammad was killed. Iraqi religious buildings in Baghdad and Mosul were targeted in August by car bombs that killed more than 12 people. In Nigeria attackers from the predominantly Christian Tarok tribe killed more than 500 people in raids on the mostly Muslim town of Yelwa in May. The raids were conducted in retaliation for the killing of almost 100 Christians in Yelwa in February, including 48 who were slain in a church. Fighting between Muslim groups and security forces in Thailand in April claimed more than 100 lives, including 32 who were killed in an attack by government troops on a mosque in Pattani. In October more than 70 Muslim men suffocated or were crushed to death as they were being taken to military barracks in army trucks after a riot in Tak Bai, Thai. Attacks by Kosovo's predominantly Muslim ethnic Albanians on Serbian Orthodox sites in March included the burning of 41 churches and 366 houses.

Such outbreaks of violence were denounced and repudiated by influential Muslim individuals and organizations. In January, Saudi Arabia's most prominent cleric, Sheikh Abdul Aziz al-Sheik, told about two million pilgrims at the Namira Mosque that terrorists who claimed to be holy warriors were an affront to the faith. Iraq's top Shi'ite cleric, Grand Ayatollah Ali al-Husseini al-Sistani (*see* BIOGRAPHIES), described the attacks on Iraqi churches as "hideous crimes." In his inaugural address in June, Iraqi Prime Minister Ayad Allawi (*see* BIOGRAPHIES), a Shi'ite, denounced Islamic militants as "the grandsons of the heretics of Islam" and said they had been "rejected by history." A gathering of about 300 Islamic scholars from 49 countries in Jakarta, Indon., in February issued a declaration condemning "acts of terrorism in all its forms and manifestations" and rejected the identification of terrorism with any religion. The Washington-based Council on American-Islamic Relations invited Muslims from around the world to sign an online petition stating that "no injustice done to Muslims can ever justify the massacre of innocent people, and no act of terror will ever serve the cause of Islam."

Homosexuality. A report prepared by an international Anglican commission, released in October, urged the U.S. Episcopal Church to apologize for having "caused deep offense" to other Anglicans with its approval in 2003 of an openly gay bishop, the Rev. V. Gene Robinson of New Hampshire. The report also said blessings of same-sex unions are not a "legitimate application" of Christian faith and urged the U.S. and Canadian churches to discontinue them. At its General Synod in St. Catharines, Ont., in June, the Canadian church affirmed the "integrity and sanctity" of same-sex relationships. Otis Charles, the retired Episcopal bishop of Utah, became the world's first bishop to wed a same-sex partner in church when he married Felipe Sanchez Paris in San Francisco in April. The Rev. Jeffrey John, an openly gay priest who had declined an appointment as a bishop in the Church of England in 2003, was installed as dean of St. Albans Cathedral in July. In April it was reported that Anglican bishops in Africa had decided not to accept money from congregations in the West that allowed the ordination of gay bishops; Anglicans in Asia, Africa, and Latin America outnumbered those in Europe and North America about two

In October a Serbian couple is married in the 19th-century St. Nicholas Serbian Orthodox Church in the predominantly ethnic Albanian city of Pristina, the capital of Kosovo. The church was gutted during ethnic violence in March.

to one but depended on large donations from congregations in the West. The 10-million-member United Methodist Church declared at its quadrennial General Conference in Pittsburgh, Pa., in May that it "does not condone the practice of homosexuality" and opposes the ordination of anyone who is a "self-avowed practicing homosexual." At its annual meeting in June in Indianapolis, Ind., the 16-million-member Southern Baptist Convention commended Pres. George W. Bush for his support of a proposed amendment to the U.S. Constitution to restrict marriage to heterosexual couples. In contrast, leaders of 26 Christian and Jewish organizations sent an open letter to Congress in June saying that the amendment proposal showed disregard for civil rights and ignored differences between religious traditions.

The Right Rev. V. Gene Robinson is invested as the ninth Episcopal bishop of New Hampshire on March 7 at St. Paul's Episcopal Church in Concord, N.H. Robinson was the first openly gay bishop in the Episcopal Church.

© Brian Snyder/Reuters/Corbis

Ecumenism and Interfaith Relations. Ecumenical Patriarch Bartholomew I, spiritual leader of the world's Eastern Orthodox Christians, accepted an apology that had been offered by Pope John Paul II in 2001 for the sacking of Constantinople in April 1204 during the Fourth Crusade. While strengthening relations with the Roman Catholic Church, Bartholomew suspended relations in May with Archbishop Christodoulos, head of Greece's Orthodox Church, in a dispute over control of Greek dioceses. The patriarch said the action had won the unanimous approval of a meeting of 41 bishops from around the world. The Southern Baptist Convention voted to sever ties with the Baptist World Alliance, which it had helped to create in 1905, to protest what it considers to be a liberal theological direction in the group of 211 denominations with a combined membership of 46 million.

In an 80-page booklet titled *The Love of Christ Towards Migrants,* the Vatican said marriage between Catholics and all non-Christians should be discouraged. Specifically citing "profound cultural and religious differences" between Christians and Muslims, it said a woman is "the least protected member of the Muslim family." The 2.5-million-member Presbyterian Church (U.S.A.) stirred the ire of several Jewish organizations when it voted at its General Synod in Richmond, Va., in June to continue financing congregations that evangelized Jews and to study whether it should divest from companies doing business in Israel to protest the Jewish state's treatment of Palestinians. The Jewish advocacy organization B'nai B'rith International said the "hostile and aggressive" positions had shattered 50 years of interfaith dialogue. The World Council of Churches and the Lutheran World Federation criticized the security wall being built by Israel to insulate itself from the West Bank as a violation of human rights, and several Christian organizations voiced concern over the Israeli government's failure to renew visas or residence permits for religious workers while taxing religious charities that had previously been exempted. Bishop Wilton Gregory, president of the U.S. Conference of Catholic Bishops, wrote to President Bush that the Israeli policies constituted "the most difficult situation in living memory for the Church in the Holy Land." In October, Interior Minister Avraham Poraz condemned incidents in which Jewish seminary students spat at Christian clergy, including Armenian Archbishop Nourhan Manougian, during processions through the Old City of Jerusalem.

At a gathering in Berlin in April, representatives of 55 countries unanimously adopted a declaration pledging to fight "new forms" of anti-Semitism and affirming that Middle East developments never justify attacks on Jews. India's Pres. Abdul Kalam announced in June that the government would adopt measures to protect religious minorities from violence and said recent elections showed that citizens reject forces of intolerance. Following the elections, leaders of the winning Congress Party chose former finance minister Manmohan Singh (*see* BIOGRAPHIES) to serve as prime minister, making him the first member of a religious minority (Sikh) to hold that position.

Church and State. Despite protest marches in several major cities around the world, the French Senate voted in March to enact a law banning religious symbols, notably Muslim head scarves, from the country's public schools. The Strasbourg, France-based European Court of Human Rights upheld a similar policy by the Turkish government in June, saying head-scarf bans in state universities were justified if they were designed to prevent "certain fundamentalist religious movements" from pressuring students. In October the Federal Administrative Court in Leipzig ruled that Germany's ban on religiously motivated clothing in schools would have to extend to nuns' habits.

The U.S. Department of State (DOS) cited Saudi Arabia, Vietnam, and Eritrea for the first time in its annual list of countries whose restrictions on religious freedom caused concern. It asserted that in Saudi Arabia, "basic religious freedoms are denied to all but those who adhere to the state-sanctioned version of Sunni Islam." In August the United States revoked a visa that had been granted to Tariq Ramadan, a prominent Swiss Muslim theologian of Egyptian descent, who had been appointed to a professorship on religion, conflict, and peacebuilding at the University of Notre Dame, South Bend, Ind. Authorities gave no explanation for the action against Ramadan, who had delivered a lecture on European Muslims in a visit to the DOS in 2003. In June, Pope John Paul II expressed disappointment that the preamble to the newly approved constitution of the European Union did not include a specific reference to Christianity despite lobbying by 7 of the union's 25 member countries. Also in June, the Moscow City Court upheld a lower court ban on activities by Jehovah's Witnesses in the Russian capital, saying its activities and beliefs promoted "alienation from traditional religions."

The U.S. Supreme Court ruled in June that the phrase "under God" may remain in the Pledge of Allegiance as recited in public-school classrooms. In overturning a federal appeals court decision, five of the eight participating justices cited procedural grounds, ruling that Michael A. Newdow, the atheist who brought the case, lacked legal standing to sue. In February the high court ruled 7–2 that the state of Washington could deny a scholarship to a student studying for the ministry. The California Supreme Court ruled 6–1 in March that Catholic Charities had to offer birth-control coverage to its employees in their health plans despite the church's position that contraception is a sin. Several U.S. bishops, as well as a senior Vatican official, Francis Cardinal Arinze, said that Catholic politicians who favoured abortion rights, including Democratic presidential candidate John Kerry, should not be given communion because their positions contradicted church teachings. Bishop Michael Sheridan of Colorado Springs, Colo., announced in May that anyone voting for a politician who supported abortion rights, same-sex marriage, stem-cell research, or euthanasia would be denied communion. Later in May, 48 Catholic Democrats in Congress signed a joint letter saying that such statements were "miring the church in partisan politics."

Sexual-Abuse Issues. Researchers commissioned by the U.S. Conference of Catholic Bishops reported in February that 4% of all U.S. priests who had served since 1950 had been accused of having sexually abused children. Bishop Gregory said the church would "do everything possible to see that it does not happen again." In November the lay review panel that monitors the bishops' efforts against clergy sexual abuse announced the start of a long-term study of the causes of the scandals. The archdiocese of Portland, Ore., and the diocese of Tucson, Ariz., filed for bankruptcy protection because of the multimillion-dollar expenses they faced as a result of such abuse cases. Desmond Cardinal Connell, archbishop of Dublin, who had drawn criticism for his handling of Ireland's priest sex scandals, was replaced in office in April; Bernard Cardinal Law, who resigned as archibishop of Boston following a sex scandal there in 2002, took up his new position as head of a basilica in Rome. In August the Vatican closed the St. Pölten Seminary outside Vienna after Austrian authorities said they found 40,000 videos and photographs of child pornography on computers at the theology school. Bishop Kurt Krenn, who had dismissed the pornography as a "childish prank," resigned in September. Also in September, the former bishop of Springfield, Mass., Thomas L. Dupre, became the first U.S. Catholic bishop to be charged with sexual abuse when he was indicted by a grand jury on child rape charges dating to the 1970s.

The Evangelical Lutheran Church in America and its seminary in Columbus,

In a still from the film **The Passion of the Christ,** *actor Jim Caviezel portrays Christ in his last hours. The controversial film stirred passions among Christians, Jews, and Muslims alike.*

© ITAR-TASS/Corbis

© Claudia Daut/Reuters/Corbis

Ecumenical Patriarch Bartholomew I (left) and Cuban Pres. Fidel Castro appear together at the consecration of the St. Nicholas Cathedral in central Havana in January. Bartholomew was the first church head to visit Cuba since the visit of Pope John Paul II in 1998.

Ohio, reached settlements totaling $32 million in molestation cases involving Gerald Patrick Thomas, a former pastor in Texas who had been sentenced to 397 years in prison in 2003. Nine plaintiffs in a separate lawsuit involving Thomas won a jury award of nearly $37 million in April. Antiochian Orthodox Bishop Demetri Khoury of Toledo, Ohio, who oversaw churches in eight states, was sentenced in April to 28 days in jail and fined $200 after he pleaded guilty for having grabbed a woman's breast in a casino in Michigan. Thomas O'Brien, the resigned Catholic bishop of Phoenix, Ariz., was sentenced to four years on probation in March for a hit-and-run accident that killed a pedestrian. He was believed to be the first U.S. Catholic bishop to have been convicted of a felony.

Religion and Popular Culture. Mel Gibson's (*see* BIOGRAPHIES) much-anticipated film *The Passion of the Christ* drew praise from Christians in the United States and Muslims in the Middle East for its portrayal of the crucifixion of Jesus. Although Jewish leaders voiced concern that the film could stir anti-Semitism, Gibson insisted that its message was about "faith, hope, love, and forgiveness." Dan Brown's (*see* BIOGRAPHIES) best-selling novel *The Da Vinci Code* (2003) prompted a spate of nonfiction books by Christian authors attempting to debunk its claims that Jesus married Mary Magdalene and fathered a child and that the Bible was commissioned by the Roman emperor Constantine for political purposes. The novel was banned by Lebanese authorities in September after Catholic leaders there said it was offensive to Christians. The Church of Jesus Christ of Latter-day Saints allowed Doubleday to publish the *Book of Mormon;* this was the first time since the scripture's initial publication in 1830 that a trade publisher had been in charge of its distribution outside Mormon circles. Madonna, a Catholic-born singer-actress, drew attention to the mystical Jewish philosophy known as Kabbala when she spoke at a conference in Tel Aviv in September. While the Los Angeles-based Kabbalah Centre drew followers such as Madonna by saying the philosophy was available to all seekers of healing, happiness, and wisdom, several Orthodox Jewish leaders said the organization's approach was unfaithful to the original intent of Kabbala as uniquely Jewish.

Personalities. George F.R. Ellis, a South African cosmologist, was the winner of the $1.4 million Templeton Prize for Progress Toward Research or Discoveries About Spiritual Realities, the world's largest monetary award to an individual. Ellis, a Quaker, was the son of atheists. The Rev. Clifton Kirkpatrick, top executive of the Presbyterian Church (U.S.A.), was the unanimous choice to be president of the World Alliance of Reformed Churches at its General Council meeting in August in Accra, Ghana. The alliance was made up of 218 church bodies with a combined constituency of 75 million people. The Rev. Jack Hayford of Van Nuys, Calif., was elected president of the four-million-member International Church of the Foursquare Gospel following the resignation of the Rev. Paul Risser in March. In the wake of $14 million in investment losses, Risser and the corporate treasurer, Brent Morgan, resigned for not having followed church governance rules. Among those sending personal greetings to Hayford at his confirmation ceremonies on October 1 was the Rev. Rick Warren, best-selling author and pastor of another huge and quickly growing international church movement. (*See* BIOGRAPHIES.)

Bartholomew became the first Orthodox patriarch to visit Latin America when he went to Havana in January to consecrate a new church and meet with Cuban Pres. Fidel Castro. Church officials said the St. Nicholas Cathedral was the first new church of any faith to be built in Cuba during Castro's 45-year rule. In October, the pope beatified five persons, including Emperor Karl I, who led the Austro-Hungarian Empire from 1916 to 1918; and Anna Katharina Emmerick, a German nun whose 19th-century visions of Christ were recounted in a book titled *The Dolorous Passion of Our Lord Jesus Christ* and were an inspiration for Gibson's movie. Dr. David Hope, the Anglican archbishop of York, Eng., announced his resignation from that post in August to serve as a parish priest in Ilkley.

Sheikh Ahmed Yassin, an Islamist leader who founded and provided spiritual inspiration for the Palestinian militant organization Hamas, was killed in an Israeli helicopter missile attack in March; the Most Rev. Ted Scott, liberal archbishop and former leader (1971–86) of the Anglican Church of Canada, died in June, and James Cardinal Hickey, the activist Roman Catholic archbishop of Washington, D.C., died in October. (*See* OBITUARIES.) Orthodox Patriarch Petros VII of Alexandria, spiritual leader of Greek Orthodox Christians in Africa, was among 17 people killed in a helicopter crash in September en route to the monastic community on Mt. Athos, Greece. Other religious figures who died in 2004 included Franz Cardinal König, retired archbishop of Vienna (1956–85) and a former president of the Vatican Secretariat for Non-Believers, in March, and dissident Russian Orthodox priest Dmitry Dudko in June.

(DARRELL J. TURNER)

THE 2004 ANNUAL MEGACENSUS OF RELIGIONS

Statistical data about religions and churches have been generated from various sources at least since 1750, and the amount of data available has been growing quickly. In addition to the religious groups' own statistics, much of the information comes from decennial governmental censuses; about half the countries of the world ask their populations to state their religions, if any. The United States has never asked a religious question in the federal censuses, which have been conducted since 1790. In its 2000 census the British government introduced a religion question for the first time since 1851, acknowledging that the information is valuable for enumerating and serving the social needs of ethnic minorities. Less-developed countries began to drop religion questions owing to the high cost of including them, but this trend seems to have been reversing in recent years.

A second major source of church membership data is the decentralized censuses taken by many religious head-

Worldwide Adherents of All Religions, Mid-2004

	Africa	Asia	Europe	Latin America	Northern America	Oceania	World	%	Number of Countries
Christians	401,717,000	341,337,000	553,689,000	510,131,000	273,941,000	26,147,000	2,106,962,000	33.0	238
Affiliated Christians	380,265,000	335,602,000	531,267,000	504,747,000	223,994,000	21,994,000	1,997,869,000	31.3	238
Roman Catholics	143,065,000	121,618,000	276,739,000	476,699,000	79,217,000	8,470,000	1,105,808,000	17.3	235
Independents	87,913,000	176,516,000	24,445,000	44,810,000	81,138,000	1,719,000	416,541,000	6.5	221
Protestants	115,276,000	56,512,000	70,908,000	53,572,000	65,881,000	7,699,000	369,848,000	5.8	232
Orthodox	37,989,000	13,240,000	158,974,000	848,000	6,620,000	756,000	218,427,000	3.4	134
Anglicans	43,404,000	733,000	25,727,000	909,000	2,986,000	4,986,000	78,745,000	1.2	163
Marginal Christians	3,269,000	3,083,000	4,425,000	10,352,000	11,384,000	630,000	33,143,000	0.5	215
Multiple affiliation	*–50,562,000*	*–34,528,000*	*–10,021,000*	*–80,962,000*	*–23,217,000*	*–2,252,000*	*–201,542,000*	*–3.2*	*163*
Unaffiliated Christians	21,437,000	5,734,000	22,395,000	5,384,000	49,947,000	4,153,000	109,050,000	1.7	232
Muslims	350,453,000	892,440,000	33,290,000	1,724,000	5,109,000	408,000	1,283,424,000	20.1	206
Hindus	2,604,000	844,593,000	1,467,000	766,000	1,444,000	417,000	851,291,000	13.3	116
Chinese universists	35,400	400,718,000	266,000	200,000	713,000	133,000	402,065,000	6.3	94
Buddhists	148,000	369,394,000	1,643,000	699,000	3,063,000	493,000	375,440,000	5.9	130
Ethnoreligionists	105,251,000	141,589,000	1,238,000	3,109,000	1,263,000	319,000	252,769,000	4.0	144
Neoreligionists	112,000	104,352,000	381,000	764,000	1,561,000	84,800	107,255,000	1.7	107
Sikhs	58,400	24,085,000	238,000	0	583,000	24,800	24,989,000	0.4	34
Jews	224,000	5,317,000	1,985,000	1,206,000	6,154,000	104,000	14,990,000	0.2	134
Spiritists	3,100	2,000	135,000	12,575,000	160,000	7,300	12,882,000	0.2	56
Baha'is	1,929,000	3,639,000	146,000	813,000	847,000	122,000	7,496,000	0.1	218
Confucianists	300	6,379,000	16,600	800	0	50,600	6,447,000	0.1	16
Jains	74,900	4,436,000	0	0	7,500	700	4,519,000	0.1	11
Shintoists	0	2,717,000	0	7,200	60,000	0	2,784,000	0.0	8
Taoists	0	2,702,000	0	0	11,900	0	2,714,000	0.0	5
Zoroastrians	900	2,429,000	89,900	0	81,600	3,200	2,605,000	0.0	23
Other religionists	75,000	68,000	257,500	105,000	650,000	10,000	1,166,000	0.0	78
Nonreligious	5,912,000	601,478,000	108,674,000	15,939,000	31,286,000	3,894,600	767,184,000	12.0	237
Atheists	585,000	122,870,000	22,048,000	2,756,000	1,997,000	400,000	150,656,000	2.4	219
Total population	**869,183,000**	**3,870,545,000**	**725,564,000**	**550,795,000**	**328,932,000**	**32,619,000**	**6,377,643,000**	**100.0**	**238**

Continents. These follow current UN demographic terminology, which now divides the world into the six major areas shown above. *See* United Nations, *World Population Prospects: The 2002 Revision* (New York: UN, 2003), with populations of all continents, regions, and countries covering the period 1950–2050, with 100 variables for every country each year. Note that "Asia" includes the former Soviet Central Asian states and "Europe" includes all of Russia eastward to the Pacific.

Countries. The last column enumerates sovereign and nonsovereign countries in which each religion or religious grouping has a numerically significant and organized following.

Adherents. As defined in the 1948 Universal Declaration of Human Rights, a person's religion is what he or she professes, confesses, or states that it is. Totals are enumerated for each of the world's 238 countries following the methodology of the *World Christian Encyclopedia,* 2nd ed. (2001), and *World Christian Trends* (2001), using recent censuses, polls, surveys, yearbooks, reports, Web sites, literature, and other data. *See* the World Christian Database <www.worldchristiandatabase.org> for more detail. Religions are ranked in order of size in mid-2004.

Christians. Followers of Jesus Christ, enumerated here under **Affiliated Christians,** those affiliated with churches (church members, with names written on church rolls, usually total number of baptized persons, including children baptized, dedicated, or undedicated); total in 2004 being 1,998,631,000, shown above divided among the six standardized ecclesiastical blocs and with (negative and italicized) figures for those persons with **Multiple affiliation** (all who are baptized members of more than one denomination) and **Unaffiliated Christians,** who are persons professing or confessing in censuses or polls to be Christians though not so affiliated.

Independents. This term here denotes members of Christian churches and networks that regard themselves as postdenominationalist and neo-apostolic and thus independent of historic, mainstream, organized, institutionalized, confessional, denominationalist Christianity.

Marginal Christians. Members of denominations who define themselves as Christians but who are on the margins of organized mainstream Christianity (e.g., Unitarians, Mormons, Jehovah's Witnesses, Christian Science, and Religious Science).

Muslims. 83% Sunnites, 16% Shi'ites, 1% other schools.

Hindus. 70% Vaishnavites, 25% Shaivites, 2% neo-Hindus and reform Hindus.

Nonreligious. Persons professing no religion, nonbelievers, agnostics, freethinkers, uninterested, or dereligionized secularists indifferent to all religion but not militantly so.

Chinese universists. Followers of a unique complex of beliefs and practices that may include: universism (yin/yang cosmology with dualities earth/heaven, evil/good, darkness/light), ancestor cult, Confucian ethics, divination, festivals, folk religion, goddess worship, household gods, local deities, mediums, metaphysics, monasteries, neo-Confucianism, popular religion, sacrifices, shamans, spirit writing, and Taoist and Buddhist elements.

Buddhists. 56% Mahayana, 38% Theravada (Hinayana), 6% Tantrayana (Lamaism).

Ethnoreligionists. Followers of local, tribal, animistic, or shamanistic religions, with members restricted to one ethnic group.

Atheists. Persons professing atheism, skepticism, disbelief, or irreligion, including the militantly antireligious (opposed to all religion).

Neoreligionists. Followers of Asian 20th-century neoreligions, neoreligious movements, radical new crisis religions, and non-Christian syncretistic mass religions.

Jews. Adherents of Judaism. For detailed data on "core" Jewish population, *see* the annual "World Jewish Populations" article in the American Jewish Committee's *American Jewish Year Book.*

Confucianists. Non-Chinese followers of Confucius and Confucianism, mostly Koreans in Korea.

Other religionists. Including a handful of religions, quasi-religions, pseudoreligions, parareligions, religious or mystic systems, and religious and semireligious brotherhoods of numerous varieties.

Total population. UN medium variant figures for mid-2004, as given in *World Population Prospects: The 2002 Revision.*

quarters. Almost all 37,000 Christian denominations ask statistical questions each year on at least some of 180 major religious subjects. All Roman Catholic bishops, for instance, are required to answer 141 statistical questions about their activities over the previous 12 months.

Each year about 27,000 new books on the religious situation in a single country, as well as some 9,000 printed annual yearbooks or official handbooks, appear in print. Although not centralized or coordinated, these publications are the third significant source of data for the megacensus of world religion.

The two tables below are the result of a combination and synthesis of these data around the major characteristic, namely individuals' religious profession and/or affiliation. The first table summarizes worldwide adherents by the 19 major or largest religions. The second goes into more detail for the United States.

(DAVID B. BARRETT, TODD M. JOHNSON, PETER F. CROSSING)

Religious Adherents in the United States of America, 1900–2005

	1900	%	mid-1970	%	mid-1990	%	mid-2000	%	mid-2005	%	Annual Change, 1990–2000 Natural	Conversion	Total	Rate (%)
Christians	**73,260,000**	**96.4**	**190,732,000**	**90.8**	**218,335,000**	**85.4**	**239,575,000**	**84.1**	**251,794,000**	**83.9**	**2,507,000**	**–378,000**	**2,129,000**	**0.93**
Affiliated Christians	54,425,000	71.6	152,874,000	72.8	175,500,000	68.6	195,798,000	68.7	205,786,000	68.6	2,016,000	18,300	2,035,000	1.10
Independents	5,850,000	7.7	35,666,000	17.0	66,900,000	26.2	76,218,000	26.7	80,286,000	26.8	766,000	166,000	932,000	1.31
Roman Catholics	10,775,000	14.2	48,305,000	23.0	56,500,000	22.1	62,970,000	22.1	65,900,000	22.0	647,000	–210	647,000	1.09
Protestants	35,000,000	46.1	58,568,000	27.9	60,216,000	23.5	60,797,000	21.3	61,295,000	20.4	690,000	–632,000	58,100	0.10
Marginal Christians	800,000	1.1	6,126,000	2.9	8,940,000	3.5	10,188,000	3.6	11,018,000	3.7	102,000	22,400	125,000	1.32
Orthodox	400,000	0.5	4,189,000	2.0	5,150,000	2.0	5,733,000	2.0	5,992,000	2.0	59,000	–670	58,300	1.08
Anglicans	1,600,000	2.1	3,196,000	1.5	2,450,000	1.0	2,325,000	0.8	2,206,000	0.7	28,100	–40,600	–12,500	–0.52
Multiple affiliation	0	0.0	–3,176,000	–1.5	–24,656,000	–9.6	–22,433,000	–7.9	–20,911,000	–7.0	–276,000	503,000	227,000	–0.98
Evangelicals	*32,068,000*	*42.2*	*35,248,000*	*16.8*	*38,400,000*	*15.0*	*42,890,000*	*15.0*	*44,825,000*	*14.9*	*440,000*	*10,000*	*450,000*	*1.11*
evangelicals	*35,000,000*	*14.5*	*45,500,000*	*21.7*	*88,449,000*	*34.6*	*98,326,000*	*34.5*	*103,513,000*	*34.5*	*1,038,000*	*488,000*	*1,527,000*	*1.57*
Unaffiliated Christians	18,835,000	24.8	37,858,000	18.0	42,835,000	16.8	43,777,000	15.4	46,009,000	15.3	491,000	–396,000	94,200	0.22
Jews	1,500,000	2.0	6,700,000	3.2	5,535,000	2.2	5,659,000	2.0	5,764,000	1.9	63,400	–51,000	12,400	0.22
Muslims	10,000	0.0	800,000	0.4	3,500,000	1.4	4,292,000	1.5	4,657,000	1.6	40,100	39,100	79,200	2.06
Black Muslims	0	0.0	200,000	0.1	1,250,000	0.5	1,650,000	0.6	1,850,000	0.6	12,700	17,300	30,000	2.29
Buddhists	30,000	0.0	200,000	0.1	1,880,000	0.7	2,517,000	0.9	2,721,000	0.9	21,500	42,100	63,700	2.96
Neoreligionists	10,000	0.0	560,000	0.3	1,155,000	0.5	1,428,000	0.5	1,509,000	0.5	13,200	14,000	27,300	2.14
Ethnoreligionists	100,000	0.1	70,000	0.0	780,000	0.3	1,083,000	0.4	1,158,000	0.4	8,900	21,400	30,300	3.34
Hindus	1,000	0.0	100,000	0.1	750,000	0.3	1,056,000	0.4	1,144,000	0.4	8,600	22,000	30,600	3.48
Baha'is	2,800	0.0	138,000	0.1	600,000	0.2	774,000	0.3	829,000	0.3	6,900	10,500	17,400	2.57
Sikhs	0	0.0	1,000	0.0	160,000	0.1	239,000	0.1	270,000	0.1	1,800	6,100	7,900	4.11
Spiritists	0	0.0	0	0.0	120,000	0.0	142,000	0.0	149,000	0.0	1,400	800	2,200	1.68
Chinese Universists	70,000	0.1	90,000	0.0	76,000	0.0	80,000	0.0	86,700	0.0	870	–430	440	0.56
Shintoists	0	0.0	0	0.0	50,000	0.0	57,600	0.0	60,600	0.0	570	180	760	1.42
Zoroastrians	0	0.0	0	0.0	42,000	0.0	54,000	0.0	58,000	0.0	490	670	1,200	2.44
Taoists	0	0.0	0	0.0	10,000	0.0	11,400	0.0	12,000	0.0	110	25	140	1.32
Jains	0	0.0	0	0.0	5,000	0.0	7,000	0.0	7,700	0.0	57	160	210	3.61
Other religionists	10,200	0.0	450,000	0.2	530,000	0.2	577,000	0.2	600,000	0.2	5,100	390	4,700	0.85
Nonreligious	1,000,000	1.3	10,070,000	4.8	21,414,000	8.4	26,123,000	9.1	27,794,000	9.3	245,000	226,000	471,000	2.01
Atheists	1,000	0.0	200,000	0.1	770,000	0.3	1,328,000	0.5	1,424,000	0.5	8,800	47,000	55,800	5.60
Total population	**75,995,000**	**100.0**	**210,111,000**	**100.0**	**255,712,000**	**100.0**	**285,003,000**	**100.0**	**300,038,000**	**100.0**	**2,929,000**	**0**	**2,929,000**	**1.13**

Methodology. This table extracts and analyzes a microcosm of the world religion table. It depicts the United States, the country with the largest number of adherents to Christianity, the world's largest religion. Statistics at five points in time from 1900 to 2005 are presented. Each religion's **Annual Change** for 1990–2000 is also analyzed by **Natural** increase (births minus deaths, plus immigrants minus emigrants) per year and **Conversion** increase (new converts minus new defectors) per year, which together constitute the **Total** increase per year. **Rate** increase is then computed as percentage per year.

Structure. Vertically the table lists 30 major religious categories. The major categories (including nonreligious) in the U.S. are listed with largest (Christians) first. Indented names of groups in the "Adherents" column are subcategories of the groups above them and are also counted in these unindented totals, so they should not be added twice into the column total. Figures in italics draw adherents from all categories of Christians above and so cannot be added together with them. Figures for Christians are built upon detailed head counts by churches, often to the last digit. Totals are then rounded to the nearest 1,000. Because of rounding, the corresponding percentage figures may sometimes not total exactly to 100%. Religions are ranked in order of size in 2005.

Christians. All persons who profess publicly to follow Jesus Christ as God and Savior. This category is subdivided into **Affiliated Christians** (church members) and **Unaffiliated** (nominal) **Christians** (professing Christians not affiliated with any church). *See also* the note on Christians to the world religion table. The first six lines under "Affiliated Christians" are ranked by size in 2005 of megabloc (Anglican, Independent, Marginal Christian, Orthodox, Protestant, and Roman Catholic).

Evangelicals/evangelicals. These two designations—italicized and enumerated separately here—cut across all of the six Christian traditions or ecclesiastical blocs listed above and should be considered separately from them. The **Evangelicals** are mainly Protestant churches, agencies, and individuals who call themselves by this term (for example, members of the National Association of Evangelicals); they usually emphasize 5 or more of 7, 9, or 21 fundamental doctrines (salvation by faith, personal acceptance, verbal inspiration of Scripture, depravity of man, Virgin Birth, miracles of Christ, atonement, evangelism, Second Advent, et al.). The **evangelicals** are Christians of evangelical conviction from all traditions who are committed to the evangel (gospel) and involved in personal witness and mission in the world but who do not belong to specifically Evangelical churches or agencies or give their primary identity as "Evangelical." Alternatively, these are all termed Great Commission Christians.

Jews. Core Jewish population relating to Judaism, excluding Jewish persons professing a different religion.

Other categories. Definitions are as given under the world religion table.

Social Protection

A new U.S. PRESCRIPTION-DRUG program was introduced by Medicare, GENOCIDE occurred in the Darfur region of The Sudan, and more than half of all displaced persons worldwide were LABOUR MIGRANTS.

BENEFITS AND PROGRAMS

North America. In the politically charged atmosphere of a presidential election year, social protection policy generated an outpouring of words but a scarcity of action in the United States in 2004. The centre of attention was Medicare, the government program that helped 41 million elderly and disabled Americans pay their medical bills. At the end of 2003, Congress had enacted the most significant changes in Medicare since its inception, adding coverage of some prescription drug costs and moving to increase the role of private health plans.

The new law was not scheduled to take full effect until 2006, but an interim scheme involving drug discount cards was implemented in mid-2004 to bridge the gap. (*See* Sidebar.) It proved to be a bridge over troubled waters. A dispute surfaced about the price tag of the Medicare Modernization Act of 2003. Originally estimated at $400 billion for 10 years, the projected cost was increased to $534 billion in Pres. George W. Bush's budget and later bumped to $576 billion. Critics charged that the White House had deliberately misled Congress in order to get the measure passed. The administration insisted that costs were higher than first predicted because of medical cost inflation.

A second controversial issue was the new law's provision of subsidies to private health care plans to encourage them to improve coverage and cut fees. President Bush, who favoured greater involvement by the private sector, said that this would give seniors more choice in their health care decisions. Democrats, however, charged it would be a giveaway to drug companies and private insurers and would siphon the healthiest beneficiaries into private plans, leaving Medicare with the sickest, most expensive patients. About one in 10 beneficiaries was in a private plan in 2004.

Seniors covered by Medicare would be able to sign up for the new drug benefits during a six-month period starting Nov. 15, 2005. Those who already had drug coverage through employers, veterans benefits, and other sources could keep it if they chose but could not have both Medicare drug benefits and outside insurance that included drug coverage. When the drug coverage program became fully implemented in January 2006, Medicare recipients who enrolled in it would pay a premium averaging $35 a month plus a $250 annual deductible. After that, they would pay 25% of their next $2,000 in prescription costs, then all of the following $2,850 in charges. Once the total tab reached $5,100, individuals would pay only 5% of charges beyond that. Low-income beneficiaries could receive additional subsidies to eliminate or reduce premiums and other costs.

Adding fuel to the fight over Medicare's future was an announcement by the trustees who monitored the program that it would run out of money in 2019 if no changes were made. That was seven years earlier than the go-broke date projected in 2003. Soaring health care costs, along with the new drug benefits and increased costs of private health plans, were cited as reasons for the revised projection.

The outlook was more positive for the other half of the safety net for seniors, Social Security. Trustees for that program said that Social Security would start paying out more than it received in payroll taxes in 2018 and would have to start dipping into its trust fund then, but the trustees estimated that the fund would not be exhausted until 2042.

Social Security also sparked spirited debate in the presidential election campaign as President Bush repeated his call to let younger workers put part of their payroll taxes into private individual retirement accounts that could be invested in stocks and bonds. Democrats opposed that idea, arguing that it would drain assets from the Social Security trust fund.

Federal Reserve Board Chairman Alan Greenspan warned that Social Security faced potentially serious problems as the baby-boom generation retired, leaving fewer workers to support retirees. Strategies suggested to combat this threat included raising the retirement age again, reducing the annual cost-of-living increase in benefits, and increasing wages subject to the payroll tax. In 2005 the maximum earnings subject to Social Security tax rose to $90,000, and the tax rate was 12.4%, shared equally by employer and employee. By law the retirement age to qualify for full benefits started rising in gradual steps in 2000 and would reach 67 in 2027 for persons born in 1960 or after.

Another casualty of partisan fighting in Congress was reauthorization of the landmark 1996 welfare-reform act that changed the face of welfare in the U.S. Instead of guaranteed benefits for the needy, it imposed a five-year limit on cash grants, required participants to

In February students from the Indiana University School of Social Work join hundreds of Indiana social workers in a rally on the grounds of the statehouse in Indianapolis. The protesters were demanding an increase in social-service funding by the state.

AP/Wide World Photos

work at least 30 hours a week, and gave states greater control of lump-sum federal grants and more flexibility in creating and experimenting with programs. Since the overhaul was enacted, welfare rolls had declined from 12.2 million to 4.9 million. The 1996 law was due to expire at the end of September 2002, but because it had passed with bipartisan support, reauthorization seemed certain. When Republicans and Democrats were unable to agree on details, however, the law was kept in force by a series of short-term extensions. The White House and Republicans generally wanted to increase the work requirements, while Democrats were intent on boosting child-care payments. Congress's failure to reach a compromise created problems for several states where spending decisions on job training, child care, and other issues involving welfare recipients were thrown into limbo. A bipartisan group of governors asked Congress to act quickly on a permanent reauthorization so that states would know what resources they had to work with.

No final action was taken on a number of other issues, including low-income housing, an increase in the minimum wage, and Bush's faith-based initiative that offered federal support to get religious organizations more involved in helping the needy. Meanwhile, the ranks of poor Americans and those without health insurance continued to grow. According to the U.S. Census Bureau, the percentage of people living below the poverty line (an annual income of $18,660 for a family of two adults and two children) rose in 2003 for the third straight year, to 12.5% or 35.9 million, 12.9 million of whom were children. Explanations for the increase included a growth in single-parent families and the lack of good jobs. The number of Americans who did not have health insurance rose to 45 million, 15.6% of the population. Rising health care costs and a drop in the number of workers in employer-sponsored plans were cited as reasons for the increase.

The government announced a 2.7% cost-of-living increase in Social Security benefits for 2005, boosting the average monthly payment for more than 47 million retired and disabled persons to $955 a month. The typical Medicare enrollee would have nearly half of the increase wiped out, however, by a 17.4% rise in Medicare premiums. The new premium for Medicare Part B, which covered doctors' services and outpatient care, jumped $11.60 to $78.20 a month, the largest increase ever in dollar terms. Social Security benefits were tied by law to the consumer price index, and Medicare premiums were adjusted to match soaring health care costs.

In Canada, as in the U.S., publicly financed health care hogged the spotlight. Long waiting times for services, shortages of doctors and nurses, especially in rural areas, and the problems of an aging population made health care a key issue in the June 2004 federal election. The ruling Liberal Party supported national health care and the establishment of a child health program and promised to keep the system accessible to all.

Since 1962 the Canadian national health system had covered all citizens with government-financed insurance that paid most medical expenses. At one time the federal government had provided about one-third of the money that the provinces spent on health care, but by 2002 Ottawa's share had been cut in half to about 16% of the total. A landmark report that year recommended increasing the federal share to 25%. In 2003 Canada had spent $121 billion on health care, 9.6% of GDP. Of that total, $85 billion came from governments and $36 billion from private sources.

Medicare's New Prescription-Drug Program

Although the new prescription-drug coverage feature of Medicare would not fully take effect until January 2006, a temporary step toward that goal was taken in 2004 with the issuance of Medicare-approved drug discount cards, which were made available to 41 million senior citizens on June 1.

Under the stopgap plan, Medicare contracted with insurance companies, pharmacy-benefit managers, health maintenance organizations (HMOs), coalitions of pharmacies, and other private sources to offer the cards to elderly beneficiaries. Altogether, 29 issuers were approved, and 73 different cards bearing Medicare's logo were issued, each with its own list of the drugs that were covered, the discounts offered, and the pharmacies and other sources from which they could be purchased. At least two cards were to be available in every area, but enrollees could sign up for only one.

While prices and covered drugs could be changed weekly by the sponsors, once a Medicare beneficiary signed up for a card, that choice could not be changed until the end of the year. The cost of a card could not exceed $30 annually. Medicare officials expected discounts to run from 10% to 25% of retail prices, with greater savings on highly competitive drugs and generic medicines. In addition, Medicare enrollees with annual incomes of $12,569 or less ($16,862 for a married couple) could receive $600 in credit on their cards in 2004 and another $600 in 2005 to spend on medicines. Low-income persons who already had drug coverage from Medicaid were not eligible for those added subsidies.

Despite the benefits and an intensive campaign to publicize and explain the discount cards, the program generated a mixed response. Medicare officials originally estimated that 7.3 million people would apply for the cards, but four months after the program began, only 4.5 million had signed up, and more than half of those had been automatically enrolled by their HMOs or other health plans. In September the administration announced that it would send discount cards to 1.8 million low-income people who were eligible but had not applied.

One of the most common criticisms was that the prices, discounts, and covered drugs changed constantly, which made it difficult for individuals to determine which card offered them the greatest savings. Officials explained that the changes occurred because sponsors kept adding new pharmacies and negotiating better prices from drugmakers. A survey by the Kaiser Family Foundation and the Harvard School of Public Health found that seniors felt ambivalent about the discount cards. They said that they appreciated the immediate help until full prescription benefits became available, but a majority felt that the cards were confusing and were not worth the trouble because they did not do enough to help people with their drug costs. (DAVID M. MAZIE)

After the election Prime Minister Paul Martin held a three-day summit meeting with premiers from the provinces and territories to plan changes in the country's health policy. The federal government's original offer to boost its contribution was rejected by provincial leaders, who said their increased outlays for health care had cut into spending on education, roads, and other needs. Eventually, the political leaders reached an agreement. Martin promised about $41 billion more over 10 years, in return for which the provinces and territories pledged to make changes that would reduce waiting times for key services and to provide greater accountability on how the money would be spent. No final action was taken on the establishment of a national pharmacare program, but the conferees agreed to set up a task force to develop a national drug strategy by 2006. (DAVID M. MAZIE)

Europe. In 2004 Italy adopted a pension-reform law that made it harder to be eligible for a seniority pension (early retirement); tax incentives were also created for those who remained longer on the job. Belgium increased by about 25% the limits on earnings that retirees or survivors age 65 (63 for women) or older were allowed to make without a reduction in their social security pensions. After April 1 in Ireland there would be no compulsion for workers entering the public sector to retire at a particular age if they wished to remain employed. To encourage the hiring of older workers, workers' and employers' organizations in Finland agreed that the country should move away from assessing employers' contributions to TEL, the mandatory pensions system for most private-sector employees, in relation to the age composition of the enterprise. Beginning in 2007 there would be uniform contribution requirements under TEL regardless of the size of the firm or the age of employees. According to a Pension Sustainability Act that was passed by the German Bundesrat (upper house of parliament), all options for taking early retirement from age 60 would be gradually phased out starting in 2006 and abolished as of 2009. Workers in Germany would not be able to take early retirement before the age of 63. (*See* WORLD AFFAIRS: *Germany.*)

An occupational pension bill that was introduced in the British House of Commons in February called for the establishment of the Pensions Regulator, a new public body to replace the Occupational Pensions Regulatory Authority, as well as a Pension Protection Fund for members of underfunded schemes or for those who were affected by employer insolvency.

The Romanian parliament passed a law in June that provided for the establishment of individual retirement accounts, and beginning on January 1 in Lithuania, employees were able to allocate part of their social security contribution to a private pension. Following the introduction in Russia of funded social security plans, confusion arose when workers were not given information on how to choose a fund manager from among the more than 50 management companies that sought to participate in the program.

On January 1 in The Netherlands, the benefit that employers were required to pay to sick workers—70% of covered earnings—doubled from 52 weeks to 104 weeks. In Sweden the government and the social partners (trade unions and employers' associations) agreed on measures that by 2008 would cut work absences related to sickness by 50%. Among other things, employers would be required to pay 15% of the cost of sick leave for employees who were ill for more than two weeks. The co-payment would not be applied if the employee returned to part-time work or worked under a rehabilitation program, and exceptions would be made for small enterprises. In the Czech Republic the employer had to pay the entire sickness benefit for the first two weeks, and in Slovakia the employer paid fully for the first 10 days; nevertheless, benefits were reduced substantially in these two countries.

Health-reform measures in France included introduction of a "gatekeeper" into the system (requiring that before seeking a specialist, people would have to see a primary physician); penalties for doctors who issued too many sickness certificates; creation of electronic medical records that would show all consultations with medical professionals; introduction of a co-payment of €1 (about $1.25) on consultations, although this would be waived for low-income households; and encouragement of the use of generic drugs.

Effective January 1 in Switzerland, each medical procedure—from simple consultations to complex surgery—would be recorded in the form of a specific number of points, with the value of a point varying from canton to canton. The changes also affected the occupational accident insurance program and led to an increase of 7% in accident insurance premiums. Switzerland also reformed its disability insurance with the fourth revision of the Federal Invalidity Insurance Act, which had four objectives: to consolidate the insurance's funding, to make targeted adjustments to benefits, to strengthen scrutiny by the federal government, and to simplify structures and procedures.

The German government's plan to replace Unemployment Assistance in 2005 with a new benefit called Unemployment Benefit II triggered major public protests. The long-term unemployed would become eligible for Unemployment Benefit II after the expiration of their regular unemployment benefit. Unlike the regular insurance-based benefit, Unemployment Benefit II would be a welfare benefit in line with social assistance. Public debate centred on restrictive eligibility tests and pressure on the unemployed to accept job offers for which the compensation was below their previous salaries.

Industrialized Asia and the Pacific. The Australian Industrial Relations Commission confirmed an agreement between the Australian Confederation of Trade Unions and various employers' organizations that revised the minimum standards on severance pay for the first time in 20 years. A person whose employment was terminated after 10 years of service would have the right to 12 weeks of severance pay; previously that person would have received no more than a colleague terminated after only 4 years.

Beginning in April, employees in New Zealand who were entitled to 5 days of sick leave annually were allowed to carry over up to 15 days of unused sick leave into the next 12-month period. In addition, more support was granted to people with children through the Working for Families package. The paid parental-leave period was extended from 12 to 14 weeks, and employers were required to keep the position open for those taking leave.

In June the Japanese House of Representatives approved the implementation in stages of a Pension Reform Act, which included measures to increase contribution rates to the Employees' Pension Insurance and the National Pension system, to provide for the division of pension rights in the case of divorce, and to improve the information-access rights of insured persons. In view of its aging population, South Korea responded by increasing the legal retirement age of 55 to age 60 by 2008 and to age 65 by 2033 and revising the equal-employment law to prohibit age discrimination in employment.

In Singapore the Parliamentary Committee for Health examined the introduction of a universal-health-insurance program to supplement the existing programs. The coverage would be limited to hospital treatment or day surgery, and deductibles and coinsurance provisions would be established. Singapore's Central Provident Fund (CPF) launched an Internet site to help members with basic investment decisions and to introduce a general program providing guidance on how to use CPF savings at different stages of life.

Emerging and Less-Developed Countries. Malaysia's Employees Provident Fund (EPF), covering most public- and private-sector employees, launched a service that permitted members to obtain information—such as options for withdrawing savings and the addresses of all EPF offices—via Short Messaging Service. Malaysia's central bank announced that it would allow the EPF and other financial institutions to invest up to 10% of their assets internationally.

In September the Indonesian House of Representatives endorsed the creation of a national social security system with five separate insurance programs—for old-age pensions, old-age savings, national health insurance, work-injury insurance, and death benefits. The reform would be implemented in stages and would be largely financed by payroll taxes imposed on employers and workers; the government would subsidize the poorest.

Thailand launched an unemployment insurance plan, and the social security office was allowed to collect its first contributions in January. With a view toward increasing labour mobility, the Thai Ministry of Finance allowed members of occupational provident funds who had terminated their employment with an employer before retirement to leave their accumulated capital with that employer for up to one year before transferring it to the scheme of another employer. Previously, they had to withdraw their savings immediately and suffer a tax penalty.

For the first time, the Chinese government established a minimum monthly wage for full-time workers and a minimum hourly wage for part-time workers; different standards were permitted within a single province, municipality, or autonomous region. Employers who violated the regulations would have to provide compensation for back pay and could face administrative sanctions.

India launched a pilot social security program to cover employees and self-employed persons in the informal economy. The voluntary scheme, which was introduced in 50 districts, provided hospitalization benefits and compensation for loss of earnings as well as old-age, disability, and survivor benefits.

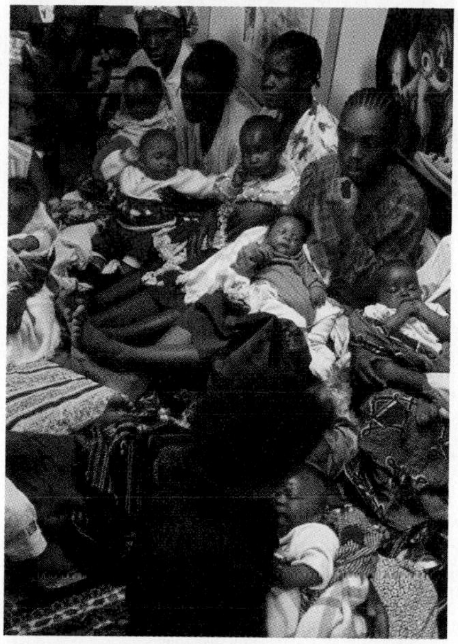

Mothers sit patiently with their babies in the overcrowded waiting room at the Nyanza provincial hospital in Kisumu, Kenya. The government was considering a national plan that would subsidize health insurance for the poor.

The Kenyan parliament discussed the legal framework for a national compulsory social health-insurance scheme with shared risk among different income groups, age groups, persons of different health status, and those residing in different geographic areas. The government would subsidize contributions of the poor with revenue gained from consumption taxes. Ghana too launched the idea of a universal health scheme and provided for the inclusion of employees in the informal economy. The Nigerian government introduced a pension-reform bill that would establish a new system of mandatory personal pensions while also abolishing the social security fund and many private-sector retirement plans. The Algerian government gave a remittance to the National Fund of Unemployment Insurance to manage a business-creation scheme for unemployed people between the ages of 35 and 50.

In Nicaragua the implementation of a 2000 law for privatizing social security appeared to be abandoned. Peru provided the new option to members of private funds to switch (back) to the publicly managed pension system. Previously, the switch could be made only in the other direction. The Chilean government announced that a reform of the 1981 private pension system was imperative. (CHRISTIANE KUPTSCH)

HUMAN RIGHTS

The problems and issues associated with the threat of terrorism dominated many important aspects of human rights in 2004. There was an increased focus on establishing the responsibility of former heads of state (such as Saddam Hussein of Iraq, Augusto Pinochet Ugarte of Chile, Luis Echeverría Álvarez of Mexico, and Slobodan Milosevic of former Yugoslavia) for major human rights abuses; the implications of the torture and abuses by American soldiers against suspected terrorists in Abu Ghraib prison in Iraq and the U.S. base at Guantánamo Bay, Cuba (*see* MILITARY AFFAIRS: Special Report); the decision by the International Court of Justice (ICJ) in The Hague that the wall being built by Israel to protect against terrorists violated international law; and an expanding recognition of the economic and social rights aspects of the human rights equation.

Terrorism. A dramatic increase in terrorism and in the fears generated by terrorist attacks affected human rights concerns more than any other single development in 2004. The increasing number and severity of terrorist attacks in the United States, Spain, Russia, Israel, and several other countries led to harsh repressive measures and major human rights challenges. Human rights impacts were especially severe for the United States, including the abuses of Iraqi prisoners in Abu Ghraib prison, the indefinite detention of suspected terrorists as "unlawful enemy combatants," and the practice of "rendition to torture"—that is, sending alleged terrorists for interrogation in other nations that use harsh techniques, such as torture, not permitted in the U.S. The U.S. Supreme Court weighed in by ruling that indefinite detention violates domestic and international law and that the president does not have unfettered discretion to declare suspected terrorists—either U.S. citizens or

© Lynsey Addario/Corbis

In The Sudan, soldiers from the Sudanese Liberation Army walk past human remains left behind after attacks allegedly by government forces on villages in the Furawiyah district. In 2004 the international community applied the term genocide *to the ongoing situation in the Darfur region.*

prisoners captured during armed conflicts who remained in U.S. control—"unlawful enemy combatants" as a basis for denying them basic due-process rights. The Abu Ghraib scandal led to military courts martial for the seven soldiers who committed the abuses. Despite a number of reports that higher-level officials in the Departments of Justice and Defense had advocated and authorized the use of moderate forms of torture on suspected terrorist detainees in order to obtain information about their activities and plans, by year's end only those prison guards immediately involved in the abuses had been placed on trial.

In a case challenging Israel's construction of a security barrier between that country and Palestinian territories through and around the West Bank, the ICJ held that portions of the wall that were built on Palestinian land violated the rights of the Palestinians, that it could not be justified by military or national security needs, and that it had to be dismantled. A similar judgment had been rendered only a week earlier by Israel's Supreme Court, which held that security needs had to be balanced against suffering caused to residents in the affected areas.

At the same time, the threat that terrorism represented to one of the most basic human rights—the right to life—came to be more widely recognized, with terrorist bombings and shootings leaving an estimated 625 people murdered and 3,646 people injured worldwide in 2003. The number of significant incidents of terrorism reported was higher than at any other time since these types of statistics were first issued by the U.S. State Department in 1982. As a result, greater recognition had been given to the fact that private groups, not just governments, could be held responsible for acts of terrorism and other major human rights abuses under international and domestic law.

Anti-impunity Efforts. The effort to hold major human rights abusers responsible for their actions received considerable support in a number of states. The trial of Milosevic continued before the International Criminal Tribunal for the Former Yugoslavia; Milosevic opened his defense in a trial that had dragged on for more than two years. The Mexican government sought to charge Echeverría with murder in connection with a massacre of political protesters by security forces in 1971. A court in Chile ruled that Pinochet could not escape prosecution by virtue of an earlier grant of immunity by that country's legislature. Saddam was taken before a special tribunal established in Iraq to prosecute war crimes and crimes against humanity that took place during his regime. In addition, the International Criminal Court (ICC), the first body applying criminal sanctions to major human rights abuses on a worldwide basis, began operations. The ICC's first two cases were brought by Uganda in January and the Democratic Republic of the Congo in March.

The progress in establishing criminal responsibility for major human rights abusers received a setback when a court in Indonesia overturned the convictions of several top officers who had been convicted of human rights abuses in breakaway East Timor (Timor-Leste). Progress was very slow in obtaining results from the new "hybrid" courts established in East Timor, Sierra Leone, and Cambodia to deal with past abuses by combining the international elements of the Yugoslavia and Rwanda tribunals and the ICC with domestic elements. The UN-backed East Timor court charged General Wiranto, one of the unsuccessful candidates in the 2004 Indonesian presidential elections, with crimes in connection with the execution of 1,500 people during demonstrations that accompanied East Timor's vote for independence in 1999. The U.S. continued its boycott of the ICC out of concern that its military and civilian personnel involved in military operations in Iraq, Afghanistan, and elsewhere might be subjected to international prosecutions.

Progress also was made in establishing the civil liability of major human rights abusers through civil damage awards to their victims. A U.S. judge ruled that a former captain in El Salvador's army could be held liable for the 1980 assassination of Archbishop Oscar Arnulfo Romero, whose execution during a church service symbolized rampant death-squad activities by the military in El Salvador and other Latin American nations during that era. The Supreme Court affirmed the availability of these kinds of civil penalties in U.S. courts under the Alien Tort Claims Act and the Torture Victims Protection Act in the case of *Sosa* v. *Alvarez-Machain.* These claims were upheld in the face of challenges by the U.S. government, which sought to prevent U.S. courts from dealing with human rights abuses committed in foreign nations. Civil damages also were authorized as part of the penalties that could be imposed by the newly functioning ICC.

Genocide in The Sudan. After what many human rights observers viewed as too long a delay, the international community officially recognized that the campaign of repression, executions, rape, and forced relocations taking place in the Darfur region of The Sudan was of a sufficient scale to be designated genocide. The attacks were carried out by the Arab militia known as Janjawid with the approval and assistance of the Sudanese government.

Though an estimated 50,000 people in Darfur had been killed and 1.2 million others had been displaced and left homeless by year's end, strong sanctions had not yet been imposed against the Sudanese government. The situation was compounded in early November when Sudanese government troops invaded and shut down two refugee camps in southern Darfur, bulldozed the temporary shelters, and forced more than 5,000 displaced residents back to their villages, where they would again be vulnerable to attack by the Janjawid.

New Emphasis on Economic and Social Rights. Additional attention was being paid to health care issues, such as HIV/AIDS, and to sex trafficking as human rights issues. An estimated 38 million people worldwide were suffering from HIV/AIDS in 2003, a substantial rise from previous years. As a result, increased pressures were placed on pharmaceutical manufacturers and developed nations to make less-expensive HIV/AIDS medications more readily available in less-developed countries (LDCs) by easing licensing and royalty restrictions. The World Health Organization reported in July that only 440,000 people infected with HIV/AIDS in LDCs were receiving life-extending drugs, a far smaller percentage than those in industrialized nations. Efforts were also made to bring attention to the threats that other diseases, such as tuberculosis and malaria, posed in LDCs. (*See* HEALTH AND DISEASE: Sidebar.)

Another important development in the HIV/AIDS front was the release from prison in July of Jiang Yanyong, a retired army surgeon who had become China's most well-known political prisoner after his arrest and confinement on June 1. Jiang was imprisoned for blowing the whistle on government efforts to downplay the increasing number of AIDS cases in that country and organizing a campaign to alert the public to the disease.

The problem of sex trafficking took centre stage with the release of a UN report estimating that "hundreds of thousands of child prostitutes" had been lured or forced into the sex trade in Asia alone, making them (and their sex partners) especially vulnerable to HIV/AIDS and other sexually transmitted diseases.

(MORTON SKLAR)

INTERNATIONAL MIGRATION

At the end of 2004, it was estimated that there were some 185 million migrants worldwide, half of whom were women. In 2004 developed states accounted for 60% of global migrant stocks, compared with 43% in 1970. As a result, migration had become an important source of demographic renewal in many industrialized countries where populations were aging and birth rates were below replacement level. In Europe net migration in 2003 accounted for more than four-fifths of the continent's total population growth.

At the end of 2003, the number of "persons of concern" to the United Nations High Commissioner for Refugees was approximately 17.1 million, which reflected a significant decline (18%) since 2002. This included 7.4 million asylum seekers, returned refugees, and certain internally displaced persons, as well as 9.7 million refugees, down from 10.6 million refugees in 2002. Sharp declines (22%) in asylum applications lodged in 30 industrialized countries were recorded in the first two quarters of 2004 compared with the same period in 2003.

General Trends. An important trend in contemporary mobility was the increasing number of people moving for employment to a country other than their own, especially on a temporary basis. More than half of all migrants worldwide were labour migrants. In developed countries a rapid decline in population as well as an aging population made foreign-labour recruitment of increasing interest to many countries. Regional and global economic integration as well as high demand for highly skilled labour in knowledge-based economies were also important factors. Many countries, notably Germany and South Korea, introduced new policies to facilitate foreign-labour recruitment. For the first time, Beijing implemented a "green card" program for foreigners to work and join family members in China. In less-developed countries (LDCs), on the other hand, population growth coupled with high rates of unemployment and underemployment continued to prompt governments to seek opportunities for their nationals abroad. By late 2004 the UN Convention on the Protection of the Rights of All Migrant Workers and Members of Their Families (in effect since July 1, 2003) had been ratified by 27 states, most of which were countries of origin for labour migrants.

In an effort to attract highly skilled foreign students into their labour market, several countries—including Switzerland, Germany, Canada, and Australia—adopted measures to facilitate immigration procedures for students as well as entry for them into domestic labour markets following completion of their studies. As a result, dramatic increases in student mobility were registered in most industrialized countries. In Europe the largest increases were in the admissions of students from LDCs. The inflow of foreign student workers in Japan increased from 10,428 in 1983 to 109,508 in 2003, mostly from other Asian countries. In Australia more than half of all visas issued under the Skilled Migration program went directly to foreign students graduating from Australian universities.

Reflecting the growth in global labour migration, migrant remittances continued to rise. In 2003 global remittance flows to LDCs totaled an estimated $93 billion through official channels alone. This figure exceeded by almost one-third the amount ($68.5 billion) that industrialized countries had spent that year on assistance to LDCs. Remittance flows were expected to reach $100 billion in 2004. Latin America received $38 billion in remittances in 2003, exceeding foreign direct investment and development-assistance flows combined.

Irregular migration continued to pose major challenges and focused increased attention on border and internal controls. Security concerns relating to international terrorism fueled this trend, especially after the March 2004 terrorist bombings in Madrid. In the U.S. there were an estimated nine million irregular migrants, at least half of whom were of Mexican origin. Though the U.S. government was considering a temporary workers' program, one had not been established by year's end. In Europe, where irregular migration figured prominently on both national and EU policy agendas, several countries, including Germany and Italy, made renewed calls to set up migrant processing centres outside Europe.

Revised figures on trafficking in persons released by the U.S. Department of State in June indicated that between 600,000 and 800,000 persons were being trafficked annually across international borders. A significant proportion of them were women and children trafficked for sexual exploitation. The two protocols (on trafficking and smuggling) to the UN Convention Against Transnational Organized Crime entered into force in December 2003 and January 2004, respectively. In April 2004 the UN Commission on Human Rights appointed a special rapporteur to focus on trafficking in persons.

Migration and Development. Given the increased awareness of the benefits migration could bring to countries of origin and destination alike, many agencies and governments called for improved integration of migration in national- and international-development frameworks. Specifically, there was greater attention to the question of how migration could be managed to maximize its contribution to the achievement of the Millennium Development Goals (MDGs)—to eradicate world poverty and promote sustainable development—agreed to by 188 heads of state at the 2000 Millennium Summit.

On June 29, 2004, the U.K. House of Commons International Development Committee issued a landmark report on migration and development that called for concerted efforts to achieve policy coherence. In the first annual report on progress toward achieving the MDGs, the World Bank and the IMF reached the same conclusion.

© Christophe Calais/In Visu/Corbis

In June a family of Hmong refugees pose with their belongings as they prepare to leave Laos for a new life in the United States.

Regional Orientations. The region that remained the most advanced in the development of harmonized approaches to migration policy and legislation was the EU. Under the successive six-month Irish and Dutch EU presidencies, the development of common policies in these areas remained a priority. The European Commission issued its assessment of the achievements of the Tampere I agenda, which had been forged in Finland five years earlier for the creation of an EU area of freedom, security, and justice. At the November 4–5 European Council, the EU's new five-year program, known as the Hague Programme, which dealt with all policy aspects in this area, was adopted. Although many feared that the joining of 10 new countries to the EU on May 1 would create a potential flood of low-cost labour from the "East" and overwhelm national labour markets, the initial migratory impact of enlargement on existing EU members was less dramatic than had been feared.

The temporary movement of unskilled and semiskilled labour in Asia was the predominant trend there. Several countries faced increasing pressures to import labour, in part because of population decline and expanding markets, while others remained major exporters of labour within the region and farther afield. In September in Manila at the Second Asian Ministerial Consultations on Labour Migration, the prime objective was to improve the management of labour migration flows from and within the region. Interstate cooperation in the area of countertrafficking and irregular migration had intensified. Several events held under the auspices of the Bali Process on People Smuggling, Trafficking in Persons and Related Transnational Crime led to greater cooperation between participating countries. Migration and health also became a priority in the wake of the SARS (severe acute respiratory syndrome) epidemic in 2003 and increased concerns in 2004 over the possibility of transmission of bird flu to humans.

In Africa the principal migration concerns included conflict-induced displacement, both internal and across international borders, migration and health issues (particularly in relation to HIV/AIDS), and the enhancement of the development potential of migration while minimizing negative consequences such as "brain drain." In March the African Union (AU), in collaboration with the International Organization for Migration (IOM) and other international agencies, drafted a comprehensive strategic framework for a policy of migration in Africa to be considered for adoption by the AU in 2005.

The May 2004 EU–Latin America and the Caribbean Guadalajara Summit in Mexico brought together 70 governments to discuss benefits and challenges of migration, remittances, brain drain, and irregular migration (particularly the trafficking and smuggling of humans).

At the third Ministerial Meeting on Migration in the Western Mediterranean (5+5 Dialogue) held in September in Algiers, participants worked on cooperative approaches to migration management. Particular attention was given to the issue of transit migration in the Maghreb, which had become a key transit area for irregular migrants trying to reach Europe.

Global Dimension. In 2004, IOM's International Dialogue on Migration explored the theme of Valuing Migration, to highlight the costs, benefits, opportunities, and challenges of migration today and in the future. Two jointly sponsored conferences were held. The first, on migration and trade (with the WTO and World Bank), looked at the temporary movement of persons across borders to provide services, and the second, on migration and health (with WHO and CDC), explored the health implications of a mobile world.

During 2004, Switzerland, in partnership with IOM, convened four regional consultations of the Berne Initiative in Africa, Europe, Asia, and the Americas to enable governments from around the world to contribute directly to the development of a migration-management resource—the International Agenda for Migration Management. On December 16–17 the Swiss government held a conference in Berne with more than 100 participating states to review the results of the regional consultations and explore the next steps in the Berne Initiative process.

On Dec. 9, 2003, UN Secretary-General Kofi Annan launched the Global Commission on International Migration (GCIM), an independent body established with the backing of Sweden and Switzerland and a core group of states from developed countries and LDCs. The mandate of the GCIM was threefold: to place international migration on the global agenda, to analyze gaps in current approaches to migration and examine interlinkages to other policy areas, and to present recommendations to the UN secretary-general and other stakeholders.

In June, at the 92nd Conference of the International Labour Organization, the ILO was charged with the development of a nonbinding multilateral framework for a rights-based approach to labour migration, to be completed by November 2005. (GERVAIS APPAVE)

Sports and Games

The OLYMPIC Games, held in Athens in August, DOMINATED the sports world in 2004, while in non-Olympic sports individuals such as cyclist Lance ARMSTRONG, race car driver Michael SCHUMACHER, golfer Vijay SINGH, and Thoroughbred colt SMARTY JONES captured headlines.

AUTOMOBILE RACING

Grand Prix Racing. The Fédération Internationale de l'Automobile (FIA) Formula 1 (F1) world drivers' championship delivered more of the same in 2004 as German Michael Schumacher (Ferrari) dominated to win an unprecedented seventh title. He posted a F1-record 13 victories, while his Brazilian teammate Rubens Barrichello won two events. The other three races featured brilliant performances, with Italy's Jarno Trulli (Renault) winning at Monaco, Finland's Kimi Räikkönen (McLaren) capturing the Belgian Grand Prix, and Colombia's Juan Pablo Montoya (Williams) edging out Räikkönen in Brazil.

Ironically, the team that made the strongest impression in 2004 was BAR, which took a superb second place to Ferrari in the constructors' championship stakes and carried British driver Jenson Button to third place in the drivers' points table. Button and BAR were a revelation. The team's emergence as a consistently competitive contender said much for the technological developments made by engine supplier Honda, which announced in November that it was purchasing a minority stake in BAR. As for Jenson, he drove superbly race after race, highlighting his season with brilliant second-place finishes to Schumacher in the San Marino and German Grand Prix. In the middle of the season, however, Button announced that he was switching to Williams in 2005; his management team cited irregularities over the way in which BAR exercised its option for the following year. Previously in such cases, discreet financial arrangements were made to ensure the transfer of the driver to the team of his choice, and most F1 insiders believed that would happen on this occasion. BAR's team principal, David Richards, however, was implacable in his determination that his team's contract with Button would prevail. He referred the matter to the FIA's Contract Recognition Board, which ruled that Button's BAR contract took priority, and Button agreed that he would, in fact, be staying with BAR.

(continued on page 296)

Bahrain International Circuit, a glamorous new $150 million Grand Prix racetrack, stands ready to host its first Formula 1 event in April. Located in Sakhir, near the Bahraini capital of Manama, the track was the world's first desert circuit and the first Formula 1 racecourse to be located in the Middle East.

Games of the XXVIII Olympiad

by Melinda C. Shepherd

On Aug. 13, 2004, the Olympic Games returned home to Greece, birthplace of the ancient Games and site of the inaugural modern Olympics. The first recorded Olympic champion was Coroebus of Elis, winner of a 192-m (210-yd) sprint race in 776 BC. Over the next century the quadrennial tournament added longer-distance races, wrestling, the five-event pentathlon, boxing, and chariot racing. The Games gradually disappeared until French educator Pierre, baron de Coubertin, revived the competition in 1896. Under the auspices of the International Olympic Committee (IOC) that he founded, the Games of the I Olympiad took place in Athens in April of that year—241 men, representing 14 countries, competed in 43 events in 9 sports (cycling, fencing, gymnastics, shooting, swimming, tennis, track and field [athletics], weight lifting, and wrestling).

The ancient Parthenon and the modern Olympic flag share the skyline over Athens, Greece.

© Reuters/Corbis

In 2004 a record 202 national Olympic committees were represented, including a returning Afghanistan and first-time participants East Timor (Timor-Leste) and Kiribati. Nearly 11,100 accredited athletes competed in 37 disciplines in 28 sports; women participated in freestyle wrestling and sabre fencing for the first time. Competitors from 75 countries took home medals, with 57 countries winning at least one gold. The United States tallied 103 (including 36 gold) of the 929 medals awarded, followed by Russia with 92 (27 gold) and China with 63 (32 gold). Greece won 16 medals, three more than at the 2000 Games in Sydney, Australia.

Serious construction delays and worries that Athens's hot, humid weather and high levels of air pollution would be detrimental to the athletes—combined with fears that terrorists might disrupt the proceedings—almost led the IOC to move the Games to another city. The heat did affect some competitors; spectator attendance was poor for many events; and more than 20 athletes were disqualified after failing tests for performance-enhancing drugs. Controversies over scoring in gymnastics and fencing even led some observers to question whether judged events should be dropped entirely from the Olympics. Nevertheless, most of the 17-day event went smoothly; the 35 competition venues were deemed excellent; and the IOC president, Jacques Rogge, declared the Athens Olympics "unforgettable, dream Games."

American swimming phenomenon Michael Phelps (*see* BIOGRAPHIES) topped the medals table with a record-tying eight (six gold and two bronze), while Ukrainian swimmer Yana Klochkova (*see* BIOGRAPHIES) continued her dominance in the individual medley. On the track, Kelly Holmes of Great Britain and Ethiopia's Hicham El Guerrouj were double gold medalists, and hurdler Liu Xiang (*see* BIOGRAPHIES) won China's first men's athletics gold. Other notable competitors included Japanese judo star Ryoko Tani (*see* BIOGRAPHIES), American all-around gymnastics titlists Paul Hamm and Carly Patterson, Russian pole vaulter Yelena Isinbayeva, and rowers Matthew Pinsent of Great Britain and Elisabeta Lipa of Romania. The concluding event, the men's marathon, was won by Stefano Baldini of Italy after the leader, Brazil's Vanderlei Lima, was assaulted by a deranged spectator about four miles from the finish line. Lima, who recovered to take the bronze, was awarded the Pierre de Coubertin medal for "his exceptional demonstration of fair play and Olympic values."

Melinda C. Shepherd is Senior Editor of Encyclopædia Britannica Yearbooks.

Archery

Event	Men	Women
Individual	M. Galiazzo (Italy)	Park Sung Hyun (S.Kor.)
Team	South Korea	South Korea

Badminton

Class	Gold Medalist
Men's singles	T. Hidayat (Indon.)
Men's doubles	South Korea
Women's singles	Zhang Ning (China)
Women's doubles	China
Mixed doubles	China

Baseball

Gold Medalist	Cuba

Basketball

Men	Argentina	**Women**	United States

Boxing

Class	Gold Medalist	Class	Gold Medalist
48 kg	Y. Bhartelemy (Cuba)	69 kg	B. Artayev (Kazakh.)
51 kg	Y. Gamboa (Cuba)	75 kg	G. Gaydarbekov (Russia)
54 kg	G. Rigondeaux (Cuba)	81 kg	A. Ward (U.S.)
57 kg	A. Tishchenko (Russia)	91 kg	O. Solis Fonte (Cuba)
60 kg	M. Kindelan (Cuba)	91+ kg	A. Povetkin (Russia)
64 kg	M. Boonjumnong (Thai.)		

Canoeing—Men

Event	Gold Medalist	Time[3]
500-m kayak singles	A. van Koeverden (Can.)	1:37.919
1,000-m kayak singles	E. Veraas Larsen (Nor.)	3:25.897
500-m kayak pairs	R. Rauhe/T. Wieskötter (Ger.)	1:27.040
1,000-m kayak pairs	H. Nilsson/M. Oscarsson (Swed.)	3:18.420
1,000-m kayak fours	Hungary	2:56.919
Slalom kayak singles	B. Peschier (Fr.)	187.96 pt
500-m Canadian singles	A. Dittmer (Ger.)	1:46.383
1,000-m Canadian singles	D. Cal (Spain)	3:46.201
500-m Canadian pairs	Meng Guanliang/Yang Wenjun (China)	1:40.278
1,000-m Canadian pairs	C. Gille/T. Wylenzek (Ger.)	3:41.802
Slalom Canadian singles	T. Estanguet (Fr.)	189.16 pt
Slalom Canadian pairs	P. Hochschorner/P. Hochschorner (Slvk.)	207.16 pt

Canoeing—Women

Event	Gold Medalist	Time[3]
500-m kayak singles	N. Janics (Hung.)	1:47.741
500-m kayak pairs	N. Janics/K. Kovacs (Hung.)	1:38.101
500-m kayak fours	Germany	1:34.340
Slalom kayak singles	E. Kaliska (Slvk.)	210.03 pt

Cycling—Men

Event	Gold Medalist	Time[3]
Road race	P. Bettini (Italy)	5:41:44
Individual time trial	T. Hamilton (U.S.)	57:31.74
1-km time trial	C. Hoy (Gr.Brit.)	1:00.711[2]
Individual pursuit	B. Wiggins (Gr.Brit.)	4:16.304
Team pursuit	Australia	3:58.233
Sprint	R. Bayley (Austl.)	
Team sprint	Germany	43.980
Points race	M. Ignatyev (Russia)	
Madison	G. Brown/S. O'Grady (Austl.)	
Keirin	R. Bayley (Austl.)	10.601
Mountain bike	J. Absalon (Fr.)	2:15.02

Cycling—Women

Event	Gold Medalist	Time[3]
Road race	S. Carrigan (Austl.)	3:24:24
Individual time trial	L. Zijlaard-van Moorsel (Neth.)	31:11.53
500-m time trial	A. Meares (Austl.)	33.952[1]
Individual pursuit	S. Ulmer (N.Z.)	3:24.537[1]
Sprint	L. Muenzer (Can.)	
Points race	O. Slyusareva (Russia)	
Mountain bike	G. Dahle (Nor.)	1:56:51

Diving—Men

Event	Gold Medalist	Score
3-m springboard	Peng Bo (China)	787.38
10-m platform	Hu Jia (China)	748.08
3-m synchronized	T. Bimis/N. Siranidis (Greece)	353.34
10-m synchronized	Tian Liang/Yang Jinghui (China)	383.88

Diving—Women

Event	Gold Medalist	Score
3-m springboard	Guo Jingjing (China)	633.15
10-m platform	C. Newbery (Austl.)	590.31
3-m synchronized	Guo Jingjing/Wu Minxia (China)	336.9
10-m synchronized	Lao Lishi/Li Ting (China)	352.14

Equestrian

Event	Individual/Horse	Team
3-day event	L. Law (Gr.Brit.)/Shear l'Eau	France
Dressage	A. van Grunsven (Neth.)/Salinero	Germany
Jumping	C. O'Connor (Ire.)/Waterford Crystal	United States

Fencing

Event	Men	Women
Individual foil	B. Guyart (Fr.)	V. Vezzali (Italy)
Team foil	Italy	
Individual épée	M. Fischer (Switz.)	T. Nagy (Hung.)
Team épée	France	Russia
Individual sabre	A. Montano (Italy)	M. Zagunis (U.S.)
Team sabre	France	

Field Hockey

Men	Australia	**Women**	Germany

Gymnastics—Men

Event	Gold Medalist	Score
Team	Japan	173.821
All-around	P. Hamm (U.S.)	57.823
Floor exercise	K. Shewfelt (Can.)	9.787
Vault	G. Deferr (Spain)	9.737
Pommel horse	Teng Haibin (China)	9.837
Rings	D. Tampakos (Greece)	9.862
Parallel bars	V. Goncharov (Ukr.)	9.787
High bar	I. Cassina (Italy)	9.812
Trampoline	Yu. Nikitin (Ukr.)	41.50

Gymnastics—Women

Event	Gold Medalist	Score
Team	Romania	114.283
All-around	C. Patterson (U.S.)	38.387
Floor exercise	C. Ponor (Rom.)	9.750
Vault	M. Rosu (Rom.)	9.656
Uneven bars	E. Lepennec (Fr.)	9.687
Balance beam	C. Ponor (Rom.)	9.787
Trampoline	A. Dogonadze (Ger.)	39.60
Indiv. rhythmic	A. Kabayeva (Russia)	108.400
Team rhythmic	Russia	51.100

Handball

Men	Croatia	**Women**	Denmark

Judo—Men

Class	Gold Medalist
60 kg	T. Nomura (Japan)
66 kg	M. Uchishiba (Japan)
73 kg	Lee Won Hee (S.Kor.)
81 kg	I. Iliadis (Greece)
90 kg	Z. Zviadauri (Geo.)
100 kg	I. Makarau (Bela.)
100+ kg	K. Suzuki (Japan)

Judo—Women

Class	Gold Medalist
48 kg	R. Tani (Japan)
52 kg	Xian Dongmei (China)
57 kg	Y. Bönisch (Ger.)
63 kg	A. Tanimoto (Japan)
70 kg	M. Ueno (Japan)
78 kg	N. Anno (Japan)
78+ kg	M. Tsukada (Japan)

Modern Pentathlon

Men	A. Moiseyev (Russia)	**Women**	Z. Voros (Hung.)

Rowing—Men

Event	Gold Medalist	Time[3]
Single sculls	O. Tufte (Nor.)	6:49.30
Double sculls	A. Hardy/S. Vielledent (Fr.)	6:29.00
Quadruple sculls	Russia	5:56.85
Coxless pairs	D. Ginn/J. Tomkins (Austl.)	6:30.76
Coxless fours	Great Britain	6:06.98
Eights	United States	5:42.48
Ltwght double sculls	T. Kucharski/R. Sycz (Pol.)	6:20.93
Ltwght fours	Denmark	6:01.39

Rowing—Women

Event	Gold Medalist	Time[3]
Single sculls	K. Rutschow-Stomporowski (Ger.)	7:18.12
Double sculls	C. Evers-Swindell/G. Evers-Swindell (N.Z.)	7:01.79
Quadruple sculls	Germany	6:29.29
Coxless pairs	G. Andrunache-Damian/V. Susanu (Rom.)	7:06.55
Eights	Romania	6:17.70
Ltwght double sculls	A. Alupei/C. Burcica (Rom.)	6:56.05

Shooting—Men

Event	Gold Medalist	Score
Rapid-fire pistol	R. Schumann (Ger.)	694.9
Free pistol	M. Nestruyev (Russia)	663.3
Air pistol	Wang Yifu (China)	690.0
10-m running target	M. Kurzer (Ger.)	682.4[1]
Small-bore rifle, 3 pos.	Jia Zhanbo (China)	1,264.5
Small-bore rifle, prone	M. Emmons (U.S.)	703.3
Air rifle	Zhu Qinan (China)	702.7[1]
Trap	A. Alipov (Russia)	149.0
Double trap	A. Almaktoum (U.A.E.)	189.0
Skeet	A. Benelli (Italy)	149.0

Shooting—Women

Event	Gold Medalist	Score
Pistol	M. Grozdeva (Bulg.)	688.2
Air pistol	O. Kostevych (Ukr.)	483.3
Small-bore rifle, 3 pos.	L. Galkina (Russia)	688.4
Air rifle	Du Li (China)	502.0
Trap	S. Balogh (Austl.)	88.0
Double trap	K. Rhode (U.S.)	146.0
Skeet	D. Igaly (Hung.)	97.0

Soccer

Men	Argentina	**Women**	United States

Softball

Gold Medalist	United States

Swimming—Men

Event	Gold Medalist	Time[3]
50-m freestyle	G. Hall (U.S.)	21.93
100-m freestyle	P. van den Hoogenband (Neth.)	48.17
200-m freestyle	I. Thorpe (Austl.)	1:44.71[2]
400-m freestyle	I. Thorpe (Austl.)	3:43.10
1,500-m freestyle	G. Hackett (Austl.)	14:43.40[2]
100-m backstroke	A. Peirsol (U.S.)	54.06
200-m backstroke	A. Peirsol (U.S.)	1:54.95[2]
100-m breaststroke	K. Kitajima (Japan)	1:00.08
200-m breaststroke	K. Kitajima (Japan)	2:09.44[2]
100-m butterfly	M. Phelps (U.S.)	51.25[2]
200-m butterfly	M. Phelps (U.S.)	1:54.04[2]
200-m individual medley	M. Phelps (U.S.)	1:57.14[2]
400-m individual medley	M. Phelps (U.S.)	4:08.26[1]
4 x 100-m freestyle relay	South Africa	3:13.17[1]
4 x 200-m freestyle relay	United States	7:07.33
4 x 100-m medley relay	United States	3:30.68[1]

Swimming—Women

Event	Gold Medalist	Time[3]
50-m freestyle	I. de Bruijn (Neth.)	24.58
100-m freestyle	J. Henry (Austl.)	53.84
200-m freestyle	C. Potec (Rom.)	1:58.03
400-m freestyle	L. Manaudou (Fr.)	4:05.34
800-m freestyle	A. Shibata (Japan)	8:24.54
100-m backstroke	N. Coughlin (U.S.)	1:00.37
200-m backstroke	K. Coventry (Zimb.)	2:09.19
100-m breaststroke	Luo Xuejuan (China)	1:06.64[2]
200-m breaststroke	A. Beard (U.S.)	2:23.37[2]
100-m butterfly	P. Thomas (Austl.)	57.72
200-m butterfly	O. Jedrzejczak (Pol.)	2:06.05
200-m individual medley	Y. Klochkova (Ukr.)	2:11.14
400-m individual medley	Y. Klochkova (Ukr.)	4:34.83
4 x 100-m freestyle relay	Australia	3:35.94[1]
4 x 200-m freestyle relay	United States	7:53.42[1]
4 x 100-m medley relay	Australia	3:57.32[1]
Synchronized duet	A. Davydova/A. Yermakova (Russia)	99.334 pt
Synchronized team	Russia	99.501 pt

Table Tennis

Event	Gold Medalist
Men's singles	Ryu Seung Min (S.Kor.)
Men's doubles	Chen Qi/Ma Lin (China)
Women's singles	Zhang Yining (China)
Women's doubles	Wang Nan/Zhang Yining (China)

Taekwondo—Men

Class	Gold Medalist
58 kg	Chu Mu Yen (Taiwan)
68 kg	H. Saei Bonehkohal (Iran)
80 kg	S. Lopez (U.S.)
80+ kg	Moon Dae Sung (S.Kor.)

Taekwondo—Women

Class	Gold Medalist
49 kg	Chen Shih Hsin (Taiwan)
57 kg	Jang Ji Won (S.Kor.)
67 kg	Luo Wei (China)
67+ kg	Chen Zhong (China)

Tennis

Event	Gold Medalist
Men's singles	N. Massu (Chile)
Men's doubles	F. González, N. Massu (Chile)
Women's singles	J. Henin-Hardenne (Belg.)
Women's doubles	Li Ting, Sun Tian Tian (China)

Track and Field (Athletics)—Men

Event	Gold Medalist	Time[3]
100 m	J. Gatlin (U.S.)	9.85
200 m	S. Crawford (U.S.)	19.79
400 m	J. Wariner (U.S.)	44.00
4 x 100-m relay	Great Britain	38.07
4 x 400-m relay	United States	2:55.91
800 m	Yu. Borzakovsky (Russia)	1:44.45
1,500 m	H. El Guerrouj (Mor.)	3:34.18
5,000 m	H. El Guerrouj (Mor.)	13:14.39
10,000 m	K. Bekele (Eth.)	27:05.10[2]
Marathon	S. Baldini (Italy)	2:10:55
110-m hurdles	Liu Xiang (China)	12.91[2]
400-m hurdles	F. Sánchez (Dom.Rep.)	47.63
Steeplechase	E. Kemboi (Kenya)	8:05.81
20-km walk	I. Brugnetti (Italy)	1:19:40
50-km walk	R. Korzeniowski (Pol.)	3:38:46
High jump	S. Holm (Swed.)	2.36 m
Long jump	D. Phillips (U.S.)	8.59 m
Triple jump	C. Olsson (Swed.)	17.79 m
Pole vault	T. Mack (U.S.)	5.95 m[2]
Shot put	Yu. Bilonog (Ukr.)	21.16 m
Discus throw	V. Alekna (Lith.)	69.89 m[2]
Javelin throw	A. Thorkildsen (Nor.)	86.50 m
Hammer throw	K. Murofushi (Japan)	82.91 m
Decathlon	R. Sebrle (Cz.Rep.)	8,893 pt[2]

Track and Field (Athletics)—Women

Event	Gold Medalist	Time[3]
100 m	Yu. Nesterenko (Bela.)	10.93
200 m	V. Campbell (Jam.)	22.05
400 m	T. Williams-Darling (Bah.)	49.41
4 x 100-m relay	Jamaica	41.73
4 x 400-m relay	United States	3:19.01
800 m	K. Holmes (Gr.Brit.)	1:56.38
1,500 m	K. Holmes (Gr.Brit.)	3:57.90
5,000 m	M. Defar (Eth.)	14:45.65
10,000 m	Xing Huina (China)	30:24.36
Marathon	M. Noguchi (Japan)	2:26:20
100-m hurdles	J. Hayes (U.S.)	12.37[2]
400-m hurdles	F. Halkia (Greece)	52.82
20-km walk	A. Tsoumeleka (Greece)	1:29:12
High jump	Ye. Slesarenko (Russia)	2.06 m[2]
Long jump	T. Lebedeva (Russia)	7.07 m
Triple jump	F. Mbango Etone (Camer.)	15.30 m
Pole vault	Ye. Isinbayeva (Russia)	4.91 m[1]
Shot put	Y. Cumba (Cuba)	19.59 m
Discus throw	N. Sadova (Russia)	67.02 m
Javelin throw	O. Menéndez (Cuba)	71.53 m[2]
Hammer throw	O. Kuzenkova (Russia)	75.02 m[2]
Heptathlon	C. Klüft (Swed.)	6,952 pt

Triathlon

Men		Women	
Men	H. Carter (N.Z.)	Women	K. Allen (Austria)

Volleyball

Event	Men	Women
Beach	E. Rego/R. Santos (Braz.)	M. May/K. Walsh (U.S.)
Indoor	Brazil	China

Water Polo

Men		Women	
Men	Hungary	Women	Italy

Weight Lifting—Men

Class	Gold Medalist	Performance
56 kg	H. Mutlu (Tur.)	295.0 kg
62 kg	Shi Zhiyong (China)	325.0 kg
69 kg	Zhang Guozheng (China)	347.5 kg
77 kg	T. Sagir (Tur.)	375.0 kg[2]
85 kg	G. Asanidze (Geo.)	382.5 kg
94 kg	M. Dobrev (Bulg.)	407.5 kg
105 kg	D. Berestov (Russia)	425.0 kg
105+ kg	H. Reza Zadeh (Iran)	472.5 kg

Weight Lifting—Women

Class	Gold Medalist	Performance
48 kg	N. Taylan (Tur.)	210.0 kg[1]
53 kg	U. Polsak (Thai.)	222.5 kg
58 kg	Chen Yanqing (China)	237.5 kg[2]
63 kg	N. Skakun (Ukr.)	242.5 kg
69 kg	Liu Chunhong (China)	275.0 kg[1]
75 kg	P. Thongsuk (Thai.)	272.5 kg
75+ kg	Tang Gonghong (China)	305.0 kg[1]

Wrestling—Men

Class	Freestyle	Greco-Roman
55 kg	M. Batirov (Russia)	I. Majoros (Hung.)
60 kg	Y. M. Quintana (Cuba)	Jung Ji Hyun (S.Kor.)
66 kg	E. Tedeyev (Ukr.)	F. Mansurov (Azer.)
74 kg	B. Saytyev (Russia)	A. Dokturishivili (Uzbek.)
84 kg	C. Sanderson (U.S.)	A. Mishin (Russia)
96 kg	K. Gatsalov (Russia)	K. Ibrahim (Egypt)
120 kg	A. Taymazov (Uzbek.)	K. Baroyev (Russia)

Wrestling—Women

Class	Freestyle
48 kg	I. Merleni (Ukr.)
55 kg	S. Yoshida (Japan)
63 kg	K. Icho (Japan)
72 kg	Wang Xu (China)

Yachting (Sailing)

Event	Gold Medalist
Men's 470	K. Burnham/P. Foerster (U.S.)
Women's 470	S. Bekatorou/A. Tsoulfa (Greece)
Men's Mistral	G. Fridman (Israel)
Women's Mistral	F. Merret (Fr.)
Men's Finn	B. Ainslie (Gr.Brit.)
Women's Europe	S. Sundby (Nor.)
Women's Yngling	Great Britain
49er (open)	X. Fernández/I. Martínez (Spain)
Laser (open)	R. Scheidt (Braz.)
Star (open)	M. Ferreira/T. Grael (Braz.)
Tornado (open)	R. Hagara/H.P. Steinacher (Austria)

[1]World record. [2]Olympic record. [3]Hr:min:sec, except as marked.

(continued from page 291)
Williams, hit by the costs involved in reaching an unsuccessful conclusion on the issue, was left casting around for another driver to pair with Australian Mark Webber in 2005.

Meanwhile, there were other issues impinging on the health of the F1 business, namely those of how to meet costs and who, in the longer term, would control the commercial-rights income, which was variously estimated at between $50 million and $800 million annually. Power broker Bernie Ecclestone's grip on those income streams suddenly appeared under greater threat than ever before when three creditor banks, which owned 75% of Ecclestone's SLEC company, took him to court in a dispute involving appointments to the board of Formula One Holdings, a subsidiary of SLEC that operated the Grand Prix circuit. In December, London's High Court ruled in favour of the banks.

Although Ecclestone remained stoic and unimpressed by the bid to undermine his control of the business, it was clear by the end of 2004 that either costs needed to be brought under control or the share of the commercial-rights income accruing to the teams needed to be radically increased. The vulnerability of F1 as a business model was also thrown into painfully sharp focus when Ford sold its Jaguar F1 team to Red Bull in November, seemingly unable to make a compelling business case for remaining in the Grand Prix game. Ford's decision seemed strangely perverse, given that it was a founding member of the GPWC Holdings BV—a company that sought a more equitable distribution of the sport's commercial-rights revenue—which collectively professed huge confidence in the long-term potential of F1. Indeed, GPWC finally tired of trying to cut a long-term deal with Ecclestone over the future income division within F1. Having agreed to a "memorandum of understanding" with SLEC in December 2003, GPWC withdrew from it in April 2004 after having concluded that Ecclestone was dragging his feet to an unacceptable degree. By the end of the year, GPWC was busy formulating its own administrative structure in plans to take over F1 after the current Concorde agreement expired at the end of 2007. It remained to be seen how long the dispute would run before a compromise solution was reached.

As far as the F1 calendar was concerned, the world's appetite for Grand Prix racing appeared insatiable. Two races were added to accommodate the spectacular new government-backed fixtures in Bahrain and Shanghai, which were based on multimillion-dollar tracks designed by Hermann Tilke, and more races were expected to be added, with Turkey joining the F1 club in 2005 and both Mexico and South Africa waiting in line for their possible chance the following year. The excitement generated by these new races and the forthcoming ban on tobacco sponsorship in F1 conspired to place many traditional European events under huge pressure. Ecclestone's continued ambivalence toward the British Racing Drivers' Club, the owners of Silverstone racecourse, placed the future of the British Grand Prix on the line as protracted negotiations ground on for much of the year to secure the venue for the event.

Wherever F1 racing took place in the future, it would almost certainly be with significantly slower cars than were seen in 2004. With 2.4-litre V8 engines and a standard control tire—probably from a single contracted supplier—due to be initiated in 2006, the four seconds or so that were trimmed from lap times during 2004 could be reversed. The FIA's president, Max Mosley, was particularly keen on such safety-driven moves, even though many of the teams questioned the efficacy of the steps the FIA had supported to reach that conclusion.

(ALAN HENRY)

U.S. Auto Racing. Top-level professional auto racing in the U.S. survived a turbulent year of change in 2004, and the National Association for Stock Car Auto Racing (NASCAR), the dominant sanctioning organization, incurred the most upheaval. Under its new president, Brian France, NASCAR inaugurated a new sponsor, Nextel Communications, and a new TV-friendly method of crowning its champion, the NASCAR Nextel Cup Chase for the Championship. Under the Chase format the top 10 drivers and those within 400 points of the leader after the 26th race of the season qualified for a 10-race point play-off, and those who fell short competed only for the considerable prize money. Kurt Busch, driving a Jack Roush Ford Taurus, edged Jimmy Johnson, in a Hendrick Chevrolet Monte Carlo, for the bonus $5.2 million in prize money. The point race lasted until extra laps of the final race, held at Homestead, Fla., in November. Busch's teammate Greg Biffle won the race and thus blocked Johnson and third-place Jeff Gordon from higher points. Busch won the title with 6,506 points, followed by Johnson (6,498) and Gordon (6,490). Chevrolet captured the manufacturer's crown with 266 points to Ford's 224, and Kasey Kahne (Dodge) was named Rookie of the Year.

In addition to modifying its rules, NASCAR continued to tinker with its schedule, moving races out of its southeast birthplace. Rockingham, N.C., was dropped from the calendar, and the final running (in Darlington, S.C.) of the Southern 500, NASCAR's oldest race, was held in November. Three stock-car classics—the Daytona 500, the Talladega (Ala.) 500, and the Brickyard 400 in Indianapolis, Ind., which were run on 4-km (2.5-mi) tracks—remained outside the Chase. Dale Earnhardt, Jr., keyed a 1–2–4–5–6 finish for Chevrolet in the season-opening Daytona 500, besting Tony Stewart (Chevrolet) and Scott Wimmer (Dodge) in the $16,003,785 race, the richest in the country. Gordon won Talladega and the Brickyard 400. The season's traditionally longest race, the Coca-Cola 600 at Lowe's Motor Speedway in Charlotte, N.C., was a repeat victory for Johnson.

NASCAR's subsidiary series continued to feed talent into the Nextel Cup, hastening the departure of such veteran stars as Rusty Wallace, Kyle Petty, and Sterling Marlin. Chevrolet's Martin Truex, Jr., beat Kyle Busch (Chevrolet), Kurt's younger brother, in the Busch Series. Bobby Hamilton (Dodge) won the Craftsman Truck Series.

The Indianapolis 500 remained the nexus of American single-seater competition. Buddy Rice won the race, which was delayed two hours and then shortened by rain. Rice, in a Rahal-Letterman Racing Team G-Force Honda, led 91 of the 180 laps run and collected $1,700,000 of the $10,250,580 purse. He was followed by six other Hondas, including second-place Tony Kanaan. Kanaan, driving for Andretti-Green, went on to capture the Indy Racing League (IRL) season crown. Honda-powered cars won 14 of 16 races in the IRL series.

Single-seater sanctioning in the U.S. remained split yet another year. The Champ Car World Series, successor to the bankrupt Champion Auto Racing Teams, staged a successful nine-race inaugural schedule by including events outside the U.S. Fittingly, Frenchman Sebastian Bourdais clinched the crown in the Mexico City finale, besting Newman-Haas teammate Bruno Junqueira of Brazil. A.J. Allmendinger of the U.S. was named Rookie of the Year.

(ROBERT J. FENDELL)

Rallies and Other Races. Sébastien Loeb (Citroën) of France won his first world rally championship (WRC) in 2004. Loeb, who had finished second to his Norwegian rival Petter Solberg (Subaru) by only one point (72–71) in 2003, totaled six victories in the 16-event 2004 season, including his second straight Monte Carlo Rally. He finished second in the Rally of Cyprus but was advanced to first after the initial winner, Marcus Grönholm (Peugeot) of Finland, was disqualified one week after the race when his car was ruled illegal in the postrace technical check. Loeb finished with 118 points, well ahead of Solberg (82 points), who won five races, and Markko Märtin (Ford) of Estonia (79 points), who won three. Loeb's dominance also helped Citroën secure its second consecutive manufacturer's title. Citroën's other driver, two-time WRC champion Carlos Sainz of Spain, captured his record-breaking 26th career victory in Argentina. At season's end the 42-year-old Sainz announced his retirement after 15 years.

The U.S.'s two road racing endurance classics, the 24 Hours of Daytona and the 12 Hours of Sebring, continued to sport rival sanctioning organizations. The Daytona, approved by the Grand American Road Racing Association, was marred by cold weather and rain that caused a three-hour stoppage. After racing resumed, NASCAR's Stewart built a three-lap lead, but mechanical problems forced him out of the race with only 20 minutes to go, which left the overall victory to the Bell Doran Pontiac driven by American Terry Borcheller, Andy Pilgrim of the U.K., Brazilian Christian Fittipaldi, and Forest Barber of the U.S. The Orbit Racing Porsche GT3 RS placed second, only 6.9 seconds ahead of the Flying Lizard GT3 Porsche.

In the 12 Hours of Sebring, an American Le Mans Series race, a record crowd watched Audi R8s continue to dominate as they finished 1–2–3. The winning Audi was driven by Allan McNish of Scotland and Germans Pierre Kaffer and Frank Biela. The second-place Audi, led by J.J. Lehto of Finland, battled through the rest of the nine-race series to win the season. In an effort to regain prestige, the Sports Car Club of America, the nation's largest organization of nonprofessional racers, added the SPEED World Challenge series. American Tommy Archer won the GT class, and his countryman Bill Auberlen claimed the touring car championship. (ROBERT J. FENDELL; MELINDA C. SHEPHERD)

Zhang Jiewen (left) and Yang Wei of China compete during the women's doubles badminton finals at the Olympic Games in Athens in August. The pair captured the gold medal over compatriots Gao Ling and Huang Sui.

BADMINTON

Chinese badminton players won the singles titles at the All England Championships, played in Birmingham in March 2004. Gong Ruina justified her number one world ranking with an easy final-round victory over compatriot Zhou Mi. In the men's singles Lin Dan proved why he held the sport's top ranking by defeating Denmark's Peter Gade in a closely contested final. Denmark was more successful, however, in the men's doubles championship, with Jens Erikson and Martin Lundgaard Hansen coming from behind to defeat Choong Tan Fook and Lee Wan Wah of Malaysia.

The Thomas Cup and the Uber Cup, team events for men and women, respectively, were held in Jakarta, Indon., in May. In the Uber Cup, China won its fourth consecutive title with a final-round win over South Korea. After a 10-year domination of the Thomas Cup by Indonesian teams, Chinese men won their first title since 1990 by defeating Denmark in the final.

At the Olympic Games in Athens, most of the top men's singles seeds lost in the early rounds. This created an opportunity for the unseeded Indonesian Taufik Hidayat, who won the gold medal with a final-round victory over South Korea's Shon Seung Mo. The men's doubles competition featured an all-South Korean gold-medal match as Kim Dong Moon and Ha Tae Kwon defeated teammates Lee Dong Soo and Yoo Yong Sung. After the early defeat of Denmark's Camilla Martin, China was hoping to win all three medals in the women's singles competition. Top-seeded Gong Ruina, however, lost her semifinal match to the Indonesian-born Dutch player Mia Audina. In the final Zhang Ning narrowly defeated Audina to claim the gold medal. The dominant mixed doubles team of the previous two years, Kim Dong Moon and Ra Kyung Min of South Korea, were also victims of an unexpected early loss. China's mixed doubles team of Zhang Jun and Gao Ling took advantage of the opening and defended the title that they had won at the 2000 Olympics in Sydney, Australia. In the women's doubles competition, the world's best teams, both from China, met in the final, with Yang Wei and Zhang Jiewen defeating Gao Ling and Huang Sui. (DONN GOBBIE)

BASEBALL

North America. In 2004 Major League Baseball established a single-season attendance record of 73,022,969 spectators, surpassing the previous record set in 2000 and marking an 8.1% increase over the 2003 total. Seven teams broke franchise records, including the New York Yankees, who led both leagues with 3,775,292. Nine teams drew more than three million spectators.

World Series. The Boston Red Sox swept the St. Louis Cardinals four games to none to capture their first World Series since 1918. The Red Sox clinched the best-of-seven series at Busch Stadium in St. Louis, Mo., on October 27 by beating the Cardinals 3–0 behind Derek Lowe, who pitched seven shutout innings. Johnny Damon hit a first-inning home run, and Trot Nixon batted in two runs in the third inning for the Red Sox, who never trailed in the World Series while extending their postseason winning streak to eight games. Manny Ramirez, Boston's power-hitting outfielder, was voted the World Series Most Valuable Player (MVP). The Cardinals, who won the National League (NL) pennant with a potent offense, batted only .190 for the World Series and scored just three runs in the last three games. The Red Sox became the third consecutive wild-card team to win a World Series. Boston gained the wild-card berth after posting the best record of any second-place team in the American League (AL).

In the World Series opener at Boston's Fenway Park on October 23, the Red Sox outslugged the Cardinals 11–9. After the Cardinals rallied from a five-run deficit, Boston's Mark Bellhorn broke a 9–9 tie with a two-run home run in the eighth inning. In game two on October 24, the Red Sox again vanquished the visiting Cardinals 6–2 as Curt Schilling (*see* BIOGRAPHIES), despite an ankle injury, pitched six innings. Jason Varitek, Orlando Cabrera, and Bellhorn each batted in two runs for the Red Sox. In game three at St. Louis on October 26, Pedro Martinez yielded just three hits over seven innings, and Ramirez hit a first-inning home run off Jeff Suppan, the losing pitcher, to propel the Red Sox to a 4–1 triumph and a three-games-to-none lead.

© Mike Segar/Reuters/Corbis

In game two of the World Series on October 24, Boston Red Sox second baseman Mark Bellhorn jumps to avoid a collision with St. Louis Cardinals runner Mike Matheny, who has just been forced out in a double play.

Play-offs. Boston routed the Yankees 10–3 in game seven of the dramatic American League Championship Series (ALCS) to win the pennant in historic fashion. The Red Sox lost the first three games of the best-of-seven series, then became the first team in postseason annals to win the next four. Damon led the Red Sox to their climactic romp in game seven at Yankee Stadium by hitting two home runs, one with the bases loaded. In the first game of the ALCS, the Yankees defeated Boston 10–7. The Yankees forged an 8–0 lead behind Mike Mussina, then held on as relief pitcher Mariano Rivera recorded the save. The Yankees won game two 3–1 as Jon Lieber outdueled Martinez and Rivera recorded another save. The Yankees then went to Boston and won their third straight by a rout of 19–8 behind 22 hits, 5 by Hideki Matsui. The Red Sox, however, won game four 6–4 in 12 innings on a two-run home run by David Ortiz, who was named MVP of the ALCS. In game five a single by Ortiz in the 14th inning provided the Red Sox a 5–4 conquest. The game lasted 5 hours 49 minutes—the longest in postseason history. The Red Sox then won their third in a row to tie the series, three victories each, by defeating the Yankees 4–2 behind the strong pitching of the ailing Schilling and a three-run home run from Bellhorn. The Yankees had advanced to the ALCS by winning their best-of-five Division Series three games to one over the Minnesota Twins, while the Red Sox had swept the Anaheim Angels three games to none.

In the National League Championship Series (NLCS), St. Louis beat the Houston Astros 5–2 in the seventh game to win the NL pennant four games to three. Scott Rolen broke a 2–2 tie in the sixth inning with a two-run home run off Roger Clemens. The Cardinals scored six runs in the sixth inning to defeat the Astros 10–7 in game one. In game two Albert Pujols and Rolen hit back-to-back home runs in the eighth inning to break a tie and provide the Cardinals with a 6–4 victory. The Astros recorded their first victory of the series when Clemens pitched seven innings in game three toward a 5–2 triumph. The Astros then tied the series at two games apiece by rallying to defeat the Cardinals 6–5 on a tie-breaking home run by Carlos Beltran. It was the fifth consecutive postseason game in which Beltran had hit a home run, a major league record. The Astros won the fifth game 3–0 on a three-run home run by Jeff Kent in the ninth inning. The Cardinals tied the series at three victories each when they defeated the Astros 6–4 in game six on a two-run home run by Jim Edmonds in the 12th inning. Pujols was named MVP of the NLCS. The Cardinals had reached the NLCS by defeating the Los Angeles Dodgers in their best-of-five Division Series three games to one. In the other NL Division Series, the Astros, the NL wild-card team, won their first postseason series by beating the Atlanta Braves three games to two.

Individual Accomplishments. Slugger Ichiro Suzuki of the Seattle Mariners won his second AL batting title with a .372 average while accumulating 262 hits to break the major league record of 257 established by George Sisler in 1920. Barry Bonds of the San Francisco Giants won the NL batting title with a .362 average and captured a record seventh MVP award. Bonds also hit 45 home runs to increase his career total to 703, third on the all-time list, behind Hank Aaron (755) and Babe Ruth (714). Anaheim's Vladimir Guerrero, playing in his first season in the AL, won the other MVP award. Ken Griffey of the Cincinnati Reds reached the 500-home-run plateau. Adrian Beltre of the Dodgers led both leagues with 48 home runs; Boston's Ramirez set the AL pace with 43. Miguel Tejada of the Baltimore Orioles led the AL in runs batted in with 150. The NL leader was the Colorado Rockies' Vinny Castilla with 131. Scott Podsednik of the Milwaukee Brewers topped both leagues in stolen bases with 70.

Schilling led AL pitchers in victories with 21; Johan Santana of Minnesota, who won the AL Cy Young Award, had 20. In the NL, Houston's Roy Oswalt led with 20, and his teammate Clemens registered 18 wins to capture a record seventh Cy Young. Rivera of the Yankees led the major league in saves with 53. Two relief pitchers in the NL recorded 47 each, Jason Isringhausen of St. Louis and Armando Benitez of the Florida Marlins. The Dodgers' Eric Gagne saw his record consecutive-save streak end at 84. Randy Johnson of the Arizona Diamondbacks, who led both leagues with 290 strikeouts, recorded the 17th perfect game in major league history, becoming at age 40 the oldest pitcher to have thrown a perfect game and just the fifth pitcher to have thrown a no-hitter in both leagues. Another veteran, Greg Maddux of the Chicago Cubs, became the 22nd pitcher to have won 300 games when he defeated the Giants on August 7. Bobby Crosby of the Oakland Athletics was voted AL Rookie of the Year, and Jason Bay of the Pittsburgh Pirates took the NL honour. Bobby Cox of Atlanta and Buck Showalter of the Texas Rangers were named the NL and AL Manager of the Year, respectively.

In the annual All-Star Game, at Minute Maid Park in Houston, the AL scored six runs in the first inning and beat the National League 9–4. After the regular season, Major League Baseball announced plans to move the Montreal Expos to the District of Columbia under their new name the Washington Nationals, effective for the 2005 season.

Little League World Series. Pabao Little League of Willemstad, Curaçao, Netherlands Antilles, defeated Conejo Valley of Thousand Oaks, Calif., 5–2 to win the Little League World Series in Williamsport, Pa. Carlos Pineda struck out 11 batters and Jurickson Profar hit a two-run homer to secure the first Little League title for Curaçao and the first for a Caribbean team. (ROBERT VERDI)

© Tim Shaffer/Reuters/Corbis

At the Little League World Series, held in Williamsport, Pa., in August, players from the Pabao Little League of Willemstad, Curaçao, Netherlands Antilles, celebrate their victory over Conejo Valley of Thousand Oaks, Calif., to win the title.

Latin America. The 2004 Caribbean Series was held in Santo Domingo, Dom.Rep., on February 1–6. The Licey Tigers (Tigres), representing the Dominican Republic, won the title with a 5–1 record. The Culiacán Tomato Growers (Tomateros), representing Mexico, finished second with a 4–2 record. The Venezuelan entry, Aragua Tigers (Tigres), had a 3–3 mark, while the Ponce Lions (Leones), from Puerto Rico, were 0–6.

In Cuba Industriales defeated Villa Clara four games to none to win the 43rd Serie Nacional (National Series) championship. Industriales defeated Sancti Spiritus in the quarterfinals and Pinar del Río in the semifinals to advance. Las Tunas outfielder Osmani Urrutia hit .469 to win his fourth consecutive batting title.

The Campeche Pirates (Piratas) defeated the Saltillo Sarape Makers (Saraperos) four games to one to win the Mexican League championship series. It was the Pirates' second league title; their first was in 1983. Campeche pitcher Francisco Campos posted a 12–2 record and won the pitching Triple Crown; he led the league during the regular season in earned run average (1.47) and strikeouts (99) and tied for most wins.

At the Olympic Games in Athens, the Cuba national team defeated Australia 6–2 in the championship game to win the gold medal. Cuba had previously won gold medals in the 1992 and 1996 games before losing in the final to the United States in 2000 in Sydney, Australia. The U.S. did not send a team to Athens, having lost in a qualifying tournament. (MILTON JAMAIL)

Japan. The Seibu Lions defeated the Chunichi Dragons four games to three in the 2004 Japan Series, winning their first title since 1992. The Pacific League (PL) champion Lions were led by pitcher Takashi Ishii, who picked up two wins over 13 scoreless innings and was named series Most Valuable Player (MVP). In September Japanese baseball players staged the first strike in the game's 70-year history after their talks with team owners failed to reach an agreement on the realignment of ball clubs. Twelve weekend games were canceled after owners approved the merger of the PL's financially troubled Osaka Kintetsu Buffaloes and Orix BlueWave. The owners, however, averted a possible second strike as they chose to admit a new team for the next season. Between the two Internet service providers that applied, Rakuten, Inc., was selected over Livedoor, Co., to run a new team that would be based in Sendai, in northern Japan.

Fukuoka Daiei Hawks infielder Nobuhiko Matsunaka became the first Triple Crown winner in 18 years as he led the PL with a .358 batting average, 44 home runs, and 120 runs batted in. Hokkaido Nippon Ham Fighters infielder Fernando Seguignol matched Matsunaka, who was named PL MVP, with 44 homers. Buffaloes pitcher Hisashi Iwakuma and Lions pitcher Daisuke Matsuzaka led the PL with 15 wins and a 2.90 earned run average, respectively. In the Central League (CL), Dragons pitcher Kenshin Kawakami was named MVP with a league-best 17 wins. Yokohama BayStars infielder

Tyrone Woods and Yomiuri Giants outfielder Tuffy Rhodes shared the home-run title with 45. Hiroshima Carp infielder Shigenobu Shima led the CL with a .337 batting average.

(HIROKI NODA)

BASKETBALL

Professional. The Detroit Pistons were the right team to cap a season of turmoil for the National Basketball Association (NBA). The Pistons stunned mighty Los Angeles in the NBA play-off finals to claim the 2003–04 crown, ousting the heavily favoured Lakers in five games. Their triumph signaled the dawn of a new pro basketball era, ending the Lakers' run of four finals appearances and three straight NBA championships in the previous five years. For Detroit Coach Larry Brown, it was doubly sweet. At 63, he became the oldest coach to have won an NBA crown and the only one to have captured titles both in the NBA and in college—Brown's University of Kansas Jayhawks took the 1988 National Collegiate Athletic Association (NCAA) championship.

The upstart Pistons wasted no time in asserting their dominance when the best-of-seven series switched to their home court after the teams split the first two games in Los Angeles. They swept all three home games, throttling their opponents with a blend of ferocious defense and aggressive rebounding. Their series-ending 100–87 romp in game five on June 15 touched off a wave of celebration in Detroit. It was the first NBA title for the Pistons since their vaunted "Bad Boys" won back-to-back championships in 1989 and 1990. Along with Lakers Coach Phil Jackson, tasting defeat for the first time as a coach in 10 NBA finals, the loss also was a bitter disappointment for veteran Karl Malone, who had ended a long career with the Utah Jazz to sign with the Lakers in 2003 in search of his first championship ring.

It was old-fashioned teamwork and defense by the Pistons that turned this play-off into a one-sided affair, to the delight of basketball purists annoyed by a new generation of jump shooters who neglected such fundamentals as passing. Brown, an old-school coach, insisted on doing things his way when he took over the Pistons after six frustrating years as head man of the Philadelphia 76ers. His players saw that playing together produced results. Five Pistons scored in double figures during the finals, with playmaker Chauncey Billups, named Most Valuable Player (MVP) of the series, skillfully directing the offense. Detroit had defeated the Indiana Pacers to win the Eastern Conference final, while in the Western Conference final Los Angeles had topped the Minnesota Timberwolves, anchored by regular-season MVP Kevin Garnett.

Few ever suspected that it would be the farewell tour for the Lakers' superstar duo of 2.16-m (7-ft 1-in) centre Shaquille O'Neal and 2.01-m (6-ft 7-in) guard Kobe Bryant. Angered by the prompt dismissal of Jackson after the play-off debacle, O'Neal forced a trade to the Miami Heat. In exchange for him, Los Angeles acquired front-line players Caron Butler, Brian Grant, and Lamar Odom from the Heat, along with a first-round draft choice. In deciding to become the central figure of the biggest NBA deal since 1975, when the Milwaukee Bucks swapped Hall of Fame centre Kareem Abdul-Jabbar to the Lakers, O'Neal put an end to the long-standing personality clash between himself and Bryant. After a brief flirtation with the Los Angeles Clippers, Bryant elected to stay put, signing a lucrative new contract with the Lakers.

In the Women's National Basketball Association (WNBA), yet another new power arose. The Seattle Storm plucked a human tornado named Betty Lennox from the dispersal draft of players from the defunct Cleveland Rockers, and she led her new team to its first league championship and Seattle's first pro sports crown in 25 years. Lennox, who had played on two WNBA teams that folded, scored a dynamic 23 points in Seattle's convincing 74–60 victory over the Connecticut Sun in the decisive third game of the WNBA finals; she was named series MVP. The Storm also got a big boost from Lauren Jackson's 13 points and seven rebounds, with Kamila Vodichkova adding 14 points. The victory made Anne Donovan the first woman to coach a WNBA champion. After the play-offs, Val Ackerman, the WNBA's only president through its first eight seasons, stepped down to spend more time with her family. The league planned to expand its finals to a best-of-five series in 2005 and hoped to grow to 15 teams with expansions in 2006 and 2007.

College. A daily double of unprecedented scope boosted the University of Connecticut men's and women's teams atop the college basketball world. On successive nights—April 5 and 6, respectively—these perennial powerhouses captured the 2004 national championships. It was the first time that the same school had won both of these prestigious tournaments.

In the men's NCAA tournament, the final rounds of which were held in San Antonio, Texas, UConn's Emeka Okafor towered over everybody, blocking shots and intimidating shooters

Detroit Pistons point guard Chauncey Billups blows past Los Angeles Lakers defenders on his way to the hoop during the first half of game four of the NBA finals on June 13. The Pistons won the title, besting the Lakers in five games.

into hurried attempts. The 2.08-m (6-ft 10-in) native of Nigeria was an obvious choice as Most Outstanding Player of the Final Four. He sparked the Huskies (33–6) to a convincing 82–73 triumph over Georgia Tech (28–10) in the title game with 24 points and 15 rebounds, giving Coach Jim Calhoun his second NCAA crown in six years. That win enabled Calhoun to join Duke's Mike Krzyzewski and Bobby Knight of Texas Tech as the only active coaches with more than one national championship.

That career-ending binge marked Okafor's 24th double-double of the season. Despite missing some playing time along the way with nagging injuries, he was the main reason why UConn became the first preseason number one pick since Kentucky in 1996 to end up in the same spot. Okafor got plenty of help as the team sprinted to an insurmountable 41–26 halftime lead over Georgia Tech, and teammate Ben Gordon added 21 points to the game's total. It was satisfying revenge for the Yellow Jackets' 77–61 rout of UConn in the preseason National Invitation Tournament.

The women's NCAA tournament final in New Orleans featured a rematch of the previous year's showdown between traditional rivals Connecticut and Tennessee. It doubled the pleasure for UConn fans, who saw the women's team roll to a second straight decision over the Volunteers and the school's second NCAA crown in as many nights. With Diana Taurasi leading the way, the Huskies (31–4) prevailed 70–61, claiming their third straight women's national title and their fourth in five years. Taurasi scored 17 points and was named the Final Four's Most Outstanding Player. Tennessee (31–4) erased most of an early 30–13 gap, pulling to within 2 points midway through the second half, but the Lady Vols never could catch up. The poised Huskies took control once more and collected their final 10 points on free throws. Shanna Zolman tallied a game-high 19 points for Tennessee.

(ROBERT G. LOGAN)

International. If the 2002 world championships had hinted at a power shift in men's international basketball, the 2004 Olympic Games in Athens confirmed it. Even with National Basketball Association (NBA) professionals on the court, the U.S. could no longer match the team-oriented play of its European and South American opponents. The U.S., which arrived in Athens as the tournament favourite, staggered into the quarterfinals after group defeats against Puerto Rico and European champion Lithuania. Puerto Rico's 92–73 win was only the U.S.'s third defeat in 111 Olympic matches (it lost to the former Soviet Union in the 1972 final and the 1988 semifinal) and its first since fielding NBA players.

Spain reached the last eight with a 5–0 group record, but the U.S.'s 102–94 quarterfinal victory, built on 31 points from Stephon Marbury, relegated the Spaniards to the seventh-place play-off. Argentina recovered from 11 points down in the second half of its quarterfinal to beat Greece 69–64. Italy defeated Puerto Rico 83–70, while Lithuania enjoyed the easiest quarterfinal, routing China 95–75.

At the 2002 world championships in Indianapolis, Ind., a U.S. group loss to Argentina had opened the door for Yugoslavia to eliminate the Americans in the quarterfinals. Argentina was too strong for the U.S. in Athens too. Emanuel Ginobili, a member of the 2003 NBA champion San Antonio Spurs, led Argentina with 29 points in the 89–81 semifinal victory. In the second semifinal Italy defeated Lithuania 100–91. Led by Gianluca Basile, who hit seven three-point shots among his 31 points, Italy completed 18 of 28 three-pointers, turning the tables on long-range specialist Lithuania, which made 15 of 35.

As in Indianapolis, where Argentina had lost the gold medal game to Yugoslavia, the Olympics produced a final that few would have predicted. Argentina won its first Olympic gold by beating Italy 84–69, with 25 points from Luis Scola. The U.S. settled for bronze, prevailing over Lithuania 104–96.

The women's tournament in Athens followed the expected script. The U.S. defeated Australia 74–63, repeating its victory over that nation at the 2000 Games in Sydney, Australia. American Tina Thompson led four players in double figures as the U.S. won its third consecutive Olympic gold—with two world championships in between. Russia overcame Brazil 71–62 for the bronze.

(RICHARD TAYLOR)

BILLIARD GAMES

Carom Billiards. After 17 years of organizing well-funded three-cushion billiards tournaments, the Billiards Worldcup Association folded in 2004 because of declining corporate sponsorships. As a result, the world's best players had to depend for income on the Union Mondiale de Billard (UMB), team leagues in several European countries, and a variety of independently produced tournaments around the world. Once again, the most successful players were Dick Jaspers of The Netherlands, Sweden's Torbjörn Blomdahl, Spain's Danny Sánchez, Semih Sayginer of Turkey, Belgium's Frédéric Caudron, and Italian Marco Zanetti. In February Sayginer, the 2003 UMB world champion and Player of the Year, won $35,000 by besting Blomdahl in the Euphony Super Cup and then teamed with countryman Tayfun Tasdemir to take the world team title for the second year in a row. At the UMB world cup in Hurghada (Al Ghardaqah), Egypt, in July, Sánchez topped Murat Coklu of Turkey. Jaspers pocketed $21,689 for winning the Crystal Kelly tournament, held in Monte-Carlo in June, for the fourth straight time, averaging 2.258 for his seven 50-point games. Belgium's Raymond Ceulemans, aged 67, played a reduced schedule and won a Belgian Grand Prix event with an average of 1.666. In May Caudron took the world cup tournament in Seville, Spain. Sánchez captured the world cup meet in Antwerp, Belg., in August, which gave him the top spot on the world-ranking list. At the final major tournament of the year, the UMB world championship in Rotterdam, Neth., in October, Jaspers prevailed in the final over the fast-rising Filippos Kasidokostas of Greece, who was only 21 years old. Among the year's best performances were 50 points in 9 innings by Zanetti and Blomdahl and a run of 26 by American national champion Pedro Piedrabuena.

The billiard world was shocked in October by the death at age 51 from cancer of South Korean-born Sang Chun Lee, the 1993 world champion. Lee won the South Korean national title 10 times before moving in 1987 to the U.S., where he won the U.S. title 12 straight times. Former Austrian champion Johann Scherz also died in 2004.

Pocket Billiards. The year began in controversy when the Billiard Congress of America (BCA) sold its not-for-profit amateur league to a commercial enterprise. Opponents of the move formed the American Cuesports Alliance. The stakes were huge, and at year's end the 532 local league operators were still being lobbied by the two sides. The BCA-sponsored championships, held in Las Vegas, Nev., in May, had 9,010 entrants vying for $840,000 in prize money. Rivaling the BCA event in size was the national

Alex Pagulayan of Canada lines up a shot during the final match of the WPA world nine-ball championships on July 18 in Taipei, Taiwan. Pagulayan prevailed over Taiwan's Chang Pei-wei to win the event.

AP/Wide World Photos

team championships organized by the American Poolplayers Association, also held in Las Vegas. With a prize fund of $750,000 and six divisions, the nine-day event, held in August, attracted 9,000 entrants.

At the Derby City Classic in January in Louisville, Ky., where spectators could find pool action almost around the clock, it was Germany's Ralf Souquet in nine-ball, Efren Reyes of the Philippines in one-pocket, and newcomer Jason Miller of the U.S. in nine-ball banks. Two high-stakes ring games attracted so much attention that they could become features at other tournaments; the two winners, Johnny Archer and Cory Deuel, both of the U.S., each pocketed $30,000.

The main American organizer of men's tournaments, the U.S. Professional Poolplayers Association, held its World Summit of Pool at New York City's Grand Central Station. Filipino Santos Sambajon won the $30,000-added event, with Americans Mike Davis second and Earl Strickland third. The World Pool-Billiard Association (WPA) world nine-ball championships, the richest event in pool with a prize fund of $350,000, was held in Taiwan after five years in Cardiff, Wales. Alex Pagulayan, a Filipino living in Canada, won $75,000 by defeating Taiwan's Chang Pei-wei. The U.S. Open, held in Chesapeake, Va., in September, saw a surprise winner, the 26-year-old Gabe Owen of the U.S., who had never finished higher than seventh in a major professional tournament. He netted $30,000 by topping Germany's Thorsten Hohmann. German Thomas Engert won the winner-take-all prize of $50,000 at the International Challenge of Champions in Uncasville, Conn., in August, adding to his victories in the Italian Open, the European championships, and the World Pool Masters in The Netherlands. Reyes dominated the Asian tour and also won the first-place prize of $20,000 in the WPA world eight-ball championships, which took place in Al-Fujayrah, U.A.E.

The popular Classic Tour events of the Women's Professional Billiard Association (WPBA) continued to be dominated by England's Allison Fisher (*see* BIOGRAPHIES) and Karen Corr of Northern Ireland, both former snooker champions. Fisher won three of the first four majors and thereby displaced Corr from the top of the rankings. In October, at the Cuetec Cues Canadian Classic in Windsor, Ont., Ireland's Julie Kelly topped Fisher in the final. Later that month, Kim Ga Young of South Korea beat Corr to take the U.S. Open in Albuquerque, N.M., and in December Kim was crowned women's world nine-ball champion. In the Cuetec Cues National in Lincoln City, Ore., it was Corr over Austria's Gerda Hofstatter, and American Jeanette Lee defeated Kelly to win the Cuetec Cues Florida Classic in Hollywood, Fla. With her fourth-place finish in Florida, Fisher overtook Corr to end the year as the WPBA's top-ranked player.

Snooker. Despite the loss of tobacco advertising, World Snooker Ltd. found other corporate sponsors to keep prize funds high. A deal was signed with Eurosport for 200 hours of coverage over three years, which would bring the game to 95 million viewers. England's Ronnie O'Sullivan earned £250,000 (about $445,000) for winning the world championship at the Crucible Theatre in Sheffield, Eng., and reclaimed his place atop the world rankings. He also won the Totesport Grand Prix in Preston, Eng., but in November lost to Stephen Maguire of Scotland in both the British Open (where fellow Scot John Higgins defeated Maguire for the title) and the season-ending U.K. championship. Maguire, a former world amateur champion, started 2004 ranked 41st and by the end of the year had climbed to 3rd place. Eddie Charlton, a 20-time winner of the Australian national title, died in November at age 75.

(ROBERT BYRNE)

BOBSLEIGH, SKELETON, AND LUGE

Bobsleigh. In bobsleigh no country was more assertive during the 2003–04 season than Germany. After finishing first in four-man and third overall in two-man competition for the season, driver André Lange easily won the World Cup combined points title. Fellow German Christoph Langen captured the two-man season points title. Lange also steered his four-man sled to a gold medal at the 2004 world championships in Königssee, Ger., with Langen's crew taking the silver. After winning the two-man gold medal at the world championships, Canadian Pierre Lueders took second in the two-man and overall season standings. After driving his four-man sled to a bronze medal at the world championships, American Todd Hays finished third overall in the combined drivers standing.

German drivers Sandra Prokoff and Susi Erdmann battled for six of the eight women's World Cup races during the season; neither competed in the last two races. Despite contending only six races, Prokoff easily finished at the top of the overall standings. American Jean Racine finished second in the season rankings, and Erdmann took third. In the women's world championships, Erdmann edged Prokoff for the gold medal, with Racine in third place.

Skeleton. In men's skeleton action, British slider Kristan Bromley won four of five World Cup races and finished atop the World Cup rankings. Canadian Duff Gibson finished second in overall season rankings and won the gold medal at the skeleton world championships in Königssee, with Germans Florian Grassi and Frank Kleber finishing second and third, respectively.

On the women's side, Canadian sliders Lindsay Alcock and Michelle Kelly had another great season. Alcock collected two gold and two silver medals on the five-race circuit, as well as a silver at the world championships, and finished atop the season standings. Kelly won one silver and three bronze to finish third overall for the season. German Diana Sartor won world championship gold and finished second overall in the World Cup rankings. (JULIE URBANSKY)

Luge. In 2003–04 Germany's Sylke Otto again dominated the luge World Cup circuit, winning five of the eight races and becoming the only women's singles slider to have won four overall titles. The world championships, held in Nagano, Japan, in February, handed Otto her lowest finish of the season, third, while her teammates Silke Kraushaar and Barbara Niedernhuber finished first and second, respectively.

Armin Zöggeler of Italy finished the men's World Cup season atop the podium only to slide to a disappointing fourth place finish at the world championships. Germany's Georg Hackl placed second in the overall World Cup standings and in Nagano finished just eight-thousandths of a second behind teammate David Möller, who captured the gold. Möller also improved his overall World Cup finish to third.

Germany's doubles team of Patric Leitner and Alexander Resch were successful in winning the world championships gold medal and the overall World Cup title. The American duo of Mark Grimmette and Brian Martin were sidelined for four races owing to injury, so the window was thus opened for Andre Florschütz and Torsten Wustlich of Germany to capture the silver in both competitions. Grimmette and Martin finished with the world championship bronze, while Italy's Christian Oberstolz and Patric Gruber took third in the overall World Cup standings. (JANELE M. URBANSKY)

The Germany 1 four-man bobsleigh team, led by driver André Lange (centre), pushes off at the start of the world championships in Königssee, Ger., on February 28. Lange steered his sled to a gold medal.

© Wolfgang Rattay/Reuters/Corbis

BOWLING

World Tenpins. The World Cup, held Sept. 27–Oct. 4, 2003, in Tegucigalpa, Honduras, was an excellent opening event for the 2003–04 bowling season. National champions from 77 member countries of the World Tenpin Bowling Association (WTBA) participated. In the men's best-of-three-games final, Christian Jan Suarez of the Philippines defeated Dutchman Marcel van den Bosch with a two-game score of 437–411 (thus eliminating the need for a third game). On the women's side, Canadian Kerry Ryan-Ciach's two-game 444–385 victory over defending champion Shannon Pluhowsky of the U.S. was even easier. The top 16 bowlers in the world were invited to compete in the World Tenpin Masters in London in April 2004. The Norwegian Tore Torgersen outclassed Tomas Leandersson of Sweden 436–415 for his third title and $30,000.

Norwich, Eng., was the venue for the final European Team Cup in early June. This championship had been inaugurated in the late 1960s, but a lack of interest and the increasing cost of holding numerous international competitions were putting an end to the event. England beat Finland 438–430 in the women's final. Finland was once again the men's champion, outclassing Germany 398–367. At the end of June, the eight top-ranked qualifiers (men and women) from each of the three world tenpin zones had a play-off in Moscow. Mohd al-Qubaisi of the U.A.E. was the men's winner, and American Diandra Asbaty (formerly Diandra Hyman) topped the women's division.

In late July participants in the world youth championships had to travel around the globe to Agana, Guam. The long distance and high travel costs were thought to have been the reason for the limited participation, with only 66 girls and 105 boys representing 27 of the WTBA national federations. Australian Jason Belmonte won three individual titles: boys' singles, all-events, and round robin, while Yannaphon Larpapharat of Thailand won the masters. The other boys' winners were Sweden (doubles) and Finland (team). American Jennifer Petrick won the girls' masters title and took second to Finland's Minna Makela in all-events. The remaining girls' champions were Kang Hyun Jin of South Korea (singles), Mexico (doubles), and the U.S. (team). (YRJÖ SARAHETE)

U.S. Tenpins. The choice of Finland's Mika Koivuniemi as the Professional Bowlers Association (PBA) Player of the Year for 2004 served as another indication of the improved caliber of bowlers from outside the U.S. The 37-year-old Koivuniemi, who had lived with his family in Ann Arbor, Mich., for several years, was chosen in a vote by PBA members. Koivuniemi led the PBA with a 222.7 average; won tournaments in Windsor Locks, Conn., and Reno, Nev.; and was second to Tom Baker of Buffalo, N.Y., in the PBA World Championship. In a televised semifinal match at Windsor Locks, Koivuniemi rolled a perfect game. Steve Jaros of Bolingbrook, Ill., who captured three PBA titles, was second in the voting, and Pete Weber of St. Ann, Mo., was third.

Koivuniemi, whose previous honours included the U.S. Open in 2001, was among the 58 bowlers who qualified for 16 of the 20 PBA tournaments in the 2004–05 season under a new system. Only this group, plus six bowlers who would be invited for various reasons each week, would be permitted to compete on the national televised tour. Each would be guaranteed a minimum prize of $2,000; it was the first time that PBA bowlers were to be provided with the equivalent of a salary. Other non-American bowlers who were guaranteed places in most of the weekly events included Venezuelan Amleto Monacelli, the PBA Player of the Year for 1989 and 1990; Torgersen; and Canadians Bill Rowe and Patrick Girard. All PBA members were eligible to compete in the men's American Bowling Congress (ABC) Masters, the U.S. Open, and the PBA World Championship. The PBA Tournament of Champions, however, was open only to the winners of other PBA meets.

After several years of negotiating, delegates to the ABC and the Women's International Bowling Congress finally voted to merge into a single organization. They were quickly joined by USA Bowling, an organization designed to train and support teams for international competition, and the Young American Bowling Alliance, for young bowlers. The unified group, to be called the United States Bowling Congress, was scheduled to begin operations on Jan. 1, 2005. (JOHN J. ARCHIBALD)

BOXING

When reigning heavyweight boxing champion Lennox Lewis (U.K.) announced his retirement on Feb. 6, 2004, it threw the sport's premier division back into the chaotic situation that had existed prior to Lewis's unification of the World Boxing Council (WBC), World Boxing Association (WBA), and International Boxing Federation (IBF) titles in 1999. Even though Lewis was widely recognized as the best heavyweight in the world and the true champion, the title was already splintered owing to the gratuitous meddling of the various governing bodies when he stepped down.

IBF titleholder Chris Byrd (U.S.) successfully defended that belt in New York City on April 17 in a 12-round draw with Andrew Golota (Pol.) and again on November 13 with a 12-round decision over Jameel McCline (U.S.), also in New York City.

The WBA version of the heavyweight title was given back to John Ruiz (U.S.) by the Venezuela-based governing body when Roy Jones, Jr. (U.S.), who had defeated Ruiz in March 2003, dropped back down to the light heavyweight division. Ruiz made the first defense of his second reign on April 17 in New York City, stopping Fres Oquendo (P.R.) in the 11th round. On November 13 Ruiz defended again, winning a 12-round decision over Golota in New York City.

Vitali Klitschko (Ukraine), who almost upset Lewis in what proved to be Lewis's final title defense, enhanced his standing by knocking out Corrie Sanders (S.Af.) on April 24 in Los Angeles to win the vacant WBC heavyweight boxing title. Klitschko took another step toward being recognized as the world's best heavyweight when on December 11 he stopped Danny Williams (U.K.) in the eighth round of a WBC title defense in Las Vegas, Nev. Williams had earned the title shot by knocking out former champion Mike Tyson (U.S.) in the fourth round on July 30 in Louisville, Ky. Tyson suffered a knee injury in the fight but was expected to continue to box in an effort to repay his debts, which had been estimated at $38 million when he filed for bankruptcy in 2003.

In one of the most dramatic falls from grace in boxing history, Jones, formerly considered one of the most gifted fighters of his era, suffered back-to-back knockout defeats. In a May 15 rematch with Antonio Tarver (U.S.) in Las Vegas, Jones was knocked out in the second round with a single left hook to the head. The upset victory earned Tarver the WBA and WBC light heavyweight titles. On September 25 in Memphis, Tenn., Jones attempted a comeback against IBF light heavyweight titleholder Glen Johnson (Jam.) but was knocked out by Johnson in the ninth round. Johnson had won the vacant IBF belt earlier in the year with a 12-round decision over Clinton Woods (U.K.) in Sheffield, Eng.

The light heavyweight division saw another shocking result when Johnson won a 12-round decision over Tarver on December 18 in Los Angeles. The WBC and the IBF had tried to prevent the bout, so Tarver and Johnson relinquished the organizations' belts in order to compete against each other in what turned out to be one of the best light heavyweight bouts in recent years.

In the biggest moneymaker of the year, undisputed middleweight champion Bernard Hopkins (*see* BIOGRAPHIES) knocked out fellow American Oscar de la Hoya with a left hook to the body in the ninth round on September 18. De la Hoya, the sport's most dependable box-office attraction, started well but was already beginning to fall behind when Hopkins delivered a textbook punch to the liver that put de la Hoya on the floor for the count of 10. Hopkins's emphatic victory was his 19th successful defense of the middleweight title, a division record. The Hopkins–de la Hoya fight was held in front of a crowd of 16,112 at the MGM Grand Garden Arena in Las Vegas, creating a live gate of more than $12 million. The pay-per-view telecast was sold to approximately one million homes, generating another $55 million in revenue. All told, it was the second largest grossing nonheavyweight fight of all time. Earlier in the year, Hopkins and de la Hoya had both fought on the same card on June 5 at the MGM Grand as part of a marketing plan to build interest in their September showdown. Hopkins scored a comprehensive 12-round decision over Robert Allen (U.S.), and de la Hoya struggled to win a close 12-round decision over Felix Sturm (Ger.).

Adding spice to the middleweight division was the comeback of Félix Trinidad (P.R.), who had not fought since May 11, 2002. The three-division former titleholder returned to action on October 2 in New York City, where he scored an eighth-round knockout of former unified welterweight champion Ricardo Mayorga (Nic.). The event drew a near-capacity crowd of 17,406 for a live gate of $4.65 million, the third highest in Madison Square Garden history. The pay-per-view event was sold to 420,000 households, generating another $21 million.

Unified welterweight champion Cory Spinks (U.S.), the son of former heavyweight champion Leon Spinks, twice retained the title, coming off the canvas to win a close 12-round decision over Zab Judah (U.S.) on April 10 in Las Vegas and comfortably outpointing Miguel Ángel González (Mex.) over 12 rounds on September 4, also in Las Vegas.

WBC heavyweight titleholder Vitali Klitschko (right) of Ukraine watches as opponent Danny Williams of the U.K. hits the canvas in the eighth round of their title bout in Las Vegas, Nev., on December 11.

Erik Morales (Mex.) improved his status as one of the best fighters among the lower weight classes by winning the WBC super featherweight title on February 28 via a 12-round decision over Jesús Chávez (Mex.) and the IBF junior lightweight belt on July 31 with a 12-round decision over Carlos Hernandez (U.S.). Both fights were held in Las Vegas. Morales, however, lost a bitterly contested bout to Marco Antonio Barrera (Mex.) in a 12-round decision on November 27 in Las Vegas. Considered by many to have been the best action fight of the year, it gave Barrera a 2–1 record against Morales.

(NIGEL COLLINS)

CHESS

In 2004 reunification of the individual chess world title system, as envisaged in the Prague Agreement of May 2002 between the Fédération Internationale des Échecs (FIDE), the world ruling body, and many, but not all, of the world's top players, continued—but in a halting fashion. A lack of sponsorship for the FIDE version of the world title was overcome when Libya, as a sign of opening itself up to the world and as a move away from its alleged association with terrorism, put up a prize fund of $1.5 million for the knockout event, which took place in Tripoli on June 18–July 13 with a field of 124 players.

Because American and Israeli players expressed doubts about their security in Libya, FIDE initially envisaged a part of the event being split off and conducted in Malta. Tripoli promised to grant visas to all participants, but the undertaking was undermined by a fiery comment, describing Israelis as "the Zionist enemy," by the son of Libyan leader Muammar al-Qaddafi. The field was finally not a representative one, lacking all but 2 of the top 10 players on the FIDE rating list.

The top seed, Veselin Topalov of Bulgaria, fell at the semifinal stage in the quickplay tiebreaker to Rustam Kasimdzhanov of Uzbekistan. The quick time limit favoured younger players, and the 24-year-old Uzbek was judged by purists to have ridden his luck in a number of clearly lost positions. The pattern continued in the final, where Kasimdzhanov pulled off a great surprise by beating the second-seeded Michael Adams of England, also in the tiebreaker, after a level 3–3 score in the initial encounters. Kasimdzhanov, a resident of Germany, was only 54th on the rating list, so this was the greatest surprise result of recent chess history and in some eyes an indictment of the knockout system.

Former world champion Bobby Fischer, who had single-handedly put an end to Soviet domination of chess with his famous defeat of Boris Spassky in Iceland in 1972, was arrested at Tokyo's Narita Airport on July 13 for holding an invalid passport. Fischer's U.S. passport had been renewed as late as 1997, in Switzerland, despite a U.S. indictment against him dating from his replay match with Spassky in 1992 in Yugoslavia, which was then under international sanctions. Fischer alleged manhandling by those who arrested him and stated from his detention cell in Tokyo, where he was awaiting extradition, that he was seeking political asylum. His checkered history—ranging from a reclusive lifestyle and the sanctions-breaking contest in 1992 to his later anti-Semitic statements in the media—had kept little sympathy for him. The judicial process, which the U.S. authorities hoped would lead to swift deportation, dragged on for months as Fischer's supporters assembled a team of lawyers whose appeal for lengthier consideration was met.

Russian Garry Kasparov had a quiet year as he concentrated on the completion of his series of books *My Great Predecessors*. Planned as a trilogy, the series had expanded to five volumes in the course of writing and was appearing in a number of languages. Kasparov played only at the tournament in Linares, Spain, held on February 19–March 9; in a friendly exhibition match, Armenia Versus the Rest of the World, held in Moscow in June in memory of former world chess champion Tigran Petrosyan of Armenia; and at the Russian Superfinal Championship in Moscow in November. At Linares Kasparov had one win and 11 draws in a double-round contest for seven players. His score of 6.5 points gained him joint second place with Peter Leko of Hungary, half a point behind Vladimir Kramnik of Russia. This result, along with the similar narrow 18.5–17.5 defeat of Armenia in June, gave further substance to commentators' belief that Kasparov's powers had weakened since he turned 40.

Kasparov was scheduled to meet Kasimdzhanov in a match in January 2005, with the victor meeting the winner of the Kramnik-Leko 14-game match in Brissago, Switz., on September 25–October 18, in an effort to complete the unification by summer 2005. Kramnik retained his world title in the 14-game match against Leko (played at the classical chess time limit). The Russian needed to win the last game to reach a 7–7 tie (2 wins each and 10 draws) and did so, repeating a feat achieved only twice in nearly a century of chess history. Shortly after the match Kramnik antagonized many by stating that he did not envisage meeting the winner of the Kasparov-Kasimdzhanov match, so undermining the Prague Agreement. Kramnik also withdrew, pleading health problems, from the Russian Superfinal, where Kasparov showed a return to form by winning with an undefeated score of 7.5 points from 10 games, a point and a half ahead of the field.

At the World Chess Olympiad, in Majorca, Spain, in October, 129 men's teams competed. This event was played at the faster FIDE time rate. Ukraine won the title for the first time, ahead of Russia, Armenia, and the U.S. In the accompanying women's event, there were 87 entries. China took the gold medal, ahead of the U.S. and Russia.

Viswanathan Anand of India won the other top tournaments of the year at Wijk aan Zee, Neth., on January 10–25 and Dortmund, Ger., on July 22–August 1. At Wijk he scored 8.5 points out of 13, half a point ahead of Leko and Adams, with Kramnik only sixth equal with 6.5 points. At Dortmund, where the high percentage (78%) of drawn games was a talking point, Anand defeated Kramnik in the final. Once again, the decision came only in a quickplay finish after games at the slower classical time limit had proved indecisive—a continuing trend in recent years. Anand was not a signatory of the Prague Agreement, and he remained outside the unification process, despite his claims to be currently the strongest player in the world.

(BERNARD CAFFERTY)

CRICKET

In the 2003–04 season—a year that was marked by two individual Test records, by Matthew Hayden of Australia and Brian Lara of the West Indies, and a revival in England's fortunes—cricket found itself at the centre of political controversy off the field in Zimbabwe. By the end of the summer season, Zimbabwe's cricket was mirroring the chaos evident elsewhere in the country, with 15 of the top players boycotting the international side to protest the corruption and increasing politicization of the Zimbabwe Cricket Union (ZCU) under Zimbabwean Pres. Robert Mugabe.

The row was sparked by the replacement of the experienced Heath Streak as captain of Zimbabwe by the black 20-year-old wicket-keeper, Tatenda Taibu, in April. The white players in the squad regarded the move as politically motivated, and led by Streak (whose father, a farmer, had been imprisoned by the government), they withdrew from the two-Test series against Sri Lanka. A scratch side was raised that was no better than club standard, with inevitable consequences, and Zimbabwe was beaten heavily in both Tests. Officials of the ZCU, under pressure from the International Cricket Council (ICC), canceled two Tests against Australia (the world champions). England, which had refused to play in Harare, Zimb., for security reasons during the 2003 World Cup, toured Zimbabwe late in the year for a series of five one-day internationals, though at least two of the England players had declined to tour.

In contrast, India's first tour of Pakistan in 14 years showed cricket's ability to overcome political divisions. The three Tests and five one-day internationals passed without incident, and India narrowly won both series in a flurry of brilliant cricket and evident goodwill. India, led by Sourav Ganguly and wisely coached by John Wright of New Zealand, laid claim to being the most attractive side in international cricket, more than matching its host in an enthralling drawn series in Australia. That series marked the retirement from international cricket of Australian captain Steve Waugh. In Waugh's final Test, a double century by Sachin Tendulkar laid the base for an enormous Indian total, and though Waugh made 80 in his final Test innings, Australia was always batting to save rather than win the game. In October all of Australia bade farewell to the legendary all-rounder Keith Miller, who died at age 84. (*See* OBITUARIES.)

Under the leadership of Michael Vaughan, England recorded an unprecedented seven consecutive Test victories at home—four against the West Indies and three against New Zealand—after winning three out of four Tests in the West Indies. Steve Harmison proved to be a bowler of real pace and bounce, while Andrew Flintoff began to justify the extravagant claims made for his talent. Harmison took 7 for 12 as the West Indies was bowled out for 47 in the first Test in Jamaica, and he ended that series with 23 wickets at an average of 14.86. In the final Test of the series, in Antigua in April, Lara became the first batsman in Test history to score 400 runs. Almost 10 years to the day since he had beaten Sir Garfield Sobers's record of 365 on the same ground, the gifted West Indies captain took just under 13 hours to break the record set by Hayden, who had flayed a second-rate Zimbabwean attack for 380 in Perth, Australia, in October 2003. Lara's record could not, however, hide the dearth of talent and poverty of spirit in West Indies cricket. The one ray of hope came in mid-September when, in conditions of near darkness, Courtney Browne and Ian Bradshaw guided the West Indies to victory in the ICC Champions Trophy in England, for the side's first international trophy in 20 years.

The battle between Shane Warne of Australia and Muttiah Muralitharan of Sri Lanka to become the leading Test wicket-taker was no less competitive. Warne, a leg-spinner, returned from a drug-related suspension in February and reached the milestone of 500 wickets on March 12, the final day of the first Test in Sri Lanka, and Murali (as Muralitharan was widely known, a less-orthodox but equally controversial off-spinner, achieved the same feat on March 16, the first day of the second Test in the same series. Both men ended the season with 527 wickets each, breaking the previous record of 519 set by former West Indian fast bowler Courtney Walsh. Not for the first time, Murali's bowling action was reported to the ICC for investigation after allegations that he threw rather than bowled a new type of delivery, nicknamed the "doosra," in which the ball turns away from a right-handed batsman. Murali was advised not to bowl that type of ball in Tests, until a new, more tolerant law on throwing was passed by the ICC in November.

Pakistan had a disappointing year with a new captain, Inzamam-ul-Haq, and a young team. Sri Lanka was overpowered by Australia but came back to rout South Africa in the second of a two-Test series, with Kumar Sangakkara batting 232, his second double century of the year. Bangladesh, the newest Test-playing nation, continued to struggle and lost four of its six Tests.

In domestic cricket in England, Warwickshire won the county championship, Gloucestershire the one-day C&G Trophy, and Leicestershire the Twenty20 Cup (the 20-over-a-side tournament that, in its second season, lured a crowd of over 25,000 to Lord's). Victoria won Australia's Pura Cup, and Western Australia took the one-day ING Cup. Eastern Province beat Gauteng in the final of the Supersport Series Shield in South Africa, while Gauteng gained revenge in the one-day Standard Bank Cup. Barbados and Guyana were champions in the West Indies, and Pakistan won the Under-19 World Cup in Dhaka, Bangladesh.

(ANDREW LONGMORE)

CURLING

In April 2004 Sweden's skip, Peter Lindholm, won the men's world curling championship for his third title in eight years; his other victories were in 2001 and 1997. In front of the home crowd in Gävle, Swed., Lindholm executed a draw to the centre of the house with his last stone for a 7–6 win over Sebastian Stock of Germany in the championship game. The Swedes went 6–3 in the round-robin to earn a playoff berth and beat Olympic gold medallist Pål Trulsen of Norway 8–6 in the semifinal. Canada's Mark Dacey went unbeaten in the round-robin at 9–0, lost 9–6 in the semifinal to Stock, and took the bronze with a 9–3 decision over Trulsen. The rest of the men's field were, in order, Scotland, Switzerland, New Zealand, Denmark, the U.S., and France.

Canada's Colleen Jones rebounded from losing the gold to the U.S. in 2003 to claim her second women's world championship in six tries (she also won in 2001). Canada doubled Norway's Dordi Nordby 8–4 in the final. Jones defeated Switzerland's Luzia Ebnöther 8–6 in one semifinal, while Nordby edged American Patti Lank 8–7 in the other. Ebnöther then beat Lank 10–5 for the bronze. The rest of the field were, in order, Scotland, Sweden, Japan, Denmark, Italy, and Finland.

Canada swept the world senior championships, held during the same week in Gävle, with Anne Dunn winning her second gold in three years and Bas Buckle taking the men's crown.

At the world junior curling championship held in March in Trois-Rivières, Que., Niklas Edin edged Switzerland's Stefan Rindlisbacher 5–4 to give Sweden its first junior gold since 1989. Norway's Linn Githmark defeated Canada's Jill Mouzar 9–6 for the women's junior crown. In January Scotland's Frank Duffy won the world wheelchair curling championship in Sursee, Switz., with a 6–3 decision over defending champion Urs Bucher of the host country. (DONNA SPENCER)

CYCLING

In 2004 American Lance Armstrong became the first person to have won cycling's premier road event, the Tour de France, six times with his victory in the three-week race, which began in Liège, Belg., on July 3 and finished on July 25 on the Champs-Élysées in Paris. Armstrong, who achieved his wins in successive years, dominated the 3,395-km (1 km = about 0.62 mi) race to finish 6 min 19 sec ahead of Germany's Andreas Klöden. The race was decided in the high mountains of the Pyrenees and Alps, where Armstrong won four of the five stages before sealing overall victory by winning the 55-km individual time trial at Besançon, France, on the penultimate day. Richard Virenque of France won the "king of the mountains" competition as the best climber for a record seventh time.

Italy's Alessandro Petacchi used his powerful sprint finish to win a record nine stages in the Tour of Italy (Giro d'Italia), which was won by his compatriot Damiano Cunego. Italian rider Paolo Bettini, who captured the road-race title at the Olympic Games in Athens, won the World Cup series for a record third time, and Spaniard Roberto Heras won a record-tying third Tour of Spain (Vuelta a España).

Three world records were set in track racing at the Olympics. Australia improved its own record for the 4,000-m men's team pursuit to 3 min 56.610 sec in the first round, going on to win the gold medal; Sarah Ulmer of New Zealand won the women's 3,000-m pursuit in a record 3 min 24.537 sec; and Anna Meares of Australia lowered the record for the women's 500-m time trial to 33.952 sec. At the world track championships in Melbourne, Australia, Yoanka González Pérez won Cuba's first world title, in the women's 10-km scratch race.

The question of drugs and doping continued to cast a shadow over the sport with police investigations carried out in a number of countries. Implicated in an inquiry into the French team Cofidis, David Millar of Great Britain admitted to having used the human growth hormone erythropoietin (EPO) in 2001 and 2003 and was banned for two years and stripped of the 2003 world individual time-trial title. The 1996 world road-race champion, Johan Museeuw, was banned for two years by Belgium's cycling authority for breaking doping regulations, and American Tyler Hamilton, who won the Olympic individual time trial, tested positive for an illegal blood transfusion during the Tour of Spain, but he was contesting the testing procedure.

Cyclist Lance Armstrong of the U.S. enters the Place de la Concorde in Paris during the final stage of the Tour de France on July 25.

AP/Wide World Photos

Italy's Marco Pantani, the winner of the Tour de France and the Tour of Italy in 1998, was found dead on February 14. (*See* OBITUARIES.)

(JOHN R. WILKINSON)

EQUESTRIAN SPORTS

Thoroughbred Racing. *United States.* Thoroughbred horse racing's long wait for another Secretariat appeared to be over in 2004 when Smarty Jones, a colt of the same chestnut hue and charismatic qualities as the 1973 Triple Crown champion, won the hearts and captured the imaginations of Americans eager to embrace a new Thoroughbred hero. On May 1 he became the first undefeated horse since Seattle Slew in 1977 to win the Kentucky Derby, and two weeks later he posted a dominating victory in the Preakness Stakes. The stage was set for Smarty Jones to become the 12th Triple Crown champion and end the 26-year drought since Affirmed won in 1978. The prohibitive 3–10 favourite to win the Belmont Stakes on June 5, Smarty Jones, under jockey Stewart Elliott, held the lead in the stretch but was passed by 36–1 longshot Birdstone, ridden by Edgar Prado, in the closing strides to lose by a length. Smarty Jones did not race again. Diagnosed with chronic bruising of the cannon bone in all four fetlock joints, he was syndicated for $39 million and retired to stud in August at Three Chimneys Farm in Midway, Ky. The Pennsylvania-bred colt won eight of nine career starts and $7,613,155 in purse money, including a $5 million bonus.

The U.S.'s jockeys made news on several fronts in 2004. California emerged as the battleground state for what was becoming a national movement on behalf of the Jockeys' Guild to raise the scale of weights. The proposal, made in response to what was perceived as a need to improve the health of riders, would raise the minimum weight of riders to 53.5 kg (118 lb) from the present 51 kg (112 lb) and would require a minimum of 5% body fat. In Kentucky a U.S. District Court judge granted a preliminary injunction to block enforcement of a state rule that banned advertising patches on jockeys. The Kentucky Horse Racing Authority then suspended the rule, and for the first time, jockeys wore ads on their pants at the Kentucky Derby. In November Churchill Downs management banned 14 jockeys from its racetrack for the balance of the autumn meet when they refused to ride because of a dispute over health-insurance coverage.

In the spring, demolition work began on the historic Gulfstream Park in Hallandale, Fla., built in 1939, as part of a two-year $120 million redevelopment plan. The 2005 racing season was to be conducted in temporary structures. Churchill Downs, Inc., bought the historic Fair Grounds in New Orleans in October. The sale price of $47 million included the track's five offtrack-wagering facilities. The Fair Grounds had been mired in bankruptcy after a district court ruled that the track owed horsemen $90 million in withheld video-poker revenue. The dispute was settled for $25 million in August.

In a move that could exert far-reaching effects, Pennsylvania Gov. Ed Rendell on July 5 signed legislation that authorized slot machines at 14 locations in the state, including the four existing racetracks. In Florida voters narrowly passed a constitutional amendment in November that would allow residents of Broward and Miami-Dade counties to vote on authorizing slot machines at racetracks. If approved, seven pari-mutuel facilities, including Gulfstream Park, would get slot machines. Voters in Oklahoma approved a referendum that paved the way for the installation of bingo machines at racetracks.

Jockey Patricia Cooksey, aged 46, the second leading female rider in history, after Hall of Fame jockey Julie Krone, retired on June 24. Plagued with illness and injury for several years, she was only the second woman to ride in the Kentucky Derby and the first to ride in the Preakness. Cooksey had 2,137 victories

Jockey Glen Boss and Makybe Diva cruised to victory in the Melbourne Cup on November 2.

from 18,266 career mounts. Two high-profile leaders of the American Thoroughbred racing industry also resigned. Tim Smith, the first and only commissioner of the National Thoroughbred Racing Association since the organization's founding in 1998, stepped down on September 1, while Barry Schwartz, chairman and CEO of the beleaguered New York Racing Association since 2000, resigned in late 2004.

Belmont Stakes winner Birdstone was retired in November owing to a bone chip in his left front ankle. He won five of nine starts and $1,575,600 in purses. Six-year-old Pleasantly Perfect, whose career earnings of $7,789,880 ranked fourth all-time behind Cigar, Skip Away, and Fantastic Light, was retired after having injured his left hind ankle during his third-place finish in the Breeders' Cup Classic on October 30 with Jerry Bailey (*see* BIOGRAPHIES), who had recently recovered from a broken wrist, on board. A multiple-stakes winner, Pleasantly Perfect won 9 of 18 career starts. Azeri, North America's top money-winning female Thoroughbred, was retired in December at age six. She had career earnings of $4,079,820 and was the 2002 Horse of the Year.

(JOHN G. BROKOPP)

International. Betting exchanges, which had revolutionized the betting industry in Britain, continued to have an expanding impact on Thoroughbred horse racing in 2004. (Betting exchanges are online sites where individuals wager against each other.) In common with so many other creations of the computer age, the exchanges challenged national boundaries, and those who controlled wagering were worried by the threat that exchanges presented. Racing authorities in Australia, where the federal government ignored the opposition of states and refused to ban them, and Hong Kong, where betting on horse racing fell for the seventh consecutive year in the season ended in June, were particularly concerned.

British racing authorities had never held control over betting, and bookmakers had customarily refused to reveal details of their business. Betfair, the biggest exchange, had begun cooperating with the British Jockey Club's security department following a 2003 agreement and helped to expose malpractices by two prominent owner-backers. The root of the controversy, however, was not dishonesty but money, both for governments and for the financing of racing.

British racing was bedeviled by stories of corruption all year, not least when jockey Kieren Fallon was one of 16 people arrested on September 1 during a race-fixing investigation. No charges were expected until 2005. Fallon was also suspended for 21 days for having failed to push Ballinger Ridge to win in a race at Lingfield Park on March 2. Betfair had alerted the Jockey Club to irregular betting patterns before the race. Fallon, a six-time champion in the previous seven years, lost his title to Lanfranco ("Frankie") Dettori. Champion in 1994 and 1995, Dettori returned to the top with the help of the Godolphin stable, for which he served as the number one jockey.

Godolphin had many bright prospects, including all but a handful of the only crop of foals sired by their best-ever horse, Dubai Millennium, before his early death in 2001. Godolphin also took over the best two-year-old in Britain, Group 1 Dewhurst Stakes winner Shamardal. The stable had no luck in the early season classics but won important prizes with Sulamani, Refuse to Bend, Rule of Law, and Doyen, which beat the American-trained Hard Buck in the King George VI and Queen Elizabeth Diamond Stakes. The stable of Coolmore Stud, on the other hand, had a miserable season, made worse by the erratic big-race performances of its best horses, Powerscourt and Antonius Pius. Oratorio, the best Coolmore two-year-old, was beaten by two and a half lengths by Shamardal in the Dewhurst. Coolmore's principal owner between about 1975 and 1990, Robert Sangster, died on April 7. (*See* OBITUARIES.)

The great success of the year in Europe was the expansion of valuable races restricted to fillies and mares. There were 39 Group races in this category in 2004, including 4 newly promoted to Group 1, compared with 20 in 2002. The aim was to encourage owners to keep fillies in training. A remarkable experiment was conducted at the Stade de France in Saint-Denis on September 18 when two trotting and two Thoroughbred races were conducted on a specially laid fibre-sand track with a 425-m (465-yd) circuit. Ioritz Mendizabal, born in the Basque region and still based in the southwestern part of the country, was France's champion jockey. He set a new French record when he won his 208th race of the year on November 16.

The most important introduction in 2004 was the Dubai (U.A.E.) International Racing Carnival at Nad al Sheba Racecourse. Nine days of racing between January 29 and March 11, with rich prizes paid in U.S. dollars rather than dirhams, led up to the Dubai World Cup meeting on March 27. The festival attracted horses from a number of countries, and South African trainer Mike de Kock had notable success with Crimson Palace, Lundy's Liability, and Victory Moon. Godolphin bought Crimson Palace after her victory on January 29, and she went on to win the Grade 1 Beverly D. Stakes at Arlington Park outside Chicago in August. Brazilian-bred Lundy's Liability won the U.A.E. Derby, and Victory Moon won twice before finishing third to the Californian pair Pleasantly Perfect and Medaglia d'Oro in the Dubai World Cup.

Godolphin's Sulamani beat the German-trained Simonas in the Canadian International, but the Canadian-trained Soaring Free won the Atto Mile at Woodbine Racetrack in Toronto. Niigon was a below-standard winner of the Queen's Plate. Makybe Diva became the fifth horse and the first filly or mare to win two Melbourne Cups. Bred in England by her Australian owners, she started favourite in a field of 24 and defeated the second favourite, Vinnie Roe, which had just won the Irish St. Leger for a record fourth consecutive year. Savabeel, which beat the 2003 winner, Fields of Omagh, in the Cox Plate, was the first three-year-old to win the Southern Hemisphere's richest weight-for-age event since 1995.

(ROBERT W. CARTER)

Harness Racing. Windsong's Legacy became the first trotter to capture the Triple Crown in 32 years when he swept the Hambletonian, Yonkers Trot, and

Kentucky Futurity in 2004; the last trotter to accomplish this harness-racing feat was Super Bowl in 1972. Windsong's Legacy was just the seventh horse to claim the trotting Triple Crown.

The newest Triple Crown winner was barely a month old in the spring of 2001 when his mother, Yankee Windsong, died after colic surgery. The orphan colt was raised drinking milk replacer out of a bottle and a bucket at Hanover Shoe Farms in Pennsylvania. He was sold as a yearling for $27,000. Raced lightly as a two-year-old in 2003, winning $30,838, Windsong's Legacy was sold on the eve of his three-year-old campaign. His Norwegian-born trainer and driver, Trond Smedshammer, had no idea that Windsong's Legacy would become a superstar, and he and his partners sold a majority interest to Fredrik Lindegaard of Norway.

Windsong's Legacy blossomed into a new horse in 2004. He won 9 of his 12 starts, with two second-place finishes and one third place. His winnings came to $1,713,806, a single-season earnings record for trotters. In all of his Triple Crown victories, Windsong's Legacy let others set the pace and then swept to victory in the homestretch. After wrapping up the Triple Crown with a victory in the Kentucky Futurity on October 9, Windsong's Legacy retired from racing. He was scheduled to begin breeding service in 2005.

The top pacer in North America was Rainbow Blue, a nearly flawless filly that crushed her opponents. As a two-year-old, she won six of her seven starts. She was unbeaten for the first several months of the 2004 racing season. She suffered a freak defeat in the Mistletoe Shalee at the Meadowlands Racetrack in East Rutherford, N.J., however, when she shied at a photographer near the track, causing her to break stride and lose her chances in the race. Otherwise, Rainbow Blue could do no wrong for trainer George W. Teague, Jr., of Delaware. She won the Breeders Crown in late October in typically effortless fashion. Rainbow Blue's regular driver, Ron Pierce, said before the coveted Little Brown Jug for three-year-old pacers that he would love to race her against colts in that event, but she was not eligible to compete. Pierce won the Little Brown Jug anyway, with Timesareachanging. Rainbow Blue ended her season with 20 wins in 21 starts and earnings of $1,195,010 for the year.

While Windsong's Legacy dominated the three-year-old trotting division, the three-year-old pacers took turns winning the big events. Mantacular won the North America Cup, Holborn Hanover captured the Meadowlands Pace, and Western Terror took the Breeders Crown.

In Europe in late January, French horsemen celebrated when one of their own, Kesaco Phedo, took the prestigious Prix d'Amerique at the Vincennes racecourse outside Paris. The marathon event (approximately 2,700 m [1⅔ mi]) historically had favoured French horses, bred for endurance. Finishing second was Abano As of Germany, while Jag de Bellouet of France was third. Four months later Kesaco Phedo was in Sweden, trying to match strides with Europe's best sprinters in the Elitlopp, a 1,600-m (1-mi) race. He was not sound at this time, however, and was never a factor as Swedish star Gidde Palema proved to be a popular winner.

In Perth, Australia, the pacing gelding Jofess scored a narrow victory in the Inter Dominion Pacing Championship Grand Final for the best harness horses "down under." Jofess led from the start and prevailed by a nose over The Falcon Strike in a furious finish. Sokyola finished third. (DEAN A. HOFFMAN)

Steeplechasing. In March 2004 Best Mate won his third consecutive Cheltenham Gold Cup, but the official handicapper still did not rate him high enough to be considered one of the all-time great steeplechasers. Irish-trained Hardy Eustace won the Champion Hurdles at both Cheltenham and Punchestown (Ireland), while Irish-trained Rule Supreme won the French Grande Course de Haies d'Auteuil. Third in the latter race was Kotkijet, winner of the Grand Steeple-Chase de Paris three weeks earlier. Amberleigh House, trained by 73-year-old Donald ("Ginger") McCain, won the Grand National at the age of 12. McCain had also trained Red Rum, a three-time winner of the race between 1973 and 1977.

(ROBERT W. CARTER)

FENCING

Without doubt the most important development in fencing in 2004 was the introduction at the Athens Olympic Games of sabre without wires, coupled with new timings for registering hits. The new system, with scoring lights also located in the side of masks, transformed the spectacle. Parallel with this advance were the growth in popularity of women's sabre to the point where it rivaled women's foil internationally and the introduction of women's sabre as an Olympic discipline. The executive of the Fédération Internationale d'Escrime (FIE), the world governing body, hoped to push through changes to foil during the 2004–05 season that would mirror the sabre innovations.

The 2004 Olympic Games saw a turning point in the world order. Although in overall rankings traditional powers Italy (with 7 of the 30 medals awarded), France (6), Russia (4), and Hungary (3) came out on top, China ranked fifth and the U.S. sixth. Women's world championships for team sabre and team foil were held separately at the Grand Prix event in New York City in June because the International Olympic Committee allowed just 10 events in Athens.

In January the Jordanian federation appeared to obstruct the entry of Israeli fencers to Jordan's World Cup event. FIE rules forbade discrimination on any grounds, and following international pressure the Jordanians relented. A problem also arose at the Olympics when a leading Hungarian referee made six errors in a final between Italy and China and failed to apply penalties appropriately. He was banned from refereeing for two years.

FIE Pres. René Roch of France was reelected to a third consecutive four-year term in December. His main contributions were forcing through the extensive modernization program and securing 200,000 Swiss francs (about $160,000) from the FIE's main sponsor, Tissot S.A., to support the world championships and Grand Prix events.

(GRAHAM MORRISON)

Aldo Montano of Italy (left) shouts with joy after defeating Zsolt Nemcsik of Hungary in the men's Olympic individual sabre final on August 14.

FOOTBALL

Association Football (Soccer). *Europe.* The outcome of Euro 2004, the quadrennial European association football (soccer) championship, produced one of the biggest upsets in the game's history as Greece—without any record of even modest achievement at the highest level—defeated the host nation, Portugal, 1–0 in the final, held on July 4 in the Estádio da Luz in Lisbon. With one previous appearance in the 1994 World Cup finals and an earlier qualification for the 1988 European championship, the Greek team had never managed to win a game. In 2004, however, Greece twice beat Portugal, as well as the defending titlist and favourite, France. The 2004 champion's sole loss was against Russia, the one opponent that, before the tournament opened, Greece might have been expected to beat.

AP/Wide World Photos

Portugal's goalkeeper Ricardo (far right) fails to block the winning goal by Greek striker Angelos Charisteas (far left) in Greece's 1–0 triumph over Portugal in the Euro 2004 association football (soccer) championship final on July 4.

In a disappointing defensive-minded, and fear-ridden competition, Greece adhered relentlessly to its strategy of sound defense, counterattacking only when the options were obvious. Greece's German-born 65-year-old coach, Otto Rehhagel, who had been appointed in 2001 with a reputation of success at domestic level in his own country, maintained a cautious policy on the field, and his emphasis on defense was completely vindicated when Greece came away the winner.

While Greece applied itself with a stifling tactical approach involving industrious man marking, its style of play was visually boring. Since the performance of the favoured teams (Italy, Spain, Germany, and France) fell below the standard expected of them, however, Greece fully deserved its success. The timing of Greece's only goal in the semifinal against the most attack-minded team, Czech Republic, could not have been better, with seconds to go before the end of the first period of extra time; it thus qualified as a silver goal and virtually ended the match at 1–0.

In the final an inswinging corner kick from Greece's Angelos Basinas in the 57th minute cleared the head of Portuguese defender Jorge Andrade, and Angelos Charisteas, who played professionally in Germany for Werder Bremen, headed the crucial goal. Despite redoubling its effort to get back into the game, Portugal, coached by Felipe Scolari (who guided Brazil to the 2002 World Cup title), found itself unable to break down the Greek resolve. Fifteen of the 23 Greek players were home-based, though many had had experience playing abroad. Another record was established when Swiss international Johan Vonlanthen, at 18 years 141 days old, became the youngest European championship scorer.

Official attendance figures of 1,165,192 for the finals showed an improvement over four years earlier (1,126,443), but the average crowd of 37,587 was well under the record 56,656 for the tournament staged in West Germany in 1988. The poor showings of Italy, Spain, Germany, and France were attributed in part to the increasing numbers of foreign players (and the attendant decrease in young home-grown talent) in these and other countries, including England, which failed to adopt the correct tactics at crucial stages in Euro 2004. Moreover, the emphasis placed on club football in those countries through the Union des Associations Européennes de Football (UEFA) Champions League and to a lesser degree the UEFA Cup had helped to reduce national team status.

Before the disappointment of losing in Euro 2004, there had been better news at club level for Portugal when FC Porto defeated AS Monaco FC 3–0 for the Champions League title. For Porto coach José Mourinho it was a double European triumph; in 2003 the club had won the UEFA Cup. In the Champions League final on May 26 in Gelsenkirchen, Ger., both Mourinho and his Monaco counterpart, Didier Deschamps, displayed unwillingness to take chances in attack and preferred defense as their chief weapon. Porto broke the deadlock in the 39th minute when Carlos Alberto took advantage of hesitancy in the Monaco rearguard to strike the ball past goalkeeper Flavio Roma. Porto's offside trap kept Monaco at bay until the 71st minute, when substitute Dmitry Alenichev of Russia made an opening for Anderson de Souza Deco, the Brazilian-born Portuguese international, to score at 2–0. Alenichev completed the scoring four minutes later, accepting a pass from Brazilian Vanderlei Fernandes Derlei.

On May 19 the UEFA Cup final in Göteborg, Swed., proved a success for Valencia of Spain against the French team Olympique Marseille but not before the incident that arguably settled the outcome. On the stroke of halftime, Marseille goalkeeper Fabien Barthez, on loan from England's Manchester United, bundled over the Spanish forward Miguel Ángel Ferrer Mista inside the penalty area and was dismissed. Jeremy Gavanon had to come on as a replacement goalkeeper, with outfield player Camel Meriem sacrificed. Vicente Rodríguez Guillen scored from the penalty and was responsible for setting up the second goal converted by Mista in the 58th minute. A low-key game underlined the second-class stamp that the tournament had been handed in recent years. In 2004–05 the introduction of a Champions League-style group stage was intended to revamp it. Valencia also provided the oldest player to win a European cup medal, Italian-born left-back Amedeo Carboni, age 39.

Both of the UEFA-tournament-winning coaches moved on to England, still considered the mecca for top mercenaries. Mourinho was drawn by the Roman Abramovich wealth of Chelsea, while Rafael Benítez moved from Valencia to Liverpool. Mourinho was quickly into trading mode and signed five players for a total of £61 million (£1 = about $1.80), the most expensive of them being the Marseille striker Didier Drogba for £24 million.

Modest Norwegian champion Rosenborg continued its remarkable consistency by qualifying for the Champions League for the ninth time in 10 years, and captain Roar Strand maintained his record of appearing in each season. Paolo Maldini of AC Milan made his 130th appearance in a European cup match.

The Fédération Internationale de Football (FIFA) decided to end the silver- and golden-goals experiment. In the future, penalty shoot-outs would be used to decide matches unresolved at the end of overtime. The world governing body also decreed an end to unlimited numbers of substitutes in noncompetitive international matches, restricting them to six only. Another innovation was the sanction of previously banned artificial pitches (playing surfaces), because of the improved technology that had been developed in preparing surfaces on which to play.

On the domestic front Lyon achieved its third successive French league title and Ajax won its 29th overall in Holland, while AC Milan took its first Serie A title in five years. Valencia achieved the La Liga championship, and Lokomotiv Plovdiv gained a notable first championship in Bulgaria. Double League and Cup winners were Graz (in Austria), FC Copenhagen, HJK Helsinki (Finland), Werder Bremen, Panathinaikos (Greece), Rosenborg, Dinamo Bucharest (Romania), Glasgow Celtic (Scotland), and Red Star Belgrade (Serbia and Montenegro).

In the English Football Association (FA), Arsenal became the third team to avoid league defeat in a season, and only the second to achieve it at top level, when it won 26 and drew 12 of 38 FA Premier League games. (Early in the 2004–05 season, Arsenal reached 43 straight victories to break the record set by Nottingham Forest in the former First Division of the Football League between November 1977 and November 1978.) Arsenal's French international Thierry Henry (*see* BIOGRAPHIES) won the Golden Shoe as Europe's top scorer (with 30 goals) and was second behind Brazilian Ronaldinho for FIFA World Player of the Year. Manchester United won the FA Cup, beating First Division Millwall 3–0. Celtic set a Scottish record with 25 consecutive wins in the Premier League. Celtic's Swedish international striker Henrik Larsson left the club after seven seasons, having scored 242 goals in 315 games. (JACK ROLLIN)

The Americas. Brazil and Argentina continued to be the giants in South American association football (soccer) in 2004, finishing the year respectively in first and third place in the Fédération Internationale de Football Association's world rankings. In July the two countries met in the final of the South American championship (Copa América), held in Peru, where Brazil, despite not fielding its strongest team, defeated Argentina 4–2 on penalties.

In club action, however, several less-fashionable teams had their day.

China's Zheng Zhi (left) and Takayuki Suzuki of Japan compete for the ball in the Asian Cup final in Beijing on August 7. Japan defeated China 3–1.

© Andrew Wong/Reuters/Corbis

Colombia's Once Caldas beat Argentina's Boca Juniors 2–0 on penalties, after a 1–1 draw in goals, to win its first Libertadores de América Cup and reached the final of the last Intercontinental Cup, losing to European Cup winners FC Porto of Portugal. (The Intercontinental Cup was to be replaced in 2005 by a club championship between continental champions.) It was an all-Costa Rican final in the CONCACAF (Confederation of North, Central American and Caribbean Association Football) Champions' Cup as Alajuelense beat Saprissa. Second division Santo André won the Brazil Cup, while Newell's Old Boys captured the opening championship in Argentina to end a run of 24 titles won by the country's big six clubs since 1992. In Uruguay modest Danubio won the 2004 title after 12 years of domination by Peñarol and Nacional. On the other hand, top club Cerro Porteño won both tournaments in Paraguay, as did UNAM Pumas in Mexico. Brazil's Santos won its second national title in three years, and Alianza Lima captured its 20th Peruvian championship. Boca Juniors ended a poor year on a positive note after capturing the South American Cup with a victory over Bolívar, the first Bolivian team to reach a continental cup final. In the U.S., D.C. United won its fourth Major League Soccer championship, defeating the Kansas City Wizards 3–2 in the MLS Cup final.

Most South American clubs continued to struggle financially and managed to keep afloat by selling their best players, mostly to Europe. In Chile, Colo Colo and Universidad de Chile, which had been declared bankrupt, were in the hands of administrators, and half a dozen clubs had points deducted for not paying players' salaries on time. (ERIC WEIL)

Africa and Asia. On Feb. 14, 2004, the final of the African Nations Cup was held in Radès, Tun., and was won by the host country, which defeated neighbours Morocco 2–1 in front of a crowd of 60,000 in the November 7 Stadium. The top player of the tournament was adjudged to have been Jay Jay Okocha of Nigeria. That country's Enyimba won the African Super Cup to confirm its status as the leading club side on the continent, beating Étoile Sahel of Tunisia 1–0 in Aba, Nigeria, on February 22.

In the Asian Cup, staged in China, Japan beat the host nation 3–1 in the final, held in Beijing on August 7 in front of a crowd of 62,000. It was Japan's third Asian Cup title in four years.

(JACK ROLLIN)

U.S. Football. *College*. The 2004–05 college football season culminated in the first-ever college game between Heisman Trophy winners, but it was a lopsided contest. The University of Southern California (USC), led by 2004 Heisman winner Matt Leinart and coach Pete Carroll, captured its second consecutive national championship and ninth overall by defeating the University of Oklahoma 55–19 in the Orange Bowl in Miami, Fla., on Jan. 4, 2005. The teams went into the game with identical 12–0 records and with two of the top-ranked defenses in Division I-A of the National Collegiate Athletic Association (NCAA). USC, however, took advantage of four Oklahoma turnovers, and Leinart threw five touchdowns, including three to Steve Smith, to extend the Trojans' winning streak to 22 games. It was the second straight defeat in a national championship game for Oklahoma quarterback Jason White, the 2003 Heisman winner, who had lost the previous year to Louisiana State University (LSU), the 2003–04 cochampion. Although teammate Adrian Peterson, the 2004 Heisman runner-up, managed only 82 yd rushing against the Trojans, that helped him set a record for freshmen of 1,925 yd rushing. Forced to pass, White, winner of the Davey O'Brien Award for top quarterback and the Maxwell Award for best player, threw three interceptions, half his regular-season total.

Auburn (13–0), the Southeastern Conference champion, was the first team in the seven-year history of the Bowl Championship Series (BCS) not to make the national championship game despite having an unbeaten record in one of the six conferences with automatic berths in the four BCS bowl games. Auburn won the Sugar Bowl, defeating Atlantic Coast Conference winner Virginia Tech (10–3), which was new to the ACC after having bolted the Big East along with the University of Miami (Fla.). Winners of the other BCS conferences were USC (13–0) in the Pacific-10, Oklahoma (12–1) in the Big 12, cochampions Michigan (9–3) and Iowa (10–2) in the Big Ten, and Pittsburgh (8–4) in the depleted Big East.

Utah (12–0) of the Mountain West and Boise State (11–1) of the Western Athletic Conference also had undefeated regular seasons. Utah, the first team from a non-BCS conference to play in a BCS bowl, beat Pittsburgh in the Fiesta Bowl, led by Urban Meyer, named Coach of the Year. The top two scoring teams were Conference USA winner Louisville (11–1) and Boise State, respectively. They met in the Liberty Bowl, where Louisville won 44–40. In other exciting bowl games, a last-play field goal in the Rose Bowl gave Texas (11–1) a 38–37 victory over Michigan in the first matchup between those traditional powerhouses, and Iowa beat LSU (9–3) 30–25 in the Capital One Bowl on a last-second 56-yd touchdown pass.

Victories by Colorado and Ohio State in the Houston Bowl and Alamo Bowl, respectively, were overshadowed by scandals off the field. At Colorado sexual assault allegations against football players led to an investigation that found the team had used sex, alcohol, and drugs as recruiting tools. Though it was never proved that he sanctioned such recruitment methods, Colorado's coach, Gary Barnett, was suspended for three months in the off-season for offensive comments he made regarding the assault cases. Ohio State suspended quarterback Troy Smith from its bowl game after allegations were made that a booster had given him benefits that violated NCAA rules.

The final rankings diverged slightly after USC, Auburn, and Oklahoma. The writers' poll chose Utah, Texas, Louisville, Georgia (10–2), Iowa, California (10–2), and Virginia Tech, in that order, but the coaches' poll reversed the order of Texas-Utah and Georgia-Louisville. Other Division I-A conference winners were Toledo (9–4) in the Mid-American and North Texas (7–5) in the Sun Belt.

In individual awards the Chuck Bednarik Award went to Georgia defensive end David Pollack, who also won the Vince Lombardi Trophy for linemen, and Derrick Johnson of Texas received the Bronko Nagurski Trophy and the Dick Butkus Award (both for defenders). The Outland Trophy, honouring interior linemen, went to Oklahoma's Jammal Brown.

Winners of the lower-budget NCAA divisions' championship tournaments were 13–2 James Madison (Va.) in Division I-AA, 13–1 Valdosta State (Ga.) in Division II, and 13–0 Linfield (Ore.) in Division III, while 12–2 Carroll (Mont.) won the National Association of Intercollegiate Athletics title.

Professional. The New England Patriots of the American Football Conference (AFC) defeated the Carolina Panthers of the National Football Conference (NFC) 32–29 to win Super Bowl XXXVIII, held in Reliant Stadium in Houston, Texas, on Feb. 1, 2004. It was their second National Football League (NFL) championship in three years. Quarterback Tom Brady (*see* BIOGRAPHIES) was named the Super Bowl Most Valuable Player (MVP) for the second time after throwing three touchdowns and moving the Patriots into position for a game-winning 41-yd field goal by Adam Vinatieri in the final seconds.

AP/Wide World Photos

On December 26 quarterback Peyton Manning of the Indianapolis Colts prepares to launch his record-breaking 49th touchdown pass of the season.

The Patriots (14–2) continued their winning streak into the 2004–05 regular season, setting a record for consecutive victories (21). The Pittsburgh Steelers and rookie quarterback Ben Roethlisberger, however, upstaged the Patriots and Brady, finishing with the fourth 15–1 record in NFL history and the first by a team that had a losing record the previous season. Roethlisberger became the starter after Tommy Maddox injured his elbow in the second game, and he led the Steelers to 13 consecutive wins before missing game 16 because of an injury. Along the way, Pittsburgh ended New England's winning streak and defeated previously unbeaten Philadelphia. Pittsburgh's defense helped the rookie by allowing league-best per-game averages of 15.7 points, 258.4 total yards, and 81.2 yd rushing.

High scoring was the theme elsewhere in a season that featured 1,268 touchdowns and 11,000 total points. With newly strict enforcement of the five-yard limit for bumping a receiver, five quarterbacks passed for at least 4,000 yd and four threw more than three times as many touchdown passes as interceptions. Peyton Manning of

Indianapolis was the game's marquee quarterback and regular season MVP, breaking Dan Marino's 20-year-old record for single-season touchdown passes (48) with 49 and Steve Young's efficiency-rating record with 121.1 points. Manning's Colts were the first team to have three players catch at least 10 touchdown passes, and Indianapolis averaged 32.6 points and 288.9 yd passing per game, both league highs. Daunte Culpepper of Minnesota led all passers with 4,717 yd and a .692 completion percentage. Quarterback Drew Brees, who had lost the starting job in 2003 owing to poor play, experienced a comeback, guiding San Diego (12–4) to its first winning season and first play-off berth in nine years. His favourite receiver, Antonio Gates, set a record for tight ends with 13 touchdown catches.

During the summer Ricky Williams of Miami abruptly retired, but the league still had plenty of exciting running backs. The Jets' Curtis Martin led the NFL with 1,697 yd, one more than Seattle's Shaun Alexander, who topped the league with 20 touchdowns. Martin and Pittsburgh's Jerome Bettis finished the season fourth and fifth, respectively, among all-time rushing leaders. Leading receivers were Kansas City's Tony Gonzalez with 102 catches, a record for tight ends, and Carolina's Muhsin Muhammad with 1,405 yd. Tory Holt of St. Louis set a record with a fifth straight season of more than 1,300 yd receiving.

The balance between the AFC and the NFC tilted heavily toward the former, where division winners Pittsburgh, New England, Indianapolis, and San Diego each won at least 12 games, and the runners-up with "wild-card" play-off berths, the New York Jets and Denver Broncos, went 10–6. In the NFC, division winners Philadelphia, Atlanta, Green Bay, and Seattle had the only winning records, while wild cards Minnesota and St. Louis made the play-offs with 8–8 records.

Two televised episodes provoked controversies that embarrassed the league. The brief exposure of singer Janet Jackson's breast punctuated a Super Bowl halftime show that featured sexually suggestive lyrics, and the carefully cropped introduction to a Monday night telecast showed TV actress Nicollette Sheridan dropping her shower towel and jumping into the arms of Philadelphia's Terrell Owens. Outside the court of public opinion, the NFL fared better when the Supreme Court declined to hear Maurice Clarett's failed challenge to the draft's eligibility rules.

Among the deaths during the year were Crazylegs Hirsch, Roosevelt Brown, and Reggie White. (*See* OBITUARIES.) (KEVIN M. LAMB)

Canadian Football. The Toronto Argonauts won the 2004 Canadian Football League (CFL) championship by defeating the B.C. Lions 27–19 in the Grey Cup on November 21 at Ottawa, behind 41-year-old quarterback Damon Allen, the game's Most Outstanding Player, with two touchdowns rushing and another passing. Allen had recovered from a broken leg in August to win his fourth championship and a league-high 15th title for Toronto. The Argonauts (10–7–1) had finished second in the East Division and reached the Grey Cup with a play-off upset of the Montreal Alouettes (14–4), the division champion.

Quarterback Casey Printers of the West Division winner Lions (13–5) was the regular-season Most Outstanding Player, leading all passers with 35 touchdowns, 10.3 yd per pass, a .658 completion percentage, and an efficiency rating of 115.0. Printers replaced injured Dave Dickenson during the regular season, but Dickenson played in the Grey Cup after Printers hurt his shoulder in the division final. Teammate Jason Clermont was named the CFL's Outstanding Canadian. Outstanding-player awards also went to Gene Makowsky of the Saskatchewan Roughriders (9–9) for linemen, Montreal's Anwar Stewart for defensive players, receiver Nikolas Lewis of the Calgary Stampeders (4–14) for rookies, and Keith Stokes of the Winnipeg Blue Bombers (7–11) for special teams. Individual leaders included kicker Sean Fleming of the Edmonton Eskimos (9–9) with 180 points and a .787 field-goal percentage and Troy Davis, who rushed for 1,628 yd for the Hamilton Tiger-Cats (9–8–1). (KEVIN M. LAMB)

Australian Football. Port Adelaide captured its first premiership in the Australian Football League (AFL) on Sept. 25, 2004. Port Adelaide, the last club to join the AFL, in 1997, scored 17.11 (113) against 10.13 (73) for the Brisbane Lions, which had won the previous three premierships. Brisbane had been strongly tipped to equal an ancient league record of four straight titles (attained by Collingwood in 1927–30). The game was played before 77,671 spectators at the Melbourne Cricket Ground, which was well short of its normal capacity because of a rebuilding program. It was the first Grand Final played between two clubs from outside Victoria, the recognized home of Australian football. The other teams to qualify for the finals were St. Kilda, Geelong, Melbourne, Sydney, West Coast, and Essendon.

Port Adelaide's Byron Pickett was judged best on the ground in the Grand Final and awarded the Norm Smith Medal. The Brownlow Medal, for the

In the Australian Football League Grand Final on September 25, Peter Burgoyne of the victorious Port Adelaide Power attempts to shake off a tackle by Martin Pike of the defending champion Brisbane Lions.

© Ryan Pierse/Getty Images

regular season's fairest and best player, was won for the first time by a West Coast Eagles player, Chris Judd. St. Kilda's Fraser Gehrig won the John Coleman Medal for the most goals (90) kicked in the regular season; when the finals were included, his total swelled to 103. Other honours went to Adelaide's Mark Ricciuto, named captain of the All-Australian team; St. Kilda's Nick Riewoldt, the AFL Players' Association Most Valuable Player; and Melbourne's Jared Rivers, the AFL Rising Star.

(GREG HOBBS)

Rugby Football. In 2003 England became the first side from the Northern Hemisphere to win the Rugby Union World Cup, but it was brought down to earth in 2004. Within 12 months of their magnificent triumph in Sydney, Australia, the English had lost two captains and their coach. Martin Johnson, the man who led England to the World Cup, quit soon after the tournament, and his successor, Lawrence Dallaglio, retired from international rugby in August, a few days before coach Clive Woodward resigned. Woodward, who was knighted in October, was selected to coach the British and Irish Lions on their trip to New Zealand in 2005. Johnson's decision to leave led to the departure of other squad members, and England proceeded to go on an awful run, surrendering its Six Nations title to France and losing five out of six games from March to June, its worst showing since the game turned professional in 1995. Under new coach Andy Robinson and new captain Jonny Wilkinson, the world champions hoped to start a new era as they headed toward the 2007 World Cup.

England's failure in 2004 was the most significant issue in the rugby world, but the year also signaled the return of the South African Springboks to the top three in the world rankings. Stung by a poor showing in the World Cup—in which they were knocked out in the quarterfinals—the Springboks appointed a new coach and captain, with startling effect, as they won the Tri-Nations, the championship of the Southern Hemisphere. Each side won its home matches in the Tri-Nations, so South Africa took the title by virtue of having grabbed more bonus points during the tournament. Significantly, it picked up one point by scoring four tries in a 40–26 thrashing of New Zealand.

In the Six Nations championship, England's failures allowed France to claim a grand slam, as it earned victories over all of the other five nations. The trophy was clinched with a 24–21 win over England in Paris. Scotland finished last and without a victory. Australia's ACT Brumbies won the Super 12, the domestic Southern Hemisphere championship, beating the Canterbury Crusaders from New Zealand 47–38 in the final. It was confirmed that the competition was to become a Super 14 in 2006, with two more teams (from Australia and South Africa) joining.

In Europe the Wasps were the dominant side, lifting the Heineken (European) Cup and the English domestic premiership title. The London-based Wasps won a sensational Heineken Cup, as they were drawing until the final moments, when scrum-half Rob Howley scored a daring try to give them a 27–20 victory over Toulouse of France.

In Rugby League the Leeds Rhinos won their first English Super League championship in 32 years, defeating the Bradford Bulls 16–8. Llanelli won the Celtic League, and in France Stade Français was league winner. In Australia the Canterbury Bulldogs beat the Sydney Roosters 16–13 in the National Rugby League grand final.

(PAUL MORGAN)

GOLF

In 2004 the dedication and hard work of Fijian golfer Vijay Singh was fully rewarded. In ending the five-year reign of American Eldrick ("Tiger") Woods as world number one, the 41-year-old Singh achieved the third major win of his career and established a level of consistency that led to record-breaking results. Singh became only the second player—Woods was the other—since Sam Snead in 1950 to have registered nine or more tournament titles in one season on the Professional Golfers' Association of America (PGA) Tour. Six of them came in his last nine starts, and, not surprisingly, Singh became the first golfer to win more than $10 million in one season. He took that to $10,905,166 at season's end, retaining the money list title by more than $5 million over South Africa's Ernie Els.

Singh had won his first professional tournament in Malaysia in 1984, but an allegation of changing his scorecard at the 1985 Indonesian Open—he always maintained that there was a misunderstanding—brought a suspension, and he became a club professional in the Borneo rainforest. He qualified for the European tour on the second attempt and after becoming one of its leading lights made the move to the U.S. and was named PGA Rookie of the Year in 1993. His first major title came at the 1998 PGA championship, and two years later he added the Masters tournament.

Fiji's Vijay Singh hits a chip shot on August 15, the final day of the PGA championship. Despite his four-over-par 76 for the day, Singh won the title in a three-hole play-off.

It was at the PGA championship that Singh triumphed again during his remarkable 2004 run. He led the final major of the season, which was staged in August at the spectacular Whistling Straits course in Kohler, Wis., by one stroke with a round to play, and despite a four-over-par 76, he qualified for a play-off against Americans Chris DiMarco and Justin Leonard; Leonard had bogeyed two of his last three holes to match their eight-under-par aggregates of 280. Singh then birdied the first of the three play-off holes, and it gave him an advantage he did not let slip. Not since Reginald Whitcombe at the 1938 British Open had someone scored as poorly in the final round of any major and still won.

In contrast, the Masters at the Augusta (Ga.) National Golf Club in April was distinguished by spectacular scoring in the closing stages. With eagles on the 8th and 13th holes of the final round, Els moved three strokes clear, but American Phil Mickelson completed a thrilling burst of five birdies in the last seven holes with a 5.5-m (18-ft) putt on the 18th to finish with a nine-under-par 279, edging Els by one stroke. The left-handed Mickelson literally jumped for joy; in 46 previous majors he had had 17 top-10 finishes but not one victory.

With two holes to play in the U.S. Open at Shinnecock Hills Golf Club in Southampton, N.Y., in June, Mickelson was out in front again. His double-bogey five at the short 17th, however, allowed South African Retief Goosen to capture his second victory in the event in four years. The championship was controversial for the increasing difficulty of the greens as the week progressed. In the final round, 28 of the 66-strong field failed to break 80, and no one broke 70. Play even had to be suspended for emergency watering of the seventh green after three of the first four players ran up triple-bogey sixes. The U.S. Golf Association was criticized for having allowed the situation to develop, but remarkably, Goosen had a mere 24 putts in his closing 71 for a total of 276, four under par.

Els, who was tied for second after three rounds, was among those who scored 80 that day, but the chance to make amends came in the British Open at Scotland's Royal Troon Golf Club in July. A birdie at the penultimate hole left him trailing Todd Hamilton by one, and he had a chance to win after the American bogeyed the last. Els missed his 3-m (10-ft) birdie putt, however, and the four-hole play-off was settled by his bogey on the third hole. Hamilton, age 38, was a PGA Tour rookie who had registered his first tour victory in March in the Honda Classic at the Country Club at Mirasol in Palm Beach Gardens, Fla.

The Ryder Cup was held in September at the Oakland Hills Country Club in Bloomfield Hills, Mich. For the first time since 1981, Europe did not have a major champion in its lineup, but it rose to the occasion, and the Americans were sent to their worst-ever defeat, a crushing 18½–9½ margin. Captain Hal Sutton paired Woods and Mickelson, his two highest-ranked players, for the opening fourballs and foursomes, but they lost both games, and the experiment was abandoned. Mickelson, who had controversially changed equipment just before the match, was then dropped, but the Europeans, led superbly by Bernhard Langer of Germany, refused to slacken the grip they had established. Top scorers were Spain's Sergio García and England's Lee Westwood with 4½ points out of 5, but all 12 players for Europe contributed at least one point. The U.S. had won only 3 of the last 10 Ryder Cup matches.

Els captured the World Golf Championships-American Express Championship at Mount Juliet in Thomastown, County Kilkenny, Ire., and then won a record sixth title in the HSBC World Match Play Championship at the Wentworth Club in Virginia Water, Surrey, Eng. Golf's richest prize of £1 million (£1 = about $1.80) was on offer again there. Els set a new record for money earned in a single season on the European tour, easily keeping his number one spot with a final figure of £2,808,907 and equaling another record on the circuit with a 12-under-par round of 60 at the Royal Melbourne Golf Club in Australia to win the Heineken Classic.

Els won two tournaments on the PGA Tour as well, but the first of those, the Sony Open at the Waialae Country Club, Honolulu, was better remembered for the performance of 14-year-old Hawaiian Michelle Wie. In May 2003 world number one Annika Sörenstam had become the first woman since 1945 to compete against men in an official event, and while the Swede failed to make the halfway cut by four strokes, Wie missed out by a single shot, beating 49 male players with her rounds of 72 and 68.

A fourth-place finish in the first of the Ladies Professional Golf Association's (LPGA's) majors, the Kraft Nabisco championship at Rancho Mirage, Calif., in March, underlined Wie's enormous potential, and in the Curtis Cup at Formby (Eng.) Golf Club, she not only became the youngest player to have competed in the match but also helped the U.S. retain the trophy with a 10–8 victory over Great Britain and Ireland's women amateurs. A fortune in the paid ranks seemingly awaited Wie, but for the time being Sörenstam remained the undisputed queen, topping the LPGA Tour for a fourth successive season and seventh in all. She also increased her number of major titles to seven by winning the McDonald's LPGA championship at DuPont Country Club in Wilmington, Del. South Korea's Grace Park won the Nabisco; American Meg Mallon captured the U.S. Open at Orchards Golf Club in South Hadley, Mass.; and England's Karen Stupples took the Women's British Open at Sunningdale, Eng., following a remarkable eagle-albatross start to her final-round 64.

Highlights of the amateur season included the world team championships at the Rio Mar Country Club in Puerto Rico. Sweden's women won the Espirito Santo Trophy, beating Canada and the U.S. by three strokes, while the U.S. men made it three wins in a row with the Eisenhower Trophy, finishing nine shots clear of Spain in an event reduced to 54 holes because of thunderstorms. American amateur champion Ryan Moore had the low individual score.

The World Cup was won by England's Luke Donald and Paul Casey at the Real Club de Golf de Sevilla in Seville, Spain. On the same November day, at the Phoenix tournament in Miyazaki, Japan, Woods finally returned to winning ways after nine months, and Sörenstam registered her 10th victory of the season and 56th in all to finish with winnings of $2,544,707.

(MARK GARROD)

GYMNASTICS

The Olympic Games, held in Athens during August 13–29, dominated the gymnastics calendar in 2004. In the men's team competition, China was favoured after having won the gold medal at the 2003 Fédération Internationale de Gymnastique (FIG) world championships, but Japan, which finished third in 2003, turned out to be the strongest team at the Games and became Olympic champion. The United States earned the silver, its first team gymnastics medal in a nonboycotted Games since 1932. Romania gained the bronze, while China finished fifth in the team competition behind South Korea.

In the men's all-around competition, American Paul Hamm, the reigning world champion, came back from a fall on vault to win the gold medal. South Korea's Kim Dae Eun and Yang Tae Young earned the silver and bronze medals, respectively. Hamm's victory turned into controversy when the South Korean gymnastics federation lodged a complaint that Yang's parallel bars routine had been given a 9.9 start value (the level of difficulty from which point deductions are taken for errors) instead of a 10.0. Under FIG rules, protests had to be filed immediately, and scores could not be changed once the meet was over. The Korean Olympic Committee took its protest to the Court of Arbitration for Sport, and in late October the court ruled to dismiss South Korea's appeal, in keeping with the original ruling by FIG.

In the men's event finals, each of the six events was won by an athlete from a different country. Canadian Kyle Shewfelt claimed the gold on floor exercise; China's Teng Haibin captured gold on pommel horse; hometown favourite Dimosthenis Tampakos of Greece won the rings title; Spain's Gervasio Deferr repeated his 2000 Olympic triumph on vault; and Valery Goncharov of Ukraine won parallel bars. Italy's Igor Cassina was awarded the gold on horizontal bar, but the event was marred by spectator protests over the low scoring for Russian defending champion Aleksey Nemov.

On August 23 Romanian gymnast Catalina Ponor pauses during her balance beam routine in the Olympic apparatus finals. Ponor captured the gold medal and another in the floor exercise about an hour later.

© Ezra Shaw/Getty Images

On the women's side, defending Olympic champion Romania won the team gold medal, slightly outdistancing the U.S. and Russia, which took the silver and bronze medals, respectively. Carly Patterson gained the all-around title to become only the second American (after Mary Lou Retton in 1984) to have accomplished this feat. Russia's Svetlana Khorkina won the silver, and Zhang Nan of China took the bronze. Romania dominated the event finals competition, with Monica Rosu winning vault and Catalina Ponor earning gold in both balance beam and floor exercise. France's Emilie Lepennec won the title on uneven bars.

In the rhythmic gymnastics competition, Russia's Alina Kabayeva, who had finished with the individual bronze medal in 2000, was able to capture the gold in 2004. Kabayeva's teammate Irina Chashina earned the silver, while Ukraine's Anna Bessonova won the bronze. In group competition, Russia won the title, with Italy and Bulgaria taking the silver and bronze.

Germany's Anna Dogonadze hit a solid routine to claim the trampoline gold medal. Canadian Karen Cockburn won the silver medal, and Huang Shanshan of China took the bronze. On the men's side, Yury Nitikin of Ukraine won the gold medal. Russia's Aleksandr Moskalenko, the defending Olympic champion in trampoline, won the silver medal, and Germany's Henrik Stehlik claimed the bronze. (LUAN PESZEK)

ICE HOCKEY

North America. The National Hockey League (NHL) once again suffered through a season hurt by poor attendance, decreasing revenue, the lowest television ratings in five years, and a huge labour problem during 2003–04. The season ended with the NHL Players Association refusing to accept the idea of a salary cap or any system that would guarantee a percentage of revenue to the owners. With neither side willing to compromise on their positions, in September the owners locked out the players. When the 2004–05 season was scheduled to begin on October 13, the lockout continued, and by year's end there seemed to be scant hope for salvaging any of the season.

During a two-day meeting that began on June 11, several NHL players said that they might sign with the reborn World Hockey Association (WHA). Created in 1971, that league lasted seven seasons and gave the game coloured pucks, among other innovations—including a salary cap. The WHA hoped to begin a comeback season in 2005. Other NHL players signed on with European teams willing to allow them an escape clause when and if NHL operations returned to normal.

The NHL also heard continued criticism for overemphasizing defense to the detriment of goal scoring, speed, and offensive excitement. Games too often decided by 2–1 or 1–0 scores were blamed for reduced attendance at a third of the NHL's arenas and for television ratings that remained the lowest of any U.S. major professional sport.

In May the NHL signed a two-year, revenue-sharing contract with NBC and a one-year $60 million deal with ESPN. Under the NBC agreement, starting in January 2005, the network would televise seven regular-season games, six play-off games, and games three through seven of the Stanley Cup final series. The ESPN deal called for the cable network to air 40 games during the 2004–05 season, 30 fewer than ESPN and its sister station ESPN2 carried in 2003–04. ESPN also held an additional two-year option, at $70 million a year. Retaining TV exposure for his game was a coup for NHL commissioner Gary Bettman, but neither agreement came close to the $120 million the NHL had made under the five-year contract it had with the ABC and ESPN networks, an agreement that ended after the 2004 Stanley Cup final.

On the ice the NHL did enjoy a better competitive balance than it had shown in several years, however, owing to the ascent of Calgary and San Jose to the Western Conference finals and the resounding success of Tampa Bay in the Eastern Conference. Anaheim and Minnesota, the Western Conference finalists of 2003, failed to make the play-offs in 2004, while New Jersey, the defending Stanley Cup champion, was ousted in the opening round of the play-offs.

The seventh game of the Stanley Cup finals epitomized the NHL season as the Tampa Bay Lightning beat the Calgary Flames 2–1, with only 15 shots on goal, to take the series four games to three. Tampa Bay's first Stanley Cup

Tampa Bay Lightning players rush across the ice to congratulate goalie Nikolai Khabibulin after the Lightning defeated the Calgary Flames in the decisive seventh game of the NHL Stanley Cup finals.

was secured when Ruslan Fedotenko, the Lightning left wing, scored twice to raise his postseason total to 12 goals. Brad Richards, who assisted on the first Fedotenko goal, won the Conn Smythe Trophy as the play-offs' Most Valuable Player (MVP). The Lightning's first championship season also brought Martin St. Louis the Art Ross Trophy as the NHL's leading scorer and the Hart Trophy, awarded to the league MVP. Tampa coach John Tortorella won the Jack Adams Award as the NHL's best coach.

Among the teams that competed through the 82-game regular season, Detroit topped the standings with 48 victories and 109 points to win its division by an 18-point margin over St. Louis (39 victories). Tampa Bay (106 points), Boston (104), San Jose (104), Philadelphia (101), and Vancouver (101) were the other division champions that qualified for the 16-team play-offs. Tampa Bay moved into the Stanley Cup finals by beating the New York Islanders four games to one, Montreal four games to none, and Philadelphia four games to three to take the Eastern Conference championship. Calgary became the Western Conference Stanley Cup finalist by defeating Vancouver four games to three and then beating Detroit and San Jose, each by four games to two.

In the 54th NHL All-Star game, which was played at breakneck speed on February 8 in St. Paul, Minn., the Eastern Conference All-Stars beat their rivals from the Western Conference 6–4. Colorado's Joe Sakic scored a hat trick (three goals) in a losing cause and was named the game's MVP. The New York Rangers' Mark Messier, at age 43, also turned in an outstanding effort in his final All-Star appearance, breaking an All-Star record with his 14th career assist and scoring a second-period goal.

International. The 2004 season could hardly have been better for the international teams of Canada. For the second straight year, the Canadian men's team won the International Ice Hockey Federation (IIHF) world championship, coming back from an 0–2 deficit to defeat Sweden 5–3 on May 9 in Prague. On April 6 Canada captured the IIHF women's world championships at Halifax, N.S., by beating the U.S. 2–0 in the tournament's gold-medal game.

The IIHF men's victory gave Canada its 23rd world title, equaling the total amassed by the Soviet Union/Russia. Team Canada's Dany Heatley, a forward for the NHL Atlanta Thrashers, led the tournament scoring with eight goals and three assists in nine games and was named MVP. That performance marked a dramatic comeback for Heatley, who had suffered a broken jaw and severe knee injury in the September 2003 auto accident that took the life of his friend and Atlanta teammate Dan Snyder. In the gold-medal game, Heatley trapped the bouncing puck with his stick, raced down the right side of the Sazka Arena ice, and flicked the puck past Swedish goalie Henrik Lundqvist to pull Team Canada to within a goal of Sweden, at 3–2. With the score deadlocked at 3–3 early in the third period, Heatley once again shot down the right side and slipped a deft pass to Jay Bouwmeester, a defenseman for the NHL Florida Panthers, for an assist on the game-winning goal. A few minutes later Matt Cooke, of the NHL Vancouver Canucks, scored to ensure Canada's victory.

The U.S. men took the bronze medal by beating Slovakia, in a penalty shoot-out, 1–0. Andy Roach, an American who had played the last four seasons for Mannheim in the unheralded German Elite League, won the game for the U.S. when his shot got past Jan Lasak, the Slovak goalie, on the third round of the shoot-out. It was only the second IIHF world championship medal won by a U.S. team since 1960. Earlier in the week the U.S. had earned an automatic berth in the 2006 Winter Olympic Games. That happened when Finland defeated Russia to boost the U.S. into the tournament quarterfinals and thereby guarantee that the U.S. would be ranked among the world's top eight teams when the world championships ended.

The Canadian women's victory brought them their eighth straight world title, each of which had come against their rivals from the U.S. Canada got the game's first goal when Hayley Wickenheiser's wrist shot beat Pam Dreyer, the U.S. goalkeeper, in the second period. Delaney Collins scored the second goal late in the third period when she pushed a loose puck past Dreyer. Canadian forward Jennifer Botterill led her team with three goals and eight assists and was named the MVP of the tournament, which set an all-time attendance record of 94,001. Finland defeated Sweden 3–2 to claim the bronze medal for the sixth time.

On April 18 Russia won the IIHF under-18 championship for the first time in three seasons by beating the U.S. 3–2 in a penalty-filled gold-medal showdown. Russia's Dimitry Shitikov scored the game-winning goal on a third-period power play. Team USA finished with the tournament's best offense, outscoring its opposition 27–10 as Phil Kessel led the way with seven goals in six games. The gold-medal game was a thriller into its final minute. Team USA pulled its goalie and with a one-skater advantage appeared to score the game-tying goal with 13 seconds left, but the goal was ultimately waved off by the officials because the goal net was dislodged. The

Czech Republic beat Canada 3–2 for the bronze medal, its second in three years. Canada had a six-on-four advantage in the dying moments of the game but could not even the score.

(RON REID)

ICE SKATING

Figure Skating. On June 6, 2004, after a yearlong tryout, the International Skating Union (ISU) approved a new scoring system that replaced the familiar 6.0 score for a perfect performance with a format based on points for technical and artistic elements. The change evolved out of the judging scandal that erupted during the pairs competition at the 2002 Winter Olympics in Salt Lake City, Utah. The new system, in which jumps, spins, edge quality, footwork choreography, and theatrics would be judged for individuality rather than as part of an overall performance, was to be introduced in the 2004–05 season.

Michelle Kwan, probably the world's best-known amateur figure skater, with five world and eight U.S. titles, had the last 6.0s awarded in an ISU competition when she received six such scores at the 2004 world championships, held in Dortmund, Ger., in March. She finished third overall, however, behind Shizuka Arakawa of Japan and Sasha Cohen, who had scored a silver behind Kwan at the U.S. nationals. Arakawa won her first world championship—the first by a Japanese skater since 1994—with a program that included six triple jumps that neither Cohen nor Kwan could match. Cohen had led the competition going into the concluding free program but suffered an awkward landing that flawed her attempt at a triple Salchow jump. She finished with the silver, her first medal in an international event. The competition started and ended badly for Kwan, whom the judges penalized for the first time in her career for taking too much time to complete her short program. Later, her free program was hardly helped when, during her warm-up, a male masked intruder leaped from the stands, skated to the centre of the ice, and stripped down to his bare chest and a tutu.

Russia's Yevgeny Plushchenko (*see* BIOGRAPHIES) won the men's world title, surviving a fall that came as he was going into his final jump, a triple loop. Before Plushchenko went sprawling—after his skate blade hit a sequin that had fallen from his costume—he had taken over first place with a bold program that included his trademark quadruple-triple-double combination jump. In a competition noteworthy for its clean programs, Plushchenko was the only skater who suffered a fall. He prevailed, however, for his third world title in four seasons and a measure of revenge against France's Brian Joubert, who had beaten his Russian rival for the gold medal at the European championships in Budapest in January. Stefan Lindemann of Germany was a surprising bronze medalist after having finished fifth in Budapest.

Russia also got gold-medal performances at the world championships from the pairs team of Tatyana Totmyanina and Maksim Marinin and the ice-dancing duo of Tatyana Navka and Roman Kostomarov. Both of the Russian couples had won their respective disciplines at the European championships, where Julia Sebestyen received the loudest cheers as the first Hungarian woman to win the women's singles gold medal. Her victory ended a Russian winning streak that had started in the event in 1996.

The 2004 season got off to a superb start for Kwan in January at the U.S. national championship in Atlanta, Ga. She skated a clean program that included six triple jumps and gained momentum over the final 45 seconds to finish ahead of Cohen and Jennifer Kirk, the 2000 world junior champion. The surprise winner of the men's gold medal was 19-year-old Johnny Weir, the 2001 world junior champion. Weir skated a clean program to take his first national title, while defending champion Michael Weiss claimed the silver medal and Matthew Savoie took the bronze. Rena Inoue and John Baldwin captured the U.S. pairs title, improving two places on their bronze-medal finish of 2003 despite a seriously flawed performance. The flawless skating of Tanith Belbin and Benjamin Agosto brought them the U.S. ice-dancing championship after three consecutive runner-up finishes.

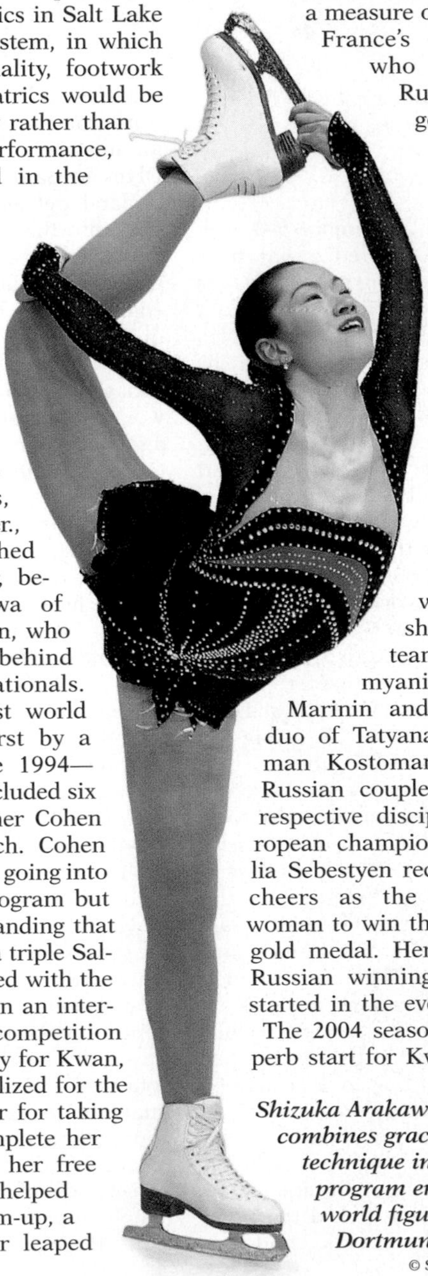

Shizuka Arakawa of Japan combines grace and flawless technique in her free-skating program en route to her first world figure-skating title in Dortmund, Ger., in March.

© Stuart Franklin/Getty Images

Speed Skating. On Feb. 8, 2004, in Hamar, Nor., Chad Hedrick, a 27-year-old Texan, became the first American in 16 years to win the world all-around speed-skating championship. Hedrick's teammate Shani Davis, who came home first in the 1,500-m final, finished second in the all-around to further reduce the usual dominance of Dutch skaters in the men's competition. Renate Groenewold, however, gave The Netherlands its first women's all-around title in 30 years. For the third year in a row, the women's 500-m final was won by American Jennifer Rodriguez, who also won the 1,500-m title. Before the competition at the Viking Ship Hall in Hamar ended, nearly 10 years to the day after the venue showcased some of the best competition of the 1994 Winter Olympics, personal best marks were achieved by 35 men and 22 women, and Eriko Ishino of Japan set a junior world record of 4 min 9.26 sec in the 3,000 m.

South Korea dominated the 24th world short-track speed-skating championships, contested March 19–21 in Göteborg, Swed., by 144 skaters representing 33 nations. The South Korean men's team captured 9 out of 10 individual gold medals. Ahn Hyun Soo led the golden haul with victories in the 1,000-, 1,500-, and 3,000-m finals and a leg that helped his team win the 5,000-m relay. In the women's competition South Korea also topped the field, thanks to victories in the 1,000- and 1,500-m finals by Choi Eun Kyung. The South Korean women finished with a wire-to-wire victory in the 3,000-m relay, beating China for the gold medal by one second.

(RON REID)

AP/Wide World Photos

Monty Lewis competes in calf roping at the Wrangler National Finals Rodeo in Las Vegas, Nev., on December 11. Lewis won the world title in the event.

RODEO

As the rodeo season ended in December 2004, the crowning of the world champions was eclipsed by the surprise resignation of Professional Rodeo Cowboys Association (PRCA) commissioner Steven Hatchell and the announcement that segments of the rodeo association had been sold to an investor group. Hatchell, who joined the PRCA as commissioner in 1998, was credited with having helped create the popular Wrangler ProRodeo Tour, which featured the sport's elite athletes in a series of televised competitions that culminated in a three-day championship finale. He also played a significant role in getting rodeo on network television after an absence of several decades. A former college football commissioner, Hatchell was to assume the presidency of the National Football Foundation and College Hall of Fame, a nonprofit educational organization.

In the waning months of his tenure, Hatchell helped to broker a $10 million deal that would transfer ownership of significant PRCA assets from the membership association to a private investors group headed by Jac Sperling, CEO of the National Hockey League franchise Minnesota Wild. The PRCA and Sperling's company, Grit Rock Ventures, LLC, agreed to create Pro Rodeo Tour, LLC, a new enterprise that would market the PRCA and its affiliates, with Grit Rock owning a majority interest. Since forming in 1936 as the Cowboys' Turtle Association, the PRCA had been owned and controlled solely by its members and its member-elected board of directors.

On the competition side, Trevor Brazile of Decatur, Texas, claimed his third consecutive world champion all-around cowboy title with earnings of $253,170. Brazile earned money in three events: steer roping, team roping, and tie-down (calf) roping. Individual world titles in rodeo, along with the all-around title, are awarded based on prize money earned during the rodeo season and at the season-ending Wrangler National Finals Rodeo (NFR), which took place December 3–12 in Las Vegas, Nev.

First-time champions were named in five of seven standard rodeo events. In bareback riding Kelly Timberman of Mills, Wyo., placed in 8 of 10 rounds at the NFR to handily win both the finals championship and the world title, with record earnings of $225,181. In calf roping Monty Lewis of Hereford, Texas, ended the nine-year run in which fellow Texans Fred Whitfield and Cody Ohl had gone back and forth, exchanging world titles. Lewis broke the string with an outstanding showing at the NFR, winning $93,672 to bring his year's total to $184,696. Other first-time champions included Kelly Kaminski of Bellville, Texas, in barrel racing ($179,373), Luke Branquinho of Los Alamos, Calif., in steer wrestling ($193,614), and Dustin Elliott of Tecumseh, Neb., in bull riding ($193,779). Veterans prevailed in the remaining two events, team roping and saddle bronc riding. In team roping Rick Skelton and Speed Williams, both of Llano, Texas, won their record-stretching eighth world championship with matching earnings of $150,427. Saddle bronc rider Billy Etbauer of Edmond, Okla., claimed his fifth world title with earnings of $222,592. (GAVIN FORBES EHRINGER)

ROWING

The Olympic Games, which returned to their birthplace in Greece in August, took pride of place in world rowing in 2004. The buildup to the Olympics was dominated by the World Cup series, which provided three opportunities (in Poznan, Pol., Munich, Ger., and Lucerne, Switz.) for countries to evaluate their final crew selections under international racing conditions. Germany (189 points) easily won the series, with Great Britain (92 points) in second place. World championships in the 10 open classes excluded from Olympic competition were held in Banyoles, Spain, in July, combined with the world junior championships.

At the Olympics eight nations shared the men's titles, but the six women's classes were dominated by Romania and Germany. Five titles were decided by less than a second. In men's events Great Britain, anchored by Matthew Pinsent and his pairs partner, James Cracknell, secured the closest verdict (0.08 sec over Canada) to retain the coxless fours and win its 10th Olympic medal in this class. Poland, in lightweight double sculls, was the only other defending Olympic champion to retain its title, finishing 0.53 sec ahead of France. Russia beat

British rowers (left to right) Steve Williams, James Cracknell, Ed Coode, and Matthew Pinsent celebrate their victory in the men's coxless fours competition at the Olympic Games in Athens on August 21.

© Shaun Botterill/Getty Images

the Czech Republic by 0.58 sec in quadruple sculls. The U.S. regained the eights title after 30 years, by 0.87 sec. The other men's winners were Australia (coxless pairs), France (double sculls), Denmark (lightweight coxless fours), and Olaf Tufte of Norway (single sculls).

Romania dominated the women's events with a triple success in coxless pairs, lightweight double sculls, and eights, in which team member Elisabeta Lipa gained a record eighth Olympic rowing medal. Germany retained the quadruple sculls and added the single sculls, won by Katrin Rutschow-Stomporowski. Twin sisters Caroline and Georgina Evers-Swindell of New Zealand beat the German pair by 0.99 sec in double sculls.

In Banyoles, Italy captured three men's events (coxed fours, coxed pairs, and lightweight quadruple sculls). France (lightweight eights), Denmark (lightweight coxless pairs), and Germany (lightweight singles) shared the other men's titles. Honours in women's events went to France (coxless fours), China (lightweight quadruple sculls), and Germany (lightweight singles). Romania excelled in the junior world championships, with four victories in men's events and one in women's. Ukraine (with two), Slovenia, and Italy were the other men's winners, while the other women's events were captured by Germany (two), Australia (two), and the Czech Republic.

The world under-23 regatta, held in Poznan in August, also provided a glimpse of the future, with Germany achieving distinction with 8 medals in the 11 events. Great Britain (5 medals) and Australia (4) were also prominent.

At the 155th Henley Royal Regatta in England, entries from six overseas countries won 8 of the 21 trophies. Crews from The Netherlands won the Grand Challenge and the Temple Challenge cups, and a crew from the U.S. won the Princess Elizabeth Cup (all eights). Ukraine took the Queen Mother Cup (quadruple sculls), while the Silver Goblets and Nickalls' Challenge Cup (coxless pairs) was captured by South Africa. The Princess Royal Cup (women's single sculls) went to American Cindy Bishop, and the Diamond Challenge Sculls (men's single sculls) was won by Marcel Hacker of Germany.

The 150th University Boat Race was preceded by a vintage re-row of the original 1829 race (the race was not an annual event in the early years and was suspended during World Wars I and II), in specially built authentic replica boats. It was followed by early drama in the battle of the "Blues" when the crews clashed in the fourth minute of the 2004 race, after Oxford had gained two-thirds of a length off the start. Oxford's bow man lost his blade for a few strokes as Cambridge surged ahead, going on to win by 18 seconds and stretch its lead in the series to 78–71.

In November British Olympic champion Matthew Pinsent announced his retirement from rowing, and at year's end he was knighted in the New Year Honours list. (KEITH L. OSBORNE)

SAILING

The Olympic Games in Athens dominated sailing in 2004, taking the regatta to Homer's "wine-dark sea" for the first time. The Olympic regatta reflected a high order of professionalism in the administrators and expertise in the sailors. Great Britain continued its world dominance, garnering five medals (two of them gold). Spain was next with three, while seven nations won two medals each. More significantly, the remaining medals were awarded to 11 different countries—an illustration of the success of the International Sailing Federation's (ISAF's) goal of spreading the sport throughout the world.

Technology continued to have major effects in sailing. Dinghies with hydrofoils proliferated in the Moth and Australian 18 classes, producing spectacular speeds when the hulls lifted completely from the water in stronger winds. In offshore sailing a similar increase in speed was provided by the technology of Canting Ballast Twin Foil (CBTF) designs. These configurations figured prominently in several major races, involving particularly the biggest boats. In 2003 *Mari-Cha IV* had used this underwater design to set a transatlantic record, and in the Sydney–Hobart race off Australia, a traditional and a canting-keel super maxi had sailed neck and neck until the last leg to the finish well ahead of the rest. Another large boat, the 26.2-m (86-ft) *Morning Glory,* took five hours off the Newport–Bermuda race record in June 2004. The CBTF concept was not new—Nat Herreshoff designed an experimental boat before 1900—but the technology to manage the enormous stresses created within the hull when the ballast is canted to windward had not been available until recently. Some of these boats produced speeds greater than the wind going to windward and routinely experienced destroyer-like speeds off the wind (more than 20 knots). In 2004 administrators of handicapping systems were scrambling to accommodate these new designs.

One result of this accommodation was a growing dissatisfaction with the scientific prediction methods of the International Measurement System (IMS), which lacked an "arbitrary correction to hit" mechanism when practice proved the prediction inaccurate. The ISAF had appointed a committee to develop an entirely new system. The English members of the committee favoured IRC, their performance-based system, which was adjusted as necessary by the English administrators. The Americans were divided but seemed still to favour their scientific approach. Meanwhile, most sailors competed under whichever system was offered locally to them.

The 2004 Newport–Bermuda race (handicapped under IMS), in which 157 boats started, featured some exciting reaching in big waves before light air filled in. The faster boats enjoyed a quick ride and won most of the silverware, and the top handicap awards went to two new designs, the cruiser-racer Swan 45 and a racing Transpac 52. The double-handed division, however, was won for the second time by a veteran Express 37.

In Britain the Rolex Commodores' Cup, an event for three-boat national teams held at Cowes, Isle of Wight, saw the British Red team come first, with *Jeronimo, Exabyte 2,* and *Bear of Britain.* The event was handicapped under the British IRC system and drew no entries from the U.S. or the Mediterranean region, where IMS still held sway.

A new single-handed-around-the-world record of 72 days 22 hr was set by Francis Joyon in a 27-m (90-ft) trimaran; a new westward record (122 days 14 hr) was set by Jean-Luc van den Heede in a monohull. The nonstop-around-the-world record fell to Steve Fossett's 38-m (125-ft) catamaran in 58 days 9 hr, cutting 5 days 23 hr off the record set by Bruno Peyron's 34-m (110-ft) catamaran *Orange* in 2004.

(JOHN B. BONDS)

SKIING

Alpine Skiing. There were several interesting story lines during the 2003–04 Alpine skiing World Cup season: Bode Miller became the first American man to win a World Cup title, the giant slalom (GS), since Phil Mahre won the overall and GS titles in 1983; Austrian Stephan Eberharter vetoed retirement to see if he could win one more World Cup downhill title at age 34; and the women's scene was unexpectedly wide open after the Croatian sensation Janica Kostelic (winner of four Olympic medals in Salt Lake City, Utah, in 2002 and two golds at the 2003 world championships, as well as the 2003 World Cup overall title) was sidelined after more knee surgeries. Nothing was more compelling during the season, however, than the return of Hermann Maier, a colossus for Austria before a fluke motorcycle mishap in August 2001 nearly cost him a leg and derailed his hopes for the 2002 Winter Olympics. After missing the entire 2001–02 season and most of the next year, Maier, who was recognized as the world's finest super-giant slalom (super G) racer before his accident, returned to form. He won three times and posted two other top-five results as he stormed to his fifth super-G title and edged two-time overall champion Eberharter by 42 points (1,265–1,223) for his fourth World Cup overall crown. Eberharter captured the downhill title, with American Daron Rahlves as runner-up in both downhill and super G.

AP/Wide World Photos

Aerials champion Alisa Camplin of Australia executes a jump at the Freestyle World Cup event in Sauze d'Oulx, Italy, on March 10.

The women's schedule turned into a rout by Sweden's Anja Pärson. Previously known as a slalom/GS racer, Pärson added super G and downhill for 2003–04, won 11 races (6 slaloms and 5 giant slaloms), and breezed to the women's title with 1,561 points. She also took the slalom and GS titles, while Austrian Renate Götschl, the overall runner-up (1,344 points), posted six victories and was downhill and super-G champion.

Nordic Skiing. Norway's Marit Bjørgen, the reigning sprint world champion in cross-country skiing, went into the 2003–04 season seeking to extend her dominance to distance races. Although she did not achieve her goal, she gave Italy's Gabriella Paruzzi a mighty challenge for the overall World Cup title. Bjørgen won seven sprints—in both classic and free technique—but Paruzzi used consistency to become women's overall champion. Paruzzi won three times and was in the top five 14 times to finish with 1,228 points to Bjørgen's 1,139. René Sommerfeldt led the resurgent Germans to three of the top five spots in the men's standings. Sommerfeldt won just 2 of the 25 World Cup races, but he was a top-five finisher nine other times and collected 956 points, while defending World Cup champion Mathias Fredriksson of Sweden won three races and was a distant runner-up with 606 points.

Finland's Hannu Manninen took charge during the second half of the season to take the Nordic combined title from defending champion Ronny Ackermann of Germany, while the World Cup jumping champion was another Finn, Janne Ahonen, who held off Norwegian veteran Roar Ljoekelsoey. Though Ljoekelsoey won five of the last nine jump meets, Ahonen had 1,316 points to 1,306 points for the Norwegian.

Freestyle Skiing. Since the 2002 Olympics, freestyle skiing had added halfpipe and ski cross (SX) to the standard aerials and moguls (including dual moguls) lineup. Olympic aerials champion Alisa Camplin of Australia, who also took the 2003 world championship, won seven times and breezed to her second consecutive World Cup title. Meanwhile, Canadian Steve Omischl, Camplin's longtime boyfriend, dominated the men's scene, winning six times en route to the aerial title. Another Canadian, Jenn Heil, was women's moguls champion, and the Finnish Olympic champion, Janne Lahtela, held off American Toby Dawson for the men's moguls championship. French skiers swept halfpipe: Mathias Wecxsteen edged teammate Laurent Favre in the men's race, and Marie Martinod earned the women's title. Ophélie David made it three titles for France, winning in women's ski cross, while Swede Jesper Brugge barely defeated yet another Frenchman, Enak Gavaggio, for the men's SX crown.

Snowboarding. In a winter with no world championships, the 2003–04 snowboarding competition was scattered more than usual, with World Cup competitions as well as non-Cup events taking place throughout the U.S. The two biggest events were the U.S. Open and ESPN television's Winter X Games, both of which were dominated by Americans. The X Games saw rising star Steve Fisher edge Olympic silver medalist Danny Kass for the men's halfpipe gold medal, while talented teen Hannah Teter beat Kelly Clark, the Olympic champion, in the women's halfpipe contest. In snowboard cross (SBX), the newest Olympic snowboard event, Swiss rider Ueli Kestenholz edged Seth Wescott, and Lindsey Jacobellis topped French great Karine Ruby. At the Open, Kass beat Fisher in the halfpipe, with Clark defeating Tricia Byrnes. On the World Cup tour, Canadian Jascy Jay Anderson won his fourth straight overall title, and Julie Pomagalski of France won her first; Austrian Siegfried Grabner and Daniela Meusli of Switzerland prevailed in parallel competition; Frenchman Xavier Delerue and Ruby captured the SBX titles; and big air was won by Sweden's Simon Ax and Japan's Soko Yamaoko. (PAUL ROBBINS)

SQUASH

When it was announced after the 2004 Olympic Games in Athens that squash was being considered for the Games program in 2012, a sense of optimism took hold that the sport might finally become an Olympic event. A decision was expected in July 2005. The other major news in 2004 was the crowning of two new champions in December. In Kuala Lumpur, Malaysia, 28-year-old Vanessa Atkinson of The Netherlands reached her first World

Open final, beating world number one Rachael Grinham of Australia in the semifinals. In the final Atkinson triumphed over Rachael's younger sister, Natalie Grinham, who was fatigued after having needed five games and 87 minutes to beat Malaysia's Nicol David in a memorable semifinal. Atkinson ended the year at number two, her highest ranking. Frenchman Thierry Lincou, aged 28 and hailing from the Indian Ocean island of Réunion, had reached the men's World Open final in 2003, but at the 2004 event in Doha, Qatar, he went one better with an exciting 83-minute win over top-seeded Lee Beachill of England. Lincou, who was taken to five games in both the quarterfinals and the semifinals, became the first French competitor to capture the crown. The Professional Squash Association, the men's player organization, had introduced 11-point games (down from 15 points) in August, and the Open became the first men's world title to use the new scoring system.

Three other world championships were staged in 2004. The men's world junior championship was held in Islamabad, Pak. Egyptian Rami Ashour beat Yasir Butt from the host nation to take the individual title, and Pakistan bested Egypt to retain the team trophy. In Amsterdam at the women's team championship, Australia, led by the Grinham sisters, defended its title by defeating England in the final. At the world doubles championship in Chennai (Madras), India, British Open winners Rachael Grinham and David Palmer of Australia won the mixed doubles event, and the Grinham sisters captured the women's title. In the men's championship, Byron Davis and Cameron White completed the Australian sweep.

(ANDREW SHELLEY)

SWIMMING

The Games of the XXVIII Olympiad, held in Athens in August, dominated swimming in 2004, and the sport was arguably the highlight of the Games. The Olympic swimming competition served to showcase the amazing talent and versatility of 19-year-old American Michael Phelps. (*See* BIOGRAPHIES.) Worldwide media pressure and the promise of a million-dollar bonus from Speedo, one of his sponsors, if he matched American Mark Spitz's seven gold medals from the 1972 Games in Munich, W.Ger., did not seem to faze Phelps. Although he fell a bit short, his eight total medals (six gold and two bronze) equaled the most won by an individual in any sport in one Olympics. The fact that Phelps gave up his spot in the final of the 4 × 100-m medley relay to a teammate only added to his reputation, though he won gold with the rest of the relay team because he had raced the preliminary heats. In all, Phelps won individual gold medals in the 100-m and 200-m butterfly and the 200-m and 400-m individual medley, setting a world record in the latter event, and an individual bronze in the 200-m freestyle. In addition to the medal in the 4 × 100-m medley, he earned gold in the 4 × 200-m freestyle relay and bronze in the 4 × 100-m freestyle relay.

Phelps, however, was not the only aquatic superstar in Athens. Australia's Ian Thorpe repeated as 400-m freestyle champion and claimed the gold in the 200-m freestyle, coming from behind to defeat Pieter van den Hoogenband of The Netherlands, the reigning Olympic champion. But van den Hoogenband, the "Flying Dutchman," defended his title in the 100-m freestyle. American Aaron Piersol, who set a world record in the 200-m backstroke at the U.S. Olympic trials in Long Beach, Calif., was a triple gold medalist in Athens. The dorsal specialist took both the 100-m and 200-m backstroke and then led off the U.S.'s winning 4 × 100-m medley relay with a world record of 53.45 sec for the 100-m backstroke; the U.S. relay team finished in the world record time of 3 min 30.68 sec. Japan's Kosuke Kitajima won both the 100-m and 200-m breaststroke, upsetting American Brendan Hansen, who had set world records in both events at the U.S. trials.

The champions from the 2000 Games in Sydney, Australia, in both the shortest and longest swimming events defended their titles, but both were pushed to the limit. Gary Hall, Jr., of the U.S. kept his crown in the 50-m freestyle by the narrowest margin possible, 0.01 sec. In the 1,500-m freestyle, Australia's Grant Hackett, unbeaten for seven years, just managed to hold off American Larsen Jensen and Briton David Davies. The U.S. men won two of the three relays, setting a world record in the 4 × 100-m medley and upsetting Australia in the 4 × 200-m freestyle. Unheralded South Africa won the 4 × 100-m freestyle relay, taking the lead on the first lap and finishing in a world-record time of 3 min 13.17 sec.

Swimmers Ian Thorpe of Australia (lane 4) and Michael Phelps of the U.S. (below, lane 3) start their 200-m freestyle semifinal at the Olympic Games in Athens on August 15. Thorpe went on to win the gold medal in the event, but Phelps emerged as the star, taking the bronze for the third of his eight medals (six gold and two bronze) in Athens.

Unlike the men, who saw swimmers from only 5 nations stand atop the victory podium, the women spread the gold around, with 10 nations sharing gold and glory. American Natalie Coughlin won five medals—more than any other woman at the Athens Games. She took the 100-m backstroke and led off the U.S.'s 4 × 200-m freestyle relay, which finished in 7 min 53.42 sec to break the previous world record, held by East

Germany. Coughlin also earned silver in the 4 × 100-m freestyle and medley relays and bronze in the 100-m freestyle.

Australian sprinter Jodie Henry was a triple winner. She captured the 100-m freestyle, posting a world record (53.52 sec) in the semifinals, and anchored Australian teams that set world records in the 4 × 100-m freestyle relay (3 min 35.94 sec) and the 4 × 100-m medley relay (3 min 57.32 sec). Ukraine's Yana Klochkova (*see* BIOGRAPHIES) swam into the record book when she won both the 200-m and 400-m individual medley for the second straight Olympics. No other woman had won both medleys in one Olympiad or had repeated as Olympic champion in either event. Kirsty Coventry of Zimbabwe won the 200-m backstroke, becoming her country's first Olympic swimming champion. She also captured silver in the 100-m backstroke and bronze in the 200-m medley. France's Laure Manaudou also claimed a medal of each colour as she won the 400-m freestyle, finished second in the 800-m freestyle, a stroke behind Japan's Ai Shibata, and placed third in the 100-m backstroke.

Otylia Jedrzejczak became the first Polish swimmer to win Olympic gold as she outdueled Petria Thomas of Australia, winner of the 100-m butterfly, in the 200-m butterfly. Jedrzejczak also captured silver medals in the 100-m butterfly and the 400-m freestyle. American Amanda Beard, who set a world record (2 min 22.44 sec) in the 200-m breaststroke at the U.S. trials, came from behind to nip Australia's Leisel Jones in that event. Beard also won silver in the 200-m individual medley and the 400-m medley relay.

There were three major short-course competitions in 2004, the American men's and women's national collegiate championships in March and the world short-course championships in Indianapolis, Ind., in October. The collegiate meets produced nine world records, while the world championships, held just six weeks after the Olympics, produced four. At the five-day Indianapolis meet, which drew some 550 swimmers from 97 countries to a state-of-the-art temporary pool inside the packed 18,000-seat Conseco Fieldhouse, Australia's Brooke Hanson, a gold and silver medalist in Athens, won an unprecedented five individual world titles—the 50-m, 100-m, and 200-m breaststroke and the 100-m and 200-m individual medley. She also swam a leg on Australia's world-record-breaking 4 × 100-m medley relay team. Jenny Thompson, the most decorated American Olympian in any sport, won two silver medals in Athens for a career total of 12 Olympic medals, and, in a fitting end to her 17-year career, she captured four medals in Indianapolis.

Diving. As expected, China dominated the diving competition at the 2004 Olympics. Challengers included a talented contingent from Australia. In contrast, the U.S., a perennial diving power, failed to win a single medal for the first time since 1912.

China's Guo Jingjing was the only diver to claim double gold; she won the 3-m springboard event over countrywoman Wu Minxia and teamed with Wu to take the 3-m springboard synchronized contest. Australia's Chantelle Newberry scored a major upset in the 10-m platform, decisively defeating favoured Lao Lishi of China. Lao teamed with Li Ting to take the 10-m platform synchronized event.

China's Peng Bo was unstoppable in the men's 3-m springboard, winning by more than 31 points over Canada's Alexandre Despatie. In the 10-m platform, Hu Jia of China earned five perfect scores of 10 on his sixth dive to clinch the gold. Australia's Matt Helm edged defending champion Tian Liang of China by less than a point for the silver. Tian and Yang Jinghui won the 10-m platform synchronized competition over Peter Waterfield and Leon Taylor, who captured Great Britain's first diving medal since 1960. The highlight of the diving competition took place in the men's 3-m springboard synchronized contest. After favoured China scored a zero for a failed dive and Russia suffered a major mishap, Greece's Nikolaos Siranidis and Thomas Bimis earned their country's first gold medal in diving, first gold medal in an aquatic sport since 1896, and first gold medal of the 2004 Games.

Synchronized Swimming. Russia again dominated the Olympic synchronized swimming competition. In the duet event, 2003 world champions Anastasiya Davydova and Anastasiya Yermakova were clearly superior in both technical merit and artistic impression, tallying a perfect score of 50 in the latter category to finish with a total of 99.334 points. Japan's Miya Tachibana and Miho Takeda were second with 98.417 points, and the American pair of Alison Bartosik and Anna Kozlova placed third with 96.918. In the team event, Russia won gold with 99.501 points, followed by Japan (98.501) and the U.S. (97.418). (PHILLIP WHITTEN)

TENNIS

A graceful all-court stylist with every essential tool in his trade, Roger Federer was in a class of his own in 2004. The fluid shotmaker from Switzerland raised his game to almost unimaginable levels, winning three of the four major tennis championships and rising incontestably to number one in the world. He was victorious in 74 of 80 matches and won 11 tournaments, the most any year-end number one had secured since Ivan Lendl of Czechoslovakia captured 11 championships in 1985. Federer also became only the fourth man to have collected three Grand Slam championships in a single year since "open" tennis commenced in 1968. Argentina's Gastón Gaudio—the French Open champion—was the only other male player to win a major.

Never before had a Russian woman prevailed at one of the Grand Slam events, but in 2004 three competitors from that nation won major championships. Anastasiya Myskina ruled on the clay courts at Roland Garros to claim the French Open crown; Mariya Sharapova was a popular winner at Wimbledon; and the formidable Svetlana Kuznetsova came away with the U.S. Open title. Belgium's Justine Henin-Hardenne (*see* BIOGRAPHIES)

Defending Wimbledon champion Roger Federer of Switzerland blasts a 167-km/hr (104-mph) serve during his first-round match on June 21.

AP/Wide World Photos

was the only woman not from Russia to triumph at a major, securing the Australian Open title as well as the Olympic gold medal later in the year. Sharapova was the highest-paid woman in tennis, earning $2,506,263, and Federer topped the men with $6,337,660.

Australian Open. For the third time in four Grand Slam tournament events, Henin-Hardenne and Kim Clijsters confronted each other in an all-Belgian final. As was the case at Roland Garros and the U.S. Open in 2003, Henin-Hardenne came through when it counted, defeating Clijsters 6–3, 4–6, 6–3 in a hard-fought battle. Henin-Hardenne built a 4–2 second-set lead but lost four straight games. With Clijsters serving at 3–4 and down break point in the final set, the umpire ruled against her on a close baseline call to give Henin-Hardenne that pivotal game. Henin-Hardenne promptly held serve to close out the contest.

Federer gave one virtuoso performance after another to take the men's title. After upending Lleyton Hewitt of Australia and Argentina's David Nalbandian, he ousted Spain's gritty Juan Carlos Ferrero and then stopped Russian Marat Safin, the 2000 U.S. Open champion, 7–6 (3), 6–4, 6–2 in the final. The resurgent Safin, who was ranked 66th at the end of 2003, was magnificent in posting five-set victories over 2003 U.S. Open champion Andy Roddick and four-time Australian Open winner Andre Agassi, both of the U.S. Safin finished 2004 as the world's number four ranked player.

French Open. Many among the cognoscenti expected Argentina's fleet-footed and cunning Guillermo Coria to claim the men's crown at the world's premier clay-court event, but number three seed Coria was beaten in a bruising final by Gaudio, a 25-year-old ranked 44th in the world. Gaudio made a gallant recovery from two sets to love down, stopping Coria 0–6, 3–6, 6–4, 6–1, 8–6. A debilitated Coria was compromised by leg cramps during the long struggle but twice reached match point in a tense fifth set. Gaudio would not surrender, though, and he became the first man since Gottfried von Cramm of Germany in 1934 to win a final at Roland Garros from match point down. The top-seeded Federer bowed in the third round, losing to three-time champion Gustavo Kuerten of Brazil 6–4, 6–4, 6–4.

Myskina celebrated the fortnight of her life, ousting four-time Grand Slam champion Venus Williams of the U.S. in the quarterfinals, 2001 Roland Garros winner American Jennifer Capriati in the penultimate round, and fellow Russian Yelena Dementyeva 6–1, 6–2 in the final. One month shy of her 23rd birthday, number six seed Myskina played unerringly when the stakes were highest. Henin-Hardenne, suffering from a virus that hurt her preparation for Paris, fell in the second round against Italy's Tathiana Garbin, becoming the first top-seeded woman to lose before the third round of the tournament.

Wimbledon. Defending champion Federer took on Roddick in a gripping final on the All-England Club's fabled Centre Court, and at the outset it seemed that the American might exploit his awesome service power and crackling forehand for an uplifting victory. Locked at one set all against the top seed, Roddick moved out in front 4–2 in the third set before rain intruded. When they returned, Federer raised his game decidedly, and his technical and tactical mastery carried him to a 4–6, 7–5, 7–6 (3), 6–4 triumph. Federer conceded only one other set in the entire tournament—to Hewitt in the quarterfinals.

Sharapova, appearing at Wimbledon for only the second time, played beautiful tennis, peaking propitiously in her last two matches. In the semifinals she was trailing 1999 champion Lindsay Davenport of the U.S. by a set and a service break when rain delayed the contest. Reprieved, Sharapova elevated her game significantly to oust Davenport 2–6, 7–6 (5), 6–1. In the final the number 13 seed produced perhaps the biggest final-round upset in the history of the women's event, stunning two-time defending champion Serena Williams of the U.S. 6–1, 6–4. Sharapova rallied from 2–4 in the second set before winning four games in a row for the championship. Serena's older sister Venus, the champion in 2000 and 2001, lost a bizarre second-round meeting with Croatia's Karolina Sprem 7–6 (5), 7–6 (6). The umpire lost track of the score in the second-set tiebreaker and inadvertently awarded a point to Sprem and failed to correct the error when he had the opportunity. Nevertheless, Venus still wasted three set points before bowing.

U.S. Open. In an immaculate exhibition of his versatility and court craft, Federer captured his first U.S. Open crown with a 6–0, 7–6 (3), 6–0 demolition of 2001 champion Hewitt at Flushing Meadows, N.Y. No one in the men's game had taken two love sets in a title match at the U.S. championships since 1884. In the opening set Federer won 24 of 29 points, setting the tone emphatically with superb shot selection. It was Federer's fourth victory without a defeat in a major final. The toughest test for Federer was his quarterfinal clash with a revitalized Agassi, who had overcome Roddick and Hewitt to win the Cincinnati, Ohio, tournament a few weeks earlier. Their duel started at night, but inclement weather forced a postponement, with Federer leading two sets to one. When they returned to the contest the following afternoon, a determined Agassi garnered the fourth set. Federer, however, was unflappable and regained the ascendancy to win in five sets.

Kuznetsova was eager, opportunistic, and poised under pressure in taking her first major. The number nine seed came from behind to oust Davenport 1–6, 6–2, 6–4 in the semifinals, erasing a 3–0 deficit in the final set to win six of the last seven games. Davenport had won 4 tournaments and 22 matches in a row, but the 28-year-old American strained a hip muscle in practice on the morning of her meeting with the Russian. In the final, Kuznetsova knocked out Dementyeva 6–3, 7–5, recouping from 2–4 down in the second set. Dementyeva held off a spirited but streaky Capriati 6–0, 2–6, 7–6 (5) after Capriati served for the match in the final set. Twice before—in 1991 and 2003—Capriati had also served for a place in the final only to lose.

Other Events. Federer closed his stellar campaign in style, dispatching Hewitt 6–3, 6–2 in the final of the Tennis Masters Cup in Houston, Texas. With that victory he ended his year on a remarkable run of 17 consecutive matches. Davenport—the top-ranked player in 1998 and 2001—finished the year ranked number one for the third time after winning a tour-leading seven singles titles.

At the Olympic Games in Athens, Henin-Hardenne and Chile's Nicolas Massu captured gold medals by taking the singles titles. Henin-Hardenne upended Amélie Mauresmo of France in a straight-set final, and Massu's tenacity carried him to a five-set final-round triumph over American Mardy Fish.

In late November Russia—led by a determined Myskina—captured the Fed Cup for the first time, defeating France 3–2 in the final in Moscow. Spain took the Davis Cup for the second time, eclipsing the U.S. 3–2 on its home clay courts in Sevilla. (STEVE FLINK)

TRACK AND FIELD SPORTS (ATHLETICS)

A doping scandal involving several top track and field athletes made negative headlines in 2004. Thrilling competition at the Olympic Games in Athens, however, produced 10 Olympic and 2 world records.

World Indoor Championships. The International Association of Athletics Federations (IAAF) rescheduled its indoor world championships from odd- to even-numbered years. On March 5–7 Budapest hosted the event as Russians set four new indoor world records and won 7 of 14 women's events. Tatyana Lebedeva equaled the world record in the triple jump and then improved it twice to post a new indoor world record of 15.36 m (50 ft 4¾ in); she later won a gold in the long jump, becoming the first athlete to win titles in both events. Pole vaulter Yelena Isinbayeva defeated Russian teammate and rival Svetlana Feofanova by breaking Feofanova's world record. The Russian women's 4 × 400-m relay squad cut 0.37 sec from the world record as Natalya Nazarova, who also set a meet record (50.19 sec) in the 400 m, ran the final leg in 49.89 sec, the fastest 400-m relay split ever run indoors. In the men's competition Swedish triple jumper Christian Olsson equaled the world record, which marked the first time since 1989 that a world record in a men's field event had been posted at the meet.

Olympic Games. The modern Olympics returned to Greece, the land of their birth, in August, and the shot put was contested at Olympia, site of the ancient Games. The men's shot put became the first field event in modern Games history in which the gold medalist was decided in a tiebreaker based on the second-best mark. On his first throw Adam Nelson of the U.S. put 21.16 m (69 ft 5¼ in), and Ukraine's Yury Bilonog nearly equaled the mark with two puts of 21.15 m (69 ft 4¾ in) as Nelson fouled his next three throws. In the last round Bilonog improved to 21.16 m (69 ft 5¼ in) and won the gold after Nelson increased his distance on his last throw but fouled. Russian Irina Korzhanenko dominated the women's shot put but was disqualified for a positive steroid test—the first of three doping disqualifications for first-place finishers—and the gold went to Cuba's Yumileidi Cumba.

In the first running final, the men's 10,000 m, Kenenisa Bekele of Ethiopia won over teammate Sileshi Sihine in an Olympic-record 27 min 5.10 sec. The old record had belonged to Haile Gebrselassie, also of Ethiopia, who finished fifth after having won the event at the two previous Olympics.

Moroccan runner Hicham El Guerrouj finally ended his Olympic jinx. Although he was the world record holder at 1,500 m and the mile and had won 86 of his last 91 finals at those distances, El Guerrouj had never captured an Olympic title. Just the second man, after Great Britain's Steve Cram, to have qualified for three Olympic 1,500-m finals, El Guerrouj took the lead at 900 m and held off Kenyan Bernard Lagat to take the gold in 3 min 34.18 sec. El Guerrouj competed in the 5,000-m final four nights later, and the Moroccan sprinted past Kenyan Eliud Kipchoge off the last turn and passed Bekele 60 m from the finish to win. El Guerrouj became the first man since Paavo Nurmi of Finland in 1924 to take gold in the 1,500 m and 5,000 m. In the women's competition Kelly Holmes of the U.K. also won the 1,500 m and 5,000 m, becoming the third woman to accomplish the feat. She took the 800 m in 1 min 56.38 sec as five women dipped under 1 min 57 sec for the first time since 1976.

Isinbayeva appeared unpressed in the pole vault as she cleared the Olympic record height of 4.65 m (15 ft 3 in), but

During the Olympic Games, Cuban shot-putter Yumileidi Cumba, the eventual gold-medal winner, pauses just before a throw in the final on August 18. Shot put was the only event held at Olympia, Greece, site of the ancient Games.

by the time the bar reached 4.80 m (15 ft 9 in), she had missed twice and needed a clearance to stay alive against Feofanova. Isinbayeva flew over that bar and the next at 4.85 m (15 ft 11 in) as Feofanova missed, and she then passed to 4.90 m (16 ft ¾ in). When Feofanova missed, a jubilant Isinbayeva had the bar raised to a world record 4.91 m (16 ft 1¼ in) and cleared with centimetres to spare.

China's Liu Xiang (*see* BIOGRAPHIES) was the only man to post a world record. In winning the 110-m hurdles, he stopped the unofficial eyebeam clock at 12.94 sec and was well into his victory lap before the reading of the digital finish photo revealed he had equaled the world record of 12.91 sec.

American pole vaulter Tim Mack (5.95 m [19 ft 6¼ in]), Lithuanian discus thrower Virgilijus Alekna (69.89 m [229 ft 3 in]), and Czech decathlete Roman Sebrle (8,893 points) also claimed men's Olympic records. American 100-m hurdler Joanna Hayes (12.37 sec), Russian high jumper Yelena Slesarenko (2.06 m [6 ft 9 in]), Russian hammer thrower Olga Kuzenkova (75.02 m [246 ft 1 in]), and Cuban javelin thrower Osleidys Menéndez (71.53 m [234 ft 8 in]) were the other women Olympic record setters. Sweeps of all three medals went to the U.S. in the men's 200 m, 400 m, and long jump. Russia's sweep of the women's long jump was the first in a women's event since 1980. Robert Korzeniowski of Poland won the 50-km walk, becoming the first athlete to have won the event three times.

Facing rumours of banned drug use, American Marion Jones, who won five medals at the 2000 Games in Sydney, Australia, placed fifth in the long jump and did not compete in the 100 m or 200 m. In the 4 × 100-m relay, Jones and teammate Lauryn Williams passed the baton outside the exchange zone, and Jones went home empty-handed.

International Competition. Olsson and women's 400-m star Tonique Williams-Darling of The Bahamas split the jackpot from the Golden League, a series that offered shares of a $1 million prize to athletes who won their events at all of its six meets. Alekna lost only one Golden League discus competition, to Hungary's Robert Fazekas in Zürich, Switz., but Fazekas was later suspended for refusing to provide an adequate doping sample at the Olympics. This led some to posit that Alekna was unfairly deprived of one-third of the prize. Olsson had one triple-jump loss outside the Golden League, to Romania's Marian Oprea in Stockholm, which ended a 29-meet win streak. Williams-Darling won eight major meets in a row but lost her last race of the season at the IAAF World Athletics Final, held in Fontvieille, Monaco, on September 18–19. Qatar's Saif Saaeed Shaheen (formerly Stephen Cherono) had the top performance at that meet, posting the fifth fastest time ever in the steeplechase, 7 min 56.94 sec. The IAAF named Bekele and Isinbayeva its Athletes of the Year.

Doping. The 2003 discovery of a previously undetectable anabolic steroid, tetrahydrogestrinone (THG), allegedly distributed by Bay Area Laboratory Cooperative (BALCO), an American nutritional supplements and testing company, continued to haunt track and field. Four athletes who tested positive for THG in 2003 were suspended in 2004, including world championship relay medalist Dwain Chambers of Great Britain (two years) and 1,500-m world indoor record holder Regina Jacobs of the U.S. (four years). Americans Kelli White, the 2003 women's world champion at 100 m and 200 m, and Alvin Harrison, the 2000 Olympic 400-m medalist, admitted to doping and accepted four-year bans that also annulled their results dating back to late 2001. Harrison's twin brother, Calvin, received a two-year ban for his second doping violation, and his results dating to early 2001 were nullified, which caused the U.S. to forfeit its 2003 world championship gold medal in the 4 × 400-m relay. American Tim Montgomery, who was Jones's boyfriend as well as the 100-m world record holder, was charged with doping and chose to plead his case before the international Court of Arbitration for Sport.

Greece was embarrassed the day before the Games began by events involving Olympic sprint medalists Konstadinos Kederis and Ekaterini Thanou. After missing their second drug test in a week, the pair turned up in a hospital claiming injuries from a motorcycle accident that police called suspicious. The sprinters withdrew from the Olympics and were criminally charged, along with their coach, with obstructing a drug test and with giving false information to police. The IAAF filed formal charges against all three in December 2004.

Cross Country and Marathon Running. The Olympic marathons were held on a historically appropriate course from Marathon to Athens. World record holder Paula Radcliffe of the U.K. took an early lead on a hot day in the women's race until Japanese Mizuki Noguchi surged ahead at 25 km (15.5 miles). An exhausted Radcliffe stopped at 36 km (22.4 mi), leaving Catherine Ndereba of Kenya to chase Noguchi, who won by 12 sec.

A spectator with a history of mental illness ran onto the course just before the 36-km (22.5-mi) mark in the men's race and knocked leader Vanderlei de Lima of Brazil into the crowd. The stunned Brazilian lost 10–15 sec in the incident and was passed by Stefano Baldini of Italy and Mebrahtom Keflezighi of the U.S. Baldini won the event, and de Lima, who took the bronze, was awarded the Pierre de Coubertin Medal by the International Olympic Committee for exemplary sportsmanship. Kenyans Felix Limo (2 hr 6 min 14 sec) and Evans Rutto (2 hr 6 min 16 sec) between them had run four of the five fastest marathons of the year but were not selected from their country's deep talent pool for the Olympics.

Ethiopia dominated rival Kenya at the world cross country championships in Brussels. Bekele won both men's senior races for the third consecutive year. Ethiopia won four of the six individual titles and five of six team titles. Kenya's only team crown was in the junior men's division. (SIEG LINDSTROM)

VOLLEYBALL

In 2004 Brazil was the world's capital for men's volleyball. Brazil's team won the men's indoor volleyball gold medal at the Olympic Games in Athens with a 25–15, 24–26, 25–20, 25–22 victory over Italy. (Russia upended the U.S. to capture the bronze.) The gold medal completed a cycle in which Brazil had won every trophy on the men's international scene, including the 2002 world championship and the 2003 World Cup and World League titles. Six weeks before the Olympics, Brazil had triumphed over Italy for its fourth World League championship (and its third in four years). Serbia and Montenegro claimed the World League bronze medal with a win over Bulgaria.

Emanuel Rego and Ricardo Santos also scored a win over Javier Bosma and Pablo Herrera of Spain to earn the gold medal for Brazil in the men's Olympic beach volleyball competition. The Swiss duo of Patrick Heuscher and Stefan Kobel downed Australia's Julien Prosser and Mark Williams for the bronze.

In women's indoor volleyball, China rallied to beat Russia 28–30, 25–27, 25–20, 25–23, 15–12 and claim its second Olympic gold medal. The victory capped an amazing year for China, which had won the 2003 women's World Cup and World Grand Prix titles. Cuba, the three-time defending women's Olympic champions, collected the bronze medal after downing Brazil. At the 2004 Grand Prix tournament, Brazil beat Italy to capture top honours, while the U.S. defeated Cuba to finish third.

The U.S. gained two medals in women's Olympic beach volleyball. Misty May and Kerri Walsh were awarded the gold following a 21–17, 21–11 triumph over Adriana Behar and Shelda Bede of Brazil. Meanwhile, Holly McPeak and Elaine Youngs scored a 21–18, 15–21, 15–9 win over Australia's Natalie Cook and Nicole Sanderson to net the bronze.

(RICHARD S. WANNINGER)

WEIGHT LIFTING

Weight lifters met at the 2004 Olympic Games in Athens for the sport's most important event of the year. A total of 249 athletes from 79 countries entered the competition: 163 men in eight body-weight classes and 86 women in seven body-weight classes. Forty three Olympic records, 14 world records, and 12 junior world records were broken.

In the women's division China topped the rankings with four medals (three gold and one silver), followed by Thailand (two gold and two bronze), Russia (one silver and two bronze), and Belarus (one silver and one bronze). Eight other countries captured one medal each. Tang Gonghong from China won the women's superheavyweight category with a 305-kg (672.4-lb) overall total, a new world record. Turkey's Nurcan Taylan and Liu Chunhong of China each set three world records to take the gold in the 48-kg and 69-kg divisions, respectively.

Russia topped the men's rankings with five medals (one gold, one silver, and three bronze), followed by China (two gold and two silver), Turkey (two gold and one bronze), and Bulgaria (one gold and one bronze). Ten other countries each won one medal. Hossein Rezazadeh from Iran, the reigning superheavyweight champion from the 2000 Olympics in Sydney, Australia, won the overall title with a 472.5-kg (1,041.7-lb) total result.

(DRAGOMIR CIOROSLAN)

WRESTLING

Freestyle and Greco-Roman. Wrestling medals were contested in three disciplines—men's freestyle, women's freestyle, and men's Greco-Roman—at the 2004 Olympic Games in Athens. Russia won the medal count in the men's freestyle competition with five, including three golds and two bronzes. The U.S. had three medals, with Cael Sanderson capturing a gold. Iran also claimed three medals—two silvers and a bronze. For the first time, women wrestlers competed in a modern Olympics, contesting freestyle events in four weight divisions—48 kg, 55 kg, 63 kg, and 72 kg. With her gold medal in the 48-kg event, Ukraine's Irini Merleni became the first female Olympic wrestling champion. Japan won the overall award tally in the women's competition with four medals, including two golds, one silver, and one bronze. The United States and France had two medals each.

In Greco-Roman competition, Russia claimed the unofficial team title with four medals, followed by Turkey and Kazakhstan with two each. The highlight was Egyptian Karam Ibrahim's victory in the 96-kg division. Ibrahim scored a 12–1 technical superiority win over Ramaz Nozadze of Georgia to give Egypt its first Olympic gold medal since 1948. In the superheavyweight competition, American Rulon Gardner, the surprise winner of the gold medal at the 2000 Games in Sydney, Australia, captured the bronze and then retired from the sport.

In American collegiate wrestling Oklahoma State University was dominant from start to finish, winning its 32nd national championship with a 41.5-point margin of victory over the University of Iowa. (ANDRÉ REDDINGTON)

Sumo. *Yokozuna* (grand champion) Asashoryu, who was born in Mongolia, won all but one of the six 15-day grand sumo tournaments in 2004. His 35 consecutive victories to start the year constituted a record eclipsed only by the great *yokozuna* Futabayama, Chiyonofuji, and Taiho. *Ozeki* (champion) Kaio won the Aki Basho in September and would have been promoted with a second consecutive *yusho* (championship) but fell short in November's Kyushu Basho.

Promising young wrestlers from Eastern Europe and Mongolia, as well as from Japan, continued to change the face of the top division of the sport, and the average weight and age decreased. The popularity of sumo continued to decline in Japan, while it increased outside the country. Tours were made to South Korea and China.

Two veteran *ozeki*, Takanonami and Musoyama, as well as former top division *rikishi* ("strong man") Oginishiki and Hamanoshima retired and accepted positions within the Japan Sumo Association. (KEN COLLER)

After winning a bronze medal in the Olympic Greco-Roman competition, superheavyweight wrestler Rulon Gardner of the U.S. walks off the mat, leaving his shoes behind in a symbolic gesture of his retirement from the sport.

© Adam Pretty/Getty Images

Sporting Record

ARCHERY

FITA Outdoor World Target Archery Championships*

Year	Men's individual Winner	Points	Men's team Winner	Points
1999	Hong Sung Chil (S.Kor.)	115	Italy	252
2001	Yeon Jung Ki (S.Kor.)	115	South Korea	247
2003	M. Frangilli (Italy)	113	South Korea	238

Year	Women's individual Winner	Points	Women's team Winner	Points
1999	Lee Eun Kyung (S.Kor.)	115	Italy	240
2001	Park Sung Hyun (S.Kor.)	111	China	232
2003	Yun Mi Jin (S.Kor.)	116	South Korea	252

*Olympic (recurve) division.

AUTOMOBILE RACING

Formula One Grand Prix Race Results, 2004

Race	Driver	Winner's time (hr:min:sec)
Australian GP	M. Schumacher (Ger.)	1:24:15.757
Malaysian GP	M. Schumacher (Ger.)	1:31:07.490
Bahrain GP	M. Schumacher (Ger.)	1:28:34.875
San Marino GP	M. Schumacher (Ger.)	1:26:19.670
Spanish GP	M. Schumacher (Ger.)	1:27:32.841
Monaco GP	J. Trulli (Italy)	1:45:46.601
European GP	M. Schumacher (Ger.)	1:32:35.101
Canadian GP	M. Schumacher (Ger.)	1:28:24.803
United States GP	M. Schumacher (Ger.)	1:40:29.914
French GP	M. Schumacher (Ger.)	1:30:18.133
British GP	M. Schumacher (Ger.)	1:24:42.700
German GP	M. Schumacher (Ger.)	1:23:54.848
Hungarian GP	M. Schumacher (Ger.)	1:35:26.131
Belgian GP	K. Räikkönen (Fin.)	1:32:35.274
Italian GP	R. Barrichello (Braz.)	1:15:18.448
Chinese GP	R. Barrichello (Braz.)	1:29:12.420
Japanese GP	M. Schumacher (Ger.)	1:24:26.985
Brazilian GP	J.P. Montoya (Colom.)	1:28:01.451

WORLD DRIVERS' CHAMPIONSHIP: M. Schumacher 148 points, Barrichello 114 points; Button 85 points. CONSTRUCTORS' CHAMPIONSHIP: Ferrari 262 points; Honda 119 points; Renault 105 points.

National Association for Stock Car Auto Racing (NASCAR) Winston Cup Champions

Year	Winner
2002	T. Stewart
2003	M. Kenseth
2004	**K. Busch**

Daytona 500

Year	Winner	Avg. speed in mph
2002	W. Burton	142.971
2003	M. Waltrip	133.870
2004	**D. Earnhardt, Jr.**	**156.345**

© Jamie Squire/Getty Images

Daytona 500 winner Dale Earnhardt, Jr.

Indy Car Champions*

Year	Driver
2002	C. da Matta (Braz.)
2003	P. Tracy (Can.)
2004	**S. Bourdais (Fr.)**

*Champ Car (formerly CART) champion.

Indianapolis 500

Year	Winner	Avg. speed in mph
2002	H. Castroneves	166.499
2003	G. de Ferran	156.291
2004*	**B. Rice (U.S.)**	**138.518**

*Race stopped because of rain after 450 mi.

Le Mans 24-Hour Grand Prix d'Endurance

Year	Car	Drivers
2002	Audi R8	F. Biela, T. Kristensen, E. Pirro
2003	Bentley	T. Kristensen, R. Capello, G. Smith
2004	**Audi R8**	**T. Kristensen, R. Capello, S. Ara**

Monte-Carlo Rally

Year	Car	Driver
2002	Subaru	T. Mäkinen (Fin.)
2003	Citroën Xsara	S. Loeb (Fr.)
2004	**Citroën Xsara**	**S. Loeb (Fr.)**

BADMINTON

All England Open Championships—Singles

Year	Men	Women
2002	Chen Hong (China)	C. Martin (Den.)
2003	Muhammad Hafiz Hashim (Malay.)	Zhou Mi (China)
2004	**Lin Dan (China)**	**Gong Ruina (China)**

Uber Cup (women)

Year	Winner	Runner-up
1999–2000	China	Denmark
2001–02	China	South Korea
2003–04	**China**	**South Korea**

Thomas Cup (men)

Year	Winner	Runner-up
1999–2000	Indonesia	China
2001–02	Indonesia	Malaysia
2003–04	**China**	**Denmark**

World Badminton Championships

Year	Men's singles	Women's singles	Men's doubles	Women's doubles	Mixed doubles
1999	Sun Jun (China)	C. Martin (Den.)	Kim Dong Moon, Ha Tae Kwon (S.Kor.)	Ge Fei, Gu Jun (China)	Kim Dong Moon, Ra Kyung Min (S.Kor.)
2001	Hendrawan (Indon.)	Gong Ruina (China)	T. Gunawan, H. Haryanto (Indon.)	Gao Ling, Huang Sui (China)	Zhang Jun, Gao Ling (China)
2003	Xia Xuanze (China)	Zhang Ning (China)	L. Paaske, J. Rasmussen (Den.)	Gao Ling, Huang Sui (China)	Kim Dong Moon, Ra Kyung Min (S.Kor.)

BASEBALL

Final Major League Standings, 2004

AMERICAN LEAGUE

East Division

Club	W.	L.	G.B.
*New York	101	61	—
*Boston	98	64	3
Baltimore	78	84	23
Tampa Bay	70	91	30½
Toronto	67	94	33½

Central Division

Club	W.	L.	G.B.
*Minnesota	92	70	—
Chicago	83	79	9
Cleveland	80	82	12
Detroit	72	90	20
Kansas City	58	104	34

West Division

Club	W.	L.	G.B.
*Anaheim	92	70	—
Oakland	91	71	1
Texas	89	73	3
Seattle	63	99	29

NATIONAL LEAGUE

East Division

Club	W.	L.	G.B.
*Atlanta	96	66	—
Philadelphia	86	76	10
Florida	83	79	13
New York	71	91	25
Montreal	67	95	29

Central Division

Club	W.	L.	G.B.
*St. Louis	105	57	—
*Houston	92	70	13
Chicago	89	73	16
Cincinnati	76	86	29
Pittsburgh	72	89	32½
Milwaukee	67	94	37½

West Division

Club	W.	L.	G.B.
*Los Angeles	93	69	—
San Francisco	91	71	2
San Diego	87	75	6
Colorado	68	94	25
Arizona	51	111	42

*Gained play-off berth.

Caribbean Series

Year	Winning team	Country
2002	Culiacán Tomato Growers	Mexico
2003	Cibao Eagles	Dominican Republic
2004	**Licey Tigers**	**Dominican Republic**

World Series*

Year	Winning team	Losing team	Results
2002	Anaheim Angels (AL)	San Francisco Giants (NL)	4–3
2003	Florida Marlins (NL)	New York Yankees (AL)	4–2
2004	**Boston Red Sox (AL)**	**St. Louis Cardinals (NL)**	**4–0**

*AL—American League; NL—National League.

Japan Series*

Year	Winning team	Losing team	Results
2002	Yomiuri Giants (CL)	Seibu Lions (PL)	4–0
2003	Fukuoka Daiei Hawks (PL)	Hanshin Tigers (CL)	4–2
2004	**Seibu Lions (PL)**	**Chunichi Dragons (CL)**	**4–3**

*CL—Central League; PL—Pacific League.

BASKETBALL

NBA Final Standings, 2003–04

EASTERN CONFERENCE

Atlantic Division

Team	Won	Lost	G.B.
*New Jersey	47	35	—
*Miami	42	40	5
*New York	39	43	8
*Boston	36	46	11
Philadelphia	33	49	14
Washington	25	57	22
Orlando	21	61	26

Central Division

Team	Won	Lost	G.B.
*Indiana	61	21	—
*Detroit	54	28	7
*New Orleans	41	41	20
*Milwaukee	41	41	20
Cleveland	35	47	26
Toronto	33	49	28
Atlanta	28	54	33
Chicago	23	59	38

WESTERN CONFERENCE

Midwest Division

Team	Won	Lost	G.B.
*Minnesota	58	24	—
*San Antonio	57	25	1
*Dallas	52	30	6
*Memphis	50	32	8
*Houston	45	37	13
*Denver	43	39	15
Utah	42	40	16

Pacific Division

Team	Won	Lost	G.B.
*L.A. Lakers	56	26	—
*Sacramento	55	27	1
Portland	41	41	15
Golden State	37	45	19
Seattle	37	45	19
Phoenix	29	53	27
L.A. Clippers	28	54	28

*Gained play-off berth.

National Basketball Association (NBA) Championship

Season	Winner	Runner-up	Results
2001–02	Los Angeles Lakers	New Jersey Nets	4–0
2002–03	San Antonio Spurs	New Jersey Nets	4–2
2003–04	**Detroit Pistons**	**Los Angeles Lakers**	**4–1**

Women's National Basketball Association (WNBA) Championship

Season	Winner	Runner-up	Results
2002	Los Angeles Sparks	New York Liberty	2–0
2003	Detroit Shock	Los Angeles Sparks	2–1
2004	**Seattle Storm**	**Connecticut Sun**	**2–1**

Division I National Collegiate Athletic Association (NCAA) Championship—Men

Year	Winner	Runner-up	Score
2002	Maryland	Indiana	64–52
2003	Syracuse	Kansas	81–78
2004	**Connecticut**	**Georgia Tech**	**82–73**

Division I National Collegiate Athletic Association (NCAA) Championship—Women

Year	Winner	Runner-up	Score
2002	Connecticut	Oklahoma	82–70
2003	Connecticut	Tennessee	73–68
2004	**Connecticut**	**Tennessee**	**70–61**

World Basketball Championship—Men

Year	Winner	Runner-up
2000*	United States	France
2002	Yugoslavia	Argentina
2004*	**Argentina**	**Italy**

*Olympic champion.

World Basketball Championship—Women

Year	Winner	Runner-up
2000*	United States	Australia
2002	United States	Russia
2004*	**United States**	**Australia**

*Olympic champion.

BILLIARD GAMES

World Three-Cushion Championship*

Year	Winner
2002	M. Zanetti (Italy)
2003	S. Sayginer (Tur.)
2004	**D. Jaspers (Neth.)**

*Union Mondiale de Billard champion.

WPA World Nine-Ball Championships

Year	Men's champion
2002	E. Strickland (U.S.)
2003	T. Hohmann (Ger.)
2004	**A. Pagulayan (Can.)**
Year	**Women's champion**
2002	Liu Shin-Mei (Taiwan)
2003	*not held*
2004	**Kim Ga Young (S.Kor.)**

World Professional Snooker Championship

Year	Winner
2002	P. Ebdon
2003	M. Williams
2004	**R. O'Sullivan**

BOBSLEIGH AND LUGE

Bobsleigh and Skeleton World Championships

Year	Two-man bobsleigh	Four-man/driver	Women's bobsleigh	Men's skeleton	Women's skeleton	Team
2002*	C. Langen, M. Zimmermann (Ger.)	Germany/A. Lange	J. Bakken, V. Flowers (U.S.)	J. Shea, Jr. (U.S.)	T. Gale (U.S.)	
2003	A. Lange, K. Kuske (Ger.)	Germany/A. Lange	S. Erdmann, A. Dietrich (Ger.)	J. Pain (Can.)	M. Kelly (Can.)	
2004	**P. Lueders, G. Zardo (Can.)**	**Germany/A. Lange**	**S. Erdmann, K. Bader (Ger.)**	**D. Gibson (Can.)**	**D. Sartor (Ger.)**	**Germany**

*Olympic champions.

Luge World Championships*

Year	Men	Women	Doubles	Team
2002†	A. Zöggeler (Italy)	S. Otto (Ger.)	P. Leitner, A. Resch (Ger.)	
2003	A. Zöggeler (Italy)	S. Otto (Ger.)	A. Linger, W. Linger (Austria)	Germany
2004	**D. Möller (Ger.)**	**S. Kraushaar (Ger.)**	**P. Leitner, A. Resch (Ger.)**	**Germany**

*Artificial track. †Olympic champions.

BOWLING

ABC Bowling Championships—Regular Division

Year	Singles	Score	All-events	Score
2002	M. Millsap	823	S.A. Hardy	2,279
2003	R. Bahr	837	S. Kloempken	2,215
2004	**J. Janawicz**	**858**	**J. Janawicz**	**2,224**

WIBC Bowling Championships—Classic Division

Year	Singles	Score	All-events	Score
2002	T. Smith	752	C. Honeychurch	2,150
2003	M. Feldman	764	M. Feldman	2,048
2004	**S. Smith**	**754**	**K. Adler**	**2,133**

World Tenpin Bowling Championships—Men

Year	Singles	Pairs	Triples	Team (fives)
1995	M. Doi (Can.)	Sweden	Netherlands	Netherlands
1999	G. Verbruggen (Belg.)	Sweden	Finland	Sweden
2003	M. Luoto (Fin.)	Sweden	United States	Sweden

World Tenpin Bowling Championships—Women

Year	Singles	Pairs	Triples	Team (fives)
1995	D. Ship (Can.)	Thailand	Australia	Finland
1999	K. Kulick (U.S.)	Australia	South Korea	South Korea
2003	Z. Glover (Eng.)	England	Philippines	Malaysia

PBA Tournament of Champions

Year	Champion
2001	*not held*
2002–03	J. Couch
2003–04	**P. Healey, Jr.**

PBA World Championship*

Year	Winner
2001–02	D. Kent
2002–03	W.R. Williams, Jr.
2003–04	**T. Baker**

*PBA National Championship until 2002.

BOXING

World Heavyweight Champions No Weight Limit

WBA

Roy Jones, Jr. (U.S.; 3/1/03)
gave up title in 2004
John Ruiz (U.S.; 2/24/04)

WBC

Lennox Lewis (U.K.; 11/17/01)
gave up title in 2004
Vitali Klitschko (Ukr.; 4/24/04)

IBF

Chris Byrd (U.S.; 12/14/02)

World Cruiserweight Champions Top Weight 200 Pounds

WBA

Jean-Marc Mormeck (Fr.; 2/23/02)

WBC

Wayne Braithwaite (Guyana; 10/11/02)

IBF

James Toney (U.S.; 4/26/03)
gave up title in 2003
Kelvin Davis (U.S.; 5/1/04)

AP/Wide World Photos

IBF junior middleweight champion Kassim Ouma of Uganda.

BOXING (continued)

World Light Heavyweight Champions
Top Weight 175 Pounds

WBA

Silvio Branco (Italy; 10/10/03)
Fabrice Tiozzo (Fr.; 3/20/04)

WBC

Roy Jones, Jr. (U.S.; 11/8/03)
Antonio Tarver (U.S.; 5/15/04)
gave up title in 2004

IBF

Antonio Tarver (U.S.; 4/26/03)
gave up title in 2003
Glencoffe Johnson (Jam.; 2/6/04)
gave up title in 2004

World Super Middleweight Champions
Top Weight 168 Pounds

WBA

Sven Ottke (Ger.; 3/15/03)
declared super champion in 2003
gave up title in 2004
Anthony Mundine (Austl.; 9/3/03)
Manny Siaca (P.R.; 5/5/04)
Mikkel Kessler (Den.; 11/12/04)

WBC

Markus Beyer (Ger.; 4/5/03)
Cristian Sanavia (Italy; 6/5/04)
Markus Beyer (Ger.; 10/9/04)

IBF

Sven Ottke (Ger.; 10/24/98)
gave up title in 2004
Jeff Lacy (U.S.; 10/2/04)

World Middleweight Champions
Top Weight 160 Pounds

WBA

Bernard Hopkins (U.S.; 12/13/03)
declared undisputed champion in 2003
Maselino Masoe (N.Z.; 5/1/04)

WBC

Bernard Hopkins (U.S.; 4/14/01)

IBF

Bernard Hopkins (U.S.; 4/29/95)

World Junior Middleweight Champions
Top Weight 154 Pounds
(also called super welterweight)

WBA

Shane Mosley (U.S.; 9/13/03)
declared super champion in 2003
Travis Simms (U.S.; 12/13/03)
Ronald ("Winky") Wright (U.S.; 3/13/04; defeated Mosley)
declared unified champion in 2004

WBC

Shane Mosley (U.S.; 9/13/03)
Ronald ("Winky") Wright (U.S.; 3/13/04)

IBF

Ronald ("Winky") Wright (U.S.; 10/12/01)
stripped of title in 2004
Verno Phillips (U.S.; 6/5/04)
Kassim Ouma (Uganda; 10/2/04)

World Welterweight Champions
Top Weight 147 Pounds

WBA

Cory Spinks (U.S.; 12/13/03)
declared undisputed champion in 2003

WBC

Cory Spinks (U.S.; 12/13/03)

IBF

Cory Spinks (U.S.; 3/22/03)

World Junior Welterweight Champions
Top Weight 140 Pounds
(also called super lightweight)

WBA

Kostya Tszyu (Austl.; 2/3/01)
declared undisputed champion in 2003
stripped of title in 2004
Diobelys Hurtado (Cuba; 5/11/02)
Vivian Harris (Guyana; 10/19/02)

WBC

Kostya Tszyu (Austl.; 8/21/99)
declared emeritus champion in 2003
Arturo Gatti (Can.; 1/24/04)

IBF

Kostya Tszyu (Austl.; 11/3/01)

World Lightweight Champions
Top Weight 135 Pounds

WBA

Leonard Dorin (Can.; 1/5/02)
stripped of title in 2003
Lakva Sim (Mong.; 4/10/04)
Juan Diaz (U.S.; 7/17/04)

WBC

Floyd Mayweather, Jr. (U.S.; 4/20/02)
gave up title in 2004
José Luis Castillo (Mex.; 6/5/04)

IBF

Javier Jauregui (Mex.; 11/22/03)
Julio Diaz (U.S.; 5/13/04)

World Junior Lightweight Champions
Top Weight 130 Pounds
(also called super featherweight)

WBA

Yodsanan Nanthachai (Thai.; 4/13/02)

WBC

Jesús Chávez (Mex.; 8/15/03)
Erik Morales (Mex.; 2/28/04)
Marco Antonio Barrera (Mex.; 11/27/04)

IBF

Carlos Hernández (El Sal.; 2/1/03)
Erik Morales (Mex.; 7/31/04)
stripped of title in 2004

World Featherweight Champions
Top Weight 126 Pounds

WBA

Juan Manuel Márquez (Mex.; 11/1/03)
declared unified champion in 2003
Chris John (Indon.; 9/26/03)

WBC

Erik Morales (Mex.; 11/16/02)
declared emeritus champion in 2003
gave up title in 2004
Chi In Jin (S.Kor.; 4/10/04)

IBF

Juan Manuel Márquez (Mex.; 2/1/03)

World Junior Featherweight Champions
Top Weight 122 Pounds
(also called super bantamweight)

WBA

Mahyar Monshipour (Fr.; 7/4/03)

WBC

Oscar Larios (Mex.; 11/1/02)

IBF

Manny Pacquiao (Phil.; 6/23/01)
gave up title in 2004
Israel Vásquez (Mex.; 3/25/04)

World Bantamweight Champions
Top Weight 118 Pounds

WBA

Johnny Bredahl (Den.; 4/19/02)
gave up title in 2004

WBC

Veeraphol Sahaprom (Thai.; 12/29/98)

IBF

Rafael Márquez (Mex.; 2/15/03)

World Junior Bantamweight Champions
Top Weight 115 Pounds
(also called super flyweight)

WBA

Alexander Muñoz (Venez.; 3/9/02)
José Martin Castillo (Mex.; 12/3/04)

WBC

Masanori Tokuyama (Japan; 8/27/00)
Katsushige Kawashima (Japan; 6/28/04)

IBF

Luis Pérez (Nic.; 1/4/03)

BOXING (continued)

World Flyweight Champions Top Weight 112 Pounds

WBA

Lorenzo Parra (Venez.; 12/6/03)

WBC

Pongsaklek Wongjongkam (Thai.; 3/2/01)

IBF

Irene Pacheco (Colom.; 4/10/99)
Vic Darchinyan (Austl.; 12/16/04)

World Junior Flyweight Champions Top Weight 108 Pounds

WBA

Rosendo Álvarez (Nic.; 3/3/01)
stripped of title in 2004

WBC

Jorge Arce (Mex.; 7/6/02)

IBF

José Víctor Burgos (Mex.; 2/15/03)

World Mini-flyweight Champions Top Weight 105 Pounds
(also called strawweight)

WBA

Noel Arambulet (Venez.; 7/29/02)
Yutaka Niida (Japan; 7/3/04)

WBC

José Antonio Aguirre (Mex.; 2/11/00)
Eagle Akakura (Kyowa) (Japan; 1/10/04)
Isaac Bustos (Mex.; 12/18/04)

IBF

Daniel Reyes (Colom.; 10/4/03)
Muhammad Rachman (Indon.; 9/14/04)

CHESS

FIDE Olympiad—Open

Year	Winner	Runner-up
2000	Russia	Germany
2002	Russia	Hungary
2004	**Ukraine**	**Russia**

FIDE Olympiad—Women

Year	Winner	Runner-up
2000	China	Georgia
2002	China	Russia
2004	**China**	**United States**

CRICKET

Cricket World Cup

Year	Result			
1996	Sri Lanka	245 for 3	Australia	241
1999	Australia	133 for 2	Pakistan	132
2003	Australia	359 for 2	India	234

Test Match Results, October 2003–September 2004

Host/Ground	Date	Scores	Result
India/Ahmedabad	Oct. 8–12	India 500 for 5 dec and 209 for 6 dec; N.Z. 340 and 272 for 6	Match drawn
India/Chandigarh	Oct. 16–20	N.Z. 630 for 6 dec; India 424 and 136 for 4	Match drawn; series drawn 0–0
Australia/Perth	Oct. 9–13	Austl. 735 for 6 dec; Zimb. 239 and 321	Austl. won by an innings and 175 runs
Australia/Sydney	Oct. 17–20	Zimb. 308 and 266; Austl. 403 and 172 for 1	Austl. won by 9 wickets; Austl. won series 2–0
Pakistan/Lahore	Oct. 17–21	S.Af. 320 and 241; Pak. 401 and 164 for 2	Pak. won by 8 wickets
Pakistan/Faisalabad	Oct. 24–28	S.Af. 278 and 371 for 8 dec; Pak. 348 and 242 for 6	Match drawn; Pak. won series 1–0
Bangladesh/Dhaka	Oct. 21–25	Bangl. 203 and 255; Eng. 295 and 164 for 3	Eng. won by 7 wickets
Bangladesh/Chittagong	Oct. 29–Nov. 1	Eng. 326 and 293 for 5 dec; Bangl. 152 and 138	Eng. won by 329 runs; Eng. won series 2–0
Zimbabwe/Harare	Nov. 4–8	Zimb. 507 for 9 dec and 200 for 7 dec; W.Ind. 335 and 207 for 9	Match drawn
Zimbabwe/Bulawayo	Nov. 12–16	W.Ind. 481 and 128; Zimb. 377 and 104	W.Ind. won by 128 runs; W.Ind. won series 1–0
Sri Lanka/Galle	Dec. 2–6	SriL. 331 and 226; Eng. 235 and 210 for 9	Match drawn
Sri Lanka/Kandy	Dec. 10–14	SriL. 382 and 279 for 7 dec; Eng. 294 and 285 for 7	Match drawn
Sri Lanka/Colombo	Dec. 18–21	Eng. 265 and 148; SriL. 628 for 8 dec	SriL. won by an innings and 215 runs; SriL. won series 1–0
Australia/Brisbane	Dec. 4–8	Austl. 323 and 284 for 3 dec; India 409 and 73 for 2	Match drawn
Australia/Adelaide	Dec. 12–16	Austl. 556 and 196; India 523 and 233 for 6	India won by 4 wickets
Australia/Melbourne	Dec. 26–30	India 366 and 286; Austl. 558 and 97 for 1	Austl. won by 9 wickets
Australia/Sydney	Jan. 2–6	India 705 for 7 dec and 211 for 2 dec; Austl. 474 and 357 for 6	Match drawn; series drawn 1–1
South Africa/Johannesburg	Dec. 12–16	S.Af. 561 and 226 for 6 dec; W.Ind. 410 and 188	S.Af. won by 189 runs
South Africa/Durban	Dec. 26–30	W.Ind. 264 and 329; S.Af. 658 for 9 dec	S.Af. won by an innings and 65 runs
South Africa/Cape Town	Jan. 2–6	S.Af. 532 and 335 for 3 dec; W.Ind. 427 and 354 for 5	Match drawn
South Africa/Centurion	Jan. 16–20	S.Af. 604 for 6 dec and 46; W.Ind. 301 and 348	S.Af. won by 10 wickets; S.Af. won series 3–0
New Zealand/Hamilton	Dec. 19–23	N.Z. 563 and 96 for 8; Pak. 463	Match drawn
New Zealand/Wellington	Dec. 26–30	N.Z. 366 and 103; Pak. 196 and 277 for 3	Pak. won by 7 wickets; Pak. won series 1–0
Zimbabwe/Harare	Feb. 19–23	Zimb. 441 and 242 for 8 dec; Bangl. 331 and 169	Zimb. won by 183 runs
Zimbabwe/Bulawayo	Feb. 26–March 1	Bangl. 168; Zimb. 210 for 2	Match drawn; Zimb. won series 1–0

CRICKET (continued)

Test Match Results, October 2003–September 2004 (continued)

Host/Ground	Date	Scores	Result
Sri Lanka/Galle	March 8–12	Austl. 220 and 512 for 8 dec; SriL. 381 and 154	Austl. won by 197 runs
Sri Lanka/Kandy	March 16–20	Austl. 120 and 442; SriL. 211 and 324	Austl. won by 27 runs
Sri Lanka/Colombo	March 24–28	Austl. 401 and 375; SriL. 407 and 248	Austl. won by 121 runs; Austl. won series 3–0
New Zealand/Hamilton	March 10–14	S.Af. 459 and 313 for 4 dec; N.Z. 509 and 39 for 1	Match drawn
New Zealand/Auckland	March 18–22	S.Af. 296 and 349; N.Z. 595 and 53 for 1	N.Z. won by 9 wickets
New Zealand/Wellington	March 26–30	N.Z. 297 and 252; S.Af. 316 and 234 for 4	S.Af. won by 6 wickets; series drawn 1–1
West Indies/Jamaica	March 11–14	W.Ind. 311 and 47; Eng. 339 and 20	Eng. won by 10 wickets
West Indies/Trinidad	March 19–23	W.Ind. 208 and 209; Eng. 319 and 99 for 3	Eng. won by 7 wickets
West Indies/Barbados	April 1–3	W.Ind. 224 and 94; Eng. 226 and 93 for 2	Eng. won by 8 wickets
West Indies/Antigua	April 10–14	W.Ind. 751 for 5 dec; Eng. 285 and 422 for 5	Match drawn; Eng. won series 3–0
Pakistan/Multan	March 28–April 1	India 675 for 5 dec; Pak. 407 and 216	India won by an innings and 52 runs
Pakistan/Lahore	April 5–8	India 287 and 241; Pak. 489 and 40 for 1	Pak. won by 9 wickets
Pakistan/Rawalpindi	April 13–16	Pak. 224 and 245; India 600	India won by an innings and 131 runs; India won series 2–1
Zimbabwe/Harare	May 6–8	Zimb. 199 and 102; SriL. 541	SriL. won by an innings and 240 runs
Zimbabwe/Bulawayo	May 14–17	Zimb. 228 and 231; SriL. 713 for 3 dec	SriL. won by an innings and 254 runs; SriL. won series 2–0
England/London (Lord's)	May 20–24	N.Z. 386 and 336; Eng. 441 and 282 for 3	Eng. won by 7 wickets
England/Leeds	June 3–7	N.Z. 409 and 161; Eng. 526 and 45 for 1	Eng. won by 9 wickets
England/Nottingham	June 10–13	N.Z. 384 and 218; Eng. 319 and 284 for 6	Eng. won by 4 wickets; Eng. won series 3–0
West Indies/St. Lucia	May 28–June 1	Bangl. 416 and 271 for 9 dec; W.Ind. 352 and 113	Match drawn
West Indies/Jamaica	June 4–8	Bangl. 284 and 176; W.Ind. 559 for 4 dec	W.Ind. won by an innings and 99 runs; W.Ind. won series 1–0
Australia/Darwin	July 1–3	Austl. 207 and 201; SriL. 97 and 162	Austl. won by 149 runs
Australia/Cairns	July 9–13	Austl. 517 and 292 for 9 dec; SriL. 455 and 183 for 8	Match drawn; Austl. won series 1–0
England/London (Lord's)	July 22–26	Eng. 568 and 325 for 5 dec; W.Ind. 416 and 267	Eng. won by 210 runs
England/Birmingham	July 29–Aug. 1	Eng. 566 for 9 dec and 248; W.Ind. 336 and 222	Eng. won by 256 runs
England/Manchester	Aug. 12–16	W.Ind. 395 and 165; Eng. 330 and 231 for 3	Eng. won by 7 wickets
England/London (the Oval)	Aug. 19–21	Eng. 470 and 4; W.Ind. 152 and 318	Eng. won by 10 wickets; Eng. won series 4–0
Sri Lanka/Galle	Aug. 4–8	SriL. 486 and 214 for 9 dec; S.Af. 376 and 203 for 3	Match drawn
Sri Lanka/Colombo	Aug. 11–15	SriL. 470 and 211 for 4 dec; S.Af. 189 and 179	SriL. won by 313 runs; SriL. won series 1–0

India's captain, Sourav Ganguly (centre), plays a sweep shot during the third Test in Rawalpindi, Pak., in April, as wicketkeeper Kamran Akmai (left) and Taufeeq Umar of Pakistan look on. India won the match and the historic series.

CURLING

World Curling Championship—Men

Year	Winner	Runner-up
2002	Canada	Norway
2003	Canada	Switzerland
2004	**Sweden**	**Germany**

World Curling Championship—Women

Year	Winner	Runner-up
2002	Scotland	Sweden
2003	United States	Canada
2004	**Canada**	**Norway**

CYCLING

Cycling Champions, 2004

Event	Winner	Country
WORLD CHAMPIONS—TRACK		
Men		
Sprint	T. Bos	Netherlands
Individual pursuit	S. Escobar Roure	Spain
Kilometre time trial	C. Hoy	Great Britain
40-km points	F. Perque	France
Team pursuit	P. Dawson, A. Hutchinson, L. Roberts, S. Wooldridge	Australia
Keirin	J. Staff	Great Britain
Team sprint	M. Bourgain, L. Gané, A. Tournant	France
50-km Madison	J. Curuchet, W. Pérez	Argentina
15-km scratch	G. Henderson	New Zealand
Women		
Sprint	S. Grankovskaya	Russia
Individual pursuit	S. Ulmer	New Zealand
500-m time trial	A. Meares	Australia
24-km points	O. Slyusareva	Russia
10-km scratch	Y. González Pérez	Cuba
Keirin	C. Sanchez	France
WORLD CHAMPIONS—ROAD		
Men		
Individual road race	O. Freire	Spain
Individual time trial	M. Rogers	Australia
Women		
Individual road race	J. Arndt	Germany
Individual time trial	K. Thürig	Switzerland
WORLD CHAMPION—CYCLO-CROSS		
Men	B. Wellens	Belgium
Women	L. Leboucher	France

Event	Winner	Country
WORLD CHAMPIONS—MOUNTAIN BIKES		
Men		
Cross-country	J. Absalon	France
Downhill	F. Barel	France
4-cross	E. Carter	United States
Women		
Cross-country	G.-R. Dahle	Norway
Downhill	V. Quin	New Zealand
4-cross	J. Horakova	Czech Republic
MAJOR ELITE ROAD-RACE WINNERS		
Tour de France	L. Armstrong	United States
Tour of Italy	D. Cunego	Italy
Tour of Spain	R. Heras	Spain
Tour of Switzerland	J. Ullrich	Germany
Milan–San Remo	O. Freire	Spain
Tour of Flanders	S. Wesemann	Germany
Paris–Roubaix	M. Backstedt	Sweden
Liège–Bastogne–Liège	D. Rebellin	Italy
Amstel Gold	D. Rebellin	Italy
HEW–Cyclassics Cup	S. O'Grady	Australia
San Sebastian Classic	M.A. Martin	Spain
Zürich Championship	J. Flecha	Spain
Paris–Tours	E. Dekker	Netherlands
Tour of Lombardy	D. Cunego	Italy
Paris–Nice	J. Jaksche	Germany
Ghent–Wevelgem	T. Boonen	Belgium
Flèche Wallonne	D. Rebellin	Italy
Tour of Romandie	T. Hamilton	United States
Dauphiné Libéré	I. Mayo	Spain
Tirreno–Adriatico	P. Bettini	Italy

EQUESTRIAN SPORTS

The Kentucky Derby

Year	Horse	Jockey
2002	War Emblem	V. Espinoza
2003	Funny Cide	J. Santos
2004	**Smarty Jones**	**S. Elliott**

The Preakness Stakes

Year	Horse	Jockey
2002	War Emblem	V. Espinoza
2003	Funny Cide	J. Santos
2004	**Smarty Jones**	**S. Elliott**

The Belmont Stakes

Year	Horse	Jockey
2002	Sarava	E. Prado
2003	Empire Maker	J. Bailey
2004	**Birdstone**	**E. Prado**

2,000 Guineas

Year	Horse	Jockey
2002	Rock of Gibraltar	J. Murtagh
2003	Refuse To Bend	P. Smullen
2004	**Haafhd**	**R. Hills**

The Derby

Year	Horse	Jockey
2002	High Chaparral	J. Murtagh
2003	Kris Kin	K. Fallon
2004	**North Light**	**K. Fallon**

The St. Leger

Year	Horse	Jockey
2002	Bollin Eric	K. Darley
2003	Brian Boru	J. Spencer
2004	**Rule of Law**	**K. McEvoy**

Triple Crown Champions—U.S.

Year	Horse
1973	Secretariat
1977	Seattle Slew
1978	Affirmed

Triple Crown Champions—British

Year	Winner
1918	Gainsborough
1935	Bahram
1970	Nijinsky

Melbourne Cup

Year	Horse	Jockey
2002	Media Puzzle	D. Oliver
2003	Makybe Diva	G. Boss
2004	**Makybe Diva**	**G. Boss**

The Hambletonian Trot

Year	Horse	Driver
2002	Chip Chip Hooray	E. Ledford
2003	Amigo Hall	M. Lachance
2004	**Windsong's Legacy**	**T. Smedshammer**

EQUESTRIAN SPORTS (continued)

Major Thoroughbred Race Winners, 2004

Race	Won by	Jockey
United States		
Acorn	Island Sand	T. Thompson
Alabama Stakes	Society Selection	C. Velasquez
American Invitational Oaks	Ticker Tape	K. Desormeaux
Apple Blossom	Azeri	M. Smith
Arlington Million	Kicken Kris	K. Desmoreaux
Ashland Stakes	Madcap Escapade	R. Douglas
Beldame	Sightseek	J. Castellano
Belmont	Birdstone	E. Prado
Beverly D.	Crimson Palace	L. Dettori
Blue Grass Stakes	The Cliff's Edge	S. Sellers
Breeders' Cup Juvenile	Wilko	L. Dettori
Breeders' Cup Juvenile Fillies	Sweet Catomine	C. Nakatani
Breeders' Cup Sprint	Speightstown	J. Velazquez
Breeders' Cup Mile	Singletary	D. Romero
Breeders' Cup Distaff	Ashado	J. Velazquez
Breeders' Cup Turf	Better Talk Now	R. Dominguez
Breeders' Cup Filly and Mare Turf	Ouija Board	K. Fallon
Breeders' Cup Classic	Ghostzapper	J. Castellano
Carter Handicap	Pico Central	A. Solis
Champagne	Proud Accolade	J. Velazquez
Cigar Mile Handicap	Lion Tamer	J. Santos
Coaching Club American Oaks	Ashado	J. Velazquez
Diana Handicap	Wonder Again	E. Prado
Donn Handicap	Medaglia d'Oro	J. Bailey
Eddie Read	Special Ring	V. Espinoza
Florida Derby	Friends Lake	R. Migliore
Flower Bowl Invitational	Riskaverse	C. Velasquez
Frizette Stakes	Balletto	C. Nakatani
Haskell Invitational Handicap	Lion Heart	J. Bravo
Hollywood Derby	Good Reward	J. Bailey
Hollywood Futurity	Declan's Moon	V. Espinoza
Hollywood Gold Cup	Total Impact	M. Smith
Hollywood Starlet	Splendid Blended	K. Desormeaux
Hollywood Turf Cup	Pellegrino	G. Stevens
Hopeful Stakes	Afleet Alex	J. Rose
Jockey Club Gold Cup	Funny Cide	J. Santos
Joe Hirsch Turf Classic	Kitten's Joy	J. Velazquez
Kentucky Derby	Smarty Jones	S. Elliott
Kentucky Oaks	Ashado	J. Velazquez
Man o' War	Magistretti	E. Prado
Matriarch Stakes	Intercontinental	J. Bailey
Metropolitan	Pico Central	A. Solis
Mother Goose	Stellar Jayne	R. Albarado
Pacific Classic	Pleasantly Perfect	J. Bailey
Personal Ensign Handicap	Storm Flag Flying	J. Velazquez
Pimlico Special	Southern Image	V. Espinoza
Preakness	Smarty Jones	S. Elliott
Queen Elizabeth II Challenge Cup	Ticker Tape	K. Desormeaux
Santa Anita Derby	Castledale	J. Valdivia, Jr.
Santa Anita Handicap	Southern Image	V. Espinoza
Secretariat Stakes	Kitten's Joy	J. Bailey
Spinster Stakes	Azeri	P. Day
Stephen Foster Handicap	Colonial Colony	R. Bejarano
Suburban Handicap	Peace Rules	J. Bailey
Travers	Birdstone	E. Prado
United Nations	Request for Parole	E. Prado
Whitney	Roses in May	E. Prado
Wood Memorial	Tapit	R. Dominguez
Woodward	Ghostzapper	J. Castellano
Yellow Ribbon Stakes	Light Jig	R. Douglas

Race	Won by	Jockey
England		
One Thousand Guineas	Attraction	K. Darley
Two Thousand Guineas	Haafhd	R. Hills
Derby	North Light	K. Fallon
Oaks	Ouija Board	K. Fallon
St. Leger	Rule of Law	K. McEvoy
Coronation Cup	Warrsan	D. Holland
Ascot Gold Cup	Papineau	L. Dettori
Coral-Eclipse Stakes	Refuse To Bend	L. Dettori
King George VI and Queen Elizabeth Diamond Stakes	Doyen	L. Dettori
Sussex Stakes	Soviet Song	J. Murtagh
Juddmonte International Stakes	Sulamani	L. Dettori
Dubai Champion Stakes	Haafhd	R. Hills
France		
Poule d'Essai des Poulains	American Post	R. Hughes
Poule d'Essai des Pouliches	Torrestrella	O. Peslier
Prix du Jockey-Club	Blue Canari	T. Thulliez
Prix de Diane	Latice	C. Soumillon
Prix Royal-Oak	Westerner	S. Pasquier
Prix Ganay	Execute	T. Gillet
Prix Jacques Le Marois	Whipper	C. Soumillon
Grand Prix de Paris	Bago	T. Gillet
Grand Prix de Saint-Cloud	Gamut	K. Fallon
Prix Vermeille	Sweet Stream	T. Gillet
Prix de l'Arc de Triomphe	Bago	T. Gillet
Prix Jean-Luc Lagardere	Oratorio	J. Spencer
Ireland		
Irish Two Thousand Guineas	Bachelor Duke	S. Sanders
Irish One Thousand Guineas	Attraction	K. Darley
Irish Derby	Grey Swallow	P. Smullen
Irish Oaks	Ouija Board	K. Fallon
Irish St. Leger	Vinnie Roe	P. Smullen
Irish Champion Stakes	Azamour	M. Kinane
Italy		
Derby Italiano	Groom Tesse	D. Vargiu
Gran Premio del Jockey Club	Shirocco	A. Suborics
Germany		
Deutsches Derby	Shirocco	A. Suborics
Grosser Preis von Baden	Warrsan	K. McEvoy
Preis von Europa	Albanova	S. Sanders
Australia		
Melbourne Cup	Makybe Diva	G. Boss
Caulfield Cup	Elvstroem	N. Rawiller
Cox Plate	Savabeel	C. Munce
United Arab Emirates		
Dubai World Cup	Pleasantly Perfect	A. Solis
Asia		
Singapore Cup	Epalo	A. Starke
Japan Cup	Zenno Rob Roy	O. Peslier
Canada		
Queen's Plate Stakes	Niigon	R. Landry
Prince of Wales Stakes	A Bit O'Gold	J. Jones
Breeders' Stakes	A Bit O'Gold	J. Jones
Canadian International	Sulamani	L. Dettori

FENCING

World Fencing Championships—Men

Year	Individual			Team		
	Foil	Épée	Sabre	Foil	Épée	Sabre
2002	S. Vanni (Italy)	P. Kolobkov (Russia)	S. Pozdnyakov (Russia)	Germany	France	Russia
2003	P. Joppich (Ger.)	F. Jeannet (Fr.)	V. Lukashenko (Ukr.)	Italy	Russia	Russia
2004*	**B. Guyart (Fr.)**	**M. Fischer (Switz.)**	**A. Montano (Italy)**	**Italy**	**France**	**France**

*Olympic champions.

World Fencing Championships—Women

Year	Individual			Team		
	Foil	Épée	Sabre	Foil	Épée	Sabre
2002	S. Boyko (Russia)	Hyun Hee (S.Kor.)	Tan Xue (China)	Russia	Hungary	Russia
2003	V. Vezzali (Italy)	N. Conrad (Ukr.)	D. Mihai (Rom.)	Poland	Russia	Italy
2004*	**V. Vezzali (Italy)**	**T. Nagy (Hung.)**	**M. Zagunis (U.S.)**	**Italy**	**Russia**	**Russia**

*Olympic champions, except for team foil and team sabre.

FIELD HOCKEY

World Cup Field Hockey Championship—Men

Year	Winner	Runner-up
1994	Pakistan	Netherlands
1998	Netherlands	Spain
2002	Germany	Australia

World Cup Field Hockey Championship—Women

Year	Winner	Runner-up
1994	Australia	Argentina
1998	Australia	Netherlands
2002	Argentina	Netherlands

FOOTBALL

FIFA World Cup—Men

Year	Result			
1994	Brazil*	0	Italy	0
1998	France	3	Brazil	0
2002	Brazil	2	Germany	0

*Won on penalty kicks.

FIFA World Cup—Women

Year	Result			
1995	Norway	2	Germany	0
1999	United States*	0	China	0
2003	Germany	2	Sweden	1

*Won on penalty kicks.

Association Football National Champions, 2004

Nation	League Champions	Cup Winners
Argentina	Newell's Old Boys (Opening)	River Plate (Closing)
Australia	Perth Glory	
Austria	Graz	Graz
Belgium	Anderlecht	FC Brugge
Bolivia	Bolivar (Opening)	The Strongest (Closing)
Brazil	Santos FC	Santo Andre
Bulgaria	Lokomotiv Plovdiv	Litex
Cameroon	Cotonsport	Mount Cameroon
Chile	Universidad de Chile (Opening)	Cobreloa (Closing)
China	Shanghai Shenhua	Beijing Hyundai
Colombia	Independiente Medellín (Opening)	Atlélico Junior (Closing)
Costa Rica	Saprissa (Opening)	Herediano (Closing)
Croatia	Hajduk Split	Dinamo Zagreb
Czech Republic	Banik Ostrava	Sparta Prague
Denmark	FC Copenhagen	FC Copenhagen
Ecuador	Deportivo Cuenca	
England	Arsenal	Manchester United
Finland	HJK Helsinki	HJK Helsinki
France	Lyon	Paris St Germain
Georgia	WIT-Georgia	Dinamo Tbilisi
Germany	Werder Bremen	Werder Bremen
Greece	Panathinaikos	Panathinaikos
Holland	Ajax	Utrecht
Hungary	Ferencvaros	Ferencvaros
Ireland	Shelbourne	Longford Town
Israel	Maccabi Haifa	Hapoel Bnei Sakhnin
Italy	AC Milan	Lazio
Japan	Yokohama Marinos	Jubilo Iwata
Mexico	Pachuca (Opening)	Pumas (Closing)
Morocco	Raja	FAR
Nigeria	Enyimba	Julius Berger
Northern Ireland	Linfield	Glentoran
Norway	Rosenborg	Rosenborg
Paraguay	Cerro Porteno	
Peru	Alianza Lima	
Poland	Wisla Krakow	Lech
Portugal	FC Porto	Benfica
Romania	Dinamo	Dinamo
Russia	Lokomotiv Moscow	Terek Grozny
Saudi Arabia	Al-Shabab	Al-Ittihad
Scotland	Celtic	Celtic
Senegal	Jeanne D'Arc	AS Douanes
Serbia & Montenegro	Red Star Belgrade	Red Star Belgrade
Slovakia	Zilina	Petrzalka
Slovenia	Gorica	Maribor
South Africa	Kaizer Chiefs	
South Korea	Songnam	Chonbuk Hyundai
Spain	Valencia	Zaragoza
Sweden	Djurgaarden	Elfsborg
Switzerland	Basle	Wil
Tunisia	Esperance	Stade Tunisien
Turkey	Fenerbahce	Trabzonspor
Ukraine	Dynamo Kiev	Shakhtar Donetsk
United States (MLS)	San Jose Earthquakes	
Uruguay	Danubio	
Venezuela	Caracas FC	

UEFA Champions League

Season	Result			
2001–02	Real Madrid (Spain)	2	Bayer 04 Leverkusen (Ger.)	1
2002–03	AC Milan (Italy)*	0	Juventus (Italy)	0
2003–04	**Porto (Port.)**	**3**	**Monaco (Fr.)**	**0**

*Won on penalty kicks.

UEFA Cup

Season	Result			
2001–02	Feyenoord (Neth.)	3	Borussia Dortmund (Ger.)	2
2002–03	Porto (Port.)*	3	Celtic (Scot.)	2
2003–04	**Valencia (Spain)**	**2**	**Olympique de Marseille (Fr.)**	**0**

*Won on "Silver Goal" in overtime.

FOOTBALL (continued)

Libertadores de América Cup

Year	Winner (country)	Runner-up (country)	Scores
2002	Olimpia (Par.)	São Caetano (Braz.)	0–1, 2–1, 4–2*
2003	Boca Juniors (Arg.)	Santos FC (Braz.)	2–0, 3–1
2004	**Once Caldas (Colom.)**	**Boca Juniors (Arg.)**	**0–0, 1–1, 2–0***

*Winner determined in penalty shoot-out.

Copa América

Year	Winner	Runner-up	Score
1999	Brazil	Uruguay	3–1
2001	Colombia	Mexico	1–0
2004	**Brazil**	**Argentina**	**2–2, 4–2***

*Winner determined in penalty shoot-out.

MLS Cup

Year	Result			
2002	Los Angeles Galaxy	1	New England Revolution	0
2003	San Jose Earthquakes	4	Chicago Fire	2
2004	**D.C. United**	**3**	**Kansas City Wizards**	**2**

U.S. College Football National Champions

Season	Champion
2002–03	Ohio State
2003–04	Louisiana State* Southern California†
2004–05	**Southern California**

*BCS champion. †AP champion.

Rose Bowl

Season	Result			
2002–03	Oklahoma	34	Washington State	14
2003–04	Southern California	28	Michigan	14
2004–05	**Texas**	**38**	**Michigan**	**37**

Orange Bowl

Season	Result			
2002–03	Southern California	38	Iowa	17
2003–04	Miami	16	Florida State	14
2004–05	**Southern California**	**55**	**Oklahoma**	**19**

Fiesta Bowl

Season	Result			
2002–03	Ohio State	31	Miami	24
2003–04	Ohio State	35	Kansas State	28
2004–05	**Utah**	**35**	**Pittsburgh**	**7**

Sugar Bowl

Season	Result			
2002–03	Georgia	26	Florida State	13
2003–04	Louisiana State	21	Oklahoma	14
2004–05	**Auburn**	**16**	**Virginia Tech**	**13**

NFL Final Standings, 2004–05

AMERICAN CONFERENCE

East Division	W	L	T	North Division	W	L	T	South Division	W	L	T	West Division	W	L	T
*New England	14	2	0	*Pittsburgh	15	1	0	*Indianapolis	12	4	0	*San Diego	12	4	0
*New York Jets	10	6	0	Baltimore	9	7	0	Jacksonville	9	7	0	*Denver	10	6	0
Buffalo	9	7	0	Cincinnati	8	8	0	Houston	7	9	0	Kansas City	7	9	0
Miami	4	12	0	Cleveland	4	12	0	Tennessee	5	11	0	Oakland	5	11	0

NATIONAL CONFERENCE

East Division	W	L	T	North Division	W	L	T	South Division	W	L	T	West Division	W	L	T
*Philadelphia	13	3	0	*Green Bay	10	6	0	*Atlanta	11	5	0	*Seattle	9	7	0
New York Giants	6	10	0	*Minnesota	8	8	0	New Orleans	8	8	0	*St. Louis	8	8	0
Dallas	6	10	0	Detroit	6	10	0	Carolina	7	9	0	Arizona	6	10	0
Washington	6	10	0	Chicago	5	11	0	Tampa Bay	5	11	0	San Francisco	2	14	0

*Qualified for play-offs.

Super Bowl

	Season	Result			
XXXVI	2001–02	New England Patriots (AFC)	20	St. Louis Rams (NFC)	17
XXXVII	2002–03	Tampa Bay Buccaneers (NFC)	48	Oakland Raiders (AFC)	21
XXXVIII	**2003–04**	**New England Patriots (AFC)**	**32**	**Carolina Panthers (NFC)**	**29**

CFL Grey Cup*

Year	Result			
2002	Montreal Alouettes (ED)	25	Edmonton Eskimos (WD)	16
2003	Edmonton Eskimos (WD)	34	Montreal Alouettes (ED)	22
2004	**Toronto Argonauts (ED)**	**27**	**British Columbia Lions (WD)**	**19**

*ED—Eastern Division; WD—Western Division.

FOOTBALL (continued)

AFL Grand Final

Year	Result			
2002	Brisbane Lions	10.15 (75)	Collingwood	9.12 (66)
2003	Brisbane Lions	20.14 (134)	Collingwood	12.12 (84)
2004	**Port Adelaide Power**	**17.11 (113)**	**Brisbane Lions**	**10.13 (73)**

Rugby Union World Cup

Year	Result			
1995	South Africa	15	New Zealand	12
1999	Australia	35	France	12
2003	England	20	Australia	17

Rugby League World Cup

Year	Result			
1992	Australia	10	Great Britain	6
1995	Australia	16	England	8
2000	Australia	40	New Zealand	12

Six Nations Championship*

Year	Result
2002	France*
2003	England*
2004	**France***

*Grand Slam winner.

GOLF

Masters Tournament

Year	Winner
2002	T. Woods (U.S.)
2003	M. Weir (Can.)
2004	**P. Mickelson (U.S.)**

United States Open Championship (men)

Year	Winner
2002	T. Woods (U.S.)
2003	J. Furyk (U.S.)
2004	**R. Goosen (S.Af.)**

British Open Tournament (men)

Year	Winner
2002	E. Els (S.Af.)
2003	B. Curtis (U.S.)
2004	**T. Hamilton (U.S.)**

U.S. Professional Golfers' Association (PGA) Championship

Year	Winner
2002	R. Beem (U.S.)
2003	S. Micheel (U.S.)
2004	**V. Singh (Fiji)**

United States Amateur Championship (men)

Year	Winner
2002	R. Barnes (U.S.)
2003	N. Flanagan (Austl.)
2004	**R. Moore (U.S.)**

British Amateur Championship (men)

Year	Winner
2002	A. Larrazabal (Spain)
2003	G. Wolstenholme (U.K.)
2004	**S. Wilson (U.K.)**

United States Women's Open Championship

Year	Winner
2002	J. Inkster (U.S.)
2003	H. Lunke (U.S.)
2004	**M. Mallon (U.S.)**

Women's British Open Championship

Year	Winner
2002	K. Webb (Austl.)
2003	A. Sörenstam (Swed.)
2004	**K. Stupples (U.K.)**

AP/Wide World Photos

Meg Mallon savours her victory in the U.S. Women's Open golf championship.

Ladies Professional Golf Association (LPGA) Championship

Year	Winner
2002	Pak Se Ri (S.Kor.)
2003	A. Sörenstam (Swed.)
2004	**A. Sörenstam (Swed.)**

United States Women's Amateur Championship

Year	Winner
2002	B. Lucidi (U.S.)
2003	V. Nirapathpongporn (Thai.)
2004	**J. Park (U.S.)**

Ladies' British Amateur Championship

Year	Winner
2002	R. Hudson (U.K.)
2003	E. Serramia (Spain)
2004	**L. Stahle (Swed.)**

World Cup (men; professional)

Year	Winner
2002	Japan (T. Izawa and S. Maruyama)
2003	South Africa (T. Immelman and R. Sabbatini)
2004	**England (P. Casey and L. Donald)**

Solheim Cup (women; professional)

Year	Result
2000	Europe 14½, United States 11½
2002	United States 15½, Europe 12½
2003	Europe 17½, United States 10½

Ryder Cup (men; professional)

Year	Result
1999	United States 14½, Europe 13½
2002	Europe 15½, United States 12½
2004	**Europe 18½, United States 9½**

GYMNASTICS

World Gymnastics Championships—Men

Year	All-around team	All-around individual	Horizontal bar	Parallel bars
2002	not held	not held	V. Maras (Greece)	Li Xiaopeng (China)
2003	China	P. Hamm (U.S.)	T. Kashima (Japan)	Li Xiaopeng (China)
2004*	**Japan**	**P. Hamm (U.S.)**	**I. Cassina (Italy)**	**V. Goncharov (Ukr.)**

Year	Pommel horse	Rings	Vault	Floor exercise
2002	M. Urzica (Rom.)	S. Csollany (Hung.)	Li Xiaopeng (China)	M. Dragulescu (Rom.)
2003	Teng Haibin (China)† T. Kashima (Japan)†	I. Iovchev (Bulg.)† D. Tampakos (Greece)†	Li Xiaopeng (China)	P. Hamm (U.S.)† I. Iovchev (Bulg.)†
2004*	**Teng Haibin (China)**	**D. Tampakos (Greece)**	**G. Deferr (Spain)**	**K. Shewfelt (Can.)**

*Olympic champions. †Tied.

World Gymnastics Championships—Women

Year	All-around team	All-around individual	Balance beam
2002	not held	not held	A. Postell (U.S.)
2003	United States	S. Khorkina (Russia)	Fan Ye (China)
2004*	**Romania**	**C. Patterson (U.S.)**	**C. Ponor (Rom.)**

Year	Uneven parallel bars	Vault	Floor exercise
2002	C. Kupets (U.S.)	Ye. Zamolodchikova (Russia)	E. Gómez (Spain)
2003	C. Memmel (U.S.)† H. Vise (U.S.)†	O. Chusovitina (Uzbek.)	D. Dos Santos (Braz.)
2004*	**E. Lepennec (Fr.)**	**M. Rosu (Rom.)**	**C. Ponor (Rom.)**

*Olympic champions. †Tied.

Olympic gymnastics all-around champion Paul Hamm of the U.S. (centre) is flanked by the South Korean silver (right) and bronze medalists.

ICE HOCKEY

NHL Final Standings, 2004

EASTERN CONFERENCE

Northeast Division	W	L	T	OTL*
†Boston	41	19	15	7
†Toronto	45	24	10	3
†Ottawa	43	23	10	6
†Montreal	41	30	7	4
Buffalo	37	34	7	4

Atlantic Division	W	L	T	OTL*
†Philadelphia	40	21	15	6
†New Jersey	43	25	12	2
†New York Islanders	38	29	11	4
New York Rangers	27	40	7	8
Pittsburgh	23	47	8	4

Southeast Division	W	L	T	OTL*
†Tampa Bay	46	22	8	6
Atlanta	33	37	8	4
Carolina	28	34	14	6
Florida	28	35	15	4
Washington	23	46	10	3

WESTERN CONFERENCE

Central Division	W	L	T	OTL*
†Detroit	48	21	11	2
†St. Louis	39	30	11	2
†Nashville	38	29	11	4
Columbus	25	45	8	4
Chicago	20	43	11	8

Northwest Division	W	L	T	OTL*
†Vancouver	43	24	10	5
†Colorado	40	22	13	7
†Calgary	42	30	7	3
Edmonton	36	29	12	5
Minnesota	30	29	20	3

Pacific Division	W	L	T	OTL*
†San Jose	43	21	12	6
†Dallas	41	26	13	2
Los Angeles	28	29	16	9
Anaheim	29	35	10	8
Phoenix	22	36	18	6

*Overtime losses, worth one point. †Qualified for play-offs.

The Stanley Cup

Season	Winner	Runner-up	Games
2001–02	Detroit Red Wings	Carolina Hurricanes	4–1
2002–03	New Jersey Devils	Anaheim Mighty Ducks	4–3
2003–04	**Tampa Bay Lightning**	**Calgary Flames**	**4–3**

World Ice Hockey Championship—Men

Year	Winner
2002	Slovakia
2003	Canada
2004	**Canada**

World Ice Hockey Championship—Women

Year	Winner
2002	*not held*
2003	*canceled*
2004	**Canada**

ICE SKATING

World Figure Skating Champions—Men

Year	Winner
2002	A. Yagudin (Russia)
2003	Ye. Plushchenko (Russia)
2004	**Ye. Plushchenko (Russia)**

World Figure Skating Champions—Women

Year	Winner
2002	I. Slutskaya (Russia)
2003	M. Kwan (U.S.)
2004	**S. Arakawa (Japan)**

World Figure Skating Champions—Pairs

Year	Winners
2002	Shen Xue, Zhao Hongbo (China)
2003	Shen Xue, Zhao Hongbo (China)
2004	**T. Totmyanina, M. Marinin (Russia)**

World Ice Dancing Champions

Year	Winners
2002	I. Lobachyova, I. Averbukh (Russia)
2003	S. Bourne, V. Kraatz (Can.)
2004	**T. Navka, R. Kostomarov (Russia)**

Dutch teammates and world speed-skating sprint champions Erben Wennemars (left) and Marianne Timmer salute the crowd.

ICE SKATING (continued)

World Ice Speed-Skating Records Set in 2004 on Major Tracks*

Event	Name	Country	Result
MEN			
all-round	Mark Tuitert	Netherlands	151.691 points
	Chad Hedrick	United States	150.478 points
team pursuit	United States National Team	United States	3 min 48.56 sec
	Netherlands National Team	Netherlands	3 min 46.44 sec
WOMEN			
team pursuit	Canada National Team	Canada	3 min 05.49 sec
	Canada National Team	Canada	3 min 03.07 sec

*May include records awaiting ISU ratification at year's end.

World Ice Speed-Skating Records Set in 2004 on Short Tracks*

Event	Name	Country	Time
MEN			
1,000 m	Li Jiajun	China	1 min 24.674 sec
WOMEN			
11,500 m	Jung Eun Ju	South Korea	2 min 18.861 sec

*May include records awaiting ISU ratification at year's end.

World All-Around Speed-Skating Champions

Year	Men	Women
2002	J. Uytdehaage (Neth.)	A. Friesinger (Ger.)
2003	G. Romme (Neth.)	C. Klassen (Can.)
2004	**C. Hedrick (U.S.)**	**R. Groenewold (Neth.)**

World Short-Track Speed-Skating Championships—Overall Winners

Year	Men	Women
2002	Kim Dong Sung (S.Kor.)	Yang Yang (A) (China)
2003	Ahn Hyun Soo (S.Kor.)	Choi Eun Kyung (S.Kor.)
2004	**Ahn Hyun Soo (S.Kor.)**	**Choi Eun Kyung (S.Kor.)**

World Speed-Skating Sprint Champions

Year	Men	Women
2002	J. Wotherspoon (Can.)	C. LeMay Doan (Can.)
2003	J. Wotherspoon (Can.)	M. Garbrecht-Enfeldt (Ger.)
2004	**E. Wennemars (Neth.)**	**M. Timmer (Neth.)**

JUDO

World Judo Championships—Men

Year	Open weights	60 kg	66 kg	73 kg
1999	S. Shinohara (Japan)	M. Poulot (Cuba)	L. Benboudaoud (Fr.)	J. Pedro (U.S.)
2001	A. Mikhaylin (Russia)	A. Lounifi (Tun.)	A. Miresmaeili (Iran)	V. Makarov (Russia)
2003	K. Suzuki (Japan)	Choi Min Ho (S.Kor.)	A. Miresmaeili (Iran)	Lee Won Hee (S.Kor.)
Year	**81 kg**	**90 kg**	**100 kg**	**+100 kg**
1999	G. Randall (U.K.)	H. Yoshida (Japan)	K. Inoue (Japan)	S. Shinohara (Japan)
2001	Cho In Chul (S.Kor.)	F. Demontfaucon (Fr.)	K. Inoue (Japan)	A. Mikhaylin (Russia)
2003	F. Wanner (Ger.)	Hwang Hee Tae (S.Kor.)	K. Inoue (Japan)	Y. Muneta (Japan)

World Judo Championships—Women

Year	Open weights	48 kg	52 kg	57 kg
1999	D. Beltran (Cuba)	R. Tamura (Japan)	N. Narasaki (Japan)	D. González (Cuba)
2001	C. Lebrun (Fr.)	R. Tamura (Japan)	Kye Sun Hui (N.Kor.)	Y. Lupetey (Cuba)
2003	Tong Wen (China)	R. Tamura (Japan)	A. Savon (Cuba)	Kye Sun Hui (N.Kor.)
Year	**63 kg**	**70 kg**	**78 kg**	**+78 kg**
1999	K. Maeda (Japan)	S. Veranes (Cuba)	N. Anno (Japan)	B. Maksymow (Pol.)
2001	G. Vandecaveye (Belg.)	M. Ueno (Japan)	N. Anno (Japan)	Yuan Hua (China)
2003	D. Krukower (Arg.)	M. Ueno (Japan)	N. Anno (Japan)	Sun Fuming (China)

ROWING

World Rowing Championships—Men

Year	Single sculls	Min:sec	Double sculls	Min:sec	Quadruple sculls	Min:sec	Coxed pairs	Min:sec
2002	M. Hacker (Ger.)	6:36.33	A. Haller, T. Peto (Hung.)	6:05.74	Germany	5:39.57	L. Krisch, A. Werner (Ger.)	6:47.93
2003	O. Tufte (Nor.)	6:46.15	A. Hardy, S. Vieilledent (Fr.)	6:13.93	Germany	6:12.26	D. Berry, M. Rich (U.S.)	7:10.11
2004*	**O. Tufte (Nor.)**	**6:49.30**	**A. Hardy, S. Vieilledent (Fr.)**	**6:29.00**	**Russia**	**5:56.85**	**M. Palmisano, M. Trombetta**	**(Italy)**

Year	Coxless pairs	Min:sec	Coxed fours	Min:sec	Coxless fours	Min:sec	Eights	Min:sec
2002	J. Cracknell, M. Pinsent (Gr.Brit.)	6:14.27	Great Britain	6:06.70	Germany	5:41.35	Canada	5:26.92
2003	D. Ginn, J. Tomkins (Austl.)	6:19.31	United States	6:04.68	Canada	5:52.91	Canada	6:00.44
2004*	**D. Ginn, J. Tomkins (Austl.)**	**6:30.76**	**Italy**	**6:11.53**	**Great Britain**	**6:06.98**	**United States**	

*Olympic champions, except coxed pairs and coxed fours.

World Rowing Championships—Women

Year	Single sculls	Min:sec	Coxless pairs	Min:sec
2002	R. Neykova (Bulg.)	7:07.71	G. Andrunache-Damian, V. Susanu (Rom.)	6:53.80
2003	R. Neykova (Bulg.)	7:18.12	C. Bishop, K. Grainger (Gt.Brit.)	7:04.88
2004*	**K. Rutschow-Stomporowski (Ger.)**	**7:18.12**	**G. Andrunache, V. Susanu (Rom.)**	**7:06.55**

Year	Double sculls	Min:sec	Coxless fours	Min:sec
2002	G. Evers-Swindell, C. Evers-Swindell (N.Z.)	6:38.78	Australia	6:26.11
2003	G. Evers-Swindell, C. Evers-Swindell (N.Z.)	6:45.79	United States	6:53.08
2004*	**G. Evers-Swindell, C. Evers-Swindell (N.Z.)**	**7:01.79**	**France**	**6:36.28**

Year	Quadruple sculls	Min:sec	Eights	Min:sec
2002	Germany	6:15.66	United States	6:04.25
2003	Australia	6:46.52	Germany	6:41.23
2004	**Germany**	**6:29.29**	**Romania**	**6:17.70**

*Olympic champions, except coxless fours.

German rower Katrin Rutschow-Stomporowski kisses her gold medal.

AP/Wide World Photos

SAILING (YACHTING)

America's Cup

Year	Winning yacht	Owner	Skipper	Losing yacht	Owner
1995	*Black Magic* (N.Z.)	P. Blake and Team New Zealand	R. Coutts	*Young America* (U.S.)	Pact 95 syndicate
2000	*Black Magic* (N.Z.)	Team New Zealand	R. Coutts	*Luna Rossa* (Italy)	Prada Challenge
2003	*Alinghi* (Switz.)	Alinghi Swiss Challenge	R. Coutts	*New Zealand* (N.Z.)	Team New Zealand

World Class Boat Champions, 2004

Class	Winner	Country
Etchells 22	P. McNeill/P. Turner/G. Torpy	Australia
Europe	S. Sundby	Norway
Finn	B. Ainslie	Great Britain
J/24	J. Hookanson	United States
Laser	R. Scheidt	Brazil
Lightning	T. González	Chile
Mistral (men's)	J. Bontemps	France
Mistral (women's)	A. Sensini	Italy
470 (men's)	N. Wilmot/M. Page	Australia
470 (women's)	T. Torgersson/V. Zachrisson	Sweden
49er	I. Martinez/X. Fernandez	Spain
2.4 metre	S. Berlin	Sweden
Optimist	Wei Ni	China
Soling	G. Warburg	Argentina
Snipe (women's)	A. Foglia/M. Foglia	Uruguay
Star	F. Loof/A. Ekstrom	Sweden
Tornado	S. Lange/C. Espinola	Argentina
Farr 40	J. Richardson	United States

Admiral's Cup

Year	Winning team
1999	Netherlands
2001	*canceled*
2003	Australia

Transpacific Race

Year	Winning yacht	Owner
1999	*Grand Illusion*	J. McDowell
2001	*Bull*	S. Radow
2003	*Alta Vita*	B. Turpin

Bermuda Race*

Year	Winning yacht	Owner
2000	*Restless*	E. Crawford
2002	*Zaraffa*	S. Sheldon
2004	***Alliance***	**D. Porco**

*St. David's Lighthouse Trophy winner from 2002.

SKIING

World Alpine Skiing Championships—Slalom

Year	Men's slalom	Men's giant slalom	Men's supergiant	Women's slalom	Women's giant slalom	Women's supergiant
2001	M. Matt (Austria)	M. von Grünigen (Switz.)	D. Rahlves (U.S.)	A. Pärson (Swed.)	S. Nef (Switz.)	R. Cavagnoud (Fr.)
2002*	J.-P. Vidal (Fr.)	S. Eberharter (Austria)	K.A. Aamodt (Nor.)	J. Kostelic (Cro.)	J. Kostelic (Cro.)	D. Ceccarelli (Italy)
2003	I. Kostelic (Cro.)	B. Miller (U.S.)	S. Eberharter (Austria)	J. Kostelic (Cro.)	A. Pärson (Swed.)	M. Dorfmeister (Austria)

*Olympic champions.

World Alpine Skiing Championships—Downhill

Year	Men	Women
2001	H. Trinkl (Austria)	M. Dorfmeister (Austria)
2002*	F. Strobl (Austria)	C. Montillet (Fr.)
2003	M. Walchhofer (Austria)	M. Turgeon (Can.)

*Olympic champions.

World Alpine Skiing Championships—Combined

Year	Men	Women
2001	K.A. Aamodt (Nor.)	M. Ertl (Ger.)
2002*	K.A. Aamodt (Nor.)	J. Kostelic (Cro.)
2003	B. Miller (U.S.)	J. Kostelic (Cro.)

*Olympic champions.

World Nordic Skiing Championships—Men

Year	Sprint	Double pursuit	10-km	15-km	30-km	50-km	Relay
2001	T.A. Hetland (Nor.)		P. Elofsson (Swed.)	P. Elofsson (Swed.)	A. Veerpalu (Est.)	J. Mühlegg (Spain)	Norway
2002*	T.A. Hetland (Nor.)		T. Alsgaard (Nor.)†‡ F. Estil (Nor.)†‡	A. Veerpalu (Est.)	C. Hoffmann (Austria)‡	M. Ivanov (Russia)	Norway
2003	T. Fredriksson (Swed.)	P. Elofsson (Swed.)		A. Teichmann (Ger.)	T. Alsgaard (Nor.)	M. Koukal (Cz.Rep.)	Norway

*Olympic champions. †Tied. ‡Original winner stripped after failed drug test.

World Nordic Skiing Championships—Women

Year	Sprint	Double pursuit	5-km	10-km	15-km	30-km	Relay
2001	P. Manninen (Fin.)		V. Kuitunen (Fin.)	B. Martinsen Skari (Nor.)	B. Martinsen Skari (Nor.)	*canceled*	Russia
2002*	Yu. Chepalova (Russia)		B. Scott (Can.)†	B. Skari (Nor.)	S. Belmondo (Italy)	G. Paruzzi (Italy)	Germany
2003	M. Bjørgen (Nor.)	K. Smigun (Est.)		B. Skari (Nor.)	B. Skari (Nor.)	O. Savyalova (Russia)	Germany

*Olympic champions. †Original winner stripped after failed drug test.

World Nordic Skiing Championships—Ski Jump

Year	Normal hill (90 m)*	Large hill (120 m)†	Team jump (normal hill)	Team jump (large hill)	Nordic combined (7.5-km)	Nordic combined (15-km)	Nordic combined Team
2001	A. Malysz (Pol.)	M. Schmitt (Ger.)	Austria	Germany	M. Baacke (Ger.)	B.E. Vik (Nor.)	Norway
2002‡	S. Ammann (Switz.)	S. Ammann (Switz.)		Germany	S. Lajunen (Fin.)	S. Lajunen (Fin.)	Finland
2003	A. Malysz (Pol.)	A. Malysz (Pol.)		Finland	J. Spillane (U.S.)	R. Ackermann (Ger.)	Austria

*95-m in 2003. †116 m in 2001. ‡Olympic champions.

Alpine World Cup

Year	Men	Women
2002	S. Eberharter (Austria)	M. Dorfmeister (Austria)
2003	S. Eberharter (Austria)	J. Kostelic (Cro.)
2004	**H. Maier (Austria)**	**A. Pärson (Swed.)**

Nordic World Cup

Year	Men	Women
2002	P. Elofsson (Swed.)	B. Martinsen Skari (Nor.)
2003	M. Fredriksson (Swed.)	B. Skari (Nor.)
2004	**R. Sommerfeldt (Ger.)**	**G. Paruzzi (Italy)**

Freestyle Skiing World Cup

Year	Men	Women
2002	E. Bergoust (U.S.)	K. Traa (Nor.)
2003	D. Arkhipov (Russia)	K. Traa (Nor.)
2004	**S. Omischl (Can.)**	**K. Traa (Nor.)**

Snowboard World Cup

Year	Men	Women
2002	J.J. Anderson (Can.)	K. Ruby (Fr.)
2003	J.J. Anderson (Can.)	K. Ruby (Fr.)
2004	**J.J. Anderson (Can.)**	**J. Pomagalski (Fr.)**

American swimmer Kaitlin Sandeno is congratulated by her teammates (Carly Piper, Natalie Coughlin, and Dana Vollmer) after she clinches the foursome's Olympic gold medal and the world record in the 4 × 200-m freestyle relay.

© Chris McGrath/Getty Images

SQUASH

British Open Championship—Men

Year	Winner
2001–02	P. Nicol (Scot.)
2002–03	D. Palmer (Austl.)
2003–04	**D. Palmer (Austl.)**

British Open Championship—Women

Year	Winner
2001–02	S. Fitz-Gerald (Austl.)
2002–03	R. Grinham (Austl.)
2003–04	**R. Grinham (Austl.)**

World Open Championship—Men

Year	Winner
2002	D. Palmer (Austl.)
2003	A. Shabana (Egypt)
2004	**T. Lincou (Fr.)**

World Open Championship—Women

Year	Winner
2002	S. Fitz-Gerald (Austl.)
2003	C. Owens (N.Z.)
2004	**V. Atkinson (Neth.)**

SWIMMING

World Swimming Records Set in 2004 in 25-m Pools*

Event	Name	Country	Time
MEN			
50-m freestyle	Frederic Bousquet	France	21.10 sec
100-m freestyle	Ian Crocker	United States	46.25 sec
50-m backstroke	Thomas Rupprath	Germany	23.27 sec
100-m backstroke	Peter Marshall	United States	50.32 sec
200-m backstroke	Aaron Peirsol	United States	1 min 50.64 sec
	Aaron Peirsol	United States	1 min 50.52 sec
200-m breaststroke	Ed Moses	United States	2 min 2.92 sec
50-m butterfly	Ian Crocker	United States	22.71 sec
100-m butterfly	Ian Crocker	United States	49.77 sec
	Ian Crocker	United States	49.07 sec
200-m individual medley	George Bovell	Trinidad and Tobago	1 min 53.93 sec
4 × 100-m medley relay	Univ. of Texas	United States	3 min 25.38 sec
	United States National Team	United States	3 min 25.09 sec
WOMEN			
800-m freestyle	Sachiko Yamada	Japan	8 min 13.35 sec
1,500-m freestyle	Laure Manaudou	France	15 min 42.39 sec
50-m breaststroke	Jade Edmistone	Australia	29.90 sec
100-m breaststroke	Tara Kirk	United States	1 min 4.79 sec
200-m butterfly	Yang Yu	China	2 min 4.04 sec
4 × 50-m freestyle relay†	Univ. of Georgia	United States	1 min 37.27 sec
4 × 50-m medley relay†	Netherlands National Team	Netherlands	1 min 48.21 sec
4 × 100-m medley relay	Australia National Team	Australia	3 min 54.95 sec

*May include records awaiting FINA ratification at year's end.
†Not an officially ratified event; best performance on record.

World Swimming Records Set in 2004 in 50-m Pools*

Event	Name	Country	Time
MEN			
100-m backstroke	Aaron Peirsol	United States	53.45 sec
200-m backstroke	Aaron Peirsol	United States	1 min 54.74 sec
100-m breaststroke	Brendan Hansen	United States	59.30 sec
200-m breaststroke	Brendan Hansen	United States	2 min 9.04 sec
50-m butterfly	Ian Crocker	United States	23.30 sec
100-m butterfly	Ian Crocker	United States	50.76 sec
400-m individual medley	Michael Phelps	United States	4 min 8.41 sec
	Michael Phelps	United States	4 min 8.26 sec
4 × 100-m freestyle relay	South Africa National Team	South Africa	3 min 13.17 sec
4 × 100-m medley relay	United States National Team	United States	3 min 30.68 sec
WOMEN			
100-m freestyle	Lisbeth Lenton	Australia	53.66 sec
	Jodie Henry	Australia	53.52 sec
200-m breaststroke	Leisel Jones	Australia	2 min 22.96 sec
	Amanda Beard	United States	2 min 22.44 sec
4 × 100-m freestyle relay	Australia National Team	Australia	3 min 35.94 sec
4 × 200-m freestyle relay	United States National Team	United States	7 min 53.42 sec
4 × 100-m medley relay	Australia National Team	Australia	3 min 57.32 sec

*May include records awaiting FINA ratification at year's end.

World Swimming and Diving Championships—Men

Year	Freestyle 50 m	100 m	200 m	400 m	800 m	1,500 m
1998	B. Pilczuk (U.S.)	A. Popov (Russia)	M. Klim (Austl.)	I. Thorpe (Austl.)		G. Hackett (Austl.)
2001	A. Ervin (U.S.)	A. Ervin (U.S.)	I. Thorpe (Austl.)	I. Thorpe (Austl.)	I. Thorpe (Austl.)	G. Hackett (Austl.)
2003	A. Popov (Russia)	A. Popov (Russia)	I. Thorpe (Austl.)	I. Thorpe (Austl.)	G. Hackett (Austl.)	G. Hackett (Austl.)

Year	Backstroke 50 m	Backstroke 100 m	Backstroke 200 m	Breaststroke 50 m	Breaststroke 100 m	Breaststroke 200 m
1998		L. Krayzelburg (U.S.)	L. Krayzelburg (U.S.)		F. De Burghgraeve (Belg.)	K. Grote (U.S.)
2001	R. Bal (U.S.)	M. Welsh (Austl.)	A. Peirsol (U.S.)	O. Lisogor (Ukr.)	R. Sludnov (Russia)	B. Hansen (U.S.)
2003	T. Rupprath (Ger.)	A. Peirsol (U.S.)	A. Peirsol (U.S.)	J. Gibson (U.K.)	K. Kitajima (Japan)	K. Kitajima (Japan)

Year	Butterfly 50 m	Butterfly 100 m	Butterfly 200 m	Individual medley 200 m	Individual medley 400 m	Team relays 4 × 100-m freestyle
1998		M. Klim (Austl.)	D. Silantyev (Ukr.)	M. Wouda (Neth.)	T. Dolan (U.S.)	United States
2001	G. Huegill (Austl.)	L. Frölander (Swed.)	M. Phelps (U.S.)	M. Rosolino (Italy)	A. Boggiatto (Italy)	Australia
2003	M. Welsh (Austl.)	I. Crocker (U.S.)	M. Phelps (U.S.)	M. Phelps (U.S.)	M. Phelps (U.S.)	Russia

Year	4 × 200-m freestyle	4 × 100-m medley	Diving 1-m springboard	3-m springboard	Platform	3-m synchronized	10-m synchronized
1998	Australia	Australia	Yu Zhuocheng (China)	D. Sautin (Russia)	D. Sautin (Russia)	China	China
2001	Australia	Australia	Wang Feng (China)	D. Sautin (Russia)	Tian Liang (China)	China	China
2003	Australia	United States	Xu Xiang (China)	A. Dobrosok (Russia)	A. Despatie (Can.)	Russia	Australia

SWIMMING (continued)

World Swimming and Diving Championships—Women

	Freestyle					
Year	50 m	100 m	200 m	400 m	800 m	1,500 m
1998	A. Van Dyken (U.S.)	J. Thompson (U.S.)	C. Poll (C.Rica)	Chen Yan (China)	B. Bennett (U.S.)	
2001	I. de Bruijn (Neth.)	I. de Bruijn (Neth.)	G. Rooney (Austl.)	Ya. Klochkova (Ukr.)	H. Stockbauer (Ger.)	H. Stockbauer (Ger.)
2003	I. de Bruijn (Neth.)	H.-M. Seppälä (Fin.)	A. Popchanka (Bela.)	H. Stockbauer (Ger.)	H. Stockbauer (Ger.)	H. Stockbauer (Ger.)

	Backstroke			Breaststroke		
	50 m	100 m	200 m	50 m	100 m	200 m
1998		L. Maurer (U.S.)	R. Maracineanu (Fr.)		K. Kowal (U.S.)	A. Kovacs (Hung.)
2001	H. Cope (U.S.)	N. Coughlin (U.S.)	D. Mocanu (Rom.)	Luo Xuejuan (China)	Luo Xuejuan (China)	A. Kovacs (Hung.)
2003	N. Zhivanevskaya (Spain)	A. Buschschulte (Ger.)	K. Sexton (U.K.)	Luo Xuejuan (China)	Luo Xuejuan (China)	A. Beard (U.S.)

	Butterfly			Individual medley		Team relays
	50 m	100 m	200 m	200 m	400 m	4 × 100-m freestyle
1998		J. Thompson (U.S.)	S. O'Neill (Austl.)	Wu Yanyan (China)	Chen Yan (China)	United States
2001	I. de Bruijn (Neth.)	P. Thomas (Austl.)	P. Thomas (Austl.)	M. Bowen (U.S.)	Ya. Klochkova (Ukr.)	Germany
2003	I. de Bruijn (Neth.)	J. Thompson (U.S.)	O. Jedrzejczak (Pol.)	Ya. Klochkova (Ukr.)	Ya. Klochkova (Ukr.)	United States

			Diving				
	4 × 200-m freestyle	4 × 100-m medley	1-m springboard	3-m springboard	Platform	3-m synchronized	10-m synchronized
1998	Germany	United States	I. Lashko (Russia)	Y. Pakhalina (Russia)	O. Zhupina (Ukr.)	Russia	Ukraine
2001	United Kingdom	Australia	B. Hartley (Can.)	Guo Jingjing (China)	Xu Mian (China)	China	China
2003	United States	China	I. Lashko (Austl.)	Guo Jingjing (China)	E. Heymans (Can.)	China	China

TABLE TENNIS

World Table Tennis Championships—Men

Year	St. Bride's Vase (singles)	Iran Cup (doubles)
1999	Liu Guoliang (China)	Kong Linghui, Liu Guoliang (China)
2001	Wang Liqin (China)	Wang Liqin, Yan Sen (China)
2003	W. Schlager (Austria)	Wang Liqin, Yan Sen (China)

World Table Tennis Championships—Women

Year	G. Geist Prize (singles)	W.J. Pope Trophy (doubles)
1999	Wang Nan (China)	Wang Nan, Li Ju (China)
2001	Wang Nan (China)	Wang Nan, Li Ju (China)
2003	Wang Nan (China)	Wang Nan, Zhang Yining (China)

World Table Tennis Championships—Mixed

Year	Heydusek Prize
1999	Ma Lin, Zhang Yingying (China)
2001	Qin Zhijian, Yang Ying (China)
2003	Ma Lin, Wang Nan (China)

World Table Tennis Championships—Team

Year	Swaythling Cup (men)	Corbillon Cup (women)
2000	Sweden	China
2001	China	China
2004	**China**	**China**

Table Tennis World Cup

Year	Men
2002	T. Boll (Ger.)
2003	Ma Lin (China)
2004	**Ma Lin (China)**

Year	Women
2002	Zhang Yining (China)
2003	Wang Nan (China)
2004	**Zhang Yining (China)**

TENNIS

Australian Open Tennis Championships—Singles

Year	Men	Women
2002	T. Johansson (Swed.)	J. Capriati (U.S.)
2003	A. Agassi (U.S.)	S. Williams (U.S.)
2004	**R. Federer (Switz.)**	**J. Henin-Hardenne (Belg.)**

Australian Open Tennis Championships—Doubles

Year	Men	Women
2002	M. Knowles, D. Nestor	M. Hingis, A. Kournikova
2003	M. Llodra, F. Santoro	S. Williams, V. Williams
2004	**M. Llodra, F. Santoro**	**V. Ruano Pascual, P. Suárez**

French Open Tennis Championships—Singles

Year	Men	Women
2002	A. Costa (Spain)	S. Williams (U.S.)
2003	J.C. Ferrero (Spain)	J. Henin-Hardenne (Belg.)
2004	**G. Gaudio (Arg.)**	**A. Myskina (Russia)**

French Open Tennis Championships—Doubles

Year	Men	Women
2002	P. Haarhuis, Ye. Kafelnikov	V. Ruano Pascual, P. Suárez
2003	B. Bryan, M. Bryan	K. Clijsters, A. Sugiyama
2004	**X. Malisse, O. Rochus**	**V. Ruano Pascual, P. Suárez**

All-England (Wimbledon) Tennis Championships—Singles

Year	Men	Women
2002	L. Hewitt (Austl.)	S. Williams (U.S.)
2003	R. Federer (Switz.)	S. Williams (U.S.)
2004	**R. Federer (Switz.)**	**M. Sharapova (Russia)**

All-England (Wimbledon) Tennis Championships—Doubles

Year	Men	Women
2002	J. Bjorkman, T. Woodbridge	S. Williams, V. Williams
2003	J. Bjorkman, T. Woodbridge	K. Clijsters, A. Sugiyama
2004	**J. Bjorkman, T. Woodbridge**	**C. Black, R. Stubbs**

TENNIS (continued)

United States Open Tennis Championships—Singles

Year	Men	Women
2002	P. Sampras (U.S.)	S. Williams (U.S.)
2003	A. Roddick (U.S.)	J. Henin-Hardenne (Belg.)
2004	**R. Federer (Switz.)**	**S. Kuznetsova (Russia)**

United States Open Tennis Championships—Doubles

Year	Men	Women
2002	M. Bhupathi, M. Mirnyi	V. Ruano Pascual, P. Suárez
2003	J. Bjorkman, T. Woodbridge	V. Ruano Pascual, P. Suárez
2004	**M. Knowles, D. Nestor**	**V. Ruano Pascual, P. Suárez**

Davis Cup (men)

Year	Winner	Runner-up	Results
2002	Russia	France	3–2
2003	Australia	Spain	3–1
2004	**Spain**	**United States**	**3–2**

Fed Cup (women)

Year	Winner	Runner-up	Results
2002	Slovakia	Spain	3–1
2003	France	United States	4–1
2004	**Russia**	**France**	**3–2**

AP/Wide World Photos

Virginia Ruano Pascual of Spain (left) and Paola Suárez of Argentina leave the court together after winning the Australian Open doubles title in January; it was the first of three Grand Slam tennis titles for the pair in 2004.

TRACK AND FIELD SPORTS (ATHLETICS)

World Outdoor Track and Field Championships—Men

Event	2001	2003
100 m	M. Greene (U.S.)	K. Collins (S.Kitts)
200 m	K. Kederis (Greece)	J. Capel (U.S.)
400 m	A. Moncur (Bahamas)	J. Young (U.S.)
800 m	A. Bucher (Switz.)	D. Saïd-Guerni (Alg.)
1,500 m	H. El Guerrouj (Mor.)	H. El Guerrouj (Mor.)
5,000 m	R. Limo (Kenya)	E. Kipchoge (Kenya)
10,000 m	C. Kamathi (Kenya)	K. Bekele (Eth.)
steeplechase	R. Kosgei (Kenya)	S.S. Shaheen (Qatar)
110-m hurdles	A. Johnson (U.S.)	A. Johnson (U.S.)
400-m hurdles	F. Sánchez (Dom.Rep.)	F. Sánchez (Dom.Rep.)
marathon	G. Abera (Eth.)	J. Gharib (Mor.)
20-km walk	R. Rasskazov (Russia)	J. Pérez (Ecua.)
50-km walk	R. Korzeniowski (Pol.)	R. Korzeniowski (Pol.)
4 × 100-m relay	United States (M. Grimes, B. Williams, D. Mitchell, T. Montgomery)	United States (J. Capel, B. Williams, D. Patton, J.J. Johnson)
4 × 400-m relay	United States (L. Byrd, A. Pettigrew, D. Brew, A. Taylor)	France (L Djhone, N. Keïta, S. Diagana, M. Raquil)*
high jump	M. Buss (Ger.)	J. Freitag (S.Af.)
pole vault	D. Markov (Austl.)	G. Gibilisco (Italy)
long jump	I. Pedroso (Cuba)	D. Phillips (U.S.)
triple jump	J. Edwards (U.K.)	C. Olsson (Swed.)
shot put	J. Godina (U.S.)	A. Mikhnevich (Bela.)
discus throw	L. Riedel (Ger.)	V. Alekna (Lith.)
hammer throw	S. Ziolkowski (Pol.)	I. Tikhon (Bela.)
javelin throw	J. Zelezny (Cz.Rep.)	S. Makarov (Russia)
decathlon	T. Dvorak (Cz.Rep.)	T. Pappas (U.S.)

*Original winner stripped after one runner failed drug test.

World Outdoor Track and Field Championships—Women

Event	2001	2003
100 m	Z. Pintusevich-Block (Ukr.)	T. Edwards (U.S.)*
200 m	M. Jones (U.S.)	A. Kapachinskaya (Russia)*
400 m	A. Mbacke Thiam (Seneg.)	A. Guevara (Mex.)
800 m	M. Mutola (Mozam.)	M. Mutola (Mozam.)
1,500 m	G. Szabo (Rom.)	T. Tomashova (Russia)
5,000 m	O. Yegorova (Russia)	T. Dibaba (Eth.)
10,000 m	D. Tulu (Eth.)	B. Adere (Eth.)
100-m hurdles	A. Kirkland (U.S.)	P. Felicien (Can.)
400-m hurdles	N. Bidouane (Mor.)	J. Pittman (Austl.)
marathon	L. Simon (Rom.)	C. Ndereba (Kenya)
20-km walk	O. Ivanova (Russia)	Ye. Nikolayeva (Russia)
4 × 100-m relay	Germany ((M. Paschke, G. Rockmeier, B. Rockmeier, M. Wagner)*	France (P. Girard, M. Hurtis, S. Félix, C. Arron)
4 × 400-m relay	Jamaica (S. Richards, C. Scott, D.-A. Parris, L. Fenton)	United States (M. Barber, D. Washington, J. Miles Clark, S. Richards)
high jump	H. Cloete (S.Afr.)	H. Cloete (S.Af.)
pole vault	S. Dragila (U.S.)	S. Feofanova (Russia)
long jump	F. May (Italy)	E. Barber (Fr.)
triple jump	T. Lebedeva (Russia)	T. Lebedeva (Russia)
shot put	Ya. Korolchik (Bela.)	S. Krivelyova (Russia)
discus throw	N. Sadova (Russia)	I. Yachenko (Bela.)
hammer throw	Y. Moreno (Cuba)	Y. Moreno (Cuba)
javelin throw	O. Menéndez (Cuba)	M. Manjani (Greece)
heptathlon	Ye. Prokhorova (Russia)	C. Klüft (Swed.)

*Original winner stripped after failed drug test.

TRACK AND FIELD SPORTS (ATHLETICS) (continued)

World Indoor Track and Field Championships—Men

Event	2003	2004
60 m	J. Gatlin (U.S.)	J. Gardener (Gr.Brit.)
200 m	M. Devonish (Gr.Brit.)	D. Demeritte (Bah.)
400 m	T. Washington (U.S.)	A. Francique (Grenada)
800 m	D. Krummenacker (U.S.)	M. Mulaudzi (S.Af.)
1,500 m	D. Maazouzi (Fr.)	P. Korir (Kenya)
3,000 m	H. Gebrselassie (Eth.)	B. Lagat (Kenya)
60-m hurdles	A. Johnson (U.S.)	A. Johnson (U.S.)
4 × 400-m relay	United States (J. Davis, J. Young, M. Campbell, T. Washington)	Jamaica (G. Haughton, L. Colquhoun, M. McDonald, D. Clarke)
high jump	S. Holm (Swed.)	S. Holm (Swed.)
pole vault	T. Lobinger (Ger.)	I. Pavlov (Russia)
long jump	D. Phillips (U.S.)	S. Stringfellow (U.S.)
triple jump	C. Olsson (Swed.)	C. Olsson (Swed.)
shot put	M. Martínez (Spain)	C. Cantwell (U.S.)
heptathlon	T. Pappas (U.S.)	R. Sebrle (Cz.Rep.)

World Indoor Track and Field Championships—Women

Event	2003	2004
60 m	Z. Block (Ukr.)	G. Devers (U.S.)
200 m	M. Collins (U.S.)	N. Safronnikova (Bela.)*
400 m	N. Nazarova (Russia)	N. Nazarova (Russia)
800 m	M. Mutola (Mozam.)	M. Mutola (Mozam.)
1,500 m	R. Jacobs (U.S.)	K. Dulecha (Eth.)
3,000 m	B. Adere (Eth.)	M. Defar (Eth.)
60-m hurdles	G. Devers (U.S.)	P. Felicien (Can.)
4 × 400-m relay	Russia (N. Antyukh, Yu. Pechonkina, O. Zykina, N. Nazarova)	Russia (O. Krasnomovets, O. Kotlyarova, T. Levina, N. Nazarova)
high jump	K. Bergqvist (Swed.)	Ye. Slesarenko (Russia)
pole vault	S. Feofanova (Russia)	Ye. Isinbayeva (Russia)
long jump	T. Kotova (Russia)	T. Lebedeva (Russia)
triple jump	A. Hansen (Gr.Brit.)	T. Lebedeva (Russia)
shot put	I. Korzhanenko (Russia)	S. Krivelyova (Russia)*
pentathlon	C. Klüft (Swed.)	N. Gomes (Port.)

*Original winner stripped after failed drug test.

2004 World Indoor Records—Men*

Event	Competitor and country	Performance
5,000 m	Kenenisa Bekele (Eth.)	12 min 49.60 sec
triple jump	Christian Olsson (Swed.)	17.83 m (58 ft 6 in)†

*May include records awaiting IAAF ratification at year's end. †Equals world record.

2004 World Indoor Records—Women*

Event	Competitor and country	Performance
500 m†	Natalya Nazarova (Russia)	1 min 07.36 sec
600 m†	Olga Kotlyarova (Russia)	1 min 23.44 sec
5,000 m	Berhane Adere (Eth.)	14 min 39.29 sec
4 × 400-m relay	Russia National Team	3 min 23.88 sec
pole vault	Yelena Isinbayeva (Russia)	4.83 m (15 ft 10 in)
	Svetlana Feofanova (Russia)	4.85 m (15 ft 11 in)
	Yelena Isinbayeva (Russia)	4.86 m (15 ft 11¼ in)
triple jump	Tatyana Lebedeva (Russia)	15.36 m (50 ft 4¾ in)

*May include records awaiting IAAF ratification at year's end. †Not an officially ratified event; best performance on record.

2004 World Outdoor Records—Men*

Event	Competitor and country	Performance
5,000 m	Kenenisa Bekele (Eth.)	12 min 37.35 sec
10,000 m	Kenenisa Bekele (Eth.)	26 min 20.31 sec
3,000-m steeplechase	Saif Saaeed Shaheen (Qatar)	7 min 53.63 sec
110-m hurdles	Liu Xiang (China)	12.91 sec†
50-km walking	Denis Nizhegorodov (Russia)	3 hr 35 min 29 sec
25-km road race	Paul Kosgei (Kenya)	1 hr 12 min 45 sec

*May include records awaiting IAAF ratification at year's end. †Equals world record.

2004 World Outdoor Records—Women*

Event	Competitor and country	Performance
5,000 m	Elvan Abeylegesse (Tur.)	14 min 24.68 sec
steeplechase	Gulnara Samitova (Russia)	9 min 1.59 sec
pole vault	Stacy Dragila (U.S.)	4.83 m (15 ft 10 in)
	Yelena Isinbayeva (Russia)	4.87 m (15 ft 11¾ in)
	Svetlana Feofanova (Russia)	4.88 m (16 ft)
	Yelena Isinbayeva (Russia)	4.89 m (16 ft ½ in)
	Yelena Isinbayeva (Russia)	4.90 m (16 ft ¾ in)
	Yelena Isinbayeva (Russia)	4.91 m (16 ft 1¼ in)
	Yelena Isinbayeva (Russia)	4.92 m (16 ft 1¾ in)
decathlon	Marie Collonvillé (Fr.)	8,150 points

*May include records awaiting IAAF ratification at year's end.

World Cross Country Championships—Men

Year	Individual	Team
2002	K. Bekele (Eth.)	Kenya
2003	K. Bekele (Eth.)	Kenya
2004	**K. Bekele (Eth.)**	**Ethiopia**

World Cross Country Championships—Women

Year	Individual	Team
2002	P. Radcliffe (U.K.)	Ethiopia
2003	W. Kidane (Eth.)	Ethiopia
2004	**B. Johnson (Austl.)**	**Ethiopia**

Boston Marathon

Year	Men	hr:min:sec
2002	R. Rop (Kenya)	2:09:02
2003	R.K. Cheruiyot (Kenya)	2:10:11
2004	**T. Cherigat (Kenya)**	**2:10:37**

Year	Women	hr:min:sec
2002	M. Okayo (Kenya)	2:20:43
2003	S. Zakharova (Russia)	2:25:20
2004	**C. Ndereba (Kenya)**	**2:24:27**

Chicago Marathon

Year	Men	hr:min:sec
2002	K. Khannouchi (U.S.)	2:05:56
2003	E. Rutto (Kenya)	2:05:50
2004	**E. Rutto (Kenya)**	**2:06:16**

Year	Women	hr:min:sec
2002	P. Radcliffe (U.K.)	2:17:18
2003	S. Zakharova (Russia)	2:23:07
2004	**C. Tomescu-Dita (Rom.)**	**2:23:45**

London Marathon

Year	Men	hr:min:sec
2002	K. Khannouchi (U.S.)	2:05:38
2003	G. Abera (Eth.)	2:07:56
2004	**E. Rutto (Kenya)**	**2:06:18**

Year	Women	hr:min:sec
2002	P. Radcliffe (U.K.)	2:18:56
2003	P. Radcliffe (U.K.)	2:15:25
2004	**M. Okayo (Kenya)**	**2:22:35**

New York City Marathon

Year	Men	hr:min:sec
2002	R. Rop (Kenya)	2:08:07
2003	M. Lel (Kenya)	2:10:30
2004	**H. Ramaala (S.Af.)**	**2:09:28**

Year	Women	hr:min:sec
2002	J. Chepchumba (Kenya)	2:25:56
2003	M. Okayo (Kenya)	2:22:31
2004	**P. Radcliffe (U.K.)**	**2:23:10**

China's gold medal-winning women's volleyball team.
AP/Wide World Photos

VOLLEYBALL

Beach Volleyball World Championships

Year	Men	Women
1999	J. Loiola, E. Rego (Braz.)	A. Behar, Shelda (Braz.)
2001	M. Baracetti, M. Conde (Arg.)	A. Behar, Shelda (Braz.)
2003	R. Santos, E. Rego (Braz.)	M. May, K. Walsh (U.S.)

World Volleyball Championships

Year	Men	Women
2000*	Yugoslavia	Cuba
2002	Brazil	Italy
2004*	**Brazil**	**China**

*Olympic champions.

WEIGHT LIFTING

World Weight Lifting Champions, 2004

MEN

Weight class	Winner and country	Performance
56 kg (123 lb)	H. Mutlu (Tur.)	295 kg (650.4 lb)
62 kg (136.5 lb)	Shi Zhiyong (China)	325 kg (716.5 lb)
69 kg (152 lb)	Zhang Gouzheng (China)	347.5kg (766.1 lb)
77 kg (169.5 lb)	T. Sagir (Tur.)	375 kg (826.7 lb)
85 kg (187 lb)	G. Asanidze (Georgia)	382.5 kg (843.3 lb)
94 kg (207 lb)	M. Dobrev (Bulg.)	407.5 kg (898.4 lb)
105 kg (231 lb)	D. Berestov (Russia)	425 kg (937 lb)
+105 kg (+231 lb)	H. Rezazadeh (Iran)	472.5 kg (1,041.7 lb)

WOMEN

Weight class	Winner and country	Performance
48 kg (105.5 lb)	N. Taylan (Tur.)	210 kg (463 lb)
53 kg (116.5 lb)	U. Polsak (Thai.)	222.5 kg (490.5 lb)
58 kg (127.5 lb)	Chen Yanqing (China)	237.5 kg (523.6 lb)
63 kg (138.5 lb)	N. Skakun (Ukr.)	242.5 kg (534.6 lb)
69 kg (152 lb)	Liu Chunhong (China)	275 kg (606.3 lb)
75 kg (165 lb)	P. Thongsuk (Thai.)	272.5 kg (600.8 lb)
+75 kg (+165 lb)	Tang Gonghong (China)	305 kg (672.4 lb)

WRESTLING

World Wrestling Championships—Freestyle

Year	55 kg	60 kg	66 kg	74 kg
2002	R. Montero (Cuba)	A. Margaryan (Arm.)	E. Tedeyev (Ukr.)	M. Hajizadeh (Iran)
2003	D. Mansurov (Uzbek.)	A.A. Yadulla (Azer.)	I. Farnyev (Russia)	B. Saytyev (Russia)
2004*	**M. Batirov (Russia)**	**Y.M. Quintana (Cuba)**	**E. Tedeyev (Ukr.)**	**B. Saytyev (Russia)**

Year	84 kg	96 kg	120 kg
2002	A. Saytyev (Russia)	E. Kurtanidze (Georgia)	D. Musulbes (Russia)
2003	S. Sazhidov (Russia)	E. Kurtanidze (Georgia)	A. Taymazov (Uzbek.)
2004*	**C. Sanderson (U.S.)**	**K. Gatsalov (Russia)**	**A. Taymazov (Uzbek.)**

*Olympic champions.

World Wrestling Championships—Greco-Roman Style

Year	55 kg	60 kg	66 kg	74 kg
2002	G. Mamedaliyev (Russia)	A. Nazaryan (Bulg.)	J. Samuelsson (Swed.)	V. Samurgashev (Russia)
2003	D. Jablonski (Pol.)	A. Nazaryan (Bulg.)	M. Kvirkelia (Georgia)	A. Glushkov (Russia)
2004*	**I. Majoros (Hung.)**	**Jung Ji Hyun (S.Kor.)**	**F. Mansurov (Azer.)**	**A. Dokturishivili (Uzbek.)**

Year	84 kg	96 kg	120 kg
2002	A. Abrahamian (Swed.)	M. Ozal (Tur.)	D. Byers (U.S.)
2003	G. Ziziashvilly (Israel)	M. Lidberg (Swed.)	K. Baroyev (Russia)
2004*	**A. Michine (Russia)**	**K. Ibrahim (Egypt)**	**K. Baroyev (Russia)**

*Olympic champions.

Sumo Tournament Champions, 2004

Tournament	Location	Winner	Winner's record
Hatsu Basho (New Year's tournament)	Tokyo	Asashoryu	15–0
Haru Basho (spring tournament)	Osaka	Asashoryu	15–0
Natsu Basho (summer tournament)	Tokyo	Asashoryu	13–2
Nagoya Basho (Nagoya tournament)	Nagoya	Asashoryu	13–2
Aki Basho (autumn tournament)	Tokyo	Kaio	13–2
Kyushu Basho (Kyushu tournament)	Fukuoka	Asashoryu	13–2

On March 12 Madrid's Cibeles Square is filled with hundreds of thousands of demonstrators expressing grief and anger at the terrorist bombings that killed almost 200 people.

AP/Wide World Photos

The World in 2004

World Affairs

INSURGENTS continued to disrupt efforts to bring peace to Iraq, Spain and Russia reeled from TERRORIST attacks, and on December 26 the deadliest TSUNAMI in history KILLED at least 225,000 people and wreaked HAVOC on about a dozen countries, notably INDONESIA, Sri Lanka, and Thailand.

UNITED NATIONS

The year 2004 was marked by tense relations between the United Nations and the United States, the world body's largest financial contributor. Much of the discontent on both sides centred on the situation in Iraq and the lack of security there. UN Secretary-General Kofi Annan's refusal to send more UN staff members into such an insecure environment greatly frustrated the administration of U.S. Pres. George W. Bush. The security situation had deteriorated substantially since the bombing in August 2003 of the UN compound in Baghdad that killed 22 UN staff members, and November 2004 was one of the deadliest months since the U.S. invasion began, in terms of both coalition forces and civilian casualties.

Tempers flared in November when Annan sent a letter to Bush, British Prime Minister Tony Blair, and Iraqi Prime Minister Ayad Allawi (*see* BIOGRAPHIES) warning that the planned military assault against insurgents in Fallujah might jeopardize the credibility of the upcoming January 2005 elections. This incident followed on the heels of an earlier one in which Annan, in an interview with the BBC in September, had irritated U.S. and British officials by suggesting that the U.S.-led invasion of Iraq had contravened the UN Charter.

As the year closed, disagreement centred on the deployment of UN personnel to assist in the preparations for the planned January 2005 elections. While pledging the UN's full support for the governance process in Iraq, Annan remained firm that for such support to be feasible, UN personnel had to be secure from violence. The situation that existed through late 2004 simply did not meet that condition.

Iraq. The year commenced on a high note following the capture of Saddam Hussein in December 2003. As 2004 wore on, however, it became clear that allegations regarding stockpiles of weapons of mass destruction simply were not to be substantiated, nor, for that matter, were claims of the U.S. and British governments that the Saddam regime had supported al-Qaeda. It was evident that it would be extremely difficult for the occupying U.S.-led coalition force to restore security and governance to the country. In April President Bush and Prime Minister Blair endorsed a proposal for the UN effort to establish an Iraqi interim government. The new regime took office on June 28.

Human security in Iraq had declined dramatically since the U.S.-led invasion in 2003. Malnutrition among children had nearly doubled, and the situation was worsened by poor sanitation, unsafe drinking water, lack of electrical power, and armed violence. In the fall of 2004, about one-quarter of the Iraqi population still relied on food rations, and about 40% of the members of this group were forced to sell at least part of their rations for other necessities. Despite the extremely dangerous conditions, UN relief agencies, such as UNICEF, the Office of the UN High Commissioner for Refugees (UNHCR), and the International Migration Organization (IMO), continued to play an important role in providing humanitarian assistance. Faced with increased violence and declining security, the United States announced on December 1 that it would increase the size of its military force to 150,000 troops by the end of the year.

Afghanistan. On October 9 presidential elections were held for the first time in Afghanistan. They had been postponed from the originally scheduled date in June. Amid allegations of voting irregularities, Afghani interim president Hamid Karzai was declared the victor, and he was officially inaugurated in December. Parliamentary elections were scheduled for April 2005. The security situation in the country continued to be somewhat precarious, with the persistence of problems related to drug trafficking, the demobilization of militias, and the traditional divisions among warlords. Secretary-General Annan urged the Security Council and the General Assembly to address these and other sources of insecurity and to consider an increase in the UN's presence and assistance.

Iran. Much of the year was characterized by contention between the Iranian government and the UN, the International Atomic Energy Agency (IAEA), and U.S. officials over the issue of uranium enrichment and other nuclear activities in Iran. In November an agreement concerning these issues was reached between European countries and the Iranian government; Iranian officials announced that they had halted all uranium-enrichment measures and would permit inspectors to verify compliance with IAEA safeguards. The IAEA, in turn, reported that it had accounted for all the declared nuclear material in Iran.

Development. The heads of state and government at the Millennium Summit in 2000 had set forth a declaration that contained eight primary goals, called the Millennium Development Goals (MDGs), for eradicating extreme poverty and the conditions associated with it by 2015. As the year 2004 came to a close, the international community was not on target for attaining any of the goals. The situation in the less-developed countries was particularly bad—half of the world's population continued to subsist on incomes of less than $2 a day. How to get and keep the MDGs process on track was to be the main focus of a special summit meeting scheduled to be held at the convening of the 60th session of the UN General Assembly in September 2005.

On a more positive note, the World Bank's *Global Economic Prospects 2005* report indicated that it was both the best of times and the worst of times for less-developed countries, depending on where they were located within the world economy. The overall economic growth rate for less-developed countries, led by spectacular increases in China and India, was 6.1%. At the same time, however, most of sub-Saharan Africa lagged far behind.

Health. HIV/AIDS remained at the top of the health agenda of the international community. The pandemic was widely recognized as much more than a global health crisis. It posed a tremendous threat to social, economic, and political stability and thus had become a top global security issue.

The UN systemwide response was led by the Joint United Nations Programme on HIV/AIDS (UNAIDS), a collaborative program that brought together 10 UN cosponsoring agencies. The primary role of UNAIDS had been that of advocate, technical adviser, coordinator, and catalyst. Its *2004 Report on the Global AIDS Epidemic* gave a sobering account of the ever-increasing toll of AIDS. (*See* HEALTH AND DISEASE.) In January the Kaiser Family Foundation joined UNAIDS in launching a new Global Media AIDS Initiative. The aim was to engage the media more fully in the fight against HIV/AIDS by focusing on increasing education and public awareness of the disease. The theme for the 2004 World AIDS Campaign was "Women, Girls, HIV, and AIDS." UNAIDS also initiated the Global Coalition on Women and AIDS.

To complement UNAIDS, the Global Fund to Fight AIDS, Tuberculosis and Malaria (GFATM) had been established in 2002 to mobilize, generate, and disperse additional funds to fight the pandemic. In 2004 GFATM approved $1.6 billion for two years and a total of $5 billion for more than five years. These sums paled in comparison with the projected cost of mounting an effective and successful campaign. UNAIDS, for example, estimated that $7 billion–$10 billion would be required annually for fighting AIDS in low- and middle-income countries.

Refugees. As of Jan. 1, 2004, there were about 17.1 million "persons of concern" who fell under the mandate of UNHCR, as compared with some 20.6 million the previous year. Well over one-half of these persons were officially classified as refugees. The vast majority of them were located in Asia, Africa, and Europe, and Asia accounted for the largest number.

Peace Operations. At the end of the year, there were 18 peace missions operating under UN auspices. Sixteen were peacekeeping operations—seven in Africa (Burundi, Democratic Republic of the Congo, Côte d'Ivoire, Ethiopia and Eritrea, Liberia, Sierra Leone, and Western Sahara), one in the Western Hemisphere (Haiti), two in Asia (East Timor and India-Pakistan), three in Europe (Cyprus, Georgia, and Kosovo), and three in the Middle East (Golan Heights, Lebanon, and the Middle East in general). In addition, there were two political missions, in Afghanistan and The Sudan. As of November 30 there were 63,909 military personnel and civilian police and 3,983 international civilian personnel serving in these operations, at an annual cost of nearly $4 billion.

Renewed fighting broke out in Haiti in early February, and by month's end embattled Pres. Jean-Bertrand Aristide had resigned and fled the country. The new interim government turned to the United Nations and requested assistance in stabilizing the situation. The UN Security Council responded and authorized the creation of the Multilateral Interim Force (MIF). The situation in Haiti worsened after the island country was ravaged by Tropical Storm Jeanne, which caused more than 1,500 deaths and left more than 200,000 homeless. Given the situation, China pledged to send 125 police officers, China's first-ever contribution to assist in a UN peace mission in the Western Hemisphere.

In February the Security Council enhanced the UN presence in strife-torn Côte d'Ivoire and established a peacekeeping operation in an effort to reinforce the peace process that was evolving there. In the final months of the year, however, it became clear that the process had broken down. Government troops launched attacks against French peacekeepers and rebel forces in the UN-patrolled "zone of confidence." In an effort to restore peace, the Security Council voted unanimously to institute an arms embargo, and it threatened economic sanctions against the regime of Pres. Laurent Gbagbo. Also in the region, the Security Council in December reinforced its previous decision to place sanctions on Liberia. The sanctions restricted trade in lumber and diamonds because profits from such trade had been used to fund violence in the region.

Civil strife raged in Darfur, in The Sudan, throughout most of the year. Janjawid militias wreaked havoc on civilians while the Sudanese government failed to act to restrain them. It was estimated that more than 70,000 people had died by early October. The UN Security Council in September called for the African Union (AU) to enhance its monitoring mission in Darfur and threatened sanctions if the Sudanese

United Nations forces stand watch as Palestinians at the Jabalya refugee camp in Gaza collect UN aid packages on October 7.

government failed to comply fully with measures to end the violence by militia forces or to cooperate fully with the AU. The Security Council took the rare step of holding a two-day session in Nairobi, Kenya, on November 18–19 to discuss the Darfur matter and to meet with AU representatives.

Digital Divide. The revolution in information and communication technology, which was propelling globalization, had led to what many termed a "digital divide" between technological haves and have-nots. A crucial issue was that of determining how to bridge the divide and make the digital revolution work for all peoples. Heads of state and their representatives met on Dec. 10–12, 2003, in Geneva for the first phase of the three-year plan of the World Summit on the Information Society (WSIS). Some progress appeared to have been made in pulling together a consensus on key principles. A plan of action was agreed upon that specified principal goals, objectives, targets, and priorities. Few real commitments ensued, however, and disagreement prevailed on several key issues, including who should govern the Internet and how the bridging of the gap would be funded. These and other critical issues were to be the focus of the second phase of the WSIS, which was to convene in Tunis, Tun., in 2005.

Administration and Finance. At the end of 2004, there were 191 UN member states, and the regular biennial budget for 2004–05 stood at more than $3.1 billion. As had been the case for years, some 40% of the UN members were in arrears in paying their dues. The peacekeeping budget approved for fiscal year 2004–05 was $3.9 billion.

Several scandals rocked the halls of UN headquarters. Foremost among them was the alleged corruption that surrounded the UN's oil-for-food program in Iraq. To investigate the allegations, an Independent Inquiry Committee chaired by Paul Volcker, former head of the U.S. Federal Reserve Board, was appointed. The committee had not completed its inquiry by year's end.

Controversy surrounding allegations of harassment and favouritism by several senior UN staff members, together with allegations of sexual abuse by a number of UN peacekeepers in the Democratic Republic of the Congo, fueled dissent within the Secretariat. On November 19 Secretary-General Annan confirmed that clear evidence existed of sexual abuse in the DRC, and he expressed his outrage at the conduct of those who were involved and pledged that appropriate action would be taken. While expressing their continuing support for Annan, the UN staff union passed a resolution harshly criticizing senior management for its failure to discipline high-level officials for their misbehaviour.

Reform. In December a report entitled *A More Secure World: Our Shared Responsibility* was issued by the High-Level Panel on Threats, Challenges and Change. This blue-ribbon panel report contained 101 recommendations for improving the capabilities of the UN to respond to shared threats. The recommendations covered a wide array of issues, proposed rules, and guidelines for the use of force. It offered recommendations for ways to increase the UN's ability to engage in peace enforcement and peacekeeping, postconflict peace building, and the protection of civilians during conflict. Nearly one-third of the recommendations focused on concrete steps to reform the institutional structure of the UN to make it more effective. With regard to the launching of preemptive war, the panel reiterated the importance of ensuring Security Council authorization for all such actions and offered a series of guidelines under which the Security Council might act rapidly and proactively to authorize states to deal with critical threats such as terrorism or the use of weapons of mass destruction. The panel offered a definition of terrorism to guide both collective and individual state action. Foremost among the recommendations for institutional reform was a proposal to enlarge the Security Council from 15 to 24 members. The panel offered two options, neither of which would expand the veto power. One option would create six new permanent seats without veto power and three nonpermanent rotating seats. The other option would provide eight four-year renewable nonpermanent seats and one new two-year nonrenewable nonpermanent seat. The report was to serve as the foundation for recommendations to be made at the high-level plenary meeting of heads of state and government to be hosted in September 2005 at the commencement of the 60th session of the General Assembly. (ROGER A. COATE)

EUROPEAN UNION

In the history books, 2004 would be remembered as the year when Europe finally said goodbye to the legacy of the Cold War. In an atmosphere of sober, thoughtful celebration—and with fireworks lighting the skies of all EU member capitals—the east-west division came to an end on May 1 when the EU, previously a club of 15 Western European nations, opened its doors to 10 new members, eight countries from the former Eastern European communist bloc (the Czech Republic, Estonia, Hungary, Latvia, Lithuania, Poland, Slovakia, and Slovenia) and the Mediterranean islands of Malta and Cyprus (although Turkish Cyprus was officially excluded). The new member countries increased the number of EU citizens from 370 million to 455 million. It was an achievement that no one had thought possible two decades before. The Italian Romano Prodi, president of the European Commission (EC), summed up the sense of fulfilment: "Five decades after our great project of European integration began, the divisions of the Cold War are gone once and for all. . . . [Our new members] bring to the union the cultures and diversity of 10 countries with distinct historical roots stretching back through the centuries."

Those driving the expansion, not content with an EU membership of 25, used the mood of optimism to talk up the prospects of further enlargement within four or five years. Bulgaria, Croatia, and Romania were mentioned as the next in line to join. An even more ambitious issue, the debate over whether to open accession negotiations with Turkey, the first predominantly Muslim applicant nation, dominated many EU council meetings for much of the rest of the year.

The upbeat rhetoric, however, hid real tensions about how an expanding community would work and what its aims should be. In the short term, many individual EU governments were worried about practical issues in such a vast border-free zone. Long-standing EU member states were concerned about how to prevent people from the poorer entrant countries, many of whom were used to much lower wages, from moving across borders en masse and throwing their own citizens out of jobs by undercutting them on the wage market. Opinion polls showed that more than 60% of Germans believed that EU expansion would lead to higher unemployment as the Poles on Germany's eastern border and EU citizens from other new member states moved in to look for better-paying work. A similar proportion of Germans feared that crime would rise after the borders came down.

There were other huge issues to resolve—both institutional and philosophical—before the 25 countries could hope to operate successfully as a unit on the world stage. A community formed in the late 1950s by six founding nations—Belgium, France, Italy, Luxembourg, The Netherlands, and West Germany—could not function in its expanded form unless it rewrote the rule book and changed and strengthened its institutions. These institutions—the European Parliament, the EC (the EU's executive arm), and the Council of Ministers—needed to be modernized so that each country could have its say and wield votes in proportion to its population. The new entrant countries were determined not to be dominated by the older members, particularly France and Germany, while Paris and Berlin did not want their traditional supremacy eroded by the newcomers.

Expansion raised many questions. How ambitious should the enlarged Europe be as a political and military entity? How much power should move from its nation-states to the EU's central administration? Should the EU try to build itself as a rival to the United States? Should it restrict its ambitions and work as Washington's partner in the fight against global terrorism and in the interests of world trade? These questions predominated as stalled efforts to draw up the EU's first written constitution resumed. After months of tense and often bitter negotiations,

Criteria for Joining the Euro Zone

When the European Union's 10 newest members (Cyprus, the Czech Republic, Estonia, Hungary, Latvia, Lithuania, Malta, Poland, Slovakia, and Slovenia) officially joined the EU on May 1, 2004, they faced many challenges, but perhaps the largest was financial—when, if ever, they would be able to meet the criteria for entry to the euro zone. The euro, the single European currency that came into being at the start of 1999, was the most ambitious project launched by the European Union in recent years. Of the EU's 15 older member states, 12 (Austria, Belgium, Finland, France, Germany, Greece, Ireland, Italy, Luxembourg, The Netherlands, Portugal, and Spain) had joined the economic and monetary union (EMU), replaced their own national currencies with the euro, and approved the European Central Bank (ECB) to monitor the single currency. As of 2004, Denmark, Sweden, and the U.K., had chosen not to join, though domestic debates continued over their future plans.

The conditions for joining the euro were set out in European Treaty articles agreed to in the early 1990s when the EU began planning a possible monetary union.

1. Government deficit must not exceed 3% of GDP. If it does exceed that level, it must have declined "substantially and continuously and have reached a level close to 3%."
2. Gross government debt must not exceed 60% of GDP. If this is not the case, the ratio must have declined significantly and be moving rapidly toward 60%.
3. The member state must have achieved exchange-rate stability for at least two years according to the rules of the European exchange-rate mechanism, which defines the permitted levels of fluctuation.
4. The nominal long-term interest rates of applicant nations must not have exceeded by more than 2% the average of the interest rates in the three member states with the best records on price stability.

In 1997 the EU agreed to a further measure to enforce fiscal and budgetary discipline inside the euro zone. This was the Stability and Growth Pact, which defined a series of checks and potential financial penalties (fines) for any euro-zone member that allowed its deficits to exceed 3% of GDP. The European Commission was granted the power to fine a member state if it failed to stay in line.

The Stability and Growth Pact, however, had proved to be highly controversial, with several countries—and even the European Commission—arguing that it was unnecessarily rigid. Both France and Germany had exceeded their 3% limits but had avoided fines. Greece had admitted not only that the cost of mounting the Olympic Games in August had pushed its annual budget deficit beyond the 3% cap every year since 2000 but also that it had used inaccurate earlier numbers in order to be admitted to the EMU in 2001. In 2004 there was heated but unresolved debate about whether the rules of the pact should be changed to allow countries to overshoot for short periods of the economic cycle if this was judged in their economic interests. The ECB, which set interest rates in the euro zone, was strongly opposed to loosening the pact's rules. Many of the new EU members expressed concern that they would be held to tighter standards than the old member states, and in November 2004 the ECB president, Jean-Claude Trichet, said that rewriting the rules would be "dangerous" and would not contribute to the "solidity and soundness" of the EMU. (TOBY HELM)

agreement was reached in June on a constitution defining the goals and beliefs of the EU and the way in which power would be shared between the member states and the EU.

The Parliament, the EC, the Council, and the European Court gained new powers. A permanent new post of EU president was created, and the EU would have its own foreign minister for the first time. The constitution ensured that the EU would have many of the trappings of a state. Its roles in justice, home affairs, and asylum and immigration policies were greatly extended. Talk of the EU's becoming a superstate was overblown, however, as the constitution also safeguarded the powers of national parliaments against further encroachment by the EU and, crucially, gave the organization no power to raise its own money through taxation.

There were bitter arguments over who should fill the principal positions in the new EC, which reflected the disagreements over the direction the community should take. A particularly unpleasant row blew up over who should succeed Prodi as EC president. Germany and France wanted Belgian Prime Minister Guy Verhofstadt, who shared both countries' desire for faster and deeper European integration. The U.K.—already enduring a period of frosty relations with Paris and Berlin because of a disagreement over the U.S.-led war in Iraq—vetoed Verhofstadt's appointment, saying that Britain did not want a man who believed in so much power's being concentrated in the EU institutions at the expense of the member states. After an extraordinary battle, British Prime Minister Tony Blair faced down the French and Germans and won. "We are operating in a Europe of 25 now, not six or two or one," said Blair's official spokesman. This statement was perceived as a message to Pres. Jacques Chirac of France and German Chancellor Gerhard Schröder. The heads of government of the 25 EU members eventually settled on Blair's suggestion of Portuguese Prime Minister José Manuel Durão Barroso as EC president.

If the writing of the constitution was divisive, its ratification might prove even more so. In many EU countries, including some of the new entrants, there was strong resentment at the way power appeared to be flowing from national capitals to the central administration in Brussels. Governments came under pressure to promise referenda on the constitution before their national parliaments agreed to sign it into law. By the end of the year, Belgium, the Czech Republic, France, Ireland, Luxembourg, The Netherlands, Spain, and the U.K. were on a growing list of nations that had promised a voter referendum. Most of these would take place in 2005, and if any one country voted "no," the constitution could not become law.

The reelection of U.S. Pres. George W. Bush in November reopened arguments that had raged before the Iraq war began in March 2003. While Blair said that Europe had to work more closely with the U.S. during a second Bush term of office, Chirac emphasized the need for the EU to strengthen itself and become an effective counterweight against U.S. dominance in the world.

By the end of the year, concerns had resurfaced about the European economy, which many observers believed was held back by overregulation, generous social security systems, and high taxation. An official report by former Dutch prime minister Wim Kok concluded that member states had failed miserably since the mid-1990s in reforming their economies. The EU's stated goal of making Europe the most dynamic economy in the world had not been reached. The 10 new members also faced special challenges if they wanted to join the euro zone by adopting the single currency that had replaced the national currencies for 12 of the 15 older members since 1999. (*See* Sidebar.)

On October 6 another historic decision was made. The EC agreed that Turkey should receive "qualified" approval to open talks on its eventual admission into the EU. This massive strategic move was urged strongly on the EU by Blair, who believed that if Turkey could be brought into the EU, a bridge would be built between Europe and the Middle East. Other European leaders pointed out that Turkey had far more to do—economically, politically, and in terms of human rights—in order to satisfy the criteria for entry. At a summit in Brussels in December, the EU announced that it would officially begin membership talks with Turkey in October 2005.

The latter months of the year were marred by a spectacular power struggle between the unelected EC and elected members of the European Parliament. Provoking a minicrisis, MEPs refused to accept Barroso's new team of commissioners because the Italian representative, Rocco Buttiglione, who had been designated to handle the justice portfolio, had called homosexuality a sin and made disparaging remarks about single mothers. The Parliament also used its power to block other suggested members, though no objections were raised to the British representative, Peter Mandelson (*see* BIOGRAPHIES), despite his controversial political history at home. On November 18 the MEPs approved Barroso's revised team by a vote of 449–149, with 82 abstentions.

(TOBY HELM)

MULTINATIONAL AND REGIONAL ORGANIZATIONS

The global preoccupation with terrorism in recent years persisted in 2004, although many multinational and regional organizations shifted their focus toward the economic and social aspects of security. Many organizations also pressed to renew the World Trade Organization's Doha negotiations to improve trade measures for less-developed nations and called for increased transparency to eliminate corruption. The Commonwealth Ministerial Action Group aggressively pursued the resumption of the Doha round with talks in Geneva, Washington, Tokyo, and Brussels. Other major groups did likewise, with particular emphasis on the need to reach agreement on agriculture.

In January the Free Trade Area of the Americas held a Special Summit of the Americas in Nuevo León, Mex.; the special meeting was called because of new leadership in many member states. The Declaration of Nuevo León issued at the summit called for continued economic growth, social development to reduce poverty and hunger, and strong democracies that were transparent and free from corruption. The declaration also called for strengthening the role of the Organization of American States (OAS) in regional development.

Events in Haiti claimed much attention in the OAS. On February 29 Haitian Pres. Jean-Bertrand Aristide fled the country after a month of violence; in June the OAS began an investigation into his ouster and called for early elections. A special mission visited Haiti in September to assess the situation and resulted in an OAS pledge to assist in a citizen registration program so that elections could be held in 2005. The June General Assembly meeting approved the Declaration of Quito on Social Development and Democracy, and the Impact of Corruption, stating that corruption undermines democracy as well as social and economic development.

The war in Iraq and rising international demand for oil pressured OPEC to control prices and ensure market stability. At February's OPEC meeting a plan to reduce production was approved. Because of the fighting in Iraq, hurricane damage in the U.S., and the legal troubles of the Russian oil company Yukos, however, OPEC production was increased in April, August, and November, reaching 27 million bbl per day, a record high to date, with the price per barrel reaching $55 in October.

The extensive focus on terrorism led the Arab League to call on the United States not to portray Islam or Arabs as supporters of terrorism, stating that such actions would alienate the Arab world and hurt efforts to promote global security. The league condemned the construction of the Israeli barrier wall for infringing on the Palestinian territory and focused significant attention on a plan for Arab participation in rebuilding Iraq.

In late November, at the Association of Southeast Asian Nations' 10th summit in Vientiane, Laos, the ASEAN Security Community Plan of Action and the Socio-Cultural Community Plan of Action were signed. Negotiations on free-trade agreements with Australia and New Zealand also were approved. The ASEAN Free Trade Area implemented the Common Effective Preferential Tariff scheme, which set tariff reductions within ASEAN but allowed members to set tariff levels against nonmembers.

The Group of Eight (G-8) industrialized nations summit at Sea Island, Ga., included leaders from Africa, Turkey, and the interim Iraqi government and focused on HIV/AIDS, alleviation of poverty through private-sector growth, development, and debt relief. Recognizing the increased international demand for peace support operations, especially complex operations, to bring stability to countries in crisis, the G-8 approved an Action Plan on Expanding Global Capability for Peace Support Operations to train and equip 75,000 troops by 2010, with particular emphasis on enhancing African peace support capabilities. Members also pledged to implement fully the Highly Indebted Poor Countries Initiative on debt relief and to work with donors to extend the initiative to 2006. In October the Group of Seven meeting of finance ministers marked China's first participation in ministerial-level discussions.

The African Union (AU) took its first major leadership role with the humanitarian crisis in The Sudan which had affected more than 2,200,000 people by late 2004, leaving more than 70,000 dead and 1,500,000 displaced. The AU meetings throughout the year with the government of The Sudan and the two rebel groups fighting in the province of Darfur led to several cease-fire agreements. The AU also sent its first peacekeeping force of 3,320 military and civilian personnel to monitor the ceasefire and provide security. The AU's unprecedented action in The Sudan marked a sharp departure from its predecessor, the Organization of African Unity, which regularly ignored crises in member countries. In addition, the AU had several other firsts during the year: the first session of the Pan-African Parliament (in March), the first Conference of the African National Human Rights Institutions (October), establishment of the Continental Peace

and Security Council (May), and the first live radio broadcast throughout the continent of the AU summit (July).
(MARGARET P. KARNS)

DEPENDENT STATES

Europe and the Atlantic. On Aug. 4, 2004, the 300th anniversary of the day that Gibraltar was captured from Spain by an Anglo-Dutch fleet, some 17,000 Gibraltarians (roughly half the colony's population) linked hands in a human chain that encircled the famous Rock. As part of the yearlong tercentenary celebration, the U.K.'s Princess Anne made a formal visit in June. British Defense Secretary Geoffrey Hoon attended the official ceremonies on August 4, despite protests from Madrid. On June 10, over the objections of the Spanish government, Gibraltarians voted in the European Parliament elections. Spanish Foreign Minister Miguel Angel Moratinos, meeting in October with British Foreign Secretary Jack Straw, acknowledged for the first time that the citizens of Gibraltar should be consulted regarding the colony's future.

The no-fly zone that Buenos Aires had instituted in late 2003, denying airplanes (mainly tourist charters from Chile) bound for the Falkland Islands/Islas Malvinas the right to fly over Argentine territory, seriously hurt the British islands' economy. In March 2004 the U.K. filed a formal protest that the Argentine ship *Almirante Irizar* had entered Falklands waters and harassed fishing vessels that were legally licensed by the Falklands government.

At a ceremony in Greenland, U.S. Secretary of State Colin Powell, Danish Foreign Minister Per Stig Møller, and Greenland's local home-rule government minister Josef Motzfeldt signed a historic agreement granting the U.S. permission to upgrade its strategically important Thule Radar Station in Greenland as part of an expanded missile-defense program. Inuit who had been evicted from the region in 1953 took their fight to regain the land to the European Court of Human Rights in May.

A divided vote in the January 20 general election in the Faroe Islands led to intense negotiations to form a new government. Although the pro-independence Republican Party had the most seats (8) in the 32-seat Lagting (parliament), on February 3 the Union, Social Democratic, and People's parties—each with 7 seats—formed a broad-based coalition, with Social Democrat leader Jóannes Eidesgaard as prime minister.
(MELINDA C. SHEPHERD)

Caribbean and Bermuda. The British colony of Montserrat decided in June 2004 to set up a regional disaster-management centre, which would facilitate experts from elsewhere in the region in conducting field-based disaster-management studies. Earlier in the year, the Royal Society had strongly criticized the U.K. government for failing to use Montserrat as a location for ongoing research into the behaviour of volcanoes. In July the European Union approved a $20 million grant to Montserrat for the construction of a new capital in Little Bay. The former capital, Plymouth, had been destroyed when the Soufrière Hills volcano first erupted in 1995.

In August the Cayman Islands government vehemently denied a report in the American press that Cuban refugees under detention had paid bribes to be released from prison. In September, Hurricane Ivan struck, with 50% of the 15,000 homes on Grand Cayman reportedly suffering some form of damage. The government strongly rejected accusations that it had covered up the scale of the destruction, which some estimated as high as $1 billion, so as not to lose its prized offshore financial-services businesses. The scheduled November 17 general election was postponed until May 2005.

The trial of former British Virgin Islands (BVI) financial secretary L. Allen Wheatley ended in January with his receiving a nine-month jail sentence for having approved an airport telecommunications contract based on inflated pricing that had cost the government $450,000. Wheatley had pleaded guilty in exchange for a lighter jail term. Former BVI budget coordinator Bevis Sylvester, former director of the Telephone Services Management Unit Berton Smith, and businessman Albion Hodge, who also were implicated in the overpricing scheme, followed Wheatley's example and were handed six-, nine-, and six-month jail terms, respectively. In an effort to help preserve the Caribbean Sea, the BVI signed a memorandum of understanding with the U.S. in August that committed the latter to helping clean up oil or other noxious substances discharged into BVI waters. Earlier in the year, some 750 litres (200 gal) of oil had spilled into the sea during oil-transfer operations by a visiting tanker.

The Netherlands Antilles faced political upheaval in 2004. In April, Prime Minister Mirna Louisa-Godett and Bernard Komproe, the current justice minister and former prime minister, were forced out of office in a parliamentary no-confidence vote. Komproe was arrested on charges of corruption, and in October he died after gastric surgery while in prison. In November, Saba voted in a referendum to break from the Netherlands Antilles and be administered separately, similar to Aruba. A 315,000-bbl-per-day oil refinery, one of Aruba's principal sources of revenue, changed hands in February when it was sold by El Paso Corp. to Valero Energy Corp. for $365 million.

After 60 years the U.S. Navy officially closed Roosevelt Roads Naval Air Station in eastern Puerto Rico in March, following the cessation of bombing practice on nearby Vieques Island in May 2003.
(DAVID RENWICK)

Pacific Ocean. Pitcairn Island became the focus of world media attention in 2004 as seven men from the island's population of 47 faced trial over sexual assaults, some dating back to the 1960s. As trials began in September, it became clear that there had been a culture of underage sex on the island for generations and that although the practice was publicly acknowledged and was usually consensual, that was not

Dependent States[1]

Country	Dependent states
Australia	Christmas Island; Cocos (Keeling) Islands; Norfolk Island
Denmark	Faroe Islands; Greenland
Finland	Åland Islands
France	French Guiana; French Polynesia; Guadeloupe; Martinique; Mayotte; New Caledonia; Réunion; Saint Pierre and Miquelon; Wallis and Futuna
Netherlands, The	Aruba; Netherlands Antilles
New Zealand	Cook Islands; Niue; Tokelau
United Kingdom	Anguilla; Bermuda; British Virgin Islands; Cayman Islands; Falkland Islands; Gibraltar; Guernsey; Isle of Man; Jersey; Montserrat; Pitcairn Island; Saint Helena, Tristan da Cunha; Turks and Caicos Islands
United States	American Samoa; Guam; Northern Mariana Islands; Puerto Rico; Virgin Islands (of the U.S.)

[1]Excludes territories (1) to which Antarctic Treaty is applicable in whole or in part, (2) without permanent civilian population, (3) without internationally recognized civilian government (Western Sahara), or (4) representing unadjudicated unilateral or multilateral territorial claims.

© Claire Harvey/Newspix/Getty Images

After a contentious and highly publicized trial on Pitcairn Island, lawyers for both the prosecution and the defense pose together on October 28. Judges found six of the seven defendants guilty of sexual assault, rape, and gross indecency.

always the case. The men faced more than 50 charges of rape, sexual assault, and gross indecency; six men no longer resident on the island also were facing charges. After lengthy preliminaries that challenged British sovereignty over the island as well as trial procedure, the trials opened on Pitcairn with judges brought in from New Zealand and a television link to New Zealand for witnesses unable or unwilling to travel to the island. After a three-week trial, six of the seven defendants were convicted; one was acquitted. Sentences ranged from community service for two men to prison terms of two to six years, but the men remained free pending appeal and the clarification of legal issues.

Cook Islands Prime Minister Robert Woonton faced a general election in September. He narrowly held his own seat, but the election was tied after electoral challenges had been resolved. Two factions emerged, each seeking to form a government with the former opposition. The government was placed in the hands of the queen's representative while negotiations continued. A recent estimate put the resident population at 13,200, which reflected a continuing migration to New Zealand, where Cook Islanders had citizenship and a right of free entry. In January Niue was devastated by Cyclone Heta, with winds reaching 300 km/hr (185 mph). The storm destroyed or badly damaged crops, the island's hospital, and most government buildings and houses. The impact of the cyclone again raised doubts about the viability of the island; only about 1,300 people remained resident, with most Niueans living in New Zealand.

U.S. Pres. George W. Bush declared the Commonwealth of the Northern Mariana Islands (CNMI) and Guam disaster areas in July after Cyclone Tingting brought heavy rain, flooding, and mud slides. Under a new funding regime, the CNMI would receive some $12.4 million for capital projects in 2005, subject to an accountability protocol. The CNMI budget for 2004 was $226 million, with a heavy emphasis on health, education, and public safety.

In French Polynesia a new statute opened the way to greater autonomy from France. Elections in June saw the defeat of longtime Pres. Gaston Flosse and, for the first time, the election of a pro-independence coalition government, led by veteran politician Oscar Temaru of the Tavini Huiraatira party. The new government lasted for less than four months before it was defeated through a vote of no confidence in the Territorial Assembly. France refused to allow new elections, which thus opened the way for Flosse's return to power. New Caledonia's economy had benefited from strong nickel prices as well as a stable tourism market.

(BARRIE MACDONALD)

Indian Ocean. The continuing negotiations over the future of the Chagos Archipelago, or British Indian Ocean Territory, focused on economic matters when British Foreign Minister Jack Straw met Mauritian Foreign Minister Jayen Cuttaree in London in October 2004. The meeting foreshadowed the possibility that British Prime Minister Tony Blair might help Mauritian Prime Minister Paul Bérenger in his dispute with the United States over sovereignty in the archipelago, which included the U.S. military base at Diego Garcia atoll. Britain maintained its position that the archipelago would be returned to Mauritius when it was no longer necessary for Europe's security. The archipelago and other Indian Ocean dependencies were not seriously damaged by the devastating December 26 tsunami.

Elections held in Réunion during 2004 saw the country divided between radicals and conservatives. The Regional Council was won by a left-wing coalition headed by Paul Vergès of the Réunion Communist Party. The General Council, however, fell comfortably into the hands of the right.

Brigitte Girardin, the French minister for overseas territories, visited Mayotte on January 24–25. Discussions during the trip were devoted to the struggle against illegal immigration, which the minister intended to stop by increasing the frontier police force by 50%. Girardin also announced plans to build an improved maritime surveillance system. Penalties for the traffickers and the employers of illegal immigrants were also increased. Girardin judged that more than a quarter of the island's population were clandestine arrivals.

Christmas Island continued to be used as a detention centre for illegal migrants seeking to enter Australia. In the 2004 election campaign, Australian Prime Minister John Howard praised Christmas Island's major role as part of the successful "Pacific solution" to stop boat people who were attempting to reach the Australian mainland.

(A.R.G. GRIFFITHS)

ANTARCTICA

Ice averaging 2,160 m (7,085 ft) in thickness covers more than about 98% of the continent of Antarctica, which has an area of 14 million sq km (5.4 million sq mi). There is no indigenous human population, and there is no land-based industry. Human activity consists mainly of scientific research. The 45-nation Antarctic Treaty is the managerial mechanism for the region south of latitude 60° S, which includes all of Antarctica. The treaty reserves the area for peaceful purposes, encourages cooperation in science, prescribes environmental protection, allows inspections to verify adherence, and defers the issue of territorial sovereignty.

The Antarctic Treaty system, after 43 years without an executive secretary, appointed its first, Jan Huber of The Netherlands, who in September 2004 took up his position in Buenos Aires,

Arg. The growth in consultative (voting) nations from 12 to 27 had made a secretariat essential to handle business and to improve public access to documents. Ukraine was admitted as the 28th consultative Antarctic Treaty country. Ukraine in 1992 had acceded to the treaty and in 1996 had begun doing research in Antarctica—a requirement for consultative status. Treaty representatives worked on measures regarding tourism and other nongovernmental activities, management plans for specially protected areas, and a liability regime related to the environment. In addition to the consultative nations, 17 nations were acceding, or nonvoting, parties.

Unprecedented construction and upgrading of research facilities in the heart of the Antarctic interior—on the vast East Antarctic Ice Sheet, a desolate region as large as the continental U.S.—was under way in 2004. China started on a year-round research station at Dome A, making a traverse there from the coast to take samples and set up a weather monitor. Dome A, at more than 4,000 m (1 m = about 3.3 ft) elevation, was the highest, driest, and coldest spot on the continent. The new station, which was scheduled to be completed by 2010, would support astrophysics, upper-atmosphere physics, ice coring, and drilling through the underlying ice sheet to study the Gamburtsev Mountains, the world's least-explored range.

Some 1,370 km (1 km = about 0.62 mi) from Dome A, France and Italy in early 2005 were to begin year-round use of their new station at Dome C, Concordia, which was 3,233 m above sea level and had been in summer use since 1996. Ice coring and astronomy were to be the science focus. At the geographic South Pole, the U.S. Amundsen-Scott research facility opened portions of a new, larger replacement station (to be finished by early 2007) to support increased astrophysics and other sciences.

Antarctic tourism in 2004 recovered from the post-2001 decline. The International Association of Antarctica Tour Operators reported that a record 19,771 tourists landed in the Antarctic in the 2003–04 austral summer on privately organized expeditions—most aboard commercial ships, some on chartered or private yachts. An additional 7,766 tourists entered the Antarctic on ships and planes that did not land. More than a third of the travelers were from the U.S.; most of the others were from Germany, the U.K., Australia, Canada, Japan, and Switzerland. This marked a significant rise in Antarctic tourism beyond the pre-2001 peak of 13,826 landed tourists in the 1999–2000 season.

Courtesy NASA/JPL-Caltech

Researchers in Greenland complete testing of the Tumbleweed rover. The wind-driven inflatable instrumented sphere was deployed on January 24 for a 70-km (40-mi) roll across Antarctica.

Fossil remains of two dinosaurs previously unknown to science were found in Antarctica. One specimen, discovered by American and Argentine scientists on James Ross Island, was a carnivore related to the tyrannosaur and the velociraptor. The remains included fragments of an upper jaw, teeth, and bones from the animal's lower legs and feet. The creature, a running dinosaur roughly 1.8–2.4 m tall, likely inhabited the northern Antarctic Peninsula during the Mesozoic Era, 248 million to 65 million years ago, when the climate and terrain were similar to the modern Pacific Northwest. American paleontologists found the pelvis of a primitive sauropod, a four-legged plant-eating dinosaur, on Mt. Kirkpatrick. The 3,900-m mountaintop had been a soft riverbed before millions of years of tectonic activity elevated it skyward. The pelvis was one metre across, and field analysis suggested that the as-yet-unnamed creature stood 1.8–2.1 m tall, was perhaps 9 m long, and lived about 200 million years ago.

Poaching of the Patagonian toothfish (usually marketed as Chilean sea bass) was a priority topic at the annual summit of the Commission for the Conservation of Antarctic Marine Living Resources, held in Hobart, Australia, in late October–early November. The 24-member commission said that illegal, unregulated, and unreported fishing for Patagonian toothfish was a serious issue and that the group would monitor global toothfish trade and implement measures to reduce the incidental capture of seabirds. Enforcement action would include development of a satellite vessel-monitoring system.

A ball-shaped robot explorer survived a 70-km surface passage across the Antarctic ice plateau, powered only by the wind. The Tumbleweed rover started from the South Pole on January 24 and finished its roll eight days later. The device, which was about two metres in diameter, relayed its position, air temperature, pressure, humidity, and light intensity to a ground station via satellite. The test confirmed the rover's durability in extreme cold, which bode well for possible use in exploring Mars and other planets. The ball reached 16 km/hr but averaged 1.3 km/hr. Such speed was unattainable in rovers such as Spirit and Opportunity that operated on Mars.

Data from U.S. satellites and a Chilean P-3 airplane showed that glaciers in West Antarctica were shrinking substantially faster than in the 1990s. The glaciers were putting 60% more ice into the Amundsen Sea than they accumulated from inland snowfall. The loss corresponded to an annual sea-level rise of 0.2 mm (1 mm = about 0.04 in), or 10% of the total global increase of 1.8 mm per year. Ice shelves in the Amundsen Sea appeared to be thinning, offering less resistance to the glaciers that formed them. The earth under the ice was found to be farther below sea level than had been assumed, so the ice was thicker than once thought, increasing the amount of ice each glacier could discharge into the ocean as its speed increased. The observed increases in velocities and thinning applied to a short period, so it was too early to tell if the accelerated thinning was part of a natural cycle or a longer-term change that could lead to a rise in sea level of as much as one metre. American and British scientists went to the area in late 2004 to make more detailed measurements. (GUY G. GUTHRIDGE)

ARCTIC REGIONS

The Arctic regions may be defined in physical terms (astronomical [north of the Arctic Circle, latitude 66° 30′ N], climatic [above the 10 °C (50 °F) July isotherm], or vegetational [above the northern limit of the tree line]) or in human terms (the territory inhabited by the circumpolar cultures—Inuit [Eskimo] and Aleut in North

A glacier looms over a fishing boat in Greenland's Ilulissat fjord, 250 km (155 mi) north of the Arctic Circle. The Ilulissat glacier was one of two Arctic sites added to the World Heritage List in 2004.

© Slim Allagui/AFP/Getty Images

America and Russia, Sami [Lapp] in northern Scandinavia and Russia, and 29 other peoples of the Russian North, Siberia, and East Asia). No single national sovereignty or treaty regime governs the region, which includes portions of eight countries: Canada, the United States, Russia, Finland, Sweden, Norway, Iceland, and Greenland (part of Denmark). The Arctic Ocean, 14.09 million sq km (5.44 million sq mi) in area, constitutes about two-thirds of the region. The land area consists of permanent ice cap, tundra, or taiga. The population (2004 est.) of peoples belonging to the circumpolar cultures is nearly 450,000 (Aleuts [in Russia and Alaska], 3,000; Athabascans [North America], 32,000; Inuits [or Eskimos, in Russian Chukhotka, North America, and Greenland], 150,000; Sami [Northern Europe], 50,000; and 40 indigenous peoples of the Russian North, totaling more than 200,000). International organizations concerned with the Arctic include the Arctic Council, institutions of the Barents Region, the Inuit Circumpolar Conference, and the Indigenous Peoples' Secretariat. International scientific cooperation in the Arctic is the focus of the International Arctic Research Center of the University of Alaska at Fairbanks.

In 2004 planning continued for the proposed natural gas pipeline from Prudhoe Bay in Alaska through Canada to the U.S. Midwest as well as for a separate Can$7 billion (U.S.$5.6 billion) gas pipeline from the Mackenzie River Delta to serve oil-sands projects in northern Alberta. In January the gas producers opened discussions with Alaska on bids to build the 1,200-km (745-mi) pipeline to the Yukon border for an estimated U.S.$6.5 billion. In March, TransCanada Corp., which since 1976 had held the right to build a natural gas pipeline to the U.S. mainland from Alaska, announced that it was prepared to lead the project. The producer's proposal was for the pipeline to deliver the gas to Chicago via a combination of new pipelines through Alaska and the Yukon and using excess capacity in TransCanada's existing pipeline system. During the year the U.S. Congress continued to debate approval of oil companies' access to the coastal plain of the Arctic National Wildlife Refuge, which was believed to hold as much as 16 billion bbl of crude oil. The refuge included calving areas for caribou and was home to polar bears and other wildlife as well as serving as an annual stopover for the migration of millions of birds. The Alaska pipeline project gained momentum in October when Congress approved a giant incentive package to support its construction, thus placing pressure on the smaller Mackenzie Valley pipeline to move faster to obtain regulatory approval and proceed with construction.

In Canada progress on the environmental-impact assessment process for the Mackenzie Delta pipeline became mired in litigation with the Deh Cho First Nations, whose traditional territory encompassed 40% of the proposed route. Both the Deh Cho and the Canadian government claimed jurisdiction but had yet to sign a land-claim agreement. The consortium of energy companies involved in the pipeline project indicated that it was ready to file an initial regulatory application, with the backing of many Northwest Territory aboriginal groups, which had a one-third stake in the project.

The U.S. and Canadian governments took steps in May toward the building of a northern railway that would connect Eielson, near Fairbanks, Alaska, with Fort Nelson in northern British Columbia and thence to the rest of Canada and the United States. The U.S. Congress approved the Alaska Railroad Corp.'s expansion of tracks to the Yukon border. It was reported in January 2004 that, thanks to the discovery of diamonds in the Northwest Territories in the 1990s, Canada had become the world's third largest producer of the gems.

In April the Russian ambassador to Canada proposed establishing an Arctic trade route between Murmansk, on Russia's Kola Peninsula, and Churchill, Man., on Hudson Bay. The proposed Arctic bridge would be the most efficient marine trading link between central North America and northern Europe. Plans were announced in June for an international study of the biological riches of the Arctic Ocean hidden beneath the polar ice. Some climatologists had predicted that within 50 to 100 years the region could be ice-free in summer owing to global warming.

Another sign of the growing impact of global climate change on the Arctic was the steady erosion of the shoreline of the Beaufort Sea. In July the residents of one community perched on the seaward edge of the Mackenzie Delta were reported to be asking the Northwest Territories government for financial assistance to strengthen the shoreline, which was retreating by as much as 2 m (6.6 ft) a year from steady permafrost erosion and from the lapping waves and storms. Scientists had predicted that as the Arctic climate warmed, plant growth on the tundra would increase, pulling carbon out of the air, locking it, and generally slowing down global warming. The results of a 20-year series of studies published in the journal *Nature* in September, however, indicated that temperature rises could cause vast stores of deep-soil carbon to escape and thus actually accelerate the warming process.

In October Canada announced a concerted effort to reinforce its jurisdiction over its largely uninhabited Arctic territory. Ottawa's "northern strategy" was aimed at protecting sovereignty over the Canadian Arctic through sustainable development initiatives in cooperation with other northern countries. Initiatives included a northern mobilization of the armed forces. Canada had conflicting territorial claims: with the U.S. in the Beaufort Sea, with Denmark over Hans Island between Greenland and Ellesmere Island, and with Russia over its drawing of the Russian continental shelf.

In June UNESCO announced the addition of two Arctic sites to its World Heritage List—Greenland's Ilulissat ice fjord, the most active glacier outside Antarctica, and the Wrangel Island Reserve in the Russian Arctic, the site of ancestral polar bear dens.

(KENNETH DE LA BARRE)

AFGHANISTAN

Area: 645,807 sq km (249,347 sq mi)
Population (2004 est.): 20,869,000 (excluding 2,150,000 Afghan refugees, numbering about 1,100,000 in Pakistan and about 850,000 in Iran at the beginning of the year)
Capital: Kabul
Chief of state and head of government: President Hamid Karzai

A new constitution was ratified in Afghanistan on Jan. 4, 2004, after weeks of contention in a constitutional Loya Jirga (Grand Assembly). The constitution called for a strong president and two vice presidents as well as a National Assembly of two houses, and it specified individual rights of the kind found in many Western democratic constitutions. It declared Afghanistan to be an Islamic republic and prohibited laws that were contrary to the tenets of Islam, but it also promised that followers of other religions would be free to exercise their faiths. It guaranteed women equal rights with men, requiring at least two female delegates per province in the Wolesi Jirga—the popular house of the National Assembly—and made specific provision for women's education and social welfare.

During the constitutional Jirga, ethnic tensions focused on recognition of official languages. Pashto and Dari were declared official, but Uzbek, Turkmen, Balochi, Pashai, Nuristani, and Pamiri were allowed third-language status, and their use was permitted in publications in areas where they predominated. International reaction was generally positive; the U.S. ambassador to Afghanistan, Zalmay Khalilzad, called the results "one of the most enlightened constitutions in the Islamic world."

Security fears and the threat of violence from terrorist groups, as well as armed disputes over regional and ethnic issues, posed a continuing problem across Afghanistan. Many attacks on civilian, military, and political targets appeared to be aimed at undermining the government of the interim president, Hamid Karzai, and interrupting scheduled elections. These attacks, often employing improvised bombs, were blamed on Taliban groups.

As the elections approached, NATO pledged to increase its International Security Assistance Force to 8,500 troops. U.S.-led forces charged with hunting down the Taliban and capturing al-Qaeda leader Osama bin Laden were enlarged to 18,500 during 2004, and their brief was expanded beyond counterterrorism to include economic, political, and social development. U.S. military officials promised an expanded program of "provincial reconstruction teams" to strengthen central and local government through village development. In July the medical relief agency Doctors Without Borders announced its withdrawal from Afghanistan, citing lack of security in the provinces, which it said had led to the death of five of its workers; linking humanitarian aid

Ballot boxes from Afghanistan's presidential election are moved hand to hand by election workers to a counting station in Kabul on October 10, the day after the election. The balloting was adjudged to have been fair, although a number of opposition leaders boycotted the election.

© Ahmad Masood/Reuters/Corbis

with military objectives, the organization said, made targets of aid providers.

With the adoption of the constitution, elections for both the president and the National Assembly were expected in June, but by late March security fears and difficulties in registering Afghanistan's estimated 10 million voters had forced a postponement until September. In July the election of a president was put back a second time, until October, and National Assembly elections were postponed until spring 2005. In August UN sources estimated that 90% of eligible voters had registered.

Interim president Karzai, a Pashtun, was favoured to win the October 9 presidential elections, and his choice of running mates—Ahmad Zia Masoud, the brother of assassinated Tajik mujahideen hero Ahmad Shah Masoud, and Hazara leader Karim Khalili—demonstrated the importance of ethnic balance in the country's new democracy. Among 17 other candidates for top offices was one woman as well as the Uzbek strongman from northern Afghanistan, Abdul Rashid Dostum, and Yunus Qanuni, a well-known Panjshiri Tajik. Voting was enthusiastic and generally peaceful, but a serious challenge from Karzai's opponents revealed that ink applied to voters' hands to prevent multiple voting could be easily removed. On November 3 Karzai was declared the winner, and he was sworn in as president on December 7.

UN sources said that 450,000 refugees had been repatriated to Afghanistan in the first half of 2004, bringing to 3,000,000 the number of Afghans returned home since 2002. Another 440,000 internally displaced persons had gone back to their homes.

Severe drought returned to many areas after improved rainfalls in 2003, and one-third of the population was expected to face unreliable food supplies. Opium production increased, and authorities feared not only the social threat posed by the illicit drug trade but also the financial support it provided for warlords and terrorists.

In September three Americans were given 8- and 10-year prison sentences for running a private prison in Kabul where Afghans were beaten and tortured. The Americans, who were said to have posed as U.S. Special Forces troops, claimed to have had the backing of high-level U.S. authorities in the Pentagon. U.S. and Afghan government officials denied having supported the group, although U.S. peacekeepers admitted there had been contacts with them. (STEPHEN SEGO)

ALBANIA

Area: 28,703 sq km (11,082 sq mi)
Population (2004 est.): 3,136,000 (not including Albanians living abroad)
Capital: Tirana
Chief of state: President Alfred Moisiu
Head of government: Prime Minister Fatos Nano

Albanian domestic politics in 2004 remained focused on the decade-old power struggle between Socialist Prime Minister Fatos Nano and his rival, former president Sali Berisha (of the Albanian Democratic Party [PD]). On February 7, police had to prevent several thousand PD protesters from entering government buildings in Tirana. Berisha called on Nano to leave office voluntarily to avoid being driven out, as Pres. Eduard Shevardnadze had been in Georgia. Two weeks later about 50,000 protesters took to the streets of the capital in what amounted to the biggest demonstration since the countrywide unrest in 1997. Nano faced tough challenges not only from the opposition but also within his own party. Ilir Meta, who had been prime minister in 2000–02, announced in September that he and 10 other parliamentary deputies had left the Socialist Party to found the Socialist Movement for Integration, which would compete with the Socialists in the 2005 general elections.

A foreign-policy blow was dealt when NATO's Istanbul summit in June ended without any firm membership date's being promised to Albania. Within the framework of the U.S.-Adriatic Charter, however, Albania was actively developing its defense cooperation with the U.S., Macedonia, and Croatia. The slow pace of domestic reforms rang alarm bells within the EU, and the government of The Netherlands, which held the rotating EU presidency, warned Albania in a statement on September 14 that more would have to be done to fight crime, corruption, and trafficking in drugs and humans and that Tirana would have to reform its electoral process if it intended to pursue an EU Stabilization and Association agreement.

In January an inflatable rubber boat carrying 32 illegal emigrants from Vlora, Alb., to the Italian coast capsized, and 21 people drowned. Police raided suspected human traffickers in Tirana and detained 24 suspected would-be immigrants. Italian and Albanian law-enforcement officers cooperated again in August when villagers from the tradi-

Relatives and neighbours from the Albanian village of Sukaj mourn a mother of three and her brother-in-law, 2 of the 21 who died when a small boat carrying illegal immigrants to Italy broke up and sank in January. Illegal human trafficking is a serious problem for both the Italian and Albanian governments.

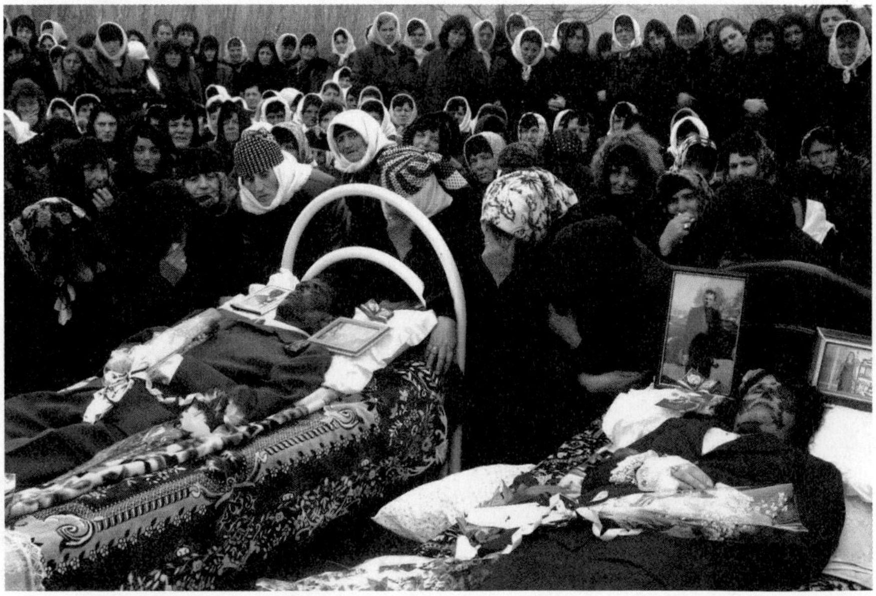

tionally rebellious town of Lazarat fired gunshots at an Italian police helicopter that was searching for cannabis fields.

Albanian-Macedonian relations improved as Macedonia pursued reforms to strengthen rights of its minorities, notably ethnic Albanians. The two foreign ministers agreed in Skopje on May 6 to open more border checkpoints and accelerate the construction of a highway and pipeline between the two countries. Prime Minister Nano and Pres. Alfred Moisiu visited Kosovo, the heavily ethnic Albanian province of the former Yugoslavia, on March 2 and April 22, respectively. Moisiu warned that delays in defining Kosovo's political status would strengthen extremists in the region, while Nano declined to support Kosovo's call for independence. In June Albania arrested two Kosovar extremists, and in July a Tirana court convicted another man of inciting ethnic hatred in Kosovo and gave him an 18-month sentence in prison.

(FABIAN SCHMIDT)

ALGERIA

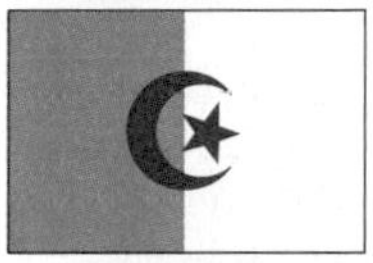

Area: 2,381,741 sq km (919,595 sq mi)
Population (2004 est.): 32,322,000
Capital: Algiers
Chief of state: President Abdelaziz Bouteflika
Head of government: Prime Minister Ahmed Ouyahia

The April presidential election was the dominant event in Algeria in 2004. Pres. Abdelaziz Bouteflika's reelection was meticulously planned and executed, although the size of his victory—85% of the vote—led to complaints of vote rigging. Despite these complaints, the result was generally accepted as reflecting popular choice. In the run-up to the elections, the complex procedures for candidate registration were effectively used to exclude Bouteflika's major rival, Ahmed Taleb Ibrahimi, which thus also eliminated any chance of the emergence of a political vehicle for supporters of the banned Islamic Salvation Front (FIS). In the aftermath the National Liberation Front (FLN), which had fielded its secretary-general, Ali Benflis, as its presidential candidate, fell into disarray, and Benflis was forced to resign. Although the FLN had joined the "presidential alliance," alongside the National Democratic Rally (RND) and the Movement for a Peaceful Society (MSP), the party itself was reduced to political impotence as factions squabbled about the FLN's future structure and role. Other opposition political parties also found themselves marginalized as a new centralized political system began to emerge.

Army Gen. Mohamed Lamari remained faithful to his 2003 promise to distance the army from the political scene and retired in August 2004. Lamari had reportedly opposed Bouteflika's ambitions for reelection, and the two had some irreconcilable differences. The changes in the army's command structure that followed, however, were minor; both the head of military security, Gen. Mohamed Medìène, and Bouteflika's military adviser, Gen. Mohamed Touati, kept their posts, as did the president's adviser, retired general and former minister of defense Larbi Belkheir, who had long been rumoured to be the real power behind the throne.

The violence that had plagued Algeria over the past decade was contained during the year; the Armed Islamic Group (GIA) was eradicated from central Algeria, and the Salafist Group for Preaching and Combat (GSPC) suffered heavy reverses in the eastern part of the country and to the east of Algiers. In August the GSPC leadership was killed close to the Soummam Valley, and for several months rural Algeria also enjoyed an uneasy calm. By October, however, a new round of attacks and ambushes had begun, despite the army's successes in Kabylia and in eastern Algeria. In late October Libya extradited Amari Saifi, the GSPC operative who had been held responsible for the 2003 kidnappings of European tourists in the Sahara. Saifi had been held by a rebel group in Tibesti, Chad, for seven months.

The draft 2005 financial law marked the beginning of a new five-year plan that called for a $50 billion investment to renew Algeria's infrastructure and economy. The president promised that by the end of his term one million new homes would be built and a vast expansion in employment would occur. After agreement with the trade union confederation (the Algerian General Workers' Union), the government was poised to launch a privatization program that would affect all but "strategic" industries, including the hydrocarbon sector. The Sonatrach Petroleum Corp., however, would operate as an autonomous state company and seek an international role.

(GEORGE JOFFÉ)

ANDORRA

Area: 464 sq km (179 sq mi)
Population (2004 est.): 67,600
Capital: Andorra la Vella
Chiefs of state: Co-princes of Andorra, the president of France and the bishop of Urgell, Spain
Head of government: Chief Executive Marc Forné Molné

Andorra in 2004 worked to develop more modern political and social institutions in order to achieve fuller alignment with those of the European Union, members of which completely surrounded Andorra. Only one-third of Andorran residents were actual citizens of the country, and residency of 25 years was required for citizenship eligibility. Noncitizens with less than 20 years of residency could own only 33% of a company. A proposed law would reduce that limitation to 10 years, however.

Andorra led the world in life expectancy at 83.5 years overall—80.6 years for males and 86.6 for females. To the disgruntlement of a few French farmers, the tiny landlocked principality increased its size by 35 ha (about 86 ac).

(ANNE ROBY)

ANGOLA

Area: 1,246,700 sq km (481,354 sq mi)
Population (2004 est.): 10,979,000
Capital: Luanda
Chief of state and head of government: President José Eduardo dos Santos, assisted by Prime Minister Fernando da Piedade Dias dos Santos

The problems in the oil-rich exclave of Cabinda, claimed by Angola but with an active independence movement, occupied the government in Luanda in

2004. In March, Roman Catholic clergy in Cabinda who sought to interpose themselves between the secessionists and the government troops formed an association called Mpalabanda. This was in response to accusations that troops pursuing the rebels were guilty of indiscriminate attacks on civilians. The association sought an accommodation with the government by negotiation rather than by forceful means, though the clergymen admitted that their ultimate goal was self-determination for Cabinda. Mpalabanda was not, they said, attempting to seize control of the province's rich oil resources, but the group expressed its deep concern that the population at large derived little benefit from the profits from oil production, a situation they blamed on the Cabinda Gulf Oil Co. as well as on the Angolan government. Recently the IMF had indicated that more than $4 billion of oil revenue for the years 1997 to 2002 could not be accounted for.

While Cabinda was the only province in Angola where peace had not been officially declared, the recovery of the rest of the country from the effects of a 27-year civil war remained slow. Early in the year, corn (maize) and bean crops in Huambo province were damaged by heavy rains, which left the region still dependent upon external aid. Although in June the UN noted a marked improvement in the overall humanitarian situation, in many parts of the country lack of funds, the inadequacy of the infrastructure—in spite of help from Brazilian construction companies—and the continuing presence of thousands of land mines still made recovery difficult. The UN had pledged to give assistance where it was needed, but crop yields continued to be inadequate, in part because of the government's refusal to admit genetically modified seed from abroad. Nor was the repatriation and resettlement of 40,000 people who had taken refuge in Zambia likely to be achieved by the end of the year as had been envisaged, despite the EU's offer in March of $9.8 million to help promote the project.

Disputes over a date for presidential and parliamentary elections continued throughout the year. In March opposition groups combined forces to try to persuade the government to reach a decision. The government's response was to announce 14 specific requirements that had to be met before elections could take place, which meant that the earliest date would likely be in 2006. In June, in response to a report produced by the Ministry of Territorial Administration, the government agreed to talks with opposition parties, an offer that was accepted enthusiastically. By August, however, the opposition was already complaining of a lack of progress, and the National Union for the Total Independence of Angola, the main opposition party, claimed that its members had been the victims of intimidation.

There was further controversy in the same month when the National Assembly prepared to vote on a new land bill. Although the government had invited civil groups to comment on a draft of the bill, opposition parties claimed that their comments had been ignored. As a result, hopes were dashed that the legislation would enable people who had been displaced from their land during the civil war to reclaim it and that they would have a new legal title that would replace their claim under the traditional system.

(KENNETH INGHAM)

ANTIGUA AND BARBUDA

Area: 442 sq km (171 sq mi)
Population (2004 est.): 68,300
Capital: Saint John's
Chief of state: Queen Elizabeth II, represented by Governor-General Sir James Carlisle
Head of government: Prime Minister Lester Bird and, from March 24, Baldwin Spencer

The Antigua Labour Party (ALP) was swept out of office in a historic general election in March 2004 and replaced by the United Progressive Party (UPP). Even ALP leader Lester Bird, whose family had ruled Antigua and Barbuda since independence in 1981, lost his seat, with the UPP grabbing 12 of the 17 electoral districts. ALP retained four, and the Barbuda seat went to the Barbuda People's Movement (BPM), which was sympathetic to the UPP. UPP leader Baldwin Spencer became the new prime minister and Robin Yearwood the new leader of the opposition.

Early good news for the new government was that Antigua and Barbuda had emerged triumphant in its dispute with the U.S. over an attempt by the U.S. to ban Internet gaming. The U.S. said it would appeal the ruling by the World Trade Organization but would, in the meantime, also try to resolve the matter through negotiations. The new government engaged a forensic accountant to investigate the alleged improper use of funds by the previous administration and halted the sale of Antigua and Barbuda passports to rich foreigners. (DAVID RENWICK)

© AP/Wide World Photos

The newly elected prime minister of Antigua and Barbuda, Baldwin Spencer, shares his joy with a United Progressive Party supporter following his victory speech in the capital, St. John's, on March 24.

ARGENTINA

Area: 2,780,092 sq km (1,073,400 sq mi)
Population (2004 est.): 39,145,000
Capital: Buenos Aires
Head of state: President Néstor Kirchner

January 2004 marked the two-year anniversary of Argentina's historic economic and political collapse. Compared with the dark days of December 2001 and January 2002, the Argentine economy and political system functioned quite well throughout 2004. Nevertheless, the use of different benchmarks, particularly economic ones, suggested that serious issues still existed, and many people remained pessimistic about the country's future despite the positive climate.

The Argentine economy experienced robust growth in 2004, fueled by the success of the agricultural sector (particularly soybean exports), increased local industrial production as consumers substituted locally manufactured products for imports (which were now prohibitively expensive, owing to the three-to-one exchange rate with the U.S. dollar), and the boom experienced by the construction sector. Though this growth began to slow during the second semester, the country's GDP increased by a healthy 8% in 2004. At the same time, the inflation rate was a tolerable 6%.

Throughout the year Pres. Néstor Kirchner of the Justicialist (Peronist) Party (PJ) consolidated his power and enjoyed the support of strong PJ majorities in both houses of the national congress. Though Kirchner was unable to marginalize his principal political rival—former president Eduardo Duhalde, leader of the PJ in the province of Buenos Aires—he was able to establish a tacit truce with Duhalde that allowed him to govern effectively.

Kirchner's failure to address several underlying economic and social problems raised serious concerns about Argentina's future. After having defaulted unilaterally 36 months earlier on its debt, Argentina had yet to come to an agreement with its creditors, a majority of whom believed that Argentina was not negotiating in good faith. Until some type of acceptable agreement was reached, foreign (as well as domestic) investment in Argentina was likely to be modest, which would thereby threaten the country's ability to maintain its current level of economic growth. At year's end the prospects for an agreement in 2005 appeared increasingly likely. The Argentine government's hostile (and at times illegal) treatment of the privatized utility companies (most of which were owned by foreign capital) had resulted in an almost complete lack of investment in energy exploration, generation, and transportation, which in turn led to electricity and natural-gas shortages during the year. These shortages could become more severe in 2005 and 2006, particularly if weather conditions proved unfavourable.

Argentina's relationship with the International Monetary Fund became increasingly conflictive in 2004, owing to Argentina's debt and utilities-related problems as well as to the Kirchner government's failure to pass legislation that would reform the banking sector and provide restitution (stemming from the 2002 devaluation) to the banks. The government's failure to reform the federal revenue-sharing system (i.e., the rules governing the fiscal relationship between the national government and the provincial governments) also complicated its relationship with the IMF.

Crime also emerged as an extremely salient issue for the Argentine public during the year, with mounting popular pressure on Kirchner to adopt a harder line toward criminals. Though

Hundreds of thousands of people fill the square in front of the Congress building in the Argentine capital, Buenos Aires, on April 1 to demand that the government do something about the high incidence of violent crime. Kidnappings in the Buenos Aires area were of special concern.

Kirchner at first resisted these demands, his declining public-approval ratings during the third quarter led to a government crackdown on many forms of criminal behaviour (especially chaotic, and often violent, street protests). The Kirchner government had only minimal success in its efforts to reduce crime, particularly in stemming the growing wave of kidnappings that plagued the Buenos Aires metropolitan area. (MARK P. JONES)

ARMENIA

Area: 29,743 sq km (11,484 sq mi). About 16% of neighbouring Azerbaijan (including the 4,400-sq-km [1,700-sq-mi] disputed region of Nagorno-Karabakh [Armenian: Artsakh]) has been under Armenian control since 1993.
Population (2004 est.): 2,991,000 (plus 130,000 in Nagorno-Karabakh)
Capital: Yerevan
Chief of state: President Robert Kocharyan
Head of government: Prime Minister Andranik Markaryan

The antagonism between the Armenian three-party coalition government and the opposition generated by the flawed presidential and parliamentary elections in 2003 continued to pervade domestic politics in 2004. On February 4 opposition deputies walked out of the parliament to protest the majority's refusal to debate proposed constitutional amendments that would have paved the way for a referendum of confidence in Pres. Robert Kocharyan. In March–April opposition leaders convened a series of protest demonstrations to call for the resignation of Kocharyan and the government. Police violently dispersed one such protest during the night of April 12–13, injuring and arresting scores of participants. The Parliamentary Assembly of the Council of Europe on April 28 condemned the violence and called for the release of persons detained after the protests and a resumption of dialogue between the authorities and the opposition.

The opposition rejected repeated government offers to resolve differences through dialogue but suspended public protests in mid-June in a search for more effective tactics. Although the opposition renewed its boycott of the fall parliament session, the authorities did not make good on their threat to strip absent deputies of their mandate.

Economic growth continued, with GDP increasing by 9.6% during the first eight months of the year. The Armenian dram strengthened against the U.S. dollar by almost 10%.

In May the U.S. government named Armenia as eligible for financial aid under the Millennium Challenge Program, and in June Armenia was formally included in the European Union's European Neighbourhood Policy. Foreign Minister Vartan Oskanyan met twice, in June and late September, with his Turkish counterpart, Abdullah Gul, but no breakthrough was reached in establishing formal diplomatic relations. During a visit to Yerevan by Iranian Pres. Mohammad Khatami, an intergovernmental agreement was signed on September 8 on construction of a 140-km (87-mi) pipeline to export Iranian gas to Armenia. Despite domestic opposition, the parliament in December approved the deployment of 46 noncombat military personnel to serve with the international peacekeeping force in Iraq.

(ELIZABETH FULLER)

AUSTRALIA

Area: 7,692,208 sq km (2,969,978 sq mi)
Population (2004 est.): 20,141,000
Capital: Canberra
Chief of state: Queen Elizabeth II, represented by Governor-General Michael Jeffery
Head of government: Prime Minister John Howard

Domestic Affairs. Australian Prime Minister John Howard won his fourth general election in a row on Oct. 9, 2004. The Liberal–Country Party coalition went into the campaign in a political climate that was overwhelmingly hostile to conservative political views, and every state government was in the hands of the Australian Labor Party (ALP). Howard, who had been prime minister for more than eight years, stood on his record, while the ALP went into battle with an untried leader, Mark Latham. (*See* BIOGRAPHIES.) Howard said that he would stay on as prime minister if his party won the election, but the ALP claimed that a vote for Howard was really a vote for Peter Costello, the federal treasurer. Both parties saw trust and integrity as key issues. Howard argued that the ALP could not be trusted to keep the economy strong, protect family interests, and lead the fight against international terrorism. Latham accused the prime minister of dishonesty and deceit and said that Australia needed to move to a new generation of national leadership. Taxation and health rather than the war on terrorism became the key issues. The ALP's tax and family policy promised a tax cut of $A 8 a week for Australians earning less than $A 52,000 a year ($A 1 = about U.S.$0.76). Latham also pledged to lift the top tax rate from $A 80,000 a year to $A 85,000 and guaranteed that the tax cuts delivered to middle-income earners in the 2004 budget would remain. Prime Minister Howard promised that if reelected he would spend $A 1.8 billion to lower the cost of doctor visits; in response, Latham pledged $A 3.4 billion "to save Medicare."

As the election drew closer, both parties softened their stances on issues on which the electorate was clearly against them. Because winning marginal seats was crucial for his victory, Howard dropped his insistence that nuclear waste could best be stored safely at Woomera, S.Aus.; Latham protested that the dump would be back on the agenda after the election. The government backed away from its tough policy on granting visas to asylum seekers and admitted to Australia a large group that had been detained on Nauru.

Although Howard supported the decriminalization of homosexual conduct, he inserted into the Marriage Act a clause banning same-sex marriages. Despite protests that the ALP had betrayed its gay and lesbian supporters, opposition legal affairs spokeswoman Nicola Roxon told a Christian forum that the ALP views were identical to the federal government's.

The Economy. The Australian economy remained solid in 2004. While global restructuring by Mitsubishi Motors Corp. cost Australian jobs, the yearly unemployment rate remained below 6%. Despite the growing balance-of-payments deficits, the Reserve Bank kept interest rates low. High fuel prices caused acute discomfort for the Australian community, and because Australia imported 40% of its oil supply, Industry and Resources Minister Ian

© Tim Wimborner/Reuters/Corbis

Demonstrators in Sydney in August protest against a ban on same-sex marriage that the government of Australian Prime Minister John Howard included in the new Marriage Act. Same-sex marriage was a top social and legal issue in many countries in 2004.

Macfarlane ordered a review of the government's legal powers to protect people from a possible major disruption of fuel supplies from Asia and the Middle East. While the short-term rise in oil prices did not cause the Reserve Bank to raise interest rates immediately, Howard was conscious of the electoral damage done as consumers blamed the government for the oil-price-driven rise in inflation. Qantas passengers in particular were not pleased by ticket surcharges levied to compensate the national airline for rising fuel costs. Qantas chief executive Geoff Dixon spoke for many when he said his concern was what the price of fuel was doing to the economy overall and whether fuel prices were going to have an impact on everything in the Australian community.

The government expected to generate dramatic growth in the economy in 2004 by signing a free-trade agreement with the United States, its major trading partner. Both Howard and U.S. Pres. George W. Bush agreed that the free-trade agreement was a milestone in the history of the Australian-U.S. alliance. The potential agreement opened up American markets—admittedly during a long time frame—to Australian farm products and allowed American investors greater access in Australia. In order to pass the free-trade agreement through the Australian Parliament, Howard was prepared to compromise with the opposition. The government accepted ALP demands that cheaper Australian generic drugs not be blocked from the market by more expensive American products. In an election year the wallets of Australian consumers were as important as the principles of free trade. Despite the last-minute amendments that limited the patent rights of American pharmaceutical companies, the agreement was scheduled to go into effect in January 2005. Government and opposition also agreed to protect local content in broadcast media by requiring the Australian Broadcasting Authority to preserve Australian voices and faces on TV and radio.

Foreign Affairs. In the lead-up to the 2004 general election, the Howard government stressed its experience and reliability as the manager of Australian foreign policy. A series of diplomatic misunderstandings undermined this strategy, however, and Australian foreign relations suffered on a number of fronts. A diplomatic row was triggered after Foreign Minister Alexander Downer told Chinese Premier Wen Jiabao that under the ANZUS Treaty in any potential conflict with China over Taiwan, Australia might not support the U.S. Howard quickly repudiated Downer's view that Australia's ANZUS commitment applied to attacks on U.S. territory but stressed that while only the U.S. could guarantee Australia's ultimate security, Australia had its own interests in Asia and a strong and growing separate relationship with China. Downer also increased tensions with North Korea by noting that Pyongyang had developed the capacity to hit Sydney with intercontinental ballistic missiles.

The secretary of Iran's National Security Council, Hassan Rowhani, visited Canberra in August and told the government that public opinion in the Middle East had turned against Australia because of its involvement with the U.S.-led coalition occupying Iraq. Rowhani's point that by withdrawing its troops from Iraq Spain had increased its standing in the region was rejected by the Australian government, which argued that the Spanish action had made Australia a more likely terrorist target. This evinced diplomatic protests from Spain, as happened also with the Philippines when Howard criticized the withdrawal of Philippine forces from Iraq in the wake of a hostage crisis. Public opinion remained opposed to the continued detention by the U.S. at Guantánamo Bay, Cuba, of two Australian citizens, David Hicks and Mamdouh Habib. In August Hicks was brought before a U.S. military commission on charges of conspiracy to commit war crimes. Habib was expected to be among the second group of prisoners put on trial.

Relationships with Malaysia improved following the retirement in late 2003 of Prime Minister Datuk Seri Mahathir bin Mohamad. Datuk Seri Abdullah Ahmad Badawi (*see* BIOGRAPHIES), the new prime minister, warmly described Australia as a friend. Howard agreed that the important business, military, and educational cooperation between the two states might in the future be expanded into a free-trade agreement. Australia signed such a free-trade agreement with Thailand as part of a strategic push to become a more central element in the Asian neighbourhood. Thailand had the fastest-growing economy in Southeast Asia, and it was expected that by 2010 approximately 98% of trade between the two countries would be tariff-free. A further positive indication in the region was that Australia for the first time received an invitation to the ASEAN (Association of Southeast Asian Nations) summit, which was held in Vientiane, Laos, in November.

(A.R.G. GRIFFITHS)

AUSTRIA

Area: 83,871 sq km (32,383 sq mi)
Population (2004 est.): 8,105,000
Capital: Vienna
Chief of state: Presidents Thomas Klestil, Andreas Khol (acting) from July 6 to 8, and, from July 8, Heinz Fischer
Head of government: Chancellor Wolfgang Schüssel

The Austrian electorate had a busy time at the ballot box in 2004, with important state elections taking place in March, a new president elected in April, and elections to the European Parliament in June. The two parties in the ruling coalition—the centre-right Austrian People's Party (ÖVP) and its junior partner, the populist far-right Freedom Party (FPÖ)—experienced contrasting fortunes, but on the whole the government ended the year in a stronger position than many had thought possible 12 months earlier.

Relations between the coalition partners improved. The degree of turbulence within the FPÖ declined, which reflected the presence of a larger number of respected figures who were willing to accept the responsibility of high office. The appointment of Hubert Gorbach, a notable representative of the FPÖ's liberal wing, as vice-chancellor in late 2003 brought stability to the coalition, as did the appointment of Ursula Haubner, a popular and respected junior minister, as the FPÖ's new leader in June. Haubner's brother was Jörg Haider, the xenophobic former party leader (who continued to apply his opportunistic style in political affairs at the federal level), but she was a moderate and showed signs of developing a constructive relationship with the ÖVP (and particularly the chancellor, Wolfgang Schüssel).

Heinz Fischer, with his wife, Margit, signals thumbs up to supporters at a rally on April 23, the final public event in Fischer's successful campaign for president of Austria.

AP/Wide World Photos

The FPÖ nevertheless struggled at the polls in 2004. Support for the party declined sharply in the Salzburg state election in March and at the European Parliament elections. The FPÖ did fare better in Carinthia, where Haider was unexpectedly reelected governor, although this was attributed to his highly personalized campaign, in which the FPÖ's name hardly featured. The main opposition Social Democratic Party (SPÖ) was victorious in the Salzburg election and in the presidential contest, where Heinz Fischer narrowly topped the ÖVP candidate, Foreign Minister Benita Ferrero-Waldner. Fischer's inauguration on July 8 was overshadowed by the death two days earlier of his predecessor, Thomas Klestil. (*See* OBITUARIES.) In June Austria gave its full support to the new EU constitutional treaty, having played a key role in defending the position of smaller member states during the lengthy negotiation process. Ferrero-Waldner began work in November as Austria's new EU commissioner with responsibility for external relations.

During 2004 the government continued to push through elements of a comprehensive structural-reform program for the economy and reached agreement on major tax cuts (in 2005), a further restructuring of the state pension system, and efficiency savings within the health care system. Opposition, particularly from trade unions, to the scale of some of the reforms was anticipated by the government, although the extent of protests was considerably more muted than had been the case in 2003. That year opposition to a major pension reform resulted in the largest public- and private-sector strikes in Austria for more than 50 years.

The global economic recovery in 2004 led to a gradual strengthening of the Austrian economy following three years of below-trend growth. Household spending remained relatively subdued, but capital investment was boosted by a government stimulus package and plans to upgrade the country's transport infrastructure, particularly to Austria's eastern neighbours following the enlargement of the EU in May. Rising demand in many of Austria's key trading-partner countries (including Germany) resulted in a modest pickup in exports, although an appreciating euro and strengthening imports meant that the foreign sector as a whole contributed little to overall growth. Protests continued throughout the year in Tyrol against the increasing amount of heavy-goods traffic and pollution following the decision by the EU to ease trucking restrictions at the end of 2003.

(NEIL PROTHERO)

AZERBAIJAN

Area: 86,600 sq km (33,400 sq mi), including the 5,500-sq-km (2,100-sq-mi) exclave of Nakhichevan and the 4,400-sq-km (1,700-sq-mi) disputed region (with Armenia) of Nagorno-Karabakh
Population (2004 est.): 8,343,000
Capital: Baku
Head of state and government: President Ilham Aliyev, assisted by Prime Minister Artur Rasizade

Despite persistent rumours of a rift within the top leadership, both veteran Prime Minister Artur Rasizade and presidential administration head Ramiz Mekhtiyev retained their posts in 2004. In September the weakened and demoralized opposition rejected an invitation from Pres. Ilham Aliyev to seek national reconciliation through dialogue. Opposition candidates fared poorly in local elections on December 17 that were marred by allegations of fraud. Aliyev dismissed Foreign Minister Vilayat Guliyev on April 2, naming Elmar Mammadyarov to succeed him, and on July 23 National Security Minister Namik Abbasov was replaced by Interior Ministry official Eldar Mahmudov.

Under pressure from the Parliamentary Assembly of the Council of Europe, President Aliyev pardoned 129 prisoners in March, 363 in May, and 264 more in September, including Alikram Gumbatov, who was sentenced to life imprisonment for having declared a secessionist republic on the border with Iran in 1993.

The trial began on May 7 of seven prominent opposition figures accused of having instigated the violent clashes in Baku on October 15–16, 2003, between police and opposition supporters protesting the perceived falsification of the October 15 presidential election. They were sentenced on October 22 to between two and a half and five years' imprisonment.

Azerbaijan's GDP grew by 10.6% during the first six months of 2004, but inflation also rose to 5.5%. The government's failure to enact key reforms impelled the IMF to withhold a loan tranche to have been released in April, but in November the government yielded to IMF pressure and raised domestic oil and gas prices.

During four meetings held between April and August, Mammadyarov and Armenian Foreign Minister Vartan Oskanyan agreed on a proposed basis for resolving the Nagorno-Karabakh conflict. Aliyev and Armenian Pres. Robert Kocharyan discussed, but failed to endorse, that framework in September.

Azerbaijan's relations with NATO proved problematic. In January three Armenian officers were denied visas to attend a planning conference in Baku for NATO-sponsored maneuvers scheduled for September, which NATO subsequently canceled when Armenian officers were denied visas to attend. Six members of the Karabakh Liberation Organization who staged a violent protest in June against the planned Armenian participation were sentenced in August to between three and five years' imprisonment; those sentences were suspended in September. In June Azerbaijan was formally included in the EU's European Neighbourhood Policy.

(ELIZABETH FULLER)

BAHAMAS, THE

Area: 13,939 sq km (5,382 sq mi)
Population (2004 est.): 317,000
Capital: Nassau
Chief of state: Queen Elizabeth II, represented by Governor-General Ivy Dumont
Head of government: Prime Minister Perry Christie

The Bahamas government announced in March 2004 that it had made "significant progress" on a key aspect of the fight against money laundering—mutual legal assistance treaties with other countries. "Positive responses" relating to legal assistance matters had been forthcoming following requests made by treaty partners.

The Inter-American Development Bank (IDB) said in May that the tourism industry, financial services, and transshipment activity would remain The Bahamas' key sources of economic growth up to 2007. It cautioned, however, that the country was vulnerable to "external shocks" of both a natural and an economic nature. True to the IDB's prediction, The Bahamas did not escape the widespread destruction wrought by hurricanes in 2004, one of the worst such seasons on record. Hurricane Frances in early September caused at least $25 million in damage to the Family Islands, and later that month Hurricane Jeanne generated additional damage, this time mostly in Freeport, Grand Bahama.

In June the government signaled that the setting up of a national lottery was "under review." It was estimated that about $100 million was being spent annually by Bahamians on the Florida Lottery.

(DAVID RENWICK)

BAHRAIN

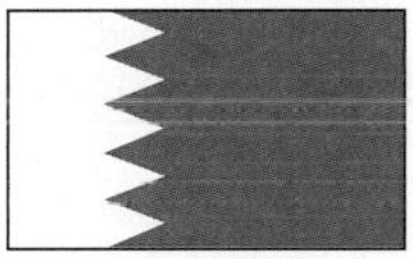

Area: 718 sq km (277 sq mi)
Population (2004 est.): 709,000
Capital: Manama
Chief of state: King Hamad ibn Isa al-Khalifah
Head of government: Prime Minister Khalifah ibn Sulman al-Khalifah

In 2004 Bahrain, lacking important oil resources, continued to establish itself as a centre of trade and finance. During the year efforts were made to attract foreign investment and encourage the establishment of private companies by offering advantages such as nondiscriminatory financial regulations and more efficient procedures for investment. Relations were strained between Bahrain and the Gulf Cooperation Council after Bahrain and the U.S. signed a free-trade accord in September. At the end of 2003, construction began on a huge billion-dollar project to modernize the port of Manama.

Debris litters the shoreline near Lucayan Harbour in Freeport, Grand Bahama; Hurricane Jeanne wreaked havoc on The Bahamas when it crossed the island nation on September 25.

Many continued to suffer from an unemployment rate in excess of 10%, and an estimated 10,000 jobs would have to be created annually to meet the needs of young Bahrainis reaching employment age. Opposition groups sought modification of the constitution to give the elected lower chamber more powers than the upper chamber, which was appointed by the king.

Bahrain and Qatar finished preliminary studies on construction of a bridge to link the two countries. In June 2004 the Bahraini government announced that it had uncovered a terrorist group allegedly linked to al-Qaeda and briefly arrested its members. This news prompted the United States to order an evacuation of most U.S. government dependents. Bahrain served as the headquarters of the U.S. Fifth Fleet, which was operating in the Persian Gulf. (LOUAY BAHRY)

BANGLADESH

Area: 147,570 sq km (56,977 sq mi)
Population (2004 est.): 135,255,000
Capital: Dhaka
Chief of state: President Iajuddin Ahmed
Head of government: Prime Minister Khaleda Zia

Tumult and violence characterized politics in Bangladesh again in 2004, with the division and mutual mistrust between the ruling Bangladesh Nationalist Party and the main opposition Awami League deepening. The Awami League stunned the nation by announcing that the government would have to step down by April 30, 2004, and that all was set for a new regime to take over on that date. The government launched a massive arrest of opposition supporters, but the deadline passed without a stir. Much more serious was a terrorist attack on an Awami League rally on August 21. At least 13 grenades were exploded, killing 21 people and seriously injuring more than 200, though the main target, Awami League leader Sheikh Hasina, escaped. The opposition was quick to blame the attacks on the government, which in return blamed the Awami League itself. International police joined the local investigators, but by year's end the identity of the attackers and the motive for the massacre were still unknown. Earlier, on May 7, Ahsanullah Master, an Awami League deputy, had been shot dead at a party conference in Tongi, and a second deputy, Momtajuddin Ahmed, was assassinated on June 7 in Natore. The British high commissioner in Dhaka had survived a grenade attack in Sylhet on May 21. In all these cases the attackers' identities and motives remained shrouded in mystery.

The political situation took on an even more sinister edge with the emergence in April of a Taliban-like anticommunist Islamist group named Jagrata Muslim Janata Bangladesh, in the northwest of the country. This group, led by Azizur Rahman, called "Bangla Bhai," was reportedly responsible for a wave of vigilante-style terrorism and the execution of some 15 persons whom it had deemed "outlaws." The group's organization and goals were murky, but there were (unproven) allegations of links to the government, and an official investigation found no evidence that such a group existed.

Parliament was also affected by the deep divide between the government and the opposition. The Awami League boycotted Parliament for most of the year, and parliamentary committees could not function because of the absence of the opposition. A new political party, Bikalpa Dhara Bangladesh, was formed during the year by former president A.Q.M. Badruddoza Chowdhury. Chowdhury's son and another legislator deserted the Bangladesh Nationalist Party and joined the Bikalpa Dhara.

Bangladesh's economy was clouted by five months of devastating floods that caused an estimated $2.1 billion in damages to agriculture and infrastructure. Damages were minimal, however, from the December 26 Indian Ocean tsunami. It was expected that GDP would be about 5%, down half a percentage point. During the first quarter of the fiscal year (July–September), revenue collection was 8.3% short of the target. Monetary growth showed an upward trend. Inflation inched up on price increases for essential items and upward adjustments of energy prices. In August the annual average inflation increased to 5.9% year-on-year. The upward trend in exports continued with year-on-year exports rising by 26.4% in July–August. The IMF released a $74 million installment for its Poverty Reduction and Growth Facility.

(INAM AHMED)

BARBADOS

Area: 430 sq km (166 sq mi)
Population (2004 est.): 273,000
Capital: Bridgetown
Chief of state: Queen Elizabeth II, represented by Governor-General Sir Clifford Husbands
Head of government: Prime Minister Owen Arthur

In February 2004 Barbados raised eyebrows in a region preparing to become a single economic unit when it referred a maritime delimitation dispute with Trinidad and Tobago for settlement by an entity outside the region—the disputes body of the UN Convention on the Law of the Sea. The two governments had been discussing an agreement that would permit fishing in each other's waters.

A no-confidence motion against the Barbados Labour Party government that had been moved by the opposition Democratic Labour Party was defeated in the House of Assembly in June. The motion was prompted by an error in a land-acquisition bill earlier passed by the House. It was the first no-confidence motion brought against any Barbados government in modern history.

In July Barbados came out ahead of every other Caribbean and Latin American state on the UN Human Development Index, placing 29th of the 177 countries surveyed. Barbados's central bank forecast in July that the country's economy would grow by 2–2.5% in 2004. In August, however, Standard & Poor's, the American credit-rating agency, cut Barbados's long-term foreign and local currency debt rating, citing growing budgetary and current-account deficits. (DAVID RENWICK)

BELARUS

Area: 207,595 sq km (80,153 sq mi)
Population (2004 est.): 9,828,000
Capital: Minsk
Head of state and government: President Alyaksandr H. Lukashenka, assisted by Prime Minister Syarhey Sidorski

The year 2004 in Belarus was dominated by a controversial referendum on whether to amend the constitution to allow Pres. Alyaksandr Lukashenka to run for a third term in office; presidential elections were scheduled for 2006. On September 7 the president announced that on Oct. 17, 2004, the day of the parliamentary election, a referendum would be held on the following question: "Do you allow the first President of the Republic of Belarus, Alyaksandr Hryhorevich Lukashenka, to participate in the presidential election as a candidate for the post of the President of the Republic of Belarus and do you accept Part 1 of Article 81 of the Constitution of the Republic of Belarus in the wording that follows: 'The President shall be elected directly by the people of the Republic of Belarus for a term of five years by universal, free, equal, direct and secret ballot?'"

After a campaign dominated by the state-backed media and harassment of opposition figures, most of whom had been debarred from participation in the parliamentary election at the registration stage, a reported 90.2% of the population took part in voting; 79.4% reportedly voted "yes" to the referendum questions. The opposition, which had argued that Lukashenka could now remain in power indefinitely, held several days of street protests after the election and cited a Gallup Poll taken at election time that indicated that only 48.4% of respondents had intended to support the motion (50% of the entire electorate had to approve the motion for it to pass). The new parliament of 110 deputies was likely to be equally compliant. No opposition figure won a seat, and only the Liberal Democrats and Communists were represented.

The year was marked generally by repressive actions on the part of the authorities. In April, Mikhail Marynich, a former minister of foreign economic relations, was arrested for illegal storage of firearms, and criminal charges were brought against him in August. Marynich, a founder of the European Choice faction and a leading opposition member, was additionally charged with stealing computers from the Business Initiative group, though these computers were supposedly a gift from the U.S. embassy in Minsk. On July 28 the authorities closed the European Humanities University, the only university in Belarus outside state control. The action was the culmination of a lengthy campaign to remove the rector, Anatol Mikhailau, a renowned scholar.

From the government's perspective, a key event of the year was the commemoration of the 60th anniversary of the liberation of Minsk from Nazi German occupation, which was marked by a military parade on July 3.

Economically, Belarus continued to enjoy high growth rates as a result of its close links with Russia. GDP grew by 11.1% in the first 11 months of the year, and industrial production rose by 15.7%—overfulfilling the respective target figures of 9% and 9–10%. The best performers were ferrous metallurgy, mechanical engineering and metalworking, pulp and paper, and fuel industries. (DAVID R. MARPLES)

BELGIUM

Area: 30,528 sq km (11,787 sq mi)
Population (2004 est.): 10,416,000
Capital: Brussels
Chief of state: King Albert II
Head of government: Prime Minister Guy Verhofstadt

Elections in mid-June 2004 in Belgium's three regions—Flanders, Wallonia, and Brussels—brought major strains to Prime Minister Guy Verhofstadt's Liberal-Socialist federal coalition government less than a year after it had come into office. Verhofstadt's own Dutch-speaking Liberal party, VLD-Vivant, fared badly and was pushed into third place in Flanders, overtaken even by the extreme right-wing Vlaams Blok. In November, however, the Supreme Court of Belgium ruled that Vlaams Blok had violated antiracism laws and was thus not a legal party. Elsewhere the main victor was the French-speaking Socialist Party, which consolidated its leading position in Wallonia and overtook the French-speaking Liberals to become the main political force in Brussels. In the complex negotiations that followed, the Socialists ended their previous government partnerships with the Liberals in Wallonia and the Belgian capital and established new coalitions in both regions with the centre-right Humanist Democratic Centre.

The political maneuvers ended the symmetry that had previously existed whereby Liberals and Socialists were driving forces at both the federal and regional levels. The change in political fortunes soon made it harder for Verhofstadt, who failed at the same time in his bid to become European Commission president, to drive through national policies, which required the cooperation of regional governments. This was demonstrated by a crisis in the autumn over the number of night flights over Brussels from Zaventem airport, located nearby in Flanders. After the federal, Flemish, and Brussels authorities failed to reach a settlement with DHL, the courier company canceled plans to expand its European hub at the airport.

The highest-profile event of the year was the three-month-long trial in the small southern town of Arlon of convicted rapist Marc Dutroux. In June, eight years after his arrest, Dutroux was sentenced to life imprisonment for the murders of two teenage girls and a male accomplice. He was also found guilty of the kidnapping, imprisonment, rape, and abuse of these young women, two eight-year-old girls (who had starved to death in an underground cell), and two other girls who survived their ordeal and testified against him in court. Dutroux's ex-wife received a 30-year sentence as an accessory, and another accomplice was sent to prison for

In April a Belgian police officer examines the underground cell where accused child rapist and murderer Marc Dutroux (later convicted) held four of his young victims.

25 years. A fourth defendant was acquitted of the kidnapping but was given a five-year sentence for drug trafficking and conspiracy to traffic human beings. Just a few weeks after Belgium's "trial of the century," the nation was again appalled when serial killer Michel Fourniret confessed to the murders of nine people, mostly young girls, between 1987 and 2001.

Sobelair, the Belgian charter airline, which had survived the bankruptcy in November 2001 of its former parent company, Sabena, itself went into liquidation in January 2004, and almost 500 jobs were lost. After Sabena, Delsey Airlines, and City Bird, it was the fourth Belgian airline to fold since 1991. Interbrew, previously the number three brewer in the world, moved to the top slot, pushing Anheuser-Busch of the U.S. into second place after the Belgian company acquired a 21.8% interest in Brazil's Ambev. Following the merger Interbrew changed its name to Inbev.

In January Belgium extended existing legislation on same-sex marriages to allow gay Belgians to marry foreign partners. Previously, the right covered only nationals from countries where same-sex marriages were legal and thus effectively enabled only Belgians and Dutch to benefit. (*See* LAW, CRIME, AND LAW ENFORCEMENT Special Report.) Between September 2002, when euthanasia was decriminalized, and the end of 2003, 259 cases of mercy killing were officially recorded. During that period, the number of cases rose from 8 to 21 per month. (RORY WATSON)

BELIZE

Area: 22,965 sq km (8,867 sq mi)
Population (2004 est.): 283,000
Capital: Belmopan
Chief of state: Queen Elizabeth II, represented by Governor-General Sir Colville Young
Head of government: Prime Minister Said Musa

The primary concern in Belize in 2004 was the heightened public debt and the manner in which the government attempted to respond to it. In an effort to meet repayment on debt owed to commercial banks, the government attempted to float a bond of $225 million on the international market. It was the first time that the government had attempted such a large bailout, and the action proved unsuccessful. The bond, together with alleged irregularities by the government in the use of Social Security funds, generated frenzied public concern, becoming so intense that seven ministers—more than half of the prime minister's cabinet—resigned their positions in August. After a few days, however, they renounced their resignations and returned to the cabinet. It was the first time in recent memory that a financial matter had galvanized interest across all sectors of the public and overcome the partisan allegiance that normally characterized Belizean public affairs.

Notwithstanding the crisis in public finance, there were praiseworthy efforts by the government to reinforce the social infrastructure. The long-awaited reopening of the Bliss Centre for the Performing Arts in Belize City ushered in a revival of music, theatre, and dance for people in all age groups, including schoolchildren.

(JOSEPH O. PALACIO)

BENIN

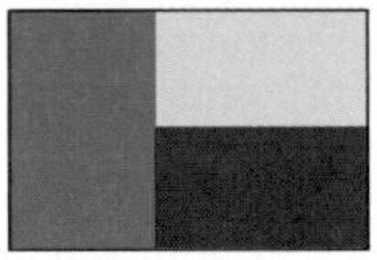

Area: 112,622 sq km (43,484 sq mi)
Population (2004 est.): 7,250,000
Capital: Porto-Novo (executive and ministerial offices remain in Cotonou)
Head of state and government: President Mathieu Kérékou

The debate over the causes of Benin's worsening economic performance grew more intense in 2004. The government's goal of a 7% growth rate in 2004 was wildly optimistic, and clearly an even larger budget deficit loomed. Prices of staple foodstuffs such as corn (maize) had doubled, while prices of cotton, the country's main export good, tumbled. Government revenue fell sharply, largely owing to a huge decline in customs duties. Nigeria's continuing ban on overland imports of goods from Benin and its crackdown on illegal exports of cheap gasoline further contributed to the crisis, as did a steep fall in the volume of trade goods passing through the port of Cotonou en route to Niger. Opposition parties blamed the deficit on corruption.

In June lengthy court proceedings in which 99 people, including 27 magistrates and 25 lawyers, were tried for embezzlement and subverting the legal system concluded. Thirty-seven defendants were found guilty and given prison terms of from 30 months to 5 years. Judges staged two strikes in June to protest the government's interference in the judicial system.

In June the United Nations granted Benin and Niger $350,000 to help offset their costs in bringing to the International Court of Justice their dispute over the course of the Niger River boundary. In another border dispute, with Nigeria, the special joint commission meeting in July made progress in adjusting land and sea frontiers, and Benin was hopeful that it would gain access to contested offshore oil sites.

(NANCY ELLEN LAWLER)

BHUTAN

Area: 38,394 sq km (14,824 sq mi)
Population (2004 est.): 700,000 (excluding more than 100,000 refugees in Nepal)
Capital: Thimphu
Head of state: Druk Gyalpo (King) Jigme Singye Wangchuk
Head of government: Prime Ministers Lyonpo Jigme Y. Thinley and, from August 18, Lyonpo Yeshey Zimba

In March protesters outside Bhutan's embassy in New Delhi demand to know the whereabouts of Indian insurgents who were captured in Bhutanese territory.

© Prakash Singh/AFP/Getty Images

Virtually untouched by terrorist activities in the past, Bhutan began 2004 with a small-scale war as its 8,000-man army was sent to flush out Indian insurgent groups such as the United Liberation Front of Assam that were hiding in Bhutanese territory. The problem of the more than 100,000 Bhutanese refugees who were languishing in camps in Nepal was nowhere close to a solution. A number of refugees formed a Bhutan Communist Party to wage war (on the Nepalese model) against the Bhutanese establishment. Following a violent incident at one refugee camp, an official Bhutanese joint verification team quit the camp and suspended the negotiations with Nepalese authorities. Exiled human rights activist Teknath Rijal traveled to Geneva to publicize the refugees' plight.

In Bhutan's traditional annual rotation of the prime ministership, Yeshey Zimba took over the post on August 18. The country's economy saw a healthy growth in 2004, and GDP climbed to about 7%. The government pursued three large hydropower projects—at Tala, Kuricchu, and Basochhu—with the goal of increasing electrical power.

(KESHAB POUDEL)

BOLIVIA

Area: 1,098,581 sq km (424,164 sq mi)
Population (2004 est.): 8,724,000
Capitals: La Paz (administrative) and Sucre (judicial)
Head of state and government: President Carlos Mesa Gisbert

The temperature of public life in Bolivia cooled somewhat in 2004 following the tumultuous events of the previous year. Pres. Carlos Mesa Gisbert, who had taken office after a popular revolt over natural-gas exports drove out his predecessor, made good his promise to submit energy policy to the people. After voters backed him in a referendum on July 18, Mesa forged ahead with legislation to strengthen state control over the gas resource. Mesa was hampered, however, by his lack of a base in Congress, and it remained unclear when Bolivians would begin to enjoy substantial benefits from the country's vast gas reserves.

Mesa submitted five initiatives to the electorate: scrapping the current energy law, affirming state ownership of oil and gas reserves, returning privatized stock to the state petroleum company, using gas as a bargaining chip in Bolivia's long-running dispute with Chile over access to the Pacific Ocean, and allowing gas exports under certain conditions. The conditions included meeting national demand first, raising taxes and royalties to 50% of production revenue, creating a domestic gas industry, and dedicating revenues to social spending. All five questions passed, and although they were ambiguous, the results were interpreted as a political victory for the president. The first bill introduced by Mesa to implement his new mandate was rejected by Congress as too weak. The revised version provided for renegotiation of contracts with foreign companies, which led to warnings that it would frighten away investors. Nevertheless, Mesa sought to increase gas exports to Bolivia's neighbours. He signed a deal with Peru and said he preferred to see liquefied Bolivian gas exported through Peru rather than Chile.

Indians and non-Indians appeared increasingly at odds. Mesa received a degree of support from powerful peasant leader Evo Morales Ayma, who approved the idea of the referendum while advocating rejection of some questions. Felipe Quispe Huanca, Morales's rival, called for a boycott of the vote. Quispe resigned from Congress in June, saying he would pursue the "revolutionary struggle" to establish an independent Aymara Indian state. The mayor of Ayo Ayo, 90 km (55 mi) south of La Paz, was assassinated by townspeople who accused him of corruption. Such developments—along with Mesa's leftward shift on energy policy—encouraged talk of secession in prosperous southeastern Bolivia, where the natural gas fields are located and where many found the concerns of highland Indians remote. In addition, in local elections in December, Indian and peasant organizations trounced traditional parties in every major Bolivian city.

The growing of coca leaf, the raw material for cocaine, continued to be a source of tension. Drug prosecutor Monica von Borries was assassinated in a car-bomb attack in March. The UN reported that coca production had declined over the previous decade but also that illegal plantings covered nearly as much acreage as legal ones, despite eradication efforts. The plight of Bolivia's impoverished tin miners was highlighted in March when a laid-off miner excluded from retirement benefits blew himself up inside the Congress chamber. Several thousand former miners were later granted monthly pensions of $60.

(PAUL KNOX)

AP/Wide World Photos

In La Paz, Bol., representatives of the Miners Union Workers Federation who have strapped dynamite to their chests, engage in a demonstration for government pension benefits for the country's tin miners.

BOSNIA AND HERZEGOVINA

Area: 51,209 sq km (19,772 sq mi)
Population (2004 est.): 3,870,000
Capital: Sarajevo
Heads of state: Nominally a tripartite presidency chaired by Dragan Covic, Sulejman Tihic from February 28, and, from October 28, Borislav Paravac; final authority resides in the Office of the High Representative, Paddy Ashdown, Baron Ashdown (U.K.)
Head of government: Prime Minister Adnan Terzic

In Bosnia and Herzegovina, as in previous years, efforts in 2004 to reintegrate and reform the two entities that make up the country—the Muslim-Croat Federation and the Serbian Republika Srpska (RS)—were pushed through by international pressure. The continuing weakness of the state and

AP/Wide World Photos

The reconstructed Old Bridge in Mostar, Bosnia and Herzegovina, awaits its official reopening on July 23. The original 16th-century stone bridge, which had been a physical and symbolic link between the Muslim and Croatian parts of the city, was destroyed in 1993.

the failure of RS to arrest a single suspect wanted by the International War Crimes Tribunal were the major obstacles blocking Bosnia and Herzegovina's eligibility for membership in NATO's Partnership for Peace program.

In January the Office of the High Representative (OHR), which administered Bosnia and Herzegovina, expressed its dissatisfaction with Mostar's inability to speed its reintegration process and reacted by combining that city's six municipal governments into a single city council with specific orders to ensure that the city remained united. High Representative Paddy Ashdown also gerrymandered the voting districts to prevent any one group from dominating. Mostar's 16th-century Old Bridge, which had been destroyed by Bosnian Croat forces in 1993, was reopened in July.

In June Ashdown clamped down on governmental foot-dragging in RS by firing 59 Bosnian Serb officials, and he issued a report the following month on the governing Serbian Democratic Party (SDS), suggesting widespread tax evasion, abuse of power, and corruption. The moves were interpreted as a direct response by the OHR to the Serbs' lack of cooperation and alleged involvement with former Bosnian Serb leader Radovan Karadzic, an indicted war criminal. The RS parliament responded by passing a resolution urging all indicted war criminals, including Karadzic, to turn themselves in or face arrest. In October both entities held local elections in 142 municipalities. For the first time since 1990 the Bosnians themselves funded and organized the balloting, and it was the first time that mayors were directly elected. Low voter turnout and apathy among younger voters, however, meant that the vast majority of offices were won by the three ruling nationalist parties.

In October a Bosnian Serb commission released its final report to the government on the 1995 massacre of some 8,000 Bosniac (Bosnian Muslim) men and boys outside Srebrenica. The Bosnian Serbs acknowledged that their armed forces had planned and carried out the executions.

Amid widespread corruption and a lacklustre economy, Bosnia continued to find ways of attracting foreign investments. In August the transnational firm LNM Holdings announced that it had purchased a 51% stake in BH Steel, Bosnia and Herzegovina's largest producer. Independent state auditors reported that the country's presidency and other officials had squandered millions of dollars of tax revenues on luxuries such as automobiles and gifts for foreign dignitaries. No laws or decrees regulating these expenses existed, and no criminal proceedings were brought against any official. The government failed to legislate reforms proposed by the EU calling for the creation of 45 new laws and 25 new agencies. At the end of the year, NATO turned over command of peacekeeping activities to the 7,000-strong EU force.

(MILAN ANDREJEVICH)

BOTSWANA

Area: 582,356 sq km (224,848 sq mi)
Population (2004 est.): 1,661,000
Capital: Gaborone
Head of state and government: President Festus Mogae

Beginning in January 2004, all patients at doctors' offices in Botswana who did not object were automatically tested for HIV. Gaborone had the largest HIV/AIDS clinic in the world; antiretroviral drugs were dispensed there free of charge in a program paid for by government and international donor agencies. In April the first cases of polio in 13 years were detected, near Maun and Francistown. The affected children were successfully treated, and an emergency national immunization campaign followed. The polio strain was identical with the one that was infecting northern Nigeria. (*See* HEALTH AND DISEASE Sidebar.)

Former inhabitants of the Central Kalahari Game Reserve took their claim for land restitution to Botswana's high court in July. The Lesetedi Commission, which reported in August, criticized irregular and possibly corrupt allocations of large plots in Gaborone to a few businesses owned by noncitizens. New diamond-polishing workshops were opened in Gaborone and Molepolole during the latter part of the year, but partial recession in the world diamond market resulted in the government's delaying expenditure on national development projects. Privatization of state assets was held back by the withdrawal of all viable bidders for Air

Botswana because of a recession in the world airline business.

In the general elections that were held on October 30, the Botswana Democratic Party captured 44 of the 57 seats in the National Assembly, while the opposition Botswana National Front gained 12 and the Botswana Congress Party secured 1. Members were elected to a five-year term in office.

(NEIL PARSONS)

BRAZIL

Area: 8,514,877 sq km (3,287,612 sq mi)
Population (2004 est.): 180,542,000
Capital: Brasília
Head of state and government: President Luiz Inácio Lula da Silva

During 2004 Pres. Luiz Inácio Lula da Silva and the federal government continued to maintain the economic stability policies implemented by the Fernando Henrique Cardoso administration (1995–2002). Despite his long history of leftist militancy and past dedication to Worker's Party (PT) social programs, Lula, a former union leader, continued the economic goals of his predecessor, such as achieving a primary budget surplus in accordance with an IMF agreement, keeping inflation in check, and pushing for budget cuts. With an eye toward the midterm municipal elections held in October, however, the government advanced little through an agenda that included a biosecurity law, reform of the regulatory agencies, judicial reform, a public-private partnership law, independence for the central bank, an increase in the minimum wage, a bankruptcy law, and an informatics law. Instead, the federal government negotiated cabinet positions and political accords in order to advance its candidates.

A cabinet reform was undertaken in January with the objective of removing ineffective ministers, strengthening the positions of PT mayoral candidates in the October elections, and bringing the Party of the Brazilian Democratic Movement (PMDB) into the PT-led governing coalition. The Lula government suffered its first major scandal in mid-February when a two-year-old videotape surfaced that showed Waldomiro Diniz da Silva—a congressional-relations assistant to José Dirceu, Lula's chief of staff—appearing to solicit campaign donations from the boss of an illegal numbers game in Rio de Janeiro. Lula immediately sacked Diniz, but the scandal continued through the rest of the year. In March the Legislative Assembly of Rio de Janeiro state created a commission to investigate Diniz's activity, and in October it recommended that he be arrested. The scandal came at an inopportune time for Lula and Dirceu, as it showed a link between a member of Dirceu's staff and gambling operators just before Lula outlawed bingo parlors and video-gaming machines. Even worse, Congress repudiated the president's action on May 6, and finally in August the Supreme Court ruled that only federal legislation could regulate bingo operations.

On June 17 Lula suffered his second major defeat of the year at the hands of the legislature when his provisional measure to raise the minimum wage to 260 reais (one real = about $0.32) a month was struck down by the Senate. On July 13 Congress approved a target budget surplus of 4.25% for 2005 and a multiyear budget plan. The Supreme Court upheld the social security reform provision that taxed retirees' pensions by 11%; judicial injunctions in January had halted such a practice in some states.

Under increasing pressure from the opposition, the administration strengthened its economic and finance team over the course of the year. On July 16 Dirceu was named coordinator of the Council of Economic Development Policy, a collegial body presided over by the finance minister. On August 16 Lula signed a measure that gave central bank president Henrique Meirelles the status of cabinet minister, with the benefit of insulating Meirelles from accusations of tax evasion and ensuring that only the Supreme Court would rule on any possible criminal conduct.

On October 3, 120 million voters cast their ballots for mayors and town councilmen. Following two rounds of elections, the PT won nine state capitals and more than doubled the number of municipalities it had won in the 2000 elections; the Brazilian Social Democratic Party (PMDB) took 841 municipalities, including 5 state capitals. Despite its gains, the PT did not win the nation's two largest cities, São Paulo and Rio de Janeiro, and suffered setbacks in Rio Grande do Sul state, losing the capital, Porto Alegre, a city it had held for 16 years. After the elections and in anticipation of another cabinet reform, in November a number of top executives were replaced, including the defense minister, the president of the Bank of Brazil, and the president of the National Social and Economic Development Bank.

Over the course of 2004, the monetary policy committee of the central bank sought to maintain its benchmark interest rate. The rate in January 2004 was 16.5%, and after successive reductions in March and April that lowered it to its lowest level in three years (16%), the rate was increased to 16.25% in September and to 17.25% by the end of November amid inflationary pressures. Cumulative inflation was 7.2% year-on-year at the end of August. In 2003 Brazilian GDP reached 1.5 trillion reais. Showing evidence of the results of fiscal restraint, declining interest rates, favourable exchange rates, primary surplus targeting, and a general economic recovery, the public-sector net debt fell from 58.7% of GDP in December 2003 to 55.3% by the end of July 2004. In the first six months of 2004, Brazilian GDP grew 4.2% year-on-year. On October 11 the Brazilian Census Bureau reported that industrial production for August 2004 was up 13.1% year-on-year. At year's end the economy was on track to grow 5.3%, and the trade surplus was a record $33.7 billion.

In April extended clashes between heavily armed Cinta Larga Indians defending their lands and unarmed illegal diamond miners resulted in the killing of at least 35 prospectors in the jungles of the huge Roosevelt Reserve in Rondônia state. President Lula sent 350 troops and federal police to defuse the situation. Meanwhile, a group of more than 100 Indians convened at the Chamber of Deputies in Brasília on April 19 to draw attention to the lack of progress in government policy for demarcation of indigenous reserves. Another violent land conflict erupted on November 19 at the encampment of the Landless Workers' Movement in Minas Gerais state. At least five hooded gunmen invaded the farm, razed the structures, and killed five people.

President Lula led a historic mission to China in late May during which several investment agreements were negotiated. A reciprocal visit to Brazil in mid-November led by Chinese Pres. Hu Jintao brought agreement by Brazil to support Chinese entry into the World Trade Organization.

(JOHN CHARLES CUTTINO)

BRUNEI

Area: 5,765 sq km (2,226 sq mi)
Population (2004 est.): 351,000
Capital: Bandar Seri Begawan
Head of state and government: Sultan and Prime Minister Haji Hassanal Bolkiah Mu'izzaddin Waddaulah

In Brunei 2004 was an eventful year. During his 58th birthday speech on July 15, Sultan Haji Hassanal Bolkiah Mu'izzaddin Waddaulah made a landmark announcement on the revitalization of the Legislative Council, which was suspended in 1984. He also stated that the 1959 constitution was being reviewed and draft amendments would soon be debated by the Legislative Council. The sultan appointed 21 Legislative Council members on September 6. Eleven were state officials, including the sultan himself and selected government ministers, while 10 were nominated members; few had served in the 1960s Legislative Council. Meanwhile, in mid-August a revised and broadened succession and regency law was announced.

A gala royal wedding took place with much pomp and pageantry as Crown Prince Haji Al-Muhtadee Billah married Sarah binti Pengiran Salleh Ab Rahaman, the daughter of a Bruneian father and a Swiss-born mother. The festivities were attended by world dignitaries, including Prince Naruhito of Japan, the king of Malaysia, the duke of Gloucester from Great Britain, and luminaries from neighbouring countries.

Malaysia and Brunei sought to finalize their maritime boundary issue. The sultan met privately with Malaysian Prime Minister Datuk Seri Abdullah Ahmad Badawi while senior officials worked out the details of a settlement.

(B.A. HUSSAINMIYA)

BULGARIA

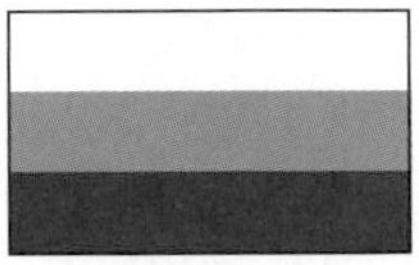

Area: 111,002 sq km (42,858 sq mi)
Population (2004 est.): 7,715,000
Capital: Sofia
Chief of state: President Georgi Purvanov
Head of government: Prime Minister Simeon Saxecoburggotski

In 2004 Bulgaria secured two major advances in its foreign-policy objectives. At the end of March, it was admitted to NATO, and there were also significant advances toward membership in the European Union. On February 19 the European Parliament's Foreign Affairs Committee reported favourably on Bulgaria's progress toward accession, and further progress was made possible when the Bulgarian assembly passed a number of amendments to the law on the judiciary. These reforms had been urgently demanded by Brussels and were aimed primarily at eliminating corruption from the judicial system. By the middle of June, negotiations had been completed, and Bulgaria's accession to the EU on Jan. 1, 2007, was virtually guaranteed, although it was also stated that the European Commission could decide to postpone the accession date for one year if it deemed there was a "serious risk" that Bulgaria might be unable to implement the remaining necessary reforms on time. That warning was partly a result of the continuing unhappiness of Pres. Georgi Purvanov and the Socialist opposition over the government's acceptance of the EU's demand for the closure of two more reactors at the Bulgarian nuclear power complex at Kozlodui.

There was a much less-happy outcome at the end of the trial of five Bulgarian nurses who, with a Palestinian doctor, were accused of having deliberately infected 426 Libyan children with HIV. The accused had been in detention since 1998 and had been maltreated in prison. Sentences were delivered on May 6, and, despite the evidence of expert witnesses from outside Libya, the accused were condemned to death. Appeals were immediately launched.

Bulgaria's involvement in Iraq created domestic tensions. Five Bulgarian soldiers had been killed in Karbala on Dec. 27, 2003, and some difficulty was later experienced in finding enough volunteers to replace the 500 troops who had finished their tour of duty early in 2004.

The government survived a motion of censure in the parliament on March 15, but the prime minister remained unpopular, mainly because the majority of the population did not feel that living standards were improving. The Bulgarian Socialist Party secured and retained a sizable lead in the opinion polls, a situation that was helped along by the weakness of the much-divided conservative factions. In July a simmering dispute between factions within the Bulgarian Orthodox Church ignited when police raided dozens of churches and detained a number of priests.

(RICHARD J. CRAMPTON)

Brunei's Crown Prince Haji Al-Muhtadee Billah, age 30, and the former Sarah Salleh, a 17-year-old half-Swiss commoner, recite a prayer during their opulent wedding ceremony on September 9.

BURKINA FASO

Area: 267,950 sq km (103,456 sq mi)
Population (2004 est.): 13,575,000
Capital: Ouagadougou
Chief of state: President Blaise Compaoré
Head of government: Prime Minister Ernest Paramanga Yonli

Preparations for the 2005 presidential elections got off to an early start after a cabinet minister revealed in January 2004 that Pres. Blaise Compaoré would be a candidate. On April 27 the National Assembly, dominated by the ruling Congress for Democracy and Progress Party, adopted a new electoral code that opposition parties claimed would make it more difficult for small parties to contest legislative and municipal elections. At a mass meeting in Ouagadougou on May 15, 14 parties comprising almost a quarter of the total number of deputies, declared themselves united in their opposition to Compaoré's reelection.

In July the government warned Côte d'Ivoire that it would fire on any of its military aircraft that flew into Burkina's airspace. On August 27 the government of Mauritania accused Burkina and Libya of having supported an abortive army coup earlier that month.

On May 17 Japan announced it would donate €2 million (about $2.4 million) to enable Burkina to purchase sufficient cereal stocks for domestic consumption. The government began an emergency distribution of insecticides as the first swarms of locusts appeared in the north of the country during the second week of August.

(NANCY ELLEN LAWLER)

BURUNDI

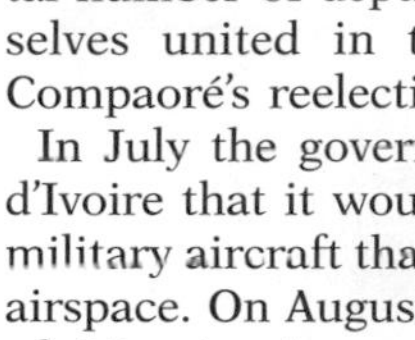

Area: 27,816 sq km (10,740 sq mi)
Population (2004 est.): 6,231,000 (excluding about 500,000 refugees in Tanzania)
Capital: Bujumbura
Head of state and government: President Domitien Ndayizeye

In late 2003 the oppositional Forces for Defense of Democracy (FDD) signed peace accords, but the Hutu rebel group, the National Liberation Front (FNL), single-handedly maintained the civil war in Burundi by continuing to attack government troops and civilians throughout most of 2004. The agreement brokered in November 2003 brought about peace to all of Burundi's 17 provinces except one, which suffered clashes between FNL forces and the country's army.

As many as 27,000 people were displaced and 21 persons were killed in April 2004 when fighting erupted between FNL rebels and the army near the capital, Bujumbura. By May the FDD had pulled out of the coalition government. In June a flood of 30,000 refugees crossed into Burundi from Bukavu in the Democratic Republic of the Congo (DRC) to escape attacks. Many of the Congolese refugees were Tutsi. On August 13 the FNL launched a well-organized nighttime assault on Gatumba camp, a UN refugee centre near Burundi's western border, from an over-the-border base in the DRC. Rebels shot or hacked to death more than 160 refugees, most of them Tutsi women and children. The FNL claimed responsibility for the assault. The Burundi and Rwandan governments threatened to invade the DRC to disarm Hutu rebels sheltered there. A month after the assault on the camp, many of the refugees returned to the DRC amid concerns from the UN that their safety was still at stake.

The coalition government, which shared power between the majority Hutu and the minority Tutsi, was dealt a blow in August in Pretoria, S.Af., when the FDD and 10 Tutsi-led groups refused to sign the power-sharing agreement. During 2004 more than 52,000 refugees returned to Burundi as part of a United Nations High Commissioner for Refugees effort to repatriate the 500,000 Burundians who had fled the country since 1993. Ahead of elections planned for October, the five-member Independent National Elections Commission was appointed in early September. The elections, later postponed until April 2005, were the final step in the three-year peace process to end the decade-long civil war.

(MARY F.E. EBELING)

CAMBODIA

Area: 181,035 sq km (69,898 sq mi)
Population (2004 est.): 13,450,000
Capital: Phnom Penh
Chief of state: Kings Norodom Sihanouk until October 6 and, from October 14, Norodom Sihamoni; acting heads of state were Chea Sim (April 10 to July 13), Nhek Bun Chhay (July 13–22), and Chea Sim (from July 22, concurrently with the king after October 14)
Head of government: Prime Minister Hun Sen

Plainclothes policemen check the bookstore in downtown Phnom Penh where prominent trade union leader Chea Vichea was gunned down on January 22. The assassination was linked to high-level political jockeying in Cambodia.

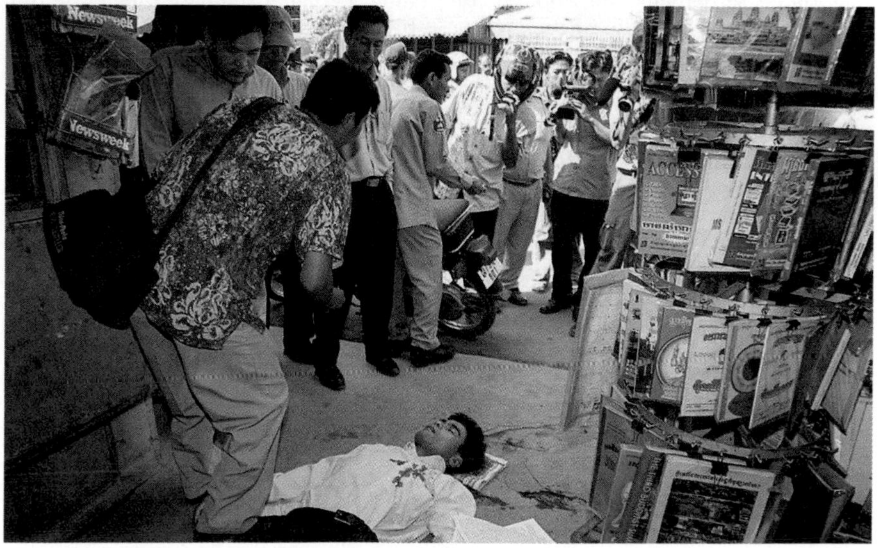

© AFP/Getty Images

Cambodia began 2004 still in the grips of the political deadlock between the majority Cambodian People's Party (CPP) of Prime Minister Hun Sen and the two other major royalist parties, National United Front for an Independent, Neutral, Peaceful and Cooperative Cambodia (Funcinpec) and the Sam Rainsy Party (SRP) on the other.

Cambodia's political deadlock began after the July 2003 elections, when constitutional requirements mandated a coalition that could not be reached. It lasted nearly a year. Although it did not seem to affect the everyday workings of the government, it meant that the National Assembly did not meet and no new ministers were appointed. Two important pieces of legislation were delayed for months and only passed when the new government was formed—the authorization of Cambodia's entry into the World Trade Organization and approval of a joint Cambodia-UN tribunal to try former Khmer Rouge leaders for genocide.

Several acts of political violence, including the assassination of labour leader Chea Vichea (*see* photo, page 375), seemed linked to the deadlocked negotiations. When a government was finally formed on June 26, 2004, by the CPP and Funcinpec, the agreement greatly increased the number of ministerial positions and thereby allowed both parties to reward supporters. The Funcinpec-SRP alliance, which originally had sought a single government of three parties, in effect ended, though the SRP was given a few minor posts.

The final agreement was questioned on constitutional grounds. Fearing that once the National Assembly was formed, legislators would abandon the negotiated settlement and appoint another prime minister, the CPP asked for a single-package vote to elect the president of the National Assembly and the prime minister, although the constitution stipulated that the National Assembly should be formed first and that its vote of confidence would enable the formation of the government. Sihanouk, absent from the country, deferred the matter to CPP leader Chea Sim, head of the Senate and acting head of state. A brief crisis materialized when, because of either constitutional issues or intraparty politics, Chea Sim also showed reluctance to sign. He too left the country temporarily—under duress, according to news reports—and the new government was signed into effect by the next in line in the Senate.

Following these events, King Sihanouk announced his intention to abdicate. The 81-year-old king was in poor health, complained of being insufficiently consulted in the formation of the government, and pushed for a clearer legal definition of royal succession to be put in place before his death. He officially left office on October 7. The National Assembly quickly enacted legislation to create a throne council, which in turn on October 14 named Norodom Sihamondi, Sihanouk's chosen successor, as king. Sihamondi, Sihanouk's son by the current queen, was formerly a ballet dancer and Cambodian representative to UNESCO.

(JOHN A. MARSTON)

CAMEROON

Area: 475,442 sq km (183,569 sq mi)
Population (2004 est.): 16,064,000
Capital: Yaoundé
Chief of state: President Paul Biya
Head of government: Prime Ministers Peter Mafany Musonge and, from December 8, Ephraim Inoni

Cameroon's main opposition parties once again faced failure in their efforts to defeat Pres. Paul Biya's bid for a third term in the election held on Oct. 11, 2004. Despite an agreement the previous year between the Social Democratic Front (SDF) and the Democratic Union of Cameroon (UDC) to unite behind a single candidate under the umbrella of the National Coalition for Reconciliation and Reconstruction, both parties nominated their own leaders. Opposition parties organized weekly protest marches in Yaoundé beginning in June. They demanded the computerization of the electoral rolls to eliminate the "ghost voters" supposedly widely employed by the government in the 1997 election. The government refused to consider such computerization, claiming that the costs of doing so would be prohibitive. The SDF suspended a demonstration called for August 30, which was intended to protest the assassination of a local SDF leader who had been killed during the night of August 20, after an election rally. Canada, the U.K., and Japan donated 63,000 transparent ballot boxes in the international effort to reduce vote fraud in the country. Turnout was high, and Biya won handily with about 75% of the vote.

Two BBC journalists were briefly imprisoned in July while visiting Cameroonian villages on the Bakassi peninsula. Both Nigeria and Cameroon claimed ownership of the oil-rich region, and under the auspices of a UN agreement, Nigeria was to withdraw by September 15. "Technical difficulties," however, forced a further delay.

President Biya attended ceremonies on August 15 marking the 60th anniversary of the liberation of Provence in southern France, in which Cameroonians, serving in the Tirailleurs Sénégalais alongside thousands of other West African troops, played a major role. On August 31 Prime Minister Peter Musonge officially opened a new floating bridge over the Mungo River to replace one that had collapsed in July. The bridge linked the francophone Cameroon with the anglophone Sud-Ouest region.

(NANCY ELLEN LAWLER)

CANADA

Area: 9,984,670 sq km (3,855,103 sq mi)
Population (2004 est.): 31,876,000
Capital: Ottawa
Chief of state: Queen Elizabeth II, represented by Governor-General Adrienne Clarkson
Head of government: Prime Minister Paul Martin

Domestic Affairs. After having won three successive majority governments since 1993, Canada's Liberal Party (LP) was humbled in a general election held on June 28, 2004. Jean Chrétien's retirement as prime minister in December 2003 had led to the selection of Paul Martin as his successor, and the LP's poor showing at the polls forced Martin to form a minority government.

The Martin administration had just begun when the auditor-general, Sheila Fraser, reported in February 2004 that she had documented serious irregularities in a program meant to enhance the federal government's image in Quebec. This program followed the 1995 referendum in which the separatist movement had been only narrowly defeated. The federal government allocated Can$250 million (Can$1 = about U.S.$0.75) to sponsor community and sporting events in Quebec. The money was disbursed through advertising and public-relations agencies friendly to the LP. It was discovered that many of these payments violated the Financial Administration Act through the use of fictitious invoices and shoddy record keeping. Martin took immediate action to deal with the scandal. A judicial inquiry was begun, and a lawyer was appointed to try to recover some of the improperly spent funds. A wave of anger, especially keen in Quebec, swept the country. The new prime minister had been Chrétien's finance minister and had successively balanced five budgets. Many Canadians therefore believed that Martin, as a senior minister from Quebec, had been aware of the misuse of public funds but had not taken action to correct it. It was against this backdrop that he announced a general election.

Martin was in a difficult position. He could not dwell on his success as finance minister, since he wanted to dissociate his government from the scandal of the previous Chrétien administration. Martin's conduct of the election campaign was uncertain, appearing to lack focus. He dwelled on his government's priority to strengthen public health care, vowed to improve the infrastructure of cities, pledged to spend more on defense and homeland security, and declared that he would accomplish all this while balancing the federal budget.

For the first time since the election of 1993, the Liberals faced a united conservative opposition. In late 2003 the two parties of the right—the historic Progressive Conservative Party and a newer group representing Western discontent, the Canadian Alliance—had merged into the Conservative Party of Canada (CP). The Alliance, formed in 2000, grew out of the Reform Party, which had been a voice for the West since 1987. On March 20, 2004, just three months before the election, the CP chose Stephen Harper (*see* BIOGRAPHIES) of the Alliance as its new leader. Harper attempted to establish a moderate tone for the new party but was hampered by extreme statements, mostly on social issues, made by some of the Western members of his organization. There was also the impression, which Harper tried to dispel, that the CP was sympathetic to introducing private medical care into the public system. The Conservatives vowed to cut taxes, both personal and corporate, and to strengthen the armed forces.

Canada's socialist New Democratic Party (NDP), led by Jack Layton, an urban reformer from Toronto, launched an ambitious agenda featuring massive spending on health care that would emphasize assistance for an improved drug plan and home care. At the same time, the NDP vowed to cut personal taxes and introduce an inheritance tax for upper-income Canadians. Opponents claimed that this agenda was unrealistic from a fiscal point of view. In Quebec the separatist Bloc Québécois (BQ) took on new life, not by preaching separatism, which it studiously avoided, but by attacking what it described as the corruption and cronyism of the LP in that province.

Public opinion polls were almost unanimous in predicting an electoral rebuke for the LP. In the voting the Canadian electorate punished the Liberals but did not take away their hold on government. Liberal MPs were reduced from 172 to 135 (with 155 of the 308 seats needed for a majority), and the party's popular vote was cut from 41% in the 2000 election to 37%. In Ontario, where the LP had held all but 3 of the province's 103 seats before the election, redistribution resulting from increased population had given the province 106 seats, of which the LP took 75. Nationally the Conservatives increased their position from 78 to 99 seats, including 24 in Ontario, mostly in the smaller towns and in rural areas. The NDP took 19 seats, including 7 in Ontario, with Layton winning a riding in downtown Toronto. The BQ, which had appeared to be in decline before the election, won almost every French-speaking constituency in Quebec, however, taking 54 of 75 seats to the LP's 21. In the Atlantic Provinces the Liberals posted a creditable showing, but they were humbled in the four Western Provinces, winning only 14 seats compared with the Conservatives' 68. In spite of the fact that a united CP had provided a strengthened opposition, voter turnout, at 60.5%, was the lowest ever in any general election.

The election results left Martin with a minority government, the first in Canada since 1979. Legislation would now have to be framed more carefully with a view to gaining support from other parties. Cooperation with the NDP seemed a reasonable course of action for the LP.

Martin reconstituted his 39-member cabinet on July 20. Six ministers had been defeated, and Martin needed to bring in new blood. Key posts were retained by close Martin associates, with Anne McLellan from Alberta continuing as deputy prime minister and minister of public safety and emergency preparedness and Ralph Goodale of Saskatchewan remaining minister of finance. Bill Graham from Toronto was moved from foreign affairs to national defense, while Pierre Pettigrew from Quebec took over the foreign-affairs portfolio.

The strengthening of Canada's prized system of public health care proved to be Prime Minister Martin's first test. During the election campaign all the parties had placed this objective as a top priority. Structural problems in the Canadian federation made changes in health care especially difficult. Canada's 140-year-old constitution alloted responsibility for the delivery of many personal and social services to the provinces, medical care being one example. Increasing medical costs meant that this responsibility had consumed an ever-larger proportion of provincial budgets. The federal government, possessing a larger taxing power, had transferred funds over the years to the provinces to help them in the delivery of health care.

The question of how to reconcile the disparity between revenues and responsibilities in the national health care system was the theme of a first ministers' conference held in Ottawa during September 13–15. Martin chaired the meeting, which was attended by first ministers from the 10 provinces and the 3 northern territories. Provinces and territories banded together to insist on larger federal transfers for health care. After three days of marathon bargaining, Martin agreed to provide larger federal grants than he had promised in his election campaign. Over the next 10 years, the federal government would contribute the massive sum of Can$41.2 billion to the provinces and territories for the delivery of medical care. An unprecedented feature of this transfer was the inclusion of an escalator clause committing Ottawa to an annual increase of 6% beginning in 2006. The escalator would provide Can$18 billion over the next six years. In an effort to reduce delays in the provision of health services, evidence-based benchmarks would be established by each province to measure its performance. A side agreement was negotiated by Quebec that would allow it to collect and share information for its own targets on reducing waiting periods.

© Larry Downing/Reuters/Corbis

Canadian Prime Minister Paul Martin (right) is shown with U.S. Pres. George W. Bush in Halifax, N.S., on December 1. Relations between the two countries remained somewhat strained in 2004.

(Quebec's provincial health plan embodied different procedures than were used in other provinces, and it was therefore allowed to work toward common national goals in its own way.) Martin defended the Quebec deal, saying that it represented a form of asymmetrical federalism that recognized the differences between the provinces. The largesse provided by the federal government at the Ottawa meeting represented a considerable financial commitment that might make it difficult for the national government to fund other promised programs.

The Economy. The Canadian economy performed well in 2004 following the shocks of the previous year. The recovery resulted from expanded trade with Canada's leading partners, the U.S., China, and Japan. High crude oil prices gave an added boost to Canada's trade position. By the middle of the year, the trade surplus had reached a three-year high. Economic growth of 2.9% was forecast for 2004. Inflation was under control, although rising energy prices were worrisome. In September the consumer price index showed an increase of 1.8% on a year-over-year basis. Employment was steady, with an unemployment rate of 7.1% recorded in September.

Goodale released the first budget of the Martin government on March 23. It was a prudent budget. New spending and minor measures of tax relief amounted to only Can$2.2 billion, lower than in previous budgets under Chrétien. The new government, in order to cut costs, promised a sweeping review of all federal operations. An office of comptroller general was reestablished to oversee government spending. Goodale took a conservative stance on a possible surplus. In October, as revenues exceeded expectations, he revised his Can$1.9 billion surplus upward to Can $9.1 billion.

Foreign Affairs. Prime Minister Martin made his first official visit to Washington for discussions with U.S. Pres. George W. Bush on April 29–30. No action was taken on bilateral commercial issues such as the U.S. duties imposed on Canadian softwood lumber and the ban on beef imports from Canada because of the "mad cow" scare in 2003 (a second case was reported in late December). In an earlier meeting between Bush and Martin in Mexico, President Bush had announced that Canada would be allowed to bid on reconstruction projects in Iraq. The U.S. also promised to consult Ottawa before Canadian citizens were deported to third countries. This decision resulted from a case in 2002 in which a Canadian citizen, suspected of links with a terrorist organization, was seized in New York and deported to Syria for questioning.

Discussions continued between the U.S. and Canada on a missile defense shield for North America. The plan aroused misgivings in Canada, mainly because critics believed it would lead to the placing of weapons in outer space. These anxieties were revealed in a debate in the House of Commons on February 24 when the BQ brought forward a motion to cut off the talks. The motion was defeated 155–71. To everyone's surprise, 30 Liberals, taking advantage of an opportunity to cast a vote free from party discipline, sided with the BQ motion. The prime minister had stated his intention to allow more free votes in Parliament. On this occasion his action revealed deep divisions within his own party.

President Bush paid his first official visit to Canada on November 30 and December 1. There were no announcements on bilateral commercial issues, although the president warmly praised Canada for having sheltered airline passengers stranded north of the border on Sept. 11, 2001. The president urged Canada to join in the controversial U.S. scheme for ballistic-missile defense. He announced his desire to promote multilateral action in international affairs provided it achieved effective results.

The dispute over softwood lumber imports into the U.S. moved toward a possible solution in 2004. During the summer it was announced that the U.S. Department of Commerce had miscalculated the costs of lumber operations in Canada and had therefore agreed to halve the 27% duties imposed in 2002. This action would not take effect until the end of the year and could be appealed in the meantime. On August 31 a panel set up under the North American Free Trade Agreement (NAFTA), composed of three American and two Canadian members, rejected the claim by American lumber producers that Canada unfairly subsidized its softwood lumber exports. The panel ruled that Canadian practices did not cause injury to American lumber interests and that the duties should be scrapped. Canadian softwood lumber exports to the U.S. were valued at Can$10 billion annually and represented a 34% share of the American lumber market.

While the Martin government moved to increase the size of the military and acquire new equipment, such as the purchase of 28 Sikorsky H-92 maritime helicopters in July, it decided that it could no longer station more than 1,600 troops abroad on peacekeeping and peace-enforcing missions. With another 8,000 soldiers preparing for overseas assignments at any one time, peacekeeping personnel accounted for one third of Canada's deployable forces. By mid-August 500 soldiers and six helicopters had been withdrawn from Haiti, although Canadian police were to be sent to train a Haitian force. The main bodies of overseas soldiers and airmen were in Afghanistan, where in November, 950 Canadians served with the International Security Assistance Force, and in Bosnia and Herzegovina, where 350 men and women were stationed. Other contingents were to be found in the Sinai and the Golan Heights.

(DAVID M.L. FARR)

CAPE VERDE

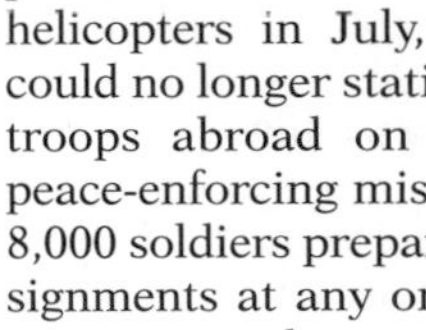

Area: 4,033 sq km (1,557 sq mi)
Population (2004 est.): 454,000
Capital: Praia
Chief of state: President Pedro Pires
Head of government: Prime Minister José Maria Neves

In 2004, because of Cape Verde's political stability and reputation for efficient government and an economy that had provided annual GDP growth averaging 7% a year for a decade, the UN Economic and Social Council decided to review its status as a "least developed country." Though the government was concerned that becoming a "medium developed county" would mean less international aid, it saw reclassification as a recognition of its success. On the UN Development Programme's Human Development Index, Cape Verde now ranked second in sub-Saharan Africa, after Mauritius. Cape Verde's main sources of income remained aid, overseas remittances (more Cape Verdeans lived abroad than in the country itself), and fish exports. The government aimed to establish a more broadly based economy. Offshore oil exploration was a possibility, and tourism was seen as a major growth area, expected to be boosted by the new international airport to open at the capital, Praia, by the end of 2004. In August, when visiting China, Prime Minister José Maria Neves said that Cape Verde hoped to become West Africa's main freight transit and financial centre. Meanwhile, locust swarms, blown from the African mainland, devoured what vegetation they could find on the islands.

(CHRISTOPHER SAUNDERS)

CENTRAL AFRICAN REPUBLIC

Area: 622,436 sq km (240,324 sq mi)
Population (2004 est.): 3,742,000
Capital: Bangui
Chief of state: President François Bozizé
Head of government: Prime Minister Célestin Gaombalet

Under increasing international pressure to restore democratic institutions to the Central African Republic (CAR), on May 25, 2004, Pres. François Bozizé, in power since the 2003 military coup, appointed 30 people to sit on the newly created Mixed Independent Electoral Commission formed to oversee legislative and presidential elections scheduled for Jan. 30 and Feb. 27, 2005. Despite being in exile in Togo, former president Ange-Félix Patassé was reelected head of the Movement for the Liberation of the Central African People at its June 6 convention, and he declared himself a candidate, but on December 31 a court ruled him ineligible to run.

The National Transitional Council (CNT) met in June and again in August to discuss proposed constitutional reform and electoral procedures. On September 3, seven opposition parties denounced both the constitution and the electoral code, claiming they did not reflect the directives agreed upon earlier. The constitution was approved in a referendum that was held on December 5.

Hundreds of former rebels rioted in April, demanding payments promised them for supporting Bozizé in the coup. Civil servants went on a three-day strike that effectively shut down the government in late August. On July 23 the IMF approved a $8.2 million credit to assist the country in stabilizing its finances and continuing its program of political reform.

(NANCY ELLEN LAWLER)

CHAD

Area: 1,284,000 sq km (495,755 sq mi)
Population (2004 est.): 9,539,000, excluding some 180,000 refugees from The Sudan
Capital: N'Djamena
Chief of state: President Lieut. Gen. Idriss Déby
Head of government: Prime Minister Moussa Faki

In 2004 Chad received the first share of royalties from the large oil project that went onstream in 2003. Estimated at about $100 million, these royalties added another 40% to the government's revenues. In theory, a citizens' committee was to review all spending, but, despite a very low standard of living in the country, the government had used much of the $25 million signing bonus it got before the completion of the pipeline to Cameroon to purchase arms. After an abortive army uprising in the capital, which Pres. Idriss Déby claimed had been organized to overthrow him, the parliament in May approved the idea of amending the constitution to allow him to seek a third term as president.

International attention focused on eastern Chad because of the humanitarian disaster caused by the genocide in the Darfur region of The Sudan, which borders Chad. By midyear there were an estimated 180,000 Sudanese refugees in some 10 large camps located in a remote part of the country. The death rate in the camps was high, and as disease spread, Chadians living nearby were affected. Meanwhile, a cholera epidemic broke out in western Chad and spread to the capital, and locusts fell on what vegetation there was in this very arid country.

From December 2003 Chad hosted a series of talks between the Sudanese government and the Darfur rebels, and a cease-fire agreement was signed in April 2004. This did not hold, however, and the Chadian government began to accuse the Janjawid militia of helping to revive the Renewed National Front of Chad (FNTR) rebel movement. The Chadian army clashed with the Janjawid militia raiding across the border. The army uprising in N'Djamena in mid-May was thought to have resulted from dissatisfaction with the relatively

Tens of thousands of refugees from the Darfur region of The Sudan poured over Chad's eastern border in 2004, including this woman and child at the UN's Bredjing camp photographed in late August.

© Jehad Nga/Corbis

conciliatory line being taken by the Chadian authorities towards the Sudanese government.

(CHRISTOPHER SAUNDERS)

CHILE

Area: 756,096 sq km (291,930 sq mi)
Population (2004 est.): 15,824,000
Capitals: Santiago (national) and Valparaíso (legislative)
Head of state and government: President Ricardo Lagos Escobar

The big story in Chile in 2004 revolved around former president Gen. Augusto Pinochet Ugarte. In July a U.S. Senate committee reported that between 1994 and 2002 the Washington, D.C.-based Riggs Bank had helped Pinochet hide millions of dollars in at least six secret bank accounts and apparently aided him in setting up phony offshore companies and illegally transferring funds to them. These unlawful activities played a significant role in changing Pinochet's image in Chile dramatically and in opening the way for his prosecution for human rights crimes. Even right-wing supporters could no longer claim that he had acted only to help his country during a turbulent time. Pinochet also damaged his case against prosecution on medical grounds by giving a lucid interview to a Miami, Fla.-based television station. As a result, Chile's Supreme Court lifted his immunity in late August, and Judge Juan Guzmán Tapia questioned the former dictator at his home in September with regard to his participation in Operation Condor, an international intelligence network formed by Southern Cone military governments in the 1970s to capture and eliminate regime opponents. Although Pinochet denied any involvement, he was considered the moving force behind the creation of Operation Condor. On December 13 Judge Guzmán ruled that Pinochet was, after all, fit for trial. Meanwhile, the report of an official commission investigating systematic torture and other abuses during the 1973–90 period was delivered to President Lagos in mid-November and published on the Internet a few weeks later. In response, Lagos announced that the government would offer lifetime pensions to some 28,000 past victims of torture.

Attention also focused increasingly on the presidential elections slated for December 2005. The big question was whether the ruling Concertación could hold on to the presidency for another six-year term or whether the right-wing Alliance for Chile candidate, Joaquín Lavín, currently mayor of Santiago, would triumph. The novelty for this election was that two of the most popular politicians were women. Foreign Minister Soledad Alvear, a Christian Democrat, had significant political experience, having served as the first minister of the National Service for Women and as minister of justice under former president Eduardo Frei. The younger and more charismatic left-wing Socialist Michelle Bachelet had much less political experience but had developed a good relationship with the military during her stint as defense minister, and she came from a military family.

Overall economic growth for the year was pegged at 5%, and inflation was low, at 3%. Trade continued to grow, partly as a result of the implementation of several new free-trade agreements (FTAs), including one with the U.S. The trade balance for the year was positive. Negotiations for an FTA with China and with New Zealand and Singapore (in the three-way Pacific Three Closer Economic Partnership) advanced significantly. In a second attempt to levy a fee on the copper industry, the government proposed another royalty-fee bill to Congress on December 15.

In late September the giant Ralco hydroelectric plant became operational after years of controversy. The plant affected not only domestic indigenous and environmental policies but also foreign affairs. A portion of the Mapuche community opposed the project because of its location on indigenous lands, and they, as well as environmental activists, decried the project's negative impact on the environment. The completion of the project was a partial answer to a burgeoning energy problem affecting relations in the region. During 2004 there was an increasing conflict with Argentina over its restrictions on the sale of natural gas to Chile; relations further deteriorated when Argentina signed an agreement to buy natural gas from Bolivia, which also forbade Argentina to sell this gas to Chile. Bolivia began rattling sabres with Chile over the loss of its access to the sea in the late 19th-century War of the Pacific.

(LOIS HECHT OPPENHEIM)

CHINA

Area: 9,572,900 sq km (3,696,100 sq mi), including Tibet and excluding Taiwan and the special autonomous regions of Hong Kong and Macau
Population (2004 est., excluding Taiwan, Hong Kong, and Macau): 1,298,848,000
Capital: Beijing
Chief of state: President Hu Jintao
Head of government: Premier Wen Jiabao

Domestic Politics. The transition of power from the third to the fourth generation of Communist Party of China (CPC) leadership had begun with the 16th party Congress, when Jiang Zemin passed his title of CPC general secretary to party Political Bureau member and Vice Pres. Hu Jintao. In March 2003 Hu became president when Jiang retired, yet Jiang retained the key position of chairman of the CPC Central Military Commission, or de facto head of the armed forces.

Jiang and his associates were actively promoting old policies, which made for some confusion in Beijing. The policies and political styles of Hu and Premier Wen Jiabao were quite different from Jiang's. Jiang, for example, favoured rapid accumulation of national wealth, while Hu and Wen tended to pay more attention to a fair distribution of wealth. Because Chinese politics still operated in a "black box" environment, the security of the new leaders' jobs was not at all certain, and it was difficult for outsiders to ascertain who was really in power, since Jiang seemed to have maintained overall control over the military and possibly over state affairs generally. Some believed that Jiang had packed the membership of the Military Commission with his protégés, which could have gravely undermined the authority of the new leadership. In the event, however, the Fourth CC Plenum in September completed the transfer of power; Jiang resigned the Military Commission post; and Hu assumed control over the military. These events were remarkable in the history of Communist China in that they represented the first peaceful leadership succession. Party, state, and military power were all now securely in Hu's hands.

In March the People's National Congress adopted landmark revisions to the 1982 constitution that would protect private property for the first time since the Communists took power in 1949—and thereby apparently abandoned one of the key pillars of communism. In other new text the state committed itself to respecting human rights. Weak and ambiguous wording, however, such as "A citizen's lawful private property is inviolable" and "The state respects and preserves human rights" did not lead one to believe these would now be the government's top priorities. Rather, the administration's immediate attention was given to problems in the countryside and to widespread official corruption.

From 1998 to 2003 net income per capita increased 9% in urban areas but only 4.3% in rural areas. The government took steps to reduce farmers' taxes and rein in overinvestment that took away arable land from the farmers. Township and village administration were merged in order to reduce redundant layers, and 7,400 local government units were eliminated. After some 8,371 corrupt functionaries had fled the country in the first half of 2003, the government cracked down on other high-ranking officials, including the governor of Hubei province and the former minister of land and resources. Strengthening the party's governing capacity—even above administrative or political reform—was the central theme of Hu's first moves after Jiang's retirement. Hu claimed that by improving the selection and oversight of party officials, corrupt and incompetent officials could be kept out of office.

The Economy. China's quickly expanding but energy-poor economy was another serious challenge facing the new leadership. Much attention was given to the question of how to ensure a soft landing for the economy and improve the energy supply. Although China enjoyed a robust 9.1% GDP growth rate in 2003, it had to import about 50% of its crude oil to fuel the overheated manufacturing sector and residential demand. The demand for oil grew by 9% in 2003, double the 1992 level, and net oil imports in 2003 were more than twice the 1998 level. Oil imports rose by nearly 40% year-on-year in the first eight months of 2004. Even so, 24 out of 31 provinces, municipalities, and regions suffered from power blackouts in the first half of the year. Fiscal policy was tightened through a series of administrative regulations that were aimed at cooling investment, especially in such sectors as property development, automotive, steel, aluminum, and cement. More than 4,800 industrial development zones were shut down, and more than 1,300 sq km (500 sq mi) of land were returned to agricultural use. Investment grew 26% year-on-year in August, down from a 43% growth in the first quarter. Although the economic growth was as high as 9.8% in the first quarter and 9.6% in the second quarter, the government was expected to bring the overall figure for the year close to 8%. The growth in retail sales—especially in telecommunications equipment and household furniture—would ease the pressure on the economic austerity, and a soft landing was projected in 2005.

To ensure smooth development, a long-overdue reform of the banking system was needed. At the beginning of 2004, the State Council injected $45 billion into the Bank of China and the China Construction Bank to encourage corporate reconstruction by transferring assets into stocks. The goal was to introduce hard budget constraint to the banking system and, among other results, to implement more fully the central "financial retrenchments" policy.

GDP per capita exceeded $1,000 in 2004, and China faced a new growing pain; as the economy entered a "golden era of development," social conflicts were expected to increase considerably. On the one hand, the better-developed coastal areas started to lose cheap labour and affordable land; on the other, increased wages put higher demand on housing, automobiles, education, leisure life, health care, and environmental protection. The increasing disparity between the advantaged and the disadvantaged in recent years had induced conflicting goals in government policies. The state had found it more difficult to satisfy different interest groups.

A quarter century of economic reform had produced a sizable middle class. A report of the Chinese Academy of Social Sciences estimated that 19% of the population had entered the middle-level income stratum, with family income between 150,000 and 300,000 yuan (about $18,000 to $36,000). This group had steadily increased by 1% annually in recent years. Those who first entered the stratum included business people in science-and-technology-oriented sectors; professionals in legal, financial, security, insurance, and accounting services; managers and executives in multinational corporations; and successful private businessmen. The Ministry of Labour and Social Security launched a new plan of training 500,000 "blue-collar high-tech experts" in the coming three years in order to meet the rising demand for labour in the manufacturing and services sectors. This group would also join the middle class in the near future.

Nonetheless, the labour market continued to face challenges from unemployment and the withering of the state economic sector. Reforms in the state sector continued to create surplus workers. The registered unemployment rate increased from 3.1% in 1998 to 4.2% in 2003. Among the 27.8 million workers laid off during this period of time, only 18.5 million had found new jobs. Under World Trade Organization regulations, the import of cheaper agricultural products would further reduce farmers' income and job opportunities in rural areas. It was estimated that there were 150 million rural workers who did not have full-time jobs, and these people continued to migrate to the cities and the south, where the economy was better.

Special Administrative Regions and Tibet. Vigourous new development in the gaming industry boosted revenue and employment in Macao. Beijing expected some $1.1 billion in tax revenues from the industry in 2004. When the government deregulated gambling, foreign investors were able to compete with local hotel and casino owners, and a plan was unveiled by Galaxy, a U.S.-Hong Kong syndicate, in December 2003 to build a $1.1 billion resort

The Sands Macao casino, developed by Las Vegas, Nev., gaming tycoon Sheldon Adelson, opened in the former Portuguese colony in May.

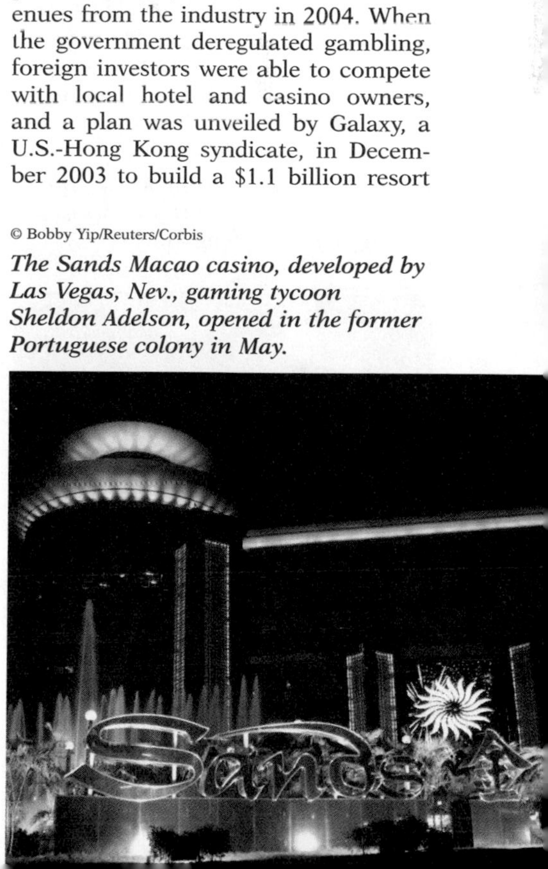

complex. Experts predicted that in the next few years, the 26.8-sq-km (10.3-sq-mi) area would attract $3.8 billion investment in the gaming industry, which was enjoying a high degree of autonomy under China's principle of "one country, two systems." Elections in Hong Kong, however, ostensibly organized under the same "one country, two systems" principle, showed more controversy than freedom of choice. Beijing was accused of trying to influence the outcome, using tactics such as recruiting Chinese Olympic medalists to appear at events just before the election to present a positive image of the central government. In the event, the pro-Beijing camp won 34 out of 60 seats.

Progress was made on resolving the status of Tibet. The Dalai Lama openly acknowledged that Tibet was a part of China and sent high-level envoys to Beijing in September to discuss the possibiliity of the Buddhist leader's return home.

Foreign Relations. A good relationship with the United States and a peaceful regional environment had been critical to China's rapid economic development. Ironically, however, the very pace of China's growth raised international concerns, which had the potential to undermine those very important pillars of Chinese foreign relations. In November 2003, speaking to the Boao Forum—an international symposium on the global economic future—Zheng Bijian, head of the Central Party School and senior adviser to President Hu, outlined a vision of China and Asia rising together in peace and prosperity. Premier Wen, visiting Harvard University a month later, introduced this "peaceful rise" concept to the American audience. Wen said that China "must more fully and more consciously depend on [its] own structural innovation, on constantly expanding the domestic market, on converting the huge savings of [its] citizens into investment, and on improving the quality of the population and scientific and technological progress to solve the problems of resources and the environment." This strategy, Wen continued, was the "essence of China's relative peaceful rise and development." Then President Hu, in his speech marking Mao Zedong's 110th birthday in December 2003 and, later, at a February 2004 "collective study" session held for the CCP Political Bureau, started to promote "peaceful development" as a state policy. At the annual United Nations Economic and Social Commission for Asia and the Pacific (UNESCAP) meeting in Shanghai in April 2004, Vice Pres. Zeng Qinghong explained to the participants that China would pursue grand cooperation and mutual benefits with other countries as its peaceful development strategy.

Election candidate Leung Kwok Hung (called "Long Hair," left) protests at a polling centre in Hong Kong on September 12.

© Ted Aljibe/AFP/Getty Images

Chinese scholars had conducted many systematic studies of historical precedents of rising powers—including the cases of pre- and post-World War II Japan and Germany—and determined how conflicts with other countries might be avoided. Government advisers emphasized the goal of a peaceful and cooperative China that would coordinate its own rapid economic growth with the needs of its neighbours in order to avoid drastic dislocations. According to this vision, China would promote an interdependent, rather than a competitive, relationship with its neighbours and the world. This notion aroused much skepticism in other countries, where analysts wondered how the world order could fail to be upset by rapid development in China. In reponse, many Chinese scholars maintained that China had already risen peacefully from its economic situation of a quarter century ago without military confrontation with any major powers.

Foreign policy is always an extension of domestic politics, and a policy shift to "peaceful development" could certainly be expected to precipitate a political struggle in Beijing. Jiang and his associates sought to make the Taiwan case an exception to "peaceful development" and, more important, believed that no new policy was needed at all, since his thoughts on the "Three Represents doctrine" adequately addressed the themes of peaceful development. In mid-May, Jiang called for either a ban on the new concept or a redefinition of it along his old policy line.

The new concept did present a significant shift in domestic and foreign policy. Jiang's group relied on nationalism and stressed the military need to ensure a prosperous and strong state. They also focused on the relationship with the U.S. to such an extent that it preempted comprehensive relations with other countries. With "peaceful development," however, Hu and Wen aimed at gaining acceptance first from neighbouring countries. They had expended much energy on developing closer political, economic, and military relationships with other Asian powers, notably a joint military exercise to be held with Russia in 2005, dialogues and trade with Central Asian countries, and collective and bilateral regional agreements with Association of South East Asian Nations countries (an open-market agreement with ASEAN was signed on November 29).

Although China had made a point of explaining how its growing economic strength would benefit the countries around it and once its border disputes with India, Vietnam, and Russia had been resolved, potentially serious territorial disputes emerged with Japan and the two Koreas. After Japan arrested seven Chinese activists who had landed on Diaoyu Island (known as Senkaku to the Japanese; about 300 km [180 mi] northeast of Taiwan), China called the arrest a violation of its sovereignty and demanded their immediate release. The ancient Koguryo kingdom flourished between 37 BC and AD 668 along the Yalu River, straddling what is now the Sino–North Korean border. Koguryo was considered the birthplace of the Korean nation but was claimed by China as a subordinate state that fell under the jurisdiction of the ancient Chinese dynasties.

On two occasions in 2004, China made efforts to bring North Korea back to the Six-Party Talks. Not much progress was made, and the fourth round scheduled for the end of September was aborted owing to reluctance of North Korea and policy uncertainty in a presidential election year in the U.S.

Chinese Vice-Premier Wu Yi met with U.S. Commerce Secretary Donald Evans in an effort to resolve a series of mutual trade problems. Agreement was reached on protection of intellectual property rights, high-technology transfers, and acceleration of plans to facilitate U.S. companies' exporting and selling directly to China. In addition, the two countries set up six working groups under the framework of the Sino-U.S. Joint Trade Commission on Commerce and Trade to study the Chinese market economy, Sino-U.S. trade resolutions, inspection of agricultural products, textile trade, intellectual property rights, and trade statistics. Newly appointed Chinese Commerce Minister Bo Xilai also encouraged Chinese investment in foreign countries. The government considered making its foreign-exchange rates more flexible, which was one of the issues discussed at the Group of Seven summit in September 2004, the first time China had been invited to participate.

(XIAOBO HU)

COLOMBIA

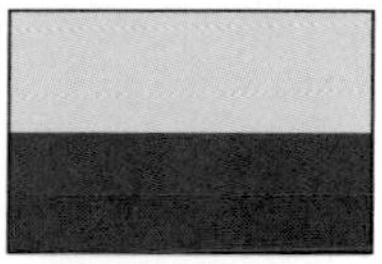

Area: 1,141,568 sq km (440,762 sq mi)
Population (2004 est.): 42,311,000
Capital: Bogotá
Head of state and government: President Álvaro Uribe Vélez

In 2004 the government of Pres. Álvaro Uribe Vélez struggled to overcome political setbacks that began in late 2003. Key political reforms in an October 2003 referendum failed to gain enough support to enter into law, mainly because of insufficient voter turnout. The government had claimed that the legal changes were necessary to give the president authority to combat corruption and to revitalize the economy.

Despite the defeat at the polls, the administration pushed ahead with its hard-line stance toward armed groups on the left and the right. According to official figures, the number of guerrillas and paramilitaries killed had risen sharply in the first year of the Uribe administration. The left-wing Revolutionary Armed Forces of Colombia (FARC) appeared unprepared for the more vigorous government approach; they had lost control over much of the countryside that the government had ceded to them, and they now chose to fight a more urban battle. The government's Patriot Plan took the fight to members of the FARC surrounding the capital, then pushed into the southeastern states of Caquetá and Guaviare.

In June 2004 the government and the National Liberation Army (ELN), a much-smaller left-wing guerrilla group, agreed to a cease-fire in order to enter into peace talks. The military had all but eliminated the group from its former strongholds of eastern Antioquia and Arauca, and right-wing paramilitaries had expelled it from Barrancabermeja, a northern oil city. Desertion among its ranks and a loss of favour with some of its European supporters seemed to bode well for a more conciliatory ELN.

Earlier in the year, talks with the United Self-Defense Forces of Colombia (AUC), a right-wing paramilitary group, led to an agreement supported by the Organization of American States (OAS). Under the plan, the AUC would be confined to a limited area in northern Colombia, and the OAS would be responsible for monitoring its disarmament (which began in late 2003). The plan went ahead despite the disappearance and presumed death of Carlos Castaño, the group's leader, in late April. AUC leaders were granted safe passage to Bogotá in order to address Congress in July, and the AUC disarmed and gave up plundered property in November and December.

Government gains against guerrillas and paramilitaries did not come without a price, however. Observers were alarmed by what they saw as ever-increasing human rights violations by the government in its war on the FARC, the ELN, and the AUC. President Uribe was seen as more interested in security than democracy, and the light-handed treatment of the AUC during the peace talks was viewed as a condoning of their past violent actions. Still, Uribe enjoyed widespread popularity, and there were continued efforts to revise the constitution to allow him to seek reelection in 2006. Colombia's economy was expected to grow by 4% during 2004, and the debt-to-GDP ratio was predicted to fall; the government's budget aimed for a deficit equal to 2.5% of GDP in 2004 and 2.4% in 2005. The October 2003 referendum would have permitted cuts in government spending by $7 billion over seven years. As it was, constitutional provisions mandated transfer of funds to local governments and other obligated spending, and the central government was left with discretion over only 10% of total expenditures. Congress was asked to expand the base of the value-added tax, increase taxes on pensions, and put a ceiling on pensions in an effort to bolster public finances. Analysts pointed out the irony that if the administration pushed for an extra term for the president, its efforts at fiscal responsibility might come to naught; Uribe might ensure his own reelection but leave himself a badly foundering economy. On November 30 Congress lifted the reelection ban.

(BRIAN F. CRISP)

COMOROS

Area: 1,862 sq km (719 sq mi), excluding the 374-sq-km (144-sq-mi) island of Mayotte, a de facto dependency of France since 1976
Population (2004 est.): 596,000 (excluding 172,000 on Mayotte)
Capital: Moroni
Chief of state and head of government: President Col. Azali Assoumani

Following the signing of the Moroni Agreement in December 2003, which mandated elections in Comoros and ironed out economic agreements, two rounds of parliamentary elections were held in April 2004. The elections had been postponed for more than a year owing to disagreements over the devolution process on the three islands—Anjouan, Grande Comore, and Mohéli. The process had been fraught with tensions since it was mandated by the Organization of African Unity in February 2001 to bring stability to the island country, which had suffered more than 20 coups since gaining independence from France in 1975. In both election rounds the party of federal Pres. Azali Assoumani suffered major setbacks, winning only 6 of the 33 national assembly seats. The majority of seats, 12, went to the parties of the autonomous islands' presidents, and the remaining 15 seats were to be appointed by the parliaments of the three islands. The new assembly finally opened in June but not without continuing tensions between the parties.

In view of the years of political instability, the IMF called for sustainable economic reforms and an immediate solution to the distribution of federal funds among the island governments.

(MARY F.E. EBELING)

CONGO, DEMOCRATIC REPUBLIC OF THE

Area: 2,344,858 sq km (905,354 sq mi)
Population (2004 est.): 54,417,000
Capital: Kinshasa
Head of state and government: President Joseph Kabila

The year 2004 began on a hopeful note in the Democratic Republic of the Congo (DRC), with a flurry of diplomatic activity aimed at improving relations with Rwanda and Uganda, but as early as February there were reports that Mai-Mai fighters who had opposed the government during the civil war were again killing people in Katanga province. Problems of another character were reported in March when the International Atomic Energy Agency called for an immediate investigation into reports that uranium and other minerals were being mined illegally at Shinkolobwe, Katanga, and sold locally to foreign businessmen who were processing them and exporting them via Zambia.

On March 28 gunmen thought to have been supporters of former president Mobutu Sese Seko attacked military installations and radio and TV stations in and around Kinshasa in what was believed to have been an attempted coup. Government forces quickly restored order. On May 14 two warring factions in the Ituri district of Orientale province signed an agreement intended to end their conflict, but fighting continued. At the end of June, UN peacekeeping forces arrested the leaders of the two groups. Early in July government envoys met with the leaders of other groups in the district with a view to achieving total disarmament of the conflicting factions, and by mid-September some progress had been made.

Potentially more serious was the seizure on June 2 of the town of Bukavu, the capital of South Kivu province, by two dissident army officers, Brig. Gen. Laurent Nkunda and Col. Jules Mutebusi. Both had commanded forces opposed to the government and had been backed by Rwanda during the civil war. They claimed their attack was aimed at protecting Tutsi from maltreatment by government soldiers. After a week UN peacekeepers helped to negotiate their withdrawal before government reinforcements arrived, but that did not prevent violent demonstrations against UN compounds in many parts of the country. The protesters were denouncing UN troops in Bukavu for not resisting the invaders.

AP/Wide World Photos

Men load cobalt ore into sacks at the Shinkolobwe mine in southeastern Democratic Republic of the Congo in April. The mine attracted international attention for possible illegal activities in 2004.

Scarcely had Bukavu been reoccupied than another putative coup took place in Kinshasa, on June 11. Pres. Joseph Kabila was quick to accuse Rwanda of being behind the capture of Bukavu, a charge that was firmly refuted by Rwandan officials. Rwandan Pres. Paul Kagame's response was to close his country's border with the DRC, but on July 3, after a meeting with President Kabila in Abuja, Nigeria, he reopened it.

Tension was heightened again in August, however, when Nkunda threatened to renew his campaign in South Kivu following the massacre of Congolese Tutsi who had taken refuge in Burundi. A group said by Nkunda to have links with the DRC government had claimed responsibility for the killing. In December intense fighting erupted in North Kivu province amid reports that Rwandan troops had entered the area. Rwanda, however, denied involvement.

Reconstruction began in eastern DRC with a limited but significant improvement in communications. The railway link between the town of Kindu in Maniema province and Lubumbashi, the provincial capital of Katanga, was reopened on June 29, and on August 7 barge traffic recommenced from Kindu for a distance of 350 km (210 mi) up the Congo River. (KENNETH INGHAM)

CONGO, REPUBLIC OF THE

Area: 342,000 sq km (132,047 sq mi)
Population (2004 est.): 3,818,000
Capital: Brazzaville
Head of state and government: President Denis Sassou-Nguesso

An improved economic and political climate resulted in a series of meetings with the International Monetary Fund, which opened consultations with the Republic of the Congo government on May 24, 2004. The IMF announced in July that it would undertake a three-year program designed to reduce poverty and increase economic growth. While inflationary pressures had eased, there was still concern over the amount of new government debt incurred as a result of continuing budget deficits.

The government admitted on June 5 that a large trade in illegal diamonds existed in the country but disclaimed all responsibility on the grounds that the diamonds were being illegally imported from neighbouring countries and then smuggled out to Switzerland and the United Arab Emirates. On July 9 the Kimberley Process Certification Scheme, the international body established to eliminate the illicit sale of so-called conflict diamonds, signaled its disbelief in the government's denials by removing the Congo from its roster of countries producing legitimate diamonds. This effectively prevented Brazzaville from selling gems on the legal world market.

On August 14 the Congo-Ocean Railway (CFCO) celebrated its 70th anniversary. Long the principal shipping artery between Brazzaville and the port of Pointe-Noire, the CFCO had seen its traffic drastically reduced during the civil wars of the past 10 years. It had received $13 million from the World Bank in January to help restore its track and rolling stock. The Democratic Republic of the Congo (DRC) signed an agreement with the Brazzaville government on September 9 to provide electricity for magnesium and aluminum plants under construction in the district of Kouilou, in southern Congo.

The country marked its 44th year of independence on August 15 with a huge military and civilian parade. The presidents of the DRC, Gabon, Ghana, and Nigeria attended the celebrations at Pointe-Noire. (NANCY ELLEN LAWLER)

COSTA RICA

Area: 51,100 sq km (19,730 sq mi)
Population (2004 est.): 4,252,000
Capital: San José
Head of state and government: President Abel Pacheco de la Espriella

For much of 2004, national attention in Costa Rica was riveted on the Central American Free Trade Agreement (CAFTA) with the United States. By late 2003 bilateral negotiations had reached an impasse, and there were growing hints that Costa Rica would be excluded from the agreement, but in January 2004 the differences were smoothed over. The main sticking point had been the U.S. insistence that Costa Rica's state-run monopolies in telecommunications—including cell phones and the Internet—as well as electric power and insurance, be opened to competition. By the terms of the agreement struck with the U.S., state monopoly status in these areas would be removed by 2011.

Pres. Abel Pacheco de la Espriella had a hard year. Although economic growth was in the 4–5% range, inflation reached an annual level of 13%—its highest rate in six years—the legislature was unable to pass a deficit-reduction package, and many sectors of the population refused to accept the terms of the CAFTA agreement. The legislature had not yet acted on CAFTA, but the agreement was stalled in the U.S. Congress as well. By August 2004 much of the country was paralyzed by a national strike that involved sectors as diverse as schoolteachers and truckers; the administration was forced to make economic concessions.

Once again in 2004 Pacheco's administration was hit by a wave of cabinet resignations. Many Costa Ricans were already focused on the February 2006 presidential election. In March 2004 former president and Nobel Peace Prize laureate Oscar Arias Sánchez announced his candidacy on a platform to transform Costa Rica into Latin America's "first developed country." In October a wave of scandals rocked the country and resulted in the arrest of two former presidents who were accused of taking bribes.

(MITCHELL A. SELIGSON)

CÔTE D'IVOIRE

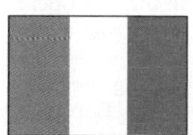

Area: 320,803 sq km (123,863 sq mi)
Population (2004 est.): 16,897,000
De facto capital: Abidjan
Chief of state: President Laurent Gbagbo
Head of government: Prime Minister Seydou Diarra

In 2004 Côte d'Ivoire remained effectively split in two as a result of the civil war that erupted in September 2002. Members of the rebellious New Force alliance (FN) continued to hold the north, while the government, assisted by 4,000 French troops and about 5,800 United Nations peacekeepers, controlled the south. Spasmodic outbreaks of ethnic and religious violence dominated the year. In late April, 10 people died when fighting broke out in the western cocoa-producing area, and in June FN adherents fired on government and French soldiers patrolling the demilitarized zone, killing at least 7 people. Government helicopters immediately retaliated by launching attacks on rebel-held country. That same day hundreds of Pres. Laurent Gbagbo's supporters demonstrated outside the French embassy in Abidjan, demanding the withdrawal of the former colonial power's forces since they appeared to be unable to prevent rebel attacks.

On May 26 Amnesty International issued a report condemning, for human rights abuses, all factions in the conflict. The United Nations launched its own inquiry on July 17 and sent a special commission to the country. On August 3 UN investigators found three mass graves near the city of Korhogo that contained at least 100 bodies of persons who likely had been killed in clashes between rival rebel factions.

Political proposals for resolving the conflict seemed to win little support. On March 25 security forces killed at least 120 opposition demonstrators and wounded several hundred more. In protest, 26 cabinet ministers representing four opposition parties and the New Forces withdrew from the power-sharing government. Following a UN-brokered summit meeting held in Accra, Ghana, in late July, opposition parties and the FN agreed to return to the government. On August 9 they attended their first cabinet meeting since March. An extraordinary session of the parliament opened on August 11 to vote on the political reforms called for by the January 2003 Marcoussis accords and the subsequent Accra agreement. With the exception of a law adopted on September 10 guaranteeing freedom of the press, the passage of any

In western Côte d'Ivoire in April, a worker gathers up cocoa beans that have been dried in the sun. Competition for land on which to grow cocoa, the country's major export, was a factor in the civil violence that split the country.

AP/Wide World Photos

other substantial legislation was stalled. In November violence flared after France, responding to an Ivorian air strike that killed nine French soldiers, destroyed Côte d'Ivoire's air force. Anti-French riots ensued, and thousands of Ivorians and French nationals and other foreigners fled the country.

The fall in GDP continued during the year and resulted in the country's inability to service its external debt. On June 17 the IMF suspended all loans to Côte d'Ivoire.

(NANCY ELLEN LAWLER)

CROATIA

Area: 56,594 sq km (21,851 sq mi)
Population (2004 est.): 4,497,000
Capital: Zagreb
Chief of state: President Stipe Mesic
Head of government: Prime Minister Ivo Sanader

Croatia entered 2004 with a new, centre-right government that assumed power on Dec. 22, 2003, following the victory of the Croatian Democratic Union (HDZ) over the incumbent centre-left coalition. Despite fears among some domestic and foreign observers that the HDZ would take the country back to the undemocratic and isolationist politics that had characterized its rule during the 1990s, the new government under Prime Minister Ivo Sanader pursued a moderate agenda. One of the government's first actions was to initiate dialogue with political representatives of the country's Serb minority, which resulted in a number of measures aimed at facilitating the return of Serb refugees as well as a cooperation agreement with the Independent Democratic Serb Party.

Relations between Croatia and the International Criminal Tribunal for the Former Yugoslavia (ICTY) also saw significant improvement. The government played a key role in securing the voluntary departure of indicted Croatian citizens to The Hague. Under indictment for war crimes allegedly committed during and after Operation Storm, the 1995 military action to regain the Krajina—Croatian territory seized by Croatian Serbs—two retired Croatian generals, Mladen Markac and Ivan Cermak, left for The Hague on March 11. On April 5 the Croatian government facilitated the transfer of six ethnic Croat leaders from Bosnia and Herzegovina. In her April report to the European Commission, ICTY chief prosecutor Carla Del Ponte congratulated the new government for its full cooperation with the tribunal.

Smoothing relations with The Hague removed an obstacle to key foreign-policy goals. On April 20 the European Commission decided that Croatia had fulfilled the political and economic criteria required for initiating negotiations on accession into the European Union. On June 18 the European Council decided to grant Croatia the status of an official candidate for the EU and scheduled accession talks for early 2005. This decision raised the hope that Croatia's most important strategic goal—membership in the EU—could be achieved by 2007. Optimism regarding Croatia's improved international status was tempered, however, when, at the June NATO summit in Istanbul, Croatia was not invited to join.

On August 22 a small right-wing group raised an unauthorized commemorative plaque to Mile Budak, a minister in Croatia's World War II fascist puppet government. The event caused domestic and international outrage. The government ordered the plaque destroyed and used the occasion also to remove a monument to another World War II fascist leader, which ironically had been erected during the previous, left-leaning government's tenure. The controversy prompted HDZ leaders to write an open letter calling for an end to the use of fascist symbols, the party's most explicit break with the legacy of Croatia's prewar and wartime ideology.

Croatia's economic picture proved less optimistic. Measures undertaken by the central bank to ease the mounting foreign debt had little impact. During the first seven months of the year, foreign debt increased by 13.4%, reaching €21.4 billion (about $25.7 billion), or almost 80% of GDP, and exceeding the limits set by the standby loan agreement Croatia had signed with the IMF. The tourist industry continued its upward trend, however, increasing by 4% over the previous year and generating nearly $5 billion in revenues.

The new government continued with large infrastructure investments. New highways to Rijeka and Split opened in early summer, and Zagreb was finally connected to Istria and the Dalmatian coast. The 2004 Olympic Games gave Croatians reason for national pride as its citizens won five medals, including a gold in handball, the most since the country gained its independence in 1992.

(DAVORKA MATIĆ)

Croatian Prime Minister Ivo Sanader (centre) and OSCE Chairman Solomon Passy (left) symbolically break bread with an elderly Croatian Serb in May. Sanader placed a high priority on repatriating Serbs who had fled Croatia during the civil war and on mending relations with the Serb population.

© Nikola Solic/Reuters/Corbis

CUBA

Area: 110,860 sq km (42,804 sq mi)
Population (2004 est.): 11,300,000
Capital: Havana
Head of state and government: President of the Council of State and President of the Council of Ministers Fidel Castro Ruz

In 2004 Cuba weathered a series of powerful hurricanes that caused serious

© AIN/Handout/Reuters/Corbis

On May 14 hundreds of thousands of Cubans, led by Pres. Fidel Castro, march to the U.S. interests section (the U.S. diplomatic presence—building upper right) in Havana to protest new measures by Washington that tighten economic pressures and travel restrictions on Cubans.

damage but little loss of life. On August 13 Pres. Fidel Castro Ruz marked his 78th birthday during Hurricane Charley, which claimed at least four lives but narrowly missed Havana. One month later Hurricane Ivan battered Pinar del Río province, forcing the evacuation of 1.9 million people, but Castro rejected a U.S. offer of $50,000 in hurricane relief aid as "hypocritical." Cuba's capable emergency management system compared favourably with some other Caribbean countries.

Oversight of the tourism industry shifted away from economic czar Carlos Lage and was moved under the control of Gen. Raúl Castro, the minister of defense and head of the armed forces. Military expenditures increased by an estimated 9%, and the government took steps to curtail self-employment and other independent economic activity. Minister of Tourism Ibrahim Ferradaz and Minister of Basic Industries Marcos Portal were dismissed. The government considered new measures to restrict access to the Internet. Havana released several dissidents who had been sentenced to long prison terms during a crackdown in 2003, including Marta Beatriz Roque, a well-known economist.

Tensions between Cuba and the United States mounted in May when the administration of Pres. George W. Bush released the 423-page report of the Commission for Assistance to a Free Cuba, chaired by Secretary of State Colin Powell. The report led to Washington's further tightening travel restrictions to Cuba, eliminating many types of educational travel, limiting family visits to once every three years (instead of once annually), and restricting remittances to close relatives not affiliated with the Communist Party. The U.S. also directed $59 million toward activities intended to undermine the Cuban government, including increased funding for anti-Castro broadcasts by Radio and TV Martí, aid to dissidents on the island, and an international public diplomacy campaign to promote the U.S. view that Cuba is a dangerous rogue state.

The Cuban government denounced the "brutal economic and political measures" and promptly shut down its U.S. dollar stores except for food and cleaning products—a move that prompted long lines to form as shelves were emptied in a spate of panic buying. The stores reopened, with higher prices, two weeks later. Fidel Castro led a massive demonstration against the U.S. interests section in Havana, with marchers waving placards comparing Bush to Adolf Hitler and showing images of U.S. soldiers humiliating Iraqi prisoners at Abu Ghraib prison in Iraq. The U.S. House of Representatives passed two amendments to reverse limits on sending gift parcels to Cuba and repeal new restrictions on Cuban-American family travel, but the White House continued to oppose efforts to ease the U.S. embargo. American agricultural sales to Cuba continued, and the island purchased $277.3 million in food sales during the first seven months of 2004. Meanwhile, the U.S. brought sanctions against a Jamaican-owned hotel company, forcing its withdrawal from Cuban investments.

Cuba's relations with Europe remained difficult, despite the election of a Socialist prime minister in Spain. Ties with Latin America were strained when Cuba narrowly lost a UN vote on its human rights conditions. In May Castro lashed out at Mexico's Pres. Vicente Fox, and the two countries briefly recalled their ambassadors before smoothing over relations. In August, Cuba broke off relations with Panama when that country pardoned four Cuban exiles convicted of having plotted to kill Castro at the Ibero-American

Summit of 2000. Ties with Venezuela, Argentina, and other states in the Caribbean remained warm, however.

The Cuban economy continued to struggle. The island expected 2.1 million tourists in 2004, but new U.S. restrictions made that figure less likely. Cuba's agricultural production was badly damaged by a severe drought in the eastern provinces. Foreign direct investment continued to dwindle, and the number of active joint ventures dropped by almost 15%. The Ministry of the Economy removed the U.S. dollar from circulation in Cuba, reversing an emergency measure that had been in effect since 1993. Offshore oil drilling by the Spanish company Repsol YPF discovered deposits but determined that the extraction was not economically viable. High nickel prices and an estimated $1.2 billion in annual remittances were among the few bright spots.

(DANIEL P. ERIKSON)

CYPRUS

Area: 9,251 sq km (3,572 sq mi) for the entire island; the area of the Turkish Republic of Northern Cyprus (TRNC), proclaimed unilaterally (1983) in the occupied northern third of the island, 3,355 sq km (1,295 sq mi)
Population (2004 est.): island 937,000; TRNC only, 211,000 (including Turkish settlers and Turkish military)
Capital: Lefkosia/Lefkosa (also known as Nicosia)
Head(s) of state and government: President Tassos Papadopoulos; of the TRNC, President Rauf Denktash

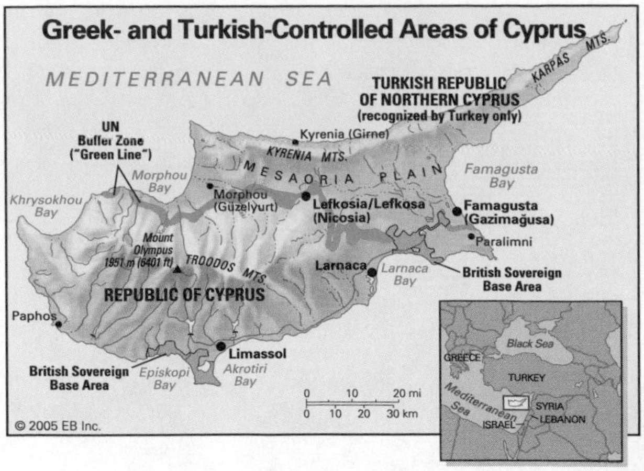

European Union membership dominated political events in Cyprus in 2004. UN-sponsored negotiations in the spring failed to produce a unification formula for the Greek and Turkish parts of the island before a last-minute referendum on the UN's compromise plan. Leaders of both sides recommended its rejection, while the EU, the UN, the U.K., and the U.S. urged acceptance. In the event, the Greeks rejected the proposal, and the island's Turks voted "yes." On May 1 the Greek side joined the EU. Cyprus participated in EU committees and elected six delegates to the European Parliament. Funding from the EU assisted the island's fishing industry and helped in the demining of the frontier, and EU regulations and supervision regulated the intercommunal border. Despite continued partition, Cyprus Turks were considered EU members. Some voted in the European elections, and international agencies planned economic relief for them.

Even while the battle of words continued, the intercommunal situation remained nonviolent. Movement between the zones eased, and telephone contact opened. Perhaps typical of the entire situation, Turkish Cyprus allowed Greeks access to Morphou, on the Turkish side, for a saint's day service. The bishop and the mayor visited their town for the first time in 30 years. The event was marred, however, by a dynamite blast in front of the church a day before the service. The incident demonstrated the passions that continued to rend the island.

Cyprus's economy continued to be strong in 2004, with considerable growth of the tourist industry in the Turkish part of the island. Economic prosperity and increased communication between the two sides of the island brought new attention to the issue of land ownership by displaced Cypriots.

(GEORGE H. KELLING)

CZECH REPUBLIC

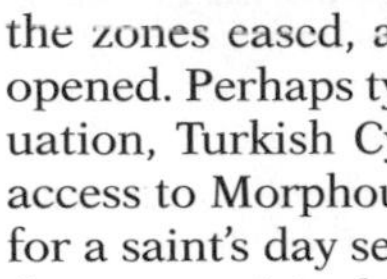

Area: 78,866 sq km (30,450 sq mi)
Population (2004 est.): 10,212,000
Capital: Prague
Chief of state: President Vaclav Klaus
Head of government: Prime Ministers Vladimir Spidla and, from July 26, Stanislav Gross

The year 2004 was marked by political upheaval and an economic upturn as the Czech Republic finally "rejoined Europe." Like its counterparts in Poland and Hungary, the left-leaning Czech government collapsed after the country's accession to the European Union on May 1, with Vladimir Spidla resigning as prime minister in July and handing over the reigns to the youthful Stanislav Gross. After weeks of uncertainty and tension, Gross's new cabinet narrowly won a parliamentary vote of confidence on August 24. Nonetheless, the new government consisted of all the same parties and most of the same ministers as the previous cabinet. Moreover, it faced all of the same problems, particularly those relating to public finance reform. The political situation was complicated further by the ruling coalition's razor-thin majority of just 101 seats in the 200-member lower house of the parliament.

The collapse of Spidla's cabinet was triggered by the humiliating defeat of the Social Democrats (CSSD) in the elections to the European Parliament (EP) that were held in the Czech Republic on June 11–12. Prior to the elections, the CSSD's popularity had been falling sharply. While some attributed that decline to the difficult impact of the first round of public finance reforms that had been approved in late 2003, others blamed it on Spidla's lacklustre leadership. In the end the three ruling parties combined won just 4 of 24 seats in the EP. While the Christian Democrats (KDU-CSL) finished in fourth place, with 9.5% of the vote, the CSSD placed fifth, winning just 8.8%, with each of the two parties gaining two seats. As expected, support for the third coalition partner, the Freedom Union (US-DEU), came in far below the 5% threshold needed to enter the parliament. In contrast, the Euroskeptic opposition Civic Democrats (ODS) and the Communists won a combined 50.3% of the vote and 15 seats, while independents picked up the remaining five mandates. Voter turnout reached just 28.3%.

Personnel changes in the Gross government did not go as far as expected. Of the 18 posts, only 6 were filled with individuals who had not served in the previous cabinet. There was some reshuffling among the various positions, and the cabinet added one member. The CSSD now held 12 of the 18 cabinet posts, up from the previous 11, with 3 of those going to nonparty members. While the KDU-CSL made no changes to its lineup, the US-DEU swapped some posts with the CSSD. The cabinet's policy statement was widely criticized as vague and lacking in new ideas.

Despite the lack of real change, public support for the CSSD and the government in general initially rose somewhat after the cabinet shake-up. That improvement could be attributed to the leadership of Gross, who had long been one of the most popular politicians in the country. According to polls by the STEM agency, Spidla's popularity had fallen from 77% in September 2002 to just 27% in July, while support for Gross dropped much less dramatically, from 85% to 56% in the two respective periods. Meanwhile, the ODS's image was damaged somewhat by allegations that the party had tried to bribe a US-DEU

Czech Prime Minister Stanislav Gross, a former railway worker, poses in front of a Czech-made locomotive in Prague in September. At 34, Gross was the youngest prime minister of any EU country and in Czech history.

© David Neff/AFP/Getty Images

deputy in an effort to persuade him to help bring down the new government.

Nonetheless, Gross did not have much time to renew the CSSD's support, given the upcoming elections to the Senate and the regional administration, both of which took place on November 5–6. With a voter turnout at an all-time low, the ODS managed to pull off an overwhelming victory in both elections, gaining majorities in 12 of the 13 regions and winning 18 of the 27 Senate seats that were up for grabs. Embarrassingly, the CSSD failed to gain a single seat in the Senate.

The economy fared better than expected in 2004, although rising inflation cut back on real wage growth and led to more caution on the part of Czech consumers. Given the country's large public finance deficit, the Czech Republic was not expected to join the euro zone before 2010, well after most of the other new EU accession countries. Even that date would be a challenge for the government. Although the Finance Ministry was expected to come up with another round of fiscal reforms, the government's ability to push through legislation was challenged by the strong right-wing slant of the Senate, regional assemblies, and presidency.

(SHARON FISHER)

DENMARK

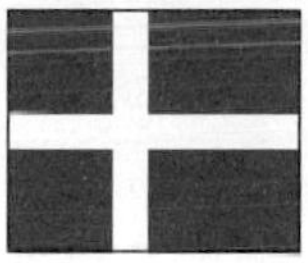

Area: 43,098 sq km (16,640 sq mi)
Population (2004 est.): 5,401,000
Capital: Copenhagen
Chief of state: Queen Margrethe II
Head of government: Prime Minister Anders Fogh Rasmussen

Denmark's involvement in Iraq, where it had 500 troops under U.K. command, continued to divide Danes in 2004. Following newspaper leaks indicating that the Danish government had deliberately ignored intelligence reports that the likelihood of finding weapons of mass destruction in Iraq was minimal, the Folketing (parliament) Foreign Policy Committee held a one-day hearing at which Prime Minister Anders Fogh Rasmussen staunchly defended Denmark's participation in the war, dismissing opposition accusations that Denmark had blindly followed the Americans and British into Iraq. In an embarrassing sequel, commanders of the Danish battalion in Iraq had to be summoned home amid an alleged abuse scandal involving Danish troops and Iraqi detainees at Denmark's base in southern Iraq, but the government reiterated its unflinching determination to maintain the Danish military presence in Iraq. The general feeling of unease about Denmark's pro-Washington stance was further exacerbated by allegations by a Danish national that he was tortured and humiliated by American soldiers in Afghanistan prior to being sent to the U.S. base at Guantánamo Bay in Cuba for two years of detention. In a vote seen as a backlash against the ruling Liberal-Conservative government for its support of the war in Iraq, the opposition Social Democrats almost doubled their support in the European Parliament in June, with their main candidate, former prime minister Poul Nyrup Rasmussen, netting an all-time record number of votes.

Denmark's ultratight immigration policies continued to attract international criticism. Council of Europe Human Rights Commissioner Álvaro Gil-Robles concluded in a report issued in July that Denmark's restrictive immigration laws—notably the notorious family-reunification requirements preventing young people from marrying or bringing in foreigners under the age of 24—were in breach of international human rights conventions. This criticism was later corroborated by the independent Danish Institute for Human Rights. A general mood of hostility toward foreigners, notably Muslims, prevailed in racially homogenous Denmark, a nominally Lutheran country where Muslims accounted for only 3% of the population, or about 170,000 people.

Aided by a spring economic-stimulus package of tax cuts designed to kick-start the economy and consumer spending after growth had slumped to a 10-year low in 2003, Denmark drew accolades from the IMF for its robust economic recovery, with growth in 2004 at a four-year high and solid current-account and state-budget surpluses. Exports stayed sluggish owing to a deterioration in competitiveness, however, and the labour market remained in the doldrums with unemployment at around 6% of the workforce.

The highlight of the year was the royal wedding of Crown Prince Frederik—elder son of Queen Margrethe and heir to the Danish throne—and Australian commoner Mary Donaldson, which took place at a glittering ceremony in Copenhagen Cathedral on May 14 and was watched by 180 million television viewers worldwide. Euphoria over the royal nuptials was dented by the announcement in September that Prince Joachim, the queen's younger son (nicknamed the "party prince" by the media for his fondness for wild partying and fast cars), and his Hong Kong-born wife, Princess Alexandra, were to separate—the first divorce in the Danish royal family in 165 years.

(CHRISTOPHER FOLLETT)

DJIBOUTI

Area: 23,200 sq km (8,950 sq mi)
Population (2004 est.): 467,000 (excluding fewer than 25,000 refugees)
Capital: Djibouti
Chief of state and head of government: President Ismail Omar Guelleh, assisted by Prime Minister Dileita Muhammad Dileita

Efforts to repatriate refugees and illegal immigrants from Djibouti continued in 2004; the initiative had begun in July 2003 after government officials told the country's estimated 100,000 illegal immigrants to either apply for asylum or leave. During February and March more than 430 Somalis returned to the self-declared Republic of Somaliland as part of a United Nations High Commissioner for Refugees operation. By June, efforts to move more than 3,000 Ethiopian returnees over the border were under way. In March, working from a tip-off that an assassination attempt was planned, German Pres. Johannes Rau abandoned his plans to visit Djibouti to meet German sailors participating in the U.S.-led Operation Enduring Freedom.

As part of a three-year plan to distribute free drugs to all HIV-positive people in Djibouti, some 40 HIV-positive patients were the first to receive free antiretroviral medicine in March. Torrential rains and flooding in mid-April killed nearly 300 people and left 3,000 homeless.

Djibouti's first prime minister after independence from France in 1977, opposition leader Ahmed Dini, died in September. (*See* OBITUARIES.) Dini had alleged election fraud when his party won no seats during the country's first multiparty parliamentary election in 2003, but he was unsuccessful in challenging the results.

(MARY F.E. EBELING)

DOMINICA

Area: 750 sq km (290 sq mi)
Population (2004 est.): 69,300
Capital: Roseau
Chief of state: President Nicholas Liverpool
Head of government: Prime Ministers Pierre Charles, Osborne Riviere (acting) from January 6, and, from January 8, Roosevelt Skerrit

Prime Minister Pierre Charles (*see* OBITUARIES), who had led Dominica since 2000, died in January 2004 of an apparent heart attack at the age of 49. Charles was succeeded by Roosevelt Skerrit, who also took over control of the Finance Ministry.

The IMF came to Dominica's aid in January with a three-year, $11.4 million credit from its Poverty Reduction and Growth Facility, which was designed, among other things, to help restore economic growth and preserve the public-sector investment program.

In March, Prime Minister Skerrit made clear that his administration "would not tolerate" ministerial corruption and that any minister caught in any "wrongdoing" would be dismissed "on the spot." After years of Dominica's fidelity to Taiwan under previous prime ministers, Skerrit did an about-face in March and recognized China instead. Beijing promptly announced a $112 million aid program for Dominica. The opposition United Workers Party condemned the change in policy.

Dominica also broke ranks with its fellow Caribbean Community and Common Market (Caricom) countries in September and called for "full engagement" with the interim regime in Haiti. Most Caricom states had distanced themselves from Haiti following what they saw as the U.S.-inspired forcible removal from office of Haitian Pres. Jean-Bertrand Aristide in February.

On October 29 Edward Oliver LeBlanc, premier of the island from 1967 to 1974, died.

(DAVID RENWICK)

DOMINICAN REPUBLIC

Area: 48,671 sq km (18,792 sq mi)
Population (2004 est.): 8,834,000
Capital: Santo Domingo
Head of state and government: Presidents Hipólito Mejía Domínguez and, from August 16, Leonel Fernández Reyna

To the surprise of almost no one, Leonel Fernández Reyna, head of the Dominican Liberation Party, defeated incumbent Pres. Hipólito Mejía Domínguez of the Dominican Revolutionary Party in the May 16, 2004, elections in the Dominican Republic. Possibly the only surprise in this bitterly contested, mudslinging presidential election was Mejía's swift recognition of defeat.

Mejía had presided over the largest contraction in the economy in more than a decade. Corruption was unchecked, and a massive banking scandal continued to damage the country's fiscal credibility. Inflation at the end of his term was running at an annualized rate of approximately 52%, and a deteriorating power infrastructure left many areas of the country without electricity for more than 12 hours a day. Without support from the IMF, the government had been unable to cover

The new president of the Dominican Republic, Leonel Fernández Reyna, appears with his wife, Margarita Cordero, before the crowd in Santo Domingo following his inauguration on August 16.

AP/Wide World Photos

overdue payments to private energy suppliers. The poor and lower-middle class were hard hit; the percentage of citizens living below the poverty line rose above 50%. The external debt, which stood at $7 billion, had almost doubled over the four years of the Mejía administration.

President Fernández had some advantages to help him lift his country out of the morass. His previous term as president (1996–2000) had coincided with the nation's strongest economic performance in 40 years. The three largest economic engines—tourism, remittances from Dominicans living abroad, and to a lesser extent the industrial free zones—survived the Mejía government intact and showed promise of powering the country back into modest growth. Tourism especially showed consistent growth. Though there was no sign of a determined campaign against government corruption, a policy to cut back government expenditures was launched with the announcement that 130 generals and admirals from the bloated armed forces were being forced into early retirement. (JOHN W. GRAHAM)

AP/Wide World Photos

Observing the first day of inspections in the court case against ChevronTexaco in August is this representative of the Secoya, one of five tribes of Ecuador's indigenous peoples affected by environmental damage and social problems allegedly caused by the American oil giant.

EAST TIMOR (TIMOR-LESTE)

Area: 14,604 sq km (5,639 sq mi)
Population (2004 est.): 925,000
Capital: Dili
Chief of state: President Xanana Gusmão
Head of government: Prime Minister Mari Alkatiri

On Dec. 10, 2003, East Timor Foreign Minister José Ramos-Horta opened an embassy in Canberra, Australia, to strengthen the new nation's close ties with its most important neighbour, but ongoing disputes over offshore gas and oil revenue kept bilateral relations strained in 2004. Australian Foreign Minister Alexander Downer welcomed the new ambassador, Jorge Teme, and pledged help to build a peaceful and prosperous future for the East Timorese people. Dili, however, refused to ratify the International Unitisation Agreement (IUA) specifying the border positioning between the two countries and consequent sovereignty over undersea resources. Were it to sign the IUA, the East Timor government believed, the deal would give East Timor only 18% of revenues from the Greater Sunrise gas field in the Timor Sea while handing Australia 82%. East Timor Prime Minister Mari Alkatiri described the argument as "literally a matter of life and death." Australia, he said, had avoided international jurisdiction and ignored the rule of law. East Timor wanted the border defined at the midpoint between the two nations and not to remain where it was in 1975. The Australian energy corporation Woodside Petroleum warned that it would scrap multibillion-dollar oil and gas developments unless the dispute was settled. (A.R.G. GRIFFITHS)

ECUADOR

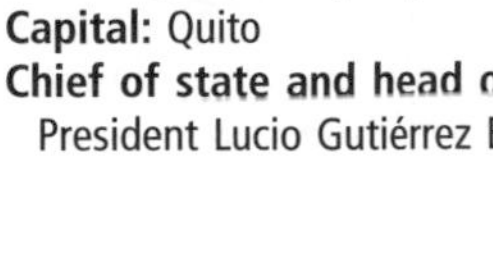

Area: 272,045 sq km (105,037 sq mi), including the 8,010-sq-km (3,093-sq-mi) Galápagos Islands
Population (2004 est.): 13,003,000 (Galápagos Islands, about 20,000)
Capital: Quito
Chief of state and head of government: President Lucio Gutiérrez Borbúa

Oil—Ecuador's economic lifeblood and its environmental nemesis—was the focus of attention in 2004. The government of Pres. Lucio Gutiérrez Borbúa tried to encourage foreign investment but was hampered by dissension within its own ranks and legal disputes involving major foreign companies.

The most contentious of these disputes was a lawsuit on behalf of 30,000 residents of the Amazon Basin lowlands, mostly Indians, against the American firm ChevronTexaco. It alleged that a Texaco subsidiary, as a minority partner with state-owned Petroecuador, polluted rivers during the 1970s and '80s by dumping contaminated water into them. Meanwhile, a dozen foreign oil firms pursued claims that their tax bills had been inflated by as much as $200 million. The government claimed that U.S.-based Occidental Petroleum violated regulations in the sale of assets to EnCana, a Canadian firm that was Ecuador's largest private oil producer. EnCana was accused of failing to fulfill its environmental obligations as lead operator of the OCP (Oleoducto de Crudos Pesados) pipeline. Its president, Gwyn Morgan, likened working in Ecuador to "a roller coaster," and the company was reported to be considering selling its stake. After several false starts, the government announced plans to auction licenses for new and producing oil fields. Gutiérrez, however, was unable to secure passage in Congress of a law reforming the oil and gas sector that some legislators believed was too generous to private-sector interests. His wife, Ximena Bohórquez, was among those members of Congress voting against the law.

Poor economic circumstances continued to induce thousands to emigrate. It was estimated that one in seven Ecuadorans lived abroad, and the money they sent home was Ecuador's second largest source of foreign exchange. Police were accused of being accomplices of migrant smugglers, and the government sought to lure migrants home with small-business incentives. Gutiérrez continued the drift toward orthodox economic policies that had alienated his Indian and leftist allies in 2003, although high world oil prices helped him stave off the most unpopular measures. He was dogged by charges of nepotism and suffered a serious blow in May with the resignation of Economy Minister Mauricio Pozo. In what looked like a desperate bid for support, Gutiérrez made overtures to former president Abdalá Bucaram, who had fled to Panama after being deposed in 1997. Bucaram's Roldosista movement maintained a significant bloc in Congress. In November Gutiérrez was almost impeached on corruption charges, and the following month Congress fired most of the country's Supreme Court judges, accusing them of favouring the opposition. (PAUL KNOX)

© Gil Cohen Magen/Reuters/Corbis

In October rescue workers search the rubble of the Taba Hilton, a resort hotel on the Red Sea near Egypt's border with Israel, following a car bomb explosion—one of three—that killed at least 33 people, most of them Israeli tourists.

EGYPT

Area: 997,739 sq km (385,229 sq mi)
Population (2004 est.): 69,261,000
Capital: Cairo
Chief of state: President Hosni Mubarak
Head of government: Prime Ministers Atef Ebeid and, from July 14, Ahmad Nazif

A 34-member Egyptian cabinet presided over by the new prime minister, Ahmad Nazif, was officially sworn in on July 14, 2004. Many of the 14 new members had been handpicked by Gamal Mubarak, Pres. Hosni Mubarak's son. Nazif promised that his government would encourage the private sector to absorb the legions of unemployed in order to relieve pressure on the bloated public sector. The new government was especially keen on training Egyptians in information technology.

President Mubarak sought to mediate between Israel and the Palestinian Authority. The Egyptians named as their envoy 'Umar Sulayman, the director of the Egyptian Intelligence Services, and he made several visits and met with Israeli and Palestinian officials. In turn, Palestinian Prime Minister Ahmad Quray made six visits to Egypt during February–September 2004. The Israeli-Palestinian conflict also loomed large during Mubarak's visit to the United States and his meeting with Pres. George W. Bush on April 12. Egypt volunteered to train up to 30,000 Palestinian security personnel to police the Gaza Strip after the expected Israeli withdrawal. Egypt canceled its participation in the ceremonies in Israel marking the 25th anniversary of the signing of the Egyptian-Israeli Peace Treaty of March 26, 1979, after the assassination in Gaza by Israeli forces of Sheikh Ahmed Yassin, the Hamas spiritual leader. (*See* OBITUARIES.)

In mid-May Egyptian authorities arrested 54 prominent members of the Muslim Brotherhood after the militant Islamist group mounted well-attended rallies following the assassinations of Yassin and another Palestinian leader, 'Abd al-'Aziz Rantisi. The Muslim Brotherhood was the most powerful opposition movement in Egypt, claiming more than two million members organized into thousands of clandestine cells. Its leader was Muhammad Mahdi 'Akif, who had earlier been in charge of the organization's covert activities.

The annual convention of the ruling National Democratic Party (NDP) was held in Cairo September 21–23. Gamal Mubarak, who chaired the powerful NDP Policies Committee, seemed clearly poised to succeed his father, whose term as president would expire in October 2005. A huge billboard showing Gamal welcoming home the Egyptian Olympic medalists was erected before the NDP convention in Cairo's Tahrir Square. Criticism by the opposition press finally got the billboard taken down but not before the message had been conveyed. The opposition held a simultaneous conference to counter the NDP gathering; it called for multicandidate presidential elections and the end of the emergency laws, which had been in force in Egypt since 1981.

Following the death of Fuad Serageddin, the leader of the New Wafd Party in August 2000, his successor, Numan Gomaa, had changed the party's liberal, democratic philosophy into a Nasserite-Islamist ideology. Early in 2004 former Wafdists founded a new party called al-Ghad ("Tomorrow") to regain the liberal and democratic ideals that had characterized Wafdism since its inception in 1918. The president of the new party was Ayman Nour, and the top three officers were all former members of the parliament. Though the Political Parties Court failed to approve the standing of the new party in September, it approved al-Ghad's formation in October.

(MARIUS K. DEEB)

© AFP/Getty Images

En route from South Africa, some 70 mercenaries, suspected of involvement in a plot to overthrow the government of Equatorial Guinea in March, were stopped at the Harare, Zimb., airport and held in a prison.

EL SALVADOR

Area: 21,041 sq km (8,124 sq mi)
Population (2004 est.): 6,698,000
Capital: San Salvador
Head of state and government: Presidents Francisco Flores Pérez and, from June 1, Elías Antonio Saca González

On March 21, 2004, following a bitter presidential campaign, Elías Antonio (Tony) Saca González (*see* BIOGRAPHIES) of the right-wing National Republican Alliance (ARENA) defeated Schafik Hándal of the leftist Farabundo Martí National Liberation Front (FMLN). Saca won the presidency with 57.7% of the vote against Hándal's 35.6% and was inaugurated on June 1. Saca's highly emotional anticommunist campaign overcame early polls that had predicted an FMLN victory. Saca argued that an FMLN victory might lead to deportation of the 2.5 million Salvadorans living in the United States, who sent about $2 billion dollars annually back to El Salvador. Factory workers also feared that an FMLN victory could drive their employers from the country and cost them their jobs. In extending ARENA's 14-year control of the presidency, Saca promised to continue the pro-business and pro-U.S. policies of his predecessor, Francisco Flores Pérez, to work toward implementation of the Central American Free Trade Agreements and to increase foreign investment. He also promised not to privatize the country's social security and health care systems.

Though higher oil prices slowed economic growth and high unemployment and unequal distribution of wealth continued to be troublesome, El Salvador continued to receive favourable investment ratings. On May 28 El Salvador signed the Central American Free Trade Agreement, along with other Central American countries and the U.S. Rising crime by youth gangs and a wave of kidnappings for ransom brought heavier law enforcement. Leaders from Central America and Mexico met in San Salvador in December to discuss ways to stem gang violence and crime in the region. Plans to increase economic cooperation and to ease border controls and customs regulations were also discussed.

The government faced increasing opposition to the presence of its troops in Iraq. After the Dominican Republic, Honduras, and Nicaragua removed their troops from Iraq during the year, El Salvador remained the only Latin American country to keep troops there, and popular opposition delayed the sending of 380 more troops to Iraq until late August. Responding to Islamic terrorist threats, the Salvadoran government asked for extra security for its foreign embassies.

In September a U.S. federal judge, acting on the basis of the 1789 Alien Tort Claims Act and the 1991 Torture Victim Protection Act, found Salvadoran Air Force Capt. Álvaro Rafael Saravía liable in the 1980 murder of Archbishop Oscar Arnulfo Romero and ordered him to pay $10 million in compensatory and punitive damages. President Saca refused to reopen the case in El Salvador (Saravía had been given amnesty as part of a 1993 peace agreement), saying, "Opening up the wounds of the past wouldn't do any good for a country that is looking to the future."

(RALPH LEE WOODWARD, JR.)

EQUATORIAL GUINEA

Area: 28,051 sq km (10,831 sq mi)
Population (2004 est.): 507,000
Capital: Malabo
Chief of state: President Brig. Gen. Teodoro Obiang Nguema Mbasogo
Head of government: Prime Ministers Cándido Muatetema Rivas and, from June 14, Miguel Abia Biteo Borico

In December 2003 news of a power struggle in Equatorial Guinea began to emerge, which seemed to be related to the illness of Pres. Teodoro Obiang Nguema Mbasogo and his plans to hand over power to his playboy son Teodorin. Various members of the armed forces, including relatives of the president, were sacked, and others were arrested. In March 2004 Obiang learned, probably from South African intelligence sources, that a coup was being planned to oust him. A group of alleged mercenaries were arrested and charged with plotting to install his rival, Severo Moto, who lived in exile. Another 70 members of the alleged plot were arrested in Zimbabwe en route to Equatorial Guinea. Efforts by Equatorial Guinea to have them extradited were not successful, perhaps in part because it was suspected that at least $35 million of oil revenues had been misappropriated by Obiang and his family and senior government officials. The mercenaries were brought to trial in August, but, after the arrest in South Africa of Mark Thatcher, son of the former British prime minister, for allegedly helping to finance the attempted coup, the trial was suspended indefinitely to allow for further investigation. (CHRISTOPHER SAUNDERS)

ERITREA

Area: 121,144 sq km (46,774 sq mi)
Population (2004 est.): 4,297,000
Capital: Asmara
Head of state and government: President Isaias Afwerki

In 2004 Eritrea settled, albeit uneasily, into a no-war–no-peace stalemate with Ethiopia. Dismayed by what it saw as yet another betrayal by the international community, the government sent delegations abroad to express its displeasure to countries as varied as Australia, Benin, Kuwait, The Gambia, Saudi Arabia, and Switzerland. The failure to attain a fair hearing internationally for its grievances against Ethiopia was due less to the merits of its case, however, than to Eritrea's deteriorating international standing—the result of violations of regional and international norms, which in turn were deftly manipulated by Ethiopia, a country that still enjoyed the esteem of African and international bodies.

In the first quarter of 2004, the government announced the demobilization of 65,000 troops who had served in the 1998–2000 border war, drafted electoral laws for regional assemblies, formulated a rent-control policy, and identified the increase of prostitution and homelessness as major social problems. In the second quarter attention was focused on the prospects that the border war with Ethiopia might resume and speculation that unrest in southwestern Eritrea might be linked to the alleged sponsorship of terrorists by The Sudan.

Fuel rationing, a crackdown on religious groups, and indiscriminate arrests of youth assumed to be draft dodgers were issues later in the year that led to international rebuke of the government. The exodus of young people, civil servants, and veteran diplomats continued throughout the year. The national development plan, called Wefri Warsay Yi'kaalo, also continued, engaging young adults in state-sponsored rural and urban projects of national reconstruction.

Inadequate rainfall in June and July exacerbated the water shortage, and locusts invaded the central highlands. International food aid arrived in Eritrea in the last two months of 2004 to stave off the spectre of famine and drought. It was estimated that more than two million Eritreans would need food aid in 2005. In November Addis Ababa announced yet another conditional acceptance of the Eritrea-Ethiopia Border Commission's resolution, which evoked a cynical response from Asmara, and the year ended with a ratcheting up of tensions.

The overall rather bleak picture in Eritrea was brightened by Zersenay Tadesse's winning bronze in the men's 10,000-m race at the 2004 Summer Games in Athens; it was the country's first Olympic medal. (RUTH IYOB)

An Estonian woman goes to the polls in Raja village to vote in the European Parliament elections on June 13. Estonia and seven other former communist countries joined the EU in 2004.

© AFP/Getty Images

ESTONIA

Area: 45,227 sq km (17,462 sq mi)
Population (2004 est.): 1,342,000
Capital: Tallinn
Chief of state: President Arnold Rüütel
Head of government: Prime Minister Juhan Parts

Prime Minister Juhan Parts's Res Publica party, the leading member of Estonia's ruling coalition, suffered a sharp decline in its political fortunes in 2004. Opinion polls showed falling support, and in the country's first elections to the European Parliament in June, Res Publica finished sixth, garnering only 7% of the vote and none of the six available seats. The results suggested that Res Publica had not delivered on its promises for a more ethical and caring government, although the public gave the party high marks for having implemented parental allowances for newborn children. The main political opposition, Edgar Savisaar's Estonian Centre Party, also endured important setbacks, including the defection of 8 of 28 members in the parliament in May and Savisaar's loss of the mayoralty in Tallinn in October following a vote of no confidence. The chief gainers were the Estonian Reform Party on the right and the Social Democratic Party (formerly the Moderates) on the left, the latter winning three seats in the European Parliament.

Estonia achieved two major foreign-policy goals in 2004 as it joined NATO on March 29 and the European Union on May 1. Nevertheless, the very low turnout for the European Parliament elections (27%) indicated that voters were perhaps not yet convinced of the importance of EU institutions. Estonia stood out among acceding EU members in that it obtained two high-profile appointments: Toomas Hendrik Ilves as a vice chairman of the European Parliament's Foreign Affairs Committee and Siim Kallas as a vice president of the European Commission.

Among the 10 new European Union countries, Estonia ranked only eighth in GDP per capita at 42% of the newly expanded EU's average. The World Economic Forum deemed Estonia's the most competitive economy among the 10 new states, however, and the econ-

Participating in an Ethiopian government plan to move millions of people from drought-stricken areas to more fertile lands in the west of the country, a man carries a sack of food at a resettlement centre southwest of Addis Ababa in April.

omy continued to display a number of other positive features, including high growth rates, a low level of public debt, and a balanced state budget.

(TOIVO U. RAUN)

ETHIOPIA

Area: 1,133,882 sq km (437,794 sq mi)
Population (2004 est.): 67,851,000
Capital: Addis Ababa
Chief of state: President Girma Wolde-Giyorgis
Head of government: Prime Minister Meles Zenawi

Ethiopia had a bumper harvest in 2004 as a result of good rains, but an estimated three million people still needed food assistance as drought affected the harvest in the Somali region and the northern highland plateau areas. A controversial resettlement scheme was launched to move people from drought-prone areas to the west of the country, where there was more regular rainfall. Approximately 300,000 people had been moved since the scheme began.

Foreign affairs were dominated by the ongoing diplomatic crisis with Eritrea. The border demarcation between Ethiopia and Eritrea necessitated by the 1998–2000 war between the two countries was still not finalized, and tensions remained high. Ethiopia rejected the border determined by the UN Boundary Commission because it was unhappy with the award of the town of Badme to Eritrea. Ethiopia called for further talks to resolve the crisis, but Eritrea wanted the demarcation to occur first. The United Nations Mission in Eritrea and Ethiopia (UNMEE), which policed the border between the two countries, was renewed. Relations with Kenya remained good despite a low-level conflict along the Kenya-Ethiopia border. The important rail line between Addis Ababa and the Red Sea port in Djibouti was to be privatized following a two-year transition period. Port access was also an important factor in continued positive Ethiopian relations with the breakaway (from Somalia) Republic of Somaliland, which controlled the port of Berbera. Ethiopia expressed an interest in rejoining the Inter Governmental Authority for Development (IGAD) talks on the status of Somalia after an absence that prevented any further diplomatic movement. The Sudan and Yemen joined with Ethiopia in announcing a pact to fight terrorism in the Horn of Africa and to crack down on Islamic militants.

Domestically, preparation for parliamentary elections scheduled for May 2005 began with the training of election officers and voter-education programs. Clashes in the Gambela region of western Ethiopia between the Anyuak people and representatives of the Ethiopian state displaced 51,000 people and led to up to 500 deaths.

Ethiopia reported an economic growth rate of 11.6% from August 2003 to July 2004, thanks to better rains. Low world coffee prices persisted, and Ethiopian coffee farmers began to replant some of their land from coffee to khat, a mild addictive stimulant traded throughout East Africa. Ethiopia reached the completion point under the Highly Indebted Poor Countries (HIPC) initiative of the World Bank and IMF. With completion, Ethiopia would receive both bilateral and multilateral debt relief of about $3.3 billion. The United States pledged to back Ethiopia's move to join the World Trade Organization. The U.S. also granted Ethiopia $18 million as part of its global initiative to fight AIDS. HIV/AIDS prevalence rates in Addis Ababa fell from a peak of 24% of the population in 1995 to 11% in 2003.

(SANDRA F. JOIREMAN)

FIJI

Area: 18,272 sq km (7,055 sq mi)
Population (2004 est.): 839,000
Capital: Suva
Chief of state: President Ratu Josefa Iloilo
Head of government: Prime Minister Laisenia Qarase

Fiji mourned the death in April 2004 of Ratu Sir Kamisese Mara, the country's first prime minister (1970–92; except for a few months in 1987) and president from 1994 until he was deposed in a coup in 2000. (*See* OBITUARIES.) Mara's wife of more than 50 years, Ro Lady Litia Mara, died in July.

The 2000 coup continued to cast a shadow in 2004; four serving politicians, including the vice president and deputy speaker, were convicted of treason and imprisoned for having taken illegal oaths of office during the coup. Courts-martial of soldiers for mutiny, also during the coup, led to several convictions. The opposition Fiji Labour Party (FLP) boycotted events during a week of national reconciliation in October. The FLP also rejected cabinet positions, forced upon Prime Minister Laisenia Qarase by the Supreme Court, because the portfolios offered were all minor and party leader Mahendra Chaudhry was excluded.

The economy continued to struggle, with a heavy dependence on tourism

© David Grey/Reuters/Corbis

A Fijian warrior in traditional dress stands guard at the funeral of former president Ratu Sir Kamisese Kapaiwai Tuimacilai Mara in April.

and, increasingly, on remittances from overseas workers (especially soldiers in UN peacekeeping roles), which reached $F 245 million (about U.S.$140 million) in 2003. The sugar industry was affected by the nonrenewal of Indian-held leases by indigenous Fijian landowners, which reduced the area under cultivation and accelerated the shift of the population to the towns.

In October, Fiji agreed to provide some 150 soldiers for UN peacekeeping in Iraq. (BARRIE MACDONALD)

FINLAND

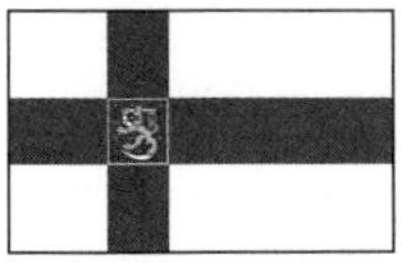

Area: 338,145 sq km (130,559 sq mi)
Population (2004 est.): 5,226,000
Capital: Helsinki
Chief of state: President Tarja Halonen
Head of government: Prime Minister Matti Vanhanen

Finnish Pres. Tarja Halonen spoke on the international stage in September 2004 when she told the United Nations that she thought the U.S.-led military intervention in Iraq was not in line with international law. Speaking to the UN General Assembly shortly after an address by U.S. Pres. George W. Bush, Halonen said that the international community had failed in advance of the Iraq war, "conflicting national interests prevailed over common will," and "there was not enough commitment to act within the boundaries of Security Council resolutions." She did not name the U.S. or its coalition of allies but said that some nations had resorted to the use of force, "which was not compatible with international law." Halonen submitted that the Security Council, and particularly its permanent members, "must display a common will" and that "other nations must show support for . . . its decisions." She added that it was now necessary for security and stability to be restored in Iraq so that democracy and prosperity could be achieved there.

Prime Minister Matti Vanhanen's government, after prompting from Halonen, had earlier announced that the country would join the Ottawa Agreement against land mines. Finland's mines, which had not been deployed but were being stockpiled, would be phased out over a long period and would be replaced with comparable anti-infantry systems.

The move aroused controversy, and a well-known political commentator remarked tartly in a letter to the press that Finland should not scrap its infantry mines until neighbouring Russia had scrapped its infantry. The two countries were evidently on good terms in 2004, although there were complaints from Moscow that Finland was delaying progress on a visa-exemption deal between Russia and the EU, of which Finland was a member.

A former senior diplomat pointed to the rapidly recovering trade with Russia and to the opportunities by rail along what he called the "Iron Silk Road," which could make Finland and its Baltic ports an expanding transit focus for freight from countries such as South Korea, Japan, and China.

Finnish unemployment persisted at around 8% without progress on the government target to raise the employment rate from 69% to 75% to ensure future welfare-state funding. Anneli Jäätteenmäki, who was unseated as the country's first woman prime minister in 2003 following a scandal over a leakage of documents, left the national parliament and won election to the European Parliament after a court trial dismissed charges against her.

(EDWARD M. SUMMERHILL)

FRANCE

Area: 543,965 sq km (210,026 sq mi)
Population (2004 est.): 60,044,000
Capital: Paris
Chief of state: President Jacques Chirac
Head of government: Prime Minister Jean-Pierre Raffarin

The year 2004 in France was dominated by domestic politics. The predominant mood was a feeling of *fin de règne* for Jacques Chirac, even though the Gaullist president's term ran until 2007. The main events of the year were the double electoral hammering meted out to his ruling Union for a Popular Movement (UMP) in the regional elections in March and the European Parliament elections in June and the growing unpopularity of everyone on the centre-right with the notable exception of Nicolas Sarkozy, whose determination to challenge Chirac for the presidency became ever more marked as the year wore on. These internal tensions helped distract the government of Prime Minister Jean-Pierre Raffarin from progress on difficult health and privatization reforms. Equally controversial was the ban on the wearing of Muslim headscarves and other ostentatious religious symbols in schools. The year was relatively undramatic for foreign policy, though French troops came under fire and suffered casualties in Côte d'Ivoire as France found it increasingly hard to keep the peace there. On the diplomatic level, Chirac once again demonstrated his belief in the desirability of a multipolar world, using various diplomatic summits to maintain his distance from U.S. policy in the Middle East and to seek rapprochement with China.

Domestic Affairs. Chirac's political difficulties started on January 30, when his former prime minister, Alain Juppé, was convicted of having used public money for party purposes. In December, on appeal, his suspended 18-month prison sentence was reduced to 14 months and the ban preventing him from holding public office was cut from 10 years to one year. The conviction was seen as implicit condemnation of Chirac—who had immunity from prosecution as long as he remained president—since the offenses took place when Juppé was a deputy to Chirac at the Paris city hall. Juppé was forced to stand down as head of the UMP later in the year, which thereby opened up this position to the ambitious Sarkozy.

Ever since Sarkozy's maneuvrings inside the neo-Gaullist movement in the mid-1990s to keep Chirac out of the presidency, relations between the two had remained strained. As a hyperactive interior minister in the lacklustre Raffarin government, however, Sarkozy shone. After the terrible performance of the UMP in the March regional elections—in which the Socialists and their allies captured 21 of France's 22 regional councils—Chirac felt he had no option but to give Sarkozy an even bigger role by making him finance minister. Sarkozy's place at interior went to Dominique de Villepin, whose job at the Foreign Ministry was filled by Michel Barnier, recalled from Brussels, where he had been serving as a member of the European Commission.

Sarkozy soon made clear his designs on the UMP post, apparently believing he could combine this job with that at the Finance Ministry. Chirac warned him he would have to choose between the two roles, arguing that such a combination would otherwise totally undermine Raffarin's position. He also used his traditional Bastille Day interview to slap Sarkozy down, saying, "I make the decisions, he [Sarkozy] executes them." Having no choice but to choose, Sarkozy eventually forsook the Finance Ministry and was elected to the party post on November 28, evidently calculating this to be the better launch pad for a presidential bid in 2007. He was replaced as finance minister by Hervé Gaymard.

Chirac's other move on Bastille Day was to announce a referendum sometime in 2005 on ratifying the new draft European Union constitution. While Chirac was expected to lead the "yes" campaign in that referendum, the outcome would depend largely on the attitude of the opposition Socialist Party, which repeated its March electoral success by easily outpolling the UMP in the June European Parliament elections. Socialist leaders split over the constitution, but in December the party's members voted to back it in the coming referendum.

The Economy. The government remained nominally committed to reducing the deficit, as promised to EU partners, but its resolve visibly weakened in tandem with its failing popularity. Despite Sarkozy's attempts to hold the line on the budget, at Chirac's behest the government announced a big new social spending program and made relatively minor savings in the health system. Sarkozy lived up to his reputation of being a relative free marketeer only by preparing Electricité de France for eventual privatization. In other ways, he displayed classic dirigiste tendencies—jawboning retailers to cut prices, directing insurers to invest in start-ups, and saving ailing companies such as the power and transport giant Alstom in the name of creating or preserving national champions.

Anti-Semitic outrages, such as the defacing of this Jewish cemetery in Herrlisheim, eastern France, in May, prompted Israeli Prime Minister Ariel Sharon to invite French Jews to immigrate to Israel.

Foreign Affairs. The most controversial piece of social legislation was the National Assembly's approval on February 10, by a sweeping 494–36, of the ban on the wearing of ostentatious religious symbols in schools. This was principally aimed at Muslim girls wearing Islamic headscarves. It might have sparked further protests when it came into effect at the start of the school year in September but for the widespread revulsion, even among French Muslims, at the kidnapping of two French journalists on August 20 in Iraq, with the kidnappers demanding that Paris repeal its ban on headscarves. Foreign Minister Barnier was dispatched to the Middle East to explain that the law was a general attempt to keep schools secular, not to victimize Muslims. The government continued to deport the more extreme of foreign-born imams in France, however, and to encourage the training of local clerics in the hope of fostering a more moderate French version of Islam. These efforts, however, did little to check the number of anti-Semitic incidents in France, which Israel Prime Minister Ariel Sharon used as justification for his appeal in July to French Jews to immigrate to Israel.

The Middle East continued to be a bone of contention with the U.S. After an amicable visit by Pres. George W. Bush to Paris on June 5–6 to celebrate the 60th anniversary of the D-Day landings, Chirac used two subsequent meetings with Bush—at the Group of Eight summit at Sea Island, Ga., and the NATO summit in Istanbul—to criticize U.S. attempts to "impose" democracy on Arab countries and to involve NATO in Iraq. This coolness toward the Bush administration contrasted with the warm reception Chirac gave Pres. Hu Jintao of China. Apart from lighting the Eiffel Tower red in honour of his guest, Chirac endorsed Beijing's "one China" policy and backed the lifting of the arms embargo on China that the EU had imposed in the wake of the Tiananmen Square massacre of 1989. In October, Chirac paid a return visit to Beijing with a large business delegation that won orders for aircraft, trains, and chemicals from the Chinese.

(DAVID BUCHAN)

GABON

Area: 267,667 sq km (103,347 sq mi)
Population (2004 est.): 1,351,000
Capital: Libreville
Chief of state: President Omar Bongo Ondimba
Head of government: Prime Minister Jean-François Ntoutoume-Emane

In January 2004 the Gabonese government closed the Omar Bongo Technical High School, the country's largest secondary educational establishment, after four days of rioting. An official inquiry found that more than 1,000 students had been admitted with falsified credentials, and in some cases bribery and sex had been used to improve grades. Although the school was reopened in March, disastrous results in the annual baccalaureate examinations underlined the overall weaknesses in the Gabonese education system.

On February 2 visiting Pres. Hu Jintao of China signed an agreement to import large quantities of Gabonese oil. China had funded and built Gabon's parliamentary complex and in July announced it would construct a national media centre in Libreville. On September 6, Pres. Omar Bongo left for a weeklong state visit to China, where he held talks with Hu at the Great Hall of the People in Beijing.

Shortly after taking off from Libreville Airport on June 8, a Gabon Express aircraft crashed into the sea, killing 19 of 30 people aboard. An investigation revealed a record of poor aircraft maintenance and inadequate corporate administration. About 200 former state employees, among 650 fired in the 1999 privatization of the state-owned railroad corporation, demonstrated on August 28. They sought full payment of promised redundancy awards. The government responded by threatening the protesters with severe reprisals should they participate in sabotage or other illegal acts. On September 9 villagers demanding the restoration of electricity supplies attacked the police station in Lébamba, 400 km (250 mi) southeast of Libreville. One gendarme was killed, and a second was seriously injured. (NANCY ELLEN LAWLER)

Georgians (foreground) and Ajarians regard each other over one of two bridges that were destroyed on May 2 by the Ajarians, who had been at odds with the central government and feared a military raid across the border.

GAMBIA, THE

Area: 10,689 sq km (4,127 sq mi)
Population (2004 est.): 1,405,000
Capital: Banjul
Head of state and government: President Col. Yahya Jammeh

In July 2004 Gambian Pres. Yahya Jammeh celebrated 10 years in office. Ceremonies were held that involved the vice president of Ghana and representatives from Swaziland, Guinea-Bissau, Burkina Faso, Mauritania, Mali, and Cape Verde. Lamin Juwara, the leader of the opposition National Democratic Action Movement, however, accused the Jammeh government of forcing many young people to flee the country because of a lack of employment opportunities and an oppressive political climate. He cited arbitrary arrests, detentions, and beatings. In October 2003 a fire was started in the main offices of the privately owned newspaper *The Independent,* which had been strongly critical of the government. Then in April, after the paper had continued with its criticisms, armed men entered a building in a suburb of Banjul and destroyed the newspaper's printing press. It was widely believed that the perpetrators were members of the State Guard, a unit providing security to the president, but appeals by the World Association of Newspapers and the World Editors Forum and others for a thorough investigation were ignored. Meanwhile, in March the president's former right-hand man, Baba Diop, was sentenced to nine years' imprisonment for economic crimes. The number of tourists increased to more than 100,000, thanks in part to a new charter service that took Spaniards to the Gambian beaches.

(CHRISTOPHER SAUNDERS)

GEORGIA

Area: 70,152 sq km (27,086 sq mi)
Population (2004 est.): 4,694,000
Capital: Tbilisi
Head of state and government: Presidents Nino Burjanadze and, from January 4, Mikhail Saakashvili assisted by Prime Minister (titled Minister of State until February 17) Zurab Zhvania

Mikhail Saakashvili (*see* BIOGRAPHIES), who led the "Rose Revolution" that culminated in the ouster of Pres. Eduard Shevardnadze in November 2003, was elected Georgian president on Jan. 4, 2004, with over 96% of the vote in a ballot deemed fair by the international community. The parliament immediately scheduled for March 28 repeat elections for the 150 parliament mandates allocated under the proportional representation system; the outcome of the Nov. 2, 2003, voting for those seats had been annulled on November 25. The ruling National Movement–Democratic Front bloc polled 67%, which gave it an overall majority of 136 seats in the 235-member legislature. On February 17 the parliament confirmed Zurab Zhvania as the new prime minister; in a cabinet reshuffle in June, Interior Minister Giorgi Baramidze was named defense minister, but he was later replaced by his successor as interior minister, Irakli Okruashvili.

At his inauguration on January 25, Saakashvili pledged to crack down on corruption and restore central government control over the breakaway regions of Ajaria, Abkhazia, and South Ossetia. Under pressure, Ajarian leader Aslan Abashidze agreed to hold parliamentary elections in March, but he was forced to step down and leave Batumi, the province's main city, for Moscow on May 5 after Tbilisi emboldened the local police and population to turn against him. Saakashvili named former fellow student Levan Varshalomidze to head the new administration; Varshalomidze was confirmed as Ajaria's prime minister following local elections on June 20. In late May, Georgia deployed Interior Ministry forces and armour to the internal border with South Ossetia, triggering a standoff that led to an exchange of fire on July 9–10 and then an abortive assault by Georgian forces on August 19 in which 16 Georgian servicemen were killed. Agreement was reached on a cease-fire and the withdrawal of all unauthorized troops from the conflict zone, but it was implemented only after a meeting between Prime Minister Zhvania and South Ossetian Pres. Eduard Kokoity on November 5. Elections in Abkhazia on October 3 for a successor to Pres. Vladislav Ardzinba resulted in a standoff between Sergey Bagapsh, officially declared the winner, and Prime Minister Raul Khadjimba. On December 6 they agreed under pressure from Russia to participate jointly in a repeat election in January.

Georgia's GDP grew by 9.5% during the first six months of 2004. The International Monetary Fund decided on June 4 to resume its assistance to Georgia; on June 16 international donors pledged $1 billion in financial aid. In June the EU included Georgia, together with Armenia and Azerbaijan, in its European Neighbourhood Policy.

(ELIZABETH FULLER)

GERMANY

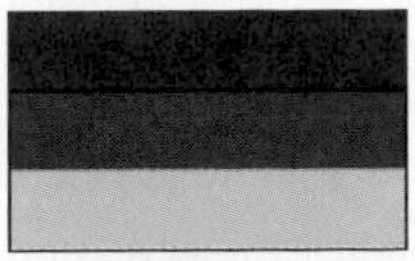

Area: 357,023 sq km (137,847 sq mi)
Population (2004 est.): 82,561,000
Capital: Berlin; some ministries remain in Bonn
Chief of state: Presidents Johannes Rau and, from July 1, Horst Köhler
Head of government: Chancellor Gerhard Schröder

The state of the German economy and the federal government's reform program were the dominant—and closely intertwined—topics of 2004. The government's economic woes were compounded by shattering results in state and European Parliament elections for the dominant coalition partner, the Social Democratic Party (SPD). The slight stirrings of economic growth remained stubbornly weak, just as the unemployment rate remained stubbornly strong at just over 10% (more than four million unemployed). Foreign affairs continued to be dominated by the German position on Iraq—and the consequences for Germany's relationship with the U.S. In the European Union tensions arose from a variety of sources, not least the row over the voting procedures set out in the draft constitutional treaty, as well as the German government's continued inability to bring its budget deficit under the ceiling set by the euro zone's Stability and Growth Pact.

Domestic Affairs. The domestic landscape was marked by continued voter disenchantment with the Schröder government's reform package, known as Agenda 2010. The reforms had a number of objectives aimed at kick-starting the sluggish economy and reducing the financial burdens imposed by Germany's generous welfare system. Displeasure was registered in a number of highly visible ways, notably in the thrashing voters dealt the SPD in state elections and in street demonstrations over the summer, particularly in eastern Germany.

The SPD registered almost universally poor results in the state elections, barely managing to retain its position as the largest party in the Brandenburg state poll, recording a mere 16% of the votes in Thuringia, and faring even worse—10.6%—in Saxony. Elections in the eastern part of the country were marked by a huge rise in support for what were effectively protest parties. The Party of Democratic Socialism (PDS), successor to East Germany's ruling communist party, achieved 28% of the vote in Thuringia, 30% in Brandenburg, and 24% in Saxony. The PDS was widely perceived as a party that gave expression to the discontent of eastern Germans with regard to the difficulties they faced after reunification, including their lesser wage rates, benefits, and pensions, and a rate of unemployment that in places was double the national average.

Observers within and outside Germany expressed greater alarm, however, over the looming possibility of a far-right resurgence in the east. In the Brandenburg election the right-wing German People's Union (DVU) won 6 seats in the state parliament, while in Saxony the German National Democratic Party (NPD) managed to win 12 seats. A measure of suspicion surrounded the politics of these two parties, particularly the NPD, which was associated with historical revisionism and incitement to racial hatred and which the government had previously sought to ban. It remained to be seen whether support for the rightists would be sustained in the future or would fade away as quickly as

In September blind demonstrators in Hannover rally around a statue of Martin Luther to protest cuts in assistance to the visually impaired in Lower Saxony state. Social benefits were targeted by budget cutters throughout Germany in 2004.

previous far-right resurgences had done as soon as economic conditions improved. In general the vote was perceived less as support for far-right policies and more as an expression of general voter discontent, especially as the Agenda 2010 reforms caused further economic hardship in the east.

For the SPD the outlook continued to be bleak as thoughts turned to the 2006 federal election. The Socialists received just 21.5% in the elections to the European Parliament, their worst showing ever in a nationwide poll. Because of a low voter turnout (43%), the results had to be treated with caution, but they were borne out by national opinion polls that suggested a gap of as much as 20 points opening up between the Christian Democratic Union/Christian Social Union (CDU/CSU) and the SPD. A key indicator would be the state election in spring 2005 in North-Rhine Westphalia, traditionally a region of strong SPD support.

Even among the ruling Social Democrats, there was a groundswell of discontent against the reform program. Grassroots supporters felt that the measures contradicted the fundamental SPD principles, and long-term supporters were turning away. The rumbles of discontent led Schröder to step down as chairman of the party in February, though this move did not affect his position as chancellor. He was replaced by Franz Müntefering, whose immediate task was to stabilize the party and win back disaffected voters. Schröder argued that it was not the reform package that was the problem but the way in which it had been communicated—or, rather, not communicated—to the citizenry. One government response was the launch of a public-relations offensive in the form of a "little red book" that laid out the basics of the reform package and was handed out at railway stations.

The CDU/CSU opposition found itself in a stronger position in 2004, though it too was hit by a general decline in the confidence of voters in the ability of both major parties to deliver. CDU leader Angela Merkel backed the reforms, but her position in the run-up to the 2006 federal elections remained somewhat insecure. Two powerful regional leaders, Roland Koch of Hesse and Edmund Stoiber of Bavaria (the candidate for chancellor in 2002), were positioning themselves to challenge her for the top nomination. Both had been involved in disputes with Merkel over Christian Democratic policy on reforms. A minor victory for the CDU/CSU came with the acceptance of the candidate it had backed to be the new president. Horst Köhler, previously the head of the International Monetary Fund, was inaugurated on July 1. Although the president's role is mainly ceremonial, he is in a position to influence national debate. Over the summer Köhler argued that the government had to have the courage to press on with the reform process despite its unpopularity.

Elsewhere in the domestic arena, plans were announced to reduce the size of the German armed forces. This came as part of a general restructuring designed to meet contemporary demands such as rapid response, peacekeeping, and conflict resolution and to move away from the Cold War confrontational model. This move immediately reignited public debate about conscription and the role of "Zivis," those young people who choose voluntary civil service instead of military service and upon whom many charities and social institutions depended.

In July a new immigration law was passed that paved the way for highly qualified foreign workers to become long-term residents in Germany. The new measures were criticized by business leaders as being insufficient to counteract the effects of an aging German population. Equally, the new legislation came in for popular criticism in light of the country's stubbornly high unemployment rate. The legislation suffered an arduous parliamentary passage, with the opposition demanding that tougher measures against terror suspects be included—an issue that became of even greater importance following the Madrid bombings in March.

The Economy. In 2003 the German economy shrank by 0.1%; in 2004 the first stirrings of growth, predominantly export-driven, could be discerned, though they remained worryingly weak. Domestic growth continued to be undermined by customers' reluctance to spend. In addition, the unemployment rate crept up again after having fallen slightly toward the end of 2003. It was clear that so far the government's reform package had failed to make much of an impact upon the weak economy. Even the tax cuts planned for 2005, rushed forward by the Schröder government to take effect on Jan. 1, 2004, had not prompted increased consumer spending.

Despite growing acceptance of the need for economic and welfare state reform, ordinary Germans were reluctant to accept the potential economic hardships or additional costs that such reforms brought. Suspicions remained about the introduction of Anglo-American-style reforms in the shape of market forces. The chancellor had effectively bet his political career on Agenda 2010's bringing about an economic recovery by the next federal elections. So far, however, the reforms had failed to deliver more than electoral setbacks and street demonstrations as citizens reacted to the immediate impact of the reforms upon their pay packets. The most unpopular elements included an increase of health care charges and the cutting of traditionally generous long-term unemployment benefits. On one Monday in August, triggered by the lowering of long-term unemployment benefits, 20,000 people demonstrated in Leipzig, with a further 15,000 on the streets in Berlin. The Schröder government remained largely firm in the face of such protests, and by autumn the momentum of the protesters had begun to fade, though disapproval continued to be registered in the state polls.

A principal objective of Agenda 2010 was to save the social security system from bankruptcy. The reforms did very little to tackle one of the most notorious brakes on the German economy, however: labour relations. The year 2004 saw a succession of threatened strikes and deals between unions and employers. In January and February there were a number of brief stoppages across the country orchestrated by Germany's largest and most influential union, IG Metall.

The unions' threats, however, were staunchly countered by the employers. The Munich-based manufacturing giant Siemens AG threatened a large-scale transfer of jobs to Hungary if IG Metall did not allow a greater use of flexible working hours. Siemens was not the only firm to challenge the restrictions of the 35-hour workweek, although it was one of the more successful. Elsewhere, the head of the Federal Labour Agency, which played a key role in the implementation of the reform package, lost his post in January after a vote of no confidence from the supervisory board and a failure to retain the backing of the government. Florian Gerster had been responsible for implementing cost-cutting measures and reforming the procedures used by the agency to find jobs for the unemployed. Rumours abounded that Gerster's sacking was more the result of resentment over his reformist policies than his alleged failure to put contracts up for bid correctly.

Economic issues were also a source of tension within the European Union, as

Germany and France continued to break the budget-deficit ceiling of the EU Stability and Growth Pact. Harsh exchanges with the European Commission led to a case heard before the European Court of Justice that challenged the legality of the EU finance ministers' decision in November 2003 not to punish member states that continued to breach the ceiling. For its part the German government argued that encouraging economic growth should take precedence over attempts to cut the deficit. France's position was similar, and both countries were criticized by other member states, particularly those that had fought hardest to meet the budget-deficit criteria. In the event, the finance ministers' ruling was overturned by the court, although it looked increasingly like a case of the European Commission's winning the battle but losing the war. Plans that featured more flexible means of assessing the budget deficits were developed to take account of periods of slow growth as well as recession. (See *European Union:* Sidebar, above.)

A clash between Anglo-American and German business cultures came to the fore in the spring. Six former directors of the telecommunications firm Mannesmann faced charges of breach of trust with regard to bonuses voted to five of them in the wake of Mannesmann's takeover by Vodafone AirTouch in 2000, the largest-ever corporate takeover at the time. The bonuses, totaling about $71 million, were of unprecedented size by German standards and were widely portrayed as evidence of corporate greed, particularly in light of the job losses that had followed the takeover. The defendants were acquitted on July 22, despite criticism of the size of the bonuses and the sloppiness of the paperwork, but the debate over the desirability for Germany of Anglo-American-style corporate governance (notably highly paid superstar CEOs) continued into the new year.

Foreign Affairs. Germany's foreign relations in 2004 were characterized by continued shakiness in its relationship with the United States. The European Union was beset by disputes and problems on a number of fronts, notably ratification of the draft constitutional treaty and the budget-deficit dispute. Germany's close relationship with France was well tended by Chancellor Schröder and French Pres. Jacques Chirac. The countries' friendship in the post-World War II period was cemented by the invitation extended to Schröder to join the 60th anniversary commemoration of the D-Day landings, the first time such an invitation had been extended to a German leader. The German chancellor's participation was generally accepted by veterans groups.

Many of the problems in the EU had to do with the issues of enlargement and the process of enacting a constitution. Ten new members acceded to the EU on May 1. Amid popular fears of a flood of cheap labour arriving from the east, Germany and some other existing member states placed restrictions on the movement of workers for a transitional period of up to seven years. Tensions with other member states were heightened when the EU "big three"—Germany, France, and the U.K.—held a summit in Berlin in February and advanced a series of proposals. Italy, in particular, took umbrage at what it saw as an attempt to dominate the European agenda and rejected the proposals out of hand. The issue of Turkey's membership in the EU was also controversial in Germany, which has a large ethnic Turkish minority. The government supported Turkey's accession, but the CDU/CSU opposed it.

The U.K., France, and Germany also reached informal consensus on a defense agreement for Europe that included plans for more structured cooperation and the creation of a military headquarters within NATO. Despite the U.K.'s strong transatlantic orientation and insistence that any defense solution for the EU be compatible with the NATO structure, the potential deal was greeted with suspicion in Washington as possibly undermining NATO. Even NATO officials seemed unclear as to how the new proposals would fit into current structures.

Berlin's relations with Washington remained on shaky ground because of Germany's staunch opposition to the U.S.-led intervention in Iraq. Chancellor Schröder and U.S. Pres. George W. Bush met in February, and the leaders sought to soft-pedal their differences by firmly emphasizing their common ground in the "war on terrorism" and particularly the role being played by Germans in Afghanistan. This did not mean, however, that the U.S. eased its ban on German firms' bidding on Iraqi reconstruction projects. Relations with the U.S. dipped again during clashes at the UN over the timetable for the handover of power to the Iraqis and the possibility of an enhanced role for NATO in Iraq. Germans were critically aware, however, that their country's hope for a permanent seat on the UN Security Council would depend in no small measure on the state of their relations with the U.S.

(ROSANNE PALMER)

GHANA

Area: 238,533 sq km (92,098 sq mi)
Population (2004 est.): 20,732,000
Capital: Accra
Head of state and government: President John Agyekum Kufuor

On Feb. 12, 2004, former president Jerry Rawlings gave evidence to the Ghanaian National Reconciliation Commission (NRC) about his alleged role in the 1982 murders of three High Court judges and an army officer. The NRC was founded in 2002 to investigate human rights abuses that occurred during the country's five military regimes, including Rawlings's (1979 and 1981–2000). As the country prepared for elections on December 7, widespread voter-registration problems were reported by the Election Commission. Turnout was massive on election day, with more than 80% of eligible voters going to the polls. Pres. John Agyekum Kufuor won reelection, garnering nearly 53% of the vote to 44% for John Atta Mills. Despite earlier reports of registration problems, observers said the vote was "transparent and in good order."

In January, Ghanaian police and British customs officers seized £80 million (about $145 million) worth of cocaine and arrested seven in Accra in one of the largest-ever international drug busts. Later in the year a tugboat off Ghana's coast was caught with two tons of cocaine, worth $50 million, for distribution in Europe.

A state of emergency was enforced from March to June in the northern Yendi district owing to ongoing political tensions over a chieftaincy. Revelations of an alleged coup plot in Equatorial Guinea in March had repercussions for Ghanaian immigrants there. Kufuor approved a major evacuation of his countrymen from the Equatorial Guinean capital of Malabo after they had been rounded up and detained by authorities. Accra played host to peace talks and a cease-fire agreement between the Côte d'Ivoire government and warring factions in July. (MARY F.E. EBELING)

GREECE

Area: 131,957 sq km (50,949 sq mi)
Population (2004 est.): 11,015,000
Capital: Athens
Chief of state: President Konstantinos Stephanopoulos
Head of government: Prime Ministers Konstantinos Simitis and, from March 10, Konstantinos Karamanlis

In 2004 Greece not only saw significant political developments at home but was also in the international limelight as the host of the 2004 Olympic Games. On March 7 parliamentary elections brought an end to 11 years of rule by the Panhellenic Socialist Movement (PASOK) and the return to power of the centre-right New Democracy (ND). With 45.4% of the vote, ND won 165 of the 300 mandates in the parliament, compared with 40.6% and 117 seats for PASOK. The Communist Party of Greece (KKE) won 5.9% and 12 seats, and the Alliance of the Left of Movements and Ecology (SYN) won 3.3% and 6 seats. Other parties, including the rightist-populist Popular Orthodox Rally (LAOS), failed to pass the 3% threshold.

Pres. Konstantinos (Kostis) Stephanopoulos asked ND leader Konstantinos (Kostas) Karamanlis (*see* BIOGRAPHIES) to form a new government. The new government was sworn in on March 10. In presenting his government's program, Karamanlis stated that the priorities were education and culture, economic policy, agricultural policy, and a more transparent and effective state administration. Although the opposition, the media, and part of the public accused his government of inaction and lethargy, Karamanlis ruled out a reshuffle. He did, however, have to replace Agriculture Minister Savvas Tsitouridis, who resigned in September after having been charged with nepotism. ND's dominant position was underlined by its success in the elections to the European Parliament on June 13, when it won 43% of the vote, compared with PASOK's 34%. KKE won 9.5%, while SYN and LAOS each received just over 4%.

The year also brought changes within several political parties. Even before the parliamentary elections, prime minister Konstantinos Simitis on January 7 resigned as PASOK president and announced that he would not stand for reelection as prime minister. He was succeeded by Foreign Minister Georgios Papandreou, who was the only candidate in direct elections by the party's members and "friends" on February 8. It soon became apparent that some leading PASOK members were at odds with Papandreou's political vision and strategy, and the party at times gave an outward image of internal disunity.

Following the European Parliament elections, SYN leader Nikos Konstantopoulos announced that having served three terms, he would not seek reelection at the party's congress in December. He was replaced as party leader by Alexandros Alavanos. Karamanlis, for his part, dominated the ND party congress in July, and his cronies were elected to leading party positions.

In February 2004 the trial of five suspected members of Revolutionary People's Struggle (ELA), an extreme-left terrorist organization, opened, with one defendant admitting having been a member of ELA and the rest denying all charges. Four were found guilty of relatively minor charges but were still sentenced to 25 years each, and one was acquitted.

The new government continued to work for good relations with Greece's neighbours, including Turkey. Athens supported the official line of Cypriot Pres. Tassos Papadopoulos against the United Nations plan for reunification of Cyprus before its accession to the European Union; in effect, Greek Cyprus alone joined the EU in May. The U.S. decision to recognize Macedonia by its constitutional name led to protests by Greek politicians and the public alike.

The Greek economy grew by an estimated 3.9%, with an inflation rate of 2.9% and 11.2% unemployment. A 5.3% budget deficit and a public debt level at 112% of GDP, however, were significantly higher than the previous government's targets. In fact, in September it was announced that the Simitis government had for years reported budget-deficit figures that were considerably below the real ones and that Greece had violated the EU Stability and Growth Pact between 2000 and 2003. The European Commission announced that it was considering legal steps against Greece.

Throughout 2004, and especially before the opening on August 13 of the 2004 Summer Olympic Games (*see* SPORTS AND GAMES: Special Report), major infrastructure projects were completed. These included the world's longest (in total length) cable-stayed suspension bridge, which linked the Peloponnesus and western mainland Greece; suburban train, subway, and tram lines in Athens; road projects; and, of course, sport venues. The Games

Construction nears completion at the Olympic Stadium in Athens on July 25, about three weeks before the Games began. Early worries that facilities would not be ready in time were largely not borne out.

A portion of the governor-general's mansion in Saint George's, Grenada, was destroyed by Hurricane Ivan on September 7. Some 39 people died in the storm, which also caused extensive damage to agriculture and the economy.

© Glen Hinkson/Reuters/Corbis

lasted until August 29 and were followed by the Paralympics in September. The events were generally hailed as a success, although attendance was at times low. The Greek public was shocked by the withdrawal of two of the country's top athletes, who failed to take a drug test shortly before the opening. Tight security (provided in part by NATO troops) proved quite effective but added an estimated €1 billion (about $1.2 billion) to the final tab for the Games. Taking everybody by surprise, the Greek national association-football (soccer) team on July 4 won the European championship. Xenophon Zolotas, a former prime minister and governor of the Bank of Greece, died on June 11 at age 100. (STEFAN KRAUSE)

GRENADA

Area: 344 sq km (133 sq mi)
Population (2004 est.): 103,000
Capital: Saint George's
Chief of state: Queen Elizabeth II, represented by Governor-General Sir Daniel Williams
Head of government: Prime Minister Keith Mitchell

Hurricane Ivan wreaked havoc in Grenada in September 2004, causing the deaths of at least 39 people and wiping out almost all the country's agriculture-based economic infrastructure as well as much of its tourism facilities. An estimated 90% of the homes were damaged, including the prime minister's official residence; the prison housing those responsible for the 1983 murder of former prime minister Maurice Bishop and several of his top officials was also damaged extensively, which allowed prisoners to escape. Overall, the damages were estimated at about $815 million. The hurricane banished any hope of Grenada's achieving the IMF forecast of 4% economic growth and a decline in the public-debt–GDP ratio during 2004.

In May the opposition National Democratic Congress called on Prime Minister Keith Mitchell to step down so that a proper inquiry could be conducted into charges that he had accepted $500,000 from Eric Resteiner, a German national, in exchange for Resteiner's appointment as a trade ambassador for Grenada. Mitchell strongly denied the accusations, though he did admit to having received $15,000 to cover legitimate expenses on behalf of the state. He also brought a libel suit against a Miami, Fla.-based online newsletter, which had first reported the allegations, but in July he agreed to set up an inquiry after Grenada's Chamber of Industry and Commerce pressed the issue.

A South Korean delegation visited the country in June to assess investment opportunities and joint ventures, including possible exploration for oil and gas.

(DAVID RENWICK)

GUATEMALA

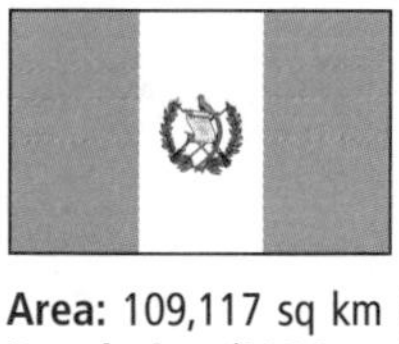

Area: 109,117 sq km (42,130 sq mi)
Population (2004 est.): 12,661,000
Capital: Guatemala City
Head of state and government: Presidents Alfonso Portillo Cabrera and, from January 14, Óscar Berger

Newly inaugurated Guatemalan Pres. Óscar Berger of the Grand National Alliance coalition promised in 2004 to increase productivity and create jobs in a country where 60% of the population lived in poverty. He also formally recognized the government's responsibility for much of the country's violence by compensating peasants for lands and lives lost during the civil war (1961–96). Berger turned over the Casa Crema—a former presidential palace and headquarters for the army for the past 40 years—to the Academy of Mayan Languages and Maya TV, which would broadcast Mayan programming. He also named Nobel laureate and indigenous peoples spokesperson Rigoberta Menchú to take charge of the implementation of the 1996 peace accords.

Nonetheless, murder, violence against women, kidnappings, land conflicts, and violations of human rights continued. Berger praised a plan for a UN-appointed special prosecutor to investigate human rights abuses, but some government and military officials delayed its progress. In January the first military officer convicted of a war crime, Col. Juan Valencia Osorio, escaped into hiding before being incarcerated. Former president Alfonso Portillo, under investigation for corruption and malfeasance after Guatemala's Constitutionality Court removed his immunity from prosecution, fled to Mexico in February. In March, however, the government placed former dictator Gen. Efraín Ríos Montt under house arrest pending trial for having organized a violent political riot during the last presidential campaign. Berger used army troops to control the rising crime while reducing the size of the army by one-third to one-half and shifting some military personnel to police duty.

Conditions for women improved in reproductive health and education, thanks to six new hospitals built and equipped by Cuba. Since 1998, in areas of Guatemala where some 200 Cuban doctors worked, the infant-mortality rate in Guatemala had fallen from 40 to

16 per 1,000 live births and the incidence of many epidemic diseases had been significantly reduced. About 600 Guatemalans were studying medicine in Havana.

Guatemala signed the Central American Free Trade Agreement with the U.S. and other Central American states on May 28. The country also took the lead in a new customs union that would integrate the Central American economies more fully.

(RALPH LEE WOODWARD, JR.)

GUINEA

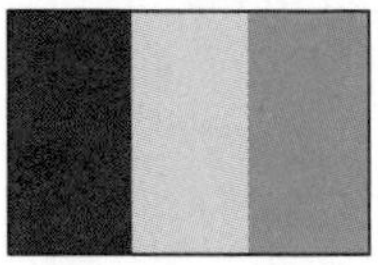

Area: 245,857 sq km (94,926 sq mi)
Population (2004 est.): 8,620,000
Capital: Conakry
Head of state and government: President Gen. Lansana Conté, assisted by Prime Ministers Lamine Sidimé, François Lonseny Fall from February 23 to April 30, and, from December 9, Cellou Dalein Diallo

In spring 2004, four months after Lansana Conté's virtually unopposed victory in the Dec. 21, 2003, presidential elections, the government of Guinea stopped former prime minister Sidya Touré and his associate Mamadou Ba from leaving the country. As leader of the opposition Union of Republican Forces in Guinea (UFR), Touré accused Conté of instigating a new campaign against his party. Several UFR members had already been taken into custody, accused of plotting a coup. Touré himself was arrested on April 26 on the same charge. François Lonseny Fall, who had been appointed prime minister in February, resigned on April 30. He cited as his reason presidential interference in his attempts to rescue the battered economy. On July 22 the Court of Appeal cleared Touré and the other members of his party of all charges.

Five years after Guinea was thought to have become completely free of polio, health experts voiced concerns over the possibility of a new epidemic. There were fears that the yearlong outbreak of the crippling disease in northern Nigeria could be spreading throughout West Africa. On August 26 the World Bank approved a $30 million credit to assist Guinea in the rebuilding and maintenance of its rural road network.

Shopkeepers in Conakry, Guinea, guard their few remaining sacks of rice on July 14; as supplies of this staple food dwindled, black market prices skyrocketed and government-imposed controls seemed unable to guarantee supplies.

AP/Wide World Photos

During the summer, riots broke out in Conakry over sharp increases in the price of the staple food, rice. Although the government responded by fixing the price at 40,000 Guinean francs per bag ($1 = about 2,000 Guinean francs), subsequent shortages saw black-market prices rise to 100,000 Guinean francs, which was more than the average monthly wage of most Guineans. University students and laid-off railway workers demonstrated in Kankan and Conakry, respectively, in September. (NANCY ELLEN LAWLER)

GUINEA-BISSAU

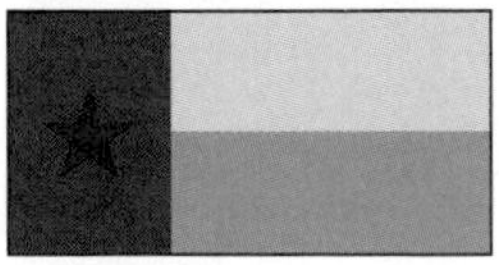

Area: 36,125 sq km (13,948 sq mi)
Population (2004 est.): 1,388,000
Capital: Bissau
Chief of state: President Henrique Pereira Rosa (acting).
Head of government: Prime Ministers Antonio Artur Sanhá and, from May 10, Carlos Gomes Júnior

In March 2004 more than 100 international observers watched as 12 political parties and three coalitions contested 102 seats in the National People's Assembly of Guinea-Bissau, fulfilling a promise—made when armed forces chief Verissimo Correia Seabra led a bloodless coup in September 2003—to hold parliamentary elections within six months. The vote was a key step toward the restoration of civilian rule, for the winning party was to replace the interim government. The caretaker president, Henrique Pereira Rosa, would remain in power, however, until presidential elections were held in 2005.

The African Party for the Independence of Guinea-Bissau and Cape Verde, which led the country for a quarter century after independence, gained the most seats, with former president Kumba Ialá's Social Renewal Party finishing second. The National Transitional Council, which would be disbanded when the results of the March poll were announced, had meanwhile approved an amnesty for those who staged the September 2003 coup.

In June defense ministers from the countries of the Community of Portuguese-Speaking Countries met in Bissau to discuss matters of common concern, including the possible creation of a joint peacekeeping force.

(CHRISTOPHER SAUNDERS)

GUYANA

Area: 215,083 sq km (83,044 sq mi)
Population (2004 est.): 752,000
Capital: Georgetown
Chief of state: President Bharrat Jagdeo
Head of government: Prime Minister Sam Hinds

In January 2004 the Guyanese opposition People's National Congress (PNC) launched a national signature campaign to force Home Affairs Minister Ronald Gajraj out of office on the basis of allegations that he had been linked to a "phantom squad" blamed for more than 40 execution-style killings over the previous 12 months. Opposition supporters also began picketing the Home Affairs Ministry in Georgetown.

The U.S. and Canadian governments barred Gajraj from entering those countries, despite his ministerial status. In May, Gajraj agreed to go on leave so that an investigation into the charges against him could proceed in a "speedy, fair, and impartial way." A commission of inquiry was set up by Pres. Bharrat Jagdeo, though it faced the difficulty of attracting information from anyone knowledgeable about the "phantom squad." George Bacchus, the key individual involved in the allegations against Gajraj, was assassinated in June. Bacchus had claimed to be a former member of the squad.

In February, Guyana formally referred its maritime border dispute with Suriname to the arbitration panel of the UN Convention on the Law of the Sea. The dispute had prevented Guyana from pursuing what was believed to be potentially lucrative oil deposits in the offshore Corentyne region.

(DAVID RENWICK)

HAITI

Area: 27,700 sq km (10,695 sq mi)
Population (2004 est.): 8,074,000
Capital: Port-au-Prince
Chief of state and government: Presidents Jean-Bertrand Aristide and, from February 29, Boniface Alexandre (provisional), assisted by Prime Ministers Yvon Neptune and, from March 12, Gérard Latortue (interim)

The long-awaited commemoration in 2004 of Haiti's bicentennial of independence was overshadowed by turmoil, violence, and disaster. By early 2004 Pres. Jean-Bertrand Aristide's grip on power had weakened considerably. Political confrontation in Port-au-Prince surged, and armed insurrectionists, who had crossed the border from the Dominican Republic, overran police stations throughout the country, releasing prisoners, gaining allies among street thugs, and attacking government officials. Following the late February refusal of President Aristide's political opponents to accept an internationally backed power-sharing agreement, Haiti's beleaguered elected leader left the country on February 29 after armed gangs, mostly affiliated with the previously disbanded Haitian army, threatened the capital.

As Aristide left Haiti on a U.S. military aircraft and questions arose whether his departure was voluntary or coerced, Supreme Court Justice Boniface Alexandre was sworn in as provisional president. Concurrently, U.S. armed forces, sanctioned under UN Security Council Resolution 1529, landed in Port-au-Prince. Joined within days by French, Canadian, and Chilean troops, the 3,600-strong Multinational Interim Force for Haiti (MIFH) stabilized the capital. The action helped pave the way for the installation of an interim government mandated to lead the country to elections in 2005 and the inauguration of a new president in February 2006. The MIFH handed over operations in June to a Brazilian-led UN Stabilization Mission in Haiti (MINUSTAH), composed of about 6,700 peacekeepers and 1,622 civilian police trainers.

Despite MINUSTAH's presence, Haiti remained in turmoil. Insurrectionists refused to disarm, calling for the restoration of the army, and the decimated Haitian National Police (HNP) yielded public security functions throughout the country to these armed groups. Overall insecurity mounted as demonstrations calling for Aristide's return sometimes turned violent, kidnappings and robberies increased, and acts of retribution against officials and supporters of the former government rose. While the interim government struggled to gain legitimacy among Haitians, deliver basic services, and fulfill its mandate, Haiti was struck in May and September by storms that took at least 5,000 lives and underscored the extent of the country's environmental devastation.

Haiti's already-weak economy suffered greatly, and its economic infrastructure was considerably damaged during the insurrection. Although international donors pledged $1.08 billion in July to assist Haiti's interim authorities in strengthening governance, promoting national dialogue and economic recovery, and improving access to basic services, by year's end no funds had been disbursed. For the

Having taken control of Gonaïves, an antigovernment group calling itself the Artibonite Resistance Front marches through the northwestern Haitian city on February 6. Rising violence forced Pres. Jean-Bertrand Aristide to flee the country at the end of the month.

most fortunate among ordinary Haitians, however, life-sustaining aid came from family members living overseas, who sent some $1 billion in remittances to Haiti in 2003. During 2004 at least 3,000 Haitian boat people were interdicted by U.S. authorities and returned home.

(ROBERT MAGUIRE)

HONDURAS

Area: 112,492 sq km (43,433 sq mi)
Population (2004 est.): 6,948,000
Capital: Tegucigalpa
Head of state and government: President Ricardo Maduro

In February 2004 the IMF issued Honduras a three-year loan of about $107 million for a Poverty Reduction and Growth Facility, ending two years of negotiations during which Honduras lacked IMF assistance. The agreement was contingent upon government compliance with spending cuts and salary freezes for government workers. Honduran workers opposed a salary freeze, however, and teachers and medical workers struck for raises. Its compliance with the IMF agreement advanced Honduras's admission process in the Heavily Indebted Poor Country Program. In August a constitutional amendment was passed by the National Congress that rescinded the immunity of government officials.

Honduran ports met a July 2004 deadline to implement security procedures required for shipping cargo to the United States, a key partner in Honduras's foreign trade, but the Honduran government pulled its troops out of the U.S.-led coalition force in Iraq. Negotiations were concluded during the year for the Central American Free Trade Agreement; the legislatures of the five Central American countries, the Dominican Republic, and the U.S. would each have to ratify the treaty before it took effect. The problem of demarcation of Honduras's border with El Salvador was finally resolved, and permanent markers were installed. The dispute resulted from the 1969 "Soccer War" and remained unsettled until International Court of Justice rulings in 1992 and 2003.

Pres. Ricardo Maduro announced his desire to freeze funds for the Central American Court of Justice and the Central American Parliament, arguing that the money would be better spent on domestic health and education programs. Constitutionally, however, the National Congress would have to renounce the relevant treaties before the president's proposal could be effected.

The World Food Programme (WFP) distributed food in drought-stricken areas of southern Honduras. The government and the WFP began a program to expand irrigation and help farmers switch from traditional corn (maize) and bean crops to sorghum, sesame, and alternate bean varieties that required less water.

(MICHELLE M. TAYLOR-ROBINSON)

HUNGARY

Area: 93,030 sq km (35,919 sq mi)
Population (2004 est.): 10,103,000
Capital: Budapest
Chief of state: President Ferenc Madl
Head of government: Prime Minister Peter Medgyessy and, from August 27, Ferenc Gyurcsany (acting until September 29)

Following the country's historic accession to the European Union on May 1, 2004, Hungary experienced a serious government crisis, which saw the resignation of a prime minister for the first time in the post-1989 period. Peter Medgyessy resigned in August after losing confidence from the governing Hungarian Socialist Party and its junior coalition partner, the Alliance of Free Democrats. His resignation came two months after the first Hungarian elections for the European Parliament (EP), which failed to confirm popular support for the governing parties. The two coalition parties received fewer seats combined than the opposition Fidesz–Hungarian Civic Alliance, which secured half of all 24 seats in the new Hungarian caucus. For more than a year, Fidesz had been leading popularity polls, and its position further strengthened after its EP election success. The fourth political party in the Hungarian assembly, the Hungarian Democratic Forum, also received one of the allotted seats in the EP.

The Hungarian turnout in the EP elections was 38.5%, which was lower than the EU average of 45% but significantly higher than the 28% average in new EU member states. The participation figures during Hungary's referendum on EU membership in April 2003 were also low—46%.

Medgyessy's resignation came amid an attempt to reshuffle his government and was directly sparked by his commitment to fire the minister of economy, whom the Alliance of Free Democrats had delegated to the government. After his departure Medgyessy implied that some core Socialist Party leaders withdrew their support for his planned personnel changes and famously said that he "would not bow before the putschists," without naming the persons he held responsible for the crisis.

His successor was announced in a matter of days by the Socialist leadership, and former minister of children, youth, and sports Ferenc Gyurcsany took over the post in September. During the 1990s, Gyurcsany stayed away from politics and focused on his businesses, gradually becoming one of Hungary's richest businessmen.

After replacing half of the government ministers, Gyurcsany pledged to focus on generating employment and improving social equality. Among other things, he promised to reduce the tax burdens on low-income families and increase taxation on banks and other financial service companies. As one of his early pledges, Gyurcsany also promised to review Hungary's military engagement in Iraq.

In September, Foreign Minister and Socialist Party Chairman Laszlo Kovacs was nominated as Hungary's new commissioner in the EU, and he received the tax portfolio in November. The opposition was critical of the choice—which had been made by Medgyessy prior to his departure—arguing that interim commissioner Peter Balazs, a technocrat, would have been more suited to representing Hungary in the EU, given his distance from domestic politics.

During the year Fidesz collected over one million signatures to press for budget amendments. The petition, launched in March, called for cutting medicine prices, concluding the privatization of state-controlled companies, restoring the system of housing subsidies that was launched during its tenure of governance, increasing agricultural subsidies, and capping annual energy price rises at 5%.

Economic growth and macroeconomic indicators remained stable throughout the year, but the Organisation for Economic Co-operation and Development suggested putting off the target date for joining the euro zone until 2009 or 2010—as opposed to the government's original plan of 2008—in view of a disappointing budget deficit in 2003. (ZSOFIA SZILAGYI)

ICELAND

Area: 102,928 sq km (39,741 sq mi)
Population (2004 est.): 292,000
Capital: Reykjavík
Chief of state: President Ólafur Ragnar Grímsson
Head of government: Prime Ministers Davíd Oddsson and, from September 15, Halldór Ásgrímsson

Iceland's economy expanded at a brisk pace in 2004, with GDP growing at a rate of 5%, following 4½% growth in the previous year. Inflation edged up slightly, to an annual rate of 3–4%. The rapid growth was primarily due to the ongoing construction project in the northeastern part of the country, where a 690-MW hydropower station was being built to provide electricity to an Alcoa aluminum plant. Together these two construction projects, which were scheduled for completion in 2006, would cost $3 billion, almost one-fourth of Iceland's normal annual GDP.

In the spring the government proposed legislation that sought to limit radio and television ownership to companies devoted solely to electronic media. Firms engaged in other lines could own only a 5% stake in broadcast media companies. The intention was to limit the opinion-shaping power of multi-industry companies. The bill was fiercely controversial but was eventually passed by the Althingi (parliament). Pres. Ólafur Ragnar Grímsson, however, refused to sign the law—the first time in the 60-year history of the Republic of Iceland that a president had exercised his veto power. Under the constitution the law still remained in force but had to be put before a national referendum. Rather than risk defeat, the government, in a special parliamentary summer session, rescinded the law.

On Sept. 15, 2004, Iceland's prime minister since 1991, Davíd Oddsson, switched posts with Foreign Minister Halldór Ásgrímsson in accordance with an agreement after the 2003 parliamentary election.
(BJÖRN MATTHÍASSON)

INDIA

Area: 3,166,414 sq km (1,222,559 sq mi)
Population (2004 est.): 1,081,229,000
Capital: New Delhi
Chief of state: President A.P.J. Abdul Kalam
Head of government: Prime Ministers Atal Bihari Vajpayee and, from May 22, Manmohan Singh

Domestic Politics. The year 2004 was one of change in India. An election in the spring yielded a mixed verdict; no major political party secured an absolute majority in the 543 member Lok Sabha, the lower house of Parliament. The ruling National Democratic Alliance (NDA) government, headed by Prime Minister Atal Bihari Vajpayee, was voted out of office after the coalition was unable to secure a clear majority. The Indian National Congress (INC), led by Sonia Gandhi, had only 145 MPs and was also unable to form a government. The Congress Party and its preelection allies, however, put together a new coalition called the United Progressive Alliance (UPA) and secured the support of the 62-member leftist bloc, which comprised an assortment of communist and radical groups. Gandhi chose not to head the government as prime minister, since her foreign origin had become a politically controversial issue. (Though Gandhi was an Indian citizen, she was born in Italy.) Consequently, she invited Manmohan Singh (*see* BIOGRAPHIES), her seniormost colleague and the leader of the INC in the Rajya Sabha (upper house of Parliament), to head the government. Singh became prime minister on May 22.

The defeat of the NDA sent its main constituent, the Bharatiya Janata Party (BJP), into a tailspin. The BJP was slow to come to terms with defeat, since most opinion and exit polls had predicted a victory for the NDA. As a result, the first session of Parliament was brought to a virtual standstill, and the BJP lurched to the political right, reinstating former deputy prime minister and party icon Lal Krishna Advani as its leader after another stunning defeat, this time in provincial elections in the state of Maharashtra. The BJP's allies became wary when the party renewed pro-Hindu religious campaigning. The 2004 elections also saw the defeat of the Telugu Desam Party (TDP) in the southern state of Andhra Pradesh. The TDP's leader, Chandrababu Naidu, was a symbol of economic reform, and his defeat reinforced the left-wing turn in Indian politics.

Apart from the clutch of elections, the other major political event in 2004 was the movement forward in peace initiatives in the troubled state of Jammu and Kashmir and in the northeastern states. The UPA government also took initiatives to resume a dialogue with other disaffected groups, such as the "Maoist" Peoples' War Group in Andhra Pradesh. Prime Minister Singh's travels to Kashmir and to Assam and Manipur in the northeast had a calming influence on political rhetoric in these states. The hope for peace was rekindled, and Singh was viewed as a sincere and caring leader who was genuinely committed to a peaceful resolution of the problem of disaffection in those parts of the country.

The Economy. The 2004 election verdict was widely interpreted by political

Prime Minister Manmohan Singh visits the Harimandir, or Golden Temple, a Sikh pilgrimage site, in the northern Indian city of Amritsar on September 1.

commentators as a vote against the NDA's "pro-urban" policies. The UPA, therefore, entered the government with a strong pro-farmer message and committed itself to providing a "New Deal" to rural India. The focus of the new government was on revitalizing the agrarian economy, stepping up investment in agriculture, providing access to credit, and improving the quality of rural infrastructure. The second message of the election outcome, it was widely believed, was that the policies aimed at increasing the economy's efficiency had to be balanced by policies that would improve equity and welfare. The government made employment generation an important feature of its agenda.

Most macroeconomic indicators were positive, however, and estimates placed the current 2004–05 fiscal year growth rate at above 6%, which followed an 8% growth rate in the previous fiscal year, mainly owing to good rainfall and a steep increase in agricultural production. There was a revival of the industrial economy, with manufacturing and electricity production rising above the previous year's growth figures. The two areas of concern had been the impact of rising world oil prices on domestic energy prices and costs and the impact of rising foreign-exchange reserves on the exchange rate of the rupee. An appreciating rupee could help in the fight against inflation, but it could also have a negative impact on exports.

The Indian stock market was booming, with increased capital flows from foreign institutional investors. Sensex, the most widely followed Bombay Stock Exchange index, hit new highs above 6300 by year's end. The Indian information-technology industry saw continued growth; international growth picked up, and global demand for Indian software services continued to increase. Though the outsourcing debate had played a role early on in the run-up to the U.S. elections, the issue later disappeared from the front pages, and Indian outsourcing business saw new activity; IBM, for example, revealed plans to do more business in India. (*See* ECONOMIC AFFAIRS: Special Report.)

Foreign Policy. The new government moved forward with the peace process with Pakistan and the negotiations on the border dispute with China. Prime Minister Singh retained the key personnel appointed by the Vajpayee government to deal with Kashmiri militants and the Naga rebels in the northeast. Early in his tenure Singh traveled to New York City for the session of the UN General Assembly, where he met with U.S. Pres. George W. Bush and Pakistani Pres. Pervez Musharraf. Both meetings were described as constructive, and the meeting with Musharraf was also dubbed historic.

Singh's foreign-policy initiatives in the first six months of his tenure were marked by major forays into regional economic diplomacy. His first visit abroad was to Bangkok, where he joined the leaders of Bangladesh, Bhutan, Myanmar (Burma), Nepal, Sri Lanka, and Thailand to launch the Bay of Bengal Initiative for Multi-Sectoral Technical and Economic Cooperation (BIMSTEC). At the UN Singh joined the heads of government of Brazil, Germany, and Japan to launch a four-nation initiative for permanent-member status in the UN Security Council. At The Hague in November, Singh participated in the India–European Union Summit meeting, at which India and the EU signed a strategic partnership agreement. Later in the month Singh participated in a summit with the Association of Southeast Asian Nations (ASEAN), at which India and ASEAN member countries signed the ASEAN-India Partnership for Peace, Progress and Shared Prosperity treaty. Singh also met with Chinese Premier Wen Jiabao and Japanese Prime Minister Junichiro Koizumi in talks that were described as important by both sides. Wen Jiabao described his upcoming 2005 visit to India as "the most important engagement on my agenda for next year."

The Indian Ocean littoral states of Kerala, Tamil Nadu, and Andhra Pradesh were hard-hit by the tsunami of December 26. (*See* DISASTERS: Sidebar.) More than 16,000 Indians died or were missing and presumed dead, including more than 5,000 on the remote and low-lying Andaman and Nicobar Islands, where criticism of the Indian government's slow response to the disaster was especially vocal. (SANJAYA BARU)

INDONESIA

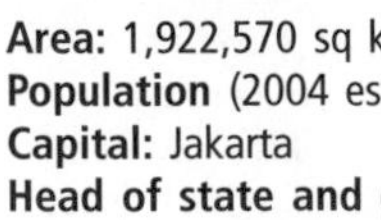

Area: 1,922,570 sq km (742,308 sq mi)
Population (2004 est.): 222,611,000
Capital: Jakarta
Head of state and government: Presidents Megawati Sukarnoputri and, from October 20, Susilo Bambang Yudhoyono

A Papuan man in traditional dress celebrates the election victory of Susilo Bambang Yudhoyono (shown on the left in the small photo with Vice President-elect Jusuf Kalla) in Jakarta on October 9.

Elections dominated Indonesian life during 2004, and the year came to a tragic close with the massive tsunami of December 26. (*See* DISASTERS: Sidebar.) The elections brought to power a new president, Susilo Bambang Yudhoyono (commonly known as SBY), and changed the dynamics of the nation's politics. The tsunami was the most lethal in modern history and devastated littoral regions of Aceh province in northern Sumatra, killing almost 100,000 people and displacing 300,000 others.

Three separate electoral processes took place during the year. Elections for the national parliament (DPR) and provincial and district legislatures were held on April 5, for which 140 million people were registered to vote (83% of whom cast a ballot). This was the world's largest simultaneous single-day election.

All the "big five" parties suffered losses. The biggest loser was Pres. Megawati Sukarnoputri's Indonesian Democratic Party of Struggle (PDI-P), which dropped to 19% of the vote from 34% in the 1999 election. This left Golkar, the electoral vehicle of the former Suharto regime, as the largest party, with 22% of the vote (down 1% on its 1999 result). Two parties made spectacular advances in the election: SBY's fledgling Democrat Party (PD), which had been formed in 2003, gained 7.5% of the vote, and the Islamic Prosperity and Justice Party

(PKS) lifted its percentage from 1.4% in 1999 to 7% in 2004.

Overall, these results pointed to greater volatility in Indonesia's electorate and indicated strong dissatisfaction with the performance of Megawati's government and the behaviour of the larger parties. Opinion polls repeatedly showed disapproval for the government's unwillingness to tackle corruption and its inability to stimulate faster economic growth. Public confidence in the parliament fell sharply after a string of graft allegations and an ever-lengthening backlog of unpassed legislation. Among the new parliament's members, 72% were serving for the first time. The April 5 poll also elected members to a newly established 128-seat Regional Representatives Council (DPD), which would have powers to review legislation relating to the regions and would also, with the 550 parliamentarians, constitute the restructured People's Consultative Assembly (MPR), Indonesia's supreme decision-making body.

The second part of the electoral process was a two-round direct presidential election, the first in Indonesia's history (the preceding four presidents had been elected by the MPR). In the first round, on July 5, SBY and Megawati emerged as the two highest-ranked candidates of the five that stood. At the runoff election on September 20, SBY won 61% of the vote to Megawati's 39%. SBY was sworn in as Indonesia's sixth president on October 20.

SBY, an ethnic Javanese, was one of four generals standing for either the presidency or the vice presidency in 2004. Much of his military career had been spent in social and political affairs, rather than on the battlefield, and he was widely seen as one of the more intellectually inclined and pro-reform generals. He had a masters degree from the United States and gained his Ph.D. shortly before being installed as president. Opinion polls indicated that he had won the election because voters saw him as honest, responsible, and better able than Megawati to overcome the nation's pressing economic and security problems.

SBY's government was a mixture of political and technocrat appointees. He gave priority to restoring economic growth to the 7% levels of the Suharto era; growth stood at 4.5%, not enough to absorb the rapid increase in the workforce. A key element of his economic policy was the need to bring in greater foreign capital. SBY was well regarded by Western governments and business, and he was seeking to use this reputation to attract overseas aid and investment.

AP/Wide World Photos

Soldiers dump the bodies of unidentified victims of the Indian Ocean tsunami into a mass grave in Banda Aceh on December 29. Aceh province, at the northern tip of the Indonesian island of Sumatra, was devastated by the massive waves.

A key challenge facing SBY was to manage emergency relief and longer-term reconstruction efforts in tsunami-hit Aceh. Most of the infrastructure in coastal regions was destroyed, and rebuilding would require billions of dollars, much of it from foreign donors.

Complicating the rebuilding of Aceh was the continuing conflict between Indonesian security forces and the separatist Free Aceh Movement (GAM). The Megawati government had launched full-scale military operations against GAM in May 2003, and the province had remained in a state of "military emergency" until May 2004. According to official figures, during 2004 more than 1,200 people had died in the conflict by the end of September. SBY had hinted that he would seek to wind back military operations in Aceh and restore full civilian control, but details were not announced.

Terrorism also still loomed as a challenge for the government. Indonesia suffered one serious attack during the year. On September 9 in Jakarta, the Australian embassy was the target of a suicide car bombing; 9 Indonesians were killed, and more than 119 were injured. Prime suspects in the masterminding of the attack were Azhari Husin and Noordin Mohamad Top, two Malaysians involved in the Indonesian-based Jemaah Islamiyah (JI) terrorist organization, which had been responsible for the 2002 Bali bombing and the 2003 Marriott Hotel bombing in Jakarta. JI had also been linked to smaller attacks in central Sulawesi. Overall, the Indonesian government had considerable success in its campaign against terrorism. In the past two years, almost 40 terrorists had been prosecuted successfully, more than in any other country. More trials were pending, and arrests of suspected terrorists continued. Nevertheless, JI and other smaller, more localized extremist groups remained a lethal threat.

A number of important reforms also took place. In late 2003 the Constitutional Court began operation with extensive powers to adjudicate disputes between government institutions, decide on electoral appeals, and advise the parliament about abuses of office by the president. Its establishment was welcomed by most legal observers in Indonesia. Soon after the Anti-Corruption Commission was formed, it took action against several prominent figures accused of corruption, including Abdullah Puteh, the governor of Aceh.

By year's end all elections had been conducted fairly and without significant unrest, and there had been a smooth transition to a new president and government. This augured well for continued democratic consolidation.

(GREGORY J. FEALY)

IRAN

Area: 1,648,200 sq km (636,374 sq mi)
Population (2004 est.): 67,503,000 (excluding about 800,000 Afghan refugees)
Capital: Tehran
Supreme political and religious authority: *Rahbar* (Spiritual Leader) Ayatollah Sayyed Ali Khamenei
Head of state and government: President Mohammad Khatami

Elections to Iran's seventh Majlis (parliament) took place on Feb. 20, 2004, in a climate of mistrust caused by the Council of Guardians, which debarred thousands of candidates whom it found inadequately committed to Islam. Widespread protests ensued, and a number of candidates were restored by the unelected council, but many more remained excluded. The result of the elections was prejudiced by the barring of reformist candidates, so overall victory was won by conservative groups. On February 23 the Interior Ministry announced that the conservatives had taken 149 seats to the reformists' 65, which left the hard-liners in undisputed control. The effect of the conservatives' takeover of the Majlis was considerable. Allegations of barefaced election rigging undermined the entire democratic basis of the regime and more than ever put its legitimacy at stake.

Indications that the conservatives' victory would soften their hard line were misleading. Social constraints, including enforcement of the dress code, were strengthened; recognition of human rights was not universal; and the media were subjected to intimidation and closure. Importantly, the national economic development plan, based on accelerated privatization of state-owned organizations and a steady modernization through the introduction of foreign investment and technology, was played down.

Foreign policy too remained antagonistic to the West, not least the United States. The U.S. and the EU showed increasing alarm at Iran's nuclear program. In January Javier Solana, representing the EU, visited Iran with a view to persuading the authorities to abandon nuclear development, while Hassan Rowhani, the head of the Iranian National Security Council, discussed nuclear issues with officials in Paris. Deep suspicion of Iran's nuclear ambitions arose in February when International Atomic Energy Agency (IAEA) inspectors announced that Iran had failed to disclose fully its program of nuclear development. Iran, it was revealed, had traded on the international black market and was involved in the manufacture of triggers for nuclear explosions.

In September Iran announced a 10-point proposal on nuclear and related security issues, including elimination of all aspects of nuclear weaponry, but this did not deter U.S. demands for immediate abandonment of its nuclear program. The situation was exacerbated by exposure of undeclared nuclear sites at Lavizan-Shian. The U.S. demanded that Iran's failure to cooperate with the IAEA be referred to the UN Security Council. Russian Pres. Vladimir Putin warned Iran in September that it had to guarantee that any weapons capability be excluded from its nuclear industry. Meanwhile, by declining to sign an Additional Safeguard Protocol to the 1968 Nuclear Non-proliferation Treaty, Iran edged ever closer to being subject to UN Security Council economic sanctions.

The weapons of mass destruction issue led to acute frictions with the U.S. and the EU. There was serious speculation that either the U.S. or Israel might attack the country's nuclear industry. Relations with the U.K. were adversely affected by antiwar rioting outside the British embassy in Tehran and by an incident in June in which three British small patrol craft were seized by the Iranians as they tried to pass through the Shatt al-Arab waterway.

Iranian policy toward the Middle East was influenced profoundly by both the U.S.-led coalition attack on Iraq and the subsequent breakdown of security in that country. When Washington severed its links with Iraqi politician Ahmad Chalabi, Iran was implicated as the recipient of secret information from Chalabi and other sources in the Iraqi Governing Council—accusations that the Iranian Foreign Ministry denied. Iran was also alleged to be supporting the revolt by Muqtada al-Sadr and other Shi'ite radicals against the coalition forces' occupation of Iraq. There was no evidence that this was the case, however, and the official Iranian policy was generally to back Ayatollah Ali al-Sistani (*see* BIOGRAPHIES), the leading Shi'ite leader in Iraq. In the Persian Gulf area, old disputes with the United Arab Emirates over the ownership of Abu Musa and the Tumb islands reemerged. Iran's relations with Turkey were soured by commercial difficulties that led to the displacement of a Turkish company managing Tehran's new Imam Khomeini International Airport and by the slow progress of joint ventures in oil pipeline development.

Iran's economy continued to prosper, supported by buoyant world oil prices. Economic growth was officially reported at 6.7% in the Iranian year ended in March, a slight fall from the foregoing year owing to poor rainfall in some farming areas. Unemployment improved to 12% against 16% the previous year, and inflation remained at 16%. Iran's foreign exchange assets were valued at $7.3 billion. The budget for the current year (to March 2005) forecast a rise in oil revenues to more than $20 billion, with exports running at two million barrels a day. (KEITH S. MCLACHLAN)

On January 18 reformist deputies to Iran's Majlis (parliament) continue their sit-in for an eighth day. They are protesting attempts by the conservative Council of Guardians to bar candidates with insufficiently Islamic views from running in the February election.

IRAQ

Area: 434,128 sq km (167,618 sq mi)
Population (2004 est.): 25,375,000
Capital: Baghdad
Head of state: occupation regime headed by Director of the Coalition Provisional Authority L. Paul Bremer III; from June 28, 2004, President Ghazi al-Yawer
Head of government: Governing Council of Iraqi leaders with a rotating presidency; from July 1, 2004, Prime Minister Ayad Allawi

The year 2004 In Iraq was marked by a sharp degradation of the security situation while the U.S.-led coalition occupation forces struggled to rebuild the Iraqi nation. (*See* Special Report.) The numbers of shadowy underground insurgent groups launching attacks against American forces and Iraqi government targets were legion. Most notorious among them was a group under the control of Abu Musab al-Zarqawi, a Jordanian-born terrorist with ties to the al-Qaeda terrorist network. These groups attracted both homegrown insurgents and non-Iraqi volunteer fighters from Arab and Islamic countries who had entered Iraq across poorly guarded borders, mainly via Syria and Iran. Insurgents also comprised remnants of the old Iraqi Ba'th regime, Arab nationalists, and Sunni Islamic fundamentalists. They were responsible for countless acts of killing, sabotage, destruction of public property, hostage taking, and suicide bombings. Their targets included hotels, police- and army-recruiting centres, electrical installations, and oil pipelines; attacks on petroleum-producing facilities effectively disrupted the export of oil from Iraq. These groups did their utmost to destabilize the new Iraqi government and inflict losses on the U.S. and other coalition forces stationed in Iraq. Several coalition partners were persuaded to withdraw their troops from Iraq; major reconstruction projects were halted; and the flow of passengers and goods to and from Syria and Jordan was disrupted. Among the prominent casualties of car-bomb attacks was Izz al-Din Salem, the president of the Iraq Governing Council, on May 11.

The insurgency was concentrated mainly in Baghdad and the Sunni areas north and west of the Iraqi capital, especially in the town of Fallujah, where the rebels dug in and in April repelled an attempt by U.S. and central government forces to regain control of the city. The military effort was renewed in November, and Fallujah was recaptured with heavy losses inflicted on the insurgents and a large part of the city destroyed.

In general, the Shi'ite areas of Iraq remained calm after fighting that lasted until September between U.S. and Iraqi forces and those of Muqtada al-Sadr, a radical young Shi'ite cleric, which took place mainly in Karbalah and Najaf. Grand Ayatollah Ali al-Sistani (*see* BIOGRAPHIES), the highest Shi'ite authority in Iraq, was able to mediate this dispute and put an end to the fighting. The ethnic Kurdish areas in northern Iraq generally remained outside the circle of violence, although Kurdish leaders were increasingly vocal in demanding greater autonomy. Ethnic and sectarian tensions, including some violence, continued between Arabs, Kurds, and Turkmen, who constituted the population of the city of Kirkuk, which was claimed by the Kurds as part of their autonomous zone.

Under pressure from the resistance movement, the U.S. authorities decided to return sovereignty to the Iraqis earlier than scheduled. The Governing Council that had been installed by the U.S. in July 2003 was dissolved, and in its place an interim administration was appointed with the task of preparing for general elections to be held by Jan. 30, 2005. UN Special Adviser Lakhdar Brahimi (*see* BIOGRAPHIES) selected Ghazi al-Yawar, a Sunni sheikh trained as an engineer, to be president and head of the interim administration. On June 8 the UN Security Council approved his appointment. Subsequently, Ayad Allawi (*see* BIOGRAPHIES) was elected prime minister of the interim Iraqi government. On June 28, two days ahead of schedule, L. Paul Bremer III, head of the Coalition Provisional Authority, handed over sovereignty to the newly created Iraqi leadership—but without any withdrawal of U.S. forces from the country. John D. Negroponte assumed some of Bremer's functions as the new U.S. ambassador to Iraq.

The Transitional Administrative Law was adopted by the Governing Council on March 8. The document proclaimed Islam as a source of legislation and granted individual rights to all Iraqis. It did not expand the Kurdish self-governing area. The new Iraqi parliament, which was supposed to be elected by the end of January 2005, would be responsible for drawing up a permanent constitution for Iraq.

Despite concentrated efforts by the U.S. to find weapons of mass destruction in Iraq, none were ever found. The

(continued on page 414)

A masked insurgent, armed with a rocket-propelled grenade launcher and carrying an Iraqi police flak jacket, pauses in front of a burning car in Mosul in November.

© Namir Noor-eldeen/Reuters/Corbis

The Character and Future of Nation Building

by Ray Salvatore Jennings

By 2004 the U.S. involvement in nation building in Afghanistan and Iraq had many people wondering whether an effort to rebuild these failed nation-states was appropriate or would succeed. Nation building, or nation-state building (a more accurate designation)—a process to resuscitate a failed or failing nation-state that has been weakened by internal disorder, natural disaster, or loss of statehood through foreign occupation—is intended to transform a country's economic, social, and political institutions. The diplomatic, development, and military communities all agree that nation-state building can be considered successful once a recovering country is again stable, has rejoined the international community, and has met the criteria for being a sovereign nation-state. This measure of success, however, has rarely been met.

Nation in the present context refers to the dominant sociopolitical culture of a country, and *state* refers to its political condition. To be a state a territory must have a permanent population, a defined terrain, a government with a monopoly of force, and the ability to order the daily affairs of the populace. It must also have the capacity to enter into relations with other states and be sovereign in its affairs at home. With a few exceptions, the 193 countries in existence claim to be nation-states or territories that meet the criteria for statehood and where one or two national cultures predominate.

A nation-state may occasionally fail; this happens largely because the criteria defining a state are unmet. In Somalia in the early 1990s, a central government with a monopoly on force within its borders was supplanted by chaotic rule by local militia groups; the state could no longer carry on relations with other countries or order the affairs of its citizens. In 2004 Afghanistan and Iraq did not meet the criteria of statehood after U.S.-led invasions removed the regimes in power. Neither country had control over its borders, a central government with a monopoly of force, or true sovereignty. The Sudan, Côte d'Ivoire, Sri Lanka, Burundi, Liberia, Bosnia and Herzegovina, Chad, Liberia, the Democratic Republic of the Congo (DRC), Haiti, and Angola can be said to be failed or failing states that lack a strong sovereign central government, sustained internal order, or consistent relations with other nation-states.

Failed nation-states pose serious problems for regional and international order. They often destabilize bordering countries and frequently displace large numbers of refugees into neighbouring states. Violations of basic human rights are common in failed and failing nation-states, and they often harbour transnational criminal activity, such as money laundering, terrorist operations, and trafficking in narcotics, weapons, and humans. Moreover, such situations seldom simply fade away on their own or are able to repair themselves without outside assistance.

Understanding the needs of a failed nation-state is a complex challenge, as is determining the most appropriate type of nation-building assistance to be provided. Sometimes, simple foreign aid by civilian agencies, the United Nations, international donor agencies, and nongovernmental organizations can help reform institutions and strengthen a country's ability to manage conflict. This is the approach being used in Sri Lanka, Angola, Rwanda, and, until recently, Côte d'Ivoire, the DRC, Burundi, and The Sudan. Military personnel now assist in nation building in the latter four countries.

In other cases of nation-state building, military forces acting in coalition or with United Nations' authorization intervene as peacekeepers to separate warring parties and provide limited reconstruction assistance while additional foreign aid is provided by civilian agencies. This is the approach that has continued in Haiti, Bosnia and Herzegovina, Kosovo, Liberia, and, for a time, Somalia and East Timor.

In yet other instances of nation-state building a stable nation-state is invaded and occupied by foreign militaries intent on displacing the regime. The sovereignty of the occupied nation-state is extinguished under military occupation, and statehood is lost until the country recovers. Foreign civilian assistance and

foreign military rule are used to support the transition back to nation-state status. This was the approach that was used in Japan and Germany after 1945 and in Grenada, Panama, Afghanistan, and Iraq in later years.

Nation building often overtly promotes the virtues of strong central security forces, democratic governance, a free-market economy, a free press, and an active civil society. Typically, however, the nation-building process is driven less by altruistic motives than by the national security concerns of the nation builders. Nation building as defined above has been attempted so far only by Western democracies that believe that political and economic systems that resemble their own are more likely to be stable and beneficial to their national security and economic interests.

Among the nation-building endeavours cited, however, only the post-World War II occupations of Japan and Germany can be considered unqualified successes. There are many causes of nation building's poor track record, including a lack of adequate planning and funding for long-term programs, flawed peace agreements, insufficient numbers of peacekeepers or occupation troops, deteriorating security environments, resistance by entrenched local elites, changes in the political climate at home, and the need to cut short assistance because of other international emergencies. Nation building in such countries as Afghanistan and Iraq, for instance, continues to be weakened by an initial lack of planning for the peace, preparation and training of forces for occupation, insufficient troop commitment, and unrealistic expectations in regard to the local populations, that have proved more hostile towards military occupation than originally anticipated by many in the U.S. administration.

Experience of the past several decades suggests that success in nation building depends on several factors. The military occupations of Japan and Germany lasted more than five years and involved the efforts of several hundred thousand trained troops, police, and civilian administrators. Intense planning began two years before each operation, and occupation handbooks were even prepared and given to soldiers and occupation administrators. Aid continued to flow to Japan and Germany in the 1950s, after they had regained statehood. In the process of occupation, the predominant national culture was transformed, as were the country's economic, social, and political institutions. In the reasonably successful cases of nation building on a small scale, as in Panama and Grenada, modest planning and small commitments of troops and funding proved adequate.

Over the course of nation-building interventions, several lessons have been learned, often the hard way. If nation building is to be undertaken, it must be adequately funded, and it should be anticipated that resources may need to be committed for as long as a decade in order to influence the character of state institutions and the national culture of the failed or failing state. Given the likelihood that nation building will be required in the future, it is critical that leading states and institutions develop standing capacities to conduct such work, especially in the area of policing. Other indicators of success are the building of international support and legitimacy prior to an intervention, the participation of local populations in the process of transforming their societies, and the undertaking of some projects that are sure to be successful within the first 18 months of an intercession.

The future of the United States' nation building—in Iraq, Afghanistan, and elsewhere—is uncertain, however. The U.S. fundamentally reshaped its doctrine of military engagement after the terrorist attacks of Sept. 11, 2001, without simultaneously reforming its commitment and capacities to stabilize and transform failed and failing states. Beneath this dissonance between an overdeveloped ability to wage and win war and an anemic facility for peace and nation building may lie the unenviable reality that rather than ameliorating global instability and misery, nation building poorly done simply contributes to it.

Ray Salvatore Jennings teaches War and Peace Transitions at Georgetown University, Washington, D.C., and is the author of The Road Ahead: Endurance, Political Will and Lessons in Nation Building from Japan, Germany and Afghanistan for Postwar Iraq *(USIP Press, 2004).*

Illustration by Mirko Ilić

(continued from page 411)
presumed possession of such weapons by deposed Iraqi president Saddam Hussein had been a principal argument used by the U.S. government to justify its invasion of Iraq. A special court was established on Dec. 9, 2003, to try Saddam Hussein and his top aides for war crimes, genocide, and crimes against humanity, and he was captured four days later. In January 2004 Saddam was declared a prisoner of war, and in July legal custody was handed over to the new Iraqi government. He was arraigned in court, where he heard the charges brought against him, publicly denied any wrongdoing, and was returned to his prison cell to await trial.

On March 20 the United States military charged several members of the U.S. Army police with assault and mistreatment of Iraqi prisoners at Abu Ghraib prison on the outskirts of Baghdad. Several of the accused military personnel were brought to trial, and some were found guilty and received punishment. (*See* MILITARY AFFAIRS: Special Report.)

Although salaries of Iraqi civil servants and some workers increased during the year, unemployment remained very high (about 60%). Components of the infrastructure, such as roads, and municipal services (sewage, water, and distribution of electricity) were further degraded owing to a shortage of funds and the worsening civil violence. The central bank, however, was able to keep the value of the Iraqi dinar stable at nearly 1,450 dinars to the dollar.

Iraqis started to enjoy rights and freedoms that had been denied them under Saddam Hussein's regime. These included the right to obtain a passport and travel abroad, freedom of the media, and the right to form professional associations and political groups. By the end of 2004, nearly 300 political parties and civil groups had emerged. Many of these aimed to compete in the January 2005 general election, but six main groups emerged. Four were pro-American—the Kurdistan Democratic Party; the Patriotic Union of Kurdistan; the Iraqi National Congress, headed by Ahmed Chalabi; and the Iraqi National Accord, headed by Prime Minister Allawi. In addition, there were two important Shi'ite religious parties, the Supreme Council of the Islamic Revolution in Iraq, led by Abd al-Aziz al-Hakim, and the Da'wa Party, which was headed by Ibrahim al-Ja'fari. A few political groups went into opposition and declared their intention to boycott the elections because Iraqis were still under foreign (i.e., U.S.) occupation. Other parties sought to form alliances before the election deadline.

(LOUAY BAHRY)

IRELAND

Area: 70,273 sq km (27,133 sq mi)
Population (2004 est.): 4,024,000
Capital: Dublin
Chief of state: President Mary McAleese
Head of government: Prime Minister Bertie Ahern

The Irish economy improved in 2004, and some private-sector analysts predicted an annual GNP growth rate of up to 5.5%. The official estimates were slightly more cautious, however; in September the Department of Finance estimated annual growth of 4.2%, up from an earlier forecast of 3%. Unemployment appeared likely to level out at 4.4% for the year and was projected to drop to 4.2% for 2005. GNP projections for 2005 were also very positive, with analysts generally predicting likely growth of between 5% and 6%. These positive trends served to allay earlier fears that Ireland's run of strong economic growth since the mid-1990s might be coming to an end. Indicators of a slowdown in 2003 had raised the prospect of treasury deficits and a return to government borrowing, which in turn prompted unhappy recollections of the economic crisis of the late 1980s. The good economic performance of 2004 reflected a strengthening global economy, but it also affirmed the effectiveness of government policies geared to restraining public spending, keeping taxation rates low, and moderating inflation.

In August census figures showed that the population of the Republic of Ireland had passed four million for the first time since 1871. Inward migration from other EU countries, notably the new entrants from Eastern Europe, contributed significantly. Former Irish emigrants also continued to return in strong numbers.

Notwithstanding the success of the economy, it was a challenging year for the coalition government of Fianna Fail and the Progressive Democrats. Ireland held the presidency of the EU from January to June, and Prime Minister Bertie Ahern led negotiations to secure agreement on the proposed EU constitution. The successful conclusion of the Brussels summit in June, confirming agreement on the constitution by the heads of government, was widely hailed as a considerable achievement for the Irish president.

Also in June, Ahern and his government hosted an EU-U.S. summit at Dromoland Castle in western Ireland.

As a consequence of the first European national law banning smoking in all workplaces, including bars and restaurants, a woman lights a cigarette outside a restaurant near Dundalk, County Louth, Ire.

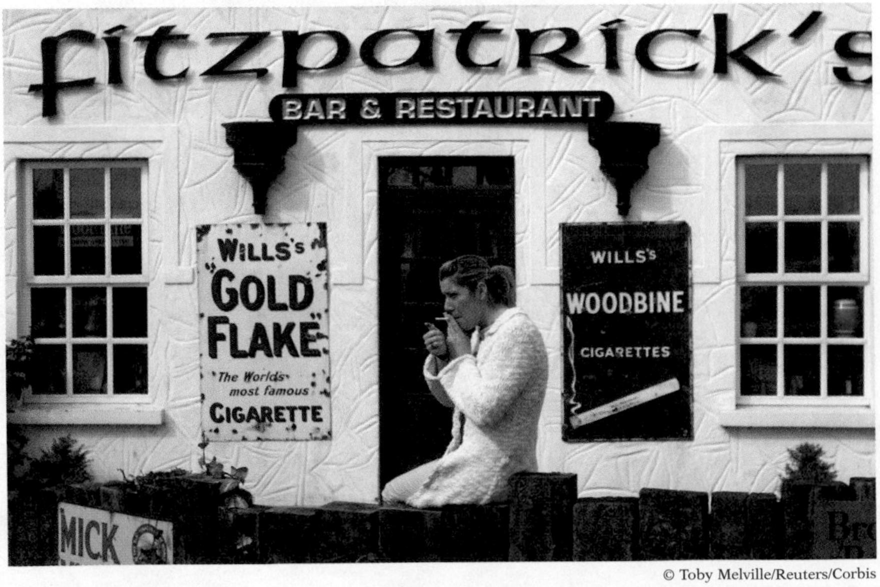

© Toby Melville/Reuters/Corbis

Pres. George W. Bush flew in for a 15-hour visit to meet EU leaders, and though there were fears that the anti-war sentiment in Ireland and across Europe (over the U.S.-led war in Iraq) would precipitate violent demonstrations, disturbances were minimal, although thousands of protesters gathered at Dromoland and at nearby Shannon International Airport.

The political impasse in Northern Ireland remained a focus of the government during the year. Although the paramilitary cease-fires continued to hold, the local administration and assembly created under the terms of the 1998 Belfast Agreement remained suspended. Unionists refused to work with Sinn Fein Republicans, led by Gerry Adams, principally because of the continuing failure of the illegal militant branch of the paramilitary Irish Republican Army (IRA) to disarm. Nationalists and Republicans accused the Unionists of sabotaging the institutions in order to avoid sharing power.

In Northern Ireland EU parliamentary elections in June, the moderate Ulster Unionist Party and the Social Democratic and Labour Party sustained heavy losses. The more extreme Democratic Unionist Party and Sinn Fein emerged as the two largest parties in Northern Ireland. With the middle ground thus eroded, the British and Irish governments brought all the parties together in September for negotiations at Leeds Castle, near London. Though progress was made toward IRA disarmament, it was not possible to achieve full agreement, and the Northern Ireland institutions remained suspended, pending further talks.

Meanwhile, in June the Fianna Fail and Progressive Democrat parties suffered severe reverses in the local and European elections within the Republic. Fianna Fail's vote collapsed in the county councils and in the urban centres as the voters sent strong messages of protest. Poor health services, inadequate public transportation, bad roads, overcrowded schools, and controversial legislation—notably a ban on smoking in the workplace—combined to create strong antigovernment sentiment. Ministers and government deputies were accused of having lost touch with ordinary people's concerns and needs. The mainstream opposition party, Fine Gael, secured some additional seats, but the bulk of the gains went to Sinn Fein.

Shaken by the Sinn Fein advance at its expense, Fianna Fail embarked on a review of policies aimed at reconnecting with the voters and generating a more caring image. In a move that was widely seen as a concession to populist disaffection and rank-and-file party anger, Ahern removed Minister for Finance Charlie McCreevy and nominated him as Ireland's European Commissioner. The Progressive Democrats and business circles were concerned, however, that the move might signal a dangerous relaxation of the disciplines that had sustained the country's economic performance.

In November Irish Pres. Mary McAleese came to the end of her first seven-year term in office. Since an Irish president could serve two terms, the popular McAleese nominated herself for a second term. Although attempts were made to run alternative candidates, they were unsuccessful, and she was returned to office unopposed.

At year's end the *Economist* magazine ranked Ireland the number one country in the world for quality of life, edging out Switzerland. (CONOR BRADY)

ISRAEL

Area: 21,671 sq km (8,367 sq mi), including the Golan Heights and disputed East Jerusalem, excluding the Emerging Palestinian Autonomous Areas
Population (2004 est.): 6,562,000
Capital: Jerusalem is the proclaimed capital of Israel (since Jan. 23, 1950) and the actual seat of government, but recognition has generally been withheld by the international community
Chief of state: President Moshe Katzav
Head of government: Prime Minister Ariel Sharon

The Emerging Palestinian Autonomous Areas (the West Bank and the Gaza Strip)
Total area under disputed administration: West Bank 5,900 sq km (2,270 sq mi); Gaza Strip 363 sq km (140 sq mi)
Population (2004 est.): West Bank 2,544,000, including 2,306,000 Arabs and 238,000 Jews; Gaza Strip 1,414,000, including 1,406,000 Arabs and 8,000 Jews
Principal administrative centres: Ram Allah and Gaza
Head of government: Presidents Yasir Arafat, Ahmad Quray (acting) from October 29, and, from November 11, Rauhi Fattouh (acting), assisted by Prime Minister Ahmad Quray

Prime Minister Ariel Sharon's plan to withdraw Israeli soldiers and settlers unilaterally from Gaza and part of the West Bank dominated the Israeli-Palestinian agenda in 2004. The emergence of a more pragmatic Palestinian leadership after the death on November 11 of Pres. Yasir Arafat (*see* OBITUARIES) raised hopes that the "disengagement plan" could lead to a negotiated Israeli-Palestinian settlement. The plan announced in late 2003 as the Palestinian uprising against Israeli occupation entered its fourth year, was presented as a significant step toward a two-state solution, with Israel and Palestine, living side by side, in accordance with the goals of the internationally approved "road map" to peace. As such, the disengagement plan received extensive international and regional backing. In Israel, however, it encountered angry right-wing opposition, and there were fears of armed clashes between radical Jewish settlers and the Israeli military.

The plan was officially launched at a White House meeting between Sharon and U.S. Pres. George W. Bush on April 14. In a letter to Sharon, Bush described the initiative as "bold and historic" and, in lieu of any negotiations with the Palestinians, seemed to give the Israeli side an American quid pro quo for the mooted withdrawal from Palestinian territory. Writing that it was unrealistic to expect Israel to return to the pre-1967 war border known as the "Green Line" and that the Palestinian refugees' right of return would be to Palestine, rather than to Israel, Bush seemed to back Israel on two of the most contentious issues in the Israeli-Palestinian conflict—that in a final settlement Israel could retain parts of the West Bank and that its Jewish character would not be threatened by a large influx of Palestinian refugees.

Despite the commitments made by the U.S., Sharon faced major opposition to the disengagement plan inside his own Likud Party. To secure party backing in the cabinet and the Knesset (parliament), he had called for a referendum of all Likud members, which he hoped the Bush letter would help him win. The party hawks, dubbing the withdrawal "a prize for terror," turned the tables on Sharon, and on May 2 the Likud voted 60% to 40% against the disengagement plan.

Undeterred, Sharon pressed ahead, winning government approval in a vote on June 7 after firing two ministers from the hawkish National Union Party and agreeing to accept an ostensibly

In the West Bank city of Ram Allah, mourners crowd around the Egyptian helicopter carrying Yasir Arafat's body. Israel granted permission for the Palestinian leader, who died in Paris in November, to be buried in Ram Allah.

modified version of his disengagement strategy. The revised plan allowed for the evacuation "in principle" of 21 settlements in Gaza and 4 in the West Bank but stipulated that Sharon would have to get renewed cabinet sanction for any actual removal of settlements and settlers. In the wake of this vote, the National Union Party (with seven seats in the Knesset) and two of the hawkish National Religious Party's six Knesset members bolted the coalition, leaving Sharon with a minority government backed by just 59 of the Knesset's 120 members.

Compounding Sharon's leadership problems, right-wingers and settlers challenged the legitimacy of his disengagement policy, claiming that it was diametrically opposed to the platform on which he had been elected. On October 26, amid public protests by settlers, the Knesset approved the revised plan 67–45 with 7 abstentions. Sharon dismissed two Likud cabinet members who had voted against it, and the four remaining national religious party Knesset members withdrew from the coalition. Opponents, led by Finance Minister (and former prime minister) Benjamin Netanyahu, insisted that Sharon renew his mandate through a nationwide referendum or national elections, but he refused and promised that the settlements in question would be evacuated in 2005. As domestic tension mounted, the Shin Bet security service reported threats by Jewish extremists on Sharon's life. Some analysts warned that armed clashes would erupt when the army and police tried to evacuate recalcitrant settlers.

In early December, however, a crisis over the state budget seemed likely to solve Sharon's coalition problems. After he fired secular Shinui cabinet ministers who voted against the budget because of a special allocation for religious Jews, the Likud central committee reversed an earlier ruling against coalition negotiations with the Labor Party, paving the way for a stable majority coalition with Labor, which strongly backed the disengagement plan, and with at least one of two ultra-Orthodox parties, Shas and United Torah Judaism.

Sharon's commitment to withdraw from some Palestinian territory failed to put an end to the *intifadah* (uprising) that had erupted in 2000. The barrier that Israel was erecting on the West Bank, however, changed the nature of Palestinian violence. It led to a marked decline in the number of suicide bombings in Israel proper, and those that occurred took place in the south of the country where the barrier was not yet in place. The Palestinians focused on firing Qassam rockets over the barrier around Gaza into Israel proper, mainly at the small Negev town of Sderot. By late summer these attacks had become an almost daily affair, and after two young children were killed on September 29 by rocket fire in Sderot, Israel launched Operation Days of Penitence, which it described as an ongoing rolling attack, targeting Palestinian militants and rocket-firing teams. Dozens of Palestinians—armed militiamen and civilians—were killed.

On July 9 the UN International Court of Justice at The Hague ruled the barrier illegal and called on Israel to dismantle it and compensate Palestinians who had suffered as a result of its construction. The ICJ was scathingly critical of the route Israel had chosen, some of it deep inside West Bank territory. Rejecting the ruling as politically motivated, Israel argued that the ICJ had failed to take into account the reason for building the fence: Palestinian terrorist attacks. Although the ruling was not binding, the Palestinians saw it as a major victory in the diplomatic battle to isolate Israel, and in mid-August 115 nonaligned nations meeting in Durban, S.Af., called for sanctions against Israel. To placate international opinion—and in line with rulings by its own Supreme Court—Israel announced that it would reroute much of the fence closer to the Green Line.

In four years of relentless fighting, more than 1,000 Israelis and nearly 3,000 Palestinians had died. Palestinian GNP plummeted to just 30% of what it had been in 1999. The economic hardship undermined the status of President Arafat's Palestinian Authority and, combined with concerns over Arafat's deteriorating health, gave rise to fears that after the Israeli withdrawal the radical Hamas might gain control of Gaza. To preempt this, Israel concentrated most of its counterterrorist activities against Hamas, assassinating most of its top leaders—cofounder Sheik Ahmed Yassin (*see* OBITUARIES) on March 22, Abdel Aziz Rantisi on April 17, the Syria-based Subhi Khalil on September 26, and Adnan al-Ghoul, the reported "father of the Qassam rocket," on October 21. The more Israel targeted Hamas, however, the more support the fundamentalist organization gained on the Palestinian street, and critics suggested that the Israeli policy might be counterproductive.

Despite ongoing Palestinian attacks, there were signs that the Israeli economy was emerging from a three-year slump. In the first half of 2004, GNP grew by 4.1%, and fixed investment rose by 2.9%, after a drop of 8.4% in the second half of 2003. Per capita consumption, often used as a measure of standard of living, was up 2.3%, following a 5.8% rise in the second half of 2003. The business sector grew by 5.9%, investment in industry increased by 4.5%, agricultural exports surged 45%, exports of goods and services rose 14.9%, and industrial exports—excluding diamonds—were up 28.5%. The recovery failed to trickle down to the weaker socioeconomic sectors, however, and unemployment reached a 12-year high above 11%. Netanyahu was accused of creating an economy for the rich, with critics pointing to the poverty statistics, which showed that despite the economic upturn, 1.3 million Israelis (one Israeli in five) and a third of Israeli children were still living below the poverty line.

(LESLIE D. SUSSER)

ITALY

Area: 301,328 sq km (116,343 sq mi)
Population (2004 est.): 57,537,000
Capital: Rome
Chief of state: President Carlo Azeglio Ciampi
Head of government: Prime Minister Silvio Berlusconi

The increasingly chaotic conflict in Iraq dominated the attention of Italians in 2004, mainly because of the possible implications of Italian military involvement in the war, highlighted by the fate of compatriots taken hostage in Iraq. As a result, domestic issues—such as the cost of living, local elections, and the proposed constitutional reform—tended to take a back seat.

Anxiety in a country dominated by family ties reached its peak in September when two female aid workers, Simona Pari and Simona Torretta, were kidnapped in Iraq, and the country remained without confirmed news of the two for more than three weeks. When the women were handed over to the Italian Red Cross in Baghdad, Italian Prime Minister Silvio Berlusconi called it a "moment of joy." He spoke of 16 separate sets of negotiations for their release. Two Iraqi colleagues captured with the "two Simonas" were also freed. Italian Foreign Minister Franco Frattini denied a British report of the payment of a $4 million ransom.

Three other hostages from Italy, snatched in separate kidnappings, were executed by their captors. Fabrizio Quattrocchi was among four private bodyguards working for a U.S.-based security firm seized in April by the hitherto unknown Green Falanges of Muhammad, which claimed that the killing was aimed at teaching Italy a lesson for refusing to withdraw its troops from Iraq. Enzo Baldoni, a freelance journalist, was executed in August after the expiry of a 48-hour ultimatum by the Islamic Army in Iraq, which was also calling for an Italian pullout. Baldoni's companions were rescued in a raid by security forces in June. Ayad Anwar Wali, a 44-year-old Iraqi businessman who had lived in Italy for 24 years, was seized in August and executed 34 days later, together with his Turkish assistant; he was accused of spying for Israel. Wali had been staying in Iraq to sell Italian tiles and furniture.

On the battlefield the heaviest clashes occurred in May around Nasiriyah in southern Iraq, the base for the Italian military contingent. Italian correspondents on the spot focused on apparently differing approaches to the fighting by Italian and other coalition forces. Under attack from militiamen firing from the windows of a hospital, Italian forces held their fire. Adm. Giampaolo Di Paola, the armed forces chief of staff, explained in Rome that Italian military tradition did not permit the causing of civilian casualties, in this case potentially among hospital patients. In the fighting one Italian soldier was killed, and troops in a key position defending a bridge over the Euphrates River were evacuated under attack. Parliament had originally dispatched the 3,275-strong contingent to Iraq on a peacekeeping mission. On a visit to Russia early in the year, Berlusconi said he considered it necessary for coalition forces to remain in Iraq; otherwise, with local contenders fighting for dominance, the country could become "another Kosovo."

On the domestic front, the ruling House of Liberties coalition led by Berlusconi tied with the centre-left opposition in European Parliament elections in June, though the share of the largest party in the coalition, Berlusconi's Forza Italia party, dropped from 25% to 21%. In partial simultaneous local elections for 63 provinces and 30 towns, the coalition lost out to the centre-left opposition, whose most spectacular victory was in the key province of Milan. The opposition also picked up 13 other provinces, as against 8 gains for Berlusconi's group. The prime minister blamed himself for the results, especially for having personally urged voters at a polling station to ignore "the small parties."

The minister of the economy, Giulio Tremonti, resigned in July against a background of popular disenchantment over rising prices but principally at the insistence of Vice Prime Minister Gianfranco Fini, leader of the right-wing National Alliance (AN) party, in a sharp disagreement over policy and spending cuts. Tremonti's replacement was Domenico Siniscalco, the top civil servant at the Treasury Ministry.

Berlusconi's government took its first steps toward a sweeping reform of Italy's constitution, in keeping with an election pledge to the Northern League, a coalition partner opposed to centralized power as "spendthrift." In March the Senate, against cries of "Shame! Shame!" from the opposition, passed the first reading of a bill that would devolve responsibility for health and education from the federal government to the country's 20 regions, transform the Senate into a regional body, substantially diminish the role of the president, and enable Italians to elect directly a prime minister with stronger powers. In October the lower house followed suit, amid opposition charges that reform would split the unity of Italy and create legislative chaos. MPs from both sides who were unconvinced of the need for reform predicted a rough passage for a packet that would require double votes of assent from both houses as well as confirmation through a national referendum. Reform of the judiciary was at the top of the agenda for many after bribery charges were dismissed against Prime Minister Berlusconi in December.

The state airline, Alitalia, which was facing bankruptcy, in October reached agreement with trade unions on a rescue plan drawn up by the airline's new chief, Giancarlo Cimoli, who was already considered to be the saviour of the once-ailing Italian railways. The scheme involved 3,679 job losses, a pledge of boosted productivity, and Alitalia's division into two separate bodies, AZ Fly and AZ Service. The agreement—the main condition for a vital loan—was at the cost of government guarantees of financial cushioning for those who were to be laid off.

In Milan in October the first of seven pretrial hearings began into the 2003 collapse of the Italian food conglomerate Parmalat, Italy's biggest company, which employed some 36,000 people worldwide. The trial, which was expected to be lengthy, represented the first chance for an estimated 135,000 injured parties, including 50,000 shareholders, to seek redress for losses. The closed-door hearing was devoted to applications by "pools" acting on their behalf to become civil parties in the case. The 29 defendants included Calisto Tanzi, Parmalat's former chief executive for some 40 years; his family relations and managers; and, initially, three of Parmalat's banks: Bank of America, Deloitte & Touche, and the Italian branch of Grant Thornton. In what was dubbed one of Europe's biggest financial scandals, involving a suspected colossal convoluted fraud, investigators had earlier found Parmalat's debts to total as much as €14.3 billion (about

$17 billion). The insolvent company had earlier been placed into administration after obtaining bankruptcy protection from the government.

Faced with continuing landings on its southern shores of boat people from Africa and elsewhere (nearly 10,000 during the year), Italy took drastic action in October against migrants who had transited through Libya before getting to the Italian island of Lampedusa by sea. Under a bilateral deal Italy initially airlifted 1,600 of them, in plastic handcuffs, back to Libya. Amnesty International branded the move a grave breach of human rights, since Italy allegedly denied the migrants' right to appeal for refugee status. The opposition in Italy called it "mass deportation" and "needlessly fierce." Italy asserted that its procedures were in keeping with international law and that, since illegal immigration was a European and not solely an Italian dilemma, it behooved European countries to tackle it jointly. In a related incident in October, 64 would-be refugees went missing when their boat, crossing from Tunisia toward Italy, snapped in two on the high seas. In June and August an estimated 301 people had lost their lives in similar tragedies. (DEREK WILSON)

JAMAICA

Area: 10,991 sq km (4,244 sq mi)
Population (2004 est.): 2,649,000
Capital: Kingston
Chief of state: Queen Elizabeth II, represented by Governor-General Sir Howard Cooke
Head of government: Prime Minister Percival J. Patterson

In March 2004 the U.S. Department of State (DOS), in its International Narcotics Control Strategy Report, gave Jamaica credit for its efforts against drug smuggling and drug-related crime but claimed that corruption continued to undermine law enforcement. In that same month Amnesty International accused Jamaican authorities of lacking the political will to end extrajudicial killings by the police. This criticism came in the wake of the collapse of a trial of a police officer charged with the murder of a 13-year-old girl. Amnesty observed that Jamaica had the dubious distinction of having one of the world's highest rates of killings by police.

Following an $80 million security upgrade, in April Jamaica's ports—the DOS focus of the drug-running business—became the first in the Caribbean to be certified under the International Maritime Organization's International Ship and Port Facility Security Code, which was designed to strengthen defenses against terrorism in port or at sea.

Finance Minister Omar Davies announced in April that 5,000 new hotel rooms would be built over the next five years to support Jamaica's burgeoning tourist industry. In September Hurricane Ivan killed at least 18 people and caused damages totaling $90 million; the estimated losses included 60% of the coffee crop, 30% of the citrus crop, 15% of the sugar-cane crop, and 20% of poultry production. In addition, 75% of the homes in one district were damaged. (DAVID RENWICK)

JAPAN

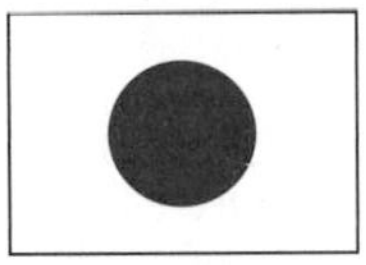

Area: 377,887 sq km (145,903 sq mi)
Population (2004 est.): 127,757,000
Capital: Tokyo
Symbol of state: Emperor Akihito
Head of government: Prime Minister Junichiro Koizumi

Domestic Affairs. The second term of Japanese Prime Minister Junichiro Koizumi continued to be stable in 2004 following the general election of November 2003, which saw the ruling coalition of the Liberal Democratic Party (LDP) and the New Komeito party lose seats but maintain its majority in the lower house of the Diet (parliament). The coalition looked so stable that in November 2004 Koizumi even allowed himself to play logic games with opposition leader Katsuya Okada of the Democratic Party of Japan (DPJ); when asked in the Diet the definition of a "noncombat zone," as prescribed in the Humanitarian Relief and Iraqi Reconstruction Special Measures Law, he retorted, "Wherever the [Japanese] Self Defense Force [SDF] troops are deployed, these are the noncombat zones." The law prohibited the deployment of Japanese troops in combat zones. The newly appointed foreign minister, Nobutaka Machimura, suggested that even the insurgent city of Fallujah was a noncombat zone, but he quickly withdrew his remarks.

Inside the LDP the so-called resistance group that opposed Prime Minister Koizumi gradually lost its clout, thanks to Koizumi's divide-and-rule tactics. The influential Hashimoto faction had breached discipline in the 2003 presidential election when many of its members voted for Koizumi over its own leader, former prime minister Ryutaro Hashimoto. For his part, Hashimoto was busy in 2004 trying to evade allegations of involvement in bribery and an illegal campaign donation of ¥100 million (about $1 million). In a cabinet reshuffle in September, shortly after the House of Councillors (upper house) election, Koizumi demonstratively gave several ministerial positions to politicians who had supported his postal-service-reform plans. Meanwhile, the hawkish LDP seemed to be gaining support for its proposals to revise Japan's arms-export regulations and pacifist constitution, traditionally one of the most delicate issues in Japanese politics.

Prime Minister Koizumi's major reform targets—pensions, the postal service, local government organization, municipal budgets, and the national security/emergency law system—were gradually but steadily being enacted; either compromises were found with those who had resisted or opposed them, or at times the opposition itself was eliminated. In 2004 the pension-reform issue was the most controversial. With the

During a visit to New York City in September, Japanese Prime Minister Junichiro Koizumi throws the first pitch before a game between Major League Baseball's New York Yankees and Boston Red Sox.

ever-increasing numbers of the elderly and an ever-diminishing birth rate, the Japanese people—young people in particular—were nervous, even doubtful, about the future of public pension plans. The Ministry of Health, Labour and Welfare reportedly postponed the announcement of the latest total fertility rate (TFR; the average number of births per childbearing woman), a record-low 1.29, until after the reform bill was passed by the Diet. Aggravating the issue, the Ministry of Internal Affairs and Communications reported in October that Japan's population (as of May 1) had decreased for the first year since it started recording the statistics in 1950.

In the House of Councillors election in July, the DPJ again increased its number of seats—this time by 12—while the share of the ruling LDP–New Komeito coalition stayed the same. Although the coalition maintained its majority, the results suggested that Koizumi's popularity was fading and that hopes for the emergence of a true two-party system might yet be realized. On the basis of the polling in this election, Kyodo News, a leading news agency, projected that had elections been held for the lower house at the same time, the DPJ would have won 308 seats and gained a majority sufficient to overthrow the coalition.

As part of a protest against government-backed pension reforms, in April opposition members in Japan's Diet (parliament) hold signs calling for cabinet ministers to disclose their own contributions to the state pension plan.

Economy. The growth of Japan's gross domestic product in the first quarter of 2004, in real terms, maintained the momentum of the last quarter of 2003, and a 3.2% growth rate was achieved. In the second and third quarters, however, the vigour disappeared, and the growth rates fell to a less-than-modest level—0.4% and 0.1%, respectively. The methodology for calculating GDP was to be slightly changed in the last quarter, and a further slowdown was expected for the year as a whole.

Corporate performances were generally satisfactory. Of 813 top companies on the Tokyo Stock Exchange, 80% recorded ordinary profit increases in their midterm earnings announcements. The stock market did not reflect this favourable environment, however. The Nikkei 225 Stock Average, the most widely followed index, drifted through the year at around 11,161, the previous calendar year's high.

In contrast to the good health of business corporations in general, Mitsubishi Motors suffered a huge loss of sales, in part because of revelations involving product-deficiency cover-ups. Yoshinoya D&C Co., Ltd., the world-wide "beef bowl" fast-food chain, experienced a substantial loss because of the ban on beef imports from the U.S. since December 2003, when a cow in the U.S. was found to be infected with bovine spongiform encephalopathy ("mad-cow" disease). Seibu Railways, a major transportation company, was delisted from the stock market for questionable business practices.

In October Daiei, Japan's supermarket giant, asked the Industrial Revitalization Corp. of Japan (IRCJ) to help support its reconstruction. The IRCJ was an official entity that had been established in 2003 to help revitalize financially troubled but salvageable companies. Daiei's finances had long been considered to be emblematic of the dangers of nonperforming loans, and the company still owed about ¥1 trillion (about $9.8 billion) in interest-bearing debts. Daiei had opted for self-reconstruction, but its banks declined financial support without IRCJ cooperation. Three major banking groups—Mizuho, Sumitomo-Mitsui, and Mitsubishi-Tokyo—finally reached their target of halving their bad-loan ratio, from a peak of 8% in March 2002.

Deflation, Japan's most serious economic concern, showed some signs of abating. In April the corporate goods price index, calculated by the Bank of Japan (BOJ), turned positive after having hovered on the negative side for 44 months. In October the BOJ forecast that the consumer price index in 2005 would turn positive for the first time in eight years. The halting in 2003 of the downward trend in real-estate prices in the metropolitan Tokyo area looked to be expanding to neighbouring cities. Announcements by the National Tax Agency in August 2004 as well as by the Ministry of Land, Infrastructure and Transport in September, however, both showed a fall in overall land prices for the 12th and 13th consecutive years, respectively.

Although the unemployment rate fell from 5% in January to 4.5% in November, private consumption remained sluggish throughout the year. The BOJ continued to maintain its "quantitative easing" and low-interest policy, the short-term rate remaining effectively at zero.

In January the Ministry of Finance reported that in 2003, Japan's exports to greater China (China, Hong Kong, and Taiwan) totaled ¥13.7 trillion (about $134 billion) and for the first time exceeded exports to the United States. Imports from greater China had surpassed U.S. imports in 2000. In September Prime Minister Koizumi and Mexican Pres. Vicente Fox Quesada signed a free-trade agreement. It was Japan's second such agreement, following one with Singapore, but the first that covered some agricultural products. The agreement was expected to accelerate similar negotiations with Southeast Asian countries.

Foreign Affairs. Japan's triad principles of pacifism, cooperation with the United Nations, and collective security with the United States had tilted in the direction of the third since the government of Prime Minister Koizumi responded quickly and offered every possible support—although under strict constitutional limitations—to the U.S.-led invasion and occupation of Iraq that began in 2003. In June 2004 the Diet passed seven additional contingency-related laws and ratified three conventions with the U.S. to facilitate security cooperation. In November, at the Asia-Pacific Economic Cooperation conference in Santiago, Chile, Koizumi suggested to U.S. Pres. George W. Bush that he would seek an extension of the mandated term of deployment of the Japanese SDF troops, which was due to expire on December 14.

In April an Iraqi armed antigovernment terrorist group kidnapped three Japanese civilians and demanded the withdrawal of the SDF troops deployed in Samawah, south of Baghdad. In October a Japanese traveler was kidnapped, and the same demands by the kidnappers were aired on local television. In neither case did Koizumi succumb to the kidnappers' demands. The three abductees were released, but the kidnapped youth was later found dead. In another case two Japanese reporters were killed in May. These violent incidents stimulated calls by the political opposition in Tokyo to withdraw SDF troops from Iraq.

In January Koizumi once again made a visit to the Yasukuni Shrine—and once again aroused China's displeasure. Along with some 2.5 million Japanese war victims, 14 convicted Class A World War II war criminals were interred at the shrine, and Koizumi's visits had been seen as marking official sanction of wartime atrocities that were committed in China and Korea, as calling into question the division of church and state, and, for some, as demonstrating the reactionary nature of his regime. Although the visit stopped short of creating an incident with Japan's neighbours, the issue remained as Koizumi's major diplomatic task to be resolved in the long run. In August, at the association football (soccer) Asian Cup final held in China, Chinese spectators booed during the Japanese national anthem, and after the game some of them mobbed a car carrying a Japanese embassy minister. Japan protested, and China maintained a low profile and apologized, although no mention was made of the alleged underlying cause of such anti-Japanese sentiment among Chinese youth. In November a Chinese nuclear submarine violated Japan's territorial waters. The director general of Japan's Defense Agency ordered a maritime alert and tracked the craft with an antisubmarine reconnaissance airplane. The submarine left Japan's territorial sea after about three hours, and China apologized.

A new type of friction emerged in the continental shelf area of the East China Sea, where the Japanese-Chinese border lies (the exact demarcation in this area had not yet been agreed upon, however). For almost a decade China had been carrying out its own research in the seabed gas field in the South China Sea, and Chinese research ships were sighted frequently in the area. In 1968 the UN had reported that the area northeast of Taiwan could turn out to be one of the world's richest oil- and gas-producing sites. Although Japan too was keenly interested in the area, research was not a top priority because of the remoteness of the area from the major consumption centres. In July, belatedly, Japan sent a research vessel to begin the exploration of seabed resources inside what it claimed to be the centre line of its exclusive economic zone (EEZ) and repeatedly requested that China share its research findings, but China declined to do so.

With a stalemate in the six-party talks—involving the U.S., China, Russia, Japan, South Korea, and North Korea—on the question of North Korea's nuclear facilities, Japan's relations with that country focused on the abduction issue. Between the 1950s and the late '90s, more than 100 Japanese citizens had allegedly been kidnapped by North Korean agents who planned to train them as spies to be reintroduced into Japan. In May Prime Minister Koizumi, apparently with the upcoming July elections for the upper house in mind, visited North Korea and met with its leader, Kim Jong Il. The meeting itself was perfunctory, but Koizumi succeeded in bringing out with him five persons, the sons and daughters of abductees who had been released and repatriated in 2002 following Kim's acknowledgement that such kidnappings had taken place and at the time of Koizumi's first visit to North Korea. In a related incident, Charles Robert Jenkins, an American who had deserted to the North from the U.S. Army in 1965 and who had subsequently married a Japanese abductee (one of the five who returned to Japan in 2002), also left North Korea during 2004 and returned via Indonesia to Japan, where he gave himself up to U.S. military authorities. No information was forthcoming about the remaining 10 Japanese abductees who had been reported dead by the North Korean government, and no substantial progress was made at working-level talks in November.

In November, Russian Pres. Vladimir Putin indicated at a cabinet meeting that he was hoping to solve his country's outstanding territorial issue with Japan, the status of four small islands of the southwestern Kurils (Chishima) claimed by Japan but occupied by the U.S.S.R./Russia since the end of World War II.

Following the December 26 Indian Ocean tsunami, Japan pledged $500 million in grant aid to the nations affected in southern Asia.

Social Life. The year 2004 would be remembered in Japan as a year of typhoons, earthquakes, and unusually hot temperatures. Among the numerous typhoons that hit the Japanese archipelago, Typhoon Songda in early September set a record for wind speed of 60.2 m per second (134.7 mph) in Hiroshima and damaged part of the Itsukushima Shrine, a World Heritage site. In October an earthquake of magnitude 6.8 shook central Niigata prefecture; 39 persons were killed, and nearly 100,000 were evacuated. The Shinkansen bullet train was derailed near the epicentre, the first such mishap since it started operation between Tokyo and Osaka in 1964. In July the temperature in Tokyo registered a record high 39.5 °C (103 °F).

High crime and suicide rates were causing concern. In June an 11-year-old girl killed her classmate with a knife; one night in August, seven family members were beaten and stabbed to death by a relative who lived nearby; in September two children were thrown from a bridge by an acquaintance of their father and drowned. Details of eerie suicides were reported frequently near the end of the year and revived unpleasant memories of several years earlier, when many similar suicide cases had been reported. Many of those who killed themselves had apparently studied Internet suicide sites and taken their lives in groups of three or four by generating carbon monoxide from charcoal stoves in tightly sealed automobiles.

Japanese athletes delivered handsomely at the Athens Olympic Games, where they won a record 37 medals, 16 of them gold. Japanese spirits were also buoyed when Ichiro Suzuki of Major League Baseball's Seattle Mariners had a league-leading .372 batting average and a record 262 hits, breaking George Sisler's 84-year-old record for number of hits in a single season (257). On a sad note, Princess Takamatsu (known as Kikuko), the 92-year-old aunt of Emperor Akihito and the first royal to campaign for changes to laws that allowed only male heirs to assume the throne, died in December.

(RINZO SAKAUCHI)

JORDAN

Area: 89,342 sq km (34,495 sq mi)
Population (2004 est.): 5,543,000 (including more than 1,750,000 Palestinian refugees, most of whom hold Jordanian citizenship)
Capital: Amman
Head of state and government: King Abdullah II, assisted by Prime Minister Faisal al-Fayez

In 2004 the Jordanian government uncovered a terrorist operation that aimed at destroying the headquarters of the Jordanian Intelligence Services in Amman and also targeted the U.S. embassy and the headquarters of the Jordanian prime minister. The authorities claimed that 17.5 tons of explosives were confiscated from five trucks that had originated in Syria. King Abdullah II expressed annoyance that despite assurances given by Syrian Pres. Bashar al-Assad about this incident, "many individuals continue to cross the borders and target the Jordanian security forces." Queen Rania led a peaceful protest march in Amman on April 29. An estimated 80,000 demonstrators proceeded to the parliament building.

© Ali Jarekji/Reuters/Corbis

A casually dressed Queen Rania (centre) leads a march against terrorism through the streets of Amman, Jordan, on April 29.

King Abdullah actively sought a solution to the Israeli-Palestinian conflict. He met with Israeli Prime Minister Ariel Sharon on March 18 and with Palestinian Prime Minister Ahmad Quray in April, May, and June. The Mideastern situation was also on the agenda when Abdullah met with U.S. Pres. George W. Bush on May 6. The king received a letter of assurance from Bush that the Israeli withdrawal from Gaza would be regarded as an integral part of the road map for peace. It was during this same meeting that President Bush publicly apologized for the U.S. abuse of Iraqi detainees at Abu Ghraib prison. Abdullah was invited to attend the Group of Eight summit in Sea Island, Ga., on June 8–10. Also, for the second consecutive year, Jordan was chosen as the venue for the World Economic Forum, which had formerly been held in Davos, Switz. The 2004 meeting was held at the Dead Sea on May 15–17 and was formally opened by the king.

On June 27, by a vote of 44–39 by the deputies present, the lower house of the parliament narrowly rejected the Personal Status Law, which would have given women the right to divorce their husbands in return for monetary compensation. Opponents of the law, which would also have raised the legal age of marriage to 18 for both sexes, argued that it would undermine family values, increase immorality, and contravene Islamic law.

On October 24 the prime minister reshuffled his cabinet, replacing 3 members who had resigned with 10 new members and thereby increasing the number of cabinet ministers from 20 to 27. The number of women serving in the cabinet was increased to 4. A new superministry was created to oversee the performance of all ministers with the objective of reforming and modernizing the public sector; this new body was to be headed by former foreign minister Marwan Muasher.

In November King Abdullah stripped his half brother and heir apparent, Prince Hamzah, of his duties as crown prince; the new heir to the throne would be Abdullah's eldest son, 10-year-old Hussein.

(MARIUS K. DEEB)

KAZAKHSTAN

Area: 2,724,900 sq km (1,052,090 sq mi)
Population (2004 est.): 15,144,000
Capital: Astana
Head of state and government: President Nursultan Nazarbayev, assisted by Prime Minister Daniyal Akhmetov

Kazakhstan faced a major political test when in September 2004 it held the first parliamentary elections following the adoption in April of controversial amendments to the country's election code. The government insisted that the changes would improve the election system and increase transparency, while opposition politicians warned that the changes, especially the introduction of electronic voting, would make it easier for election results to be falsified. The election, held on September 19, resulted in Otan, the party of Pres. Nursultan Nazarbayev, winning the largest number of seats (42) in the new Parliament. A bloc formed by two pro-presidential parties obtained 11 seats; Asar, the party of the president's daughter Dariga, won 4 seats; and the moderate opposition party Ak Zhol obtained only 1. A bloc formed by the opposition Communist Party and the Democratic Choice of Kazakhstan Party, which had succeeded in registering with the Justice Ministry

© Antony Njuguna/Reuters/Corbis

Constitutional conference delegates celebrate the delivery of Kenya's draft constitution on March 23.

in time to take part in the election, won no seats and immediately protested that the voting had been marred by widespread violations of election rules. Foreign observer teams agreed that the election had fallen short of international standards, but even so, the outcome indicated that the Kazakh opposition was not as influential as it believed itself to be.

In late April President Nazarbayev ended controversy between the government and the independent media over a draft media law when he unexpectedly vetoed the legislation after Parliament had approved it. Dariga Nazarbayeva attributed her father's veto to the pressure of public opinion. In July the president appointed Altynbek Sarsenbayev, Ak Zhol cochairman, to the post of information minister. Sarsenbayev immediately promised that a radically different media law would be drafted with input from journalists and the public. He also said that if his party considered the parliamentary election to be unfair, he would resign the following day. Consequently, he handed in his resignation on September 20 and was replaced by a Nazarbayev crony.

In July the World Bank and the IMF advised Kazakhstan to use its oil profits to develop other sectors of the national economy, especially services and small and medium businesses. President Nazarbayev continued in his efforts to attract foreign investment to nonextractive sectors of the economy and hoped that Kazakhstan could become a centre of high-tech industry. In the first six months of 2004, the U.S. remained the top foreign investor in the Kazakh economy, followed by European states. Economic and security ties with Russia grew during the year, as did ties with China.

(BESS BROWN)

KENYA

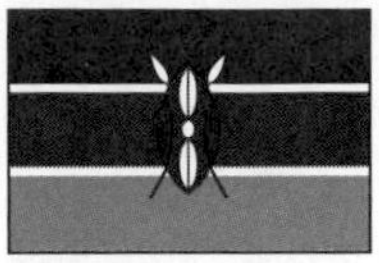

Area: 582,646 sq km (224,961 sq mi)
Population (2004 est.): 32,022,000
Capital: Nairobi
Head of state and government: President Mwai Kibaki

Three men accused of having conspired to shoot down an Israeli aircraft over Mombasa in November 2002 went on trial in Kenya in January 2004. Early in March a fire in the Nairobi city hall, which destroyed most of the records relating to the city council's activities over the previous 20 years, was widely linked in popular opinion to the inquiry recently begun by a special anticorruption squad into irregularities in the council's work. Transparency International, an international organization monitoring governmental corruption, had earlier concluded that bribes were demanded in almost 70% of dealings with Kenyan public officials—not least with the police—although there had been some improvement in that quarter as a result of the doubling of police salaries.

On April 5 Pres. Mwai Kibaki dismissed Police Commissioner Edwin Nyasede after a series of complaints in the press about the rising incidence of crime, especially in Nairobi. Nyasede was succeeded by Brig. Mohammed Hussein Ali, who removed 57 senior police officers in May to sustain the campaign for greater efficiency. Eight days later the president himself continued his anticorruption campaign by suspending four senior officials in connection with scandals in the Immigration Department relating to the sale of passports.

On March 15 a commission set up to draft a new constitution recommended the creation of a post of prime minister with strong executive powers, leaving the president with an essentially ceremonial role. The proposal had support from the Liberal Democratic Party (LDP), which formed part of the ruling coalition and whose leader, Raila Odinga, was widely believed to be a strong candidate for the new post. The minister of constitutional affairs responded by saying that the government intended to withdraw support from the Review Commission. The matter went to the High Court, which ruled that the draft constitution had to be approved by a public referendum and not solely by a vote by the members of the parliament.

Early in the year the promising state of the country's economy had resulted in the recommencement of external aid. President Kibaki had sought to strengthen his position by introducing a number of opposition members into his cabinet. Some of the new cabinet members, however, were suspected of having committed financial malpractices when they were members of former president Daniel arap Moi's government, and in May external donors again withheld aid. The situation became still more serious in October when, apparently discounting the president's efforts at reform, a United Nations report claimed that Kenya was one of the most corrupt countries in Africa.

Against this turbulent background, Kibaki's meeting with the presidents of Tanzania and Uganda to try once again to promote the economic integration of the three countries passed almost unnoticed. On March 15 an agreement was signed to accept a common tariff on imported goods and to remove duties from goods imported into Kenya from Tanzania and Uganda. The measures could not take immediate effect, however, because they required the approval of the parliaments of the countries involved and because there was a need to consider their possible impact on other African trading blocs with which the territories were variously linked.

Kenyan Wangari Maathai, an environmental activist and feminist leader, was awarded the 2004 Nobel Prize for Peace. (*See* NOBEL PRIZES.) Maathai, the first African woman and first environmentalist to be so honoured, had been a political thorn in the side of former president Moi; she was elected to the parliament and became an assistant environment minister after he retired from office.

(KENNETH INGHAM)

KIRIBATI

Area: 811 sq km (313 sq mi)
Population (2004 est.): 89,100
Capital: Bairiki, on Tarawa
Head of state and government: President Anote Tong

Relations remained strained between Kiribati and China in 2004. After the newly elected government of Pres. Anote Tong recognized Taiwan in November 2003, China severed diplomatic links and dismantled its satellite-tracking station on South Tarawa Island. The switch of diplomatic allegiance was criticized by the parliamentary opposition led by Harry Tong, the president's brother. Taiwan had offered scholarships and technical assistance to Kiribati, together with aid for infrastructure projects and the development of sports facilities.

The economy, which had traditionally relied heavily on investment income from funds accumulated during the life of the now-defunct phosphate industry and remittances from merchant seamen working overseas, suffered a decline in export revenue from fishing and coconut products (mostly copra) and from the licensing of foreign fishing fleets to work in the Kiribati exclusive economic zone.

At the UN in September, President Tong urged other governments to support the Kyoto Protocol on climate change, emphasizing the risk to small island states of global warming and the consequent increased hurricane risk and rising sea levels. The government introduced legislation to end the investor passport scheme introduced by its predecessor. A number of airlines operating in the central Pacific combined to upgrade Cassidy Airfield on Christmas Island for emergency use after the closure of the former U.S. military airfield on Johnston Atoll.

(BARRIE MACDONALD)

KOREA, DEMOCRATIC PEOPLE'S REPUBLIC OF

Area: 122,762 sq km (47,399 sq mi)
Population (2004 est.): 22,698,000
Capital: Pyongyang
Head of state and government: Chairman of the National Defense Commission Kim Jong Il

The dominant issue in North Korea in 2004 was the development of nuclear weapons and negotiations to abandon that program. Six-party talks were held in February in Beijing, where the two Koreas, China, the United States, Japan, and Russia met to find a negotiated end to the confrontation over nuclear weapons on the Korean peninsula. The February talks were the second round; the first round had been held in August 2003. The third round was held in June 2004, and the fourth round planned for October was postponed and not rescheduled. It appeared that North Korea had decided to wait for the outcome of the U.S. presidential election before meeting again. With the reelection of Pres. George W. Bush, the United States sent the message that there would be no changes in the U.S. position regarding the dismantling of North Korea's nuclear program.

In April North Korean leader Kim Jong Il made a trip to China. Though the trip was dubbed "unofficial," Kim met with the top leadership of China in talks over North Korea's nuclear-weapons program. On April 21, within hours after Kim's special presidential train had passed through the border town of Ryongchon, the train station there was rocked by a huge explosion after two fuel trains collided. At least 161 people were killed, thousands were injured, 1,850 homes were destroyed, and another 6,350 were damaged. Though speculation grew that the explosion was an attempt on Kim's life, other explanations were offered, including the idea that the blast was an accident or a coincidence.

Relations with Japan improved with the visit of Japanese Prime Minister Junichiro Koizumi. He was able to take back to Japan with him children of Japanese citizens who had been kidnapped in the 1970s and '80s. North Korea had admitted having abducted Japanese citizens to teach Japanese in North Korea and had allowed the abductees to return home 19 months earlier.

Near year's end it was reported that many of the publicly displayed portraits of Kim had begun to disappear. Many wondered whether Kim had ordered the action to dispel the cult of personality that surrounded him; the "Dear Leader" honorific title was also dropped by state-run media.

(MARK PETERSON)

© World Food Program/Reuters/Corbis

Among those killed in the massive explosion on April 21 at Ryongchon train station in North Korea were at least 76 grade-school pupils, some of whose book bags and papers are shown here.

KOREA, REPUBLIC OF

Area: 99,900 sq km (38,572 sq mi)
Population (2004 est.): 48,199,000
Capital: Seoul
Head of state and government: President Roh Moo Hyun (except Goh Kun [acting] from March 12 to May 14), assisted by Prime Ministers Goh Kun, Lee Hun Jai from May 25, and, from June 30, Lee Hai Chan

South Korea's newly elected Pres. Roh Moo Hyun was at the centre of controversy as 2004 began, but by the second half of the year, he was in a stronger position than ever before. In January Foreign Minister Yoon Young Kwan was forced to resign for taking a pro-American stance in regard to North Korea and criticizing the Roh administration's position, which was one of cautious engagement; the United States had taken a hard line, especially in regard to nuclear weapons.

Roh had been elected by a majority of younger voters who viewed South Korea's traditionally strong ties with the U.S. as an impediment to working out diplomatic initiatives with North Korea. For the first time, opinion polls indicated that more people feared that war would be caused by the U.S. than by North Korea. In a speech on the holiday commemorating the March First Movement, Korea's 1919 protests against Japanese colonial rule, Roh reiterated his call for a foreign policy independent of the U.S. and said that South Korea should strengthen its independence step by step.

The conservative political party, the Grand National Party (GNP), and the moderate elements of the Millennium Democratic Party (MDP)—the party Roh had belonged to but from which he split to join the Uri Party—joined in the parliament to pass a bill of impeachment against Roh on March 12. The vote was 11 votes greater than the required two-thirds, with most of Roh's supporters boycotting the vote. Under the terms of the constitution, the president stepped down while the Constitutional Court heard the case. While the Constitutional Court was deliberating—it was required to make a decision within six months, and it stated that a decision would be made as quickly as possible—elections for the parliament were scheduled.

The results of the April 15 election for the National Assembly were a stunning show of support for Roh. His party, only six months old, took 152 seats in the new 299-seat parliament. The other parties suffered a great defeat. The GNP lost 16 seats, which left it with 121 seats, and the MDP lost 53 seats, which left it with only 9 seats. A new party, the Democratic Labour Party, appeared on the scene with 10 seats. Just prior to the election, the GNP had named a new party leader, Park Kun Hye, the daughter of Gen. Park Chung Hee, who had served as the country's president from 1961 to 1979 and who had been credited with the economic development of South Korea.

On May 14 the Constitutional Court ruling on Roh's impeachment was handed down; Roh was found not guilty of the charges made, and he was reinstated as president. The reinstatement and the new majority in the parliament gave Roh the mandate to move forward with his agenda for new leadership in South Korea.

Roh's independent foreign policy did not interfere with a U.S. request that South Korea send additional troops to Iraq; a force of 3,000 was dispatched to help with the rebuilding of Iraq. A terrorist group kidnapped a South Korean translator, and he was beheaded after a videotape was released showing him pleading for his life. The experience was traumatic for the South Korean public and led to protests against the then impending dispatch of South Korean troops to Iraq.

South Korea opened its high-speed rail line from Seoul to Pusan. The trains, capable of travel of up to 322 km/hr (about 200 mph), were expected to shrink the travel time to provincial cities by half and make rail travel competitive with domestic air travel.

(MARK PETERSON)

KUWAIT

Area: 17,818 sq km (6,880 sq mi)
Population (2004 est.): 2,586,000
Capital: Kuwait
Head of state and government: Emir Sheikh Jabir al-Ahmad al-Jabir al-Sabah, assisted by Prime Minister Sheikh Sabah al-Ahmad al-Jabir al-Sabah

The year 2004 saw a major shift in Kuwait's policy toward Iraq. Traditionally, the two neighbours entertained considerable suspicion—even animosity—toward one another, but the changing situation in Iraq induced Kuwait to call for friendly ties. Kuwaiti businesses sought commerce with Iraq and hoped to help in Iraq's reconstruction. At the end of July, Iraqi Prime Minister Ayad Allawi (*see* BIOGRAPHIES) made a historic state visit to Kuwait during which he asked for relief of the $15 billion that Iraq owed from its invasion of Kuwait in 1990–91. On June 28 Kuwait's prime minister, Sheikh Sabah al-Ahmad al-Jabir al-Sabah, announced the restoration of full diplomatic ties with Iraq and said he planned to open an embassy in Baghdad as soon as the security situation permitted.

During the year the government announced the arrest of several Islamic extremists who had published articles or spoken out against Kuwait's pro-American policies. Several were caught trying to enter Iraq to join the anti-American insurgency there. In September a number of Shi'ite religious leaders petitioned the government to allow the teaching of their theology in Kuwait's public schools. Shi'ites constituted about 30% of Kuwait's population.

In June liberal deputies in the parliament introduced a bill to reduce the number of electoral districts from 25 to 10; the existing distribution was felt to favour sectarianism and tribalism. The plan met with stiff resistance, however, and was effectively delayed until 2005. In October the government sent a measure to the parliament that would give women the right to vote in general elections, but the proposal was expected to meet with vigorous opposition from Islamist and tribal deputies. Privatization was a top economic priority, and the government turned its eye toward state-owned companies, including Kuwaiti Airways and several communications firms. It also set up a mainly private company to manage 40 of the country's 110 gas stations.

(LOUAY BAHRY)

KYRGYZSTAN

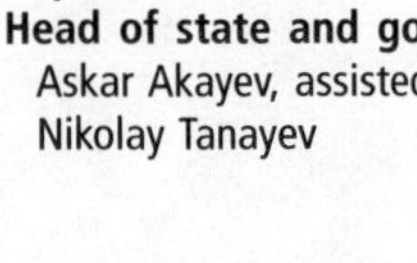

Area: 199,945 sq km (77,199 sq mi), including about 1,250 sq km (480 sq mi) ceded to China in May 2002
Population (2004 est.): 5,081,000
Capital: Bishkek
Head of state and government: President Askar Akayev, assisted by Prime Minister Nikolay Tanayev

Throughout 2004 political life in Kyrgyzstan remained polarized between supporters and opponents of Pres. Askar Akayev. Pleas by Akayev to opposition forces not to begin parliamentary and presidential election campaigns prematurely (both elections were scheduled for 2005) were largely ignored. Akayev stated repeatedly in public that he would not seek another term in office, but pro-government politicians and parties urged him to reconsider. In January primitive listening devices were discovered in the offices of six opposition members of the parliament. Although national security chief Kalyk Imankulov denied that any government agency had been involved in the bugging, the opposition politicians called for the resignation of Imankulov and other security officials and laid ultimate blame for the affair on Akayev and his supporters. Relations between the government and opposition worsened after the decision by the Supreme Court in mid-April to acquit the officials who had been held responsible for the killings of demonstrators in southern Kyrgyzstan in 2002.

In April police broke up a rally of members of the prominent opposition Ar-Namys party in Bishkek. The party was seeking to draw attention to the continued imprisonment of its leader, former vice president Feliks Kulov, who was serving a jail term on charges of abuse of office that his supporters said were politically motivated. Ar-Namys activists became convinced that Kulov would be released, but only after parliamentary elections scheduled for February 2005. The party and independent journalists also accused the government of restricting freedom of the media by closing down the independent Pyramida TV and Osh TV stations; U.S. financier George Soros intervened personally with the Kyrgyz president, and Pyramida was back on the air by the end of April.

In early May Akayev called on the newly formed Consultative Council for Fair Management to make a genuine effort to fight the corruption that was widely acknowledged to be damaging the country's economic development. A television report noted that 284 officials were facing charges of corruption and abuse of office. By mid-July the president was boasting to a conference attended by international donors that direct foreign investment in the first six months of 2004 had reached the high point achieved in 1996 and that foreign investors were shifting their interest from extractive industries to other sectors of the economy.

(BESS BROWN)

LAOS

Area: 236,800 sq km (91,429 sq mi)
Population (2003 est.): 5,657,000
Capital: Vientiane
Chief of state: President Khamtay Siphandone
Head of government: Prime Minister Bounngang Vorachith

Issues of regional integration were topmost among the priorities for Laos in 2004. In November, for the first time, Laos was host of the annual summit of the Association of Southeast Asian Nations (ASEAN)—an event that was, despite the logistic and financial challenges, a landmark for Laos's relations with its neighbours. In March, the first Thai-Lao joint cabinet retreat had taken place in Pakse, southern Laos, led by the two countries' prime ministers. The meeting marked the official start of the construction of the second Lao-Thai Friendship Bridge between the towns of Savannakhet, Laos, and Mukdahan, Thai.; the first Friendship Bridge connected Vientiane with Nongkhai. Earlier in the same month, the Thai government approved partial funding for the construction of a third bridge, linking Huay Xai, Laos, and Chiang Rai, Thai. Additional investment was expected from China. The Laotian government and various donors (notably the Asian Development Bank) hoped that the building of such infrastructure would turn Laos into the transportation hub of mainland Southeast Asia. Perhaps as a consequence of warmer relations between the two countries, the 16 Lao dissidents who participated in an attack against a customs checkpoint in southern Laos in 2000 were extradited to Laos in July.

In late February there appeared to be some respite in the conflict between the Laotian government and groups of what it called Hmong resistance fighters, with Hmong surrendering allegedly in exchange for amnesty and allotments of land. The Hmong people had clashed with the Lao army over many years for reasons that were linked both with the government's development projects and with past history (some Hmong were entangled in a proxy alliance with the United States and fought against the Lao communists during the Vietnam War). Reports of the brutal

Workers lay paving stones at the Arch of Triumph in Vientiane in September, before the ASEAN summit meeting in November, which was held in the Laotian capital for the first time.

killing of Hmong teenagers by a group of Laotian soldiers in September reignited serious concerns within the international community over authorities' handling of the Hmong issue.

The World Bank hosted an unprecedented series of public consultations between August and September in five capitals (Bangkok, Tokyo, Paris, Washington, and Vientiane) over Laos's controversial Nam Theun 2 hydropower project. A final decision was expected from the bank by early 2005.

(VATTHANA PHOLSENA)

LATVIA

Area: 64,589 sq km (24,938 sq mi)
Population (2004 est.): 2,312,000
Capital: Riga
Chief of state: President Vaira Vike-Freiberga
Head of government: Prime Ministers Einars Repse, Indulis Emsis from March 9, and, from December 2, Aigars Kalvitis

Having joined NATO on March 29 and the European Union on May 1, Latvia in 2004 achieved its main foreign-policy goals since regaining independence.

Riga contributed to international missions in Iraq, Afghanistan, the Balkans, and Georgia and generally maintained good relations with the rest of the world.

Relations with Russia remained a challenge, however. Moscow objected to NATO's patrolling airspace over the Baltic States and insisted that EU enlargement and the new EU-Russia Partnership and Cooperation Agreement be contingent upon concessions from both the EU and the Baltic States. In April Riga expelled a Russian diplomat suspected of espionage, and Moscow reciprocated in kind. The EU rejected Moscow's accusations that the rights of Russian-speaking minorities in Latvia and Estonia were being violated, especially in education, and by September some 60% of 10th-grade courses in minority-language schools were being taught in Latvian without major problems.

Indulis Emsis of the Green and Farmers' Party became prime minister in March after the tension-ridden coalition government of Einars Repse (New Era) resigned. People's Party deputies decided not to endorse the 2005 budget, which led to the fall of Emsis's government on October 28. After numerous political machinations, Aigars Kalvitis of the People's Party formed a minority centre-right government.

Latvia's GDP grew about 8%, and midyear revenues permitted raising the income of some of the neediest members of society. Teachers' salaries, pensions, and child-care payments grew, but not the wages of doctors and nurses, who began a crippling strike on November 1. Latvia remained among the poorest EU countries in terms of GDP per capita (42% of the EU average) and inflation rate (about 7%), but unemployment was at about the EU average of 9%. (DZINTRA BUNGS)

LEBANON

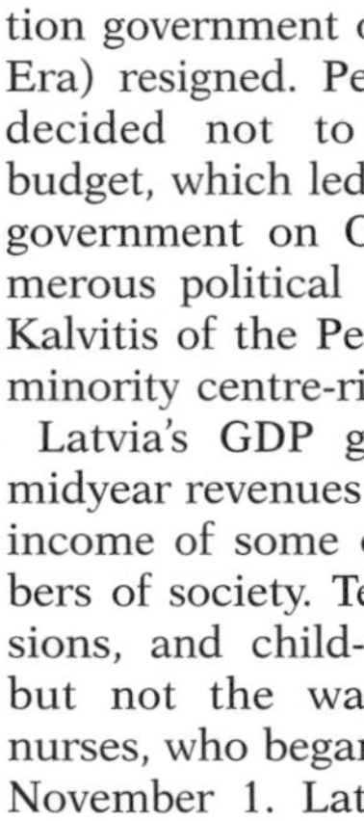

Area: 10,400 sq km (4,016 sq mi)
Population (2004 est.): 3,777,000 (excluding unnaturalized Palestinian refugees estimated to number nearly 300,000)
Capital: Beirut
Chief of state: President Gen. Émile Lahoud
Head of government: Prime Ministers Rafiq al-Hariri and, from October 21, Omar Karami

Lebanon had a very eventful year in 2004. In August, under strong pressure from Syria, the Lebanese parliament extended for three more years the term in office of Pres. Émile Lahoud. On September 2 the UN Security Council passed Resolution 1559, which called on all "foreign forces" to leave Lebanon. Shortly after the resolution, Syrian troops redeployed to the eastern part of the country and reduced their number to 14,000. The resolution also called for the Lebanese government to deploy its army in the south and disband all militias active in the country. This last point was interpreted to mean Hezbollah, the main Lebanese resistance force in the south. In a follow-up report on October 2, UN Secretary-General Kofi Annan concluded that Syria and Lebanon had not met the requirements of Resolution 1559. He said that Syrian troops were still in the country and that the constitutional amendment that provided a three-year extension of President Lahoud's term in office implied "a direct intervention" by the government of Syria. On November 7 Hezbollah launched its first pilotless reconnaissance drone into Israel in retaliation for what it said were repeated violations of Lebanese airspace by Israel. Though the Lebanese government justified the action, the UN representative in southern Lebanon considered both Israeli and Hezbollah overflights unjustified.

The Lebanese government said that the Syrian presence was a result of joint Syrian-Lebanese official agreements and that the extension of the term of the president was a sovereign act. Many linked strained Lebanese-U.S. relations to Beirut's refusal of a suggestion made in August by a visiting U.S. congressional delegation to settle permanently the Palestinian refugees in Lebanon.

On October 1 an attempt to assassinate Marwan Hamade, the former minister of the economy, failed, although one of his guards was killed in the bomb blast. Hamade, a member of Druze leader Walid Jumblatt's parliamentary bloc, a week earlier had resigned from the cabinet to protest Lahoude's extended term. Jumblatt became the most vocal critic of the extension and of the state of relations between Syria and Lebanon.

The economy improved. The central bank declared that it had $12 billion in foreign currency reserves; the tourism industry enjoyed a robust recovery; and MEA, the Lebanese national airline, made more than $20 million in profits.

An elderly woman walks past an armoured personnel carrier in Zibdin in early October. Violence between local militias continued in Lebanon throughout the year.

A row occurred, however, when Minister of Finance Fouad Siniora presented his 2005 draft budget, which proposed sweeping reforms, including the elimination of the Ministry of the Displaced, the Council of the South, and the state security apparatus. MPs close to Prime Minister Rafiq al-Hariri supported the budget, while those close to President Lahoud criticized it. The cabinet, however, which was installed in November under Prime Minister Omar Karami, was expected to approve some of these measures.

Ismail al-Khatib, an alleged operative of al-Qaeda who was accused of recruiting people to carry out anti-American acts of sabotage in Iraq, was captured in late September and died of a heart attack a week later. Residents in his hometown of Majdal Anjar, in eastern Lebanon, staged three-day riots accusing the Ministry of Interior of having tortured him and then made up the whole story about al-Qaeda in order to appease the U.S.

(MAHMOUD HADDAD)

LESOTHO

Area: 30,355 sq km (11,720 sq mi)
Population (2004 est.): 1,800,000
Capital: Maseru
Chief of state: King Letsie III
Head of government: Prime Minister Bethuel Pakalitha Mosisili

In February and March 2004, Lesotho briefly grabbed international headlines when Prince Harry, the younger son of Britain's Prince Charles, spent two months in the mountain kingdom, some of it working at an orphanage south of Maseru, the capital. His purpose was in part to give publicity to the related crises of HIV/AIDS and food shortages affecting the small landlocked country. According to UNAIDS, some 360,000 of the 2,000,000 people in Lesotho were living with HIV, and 100,000 orphans had lost parents to HIV/AIDS. Prime Minister Pakalitha Mosisili became one of the first heads of government to be tested publicly for HIV when he launched a free national HIV-testing program, the first in Africa. In May he opened the country's first health centre to provide antiretroviral therapy. A National AIDS Commission was established, but Lesotho lacked the resources and capacity to fight the pandemic effectively.

By midyear three multinational companies had been convicted of having given bribes in order to secure contracts for the Highlands Water Project. Lesotho's term as chair of the Southern African Development Community's Organ on Politics, Defence and Security ended with nothing having been achieved on the Zimbabwe issue.

(CHRISTOPHER SAUNDERS)

LIBERIA

Area: 97,754 sq km (37,743 sq mi)
Population (2004 est.): 3,391,000 (including about 325,000 refugees in neighbouring countries)
Capital: Monrovia
Head of state and government: Chairman of the National Transitional Government Charles Gyude Bryant

Most of 2004 was spent rebuilding Liberia after 14 years of civil war that had killed thousands of people, displaced 300,000, created a generation of child soldiers, destabilized Liberian society, and devastated the national economy. Demobilization efforts were threatened in late January when the leaders from Liberia's two rebel movements, the Liberians United for Reconciliation and Democracy and the Movement for Democracy in Liberia, issued a joint statement declaring that their soldiers would not disarm until transitional leader Charles Gyude Bryant had stepped down. The statement was considered an attempt to derail the UN disarmament program of 40,000 former combatants and the peace process. By April, however, more than 18,000 former combatants had been disarmed and 10,600 weapons collected. Demobilized soldiers rioted against the disarmament program in Monrovia owing to a dispute over insufficient payment for turning in their weapons. Bryant swore in the new 21-member cabinet that would lead the country until March 2005 elections.

At a Lagos, Nigeria, conference of international leaders in February, the UN, the U.S., and the European Union pledged $520 million over a two-year period to rebuild Liberia. The UN Security Council passed a resolution in March freezing the assets of exiled former Liberian president Charles Taylor. Despite arguments by Taylor's lawyers that a court in one country did not have the right to try the head of state of another, in late May a UN-backed court in Sierra Leone ruled that Taylor could be tried by an international war-crimes tribunal on 17 counts of crimes against humanity for his alleged role in arming and supporting rebels in Sierra Leone. In May a Nigerian court began reviewing Taylor's right to asylum, and in September Amnesty International, in a brief given to Nigeria's Federal High Court, maintained that Nigeria was breaking an international law by harbouring Taylor.

(MARY F.E. EBELING)

Great Britain's Prince Harry, taking a year away from his studies, helps a young boy plant a fruit tree at a children's home in Lesotho in March.

AP/Wide World Photos

LIBYA

Area: 1,759,540 sq km (679,362 sq mi)
Population (2004 est.): 5,659,000
Capital: Tripoli (policy-making body intermittently meets in Surt)
Chief of state: (de facto) Col. Muammar al-Qaddafi; (nominal) Secretary of the General People's Congress Zentani Muhammad al-Zentani
Head of government: Secretary of the General People's Committee (Prime Minister) Shokri Ghanem

In 2004 Libyan leader Muammar al-Qaddafi (*see* BIOGRAPHIES) realized the

PA Photos

British Prime Minister Tony Blair visits Libyan leader Muammar al-Qaddafi (right) in March. Libya's relations with the United States and European countries improved greatly after December 2003.

rapprochement with the United States and its European allies that he had been signaling for more than a decade. The cost paid by Libya to rejoin the international community was high, although it was small compared with the cost of the damaging trade sanctions of the 1990s. Libya's penalty payments included $2.7 billion compensation for the 270 victims of the December 1988 Pan Am disaster over Lockerbie, Scot., $170 million for the 170 victims of the 1989 UTA flight, and $35 million for more than 160 non-American victims of the 1986 Berlin disco bombing. Following the lifting of sanctions by the UN Security Council in 2003, EU countries had intensified their trading activities in Libya, a process that significantly accelerated in 2004. In September 2004 U.S. Pres. George W. Bush lifted the ban on U.S. commercial air services to Libya and released $1.3 billion of frozen assets in recognition of Libya's significant steps in eliminating its weapons programs. Other international airlines had already reestablished air services to Tripoli in 2003.

Other gestures from Libya, such as its promise in December 2003 to eliminate all weapons of mass destruction, were welcomed by the international community. The initiative prompted a visit to Tripoli by British Prime Minister Tony Blair in the spring of 2004. In February, Libyan Prime Minister Shokri Ghanem stated that several instances of alleged Libyan wrongdoing had not been proved and that the compensation payments were not an admission of guilt. His diplomatic gaffe was quickly repaired by the foreign minister in terms that satisfied the international community, if not the relatives of the victims.

With world oil prices above $50 a barrel, both the Libyan leadership and the people felt very confident about their immediate economic future. Public debates on the restructuring of the economy intensified, and Qaddafi seemed comfortable with the change from an economy that was mainly dependent on government subsidy and intervention to one in which private initiative and international private-sector synergies would drive economic expansion. (J.A. ALLAN)

LIECHTENSTEIN

Area: 160 sq km (62 sq mi)
Population (2004 est.): 34,500
Capital: Vaduz
Chief of state: Prince Hans Adam II
Head of government: Otmar Hasler

On Aug. 15, 2004, Prince Hans Adam II, age 59, formally transferred day-to-day governing power in Liechtenstein to his 36-year-old son, Crown Prince Alois, and invited the entire country to the garden-party celebration. Prince Hans Adam retained overall authority over the country, which his family had ruled for almost 300 years.

The reopening of the Liechtenstein Museum in Vienna on March 28 was cause for celebration. The 1,600 paintings and many Italian bronzes and decorative objects constituted one of the largest and most valuable private collections in the world, assembled over four centuries by the Liechtenstein princely family, which fully financed the €23 million (about $27.8 million) renovations of the museum's Baroque Garden Palace. Foremost in the Princely Collections were important paintings by Peter Paul Rubens, including *The Assumption of the Virgin*, and works by Jan Brueghel the Elder, Raphael, and Rembrandt. The Austrian museum had been closed since 1938 after the Nazis had claimed the collection. Then museum director Gustav Wilhelm had switched labels on the most precious works and, renting trucks and buses from Switzerland, had transported the art under cover of darkness to the royal palace in Vaduz, where it remained safe. Although some of the works had been exhibited in Vaduz, most of the collection had been closed to public view for 66 years. (ANNE ROBY)

LITHUANIA

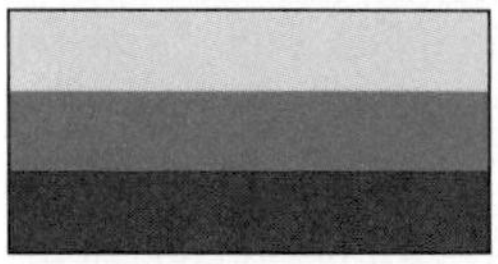

Area: 65,300 sq km (25,212 sq mi)
Population (2004 est.): 3,439,000
Capital: Vilnius
Chief of state: Presidents Rolandas Paksas, Arturas Paulauskas (acting) from April 6, and, from July 12, Valdas Adamkus
Head of government: Prime Minister Algirdas Brazauskas

Lithuania became a member of NATO on April 2, 2004, and joined the European Union on May 1. On April 6 Pres. Rolandas Paksas was impeached, with 86 of the 141 members of the Seimas (parliament) voting to remove him from office (85 votes were required). The Constitutional Court confirmed that the president had violated the constitution on at least three occasions, notably when he granted Lithuanian citizenship to a Russian-born financial supporter. Declassified transcripts linked Paksas advisers and major election-campaign donors with Russian organized crime. After the impeachment Arturas Paulauskas, chairman of the Seimas, became acting president. Former president Valdas Adamkus won the special presidential election, with 30% of the vote in the first round on June 13 and 52% in the runoff on June 27.

The country's first election to the European Parliament also took place on June 13. Five of the 13 MEP seats that Lithuania had been allocated were won by the newly established pro-Russia populist Labour Party. The So-

Petras Malukas/AFP/Getty Images

Valdas Adamkus poses for a photo after his second inauguration as Lithuania's president on July 12. He replaced Rolandas Paksas, who was impeached less than a month before the country joined the European Union.

cial Democrats, conservative Homeland Union, and Liberal and Centre Union (LCS) each captured two seats, with the Farmers Union and Paksas's Liberal Democratic Party dividing the last two.

In June, Russia refused to make an apology for the occupation of Lithuania, Latvia, and Estonia, and at the end of September, it surprisingly demanded $3 billion in compensation for its withdrawal from the Baltic States. In response, Vilnius reminded Moscow that damages during the Soviet occupation of Lithuania could be estimated at $27 billion. Lithuania's GDP continued to grow beyond 7%, one of the fastest rates in the EU, while inflation remained low.

In Lithuania's two-round general election, held on October 10 and 24, the Labour Party gained the most seats (39), followed by Prime Minister Algirdas Brazauskas's ruling coalition (31), the Homeland Union (25), and the LCS (18). A left-wing coalition was formed, embracing Brazauskas's coalition (comprising the Social Democrats and the Social Liberals), the Labour Party, and the Farmers Union.

(DARIUS FURMONAVIČIUS)

LUXEMBOURG

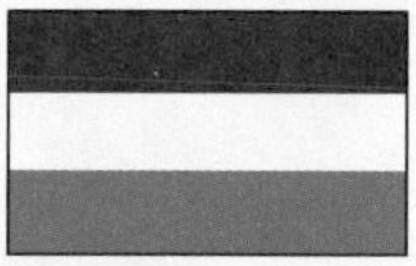

Area: 2,586 sq km (999 sq mi)
Population (2004 est.): 454,000
Capital: Luxembourg
Chief of state: Grand Duke Henri
Head of government: Prime Minister Jean-Claude Juncker

In Luxembourg's parliamentary elections, held on June 13, 2004, the Christian Social People's Party again came in first, winning 36.11% of the vote and 24 of the 60 seats in the Chamber of Deputies. The Luxembourg Socialist Workers' Party captured 14 seats (23.37%), followed by the Democratic Party with 10 seats (16.05%), the Greens (7 seats; 11.58%), and the Action Committee for Democracy and Pension Justice (5 seats; 9.95%). Jean-Claude Juncker, first appointed in January 1995, continued as prime minister. Major issues in the election were the country's position in the enlarged European Union, of which Luxembourg was a founding member, and concerns about increased illegal immigration, domestic security, and the economy.

The economy, based on private banking services and investment businesses, continued to thrive, however. *The Economist* reported that Luxembourg had the highest GDP per capita in the world (followed by the U.S. and Norway).

In September EU finance ministers appointed Juncker "Mr. Euro," the first permanent president of the 12 euro-zone nations. This renewable two-year appointment replaced the previous system, in which the chair of the euro group changed every six months along with the EU's rotating presidency. Juncker was to take up this additional post on Jan. 1, 2005.

(ANNE ROBY)

MACEDONIA

Area: 25,713 sq km (9,928 sq mi)
Population (2004 est.): 2,035,000
Capital: Skopje
Chief of state: Presidents Boris Trajkovski, Ljubco Jordanovski (acting) from February 26, and, from May 12, Branko Crvenkovski
Head of government: Prime Ministers Branko Crvenkovski, Radmila Sekerinska (acting) from May 12, Hari Kostov from June 2, Sekerinska (acting) from November 18, and, from December 17, Vlado Buckovski

Macedonia was thrown into a state of shock on Feb. 26, 2004, when Pres. Boris Trajkovski was killed in a plane crash near Mostar, Bosnia and Herzegovina. (*See* OBITUARIES.) According to the official Bosnian investigation report, the plane in which Trajkovski, six of his staff, and two crew members had been traveling went down in bad weather owing to pilot error. On March 6, one day after Trajkovski's state funeral, the Constitutional Court declared the end of his term in office, paving the way for early presidential elections.

The first round of the presidential elections was held on April 14. Prime Minister Branko Crvenkovski of the Social Democratic Union of Macedonia and Sasko Kedev of the Internal Macedonian Revolutionary Organization–Democratic Party of Macedonian National Unity (VMRO-DPMNE) advanced to the second round, leaving behind two ethnic Albanian candidates. Former interior minister Ljube Boskovki (VMRO-DPMNE) was barred from running as an independent because he had not fulfilled a constitutional residency requirement, while the chairman of the Democratic Party of Albanians, Arben Xhaferi, withdrew. Crvenkovski won the runoff on April 28 with 62.7% of the vote and was sworn in as president on May 12. Interior Minister Hari Kostov succeeded him as prime minister; Kostov's government was sworn in on June 2 after the parliament voted confidence in it. On November 15 Kostov resigned, citing corruption and nepotism within one of the coalition partners as the reason. He was replaced by Defense Minister Vlado Buckovski, who also took over as SDSM chairman. Buckovski's government was approved by a parliamentary vote of confidence on December 17.

AP/Wide World Photos

On November 6 citizens in Skopje celebrate the decision of the U.S. to recognize their country under the name Macedonia despite the strong objections of Greek political and religious leaders.

The main domestic issue was the government's local-government reform plan, which included the reduction of the number of municipalities. Because the necessary redistricting would have changed the ethnic balance of many municipalities, the plan met with resistance from local communities and opposition parties. Amid protests—some violent—the government parties agreed on a redistricting plan, and the parliament approved the new Law on Territorial Organization on August 11. A coalition of ethnic Macedonian parties and nongovernmental organizations demanded and got a referendum, which was called for November 7. The referendum failed owing to insufficient turnout.

On January 21 the parliament passed a law legalizing the Albanian-language university in Tetovo and transforming it into a state university. The dispute between the Macedonian Orthodox Church (MPC) and its Serbian counterpart remained unresolved, and some monasteries and clerics left the MPC to join the revived Serbian archbishopric of Ohrid. Bishop Jovan, the highest-ranking cleric to join the Serbian Orthodox Church, was sentenced on August 19 to 18 months in jail for inciting religious and ethnic hatred. On March 22 the Macedonian government submitted its application for European Union membership. The Stabilization and Association Agreement between Macedonia and the EU took effect on April 1. On November 4 the United States recognized Macedonia under its constitutional name.

Macedonia's economy remained in a precarious situation, with negative GDP growth (–3.6% in the first quarter of 2004), an unemployment rate above 35%, a drop in industrial production of more than 20%, and a trade deficit of about $600 million in the first half of the year. Throughout the year civil servants, schoolteachers, and railway workers, among others, staged strikes and protests against the government's economic policy.

(STEFAN KRAUSE)

MADAGASCAR

Area: 587,041 sq km (226,658 sq mi)
Population (2004 est.): 17,082,000
Capital: Antananarivo
Chief of state and head of government: President Marc Ravalomanana

Two major cyclones hit Madagascar in January and March 2004, killing 295 people, ruining rice fields, and destroying infrastructure. High world oil prices and a collapse of the Malagasy franc helped force up the price of rice, the major staple, which led to mass street demonstrations. With three-quarters of the population living on less than a dollar a day, the government was forced to import cheap rice to try to stabilize prices. Meanwhile, the government of Pres. Marc Ravalomanana continued to consolidate its position in the aftermath of the 2002 crisis. It engaged in months of negotiations with the World Bank and International Monetary Fund to secure a write-off of part of the country's debt. Its Poverty Reduction Strategy Paper pledged good governance, budgetary control, and more privatization. In October it was announced that the institutions would write off $1.9 billion of the total $4 billion debt in accordance with the Heavily Indebted Poor Countries Initiative. While open opposition to Ravalomanana decreased, critics of the government denounced the terms on which the debt relief was secured.

The extension of trade benefits in the version of the African Growth and Opportunity Act signed by U.S. Pres. George W. Bush in July boosted the textile industry and saved thousands of jobs that had been threatened in Madagascar's manufacturing and export sectors. On the other hand, inequality and poverty increased, and the prevalence of HIV/AIDS rose. Madagascar wanted to attract as many tourists as Mauritius and the Seychelles did, but poor facilities hampered this. With new emphasis put on ecotourism and adventure, however, 120,000 tourists arrived in the first half of 2004, nearly as many as in all of 2003.

(CHRISTOPHER SAUNDERS)

MALAWI

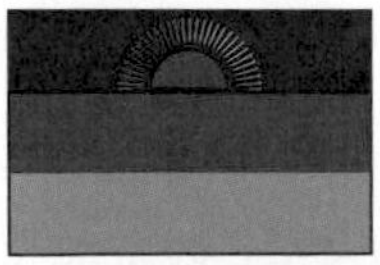

Area: 118,484 sq km (45,747 sq mi)
Population (2004 est.): 11,907,000
Capital: Lilongwe; judiciary meets in Blantyre
Head of state and government: Presidents Bakili Muluzi and, from May 24, Bingu na Mutharika

On Jan. 1, 2004, Malawi's Vice Pres. Justin Malewezi caused a stir by resigning from the ruling United Democratic Front (UDF) and joining an opposition party. Victory for the UDF in the spring parliamentary elections was not a foregone conclusion because of widespread discontent over official corruption, the government's inadequate handling of the economy, and its failure to deal with the problem of HIV/AIDS.

In the event, which took place on May 20, Bingu wa Mutharika, the UDF presidential candidate, was victorious but polled fewer than 40% of the votes cast. The UDF fared badly in general, winning only 49 of the 193 seats in the National Assembly and having to face a challenge by opposition parties that claimed that the run-up to the elections had been unfairly conducted. The UDF received quick and unexpected reinforcements, however, when three opposition parties agreed to a merger and were joined by at least 26 independent delegates.

The continuing steep rise in the price of essentials such as corn (maize) meal, meat, charcoal, and house rents, unaccompanied by any commensurate rise in wages, and the overall shortage of food were only some of the serious problems faced by the new government.

(KENNETH INGHAM)

MALAYSIA

Area: 329,847 sq km (127,355 sq mi)
Population (2004 est.): 25,584,000
Capital: Kuala Lumpur; some government offices have moved to Putrajaya (the new planned capital)
Chief of state: *Yang di-Pertuan Agong* (Paramount Ruler) Tuanku Syed Sirajuddin ibni al-Marhum Tuanku Syed Putra Jamalullail
Head of government: Prime Minister Datuk Seri Abdullah Ahmad Badawi

On Sept. 2, 2004, the High Court in Malaysia ended one of the country's most wrenching controversies when it released Anwar Ibrahim, the former deputy prime minister imprisoned since 1998 on questionable charges. The court, having previously rejected repeated appeals from Anwar, overturned his conviction for sodomy, belatedly citing evidence that the prosecution's key witness was unreliable. The move was widely attributed to the anticorruption campaign of Prime Minister Abdullah Ahmad Badawi. (*See* BIOGRAPHIES.) The arrests in February of a government minister and a prominent businessman on fraud charges gave early promise of Abdullah's success in combating corruption. Despite claims that further prosecutions were imminent, the effort appeared to have stalled in the months before Anwar's release. Nevertheless, Abdullah's anticorruption stance clearly resonated with Malaysians, who gave his United Malays National Organization (UMNO) a landslide victory in general elections held on March 21. The ruling National Front coalition, led by the UMNO, gained control of more than 90% of the seats in the federal parliament.

In 2004 Malaysia's government struggled to combat rising crime rates. In January, following the rape and murder of two girls within one week, the government considered introducing public flogging as a punishment for child rape. Flogging demonstrations in Malaysian schools, launched in May to deter juvenile delinquency, were quickly discontinued following warnings that such demonstrations legitimized violence in the eyes of children. In February and March 85,000 teenagers reported for training in the country's new national service program, created to foster goodwill between ethnic groups and discipline among youth. By April, however, the program had started to founder amid reports of ethnic gang violence, sexual assaults, extortion, and drug abuse in its training camps. In August a royal commission reported that Malaysia's police force was riddled with corruption and brutality.

Malaysia's economy continued to thrive in 2004, with estimated growth of 7% coupled with low inflation. The manufacturing and services sectors led the economy. High rates of consumer spending and a record number of tourist arrivals spurred growth in the services sector. The country was expected to maintain a positive overall balance of payments for the fourth consecutive year.

Malaysia sought to foster greater cooperation between Asian nations in 2004. In an address before the East Asian Congress in June, the prime minister urged the formation of an Asian economic union. Malaysia, Singapore, and Indonesia began coordinating naval patrols in the Strait of Malacca in July. In October Abdullah

Little remains of the town of Antalaha in northeastern Madagascar after it was struck by Cyclone Gafilo on March 7. The year saw an unusually large number of major natural disasters worldwide.

AP/Wide World Photos

met with Thailand's prime minister to discuss increasing security along the Thai border, where Thai Muslim separatists had launched several attacks. Malaysia also partook of its share of controversy in the international sphere. In February, U.S. Pres. George W. Bush accused Malaysia of trafficking in nuclear secrets, a charge vehemently denied by the government. Suspected terrorists imprisoned in Malaysia started a hunger strike in March to protest the country's internal security laws, which permitted the indefinite detention of suspects without charge. In April the New York-based Human Rights Watch charged Malaysia with mistreating refugees who were fleeing fighting in Aceh province, Indon. (JANET MOREDOCK)

MALDIVES

Area: 298 sq km (115 sq mi)
Population (2004 est.): 289,000
Capital: Male
Head of state and government: President Maumoon Abdul Gayoom

In 2004 the very survival of Maldives was threatened by the tsunami that swept across the Indian Ocean in late December. Waves submerged many of the nation's low-lying coral islands, at least 50 of which were either severely damaged or completely destroyed. Only a sea wall built to protect Male saved the capital city itself from catastrophic damage. Relief workers and government officials believed the death toll would exceed 100 persons. The economic cost of the disaster was estimated at hundreds of millions of dollars, and socioeconomic development was set back "by at least two decades," a government spokesman said. Earlier in the year, the government of Pres. Maumoon Abdul Gayoom had faced an unprecedented challenge from political dissidents led by former minister Ibrahim Hussein Zaki, who demanded greater democratization of Maldives. This culminated in a protest by some 3,000 people in Male on August 12–13, which the government considered as an attempt to overthrow the democratic regime and disrupt the economy. President Gayoom responded by declaring an emergency and arresting many pro-democracy leaders, including Zaki and some members of the People's Majlis (parliament) and Special Majlis. The emergency continued until October 10. It was lifted mainly under pressure from the European Union and the Maldivian Human Rights Commission.

(PONMONI SAHADEVAN)

MALI

Area: 1,248,574 sq km (482,077 sq mi)
Population (2004 est.): 11,957,000
Capital: Bamako
Chief of state: President Amadou Toumani Touré
Head of government: Prime Ministers Ahmed Mohamed Ag Hamani and, from April 30, Ousmane Issoufi Maïga

No single party or alliance dominated Mali's municipal elections held on May 30, 2004, when 10,789 councillors were selected to serve on 703 urban and rural district assemblies throughout the country. The Alliance for Democracy in Mali (ADEMA), the party of former president Alpha Konaré, topped the field by taking 28% of the seats that were being contested; the Union for the Republic and Democracy garnered 14%; and independent candidates gained 9%. The latter were generally assumed to be supporters of Pres. Amadou Toumani Touré's policy of consensus. Although only a quarter of registered voters took part, the poll was significant in that it marked the first local elections in which all parties participated.

On September 1 the two largest parties in the National Assembly, ADEMA and the Assembly for Mali (RPM), announced that they were attempting to work together in the parliament; the RPM had split off from ADEMA just before the 2002 presidential elections.

Over a period of five years, skirmishing between the Kounta and a group vaguely identified as "Arab" had occurred intermittently. On September 6, 16 Kounta and Arab prisoners, who had been jailed for fighting, broke out of prison in Gao. In a major flare-up on September 11 in Bamba, 220 km (137 mi) west of Gao, 13 people were reported dead.

A bilateral commission set up to improve cooperation between South Africa and Mali in economic and security matters had its inaugural session in Pretoria, S.Af., on August 10. Malian Foreign Minister Moctar Ouane invited South Africans to invest in his country's agriculture and mining sectors.

The plague of locusts infesting West Africa swept into Mali during the summer. On September 3 President Touré, Prime Minister Ousmane Issoufi Maïga, and all the cabinet ministers donated one month's salary to the fight to eradicate the pests. Despite efforts to control the invasion, it was estimated that one-third of Mali's grain crop would be destroyed.

(NANCY ELLEN LAWLER)

A Tuareg nomad stands before a 13th-century mosque in Timbuktu, Mali. The presence of U.S. Special Forces instructors in the area alarmed the Tuareg, whose livelihood depended in large part on tourism.

MALTA

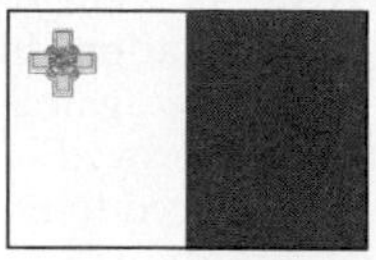

Area: 315 sq km (122 sq mi)
Population (2004 est.): 401,000
Capital: Valletta
Chief of state: Presidents Guido de Marco and, from April 4, Eddie Fenech Adami
Head of government: Prime Ministers Eddie Fenech Adami and, from March 23, Lawrence Gonzi

Following the successful referendum and general election held in Malta in 2003, the country became a member of the European Union on May 1, 2004. Celebrations were organized on the eve of Malta's accession to commemorate this momentous event.

In February, Prime Minister Eddie Fenech Adami gave up his leadership of the Nationalist Party (NP), and Deputy Prime Minister Lawrence Gonzi was elected as the new party leader. On March 23 Fenech Adami handed in his resignation as prime minister, and Gonzi succeeded him. The next month the parliament elected Fenech Adami president in succession to Guido de Marco, who had ended his term of office.

The election of Malta's five members of the European Parliament was held in June. The NP obtained two seats, while the opposition Labour Party won three. The turnout was 82%, compared with 91% for the EU referendum and 96% for the 2003 general election. Ireland, which held the EU presidency, submitted for discussion at the EU summit a proposal that Malta have a sixth seat. In August Joseph Borg, Malta's former foreign minister, was appointed EU Commissioner for Fisheries and Maritime Affairs.

Illegal immigration from Libya, mostly of Arabs and black Africans, created a serious problem. In September the EU endorsed a proposal by Italy and Malta to lift the arms embargo on Libya. Later Gonzi led a delegation to Libya to discuss the migration issue and other matters of mutual interest.

(ALBERT GANADO)

MARSHALL ISLANDS

Area: 181 sq km (70 sq mi)
Population (2004 est.): 54,600
Capital: Majuro
Head of state and government: President Kessai Note

In January 2004 Kessai Note was inaugurated president of the Marshall Islands by the Nitijela (Congress) after having been reelected in November 2003. Vice Pres. Ruben Zackhras was also inaugurated.

The 2004–05 budget was at record levels, with two-thirds of the $114 million revenue coming from the U.S. government, either directly or through federal programs. The balance was derived from shipping registry fees, license fees from foreign fishing fleets, and local taxes. A proposed Taiwanese venture to establish a ship-repair facility and floating dock in Majuro was expected to attract more fishing vessels to the region. Under the revised Compact of Free Association, an investment fund was established to provide long-term revenue. The fund was founded with $25 million from the Marshall Islands and $7.6 million from the U.S., which agreed to add $500,000 a year until 2023. It was expected that the fund would be supplemented by $40 million in grants from Taiwan over 20 years.

In a major report in September, the Asian Development Bank identified economic dependence on the U.S. and public health on Majuro Atoll as significant issues. On Majuro, rapid urbanization had led to overcrowding, inadequate infrastructure, contaminated water supplies, and poor waste disposal. (BARRIE MACDONALD)

MAURITANIA

Area: 1,030,700 sq km (398,000 sq mi)
Population (2004 est.): 2,774,000
Capital: Nouakchott
Chief of state: President Col. Maaouya Ould Sid'Ahmed Taya
Head of government: Prime Minister Sghair Ould M'Barek

On Aug. 10, 2004, the government of Mauritania claimed that it had prevented an army coup aimed at assassinating Pres. Maaouya Ould Taya a few days before his official visit to France. At least 20–30 soldiers, many of them high-ranking officers in the elite National Guard, were arrested. Defense Minister Baba Ould Sidi accused the plotters of having close links with the failed coup of June 2003, for which 123 men remained in detention. There was apparently considerable discontent in

A young farmer in Mauritania looks on as a dense swarm of desert locusts descends on his crops in August. UN Food and Agriculture Organization officials estimated that Mauritania lost about half its 2004 cereal crop to the locust infestation.

the army over issues ranging from low pay to the government's maintenance of diplomatic relations with Israel. On August 27 Chief of Police Sidi Ould Riha charged that the governments of Burkina Faso and Libya had supported the coup and had allowed rebel commando units to live and train on their territory.

Mauritania, among the world's poorest nations, saw prices rise sharply and the value of its currency plummet by 30% beginning in May. On July 26, as part of a purge affecting those responsible for economic policy, Pres. Taya reshuffled his cabinet and fired nine senior members, as well as the governor of the central bank. On August 3 the World Bank announced a grant of $15 million to Mauritania to modernize its education sector. An Australian corporation announced on May 31 that it would invest $600 million to develop the Chinguetti offshore oil field, thought to be Mauritania's most promising petroleum site.

In August the government appealed to the global community for planes and insecticides to combat a locust plague; massive infestations of the pests were devastating many of Mauritania's fields and pastures, and a major food crisis seemed inevitable.

(NANCY ELLEN LAWLER)

MAURITIUS

Area: 2,040 sq km (788 sq mi)
Population (2004 est.): 1,233,000
Capital: Port Louis
Chief of state: President Sir Anerood Jugnauth
Head of government: Prime Minister Paul Bérenger

The Mauritian government averted economic disaster in 2004 when it settled two lawsuits brought in February by U.S.-based Polo Ralph Lauren Corp., which alleged that a local manufacturer did not have permission to produce and sell clothing under the Polo label. The country's economy relied heavily on the textile manufacturing and retailing industries, which had generated £8 million (about $14.5 million) in revenue and eliminated unemployment. The government brokered an agreement between Ralph Lauren and local outlets.

A diplomatic row erupted in June with the United Kingdom over the sovereignty of the Chagos Archipelago, or British Indian Ocean Territory, 60 islands 965 km (600 mi) north of Mauritius, and the right of the Ilois—who had been forcibly removed by the U.K. after it bought the islands from Mauritius in 1965—to return. The disputed archipelago included Diego Garcia, an atoll that the British had cleared of all inhabitants to enable the construction of a U.S. naval support base. Prime Minister Paul Bérenger visited London to discuss the dispute with Commonwealth Secretary-General Don McKinnon and to visit British Prime Minister Tony Blair, who rebuffed Bérenger. The Group of 90, a coalition of the world's less-developed countries, met in Mauritius to discuss international trade.

(MARY F.E. EBELING)

MEXICO

Area: 1,964,375 sq km (758,449 sq mi)
Population (2004 est.): 105,447,000
Capital: Mexico City
Head of state and government: President Vicente Fox Quesada

Political topics dominated the agenda in Mexico during 2004. Highly public maneuvering in advance of the 2006 presidential election gave a premature lame-duck cast to the administration of Pres. Vicente Fox Quesada. The failure of President Fox's centre-right National Action Party (PAN) to win a congressional majority in the 2003 midterm elections, as well as growing frustration with his inability to secure congressional approval for his principal policy initiatives, eroded Fox's public credibility despite the fact that his personal-approval ratings remained comparatively strong.

However, the events that sparked the greatest controversy—and deprived the government of political oxygen for an extended period—were repeated comments by Martha Sahagún de Fox suggesting that she aspired to succeed her husband in the presidency. Although Sahagún maintained that she was the victim of gender discrimination in a male-dominated political culture, widespread opposition to her candidacy also reflected deeply held Mexican beliefs about the threat posed by an individual's (or a family's) perpetuation in power. The political reaction against Sahagún's possible candidacy proved so strong that in July she was forced to renounce her presidential ambitions.

Although Sahagún was forced to withdraw, her actions encouraged other presidential aspirants to initiate their own campaigns scarcely more than halfway through Fox's term in office. Secretary of Energy Felipe Calderón was forced to resign his cabinet post in May after he appeared at a public rally backing his candidacy, but he remained a contender for the PAN's presidential nomination. In addition, Jorge G. Castañeda, Fox's first secretary of foreign relations, launched an independent presidential bid.

Although the PAN remained more united than its main partisan rivals, the party's prospects for retaining the presidency dimmed as the Institutional Revolutionary Party (PRI, the party that had held national power for 71 years until its defeat in 2000) regained ground. During 2004 the PRI won important gubernatorial races in Chihuahua, Durango, Oaxaca, and Veracruz. PRI victories in northern states hitherto identified with the PAN were serious blows to the latter party. Internal rivalries continued to divide the PRI, however, and there remained a distinct possibility that nominating party leader Roberto Madrazo (who had been charged with serious electoral fraud in his successful 1994 gubernatorial campaign in Tabasco) for the presidency might crush the party's renewed hopes under the weight of the past. The PRI remained the party with the strongest national organizational base and the largest group of core supporters, however, and was thus a serious contender for the presidency in 2006.

One of the year's greatest political controversies involved Andrés Manuel López Obrador, the popular governor of the Federal District. Even in the wake of sensational corruption scandals involving other Party of the Democratic Revolution (PRD) officials, public opinion polls consistently favoured López Obrador to win the 2006 presidential race. His candidacy was, however, endangered by judicial charges stemming from his decision—in defiance of a court order—to construct across private land a public-access road to a hospital. In May the federal attorney general initiated legal proceedings against López Obrador by requesting that the Chamber of Deputies lift his immunity from prosecution as an elected public official, an action that might eventually lead to his formal conviction, removal from office, and ineligibility to hold future public office. These actions touched off a political firestorm, with the PRD and its allies arguing that the Fox administration was manipulating the judicial process in order to eliminate its most visible partisan rival (and the PRD's best-ever chance of winning the presidency).

The past also featured prominently in the year's political struggles. In July the special prosecutor appointed to investigate human rights crimes committed during Mexico's "dirty war" of the late 1960s and early 1970s filed an indictment against former president Luis Echeverría (1970–76) and several other retired military and security officials. The prosecutor formally charged Echeverría with the crime of genocide for his involvement in a government-trained paramilitary group's violent repression of a protest march in Mexico City on June 10, 1971, an action in which some two dozen demonstrators were killed. Leftist groups and human rights organizations applauded the action as an important step toward breaking Mexico's long tradition of official impunity. However, the PRI and the armed forces immediately closed ranks in defense of Echeverría and his co-defendants, arguing that consolidating Mexico's new democratic order required all parties to set aside divisive controversies over the past. A judge overturned the indictment principally on the grounds that the statute of limitations on the alleged crimes had expired, and the special prosecutor then appealed the case to the Supreme Court.

In international affairs the year's most important development was the temporary rupture of diplomatic relations between Mexico and Cuba. Relations between the two governments had remained tense since early 2002, when President Fox asked Cuban Pres. Fidel Castro to depart early from the UN International Conference on Financing for Development in Monterrey, Mex. (so as not to overlap with the visit of U.S. Pres. George W. Bush), and when Mexico reversed its long-standing diplomatic position by aligning itself with international critics of the Castro regime's human rights record. In May the Fox government accused Cuban officials of intervening in Mexico's internal affairs. Mexico withdrew its own ambassador to Cuba and ordered Cuba's ambassador to leave Mexico. Formal relations were restored in July, but the bilateral relationship remained awkward.

On the economic front a recovery gained momentum as Mexico achieved an inflation-adjusted growth rate of 4.4% (compared with 1.3% in 2003). Mexico benefited from economic recovery in the United States (the country's principal export market) and high international oil prices. Government officials maintained tight budgetary discipline, however, and sought to use the petroleum-export earnings windfall to pay down the country's external debt rather than to increase public expenditures. The need to generate sufficient employment to meet the country's pressing human needs remained a particularly serious concern.

(KEVIN J. MIDDLEBROOK)

MICRONESIA, FEDERATED STATES OF

Area: 701 sq km (271 sq mi)
Population (2004 est.): 114,000
Capital: Palikir, on Pohnpei
Head of state and government: President Joseph J. Urusemal

The Federated States of Micronesia (FSM) ratified its renegotiated Compact of Free Association with the U.S. in May 2004. The Compact provided for an investment fund to be built with U.S. contributions of $800,000 a year until the fund reached an estimated $16 million by 2023, at which time income from the fund was expected to replace grants from the U.S. The Asian Development Bank had agreed to provide $800,000 in technical assistance for the management of the fund. Under a new licensing arrangement with the European Union, up to 18 EU vessels would be given approval to fish in the FSM exclusive economic zone from 2005.

Tensions between the FSM Congress and Pres. Joseph Urusemal heightened in October when the president vetoed legislation that would have given Congress additional staff to provide independent economic and financial advice. The governors of several states indicated that they would block legislation intended to provide an amnesty for criminal offenses by members of Congress and senior government officials. In late 2003, 14 FSM congressional leaders and senior officials had been indicted in a $1.2 million purchasing scam. In August 2004 former speaker of Congress Jack Fritz was found guilty of unrelated fraud and theft charges.

(BARRIE MACDONALD)

MOLDOVA

Area: 33,845 sq km (13,068 sq mi)
Population (2004 est.): 4,216,000 (including more than a half million persons working abroad and about 600,000 persons in Transnistria)
Capital: Chisinau
Chief of state: President Vladimir Voronin
Head of government: Prime Minister Vasile Tarlev

In July 2004 a serious crisis erupted between the Moldovan government and the self-proclaimed territory of Transnistria, which had seceded in 1992. Although some 40% of Transnistria's population spoke Romanian as its first language, the authorities in Tiraspol, the capital, forcibly closed six schools for teaching Romanian in the Latin rather than the Cyrillic script. On August 1 Moldova imposed economic sanctions and severed transport links with Transnistria, despite an earlier warning from the Russian Foreign Ministry not to take such steps. The Organization for Security and Co-operation in Europe (OSCE), which had promoted a federal solution, accused Transnistrian leader Igor Smirnov of carrying out "linguistic cleansing." The situation had already prompted U.S. Secretary of Defense Donald Rumsfeld to visit Moldova on June 26, when he added his voice to calls for Russia to abide by the 1999 OSCE agreement and withdraw its forces from Transnistria.

Meanwhile, previously tense bilateral relations with Romania (which had ruled nearly all of Moldova from 1918 to 1940) improved somewhat, and on May 27 the two heads of state met and decided to reactivate a joint commission meant to analyze all "serious issues" between them. Moldova, however, declined to participate in the ceremonies held across the border in Putna, Rom., on the first weekend of July to commemorate the 500th anniversary of the death of Moldavian Prince Stephen the Great, whom the Orthodox Church had recently proclaimed a saint.

Moldova's ruling Communist Party enjoyed 67.76% popular support, according to a poll published in May, but 48.5% of respondents also stated their belief that the poverty-stricken country, seen by some as showing some hallmarks of a failed state, was heading in the wrong direction.

(TOM GALLAGHER)

MONACO

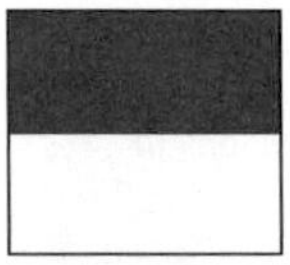

Area: 1.95 sq km (0.75 sq mi)
Population (2004 est.): 32,600
Chief of state: Prince Rainier III
Head of government: Minister of State Patrick Leclercq

The year 2004 began in Monaco with renewed concern about the health of Prince Rainier III, who was admitted to a hospital cardiac unit in December 2003 and again on Jan. 2, 2004, suffering "general fatigue." The 80-year-old prince was hospitalized again for several days in February and October.

Although Rainier's son and heir, Prince Albert, remained unmarried, worries over Monaco's future had been eased with the revised constitution of 2002, which included female siblings and their legitimate children in the line of succession. Therefore, in 2004 Princess Caroline's elder son, 20-year-old Andrea Casiraghi, stood third in line to the throne, after Albert and Caroline. Meanwhile, Rainier's youngest child, Princess Stephanie, was divorced from her husband of less than a year, Portuguese circus acrobat Adans Lopez Peres.

On May 4 Monaco signed a cooperative agreement with Andorra to combat money laundering. This agreement, the 15th such bilateral accord reached by Monaco, marked the principality's commitment to international cooperation in the fight against money laundering and the financing of terrorism.

Twelve new stands opened in time for the 2004 Monaco Grand Prix Formula 1

© Jean-Paul Pelissier/Reuters/Corbis

Prince Rainier and Princess Caroline of Monaco watch a football match in April.

auto race in late May. The rebuilt stands provided seating for 6,000 spectators, and a widened esplanade afforded new underground premises that would be used for offices, shops, and restaurants. The total area gained was 5,000 sq m (about 54,000 sq ft).

(ANNE ROBY)

MONGOLIA

Area: 1,564,116 sq km (603,909 sq mi)
Population (2004 est.): 2,519,000
Capital: Ulaanbaatar
Chief of state: President Natsagiyn Bagabandi
Head of government: Prime Ministers Nambaryn Enhbayar, Chultemiyn Ulaan from August 13, and, from August 20, Tsahiagiyn Elbegdorj

The June 27, 2004, general elections marked a turning point in Mongolia's post-Soviet history and a challenge to its emerging democracy. The ruling Mongolian People's Revolutionary Party (MPRP) went to the polls full of confidence. On the last day of 2003, the MPRP government had announced the payment of $250 million in final settlement of the "big debt" of 11.4 billion transferable rubles owed to Russia for Soviet aid 1947–91. With its 72 to 4 majority, the MPRP commanded the Great Hural (parliament), and with its control of the state-owned media, it also dominated the election campaign.

Nonetheless, the "Motherland-Democracy" (MD) coalition of the Democratic Party (DP) and the "Motherland"–Mongolian Democratic New Socialist Party was joined by the Civil Courage–Republican Party and overturned the MPRP's monopoly of power. The elections resulted in an impasse, however; neither the MD nor the MPRP won enough seats for an overall majority of 39. Eventually they agreed to form a "grand coalition," but there was much mutual antagonism during protracted negotiations.

While 74 new Great Hural members were sworn in on July 26, results in two constituencies were being contested in the courts. On August 13 Nambaryn Enhbayar (prime minister 2000–04) was elected the Hural's chairman (speaker), and Hural standing committees were formed. On August 20 the new prime minister was appointed: Tsahiagiyn Elbegdorj, not an election candidate but a member of the DP National Consultative Council who had been prime minister in 1998. After

Supporters of Mongolia's opposition "Motherland-Democracy" coalition parade in a pasture south of Ulaanbataar in June, before the country's parliamentary elections, which unseated the ruling party.

© Guang Niu/Reuters/Corbis

lengthy discussion between the MD and MPRP on "grand coalition" policy, the new government was formed on September 28. The 16 members were a mix of MD and MPRP former ministers such as Deputy Prime Minister Chultemiyn Ulaan, but the new faces included Badarchiyn Erdenebat (defense minister), Norovyn Altanhuyag (finance minister), and Tsendiyn Monh-Orgil (foreign minister).

(ALAN J.K. SANDERS)

MOROCCO

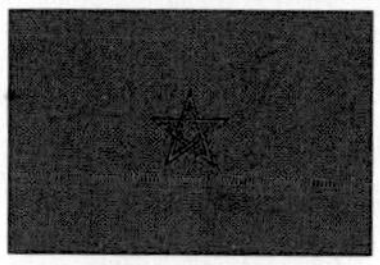

Area: 710,850 sq km (274,461 sq mi), including the 252,120-sq-km (97,344-sq-mi) area of the disputed Western Sahara annexation
Population (2004 est.): 30,569,000, of which Western Sahara 267,000 (excluding 165,000 Saharawi refugees living near Tindouf, Alg., from 1975)
Capital: Rabat
Head of state and government: King Muhammad VI, assisted by Prime Minister Driss Jettou

For Moroccan King Muhammad VI, 2004 was a year full of worries. There was a good harvest, but the rise in global oil prices adversely affected the external account, and domestic economic growth continued to be inadequate to mitigate the social and political consequences of poverty. Though Morocco had signed a free-trade agreement with the United States on June 15, Washington still seemed to look with favour on Algiers, and the situation in the Western Sahara and relations with neighbouring Algeria continued to be worrisome. Despite efforts to root out Islamic extremism in the aftermath of the Casablanca suicide bombings in mid-May 2003, Moroccans were deeply implicated in the March 2004 bombings of the Madrid suburban railway system that caused at least 200 deaths. Despite toughened legislation and renewed vigilance by the security forces, urban violence and support for Islamist extremists increased alarmingly in Morocco.

In June King Muhammad VI reappointed his technocrat Prime Minister Driss Jettou and surrounded him with a more nonpartisan, technocratic cabinet than in the past. Some major political figures, such as Khalid Alioua, moved to the private sector, but the major political parties maintained their cabinet presence. The objective of the reshuffle was clearly linked to the need to stimulate the economy in relatively adverse conditions as growth proved to be sluggish, despite a cereals harvest of 8.3 million metric tons. Morocco's foreign currency reserves also rose by 21.5% by midyear to $14 billion, but GDP growth stubbornly remained at 5.5% and was predicted to fall to 3.5% in 2005. The World Bank provided a $100 million loan for administrative reform in July.

© Abdelhak Senna/AFP/Getty Images

Asma Chaabi, Morocco's only female mayor, attends a ceremony marking the fifth anniversary of King Muhammad VI's enthronement in July. The country passed a family law in 2004 that made women and men legally equal.

Morocco was increasingly eager to resolve the Western Sahara dispute in the wake of James Baker's resignation as UN special envoy and, in the light of increased French and Spanish support, had been pushing Algeria to bring pressure to bear on the Polisario Front, the Western Saharan liberation movement based in Algeria. Regional tensions over the issue hardened as Morocco accused Algeria of supplying military aid to the Polisario Front and South Africa recognized the Saharawi Arab Democratic Republic in September.

In January the parliament approved Morocco's new family law, the Mudawwanah, which effectively rendered the status of males and females equal before the law. The government was eager to extend its privatization program as part of renewed economic restructuring designed to address the problem of job creation; during the year an estimated $1.5 billion was earned from sales of public assets.

(GEORGE JOFFÉ)

MOZAMBIQUE

Area: 812,379 sq km (313,661 sq mi)
Population (2004 est.): 18,812,000
Capital: Maputo
Head of state and government: President Joaquim Chissano, assisted by Prime Ministers Pascoal Mocumbi and, from February 17, Luisa Diogo

On Feb. 17, 2004, Pres. Joaquim Chissano announced the dismissal of Prime Minister Pascoal Mocumbi, who had held office since 1994. Mocumbi was replaced by Luisa Diogo, minister of planning and finance, an office that she retained.

Floods in March in the central Sofala province left thousands of families stranded, and the late arrival of rains in the drought-stricken southern districts of the country raised serious concern about the food supply. Although harvests were uneven in different regions, the overall results were better than in the previous three years. In general the corn (maize) harvest was good, and there was an increase in both the quantity and the range of cash crops that provided the growers with money to buy food and other essentials. It was estimated, however, that 200,000 people would require food aid, more than half of them until the next harvest and the rest for an indefinite period. Deaths from HIV/AIDS were also causing a serious decline in the number of agricultural workers who were familiar with the problems of farming in the climatic and soil conditions peculiar to the country.

Although a considerable number of South African businessmen were working to help stimulate the economy, they provided relatively few secure jobs for local people. Nevertheless, South African investment was broadening the country's revenue base and was providing a more reliable supply of a wider range of goods. On June 21 the Executive Board of the IMF approved a three-year $16.66 million arrangement under the Poverty Reduction and Growth Facility for Mozambique to support the government's economic program until 2006. From having been the poorest country in the world, Mozambique had become a popular destination for outside investors.

In July, however, there were reports of beatings and killings by former Mozambique National Resistance (Renamo) guerrillas, about 150 of whom had been retained as guards to their former leader and presidential candidate Afonso Dhlakama, in Maringue, 150 km (93 mi) northwest of Beira. The attacks were feared to be indicative of continuing distrust between the opposition Renamo and the ruling Frelimo party and were deemed to be a bad augury for the general election to be held in December. In the event, Frelimo's Armando Guebuza (President Chissano had stood down after serving his statutory two terms in office) scored a decisive victory over Renamo candidate Dhlakama. In only the country's third presidential and parliamentary election since independence in 1975, observers from independent monitoring agencies deemed the election fair but noted a low voter turnout of less than 50%.

(KENNETH INGHAM)

MYANMAR (BURMA)

Area: 676,577 sq km (261,228 sq mi)
Population (2004 est.): 42,720,000
Capital: Yangon (Rangoon)
Head of state and government: Chairman of the State Peace and Development Council Gen. Than Shwe, assisted by Prime Ministers Gen. Khin Nyunt and, from October 19, Lieut. Gen. Soe Win

In 2004 Myanmar's growing isolation and international pressure for political reform created fissures inside the military junta, known as the State Peace and Development Council (SPDC), forcing it to consolidate its control over power and neutralize domestic and external threats. After 14 months in office, the intelligence chief and prime minister, Gen. Khin Nyunt, was sacked on October 19 and put under house arrest on corruption charges. He was replaced by a hard-liner, Lieut. Gen. Soe Win.

Khin Nyunt had promoted a "road map to democracy" in UN-brokered contacts between the government and Aung San Suu Kyi's National League for Democracy. The talks reached a stalemate, however, and critics accused the junta of using stalling tactics to retain its monopoly over power. Despite repeated assurances, the junta excluded the political parties from the constitutional drafting process and kept Suu Kyi under detention. Yangon also refused entry to both Kofi Annan's special envoy for political reform in Myanmar and the UN human rights envoy for Myanmar. The junta sentenced three Burmese citizens to death for having contacted representatives of the International Labour Organization.

In 2004 the United States and the European Union imposed tough new sanctions that extended a visa blacklist for all of Myanmar's military leaders, froze their overseas assets, and banned all commercial links. These measures had a severe impact on the garments and textiles sector. Myanmar's Association of Southeast Asian Nations neighbours, China and India, refused to cut off commercial ties with Yangon, however. Regional trade gave the military government just enough income to maintain its hold on power. Myanmar exported nearly a billion dollars a year in natural gas—well over twice the potential windfall from trade with the U.S. or the EU. In early 2004, rice exports were banned, apparently to curb inflation. Industry continued to suffer from acute power shortages. On the positive side, opium production in Myanmar was expected to fall in 2004 by 50%, largely owing to a combination of factors such as bad weather, police crackdowns, and public-awareness campaigns. Following a last-minute compromise whereby the government agreed to send a lower-level delegation to the Asia-Europe Meeting held in Hanoi in early October, Myanmar was finally admitted into the ASEM.

(MOHAN MALIK)

NAMIBIA

Area: 825,118 sq km (318,580 sq mi)
Population (2004 est.): 1,954,000
Capital: Windhoek
Chief of state and head of government: President Sam Nujoma, assisted by Prime Minister Theo-Ben Gurirab

Until the South West African People's Organization (SWAPO) held an extraordinary congress in May 2004, there was intense competition over the successor to Sam Nujoma as president of Namibia. One of the leading contenders, Hidipo Hamutenya, was dismissed by Nujoma from his government on the eve of the congress. After Nujoma made clear that he favoured Hifikepunye Pohamba as his successor, the congress ratified the decision, and few were surprised that Pohamba won the election held in mid-November. Nujoma, who was voted a very generous retirement package by the parliament, was to remain SWAPO president after he stepped down as president of the country in March 2005.

The issue of land redistribution continued to arouse much controversy. The government now claimed that some

Namibia commemorated the centenary of a three-year uprising in 1904–07 in which German colonialists massacred thousands of Herero tribesmen. The photo shows a reenactment of the treatment of Herero in Okakarara in August.

EPA Photos

white farmers were unwilling to sell their land and began to use its powers to expropriate farms. An evaluation of commercial farmland was conducted, and on this basis a land tax was to be imposed to help fund the state's acquisition of agricultural land for resettling the estimated quarter of a million people who wanted such land. It remained unclear, however, how resettlement would work in a country as arid as Namibia.

Some Herero people placed hope in the legal action they had brought against the German government. They sought recompense for the genocide carried out by the Germans against them after the Herero uprising of 1904. A German minister who attended the centenary commemoration of the genocide in August apologized for what had happened, but both the German and Namibian governments remained firmly opposed to the payment of reparations.

(CHRISTOPHER SAUNDERS)

NAURU

Area: 21.2 sq km (8.2 sq mi)
Population (2004 est.): 10,100
Capital: Government offices in Yaren district
Head of state and government: Presidents René Harris and, from June 22, Ludwig Scotty

Constitutional problems combined with a funding crisis to cripple Nauru's economy in 2004. Early in the year, while Pres. René Harris and Finance Minister Kinza Clodumar were on a prolonged financial aid-seeking trip to Australia, Parliament passed laws to prevent the government from spending money without prior parliamentary approval. For six weeks Nauru's Parliament was unable to pass the budget because neither the government nor the opposition (each with nine seats) was prepared to lose a vote by nominating a speaker. In late May the opposition suddenly elected David Adeang parliamentary speaker and passed several private members' bills, including one regarding the examination of allegations of illegal passport sales and another that required all MPs to divulge property holdings and business interests.

On June 22 Harris's government collapsed in a vote of no-confidence after one of his supporters changed sides, and former president Ludwig Scotty was returned to office. At the Pacific Islands Forum in Samoa in August, the new president told Australian Prime Minister John Howard that the Nauruan economy would be badly affected if Australia did not increase its $A 60 million (about U.S.$42 million) aid package. The financial plight of Nauru was worsened by the failure of property-development schemes and the Australian decision to reduce reliance on Nauru as an offshore point of detention for asylum seekers.

On October 1 President Scotty abruptly dissolved the government, announced a state of emergency, and called a snap election for October 23. His supporters captured a solid majority with 15 of the 18 seats, and Scotty immediately announced a new cabinet with Adeang as both finance minister and foreign minister. A tough reformist budget was approved on October 27.

(A.R.G. GRIFFITHS)

NEPAL

Area: 147,181 sq km (56,827 sq mi)
Population (2004 est.): 24,692,000
Capital: Kathmandu
Head of state: King Gyanendra Bir Bikram Shah Dev
Head of government: Prime Minister Surya Bahadur Thapa and, from June 3, Sher Bahadur Deuba

© Gopal Chitrakar/Reuters/Corbis

Nepalese police arrest antimonarchist activists at a demonstration in the capital, Kathmandu, on April 9. Popular dissatisfaction with the king and his government increased during the year, and Maoist rebels were also inciting insurrection throughout the country.

Kathmandu experienced unprecedented street violence in 2004 following the killing of 12 Nepalese workers in Iraq by a terrorist group. The protesters tried to set fire to the two mosques in the capital on September 1. Homegrown violence escalated in rural areas as Maoist forces attacked two district police headquarters in April, and the guerrillas began targeting the economy by calling for strikes and plant closures. As of September 30, more than 10,500 people had died in the violence.

In the capital, political chaos and uncertainty continued. King Gyanendra appointed Sher Bahadur Deuba prime minister on June 2. Deuba was instructed to hold elections by April 2005 in conditions of peace, and he invited the Maoists to peace negotiations. The Maoists rejected the invitation and launched deadly new attacks near year's end. Government forces responded, killing 22 guerrillas.

A meeting of Nepal's international donors in May agreed to increase foreign assistance to $500 million a year. On April 23 Nepal became the first least-developed country to be granted full membership in the World Trade Organization.

Two Nepalese set world records on Mt. Everest in 2004. Pemba Dorji Sherpa ascended in a record 8 hr 10 min in May, while Appa Sherpa scaled Everest for a record 14th time. (KESHAB POUDEL)

NETHERLANDS, THE

Area: 41,528 sq km (16,034 sq mi)
Population (2004 est.): 16,275,000
Capital: Amsterdam; seat of government, The Hague
Chief of state: Queen Beatrix
Head of government: Prime Minister Jan Peter Balkenende

In 2004, the year that marked the 40th anniversary of the arrival of the first Turkish migrant workers, The Netherlands continued to struggle with issues of diversity and integration. A parliamentary commission in January concluded that government policies and procedures of the past 30 years had been at best partially effective in accomplishing integration of immigrants. The Blok Commission's report was met with criticism in a negatively charged political atmosphere. The same month, Rita Verdonk, minister for integration and immigration, announced the one-time approval of 2,334 long-standing applications for residence permits. In a move that was met with widespread consternation, the government also announced that within the next three years some 26,000 rejected asylum seekers who had exhausted all appeals would be returned to countries in which their safety was not deemed endangered. The murder of filmmaker Theo van Gogh, threats against politicians Ayaan Hirsi Ali (van Gogh's collaborator on *Submission,* a film some people considered derisive of Islam) and Geert Wilders (for controversial political proposals about immigration policy), along with the ensuing upheaval—including violent attacks on Muslim and Christian schools and houses of worship—underscored the view that ethnic and religious factions remained a significant concern, warranting additional efforts and eliciting vigorous ongoing debates.

The Netherlands played a significant international role during the year. In January former foreign minister Jaap de Hoop Scheffer became NATO secretary-general. (*See* BIOGRAPHIES.) After the terrorist attacks in Madrid in March, law-enforcement agencies throughout Europe began to coordinate their efforts more closely. As of August 10, the Crimes of Terrorism Act made it a criminal offense to recruit for a jihad or to conspire to commit a serious terrorist crime and raised the penalties for serious crimes committed with terrorist intent. Two Dutch soldiers lost their lives in Iraq during the year, which prompted the deployment of additional armoured vehicles and four-wheel-drive vehicles fitted with machine guns, as well as approximately 60 additional troops. The Netherlands held the rotating six-month EU presidency from July 1 to December 31.

The Dutch royal family experienced a turbulent year. Princess Juliana, former monarch and mother of Queen Beatrix, died on March 20; Juliana's husband, Prince Bernhard, died on December 1. (*See* OBITUARIES.) Prince Johan Friso, Queen Beatrix's second son, married Mabel Wisse Smit on April 24 in Delft and relinquished his claim to the throne. The christening on June 12 of Princess Catharina-Amalia Beatrix Carmen Victoria (born Dec. 7, 2003), the daughter of Crown Prince Willem-Alexander and his wife, Princess Máxima, signaled a shift in attitudes. Although the baptism of the future queen was a private, rather than a state, affair, it marked the first public appearance in The Netherlands of Princess Máxima's father, Jorge Zorreguieta, whose political past in Argentina had been a delicate issue in the approval of the crown prince's marriage. A poll showed that 84% of the Dutch approved of Zorreguieta's presence at the christening.

(JOLANDA VANDERWAL TAYLOR)

NEW ZEALAND

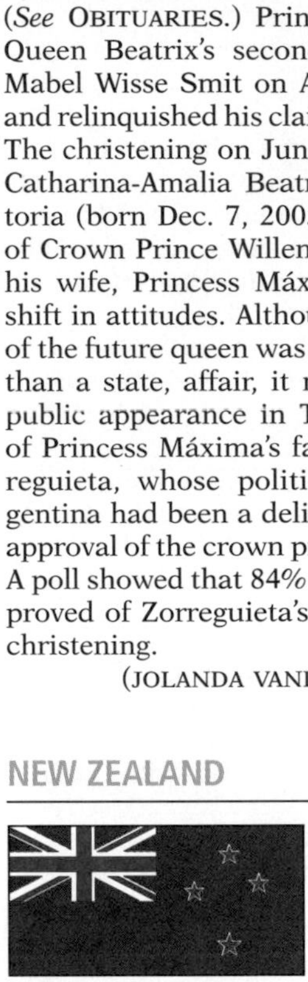

Area: 270,534 sq km (104,454 sq mi)
Population (2004 est.): 4,060,000
Capital: Wellington
Chief of state: Queen Elizabeth II, represented by Governor-General Dame Silvia Cartwright
Head of government: Prime Minister Helen Clark

New Zealand was sustained in 2004 by a buoyant economy and strong domestic growth, which enabled Finance Minister Michael Cullen's May 27 budget to predict government surpluses exceeding \$NZ 5 billion (\$NZ 1 = about U.S.\$0.65) annually to 2007–08 and to project economic growth of 2.8% to March 2005. New commitments included \$NZ 221 million in targeted family assistance, plans to upgrade Auckland's infrastructure and rail networks over the next decade, and \$NZ 500 million over four years for economic development and export incentives. To contain inflation, the Reserve Bank of New Zealand incrementally increased the official cash rate from 5% on January 1 to 6.5% on October 28. Wellington and Beijing agreed to begin negotiations in early 2005 for a New Zealand–China free-trade agreement. Prime Minister Helen Clark's administration also advanced talks for better trade access with Thailand, Mexico, Singapore, Chile, and Hong Kong and lobbied for a free-trade arrangement with the U.S.

Race relations dominated politics after opposition National Party leader Donald Brash alleged that Clark's Labour-led government was running policies with a pro-Maori bias. Responding to opinion polls supporting Brash's stance, Clark appointed Trevor Mallard coordinating minister on race relations to review policies with racial preferences. Having rejected Maori claims to title of the nation's foreshore and seabed and ignored a two-week protest march by thousands of Maori demonstrators that ended on May 5, Parliament enacted government-sponsored legislation in November confirming public ownership. In protest against the Foreshore and Seabed bill, junior cabinet minister Tariana Turia resigned from the Labour Party and the House of Representatives,

The shearing of Shrek, a nine-year-old New Zealand merino wether, was an international media event in April.

AP/Wide World Photos

forcing a by-election on July 10, which she won overwhelmingly on behalf of the new Maori Party. Veteran parliamentarian Richard Prebble quit as leader of the ACT political party, which held 8 seats in the 120-seat House, and was succeeded by Rodney Hide in June.

Destiny New Zealand, a new church-based political party, organized rallies on family and moral issues in Auckland and Wellington, where police estimated 7,500 attendees. The party also protested legalized prostitution, abortion, and government-sponsored legislation to solemnize and register relationships and civil unions between same-sex couples. (*See* LAW, CRIME, AND LAW ENFORCEMENT: Special Report.)

Floods devastated farmland in the lower part of North Island in February and the Bay of Plenty region in July. Officials calculated that damage from the February storms exceeded $NZ 250 million. Farming leaders estimated that 500,000 newborn lambs perished in September snows in Otago and Southland. The government began negotiations with pastoral leaseholders in the South Island high country to create a network of up to 20 conservation parks and reserves over 200,000 ha (almost 500,000 ac) of tussock grasslands, designating $NZ 79 million for the purpose. A nine-year-old Merino wether nicknamed Shrek was accorded international celebrity status during the year. The renegade "hermit sheep," which was believed to have evaded the annual muster for six years by hiding in a cave, had grown a 27.5-kg (60-lb) fleece with wool staples 380 mm (15 in) in length. Shrek's April 28 shearing on live television was broadcast worldwide, and most of the fleece was auctioned for charity.

Internationally acclaimed author Janet Frame died on January 29 at age 79. Just two months later Frame's biographer, eminent historian Michael King, was killed in a road accident. (*See* OBITUARIES.) (NEALE MCMILLAN)

NICARAGUA

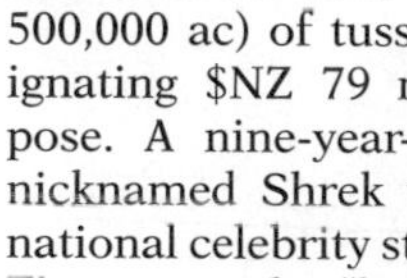

Area: 130,373 sq km (50,337 sq mi)
Population (2004 est.): 5,360,000
Capital: Managua
Head of state and government: President Enrique Bolaños Geyer

In February 2004 National Assembly deputies loyal to former president Arnoldo Alemán Lacayo, who had been sentenced to 20 years in prison for money laundering and other crimes, failed to pass an amnesty bill overturning his 2003 conviction.

Politics was dominated by a three-way struggle between Pres. Enrique Bolaños Geyer, the Constitutionalist Liberal Party (PLC), and the Sandinista Front (FSLN). In November municipal elections, the FSLN won 87 of the 152 municipalities, including Managua. The PLC won 57 municipalities, and a conservative alliance (APRE) formed to back President Bolaños placed a distant third. An ongoing dispute over a new judicial career law led to a two-day strike by judges and court workers and a physical confrontation in the National Assembly in March. In November President Bolaños garnered international support against FSLN and PLC threats to remove him from the presidency for having committed electoral crimes during the 2001 presidential campaign.

The economy grew 4% in 2004. Remittances from family members overseas amounted to more than $800 million, about one-third of the GNP, and they outsized exports. In January Nicaragua was approved for the IMF's Highly Indebted Poor Country initiative, which reduced the country's foreign debt by 80%. In February, however, the Civil Coordinator, representing 300 organizations, said that the budget sent to the National Assembly and the version sent to the IMF differed by $650 million and that sum was spent paying the internal debt rather than reducing poverty. In September the government of the North Atlantic Autonomous Region—one of the poorest regions in the country—declared a state of emergency following torrential rains that killed 24 persons in July.

In February the soldiers who had been sent to Iraq returned. Under pressure from the U.S., President Bolaños ordered the destruction of all surface-to-air missiles, and by December about half of them had been destroyed. Four police officers were killed and one was seriously injured in May during a raid of a police station in Bluefields; the attack was blamed on drug traffickers and organized crime. A free-trade agreement between Central America and the U.S. was signed in Washington in May and presented to the National Assembly in November.

(NADINE JUBB)

NIGER

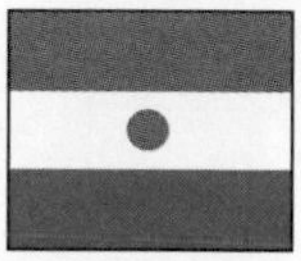

Area: 1,189,546 sq km (459,286 sq mi)
Population (2004 est.): 11,679,000
Capital: Niamey
Head of state and government: President Tandja Mamadou, assisted by Prime Minister Hama Amadou

Niger held municipal elections on July 24, 2004, with voters choosing 3,747 candidates to serve four-year terms on 265 rural and urban local councils. Pres. Mamadou Tandja, leader of the ruling National Movement for Society and Development, won a second term in office, garnering more than 65% of the vote in a runoff ballot held on December 4. He had failed to win a clear majority in the initial round of balloting held on November 16. Challenger Mahamadou Issoufou, leader of the main opposition Party for Democracy and Socialism, claimed 34.5% of the vote in the runoff. International observers, while pointing out some minor problems, deemed the elections overall to have been free and fair.

During the summer, armed bandits conducted a series of raids on civilian buses and trucks in the northern Tuareg area. The most serious incident occurred on August 11, when raiders stopped a bus on the Trans-Sahara Highway, robbing its passengers and leaving three dead, one a two-year-old child. On August 12 journalist Moussa Kaka was arrested for having broadcast an interview with fugitive Tuareg leader Mohammed Boula, who proclaimed that his rebel group had carried out this latest attack. Kaka was released on August 16.

Niger remained one of the poorest countries in the world, but international donors expressed guarded approval of the government's attempts to lift the standard of living of its people and, in particular, subsistence farmers. Financed by the United Nations, the two-year-old poverty-reduction strategy had seen the construction of hundreds of new classrooms and clinics, as well as new dams and good wells. Primary-school enrollment was estimated to have risen by at least 10% in rural areas. On October 5 the first ingot was extracted from the new Samira gold mine in southwestern Niger, marking the launch of modern commercial extraction of the ore.

(NANCY ELLEN LAWLER)

NIGERIA

Area: 923,768 sq km (356,669 sq mi)
Population (2004 est.): 128,254,000
Capital: Abuja
Head of state and government: President Olusegun Obasanjo

Several bouts of violence and civil unrest plagued Nigeria throughout 2004 and threatened to collapse the country's fragile democracy. The overwhelming victory by the ruling People's Democratic Party in the March municipal elections was marred by allegations of fraud and by violent clashes at polling stations that claimed some 50 lives. In April several military officers were arrested after a plan to oust Pres. Olusegun Obasanjo was foiled.

During much of the year, religious violence preoccupied Nigeria, which had not experienced such heightened unrest since similar bouts of religious conflict occurred in 2001. During the first three months, 350 people were killed and thousands were displaced by the clashes. In May the government declared a state of emergency in Plateau state following religious-based violence that left more than 1,000 persons dead and 70,000 displaced. Christian militias in six Plateau villages attacked mosques and killed an estimated 600 people and left more than 1,000, mostly Muslims, wounded; the most horrific atrocities occurred in Yelwa. These attacks led to reprisals by Muslims in Kano, Nigeria's second largest city, where an estimated 600 people, predominately Christians, were killed. Moreover, many observers emphasized that the violence could not be attributed to religion alone and that the causes were complex. Land disputes between Tarok farmers and Fulani cattle herders were cited as one of the causes. Similar but smaller religious attacks occurred in early June in Numan, near the Cameroon border. Two police crackdowns on antigovernment protests in Abuja and Lagos led to the arrests of more than 200 demonstrators, including Nobel laureate playwright and novelist Wole Soyinka. More than 10,000 people had died in religious, ethnic, and political clashes since 1999, when Nigeria officially ended 15 years of military rule. In August Swiss authorities agreed to release $500 million of former dictator Sani Abacha's assets that were being held in a Swiss bank.

AP/Wide World Photos

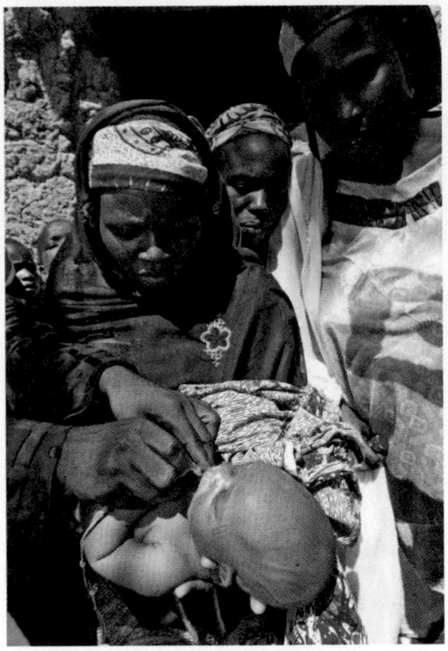

In July a baby is immunized against polio in the Nigerian state of Kano, where fears among the populace that the vaccinations could cause AIDS or infertility had induced the governor to suspend vaccinations in August 2003.

Kano state was hit hard by a serious polio outbreak that swept across nine West and Central African countries and was believed to have originated in Nigeria. The Kano state government refused to participate in the immunization program led by the World Health Organization, citing that the shots were unsafe. The boycott resulted in 257 polio-afflicted Nigerian children's becoming paralyzed. (*See* HEALTH: Sidebar.)

Nigeria's oil-rich Niger delta was fraught with continued violence and targeted attacks on oil-production sites. Fighting between ethnic militias left more than 12 people dead in January, and at least 5 persons were killed in March. In September the Niger Delta People's Volunteer Force (NDPVF) threatened war on the Nigerian government and warned the oil companies that they should leave. The crisis deepened later that month when violence peaked in Port Harcourt, leaving close to 500 people dead. That same month 50 people were killed in a pipeline explosion near Lagos. In October union leaders staged a four-day oil strike that virtually shut down Lagos, and the NDPVF surrendered many weapons to the government as part of a money-for-guns exchange.

Several foreign oil companies operating in Nigeria faced lawsuits and continued attacks, as a result of ongoing conflict over land and extraction rights. The U.S.-based oil multinational ChevronTexaco suspended operations in April after seven people, including two of its workers, were killed in an attack. Oil giant Shell, dogged by investigations after having admitted that it had falsified oil-reserve estimates, was sued by the Nigerian government for £840 million (about $1.55 billion) for the environmental damage it had caused in the Niger delta. The company had a bitter history in Nigeria owing to allegations of oil spills, security-force brutality, and corruption. American oil-services company Halliburton was under investigation as part of a $180 million bribery case that alleged that the company had funneled bribes to local officials from 1995 to 2000.

(MARY F.E. EBELING)

NORWAY

Area: 323,758 sq km (125,004 sq mi)
Population (2004 est.): 4,591,000
Capital: Oslo
Chief of state: King Harald V
Head of government: Prime Minister Kjell Magne Bondevik

Norway's favourable trade balance continued in 2004, thanks to strong oil and gas exports, and the Government Petroleum Fund continued to grow because of high oil prices. Despite these positive trends, Norwegians worried about the decrease in industrial employment. In 2004 this declining trend halted for a while as new investments in oil-related, metallurgical, and consumer-based industries had an effect, but many companies continued to move their production abroad to countries where costs were lower. (*See* ECONOMIC AFFAIRS: Special Report.) Norwegian communities were often vulnerable because they were based on one factory, and many industrial workers had lost their jobs or had been handed early-retirement arrangements. The national average unemployment, however, remained stable at 4.5%.

Meanwhile, some Norwegian companies had hired cheaper employees from other countries for jobs in Norway. In response, the unions claimed minimum wages, something that had been approved in sectors such as transport and construction. The globalization of the economy was also reflected in discussions about the retirement-pension and sickness-allowance schemes. The centre-right government's policies, which emphasized reducing government budgets, seemed to some to be in conflict with the traditional welfare-state policies of previous decades.

From the outside these problems might seem rather small. On the index of human development issued by the UN Development Programme, Norway was ranked as having the highest standard of living in the world. The annual ranking was based largely on average levels of education and income combined with expected length of lifetime (78.9 years in Norway). The political left, however, pointed to the growing number of poor Norwegians. On the basis of the Organisation for Economic Co-operation and Development standard, Norway had 90,000 poor people, while according to the EU criteria, the number was approximately 400,000.

Since the election in 2001, the minority government of Prime Minister Kjell Magne Bondevik had received case by case support from the Storting (parliament). A Gallup Poll in October showed that two of the three parties in the ruling coalition had very low support. The Christian People's Party had about 7%, and the Liberal Party had 3%, while the Conservative Party remained the strongest of the governing parties, with about 18% support. Parties were already lining up for the general election in September 2005. For the first time the Norwegian Labour Party announced that it would negotiate with the Socialist Left and Centre parties to form a coalition after the 2005 election. According to the results of the October poll, this prospective red-green alliance would have more than 50% of the vote.

In the middle of December, the Storting accepted the government's budget proposal. A deficit of nearly 69 billion kroner (1 krone = about $0.16) was covered by taking the money from the steadily growing Government Petroleum Fund, which totaled nearly 1 trillion kroner at year's end.

On January 21 Crown Princess Mette-Marit gave birth to a daughter. The new princess, who was baptized Ingrid Alexandra on April 17, was the second in line to the throne behind her father, Crown Prince Haakon. The crown prince filled in as regent during King Harald's four-month recuperation after a December 2003 cancer operation. The king resumed his duties on April 13. Princess Märtha Louise and her husband, Ari Behn, announced that they were expecting their second child in April 2005. (HILDE SANDVIK)

Pascal Le Segretain/Getty Images

Norway's Crown Princess Mette-Marit, with her husband, Crown Prince Haakon, and her son, Marius Hoiby, introduces Princess Ingrid Alexandra to the public on the occasion of the baby's christening in April.

OMAN

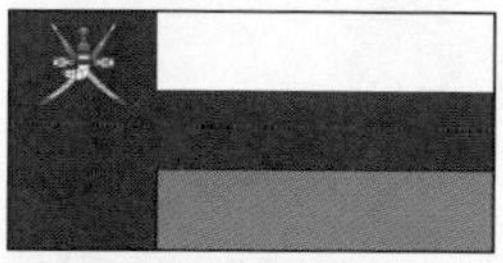

Area: 309,500 sq km (119,500 sq mi)
Population (2004 est.): 2,350,000
Capital: Muscat
Head of state and government: Sultan and Prime Minister Qaboos bin Said (Qabus ibn Sa'id)

In 2004 Oman continued on its path of incrementally privatizing sectors of its economy, replacing increasing numbers of foreign workers with citizens, and taking additional steps to further liberalize the climate for encouraging international investment. Dramatically higher oil prices alleviated predictions of negative economic growth, and the accompanying spike in official revenues not only lessened earlier pressures to increase revenue by raising rates for water, electricity, and gasoline but also produced a surplus in the balance of trade by year's end. In addition, investors in neighbouring United Arab Emirates sought to provide much of the $800 million destined for a new 7.2-km (4.5-mi) beachfront-development scheme west of the capital.

In a regional first, women were appointed to head the Ministries of Tourism, Social Development, and Higher Education. In addition, all 83 members of the national consultative assembly were elected directly for the first time. Previously, the government had selected the voters, and only 25% of the electorate could vote in a given election. The number of members in the country's appointed state council was expanded to 57, and the terms of both the elected and appointed councils were extended from three to four years.

Oman remained apprehensive of U.S. and Israeli threats to neighbouring Iran regarding its nuclear program and expressed displeasure at stated U.S. intentions to pressure Arab and Islamic governments in general to conform to Western notions of governance. Oman declined to commit troops to Iraq and questioned the legitimacy of Baghdad's new leaders. Oman and Yemen agreed

Mohammed Mahjoub/AFP/Getty Images

Minister for Social Development Sherifa bint Khalfan bin Nasser al-Yahieyaiah was one of three women in 2004 named to head ministries in Oman's government.

on the demarcation of their maritime boundary, completing the delineation of their borders on land and sea, and the two countries launched discussions to establish a free-trade zone.

(JOHN DUKE ANTHONY)

PAKISTAN

Area: 796,096 sq km (307,374 sq mi), excluding the 84,159-sq-km Pakistani-administered portion of Jammu and Kashmir
Population (2004 est.): 151,600,000 (excluding 4,250,000 residents of Pakistani-administered Jammu and Kashmir as well as 1,100,000 Afghan refugees)
Capital: Islamabad
Head of state and government: President and Chief Executive Gen. Pervez Musharraf, assisted by Prime Ministers Mir Zafarullah Khan Jamali, Chaudry Shujaat Hussain from June 30, and, from August 28, Shaukat Aziz

Pakistan remained a troubled country in 2004. In January at the Islamabad South Asian Association for Regional Cooperation conference, steps were taken to improve Indo-Pakistani relations, but terrorism remained the overriding concern. On January 1 Pres. Pervez Musharraf was accorded a vote of confidence by a parliamentary electoral college. The unprecedented vote was held under a new constitutional amendment that accorded legitimacy to the military presidency after more than a year of opposition protests had paralyzed the assembly. Musharraf accepted an arrangement to remain president until November 2007 but agreed to relinquish the post of chief of the army staff by Dec. 31, 2004. Late in the summer, however, faced with fierce fighting near the Afghan border in South Waziristan (*see* Map), the government floated a discussion about extending Musharraf's army tenure. The "dual-office" bill that allowed Musharraf to keep both positions passed both houses of parliament, and on December 1 the bill, which had been kept pending until Musharraf was abroad on an extended tour, was signed into law by the acting president.

In May thousands of protesters battled with police after the government prevented Shahbaz Sharif, a brother of deposed prime minister Nawaz Sharif, from returning to Pakistan. Out of concern that his appearance posed a threat to Musharraf's presidency, Sharif was returned to his exile in Saudi Arabia.

Sectarian and terrorist violence continued throughout the year. The suicide bombing of a Shi'ite mosque in Karachi in which 25 people were killed and 200 wounded ignited six weeks of Shi'ite-Sunni bloodletting. In June Karachi's military commander escaped an assassination attempt, but 11 others died in the incident; Musharraf laid blame for the rising violence in Karachi to the Jund Allah, an al-Qaeda affiliate. On October 1 a Shi'ite mosque in Sialkot was bombed, and more than 30 were killed; six days later a car bomb killed more than 40 people at a Sunni meeting in Multan. All religious gatherings were subsequently banned in the country.

With young Pakistanis ever more drawn to militant religious organizations and amid reports that the police and army structures had been infiltrated by jihadi recruiters, on June 27 Prime Minister Mir Zafarullah Khan Jamali resigned and was succeeded temporarily by the leader of the Pakistan Muslim League, Chaudry Shujaat Hussain, and a few weeks later by Finance Minister Shaukat Aziz. The civil terror continued, however, and in late July a suicide bomber exploded a device near Aziz's vehicle, killing the driver and several others. The incident came hours after the capture of Ahmed Khalfan Ghailani, a senior al-Qaeda operative, and shortly after UN Secretary-General Kofi Annan revealed that he had selected Pakistani diplomat Ashraf Jehangir Qazi to be his top envoy in Iraq. In August the government reported that it had foiled a terrorist plot to kill Musharraf and bomb the parliament and the U.S. embassy. On September 28 the government announced the killing of Amjad Hussain Farooqui, the alleged mastermind of the plot. Six members of Jaish-i-Mohammad were arrested in connection with the December 2003 assassination attempts on Musharraf.

On September 22 Musharraf addressed the UN General Assembly, warning about an "iron curtain" descending between the Islamic world and the West. In New York City he also had conversations with Manmohan Singh (*see* BIOGRAPHIES), the new Indian prime minister, and on his way back to Pakistan he met with the pope in the Vatican. In early December he met with U.S. Pres. George W. Bush and British Prime Minister Tony Blair.

On February 1 'Abd al-Qadir Khan, an internationally known physicist and

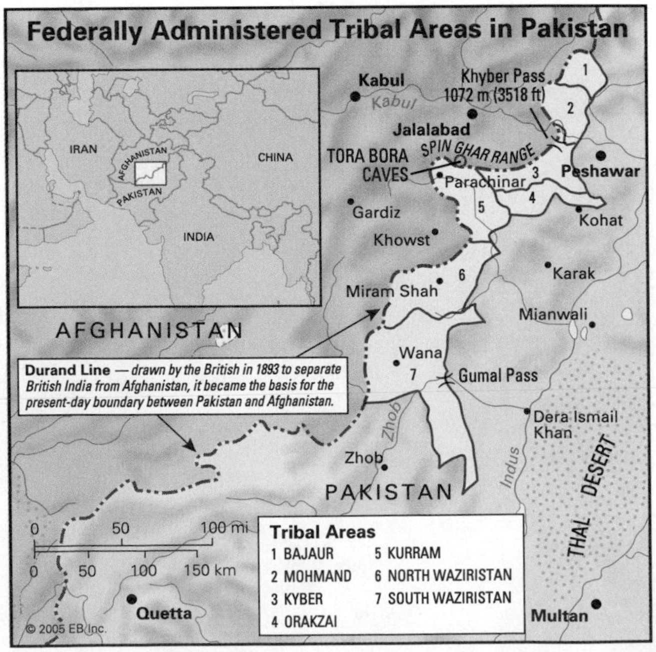

leader of Pakistan's nuclear weapons program, admitted that he had run an international network that marketed nuclear technology to Libya, Iran, and North Korea. Khan asserted that he had done nothing illegal, but he made a public confession nonetheless and was granted a pardon. Efforts by the International Atomic Energy Agency to talk to the scientist were rebuffed by the government. (LAWRENCE ZIRING)

PALAU

Area: 488 sq km (188 sq mi)
Population (2004 est.): 20,700
Provisional capital: Koror; new capital buildings at Melekeok (on Babelthuap) had not been completed as of late 2004
Head of state and government: President Tommy Remengesau, Jr.

In June 2004 Palauan Pres. Tommy Remengesau declared his intention to seek another four-year term in office, running on a platform of "preserving the best while improving the rest." He said that despite outside factors—such as global terrorism, which hurt tourism, the wars in Iraq and Afghanistan, the recent outbreaks of SARS (severe acute respiratory syndrome), and the Asian economic decline—Palau had a positive economic and social outlook. In the general election on November 2, Remengesau easily won reelection.

Remengesau visited Taiwan to attend Pres. Chen Shui-ban's inauguration in May and reiterated that a key objective in Palau's foreign policy was to support Taiwan actively. At a summit meeting in Guam in July, Remengesau pledged cooperation with three other Pacific island governments to boost tourism in the region, find alternative sources of energy, and develop solid-waste-management facilities. Palau also took effective steps to protect its valuable tuna-fishing industry in a multinational law-enforcement operation called Island Chief 2004. The operation, which used four ships, including the Palau-owned Pacific-class patrol boat *President H.I. Remeliik,* lasted three weeks. The successful exercise was supported by the U.S., Australia, New Zealand, and Canada and used Canadian satellite support as well as surveillance by New Zealand P3 and U.S. C130 aircraft to detect illegal fisheries.

(A.R.G. GRIFFITHS)

Martín Torrijos, with his wife, Vivian, campaigns for president of Panama. Torrijos easily defeated former president Guillermo Endara and led the opposition Democratic Revolutionary Party to victory in the May 2 national elections.

PANAMA

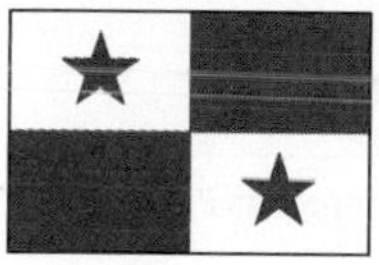

Area: 75,040 sq km (28,973 sq mi)
Population (2004 est.): 3,172,000
Capital: Panama City
Head of state and government: Presidents Mireya Moscoso and, from September 1, Martín Torrijos

The national elections of May 2, 2004, and the transition from one administration to another dominated Panamanian politics in 2004. The outgoing administration of Pres. Mireya Moscoso had been accused of being one of the most corrupt in Panamanian history, with charges ranging from nepotism to buying votes in the Legislative Assembly. In the event, Martín Torrijos, son of former military strongman Gen. Omar Torrijos and candidate of the main opposition Democratic Revolutionary Party (PRD), won more than 47% of the vote and easily defeated the second-place finisher, former president Guillermo Endara, who received 31% of the vote and represented the Solidarity Party. In the final tally the PRD controlled 42 seats, which gave it a majority in the Legislative Assembly.

During the summer Torrijos and his allies in the Legislative Assembly proposed a series of controversial constitutional amendments. The reforms included reducing the number of legislators, increasing the autonomy of the Electoral Tribunal, changing the manner in which a national constitutional convention could be called, and reducing the time for the presidential transition. The amendments awaited the approval of the new Legislative Assembly sworn in on September 1.

In the realm of foreign policy, Panama and the U.S. held a series of meetings to negotiate a bilateral free-trade agreement. Ranching and agricultural interests could lose significant government protection if Panama's market was opened to U.S. agricultural products. In its report on international trafficking in humans, the U.S. Department of State alleged that "Panama is a transit and destination country for women and girls, primarily from Colombia and the Dominican Republic, trafficked for sexual exploitation." Panamanian government officials vehemently questioned the veracity of the report.

Although several former officials connected with the Moscoso administration were denied U.S. entry visas, Panama continued to cooperate with the U.S. on the defense of the Panama Canal.

(ORLANDO J. PÉREZ)

PAPUA NEW GUINEA

Area: 462,840 sq km (178,704 sq mi)
Population (2004 est.): 5,695,000
Capital: Port Moresby
Chief of state: Queen Elizabeth II, represented by Governors-General Bill Skate (acting) until March 3 and from March 5, Jeffrey Nape (acting) from May 28, and, from June 29, Sir Paulias Matane
Head of government: Prime Minister Sir Michael Somare

Papua New Guinean Prime Minister Michael Somare faced the prospect of no-confidence motions when the 18-month postelection grace period that had kept him immune from parliamentary challenges expired in February 2004. On January 21 he adjourned Parliament for five months while he tried to have his period of immunity extended to three years. In a move to improve stability, opposition leader Sir Mekere Morauta joined Somare's government in May. Parliament reconvened on June 29, but in early August Somare, citing concerns about security, declared another adjournment until November.

The search for a new governor-general continued for months after the Supreme Court ruled that the elections of Sir Albert Kipalan and Sir Pato Kakaraya were null and void. Acting Gov.-Gen. (and former prime minister) Bill Skate, who was acquitted on charges of misappropriation, stepped down during his two-day trial in March; he resigned in May. Sir Paulius Matane was elected by 50 members of Parliament as the new governor-general in May. He moved into the official residence with a mat, comb, razor blade, and clothes and pledged to leave with nothing more.

On June 29 Papua New Guinea and Australia formalized an Enhanced Cooperation Program worth $A 800 million (about U.S.$550 million) over five years. Some 300 Australian experts would work with Papua New Guineans in the local police, courts, and treasury and in the areas of health, border protection, immigration, customs, and civil aviation. In October delegates reached agreement on a draft constitution for the secessionist province of Bougainville. (A.R.G. GRIFFITHS)

© Reuters/Corbis

The fire-damaged food court of a supermarket in Asunción, Paraguay, sits empty on August 4, three days after a devastating blaze in which at least 300 people died and hundreds were injured when locked exits prevented their escape.

PARAGUAY

Area: 406,752 sq km (157,048 sq mi)
Population (2004 est.): 5,773,000
Capital: Asunción
Head of state and government: President Nicanor Duarte Frutos

Pres. Nicanor Duarte Frutos's reputation as a reformer intent on cleaning up cronyism, corruption, and contraband in Paraguay was seriously put to the test in 2004. In early February Duarte's plans to purge and modernize Paraguay's national police force were stymied as state prosecutors charged that top police officers who were investigating the robbery of $500,000 from the state-owned National Development Bank had plotted to steal part of the recovered booty. In March Duarte's campaign to reform the judiciary by retiring six of the nine Supreme Court justices ended in a disappointing throwback to the old backroom practice of political-party quotas and a division of high-court seats. The ruling Colorado Party took two seats, as did the main opposition party, the Authentic Radical Liberal Party, while a fifth seat went to Patria Querida. The latter seat was initially intended for the National Union of Ethical Citizens, the Colorado splinter group that followed cashiered and exiled Gen. Lino Oviedo.

General Oviedo had been charged with having masterminded the 1999 assassination of Vice Pres. Luis María Argaña and had been convicted on charges surrounding an attempted coup in 1996. Oviedo returned in June from exile in Brazil to contest the charges and reenter politics and was greeted by a tumultuous welcome from party supporters. The government promptly clapped Oviedo in prison to serve out his 10-year sentence for the 1996 coup attempt.

On August 1 a fire that raged through an Asunción supermarket crowded with weekend shoppers killed more than 300 people and injured hundreds, many of them children. Interior Ministry officials investigating the disaster said that many victims had been unable to escape the intense smoke and flames because the exits were locked, possibly to avoid robberies and prevent theft, a claim that the supermarket's owner denied. Investigators concluded that the fire started in a chimney in the food court. They focused on a possible short circuit and accidental fire, although the possibility of arson was not ruled out.

The year ended with former president Juan Carlos Wasmosy's charging that the U.S. embassy in Asunción was eavesdropping on the presidential residence, which was located across the street. (PAUL C. SONDROL)

PERU

Area: 1,285,216 sq km (496,225 sq mi)
Population (2004 est.): 27,544,000
Capital: Lima
Head of state and government: President Alejandro Toledo

In 2004 Peru exemplified a classic case of a less-developed country where the macro-level economic picture was bright but day-to-day political life posed enormous problems for its president, Alejandro Toledo. Most of Peru's economic indicators attested that the country was doing well. The GNP had been growing steadily between 3.5% and 4% annually for more than three years. Inflation was nowhere in sight, tax revenues were growing steadily, foreign reserves were at or near an all-time high, and as a general rule, foreign investors and international watchdogs, including the IMF, saw the country's prospects in a positive light overall. The long-awaited Camisea gas pipeline went on line in August, promising more revenues, and Peru was in the midst of multilateral discussions with the U.S. for a free-trade pact.

In political and social terms, however, the country was under considerable strain. President Toledo, whose term was due to expire in 2006, was surrounded by rumours and accusations of misconduct, including having had knowledge of the alleged falsification of signatures needed for his political party, Peru Posible, to meet legal requirements to appear on the 2000 presidential ballot. Several of his siblings were also under investigation for a variety of alleged wrongdoings. Moreover, some high-ranking members of his party had either bolted from the party or were threatening to do so. Roughly half the population continued to live below the poverty line, and unemployment and underemployment were constant concerns for many more. As a result, Toledo's approval ratings were frequently in the single digits, and a variety of newspapers and media outlets debated his right to serve or called for him to resign. Several polls taken during the year showed former president Alberto Fujimori finishing first or second among voters looking toward the 2006 elections. That Fujimori was a fugitive from justice, wanted on serious charges and being sought for extradition from Japan to Peru, made his popularity all the more unsettling.

In April special police arrive to take control of Ilave, where residents, protesting corruption in the municipal government, had kidnapped several people and lynched the mayor.

© Lino Chipana/El Comercio/Reuters/Corbis

The rule of law was also problematic in some areas. In April some Aymara residents of Ilave, a small city in the highland district of Puno near the Bolivian border, became outraged with the behaviour of their mayor and lynched him. At least partially as a result of this incident, Law 28222 was passed by the Peruvian Congress, allowing the military to take command over local police in cases of public disorder. The Ilave event was taken by some observers as evidence of the weakness of the Peruvian state and the inability to extend the rule of law into indigenous areas. Throughout much of the year, strikes and demonstrations took place, notably a march by coca farmers in early May, a strike by labour unions in July, and a prolonged strike by employees of the nation's judicial system.

Peru also saw some difficulties and contretemps in its foreign relations. A major dispute over the construction of a gas pipeline from Bolivia through Chile to the Pacific coast brought about severe political disruptions in Bolivia and resulted in negotiations between Bolivia and Peru about building the pipeline through Peruvian territory. (See: *Bolivia,* above.) Peru and Chile also had disagreements over maritime rights. In May Peru severed relations with Cuba after Cuban Pres. Fidel Castro criticized Lima for voting against Cuba's human rights record at the UN Human Rights Commission and for taking orders from the U.S. regarding its foreign policy. (HENRY A. DIETZ)

PHILIPPINES

Area: 316,076 sq km (122,121 sq mi)
Population (2004 est.): 82,670,000
Capital: Quezon City (designated national government centre and the location of the lower house of the legislature and some ministries); many government offices are in Manila or other suburbs
Head of state and government: President Gloria Macapagal Arroyo

Gloria Macapagal Arroyo was sworn in June 30, 2004, as president for a full six-year term after she defeated Fernando Poe, Jr., by more than a million votes in the May 10 Philippine election. She had already served three years as president. Arroyo campaigned on her record and on promises to improve the economy and reduce corruption. Poe, a movie star, was a high-school dropout with no political experience. He campaigned with other celebrities without offering a political program or being willing to debate issues. With politics in the Philippines widely being seen as show business, Arroyo chose a popular television newsman as her vice presidential candidate. Arroyo's record as president was widely criticized as inadequate, but Poe was considered by many as a front man for ousted former president Joseph Estrada and for supporters of another ousted president, the late Ferdinand Marcos. Church groups and regional leaders rallied to Arroyo during a violent campaign in which 115 people died in election-related bombings, assassinations, and brawls. Poe was defeated, but he argued that vote rigging and other illegal methods had been used by Arroyo. Not until

© Erik De Castro/Reuters/Corbis

Philippine Pres. Gloria Macapagal Arroyo, who was reelected to a full six-year term in the May 10 balloting, salutes during her formal inauguration ceremony in June.

a recount, a court rejection of Poe's protests, and an all-night session of the nation's Congress was Arroyo declared elected on June 24. Poe died of a stroke on December 13. (*See* OBITUARIES.)

In her inaugural speech Arroyo promised to crack down on widespread tax evasion; later, in a state of the nation address, she asked Congress to pass eight new tax bills in order to cut a public debt of more than $60 billion. She warned that the Philippines faced a financial crisis because of the government's spending 4–5% more than it brought in. Unemployment was estimated at 11%, and some eight million Filipinos had to go abroad to find jobs. Arroyo's efforts to push new taxes through Congress were seen by political observers as a test of both her leadership and the viability of the political system. Congress had in recent years been more absorbed in personal politics than in passing legislation. Both Arroyo and Poe advocated a constitutional change from the Philippines' American-style presidential system to one that included a prime minister who might better lead a legislature that operated with clear-cut party factions instead of shifting personal alliances.

Abu Sayyaf, a terrorist group that sought a separate Islamic state in the southern Philippines, exploded a bomb on a new ferry, the owners of which, officials said, refused to pay the terrorists protection money. The ferry sank in Manila Bay on February 26. Of some 900 persons aboard, 116 were killed or were missing. Officials said that the terrorists had trained with Jemaah Islamiyah, a Southeast Asian branch of al-Qaeda. Two terrorists were captured, including a man accused of having kidnapped three Americans in 2001 and beheaded one of them. In March police captured four Abu Sayyaf militants accused of planning to bomb shopping centres and trains around Manila. On April 8 in the far south, soldiers killed a top Abu Sayyaf commander. Abu Sayyaf militants and others escaped from a prison in the area two days later, despite army warnings of an escape plot, but some fugitives were soon killed or captured. Four storms raked the Philippines with heavy rain in late November and early December. They caused floods and mud slides along the country's Pacific coast east of Manila. Civil defense officials in mid-December indicated that the storms had killed 1,062 people and that 552 others were missing. (HENRY S. BRADSHER)

POLAND

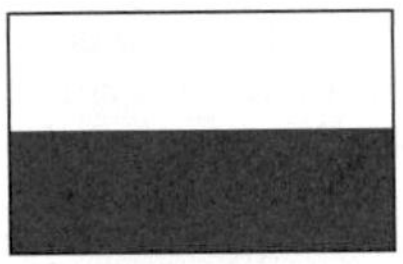

Area: 312,685 sq km (120,728 sq mi)
Population (2004 est.): 38,176,000
Capital: Warsaw
Chief of state: President Aleksander Kwasniewski
Head of government: Prime Ministers Leszek Miller and, from May 2, Marek Belka

Public debate in Poland in early 2004 focused on the country's place in the European Union, which it joined on May 1, and the new "double majority" voting system that would have reduced Poland's (and Spain's) voting powers in the EU. This issue united the political opposition against the ruling Democratic Left Alliance (SLD) for taking too soft a stance in the EU membership negotiations. SLD support had been declining anyway. Sleaze and political scandals had become hallmarks of Prime Minister Leszek Miller's government, which ironically had won office on an anticorruption platform. The party itself was beset by tensions, and in March a new left-wing group, the Polish Social Democracy party, split off. Miller stepped down, first as SLD chairman and later as prime minister, and former finance minister Marek Belka took over on May 2. Many people, however, felt that the SLD had lost its legitimacy and that therefore no socialist government would be acceptable, Belka won a parliamentary vote of confidence in June, but on the condition that another vote would be taken in October. Early elections were scheduled for May 2005 anyway, and opposition politicians immediately switched to election-campaign mode with populist declarations and attacks on the incumbents.

In September, in an almost unanimous vote, the Sejm (lower house of parliament) passed a resolution that the government should call for Germany to pay war reparations. From a legal point of view, such claims had no chance to be recognized, but, as subsequently revealed in a poll by *Rzeczpospolita,* a leading daily newspaper, 64% of Poles were in favour of extracting compensation for the Nazi depredations. Polish citizens were reacting to declarations of the right-wing Prussian Trust formed in Germany to secure and support claims by displaced Germans seeking damages for lost property in an area that was now part of Poland (parts of Silesia, Pomerania, and East Prussia). The Polish government, concerned about its cool relations with Germany (in part because of Poland's support of the U.S.-led war in Iraq), did not approve the parliamentary decision. A trip by Belka to Berlin and a follow-up visit by German Chancellor Gerhard Schröder with Belka in Krakow in November helped to ease these tensions. Pres. Aleksander Kwasniewski's visit to Russia in late September, however, could not warm relations with this important commercial partner that was unhappy about Poland's membership in the EU and NATO.

Farmers—formerly Euro-skeptics—happily welcomed the positive consequences of Poland's membership in the EU as the opening of new markets and broader demand for their products, and they eagerly awaited the first EU agricultural subsidy payments. There were also some signs that after years of stagnation the economy had started to pick up, even if improvement was mainly due to the depreciation of the zloty, which was keeping labour costs down. Poland's GDP rose by 6.9% year-on-year

Szymon Bolivar/AFP/Getty Images

In Warsaw potential investors eagerly await the chance to buy shares in the October initial public offering of the partially privatized PKO BP, Poland's largest bank.

in the first quarter of 2004 (up from 4.7% in the last three months of 2003) and by about 6% in the second half of the year. In mid-September, for the first time in three years, the number of unemployed sank below three million, or to 19%. In October the treasury floated 30% of Poland's largest bank, the state-owned PKO BP; this was the largest offering in the history of the fast-growing Warsaw Securities Exchange. A public-service regulation bill passed by the Council of Ministers provided for clearer and more competitive recruitment procedures for some 300,000 civil service positions. At almost the same time, the parliament heard the final report of the parliamentary committee investigating corruption at the government level, which confirmed the existence of a "group holding power" that included the closest associates of then prime minister Miller. PKN Orlen, Poland's largest fuel company, was the subject of another parliamentary investigation that found suspicious interconnections among business leaders, politicians, and top prosecutors.

In 2004 the world mourned the death of two outstanding Poles, Solidarity leader Jacek Kuron and Nobel Prize-winning author Czeslaw Milosz (*see* OBITUARIES) and bestowed top international prizes on two others, writer Adam Zagajewski and philosopher Leszek Kolakowski (*see* BIOGRAPHIES).

(IWONA GRENDA)

PORTUGAL

Area: 92,152 sq km (35,580 sq mi)
Population (2004 est.): 10,524,000
Capital: Lisbon
Chief of state: President Jorge Sampaio
Head of government: Prime Ministers José Manuel Durão Barroso and, from July 17, Pedro Santana Lopes

The year 2004 started off on a strong note in Portugal as the economy slowly began emerging from five quarters of recession and got an extra dose of optimism from two major events: the Rock in Rio international music festival in Lisbon from May 28 to June 6 and then the monthlong Euro 2004 European association football (soccer) championship. Portugal saw the organization and logistics of these crowd-pleasing events broadly praised by most international observers. Euro 2004 in particular brought a wave of patriotism as people decked their homes and cars with the national flag; the only bitter pill came in the final, held in Lisbon on July 4, in which Portugal was defeated 1–0 by underdog Greece. Despite that loss, the Portuguese considered the championship a success, as it brought in additional visitors and shone a favourable international spotlight on the country for the tournament's duration. Seven modern stadiums were purpose-built for Euro 2004 and another three totally renovated, vastly expanding the country's network of modern sports facilities.

On the political front, things were more complicated. After months of difficult, often heated negotiations to find a European Commission president to replace the outgoing Romano Prodi, the European Union finally turned to a candidate who had consensual support among the member states: Portuguese Prime Minister José Manuel Durão Barroso. (See *European Union,* above.) Barroso accepted, setting off a political crisis at home as his centre-right coalition squabbled with the three main opposition parties over the rules of succession. As Barroso left in midterm, his Social Democratic Party (PSD) and its Partido Popular (PP) coalition partner argued that they should be allowed to form a new government. The main opposition Socialist Party (PS), as well as the Portuguese Communist Party (PCP) and the Bloco Esquerda (BE), argued for a snap election to resolve the issue. It fell to Pres. Jorge Sampaio to make the final call, and after two weeks of consultations with party heads, constitutional experts, and other key public figures, Sampaio decided to let the ruling PSD/PP name a new government. Former Lisbon mayor and PSD vice president Pedro Santana Lopes was tapped as prime minister, and the coalition government included four ministers—including Finance Minister Antonio Bagão Félix—from the PP's ranks. Political analysts expected the new government to follow the broad outlines of policy set out by Barroso, though it was clear from a number of policy initiatives from the Santana Lopes government that a move was on to take advantage of a slightly stronger economy to deliver on some populist promises. While the draft budget for 2005 stressed the need for further fiscal consolidation and targeted a budget deficit of below 3% of GDP, it also included an above-inflation raise for public-sector workers and a small cut in income taxes. Economists and observers, including the Bank of Portugal, warned that any tax cuts would increase the risk of the budget deficit's swelling out of control. Bagão Félix said that there would be no recourse to one-off measures to keep the deficit below the EU's limit of 3% of GDP, which made it increasingly likely that the target would not be met in 2005.

Santana Lopes and the PSD/PP coalition faced the difficult task of balancing the need to bolster their slipping popularity in the polls while keeping the fragile economy on a recovery path and trying to implement much-needed reforms, such as overhauls of the health care and social security systems. The opposition PS, meanwhile, was gaining electoral momentum, even though the next scheduled general elections were not until 2006.

(ERIK T. BURNS)

QATAR

Area: 11,427 sq km (4,412 sq mi)
Population (2004 est.): 754,000
Capital: Doha
Head of state and government: Emir Sheikh Hamad ibn Khalifah al-Thani, assisted by Prime Minister Sheikh Abdullah ibn Khalifah al-Thani

Several achievements in 2004 underscored Qatar's continuing robust economic, social, and political development together with the further modernization of its system of governance. Qatar signed a Trade and Investment Framework Agreement with the U.S., an essential stepping-stone to a bilateral free-trade accord. The potential benefits—for the U.S. an assured long-term supply of the world's most prodigious and least-expensive sources of natural gas and for Qatar a deepening strategic energy relationship with the world's largest economy—highlighted the growing depth and diversity of their bilateral cooperation. In the educational and social fields, the establishment of branch campuses of five of the U.S.'s most prominent universities in Qatar's new Education City surpassed the previous norm for cooperative academic arrangements between countries worldwide. Qatar was also importing and applying these universities' exact standards for measuring academic achievement and awarding degrees in the fields of engineering, medicine, information technology, business administration, design, and educational planning. The breakthrough represented a first not only for the Arab countries, the Middle East, and the Islamic world but also for less-developed countries in general.

Qatar hosted the fourth annual international Conference on Free Trade and Democracy; the largest percentage of featured speakers and participants among the record 480 attendees were from Great Britain and France. The annual conference complemented other Qatari efforts involving the U.S. Middle East Partnership Initiative, which provided support for expanding education and economic reforms as well as human rights and democracy among Arab and Islamic countries.

(JOHN DUKE ANTHONY)

ROMANIA

Area: 238,391 sq km (92,043 sq mi)
Population (2004 est.): 21,549,000
Capital: Bucharest
Chief of state: Presidents Ion Iliescu and, from December 20, Traian Basescu
Head of government: Prime Ministers Adrian Nastase, Eugen Bejinariu (acting) from December 21, and, from December 29, Calin Popescu-Tariceanu

Romania's ruling Social Democratic Party (PSD) suffered unexpected heavy losses in local elections held on June 6 and 20, 2004. The winner by a narrow margin was the Truth and Justice Alliance, a centrist formation that appealed mainly to urban voters. Romania's entry into NATO in April and four years of improving economic indicators had little impact on social conditions. Most Romanians, including the professional middle class, survived on low incomes. Public corruption was endemic, and the average citizen spent about 10% of earnings on bribes.

The rhetorically left-wing PSD doubled as the party of the economic elite; about 300 people with close ties to the PSD controlled approximately one-quarter of GDP. In August the PSD nominated Prime Minister Adrian Nastase as its candidate for the November 28 presidential elections. The PSD's chief support base was found in rural and small-town communities in southern and eastern Romania, where the PSD (like the Communist Party before it) controlled nearly all the levers of local power.

Nastase received a boost in October when the European Union decided that Romania had acquired a functioning market economy, which paved the way for the completion of negotiations for EU entry. In November, however, the government was shaken by the revelation that the debts of the partly privatized oil industry, with a valuation of €400 million (about $520 million), had been covered up by the state since 2001. On November 24–25 Nastase suffered a reverse with the publication of transcripts of PSD meetings at which top officials had discussed how to suppress corruption charges against party notables by interfering in the justice system and how to utilize the state machinery to ensure the PSD's electoral victory.

In the November 28 election, the Alliance nearly doubled its percentage of the vote for the Chamber of Deputies to 31.3%, while the PSD and a small ally obtained 36.6% of the vote. Weaknesses in the electoral law, however, allowed widespread multiple voting on supplementary lists that catered to voters away from their home district on election day. Since no candidate had obtained an absolute majority, presidential elections went to a second round on December 12. The winner by the narrowest of margins was the Alliance's Traian Basescu, the mayor of Bucharest and a former sea captain.

Before taking office on December 20, Basescu said that defeating corruption would be the focus of his national security strategy. On December 16 Pres. Ion Iliescu had announced an amnesty for rapists, human traffickers, and individuals found guilty of repression in the 1989 revolution, which had brought about the collapse of communism. On December 17, however, he revoked the amnesty in the face of popular fury over the inclusion of Miron Cozma, who in 1999 had been sentenced to 18 years in prison for leading several attacks on public offices in the capital. Calin Popescu-Tariceanu of the Alliance was asked to form a government on December 21, and the new cabinet was approved by the parliament on December 28 and sworn in the following day. Top priorities included modernizing the country and reducing poverty.

(TOM GALLAGHER)

RUSSIA

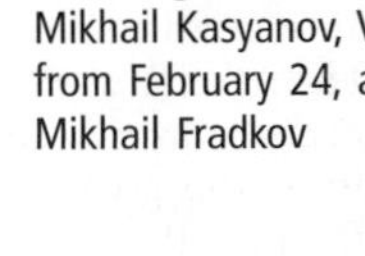

Area: 17,075,400 sq km (6,592,800 sq mi)
Population (2004 est.): 144,315,000
Capital: Moscow
Chief of state: President Vladimir Putin
Head of government: Prime Ministers Mikhail Kasyanov, Viktor Khristenko (acting) from February 24, and, from March 5, Mikhail Fradkov

Domestic Politics. Major political events in 2004 included a presidential election and a series of terrorist atrocities that provoked proposals for a sweeping consolidation of presidential power. In

© Gleb Garanich/Reuters/Corbis

In the village of Yar-Sale, north of the Arctic Circle, a Nenets woman votes for president on March 11. Citizens in remote regions of Russia cast their ballots in advance of the March 14 election.

March, Vladimir Putin was elected to a second presidential term. The outcome of the election was never in doubt, since none of the other five candidates represented serious opposition. Putin won handsomely in the first round with more than 70% of the votes cast (compared with 53% in 2000). International observers praised the professionalism with which the election had been organized but criticized the state-controlled media for their pro-Putin bias. Such criticisms aside, no one doubted that the election outcome accurately reflected the will of the majority of the Russian population.

In a surprise move three weeks before the election, Putin sacked the entire government. He appointed as prime minister a little-known technocrat, Mikhail Fradkov, who was associated with no political party. Commentators explained the move in terms of Putin's determination to conduct his second term in office standing on his own legs. Putin had come to power in 2000 as the anointed successor of Pres. Boris Yeltsin, and during his first term in office he had worked with members of the so-called Yeltsin "family," notably the outgoing prime minister, Mikhail Kasyanov, and the head of the Presidential Administration, Aleksandr Voloshin. Now Putin was his own man and no longer owed his position to Yeltsin. The policies he began to implement in his second term indicated that he was indeed a very different leader from his predecessor.

Putin's landslide victory put him in an extremely powerful position. The victory of the pro-presidential United Russia party in the December 2003 elections to the State Duma had already given his supporters a two-thirds majority in the lower house of the parliament and assured Putin of parliamentary approval for his legislative initiatives. Opposition parties were virtually eliminated. Liberals lamented the emasculation of the parliament and government and warned that while it might make it easier for the Kremlin to enact reforms, it would make it harder to ensure that the policies adopted were the right ones and, if they were not, to correct them after they had been adopted. The Kremlin's tightening grip on power, these observers argued, was incompatible with political pluralism and mature democracy. Other commentators pointed the finger not at Putin's centralizing policies but at the continuing weakness of civil society and the political indifference of the Russian population; in these circumstances, it was argued, strong central government was both inevitable and desirable. When Fradkov unveiled his new government, however, it turned out that many members of the former government had changed their titles but kept their jobs. In particular, the teams running the economic ministries and the security agencies remained in place. The stage was accordingly set for continuing clashes of opinion between liberal reformers, who advocated the lowest-possible level of state intervention in society and the economy, and the so-called *siloviki* ("men of power"), who favoured the reassertion of state control over the "commanding heights" of the economy.

In his annual address to the parliament on May 26, Putin laid out his priorities for his second term. These included consolidating the political stability established during his first four-year term and boosting economic growth to ensure that all members of the population would begin to benefit. Putin called on the government to raise the living standards of the poorest sections of society, modernize education and health care, create an affordable housing market, and establish an effective mortgage-finance system. Putin spoke of the importance of democracy but at the same time accused human rights groups that had been critical of his record of "receiving funding from influential foreign and domestic foundations" and "serving dubious groups and commercial interests."

Human rights activists and liberal journalists were particularly critical of what they saw as the Kremlin's efforts to control the mass media, which led during the summer to the cancellation of Russian TV's last live discussion program. Following a terrorist attack on a Russian school in September, the editor of one of Russia's leading newspapers was forced to resign on the grounds that his paper had published information that could have aided the terrorists. In another blow to media freedom—though there was no suggestion of Kremlin involvement in this event—Paul Klebnikov, editor of the Russian edition of *Forbes* magazine, was gunned down in Moscow in July; Klebnikov was the first Western journalist to have been killed in Russia since 1996.

There was no letup in the separatist conflict in the North Caucasus republic of Chechnya. Moscow continued its policy of "Chechenization"—that is, the gradual transfer of responsibility for public administration to Moscow-approved members of the Chechen community. February saw the assassination in Qatar of exiled Chechen separatist Zelimkhan Yanderbiyev; two Russian intelligence officers were tried and sentenced to life imprisonment for the murder. In May, Chechnya's pro-Moscow president, Akhmad Kadyrov, was assassinated by a bomb in the republic's capital, Grozny. An election for a new president was held on August 29 and was won by a landslide by Moscow's

© Eduard Kornienko/Reuters/Corbis

Chechen Pres. Alu Alkhanov is shown at his inauguration in Grozny, the capital, on October 5. Alkhanov's predecessor and a leading Chechen rebel leader were assassinated during the year.

preferred candidate, former interior minister Alu Alkhanov.

The summer saw an escalation of terrorist attacks on Russian targets. In each case Chechen separatists claimed responsibility. These included the nearly simultaneous midair explosions in August of two Russian commercial aircraft that killed all 90 people aboard, an August suicide bombing outside a Moscow subway station, and in September a siege at a provincial school in Beslan, North Ossetia, in which over 1,000 people were held hostage and more than 330 died, nearly half of them children. The scale of the violence at Beslan, and, in particular, the fact that the terrorists deliberately targeted young children, traumatized public opinion and horrified the outside world. The failure of the law-enforcement agencies to prevent these atrocities shook public confidence, and there was even some muted criticism of Putin himself.

In September, following the Beslan massacre, Putin proposed a set of measures that would, he said, strengthen the Russian state against the terrorist threat. These included a proposal that regional governors no longer be popularly elected but instead be appointed by the president, subject to endorsement by regional legislatures, which the president would be empowered to dissolve if they rejected his nominations on two occasions. The legislation, which was approved by overwhelming majorities in both houses of the parliament, returned Russia to the unitary system of government that had existed prior to the collapse of the U.S.S.R. in 1991. It was therefore seen as a sign that Putin was abandoning the attempts made by Yeltsin to turn Russia into a federation in substance as well as in name. Putin also proposed that candidates standing on party lists only, and not independents, in the future be allowed to run for the parliament. These proposals were met with dismay by many both inside and outside Russia. Liberals warned that they would remove the last checks on presidential power, that Russia was too large and ethnically diverse to be ruled from a single centre, and that in a country where parties were weakly developed, confining elections to party lists could weaken democracy.

In July 17-year-old Mariya Sharapova became the first Russian woman to win the singles All-England (Wimbledon) tennis championships, while in September 19-year-old Svetlana Kuznetsova became the first Russian tennis player to win the U.S. Open women's championship.

The Economy. The economy recorded its sixth consecutive year of growth since the prolonged output collapse of 1989–98. For 2004 as a whole, GDP was projected to grow at a rate of 6.6%, compared with the 7.3% achieved in 2003. Growth was boosted by record world oil prices, which generated big export revenues for Russia. High energy prices were the result partly of growing demand, partly of uncertainty over supplies from the conflict-ridden Middle East, and partly, ironically enough, of nervousness over the fate of Russian oil giant Yukos. As a result, Russia maintained a high trade surplus and was able to meet its external-debt repayments ahead of schedule. Inflation continued to decline, albeit slowly, and was projected at somewhat over 11% over the year. The state budget recorded its fifth successive surplus. For much of the year, Russia continued to accumulate foreign-currency reserves, which exceeded a year's supply of merchandise imports. At the same time, sovereign foreign debt fell relative to GDP and was below a quarter of the national income. Thus, the economy not only was growing robustly but also had high international liquidity, which made it sounder than at any other time since 1991.

Behind the impressive macroeconomic headlines, however, there was growing concern about the Putin leadership's turn toward a more interventionist economic policy. Dominating the year was the trial, on charges of fraud and tax evasion, of Mikhail Khodorkovsky, former CEO of Yukos. Liberals criticized the trial as politically motivated and legally unsound. They accused the Kremlin of seeking to bankrupt or break up the oil company in order to reestablish control over the "commanding heights" of the Russian economy—that is, the key natural resource-exporting branches: oil, gas, and metals. This raised as-yet-unanswered questions about the Kremlin's attitude toward big business as a whole. During the summer there were indeed signs that the Kremlin was tightening rather than loosening its control as officials from the presidential administration replaced government officials in leading posts in the energy and other sectors, and the end of the year saw the state effectively renationalize Yukos's core assets.

© Eduard Kornienko/Reuters/Corbis

Russian women tennis players dominated international competition in 2004. Shown here in Los Angeles in November are (left to right) Vera Zvonareva, Svetlana Kuznetsova, Mariya Sharapova, and Anastasiya Myskina.

Concern was also raised when regions were stripped of the right to issue licenses to exploit subsoil resources, particularly oil, gas, and ores. Liberals saw this too as an indication that the Putin administration intended to centralize economic management, and some analysts detected signs of an increase in capital flight. A sustained increase in capital flight would tend to reduce the growth of investment and ultimately of output.

Putin put his main focus on the economy when he delivered his annual address to the parliament in May. He repeated the pledge, which he had first made in 2003, to double Russia's GDP within 10 years (though the precise target date was never specified) and to improve the living conditions of the many Russians who had yet to feel the benefit of the market reforms of the 1990s. Meeting Putin's target would require an average annual growth rate of 7.5%. (Doubling GDP by 2010 would bring Russia within striking distance of current living standards in European countries such as the Czech Republic, Hungary, and Slovenia, but it would have to double its GDP once again before it would catch up with current levels in leading industrialized nations such as Denmark, Switzerland, or The Netherlands.) Putin also called on the government to ensure that the ruble would become fully convertible by 2006, average annual incomes would grow by 150% by 2008, and at least one-third of Russians would have the opportunity to purchase affordable housing by 2010. He urged the government to work harder to push inflation to 3%—well below its target of 10% for 2004. He promised to maintain low rates of taxation but called for further reform of the tax system to prevent the abuse of so-called tax-optimization schemes.

Significant progress was made in 2004 toward Russia's accession to the World Trade Organization (WTO). In May Moscow secured the approval of the EU; this was expected to facilitate negotiations with leading WTO members, including the United States. Following the agreement with the EU, Russia ratified the Kyoto Protocol, an international agreement intended to control the emission of greenhouse gases believed to cause global warming. Putin also announced that in exchange for an EU undertaking to minimize the negative consequences of EU enlargement for the Russian economy, Russia would reduce import duties, open its banking, telecommunications, and insurance markets to European companies, and gradually increase domestic gas prices. Meanwhile, Moscow secured China's provisional agreement to Russia's WTO accession in a deal reported to include promises of a pipeline to China and low oil prices.

July saw the parliament approve controversial legislation to replace social benefits dispensed in kind, such as free transportation and prescription drugs, with monetary payments. The legislation was unpopular with many sections of the population, especially pensioners, veterans, and the disabled. It was also unwelcome for regional governments, because it put most of the burden of financing such payments onto them. The changes in the way social benefits were awarded provoked angry demonstrations in many parts of the country. Eventually a compromise was reached in which the monetary value of the benefits was increased and recipients were given the choice of taking the benefits, as of 2006, in money or kind.

Foreign, Military, and Security Policy. On the whole, Russia's relations with the outside world remained good. President Putin continued to place the greatest emphasis on rebuilding close relations with the other 11 members of the Commonwealth of Independent States (CIS)—that is, the other former Soviet states on or close to Russia's borders (the Baltic states of Estonia, Latvia, and Lithuania excepted). He did so, however, not through the unwieldy mechanism of the CIS itself but through the pursuit of smaller bilateral or multilateral alliances within the CIS framework, such as the Single Economic Space consisting of Russia, Belarus, Kazakhstan, and Ukraine. Relations with neighbouring Georgia remained volatile.

Moscow responded calmly in the spring when the three Baltic states, which had until 1991 been part of the U.S.S.R., joined the EU and NATO. Under the impact of the Chechen terrorist atrocities, Russia's relations with several leading Western states came under strain. Following the Beslan siege, Russia announced that it reserved the right to take preemptive action—the use of nuclear weapons alone excepted—against terrorists inside or outside Russia; commentators pointed out that this was not a new departure. Despite Putin's emotional reaction immediately following the Beslan siege, when he accused foreign states of encouraging terrorism in order to dismantle the Russian Federation, he enthusiastically endorsed the reelection of U.S. Pres. George W. Bush in November. At the end of the year, however, Russia's relations with both the U.S. and the EU were strained by mutual accusations of interference in Ukraine's fiercely contested presidential election.

Russia's security and intelligence services preserved their dominant position in the Kremlin corridors of power. Amendments to the Law on Defense seemed set to change the structure of the military high command by significantly reducing the role of the General Staff in controlling the armed forces; until then, the General Staff had been effectively coequal with the Ministry of Defense, and infighting between the two had hindered efforts at military reform. At the beginning of the year, a law on alternative service came into effect that allowed conscripts for the first time to choose civilian instead of military service. (ELIZABETH TEAGUE)

RWANDA

Area: 26,338 sq km (10,169 sq mi)
Population (2004 est.): 8,380,000
Capital: Kigali
Head of state and government: President Maj. Gen. Paul Kagame, assisted by Prime Minister Bernard Makuza

The year 2004 marked the 10th anniversary of the genocide in Rwanda that killed nearly a million Tutsi and moderate Hutu. Solemn commemorations attended by Rwandans and African leaders, with Europe and the United States represented by junior officials, were held in locations throughout the country during April, the month in which the 100-day massacre began. The French junior foreign minister, Renaud Muselier, cut short his visit during commemorations after Pres. Paul Kagame accused France of complicity in the genocide. Former higher education minister Jean de Dieu Kamuhanda received a life sentence for genocide in January at the International Criminal Tribunal for Rwanda (ICTR) in Arusha, Tanz. Several high-profile genocide suspects were captured or sentenced during the year, including senior Interahamwe (Hutu terrorist militia) councillor Ephrem Nkezabera, who was arrested in June.

© Gianluigi Guercia/AFP/Getty Images

Rwandan Pres. Paul Kagame (left) and Yoweri Museveni, his Ugandan counterpart, hold roses to be placed on the graves at the Gisozi Genocide Memorial on April 7 during the 10th-anniversary commemoration of the 1994 genocide.

Nine people were sentenced to death and one to life imprisonment for the killing of a genocide survivor who had been scheduled to testify at the ICTR.

Thirty thousand accused prisoners were granted amnesty and freed in March after they confessed guilt and asked forgiveness for having committed acts of genocide. Rwandan prisons still held nearly 90,000 alleged *genocidaires.* Amnesties were not wholly supported by survivors, who believed that those who confessed were not genuinely sorry for what they had done but used the amnesty to escape justice.

Rwanda came close to war with the Democratic Republic of the Congo (DRC) in June when Congolese rebels captured Bukavu, a DRC town near the Rwandan border. DRC Pres. Joseph Kabila accused Rwanda of backing the rebels, an accusation vigorously denied by the Rwandans. Tensions between the two countries had continued since 1998, when Rwanda's military occupied eastern Congo. British and American envoys were sent to the DRC in late June to quell violence and smooth relations. A UN report later accused Rwanda of breaching an arms embargo and of supporting the rebels. Both Burundi and Rwanda threatened to invade the DRC to disarm rebels after the August massacre of ethnically Tutsi Congolese refugees by a DRC militia in a Burundi camp. The Kinshasa and Kigali governments attempted to repair relations by agreeing to disarm groups in both countries and to address border security during August and September, but these efforts were jeopardized late in September by renewed attacks in the eastern DRC allegedly carried out by a Rwandan Hutu extremist militia based in the area. In December Rwanda made several invasion threats amid reports that its soldiers had already entered the DRC. Rwanda denied troop involvement and later backed off its threats.

(MARY F.E. EBELING)

SAINT KITTS AND NEVIS

Area: 269 sq km (104 sq mi)
Population (2004 est.): 46,300
Capital: Basseterre
Chief of state: Queen Elizabeth II, represented by Governor-General Sir Cuthbert Montraville Sebastian
Head of government: Prime Minister Denzil Douglas

In August 2004 the Kuwait Fund for Arab Economic Development agreed to provide about $5.5 million to Saint Kitts and Nevis for a second cruise-ship pier at Port Zante. Prime Minister Denzil Douglas noted that the pier would enhance the territory's tourism industry. In September Saint Kitts and Nevis accepted a $1.4 million check from Taiwan to help fund construction of a new world-class sports complex. The money was the first installment of a $12 million assistance package agreed to during Douglas's visit to Taiwan in November 2003.

Tough new anticrime measures were announced in August in an attempt to curb a growing wave of lawlessness. The previous month an armed gang had attacked a Brinks security vehicle and stolen more than $133,000 (a record haul in Saint Kitts), while 17 murders had been committed in the first eight months of the year. The government's response was to institute joint police-army patrols, stop-and-search operations, and expanded sea surveillance.

Douglas won reelection to a third term in National Assembly voting on October 25 as his Saint Kitts-Nevis Labour Party captured seven of Saint Kitts's eight seats. The Concerned Citizens Movement gained two of the three seats on Nevis. (DAVID RENWICK)

SAINT LUCIA

Area: 617 sq km (238 sq mi)
Population (2004 est.): 164,000
Capital: Castries
Chief of state: Queen Elizabeth II, represented by Governor-General Dame Pearlette Louisy
Head of government: Prime Minister Kenny Anthony

Like many other states in the region, Saint Lucia found itself in the path of Hurricane Ivan, the most destructive storm of the 2004 hurricane season. Though the hurricane changed course and hit Grenada instead, as much as 35% of the vital banana crop was destroyed by tropical-storm-force winds.

Antiabortion activists wrote to Pope John Paul II to request that a papal honour not be conferred on Julian R. Hunte, the country's minister of external affairs, in September. Though a staunch Roman Catholic, Hunte, as a member of Saint Lucia's parliament, had been instrumental in the passage of amendments to the criminal code that made abortion legal under certain circumstances. Hunte had a high international profile and in September completed his term as president of the 58th session of the UN General Assembly. He was replaced as minister of external affairs and returned to his previous role as St. Lucia's ambassador to the UN.

A sharp disagreement over the role of external institutions and governments in the financing of political parties in Saint Lucia arose in September when Prime Minister Kenny Anthony challenged Vaughan Lewis, leader of the opposition United Workers' Party (UWP), over a letter the latter had written to a political organization in the U.S., requesting support for the UWP. Anthony strongly cautioned against the practice.

Saint Lucia signed an economic and technological cooperation agreement with Beijing in September. The deal, which included $3.65 million in aid from China, was the latest in the seven-year diplomatic relationship between the two countries. (DAVID RENWICK)

SAINT VINCENT AND THE GRENADINES

Area: 389 sq km (150 sq mi)
Population (2004 est.): 113,000
Capital: Kingstown
Chief of state: Queen Elizabeth II, represented by Governor-General Sir Frederick Ballantyne
Head of government: Prime Minister Ralph Gonsalves

During 2004 Saint Vincent and the Grenadines continued to be an attractive location for international business companies (IBCs), which operated under generous tax incentives. By the end of April, according to an official count, 357 new IBCs had been registered in the country, compared with 194 in 2003.

The country drew closer to Taiwan, even though this flew in the face of majority opinion among Caribbean states, most of which had long accepted Beijing as the legitimate government of China. In August–September a private-sector delegation visited Taiwan to drum up investment. The delegation also included representatives from National Investment Promotion Inc., an agency set up as a one-stop shop for direct foreign investment in Saint Vincent and the Grenadines. In October, Prime Minister Ralph Gonsalves traveled to Taipei to meet with Taiwanese Pres. Chen Shui-bian.

Compared with other Caribbean territories such as Haiti, Jamaica, and Grenada, Saint Vincent and the Grenadines was lucky to escape the worst of Hurricane Ivan's wrath in September. Houses, bridges, and roads did suffer some damage, however, and Prime Minister Gonsalves said he would ask the World Bank and the Caribbean Development Bank to assess the cost of reconstructing public assets. (DAVID RENWICK)

SAMOA

Area: 2,831 sq km (1,093 sq mi)
Population (2004 est.): 183,000
Capital: Apia
Chief of state: *O le Ao o le Malo* (Head of State) Malietoa Tanumafili II
Head of government: Prime Minister Tuila'epa Sa'ilele Malielegaoi

In January 2004 Cyclone Heta brushed Samoa, causing serious damage, though little loss of life, on coastal Savai'i. Most of the damage was to crops and houses; many Samoans were left homeless, and food shortages occurred. The disaster prompted China to offer $120,000 in aid. The cyclone (and the severe drought conditions later in the year) contributed to a continuing economic decline that had seen Samoan GDP growth fall from 6% to 2% over recent years. Exports had fallen by 10% in 2003 compared with 2002, with fishing and tourism most affected. Despite increased returns from the garment industry, the balance of trade declined. In August workers broke ground for a much-anticipated hotel complex on Taumeasina Island.

In July thousands of demonstrators protested the refusal of New Zealand, a former administering power, to repeal a law that had stripped Samoans of their dual citizenship and denied them visa-free entry. On August 5–7 Samoa hosted the Pacific Islands Forum, which focused on the economic collapse of Nauru, the rebuilding of a government in Solomon Islands, and concerns over the ability of small island states to maintain border security. In October the UN-sponsored regional forum on Reinventing Government in the Pacific Islands was held in Apia. (BARRIE MACDONALD)

SAN MARINO

Area: 61.2 sq km (23.6 sq mi)
Population (2004 est.): 29,400
Capital: San Marino
Heads of state and government: The republic is governed by two *capitani reggenti* (coregents) appointed every six months by a popularly elected Great and General Council.

Oceanian leaders gather for a group photograph on August 7, during the 35th Pacific Islands Forum meeting in Apia, Samoa. The group discussed a number of economic and political problems.

© Kym Smith/Newspix via Getty Images

In October 2004 a congress was held that brought together delegates from the 24 San Marino "communities" abroad. The congress was intended to forge stronger links between the republic and the extensive expatriate community, distributed among such wide-ranging locations as Argentina and the U.S. Not only were citizens who lived abroad pressing for a greater voice in domestic political affairs, but so were women. Only 10 women sat on San Marino's 60-seat legislative assembly, the Great and General Council, and various calls were made for incentives to be given to political parties that were successful in promoting women candidates.

Delegates from San Marino attended the meeting of the Inter-Parliamentary Union, held September 28–October 1 in Geneva. The IPU brought together 112 sovereign states in order to press for worldwide advocacy of such issues as biodiversity and multilateral disarmament.

San Marino continued to be an economic oasis in the turbulent Italian peninsula, although its unemployment rate, while still half the EU average, had increased since 2001. Part of this rise was ascribed to setbacks in the crucial banking sector, prompted by increasing competition and a recent tax amnesty that encouraged Italians to withdraw their savings from San Marino banks. (GREGORY O. SMITH)

SÃO TOMÉ AND PRÍNCIPE

Area: 1,001 sq km (386 sq mi)
Population (2004 est.): 142,000
Capital: São Tomé
Chief of state: President Fradique de Menezes
Head of government: Prime Ministers Maria das Neves and, from September 18, Damião Vaz d'Almeida

After a failed army coup in the summer of 2003, São Tomé and Príncipe Pres. Fradique de Menezes gradually reestablished his authority in the small, potentially oil-rich country. He entered into especially close relations with neighbouring Nigeria, and the two countries set up an agency to administer the Joint Development Zone (JDZ) between them. In July 2004 de Menezes and Nigerian Pres. Olusegun Obasanjo signed a pact on governance in the JDZ that required all payments by oil companies to be made public.

With the army now seen as a priority, military pay was increased and the main barracks were improved. The United States, much concerned with oil exports from the Gulf of Guinea, organized military exercises and training for the army. Portugal and Angola supplied equipment and training. In July President de Menezes accused the ruling party of trying to undermine good relations with Angola. This was after party leader Manuel Pinto da Costa had said that the poverty that engulfed more than half of the country's population was creating an explosive situation. Political tension within the ruling elite further increased when the attorney general opened an anticorruption inquiry into the office managing foreign-aid funds. (CHRISTOPHER SAUNDERS)

SAUDI ARABIA

Area: 2,149,690 sq km (830,000 sq mi)
Population (2004 est.): 24,580,000
Capital: Riyadh
Head of state and government: King Fahd, assisted by Crown Prince Abdullah

The issue that dominated Saudi Arabian internal affairs in 2004 was the official campaign against anti-Western Islamist groups accused of carrying out acts of sabotage in the kingdom and abroad. The authorities even cracked down on charitable organizations accused of funding suspected radical groups. The al-Haramain Islamic Foundation, one of the largest nongovernmental charitable organizations in Saudi Arabia, was disbanded in early October, and its 250 employees were sacked. The organization, which was founded in Pakistan by Aqil al-Aqil, had first been accused of funding terrorism in 2002 by the U.S. authorities. The terrorist organization al-Qaeda was linked to the killings of a number of Westerners in Saudi Arabia throughout the year, including three Americans in June, and al-Qaeda leaders declared that such killings were a message for foreigners to leave Saudi territory. Saudi security forces killed a number of al-Qaeda operatives, and a few high-profile members gave themselves up under a limited amnesty offer. Muslim militants stormed the U.S. consulate in Jeddah on December 6 and killed five non-American staff members before Saudi forces shot dead three attackers and captured two to regain control.

The government carried on with its program for internal reform in two ways. The first was to agree to hold municipal elections, the first in decades, in various parts of the country from February 10 to April 21, 2005. Women, however, would still not be allowed to

© Sultan al-Fahd/Reuters/Corbis

On April 21 a rescue worker surveys the damage done by a suicide car bomber to a government security forces building in Riyadh, Saudi Arabia. Sporadic anti-Western acts of violence took place throughout the year.

vote. The second measure was to combat militant Islamism by creating new jobs. This was to be done, according to news reports, by making jobs in the private sector traditionally held by foreigners more available to Saudis. At present only 13% of the private-sector workforce—800,000 people—was Saudi, far below the 45% goal of the government for 2004.

Although the beginning of 2004 witnessed some strain in Saudi-American relations, there was a thaw in tensions by midyear. In September the U.S. Department of State added Saudi Arabia to its list of the world's most religiously intolerant nations, though Secretary of State Colin Powell tried to soft-pedal the message and mollify the Saudis.

A budget surplus of about $35 billion was forecast in 2004. Economists welcomed a government decision to earmark $11 billion in windfall oil revenues to development projects and to allocate $8 billion into a safety reserve fund with the aim of protecting the budget against drops in oil revenues in the future. Most of the remaining surplus was to be spent on repaying part of the public debt, which reached $176 billion, or about 90% of GDP. The country posted a $12 billion surplus for the 2003 fiscal year, the first nondeficit budget since 2000. After the steep rise in prices of crude oil in the summer, the Saudi authorities announced that the kingdom would increase production capacity from 9.5 million to 11 million bbl a day starting in early October.

(MAHMOUD HADDAD)

SENEGAL

Area: 196,722 sq km (75,955 sq mi)
Population (2004 est.): 10,339,000
Capital: Dakar
Chief of state: President Abdoulaye Wade, assisted by Prime Ministers Idrissa Seck and, from April 21, Macky Sall

Citing the need to restore unity in the government, Pres. Abdoulaye Wade sacked Prime Minister Idrissa Seck on April 21, 2004, and replaced him with former interior minister Macky Sall. Seck had been increasingly portrayed in the media as a possible challenger to

On August 23 in Dakar, the Senegalese capital, a statue is unveiled to celebrate the participation of African riflemen in the French military during World War II.

Wade's leadership. In June President Wade announced that, effective in 2005, he would introduce legislation to provide public funding of political parties. On July 9 Madiambal Diagne, editor of the newspaper *Le Quotidien,* was arrested after having published an article about government corruption. In protest, on July 12 all of Senegal's privately owned newspapers ceased publication, and private radio stations canceled their newscasts. In July Senegal battled swarms of locusts that had invaded the country.

On May 27 the cabinet unanimously approved the principle of granting amnesty to members of the secessionist Movement of the Democratic Forces of Casamance (MFDC). Relevant legislation would be put before the National Assembly at its next session. The World Bank announced on September 9 that it would give Senegal a $20 million credit to assist in the reconstruction of the Casamance region and the demobilization and reintegration into society of an estimated 2,000 MFDC fighters and their families. On December 30 the government and the MFDC signed a peace deal, though several factions within the movement opposed the accord. President Wade attended ceremonies in Toulon, France, to commemorate the 60th anniversary of the liberation of Provence and called on the French government to give African combat veterans pensions equal to those of their French comrades. On August 13 Wade announced the establishment of an annual Day of the Senegalese Rifles to honour the generations of African soldiers whose history had been ignored or unknown to most of the people of France.

(NANCY ELLEN LAWLER)

SERBIA AND MONTENEGRO

Area: 102,173 sq km (39,449 sq mi)
Population (2004 est.): 10,826,000, including 1,900,000 persons in the UN interim-administrated region of Kosovo
Administrative centres: Belgrade (Serbia) and Podgorica (Montenegro)
Chief of state: President Svetozar Marovic
Head of government: Prime Ministers Zoran Zivkovic and, from March 3, Vojislav Kostunica (Serbia) and Milo Djukanovic (Montenegro)

Some promising signs of political stability emerged in Serbia in 2004 amid the worst outbreak of interethnic violence since 1999 in the predominantly ethnic Albanian Kosovo area. Despite the obvious split among Serbs, Montenegrins, ethnic Albanians, and other minorities, the results of presidential and local elections indicated that Serbia's fragile political landscape continued to follow the reform-oriented direction it had adopted after Slobodan Milosevic's ouster in October 2000. Major Serbian leaders continued to withhold cooperation with the United Nations International Criminal Tribunal for the Former Yugoslavia. A growing number of government officials, however, were eager to win Serbia's entry into the EU and NATO and were pushing for cooperation with international investigators.

In March the first formal talks took place between representatives of Serbia and Kosovo since the end of the 1999 war; the focus of the talks was on issues such as low energy supplies, missing persons, the return of Serbian refugees to Kosovo, and trade between

© Ermal Meta/AFP/Getty Images

A NATO Kosovo Force armoured personnel carrier patrols the streets of Pristina, Kosovo, on October 22, the day before elections were held for a new parliament. The balloting was boycotted by most Serbs.

the two entities. Ethnic Albanian and Serbian leaders remained divided over Kosovo's final status. Though the region was under UN administration and under the protection of some 19,000 NATO peacekeepers, the ethnic Albanian majority continued to insist on independence, while Serbia fiercely opposed the idea. Serbian Prime Minister Vojislav Kostunica reaffirmed Belgrade's position that Serbia would not let Kosovo gain independence and proposed a "partition or cantonization," which he called the "decentralization" of Kosovo along ethnic lines. The Albanians rejected the idea on the grounds that it would have led to Kosovo's partition and given Serbs the mineral-rich north region of (Kosovska) Mitrovica, where about 60,000 Serbs lived and Albanians were a minority.

Kostunica's plan came on the heels of three days of violence in early March that drove more than 4,000 Serbs and Roma (Gypsies) from their homes and claimed some 30 lives, mostly those of Serbs. NATO commanders likened the violence to ethnic cleansing, and the UN's top official in Kosovo, Harri Holkeri, stated that the violence had been "orchestrated" by Albanian extremists. A report in May by the Organization for Security and Co-operation in Europe accused major Albanian-language broadcasters of having incited the vengeful mood and violence through "sloppy and biased reporting." The Serbs responded by boycotting the October parliamentary elections, which analysts said could deprive the Serbs of legitimate leaders to participate in any future talks on Kosovo's status. In the balloting for the 120-seat Kosovo assembly, Pres. Ibrahim Rugova's party, the pro-independence Democratic League of Kosovo, won the most seats but not enough for a parliamentary majority. In December, Ramush Haradinaj, a former rebel commander, was elected prime minister of Kosovo. The Serbs objected, but the UN refused to annul the election, and Belgrade broke off formal negotiations with the ethnic Albanians.

The events also raised concerns about how deep the divisions had become after several years of international efforts, at a cost estimated at some $40 billion, to rebuild the infrastructure and reconcile hostilities. Unemployment fluctuated around 60–70%, and pervasive poverty exacerbated ethnic tensions. The attempt to make a smoother transition from a socialist to a market-oriented economy was also complicated by Kosovo's ambivalent legal position. International investors saw Kosovo's unresolved political status as far too risky.

In June—after four failed attempts within two years—Boris Tadic was elected president of Serbia. Tadic, who had succeeded Zoran Djindjic as leader of the opposition Democratic Party after Djindjic was assassinated in March 2003, defeated Tomislav Nikolic of the nationalist Serbian Radical Party. Both parties effectively divided power between them in municipal elections held in September and October.

Tadic's victory was expected to boost the country's stalled reform initiatives, help stabilize the overall political situation, and give a jump start to Kostunica's reform efforts. Tadic's pledge to build a pro-democracy consensus was backed by Kostunica, head of the conservative Democratic Party of Serbia. Tadic and Kostunica pledged not to call early elections but rather to work on adopting a new constitution, but by year's end their cooperative spirit was beset by disagreements.

Few analysts believed that the new government could quickly halt the slide into deeper recession. After payment of enormous sums of money to social services agencies and support for indebted state companies, a budget surplus was not expected for 2004. Unemployment officially stood at 30%, but economists warned that the true rate was higher than 40%. Foreign investment fell, though Serbia still attracted some $500 million, notably as a result of the sale of state tobacco companies to Philip Morris and British American Tobacco. It was not clear how much Belgrade paid on the more than $700 million due to service its $13 billion foreign debt.

The state union of Serbia and Montenegro yielded little progress in reconciling differences over the future relations of the two republics. They failed to take steps toward creating a single-market economy, implementing joint reforms to the judiciary and police, or cooperating with the UN war crimes tribunal, all required for EU membership. The Montenegrin government was forced to shelve plans for a referendum on independence; polls showed a steady decline of support among Montenegrins, and the EU imposed an indefinite ban on such a move.

In July progress was reported as the state union adopted a new defense doctrine in which Serbia and Montenegro agreed to focus its defense strategy entirely on integration with the West and stressed Belgrade's new determination to join NATO's Partnership for Peace. The new defense doctrine identified terrorism and organized crime as the biggest security threats facing the state union. As part of a broader defense-reform plan, Belgrade also started reducing the number of military facilities and personnel, as well as cutting back on equipment.

(MILAN ANDREJEVICH)

SEYCHELLES

Area: 455 sq km (176 sq mi)
Population (2004 est.): 81,800
Capital: Victoria
Head of state and government: Presidents France-Albert René and, from April 14, James Michel

On Feb. 24, 2004, Pres. France-Albert René, who had served as the president of Seychelles for 27 years and was the longest-serving head of state in the Commonwealth, announced to the parliament that he would leave office early. The news came as a surprise; President René had declared in 2003 that he would step down from office in 2006, at the end of his third term. René had come to power in 1977 after mounting a coup against James Mancham, Seychelles's first democratically elected president. Since 1993 Seychelles had embraced a multiparty democracy. Vice Pres. James Michel was sworn into office on April 14 to replace René. President Michel inherited a serious budget deficit and a national economy that had been in recession for more than 10 years, a condition that critics blamed on years of René's socialist policies. The opposition Seychelles National Party (PNS) welcomed the new president but warned that the worsening economy needed to be addressed. René remained chairman of the ruling party, the Seychelles People's Progressive Front (FPPS), which held 23 of the 34 seats in the National Assembly. As part of a crackdown on Seychelles's illegal trade in endangered wildlife, in May six men were sentenced to prison for poaching rare sea turtles. In late December the country was struck by a tsunami that caused some $30 million in damages.

(MARY F.E. EBELING)

SIERRA LEONE

Area: 71,740 sq km (27,699 sq mi)
Population (2004 est.): 5,168,000
Capital: Freetown
Head of state and government: President Ahmad Tejan Kabbah

During most of 2004 Sierra Leone, with the help of the UN, was preoccupied with the Special Court for Sierra Leone (SCSL) war-crimes tribunal. A number of cases were heard involving the leading members of the rebel Revolutionary United Front (RUF) and the government's Civil Defence Force (CDF)—those most responsible for the atrocities that had been committed on civilians during the 11-year civil war that ended in 2002 after having claimed more than 50,000 lives and left 500,000 others directly affected by violence. In mid-March the tribunal faced a crisis when its president, Geoffrey Robertson, was asked to step down because of alleged bias. Prior to his appointment to the tribunal, Robertson, a British human rights lawyer, had written a book that severely criticized the atrocities committed by the RUF. He ultimately retained a position on the court after agreeing to not hear the cases of RUF detainees. After the court officially began hearings on June 3, some of the most shocking cases of brutality were heard during the trial of Sam Hinga Norman, whose government forces were accused of hacking off the limbs, ears, and lips of civilians as well as practicing widespread forced conscription of children, who were used either as soldiers or as sex slaves. These horrendous methods became the signature of the RUF, but they were also widely used by government forces. Some of the most notorious of those indicted had not stood before the court. Two of the accused were dead; Foday Sankoh, leader of the RUF, died in custody in 2003, and RUF commander Sam Bockarie was killed in Liberia in May 2003. Johnny Paul Koroma, who had led the military junta in 1997, was in hiding, and former Liberian president Charles Taylor, accused of backing the RUF, had sought asylum in Nigeria. The SCSL ruled in May 2004, however, that Taylor was not immune from standing trial.

In May the tribunal decided that for the first time under international law, cases involving forced marriages of women and girls would be tried as crimes against humanity. Widespread kidnapping and rape were common during the war. The human rights panel, the Truth and Reconciliation Commission, mandated under the 1999 peace accords, was approved by Parliament in May. A UN helicopter carrying 24 people, including peacekeepers, crashed into a hillside in June, killing all aboard.

(MARY F.E. EBELING)

© Luc Gnago/Reuters/Corbis

As the UN-backed war-crimes tribunal opens on June 3, a UN peacekeeper guards the courthouse in Freetown, Sierra Leone, where inquiries into atrocities committed during the decade-long civil war are being heard.

SINGAPORE

Area: 697 sq km (269 sq mi)
Population (2004 est.): 4,229,000
Head of state: President S.R. Nathan
Head of government: Prime Ministers Goh Chok Tong and, from August 12, Lee Hsien Loong

Following months of speculation, it was finally announced that on Aug. 12, 2004, Prime Minister Goh Chok Tong, who had held office since 1990, would hand over power to Lee Hsien Loong (*see* BIOGRAPHIES), the deputy prime minister and son of Lee Kuan Yew, Singapore's first prime minister (1959–90). Goh remained in the cabinet, however, and assumed the position of senior minister, a post hitherto occupied by the elder Lee, who in turn became minister mentor—a new title created to reflect his role. Lee Hsien Loong broke with tradition by having his inauguration outdoors, in a ceremony attended not only by high officials but also by ordinary citizens, such as cooks, students, and shopkeepers.

A month before the leadership change, Singapore catapulted into the international headlines when then deputy prime minister Lee paid what was billed as a "private and unofficial" visit to Taiwan, with which Singapore had close commercial and military ties but did not officially recognize. Beijing took severe umbrage and demanded "concrete actions" as proof of redress. Singapore insisted that the visit was within its sovereign rights.

Ties with Taiwan deteriorated soon after, however, when Taipei became angered when Singapore called the Taiwanese push toward independence "dangerous." In one angry outburst, Taiwanese Foreign Minister Mark Chen called Singapore "a tiny country the size of a piece of snot."

On the domestic front, the issue that generated the most debate was whether to have a casino. The idea split the country down the middle, and a consensus appeared unlikely. Meanwhile, the economy improved over that of 2003, with unemployment falling from 4.5% to 3.4% in the third quarter. The struggle to keep jobs within the country remained; the government continued efforts to retrain workers and secure free-trade agreements that would bring down tariff walls and thus increase exports. In the public sector, as part of an efficiency drive that had begun a few years earlier, ministries were asked to cut their staffs by 3% every year for the next three years to bring the head count down to 1996 levels. Ministries that did not comply would have to pay S$10,000 (about $6,000) annually into government coffers for each extra officer they had above the limit. (LEE HOONG CHUA)

SLOVAKIA

Area: 49,035 sq km (18,933 sq mi)
Population (2004 est.): 5,383,000
Capital: Bratislava
Chief of state: Presidents Rudolf Schuster and, from June 15, Ivan Gasparovic
Head of government: Prime Minister Mikulas Dzurinda

The year 2004 was a very successful one for Slovakia; the country acceded to both NATO and the European Union (EU) and won international praise as a reform leader. Despite the political squabbling that had caused the ruling coalition to lose its parliamentary majority in late 2003, the cabinet managed to push through legislation on health care reform and fiscal decentralization and thereby wrapped up the key points of its program within the first two years of its term. Given the progress that Slovakia had made since 1998, the World Bank's *Doing Business in 2005* report ranked the country as the world's top reformer and listed it as one of the top 20 economies in regard to "the ease of doing business." The reforms attracted new investment projects, including an automobile manufacturing plant by Hyundai affiliate Kia Motors, scheduled to open in 2006.

One challenge faced by the cabinet in 2004 was a referendum on early parliamentary elections that was organized on the basis of a petition drive by opposition parties and trade unions, which claimed that government-led reforms had contributed to a worsening social situation. Held on April 3, the referendum failed, since turnout was well below the required 50% threshold. Although the referendum results marked a victory for Prime Minister Mikulas Dzurinda, the cabinet received a major blow in the presidential elections that were held the same day, as the ruling parties' candidates unexpectedly failed to make it past the first round. In the second-round runoff, former speaker of the parliament Ivan Gasparovic prevailed over former prime minister Vladimir Meciar.

A huge storm in Slovakia's Tatra Mountains on November 19 leveled an estimated 3 million cu m (1.3 billion bd ft) of timber. An official called it the country's worst natural disaster in 100 years.

© AFP/Getty Images

The ruling parties fared better than had been expected in Slovakia's first elections to the European Parliament (EP) on June 13; they won a combined 8 out of 14 seats. A major concern was the disappointingly low turnout, just under 17% of eligible voters, the lowest in EU history. Still, the failure of the referendum combined with the EP elections helped to strengthen Dzurinda's position, even as the prime ministers in three neighbouring countries lost their jobs.

The year also brought more rapid economic growth. Though the 2003 increase in GDP had been based entirely on an improvement in net exports, growth was much more balanced in 2004, with a recovery in investment and household demand, signaling that Slovaks were adjusting well to the sweeping changes in taxation that had taken effect at the start of the year.

(SHARON FISHER)

SLOVENIA

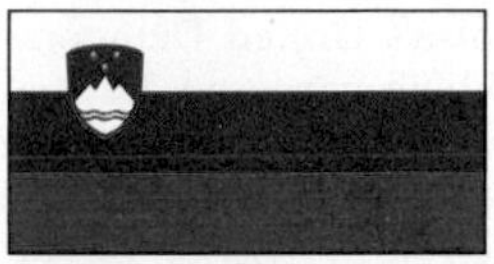

Area: 20,273 sq km (7,827 sq mi)
Population (2004 est.): 1,997,000
Capital: Ljubljana
Chief of state: President Janez Drnovsek
Head of government: Prime Ministers Anton Rop and, from November 9, Janez Jansa

The year 2004 was a significant one for Slovenia. It became a member of NATO on March 29 and of the European Union on May 1. Full membership in both organizations was the primary foreign-policy goal and was supported by all major political parties. Slovenia was to host the meeting of NATO members scheduled for the spring of 2005 and would hold the presidency of the EU for the first half of 2008.

On June 13 Slovenia took part for the first time in EU-wide parliamentary elections. Turnout was low—only about 28% of voters went to the polls. Of the seven deputies that the country was entitled to send to the European Parliament, four were from conservative opposition parties, a harbinger of the results in the October 3 quadrennial parliamentary election. The major victor in that election was the Slovenian Democrat Party, which won 29 of the 90 seats. The party's leader, Janez Jansa, who had served as defense minister during the country's brief war for independence from Yugoslavia in 1991, became prime minister in November and formed a four-party centre-right coalition government in December. This ended a 12-year period of centre-left governments (except for six months in 2000) that were dominated by the leftist Liberal Democrat Party.

A predominantly Roman Catholic country, Slovenia markedly improved its relations with the Vatican during the year. In January the parliament ratified an agreement with the Vatican—negotiated in 2001—that delineated the legal status of the church in Slovenia. In February, Archbishop Franc Rode of Ljubljana, who had led the church in Slovenia since 1997 and had spoken out often and in strong terms in defense of its rights, was appointed to a major post in the Vatican. His successor, Alojz Uran, appointed on October 25, was seen as both a less-controversial and a more popular leader than Rode.

Slovenia's relations with Croatia, its southern neighbour, remained strained, owing primarily to the still-unresolved demarcation of the sea and land border between them. Several conflicts over fishing rights occurred, and it seemed likely that only some form of international arbitration could settle the issues.

The country's economy remained stable during the year. Unemployment and inflation declined. Slovenia declared its intention to adopt the euro as soon as feasible, by 2008 at the latest, and to make the reforms necessary to achieve this goal. (See *European Union:* Sidebar, above.) (RUDOLPH M. SUSEL)

SOLOMON ISLANDS

Area: 28,370 sq km (10,954 sq mi)
Population (2004 est.): 461,000
Capital: Honiara
Chief of state: Queen Elizabeth II, represented by Governors-General Sir John Lapli and, from July 7, Nathaniel Waena
Head of government: Prime Minister Sir Allan Kemakeza

Solomon Islands continued to make progress toward normalcy in 2004 after having endured civil disturbances over the previous few years. Peacekeepers were withdrawn from the Weather Coast of Guadalcanal beginning in February, but there were outbreaks of violence in the centre of the island later in the year. One government minister was charged with having committed violent offenses in 2000 as a member of one of the warring militias. Police leadership in four provinces was strengthened with expatriate command appointments, and steps were taken to curtail the practices that had seen some SI$55 million (U.S.$1 = about SI$7.35) in illegal police payments during 2002–03.

The budgetary situation also showed improvement, which reflected the steps taken to cleanse the public-service payroll, clamp down on illegal payments, and improve financial controls. The 2003 expenditure budget of SI$259 million was exceeded by SI$74 million, but the budget showed a SI$30 million surplus in the final quarter of 2004. The central bank projected GDP growth of 4% for the year. In October the central bank began to repay development bank depositors whose accounts had been frozen a year earlier because of insufficient funds.

In a midyear cabinet reshuffle, the leader of the opposition, John Garo, joined the government of Prime Minister Sir Allan Kemakeza. He was replaced as opposition leader by former prime minister Francis Billy Hilly.

(BARRIE MACDONALD)

SOMALIA

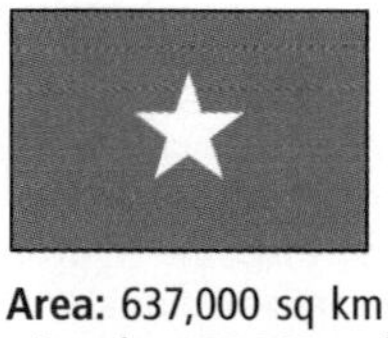

Area: 637,000 sq km (246,000 sq mi), including the 176,000-sq-km (68,000-sq-mi) area of the unilaterally declared (in 1991) and unrecognized Republic of Somaliland
Population (2004 est.): 8,305,000 (including Somaliland); about 275,000 refugees are registered in neighbouring countries
Capital: Mogadishu; Hargeysa is the capital of Somaliland
Head of state and government: Somalia's government under President Abdiqassim Salad Hassan was barely functioning in 2004; a new transitional government was formed in exile, comprising President Abdullahi Yusuf Ahmed from October 14, assisted by Prime Minister Ali Muhammad Ghedi from November 3.

© Antony Njuguna/Reuters/Corbis

Abdullahi Yusuf Ahmed (left), the new president of Somalia, presents his prime minister, Ali Muhammad Ghedi, to the press in Nairobi, Kenya, on November 3. Somalia had been virtually without a functioning government for years.

The two-year peace and reconciliation conference between Somalia's warring factions culminated in January 2004 with the signing of a peace agreement in Nairobi, Kenya. In October a new transitional federal government was formed that was intended to bring to an end the 13 years of anarchy that had roiled the country since the fall of dictator Muhammad Siad Barre. The new government, however, was based outside Somalia in the Kenyan capital of Nairobi and had yet to establish its power on the ground.

The peace conference was held near Nairobi and was sponsored by the Intergovernmental Authority on Development, a subregional organization made up of Djibouti, Eritrea, Ethiopia, Kenya, The Sudan, Uganda, and nominally Somalia itself. In the two years since its inception, the conference had frequently seemed on the verge of collapse; in August, however, delegates finally formed a 275-member transitional federal parliament, in which each of Somalia's four major clans was allocated 61 seats, and an alliance of smaller groups was awarded 31 seats. Though 22 women MPs were appointed, women's rights activists complained that this did not fulfill the quota (12% of MPs were to be women) stipulated in the interim charter.

On October 10 the parliament elected as transitional president Abdullahi Yusuf Ahmed, who since 1998 had been president of the northeastern semiautonomous region of Puntland. (Puntland's former vice president, Mohammed Abdi Haashi, took his place there.) A rival candidate was Abdiqassim Salad Hassan, the president of the previous Transitional National Government, which had never succeeded in establishing its authority anywhere except in a part of the capital, Mogadishu, and some territory in the south of the country.

Several faction leaders remained opposed to the new federal government, notably Gen. Muhammad Siad Hersi "Morgan," who quit the conference and appeared to be preparing to attack the port city of Kismayo, his former stronghold. Meanwhile, outbreaks of fighting between rival clans continued throughout the year in Mogadishu and elsewhere.

The self-declared republic of Somaliland in the northwest, under its president, Dahir Riyale Kahin, boycotted the conference and refused to join the federation. Though Somaliland had not attained international recognition as a state, it remained stable and mainly peaceful. The murder of three well-known aid workers in October 2003 and two others in March 2004 remained unsolved, however.

A prolonged drought led to severe food shortages in the central and northeastern regions, including parts of Somaliland and Puntland. In July aid agencies estimated that up to one million people needed help. This was exacerbated by fighting between rival clans in the central Galguduud region and even more by the standoff in the Sool and Sanaag regions, which were claimed by both Puntland and Somaliland. There were clashes over the territory in January and September.

The UN estimated that throughout Somalia and Somaliland 750,000 people, including 350,000 internally displaced persons, were living in a state of chronic humanitarian need. Conditions worsened in December when a tsunami hit the country. Puntland suffered extensive damage, and several hundred Somalis were killed. (VIRGINIA LULING)

SOUTH AFRICA

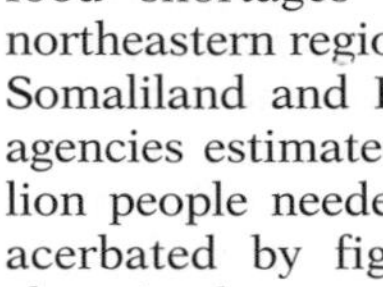

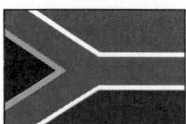

Area: 1,219,090 sq km (470,693 sq mi)
Population (2004 est.): 46,587,000
Capitals (de facto): Pretoria/Tshwane (executive); Bloemfontein/Mangaung (judicial); Cape Town (legislative)
Head of state and government: President Thabo Mbeki

Domestic Affairs. As South Africa celebrated 10 years of democracy, the African National Congress (ANC) was overwhelmingly returned to power in the national and provincial elections held on April 14, 2004, which led to the inauguration of Pres. Thabo Mbeki for a second term. The ANC received 69.8% of the vote, compared with 66.35% in 1999. The Democratic Alliance (DA), led by Tony Leon, continued as the official opposition, with 12.3% of the vote, up from 9.56% in 1999. Mangosutho Buthelezi's Inkatha Freedom Party (IFP) obtained 6.97% of the vote, down from 8.58% in 1999. For the first time, the ANC took office on its own, or as senior partner, in all nine provinces. Members of the IFP, the New National Party (NNP), and the Azanian People's Organization were included in Mbeki's cabinet, which had 12 women.

The old apartheid-era ruling party, Marthinus van Schalkwyk's NNP, had an election pact with the ANC but received a paltry 1.65% of the vote, down from 6.87% in 1999, and was beaten by Bantu Holomisa's United Democratic Movement, which garnered 2.2% of the vote (3.42% in 1999), and Patricia de Lille's newly formed Independent Democrats, which won 1.73%. In August the dissolution of the NNP was sealed when van Schalkwyk announced that he would be joining the ANC, and he invited other NNP members to do the same. Former president F.W. de Klerk refused. During the "floor-crossing window" in September, when elected officials at the local level were permitted to change parties, two-thirds of NNP councillors joined the ANC. After the election the coalition between the DA and the IFP appeared unlikely to continue.

On February 6 President Mbeki delivered a state of the nation speech to Parliament in which he highlighted the accomplishments of his administration—the lowest rate of inflation (4%) in more than 30 years, sustained economic growth for 20 quarters, and political stability. Since 1994 the government had built 1.6 million homes and 56,000 new classrooms and had delivered potable water to 9 million people and sanitation to 6.4 million people. Leon claimed that Mbeki's speech had failed to include mention of the millions of unemployed in the country, the millions of victims of crime, and the hundreds of thousands of people with HIV/AIDS. Commentators noted that Mbeki had not addressed the problem

© Andreas Meier./Reuters/Corbis

A joyful Nelson Mandela, former president, clutches the association football (soccer) World Cup trophy on May 15 as it is announced that South Africa has been chosen to host the World Cup competition in 2010.

of human rights abuses in Zimbabwe. In his inauguration speech Mbeki concentrated on the need for the eradication of poverty, and in his second state of the nation speech he gave concrete target dates to deliver on his promises.

In these and other speeches made by Mbeki and his ministers during the year, there was a noticeable if subtle shift of emphasis from market-led to state-led policies for economic growth. An expanded public-works program was launched, which was to improve the transportation infrastructure. With regard to privatization, further sales of shares of big parastatals such as Eskom (electricity), Transnet (transport), and Denel (arms) were ruled out in favour of encouragement of parastatal investment with public-private partnerships. In addition, in pursuit of a long-term aim, the ANC government obliged all economic sectors to draw up "charters" committing themselves to policies of black economic empowerment (affirmative action). In June former president Nelson Mandela officially retired from public life.

Following the fallout from the 1999 arms deal, in January the Hefer Commission reported to Mbeki that Bulelani Ngcuka, the national director of prosecutions, was "probably never" an apartheid-era spy, but no disciplinary action was taken by the ANC against Schabir Shaik, a financial adviser to Deputy Pres. Jacob Zuma, or former transport minister Mac Maharaj, who had initiated the allegations. At the end of January, however, Zuma complained to Public Protector Lawrence Mushwana that Ngcuka had abused his powers in 2003 by claiming that there was prima facie evidence of corruption against Zuma. In late May Mushwana reported that Ngcuka's claim was "unfair" and "improper" and that it violated Zuma's right to dignity. Ngcuka and Justice Minister Penuell Maduna declared that Mushwana's statement was "preposterous ... thoroughly unconsidered, and without substance." In July Ngcuka resigned his post. In February Shaik had been indicted on charges of bribery relating to the arms deal, and his trial commenced in October. For the remainder of the year, the defense mounted its case again Shaik, whose defense was expected to commence in 2005.

In June public investigations were launched into what was described as a multimillion-rand scam, which involved MPs making fraudulent travel claims on free vouchers. On September 3, members of eight civil-service unions, including teachers, nurses, and police, marched on Parliament in a dispute with the government over wages, and on September 16 at least 800,000 civil servants of all colours walked off their jobs in the largest such strike in South African history. A settlement was reached over the following weekend, and further strike action was averted.

In May countrywide celebrations greeted the announcement that the association football (soccer) World Cup would be held in South Africa in 2010. In June, however, a number of senior referees were arrested on charges of fixing football matches.

Among the notable deaths during the year were those of Transport Minister Dullah Omar (*see* OBITUARIES), pop icon Brenda Fassie (*see* OBITUARIES), and antiapartheid-struggle stalwarts Ray Alexander, Vella Pillay, Ethel de Keyser, and Beyers Naude.

Economy. By the first quarter of 2004, the economy had sped up to 3.6%, and it increased to 3.9% in the second quarter. Manufacturing production grew by 2.7%, having recovered in the first quarter from three successive quarters of decline. The growth was attributed to increased state spending on infrastructure, lowered interest rates, and increased consumer demand. Unemployment remained high, with the official rate at 27.8% in March 2004. Inflation slowed to its lowest recorded level (3.7%) in August.

The budget increased the child-support grant to 170 rand (1 rand = about $0.16) a month and provided modest tax relief and provided for 15 billion rand to be set aside over five years for the extended public-works program. The anticipated budget deficit for 2004–05 would increase to 3.1% of GDP, compared with some 2.6% for 2003–04. Total spending would be 370 billion rand, and revenue would amount to 327 billion rand.

The current balance of payment account turned from a surplus in 2002 to record deficits—2.84% of GDP in the fourth quarter of 2003 and 3.7% of GDP in the second quarter of 2004. The real value of imports had risen sharply, while the volume of exports had declined, which reflected the continued strength of the rand. This deficit was neutralized by a large surplus on the financial account of the balance of payments, which caused foreign reserves to rise and reflected foreign bank loans and deposits, portfolio capital, and the takeover of some domestic companies.

Foreign Relations. In January President Mbeki attended the bicentennial of the independence of Haiti. Deposed Haitian president Jean-Bertrand Aristide sought exile in South Africa and arrived at the end of May.

Though South Africa continued to be involved in peace-brokering exercises in Burundi and in Zimbabwe, no significant negotiations took place between the ruling Zimbabwe African National Union–Patriotic Front and the opposition Movement for Democratic Change.

In March 70 alleged South African mercenaries were arrested in Zimbabwe, along with 18 others in Equatorial Guinea, on charges related to involvement in a planned coup in the latter country. By September 65 of those in Zimbabwe had received 12-month prison sentences, 2 persons had been sentenced to 16 months, and the leader of the coup, Simon Mann, had been sentenced to 7 years. The plot had allegedly been partially financed by Sir Mark Thatcher, son of former British prime minister Margaret Thatcher. He was arrested in South Africa and released on bail of 2 million rand. In a November court appearance, he was not asked to plead, and the trial was postponed until 2005.

(MARTIN LEGASSICK)

SPAIN

Area: 505,988 sq km (195,363 sq mi)
Population (2004 est.): 43,768,000
Capital: Madrid
Chief of state: King Juan Carlos I
Head of government: Prime Ministers José María Aznar López and, from April 17, José Luis Rodríguez Zapatero

Spain suffered its worst terrorist attack ever on the morning of March 11, 2004, when 13 bombs exploded on four packed commuter trains heading toward Atocha station in central Madrid, leaving more than 190 dead and more than 1,500 injured. Coming just three days before the general elections, the attack was bound to have major political consequences. The nature of these consequences, however, depended on the identity of the terrorists and the way that the conservative Popular Party (PP) government of Prime Minister José María Aznar handled the situation.

Understandably, after more than 30 years of violence and at least 800 deaths at the hands of the armed Basque separatist organization Euzkadi Ta Askatasuna (ETA), both the government and the media immediately attributed the bombings to ETA. The following day an estimated 11 million Spaniards turned out to nationwide government-sponsored demonstrations. This display of national unity rapidly broke down, however, as the police investigation began to focus on the Islamist militant group al-Qaeda. On March 13, as the first arrests of Islamist suspects were being made, the government continued to point the finger at ETA. That evening spontaneous, illegal protests took place in Madrid, Barcelona, and other cities as demonstrators chanted, "We want to know the truth before we vote." With some 90% of Spaniards opposed to Aznar's support for the U.S.-led invasion of Iraq, the Islamic connection inevitably put Iraq back on top of the political agenda, which thereby favoured the opposition Socialist Party (PSOE), which had strongly opposed the war.

The March 11 attack and the government's bungled response to it undoubtedly contributed to the Socialists' surprise electoral victory on March 14. The PSOE took 42.6% of the vote and 164 of the 350 seats in the Congress of Deputies, compared with the PP's 37.6% and 148 seats. The Socialists easily negotiated the support of various minority leftist and nationalist parties for the investiture of their young leader, José Luis Rodríguez Zapatero (*see* BIOGRAPHIES), as prime minister. Zapatero was formally sworn in by King Juan Carlos on April 17.

On April 17 Prime Minister José Luis Rodríguez Zapatero poses in front of the names of those killed in commuter train bombings in Madrid on March 11. Zapatero won Spain's general elections just three days after the terrorist attack.

© Sergio Perez/Reuters/Corbis

Police investigations and a subsequent parliamentary inquiry confirmed the al-Qaeda connection and identified possible intelligence and security failings prior to March. More suspects, mainly Moroccans and Algerians, were arrested in October, and plans were uncovered for additional attacks on other targets in Madrid.

The new government lost no time in carrying out one of its main electoral pledges, withdrawing the 1,300 Spanish troops stationed in Iraq. This and the Socialists' realignment with the "Old Europe" of France and Germany inevitably damaged relations with Washington. The breach appeared to widen in September when Zapatero gave a speech in Tunisia encouraging other countries to follow Spain's example. In October the U.S. ambassador's failure to attend the military parade and reception held to celebrate Spain's national holiday confirmed the strains in bilateral relations. The government put on a brave face after the reelection of U.S. Pres. George W. Bush on November 2, emphasizing Zapatero's desire for renewed cooperation between the two countries.

Amid signs of coordination problems, the Socialists also moved rapidly on a wide range of internal issues. Responding to public concern about domestic violence, the first bill the new government presented to the parliament introduced tougher sentences for perpetrators (although, controversially, only in the case of men) and increased support and protection for victims. The government froze the PP's educational reforms, which among other things had boosted the status of religious teaching in schools, and announced laws introducing gay marriage and adoption as well as measures to facilitate the regularization of Spain's estimated 800,000 illegal immigrants.

In October Zapatero hosted a summit of the presidents of Spain's 17 regional governments. The first such occasion in the history of Spain's young democracy, the meeting symbolized the Socialists' more conciliatory approach to the demands of Basque and Catalan nationalists, including a willingness to modify the constitution to permit effective cooperation between the central and regional governments. In part ideological, the Socialists' position was also pragmatic, given their need for the votes of nationalists both in the Congress in Madrid and in the Catalan regional parliament.

Neither the obdurate opposition of the PP nor the Roman Catholic Church's protests against changes in education and marriage laws as well as talk of reviewing state funding for the church seemed to dent support for the new government. With inflation running at around 3%, however, the European Commission reduced the optimistic Spanish estimates of 2.8% GDP growth in 2004 and 3.2% in 2005 to 2.6% in both years. The lowered projections provoked fears of increased unemployment and a possible collapse in rocketing house prices. The issue of Basque independence also remained a pressing issue, especially after the Basque parliament approved a plan in December that would give the region greater autonomy. (JUSTIN BYRNE)

AP/Wide World Photos

In Telwatta, Sri Lanka, about 19 km (12 mi) from the town of Galle on the Indian Ocean, an aerial photograph shows villagers surveying the wreckage of a train demolished by the December 26 tsunami. The Samudradevi *("Queen of the Sea") was traveling from the capital, Colombo, to Galle when it was struck by a giant wave and thrown off the track. It was Sri Lanka's biggest single tragedy on that day, with at least 800 of the more than 1,000 passengers onboard killed.*

SRI LANKA

Area: 65,610 sq km (25,332 sq mi)
Population (2004 est.): 19,218,000
Capitals: Sri Jayawardenepura Kotte (legislative and judicial); Colombo (executive)
Head of state and government: President Chandrika Kumaratunga, assisted by Prime Ministers Ranil Wickremesinghe and, from April 6, Mahinda Rajapakse

In 2004 Sri Lanka experienced political turmoil, violence, and frustration over the seemingly endless complications of trying to arrange negotiations between the government and the Liberation Tigers of Tamil Eelam (LTTE) to end the conflict that had raged sporadically since 1983 and cost more than 60,000 lives. Then on December 26 coastal areas were swept by a tsunami that killed more than 30,000 Sri Lankans. (*See* DISASTERS: *Sidebar*.)

The bitterly personal conflict between Pres. Chandrika Kumaratunga and Prime Minister Ranil Wickremesinghe, who uncomfortably shared power in Sri Lanka's complex political system until April, continued to dominate national politics. In January, Kumaratunga's People's Alliance (PA) struck an accord with the left-wing People's Liberation Front (JVP), and on February 7 Kumaratunga dissolved Parliament and called for an election on April 2. The LTTE expressed dismay, and the Colombo stock exchange fell 10.5%, its largest one-day loss ever. The election included more than 6,000 candidates from 24 parties and 192 independent groups in competition for 225 seats. During the campaign Kumaratunga stirred fears in the majority Sinhalese community by calling Wickremesinghe's government soft on the Tamil separatists. Other issues under debate included employment, inflation, and the impact of globalization in formerly socialist Sri Lanka.

In a generally peaceful vote on April 2, Kumaratunga's United People's Freedom Alliance won 105 seats and replaced Wickremesinghe's United National Front, whose allotment fell to 82 seats, as the strongest party in Parliament. When Parliament reconvened, support for the new minority government proved unreliable; differences between its two principal factions persisted, and minor parties offered or withdrew their support. On the critical issue of peace negotiations, repeated efforts by Norwegian mediators to bring the parties to the bargaining table proved fruitless. Even the $4.5 billion in potential foreign assistance that was offered by donors in 2003 conditional on a peace settlement could not induce negotiations.

On July 7 a suicide bomber blew herself up, killing four policemen, after trying to assassinate a government minister. It was the first suicide bombing in nearly three years.

Despite the unresolved conflict with the LTTE and the damage the tsunami did to the fishing and tourism industries, annual growth appeared to be running at 5–5.5%. Manufacturing was the most dynamic export sector, while agriculture provided the most employment. Several global service companies launched operations in Sri Lanka. The World Bank made two loans in support of rural development and the tsunami prompted relief contributions, but significant foreign aid and private investment both remained dependent on the elusive peace settlement.

(DONALD SNODGRASS)

SUDAN, THE

Area: 2,503,890 sq km (966,757 sq mi)
Population (2004 est.): 39,148,000, including more than 600,000 Sudanese refugees in African countries, including nearly 200,000 in Chad
Capitals: Khartoum (executive and ministerial) and Omdurman (legislative)
Head of state and government: President and Prime Minister Lieut. Gen. Omar Hassan Ahmad al-Bashir

On May 26, 2004, a peace deal was signed between the Sudanese government in Khartoum and the Sudan People's Liberation Movement, and a 20-year civil war was thus ended. The pact incorporated two earlier agreements on the constitutional future of the south and the allocation of oil revenues between the north and the south, as well as agreement on the nature of power sharing in the central government and on setting up a 39,000-strong army.

The satisfaction that came from forging an agreement, however, was quickly overshadowed by events in the western province of Darfur, which was not included in the deal. With most of its troops engaged in the war in the south, the government had enlisted and armed Arab militias to quell the revolt of black subsistence farmers that had begun in February 2003. As a result, more than a million black civilians were forced to seek safety in refugee camps, and an estimated 70,000 others had been killed or had died as a result of disease and/or hardship. Aid agencies complained that obstacles were impeding their access to the camps, but the government insisted that it was committed to securing a just and peaceful settlement of the conflict. On April 8, under the auspices of UN Secretary-General Kofi Annan, the Sudanese government and two rebel groups agreed to a cease-fire, but it was ignored.

Senior diplomats from the U.S., the U.K., Germany, and France visited Khartoum and urged the government to take action to curb the militias and what some had referred to as genocide, but their pleas only strengthened the government's resistance to foreign intervention. Successive resolutions by the UN Security Council on June 11, on July 30, and again in mid-September, threatening action if the government did not call a halt to the conflict, produced little result and were seriously weakened by the abstentions of China, Pakistan, Russia, and Algeria. In September China, which had invested millions of dollars in the development of The Sudan's oil resources, threatened to veto any resolutions seeking to impose sanctions on the oil industry.

In August the Sudanese government accepted the deployment in Darfur of 300 troops offered by the African Union (AU) to protect observers and aid workers. The AU also called on the government to arrest those responsible for the violence. Talks between the opposing parties, which began in mid-August in Abuja, Nigeria, broke down after three weeks but were resumed in October, with the AU serving as mediator; nonetheless, fighting continued between the government and the rebels in Darfur despite repeated efforts to reach an agreement. The AU also offered 3,000 more troops to be deployed as peacekeepers, but only 800 of them had been deployed by mid-December.

(KENNETH INGHAM)

© Luc Gnago/Reuters/Corbis

A Sudanese woman, waiting to receive food aid in the Am Nabak refugee camp in Chad, has her fingers dipped into ink as a form of identification.

SURINAME

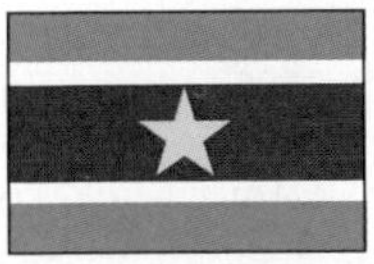

Area: 163,820 sq km (63,251 sq mi)
Population (2004 est.): 437,000
Capital: Paramaribo
Head of state and government: President Ronald Venetiaan, assisted by Prime Minister Jules Rattankoemar Ajodhia

In 2004 Suriname enjoyed another good year, with growth near 5%. This was the second buoyant year in a row after prolonged periods of maladministration that had followed the civil conflict of the 1980s. A flourishing underground economy, a Chinese-backed palm-oil project, and a new gold mine, funded by Canadian entrepreneurs, fueled the economy, along with steady returns from the staple bauxite industry.

Pres. Ronald Venetiaan's skill, together with uncharacteristic trade-union restraint, helped contain spiraling wage demands and corrosive inflation levels. Equally successful was the conversion of the Suriname guilder to the Suriname dollar, which reinforced foreign-exchange-rate stabilization. The government of The Netherlands, the Inter-American Development Bank, and other donors responded positively with development programs.

Despite a much-improved outlook for Suriname, problems remained. The government was unable to cut back thriving criminal industries in drugs, gold smuggling, and human trafficking; no solution was in sight for the maritime boundary dispute with Guyana that was blocking Guyana's oil exploration; and polls suggested that President Venetiaan's two major rivals for the 2005 presidential elections had overtaken him in popular support. This news was galling for Venetiaan; the two contenders were former military dictator Dési Bouterse and former president Jules Wijdenbosch, both of whom had managed corrupt and incompetent administrations. (JOHN W. GRAHAM)

SWAZILAND

Area: 17,364 sq km (6,704 sq mi)
Population (2004 est.): 1,083,000
Capitals: Mbabane (administrative and judicial); Lozitha and Ludzidzini (royal); Lobamba (legislative)
Chief of state: King Mswati III, with much power shared by his mother, Queen Mother Ntombi Latfwala
Head of government: Prime Minister Absalom Themba Dlamini

By October 2004 significant advances had been made in two closely related issues that dominated political life in

Swaziland—the review of the country's constitution and the restoration of the rule of law. Most of the year was spent trying to reach the rural Swazi population in accordance with a resolution made in June at the National Dialogue to increase participation in drawing up the new constitution. King Mswati III also came under international pressure at various meetings he attended to complete the draft, which he announced would be finished before the end of 2004.

The king summoned the Swazi nation to the Sibaya, a traditional "people's parliament" in the sacred cattle kraal at Ludzidzini, where deliberations on the constitution lasted two weeks. Prince David Dlamini, minister of justice and constitutional affairs, indicated that 80% of the people supported a continuation of the royal system of government and that the document was ready for the parliament. It was generally expected that the constitution would not guarantee the establishment of political parties. The Peoples' United Democratic Movement did not participate in the constitutional proceedings but rallied its youth to effect change at its Swaziland Youth Congress, held in South Africa.

Restoration of the rule of law was dealt a setback in February when the speaker of the National Assembly was forced to resign. Prince David later moved a bill in the parliament that paved the way for the restoration in November of the rule of law and the Supreme Court, which had been vacated in 2002. Meanwhile, the country suffered from a four-year drought and the highest HIV rate among adults in Africa. (ACKSON M. KANDUZA)

SWEDEN

Area: 450,295 sq km (173,860 sq mi)
Population (2004 est.): 8,991,000
Capital: Stockholm
Chief of state: King Carl XVI Gustaf
Head of government: Prime Minister Göran Persson

The Swedish economy performed well in 2004, but the Social Democratic government under Prime Minister Göran Persson failed to reap the political benefits as unemployment and problems in public services dominated the news.

Boosted by strong exports, the country's economy was expected to have grown by 3.5% in 2004. Although the strong U.S. dollar might slow Swedish exports in 2005, tax cuts and increased public spending were expected to stimulate domestic demand, and economic growth was projected to remain above 3%.

Swedish voters had elected to stay outside the euro zone in a national referendum in 2003, but interest rates continued to fall in 2004, reaching 2% in April in line with those set by the European Central Bank. Unlike many of its European Union colleagues, Sweden's public finances remained largely in balance. While Swedish industry continued to be competitive in sectors ranging from telecommunications to automotive, however, there were few new jobs. Open unemployment was expected to reach 5.6% of the workforce, well above the government's 4% target.

Away from the economy, the country still struggled to come to terms with the murder of Anna Lindh, the country's foreign minister who was stabbed to death on a private shopping trip in central Stockholm in September 2003. Mijailo Mijailovic, a 25-year-old Swede of Serbian parentage, was convicted in March 2004 of the murder of Lindh, who had been heavily tipped to be the country's next prime minister. At Mijailovic's trial most of the details of the killing were undisputed, but Swedes were left with little idea of the motive for the attack. Initially the court sentenced him to life imprisonment, but he was later placed under psychiatric care. After a legal battle, the Supreme Court ruled in December that Mijailovic would serve his life sentence in jail.

It had been thought that Persson might step down in 2004, but with his obvious successor gone, he had little choice but to continue as leader of the Social Democrats. Still stung from the political defeat he had suffered in the euro referendum, Persson seemed to lack enthusiasm for political debate in the early part of the year. The Social Democrats' poor showing in the European Parliamentary election in June, his own health problems, and a bruising row over the nomination of the country's European commissioner did little to improve the prime minister's temper.

In the autumn, after a long summer break and a hip operation, Persson returned to the political fray with renewed vigour, reshuffled his government, and pledged to remain party leader through the next general election in 2006. The prime minister would have his work cut out, however, if the Social Democrats were to secure a fourth consecutive election victory. The opposition, headed by Fredrik Reinfeldt, the leader of the conservative Moderate Party, spent 2004 moving toward the political centre ground, and by December it had been rewarded with a steady lead in the opinion polls. Reinfeldt had toned down promises of large-scale tax cuts, instead insisting that a nonsocialist government would better run public services such as health and education.

Sweden was severely affected by the December tsunami disaster in Southeast Asia. A large number of Swedes were vacationing in the area, and it was feared that the Swedish death toll could reach 1,000. (*See* DISASTERS: *Sidebar.*) (NICHOLAS GEORGE)

SWITZERLAND

Area: 41,284 sq km (15,940 sq mi)
Population (2004 est.): 7,392,000
Capitals: Bern (administrative) and Lausanne (judicial)
Head of state and government: President Joseph Deiss

An anti-immigrant campaign poster on a street in Zürich proclaims "Mass Naturalization?—No to the naturalization proposals."

© Siggi Bucher/Reuters/Corbis

As 10 new members joined the European Union on May 1, 2004, Switzerland remained resolutely outside, but the country was prodded into concessions toward greater European integration by economic, trade, and political realities. The EU and Switzerland in March signed a bilateral package to make it harder for EU citizens to evade domestic taxes by having a Swiss bank account. Switzerland agreed to impose taxes on deposits of EU citizens—starting at 15% and rising to 35% after 2010—and to transfer the revenue in lump sums to the respective European nations, which would thereby preserve the anonymity of the depositors and uphold cherished Swiss banking secrecy. In return, Swiss citizens won the right to travel more freely in the EU. The EU was forced to postpone the starting date of the clampdown on cross-border tax evasion by six months to July 1, 2005, because Switzerland and Liechtenstein said that they needed more time to prepare.

EU frustration was aggravated by Switzerland's new justice minister, Christoph Blocher, an outspoken critic of the EU and the UN. Blocher had been named to the seven-member federal executive in December 2003 after his nationalist Swiss People's Party (SVP) made sweeping gains in the October 2003 general elections. His ministerial responsibilities were expected to give Blocher a pivotal role in the anticipated June 2005 referendum on the so-called Schengen/Dublin agreements on border controls.

The presence of Blocher—a combative billionaire industrialist—crippled the consensus politics that had shaped cabinet decisions since 1959. This was particularly evident in a September 26 referendum in which an unexpected 57% majority rejected government proposals to give automatic citizenship to some 80,000 third-generation immigrants and 52% voted against making it easier for nearly 120,000 longtime residents to gain Swiss nationality. About one in five of Switzerland's 7.4 million inhabitants was a foreigner, partly because of the strict citizenship laws. In the run-up to the referendum, Blocher's SVP successfully played on simmering resentment against immigrants from the Balkans—ethnic Albanians in particular—as well as fear of terrorism. The other three coalition parties were furious, and Economics Minister (and former president) Pascal Couchepin, of the centrist Radical Democrats, accused Blocher of being a threat to Swiss democracy.

© Khaled al Hariri/Reuters/Corbis

A Syrian security officer stands guard near the sand barrier that marks the border with Iraq. In response to U.S. demands, Syria agreed to increase measures to prevent foreign fighters from crossing the frontier into Iraq.

Swiss authorities made arrests of at least eight alleged al-Qaeda members suspected of involvement in attacks against foreigners in Saudi Arabia. Officials also handed over a number of bank documents to the U.S. in connection with the war on terrorism, although there were no signs that the Swiss financial centre had acted as a major conduit for terrorist funds. Authorities froze some 180 million Swiss francs (about $150 million) in Iraqi assets following a UN Security Council decision to widen sanctions against people with suspected links to former Iraqi president Saddam Hussein.

The official State Secretariat for the Economy predicted a growth rate of 1.8% for 2004, with a stronger performance expected for 2005. Major Swiss-based concerns, such as Nestlé foods, pharmaceutical giants Novartis and Roche, and the Credit Suisse and UBS banking groups, reported healthy third-quarter results. (CLARE KAPP)

SYRIA

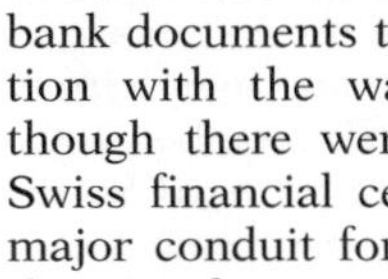

Area: 185,180 sq km (71,498 sq mi)
Population (2004 est.): 18,017,000
Capital: Damascus
Head of state and government: President Bashar al-Assad, assisted by Prime Minister Muhammad Naji al-Otari

Syria's leaders faced a succession of major challenges during 2004. As the year opened, more than 1,000 prominent intellectuals signed and circulated a petition that called for an end to martial law, the release of all prisoners of conscience, and the repatriation of exiled activists. Just before the petition was to be presented to the authorities, violence erupted at an association football (soccer) match in Al-Qamishli between Kurdish spectators, who reportedly displayed a Kurdish flag and pictures of U.S. Pres. George W. Bush, and a group of fans from outside the district who chanted slogans in praise of Saddam Hussein and waved banners that bore his portrait. When residents of the city attacked the interlopers, police shot into the crowd, killing a dozen Kurds.

Rioting spread quickly through Kurdish communities across the northeast, leaving behind burnt-out government offices and looted shops. Rumours that the whole incident had been set up by the security services to justify the state of emergency prompted a demonstration by a coalition of human rights groups in front of the People's Assembly in Damascus. Confrontations between protesters and police followed in Aleppo, Ras al-ʿAin, and ʿAfrin; some 1,200 Kurds were arrested before the disorder subsided. At the end of April, a dozen bombs were detonated simultaneously in the capital. Proponents of greater political liberalization, including advisers close to Pres. Bashar al-Assad, voiced exasperation that the situation had become so volatile, and in June the president expressed a desire to renew efforts to reform the Ba'th Party-led political system. Nevertheless, the government reiterated the ban on political activities by all unlicensed organizations. A month earlier longtime Minister of Defense Mustafa Tlas had stepped down. An officer who had gained notoriety for his toughness in imposing order in Lebanon, Gen. Ghazi Kan'an, took over as minister of the interior in October.

Syrian overtures to Israel at the start of the year elicited no response and collapsed when Israeli troops skirmished with Palestinian and Lebanese-based Hezbollah guerrillas along the Syrian-Lebanese-Israeli border in March. Two months later Israeli agents who had infiltrated Syria to assassinate a leader of the radical Islamist Hamas were discovered and arrested. In September a senior Hamas commander was killed by a car bomb in Damascus.

Relations between Damascus and Washington remained almost as tense. In May the U.S. imposed sanctions against Syria that included an embargo on most trade and a ban on transactions with the commercial bank of Syria. U.S. forces in Iraq took up positions on the Syrian border in August and deployed drone aircraft to keep track of movement across the frontier. U.S. officials then shepherded a resolution through the UN Security Council that demanded the withdrawal of Syrian troops from Lebanon and the disarming of Lebanese militias. U.S. Secretary of State Colin Powell welcomed the evacuation of Syrian military encampments around Beirut in September; he then met Syrian Foreign Minister Faruq al-Shar' at the UN to discuss ways to coordinate patrols along the Syrian-Iraqi border.

(FRED H. LAWSON)

TAIWAN

Area: 36,188 sq km (13,972 sq mi)
Population (2004 est.): 22,640,000
Capital: Taipei
Chief of state: President Chen Shui-bian
Head of government: President of the Executive Yuan (Premier) Yu Shyi-kun

The year 2004 was an eventful one in Taiwan. Pres. Chen Shui-bian was reelected, and his efforts and those of his Democratic Progressive Party (DPP) to move the island to independence from China aroused both internal and external resistance.

The presidential race was very close. Two former presidential candidates, Lien Chan of the Nationalist Party (KMT) and James Soong of the People's First Party (PFP), joined forces against Chen. In the 2000 presidential election, Lien had won 23% of the popular vote, while Soong had captured 37% of the vote. Counting on the support that the two parties had four years earlier, the KMT-PFP alliance hoped to deliver a 2004 election victory to the pan-blue camp (so called because blue was the colour of the KMT). Of the more than 150,000 businesspeople who flew back to Taiwan to cast their ballots, between 80% and 90% were supporters of the KMT-PFP pan-blue alliance. Nonetheless, four years under President Chen had given the DPP advantages in mobilizing supporters, especially young ones, and capitalizing on ethnic issues, particularly the division between the mainlanders who had migrated to the island in the late 1940s and those whose families had migrated generations earlier. By election day the island was seriously torn apart, primarily on issues of independence.

While campaigning the day before the March 20 election in the strongly pro-DPP area of Tainan, both Chen and Vice Pres. Annette Lu were shot and slightly wounded, which added much emotion and terror to the already heavily divided population, as well as skepticism in the minds of at least half of the population. All military personnel, more of them pan-blue supporters than not, were called back into position, although the national-security-alert level remained unchanged. Amid protests by pan-blue candidates and supporters, incumbent candidates Chen and Lu declared a narrow victory with 6,471,970 votes, 29,518 more votes (or 0.2%) than the pan-blue candidates (337,297 ballots had been invalidated). Voter turnout was 80.28%. Lien immediately filed a legal challenge and demanded a recount. In addition, he requested that the government set up an investigation commission to look into the suspicious assassination attempt on Chen in Tainan.

An independent group of foreign experts commissioned by the government discounted the possibility of a political assassination but claimed that further investigation would be difficult because the crime scene had not been protected. Dissatisfied with the ambiguity of the official report, the opposition parties hired their own international experts, who concluded that the wounds were possibly surgical but not from gunshots. An official investigation commission was not established until early October, yet the DPP still boycotted it.

Voters also decided on two referenda that would have authorized the govern-

In Taipei, Taiwan, Pres. Chen Shui-bian (right) and Vice Pres. Annette Lu, protected by a bullet-proof shield, celebrate their reelection on March 20. The pair had been slightly wounded in an assassination attempt the previous day.

© Ray Li/Reuters/Corbis

ment to build up the military to counter Beijing's forces and to negotiate with Beijing on the status of the island. Since only 45% of voters cast ballots, a level short of the 50% legal requirement, the referenda were rendered ineffective. This was the first time Taiwan had used a referendum for policy making.

Weapons imports remained a political as well as an economic issue after the election. The government was seeking legislative approval for a controversial $19 billion special-defense budget to purchase six American-made Pac-3 antimissile systems, eight conventional submarines, and a fleet of submarine-hunting P-3C aircraft. Division fell along partisan lines, with DPP demonstrations calling for "military purchase to protect Taiwan" and KMT-PFP hunger strikers rallying for "saving Taiwan from military spending." By year's end the military budget bill had been voted down 10 times.

In other pro-independence moves, the Taiwanese government began adding the word *Taiwan* to ROC (Republic of China) in its diplomatic documents in order to separate it from the ROC that used to rule the territory including the mainland, and Chen maintained that China should not be included in the national history or geography taught in Taiwan. Beijing protested against Chen's maneuvers vehemently, while the United States maintained that it did not recognize Taiwan as an independent country. In the December parliamentary elections, Chen's government and the independence movement received an unexpected setback when the DPP and its allies failed to win a majority. Several days later Chen announced that he would be stepping down as DPP chairman. (XIAOBO HU)

TAJIKISTAN

Area: 143,100 sq km (55,300 sq mi)
Population (2004 est.): 6,606,000
Capital: Dushanbe
Chief of state: President Imomali Rakhmonov
Head of government: Prime Minister Akil Akilov

During 2004 political life in Tajikistan was marked by growing tensions between Pres. Imomali Rakhmonov, his supporters, and opposition political parties, who accused the president of turning increasingly to authoritarian rule in the run-up to parliamentary elections scheduled for February 2005. In July Rakhmonov signed a controversial new election law, despite threats from four political parties to boycott the upcoming poll. Their criticism of the new law focused on the exclusion of party representatives from election commissions and on the high registration fee for candidates.

Leaders of the Islamic Renaissance Party—which under the peace accords that ended the 1992–97 civil war was one of the opposition groups entitled to a certain percentage of government posts at all levels—asserted that Rakhmonov was unfairly dismissing party members from their official positions. It was not only the opposition that felt the effects of presidential disapproval. In February former interior minister Yakub Salimov, who had been one of Rakhmonov's main supporters during the civil war, was extradited to Tajikistan from Russia to face charges of treason and abuse of office. In August Gaffor Mirzoyev, head of the Tajik Drug Control Agency and one of Rakhmonov's field commanders during the civil war, was arrested on charges of having committed a number of serious crimes, including murder and illegal possession of firearms.

Tajikistan's independent media also found it progressively more difficult to work as the election approached. Several publications that had been critical of the government were denied the use of printing facilities on various pretexts, and in July Rajab Mirzo, chief editor of the independent weekly *Ruzi Nav,* was badly beaten by an unidentified assailant.

Large numbers of Tajiks—possibly as many as one million or more—continued to go abroad, primarily to Russia, in search of work. Tajik economists estimated that the amount of remittances sent back home by the labour migrants equaled the national budget. Many Tajik job seekers were deported from Russia for violations of the immigration rules, and the Tajik government and various international organizations began opening information offices to educate potential labour migrants about immigration requirements. In October Russia signed a deal granting all Tajik migrants legal status and medical insurance.

Tajikistan continued to be a major transit area for illegal drugs to Russia and Europe from Afghanistan. In early August Russian border troops stationed in Tajikistan found a cache containing one ton of heroin and 72 kg (about 158 lb) of raw opium—the largest single haul of drugs to date. Such finds provided substance to Russian officials' claim that Tajik border troops were not ready to assume full responsibility for controlling the Tajik-Afghan border. Rakhmonov agreed to extend the Russian guards' stay until the end of 2006. (BESS BROWN)

TANZANIA

Area: 945,090 sq km (364,901 sq mi)
Population (2004 est.): 35,078,000
De facto capital: Dar es Salaam; Dodoma is the longtime planned capital
Chief of state and head of government: President Benjamin William Mkapa, assisted by Prime Minister Frederick Tulway Sumaye

The most significant event in Tanzania in 2004 was the government's decision in February to launch a $27.6 million project to draw water from Lake Victoria to supply hundreds of villages in the western Shinyanga region. The announcement that the contract for laying the pipeline had been awarded to a Chinese company brought an immediate protest from Egypt, which claimed that Tanzania was in breach of a 1929 treaty that had determined the distribution of the water that flowed from the lake to Egypt through the Nile River to be in perpetuity. On March 8 an emergency meeting took place in Uganda, where representatives gathered from 10 countries reliant upon Nile River water, and a majority of them agreed that the treaty should be updated.

On March 2 a meeting of the presidents of Tanzania, Kenya, and Uganda to sign an agreement preparing the way for an East African customs union passed off more quietly. Tanzanian businessmen, however, were anxious that the proposals would favour Kenya, which already exported far more goods to Tanzania than it imported. The protection of Tanzania's developing tea industry was a case in point; about 30% of the tea sold in Tanzania had been smuggled in from Kenya and Burundi.

On July 21 the Ubongo power station in Dar es Salaam, which was financed by the U.S. and created electricity from natural gas, began producing power. Nonetheless, the vast majority of the population still relied on firewood to produce heat, which had disastrous consequences for the country's forests.

Despite rainfall in areas that had been affected by drought, there was little improvement in the overall availability of food, and it was estimated that 3.5 million people would require food aid by May. In February the IMF approved a loan of $4.2 million to assist the country's poverty-reduction program, and on March 2 the Japanese government rescheduled a debt of some $115 million.

The nearly 400,000 officially registered refugees from Burundi, along with another 400,000 who were undocumented and living in refugee circumstances, continued to impose a heavy financial and administrative burden on the country. As a result, Pres. Benjamin William Mkapa held a number of meetings in August with other regional heads of state in an effort to achieve a settlement of the conflicts in Burundi.

There were problems too for the Civil Service Department. Although the government raised the salaries of civil servants in July, many of the recipients claimed that their incomes were still inadequate and denounced the huge gap between the salaries at the top and at the bottom of the pay scale.

On the island of Zanzibar, March proved to be a turbulent month. A spate of bombings and protests took place, but they suddenly died down. The police were unable to pinpoint the reason for the outburst or the culprit behind it; the Tanzanian government believed the violence to have been politically motivated, but the police were unable to rule out religious extremism. Zanzibar also attracted attention in April when the island's parliament unanimously approved a bill outlawing homosexuality, with penalties of up to 25 years' imprisonment for breach of the law.

(KENNETH INGHAM)

THAILAND

Area: 513,115 sq km (198,115 sq mi)
Population (2004 est.): 64,485,000
Capital: Bangkok
Chief of state: King Bhumibol Adulyadej
Head of government: Prime Minister Thaksin Shinawatra

The year 2004 started and ended inauspiciously in Thailand. On January 4 a spate of violent incidents—arson attacks on schools, murders, and a militant assault on an arms depository—erupted in three southern provinces where 70–80% of the people were Muslims. These incidents, reportedly instigated by Muslim separatists-turned-bandits, led Prime Minister Thaksin Shinawatra to put the southern provinces under martial law. On April 28 more Muslim-led attacks provoked the military into storming the famous Krue Se mosque in Pattani province, where the bandits took refuge. More than 100 people were killed, including 32 inside the mosque. By October the number of casualties had exceeded 350. Then on December 26 Thailand was struck by a tsunami that severely damaged much of the south and caused the death of thousands of people, including many tourists. (*See* DISASTERS: *Sidebar.*)

Another grave concern for Bangkok was the outbreak of bird flu in January. The government killed millions of infected chickens. Several countries put a ban on the import of Thai chickens. Although Thaksin declared an end to the epidemic in May, it resurfaced in July. During the year 12 people died of infection, and the damage to the poultry industry totaled an estimated several billion baht.

Persistent unrest in the south and bird flu, coupled with rising oil prices and the U.S. imposition in August of antidumping duties (6.39%) on Thai shrimp exports, slowed down the economy, which had been showing signs of robust growth. The damage was not devastating, however. The economy, buoyed by rising consumer spending and a construction boom, registered a respectable growth rate of some 6%.

Known for his intolerance to opposition, Prime Minister Thaksin continued to meddle in the media. The editors of the *Bangkok Post* and *Siamrath* were pressured to resign for having reported "biased" criticisms of him. ITV, a broadcasting station in which his family-owned Shin Corp. had a more than 50% stake, similarly sacked dozens of people, including its news editor.

Despite these problems, Thaksin's political position was strengthened. The wealthy telecom tycoon used his unrivaled financial resources to co-opt several opposition Democrat Party members into his Thai Rak Thai party (TRT). In July the Chart Pattana Party rejoined his coalition government. These developments gave TRT a comfortable majority (more than 70%) in the 500-seat lower house and prepared Thaksin for the general election scheduled to take place by February 2005. Unfettered by opposition, he resumed a

As part of a nationwide sympathy campaign for the families of those killed during recent unrest in Thailand's predominantly Muslim south, Buddhists and Roman Catholics hang paper doves, a symbol of peace, in a Buddhist temple near Bangkok.

war on drug dealers in October—a war that had claimed the lives of some 2,500 people in 2003. Intellectuals, human rights activists, and middle-class people in Bangkok branded him an arrogant dictator who endangered democracy. In one reflection of public discontent, Apirak Kosayodhin, a Democrat Party member, won a landslide victory in Bangkok's gubernatorial election in August over Paveena Hongsakul, who was supported by TRT. Mounting opposition in Bangkok notwithstanding, Thaksin remained popular in the countryside, where, since assuming office in 2001, he had implemented a series of pro-rural-sector policies, including debt relief and inexpensive public-health services, that benefited mainly low-income people, his strongest supporters.

(YOSHINORI NISHIZAKI)

TOGO

Area: 56,785 sq km (21,925 sq mi)
Population (2004 est.): 5,557,000
Capital: Lomé
Chief of state: President Gen. Gnassingbé Eyadéma
Head of government: Prime Minister Koffi Sama

Efforts to regain assistance from the European Union (EU)—which had stopped all aid in 1993 after citing Togo's undemocratic regime and its record of human rights abuses—dominated Togo's political agenda for 2004. In April, Pres. Gnassingbé Eyadéma ordered his ministers to promote political freedom. All parties were invited to participate in a national dialogue that was officially opened by Eyadéma on May 27, just six days before an expected visit by an EU delegation. Further evidence of the president's desire to normalize relations with major international donors was provided when exiled opposition leader Gilchrist Olympio—son of Togo's first president, Sylvanus Olympio—was finally granted a passport on July 28.

On August 24 the National Assembly amended the nation's press code. Among other changes, prison terms were abolished for journalists convicted of defaming the government. Although the opposition welcomed the reforms, relations soon deteriorated when the government denounced the private press for continuing to attack the regime. On October 12 two human rights organizations, the International Federation of the Rights of Man and Reporters Without Borders, accused the government of having initiated death threats against journalist Jean-Baptiste Dzilan.

Though Justice Minister Foli Bazi-Katare had stated on May 17 that Togo had no political detainees, on August 18 Eyadéma pardoned some 500 prisoners, including 7 opposition party members. On September 7, pardons were issued for 14 University of Lomé students who had been imprisoned for their role in a series of protests over grants and living conditions. The demonstrations had resulted in the closure of the university on May 2; though the university reopened on May 27, students boycotted their exams as a further protest.

(NANCY ELLEN LAWLER)

TONGA

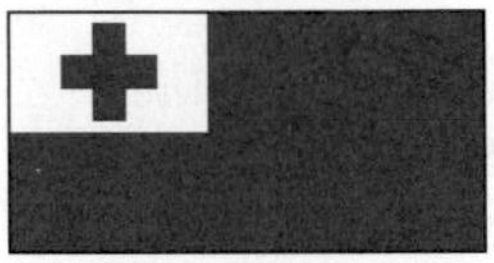

Area: 750 sq km (290 sq mi)
Population (2004 est.): 98,400
Capital: Nuku'alofa
Head of state and government: King Taufa'ahau Tupou IV, assisted by Prime Minister of Privy Council Prince 'Ulukalala Lavaka Ata

The year 2004 was marked by a number of challenges to the Tongan government, which, like the legislature, was dominated by royal appointees and nobles. Pro-democracy movements and the press promoted reforms of government structure and changes in policy, notably the restrictive media legislation passed by the government in 2003 and challenged successfully in court. After the Supreme Court struck down the law in October, newspapers—those published locally or imported—gained much greater freedom to comment on political affairs without fear of closure.

The government-owned Royal Tongan Airlines collapsed after its sole aircraft used for international flights was repossessed in April and it lacked the funds to repair its sole domestic aircraft in May. The airline was reported to have accumulated debts of $20 million. In its wake two small airlines emerged until the Ministry of Civil Aviation awarded a monopoly license to the company owned by King Taufa'ahau Tupou IV's eldest son, Crown Prince Tupoutoa. The airline used two leased World War II-vintage DC3 aircraft. The three ministers who opposed the decision were dismissed from office.

The economy suffered when tourism declined in the wake of the collapse of Royal Tongan Airlines. With a narrow export base, high imports, and pressure on the currency because of high imported inflation, domestic inflation was running at 12% for the year.

(BARRIE MACDONALD)

TRINIDAD AND TOBAGO

Area: 5,128 sq km (1,980 sq mi)
Population (2004 est.): 1,286,000
Capital: Port of Spain
Chief of state: President Maxwell Richards
Head of government: Prime Minister Patrick Manning

Trinidad and Tobago's labour minister, Larry Achong, resigned from Prime Minister Patrick Manning's cabinet in March 2004 because of the government's failure to enact a special minimum wage for the heavy construction (energy) sector, which had been opposed by business groups. Achong had publicly backed the measure and felt he had been compromised. He continued to support the Manning government in Parliament, however.

At a conference held in Tobago in April, Manning told Western Hemisphere energy ministers that Trinidad and Tobago was planning to add two more liquefied natural gas (LNG) plants after the processing unit Train IV came onstream in early 2006. This reflected a determination on the country's part to remain the leading supplier of LNG to the U.S.

Trinidad and Tobago's rapid pace of heavy industrial development reached a new milestone in May when the world's largest aluminum company, Alcoa Inc., announced that it would build a new smelter in the country. The complex, which was to include a new power plant and downstream fabrication, would cost $1 billion to construct.

In July former U.S. secretary of state Henry Kissinger paid a flying visit to discuss U.S.–Trinidad and Tobago energy relations and other matters with

Manning. In September Manning was quoted as having said that the Trinidad and Tobago Coast Guard could patrol the Caribbean Sea as far north as Antigua, to protect against drug traffickers taking advantage of vulnerable regional economies, once the U.S. government was prepared to foot the bill.

(DAVID RENWICK)

TUNISIA

Area: 163,610 sq km (63,170 sq mi)
Population (2004 est.): 9,975,000
Capital: Tunis
Chief of state: President Gen. Zine al-Abidine Ben Ali
Head of government: Prime Minister Mohamed Ghannouchi

On Oct. 24, 2004, Tunisia held its simultaneous quinquennial presidential and legislative elections. A special constitutional amendment had been passed that allowed candidates to stand for reelection more than three times consecutively so that incumbent Pres. Gen. Zine al-Abidine Ben Ali could take part in the presidential election. As expected, he won a massive majority, capturing 94.49% of the vote, which reflected a turnout of 91.52% of Tunisia's 4.88 million voters.

Running against President Ben Ali were Popular Union Party (PUP) leader Mohammed Bouchiha; Mohammed Ali Halouani, the leader of Ettajdid, Tunisia's communist party; and Mohammed Mounir Beji, head of the centrist Liberal Social Party (PSL). Another candidate, lawyer Ahmed Nejib Chebbi, was disqualified when he failed to gain the endorsement of 30 members of the parliamentary assembly—undoubtedly because he had declared that the elections would not be democratic. The other three opposition candidates were prevented from handing out election material and officially withdrew from the race, but two of the three agreed in withdrawing to endorse the president.

In the legislative elections the ruling Democratic Constitutional Assembly (RCD)—effectively Tunisia's single political party—won all 152 constituency seats outright. In the special national list—reserved to compensate opposition parties that could not confront the RCD—the Democratic Socialist Movement (MDS) gained 14 seats, followed by the PUP with 11; the Unionist Democratic Union (UDU), 7; Ettajdid, 3; and the Liberal Social Party (PSL), 2. Independents failed to gain any representation.

International disquiet about the nature of the electoral process in Tunisia reflected the wider disquiet over the state of human rights in the country. Both U.S. Pres. George W. Bush and Secretary of State Colin Powell brought the matter to President Ben Ali's personal attention during his visit to the United States in February. Human rights organizations estimated that Tunisia still had about 500 political prisoners.

The Tunisian economy continued to show strong growth, with GDP expected to grow by 5.6% in 2004 and by 6% in 2006. Unemployment, however, remained high at 14%, and anxieties were expressed about the slow rate of microeconomic reform in the country, despite government promises that it would be sped up. The privatization program remained stagnant during the year but was expected to accelerate in the future. Although Tunisia had not yet negotiated a free-trade-area agreement with the U.S., Washington established its regional Middle East Partnership Initiative office for North Africa in Tunis.

(GEORGE JOFFÉ)

TURKEY

Area: 774,815 sq km (299,158 sq mi)
Population (2004 est.): 71,617,000
Capital: Ankara
Chief of state: President Ahmet Necdet Sezer
Head of government: Prime Minister Recep Tayyip Erdogan

The prospect of securing a firm date from the European Union for the opening of negotiations on Turkey's accession dominated domestic politics and foreign policy in 2004. Although a settlement of the Cyprus problem was not formally a precondition, Prime Minister Recep Tayyip Erdogan, leader of the ruling Justice and Development Party (AKP), sought to satisfy the EU request that Turkey encourage the Turkish Cypriot leadership to agree to a referendum on the settlement proposals put forward by UN Secretary-General Kofi Annan. When Erdogan visited (January 26–31) the U.S., Secretary of State Colin Powell promised to persuade Annan to restart negotiations between the two Cypriot communities. Though the two sides failed to agree on a common settlement plan, on April 7 both Turkey and Greece announced that they would support a referendum on the island on April 24 on the text finalized by Annan. The plan was endorsed by the Turkish Cypriots but rejected by Greek Cypriots. The Turkish government secured promises from both Brussels and Washington that the Turkish Cypriots would be rewarded for their positive attitude, even though their area in northern Cyprus remained outside the EU, when the republic of Cyprus became a full member on May 1. Erdogan then concentrated on domestic reforms to satisfy the political criteria for Turkey's accession negotiations. His task was eased when on June 9 the court of appeal in Ankara ordered the release, pending a retrial, of four Kurdish nationalist members of the parliament, including writer Leyla Zana, winner of the 1995 Council of Europe's Sakharov Prize for Freedom of Thought; she had spent 10 years in jail on charges of collusion with the Kurdistan Workers Party (PKK) terrorist organization and until October 14 had been unable to accept her prize. On June 7 Turkish public-service television started broadcasting in minority languages, including two Kurdish dialects. The parliament in Ankara approved another major reform

Former Nobel Peace Prize nominee Leyla Zana (centre), with former Kurdish lawmakers, waves to a cheering crowd in Diyarbakir on June 13.

on September 26, when it amended the Turkish penal code in line with EU standards. At its meeting on December 16–17, the European Council decided to begin EU membership talks for Turkey in 2005.

Erdogan's ability to make major changes in domestic and foreign policy was enhanced by the results of local polls on March 28. In provincial councils the AKP increased its share of the poll to 42% (from 34%); the main opposition Republican People's Party (CHP) trailed with 18%. In mayoral elections the AKP retained control of Istanbul and Ankara and made gains at the expense of the Kurdish Nationalist Democratic People's Party (DEHAP) in the Kurdish-speaking southeastern provinces. This did not prevent a renewal of terrorism, however; at a meeting in northern Iraq, the leadership of the PKK—renamed the People's Congress of Kurdistan (KONGRA-GEL)—announced that it would resume armed attacks on June 1. The terrorist threat topped the agenda of the NATO summit meeting held in Istanbul on June 28–29. When U.S. Pres. George W. Bush stopped over in Ankara on his way to Istanbul, the Turkish government pressed him once again to take action against KONGRA-GEL terrorists based in northern Iraq. NATO leaders declared that terrorist activities in and from Iraq threatened the security of its neighbours. Although Iraqi Kurdish leaders Jalal Talabani and Mas'ud al-Barzani said that they would not allow any attacks on Turkey from territory under their control, KONGRA-GEL terrorists continued to infiltrate into Turkey from northern Iraq; more than 20 Turkish soldiers and policemen had been killed by early September. The major threat to Turkey, however, came from Iraq, where Islamist terrorists murdered more than 60 Turks—mainly truck drivers—in an effort to force Turkish companies to abandon the reconstruction program.

The Turkish economy performed strongly; the GNP grew by nearly 10% in the first three quarters of 2004 year-on-year; by the end of November, consumer price inflation had dropped to 10% year-on-year (against 19% for the same period in 2002–03); exports and imports increased, respectively, by 31% and 40% in the first 10 months; and the number of visitors from abroad rose by 28% in the first nine months. The stabilization of the economy was symbolized by the "new lira," a unit of currency worth one million old liras that was to be launched in January 2005.

(ANDREW MANGO)

TURKMENISTAN

Area: 488,100 sq km (188,500 sq mi)
Population (2004 est.): 4,940,000
Capital: Ashgabat
Head of state and government: President Saparmurad Niyazov

Throughout 2004 Turkmenistan's Pres. Saparmurad Niyazov continued to astonish the country's inhabitants as well as the outside world with his erratic policies, which were intended to turn Turkmenistan into a great nation. In response to international ridicule of his all-pervasive personality cult, Niyazov had some portraits and statues of himself removed from public places, but the spirit of the cult remained.

As a gesture to international critics of his human rights record, in January Niyazov abolished the requirement that citizens obtain exit visas in order to leave the country. The exit-visa requirement had been abolished once before, in 2001, but was restored after an alleged assassination attempt in 2002. In 2004 exit visas were replaced by a blacklist of persons who, for a wide variety of reasons, were forbidden to leave the country. In early May, after the U.S. Commission on International Religious Freedom published a report sharply critical of Turkmenistan, President Niyazov revoked the criminalization of religious activity by unregistered religious groups, and in subsequent months he allowed four groups that had long been denied legal registration to at last obtain it. Later in the year, however, members of some confessions that had been allowed to register, including Baptists, Adventists, and Pentecostalists, reported that law-enforcement officers were preventing them from worshipping together, even in private homes.

Niyazov continued to reorganize the educational system in Turkmenistan, using limitations placed on education as a tool to further isolate the country. According to official figures, fewer than 4,000 new students were admitted to higher education in 2004, and private study abroad became almost impossible after health officials were instructed not to provide health certificates to persons wishing to study outside Turkmenistan without official sponsorship. Niyazov ordered that degrees obtained at educational institutions outside Turkmenistan since 1993 be invalidated, with a few exceptions, including some degrees earned in Turkey. The result was a further loss for Turkmenistan of qualified educational personnel.

In September Niyazov presented the country with a second volume of his rambling discourse on Turkmen history and culture, the *Ruhnama,* which had been declared officially to be as important as the Qur'an and had become the most important text taught in schools at all levels.

During the summer Turkmenistan's relations with Uzbekistan and Kazakhstan were strained by the Turkmen refusal to admit that there was an outbreak of plague in the northern part of the country. Turkmen doctors revealed that they had been warned unofficially not to report the existence of cases of serious diseases.

(BESS BROWN)

TUVALU

Area: 25.6 sq km (9.9 sq mi)
Population (2004 est.): 9,600
Capital: Government offices in Vaiaku, Fongafale islet, of Funafuti Atoll
Chief of state: Queen Elizabeth II, represented by Governor-General Faimalaga Luka
Head of government: Prime Ministers Saufatu Sopoanga and, from August 27, Maatia Toafa (acting until October 11)

Prime Minister Saufatu Sopoanga was defeated by a vote of no confidence in August 2004. Because all seats in the 15-member legislature had to be filled before a vote for prime minister could be taken, Sopoanga resigned his seat to buy more time for negotiating a return to power. He was successful in the subsequent by-election, but former deputy prime minister Maatia Toafa, from Nanumea Atoll, defeated him 8–7 in the vote for prime minister.

Tuvalu, comprising low coral atolls and reef islands vulnerable to rising sea levels, was a strong campaigner for the Kyoto Protocol on climate change and had regularly sought resettlement options for its people. In February unusually high "king tides" caused flooding on much of Funafuti Atoll. In July Tuvalu joined the International Whaling

Commission but denied that it had received additional aid from Japan as a consequence.

The Tuvalu economy relied heavily on its investment fund, the licensing of its Internet top-level domain name (.tv), and remittance income from merchant seamen and workers in the phosphate industry in Nauru. The financial collapse of Nauru and its phosphate corporation forced Tuvalu to repatriate some 200 workers who had not been paid and to consider financial assistance for the remaining 100.

(BARRIE MACDONALD)

UGANDA

Area: 241,038 sq km (93,065 sq mi)
Population (2004 est.): 26,335,000
Capital: Kampala
Head of state and government: President Yoweri Museveni, assisted by Prime Minister Apolo Nsibambi

Long before 2004 began, Uganda had become virtually two countries. In the south, bolstered by vast sums of external aid, the economy remained on a sound basis, and the government's campaign to control the spread of HIV/AIDS continued to meet with remarkable success and acclaim; the U.S. in June provided an additional grant of $51 million to assist in the work. In the north, although the Ugandan army was no longer engaged in promoting civil war in the Democratic Republic of the Congo (DRC), the population still suffered the ravages of the Lord's Resistance Army (LRA) led by Joseph Kony; at the beginning of the year, there were still more than one million people living in refugee camps. On February 21 the LRA attacked one of the camps near Lira, in Lango district, killing nearly 200 people. After visiting the camp, Pres. Yoweri Museveni blamed mistakes by the army for the massacre and recalled the officer in command. Shortly afterward, a protest march in Lira, in which accusers charged the government with inaction and with having failed to protect civilians, was broken up by police and soldiers who fired on the marchers and killed at least eight of them. In their frustration some of the protesters then attacked property owned by Acholi businessmen resident in the town because, they said, the LRA was made up of Acholi.

Children sleep in a Catholic Relief Service shelter in Gulu to avoid being kidnapped at night by the rebel Lord's Resistance Army.

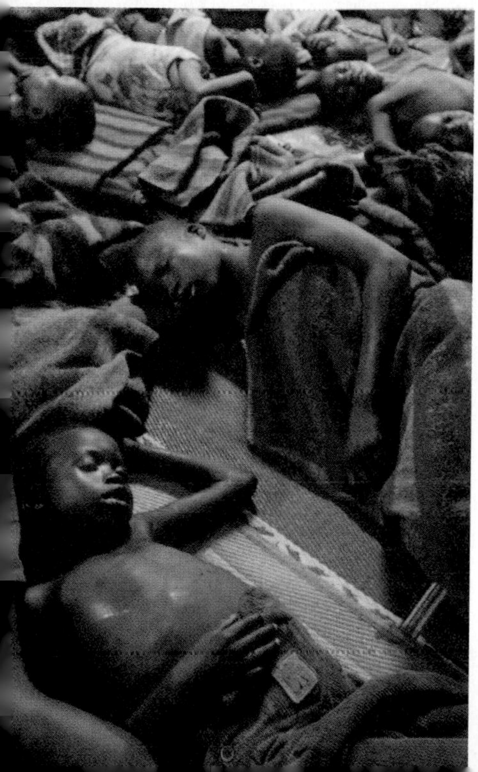

Later in the year the army claimed successes against the LRA, killing a number of the rebels and inducing others to surrender. Kony narrowly escaped capture in July. Nevertheless, LRA attacks on unprotected civilians continued, and in August an advance team from the International Criminal Court arrived in the country to prepare for an investigation into crimes committed in the course of the conflict. A cease-fire in November in a restricted area did not last, and in December part of the Ugandan army was deployed once more on the border of the DRC.

There were conflicting developments on the constitutional front. On June 24 the government announced that it would relax the restrictions imposed by the ruling National Resistance Movement on the activities of other political parties and that it would hold a referendum in February to determine whether the country should revert to full multiparty politics in preparation for presidential and parliamentary elections to be held in February or March 2006. It was also stated, however, that the referendum would decide whether the president could serve another term. The following day the opposition, which resisted any extension of the president's rule, won an important victory when the Constitutional Court ruled null and void the referendum in 2000 that had prolonged "nonparty" government and stated that any future referendum would be illegal. Museveni, desperate to stay in office, responded angrily that the courts would not be allowed to usurp the power of the people and appealed to the Supreme Court to overrule the judgment of the Constitutional Court.

(KENNETH INGHAM)

UKRAINE

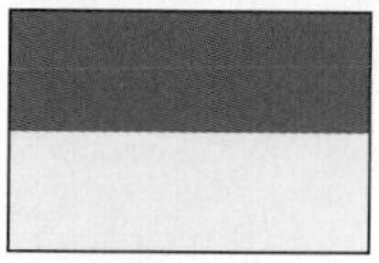

Area: 603,628 sq km (233,062 sq mi)
Population (2004 est.): 47,470,000
Capital: Kiev
Chief of state: President Leonid Kuchma
Head of government: Prime Minister Viktor Yanukovich

The year 2004 in Ukraine ended in political turmoil in connection with the presidential elections that took place in late October through December. In late 2003 a bill to change the constitution to give more authority to the parliament over the president had been initiated by Pres. Leonid Kuchma's chief of staff, Viktor Medvedchuk, and Communist Party leader Petro Symonenko. The bill anticipated the election of the president directly by the parliament. On March 5, 2004, the parliament accepted a first draft of a law that would introduce a system of proportional representation for parliamentary elections, but on April 8 the draft constitutional reform bill fell just short of the required 300 votes.

The Constitutional Court also paved the way for a possible third term for President Kuchma by dating his presidency from the entry into force of the constitution in 1996. By mid-April, however, Kuchma's supporters in the parliament had agreed to nominate Prime Minister Viktor Yanukovich, a former Donetsk governor, as their presidential candidate, clearly with the president's backing. Our Ukraine leader Viktor Yushchenko emerged as the chief opposition candidate, backed by Yuliya Tymoshenko, leader of the Tymoshenko bloc.

Spring and summer saw an apparent victory for Our Ukraine candidate Viktor Baloha in the election for mayor in Mukachiv city in Transcarpathia

© Gleb Garanich/Reuters/Corbis

© Vasily Fedosenko/Reuters/Corbis

Photographs of Ukrainian presidential candidate Viktor Yushchenko taken on January 21 (left) and November 23 show the disfiguring effects of dioxin poisoning.

overturned in favour of Ernest Nuser, who was supported by Medvedchuk and the United Social Democratic Party, and the use of skinhead thugs to attack Our Ukraine supporters. A government inquiry later overturned Nuser's "victory." In June, Investment-Metallurgical Union, the company of the president's son-in-law, was allowed to purchase Kryvorizhstal, the country's largest steel producer, at a price of about $800 million, believed to be less than one-fifth of the market value.

The election campaign saw impediments put in the way of Yushchenko, including physical prevention from campaigning in Donetsk and other eastern cities. In early September Yushchenko had to interrupt his campaign after he became ill with what was termed "acute poisoning." The illness became a campaign issue as Yushchenko's face became disfigured and pockmarked. Russia took a partisan stance during the campaign. Yanukovich was invited to Moscow to celebrate Pres. Vladimir Putin's birthday on October 7, and Putin made two visits to Kiev during the elections.

Twenty-four candidates ran in the first round on October 31. The Central Election Commission (CEC) initially put Yanukovich slightly ahead of Yushchenko, 39.88% to 39.22%. Ten days later, when counting was completed, however, Yushchenko's portion rose to 39.87% and Yanukovich's fell to 39.32%. The runoff round saw Yanukovich and Yushchenko in a direct contest. Though exit polls suggested that the opposition leader led by about nine points, the CEC announced that Yanukovich had won, with 49.42% compared with Yushchenko's 46.7%. These results were recognized by Russia and Belarus but not by the EU or the U.S.

Yushchenko's supporters maintained that the results were fabricated, and mass protests began in Kiev's Independence Square on November 22. Tymoshenko called for a nationwide strike. The protesters pitched tents along Kreshchatyk, the main street, and blocked entrances to government buildings. Several provinces, particularly in western Ukraine, recognized Yushchenko as the winner, and the candidate was sworn in as president in an informal session of the parliament. Gradually the television stations formerly controlled by Kuchma, as well as security and military leaders, switched support to the Yushchenko campaign. Meanwhile, in Severodonetsk a meeting of leaders of eastern Ukrainian regions recognized Yanukovich as president and postulated a referendum on whether these regions should become autonomous and eventually secede from Ukraine and join Russia.

The impasse continued for two weeks. On December 3 the Supreme Court declared the election results to be invalid and ordered a rerun of the second round. For their part the Yushchenko supporters agreed to recognize the main points of the constitutional reform bill that would limit the powers of the president, reform local government, and elect the parliament by proportional representation. The CEC was replaced and an agreement made that the rerun would be monitored closely by the Organization for Security and Co-operation in Europe.

Tensions rose again on December 12 when doctors in Vienna confirmed that Yushchenko's blood contained levels of dioxin that were more than 1,000 times the norm and concluded that he had been poisoned at the early stages of the election campaign.

On December 26 the runoff election was held, and preliminary results revealed Yushchenko as the winner. Yanukovich, however, legally challenged the results, and the matter was not expected to be resolved until early 2005.

(DAVID R. MARPLES)

UNITED ARAB EMIRATES

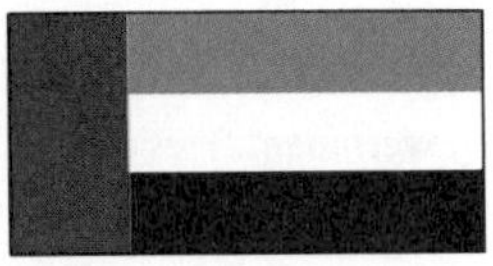

Area: 83,600 sq km (32,280 sq mi)
Population (2004 est.): 4,298,000, of whom about 750,000 are citizens
Capital: Abu Dhabi
Chief of state: Presidents Sheikh Zayid ibn Sultan Al Nahyan, Sheikh Maktum ibn Rashid al-Maktum (acting) from November 2, and, from November 3, Sheikh Khalifah ibn Zayid Al Nahyan
Head of government: Prime Minister Sheikh Maktum ibn Rashid al-Maktum

In November 2004 Sheikh Zayid ibn Sultan Al Nahyan (*see* OBITUARIES), the ruler of Abu Dhabi since 1966 and the president of the United Arab Emirates since it was founded in 1971, passed away. He was universally loved throughout the country and respected throughout the region and internationally; his passing marked a milestone in the country's history. His eldest son, Sheikh Khalifah ibn Zayid, crown prince of Abu Dhabi, immediately became ruler of that emirate, and another son, Sheikh Muhammad ibn Zayid, became its crown prince. Sheikh Khalifah was also elected president of the U.A.E.; he thus held the same two positions that his father had. The transition went very smoothly.

In 2004 the U.A.E. continued to enjoy a remarkably strong economy. It maintained a high per capita income level,

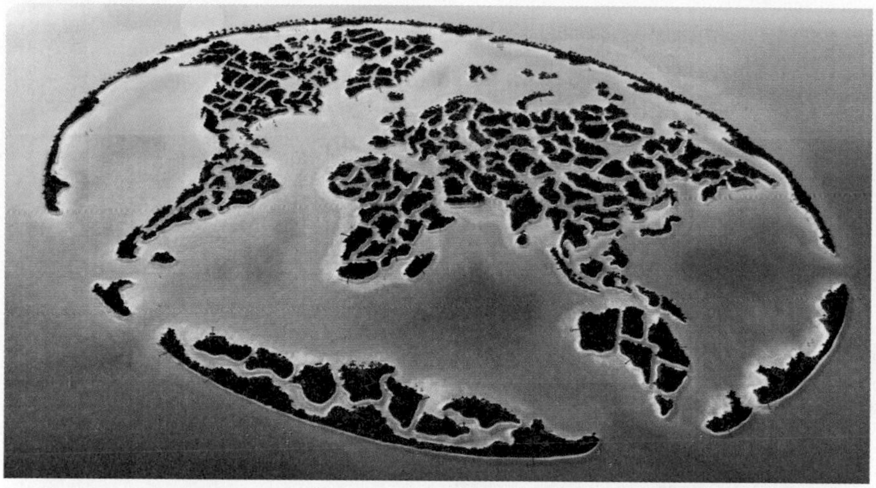

A graphic image illustrates the final plan for a luxury retreat being constructed in the Persian Gulf near Dubai, U.A.E. The 300 man-made islands, which would be sold to private individuals, were being laid out in the shape of a world map.

over $18,200 at the beginning of 2004, the second highest per capita income in the Middle East, after Qatar, and one of the highest in the world. The main cause was a $12.1% growth in GDP in 2003 to $80 billion. During 2004 the economy grew at a rate of 7%.

The U.A.E. economy benefited from high oil prices, and significantly, it suffered very little from the Iraq war and regional tension; in fact, the economy benefited from Iraq trade after the war. The London-based Business Monitor International ranked the U.A.E. as the top long-term performer in the Middle East.

The high per capita income was especially striking because it was calculated on the basis of the total population, including noncitizen guest workers, who accounted for more than three-quarters of the total population and who substantially increased their numbers in the U.A.E. in 2004. Citizens of South Asian countries and Iran made up 40% of the total. In 2003 the population grew at 7.6%, one of the highest rates in the world. (WILLIAM A. RUGH)

UNITED KINGDOM

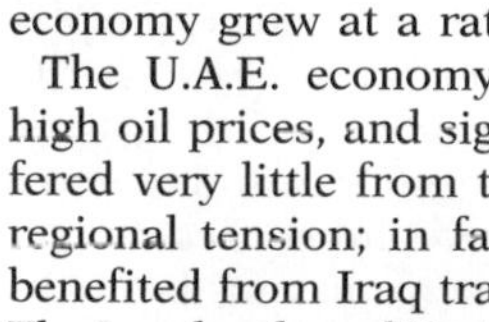

Area: 242,910 sq km (93,788 sq mi)
Population (2004 est.): 59,561,000
Capital: London
Chief of state: Queen Elizabeth II
Head of government: Prime Minister Tony Blair

Domestic Affairs. Throughout 2004 United Kingdom domestic politics was overshadowed by disputes over Britain's involvement in Iraq. These disputes concerned both the deployment of British troops in Iraq and whether government ministers had told the truth when they said before the war that Pres. Saddam Hussein had weapons of mass destruction (WMD) at the time of the 2003 U.S.-led invasion of Iraq.

On January 28 Lord Hutton, a senior judge, published his report on the circumstances that led to the suicide in July 2003 of David Kelly, a government expert on WMD. Kelly had been the source of a controversial allegation by a BBC reporter that the government had deliberately misled the public about WMD. Hutton exonerated ministers and criticized the BBC. The BBC's chairman and director-general, as well as the reporter who had broadcast the initial allegation, all resigned. Public opinion polls showed that most Britons considered the Hutton report a whitewash and thought that ministers deserved far more criticism than the BBC.

To address the continuing public debate about the quality of the intelligence about WMD, Prime Minister Tony Blair established a fresh inquiry led by Lord Butler, a former cabinet secretary. On July 14 Butler published his report. He found that much of the intelligence was either wrong or greatly exaggerated, most notably the claim that Saddam had the ability to unleash WMD within 45 minutes of an order's being given to use them. More generally, Butler found that the initial highly tentative and qualified assertions about WMD prepared within the intelligence services had been wrongly converted into hard, unqualified statements by the time they were issued to the general public, most notably in a September 2002 dossier that had highlighted the 45-minute claim.

Blair endorsed Butler's conclusions and accepted responsibility for what had happened, but the prime minister was reluctant to apologize for anything, least of all for having taken Britain to war, and he continued to insist that Saddam had been intent on developing WMD, that Saddam had repeatedly acted in defiance of the UN Security Council, and that—despite Iraq's continuing problems—the country was far better off without Saddam. On October 13 Blair issued a narrowly worded apology "for any information given in good faith that has subsequently turned out to be wrong."

Blair's lack of penitence upset not only opponents of the war but also many voters. The prime minister was increasingly seen as arrogant and untrustworthy, and the Labour Party he headed suffered a series of electoral reverses. It lost 479 seats (out of 6,000 contested) in local elections held on June 10. In the countrywide elections held on the same day to elect the U.K.'s members of the European Parliament, Labour's share of the vote fell to 23%, five points down on its share in the previous European elections in 1999 and by far its lowest in any national election in over 80 years. Even taking into account the proportional voting system, which helped smaller parties, Labour's share of the vote was little short of disastrous. Labour's vote also fell sharply in three parliamentary by-elections, two in July and one in September. Labour's one consolation was that it was the Liberal Democrats, the third largest party in Parliament, rather than the main opposition Conservative Party, that gained ground.

In the European elections Conservative support fell to 27%, down from 36% in 1999, as many of the party's traditional voters switched to the previously tiny UK Independence Party (UKIP), which advocated complete withdrawal from the European Union. UKIP won 16% support and secured 12 of the U.K.'s 78 seats in the European Parliament. UKIP's vote reflected not only disenchantment among many voters with the EU and the Conservative Party but also support for the candidacy of Robert Kilroy-Silk, a Labour MP in the 1970s who had spent 18 years

© Scott Barbour/Getty Images

On September 13 a costumed protester from Fathers 4 Justice, having eluded guards and scaled a wall at Buckingham Palace, demands rights for fathers. The incident at Queen Elizabeth II's London residence raised concerns about a lack of security in the U.K.

as a daytime-television personality and newspaper columnist. On October 27, however, Kilroy-Silk resigned from the UKIP group in the European Parliament following a failed attempt to call for a vote to replace Roger Knapman as UKIP's leader.

The Conservatives hoped that UKIP's support would melt away as the next general election, expected in 2005, approached. In the September by-election in Hartlepool, triggered by the departure of Labour MP Peter Mandelson (*see* BIOGRAPHIES) to become a European commissioner, however, UKIP's candidate overtook the Conservative hopeful, who came in fourth. The Conservatives' poor performance was bad news for party leader Michael Howard (*see* BIOGRAPHIES), but there was no appetite within the party for replacing Howard just one year after the previous Conservative leader, Iain Duncan Smith, had been deposed for failing to attract enough voters.

Labour's only clear electoral triumph in 2004 was in London, where Ken Livingstone was comfortably reelected mayor. Even this was a mixed blessing for Blair, who had long been a committed foe of Livingstone, a left-winger who opposed the Iraq war.

Although Blair was only 50 at the start of 2004, speculation persisted that he might resign before the next general election, which was expected to be held in 2005. On September 30, on the eve of a minor hospital procedure to treat an irregular heartbeat, Blair announced that he would remain prime minister through the following Parliament (assuming Labour remained in office) but would step down before the election after that. On December 15 Blair suffered a severe setback when one of his closest allies, David Blunkett, resigned as home secretary. Blunkett, blind from birth and from a poor background, had provided a notable role model for Blair's "opportunity for all" political platform. Following a messy and well-publicized fallout from a failed love affair, however, Blunkett admitted that his staff at the Home Office had acted wrongly in speeding up a visa application for his former lover's nanny. This admission made it impossible for him to remain in office. He was replaced by Education Secretary Charles Clarke.

Meanwhile, the government continued to provoke controversy with its strategy of public-service reform. The most contentious issue concerned higher education. In January the government published a bill to give universities the freedom to charge students fees of up to £3,000 (£1 = about $1.80) a year, compared with the £1,100 then being charged. Clarke said that the money was needed to allow British universities to improve and expand. To offset the pain, he also announced that students could borrow the whole sum at heavily subsidized rates of interest and need start repaying the loan only once their future annual earnings had reached £15,000. When the bill was debated in the House of Commons on January 27, however, 72 Labour MPs voted against the government, which left a majority (normally more than 160) of just 5.

A different kind of controversy involved plans to ban fox hunting. This traditional pastime was defended on the grounds that it was a form of pest control that brought jobs and pleasure to many in rural areas, but opponents condemned it on the grounds that it was cruel for dogs to pursue foxes to their death. On a number of occasions, the House of Commons had voted to ban hunting with dogs, only to be thwarted by a contrary vote in the House of Lords. In September the government announced that it would invoke the Parliament Act, which allowed the House of Commons to overrule the House of Lords after a year's delay. On November 18 the Hunting Bill became law, banning fox hunting from February 2005.

While MPs were debating the Hunting Bill on September 15, a group of pro-hunting protesters managed to enter the chamber of the House of Commons, having evaded Parliament's security systems by masquerading as builders. This was the third security lapse of the year. On May 19 a bag of purple-coloured flour had been hurled at the prime minister from the VIP gallery. The protest, by a group wanting extra rights for divorced fathers, came despite a thick screen's having been installed in front of the public gallery to prevent such attacks. On September 13 a member of the same group, dressed as the comic book hero Batman, evaded police to climb into Buckingham Palace—Queen Elizabeth II's London residence—and onto a palace balcony. These incidents led to debates over whether security in London should be tightened further, to prevent terrorists from repeating these escapades with more sinister intentions.

Economic Affairs. Economic growth, which had started to accelerate in 2003, slowed in the second half of 2004. The chancellor of the Exchequer, however, was able to boast toward the end of the year that the economy had grown in each of the 30 quarters since Labour returned to power in May 1997. Both unemployment (at about 5%) and inflation (approximately 2%) remained low. Tax revenues proved to be less than forecast, with the result that the government had to borrow more than it had predicted. The amount borrowed rose to £36.5 billion in the year to March 2004—just over 3% of national income.

One continuing issue for Britain's economy was the divergence between different sectors of the economy. Output of services continued to grow strongly, while manufacturing output started to decline in the middle of 2004. Companies relying on exports were especially hurt by the weakness of the U.S. dollar. In September Jaguar Cars (a subsidiary of Ford Motor Co. since 1990) closed its historic Coventry factory, where it had made cars since 1928.

One reason for the reduction in economic growth was the sequence of decisions by the Bank of England to raise interest rates. The benchmark "repo" rate started the year at 3.75%. Four quarter-point increases between February and August took the rate to 4.75%—still low by historical standards but a significant increase for people, especially homeowners, who borrowed money. One effect was to end the rise in house prices. In 2002 and 2003 prices had risen at the rate of 15–20% a year. By October 2004 the main house price indexes were showing slight month-on-month declines.

Foreign Affairs. On April 20 Prime Minister Blair announced that a referendum would be held in due course on the EU's new constitution. This announcement was significant for two reasons. First, it represented a reversal of government policy. Blair had previously insisted that the new constitution was merely a "tidying up" exercise and that Parliament alone should decide whether the U.K. ratified it. Second, EU rules required that new treaties (of which the proposed constitution was one) obtain the unanimous consent of all member states. Opinion polls showed that the British public was divided two-to-one against the constitution. By agreeing to a referendum, Blair increased the danger that the U.K. would be unable to ratify it—and therefore would provoke a crisis for the EU as a whole.

In Iraq, Britain contributed more than 8,000 troops to the multinational force seeking to restore order and prepare the country for elections in 2005. Britain's forces, second in size to those of the U.S., were based in Basra and adjacent parts of southern Iraq. In October 850 troops and support staff from the 1st Battalion, the Black Watch, were sent nearer to Baghdad, for two months, at the request of U.S. military commanders, in order to relieve U.S. troops preparing to assault the rebel-held town of Fallujah.

The issue of climate change moved up Britain's political agenda in 2004. On September 15 Blair delivered a major speech in which he described global warming as the world's "greatest environmental challenge" and said that the richest nations needed to take the lead in acting together to prevent dire consequences from being felt in 20–30 years. This was, in part, an implied call for the U.S. to do more; although Blair enjoyed close relations with U.S. Pres. George W. Bush over many issues, not least Iraq, there was a gulf between the two leaders on how to combat climate change.

Northern Ireland. Northern Ireland's main political institution, the 108-member Assembly, remained inactive throughout 2004, as the largest party, the (Protestant, antirepublican) Democratic Unionist Party (DUP), refused to work with the second largest, (Catholic, republican) Sinn Fein. As the Assembly's rules required a significant degree of co-operation, it remained suspended, and the province was ruled from London.

On February 3 Paul Murphy, the U.K.'s Northern Ireland secretary, launched a review into the 1998 Good Friday Agreement. With the DUP, which had always opposed the Good Friday Agreement, calling for its repeal and Sinn Fein demanding a withdrawal of all remaining British troops from Northern Ireland, however, progress was inevitably slow. Matters were complicated further on February 20 when attempts were made to abduct an anti-Sinn Fein republican in Belfast. Four men arrested in connection with the abduction were members of the Provisional Irish Republican Army (IRA), which was closely linked to Sinn Fein. Unionists accused Sinn Fein of condoning a breach of the Good Friday Agreement. On March 2 former first minister David Trimble, the leader of the second largest Unionist party, withdrew his party's support for the Good Friday Agreement and the review talks.

Talks resumed on June 15, though with little sign of a breakthrough. On June 25, following meetings between Blair and Irish Prime Minister Bertie Ahern, Blair announced that all the parties would be invited to meet in September, with each other and with the two prime ministers, to seek a way forward. These talks, which took place September 16–18 at Leeds Castle in Kent, failed to secure agreement. Blair and Ahern offered to restore the Assembly in return for the IRA's giving up its remaining arms; for their part the two unionist parties would have had to agree to share power with Sinn Fein and the more moderate nationalist Social Democratic and Labour Party. Sinn Fein accepted these proposals, but DUP leader Ian Paisley did not. He insisted that the Good Friday Agreement would have to be changed significantly.

Further attempts to break the deadlock took place in November and early December and involved negotiations in London, Belfast, and Dublin. Agreement was reached on the future of power sharing and the Northern Ireland Assembly, but agreement could not be reached over the decommissioning of the IRA's arms. The IRA indicated its willingness to put all its weapons beyond use by the end of 2004 and for this process to be supervised by Sir John de Chastelain's Independent International Commission on Decommissioning and other witnesses, including at least one nominated by the DUP. The DUP however, insisted that photographs be taken of the destruction of the remaining weapons. On December 8, following the IRA's refusal to accept this condition, Blair announced that the talks had failed; speaking at a joint press conference with Ahern in Belfast, however, he called for an "extra effort to finish the journey" toward a final settlement. (PETER KELLNER)

Ian Paisley, leader of Northern Ireland's Protestant Democratic Unionist Party, displays a December 8 Belfast newspaper headline reporting that the Provisional Irish Republican Army has refused to allow photographic proof of IRA disarmament.

UNITED STATES

Area: 9,366,008 sq km (3,616,236 sq mi), including 204,083 sq km of inland water but excluding the 156,049 sq km of the Great Lakes that lie within U.S. boundaries
Population (2004 est.): 293,850,000
Capital: Washington, D.C.
Head of state and government: President George W. Bush

For a third consecutive year, the strategic response to the Sept. 11, 2001, terrorist attacks by the administration of Pres. George W. Bush (*see* BIOGRAPHIES) dominated world affairs. The U.S. plan included two highly controversial initiatives—a proclaimed right of preemptive attack, to forestall perceived threats against U.S. interests, and a long-term objective of exporting democracy worldwide, to bring human rights to such areas as Afghanistan and Iraq, which had previously known mainly tyranny and despotism.

The administration's initiatives caused deep divisions abroad. Support came from the U.K., Australia, and emerging Eastern Europe, but other nations voiced strong opposition and resentment. At home the body politic was also split, and President Bush's foreign policies, particularly the occupation and rehabilitation of Iraq, became the central issue in the 2004 national elections.

Costs of the Iraq intervention continued to mount during the year. At times the U.S.-led effort appeared greatly overextended, putting unsustainable strain on U.S. resources, even the well-functioning U.S. economy. Domestic critics were unable to put forward an attractive alternative path as, in one sense, the November election became a referendum on the Bush terrorism strategy. In a high turnout of more than 60% by U.S. voters, Bush won reelection by a relatively narrow margin, 51–48%. (*See* Special Report.)

War on Terrorism. The Bush administration could point to substantial progress in Iraq, from construction and infrastructure rebuilding to election preparations, but the U.S. was again on the defensive for most of 2004. Pentagon officials reported that 848 Americans died in Iraq during the year, and another 6,000 were wounded, a casualty rate nearly twice as high as 2003, which included the military invasion that had toppled Saddam Hussein.

Early in 2004, in an assessment that cast a pall over the administration's rationale for the war, former U.S. arms inspector David Kay reported that allied prewar intelligence on Iraqi weapons of mass destruction was "almost all wrong." Under pressure, President Bush reluctantly agreed to appoint a bipartisan commission to study the 9/11 attacks and their aftermath. The commission, headed by Republican former New Jersey governor Thomas Kean, proved activist and highly critical, and its periodic public hearings and reports roiled the domestic political landscape through the year.

In late March, as the U.S.-dominated occupation attempted to prepare Iraq for elections and a handover to Iraqi control, authorities in Baghdad closed down a newspaper controlled by Muqtada al-Sadr, a militant Shi'ite cleric. A few days later four U.S. security contractors were ambushed and killed while driving in Fallujah, a city controlled by Islamic militants, and their bodies were publicly defiled. Militia forces loyal to Sadr then launched coordinated attacks in five Iraqi cities. The rebellion was particularly disheartening because Shi'ites, who had long been suppressed, were widely expected to be the major beneficiaries of the transition to democracy.

Allied forces eventually decimated the militia, retook several cities, and, with tacit backing of a more senior Shi'ite cleric, Ayatollah Ali al-Sistani (*see* BIOGRAPHIES), arranged a cease-fire with Sadr. Allied plans to pacify Fallujah, however, the apparent heart of the opposition, proved highly divisive, which prompted the resignation of two Iraqi Governing Council members. In a controversial step, the U.S. then postponed a planned major offensive on Fallujah.

In late April photographs showing apparent U.S. military abuse of detainees at the notorious Abu Ghraib prison in Baghdad began circulating on the Internet, setting off a firestorm of criticism around the world against the U.S. occupation. The photos, taken by fellow soldiers, became key to a dozen investigations, including inquiries by both houses of Congress. Seven U.S. military personnel, most of them low-ranking, were prosecuted on abuse charges. One report called the Abu Ghraib abuse the result of "fundamental failures" in military oversight, but claims by some critics that the abuse stemmed from official U.S. policy, approved by Bush appointees, were never proved. (*See* MILITARY AFFAIRS: *Special Report*.)

Coalition authorities handed over nominal control of Iraq on June 28, two days ahead of schedule, to an Iraqi interim government headed by Prime Minister Ayad Allawi (*see* BIOGRAPHIES), a neurosurgeon allied with the U.S. Under the unusual arrangement, the U.S. forces continued to lead security operations but operated technically under Iraqi supervision. The arrangement proved workable but did little to slow a continuing, apparently growing guerrilla insurgency, especially in Sunni areas.

On November 3 an American peacekeeper stationed in Bosnia and Herzegovina, on his way to watch the presidential election returns in a TV room at U.S. Eagle Base, near Tuzla, passes a sign reminding him to vote.

AP/Wide World Photos

© Joe Skipper/Reuters/Corbis

Little of any use remained of this beach house in Gulf Shores, Ala., after Hurricane Ivan slammed into the area on September 16. Four major hurricanes struck the islands of the West Indies and the U.S. Gulf Coast in a few weeks' time in 2004.

In early September, in a tacit acknowledgement of ongoing problems, the Bush administration asked Congress to reprogram funds designated for Iraqi reconstruction and shift $3.5 billion to law enforcement and security accounts. At that point, largely owing to dangerous conditions, only 6% of the $18.4 billion appropriated in 2003 for rebuilding had been actually spent.

Less than a week after the U.S. election, some 10,000 U.S. troops surrounded Fallujah and began a house-to-house campaign to uproot heavily armed insurgents. The assault took little more than a week to overrun the rebel area, and authorities announced that some 1,600 suspected insurgents had been killed, but most resistance leaders escaped the allied dragnet.

Bombings, surprise attacks, and even frontal military assaults continued at a high level through the end of 2004. U.S. authorities, under continuing criticism for failing to supply adequate troop strength and supplies, including body and vehicle armour, announced plans to increase the U.S. presence to 150,000 in early 2005.

Domestic Policy. In 2004 numerous bills bogged down in partisan wrangling as both political parties maneuvered for electoral advantage, and congressional productivity was light.

Democrats continued to throw up roadblocks to Bush appellate court nominees deemed excessively conservative, preventing 10 of 34 named by Bush during his first term from gaining an up-or-down vote on the Senate floor. The gridlock became an issue in the fall elections, with Senate Majority Leader Bill Frist, in a break from tradition, traveling in May to South Dakota, the home state of Sen. Tom Daschle, his Democratic counterpart, to campaign for Daschle's GOP opponent. Daschle was defeated. Following the election, Republican Sen. Arlen Specter of Pennsylvania, slated to become chairman of the Senate Judiciary Committee, seemed to warn President Bush in an interview against nominating antiabortion judges; following a storm of protest that reached his Senate colleagues, Specter withdrew his statement.

With few exceptions, only relatively minor legislation was approved prior to November. One significant election-eve law awarded $140 billion in tax relief to U.S. business, including a $10 billion buyout for tobacco growers. Another bill extended temporarily four middle-class tax cuts previously won by the Bush administration but scheduled to expire, including a $1,000-per-couple child tax credit, expansion of the lowest (10%) tax bracket, exceptions for the alternative minimum tax, and relief from the so-called marriage penalty for two-income families.

Reacting to increased abuse in the computer age, Congress increased penalties for identity theft, a growing source of fraud. At the urging of the Bush administration, and over objections of abortion rights advocates, Congress also specified that an individual alleged to have committed a violent crime against a pregnant woman could also be charged with a second offense, against the unborn child.

Four hurricanes—Charley, Frances, Ivan, and Jeanne—rolled over Florida, a hotly contested presidential battleground state, during a six-week period in the fall, causing an estimated $50 billion in property damage. Congress responded with a $2 billion disaster-relief appropriation for the Federal Emergency Management Agency, followed later by another $11 billion in hurricane aid.

As Massachusetts became the first state to legalize same-sex marriage, Congress struggled to fashion a federal legislative response. A proposed U.S. constitutional amendment defining marriage as only between a man and a woman went nowhere; the House approved the measure by only 227–186, less than the two-thirds required, and the Senate also failed, by 48–50, even to gain sufficient votes to stop debate on the measure. The House pursued an alternative idea, approving a measure to prohibit federal courts from hearing challenges to the 1997 Defense of Marriage Act. The Senate, however, never took up the bill. (*See* LAW, CRIME, AND LAW ENFORCEMENT: *Special Report*.)

Numerous congressional bills died or were postponed, including ones regarding bankruptcy reform, the banning of assault weapons, welfare reform, asbestos lawsuits, class-action and medical-malpractice legislation, and increased funding for federal highway construction.

Congress adjourned in early October without having made major changes to the highly decentralized U.S. intelligence structure. Pressure generated by the 9/11 commission, however, helped prompt a congressional lame-duck session in early December. The result was a bipartisan reorganization of national intelligence operations under a single director, along with new surveillance and antiterrorism powers for the new agency.

The Economy. World turmoil impacted the nation's domestic business climate but failed to stop a continued expansion of the resilient U.S. economy. Dramatically higher oil prices provided a damper on strong United States economic growth. The U.S., spending heavily at home and abroad, resumed its place as the world's main economic engine in 2004, at least temporarily shrugging off heavy costs associated with homeland security and the war on terrorism, and finally reversing a decline in employment that had started with the 2001 recession.

As the year began, the economy was growing at a robust pace. Expansion was stimulated by federal tax cuts and outlays from a record federal budget deficit and aided by low interest rates, modest inflation, and oil selling for $32.50 per barrel. Energy supplies, however, tightened under demand pressure from growing economies worldwide, especially in China. The growing insurgency in Iraq threatened supplies, as did less-violent uncertainty during the year in other major petroleum-producing countries, including Saudi Arabia, Russia, Nigeria, and Venezuela. By late October oil topped $55 per barrel, which acted as a major drain on the U.S. economy and helped turn what might have been an extraordinary economic year into a mere solid one.

The U.S. GDP grew by 4.5% in the first quarter and readily topped 3.5% for the remainder of the year. The Federal Reserve Board increased historically low short-term interest rates by a modest 0.25% on five separate occasions, ending the year at 2.25%. The consumer price index rose by more than 3.5% for the year, higher than in recent years, but nearly half of that increase was attributable to higher energy prices.

The national prosperity was fueled in part by unprecedented and disquieting red ink. The 2004 federal budget deficit, impacted by war, homeland security, and tax-cut measures, was $422 billion, less than forecast early in the year but easily topping the previous record 2003 deficit of $377 billion. U.S. imports of petroleum and Asian consumer goods paced record trade deficits that exceeded $50 billion a month through the year, another record pace. The weight of both deficits helped drive down the value of the U.S. dollar, a drop that accelerated after the November elections. The dollar finished the year at a historic low against the euro.

Unemployment drifted lower during 2004, from 5.7% to 5.4%. About two million new jobs were created in the U.S. during the year, a creditable performance but not sufficient to fully offset jobs lost during the recession. In addition, jobs were also being "offshored" to countries that had lower labour costs. (*See* ECONOMIC AFFAIRS: *Special Report*.)

The nation's equity markets followed a major bounce back in 2003 with a solid, if unspectacular, upward move in 2004. Broad indicators demonstrated that overall, share prices rose nearly 10% during the year, but some indexes were lower. The Dow Jones Industrial Average started the year above 10,400, but energy price increases and election uncertainty caused a sell-off to 9750 in late October. With election jitters settled, the Dow started a year-end rally and finished at 10,783, a gain of 3%.

Business news was dominated by continued fallout from 2001–02 corporate scandals. Two onetime business titans, Kenneth Lay of Enron and Bernie Ebbers of WorldCom, were indicted for their roles in accounting irregularities that afflicted their companies. John Rigas, CEO of Adelphia, a major cable company, was convicted on 18 felony counts for misappropriation of corporate funds. Martha Stewart, head of a successful marketing and publishing company carrying her name, was convicted of having lied about stock trades and sentenced to five months' imprisonment. Stewart appealed the decision but began serving the sentence in October at a West Virginia penal facility in hopes of limiting damage to her firm.

New York Attorney General Eliot Spitzer (*see* BIOGRAPHIES), who had rocked the mutual-fund industry in 2003 with allegations of after-hours trading and other improprieties, turned his attention to insurance in 2004. In a wide-ranging investigation affecting almost all types of insurance, Spitzer charged two companies with civil fraud for alleged bid rigging and steering business. At year-end, several insurers, while acknowledging problems in their industry, called for Congress to take over for state regulation of insurance companies.

Foreign Policy. With maneuvering ability almost nonexistent, owing to the war in Iraq, and constricted by domestic political considerations, U.S. diplomacy struggled through a dark 2004. Resentment toward perceived U.S. unilateralism coloured relationships with several countries, and despite earnest efforts, only marginal progress was recorded in expanding international participation in Iraq's security and reconstruction. The year saw some bright moments, particularly in nurturing democracy in Afghanistan, Indonesia, and Ukraine, but overall the year was replete with frustrations.

U.S. attempts to stop Iran's and North Korea's progress in their development of nuclear weapons capability met little success. Early in the year Iran reneged on 2003 promises to cease uranium enrichment that can produce either low-grade nuclear fuel or raw material for nuclear weapons. The U.S. pressed the International Atomic Energy Agency for punitive sanctions. The U.K., France, and Germany, however, offered Iran a trade pact with the European Union instead. Iran eventually agreed to a temporary halt in enrichment activities, one that critics said would be meaningless in the country's drive for weapons capability.

A long-running effort to dismantle North Korean nuclear designs made even less progress during 2004. The United States again refused North Korean demands for bilateral negotiations,

U.S. National Security Advisor Condoleezza Rice chats with Secretary of State Colin Powell at the White House in May; on November 16 Rice was nominated to succeed Powell as secretary of state.

© AP/Wide World Photos

insisting instead on six-party talks that included Japan, Russia, China, South Korea, North Korea, and the U.S. A June meeting produced no notable result, and North Korea then refused further negotiations, openly suggesting that the U.S. election might produce a new U.S. administration. The talks remained stalled at year's end.

The brightest chapter in international cooperation came in Afghanistan, which had lacked a democratic tradition. With the assistance of numerous countries, however, Afghans set up a voter-registration system and attracted nearly eight million voters, with substantial participation by previously disenfranchised women. The Afghan success, along with democratic electoral progress in Indonesia and Ukraine, was considered a major accomplishment in the Bush administration's campaign to spread democracy worldwide.

U.S. relations with Russia deteriorated amid charges that Russian Pres. Vladimir Putin was eroding democratic reforms, confiscating private property, and interfering in the internal affairs of European neighbours. In the Middle East, Russia was also suspected of providing assistance to Iran in its nuclear ambitions. U.S. authorities maintained a public facade of cooperation with the Putin regime but expressed private dismay over a variety of Russian actions, including nationalization of the giant Yukos oil company and heavy-handed—and ultimately unsuccessful—attempts to influence the election in Ukraine. (See *Ukraine*, above.)

Bush administration relations with the UN were also superficially correct but deteriorated significantly. The international organization was rocked by scandal, ranging from harassment allegations against ranking officials at the UN headquarters in New York to sexual mistreatment of women and girls by UN peacekeepers in the Democratic Republic of the Congo to culpability in having allowed Saddam Hussein to divert an estimated $21 billion from the "oil for food" program. A Republican-led congressional inquiry into oil for food was largely stonewalled by UN officials, and prominent U.S. legislators publicly called for the resignation of UN Secretary-General Kofi Annan.

The U.S. also fumed over lack of UN support for Iraq. UN relief officials had largely departed from Iraq in 2003 following a bombing attack on their headquarters and, citing ongoing security concerns, failed to return in 2004. In a notable interview in mid-September, only weeks before U.S. elections, Annan declared the 2003 U.S.-led invasion of Iraq to have been an illegal act, a declaration that Bush officials judged excessively political.

The UN's largely ineffectual response to humanitarian concerns in the Darfur region of The Sudan was yet another issue. More than 100,000 largely Christian Darfur residents were driven out of their homes by Islamic Sudanese, and thousands died. U.S. Secretary of State Colin Powell called the situation "genocide" and facilitated U.S. aid, but UN efforts to stop the ethnic disruption were minimal.

The tsunami disaster that followed the December 26 earthquake near Sumatra, Indon., also strained U.S.-UN relations. As the magnitude of the disaster began to unfold, the U.S. pledged an initial $15 million to the relief effort, and a ranking UN official labeled donations by wealthy countries as "stingy." Within hours of the disaster, however, the U.S. began deploying military resources and mounted a major humanitarian-relief campaign to affected areas in conjunction with Australia and Japan, often bypassing the UN relief bureaucracy. The U.S. contributed $350 million to the relief effort, and Americans gave more than $200 million in private funds; donations were rising at year's end. (*See* DISASTERS: *Sidebar*.)

The long-stalled Middle East peace process appeared close to renewal in October with the death of Palestinian leader Yasir Arafat (*see* OBITUARIES), whose intransigence and encouragement of violence against Israel were widely blamed for the breakdown of a key 2000 U.S.-sponsored peace accord.

(DAVID C. BECKWITH)

DEVELOPMENTS IN THE STATES

A long-awaited economic expansion finally ended a serious budget crisis in U.S. state governments in 2004. Although the recovery was modest and allowed replenishment of exhausted accounts, there was little expansion of services. States continued to wrestle with the federal government over education, health care, and prescription-drug reimbursement, among other problems.

Party Strengths. Democrats made notable gains in 2004 in state legislative elections, and Republicans appeared to increase their control of governorships. The results left the two parties at virtual parity in state governments nationwide at year's end. In 2005 Republicans would control both state legislative chambers in 20 states, down from 21 in 2004, and Democrats would dominate both bodies in 19 states, up from 17 in 2003. Ten states were split, with neither party organizing both chambers, and Nebraska had a nonpartisan legislature.

Republicans enjoyed a 28–22 edge in governorships for most of the year. In the November balloting Democrats took away GOP seats in Montana and New Hampshire, but Republicans were awarded previously Democratic governorships in Indiana and Missouri. In Washington, after the closest gubernatorial election in state history, it appeared after the first recount of 2.9 million ballots that Republican Dino Rossi had bested Democrat Christine Gregoire by 42 votes, but the Democrats challenged the results. Following a second recount, Gregoire was declared the winner by 129 votes in December. That left the Republican prospective advantage for 2005 at 28–22.

AP/Wide World Photos

Christine Gregoire, the Democratic candidate for governor of the state of Washington, speaks at a news conference on December 23 after a hand recount of ballots showed that she won the election by 129 votes.

Structures, Powers. An attempt to divide Colorado's presidential votes in the electoral college proportionately, abandoning the winner-take-all system, was soundly defeated in November voting. Citizens in Arkansas and Montana rejected November ballot proposals to relax term-limit laws for state officials. Wyoming's Supreme Court invalidated that state's term-limit law just as it began to take effect. Of 21 state laws approving term-limit laws over recent years, 6 were thrown out or repealed.

Numerous states expanded early-voting opportunities, and Missouri, North

(continued on page 486)

The U.S. Election of 2004

by David C. Beckwith

Incumbent Pres. George W. Bush (*see* BIOGRAPHIES) won a second term in 2004 over Sen. John F. Kerry (*see* BIOGRAPHIES) of Massachusetts by 3.3 million votes, with the narrowest popular-ballot percentage of any incumbent since 1916, in an election that was remarkable for an extremely polarized electorate, unprecedented spending, and high voter turnout.

As the year began, former Vermont governor Howard Dean was the front-runner for the Democratic nomination, but he faded rapidly. Dean was knocked out in the first major event, the January 19 Iowa caucuses. Dean fielded thousands of volunteer workers nationwide but finished with only 18% of the caucus vote, compared with 32% for first-term Sen. John Edwards (*see* BIOGRAPHIES) of North Carolina and 38% for Kerry. Dean sealed his fate that evening, capping a defiant address to a raucous crowd of supporters with a primal yell in what became known as the "I Have a Scream" speech.

Kerry won all but three Democratic primaries, sewing up the nomination by mid-March. He eventually selected as his running mate rival Edwards, a former trial lawyer who had gained good reviews for his populist "two Americas" message. Early on, independent candidate Ralph Nader appeared poised again to be a spoiler, but Democrats successfully kept him off the general-election ballot in 16 states.

The president's reelection strategy was overseen by Karl Rove, a canny longtime Bush aide from Texas. Bush pointed to significant domestic accomplishments during his first term: a major tax reduction, prescription-drug assistance for seniors, an expansion of federal assistance to public schools, and a real if less-than-robust recovery from the 2001 recession. In contrast to Kerry, Bush also endorsed a constitutional amendment banning same-sex marriage, which energized religious and conservative voters.

Kerry faulted the administration's health and education spending records as puny, vowed to raise taxes on the wealthiest Americans to finance a more muscular expansion, and taunted Bush repeatedly as the first president since Herbert Hoover to preside over a net loss of jobs during his term.

The central campaign issue was Bush's response to the Sept. 11, 2001, terrorist attacks, an aggressive approach that split the country virtually down the middle. Bush claimed the strategy was working and promised continuity. Kerry's position was critical of Bush and more nuanced.

Kerry had been launched into politics by his opposition to the Vietnam War in the early 1970s. As a U.S. senator, he had voted against the 1991 Gulf War, for the resolution authorizing the 2003 U.S.-led invasion of Iraq, but against an appropriation bill funding Iraq's occupation and rebuilding. At one point, attempting to explain, he noted that he had voted both for and against that funding bill—playing into Bush campaign charges that Kerry was an inveterate "flip-flopper."

Many of his supporters opposed the Iraq incursion, but a majority of Americans favoured tough antiterrorism policies, so Kerry walked a narrow ledge. His campaign settled on a strategy: Kerry would underscore his decorated 1968–69 military service as a navy lieutenant in Vietnam, background that contrasted favourably with President Bush's service in the Texas Air National Guard, to demonstrate that Kerry had superior qualifications to be in charge during perilous times.

The late July Democratic convention in Boston became a paean to Kerry's role in Vietnam. Kerry traveled accompanied by his "band of brothers," shipmates from his Vietnam experience.

In early August, as Kerry nursed a small lead in public opinion polls, a new ad-hoc group, Swift Boat Veterans for Truth, composed of navy officers who had also served in Vietnam, produced anti-Kerry television ads in three states. The commercials challenged Kerry's account of his medal-winning experiences and blasted his later antiwar activism as disloyalty to his comrades in arms. Many major news outlets were slow to cover the Swift Boaters, but conservative Internet "bloggers," writers of so-called Web logs, helped whip up attention to their claims.

This was the first election contested under the 2002 McCain-Feingold campaign-finance-reform legislation designed to reduce the role of money in politics. The law made "soft-money" contributions from corporations and unions to party organizations illegal but opened the door to "527" groups such as the Swift Boaters operating independently of the campaign. By one estimate total election spending increased by nearly a third, to $3.9 billion, since 2000. Democratic-oriented groups were far quicker to organize under the new rules, and 527s poured about $400 million into the race, helping Democrats overcome a marked Republican-funding advantage.

By late August, when Republicans gathered in New York City for their convention, Bush had regained a significant polling lead. Moderate Republican stars, including California Gov. Arnold Schwarzenegger and former New York City mayor Rudy Giuliani, and disaffected Democrats such as U.S. Sen. Zell Miller of Georgia, extolled Bush's conduct of the war on terrorism and attacked Kerry's leadership ability.

Kerry's campaign floundered under the assault, and Bush seemed headed to a comfortable victory—until the two candidates met on September 30 in Miami, Fla., for the first of three debates. Bush's aides had insisted that the first debate cover foreign policy, thought to be Bush's strong suit. The strategy backfired when Bush appeared on the defensive, finding it difficult to explain his positions and often repeating himself. Of the war on terrorism, Bush said some version of "It's hard work" on 11 occasions. Kerry, by contrast, spoke smoothly and authoritatively and, for the first time, emerged as a plausible alternative.

Within days Bush's lead had almost entirely evaporated. Both candidates

U.S. ELECTION 2004

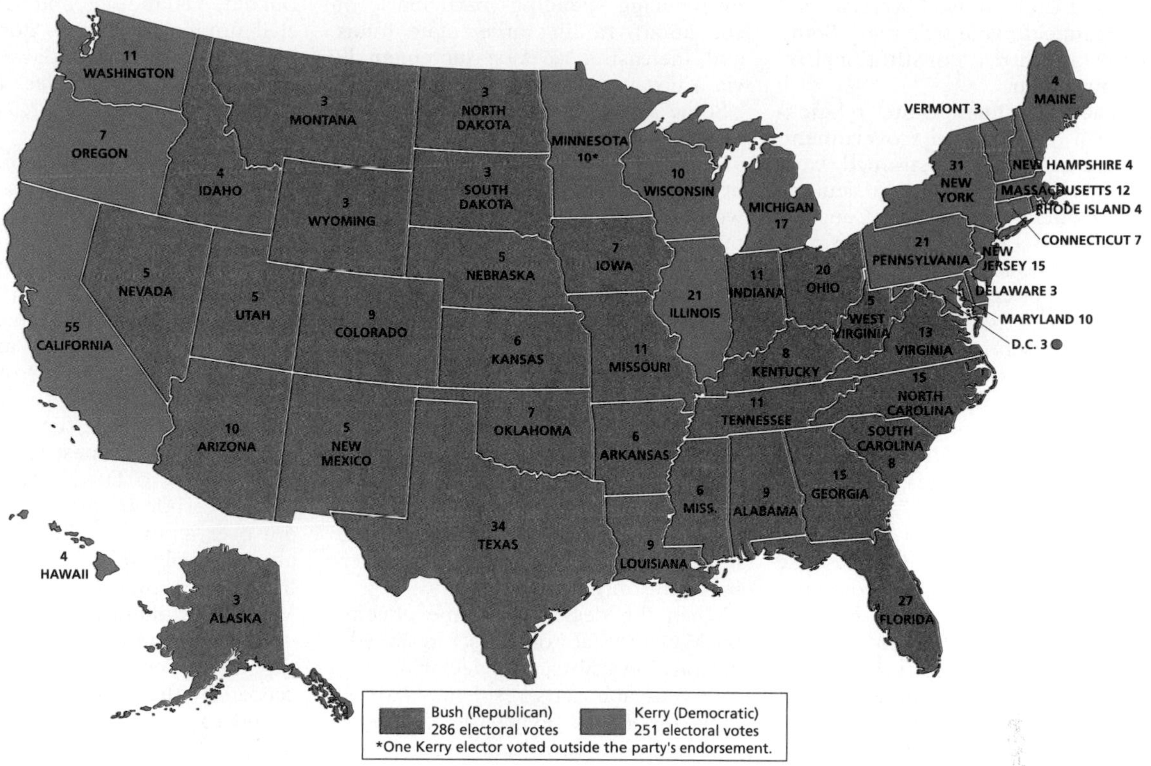

spent the final campaign weeks fighting in 14 "battleground" states, with imperceptible movement in the polls. Bush stepped up his game markedly in the second and third debates and thereby halted his slide in the polls and stabilized the race. Potential voters in the 14 battlegrounds were bombarded with repeated candidate visits, saturation media advertising, and multiple phone calls and mail from both campaigns and allied groups.

To all indications the country was heading toward a second consecutive 50–50 election. Kerry's operation, aided significantly by 527s such as America Coming Together, used a small army of paid staffers to register new voters, identify sympathizers, and get them to the polls. Bush's campaign was more centralized, relying heavily on volunteers who worked their own neighbourhoods to identify and turn out Republican voters.

Of the most closely watched battlegrounds, Pennsylvania went to Kerry by a small but comfortable margin. Florida, well organized by Gov. Jeb Bush, the president's brother, went clearly for the incumbent. That left Ohio, ordinarily GOP-leaning but hard hit by manufacturing job losses, as the decisive major swing state. Shortly after midnight it appeared that Ohio belonged to Bush by about 135,000 votes—but tens of thousands of "provisional ballots" cast by voters whose registration was in question made the results "within the margin of litigation." As most voters went to bed, it appeared possible the election would again be decided only after court battles. By Wednesday morning, however, the Bush advantage appeared insurmountable, and Kerry delivered a gracious concession speech.

Political maps again popularized the terms "red states" for Republicans and "blue states" for Democrats. Only three states switched colour from 2000 to 2004: New Hampshire went from red to blue, and Iowa and New Mexico shifted from blue to red. Bush won 8 of the 14 battleground states. Nader, whose 2.9 million votes in 2000 might have cost Democrat Al Gore the race, was not a factor in 2004.

In the end Kerry and allies were wildly successful in turning out voters to oppose Bush. The Democrat won 57.3 million votes, nearly 7 million more than Gore in 2000 and significantly more than any previous presidential candidate of either party in U.S. history. Nonetheless, Kerry received only 48% of the vote; it was the seventh consecutive presidential election in which the Democratic candidate had failed to top 50%.

The GOP turnout effort was even better. Targeting infrequent voters in suburban, exurban, and rural areas, Bush attracted 60.6 million votes, some 10.2 million more than he had earned in 2000, a 51% share of the electorate. The 120.3 million total votes was nearly 15 million more than in 2000. Bush's margin of victory, while narrow in a reelection contest, was larger than predicted by public opinion polls.

In another unusual result, the incumbent's party added seats in both houses of Congress, increasing the number of Republican U.S. senators from 51 to 55. Bush had surprised many analysts by pursuing an aggressive agenda following his narrow 2000 win. At year's end Bush reshuffled his cabinet, replacing 9 of its 15 members, and again claimed a mandate for an activist agenda, including self-sustaining private accounts in social security, reform of the income-tax system, and staying the course in Iraq.

David C. Beckwith is Vice President of the National Cable Television Association.

(continued from page 483)
Dakota, and Utah allowed overseas military personnel to vote by e-mail. South Dakota established a constitutional review commission.

Government Relations. State relationships with the federal government, which had always been strained, were tumultuous during 2004, particularly on public-education policy. Congress again extended a ban on state taxation of Internet services, this time until 2008. In another controversial action, a federal ban on the manufacture and sale of certain semiautomatic weapons was allowed to expire; only five states had enacted curbs on so-called assault rifles.

The U.S. Supreme Court, in a 5–4 decision affecting 13 states, prohibited judges from considering aggravating factors and extending jury sentencing verdicts. In a bow to seven states that failed to impose a personal income tax, Congress approved a two-year measure to allow optional deduction of sales taxes on federal income-tax returns.

Finances. Pressure on state budgets eased markedly in 2004 as the national economy recovered, and this led to an uneventful year for tax legislation. States still faced substantial budget shortfalls, but most were able to balance their books without raising taxes or substantially cutting state spending. With budgets tight, few states expanded social services.

Only nine states raised taxes during the year. Arkansas and Virginia increased their sales taxes. Alabama, Colorado, Michigan, Oklahoma, and Rhode Island raised their tobacco tax. Two states boosted personal-income levies on their highest-income taxpayers; California dedicated the added revenue to expanding mental health programs, and New Jersey funded a property-tax-rebate plan. Oregon voters repealed substantial personal and corporate tax increases approved by the 2003 legislature, and legislators in Iowa and New Hampshire reduced state sales taxes.

Overall, states began rebuilding "rainy-day" funds and repaying accounts that had been used to steer state budgets through the 2001–03 down cycle. In recent years California, which was particularly hard-hit by the bursting of the dot-com bubble, had accounted for nearly 40% of state budget shortfalls. At the urging of California Gov. Arnold Schwarzenegger, voters extended resolution of the crisis via a $15 billion bond issue early in the year. The state worked through the down period by reducing spending (particularly on education), raiding other state funds, and increasing revenue incrementally via a tax-amnesty plan.

Some 35 legislatures considered bills designed to curb outsourcing of jobs abroad, usually by banning out-of-state or foreign companies from doing state work. Only Tennessee enacted an anti-outsourcing law, however, while governors in Maryland and Massachusetts vetoed similar measures. (*See* ECONOMIC AFFAIRS: *Special Report*.)

Marriage. Fallout from the November 2003 Massachusetts Supreme Judicial Court decision making single-sex marriage a state constitutional right created turmoil nationwide throughout the year. Backers of traditional marriage took vigorous steps to overturn the decision and to limit its effect to Massachusetts, but their efforts were met with only partial success.

When the decision became effective on May 17, state officials forestalled a nationwide influx by declaring that only Massachusetts residents were eligible for marriage licenses. The state legislature took initial steps toward placing the issue on the 2006 statewide ballot, obtaining 105 votes (with 101 required) for a constitutional amendment permitting civil unions but not same-sex marriage. Another legislative vote in 2005 was required before the ballot measure would be scheduled.

Reaction in some states was sympathetic. New Jersey, anticipating a similar court decision in an ongoing lawsuit, joined Vermont in recognizing same-sex civil unions. Two lower court decisions in Washington state also declared the state ban on same-sex marriage to be unconstitutional, but the case was appealed. Local authorities in several jurisdictions, including San Francisco and Portland, Ore., began issuing same-sex marriage licenses before state authorities intervened; the San Francisco action was voided by the state Supreme Court.

Other states began taking legal steps to prevent the Massachusetts decision from being recognized under the U.S. Constitution's "full faith and credit" clause. Louisiana and Missouri voters and state legislators in Wisconsin joined four other states in amending their state constitutions to ban same-sex marriages. On November 2, voters in 11 additional states overwhelmingly approved constitutional amendments: Oregon, Mississippi, and Montana barred same-sex marriages; Arkansas, Georgia, Kentucky, Michigan, North Dakota, Oklahoma, and Utah banned civil unions as well as domestic partnerships; and Ohio outlawed any benefits to same-sex couples. (*See* CRIME AND LAW ENFORCEMENT: *Law:* Special Report.)

Ethics. Two governors, John Rowland of Connecticut and James McGreevey of New Jersey, were forced to resign under a cloud of scandal during the year. Rowland, a Republican, quit June 21 as a federal grand jury probed multiple charges that he had steered state contracts to favoured firms and received free remodeling services from state contractors. In December Rowland pleaded guilty to a single felony count of conspiracy to steal honest service.

McGreevey, a Democrat, became the first governor in history to be forced out over a sex scandal. On August 12, after a male former aide threatened him with sexual-harassment litigation, McGreevey announced that "I am a gay American" and declared that he would quit three months later. He was succeeded by the state Senate president, a Democrat, who would serve until January 2006; if McGreevey had left immediately, a special election in November would have filled the vacancy.

Law and Justice. States moved aggressively to combat escalating medical-malpractice insurance premiums, which were widely blamed on personal-injury lawsuits. Thirteen legislatures approved malpractice-relief bills, but governors in three states (Connecticut, Iowa, and Missouri) vetoed them. Florida voters approved a far-reaching plan to curb lawsuits and place a ceiling on noneconomic damage awards, and Nevada voters embraced a cap on noneconomic damages, but similar measures in Oregon and Wyoming were rejected in November balloting.

Ohio became the first jurisdiction to reform asbestos-exposure litigation, which in recent years had led to the bankruptcy of more than 70 corporations. The new law required that plaintiffs prove that they were actually ill before they could receive compensation; up to two-thirds of current asbestos claimants had not been diagnosed with cancer or other diseases.

Voters in Alaska rejected a proposal to effectively legalize and regulate marijuana use. Montana became the 11th state, most of them in the West, to allow the use of marijuana for medicinal purposes, but Oregon voters rejected an expansion of the state's similar program. Voters in Alaska and Maine

AP/Wide World Photos

A voter outside a courthouse in Tucson calls for federal judges to remove a temporary restraining order on Arizona's Proposition 200. The measure, which had earlier been approved by voters and was cleared by the court on December 22, denied some public benefits to illegal immigrants.

turned down proposals to stop using baited traps in the hunting of bears.

State-sponsored gambling enjoyed mixed luck during the year. Oklahoma and Pennsylvania allowed slot machines or video lottery terminals at horse-racing tracks. Oklahoma voters approved a new state lottery, with proceeds dedicated to education. Michigan voters, however, demanded veto power over any further expansion of gambling. Nebraska voters rejected a casino gambling plan approved by the state legislature, and California and Washington voters turned down revenue plans funded by expansion of Native American casinos.

Loopholes exposed in the highly publicized case involving basketball player Kobe Bryant of the Los Angeles Lakers prompted California and Colorado to strengthen their shield laws protecting the identity of rape victims. Wisconsin barred police from requiring that rape victims submit to a lie-detector test.

California became the first state to order suspects to submit DNA samples for testing after a felony arrest. Voters also narrowly defeated a proposal to relax the state's "three strikes" law, which mandated life imprisonment on a third felony conviction. A downward trend in application of the death penalty continued during 2004. During the year only 59 convicts were executed nationwide, down from 98 in 1999.

Health and Welfare. Conflict between state and federal approaches to health care policy was high during 2004, particularly over prescription drugs. A growing number of states—including Illinois, Minnesota, North Dakota, New Hampshire, and Wisconsin—actively defied a Food and Drug Administration (FDA) ban on the importation of drugs from abroad, particularly Canada, by setting up Internet sites to assist with such purchases. Oregon floated a plan to license foreign pharmacies; Minnesota waived co-payments for state employees and ordered Canadian drugs; and Vermont filed a lawsuit against the U.S. government seeking permission to import drugs directly. At year's end the FDA was continuing to battle the state action, asserting that uninspected imported drugs were not safe.

The limits imposed by the administration of Pres. George W. Bush on federal stem-cell research were challenged in several states. New Jersey expanded funding for a state stem-cell institute, and in November California voters approved $3 billion in state bonds to support embryonic stem-cell research over 10 years. Delaware established a novel $10 million anticancer research program, which would guarantee health benefits for uninsured patients.

States reacted warily as initial benefits began flowing from the federal government's 2003 reform of Medicare. Prescription-drug discount cards were offered to seniors nationwide, which created some confusion in 22 states that assisted with drugs via discount or subsidy programs. Twelve states approved new legislation to help transition seniors into expanded federal drug benefits expected in early 2006. (*See* SOCIAL PROTECTION: *Sidebar*.)

Georgia and Wisconsin became the first states to grant a major tax credit to encourage organ donation. Illinois allowed organ transfers from HIV donors to HIV-infected patients. Colorado, Tennessee, and Washington joined four other states that restricted student access to candy-, snack-, and soda-vending machines in public schools.

State spending on Medicaid low-income health assistance—the states' fastest-growing program—continued to strain budgets, with a fourth consecutive year of double-digit increases. States continued to react by trimming benefits and eligibility, and Tennessee contemplated a wholesale revamping of its signature TennCare plan.

California issued regulations aimed at fighting global warming by mandating reduced greenhouse-gas emissions, including carbon dioxide, in automobiles. Seven northeastern states tied their emission standards to California's. Arizona voters approved a law barring undocumented aliens from voting or applying for social services.

Education. State officials chafed under increasing pressure of the 2002 federal No Child Left Behind Act, which mandated gradually increasing standards for teachers and students. One-quarter of public schools failed initial testing requirements, and states sought exemptions from requirements for stepped-up teacher certification and achievement for at-risk and minority students. Protests against the estimated $9 billion annual costs, penalties, and unprecedented federal oversight were introduced in more than 20 legislatures. Only Maine and Utah, however, enacted legislation promising critical review of the Bush administration initiative.

Consumer Protection. Utah became the first state to ban "spyware," software installed on a computer without the owner's consent. New Jersey joined New York in banning the use of handheld cellular phones while driving. Massachusetts became the sixth state to outlaw smoking in virtually all public places, and Idaho also approved public-smoking curbs, with the exception of bars. (DAVID C. BECKWITH)

URUGUAY

Area: 176,215 sq km (68,037 sq mi)
Population (2004 est.): 3,399,000
Capital: Montevideo
Head of state and government: President Jorge Batlle Ibáñez

The year 2004 was an exciting one in Uruguay. After four years of sharply negative growth, the economy—aided by recovery in Argentina, strong growth in Brazil, and excellent commodity prices—grew by a robust 13.6% in the first half of the year. Unfortunately for the ruling Colorado Party (CP), little of this positive macroeconomic performance filtered down to Uruguay's poor or to the middle class. Unemployment remained above 13%, and more than one-third of Uruguayans lived in poverty.

In this context the presidential and congressional elections that took place on October 31 marked a sea change in Uruguayan politics. During the year the polls showed that the leftist coalition known as the Broad Front–Progressive Encounter was the largest party in the country. The question that remained was whether it would secure the 50% + 1 vote it needed in order to avoid a runoff with one of the traditional parties, the Blanco Party (PN) or the CP. In the last two weeks before the election, all of Uruguay's polls agreed that the socialists had reached the magical number needed to avoid a second round and that Tabaré Ramón Vázquez Rosas would be president. In the election, the left received just over 50% of the vote, followed by the PN (34%) and the CP (10%). Vázquez was to assume office on March 1, 2005.

The historic victory by Vázquez and the left was seen by many to further strengthen the hand of Brazilian Pres. Luiz Inácio Lula da Silva as he sought to turn Mercosur (the Southern Cone Common Market, consisting of Argentina, Brazil, Paraguay, and Uruguay) into the major voice for Latin American economic integration and the chief interlocutor with both the European Union and the United States in trade negotiations. Vázquez's victory was the latest example in South America of the move to the centre-left since the start of the new millennium.

(MARTIN WEINSTEIN)

Outgoing Uruguayan Pres. Jorge Batlle Ibáñez (right) meets with his successor, Tabaré Ramón Vázquez Rosas, at the presidential residence in Montevideo on November 10. President-elect Vázquez was to be inaugurated on March 1, 2005.

AP/Wide World Photos

UZBEKISTAN

Area: 447,400 sq km (172,700 sq mi)
Population (2004 est.): 26,009,000
Capital: Tashkent
Chief of state and head of government: President Islam Karimov, assisted by Prime Minister Shavkat Mirziyayev

Two terrorist episodes in 2004 drew international attention to the unstable security situation in Uzbekistan. In late March and early April, a series of blasts in Tashkent and Bukhara were carried out by suicide bombers—the country's first instances involving them—and according to official figures, these attacks on police stations resulted in the death of 28 persons and injuries to 50 others. Pres. Islam Karimov, whose repressive policies almost certainly bore some responsibility for the disaffection of the terrorists, blamed international terrorists and the Muslim extremist group Hizb ut-Tahrir for having inspired the attacks. At the end of July, the U.S. and Israeli embassies, along with the prosecutor-general's office, were targets of bomb attacks. Seven people were killed, including the three bombers themselves. In response to the attacks, hundreds of persons were arrested throughout the country, many of whom were pious Muslims who denied that they had any connection with terrorism.

Uzbekistan came under increasing criticism from the international community for its failure to register opposition political parties, its harassment of independent journalists, and its apparent inability to end torture of suspects in police stations and prisoners in correctional institutions. The country's oldest opposition group, Birlik, had its application for registration as a political party turned down in late June, which excluded it from participation in the December parliamentary elections. After a review of Uzbekistan's progress in implementing international human rights standards, Washington cut part of its assistance to the country while insisting that the U.S. wished to continue to cooperate in the struggle against terrorism. Apparently in retaliation, Tashkent refused to register American nongovernmental organizations working on political-party development and human rights.

Relations with Russia improved with the signing of deals for Russian firms to develop the Uzbek natural gas industry; international observers speculated that Russia was seeking to take advantage of Uzbekistan's annoyance with the U.S. over American criticism of the Uzbek human rights record. In June the Uzbek promise to start removing land mines planted on its borders with Kyrgyzstan and Tajikistan was hailed by the two countries. That same month Kazakh television reported that President Karimov had dismissed the border protection chief, Gafurjon

Teshayev, after a Kazakh citizen was shot dead by Uzbek border guards. The officers involved in the incident were prosecuted, and Tashkent admitted that the use of weapons had been unnecessary; previously, the Uzbek reaction to such incidents had been a defense of the border guards' right to use firearms.

(BESS BROWN)

VANUATU

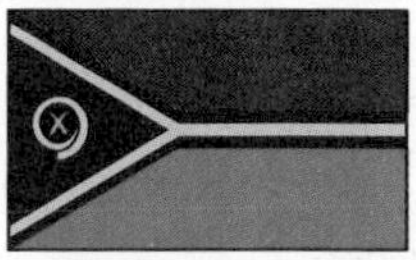

Area: 12,190 sq km (4,707 sq mi)
Population (2004 est.): 216,000
Capital: Vila
Chief of state: Presidents John Bernard Bani, Roger Abuit (acting) from March 24, Alfred Maseng from April 12, Abuit (acting) from May 11, Josias Moli (acting) from July 29, and, from August 16, Kalkot Mataskelekele
Head of government: Prime Ministers Edward Natapei and, from July 29, Serge Vohor

After a long period of instability in Vanuatu, during which the cabinet was reshuffled several times and the president dismissed because of his criminal record, Prime Minister Edward Natapei of the Vanua'aku Party called a snap election in July 2004 rather than face a no-confidence vote in Parliament. He was defeated at the polls, and former prime minister Serge Vohor of the Union of Moderate Parties joined with the National United Party, minor parties, and independents to form a coalition government. The new government was immediately tested by a vote of no confidence, which it won 31–21 in the 52-member house. There was continuing political tension, however, with the police commissioner being suspended for issuing an arrest warrant against the prime minister for contempt in regard to remarks that were covered by parliamentary privilege. In November Vohor and the cabinet clashed over the prime minister's diplomatic recognition of Taiwan.

In February the northern and central islands of Vanuatu were lashed by Cyclone Ivy, which caused damage to buildings and crops but no deaths. In September 120 kg (265 lb) of cocaine with a potential street value of $25 million was found buried on a beach just outside the capital, Vila.

(BARRIE MACDONALD)

AP/Wide World Photos

Pope John Paul II (right) receives U.S. Pres. George W. Bush at the Vatican on June 4. Bush presented the pontiff with the Presidential Medal of Freedom during the visit.

VATICAN CITY STATE

Area: 44 ha (109 ac)
Population (2004 est.): 800; about 3,000 workers live outside the Vatican
Chief of state: (sovereign pontiff) Pope John Paul II
Head of administration: Secretary of State Angelo Cardinal Sodano, who heads a pontifical commission of five cardinals

High on the agenda of the Vatican in 2004 was peace in an increasingly interrelated world. Pope John Paul II spoke out repeatedly against war and unilateral action by individual countries and in support of the concerted action of all nations, under the aegis of the UN. In early June, U.S. Pres. George W. Bush met with the pope and presented him with the Presidential Medal of Freedom, the highest U.S. civilian honour. Pope John Paul called for an end to the U.S.-led war in Iraq and a "speedy return of Iraq's sovereignty" but praised the president for his "promotion of moral values in American society."

The year was punctuated with rumours of terrorist threats directed at the pontiff. While the pope had refused to change his habit of mixing with the public, press statements indicated that some members of the Swiss Guard charged with his defense had traded their traditional pikes for automatic weapons to provide a more effective deterrent. The Vatican reportedly also installed surveillance cameras and metal detectors at entrances and issued wireless computer equipment to some security guards.

The Vatican continued its efforts to create unity among the Christian faithful, including those in the Russian Orthodox Church, with which relations appeared to have warmed. The return of the much-venerated icon of Our Lady of Kazan to the Russian Orthodox Church in Moscow played a role in this strategy of rapprochement.

The pope expressed his full advocacy of a united Europe, stating at the same time disappointment that the new EU constitution did not include an explicit mention of Europe's Christian roots. Some EU member countries, notably Italy, continued to push for inclusion of this mention. Despite his declining health, Pope John Paul traveled to Switzerland in June and in August made his second pilgrimage to the shrine at Lourdes, France.

(GREGORY O. SMITH)

© Jose Miguel Gomez/Reuters/Corbis

Venezuelan Pres. Hugo Chávez Frías (right) and Vice Pres. José Vicente Rangel wave to the crowd on August 16 after it has become clear that they have survived a contentious recall referendum.

VENEZUELA

Area: 916,445 sq km (353,841 sq mi)
Population (2004 est.): 26,170,000
Capital: Caracas
Head of state and government: President Hugo Chávez Frías

The regional and municipal elections held on Oct. 31, 2004, gave Pres. Hugo Chávez Frías unprecedented control over Venezuela. His Fifth Republic Movement and its allies captured 20 of the 22 governorships, as well as the office of mayor in metropolitan Caracas. Pro-government political parties won control of 270 municipalities (80% of the total). The total vote for all candidates fielded by Democratic Action (AD), the major opposition party, was slightly more than one-fourth of that received by government-backed candidates. The AD elected a governor only in the small island state of Nueva Esparta. In the aftermath of this resounding victory, Vice Pres. José Vicente Rangel announced that the government would accelerate the leftist social experiment known as the Bolivarian Revolution, which was launched following the presidential election of Dec. 6, 1998.

The government's victory in the October regional and municipal elections flowed from the opposition's failure to oust President Chávez in the recall referendum on August 15; of those voting in the referendum, 59% supported Chávez and 41% opted to remove him. This result, coming after a protracted campaign to oust Chávez, shocked his opponents. Public-opinion polls in the first quarter of 2004 indicated that voters favoured removing the president from office. The government, however, delayed the referendum for eight months, and Chávez spent petroleum income to fund social programs that changed attitudes toward his rule. The government's victory discredited and embittered the opposition. Some asserted that Chávez had manipulated voting in the referendum and the regional elections, even though international observers declared the results valid. Some opponents went so far as to state publicly that regaining power by democratic means was impossible, which moved the political situation into uncharted waters.

By early November Venezuela's economy appeared on track to grow at an annual rate of 12%. This increase followed two consecutive years in which the economy had contracted, by 9.3% (2003) and by 9% (2002). The turnabout resulted from the government's drawing down of foreign exchange to invest in social programs as well as from increased revenue from petroleum sales (prices for Venezuelan crude oils had surged to more than $40 a barrel, almost double the amount during 2002). At $40 a barrel, additional production (roughly 500,000 bbl a day) of viscous petroleum from the Orinoco tar belt became profitable. Correspondingly, the Chávez government increased the tax on foreign companies operating in the tar belt from 1% to 16.6% of the value of their production.

Continuity as well as change characterized Venezuelan foreign policy. President Chávez continued his support for Cuban Pres. Fidel Castro, supplying petroleum to Cuba at cut-rate prices. Chávez remained determined to reduce U.S. economic influence in South America; he opposed the Free Trade Area of the Americas initiative and committed Venezuela to associate membership in the Southern Cone Common Market (Mercosur). Nevertheless, Chávez's hostility was muted toward the U.S. after George W. Bush's administration accepted Chávez's victory in the August 15 referendum. Following President Bush's reelection in November, Chávez opined that he hoped for better relations with the Bush administration in its second term. On November 9 Chávez traveled to Cartagena, where he met with Colombian Pres. Álvaro Uribe. Directly addressing concerns that Venezuela was sympathetic toward Colombia's guerrillas, Chávez stated his support for Uribe's pacification efforts. The two presidents agreed to cooperate on matters of mutual interest, such as tightening security along their 2,200-km (1,400-mi) border, cracking down on drug trafficking, and coordinating energy policy.

(DAVID J. MYERS)

VIETNAM

Area: 332,501 sq km (128,379 sq mi)
Population (2004 est.): 81,839,000
Capital: Hanoi
Chief of state: President Tran Duc Luong
Head of government: Prime Minister Phan Van Khai

On Feb. 3, 2004, the Vietnam Communist Party's (VCP's) Central Committee declared, "International reactionary forces are likely to intensify their schemes of using issues related to 'democracy,' 'human rights,' ethnicity, and religion while aiding and abetting reactionaries and extremists at home to cause sociopolitical instability as a pretext for intervention." This dire assessment was seemingly borne out on April 10–11 when a demonstration of more than 10,000 ethnic minorities in the Central Highlands turned violent. Western human rights organizations claimed that dozens of highlanders were killed and hundreds injured by security forces who reportedly responded in a heavy-handed fashion. Vietnamese authorities were quick to accuse the South Carolina-based Montagnard Foundation of having instigated unrest.

In January the ninth plenum of the VCP Central Committee reprimanded Ksor Phuoc, the secretary of the Gia Lai province party committee and chairman of the Committee for Ethnic Minority and Mountainous Area Affairs, for having failed to deal in an effective way with similar ethnic-minority unrest in February 2001. The plenum conducted a midterm review of socioeconomic policies that had been adopted by the ninth national party congress in April 2001 and identified six priority goals: accelerating economic growth; developing capital, labour markets, and real estate; reducing poverty; gaining membership in the World Trade Organization; party building; and enhancing national defense and security. The plenum acknowledged that not all of Vietnam's domestic problems could be attributed to international reactionary forces. The plenum identified corruption, financial irresponsibility, and bureaucracy as serious problems. Two other senior provincial-party officials were reprimanded for fraud and "internal party discord." The plenum also issued a warning to Le Huy Ngo, minister of agriculture and rural development, for failing to prevent large-scale embezzlement by his employees.

The issues of corruption and administrative incompetence were featured at the fifth session (11th legislature) of the National Assembly, which met May 11–June 15. On the advice of Prime Minister Phan Van Khai, Ngo was summarily dismissed from the cabinet. Deputies grilled the ministers responsible for public health, planning and investment, transport and communications, natural resources and environment, culture and information, education and training, and physical training and sport for mismanaging their portfolios. Each minister conceded shortcomings and was spared a no-confidence vote.

In midyear the VCP was rocked by allegations of abuse of power by the military-intelligence service and political factionalism within the party itself. These charges were contained in a letter written by a retired major general, Nguyen Nam Khanh, a pillar of the establishment. Khanh was the former head of the Central Committee's Propaganda and Training Department, political officer for Military Region 5, and deputy head of the army's General Political Department.

Khanh's letter was timed to influence the deliberations of the Central Committee's 10th plenum that met July 5–10. Secretary General Nong Duc Manh, in his address to this meeting, noted that there was "degradation of ideological thinking, morality, and lifestyle among some officials, party members, and people and the gravity of red tape, corruption, wastefulness, social evils, and other negative phenomena." Manh then concluded that the people were losing confidence in the party and the state. In an effort to rectify this unwelcome trend, the Central Committee adopted a policy resolution on dealing with ideological and cultural issues. The plenum also initiated preparations for the holding of the 10th national party congress, scheduled for the second quarter of 2006.

On June 15 the National Assembly ratified the China-Vietnam agreement that had been signed in December 2000 on demarcation of the territorial sea, exclusive economic zones, and the continental shelf in the Gulf of Tonkin. In October Vietnam hosted the fifth Asia-Europe Summit Meeting after skillful diplomacy averted a threatened boycott by European countries over Myanmar's (Burma's) presence at the table.

(CARLYLE A. THAYER)

YEMEN

Area: 555,000 sq km (214,300 sq mi)
Population (2004 est.): 20,733,000
Capital: Sanaa
Chief of state: President Maj. Gen. ʿAli ʿAbdallah Salih
Head of government: Prime Minister ʿAbd al-Qadir al-Ba Jamal

The Yemeni government continued to confront hostile elements that were using violence against the regime, but during 2004 progress was made in achieving greater internal security. The Yemeni military and law-enforcement authorities successfully shut down a number of small terrorist groups. Socialist leader Jarallah Omar's assassin was tried and condemned to death. Reliable details about the terrorist groups were scarce, but some of them probably had loose connections with al-Qaeda. The government's cooperation with Washington in antiterrorism efforts continued. In September a Yemeni judge sentenced two men to death and four others to terms of up to 10 years in prison for the 2000 bombing attack on the U.S. destroyer *Cole*.

A separate internal security problem arose in early 2004 when a royalist, Hussein al-Houthi, started a rebellion in the north near the town of Saada, demanding a return to the imamate that had been abolished in 1962 with the establishment of a republican form of government. He was rumoured to be enjoying financial support from Iranians because he was a Shiʿite Muslim. After a five-month insurgency, in which some 200 persons were killed, in October government forces found Houthi hiding in a cave and killed him. Meanwhile, political leaders were already preparing for local and presidential elections in 2005. (WILLIAM A. RUGH)

ZAMBIA

Area: 752,612 sq km (290,585 sq mi)
Population (2004 est.): 10,462,000
Capital: Lusaka
Head of state and government: President Levy Mwanawasa

The budget, which was presented in February 2004, provoked widespread but peaceful protest in Zambia; the government, under pressure from the IMF to cut spending, proposed to freeze public-service salaries and to tax them at source. In August, as the impact of the measures became more apparent, the Civil Servants and Allied Workers Union threatened strike action unless the government agreed to increase the wages of lower-paid staff.

On a more promising note, the corn (maize) harvest produced a generous surplus, but food aid was still required in some areas of the country because much of the surplus was produced by commercial farmers who sought to take advantage of the huge demand for their crop in Zimbabwe and other neighbouring countries.

The death sentences that had been imposed in 1999 on 44 soldiers found guilty of having planned a 1997 coup against the government of former president Frederick Chiluba were in February commuted to terms of imprisonment by Pres. Levy Mwanawasa; 14 of the soldiers were set free in June. The leader of the coup was also released on medical grounds but died on August 18.

Mwanawasa's anticorruption campaign suffered a setback in August when the cases against Xavier Chungu, former director of intelligence services, and Atan Shansonga, former ambassador to the U.S., were dismissed because

AP/Wide World Photos

Roy Clarke, a British journalist in Zambia, greets well-wishers after the Zambian High Court reversed a deportation order from the government he had received because he allegedly insulted Pres. Levy Mwanawasa in a newspaper article.

both men were deemed to be beyond the jurisdiction of Zambia's courts, the former having disappeared and the latter having fled to England. As a result, the case against former president Chiluba, charged along with the other two, could no longer be prosecuted in its original form, but he was rearrested on a revised charge immediately after his release.

Another court case that attracted considerable attention arose from the deportation order issued against Roy Clarke, a British journalist who was accused of having insulted President Mwanawasa and some of his ministers in a satiric article published in *The Post* newspaper on New Year's Day. The order was quashed by the High Court in April, but Mwanawasa was sufficiently incensed to state that he intended to lodge an appeal.

Throughout the year the people of what was formerly Barotseland, now Western Province, continued to press for the restoration of a greater measure of autonomy, but their hopes that the August summit meeting of the Southern African Development Community might address their problem proved groundless. (KENNETH INGHAM)

ZIMBABWE

Area: 390,757 sq km (150,872 sq mi)
Population (2004 est.): 11,821,000, of which about 3 million people might be living outside the country
Capital: Harare
Head of state and government: President Robert Mugabe

Zimbabwe's international status remained controversial as 2004 began. Its withdrawal from the Commonwealth of Nations in December 2003 had won the sympathy of many African leaders who regarded Pres. Robert Mugabe's action as a justifiable response to the arrogance of the white members of the Commonwealth. South African Pres. Thabo Mbeki, who was not unaware of the situation in Zimbabwe, nevertheless considered that the majority of the Commonwealth heads of government had acted high-handedly in prolonging Zimbabwe's suspension from membership, first issued in March 2002 as a one-year suspension. Mugabe's popularity in South Africa was reflected in the loud cheers and standing ovation that greeted him in Pretoria when he attended the swearing in of Mbeki to a second term of office in April 2004.

Meanwhile, Mugabe continued to suppress dissent at home and to dismiss criticism from abroad. In January the government ignored a court ruling that the *Daily News* newspaper should be permitted to resume publication and ordered the arrest of three journalists for the *Independent* weekly for allegedly having printed lies about Mugabe.

In March the arrest of a British former SAS officer and leader of 67 mercenaries who were believed to be planning a coup in Equatorial Guinea was a propaganda boost for Mugabe. In May he cut short a UN mission engaged in assessing Zimbabwe's food requirements. Two days later the minister for labour and social welfare, Paul Mangwana, stated that Zimbabwe had no need of foreign food aid despite the fact that independent consultants had predicted a serious shortfall in the country's food production. In the event, observers claimed that huge quantities of corn (maize) were being imported from Zambia, while the South African grain-information service reported that an additional 150,000 metric tons were imported via South Africa.

Early in June, John Nkomo, the minister responsible for overseeing the government's land-reform program, announced that all productive farmland would be nationalized, with title deeds replaced by 99-year leases. President Mugabe stated that the government would take a half share in all mining enterprises and that he would not permit representatives of former imperial powers to oversee elections in his country. In August a draft bill was published banning all foreign human rights groups from operating in Zimbabwe and requiring Zimbabwe's own voluntary organizations to register with a new state-controlled council that would have the right to withdraw licenses and to appoint trustees.

To the consternation of some foreign sympathizers, the opposition Movement for Democratic Change (MDC) decided in August to boycott future elections unless the government abided by the charter on holding democratic polls that had recently been adopted at a summit meeting of southern African leaders. The MDC was heartened, however, when in October its leader, Morgan Tsvangirai, was acquitted of having plotted to kill Mugabe. Although Tsvangirai remained charged with other treasonable offenses, his passport was restored, and he immediately resumed his efforts to win support from other African countries for his campaign for free elections. In November Mugabe tightened his hold on power by suspending Zimbabwe's constitution and forcing a number of repressive laws through the House of Assembly, and in early December he suspended seven up-and-coming members of his party, accusing them of plotting to choose his successor. (KENNETH INGHAM)

Ahmed, Inam. News Editor, *The Daily Star*, Bangladesh. Contributor to *Rivers of Life*. •WORLD AFFAIRS: *Bangladesh*

Alexander, Steve. Freelance Technology Writer. •COMPUTERS AND INFORMATION SYSTEMS

Allaby, Michael. Freelance Writer. Author of *Encyclopedia of Weather and Climate* and *Basics of Environmental Science*. •THE ENVIRONMENT: *Environmental Issues; International Activities*

Allan, J.A. Professor of Geography, School of Oriental and African Studies, University of London. Author of *The Middle East Water Question: Hydropolitics and the Global Economy*. •BIOGRAPHIES *(in part)*; WORLD AFFAIRS: *Libya*

Andrejevich, Milan. Adjunct Professor of Communications and History, Valparaiso (Ind.) University and Indiana University Northwest. Author of *The Sandžak: A Perspective of Serb-Muslim Relations*. •WORLD AFFAIRS: *Bosnia and Herzegovina; Serbia and Montenegro*

Anthony, John Duke. President and CEO, National Council on U.S.-Arab Relations; Secretary, U.S. Gulf Cooperation Council Corporate Cooperation Committee; Consultant to U.S. Departments of Defense and State. •WORLD AFFAIRS: *Oman; Qatar*

Appave, Gervais. Director, Migration Policy and Research, International Organization for Migration. •SOCIAL PROTECTION: *International Migration*

Archibald, John J. Retired Feature Writer, *St. Louis* (Mo.) *Post-Dispatch*. Member of the American Bowling Congress Hall of Fame. •SPORTS AND GAMES: *Bowling:* U.S. Tenpins

Aurora, Vincent. Lecturer in French and Romance Philology, Columbia University, New York City. Author of *Michel Leiris' Failles: immobile in mobili*. •LITERATURE: *French:* France

Bahry, Louay. Adjunct Professor of Political Science, University of Tennessee. Author of *The Baghdad Bahn*. •BIOGRAPHIES *(in part)*; WORLD AFFAIRS: *Bahrain; Iraq; Kuwait*

Balaban, Avraham. Professor of Modern Hebrew Literature, University of Florida. Author of *Mourning a Father Lost: A Kibbutz Childhood Remembered*. •LITERATURE: *Jewish:* Hebrew

Bamia, Aida A. Professor of Arabic Language and Literature, University of Florida. Author of *The Graying of the Raven: Cultural and Sociopolitical Significance of Algerian Folk Poetry*. Associate Editor of *Encyclopedia of African Literature, 2003*. •LITERATURE: *Arabic*

Barrett, David B. Research Professor of Missiometrics, Regent University, Virginia Beach, Va. Author of *World Christian Encyclopedia* and *Schism and Renewal in Africa*. Coauthor of *World Christian Trends, AD 30–AD 2200: Interpreting the Annual Christian Megacensus*. •RELIGION: *Tables (in part)*

Baru, Sanjaya. Media Adviser to Prime Minister, Government of India. Author of *The Political Economy of Indian Sugar: State Intervention and Structural Change*. •BIOGRAPHIES *(in part)*; WORLD AFFAIRS: *India*

Bauer, Patricia. Assistant Editor, Encyclopædia Britannica. •CALENDAR; DISASTERS; OBITUARIES *(in part)*

Beckwith, David C. Vice President, National Cable Television Association. •WORLD AFFAIRS: *United States; United States:* SPECIAL REPORT: The U.S. Election of 2004; *United States:* State and Local Affairs

Benedetti, Laura. Laura and Gaetano De Sole Associate Professor of Contemporary Italian Culture, Georgetown University, Washington, D.C. Author of *La sconfitta di Diana: un percorso per la Gerusalemme liberata*. •LITERATURE: *Italian*

Bernstein, Ellen. Freelance Writer and Editor, specializing in health and medicine. •HEALTH AND DISEASE; HEALTH AND DISEASE: Sidebar

Berris, Linda. Freelance Journalist. •OBITUARIES *(in part)*

Bird, Thomas E. Professor of European Languages, the Jewish Studies Program, Queens College, City University of New York. Coeditor of *Hryhorij Savyč Skovoroda: An Anthology of Critical Articles*. •LITERATURE: *Jewish:* Yiddish

Bonds, John B. Visiting Assistant Professor of History, The Citadel, Charleston, S.C. Author of *Bipartisan Strategy: Selling the Marshall Plan*. •SPORTS AND GAMES: *Sailing (Yachting)*

Bradsher, Henry S. Foreign Affairs Analyst, Author, and Lecturer. •WORLD AFFAIRS: *Philippines*

Brady, Conor. Editor Emeritus, *The Irish Times*, Dublin. •WORLD AFFAIRS: *Ireland*

Brecher, Kenneth. Professor of Astronomy and Physics; Director, Science and Mathematics Education Center, Boston University. •PHYSICAL SCIENCES: *Astronomy*

Brockmann, Stephen. Associate Professor of German, Carnegie Mellon University, Pittsburgh, Pa. Editor of *The Brecht Yearbook*. Author of *Literature and German Reunification and German Literary Culture at the Zero Hour: Studies in German Literature, Linguistics, and Culture*. •LITERATURE: *German*

Brokopp, John G. Media Relations Consultant; Freelance Journalist; Syndicated Columnist on casino gambling. Author of *Thrifty Gambling* and *Insider's Guide to Internet Gambling: Your Sourcebook for Safe and Profitable Gambling*. •BIOGRAPHIES *(in part)*; SPORTS AND GAMES: *Equestrian Sports:* Thoroughbred Racing: *United States*

Brown, Bess. Consultant on Central Asia, Munich, Ger. Author of *Authoritarianism in the New States of Central Asia*. •WORLD AFFAIRS: *Kazakhstan; Kyrgyzstan; Tajikistan; Turkmenistan; Uzbekistan*

Buchan, David. Foreign Editorial Writer, *Financial Times*, London. Author of *The Single Market and Tomorrow's Europe: A Progress Report from the European Commission*. •WORLD AFFAIRS: *France*

Bungs, Dzintra. Senior Research Fellow, Latvian Institute of International Affairs, Riga. Author of *The Baltic States: Problems and Prospects of Membership in the European Union*. •WORLD AFFAIRS: *Latvia*

Burns, Erik T. Bureau Chief, Dow Jones Newswires, Lisbon. •WORLD AFFAIRS: *Portugal*

Byrne, Justin. Researcher, Center for Advanced Study in the Social Sciences, Instituto Juan March de Estudios e Investigaciones, Madrid. •BIOGRAPHIES *(in part)*; WORLD AFFAIRS: *Spain*

Byrne, Robert. Writer. Member of the Billiard Congress of America's Hall of Fame. Author of *Byrne's Complete Book of Pool Shots: 350 Moves Every Player Should Know* and others. •SPORTS AND GAMES: *Billiard Games*

Cafferty, Bernard. Associate Editor, *British Chess Magazine*. Author of *The Soviet Championships*. •SPORTS AND GAMES: *Chess*

Campbell, Robert. Architect and Architecture Critic. Author of *Cityscapes of Boston: An American City Through Time*. •ARCHITECTURE AND CIVIL ENGINEERING: *Architecture*

Caplan, Marla. Programs Associate, International Center of Photography, New York City. •ART AND ART EXHIBITIONS: *Photography*

Carter, Robert W. Journalist. •SPORTS AND GAMES: *Equestrian Sports:* Steeplechasing; Thoroughbred Racing: *International*

Chappell, Duncan. President, Mental Health Review Tribunal, Sydney, Australia. Author of *Preventing and Responding to Violence at Work*. •LAW, CRIME, AND LAW ENFORCEMENT: *Crime*

Cheuse, Alan. Writing Faculty, English Department, George Mason University, Fairfax, Va.; Book Commentator, National Public Radio. Author of *The Light Possessed* and *Listening to the Page: Adventures in Reading and Writing*. •LITERATURE: *English:* United States

Chua Lee Hoong. Features Editor, *The Straits Times*, Singapore. •WORLD AFFAIRS: *Singapore*

Cioroslan, Dragomir. USAW Board of Directors Member; Executive Board Member, International Weightlifting Federation. Coauthor of *Banish Your Belly*. •SPORTS AND GAMES: *Weight Lifting*

Clark, David Draper. Editor in Chief, *World Literature Today*. •LITERATURE: *English:* Other Literature in English

Clark, Janet H. Editor, Independent Analyst, and Writer on economic and financial topics. •NOBEL PRIZES *(in part)*

Coate, Roger A. Professor of International Organization, University of South Carolina. Coauthor of *The United Nations and Changing World Politics*. •WORLD AFFAIRS: *United Nations*

Coller, Ken. President, West Seattle Productions. •SPORTS AND GAMES: *Wrestling:* Sumo

Collins, Nigel. Editor in Chief, *The Ring, KO, World Boxing*, and *Boxing 2004*. •BIOGRAPHIES *(in part)*; SPORTS AND GAMES: *Boxing*

Cooper, Peter. Music Journalist, *The Tennessean*. •PERFORMING ARTS: *Music:* Popular (United States)

Cosgrave, Bronwyn. Author, Journalist, Broadcaster. Author of *Costume and Fashion: A Complete History* and *Sample* (forthcoming in 2005). •BIOGRAPHIES *(in part)*; FASHIONS

Coveney, Michael. Theatre Critic in London. Author of *Maggie Smith; The World According to Mike Leigh; The Andrew Lloyd Webber Story*. •PERFORMING ARTS: *Theatre:* Great Britain and Ireland

Craine, Anthony G. Writer. •BIOGRAPHIES *(in part)*

Crampton, Richard J. Professor of East European History, University of Oxford. Author of *A Concise History of Bulgaria* and *The Balkans Since the Second World War*. •WORLD AFFAIRS: *Bulgaria*

Crisp, Brian F. Associate Professor of Political Science, Washington University, St. Louis, Mo. Author of *Democratic Institutional Design*. •WORLD AFFAIRS: *Colombia*

Crossing, Peter F. Associate Editor, *World Christian Encyclopedia*; Missions Information Coordinator, Sydney Centre for World Mission, Australia. •RELIGION: *Tables (in part)*

Cullen, Dan. Director, American Booksellers Association, Information Department. •MEDIA AND PUBLISHING: *Book Publishing* (United States)

Curwen, Peter. Professor of Telecommunications, Strathclyde University, Glasgow, Scot. Author of *The U.K. Publishing Industry* and others. •MEDIA AND PUBLISHING: *Book Publishing* (international)

Cuttino, John Charles. Lyndon B. Johnson School of Public Affairs, University of Texas at Austin. •WORLD AFFAIRS: *Brazil*

Deeb, Marius K. Professor of Middle East Studies, SAIS, Johns Hopkins University, Washington, D.C. Author of *Syria's Terrorist War on Lebanon and the Peace Process*. •WORLD AFFAIRS: *Egypt; Jordan*

de la Barre, Kenneth. Fellow, Arctic Institute of North America; Research Associate, Yukon College, Northern Research Institute. •WORLD AFFAIRS: *Arctic Regions*

Denselow, Robin. Correspondent, BBC Television's *Newsnight*. Author of *When the Music's Over: The Story of Political Pop*. •PERFORMING ARTS: *Music:* Popular (international)

Dietz, Henry A. Professor, Department of Government, University of Texas at Austin. •WORLD AFFAIRS: *Peru*

Dooling, Dave. Education and Public Outreach Officer, National Solar Observatory, Sacramento Peak, New Mexico. Coauthor of *Engineering Tomorrow*. •PHYSICAL SCIENCES: *Space Exploration; Space Exploration:* SPECIAL REPORT: The Mystique of Mars

Dowd, Siobhan. Columnist, *Glimmer Train* (U.S.). Author of *This Prison Where I Live* and *Roads of the Roma*. •BIOGRAPHIES *(in part)*

Ebeling, Mary F.E. Department of Sociology, University of Surrey, Guildford, Eng. •WORLD AFFAIRS: *Burundi; Comoros; Djibouti; Ghana; Liberia; Mauritius; Nigeria; Rwanda; Seychelles; Sierra Leone*

Ehringer, Gavin Forbes. Sports Columnist, *Rocky Mountain News* and *Western Horseman*. Author of *Rodeo Legends*. •SPORTS AND GAMES: *Rodeo*

Erikson, Daniel P. Director, the Cuba Program, Inter-American Dialogue, Washington, D.C. •WORLD AFFAIRS: *Cuba*

Esteban, Verónica. Journalist and Bilingual Editor. •LITERATURE: *Spanish:* Spain

Fagan, Brian. Professor of Anthropology, University of California, Santa Barbara. Author of *The Little Ice Age: How Climate Made History, 1300–1850; Floods, Famines, and Emperors: El Niño and the Fate of Civilizations;* and *The Long Summer: How Climate Changed Civilization*. •ANTHROPOLOGY AND ARCHAEOLOGY: *Archaeology:* Western Hemisphere

Farr, David M.L. Professor Emeritus of History, Carleton University, Ottawa. •BIOGRAPHIES *(in part);* WORLD AFFAIRS: *Canada*

Fealy, Greg. Research Fellow and Lecturer in Indonesian Politics, The Australian National University, Canberra. Author of *The Release of Indonesia's Political Prisoners: Domestic Versus Foreign Policy, 1975–1979.* •WORLD AFFAIRS: *Indonesia*

Fendell, Robert J. Freelance Writer on automobiles and racing. Author of *The Encyclopedia of Auto Racing Greats.* •SPORTS AND GAMES: *Automobile Racing:* U.S. Auto Racing *(in part);* Rallies and Other Races *(in part)*

Fisher, Martin. Editor, *Oryx;* Coeditor, *The Natural History of Oman: A Festschrift for Michael Gallagher.* •THE ENVIRONMENT: *Wildlife Conservation*

Fisher, Sharon. Central European Specialist, Global Insight, Inc., Washington, D.C. •WORLD AFFAIRS: *Czech Republic; Slovakia*

Flink, Steve. Senior Correspondent, *Tennis Week.* Author of *The Greatest Tennis Matches of the Twentieth Century.* •BIOGRAPHIES *(in part);* SPORTS AND GAMES: *Tennis*

Flores, Ramona Monette Sargan. Professor, Department of Speech Communication and Theatre Arts, University of the Philippines, Quezon City; Freelance Journalist. •MEDIA AND PUBLISHING: *Radio, Television* (international)

Follett, Christopher. Denmark Correspondent, *The Times;* Editor, *Copenhagen This Week.* •WORLD AFFAIRS: *Denmark*

Fridovich-Keil, Judith L. Associate Professor, Department of Human Genetics, Emory University School of Medicine, Atlanta, Ga. •LIFE SCIENCES: *Molecular Biology and Genetics*

Fuller, Elizabeth. Editor, *Newsline,* Radio Free Europe/Radio Liberty, Prague. •BIOGRAPHIES *(in part);* WORLD AFFAIRS: *Armenia; Azerbaijan; Georgia*

Furmonavičius, Darius. Doctor and Research Fellow, Department of Languages and European Studies, University of Bradford, Eng. •WORLD AFFAIRS: *Lithuania*

Gallagher, Tom. Professor of Ethnic Peace and Conflict, University of Bradford, Eng. Author of *Modern Romania: The End of Communism, the Failure of Democratic Reform, and the Theft of a Nation; The Balkans After the Cold War: From Tyranny to Tragedy;* and others. •WORLD AFFAIRS: *Moldova; Romania*

Ganado, Albert. Lawyer; Chairman, Malta National Archives Advisory Committee; Vice President, Malta Historical Society. Author of *Valletta Città Nuova: A Map History (1566–1600).* •WORLD AFFAIRS: *Malta*

Garrod, Mark. Golf Correspondent, PA Sport, U.K. •SPORTS AND GAMES: *Golf*

Gaughan, Thomas. Library Director, Muhlenberg College, Allentown, Pa. •LIBRARIES AND MUSEUMS: *Libraries*

George, Nicholas. Nordic Correspondent, *Financial Times.* •WORLD AFFAIRS: *Sweden*

Gibbons, J. Whitfield. Professor of Ecology, Savannah River Ecology Laboratory, University of Georgia. Coauthor of *Ecoviews: Snakes, Snails, and Environmental Tales.* •LIFE SCIENCES: *Zoology*

Gill, Martin J. Executive Director, Food Certification (Scotland) Ltd. •AGRICULTURE AND FOOD SUPPLIES: *Fisheries*

Gobbie, Donn. CEO, American Badminton League. •SPORTS AND GAMES: *Badminton*

Graham, John W. Chair, Canadian Foundation for the Americas; Former Canadian Ambassador. •WORLD AFFAIRS: *Dominican Republic; Suriname*

Grenda, Iwona. Senior Lecturer in English, the Faculty of Law and Administration, Adam Mickiewicz University, Poznan, Pol. •WORLD AFFAIRS: *Poland*

Greskovic, Robert. Dance Writer, *The Wall Street Journal.* Author of *Ballet 101.* •PERFORMING ARTS: *Dance:* North America

Griffiths, A.R.G. Associate Professor in History, Flinders University of South Australia. Author of *Contemporary Australia* and *Beautiful Lies.* •WORLD AFFAIRS: *Australia; Dependent States: Indian Ocean and Southeast Asia; East Timor; Nauru; Palau; Papua New Guinea*

Guthridge, Guy G. Manager, Antarctic Information Program, U.S. National Science Foundation. •WORLD AFFAIRS: *Antarctica*

Haddad, Mahmoud. Associate Professor of History, the University of Balamand, Lebanon. Contributor to *Altruism and Imperialism: Western Cultural and Religious Missions in the Middle East.* •WORLD AFFAIRS: *Lebanon; Saudi Arabia*

Halman, Talat Sait. Professor and Chairman, Department of Turkish Literature, Bilkent University, Ankara, Turkey. Author of *Aklın Yolu Bindir.* •LITERATURE: *Turkish*

Hammer, William R. Professor and Chair, Department of Geology, Augustana College, Rock Island, Ill. Author of *Gondwana Dinosaurs from the Jurassic of Antarctica.* •LIFE SCIENCES: *Paleontology*

Hayes, David C. Science Editor, Encyclopædia Britannica. •OBITUARIES (in part)

Helm, Toby. Chief Political Correspondent, *The Daily Telegraph.* •WORLD AFFAIRS: *European Union; European Union:* Sidebar

Hennelly, James. Associate Editor, Encyclopædia Britannica. •BIOGRAPHIES *(in part);* OBITUARIES *(in part)*

Henry, Alan. Grand Prix Editor, *Autocar* (London); Motor Racing Correspondent, *The Guardian.* Author of *50 Years of World Championship Grand Prix Motor Racing* and *Four Seasons at Ferrari: The Lauda Years.* •SPORTS AND GAMES: *Automobile Racing:* Grand Prix Racing

Hobbs, Greg. Senior Writer, *AFL Record.* Author of *One Hundred and Twenty-Five Years of the Melbourne Demons.* •SPORTS AND GAMES: *Football:* Australian

Hoffman, Dean A. Executive Editor, *Hoof Beats.* Author of *Quest for Excellence: Hanover Shoe Farms: The First 75 Years* and *The Hambletonian: America's Trotting Classic.* •SPORTS AND GAMES: *Equestrian Sports:* Harness Racing

Hollar, Sherman. Associate Editor, Encyclopædia Britannica. •BIOGRAPHIES *(in part);* OBITUARIES *(in part)*

Homel, David. Freelance Writer; Lecturer, Concordia University, Montreal. Author of *The Speaking Cure: A Novel* and others. •LITERATURE: *French:* Canada

Hope, Thomas W. Owner, Hope Reports; Former Film Producer. Contributor to *The Optics Encyclopedia: Basic Foundations and Practical Applications* and *Encyclopedia of Imaging Science and Technology.* •PERFORMING ARTS: *Motion Pictures:* Nontheatrical Films

Hosch, William L. Editor, Encyclopædia Britannica. •THE ENVIRONMENT: Sidebar; OBITUARIES *(in part)*

Hu, Xiaobo. Associate Professor of Political Science, Clemson (S.C.) University. Coeditor of *China After Jiang.* •WORLD AFFAIRS: *China; Taiwan*

Hussainmiya, B.A. Associate Professor, Department of History, University of Brunei Darussalam. Author of *The Brunei Constitution of 1959: An Inside History.* •WORLD AFFAIRS: *Brunei*

IEIS. International Economic Information Services. •ECONOMIC AFFAIRS: *World Economy; Stock Markets* (international)

Ingham, Kenneth. Emeritus Professor of History, University of Bristol, Eng. Author of *Politics in Modern Africa: The Uneven Tribal Dimension* and others. •WORLD AFFAIRS: *Angola; Congo, Democratic Republic of the; Kenya; Malawi; Mozambique; Sudan, The; Tanzania; Uganda; Zambia; Zimbabwe*

Isaacson, Lanae Hjortsvang. Editor, *Nordic Women Writers.* •LITERATURE: *Danish*

Iyob, Ruth. Associate Professor of Political Science, University of Missouri at St. Louis; Fellow, Center for International Studies. Contributor to *African Foreign Policies: Power and Process.* •WORLD AFFAIRS: *Eritrea*

Jamail, Milton. Lecturer, Department of Government, University of Texas at Austin. Author of *Full Count: Inside Cuban Baseball.* •SPORTS AND GAMES: *Baseball:* Latin America

Jennings, Ray Salvatore. Associate Professor, Georgetown University, Washington, D.C.; Freelance Field Practicioner in Post-Conflict Reconstruction. Author of "The Road Ahead: Lessons in Nation Building from Japan, Germany, and Afghanistan for Postwar Iraq" (Peaceworks Reports #49, 2003) •WORLD AFFAIRS: *Special Report:* The Character and Future of Nation Building

Joffé, George. Research Fellow, Centre of International Studies, University of Cambridge; Visiting Professor, Department of Geography, King's College, University of London. Editor, *Jordan in Transition.* •WORLD AFFAIRS: *Algeria; Morocco; Tunisia*

Johnson, Steve. Television Critic, *Chicago Tribune.* •MEDIA AND PUBLISHING: *Radio* (U.S.); *Radio:* Sidebar; *Television* (U.S.)

Johnson, Todd M. Director, Center for the Study of Global Christianity. Coauthor of *World Christian Encyclopedia.* •RELIGION: *Tables (in part)*

Joireman, Sandra F. Associate Professor of Politics and International Relations, Wheaton (Ill.) College. Author of *Property Rights and Political Development in Ethiopia and Eritrea.* •WORLD AFFAIRS: *Ethiopia*

Jones, David G.C. Tutor, Department of Continuing Education, University of Aberystwyth, Wales. Author of *Atomic Physics.* •PHYSICAL SCIENCES: *Physics*

Jones, Mark P. Associate Professor of Political Science, Rice University, Houston, Texas. Author of *Electoral Laws and the Survival of Presidential Democracies.* •WORLD AFFAIRS: *Argentina*

Jubb, Nadine. Political Scientist; Research Associate, Centre for Research on Latin America and the Caribbean, York University, Toronto. •WORLD AFFAIRS: *Nicaragua*

Kanduza, Ackson M. Associate Professor, Department of History, University of Swaziland. Author of *Political Economy of Democratisation in Swaziland* and "Tackling HIV/AIDS and Related Stigma in Swaziland Through Education" (*Eastern Africa Social Science Research Review,* XIX, no. 2, June 2003). •WORLD AFFAIRS: *Swaziland*

Kapp, Clare. Freelance Journalist; Contributor to *The Lancet.* •WORLD AFFAIRS: *Switzerland*

Karimi-Hakkak, Ahmad. Professor and Founding Director, The Center for Persian Studies, University of Maryland. •LITERATURE: *Persian*

Karns, Margaret P. Professor of Political Science, University of Dayton, Ohio. Coauthor of *International Organizations: The Politics and Processes of Global Governance.* •WORLD AFFAIRS: *Multinational and Regional Organizations*

Kazamaru, Yoshihiko. Literary Critic. •LITERATURE: *Japanese*

Kelling, George H. Lieutenant Colonel, U.S. Army (ret.). Author of *Countdown to Rebellion: British Policy in Cyprus 1939–1955.* •WORLD AFFAIRS: *Cyprus*

Kellner, Peter. Chairman, YouGov Ltd. Author of *The New Mutualism* and others. •BIOGRAPHIES *(in part);* WORLD AFFAIRS: *United Kingdom*

King, James Thaddeus. Research Editor, Encyclopædia Britannica. •OBITUARIES *(in part)*

Knox, Paul. Foreign Editor, *The Globe and Mail,* Toronto. •WORLD AFFAIRS: *Bolivia; Ecuador*

Kobliner, Beth. Journalist. Author of *Get a Financial Life.* •ECONOMIC AFFAIRS: *Stock Markets:* Canada, U.S.

Koper, Keith. Assistant Professor of Geophysics, Saint Louis (Mo.) University. •EARTH SCIENCES: *Geophysics*

Koppelman, Andrew. Professor of Law and Political Science, Northwestern University, Chicago. Author of *The Gay Rights Question in Contemporary American Law.* •LAW, CRIME, AND LAW ENFORCEMENT: *Special Report:* The Legal Debate over Same-Sex Marriages

Krause, Stefan. Freelance Analyst. •BIOGRAPHIES *(in part);* WORLD AFFAIRS: *Greece; Macedonia*

Kuhn, Steven. Associate Professor, Department of Anthropology, University of Arizona. Coauthor of "Thinking Small: Global Perspectives on Microlithization" *(Archeological Papers of the American Anthropological Association).* •ANTHROPOLOGY AND ARCHAEOLOGY: *Anthropology:* Sidebar

Kuiper, Kathleen. Senior Editor, Encyclopædia Britannica. Editor, *Merriam-Webster's Encyclopedia of Literature*. •BIOGRAPHIES *(in part)*; OBITUARIES *(in part)*

Kuptsch, Christiane. Research Officer, International Institute for Labour Studies, International Labour Office. Coeditor of *Social Security at the Dawn of the 21st Century*. •SOCIAL PROTECTION (international)

Lamb, Kevin M. Health and Medical Writer, *Dayton* (Ohio) *Daily News*. Author of *Quarterbacks, Nickelbacks & Other Loose Change*. •SPORTS AND GAMES: *Football:* Canadian, U.S.

Lawler, Nancy Ellen. Professor Emeritus, Oakton Community College, Des Plaines, Ill. Author of *Soldiers, Airmen, Spies, and Whisperers: The Gold Coast in World War II*. •WORLD AFFAIRS: *Benin; Burkina Faso; Cameroon; Central African Republic; Congo, Republic of the; Côte d'Ivoire; Gabon; Guinea; Mali; Mauritania; Niger; Senegal; Togo*

Lawson, Fred H. Professor of Government, Mills College, Oakland, Calif. Author of *Why Syria Goes to War*. •WORLD AFFAIRS: *Syria*

Le Comte, Douglas. Meteorologist, Climate Prediction Center, National Oceanic and Atmospheric Administration. •EARTH SCIENCES: *Meteorology and Climate*

Legassick, Martin. Professor of History, University of the Western Cape, Bellville, S.Af. Author of *Skeletons in the Cupboard: South African Museums and the Trade in Human Remains 1907–1917*. •WORLD AFFAIRS: *South Africa*

Lindstrom, Sieg. Managing Editor, *Track & Field News*. •BIOGRAPHIES *(in part)*; SPORTS AND GAMES: *Track and Field Sports (Athletics)*

Litweiler, John. Jazz Critic. Author of *The Freedom Principle: Jazz After 1958* and *Ornette Coleman: A Harmolodic Life*. •BIOGRAPHIES *(in part)*; OBITUARIES *(in part)*; PERFORMING ARTS: *Music:* Jazz

Logan, Robert G. Sports Journalist. Author of *Bob Logan's Tales from Chicago Sports: Cubs, Bulls, Bears, and Other Animals*. Coauthor of *Gerry Faust's Tales from the Notre Dame Sideline*. •SPORTS AND GAMES: *Basketball:* United States

Longmore, Andrew. Senior Sports Writer, *Sunday Times;* Former Assistant Editor, *The Cricketer*. Author of *The Complete Guide to Cycling*. •SPORTS AND GAMES: *Cricket*

Luling, Virginia. Independent Researcher. Author of *Somali Sultanate: The Geledi City-State over 150 Years*. •WORLD AFFAIRS: *Somalia*

Lundin, Immi. Freelance Journalist and Literary Critic. •LITERATURE: *Swedish*

Macdonald, Barrie. Professor of History, Massey University, Palmerston, N.Z. •WORLD AFFAIRS: *Dependent States:* Pacific; *Fiji; Kiribati; Marshall Islands; Micronesia, Federated States of; Samoa; Solomon Islands; Tonga; Tuvalu; Vanuatu*

Macdonald, Stuart. Lecturer in Law, University of Southampton, Eng. •LAW, CRIME, AND LAW ENFORCEMENT: *Death Penalty*

Maguire, Robert. Director, Trinity College Haiti Program, Washington, D.C. Author of *Haiti Held Hostage: International Responses to the Quest for Nationhood 1986–1996*. •WORLD AFFAIRS: *Haiti*

Malik, Mohan. Professor, Asia-Pacific Center for Security Studies, Honolulu. Author of *Dragon on Terrorism: Assessing China's Tactical Gains and Strategic Losses Post-September 11*. •WORLD AFFAIRS: *Myanmar (Burma)*

Mango, Andrew. Foreign Affairs Analyst. Author of *Atatürk: The Biography of the Founder of Modern Turkey*. •WORLD AFFAIRS: *Turkey*

Marples, David R. Professor of History, University of Alberta. Author of *Belarus: A Denationalized Nation* and *Motherland: Russia in the Twentieth Century*. •WORLD AFFAIRS: *Belarus; Ukraine*

Marston, John A. Professor, Centro de Estudios de Asia y África, El Colegio de México. Coeditor of *History, Buddhism, and New Religious Movements in Cambodia*. •WORLD AFFAIRS: Cambodia

Matić, Davorka. Assistant Professor, Department of Sociology, Faculty of Philosophy, University of Zagreb, Croatia. •WORLD AFFAIRS: *Croatia*

Matthíasson, Björn. Economist, Ministry of Finance, Iceland. •WORLD AFFAIRS: *Iceland*

Mazie, David M. Freelance Journalist. •SOCIAL PROTECTION: *Benefits and Programs:* North America; SOCIAL PROTECTION: Sidebar

McLachlan, Keith S. Professor Emeritus, School of Oriental and African Studies, University of London. Coeditor of *Landlocked States of Africa and Asia*. Author of *Boundaries of Modern Iran*. •WORLD AFFAIRS: *Iran*

McMillan, Neale. Managing Editor, South Pacific News Service. Author of *Top of the Greasy Pole: New Zealand Prime Ministers of Recent Times*. •WORLD AFFAIRS: *New Zealand*

Michael, Tom. Editor, Encyclopædia Britannica. •BIOGRAPHIES *(in part)*; OBITUARIES *(in part)*

Middlebrook, Kevin J. Reader in Latin American Politics, Institute for the Study of the Americas, University of London. Editor, *Dilemmas of Political Change in Mexico*. •WORLD AFFAIRS: *Mexico*

Moredock, Janet. Freelance Writer and Editor. •BIOGRAPHIES *(in part)*; WORLD AFFAIRS: *Malaysia*

Morgan, Paul. Editor, *Rugby World*. •SPORTS AND GAMES: *Football:* Rugby Football

Morrison, Graham. Press Officer, British Fencing Association; Correspondent, *Daily Telegraph* and *Country Life*. •SPORTS AND GAMES: *Fencing*

Myers, David J. Professor of Political Science, Pennsylvania State University. Coauthor of *Capital City Politics in Latin America: Democratization and Empowerment*. •WORLD AFFAIRS: *Venezuela*

Naka-Michaeli, Kimiyo. International Editorial Project Coordinator, Encyclopædia Britannica. •BIOGRAPHIES *(in part)*

Nishizaki, Yoshinori. Ph.D. Candidate, University of Washington. •WORLD AFFAIRS: *Thailand*

Noda, Hiroki. Major League Baseball News Editor, International Sports and Marketing Company, Tokyo. •SPORTS AND GAMES: *Baseball:* Japan

O'Leary, Christopher. Assistant Managing Editor, *Investment Dealers Digest*. •BIOGRAPHIES *(in part)*; ECONOMIC AFFAIRS: *Business Overview;* ECONOMIC AFFAIRS: Sidebar; ECONOMIC AFFAIRS: *Special Report:* Offshoring

Oppenheim, Lois Hecht. Professor of Political Science, University of Judaism, Los Angeles. Author of *Politics in Chile: Democracy, Authoritarianism, and the Search for Development*. •WORLD AFFAIRS: *Chile*

O'Quinn, Jim. Editor in Chief, *American Theatre*. •BIOGRAPHIES *(in part)*; PERFORMING ARTS: *Theatre:* U.S. and Canada

Orwig, Sarah Forbes. Associate Editor, Encyclopædia Britannica. Contributor to *The Next Phase of Business Ethics: Integrating Psychology and Ethics*. •BIOGRAPHIES *(in part)*

Osborne, Keith L. Editor, *British Rowing Almanack*. Author of *1000 Years of Rowing on the Dee; Berlin or Bust, Boat Racing in Britain, 1715–1975;* and others. •SPORTS AND GAMES: *Rowing*

Paarlberg, Philip L. Professor of Agricultural Economics, Purdue University, West Lafayette, Ind. •AGRICULTURE AND FOOD SUPPLIES: *Agriculture*

Palacio, Joseph O. Ph.D. Former Resident Tutor and Head, University Centre, University of the West Indies School of Continuing Studies, Belize. Author of *Development in Belize, 1960–1980: Initiatives at the State and Community Levels*. •WORLD AFFAIRS: *Belize*

Palmer, Rosanne. Research Fellow, Institute for German Studies, University of Birmingham, Eng. •WORLD AFFAIRS: *Germany*

Parsons, Neil. Professor of History, University of Botswana. Author of *King Khama, Emperor Joe, and the Great White Queen*. •WORLD AFFAIRS: *Botswana*

Peaker, Carol. D.Phil. Candidate, Wolfson College, Oxford. Author of *The Penguin Modern Painters: A History*. •LITERATURE: *English:* United Kingdom

Pérez, Orlando J. Associate Professor of Political Science, Central Michigan University. Editor of *Post-Invasion Panama: The Challenges of Democratization in the New World Order* and others. •WORLD AFFAIRS: *Panama*

Peszek, Luan. Publications Director and Editor, *U.S.A. Gymnastics*. Author of *Gymnastics Almanac*. •SPORTS AND GAMES: *Gymnastics*

Peterson, Mark. Associate Professor of Korean Studies, Brigham Young University, Provo, Utah. Author of *Korean Adoption and Inheritance* and others. •WORLD AFFAIRS: *Korea, Democratic People's Republic of; Korea, Republic of*

Phillips, Sam. Assistant Editor, *Royal Academy of Arts Magazine*, London. •LIBRARIES AND MUSEUMS: *Museums*

Phillips, Stephen J. United States Correspondent, *The Times Educational Supplement*, London. •AGRICULTURE AND FOOD SUPPLIES: Sidebar; BIOGRAPHIES *(in part)*

Pholsena, Vatthana. Visiting Fellow, Southeast Asian Studies Programme, National University of Singapore. •WORLD AFFAIRS: Laos

Ponmoni Sahadevan. Associate Professor, Jawaharlal Nehru University, New Delhi. Author of *Conflict and Peacemaking in South Asia*. •WORLD AFFAIRS: *Maldives*

Poplawska, Anna. Freelance Writer; Art Critic; Chicago Art Critics Association Member; Arts and Culture Committee Member, C.G. Jung Institute of Chicago. •BIOGRAPHIES *(in part)*

Poudel, Keshab. Freelance Journalist. •WORLD AFFAIRS: *Bhutan; Nepal*

Prothero, Neil. Editor and Economist, Economist Intelligence Unit, Europe. •WORLD AFFAIRS: *Austria*

Rauch, Robert. Freelance Editor and Writer. •BIOGRAPHIES *(in part)*; NOBEL PRIZES *(in part)*; OBITUARIES *(in part)*

Raun, Toivo U. Professor of Central Eurasian Studies, Indiana University. Author of *Estonia and the Estonians*. Contributor to *Nations and Nationalism*. •WORLD AFFAIRS: *Estonia*

Ray, Michael. Copy Editor, Encyclopædia Britannica. Contributor to *Trimtab* (the newsletter of the Buckminster Fuller Institute). •BIOGRAPHIES *(in part)*; LITERATURE: Sidebar; OBITUARIES *(in part)*

Rebelo, L.S. Professor Emeritus, Department of Portuguese Studies, King's College, University of London. Author of *Lilia Pegado: Painter of the Future* and *A concepção do poder em Fernão Lopes*. •LITERATURE: *Portuguese:* Portugal

Reddington, André. Assistant Editor, *Amateur Wrestling News*. •SPORTS AND GAMES: *Wrestling:* Freestyle and Greco-Roman

Reid, Ron. Staff Writer, *Philadelphia Inquirer*. •SPORTS AND GAMES: *Ice Hockey; Ice Skating*

Renwick, David. Freelance Journalist. •WORLD AFFAIRS: *Antigua and Barbuda; Bahamas, The; Barbados; Dependent States:* Caribbean and Bermuda; *Dominica; Grenada; Guyana; Jamaica; Saint Kitts and Nevis; Saint Lucia; Saint Vincent and the Grenadines; Trinidad and Tobago*

Robbins, Paul. Freelance Writer; Correspondent, *Ski Trax* and *Ski Racing*. •SPORTS AND GAMES: *Skiing*

Robinson, David. Film Critic and Historian. Author of *A History of World Cinema* and others. •PERFORMING ARTS: *Motion Pictures*

Roby, Anne. Freelance Journalist; Program Associate, Institute for Mathematics and Science Education, University of Illinois at Chicago. •WORLD AFFAIRS: *Andorra; Liechtenstein; Luxembourg; Monaco*

Rollin, Jack. Editor, *Sky Sports Football Yearbook* and *Playfair Football Annual*. Author of *The World Cup 1930–1990: Sixty Glorious Years of Soccer's Premier Event* and others. •BIOGRAPHIES *(in part)*; SPORTS AND GAMES: *Football:* Association Football (Soccer): *Africa and Asia; Europe*

Rugh, William A. Associate, Georgetown University Institute for the Study of Diplomacy, Washington, D.C.; Former President and CEO, AMIDEAST; Former U.S. Ambassador to Yemen and the United Arab Emirates. Author of *The Arab Press*. •WORLD AFFAIRS: *United Arab Emirates; Yemen*

Sabo, Anne G. Assistant Professor of Norwegian, St. Olaf College, Northfield, Minn.; Contributor to *NORA: Nordic Journal of Women's Studies, Journal of European Studies, Scandinavian Studies*, and others. •LITERATURE: *Norwegian*

Sakauchi, Rinzo. Staff Writer, Encyclopædia Britannica, Japan. •WORLD AFFAIRS: *Japan*

Sanders, Alan J.K. Freelance Mongolist; Former Lecturer in Mongolian Studies, School of Oriental and African Studies, University of London. Author of *Historical Dictionary of Mongolia;* Coauthor of *Colloquial Mongolian.* •WORLD AFFAIRS: *Mongolia*

Sandvik, Hilde. Dr. Philos, Associate Professor, Department of History, University of Oslo. Author of *Norsk historie 1300–1625.* •WORLD AFFAIRS: *Norway*

Saracino, Peter. Freelance Defense Journalist; Contributor to *PEJ News,* Victoria, B.C. •BIOGRAPHIES *(in part);* MILITARY AFFAIRS; MILITARY AFFAIRS: *Special Report:* POWs and the Global War on Terrorism

Sarahete, Yrjö. Secretary Emeritus, Fédération Internationale des Quilleurs. •SPORTS AND GAMES: *Bowling:* World Tenpins

Saunders, Christopher. Professor of Historical Studies, University of Cape Town. Coauthor of *Historical Dictionary of South Africa* and *South Africa: A Modern History.* •WORLD AFFAIRS: *Cape Verde; Chad; Equatorial Guinea; Gambia, The; Guinea-Bissau; Lesotho; Madagascar; Namibia; São Tomé and Príncipe*

Schiavo, Leda. Professor Emerita, University of Illinois at Chicago. Author of *El éxtasis de los límites: temas y figuras del decadentismo.* •LITERATURE: *Spanish:* Latin America

Schmidt, Fabian. Head of the Bosnian Program, Deutsche Welle. •WORLD AFFAIRS: *Albania*

Schreiber, Barbara A. Editorial Assistant, Encyclopædia Britannica. •BIOGRAPHIES *(in part);* OBITUARIES *(in part)*

Schuster, Angela M.H. Editor in Chief, *ICON;* Editor, *The Explorers Journal;* Contributing Editor, *Archaeology;* Science Correspondent, *Corriere della Sera* (Italy); Contributor, *New York Times.* •ANTHROPOLOGY AND ARCHAEOLOGY: *Archaeology:* Eastern Hemisphere

Sego, Stephen. Freelance Journalist; Former Director, Radio Free Afghanistan. •WORLD AFFAIRS: *Afghanistan*

Seligson, Mitchell A. Centennial Professor of Political Science, Vanderbilt University, Nashville, Tenn. Editor of *Elections and Democracy in Central America, Revisited.* •WORLD AFFAIRS: *Costa Rica*

Serafin, Steven R. Director, Writing Center, Hunter College, City University of New York. Coeditor of *The Continuum Encyclopedia of American Literature* and *The Continuum Encyclopedia of British Literature.* •NOBEL PRIZES *(in part)*

Shelley, Andrew. Executive Director, Women's International Squash Players Association; Technical Director, World Squash Federation. Author of *Squash Rules: A Players Guide.* •SPORTS AND GAMES: *Squash*

Shepherd, Melinda C. Senior Editor, Encyclopædia Britannica. •OBITUARIES *(in part);* SPORTS AND GAMES: *Automobile Racing:* Rallies and Other Races *(in part);* SPORTS AND GAMES: *Special Report:* Games of the XXVIII Olympiad; WORLD AFFAIRS: *Dependent States:* Europe and the Atlantic

Shubinsky, Valery. Freelance Critic and Journalist. Author of *Nikolay Gumilyov: Zhizn poeta.* •LITERATURE: *Russian*

Siler, Shanda. Freelance Writer. •BIOGRAPHIES *(in part)*

Simons, Paul. Freelance Journalist. Author of *The Action Plant.* •LIFE SCIENCES: *Botany*

Simpson, Jane. Freelance Writer. •PERFORMING ARTS: *Dance:* European

Sklar, Morton. Executive Director, World Organization for Human Rights USA; Judge, Administrative Labor Tribunal, Organization of American States. Editor, *The Status of Human Rights in the United States* and *Torture in the U.S.* Author of *The Right to Travel* and others. •SOCIAL PROTECTION: *Human Rights*

Smentkowski, Brian. Professor of Political Science and Assistant Director, Center for Scholarship in Teaching and Learning, Southeast Missouri State University. •LAW, CRIME, AND LAW ENFORCEMENT: *Court Decisions*

Smith, Gregory O. Academic Director, European School of Economics, Rome. •WORLD AFFAIRS: *San Marino; Vatican City State*

Snodgrass, Donald. Institute Fellow Emeritus, Harvard University. Coauthor of *Economics of Development,* 5th ed. •WORLD AFFAIRS: *Sri Lanka*

Sondrol, Paul C. Associate Professor of Political Science, University of Colorado at Colorado Springs. Author of "The 'English' Patient: General Augusto Pinochet and International Law" (Pew Case Studies in International Affairs #230, 2000). •WORLD AFFAIRS: *Paraguay*

Sparks, Karen J. Editor, Encyclopædia Britannica. •BIOGRAPHIES *(in part);* OBITUARIES *(in part)*

Spencer, Donna. Journalist, The Canadian Press. •SPORTS AND GAMES: Curling

Stern, Irwin. Lecturer in Foreign Languages, North Carolina State University. Editor of *Dictionary of Brazilian Literature.* Coauthor of *Paso a Paso: Spanish for Health Professionals.* •LITERATURE: *Portuguese:* Brazil

Stewart, Alan. Freelance Journalist. Author of *Gathering the Clans: Tracing Scottish Ancestry on the Internet.* •COMPUTERS AND INFORMATION SYSTEMS: Sidebar

Subotnick, Ali J. Independent Curator, Writer, Editor. Cofounder of The Wrong Gallery, New York; Cofounder and Editor of the contemporary art publication series *Charley;* Cocurator of the 4th Berlin Biennial for Contemporary Art (2006). •ART AND ART EXHIBITIONS: *Art; Art Exhibitions;* BIOGRAPHIES *(in part)*

Summerhill, Edward M. Lead Editor of the News Bulletin, Finnish News Agency. •WORLD AFFAIRS: *Finland*

Sumner, David E. Professor of Journalism and Head of the Magazine Program, Ball State University, Muncie, Ind. General Editor, Peter Lang Media Industry Series; Coauthor of *Feature and Magazine Writing: Action, Angle and Anecdotes.* •MEDIA AND PUBLISHING: *Magazines*

Sumrall, Harry. Editor in Chief, RedLudwig.com; Classical Music Editor, Gracenote, Inc. •PERFORMING ARTS: *Music:* Classical

Susel, Rudolph M. Editor, *American Home.* •WORLD AFFAIRS: *Slovenia*

Susser, Leslie D. Diplomatic Correspondent, *The Jerusalem Report.* Coauthor of *Shalom Friend: The Life and Legacy of Yitzhak Rabin.* •WORLD AFFAIRS: *Israel*

Szilagyi, Zsofia. Freelance Writer. •WORLD AFFAIRS: *Hungary*

Taylor, Jolanda Vanderwal. Associate Professor of Dutch and German, University of Wisconsin at Madison. Author of *A Family Occupation: Children of the War and the Memory of World War II in Dutch Literature of the 1980s.* •LITERATURE: *Netherlandic;* WORLD AFFAIRS: *The Netherlands*

Taylor, Richard. Basketball Correspondent, *The Independent;* Production Editor, Midland Weekly Media (Trinity Mirror). •SPORTS AND GAMES: *Basketball:* International

Taylor-Robinson, Michelle M. Associate Professor of Political Science, Texas A&M University. Coauthor of *Negotiating Democracy: Transitions from Authoritarian Rule.* •WORLD AFFAIRS: *Honduras*

Teague, Elizabeth. Ministry of Defence, London. (The opinions expressed are personal and do not necessarily represent those of the British government.) •WORLD AFFAIRS: *Russia*

Thayer, Carlyle A. Professor of Politics, Australian Defence Force Academy, Canberra. Author of *The Vietnam People's Army Under Doi Moi.* •WORLD AFFAIRS: *Vietnam*

Thomas, R. Murray. Professor Emeritus of Education, University of California, Santa Barbara. Author of *Recent Theories of Human Development* and *Folk Psychologies Across Cultures.* •EDUCATION

Tikkanen, Amy. Freelance Writer and Editor. •BIOGRAPHIES *(in part);* OBITUARIES *(in part)*

Trumbull, Charles. Director of Yearbooks, Encyclopædia Britannica, and aspiring poet. •BIOGRAPHIES *(in part);* OBITUARIES *(in part)*

Turner, Darrell J. Freelance Writer; Former Religion Writer, *Fort Wayne* (Ind.) *Journal Gazette;* Former Associate Editor, Religion News Service. •BIOGRAPHIES *(in part);* RELIGION

Urbansky, Janele M. Account Executive, Crowley Webb & Associates. •SPORTS AND GAMES: *Bobsleigh, Skeleton, and Luge:* Luge

Urbansky, Julie. Communications and Promotions Coordinator, Hersheypark Sports and Entertainment. •SPORTS AND GAMES: *Bobsleigh, Skeleton, and Luge:* Bobsleigh; Skeleton

Verdi, Robert. Senior Writer, *Golf Digest, Golf World;* Contributing Columnist, *Chicago Tribune.* •SPORTS AND GAMES: *Baseball* (U.S. and Canada)

Wallenfeldt, Jeff. Senior Editor, Encyclopædia Britannica. •BIOGRAPHIES *(in part);* OBITUARIES *(in part)*

Wang Xiaoming. Professor of Modern Chinese Literature; Director, Center for Contemporary Culture Studies, Shanghai University. Author of *The Cold Face of Reality: A Biography of Lu Xun.* •LITERATURE: *Chinese*

Wanninger, Richard S. Freelance Journalist. •SPORTS AND GAMES: *Volleyball*

Watson, Rory. Freelance Journalist in European Union affairs; Brussels Correspondent, *The Times.* Coauthor of *The American Express Guide to Brussels.* Contributor to *The European Union: How Does It Work?* •WORLD AFFAIRS: *Belgium*

Weil, Eric. Columnist and Contributor, *Buenos Aires* (Arg.) *Herald;* South America Correspondent, *World Soccer Magazine;* Contributor to *FIFA Magazine.* •SPORTS AND GAMES: *Football:* Association Football (Soccer): *The Americas*

Weinstein, Martin. Professor of Political Science, William Paterson University of New Jersey. Author of *Uruguay: Democracy at the Crossroads.* •WORLD AFFAIRS: *Uruguay*

White, Martin L. Freelance Writer. •BIOGRAPHIES *(in part);* OBITUARIES *(in part)*

Whitney, Barbara. Copy Supervisor, Encyclopædia Britannica. •BIOGRAPHIES *(in part);* OBITUARIES *(in part)*

Whitten, Phillip. Editor in Chief, Swiminfo.com, *Swimming World, Swim,* and *Swimming Technique* magazines. Author of *The Complete Book of Swimming* and others. •SPORTS AND GAMES: *Swimming*

Wilkinson, Earl J. Executive Director and Chief Executive Officer, International Newspaper Marketing Association. Author of *Branding and the Newspaper Consumer.* •MEDIA AND PUBLISHING: *Newspapers*

Wilkinson, John R. Sportswriter, Coventry Newspapers. •SPORTS AND GAMES: *Cycling*

Williams, Victoria C. Assistant Professor of the Humanities, Alvernia College, Reading, Pa.; Independent Consultant on international affairs. •LAW, CRIME, AND LAW ENFORCEMENT: *International Law*

Wilson, Derek. Former Correspondent, BBC. Author of *Rome, Umbria and Tuscany.* •WORLD AFFAIRS: *Italy*

Wood, Sara. Freelance Writer. •BIOGRAPHIES *(in part)*

Woods, Elizabeth Rhett. Writer. Author of *Family Fictions; If Only Things Were Different (I): A Model for a Sustainable Society; Bird Salad;* and others. •BIOGRAPHIES *(in part);* LITERATURE: *English:* Canada; OBITUARIES *(in part)*

Woods, Michael. Science Editor, *Toledo* (Ohio) *Blade.* Author of *Ancient Technology.* •PHYSICAL SCIENCES: *Chemistry;* NOBEL PRIZES *(in part)*

Woodward, Ralph Lee, Jr. Emeritus Professor of Latin American History, Tulane University, New Orleans. Author of *Central America, a Nation Divided.* •BIOGRAPHIES *(in part);* WORLD AFFAIRS: *El Salvador; Guatemala*

Wyllie, Peter J. Emeritus Professor of Geology, California Institute of Technology. Author of *The Dynamic Earth* and *The Way the Earth Works.* •EARTH SCIENCES: *Geology and Geochemistry*

Zegura, Stephen L. Professor of Anthropology, University of Arizona. •ANTHROPOLOGY AND ARCHAEOLOGY: *Anthropology*

Ziring, Lawrence. Arnold E. Schnieder Professor of Political Science, Western Michigan University. Author of *Pakistan in the Twentieth Century: A Political History* and *Pakistan: At the Crosscurrent of History.* •WORLD AFFAIRS: *Pakistan*

© Gleb Garanich/Reuters/Corbis

World Data

Thousands of Ukrainians, standing in frigid temperatures, protested the results of the Nov. 21, 2004, presidential runoff election. In elections held all over the world, people came out in record numbers.

CONTENTS

INTRODUCTION

Britannica World Data provides a statistical portrait of some 217 countries and dependencies of the world, at a level appropriate to the significance of each. It contains 214 country statements (the "Nations of the World" section), ranging in length from one to six pages, and permits, in the 20 major thematic tables (the "Comparative National Statistics" [CNS] section), comparisons among these larger countries and 4 other states.

Updated annually, *Britannica World Data* is particularly intended as direct, structured support for many of Britannica's other reference works—encyclopaedias, yearbooks, atlases—at a level of detail that their editorial style or design do not permit.

Like the textual, graphic, or cartographic modes of expression of these other products, statistics possess their own inherent editorial virtues and weaknesses. Two principal goals in the creation of *Britannica World Data* were up-to-dateness and comparability, each possible to maximize separately, but not always possible to combine. If, for example, research on some subject is completed during a particular year (x), figures may be available for 100 countries for the preceding year ($x - 1$), for 140 countries for the year before that ($x - 2$), and for 180 countries for the year before that ($x - 3$).

Which year should be the basis of a thematic compilation for 217 countries so as to give the best combination of up-to-dateness and comparability? And, should $x - 1$ be adopted for the thematic table, ought up-to-dateness in the country table (for which year x is already available) be sacrificed for agreement with the thematic table? In general, the editors have opted for maximum up-to-dateness in the country statistical boxes and maximum comparability in the thematic tables.

Comparability, however, also resides in the meaning of the numbers compiled, which may differ greatly from country to country. The headnotes to the thematic tables explain many of these methodological problems; the Glossary serves the same purpose for the country statistical pages. Published data do not always provide the researcher or editor with a neat, unambiguous choice between a datum compiled on two different bases (say, railroad track length, or route length), one of which is wanted and the other not. More often a choice must be made among a variety of official, private, and external intergovernmental (UN, FAO, IMF) sources, each reporting its best data but each representing a set of problems: (1) of methodological variance from (or among) international conventions; (2) of analytical completeness (data for a single year may, successively, be projected [based on 10 months' data], preliminary [for 12 months], final, revised or adjusted, etc.); (3) of time frame, or accounting interval (data may represent a full Gregorian calendar year [preferred], a fiscal year, an Islamic or other national or religious year, a multiyear period or average [when a one-year statement would contain unrepresentative results]); (4) of continuity with previous data; and the like. Finally, published data on a particular subject may be complete and final but impossible to summarize in a simple manner. The education system of a single country may include, for example, public and private sectors; local, state, or national systems; varying grades, tracks, or forms within a single system; or opportunities for double-counting or fractional counting of a student, teacher, or institution. When no recent official data exist, or they exist, but may be suspect, the tables may show unofficial estimates, a range (of published opinion), analogous data, or no data at all.

The published basis of the information compiled is the statistical collections of Encyclopædia Britannica, Inc., some of the principal elements of which are enumerated in the Bibliography. Holdings for a given country may include any of the following: the national statistical abstract; the constitution; the most recent censuses of population; periodic or occasional reports on vital statistics, social indicators, agriculture, mining, labour, manufacturing, domestic and foreign trade, finance and banking, transportation, and communications. Further information is received in a variety of formats—telephone, letter, fax, microfilm and microfiche, and most recently, in electronic formats such as computer disks, CD-ROMs, and the Internet. So substantial has the resources of the Internet become that it was decided to add uniform resource locators (URLs) to the great majority of country pages and a number of the CNS tables (summary world sites with data on all countries still being somewhat of a rarity) so as to apprise the reader of the possibility and means to access current information on these subjects year-round.

The recommendations offered are usually to official sites (national statistical offices, general national governments, central banks, embassies, intergovernmental organizations [especially the UN Development Programme], and the like). Though often dissimilar in content, they will usually be updated year-round, expanded as opportunity permits, and lead on to related sites, such as parliamentary offices, information offices, diplomatic and consular sites, news agencies and newspapers, and, beyond, to the myriad academic, commercial, and private sites now accessible from the personal computer. While these URLs were correct and current at the time of writing, they may be subject to change.

The great majority of the social, economic, and financial data contained in this work should not be interpreted in isolation. Interpretive text of long perspective, such as that of the *Encyclopædia Britannica* itself; political, geographic, and topical maps, such as those in the *Britannica Atlas;* and recent analysis of political events and economic trends, such as that contained in the articles of the *Book of the Year,* will all help to supply analytic focus that numbers alone cannot. By the same token, study of those sources will be made more concrete by use of *Britannica World Data* to supply up-to-date geographic, demographic, and economic detail.

GLOSSARY

A number of terms that are used to classify and report data in the "Nations of the World" section require some explanation.

Those italicized terms that are used regularly in the country compilations to introduce specific categories of information (*e.g., birth rate, budget*) appear in this glossary in italic boldface type, followed by a description of the precise kind of information being offered and how it has been edited and presented.

All other terms are printed here in roman boldface type. Many terms have quite specific meanings in statistical reporting, and they are so defined here. Other terms have less specific application as they are used by different countries or organizations. Data in the country compilations based on definitions markedly different from those below will usually be footnoted.

Terms that appear in small capitals in certain definitions are themselves defined at their respective alphabetical locations.

Terms whose definitions are marked by an asterisk (*) refer to data supplied only in the larger two- to four-page country compilations.

access to services, a group of measures indicating a population's level of access to public services, including electrical power, treated public drinking water, sewage removal, and fire protection.*

activity rate, *see* participation/activity rates.

age breakdown, the distribution of a given population by age, usually reported here as percentages of total population in 15-year age brackets. When substantial numbers of persons do not know, or state, their exact age, distributions may not total 100.0%.

area, the total surface area of a country or its administrative subdivisions, including both land and inland (nontidal) water area. Land area is usually calculated from "mean low water" on a "plane table," or flat, basis.

area and population, a tabulation usually including the first-order administrative subdivisions of the country (such as the states of the United States), with capital (headquarters, or administrative seat), area, and population. When these subdivisions are especially numerous or, occasionally, nonexistent, a planning, electoral, census, or other nonadministrative scheme of regional subdivisions has been substituted.

associated state, *see* state.

atheist, in statements of religious affiliation, one who professes active opposition to religion; "nonreligious" refers to those professing only no religion, nonbelief, or doubt.

balance of payments, a financial statement for a country for a given period showing the balance among: (1) transactions in goods, services, and income between that country and the rest of the world, (2) changes in ownership or valuation of that country's monetary gold, SPECIAL DRAWING RIGHTS, and claims on and liabilities to the rest of the world, and (3) unrequited transfers and counterpart entries needed (in an accounting sense) to balance transactions and changes among any of the foregoing types of exchange that are not mutually offsetting. Detail of national law as to what constitutes a transaction, the basis of its valuation, and the size of a transaction visible to fiscal authorities all result in differences in the meaning of a particular national statement.*

balance of trade, the net value of all international goods trade of a country, usually excluding reexports (goods received only for transshipment), and the percentage that this net represents of total trade.

Balance of trade refers only to the "visible" international trade of goods as recorded by customs authorities and is thus a segment of a country's BALANCE OF PAYMENTS, which takes all visible and invisible trade with other countries into account. (Invisible trade refers to imports and exports of money, financial instruments, and services such as transport, tourism, and insurance.) A country has a favourable, or positive (+), balance of trade when the value of exports exceeds that of imports and negative (–) when imports exceed exports.

barrel (bbl), a unit of liquid measure. The barrel conventionally used for reporting crude petroleum and petroleum products is equal to 42 U.S. gallons, or 159 litres. The number of barrels of crude petroleum per metric ton, ranging typically from 6.20 to 8.13, depends upon the specific gravity of the petroleum. The world average is roughly 7.33 barrels per ton.

birth rate, the number of live births annually per 1,000 of midyear population. Birth rates for individual countries may be compared with the estimated world annual average of 22.5 births per 1,000 population in 2000.

budget, the annual receipts and expenditures—of a central government for its activities only;

Abbreviations

Measurements

cu m	cubic metre(s)
kg	kilograms(s)
km	kilometre(s)
kW	kilowatt(s)
kW-hr	kilowatt-hour(s)
metric ton-km	metric ton-kilometre(s)
mi	mile(s)
passenger-km	passenger-kilometre(s)
passenger-mi	passenger-mile(s)
short ton-mi	short ton-mile(s)
sq km	square kilometre(s)
sq m	square metre(s)
sq mi	square mile(s)
troy oz	troy ounce(s)
yr	year(s)

Political Units and International Organizations

CACM	Central American Common Market
Caricom	Caribbean Community and Common Market
CFA	Communauté Financière Africaine
CFP	Comptoirs Françaises du Pacifique
CIS	Commonwealth of Independent States
CUSA	Customs Union of Southern Africa
EC	European Communities
ESCWA	Economic and Social Commission for Western Asia
EU	European Union
FAO	United Nations Food and Agriculture Organization
IMF	International Monetary Fund
OECD	Organization for Economic Cooperation and Development
OECS	Organization of Eastern Caribbean States
U.A.E.	United Arab Emirates
U.K.	United Kingdom
UNDP	United Nations Development Programme
U.S.	United States
U.S.S.R.	Union of Soviet Socialist Republics

Months

Jan.	January	Oct.	October
Feb.	February	Nov.	November
Aug.	August	Dec.	December
Sept.	September		

Miscellaneous

AIDS	Acquired Immune Deficiency Syndrome
avg.	average
c.i.f.	cost, insurance, and freight
commun.	communications
CPI	consumer price index
est.	estimate(d)
excl.	excluding
f.o.b.	free on board
GDP	gross domestic product
GNP	gross national product
govt.	government
incl.	including
mo.	month(s)
n.a.	not available (in text)
n.e.s.	not elsewhere specified
no.	number
pl.	plural
pos.	position
pub. admin.	public administration
SDR	Special Drawing Right
SITC	Standard International Trade Classification
svcs.	services
teacher tr.	teacher training
transp.	transportation
VAT	value-added taxes
voc.	vocational
$	dollar (of any currency area)
£	pound (of any currency area)
...	not available (in tables)
—	none, less than half the smallest unit shown, or not applicable (in tables)

does not include state, provincial, or local governments or semipublic (parastatal, quasi-nongovernmental) corporations unless otherwise specified. Figures for budgets are limited to ordinary (recurrent) receipts and expenditures, wherever possible, and exclude capital expenditures—*i.e.,* funds for development and other special projects originating as foreign-aid grants or loans.

When both a recurrent and a capital budget exist for a single country, the former is the budget funded entirely from national resources (taxes, duties, excises, etc.) that would recur (be generated by economic activity) every year. It funds the most basic governmental services, those least able to suffer interruption. The capital budget is usually funded by external aid and may change its size considerably from year to year.

capital, usually, the actual seat of government and administration of a state. When more than one capital exists, each is identified by kind; when interim arrangements exist during the creation or movement of a national capital, the de facto situation is described.

Anomalous cases are annotated, such as those in which (1) the de jure designation under the country's laws differs from actual local practice (*e.g.,* Benin's designation of one capital in constitutional law, but another in actual practice), (2) international recognition does not validate a country's claim (as with the proclamation by Israel of a capital on territory not internationally recognized as part of Israel), or (3) both a state and a capital have been proclaimed on territory recognized as part of another state (as with the Turkish Republic of Northern Cyprus).

capital budget, *see* budget.

causes of death, as defined by the World Health Organization (WHO), "the disease or injury which initiated the train of morbid events leading directly to death, or the circumstances of accident or violence which produced the fatal injury." This principle, the "underlying cause of death," is the basis of the medical judgment as to cause; the statistical classification system according to which these causes are grouped and named is the *International List of Causes of Death*, the latest revision of which is the Tenth. Reporting is usually in terms of events per 100,000 population. When data on actual causes of death are unavailable, information on morbidity, or illness rate, usually given as reported cases per 100,000 of infectious diseases (notifiable to WHO as a matter of international agreement), may be substituted.

chief of state/head of government, paramount national governmental officer(s) exercising the highest executive and/or ceremonial roles of a country's government. In general usage, the chief of state is the formal head of a national state. The primary responsibilities of the chief of state may range from the purely ceremonial—convening legislatures and greeting foreign officials—to the exercise of complete national executive authority. The head of government, when this function exists separately, is the officer nominally charged (by the constitution) with the majority of actual executive powers, though they may not in practice be exercised, especially in military or single-party regimes in which effective power may reside entirely outside the executive governmental machinery provided by the constitution. A prime minister, for example, usually the actual head of government, may in practice exercise only Cabinet-level authority.

In communist countries an official identified as the chief of state may be the chairman of the policy-making organ, and the official given as the head of government the chairman of the nominal administrative/executive organ.

c.i.f. (trade valuation): *see* imports.

colony, an area annexed to, or controlled by, an independent state but not an integral part of it; a non-self-governing territory. A colony has a charter and may have a degree of self-government. A crown colony is a colony originally chartered by the British government.

commonwealth (U.K. and U.S.), a self-governing political entity that has regard to the common weal, or good; usually associated with the United Kingdom or United States. Examples include the Commonwealth (composed of independent states [from 1931 onward]), Puerto Rico since 1952, and the Northern Marianas since 1979.

communications, collectively, the means available for the public transmission of information within a country. Data are tabulated for: daily newspapers and their total circulation; radio and television as total numbers of receivers; telephone data as "main lines," or the number of subscriber lines (not receivers) having access to the public switched network; cellular telephones as number of subscribers; and facsimile machines and personal computers as number of units. For each, a rate per 1,000 persons is given.

constant prices, an adjustment to the members of a financial time series to eliminate the effect of inflation year by year. It consists of referring all data in the series to a single year so that "real" change may be seen.

constitutional monarchy, *see* monarchy.

consumer price index (CPI), also known as the retail price index, or the cost-of-living index, a series of index numbers assigned to the price of a selected "basket," or assortment, of basic consumer goods and services in a country, region, city, or type of household in order to measure changes over time in prices paid by a typical household for those goods and services. Items included in the CPI are ordinarily determined by governmental surveys of typical household expenditures and are assigned weights relative to their proportion of those expenditures. Index values are period averages unless otherwise noted.

coprincipality, *see* monarchy.

current prices, the valuation of a financial aggregate as of the year reported.

daily per capita caloric intake (supply), the calories equivalent to the known average daily supply of foodstuffs for human consumption in a given country divided by the population of the country (and the proportion of that supply provided, respectively, by vegetable and animal sources). The daily per capita caloric intake of a country may be compared with the corresponding recommended minimum daily requirement. The latter is calculated by the Food and Agriculture Organization of the United Nations from the age and sex distributions, average body weights, and environmental temperatures in a given region to determine the calories needed to sustain a person there at normal levels of activity and health. The daily per capita caloric requirement ranges from 2,200 to 2,500.

de facto population, for a given area, the population composed of those actually present at a particular time, including temporary residents and visitors (such as immigrants not yet granted permanent status, "guest" or expatriate workers, refugees, or tourists), but excluding legal residents temporarily absent.

de jure population, for a given area, the population composed only of those legally resident at a particular time, excluding temporary residents and visitors (such as "guest" or expatriate workers, refugees, or tourists), but including legal residents temporarily absent.

deadweight tonnage, the maximum weight of cargo, fuel, fresh water, stores, and persons that may safely by carried by a ship. It is customarily measured in long tons of 2,240 pounds each, equivalent to 1.016 metric tons. Deadweight tonnage is the difference between the tonnage of a fully loaded ship and the fully unloaded tonnage of that ship.

See also gross ton.

death rate, the number of deaths annually per 1,000 of midyear population. Death rates for individual countries may be compared with the estimated world annual average of 9.0 deaths per 1,000 population in 2000.

density (of population), usually, the DE FACTO POPULATION of a country divided by its total area. Special adjustment is made for large areas of inland water, desert, or other uninhabitable areas—*e.g.,* excluding the ice cap of Greenland.

dependent state, constitutionally or statutorily organized political entity outside of and under the jurisdiction of an independent state (or a federal element of such a state) but not formally annexed to it (*see* Table).

Dependent states[1]

Australia
Christmas Island
Cocos (Keeling) Islands
Norfolk Island

Denmark
Faroe Islands
Greenland

France
French Guiana
French Polynesia
Guadeloupe
Martinique
Mayotte
New Caledonia
Réunion
Saint Pierre and Miquelon
Wallis and Futuna

Netherlands, The
Aruba
Netherlands Antilles

New Zealand
Cook Islands
Niue
Tokelau

United Kingdom
Anguilla
Bermuda
British Virgin Islands
Cayman Islands
Falkland Islands
Gibraltar
Guernsey
Isle of Man
Jersey
Montserrat
Pitcairn Island
Saint Helena and Dependencies
Turks and Caicos Islands

United States
American Samoa
Guam
Northern Mariana Islands
Puerto Rico
Virgin Islands (of the U.S.)

[1]Excludes territories (1) to which Antarctic Treaty is applicable in whole or in part, (2) without permanent civilian population, (3) without internationally recognized civilian government (Western Sahara, Gaza Strip), or (4) representing unadjudicated unilateral or multilateral territorial claims.

direct taxes, taxes levied directly on firms and individuals, such as taxes on income, profits, and capital gains. The *immediate* incidence, or burden, of direct taxes is on the firms and individuals thus taxed; direct taxes on firms may, however, be passed on to consumers and other economic units in the form of higher prices for goods and services, blurring the distinction between direct and indirect taxation.

distribution of income/wealth, the portion of personal income or wealth accruing to households or individuals constituting each respective decile (tenth) or quintile (fifth) of a country's households or individuals.*

divorce rate, the number of legal, civilly recognized divorces annually per 1,000 population.

doubling time, the number of complete years required for a country to double its population at its current rate of natural increase.

earnings index, a series of index numbers comparing average wages in a collective industrial sample for a country or region with the same industries at a previous period to measure changes over time in those wages. It is most commonly reported for wages paid on a daily, weekly, or monthly basis; annual figures may represent total income or averages of these shorter periods. The scope of the earnings index varies from country to country. The index is often limited to earnings in manufacturing industries. The index for each country applies to all wage earners in a designated group and ordinarily takes into account basic wages (overtime is normally distinguished), bonuses, cost-of-living allowances, and contributions toward social security. Some countries include payments in kind. Contributions toward social security by employers are usually excluded, as are social security benefits received by wage earners.

economically active population, *see* population economically active.

education, tabulation of the principal elements of a country's educational establishment, classified as far as possible according to the country's own system of primary, secondary, and higher levels (the usual age limits for these levels being identified in parentheses), with total number of schools (physical facilities) and of teachers and students (whether full- or part-time). The student-teacher ratio is calculated whenever available data permit.

educational attainment, the distribution of the population age 25 and over with completed educations by the highest level of formal education attained or completed; it must sometimes be reported, however, for age groups still in school or for the economically active only.

emirate, *see* monarchy.

enterprise, a legal entity formed to conduct a business, which it may do from more than one establishment (place of business or service point).

ethnic/linguistic composition, ethnic, racial, or linguistic composition of a national population, reported here according to the most reliable breakdown available, whether published in official sources (such as a census) or in external analysis (when the subject is not addressed in national sources).

exchange rate, the value of one currency compared with another, or with a standardized unit of account such as the SPECIAL DRAWING RIGHT, or as mandated by local statute when one currency is "tied" by a par value to another. Rates given usually refer to free market values when the currency has no, or very limited, restrictions on its convertibility into other currencies.

exports, material goods legally leaving a country (or customs area) and subject to customs regulations. The total value and distribution by percentage of the major items (in preference to groups of goods) exported are given, together with the distribution of trade among major trading partners (usually single countries or trading blocs). Valuation of goods exported is free on board (f.o.b.) unless otherwise specified. The value of goods exported and imported f.o.b. is calculated from the cost of production and excludes the cost of transport.

external debt, public and publicly guaranteed debt with a maturity of more than one year owed to nonnationals of a country and repayable in foreign currency, goods, or services. The debt may be an obligation of a national or subnational governmental body (or an agency of either), of an autonomous public body, or of a private debtor that is guaranteed by a public entity. The debt is usually either outstanding (contracted) or disbursed (drawn).

external territory (Australia), *see* territory.

federal, consisting of first-order political subdivisions that are prior to and independent of the central government in certain functions.

federal republic, *see* republic.

federation, union of coequal, preexisting political entities that retain some degree of autonomy and (usually) right of secession within the union.

fertility rate, *see* total fertility rate.

financial aggregates, tabulation of seven-year time series, providing principal measures of the financial condition of a country, including: (1) the exchange rate of the national crurency against the U.S. dollar, the pound sterling, and the International Monetary Fund's SPECIAL DRAWING RIGHT (SDR), (2) the amount and kind of international reserves (holdings of SDRs, gold, and foreign currencies) and reserve position of the country in the IMF, and (3) principal economic rates and prices (central bank discount rate, government bond yields, and industrial stock [share] prices). For BALANCE OF PAYMENTS, the origin in terms of component balance of trade items and balance of invisibles (net) is given.*

fish catch, the live-weight equivalent of the aquatic animals (including fish, crustaceans, mollusks, etc., but excluding whales, seals, and other aquatic mammals) caught in freshwater or marine areas by national fleets and landed in domestic or foreign harbours for commercial, industrial, or subsistence purposes.

f.o.b. (trade valuation), *see* exports.

food, *see* daily per capita caloric intake.

form of government/political status, the type of administration provided for by a country's constitution—whether or not suspended by extralegal military or civil action, although such de facto administrations are identified—together with the number of members (elected, appointed, and ex officio) for each legislative house, named according to its English rendering. Dependent states (*see* Table) are classified according to the status of their political association with the administering country.

gross domestic product (GDP), the total value of the final goods and services produced by residents and nonresidents within a given country during a given accounting period, usually a year. Unless otherwise noted, the value is given in current prices of the year indicated. The *System of National Accounts* (SNA, published under the joint auspices of the UN, IMF, OECD, EC, and World Bank) provides a framework for international comparability in classifying domestic accounting aggregates and international transactions comprising "net factor income from abroad," the measure that distinguishes GDP and GNP.

gross national product (GNP), the total value of final goods and services produced both from within a given country *and* from external (foreign) transactions in a given accounting period, usually a year. Unless otherwise noted, the value is given in current prices of the year indicated. GNP is equal to GROSS DOMESTIC PRODUCT (*q.v.*) adjusted by net factor income from abroad, which is the income residents receive from abroad for factor services (labour, investment, and interest) less similar payments made to nonresidents who contribute to the domestic economy.

gross ton, volumetric unit of measure (equaling 100 cubic feet [2.83 cu m]) of the permanently enclosed volume of a ship, above and below decks available for cargo, stores, or passenger accommodation. Net, or register, tonnage exempts certain nonrevenue spaces—such as those devoted to machinery, bunkers, crew accommodations, and ballast—from the gross tonnage. *See also* deadweight tonnage.

head of government, *see* chief of state/head of government.

health, a group of measures including number of accredited physicians currently practicing or employed and their ratio to the total population; total hospital beds and their ratio; and INFANT MORTALITY RATE.

household, economically autonomous individual or group of individuals living in a single dwelling unit. A family household is one composed principally of individuals related by blood or marriage.

household income and expenditure, data for average size of a HOUSEHOLD (by number of individuals) and median household income. Sources of income and expenditures for major items of consumption are given as percentages.

In general, household income is the amount of funds, usually measured in monetary units, received by the members (generally those 14 years old and over) of a household in a given time period. The income can be derived from (1) wages or salaries, (2) nonfarm or farm SELF-EMPLOYMENT, (3) transfer payments, such as pensions, public assistance, unemployment benefits, etc., and (4) other income, including interest and dividends, rent, royalties, etc. The income of a household is expressed as a gross amount before deductions for taxes. Data on expenditure refer to consumption of personal or household goods and services; they normally exclude savings, taxes, and insurance; practice with regard to inclusion of credit purchases differs markedly.

immigration, usually, the number and origin of those immigrants admitted to a nation in a legal status that would eventually permit the granting of the right to settle permanently or to acquire citizenship.*

imports, material goods legally entering a country (or customs area) and subject to customs regulations; excludes financial movements. The total value and distribution by percentage of the major items (in preference to groups of goods) imported are given, together with the direction of trade among major trading partners (usually single countries), trading blocs (such as the European Union), or customs areas (such as Belgium-Luxembourg). The value of goods imported is given free on board (f.o.b.) unless otherwise specified; f.o.b. is defined above under EXPORTS.

The principal alternate basis for valuation of goods in international trade is that of cost, insurance, and freight (c.i.f.); its use is restricted to imports, as it comprises the principal charges needed to bring the goods to the customs house in the country of destination. Because it inflates the value of imports relative to exports, more countries have, latterly, been estimating imports on an f.o.b. basis as well.

incorporated territory (U.S.), *see* territory.

independent, of a state, autonomous and controlling both its internal and external affairs. Its date usually refers to the date from which the country was in effective control of these affairs within its present boundaries, rather than the date independence was proclaimed or the date recognized as a de jure act by the former administering power.

indirect taxes, taxes levied on sales or transfers of selected intermediate goods and services, including excises, value-added taxes, and tariffs, that are ordinarily passed on to the ultimate consumers of the goods and services. Figures given for individual countries are limited to indirect taxes levied by their respective central governments unless otherwise specified.

infant mortality rate, the number of children per 1,000 live births who die before their first birthday. Total infant mortality includes neonatal mortality, which is deaths of children within one month of birth.

invisibles (invisible trade), *see* balance of trade.

kingdom, *see* monarchy.

labour force, portion of the POPULATION ECONOMICALLY ACTIVE (PEA) comprising those most fully employed or attached to the labour market (the unemployed are considered to be "attached" in that they usually represent persons previously employed seeking to be reemployed), particularly as viewed from a short-term perspective. It normally includes those who are self-employed, employed by others (whether full-time, part-time, seasonally, or on some other less than full-time, basis), and, as noted above, the unemployed (both those previously employed and those seeking work for the first time). In the "gross domestic product and labour force" table, the majority of the labour data provided refer to population economically active, since PEA represents the longer-term view of working population and, thus, subsumes more of the marginal workers who are often missed by shorter-term surveys.

land use, distribution by classes of vegetational cover or economic use of the land area only (excluding inland water, built-up areas, and wasteland), reported as percentages. The principal categories utilized include: (1) arable land under temporary cultivation including land left fallow less than five years, (2) land under permanent cultivation (significantly tree crops but also grapes, pineapples, and bananas), (3) pastures and rangeland, which includes land in temporary or permanent use whose principal purpose is the growing of animal fodder, and (4) forest areas, whose definition overlaps with other land use classes per the FAO *State of the World's Forests;* forest areas include scrub forests, forest plantations, and recently afforested or reforested land.

life expectancy, the number of years a person born within a particular population group (age cohort) would be expected to live, based on actuarial calculations.

literacy, the ability to read and write a language with some degree of competence; the precise degree constituting the basis of a particular national statement is usually defined by the national census and is often tested by the census enumerator. Elsewhere, particularly where much adult literacy may be the result of literacy campaigns rather than passage through a formal educational system, definition and testing of literacy may be better standardized.

major cities, usually the five largest cities proper (national capitals are always given, regardless of size); fewer cities may be listed if there are fewer urban localities in the country. For multipage tables, 10 or more may be listed.* Populations for cities will usually refer to the city proper—*i.e.,* the legally bounded corporate entity, or the most compact, contiguous, demographically urban portion of the entity defined by the local authorities. Occasionally figures for METROPOLITAN AREAS are cited when the relevant civil entity at the core of a major agglomeration had an unrepresentatively small population.

manufacturing, mining, and construction enterprises/retail sales and service enterprises, a detailed tabulation of the principal industries in these sectors, showing for each industry the number of enterprises and employees, wages in that industry as a percentage of the general average wage, and the value of that industry's output in terms of value added or turnover.*

marriage rate, the number of legal, civilly recognized marriages annually per 1,000 population.

material well-being, a group of measures indicating the percentage of households or dwellings possessing certain goods or appliances, including automobiles, telephones, television receivers, refrigerators, air conditioners, and washing machines.*

merchant marine, the privately or publicly owned ships registered with the maritime authority of a nation (limited to those in Lloyd's of London statistical reporting of 100 or more GROSS TONS) that are employed in commerce, whether or not owned or operated by nationals of the country.

metropolitan area, a city and the region of dense, predominantly urban, settlement around the city; the population of the whole usually has strong economic and cultural affinities with the central city.

military expenditure, the apparent value of all identifiable military expenditure by the central government on hardware, personnel, pensions, research and development, etc., reported here both as a percentage of the GNP, with a comparison to the world average, and as a per capita value in U.S. dollars.

military personnel, *see* total active duty personnel.

mobility, the rate at which individuals or households change dwellings, usually measured between censuses and including international as well as domestic migration.*

monarchy, a government in which the CHIEF OF STATE holds office, usually hereditarily and for life, but sometimes electively for a term. The state may be a coprincipality, emirate, kingdom, principality, sheikhdom, or sultanate. The powers of the monarch may range from absolute (*i.e.,* the monarch both reigns and rules) through various degrees of limitation of authority to nominal, as in a constitutional monarchy, in which the titular monarch reigns but others, as elected officials, effectively rule.

monetary unit, currency of issue, or that in official use in a given country; name, spelling, and abbreviation in English according to International Monetary Fund recommendations or local practice; name of the lesser, usually decimal, monetary unit constituting the main currency; and valuation in U.S. dollars and U.K. pounds sterling, usually according to free-market or commercial rates.

See also exchange rate.

natural increase, also called natural growth, or the balance of births and deaths, the excess of births over deaths in a population; the rate of natural increase is the difference between the BIRTH RATE and the DEATH RATE of a given population. The estimated world average during 2000 was 13.5 per 1,000 population, or 1.35% annually. Natural increase is added to the balance of migration to calculate the total growth of that population.

net material product, *see* material product.

nonreligious, *see* atheist.

official language(s), that (or those) prescribed by the national constitution for day-to-day conduct and publication of a country's official business or, when no explicit constitutional provision exists, that of the constitution itself, the national gazette (record of legislative activity), or like official documents. Other languages may have local protection, may be permitted in parliamentary debate or legal action (such as a trial), or may be "national languages," for the protection of which special provisions have been made, but these are not deemed official. The United States, for example, does not yet formally identify English as "official," though it uses it for virtually all official purposes.

official name, the local official form(s), short or long, of a country's legal name(s) taken from the country's constitution or from other official documents. The English-language form is usually the protocol form in use by the country, the U.S. Department of State, and the United Nations.

official religion, generally, any religion prescribed or given special status or protection by the constitution or legal system of a country. Identification as such is not confined to constitutional documents utilizing the term explicitly.

organized territory (U.S.), *see* territory.

overseas department (France), *see* department.

overseas territory (France), *see* territory.

parliamentary state, *see* state.

part of a realm, a dependent Dutch political entity with some degree of self-government and having a special status above that of a colony (*e.g.,* the prerogative of rejecting for local application any law enacted by The Netherlands).

participation/activity rates, measures defining differential rates of economic activity within a population. Participation rate refers to the percentage of those employed or economically active who possess a particular characteristic (sex, age, etc.); activity rate refers to the fraction of the total population who *are* economically active.

passenger-miles, or **passenger-kilometres,** aggregate measure of passenger carriage by a specified means of transportation, equal to the number of passengers carried multiplied by the number of miles (or kilometres) each is transported. Figures given for countries are often calculated from ticket sales and ordinarily exclude passengers carried free of charge.

people's republic, *see* republic.

place of birth/national origin, if the former, numbers of native- and foreign-born population of a country by actual place of birth; if the latter, any of several classifications, including those based on origin of passport at original admission to country, on cultural heritage of family name, on self-designated (often multiple) origin of (some) ancestors, and on other systems for assigning national origin.*

political status, *see* form of government/political status.

population, the number of persons present within a country, city, or other civil entity at the date of a census of population, survey, cumulation of a civil register, or other enumeration. Unless otherwise specified, populations given are DE FACTO, referring to those actually present, rather than DE JURE, those legally resident but not necessarily present on the referent date. If a time series, noncensus year, or per capita ratio referring to a country's total population is cited, it will usually refer to midyear of the calendar year indicated.

population economically active, the total number of persons (above a set age for economic labour, usually 10–15 years) in all employment statuses—self-employed, wage- or salary-earning, part-time, seasonal, unemployed, etc. The International Labour Organisation defines the economically active as "all persons of either sex who furnish the supply of labour for the production of economic goods and services." National practices vary as regards the treatment of such groups as armed forces, inmates of institutions, persons seeking their first job, unpaid family workers, seasonal workers and persons engaged in part-time economic activities. In some countries, all or part of these groups may be included among the economically active, while in other countries the same groups may be treated as inactive. In general, however, the data on economically active population do not include students, persons occupied solely in family or household work, retired persons, persons living entirely on their own means, and persons wholly dependent upon others.

See also labour force.

population projection, the expected population in the years 2010 and 2020, embodying the country's own projections wherever possible. Estimates of the future size of a population are usually based on assumed levels of fertility, mortality, and migration. Projections in the tables, unless otherwise specified, are medium (*i.e.,* most likely) variants, whether based on external estimates by the United Nations, World Bank, or U.S. Department of Commerce or on those of the country itself.

price and earnings indexes, tabulation comparing the change in the CONSUMER PRICE INDEX over a period of seven years with the change in the general labour force's EARNINGS INDEX for the same period.

principality, *see* monarchy.

production, the physical quantity or monetary value of the output of an industry, usually tabulated here as the most important items or groups of items (depending on the available detail) of primary (extractive) and secondary (manufactured) production, including construction. When a single consistent measure of value, such as VALUE ADDED, can be obtained, this is given, ranked by value; otherwise, and more usually, quantity of production is given.

public debt, the current outstanding debt of all periods of maturity for which the central government and its organs are obligated. Publicly guaranteed private debt is excluded. For countries that report debt under the World Bank Debtor Reporting System (DRS), figures for outstanding, long-term EXTERNAL DEBT are given.

quality of working life, a group of measures including weekly hours of work (including overtime); rates per 100,000 for job-connected injury, illness, and mortality; coverage of labour force by insurance for injury, permanent disability, and death; workdays lost to labour strikes and stoppages; and commuting patterns (length of journey to work in minutes and usual method of transportation).*

railroads, mode of transportation by self-driven or locomotive-drawn cars over fixed rails. Length-of-track figures include all mainline and spurline running track but exclude switching sidings and yard track. Route length, when given, does not compound multiple running tracks laid on the same trackbed.

recurrent budget, *see* budget.

religious affiliation, distribution of nominal religionists, whether practicing or not, as a percentage of total population. This usually assigns to children the religion of their parents.

republic, a state with elected leaders and a centralized presidential form of government, local subdivisions being subordinate to the national government. A *federal republic* (as distinguished from a unitary republic) is a republic in which power is divided between the central government and the constituent subnational administrative divisions (*e.g.,* states, provinces, or cantons) in whom the central government itself is held to originate, the division of power being defined in a written constitution and jurisdictional disputes usually being settled in a court; sovereignty usually rests with the authority that has the power to amend the constitution. A *unitary republic* (as distinguished from a federal republic) is a republic in which power originates in a central authority and is not derived from constituent subdivisions. A *people's republic,* in the dialectics of Communism, is the first stage of development toward a communist state, the second stage being a *socialist republic.* An *Islamic republic* is structured around social, ethical, legal, and religious precepts central to the Islamic faith.

retail price index, *see* consumer price index.

retail sales and service enterprises, *see* manufacturing, mining, and construction enterprises/retail sales and service enterprises.

roundwood, wood obtained from removals from forests, felled or harvested (with or without bark), in all forms.

rural, *see* urban-rural.

self-employment, work in which income derives from direct employment in one's own business, trade, or profession, as opposed to work in which salary or wages are earned from an employer.

self-governing, of a state, in control of its internal affairs in degrees ranging from control of most internal affairs (though perhaps not of public order or of internal security) to complete control of all internal affairs (*i.e.,* the state is autonomous) but having no control of external affairs or defense. In this work the term self-governing refers to the final stage in the successive stages of increasing self-government that generally precede independence.

service/trade enterprises, *see* manufacturing, mining, and construction enterprises/retail sales and service enterprises.

sex distribution, ratios, calculated as percentages, of male and female population to total population.

sheikhdom, *see* monarchy.

social deviance, a group of measures, usually reported as rates per 100,000 for principal categories of socially deviant behaviour, including specified crimes, alcoholism, drug abuse, and suicide.*

social participation, a group of measures indicative of the degree of social engagement displayed by a particular population, including rates of participation in such activities as elections, voluntary work or memberships, trade unions, and religion.*

social security, public programs designed to protect individuals and families from loss of income owing to unemployment, old age, sickness or disability, or death and to provide other services such as medical care, health and welfare programs, or income maintenance.

socialist republic, *see* republic.

sources of income, *see* household income and expenditure.

Special Drawing Right (SDR), a unit of account utilized by the International Monetary Fund (IMF) to denominate monetary reserves available under a quota system to IMF members to maintain the value of their national currency unit in international transactions.*

state, in international law, a political entity possessing the attributes of: territory, permanent civilian population, government, and the capacity to conduct relations with other states. Though the term is sometimes limited in meaning to fully independent and internationally recognized states, the more general sense of an entity possessing a *preponderance* of these characteristics is intended here. It is, thus, also a first-order civil administrative subdivision, especially of a federated union. An associated state is an autonomous state in free association with another that conducts its external affairs and defense; the association may be terminated in full independence at the instance of the autonomous state in consultation with the administering power. A *parliamentary state* is an independent state of the Commonwealth that is governed by a parliament and that may recognize the British monarch as its titular head.

structure of gross domestic product and labour force, tabulation of the principal elements of the national economy, according to standard industrial categories, together with the corresponding distribution of the labour force (when possible POPULATION ECONOMICALLY ACTIVE) that generates the GROSS DOMESTIC PRODUCT.

sultanate, *see* monarchy.

territory, a noncategorized political dependency; a first-order administrative subdivision; a dependent political entity with some degree of self-government, but with fewer rights and less autonomy than a colony because there is no charter. An *external territory* (Australia) is a territory situated outside the area of the country. An *organized territory* (U.S.) is a territory for which a system of laws and a settled government have been provided by an act of the United States Congress. An *overseas territory* (France) is an overseas subdivision of the French Republic with elected representation in the French Parliament, having individual statutes, laws, and internal organization adapted to local conditions.

ton-miles, or **ton-kilometres,** aggregate measure of freight hauled by a specified means of transportation, equal to tons of freight multiplied by the miles (or kilometres) each ton is transported. Figures are compiled from waybills (nationally) and ordinarily exclude mail, specie, passengers' baggage, the fuel and stores of the conveyance, and goods carried free.

total active duty personnel, full-time active duty military personnel (excluding militias and part-time, informal, or other paramilitary elements), with their distribution by percentages among the major services.

total fertility rate, the sum of the current age-specific birth rates for each of the child-bearing years (usually 15–49). It is the probable number of births, given present fertility data, that would occur during the lifetime of each woman should she live to the end of her child-bearing years.

tourism, service industry comprising activities connected with domestic and international travel for pleasure or recreation; confined here to international travel and reported as expenditures in U.S. dollars by tourists of all nationalities visiting a particular country and, conversely, the estimated expenditures of that country's nationals in all countries of destination.

transfer payments, *see* household income and expenditure.

transport, all mechanical methods of moving persons or goods. Data reported for national establishments include: for railroads, length of track and volume of traffic for passengers and cargo (but excluding mail, etc.); for roads, length of network and numbers of passenger cars and of commercial vehicles (*i.e.,* trucks and buses); for merchant marine, the number of vessels of more than 100 gross tons and their total deadweight tonnage; for air transport, traffic data for passengers and cargo and the number of airports with scheduled flights.

unincorporated territory (U.S.), *see* territory.

unitary republic, *see* republic.

urban-rural, social characteristic of local or national populations, defined by predominant economic activities, "urban" referring to a group of largely nonagricultural pursuits, "rural" to agriculturally oriented employment patterns. The distinction is usually based on the country's own definition of urban, which may depend only upon the size (population) of a place or upon factors like employment, administrative status, density of housing, etc.

value added, also called value added by manufacture, the gross output value of a firm or industry minus the cost of inputs—raw materials, supplies, and payments to other firms—required to produce it. Value added is the portion of the sales value or gross output value that is actually created by the firm or industry. Value added generally includes labour costs, administrative costs, and operating profits.

The Nations of the World

Afghanistan

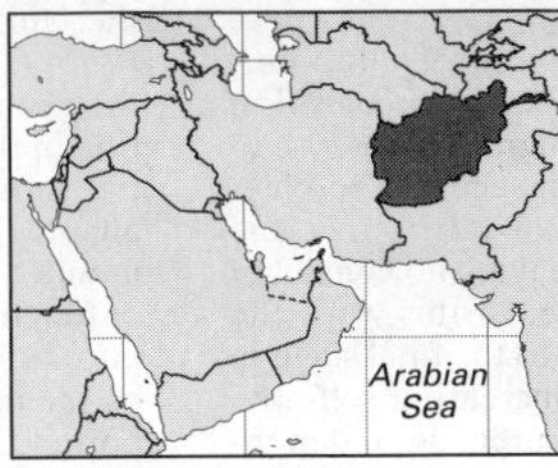

Official name: Islamic Republic of Afghanistan (Jomhūrī-ye Eslāmī-ye Afghānestān [Dari (Persian)]); Da Afghanestan Eslami Jamhuriyat (Pashto)[1].
Form of government: Islamic republic[1].
Head of state and government: President.
Capital: Kabul.
Official languages: Dari (Persian); Pashto[2].
Official religion: Islam.
Monetary unit: 1 (new) afghani (Af) = 100 puls (puli); valuation (Sept. 1, 2004) 1 U.S.$ = Af 43.00; 1 £ = Af 77.35[3].

Population (2003–04 estimate)

Province	population ('000)	Province	population ('000)	Province	population ('000)
Badakhshān	725.7	Jowzjān	447.5	Nūrestān	111.0
Bādghīs	305.6	Kābol (Kabul)	3,445.0	Paktīā	401.3
Bāghlān	726.6	Kandahār	913.9	Paktīkā	357.3
Balkh	949.6	Kāpīsā	364.9	Parvān[4]	737.2
Bāmīān	391.7	Khowst	304.6	Samangān	318.5
Farāh	343.4	Konar	328.1	Sar-e Pol	474.8
Fāryāb	794.1	Kondūz	833.2	Takhār	761.4
Ghaznī	914.8	Laghmān	378.1	Uruzgān	636.0
Ghowr	492.4	Lowgar	315.4	Vardak	448.7
Helmand	756.4	Nangarhār	1,105.7	Zābol	249.1
Herāt	1,208.0	Nīmrūz	151.5	TOTAL	20,691.5

Demography

Area: 249,347 sq mi, 645,807 sq km.
Population (2004): 20,869,000[5].
Density (2004): persons per sq mi 83.7, persons per sq km 32.3.
Urban-rural (2003): urban 22.4%; rural 77.6%.
Sex distribution (2003): male 51.17%; female 48.83%.
Age breakdown (2003): under 15, 44.8%; 15–29, 26.8%; 30–44, 15.9%; 45–59, 8.5%; 60–74, 3.4%; 75 and over, 0.6%.
Population projection: (2010) 26,149,000; (2020) 33,546,000.
Doubling time: 27 years.
Ethnolinguistic composition (early 1990s): Pashtun 52.4%; Tajik 20.4%; Ḥazāra 8.8%; Uzbek 8.8%; Chahar Aimak 2.8%; Turkmen 1.9%; other 4.9%.
Religious affiliation (2000): Sunnī Muslim 89.2%; Shīʿī Muslim 8.9%; Zoroastrian 1.4%; Hindu 0.4%; other 0.1%.
Major cities (2003–04): Kabul 2,799,300[6]; Kandahār (Qandahār) 323,900; Herāt 254,800; Mazār-e Sharīf 187,700; Jalālābād 97,900.

Vital statistics

Birth rate per 1,000 population (2003): 47.5 (world avg. 21.3).
Death rate per 1,000 population (2003): 21.5 (world avg. 9.1).
Total fertility rate (avg. births per childbearing woman; 2003): 6.8.
Life expectancy at birth (2003): male 41.8 years; female 42.2 years.

National economy

Budget (2003–04). Revenue: U.S.$208,000,000[7] (tax revenue 63.0%, of which import duties 53.4%; nontax revenue 37.0%). Expenditures: U.S.$2,826,000,000 (development expenditure 84.0%; current expenditure 16.0%).
Gross domestic product (2003): U.S.$7,000,000,000[8] (U.S.$340 per capita).

Structure of gross domestic product and labour force

	2003		1992–93	
	in value U.S.$'000,000	% of total value	labour force	% of labour force
Agriculture (legal)	2,310	33.0	4,276,100	67.2
Opium (illegal)	2,450	35.0		
Mining	—	—	298,900	4.7
Manufacturing	630	9.0		
Public utilities Transp. and commun.	560	8.0		
Transp. and commun.			139,900	2.2
Construction	210	3.0	81,400	1.3
Trade	420	6.0	420,600	6.6
Pub. administration	210	3.0	929,300	14.6
Services	210	3.0		
Other	—	—	214,300	3.4
TOTAL	7,000	100.0	6,360,500	100.0

Public debt (external, outstanding; 2000): U.S.$5,319,000,000.
Production (metric tons except as noted). Agriculture, forestry, fishing (2002): wheat 2,686,000, rice 388,000, grapes 365,000, barley 345,000, corn (maize) 298,000, potatoes 240,000, apricots 38,000, opium poppy 3,400[9]; livestock (number of live animals; 2003) 8,700,000 sheep, 7,200,000 goats, 3,600,000 cattle; roundwood (2002) 1,404,208 cu m; fish catch (2001) 2,000. Mining and quarrying (2000): salt 13,000; copper (metal content) 5,000. Manufacturing (by production value in Af '000,000; 1988–89): food products 4,019; leather and fur products 2,678; textiles 1,760; printing and publishing 1,070; industrial chemicals 1,053. Energy production (consumption): electricity (kW-hr; 2002) 557,000,000 ([2000] 480,000,000); coal (metric tons; 2000) 2,000 (2,000); petroleum products (metric tons; 2000) none (206,000); natural gas (cu m; 2000) 116,603,000 (116,603,000).
Household income and expenditure (2003). Average household size 8.0; sources of income: wages and salaries 49%, self-employed 47%, other 4%.
Population economically active (1994)[10]: total 5,557,000; activity rate of total population 29.4% (participation rates: female 9.0%; unemployed [1995] *c.* 8%).

Price index (March 2001 = 100)

	2001	2002	2003	2004
Consumer price index[11]	100.0	143.4	218.4	241.3

Tourism (1997): receipts U.S.$1,000,000; expenditures U.S.$1,000,000.
Land use as % of total land area (2000): in temporary crops 12.1%, in permanent crops 0.2%, in pasture 46.0%; overall forest area 2.1%.

Foreign trade[12]

Balance of trade (current prices)

	1997	1998	1999	2000	2001	2002
U.S.$'000,000	–424	–356	–450	–503	–627	–783
% of total	59.2%	55.6%	60.0%	65.4%	77.3%	89.0%

Imports (2002–03): U.S.$880,000,000 (machinery 36.8%, consumer goods and medicine 26.8%, clothing 14.9%, food 8.9%). *Major import sources:* Pakistan 23.5%; South Korea 12.8%; Japan 9.7%; Kenya 6.5%; Turkmenistan 5.6%; Germany 5.6%.
Exports (2002–03): U.S.$97,000,000 (carpets and rugs 47.4%, dried fruits and nuts 40.5%). *Major export destinations:* India 27.8%; Pakistan 23.7%; Germany 6.2%; Finland 6.2%; UAE 5.2%.

Transport and communications

Transport. Railroads (2003): none operational. Roads (2001): total length 20,720 km (paved 12%). Vehicles (2000): passenger cars 39,707; trucks and buses 7,000. Air transport[13]: passenger-km (1999) 129,000,000; metric ton-km cargo 19,000,000; airports (2002) 2.

Communications

Medium	date	unit	number	units per 1,000 persons
Daily newspapers	2000	circulation	129,000	5.0
Radio	2000	receivers	2,950,000	114
Television	2000	receivers	362,000	14
Telephones	2002	main lines	33,100	1.6
Cellular telephones	2002	subscribers	12,000	0.6
Internet	2002	users	1,000	0.04

Education and health

Educational attainment: n.a. *Literacy* (2003)[10]: total population age 15 and over literate 29%; males 43%; females 14%.

Education (2003)

	schools	teachers	students	student/ teacher ratio
Primary	...	...	3,900,000	...
Secondary	...	...	400,000	...
Higher[14]	1	462	13,000	28.1

Health: physicians (2002) 2,880 (1 per 7,128 persons); hospital beds, n.a.; infant mortality rate per 1,000 live births (2003) 115.0.
Food (1999): daily per capita caloric intake 1,755 (vegetable products 79%, animal products 21%); 72% of FAO recommended minimum requirement.

Military

Total active duty personnel (August 2004): 13,000 (army 100%); size of planned army is 65,000, size of planned air force 8,000[15].

[1]From promulgation of new constitution on Jan. 26, 2004. [2]Six additional locally official languages per the 2004 constitution are Uzbek, Turkmen, Balochi, Kafiri (Nuristani), Pashai, and Pamiri. [3]The afghani was re-denominated on Oct. 7, 2002; from that date 100 (old) afghanis equaled 1 (new) afghani. [4]Includes Panjsher province created May 2004. [5]Excludes Afghan refugees in Pakistan and Iran and other Afghans abroad. [6]Urban agglomeration. [7]Domestic revenue only; excludes heavy reliance on foreign assistance. [8] 1/3 of which is illegal opiate receipts. [9]Represents 74% of world production. [10]Based on settled population only. [11]March 21 to March 20 fiscal year. [12]Exports are f.o.b. and imports are c.i.f. [13]Ariana Afghan Airlines only. [14]University of Kabul only. [15]Foreign troops (September 2004): 8,000-member, NATO-controlled, 31-nation International Security Assistance Force (ISAF) and more than 18,000-member, non-ISAF U.S. troops searching for al-Qaeda and Taliban fighters.

Albania

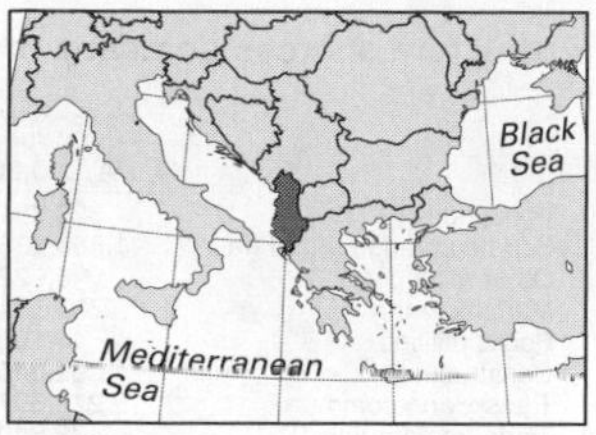

Official name: Republika e Shqipërisë (Republic of Albania).
Form of government: unitary multiparty republic with one legislative house (Assembly [140]).
Chief of state: President.
Head of government: Prime Minister.
Capital: Tirana (Tiranë).
Official language: Albanian.
Official religion: none.
Monetary unit: 1 lek = 100 qindars; valuation (Sept. 1, 2004) 1 U.S.$ = 103.55 leks; 1 £ = 186.28 leks.

Area and population

		area		population
Provinces	**Capitals**	sq mi	sq km	2001 census
Berat	Berat	353	915	127,837
Bulqizë	Bulqizë	277	718	42,968
Delvinë	Delvinë	142	367	10,765
Devoll	Bilisht	166	429	34,641
Dibër	Peshkopi	294	761	85,699
Durrës	Durrës	176	455	181,662
Elbasan	Elbasan	498	1,290	221,635
Fier	Fier	328	850	199,082
Gjirokastër	Gjirokastër	439	1,137	54,647
Gramsh	Gramsh	268	695	35,750
Has	Krumë	144	374	19,660
Kavajë	Kavajë	152	393	78,179
Kolonjë	Ersekë	311	805	17,161
Korçë	Korçë	676	1,752	142,909
Krujë	Krujë	144	372	63,517
Kuçovë	Kuçovë	43	112	35,338
Kukës	Kukës	369	956	63,786
Kurbin[1]	Laç	91	235	54,392
Lezhë	Lezhë	185	479	67,734
Librazhd	Librazhd	425	1,102	72,387
Lushnjë	Lushnjë	275	712	143,933
Malësi e Madhe	Koplic	346	897	36,692
Mallakastër	Ballsh	125	325	39,529
Mat	Burrel	397	1,028	61,187
Mirditë	Rrëshen	335	867	37,056
Peqin	Peqin	74	191	32,964
Përmet	Përmet	359	929	25,780
Pogradec	Pogradec	280	725	70,471
Pukë	Pukë	399	1,034	34,386
Sarandë	Sarandë	282	730	35,089
Shkodër	Shkodër	630	1,631	185,395
Skrapar	Çorovoda	299	775	29,845
Tepelenë	Tepelenë	315	817	32,404
Tiranë	Tirana (Tiranë)	461	1,193	519,720
Tropojë	Bajram	403	1,043	27,947
Vlorë	Vlorë	621	1,609	147,128
TOTAL		11,082	28,703	3,069,275

Demography

Population (2004): 3,136,000.
Density (2004): persons per sq mi 283.0, persons per sq km 109.3.
Urban-rural (2001): urban 42.1%; rural 57.9%.
Sex distribution (2001): male 49.88%; female 50.12%.
Age breakdown (2003): under 15, 27.1%; 15–29, 26.0%; 30–44, 20.6%; 45–59, 14.6%; 60–74, 8.8%; 75 and over, 2.9%.
Population projection: (2010) 3,275,000; (2020) 3,484,000.
Doubling time: 58 years.
Ethnic composition (2000): Albanian 91.7%; Vlach (Aromanian) 3.6%; Greek 2.3%; other 2.4%.
Religious affiliation (2000): Muslim 38.8%; Roman Catholic 16.7%; nonreligious 16.6%; Albanian Orthodox 10.4%; other Orthodox 5.7%; other 11.8%.
Major cities (2001): Tirana (Tiranë) 343,078; Durrës 99,546; Elbasan 87,797; Shkodër 82,455.

Vital statistics

Birth rate per 1,000 population (2002): 18.6 (world avg. 21.3).
Death rate per 1,000 population (2002): 6.5 (world avg. 9.1).
Natural increase rate per 1,000 population (2002): 12.1 (world avg. 12.2).
Total fertility rate (avg. births per childbearing woman; 2002): 2.3.
Marriage rate per 1,000 population (1998): 7.4.
Life expectancy at birth (2002): male 69.3 years; female 75.1 years.

National economy

Budget (2002). Revenue: 149,487,000,000 leks (taxes 86.3%, of which value-added tax 30.8%, social security contributions 17.1%, income tax 14.0%, import duties and export taxes 9.0%, other taxes 15.4%; nontax revenue 13.7%). Expenditures: 196,549,000,000 leks (current expenditure 78.7%, of which wages 21.4%, social security 20.4%, interest on debt 12.6%, government operations 10.4%, other 13.9%; capital expenditure 21.3%).
Public debt (2002): U.S.$1,187,000,000.
Production (metric tons except as noted). Agriculture, forestry, fishing (2002): vegetables and melons 650,000 (mainly beans, peas, onions, tomatoes, cabbage, eggplants, and carrots), cereals 472,500, watermelons 293,000, potatoes 163,100; livestock (number of live animals) 1,844,000 sheep, 929,000 goats, 690,000 cattle, 4,446,000 poultry; roundwood (2002) 304,800 cu m; fish catch (2001) 3,596. Mining and quarrying (2001): chromium ore 165,000; copper ore 45,000. Manufacturing (value added in U.S.$'000,000; 2001): textiles 17; glass products 14; leather (all forms) 11; iron and steel 11; office machinery 9. Energy production (consumption): electricity (kW-hr; 2002) 3,880,000,000 (3,880,000,000); lignite (metric tons; 2001) 17,300 (17,300); crude petroleum (barrels; 2001) 2,136,000 ([2000] 2,090,000); petroleum products (metric tons; 2000) 228,000 (390,000); natural gas (cu m; 2001) 10,000,000 (10,000,000).
Gross national product (2003): U.S.$5,517,000,000 (U.S.$1,740 per capita).

Structure of gross domestic product and labour force

	2002		2001	
	in value '000,000 leks	% of total value	labour force	% of labour force
Agriculture	219,100	33.3	767,000	61.7
Manufacturing, mining, public utilities	84,200	12.8	55,000	4.4
Construction	71,100	10.8	13,000	1.0
Transp. and commun. }	69,700	10.6	24,000	1.9
Trade }			56,000	4.5
Pub. admin., defense }	214,000	32.5	148,000 }	11.9
Services }				
Other }			181,000[2]	14.5[2]
TOTAL	658,100	100.0	1,244,000	100.0[3]

Population economically active (2001): total 1,244,000; activity rate of total population 40.3% (participation rates: ages 15–64, 55.4%; female 49.8%; unemployed [2002] 15.8%).

Price index (2000 = 100)

	1997	1998	1999	2000	2001	2002	2003
Consumer price index	82.5	99.6	100.0	100.0	103.1	111.1	111.7

Household income and expenditure. Average household size (2002): 4.2.
Tourism (2002): receipts U.S.$487,000,000; expenditures U.S.$366,000,000.
Land use as % of total land area (2000): in temporary crops 21.1%, in permanent crops 4.4%, in pasture 16.2%; overall forest area 36.2%.

Foreign trade

Balance of trade (current prices)

	1997	1998	1999	2000	2001	2002
U.S.$'000,000	–535	–604	–663	–814	–1,033	–1,157
% of total	62.8%	59.2%	54.6%	61.4%	62.9%	63.6%

Imports (2002): U.S.$1,487,000,000 (food and beverages 20.0%; nonelectrical and electrical machinery 16.2%; mineral fuels 12.9%; textiles and clothing 11.0%; base and fabricated metals 8.9%). *Major import sources:* Italy 47.9%; Greece 34.3%; Germany 6.3%; United Kingdom 3.6%.
Exports (2002). U.S.$330,000,000 (textiles and clothing 37.7%; footwear and related products 28.9%; base and fabricated metals 9.3%). *Major export destinations:* Italy 71.7%; Greece 12.8%; Germany 5.5%; Yugoslavia 1.5%.

Transport and communications

Transport. Railroads (2001): length 670 km; passenger-km 138,000,000; metric ton-km cargo 19,000. Roads (2000): total length 18,000 km (paved 30%). Vehicles (2001): passenger cars 133,533; trucks and buses 70,413. Air transport (2001)[4]: passenger-km 82,298,000, passenger-mi 56,370,000; short ton-mi, none, metric ton-km, none; airports (2002) 1.

Communications

Medium	date	unit	number	units per 1,000 persons
Daily newspapers	2000	circulation	109,000	35
Radio	2000	receivers	756,000	243
Television	2001	receivers	480,000	157
Telephones	2003	main lines	255,000	83
Cellular telephones	2003	subscribers	1,100,000	358
Internet	2003	users	30,000	9.8

Education and health

Educational attainment (1989). Population age 10 and over having: primary education 65.3%; secondary 29.1%; higher 5.6%. *Literacy* (2001): total population age 10 and over literate 85.3%; males 92.5%; females 77.8%.

Education (2000–01)

	schools	teachers	students[5]	student/ teacher ratio
Primary (age 6–13)	1,782[6]	28,293	523,253	...
Secondary (age 14–17)	...	5,760	100,082	...
Voc., teacher tr.	...	2,174[7]	18,495	8.5[7]
Higher	10	1,683	42,160	24.3

Health (1999): physicians 4,325 (1 per 724 persons); hospital beds 10,237 (1 per 306 persons); infant mortality rate per 1,000 live births (2002) 38.6.
Food (2001): daily per capita caloric intake 2,900 (vegetable products 72%, animal products 28%); 110% of FAO recommended minimum requirement.

Military

Total active duty personnel (2003): 22,000 (army 72.7%, navy 11.4%, air force 15.9%). *Military expenditure as percentage of GNP* (1999): 1.3% (world 2.4%); per capita expenditure U.S.$21.

[1]Name changed from Laç to Kurbin in 1999. [2]Unemployed. [3]Detail does not add to total given because of rounding. [4]Albanian Air only. [5]2001–02. [6]1995. [7]1996.

Internet resources for further information:
- **Albanian Economic Development Agency http://www.aeda.gov.al**
- **Instituti i Statistikës http://www.instat.gov.al**

Algeria

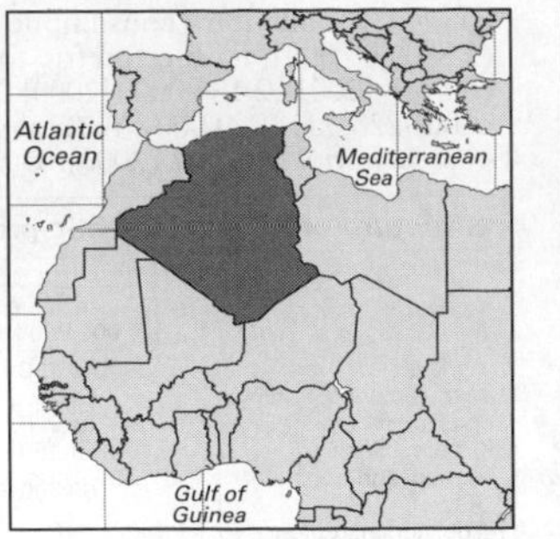

Official name: Al-Jumhūrīyah al-Jazā'irīyah ad-Dīmuqrāṭīyah ash-Sha'bīyah (Arabic) (People's Democratic Republic of Algeria).
Form of government: multiparty republic with two legislative bodies (Council of the Nation [144][1]; National People's Assembly [389]).
Chief of state: President.
Head of government: Prime Minister.
Capital: Algiers.
Official language: Arabic[2].
Official religion: Islam.
Monetary unit: 1 Algerian dinar (DA) = 100 centimes; valuation (Sept. 1, 2004) 1 U.S.$ = DA 72.28; 1 £ = DA 130.02.

Population (1998 census)

Provinces	population	Provinces	population	Provinces	population
Adrar	313,417	El-Bayadh	172,957	Ouargla	444,683
Aïn Defla	658,897	El-Oued	525,083	Oum el-Bouaghi	529,540
Aïn Temouchent	337,570	Et-Tarf	350,789	Relizane	646,175
Alger	2,423,694	Ghardaïa	311,678	Saïda	313,351
Annaba	559,898	Guelma	444,231	Sétif	1,299,116
Batna	987,475	Illizi	34,189	Sidi bel-Abbès	535,634
Béchar	232,012	Jijel	582,865	Skikda	793,146
Bejaïa	836,301	Khenchela	345,009	Souk Ahras	365,106
Biskra	568,701	Laghouat	326,862	Tamanrasset	138,704
Blida	796,616	Mascara	651,239	Tébessa	565,125
Bordj Bou Arreridj	561,471	Médéa	859,273	Tiaret	770,194
Bouira	637,042	Mila	663,578	Tindouf	27,053
Boumerdes	608,806	Mostaganem	636,884	Tipaza	507,959
Constantine	807,371	M'Sila	835,701	Tissemsilt	274,380
Djelfa	805,298	Naâma	131,846	Tizi Ouzou	1,100,297
Ech-Cheliff	874,917	Oran	1,208,171	Tlemcen	873,039
				TOTAL	29,273,343

Demography

Area: 919,595 sq mi, 2,381,741 sq km.
Population (2004): 32,322,000.
Density (2004): persons per sq mi 35.1, persons per sq km 13.6.
Urban-rural (1998): urban 80.8%; rural 19.2%.
Sex distribution (2003): male 50.40%; female 49.60%.
Age breakdown (1998): under 15, 29.9%; 15–29, 30.6%; 30–44, 17.7%; 45–59, 8.9%; 60–74, 5.1%; 75 and over, 1.5%.
Population projection: (2010) 35,549,000; (2020) 40,479,000.
Doubling time: 51 years.
Ethnic composition (2000): Algerian Arab 59.1%; Berber 26.2%, of which Arabized Berber 3.0%; Bedouin Arab 14.5%; other 0.2%.
Religious affiliation (2000): Muslim 99.7%, of which Sunnī 99.1%, Ibāḍīyah 0.6%; Christian 0.3%.
Major cities (1998): Algiers 1,519,570; Oran 692,516; Constantine 462,187; Annaba 348,554; Batna 242,514; Blida 226,512; Sétif 211,859.

Vital statistics

Birth rate per 1,000 population (2003): 18.3 (world avg. 21.3).
Death rate per 1,000 population (2003): 4.6 (world avg. 9.1).
Natural increase rate per 1,000 population (2003): 13.7 (world avg. 12.2).
Total fertility rate (avg. births per childbearing woman; 2003): 2.2.
Marriage rate per 1,000 population (2000): 5.8.
Life expectancy at birth (2003): male 71.0 years; female 74.0 years.
Notified cases of infectious diseases per 100,000 population (1996): measles 67.8; typhoid fever 15.2; hepatitis 11.3; dysentery 10.1; meningitis 9.4.

National economy

Budget (2002). Revenue: DA 1,603,200,000,000 (taxes on hydrocarbons 62.9%, value-added taxes 7.0%, other 30.1%). Expenditures: DA 1,550,600,000,000 (current expenditure 70.8%, development expenditure 29.2%).
Land use as % of total land area (2000): in temporary crops 3.2%, in permanent crops 0.2%, in pasture 13.4%; overall forest area 0.9%.
Production (metric tons except as noted). Agriculture, forestry, fishing (2002): wheat 1,502,000, potatoes 1,000,000, tomatoes 830,000, barley 550,000, dates 437,000, onions 430,000, oranges 330,000, olives 200,000, grapes 196,000; livestock (number of live animals) 17,300,000 sheep, 3,200,000 goats; roundwood (2002) 7,526,000 cu m; fish catch (2001) 100,300. Mining and quarrying (2002): iron ore 1,202,000; phosphate rock 740,000; zinc (metal content) 8,576; mercury 307. Manufacturing (value added in U.S.$'000,000; 1997): food products 463; cement, bricks, and tiles 393; iron and steel 118; tobacco products 114; paints, soaps, and related products 105; electrical machinery 79. Energy production (consumption): electricity (kW-hr; 2001) 24,690,000,000 (22,900,000,000); coal (metric tons; 2000) 25,000 (583,000); crude petroleum (barrels; 2001) 305,599,000 ([2000] 168,338,000); petroleum products (metric tons; 2000) 44,689,000 (10,584,000); natural gas (cu m; 2001) 80,300,000,000 (22,320,000,000).
Household income and expenditure. Average household size (2000) 6.3; income per household (2001) *c.* U.S.$6,700; sources of income (2001): wages and salaries 39.9%, self-employment 39.2%, transfers 20.9%; expenditure (2001): food and beverages 44.1%, clothing and footwear 11.6%, transportation and communications 11.5%, furniture 6.8%, education 6.5%.
Gross national product (2003): U.S.$60,221,000,000 (U.S.$1,890 per capita).

Structure of gross domestic product and labour force

	2000		2002	
	in value DA '000,000	% of total value	labour force	% of labour force
Agriculture	325,751	8.0	1,438,000	15.5
Petroleum and natural gas	1,666,236[3]	40.9[3]	} 504,000	} 5.4
Other mining	5,022	0.1		
Manufacturing	234,624[3]	5.8[3]		
Public utilities	44,108	1.0		
Construction	292,046	7.2	860,000	9.2
Transp. and commun.	272,697	6.7	} 1,157,000	} 12.4
Trade, restaurants	478,840	11.7		
Finance, real estate / Services	194,698	4.8		
Pub. admin., defense	359,744	8.8	1,476,000	15.9
Other	204,909[4]	5.0[4]	3,868,000[5]	41.6[5]
TOTAL	4,078,675	100.0	9,303,000	100.0

Population economically active (2002): total 9,303,000; activity rate of population 29.2% (participation rates: ages 15–64 [1998] 52.6%; female, n.a.; unemployed [2002] 25.9%).

Price index (2000 = 100)

	1997	1998	1999	2000	2001	2002	2003
Consumer price index	92.5	97.1	99.7	100.0	104.2	105.7	108.4

Public debt (external, outstanding; 2002): U.S.$21,255,000,000.
Tourism: receipts from visitors (2002) U.S.$133,000,000; expenditures by nationals abroad (2000) U.S.$193,000,000.

Foreign trade[6]

Balance of trade (current prices)

	1996	1997	1998	1999	2000	2001
U.S.$'000,000	+1,994	+5,206	+435	+3,363	+12,879	+9,609
% of total	9.9%	23.1%	2.4%	15.5%	41.3%	33.6%

Imports (2001): U.S.$9,482,000,000 (industrial equipment 34.7%, food 24.7%, semifinished products 18.4%, consumer goods 14.8%). *Major import sources* (2002): France 22.7%; U.S. 9.8%; Italy 9.6%; Germany 7.2%; Spain 5.3%.
Exports (2001): U.S.$19,091,000,000 (crude petroleum 38.9%, natural and manufactured gas 36.6%, refined petroleum 17.1%). *Major export destinations* (2002): Italy 20.1%; U.S. 14.2%; France 13.6%; Spain 12.1%; The Netherlands 9.0%; Turkey 5.1%; Canada 5.0%.

Transport and communications

Transport. Railroads (2003): route length 2,468 mi, 3,973 km; (2000) passenger-km 1,142,000,000; metric ton-km cargo 2,029,000,000. Roads (1999): total length 64,600 mi, 104,000 km (paved 69%). Vehicles (2001): passenger cars 1,692,148; trucks and buses 948,553. Air transport (2003)[7]: passenger-km 3,343,000,000; metric ton-km cargo 19,091,000; airports (1996) 28.

Communications

Medium	date	unit	number	units per 1,000 persons
Daily newspapers	2000	circulation	817,000	27
Radio	2000	receivers	7,380,000	244
Television	2000	receivers	3,300,000	110
Telephones	2003	main lines	2,199,600	69
Cellular telephones	2003	subscribers	1,447,310	45
Personal computers	2003	units	242,000	7.6
Internet	2002	users	500,000	16.0

Education and health

Educational attainment (1998). Percentage of economically active population age 6 and over having: no formal schooling 30.1%; primary education 29.9%; lower secondary 20.7%; upper secondary 13.4%; higher 4.3%; other 1.6%. *Literacy* (1998): total population age 10 and over literate 15,314,109 (68.1%); males literate 8,650,719 (76.3%); females literate 6,663,392 (59.7%).

Education (1996–97)

	schools	teachers	students	student/ teacher ratio
Primary (age 6–11)	15,426	170,956	4,674,947	27.3
Secondary (age 12–17)	3,954[8]	151,948	2,618,242	17.2
Higher[8]	...	19,910	347,410	17.4

Health (1996): physicians 27,650 (1 per 1,015 persons); hospital beds 34,544 (1 per 812 persons); infant mortality rate per 1,000 live births (2003) 33.4.
Food (2000): daily per capita caloric intake 2,987 (vegetable products 90%, animal products 10%); 124% of FAO recommended minimum requirement.

Military

Total active duty personnel (2003): 127,500 (army 86.3%, navy 5.9%, air force 7.8%). *Military expenditure as percentage of GNP* (1999): 4.0% (world 2.4%); per capita expenditure U.S.$60.

[1]Includes 48 nonelected seats appointed by the president. [2]The Berber language, Tamazight, became a national language in April 2002. [3]Petroleum and natural gas includes (and Manufacturing excludes) refined petroleum and manufacture of hydrocarbons. [4]Import taxes and duties. [5]Includes 2,412,000 unemployed and 1,456,000 military draft and irregular employment. [6]Imports c.i.f.; exports f.o.b. [7]Air Algérie. [8]1995–96.

Internet resources for further information:
- **Statistiques Algérie http://www.ons.dz/them_sta.htm**

American Samoa

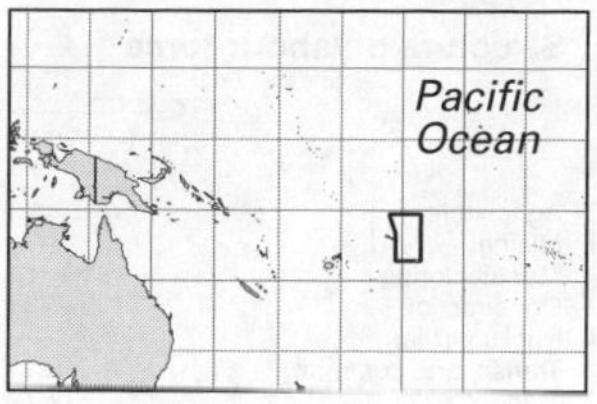

Official name: American Samoa (English); Amerika Samoa (Samoan).
Political status: unincorporated and unorganized territory of the United States with two legislative houses (Senate [18]; House of Representatives [20]).
Chief of state: President of the United States.
Head of government: Governor.
Capital: Fagatogo[1] (legislative and judicial) and Utulei (executive).
Official languages: English; Samoan.
Official religion: none.
Monetary unit: 1 dollar (U.S.$) = 100 cents; valuation (Sept. 1, 2004) 1 U.S.$ = £0.56.

Area and population

Districts and islands	area sq mi	area sq km	population 2000 census
Eastern District	25.9	67.1	23,441
Tutuila Island (part)	25.3	65.5	21,673
Aunu'u Island	0.6	1.6	1,768
Western District	28.8	74.6	32,435
Tutuila Island (part)	28.8	74.6	32,435
Manu'a District (Manu'a Islands)	21.9	56.7	1,378
Ofu Island	2.8	7.2	289
Olosega Island	2.0	5.2	216
Ta'u Island	17.1	44.3	873
Rose Island[2]	0.1	0.3	0
Swains Island[2]	0.6	1.5	37
LAND AREA	77.3	200.2	—
INLAND WATER (HARBOUR) AREAS	7.1	18.4	—
TOTAL AREA	84.4	218.6	57,291

Demography

Population (2004): 62,700.
Density (2004)[3]: persons per sq mi 811.1, persons per sq km 313.2.
Urban-rural (2000): urban 53.4%; rural 46.6%.
Sex distribution (2000): male 51.08%; female 48.92%.
Age breakdown (2000): under 15, 38.8%; 15–29, 25.5%; 30–44, 19.4%; 45–59, 10.8%; 60–74, 4.5%; 75 and over, 1.0%.
Population projection: (2010) 61,800; (2020) 58,400.
Doubling time: 30 years.
Ethnic composition (2000): Samoan 88.2%; Tongan 2.8%; Asian 2.8%; Caucasian 1.1%; other 5.1%.
Religious affiliation (1995): 4 major Protestant groups 60.1%; Roman Catholic 19.4%; Mormon 12.5%; other 8.0%.
Major villages (2000): Tafuna 8,406; Nu'uuli 5,154; Pago Pago 4,278 (urban agglomeration [2001] 15,000); Leone 3,568; Fagatogo 2,096[1].

Vital statistics

Birth rate per 1,000 population (2003): 25.9 (world avg. 21.3); legitimate (2001) 71.7%; illegitimate 28.3%.
Death rate per 1,000 population (2003): 3.4 (world avg. 9.1).
Natural increase rate per 1,000 population (2003): 22.5 (world avg. 12.2).
Total fertility rate (avg. births per childbearing woman; 2003): 3.6.
Marriage rate per 1,000 population (2000): 4.7.
Divorce rate per 1,000 population (1993): 0.5.
Life expectancy at birth (2003): male 71.8 years; female 79.2 years.
Major causes of death per 100,000 population (2000): heart diseases 89; malignant neoplasms (cancers) 61; cerebrovascular diseases 31; accidents 28; other causes 72.

National economy

Budget (1997). Revenue: U.S.$144,438,095 (U.S. government grants 67.4%; taxes 23.6%; insurance claims 4.9%; other 4.1%). Expenditures: U.S.$152,912,308 (education and culture 28.5%; health and welfare 27.3%; general government 14.1%; public works and parks 12.8%; public safety 6.9%; economic development 6.1%; capital projects 3.4%; debt 0.9%).
Gross national product (1997): U.S.$253,000,000 (U.S.$4,300 per capita).

Structure of labour force

	2000 labour force	2000 % of labour force
Agriculture, forestry, and fishing	517	2.9
Manufacturing	5,900	33.4
Construction	1,066	6.0
Transp. and commun.	1,036	5.9
Trade	1,790	10.1
Finance, real estate	311	1.8
Public administration	1,550	8.8
Services	4,548	25.7
Other	946[4]	5.4
TOTAL	17,664	100.0

Production (metric tons except as noted). Agriculture, forestry, fishing (2002): coconuts 4,700, taros 1,500, fruits (excluding melons) 1,200, bananas 750, vegetables and melons 470; livestock (number of live animals; 2002) 10,700 pigs, 37,000 chickens; forestry, n.a.; fish catch (2000) 866, of which tunas, bonitos, and billfish 820. Mining and quarrying: n.a. Manufacturing (value of export in U.S.$; 2003): canned tuna 467,700,000; pet food 9,800,000; other manufactures include garments, handicrafts, soap, and alcoholic beverages. Construction (value of building permits in U.S.$; 2000) 12,801,000. Energy production (consumption): electricity (kW-hr; 2001) 171,101,000 (148,109,000); coal, none (n.a.); crude petroleum, none (n.a.); petroleum products (metric tons; 1999) none (93,000); natural gas, none (n.a.).
Public debt: n.a.
Population economically active (2000): total 17,664, activity rate of total population 30.8% (participation rates: ages 16 and over 52.0%; female 41.5%; unemployed 5.1%).

Price index (1990 = 100)

	2000	2001	2002	2003	2004[5]
Consumer price index[6]	125.7	127.5	130.1	136.5	140.2

Household income and expenditure. Average household size (2000) 6.0; income per household (2000): U.S.$24,000; sources of income: n.a.; expenditure (1995): food and beverages 30.9%, housing and furnishings 25.8%, church donations 20.7%, transportation and communications 9.4%, clothing 2.9%, other 10.3%.
Tourism: receipts from visitors (1997) U.S.$10,000,000; expenditures by nationals abroad (1996) U.S.$2,000,000.
Land use as % of total land area (2000): in temporary crops *c.* 10%, in permanent crops *c.* 15%, in pasture, n.a.; overall forest area *c.* 60%.

Foreign trade[7]

Balance of trade (current prices)

	1996	1997	1998	1999	2000	2001
U.S.$'000,000	–157.8	–104.3	–83.4	–107.5	–159.6	–203.0
% of total	20.1%	10.9%	9.1%	13.5%	18.7%	24.2%

Imports (2001): U.S.$520,000,000 (fish for cannery 50.9%, consumer goods 16.4%, other food 12.8%, mineral fuels 5.0%). *Major import sources* (2000): United States 56.7%; Australia 14.9%; New Zealand 11.1%; Fiji 5.7%; Samoa 3.1%.
Exports (2001)[7]: U.S.$317,000,000 (tuna in airtight containers 86.3%, fish meal 8.9%, pet food 4.8%). *Major export destinations* (2000): United States 99.6%.

Transport and communications

Transport. Railroads: none. Roads (1991): total length 217 mi, 350 km (paved, 43%). Vehicles (2001): passenger cars 6,579; trucks and buses 625. Merchant marine (1990): vessels (100 gross tons and over) 3; total deadweight tonnage 143. Air transport (2001): incoming flights 7,805; incoming passengers 74,543; incoming cargo 890 metric tons; airports (2000) with scheduled flights 3.

Communications

Medium	date	unit	number	units per 1,000 persons
Daily newspapers	1996	circulation	5,000	85
Radio	1997	receivers	57,000	929
Television	2000	receivers	13,200	211
Telephones	2002	main lines	14,700	252
Cellular telephones	2001	subscribers	2,156	38

Education and health

Educational attainment (2000). Percentage of population age 25 and over having: no formal schooling to some secondary education 33.9%; completed secondary 39.3%; some college 19.4%; undergraduate degree 4.8%; graduate degree 2.6%. *Literacy* (2000): total population age 10 and over literate 33,993 (99.4%); males literate 17,704 (99.4%); females literate 16,589 (99.5%).

Education (2001)

	schools[8]	teachers	students	student/teacher ratio
Primary (age 6–14)	32	...	11,343	...
Secondary (age 14–18)	10	...	4,217	...
Vocational[9]	...	21	160	7.6
Higher[10]	1	77	1,178	15.3

Health (1991): physicians 26 (1 per 1,888 persons); hospital beds (1995) 140 (1 per 4.7 persons); infant mortality rate per 1,000 live births (2003) 9.7.
Food: daily per capita caloric intake, n.a.

Military

Military defense is the responsibility of the United States.

[1]The seat of the legislature, as defined by the Constitution of American Samoa, is at Fagatogo, one of a number of villages within an urban agglomeration collectively known as Pago Pago. [2]Not within district administrative structure. Swains Island is administered by a village government and a representative of the governor. [3]Based on land area. [4]Includes 909 unemployed and 37 in military. [5]March. [6]Excludes rent. [7]Based on exports to the United States only. [8]1999–2000. [9]1997–98. [10]American Samoa Community College at Mapusaga.

Internet resources for further information:

- **U.S. Department of the Interior: Pacific Web http://www.pacificweb.org**
- **Bank of Hawaii: Economics Research Center http://www.boh.com/econ/pacific**
- **American Samoa Government Department of Commerce http://www.amsamoa.com**

Andorra

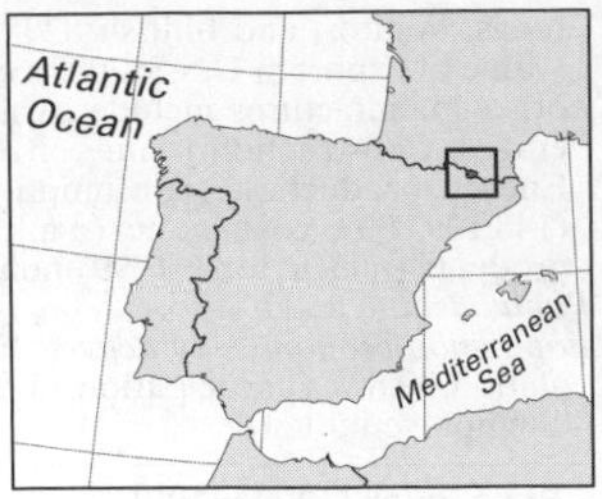

Official name: Principat d'Andorra (Principality of Andorra).
Form of government: parliamentary coprincipality with one legislative house (General Council [28]).
Chiefs of state: President of France; Bishop of Urgell, Spain.
Head of government: Head of Government.
Capital: Andorra la Vella.
Official language: Catalan.
Official religion: none[1].
Monetary unit[2]: 1 euro (€) = 100 cents; valuation (Sept. 1, 2004) 1 U.S.$ = €0.82; 1 £ = €1.48.

Area and population

Parishes	Capitals	area sq mi	area sq km	population 2003[3] estimate
Andorra la Vella	Andorra la Vella	23[4]	59[4]	20,724
Canillo	Canillo	47	121	3,205
Encamp	Encamp	29	74	10,772
La Massana	La Massana	23	61	6,660
Les Escaldes–Engordany	—	4	4	15,528
Ordino	Ordino	34	89	2,485
Sant Julià de Lòria	Sant Julià de Lòria	23	60	7,785
TOTAL		179	464	67,159

Demography

Population (2004): 67,600.
Density (2004): persons per sq mi 377.7, persons per sq km 145.7.
Urban-rural (2003): urban 93%; rural 7%.
Sex distribution (2002): male 51.82%; female 48.18%.
Age breakdown (2002): under 15, 15.1%; 15–29, 18.0%; 30–44, 29.1%; 45–59, 20.5%; 60–74, 11.1%; 75 and over, 6.2%.
Population projection: (2010) 70,000; (2020) 73,000.
Doubling time: 89 years.
Ethnic composition (by nationality; 2000): Spanish 40.6%; Andorran 36.0%; Portuguese 10.2%; French 6.5%; British 1.4%; Moroccan 0.7%; German 0.5%; other 4.1%.
Religious affiliation (2000): Roman Catholic 89.1%; other Christian 4.3%; Muslim 0.6%; Hindu 0.5%; nonreligious 5.0%; other 0.5%.
Major urban areas (2002[3]): Andorra la Vella 20,787; Les Escaldes–Engordany 15,519; Encamp 10,627.

Vital statistics

Birth rate per 1,000 population (2002): 11.1 (world avg. 21.3).
Death rate per 1,000 population (2002): 3.3 (world avg. 9.1).
Natural increase rate per 1,000 population (2002): 7.8 (world avg. 12.2).
Total fertility rate (avg. births per childbearing woman; 2003): 1.3.
Marriage rate per 1,000 population (2002): 2.8.
Life expectancy at birth (2003): male 80.6 years; female 86.6 years.
Major causes of death per 100,000 population (1996–2000 avg.): cancers (neoplasms) 103.2; diseases of the circulatory system 90.0; diseases of the respiratory system 28.6; accidents and violence 24.3; diseases of the digestive system 16.9.

National economy

Budget (2003). Revenue: €246,610,000 (indirect taxes 75.0%, taxes from government enterprises 15.6%, revenue from capital 9.4%). Expenditures: €253,835,000 (current expenditures 51.3%, of which education 13.9%, tourism 7.7%, public order 6.5%, health 4.3%, environment 3.5%; development expenditures 48.7%).
Production. Agriculture (2002): tobacco 321 metric tons; other traditional crops include hay, potatoes, and grapes; livestock (number of live animals; 2002) 2,683 sheep[5], 1,194 cattle, 741 horses, 362 goats. Quarrying: small amounts of marble are quarried. Manufacturing (value of recorded exports in €'000; 2000): electrical machinery and apparatus 11,090; motor vehicles and parts 8,500; newspapers and periodicals 4,690; clothing 2,180; other products include furniture, cigarettes, and liqueurs. Construction (approved new building construction; 2002): 309,918 sq m. Energy production (consumption): electricity (kW-hr; 1997) 116,000,000 ([2002] 463,000,000); coal, none (n.a.); crude petroleum, none (n.a.); petroleum products, none ([2000] 201,677,000 litres); natural gas, none (n.a.).
Household expenditure (1997)[6]: food, beverages, and tobacco 25.5%, housing and energy 19.4%, transportation 17.7%, clothing and footwear 9.2%.
Land use as % of total land area (2000): in temporary and permanent crops *c.* 4%, in pasture *c.* 45%; overall forest area *c.* 35%.
Population economically active (2002): total 44,058; activity rate of total population 66.4% (participation rates: ages 15–64 [2000] 72.6%; female, n.a.; unemployed, none[7]).

Price and earnings indexes (1997 = 100)[8]

	1996	1997	1998	1999	2000	2001	2002
Consumer price index	...	100.0	101.6	104.3	108.9	111.9	115.7
Annual earnings index	98.6	100.0	101.6	103.7	105.8	...	...

Gross domestic product (at current market prices; 2001): U.S.$1,462,000,000 (U.S.$22,120 per capita)[9].

Structure of labour force[10]

	2002 labour force	2002 % of labour force
Agriculture, Mining	132	0.4
Manufacturing	1,141	3.0
Construction	6,226	16.6
Public utilities	...	...
Transp. and commun.	...	...
Trade	7,057	18.8
Restaurants, hotels	6,524	17.4
Finance, real estate, insurance	1,537	4.1
Pub. admin., defense	4,749	12.7
Services	7,182	19.1
Other	2,967	7.9
TOTAL	37,515	100.0

Public debt (1995): *c.* U.S.$500,000,000.
Tourism (2002): 11,500,698 visitors; number of hotels 271.

Foreign trade

Balance of trade (current prices)

	1996	1997	1998	1999	2000	2001
€'000,000	–779	–902	–918	–989	–1,057	–1,204
% of total	91.7%	91.4%	89.8%	92.4%	91.4%	90.3%

Imports (2002): €1,269,200,000 (food, beverages, and tobacco 19.2%; machinery and apparatus 19.1%; chemicals and chemical products 10.0%; transport equipment 9.9%; textiles and wearing apparel 8.4%; photographic and optical goods and watches and clocks 5.7%). *Major import sources:* Spain 50.0%; France 24.5%; Germany 5.1%; Italy 3.2%; U.K. 2.0%.
Exports (2002): €64,900,000 (motor vehicles and parts 29.7%; optical and photo equipment 17.7%; electrical machinery and apparatus 16.3%; chemicals and chemical products 7.0%; clothing 4.8%). *Major export destinations:* Spain 54.8%; France 30.3%; Germany 9.8%; Hong Kong 3.2%.

Transport and communications

Transport. Railroads: none; however, both French and Spanish railways stop near the border. Roads (1999): total length 167 mi, 269 km (paved 74%). Vehicles (2002): passenger cars 63,616; trucks and buses 4,809. Airports with scheduled flights: none.

Communications

Medium	date	unit	number	units per 1,000 persons
Daily newspapers	1996	circulation	4,000	62
Radio	1997	receivers	16,000	247
Television	2000	receivers	30,400	458
Telephones	2002	main lines	43,561	653
Cellular telephones	2002	subscribers	31,323	469
Internet	2001	users	7,000	88

Education and health

Educational attainment (mid-1980s). Percentage of population age 15 and over having: no formal schooling 5.5%; primary education 47.3%; secondary education 21.6%; postsecondary education 24.9%; unknown 0.7%. *Literacy:* resident population is virtually 100% literate.

Education (1999–2000)

	schools	teachers	students	student/teacher ratio
Primary/lower secondary (age 7–15)	12	...	5,996	...
Upper secondary	6	...	1,136	...
Higher	1	...	1,341	...

Health (1999): physicians 218 (1 per 303 persons); hospital beds 203 (1 per 323 persons); infant mortality rate per 1,000 live births (1999–2001 avg.) 4.1.
Food: n.a.

Military

Total active duty personnel: none. France and Spain are responsible for Andorra's external security; the police force is assisted in alternate years by either French gendarmerie or Barcelona police.

[1]Roman Catholicism enjoys special recognition in accordance with Andorran tradition. [2]The French franc and Spanish peseta were the former monetary units; on Jan. 1, 2002, F 6.56 = €1 and Pta 166.39 = €1. [3]January 1. [4]Andorra la Vella includes Les Escaldes–Engordany. [5]Large herds of sheep and goats from Spain and France feed in Andorra in the summer. [6]Weights of consumer price index components. [7]The restricted size of the indigenous labour force has in the near past necessitated immigration to serve the tourist trade. [8]All indexes are end of year. [9]Tourism (including winter-season sports, fairs, festivals, and income earned from low-duty imported manufactured items) and the banking system are the primary sources of GDP. [10]Labour force receiving wages only.

Internet resources for further information:
- **Andorra National Information Centre http://www.andorra.ad**
- **Department d'Estudis i d'Estadística http://www.finances.ad**

Angola

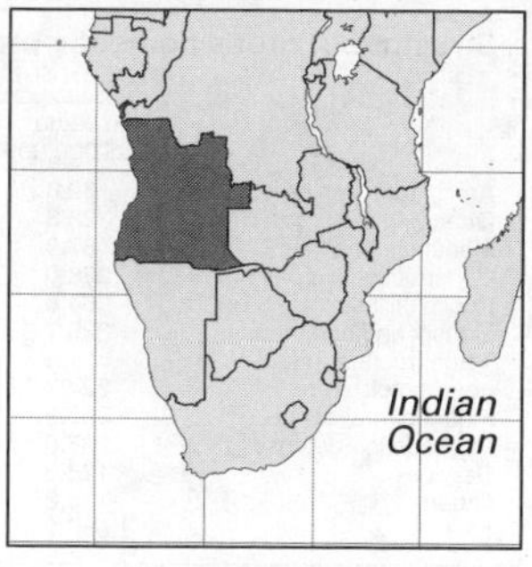

Official name: República de Angola (Republic of Angola).
Form of government: unitary multiparty republic with one legislative house (National Assembly [220])[1].
Head of state and government: President assisted by Prime Minister[2].
Capital: Luanda.
Official language: Portuguese.
Official religion: none.
Monetary unit: 1 refloated kwanza (Kz) = 100 lwei; valuation (Sept. 1, 2004), 1 U.S.$ = refloated kwanza 79.03; 1 £ = refloated kwanza 145.95.

Area and population

Provinces	Capitals	area sq mi	area sq km	population 2003 estimate
Bengo	Caxito	12,112	31,371	...
Benguela	Benguela	12,273	31,788	...
Bié	Kuito	27,148	70,314	...
Cabinda	Cabinda	2,807	7,270	...
Cunene	N'Giva	34,495	89,342	...
Huambo	Huambo	13,233	34,274	...
Huíla	Lubango	28,958	75,002	...
Kuando Kubango	Menongue	76,853	199,049	...
Kuanza Norte	N'Dalatando	9,340	24,190	...
Kuanza Sul	Sumbe	21,490	55,660	...
Luanda	Luanda	934	2,418	...
Lunda Norte	Lucapa	39,685	102,783	...
Lunda Sul	Saurimo	17,625	45,649	...
Malanje	Malanje	37,684	97,602	...
Moxico	Lwena	86,110	223,023	...
Namibe	Namibe	22,447	58,137	...
Uíge	Uíge	22,663	58,698	...
Zaire	M'Banza Kongo	15,494	40,130	...
TOTAL		481,354[3]	1,246,700	10,766,000

Demography

Population (2004): 10,979,000.
Density (2004): persons per sq mi 22.8, persons per sq km 8.8.
Urban-rural (2001): urban 34.9%; rural 65.1%.
Sex distribution (2003): male 50.53%; female 49.47%.
Age breakdown (2003): under 15, 43.5%; 15–29, 26.5%; 30–44, 16.8%; 45–59, 8.5%; 60–74, 4.1%; 75 and over, 0.6%.
Population projection: (2010) 12,250,000; (2020) 14,473,000.
Doubling time: 35 years.
Ethnic composition (2000): Ovimbundu 25.2%; Kimbundu 23.1%; Kongo 12.6%; Lwena (Luvale) 8.2%; Chokwe 5.0%; Kwanyama 4.1%; Nyaneka 3.9%; Luchazi 2.3%; Ambo (Ovambo) 2.0%; Mbwela 1.7%; Nyemba 1.7%; other 10.2%.
Religious affiliation (2001): Christian 94.1%, of which Roman Catholic 62.1%, Protestant 15.0%; traditional beliefs 5.0%; other 0.9%.
Major cities (2004): Luanda 2,783,000; Huambo 173,600; Lobito 137,400; Benguela 134,500; Namibe 132,900.

Vital statistics

Birth rate per 1,000 population (2003): 45.6 (world avg. 21.3).
Death rate per 1,000 population (2003): 25.8 (world avg. 9.1).
Natural increase rate per 1,000 population (2003): 19.8 (world avg. 12.2).
Total fertility rate (avg. births per childbearing woman; 2003): 6.4.
Life expectancy at birth (2003): male 36.1 years; female 37.8 years.
Major causes of death (percentage of total deaths; 1990): diarrheal diseases 25.8%; malaria 19.4%; cholera 7.3%; acute respiratory infections 6.8%.

National economy

Budget (2002). Revenue: U.S.$4,367,000,000 (oil revenue 76.7%; non-oil revenue 23.3%, of which tax on goods 7.7%, income tax 6.6%, import duties 5.6%, other 3.4%). Expenditure: U.S.$5,370,000,000 (defense and internal security 15.0%, social security 7.0%, education 6.0%, economic services 5.2%, health 4.0%, interest payment 2.1%, other 60.7%).
Public debt (external, outstanding; 2002): U.S.$8,883,000,000.
Household income and expenditure. Average household size (2000) 4.7; annual income per household: n.a.; sources of income: n.a.; expenditure: n.a.
Production (metric tons except as noted). Agriculture, forestry, fishing (2002): cassava 5,400,000, corn (maize) 430,000, sugarcane 360,000, sweet potatoes 355,000, bananas 300,000, oil palm fruit 280,000, millet 100,000, dry beans 89,000, pineapples 40,000, peanuts (groundnuts) 27,000, coffee 2,160; livestock (number of live animals) 4,150,000 cattle, 2,050,000 goats, 780,000 pigs, 340,000 sheep, 6,800,000 chickens; roundwood (2002) 4,436,271 cu m; fish catch (2001) 252,518. Mining and quarrying (2002): diamonds 5,022,000 carats. Manufacturing (1999): bread 87,500; frozen fish 57,700; wheat flour 57,500; soap 8,565; salt 7,803; leather shoes 25,000 pairs; beer 160,900 hectolitres; fabric 316,000 sq m. Energy production (consumption): electricity (kW-hr; 2002) 1,710,000,000 ([2000] 1,235,000,000); coal, none (none); crude petroleum (barrels; 2001) 270,800,000 ([2000] 14,114,000); petroleum products (metric tons; 2000) 1,658,000 (976,000); natural gas (cu m; 2001) 710,000,000 (710,000,000).
Tourism: receipts from visitors (2002) U.S.$60,000,000; expenditures by nationals abroad (2001) U.S.$66,000,000.
Gross national product (at current market prices; 2003): U.S.$10,004,000,000 (U.S.$740 per capita).

Structure of gross domestic product and labour force

	2003 in value Kz '000,000	2003 % of total value	1999 labour force	1999 % of labour force
Agriculture	79,579	7.7	4,132,000 (Agriculture and Mining)	72.1
Mining	549,284	53.0		
Manufacturing	37,063	3.6	1,597,000 (Manufacturing through Services)	27.9
Construction	34,413	3.3		
Finance, Trade, Public utilities, Transp. and commun.	154,772	14.9		
Pub. admin., defense, Services	155,832	15.0		
Other	26,097	2.5	...	...
TOTAL	1,037,040	100.0	5,729,000	100.0

Population economically active (1999): total 5,729,000; activity rate of total population 57.7% (participation rates over age 10 [1991] 60.1%; female 38.4%; unemployed [2002] 70%).

Price and earnings indexes (2000 = 100)

	2000	2001	2002	2003
Consumer price index	100.0	241.2	527.6	1,045.8
Monthly earnings index	...	...	...	...

Land use as % of total land area (2000): in temporary crops 2.4%, in permanent crops 0.2%, in pasture 43.3%; overall forest area 56.0%.

Foreign trade

Balance of trade (current prices)

	1996	1997	1998	1999	2000	2001
U.S.$'000,000	+3,055	+2,410	+1,464	+2,077	+4,881	+3,355
% of total	42.8%	31.7%	26.0%	24.1%	44.5%	34.6%

Imports (2001): U.S.$3,179,000,000 (consumer goods 68.4%, capital goods 22.1%, intermediate goods 9.5%). *Major import sources* (2001): South Korea 22.4%; Portugal 14.5%; South Africa 12.3%; U.S. 8.9%; France 4.8%.
Exports (2001): U.S.$6,534,000,000 (crude petroleum 90.5%, diamonds 7.6%, refined petroleum 1.4%, coffee 0.1%). *Major export destinations* (2001): U.S. 44.3%; China 18.7%; France 9.0%; Belgium 8.8%; Taiwan 6.8%.

Transport and communications

Transport. Railroads (2001): route length 1,722 mi, 2,771 km; (1991) passenger-mi 153,000,000, passenger-km 246,200,000; short ton-mi cargo 28,100,000, metric ton-km cargo 45,300,000. Roads (1998): total length 45,128 mi, 72,626 km (paved 25%). Vehicles (1997): passenger cars 207,000; trucks and buses 25,000. Air transport (2001)[4]: passenger-mi 455,400,000, passenger-km 732,968,000; short ton-mi cargo 35,800,000, metric ton-km cargo 57,662,000; airports (1999) with scheduled flights 17.

Communications

Medium	date	unit	number	units per 1,000 persons
Daily newspapers	2000	circulation	111,000	11
Television	2000	receivers	193,000	19
Telephones	2003	main lines	96,300	6.7
Cellular telephones	2002	subscribers	130,000	9.3
Personal computers	2002	units	27,000	1.9
Internet	2002	users	41,000	2.9

Education and health

Educational attainment: n.a. *Literacy* (1998): percentage of population age 15 and over literate 41.7%; males literate 55.6%; females literate 28.5%.

Education (1997–98)

	schools	teachers	students	student/ teacher ratio
Primary (age 7–10)	...	31,062[5]	1,342,116	...
Secondary (age 11–16)	...	5,138[6]	267,399	...
Voc., teacher tr.	...	566[6]	...	...
Higher	...	776	8,337	10.7

Health (1997): physicians 736 (1 per 12,985 persons); hospital beds (1990) 11,857 (1 per 845 persons); infant mortality rate per 1,000 live births (2003) 193.8.
Food (2000): daily per capita caloric intake 1,953 (vegetable products 92%, animal products 8%); 81% of FAO recommended minimum requirement.

Military

Total active duty personnel (2003): 131,000 (army 91.6%, navy 2.3%, air force 6.1%). *Military expenditure as percentage of GNP* (1999): 21.2% (world 2.4%); per capita expenditure U.S.$248.

[1]Civil war begun in 1975 was officially declared over on Aug. 2, 2002. A cease-fire agreement had been signed earlier in April 2002. [2]Post of Prime Minister abolished in January 1999 and reinstated in December 2002. [3]Detail does not add to total given because of rounding. [4]TAAG airline. [5]1991–92. [6]1989–90.

Internet resources for further information:
- **Official Home Page of the Republic of Angola http://www.angola.org**
- **Bank of Angola http://www.bna.ao**

Antigua and Barbuda

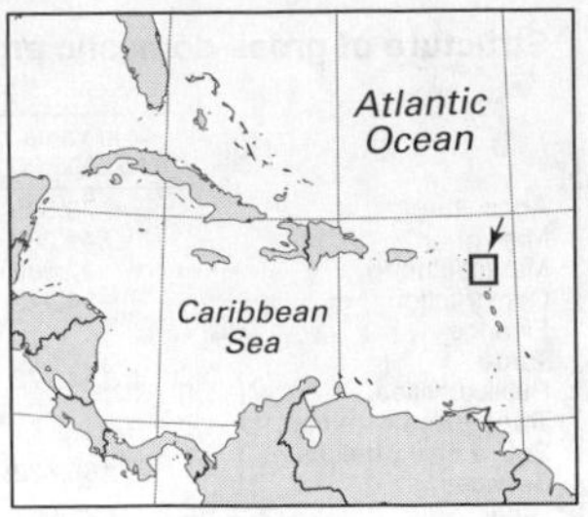

Official name: Antigua and Barbuda.
Form of government: constitutional monarchy with two legislative houses (Senate [17]; House of Representatives [17[1]]).
Chief of state: British Monarch represented by Governor-General.
Head of government: Prime Minister.
Capital: Saint John's.
Official language: English.
Official religion: none.
Monetary unit: 1 Eastern Caribbean dollar (EC$) = 100 cents; valuation (Sept. 1, 2004) 1 U.S.$ = EC$2.70; 1 £ = EC$4.86.

Area and population

	area		population
			2001
Parishes (of Antigua)[2]	sq mi	sq km	census[3]
Saint George	9.3	24.1	} 74,324
Saint John's	28.5	73.8	
Saint Mary	22.0	57.0	
Saint Paul	18.5	47.9	
Saint Peter	12.7	32.9	
Saint Phillip	17.0	44.0	
Other islands[2]			
Barbuda	62.0	160.6	1,417
Redonda	0.5	1.3	0
TOTAL	170.5	441.6	75,741

Demography

Population (2004): 68,300.
Density (2004): persons per sq mi 399.4, persons per sq km 154.5.
Urban-rural (2001): urban 36.9%; rural 63.1%.
Sex distribution (2001): male 48.25%; female 51.75%.
Age breakdown (2001): under 15, 26.4%; 15–29, 25.4%; 30–44, 23.9%; 45–59, 13.9%; 60 and over, 10.4%.
Population projection: (2010) 71,000; (2020) 74,000.
Doubling time: 56 years.
Ethnic composition (2000): black 82.4%; U.S. white 12.0%; mulatto 3.5%; British 1.3%; other 0.8%.
Religious affiliation (1991): Protestant 73.7%, of which Anglican 32.1%, Moravian 12.0%, Methodist 9.1%, Seventh-day Adventist 8.8%; Roman Catholic 10.8%; Jehovah's Witness 1.2%; Rastafarian 0.8%[4]; other religion/no religion/not stated 13.5%.
Major city (2004): Saint John's 23,600[5].

Vital statistics

Birth rate per 1,000 population (2003): 18.2 (world avg. 21.3).
Death rate per 1,000 population (2003): 5.6 (world avg. 9.1).
Natural increase rate per 1,000 population (2003): 12.6 (world avg. 12.2).
Total fertility rate (avg. births per childbearing woman; 2003): 2.3.
Marriage rate per 1,000 population (1995): 22.1.
Divorce rate per 1,000 population (1988): 0.2.
Life expectancy at birth (2003): male 69.0 years; female 73.8 years.
Major causes of death per 100,000 population (1993–95): diseases of the circulatory system 258.1, of which cerebrovascular disease 103.3, diseases of pulmonary circulation and other forms of heart disease 76.9; malignant neoplasms (cancers) 104.9; endocrine and metabolic disorders 73.7.

National economy

Budget (2002). Revenue: EC$418,000,000 (tax revenue 92.9%, of which taxes on international transactions 49.8%, consumption taxes 18.9%, corporate income taxes 14.7%; grants 4.3%; other 2.8%). Expenditures: EC$535,500,000 (current expenditures 94.5%, of which interest payments 10.8%; development expenditures 5.5%).
Public debt (external, outstanding; 2004): more than U.S.$740,000,000.
Production (metric tons except as noted). Agriculture, forestry, fishing (2002): tropical fruit (including papayas, guavas, soursops, and oranges) 6,750, mangoes 1,400, eggplants 270, lemons and limes 230, carrots 220, "Antiguan Black" pineapples 150; livestock (number of live animals) 18,500 sheep, 13,800 cattle; roundwood, n.a.; fish catch (2000) 1,481. Mining and quarrying: crushed stone for local use. Manufacturing (1994): beer and malt 166,000 cases; T-shirts 179,000 units; other manufactures include cement, handicrafts, and furniture, as well as electronic components for export. Energy production (consumption): electricity (kW-hr; 2002) 110,000,000 (110,000,000); coal, none (none); crude petroleum, none (none); petroleum products (metric tons; 2000) negligible (115,000); natural gas, none (none).
Population economically active (1991): total 26,753; activity rate of total population 45.1% (participation rates: ages 15–64, 69.7%; female 45.6%; unemployed [2000] 11.0%).

Price and earnings indexes (1996 = 100)

	1996	1997	1998	1999	2000	2001
Consumer price index	100.0	98.9	103.6	104.4	104.6	106.3
Annual earnings index[6]	100.0	100.0	106.0	106.0	106.0	106.0

Household income and expenditure. Average household size (2001) 3.1; income per household: n.a.; sources of income: n.a.; expenditure: n.a.
Gross national product (2003): U.S.$719,000,000 (U.S.$9,160 per capita).

Structure of gross domestic product and labour force

	2002		1991	
	in value EC$'000,000	% of total value	labour force	% of labour force
Agriculture, fishing	62.6	3.8	1,040	3.9
Quarrying	28.3	1.7	64	0.2
Manufacturing	37.9	2.2	1,444	5.4
Construction	228.6	13.8	3,109	11.6
Public utilities	64.8	3.9	435	1.6
Transp. and commun.	325.7	19.6	2,395	9.0
Trade, restaurants, and hotels	324.7	19.6	8,524	31.9
Finance, real estate	282.3	17.0	1,454	5.4
Pub. admin., defense	297.8	17.9	2,572	9.6
Services	123.8	7.5	5,207	19.5
Other	–116.2[7]	–7.0[7]	509	1.9
TOTAL	1,660.3	100.0	26,753	100.0

Land use as % of total land area (2000): in temporary crops *c.* 18%, in permanent crops *c.* 5%, in pasture *c.* 9%; overall forest area *c.* 20%.
Tourism: receipts from visitors (2001) U.S.$272,000,000; expenditures by nationals abroad U.S.$32,000,000.

Foreign trade[8]

Balance of trade (current prices)

	1996	1997	1998	1999	2000	2001
U.S.$'000,000	–302	–297	–304	–335	–322	–318
% of total	90.0%	91.9%	91.1%	91.4%	90.8%	90.4%

Imports (1999): U.S.$356,000,000 (machinery and equipment 32.2%, agricultural products 24.7%, basic manufactures 15.4%, petroleum products 10.5%). *Major import sources:* United States 49.5%; Japan 10.2%; United Kingdom 6.3%; Trinidad and Tobago 6.0%; Netherlands Antilles 5.5%.
Exports (1999): U.S.$37,800,000 (reexports [significantly, petroleum products reexported to neighbouring islands] 60.3%, domestic exports 39.7%). *Major export destinations* (1998): Barbados 9.5%; Trinidad and Tobago 7.3%; St. Lucia 7.3%; United Kingdom 6.1%; unspecified 52.5%.

Transport and communications

Transport. Railroad[9]. Roads (1998): total length 155 mi, 250 km (paved, n.a.). Vehicles (1995): passenger cars 13,588; trucks and buses 1,342. Air transport (1999): passenger-mi 172,000,000, passenger-km 276,300,000; short ton-mi cargo 205,000, metric ton-km cargo 300,000; airports (2001) with scheduled flights 2.

Communications

Medium	date	unit	number	units per 1,000 persons
Daily newspapers	1996	circulation	6,000	87
Radio	1997	receivers	36,000	523
Television	1999	receivers	33,000	501
Telephones	2002	main lines	38,000	488
Cellular telephones	2002	subscribers	38,200	490
Internet	2002	users	10,000	128

Education and health

Educational attainment (1991). Percentage of population age 25 and over having: no formal schooling 1.1%; primary education 50.5%; secondary 33.4%; higher (not university) 5.4%; university 6.2%; other/unknown 3.4%. *Literacy* (2000): percentage of total population age 15 and over literate 86.6%.

Education (2000–01)

	schools	teachers	students	student/ teacher ratio
Primary (age 5–11)	55	525	10,427	19.9
Secondary (age 12–16)	14	361	5,794	16.0
Higher[10]	1	16	46	2.9

Health (1996): physicians 75 (1 per 915 persons); hospital beds 255 (1 per 269 persons); infant mortality rate per 1,000 live births (2003) 20.9.
Food (2000): daily per capita caloric intake 2,381 (vegetable products 67%, animal products 33%); 102% of FAO recommended minimum requirement.

Military

Total active duty personnel (2003): a 170-member defense force (army 73.5%, navy 26.5%) is part of the Eastern Caribbean regional security system. *Military expenditure as percentage of GNP* (1998): 0.7%[11] (world 2.5%); per capita expenditure U.S.$57.

[1]Directly elected seats only; attorney general and speaker may serve ex officio if they are not elected to House of Representatives. [2]Community councils on Antigua and the local government council on Barbuda are the organs of local government. [3]Preliminary figures; a second preliminary figure equals 72,309. [4]Increased to more than 3% of population by 2000. [5]Large settlements include (1991): All Saints 2,230; Liberta 1,473; Codrington 814. [6]Public sector only. [7]Net indirect taxes less imputed bank service charges. [8]Balance of trade excludes reexports; data for commodities and destinations includes reexports. [9]Mostly nonoperative privately owned tracks. [10]1994–95. [11]Estimated percentage.

Internet resources for further information:
- **Eastern Caribbean Central Bank**
  http://www.eccb-centralbank.org
- **Ministry of Foreign Affairs**
  http://www.foreignaffairs.gov.ag

Argentina

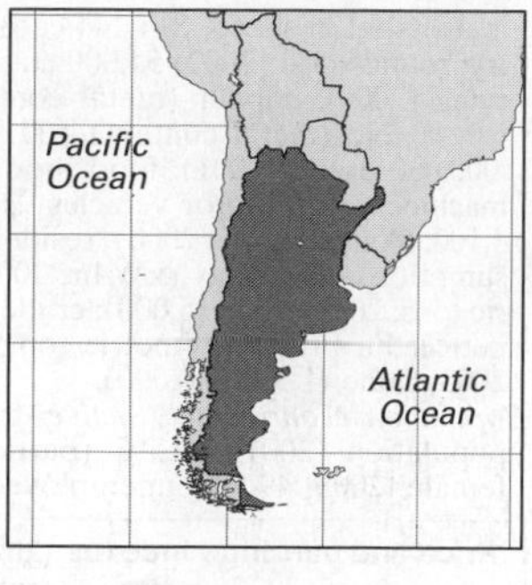

Official name: República Argentina (Argentine Republic).
Form of government: federal republic with two legislative houses (Senate [72]; Chamber of Deputies [257]).
Head of state and government: President[1].
Capital: Buenos Aires.
Official language: Spanish.
Official religion: Roman Catholicism.
Monetary unit: 1 peso (pl. pesos) (Arg$) = 100 centavos; valuation (Sept. 1, 2004) 1 U.S.$ = Arg$3.00; 1 £ = Arg$5.39.

Area and population

Provinces	Capitals	area sq mi	area sq km	population 2001 census
Buenos Aires	La Plata	118,754	307,571	13,827,203
Catamarca	Catamarca	39,615	102,602	334,568
Chaco	Resistencia	38,469	99,633	984,446
Chubut	Rawson	86,752	224,686	413,237
Córdoba	Córdoba	63,831	165,321	3,066,801
Corrientes	Corrientes	34,054	88,199	930,991
Entre Ríos	Paraná	30,418	78,781	1,158,147
Formosa	Formosa	27,825	72,066	486,559
Jujuy	San Salvador de Jujuy	20,548	53,219	611,888
La Pampa	Santa Rosa	55,382	143,440	299,294
La Rioja	La Rioja	34,626	89,680	289,983
Mendoza	Mendoza	57,462	148,827	1,579,651
Misiones	Posadas	11,506	29,801	965,522
Neuquén	Neuquén	36,324	94,078	474,155
Río Negro	Viedma	78,384	203,013	552,822
Salta	Salta	60,034	155,488	1,079,051
San Juan	San Juan	34,614	89,651	620,023
San Luis	San Luis	29,633	76,748	367,933
Santa Cruz	Río Gallegos	94,187	243,943	196,958
Santa Fe	Santa Fe	51,354	133,007	3,000,701
Santiago del Estero	Santiago del Estero	52,645	136,351	804,457
Tierra del Fuego[2]	Ushuaia	8,210	21,263	101,079
Tucumán	San Miguel de Tucumán	8,697	22,524	1,338,523
Autonomous city				
Buenos Aires	—	77	200	2,776,138
TOTAL		1,073,400[3]	2,780,092	36,260,130

Demography

Population (2004): 39,145,000.
Density (2004): persons per sq mi 36.5, persons per sq km 14.1.
Urban-rural (2000): urban 89.6%; rural 10.4%.
Sex distribution (2001): male 48.70%; female 51.30%.
Age breakdown (2001): under 15, 28.3%; 15–29, 25.0%; 30–44, 18.6%; 45–59, 14.7%; 60–74, 9.3%; 75 and over, 4.1%.
Population projection: (2010) 41,405,000; (2020) 44,524,000.
Ethnic composition (2000): European extraction 86.4%; mestizo 6.5%; Amerindian 3.4%; Arab 3.3%; other 0.4%.
Religious affiliation (2000): Roman Catholic 79.8%; Protestant 5.4%; Muslim 1.9%; Jewish 1.3%; other 11.6%.
Major cities (2001): Buenos Aires 2,768,772 (16,603,341[4]); Córdoba 1,267,774; San Justo 1,256,724; Rosario 906,004; La Plata 553,002; Mar del Plata 541,807.

Vital statistics

Birth rate per 1,000 population (2003): 17.5 (world avg. 21.3).
Death rate per 1,000 population (2003): 7.6 (world avg. 9.1).
Natural increase rate per 1,000 population (2003): 9.9 (world avg. 12.2).
Total fertility rate (avg. births per childbearing woman; 2003): 2.3.
Life expectancy at birth (2003): male 71.7 years; female 79.4 years.
Major causes of death per 100,000 population (1998): diseases of the circulatory system 265.8; neoplasms (cancers) 146.3; diseases of the respiratory system 91.0; accidents 30.5.

National economy

Budget (2001). Revenue: Arg$37,093,900,000 (tax revenue 90.3%, of which sales tax 36.0%, social security tax 22.8%, income tax 17.9%, property tax 9.3%; nontax revenue 9.7%). Expenditure: Arg$46,013,400,000 (social security 47.8%; debt service 22.1%; education 5.7%; defense 3.8%; health 1.8%).
Public debt (external, outstanding; 2002): U.S.$74,661,000,000.
Gross national product (at current market prices; 2003): U.S.$140,113,000,000 (U.S.$3,650 per capita).

Structure of gross domestic product and labour force

	2001 in value Arg$'000,000	2001 % of total value	1996 labour force	1996 % of labour force
Agriculture	12,276	4.6	190,300[5]	1.5[5]
Mining	6,657	2.5		
Manufacturing	43,242	16.1	1,999,600	15.9
Construction	11,597	4.3	1,217,400	9.7
Public utilities	6,332	2.4	115,700	0.9
Transp. and commun.	22,873	8.5	873,300	6.9
Trade, restaurants	40,139	14.9	2,523,800	20.0
Finance, real estate	56,459	21.0	1,021,800	8.1
Pub. admin., defense	55,401	20.6	1,010,500	8.0
Services			3,573,000	28.4
Other	13,721[6]	5.1[6]	63,500	0.5
TOTAL	268,697	100.0	12,588,900[5]	100.0[3]

Production (metric tons except as noted). Agriculture, forestry, fishing (2002): soybeans 30,000,000, sugarcane 16,500,000, corn (maize) 14,710,000, wheat 12,500,000, sunflower seeds 3,843,600, grapes 2,460,000, potatoes 2,132,500; livestock (number of live animals) 50,669,000 cattle, 14,000,000 sheep; roundwood (2002) 9,307,000 cu m; fish catch (2001) 924,700. Mining and quarrying (2001): silver 152,802 kg; gold 30,630 kg. Manufacturing (value added in U.S.$'000,000; 1999): food products 5,601; beverages 2,146; refined petroleum products 1,361; fabricated metal products 1,321; plastic products 985. Energy production (consumption): electricity (kW-hr; 2002) 81,390,000,000 ([2000] 89,014,000,000); coal (2000) 259,000 (1,058,000); crude petroleum (barrels; 2001) 277,000,000 ([2000] 191,379,000); petroleum products (metric tons; 2000) 23,197,000 (20,460,000); natural gas (cu m; 2001) 53,298,000,000 ([2000] 40,817,400,000).
Land use as % of total land area (2000): in temporary crops 12.2%, in permanent crops 0.5%, in pasture 51.9%; overall forest area 12.7%.
Tourism (2002): receipts U.S.$1,476,000,000; expenditures U.S.$2,256,000,000.
Population economically active (2001): total 15,264,783; activity rate of total population 42.1% (participation rates: ages 14 and over 57.2%; female 40.9%; unemployed [2004] c. 12%).

Price and earnings indexes (2000 = 100)

	1998	1999	2000	2001	2002	2003	2004[7]
Consumer price index	102.1	100.9	100.0	98.9	124.5	141.3	146.7
Monthly earnings index	...	...	...	...	...	...	...

Household size and expenditure. Average household size (2001) 3.6.

Foreign trade[8]

Balance of trade (current prices)

	1998	1999	2000	2001	2002	2003
U.S.$'000,000	−3,097	−794	+2,558	+7,385	+17,236	+16,277
% of total	5.5%	1.7%	5.1%	16.2%	50.4%	36.0%

Imports (2001): U.S.$20,311,600,000 (chemicals and chemical products 17.8%, nonelectrical machinery 17.4%, electrical machinery 12.6%, transport equipment 10.5%). *Major import sources:* Brazil 26.0%; U.S. 18.6%; Germany 5.2%; China 5.2%; Italy 4.1%; Japan 3.8%.
Exports (2001): U.S.$26,655,200,000 (food products and live animals 44.2%, crude petroleum and petroleum products 16.9%, road vehicles 8.3%, nonelectrical machinery 4.3%). *Major export destinations:* Brazil 23.3%; U.S. 10.9%; Chile 10.7%; China 4.2%; Spain 4.1%.

Transport and communications

Transport. Railroads: (2000) route length 35,753 km; (2001) passenger-km 7,934,000,000; (2001) metric ton-km cargo 8,989,000,000. Roads (1999): total length 133,890 mi, 215,471 km (paved 29%). Vehicles: passenger cars (2000) 5,386,700; commercial vehicles and buses (1998) 1,496,567. Air transport (2003)[9]: passenger-km 9,514,000,000; metric ton-km cargo 103,435,000.

Communications

Medium	date	unit	number	units per 1,000 persons
Daily newspapers	2000	circulation	1,320,000	37
Radio	2000	receivers	24,300,000	681
Television	2000	receivers	10,500,000	293
Telephones	2002	main lines	8,009,400	219
Cellular telephones	2002	subscribers	6,500,000	178
Personal computers	2002	units	3,000,000	82
Internet	2002	users	4,100,000	112

Education and health

Educational attainment (2001). Percentage of population age 15 and over having: no formal schooling 3.7%; incomplete primary education 14.2%; complete primary 28.0%; secondary 37.1%; some higher 8.3%; complete higher 8.7%. *Literacy* (2001): percentage of total population age 10 and over literate 97.4%; males literate 97.4%; females literate 97.4%.

Education (1999–2000)

	schools	teachers	students	student/ teacher ratio
Primary (age 6–12)	22,283	307,874	4,609,077	15.0
Secondary (age 13–17)[10]	21,492	127,718	3,281,512	25.7
Higher	1,744	126,224	1,336,800	10.6

Health: physicians (1992) 88,800 (1 per 376 persons); hospital beds (1996) 115,803 (1 per 304 persons); infant mortality rate (2003) 16.2.
Food (2001): daily per capita caloric intake 3,171 (vegetable products 70%, animal products 30%); 135% of FAO recommended minimum requirement.

Military

Total active duty personnel (2003): 71,400 (army 58.0%, navy 24.5%, air force 17.5%). *Military expenditure as percentage of GNP* (1999): 1.6% (world 2.4%); per capita expenditure U.S.$118.

[1]Assisted by the cabinet chief (ministerial coordinator) who exercises general administration of the country. [2]Area of Tierra del Fuego excludes claims to British-held islands in the South Atlantic Ocean. [3]Detail does not add to total given because of rounding. [4]Combined population of Gran Buenos Aires and Buenos Aires city. [5]Based on October survey; data for agriculture and mining sectors are incomplete. [6]Import duties less imputed bank service charges. [7]May. [8]Import figures are f.o.b. in balance of trade and c.i.f. in commodities and trading partners. [9]Aerolineas Argentinas. [10]Secondary includes vocational and teacher training.

Internet resources for further information:
- **National Institute of Statistics and Censuses http://www.indec.mecon.ar**

Armenia

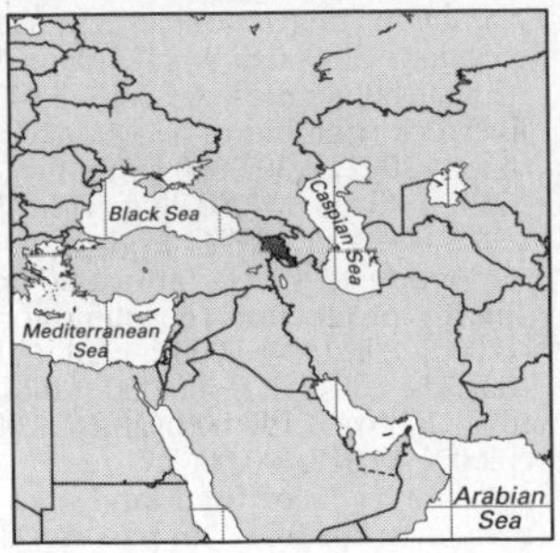

Official name: Hayastani Hanrapetut'yun (Republic of Armenia).
Form of government: unitary multiparty republic with a single legislative body (National Assembly [131]).
Head of state: President.
Head of government: Prime Minister.
Capital: Yerevan.
Official language: Armenian.
Official religion: none[1].
Monetary unit: 1 dram = 100 lumas; valuation (Sept. 1, 2004) 1 U.S.$ = 516.50 drams; 1 £ = 929.16 drams.

Area and population

Districts	Centres	area sq mi	area sq km	population 2001 census
Aragatsotn	Ashtarak	1,063	2,753	126,278
Ararat	Artashat	809	2,096	252,665
Armavir	Armavir	480	1,242	255,861
Gegharkunik	Gavar	2,065[2]	5,348[2]	215,371
Kotayk	Hrazdan	807	2,089	241,337
Lori	Vanadzor	1,463	3,789	253,351
Shirak	Gyumri	1,035	2,681	257,242
Syunik	Kapan	1,740	4,506	134,061
Tavush	Ijevan	1,044	2,704	121,963
Vayots-Dzor	Yeghegnadzor	891	2,308	53,230
City				
Yerevan	—	88	227	1,091,235
TOTAL		11,484[3, 4]	29,743[3]	3,002,594[5]

Demography

Population (2004): 2,991,000.
Density (2004): persons per sq mi 260.4, persons per sq km 100.6.
Urban-rural (2001): urban 64.8%; rural 35.2%.
Sex distribution (2001): male 46.87%; female 53.13%.
Age breakdown (2001): under 15, 24.8%; 15–29, 24.9%; 30–44, 21.8%; 45–59, 13.6%; 60–74, 12.1%; 75 and over, 2.8%.
Population projection: (2010) 2,967,000; (2020) 3,017,370.
Ethnic composition (2001): Armenian 97.9%; Kurdish 1.3%; Russian 0.5%; other 0.3%.
Religious affiliation (1995): Armenian Apostolic 64.5%; other Christian 1.3%; other (mostly nonreligious) 34.2%.
Major cities (2001[5]): Yerevan 1,091,235; Gyumri 150,917; Vanadzor (Kirovakan) 107,394; Vagharshapat 56,388; Hrazdan 52,808.

Vital statistics

Birth rate per 1,000 population (2002): 10.1 (world avg. 21.3); legitimate 86.8%; illegitimate 13.2%.
Death rate per 1,000 population (2002): 8.0 (world avg. 9.1).
Natural increase rate per 1,000 population (2002): 2.1 (world avg. 12.2).
Total fertility rate (avg. births per childbearing woman; 2001): 1.1.
Marriage rate per 1,000 population (2002): 4.3.
Divorce rate per 1,000 population (2002): 0.5.
Life expectancy at birth (2002): male 70.0 years; female 76.1 years.
Major causes of death per 100,000 population (2002): diseases of the circulatory system 436.8; malignant neoplasms (cancers) 131.8; diabetes mellitus 47.3; diseases of the respiratory system 45.5; accidents and violence 33.3.

National economy

Budget (2002). Revenue: 228,317,000,000 drams (tax revenue 87.0%, of which value-added tax 41.6%, excise tax 15.5%, enterprise profit tax 7.6%, stamp duties 5.8%; nontax revenue 13.0%). Expenditures: 263,912,000,000 drams (public services and social welfare 18.2%, defense 13.9%, education 11.0%, housing and energy 6.4%, public health 6.0%, unspecified 27.2%).
Public debt (external, outstanding; 2002): U.S.$920,000,000.
Tourism (2002): receipts from visitors U.S.$162,000,000; expenditures by nationals abroad U.S.$54,000,000.
Land use as % of total land area (2000): in temporary crops 17.6%, in permanent crops 2.3%, in pasture 28.4%; overall forest area 12.4%.
Gross national product (2003): U.S.$2,910,000,000 (U.S.$950 per capita).

Structure of net material product and labour force

	2001		2002	
	in value '000,000 drams	% of total value	labour force	% of labour force
Agriculture	293,872	25.0	500,800	40.4
Manufacturing, mining; Public utilities	237,668	20.2	143,100	11.5
Construction	125,777	10.7	36,100	2.9
Transp. and commun.	88,162	7.5	40,200	3.2
Trade	115,198	9.8	99,600	8.0
Finance	…	…	35,400	2.9
Pub. admin., defense; Services	…	…	251,200	20.3
Other	314,810	26.8	133,700[6]	10.8[6]
TOTAL	1,175,487	100.0	1,240,100	100.0

Production (metric tons except as noted). Agriculture, forestry, fishing (2002): potatoes 374,263, wheat 280,477, tomatoes 171,000, barley 113,332, grapes 103,962, watermelons 89,727, apples 35,200; livestock (number of live animals) 546,136 sheep, 514,244 cattle, 97,884 pigs, 45,950 goats, 4,400,000 poultry; roundwood (2002) 54,000 cu m; fish catch (2001) 2,100. Mining and quarrying (2000): copper (metal content) 14,000; molybdenum (metal content) 6,044; gold (metal content) 400 kg. Manufacturing (value of production in '000,000 drams; 2001): food products 109,300; metals 24,600; jewelry 16,600; machinery and motor vehicles 9,600; chemicals 9,300; tobacco 8,600; textiles 4,100. Construction (2000): residential 195,000 sq m. Energy production (consumption): electricity (kW-hr; 2002) 5,519,000,000 (5,519,000,000); coal (metric tons; 2001) none (5,000); crude petroleum (barrels; 1998) none (1,035,000); petroleum products (metric tons; 2000) none (273,000); natural gas (cu m; 2000) none (1,336,000,000).
Population economically active: total (2003) 1,232,400; activity rate of total population (2001) 49.5% (participation rates [2001]: ages 15–64, 72.1%; female [2003] 49.5%; unemployed [2003] 10.1%).

Price and earnings indexes (2000 = 100)

	1998	1999	2000	2001	2002	2003
Consumer price index	100.2	100.8	100.0	103.1	104.3	109.2
Earnings index	…	…	…	…	…	…

Household income and expenditure. Average household size (2001) 4.1; income per household (2002) 750,400 drams (U.S.$1,300); sources of income (1999): agricultural income 32.1%, wages and salaries 24.6%, transfers 19.3%, help from abroad 12.8%, self-employment 10.6%, other 0.6%; expenditure (1999): food 67.0%, beverages and tobacco 19.2%, services 12.4%, other 1.4%.

Foreign trade[7]

Balance of trade (current prices)

	1996	1997	1998	1999	2000	2001
U.S.$'000,000	–467	–547	–574	–471	–482	–536
% of total	44.6%	54.0%	56.5%	50.4%	45.0%	44.0%

Imports (2001): U.S.$877,434,000 (2000; mineral fuels 20.8%; food 20.6%, of which cereals 9.8%; rough diamonds 11.0%; nonelectrical machinery 10.9%). *Major import sources* (2001): Russia 19.5%; U.K. 10.4%; U.S. 9.6%; Iran 8.9%; U.A.E. 5.4%; Belgium 4.8%.
Exports (2001): U.S.$341,836,000 (2000; cut diamonds 33.5%; alcoholic beverages 7.5%; electric current 7.0%; metal scrap 6.8%; nonelectrical machinery 6.4%). *Major export destinations* (2001): Russia 17.7%; U.S. 15.3%; Belgium 13.6%; Iran 9.5%; U.K. 5.9%.

Transport and communications

Transport. Railroads (2003): length 442 mi, 711 km; (2002) passenger-mi 30,074,000, passenger-km 48,400,000; short ton-mi cargo 309,140,000, metric ton-km cargo 451,800,000. Roads (2003): length 4,677 mi, 7,527 km (paved 100%). Vehicles (1996): passenger cars 1,300; trucks and buses 4,460. Air transport (2002): passenger-mi 469,300,000, passenger-km 755,300,000; short ton-mi cargo 3,969,000, metric ton-km cargo 5,800,000; airports (2003) 1.

Communications

Medium	date	unit	number	units per 1,000 persons
Daily newspapers	2000	circulation	18,700	6.2
Radio	2000	receivers	700,000	225
Television	2000	receivers	759,000	244
Telephones	2003	main lines	562,600	148
Cellular telephones	2003	subscribers	114,400	30
Personal computers	2002	units	60,000	16
Internet	2003	users	150,000	39

Education and health

Educational attainment (2001). Percentage of population age 26 and over having: no formal schooling 0.7%; primary education 13.0%; completed secondary and some postsecondary 66.0%; higher 20.3%. *Literacy* (2001): total population age 15 and over literate 99.4%; male 99.7%; female 99.2%.

Education (2002–03)

	schools	teachers	students	student/teacher ratio
Primary (age 6–13); Secondary (age 14–17)	1,481	54,300	520,600	9.6
Voc., teacher tr.	77	3,198	27,600	8.6
Higher	20	5,917	54,100	9.1

Health (2002): physicians 11,508 (1 per 279 persons); hospital beds 13,968 (1 per 230 persons); infant mortality rate per 1,000 live births (2002) 14.0.
Food (2001): daily per capita caloric intake 1,991 (vegetable products 84%, animal products 16%); 80% of FAO recommended minimum requirement.

Military

Total active duty personnel (2003): 44,660 (army 92.9%, air force 7.1%); Russian troops (August 2004) 3,500. Russian troops (August 2004) 3,500. *Military expenditure as percentage of GNP* (1999): 5.8% (world 2.4%); per capita expenditure U.S.$170.

[1]The Armenian Apostolic Church (Armenian Orthodox Church) has special status per 1991 religious law. [2]Includes area of Lake Sevan. [3]In addition, about 16% of neighbouring Azerbaijan (including the 4,400-sq km geographic region of Nagorno-Karabakh [Armenian: Artsakh]) has been occupied by Armenian forces since 1993. [4]Detail does not add to total given because of rounding. [5]De facto population. [6]Unemployed. [7]Imports f.o.b. in balance of trade and c.i.f. in commodities and trading partners.

Internet resources for further information:
- **National Statistical Service http://www.armstat.am**

Aruba

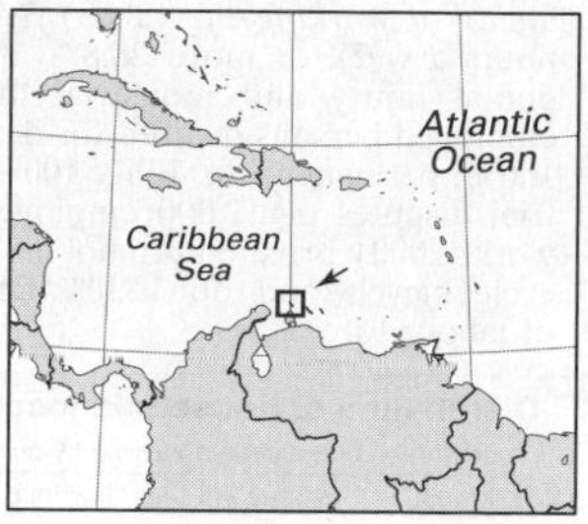

Official name: Aruba.
Political status: nonmetropolitan territory of The Netherlands with one legislative house (States of Aruba [21]).
Chief of state: Dutch Monarch represented by Governor.
Head of government: Prime Minister.
Capital: Oranjestad.
Official language: Dutch.
Official religion: none.
Monetary unit: 1 Aruban florin[1] (Af.) = 100 cents; valuation (Sept. 1, 2004) 1 U.S.$ = Af. 1.79; 1 £ = Af. 3.22.

Area and population

Census region	area[2] sq mi	area[2] sq km	population 2000 census
Noord/Tanki Leendert	14	37	16,944
Oranjestad East	5	13	14,224
Oranjestad West	4	10	12,131
Paradera	10	25	9,037
San Nicolas North	9	23	10,118
San Nicolas South	4	10	5,730
Santa Cruz	18	47	12,326
Savaneta	11	28	9,996
TOTAL	75	193	90,506

Demography

Population (2004): 95,600.
Density (2004): persons per sq mi 1,274.7, persons per sq km 495.3.
Urban-rural (2001): urban 67.0%; rural 33.0%.
Sex distribution (2002): male 47.81%; female 52.19%.
Age breakdown (2002): under 15, 22.9%; 15–29, 19.4%; 30–44, 27.5%; 45–59, 18.7%; 60–74, 8.7%; 75 and over, 2.7%; unknown 0.1%.
Population projection: (2010) 100,000; (2020) 108,000.
Linguistic composition (2000): Papiamento 69.4%; Spanish 13.2%; English 8.1%; Dutch 6.1%; Portuguese 0.3%; other 2.0%; unknown 0.9%.[3]
Religious affiliation (2000): Christian 96.2%, of which Roman Catholic 81.9%, Protestant 7.3%, other Christian (Jehovah's Witness) 1.3%; Spiritist 1.0%; nonreligious 1.4%; other 1.4%.
Major urban areas (2000): Oranjestad 26,355[4]; San Nicolas 15,848[5].

Vital statistics

Birth rate per 1,000 population (2002): 14.6 (world avg. 21.3); legitimate 52.5%; illegitimate 47.5%.
Death rate per 1,000 population (2002): 5.2 (world avg. 9.1).
Natural increase rate per 1,000 population (2002): 9.4 (world avg. 12.2).
Total fertility rate (avg. births per childbearing woman; 2002): 1.8.
Marriage rate per 1,000 population (2002): 6.9.
Divorce rate per 1,000 population (2002): 5.2.
Life expectancy at birth (2002): male 70.0 years; female 76.0 years.
Major causes of death per 100,000 population (2001): diseases of the circulatory system 151.9, malignant neoplasms (cancers) 109.1, infectious and parasitic diseases/diseases of the respiratory system 48.1.

National economy

Budget (2002). Revenue: Af. 751,200,000 (tax revenue 81.2%, of which taxes on income and profits 40.1%, sales tax 28.4%; nontax revenue 13.8%; grants 5.0%). Expenditures: Af. 816,400,000 (wages 32.1%, goods and services 18.3%, subsidies 13.2%, social security contributions 8.1%).
Production (metric tons except as noted). Agriculture, forestry, fishing: aloes are cultivated for export; small amounts of tomatoes, beans, cucumbers, gherkins, watermelons, and lettuce are grown on hydroponic farms; divi-divi pods, sour orange fruit, sorghum, and peanuts (groundnuts) are nonhydroponic crops of limited value; livestock (number of live animals) Aruba has very few livestock; roundwood, n.a.; fish catch (2001) 163. Mining and quarrying: excavation of sand for local use. Manufacturing[6]: rum, cigarettes, aloe products, and soaps. Construction (value of residential and nonresidential construction permits; 2000): Af. 183,300,000. Energy production (consumption): electricity (kW-hr; 2002) 824,649,000 (690,129,000); coal, none (none); crude petroleum (barrels; 2000) none (2,382,000); petroleum products (metric tons; 2000) none (302,000); natural gas, none (none).
Gross domestic product (2003): U.S.$2,011,000,000 (U.S.$21,160 per capita).

Structure of gross domestic product and labour force

	1998 in value Af. '000,000	1998 % of total value	2000 labour force	2000 % of labour force
Agriculture / Mining	11	0.4	212 / 38	0.5 / 0.1
Manufacturing	77	2.6	2,440	5.4
Construction	218	7.5	3,892	8.6
Public utilities	193	6.6	500	1.1
Transp. and commun.	234	8.0	2,905	6.5
Trade, restaurants	692	23.7	14,763	32.8
Finance, real estate	772	26.4	5,206	11.6
Pub. admin., defense	364	12.5	3,528	7.8
Services	285	9.8	8,129	18.1
Other	77	2.6	3,423[7]	7.6[7]
TOTAL	2,923	100.0[8]	45,036	100.0[8]

Population economically active (2000): total 45,036; activity rate of total population 49.5% (participation rates: ages 15–64, 71.9%; female 46.6%; unemployed [2003] 8.0%).

Price and earnings indexes (2000 = 100)[9]

	2000	2001	2002	2003	2004
Consumer price index	100.0	102.6	106.8	109.2	111.6[10]
Earnings index	...	...	...	...	...

Public debt (external, outstanding; 2003): U.S.$407,800,000.
Household income and expenditure (1999): average household size 3.6; average annual income per household: Af. 39,000 (U.S.$21,800); sources of income: n.a.; expenditure (1994)[11]: transportation and communications 20.7%, food and beverages 18.4%, clothing and footwear 11.3%, household furnishings 10.4%, housing 9.8%.
Tourism: receipts from visitors (2003) U.S.$844,000,000; expenditures by nationals abroad (2002) U.S.$154,000,000.
Land use as % of total land area (2000): in temporary crops *c.* 11%, in permanent crops, none, in pasture, negligible; overall forest area, negligible.

Foreign trade

Balance of trade (current prices)

	1996	1997	1998	1999	2000	2001
U.S.$'000,000	–308	–391	–354	–594	–35	+77
% of total	8.1%	10.2%	13.2%	17.3%	0.7%	1.6%

Imports (2001): U.S.$2,362,000,000 (petroleum [all forms] and free-zone imports 68.8%, food and beverages 7.1%, electrical and nonelectrical machinery 5.5%). *Major import sources*[12]: United States 61.9%; The Netherlands 11.6%; Netherlands Antilles 3.6%; Venezuela 3.1%.
Exports (2001): U.S.$2,439,000,000 (petroleum [all forms] and free-zone exports 98.8%, food and beverages 0.5%). *Major export destinations*[12]: United States 25.9%; Venezuela 21.3%; Netherlands Antilles 19.8%; The Netherlands 14.5%.

Transport and communications

Transport. Railroads: none. Roads (1995): total length 497 mi, 800 km (paved 64%). Vehicles (2002): passenger cars 42,802; trucks and buses 1,072. Air transport (2001)[13]: passenger-mi 497,000,000, passenger-km 800,000,000; metric ton-mi cargo, n.a.; airports (2001) with scheduled flights 1.

Communications

Medium	date	unit	number	units per 1,000 persons
Daily newspapers	1996	circulation	73,000	851
Radio	2000	receivers	51,000	562
Television	2000	receivers	20,000	224
Telephones	2001	main lines	37,100	350
Cellular telephones	2001	subscribers	53,000	500
Internet	2001	users	24,000	226

Education and health

Educational attainment (2000). Percentage of population age 25 and over having: no formal schooling or incomplete primary education 9.7%; primary education 33.9%; secondary/vocational 39.2%; advanced vocational/higher 16.2%; unknown status 1.0%. *Literacy* (2000): percentage of total population age 13 and over literate 97.3%.

Education (2001)

	schools	teachers	students	student/ teacher ratio
Primary (age 6–12)	33	437	9,245	21.2
Secondary (age 12–17) / Voc., teacher tr.	12	533	7,924	14.9
Higher	2	49	437	8.9

Health (2002): physicians 99 (1 per 944 persons); hospital beds 305 (1 per 306 persons); infant mortality rate per 1,000 live births (2000) 6.5.

Military

Total active duty personnel (2003): a small Dutch naval/coast guard contingent is stationed in Aruba and the Netherlands Antilles to combat organized crime and drug smuggling.

[1]The Aruban florin (Af.) is pegged to the U.S. dollar at a fixed rate of Af. 1.79 = 1 U.S.$. [2]Areas for census regions are approximate. [3]Most Arubans are racially and ethnically mixed; ethnic composition (1998): Amerindian/other 80%; other (primarily Dutch, Spanish and/or black) 20%. [4]Combined population of Oranjestad East and Oranjestad West. [5]Combined population of San Nicolas North and San Nicolas South. [6]Service facilities include a free zone, offshore corporate banking facilities, casino/resort complexes, a petroleum transshipment terminal, a cruise ship terminal, and ship repair and bunkering facilities. [7]Includes 3,118 unemployed. [8]Detail does not add to total given because of rounding. [9]All end of year unless otherwise indicated. [10]End of June. [11]Weights of consumer price index components. [12]Excludes petroleum (all forms) and free-zone trade. [13]Air Aruba only.

Internet resources for further information:
- **Centrale Bank van Aruba**
http://www.cbaruba.org

Australia

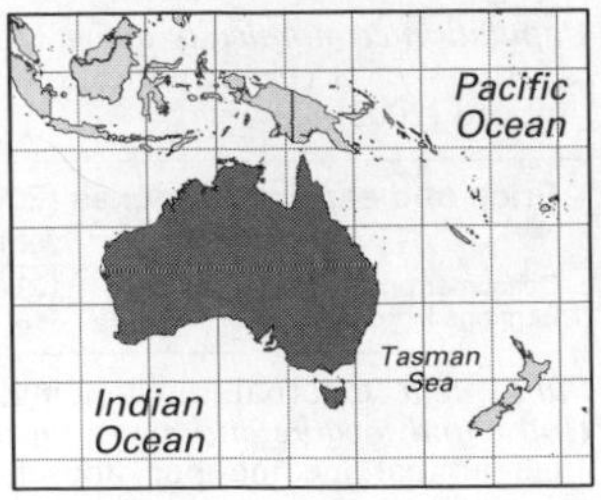

Official name: Commonwealth of Australia.
Form of government: federal parliamentary state (formally a constitutional monarchy) with two legislative houses (Senate [76]; House of Representatives [150]).
Chief of state: British Monarch represented by Governor-General.
Head of government: Prime Minister.
Capital: Canberra.
Official language: English.
Official religion: none.
Monetary unit: 1 Australian dollar ($A) = 100 cents; valuation (Sept. 1, 2004) 1 U.S.$ = $A 1.42; 1 £ = $A 2.55.

Area and population

		area[1]		population
States	Capitals	sq mi	sq km	2004 estimate[2]
New South Wales	Sydney	309,130	800,642	6,716,277
Queensland	Brisbane	668,207	1,730,648	3,840,111
South Australia	Adelaide	379,725	983,482	1,531,375
Tasmania	Hobart	26,410	68,401	479,958
Victoria	Melbourne	87,806	227,416	4,947,985
Western Australia	Perth	976,790	2,529,875	1,969,046
Territories[3]				
Australian Capital Territory	Canberra	910	2,358	322,579
Christmas Island	The Settlement	52	135	}
Cocos (Keeling) Islands	West Island	5	14	} 2,646
Jervis Bay	—	28	73	}
Norfolk Island	Kingston	13	35	2,037[4]
Northern Territory	Darwin	520,902	1,349,129	198,700
TOTAL		2,969,978	7,692,208	20,010,714[4]

Demography

Population (2004): 20,141,000.
Density (2004): persons per sq mi 6.8, persons per sq km 2.6.
Urban-rural (2002): urban 85.0%; rural 15.0%.
Sex distribution (2003): male 49.80%; female 50.20%.
Age breakdown (2003): under 15, 20.3%; 15–29, 20.7%; 30–44, 22.7%; 45–59, 19.3%; 60–74, 11.0%; 75 and over, 6.0%.
Population projection: (2010) 21,107,000; (2020) 22,765,000.
Ethnic composition (2001): white *c.* 92%; Asian *c.* 6%; aboriginal *c.* 2%.
Religious affiliation (2001): Christian 68.0%, of which Roman Catholic 26.6%, Anglican Church of Australia 20.7%, other Protestant 15.8% (Uniting Church 6.7%, Presbyterian 3.4%), Orthodox 2.8%, other Christian 2.1%; Buddhist 1.9%; Muslim 1.5%; Hindu 0.5%; Jewish 0.4%; no religion 15.5%; other 12.2%.
Metropolitan areas (2001): Sydney 3,997,321; Melbourne 3,366,542; Brisbane 1,627,535; Perth 1,339,993; Adelaide 1,072,585; Newcastle 470,610; Gold Coast 444,077; Canberra 353,149; Wollongong 257,510; Caloundra 192,397; Hobart 191,169.
Place of birth (2001): 76.9% native-born; 23.1% foreign-born, of which Europe 9.7% (United Kingdom and Republic of Ireland 5.5%, Italy 1.2%, Greece 0.7%, Germany 0.7%, The Netherlands 0.5%, other Europe 1.1%), Asia and Middle East 3.9%, New Zealand 1.9%, Africa, the Americas, and other 7.6%.
Mobility (1995–96). Population age 15 and over living in the same residence as in 1994: 81.6%; different residence between states, regions, and neighbourhoods 18.4%.
Households (2000). Total number of households 7,510,000. Average household size 3.0; 1 person 25.1%, 2 persons 33.4%, 3 or more persons 41.5%. Family households 5,367,000 (71.5%), nonfamily 2,143,000 (28.5%), of which 1-person 25.1%.
Immigration (2001–02): permanent immigrants admitted 88,900, from New Zealand 17.6%, United Kingdom and Ireland 10.4%, China 7.5%, India 5.7%, Indonesia 4.7%, South Africa 4.0%, Vietnam 2.3%, Philippines 2.3%, former Yugoslavia 2.3%, Sri Lanka 2.3%. Refugee arrivals (2001–02): 12,349. Emigration (2001–02): 48,241.

Vital statistics

Birth rate per 1,000 population (2003): 12.6 (world avg. 21.3); (2000) legitimate 69.3%; illegitimate 30.7%.
Death rate per 1,000 population (2003): 7.3 (world avg. 9.1).
Natural increase rate per 1,000 population (2003): 5.3 (world avg. 12.2).
Total fertility rate (avg. births per childbearing woman; 2003): 1.8.
Marriage rate per 1,000 population (2001): 5.3.
Divorce rate per 1,000 population (2001): 2.8.
Life expectancy at birth (2003): male 77.3 years; female 83.1 years.
Major causes of death per 100,000 population (2001): diseases of the circulatory system 219.0; cancers 162.0; respiratory diseases 48.0; accidents, poisoning, and violence 27.0; diabetes 13.0; suicides 13.0.

Social indicators

Educational attainment (1999). Percentage of population age 15 to 64 having: no formal schooling and incomplete secondary education 38.0%; completed secondary 18.3%; postsecondary, technical, or other certificate/diploma 28.3%; university 15.4%.
Quality of working life (2003). Average workweek: 34.7 hours. Working 50 hours a week or more 28.8%. Annual rate per 100,000 workers for: accidental injury and industrial disease, 3,200[5]; death, n.a. Proportion of employed persons insured for damages or income loss resulting from: injury 100%; permanent disability 100%; death 100%. Working days lost to industrial disputes per 1,000 employees (2000): 52. Means of transportation to work (2000): private automobile 76.0%; public transportation 12.0%; motorcycle, bicycle, and foot 12.0%. Discouraged job seekers (2002): 78,000 (0.8% of labour force).

Distribution of household income (1999–2000)

percentage of household income by quintile				
lowest	second	third	fourth	highest
3.8%	9.0%	15.0%	23.8%	48.4%

Social participation. Eligible voters participating in last national election (2001): 95.0%; voting is compulsory. Trade union membership in total workforce (2002): 23.1%.
Social deviance (2003). Offense rate per 100,000 population for: murder 1.5; sexual assault 92; assault 798; auto theft 497; burglary and housebreaking 1,776; armed robbery 99. Incidence per 100,000 in general population of: prisoners 139[6]; suicide 13.0[6].
Material well-being (1995). Households possessing: automobile 85%; telephone 95%; refrigerator 99.7%; washing machine 90.0%.

National economy

Gross national product (2003): U.S.$430,533,000,000 (U.S.$21,650 per capita).

Structure of gross domestic product and labour force

	2001			
	in value $A '000,000[7]	% of total value	labour force	% of labour force
Agriculture	19,005	3.1	433,500	4.4
Mining	26,183	4.2	68,300	0.8
Manufacturing	75,560	12.2	1,109,100	11.3
Construction	34,434	5.5	678,300	6.9
Public utilities	11,314	1.8	67,400	0.7
Transportation and communications	54,049	8.7	600,900	6.1
Trade[8]	122,282	19.7	2,254,200	23.0
Finance, real estate	114,389	18.4	1,433,300	14.6
Pub. admin., defense	22,702	3.7	480,400	4.9
Services	95,079	15.3	1,998,500	20.4
Other	45,966[9]	7.4[9]	666,700[10]	6.8[10]
TOTAL	620,963	100.0	9,790,600	100.0[11]

Budget (2002–03). Revenue: $A 175,014,000,000 (tax revenue 93.2%, of which individual 52.5%, corporate 19.1%, excise duties and sales tax 15.6%; nontax revenue 6.8%). Expenditures: $A 169,247,000,000 (social security and welfare 42.1%; health 17.4%; defense 7.9%; public services 7.7%; economic services 7.5%; education 7.2%; interest on public debt 2.7%; other 7.5%).
Public debt (2002–03): $A 69,926,000,000.
Tourism (2002): receipts from visitors U.S.$8,087,000,000; expenditures by nationals abroad U.S.$6,116,000,000.

Retail and service enterprises

	no. of establishments	no. of employees	total wages and salaries ($A '000,000)	annual turnover ($A '000,000)
Retail[12]				
Motor vehicle dealers, gasoline and tire dealers	37,305	220,661	...	44,954
Food stores	53,166	406,299	...	63,340[13]
Department and general stores	459	87,148	...	13,714[13]
Clothing, fabric, and furniture stores	21,688	91,138	...	11,005[13]
Household appliances and hardware stores	14,268	75,355	629	20,554[13]
Recreational goods	...	...	...	7,393[13]
Services				
Real estate agents[14]	7,589	52,079	1,847.5	3,902.7
Pubs, taverns, and bars	4,792[15]	81,724[15]	...	9,007.2[13]
Dental services[15]	5,257	24,108	568.4	1,685.2
Consulting engineering services[16]	5,514	30,736	1,242	3,233.3
Legal services[14]	10,819	73,186	2,181.0	7,034.3
Accounting services[16]	8,389	66,792	...	4,939.1
Computing services[14]	14,731	74,395	4,065.0	10,474.0
Travel agency services[17]	3,266	24,451	647.9	1,979.5
Market research services[14]	272	10,744	203.4	455.8
Private security services[14]	1,714	31,752	756.2	1,394.8

Production (gross value in $A '000 except as noted). Agriculture, forestry, fishing (1999–2000): livestock[18] 7,946,900 (cattle 5,050,900, sheep and lambs 1,053,900, poultry 1,031,000, pigs 791,700); wheat 4,831,200, wool 2,149,000, vegetables 1,861,900, fruits and nuts 1,761,100, seed cotton 1,400,000, grapes 1,118,200, sugarcane 881,900, barley 864,800, canola 638,000, oats 118,400, sunflower seeds 74,000, corn (maize) 60,000, tobacco 40,000, other cereal crops 4,735,100; livestock (number of live animals; 2002) 113,000,000 sheep, 30,500,000 cattle, 2,912,000 pigs, 93,000,000 poultry; roundwood (2002) 31,212,000 cu m; fish catch (2001) 236,300 metric tons. Mining and quarrying (metric tons except as noted; 2001): iron ore 112,592,000 (world rank: 2), bauxite 53,285,000 (world rank: 1), ilmenite 2,017,000, zinc (metal content) 1,519,000, copper (metal content) 873,000 (world rank: 4), lead (metal content) 432,000, rutile 206,000, nickel (metal content) 205,000, cobalt (metal content) 6,100, opal (value of production) U.S.$140,000,000, sapphire (value of production) U.S.$40,000,000; gem diamonds 14,397,000 carats, gold 285,030 kilograms (world rank: 3). Manufacturing (value added in $A '000,000; 2000–01): food products 11,026; printing and publishing 6,599; chemicals and chemical products 5,756; nonferrous base metals 5,678; fabricated metal products 5,402; motor vehicles and parts 4,657; electrical machinery and apparatus 3,366; beverages 3,185. Construction (buildings completed, by value in $A '000; 2002): new dwellings 15,043,000; alterations and additions to dwellings 4,081,000; nonresidential (1998–99) 14,016,000.

Population economically active (2003): total 10,066,000; activity rate of total population 50.6% (participation rates: ages 15–64, 74.2%; female 44.8%; unemployed [September 2003–August 2004] 5.7%).

Price and earnings indexes (2000 = 100)

	1997	1998	1999	2000	2001	2002	2003
Consumer price index	93.5	94.3	95.7	100.0	104.4	107.5	110.5
Weekly earnings index	89.2	92.8	95.3	100.0	105.0	110.3	116.5

Household income and expenditure (1999–2000). Average household size (2002) 3.0; average annual income per household $A 37,752 (U.S.$20,600); sources of income: wages and salaries 56.7%, transfer payments 28.0%, self-employment 6.0%, other 9.3%; expenditure (1998–99): food and nonalcoholic beverages 18.2%, transportation and communications 16.9%, housing 13.9%, recreation 12.7%, household durable goods 6.0%.

Financial aggregates

	1997	1998	1999	2000	2001	2002	2003
Exchange rate, $A 1.00 per[19]:							
U.S. dollar	0.74	0.63	0.65	0.58	0.51	0.57	0.75
£	0.45	0.38	0.40	0.38	0.35	0.38	0.42
SDR	0.48	0.44	0.48	0.43	0.41	0.42	0.50
International reserves (U.S.$)[19]							
Total (excl. gold; '000,000)	16,845	14,641	21,212	18,118	17,955	20,689	32,189
SDRs ('000,000)	19	18	72	94	109	136	170
Reserve pos. in IMF ('000,000)	727	1,256	1,633	1,243	1,412	1,934	2,053
Foreign exchange ('000,000)	16,099	13,366	19,507	16,782	16,434	18,618	29,966
Gold ('000,000 fine troy oz)	2.56	2.56	2.56	2.56	2.56	2.56	2.56
% world reserves	0.3	0.3	0.3	0.3	0.3	0.3	0.3
Interest and prices							
Govt. bond yield (short-term; %)	6.00	5.02	5.55	6.18	4.97	5.30	4.90
Industrial share prices (2000 = 100)	79.9	83.8	92.7	100.0	103.2	100.2	96.0
Balance of payments[19] (U.S.$'000,000)							
Balance of visible trade	+1,849	–5,332	–9,761	–4,813	+1,786	–5,431	–15,369
Imports, f.o.b.	63,044	61,215	65,857	68,865	61,890	70,530	85,946
Exports, f.o.b.	64,893	55,884	56,096	64,052	63,676	65,099	70,577
Balance of invisibles	–14,233	–12,682	–12,534	–10,668	–10,498	–11,955	–15,306
Balance of payments, current account	–12,384	–18,014	–22,295	–15,481	–8,712	–17,386	–30,675

Energy production (consumption): electricity (kW-hr; 2002) 210,320,000,000 (210,320,000,000), hard coal (metric tons; 2001) 264,680,000 ([1999] 60,643,000); lignite (metric tons; 2001) 70,000,000 (70,000,000); crude petroleum (barrels; 2000) 187,500,000 (224,810,000); petroleum products (metric tons; 1999) 34,381,000 (32,001,000); natural gas (cu m; 2002) 31,188,000,000 ([2000] 24,095,000,000).

Land use as % of total land area (2000): in temporary crops 6.5%, in permanent crops 0.04%, in pasture 52.7%; overall forest area 20.1%.

Foreign trade[20]

Balance of trade (current prices)

	1996	1997	1998	1999	2000	2001
$A '000,000	–1,424	+1,422	–7,746	–14,551	–6,376	+5,307
% of total	0.9%	0.8%	4.2%	7.7%	2.8%	2.2%

Imports (2000–01): $A 118,264,000,000 (machinery and transport equipment 45.2%, of which road motor vehicles 12.1%, office machines and automatic data-processing equipment 7.0%, telecommunications equipment 6.7%; chemicals and related products 12.0%, of which medicines and pharmaceuticals 3.7%; mineral fuels and lubricants 8.9%; food and live animals 3.6%). *Major import sources:* U.S. 18.9%; Japan 13.0%; China 8.4%; U.K. 5.3%; Germany 5.2%; South Korea 4.0%; New Zealand 3.9%; Malaysia 3.5%; Singapore 3.3%; Taiwan 2.8%.

Exports (2000–01): $A 119,602,000,000 (mineral fuels 21.1%, of which coal [all forms] 9.1%, petroleum products and natural gas 9.1%; crude materials excluding fuels 19.7%, of which metalliferous ores and metal scrap [mostly iron ore and alumina] 12.3%, textile fibres 4.7%; food 16.8%, of which meat and meat preparations 4.8%, cereals and cereal preparations 4.5%; nonferrous metals 7.9%). *Major export destinations:* Japan 19.6%; U.S. 9.7%; South Korea 7.7%; China 5.7%; New Zealand 5.7%; Singapore 5.0%; Taiwan 4.9%; U.K. 3.9%; Hong Kong 3.3%; Indonesia 2.6%.

Trade by commodity group (1999–2000)

	imports		exports	
SITC Group	U.S.$'000,000	%	U.S.$'000,000	%
00 Food and live animals	2,488	3.6	10,570	17.3
01 Beverages and tobacco	445	0.6	988	1.6
02 Crude materials, excluding fuels	1,162	1.7	11,556	18.9
03 Mineral fuels, lubricants, and related materials	4,832	7.0	11,366	18.6
04 Animal and vegetable oils, fat, and waxes	174	0.3	190	0.3
05 Chemicals and related products, n.e.s.	7,863	11.4	2,638	4.3
06 Basic manufactures	8,614	12.4	7,746	12.7
07 Machinery and transport equipment	32,305	46.6	7,302	11.9
08 Miscellaneous manufactured articles	9,759	14.1	2,409	3.9
09 Goods not classified by kind	1,614	2.3	6,421	10.5
TOTAL	69,256	100.0	61,186	100.0

Direction of trade (1999–2000)

	imports		exports	
	U.S.$'000,000	%	U.S.$'000,000	%
Africa	627	0.9	1,363	2.2
Asia	31,198	45.1	37,117	60.7
Japan	8,895	12.8	11,828	19.3
South America	403	0.6	498	0.8
North and Central America	16,018	23.1	7,020	11.5
United States	14,462	20.9	6,025	9.8
Europe	16,512	23.8	8,254	13.5
European Union	15,321	22.1	7,573	12.4
Russia	37	—	119	0.2
Other Europe	1,154	1.7	562	0.9
Oceania	4,220	6.1	5,663	9.2
New Zealand	2,750	4.0	4,235	6.9
Other	278	0.4	1,271	2.1
TOTAL	69,256	100.0	61,186	100.0

Transport and communications

Transport. Railroads (1999–2000)[21]: route length 22,233 mi, 35,780 km; passengers carried 629,200,000; short ton-mi cargo 91,825,000,000, metric ton-km cargo 134,200,000,000. Roads (2000): total length 502,356 mi, 808,465 km (paved 40%). Vehicles (2002): passenger cars 10,100,000; trucks and buses 2,355,400. Merchant marine (1999): vessels (150 gross tons and over) 77; total deadweight tonnage 2,505,369. Air transport (2002)[22]: passenger-mi 45,292,014,000, passenger-km 72,890,571,000; short ton-mi cargo 1,004,770,000, metric ton-km cargo 1,466,937,000; airports (1996) with scheduled flights 400.

Communications

Medium	date	unit	number	units per 1,000 persons
Daily newspapers	2000	circulation	5,630,000	293
Radio	2000	receivers	36,700,000	1,908
Television	2000	receivers	14,200,000	738
Telephones	2003	main lines	10,815,000	542
Cellular telephones	2003	subscribers	14,347,000	720
Personal computers	2002	units	11,100,000	564
Internet	2002	users	9,472,000	482

Education and health

Literacy (1996): total population literate, virtually 100%[23].

Education (2001)

	schools	teachers	students	student/ teacher ratio
Primary (age 6–12)	9,596	114,400	1,384,866	16.9
Secondary (age 13–17)		110,900	863,353	12.5
Vocational[24]	541[25]	26,345[25]	1,757,000	...
Higher	43	78,228	795,000	18.3

Health: physicians (2001) 48,211 (1 per 404 persons); hospital beds (2001) 79,900 (1 per 244 persons); infant mortality rate per 1,000 live births (2003) 4.8.

Food (2001): daily per capita caloric intake 3,126 (vegetable products 66%, animal products 34%); 117% of FAO recommended minimum requirement.

Military

Total active duty personnel (2003): 53,650 (army 49.5%, navy 24.0%, air force 26.5%). *Military expenditure as percentage of GNP* (1999): 1.8% (world 2.4%); per capita expenditure U.S.$372.

[1]Mainland and island areas only; excludes coastal water. [2]January 1. [3]With permanent civilian population only. [4]Total includes 2001 census population for Norfolk Island. [5]1992–93. [6]2001. [7]At 1996–97 prices. [8]Trade includes hotels and restaurants. [9]Import duties less imputed bank service charges. [10]Mostly unemployed. [11]Detail does not add to total given because of rounding. [12]1991–92. [13]2001–02. [14]1998–99. [15]1997–98. [16]1995–96. [17]1996–97. [18]Slaughtered value. [19]At end of year. [20]Imports f.o.b.; exports c.i.f. [21]Government railways only. [22]Qantas only. [23]A national survey conducted in 1996 put the number of persons who had very poor literacy and numeracy skills at about 17% of the total population (age 15 to 64). [24]Includes special education. [25]1996.

Internet resources for further information:

- **Australian Bureau of Statistics http://www.abs.gov.au**

Austria

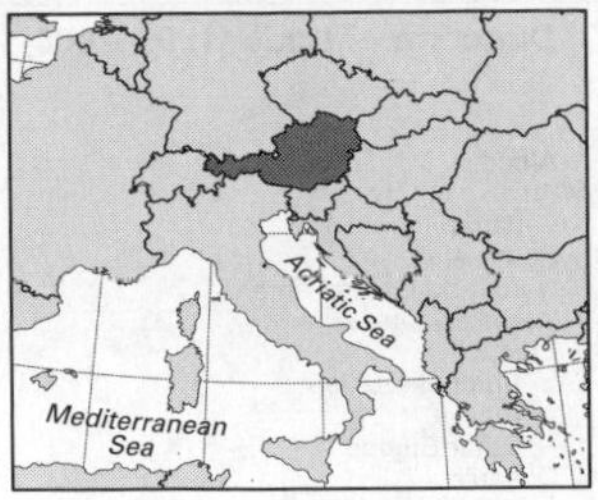

Official name: Republik Österreich (Republic of Austria).
Form of government: federal state with two legislative houses (Federal Council [64]; National Council [183]).
Chief of state: President.
Head of government: Chancellor.
Capital: Vienna.
Official language: German.
Official religion: none.
Monetary unit: 1 euro (€) = 100 cents; valuation (Sept. 1, 2004) 1 U.S.$ = €0.82; 1 £ = €1.48[1].

Area and population

		area		population
States	Capitals	sq mi	sq km	2001 census
Burgenland	Eisenstadt	1,531	3,965	277,569
Kärnten	Klagenfurt	3,682	9,536	559,404
Niederösterreich	Sankt Pölten	7,404	19,178	1,545,804
Oberösterreich	Linz	4,626	11,982	1,376,797
Salzburg	Salzburg	2,762	7,154	515,327
Steiermark	Graz	6,329	16,392	1,183,303
Tirol	Innsbruck	4,883	12,648	673,504
Vorarlberg	Bregenz	1,004	2,601	351,095
Wien (Vienna)	—	160	415	1,550,123
TOTAL		32,383[2]	83,871	8,032,926

Demography

Population (2004): 8,105,000.
Density (2004): persons per sq mi 250.3, persons per sq km 96.6.
Urban-rural (2001): urban 66.8%; rural 33.2%.
Sex distribution (2001): male 48.41%; female 51.59%.
Age breakdown (2001): under 15, 16.9%; 15–29, 18.6%; 30–44, 24.9%; 45–59, 18.6%; 60–74, 13.8%; 75 and over, 7.2%.
Population projection: (2010) 8,255,000; (2020) 8,401,000.
Ethnic composition (national origin; 1998): Austrian 91.2%; citizens of former Yugoslavia 4.0%; Turkish 1.6%; other 3.2%.
Religious affiliation (1995): Roman Catholic 75.1%; nonreligious and atheist 8.6%; Protestant (mostly Lutheran) 5.4%; Muslim 2.1%; Eastern Orthodox 0.7%; Jewish 0.1%; other 1.9%; unknown 6.1%.
Major cities (2001): Vienna 1,550,123 (urban agglomeration 2,179,000[3]); Graz 226,244; Linz 183,504; Salzburg 142,662; Innsbruck 113,392; Klagenfurt 90,141.

Vital statistics

Birth rate per 1,000 population (2002): 9.7 (world avg. 21.3); (2002) legitimate 73.6%; illegitimate 26.4%.
Death rate per 1,000 population (2002): 9.5 (world avg. 9.1).
Natural increase rate per 1,000 population (2002): 0.2 (world avg. 12.2).
Total fertility rate (avg. births per childbearing woman; 2002): 1.3.
Marriage rate per 1,000 population (2002): 4.5.
Divorce rate per 1,000 population (2002): 2.5.
Life expectancy at birth (2002): male 75.8 years; female 81.7 years.
Major causes of death per 100,000 population (2002): diseases of the circulatory system 458.3; malignant neoplasms (cancers) 237.3.

National economy

Budget (2003). Revenue: €57,414,000,000 (tax revenue 93.6%, of which individual income taxes 29.3%, turnover tax 28.4%, corporate income tax 7.1%, other taxes 28.8%; nontax revenue 6.4%). Expenditures: €61,355,000,000 (social security, health, and welfare 34.3%; education 14.3%; interest 14.2%; transportation 9.9%; public safety 6.6%; defense 2.6%).
Public debt (2001): U.S.$117,420,000,000.
Production (metric tons except as noted). Agriculture, forestry, fishing (2002): sugar beets 3,005,000, corn (maize) 2,000,000, wheat 1,460,000, barley 946,000, potatoes 684,000, apples 480,844, grapes 350,000, rye 200,000, triticale 190,000, rapeseed 150,000; livestock (number of live animals) 3,440,405 pigs, 2,118,454 cattle, 11,000,000 chickens; roundwood (2002) 14,845,000 cu m; fish catch (2001) 2,755. Mining and quarrying (2002): iron ore 1,941,800; magnesite 728,200; talc 140,000. Manufacturing (value added in U.S.$'000,000; 2000): nonelectrical machinery and apparatus 3,907; electrical machinery and apparatus 3,786; food products and beverages 3,112; fabricated metals 2,896; chemicals and chemical products 2,246; base metals 2,050. Energy production (consumption): electricity (kW-hr; 2002) 58,490,000,000 ([2001] 62,250,000,000); hard coal (metric tons; 2002) negligible ([2000] 3,710,000); lignite (metric tons; 2002) 1,411,800 ([2000] 1,290,000); crude petroleum (barrels; 2001) 7,139,000 ([2000] 58,639,000); petroleum products (metric tons; 2000) 7,461,000 (10,297,000); natural gas (cu m; 2002) 2,014,600,000 ([2001] 7,333,000,000).
Tourism (U.S.$'000,000; 2002): receipts U.S.$11,237; expenditures U.S.$9,391.
Population economically active (2002): total 3,996,700; activity rate of total population 49.6% (participation rates: ages 15–64 [2001] 72.0%; female 44.4%; unemployed [April 2003–March 2004] 7.1%).

Price index (2000 = 100)

	1998	1999	2000	2001	2002	2003
Consumer price index	94.2	94.8	100.0	102.7	104.5	105.9

Gross national product (2003): U.S.$215,372,000,000 (U.S.$26,720 per capita).

Structure of gross domestic product and labour force

	2002			
	in value €'000,000	% of total value	labour force	% of labour force
Agriculture, forestry	4,685	2.1	215,300	5.4
Mining	744	0.3	8,300	0.2
Manufacturing	42,219	19.3	747,100	18.7
Construction	15,151	6.9	338,000	8.5
Public utilities	4,477	2.1	35,200	0.9
Transp. and commun.	14,791	6.8	251,800	6.3
Trade, restaurants	34,133	15.6	818,900	20.5
Finance, real estate	48,538	22.2	436,200	10.9
Pub. admin., defense	11,835	5.4	248,400	6.2
Services	29,005	13.3	736,500	18.4
Other	12,755[4]	5.8[4]	161,000	4.0
TOTAL	218,333	100.0[2]	3,996,700	100.0

Household income and expenditure. Average household size (2001) 2.4; sources of income (1995): wages and salaries 54.8%, transfer payments 25.9%; expenditure (2001): housing and energy 19.3%, transportation 12.6%, food and nonalcoholic beverages 12.6%, cafe and hotel expenditures 12.2%, recreation 11.5%, household furnishings 8.3%.
Land use as % of total land area (2000): in temporary crops 16.9%, in permanent crops 0.9%, in pasture 23.2%; overall forest area 47.0%.

Foreign trade[5]

Balance of trade (current prices)

	1999	2000	2001	2002
€'000,000,000	–5.05	–5.25	–4.44	+0.30
% of total	4.0%	3.6%	2.9%	0.2%

Imports (2002): €77,104,000,000 (machinery and transport equipment 38.9%, of which road vehicles 11.2%, electrical machinery and apparatus 7.6%; chemicals and related products 11.3%; mineral fuels 7.4%; food products 5.2%). *Major import sources:* Germany 40.3%; Italy 7.2%; United States 4.8%; France 3.9%; Hungary 3.3%; Switzerland 3.3%.
Exports (2002): €77,400,000,000 (machinery and apparatus 32.9%; chemical products 10.2%; transportation equipment 9.8%; paper and paper products 4.6%; fabricated metals 4.3%; iron and steel 4.1%). *Major export destinations:* Germany 32.0%; Italy 8.5%; Switzerland 5.3%; United States 5.2%; United Kingdom 4.7%; France 4.4%; Hungary 4.3%.

Transport and communications

Transport. Railroads[6]: (2002) length 5,616 km; (2000) passenger-km 8,206,000,000; (2001) metric ton-km cargo 17,387,000,000. Roads (2001): total length 210,483 km (paved 100%). Vehicles (2002): passenger cars 3,987,093; trucks and buses 313,434. Air transport (2003)[7]: passenger-km 17,965,000,000; metric ton-km cargo 442,549,000; airports (2002) with scheduled flights 6.

Communications

Medium	date	unit	number	units per 1,000 persons
Daily newspapers	2000	circulation	2,380,000	296
Radio	2000	receivers	6,050,000	753
Television	2000	receivers	4,310,000	536
Telephones	2003	main lines	3,881,000	481
Cellular telephones	2003	subscribers	7,094,500	879
Personal computers	2002	units	3,013,000	374
Internet	2003	users	3,730,000	462

Education and health

Educational attainment (1993). Percentage of population age 25 and over having: lower-secondary education 37.5%; vocational education ending at secondary level 44.6%; completed upper secondary 6.1%; higher vocational 5.5%; higher 6.3%. *Literacy:* virtually 100%.

Education (2002–03)

	schools	teachers	students	student/teacher ratio
Primary/lower secondary (age 6–13)	4,458	67,152	649,198	9.7
Upper secondary/voc. (age 14–17)	734	41,840	326,891	7.8
Higher[8]	19	16,099	242,598	15.1

Health: physicians (2003) 36,531[9] (1 per 213 persons); hospital beds (2002) 66,299[9] (1 per 118 persons); infant mortality rate per 1,000 live births (2002) 4.1.
Food (2001): daily per capita caloric intake 3,799 (vegetable products 67%; animal products 33%); 144% of FAO recommended minimum requirement.

Military

Total active duty personnel (2003): 34,600 (army 80.2%; air force 19.8%). *Military expenditure as percentage of GNP* (1999): 0.8% (world 2.4%); per capita expenditure U.S.$208.

[1]The Austrian Schilling (S) was the former monetary unit; on Jan. 1, 2002, S 13.76 = €1. [2]Detail does not add to total given because of rounding. [3]2003. [4]Value-added tax less imputed bank service charges and subsidies. [5]Imports c.i.f., exports f.o.b. [6]Federal railways only. [7]Austrian Airlines Group. [8]Universities only. [9]January 1.

Internet resources for further information:
- **Austrian Central Office of Statistics http://www.statistik.at**
- **Austrian Press and Information Service (Washington, D.C.) http://www.austria.org/index.html**

Azerbaijan

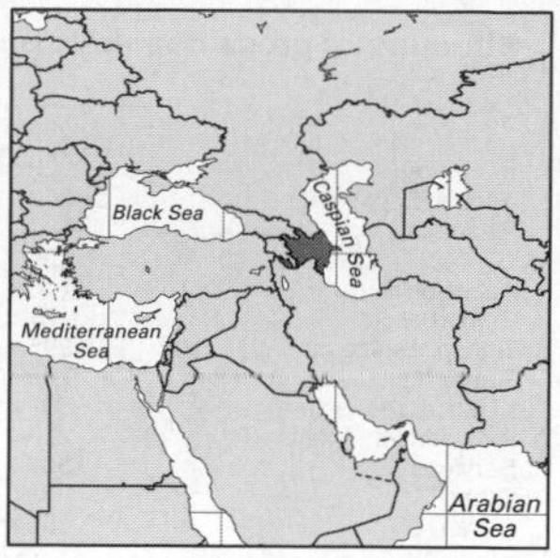

Official name: Azərbaycan Respublikası (Republic of Azerbaijan).
Form of government: unitary multiparty republic with a single legislative body (National Assembly [124[1]]).
Head of state and government: President assisted by Prime Minister.
Capital: Baku (Azerbaijani: Bakı).
Official language: Azerbaijani.
Official religion: none.
Monetary unit: 1 manat (A.M.) = 100 gopik; valuation (Sept. 1, 2004) free rate, 1 U.S.$ = A.M. 4,911; 1 £ = A.M. 8,835.

Area and population

	area	population
Economic regions[2]	sq km	2000 estimate
Absheron	5,400	2,182,000
Gyadza	5,400	529,000
Kazakh	7,100	568,000
Kelbadjar	7,400	259,000
Khachmas	7,000	455,000
Lenkoran	6,100	744,000
Mil-Karabakh	6,500	696,000
Mugan-Salyan	9,000	621,000
Priarak	4,300	323,000
Sheki	9,000	531,000
Shirvan	11,200	661,000
Upper-Karabakh[3]	2,700	143,000
Autonomous republic		
Nakhchivan	5,500	363,000
TOTAL	86,600	8,075,000[4]

Demography

Population (2004): 8,343,000.
Density (2004): persons per sq mi 249.8, persons per sq km 96.3.
Urban-rural (2004)[5]: urban 50.6%; rural 49.4%.
Sex distribution (2001): male 48.94%; female 51.06%.
Age breakdown (2004)[5]: under 15, 27.4%; 15–29, 27.1%; 30–44, 24.5%; 45–59, 11.5%; 60 and over, 9.5%.
Population projection: (2010) 8,865,000; (2020) 9,746,000.
Doubling time: 87 years.
Ethnic composition (1995): Azerbaijani 89.0%; Russian 3.0%; Lezgian 2.2%; Armenian 2.0%; other 3.8%.
Religious affiliation (1995): Muslim 93.4%, of which Shīʿī 65.4%, Sunnī 28.0%; Russian Orthodox 1.1%; Armenian Apostolic (Orthodox) 1.1%; other 4.4%.
Major cities (2003): Baku 1,828,800; Gäncä 302,200; Sumqayıt (Sumgait) 289,700; Mingäçevir (Mingechaur) 94,900; Äli Bayramlı (2002) 68,700.

Vital statistics

Birth rate per 1,000 population (2004): 14.0 (world avg. 21.3); (2003) legitimate 92.4%; illegitimate 7.6%.
Death rate per 1,000 population (2004): 6.0 (world avg. 9.1).
Natural increase rate per 1,000 population (2004): 8.0 (world avg. 12.2).
Total fertility rate (avg. births per childbearing woman; 2001): 1.6.
Life expectancy at birth (2003): male 69.5 years; female 75.1 years.
Major causes of death per 100,000 population (2003): diseases of the circulatory system 344.1; malignant neoplasms (cancers) 76.1; diseases of the respiratory system 41.5; accidents, poisoning, and violence 24.3.

National economy

Budget (2003). Revenue: A.M. 6,131,900,000,000 (tax revenue 82.5%, of which value-added tax 33.4%, enterprise profits tax 14.5%, personal income tax 12.3%, import duties 7.6%, excise taxes 5.5%; nontax revenue 17.5%). Expenditures: A.M. 6,173,000,000,000 (national economy 19.7%; education 19.0%; social security 17.3%; defense 9.8%; health 5.0%).
Public debt (external, outstanding; 2002): U.S.$964,000,000.
Production (metric tons except as noted). Agriculture, forestry, fishing (2003): cereals 2,057,800, vegetables (except potatoes) 1,046,300, potatoes 769,000, fruit (except grapes) 572,100, sugar beets 128,900, cotton 99,600, grapes 65,000, tobacco leaves 4,700, tea 900; livestock (number of live animals) 7,280,100 sheep and goats, 2,241,800 cattle; roundwood (2002) 13,500 cu m; fish catch (2001) 11,063. Mining and quarrying (2000): alumina 200,000; gypsum 60,000. Manufacturing (gross value of production in A.M. '000,000; 2003): food, beverages, and tobacco products 4,216,600; petroleum products 3,162,800; chemicals and chemical products 697,000; fabricated metal products 684,100. Energy production (consumption): electricity (kW-hr; 2002) 18,708,000,000 ([2001] 19,193,000,000); coal (metric tons; 2002) none (1,000); crude petroleum (barrels; 2002) 113,418,000 (63,384,000); petroleum products (metric tons; 2003) 5,476,000 ([1999] 5,030,000); natural gas (cu m; 2003) 5,100,000,000 (5,100,000,000).
Household income and expenditure. Average household size (2000) 5.3; income per household (2000) U.S.$460; sources of money income (2003): self-employment 55.2%, wages and salaries 7.5%, transfers 7.5%, other 29.8%; expenditure, n.a.
Tourism (2002): receipts U.S.$51,000,000; expenditures U.S.$106,000,000.
Gross national product (at current market prices; 2003): U.S.$6,709,000,000 (U.S.$810 per capita).

Structure of gross domestic product and labour force

	2003			
	in value A.M. '000,000	% of total value	labour force	% of labour force
Agriculture	4,592,000	13.1	1,499,600	39.5
Petroleum and natural gas	10,025,300	28.6	42,300	1.1
Manufacturing	2,839,300	8.1	169,900	4.5
Public utilities	385,600	1.1	39,800	1.0
Construction	4,241,500	12.1	180,000	4.7
Transp. and commun.	3,330,100	9.5	178,500	4.7
Trade	2,769,200	7.9	630,100	16.6
Finance, real estate			110,500	2.9
Pub. admin., defense	4,416,700	12.6	330,000	8.7
Services			566,300	14.9
Other	2,453,700[6]	7.0[6]	54,400[7]	1.4[7]
TOTAL	35,053,400	100.0	3,801,400	100.0

Population economically active (2003): total 3,801,400; activity rate of total population 46.3% (participation rates: ages 15–64, 75.6%; female 47.7%; unemployed 1.4%).

Price index (2000 = 100)

	1997	1998	1999	2000	2001	2002	2003
Consumer price index	108.2	107.3	98.2	100.0	101.5	104.4	106.7

Land use as % of total land area (2000): in temporary crops 19.2%, in permanent crops 2.8%, in pasture 29.6%; overall forest area 13.1%.

Foreign trade

Balance of trade (current prices)

	1997	1998	1999	2000	2001	2002
U.S.$'000,000	–567	–470	–106	+573	+883	+502
% of total	26.0%	28.0%	5.4%	19.6%	23.6%	13.1%

Imports (2002): U.S.$1,665,000,000 (machinery and equipment 23.8%, natural gas 12.9%, iron and steel 11.6%, food 10.3%, transport equipment 7.4%). *Major import sources* (2002): Russia 16.9%; Turkey 9.4%; Kazakhstan 9.0%; Turkmenistan 7.2%; France 7.1%; U.S. 5.9%.
Exports (2002): U.S.$2,167,000,000 (crude petroleum 68.1%, refined petroleum 19.6%, food products 1.8%). *Major export destinations* (2002): Italy 50.0%; France 7.7%; Israel 7.1%; Spain 4.8%; Russia 4.4%.

Transport and communications

Transport. Railroads (2003): length 2,116 km; passenger-km 636,000,000; metric ton-km cargo 7,696,000,000. Roads (2002): total length 45,870 km (paved 94%). Vehicles (2003): passenger cars 370,439; trucks and buses 95,800. Air transport (2003)[8]: passenger-km 755,000,000; metric ton-km cargo 67,109,000; airports (2002) 3.

Communications

Medium	date	unit	number	units per 1,000 persons
Daily newspapers	2000	circulation	217,000	27
Radio	2000	receivers	177,000	22
Television	2000	receivers	2,080,000	259
Telephones	2003	main lines	976,500	119
Cellular telephones	2003	subscribers	1,055,000	128
Internet	2002	users	300,000	37

Education and health

Educational attainment (1995). Percentage of population age 15 and over having: primary education or no formal schooling 12.1%; some secondary 9.1%; completed secondary and some postsecondary 27.5%; higher 7.6%. *Literacy* (1995): percentage of total population 15 and over literate 99.6%.

Education (2003–04)

	schools	teachers	students	student/ teacher ratio
Primary (age 6–13) / Secondary (age 14–17)	4,565	171,725	1,680,424	9.8
Voc., teacher tr.	60	6,547	53,694	8.2
Higher	42	13,032	121,535	9.3

Health (2003): physicians 29,500 (1 per 280 persons); hospital beds 68,600 (1 per 120 persons); infant mortality rate per 1,000 live births (2003) 12.8.
Food (2001): daily per capita caloric intake 2,474 (vegetable products 86%, animal products 14%); 96% of FAO recommended minimum requirement.

Military

Total active duty personnel (2003): 66,490 (army 85.5%, navy 2.6%, air force 11.9%). *Military expenditure as percentage of GNP* (1999): 6.6% (world 2.4%); per capita expenditure U.S.$120.

[1]Excludes one vacant seat reserved for Nagorno-Karabakh representative. [2]Administratively, Azerbaijan is divided into 59 regions, 7 cities, and 1 autonomous republic. [3]Controlled in part by Armenian forces from 1993. [4]Sum of grossly rounded parts; beginning of year 2003 population estimate is 8,202,500. [5]January 1. [6]Taxes and subsidies on goods and services. [7]Unemployed. [8]Azerbaijan Airlines.

Internet resources for further information:
- **The National Bank of Azerbaijan Republic http://www.nba.az/eng**
- **The State Statistical Committee of Azerbaijan Republic http://www.azstat.org**

Bahamas, The

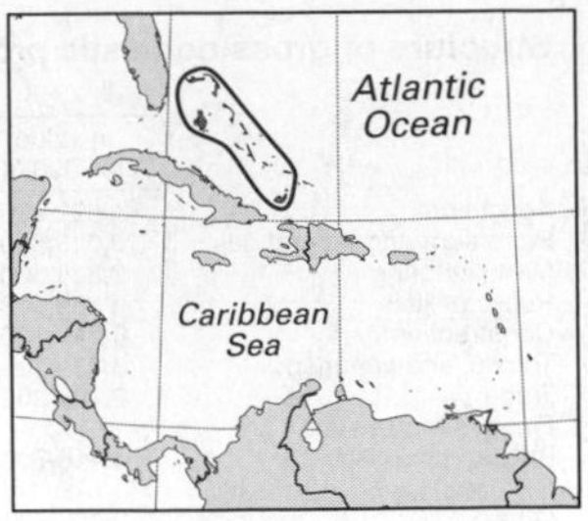

Official name: The Commonwealth of The Bahamas.
Form of government: constitutional monarchy with two legislative houses (Senate [16]; House of Assembly [40]).
Chief of state: British Monarch represented by Governor-General.
Head of government: Prime Minister.
Capital: Nassau.
Official language: English.
Official religion: none.
Monetary unit: 1 Bahamian dollar (B$) = 100 cents; valuation (Sept. 1, 2004) 1 U.S.$ = B$1.00; 1 £ = B$1.80.

Area and population

	area[1]		population
Islands and Island Groups[2]	sq mi	sq km	2000 census
Abaco, Great and Little	649	1,681	13,170
Acklins	192	497	428
Andros	2,300	5,957	7,686
Berry Islands	12	31	709
Bimini Islands	9	23	1,717
Cat Island	150	388	1,647
Crooked and Long Cay	93	241	350
Eleuthera	187	484	7,999
Exuma, Great, and Exuma Cays	112	290	3,571
Grand Bahama	530	1,373	46,994
Harbour Island	3	8	1,639
Inagua, Great and Little	599	1,551	969
Long Island	230	596	2,992
Mayaguana	110	285	259
New Providence	80	207	210,832
Ragged Island	14	36	72
Rum Cay	30	78	80
San Salvador	63	163	970
Spanish Wells	10	26	1,527
Other uninhabited cays and rocks	9	23	—
TOTAL	5,382	13,939[3]	303,611

Demography

Population (2004): 317,000.
Density (2004)[4]: persons per sq mi 81.5, persons per sq km 31.5.
Urban-rural (2000): urban 88.4%; rural 11.6%.
Sex distribution (2000): male 48.65%; female 51.35%.
Age breakdown (2000): under 15, 29.6%; 15–29, 25.8%; 30–44, 24.2%; 45–59, 12.6%; 60–74, 5.9%; 75 and over, 1.9%.
Population projection: (2010) 336,000; (2020) 363,000.
Doubling time: 70 years.
Ethnic composition (2000): local black 67.5%; mulatto 14.2%; British 12.0%; Haitian black 3.0%; U.S. white 2.4%; other 0.9%.
Religious affiliation (1995): non-Anglican Protestant 45.4%, of which Baptist 17.5%; Roman Catholic 16.8%; Anglican 10.8%; nonreligious 5.3%; Spiritist 1.5%; other (mostly independent and unaffiliated Christian) 20.2%.
Major cities (2002): Nassau 179,300; Freeport 42,600; West End 7,800; Cooper's Town 5,700; Marsh Harbour 3,600.

Vital statistics

Birth rate per 1,000 population (2003): 18.6 (world avg. 21.3); (2000) legitimate 43.2%; illegitimate 56.8%.
Death rate per 1,000 population (2003): 8.7 (world avg. 9.1).
Natural increase rate per 1,000 population (2003): 9.9 (world avg. 12.2).
Total fertility rate (avg. births per childbearing woman; 2003): 2.3.
Marriage rate per 1,000 population (2000): 7.8.
Life expectancy at birth (2003): male 62.3 years; female 69.2 years.
Major causes of death per 100,000 population (2000): diseases of the circulatory system 145.0; HIV/AIDS 80.7; malignant neoplasms (cancers) 73.8; accidents and violence 71.8; diabetes 34.6.

National economy

Budget (2003). Revenue: B$991,503,000 (import taxes 45.0%, stamp taxes from imports 11.3%, departure taxes 6.6%, business and professional licenses 5.5%). Expenditures: B$1,088,643,000 (education 19.2%, health 15.9%, public order 11.6%, interest on public debt 10.3%, defense 3.1%).
National debt (2003): U.S.$1,647,600,000.
Production (value of production in B$'000 except as noted). Agriculture, forestry, fishing (2001): crayfish 56,500, poultry products 28,300[5], citrus and other fruit 21,300[5], conch 4,300; roundwood (2002) 17,000 cu m. Mining and quarrying (value of export production; 2000): aragonite 26,086; salt 12,447. Manufacturing (value of export production; 2000): chemical products 42,787; rum 18,856. Energy production (consumption): electricity (kW-hr; 2003) 1,797,029,000 (1,656,600,000); petroleum products (metric tons; 2000) none (584,000).
Tourism (U.S.$'000,000): receipts (2003) 1,763; expenditures (2001) 297.
Household income and expenditure. Average household size (2000) 3.5; income per household (1996) B$27,252 (U.S.$27,252); sources of income: n.a.; expenditure (1995)[6]: housing 32.8%, transportation and communications 14.8%, food and beverages 13.8%, household furnishings 8.9%.
Gross national product (at current market prices; 2002): U.S.$4,684,000,000 (U.S.$14,920 per capita).

Structure of gross domestic product and labour force

	1995		2000	
	in value B$'000,000	% of total value	labour force	% of labour force
Agriculture, fishing	100	3.3	5,058	3.3
Manufacturing	80	2.6	6,108	4.0
Mining	26	0.8	412	0.2
Public utilities	116	3.8	1,813	1.2
Construction	71	2.3	16,980	11.0
Transp. and commun.	295	9.6	10,776	7.0
Trade, restaurants	705	23.0	46,908	30.4
Finance, real estate	599	19.5	15,900	10.3
Pub. admin., defense	210	6.8	13,069	8.5
Services	301	9.8	29,630	19.2
Other	568[7]	18.5[7]	7,742[8]	5.0[8]
TOTAL	3,069[3]	100.0	154,396	100.0[3]

Population economically active (2000): total 154,396; activity rate of total population 50.9% (participation rates: ages 15–64, 76.6%; female 47.5%; unemployed [2001] 6.9%).

Price index (2000 = 100)

	1997	1998	1999	2000	2001	2002	2003
Consumer price index	95.9	97.2	98.4	100.0	102.0	104.2	107.3

Land use as % of total land area (2000): in temporary crops 0.7%, in permanent crops 0.4%, in pasture 0.2%; overall forest area 84.1%.

Foreign trade[9]

Balance of trade (current prices)

	1997	1998	1999	2000	2001
B$'000,000	–1,441	–1,515	–1,325	–1,447	–1,551
% of total	79.9%	71.6%	60.9%	56.6%	67.4%

Imports (2001): B$1,927,000,000 (machinery and apparatus 16.0%; food products 14.2%; refined petroleum 14.1%; transport equipment 10.3%). *Major import sources:* U.S. 83.3%; Venezuela 5.5%; Netherlands Antilles 2.6%; Japan 1.2%.
Exports (2001): B$376,000,000 (crustaceans and mollusks [primarily crayfish] 19.1%; polystyrene 19.1%; refined petroleum 18.3%; alcoholic beverages 10.5%). *Major export destinations:* U.S. 77.5%; France 5.7%; Germany 3.9%; Spain 3.3%.

Transport and communications

Transport. Railroads: none. Roads (2000): total length 1,673 mi, 2,693 km (paved 57%). Vehicles (1998): passenger cars 67,400; trucks and buses 16,800. Air transport (2001)[10]: passenger-mi 232,000,000, passenger-km 374,000,000; short ton-mi cargo 1,208,000, metric ton-km cargo 1,764,000; airports (1997) with scheduled flights 22.

Communications

Medium	date	unit	number	units per 1,000 persons
Daily newspapers	1996	circulation	28,000	99
Radio	1997	receivers	215,000	744
Television	2000	receivers	75,200	247
Telephones	2003	main lines	131,700	419
Cellular telephones	2002	subscribers	121,800	390
Internet	2003	users	84,000	264

Education and health

Educational attainment (2000). Percentage of population age 15 and over having: no formal schooling 1.5%; primary education 8.7%; incomplete secondary 19.9%; complete secondary 53.7%; incomplete higher 8.1%; complete higher 7.1%; not stated 1.0%. *Literacy* (2001): total percentage age 15 and over literate 95.5%; males literate 94.6%; females literate 96.3%.

Education (1996–97)

	schools	teachers	students	student/teacher ratio
Primary (age 5–10)	113	1,540	34,199	22.2
Secondary (age 11–16)[11]	...	1,352	27,970	20.7
Higher[12]	1	160	3,463	21.6

Health (2001): physicians 458 (1 per 672 persons); hospital beds 1,540 (1 per 200 persons); infant mortality rate per 1,000 live births (2000) 17.0.
Food (2001): daily per capita caloric intake 2,777 (vegetable products 67%, animal products 33%); 104% of FAO recommended minimum requirement.

Military

Total active duty personnel (2003): 860 (paramilitary coast guard 100%). *Military expenditure as percentage of GNP* (2000): 0.6% (world, n.a.); per capita expenditure U.S.$85.

[1]Includes areas of lakes and ponds, as well as lagoons and sounds almost entirely surrounded by land; area of land only is about 3,890 sq mi (10,070 sq km). [2]For local administrative purposes, The Out Islands of the Bahamas are divided into 31 districts; New Providence Island is administered directly by the national government. [3]Detail does not add to total given because of rounding. [4]Land area only. [5]1998. [6]Weights of retail price index components. [7]Includes net indirect taxes (B$503,000,000) and statistical discrepancy (B$65,000,000). [8]Includes 552 not adequately defined and 7,190 unemployed. [9]Imports c.i.f.; exports f.o.b. [10]Bahamasair only. [11]Public sector only. [12]College of The Bahamas only; 1997–98.

Internet resources for further information:
- **The Central Bank of The Bahamas http://www.bahamascentralbank.com**

Bahrain

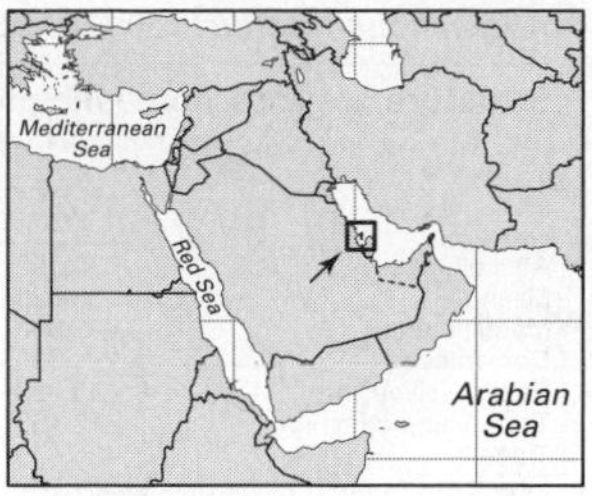

Official name: Mamlakat al-Baḥrayn (Kingdom of Bahrain).
Form of government: constitutional monarchy with a parliament comprising two bodies (Chamber of Deputies [40]; Consultative Council [40])[1].
Chief of state: Monarch.
Head of government: Prime Minister.
Capital: Manama.
Official language: Arabic.
Official religion: Islam.
Monetary unit: 1 Bahrain dinar (BD) = 1,000 fils; valuation (Sept. 1, 2004) 1 BD = U.S.$2.66 = £1.48.

Area and population

		area		population
				2001
Governorates[2]	Principal cities	sq mi	sq km	census
Capital	Manama	...	...	163,696
Central	Ar-Rifā'	...	...	167,691
Muharraq[3]	Muharraq[3]	...	...	103,576
Northern	Madīnat Ḥamad	...	...	166,824
Southern	'Awālī	...	...	44,764
TOTAL		277.0[4]	717.5[4]	650,604[5]

Demography

Population (2004): 709,000.
Density (2004): persons per sq mi 2,559.6, persons per sq km 988.2.
Urban-rural (2001): urban 88.4%; rural 11.6%.
Sex distribution (2002): male 57.46%; female 42.54%.
Age breakdown (2001): under 15, 27.9%; 15–29, 27.5%; 30–44, 29.6%; 45–59, 11.0%; 60–74, 3.2%; 75 and over, 0.8%.
Population projection: (2010) 795,000; (2020) 930,000.
Doubling time: 41 years.
Ethnic composition (2000): Bahraini Arab 63.9%; Indo-Pakistani 14.8%, of which Urdu 4.5%, Malayali 3.5%; Persian 13.0%; Filipino 4.5%; British 2.1%; other 1.7%.
Religious affiliation (2000): Muslim 82.4%, of which Shīʿī *c.* 41%, Sunnī *c.* 41%; Christian 10.5%; Hindu 6.3%; other 0.8%.
Major urban areas (2001): Manama 143,035; Muharraq 91,307; Ar Rifāʿ 79,550; Madīnat Ḥamad 52,718; Madīnat ʿIsā 36,833.

Vital statistics

Birth rate per 1,000 population (2002): 20.2 (world avg. 21.3).
Death rate per 1,000 population (2002): 3.0 (world avg. 9.1).
Natural increase rate per 1,000 population (2002): 17.2 (world avg. 12.2).
Total fertility rate (avg. births per childbearing woman; 2002): 3.0.
Marriage rate per 1,000 population (2002): 7.3.
Divorce rate per 1,000 population (2002): 1.2.
Life expectancy at birth (2002): male 73.2 years; female 76.2 years.
Major causes of death per 100,000 population (2000): diseases of the circulatory system 77.6; injury and poisoning 44.9; malignant neoplasms (cancers) 35.8; metabolic and immunity diseases 20.3; diseases of the respiratory system 12.2; diseases of the digestive system 10.6; congenital anomalies 7.2.

National economy

Budget (2002). Revenue: BD 1,026,800,000 (petroleum revenue 67.3%, non-petroleum revenue 32.7%). Expenditures: BD 1,031,000,000 (infrastructure 35.4%, general administration and public order 26.3%, social services 18.3%, transfers 12.9%, economic services 5.8%, other 1.3%).
Production (metric tons except as noted). Agriculture, forestry, fishing (2002): dates 16,508, fruit (excluding dates) 8,336, vegetables 7,922 (of which tomatoes 2,048, onions 1,213), hen's eggs 1,186, cow's milk 6,200 litres; livestock (number of live animals; 2003) 17,500 sheep, 16,000 goats, 13,000 cattle; roundwood, n.a.; fish catch (2002) 11,204. Manufacturing (barrels; 2002): gas oil 31,575,000; fuel oil 18,878,000; kerosene and jet fuel 18,804,000; naphtha 13,611,000; gasoline 6,366,000; aluminum (2003) 531,000 metric tons. Energy production (consumption): electricity (kW-hr; 2002) 7,278,000,000 (6,454,658,000); crude petroleum (barrels; 2003) 68,900,000[6] ([2000] 93,886,000); petroleum products (metric tons; 2000) 11,105,000 (913,000); natural gas (cu m; 2002) 9,429,000,000 (9,429,000,000).
Public debt (2001): BD 773,600,000 (U.S.$2,057,800,000).
Gross national product (2002): U.S.$7,977,000,000 (U.S.$11,900 per capita).

Structure of gross domestic product and labour force

	2002		2001	
	value in BD '000,000	% of total value	labour force[7]	% of labour force[7]
Agriculture, fishing	21.0	0.7	4,483	1.5
Mining	779.7	25.0	2,780	0.9
Manufacturing	375.3	12.0	49,979	16.2
Construction	134.3	4.3	26,416	8.6
Public utilities	43.8	1.4	2,515	0.8
Transp. and commun.	248.9	8.0	13,769	4.5
Trade, restaurants	353.7	11.3	47,570	15.5
Finance, real estate[8]	862.5	27.7	24,797	8.1
Pub. admin., defense }			52,389	17.0
Services[8] }	298.7	9.6	61,256	19.9
Other }			21,560[9]	7.0[9]
TOTAL	3,117.9	100.0	307,514	100.0[10]

Population economically active (2002): total 319,000; activity rate of total population 46.3% (participation rates: ages 15 and over 64.1%; female 21.7%; unemployed [2001] 5.5%).

Price index (2000 = 100)

	1997	1998	1999	2000	2001	2002
Consumer price index	102.4	102.2	100.7	100.0	100.2	101.5

Tourism (2002): receipts from visitors U.S.$741,000,000; expenditures by nationals abroad U.S.$378,000,000.
Household income and expenditure. Average household size (2001) 6.2; expenditure (1984): food and tobacco 33.3%, housing 21.2%, household durable goods 9.8%, transportation and communications 8.5%, recreation 6.4%, clothing and footwear 5.9%.
Land use as % of total land area (2000): in temporary crops *c.* 3%, in permanent crops *c.* 6%, in pasture *c.* 6%; overall forest area, negligible.

Foreign trade[11]

Balance of trade (current prices)

	1998	1999	2000	2001	2002	2003
BD '000,000	–111.3	+166.5	+420.0	+482.0	+297.5	+454.1
% of total	4.3%	5.6%	10.8%	13.1%	7.3%	10.1%

Imports (2002): BD 1,881,300,000 (petroleum products 33.4%, machinery and transport equipment 23.6%, food, beverages, and tobacco products 11.1%). *Major import sources*[12] (2001): Australia 10.0%; Saudi Arabia 9.0%; Japan 8.3%; U.S. 7.8%; U.K. 6.4%; Germany 6.0%.
Exports (2002): BD 2,178,800,000 (petroleum products 68.3%, aluminum [all forms] 15.0%, textiles and clothing 7.8%). *Major export destinations*[12] (2001): U.S. 23.8%; Saudi Arabia 14.2%; Taiwan 9.8%; Malaysia 4.3%; India 4.2%.

Transport and communications

Transport. Railroads: none. Roads (2002): total length 3,459 km (paved 79%). Vehicles (2002): passenger cars 176,261; trucks and buses 36,231. Air transport (2003)[13]: passenger-km 3,369,800,000; metric ton-km cargo 140,000,000; airports (2002) with scheduled flights 1.

Communications

Medium	date	unit	number	units per 1,000 persons
Daily newspapers	1996	circulation	67,000	117
Radio	2000	receivers	48,500	76
Television	2000	receivers	256,000	402
Telephones	2003	main lines	185,800	268
Cellular telephones	2003	subscribers	443,100	638
Personal computers	2002	units	108,000	159
Internet	2003	users	195,700	282

Education and health

Educational attainment (2001). Percentage of population age 15 and over having: no formal education 24.0%; primary education 37.1%; secondary 26.4%; higher 12.5%. *Literacy* (2001): percentage of population age 15 and over literate 87.7%; males literate 92.5%; females literate 83.0%.

Education (2001–02)

	schools	teachers	students	student/ teacher ratio
Primary (age 6–11) } Secondary (age 12–17) }	241	9,970	150,054	15.1
Higher[14]	2	696	14,187	20.4

Health (2002): physicians 1,189 (1 per 565 persons); hospital beds 1,814 (1 per 371 persons); infant mortality rate per 1,000 live births (2001) 8.7.

Military

Total active duty personnel (2003): 11,200 (army 75.9%, navy 10.7%, air force 13.4%)[15]. *Military expenditure as percentage of GNP* (1999): 8.1% (world 2.4%); per capita expenditure U.S.$666.

[1]Constitutional monarchy declared Feb. 14, 2002. Seats of Chamber of Deputies are elected, and seats of the Consultative Council are appointed by the monarch. [2]As of the administrative reorganization announced July 2002. [3]Official name is Al-Muḥarraq. [4]Includes the area of Ḥawār island and other nearby islets awarded to Bahrain by the International Court of Justice in 2001. [5]Includes 4,053 living abroad. [6]Including offshore production totaling 55,100,000 barrels. [7]Excludes small number of unemployed non-Bahrainis. [8]Finance includes Services. [9]Includes 5,424 inadequately defined and 16,136 unemployed Bahrainis. [10]Of which *c.* 59% non-Bahrainis. [11]Imports c.i.f. [12]Excludes trade in petroleum. [13]One-fourth apportionment of international flights of Gulf Air (jointly administered by the governments of Bahrain, Oman, Qatar, and the United Arab Emirates). [14]Bahrain and Arabian Gulf universities only. [15]U.S. troops in Bahrain (2004): 4,500.

Internet resources for further information:
- **Bahrain Government Homepage http://www.bahrain.gov.bh/english/index.asp**
- **Bahrain Monetary Agency http://www.bma.gov.bh**

Bangladesh

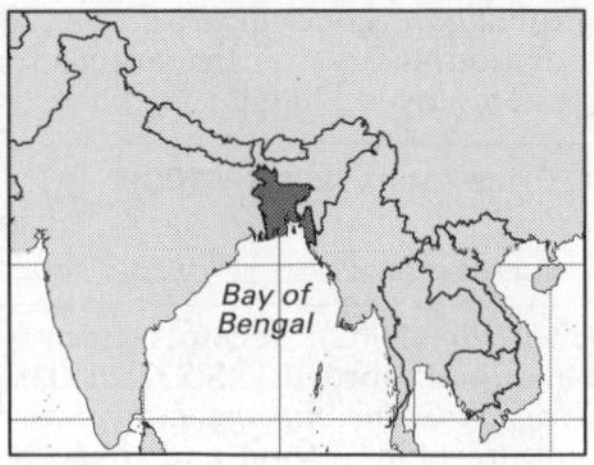

Official name: Gana Prajatantri Bangladesh (People's Republic of Bangladesh).
Form of government: unitary multiparty republic with one legislative house (Parliament [300[1]]).
Chief of state: President.
Head of government: Prime Minister.
Capital: Dhaka.
Official language: Bengali (Bangla).
Official religion: Islam.
Monetary unit: 1 Bangladesh taka (Tk) = 100 paisa; valuation (Sept. 1, 2004) 1 U.S.$ = Tk 59.43; 1 £ = Tk 106.90.

Area and population

Divisions	Administrative centres	area sq mi	area sq km	population 2001 census[2]
Barisal	Barisal	5,134	13,297	8,514,000
Chittagong	Chittagong	7,906	20,476	23,796,682
Dhaka	Dhaka	12,015	31,119	40,592,431
Khulna	Khulna	8,600	22,274	15,185,026
Rajshahi	Rajshahi	13,326	34,513	31,477,606
Sylhet	Sylhet	4,863	12,596	8,290,857
Tribal region				
Chittagong Hill Tracts[3]	Rangamati	5,133	13,295	1,390,631
TOTAL		56,977[4]	147,570[4]	129,247,233

Demography

Population (2004): 135,255,000.
Density (2004)[5]: persons per sq mi 2,514.2, persons per sq km 970.7.
Urban-rural (2001): urban 23.4%; rural 76.6%.
Sex distribution (2003): male 51.30%; female 48.70%.
Age breakdown (2003): under 15, 34.1%; 15–29, 32.4%; 30–44, 18.0%; 45–59, 10.2%; 60–74, 4.3%; 75 and over, 1.0%.
Population projection: (2010) 146,939,000; (2020) 168,698,000.
Doubling time: 33 years.
Ethnic composition (1997): Bengali 97.7%; tribal 1.9%, of which Chakma 0.4%, Saontal 0.2%, Marma 0.1%; other 0.4%.
Religious affiliation (2000): Muslim 85.8%; Hindu 12.4%; Christian 0.7%; Buddhist 0.6%; other 0.5%.
Major cities/urban agglomerations (2001): Dhaka 5,644,235/10,403,597; Chittagong 2,199,590/3,361,244; Khulna 811,490/1,287,987; Rajshahi 402,646/678,728.

Vital statistics

Birth rate per 1,000 population (2003): 29.9 (world avg. 21.3).
Death rate per 1,000 population (2003): 8.6 (world avg. 9.1).
Natural increase rate per 1,000 population (2003): 21.3 (world avg. 12.2).
Total fertility rate (avg. births per childbearing woman; 2003): 3.2.
Marriage rate per 1,000 population (1998): 9.2.
Life expectancy at birth (2003): male 61.5 years; female 61.2 years.
Major causes of death (1990; percentage of recorded deaths): typhoid fever 19.8%; old age 14.8%; tetanus 10.1%; tuberculosis and other respiratory diseases 8.7%; diarrhea 6.4%; suicide, accidents, and poisoning 5.1%; high blood pressure and heart diseases 5.0%.

National economy

Budget (2002–03). Revenue: Tk 326,000,000,000 (value-added tax 39.3%, international trade 36.2%, income taxes 14.7%, other 9.8%). Expenditures: Tk 448,000,000,000 (development program 42.4%, wages 16.5%, subsidies 14.7%, interest payments 10.3%, goods and services 8.3%, other 7.8%).
Production (metric tons except as noted). Agriculture, forestry, fishing (2002): paddy rice 38,134,000, sugarcane 6,502,000, potatoes 3,216,000, wheat 1,606,000, jute 858,740, bananas 606,000, sweet potatoes 346,000, oilseeds 279,100, mangoes 188,000, tea 52,000; livestock (number of live animals) 34,400,000 goats, 24,000,000 cattle, 1,143,000 sheep, 830,000 water buffalo, 140,000,000 chickens, 13,000,000 ducks; roundwood (2002) 28,386,000 cu m; fish catch (2001) 1,687,000. Mining and quarrying (2002): marine salt 350,000; industrial limestone 32,000. Manufacturing (value added in U.S.$'000,000; 1998): wearing apparel 839; tobacco products 634; textiles 567; industrial chemicals 499; food products 382; footwear 315; iron and steel 153. Energy production (consumption): electricity (kW-hr; 2002) 17,021,000,000 (17,021,000,000); coal (metric tons; 2000) none (660,000); crude petroleum (barrels; 2000) none (10,054,000); petroleum products (metric tons; 2002) 1,323,000 (3,769,000); natural gas (cu m; 2002) 6,568,000,000 (3,096,000,000).
Household income. Average household size (2000) 5.7; average annual income per household Tk 52,389 (U.S.$1,277); sources of income: self-employment 56.9%, wages and salaries 28.1%, transfer payments 9.1%, other 5.9%; expenditure (2002–03): food and drink 64.5%, housing and energy 15.0%, clothing and footwear 5.9%, transport 3.3%, other 11.3%.
Population economically active (2000): total 52,847,000; activity rate of total population 47.3% (participation rates: over age 15, 58.8%; female 37.5%; unemployed 2.0%[6]).

Price index (2000 = 100)

	1997	1998	1999	2000	2001	2002	2003
Consumer price index	85.1	92.2	97.8	100.0	102.0	105.4	111.4

Public debt (external, outstanding; 2002): U.S.$16,445,000,000.

Gross national product (2003): U.S.$54,587,000,000 (U.S.$400 per capita).

Structure of gross domestic product and labour force

	2002–03 in value Tk '000,000	2002–03 % of total value	2000 labour force	2000 % of labour force
Agriculture	630,590	21.1	32,171,000	60.9
Mining	33,020	1.1	295,000	0.6
Manufacturing	462,380	15.4	3,783,000	7.1
Construction	234,830	7.8	1,099,000	2.1
Public utilities	40,350	1.3	134,000	0.3
Transp. and commun.	312,150	10.4	2,509,000	4.7
Trade	406,810	13.5	6,276,000	11.9
Finance	301,660	10.0	403,000	0.8
Public admin., defense	77,850	2.6	5,095,000	9.6
Services	402,000	13.4		
Other	103,210[7]	3.4[7]	1,082,000[8]	2.0[8]
TOTAL	3,004,850	100.0	52,847,000	100.0

Land use as % of total land area (2000): in temporary crops 62.5%, in permanent crops 2.7%, in pasture 4.6%; overall forest area 10.2%.
Tourism (2002): receipts U.S.$57,000,000; expenditures U.S.$202,000,000.

Foreign trade[9]

Balance of trade (current prices)

	1997–98	1998–99	1999–2000	2000–01	2001–02	2002–03
U.S.$'000,000	–1,611	–1,904	–1,814	–1,963	–1,711	–2,151
% of total	13.5%	15.2%	13.6%	13.2%	12.5%	14.1%

Imports (2002–03): U.S.$9,648,000,000 (capital goods 28.3%; textile yarn, fabrics, and made-up articles 14.3%; imports for export processing zone 7.5%; rice and wheat 4.3%; cotton 4.1%). *Major import sources* (2001): China 11.0%; India 10.9%; Singapore 8.1%; Japan 7.3%; South Korea 6.5%; Hong Kong 6.2%.
Exports (2002–03): U.S.$6,548,000,000 (ready-made garments 49.8%; hosiery and knitwear 25.3%; frozen fish and shrimp 4.9%; jute manufactures 3.9%). *Major export destinations* (2001): U.S. 39.0%; Germany 11.1%; U.K. 8.8%; France 5.7%; The Netherlands 5.3%.

Transport and communications

Transport. Railroads (1998–99): route length 1,699 mi, 2,734 km; passenger-mi 3,094,000,000, passenger-km 4,980,000,000; short ton-mi cargo 567,000,000, metric ton-km cargo 828,000,000. Roads (1999): total length 128,925 mi, 207,486 km (paved 10%). Vehicles (1999): passenger cars 66,723; trucks and buses 82,025. Air transport (2002)[10]: passenger-mi 2,848,000,000, passenger-km 4,584,000,000; short ton-mi cargo 140,883,000, metric ton-km cargo 205,896,000; airports with scheduled flights (2001) 8.

Communications

Medium	date	unit	number	units per 1,000 persons
Daily newspapers	2000	circulation	6,880,000	53
Radio	2000	receivers	6,360,000	49
Television	2000	receivers	909,000	7.0
Telephones	2003	main lines	740,000	5.5
Cellular telephones	2003	subscribers	1,365,000	10.1
Personal computers	2002	units	450,000	3.0
Internet	2003	users	243,000	1.8

Education and health

Educational attainment (1991). Percentage of population age 25 and over having: no formal schooling 65.4%; primary education 17.1%; secondary 13.8%; postsecondary 3.7%. *Literacy* (2000): total population age 15 and over literate 41.3%; males literate 52.3%; females literate 29.9%.

Education (2000)

	schools	teachers	students	student/ teacher ratio
Primary (age 6–10)[11]	66,235	250,990	17,627,000	70.2
Secondary (age 11–17)	16,095	187,338	7,746,885	41.4
Voc., teacher tr.	138	2,560	44,832	17.5
Higher[12]	13	5,172	85,224	16.5

Health (1999): physicians 30,864 (1 per 4,150 persons); hospital beds 44,374 (1 per 2,886 persons); infant mortality rate per 1,000 live births (2002) 68.0.
Food (2001): daily per capita caloric intake 2,187 (vegetable products 97%, animal products 3%); 95% of FAO recommended minimum requirement.

Military

Total active duty personnel (2003): 125,500 (army 87.6%, navy 7.2%, air force 5.2%). *Military expenditure as percentage of GNP* (1999): 1.4% (world 2.4%); per capita expenditure U.S.$5.

[1]Excludes 45 seats reserved for women to be reinstated as of 2006 elections. [2]Preliminary figure. [3]Autonomous region for non-Bengali tribal people was created by accord signed in December 1997 and formally established in May 1999. [4]The total area excluding the river area equals 53,797 sq mi (139,334 sq km). [5]Based on the total area excluding the river area. [6]Excluding underemployment. [7]Import duties. [8]Unemployed. [9]Import figures are f.o.b. in balance of trade and c.i.f. in commodities and trading partners. [10]Bangladesh Biman only. [11]1997–98. [12]Universities only.

Internet resources for further information:
- **National Data Bank http://www.bbsgov.org**
- **Bangladesh Bank http://www.bangladesh-bank.org**

Barbados

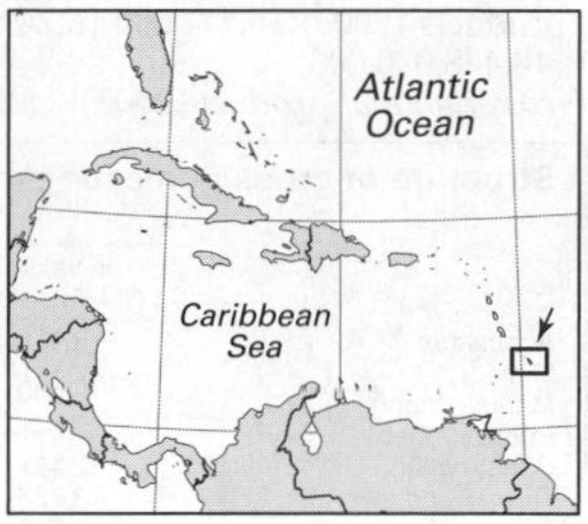

Official name: Barbados.
Form of government: constitutional monarchy with two legislative houses (Senate [21]; House of Assembly [30]).
Chief of state: British Monarch represented by Governor-General.
Head of government: Prime Minister.
Capital: Bridgetown.
Official language: English.
Official religion: none.
Monetary unit: 1 Barbados dollar (BDS$) = 100 cents; valuation (Sept. 1, 2004) 1 U.S.$ = BDS$2.00; 1 £ = BDS$3.60.

Area and population

	area		population
Parishes[1]	sq mi	sq km	1990 census
Christ Church	22	57	47,050
St. Andrew	14	36	6,346
St. George	17	44	17,905
St. James	12	31	21,001
St. John	13	34	10,206
St. Joseph	10	26	7,619
St. Lucy	14	36	9,455
St. Michael[2]	15	39	97,516
St. Peter	13	34	11,263
St. Philip	23	60	20,540
St. Thomas	13	34	11,590
TOTAL	166	430[3]	260,491

Demography

Population (2004): 273,000.
Density (2004): persons per sq mi 1,645, persons per sq km 634.9.
Urban-rural (2001): urban 50.5%; rural 49.5%.
Sex distribution (2003): male 48.26%; female 51.74%.
Age breakdown (2003): under 15, 21.2%; 15–29, 23.1%; 30–44, 25.8%; 45–59, 17.8%; 60–74, 8.1%; 75 and over, 4.0%.
Population projection: (2010) 278,000; (2020) 283,000.
Ethnic composition (2000): local black 87.1%; mulatto 6.0%; British expatriates 4.3%; U.S. white 1.2%; Indo-Pakistani 1.1%; other 0.3%.
Religious affiliation (1995): Protestant 63.0%, of which Anglican 26.3%, Pentecostal 10.6%, Methodist 5.7%; Roman Catholic 4.8%; other Christian 2.0%; nonreligious/other 30.2%.
Major cities (1990): Bridgetown 6,070 (urban agglomeration [2003] 140,000); Speightstown, *c.* 3,500.

Vital statistics

Birth rate per 1,000 population (2001): 15.0 (world avg. 21.3).
Death rate per 1,000 population (2001): 8.9 (world avg. 9.1).
Natural increase rate per 1,000 population (2001): 6.1 (world avg. 12.2).
Total fertility rate (avg. births per childbearing woman; 2000): 1.6.
Marriage rate per 1,000 population (1995): 13.5.
Divorce rate per 1,000 population (1995): 1.5.
Life expectancy at birth (2000): male 70.4 years; female 75.6 years.
Major causes of death per 100,000 population (1995): diseases of the circulatory system 369.7; malignant neoplasms (cancers) 163.6; endocrine and metabolic disorders 151.3; diseases of the respiratory system 56.3; accidents, poisonings, and violence 36.4; diseases of the digestive system 34.5.

National economy

Budget (2003). Revenue: BDS$1,843,800,000[4] (tax revenue *c.* 94%, of which personal income and company taxes 31.4%, value-added tax 29.8%, import duties 9.3%; nontax revenue *c.* 6%). Expenditures: BDS$2,009,200,000 (current expenditure 86.4%, of which wages and salaries 31.5%, debt payment 13.5%; capital expenditure 13.6%).
Public debt (external, outstanding; 2002): U.S.$958,000,000.
Production (metric tons except as noted). Agriculture, forestry, fishing (2002): raw sugar 50,000, sweet potatoes 5,300, yams 1,450, cucumbers and gherkins 1,350, cabbage 1,275, pumpkins, squash, and gourds 1,050, cassava 830, carrots 810, tomatoes 720; livestock (number of live animals) 41,300 sheep, 35,000 pigs, 21,000 cattle; roundwood (2002) 5,000; fish catch (2001) 2,676. Manufacturing (value added in U.S.$'000,000; 1997): industrial chemicals 87; food products 63; beverages (significantly rum and beer) 58; paper and paper products 32; fabricated metal products 23. Energy production (consumption): electricity (kW-hr; 2002) 741,300,000 (741,300,000); crude petroleum (barrels; 2002) 390,600 ([2000] 1,778,000); petroleum products (metric tons; 2000) 1,000 (332,000); natural gas (cu m; 2001) 34,900,000 (34,900,000).
Household income and expenditure. Average household size (2000) 2.8; income per household (1988) BDS$13,455 (U.S.$6,690); sources of income: n.a.; expenditure (1994): food 39.4%, housing 16.8%, transportation 10.5%, household operations 8.1%, alcohol and tobacco 6.4%, fuel and light 5.2%, clothing and footwear 5.0%, other 8.6%.
Tourism: receipts from visitors (2002) U.S.$648,000,000; expenditures by nationals abroad (2001) U.S.$101,000,000.
Population economically active (2002): total 143,200; activity rate of total population 52.8% (participation rates: ages 15 and over, 68.5%; female 48.4%; unemployed 10.3%).

Price index (2000 = 100)

	1997	1998	1999	2000	2001	2002	2003
Consumer price index	97.4	96.1	97.6	100.0	102.6	102.7	104.4

Gross national product (2003): U.S.$2,512,000,000 (U.S.$9,270 per capita).

Structure of gross domestic product and labour force

	2003[5]		2002	
	in value BDS$'000,000	% of total value	labour force	% of labour force
Agriculture, fishing	50	5.1	5,700	4.0
Mining	7	0.7	...	...
Manufacturing	81	8.2	10,020	7.0
Construction	75	7.7	14,750	10.3
Public utilities	41	4.1	2,150	1.5
Transp. and commun.	82	8.3	5,300	3.7
Trade, restaurants	345	35.2	37,650	26.3
Finance, real estate	6	6	12,200	8.5
Pub. admin., defense	138	14.1	55,400	38.7
Services	163[6]	16.6[6]		
TOTAL	981[3]	100.0	143,200[3]	100.0

Land use as % of total land area (2000): in temporary crops *c.* 37%, in permanent crops *c.* 2%, in pasture *c.* 5%; overall forest area *c.* 5%.

Foreign trade[7]

Balance of trade (current prices)

	1999	2000	2001	2002	2003
BDS$'000,000	–1,430	–1,488	–1,362	–1,404	–1,647
% of total	56.6%	56.5%	55.7%	58.3%	60.3%

Imports (2003): BDS$2,050,000,000 (capital goods 20.9%; food and beverages 15.5%; mineral fuels 11.1%; chemicals and chemical products 5.1%). *Major import sources* (2002): U.S. 44.1%; Trinidad and Tobago 11.7%; U.K. 7.9%; Japan 4.5%; Canada 3.7%.
Exports (2003): BDS$542,000,000 (food and beverages 25.3%, of which sugar and molasses 9.2%, rum 7.0%; chemicals and chemical products 8.3%; electrical components 5.2%; other manufactures 17.5%). *Major export destinations* (2002): U.S. 16.5%; U.K. 11.9%; Trinidad and Tobago 11.0%; Jamaica 7.0%; bunkers and ships' stores 9.3%.

Transport and communications

Transport. Railroads: none. Roads (2000): total length 9,942 mi, 1,600 km (paved 99%). Vehicles (2001): passenger cars 64,900; trucks and buses 11,400. Air transport: (2001) passenger arrivals and departures 1,760,000; (2000) cargo unloaded and loaded 14,000 metric tons; airports (2002) with scheduled flights 1.

Communications

Medium	date	unit	number	units per 1,000 persons
Daily newspapers	1996	circulation	53,000	199
Radio	2001	receivers	202,000	749
Television	2001	receivers	83,700	310
Telephones	2003	main lines	134,000	497
Cellular telephones	2003	subscribers	140,000	519
Personal computers	2002	units	28,000	104
Internet	2003	users	100,000	371

Education and health

Educational attainment (1990). Percentage of population age 25 and over having: no formal schooling 0.4%; primary education 23.7%; secondary 60.3%[8]; higher 11.2%; other 4.4%. *Literacy* (1995): total population age 15 and over literate 97.4%; males literate 98.0%; females literate 96.8%.

Education (2002)

	schools	teachers	students	student/ teacher ratio
Primary (age 3–11)	109	1,823	29,502	16.2
Secondary (age 12–16)	32	1,389	21,436	15.4
Higher	4	339	11,226	33.1

Health: physicians (2002) 376 (1 per 721 persons); hospital beds (1992) 1,966 (1 per 134 persons); infant mortality rate per 1,000 live births (2002) 12.6.
Food (2001): daily per capita caloric intake 2,992 (vegetable products 75%, animal products 25%); 124% of FAO recommended minimum requirement.

Military

Total active duty personnel (2003): 500 (army 82.0%, navy 18.0%). *Military expenditure as percentage of GNP* (1999): 0.5% (world 2.4%); per capita expenditure U.S.$44.

[1]Parishes and city of Bridgetown have no local administrative function. [2]Includes city of Bridgetown. [3]Detail does not add to total given because of rounding. [4]Current revenue only. [5]In 1974 prices at factor cost. [6]Finance, real estate is included with Services. [7]Imports c.i.f.; exports f.o.b. [8]Includes composite senior.

Internet resources for further information:
- **Central Bank of Barbados http://www.centralbank.org.bb**
- **Profile of Barbados http://labour.gov.bb/blmis2/WEBDOC/trends/profile_of_barbados.asp?stats-quart**

Belarus

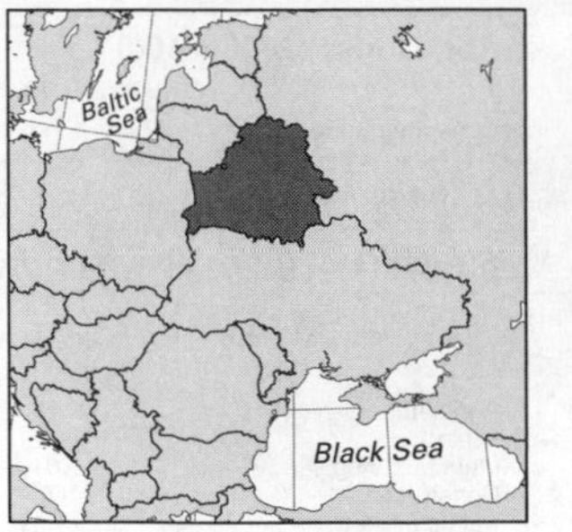

Official name: Respublika Belarus (Republic of Belarus).
Form of government: republic with two legislative bodies (Council of the Republic [62[1]]; House of Representatives [110[1]]).
Head of state and government: President assisted by Prime Minister.
Capital: Minsk.
Official languages: Belarusian; Russian.
Official religion: none.
Monetary unit: rubel[2] (Rbl; plural rubli); valuation (Sept. 1, 2004), 1 U.S.$ = (new) Rbl 2,165; 1 £ = (new) Rbl 3,895.

Area and population

		area		population
Provinces	**Capitals**	sq mi	sq km	2002 estimate
Brest	Brest	12,700	32,800	1,477,200
Homyel (Gomel)	Homyel	15,600	40,400	1,527,500
Hrodna (Grodno)	Hrodna	9,700	25,100	1,166,200
Mahilyow (Mogilyov)	Mahilyow	11,200	29,100	1,191,800
Minsk (Myensk)	Minsk	15,500[3]	40,200[3]	1,527,300
Vitsyebsk (Vitebsk)	Vitsyebsk	15,500	40,000	1,348,300
City				
Minsk (Myensk)	—	[3]	[3]	1,712,600
TOTAL		80,200[4]	207,600[4]	9,950,900

Demography

Population (2004): 9,828,000.
Density (2004): persons per sq mi 122.6, persons per sq km 47.3.
Urban-rural (2004): urban 71.5%; rural 28.5%.
Sex distribution (2004): male 46.61%; female 53.39%.
Age breakdown (2003): under 15, 16.8%; 15–29, 23.5%; 30–44, 22.7%; 45–59, 18.1%; 60–74, 13.4%; 75 and over, 5.5%.
Population projection: (2010) 9,587,000; (2020) 9,184,000.
Ethnic composition (1999): Belarusian 81.2%; Russian 11.4%; Polish 3.9%; Ukrainian 2.4%; Jewish 0.3%; other 0.8%.
Religious affiliation (1995): Belarusian Orthodox 31.6%; Roman Catholic 17.7%; other (mostly nonreligious) 50.7%.
Major cities (2004): Minsk 1,682,900; Homyel 497,200; Mahilyow 365,400; Vitsyebsk 355,200; Hrodna 315,500.

Vital statistics

Birth rate per 1,000 population (2003): 10.1 (world avg. 21.3); (2000) legitimate 81.4%; illegitimate 18.6%.
Death rate per 1,000 population (2003): 14.1 (world avg. 9.1).
Natural increase rate per 1,000 population (2003): –4.0 (world avg. 12.2).
Total fertility rate (avg. births per childbearing woman; 2003): 1.3.
Marriage rate per 1,000 population (2000): 6.2.
Divorce rate per 1,000 population (2000): 4.3.
Life expectancy at birth (2003): male 62.5 years; female 74.6 years.
Major causes of death per 100,000 population (2000): diseases of the circulatory system 722.6; malignant neoplasms (cancers) 195.3; accidents and violence 157.8; diseases of the respiratory system 66.7.

National economy

Budget (2003). Revenue: Rbl 12,154,223,000,000 (tax revenue 76.8%, of which value-added tax 23.8%, income tax 8.4%, profit tax 7.7%, excise tax 6.9%, property tax 6.0%, other 24.0%; nontax revenue 23.2%). Expenditures: Rbl 12,646,135,000,000 (education 18.5%, target budgetary fund 15.3%, health 14.3%, subsidies 7.4%, public order 5.2%, capital expenditure 4.2%, defense 3.0%).
Public debt (external, outstanding; 2002): U.S.$709,500,000.
Household income and expenditure. Average household size (2000) 3.4; income per household, n.a.; sources of money income (2003): wages and salaries 49.2%, business activities 31.6%, transfers 18.1%; expenditure (2001): food and nonalcoholic beverages 53.6%, clothing and footwear 9.4%, housing and energy 7.2%, transport 6.3%, alcoholic beverages and tobacco products 5.9%.
Population economically active (2003): 4,446,000; activity rate of total population 45.1% (participation rate: ages 16–59 [male], 16–54 [female] 74.0%; female 53.5%; unemployed 3.1%).

Price and earnings indexes (2000 = 100)

	1998	1999	2000	2001	2002	2003
Consumer price index	9.4	37.2	100.0	161.1	229.6	294.8
Annual earnings index	7.9	33.2	100.0	208.8	321.1	346.5

Production (metric tons except as noted). Agriculture, forestry, fishing (2003): potatoes 8,649,000, maize for forage 6,500,000, sugar beets 1,920,000, barley 1,770,000, rye 1,400,000, wheat 1,100,000, cabbages 685,000, apples 300,000; livestock (number of live animals) 3,921,000 cattle, 3,277,000 pigs, 192,000 horses, 30,600,000 poultry; roundwood (2002) 6,947,000 cu m; fish catch (2001) 5,609. Mining and quarrying (2000): potash 3,400,000; peat 2,211,000. Manufacturing (value of production in [old] Rbl '000,000; 1994): machine-building equipment 1,086,650; chemical products 659,438; food products 562,438; construction materials 142,555. Energy production (consumption): electricity (kW-hr; 2003) 26,615,000,000 (33,228,000,000); coal (2000) none (504,000); crude petroleum (barrels; 2000) 13,600,000 (98,640,000); petroleum products (2003) 15,774,000 (6,240,000); natural gas (cu m; 2003) 254,000,000 (18,448,000,000).
Gross national product (2003): U.S.$15,700,000,000 (U.S.$1,590 per capita).

Structure of gross domestic product and labour force

	2003			
	in value Rbl '000,000	% of total value	labour force	% of labour force
Agriculture	2,985	8.3	493,000	11.1
Mining / Manufacturing	9,180	25.5	987,000	22.2
Public utilities	[5]	[5]	171,000	3.8
Construction	2,151	6.0	231,000	5.2
Transp. and commun.	3,735	10.4	265,000	6.0
Trade	3,560	9.9	257,000	5.8
Finance			57,000	1.3
Public admin., defense / Services	14,319[5]	39.9[5]	1,050,000	23.6
Other			935,000[6]	21.0[6]
TOTAL	35,930	100.0	4,446,000	100.0

Tourism (2002): receipts U.S.$193,000,000; expenditures U.S.$559,000,000.
Land use as % of total land area (2000)[7]: in temporary crops 29.6%, in permanent crops 0.6%, in pasture 14.4%; overall forest area 45.3%.

Foreign trade[8]

Balance of trade (current prices)

	1998	1999	2000	2001	2002	2003
U.S.$'000,000	–1,479	–765	–1,320	–835	–882	–1,541
% of total	9.5%	6.1%	8.3%	5.3%	5.2%	7.2%

Imports (2002): U.S.$8,980,000,000 (crude petroleum 16.8%, machinery and apparatus 15.5%, chemicals and chemical products 10.2%, food and beverages 8.8%, natural and manufactured gas 6.3%, iron and steel 6.2%). *Major import sources:* Russia 65.1%; Germany 7.7%; Ukraine 3.2%; Poland 2.4%; Italy 2.4%.
Exports (2002): U.S.$8,098,000,000 (refined petroleum 18.3%, road vehicles 8.9%, nonelectrical machinery 8.3%, food 6.7%, potassium chloride 5.7%, electrical machinery 5.7%). *Major export destinations:* Russia 50.1%; Latvia 6.4%; United Kingdom 6.1%; Germany 4.3%; The Netherlands 3.4%.

Transport and communications

Transport. Railroads (2002): length 5,533 km; passenger-km 14,349,000,000; metric ton-km cargo 34,169,000,000. Roads (2000): total length 74,400 km (paved 89.0%). Vehicles (2001): passenger cars 1,448,461; trucks and buses 85,791. Air transport (2002): passenger-km 553,000,000; metric ton-km cargo 37,000,000; airports 1.

Communications

Medium	date	unit	number	units per 1,000 persons
Daily newspapers	2000	circulation	1,550,000	155
Radio	2000	receivers	2,990,000	299
Television	2000	receivers	3,420,000	342
Telephones	2003	main lines	3,071,300	311
Cellular telephones	2003	subscribers	1,118,000	113
Internet	2003	users	1,391,900	141

Education and health

Education (2003–04)

	schools	teachers	students	student/teacher ratio
Primary (age 6–13) / Secondary (age 14–17)	4,460	138,744	1,369,000	9.9
Voc., teacher tr.[9]	248	14,772	138,593	9.4
Higher	58	21,684	337,000	15.5

Literacy (2001): total population age 15 and over literate 99.7%; males literate 99.8%; females literate 99.6%.
Health: physicians (2003) 44,800 (1 per 220 persons); hospital beds (2000) 126,209 (1 per 79 persons); infant mortality rate per 1,000 live births (2003) 7.7.
Food (2001): daily per capita caloric intake 2,925 (vegetable products 72%, animal products 28%); 113% of FAO recommended minimum requirement.

Military

Total active duty personnel (2003): 72,940 (army 40.6%, air force and air defense 24.9%, other 34.5%). *Military expenditure as percentage of GNP* (1999): 1.3% (world 2.4%); per capita expenditure U.S.$89.

[1]Statutory number. [2]Rubel re-denominated Jan. 1, 2000; 1,000 (old) rubli = 1 (new) rubel. [3]Minsk province includes Minsk city. [4]Rounded area figures; exact area figures are 80,153 sq mi (207,595 sq km). [5]Public utilities included with Services. [6]Includes 136,000 registered unemployed and 799,000 undistributed self-employed and unregistered unemployed. [7]25% of Belarusian territory severely affected by radioactive fallout from Chernobyl. [8]Imports c.i.f.; exports f.o.b. [9]2000–01.

Internet resources for further information:
- **Ministry of Statistics and Analysis**
  http://president.gov.by/Minstat/en/main.html
- **National bank of the Republic of Belarus**
  http://www.nbrb.by

Belgium

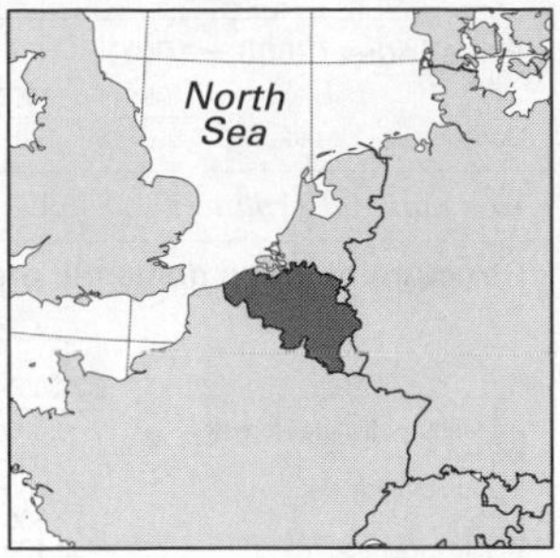

Official name: Koninkrijk België (Dutch); Royaume de Belgique (French) (Kingdom of Belgium).
Form of government: federal constitutional monarchy with a Parliament composed of two legislative chambers (Senate [71[1]]; House of Representatives [150]).
Chief of state: Monarch.
Head of government: Prime Minister.
Capital: Brussels.
Official languages: Dutch; French; German.
Official religion: none.
Monetary unit: 1 euro (€) = 100 cents; valuation (Sept. 1, 2004) 1 U.S.$ = €0.82; 1£ = €1.48[2].

Area and population

Regions[3] Provinces	Capitals	area sq mi	area sq km	population 2004[4] estimate
Brussels[5]	—	62	161	999,899
Flanders	—	5,221[6]	13,522	6,016,024
Antwerp	Antwerp	1,107	2,867	1,668,812
East Flanders	Ghent	1,151	2,982	1,373,720
Flemish Brabant	Leuven	813	2,106	1,031,904
Limburg	Hasselt	935	2,422	805,786
West Flanders	Brugge	1,214	3,145	1,135,802
Wallonia	—	6,504[6]	16,844[6]	3,380,498
Hainaut	Mons	1,462	3,786	1,283,200
Liège	Liège	1,491	3,862	1,029,605
Luxembourg	Arlon	1,714	4,440	254,120
Namur	Namur	1,415	3,666	452,856
Walloon Brabant	Wavre	421	1,091	360,717
TOTAL		11,787	30,528[6]	10,396,421

Demography

Population (2004): 10,416,000.
Density (2004): persons per sq mi 883.7, persons per sq km 341.9.
Urban-rural (2002): urban 97.0%; rural 3.0%.
Sex distribution (2003): male 48.95%; female 51.05%.
Age breakdown (2003): under 15, 17.2%; 15–29, 18.2%; 30–44, 22.5%; 45–59, 20.1%; 60–74, 14.1%; 75 and over, 7.9%.
Population projection: (2010) 10,506,000; (2020) 10,577,000.
Ethnic composition (2000): Flemish 53.7%; Walloon (French) 31.6%; Italian 2.6%; French 2.0%; Arab 1.8%; German 1.5%; Berber 0.9%; other 5.9%.
Religious affiliation (1995): Roman Catholic 87.9%; Muslim 2.5%; other Christian 2.4%, of which Protestant 1.0%; Jewish 0.3%; other 6.9%.
Major cities (2004[4]): Brussels 999,899[5]; Antwerp 455,148; Ghent 229,344; Charleroi 200,608; Liège 185,488; Brugge 117,025.

Vital statistics

Birth rate per 1,000 population (2003): 10.7 (world avg. 21.3).
Death rate per 1,000 population (2003): 10.2 (world avg. 9.1).
Natural increase rate per 1,000 population (2003): 0.5 (world avg. 12.2).
Total fertility rate (avg. births per childbearing woman; 2003): 1.6.
Marriage rate per 1,000 population (2001): 4.1.
Divorce rate per 1,000 population (2000): 2.6.
Life expectancy at birth (2002): male 75.1 years; female 81.6 years.
Major causes of death per 100,000 population (1992): diseases of the circulatory system 383.3; malignant neoplasms (cancers) 272.6; diseases of the respiratory system 90.6; accidents and violence 40.9.

National economy

Budget (2003). Revenue: €137,781,000,000 (social security contributions 28.4%, income tax 24.5%, taxes on goods and services 21.9%, property tax 6.7%). Expenditures: €137,348,000,000 (social security payments 25.7%, wages 23.5%, health 12.1%, interest on debt 11.0%, capital expenditure 6.1%).
Public debt (2001): U.S.$244,540,000,000.
Production (metric tons except as noted). Agriculture, forestry, fishing (2003): sugar beets 6,450,000, potatoes 2,522,000, wheat 1,640,000, apples 274,000, barley 271,000, tomatoes 235,000; livestock (number of live animals) 6,539,000 pigs, 2,778,000 cattle; roundwood (2002) 4,500,000 cu m; fish catch (2001)[7] 31,839. Mining and quarrying (2002): limestone 30,000,000; granite (Belgium bluestone) 1,200,000 cu m. Manufacturing (value added in U.S.$'000,000; 1997): chemicals and chemical products 7,702; food products 4,513; motor vehicles and parts 3,287; electrical machinery 3,278; base metals 3,126; value of traded diamonds handled in Antwerp (2002) U.S.$26,000,000,000. Energy production (consumption): electricity (kW-hr; 2002) 76,580,000,000 ([2000] 88,225,000,000); coal (metric tons; 2000) 375,000 (11,266,000); crude petroleum (barrels; 2000) none (248,700,000); petroleum products (metric tons; 2000) 29,525,000 (15,991,000); natural gas (cu m; 2000) 3,017,000 (19,544,000,000).
Household income and expenditure. Avg. household size (2000) 2.5; sources of income (2003): wages and transfer payments 69.3%, property income 11.1%, mixed income 19.6%; expenditure (1992): food 18.0%, housing 17.0%, transportation 13.3%, health 11.8%, durable goods 10.7%, clothing 7.7%.
Tourism (2002): receipts U.S.$6,892,000,000; expenditures U.S.$10,435,000,000.
Population economically active (2003): total 4,708,000; activity rate 45.5% (participation rates: ages 15–64, 69.3%; female [2000] 43.1%; unemployed 11.4%).

Price index (2000 = 100)

	1997	1998	1999	2000	2001	2002	2003
Consumer price index	95.4	96.3	97.4	100.0	102.5	104.2	105.8

Gross national product (2003): U.S.$267,227,000,000 (U.S.$25,820 per capita).

Structure of gross domestic product and labour force

	2001 in value €'000,000	% of total value	labour force[8]	% of labour force[8]
Agriculture	3,413.8	1.3	28,400	0.7
Mining	346.8	0.1	3,500	0.1
Manufacturing	43,174.2	17.0	622,000	16.0
Construction	11,879.8	4.7	189,400	4.9
Public utilities	5,942.3	2.3	26,700	0.7
Transp. and commun.	16,307.3	6.4	260,700	6.7
Trade	31,484.2	12.4	544,800	14.1
Finance	66,112.6	26.0	502,200	13.0
Pub. admin., defense	18,701.2	7.4	419,800	10.8
Services	38,454.0	15.1	918,200	23.7
Other	18,466.2[9]	7.3[9]	360,000[10]	9.3[10]
TOTAL	254,282.4	100.0	3,875,700	100.0

Land use as % of total land area (2000): in temporary crops 25.6%, in permanent crops 0.7%, in pasture 20.5%; overall forest area 21.1%.

Foreign trade[11]

Balance of trade (current prices)

	1998	1999	2000	2001	2002	2003
€'000,000	+11,600	+13,500	+14,600	+12,500	+18,841	+17,700
% of total	3.7%	4.2%	3.8%	3.1%	4.3%	4.0%

Imports (2002): €209,720,700,000 (machinery and apparatus 16.3%, road vehicles 12.0%, medicine and pharmaceuticals 10.6%, food 6.8%). *Major import sources:* Germany 17.3%; The Netherlands 15.8%; France 12.6%; U.K. 7.5%; Ireland 7.0%.
Exports (2002): €228,561,700,000 (machinery and apparatus 14.0%, road vehicles 13.8%, pharmaceuticals 10.1%, food 7.6%, organic chemicals 5.9%). *Major export destinations:* Germany 18.6%; France 16.3%; The Netherlands 11.7%; U.K. 9.6%; U.S. 7.8%.

Transport and communications

Transport. Railroads (2001): route length 3,380 km; passenger-km 8,038,000,000; metric ton-km cargo 7,080,000,000. Roads (1997): total length 143,800 km (paved 97%). Vehicles (2001): passenger cars 4,739,850; trucks and buses 541,056. Air transport (2000)[12]: passenger-km 19,378,689,000; metric ton-km cargo 568,244,000; airports 2.

Communications

Medium	date	unit	number	units per 1,000 persons
Daily newspapers	2000	circulation	1,640,000	160
Radio	2000	receivers	8,130,000	793
Television	2000	receivers	5,550,000	541
Telephones	2002	main lines	5,120,400	494
Cellular telephones	2002	subscribers	8,135,500	786
Personal computers	2002	units	2,500,000	242
Internet	2002	users	3,400,000	329

Education and health

Educational attainment (1991). Percentage of population age 18 and over having: less than secondary education 46.8%; lower secondary 16.6%; upper secondary 21.6%; teacher's college 3.7%; university 11.3%.

Education (2002–03)

	schools	teachers	students	student/ teacher ratio
Primary (age 6–12)	4,596	89,445[13, 14]	755,447	...
Secondary (age 12–18)	1,911	112,487	795,590	7.1
Higher	226	26,454	298,387	11.3

Health: physicians (2002) 46,268 (1 per 223 persons); hospital beds (2001) 71,907 (1 per 143 persons); infant mortality rate (2001) 5.1.
Food (2001)[7]: daily per capita caloric intake 3,682 (vegetable products 69%, animal products 31%); 140% of FAO recommended minimum requirement.

Military

Total active duty personnel (2003): 40,800 (army 60.8%, navy 6.0%, air force 25.1%, medical service 4.4%, other 3.7%). *Military expenditure as percentage of GNP* (1999): 1.4% (world 2.4%); per capita expenditure U.S.$352.

[1]Excludes children of the monarch serving ex officio from age 18. [2]The Belgian franc (BF) was the former monetary unit; on Jan. 1, 2002, BF 40.34 = €1. [3]Corresponding to three language-based federal community councils: Dutch (Flanders), French (Wallonia), and bilingual (Brussels) having authority in cultural affairs; a fourth (German) community council (within Wallonia; 2002 population 71,287) lacks expression as an administrative region. [4]January 1. [5]Officially, Brussels Capital Region. [6]Detail does not add to total given because of rounding. [7]Includes Luxembourg. [8]Annual average. [9]Taxes on products less subsidies on products. [10]Unemployed. [11]Imports c.i.f.; exports f.o.b. [12]Sabena airlines only; shut down November 2001. SN Brussels Airlines was founded in February 2002. [13]Includes preschool teachers. [14]2001–02.

Internet resources for further information:

- **Belgian Federal Government On Line http://belgium.fgov.be**
- **National Bank of Belgium http://www.bnb.be/sg/index.htm**

Belize

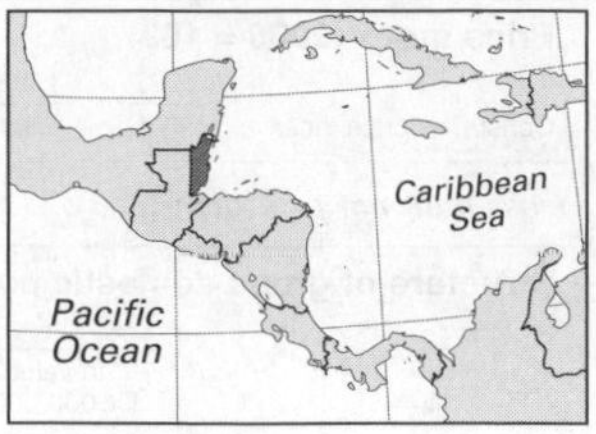

Official name: Belize.
Form of government: constitutional monarchy with two legislative houses (Senate [8[1]]; House of Representatives [29[2]]).
Chief of state: British Monarch represented by Governor-General.
Head of government: Prime Minister.
Capital: Belmopan.
Official language: English.
Official religion: none.
Monetary unit: 1 Belize dollar (BZ$) = 100 cents; valuation (Sept. 1, 2004) 1 U.S.$ = BZ$2.00; 1 £ = BZ$3.60.

Area and population

Districts	Capitals	area sq mi	area sq km	population 2004 estimate
Belize	Belize City	1,663	4,307	84,200
Cayo	San Ignacio/Santa Elena	2,006	5,196	63,900
Corozal	Corozal	718	1,860	35,000
Orange Walk	Orange Walk	1,790	4,636	43,800
Stann Creek	Dangriga	986	2,554	28,900
Toledo	Punta Gorda	1,704	4,413	26,800
TOTAL		8,867[3]	22,965[3, 4]	282,600

Demography

Population (2004): 283,000.
Density (2004): persons per sq mi 31.9, persons per sq km 12.3.
Urban-rural (2004): urban 49.9%; rural 50.1%.
Sex distribution (2004): male 50.50%; female 49.50%.
Age breakdown (2004): under 15, 40.8%; 15–29, 27.7%; 30–44, 17.4%; 45–59, 8.1%; 60–74, 4.3%; 75 and over, 1.7%.
Population projection: (2010) 315,000; (2020) 381,000.
Doubling time: 30 years.
Ethnic composition (2000): mestizo (Spanish-Indian) 48.7%; Creole (predominantly black) 24.9%; Mayan Indian 10.6%; Garifuna (black-Carib Indian) 6.1%; white 4.3%; East Indian 3.0%; other or not stated 2.4%.
Religious affiliation (2000): Roman Catholic 49.6%; Protestant 31.8%, of which Pentecostal 7.4%, Anglican 5.3%, Seventh-day Adventist 5.2%, Mennonite 4.1%; other Christian 1.9%; nonreligious 9.4%; other 7.3%.
Major cities (2004): Belize City 59,400; San Ignacio/Santa Elena 16,100; Orange Walk 15,000; Belmopan 12,300; Dangriga 10,400.

Vital statistics

Birth rate per 1,000 population (2002): 27.7 (world avg. 21.3); (1997) legitimate 40.3%; illegitimate 59.7%.
Death rate per 1,000 population (2002): 4.8 (world avg. 9.1).
Natural increase rate per 1,000 population (2002): 22.9 (world avg. 12.2).
Total fertility rate (avg. births per childbearing woman; 2003): 3.9.
Marriage rate per 1,000 population (2002): 6.1.
Divorce rate per 1,000 population (2002): 0.2.
Life expectancy at birth (2003): male 65.2 years; female 69.6 years.
Major causes of death per 100,000 population (1995): diseases of the circulatory system 119.8; accidents and violence 57.1; diseases of the respiratory system 47.8; malignant neoplasms 38.1; infectious and parasitic diseases 23.7.

National economy

Budget (2002–03). Revenue: BZ$431,300,000 (tax revenue 83.4%, of which import duties 38.3%, general sales tax 26.3%, income tax 18.3%; nontax revenue 12.2%; grants 4.4%). Expenditures: BZ$600,900,000 (current expenditure 60.2%; capital expenditure 39.8%).
Production (metric tons except as noted). Agriculture, forestry, fishing (2002): sugarcane 1,150,656, oranges 168,652, grapefruits 44,762, bananas 43,030, corn (maize) 33,459, plantain 28,000, papayas (2003) 13,356; livestock (number of live animals; 2002) 56,949 cattle, 22,874 pigs, 1,400,000 chickens; roundwood (2002) 187,600 cu m; fish catch (2001) 18,830, of which marine fish 10,155, crustaceans 4,983. Mining and quarrying (2002): limestone 700,000; sand and gravel 415,000. Manufacturing (2002): sugar 107,209; molasses 35,633; flour 26,078; orange concentrate 165,000 hectolitres; beer 90,000 hectolitres; cigarettes 84,000,000 units; garments 1,183,000 units. Energy production (consumption): electricity (kW-hr; 2000) 137,000,000 (162,000,000); coal, none (none); crude petroleum, none (none); petroleum products (metric tons; 2000) none (258,000); natural gas, none (none).
Household income and expenditure. Average household size (2000) 4.5; average annual income of employed head of household (1993) BZ$6,450[5] (U.S.$3,225[5]); sources of income, n.a.; expenditure (1990): food, beverages, and tobacco 34.0%, transportation 13.7%, energy and water 9.1%, housing 9.0%, clothing and footwear 8.8%, household furnishings 8.0%.
Tourism (2002): receipts from visitors U.S.$132,800,000; expenditures by nationals abroad U.S.$43,000,000.
Land use as % of total land area (2000): in temporary crops 2.8%, in permanent crops 1.7%, in pasture 2.2%; overall forest area 59.1%.
Population economically active (2002): total 94,172; activity rate of total population 35.5% (participation rates: ages 14 and over 58.4%; female [2001] 29.6%; unemployed 10.0%).

Price index (2000 = 100)

	1999	2000	2001	2002	2003
Consumer price index	99.4	100.0	101.2	103.4	106.1

Gross national product (2002): U.S.$807,000,000 (U.S.$3,190 per capita).

Structure of gross domestic product and labour force

	2002 in value BZ$'000	2002 % of total value	2001 labour force	2001 % of labour force
Agriculture, fishing, forestry	240,000	12.9	23,610	24.7
Mining	9,000	0.5	315	0.3
Manufacturing	155,200	8.4	8,170	8.5
Construction	87,600	4.7	5,055	5.3
Public utilities	62,100	3.3	1,135	1.2
Transp. and commun.	187,000	10.1	4,685	4.9
Trade, restaurants	371,200	20.0	19,965	20.9
Finance, real estate, insurance	247,600	13.3	3,285	3.4
Pub. admin., defense	186,100	10.0	20,315	21.2
Services	109,400	5.9		
Other	201,400[6]	10.8[6]	9,155[7]	9.6[7]
TOTAL	1,856,600	100.0[4]	95,690	100.0

Public debt (external, outstanding; 2002): U.S.$789,600,000.

Foreign trade

Balance of trade (current prices)

	1999	2000	2001	2002
BZ$'000,000	–205.1	–346.4	–382.9	–376.5
% of total	16.3%	23.1%	26.2%	23.3%

Imports (2002): BZ$995,900,000 (machinery and transport equipment 19.4%; mineral fuels and lubricants 13.0%; manufactured goods 11.9%; food 10.0%; chemicals and chemical products 7.9%). *Major import sources:* U.S. 43.3%; EU 7.9%; Mexico 7.8%; Canada 3.1%; Caricom 3.0%.
Exports (2002): BZ$619,400,000 (domestic exports 51.6%, of which seafood products [significantly shrimp] 11.8%, raw sugar 11.3%, citrus concentrate 9.3%, bananas 7.0%, garments 5.1%; reexports [principally to Mexico] 48.4%). *Major export destinations*[8]: U.S. 49.0%; U.K. 22.7%; other EU 8.6%; Caricom 6.5%.

Transport and communications

Transport. Railroads: none. Roads (1999): total length 1,785 mi, 2,872 km (paved 18%). Vehicles (1998): passenger cars 9,929; trucks and buses 11,755. Air transport (2001)[9]: passenger arrivals 256,564, passenger departures 240,900; cargo loaded 186 metric tons, cargo unloaded 1,272 metric tons. Airports (1997) with scheduled flights 9.

Communications

Medium	date	unit	number	units per 1,000 persons
Radio	1997	receivers	133,000	571
Television	1998	receivers	42,000	183
Telephones	2003	main lines	33,300	113
Cellular telephones	2003	subscribers	60,400	205
Personal computers	2002	units	35,000	138
Internet	2002	users	30,000	109

Education and health

Educational attainment (2000). Percentage of population age 25 and over having: no formal schooling 36.6%; primary education 40.9%; secondary 11.7%; postsecondary/advanced vocational 6.4%; university 3.8%; other/unknown 0.6%. *Literacy* (2001): total population age 14 and over literate 93.4%; males 93.6%; females 93.3%.

Education (2003–04)

	schools	teachers	students	student/ teacher ratio
Primary (age 5–12)	275	2,618	62,074	23.7
Secondary (age 13–16)	43	1,074	15,344	14.3
Higher[10]	12	228	2,853	12.1

Health (1998): physicians 155 (1 per 1,558 persons); hospital beds 554 (1 per 435 persons); infant mortality rate per 1,000 live births (2003) 27.1.
Food (2001): daily per capita caloric intake 2,885 (vegetable products 79%, animal products 21%); 128% of FAO recommended minimum requirement.

Military

Total active duty personnel (2003): 1,050 (army 100%).[11] *Military expenditure as percentage of GNP* (1999): 1.6% (world 2.4%); per capita expenditure U.S.$47.

[1]Excludes president of the Senate, who may be elected by the Senate from outside its appointed membership. [2]Excludes speaker of the House of Representatives, who may be elected by the House from outside its elected membership. [3]Includes offshore cays totaling 266 sq mi (689 sq km). [4]Detail does not add to total given because of rounding. [5]Estimated figure for about 33,000 employed heads of household. [6]Taxes less subsidies on products. [7]Includes 245 not adequately defined and 8,910 unemployed. [8]Domestic exports only. [9]Belize international airport only. [10]1997–98. [11]Foreign forces (2003): British army 30.

Internet resources for further information:
- **Government of Belize http://www.belize.gov.bz**
- **Central Statistical Office—Belize http://www.cso.gov.bz**

Benin

Official name: République du Bénin (Republic of Benin).
Form of government: multiparty republic with one legislative house (National Assembly [83]).
Head of state and government: President, assisted by Prime Minister[1].
Capital[2]: Porto-Novo.
Official language: French.
Official religion: none.
Monetary unit: 1 CFA franc (CFAF) = 100 centimes; valuation (Sept. 1, 2004) 1 U.S.$ = CFAF 539.75; 1 £ = CFAF 970.98[3].

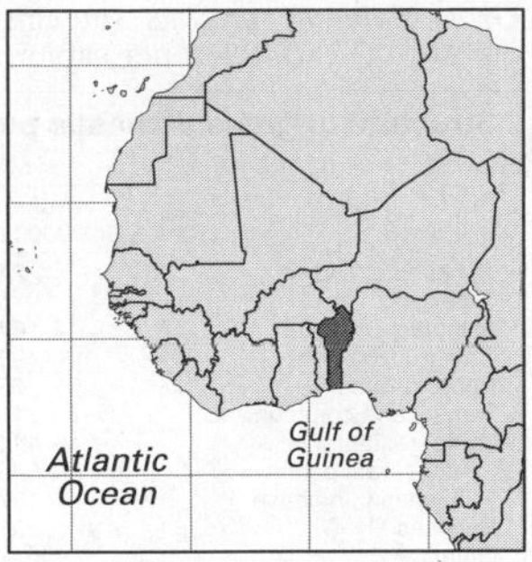

Area and population

Departments	Capitals	area sq mi	area sq km	population 2002[4] census
Alibori	Kandi	9,916	25,683	522,619
Atacora	Natitingou	7,899	20,459	543,929
Atlantique	Ouidah	1,248	3,233	805,986
Borgou	Parakou	9,772	25,310	720,287
Collines	Savalou	5,236	13,561	535,671
Couffo	Dogbo	928	2,404	522,904
Donga	Djougou	4,128	10,691	351,913
Littoral	Cotonou	31	79	658,572
Mono	Lokossa	539	1,396	358,467
Ouémé	Porto-Novo	1,095	2,835	728,718
Plateau	Sakété	720	1,865	406,715
Zou	Abomey	1,971	5,106	596,788
TOTAL		43,483	112,622	6,752,569

Demography

Population (2004): 7,250,000.
Density (2004): persons per sq mi 166.7, persons per sq km 64.4.
Urban-rural (2002): urban 43.0%; rural 57%.
Sex distribution (2003): male 49.36%; female 50.64%.
Age breakdown (2003): under 15, 47.1%; 15–29, 27.7%; 30–44, 14.5%; 45–59, 7.0%; 60–74, 3.1%; 75 and over, 0.6%.
Population projection: (2010) 8,504,000; (2020) 10,647,000.
Doubling time: 24 years.
Ethnic composition (1992): Fon 39.7%; Yoruba (Nago) 12.1%; Adjara 11.1%; Bariba 8.6%; Aïzo 8.6%; Somba (Otomary) 6.6%; Fulani 5.6%; other 7.7%.
Religious affiliation (1992): Christian 35.4%, of which Roman Catholic 25.9%, Protestant 9.5%; traditional beliefs, including voodoo 35.0%; Muslim 20.6%; other 9.0%.
Major cities (2004): Cotonou 818,100; Porto-Novo 234,300; Parakou 227,900; Djougou 206,500; Abomey 126,800.

Vital statistics

Birth rate per 1,000 population (2003): 43.2 (world avg. 21.3).
Death rate per 1,000 population (2003): 13.7 (world avg. 9.1).
Natural increase rate per 1,000 population (2003): 29.5 (world avg. 12.2).
Total fertility rate (avg. births per childbearing woman; 2003): 6.0.
Life expectancy at birth (2003): male 50.4 years; female 51.8 years.

National economy

Budget (2002). Revenue: CFAF 300,200,000,000 (tax revenue 80.5%, of which tax on international trade 44.3%, income tax 19.8%, sales tax 16.3%; nontax revenue 12.8%; grants 6.7%). Expenditures: CFAF 352,800,000,000 (current expenditures 61.6%, of which salaries 22.9%, pensions and other transfers 17.6%, interest on debt 4.3%; development expenditure 38.4%).
Production (metric tons except as noted). Agriculture, forestry, fishing (2002): cassava 2,452,050, yams 1,785,000, corn (maize) 622,136, seed cotton 485,522, oil palm fruit 220,000, sorghum 195,468, peanuts (groundnuts) 146,214, tomatoes 141,301, dry beans 100,462, pineapples 86,700, karité nuts (shea nuts) 21,000; livestock (number of live animals; 2002) 1,550,000 cattle, 1,270,000 goats, 670,000 sheep, 550,000 pigs, 10,000,000 chickens; roundwood (2002) 6,297,969 cu m; fish catch (2001) 38,415. Mining (2002): gold 20 kg. Manufacturing (value added in U.S.$'000,000; 1999): food products 74; textiles 42; beverages 36; bricks, tiles, and cement 21. Energy production (consumption): electricity (kW-hr; 2001) 55,888,000 (413,587,000); coal, none (none); crude petroleum (barrels; 2001) 365,000 (negligible); petroleum products (metric tons; 2001) none (150,000); natural gas, none (none).
Gross national product (2003): U.S.$2,990,000,000 (U.S.$440 per capita).

Structure of gross domestic product and labour force

	2001		1992	
	in value CFAF '000,000,000	% of total value	labour force[5]	% of labour force[5]
Agriculture	617.7	35.5	1,147,746	55.0
Mining	4.0	0.2	661	0.0
Manufacturing	159.7	9.2	160,406	7.7
Public utilities	16.6	1.0	1,176	0.1
Construction	70.7	4.1	51,655	2.5
Transp. and commun.	139.8	8.0	52,837	2.5
Trade	318.0	18.3	432,501	20.7
Finance	167.5	9.6	3,106	0.1
Pub. admin., defense Services	106.8	6.1	164,544	7.9
Other	137.8[6]	7.9[6]	70,814	3.4
TOTAL	1,738.6	100.0[7]	2,085,446	100.0[7]

Public debt (external, outstanding; 2002): U.S.$1,690,000,000.
Population economically active (1997): total 2,608,000; activity rate of total population 44.2% (participation rates: ages 15–64, 84.3%; female 48.3%; unemployed, n.a.).

Price index (2000 = 100)

	1997	1998	1999	2000	2001	2002
Consumer price index	71.7	81.6	94.8	100.0	103.4	106.0

Household income and expenditure. Average household size (2000) 6.1; income per household: n.a.; sources of income: n.a.; expenditure: n.a.
Land use as % of total land area (2000): in temporary crops 17.6%, in permanent crops 2.4%, in pasture 5.0%; overall forest area 24.0%.
Tourism (2002): receipts from visitors U.S.$60,000,000; expenditures by nationals abroad U.S.$7,000,000.

Foreign trade[8]

Balance of trade (current prices)

	1997	1998	1999	2000	2001	2002
CFAF '000,000,000	–89.2	–93.4	–131.6	–88.1	–131.8	–128.4
% of total	15.3%	16.0%	20.2%	13.6%	19.3%	19.7%

Imports (2002): CFAF 389,800,000,000 (food products 27.6%; petroleum products 22.4%; machinery and transport equipment 18.0%). *Major import sources* (2001): France *c.* 23%; China *c.* 8%; free trade zones *c.* 6%; Côte d'Ivoire *c.* 5%; Ghana *c.* 5%; Nigeria *c.* 5%.
Exports (2002): CFAF 261,400,000,000 (domestic exports 60.2%, of which cotton yarn 33.3%; reexports 39.8%). *Major export destinations* (2001): India *c.* 31%; Brazil *c.* 6%; Indonesia *c.* 6%; Ghana *c.* 6%; Nigeria *c.* 5%.

Transport and communications

Transport. Railroads (2000): length 359 mi, 578 km; passenger-mi 97,306,000, passenger-km 156,600,000; short ton-mi cargo 95,194,000, metric ton-km cargo 153,200,000. Roads (1999): total length 4,217 mi, 6,787 km (paved 20.0%). Vehicles (1996): passenger cars 37,772; trucks and buses 8,058. Air transport[9]: n.a.; airports (2002) with scheduled flights 1.

Communications

Medium	date	unit	number	units per 1,000 persons
Daily newspapers	2000	circulation	12,900	2
Radio	2000	receivers	2,820,000	439
Television	2000	receivers	289,000	45
Telephones	2003	main lines	66,500	9.5
Cellular telephones	2003	subscribers	236,200	34
Personal computers	2003	units	26,000	3.7
Internet	2003	users	70,000	10.0

Education and health

Educational attainment (1992). Percentage of population age 25 and over having: no formal schooling 78.5%; primary education 10.8%; some secondary 8.2%; secondary 1.2%; postsecondary 1.3%. *Literacy* (1998): total percentage of population age 15 and over literate 37.7%; males literate 53.8%; females literate 22.6%.

Education (1999–2000)

	schools	teachers	students	student/ teacher ratio
Primary	4,178	17,710	932,424	52.6
Secondary	145[10]	4,447[11]	188,035[11]	42.0[11]
Voc., teacher tr.[10]	14	283	4,873	17.2
Higher	16[10]	962[12]	14,085[12]	14.6[12]

Health: physicians (1995) 313 (1 per 17,520 persons); hospital beds (1994) 1,230 (1 per 4,342 persons); infant mortality rate per 1,000 live births (2003) 86.7.
Food (2001): daily per capita caloric intake 2,455 (vegetable products 96%, animal products 4%); 107% of FAO recommended minimum requirement.

Military

Total active duty personnel (2003): 4,550 (army 94.5%, navy 2.2%, air force 3.3%). *Military expenditure as percentage of GNP* (1999): 1.4% (world 2.4%); per capita expenditure U.S.$5.

[1]Office of Prime Minister vacant from May 1998. [2]Porto-Novo, the official capital established under the constitution, is the seat of the legislature, but the president and most government ministers reside in Cotonou. [3]Formerly pegged to the French franc and since Jan. 1, 2002, to the euro at the rate of €1 = CFAF 655.96. [4]Preliminary. [5]Age 10 years and over. [6]Indirect taxes. [7]Detail does not add to total given because of rounding. [8]Import figures are f.o.b. in balance of trade and commodities and c.i.f. in trading partners. [9]Air Afrique, an airline jointly owned by 11 African countries (including Benin) was declared bankrupt in February 2002. [10]1993–94. [11]1997–98. [12]1996–97.

Internet resources for further information:
- **Embassy of Benin in Paris, France**
  http://www.ambassade-benin.org
- **La Banque de France: La Zone Franc**
  http://www.banque-france.fr/fr/zonefr/main.htm

Bermuda

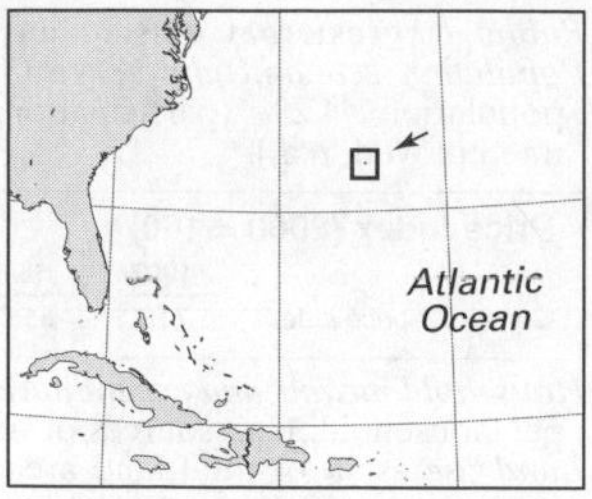

Official name: Bermuda.
Political status: colony (United Kingdom) with two legislative houses (Senate [11]; House of Assembly [36]).
Chief of state: British Monarch, represented by Governor.
Head of government: Premier.
Capital: Hamilton.
Official language: English.
Official religion: none.
Monetary unit: 1 Bermuda dollar (Bd$) = 100 cents; valuation (Sept. 1, 2004) 1 U.S.$ = Bd$1.00[1]; 1 £ = Bd$1.80.

Area and population

Municipalities	area sq mi	area sq km	population 2000 census
Hamilton	0.3	0.8	969
St. George	0.5	1.3	1,752
Parishes			
Devonshire	2.0	5.1	7,307
Hamilton	2.0	5.1	5,270
Paget	2.1	5.3	5,088
Pembroke[2]	1.8	4.6	10,337
St. George's[3, 4]	3.5	8.0	3,699
Sandys	2.1	5.4	7,275
Smith's	1.8	4.7	5,658
Southampton	2.2	5.6	6,117
Warwick	2.0	5.1	8,587
TOTAL	20.5[5, 6]	53.1[5, 6]	62,059[7]

Demography

Population (2004): 64,000.
Density (2004): persons per sq mi 3,048, persons per sq km 1,185.
Urban-rural (2003): urban 100.0%; rural, none.
Sex distribution (2000): male 48.03%; female 51.97%.
Age breakdown (2000): under 15, 19.1%; 15–29, 18.4%; 30–44, 27.9%; 45–59, 19.6%; 60–74, 10.9%; 75 and over, 4.1%.
Population projection: (2010) 66,000; (2020) 69,000.
Ethnic composition (2000): black 50.4%; British expatriates 29.0%; mulatto 10.0%; U.S. white 6.0%; Portuguese 4.5%; other 0.1%.
Religious affiliation (2000): Protestant 64.3%, of which Anglican 22.6%, Methodist 14.9%; Roman Catholic 14.9%; nonreligious 13.8%; other 6.0%; unknown 1.0%.
Major cities (2000): St. George 1,752; Hamilton 969.

Vital statistics

Birth rate per 1,000 population (2001): 13.2 (world avg. 21.3); legitimate 62.3%; illegitimate 37.7%.
Death rate per 1,000 population (2001): 7.0 (world avg. 9.1).
Natural increase rate per 1,000 population (2001): 6.2 (world avg. 12.2).
Total fertility rate (avg. births per childbearing woman; 2000): 1.8.
Marriage rate per 1,000 population (2001): 14.6.
Divorce rate per 1,000 population (2000): 3.5.
Life expectancy at birth (2000): male 74.9 years; female 78.9 years.
Major causes of death per 100,000 population (1998): diseases of the circulatory system 313.9; malignant neoplasms (cancers) 252.7; accidents and violence 38.6; AIDS 27.4.

National economy

Budget (2002). Revenue: Bd$631,100,000 (customs duty 30.1%; payroll tax 27.1%; tax on international companies 7.2%; land tax 6.3%; stamp duties 4.5%; other 24.8%). Expenditures: Bd$607,500,000 (current expenditure 89.4%, of which wages 41.9%, goods and services 25.6%, grants and contributions 21.9%; development expenditure 10.6%).
Production (value in Bd$'000 except as noted). Agriculture, forestry, fishing (1999): vegetables 3,000, milk 1,657, fruits 900, eggs 435, honey 160; livestock (number of live animals; 2002) 900 horses, 600 cattle, 45,000 chickens; roundwood, n.a.; fish catch (metric tons; 2001) 315, of which crustaceans and mollusks 25. Mining and quarrying: crushed stone for local use. Manufacturing: industries include pharmaceuticals, cosmetics, electronics, fish processing, handicrafts, and small boat building[8]. Energy production (consumption): electricity (kW-hr; 2003) 664,000,000 (664,000,000); coal, none (none); crude petroleum, none (none); petroleum products (metric tons; 2000) none (151,000); natural gas, none (none).
Land use as % of total land area (2000): in temporary crops, n.a., in permanent crops, n.a., in pasture, n.a.; overall forest area, n.a.
Tourism: receipts from visitors (2003) U.S.$342,000,000; expenditures by nationals abroad (1997) U.S.$148,000,000.
Population economically active (2002): total 37,815; activity rate of total population 59.1% (participation rates [2000]: ages 15–64, 88.1%; female 49.0%; unemployed 2.9%).

Price and earnings indexes (1995 = 100)

	1996	1997	1998	1999	2000	2001	2002
Consumer price index	102.5	104.6	106.7	109.3	112.3	115.1	119.6
Weekly earnings index	103.2	106.5	109.8	113.1	...	...	...

Gross domestic product (at current market prices; 2000–01): U.S.$3,023,000,000 (U.S.$48,580 per capita).

Structure of gross domestic product and labour force

	2001–02 in value Bd$'000,000	% of total value	labour force	% of labour force
Agriculture, fishing	24	0.8	648	1.7
Quarrying	5	0.2		
Manufacturing	67	2.2	1,107	2.9
Construction	193	6.4	2,917	7.7
Public utilities	75	2.5	412	1.1
Transp. and commun.	217	7.2	2,859	7.6
Trade, restaurants	444	14.8	8,572	22.7
Finance, real estate	1,526	50.7	3,373	8.9
Pub. admin., defense	167	5.6	3,896	10.3
Services	291	9.7	12,556	33.2
Other	—	—	1,475[9]	3.9[9]
TOTAL	3,009	100.0[6]	37,815	100.0

Public debt (external, outstanding): n.a.
Household income and expenditure. Average household size (2000) 2.4; average annual income per household (2001) Bd$72,500 (U.S.$72,500); sources of income (1993): wages and salaries 65.3%, imputed income from owner occupancy 10.6%, self-employment 9.0%, net rental income 4.8%, other 10.3%; expenditure (2002): housing 26.1%, food and nonalcoholic beverages 16.0%, household furnishings 15.0%, clothing and footwear 4.2%, other goods and services 38.7%.

Foreign trade

Balance of trade (current prices)

	1997	1998	1999	2000	2001	2002
Bd$'000,000	–554	–564	–661	–668	–671	–696
% of total	81.0%	80.3%	86.6%	86.5%	87.0%	86.7%

Imports (2002): Bd$746,000,000 (food, beverages, and tobacco 20.2%; machinery 16.5%; chemicals and chemical products 13.9%; mineral fuels 7.8%; transport equipment 6.0%). *Major import sources:* United States 76%; Canada 5%; United Kingdom 5%; Caribbean countries (mostly Netherlands Antilles) 3%.
Exports (2002): Bd$57,000,000 (nearly all reexports; diamond market was established in 1990s). *Major export destinations* (2002): mostly United States, United Kingdom, Norway, and Spain.

Transport and communications

Transport. Railroads: none. Roads (2000): total length 140 mi, 225 km (paved 100%)[10]. Vehicles (2002): passenger cars 21,594; trucks and buses 3,768. Air transport (2001): passenger arrivals 826,000, passenger departures 826,000; cargo loaded and unloaded 4,200 metric tons; airports (2002) with scheduled flights 1.

Communications

Medium	date	unit	number	units per 1,000 persons
Daily newspapers	1996	circulation	17,000	277
Radio	1997	receivers	82,000	1,328
Television	1997	receivers	66,000	1,069
Telephones	2001	main lines	56,300	872
Cellular telephones	2001	subscribers	13,300	206
Personal computers	2001	units	32,000	495
Internet	2001	users	30,000	464

Education and health

Educational attainment (2000). Percentage of total population age 16 and over having: no formal schooling 0.4%; primary education 7.0%; secondary 39.3%; postsecondary technical 25.7%; higher 26.8%; not stated 0.8%. *Literacy* (1997): total population age 15 and over literate, 98%.

Education (2002)

	schools	teachers	students	student/ teacher ratio
Primary (age 5–11) / Secondary (age 12–16)	...	1,291[11]	10,474	...
Higher	1	...	544	...

Health (2002): physicians 122 (1 per 524 persons); hospital beds 226 (1 per 283 persons); infant mortality rate per 1,000 live births (2003) 9.1.
Food (2001): daily per capita caloric intake 2,904 (vegetable products 74%, animal products 26%); 115% of FAO recommended minimum requirement.

Military

Total active duty personnel (2003): 700; part-time defense force assists police and is drawn from Bermudian conscripts.

[1]The Bermuda dollar is at par with the U.S. dollar. [2]Excludes the area and population of the city of Hamilton. [3]Excludes the area and population of the town of St. George. [4]Includes the 2.0 sq mi (5.2 sq km) area of the former U.S. military base closed in 1995. [5]Includes 0.4 sq mi (1.1 sq km) of uninhabited islands. [6]Detail does not add to total given because of rounding. [7]Excludes 8,335 short-term visitors, 901 institutionalized persons, and 39 transients. [8]The economy of Bermuda is overwhelmingly based on service industries such as tourism, insurance companies, offshore financial centres, e-commerce companies, and ship repair facilities. [9]Unemployed. [10]Excludes 138 mi (222 km) of paved private roads. [11]Includes preschool teachers.

Internet resources for further information:
- **Bermuda Online: Economy http://bermuda-online.org/economy.htm**

Bhutan

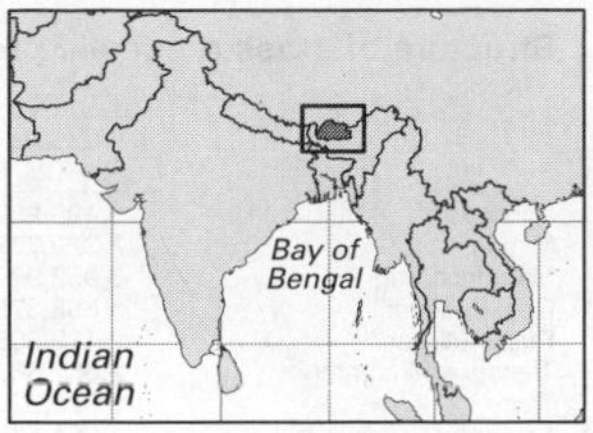

Official name: Druk-Yul (Kingdom of Bhutan).
Form of government: monarchy[1] with one legislative house (National Assembly [152[2]]).
Chief of state: Monarch[1].
Head of government: Prime Minister[1].
Capital: Thimphu.
Official language: Dzongkha (a Tibetan dialect).
Official religion: Mahāyāna Buddhism.
Monetary unit: 1 ngultrum[3] (Nu) = 100 chetrum; valuation (Sept. 1, 2004) 1 U.S.$ = Nu 46.35; 1 £ = Nu 83.37.

Area and population

		area		population
Districts	Capitals	sq mi	sq km	2000 estimate
Bumthang	Jakar	...	...	...
Chhukha	Chhukha	...	...	...
Chirang	Damphu	...	...	...
Dagana	Dagana	...	...	...
Gasa	...	...	...	...
Gaylegphug	Gaylegphug	...	...	...
Ha	Ha	...	...	...
Lhuntshi	Lhuntshi	...	...	...
Mongar	Mongar	...	...	...
Paro	Paro	...	...	...
Pema Gatsel	Pema Gatsel	...	...	...
Punakha	Punakha	...	...	...
Samchi	Samchi	...	...	...
Samdrup Jongkhar	Samdrup Jongkhar	...	...	...
Shemgang	Shemgang	...	...	...
Tashi Yangtse	Tashi Yangtse	...	...	...
Tashigang	Tashigang	...	...	...
Thimphu	Thimphu	...	...	...
Tongsa	Tongsa	...	...	...
Wangdi Phodrang	Wangdi Phodrang	...	...	...
TOTAL		14,824	38,394	677,932

Demography

Population (2004): 700,000.
Density (2004): persons per sq mi 47.2, persons per sq km 18.2.
Urban-rural (2000): urban 21.0%; rural 79.0%.
Sex distribution (2003): male 50.50%; female 49.50%.
Age breakdown (2003): under 15, 42.1%; 15–29, 23.7%, 30–44, 16.4%, 45–59, 10.6%; 60–74, 5.9%; 75 and over, 1.3%.
Population projection: (2010) 793,000; (2020) 965,000.
Doubling time: 27 years.
Ethnic composition (1993): Bhutiā (Ngalops) 50.0%; Nepalese (Gurung) 35.0%; Sharchops 15.0%.
Religious affiliation (2000): Buddhist 74.0%; Hindu 20.5%; other 5.5%.
Major cities (2002): Thimphu 45,000; Phuntsholing (1997) 45,000.

Vital statistics

Birth rate per 1,000 population (2002): 34.9 (world avg. 21.3).
Death rate per 1,000 population (2002): 8.7 (world avg. 9.1).
Natural increase rate per 1,000 population (2002): 26.2 (world avg. 12.2).
Total fertility rate (avg. births per childbearing woman; 2003): 4.9.
Life expectancy at birth (2002): male 62.0 years; female 64.0 years.
Major causes of death (percentage distribution; 1989): respiratory tract infections 19.5%; diarrhea/dysentery 15.2%; skin infections 12.2%; parasitic worm infestations 10.0%; malaria 9.4%.

National economy

Budget (2003–04). Revenue: Nu 11,154,500,000 (domestic revenue 46.8%, grants 44.6%, other 8.6%). Expenditures: Nu 11,537,700,000 (capital expenditures 54.4%, current expenditures 43.3%, repayments 2.3%).
Public debt (external, outstanding; 2002): U.S.$376,900,000.
Production (metric tons except as noted). Agriculture, forestry, fishing (2002): corn (maize) 48,500, rice 44,300, oranges 30,000, potatoes 22,000, sugarcane 12,800, apples 5,100, wheat 4,350, millet 3,800, green peppers and chilies 2,900, barley 1,700, pulses 1,600; livestock (number of live animals) 355,400 cattle, 41,400 pigs, 31,300 goats, 29,900 horses, 22,880 sheep; roundwood (2002) 4,482,000 cu m; fish catch (2001) 330. Mining and quarrying (2001): limestone 434,900; dolomite 283,700; gypsum 87,000; iron ore 3,100. Manufacturing (value in Nu '000,000; 2000): cement 696.7; chemical products 474.6; alcoholic beverages 255.0; wood board products 228.6; processed fruits 108.5. Energy production (consumption): electricity (kW-hr; 2002) 2,059,400,000 (489,260,000); coal (metric tons; 2000) 50,000 (66,000); crude petroleum, none (n.a.); petroleum products (metric tons; 2000) none (47,000); natural gas, none (n.a.).
Household income and expenditure. Average household size (2000) 5.5; income per household: n.a.; sources of income: n.a.; expenditure: n.a.
Population economically active (1999): total 358,950; activity rate of total population 52.9% (participation rates: ages 15 and over 69.6%; female, n.a.; unemployed 1.4%).

Price index (2000 = 100)

	1997	1998	1999	2000	2001	2002	2003
Consumer price index	81.4	90.0	96.1	100.0	103.4	106.0	108.8

Gross national product (2003): U.S.$578,000,000 (U.S.$660 per capita).

Structure of gross domestic product and labour force

	2002		1999	
	in value Nu '000,000	% of total value	labour force	% of labour force
Agriculture	9,325.5	33.9	...	...
Mining	472.8	1.7	...	...
Manufacturing	2,225.9	8.1	...	...
Construction	4,836.3	17.6	...	...
Trade	1,910.8	0.9	...	...
Public utilities	2,756.5	10.0	...	...
Transportation and communications	2,463.1	8.9	...	...
Finance	1,921.6	7.0	...	...
Pub. admin., defense / Services	2,393.4	8.7	...	...
Other	–773.2[4]	–2.8[4]	...	...
TOTAL	27,532.7	100.0	358,950	100.0

Tourism (2002): receipts from visitors U.S.$8,000,000; expenditures by nationals abroad, n.a.
Land use as % of total land area (2000): in temporary crops 3.0%, in permanent crops 0.4%, in pasture 8.8%; overall forest area 64.2%.

Foreign trade[5]

Balance of trade (current prices)

	1997–98	1998–99	1999–2000	2000–01	2001–02
U.S.$'000,000	–24.7	–57.5	–70.7	–103.0	–90.6
% of total	10.0%	21.5%	23.6%	31.4%	31.6%

Imports (2001): U.S.$188,300,000 (1999; machinery and transport equipment 41.7%, of which computers and related goods 11.0%, road vehicles 10.5%; food 13.9%, of which cereals 7.6%; refined petroleum 7.2%). *Major import sources* (2001): India 81.1%; Japan 7.2%; Thailand 3.4%; Singapore 2.5%.
Exports (2001): U.S.$97,700,000 (electricity 48.1%, calcium carbide 13.3%, ferro-silicon 12.6%, cement 9.6%). *Major export destinations* (2001): India 94.1%; Bangladesh 4.5%; Nepal 0.8%.

Transport and communications

Transport. Railroads: none. Roads (2003): total length 2,489 mi, 4,007 km (paved 60%). Vehicles (2003): passenger cars 10,574; trucks and buses 3,852. Air transport (1999): passenger-mi 30,000,000, passenger-km 49,000,000; short ton-mi cargo 2,700,000, metric ton-km cargo 4,000,000; airports (2002) with scheduled flights 1.

Communications

Medium	date	unit	number	units per 1,000 persons
Radio	1997	receivers	37,000	19
Television	1999	receivers	13,000	20
Telephones	2002	main lines	20,168	33
Personal computers	2002	units	10,000	15
Internet	2002	users	17,980	27

Education and health

Educational attainment: n.a. *Literacy* (1995 est.): total population age 15 and over literate 42.2%; males literate 56.2%; females literate 28.1%.

Education (2003)

	schools	teachers	students	student/ teacher ratio
Primary (age 7–11) / Secondary (age 12–16)	412	4,005	129,160	32.2
Institutes	14	313	3,251	10.4

Health (2002): physicians 122 (1 per 6,019 persons); hospital beds 1,023 (1 per 696 persons); infant mortality rate per 1,000 live births 55.0.
Food: daily per capita caloric intake, n.a.

Military

Total active duty personnel (2002): about 6,000 (army 100%).

[1]Constitution commissioned by the monarch is to become effective in 2005; reforms in July 1998 curtailed the powers of the monarchy. [2]Includes 36 nonelective seats occupied by representatives of the King and religious groups. [3]Indian currency is also accepted legal tender; the ngultrum is at par with the Indian rupee. [4]Imputed bank service charges. [5]Imports c.i.f.; exports f.o.b.

Internet resources for further information:
- **Planning Commission: Royal Government of Bhutan http://www.dop.gov.bt**
- **Royal Monetary Authority of Bhutan http://www.rma.org.bt**

Bolivia

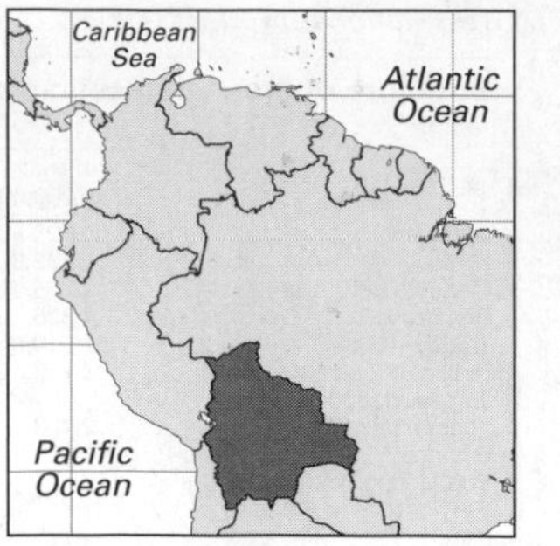

Official name: República de Bolivia (Republic of Bolivia).
Form of government: unitary multiparty republic with two legislative houses (Chamber of Senators [27]; Chamber of Deputies [130]).
Head of state and government: President.
Capitals: La Paz (administrative); Sucre (judicial).
Official languages: Spanish; Aymara; Quechua.
Official religion: Roman Catholicism.
Monetary unit: 1 boliviano (Bs) = 100 centavos; valuation (Sept. 1, 2004) 1 U.S.$ = Bs 7.97; 1 £ = Bs 14.34.

Area and population

Departments	Capitals	area sq mi	area sq km	population 2001 census
Beni	Trinidad	82,458	213,564	362,521
Chuquisaca	Sucre	19,893	51,524	531,522
Cochabamba	Cochabamba	21,479	55,631	1,455,711
La Paz	La Paz	51,732	133,985	2,350,466
Oruro	Oruro	20,690	53,588	391,870
Pando	Cobija	24,644	63,827	52,525
Potosí	Potosí	45,644	118,218	709,013
Santa Cruz	Santa Cruz	143,098	370,621	2,029,471
Tarija	Tarija	14,526	37,623	391,226
TOTAL		424,164	1,098,581	8,274,325

Demography

Population (2004): 8,724,000.
Density (2004): persons per sq mi 20.6, persons per sq km 7.9.
Urban-rural (2001): urban 62.4%; rural 37.6%.
Sex distribution (2003): male 49.81%; female 50.19%.
Age breakdown (2001): under 15, 38.6%; 15–29, 27.4%; 30–44, 17.0%; 45–59, 10.0%; 60–74, 5.2%; 75 and over, 1.8%.
Population projection: (2010) 9,499,000; (2020) 10,747,000.
Doubling time: 40 years.
Ethnic composition (2000): Amerindian *c.* 65%, of which Quechua *c.* 40%, Aymara *c.* 24%; mestizo *c.* 27%; white 8%, of which German 3%.
Religious affiliation (1995): Roman Catholic 88.5%; Protestant 9.0%; other 2.5%.
Major cities (2001): Santa Cruz 1,116,059; La Paz 789,585 (urban agglomeration [2003] 1,477,000); El Alto 647,350[1]; Cochabamba 516,683; Oruro 201,230; Sucre 193,873.

Vital statistics

Birth rate per 1,000 population (2003): 25.5 (world avg. 21.3).
Death rate per 1,000 population (2003): 7.9 (world avg. 9.1).
Natural increase rate per 1,000 population (2003): 17.6 (world avg. 12.2).
Total fertility rate (avg. births per childbearing woman; 2003): 3.2.
Life expectancy at birth (2003): male 62.2 years; female 67.4 years.
Major causes of death: n.a.

National economy

Budget (2002). Revenue: Bs 13,558,000,000 (tax revenue 74.3%, of which value-added taxes 25.2%, taxes on hydrocarbons 19.3%, import duties 12.7%; nontax revenue 11.3%; foreign grants 9.4%; other 5.0%). Expenditures: Bs 18,857,000,000 (current expenditure 75.1%; capital expenditure 24.9%).
Production (metric tons except as noted). Agriculture, forestry, fishing (2002): sugarcane 4,320,784, soybeans 1,166,660, potatoes 944,216, corn (maize) 724,613, bananas 714,191, cassava 519,763, rice 248,211, sunflower seeds 193,812, sorghum 165,557, wheat 143,480; livestock (number of live animals) 8,901,631 sheep, 6,576,277 cattle, 2,850,547 pigs, 1,500,500 goats, 632,000 asses, 323,000 horses; roundwood (2002) 10,237,753 cu m; fish catch (2001) 6,260. Mining and quarrying (metric tons of pure metal; 2003): zinc 145,490; tin 16,386; lead 9,353; silver 466; gold 9,361 kg. Manufacturing (value added in U.S.$'000,000; 1998): petroleum products 399; food products 222; beverages 141; nonmetal mineral products 75; textiles 30; printing and publishing 24; nonferrous metals 20. Energy production (consumption): electricity (kW-hr; 2003) 4,318,000,000 (2,905,000,000); coal, none (none); crude petroleum (barrels; 2000) 11,877,000 (11,877,000); petroleum products (metric tons; 2000) 1,345,000 (1,641,000); natural gas (cu m; 2000) 3,904,000,000 (1,815,000,000).
Population economically active (2002): total 3,823,500; activity rate of total population 44.5% (participation rates: ages 10 and over 78.2%; female 45.9%; unemployed [2000] 7.4%).

Price and earnings indexes (2000 = 100)

	1998	1999	2000	2001	2002	2003
Consumer price index	93.6	95.6	100.0	101.6	102.5	106.0
Monthly earnings index	...	...	...	...	...	...

Tourism: receipts (2002) U.S.$104,000,000; expenditures (2001) U.S.$118,000,000.
Gross national product (at current market prices; 2003): U.S.$7,985,000,000 (U.S.$890 per capita).

Structure of gross domestic product and labour force

	2003 in value Bs '000[2]	2003 % of total value[2]	2002 labour force[3]	2002 % of labour force[3]
Agriculture	3,493,253	14.7	1,609,700	42.1
Mining	2,329,777	9.8	38,200	1.0
Manufacturing	3,952,929	16.6	435,900	11.4
Construction	668,375	2.8	206,500	5.4
Public utilities	479,608	2.0	7,700	0.2
Transp. and commun.	2,657,867	11.2	175,900	4.6
Trade	2,725,020	11.4	722,600	18.9
Finance	3,061,518	12.8	95,600	2.5
Pub. admin., defense	2,256,926	9.5	68,800	1.8
Services	1,101,000	4.6	462,600	12.1
Other	1,110,364[4]	4.6[4]	—	—
TOTAL	23,836,637	100.0	3,823,500	100.0

Public debt (external, outstanding; 2002): U.S.$3,378,000,000.
Household income and expenditure. Average household size (2000): 4.0; expenditure (1988): food 35.5%, transportation and communications 17.7%, housing 14.8%, household durable goods 7.3%, clothing and footwear 5.1%, beverages and tobacco 4.5%, recreation 2.7%, health 2.1%.
Land use as % of total land area (2000): in temporary crops 2.7%, in permanent crops 0.2%, in pasture 31.2%; overall forest area 48.9%.

Foreign trade[5]

Balance of trade (current prices)

	1998	1999	2000	2001	2002	2003
U.S.$'000,000	–721.0	–487.9	–375.0	–212.7	–253.6	+158.8
% of total	24.6%	18.8%	13.2%	7.6%	9.0%	5.3%

Imports (2001): U.S.$1,706,800,000 (machinery and transport equipment 27.6%; chemicals and chemical products 17.0%; food 11.4%; refined petroleum 6.2%; iron and steel 5.8%). *Major import sources:* Argentina 16.9%; U.S. 16.6%; Brazil 16.2%; Chile 8.4%; Peru 6.3%.
Exports (2001): U.S.$1,351,200,000 (food 20.7%, of which soybean oilcake 13.7%; natural gas 17.9%; zinc ores and concentrates 8.9%; soybean oil 5.5%; gold 3.7%). *Major export destinations:* Brazil 22.1%; Colombia 14.1%; U.S. 13.9%; Switzerland 13.0%; Venezuela 7.3%.

Transport and communications

Transport. Railroads (2000): route length 2,242 mi, 3,608 km; (1997) passenger-mi 139,746,000, passenger-km 224,900,000; short ton-mi cargo 574,600,000, metric ton-km cargo 838,900,000. Roads (2001): total length 33,100 mi, 53,259 km (paved 6%). Vehicles (2001): passenger cars 254,175; trucks and buses 194,510. Air transport (2003): passenger-mi 1,058,800,000, passenger-km 1,704,000,000; short ton-mi cargo 16,660,000, metric ton-km cargo 24,348,000; airports (2000) with scheduled flights 14.

Communications

Medium	date	unit	number	units per 1,000 persons
Daily newspapers	2000	circulation	448,000	65
Radio	2000	receivers	5,510,000	676
Television	2000	receivers	970,000	119
Telephones	2003	main lines	600,100	71
Cellular telephones	2003	subscribers	1,401,500	167
Personal computers	2002	units	190,000	23
Internet	2002	users	270,000	32

Education and health

Educational attainment (1992). Percentage of population age 25 and over having: no formal schooling 23.3%; some primary 20.3%; primary education 21.7%; some secondary 9.0%; secondary 6.5%; some higher 5.0%; higher 4.8%; not specified 9.4%. *Literacy* (2001): total population age 15 and over literate 86.0%; males literate 92.3%; females literate 79.9%.

Education (2001)

	schools	teachers	students	student/ teacher ratio
Primary (age 6–13)	...	66,339	1,666,150	25.1
Secondary (age 14–17)	...	16,507	398,360	24.1
Higher[6]	12	11,836	261,411	22.1

Health (2002): physicians 2,987 (1 per 2,827 persons); hospital beds 11,921 (1 per 708 persons); infant mortality rate per 1,000 live births (2003) 56.1.
Food (2001): daily per capita caloric intake 2,267 (vegetable products 84%, animal products 16%); 95% of FAO recommended minimum requirement.

Military

Total active duty personnel (2003): 31,500 (army 79.4%, navy 11.1%, air force 9.5%). *Military expenditure as percentage of GNP* (1998): 1.8% (world 2.5%); per capita expenditure U.S.$18.

[1]Within La Paz urban agglomeration. [2]In 1990 prices. [3]Population 10 years of age and over. [4]Imputed bank service charges. [5]Import figures are f.o.b. in balance of trade and c.i.f. for commodities and trading partners. [6]2000.

Internet resources for further information:
- **Instituto Nacional de Estadística http://www.ine.gov.bo**
- **Banco Central de Bolivia http://www.bcb.gov.bo/sitio/introduccion_f.html**

Bosnia and Herzegovina[1]

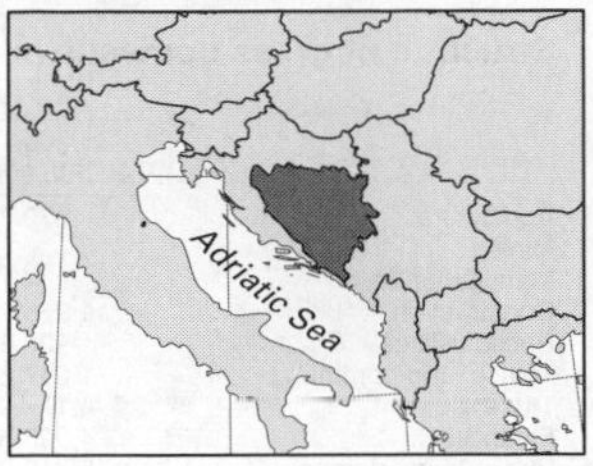

Official name: Bosna i Hercegovina (Bosnia and Herzegovina).
Form of government: federal multiparty republic with bicameral legislature (House of Peoples [15[2]]; House of Representatives [42]).
Chiefs of state: nominally a tripartite presidency.
International authority: High Representative[1].
Head of government: Prime Minister (Chairman of the Council of Ministers).
Capital: Sarajevo.
Official language: Bosnian.
Official religion: none.
Monetary unit: 1 marka[3, 4, 5] (KM) = 100 fenning; valuation (Sept. 1, 2004) 1 U.S.$ = KM 1.53; 1 £ = KM 2.83.

Area and population

		area		population
				2002[6]
Autonomous regions	**Principal cities**	sq mi	sq km	estimate
Cantons				
Federation of Bosnia and Herzegovina	Sarajevo	10,081	26,110	2,312,000
Central Bosnia	Travnik	1,231	3,189	240,000
Goražde	Goražde	195	505	35,000
Neretva	Mostar	1,699	4,401	217,000
Posavina	Orašje	125	325	44,000
Sarajevo	Sarajevo	493	1,277	401,000
Tuzla-Podrinje	Tuzla	1,023	2,649	507,000
Una-Sava	Bihać	1,593	4,125	306,000
Western Bosnia	Livno	1,905	4,934	84,000
Western Herzegovina	Ljubuški	526	1,362	81,000
Zenica-Doboj	Zenica	1,291	3,343	397,000
Republika Srpska	Banja Luka	9,496	24,594	1,392,000[7]
District				
Br ko	Br ko	190	493	85,000
WATER		5	12	—
TOTAL		19,772	51,209	3,789,000

Demography

Population (2004)[8]: 3,870,000.
Density (2004)[8]: persons per sq mi 195.7, persons per sq km 75.6.
Urban-rural (2002): urban 43.4%; rural 56.6%.
Sex distribution (2002): male 48.80%; female 51.20%.
Age breakdown (2002): under 15, 18.4%; 15–29, 21.8%; 30–44, 23.0%; 45–59, 18.5%; 60–74, 15.2%; 75 and over, 3.1%.
Population projection: (2010) 3,962,000; (2020) 4,039,000.
Ethnic composition (1999): Bosniac 44.0%; Serb 31.0%; Croat 17.0%; other 8.0%.
Religious affiliation (1999): Sunnī Muslim 43.0%; Serbian Orthodox 30.0%; Roman Catholic 18.0%; other (mostly nonreligious) 9.0%.
Major cities (2004): Sarajevo 428,600 (urban agglomeration 602,500); Banja Luka 170,000; Zenica 139,800; Tuzla 123,500; Mostar 94,100.

Vital statistics

Birth rate per 1,000 population (2002): 9.5 (world avg. 21.3); (2001) legitimate 89.4%; illegitimate 10.6%.
Death rate per 1,000 population (2002): 8.0 (world avg. 9.1).
Natural increase rate per 1,000 population (2002): 1.5 (world avg. 12.2).
Total fertility rate (avg. births per childbearing woman; 2002): 1.4.
Marriage rate per 1,000 population (2002): 5.4.
Life expectancy at birth (2001): male 64.6 years; female 70.2 years.
Major causes of death per 100,000 population (2002): circulatory diseases 418.1; malignant neoplasms (cancers) 138.1; accidents, violence, and poisoning 25.7; digestive system diseases 21.4; respiratory diseases 21.3.

National economy

Budget (2001)[9]. Revenue: KM 1,653,100,000 (tax revenue 90.8%, nontax revenue 6.4%, grants 2.8%). Expenditures: KM 1,887,600,000 (wages and contributions 24.1%, transfers to households 22.6%, defense 15.4%).
Gross national product (2003): U.S.$6,386,000,000 (U.S.$1,540 per capita).

Structure of gross domestic product and labour force

	2002		1990	
	in value KM '000,000	% of total value	labour force[10]	% of labour force[10]
Agriculture	1,144	9.8	39,053	3.8
Manufacturing, mining	1,383	11.9	496,190	48.3
Construction	482	4.1	74,861	7.3
Public utilities	592	5.1	22,345	2.2
Transp. and commun.	1,045	9.0	68,798	6.7
Trade, restaurants	1,463	12.5	130,914	12.8
Finance, real estate	612	5.3	38,686	3.8
Pub. admin., defense	1,450	12.4	}	
Services	1,270	10.9	155,411	15.1
Other	2,210[11]	19.0[11]	}	
TOTAL	11,651	100.0	1,026,258	100.0

Production (metric tons except as noted). Agriculture, forestry, fishing (2002): corn (maize) 530,000, potatoes 310,000, wheat 297,000, cabbages 60,000, oats 55,000, plums 27,000, tobacco 3,444; livestock (number of live animals) 670,000 sheep, 440,000 cattle, 300,000 pigs; roundwood (2002) 4,226,000 cu m; fish catch (2001) 2,500. Mining (2001): iron ore (gross weight) 100,000; bauxite 75,000; kaolin 3,000; barite (concentrate) 2,000. Manufacturing (2001): cement 300,000; crude steel 80,000; pig iron 60,000. Energy production (consumption): electricity (kW-hr; 2000) 10,429,000,000 (9,365,000,000); hard coal (metric tons; 2000) 3,553,000 (3,553,000); lignite (metric tons; 2000) 5,330,000 (5,330,000); crude petroleum, none (none); petroleum products (metric tons; 2000) none (842,000); natural gas (cu m; 2000) none (276,800,000).
Public debt (external, outstanding; 2002): U.S.$2,282,000,000.
Population economically active (2001): total 1,015,169; activity rate of total population 27.4% (participation rates: ages 15–64 [1991] 35.6%; female [1990] 37.7%; unemployed [2002] 42.7%[12]).

Price index (2000 = 100)

	1998	1999	2000	2001	2002	2003
Retail price index	108.1	99.0	100.0	98.4	95.8	95.7

Household income and expenditure. Average household size (1991) 3.4; income per household: n.a.; sources of income (1990): wages 53.2%, transfers 18.2%, self-employment 12.0%, other 16.6%; expenditure: n.a.
Tourism (2002): receipts from visitors U.S.$112,000,000; expenditures by nationals abroad U.S.$49,000,000.
Land use as % of total land area (2000): in temporary crops 13.0%, in permanent crops 3.0%, in pasture 23.7%; overall forest area 44.6%.

Foreign trade

Balance of trade (current prices)

	1998	1999	2000	2001	2002	2003
KM '000,000	–4,077	–4,673	–4,317	–4,692	–5,805	–5,571
% of total	66.2%	63.0%	48.8%	49.7%	58.1%	54.2%

Imports (2003): KM 7,920,191,000. *Major import sources:* Croatia 17.3%; Germany 13.2%; Italy 9.6%; Slovenia 9.6%; Serbia and Montenegro 7.6%.
Exports (2003): KM 2,349,189,000. *Major export destinations:* Croatia 17.9%; Germany 15.4%; Serbia and Montenegro 15.3%; Italy 13.4%; Slovenia 9.7%.

Transport and communications

Transport. Railroads (2001)[13]: length 1,031 km; passenger-km 38,740,000; metric ton-km cargo 239,138,000. Roads (2001): total length 21,846 km (paved 64%). Vehicles (1996): passenger cars 96,182; trucks and buses 10,919. Air transport (2000): passenger-km 48,000,000; metric ton-km, n.a.; airports (2000) with scheduled flights 1.

Communications

Medium	date	unit	number	units per 1,000 persons
Daily newspapers	2000	circulation	563,000	152
Radio	2000	receivers	900,000	243
Television	2000	receivers	411,000	111
Telephones	2003	main lines	938,000	244
Cellular telephones	2003	subscribers	1,050,000	274
Internet	2002	users	100,000	24

Education and health

Educational attainment: n.a. *Literacy:* n.a.

Education (2002–03)

	schools[14]	teachers	students	student/ teacher ratio
Primary (age 7–14)	955	20,874	363,072	17.4
Secondary (age 15–18)	184	10,792	169,497	15.7
Higher	55	2,833	34,477	13.4

Health: physicians (2000) 5,293 (1 per 714 persons); hospital beds (1999) 13,783 (1 per 270 persons); infant mortality rate per 1,000 live births (2002) 23.5.
Food (2001): daily per capita caloric intake 2,845 (vegetable products 85%, animal products 15%); 112% of FAO recommended minimum requirement.

Military

Total active duty personnel: n.a.; EU peacekeeping troops[15] (December 2004) 7,000. *Military expenditure as percentage of GNP* (1999): 4.5% (world 2.4%); per capita expenditure U.S.$75.

[1]Government structure provided for by Dayton accords and constitutions of 1993 and 1994 is being implemented in stages since formal signing of peace accord on Dec. 14, 1995. [2]All seats are nonelective. [3]An interim currency, the marka (or "convertible mark"; KM), was introduced on June 22, 1998, to replace another interim currency, the Bosnian dinar (BD), at a rate of 1 KM to 100 BD. [4]The KM is pegged to the euro from Jan. 1, 2002. [5]The euro also circulates as semiofficial legal tender. [6]January 1. [7]Estimated figure by Republika Srpska government. [8]Excludes refugees in adjacent countries and Western Europe. [9]Combined total for the separately constructed budgets of the Federation of Bosnia and Herzegovina and Republika Srpska. [10]Excludes 28,000 workers in the private sector. [11]Taxes on products and imports less subsidies. [12]December. [13]1991–95 war destroyed much infrastructure; limited service resumed in 1998. [14]1997–98. [15]Also includes Canadian and Turkish troops.

Internet resources for further information:
- **Central Bank of Bosnia and Herzegovina http://www.cbbh.gov.ba**
- **NATO Stabilization Force http://www.nato.int/sfor**

Botswana

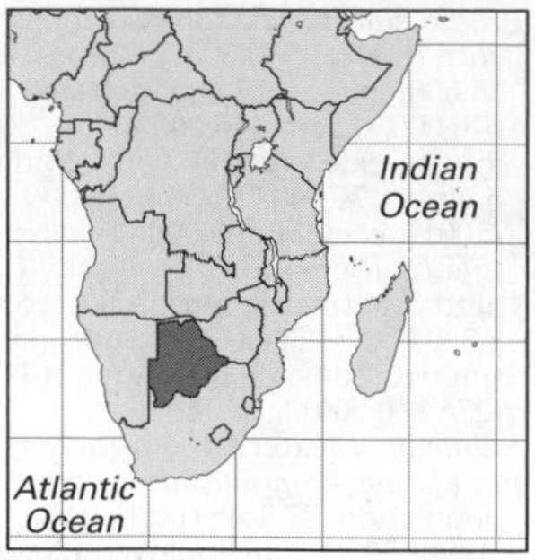

Official name: Republic of Botswana.
Form of government: multiparty republic with one legislative body[1] (National Assembly [63[2]]).
Head of state and government: President.
Capital: Gaborone.
Official language: English[3].
Official religion: none.
Monetary unit: 1 pula (P) = 100 thebe; valuation (Sept. 1, 2004) 1 U.S.$ = P 4.86; 1 £ = P 8.75.

Area and population

Districts	Capitals	area sq mi	area sq km	population 2001 census
Central	Serowe	57,039	147,730	501,381
Ghanzi	Ghanzi	45,525	117,910	33,170
Kgalagadi	Tsabong	41,290	106,940	42,049
Kgatleng	Mochudi	3,073	7,960	73,507
Kweneng	Molepolole	13,857	35,890	230,335
North East	Masunga	1,977	5,120	49,399
North West				
Chobe	Maun	8,031	20,800	18,258
Ngamiland	Maun	33,359	86,400	75,070
Okavango	Maun	8,776	22,730	49,642
South East	Ramotswa	687	1,780	60,623
Southern	Kanye	10,991	28,467	171,652
Towns				
Francistown	—	31	79	83,023
Gaborone	—	65	169	186,007
Jwaneng	—	39	100	15,179
Lobatse	—	16	42	29,689
Orapa	—	7	17	9,151
Selebi-Pikwe	—	23	60	49,849
Sowa	—	61	159	2,879
TOTAL		224,848[4]	582,356[4]	1,680,863

Demography

Population (2004): 1,661,000.
Density (2004): persons per sq mi 7.3, persons per sq km 2.9.
Urban-rural (2002): urban 49.4%; rural 50.6%.
Sex distribution (2001): male 48.40%; female 51.60%.
Age breakdown (2000): under 15, 40.6%; 15–29, 30.8%; 30–44, 15.0%; 45–59, 7.7%; 60–74, 4.3%; 75 and over, 1.6%.
Population projection: (2010) 1,505,000; (2020) 1,220,000.
Ethnic composition (2000): Tswana 66.8%; Kalanga 14.8%; Ndebele 1.7%; Herero 1.4%; San (Bushman) 1.3%; Afrikaner 1.3%.
Religious affiliation (2000): traditional beliefs 38.8%; African Christian 30.7%; Protestant 10.9%; Roman Catholic 3.7%.
Major cities (2001): Gaborone 186,007; Francistown 83,023; Molepolole 54,561; Selebi-Pikwe 49,849; Maun 43,776.

Vital statistics

Birth rate per 1,000 population (2002): 28.0 (world avg. 21.3).
Death rate per 1,000 population (2002): 26.3 (world avg. 9.1).
Natural increase rate per 1,000 population (2002): 1.7 (world avg. 12.2).
Total fertility rate (avg. births per childbearing woman; 2002): 3.6.
Marriage rate per 1,000 population: n.a.
Life expectancy at birth (2002): male 36.9 years; female 37.6 years.
Adult population (ages 15–49) *living with HIV* (2004[5]): 37.3% (world avg. 1.1%).

National economy

Budget (2002–03). Revenue: P 14,311,000,000 (tax revenue 85.7%, of which mineral royalties 52.4%, income tax 12.9%, value-added tax 8.8%; nontax revenue 13.7%, of which property income 7.4%; grants 0.6%). Expenditures: P 15,710,100,000 (education 22.6%, health 8.8%, defense 8.3%, public order 4.0%).
Public debt (external, outstanding; 2002): U.S.$463,900,000.
Population economically active (2000): total 574,160; activity rate of total population 35.1% (participation rates: ages 15–64, 58.3%; female 44.3%; unemployed 15.8%).

Price index (2000 = 100)

	1997	1998	1999	2000	2001	2002	2003
Consumer price index	80.1	85.5	92.1	100.0	106.6	115.1	125.7

Production (metric tons except as noted). Agriculture, forestry, fishing (2002): sorghum 32,298, pulses 17,500, corn (maize) 10,000; livestock (number of live animals) 2,250,000 goats, 1,700,000 cattle, 370,000 sheep; roundwood 749,515 cu m; fish catch (2001) 118. Mining and quarrying (2003): soda ash 234,520; nickel ore (metal content) 27,400; copper ore (metal content) 24,289; diamonds 30,371,000 carats. Manufacturing (value added in U.S.$'000,000; 1997): motor vehicles 33; beverages 26; bricks, cement, and tiles 20; rubber products 15. Energy production (consumption): electricity (kW-hr; 2003) 624,000,000 ([2000] 1,450,000,000); coal (metric tons; 2003) 822,780 ([2000] 971,000); crude petroleum (2001) none (n.a.); natural gas (2000) none (none).
Tourism: receipts (2002) U.S.$309,000,000; expenditures U.S.$184,000,000.
Gross national product (at current market prices; 2003): U.S.$5,911,000,000 (U.S.$3,430 per capita).

Structure of gross domestic product and labour force

	2002–03 in value P '000,000	2002–03 % of total value	2000 labour force	2000 % of labour force
Agriculture	870.7	2.4	95,283	16.6
Mining	14,185.2	39.0	11,219	2.0
Manufacturing			42,626	7.4
Construction	1,976.2	5.4	44,940	7.8
Public utilities	926.8	2.6	2,222	0.4
Transp. and commun.	1,287.8	3.6	13,800	2.4
Trade, hotels	4,177.9	11.5	73,446	12.8
Finance	4,096.3	11.3	22,068	3.8
Pub. admin., defense	5,818.0	16.0	73,217	12.8
Services	1,394.3	3.8	104,613	18.2
Other	1,604.3[6]	4.4[6]	90,728[7]	15.8[7]
TOTAL	36,337.5	100.0	574,160[4]	100.0

Household income and expenditure. Average household size (2001) 4.2; average annual income per household, n.a.; sources of income, n.a.; expenditure (2000): food and nonalcoholic beverages 30.6%, housing and energy 13.4%, alcoholic beverages and tobacco 12.3%, education 7.0%, transportation 5.7%.
Land use as % of total land area (2000): in temporary crops 0.7%, in permanent crops 0.01%, in pasture 45.2%; overall forest area 21.9%.

Foreign trade[8]

Balance of trade (current prices)

	1997	1998	1999	2000	2001	2002
P '000,000	+2,135	–816	+2,063	+3,222	+3,750	+4,814
% of total	11.4%	4.5%	9.2%	13.2%	15.1%	19.1%

Imports (2002): P 10,169,000,000 (machinery and apparatus 19.6%; food, beverages, and tobacco 13.9%; transport equipment 12.1%; chemical and rubber products 10.3%; wood and paper products 8.8%). *Major import sources* (2001): Customs Union of Southern Africa (CUSA) 77.6%; Europe 12.3%, of which U.K. 4.4%; Zimbabwe 3.2%; U.S. 1.8%.
Exports (2002): P 14,983,000,000 (diamonds 83.3%; copper-nickel matte 3.2%; textiles 2.0%; meat products 1.9%). *Major export destinations* (2001): U.K. 85.9%; CUSA 6.5%; Zimbabwe 2.6%.

Transport and communications

Transport. Railroads (2000–01): length 705 mi, 1,135 km; passenger-km 106,000,000; metric ton-km cargo 747,000. Roads (2002): total length 6,541 mi, 10,528 km (paved 55%). Vehicles (2003): passenger cars 64,681; trucks and buses 70,923. Air transport (2002)[9]: passenger-km 96,000,000; metric ton-km cargo 300,000; airports (1998) 7.

Communications

Medium	date	unit	number	units per 1,000 persons
Daily newspapers	2000	circulation	44,200	27
Radio	2000	receivers	254,000	155
Television	2000	receivers	40,900	25
Telephones	2002	main lines	142,400	83
Cellular telephones	2002	subscribers	435,000	253
Personal computers	2002	units	70,000	41
Internet	2002	users	60,000	35

Education and health

Educational attainment (1993). Percentage of population age 25 and over having: no formal schooling 34.7%; primary education 44.1%; some secondary 19.8%; postsecondary 1.4%. *Literacy* (2001): total population over age 15 literate 78.1%; males literate 75.3%; females literate 80.6%.

Education (2003)

	schools	teachers	students	student/ teacher ratio
Primary (age 6–13)	770	13,153	328,825	25.0
Secondary (age 14–18)	275	9,597	205,093	21.4
Teacher training	...	...	2,899	...
Higher	1	697[10]	12,286	...

Health (2003): physicians 510 (1 per 3,261 persons); hospital beds 3,088 (1 per 539 persons); infant mortality rate per 1,000 live births (2002) 64.7.
Food (2001): daily per capita caloric intake 2,292 (vegetable products 83%, animal products 17%); 99% of FAO recommended minimum requirement.

Military

Total active duty personnel (2003): 9,000 (army 94.4%, navy, none [land locked], air force 5.6%). *Military expenditure as percentage of GNP* (1999): 4.7% (world 2.4%); per capita expenditure U.S.$142.

[1]In addition, the House of Chiefs, a 15-member body consisting of chiefs, subchiefs, and associated members, serves in an advisory capacity to the government. [2]Includes 4 specially elected members. [3]Tswana is the national language. [4]Detail does not add to total given because of rounding. [5]Beginning of year. [6]Imputed bank service charge. [7]Unemployed. [8]Imports c.i.f.; exports f.o.b. [9]Air Botswana only. [10]1999.

Internet resources for further information:
- **Central Statistical Office http://www.cso.gov.bw**
- **Bank of Botswana http://www.bankofbotswana.bw**

Brazil

Official name: República Federativa do Brasil (Federative Republic of Brazil).
Form of government: multiparty federal republic with 2 legislative houses (Federal Senate [81]; Chamber of Deputies [513]).
Chief of state and government: President.
Capital: Brasília.
Official language: Portuguese.
Official religion: none.
Monetary unit: 1 real[1] (R$; plural reais) = 100 centavos; valuation (Sept. 1, 2004) 1 U.S.$ = 2.93 reais; 1 £ = 5.28 reais.

Area and population

		area		population
States	Capitals	sq mi	sq km	2003 estimate
Acre	Rio Branco	58,912	152,581	600,595
Alagoas	Maceió	10,721	27,768	2,917,664
Amapá	Macapá	55,141	142,815	534,835
Amazonas	Manaus	606,468	1,570,746	3,031,068
Bahia	Salvador	218,029	564,693	13,435,612
Ceará	Fortaleza	57,462	148,826	7,758,441
Espírito Santo	Vitória	17,791	46,078	3,250,219
Goiás	Goiânia	131,308	340,087	5,306,459
Maranhão	São Luís	128,179	331,983	5,873,655
Mato Grosso	Cuiabá	348,788	903,358	2,651,335
Mato Grosso do Sul	Campo Grande	137,887	357,125	2,169,688
Minas Gerais	Belo Horizonte	226,460	586,528	18,553,312
Pará	Belém	481,736	1,247,690	6,574,993
Paraíba	João Pessoa	21,792	56,440	3,518,595
Paraná	Curitiba	76,956	199,315	9,906,866
Pernambuco	Recife	37,958	98,312	8,161,862
Piauí	Teresina	97,116	251,529	2,923,725
Rio de Janeiro	Rio de Janeiro	16,871	43,696	14,879,118
Rio Grande do Norte	Natal	20,385	52,797	2,888,058
Rio Grande do Sul	Porto Alegre	108,784	281,749	10,510,992
Rondônia	Porto Velho	91,729	237,576	1,455,907
Roraima	Boa Vista	86,602	224,299	357,302
Santa Catarina	Florianópolis	36,813	95,346	5,607,233
São Paulo	São Paulo	95,834	248,209	38,709,320
Sergipe	Aracaju	8,459	21,910	1,874,613
Tocantins	Palmas	107,190	277,621	1,230,181
Federal District				
Distrito Federal	Brasília	2,240	5,802	2,189,789
TOTAL		3,287,612[2]	8,514,877[2, 3]	176,871,437

Demography

Population (2004): 180,542,000.
Density (2004): persons per sq mi 54.9, persons per sq km 21.2.
Urban-rural (2000): urban 81.2%; rural 18.8%.
Sex distribution (2000): male 49.21%; female 50.79%.
Age breakdown (2000): under 15, 29.6%; 15–29, 28.2%; 30–44, 21.1%; 45–59, 12.5%; 60–74, 6.5%; 75 and over, 2.1%.
Population projection: (2010) 192,879,000; (2020) 209,793,000.
Doubling time: 55 years.
Racial composition (1999)[4]: white 54.0%; mulatto and mestizo 39.9%; black and black/Amerindian 5.4%; Asian 0.5%; Amerindian 0.2%.
Religious affiliation (1995)[5]: Catholic 74.3%[6], of which Roman Catholic 72.3%[6]; Protestant 23.2%, of which Pentecostal 19.1%; other Christian 0.9%; New-Religionist 0.3%; Buddhist 0.3%; Jewish 0.2%; Muslim 0.1%; other 0.7%.
Major cities[7] *and metropolitan areas* (2003): São Paulo 10,041,500 (18,628,444); Rio de Janeiro 5,974,100 (11,226,729); Salvador 2,555,400 (3,183,327); Belo Horizonte 2,305,800 (5,100,359); Fortaleza 2,256,200 (3,164,225); Brasília 2,094,100 (3,199,451); Curitiba 1,671,200 (2,930,772); Manaus 1,517,500 (1,527,314); Recife 1,461,300 (3,466,214); Porto Alegre 1,353,300 (3,815,447); Belém 1,333,500 (1,916,982); Goiânia 1,138,600 (1,766,588); Guarulhos 1,135,500[8]; Campinas 990,100 (2,483,594).

Other principal cities[7] (2003)

	population		population		population
Aracaju	479,800	Maceió	847,700	São Gonçalo	925,400[8]
Campo Grande	697,800	Natal	744,800	São Jose dos Campos	562,200
Contagem	560,300[9]	Nova Iguaçu	792,200[10]	São Luís	889,100
Cuiabá	501,000	Osasco	678,600[8]	Sorocaba	521,500
Duque de Caxias	805,400[10]	Ribeirão Preto	525,500	Teresina	711,700
Jaboatão	596,900[11]	Santo André	659,300[8]	Uberlândia	529,300
João Pessoa	628,800	São Bernardo do Campo	732,200[8]		
Juiz de Fora	474,600				

Families (1999). Average family size 3.3; (1996) 1–2 persons 25.2%, 3 persons 20.3%, 4 persons 22.2%, 5–6 persons 23.3%, 7 or more persons 9.0%.
Number of emigrants/immigrants (1986–96): 2,355,057/169,303. Emigrants' most popular destinations in order of preference are the United States, Japan, and the United Kingdom.

Vital statistics

Birth rate per 1,000 population (2003): 19.5 (world avg. 21.3).
Death rate per 1,000 population (2003): 6.7 (world avg. 9.1).
Natural increase rate per 1,000 population (2003): 12.8 (world avg. 12.2).
Total fertility rate (avg. births per childbearing woman; 2003): 2.2.
Marriage rate per 1,000 population (2002): 4.1.
Divorce rate per 1,000 population (2001): 0.7.
Life expectancy at birth (2003): male 67.2 years; female 75.3 years.
Major causes of death per 100,000 population (1998; based on incomplete registration of deaths): diseases of the circulatory system 153.2; accidents, murder, and violence 70.3; malignant neoplasms (cancers) 66.2; diseases of the respiratory system 55.0; infectious and parasitic diseases 29.1; diseases of the digestive system 24.3; endocrine, metabolic, and nutritional disorders 23.8; ill-defined conditions 82.8.

Social indicators

Educational attainment (1996). Percentage of population age 25 and over having: no formal schooling or less than one year of primary education 17.7%; lower primary only 19.1%; upper primary 30.7%; complete primary to some secondary 11.6%; complete secondary to some higher 13.9%; complete higher 6.2%; unknown 0.8%.

Distribution of income (1998)

percentage of national income by decile/quintile

1	2	3	4	5	6	7	8	9	10 (highest)
0.7	1.5	—5.4—		—10.1—		—18.3—		16.1	48.0

Quality of working life. Proportion of employed population receiving minimum wage (2002): 53.5%. Number and percentage of children (age 5–17) working: 5,400,000 (12.6% of age group).
Access to services (1999)[4]. Proportion of households having access to: electricity 94.8%, of which urban households having access 99.2%, rural households having access 75.4%; safe public (piped) water supply 79.8%, of which urban households having access 92.3%, rural households having access 24.9%; public (piped) sewage system 43.6%, of which urban households having access 52.5%, rural households having access 4.5%; no sewage disposal 8.5%, of which urban households having no disposal 2.9%, rural households having no disposal 32.9%.
Social participation. Voting is mandatory for national elections; abstention is punishable by a fine. Trade union membership in total workforce (2001): 19,500,000. Practicing Roman Catholic population in total affiliated Roman Catholic population (2000): large cities 10–15%; towns and rural areas 60–70%.
Social deviance. Annual murder rate per 100,000 population (1996): Brazil 23, Rio de Janeiro only 69, São Paulo only 55.
Leisure. Favourite leisure activities include: playing soccer, dancing, rehearsing all year in neighbourhood samba groups for celebrations of Carnival, and competing in water sports, volleyball, and basketball.
Material well-being (1999)[4]. Households possessing: television receiver 87.7%, of which urban 93.2%, rural 63.8%; refrigerator 82.8%, of which urban 89.7%, rural 52.5%; washing machine 32.8%, of which urban 38.0%, rural 10.0%.

National economy

Gross national product (at current market prices; 2003): U.S.$478,922,000,000 (U.S.$2,710 per capita).

Structure of gross domestic product and labour force

	2000			
	in value R$'000,000	% of total value	labour force[4, 12]	% of labour force
Agriculture	74,426	6.8	12,119,389	15.6
Mining	24,270	2.2	234,869	0.3
Public utilities	34,071	3.2	328,918	0.4
Manufacturing	216,388	19.9	8,757,040	11.3
Construction	88,227	8.1	4,568,396	5.9
Transportation and communications	60,084	5.5	3,318,814	4.3
Trade[13]	69,986	6.4	13,970,811	18.0
Finance, real estate	176,888	16.3	4,587,510	5.9
Pub. admin., defense	159,443	14.7	3,522,868	4.5
Services	224,133	20.6	14,221,277	18.4
Other	–41,216[14]	–3.8[14]	11,837,581[15]	15.3[15]
TOTAL	1,086,700	100.0[3]	77,467,473	100.0[3]

Budget (1998). Revenue R$237,187,000,000 (current revenue 95.8%, of which social contributions 32.6%, sales tax 20.3%, tax on income and profit 19.4%, nontax revenue 16.3%; capital revenue 4.2%). Expenditures: R$245,032,-100,000 (social security and welfare 47.3%; interest on debt 14.3%; defense and public order 6.6%; health 6.2%; education 6.1%; economic affairs 4.8%; other 14.7%).
Public debt (external, outstanding; 2002): U.S.$96,565,000,000.
Production ('000 metric tons except as noted). Agriculture, forestry, fishing (2002): sugarcane 360,566, soybeans 41,903, corn (maize) 35,479, cassava 23,108, oranges 18,694, rice 10,489, bananas 6,369, tomatoes 3,518, dry beans 3,017, wheat 2,926, potatoes 2,865, coconuts 2,695, coffee 2,390, seed cotton 2,172, cashew apples 1,600, papayas 1,500, pineapples 1,469, onions 1,132, grapes 1,099, apples 858, sorghum 814, tobacco 654, lemons and limes 580, maté 535, oil palm fruit 450, peanuts (groundnuts) 192, cashews 184, sisal 177, cacao beans 172, garlic 113, natural rubber 96, Brazil nuts 26; livestock (number of live animals) 176,000,000 cattle, 30,000,000 pigs, 15,000,000 sheep, 5,900,000 horses; roundwood (2002) 237,467,063 cu m, of which fuelwood 134,473,063 cu m, sawlogs and veneer logs 49,290,000 cu m, pulpwood 45,860,000 cu m; fish catch (2001) 847, of which freshwater fishes 299. Mining and quarrying (value of export production in U.S.$'000,000; 1998): iron ore 3,066; ferroniobium 242; silicon 135; bauxite 122; kaolin (clay) 106; ferrosilicon 101; granite (1996) 97; copper 89; manganese 52; nickel 52; gold production for both domestic use and export 1,594,000 troy oz; Brazil is also a world-leading producer of high-quality grade quartz and tantalum. Manufacturing (value added in U.S.$'000,000; 2001): food products 15,387; petroleum products 11,046; transport equipment 10,632, of which cars 8,103;

electrical machinery 7,248; iron, steel, and nonferrous metals 7,209; industrial chemicals 5,457; paper and paper products 4,740; printing and publishing 4,304; plastics and rubber products 4,201.

Land use as % of total land area (2000): in temporary crops 6.8%, in permanent crops 0.9%, in pasture 23.2%; overall forest area 64.3%.

Manufacturing enterprises (2001)

	number of employees	wages of employers as a % of avg. of all mfg. wages	value added at factor cost (in U.S.$'000,000)
Food products	894,457	67.1	15,387
Petroleum products	23,385	494.9	11,046
Transport equipment	323,485	184.9	10,632
Nonelectrical machinery and apparatus	368,050	132.8	8,855
Paints, soaps, pharmaceuticals, and related products	226,848	181.6	8,016
Electrical machinery and apparatus	216,030	160.5	7,248
Industrial chemicals	72,088	229.8	5,457
Iron and steel	97,513	184.9	5,151
Beverages	137,197	106.1	5,115
Paper and paper products	138,268	131.8	4,740
Clothing and footwear	762,034	44.4	4,727
Fabricated metal products	315,417	87.8	4,310
Printing and publishing	194,903	125.4	4,304
Bricks, tiles, cement, and related products	262,184	67.3	4,042
Plastics	210,099	90.3	2,976
Textiles	244,882	71.5	2,831
Nonferrous base metals	40,262	165.5	2,058
Furniture	193,388	56.2	1,479
Rubber products	69,630	117.2	1,225

Population economically active (2000)[4, 12]: total 77,467,473; activity rate of total population 45.6% (participation rates: ages 15–59, 73.8%; female [1999] 40.2%; unemployed [July 2004] 11.2%).

Price and earnings indexes (2000 = 100)

	1997	1998	1999	2000	2001	2002	2003
Consumer price index	86.3	89.1	93.4	100.0	106.8	115.9	132.9
Monthly earnings index	79.4	85.7	90.7	100.0	...	...	...

Tourism (2002): receipts from visitors U.S.$3,120,000,000; expenditures by nationals abroad U.S.$2,380,000,000.

Retail trade enterprises (1996)

	no. of businesses	total no. of employees	annual wage as a % of all trade wages	annual values of sales in R$'000,000[1]
General merchandise stores (including food products)	10,382	437,452	131.2	35,766
Vehicles, new and used	9,348	202,892	229.9	30,926
Gas stations	20,388	210,250	124.7	23,199
Electronics, kitchen equipment, musical instruments	18,245	158,755	143.7	14,855
Metal products, lumber, glass, and construction materials	81,303	386,285	90.1	14,047
Vehicles, parts	55,534	252,731	110.6	10,881
Pharmaceutical and cosmetic products	50,778	240,633	94.2	9,658
Clothing and apparel	128,908	428,150	76.4	9,023
Food, beverages, and tobacco	135,672	378,102	60.7	6,900

Households. Average household size (2002) 3.8.

Family income and expenditure. Average family size (1999) 3.3[4]; annual income per family (1999) R$10,500 (U.S.$5,900[4]); sources of income, n.a.; expenditure (1995–96)[16]: housing, energy, and household furnishings 28.8%, food and beverages 23.4%, transportation and communications 13.8%, health care 9.2%, education and recreation 8.4%.

Financial aggregates[17]

	1998	1999	2000	2001	2002	2003
Exchange rate, reais per:						
U.S. dollar	1.209	1.789	1.955	2.320	3.533	2.888
£	2.011	2.892	2.917	3.365	2.355	1.618
SDR	1.702	2.455	2.547	2.916	4.804	4.292
International reserves (U.S.$)						
Total (excl. gold; '000,000)	42,580	34,796	32,488	35,740	37,683	49,111
SDRs ('000,000)	2	10	—	11	275	2
Reserve pos. in IMF ('000,000)	—	—	—	—	—	—
Foreign exchange ('000,000)	42,578	34,786	32,488	35,729	37,409	49,108
Gold ('000,000 fine troy oz)	4.60	3.17	1.89	0.46	0.44	0.45
% world reserves	0.48	0.44	0.20	0.05	0.05	0.05
Interest and prices						
Central bank discount (%)	39.41	21.37	18.52	21.43	18.52	23.92
Govt. bond yield (%)	...	...	...	...	...	...
Industrial share prices	...	...	...	...	...	...
Balance of payments (U.S.$'000,000)						
Balance of visible trade	–6,603	–1,260	–696	+2,645	+13,143	+24,831
Imports, f.o.b.	57,739	49,272	55,783	55,579	47,219	48,253
Exports, f.o.b.	51,136	48,012	55,087	58,224	60,362	73,084
Balance of invisibles	–27,226	–24,140	–23,936	–25,853	–20,829	...
Balance of payments, current account	–33,829	–25,400	–24,632	–23,208	–7,696	...

Energy production (consumption): electricity (kW-hr; 2000) 349,000,000,000 (393,000,000,000); coal (metric tons; 2001) 6,600,000 ([2000] 20,270,000); crude petroleum (barrels; 2002) 536,000,000 ([2000] 583,000,000); petroleum products (metric tons; 2000) 67,910,000 (71,664,000); natural gas (cu m; 2002) 15,517,000,000 ([2000] 7,938,000,000).

Foreign trade[18]

Balance of trade (current prices)

	1998	1999	2000	2001	2002	2003
U.S.$'000,000	–6,623	–1,284	–753	+2,642	+13,121	+24,831
% of total	6.1%	1.4%	0.7%	2.3%	12.2%	20.5%

Imports (2001): U.S.$55,581,000,000 (machinery and apparatus 43.0%; chemicals and chemical products 18.1%; mineral fuels 14.4%; motor vehicles 9.5%; food products 5.0%). *Major import sources* (2002): United States 21.8%; Argentina 10.1%; Germany 9.3%; Japan 5.0%; Italy 3.7%; France 3.7%; China 3.3%; U.K. 2.8%; Algeria 2.3%; South Korea 2.3%.

Exports (2001): U.S.$58,223,000,000 (food products 20.0%, of which meat 5.0%, sugar 4.1%, animal food 3.7%, coffee 3.0%; transportation equipment 13.6%, of which road vehicles 7.4%; machinery and apparatus 13.1%; iron and steel 5.5%; chemicals and chemical products 5.4%; iron ore and concentrates 5.0%; soybeans 4.7%). *Major export destinations* (2002): United States 25.4%; The Netherlands 5.3%; Germany 4.2%; China 4.2%; Argentina 3.9%; Mexico 3.9%; Japan 3.5%; Belgium 3.1%; United Kingdom 2.9%; France 2.5%.

Transport and communications

Transport. Railroads (2000)[19]: route length 18,196 mi, 29,283 km; passenger-mi 3,636,000,000, passenger-km 5,852,000,000; short ton-mi cargo 106,077,000,000, metric ton-km cargo 154,870,000,000. Roads (2000): total length 1,071,816 mi, 1,724,924 km (paved 10%). Vehicles (2001): passenger cars 23,241,966; trucks and buses 3,897,140. Air transport (2002)[20]: passenger-mi 25,390,000,000, passenger-km 40,861,000,000; short ton-mi cargo 909,000,000, metric ton-km cargo 1,327,000,000; airports (1995) with scheduled flights 139.

Communications

Medium	date	unit	number	units per 1,000 persons
Daily newspapers	2000	circulation	7,390,000	43
Radio	2000	receivers	74,400,000	433
Television	2000	receivers	58,900,000	343
Telephones	2002	main lines	38,810,000	223
Cellular telephones	2003	subscribers	46,373,000	264
Personal computers	2002	units	13,000,000	75
Internet	2002	users	14,300,000	82

Education and health

Literacy (2000): total population age 15 and over literate 86.4%.

Education (2002)

	schools	teachers	students	student/ teacher ratio
Primary (age 7–14)	172,508	1,581,044	35,150,362	22.2
Secondary (age 15–17)	21,304	468,310	8,710,584	18.6
Higher	1,180	197,712	2,694,245	13.6

Health: physicians (1999) 429,808 (1 per 395 persons); hospital beds (1999) 484,945 (1 per 343 persons); infant mortality rate per 1,000 live births (2002) 31.8.

Food (2001): daily per capita caloric intake 3,002 (vegetable products 80%, animal products 20%); 126% of FAO recommended minimum requirement.

Military

Total active duty personnel (2003): 287,600 (army 65.7%, navy 16.9%, air force 17.4%). *Military expenditure as percentage of GNP* (1999): 1.9% (world 2.4%); per capita expenditure U.S.$59.

[1]The real (R$) replaced the cruzeiro real (CR$) on July 1, 1994, at a rate of 2,750 cruzeiros reais to 1 real (a rate par to the U.S.$ on that date). [2]Total area including inland water per survey of 2002. [3]Detail does not add to total given because of rounding. [4]Excludes rural population of Acre, Amapá, Amazonas, Pará, Rondônia, and Roraima. [5]Christian data include nominal Christians. [6]Includes syncretic Afro-Catholic cults having Spiritist beliefs and rituals. [7]Populations are for *municípios,* which may include adjacent urban or rural districts. [8]Within São Paulo metropolitan area. [9]Within Belo Horizonte metropolitan area. [10]Within Rio de Janeiro metropolitan area. [11]Within Recife metropolitan area. [12]Excludes members of armed forces in barracks. [13]Includes restaurants and hotels. [14]Less imputed bank service charges. [15]Unemployed. [16]Based on survey of 11 metropolitan areas only. [17]End-of-period figures. [18]Imports f.o.b. [19]Includes suburban services. [20]TAM, VARIG, and VASP airlines only.

Internet resources for further information:

- **IBGE: Instituto Brasileiro de Geografia e Estatística**
  http://www.ibge.gov.br/english/default.php
- **Central Bank of Brazil: Economic Data**
  http://www.bcb.gov.br/defaulti.htm

Brunei

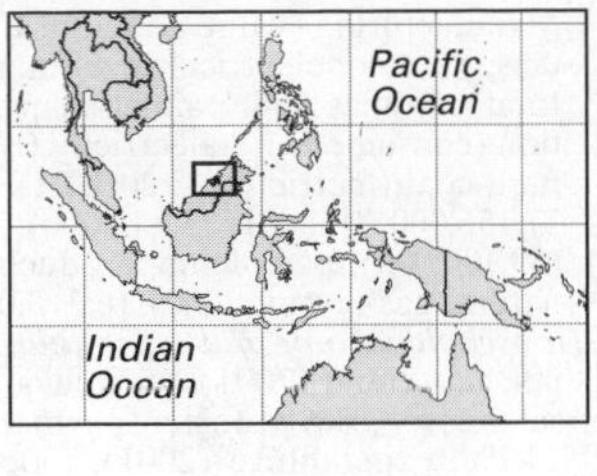

Official name: Negara Brunei Darussalam (State of Brunei, Abode of Peace).
Form of government: monarchy (sultanate) with one advisory body (Legislative Council [21][1]).
Head of state and government: Sultan.
Capital: Bandar Seri Begawan.
Official language: Malay[2].
Official religion: Islam.
Monetary unit: 1 Brunei dollar (B$) = 100 cents; valuation (Sept. 1, 2004) 1 U.S.$ = B$1.71; 1 £ = B$3.08.

Area and population

		area		population
				2001
Districts	Capitals	sq mi	sq km	census
Belait	Kuala Belait	1,052	2,724	55,602
Brunei and Muara	Bandar Seri Begawan	220	571	230,030
Temburong	Bangar	504	1,304	8,563
Tutong	Tutong	450	1,166	38,649
TOTAL		2,226	5,765	332,844

Demography

Population (2004): 351,000.
Density (2004): persons per sq mi 157.7, persons per sq km 60.9.
Urban-rural (2002): urban 73.0%; rural 27.0%.
Sex distribution (2002): male 52.35%; female 47.65%.
Age breakdown (2002): under 15, 30.2%; 15–29, 27.0%; 30–44, 25.2%; 45–59, 13.2%; 60–74, 3.6%; 75 and over, 0.8%.
Population projection: (2010) 393,000; (2020) 458,000.
Doubling time: 42 years.
Ethnic composition (2001): Malay 66.8%; Chinese 11.1%; other indigenous 3.5%; other 18.6%.
Religious affiliation (2000): Muslim 64.4%; traditional beliefs 11.2%; Buddhist 9.1%; Christian 7.7%; other religions and nonreligious 7.6%.
Major cities: Bandar Seri Begawan (2001) 27,285 (urban agglomeration [2002] 74,700); Kuala Belait (2002) 27,200; Seria (2002) 23,200.

Vital statistics

Birth rate per 1,000 population (2002): 20.1 (world avg. 21.3).
Death rate per 1,000 population (2002): 3.4 (world avg. 9.1).
Natural increase rate per 1,000 population (2002): 16.7 (world avg. 12.2).
Total fertility rate (avg. births per childbearing woman; 2002): 2.4.
Marriage rate per 1,000 population (2000): 6.7.
Divorce rate per 1,000 population (2000): 1.1.
Life expectancy at birth (2002): male 71.7 years; female 76.6 years.
Major causes of death per 100,000 population (1999): cardiovascular disease 70.0; malignant neoplasms (cancers) 50.0; diseases of the respiratory system 28.2; accidents, poisoning, and violence 15.5; congenital anomalies 7.6.

National economy

Budget (2000). Revenue: B$5,084,000,000 (nontax revenue 52.1%, of which government property income 39.7%, commercial receipts 12.4%; tax revenue 47.6%). Expenditures: B$4,196,000,000 (current expenditure 83.5%; capital expenditure 9.1%; other 7.4%).
Public debt (external, outstanding; 1999): U.S.$902,000,000.
Tourism (1998): receipts from visitors U.S.$37,000,000; expenditures by nationals abroad U.S.$1,000,000.
Production (metric tons except as noted). Agriculture, forestry, fishing (2002): vegetables and melons 9,800, fruits (excluding melons) 4,150, cassava 1,800, pineapples 900, bananas 640, rice 360; livestock (number of live animals) 7,000 buffalo, 6,500 pigs, 12,500,000 chickens; roundwood (2001) 228,550 cu m; fish catch (2001) 1,591. Mining and quarrying: other than petroleum and natural gas, none except sand and gravel for construction. Manufacturing (2003): gasoline 1,717,000 barrels; kerosene 634,000 barrels; distillate fuel oils 1,195 barrels. Energy production (consumption): electricity (kW-hr; 2000) 2,434,000,000 (2,434,000,000); coal, none (none); crude petroleum (barrels; 2003) 75,600,000 ([2000] 1,700,000); petroleum products (metric tons; 2000) 985,000 (987,000); natural gas (cu m; 2003) 12,000,000,000 ([2001] 1,371,000,000).
Gross national product (at current market prices; 2001): U.S.$8,169,000,000 (U.S.$24,630 per capita).

Structure of gross domestic product and labour force

	2001		1995	
	in value B$'000,000	% of total value	labour force	% of labour force
Agriculture	210.0	2.6	1,976	1.7
Mining / Manufacturing	3,140.9	41.2	9,959[3]	8.8[3]
Construction	425.2	5.6	38,128	33.5
Public utilities	65.2	0.9	3	3
Transportation and communications	434.4	5.7	4,320	3.8
Trade	705.0	9.3	11,821	10.4
Finance	701.0	9.2	5,149	4.5
Services	2,138.7	28.1	42,333[4]	37.3[4]
Other	−201.2[5]	−2.6[5]	...	...
TOTAL	7,619.2	100.0	113,686	100.0

Population economically active (2001): total 145,600; activity rate of total population 43.9% (participation rates: ages 15–64, 65.9%; female 41.4%; unemployed [2002] 4.6%).

Price index (2000 = 100)

	1998	1999	2000	2001	2002	2003
Consumer price index	98.8	98.7	100.0	100.6	98.3	98.6

Household income and expenditure. Average household size (2000) 6.1; income per household: n.a.; sources of income: n.a.; expenditure (1990): food 38.7%, transportation and communications 19.9%, housing 18.6%, clothing 6.4%, other 16.4%.
Land use as % of total land area (2000): in temporary crops 0.6%, in permanent crops 0.8%, in pasture 1.1%; overall forest area 83.9%.

Foreign trade[6]

Balance of trade (current prices)

	1996	1997	1998	1999	2000	2001
B$'000,000	+153	+819	+856	+2,074	+4,826	+4,446
% of total	2.1%	11.5%	15.5%	31.5%	55.8%	51.7%

Imports (2001): B$2,076,000,000 (basic manufactures 30.7%, machinery and transport equipment 30.3%, food and live animals 16.4%, chemicals and chemical products 7.6%). *Major import sources:* Singapore 23.4%; Malaysia 22.0%; United States 9.2%; Japan 6.4%; Hong Kong 5.0%.
Exports (2001): B$6,522,000,000 ([1999] crude petroleum and partly refined petroleum 43.4%, natural gas 37.7%, petroleum products 2.2%). *Major export destinations* (2001): Japan 46.0%; South Korea 11.9%; Thailand 11.8%; Singapore 8.4%; United States 7.5%.

Transport and communications

Transport. Railroads[7]: length 12 mi, 19 km. Roads (2000): total length 2,033 mi, 3,272 km (paved 73%). Vehicles (2001): passenger cars 188,720; trucks and buses 17,828. Air transport (2003)[8]: passenger-mi 2,229,000,000, passenger-km 3,588,000,000; short ton-mi cargo 101,853,000, metric ton-km cargo 148,703,000; airports (2001) with scheduled flights 1.

Communications

Medium	date	unit	number	units per 1,000 persons
Daily newspapers	2002	circulation	72,000	213
Radio	2000	receivers	362,712	1,120
Television	2000	receivers	216,223	668
Telephones	2002	main lines	90,000	250
Cellular telephones	2001	subscribers	137,000	401
Personal computers	2002	units	27,000	77
Internet	2001	users	35,000	102

Education and health

Educational attainment (1991). Percentage of population age 25 and over having: no formal schooling 17.0%; primary education 43.3%; secondary 26.3%; postsecondary and higher 12.9%; not stated 0.5%. *Literacy* (2000): percentage of total population age 15 and over literate 91.5%; males literate 95.0%; females literate 88.0%.

Education (2001)

	schools	teachers	students	student/ teacher ratio
Primary (age 5–11)[9]	186	3,806	59,369	15.6
Secondary (age 12–20)	40	2,891	34,809	12.0
Voc., teacher tr.	6	505	2,509	5.0
Higher	3	403	3,885	9.6

Health (2001): physicians 371 (1 per 929 persons); hospital beds 908 (1 per 379 persons); infant mortality rate per 1,000 live births (2002) 14.0.
Food (2001): daily per capita caloric intake 2,814 (vegetable products 80%, animal products 20%); 120% of FAO recommended minimum requirement.

Military

Total active duty personnel (2003): 7,000 (army 70.0%, navy 14.3%, air force 15.7%). British troops (a Gurkha batallion): 1,100. *Military expenditure as percentage of GNP* (1999): 4.0% (world 2.4%); per capita expenditure U.S.$897.

[1]Legislative Council (suspended from 1984) reinstated September 2004; all seats are nonelected. [2]All official documents that must be published by law in Malay are also required to be issued in an official English version. [3]Mining and Manufacturing includes Public utilities. [4]Includes 38,068 government employees. [5]Less imputed bank service charge. [6]Imports c.i.f.; exports f.o.b. [7]Privately owned. [8]Royal Brunei Airlines. [9]Includes preprimary.

Internet resources for further information:

- **The Government of Brunei Darussalam http://www.brunei.gov.bn/index.htm**

Bulgaria

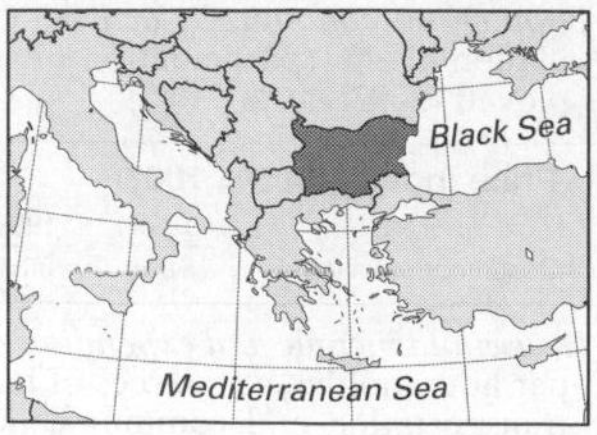

Official name: Republika Bŭlgaria (Republic of Bulgaria).
Form of government: unitary multiparty republic with one legislative body (National Assembly [240]).
Chief of state: President.
Head of government: Prime Minister.
Capital: Sofia.
Official language: Bulgarian.
Official religion: none[1].
Monetary unit: 1 lev (Lw; leva)[2] = 100 stotinki; valuation (Sept. 1, 2004) 1 U.S.$ = 1.61 leva; 1 £ = 2.90 leva.

Area and population

Districts	area sq km	population 2002[3] estimate	Districts	area sq km	population 2002[3] estimate
Blagoevgrad	6,449	339,790	Ruse	2,803	266,894
Burgas	7,748	422,458	Shumen	3,390	203,383
Dobrich	4,720	213,325	Silistra	2,846	140,784
Gabrovo	2,023	142,850	Sliven	3,544	217,226
Khaskovo	5,533	275,183	Smolyan	3,193	138,802
Kurdzhali	3,209	163,341	Sofiya[4]	7,062	270,459
Kyustendil	3,052	160,702	Sofiya-Grad[5]	1,349	1,178,579
Lovech	4,129	167,931	Stara Zagora	5,151	368,771
Montana	3,636	179,741	Targovishte	2,559	140,860
Pazardzhik	4,457	308,719	Varna	3,819	461,174
Pernik	2,394	148,251	Veliko Turnovo	4,662	291,121
Pleven	4,335	325,531	Vidin	3,033	128,050
Plovdiv	5,973	714,779	Vratsa	3,938	223,358
Razgrad	2,640	144,818	Yambol	3,355	154,215
			TOTAL	111,002	7,891,095

Demography

Population (2004): 7,715,000.
Density (2004): persons per sq mi 180.0, persons per sq km 69.5.
Urban-rural (2001): urban 69.0%; rural 31.0%.
Sex distribution (2002): male 48.68%; female 51.32%.
Age breakdown (2002)[3]: under 15, 15.0%; 15–29, 21.3%; 30–44, 20.4%; 45–59, 20.9%; 60–74, 16.1%; 75 and over, 6.3%.
Population projection: (2010) 7,353,000; (2020) 6,781,000.
Ethnic composition (2001): Bulgarian 83.9%; Turkish 9.4%; Rom (Gypsy) 4.7%; other 2.0%.
Religious affiliation (2001): Christian 83.7%, of which Bulgarian Orthodox *c.* 72%, independent Christian *c.* 7%; Sunnī Muslim 12.2%; other/nonreligious 4.1%.
Major cities (2001): Sofia 1,099,507; Plovdiv 340,122; Varna 313,408; Burgas 193,316; Ruse 162,128.

Vital statistics

Birth rate per 1,000 population (2001): 8.6 (world avg. 21.3).
Death rate per 1,000 population (2001): 14.2 (world avg. 9.1).
Natural increase rate per 1,000 population (2001): –5.6 (world avg. 12.2).
Total fertility rate (avg. births per childbearing woman; 2001): 1.2.
Life expectancy at birth (2001): male 68.5 years; female 75.2 years.
Major causes of death per 100,000 population (2001): diseases of the circulatory system 944.2; malignant neoplasms (cancers) 195.7; accidents, poisoning, and violence 55.1; diseases of the respiratory system 46.6.

National economy

Budget (2003). Revenue: 13,222,000,000 leva (tax revenue 77.7%, of which value-added tax 23.5%, social insurance 21.2%, income and profit tax 16.8%; nontax revenue 20.0%; grants 2.3%). Expenditures: 13,221,000,000 leva (social insurance 35.0%; capital expenditure 10.3%; health 9.5%; administration and defense 8.4%; interest on debt 5.5%).
Public debt (external, outstanding; 2002): U.S.$7,474,000,000.
Gross national product (2003): U.S.$16,639,000,000 (U.S.$2,130 per capita).

Structure of gross domestic product and labour force

	2002 in value '000,000 leva	% of total value	labour force	% of labour force
Agriculture, forestry, and fishing	3,557	11.0	767,134	21.3
Manufacturing, mining	5,284	16.3	648,842	18.0
Construction	1,264	3.9	128,558	3.6
Transp. and commun.	4,458	13.8	221,870	6.2
Trade	2,332	7.2	470,205	13.1
Public utilities, housing	1,381	4.3	58,462	1.6
Finance, real estate	923	2.9	168,662	4.7
Pub. admin., defense	9,834[6]	30.4[6]	98,939	2.7
Services			429,608	12.0
Other	3,291[7]	10.2[7]	602,484[8]	16.8[8]
TOTAL	32,324	100.0	3,594,764	100.0

Production (metric tons except as noted). Agriculture, forestry, fishing (2002): wheat 4,888,648, corn (maize) 1,206,000, barley 1,187,859, sunflower seeds 523,000, grapes 400,000, tomatoes 390,000; livestock (number of live animals) 2,418,490 sheep, 1,013,740 pigs, 898,559 goats, 634,540 cattle; roundwood (2002) 4,833,000 cu m; fish catch (2001) 8,100. Mining and quarrying (2000): iron (metal content) 178,000; copper (metal content) 107,000; gold 2,347 kg. Manufacturing (value added in U.S.$'000,000; 2001): refined petroleum products, n.a.; nonelectrical machinery and apparatus 188; wearing apparel 168; food products 158; paints, soaps, and pharmaceuticals 122. Energy production (consumption): electricity (kW-hr; 2001) 43,968,000,000 (43,968,000,000); hard coal (metric tons; 2000) 118,000 (3,379,000); lignite (metric tons; 2003) 27,156,000 ([2000] 25,844,000); crude petroleum (barrels; 2000) 308,000 (39,100,000); petroleum products (metric tons; 2000) 4,459,000 (3,064,000); natural gas (cu m; 2000) 16,313,000 (3,883,000,000).
Household income and expenditure. Average household size (2001) 3.0; income per household (2001) 4,532 leva (U.S.$2,280); sources of income: wages and salaries 37.8%, transfer payments 24.4%, self-employment in agriculture 14.2%; expenditure (2001): food 42.7%, housing and energy 11.5%, transportation 5.0%, health 3.7%, clothing 3.4%.
Population economically active (2003): total 3,237,100; activity rate of total population 41.5% (participation rates [2001] age 16–59 [male], 16–54 [female] 54.2%; female [2001] 46.4%; unemployed 12.7%).

Price index (2000 = 100)

	1997	1998	1999	2000	2001	2002	2003
Consumer price index	74.5	88.4	90.6	100.0	107.4	113.6	116.0

Tourism (2002): receipts U.S.$1,344,000,000; expenditures U.S.$616,000,000.
Land use as % of total land area (2000): in temporary crops 40.0%, in permanent crops 1.9%, in pasture 14.6%; overall forest area 33.4%.

Foreign trade[9]

Balance of trade (current prices)

	1998	1999	2000	2001	2002	2003
U.S.$'000,000	–381	–1,081	–1,175	–1,576	–1,619	–2,474
% of total	4.3%	11.9%	10.9%	13.4%	12.7%	14.3%

Imports (2003): U.S.$10,836,000,000 (textiles 13.7%; crude petroleum and natural gas 13.6%; machinery and apparatus 13.1%; transport equipment 9.4%; plastics and rubber 4.6%). *Major import sources:* Germany 14.3%; Russia 12.6%; Italy 10.2%; Turkey 6.1%; France 5.6%.
Exports (2003): U.S.$7,520,000,000 (clothing and footwear 21.9%; base and fabricated metals 16.1%, of which iron and steel 8.1%; machinery and transport equipment 10.3%; mineral fuels 8.4%, of which petroleum products 5.8%). *Major export destinations:* Italy 14.0%; Germany 10.8%; Greece 10.4%; Turkey 9.2%; Belgium 6.1%; France 5.1%.

Transport and communications

Transport. Railroads (2002): track length 6,384 km; passenger-km 2,598,-000,000; metric ton-km cargo 4,628,000,000. Roads (2001): length 37,296 km (paved 92%). Vehicles (2001): cars 2,085,730; trucks and buses 288,832. Air transport (2001): passenger-km 1,795,400,000; metric ton-km cargo 2,335,000; airports (2000) with scheduled flights 3.

Communications

Medium	date	unit	number	units per 1,000 persons
Daily newspapers	2000	circulation	2,060,000	257
Radio	2001	receivers	4,340,000	543
Television	2002	receivers	3,620,000	453
Telephones	2002	main lines	2,868,200	368
Cellular telephones	2002	subscribers	2,597,500	330
Personal computers	2002	units	405,000	52
Internet	2002	users	630,000	81

Education and health

Educational attainment (1992). Percentage of population age 25 and over having: no formal schooling 4.7%; incomplete primary education 12.5%; primary 31.9%; secondary 35.7%; higher 15.0%. *Literacy* (2001): total population age 15 and over literate 98.5%; males 99.0%; females 98.0%.

Education (2002–03)

	schools	teachers	students	student/ teacher ratio
Primary (age 6–14) / Secondary (age 15–17)	2,720	61,354	825,668	13.5
Voc., teacher tr.	513	21,103	217,313	10.3
Higher	42	18,710	215,712	11.5

Health (2002): physicians 27,186 (1 per 290 persons); hospital beds 56,984 (1 per 138 persons); infant mortality rate per 1,000 live births (2001) 13.5.
Food (2001): daily per capita caloric intake 2,626 (vegetable products 73%, animal products 27%); 105% of FAO recommended minimum requirement.

Military

Total active duty personnel (2003): 51,000 (army 49.0%, navy 8.6%, air force 25.7%, other 16.7%). *Military expenditure as percentage of GNP* (1999): 3.0% (world 2.4%); per capita expenditure U.S.$158.

[1]Bulgaria has no official religion; the 1991 constitution, however, refers to Eastern Orthodoxy as the "traditional" religion. [2]The lev was re-denominated as of July 5, 1999; as of this date 1,000 (old) leva = 1 (new) lev. [3]January 1. [4]District nearly encircles Sofiya-Grad district on north, east, and south. [5]Sofiya-Grad includes Sofia city and immediately adjacent urban and rural areas. [6]Includes hotels, restaurants (usually included with Trade). [7]Taxes on products and import duties less bank service charges. [8]Unemployed. [9]Imports f.o.b. in balance of trade and c.i.f. for commodities and trading partners.

Internet resources for further information:
- **National Statistical Institute http://www.nsi.bg**
- **Bulgarian National Bank http://www.bnb.bg**

Burkina Faso

Official name: Burkina Faso (Burkina Faso).
Form of government: multiparty republic with one legislative body (National Assembly [111]).
Chief of state: President.
Head of government: Prime Minister.
Capital: Ouagadougou.
Official language: French.
Official religion: none.
Monetary unit: 1 CFA franc (CFAF) = 100 centimes; valuation (Sept. 1, 2004) 1 U.S.$ = CFAF 539.75; 1 £ = CFAF 970.98[1].

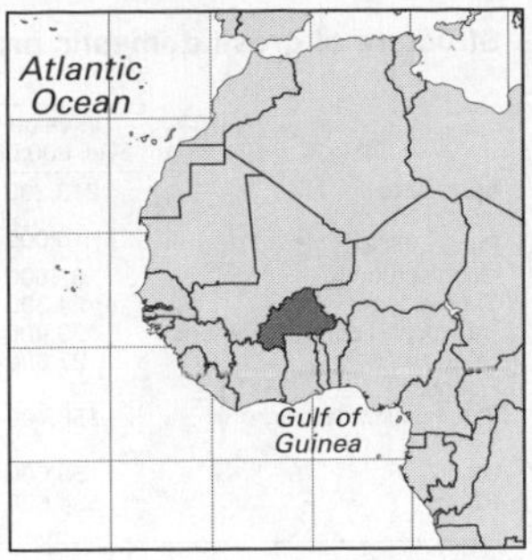

Population[2]

Provinces	population	Provinces	population	Provinces	population
Balé	169,543	Komondjari	49,389	Passoré	271,216
Bam	212,295	Kompienga	73,949	Poni	196,568
Banwa	214,234	Kossi	217,866	Sanguié	249,169
Bazèga	214,450	Koulpélogo	188,760	Sanmatenga	460,684
Bougouriba	76,444	Kouritenga	250,699	Séno	202,972
Boulgou	415,414	Kourwéogo	117,370	Sissili	153,560
Boulkiemdé	421,083	Léraba	93,351	Soum	253,867
Comoé	240,942	Loroum	111,707	Sourou	189,726
Ganzourgou	257,707	Mouhoun	237,048	Tapoa	235,288
Gnagna	307,386	Nahouri	121,314	Tuy	160,249
Gourma	221,956	Namentenga	251,909	Yagha	116,985
Houet	674,916	Nayala	136,273	Yatenga	443,967
Ioba	159,422	Noumbiel	51,449	Ziro	117,774
Kadiogo	976,513	Oubritenga	198,130	Zondoma	127,580
Kénédougou	198,936	Oudalan	136,583	Zoundwéogo	196,698
				TOTAL	10,373,341

Demography

Area: 103,456 sq mi, 267,950 sq km.
Population (2004): 13,575,000.
Density (2004): persons per sq mi 131.2, persons per sq km 50.7.
Urban-rural (2002): urban 16.9%; rural 83.1%.
Sex distribution (2003): male 49.26%; female 50.74%.
Age breakdown (2003): under 15, 46.1%; 15–29, 27.4%; 30–44, 14.8%; 45–59, 7.4%; 60–74, 3.7%; 75 and over, 0.8%.
Population projection: (2010) 15,748,000; (2020) 19,965,000.
Ethnic composition (1995): Mossi 47.9%; Fulani 10.3%; Lobi 6.9%; Bobo 6.9%; Mande 6.7%; Senufo 5.3%; Grosi 5.0%; Gurma 4.8%; Tuareg 3.1%.
Religious affiliation (2000): Muslim 48.6%; traditional beliefs 34.1%; Christian 16.7%, of which Roman Catholic 9.5%.
Major cities (1996): Ouagadougou 709,736; Bobo-Dioulasso 309,771; Koudougou 72,490; Ouahigouya 52,193; Banfora 49,724.

Vital statistics

Birth rate per 1,000 population (2003): 44.8 (world avg. 21.3).
Death rate per 1,000 population (2003): 18.8 (world avg. 9.1).
Natural increase rate per 1,000 population (2003): 26.0 (world avg. 12.2).
Total fertility rate (avg. births per childbearing woman; 2003): 6.3.
Life expectancy at birth (2003): male 43.0 years; female 45.9 years.
Adult population (ages 15–49) *living with HIV* (2004[3]): 4.2% (world avg. 1.1%).

National economy

Budget (2002). Revenue: CFAF 377,000,000,000 (tax revenue 63.9%, of which sales tax 34.5%, income taxes 16.4%, import duties 11.2%; grants 31.5%; nontax revenue 4.6%). Expenditures: CFAF 489,100,000,000 (current expenditure 52.9%, of which wages and salaries 21.1%, transfers 14.3%, goods and services 12.8%, debt service 3.4%; investment expenditure 47.1%).
Public debt (external, outstanding; 2002): U.S.$1,399,000,000.
Household income and expenditure. Average household size (2000) 6.0; average annual income per household: n.a.; sources of income: n.a.; expenditure (1998)[4]: food 33.9%, transportation 15.6%, electricity and fuel 10.5%, clothing 6.4%, health 4.2%, education 3.4%.
Production (metric tons except as noted). Agriculture, forestry, fishing (2002): sorghum 1,373,300, millet 994,700, corn (maize) 653,100, sugarcane 420,000, seed cotton 400,000, peanuts (groundnuts) 323,600, shea nuts 110,500, rice 89,100, sesame 34,400; livestock (number of live animals) 9,450,000 goats, 7,411,000 sheep, 5,092,000 cattle, 23,000,000 chickens; roundwood (2002) 11,994,000 cu m; fish catch (2001) 8,505. Mining and quarrying (2002): gold 624 kg[5]. Manufacturing (2002): sugar 47,743; edible oils 19,636; flour 10,005; soap 9,923; beer 546,000 hectolitres; soft drinks 250,000 hectolitres; bicycles 20,849 units; mopeds 19,702 units; cigarettes 78,000,000 packets. Construction (value added in CFAF; 1995): 62,400,000,000. Energy production (consumption): electricity (kW-hr; 2002) 361,000,000 (361,000,000); crude petroleum (barrels; 2000) none (none); petroleum products (metric tons; 2001) none (294,000).
Tourism: receipts (2002) U.S.$39,000,000; expenditures (1994) U.S.$23,000,000.
Population economically active (1996): total 5,075,615; activity rate 49.2% (participation rates: over age 10, 70.0%; female 48.2%; unemployed 1.4%).

Price index (2000 = 100)

	1997	1998	1999	2000	2001	2002	2003
Consumer price index	96.5	101.4	100.3	100.0	105.0	107.3	109.5

Gross national product (at current market prices; 2003): U.S.$3,587,000,000 (U.S.$300 per capita).

Structure of gross domestic product and labour force

	2002		1996	
	in value CFAF '000,000	% of total value	labour force	% of labour force
Agriculture	692,600	31.8	4,513,868	88.9
Mining }	274,600	12.6	3,979	0.1
Manufacturing }			71,565	1.4
Construction	96,600	4.4	21,076	0.4
Public utilities	31,700	1.4	2,813	0.1
Transp. and commun.	84,000	3.9	20,580	0.4
Trade	306,800	14.1	224,581	4.4
Finance	...	...	13,131	0.3
Pub. admin., defense }	671,900	30.8	103,926	2.0
Services }				
Other	21,000[6]	1.0[6]	100,096[7]	2.0[7]
TOTAL	2,179,200	100.0	5,075,615	100.0

Land use as % of total land area (2000): in temporary crops 13.9%, in permanent crops 0.2%, in pasture 21.9%; overall forest area 25.9%.

Foreign trade

Balance of trade (current prices)

	1997	1998	1999	2000	2001	2002
CFAF '000,000,000	–164.0	–183.8	–201.2	–222.4	–204.5	–217.5
% of total	38.0%	32.5%	39.2%	43.2%	37.7%	39.8%

Imports (2002): CFAF 381,700,000,000 (capital equipment 32.6%, petroleum products 18.6%, food products 12.7%, raw materials 10.1%). *Major import sources:* France 19.6%; Côte d'Ivoire 18.8%; Japan 9.3%; Germany 6.0%; U.S. 3.3%.
Exports (2002): CFAF 164,200,000,000 (raw cotton 54.1%, hides and skins 11.0%, live animals 8.8%, shea nuts 2.6%, gold 2.0%). *Major export destinations:* France 45.3%; Côte d'Ivoire 9.2%; Singapore 5.1%; Mali 4.0%; Japan 3.0%.

Transport and communications

Transport. Railroads: (2002) route length 386 mi, 622 km; (1995)[8] passenger-km 202,000,000; (1995)[8] metric ton-km cargo 45,000,000. Roads (1999): total length 6,505 mi, 10,469 km (paved 19%). Vehicles (1999): passenger cars 26,300; trucks and buses 19,600. Air transport (2000)[9]: passenger-km 247,000,000; metric ton-km cargo, n.a.; airports 2.

Communications

Medium	date	unit	number	units per 1,000 persons
Daily newspapers	2000	circulation	12,200	1.0
Radio	2000	receivers	428,000	35
Television	2000	receivers	147,000	12
Telephones	2003	main lines	65,400	5.3
Cellular telephones	2003	subscribers	227,000	19
Personal computers	2003	units	26,000	2.1
Internet	2003	users	48,000	3.9

Education and health

Educational attainment (1985). Percentage of population age 10 and over having: no formal schooling 86.1%; some primary 7.3%; general secondary 2.2%; specialized secondary and postsecondary 3.8%; other 0.6%. *Literacy* (2000): percentage of total population age 15 and over literate 23.9%; males literate 33.9%; females literate 14.1%.

Education (1995–96)

	schools	teachers	students[9]	student/ teacher ratio
Primary (age 7–12)	3,568	14,037	816,393	50.0
Secondary (age 13–19)	252	4,162 }	173,200	33.0
Vocational	41	731 }		13.0
Higher	9	632	9,900	15.1

Health (1995): physicians 361 (1 per 29,385 persons); hospital beds (1991) 5,041 (1 per 1,837 persons); infant mortality rate per 1,000 live births (2003) 99.8.
Food (2001): daily per capita caloric intake 2,485 (vegetable products 95%, animal products 5%); 105% of FAO recommended minimum requirement.

Military

Total active duty personnel (2003): 10,800 (army 98.1%, air force 1.9%). *Military expenditure as percentage of GNP* (1999): 1.6% (world 2.4%); per capita expenditure U.S.$4.

[1]Formerly pegged to the French franc and since Jan. 1, 2002, to the euro at the rate of €1 = CFAF 655.96. [2]As of October 1996 census. [3]January 1. [4]Weights of consumer price index components; Ouagadougou only. [5]Officially marketed gold only; does not include substantial illegal production. [6]Includes indirect taxes less imputed bank service charges and subsidies. [7]Includes 71,280 unemployed. [8]Passenger-km and metric ton-km cargo figures are based on traffic between Abidjan, Côte d'Ivoire, and Ouagadougou. [9]Air Afrique, an airline jointly owned by 11 African countries (including Burkina Faso), was declared bankrupt in February 2002. [10]1998–99.

Internet resources for further information:
- **Embassy of Burkina Faso**
  http://www.burkinaembassy-usa.org
- **La Banque de France: La Zone Franc**
  http://www.banque-france.fr/fr/zonefr/main.htm

Burundi

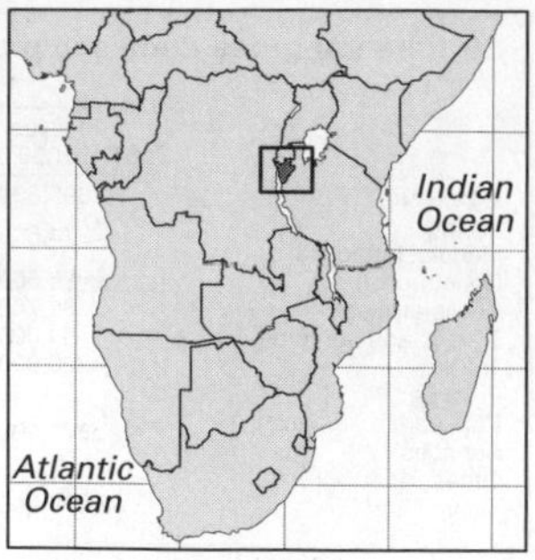

Official name: Republika y'u Burundi (Rundi); République du Burundi (French) (Republic of Burundi).
Form of government: transitional regime[1] with one legislative body (Transitional Assembly[2] [178]).
Head of state and government: President assisted by Vice President.
Capital: Bujumbura.
Official languages: Rundi; French.
Official religion: none.
Monetary unit: 1 Burundi franc (FBu) = 100 centimes; valuation (Sept. 1, 2004) 1 U.S.$ = FBu 1,060; 1 £ = FBu 1,907.

Area and population

Provinces	Capitals	area sq mi	area sq km	population 1990 census
Bubanza	Bubanza	420	1,089	222,953
Bujumbura	Bujumbura	476[3]	1,232[3]	608,931[4]
Bururi	Bururi	952	2,465	385,490
Cankuzo	Cankuzo	759	1,965	142,707
Cibitoke	Cibitoke	631	1,636	279,843
Gitega	Gitega	764	1,979	565,174
Karuzi	Karuzi	563	1,457	287,905
Kayanza	Kayanza	476	1,233	443,116
Kirundo	Kirundo	658	1,703	401,103
Makamba	Makamba	757	1,960	223,799
Muramvya	Muramvya	269	696	441,653[5]
Muyinga	Muyinga	709	1,836	373,382
Mwaro	Mwaro	324	840	[5]
Ngozi	Ngozi	569	1,474	482,246
Rutana	Rutana	756	1,959	195,834
Ruyigi	Ruyigi	903	2,339	238,567
Urban Province				
Bujumbura	—	34	87	[4]
TOTAL LAND AREA		10,020	25,590	
INLAND WATER		721	1,867	
TOTAL		10,740[6]	27,816[6]	5,292,703

Demography

Population (2004): 6,231,000.
Density (2004)[7]: persons per sq mi 621.9, persons per sq km 243.5.
Urban-rural (2002): urban 9.3%; rural 90.7%.
Sex distribution (2003): male 49.57%; female 50.43%.
Age breakdown (2003): under 15, 46.7%; 15–29, 28.8%; 30–44, 13.4%; 45–59, 7.1%; 60–74, 3.1%; 75 and over, 0.9%.
Population projection: (2010) 7,296,000; (2020) 9,174,000.
Doubling time: 32 years.
Ethnic composition (2000): Hutu 80.9%; Tutsi 15.6%; Lingala 1.6%; Twa Pygmy 1.0%; other 0.9%.
Religious affiliation (2000): Roman Catholic 57.2%; Protestant 19.5%; unaffiliated Christian 14.7%; traditional beliefs 6.7%; Muslim 1.4%; other 0.5%.
Major cities (2004): Bujumbura 340,300; Gitega 46,900; Muyinga 45,300; Ngozi 40,200; Ruyigi 36,800.

Vital statistics

Birth rate per 1,000 population (2003): 39.7 (world avg. 21.3).
Death rate per 1,000 population (2003): 17.8 (world avg. 9.1).
Natural increase rate per 1,000 population (2003): 21.9 (world avg. 12.2).
Total fertility rate (avg. births per childbearing woman; 2003): 6.0.
Life expectancy at birth (2003): male 42.5 years; female 43.9 years.
Adult population (ages 15–49) *living with HIV* (2004[8]): 6.0% (world avg. 1.1%).

National economy

Budget (2002). Revenue: FBu 118,400,000,000 (tax revenue 88.5%, of which taxes on goods and services 43.8%, income tax 24.8%, taxes on international trade 19.6%; nontax revenue 11.5%). Expenditures: FBu 151,600,000,000 (current expenditure 79.0%; capital expenditure 21.0%).
Public debt (external, outstanding; 2002): U.S.$1,095,000,000.
Production (metric tons except as noted). Agriculture, forestry, fishing (2003): bananas 1,600,000, sweet potatoes 835,000, cassava 750,000, dry beans 245,000, sugarcane 200,000, corn (maize) 127,000, yams and taros 95,700, coffee 36,155, tea 8,625; livestock (number of live animals) 750,000 goats, 325,000 cattle, 230,000 sheep, 4,300,000 chickens; roundwood (2002) 8,428,000 cu m; fish catch (2001) 9,064. Mining and quarrying (2001): gemstones 16,500 kg; gold 415 kg. Manufacturing (2003): beer 580,226 hectolitres; carbonated beverages 82,367 hectolitres; cottonseed oil 25,000 litres; sugar 8,859 tons; cigarettes 234,800,000 units; blankets 84,292 units; fabrics 6,000,000 sq m. Energy production (consumption): electricity (kW-hr; 2001) 107,774,000 (108,800,000); coal, none (none); crude petroleum, none (none); petroleum products (metric tons; 2001) none (48,093); natural gas, none (none); peat (metric tons; 2000) 12,000 (12,000).
Household income and expenditure. Average household size (2000) 5.1; income per household: n.a.; sources of income: n.a.; expenditure[9]: (1991) food 51.9%, energy and housing 27.0%, transportation 5.3%, clothing 5.3%.
Land use as % of total land area (2000): in temporary crops 35.0%, in permanent crops 14.0%, in pasture 36.4%; overall forest area 3.7%.
Gross national product (at current market prices; 2003): U.S.$702,000,000 (U.S.$100 per capita).

Structure of gross domestic product and labour force

	2002 in value FBu '000,000	2002 % of total value	1990 labour force	1990 % of labour force
Agriculture	213,200	36.5	2,574,443	93.1
Mining } Public utilities	6,000	1.0	1,419	—
			1,672	0.1
Manufacturing	67,500	11.5	33,867	1.2
Construction	24,300	4.2	19,737	0.7
Transp. and communications	29,000	5.1	8,504	0.3
Trade	27,600	4.7	25,822	0.9
Finance			2,005	0.1
Pub. admin., defense } Services	158,400	27.0	85,191	3.1
Other	58,600[10]	10.0[10]	13,270	0.5
TOTAL	584,600	100.0	2,765,945[6]	100.0

Population economically active (1997): total 3,475,000; activity rate of total population 63.1% (participation rates [1991]: ages 15–64, 91.4%; female 48.9%; unemployed, n.a.).

Price index (2000 = 100)

	1997	1998	1999	2000	2001	2002	2003
Consumer price index	69.2	77.8	80.4	100.0	109.2	112.9	119.3

Tourism (2002): receipts from visitors U.S.$1,100,000; expenditures by nationals abroad U.S.$14,000,000.

Foreign trade

Balance of trade (current prices)

	1998	1999	2000	2001	2002
U.S.$'000,000	–59.7	–42.3	–58.7	–69.2	–72.7
% of total	31.8%	27.8%	37.4%	46.9%	53.8%

Imports (2002): U.S.$103,900,000 (consumption goods 45.0%, of which food and food products 12.4%; capital goods 30.8%; petroleum products 15.3%). *Major import sources:* Belgium 16.4%; Kenya 12.1%; Tanzania 10.3%; France 7.0%; Japan 5.7%.
Exports (2002): U.S.$31,200,000 (coffee 53.9%, tea 28.5%, manufactured products 12.9%). *Major export destinations:* United Kingdom 18.9%; Kenya 18.7%; Rwanda 10.1%; Belgium 8.5%; The Netherlands 5.2%.

Transport and communications

Transport. Railroads: none. Roads (1999): total length 8,997 mi, 14,480 km (paved 7%). Vehicles (1999): passenger cars 6,900; trucks and other vehicles 9,300. Air transport (2000)[11]: passenger arrivals and departures 58,402; cargo loaded and unloaded 3,905 metric tons; airports (2002) 1.

Communications

Medium	date	unit	number	units per 1,000 persons
Daily newspapers	1996	circulation	20,000	3.2
Radio	2000	receivers	1,260,000	220
Television	2002	receivers	220,000	31
Telephones	2003	main lines	23,900	3.4
Cellular telephones	2003	subscribers	64,000	9.0
Internet	2003	users	14,000	1.8

Education and health

Educational attainment: n.a. *Literacy* (2000): percentage of total population age 15 and over literate 48.0%; males literate 56.2%; females literate 40.4%.

Education (1998)

	schools	teachers	students	student/teacher ratio
Primary (age 6–11)	1,512	12,107	557,344	46.0
Secondary (age 12–18) } Vocational and teacher training	400	3,548	56,872	16.0
Higher	...	379	5,037	13.3

Health (1999): physicians 357 (1 per 15,695 persons); hospital beds 3,380 (1 per 1,657 persons); infant mortality rate per 1,000 live births (2003) 71.5.
Food (2001): daily per capita caloric intake 1,612 (vegetable products 98%, animal products 2%); 72% of FAO recommended minimum requirement.

Military

Total active duty personnel (2003): 50,500 (army 100%); UN peacekeeping troops (July 2004) 2,700. *Military expenditure as percentage of GNP* (1999): 7.0% (world 2.4%); per capita expenditure U.S.$8.

[1]Transitional government from November 2001 extended to April 2005 per October 2004 announcement. [2]"New" transitional body installed January 2002. [3]Unverified figure. [4]Bujumbura (province) includes Bujumbura urban province. [5]Muramvya includes Mwaro. [6]Detail does not add to total given because of rounding. [7]Based on land area. [8]Beginning of year. [9]Weights of consumer price index components. [10]Indirect taxes less subsidies. [11]Figures for Bujumbura airport only.

Cambodia

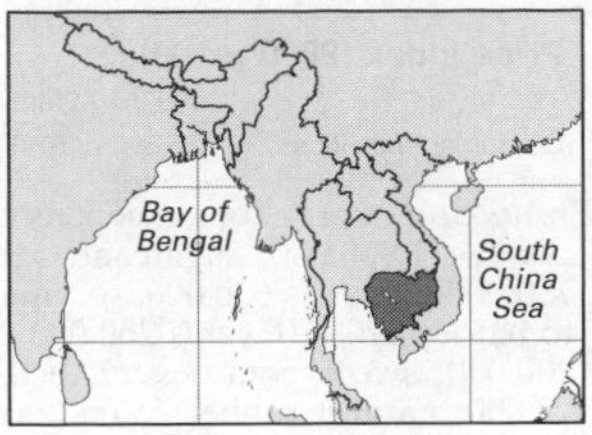

Official name: Preah Reach Ana Pak Kampuchea (Kingdom of Cambodia).
Form of government: constitutional monarchy with two legislative houses (Senate [61[1]]; National Assembly [123]).
Chief of state: King.
Head of government: Prime Minister.
Capital: Phnom Penh.
Official language: Khmer.
Official religion: Buddhism.
Monetary unit: 1 riel = 100 sen; valuation (Sept. 1, 2004) 1 U.S.$ = 3,845 riels; 1 £ = 6,917 riels.

Area and population

		area		population
				1998
Provinces	**Capitals**	sq mi	sq km	census
Banteay Mean Chey	Sisophon	2,579	6,679	577,772
Bat Dambang	Bat Dambang	4,518	11,702	793,129
Kampong Cham	Kampong Cham	3,783	9,799	1,608,914
Kampong Chhnang	Kampong Chhnang	2,132	5,521	417,693
Kampong Spueu	Kampong Spueu	2,709	7,017	598,882
Kampong Thum	Kampong Thum	5,334	13,814	569,060
Kampot	Kampot	1,881	4,873	528,405
Kandal	Ta Khmau	1,378	3,568	1,075,125
Kaoh Kong	Krong Kaoh Kong	4,309	11,160	132,106
Kracheh	Kracheh	4,283	11,094	263,175
Mondol Kiri	Senmonorom	5,517	14,288	32,407
Otdar Mean Cheay	Phumi Samraong	2,378	6,158	68,279
Pousat	Pousat	4,900	12,692	360,445
Preah Vihear	Phum Tbeng Mean Cheay	5,324	13,788	119,261
Prey Veaeng	Prey Veaeng	1,885	4,883	946,042
Rotanak Kiri	Lumphat	4,163	10,782	94,243
Siem Reab	Siem Reab	3,976	10,299	696,164
Stueng Traeng	Stueng Traeng	4,283	11,092	81,074
Svay Rieng	Svay Rieng	1,145	2,966	478,252
Takaev	Takaev	1,376	3,563	790,168
Municipalities				
Kaeb	—	130	336	28,660
Pailin	—	310	803	22,906
Phnom Penh	—	112	290	999,804
Preah Sihanouk	—	335	868	155,690
TOTAL LAND AREA		68,740	178,035	
INLAND WATER		1,158	3,000	
TOTAL		69,898	181,035	11,437,656

Demography

Population (2004): 13,470,000.
Density (2004)[2]: persons per sq mi 196.0, persons per sq km 75.7.
Urban-rural (2002): urban 17.0%; rural 83.0%.
Sex distribution (2003): male 48.60%; female 51.40%.
Age breakdown (2003): under 15, 39.3%; 15–29, 28.8%; 30–44, 18.5%; 45–59, 8.8%; 60–74, 3.7%; 75 and over, 0.9%.
Population projection: (2010) 14,971,000; (2020) 17,768,000.
Ethnic composition (2000): Khmer 85.2%; Chinese 6.4%; Vietnamese 3.0%; Cham 2.5%; Lao 0.6%; other 2.3%.
Religious affiliation (2000): Buddhist 84.7%; Chinese folk religionist 4.7%; traditional beliefs 4.3%; Muslim 2.3%; Christian 1.1%; other 2.9%.
Major urban areas (1998): Phnom Penh (2003) 1,157,000; Bat Dambang 124,290; Sisophon 85,382; Siem Reab 83,715; Preah Sihanouk 66,723.

Vital statistics

Birth rate per 1,000 population (2003): 27.3 (world avg. 21.3).
Death rate per 1,000 population (2003): 9.3 (world avg. 9.1).
Natural increase rate per 1,000 population (2003): 18.0 (world avg. 12.2).
Total fertility rate (avg. births per childbearing woman; 2003): 3.7.
Life expectancy at birth (2003): male 55.5 years; female 60.5 years.
Major causes of death per 100,000 population: n.a.; however, major health problems include tuberculosis, malaria, and pneumonia. Violence and military ordnance (especially unexploded mines) remain hazards.

National economy

Budget (2001). Revenue: 1,520,000,000,000 riels (indirect taxes 37.6%, of which value-added taxes 26.5%; taxes on international trade 24.7%; nontax revenue 27.9%). Expenditures: 2,329,000,000,000 riels (current expenditure 58.1%, of which civil administration 30.2%, defense and security 16.7%; development expenditure 41.9%).
Public debt (external, outstanding; 2002): U.S.$2,594,000,000.
Production (metric tons except as noted). Agriculture, forestry, fishing (2002): rice 3,740,002, cassava 186,800, corn (maize) 168,700, sugarcane 168,650, bananas 146,000, coconuts 70,000, oranges 63,000, rubber 32,365, soybeans 21,250, tobacco leaves 4,692; livestock (number of live animals) 2,924,457 cattle, 2,105,435 pigs, 625,912 buffalo; roundwood (2002) 9,858,000 cu m; fish catch (2001) 412,700. Mining and quarrying: legal mining is confined to fertilizers, salt, and construction materials. Manufacturing (value added in U.S.$'000,000; 2000): wearing apparel 626; textiles 479; leather products 105; food products 81; rubber products 66. Energy production (consumption): electricity (kW-hr; 2000) 229,000,000 (229,000,000); petroleum products (metric tons; 2000) negligible (173,000); crude petroleum, none (none); natural gas, none (none).
Household income and expenditure. Average household size (2000) 5.7; household expenditure (2002): food, beverages, and tobacco 62.6%, housing and energy 19.7%, health 6.0%, transportation and communications 3.4%.

Gross national product (2003): U.S.$4,105,000,000 (U.S.$310 per capita).

Structure of gross domestic product and labour force

	2002			
	in value '000,000,000 riels	% of total value	labour force	% of labour force
Agriculture	5,231.8	33.4	4,479,773	70.0
Mining	46.6	0.3	10,751	0.2
Manufacturing	2,969.5	19.0	556,388	8.7
Construction	1,023.1	6.5	100,123	1.6
Public utilities	75.8	0.5	4,704	0.1
Transp. and commun.	960.0	6.0	174,711	2.7
Trade	2,140.2	13.7	661,406	10.3
Finance	964.8	6.2	16,224	0.3
Public admin., defense	390.5	2.5	143,513	2.2
Services	902.9	5.8	252,084	3.9
Other	962.0[3]	6.1[3]	—	—
TOTAL	15,667.2	100.0	6,399,677	100.0

Population economically active (2002): total 6,399,677; activity rate of total population 48.8% (participation rates [2000]: ages 15 and over, 69.9%; female 54.6%; unemployed 5.3%).

Price index (2000 = 100)

	1997	1998	1999	2000	2001	2002	2003
Consumer price index	84.4	96.9	99.4	100.0	102.4	102.6	103.8

Tourism (2002): receipts U.S.$379,000,000; expenditures U.S.$38,000,000.
Land use as % of total land area (2000): in temporary crops 21.0%, in permanent crops 0.6%, in pasture 8.5%; overall forest area 52.9%.

Foreign trade

Balance of trade (current prices)

	1997	1998	1999	2000	2001	2002
U.S.$'000,000	−264	−264	−292	−452	−476	−564
% of total	14.4%	13.2%	11.7%	14.0%	13.9%	13.9%

Imports (2001): U.S.$1,951,000,000 (retained imports 91.1%; imports for reexport 8.9%). *Major import sources* (2002): Thailand 30.2%; Singapore 21.5%; Hong Kong 10.2%; China 7.7%; Vietnam 6.6%.
Exports (2001): U.S.$1,475,000,000 (domestic exports 87.8%, of which garments *c.* 75%, rubber 3.4%[4], sawn timber and logs 2.2%[4]; reexports 12.2%). *Major export destinations* (2002): U.S. 61.4%; Germany 8.9%; U.K. 7.2%.

Transport and communications

Transport. Railroads (1999): length 403 mi, 649 km; passenger-km 49,894,000; metric ton-km 76,171,000. Roads (1999): total length 22,226 mi, 35,769 km (paved 12%). Vehicles (2002): passenger cars 209,128; trucks and buses 33,164. Air transport (2002)[5]: passenger-km 60,900,000; metric ton-km cargo 4,100,000; airports (1997) with scheduled flights 8.

Communications

Medium	date	unit	number	units per 1,000 persons
Daily newspapers	2000	circulation	24,000	2.0
Radio	2000	receivers	1,480,000	119
Television	2000	receivers	99,500	8.0
Telephones	2002	main lines	35,400	2.6
Cellular telephones	2002	subscribers	380,000	28
Personal computers	2002	units	27,000	2.0
Internet	2002	users	30,000	2.2

Education and health

Educational attainment (1998). Percentage of population age 25 and over having: no formal schooling 2.1%; some primary education 56.6%; primary 24.7%; some secondary 11.8%; secondary and above 4.8%. *Literacy* (2000): percentage of total population age 15 and over literate 68.5%; males literate 79.8%; females literate 57.1%.

Education (2001–02)

	schools	teachers	students	student/teacher ratio
Primary (age 6–10)	5,471	54,519	2,705,453	49.6
Secondary (age 11–16)	542	24,884	465,039	18.7
Voc., teacher tr.[6]	...	2,315	9,983	4.3
Higher[6]	...	1,001	8,901	8.9

Health (2001): physicians 2,047 (1 per 5,862 persons); hospital beds 10,900 (1 per 1,100 persons); infant mortality rate per 1,000 live births (2003) 75.9.
Food (2001): daily per capita caloric intake 1,967 (vegetable products 91%, animal products 9%); 89% of FAO recommended minimum requirement.

Military

Total active duty personnel (2003)[7]: 125,000 (army 60.0%, navy 2.4%, air force 1.6%, provincial forces 36.0%). *Military expenditure as percentage of GNP* (1999): 4.0% (world 2.4%); per capita expenditure U.S.$28.

[1]All seats appointed in 1999; future Senate membership to be elected in 2005 or 2006. [2]Based on land area. [3]Indirect taxes less imputed bank service charge. [4]Includes estimates for illegal exports. [5]Combined total of Imtrec Aviation, Phnom Penh Airways, President Airlines, and Siem Reap Airways. [6]1997–98. [7]Figures exclude paramilitary forces.

Internet resources for further information:
- **National Institute of Statistics http://www.nis.gov.kh**

Cameroon

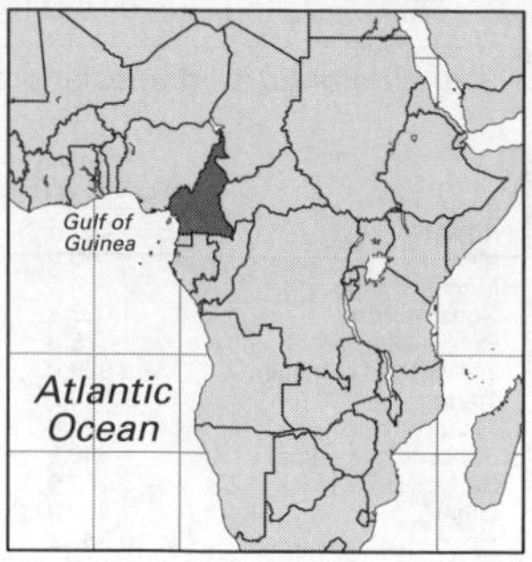

Official name: République du Cameroun (French); Republic of Cameroon (English).
Form of government: unitary multiparty republic with one legislative house (National Assembly [180]).
Chief of state: President.
Head of government: Prime Minister.
Capital: Yaoundé.
Official languages: French; English.
Official religion: none.
Monetary unit: 1 CFA franc (CFAF) = 100 centimes; valuation (Sept. 1, 2004) 1 U.S.$ = CFAF 539.75; 1 £ = CFAF 970.98[1].

Area and population

		area		population
Regions	Capitals	sq mi	sq km	1990 estimate
Adamoua	Ngaoundéré	24,591	63,691	538,000
Centre	Yaoundé	26,613	68,926	1,901,000
Est	Bertoua	42,089	109,011	553,000
Extrême-Nord	Maroua	13,223	34,246	1,917,000
Littoral	Douala	7,814	20,239	1,669,000
Nord	Garoua	25,319	65,576	946,000
Nord-Ouest	Bamenda	6,877	17,810	1,277,000
Ouest	Bafoussam	5,356	13,872	1,408,000
Sud	Ebolowa	18,189	47,110	380,000
Sud-Ouest	Buea	9,448	24,471	897,000
LAND AREA		179,519	464,952	
INLAND WATER		4,051	10,492	
TOTAL		183,569[2]	475,442[2]	11,486,000

Demography

Population (2004): 16,064,000.
Density (2004)[3]: persons per sq mi 89.5, persons per sq km 34.5.
Urban-rural (2002): urban 49.7%; rural 50.3%.
Sex distribution (2003): male 50.27%; female 49.73%.
Age breakdown (2003): under 15, 42.3%; 15–29, 29.0%; 30–44, 15.3%; 45–59, 8.4%; 60–74, 4.0%; 75 and over, 0.9%.
Population projection: (2010) 17,938,000; (2020) 20,946,000.
Doubling time: 34 years.
Ethnic composition (1983): Fang 19.6%; Bamileke and Bamum 18.5%; Duala, Luanda, and Basa 14.7%; Fulani 9.6%; Tikar 7.4%; Mandara 5.7%; Maka 4.9%; Chamba 2.4%; Mbum 1.3%; Hausa 1.2%; French 0.2%; other 14.5%.
Religious affiliation (2000): Roman Catholic 26.4%; traditional beliefs 23.7%; Muslim 21.2%; Protestant 20.7%.
Major cities (2002): Douala 1,239,100; Yaoundé 1,122,500; Garoua 185,800; Maroua 169,200; Bafoussam 151,800.

Vital statistics

Birth rate per 1,000 population (2003): 35.5 (world avg. 21.3).
Death rate per 1,000 population (2003): 15.3 (world avg. 9.1).
Natural increase rate per 1,000 population (2003): 20.2 (world avg. 12.2).
Total fertility rate (avg. births per childbearing woman; 2003): 4.6.
Life expectancy at birth (2003): male 47.2 years; female 49.0 years.
Adult population (ages 15–49) *living with HIV* (2004[4]): 6.9% (world avg. 1.1%).

National economy

Budget (2000–01). Revenue: CFAF 1,326,000,000,000 (oil revenue 33.0%; taxes on goods and services 32.9%; income tax 16.6%; customs duties 11.2%). Expenditures: CFAF 1,175,000,000,000 (current expenditure 80.9%, of which wages and salaries 28.8%, debt service 20.9%, goods and services 20.0%, transfers 11.3%; capital expenditure 19.1%).
Public debt (external, outstanding; 2002): U.S.$7,240,000,000.
Gross national product (2003): U.S.$10,287,000,000 (U.S.$640 per capita).

Structure of gross domestic product and labour force

	2000–01		1985	
	in value CFAF '000,000,000	% of total value	labour force	% of labour force
Agriculture	2,699	42.7	2,900,871	74.0
Mining	246	3.9	1,793	0.1
Manufacturing	669	10.6	174,498	4.5
Construction	229	3.6	66,684	1.7
Public utilities	95	1.5	3,522	0.1
Transp. and commun.			51,688	1.3
Trade			154,014	3.9
Finance	2,205	34.9	8,009	0.2
Services			292,922	7.5
Public admin., defense				
Other	177[5]	2.8[5]	263,634	6.7
TOTAL	6,320	100.0	3,917,635	100.0

Household income and expenditure. Average household size (2000) 5.5; average annual income per household: n.a.; sources of income: n.a.; expenditure (1993)[6]: food 49.1%, housing 18.0%, transportation and communications 13.0%, health 8.6%, clothing 7.6%, recreation 2.4%.
Tourism (2000): receipts U.S.$39,000,000; expenditures (1995) U.S.$105,000,000.
Population economically active (1991): total 4,740,000; activity rate of total population 40.0% (participation rates [1985]: ages 15–69, 66.3%; female 38.5%; unemployed, n.a.).

Price index (2000 = 100)

	1997	1998	1999	2000	2001	2002
Consumer price index	86.5	97.2	98.9	100.0	104.5	107.4

Production (metric tons except as noted). Agriculture, forestry, fishing (2002): cassava 1,900,000, sugarcane 1,350,000, plantains 1,200,000, corn (maize) 750,000, bananas 630,000, sorghum 450,000, vegetables and melons 450,000, tomatoes 370,000, yams 260,000, seed cotton 200,000, peanuts (groundnuts) 200,000, sweet potatoes 175,000, palm oil 150,000, cacao 125,000, coffee 78,000, natural rubber 55,000, avocados 52,000; livestock (number of live animals) 5,900,000 cattle, 4,400,000 goats, 3,800,000 sheep; roundwood (2002) 10,526,000 cu m; fish catch (2001) 111,100. Mining and quarrying (2002): pozzolana 620,000; aluminum 80,000; gold 1,000 kg. Manufacturing (value added in U.S.$'000; 1999): beverages 182; food products 149; textiles 112; wood products excluding furniture 68; nonferrous base metals 41; rubber products 38. Energy production (consumption): electricity (kW-hr; 2000) 3,441,000,000 (3,441,000,000); coal (metric tons; 2000) 1,000 (1,000); crude petroleum (barrels; 2000) 52,000,000 (10,700,000); petroleum products (metric tons; 2000) 1,530,000 (898,000); natural gas, none (none).
Land use as % of total land area (2000): in temporary crops 12.8%, in permanent crops 2.6%, in pasture 4.3%; overall forest area 51.3%.

Foreign trade

Balance of trade (current prices)

	1996–97	1997–98	1998–99	1999–2000	2000–01	2001–02
CFAF '000,000,000	+380.5	+295.8	+205.8	+460.5	+382.4	+159.5
% of total	21.3%	13.9%	11.0%	20.3%	14.2%	7.1%

Imports (2000–01): CFAF 1,157,800,000,000 (minerals and other raw materials *c.* 21%, semifinished goods *c.* 16%, industrial equipment *c.* 13%, food and beverages *c.* 11%, transport equipment *c.* 10%). *Major import sources:* France *c.* 24%; Nigeria *c.* 20%; Germany *c.* 5%; U.S. *c.* 5%; Japan *c.* 5%; Belgium-Luxembourg *c.* 5%.
Exports (2000–01): CFAF 1,540,200,000,000 (crude petroleum 50.6%, lumber 13.4%, cocoa beans 6.3%, aluminum 4.6%, cotton 4.2%, coffee 3.7%). *Major export destinations:* Italy *c.* 24%; France *c.* 9%; Spain *c.* 9%; The Netherlands *c.* 7%; China *c.* 7%; Taiwan *c.* 7%.

Transport and communications

Transport. Railroads (2001): route length 631 mi, 1,016 km; passenger-km 237,800,000; metric ton-km cargo 854,600,000. Roads (1999): total length 30,630 mi, 49,300 km (paved 8%). Vehicles (1997): passenger cars 98,000; trucks and buses 64,350. Air transport (2001): passenger-km 796,567,000; metric ton-km cargo 23,255,000; airports (1998) with scheduled flights 5.

Communications

Medium	date	unit	number	units per 1,000 persons
Daily newspapers	2000	circulation	104,000	7.0
Radio	2000	receivers	2,410,000	163
Television	2000	receivers	503,000	34
Telephones	2002	main lines	110,900	7.0
Cellular telephones	2003	subscribers	1,077,000	66
Personal computers	2002	units	90,000	5.7
Internet	2002	users	60,000	3.8

Education and health

Educational attainment: n.a. *Literacy* (2001): percentage of total population age 15 and over literate 72.5%; males literate 79.9%; females literate 65.1%.

Education (1998)

	schools	teachers	students	student/ teacher ratio
Primary (age 6–14)	9,459	41,142	2,133,707	51.9
Secondary (age 15–24)	700[7]	19,515	341,439	17.5
Vocational	324[7]	7,245[7]	122,122	...
Higher[8]	6	2,645	66,902	25.3

Health: physicians (1996) 1,031 (1 per 13,510 persons); hospital beds (1988) 29,285 (1 per 371 persons); infant mortality rate per 1,000 live births (2003) 70.1.
Food (2001): daily per capita caloric intake 2,242 (vegetable products 94%, animal products 6%); 97% of FAO recommended minimum requirement.

Military

Total active duty personnel (2003): 14,100 (army 88.7%, navy 9.2%, air force 2.1%). *Military expenditure as percentage of GNP* (1999): 1.8% (world 2.4%); per capita expenditure U.S.$10.

[1]Formerly pegged to the French franc and since Jan. 1, 2002, to the euro at the rate of 1 € = CFAF 655.96. [2]Detail does not add to total given because of rounding. [3]Based on land area. [4]Beginning of year. [5]Indirect taxes. [6]Weights of consumer price index components. [7]1995–96. [8]1990–91.

Internet resources for further information:
- **La Banque de France: La Zone Franc**
http://www.banque-france.fr/fr/zonefr/main.htm

Canada

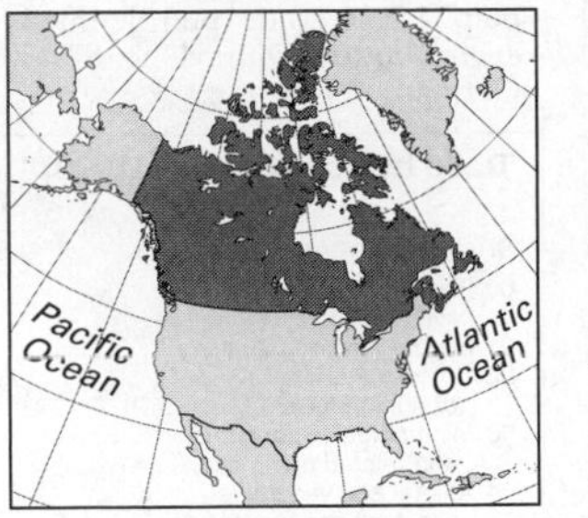

Official name: Canada.
Form of government: federal multiparty parliamentary state with two legislative houses (Senate [105]; House of Commons [308]).
Chief of state: Queen of Canada (British Monarch).
Representative of chief of state: Governor-General.
Head of government: Prime Minister.
Capital: Ottawa.
Official languages: English; French.
Official religion: none.
Monetary unit: 1 Canadian dollar (Can$) = 100 cents; valuation (Sept. 1, 2004) 1 U.S.$ = Can$1.32; 1 £ = Can$2.37.

Area and population

		area		population
Provinces	Capitals	sq mi	sq km	2003 estimate[1]
Alberta	Edmonton	255,541	661,848	3,153,700
British Columbia	Victoria	364,764	944,735	4,146,600
Manitoba	Winnipeg	250,116	647,797	1,162,800
New Brunswick	Fredericton	28,150	72,908	750,600
Newfoundland and Labrador	St. John's	156,453	405,212	519,600
Nova Scotia	Halifax	21,345	55,284	936,000
Ontario	Toronto	415,599	1,076,395	12,238,300
Prince Edward Island	Charlottetown	2,185	5,660	137,800
Quebec	Quebec	595,391	1,542,056	7,487,200
Saskatchewan	Regina	251,367	651,036	994,800
Territories				
Northwest Territories	Yellowknife	519,735	1,346,106	41,900
Nunavut[2]	Iqaluit	808,185	2,093,190	29,400
Yukon Territory	Whitehorse	186,272	482,443	31,100
TOTAL		3,855,103	9,984,670	31,629,800

Demography

Population (2004): 31,876,000.
Density (2004)[3]: persons per sq mi 9.0, persons per sq km 3.5.
Urban-rural (2001): urban 78.9%; rural 21.1%.
Sex distribution (2003): male 49.51%; female 50.49%.
Age breakdown (2003): under 15, 18.3%; 15–29, 20.3%; 30–44, 23.4%; 45–59, 20.7%; 60–74, 11.3%; 75 and over, 6.0%.
Population projection: (2010) 33,296,000; (2020) 35,390,000.
Ethnic origin (2000): Anglo-Canadian 45.5%; French-Canadian 23.5%; Chinese 3.4%; British expatriates 3.3%; Indo-Pakistani 2.6%, of which Punjabi 2.3%; German 2.4%; Italian 2.2%; U.S. white 1.8%; Métis (part-Indian) 1.8%; Indian 1.5%, of which detribalized 0.5%; Jewish 1.4%; Arab 1.3%; Ukrainian 1.2%; Eskimo (Inuit) 0.1%; other 8.0%.
Religious affiliation (2001): Christian 77.1%, of which Roman Catholic 43.2%, Protestant 28.3%, unspecified Christian 2.6%, Orthodox 1.7%, other Christian 1.3%; Muslim 2.0%; Jewish 1.1%; Hindu 1.0%; Buddhist 1.0%; Sikh 0.9%; nonreligious 16.5%; other 0.4%.
Major metropolitan areas (2002): Toronto 5,029,900; Montreal 3,548,800; Vancouver 2,122,700; Ottawa-Hull 1,128,900; Calgary 993,200; Edmonton 967,200; Quebec 697,800; Hamilton 686,900; Winnipeg 685,500; Kitchener 438,000.

Other metropolitan areas (2002)

	population		population		population
Chicoutimi-Jonquière	156,900	Regina	197,000	Sherbrooke	156,500
Halifax	363,200	St. Catharines–Niagara	392,300	Sudbury	155,900
London	427,300	St. John's	177,200	Trois Rivières	141,400
Oshawa	310,000	Saskatoon	231,800	Victoria	318,900
				Windsor	319,900

Place of birth (2001): 81.6% native-born; 18.4% foreign-born, of which U.K. 2.0%, other European 5.7%, Asian countries 5.8%, U.S. 0.8%, other 4.1%.
Mobility (2001). Population living in the same residence as in 1996: 58.1%; different residence, same municipality 22.4%; same province, different municipality 3.3%; different province 12.7%; different country 3.5%.
Households. Total number of households (2002) 11,657,730. Average household size (2002) 2.7; 1 person (1997) 25.2%, 2 persons 33.0%, 3 persons 16.7%, 4 persons 16.3%, 5 or more persons 8.8%. Family households (2001): 8,371,020 (72.4%), nonfamily 3,191,955 (27.6%, of which 1 person 75.6%).
Immigration (2002): permanent immigrants admitted 222,447; (2000) from Asia 62.1%, of which India 11.6%, Philippines 5.6%, Vietnam 0.7%, Hong Kong 0.3%; United States 2.4%; United Kingdom 2.1%; refugee arrivals (2002) 27,899.

Vital statistics

Birth rate per 1,000 population (2003): 10.5 (world avg. 21.3); (1997) legitimate 72.3%; illegitimate 27.7%.
Death rate per 1,000 population (2003): 7.2 (world avg. 9.1).
Natural increase rate per 1,000 population (2003): 3.3 (world avg. 12.2).
Total fertility rate (avg. births per childbearing woman; 2002): 1.6.
Marriage rate per 1,000 population (2003): 4.8.
Divorce rate per 1,000 population (2003): 2.2.
Life expectancy at birth (2003): male 76.4 years; female 83.4 years.
Major causes of death per 100,000 population (1998): diseases of the circulatory system 214.8; malignant neoplasms (cancers) 183.5; diseases of the respiratory system 55.7; accidents and violence 29.0 (including suicide 12.0).

Social indicators

Educational attainment (2001). Percentage of population age 15 and over having: incomplete primary education 2.2%; complete primary education 7.6%; some secondary and complete secondary 49.5%; postsecondary 25.3%; undergraduate degree 10.1%; graduate degree 5.3%.

Distribution of income (1999)

percentage of household income by quintile

1	2	3	4	5 (highest)
7.4%	11.6%	15.3%	24.2%	41.5%

Quality of working life. Average workweek (2000): 31.6 hours. Annual rate per 100,000 workers for (1997): injury, accident, or industrial illness 1,330; death 2.7. Average days lost to labour stoppages per 1,000 employee-workdays (2001): 0.7. Average commuting distance (2001): 4.5 mi, 7.2 km; mode of transportation: automobile 80.7%, public transportation 10.5%, walking 6.6%, other 2.2%. Labour force covered by a pension plan (2001): 33.6%.
Access to services. Proportion of households having access to: electricity (2002) 100.0%; public water supply (1996) 99.8%; public sewage collection (1996) 99.3%.
Social participation. Eligible voters participating in last national election (June 2004): 60.5%. Population over 18 years of age participating in voluntary work (2000): 26.7%. Union membership as percentage of civilian labour force (2003) 25.0%. Attendance at religious services on a weekly basis (2001): 20.0%.
Social deviance (2003). Offense rate per 100,000 population for: violent crime 962.8, of which assault 746.5, sexual assault 74.1, homicide 1.7; property crime 4,121, of which auto theft 541, burglary 900.
Leisure (1998). Favourite leisure activities (hours weekly): television (2002) 21.6; social time 13.3; reading 2.8; sports and entertainment 1.4.
Material well-being (1999). Households possessing: automobile 64.4%; telephone 98.2%; cellular phone 31.9%; colour television 99.9%; central air conditioner 34.0%; cable television 73.3%; home computers 49.8%; Internet access 33.1%.

National economy

Gross national product (2003): U.S.$756,770,000,000 (U.S.$23,930 per capita).

Structure of gross domestic product and labour force

	2003			
	in value Can$'000,000[4]	% of total value	labour force	% of labour force
Agriculture	22,626	2.2	629,200 (Agriculture and Mining)	3.7
Mining	35,908	3.6		
Manufacturing	173,664	17.2	2,294,000	13.4
Construction	54,389	5.4	931,400	5.5
Public utilities	25,412	2.5	131,500	0.8
Transportation	45,844	4.5	766,800	4.5
Trade	119,443	11.8	2,460,700	14.4
Finance	187,218	18.5	936,200	5.5
Pub. admin., defense	58,263	5.8	815,200	4.8
Services[5]	287,867	28.5	6,781,000	39.8
Other	—	—	1,300,800[6]	7.6[6]
TOTAL	1,010,634[7]	100.0	17,046,800	100.0

Budget (2003–04)[8]. Revenue: Can$204,075,000,000 (income tax 60.8%, sales tax 21.6%, contributions to social security 10.8%, other 6.8%). Expenditures: Can$197,296,000,000 (social services and welfare 37.9%, defense and social protection 13.0%, public debt interest 12.1%, economy 3.9%, health 3.1%, education 2.4%).
Public debt (2001): U.S.$406,000,000,000.
Tourism (2002): receipts U.S.$9,700,000,000; expenditures U.S.$9,929,000,000.

Manufacturing, mining, and construction enterprises (2000)

	no. of employees	weekly wages as a % of avg. of all wages[9]	annual value added (Can$'000,000)[10]
Manufacturing			
Transport equipment	255,500	148.4	27,656
Food and beverages	239,500	100.2	21,577[11]
Chemicals and related products	95,700	147.5	14,884
Electrical and electronic products	139,700	140.1	13,264
Metal fabricating	191,500	123.2	11,418
Primary metals	87,300	153.9	11,171
Wood products (excl. furniture)	150,700	111.9	11,160
Paper and related products	105,400	154.4	11,132
Nonelectrical machinery	95,700	145.9	9,756
Rubber and plastic products	98,700	111.3	9,271
Furniture and fixtures	67,300	99.7	4,928
Nonmetallic mineral products	54,300	121.5	4,362
Printing, publishing, and related products	157,100	109.6	4,184
Wearing apparel	93,200	72.6	2,799
Textiles	54,700	101.9	2,048
Petroleum and coal products	15,400	186.1	1,815
Tobacco products industries	4,400	201.3	[11]
Mining	140,900	180.5	36,517
Construction	557,700	115.4	51,117

Production (metric tons except as noted). Agriculture, forestry, fishing (2002): wheat 15,689,000, corn (maize) 9,069,000, barley 7,282,600, potatoes 4,645,000, rapeseed 3,577,100, oats 2,748,000, vegetables 2,435,000 (of which tomatoes 690,000, carrots 280,000, onions 190,000, cabbage 160,000), soybeans 2,334,000, dry peas 1,365,000, linseed 679,400, sugar beets 540,000, apples 460,000; livestock (number of live animals) 14,367,100 pigs, 13,699,500 cattle, 993,600 sheep; roundwood (2002) 193,168,000 cu m; fish catch (2001) 1,116,902. Mining and quarrying (value of production in Can$'000,000; 2002): gold 2,292; nickel 1,883; potash 1,598; copper 1,419; iron ore 1,392; zinc 1,090; sand and gravel 1,047; stone 972; diamonds 802. Manufacturing (value of shipments in Can$'000,000; 2002): transportation equipment 119,746; food 62,911; chemicals 37,679; paper products 32,726; petroleum and coal 32,250; primary metals 32,216; wood industries 29,498; fabricated metal products 27,510; machinery 24,113; rubber and plastic products 23,002; computers and electronic products 21,255.

Retail trade (2002)

	no. of employees[12]	weekly wages as a % of all wages[9, 12]	annual sales (Can$'000,000)
Motor vehicle dealers	326,400[13]	143.5	89,979.0
Food stores	496,700	84.2	66,424.8
Clothing and footwear stores	144,600	79.4	27,229.0
Home furnishings and electronics	173,200	81.7	24,501.5
Automotive stores	[13]	143.5	23,078.5
Service stations	[13]	143.5	22,679.5
Furniture and appliance stores	87,000	119.2	18,275.9
Pharmacies	54,200	…	14,356.7
Sporting goods	…	…	11,686.9
Hardware stores	…	81.7	8,113.0
Electronics, including computers	[14]	92.0	8,108.2
Personal care products	[14]	79.4	7,620.0
Other	235,300[14]	92.0	53,767.7

Energy production (consumption): electricity (kW-hr; 2000) 590,134,000,000 (554,411,000,000); hard coal (metric tons; 2000) 33,804,000 (21,620,000); lignite (metric tons; 2000) 35,359,000 (40,459,000); crude petroleum (barrels; 2000) 655,400,000 (554,300,000); petroleum products (metric tons; 2000) 103,972,000 (88,296,000); natural gas (cu m; 2000) 164,352,000,000 (76,277,000,000).

Population economically active (2003): total 17,046,800; activity rate of total population 54.0% (participation rates: ages 15 and over 67.5%; female 46.4%; unemployed [August 2004] 7.2%).

Price and earnings indexes (2000 = 100)

	1997	1998	1999	2000	2001	2002	2003
Consumer price index	94.7	95.7	97.3	100.0	102.5	104.0	107.7
Hourly earnings index[15]	94.3	96.2	97.5	100.0	101.6	104.7	107.8

Household income and expenditure (2002). Average household size 2.6; average annual income per family (2002) Can$73,200 (U.S.$46,340); sources of income (1995): wages and salaries 57.0%, transfer payments 20.7%, property and entrepreneurial income 13.7%, profits 8.6%; expenditure (2002): housing 25.9%, food, alcohol, and tobacco 18.9%, transportation and communications 19.5%, recreation 8.2%, utilities 6.4%, clothing 5.7%, household durable goods 4.1%, health 3.7%, education 2.1%, other 5.5%.

Financial aggregates

	1998	1999	2000	2001	2002	2003
Exchange rate, Can$ per:						
U.S. dollar	1.53	1.44	1.50	1.59	1.58	1.40
£	2.55	2.33	2.24	2.29	2.37	2.29
SDR	2.16	1.98	1.95	2.00	2.15	1.92
International reserves (U.S.$)						
Total (excl. gold; '000,000)	23,308	28,126	31,924	33,962	36,984	36,222
SDRs ('000,000)	1,098	527	574	614	719	838
Reserve pos. in IMF ('000,000)	2,299	3,168	2,509	2,863	3,580	3,847
Foreign exchange ('000,000)	19,991	24,432	28,841	30,484	32,685	31,537
Gold ('000,000 fine troy oz)	2.49	1.81	1.18	1.05	0.60	0.11
% world reserves	0.26	0.18	0.12	0.11	0.06	0.11
Interest and prices						
Central bank discount (%)	5.25	5.00	6.00	2.50	3.00	3.00
Govt. bond yield (%)	5.47	5.69	5.89	5.78	5.66	5.28
Industrial share prices (2000 = 100)	70.3	73.5	100.0	80.5	73.2	74.5
Balance of payments (U.S.$'000,000)						
Balance of visible trade, of which:	+15,922	+28,291	+45,579	+45,864	+36,838	+47,324
Imports, f.o.b.	204,617	220,203	243,899	226,495	227,240	334,331
Exports, f.o.b.	220,539	248,494	289,468	272,359	264,078	381,655
Balance of invisibles	–23,761	–26,526	–24,974	–28,442	–21,929	–30,056
Balance of payments, current account	–7,839	+1,765	+20,595	+17,442	+14,909	+17,268

Land use as % of total land area (2000): in temporary crops 4.9%, in permanent crops 0.02%, in pasture 3.1%; overall forest area 26.5%.

Foreign trade

Balance of trade (current prices)

	1998	1999	2000	2001	2002	2003
Can$'000,000,000	+19.8	+35.1	+56.3	+58.9	+47.8	+47.3
% of total	3.2%	5.2%	7.3%	7.9%	6.4%	6.6%

Imports (2002): Can$348,198,000,000 (machinery and apparatus 27.8%; transport equipment 21.5%, of which road vehicles 19.1%; chemicals and chemical products 9.4%; food products 5.1%; crude petroleum 3.4%). *Major import sources:* U.S. 62.6%; China 4.6%; Japan 4.4%; Mexico 3.6%; U.K. 2.8%; Germany 2.4%; France 1.7%.

Exports (2002): Can$396,020,000,000 (transport equipment 24.8%, of which road vehicles 21.4%; machinery and apparatus 13.3%; food products 6.4%; chemicals and chemical products 5.9%; natural gas 5.2%; wood and wood pulp 4.7%; crude petroleum 4.5%; paper and paperboard 4.4%). *Major export destinations:* U.S. 87.2%; Japan 2.1%; U.K. 1.1%; China 1.0%; Germany 0.7%.

Trade by commodities (1998)

	imports		exports	
SITC Group	U.S.$'000,000	%	U.S.$'000,000	%
00 Food and live animals	9,629.6	4.8	12,443.0	5.8
01 Beverages and tobacco	1,065.2	0.5	1,039.0	0.5
02 Crude materials, excluding fuels	5,718.0	2.8	19,337.5	9.0
03 Mineral fuels, lubricants, and related materials	6,847.8	3.5	17,584.3	8.2
04 Animal and vegetable oils, fats, and waxes	…	…	…	…
05 Chemicals and related products, n.e.s.	16,363.1	8.1	11,792.8	5.5
06 Basic manufactures	27,121.9	13.5	34,591.1	16.1
07 Machinery and transport equipment	105,052.9	52.2	88,180.3	41.2
08 Miscellaneous manufactured articles	23,369.9	11.6	13,996.2	6.5
09 Goods not classified by kind	5,568.9	2.8	14,280.2	6.7
TOTAL	201,219.3[16]	100.0[16]	214,187.9[16]	100.0[16]

Direction of trade (1999)

	imports		exports	
	U.S.$'000,000	%	U.S.$'000,000	%
Africa	1,440	0.7	993	0.4
Asia	28,838	13.8	11,587	4.9[16]
China	6,017	2.9	1,673	0.7
Japan	10,104	4.8	5,254	2.2
Taiwan	3,100	1.5	740	0.3
Other	9,617	4.6	3,920	1.6
Americas	153,335	73.2	211,454	89.4
Mexico	6,263	3.0	1,025	0.4
United States	143,498	68.5	208,013	88.0
Other Americas	3,574	1.7	2,416	1.0
Europe	24,904	11.9	11,587	4.9
EU	21,524	10.3	10,427	4.4
Other Europe	3,380	1.6	1,160	0.5
Oceania	1,077	0.5	758	0.3
TOTAL	214,161[16, 17]	100.0[16, 17]	237,337[16]	100.0[16]

Transport and communications

Transport. Railroads (2000): length 65,403 km; passenger-km 1,571,000,000; metric ton-km cargo 319,382,000,000. Roads (1999): total length 901,903 km (paved 35%). Vehicles (1998): passenger cars 13,887,270; trucks and buses 3,694,125. Air transport (2003): passenger-km 59,016,000,000; metric ton-km cargo 1,284,800,000; airports (1997) 269.

Communications

Medium	date	unit	number	units per 1,000 persons
Daily newspapers	2000	circulation	4,890,000	159
Radio	2000	receivers	32,200,000	1,047
Television	2000	receivers	21,700,000	691
Telephones	2003	main lines	19,950,900	658
Cellular telephones	2003	subscribers	13,221,800	417
Personal computers	2002	units	15,300,000	487
Internet	2002	users	16,110,000	513

Education and health

Literacy (2003): total population age 15 and over literate virtually 100%.

Education (1999–2000)

	schools	teachers	students	student/ teacher ratio
Primary (age 6–14) } Secondary (age 14–18) }	15,595	302,977	5,397,000	17.8
Postsecondary[18]	199	27,832	407,000	14.6
Higher[19]	75	33,801	591,000	17.5

Health: physicians (2000) 60,559 (1 per 508 persons); hospital beds (1997) 161,867 (1 per 185 persons); infant mortality rate per 1,000 live births (2001) 5.0.

Food (2001): daily per capita caloric intake 3,176 (vegetable products 70%, animal products 30%); 121% of FAO recommended minimum requirement.

Military

Total active duty personnel (2003): 52,300 (army 36.9%, navy 17.2%, air force 25.8%, not identified by service 20.1%). *Military expenditure as percentage of GNP* (1999): 1.4% (world 2.4%); per capita expenditure U.S.$269.

[1]July 1 estimate based on adjusted 2001 census figure. [2]Nunavut came into existence on April 1, 1999. [3]Based on land area of 3,551,023 sq mi (9,093,507 sq km). [4]At prices of 1997. [5]Services includes communications and hotels and restaurants. [6]Unemployed. [7]GDP at current values in 2003 was Can$1,181,900,000. [8]Federal government revenue and expenditure. [9]Excludes agriculture, fishing and trapping, private household services, religious organizations, and the military. [10]For 2002 in constant dollars of 1997. [11]Food and beverages includes tobacco. [12]2000. [13]Motor vehicle dealers includes Service stations and Automotive stores. [14]Other includes Electronics and Personal care products. [15]Manufacturing only. [16]Detail does not add to total because of discrepancies in estimates. [17]Total for imports includes U.S.$3,299,000,000 (1.7% of total imports; mostly special transactions) not distributable by region. [18]Community colleges. [19]Universities only.

Internet resources for further information:
- **Statistics Canada http://www.statcan.ca**

Cape Verde

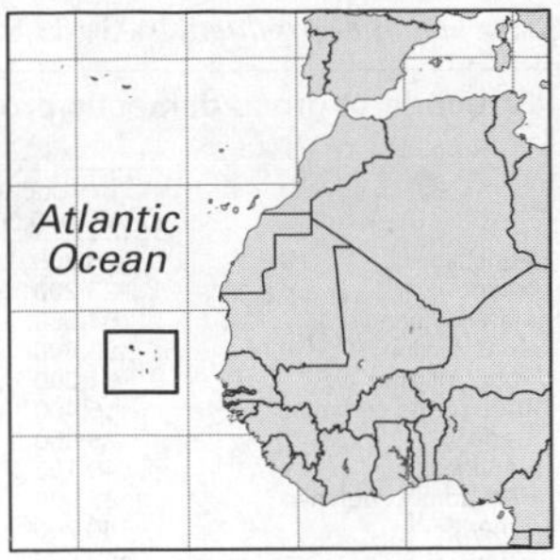

Official name: República de Cabo Verde (Republic of Cape Verde).
Form of government: multiparty republic with one legislative house (National Assembly [72]).
Chief of state: President.
Head of government: Prime Minister.
Capital: Praia.
Official language: Portuguese.
Official religion: none.
Monetary unit: 1 escudo (C.V.Esc.)[1] = 100 centavos; valuation (Sept. 1, 2004) 1 U.S.$ = C.V.Esc. 91.90; 1 £ = C.V.Esc. 165.32.

Area and population

Island Groups / Islands/Counties[2] / Counties	Capitals	area sq mi	area sq km	population 2000 census
Leeward Islands		696[3]	1,803	287,323
Brava	Nova Sintra	26	67	6,820
Fogo				
Mosteiros[4]	Mosteiros	184	476	9,479
São Filipe	São Filipe			27,930
Maio	Porto Inglês	104	269	6,742
Santiago		383	991	236,352
Praia	Praia	153	396	106,052
Santa Catarina	Assomada	94	243	49,970
Santa Cruz	Pedra Badejo	58	149	32,822
São Domingos[4]	São Domingos	78	203	13,296
São Miguel[4]	São Miguel			16,153
Tarrafal	Tarrafal			18,059
Windward Islands		861[3]	2,230	147,489
Boa Vista	Sal Rei	239	620	4,193
Sal	Santa Maria	83	216	14,792
Santo Antão		300	779	47,124
Paúl	Pombas	21	54	8,325
Porto Novo	Porto Novo	215	558	17,239
Ribeira Grande	Ponta do Sol	64	167	21,560
São Nicolau	Ribeira Brava	150	388	13,536
São Vicente[5]	Mindelo	88	227	67,844
TOTAL		1,557	4,033	434,812

Demography

Population (2004): 454,000.
Density (2004): persons per sq mi 291.6, persons per sq km 112.6.
Urban-rural (2002): urban 63.5%; rural 36.5%.
Sex distribution (2003): male 48.39%; female 51.61%.
Age breakdown (2003): under 15, 41.0%; 15–29, 26.7%; 30–44, 17.0%; 45–59, 6.8%; 60–74, 5.8%; 75 and over, 2.7%.
Population projection: (2010) 472,000; (2020) 491,000.
Doubling time: 35 years.
Ethnic composition (2000): Cape Verdean *mestico* (black-white admixture) 69.6%; Fulani 12.2%; Balanta 10.0%; Mandyako 4.6%; Portuguese white 2.0%; other 1.6%.
Religious affiliation (2000): Roman Catholic 91.4%; Muslim 2.8%; other 5.8%.
Major cities (2000): Praia 94,757; Mindelo 62,970; São Filipe 7,894.

Vital statistics

Birth rate per 1,000 population (2003): 27.0 (world avg. 21.3); (1989) legitimate 28.9%; illegitimate 71.1%.
Death rate per 1,000 population (2002): 6.9 (world avg. 9.1).
Natural increase rate per 1,000 population (2002): 20.1 (world avg. 12.2).
Total fertility rate (avg. births per childbearing woman; 2003): 3.8.
Marriage rate per 1,000 population (1994): 3.1.
Life expectancy at birth (2003): male 66.5 years; female 73.2 years.
Major causes of death per 100,000 population (1987): enteritis and other diarrheal diseases 97.4; heart disease 77.9; malignant neoplasms (cancers) 47.9; pneumonia 46.4; accidents, poisoning, and violence 44.0.

National economy

Budget (2001). Revenue: C.V.Esc. 14,900,000,000 (tax revenue 87.2%, of which taxes on international trade 35.6%, income taxes 32.2%, sales taxes 14.1%; nontax revenue 12.8%). Expenditures: C.V.Esc. 21,200,000,000 (current expenditure 69.8%, of which wages and salaries 31.1%, transfers 26.9%, public debt 6.6%, goods and services 2.9%; capital expenditure 30.2%).
Public debt (external, outstanding; 2002): U.S.$385,000,000.
Production (metric tons except as noted). Agriculture, forestry, fishing (2002): corn (maize) 20,000, sugarcane 14,000, bananas 6,000, coconuts 6,000, vegetables (including melons) 5,000, fruits (except melons) 4,700, sweet potatoes 3,800; livestock (number of live animals) 200,000 pigs, 112,000 goats, 22,000 cattle; roundwood, n.a.; fish catch (2000) 10,821. Mining and quarrying (2000): salt 2,000. Manufacturing (1999): flour 15,901; bread 5,628[6]; soap 833; paint 628[7]; canned tuna 337[6]; cigarettes 41 kg; beer 4,104,546 litres; soft drinks 922,714[7] litres. Energy production (consumption): electricity (kW-hr; 2001) 43,000,000 (43,000,000); coal, none (none); crude petroleum, none (none); petroleum products (metric tons; 2001) none (101,619); natural gas, none (none).
Tourism (2002): receipts from visitors U.S.$66,000,000; expenditures by nationals abroad U.S.$56,000,000.
Land use as % of total land area (2000): in temporary crops 9.7%, in permanent crops 0.5%, in pasture 6.2%; overall forest area 21.1%.

Gross national product (2003): U.S.$701,000,000 (U.S.$1,490 per capita).

Structure of gross domestic product and labour force

	2001		1990	
	in value C.V.Esc. '000,000	% of total value	labour force	% of labour force
Agriculture	6,888.7	10.3	29,876	24.7
Manufacturing	6,098.3	9.1	5,520	4.6
Public utilities			883	0.7
Mining			410	0.3
Construction	5,196.2	7.8	22,722	18.9
Transp. and commun.	12,197.7	18.3	6,138	5.1
Trade	12,402.2	18.6	12,747	10.6
Finance	7,686.1	11.5	821	0.7
Pub. admin., defense	9,311.9	14.0	17,358	14.4
Services	1,967.8	3.0		
Other	4,946.1[8]	7.4[8]	24,090	20.0
TOTAL	66,695	100.0	120,565	100.0

Population economically active (2000): total 174,644; activity rate of total population 40.2% (participation rates: ages 15–64 [1990] 64.3%; female 39.0%; unemployed 17.4%).

Price index (2000 = 100)

	1997	1998	1999	2000	2001	2002	2003
Consumer price index	94	98	103	100	103	105	106

Household income and expenditure. Average household size (2000) 4.6; income per household: n.a.; sources of income: n.a.; expenditure (1988): food 51.1%, housing, fuel, and power 13.5%, beverages and tobacco 11.8%, transportation and communications 8.8%, household durable goods 6.9%, other 7.9%.

Foreign trade[9]

Balance of trade (current prices)

	1997	1998	1999	2000	2001
C.V.Esc. '000,000	−20,469	−21,582	−25,746	−26,313	−29,317
% of total	88.8%	91.4%	91.7%	91.2%	92.4%

Imports (2000): C.V.Esc. 27,585,000,000 (food 32.8%, machinery and apparatus 16.1%, transport equipment 9.5%, base and fabricated metals 6.5%). *Major import sources* (2001–02): Portugal 54.8%; The Netherlands 13.4%; Spain 4.9%; Belgium 4.1%; Brazil 3.6%.
Exports (2000): C.V.Esc. 1,272,000,000 (shoes and shoe parts 51.8%, clothing 35.1%, fish 4.8%). *Major export destinations* (2001–02): Portugal 91.7%; United States 2.1%; Germany 1.6%.

Transport and communications

Transport. Railroads: none. Roads (1999): total length 684 mi, 1,100 km (paved [1996] 78%). Vehicles (2000): passenger cars 13,473; trucks and buses 3,085. Air transport (2001)[10]: passenger-mi 171,000,000, passenger-km 276,000,000; short ton-mi cargo (1998) 16,200,000, metric ton-km cargo 26,000,000; airports (1997) with scheduled flights 9.

Communications

Medium	date	unit	number	units per 1,000 persons
Radio	1997	receivers	71,000	179
Television	2000	receivers	2,000	4.6
Telephones	2003	main lines	71,700	156
Cellular telephones	2003	subscribers	53,300	116
Personal computers	2002	units	35,000	78
Internet	2003	users	20,400	44

Education and health

Educational attainment (1990). Percentage of population age 25 and over having: no formal schooling 47.9%; primary 40.9%; incomplete secondary 3.9%; complete secondary 1.4%; higher 1.5%; unknown 4.4%. *Literacy* (2000): total population age 15 and over literate 73.8%; males 84.5%; females 65.7%.

Education (1997–98)

	schools	teachers	students	student/ teacher ratio
Primary (age 7–12)	370[11]	3,219	91,636[12]	...
Secondary (age 13–17) / Vocational	...	1,372	40,214[12]	...
Higher	...	...	1,600[13]	...

Health (2000): physicians 102 (1 per 4,274 persons); hospital beds 689 (1 per 631 persons); infant mortality rate per 1,000 live births (2002) 50.5.
Food (2001): daily per capita caloric intake 3,308 (vegetable products 85%, animal products 15%); 141% of FAO recommended minimum requirement.

Military

Total active duty personnel (2003): 1,200 (army 83.3%, air force 8.3%, coast guard 8.4%). *Military expenditure as percentage of GNP* (1999): 0.9% (world 2.4%); per capita expenditure U.S.$13.

[1]Formerly pegged to the Portuguese escudo and since Jan. 1, 2002, to the euro at the rate of €1 = C.V.Esc. 110.27. [2]Island/county areas are coterminous except Fogo, Santiago, and Santo Antão islands. [3]Detail does not add to total given because of rounding. [4]Created after the 1990 census. [5]Includes Santa Luzia Island, which is uninhabited. [6]1995. [7]1996. [8]Taxes and duties on imports. [9]Imports c.i.f., exports f.o.b.; excludes reexports of fuel. [10]TACV airline only. [11]1991. [12]1999–2000. [13]Students abroad in 1996–97.

Internet resources for further information:
- **Instituto Nacional de Estatística de Cabo Verde http://www.ine.cv**
- **Banco de Cabo Verde http://www.bcv.cv**

Central African Republic

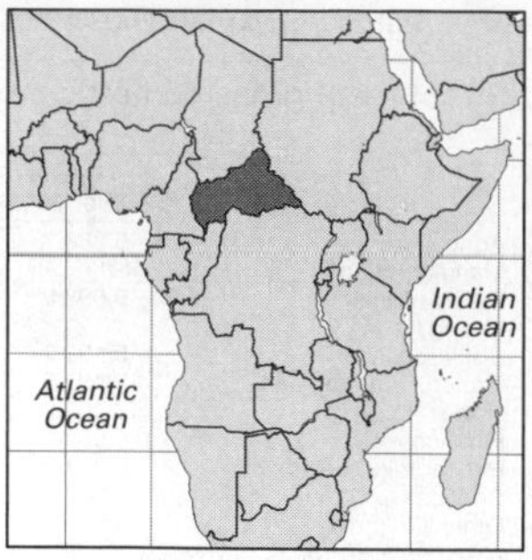

Official name: République Centrafricaine (Central African Republic).
Form of government: military regime with one advisory body (National Transitional Council [63])[1].
Chief of state: President assisted by Prime Minister[1].
Capital: Bangui.
Official languages: French; Sango.
Official religion: none.
Monetary unit: 1 CFA franc (CFAF) = 100 centimes; valuation (Sept. 1, 2004) 1 U.S.$ = CFAF 539.75; 1 £ = CFAF 970.98[2].

Area and population

		area		population
Prefectures	**Capitals**	sq mi	sq km	1988 census
Bamingui-Bangoran	Ndélé	22,471	58,200	28,643
Basse-Kotto	Mobaye	6,797	17,604	194,750
Haut-Mbomou	Obo	21,440	55,530	27,113
Haute-Kotto	Bria	33,456	86,650	58,838
Kemo	Sibut	6,642	17,204	82,884
Lobaye	Mbaïki	7,427	19,235	169,554
Mambéré-Kadéï	Berbérati	11,661	30,203	230,364
Mbomou	Bangassou	23,610	61,150	119,252
Nana-Gribizi	Kaga-Bandoro	7,721	19,996	95,497
Nana-Mambéré	Bouar	10,270	26,600	191,970
Ombella-M'poko	Boali	12,292	31,835	180,857
Ouaka	Bambari	19,266	49,900	208,332
Ouham	Bossangoa	19,402	50,250	262,950
Ouham-Pendé	Bozoum	12,394	32,100	287,653
Sangha-Mbaéré	Nola	7,495	19,412	65,961
Vakaga	Birao	17,954	46,500	32,118
Autonomous commune				
Bangui	Bangui	26	67	451,690
TOTAL		240,324	622,436	2,688,426

Demography

Population (2004): 3,742,000.
Density (2004): persons per sq mi 15.6, persons per sq km 6.0.
Urban-rural (2002): urban 41.7%; rural 58.3%.
Sex distribution (2003): male 49.47%; female 50.53%.
Age breakdown (2003): under 15, 43.1%; 15–29, 28.9%; 30–44, 14.6%; 45–59, 8.2%; 60–74, 4.2%; 75 and over, 1.0%.
Population projection: (2010) 4,073,000; (2020) 4,557,000.
Doubling time: 44 years.
Ethnolinguistic composition (1988): Gbaya (Baya) 23.7%; Banda 23.4%; Mandjia 14.7%; Ngbaka 7.6%; Sara 6.5%; Mbum 6.3%; Kare 2.4%; French 0.1%; other 15.3%.
Religious affiliation (2000): Christian 67.8%, of which Roman Catholic 18.4%, Protestant 14.4%, African Christian 11.6%, other Christian 23.4%; Muslim 15.6%; traditional beliefs 15.4%; other 1.2%.
Major cities (1994): Bangui 524,000; Berbérati 47,000; Bouar 43,000; Bambari 41,000; Carnot 41,000; Bossangoa 33,000.

Vital statistics

Birth rate per 1,000 population (2003): 35.9 (world avg. 21.3).
Death rate per 1,000 population (2003): 19.7 (world avg. 9.1).
Natural increase rate per 1,000 population (2003): 16.2 (world avg. 12.2).
Total fertility rate (avg. births per childbearing woman; 2003): 4.7.
Life expectancy at birth (2003): male 40.2 years; female 43.3 years.
Adult population (ages 15–49) *living with HIV* (2004[3]): 13.5% (world avg. 1.1%).

National economy

Budget (2001). Revenue: CFAF 63,200,000,000 (1999; taxes 88.0%, of which international trade tax 38.0%, indirect domestic tax 30.1%, taxes on income and profits 19.9%; nontax receipts 12.0%). Expenditures: CFAF 97,200,000,000 (current expenditure 61.2%, of which wages 30.5%; public investment program 38.8%).
Public debt (external, outstanding; 2002): U.S.$980,000,000.
Production (metric tons except as noted). Agriculture, forestry, fishing (2002): cassava 563,000, yams 400,000, peanuts (groundnuts) 127,800, bananas 118,000, corn (maize) 113,000, taro 110,000, sugarcane 90,000, plantains 83,000, sorghum 52,900, sesame seeds 39,400, pulses 32,000, seed cotton 30,000, paddy rice 27,400, coffee 13,000; livestock (number of live animals; 2002) 3,273,000 cattle, 2,921,000 goats, 738,000 pigs, 4,575,000 chickens; roundwood (2001) 3,058,000 cu m; fish catch (2001) 15,125. Mining and quarrying (2002): gold 20 kg, diamonds 415,000 carats[4]. Manufacturing (value added in U.S.$'000; 1994): food, beverages, and tobacco 19,000; chemical products 3,000; wood products 2,000; textiles, wearing apparel, and leather products 1,000; transport equipment 1,000. Energy production (consumption): electricity (kW-hr; 2000) 107,000,000 (107,000,000); coal, none (none); crude petroleum, none (none); petroleum products (metric tons; 2000) none (88,000); natural gas, none (none).
Household income and expenditure. Average household size (2000) 5.9; average annual income per household (1988) CFAF 91,985 (U.S.$435); sources of income: n.a.; expenditure (1991)[5]: food 70.5%, clothing 8.5%, other manufactured products 7.6%, energy 7.3%, services (including transportation and communications, recreation, and health) 6.1%.

Gross national product (2003): U.S.$1,019,000,000 (U.S.$260 per capita).

Structure of gross domestic product and labour force

	1999		1988	
	in value CFAF '000,000	% of total value	labour force	% of labour force
Agriculture	326,800	50.1	1,113,900	80.4
Mining	26,200	4.0	15,400	1.1
Manufacturing	54,500	8.4	22,400	1.6
Construction	29,500	4.5	7,000	0.5
Public utilities	4,600	0.7	1,500	0.1
Transp. and commun.	15,400	2.4	1,500	0.1
Trade	78,800	12.1	118,000	8.5
Services	40,100	6.1	15,600	1.1
Pub. admin., defense	35,900	5.5	91,700	6.6
Other	40,700[6]	6.2[6]	—	—
TOTAL	652,500	100.0	1,387,000	100.0

Population economically active (2000): total 1,752,000; activity rate of total population 50.0% (participation rates [1988]: ages 15–64, 78.3%; female 46.8%; unemployed, n.a.).

Price index (2000 = 100)

	1997	1998	1999	2000	2001	2002	2003
Consumer price index	100.2	98.3	96.9	100.0	103.4	106.9	110.2

Land use as % of total land area (2000): in temporary crops 3.1%, in permanent crops 0.1%, in pasture 5.0%; overall forest area 36.8%.
Tourism (2002): receipts U.S.$3,000,000; expenditures U.S.$29,000,000.

Foreign trade

Balance of trade (current prices)

	1996	1997	1998	1999	2000	2001
CFAF '000,000,000	–3.1	+9.1	+2.9	+9.4	+31.0	+15.7
% of total	3.1%	5.3%	1.7%	5.5%	15.7%	8.5%

Imports (2001): CFAF 84,800,000,000 (1996; road vehicles 18.3%, machinery and apparatus 15.8%, raw cotton 9.7%, refined petroleum 8.0%, food 7.0%). *Major import sources* (1999): France *c.* 34%; Cameroon *c.* 12%; Belgium *c.* 7%; U.K. *c.* 4%; Japan *c.* 3%.
Exports (2001): CFAF 100,500,000,000 (wood 41.3%, diamonds 41.0%, cotton 7.4%, coffee 1.8%). *Major export destinations* (1999): Belgium *c.* 65%; Spain *c.* 6%; Indonesia *c.* 4%; France *c.* 3%; United Kingdom *c.* 3%.

Transport and communications

Transport. Railroads: none. Roads (1999): total length 14,795 mi, 23,810 km (paved 3%). Vehicles (1996): passenger cars 8,900; trucks and buses 7,000. Air transport (1998)[7]: passenger-km 258,000,000; metric ton-km cargo 38,000,000; airports (2001) 1.

Communications

Medium	date	unit	number	units per 1,000 persons
Daily newspapers	2000	circulation	7,000	2.0
Radio	2000	receivers	280,000	80
Television	2002	receivers	22,800	6.0
Telephones	2002	main lines	9,000	2.3
Cellular telephones	2002	subscribers	13,000	3.1
Personal computers	2002	units	8,000	2.0
Internet	2002	users	5,000	1.3

Education and health

Educational attainment (1988). Percentage of population age 10 and over having: no formal schooling 59.3%; primary education 29.6%; lower secondary 7.5%; upper secondary 2.3%; higher 1.3%. *Literacy* (2000): total population age 15 and over literate 46.7%; males literate 59.7%; females literate 34.9%.

Education (1998)

	schools	teachers	students	student/ teacher ratio
Primary (age 6–11)	...	3,125	284,398	91.0
Secondary (age 12–18)	46[8]	845[8]	42,263[9]	...
Vocational	[10]	[10]	1,477[9]	...
Higher[11]	1	300	6,229	20.8

Health (1995): physicians 112 (1 per 28,600 persons); hospital beds (1998) 3,044 (1 per 1,111 persons); infant mortality rate (2003) 93.3.
Food (2002): daily per capita caloric intake 1,980 (vegetable products 90%, animal products 10%); 86% of FAO recommended minimum requirement.

Military

Total active duty personnel (2003): 2,550 (army 54.9%; navy, none; air force 5.9%; paramilitary [gendarmerie] 39.2%). *Military expenditure as percentage of GNP* (1999): 2.8% (world 2.4%); per capita expenditure U.S.$8.

[1]From March 15, 2003, coup d'état; expect transitional government until February 2005. [2]Formerly pegged to the French franc and since Jan. 1, 2002, to the euro at the rate of €1 = CFAF 655.96. [3]January 1. [4]Official figure; at least an equal amount was smuggled out of the country in 2002. [5]Weights of consumer price index components. [6]Indirect taxes and customs duties. [7]Air Afrique, an airline jointly owned by 11 African countries (including the Central African Republic), was declared bankrupt in February 2002. [8]1990–91. [9]1991–92. [10]Included with secondary. [11]University of Bangui only.

Internet resources for further information:
- **Le Banque de France: La Zone Franc**
http://www.banque-france.fr/fr/zonefr/main.htm

Chad

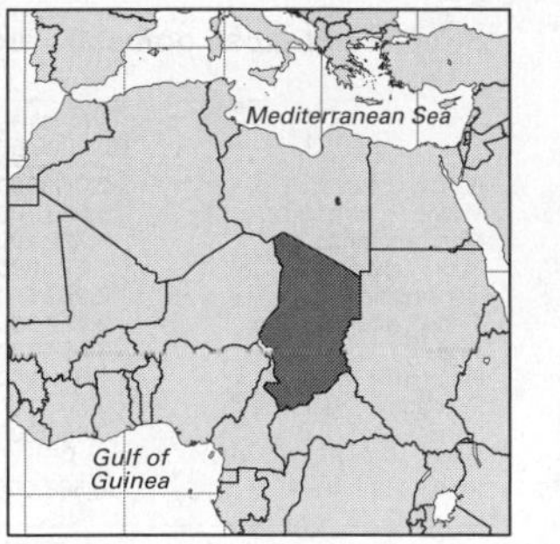

Official name: Jumhūrīyah Tshad (Arabic); République du Tchad (French) (Republic of Chad).
Form of government: unitary republic with one legislative body (National Assembly [155]).
Chief of state: President.
Head of government: Prime Minister.
Capital: N'Djamena.
Official languages: Arabic; French.
Official religion: none.
Monetary unit: 1 CFA franc (CFAF) = 100 centimes; valuation (Sept. 1, 2004) 1 U.S.$ = CFAF 539.75; 1 £ = CFAF 970.98[1].

Area and population

Préfectures[2]	Capitals	area sq mi	area sq km	population 1993 census
Batha	Ati	34,285	88,800	288,458
Biltine	Biltine	18,090	46,850	184,807
Borkou-Ennedi-Tibesti	Faya Largeau	231,795	600,350	73,185
Chari-Baguirmi	N'Djamena	32,010	82,910	1,251,906
Guéra	Mongo	22,760	58,950	306,253
Kanem	Mao	44,215	114,520	279,927
Lac	Bol	8,620	22,320	252,932
Logone Occidental	Moundou	3,357	8,695	455,489
Logone Oriental	Doba	10,825	28,035	441,064
Mayo-Kebbi	Bongor	11,625	30,105	825,158
Moyen-Chari	Sarh	17,445	45,180	738,595
Ouaddaï	Abéché	29,436	76,240	543,900
Salamat	Am Timan	24,325	63,000	184,403
Tandjilé	Laï	6,965	18,045	453,854
TOTAL		495,755[3]	1,284,000	6,279,931

Demography

Population (2004): 9,539,000.
Density (2004): persons per sq mi 19.2, persons per sq km 7.4.
Urban-rural (2002): urban 24.1%; rural 75.9%.
Sex distribution (2002): male 48.62%; female 51.38%.
Age breakdown (2002): under 15, 47.8%; 15–29, 26.2%; 30–44, 14.1%; 45–59, 7.5%; 60–74, 3.6%; 75 and over, 0.8%.
Population projection: (2010) 11,302,000; (2020) 14,671,000.
Doubling time: 23 years.
Ethnolinguistic composition (1993): Sara 27.7%; Sudanic Arab 12.3%; Mayo-Kebbi peoples 11.5%; Kanem-Bornu peoples 9.0%; Ouaddaï peoples 8.7%; Hadjeray (Hadjaraï) 6.7%; Tangale (Tandjilé) peoples 6.5%; Gorane peoples 6.3%; Fitri-Batha peoples 4.7%; Fulani (Peul) 2.4%; other 4.2%.
Religious affiliation (1993): Muslim 53.9%; Christian 34.7%, of which Roman Catholic 20.3%, Protestant 14.4%; traditional beliefs 7.4%; other 4.0%.
Major cities (1993): N'Djamena 530,965; Moundou 282,103; Bongor 196,713; Sarh 193,753; Abéché 187,936; Doba 185,461.

Vital statistics

Birth rate per 1,000 population (2003): 47.1 (world avg. 21.3).
Death rate per 1,000 population (2003): 16.4 (world avg. 9.1).
Natural increase rate per 1,000 population (2003): 30.7 (world avg. 12.2).
Total fertility rate (avg. births per childbearing woman; 2003): 6.4.
Life expectancy at birth (2003): male 47.0 years; female 50.1 years.
Adult population (ages 15–49) *living with HIV* (2004[4]): 4.8% (world avg. 1.1%).

National economy

Budget (2000). Revenue: CFAF 128,200,000,000 (tax revenue 53.3%, of which income tax 19.0%, taxes on international trade 17.0%, taxes on goods and services 14.7%, other taxes 2.6%; grants 37.4%; nontax revenue 9.3%). Expenditures: CFAF 203,200,000,000 (current expenditure 49.2%, of which government salaries 19.7%, materials and supply 10.2%, defense 7.5%, transfer payments 5.9%, debt service 5.1%, other 0.8%; capital expenditure 50.8%).
Tourism (2001): receipts from visitors U.S.$23,000,000; expenditures by nationals abroad U.S.$56,000,000.
Production (metric tons except as noted). Agriculture, forestry, fishing (2002): peanuts (groundnuts) 448,089, sorghum 428,000, millet 369,000, cassava 310,000, yams 230,000, seed cotton 170,000, corn (maize) 115,000, rice 115,000; livestock (number of live animals) 5,900,000 cattle, 5,500,000 goats, 2,450,000 sheep, 725,000 camels, 5,000,000 chickens; roundwood (2001) 6,761,676 cu m; fish catch (2001) 84,000. Mining and quarrying (1997): aggregate (gravel) 170,000; limited commercial production of natron (10,000) and salt; artisanal gold production. Manufacturing (2000): cotton fibre (1998) 86,260; refined sugar 27,000; gum arabic 3,420; woven cotton fabrics 1,000,000 metres; beer 78,000,000 hectolitres; edible oil 10,000,000 hectolitres; cigarettes 30,000,000 packs; bicycles (1998) 3,444 units. Energy production (consumption): electricity (kW-hr; 2000) 92,000,000 (92,000,000); coal, none (none); crude petroleum (barrels; 2003) 50,000[5] (none); petroleum products (metric tons; 2000) none (41,000); natural gas, none (none).
Household income and expenditure. Average household size (2000) 4.2; average annual income per household (1993) CFAF 96,806 (U.S.$458); sources of income (1995–96; urban): informal-sector employment and entrepreneurship 36.7%, transfers 24.8%, wages 23.6%, ownership of real estate 8.6%; expenditure (1983)[6]: food 45.3%, health 11.9%, energy 5.8%, clothing 3.3%.
Population economically active (1997): total 3,433,000; activity rate of total population 47.9% (participation rates: over age 15, 72.3%; female 44.5%; unemployed [1993] 0.6%).

Price index (2000 = 100)

	1997	1998	1999	2000	2001	2002	2003
Consumer price index	92.2	103.4	96.5	100.0	112.4	118.3	116.0

Public debt (external, outstanding; 2002): U.S.$1,148,000,000.
Gross national product (2003): U.S.$2,104,000,000 (U.S.$250 per capita).

Structure of gross domestic product and labour force

	2000		1993	
	in value CFAF '000,000	% of total value	labour force	% of labour force
Agriculture	349,000	34.8	1,903,492	83.0
Mining	31,200	3.1	...	...
Manufacturing	108,400	10.8	33,670	1.5
Construction	19,700	2.0	10,885	0.5
Public utilities	5,900	0.6	756	—
Transp. and commun.	244,600	24.4	13,252	0.6
Trade and finance			179,169	7.8
Pub. admin., defense	114,700	11.4	61,875	2.7
Services	96,400	9.6	79,167	3.4
Other	32,500[7]	3.2[7]	9,311	0.4
TOTAL	1,002,400	100.0[3]	2,291,577	100.0[3]

Land use as % of total land area (2000): in temporary crops 2.8%, in permanent crops 0.02%, in pasture 35.7%; overall forest area 10.1%.

Foreign trade

Balance of trade (current prices)

	1996	1997	1998	1999	2000	2001
CFAF '000,000,000	–3.2	+3.2	–11.5	–22.1	–35.5	–199.1
% of total	1.3%	1.2%	3.6%	7.3%	12.0%	43.4%

Imports (2001): CFAF 328,700,000,000 (petroleum sector 61.3%; non-petroleum sector 38.7%). *Major import sources* (1999): France *c.* 37%; Cameroon *c.* 22%; Nigeria *c.* 10%; India *c.* 4%.
Exports (2001): CFAF 129,600,000,000 (cattle, sheep, and goats 39.5%; cotton fibre 37.2%; other 23.3%). *Major export destinations* (1999): Portugal *c.* 29%; Germany *c.* 15%; Taiwan *c.* 8%; U.S. *c.* 7%; France *c.* 5%; Brazil *c.* 5%.

Transport and communications

Transport. Railroads (2002): none. Roads (1999): total length 33,400 km (paved 1%). Vehicles (1996): passenger cars 10,560; trucks and buses 14,550. Air transport (1996)[8]: passenger-km 233,000,000; metric ton-km cargo 37,000,000; airports (2000) with scheduled flights 1.

Communications

Medium	date	unit	number	units per 1,000 persons
Daily newspapers	1997	circulation	2,000	0.2
Radio	2000	receivers	1,990,000	236
Television	2002	receivers	16,600	2.0
Telephones	2002	main lines	11,800	1.5
Cellular telephones	2003	subscribers	65,000	8.0
Personal computers	2002	units	13,000	1.7
Internet	2002	users	15,000	1.9

Education and health

Educational attainment (1993). Percentage of economically active population age 15 and over having: no formal schooling 81.1%; Qur'anic education 4.2%; primary education 11.2%; secondary education 2.7%; higher education 0.3%; professional education 0.5%. *Literacy* (2000): percentage of total population age 15 and over literate 42.6%; males 51.6%; females 34.0%.

Education (1996–97)

	schools	teachers	students	student/ teacher ratio
Primary (age 6–12)	2,660	10,151	680,909	67.1
Secondary (age 13–19)	153	2,598	97,011	37.3
Voc., teacher tr.	18	194	2,778	14.5
Higher[9]	8	288	3,274	11.4

Health (2000): physicians 1,667 (1 per 4,471 persons); hospital beds (1993) 3,962 (1 per 1,521 persons); infant mortality rate (2002) 96.7.
Food (2001): daily per capita caloric intake 2,245 (vegetable products 94%, animal products 6%); 94% of FAO recommended minimum requirement.

Military

Total active duty personnel (2003): 30,350[9] (army 82.4%; air force 1.2%; paramilitary [gendarmerie] 16.4%); French peacekeeping troops (August 2004) *c.* 1,000. *Military expenditure as percentage of GNP* (1999): 2.4% (world 2.4%); per capita expenditure U.S.$5.

[1]Formerly pegged to the French franc and since Jan. 1, 2002, to the euro at the rate of €1 = CFAF 655.96. [2]Chad was administratively reorganized into 28 departments and 1 commune in 1999; area and population details are not available. [3]Detail does not add to total given because of rounding. [4]January 1. [5]Production began in July 2003 at 50,000 barrels per day and was expected to increase to 225,000 barrels per day by the end of the first quarter 2004. [6]Capital city only. [7]VAT and import taxes. [8]One-eleventh portion of total traffic of Air Afrique; Air Afrique, an airline jointly owned by 11 African countries (including Chad), was declared bankrupt in February 2002. [9]Universities and equivalent institutions only. [10]Excludes 900 French troops.

Internet resources for further information:
- **Embassy of Chad in the U.S. http://www.chadembassy.org**
- **La Banque de France: La Zone Franc http://www.banque-france.fr/fr/zonefr/main.htm**

Chile

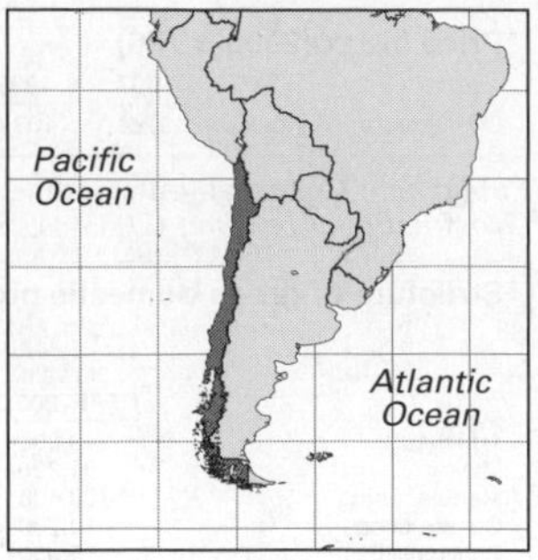

Official name: República de Chile (Republic of Chile).
Form of government: multiparty republic with two legislative houses (Senate [48[1]]; Chamber of Deputies [120]).
Head of state and government: President.
Capital: Santiago[2].
Official language: Spanish.
Official religion: none.
Monetary unit: 1 peso (Ch$) = 100 centavos; valuation (Sept. 1, 2004) 1 U.S.$ = Ch$624.35; 1 £ = Ch$1,123.

Area and population[3]

Regions	Capitals	area sq mi	area sq km	population 2002 census[4]
Aisén del General Carios Ibáñez del Campo	Coihaique	41,890	108,495	91,492
Antofagasta	Antofagasta	48,668	126,049	493,984
Araucanía	Temuco	12,294	31,842	869,535
Atacama	Copiapó	29,026	75,176	254,336
Bío-Bío	Concepción	14,310	37,063	1,861,562
Coquimbo	La Serena	15,668	40,580	603,210
Libertador General Bernardo O'Higgins	Rancagua	6,327	16,387	780,627
Los Lagos	Puerto Montt	25,874	67,013	1,073,135
Magallanes y Antártica Chilena	Punta Arenas	51,080	132,297	150,826
Maule	Talca	11,697	30,296	908,097
Región Metropolitana	Santiago	5,947	15,403	6,061,185
Tarapacá	Iquique	22,818	59,099	428,594
Valparaíso	Valparaíso	6,331	16,396	1,539,852
TOTAL		291,930	756,096	15,116,435

Demography

Population (2004): 15,824,000.
Density (2004): persons per sq mi 54.2, persons per sq km 20.9.
Urban-rural (2002): urban 86.6%; rural 13.4%.
Sex distribution (2002): male 49.27%; female 50.73%.
Age breakdown (2002): under 15, 25.7%; 15–29, 24.3%; 30–44, 23.6%; 45–59, 15.0%; 60–74, 8.3%; 75 and over, 3.1%.
Population projection: (2010) 16,720,000; (2020) 18,008,000.
Doubling time: 67 years.
Ethnic composition (2000): mestizo 72.4%; local white 20.8%; Araucanian (Mapuche) 4.7%; European 1.0%; other 1.1%.
Religious affiliation (2002)[5]: Roman Catholic 70.0%; Protestant 15.4%; other Christian 2.1%; atheist/nonreligious 4.6%; other 7.9%.
Major cities[6] (2002): Greater Santiago 4,647,444; Puente Alto 501,042; Concepción 376,043; Viña del Mar 298,828; Antofagasta 298,153; Valparaíso 270,242.

Vital statistics

Birth rate per 1,000 population (2003): 16.1 (world avg. 21.3).
Death rate per 1,000 population (2003): 5.7 (world avg. 9.1).
Natural increase rate per 1,000 population (2003): 10.4 (world avg. 12.2).
Total fertility rate (avg. births per childbearing woman; 2003): 2.1.
Life expectancy at birth (2003): male 72.9 years; female 79.6 years.
Major causes of death per 100,000 population (1999): diseases of the circulatory system 155.7; malignant neoplasms (cancers) 122.5; diseases of the respiratory system 78.6; accidents and adverse effects 25.2.

National economy

Budget (2001). Revenue: Ch$9,537,200,000,000 (income from taxes 76.2%, nontax revenue 23.5%, capital 0.3%). Expenditures: Ch$9,932,200,000,000 (pensions 29.5%, wages 19.0%, capital expenditure 15.0%, interest 2.1%).
Population economically active (1999): total 5,822,700; activity rate of total population 38.6% (participation rates [1995]: ages 15–64, 58.6%; female 32.4%; unemployed [2002] 9.0%).

Price and earnings indexes (2000 = 100)

	1997	1998	1999	2000	2001	2002	2003
Consumer price index	88.7	93.2	96.3	100.0	103.6	106.1	109.1
Hourly earnings index	83.2	89.7	95.0	100.0	105.2	110.0	114.2

Production (metric tons except as noted). Agriculture, forestry, fishing (2003): sugar beets 2,100,000, wheat 1,797,084, grapes 1,750,000, tomatoes 1,300,000, corn (maize) 1,189,729, apples 1,100,000, potatoes 1,093,728, oats 488,050, onions (dry) 290,000; livestock (number of live animals) 4,105,000 sheep, 3,927,000 cattle, 3,100,000 pigs; roundwood (2001) 37,790,000 cu m; fish catch (2001) 3,717,000. Mining (metal content; 2002): iron ore 5,520,000[7]; copper 4,580,600; molybdenum 29,500; zinc 36,200; silver 1,210,500 kg; gold 38,700 kg. Manufacturing (value added in U.S.$'000,000; 2000): food products 3,251; nonferrous base metals 1,947; paints, soaps, pharmaceuticals 1,206; beverages 1,169; industrial chemicals 1,047; paper and paper products 1,020; refined petroleum 705. Energy production (consumption): electricity (kW-hr; 2001) 41,292,000,000 (41,292,000,000); coal (metric tons; 2001) 480,000 ([2000] 4,590,000); crude petroleum (barrels; 2000) 2,027,000 (72,771,000); petroleum products (metric tons; 2000) 8,943,000 (10,270,000); natural gas (cu m; 2000) 2,188,300,000 (6,407,400,000).
Gross national product (2003): U.S.$69,193,000,000 (U.S.$4,390 per capita).

Structure of gross domestic product and labour force

	2001 in value Ch$'000,000[9]	2001 % of total value[9]	1998[8] labour force	1998[8] % of labour force
Agriculture	2,052,900	5.6	770,000	13.1
Mining	3,050,700	8.3	70,300	1.2
Manufacturing	5,722,100	15.7	754,200	12.9
Public utilities	1,214,800	3.3	28,400	0.5
Construction	2,952,500	8.1	406,100	6.9
Transp. and commun.	2,727,900	7.5	430,200	7.3
Trade	3,904,100	10.7	995,500	17.0
Finance	4,557,200	12.5	425,800	7.3
Pub. admin., defense; Services; Other	10,350,800[10]	28.3[10]		
Pub. admin., defense; Services			1,494,200	25.5
Other			489,400[11]	8.3[11]
TOTAL	36,583,000[12]	100.0	5,864,100	100.0

Public debt (external, outstanding; 2002): U.S.$6,792,000,000.
Household income and expenditure. Average household size (2002) 3.4; average annual income per household (1994) Ch$5,981,706 at November prices (U.S.$12,552); sources of income (1990): wages and salaries 75.1%, transfer payments 12.0%, other 12.9%; expenditure (1989): food 27.9%, clothing 22.5%, housing 15.2%, transportation 6.4%.
Tourism (2002): receipts U.S.$845,000,000; expenditures U.S.$793,000,000.
Land use as % of total land area (2000): in temporary crops 2.6%, in permanent crops 0.4%, in pasture 17.3%; overall forest area 20.7%.

Foreign trade[13]

Balance of trade (current prices)

	1997	1998	1999	2000	2001	2002[14]
U.S.$'000,000	−1,396	−2,010	+2,459	+2,155	+2,093	+2,238
% of total	3.8%	5.8%	7.7%	5.9%	6.0%	7.1%

Imports (2001): U.S.$17,181,000,000 (machinery and fabricated metals 29.4%; chemical products and mineral fuels 19.7%; copper 12.5%). *Major import sources:* Argentina 17.8%; U.S. 16.8%; Brazil 8.7%; Germany 4.0%; Japan 3.3%.
Exports (2001): U.S.$17,620,000,000 (copper 37.9%; food products 24.8%, of which raw fruit 7.8%; paper and paper products 6.4%). *Major export destinations:* U.S. 19.4%; Japan 12.1%; U.K. 7.0%; Brazil 4.8%; France 3.4%.

Transport and communications

Transport. Railroads (2001): route length 5,282 mi, 8,501 km; passenger-km 870,836,000; metric ton-km cargo 3,318,000,000. Roads (1996): total length 49,590 mi, 79,800 km (paved 14%). Vehicles (2001): passenger cars 1,351,900; trucks and buses 693,000. Air transport (1999): passenger-km 10,650,500,000; metric ton-km cargo 2,107,000,000; airports (1998) with scheduled flights 23.

Communications

Medium	date	unit	number	units per 1,000 persons
Daily newspapers	2000	circulation	1,450,000	98
Radio	2000	receivers	5,230,000	354
Television	2000	receivers	3,580,000	242
Telephones	2002	main lines	3,467,200	230
Cellular telephones	2002	subscribers	6,446,000	428
Personal computers	2002	units	1,796,000	119
Internet	2002	users	3,575,000	236

Education and health

Educational attainment (1992). Percentage of population age 25 and over having: no formal schooling 5.7%; primary education 44.2%; secondary 42.2%; higher 7.9%. *Literacy* (1995): total population age 15 and over literate 95.2%; males literate 95.4%; females literate 95.0%.

Education (1995)

	schools	teachers	students	student/teacher ratio
Primary (age 6–13)	8,702	80,155	2,149,501	26.8
Secondary (age 14–17)[15]	...	51,042	679,165	13.3
Higher	...	18,084[16]	367,094	...

Health: physicians (2000) 17,720 (1 per 834 persons); hospital beds (1999) 42,163 (1 per 346 persons); infant mortality rate (2003) 9.3.
Food (2001): daily per capita caloric intake 2,868 (vegetable products 78%, animal products 22%); 118% of FAO recommended minimum requirement.

Military

Total active duty personnel (2003): 77,300 (army 61.7%, navy 24.6%, air force 13.7%). *Military expenditure as percentage of GNP* (1999): 3.0% (world 2.4%); per capita expenditure U.S.$133.

[1]Includes 9 nonelective seats, excludes one former president serving as Senator-for-life. [2]Legislative bodies meet in Valparaíso. [3]Excludes the 480,000-sq mi (1,250,000-sq km) section of Antarctica claimed by Chile (and administered as part of Magallanes y Antártica Chilena region) and "inland" (actually tidal) water areas. The 2002 census population of Chilean-claimed Antarctica is 130. [4]Final. [5]For population age 15 years and older. [6]Preliminary census populations of single communes except Greater Santiago and Concepción, which is a total for 3 communes. [7]2001. [8]Excludes all or some classes or elements of the military. [9]In constant prices of 1996. [10]Less imputed bank service charges, import duties, and value-added tax on imports. [11]Unemployed. [12]Detail does not add to total given because of rounding. [13]Imports f.o.b. in balance of trade and c.i.f. in commodities and trading partners. [14]Excludes December. [15]Includes vocational. [16]Universities only.

Internet resources for further information:
- **Instituto Nacional de Estadísticas http://www.ine.cl**
- **Banco Central de Chile http://www.bcentral.cl/eng**

China

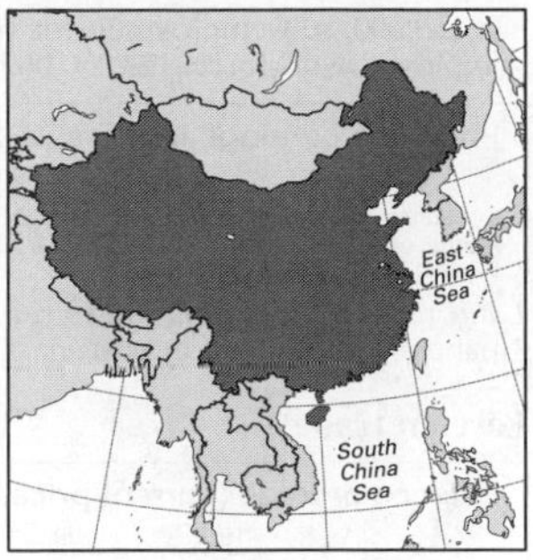

Official name: Chung-hua Jen-min Kung-ho-kuo (People's Republic of China).
Form of government: single-party people's republic with one legislative house (National People's Congress [2,985[1]]).
Chief of state: President.
Head of government: Premier.
Capital: Peking (Beijing).
Official language: Mandarin Chinese.
Official religion: none.
Monetary unit: 1 Renminbi (yuan) (Y) = 10 jiao = 100 fen; valuation (Sept. 1, 2004) 1 U.S.$ = Y 8.28; 1 £ = Y 14.89.

Area and population[2, 3]

		area[4]		population
Provinces	Capitals	sq mi	sq km	2002[5] estimate
Anhwei (Anhui)	Ho-fei (Hefei)	54,000	139,900	63,380,000
Chekiang (Zhejiang)	Hang-chou (Hangzhou)	39,300	101,800	46,470,000
Fukien (Fujian)	Fu-chou (Fuzhou)	47,500	123,100	34,660,000
Hainan (Hainan)	Hai-k'ou (Haikou)	13,200	34,300	8,030,000
Heilungkiang (Heilongjiang)	Harbin	179,000	463,600	38,130,000
Honan (Henan)	Cheng-chou (Zhengzhou)	64,500	167,000	96,130,000
Hopeh (Hebei)	Shih-chia-chuang (Shijiazhuang)	78,200	202,700	67,350,000
Hunan (Hunan)	Ch'ang-sha (Changsha)	81,300	210,500	66,290,000
Hupeh (Hubei)	Wu-han (Wuhan)	72,400	187,500	59,880,000
Kansu (Gansu)	Lan-chou (Lanzhou)	141,500	366,500	25,930,000
Kiangsi (Jiangxi)	Nan-ch'ang (Nanchang)	63,600	164,800	42,220,000
Kiangsu (Jiangsu)	Nanking (Nanjing)	39,600	102,600	73,810,000
Kirin (Jilin)	Ch'ang-ch'un (Changchun)	72,200	187,000	26,990,000
Kwangtung (Guangdong)	Canton (Guangzhou)	76,100	197,100	78,590,000
Kweichow (Guizhou)	Kuei-yang (Guiyang)	67,200	174,000	38,370,000
Liaoning (Liaoning)	Shen-yang (Shenyang)	58,300	151,000	42,030,000
Shansi (Shanxi)	T'ai-yüan (Taiyuan)	60,700	157,100	32,940,000
Shantung (Shandong)	Chi-nan (Jinan)	59,200	153,300	90,820,000
Shensi (Shaanxi)	Sian (Xi'an)	75,600	195,800	36,740,000
Szechwan (Sichuan)	Ch'eng-tu (Chengdu)	188,000	487,000	86,730,000
Tsinghai (Qinghai)	Hsi-ning (Xining)	278,400	721,000	5,290,000
Yunnan (Yunnan)	K'un-ming (Kunming)	168,400	436,200	43,330,000
Autonomous regions				
Inner Mongolia (Nei Monggol)	Hu-ho-hao-t'e (Hohhot)	454,600	1,177,500	23,790,000
Kwangsi Chuang (Guangxi Zhuang)	Nan-ning (Nanning)	85,100	220,400	48,220,000
Ningsia Hui (Ningxia Hui)	Yin-ch'uan (Yinchuan)	25,600	66,400	5,720,000
Sinkiang Uighur (Xinjiang Uygur)	Wu-lu-mu-c'hi (Urumqi)	635,900	1,646,900	19,050,000
Tibet (Xizang)	Lhasa	471,700	1,221,600	2,670,000
Municipalities				
Chungking (Chongqing)	—	31,700	82,000	31,070,000
Peking (Beijing)	—	6,500	16,800	14,230,000
Shanghai (Shanghai)	—	2,400	6,200	16,250,000
Tientsin (Tianjin)	—	4,400	11,300	10,070,000
TOTAL		3,696,100[4]	9,572,900[4]	1,275,180,000

Demography

Population (2004): 1,298,848,000.
Density (2004): persons per sq mi 351.4, persons per sq km 135.7.
Urban-rural (2002): urban 37.7%; rural 62.3%.
Sex distribution (2002): male 51.46%; female 48.54%.
Age breakdown (2000): under 15, 22.9%; 15–29, 25.4%; 30–44, 25.6%; 45–59, 15.7%; 60–74, 8.2%; 75 and over, 2.2%.
Population projection: (2010) 1,347,563,000; (2020) 1,430,533,000.
Ethnic composition (2000): Han (Chinese) 91.53%; Chuang 1.30%; Manchu 0.86%; Hui 0.79%; Miao 0.72%; Uighur 0.68%; Tuchia 0.65%; Yi 0.62%; Mongolian 0.47%; Tibetan 0.44%; Puyi 0.24%; Tung 0.24%; Yao 0.21%; Korean 0.15%; Pai 0.15%; Hani 0.12%; Kazakh 0.10%; Li 0.10%; Tai 0.09%; other 0.54%.
Religious affiliation (2000): nonreligious 42.1%; Chinese folk-religionist 28.5%; Buddhist 8.4%; atheist 8.1%; Christian 7.1%; traditional beliefs 4.3%; Muslim 1.5%.
Major cities (2003[6]): Shanghai 10,030,800; Beijing 7,699,300; Tianjin 4,933,100; Guangzhou 4,653,100; Wuhan 4,593,400; Chongqing 4,239,700; Shenyang 3,995,500; Nanjing 2,966,000; Harbin 2,735,100; Chengdu 2,664,000; Xi'an 2,657,900; Jinan 2,346,000; Changchun 2,283,800; Dalian 2,181,600; Hangzhou 2,059,800; Shijiazhuang 1,971,000; Taiyuan 1,970,300; Qingdao 1,930,200; Zhengzhou 1,770,800; Kunming 1,597,800; Lanzhou 1,576,400; Changsha 1,562,200; Zibo 1,519,300.
Households. Average household size (2000) 3.4; total households 351,233,698, of which family households 340,491,197 (96.9%), collective 10,742,501 (3.1%).

Vital statistics

Birth rate per 1,000 population (2003): 13.0 (world avg. 21.3).
Death rate per 1,000 population (2003): 6.9 (world avg. 9.1).
Natural increase rate per 1,000 population (2003): 6.1 (world avg. 12.2).
Total fertility rate (avg. births per childbearing woman; 2003): 1.7.
Marriage rate per 1,000 population (2001): 6.3.
Divorce rate per 1,000 population (2001): 1.0.
Life expectancy at birth (2003): male 70.1 years; female 73.3 years.
Major causes of death per 100,000 population (2002)[7]: malignant neoplasms (cancers) 119.7; cerebrovascular disease 88.4; diseases of the respiratory system 78.1; heart diseases 74.1; accidents, violence, and poisoning 43.5.

Social indicators

Educational attainment (2000). Percentage of population age 15 and over having: no schooling and incomplete primary 15.6%; completed primary 35.7%; some secondary 34.0%; complete secondary 11.1%; some postsecondary through advanced degree 3.6%.

Distribution of urban household income (1996)

avg. per capita income by quintile (avg. Y 4,845 [U.S.$583])

first quintile	second quintile	third quintile	fourth quintile	fifth quintile
Y 2,801	Y 3,780	Y 4,580	Y 5,599	Y 8,039

Quality of working life. Average workweek (1998): 40 hours. Annual rate per 100,000 workers for (1997)[8]: injury or accident 0.7; industrial illness, n.a.; death 1.4. Funds for pensions and social welfare relief (2001): Y 26,668,000,000.
Access to services. Proportion of communes having access to electricity (1979) 87.1%. Percentage of urban population with: safe public water supply (1996) 95.0%; public sewage collection, n.a.; public fire protection, n.a.
Social participation. Eligible voters participating in last national election: n.a. Population participating in voluntary work: n.a. Trade union membership in total labour force (1996): 14.7%. Practicing religious population in total affiliated population: n.a.
Social deviance. Annual reported arrest rate per 100,000 population (1986) for: property violation 20.7; infringing personal rights 7.2; disruption of social administration 3.3; endangering public security 1.0[9].
Material well-being. Urban households possessing (number per household; 2002[6]): bicycles 1.6; colour televisions 1.2; washing machines 0.9; refrigerators 0.8; cameras 0.4. Rural families possessing (number per family; 2002): bicycles 1.2; colour televisions 0.5; washing machines 0.3; refrigerators 0.1; cameras 0.03.

National economy

Gross national product (2003): U.S.$1,417,301,000,000 (U.S.$1,100 per capita).

Structure of gross domestic product and labour force

	2001			
	in value Y '000,000	% of total value	labour force ('000)	% of labour force
Agriculture	1,460,990	15.2	329,740	44.3
Mining	4,260,710	44.4	5,610	0.8
Manufacturing			80,830	10.9
Construction	646,200	6.7	36,690	4.9
Public utilities	...	...	2,880	0.4
Transp. and commun.	522,210	5.5	20,370	2.7
Trade	782,350	8.2	47,370	6.3
Finance	...	...	4,430	0.6
Pub. admin.	...	...	11,010	1.5
Services	1,920,870	20.0	205,390[10]	27.6[10]
Other	...	...	...	...
TOTAL	9,593,330	100.0	744,320	100.0

Budget (2001). Revenue: Y 1,638,604,000,000 (tax revenue 93.4%, of which VAT 32.7%, corporate income taxes 12.6%, consumption tax 5.6%; nontax revenue 6.6%). Expenditures: Y 1,890,258,000,000 (economic development 34.2%; education, health, and science 27.6%; administration 18.9%; debt payment 10.6%; defense 7.6%; other 1.1%).
Public debt (external, outstanding; 2002): U.S.$88,531,000,000.
Tourism (2002): receipts from visitors U.S.$20,385,000,000; expenditures by nationals abroad U.S.$15,398,000,000.

Retail and catering enterprises (1996)

	no. of enter-prises	no. of employees	annual wage as a % of all wages	annual gross output value (Y '000,000)
Retail trade	13,963,162	31,892,181	...	...
Food, beverage, and tobacco	5,177,416	10,738,924	...	241,350
Articles for daily use	3,242,769	8,614,944	...	88,470
Textile goods, garments, shoes, and hats	2,018,136	4,030,888	...	125,250
Sundry goods for daily use	799,486	1,670,984	...	...
Hardware, electrical appliances, and chemicals	583,466	1,828,788	...	...
Medicines and medical appliances	123,534	405,424	...	57,980
Books and newspapers	140,856	365,424	...	23,110
Other	1,877,499	4,236,805	...	...
Catering trade	2,587,730	7,753,108	...	...
Restaurants	1,181,732	4,321,824	...	...
Fast-food eateries	397,561	1,049,829	...	...
Other	1,008,437	2,381,455	...	...

Production (metric tons except as noted). Agriculture, forestry, fishing (2002): grains—rice 176,553,000, corn (maize) 123,175,000, wheat 91,290,000, sorghum 2,731,000, barley 2,470,000, millet 2,071,000; oilseeds—soybeans 16,900,000, peanuts (groundnuts) 15,006,000, rapeseed 10,530,000, sunflower seeds 1,900,000; fruits and nuts—watermelons 57,530,000, apples 20,435,000, pears 9,091,000, cantaloupes 8,631,000, oranges 3,676,000; other—sweet potatoes 114,289,000, sugarcane 82,278,000, potatoes 65,052,000, cabbage 26,812,000, tomatoes 25,466,000, cucumbers 22,924,000, onions 15,622,000, eggplants 15,430,000, seed cotton 14,760,000, sugar beets 11,562,000, garlic 8,694,000, tobacco leaves 2,394,000, tea 760,000; livestock (number of live animals) 464,695,000 pigs, 161,492,000 goats, 136,972,000 sheep, 106,175,000 cattle, 22,249,000 water buffalo, 8,815,000 asses, 8,262,000 horses, 3,923,600,000 chickens, 661,250,000 ducks; roundwood (2001) 284,910,000 cu m; fish catch (2002) 44,320,000, of which aquaculture 27,767,000. Mining and quarrying (2002): metal content of mine output—zinc 1,550,000, lead 641,000, copper 568,000, antimony 100,000, tin 62,000, tungsten 49,500; metal ores—iron ore 231,000,000, bauxite 11,000,000, manganese ore 4,500,000, vanadium 33,000, silver 2,950, gold 192; nonmetals—salt 36,024,000, soda ash 10,330,000, gypsum 6,850,000, magnesite 3,700,000, talc 3,600,000, barite 3,100,000, fluorspar 2,450,000, asbestos 270,000. Manufacturing (2001): cement 661,040,000; steel products 160,676,000; pig iron 155,554,000; rolled steel 151,634,000; paper and paperboard 37,771,000; chemical fertilizer 33,830,000; sulfuric acid 22,300,000; cotton fabrics 11,716,000; cotton yarn 7,606,000; sugar 6,531,000; colour television sets 40,937,000 units; bicycles 29,023,000 units; household refrigerators 13,513,000 units; household washing machines 13,416,000 units; motor vehicles 2,342,000 units. Distribution of industrial production (percentage of total value of output by sector; 2001): state-operated enterprises 26.8%; urban collectives 16.6%; rural collectives 23.2%; privately operated enterprises 33.4%. Retail sales (percentage of total sales by sector; 2001): state-operated enterprises 25.3%; collectives 29.8%; privately operated enterprises 44.9%.

Manufacturing and mining enterprises (1996)

	no. of enter-prises	no. of employees[11]	annual wages as a % of avg. of all wages	annual gross output value (Y '000,000)
Manufacturing				
Machinery, transport equipment, and metal manufactures,	23,032	21,560	...	880,886
of which,				
Metal products	2,641	1,810,000	...	23,593
Industrial equipment	8,875	7,020,000	...	183,951
Transport equipment	4,303	3,540,000	...	187,581
Electronic goods	1,579	1,630,000	...	70,046
Measuring equipment	1,179	820,000	...	14,738
Textiles	4,031	6,340,000	...	161,949
Garments	1,177	1,680,000	...	11,359
Foodstuffs,	18,191	4,710,000	...	383,264
of which,				
Food processing	14,520	3,170,000	...	196,393
Beverages	3,367	1,210,000	...	70,368
Tobacco manufactures	304	330,000	...	116,503
Chemicals,	10,707	8,140,000	...	537,768
of which,				
Pharmaceuticals	2,044	1,020,000	...	53,749
Plastics	1,667	1,050,000	...	15,167
Secondary forest products (including paper and stationery)	3,664	2,310,000	...	51,238
Primary forest products	877	1,140,000	...	16,750
Mining				
Nonferrous and ferrous metals	1,163	810,000	...	22,711
Crude petroleum	71	1,250,000	...	149,525
Coal	2,011	5,050,000	...	105,946

Energy production (consumption): electricity (kW-hr; 2003) 1,838,748,000,000 ([2002] 1,602,156,000,000); coal (metric tons; 2003) 1,315,224,000 ([2000] 981,776,000); crude petroleum (barrels; 2003) 1,247,679,000 ([2000] 1,565,-236,000); petroleum products (metric tons; 2000) 157,629,000 (174,016,000); natural gas (cu m; 2003) 34,243,412,000 ([2000] 33,542,000,000).

Financial aggregates[12]

	1996	1997	1998	1999	2000	2001	2002
Exchange rate, Y per:							
U.S. dollar	8.30	8.28	8.28	8.28	8.28	8.28	8.28
£	12.95	13.58	13.74	13.41	12.59	11.92	12.42
SDR	11.93	11.17	11.66	11.36	10.78	10.40	11.25
International reserves (U.S.$)							
Total (excl. gold; '000,000)	107,039	142,762	149,188	157,728	168,278	215,605	291,128
SDRs ('000,000)	614	602	676	741	798	851	998
Reserve pos. in IMF ('000,000)	1,396	2,270	3,553	2,312	1,905	2,590	3,723
Foreign exchange	105,029	139,890	144,959	154,675	165,574	212,165	286,407
Gold ('000,000 fine troy oz)	12.7	12.7	12.7	12.7	12.7	16.1	19.3
% world reserves	1.4	1.4	1.4	1.3	1.3	1.7	2.1
Interest and prices							
Central bank discount (%)	9.00	8.55	4.59	3.24	3.24	3.24	2.70
Govt. bond yield (%)	...	...	...	...	...	...	...
Industrial share prices	...	...	...	...	...	...	...
Balance of payments (U.S.$'000,000)							
Balance of visible trade,	+19,535	+46,222	+46,614	+35,982	+34,474	+34,017	+44,167
of which:							
Imports, f.o.b.	−131,542	−136,448	−136,915	−158,734	−214,657	−232,058	−281,484
Exports, f.o.b.	151,077	182,670	183,529	194,716	249,131	266,075	325,651
Balance of invisibles	−12,292	−9,259	−15,142	−20,540	−13,956	−16,616	−8,745
Balance of payments, current account	+7,243	+36,963	+31,472	+21,115	+20,518	+17,401	+35,422

Household income and expenditure. Average household size (2001) 3.5; rural households 4.4, urban households 3.1. Average annual per capita income of household (2001): rural households Y 2,366 (U.S.$286), urban households Y 6,907 (U.S.$834). Sources of income (2001): rural households—income from household businesses 77.9%, wages 16.6%, transfers 4.3%, other 1.2%; urban households—wages 73.9%, transfers 19.7%, business income 5.8%, other 0.6%. Expenditure: rural (urban) households—food 47.7% (37.9%), housing 16.0% (10.3%), education and recreation 11.1% (13.0%), transportation and communications 6.3% (8.6%), clothing 5.7% (10.1%), health and personal effects 5.6% (6.5%), household furnishings 4.4% (8.3%).

Population economically active (2001): total 744,320,000; activity rate of total population 58.5% (participation rates: over age 15, 77.7%; female 37.8%; registered unemployed in urban areas 3.6%). Urban employed workforce (2001): 239,400,000; by sector: state enterprises 76,400,000, collectives 28,130,000, self-employment or privately run enterprises 134,870,000. Rural employed workforce 490,850,000.

Price and earnings indexes (2000 = 100)

	1998	1999	2000	2001	2002	2003
Consumer price index	98.9	100.3	100.0	100.5	99.7	100.9
Annual earnings index[13]	94.9	99.4	100.0	103.3	...	...

Land use as % of total land area (2000): in temporary crops 14.7%, in permanent crops 1.2%, in pasture 42.9%; overall forest area 17.5%.

Foreign trade[14]

Balance of trade (current prices)

	1997	1998	1999	2000	2001	2002
U.S.$'000,000	+46,222	+46,614	+35,982	+34,474	+34,017	+44,167
% of total	14.5%	14.5%	10.2%	7.4%	6.8%	7.3%

Imports (2000): U.S.$225,094,000,000 (machinery and apparatus 38.0%, of which transistors/microcircuits 9.4%, telecommunications equipment 5.5%; crude petroleum 6.6%; artificial resins and plastic materials 5.8%; textile yarn, fabrics, and made-up articles 5.8%; iron and steel 4.4%). *Major import sources:* Japan 18.4%; unspecified Asia (mostly Taiwan) 11.3%; South Korea 10.3%; United States 9.9%; Germany 4.6%; Hong Kong 4.2%; free zones 3.2%; Russia 2.6%; Malaysia 2.4%; Singapore 2.2%.

Exports (2000): U.S.$249,203,000,000 (machinery and apparatus 29.5%, of which computers and related units 7.5%, telecommunications equipment and related parts 5.0%; wearing apparel 14.5%; textile yarn, fabrics, and made-up articles 6.5%; toys, games, and sporting goods 4.1%). *Major export destinations:* United States 20.9%; Hong Kong 17.9%; Japan 16.7%; South Korea 4.5%; Germany 3.7%; The Netherlands 2.7%; United Kingdom 2.5%; Singapore 2.3%.

Transport and communications

Transport. Railroads (2001): route length 43,531 mi, 70,057 km; passenger-mi 296,195,000,000, passenger-km 476,680,000,000; short ton-mi cargo 998,313,-000,000, metric ton-km cargo 1,457,510,000,000. Roads (2001): total length 1,055,094 mi, 1,698,012 km (paved, n.a.). Vehicles (2001): passenger cars 9,939,600; trucks and buses 7,652,400. Air transport (2001): passenger-mi 67,816,000,000, passenger-km 109,140,000,000; short ton-mi cargo 2,995,-000,000, metric ton-km cargo 4,372,000,000; airports (1996) with scheduled flights 113.

Communications

Medium	date	unit	number	units per 1,000 persons
Daily newspapers	1994	circulation	27,790,000	23
Radio	2000	receivers	428,000,000	339
Television	2000	receivers	448,000,000	350
Telephones	2003	main lines	263,000,000	209
Cellular telephones	2003	subscribers	269,000,000	214
Personal computers	2002	units	35,500,000	28
Internet	2003	users	79,500,000	63

Education and health

Literacy (2000): total population age 15 and over literate 90.9%; males literate 95.1%; females literate 86.5%.

Education (2001)

	schools	teachers	students	student/ teacher ratio
Primary (age 7–13)	491,273	5,798,000	125,435,000	21.6
Secondary (age 13–17)	80,432	4,188,000	78,360,000	18.7
Secondary specialized	2,690	184,000	3,917,000	21.3
Voc., teacher tr.	8,372	352,000	5,326,000	15.1
Higher	1,225	532,000	7,191,000	13.5

Health (2004[6]): physicians 1,830,000 (1 per 708 persons); hospital beds 2,900,-000 (1 per 447 persons); infant mortality rate per 1,000 live births (2003) 26.4.

Food (2002): daily per capita caloric intake 2,951 (vegetable products 79%, animal products 21%); 125% of FAO recommended minimum requirement.

Military

Total active duty personnel (2003): 2,250,000 (army 75.6%, navy 11.1%, air force 13.3%). *Military expenditure as percentage of GNP* (1999): 2.3% (world 2.4%); per capita expenditure U.S.$71.

[1]As of March 2003; 36 seats are allotted to Hong Kong and 12 to Macau. [2]Names of the provinces, autonomous regions, and municipalities are stated in conventional form, followed by Pinyin transliteration; names of capitals are stated in conventional form or Wade-Giles transliteration, followed by Pinyin transliteration. [3]Data for Taiwan, Quemoy, and Matsu (parts of Fukien province occupied by Taiwan); Hong Kong (which reverted to China from British administration on July 1, 1997) and Macau (which reverted to China from Portuguese administration on Dec. 20, 1999) are excluded. [4]Estimated figures. [5]July 1. [6]January 1. [7]Based on urban sample population. [8]Reported cases. [9]Excludes arrests for anti-Communist activities. [10]Includes 6,810,000 registered unemployed. [11]In state-owned and collective-owned industries only. [12]Exchange rates and international reserves are period average figures. [13]Average annual wage in industrial establishments in urban areas. [14]Imports f.o.b. in balance of trade and c.i.f. in commodities and trading partners.

Internet resource for further information:

- **Embassy of The People's Republic of China http://www.china-embassy.org**
- **China Statistical Information Net http://www.stats.gov.cn/english**

Colombia

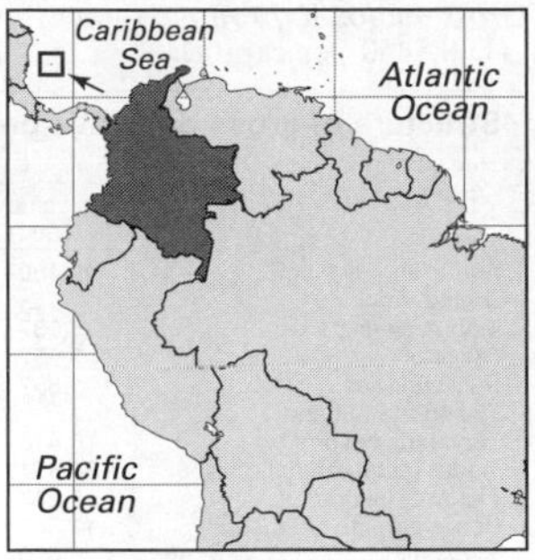

Official name: República de Colombia (Republic of Colombia).
Form of government: unitary, multiparty republic with two legislative houses (Senate [102]; House of Representatives [166[1]]).
Head of state and government: President.
Capital: Bogotá.
Official language: Spanish.
Official religion: none.
Monetary unit: 1 peso (Col$) = 100 centavos; valuation (Sept. 1, 2004) 1 U.S.$ = Col$2,539; 1 £ = Col$4,568.

Area and population

		area		population
Departments	**Capitals**	sq mi	sq km	1999 estimate
Antioquia	Medellín	24,445	63,912	5,300,000
Atlántico	Barranquilla	1,308	3,388	2,081,000
Bolívar	Cartagena	10,030	25,978	1,951,000
Boyacá	Tunja	8,953	23,189	1,355,000
Caldas	Manizales	3,046	7,888	1,094,000
Caquetá	Florencia	34,349	88,965	410,000
Cauca	Popayán	11,316	29,308	1,234,000
Cesar	Valledupar	8,844	22,905	944,000
Chocó	Quibdó	17,965	46,530	406,000
Córdoba	Montería	9,660	25,020	1,308,000
Cundinamarca	Bogotá, D.C.	8,735	22,623	2,099,000
Huila	Neiva	7,680	19,890	911,000
La Guajira	Riohacha	8,049	20,848	475,000
Magdalena	Santa Marta	8,953	23,188	1,260,000
Meta	Villavicencio	33,064	85,635	686,000
Nariño	Pasto	12,845	33,268	1,603,000
Norte de Santander	Cúcuta	8,362	21,658	1,316,000
Orinoquía-Amazonía[2]	...	186,519	483,083	1,162,000
Quindío	Armenia	712	1,845	552,000
Risaralda	Pereira	1,598	4,140	928,000
San Andrés y Providencia	San Andrés	17	44	71,000
Santander	Bucaramanga	11,790	30,537	1,939,000
Sucre	Sincelejo	4,215	10,917	779,000
Tolima	Ibagué	9,097	23,562	1,293,000
Valle	Cali	8,548	22,140	4,104,000
Capital District				
Bogotá		613	1,587	6,276,000
TOTAL		440,762[3]	1,141,568[3]	41,537,000[4]

Demography

Population (2004): 42,311,000[5].
Density (2004): persons per sq mi 96.0, persons per sq km 37.1.
Urban-rural (2003): urban 76.5%; rural 23.5%.
Sex distribution (2003): male 49.08%; female 50.92%.
Age breakdown (2003): under 15, 31.3%; 15–29, 25.8%; 30–44, 22.8%; 45–59, 12.8%; 60–74, 5.8%; 75 and over, 1.5%.
Population projection: (2010) 46,109,000; (2020) 52,199,000.
Doubling time: 44 years.
Ethnic composition (2000): mestizo 47.3%; mulatto 23.0%; white 20.0%; black 6.0%; black-Amerindian 1.0%; Amerindian/other 2.7%.
Religious affiliation (1995): Roman Catholic 91.9%; other 8.1%.
Major cities (1999): Bogotá, D.C., 6,276,428; Cali 2,110,571; Medellín 1,957,928; Barranquilla 1,226,292; Bucaramanga 520,874.

Vital statistics

Birth rate per 1,000 population (2003): 21.6 (world avg. 21.3).
Death rate per 1,000 population (2003): 5.6 (world avg. 9.1).
Natural increase rate per 1,000 population (2003): 16.0 (world avg. 12.2).
Total fertility rate (avg. births per childbearing woman; 2003): 2.6.
Life expectancy at birth (2003): male 67.3 years; female 75.1 years.
Major causes of death per 100,000 population (1997): violence and suicides 85.6; malignant neoplasms (cancers) 84.8; ischemic heart disease 71.4; cerebrovascular diseases 44.8; accidents 43.6.

National economy

Budget (1999)[6]. Revenue: Col$41,457,000,000,000 (tax revenue 61.7%, nontax revenue 38.3%). Expenditures: Col$50,441,000,000,000 (current expenditure 73.6%, capital expenditure 26.4%).
Public debt (external, outstanding; 2002): U.S.$21,177,000,000.
Population economically active (2000): total 15,417,000; activity rate 38.8% (participation rates: ages 15–69, 64.3%; female 38.0%; unemployed 20.2%).

Price index (2000 = 100)

	1997	1998	1999	2000	2001	2002	2003
Consumer price index	69.6	82.6	91.6	100.0	108.0	114.8	123.0

Production (metric tons except as noted). Agriculture, forestry, fishing (2002): sugarcane 38,200,000, plantains 2,827,024, potatoes 2,697,980, rice 2,353,440, cassava 2,214,990, bananas 1,650,000, corn 1,331,160, coffee 660,000; livestock (number of live animals) 27,000,000 cattle, 2,260,000 sheep, 2,150,000 pigs; roundwood (2001) 12,501,000 cu m; fish catch (2001) 190,000. Mining and quarrying (2001): nickel (metal content) 52,962; gold 21,813 kg; emeralds 5,500,000 carats. Manufacturing (value added in Col$'000,000; 1997): processed food 11,133,000; beverages 3,165,400; petroleum products 2,483,600; textiles 2,244,200; transport equipment 2,186,600; chemicals 2,170,300; machinery and electrical apparatus 1,707,300; paper products 1,649,000; fabricated metal products 1,334,500. Energy production (consumption): electricity (kW-hr; 2000) 43,943,000,000 (43,983,000,000); coal (metric tons; 2000) 38,365,000 (4,551,000); crude petroleum (barrels; 2001) 243,208,000 ([2000] 110,482,000); petroleum products (metric tons; 2000) 13,050,000 (8,656,000); natural gas (cu m; 2000) 7,337,400,000 (7,337,400,000).
Gross national product (2003): U.S.$80,488,000,000 (U.S.$1,810 per capita).

Structure of gross domestic product and labour force

	2000			
	in value Col$'000,000	% of total value	labour force	% of labour force
Agriculture	21,745,142	12.8	3,221,000	20.9
Mining	12,998,058	7.7	359,000[7]	2.3[7]
Manufacturing	21,761,444	12.8	1,951,000	12.7
Construction	6,216,386	3.7	700,000	4.5
Public utilities	6,992,144	4.1	[7]	[7]
Transp. and commun.	12,551,115	7.4	842,000	5.5
Trade	18,803,503	11.1	3,469,000	22.5
Finance	24,898,482	14.7	621,000	4.0
Pub. admin., defense / Services	38,204,472	22.5	4,240,000	27.5
Other	5,533,202[8]	3.3[8]	14,000[9]	0.1[9]
TOTAL	169,703,948	100.0[3]	15,417,000	100.0

Land use as % of total land area (2000): in temporary crops 2.7%, in permanent crops 1.7%, in pasture 39.4%; overall forest area 47.8%.
Household income and expenditure. Average household size (2000) 5.0; expenditure (1992): food 34.2%, transportation 18.5%, housing 7.8%, health care 6.4%.
Tourism (2002): receipts U.S.$962,000,000; expenditures U.S.$1,072,000,000.

Foreign trade[10]

Balance of trade (current prices)

	1997	1998	1999	2000	2001	2002
U.S.$'000,000	–3,855	–3,782	+917	+1,502	–577	–790
% of total	14.3%	14.8%	4.1%	6.1%	2.3%	3.2%

Imports (2002): U.S.$12,690,000,000 (capital goods 32.5%, consumer goods 21.3%). *Major import sources:* U.S. 31.7%; Venezuela 6.2%; Mexico 5.3%; Brazil 5.1%; Japan 4.9%.
Exports (2002): U.S.$11,900,000,000 (crude and refined petroleum 27.5%, chemicals and chemical products 12.4%, coal 8.3%, food, beverages, and tobacco 7.9%, machinery and equipment 7.6%, coffee 6.5%). *Major export destinations:* U.S. 43.0%; Venezuela 9.4%; Ecuador 6.8%; Peru 2.9%; Germany 2.8%.

Transport and communications

Transport. Railroads (2000): route length 1,960 mi, 3,154 km; passenger-km (1992) 15,524,000; metric ton-km cargo (1999) 473,000,000. Roads (1999): total length 71,400 mi, 114,912 km (paved 14%). Vehicles (1999): cars 762,000; trucks 672,000. Air transport (2001): passenger-km 5,858,369,000; metric ton-km cargo 33,037,000; airports (1998) 43.

Communications

Medium	date	unit	number	units per 1,000 persons
Daily newspapers	1996	circulation	1,800,000[11]	46[11]
Radio	2001	receivers	25,968,000	549
Television	2002	receivers	13,241,000	303
Telephones	2003	main lines	8,768,000	200
Cellular telephones	2003	subscribers	6,186,000	141
Personal computers	2002	units	2,133,000	49
Internet	2003	users	2,732,000	62

Education and health

Educational attainment (1985). Percentage of population age 25 and over having: no schooling 15.3%; primary education 50.1%; secondary 25.4%; higher 6.8%; not stated 2.4%. *Literacy* (2002): population age 15 and over literate 92.1%; males literate 92.1%; females literate 92.2%.

Education (1999)

	schools	teachers	students	student/ teacher ratio
Primary (age 6–10)	60,183	214,911	5,162,260	24.0
Secondary (age 11–16)	13,421	200,337	3,594,083	17.9
Higher[12]	266	75,568	673,353	8.9

Health (2003): physicians 57,000 (1 per 729 persons); hospital beds 49,000 (1 per 850 persons); infant mortality rate 24.2.
Food (2001): daily per capita caloric intake 2,580 (vegetable products 84%, animal products 16%); 111% of FAO recommended minimum requirement.

Military

Total active duty personnel (2003): 200,000 (army 89.0%, navy 7.5%, air force 3.5%). *Military expenditure as percentage of GNP* (1999): 3.2% (world 2.4%); per capita expenditure U.S.$68.

[1]Two seats are occupied by representatives from indigenous communities. [2]Geographic designation for eight political entities in eastern Colombia elevated to departmental status in the early 1990s. [3]Detail does not add to total given because of rounding. [4]De jure estimates. [5]Excludes at least 2,000,000 Colombians who left the country since 1997 because of the violence and high unemployment. [6]Preliminary. [7]Mining includes Public utilities. [8]Import duties and VAT, less imputed bank service charges. [9]Activities not adequately described. [10]Imports c.i.f., exports f.o.b. [11]Circulation for 26 newspapers only. [12]1996.

Internet resources for further information:
- **National Administration Department of Statistics http://www.dane.gov.co**

Comoros[1]

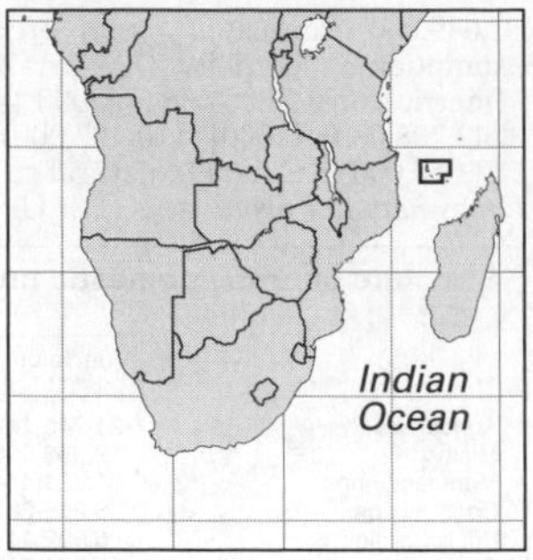

Official name: L'Union des Comores (French); Udzima wa Komori (Comorian); (Union of the Comoros)[2].
Form of government: federal republic with one legislative house (Federal Assembly [33[3]]).
Head of state and government: President assisted by Vice Presidents.
Capital: Moroni.
Official languages: Comorian (Shikomor); Arabic; French.
Official religion: Islam.
Monetary unit: 1 Comorian franc[4] (CF) = 100 centimes; valuation (Sept. 1, 2004) 1 U.S.$ = CF 404.81; 1 £ = CF 728.24.

Area and population

		area		population
Autonomous islands	Capitals	sq mi	sq km	2003 census[5]
Mwali (Mohéli)	Fomboni	112	290	35,400
Ngazidja (Grande Comore)	Moroni	443	1,148	295,700
Nzwani (Anjouan)	Mutsamudu	164	424	259,100
TOTAL		719	1,862	590,200

Demography

Population (2004): 596,000[6].
Density (2004): persons per sq mi 828.9, persons per sq km 320.1.
Urban-rural (2002): urban 33.8%; rural 66.2%.
Sex distribution (2002): male 49.62%; female 50.38%.
Age breakdown (2002): under 15, 42.9%; 15–29, 27.8%; 30–44, 16.6%; 45–59, 8.1%; 60–74, 3.9%; 75 and over, 0.7%.
Population projection: (2010) 672,000; (2020) 822,000.
Doubling time: 23 years.
Ethnic composition (2000): Comorian (a mixture of Bantu, Arab, Malay, and Malagasy peoples) 97.1%; Makua 1.6%; French 0.4%; Arab 0.1%; other 0.8%.
Religious affiliation (2000): Sunnī Muslim 98.0%; Christian 1.2%; other 0.8%.
Major cities (1991): Moroni (2003) 41,557 (urban agglomeration [2001] 49,000); Mutsamudu 16,785; Domoni 10,400; Fomboni 5,633.

Vital statistics

Birth rate per 1,000 population (2003): 38.5 (world avg. 21.3).
Death rate per 1,000 population (2003): 8.9 (world avg. 9.1).
Natural increase rate per 1,000 population (2003): 29.6 (world avg. 12.2).
Total fertility rate (avg. births per childbearing woman; 2002): 5.2.
Marriage rate per 1,000 population: n.a.[7]
Divorce rate per 1,000 population: n.a.
Life expectancy at birth (2003): male 58.9 years; female 63.5 years.
Major causes of death per 100,000 population: n.a.; however, major diseases include malaria (afflicts 80–90% of the adult population), tuberculosis, leprosy, and kwashiorkor (a nutritional deficiency disease).

National economy

Budget (2000). Revenue: CF 15,557,000,000 (tax revenue 62.5%, of which taxes on international trade 40.9%, income and profit taxes 12.2%, sales tax 7.7%; grants 29.2%; nontax revenue 8.3%). Expenditures: CF 17,649,000,000 (current expenditures 68.4%, of which wages 34.5%, goods and services 23.3%, interest on debt 5.4%, transfers 4.8%; development expenditures 31.6%).
Public debt (external, outstanding; 2002): U.S.$239,900,000.
Production (metric tons except as noted). Agriculture, forestry, fishing (2002): coconuts 76,000, bananas 60,000, cassava 55,000, rice 17,000, taro 9,000, corn (maize) 4,000, cloves 2,700, vanilla 140, ylang-ylang essence 40; other export crops grown in small quantities include coffee, cinnamon, and tuberoses; livestock (number of live animals; 2002) 115,000 goats, 52,000 cattle, 21,000 sheep; roundwood (2001) 8,650; fish catch (2002) 12,200. Mining and quarrying: sand, gravel, and crushed stone from coral mining for local construction. Manufacturing: products of small-scale industries include processed vanilla and ylang-ylang, cement, handicrafts, soaps, soft drinks, woodwork, and clothing. Energy production (consumption): electricity (kW-hr; 2001) 36,578,000 (19,780,000); coal, none (none); crude petroleum, none (none); petroleum products (metric tons; 2000) none (26,000); natural gas, none (none).
Population economically active (2000): total 156,000; activity rate of total population 28.4% (participation rates: [1991] ages 10 years and over, 57.8%; female 40.0%; unemployed [2000] 20%).

Price index (2000 = 100)

	1997	1998	1999	2000	2001
Consumer price index	89.1	92.2	95.4	100.0	105.9

Tourism: receipts from visitors (2002) U.S.$11,000,000; expenditures by nationals abroad (1998) U.S.$3,000,000.
Household income and expenditure. Average household size (1995) 6.3[8]; average annual income per household (1995) CF 188,985 (U.S.$505)[8]; sources of income: n.a.; expenditure (1993)[9]: food and beverages 67.3%, clothing and footwear 11.6%, tobacco and cigarettes 4.1%, energy 3.8%, health 3.2%, education 2.5%, transportation 2.2%, other 5.3%.

Gross national product (at current market prices; 2003): U.S.$269,000,000 (U.S.$450 per capita).

Structure of gross domestic product and labour force

	2001		1980	
	in value CF '000,000	% of total value	labour force[10]	% of labour force[10]
Agriculture, fishing	49,480	40.9	53,063	53.3
Mining	...	...	62	0.1
Manufacturing	5,037	4.2	3,946	4.0
Construction	7,557	6.2	3,267	3.3
Public utilities	1,857	1.5	129	0.1
Transportation and communications	6,415	5.3	2,118	2.1
Trade, restaurants, hotels	30,481	25.2	1,873	1.9
Finance, insurance	5,217	4.3	237	0.2
Public admin., defense	17,309	14.3	2,435	2.5
Services	668	0.6	4,646	4.7
Other	–3,018[11]	–2.5[11]	27,687[12]	27.8[12]
TOTAL	121,003	100.0	99,463	100.0

Land use as % of total land area (2000)[13]: in temporary crops *c.* 36%, in permanent crops *c.* 22%, in pasture *c.* 7%; overall forest area *c.* 4%.

Foreign trade[14]

Balance of trade (current prices)

	1996	1997	1998	1999	2000	2001
CF '000,000,000	–22.2	–23.6	–19.6	–20.7	–16.7	–18.6
% of total	82.0%	81.8%	78.8%	70.9%	57.0%	50.5%

Imports (2001): CF 27,776,000,000 (food products 28.1%, of which rice 11.3%, meat and fish 8.0%; vehicles 15.6%; petroleum products 15.3%; unspecified 30.1%). *Major import sources:* EU *c.* 49%; United Arab Emirates *c.* 11%; South Africa *c.* 10%; Pakistan *c.* 9%.
Exports (2001): CF 9,144,000,000 (vanilla 59.1%, cloves 26.6%, ylang-ylang 10.9%). *Major export destinations:* France *c.* 47%; United States *c.* 30%.

Transport and communications

Transport. Railroads: none. Roads (1996): total length 559 mi, 900 km (paved 76%). Vehicles (1996): passenger cars 9,100; trucks and buses 4,950. Merchant marine (1992): vessels (100 gross tons and over) 6; total deadweight tonnage 3,579. Air transport (1996): passenger-mi 1,900,000, passenger-km 3,000,000; short ton-mi cargo, n.a., metric ton-mi cargo, n.a.; airports (2002) with scheduled flights 4.

Communications

Medium	date	unit	number	units per 1,000 persons
Daily newspapers	1997	circulation	0	0
Radio	1997	receivers	90,000	170
Television	1997	receivers	1,000	1.8
Telephones	2003	main lines	13,200	17
Cellular telephones	2003	subscribers	2,000	2.5
Personal computers	2003	units	5,000	5.8
Internet	2003	users	5,000	5.8

Education and health

Educational attainment (1980). Percentage of population age 25 and over having: no formal schooling 56.7%; Qurʾanic school education 8.3%; primary 3.6%; secondary 2.0%; higher 0.2%; not specified 29.2%. *Literacy* (2000): total population age 15 and over literate 55.9%; males literate 63.2%; females literate 48.7%.

Education (1998)

	schools	teachers	students	student/ teacher ratio
Primary (age 7–12)	348	2,381	82,789	34.8
Secondary (age 13–19)	...	591	28,599	48.4
Higher	...	67	649	9.7

Health (1995): physicians 64[15] (1 per 7,800[15] persons); hospital beds 1,450[15] (1 per 342[15] persons); infant mortality rate per 1,000 live births (2003) 79.5.
Food (2002): daily per capita caloric intake 1,754 (vegetable products 95%, animal products 5%); 75% of FAO recommended minimum requirement.

Military

Total active duty personnel (1997): 1,500. *Military expenditure as percentage of GNP:* n.a.

[1]Excludes Mayotte, an overseas possession of France, unless otherwise indicated. [2]New official name effective with the swearing in of the first president of the new union on May 26, 2002. [3]Includes 15 nonelected seats. [4]Formerly pegged to the French franc and since Jan. 1, 2002, to the euro at the rate of €1 = CF 491.97. [5]Preliminary. [6]Includes Comorians living abroad in France or Mayotte. [7]In the early 1990s, 20% of adult men had more than one wife. [8]Based on sample survey of 2,004 households on all three islands. [9]Weights of consumer price index components for Moroni. [10]The wage labour force was very small in 1995; total of less than 7,000 including government employees, and less than 2,000 excluding them. [11]Less imputed bank service charge. [12]Not adequately defined. [13]Includes Mayotte. [14]Imports c.i.f.; exports f.o.b. [15]Estimated figure.

Internet resources for further information:
- **Indian Ocean Commission http://www.coi-info.org**
- **UN Development Programme http://www.km.undp.org**
- **La Banque de France: La Zone Franc http://www.banque-france.fr/fr/zonefr/main.htm**

Congo, Democratic Republic of the

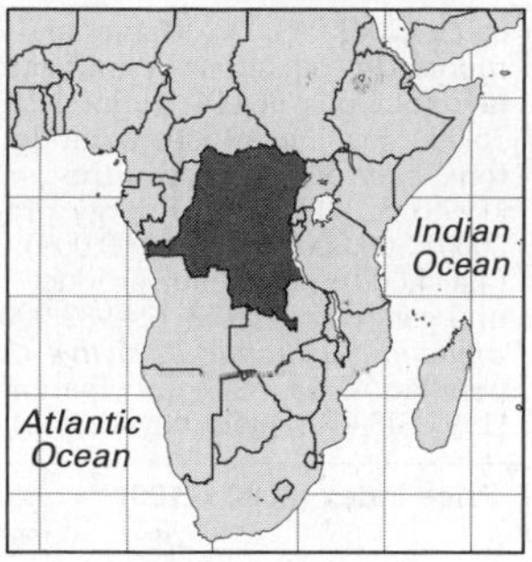

Official name: République Democratique du Congo (Democratic Republic of the Congo).
Form of government: transitional regime[1] with two legislative bodies (Senate [120]; National Assembly [500]).
Head of state and government: President assisted by Vice Presidents[1].
Capital: Kinshasa.
Official languages: French; English.
Official religion: none.
Monetary unit: Congo franc (FC)[2]; valuation (Sept. 1, 2004) 1 U.S.$ = FC 378.00; 1 £ = FC 698.05.

Area and population

		area		population
Provinces	**Capitals**	sq mi	sq km	1998 estimate
Bandundu	Bandundu	114,154	295,658	5,201,000
Bas-Congo	Matadi	20,819	53,920	2,835,000
Equateur	Mbandaka	155,712	403,292	4,820,000
Kasai-Occidental	Kananga	59,746	154,742	3,337,000
Kasai-Oriental	Mbuji-Mayi	65,754	170,302	3,830,000
Katanga	Lubumbashi	191,845	496,877	4,125,000
Maniema	Kindu	51,062	132,250	1,246,787
Nord-Kivu	Goma	22,967	59,483	3,564,434
Orientale	Kisangani	194,302	503,239	5,566,000
Sud-Kivu	Bukavu	25,147	65,130	2,837,779
City				
Kinshasa	—	3,848	9,965	4,787,000
TOTAL		905,354[3]	2,344,858	42,150,000

Demography

Population (2004): 54,417,000[4].
Density (2004): persons per sq mi 60.1, persons per sq km 23.2.
Urban-rural (2002): urban 30.7%; rural 69.3%.
Sex distribution (2002): male 49.38%; female 50.62%.
Age breakdown (2002): under 15, 48.3%; 15–29, 27.2%; 30–44, 13.6%; 45–59, 6.9%; 60–74, 3.2%; 75 and over, 0.8%.
Population projection: (2010) 64,714,000; (2020) 84,418,000.
Ethnic composition (1983): Luba 18.0%; Kongo 16.1%; Mongo 13.5%; Rwanda 10.3%; Azande 6.1%; Bangi and Ngale 5.8%; Rundi 3.8%; Teke 2.7%; Boa 2.3%; Chokwe 1.8%; Lugbara 1.6%; Banda 1.4%; other 16.6%.
Religious affiliation (1995): Roman Catholic 41.0%; Protestant 32.0%; indigenous Christian 13.4%, of which Kimbanguist 13.0%; other Christian 0.8%; Muslim 1.4%; traditional beliefs and other 11.4%.
Major cities (1994): Kinshasa 4,655,313; Lubumbashi 851,381; Mbuji-Mayi 806,475; Kolwezi 417,800; Kisangani 417,517; Kananga 393,030.

Vital statistics

Birth rate per 1,000 population (2003): 45.1 (world avg. 21.3).
Death rate per 1,000 population (2003): 14.9 (world avg. 9.1).
Natural increase rate per 1,000 population (2003): 30.2 (world avg. 12.2).
Total fertility rate (avg. births per childbearing woman; 2003): 6.7.
Life expectancy at birth (2003): male 46.8 years; female 51.1 years.
Adult population (ages 15–49) *living with HIV* (beginning of 2004): 4.2% (world avg. 1.1%).

National economy

Budget (2000). Revenue: FC 15,091,000,000 (tax revenue 83.3%, of which sales tax 24.4%, taxes on international trade 23.8%, corporate tax 23.8%; nontax revenue 16.7%). Expenditures: FC 32,988,000,000 (goods and services 45.4%; wages and salaries 22.2%; interest on debt 18.7%).
Public debt (external, outstanding; 2002): U.S.$7,391,000,000.
Production (metric tons except as noted). Agriculture, forestry, fishing (2002): cassava 14,929,410, sugarcane 1,550,000, plantains 1,200,000, corn (maize) 1,153,990, oil palm fruit 900,000, peanuts (groundnuts) 355,180, rice 314,614, bananas 313,382, sweet potatoes 219,926, papayas 210,000, yams 200,000, pineapples 192,080, coffee 32,077, seed cotton 30,000, natural rubber 7,000; livestock (number of live animals) 4,003,880 goats, 953,066 pigs; roundwood (2001) 69,733,688 cu m; fish catch (2001) 208,848. Mining and quarrying (2002): copper (metal content) 30,000; cobalt (metal content) 3,000; zinc (metal content) 1,300[5]; gold 20 kg; diamonds 18,556,000 carats. Manufacturing (2000): butter 2,052,000; steel 259,000; explosives 246,000; cement 169,000; sugar 80,000; soap 28,000; tires 107,000 units; printed fabrics 14,334,000 sq m; cotton fabrics 2,361,000 sq m; shoes 962,000 pairs; beer 1,710,000 hectolitres; soft drinks 810,000 hectolitres. Energy production (consumption): electricity (kW-hr; 2000) 5,458,000,000 (4,414,000,000); coal (metric tons; 2000) 986,000 (136,000); crude petroleum (barrels; 2000) 9,553,000 (1,358,000); petroleum products (metric tons; 2000) 176,000 (612,000); natural gas, none (none).
Household income and expenditure. Average household size (1998) 2.3; expenditure (1985): food 61.7%, housing and energy 11.5%, clothing and footwear 9.7%, transportation 5.9%, furniture and utensils 4.9%.
Gross national product (at current market prices; 2002): U.S.$5,369,000,000 (U.S.$100 per capita).

Structure of gross domestic product and labour force

	2001		2000	
	in value FC '000,000	% of total value	labour force	% of labour force
Agriculture	824,300	56.3	13,074,000	63.2
Mining	142,000	9.7		
Manufacturing	57,100	3.9		
Construction	64,400	4.4		
Public utilities	11,700	0.8		
Transp. and commun.	39,500	2.7	7,612,000	36.8
Trade	218,200	14.9		
Pub. admin., defense	26,400	1.8		
Finance and services	60,200	4.1		
Other	20,200[6]	1.4[6]		
TOTAL	1,464,000	100.0	20,686,000	100.0

Population economically active (2000): total 20,686,000; activity rate 42.6% (participation rates: over age 10, n.a.; female, n.a.).

Price index (2000 = 100)

	1997	1998	1999	2000	2001	2002
Consumer price index	3.3	4.2	16.3	100.0	459.9	604.9

Tourism (1998): receipts U.S.$2,000,000; expenditures (1997) U.S.$7,000,000.
Land use as % of total land area (2000): in temporary crops 3.0%, in permanent crops 0.5%, in pasture 6.6%; overall forest area 59.6%.

Foreign trade

Balance of trade (current prices)

	1996	1997	1998	1999	2000	2001[7]
U.S.$'000,000	+249	+56	−50	−175	−212	+73
% of total	8.2%	2.2%	2.1%	8.6%	13.5%	4.3%

Imports (2000): U.S.$680,000,000 (non-petroleum sector 92.9%, petroleum sector 7.1%). *Major import sources* (2001): Belgium 17.5%; South Africa 15.9%; Nigeria 10.3%; France 5.1%; Kenya 5.0%.
Exports (2000): U.S.$892,000,000 (diamonds 52.5%, crude petroleum 22.8%, cobalt 8.0%, coffee 6.2%, copper 4.8%, gold 2.4%). *Major export destinations* (2001): Belgium 62.1%; U.S. 14.7%; Finland 8.0%; India 4.8%; Italy 2.0%.

Transport and communications

Transport. Railroads (1996)[8]: length 5,138 km; passenger-km 29,000,000[9]; metric ton-km cargo 176,000,000[9]. Roads (1996): total length 154,027 km (paved 2%). Vehicles (1996): passenger cars 787,000; trucks and buses 60,000. Air transport (1996): passenger-km 279,000,000; metric ton-km cargo 42,000,000; airports (1997) with scheduled flights 22.

Communications

Medium	date	unit	number	units per 1,000 persons
Daily newspapers	1996	circulation	124,000	2.7
Radio	2000	receivers	18,700,000	386
Television	1997	receivers	6,478,000	135
Telephones	2002	main lines	10,000	0.2
Cellular telephones	2003	subscribers	1,000,000	19
Internet	2002	users	50,000	0.9

Education and health

Educational attainment: n.a. *Literacy* (2000): percentage of total population age 15 and over literate 61.4%; males literate 73.1%; females literate 50.2%.

Education (1998)

	schools	teachers	students	student/teacher ratio
Primary (age 6–11)	17,585	154,618	4,022,411	26.0
Secondary (age 12–17) Voc., teacher tr.	6,007	89,461	1,234,528	13.8
Higher	...	3,788	60,341	15.9

Health: physicians (1996) 3,129 (1 per 14,494 persons); hospital beds, n.a.; infant mortality rate per 1,000 live births (2003) 96.6.
Food (2001): daily per capita caloric intake 1,535 (vegetable products 98%, animal products 2%); 68% of FAO recommended minimum requirement.

Military

Total active duty personnel: new national army being created from August 2003; UN peacekeepers (August 2004): 10,000. *Military expenditure as percentage of GNP* (1997): 14.4% (world 2.4%); per capita expenditure U.S.$102.

[1]Per signing of Sun City accord, ending nearly five years of civil war beginning in August 1998; transitional constitution effective from April 5–6, 2003, created a two-year interim administration. [2]The Congo franc (FC) replaced the new zaïre (NZ) at a rate of FC 1 to NZ 100,000 on July 1, 1998. [3]Detail does not add to total given because of rounding. [4]2004 population estimate adjusted for about 3 million deaths associated with the civil war and other civil unrest between 1998 and 2003. [5]2001. [6]Import duties. [7]Preliminary data. [8]Traffic statistics are for services operated by the Zaire National Railways (SNCZ), which controls more than 90% of the country's total rail facility. [9]1994.

Internet resources for further information:
- **Permanent Mission of the Democratic Republic of the Congo http://www.un.int/drcongo**

Congo, Republic of the

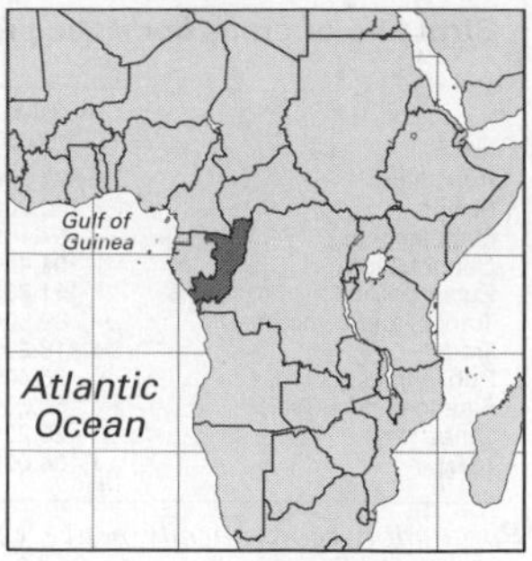

Official name: République du Congo (Republic of the Congo).
Form of government: republic with two legislative houses (Senate [66[1]]; National Assembly [137[1]]).
Chief of state and government: President.
Capital: Brazzaville.
Official language: French[2].
Official religion: none.
Monetary unit: 1 CFA franc (CFAF) = 100 centimes; valuation (Sept. 1, 2004) 1 U.S.$ = CFAF 539.75; 1 £ = CFAF 970.98[3].

Area and population

Regions	Capitals	area sq mi	area sq km	population 1992 estimate
Bouenza	Madingou	4,733	12,258	177,357
Cuvette Est	Owando	18,861	48,850	151,839
Cuvette Ouest	Ewo	10,039	26,000	
Kouilou	Pointe-Noire	5,270	13,650	89,296
Lékoumou	Sibiti	8,089	20,950	74,420
Likouala	Impfondo	25,500	66,044	70,675
Niari	Dolisie[4]	10,007	25,918	120,077
Plateaux	Djambala	14,826	38,400	119,722
Pool	Kinkala	13,110	33,955	182,671
Sangha	Ouesso	21,542	55,795	35,961
Communes				
Brazzaville	—	39	100	937,579
Dolisie[4]	—	7	18	83,605
Mossendjo	—	2	5	16,405
Nkayi	—	3	8	42,465
Ouesso	—	2	5	16,171
Pointe-Noire	—	17	44	576,206
TOTAL		132,047	342,000	2,694,449

Demography

Population (2004): 3,818,000.
Density (2004): persons per sq mi 28.9, persons per sq km 11.2.
Urban-rural (2002): urban 66.1%; rural 33.9%.
Sex distribution (2002): male 49.36%; female 50.64%.
Age breakdown (2002): under 15, 38.9%; 15–29, 29.6%; 30–44, 17.7%; 45–59, 8.4%; 60–74, 4.4%; 75 and over, 1.0%.
Population projection: (2010) 4,532,000; (2020) 5,960,000.
Doubling time: 47 years.
Ethnic composition (1983): Kongo 51.5%; Teke 17.3%; Mboshi 11.5%; Mbete 4.9%; Punu 3.0%; Sango 2.7%; Maka 1.8%; Pygmy 1.5%; other 5.8%.
Religious affiliation (2000): Roman Catholic 49.3%; Protestant 17.0%; African Christians 12.6%; unaffiliated Christians 11.9%; traditional beliefs 4.8%; other 4.4%.
Major cities (1992): Brazzaville (urban agglomeration; 2001) 1,360,000; Pointe-Noire (1996) 455,131; Dolisie[4] 83,605; Nkayi 42,465; Mossendjo 16,405.

Vital statistics

Birth rate per 1,000 population (2003): 29.5 (world avg. 21.3).
Death rate per 1,000 population (2003): 14.2 (world avg. 9.1).
Natural increase rate per 1,000 population (2002): 15.3 (world avg. 12.2).
Total fertility rate (avg. births per childbearing woman; 2003): 3.7.
Life expectancy at birth (2003): male 49.0 years; female 51.0 years.
Adult population (ages 15–49) *living with HIV* (beginning of 2004): 4.9% (world avg. 1.1%).

National economy

Budget (2001). Revenue: CFAF 631,800,000,000 (petroleum revenue 68.2%; nonpetroleum receipts 31.2%; grants 0.6%). Expenditures: CFAF 645,900,-000,000 (current expenditure 68.2%, of which debt service 23.5%, salaries 18.3%, transfers and subsidies 11.3%; capital expenditure 31.8%).
Public debt (external, outstanding; 2002): U.S.$3,974,000,000.
Household income and expenditure. Average household size (1984) 5.2.
Gross national product (at current market prices; 2002): U.S.$2,407,000,000 (U.S.$640 per capita).

Structure of gross domestic product and labour force

	2000 in value CFAF '000,000	2000 % of total value	1991 labour force	1991 % of labour force
Agriculture, forestry, fishing	121,600	5.3	471,000	59.1
Petroleum	1,502,300	65.5	101,000	12.7
Manufacturing, mining	79,700	3.5		
Construction	56,500	2.5		
Public utilities	15,600	0.7	225,000	28.2
Trade	138,500	6.0		
Transp. and commun.	86,000	3.8		
Pub. admin., defense	125,100	5.5		
Services	113,400	4.9		
Other	53,800[5]	2.3[5]	—	—
TOTAL	2,292,500	100.0	797,000	100.0

Production (metric tons except as noted). Agriculture, forestry, fishing (2002): cassava 862,000, sugarcane 459,000, oil palm fruit 90,000, bananas 84,000, plantains 71,000, mangoes 25,000, peanuts (groundnuts) 24,000, coffee 1,687, cacao beans 1,253, rubber 1,200; livestock (number of live animals) 294,000 goats, 96,000 sheep, 93,000 cattle; roundwood (2001) 2,420,000 cu m; fish catch (2002) 43,000. Mining and quarrying (2002): gold 10 kg; diamonds, no reported production[6]. Manufacturing (2000): residual fuel oil 262,000; distillate fuel oils 96,000; refined sugar 74,726; aviation gas 50,000; kerosene 36,000; gasoline 35,000; wheat flour 1,636; soap 1,620; cigarettes 4,000,000 cartons; beer 526,000 hectolitres; soft drinks 290,000 hectolitres; veneer sheets (1998) 52,000 cu m. Energy production (consumption): electricity (kW-hr; 2000) 300,000,000 (490,000,000); crude petroleum (barrels; 2000) 99,200,000 (4,444,000); petroleum products (metric tons; 2001) 383,000 (165,400); natural gas (cu m; 2000) 124,983,000 (124,983,000).
Population economically active (2000): total 1,232,000; activity rate of total population 35.7% (participation rates [1984]: ages 15–64, 54.0%; female [1997] 43.4%; unemployed, n.a.).

Price index (2000 = 100)

	1997	1998	1999	2000	2001	2002	2003
Consumer price index	...	95.7	100.9	100.0	100.1	104.7	103.8

Land use as % of total land area (2000): in temporary crops 0.5%, in permanent crops 0.1%, in pasture 29.3%; overall forest area 64.6%.
Tourism (2002): receipts U.S.$25,000,000; expenditures U.S.$70,000,000.

Foreign trade

Balance of trade (current prices)

	1996	1997	1998	1999	2000	2001
CFAF '000,000,000	+574.2	+502.4	+477.6	+638.7	+1,432.9	+957.0
% of total	48.9%	39.9%	42.0%	49.8%	62.8%	49.6%

Imports (2001): CFAF 486,200,000,000 (non-petroleum sector 84.0%; petroleum sector 16.0%). *Major import sources* (1999): France *c.* 23%; U.S. *c.* 8%; Italy *c.* 8%; Hong Kong *c.* 5%; Belgium *c.* 4%.
Exports (2001): CFAF 1,443,200,000,000 (crude petroleum 89.6%, wood and wood products 5.1%, petroleum products 1.3%, sugar 0.7%). *Major export destinations* (1999): Taiwan *c.* 32%; U.S. *c.* 23%; South Korea *c.* 15%; Germany *c.* 7%; China *c.* 3%.

Transport and communications

Transport. Railroads: (1998) length 894 km; passenger-km 242,000,000; metric ton-km cargo 135,000,000. Roads (2001): total length 17,244 km (paved 7%). Vehicles (1997): passenger cars 37,240; trucks and buses 15,500. Air transport (1998)[7]: passenger-km 258,272,000; metric ton-km cargo 13,524,000; airports (1998) with scheduled flights 10.

Communications

Medium	date	unit	number	units per 1,000 persons
Daily newspapers	2000	circulation	10,300	3.0
Radio	2000	receivers	403,300	109
Television	2000	receivers	114,000	13
Telephones	2003	main lines	7,000	2.0
Cellular telephones	2003	subscribers	330,000	94
Personal computers	2003	units	15,000	4.3
Internet	2003	users	15,000	4.3

Education and health

Educational attainment (1984). Percentage of population age 25 and over having: no formal schooling 58.7%; primary education 21.4%; secondary education 16.9%; postsecondary 3.0%. *Literacy* (2000): total population age 15 and over literate 80.7%; males literate 87.5%; females literate 74.4%.

Education (1998)

	schools	teachers	students	student/ teacher ratio
Primary (age 6–13)	1,168	4,515	270,451	59.9
Secondary (age 14–18)	...	5,094	114,450	22.5
Voc., teacher tr.[8]	...	1,746	23,606	13.5
Higher	...	1,341[8]	16,862	12.4

Health: physicians (1995) 632 (1 per 4,083 persons); hospital beds (1989) 4,817 (1 per 446 persons); infant mortality rate per 1,000 live births (2003) 95.3.
Food (2002): daily per capita caloric intake 2,162 (vegetable products 94%, animal products 6%); 97% of FAO recommended minimum requirement.

Military

Total active duty personnel (2003): 10,000 (army 80.0%, navy 8.0%, air force 12.0%). *Military expenditure as percentage of GNP* (1999): 3.5% (world 2.4%); per capita expenditure U.S.$21.

[1]Includes vacant seats. [2]"Functional" national languages are Lingala and Monokutuba. [3]Formerly pegged to the French franc and since Jan. 1, 2002, to the euro at a rate of €1 = CFAF 655.96. [4]Known as Loubomo between 1980 and 2000. [5]Import duties. [6]Annual volume of large-scale diamond smuggling as of July 2004 equaled 5,200,000 carats. [7]Represents 1/11 of the traffic of Air Afrique; Air Afrique, an airline jointly owned by 11 African countries (including Republic of the Congo), was declared bankrupt in February 2002. [8]1996–97.

Internet resources for further information:

- **La Banque de France: La Zone Franc http://www.banque-france.fr/fr/zonefr/main.htm**

Costa Rica

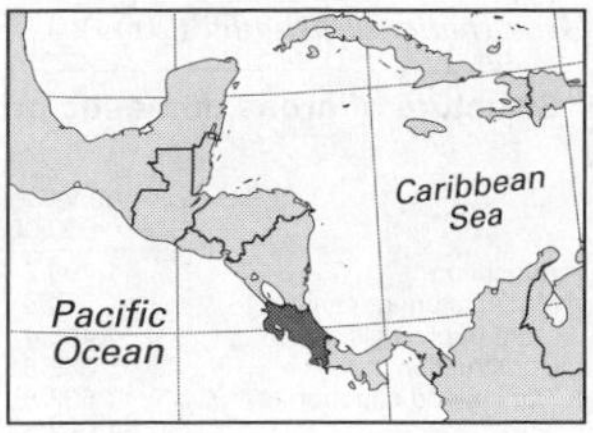

Official name: República de Costa Rica (Republic of Costa Rica).
Form of government: unitary multiparty republic with one legislative house (Legislative Assembly [57]).
Head of state and government: President.
Capital: San José.
Official language: Spanish.
Official religion: Roman Catholicism.
Monetary unit: 1 Costa Rican colón (₡) = 100 céntimos; valuation (Sept. 1, 2004) 1 U.S.$ = ₡444.60; 1 £ = ₡799.81.

Area and population

		area		population
Provinces	**Capitals**	sq mi	sq km	2000 census
Alajuela	Alajuela	3,766	9,753	716,286
Cartago	Cartago	1,207	3,125	432,395
Guanacaste	Liberia	3,915	10,141	264,238
Heredia	Heredia	1,026	2,657	354,732
Limón	Limón	3,547	9,188	339,295
Puntarenas	Puntarenas	4,354	11,277	357,483
San José	San José	1,915	4,959	1,345,750
TOTAL		19,730	51,100	3,810,179[1]

Demography

Population (2004): 4,252,000.
Density (2004): persons per sq mi 215.5; persons per sq km 83.2.
Urban-rural (2003): urban 60.6%; rural 39.4%.
Sex distribution (2003): male 50.86%; female 49.14%.
Age breakdown (2002): under 15, 30.7%; 15–29, 27.3%; 30–44, 21.7%; 45–59, 12.5%; 60–74, 5.7%; 75 and over, 2.1%.
Population projection: (2010) 4,732,000; (2020) 5,474,000.
Doubling time: 47 years.
Ethnic composition (2000): white 77.0%; mestizo 17.0%; black/mulatto 3.0%; East Asian (mostly Chinese) 2.0%; Amerindian 1.0%.
Religious affiliation (1995): Roman Catholic 86.0%; Protestant 9.3%, of which Pentecostal 4.9%; other Christian 2.4%; other 2.3%.
Major cities (2000): San José 309,672[2] (urban agglomeration 983,000[3]); Limón 60,298[4]; Alajuela 42,889[4]; San Isidro de El General 41,221[4]; Cartago 39,958[5]; Liberia 39,242[4].

Vital statistics

Birth rate per 1,000 population (2003): 19.4 (world avg. 21.3); (1999) legitimate 51.0%; illegitimate 49.0%.
Death rate per 1,000 population (2003): 4.3 (world avg. 9.1).
Natural increase rate per 1,000 population (2003): 15.1 (world avg. 12.2).
Total fertility rate (avg. births per childbearing woman; 2003): 2.4.
Marriage rate per 1,000 population (1999): 7.1.
Divorce rate per 1,000 population (1995): 1.4.
Life expectancy at birth (2003): male 73.9 years; female 79.1 years.
Major causes of death per 100,000 population (1999): diseases of the circulatory system 127.6; malignant neoplasms (cancers) 87.2; accidents and violence 50.1; diseases of the respiratory system 44.5.

National economy

Budget (2000). Revenue: ₡610,138,000,000 (taxes on goods and services 63.8%, income and profit taxes 21.8%, import duties 7.7%, other 6.7%). Expenditures: ₡761,306,000,000 (current expenditures 90.1%, of which transfers 30.5%, wages 29.7%, interest on debt 23.0%; development expenditures 9.9%).
Public debt (external, outstanding; 2002): U.S.$3,139,000,000.
Gross national product (2003): U.S.$17,157,000,000 (U.S.$4,280 per capita).

Structure of gross domestic product and labour force

	2000			
	in value ₡'000,000	% of total value	labour force	% of labour force
Agriculture, forestry, fishing	420,369	8.6	269,200	19.4
Mining	6,954	0.1	2,610	0.2
Manufacturing	1,085,501	22.2	190,260	13.7
Construction	176,270	3.6	89,720	6.4
Public utilities	118,136	2.4	10,000	0.8
Transp. and commun.	371,182	7.6	78,830	5.7
Trade, restaurants	882,631	18.0	266,830	19.2
Finance, real estate	225,756	4.6	64,260	4.6
Public administration	173,155	3.5	337,090	24.2
Services	817,425	16.7		
Other	618,071[6]	12.6[6]	80,880[7]	5.8[7]
TOTAL	4,895,450	100.0[8]	1,390,560	100.0

Production (metric tons except as noted). Agriculture, forestry, fishing (2003): sugarcane 3,923,870, bananas 1,862,978, green coffee 731,126, pineapples 725,224, oil palm fruit 700,000, oranges 367,000, cantaloupes/other melons 215,000, rice 179,987, cassava 94,248, potatoes 81,678; livestock (number of live animals) 1,150,000 cattle, 500,000 pigs, 18,500,000 chickens; roundwood (2001) 5,140,781 cu m; fish catch (2001) 35,000. Mining and quarrying (2002): limestone 900,000; gold 100 kg. Manufacturing (value added in U.S.$'000,000; 2001): food products 777; beverages 211; paints, soaps, and pharmaceuticals 148; plastic products 111; paper and paper products 100; bricks, tiles, and cement 93; industrial chemicals 72. Energy production (consumption): electricity (kW-hr; 2000) 7,227,000,000 (7,226,000,000); coal, none (none); crude petroleum (barrels; 2000) none (80,630); petroleum products (metric tons; 2000) 6,000 (1,597,000); natural gas, none (none).
Population economically active (2000): total 1,390,560; activity rate of total population 39.9% (participation rates: ages 12–59, 53.4%; female 32.1%; unemployed 5.2%).

Price and earnings indexes (2000 = 100)

	1997	1998	1999	2000	2001	2002	2003
Consumer price index	73.3	81.9	90.1	100.0	111.2	121.4	132.9
Monthly earnings index	71.2	81.1	89.6	100.0	124.2	...	...

Tourism (2002): receipts U.S.$1,078,000,000; expenditures U.S.$367,000,000.
Household income and expenditure. Average household size (2000) 4.1; average annual household income (1997) ₡1,468,597 (U.S.$6,314); sources of income (1987–88): wages and salaries 61.0%, self-employment 22.6%, transfers 9.6%; expenditure (1987–88): food and beverages 39.1%, housing and energy 12.1%, transportation 11.6%, household furnishings 10.9%.
Land use as % of total land area (2000): in temporary crops 4.4%, in permanent crops 5.9%, in pasture 45.8%; overall forest area 38.5%.

Foreign trade[9]

Balance of trade (current prices)[10]

	1997	1998	1999	2000	2001	2002
U.S.$'000,000	–764	–713	+308	–483	–1,548	–1,922
% of total	8.3%	6.1%	2.3%	3.9%	13.4%	15.5%

Imports (2000): U.S.$6,380,000,000 ([11]general merchandise 68%; goods for reassembly 32%). *Major import sources:* U.S. 53.1%; Mexico 6.2%; Venezuela 5.3%; Japan 3.4%; Spain 2.3%.
Exports (2000): U.S.$5,897,000,000 (components for microprocessors 28.0%, bananas 9.0%, processed food and tobacco products 6.5%, coffee 4.7%, tropical fruit 3.4%). *Major export destinations:* U.S. 51.8%; The Netherlands 6.7%; U.K. 5.1%; Guatemala 3.3%; Nicaragua 3.0%.

Transport and communications

Transport. Railroads[12]. Roads (1999): total length 22,292 mi, 35,876 km (paved 17%). Vehicles (1999): passenger cars 326,524; trucks and buses 181,272. Air transport (2001)[13]: passenger-mi 1,332,000,000, passenger-km 2,143,000,000; short-ton mi cargo (1999) 58,013,000, metric ton-km cargo 84,697,000; airports (1996) 14.

Communications

Medium	date	unit	number	units per 1,000 persons
Daily newspapers	1996	circulation	320,000	94
Radio	2000	receivers	3,200,000	816
Television	2000	receivers	907,000	231
Telephones	2002	main lines	1,038,000	251
Cellular telephones	2003	subscribers	459,800	141
Personal computers	2002	units	800,000	193
Internet	2002	users	817,000	197

Education and health

Educational attainment (1996). Percentage of population age 5 and over having: no formal schooling 11.7%; incomplete primary education 28.5%; complete primary 25.8%; incomplete secondary 16.0%; complete secondary 9.0%; higher 8.5%; other/unknown 0.5%. *Literacy* (2002): total population age 15 and over literate 95.8%; males literate 95.7%; females literate 95.9%.

Education (1999)

	schools	teachers	students	student/ teacher ratio
Primary (age 7–12)	3,768	20,185	535,057	26.5
Secondary (age 13–17)	468	11,891	235,425	19.8
Higher	52	...	59,947	...

Health (2003): physicians (2000) 6,800 (1 per 625 persons); hospital beds 6,000 (1 per 700 persons); infant mortality rate per 1,000 live births 10.6.
Food (2001): daily per capita caloric intake 2,761 (vegetable products 80%, animal products 20%); 123% of FAO recommended minimum requirement.

Military

Paramilitary expenditure as percentage of GNP (1999): 0.5% (world 2.4%); per capita expenditure U.S.$19. The army was officially abolished in 1948. Paramilitary (police) forces had 8,400 members in 2003.

[1]Adjusted census total for underenumeration equals 3,925,331. [2]Population of San José canton. [3]2001 estimate. [4]District population. [5]Population of three districts. [6]Taxes less imputed bank service charge. [7]Includes 8,940 not adequately defined and 71,940 unemployed. [8]Detail does not add to total given because of rounding. [9]Imports c.i.f.; exports f.o.b. [10]Includes goods imported for reassembly and reexported. [11]Estimated figures. [12]National rail service was not in regular service from 1995 through 2000. [13]Lacsa (Costa Rican Airlines) only.

Internet resources for further information:

- **Central Bank of Costa Rica: Economic Indicators http://websiec.bccr.fi.cr**
- **Government of Costa Rica http://www.casapres.go.cr**

Côte d'Ivoire

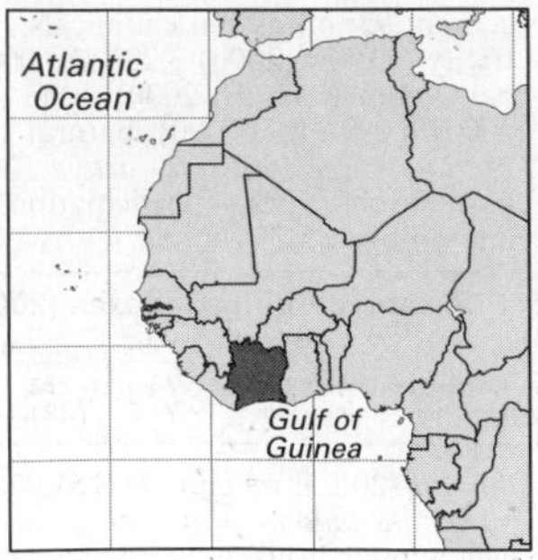

Official name: République de Côte d'Ivoire (Republic of Côte d'Ivoire [Ivory Coast][1]).
Form of government: republic[2] with one legislative house (National Assembly [225[3]]).
Chief of state and government: President assisted by Prime Minister.
De facto capital: Abidjan.
Official language: French.
Official religion: none.
Monetary unit: 1 CFA franc (CFAF) = 100 centimes; valuation (Sept. 1, 2004) 1 U.S.$ = CFAF 539.75; 1 £ = CFAF 970.98.[4]

Area and population

		area		population
Regions	Capitals	sq mi	sq km	2000 estimate
Agnebi	Agboville	3,510	9,080	641,400
Bafing	Touba	3,370	8,720	158,700
Bas-Sassandra	San-Pédro	9,960	25,800	937,700
Denguélé	Odienné	7,950	20,600	246,400
Dix-huit Montagnes	Man	6,410	16,600	1,051,600
Fromager	Gagnoa	2,660	6,900	604,800
Haut-Sassandra	Daloa	5,870	15,200	1,055,600
Lacs	Yamoussoukro	3,450	8,940	531,600
Lagunes	Abidjan	5,480	14,200	3,894,300
Marahoué	Bouaflé	3,280	8,500	579,800
Moyen-Cavally	Guiglo	5,460	14,150	394,200
Moyen-Comoé	Abengourou	2,660	6,900	434,200
Nzi-Comoé	Dimbokro	7,550	19,560	809,400
Savanes	Korhogo	15,570	40,323	1,081,000
Sud-Bandama	Divo	4,110	10,650	735,100
Sud-Comoé	Aboisso	2,410	6,250	328,500
Vallée du Bandama	Bouaké	11,020	28,530	1,188,000
Worodougou	Séguéla	8,460	21,900	356,000
Zanzan	Bondoukou	14,670	38,000	746,300
TOTAL		123,863[5]	320,803	15,774,600

Demography

Population (2004): 16,897,000.
Density (2004): persons per sq mi 136.4, persons per sq km 52.7.
Urban-rural (2003): urban 44.9%; rural 55.1%.
Sex distribution (2002): male 50.28%; female 49.72%.
Age breakdown (2002): under 15, 45.6%; 15–29, 28.7%; 30–44, 14.4%; 45–59, 7.6%; 60–74, 3.0%; 75 and over, 0.7%.
Population projection: (2010) 18,526,000; (2020) 21,026,000.
Ethnolinguistic composition (1998)[6]: Akan 42.1%; Mande 26.5%; other 31.4%.
Religious affiliation (1998): Muslim 38.6%; Christian 30.4%; nonreligious 16.7%; animist 11.9%; other 2.4%.
Major cities (1998): Abidjan (1999) 3,199,000; Bouaké 462,000; Daloa 173,000; Yamoussoukro 110,000.

Vital statistics

Birth rate per 1,000 population (2002): 40.4 (world avg. 21.3).
Death rate per 1,000 population (2001): 18.4 (world avg. 9.1).
Natural increase rate per 1,000 population (2002): 22.0 (world avg. 12.2).
Total fertility rate (avg. births per childbearing woman; 2002): 5.6.
Life expectancy at birth (2002): male 40.4 years; female 45.3 years.
Adult population (ages 15–49) *living with HIV* (2004[7]): 7.0% (world avg. 1.1%).

National economy

Budget (2000). Revenue: CFAF 1,237,100,000,000 (tax revenue 87.1%, of which import taxes and duties 29.2%, export taxes 13.2%, taxes on profits 11.6%, income tax 10.2%; nontax revenue 12.9%). Expenditures: CFAF 1,358,200,000,000 (wages and salaries 33.0%; debt service 22.7%; capital expenditure 15.4%; transfers 13.1%; other 15.8%).
Production (metric tons except as noted). Agriculture, forestry, fishing (2002): yams 3,000,000, cassava 1,700,000, plantains 1,410,000, oil palm fruit 1,400,000, cacao beans 1,000,000, rice 818,000, corn (maize) 625,000, cotton seed 280,000, bananas 270,000, coffee 198,000, rubber 123,000; livestock (number of live animals) 1,522,000 sheep, 1,476,000 cattle, 1,191,000 goats, 32,625,000 chickens; roundwood (2001) 12,083,092 cu m; fish catch (2001) 74,581. Mining and quarrying (2002): gold 2,000 kg; diamonds 306,500 carats. Manufacturing (value added in CFAF '000,000,000; 1997): food 156.6, of which cocoa and chocolate 72.4, vegetable oils 62.7; chemicals 60.2; wood products 55.9; refined petroleum 46.0; textiles 37.9; tobacco 27.6; fabricated metal products 25.9. Energy production (consumption): electricity (kW-hr; 2000) 3,619,000,000 (3,619,000,000); crude petroleum (barrels; 2000) 11,270,000 (30,087,000); petroleum products (metric tons; 2000) 2,801,000 (1,242,000); natural gas (cu m; 2000) 1,510,400,000 (1,510,400,000).
Household income and expenditure. Average household size (2000) 7.8; expenditure (1992–93)[8]: food 48.0%, transportation 12.2%, clothing 10.1%, energy and water 8.5%, housing 7.8%, household equipment 3.4%.
Population economically active (2000): total 6,531,000; activity rate of total population 40.9% (participation rates [1994] over ages 10, 64.3%; female 33.0%; unemployed [1996] 38.8%).

Price index (2000 = 100)

	1997	1998	1999	2000	2001	2002	2003
Consumer price index	92.5	96.8	97.6	100.0	104.3	107.5	111.1

Gross national product (2003): U.S.$11,159,000,000 (U.S.$660 per capita).

Structure of gross domestic product and labour force

	1999		2000	
	in value CFAF '000,000,000	% of total value	labour force	% of labour force
Agriculture	1,795.2	26.0	3,211,000	49.2
Manufacturing, mining, and public utilities	1,466.4	21.3		
Construction	352.8	5.1		
Transp. and commun.	592.8	8.6		
Trade	1,042.6	15.1	3,320,000	50.8
Public admin., defense	525.8	7.6		
Services	875.5	12.7		
Other (customs receipts)	248.6	3.6		
TOTAL	6,899.7	100.0	6,531,000	100.0

Public debt (external, outstanding; 2002): U.S.$9,110,000,000.
Tourism (2001): receipts U.S.$48,000,000; expenditures U.S.$192,000,000.
Land use as % of total land area (2000): in temporary crops 9.7%, in permanent crops 13.8%, in pasture 40.9%; overall forest area 22.4%.

Foreign trade[9]

Balance of trade (current prices)

	1996	1997	1998	1999	2000	2001
CFAF '000,000,000	+933	+1,046	+1,015	+1,167	+1,058	+1,123
% of total	25.8%	25.2%	23.0%	25.5%	23.6%	24.1%

Imports (2001): CFAF 1,768,000,000,000 (crude and refined petroleum 28.8%, food products 22.5%, machinery and transport equipment 20.4%). *Major import sources* (2000): Nigeria 26.6%; France 20.3%; Belgium 4.0%; Italy 3.6%; Germany 3.6%.
Exports (2001): CFAF 2,891,000,000,000 (cocoa beans and products 33.2%, crude petroleum and petroleum products 13.7%, wood and wood products 7.1%, coffee beans 3.6%). *Major export destinations* (2000): France 14.9%; The Netherlands 9.7%; United States 8.3%; Mali 5.7%; Italy 4.8%; Senegal 4.0%.

Transport and communications

Transport. Railroads (1999): route length 655 km; passenger-km 93,100,000; metric ton-km cargo 537,600,000. Roads (1999): total length 50,400 km (paved 9.7%). Vehicles (1999): passenger cars 109,600; trucks and buses 54,100. Air transport (1998): passenger-km 318,000,000; metric ton-km cargo 44,000,000; airports (1999) 5.

Communications

Medium	date	unit	number	units per 1,000 persons
Daily newspapers	2000	circulation	1,440,000	91
Radio	2001	receivers	3,053,000	185
Television	2002	receivers	1,007,000	61
Telephones	2003	main lines	328,000	20
Cellular telephones	2003	subscribers	1,236,000	74
Personal computers	2002	units	154,000	9.3
Internet	2002	users	90,000	5.5

Education and health

Educational attainment (1988). Percentage of population age 6 and over having: no formal schooling 60.0%; Koranic school 3.6%; primary education 24.8%; secondary 10.7%; higher 0.9%. *Literacy* (2000): percentage of population age 15 and over literate 46.8%; males 54.5%; females 38.6%.

Education (1998–99)

	schools	teachers	students	student/ teacher ratio
Primary (age 7–12)	7,599[10]	40,529[10]	1,910,820	...
Secondary (age 13–19)	147[10]	15,959[10]	565,856	...
Vocational[11]	...	1,424	11,037	7.8
Higher	7[11]	1,657[11]	47,187	...

Health: physicians (1996) 1,318 (1 per 11,111 persons); hospital beds (1993) 7,928 (1 per 1,698 persons); infant mortality rate per 1,000 live births (2001) 99.6.
Food (2001): daily per capita caloric intake 2,594 (vegetable products 97%, animal products 3%); 112% of FAO recommended minimum requirement.

Military

Total active duty personnel: 12. *Military expenditure as percentage of GNP* (1999): 0.8% (world avg. 2.4%); per capita expenditure U.S.$5.

[1]Since 1986, Côte d'Ivoire has requested that the French form of the country's name be used as the official protocol version in all languages. [2]Côte d'Ivoire has been split between a government-controlled south and a rebel-held north from September 2002 through early October 2004. [3]Includes vacant/unoccupied seats. [4]Formerly pegged to the French franc and since Jan. 1, 2002, to the euro at the rate of €1 = CFAF 655.96. [5]Detail does not add to total given because of rounding. [6]Local population only; in 1998 foreigners constituted 26% of the population and two-thirds of all foreigners were from Burkina Faso. [7]January 1. [8]Weights of consumer price index components for a worker's family living in the capital city. [9]Imports are f.o.b. in balance of trade and commodities and c.i.f. for trading partners. [10]1996–97. [11]1994–95. [12]New national army to be created pending final resolution of 2002–03 civil war. Peacekeeping troops (August 2004): UN 5,800; French 4,000.

Internet resources for further information:

- **La Banque de France: La Zone Franc**
  http://www.banque-france.fr/fr/zonefr/main.htm

Croatia

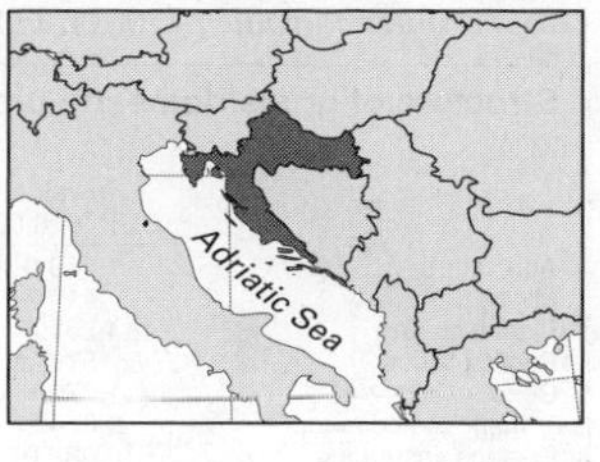

Official name: Republika Hrvatska (Republic of Croatia).
Form of government: multiparty republic with one legislative house (House of Representatives [152[1]])[2].
Head of state: President.
Head of government: Prime Minister.
Capital: Zagreb.
Official language: Croatian (Serbo-Croatian).
Official religion: none.
Monetary unit: 1 kuna (HrK; plural kune) = 100 lipa; valuation (Sept. 1, 2004) 1 U.S.$ = HrK 6.06; 1 £ = HrK 10.91.

Area and population

Counties	area sq km	population 2001 census
Bjelovar-Bilogora	2,640	133,084
Dubrovnik-Neretva	1,781	122,870
Istria	2,813	206,344
Karlovac	3,626	141,787
Koprivnica-Križevci	1,748	124,467
Krapina-Zagorje	1,229	142,432
Lika-Senj	5,353	53,677
Medimurje	729	118,426
Osijek-Baranja	4,155	330,506
Požega-Slavonia	1,823	85,831
Primorje-Gorski kotar	3,588	305,505
Šibenik-Knin	2,984	112,891
Sisak-Moslavina	4,468	185,387
Slavonski Brod-Posavina	2,030	176,765
Split-Dalmatia	4,540	463,676
Varaždin	1,262	184,769
Virovitica-Podravina	2,024	93,389
Vukovar-Srijem	2,454	204,768
Zadar	3,646	162,045
Zagreb	3,060	309,696
City		
Zagreb	641	779,145
TOTAL	56,594	4,437,460

Demography

Population (2004): 4,497,000.
Density (2004): persons per sq mi 206.0, persons per sq km 79.5.
Urban-rural (2002): urban 59.0%; rural 41.0%.
Sex distribution (2001): male 48.13%; female 51.87%.
Age breakdown (2001): under 15, 17.1%; 15–29, 20.4%; 30–44, 21.4%; 45–59, 19.5%; 60–74, 16.3%; 75 and over, 5.3%.
Population projection: (2010) 4,487,000; (2020) 4,427,000.
Ethnic composition (2001): Croat 89.6%; Serb 4.5%; Bosniac 0.5%; Italian 0.4%; Hungarian 0.4%; other 4.6%.
Religious affiliation (2000): Christian 95.2%, of which Roman Catholic 88.5%, Eastern Orthodox 5.6%, Protestant 0.6%; Sunnī Muslim 2.3%; nonreligious/atheist 2.5%.
Major cities (2001): Zagreb 691,724; Split 175,140; Rijeka 143,800; Osijek 90,411; Zadar 69,556.

Vital statistics

Birth rate per 1,000 population (2003): 9.5 (world avg. 21.3); (1999) legitimate 91.8%; illegitimate 8.2%.
Death rate per 1,000 population (2003): 11.2 (world avg. 9.1).
Natural increase rate per 1,000 population (2001): –1.7 (world avg. 12.2).
Total fertility rate (avg. births per childbearing woman; 2003): 1.4.
Marriage rate per 1,000 population (2001): 5.0.
Divorce rate per 1,000 population (2001): 1.1.
Life expectancy at birth (2003): male 69.6 years; female 78.3 years.
Major causes of death per 100,000 population (2001): diseases of the circulatory system 540.0; malignant neoplasms (cancers) 240.0; accidents, violence, and poisoning 50.0; diseases of the digestive system 50.0; diseases of the respiratory system 40.0.

National economy

Budget (2001). Revenue: HrK 55,303,800,000 (tax revenue 84.9%, of which sales tax 40.7%, excise taxes 14.2%, income tax 6.8%; nontax revenue 15.1%). Expenditures: HrK 57,308,100,000 (social security and welfare 43.2%; education 10.7%; public order 8.3%; defense 7.4%).
Population economically active (2001): total 1,728,503; activity rate 39.0% (participation rates: ages 15–64, 57.9%; female 43.0%; unemployed 22.0%).

Price and earnings indexes (2000 = 100)

	1997	1998	1999	2000	2001	2002	2003
Consumer price index	86.3	91.8	95.0	100.0	104.8	106.5	106.7
Annual earnings index	71.5	80.6	91.9	100.0	106.5	111.8	118.4

Production (metric tons except as noted). Agriculture, forestry, fishing (2002): corn (maize) 2,502,000, sugar beets 1,183,000, wheat 988,000, potatoes 736,000, grapes 371,000, barley 171,000, soybeans 129,000, cabbage 128,000, tomatoes 71,000, sunflower seed 63,000, apples 59,000, plums 21,000; livestock (number of live animals) 1,286,000 pigs, 580,000 sheep, 417,000 cattle, poultry 11,665,000; roundwood (2001) 3,468,000 cu m; fish catch (2002) 30,000. Mining and quarrying (2002): gypsum 145,000; ornamental stone 1,128,000 sq m. Manufacturing (value added in U.S.$'000,000; 1996): food products 895; transport equipment 425; electrical machinery 362; textiles 285; wearing apparel 260. Energy production (consumption): electricity (kW-hr; 2001) 11,674,000,000 ([2000] 14,702,000,000); hard coal (metric tons; 2000) none (623,000); lignite (metric tons; 2000) none (80,000); crude petroleum (barrels; 2000) 8,158,000 (37,845,000); petroleum products (metric tons; 2000) 4,827,000 (3,534,000); natural gas (cu m; 2001) 2,009,000,000 ([2000] 2,633,994,000).

Gross national product (2003): U.S.$23,839,000,000 (U.S.$5,350 per capita).

Structure of gross domestic product and labour force

	2001			
	in value HrK '000,000	% of total value	labour force	% of labour force
Agriculture	13,113	7.8	111,233	6.4
Mining			7,733	0.4
Manufacturing	38,008	22.5	287,030	16.6
Public utilities			27,655	1.6
Construction	8,186	4.8	90,222	5.2
Transp. and commun.	15,105	8.9	96,768	5.6
Trade	24,002	14.2	282,235	16.3
Finance, real estate	20,266	12.0	99,378	5.7
Pub. admin., defense	28,528	16.9	121,332	7.0
Services			224,722	13.0
Other	21,764[3]	12.9[3]	380,195[4]	22.0[4]
TOTAL	168,972	100.0	1,728,503	100.0[5]

Public debt (external, outstanding; 2002): U.S.$7,679,000,000.
Household income and expenditure. Average household size (2001) 3.0; income per household HrK 64,288 (U.S.$8,700); sources: wages 42.8%, self-employment 22.5%, pension 20.6%, other 14.1%; expenditure (2001): food and nonalcoholic beverages 33.7%, housing and energy 13.4%, transportation 11.5%, clothing 9.1%, recreation and culture 5.9%, household furnishings 5.6%, alcoholic beverages and tobacco 4.1%, other 16.7%.
Tourism (2002): receipts U.S.$3,811,000,000; expenditures U.S.$781,000,000.
Land use as % of total land area (2000): in temporary crops 26.1%, in permanent crops 2.3%, in pasture 28.1%; overall forest area 31.9%.

Foreign trade[6]

Balance of trade (current prices)

	1996	1997	1998	1999	2000	2001
U.S.$'000,000	–3,623	–5,196	–4,147	–3,299	–3,204	–4,012
% of total	28.5%	38.2%	31.1%	27.3%	26.0%	29.7%

Imports (2001): U.S.$9,044,000,000 (machinery and transport equipment 33.2%, chemical products 11.5%, base and fabricated metals 10.1%, crude and refined petroleum 9.2%). *Major import sources:* Germany 17.1%; Italy 16.9%; Slovenia 7.9%; Russia and other countries of former U.S.S.R. 7.2%; Austria 7.0%.
Exports (2001): U.S.$4,659,000,000 (machinery and transport equipment 29.4%, chemical and chemical products 10.6%, clothing 10.5%, crude petroleum and petroleum products 7.4%, food 6.9%). *Major export destinations:* Italy 23.7%; Germany 14.8%; Bosnia and Herzegovina 12.0%; Slovenia 9.1%; Austria 5.7%.

Transport and communications

Transport. Railroads (2001): length 2,726 km; passenger-km 1,234,000,000; metric ton-km cargo 2,148,000,000. Roads (2001): total length 28,275 km (paved 82%). Vehicles (2001): passenger cars 1,195,450; trucks and buses 124,669. Air transport (2001): passenger-km 921,053,000; metric ton-km cargo 3,597,000; airports (2001) 4.

Communications

Medium	date	unit	number	units per 1,000 persons
Daily newspapers	1996	circulation	515,000	118
Radio	2000	receivers	1,120,000	252
Television	2000	receivers	1,693,000	380
Telephones	2002	main lines	1,825,000	417
Cellular telephones	2003	subscribers	2,553,000	584
Personal computers	2002	units	760,000	174
Internet	2003	users	1,014,000	232

Education and health

Educational attainment (1991). Percentage of population age 15 and over having: no schooling or unknown 10.1%; less than full primary education 21.2%; primary 23.4%; secondary 36.0%; postsecondary and higher 9.3%. *Literacy* (1999): population age 15 and over literate 98.2%; males 99.3%; females 97.1%.

Education (2001–02)

	schools	teachers	students	student/ teacher ratio
Primary (age 7–14)	2,134	27,502	400,100	14.5
Secondary (age 15–18)	645	19,718	195,000	9.9
Higher	89	7,622	100,297	13.2

Health (1999): physicians 8,046 (1 per 529 persons); hospital beds 27,000 (1 per 158 persons); infant mortality rate per 1,000 live births (2003) 7.1.
Food (2002): daily per capita caloric intake 2,799 (vegetable products 81%, animal products 19%); 110% of FAO recommended minimum requirement.

Military

Total active duty personnel (2003): 20,800 (army 67.5%, navy 12.0%, air force and air defense 11.1%, headquarters staff 9.4%). *Military expenditure as percentage of GNP* (1999): 6.4% (world 2.4%); per capita expenditure U.S.$491.

[1]Includes 6 seats representing Croatians abroad and 2 seats for minorities. [2]A constitutional amendment in March 2001 abolished the former upper house (House of Counties). [3]Import and turnover taxes less imputed bank service charges. [4]Unemployed. [5]Detail does not add to total given because of rounding. [6]Imports f.o.b. in balance of trade and c.i.f. for commodities and trading partners.

Internet resources for further information:
- **Croatian Bureau of Statistics http://www.dzs.hr/Eng/ouraddress.htm**
- **Ministry of Foreign Affairs http://www.mfa.hr/MVP.asp?pcpid=1612**

Cuba

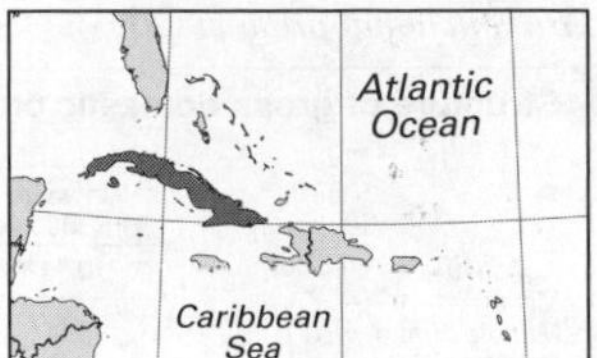

Official name: República de Cuba (Republic of Cuba).
Form of government: unitary socialist republic with one legislative house (National Assembly of the People's Power [609]).
Head of state and government: President.
Capital: Havana.
Official language: Spanish.
Official religion: none.
Monetary unit: 1 Cuban peso (CUP) = 100 centavos; valuation (Sept. 1, 2004) 1 U.S.$ = 21.00 CUP[1]; 1 £ = 37.78 CUP[1].

Area and population

		area[2]		population
				2002[3]
Provinces	**Capitals**	sq mi	sq km	estimate
Camagüey	Camagüey	6,174	15,990	792,800
Ciego de Avila	Ciego de Avila	2,668	6,910	414,500
Cienfuegos	Cienfuegos	1,613	4,178	399,000
Ciudad de la Habana	—	281	727	2,175,900
Granma	Bayamo	3,232	8,372	837,200
Guantánamo	Guantánamo	2,388	6,186	517,400
Holguín	Holguín	3,591	9,301	1,037,700
La Habana[4]	Havana	2,213	5,731	713,100
Las Tunas	Las Tunas	2,544	6,589	533,600
Matanzas	Matanzas	4,625	11,978	666,000
Pinar del Río	Pinar del Río	4,218	10,925	740,200
Sancti Spíritus	Sancti Spíritus	2,604	6,744	463,500
Santiago de Cuba	Santiago de Cuba	2,382	6,170	1,043,200
Villa Clara	Santa Clara	3,345	8,662	836,200
Special municipality				
Isla de la Juventud	Nueva Gerona	926	2,398	80,700
TOTAL		42,804	110,861	11,251,000

Demography

Population (2004): 11,300,000.
Density (2004): persons per sq mi 264.0, persons per sq km 101.9.
Urban-rural (2003): urban 75.6%; rural 24.4%.
Sex distribution (2003): male 50.02%; female 49.98%.
Age breakdown (2003): under 15, 20.5%; 15–29, 21.2%; 30–44, 27.7%; 45–59, 16.5%; 60–74, 9.9%; 75 and over, 4.2%.
Population projection: (2010) 11,447,000; (2020) 11,528,000.
Ethnic composition (1994): mixed 51.0%; white 37.0%; black 11.0%; other 1.0%.
Religious affiliation (1995): Roman Catholic 39.5%; Protestant 2.4%; other Christian 0.2%; other (mostly Santería) 57.9%.
Major cities (1999): Havana (2002)[3] 2,175,900; Santiago de Cuba 441,524; Camagüey 306,049; Holguín 259,300; Santa Clara 210,100; Guantánamo 208,030.

Vital statistics

Birth rate per 1,000 population (2003): 12.4 (world avg. 21.3).
Death rate per 1,000 population (2003): 7.2 (world avg. 9.1).
Natural increase rate per 1,000 population (2003): 5.2 (world avg. 12.2).
Total fertility rate (avg. births per childbearing woman; 2003): 1.7.
Marriage rate per 1,000 population (2001): 4.8.
Divorce rate per 1,000 population (2001): 2.3.
Life expectancy at birth (2003): male 74.6 years; female 79.2 years.
Major causes of death per 100,000 population (1998): heart disease 142.6; malignant neoplasms (cancers) 111.0; cerebrovascular disease 52.9; accidents 39.0; influenza and pneumonia 31.3; diseases of the blood vessels 21.9.

National economy

Budget (2000). Revenue: CUP 14,505,000,000. Expenditures: CUP 15,243,000,000 (capital expenditure 18.0%, education 13.9%, health 11.3%, defense 6.1%, other 50.7%).
Public debt (external, outstanding; 2002): U.S.$12,300,000,000.
Production (metric tons except as noted). Agriculture, forestry, fishing (2003): sugarcane 22,901,600, fresh vegetables 1,930,870, plantains 797,200, rice 715,800, cassava 682,522, tomatoes 643,700, sweet potatoes 503,400, oranges 492,200, tobacco leaves 34,494; livestock (number of live animals) 4,025,000 cattle, 3,121,000 sheep, 1,684,000 pigs, 23,210,000 chickens; roundwood (2003) 3,597,000 cu m; fish catch (2001) 110,330. Mining and quarrying (2001): nickel (metal content) 72,619; cobalt (metal content) 3,910. Manufacturing (value added in U.S.$'000,000; 1990): tobacco products 2,629; food products 1,033; beverages 358; chemical products 354; transport equipment 225; nonelectrical machinery 176. Energy production (consumption): electricity (kW-hr; 2001) 15,301,000,000 (15,301,000,000); coal (metric tons; 2000) none (15,000); crude petroleum (2003) 26,020,000 ([2000] 28,240,000); petroleum products (metric tons; 2000) 2,068,000 (5,888,000); natural gas (cu m; 2003) 653,000,000 ([2000] 574,000,000).
Population economically active (2002): total 4,300,000; activity rate 38.2% (participation rates: n.a.; female [1998] 37.0%; unemployed [2002] 3.5%).

Price and earnings indexes (2000 = 100)

	1996	1997	1998	1999	2000	2001	2002
Consumer price index	90.1	91.8	94.4	97.2	100.0	...	...
Monthly earnings index	86.3	88.0	88.5	94.9	100.0	104.7	111.5

Gross domestic product (2002): U.S.$25,900,000,000 (U.S.$2,300 per capita).

Structure of gross domestic product and labour force

	2001		1989	
	in value CUP '000,000[5]	% of total value	labour force	% of labour force
Agriculture	1,768.0	6.5	721,100	20.4
Mining	417.7	1.5		
Manufacturing	4,751.6	17.4	767,500	21.8
Public utilities	576.3	2.1		
Construction	1,779.5	6.5	344,300	9.8
Transp. and commun.	2,874.9	10.5	235,900	6.7
Finance, insurance	2,039.0	7.4	21,700	0.6
Trade	7,608.4	27.8	395,300	11.2
Public administration	—	—	151,700	4.3
Services	5,123.0	18.7	835,700	23.7
Other	435.3[6]	1.6[6]	53,400	1.5
TOTAL	27,373.7	100.0	3,526,600	100.0

Household income and expenditure. Average household size (2000) 3.6; average annual income per household, n.a.; sources of income, n.a.
Tourism (2002): U.S.$1,633,000,000; expenditures by nationals abroad, n.a.
Land use as % of total land area (2000): in temporary crops 33.1%, in permanent crops 7.6%, in pasture 20.0%; overall forest area 21.4%.

Foreign trade[7]

Balance of trade (current prices)

	1997	1998	1999	2000	2001[8]
U.S.$'000,000	–1,200	–1,300	–1,800	–1,600	–3,000
% of total	25.2%	25.5%	39.1%	30.8%	45.5%

Imports (1996): U.S.$3,481,000,000 (refined petroleum 20.2%; food and live animals 19.8%, of which cereals 11.4%; machinery and transport equipment 16.1%, of which power-generating machinery 7.4%; crude petroleum 7.2%). *Major import sources* (2001): Spain 12.7%; France 6.5%; Canada 5.7%; China 5.3%; Italy 5.0%.
Exports (1996): U.S.$1,849,000,000 (raw sugar 51.5%; nickel [all forms] 22.6%; fresh and frozen fish 6.7%; raw tobacco and tobacco products 5.9%; medicinal and pharmaceutical products 2.8%). *Major export destinations* (2001): The Netherlands 22.4%; Russia 13.3%; Canada 13.3%; Spain 7.3%; China 6.2%.

Transport and communications

Transport. Railroads (2001): length 2,987 mi, 4,807 km; (1997) passenger-km 1,684,000; metric ton-km cargo 821,500,000. Roads (1997): total length 37,815 mi, 60,858 km (paved 49%). Vehicles (1998): passenger cars 172,574; trucks and buses 185,495. Air transport (2000): passenger-km 2,769,162,000; metric ton-km cargo 49,294,000; airports with scheduled flights (1999) 14.

Communications

Medium	date	unit	number	units per 1,000 persons
Daily newspapers	2000	circulation	1,280,000	114
Radio	2001	receivers	2,091,000	185
Television	2000	receivers	3,580,000	242
Telephones	2001	main lines	574,000	51
Cellular telephones	2002	subscribers	179,000	1.6
Personal computers	2002	units	359,000	32
Internet	2001	users	120,000	11

Education and health

Educational attainment: n.a. *Literacy* (2004): total population age 15 and over literate 96.9%; males 97.0%; females 96.8%.

Education (2000–01)

	schools	teachers	students	student/ teacher ratio
Primary (age 6–11)	8,868	75,900	950,400	12.5
Secondary (age 12–17)	1,887	76,000	911,100	12.0
Voc., teacher tr.	...	27,267[9]	244,253[9]	9.0[9]
Higher	48	20,800	116,700	5.6

Health (2002): physicians 67,000 (1 per 168 persons); hospital beds 70,424 (1 per 161 persons); infant mortality rate per 1,000 live births 6.5.
Food (2001): daily per capita caloric intake 2,564 (vegetable products 86%, animal products 14%); 111% of FAO recommended minimum requirement.

Military

Total active duty personnel (2003): 46,000 (army 76.1%, navy 6.5%, air force 17.4%). *Military expenditure as percentage of GDP* (1999): 1.9% (world 2.4%); per capita expenditure: U.S.$57.

[1]Unofficial rate for domestic use; official rate for international transactions is 1 U.S.$ = 1.00 CUP; 1 £ = 1.80 CUP. [2]Geographic areas: island of Cuba 40,520 sq mi (104,945 sq km); Isla de la Juventud 850 sq mi (2,200 sq km); numerous adjacent cays (administratively a part of provinces or the Isla de la Juventud) 1,434 sq mi (3,715 sq km). [3]June 30. [4]Province bordering Ciudad de la Habana on the east, south, and west. [5]At constant 1981 prices. [6]Import duties. [7]Imports are f.o.b. in balance of trade and trading partners and c.i.f. for commodities. [8]Based on balance of estimated imports for 2001 and estimated exports for 2002. [9]1995–96.

Internet resources for further information:
- **Oficina Nacional de Estadísticas**
  http://www.cubagob.cu/otras_info/estadisticas.htm
- **Naciones Unidas en Cuba**
  http://www.onu.org.cu/uunn/homepage/index2.html

Cyprus

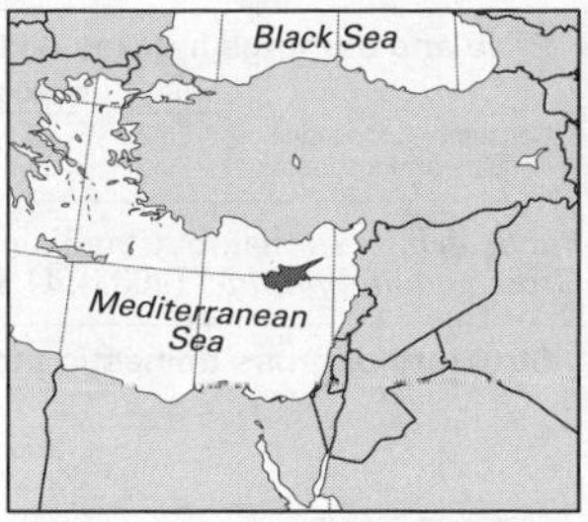

Island of Cyprus

Area: 3,572 sq mi, 9,251 sq km.
Population (2004): 937,000[1].

Two de facto states currently exist on the island of Cyprus: the Republic of Cyprus (ROC), predominantly Greek in character, occupying the southern two-thirds of the island, which is the original and still the internationally recognized de jure government of the whole island; and the Turkish Republic of Northern Cyprus (TRNC), proclaimed unilaterally Nov. 15, 1983, on territory originally secured for the Turkish Cypriot population by the July 20, 1974, intervention of Turkey. Only Turkey recognizes the TRNC, and the two ethnic communities have failed to reestablish a single state. Provision of separate data below does not imply recognition of either state's claims but is necessitated by the lack of unified data.

Republic of Cyprus

Official name: Kipriakí Dhimokratía (Greek); Kıbrıs Cumhuriyeti (Turkish) (Republic of Cyprus).
Form of government: unitary multiparty republic with a unicameral legislature (House of Representatives [80[2]]).
Head of state and government: President.
Capital: Lefkosia (Nicosia).
Official languages: Greek; Turkish.
Monetary unit: 1 Cyprus pound (£C) = 100 cents; valuation (Sept. 1, 2004) 1 £C = U.S.$2.10 = £1.17.

Demography

Area[3]: 2,276 sq mi, 5,896 sq km.
Population (2004): 726,000[4].
Urban-rural (2001): urban 68.8%; rural 31.2%.
Age breakdown (2002)[5]: under 15, 21.5%; 15–29, 22.6%, 30–44, 22.0%; 45–59, 17.8%; 60–74, 11.2%; 75 and over, 4.9%.
Ethnic composition (2000): Greek Cypriot 91.8%; Armenian 3.3%; Arab 2.9%, of which Lebanese 2.5%; British 1.4%; other 0.6%.
Religious affiliation (2001): Greek Orthodox 94.8%; Roman Catholic 2.1%, of which Maronite 0.6%; Anglican 1.0%, Muslim 0.6%; other 1.5%.
Urban areas (2001): Lefkosia 200,686[6]; Limassol 156,939; Larnaca 70,502.

Vital statistics

Birth rate per 1,000 population (2003): 11.2 (world avg. 21.3).
Death rate per 1,000 population (2003): 7.2 (world avg. 9.1).
Natural increase rate per 1,000 population (2003): 4.0 (world avg. 12.2).
Life expectancy at birth (2002–03): male 77.0 years; female 81.4 years.

National economy

Budget (2001). Revenue: £C 2,073,100,000 (indirect taxes 34.8%, direct taxes 31.8%, social security contributions 19.7%). Expenditures: £C 2,239,700,000 (current expenditures 90.0%, development expenditures 10.0%).
Tourism (2002): receipts U.S.$1,863,000,000; expenditures U.S.$424,000,000.
Household expenditure (2000): housing and energy 21.3%, food and beverages 20.0%, transportation and communications 19.2%.
Gross national product (2003): U.S.$9,373,000,000 (U.S.$12,320 per capita).

Structure of gross domestic product and labour force

	2001			
	in value £C '000,000	% of total value	labour force	% of labour force
Agriculture, fishing	219.4	3.7	24,700	7.6
Mining	15.0	0.3	600	0.2
Manufacturing	562.7	9.6	37,200	11.4
Construction	398.5	6.8	26,900	8.2
Public utilities	115.2	2.0	1,500	0.5
Transportation and communications	557.8	9.5	22,200	6.8
Trade	1,267.7	21.6	88,200	27.0
Finance, insurance	1,194.3	20.3	31,100	9.5
Pub. admin., defense	805.6	13.7	74,700	22.9
Services	467.0	8.0		
Other	264.0[7]	4.5[7]	19,100[8]	5.9[8]
TOTAL	5,867.2	100.0	326,200	100.0

Production. Agriculture (in '000 metric tons; 2002): potatoes 142.0, barley 125.7, grapes 88.0, oranges 36.5, grapefruit 27.8, olives 17.5. Manufacturing (value added in £C '000,000; 1999): food 102.7; cement, bricks, and tiles 47.1; tobacco products 46.3; beverages 45.3; fabricated metal products 35.1. Energy production: electricity (kW-hr; 2001) 3,552,000,000.

Foreign trade[9]

Imports (2001): £C 2,528,700,000 (consumer goods 24.4%; for reexport 13.9%; mineral fuels 10.5%; capital goods 10.2%). *Major import sources:* U.S. 9.4%; Greece 8.9%; U.K. 8.8%; Italy 8.8%; Germany 6.8%; Japan 6.1%.
Exports (2001): £C 628,000,000 (reexports 53.7%[10]; domestic exports 37.2%, of which pharmaceuticals 6.3%, clothing 3.1%; ships' stores 9.1%). *Major export destinations:* U.K. 18.7%; Russia 8.6%; Greece 8.4%; U.A.E. 7.8%; Syria 6.0%.

Transport and communications

Transport. Roads (2001): total length 11,408 km (paved 58%). Vehicles (2001): cars 268,200; trucks and buses 136,200. Air transport (2002)[11]: passenger-km 3,276,000,000; metric ton-km cargo 40,392,000; airports (2000) 2.

Communications

Medium	date	unit	number	units per 1,000 persons
Television	1999	receivers	120,000	180
Telephones	2002	main lines	492,000	688
Cellular telephones	2002	subscribers	417,900	597
Personal computers	2002	units	193,000	270
Internet	2002	users	210,000	294

Education and health

Educational attainment (2001). Percentage of population age 15 and over having: no formal schooling 2.1%; incomplete primary 6.4%; complete primary 20.6%; secondary 48.3%; higher education 22.3%; not stated 0.3%.

Education (1997–98)

	schools	teachers	students	student/teacher ratio
Primary (age 6–11)	372	3,521	64,592	18.3
Secondary (age 12–17) / Vocational	125	5,032	61,703	12.3
Higher	34	835	10,527	12.6

Health (2002): physicians 1,864 (1 per 381 persons); hospital beds 3,092 (1 per 229 persons); infant mortality rate per 1,000 live births (2003) 4.1.

Internet resources for further information:
- **Central Bank of Cyprus http://www.centralbank.gov.cy**
- **Rep. of Cyprus Statistical Service http://www.mof.gov.cy/mof/cystat/statistics.nsf/index_en/index_en?OpenDocument**

Turkish Republic of Northern Cyprus

Official name: Kuzey Kıbrıs Türk Cumhuriyeti (Turkish) (Turkish Republic of Northern Cyprus).
Capital: Lefkoşa (Nicosia).
Official language: Turkish.
Monetary unit: 1 Turkish lira (TL) = 100 kurush; valuation (Sept. 1, 2004) 1 U.S.$ = TL 1,503,500; 1 £ = TL 2,704,722.
Population (2004): 211,000[1] (Lefkoşa 39,176[12]; Gazimağusa [Famagusta] 27,637[12]; Girne [Kyrenia] 14,205[12]).
Ethnic composition (1996): Turkish Cypriot/Turkish 96.4%; other 3.6%.

Structure of gross domestic product and labour force

	2002			
	in value TL '000,000,000	% of total value	labour force	% of labour force
Agriculture and fishing	125,668.9	9.3	14,632	15.6
Mining and manufacturing	82,002.3	6.0	7,510	7.9
Construction	62,013.0	4.6	15,786	16.7
Public utilities	75,574.2	5.5	1,381	1.4
Transportation and communications	185,264.8	13.6	8,310	8.8
Trade, restaurants	215,553.6	15.9	10,520	11.1
Pub. admin.	227,867.1	16.8	18,084	19.1
Finance, real estate	131,384.2	9.7	2,397	2.5
Services	138,860.1	10.2	14,494	15.3
Other	113,513.4[13]	8.4[13]	1,535[14]	1.6[14]
TOTAL	1,357,701.6	100.0	94,649	100.0

Budget (2001). Revenue: U.S.$418,200,000 (foreign aid 46.8%, direct taxes 24.2%, indirect taxes 18.8%, loans 6.4%). Expenditures: U.S.$418,200,000 (wages 32.9%, social transfers 29.8%, defense 8.3%, investments 8.2%).
Imports (2001): U.S.$272,000,000 (machinery and transport equipment 21.7%, food 21.7%). *Major import sources:* Turkey 63.7%; U.K. 10.5%.
Exports (2001): U.S.$34,600,000 (ready-made garments 32.1%, citrus fruits 28.6%). *Major export destinations:* Turkey 37.0%; U.K. 33.2%.

Education (2001–02)

	schools	teachers	students	student/teacher ratio
Primary (age 7–11)	94	1,177	15,584	13.2
Secondary (age 12–17)	52	1,442	15,631	10.8
Vocational	13	438	2,177	5.0
Higher	6	884[15]	26,321	24.8[15]

Health (2002): physicians 523 (1 per 408 persons); hospital beds 1,121 (1 per 190 persons); infant mortality rate per 1,000 live births (1999) 3.7.

Internet resources for further information:
- **Turkish Republic of Northern Cyprus http://www.cypnet.com/.ncyprus/root.html**

[1]Includes 80,000 "settlers" from Turkey and 38,000 Turkish military in the TRNC; excludes 3,300 British military in the Sovereign Base Areas (SBA) in the ROC and 1,200 UN peacekeeping forces. [2]Twenty-four seats reserved for Turkish Cypriots are not occupied. [3]Area includes 99 sq mi (256 sq km) of British military SBA and *c.* 107 sq mi (*c.* 278 sq km) of the UN Buffer Zone. [4]Excludes British and UN military forces. [5]January 1. [6]ROC only. [7]Import duties less imputed bank service charges. [8]Includes 3,200 unemployed. [9]Imports c.i.f.; exports f.o.b. [10]Mainly cigarettes, vehicles, and consumer electronics. [11]Cyprus Airways. [12]1996 census. [13]Import duties. [14]Unemployed. [15]1998–99.

Czech Republic

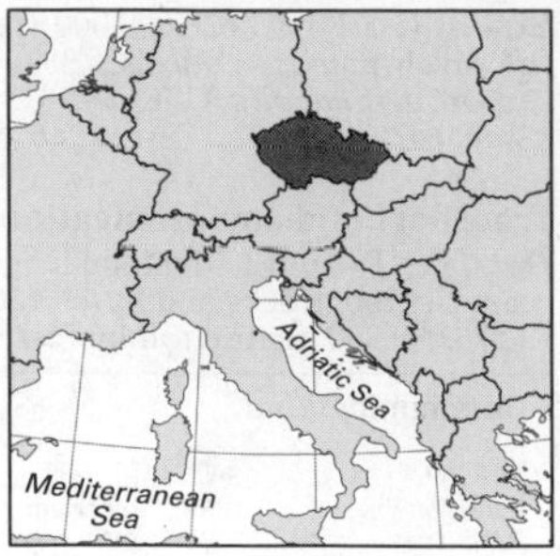

Official name: Česká Republika (Czech Republic).
Form of government: unitary multiparty republic with two legislative houses (Senate [81]; Chamber of Deputies [200]).
Chief of state: President.
Head of government: Prime Minister.
Capital: Prague.
Official language: Czech.
Official religion: none.
Monetary unit: 1 koruna (Kč) = 100 halura; valuation (Sept. 1, 2004) 1 U.S.$ = Kč 26.28; 1 £ = Kč 47.27.

Area and population

Regions[1]	area sq km	population 2001 census	Regions[1]	area sq km	population 2001 census
Brno	7,067	1,127,718	Pardubice	4,519	508,281
Budejovice	10,056	625,267	Plzeň	7,560	550,688
Hradec Králové	4,757	550,724	Střed	11,014	1,122,473
Jihlava	6,925	519,211	Ústí	5,335	820,219
Karlovy Vary	3,315	304,343	Zlín	3,965	595,010
Liberec	3,163	428,184	**Capital city**		
Olomouc	5,139	639,369	Prague (Praha)	496	1,169,106
Ostrava	5,555	1,269,467	TOTAL	78,866	10,230,060

Demography

Population (2004): 10,212,000.
Density (2004): persons per sq mi 335.4, persons per sq km 129.5.
Urban-rural (2003): urban 74.3%; rural 25.7%.
Sex distribution (2002): male 48.68%; female 51.32%.
Age breakdown (2001): under 15, 16.3%; 15–29, 23.5%; 30–44, 20.1%; 45–59, 21.8%; 60–74, 12.8%; 75 and over, 5.5%.
Population projection: (2010) 10,167,000; (2020) 9,980,000.
Ethnic composition (2001): Czech 90.4%; Moravian 3.7%; Slovak 1.9%; Polish 0.5%; German 0.4%; Silesian 0.1%; Rom (Gypsy) 0.1%; other 2.9%.
Religious affiliation (2000): Catholic 43.8%, of which Roman Catholic 40.4%, Hussite Church of the Czech Republic 2.2%; nonreligious 31.9%; atheist 5.0%; Protestant 3.1%; Orthodox Christian 0.6%; Jewish 0.1%; other (mostly unaffiliated Christian) 15.5%.
Major cities (2003): Prague 1,161,938; Brno 370,505; Ostrava 314,102; Plzeň 163,791; Olomouc 101,624.

Vital statistics

Birth rate per 1,000 population (2003): 9.2 (world avg. 21.3); (2002) legitimate 74.5%; illegitimate 25.5%.
Death rate per 1,000 population (2003): 10.9 (world avg. 9.1).
Natural increase rate per 1,000 population (2003): –1.7 (world avg. 12.2).
Total fertility rate (avg. births per childbearing woman; 2001): 1.1.
Marriage rate per 1,000 population (2003): 4.8.
Divorce rate per 1,000 population (2003): 3.2.
Life expectancy at birth (2002): male 72.1 years; female 78.5 years.
Major causes of death per 100,000 population (2001): diseases of the circulatory system 532.7; malignant neoplasms (cancers) 264.1; accidents, poisoning, and violence 64.1; diseases of the respiratory system 43.2.

National economy

Budget (2001). Revenue: Kč 626,216,000,000 (tax revenue 95.6%, of which social security contributions 37.4%, value-added tax 18.6%, personal income tax 13.4%, corporate tax 9.4%, excise tax 9.3%; nontax revenue 4.4%). Expenditures: Kč 693,920,000,000 (social security and welfare 39.3%; education 11.6%; health 6.1%; defense 5.4%; police 3.9%).
Production (metric tons except as noted). Agriculture, forestry, fishing (2002): cereals 6,771,000 (of which wheat 3,867,000, barley 1,793,000, corn [maize] 616,000), sugar beets 3,833,000, potatoes 901,000, rapeseed 710,000; livestock (number of live animals) 3,363,000 pigs, 1,474,000 cattle, 96,000 sheep, 16,564,000 chickens; roundwood (2001) 14,374,000 cu m; fish catch (2002) 24,000. Mining and quarrying (2001): kaolin 6,300,000; feldspar 410,000. Manufacturing (value added in Kč '000,000,000; 1998): nonelectrical machinery and apparatus 47.0; food products 37.4; fabricated metals 35.2; motor vehicles 34.2; electrical machinery and apparatus 31.1; iron and steel 25.5. Construction (2001): Kč 196,700,000,000. Energy production (consumption): electricity (kW-hr; 2001) 74,647,000,000 (65,108,000,000); hard coal (metric tons; 2001) 15,138,000 (15,138,000); lignite (metric tons; 2001) 50,968,000 (50,968,000); crude petroleum (barrels; 2000) 1,186,500 (39,771,000); petroleum products (metric tons; 2000) 6,132,000 (7,998,000); natural gas (cu m; 2000) 238,462,000 (10,564,000,000).
Household income and expenditure. Average household size (2001) 2.5; disposable income per household (2000) Kč 286,920 (U.S.$8,900); sources of income (2001): wages and salaries 67.4%, transfer payments 21.5%, self-employment 6.7%, other 4.4%; expenditure (2001): food and beverages 25.3%, housing and utilities 19.8%, transportation and communications 14.4%, recreation 10.5%, household furnishings 6.9%.
Population economically active (2002): total 4,769,727; activity rate of total population 46.6% (participation rates: ages 15–64, 60.9%; female 44.3%; unemployed [2003] 9.9%).

Price and earnings indexes (2000 = 100)

	1997	1998	1999	2000	2001	2002	2003
Consumer price index	85.2	94.2	96.2	100.0	104.7	106.6	106.7
Annual earnings index	79.3	86.7	94.0	100.0	108.7	116.5	124.3

Public debt (external, outstanding; 2002): U.S.$6,904,000,000.
Gross national product (2003): U.S.$68,711,000,000 (U.S.$6,740 per capita).

Structure of gross domestic product and labour force

	2001		2002	
	in value Kč '000,000	% of total value	labour force	% of labour force
Agriculture, forestry	82,600	3.8	195,264	4.1
Mining	[2]	[2]	56,030	1.2
Manufacturing	652,100[2]	30.2[2]	1,389,903	29.1
Construction	141,900	6.6	367,706	7.7
Public utilities	[2]	[2]	68,870	1.4
Transportation and communications	162,900	7.6	349,018	7.3
Trade, hotels	337,400	15.6	906,093	19.0
Finance, real estate	311,400	14.4	518,484	10.9
Pub. admin., defense } Services	296,900	13.8	195,066	4.1
			723,293	15.2
Other	172,600[3]	8.0[3]	—	—
TOTAL	2,157,800	100.0	4,769,727	100.0

Tourism (2002): receipts from visitors U.S.$2,941,000,000; expenditures by nationals abroad U.S.$1,575,000,000.
Land use as % of total land area (2000): in temporary crops 39.9%, in permanent crops 3.1%, in pasture 12.4%; overall forest area 34.1%.

Foreign trade

Balance of trade (current prices)

	1997	1998	1999	2000	2001	2002
Kč '000,000	–139,269	–76,319	–64,413	–120,825	–116,685	–74,455
% of total	8.8%	4.3%	3.4%	5.1%	4.4%	2.9%

Imports (2002): Kč 1,326,339,000,000 (machinery and apparatus 31.2%; base and fabricated metals 10.9%; chemicals and chemical products 10.4%; motor vehicles 9.7%). *Major import sources:* Germany 32.5%; Italy 5.4%; Slovakia 5.2%; France 4.8%; China 4.6%; Russia 4.5%.
Exports (2002): Kč 1,251,884,000,000 (machinery and apparatus 31.9%, of which computers 6.2%; motor vehicles 16.7%; fabricated metals 6.5%; base metals 5.4%; chemicals and chemical products 5.4%). *Major export destinations:* Germany 36.5%; Slovakia 7.7%; United Kingdom 5.8%; Austria 5.5%; Poland 4.7%; France 4.7%.

Transport and communications

Transport. Railroads (2001): length 9,444 km; passenger-km 7,299,000,000; metric ton-km cargo 16,882,000,000. Roads (2001): total length 125,905 km (paved, n.a.). Vehicles (2001): passenger cars 3,529,791; trucks and buses 381,876. Air transport (2001): passenger-km 6,398,920,000; metric ton-km 29,209,000; airports (2001) with scheduled flights 2.

Communications

Medium	date	unit	number	units per 1,000 persons
Daily newspapers	2000	circulation	1,210,000	118
Television	2000	receivers	3,289,000	341
Telephones	2003	main lines	3,626,000	360
Cellular telephones	2003	subscribers	9,709,000	965
Personal computers	2002	units	1,800,000	177
Internet	2003	users	2,700,000	268

Education and health

Educational attainment (2001). Percentage of population age 15 and over having: no formal schooling 0.2%; primary education 21.6%; secondary 68.7%; higher 9.5%. *Literacy* (2001): 99.8%.

Education (2001–02)

	schools	teachers	students	student/teacher ratio
Primary (age 6–14)	4,263	67,594	1,028,000	15.2
Secondary (age 15–18)	346	11,000	136,729	12.4
Voc., teacher tr.	1,388	10,669	197,229	18.5
Higher[4]	24	13,332	219,514	16.5

Health (2002): physicians 43,824 (1 per 233 persons); hospital beds 66,668 (1 per 153 persons); infant mortality rate per 1,000 live births (2003) 3.9.
Food (2002): daily per capita caloric intake 3,171 (vegetable products 73%, animal products 27%); 128% of FAO recommended minimum requirement.

Military

Total active duty personnel (2003): 57,050 (army 69.9%, air force 23.0%, ministry of defense 7.1%). *Military expenditure as percentage of GNP* (1999): 2.3% (world 2.4%); per capita expenditure: U.S.$292.

[1]New local government structure as of November 2000 elections. [2]Manufacturing includes Mining and Public utilities. [3]Taxes less subsidies and imputed bank charges. [4]Universities only.

Internet resources for further information:
- **Czech Statistical Office http://www.czso.cz**

Denmark

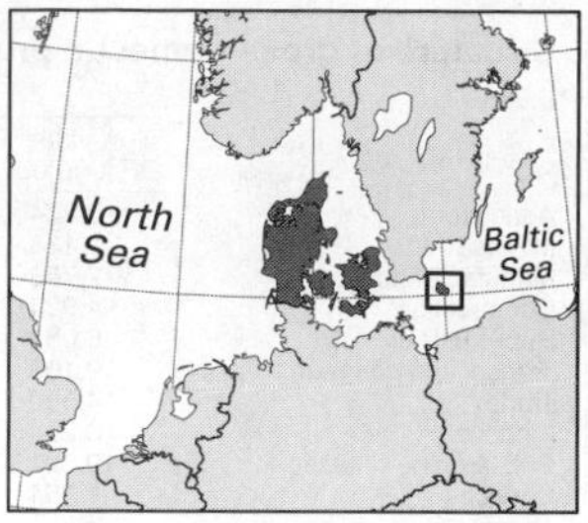

Official name: Kongeriget Danmark (Kingdom of Denmark).
Form of government: parliamentary state and constitutional monarchy with one legislative house (Folketing [179]).
Chief of state: Danish Monarch.
Head of government: Prime Minister.
Capital: Copenhagen.
Official language: Danish.
Official religion: Evangelical Lutheran.
Monetary unit: 1 Danish krone (Dkr; plural kroner) = 100 øre; valuation (Sept. 1, 2004) 1 U.S.$ = Dkr 6.12; 1 £ = Dkr 11.01.

Area and population[1]

		area		population
Counties	**Capitals**	sq mi	sq km	2004 estimate
Århus	Århus	1,761	4,561	654,426
Frederiksborg	Hillerød	520	1,347	374,658
Fyn	Odense	1,346	3,486	475,377
København	—	204	528	617,537
Nordjylland	Ålborg	2,383	6,173	495,173
Ribe	Ribe	1,209	3,132	224,747
Ringkøbing	Ringkøbing	1,874	4,854	275,009
Roskilde	Roskilde	344	891	237,720
Sønderjylland	Åbenrå	1,521	3,939	253,173
Storstrøm	Nykøbing Falster	1,312	3,398	262,098
Vejle	Vejle	1,157	2,997	356,772
Vestsjælland	Sorø	1,152	2,984	303,722
Viborg	Viborg	1,592	4,122	234,716
Municipalities				
Bornholm	Rønne	227	589	43,645
Copenhagen (København)	—	34	88	500,980
Frederiksberg	—	3	9	91,424
TOTAL		16,640[2]	43,098	5,401,177

Demography

Population (2004): 5,401,000.
Density (2004): persons per sq mi 324.6, persons per sq km 125.3.
Urban-rural (2003): urban 85.3%; rural 14.7%.
Sex distribution (2003): male 49.46%; female 50.54%.
Age breakdown (2003): under 15, 18.8%; 15–29, 17.9%; 30–44, 22.3%; 45–59, 20.9%; 60–74, 13.1%; 75 and over, 7.0%.
Population projection: (2010) 5,421,000; (2020) 5,431,000.
Ethnic composition (2001)[3]: Danish 95.2%; Asian 1.7%, of which Turkish 0.7%; residents of pre-1992 Yugoslavia 0.7%; African 0.5%; German 0.2%; English 0.2%; other 1.5%.
Religious affiliation (1998): Christian 87.5%, of which Evangelical Lutheran 85.8%; Muslim 2.2%; other/nonreligious 10.3%.
Major urban areas (2003): Greater Copenhagen 1,085,813; Århus 222,559; Odense 145,374; Ålborg 121,100; Esbjerg 72,613.

Vital statistics

Birth rate per 1,000 population (2003): 12.0 (world avg. 21.3).
Death rate per 1,000 population (2003): 10.7 (world avg. 9.1).
Natural increase rate per 1,000 population (2003): 1.3 (world avg. 12.2).
Total fertility rate (avg. births per childbearing woman; 2003): 1.8.
Marriage rate per 1,000 population (2003): 6.5.
Divorce rate per 1,000 population (2003): 2.9.
Life expectancy at birth (2003): male 74.9 years; female 79.5 years.
Major causes of death per 100,000 population (1999): diseases of the circulatory system 400.2; malignant neoplasms (cancers) 300.0.

National economy

Budget (2002). Revenue: Dkr 498,382,000,000 (tax revenue 82.8%, nontax revenue 11.9%, other 5.3%). Expenditures: Dkr 482,437,000,000 (health and social protection 39.6%, education 12.9%, economic affairs 7.1%, defense 4.8%, public order 2.7%).
National debt (end of year; 2001): Dkr 679,957,000,000.
Tourism (2002): receipts U.S.$5,785,000,000; expenditures U.S.$6,856,000,000.
Population economically active (2002): total 2,892,800; activity rate of total population 53.9% (participation rates: ages 16–66, 77.8%; female 46.9%; unemployed 3.8%).

Price and earnings indexes (2000 = 100)

	1997	1998	1999	2000	2001	2002	2003
Consumer price index	93.1	99.3	97.2	100.0	102.4	104.8	107.0
Hourly earnings index	87.2	97.8	95.6	100.0	104.4	106.2	...

Household income and expenditure. Average household size (2001) 2.2; annual disposable income per household (2000) Dkr 259,589 (U.S.$32,115); expenditure (2000): housing 22.3%, transportation and communications 16.1%, food 11.3%, recreation 11.1%, energy 6.8%, household furnishings 6.3%.
Production (in Dkr '000,000 except as noted). Agriculture, forestry, fishing (value added; 2001): meat 24,884 (of which pork 21,069, beef 2,178), milk 11,327, cereals 8,095 (of which wheat 4,012, barley 3,469), furs 2,659, flowers and plants 2,535; livestock (number of live animals) 12,732,035 pigs, 1,796,118 cattle; roundwood (2002) 1,446,000 cu m; fish catch (2001) 1,552,000 metric tons. Mining and quarrying (2001): sand and gravel 23,000,000 cu m; chalk 410,000 metric tons. Manufacturing (value added in U.S.$'000,000; 1998): nonelectrical machinery and apparatus 3,874; food products 3,848; fabricated metals 2,228; printing and publishing 2,177; plastic and rubber products 1,114; furniture 1,089. Energy production (consumption): electricity (kW-hr; 2003) 43,752,000,000 ([2000] 44,284,000,000); coal (metric tons; 2001) none (6,984,000); crude petroleum (barrels; 2003) 140,800,000 ([2000] 61,812,000); petroleum products (metric tons; 2001) 8,860,000 (7,547,000); natural gas (cu m; 2003) 4,427,000,000 ([2001] 4,366,000,000).
Gross national product (2003): U.S.$181,825,000,000 (U.S.$33,750 per capita).

Structure of gross domestic product and labour force

	2002			
	in value Dkr '000,000	% of total value	labour force	% of labour force
Agriculture, fishing	29,998	2.6	102,300	3.5
Mining	29,739	2.6		
Manufacturing	192,338	16.5	453,800	15.7
Construction	57,625	5.0	173,300	6.0
Public utilities	25,888	2.2	14,400	0.5
Transp. and commun.	94,249	8.1	179,000	6.2
Trade, restaurants	165,560	14.2	494,900	17.1
Finance, real estate	293,019	25.2	375,600	13.0
Pub. admin., defense; Services	314,829	27.1	974,300	33.7
Other	–40,869[4]	–3.5[4]	125,200[5]	4.3[5]
TOTAL	1,162,377[2]	100.0	2,892,800	100.0

Land use as % of total land area (2000): in temporary crops 53.8%, in permanent crops 0.2%, in pasture 8.4%; overall forest area 10.7%.

Foreign trade[6]

Balance of trade (current prices)

	1997	1998	1999	2000	2001	2002
Dkr '000,000	+24,353	+13,776	+32,418	+46,201	+53,295	+57,884
% of total	4.0%	2.2%	5.0%	6.1%	6.7%	7.0%

Imports (2001): Dkr 369,582,000,000 (machinery and apparatus [including parts] 22.9%; transport equipment and parts 10.5%; food, beverages, and tobacco 8.5%; clothing and footwear 5.0%; fuels 4.7%). *Major import sources:* Germany 22.0%; Sweden 12.0%; U.K. 7.5%; The Netherlands 7.0%; France 5.7%.
Exports (2001): Dkr 422,877,000,000 (machinery and apparatus 27.5%; agricultural products 19.2%, of which swine 5.7%; mineral fuels and lubricants 6.8%; pharmaceuticals 6.7%; furniture 3.8%). *Major export destinations:* Germany 19.7%; Sweden 11.7%; U.K. 9.4%; U.S. 7.0%; Norway 5.6%; France 5.1%.

Transport and communications

Transport. Railroads (2001): route length 2,743 km; passenger-km 5,318,000,000; metric ton-km cargo 2,025,000,000. Roads (2001): total length 71,663 km (paved 100%). Vehicles (2001): passenger cars 1,854,060; trucks and buses 335,690. Air transport (2001)[7]: passenger-km 8,942,000,000; metric ton-km cargo 183,152,000; airports (1996) with scheduled flights 13.

Communications

Medium	date	unit	number	units per 1,000 persons
Daily newspapers	2000	circulation	1,510,000	283
Radio	2000	receivers	7,200,000	1,349
Television	2000	receivers	4,310,000	807
Telephones	2003	main lines	3,610,100	669
Cellular telephones	2003	subscribers	4,785,300	887
Personal computers	2002	units	2,756,000	513
Internet	2002	users	3,100,000	577

Education and health

Educational attainment (2000). Percentage of population age 25–69 having: completed lower secondary or not stated 34.6%; completed upper secondary or vocational 42.3%; undergraduate 17.6%; graduate 5.5%. *Literacy:* 100%.

Education (2001)

	schools	teachers[8]	students	student/teacher ratio
Primary/lower secondary (age 7–15)	3,036	58,500	664,224	...
Upper secondary (age 16–18)	154	11,000	64,451	...
Vocational	165	12,000	174,827	...
Higher	154	8,000	174,615	...

Health: physicians (2002) 19,600 (1 per 276 persons); hospital beds (2001) 22,604 (1 per 239 persons); infant mortality rate per 1,000 live births (2003) 4.0.
Food (2001): daily per capita caloric intake 3,454 (vegetable products 60.5%, animal products 39.5%); 128% of FAO recommended minimum requirement.

Military

Total active duty personnel (2003): 22,880 (army 64.2%, navy 17.5%, air force 18.3%). *Military expenditure as percentage of GNP* (1999): 1.6% (world 2.4%); per capita expenditure U.S.$524.

[1]Excludes the Faroe Islands and Greenland. [2]Detail does not add to total given because of rounding. [3]Based on nationality. [4]Taxes on products less imputed bank service charges. [5]Includes 14,700 not adequately defined and 110,500 unemployed. [6]Imports c.i.f., exports f.o.b. [7]Danish share of Scandinavian Airlines System (scheduled air service only) and Maersk Air. [8]1993–94.

Internet resources for further information:
- **Statistics Denmark http://www.dst.dk/yearbook**
- **StatBank Denmark http://www.statbank.dk**

Djibouti

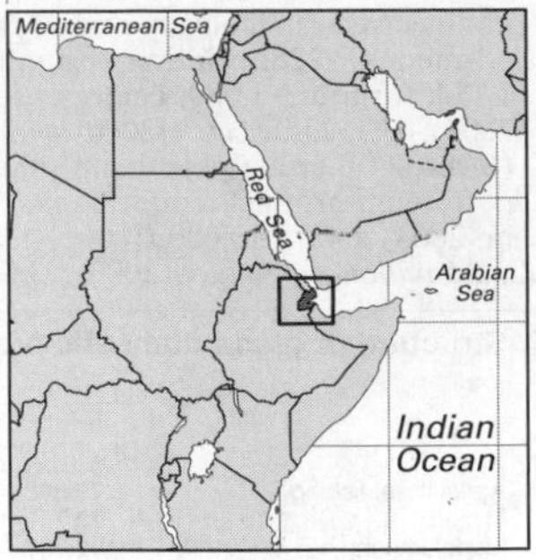

Official name: Jumhūrīyah Jībūtī (Arabic); République de Djibouti (French) (Republic of Djibouti).
Form of government: multiparty republic with one legislative house (National Assembly [65]).
Head of state and government: President.
Capital: Djibouti.
Official languages: Arabic; French.
Official religion: none.
Monetary unit: 1 Djibouti franc (DF) = 100 centimes; valuation (Sept. 1, 2004) 1 U.S.$ = DF 177.72; 1 £ = DF 319.72.

Area and population

Districts	Capitals	area[1] sq mi	area[1] sq km	population 1991 estimate
ʿAlī Sabīḥ (Ali-Sabieh)	ʿAlī Sabīḥ	925	2,400	45,900
Dikhil	Dikhil	2,775	7,200	52,900
Djibouti	Djibouti	225	600	329,300
Obock	Obock	2,200	5,700	20,700
Tadjoura (Tadjourah)	Tadjoura	2,825	7,300	45,100
TOTAL		8,950	23,200	493,900[2]

Demography

Population (2004): 467,000.
Density (2004): persons per sq mi 52.2, persons per sq km 20.1.
Urban-rural (2003): urban 83.7%; rural 16.3%.
Sex distribution (2002): male 51.55%; female 48.45%.
Age breakdown (2002): under 15, 43.0%; 15–29, 28.1%; 30–44, 13.2%; 45–59, 10.5%; 60–74, 4.6%; 75 and over, 0.6%.
Population projection: (2010) 526,000; (2020) 627,000.
Doubling time: 33 years.
Ethnic composition (2000): Somali 46.0%; Afar 35.4%; Arab 11.0%; mixed African and European 3.0%; French 1.6%; other/unspecified 3.0%.
Religious affiliation (1995): Sunnī Muslim 97.2%; Christian 2.8%, of which Roman Catholic 2.2%, Orthodox 0.5%, Protestant 0.1%.
Major city and towns (1991): Djibouti 465,300[3]; ʿAlī Sabīḥ 8,000; Tadjoura 7,500; Dikhil 6,500.

Vital statistics

Birth rate per 1,000 population (2003): 40.8 (world avg. 21.3).
Death rate per 1,000 population (2003): 19.5 (world avg. 9.1).
Natural increase rate per 1,000 population (2003): 21.3 (world avg. 12.2).
Total fertility rate (avg. births per childbearing woman; 2003): 5.6.
Life expectancy at birth (2003): male 41.8 years; female 44.5 years.
Major causes of death (percentage of total deaths [infants and children to age 10, district of Djibouti only]; 1984): diarrhea and acute dehydration 16.0%; malnutrition 16.0%; poisoning 11.0%; tuberculosis 6.0%; acute respiratory disease 6.0%; malaria 6.0%; anemia 6.0%; heart disease 2.0%; kidney disease 1.0%; other ailments 19.0%; no diagnosis 11.0%.

National economy

Budget (2000). Revenue: DF 23,739,000,000 (tax revenue 91.2%, of which indirect taxes 45.3%, direct taxes 38.9%, income and profit tax 6.7%; nontax revenue 8.8%). Expenditures: DF 32,813,000,000 (current expenditures 92.0%, of which general administration 22.7%, defense 13.7%, education 10.0%, health 4.6%; capital expenditures 8.0%).
Tourism (1998): receipts from visitors U.S.$4,000,000; expenditures by nationals abroad U.S.$4,000,000.
Production (metric tons except as noted). Agriculture, forestry, fishing (2002): vegetables and melons 24,000 (of which tomatoes 1,100, onions 110, eggplant 33), lemons and limes 1,800, tropical fruit 1,100; livestock (number of live animals) 512,000 goats, 475,000 sheep, 270,000 cattle, 68,000 camels, 8,700 asses; roundwood, n.a.; fish catch (2001) 350. Mining and quarrying: mineral production limited to locally used construction materials and evaporated salt (2001) 173,000. Manufacturing (2000): structural detail, n.a.; main products include furniture, nonalcoholic beverages, meat and hides, light electromechanical goods, and mineral water. Energy production (consumption): electricity (kW-hr; 2001) 235,262,000 (182,870,000); coal, none (none); crude petroleum, none (none); petroleum products (metric tons; 2000) none (126,000); natural gas, none (none); geothermal, wind, and solar resources are substantial but largely undeveloped.
Population economically active (1991): total 282,000; activity rate of total population 61.5% (participation rates: over age 10, 70.4%; female 40.8%; unemployed [2000] *c.* 50%).

Price index (2000 = 100)

	1999[4]	2000	2001	2002
Consumer price index	97.7	100.0	101.3	102.6

Household income and expenditure. Average household size (2000) 5.3; income per household: n.a.; sources of income: n.a.; expenditure (expatriate households; 1984): food 50.3%, energy 13.1%, recreation 10.4%, housing 6.4%, clothing 1.7%, personal effects 1.4%, health care 1.0%, household goods 0.3%, other 15.4%.
Gross national product (2003): U.S.$643,000,000 (U.S.$910 per capita).

Structure of gross domestic product and labour force

	2000 in value DГ '000,000[5]	2000 % of total value[5]	1991 labour force	1991 % of labour force
Agriculture	3,274	4.0	212,000	75.2
Mining	138	0.2		
Manufacturing	2,750	3.4	31,000	11.0
Construction	4,924	6.1		
Public utilities	5,083	6.3		
Transp. and commun.	19,105	23.6		
Trade	14,530	18.0		
Finance	10,258	12.7	39,000	13.8
Pub. admin., defense	19,392	24.0		
Services	1,354	1.7		
Other	—	—	...	...
TOTAL	80,808	100.0	282,000	100.0

Public debt (external, outstanding; 2002): U.S.$305,200,000.
Land use as % of total land area (2000): in temporary crops, negligible, in permanent crops, negligible, in pasture 56.1%; overall forest area 0.3%.

Foreign trade

Balance of trade (current prices)[6]

	1996	1997	1998	1999	2000	2001
U.S.$'000,000	–161.1	–161.4	–180.5	–182.5	–194.9	–187.4
% of total	67.0%	65.3%	60.4%	56.9%	56.4%	55.3%

Imports (1999): U.S.$152,700,000[7] (food and beverages 25.0%; machinery and electric appliances 12.5%; khat 12.2%; petroleum products 10.9%; transport equipment 10.3%). *Major import sources* (2001): Saudi Arabia 18.5%; France 16.1%; Ethiopia 10.3%; China 8.1%; Italy 3.8%.
Exports (2001): U.S.$10,200,000[7] (aircraft parts 24.5%; hides and skins of cattle, sheep, goats, and camels 20.6%; unspecified special transactions 8.8%; leather 7.8%; live animals 6.9%). *Major export destinations* (2001): Somalia 44.8%; France 23.5%; Yemen 19.2%; Ethiopia 3.5%; United Arab Emirates 3.3%.

Transport and communications

Transport. Railroads (2000): length 62 mi, 100 km; (1999) passenger-mi 50,331,000, passenger-km 81,000,000; short ton-mile cargo 165,347,000, metric ton-km cargo 266,100,000. Roads (1999): total length 1,796 mi, 2,890 km (paved 13%). Vehicles (1996): passenger cars 9,200; trucks and buses 2,040. Merchant marine (2000): vessels (100 gross tons and over) 13; total deadweight tonnage 4,356. Air transport (2001): passengers handled 94,590; metric tons of freight handled 6,652; airports (2000) with scheduled flights 1.

Communications

Medium	date	unit	number	units per 1,000 persons
Daily newspapers	1995	circulation	500	0.8
Radio	1997	receivers	52,000	84
Television	2000	receivers	45,000	104
Telephones	2003	main lines	9,500	14
Cellular telephones	2003	subscribers	23,000	34
Personal computers	2003	units	15,000	22
Internet	2003	users	6,500	9.7

Education and health

Educational attainment: n.a. *Literacy* (2000): percentage of population age 15 and over literate 64.6%; males literate 75.6%; females literate 54.4%.

Education (2000–01)

	schools	teachers	students	student/ teacher ratio
Primary (age 6–11)	73	1,127	37,938	33.7
Secondary (age 12–18) / Voc., teacher tr.	26[8]	628[9]	16,121	...
Higher	1[8]	13[8]	478	...

Health: physicians (1996) 60 (1 per 7,100 persons); hospital beds[10] (1990) 930 (1 per 394 persons); infant mortality rate per 1,000 live births (2003) 107.0.
Food (2002): daily per capita caloric intake 2,220 (vegetable products 87%, animal products 13%); 96% of FAO recommended minimum requirement.

Military

Total active duty personnel (2003): 9,850[11] (army 81.3%, navy 2.0%, air force 2.5%, paramilitary 14.2%). Foreign troops (March 2004): French 2,700; U.S. 1,800; German 800. *Military expenditure as percentage of GNP* (1999): 4.3% (world 2.4%); per capita expenditure U.S.$51.

[1]Original figures are those given in sq km; sq mi equivalent is rounded to appropriate level of generality. [2]Includes refugees. [3]2004 estimate. [4]March 1 through October 31 only. [5]At factor cost. [6]Includes trade with Ethiopia (via rail) comprising *c.* 20% of all imports and *c.* 75% of all exports. [7]Excludes Ethiopian trade via rail. [8]1991. [9]1995–96. [10]Public health facilities only. [11]Excluding foreign troops.

Internet resources for further information:
- **Banque Centrale de Djibouti http://www.banque-centrale.dj**

Dominica

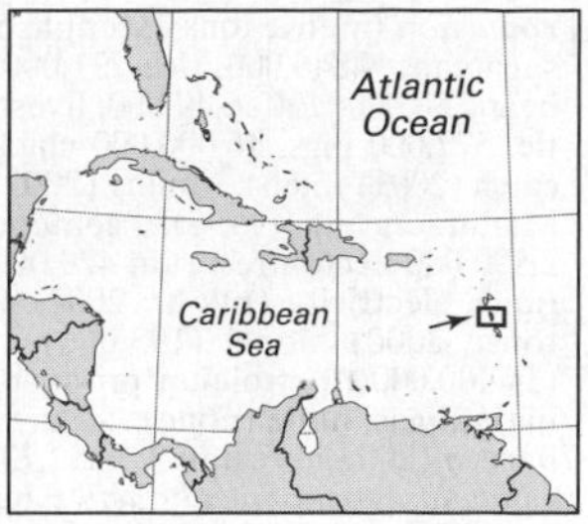

Official name: Commonwealth of Dominica.
Form of government: multiparty republic with one legislative house (House of Assembly [32[1]]).
Chief of state: President.
Head of government: Prime Minister.
Capital: Roseau.
Official language: English.
Official religion: none.
Monetary unit: 1 East Caribbean dollar (EC$) = 100 cents; valuation (Sept. 1, 2004) 1 U.S.$ = EC$2.70; 1 £ = EC$4.86.

Area and population

	area		population
			1991
Parishes	sq mi	sq km	census
St. Andrew	69.3	179.6	11,106
St. David	49.0	126.8	6,977
St. George	20.7	53.5	20,365
St. John	22.5	58.5	4,990
St. Joseph	46.4	120.1	6,183
St. Luke	4.3	11.1	1,552
St. Mark	3.8	9.9	1,943
St. Patrick	32.6	84.4	8,929
St. Paul	26.0	67.4	7,495
St. Peter	10.7	27.7	1,643
TOTAL	285.3[2]	739.0[2]	71,183[3]

Demography

Population (2004): 69,300.
Density (2004)[2]: persons per sq mi 239.0, persons per sq km 92.4.
Urban-rural (2003): urban 72.0%; rural 28.0%.
Sex distribution (2003): male 50.33%; female 49.67%.
Age breakdown (2002): under 15, 27.8%; 15–29, 24.8%; 30–44, 26.3%; 45–59, 10.7%; 60–74, 7.0%; 75 and over, 3.4%.
Population projection: (2010) 70,000; (2020) 75,000.
Doubling time: 64 years.
Ethnic composition (2000): black 88.3%; mulatto 7.3%; black-Amerindian 1.7%; British expatriates 1.0%; Indo-Pakistani 1.0%; other 0.7%.
Religious affiliation (1991): Roman Catholic 70.1%; six largest Protestant groups 17.2%, of which Seventh-day Adventist 4.6%, Pentecostal 4.3%, Methodist 4.2%; other 8.9%; nonreligious 2.9%; unknown 0.9%.
Major towns (1991): Roseau 15,853; Portsmouth 3,621; Marigot 2,919; Atkinson 2,518; Mahaut 2,372.

Vital statistics

Birth rate per 1,000 population (2003): 17.8 (world avg. 21.3); (1991) legitimate 24.1%; illegitimate 75.9%.
Death rate per 1,000 population (2003): 7.0 (world avg. 9.1).
Natural increase rate per 1,000 population (2003): 10.8 (world avg. 12.2).
Total fertility rate (avg. births per childbearing woman; 2003): 2.0.
Marriage rate per 1,000 population (1996): 3.1.
Divorce rate per 1,000 population (1996): 0.7.
Life expectancy at birth (2002): male 71.0 years; female 75.8 years.
Major causes of death per 100,000 population (1994): diseases of the circulatory system 237.8, of which hypertensive disease 93.8, diseases of pulmonary circulation and other forms of heart disease 72.0; malignant neoplasms (cancers) 125.0; endocrine and metabolic disorders 59.8; infectious and parasitic diseases 46.2; diseases of the respiratory system 38.0.

National economy

Budget (2000–01). Revenue: EC$194,900,000 (tax revenue 79.2%, of which consumption taxes on imports 39.1%, income taxes 19.9%; nontax revenue 13.8%; grants 7.0%). Expenditures: EC$270,800,000 (current expenditures 84.2%, of which wages 42.8%, debt payment 13.6%; development expenditures 15.8%).
Tourism: receipts from visitors (2002) U.S.$45,000,000; expenditures by nationals abroad (2001) U.S.$9,000,000.
Gross national product (2003): U.S.$239,000,000 (U.S.$3,360 per capita).

Structure of gross domestic product and labour force

	2000		1997	
	in value EC$'000,000[4]	% of total value[4]	labour force	% of labour force
Agriculture	110.6	18.0	6,100	18.2
Mining	5.2	0.8	...	...
Manufacturing	54.7	8.9	2,250	6.7
Construction	52.2	8.5	2,150	6.4
Public utilities	33.5	5.5	280	0.8
Transportation and communications	104.2	17.0	1,500	4.5
Trade, hotels, restaurants	88.2	14.4	5,030	15.1
Finance, real estate	91.5	14.9	1,390	4.2
Services	9.7	1.6	4,370	13.1
Pub. admin., defense	119.4	19.4	1,530	4.6
Other	–55.3[5]	–9.0[5]	8,820[6]	26.4[6]
TOTAL	613.9	100.0	33,420	100.0

Land use as % of total land area (2000): in temporary crops *c.* 7%, in permanent crops *c.* 19%, in pasture *c.* 3%; overall forest area *c.* 61%.

Public debt (external, outstanding; 2002): U.S.$178,300,000.
Population economically active (1997): total 33,420; activity rate of total population 45.8% (participation rates: ages 15–64 [1991] 62.4%; female 45.8%; unemployed 23.1%).

Price index (2000 = 100)

	1997	1998	1999	2000	2001	2002	2003
Consumer price index	97.0	98.0	99.2	100.0	101.5	101.8	103.3

Household income and expenditure. Average household size (1991) 3.6; income per household: n.a.; sources of income: n.a.; expenditure (1984)[7]: food and nonalcoholic beverages 43.1%, housing and utilities 16.1%, transportation 11.6%, clothing and footwear 6.5%, household furnishings 6.0%.
Production (metric tons except as noted). Agriculture, forestry, fishing (2003): bananas 29,000, root crops 23,750 (of which taro 11,200, yams 8,000, yautia 4,550), grapefruit and pomelos 17,000, coconuts 11,500, oranges 7,200, plantains 5,700, sugarcane 4,400, sweet potatoes 1,850; livestock (number of live animals; 2003) 13,400 cattle, 9,700 goats, 7,600 sheep; roundwood, n.a.; fish catch (2001) 1,157. Mining and quarrying: pumice, limestone, and sand and gravel are quarried primarily for local consumption. Manufacturing (value of production in EC$'000; 2000): toilet and laundry soap 18,815; toothpaste 10,063; crude coconut oil 1,758; other products include fruit juices, beer, garments, bottled spring water, and cardboard boxes. Energy production (consumption): electricity (kW-hr; 2000) 77,000,000 (77,000,000); coal, none (none); crude petroleum, none (none); petroleum products (metric tons; 2000) none (33,000); natural gas, none (none).

Foreign trade[8]

Balance of trade (current prices)

	1996	1997	1998	1999	2000	2001
EC$'000,000	–212.4	–193.3	–196.8	–233.6	–251.6	–268.7
% of total	43.4%	40.3%	36.6%	44.4%	46.3%	48.1%

Imports (2000): EC$397,700,000 (food and beverages 19.3%; machinery and apparatus 17.7%; refined petroleum 8.6%; road vehicles 8.3%). *Major import sources:* U.S. 37.5%; Trinidad and Tobago 16.3%; U.K. 7.7%; Japan 6.3%; Canada 4.2%.
Exports (2000): EC$147,300,000 (agricultural exports 37.5%, of which bananas 25.9%; coconut-based soaps 25.0%; perfumery and cosmetics 13.7%). *Major export destinations:* U.K. 24.8%; Jamaica 23.7%; France (significantly Guadeloupe) 8.5%; U.S. 7.4%; Antigua and Barbuda 7.4%.

Transport and communications

Transport. Railroads: none. Roads (1999): total length 485 mi, 780 km (paved 50%). Vehicles (1998): passenger cars 8,700; trucks and buses 3,400. Air transport: (1997) passenger arrivals and departures 74,100; (1997) cargo unloaded 575 metric tons, cargo loaded 363 metric tons; airports (1996) with scheduled flights 2.

Communications

Medium	date	unit	number	units per 1,000 persons
Radio	1997	receivers	46,000	608
Television	2000	receivers	15,700	220
Telephones	2002	main lines	23,700	265
Cellular telephones	2002	subscribers	9,400	120
Personal computers	2002	units	7,000	90
Internet	2002	users	12,500	160

Education and health

Educational attainment (1991). Percentage of population age 25 and over having: no formal schooling 4.2%; primary education 78.4%; secondary 11.0%; higher vocational 2.3%; university 2.8%; other/unknown 1.3%. *Literacy* (1996): total population age 15 and over literate, 94.0%.

Education (1997–98)

	schools	teachers	students	student/ teacher ratio
Primary	63	587	13,636	23.2
Secondary	15	293	5,455	18.6
Higher[9]	2	34	484	14.2

Health (2002): physicians 34 (1 per 2,041 persons); hospital beds 270 (1 per 257 persons); infant mortality rate per 1,000 live births 15.9.
Food (2001): daily per capita caloric intake 2,995 (vegetable products 77%, animal products 23%); 124% of FAO recommended minimum requirement.

Military

Total active duty personnel (2003): none[10].

[1]Includes 22 seats that are elective (including speaker if elected from outside of the House of Assembly) and 10 seats that are nonelective (including 9 appointees of the president and the attorney general serving ex officio). [2]Total area of Dominica per more recent survey is 290 sq mi (750 sq km). [3]March 2001 preliminary census total equals 71,727. [4]At current factor cost. [5]Less imputed banking service charge. [6]Includes 7,720 unemployed and 1,100 unclassified by economic activity. [7]Weights of consumer price index components. [8]Imports c.i.f.; exports f.o.b. [9]1992–93. [10]300-member police force includes a coast guard unit.

Internet resources for further information:
- **Eastern Caribbean Central Bank http://www.eccb-centralbank.org**

Dominican Republic

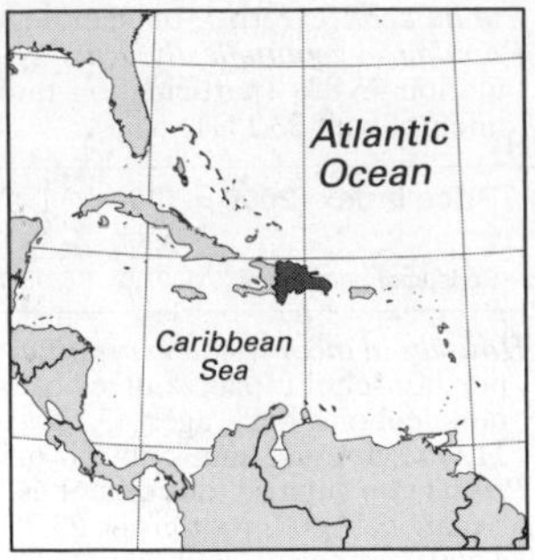

Official name: República Dominicana (Dominican Republic).
Form of government: multiparty republic with two legislative houses (Senate [32]; Chamber of Deputies [150]).
Head of state and government: President.
Capital: Santo Domingo.
Official language: Spanish.
Official religion: none[1].
Monetary unit: 1 Dominican peso (RD$) = 100 centavos; valuation (Sept. 1, 2004) 1 U.S.$ = RD$37.50; 1 £ = RD$67.46.

Area and population

	area	population		area	population
		2002 final			2002 final
Provinces	sq km	census	**Provinces**	sq km	census
Azua	2,532	208,857	Peravia	998	232,233[2]
Baoruco	1,283	91,480	Puerto Plata	1,857	312,706
Barahona	1,739	179,239	Salcedo	440	96,356
Dajabón	1,021	62,046	Samaná	854	91,875
Duarte	1,605	283,805	San Cristóbal	1,265	532,880
El Seíbo (El Seybo)	1,786	89,261	San José de Ocoa	650	[2]
Elías Piña	1,424	63,879	San Juan	3,571	241,105
Espaillat	838	225,091	San Pedro de Macorís	1,255	301,744
Hato Mayor	1,329	87,631	Sánchez Ramírez	1,196	151,179
Independencia	2,008	50,833	Santiago	2,836	908,250
La Altagracia	3,010	182,020	Santiago Rodríguez	1,112	59,629
La Romana	654	219,812	Santo Domingo	1,296	2,731,294[3]
La Vega	2,286	385,101	Valverde	823	158,293
María Trinidad Sánchez	1,271	135,727			
Monseñor Nouel	992	167,618	**National district**		
Monte Cristi	1,925	111,014	Santo Domingo (city)	104	[3]
Monte Plata	2,633	180,376	TOTAL	48,671[4, 5]	8,562,541
Pedernales	2,077	21,207			

Demography

Population (2004): 8,834,000.
Density (2004): persons per sq mi 470.1, persons per sq km 181.5.
Urban-rural (2002): urban 63.6%; rural 36.4%.
Sex distribution (2002): male 49.81%; female 50.19%.
Age breakdown (2002): under 15, 34.0%; 15–29, 27.1%; 30–44, 20.2%; 45–59, 11.2%; 60–74, 5.9%; 75 and over, 1.6%.
Population projection: (2010) 9,521,000; (2020) 10,625,000.
Doubling time: 45 years.
Ethnic composition (2000): mulatto 69.5%; white 17.0%; local black 9.4%; Haitian black 2.4%; other/unknown 1.7%.
Religious affiliation (1995): Roman Catholic 81.8%; Protestant 6.4%; other Christian 0.6%; other 11.2%.
Major urban centres (2004): Santo Domingo 1,817,754; Santiago 505,600; La Romana 171,500; San Francisco de Macorís 152,600; San Cristóbal 120,200.

Vital statistics

Birth rate per 1,000 population (2003): 23.0 (world avg. 21.3).
Death rate per 1,000 population (2003): 7.2 (world avg. 9.1).
Natural increase rate per 1,000 population (2003): 15.8 (world avg. 12.2).
Total fertility rate (avg. births per childbearing woman; 2003): 2.7.
Marriage rate per 1,000 population (2001): 2.9.
Divorce rate per 1,000 population (2001): 1.0.
Life expectancy at birth (2003): male 66.4 years; female 69.6 years.
Major causes of death per 100,000 population (1997): diseases of the circulatory system 172; infectious and parasitic diseases 64; malignant neoplasms (cancers) 62; accidents and violence 47.

National economy

Budget (2002). Revenue: RD$67,009,000,000 (tax revenue 94.5%, of which taxes on goods and services 45.5%, income taxes 25.0%, import duties 21.2%; nontax revenue 5.5%). Expenditures: RD$75,789,000,000 (current expenditures 63.1%; development expenditures 36.9%).
Public debt (external, outstanding; 2002): U.S.$4,035,000,000.
Gross national product (2003): U.S.$18,078,000,000 (U.S.$2,070 per capita).

Structure of gross domestic product and labour force

	2002		1997	
	in value RD$'000,000	% of total value	labour force	% of labour force
Agriculture	46,931	11.8	529,000	16.7
Mining	5,719	1.4	8,400	0.3
Manufacturing	63,920	16.1	483,300	15.3
Construction	50,743	12.8	153,600	4.9
Public utilities	9,980	2.5	20,300	0.6
Transp. and commun.	55,061	13.9	202,700	6.4
Trade, restaurants	50,928	12.9	647,600	20.5
Finance, real estate	31,287	7.9	34,000	1.1
Pub. admin., defense	30,726	7.8	125,400	4.0
Services, other	50,822	12.9	447,500	14.2
Unemployed	—	—	503,700	16.0
TOTAL	396,117	100.0	3,155,500	100.0

Household income and expenditure. Average household size (2002) 3.5.

Production (metric tons except as noted). Agriculture, forestry, fishing (2002): sugarcane 4,846,000, rice 731,000, bananas 503,000, plantains 192,000, cacao beans 50,000, coffee 49,000; livestock (number of live animals) 2,160,000 cattle, 577,000 pigs, 46,000,000 chickens; roundwood (2001) 562,000 cu m; fish catch (2001) 15,864. Mining (2002): nickel (metal content) 38,859; gold, none[6]. Manufacturing (1998)[7]: cement 1,872,000; refined sugar 105,000; beer 2,990,000 hectolitres; rum 420,000 hectolitres. Energy production (consumption): electricity (kW-hr; 2002) 10,449,000,000 (6,808,000,000); coal (metric tons; 2000) none (193,000); crude petroleum (barrels; 2002) none (14,400,000); petroleum products (metric tons; 2000) 1,859,000 (7,325,000); natural gas, none (none).
Tourism (2002): receipts U.S.$2,738,000,000; expenditures U.S.$295,000,000.
Population economically active (1997): total 3,155,500; activity rate of total population 39.5% (participation rates: ages 15–64 [1993] 54.3%; female [1993] 24.9%; unemployed [2002] 16.1%).

Price and earnings indexes (2000 = 100)

	1997	1998	1999	2000	2001	2002	2003
Consumer price index	83.2	87.2	92.8	100.0	108.9	114.6	146.0
Annual earnings index[8]	...	87.0	100.0	100.0	118.0	127.6	...

Land use as % of total land area (2000): in temporary crops 22.7%, in permanent crops 10.3%, in pasture 43.4%; overall forest area 28.4%.

Foreign trade[9]

Balance of trade (current prices)

	1997	1998	1999	2000	2001	2002
U.S.$'000,000	–1,995	–2,616	–2,905	–3,741	–3,503	–3,699
% of total	17.8%	20.8%	22.0%	24.6%	24.9%	26.3%

Imports (2002): U.S.$8,882,000,000 (imports for free zones 29.8%, refined petroleum 14.6%, machinery and apparatus 11.4%, transport equipment 10.5%, food 5.4%). *Major import sources* (1998): U.S. *c.* 65%; Venezuela *c.* 6%; Mexico *c.* 4%; Japan *c.* 3%.
Exports (2002): U.S.$5,183,000,000 (reexports of free zones 83.6%, ferronickel 3.0%, ships' stores 2.2%, raw sugar 1.4%, cacao and cocoa 1.3%). *Major export destinations* (1998): U.S. *c.* 87%; Belgium-Luxembourg *c.* 2%; U.K. *c.* 2%.

Transport and communications

Transport. Railroads (1997)[10]: route length 1,083 mi, 1,743 km. Roads (1999): total length 7,829 mi, 12,600 km (paved 49%). Vehicles (1998): passenger cars 353,177; trucks and buses 200,347. Air transport (1997)[11]: passenger-mi 9,823,000, passenger-km, 15,808,000; short ton-mi cargo 7,962,000, metric ton-km cargo 11,624,000; airports (2002) 6.

Communications

Medium	date	unit	number	units per 1,000 persons
Daily newspapers	1996	circulation	416,000	53
Radio	2000	receivers	1,510,000	181
Television	2000	receivers	810,000	97
Telephones	2003	main lines	901,800	115
Cellular telephones	2003	subscribers	2,120,400	271
Internet	2003	users	500,000	64

Education and health

Educational attainment: n.a. *Literacy* (1995): total population age 15 and over literate, *c.* 4,164,000 (82.1%); males literate, *c.* 2,118,000 (82.0%); females literate, *c.* 2,046,000 (82.2%).

Education (1996–97)

	schools	teachers	students	student/ teacher ratio
Primary (age 6–13)	4,001[12]	39,860	1,360,044	34.1
Secondary (age 14–17)	...	11,033	329,944	29.9
Voc. teacher tr.	...	1,297	22,795	17.6
Higher	...	9,041	176,995	19.6

Health (1999): physicians 15,422 (1 per 526 persons); hospital beds 16,234 (1 per 500 persons); infant mortality rate per 1,000 live births (2003) 34.2.
Food (2002): daily per capita caloric intake 2,347 (vegetable products 85%, animal products 15%); 104% of FAO recommended minimum.

Military

Total active duty personnel (2003): 24,500 (army 61.2%, navy 16.3%, air force 22.4%). *Military expenditure as percentage of GNP* (1999): 0.7% (world 2.4%); per capita expenditure U.S.$15.

[1]Roman Catholicism is the state religion per concordat with Vatican City. [2]Peravia total includes San José de Ocoa; San José de Ocoa preliminary census total equals 59,335. [3]Santo Domingo (province) total includes Santo Domingo (city); Santo Domingo (city) preliminary census total equals 916,398. [4]Detail does not add to total given because of rounding. [5]Mainland total is 48,512 sq km and offshore islands total is 159 sq km. [6]The mining of gold was suspended from 1999 through late 2003. [7]Excludes free-zone sector for reexport (significantly ready-made garments but also services, cigars, and footwear) employing (2000) 195,000. [8]Minimum wage for medium-sized businesses in private sector. [9]Includes free zones. [10]Most track is privately owned and serves the sugar industry only. [11]Aerochago and Dominair airlines. [12]1994–95.

Internet resources for further information:
- **Banco Central de la República Dominicana http://www.bancentral.gov.do**

East Timor[1]

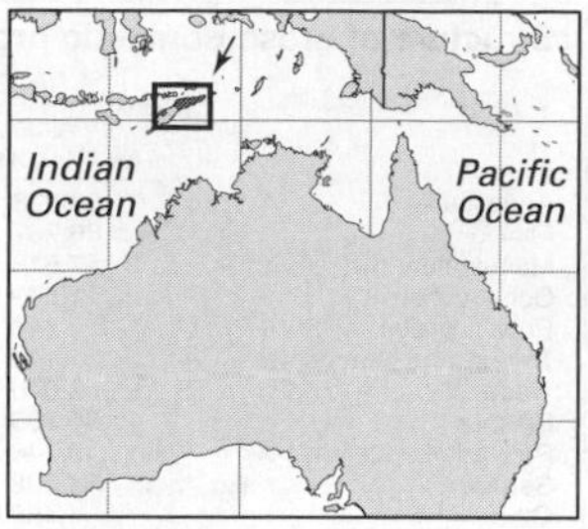

Official name: Repúblika Demokrátika Timor Lorosa'e (Tetum); República Democrática de Timor-Leste (Portuguese) (Democratic Republic of Timor-Leste)[1].
Form of government: republic with one legislative body (National Parliament [88]).
Chief of state: President.
Head of government: Prime Minister.
Capital: Dili.
Official languages: Tetum; Portuguese[2].
Official religion: none.
Monetary unit: 1 United States dollar (U.S.$) = 100 centavos[3] (100 U.S. cents); valuation (Sept. 1, 2004) 1 U.S.$ = £0.56.

Area and population

		area		population
Districts	**Capitals**	sq mi	sq km	1999 census[4]
Aileu	Aileu	281	729	32,500
Ainaro	Ainaro	308	797	44,100
Ambeno (Ocussi) exclave	Pante Macassar	315	815	54,500
Baucau (Baukau)	Baucau	577	1,494	97,600
Bobonaro	Maliana	528	1,368	90,700
Cova Lima	Suai	473	1,226	63,900
Dili	Dili	144	372	179,600
Ermera	Ermera	288	746	89,500
Lautem	Los Palos	657	1,702	52,100
Liquiça	Liquiça	210	543	54,800
Manatuto	Manatuto	659	1,706	34,900
Manufahi	Same	512	1,325	37,200
Viqueque	Viqueque	688	1,781	59,600
TOTAL		5,639[5]	14,604	891,000

Demography

Population (2004): 925,000.
Density (2004): persons per sq mi 164.0, persons per sq km 63.3.
Urban-rural (2001): urban 24.0%; rural 76.0%.
Sex distribution (2003): male 50.94%; female 49.06%.
Age breakdown (2003): under 15, 38.7%; 15–29, 26.9%; 30–44, 19.0%; 45–59, 10.6%; 60–74, 4.0%; 75 and over, 0.7%.
Population projection: (2010) 1,101,000; (2020) 1,284,000.
Doubling time: 33 years.
Ethnic composition (1999): East Timorese *c.* 80%; other (nearly all Indonesian, and particularly West Timorese) *c.* 20%.
Religious affiliation (2000): Roman Catholic *c.* 87%; Protestant *c.* 5%; Muslim *c.* 3%; traditional beliefs *c.* 3%; other *c.* 2%.
Major cities (2000): Dili 48,200; Dare 17,100; Baucau 14,200; Maliana 12,300; Ermera 12,000.

Vital statistics

Birth rate per 1,000 population (2003): 27.7 (world avg. 21.3).
Death rate per 1,000 population (2003): 6.4 (world avg. 9.1).
Natural increase rate per 1,000 population (2003): 21.3 (world avg. 12.2).
Total fertility rate (avg. births per childbearing woman; 2003): 3.8.
Marriage rate per 1,000 population (1997–98): 0.4.
Divorce rate per 1,000 population (1997–98): 0.1.
Life expectancy at birth (2003): male 63.0 years; female 67.0 years.
Major causes of death per 100,000 population (2002): n.a.[6]

National economy

Budget (2002–03). Revenue: U.S.$77,100,000 (tax revenue 52.0%, grants 42.8%; nontax revenue 5.2%). Expenditures: U.S.$70,500,000 (education 24.3%, economic affairs 23.3%, general public services 17.0%, public order 13.9%, health 10.5%, defense 7.0%).
Public debt (external, outstanding; 2001): n.a.
Production (metric tons except as noted). Agriculture, forestry, fishing (2003): corn (maize) 70,200, rice 65,400, cassava 41,500, sweet potatoes 26,000, coffee 14,000, coconuts 14,000, peanuts (groundnuts) 4,000, candlenut (1997) 1,055, spices 425; livestock (number of live animals; 2003) 345,000 pigs, 170,000 cattle, 75,000 buffalo, 1,300,000 chickens; roundwood, n.a.; sandalwood exports were formerly more significant; fish catch (2001) 356. Mining and quarrying (2001): commercial quantities of marble are exported. Manufacturing (2001): principally the production of textiles, garments, handicrafts, bottled water, and processed coffee. Energy production (consumption): electricity (kW-hr; 1998) 40,000,000 (n.a.); coal, n.a. (n.a.); crude petroleum, n.a. (n.a.); petroleum products, n.a. (n.a.); natural gas, n.a. (n.a.).
Household income and expenditure. Average household size (1995) 4.9; average annual income per household, n.a.[7]; sources of income, n.a.; expenditure, n.a.
Population economically active (2001): total 232,000[8]; activity rate of total population 28%[8] (participation rates: ages 15–64, 57%[8]; female, n.a.; unemployed, n.a.).

Price index (2000 = 100)

	2000	2001	2002	2003[9]
Consumer price index	100.0	113.5	113.1	116.6

Gross national product (2003): U.S.$351,000,000 (U.S.$430 per capita).

Structure of gross domestic product and labour force

	2002		1998	
	in value U.S.$'000,000	% of total value	labour force	% of labour force
Agriculture	102.6	27.1	...	75.0
Mining	3.5	0.9	...	...
Manufacturing	10.4	2.8	...	...
Public utilities	3.1	0.8	...	...
Construction	57.7	15.3	...	...
Transp. and commun.	30.7	8.1	...	...
Trade, hotels	34.0	9.0	...	...
Finance, insurance	26.1	6.9	...	...
Services	2.6	0.7	...	...
Pub. admin., defense	107.3	28.4	...	13.0
Other	—	—	...	12.0
TOTAL	378.0	100.0	...	100.0

Tourism: receipts, n.a.; expenditures, n.a.; available beds for tourists (1998) 580.
Land use as % of total land area (2000): in temporary crops 4.7%, in permanent crops 0.7%, in pasture 10.1%; overall forest area 34.3%.

Foreign trade

Balance of trade (current prices)

	1997	1998	1999	2000	2001	2002
U.S.$'000,000	−90	−80	−36	−84	−229	−180
% of total	46.4%	42.1%	28.1%	...	93.5%	93.8%

Imports (1998): U.S.$135,000,000 (foodstuffs 26%, of which rice 10%; construction materials 15%; petroleum products 10%; unspecified 49%). *Major import sources* (2003): Australia 44.0%, Indonesia 16.8%, Singapore 12.9%, Japan 7.3%, Portugal 4.3%.
Exports (1998): U.S.$55,000,000 (agricultural products 93%, of which nonfood crops [nearly all coffee] 51%, livestock 22%, food crops 15%; garments, bottled water, handicrafts, and other manufactured goods 5%). *Major export destinations:* Indonesia 96%.

Transport and communications

Transport. Railroads: none. Roads (December 1999): total length 879 mi (1,414 km)[10]. Vehicles (1998): passenger cars 3,156; trucks and buses 7,140. Air transport: airports (2001) with scheduled flights 2.

Communications

Medium	date	unit	number	units per 1,000 persons
Daily newspaper	2002	circulation	1,500	1.8
Television	2002[11]	receivers	...	...
Telephones	1006	main lines	6,600	8.0

Education and health

Educational attainment (2001). Percentage of adult population having: no formal education *c.* 57%, primary education *c.* 23%, secondary *c.* 18%, higher 1.4%. *Literacy* (2001): total population age 15 and over literate 203,000 (48%); males literate, n.a.; females literate, n.a.

Education (2003)

	schools	teachers	students	student/ teacher ratio
Primary (age 7–12)	...	4,080	183,600[12]	45.0[12]
Lower secondary (age 13–15)	...	1,103	38,180	34.6
Upper secondary (age 16–18)	...	...	...	...
Higher[13]	1	...	4,500	...

Health: physicians (1996–97) 122 (1 per 6,590 persons); hospital beds (1999) 560 (1 per 1,277 persons); infant mortality rate (2003) 50.5.

Military

Total active duty personnel (2003): 650 (army 94.3%, naval element 5.7%); UN peacekeeping troops (August 2004) 425[14].
Military expenditure as percentage of GNP: n.a.

[1]Per U.S. Board on Geographic Names: conventional short-form name is East Timor, conventional long-form name is Democratic Republic of Timor-Leste. [2]Indonesian and English are "working" languages. [3]Minor currency coins introduced in November 2003 at par with U.S. coins; the U.S. dollar is the official currency. [4]Per Indonesian source. [5]Detail does not add to total given because of rounding. [6]The health sector faces immense difficulties; malaria is endemic and prevalence rates for tuberculosis and leprosy are 2.4% and 1.2%, respectively. [7]Minimum annual wage (1999) U.S.$276; average public administration wage (2003) U.S.$1,500. [8]Estimated figures. [9]April. [10]57% of paved roads were in poor or damaged condition in late 1999; gravel roads were not usable for most vehicles. [11]Locally produced television service commenced in May 2002. [12]Rounded figures. [13]2001. [14]UN presence expected to end in May 2005 per May 2004 announcement.

Internet resources for further information:
- **Asia Observer**
  http://www.asiaobserver.com
- **Asian Development Bank: Key Indicators**
  http://www.adb.org/Documents/Books/Key_Indicators/2003/default.asp
- **Boletine Económico do Banco Central de Timor-Leste**
  http://pascal.iseg.utl.pt/~cesa

Ecuador

Official name: República del Ecuador (Republic of Ecuador).
Form of government: unitary multiparty republic with one legislative house (National Congress [125]).
Head of state and government: President.
Capital: Quito.
Official language: Spanish[1].
Official religion: none.
Monetary unit[2]: 1 dollar (U.S.$); valuation (Sept. 1, 2004) 1 U.S.$ = £ 0.56.

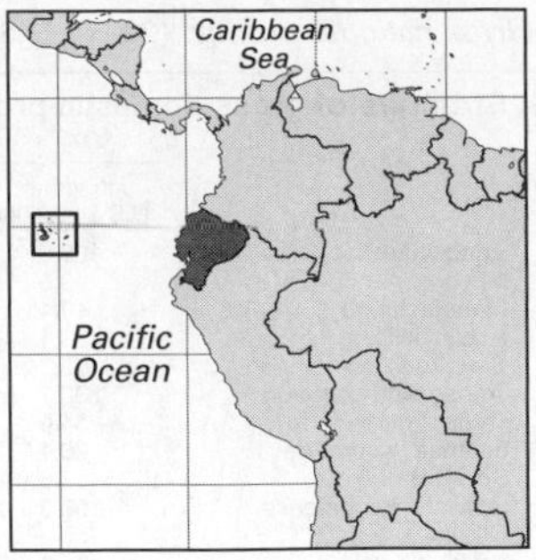

Area and population

Regions / Provinces	area sq km	population 2001 census	Regions / Provinces	area sq km	population 2001 census
Amazonica			Insular		
Morona-Santiago	33,930	115,412	Galápagos	8,010	18,640
Napo	25,690	79,139	Sierra		
Orellana		86,493	Azuay	8,125	599,546
Pastaza	29,774	61,779	Bolívar	3,940	169,370
Sucumbíos	18,327	128,995	Cañar	3,122	206,981
Zamora-Chinchipe	23,111	76,601	Carchi	3,605	152,939
Costa			Chimborazo	6,569	403,632
El Oro	5,850	525,763	Cotopaxi	6,072	349,540
Esmeraldas	15,239	385,223	Imbabura	4,559	344,044
Guayas	20,503	3,309,034	Loja	11,026	404,835
Los Ríos	7,175	650,178	Pichincha	12,915	2,388,817
Manabí	18,879	1,186,025	Tungurahua	3,335	441,034
			TOTAL	272,045[3]	12,156,608[4]

Demography

Population (2004): 13,213,000.
Density (2004): persons per sq mi 125.8, persons per sq km 48.6.
Urban-rural (2003): urban 61.8%; rural 38.2%.
Sex distribution (2003): male 49.99%; female 50.01%.
Age breakdown (2003): under 15, 34.4%; 15–29, 28.6%; 30–44, 19.1%; 45–59, 10.9%; 60–74, 5.1%; 75 and over, 1.9%.
Doubling time: 36 years.
Population projection: (2010) 14,245,000; (2020) 16,178,000.
Ethnic composition (2000): mestizo 42.0%; Amerindian 40.8%; white 10.6%; black 5.0%; other 1.6%.
Religious affiliation (2000): Roman Catholic 94.1%; Protestant 1.9%; other 4.0%.
Major cities (2001): Guayaquil 1,985,379; Quito 1,399,378; Cuenca 277,374; Machala 204,578; Santo Domingo de los Colorados 200,421; Manta 183,166.

Vital statistics

Birth rate per 1,000 population (2003): 23.7[5] (world avg. 21.3).
Death rate per 1,000 population (2003): 4.3[5] (world avg. 9.1).
Natural increase rate per 1,000 population (2003): 19.4[5] (world avg. 12.2).
Total fertility rate (avg. births per childbearing woman; 2003): 2.8.
Life expectancy at birth (2003): male 73.0 years; female 78.8 years.
Major causes of death per 100,000 population (2002): diseases of the circulatory system 153.1; malignant neoplasms (cancers) 82.3; communicable diseases 76.1; accidents 46.7.

National economy

Budget (2002). Revenue: U.S.$4,526,000,000 (nonpetroleum revenue 72.4%, of which value-added tax 33.8%, income tax 14.8%; petroleum revenue 27.6%). Expenditures: U.S.$4,694,000,000 (current expenditure 73.9%; capital expenditure 26.1%).
Public debt (external, outstanding; 2002): U.S.$13,828,000,000.
Production (metric tons except as noted). Agriculture, forestry, fishing (2002): sugarcane 5,690,895, bananas 5,609,460, fruit palm oil 1,450,000, rice 1,235,967, plantains 860,000, corn (maize) 677,479; livestock (live animals) 4,794,000 cattle, 3,007,000 pigs, 2,645,000 sheep, 142,000,000 chickens; roundwood (2001) 10,919,709 cu m; fish catch (2001) 654,539. Mining and quarrying (2000): limestone 3,147,000; gold 2,823 kg. Manufacturing (value added in U.S.$'000,000; 1999): food products 497; refined petroleum 413; beverages 223; nonmetallic mineral products 103; paper and paper products 81. Energy production (consumption): electricity (kW-hr; 2000) 10,607,000,000 (10,607,000,000); crude petroleum (barrels; 2001) 146,200,000 ([2000] 61,026,000); petroleum products (metric tons; 2000) 7,567,000 (5,723,000); natural gas (cu m; 2000) 569,500,000 (569,500,000).
Household income and expenditure. Average household size (2001) 4.1; average annual income per household (1995) S/. 9,825,610 (U.S.$3,830); sources of income (1995): self-employment 70.9%, wages 16.0%, transfer payments 6.7%, other 6.4%; expenditure (1995): food and tobacco 37.9%, transportation and communications 15.0%, clothing 9.2%, household furnishings 6.5%.
Population economically active (2001): total 4,124,185; activity rate of total population 49.6% (participation rates: ages 15 and over, 72.8%; female 42.3%; unemployed 13.3%).

Price and earnings indexes (2000 = 100)

	1997	1998	1999	2000	2001	2002	2003
Consumer price index	24.6	33.5	51.0	100.0	137.7	154.9	167.1
Monthly earnings index	...	172.0	108.5	100.0	147.6	170.2	...

Gross national product (2003): U.S.$23,347,000,000 (U.S.$1,790 per capita).

Structure of gross domestic product and labour force

	2000		2001	
	in value S/. '000,000	% of total value	labour force	% of labour force
Agriculture	33,928	10.0	391,300	9.5
Mining	66,767	19.6	18,300	0.4
Manufacturing	57,518	16.9	610,600	14.8
Construction	11,500	3.4	234,900	5.7
Public utilities	848	0.2	27,800	0.7
Transp. and commun.	31,144	9.2	244,600	5.9
Trade	58,046	17.1	1,184,900	28.7
Finance	30,386	8.9	191,700	4.6
Pub. admin., defense	19,746	5.8	159,900	3.9
Services	34,608	10.2	511,700	12.4
Other	–4,469[6]	–1.3[6]	548,300[7]	13.3[7]
TOTAL	340,022	100.0	4,124,000	100.0[8]

Land use as % of total land area (2000): in temporary crops 5.8%, in permanent crops 4.9%, in pasture 18.4%; overall forest area 38.1%.
Tourism (2002): receipts U.S.$447,000,000; expenditures U.S.$364,000,000.

Foreign trade[9]

Balance of trade (current prices)

	1997	1998	1999	2000	2001	2002
U.S.$'000,000	+744	–810	+1,714	+1,526	–258	–955
% of total	7.6%	8.8%	23.8%	18.3%	2.7%	8.7%

Imports (2000): U.S.$3,446,000,000 (chemicals and chemical products 23.5%; machinery and apparatus 21.1%; mineral fuels and lubricants 8.2%; food and live animals 7.6%). *Major import sources* (2001): U.S. 29.4%; Colombia 10.3%; Japan 8.2%; Venezuela 4.7%; Chile 4.5%.
Exports (2000): U.S.$4,822,000,000 (mineral fuels and lubricants 50.7%, of which crude petroleum 44.5%; food 35.7%, of which bananas 17.0%, fish and crustaceans 11.8%; cut flowers 3.2%). *Major export destinations* (2001): U.S. 36.2%; Colombia 5.0%; South Korea 4.6%; Germany 4.3%; Japan 4.0%.

Transport and communications

Transport. Railroads (2000): route length 956 km; passenger-km 5,000,000; metric ton-km cargo, less than 500,000. Roads (1999): total length 43,197 km (paved 19%). Vehicles (1999): passenger cars 322,300; trucks and buses 272,000. Air transport (2001)[10]: passenger-km 901,000,000; metric ton-km cargo 14,344,000.

Communications

Medium	date	unit	number	units per 1,000 persons
Daily newspapers	1996	circulation	820,000	70
Radio	2001	receivers	5,130,000	422
Television	2002	receivers	3,034,000	237
Telephones	2003	main lines	1,549,000	119
Cellular telephones	2003	subscribers	2,394,400	184
Personal computers	2002	units	403,000	31
Internet	2003	users	569,700	44

Education and health

Educational attainment (1990). Percentage of population age 25 and over having: no formal schooling 2.2%; incomplete primary 54.3%; primary 28.0%; postsecondary 15.5%. *Literacy* (2001): total population age 15 and over literate 91.0%; males 92.3%; females 89.7%.

Education (1996–97)

	schools	teachers	students[11]	student/ teacher ratio
Primary (age 4–12)	17,367	74,601	2,147,446	...
Secondary (age 12–18) / Vocational	...	62,630[12]	950,834	...
Higher	...	12,856[13]	115,554	...

Health (2000): physicians 18,335 (1 per 456 persons); hospital beds 19,564 (1 per 427 persons); infant mortality rate (2003) 25.4.
Food (2001): daily per capita caloric intake 2,333 (vegetable products 86%, animal products 14%); 103% of FAO recommended minimum requirement.

Military

Total active duty personnel (2003): 59,500 (army 84.0%, navy 9.3%, air force 6.7%). *Military expenditure as percentage of GNP* (1999): 3.7% (world 2.4%); per capita expenditure U.S.$38.

[1]Quechua and Shuar are also official languages for the indigenous peoples. [2]The United States dollar was formally adopted as the national currency on Sept. 9, 2000; the pegged value of the Sucre (S/.), the former national currency, to the U.S. dollar was S/. 25,000 = 1 U.S.$. [3]Includes 884 sq mi (2,289 sq km) in nondelimited areas. [4]Total includes 72,588 persons in nondelimited areas. [5]Excluding nomadic Indian tribes. [6]Minus imputed bank service charges plus gross import duties. [7]Unemployed. [8]Detail does not add to total given because of rounding. [9]Import figures are f.o.b. in balance of trade and c.i.f. for commodities and trading partners. [10]Ecuatoviana and TAME airlines. [11]2000. [12]1992–93. [13]1990–91.

Internet resources for further information:

- **Instituto Nacional de Estadística y Censos http://www.inec.gov.ec**
- **Banco Central del Ecuador http://www.bce.fin.ec**

Egypt

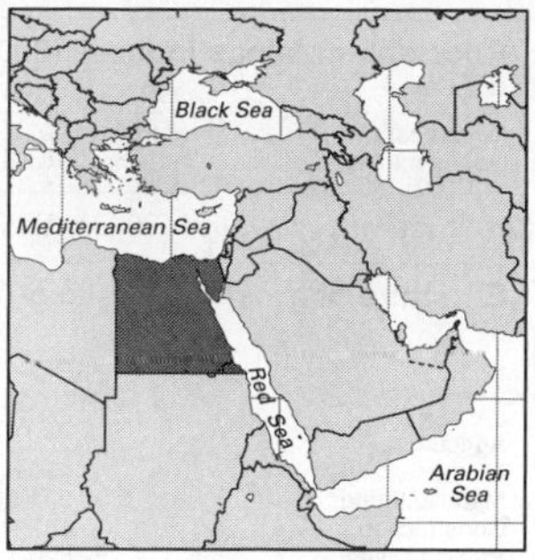

Official name: Jumhūrīah Miṣr al-ʿArabīyah (Arab Republic of Egypt).
Form of government: republic with one legislative house (People's Assembly [454[1]]).
Chief of state: President.
Head of government: Prime Minister.
Capital: Cairo.
Official language: Arabic.
Official religion: Islam.
Monetary unit: 1 Egyptian pound (£E) = 100 piastres; valuation (Sept. 1, 2004) 1 U.S.$ = £E 6.23; 1 £ = £E 11.21.

Area and population

Regions / Governorates	Capitals	area sq mi	area sq km	population 2004[2] estimate
Frontier				
Al-Baḥr al-Aḥmar	Al-Ghurdaqah	78,643	203,685	182,526
Janūb Sīnāʾ	Aṭ-Ṭūr	12,796	33,140	63,834
Maṭrūḥ	Marsā Maṭrūḥ	81,897	212,112	262,210
Shamāl Sīnāʾ	Al-ʿArish	10,646	27,574	302,077
Al-Wādī al-Jadīd	Al-Kharijah	145,369	376,505	166,211
Lower Egypt				
Al-Buḥayrah	Damanhūr	3,911	10,130	4,604,443
Ad-Daqahlīyah	Al-Manṣūrah	1,340	3,471	4,839,359
Dumyāṭ	Damietta	227	589	1,056,324
Al-Gharbīyah	Ṭanṭā	750	1,942	3,859,378
Al-Ismāʿīlīyah (Ismailia)	—	557	1,442	844,091
Kafr ash-Shaykh	Kafr ash-Shaykh	1,327	3,437	2,541,124
Al-Minūfīyah	Shibīn al-Kawm	592	1,532	3,171,058
Al-Qalyūbīyah	Banhā	387	1,001	3,804,188
Ash-Sharqīyah	Az-Zaqāzīq	1,614	4,180	5,009,690
Upper Egypt				
Aswān	Aswān	262	679	1,098,870
Asyūṭ	Asyūṭ	600	1,553	3,351,057
Banī Suwayf	Banī Suwayf	510	1,322	2,208,082
Al-Fayyūm	Al-Fayyūm	705	1,827	2,371,780
Al-Jīzah	Al-Jīzah	32,877	85,153	5,535,498
Al-Minyā	Al-Minyā	873	2,262	3,960,656
Qinā	Qinā	715	1,851	2,876,746
Sawhāj	Sawhāj	597	1,547	3,730,894
Urban				
Būr Saʿīd (Port Said)	—	28	72	529,684
Al-Iskandarīyah (Alexandria)	—	1,034	2,679	3,755,901
Al-Qāhirah (Cairo)	—	83	214	7,029,866
Al-Uqṣur (Luxor)	—	21	55	414,389
As-Suways (Suez)	—	6,888	17,840	478,553
TOTAL		385,229[3]	997,739[3]	70,548,718[4]

Demography

Population (2004): 69,261,000.
Density (2004): persons per sq mi 179.8, persons per sq km 69.4.
Urban-rural (2002): urban 45.0%; rural 55.0%.
Sex distribution (2003): male 50.46%; female 49.54%.
Age breakdown (2003): under 15, 33.9%; 15–29, 28.1%; 30–44, 19.4%; 45–59, 12.0%; 60–74, 5.5%; 75 and over, 1.1%.
Population projection: (2010) 76,751,000; (2020) 88,531,000.
Doubling time: 37 years.
Ethnic composition (2000): Egyptian Arab 84.1%; Sudanese Arab 5.5%; Arabized Berber 2.0%; Bedouin 2.0%; Rom (Gypsy) 1.6%; other 4.8%.
Religious affiliation (2000): Muslim 84.4%[5]; Christian 15.1%, of which Orthodox 13.6%, Protestant 0.8%, Roman Catholic 0.3%; nonreligious 0.5%.
Major cities ('000; 1996): Cairo 6,789 (10,834[6]); Alexandria 3,328; Al-Jīzah 2,222; Shubrā al-Khaymah 871; Port Said 470; Suez 418.

Vital statistics

Birth rate per 1,000 population (2003): 24.4 (world avg. 21.3).
Death rate per 1,000 population (2003): 5.4 (world avg. 9.1).
Natural increase rate per 1,000 population (2003): 19.0 (world avg. 12.2).
Total fertility rate (avg. births per childbearing woman; 2003): 3.0.
Life expectancy at birth (2003): male 67.9 years; female 73.0 years.

National economy

Budget (2000–01). Revenue: £E 97,938,000,000 (income and profits taxes 28.4%, sales taxes 18.4%, customs duties 13.3%, oil revenue 4.7%, Suez Canal fees 3.6%). Expenditures: £E 111,669,000,000 (current expenditure 76.7%; capital expenditure 23.3%).
Public debt (external, outstanding; 2002): U.S.$26,624,000,000.
Population economically active (1999–2000): total 18,818,000; activity rate 29.7% (participation rates [1998]: ages 15–64, 45.9%; female 21.4%; unemployed 8.1%).

Price index (2000 = 100)

	1997	1998	1999	2000	2001	2002
Consumer price index	91.0	94.5	97.4	100.0	102.3	105.1

Production ('000; metric tons except as noted). Agriculture, forestry, fishing (2003): sugarcane 12,000, corn (maize) 6,400, tomatoes 6,350, wheat 6,150, rice 5,800, sugar beets 2,900, potatoes 1,900, oranges 1,725, dates 1,115, grapes 1,104, seed cotton 800; livestock ('000, number of live animals) 4,672 sheep, 3,810 cattle, 3,560 buffalo; roundwood (2003) 16,905,059 cu m; fish catch (2001) 772. Mining and quarrying (1999–2000): gypsum 3,027; iron ore 2,932; salt 1,990; phosphate rock 1,177; kaolin 205. Manufacturing (value added in U.S.$'000,000; 1998): chemicals (all forms) 1,535; food products 958; textiles 828; bricks, cement, ceramics 683; iron and steel 365. Energy production (consumption): electricity ('000,000 kW-hr; 2000) 76,282 (76,282); coal ('000 metric tons; 2000) none (458); crude petroleum ('000 barrels; 2001) 243,400 ([2000] 239,400); petroleum products ('000 metric tons; 2000) 28,815 (21,512); natural gas ('000,000 cu m; 2000) 21,000 (21,000).
Gross national product (2003): U.S.$93,850,000,000 (U.S.$1,390 per capita).

Structure of gross domestic product and labour force

	2000–01[7] in value £E '000,000	2000–01[7] % of total value	1998 labour force	1998 % of labour force
Agriculture	49,110	16.1	4,807,000	26.4
Mining (petroleum)	78,871	25.8	47,400	0.3
Manufacturing			2,207,600	12.1
Construction	18,261	6.0	1,320,100	7.2
Public utilities	5,634	1.8	207,000	1.1
Transp. and commun.	27,616[8]	9.0[8]	1,060,200	5.8
Trade, hotels	72,719[9]	23.8[9]	2,319,800	12.7
Finance	[9]	[9]	458,400	2.5
Pub. admin., defense	23,252	7.6	1,631,700	9.0
Services	30,308	9.9	2,691,500	14.8
Other	—	—	1,480,000[10]	8.1[10]
TOTAL	305,771	100.0	18,230,700	100.0

Land use as % of total land area (2000): in temporary crops 2.8%, in permanent crops 0.5%, in pasture, n.a.; overall forest area 0.1%.
Household income and expenditure. Average household size (2000) 4.7; average annual income per household: n.a.; sources of income: n.a.; expenditure: n.a.
Tourism (2002): receipts U.S.$3,764,000,000; expenditures U.S.$1,278,000,000.

Foreign trade[11]

Balance of trade (current prices)

	1999–2000	2000–01	2001–02
U.S.$'000,000	–11,472	–9,363	–8,001
% of total	47.3%	39.8%	37.6%

Imports (1999): U.S.$15,962,000,000 (machinery and apparatus 22.6%; food 18.3%, of which cereals 8.1%; chemicals and chemical products 11.5%; iron and steel 5.6%). *Major import sources* (2001): U.S. 18.6%; Italy 6.6%; Germany 6.5%; France 4.9%; China 4.4%.
Exports (1999): U.S.$3,501,000,000 (crude petroleum 27.4%; refined petroleum 8.4%; food 7.9%; wearing apparel 7.9%; raw cotton 6.8%). *Major export destinations* (2001): Italy 15.0%; U.S. 14.4%; U.K. 9.3%; France 4.7%; Germany 4.1%.

Transport and communications

Transport. Railroads (1999): length 4,810 km; passenger-km (1998) 56,667,000,000; metric ton-km cargo (1996) 4,117,000,000. Roads (1999): length 64,000 km (paved 78%). Vehicles (1998): passenger cars 1,154,753; trucks and buses 510,766. Inland water (2000): Suez Canal, number of transits 14,141; metric ton cargo 438,962,000. Air transport (2001): passenger-km 8,892,000,000; metric ton-km cargo 239,040,000; airports (1998) 11.

Communications

Medium	date	unit	number	units per 1,000 persons
Daily newspapers	2000	circulation	2,780,000	43
Radio	2000	receivers	21,900,000	418
Television	2002	receivers	15,206,000	229
Telephones	2003	main lines	8,735,700	127
Cellular telephones	2003	subscribers	5,797,500	85
Personal computers	2003	units	1,500,000	22
Internet	2003	users	2,700,000	39

Education and health

Literacy (2000): total population age 15 and over literate 55.3%; males 66.6%; females 43.8%.

Education (1999–2000)

	schools	teachers	students	student/ teacher ratio
Primary (age 6–11)[12, 13]	15,533	314,528	7,224,989	23.0
Secondary (age 12–17)[12, 13]	9,149	272,687	5,385,314	19.7
Vocational	1,826	140,050	1,913,022	13.7
Higher	356[14]	...	1,316,491[15]	...

Health (2002–03): physicians 145,000 (1 per 464 persons); hospital beds 143,100 (1 per 470 persons); infant mortality rate (2003) 35.3.
Food (2001): daily per capita caloric intake 3,385 (vegetable products 92%, animal products 8%); 133% of FAO recommended minimum requirement.

Military

Total active duty personnel (2003): 450,000 (army 71.1%, navy 4.4%, air force [including air defense] 24.5%). *Military expenditure as percentage of GNP* (1999): 2.7% (world 2.4%); per capita expenditure U.S.$36.

[1]Includes 10 nonelective seats. [2]January 1. [3]Detail does not add to total given because of rounding. [4]Includes 1,900,229 Egyptians temporarily abroad. [5]Nearly all Sunnī; Shīʿī comprise less than 1% of population. [6]2003 urban agglomeration. [7]At 1996–97 factor cost. [8]Transportation includes earnings from traffic on the Suez Canal. [9]Trade, hotels includes Finance. [10]Unemployed. [11]Imports c.i.f.; exports f.o.b. [12]Data exclude 2,631 primary and 1,081 secondary schools, and 707,633 primary and 269,469 secondary students in the Al-Azhar education system. [13]Includes preparatory. [14]1998–99. [15]1996–97.

Internet resources for further information:
- **Egypt State Information Service http://www.sis.gov.eg**
- **Central Bank of Egypt http://www.cbe.org.eg**

El Salvador

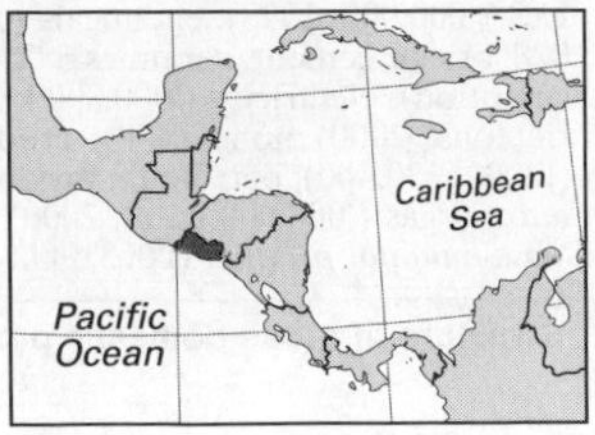

Official name: República de El Salvador (Republic of El Salvador).
Form of government: republic with one legislative house (Legislative Assembly [84]).
Chief of state and government: President.
Capital: San Salvador.
Official language: Spanish.
Official religion: none[1].
Monetary unit: 1 dollar (U.S.$)[2] = 100 cents; valuation (Sept. 1, 2004) 1 U.S.$ = £0.56.

Area and population

		area		population
				2000
Departments	**Capitals**	sq mi	sq km	estimate
Ahuachapán	Ahuachapán	479	1,240	319,781
Cabañas	Sensuntepeque	426	1,104	152,842
Chalatenango	Chalatenango	779	2,017	196,587
Cuscatlán	Cojutepeque	292	757	202,951
La Libertad	Nueva San Salvador	638	1,653	682,093
La Paz	Zacatecoluca	474	1,228	292,887
La Unión	La Unión	801	2,074	289,022
Morazán	San Francisco	559	1,447	173,501
San Miguel	San Miguel	802	2,077	480,276
San Salvador	San Salvador	342	886	1,985,294
San Vicente	San Vicente	456	1,181	161,104
Santa Ana	Santa Ana	781	2,023	550,209
Sonsonate	Sonsonate	473	1,226	450,118
Usulután	Usulután	822	2,130	338,334
TOTAL		8,124	21,042[3]	6,274,999

Demography

Population (2004): 6,698,000.
Density (2004): persons per sq mi 824.5, persons per sq km 318.3.
Urban-rural (2003): urban 59.6%; rural 40.4%.
Sex distribution (2002): male 48.67%; female 51.33%.
Age breakdown (2002): under 15, 37.1%; 15–29, 28.7%; 30–44, 17.2%; 45–59, 9.8%; 60–74, 5.0%; 75 and over 2.2%.
Population projection: (2010) 7,269,000; (2020) 8,133,000.
Doubling time: 32 years.
Ethnic composition (2000): mestizo 88.3%; Amerindian 9.1%, of which Pipil 4.0%; white 1.6%; other/unknown 1.0%.
Religious affiliation (1995): Roman Catholic 78.2%; Protestant 17.1%, of which Pentecostal 13.3%; other Christian 1.9%; other 2.8%.
Major cities (2000): San Salvador 479,600 (urban agglomeration 1,959,036); Soyapango 285,300[4]; Mejicanos 172,500[4]; Santa Ana 164,500; San Miguel 159,700.

Vital statistics

Birth rate per 1,000 population (2003): 27.9 (world avg. 21.3); (1998) legitimate 27.2%; illegitimate 72.8%.
Death rate per 1,000 population (2003): 6.0 (world avg. 9.1).
Natural increase rate per 1,000 population (2003): 21.9 (world avg. 12.2).
Total fertility rate (avg. births per childbearing woman; 2003): 3.2.
Marriage rate per 1,000 population (2001): 4.6.
Life expectancy at birth (2003): male 67.0 years; female 74.4 years.
Major causes of death per 100,000 population (1998)[5]: accidents and violence 118; diseases of the circulatory system 89; diseases of the respiratory system 60; malignant neoplasms (cancers) 58; ill-defined conditions 116.

National economy

Budget. Revenue (2001): U.S.$1,499,400,000 (sales taxes 57.2%, corporate taxes 13.1%, individual income taxes 11.4%, import duties 9.7%). Expenditures: U.S.$1,968,600,000 (education 23.3%, police 15.7%, economic services 14.7%, social services 12.7%, health 11.1%, defense 6.6%).
Public debt (external, outstanding; 2002): U.S.$4,712,000,000.
Production (metric tons except as noted). Agriculture, forestry, fishing (2002): sugarcane 4,933,000, corn (maize) 637,000, sorghum 139,000, coffee 92,000, dry beans 82,000, bananas 65,000, yautia 52,000, avocados 40,000, tobacco 1,100; livestock (number of live animals) 1,392,000 cattle, 153,000 pigs; roundwood (2001) 5,200,000 cu m; fish catch (2001) 18,142. Mining and quarrying (2002): limestone 3,200,000. Manufacturing (value added in U.S.$'000,000; 1998): food products 306; wearing apparel 249; drugs and medicines 128; textiles 120; beverages 112; soaps, cleansers, and cosmetics 92; nonmetallic mineral products 76. Energy production (consumption): electricity (kW-hr; 2000) 3,546,000,000 (4,242,000,000); coal, none (none); crude petroleum (barrels; 2000) none (7,147,000); petroleum products (metric tons; 2000) 901,000 (1,723,000); natural gas, none (none).
Household income and expenditure. Average household size (2000) 4.5; average income per household (1992–93) ₡22,930 (U.S.$2,562); expenditure (1990–91)[6]: food and beverages 37.0%, housing 12.1%, transportation and communications 10.2%, clothing and footwear 6.7%.
Land use as % of total land area (2000): in temporary crops 30.9%, in permanent crops 12.1%, in pasture 38.3%; overall forest area 5.8%.
Population economically active (1999): total 2,444,900; activity rate of total population 40.1% (participation rates: ages 15–64 (1995) 62.9%; female 40.7%; unemployed 7.0%).

Price and earnings indexes (2000 = 100)

	1997	1998	1999	2000	2001	2002	2003
Consumer price index	94.9	97.3	97.8	100.0	103.8	105.7	107.9
Hourly earnings index[7]	...	101.8	105.8	100.0	...	...	...

Gross national product (2003): U.S.$14,387,000,000 (U.S.$2,200 per capita).

Structure of gross domestic product and labour force

	2000		1999	
	in value ₡'000,000	% of total value	labour force	% of labour force
Agriculture	11,121.0	9.6	503,300	20.6
Mining	496.0	0.4	1,800	0.1
Manufacturing	27,234.6	23.6	426,600	17.4
Construction	5,107.7	4.4	130,900	5.4
Public utilities	2,520.1	2.2	8,500	0.3
Transp. and commun.	9,736.9	8.4	100,300	4.1
Trade	21,692.0	18.8	578,500	23.7
Finance, real estate	18,580.4	16.1	84,500	3.5
Public admin., defense	8,710.0	7.5	113,100	4.6
Services	7,642.2	6.6	327,200	13.4
Other	2,769.2[8]	2.4[8]	170,200[9]	7.0[9]
TOTAL	115,610.1	100.0	2,444,900	100.0[3]

Tourism (2002): receipts U.S.$342,000,000; expenditures U.S.$229,000,000.

Foreign trade[10]

Balance of trade (current prices)

	1997	1998	1999	2000	2001	2002
U.S.$'000,000	–1,318	–1,527	–1,585	–2,006	–2,163	–2,198
% of total	21.4%	23.8%	24.0%	25.4%	27.4%	26.9%

Imports (2000): U.S.$4,947,000,000 (imports for reexport 23.3%; machinery and apparatus 15.5%; chemicals and chemical products 11.2%; food 10.4%; petroleum [all forms] 10.3%). *Major import sources* (2002): U.S. 49.6%; Guatemala 8.1%; Honduras 3.0%; Costa Rica 2.9%; unspecified 30.4%.
Exports (2000): U.S.$2,941,000,000 (reexports [mostly clothing] 54.4%; coffee 10.1%; paper and paper products 2.8%; yarn, fabrics, made-up articles 2.7%). *Major export destinations:* U.S. 67.0%; Guatemala 11.5%; Honduras 5.9%; Nicaragua 3.8%; unspecified 6.9%.

Transport and communications

Transport. Railroads (2001): operational route length 283 km; (1999) passenger-km 8,000,000; metric ton-km cargo 19,000,000. Roads (1999): total length 10,029 km (paved 20%). Vehicles (2000): passenger cars 148,000; trucks and buses 250,800. Air transport (2001)[11]: passenger-km 6,150,000,000; metric ton-km cargo 379,000; airports (2001) with scheduled flights 1.

Communications

Medium	date	unit	number	units per 1,000 persons
Daily newspapers	2000	circulation	217,000	35
Radio	2000	receivers	2,970,000	478
Television	2000	receivers	1,250,000	201
Telephones	2003	main lines	752,600	116
Cellular telephones	2003	subscribers	1,149,800	177
Personal computers	2002	units	163,000	25
Internet	2003	users	550,000	84

Education and health

Educational attainment (1992). Percentage of population over age 25 having: no formal schooling 34.7%; incomplete primary education 37.6%; complete primary[12] 10.8%; secondary 9.4%; higher technical 2.4%; incomplete undergraduate 1.1%; complete undergraduate 2.9%; other/unknown 1.1%.
Literacy (1999): total population age 15 and over literate 78.3%; males literate 81.3%; females literate 75.6%.

Education (2000)

	schools	teachers	students	student/ teacher ratio
Primary (age 7–15)	5,090	26,209	1,212,622	46.3
Secondary (age 16–18)	...	9,255[13]	147,867	15.5[13]
Higher	...	7,501	114,675	15.3

Health (2002): physicians 8,212 (1 per 794 persons); hospital beds 4,562 (1 per 1,429 persons); infant mortality rate per 1,000 live births (2003) 26.8.
Food (2002): daily per capita caloric intake 2,584 (vegetable products 87%, animal products 13%); 113% of FAO recommended minimum requirement.

Military

Total active duty personnel (2003): 15,500 (army 89.4%, navy 4.5%, air force 6.1%). *Military expenditure as percentage of GNP* (1999): 0.9% (world 2.4%); per capita expenditure U.S.$18.

[1]Roman Catholicism, although not official, enjoys special recognition in the constitution. [2]The U.S. dollar was legal tender in El Salvador from Jan. 1, 2001 (along with the colón) at a pegged rate of 1 U.S.$ = ₡8.75; the colón was hardly used by mid-2004. [3]Detail does not add to total given because of rounding. [4]Within San Salvador urban agglomeration. [5]Projected rates based on about 78% of total deaths. [6]536,628 urban households only. [7]Manufacturing only. [8]Import duties. [9]Unemployed. [10]Imports c.i.f., exports f.o.b. (including assembled components for reexport). [11]TACA International Airlines only. [12]Education completed through ninth grade. [13]1996.

Internet resources for further information:
- **Banco Central de Reserva de El Salvador http://www.bcr.gob.sv**
- **Ministerio de Economía http://www.minec.gob.sv**

Equatorial Guinea

Official name: República de Guinea Ecuatorial (Spanish); République du Guinée Équatoriale (French) (Republic of Equatorial Guinea).
Form of government: republic with one legislative house (House of Representatives of the People [100]).
Chief of state: President.
Head of government: Prime Minister.
Capital: Malabo[1].
Official languages: Spanish; French.
Official religion: none.
Monetary unit: 1 CFA franc (CFAF) = 100 centimes; valuation (Sept. 1, 2004) 1 U.S.$ = CFAF 539.75; 1 £ = CFAF 970.98[2].

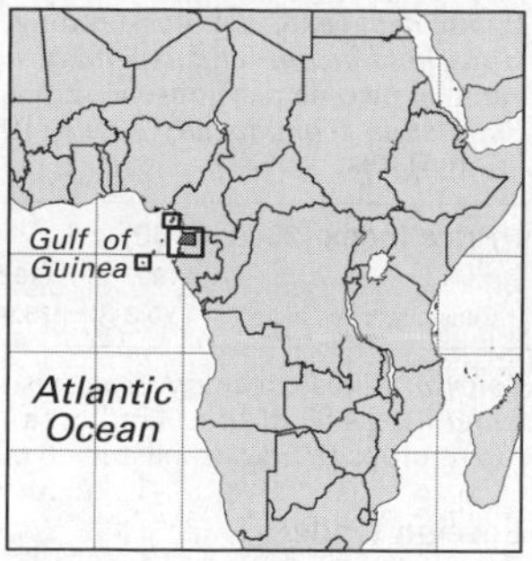

Area and population

Regions / Provinces	Capitals	area sq mi	area sq km	population 1994 census
Insular		785[3]	2,034	90,500
Annobón	Palé	7	17	2,800
Bioko Norte	Malabo	300	776	75,100
Bioko Sur	Luba	479	1,241	12,600
Continental		10,045[3]	26,017	315,600
Centro-Sur	Evinayong	3,834	9,931	60,300
Kie-Ntem	Ebebiyin	1,522	3,943	92,800
Litoral[4]	Bata	2,573	6,665	100,000
Wele-Nzas	Mongomo	2,115	5,478	62,500
TOTAL		10,831[3]	28,051	406,200[3]

Demography

Population (2004): 507,000.
Density (2004): persons per sq mi 46.8, persons per sq km 18.1.
Urban-rural (2003): urban 48.1%; rural 51.9%.
Sex distribution (2002): male 48.77%; female 51.23%.
Age breakdown (2002): under 15, 42.4%; 15–29, 27.0%; 30–44, 16.2%; 45–59, 8.3%; 60–74, 4.8%; 75 and over, 1.3%.
Population projection: (2010) 590,000; (2020) 736,000.
Doubling time: 29 years.
Ethnic composition (1995): Fang 82.9%; Bubi 9.6%; other 7.5%.
Religious affiliation (2000): Roman Catholic 80.1%; Muslim 4.0%; African Christian 3.7%; Protestant 3.1%; other 9.1%.
Major cities (2003): Malabo 92,900; Bata 66,800; Mbini 11,600; Ebebiyin 9,100; Luba 6,800.

Vital statistics

Birth rate per 1,000 population (2003): 36.9 (world avg. 21.3).
Death rate per 1,000 population (2003): 12.5 (world avg. 9.1).
Natural increase rate per 1,000 population (2003): 24.4 (world avg. 12.2).
Total fertility rate (avg. births per childbearing woman; 2003): 4.7.
Life expectancy at birth (2003): male 52.6 years; female 56.9 years.
Major causes of death per 100,000 population: n.a.; however, major diseases include malaria (about 24% of total mortality), respiratory infections (about 12% of mortality), cholera, leprosy, trypanosomiasis (sleeping sickness), and waterborne (especially gastrointestinal) diseases.

National economy

Budget (2002). Revenue: CFAF 414,484,000,000 (oil revenue 81.6%, of which royalties 41.5%; tax revenue 15.3%; nontax revenue 3.1%). Expenditures: CFAF 227,236,000,000 (capital expenditure 55.7%; current expenditure 44.3%).
Public debt (external, outstanding; 2002): U.S.$209,100,000.
Gross national product (at current market prices; 2003): U.S.$2,200,000,000[5] (U.S.$4,400[5] per capita).

Structure of gross domestic product and labour force

	2002 in value CFAF '000,000	2002 % of total value	1997 labour force	1997 % of labour force
Agriculture, fishing	41,900	2.8	...	...
Forestry	31,800	2.1	...	...
Crude petroleum	1,291,600	86.9	...	...
Manufacturing	1,000	0.1	...	...
Construction	32,200	2.2	...	...
Public utilities	5,200	0.4	...	...
Transportation and communications	4,900	0.3	...	...
Trade	24,600	1.7	...	...
Finance, real estate	7,200	0.5	...	...
Pub. admin., defense	31,100	2.1	...	...
Services	8,900	0.6	...	...
Other	4,700[6]	0.3[6]	...	...
TOTAL	1,485,500[3]	100.0	177,000	100.0

Production (metric tons except as noted). Agriculture, forestry, fishing (2002): roots and tubers 105,000 (of which cassava 45,000, sweet potatoes 36,000), palm oil 35,000, bananas 20,000, coconuts 6,000, cacao beans 4,000, coffee 3,500; livestock (number of live animals) 38,000 sheep, 9,000 goats, 6,100 pigs, 5,000 cattle; roundwood (2003) 811,000 cu m, of which saw logs and veneer logs 364,000; fish catch (2001) 3,500. Mining and quarrying: gold (2002) 500 kg. Manufacturing: methanol (2002) 719,000. Energy production (consumption): electricity (kW-hr; 2000) 23,000,000 (23,000,000); coal, none (none); crude petroleum (barrels; 2003) 97,601,000 ([2000] 102,600); petroleum products (metric tons; 2000) none (53,000); natural gas (2002) 1,050,000,000 (n.a.).
Population economically active (1997): total 177,000; activity rate of total population 40.0% (participation rates: ages 15–64, 74.7%; female 35.4%; unemployed, n.a.).

Price index (2000 = 100)

	2000	2001	2002
Consumer price index	100.0	108.8	117.0

Household income and expenditure. Average household size, n.a.; income per household: n.a.; sources of income (1988): wages and salaries 57.0%, business income 42.0%, other 1.0%; expenditure (2000)[7]: food and beverages 60.4%, clothing 14.7%; household furnishings 8.6%.
Tourism: tourism is a government priority but remains undeveloped.
Land use as % of total land area (2000): in temporary crops 4.6%, in permanent crops 3.6%, in pasture 3.7%; overall forest area 62.5%.

Foreign trade[8]

Balance of trade (current prices)

	1996	1997	1998	1999	2000	2001
CFAF '000,000,000	–16.3	+76.1	–5.5	+167.5	+532.3	+753.3
% of total	6.9%	15.3%	1.1%	23.7%	42.2%	38.8%

Imports (2001): CFAF 593,400,000,000 (for petroleum sector 80.8%; other machinery and apparatus 11.6%; petroleum products 4.8%). *Major import sources* (1999): United States *c.* 60%; France *c.* 12%; Spain *c.* 8%; Italy *c.* 6%; Cameroon *c.* 3%.
Exports (2001): CFAF 1,346,700,000,000 (crude petroleum 91.6%; methanol 4.5%; wood 2.9%; cocoa beans 0.1%). *Major export destinations* (1999): Spain *c.* 46%; China *c.* 24%; Japan *c.* 7%; United States *c.* 7%; Chile *c.* 5%.

Transport and communications

Transport. Railroads: none. Roads (1999): total length 1,790 mi, 2,880 km (paved 13%). Vehicles (1994): passenger cars 6,500; trucks and buses 4,000. Air transport (1998): passenger-km 4,000,000; metric ton-km cargo, n.a.; airports (2003) with scheduled flights 3.

Communications

Medium	date	unit	number	units per 1,000 persons
Daily newspapers	1996	circulation	2,000	4.9
Radio	1997	receivers	180,000	428
Television	1997	receivers	4,000	9.8
Telephones	2003	main lines	9,600	18
Cellular telephones	2003	units	41,500	76
Personal computers	2002	units	4,000	6.9
Internet	2002	users	1,800	3.6

Education and health

Educational attainment (1983). Percentage of population age 15 and over having: no schooling 35.4%; some primary education 46.6%; primary 13.0%; secondary 2.3%; postsecondary 1.1%; not specified 1.6%. *Literacy* (2000): percentage of total population age 15 and over literate 83.2%; males literate 92.5%; females literate 74.4%.

Education (1998)

	schools	teachers	students	student/ teacher ratio
Primary (age 6–11)	483	1,322	74,940	56.7
Secondary (age 12–17)	...	763	18,802	24.6
Voc., teacher tr.[9]	...	122	2,105	17.3
Higher[9]	...	58	578	10.0

Health: physicians (1996) 106 (1 per 4,065 persons); hospital beds (1990) 992 (1 per 350 persons); infant mortality rate per 1,000 live births (2003) 89.0.

Military

Total active duty personnel (2003): 1,320 (army 83.3%, navy 9.1%, air force 7.6%). *Military expenditure as percentage of GNP* (1999): 3.2% (world 2.4%); per capita expenditure U.S.$40.

[1]Construction work on new capital complex in Malabo suburbs underway in late 2003. [2]Formerly pegged to the French franc and since Jan. 1, 2002, to the euro at the rate of CFAF 655.96 = €1. [3]Detail does not add to total given because of rounding. [4]Includes three islets in Corisco Bay. [5]Estimated figure of the Bank of Central African States. [6]Import duties. [7]Weights of consumer price index components. [8]Imports c.i.f.; exports f.o.b. [9]1993–94.

Internet resources for further information:
- **La Banque de France: La Zone Franc http://www.banque-france.fr/fr/zonefr/main.htm**

Eritrea

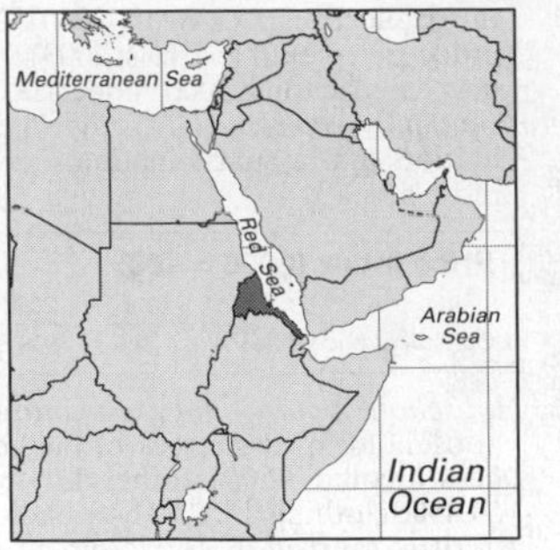

Official name: State of Eritrea.
Form of government: transitional regime with one interim legislative body (Transitional National Assembly [150][1]).
Head of state and government: President.
Capital: Asmara.
Official language: none.
Official religion: none.
Monetary unit: 1 nakfa (Nfa) = 100 cents; valuation (Sept. 1, 2004) 1 U.S.$ = Nfa 13.79; 1 £ = Nfa 24.81.

Area and population

		area[2]		population
Regions	**Capitals**	sq mi	sq km	2002 estimate[3]
Anseba	Keren	8,960	23,200	580,700
Debub	Mendefera	3,090	8,000	1,018,000
Debub-Keih-Bahri	Asseb (Aseb)	10,660	27,600	274,800
Gash-Barka	Barentu	12,820	33,200	747,200
Maekel	Asmara (Asmera)	500	1,300	727,800
Semien-Keih-Bahri	Massawa (Mitsiwa)	10,730	27,800	569,000
TOTAL		46,760	121,100	3,917,500

Demography

Population (2004): 4,297,000[4].
Density (2004)[5]: persons per sq mi 110.2, persons per sq km 42.5.
Urban-rural (2003): urban 19.9%; rural 80.1%.
Sex distribution (2003): male 49.75%; female 50.25%.
Age breakdown (2003): under 15, 44.7%; 15–29, 27.2%; 30–44, 14.1%; 45–59, 8.7%; 60–74, 4.3%; 75 and over, 1.0%.
Population projection[4]: (2010) 5,256,000; (2020) 6,584,000.
Doubling time: 27 years.
Ethnolinguistic composition (2000): Tigrinya (Tigray) 51.8%; Tigré 17.9%; Afar 8.1%; Saho 4.3%; Kunama 4.1%; other 13.8%.
Religious affiliation (2000): Christian 50.5%, of which Eritrean Orthodox 46.1%; Muslim 44.7%; other 4.8%.
Major cities (2000): Asmara (2001) 503,000; Keren 70,000; Mendefera 65,000; Asseb (2003) 56,300; Massawa 35,000.

Vital statistics

Birth rate per 1,000 population (2003): 39.4 (world avg. 21.3).
Death rate per 1,000 population (2003): 13.2 (world avg. 9.1).
Natural increase rate per 1,000 population (2003): 26.2 (world avg. 12.2).
Total fertility rate (avg. births per childbearing woman; 2003): 5.7.
Marriage rate per 1,000 population (1992): 6.8.
Divorce rate per 1,000 population: n.a.
Life expectancy at birth (2003): male 51.5 years; female 54.9 years.
Major causes of death per 100,000 population: n.a.; morbidity (principal causes of illness) arises mainly in malaria and other infectious diseases, parasitic infections, malnutrition, diarrheal diseases, and dysenteries.

National economy

Budget (2001). Revenue: Nfa 3,361,900,000 (grants 40.9%; tax revenue 38.0%, of which direct taxes 17.0%, import duties 12.2%; nontax revenue 15.9%; extraordinary revenue 5.2%). Expenditures: Nfa 4,545,300,000 (current expenditure 72.3%; capital expenditure 27.7%).
Production (metric tons except as noted). Agriculture, forestry, fishing (2003): roots and tubers 85,000, sorghum 64,000, potatoes 33,000, pulses 25,000, vegetables 23,000, millet 16,900, oilseeds 15,000, barley 8,600, cereals 7,200, wheat 4,800, vetches 4,500, corn (maize) 4,500; livestock (number of live animals; 2003) 2,100,000 sheep, 1,927,500 cattle, 1,700,000 goats, 75,000 camels, 1,370,000 chickens; roundwood (2003) 2,366,117; fish catch (2001) 8,820. Mining and quarrying (2001): salt 200,000; marble and granite are quarried, as are sand and aggregate (gravel) for construction. Manufacturing (value added in U.S.$'000,000; 2001): beverages 17; food products 6; tobacco products 5; furniture 4; leather products and shoes 3; printing and publishing 3. Energy production (consumption): electricity (kW-hr; 2002) 249,117,000 (194,161,000); crude petroleum, none (none); petroleum products (metric tons; 2000) n.a. (191,000); natural gas, none (none).
Gross national product (at current market prices; 2002): U.S.$850,000,000 (U.S.$190 per capita).

Structure of gross domestic product

	2002	
	in value Nfa '000,000	% of total value
Agriculture	941.3	10.4
Manufacturing / Mining	942.4	10.4
Public utilities	100.8	1.1
Construction	954.0	10.6
Transp. and commun.	1,071.3	11.9
Trade	1,672.4	18.5
Finance	448.0	5.0
Pub. admin., defense	1,387.6	15.4
Services	528.0	5.8
Other	985.4[7]	10.9[7]
TOTAL	9,031.2	100.0

Public debt (external, outstanding; 2002): U.S.$496,400,000.
Household income and expenditure. Average household size (2000) 5.3; average annual income per household: n.a.; sources of income: n.a.; expenditure: n.a.
Population economically active (1996): 1,649,000; activity rate of total population 41.4%.

Price index (2000 = 100)

	1997	1998	1999	2000	2001	2002
Consumer price index	70.3	76.9	83.4	100.0	114.6	134.0[6]

Tourism (2002): receipts from visitors U.S.$73,000,000.
Land use as % of total land area (2000): in temporary crops 5.0%, in permanent crops 0.03%, in pasture 69.0%; overall forest area 13.5%.

Foreign trade[8]

Balance of trade (current prices)

	1997	1998	1999	2000	2001	2002
U.S.$'000,000	–441	–499	–481	–309	–404	–486
% of total	80.4%	89.9%	90.2%	89.2%	91.4%	82.4%

Imports (2002): U.S.$538,000,000 (food and live animals 28.4%, of which cereals [all forms] 13.6%, raw sugar 7.9%; machinery and apparatus 17.5%; road vehicles 11.5%; chemicals and chemical products 6.6%; iron and steel 6.2%). *Major import sources* (2001): Italy 18.7%; Saudi Arabia 16.6%; United Arab Emirates 15.3%; United States 4.8%.
Exports (2002): U.S.$52,000,000 (raw sugar 60.8%; synthetic woven fabrics 4.4%; vegetables and fruits 3.3%; fish 2.9%; sesame 2.7%). *Major export destinations* (2001): The Sudan 48.9%; Italy 8.2%; Germany 3.5%.

Transport and communications

Transport. Railroads (2001): part of the 190-mi (306-km) rail line that formerly connected Massawa and Agordat is under reconstruction; the 73-mi (118-km) section between Massawa and Asmara was reopened in 2003. Roads (1999): total length 2,491 mi, 4,010 km (paved 22%). Vehicles (1996): automobiles 5,940, trucks and buses, n.a. Air transport (2001)[9]: passenger arrivals 39,266, passenger departures 46,448; freight loaded 202 metric tons, freight unloaded 1,548 metric tons; airports (2000) with scheduled flights 2.

Communications

Medium	date	unit	number	units per 1,000 persons
Daily newspapers	2000	circulation	104,000	28
Radio	2001	receivers	1,763,000	464
Television	2002	receivers	215,000	50
Telephones	2003	main lines	38,100	9.2
Personal computers	2003	units	12,000	2.9
Internet	2003	users	9,500	2.3

Education and health

Literacy (2003): total population age 15 and over literate, 58.6%; males 69.9%; females 47.6%.

Education (1996–97)

	schools	teachers	students	student/ teacher ratio
Primary (age 7–12)	549	5,476	240,737	44.0
Secondary (age 13–18)	86[10]	1,959	88,054	44.9
Voc., teacher tr.	4[10]	112	1,145	10.2
Higher[11]	1	198	3,096	15.6

Health (2000): physicians 173 (1 per 21,457 persons); hospital beds: 3,126 (1 per 1,187 persons); infant mortality rate per 1,000 live births (2003) 76.3.
Food (2001): daily per capita caloric intake 1,690 (vegetable 94%, animal products 6%); 76% of FAO recommended minimum requirement.

Military

Total active duty personnel (2002): 172,200 (army 98.7%, navy 0.8%, air force 0.5%). UN peacekeeping force along Eritrean-Ethiopian border (September 2004) 3,900. *Military expenditure as percentage of GNP* (1999): 27.4% (world 2.4%); per capita expenditure U.S.$52.

[1]New constitution adopted in May 1997 was still not implemented in mid-2004. [2]Approximate figures. The published total area is 46,774 sq mi (121,144 sq km); water area is 7,776 sq mi (20,140 sq km). [3]Unofficial figures. [4]Estimate of the UN *World Population Prospects* (2002 revision). [5]Based on land area only. [6]Estimate. [7]Including indirect taxes less subsidies. [8]Imports c.i.f.; exports f.o.b. [9]Asmara airport only. [10]1992–93. [11]1997–98.

Estonia

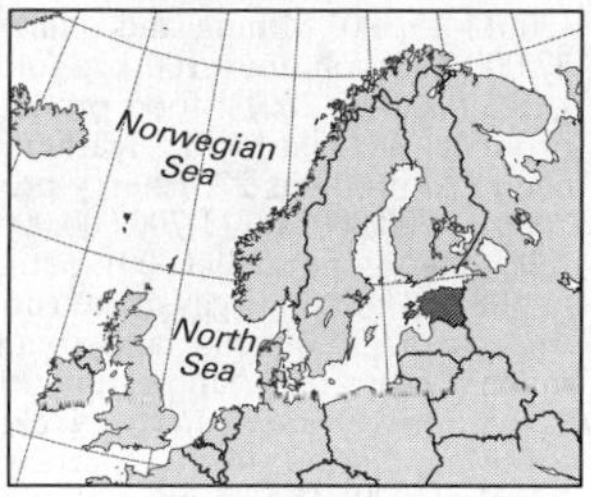

Official name: Eesti Vabariik (Republic of Estonia).
Form of government: unitary multiparty republic with a single legislative body (Riigikogu[1] [101]).
Chief of state: President.
Head of government: Prime Minister.
Capital: Tallinn.
Official language: Estonian.
Official religion: none.
Monetary unit: 1 kroon (EEK) = 100 senti; valuation (Sept. 1, 2004) 1 U.S.$ = EEK 12.87; 1 £ = EEK 23.16.

Area and population

Counties	Capitals	area sq mi	area sq km	population 2003 estimate[2]
Harju	Tallinn	1,672	4,332	522,252
Hiiu	Kärdla	395	1,023	10,348
Ida-Viru	Jõhvi	1,299	3,364	176,181
Järva	Paide	1,013	2,623	38,408
Jõgeva	Jõgeva	1,005	2,604	37,886
Lääne	Haapsalu	920	2,383	28,232
Lääne-Viru	Rakvere	1,338	3,465	67,052
Pärnu	Pärnu	1,856	4,806	90,127
Põlva	Põlva	836	2,165	32,121
Rapla	Rapla	1,151	2,980	37,270
Saare	Kuressaare	1,128	2,922	35,584
Tartu	Tartu	1,156	2,993	148,992
Valga	Valga	789	2,044	35,242
Viljandi	Viljandi	1,321	3,422	57,148
Võru	Võru	890	2,305	39,202
TOTAL		16,769[3, 4, 5]	43,431[3, 4, 5]	1,356,045

Demography

Population (2004): 1,342,000.
Density (2004)[3]: persons per sq mi 76.9, persons per sq km 29.7.
Urban-rural (2002): urban 69.4%; rural 30.6%.
Sex distribution (2003[2]): male 46.09%; female 53.91%.
Age breakdown (2002): under 15, 15.8%; 15–29, 22.7%; 30–44, 21.5%; 45–59, 19.1%; 60–74, 14.9%; 75 and over, 6.0%.
Population projection: (2010) 1,291,000; (2020) 1,203,000.
Ethnic composition (2000): Estonian 67.9%; Russian 25.6%; Ukrainian 2.1%; Belarusian 1.3%; Finnish 0.9%; other 2.2%.
Religious affiliation (1995): Christian 38.1%, of which Orthodox 20.4%, Evangelical Lutheran 13.7%; other (mostly nonreligious) 61.9%.
Major cities (2003): Tallinn 400,378; Tartu 101,169; Narva 67,752[2]; Kohtla-Järve 46,765[2]; Pärnu 44,781[2].

Vital statistics

Birth rate per 1,000 population (2002): 9.6 (world avg. 21.3); legitimate 43.7%; illegitimate 56.3%.
Death rate per 1,000 population (2002): 13.5 (world avg. 9.1).
Natural increase rate per 1,000 population (2002): –3.9 (world avg. 12.2).
Total fertility rate (avg. births per childbearing woman; 2002): 1.4.
Marriage rate per 1,000 population (2002): 4.3.
Divorce rate per 1,000 population (2002): 3.0.
Life expectancy at birth (2002): male 64.4 years; female 76.6 years.
Major causes of death per 100,000 population (2002): diseases of the circulatory system 734.8; malignant neoplasms (cancers) 252.2; accidents, violence, and homicide 147.9; diseases of the digestive system 49.5.

National economy

Budget (2001). Revenue: EEK 36,881,000,000 (social security contributions 31.2%, value-added taxes 23.4%, personal income taxes 19.2%, excise taxes 9.3%). Expenditures: EEK 36,548,000,000 (social security and welfare 31.5%, health 16.3%, education 7.3%, police 7.2%, defense 5.0%).
Public debt (external, outstanding; 2002): U.S.$482,000,000.
Production (metric tons except as noted). Agriculture, forestry, fishing (2002): barley 249,400, potatoes 210,900, wheat 74,400, rapeseed 63,900, oats 61,700, rye 41,500; livestock (number of live animals) 345,000 pigs, 260,500 cattle; roundwood (2001) 10,200,000 cu m; fish catch (2001) 105,634. Mining and quarrying (2002): oil shale 12,400,000; peat 1,518,600. Manufacturing (value of production in EEK '000,000; 2001): food products 9,282; wood products (excluding furniture) 7,321; fabricated metal products 4,251; furniture 4,143; textiles 3,554; printing and publishing 2,618. Energy production (consumption): electricity (kW-hr; 2002) 8,527,000,000 (5,686,000,000); hard coal (metric tons; 2002) none (60,000); lignite (metric tons; 2000) 11,727,000 (13,232,000); crude petroleum, none (n.a.); petroleum products (metric tons; 2000) none (736,000); natural gas (cu m; 2002) none (743,000,000).
Tourism (2002): receipts U.S.$555,000,000; expenditures U.S.$231,000,000.
Population economically active (2002): total 652,700; activity rate of total population 48.0% (participation rates: ages 15–74, 62.3%; female 48.9%; unemployed 10.3%).

Price and earnings indexes (2000 = 100)

	1997	1998	1999	2000	2001	2002	2003
Consumer price index	86.0	93.1	96.1	100.0	105.7	109.5	111.0
Annual earnings index	73.1	83.9	90.4	100.0	112.9	...	...

Household income and expenditure (2002). Average household size (2000) 2.2; average disposable income per household (1998) EEK 53,049 (U.S.$3,769); sources of income: wages and salaries 64.5%, transfers 25.0%, self-employment 5.2%, other 5.3%; expenditure: food and beverages 32.6%, housing 15.7%, transportation and communications 13.1%, clothing and footwear 6.2%.
Gross national product (2003): U.S.$6,699,000,000 (U.S.$4,960 per capita).

Structure of gross domestic product and labour force

	2003 in value EEK '000,000	2003 % of total value	2002 labour force	2002 % of labour force
Agriculture, fishing, forestry	4,992.4	4.0	38,800	5.9
Mining	1,097.8	0.9	5,700	0.9
Manufacturing	20,029.9	15.9	128,200	19.6
Public utilities	3,170.8	2.5	10,500	1.6
Construction	7,392.8	5.9	38,900	6.0
Trade, restaurants	15,765.9	12.5	104,200	16.0
Transp. and commun.	16,969.1	13.5	54,500	8.3
Finance, real estate	23,620.1	18.8	52,200	8.0
Pub. admin., defense	5,514.3	4.4	33,200	5.1
Services	14,412.8	11.4	117,300	18.0
Other	12,866.8[6]	10.2[6]	69,200[7]	10.6[7]
TOTAL	125,832.7	100.0	652,700	100.0

Land use as % of total land area (2000): in temporary crops 26.5%, in permanent crops 0.3%, in pasture 7.1%; overall forest area 48.7%.

Foreign trade[8]

Balance of trade (current prices)

	1997	1998	1999	2000	2001	2002
EEK '000,000	–20,925	–20,945	–17,070	–18,985	–17,241	–22,609
% of total	20.4%	19.2%	16.5%	15.1%	13.0%	16.6%

Imports (2001): EEK 75,073,000,000 (electrical and nonelectrical machinery 33.5%, textiles and apparel 10.3%, foodstuffs 9.4%, transport equipment 8.9%). *Major import sources:* Finland 29.9%; Germany 11.2%; Sweden 10.0%; Russia 7.8%; Latvia 4.0%.
Exports (2001): EEK 57,832,000,000 (electrical and nonelectrical machinery 33.1%, wood and paper products 15.2%, textiles and apparel 14.0%). *Major export destinations:* Finland 33.9%; Sweden 14.0%; Germany 6.9%; Latvia 6.9%; United Kingdom 4.2%.

Transport and communications

Transport. Railroads (2002): route length 963 km; passenger-km 177,000,000; metric ton-km cargo 9,697,000,000. Roads (2000): total length 16,430 km (paved 51%). Vehicles (2002): passenger cars 400,700; trucks and buses 85,700. Air transport (2002)[9]: passenger-km 355,000,000; metric ton-km cargo 5,000,000; airports (2001) 1.

Communications

Medium	date	unit	number	units per 1,000 persons
Daily newspapers	1996	circulation	255,000	174
Radio	2001	receivers	1,590,000	1,136
Television	2002	receivers	702,000	502
Telephones	2003	main lines	464,000	343
Cellular telephones	2003	subscribers	1,050,200	776
Personal computers	2002	units	285,000	210
Internet	2002	users	444,000	328

Education and health

Education (2002–03)

	schools	teachers	students	student/ teacher ratio
Primary (age 7–12) / Secondary (age 13–17)	592	15,762[10]	200,500	13.5[10]
Vocational	79	1,279[10]	28,100	24.1[10]
Higher[11]	14	...	46,801	...

Health (2002): physicians 4,190 (1 per 324 persons); hospital beds 8,088 (1 per 168 persons); infant mortality rate per 1,000 live births (2002) 5.7.
Food (2001): daily per capita caloric intake 3,048 (vegetable products 75%, animal products 25%); 119% of FAO recommended minimum requirement.

Military

Total active duty personnel (2003): 5,510 (army 88.0%, navy 8.0%, air force 4.0%). *Military expenditure as a percentage of GNP* (1999): 1.5% (world 2.4%); per capita expenditure U.S.$120.

[1]Official legislation bans translation of parliament's name. [2]As of January 1. [3]Based on area used by Estonian government to calculate population densities. [4]Total area including the Estonian portion of Lake Peipus (590 sq mi [1,529 sq km]), Lake Võrtsjärv, and Muuga harbour is 17,462 sq mi (45,227 sq km). [5]Total includes 1,596 sq mi (4,133 sq km) of Baltic Sea islands. [6]Includes net taxes (EEK 14,557,700,000) less imputed bank service charges (EEK 1,690,900,000). [7]Includes 2,000 not adequately defined and 67,200 unemployed. [8]Imports c.i.f.; exports f.o.b. [9]Estonian Air. [10]2000–01. [11]Universities only.

Internet resources for further information:

- **Statistical Office of Estonia http://www.stat.ee**

Ethiopia

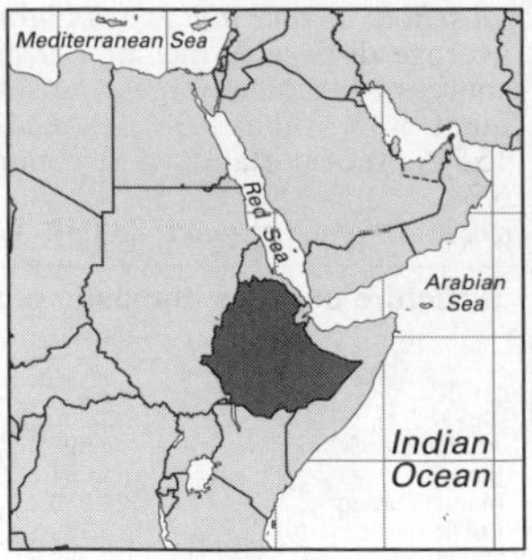

Official name: Federal Democratic Republic of Ethiopia.
Form of government: federal republic with two legislative houses (Federal Council [108]; Council of People's Representatives [546]).
Chief of state: President.
Head of government: Prime Minister.
Capital: Addis Ababa.
Official language: none[1].
Official religion: none.
Monetary unit: 1 birr (Br) = 100 cents; valuation (Sept. 1, 2004) 1 U.S.$ = Br 8.65; 1 £ = Br 15.56.

Area and population

		area		population
				1994
Regional states	**Capitals**	sq mi	sq km	census
Afar	Aysaita	37,339	96,708	1,106,383
Amhara	Bahir Dar	60,603	156,960	13,834,297
Benishangul/ Gumuz	Asosa	19,401	50,248	460,459
Gambela	Gambela	9,795	25,369	181,862
Harer Zuriya	Harer (Harar)	144	374	131,139
Oromiya	Addis Ababa	136,538	353,632	18,732,525
Somali	Jijiga	107,820	279,252	3,383,165
Southern Nations, Nationalities and Peoples'	Awasa	43,524	112,727	10,377,028
Tigray	Mekele	19,415	50,286	3,136,267
Cities				
Addis Ababa	...	211	546	2,112,737
Dire Dawa	...	396	1,025	251,864
TOTAL		435,186	1,127,127	53,707,726[2]

Demography

Population (2004): 67,851,000.
Density (2004): persons per sq mi 155.0, persons per sq km 59.8.
Urban-rural (2002): urban 15.6%; rural 84.4%.
Sex distribution (2002): male 50.14%; female 49.86%.
Age breakdown (2002): under 15, 44.9%; 15–29, 28.0%; 30–44, 14.5%; 45–59, 8.2%; 60–74, 3.7%; 75 and over, 0.7%.
Population projection: (2010) 75,066,000; (2020) 85,965,000.
Doubling time: 29 years.
Ethnolinguistic composition (1994): Oromo 31.8%; Amharic 29.3%; Somali 6.2%; Tigrinya 5.9%; Walaita 4.6%; Gurage 4.2%; Sidamo 3.4%; Afar 1.9%; Hadya-Libide 1.7%; other 11.0%.
Religious affiliation (1994): Ethiopian Orthodox 50.3%; Muslim 32.9%; Protestant 10.1%; traditional beliefs 4.8%; Roman Catholic 0.6%; other 1.3%.
Major cities (1994): Addis Ababa 2,112,737; Dire Dawa 164,851; Nazret 127,842; Gonder 112,249; Dese 97,314; Mekele 96,938.

Vital statistics

Birth rate per 1,000 population (2003): 39.9 (world avg. 21.3).
Death rate per 1,000 population (2003): 15.5 (world avg. 9.1).
Natural increase rate per 1,000 population (2003): 24.4 (world avg. 12.2).
Total fertility rate (avg. births per childbearing woman; 2003): 5.6.
Life expectancy at birth (2003): male 47.3 years; female 49.7 years.
Adult population (ages 15–49) *living with HIV* (beginning of 2004): 4.4% (world avg. 1.1%).

National economy

Budget (1999–2000). Revenue: Br 11,222,000,000 (tax revenue 57.8%, of which import duties 22.5%, income and profit tax 19.3%, sales tax 12.8%, export duties 1.3%; nontax revenue 26.9%; grants 15.3%). Expenditures: Br 17,184,000,000 (current expenditure 80.0%, of which defense 39.8%, wages 20.5%, education and health 12.2%, debt payment 6.5%; capital expenditure 20.0%).
Public debt (external, outstanding; 2002): U.S.$6,313,000,000.
Tourism (2002): receipts U.S.$77,000,000; expenditures U.S.$45,000,000.
Gross national product (2003): U.S.$6,325,000,000 (U.S.$90 per capita).

Structure of gross domestic product and labour force

	2000–01		1995[3]	
	in value Br '000,000[4]	% of total value	labour force	% of labour force
Agriculture	7,831	45.1	21,605,317	87.8
Manufacturing, mining	1,158	6.7	401,535	1.6
Construction	431	2.5	61,232	0.2
Public utilities	243	1.4	17,066	0.1
Transp. and commun.	1,081	6.2	103,154	0.4
Trade	1,469	8.5	935,937	3.8
Finance	1,207	7.0	19,451	0.1
Pub. admin., defense	2,513	14.5	1,252,224	5.1
Services	1,424	8.2		
Other	—	—	210,184[5]	0.9[5]
TOTAL	17,357	100.0[6]	24,606,100	100.0

Production (metric tons except as noted). Agriculture, forestry, fishing (2002): corn (maize) 2,600,000, sugarcane 2,500,000, sorghum 1,820,000, wheat 1,250,000, barley 830,000, potatoes 415,000, millet 378,000, coffee 235,000, seed cotton 45,500, sesame seed 12,000; livestock (number of live animals) 35,500,000 cattle, 11,438,000 sheep, 9,622,000 goats, 5,298,000 horses, mules, and asses, 326,000 camels; roundwood (2001) 91,283,000 cu m; fish catch (2001) 15,390. Mining and quarrying (2001–02): rock salt 61,000; tantalum 37,000 kg; niobium 6,100 kg; gold 5,300 kg. Manufacturing (value added in U.S.$'000,000; 2001): food products 143; beverages 95; nonmetallic mineral products 38; textiles 32; leather products and footwear 23; chemicals and chemical products 22. Energy production (consumption): electricity (kW-hr; 2000) 1,700,000,000 (1,700,000,000); coal, none (n.a.); crude petroleum (barrels; 2000) none (5,498,000); petroleum products (metric tons; 2000) 611,000 (1,508,000); natural gas, none (none).
Land use as % of total land area (2000): in temporary crops 10.0%, in permanent crops 0.7%, in pasture 20.0%; overall forest area 4.2%.
Population economically active (2000): total 27,781,000; activity rate of total population 44.3% (participation rates [1999]: ages over 15, 80.5%; female [1999] 45.5%; unemployed, n.a.).

Price index (2000 = 100)

	1998	1999	2000	2001	2002	2003
Consumer price index	92.1	99.3	100.0	91.9	93.3	109.9

Household income and expenditure. Average household size (2000) 5.2.

Foreign trade[7]

Balance of trade (current prices)

	1996	1997	1998	1999	2000	2001
U.S.$'000,000	–586	–414	–800	–920	–645	–1,193
% of total	41.3%	26.0%	41.7%	49.6%	39.9%	57.9%

Imports (2000): U.S.$1,260,000,000 (machinery and apparatus 19.8%, refined petroleum 19.6%, road vehicles 12.0%, chemicals and chemical products 11.3%, iron and steel 5.6%). *Major import sources:* Yemen 19.1%; Italy 8.9%; Japan 8.2%; China 7.7%; India 5.2%; Germany 5.2%.
Exports (2000): U.S.$482,000,000 (coffee 53.0%, leather 8.5%, nonmonetary gold 5.7%, sesame seeds 4.6%). *Major export destinations:* Germany 19.6%; Japan 11.7%; Djibouti 10.7%; Saudi Arabia 8.1%; Italy 6.7%; Somalia 6.1%.

Transport and communications

Transport. Railroads (2001): length 681 km[8]; (1998–99) passenger-km 151,000,000[9]; (1998–99) metric ton-km cargo 90,000,000[9]. Roads (2001): total length 29,799 km (paved 13%). Vehicles (1999): passenger cars 54,240; trucks and buses 34,333. Air transport (2003)[10]: passenger-km 3,573,000,000; metric ton-km cargo 93,000,000; airports (1997) 31.

Communications

Medium	date	unit	number	units per 1,000 persons
Daily newspapers	1997	circulation	86,000	1.5
Radio	2000	receivers	11,800,000	189
Television	2000	receivers	376,000	6.0
Telephones	2003	main lines	435,000	6.3
Cellular telephones	2003	subscribers	97,800	1.4
Personal computers	2003	units	150,000	2.2
Internet	2003	users	75,000	1.1

Education and health

Educational attainment: n.a. *Literacy* (2000): total population age 15 and over literate 39.1%; males 47.2%; females 30.9%.

Education (1999–2000)

	schools	teachers	students	student/ teacher ratio
Primary (age 7–12)	11,490	115,777	6,462,503	55.8
Secondary (age 13–18)	410	13,154	571,719	43.5
Voc., teacher tr.	62	1,309	12,551	9.6
Higher	6	1,779	40,894	23.0

Health (2001–02): physicians: 1,833 (1 per 35,604 persons); hospital beds: 11,367 (1 per 5,740 persons); infant mortality rate (2003) 98.6.
Food (2002): daily per capita caloric intake 1,857 (vegetable products 95%, animal products 5%); 80% of FAO recommended minimum requirement.

Military

Total active duty personnel (2003): 162,500 (army 98.5%, air force 1.5%); UN peacekeeping personnel along Ethiopian-Eritrean border (August 2004): 3,900. *Military expenditure as percentage of GNP* (1999): 8.8% (world 2.4%); per capita expenditure U.S.$9.

[1]Amharic is the "working" language. [2]Represents sum of regional state populations; reported census total is 53,477,265. [3]For ages 10 and up. [4]At 1980–81 factor cost. [5]First-time job seekers. [6]Detail does not add to total given because of rounding. [7]Imports f.o.b. in balance of trade and c.i.f. for commodities and trading partners. [8]Length of Ethiopian segment of Addis Ababa–Djibouti railroad. [9]Includes Djibouti part of Addis Ababa–Djibouti railroad. [10]Ethiopian Airlines only.

Internet resources for further information:
- **Ethiopian Embassy (Washington, D.C.)**
http://www.ethiopianembassy.org
- **National Bank of Ethiopia**
http://www.nbe.gov.et

Faroe Islands[1]

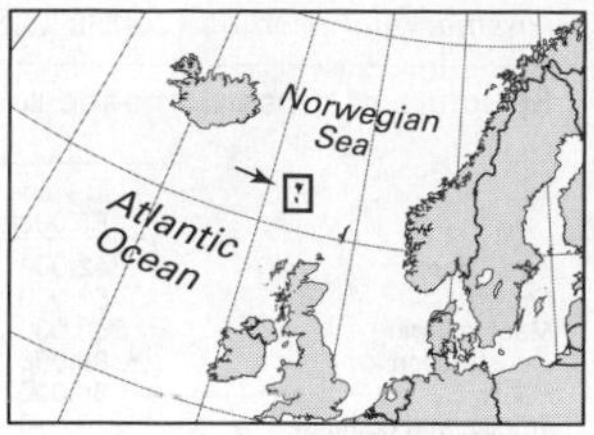

Official name: Føroyar (Faroese); Færøerne (Danish) (Faroe Islands).
Political status: self-governing region of the Danish realm with a single legislative body (Lagting [32]).
Chief of state: Danish Monarch represented by High Commissioner.
Head of home government: Prime Minister.
Capital: Tórshavn (Thorshavn).
Official languages: Faroese; Danish.
Official religion: Evangelical Lutheran.
Monetary unit: 1 Danish krone[2] (Dkr) = 100 øre; valuation (Sept. 1, 2004) 1 U.S.$ = Dkr 6.12; 1£ = Dkr 11.01.

Area and population

		area		population
Districts	Capitals	sq mi	sq km	2003[3] estimate
Klaksvík	Klaksvík	4.9	12.7	5,247
Nordhara Eysturoy (Østerø Nordre)	Eidhi	48.4	125.4	1,608
Nordhoy (Norderøernes)	...	88.1	228.1	746
Sandoy (Sandø)	Húsavík	48.1	124.7	1,455
Streymoy (Strømø)	Vestmanna	145.6	377.0	3,313
Sudhuroy (Suderø)	Tvøroyri	64.4	166.8	5,134
Sydhra Eysturoy (Østerø Søndre)	Runavík	62.1	160.9	8,978
Tórshavn (Thorshavn)	Tórshavn	5.9	15.3	18,420
Vágar (Vágø)	Midvágs	72.6	187.9	2,803
TOTAL		540.1	1,398.8	47,704

Demography

Population (2004): 48,500.
Density (2004): persons per sq mi 89.8, persons per sq km 34.7.
Urban-rural (2003[3]): urban[4] 38.6%; rural 61.4%.
Sex distribution (2003[3]): male 51.90%; female 48.10%.
Age breakdown (2003[3]): under 15, 23.6%; 15–29, 19.4%; 30–44, 20.9%; 45–59, 18.4%; 60–74, 11.3%; 75 and over, 6.4%.
Population projection: (2010) 50,000; (2020) 53,000.
Ethnic composition (2000): Faroese 97.0%; Danish 2.5%; other Scandinavian 0.4%; other 0.1%.
Religious affiliation (1995): Evangelical Lutheran Church of Denmark 80.8%; Plymouth Brethren 10.1%; Roman Catholic 0.2%; other (mostly nonreligious) 8.9%.
Major towns (2003[3]): Tórshavn 18,420; Klaksvík 4,794; Runavík 2,557; Tvøroyri 1,867.

Vital statistics

Birth rate per 1,000 population (2002): 15.0 (world avg. 21.3); (1998) legitimate 62.0%; illegitimate 38.0%.
Death rate per 1,000 population (2002): 8.3 (world avg. 9.1).
Natural increase rate per 1,000 population (2002): 6.7 (world avg. 12.2).
Total fertility rate (avg. births per childbearing woman; 2002): 2.5.
Marriage rate per 1,000 population (2002): 5.2.
Divorce rate per 1,000 population (2002): 1.1.
Life expectancy at birth (2003): male 75.4 years; female 82.4 years.
Major causes of death per 100,000 population (1999): diseases of the circulatory system 339.2; malignant neoplasms (cancers) 257.2; diseases of the respiratory system 48.8; accidents 39.9; other 166.3, of which suicide 2.2.

National economy

Budget (2002). Revenue: Dkr 3,762,060,000 (income taxes 44.5%, customs and excise duties 32.9%, transfers from the Danish government 16.7%). Expenditures: Dkr 3,586,220,000 (health and social welfare 46.6%, education 17.6%, debt service 10.5%, agriculture, fishing, and commerce 4.1%).
Gross national product (at current market prices; 2002): U.S.$1,290,000,000 (U.S.$27,270 per capita).

Structure of gross domestic product and labour force

	2001		2002	
	in value Dkr '000,000	% of total value	labour force	% of labour force
Agriculture	57	0.7	...	...
Fishing[5]	1,865	21.7	...	...
Mining	497	5.8	...	...
Manufacturing[6]	290	3.4	...	...
Construction	471	5.5	...	...
Public utilities	186	2.2	...	...
Transp. and commun.	711	8.3	...	...
Trade, hotels	959	11.2	...	...
Finance and real estate	1,205	14.0	...	...
Pub. admin., defense	1,800	20.9	...	...
Services	305	3.5	...	...
Other	250	2.9	...	...
TOTAL	8,598[7]	100.0[7]	29,540	100.0

Production (metric tons except as noted). Agriculture, forestry, fishing (2002): potatoes 1,500, other vegetables, grass, hay, and silage are produced; livestock (number of live animals) 70,000 sheep, 2,398 cattle; fish catch (2001) 524,837 (of which blue whiting 259,761, saithe 45,792, cod 38,706, herring 35,172, capelin 32,110, mackerel 24,005, prawns, shrimps, and other crustaceans 20,239). Mining and quarrying: negligible[8]. Manufacturing (value added in Dkr '000,000; 1999): processed fish 393; all other manufacturing 351; important products include handicrafts and woolen textiles and clothing. Energy production (consumption): electricity (kW-hr; 2002) 239,644,000 ([2001] 223,000,000); coal, none (none); crude petroleum, none (none); petroleum products (metric tons; 2001) none (285,603); natural gas, none (none).
Population economically active (2002): total 29,540; activity rate of total population *c.* 62% (participation rates: ages 14–64, n.a.; female [1997] *c.* 46%; unemployed *c.* 2%).

Price and earnings indexes (2000 = 100)

	1997	1998	1999	2000	2001	2002	2003[9]
Consumer price index	88.7	91.7	95.8	100.0	107.6	107.9	109.7
Hourly wage index	92.9	93.8	95.5	100.0	...	...	...

Public debt (to Denmark; end of 2001): none.
Household income and expenditure. Average household size: n.a.; average annual income per household: n.a.; sources of income: n.a.; expenditure (1998)[10]: food and beverages 25.1%, transportation and communications 17.7%, housing 12.5%, recreation 11.9%, energy 7.7%.
Land use as % of total land area (1997): in temporary crops *c.* 2%, in permanent crops, n.a., in pasture *c.* 93%; overall forest area, negligible.

Foreign trade

Balance of trade (current prices)

	1997	1998	1999	2000	2001	2002
Dkr '000,000	+234	+361	–38	–485	+123	+211
% of total	4.7%	6.5%	0.6%	6.0%	1.5%	2.6%

Imports (2002): Dkr 3,896,000,000 (goods for household consumption 28.3%, machinery and transport equipment 21.3%, goods for industries 19.0%). *Major import sources:* Denmark 31.4%; Norway 18.7%; Germany 7.6%; Sweden 6.5%; United Kingdom 4.6%.
Exports (2002): Dkr 4,107,000,000 (chilled and frozen fish [excluding salmon] 50.4%, salted fish 16.3%, salmon 14.8%, prawns 5.7%, fish meal and fish oil 4.8%, trout 3.2%). *Major export destinations:* United Kingdom 24.4%; Denmark 20.5%; Spain 11.7%; France 8.2%; Germany 6.9%; Norway 6.5%.

Transport and communications

Transport. Railroads: none. Roads (2001): total length 288 mi, 464 km (paved, n.a.). Vehicles (2001): passenger cars 15,615; trucks, vans, and buses 3,698. Merchant marine (2001): vessels (20 gross tons and over) 251; total gross tonnage 104,711. Air transport (2001): airports with scheduled flights 1.

Communications

Medium	date	unit	number	units per 1,000 persons
Daily newspapers	1996	circulation	6,000	136
Radio	2000	receivers	102,000	2,222
Television	2000	receivers	46,800	1,022
Telephones	2002	main lines	23,000	482
Cellular telephones	2002	subscribers	30,700	644
Internet	2002	users	25,000	524

Education and health

Education (2001–02)

	schools	teachers	students	student/teacher ratio
Primary (age 6–14)	38	...	5,579	...
Secondary (age 15–17)	23	...	2,019	...
Voc., teacher tr.	11	...	2,195[11]	...
Higher[12]	1	19	173	9.1

Health (2001): physicians 90 (1 per 518 persons); hospital beds (2002) 290 (1 per 163 persons); infant mortality rate per 1,000 live births (2003) 6.5.
Food: n.a.

Military

Defense responsibility lies with Denmark.

[1]English-language alternative spelling is Faeroe Islands. [2]The local currency, the Faroese króna (Fkr), is equivalent to the Danish krone. Banknotes used are Faroese or Danish; coins are Danish. [3]January 1. [4]Tórshavn only. [5]Fishing includes fish processing. [6]Manufacturing excludes fish processing. [7]Detail does not add to total given because of rounding. [8]The maritime boundary demarcation agreement between the Shetland Islands (U.K.) and the Faroes in May 1999 allowed for the exploration of deep-sea petroleum. [9]April only. [10]Weights of consumer price index. [11]1996–97. [12]University of the Faroe Islands.

Internet resources for further information:

- **Faroe Islands in Figures**
  http://www.hagstova.fo/pls/portal/docs/PAGE/HAGSTOVA_FOROYA_FO/HEIM_VERS_03/PUBL_NEW/FAROE_ISLAND_IN_FIGURES/UPPSETING_GRON_ENDALIGT_0404.PDF
- **Danmarks Statistik**
  http://www.dst.dk/HomeUK.aspx

Fiji

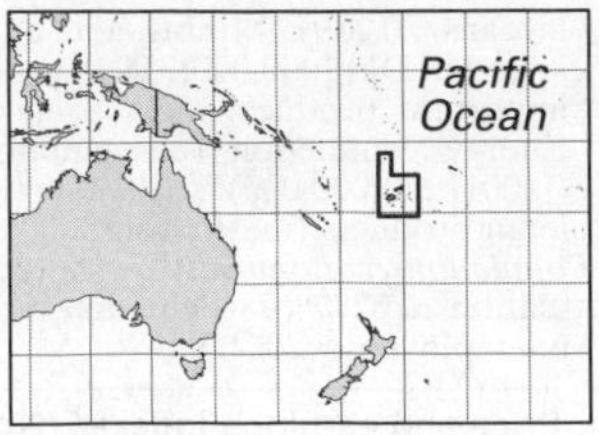

Official name: Republic of the Fiji Islands[1].
Form of government: multiparty republic with two legislative houses (Senate [32[2]]; House of Representatives [72]).
Chief of state: President.
Head of government: Prime Minister.
Capital: Suva.
Official languages: [3].
Official religion: none.
Monetary unit: 1 Fiji dollar (F$) = 100 cents; valuation (Sept. 1, 2004) 1 U.S.$ = F$1.78; 1 £ = F$3.21.

Area and population

Divisions / Provinces	Capitals	area sq mi	area sq km	population 1996 census
Central	Suva			
Naitasiri	—	643	1,666	126,641
Namosi	—	220	570	5,742
Rewa	—	105	272	101,547
Serua	—	320	830	15,461
Tailevu	—	369	955	48,216
Eastern	Levuka			
Kadavu	—	185	478	9,535
Lau	—	188	487	12,211
Lomaiviti	—	159	411	16,214
Rotuma	—	18	46	2,810
Northern	Labasa			
Bua	—	532	1,379	14,988
Cakaudrove	—	1,087	2,816	44,321
Macuata	—	774	2,004	80,207
Western	Lautoka			
Ba	—	1,017	2,634	212,197
Nadroga-Navosa	—	921	2,385	54,083
Ra	—	518	1,341	30,904
TOTAL	—	7,055[4]	18,272[4]	775,077

Demography

Population (2004): 839,000.
Density (2004): persons per sq mi 118.9, persons per sq km 45.9.
Urban-rural (2003): urban 51.7%; rural 48.3%.
Sex distribution (2003): male 50.21%; female 49.79%.
Age breakdown (2003): under 15, 32.1%; 15–29, 28.8%; 30–44, 19.9%; 45–59, 12.8%; 60–74, 5.6%; 75 and over, 0.8%.
Population projection: (2010) 882,000; (2020) 932,000.
Doubling time: 40 years.
Ethnic composition (2000): Fijian 52.0%; Indian 41.5%[5]; other 6.5%.
Religious affiliation (2000): Christian 56.8%, of which Protestant 37.1%, independent Christian 8.5%, Roman Catholic 8.4%; Hindu 33.3%; Muslim 6.9%; nonreligious 1.3%; Sikh 0.7%; other 1.0%.
Major cities (1996; "urban centres"): Suva 167,421; Lautoka 42,917; Nadi 30,791; Labasa 24,187; Nausori 21,645.

Vital statistics

Birth rate per 1,000 population (2003): 23.1 (world avg. 21.3).
Death rate per 1,000 population (2003): 5.7 (world avg. 9.1).
Natural increase rate per 1,000 population (2003): 17.4 (world avg. 12.2).
Total fertility rate (avg. births per childbearing woman; 2003): 2.8.
Life expectancy at birth (2003): male 66.4 years; female 71.4 years.
Major causes of death per 100,000 population (2001): diseases of the circulatory system 330.0; diseases of the respiratory system 50.2; infectious and parasitic diseases 45.8; neoplasms (cancers) 38.0; accidents, poisoning, and violence 31.7.

National economy

Budget (2002). Revenue: F$949,388,000 (customs duties 54.9%, income and estate taxes 29.0%, fees and royalties 5.6%). Expenditures: F$1,345,300,000 (goods and services 42.5%, debt redemption 14.2%, education 12.5%, defense 4.2%).
Production (metric tons except as noted). Agriculture, forestry, fishing (2003): sugarcane 3,300,000, coconuts 170,000, taro 38,000, cassava 33,000, rice 16,000, bananas 6,500, sweet potatoes 6,200, yams 5,200; livestock (number of live animals) 320,000 cattle, 248,000 goats, 139,000 pigs; roundwood (2003) 383,000 cu m; fish catch (2001) 44,689. Mining and quarrying (2003): gold 3,517 kg; silver 1,247 kg. Manufacturing (2002): raw sugar 317,000; cement 102,000; flour 59,000; coconut oil 9,000. Energy production (consumption): electricity (kW-hr; 2000) 545,000,000 (545,000,000); coal (metric tons; 2000) none (18,000); petroleum products (metric tons; 2000) none (205,000).
Tourism: receipts from visitors (2002) U.S.$261,000,000; expenditures by nationals abroad (2000) U.S.$78,000,000.
Land use as % of total land area (2000): in temporary crops 10.9%, in permanent crops 4.7%, in pasture 9.6%; overall forest area 44.6%.
Population economically active (1996): total 297,770; activity rate of total population 38.4% (participation rates: ages 15–64, 60.6%; female 32.8%; unemployed [2000] 12.2%).

Price and earnings indexes (2000 = 100)

	1997	1998	1999	2000	2001	2002	2003
Consumer price index	91.8	97.0	98.9	100.0	104.3	105.1	109.5
Earnings index	98.8	94.6	99.0	100.0	104.3	105.2	109.5

Gross national product (2003): U.S.$1,969,000,000 (U.S.$2,360 per capita).

Structure of gross domestic product and labour force

	2000		1996	
	in value F$'000[6]	% of total value[6]	labour force	% of labour force
Agriculture	342,000	16.8	132,676	44.6
Mining	51,000	2.5	2,507	0.8
Manufacturing	296,000	14.6	29,043	9.8
Construction	88,000	4.3	10,639	3.6
Public utilities	88,000	4.3	2,107	0.7
Transp. and commun.	270,000	13.3	16,722	5.6
Trade, hotels	382,000	18.8	32,175	10.8
Finance, real estate	248,000	12.2	7,812	2.6
Pub. admin., defense	393,000	19.3	15,854	5.3
Services			28,766	9.7
Other	–126,000[7]	–6.2[7]	19,469[8]	6.5[8]
TOTAL	2,032,000	100.0[4]	297,770	100.0

Public debt (external, outstanding; 2002): U.S.$165,400,000.
Household income and expenditure. Average household size (2000) 6.1; income per household: n.a.; sources of income: n.a.; expenditure (1991[9]): food, beverages, and tobacco 41.5%, housing and energy 21.4%, transportation and communications 12.9%, household durable goods 6.5%.

Foreign trade[10, 11]

Balance of trade (current prices)

	1998	1999	2000	2001	2002	2003
F$'000,000	–418	–623	–513	–584	–758	–941
% of total	17.5%	20.4%	17.1%	19.3%	24.0%	27.0%

Imports (2003): F$2,215,000,000 (transport equipment 16.1%, mineral fuels 15.0%, machinery and apparatus 13.8%, textiles and wearing apparel 10.7%, live animals and animal products 6.2%). *Major import sources:* Australia 37.5%; New Zealand 18.8%; United States 9.2%; Singapore 6.4%; Japan 5.4%.
Exports (2003): F$1,273,000,000 (reexports [mostly petroleum products] 26.0%, clothing 19.8%, sugar 18.1%, fish 6.7%, gold 6.0%). *Major export destinations:* Australia 27.4%; United States 24.5%; United Kingdom 19.5%; New Zealand 5.6%; Japan 4.5%.

Transport and communications

Transport. Railroads (1999)[12]: length 370 mi, 595 km. Roads (1999): total length 2,140 mi, 3,440 km (paved 49%). Vehicles (2000): passenger cars 50,005; trucks and buses 35,038. Air transport (2003)[13]: passenger-km 2,190,000,000; metric ton-km cargo 62,692,000; airports (1997) with scheduled flights 13.

Communications

Medium	date	unit	number	units per 1,000 persons
Daily newspapers	2001	circulation	49,000	60
Radio	1997	receivers	500,000	636
Television	2000	receivers	92,000	114
Telephones	2003	main lines	102,000	124
Cellular telephones	2003	subscribers	109,900	133
Personal computers	2002	units	40,000	49
Internet	2003	users	55,000	67

Education and health

Educational attainment (1996): Percentage of population age 25 and over having: no formal schooling 4.4%; some education 22.3%; incomplete secondary 47.7%; complete secondary 17.0%; some higher 6.7%; university degree 1.9%. *Literacy* (2001): total population age 15 and over literate 93.2%; males 95.2%; females 91.2%.

Education (2000)

	schools	teachers	students	student/ teacher ratio
Primary (age 5–15)	709[14]	5,082	142,912	28.1
Secondary (age 16–19)	146[14]	3,696	66,905	18.1
Voc., teacher tr.	35[14]	864[15]	9,997[15]	...
Higher[16]	1	355	4,000	11.3

Health (2003): physicians 373 (1 per 2,229 persons); hospital beds (1999) 2,097 (1 per 385 persons); infant mortality rate per 1,000 live births 13.4.
Food (2002): daily per capita caloric intake 2,894 (vegetable products 84%, animal products 16%); 127% of FAO recommended minimum requirement.

Military

Total active duty personnel (2003): 3,500 (army 91.4%, navy 8.6%, air force, none). *Military expenditure as percentage of GNP* (1999): 2.0% (world 2.4%); per capita expenditure U.S.$42.

[1]The long-form name in Fijian is Kai Vakarairai ni Fiji. [2]All seats are nonelected. [3]English, Fijian, and Hindustani (Fijian Hindi) have equal status per 1998 constitution. [4]Detail does not add to total given because of rounding. [5]The emigration of Indian population after the coup in 1987 has resulted in the reemergence of a Fijian majority. [6]Constant 1989 prices. [7]Less imputed bank service charges. [8]Includes 2,204 not stated and 17,265 unemployed. [9]Weights of consumer price index components based on 3,000 urban households. [10]Imports c.i.f.; exports f.o.b. [11]All export data include reexports. [12]Owned by the Fiji Sugar Corporation. [13]Air Pacific only. [14]1995. [15]1998. [16]University of the South Pacific only.

Internet resources for further information:
- **Fiji Islands Bureau of Statistics http://www.spc.int/prism/Country/FJ/stats/index.htm**
- **Reserve Bank of Fiji http://www.reservebank.gov.fj**

Finland

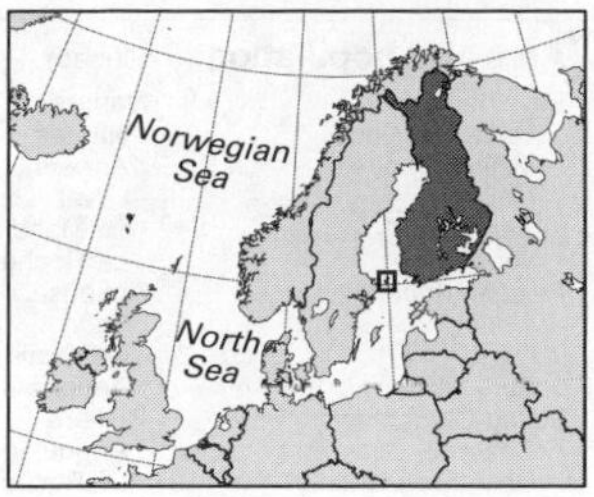

Official names[1]: Suomen Tasavalta (Finnish); Republiken Finland (Swedish) (Republic of Finland).
Form of government: multiparty republic with one legislative house (Parliament [200]).
Chief of state: President.
Head of government: Prime Minister.
Capital: Helsinki.
Official languages: none[1].
Official religion: none.
Monetary unit: 1 euro (€) = 100 cents; valuation (Sept. 1, 2004) 1 U.S.$ = €0.82; 1 £ = €1.48[2].

Area and population

		area		population
Provinces	Capitals	sq mi	sq km	2004 estimate[3]
Eastern Finland	Mikkeli	23,444	60,720	582,781
Lapland	Rovaniemi	38,203	98,946	186,917
Oulu	Oulu	23,773	61,572	458,504
Southern Finland	Hämeenlinna	13,273	34,378	2,116,914
Western Finland	Turku	31,265	80,976	1,848,269
Autonomous Territory				
Åland (Ahvenamaa)[4]	Mariehamn (Maarianhamina)	599	1,552	26,347
TOTAL		130,559[5, 6]	338,145[5, 6]	5,219,732

Demography

Population (2004): 5,226,000.
Density (2004)[7]: persons per sq mi 44.5, persons per sq km 17.2.
Urban-rural (2003[3]): urban 83.3%; rural 16.7%.
Sex distribution (2003[3]): male 48.88%; female 51.12%.
Age breakdown (2003[3]): under 15, 17.8%; 15–29, 18.6%; 30–44, 20.6%; 45–59, 22.5%; 60–74, 13.6%; 75 and over, 6.9%.
Population projection: (2010) 5,267,000; (2020) 5,317,000.
Ethnic composition (2000): Finnish 91.9%; Swedish 5.9%; Karelian 0.8%; Russian 0.2%; other 1.2%.
Religious affiliation (2002[3]): Evangelical Lutheran 84.9%; Finnish (Greek) Orthodox 1.1%; nonreligious 12.9%; other 1.1%.
Major cities (2003[3]): Helsinki 559,716 (urban agglomeration 1,075,000); Espoo 221,097[8]; Tampere 199,823; Vantaa 181,890[8]; Turku 174,618; Oulu 124,588.

Vital statistics

Birth rate per 1,000 population (2002): 10.7 (world avg. 21.3); (2000) legitimate 60.8%; illegitimate 39.2%.
Death rate per 1,000 population (2002): 9.5 (world avg. 9.1).
Natural increase rate per 1,000 population (2002): 1.2 (world avg. 12.2).
Total fertility rate (avg. births per childbearing woman; 2002): 1.7.
Marriage rate per 1,000 population (2002): 5.3.
Divorce rate per 1,000 population (2002): 2.6.
Life expectancy at birth (2002): male 74.6 years; female 81.6 years.
Major causes of death per 100,000 population (2001): diseases of the circulatory system 400.7, of which ischemic heart disease 239.6, cerebrovascular diseases 93.9; malignant neoplasms (cancers) 204.5; accidents and violence 80.3; diseases of the respiratory system 74.0.

National economy

Budget (2003). Revenue: €35,755,000,000 (income and property taxes 36.6%, value-added taxes 27.4%, excise duties 13.7%). Expenditures: €35,755,000,000 (social security and health 23.8%, education 16.4%, interest on state debt 9.6%, agriculture and forestry 7.2%, defense 5.5%).
Production (metric tons except as noted). Agriculture, forestry, fishing (2002): silage 6,842,500, barley 1,738,700, oats 1,507,800, sugar beets 1,066,300, potatoes 780,100, spring wheat 483,900; livestock (number of live animals; 2002) 1,315,000 pigs, 1,025,400 cattle, 200,000 reindeer; roundwood (2002) 52,210,000 cu m; fish catch (2001) 165,835. Mining and quarrying (2002): chromite (concentrate) 340,000; zinc (metal content) 61,580; gold 4,666 kg. Manufacturing (value added in €'000,000; 2000): radio, television, and communications equipment 6,289; wood pulp, paper, and paper products 5,472; nonelectrical machinery and equipment 3,183; fabricated metals 1,827; food and beverages 1,784; chemicals and chemical products 1,623; printing and publishing 1,616. Energy production (consumption): electricity (kW-hr; 2001) 71,229,000,000 (81,188,000,000); coal (metric tons; 2000) none (5,131,000); crude petroleum (barrels; 2000) none (78,409,000); petroleum products (metric tons; 2000) 12,131,000 (9,305,000); natural gas (cu m; 2000) none (4,079,844,000).
Population economically active (2002): total 2,610,000; activity rate of total population 50.2% (participation rates: ages 15–64, 74.5%; female 47.9%; unemployed 9.1%).

Price and earnings indexes (2000 = 100)

	1998	1999	2000	2001	2002	2003	2004
Consumer price index	95.6	96.7	100.0	102.6	104.2	105.1	105.1[9]
Hourly earnings index	93.6	96.1	100.0	104.5	108.2	112.6	...

Household income and expenditure (2001). Average household size 2.2; disposable income per household €28,807 (U.S.$25,387); sources of gross income (2000): wages and salaries 55.4%, transfer payments 24.3%, other 20.3%; expenditure: housing and energy 28.7%, transportation and communications 18.0%, food, beverages, and tobacco 16.0%.

Gross national product (2003): U.S.$140,755,000,000 (U.S.$27,020 per capita).

Structure of gross domestic product and labour force

	2002			
	in value €'000,000	% of total value	labour force	% of labour force
Agriculture, fishing	1,803	1.3	106,000	4.0
Forestry	2,490	1.8	21,000	0.8
Mining	334	0.2	491,000	18.8
Manufacturing	29,189	20.9		
Public utilities	2,468	1.8	...	...
Construction	6,729	4.8	148,000	5.7
Transp. and commun.	13,185	9.4	169,000	6.5
Trade, restaurants	14,384	10.3	363,000	13.9
Finance, real estate	22,047	15.8	308,000	11.8
Pub. admin., defense	22,090	15.8	117,000	4.5
Services	4,349	3.1	642,000	24.6
Other	20,648[10]	14.8[10]	245,000[11]	9.4[11]
TOTAL	139,716	100.0	2,610,000	100.0

Public debt (2001): U.S.$52,850,000,000.
Tourism (in U.S.$'000,000; 2002): receipts 1,573; expenditures 2,002.
Land use as % of total land area (2000): in temporary crops 7.2%, in permanent crops 0.03%, in pasture 0.07%; overall forest area 72.0%.

Foreign trade[12]

Balance of trade (current prices)

	1998	1999	2000	2001	2002	2003
€'000,000	+9,713	+9,554	+12,647	+11,910	+11,634	+9,603
% of total	14.3%	13.9%	14.7%	14.3%	14.0%	11.5%

Imports (2001): €35,891,000,000 (electrical machinery and apparatus 18.2%; nonelectrical machinery and apparatus 13.8%; mineral fuels 11.6%; automobiles 7.0%). *Major import sources:* Germany 14.5%; Sweden 10.2%; Russia 9.5%; U.S. 6.8%; U.K. 6.4%; France 4.5%.
Exports (2001): €47,800,000,000 (electrical machinery and apparatus 24.3%; paper and paper products 18.8%; nonelectrical machinery and apparatus 11.6%; wood and wood products [excluding furniture] 5.1%). *Major export destinations:* Germany 12.3%; U.S. 9.7%; U.K. 9.6%; Sweden 8.4%; Russia 5.9%; France 4.6%.

Transport and communications

Transport. Railroads: route length (2002) 5,850 km; passenger-km 3,305,000,000; metric ton-km cargo 9,664,000,000. Roads (2002[3, 13]): total length 78,137 km (paved 64%). Vehicles (2002[3]): passenger cars 2,194,683; trucks and buses 319,699. Air transport (2003)[14]: passenger-km 12,971,000,000; metric ton-km cargo 314,500,000; airports (2001) 27.

Communications

Medium	date	unit	number	units per 1,000 persons
Daily newspapers	2000	circulation	2,360,000	456
Radio	2000	receivers	8,400,000	1,623
Television	2000	receivers	3,580,000	692
Telephones	2002	main lines	2,850,000	547
Cellular telephones	2002	subscribers	4,400,000	845
Personal computers	2002	units	2,300,000	442
Internet	2002	users	2,650,000	509

Education and health

Educational attainment (end of 2000). Percentage of population age 25 and over having: incomplete upper-secondary education 38.6%; complete upper secondary or vocational 34.5%; higher 26.9%. *Literacy:* virtually 100%.

Education (1999–2000)

	schools	teachers	students	student/ teacher ratio
Primary/lower secondary (age 7–15)	4,101	41,631[15]	591,272	...
Upper secondary (age 16–18)	456	6,693[15]	130,624	...
Voc. (incl. higher)	398	...	258,845	...
Higher[16]	20	7,252[15]	152,466	...

Health (2002): physicians 16,446 (1 per 316 persons); hospital beds 38,025 (1 per 137 persons); infant mortality rate per 1,000 live births 3.6.
Food (2001): daily per capita caloric intake 3,202 (vegetable products 64.3%, animal products 35.7%); 118% of FAO recommended minimum requirement.

Military

Total active duty personnel (2003): 27,000 (army 71.1%, navy 18.5%, air force 10.4%). *Military expenditure as percentage of GNP* (1999): 1.4% (world 2.4%); per capita expenditure U.S.$344.

[1]Finnish and Swedish are national (not official) languages. [2]The Finnish markka (Fmk) was the former monetary unit; on Jan. 1, 2002, Fmk 5.95 = €1. [3]January 1. [4]Has increased autonomy in relationship to Finland from 1993. [5]Detail does not add to total given because of rounding. [6]Total includes land area of 117,558 sq mi (304,473 sq km) and inland water area of 13,001 sq mi (33,672 sq km). [7]Based on land area only. [8]Within Helsinki urban agglomeration. [9]June. [10]Taxes less subsidies and imputed bank service charges. [11]Includes 237,000 unemployed persons not previously employed and 8,000 not adequately defined. [12]Imports c.i.f., exports f.o.b. [13]Excludes Åland Islands. [14]Finnair. [15]1998–99. [16]Universities only.

Internet resources for further information:
- **Embassy of Finland (Washington, D.C.) http://www.finland.org**
- **Statistics Finland http://www.stat.fi/index_en.html**

France

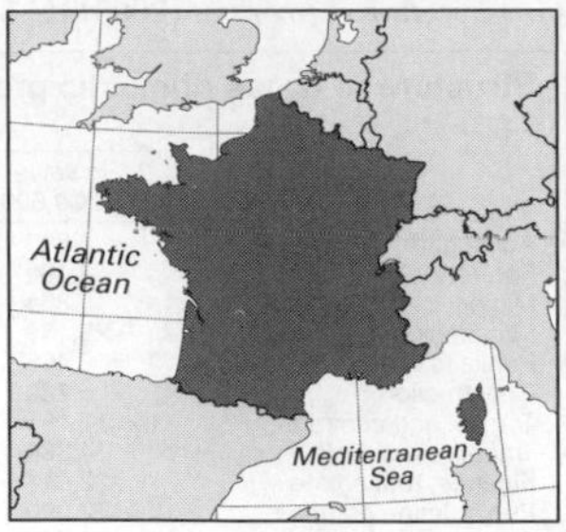

Official name: République Française (French Republic).
Form of government: republic with two legislative houses (Parliament; Senate [321], National Assembly [577]).
Chief of state: President.
Head of government: Prime Minister.
Capital: Paris.
Official language: French.
Official religion: none.
Monetary unit: 1 euro (€) = 100 cents; valuation (Sept. 1, 2004) 1 U.S.$ = €0.82; 1 £ = €1.48[1].

Area and population

Regions / Departments	Capitals	area sq mi	area sq km	population 2003 estimate[2]
Alsace	Strasbourg			1,775,390
Bas-Rhin	Strasbourg	1,836	4,755	1,052,698
Haut-Rhin	Colmar	1,361	3,525	722,692
Aquitaine	Bordeaux			2,988,395
Dordogne	Périgueux	3,498	9,060	392,291
Gironde	Bordeaux	3,861	10,000	1,330,683
Landes	Mont-de-Marsan	3,569	9,243	341,254
Lot-et-Garonne	Agen	2,070	5,361	309,993
Pyrénées-Atlantiques	Pau	2,952	7,645	614,174
Auvergne	Clermont-Ferrand			1,314,476
Allier	Moulins	2,834	7,340	342,307
Cantal	Aurillac	2,211	5,726	148,359
Haute-Loire	Le Puy-en-Velay	1,922	4,977	213,993
Puy-de-Dôme	Clermont-Ferrand	3,077	7,970	609,817
Basse-Normandie	Caen			1,436,134
Calvados	Caen	2,142	5,548	659,893
Manche	Saint-Lô	2,293	5,938	484,967
Orne	Alençon	2,356	6,103	291,274
Bourgogne (Burgundy)	Dijon			1,612,397
Côte-d'Or	Dijon	3,383	8,763	510,334
Nièvre	Nevers	2,632	6,817	222,298
Saône-et-Loire	Mâcon	3,311	8,575	543,848
Yonne	Auxerre	2,868	7,427	335,917
Bretagne (Brittany)	Rennes			2,977,932
Côtes-d'Armor	Saint-Brieuc	2,656	6,878	553,969
Finistère	Quimper	2,600	6,733	863,798
Ille-et-Vilaine	Rennes	2,616	6,775	894,625
Morbihan	Vannes	2,634	6,823	665,540
Centre	Orléans			2,466,617
Cher	Bourges	2,793	7,235	312,277
Eure-et-Loir	Chartres	2,270	5,880	412,094
Indre	Châteauroux	2,622	6,791	230,954
Indre-et-Loire	Tours	2,366	6,127	563,062
Loir-et-Cher	Blois	2,449	6,343	318,853
Loiret	Orléans	2,616	6,775	629,377
Champagne-Ardenne	Châlons su Marne			1,336,741
Ardennes	Charleville-Mézières	2,019	5,229	288,806
Aube	Troyes	2,318	6,004	293,925
Haute-Marne	Chaumont	2,398	6,211	190,983
Marne	Châlons-en-Champagne	3,151	8,162	563,027
Corse[2] (Corsica)	Ajaccio			265,999
Corse-du-Sud	Ajaccio	1,550	4,014	121,371
Haute-Corse	Bastia	1,802	4,666	144,628
Franche-Comté	Besançon			1,130,532
Doubs	Besançon	2,021	5,234	505,557
Haute-Saône	Vesoul	2,070	5,360	232,283
Jura	Lons-le-Saunier	1,930	4,999	253,309
Territoire de Belfort	Belfort	235	609	139,383
Haute-Normandie	Rouen			1,787,319
Eure	Évreux	2,332	6,040	550,056
Seine-Maritime	Rouen	2,424	6,278	1,237,263
Île-de-France	Paris			11,131,412
Essonne	Évry	696	1,804	1,153,434
Hauts-de-Seine	Nanterre	68	176	1,470,706
Paris	Paris	40	105	2,147,274
Seine-et-Marne	Melun	2,284	5,915	1,232,467
Seine-Saint-Denis	Bobigny	91	236	1,396,122
Val-de-Marne	Créteil	95	245	1,239,352
Val-d'Oise	Pontoise	481	1,246	1,121,614
Yvelines	Versailles	882	2,284	1,370,443
Languedoc-Roussillon	Montpellier			2,401,838[3]
Aude	Carcassonne	2,370	6,139	321,734
Gard	Nîmes	2,260	5,853	648,522
Hérault	Montpellier	2,356	6,101	945,901
Lozère	Mende	1,995	5,167	74,234
Pyrénées-Orientales	Perpignan	1,589	4,116	411,447
Limousin	Limoges			710,645
Corrèze	Tulle	2,261	5,857	234,144
Creuse	Guéret	2,149	5,565	122,713
Haute-Vienne	Limoges	2,131	5,520	353,788
Lorraine	Metz			2,319,109
Meurthe-et-Moselle	Nancy	2,024	5,241	718,250
Meuse	Bar-le-Duc	2,400	6,216	191,728
Moselle	Metz	2,400	6,216	1,027,854
Vosges	Épinal	2,268	5,874	381,277
Midi-Pyrénées	Toulouse			2,637,957
Ariège	Foix	1,888	4,890	139,612
Aveyron	Rodez	3,373	8,736	266,940
Gers	Auch	2,416	6,257	175,055
Haute-Garonne	Toulouse	2,436	6,309	1,102,919
Haute-Pyrénées	Tarbes	1,724	4,464	224,053
Lot	Cahors	2,014	5,217	164,413
Tarn	Albi	2,223	5,758	350,477
Tarn-et-Garonne	Montauban	1,435	3,718	214,488
Nord-Pas-de-Calais	Lille			4,013,107
Nord	Lille	2,217	5,742	2,561,800
Pas-de-Calais	Arras	2,576	6,671	1,451,307

Area and population (continued)

Regions / Departments	Capitals	area sq mi	area sq km	population 2003 estimate[2]
Pays de la Loire	Nantes			3,312,473
Loire-Atlantique	Nantes	2,631	6,815	1,174,120
Maine-et Loire	Angers	2,767	7,166	745,486
Mayenne	Laval	1,998	5,175	290,780
Sarthe	Le Mans	2,396	6,206	536,857
Vendée	La Roche-sur-Yon	2,595	6,720	565,230
Picardie (Picardy)	Amiens			1,869,386
Aisne	Laon	2,845	7,369	535,326
Oise	Beauvais	2,263	5,860	776,999
Somme	Amiens	2,382	6,170	557,061
Poitou-Charentes	Poitiers			1,668,337
Charente	Angoulême	2,300	5,956	341,275
Charente-Maritime	La Rochelle	2,650	6,864	576,855
Deux-Sèvres	Niort	2,316	5,999	347,652
Vienne	Poitiers	2,699	6,990	402,555
Provence-Alpes–Côte d'Azur	Marseille			4,665,051
Alpes-de-Haute-Provence	Digne	2,674	6,925	144,508
Alpes-Maritimes	Nice	1,660	4,299	1,045,973
Bouches-du-Rhône	Marseille	1,964	5,087	1,883,645
Hautes-Alpes	Gap	2,142	5,549	126,810
Var	Toulon	2,306	5,973	946,305
Vaucluse	Avignon	1,377	3,567	517,810
Rhône-Alpes	Lyon			5,813,733
Ain	Bourg-en-Bresse	2,225	5,762	539,006
Ardèche	Privas	2,135	5,529	294,933
Drôme	Valence	2,521	6,530	452,652
Haute-Savoie	Annecy	1,694	4,388	663,810
Isère	Grenoble	2,869	7,431	1,128,755
Loire	Saint-Étienne	1,846	4,781	726,613
Rhône	Lyon	1,254	3,249	1,621,718
Savoie	Chambéry	2,327	6,028	386,246
TOTAL		210,026	543,965	59,634,980

Demography

Population (2004): 60,044,000.
Density (2004): persons per sq mi 285.9, persons per sq km 110.4.
Urban-rural (2003): urban 76.3%; rural 23.7%.
Sex distribution (2003): male 48.77%; female 51.23%.
Age breakdown (2003): under 15, 18.6%; 15–29, 19.4%; 30–44, 21.6%; 45–59, 19.8%; 60–74, 12.8%; 75 and over, 7.8%.
Population projection: (2010) 61,499,000; (2020) 63,196,000.
Ethnic composition (2000): French 76.9%; Algerian and Moroccan Berber 2.2%; Italian 1.9%; Portuguese 1.5%; Moroccan Arab 1.5%; Fleming 1.4%; Algerian Arab 1.3%; Basque 1.3%; Jewish 1.2%; German 1.2%; Vietnamese 1.0%; Catalan 0.5%; other 8.1%.
Religious affiliation (2000): Roman Catholic 82.3%; Muslim 7.1%; atheist 4.4%; Protestant 3.7%; Orthodox 1.1%; Jewish 1.0%; other 0.4%.
Major cities (1999): Paris 2,125,246 (metropolitan area 9,644,507); Marseille 798,430 (1,349,772); Lyon 445,452 (1,348,832); Toulouse 390,350 (761,090); Nice 342,738 (888,784); Nantes 270,251 (544,932); Strasbourg 264,115 (427,245); Montpellier 225,392 (287,981); Bordeaux 215,363 (753,931); Rennes 206,229 (272,263); Le Havre 190,905 (248,547); Reims 187,206 (215,581); Lille 184,493 (1,000,900); Saint-Étienne 180,210 (291,960); Toulon 160,639 (519,640).
Mobility (1990). Population living in same residence as in 1982: 51.4%; same region 89.0%; different region 8.8%; different country 2.2%.
Households (1999). Average household size 2.4; 1 person 31.0%, 2 persons 31.1%, 3 persons 16.2%, 4 persons 13.8%, 5 persons or more 7.9%. Family households (1999): 15,942,369 (67.0%); nonfamily 7,865,703 (33.0%).
Immigration (2000): immigrants admitted 53,879 (from Africa 56.0%, of which Algerian 16.9%; from Europe 23.1%; from Asia 12.4%).

Vital statistics

Birth rate per 1,000 population (2003): 12.5 (world avg. 21.3); (2002) legitimate 54.8%; illegitimate 45.2%.
Death rate per 1,000 population (2003): 9.1 (world avg. 9.1).
Natural increase rate per 1,000 population (2003): 3.4 (world avg. 12.2).
Total fertility rate (avg. births per childbearing woman; 2003): 1.9.
Marriage rate per 1,000 population (2002): 4.7.
Divorce rate per 1,000 population (2002): 2.2.
Life expectancy at birth (2003): male 75.6 years; female 83.1 years.
Major causes of death per 100,000 population (1999): diseases of the circulatory system 281.3; malignant neoplasms (cancers) 253.5; diseases of the respiratory system 74.8; accidents and violence 74.7; diseases of the digestive system 43.5; endocrine, metabolic, and nutritional disorders 29.4.

Social indicators

Educational attainment (2001). Percentage of population age 25–64 with at least upper secondary education 63.2%.
Quality of working life. Average workweek (2001): 38.4 hours. Annual rate per 100,000 workers for (1999): injury or accident 4,432 (deaths 0.1%); accidents in transit to work (1994) 708 (deaths 68.3). Average days lost to labour stoppages per 1,000 workers (1994): 21.0. Trade union membership (2003): 1,900,000 (*c.* 8% of labour force).
Access to services (1992). Proportion of dwellings having: central heating 86.0%; piped water 97.0%; indoor plumbing 95.8%.
Social participation. Eligible voters participating in last (June 2002) national election: 64.4%. Population over 15 years of age participating in voluntary associations (1997): 28.0%.
Social deviance. Offense rate per 100,000 population (1998) for: murder 1.6, rape 13.4, other assault 583.8; theft (including burglary and housebreaking) 6,107.6. Incidence per 100,000 in general population of: homicide (2000) 0.9; suicide (2000) 16.8.
Material well-being (2002). Households possessing: automobile 79%; colour television 94%; VCR (2001) 70%; microcomputer 37%; washing machine 91%; microwave 68%; dishwasher (2001) 39%.

National economy

Gross national product (2003): U.S.$1,523,025,000,000 (U.S.$24,770 per capita).

Structure of gross domestic product and labour force

	2001			
	in value €'000,000	% of total value	labour force[4]	% of labour force[4]
Agriculture	37,781	2.6	348,200	1.6
Mining	...	...	49,500	0.2
Manufacturing	235,769	16.1	3,919,800	17.6
Construction	63,322	4.3	1,256,000	5.6
Public utilities	35,995	2.5	210,100	0.9
Transp. and commun.	56,795	3.9	1,563,100	7.0
Trade, hotels	138,081	9.4	3,659,300	16.4
Finance, real estate	225,463	15.4	3,542,600	15.9
Pub. admin., defense	116,780	8.0	2,353,700	10.6
Services	440,738	30.1	4,955,400	22.2
Other	112,998[5]	7.7[5]	441,700[6]	2.0[6]
TOTAL	1,463,722	100.0	22,302,800[7]	100.0

Budget (2001). Revenue: €244,846,800,000 (value-added taxes 55.7%, personal income tax 21.8%, corporate income tax 20.1%). Expenditures: €268,669,600,000 (current expenditure 89.9%, of which public debt 14.9%, pensions 11.3%, social services 11.3%; development expenditure 10.1%).
Public debt (2001): U.S.$756,080,000,000.

Manufacturing enterprises (1995)

	no. of enterprises[8]	no. of employees	annual salaries as a % of avg. of all salaries[8]	annual value added (F '000,000)
Food products	55,197	545,900	87	208,065
Transport equipment	4,293	508,700	108	167,357
Electrical machinery	15,620	433,600	118	156,221
Iron and steel	27,847	403,800	96	131,376
Mechanical equipment	32,134	390,300	104	127,637
Petroleum refineries	180	46,200	174	117,041
Printing, publishing	30,359	231,900	125	83,083
Textiles and wearing apparel	29,701	281,500	78	63,633
Rubber products	5,875	204,200	94	57,758
Chemical products	1,442	102,100	128	51,146
Paper and paper products	1,916	101,500	102	38,585
Metal products	442	43,700	103	28,115
Glass products	1,536	52,400	104	16,638
Footwear	4,236	55,400	75	12,970

Production (metric tons except as noted). Agriculture, forestry, fishing (2003): corn (maize) 59,170,000, wheat 30,582,000, sugar beets 29,238,000, barley 9,818,000, potatoes 6,235,000, grapes 6,178,000, rapeseed 3,341,000, apples 2,402,000, dry peas 1,617,000, sunflower seeds 1,494,000, triticale 1,291,000, tomatoes 834,000, carrots 682,000, oats 555,000, lettuce 426,000, green peas 396,000, dry onions 393,000, cauliflower 390,000, string beans 373,000; livestock (number of live animals) 19,517,000 cattle, 15,058,000 pigs, 9,204,000 sheep, 220,000,000 chickens; roundwood 36,850,000 cu m; fish catch 877,995. Mining and quarrying (2001): gypsum 4,500,000; kaolin 375,000; potash 257,000; gold 80,700 troy oz. Manufacturing (value added in U.S.$'000,000; 2000[9]): motor vehicles, trailers, and motor vehicle parts 17,157; pharmaceuticals, soaps, and paints 16,360; fabricated metal products 12,996; general purpose machinery 7,064; basic chemicals 6,378; aircraft and spacecraft 6,045; plastic products 6,014; publishing 5,184; medical, measuring, and testing appliances 4,765; telecommunications equipment 4,615.

Financial aggregates

	1998	1999	2000	2001	2002	2003
Exchange rate, F per:[10]						
U.S. dollar	5.62	1.00	1.07	1.13	0.95	0.79
£	9.35	1.62	1.60	1.65	1.43	1.41
SDR	7.92	1.37	1.40	1.43	1.30	1.18
International reserves (U.S.$)						
Total (excl. gold; '000,000)	44,312	39,701	37,039	31,749	28,365	30,186
SDRs ('000,000)	1,107	347	402	492	622	761
Reserve pos. in IMF ('000,000)	4,452	5,241	4,522	4,894	5,778	6,303
Foreign exchange	38,753	33,933	32,114	26,363	21,965	23,122
Gold ('000,000 fine troy oz)	102.37	97.24	97.25	97.25	97.25	97.25
% world reserves	10.6	10.1	10.2	10.3	10.5	10.7
Interest and prices						
Central bank discount (%)	...	...	...	...	...	...
Govt. bond yield (%)	4.72	4.69	5.45	5.05	4.93	4.18
Industrial share prices (2000 = 100)	59.8	74.0	100.0	80.1	60.4	...
Balance of payments (U.S.$'000,000)						
Balance of visible trade	+24,940	+17,990	–3,620	+2,840	+6,920	+1,040
Imports, f.o.b.	278,080	282,060	301,820	291,780	300,740	360,830
Exports, f.o.b.	303,020	300,050	298,200	294,620	307,660	361,870
Balance of invisibles	+12,760	+13,880	+22,200	+25,920	+6,870	+3,340
Balance of payments, current account	+37,700	+31,870	+18,580	+28,760	+13,790	+4,380

Retail trade enterprises (1995[2])

	no. of enterprises	no. of employees	weekly wages as a % of all wages	annual turnover (F '000,000)
Large food stores	4,373	385,402	...	617,222
Clothing stores	51,873	195,535	...	126,504
Pharmacies	22,301	126,508	...	121,980
Small food stores	64,565	163,474	...	110,928
butcher shops	21,548	59,962	...	36,732
Furniture stores	7,179	53,080	...	54,390
Electrical and electronics stores	10,990	55,560	...	43,995
Department stores	736	35,074	...	27,741
Publishing and paper	15,083	40,375	...	24,591
Gas, coal, and other energy products	6,042	25,375	...	19,204

Energy production (consumption)[11]: electricity (kW-hr; 2001) 520,000,000,000 ([2000] 477,288,000,000); hard coal (metric tons; 2001) 2,400,000[12] ([2000] 21,090,000); lignite (metric tons; 2000) 296,000 (335,000); crude petroleum (barrels; 2001) 11,027,000 ([1999] 608,200,000); petroleum products (metric tons; 2000) 76,665,000 (71,631,000); natural gas (cu m; 2001) 1,982,000,000 ([2000] 43,555,000,000).
Population economically active (2001): total 27,812,600; activity rate of total population 47.0% (participation rates: ages 15–64 [1994] 67.6%; female [2001] 47.9%; unemployed 12.1%).

Price and earnings indexes (2000 = 100)

	1997	1998	1999	2000	2001	2002	2003
Consumer price index	97.2	97.8	98.3	100.0	101.6	103.6	105.8
Earnings index	91.0	93.6	95.7	100.0	104.5	108.4	112.8

Household income and expenditure. Average household size (1999) 2.5; average disposable income per household (2001) €26,570 (U.S.$23,776); sources of income (1995): wages and salaries 70.0%, self-employment 24.4%, social security 5.6%; expenditure (2001): housing and energy 23.4%, transportation 15.2%, food and nonalcoholic beverages 14.4%, recreation 8.9%, restaurants and hotels 7.6%.
Tourism (in U.S.$'000,000; 2002): receipts U.S.$32,329; expenditures U.S.$19,460.
Land use as % of total land area (2000): in temporary crops 33.5%, in permanent crops 2.1%, in pasture 18.4%; overall forest area 27.9%.

Foreign trade[13]

Balance of trade (current prices)

	1998	1999	2000	2001	2002	2003
U.S.$'000,000,000	+14.6	+9.4	–8.7	–4.3	+1.1	–3.9
% of total	2.5%	1.7%	1.4%	0.7%	0.2%	0.5%

Imports (2002)[14]: U.S.$303,800,000,000 (machinery and apparatus 24.2%; transport equipment 13.5%; chemicals and chemical products 12.9%; petroleum [all forms] 9.2%; food 7.0%). *Major import sources:* Germany 17.2%; Italy 9.0%; U.S. 8.0%; U.K. 7.3%; Spain 7.2%; Belgium 6.6%; The Netherlands 4.7%; China 3.5%; Japan 3.2%; Switzerland 2.2%; Ireland 2.0%.
Exports (2002)[14]: U.S.$304,900,000,000 (machinery and apparatus 23.2%; transport equipment 20.5%, of which road vehicles 14.0%, aircraft and spacecraft 5.6%; chemicals and chemical products 14.9%, of which pharmaceuticals 4.9%; food 7.9%; iron and steel 3.2%; perfumes, cosmetics, and toiletries 2.9%). *Major export destinations:* Germany 14.5%; U.K. 10.3%; Spain 9.7%; Italy 9.1%; U.S. 8.1%; Belgium 7.2%; The Netherlands 4.0%; Switzerland 3.2%; Japan 1.7%; Portugal 1.5%.

Transport and communications

Transport. Railroads (2002): route length 32,008 km; (2000) passenger-km 69,870,000,000; metric ton-km cargo 55,370,000,000. Roads (1999[2]): total length 893,300 km (paved 100%). Vehicles (2000): passenger cars 28,060,000; trucks and buses 5,673,000. Air transport (2003)[15]: passenger-km 99,122,000,000; metric ton-km cargo 4,875,000,000; airports (1996) 61.

Communications

Medium	date	unit	number	units per 1,000 persons
Daily newspapers	2000	circulation	11,800,000	201
Radio	2000	receivers	55,900,000	950
Television	2000	receivers	37,000,000	628
Telephones	2003	main lines	33,905,400	566
Cellular telephones	2003	subscribers	41,683,100	696
Personal computers	2002	units	20,700,000	347
Internet	2003	users	21,900,000	366

Education and health

Education (2000–01)

	schools	teachers	students	student/ teacher ratio
Primary (age 6–10)	39,131[16]	211,192	3,839,770	18.2
Secondary (age 11–18) } Voc., teacher tr. }	11,052[16]	483,493	5,399,433	11.2
Higher[17]	...	46,196	1,400,393	30.3

Health: physicians (2002) 199,000 (1 per 301 persons); hospital beds (2001) 477,000 (1 per 126 persons); infant mortality rate (2003) 4.4.
Food (2001): daily per capita caloric intake 3,629 (vegetable products 63%, animal products 37%); 129% of FAO recommended minimum requirement.

Military

Total active duty personnel (2003): 259,050 (army 52.9%, navy 17.1%, air force 24.7%, unallocated 5.3%). *Military expenditure as percentage of GNP* (1999): 2.7% (world 2.4%); per capita expenditure U.S.$658.

[1]The French franc was the former monetary unit; on Jan. 1, 2002, F 6.56 = €1. [2]January 1. [3]Experienced evolving autonomy from central government between 2001 and 2004. [4]Paid employees only; excludes 2,140,300 non-salaried workers and 3,369,500 unemployed. [5]Includes value-added tax and import duties less subsidies and imputed bank service charges. [6]Private households with employed persons. [7]Detail does not add to total given because of rounding. [8]1991. [9]Data unavailable for production of food, beverages, and tobacco products. [10]Beginning in 1999 exchange rates expressed in euros. [11]Consumption data includes Monaco. [12]Last coal-producing mine closed in April 2004. [13]Imports c.i.f.; exports f.o.b. [14]Includes Monaco. [15]Air France only. [16]1996–97. [17]Universities only.

Internet resources for further information:
- **INSEE http://www.insee.fr/fr/home/home_page.asp**
- **La France en Faits en Chiffres http://www.insee.fr/fr/ffc/accueil_ffc.asp**

French Guiana

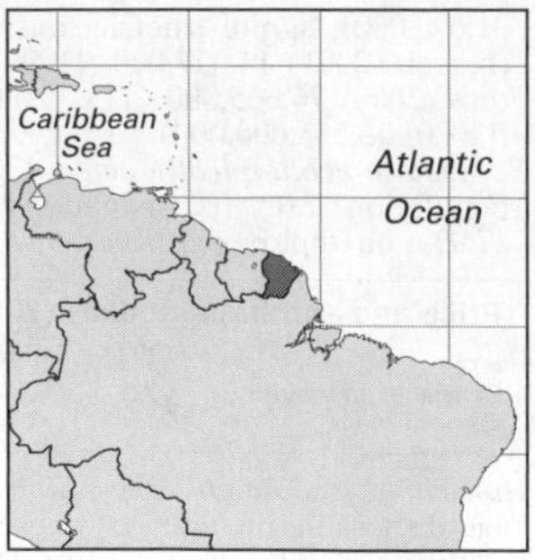

Official name: Département de la Guyane française (Department of French Guiana).
Political status: overseas department of France with two legislative houses (General Council [19]; Regional Council [31]).
Chief of state: President of France.
Heads of government: Prefect (for France); President of the General Council (for French Guiana); President of the Regional Council (for French Guiana).
Capital: Cayenne.
Official language: French.
Official religion: none.
Monetary unit: 1 euro (€) = 100 cents; valuation (Sept. 1, 2004) 1 U.S.$ = €0.82; 1 £ = €1.48[1].

Area and population

Arrondissements	Capitals	area sq mi	area sq km	population 1999 census
Cayenne	Cayenne	17,727	45,913	119,660
Saint-Laurent-du-Maroni	Saint-Laurent-du-Maroni	14,526	37,621	37,553
TOTAL		32,253	83,534	157,213

Demography

Population (2004): 182,000.
Density (2004): persons per sq mi 5.6, persons per sq km 2.2.
Urban-rural (2003): urban 75.4%; rural 24.6%.
Sex distribution (1999): male 50.36%; female 49.64%.
Age breakdown (1999): under 15, 34.0%; 15–29, 24.2%; 30–44, 23.3%; 45–59, 12.5%; 60–74, 4.3%; 75 and over, 1.7%.
Population projection: (2010) 208,000; (2020) 252,000.
Doubling time: 42 years.
Ethnic composition (2000): Guianese Mulatto 37.9%; French 8.0%; Haitian 8.0%; Surinamese 6.0%; Antillean 5.0%; Chinese 5.0%; Brazilian 4.9%; East Indian 4.0%; other (other West Indian, Hmong, other South American) 21.2%.
Religious affiliation (2000): Christian 84.6%, of which Roman Catholic 80.0%, Protestant 3.9%; Chinese folk-religionist 3.6%; Spiritist 3.5%; nonreligious/atheist 3.0%; traditional beliefs 1.9%; Hindu 1.6%; Muslim 0.9%; other 0.9%.
Major cities (1999)[2]: Cayenne 50,594 (urban agglomeration 84,181); Saint-Laurent-du-Maroni 19,211; Kourou 19,107; Matoury 18,032[3]; Rémire-Montjoly 15,555[3].

Vital statistics

Birth rate per 1,000 population (2003): 21.3 (world avg. 21.3); (2000) legitimate 17.6%; illegitimate 82.4%.
Death rate per 1,000 population (2003): 4.8 (world avg. 9.1).
Natural increase rate per 1,000 population (2003): 16.5 (world avg. 12.2).
Total fertility rate (avg. births per childbearing woman; 2003): 3.1.
Marriage rate per 1,000 population (1999): 3.5.
Divorce rate per 1,000 population (1998): 1.0.
Life expectancy at birth (2003): male 73.4 years; female 80.2 years.
Major causes of death per 100,000 population (1999): diseases of the circulatory system *c.* 100; violence and accidents *c.* 71; malignant neoplasms (cancers) *c.* 54[4]; infectious and parasitic diseases *c.* 33, of which HIV/AIDS *c.* 16; diseases of the digestive system *c.* 16; endocrine and metabolic disorders *c.* 16.

National economy

Budget (2000). Revenue: €141,000,000 (direct taxes 32.6%, indirect taxes 29.8%, revenue from French central government 17.7%, development receipts 15.6%). Expenditures: €141,000,000 (current expenditures 83.0%, capital expenditures 17.0%).
Production (metric tons except as noted). Agriculture, forestry, fishing (2002): rice 19,900, cassava 10,375, cabbages 6,350, bananas 4,495, taro 4,095, tomatoes 3,770; livestock (number of live animals) 10,500 pigs, 9,200 cattle; roundwood (2001) 139,000 cu m; fish catch (2001) 5,231. Mining and quarrying (2001): stone, sand, and gravel 1,500; gold 127,671 troy oz. Manufacturing (2001): pork 1,245; chicken meat 560; finished wood products 3,172 cu m[5]; rum (2000) 3,072 hectolitres; other products include leather goods, clothing, rosewood essence, yogurt, and beer. Number of satellites launched from the Kourou Space Centre (2002): 12[6]. Energy production (consumption): electricity (kW-hr; 2000) 455,000,000 (455,000,000); coal, none (none); crude petroleum, none (none); petroleum products (metric tons; 2000) none (292,000); natural gas, none (none).
Household income and expenditure. Average household size (1999) 3.3; income per household (1997) €31,203 (U.S.$33,244); sources of income (1997): wages and salaries and self-employed 72.9%, transfer payments 20.2%; expenditure (1994)[7]: food and beverages 28.7%, housing 11.7%, energy 9.0%, clothing and footwear 6.4%, health 2.7%, other 41.5%.
Land use as % of total land area (2000): in temporary crops 0.14%, in permanent crops 0.05%, in pasture 0.08%; overall forest area 89.9%.
Gross national product (2000): U.S.$2,360,000,000 (U.S.$14,370 per capita).

Structure of gross domestic product and labour force

	2000 in value €'000,000	2000 % of total value	2002 labour force[8]	2002 % of labour force[8]
Agriculture, forestry, fishing	81	5.1	1,024	2.1
Mining	30	1.9	409	0.8
Manufacturing	158	9.9	1,053	2.1
Construction	147	9.2	2,583	5.2
Public utilities	22	1.4	644	1.3
Finance, real estate[9]	379	23.8	830	1.7
Transp. and commun.	–165	–10.4	2,134	4.3
Trade, restaurants, hotels	245	15.4	4,815	9.8
Pub. admin., defense	256	16.1	9,758	19.8
Services	439	27.6	14,975	30.4
Other	—	—	11,095	22.5
TOTAL	1,592	100.0	49,320	100.0

Population economically active (1999): total 62,634; activity rate of total population 39.4% (participation rates: age 15 and over 60.5%; female 43.8%; unemployed [March 2003] 22.8%).

Price and earnings indexes (2000 = 100)

	1997	1998	1999	2000	2001	2002	2003
Consumer price index	97.9	98.4	98.6	100.0	101.6	103.1	...
Monthly earnings index[10, 11]	...	...	99.4	100.0	101.6	102.6	102.6

Tourism (2002): receipts U.S.$45,000,000; expenditures, n.a.

Foreign trade

Balance of trade (current prices)

	1997	1998	1999	2000	2001	2002
€'000,000	–384	–437	–421	–499	–515	–514
% of total	64.4%	70.8%	68.2%	67.3%	66.3%	66.6%

Imports (2002): €643,000,000 (food products 21.8%, road vehicles 12.8%, refined petroleum 9.0%, nonelectrical machinery 8.6%). *Major import sources:* France 51.5%; Trinidad and Tobago 8.7%; The Netherlands 2.5%; Germany 2.5%; Japan 2.5%.
Exports (2002): €129,000,000 (nonferrous metals [nearly all gold] 70.5%, food products [mostly fish, shrimp, and rice] 12.5%, parts for air and space vehicles 3.1%). *Major export destinations:* France 62.8%; Belgium 10.1%; Switzerland 9.3%; Brazil 3.9%; Guadeloupe 3.1%.

Transport and communications

Transport. Railroads: none. Roads (1996): total length 774 mi, 1,245 km (paved, n.a.). Vehicles (1999): passenger cars 32,900; trucks and buses 11,900. Air transport (2002): passenger arrivals 186,920; passenger departures 192,764; cargo unloaded 4,569 metric tons, cargo loaded 2,119 metric tons; airports (2001) with scheduled flights 1.

Communications

Medium	date	unit	number	units per 1,000 persons
Daily newspapers	1996	circulation	2,000	14
Radio	1997	receivers	104,000	702
Television	1998	receivers	37,000	202
Telephones	1999	main lines	49,000	308
Cellular telephones	2002	subscribers	138,200	781
Personal computers	1999	units	23,000	145
Internet	2001	users	3,200	17

Education and health

Educational attainment (1990). Percentage of population age 25 and over having: incomplete primary education or no declaration 61.7%; completed primary 5.3%; some secondary 15.9%; completed secondary 8.2%; some higher 4.9%; completed higher 4.0%. *Literacy:* n.a.

Education (2000–01)

	schools	teachers	students	student/ teacher ratio
Primary (age 6–11)	86	1,718	20,826	12.1
Secondary (age 12–18)	35	1,385	20,585	14.9
Higher[12]	1	...	666	...

Health (2000): physicians 219 (1 per 737 persons); hospital beds 750 (1 per 215 persons); infant mortality rate per 1,000 live births (2003) 12.8.
Food (1992): daily per capita caloric intake 2,900 (vegetable products 70%, animal products 30%); 128% of FAO recommended minimum requirement.

Military

Total active duty personnel (2003): French troops 3,100.

[1]The French franc (F) was replaced by the euro (on Jan. 1, 2002, F 6.56 = €1). [2]Commune population. [3]Within Cayenne urban agglomeration. [4]Excludes breast and lung neoplasms (cancers). [5]1996. [6]In 1991 the European Space Agency accounted for 28.7% of GDP, 28.2% of employed labour force, and 70.9% of imports. [7]Weights of consumer price index components. [8]Employed only. [9]Includes insurance. [10]Index based on end-of-year figures. [11]Based on minimum-level wage in public administration. [12]Université des Antilles et de la Guyane, Cayenne campus.

Internet resources for further information:
- **Chambre de Commerce et l'Industrie: Guyane http://www.guyane.cci.fr**

French Polynesia

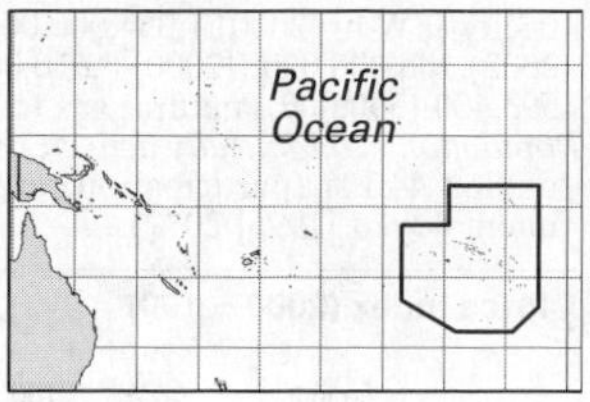

Official name: Polynésie française (French); Polynesia Farani (Tahitian) (French Polynesia).
Political status: overseas country[1] (France) with one legislative house (Assembly [57]).
Chief of state: President of France represented by High Commissioner.
Head of government: President.
Capital: Papeete.
Official languages: French; Tahitian.
Official religion: none.
Monetary unit: 1 Franc de la Comptoirs française du pacifique (CFPF) = 100 centimes; valuation (Sept. 1, 2004)[2] 1 U.S.$ = CFPF 98.12; 1 £ = CFPF 176.52.

Area and population

Administrative subdivisions	Capitals	area sq mi	area sq km	population 2002 census
Austral (Tubuai) Islands	Mataura	57	148	6,386
Leeward Islands	Uturoa	156	404	30,221
Marquesas Archipelago	Taiohae	405	1,049	8,712
Tuamotu-Gambier Islands	Papeete	280	726	15,973
Windward Islands	Papeete	461	1,194	184,224
TOTAL		1,544[3]	4,000[3]	245,516

Demography

Population (2004): 252,000.
Density (2004)[4]: persons per sq mi 185.4, persons per sq km 71.6.
Urban-rural (2002): urban 52.1%; rural 47.9%.
Sex distribution (2002): male 51.39%; female 48.61%.
Age breakdown (2002): under 15, 29.9%; 15–29, 26.0%; 30–44, 23.5%; 45–59, 13.3%; 60–74, 5.9%; 75 and over, 1.4%.
Population projection: (2010) 275,000; (2020) 308,000.
Doubling time: 47 years.
Ethnic composition (1996): Polynesian and part-Polynesian 82.8%; European (mostly French) 11.9%; Asian (mostly Chinese) 4.7%; other 0.6%.
Religious affiliation (1995): Protestant 50.2%, of which Evangelical Church of French Polynesia (Presbyterian) 46.1%; Roman Catholic 39.5%; other Christian 9.9%, of which Mormon 5.9%; other 0.4%.
Major communes (2002): Faaa 28,339[5]; Papeete 26,181 (urban agglomeration [2002] 124,864); Punaauia 23,706[5]; Moorea-Maiao 14,550; Pirae 14,499[5].

Vital statistics

Birth rate per 1,000 population (2002): 19.6 (world avg. 21.3); (1996) legitimate 35.4%; illegitimate 64.6%.
Death rate per 1,000 population (2002): 4.5 (world avg. 9.1).
Natural increase rate per 1,000 population (2002): 15.1 (world avg. 12.2).
Total fertility rate (avg. births per childbearing woman; 2003): 2.1.
Marriage rate per 1,000 population (2000): 4.6.
Life expectancy at birth (2003): male 73.1 years; female 77.9 years.
Major causes of death per 100,000 population (2002): diseases of the circulatory system 113; malignant neoplasms (cancers) 102; accidents, suicide, and violence 54; respiratory diseases 46; diseases of the digestive system 13.

National economy

Budget (2001). Revenue: CFPF 108,036,000,000 (indirect taxes 55.1%, direct taxes and nontax revenue 44.9%). Expenditures: CFPF 140,709,000,000 (current expenditure 68.1%, capital expenditure 31.9%).
Public debt (external, outstanding; 1999): U.S.$542,000,000.
Production (metric tons except as noted). Agriculture, forestry, fishing (2002): coconuts 88,000, copra 9,416, cassava 6,000, roots and tubers 5,500, pineapples 3,500, sugarcane 3,200, tomatoes 1,100, watermelon 1,000, cucumbers 1,000, bananas 500; livestock (number of live animals) 34,000 pigs, 16,500 goats, 10,800 cattle; roundwood, n.a.; fish catch (2001) 15,470; export production of black pearls (1998) 6,050 kg. Mining and quarrying: estimated annual production of phosphates ranges from 1,000,000 to 1,200,000 tons. Manufacturing (1999): coconut oil 6,386; other manufactures include *monoï* oil (primarily refined coconut and sandalwood oils), beer, printed cloth, and sandals. Energy production (consumption): electricity (kW-hr; 2001) 495,000,000 (495,000,000); coal, none (none); crude petroleum, none (none); petroleum products (metric tons; 2000) none (177,000); natural gas, none (none).
Population economically active (1996): total 87,121; activity rate of total population 39.7% (participation rates: ages 14 and over, 68.3%; female 38.7%; unemployed 13.2%).

Price and earnings indexes (2000 = 100)

	1997	1998	1999	2000	2001	2002	2003
Consumer price index	96.9	98.2	99.0	100.0	101.0	103.9	104.3
Earnings index[6]	90.4	93.1	97.0	100.0	102.0	105.2	106.0

Tourism (1999): receipts from visitors U.S.$394,000,000; expenditures by nationals abroad, n.a.
Gross national product (at current market prices; 2001): U.S.$4,100,000,000 (U.S.$17,290 per capita).

Structure of gross domestic product and labour force

	1997 in value CFPF '000,000	1997 % of total value	1996 labour force	1996 % of labour force
Agriculture, fishing	15,534	4.1	10,888	12.5
Manufacturing[7]	26,360	7.0	6,424	7.4
Construction	20,104	5.3	4,777	5.5
Public utilities[7]	12,221	3.2	459	0.5
Transp. and commun.	27,832	7.4	3,788	4.4
Trade	81,054	21.0	9,357	10.7
Finance, real estate[8]	...	...	1,865	2.1
Pub. admin., defense	97,238	25.7	13,475	15.5
Services[8]	97,360	25.7	23,514	27.0
Other	—	...	12,574[9]	14.4[9]
TOTAL	378,503	100.0	87,121	100.0

Household income and expenditure (1986). Average household size (1996) 4.3; average annual income per household CFPF 2,153,112 (U.S.$17,831); sources of income (1993): salaries 61.9%, self-employment 21.5%, transfer payments 16.6%; expenditure: food and beverages 32.1%, household furnishings 12.3%, transportation 12.2%, energy 8.1%, recreation and education 6.9%, clothing 6.3%.
Land use as % of total land area (2000): in temporary crops 0.8%, in permanent crops 5.5%, in pasture 5.5%; overall forest area 28.7%.

Foreign trade[10]

Balance of trade (current prices)

	1997	1998	1999	2000	2001	2002[11]
CFPF '000,000	–82,819	–82,685	–78,463	–97,343	–116,892	–110,297
% of total	71.5%	61.0%	64.8%	67.5%	75.8%	80.7%

Imports (2001): CFPF 135,569,000,000 (machinery and apparatus 19.7%; consumer goods 16.0%; mineral fuels 8.5%). *Major import sources* (2000): France 35.9%; U.S. 13.9%; Australia 9.3%; New Zealand 7.4%; Germany 4.8%.
Exports (2001): CFPF 18,677,000,000 (pearl products 80.0%, of which black cultured pearls 76.1%; fish 7.3%; *nono* fruit 4.6%; coconut oil 1.6%; *monoï* oil 0.8%). *Major export destinations* (2000): Japan 36.9%; Hong Kong 20.9%; France 14.5%; U.S. 12.1%; New Caledonia 5.0%.

Transport and communications

Transport. Railroads: none. Roads (1996): total length 549 mi, 884 km (paved 44%). Motor vehicles: passenger cars (1996) 47,300; trucks and buses (1993) 15,300. Air transport (2001): passengers carried 1,453,513; freight handled 9,834 metric tons; airports (1994) with scheduled flights 17.

Communications

Medium	date	unit	number	units per 1,000 persons
Daily newspapers	1996	circulation	24,000	110
Radio	1997	receivers	128,000	574
Television	2000	receivers	44,500	189
Telephones	2002	main lines	52,000	219
Cellular telephones	2002	subscribers	90,000	375
Personal computers	2002	units	70,000	292
Internet	2002	users	35,000	146

Education and health

Educational attainment (1996). Percentage of population age 15 and over having: no formal schooling 4.9%; primary education 37.4%; secondary 49.0%; higher 8.7%. *Literacy* (2000): total population age 15 and over literate, almost 100%.

Education (1998–99)

	schools	teachers	students	student/teacher ratio
Primary (age 6–10)[12]	255	2,751	...	...
Secondary (age 11–17) / Vocational	82	2,059	30,473	14.8
Higher[13]	1	54	1,600	29.6

Health (2002): physicians 429 (1 per 568 persons); hospital beds (2003) 971 (1 per 256 persons); infant mortality rate per 1,000 live births 9.0.
Food (2001): daily per capita caloric intake 2,889 (vegetable products 72%, animal products 28%); 127% of FAO recommended minimum.

Military

Total active duty personnel (2003): 2,400 French military personnel. *Military expenditure as percentage of GNP:* n.a.

[1]Status change to "overseas country" in effect from Feb. 27, 2004. [2]Pegged to the euro on Jan. 1, 2002, at the rate of €1 = CFPF 119.25. [3]Approximate total area including inland water; total land area is 1,359 sq mi (3,521 sq km). [4]Based on land area. [5]Part of Papeete urban agglomeration. [6]Guaranteed minimum wage. [7]The manufacture of energy-generating products is included in Public utilities. [8]Services includes Finance, real estate. [9]Includes not adequately defined and unemployed. [10]Imports c.i.f.; exports f.o.b. [11]First nine months only. [12]Includes preprimary. [13]University of French Polynesia only; 2000–01.

Internet resources for further information:
- **Institut de la Statistique de la Polynésie Francaise http://www.ispf.pf**

Gabon

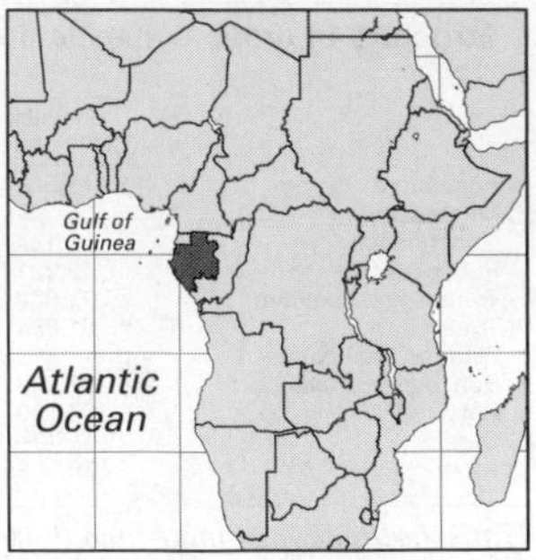

Official name: République Gabonaise (Gabonese Republic).
Form of government: unitary multiparty republic with a Parliament comprising two legislative houses (Senate [91]; National Assembly [120]).
Chief of state: President.
Head of government: Prime Minister.
Capital: Libreville.
Official language: French.
Official religion: none.
Monetary unit: 1 CFA franc (CFAF) = 100 centimes; valuation (Sept. 1, 2004) 1 U.S.$ = CFAF 539.75; 1 £ = CFAF 970.98[1].

Area and population

		area		population
Provinces	Capitals	sq mi	sq km	2002 estimate
Estuaire	Libreville	8,008	20,740	597,200
Haut-Ogooué	Franceville	14,111	36,547	134,500
Moyen-Ogooué	Lambaréné	7,156	18,535	54,600
Ngounié	Mouila	14,575	37,750	100,300
Nyanga	Tchibanga	8,218	21,285	50,800
Ogooué-Ivindo	Makokou	17,790	46,075	63,000
Ogooué-Lolo	Koulamoutou	9,799	25,380	56,600
Ogooué-Maritime	Port-Gentil	8,838	22,890	126,200
Woleu-Ntem	Oyem	14,851	38,465	125,400
TOTAL		103,347[2]	267,667	1,308,600

Demography

Population (2004): 1,351,000.
Density (2004): persons per sq mi 13.1, persons per sq km 5.0.
Urban-rural (2003): urban 83.8%; rural 16.2%.
Sex distribution (2003): male 49.59%; female 50.41%.
Age breakdown (2003): under 15, 42.3%; 15–29, 26.3%; 30–44, 16.6%; 45–59, 8.7%; 60–74, 4.8%; 75 and over, 1.3%.
Population projection: (2010) 1,509,000; (2020) 1,781,000.
Doubling time: 28 years.
Ethnic composition (2000): Fang 28.6%; Punu 10.2%; Nzebi 8.9%; French 6.7%; Mpongwe 4.1%.
Religious affiliation (2000): Christian 90.6%, of which Roman Catholic 56.6%, Protestant 17.7%; Muslim 3.1%; traditional beliefs 1.7%.
Major cities (2003): Libreville 420,000; Port-Gentil 88,000; Franceville (1993) 30,246; Oyem 23,000; Moanda (1993) 21,921.

Vital statistics

Birth rate per 1,000 population (2003): 36.5 (world avg. 21.3).
Death rate per 1,000 population (2003): 11.2 (world avg. 9.1).
Natural increase rate per 1,000 population (2003): 25.3 (world avg. 12.2).
Total fertility rate (avg. births per childbearing woman; 2003): 4.8.
Life expectancy at birth (2003): male 55.5 years; female 58.8 years.
Adult population (ages 15–49) *living with HIV* (2004[3]): 8.1% (world avg. 1.1%).

National economy

Budget (2001). Revenue: CFAF 1,190,100,000,000 (oil revenues 65.7%; taxes on international trade 17.7%; income tax 8.3%; value-added tax 5.1%; other revenues 3.2%). Expenditures: CFAF 976,200,000,000 (current expenditure 81.0%, of which service on public debt 31.0%, wages and salaries 21.9%, transfers 14.3%; capital expenditure 19.0%).
Public debt (external, outstanding; 2002): U.S.$3,231,000,000.
Tourism: receipts from visitors (2001) U.S.$7,000,000; expenditures by nationals abroad (2002) U.S.$219,000,000.
Gross national product (2003): U.S.$4,813,000,000 (U.S.$3,580 per capita).

Structure of gross domestic product and labour force

	2001		1993	
	in value CFAF '000,000	% of total value	labour force	% of labour force
Agriculture, forestry, fishing	234,400	6.9	156,000[4]	41.6
Mining	1,481,200	43.7	43,000[4]	11.5
Manufacturing	173,500	5.1		
Construction	62,400	1.8		
Public utilities	35,000	1.0		
Transp. and commun.	157,400	4.6	115,000[4]	30.7
Trade	244,900	7.2		
Finance	19,600	0.6		
Services	384,600	11.4		
Pub. admin., defense	300,300	8.9	61,000[4]	16.2
Other	294,100[5]	8.7[5]	...	...
TOTAL	3,387,400	100.0[2]	376,000[2]	100.0

Production (metric tons except as noted). Agriculture, forestry, fishing (2003): plantains 170,000, yams 155,000, sugarcane 135,000, cassava 130,000, taro 19,000, oil palm fruit 12,000, bananas 12,000, corn (maize) 11,000, natural rubber 11,000, peanuts (groundnuts) 10,000; livestock (number of live animals) 212,000 pigs, 195,000 sheep; roundwood (2003) 3,106,710 cu m; fish catch (2001) 40,559. Mining and quarrying (2002): manganese ore 1,816,000; gold 70 kg[6]. Manufacturing (value added in U.S.$'000,000; 1995): wood products (excluding furniture) 44; refined petroleum products 25; food products 22; fabricated metals 21; beverages 17. Energy production (consumption): electricity (kW-hr; 2000) 1,354,000,000 (1,354,000,000); crude petroleum (barrels; 2002) 108,000,000 ([2000] 5,610,000); petroleum products (metric tons; 2000) 593,400 (590,000); natural gas (cu m; 2000) 810,000,000 (810,000,000).
Population economically active (2000): total 555,000; activity rate of total population 44.1% (participation rates [1985] ages 15–64, 68.2%; female 44.5%; unemployed [1996] 20%).

Price index (2000 = 100)

	1997	1998	1999	2000	2001	2002	2003
Consumer price index	96.7	100.1	99.4	100.0	102.1	102.3	104.4

Household income and expenditure. Average household size (2000) 6.1; income per household: n.a.; sources of income: n.a.; expenditure: n.a.
Land use as % of total land area (2000): in temporary crops 1.3%, in permanent crops 0.7%, in pasture 18.1%; overall forest area 84.7%.

Foreign trade

Balance of trade (current prices)

	1998	1999	2000	2001	2002	2003
CFAF '000,000,000	+439	+978	+1,796	+1,295	+1,141	+1,240
% of total	24.3%	46.6%	61.2%	51.0%	46.2%	50.7%

Imports (2003): CFAF 602,000,000,000 (for petroleum sector 27.9%, other unspecified 72.1%). *Major import sources* (2000): France *c.* 44%; U.S. *c.* 11%; The Netherlands *c.* 5%; Germany *c.* 3%; Spain *c.* 3%.
Exports (2003): CFAF 1,842,000,000,000 (crude petroleum and petroleum products 80.5%, wood 10.2%, manganese ore and concentrate 4.8%). *Major export destinations* (2000): U.S. *c.* 63%; China *c.* 7%; Australia *c.* 6%; France *c.* 4%; South Korea *c.* 4%.

Transport and communications

Transport. Railroads (2002): route length 506 mi, 814 km; (2002) passenger-km 97,500,000; (2002) metric ton-km cargo carried 1,553,000,000. Roads (1996): total length 4,760 mi, 7,670 km (paved 8%). Vehicles (1997): passenger cars 24,750; trucks and buses 16,490. Air transport (2000): passenger-km 1,204,000,000; metric ton-km cargo, n.a.; airports (1997) 17.

Communications

Medium	date	unit	number	units per 1,000 persons
Daily newspapers	1997	circulation	33,000	30
Radio	2000	receivers	630,000	501
Television	2002	receivers	400,000	308
Telephones	2003	main lines	38,400	29
Cellular telephones	2003	subscribers	300,000	224
Personal computers	2003	units	30,000	22
Internet	2003	users	35,000	26

Education and health

Educational attainment of economically active population (1993): no formal schooling and incomplete primary education 37.7%; complete primary 32.1%; complete secondary 16.4%; postsecondary certificate or degree 13.8%. *Literacy* (2000): total population age 15 and over literate 71%; males literate 80%; females literate 62%.

Education (1998)

	schools	teachers	students	student/ teacher ratio
Primary	1,175	6,022	265,244	44.0
Secondary	88[7]	3,078	80,282	...
Voc., teacher tr.	11[7]		6,161	...
Higher[8]	2[7]	585	7,473	12.8

Health: physicians (1995) 321 (1 per 3,455 persons); hospital beds (1995) 4,631 (1 per 240 persons); infant mortality rate per 1,000 live births (2003) 55.1.
Food (2001): daily per capita caloric intake 2,602 (vegetable products 87%, animal products 13%); 111% of FAO recommended minimum requirement.

Military

Total active duty personnel (2003): 4,700 (army 68.1%, navy 10.6%, air force 21.3%); French troops (2003) 800. *Military expenditure as percentage of GNP* (1999): 2.4% (world 2.4%); per capita expenditure U.S.$78.

[1]Formerly pegged to the French franc and since Jan. 1, 2002, to the euro at the rate of 1 € = CFAF 655.96. [2]Detail does not add to total given because of rounding. [3]Beginning of year. [4]Derived values. [5]Import duties. [6]Excludes about 400 kg of illegally mined gold smuggled out of Gabon. Uranium mining ceased in 1999. [7]1995–96. [8]Universities only.

Internet resources for further information:
- **Afristat http://www.afristat.org**
- **Investir en Zone Franc http://www.izf.net/izf/Guide/Gabon/Default.htm**
- **PNUD au GABON http://mirror.undp.org/gabon**

Gambia, The

Official name: The Republic of The Gambia.
Form of government: multiparty republic with one legislative house (National Assembly [53[1]]).
Head of state and government: President.
Capital: Banjul.
Official language: English.
Official religion: none.
Monetary unit: 1 dalasi (D) = 100 butut; valuation (Sept. 1, 2004) 1 U.S.$ = D 29.88; 1 £ = D 53.74.

Area and population

		area		population
Divisions	Capitals	sq mi	sq km	2003 census[2]
Basse	Basse	799	2,069	183,033
Brikama	Brikama	681	1,764	392,987
Janjanbureh	Janjanbureh	494	1,280	106,799
Kanifing[3, 4]	Kanifing	29	76	322,410
Kerewan	Kerewan	871	2,256	172,806
Kuntaur	Kuntaur	623	1,614	79,098
Mansakonko	Mansakonko	625	1,618	72,546
City				
Banjul[4]	—	5	12	34,828
TOTAL		4,127[5]	10,689[5]	1,364,507

Demography

Population (2004): 1,405,000.
Density (2004)[6]: persons per sq mi 422.6, persons per sq km 163.1.
Urban-rural (2003): urban 26.1%; rural 73.9%.
Sex distribution (2003): male 49.59%; female 50.41%.
Age breakdown (2003): under 15, 44.9%; 15–29, 26.4%; 30–44, 15.5%; 45–59, 8.8%; 60–74, 3.6%; 75 and over, 0.8%.
Population projection: (2010) 1,617,000; (2020) 1,939,000.
Doubling time: 25 years.
Ethnic composition (1993): Malinke 34.1%; Fulani 16.2%; Wolof 12.6%; Diola 9.2%; Soninke 7.7%; other 20.2%.
Religious affiliation (1993): Muslim 95.0%; Christian 4.1%; traditional beliefs and other 0.9%.
Major cities/urban areas (2003): Kanifing 322,410[3]; Brikama 63,000; Banjul 34,828 (Greater Banjul 523,589[4]).

Vital statistics

Birth rate per 1,000 population (2003): 40.8 (world avg. 21.3).
Death rate per 1,000 population (2003): 12.4 (world avg. 9.1).
Natural increase rate per 1,000 population (2003): 28.4 (world avg. 12.2).
Total fertility rate (avg. births per childbearing woman; 2002): 5.5.
Marriage rate per 1,000 population: n.a.
Life expectancy at birth (2003): male 52.4 years; female 56.4 years.
Major causes of death per 100,000 population: n.a.; however, major infectious diseases include malaria, gastroenteritis and dysentery, pneumonia and bronchitis, measles, schistosomiasis, and whooping cough.

National economy

Budget (2002). Revenue: D 1,528,700,000 (tax revenue 68.0%, of which taxes on international trade 39.1%, corporate taxes 11.6%; grants 21.4%; nontax revenue 10.6%). Expenditures: D 1,870,700,000 (current expenditure 70.5%, of which interest payments 19.8%; capital expenditure 29.5%).
Production (metric tons except as noted). Agriculture, forestry, fishing (2002): millet 84,618, peanuts (groundnuts) 71,526, paddy rice 20,452, corn (maize) 18,850, sorghum 15,209, fresh vegetables 9,000, cassava 7,500, pulses (mostly beans) 3,200, palm oil 3,000; livestock (number of live animals) 327,000 cattle, 262,000 goats, 146,000 sheep; roundwood (2001) 724,000 cu m; fish catch (2001) 34,527, of which Atlantic Ocean 32,037, inland water 2,490. Mining and quarrying: sand, clay, and gravel are excavated for local use. Manufacturing (value added in U.S.$; 1995): food products and beverages 6,000,000; textiles, clothing, and footwear 750,000; wood products 550,000. Construction: n.a. Energy production (consumption): electricity (kW-hr; 2001) 134,000,000 (134,000,000); coal, none (none); crude petroleum, none (none); petroleum products (metric tons; 2000) none (88,000); natural gas, none (none).
Population economically active (1998): total 575,140; activity rate of total population 47.3% (participation rates: ages 15–64, 86.6%; female 40.0%; unemployed, n.a.).

Price and earnings indexes (2000 = 100)

	1997	1998	1999	2000	2001	2002	2003
Consumer price index[7]	95.5	97.7	99.2	100.0	104.5	113.5	132.8
Daily earnings index[8]	...	100.0	100.0	100.0	100.0	106.0	132.5

Tourism (2000): receipts from visitors U.S.$48,000,000; expenditures by nationals abroad (1997) U.S.$16,000,000.
Household income and expenditure. Average household size (2000) 7.9; income per household: n.a.; sources of income: n.a.; expenditure (1991)[7]: food and beverages 58.0%, clothing and footwear 17.5%, energy and water 5.4%, housing 5.1%, education, health, transportation and communications, recreation, and other 14.0%.

Public debt (external, outstanding; 2002): U.S.$503,600,000.
Gross national product (at current market prices; 2003): U.S.$442,000,000 (U.S.$310 per capita).

Structure of gross domestic product and labour force

	1999		1993	
	in value D '000,000	% of total value	labour force	% of labour force
Agriculture	1,466.5	29.6	181,752	52.6
Mining	[9]	[9]	398	0.1
Manufacturing	234.6	4.7	21,682	6.3
Construction	236.2[9]	4.8[9]	9,679	2.8
Public utilities	82.0	1.7	1,858	0.5
Transp. and commun.	717.6	14.5	14,203	4.1
Trade	735.0	14.8	54,728	15.8
Finance	299.8	6.0	2,415	0.7
Public administration	421.6	8.5	41,254	11.9
Services	204.4	4.1		
Other	557.9[10]	11.3[10]	17,412[11]	5.0[11]
TOTAL	4,955.6	100.0	345,381	100.0[12]

Land use as % of total land area (2000): in temporary crops 23.0%, in permanent crops 0.5%, in pasture 45.9%; overall forest area 48.1%.

Foreign trade[13]

Balance of trade (current prices)

	1998	1999	2000	2001	2002	2003
U.S.$'000,000	–78.9	–68.7	–63.3	–43.1	–49.1	–51.8
% of total	23.2%	21.5%	20.0%	17.5%	18.0%	20.3%

Imports (2002): U.S.$160,100,000[14] (food and live animals 23.5%; machinery and transport equipment 17.0%; petroleum products 10.6%). *Major import sources:* EU 31.0%; China 22.3%; Senegal 9.2%.
Exports (2002): U.S.$111,000,000 (reexports 70.4%; peanuts [groundnuts] 21.6%; fruits and vegetables 3.7%; fish and fish products 2.6%). *Major export destinations:* EU 76.6%; Asian countries 16.7%.

Transport and communications

Transport. Railroads: none. Roads (1999): total length 1,678 mi, 2,700 km (paved 35%). Vehicles (1997): passenger cars 7,267; trucks and buses (1996) 9,000. Air transport (2001)[15]: passenger arrivals 300,000, passenger departures 300,000; cargo loaded and unloaded 2,700 metric tons; airports (2000) with scheduled flights 1.

Communications

Medium	date	unit	number	units per 1,000 persons
Daily newspapers	2000	circulation	39,400	30
Radio	2000	receivers	520,000	396
Television	2000	receivers	3,940	3.0
Telephones	2002	main lines	38,400	29
Cellular telephones	2002	subscribers	100,000	75
Personal computers	2002	units	19,000	14
Internet	2002	users	25,000	19

Education and health

Educational attainment: n.a. *Literacy* (1998): total population age 15 and over literate 34.6%; males literate 41.9%; females literate 27.5%.

Education (1998–99)

	schools	teachers	students	student/ teacher ratio
Primary (age 8–14)	331	4,572	150,403	32.9
Secondary (age 15–21)[16]	85	1,936	46,769	24.2
Postsecondary	4	155[17]	1,082[17]	7.0[17]

Health (2000): physicians 105 (1 per 12,977 persons); hospital beds 1,140 (1 per 1,199 persons); infant mortality rate per 1,000 live births (2003) 74.9.
Food (2002): daily per capita caloric intake 2,273 (vegetable products 94%, animal products 6%); 96% of FAO recommended minimum requirement.

Military

Total active duty personnel (2003): 800 (army 100%). *Military expenditure as percentage of GNP* (1999): 1.3% (world 2.4%); per capita expenditure U.S.$12.

[1]Includes 5 nonelective seats. [2]Preliminary. [3]Kanifing includes the urban areas of Serekunda and Bakau. [4]Kanifing and Banjul make up most of Greater Banjul. [5]Includes inland water area of 802 sq mi (2,077 sq km). [6]Based on land area only. [7]Low-income population in Banjul and Kanifing only; weights of consumer price index components. [8]Minimum wage. [9]Construction includes mining. [10]Indirect taxes. [11]Not adequately defined. [12]Detail does not add to total given because of rounding. [13]Imports c.i.f.; exports f.o.b. [14]Imports for reexport comprise 36.0% of total. [15]Yumdum International Airport at Banjul. [16]Includes teacher training and vocational. [17]1994.

Internet resources for further information:

- **Official WWW Site of The Republic of The Gambia**
  http://www.gambia.gm

Georgia

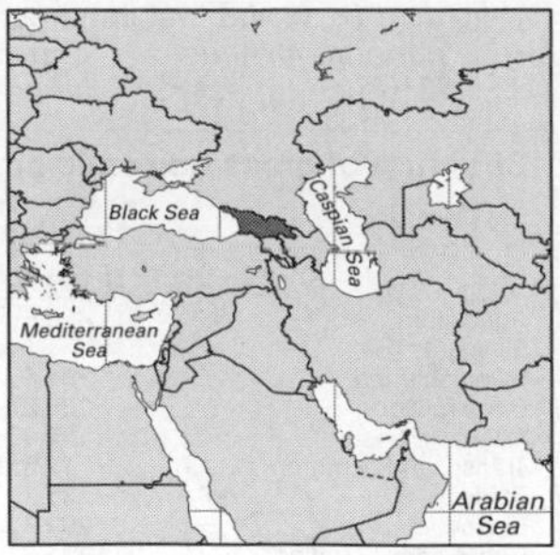

Official name: Sak'art'velo (Georgia).
Form of government: unitary multiparty republic with a single legislative body (Parliament [235]).
Head of state and government: President, assisted by Prime Minister.
Capital: Tbilisi.
Official language: Georgian[1].
Official religion: none[2].
Monetary unit: 1 Georgian lari = 100 tetri; valuation (Sept. 1, 2004) 1 U.S.$ = 2.12 lari; 1 £ = 3.92 lari.

Area and population

		area		population
Autonomous republics	**Capitals**	sq mi	sq km	2002 census[3]
Abkhazia[4]	Sokhumi (Sukhumi)	3,336	8,640	...[5]
Ajaria (Adjara)	Bat'umi	1,112	2,880	376,016
Regions				
Guria	Ozurget'i	785	2,032	143,357
Imereti	K'ut'aisi	2,500	6,475	699,666
Kakheti	T'elavi	4,367	11,311	407,182
Kvemo Kartli	Rust'avi	2,344	6,072	497,530
Mtskheta-Mtianeti	Mts'khet'a	2,620	6,786	125,443
Racha-Lechkhumi & Kvemo Svaneti	Ambrolauri	1,927	4,990	50,969
Samegrelo & Zemo Svaneti	Zugdidi	2,873	7,440	466,100
Samtskhe-Javakheti	Akhalts'ikhe	2,476	6,413	207,598
Shida Kartli[6]	Gori	2,212[6]	5,729[6]	314,039[7]
City				
Tbilisi (T'bilisi)	—	534	1,384	1,081,679
TOTAL		27,086	70,152	4,369,579[3]

Demography

Population (2004): 4,694,000.
Density (2004): persons per sq mi 174.4, persons per sq km 67.3.
Urban-rural (2002): urban 52.3%; rural 47.7%.
Sex distribution (2002): male 47.16%; female 52.84%.
Age breakdown (2002): under 15, 21.0%; 15–29, 22.8%; 30–44, 21.9%; 45–59, 15.6%; 60–74, 14.6%; 75 and over, 4.1%.
Population projection: (2010) 4,601,000; (2020) 4,440,000.
*Ethnic composition (*2000): Georgian 57.9%; Mingrelian 9.1%; Armenian 8.1%; Russian 6.3%; Azerbaijani 5.7%; Ossetian 3.0%; Greek 1.9%; Abkhazian 1.8%; other 6.2%.
Religious affiliation (1995): Christian 46.2%, of which Georgian Orthodox 36.7%, Armenian Apostolic 5.6%, Russian Orthodox 2.7%, other Christian 1.2%; Sunnī Muslim 11.0%; other (mostly nonreligious) 42.8%.
Major cities (2002): Tbilisi 1,081,679; K'ut'aisi 185,965; Bat'umi 121,806; Rust'avi 116,348; Sokhumi (1994) 112,000.

Vital statistics

Birth rate per 1,000 population (2003): 10.0 (world avg. 21.3).
Death rate per 1,000 population (2003): 8.9 (world avg. 9.1).
Natural increase rate per 1,000 population (2003): 1.1 (world avg. 12.2).
Total fertility rate (avg. births per childbearing woman; 2003): 1.4.
Marriage rate per 1,000 population (2001): 2.7.
Divorce rate per 1,000 population (2001): 0.4.
Life expectancy at birth (2003): male 72.1 years; female 79.2 years.
Major causes of death per 100,000 population (2002): diseases of the circulatory system 914.4; malignant neoplasms (cancers) 105.0; accidents, poisoning, and violence 31.9; diseases of the respiratory system 25.6.

National economy

Budget (2002). Revenue: 928,600,000 lari (tax revenue 83.1%, of which value-added tax 40.4%, social security tax 17.4%, excise tax 11.3%; nontax revenue 8.5%; grants 8.4%). Expenditures: 920,500,000 lari (current expenditure 99.7%, of which social security and welfare 30.0%, public order 9.1%, health 4.5%, defense 4.4%, education 4.1%; capital expenditure 0.3%).
Public debt (external, outstanding; 2002): U.S.$1,444,000,000.
Population economically active (2000): total 1,748,800[8]; activity rate of total population 35.1% (participation rates [1993]: ages 16–65 [male], 16–60 [female] 55.6%; female 47.8%; unemployed [2000] 12.0%).

Price and earnings indexes (2000 = 100)

	1996	1997	1998	1999	2000	2001	2002
Consumer price index	72.3	77.8	80.6	96.1	100.0	104.6	110.5
Annual earnings index	34.5	51.6	69.4	88.0	100.0	134.0	...

Production (metric tons except as noted). Agriculture, forestry, fishing (2002): potatoes 414,000, wheat 306,000, corn (maize) 290,000, tomatoes 150,000, grapes 150,000, apples 65,000, tea 20,000; livestock (number of live animals) 1,180,000 cattle, 568,000 sheep; fish catch (2001) 1,910. Mining and quarrying (2001): manganese ore 98,300. Manufacturing (value of production in U.S.$'000,000; 2001)[9]: food products 139.6, basic metals 36.5, transport equipment 27.0, nonmetallic mineral products 25.3. Energy production (consumption): electricity (kW-hr; 2001) 5,700,000,000 (5,700,000,000); coal (metric tons; 2000) 7,000 (27,000); crude petroleum (barrels; 2001) 719,000 (719,000); petroleum products (metric tons; 2000) 10,600 (1,305,000); natural gas (cu m; 2000) 59,019,000 (1,002,000,000).

Gross national product (2003): U.S.$3,780,000,000 (U.S.$830 per capita).

Structure of net material product and labour force

	2000			
	in value '000,000 lari	% of total value	labour force[10]	% of labour force[10]
Agriculture	1,191.0	20.0	911,200	52.1
Mining }			6,300	0.4
Manufacturing }	833.7	14.0	103,900	5.9
Public utilities }			29,100	1.7
Construction	226.3	3.8	32,000	1.8
Transp. and commun.	857.5	14.4	71,900	4.1
Trade, restaurants	899.2	15.1	189,800	10.9
Finance, real estate	101.2	1.7	46,700	2.7
Pub. admin., defense	190.6	3.2	105,800	6.0
Services	518.1	8.7	244,700	14.0
Other	1,137.5	19.1	7,400	0.4
TOTAL	5,955.1	100.0	1,748,800	100.0

Household income and expenditure. Average household size (2000) 4.6; income per household: n.a.; sources of income (1993): wages and salaries 34.5%, benefits 21.9%, agricultural income 21.6%, other 22.0%; expenditure (1993): taxes 42.5%, retail goods 32.3%, savings 16.4%, transportation 4.2%.
Tourism (U.S.$'000,000; 2002): receipts 472; expenditures 174.
Land use as % of total land area (2000): in temporary crops 11.4%, in permanent crops 3.9%, in pasture 27.9%; overall forest area 43.7%.

Foreign trade[11]

Balance of trade (current prices)

	1996	1997	1998	1999	2000	2001
U.S.$'000,000	–488	–704	–608	–364	–321	–364
% of total	55.1%	59.5%	64.1%	43.3%	32.7%	36.3%

Imports (2001): U.S.$684,000,000 (food [all forms] 23.8%; mineral fuels 22.7%; machinery and apparatus 18.3%; transport equipment 7.1%). *Major import sources:* Turkey 15.4%; Russia 13.3%; Azerbaijan 10.7%; Germany 10.1%; Ukraine 7.2%.
Exports (2001): U.S.$320,000,000 (beverages [including wine] 16.7%; iron and steel 15.9%; aircraft and parts 11.3%; food [all forms] 8.8%; mineral fuels 8.6%). *Major export destinations:* Russia 23.0%; Turkey 21.5%; Turkmenistan 9.0%; United Kingdom 7.2%; Switzerland 4.9%.

Transport and communications

Transport. Railroads (2001): 1,546 km; passenger-km 398,000,000; metric ton-km cargo 4,473,000,000. Roads (2001): 20,215 km (paved 93.5%). Vehicles (1999): passenger cars 247,872; trucks and buses 43,421. Air transport (2001): passenger-km 241,000,000; metric ton-km cargo 3,000,000; airports with scheduled flights 1.

Communications

Medium	date	unit	number	units per 1,000 persons
Radio	2000	receivers	2,790,000	556
Television	2002	receivers	1,856,000	357
Telephones	2003	main lines	650,500	133
Cellular telephones	2003	subscribers	522,300	107
Personal computers	2002	units	156,000	31
Internet	2003	users	150,500	31

Education and health

Education (2000–01)

	schools	teachers	students	student/ teacher ratio
Primary (age 6–9)	1,505 }	73,000	271,000 }	9.6
Secondary (age 10–16)	1,652 }		429,000 }	
Voc., teacher tr.	140	2,146[12]	32,500	...
Higher	23[12]	25,549[12]	139,000	...

Food (2002): daily per capita caloric intake 2,354 (vegetable products 82%, animal products 18%); 92% of FAO recommended minimum requirement.
Health (2001): physicians 22,000 (1 per 213 persons); hospital beds 24,520 (1 per 208 persons); infant mortality rate per 1,000 live births (2002) 23.3.

Military

Total active duty personnel (2003): 17,500 (army 49.3%, air force 7.1%, navy 10.5%, paramilitary 33.1%).[13] *Military expenditure as percentage of GNP* (1999): 1.2% (world 2.4%); per capita expenditure U.S.$33.

[1]Locally Abkhazian, in Abkhazia. [2]Special recognition is given to the Georgian Orthodox Church. [3]Excludes Abkhazia and South Ossetia; alternate census total is 4,371,534. [4]Abkhazia has had de facto autonomy from Georgia since 1993. Its final status was unresolved in October 2004. [5]2002 population estimate is 160,000. [6]Includes the 1,505-sq-mi (3,900-sq-km) area of the autonomous region (from 1992) of South Ossetia; the final status of South Ossetia was unresolved in March 2004. [7]Excludes 2002 population estimate for South Ossetia equaling 70,000. [8]Excludes informal sector, which was about 750,000 persons in 1998. [9]Excludes Abkhazia and South Ossetia. [10]Employed persons in formal sector only. [11]Imports c.i.f.; exports f.o.b. [12]1996–97. [13]About 3,000 Russian troops acting as a buffer force between Georgians and Abkhazians were in Abkhazia in August 2004 along with about 125 UN peacekeeping troops.

Internet resources for further information:
- **National Bank of Georgia**
  http://www.nbg.gov.ge/NBG_New/home_nf1.htm
- **State Department for Statistics of Georgia**
  http://www.statistics.ge/bottom_eng.htm

Germany

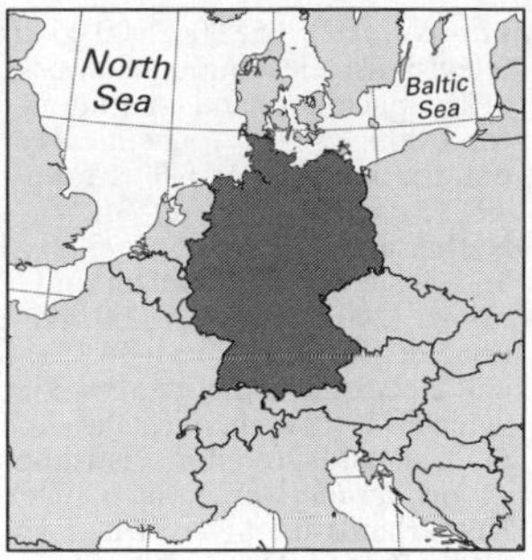

Official name: Bundesrepublik Deutschland (Federal Republic of Germany).
Form of government: federal multiparty republic with two legislative houses (Federal Council [69]; Federal Diet [603]).
Chief of state: President.
Head of government: Chancellor.
Capital: Berlin, some ministries remain in Bonn.
Official language: German.
Official religion: none.
Monetary unit: 1 euro (€) = 100 cents; valuation (Sept. 1, 2004) 1 U.S.$ = €0.82; 1 £ = €1.48[1].

Area and population

States[2] Administrative districts	Capitals	area sq mi	area sq km	population 2002[3] estimate
Baden-Württemberg	Stuttgart	13,804[4]	35,752	10,600,900[4]
Freiburg	Freiburg im Breisgau	3,613	9,357	2,156,900
Karlsruhe	Karlsruhe	2,671	6,919	2,701,400
Stuttgart	Stuttgart	4,076	10,558	3,964,200
Tübingen	Tübingen	3,443	8,918	1,778,500
Bavaria	Munich	27,240	70,550	12,329,700
Mittelfranken	Ansbach	2,798	7,246	1,698,300
Niederbayern	Landshut	3,988	10,330	1,185,500
Oberbayern	Munich	6,768	17,530	4,138,400
Oberfranken	Bayreuth	2,792	7,230	1,113,800
Oberpfalz	Regensburg	3,742	9,691	1,085,600
Schwaben	Augsburg	3,858	9,992	1,767,200
Unterfranken	Würzburg	3,294	8,531	1,340,900
Berlin	—	344	892	3,388,400
Brandenburg	Potsdam	11,381	29,476	2,593,000
Bremen	Bremen	156	404	659,700
Hamburg	Hamburg	292	755	1,726,400
Hessen	Wiesbaden	8,152	21,114	6,077,800
Darmstadt	Darmstadt	2,874	7,444	3,740,900
Giessen	Giessen	2,078	5,381	1,065,000
Kassel	Kassel	3,200	8,289	1,265,900
Lower Saxony	Hannover	18,385	47,616	7,956,400
Braunschweig	Braunschweig	3,127	8,098	1,666,900
Hannover	Hannover	3,493	9,047	2,163,900
Lüneburg	Lüneburg	5,987	15,506	1,683,400
Weser-Ems	Oldenburg	5,778	14,965	2,442,200
Mecklenburg-West Pomerania	Schwerin	8,947	23,173	1,759,900
North Rhine-Westphalia	Düsseldorf	13,159[4]	34,082[4]	18,052,100[4]
Arnsberg	Arnsberg	3,090	8,002	3,803,300
Cologne (Köln)	Cologne (Köln)	2,843	7,364	4,310,000
Detmold	Detmold	2,517	6,518	2,063,200
Düsseldorf	Düsseldorf	2,042	5,290	5,255,300
Münster	Münster	2,666	6,906	2,620,200
Rhineland-Palatinate	Mainz	7,663	19,846	4,049,100
Saarland	Saarbrücken	992	2,568	1,066,500
Saxony	Dresden	7,109	18,413[4]	4,384,200[4]
Chemnitz	Chemnitz	2,354	6,097	1,602,000
Dresden	Dresden	3,062	7,931	1,695,700
Leipzig	Leipzig	1,693	4,386	1,085,500
Saxony-Anhalt	Magdeburg	7,895[4]	20,447	2,580,600
Schleswig-Holstein	Kiel	6,085	15,761	2,804,200
Thuringia	Erfurt	6,244	16,172	2,411,400
TOTAL		137,847[4]	357,023[4]	82,440,300

Demography

Population (2004): 82,561,000.
Density (2004): persons per sq mi 598.9, persons per sq km 231.2.
Urban-rural (2003): urban 88.1%; rural 11.9%.
Population projection: (2010) 82,419,000; (2020) 81,471,000.
Major cities (2002; *urban agglomerations*[5]): Berlin 3,388,434[6]; Hamburg 1,726,363 (2,664,000); Munich 1,227,958 (2,291,000); Cologne 967,940 (3,050,000); Frankfurt am Main 641,076 (3,681,000); Essen 591,889 (6,531,000[7]); Dortmund 589,240 (6,531,000[7]); Stuttgart 587,152 (2,672,000); Düsseldorf 570,765 (3,233,000); Bremen 540,950 (880,000); Hannover 516,415 (1,283,000); Duisburg 512,030 (6,531,000[7]); Leipzig 493,052; Nuremberg (Nürnberg) 491,307 (1,189,000).

Other principal cities (2002)

	population		population		population
Aachen	245,778	Heidelberg	141,509	Neuss	150,957
Augsburg	257,836	Herne	174,018	Oberhausen	221,619
Bielefeld	323,373	Karlsruhe	279,578	Oldenburg	155,908
Bochum	390,087	Kassel	194,748	Osnabrück	164,195
Bonn	306,016	Kiel	232,242	Paderborn	140,869
Braunschweig	245,516	Krefeld	239,559	Potsdam	130,435
Chemnitz	255,798	Leverkusen	160,829	Recklingshausen	124,587
Darmstadt	138,457	Lübeck	213,496	Regensburg	127,198
Dresden	478,631	Ludwigshafen		Rostock	198,964
Erfurt	200,126	am Rhein	162,458	Saarbrücken	182,858
Freiburg		Magdeburg	229,755	Solingen	165,032
im Breisgau	208,294	Mainz	185,293	Wiesbaden	271,076
Gelsenkirchen	276,740	Mannheim	308,385	Wuppertal	364,784
Göttingen	123,822	Mönchengladbach	262,963	Würzburg	129,915
Hagen	202,060	Mülheim			
Halle	243,045	an der Ruhr	172,332		
Hamm	183,805	Münster	267,197		

Sex distribution (2003[3]): male 48.78%; female 51.22%.
Ethnic composition (by nationality; 2000): German 88.2%; Turkish 3.4% (including Kurdish 0.7%); Italian 1.0%; Greek 0.7%; Serb 0.6%; Russian 0.6%; Polish 0.4%; other 5.1%.
Age breakdown (2003): under 15, 14.9%; 15–29, 17.0%; 30–44, 24.3%; 45–59, 19.3%; 60–74, 16.9%; 75 and over, 7.6%.
Religious affiliation (2000): Christian 75.8%, of which Protestant 35.6% (including Lutheran 33.9%), Roman Catholic 33.5%, Orthodox 0.9%, independent Christian 0.9%, other Christian 4.9%; Muslim 4.4%; Jewish 0.1%; nonreligious 17.2%; atheist 2.2%; other 0.3%.
Households (2000). Number of households 38,124,000; average household size 2.2; 1 person 36.0%, 2 persons 33.4%, 3 persons 14.7%, 4 persons 11.5%, 5 or more persons 4.4%.

Vital statistics

Birth rate per 1,000 population (2003): 8.6 (world avg. 21.3); legitimate 73.0%; illegitimate 27.0%.
Death rate per 1,000 population (2003): 10.3 (world avg. 9.1).
Natural increase rate per 1,000 population (2003): –1.7 (world avg. 12.2).
Total fertility rate (avg. births per childbearing woman; 2003): 1.4.
Marriage rate per 1,000 population (2003): 4.6.
Divorce rate per 1,000 population (2003): 2.6.
Life expectancy at birth (2003): male 75.5 years; female 81.6 years.
Major causes of death per 100,000 population (2002): diseases of the circulatory system 477.3; malignant neoplasms (cancers) 254.6; diseases of the respiratory system 65.0; diseases of the digestive system 50.7.

Social indicators

Educational attainment (2000). Percentage of population age 25 and over having: primary and lower secondary 50.6%; intermediate secondary 17.9%; vocational secondary 8.7%; post-secondary and higher (all levels) 22.8%.
Quality of working life. Average workweek (2002): 37.9 hours. Annual rate per 100,000 workers (1993) for: injuries or accidents at work 4,808; deaths, including commuting accidents, 6.7. Proportion of labour force insured for damages of income loss resulting from: injury, virtually 100%; permanent disability, virtually 100%; death, virtually 100%. Average days lost to labour stoppages per 1,000 workers (2000): 0.3.
Access to services. Proportion of dwellings (2002) having: electricity, virtually 100%; piped water supply, virtually 100%; flush sewage disposal (1993) 98.4%; public fire protection, virtually 100%.
Social participation. Eligible voters participating in last (September 2002) national election 79.1%. Trade union membership in total workforce (2003): *c.* 18%. Practicing religious population (1994): 5% of Protestants and 25% of Roman Catholics "regularly" attend religious services.
Social deviance (2000). Offense rate per 100,000 population for: murder and manslaughter 3.8; sexual abuse 37.0, of which rape and forcible sexual assault 11.7, child molestation 10.2; assault and battery 153.2; theft 754.2.
Material well-being (2001[3]; median income). Households possessing: automobile 75.1%; telephone 96.4%; mobile telephone 55.7%; colour television 95.9%; washing machine 95.1%; clothes dryer 33.3%; personal computer 53.4%; dishwasher 51.3%; high-speed internet access 12.0%.

National economy

Budget (2001). Revenue: €922,472,000,000 (taxes 87.9%, loan interest 2.7%, other 9.4%). Expenditures: €972,104,000,000 (current expenditure 66.1%, of which purchase of current goods and services 22.2%, personnel costs 18.6%; capital expenditure 33.9%).
Total public debt (2001): U.S.$1,109,680,000,000.
Production (value of production in € except as noted; 2002). Agriculture, forestry, fishing: cereal grains 4,265,000,000, fodder plants 4,148,000,000, flowers and ornamental plants 2,797,000,000, vegetables 1,334,000,000, sugar beets 1,267,000,000, potatoes 939,000,000, grapes for wine 929,000,000, oilseeds 876,000,000, fruits 628,000,000; livestock (number of live animals; 2003) 26,251,000 pigs, 13,732,000 cattle, 2,658,000 sheep, 110,000,000 chickens; roundwood 42,380,000 cu m; fish catch (metric tons; 2001) 266,000. Mining and quarrying (metric tons; 2001): potash (potassium oxide content) 3,549,000; feldspar 500,000. Manufacturing (value added in U.S.$'000,000; 2000): motor vehicles 72,300; nonelectrical machinery and apparatus 71,800; chemicals (including pharmaceuticals) 62,900; food and beverages 44,700; electrical machinery and apparatus [excluding telecommunications, electronics] 38,600; fabricated metal products 37,000; petroleum products and coal derivatives 28,200; printing and publishing 25,400; rubber products and plastic products 23,700; base metals 22,100. Construction (newly completed buildings, sq m; 2000): residential 34,354,000; nonresidential 44,404,000.

Manufacturing enterprises (2000)

	no. of enter-prises	no. of employees	wages as a % of avg. of all wages	annual value added (€'000,000)
Manufacturing	40,052	6,424,000	100.0	600,009
of which				
Machinery (electrical and nonelectrical)	7,996	1,480,000	110.0	119,652
Transport equipment	1,239	967,000	117.8	90,538
Chemical products	1,282	481,000	119.9	68,313
Fabricated metals	7,211	855,000	95.4	63,945
Food and beverages	5,448	599,000	68.2	48,538
Refined petroleum, coke	48	23,000	130.9	30,453
Publishing and printing	2,679	274,000	105.5	27,594
Rubber and plastic products	2,708	359,000	85.5	26,022
Wood and wood products	3,688	329,000	79.7	21,427
Glass and ceramics	2,203	248,000	88.1	20,847
Professional and scientific equipment	1,930	224,000	100.0	17,930
Radio and television	514	161,000	115.4	17,269

Energy production (consumption): electricity (kW-hr; 2001) 565,284,000,000 ([2000] 583,415,000,000); hard coal (metric tons; 2002) 26,364,000 ([2000] 64,357,000); lignite (metric tons; 2002) 181,416,000 ([2000] 169,942,000); crude petroleum (barrels; 2003) 30,003,000 ([2000] 775,820,000); petroleum products (metric tons; 2000) 98,024,000 (104,149,000); natural gas (cu m; 2002) 24,158,000,000 ([2000] 109,387,000,000).

Gross national product (at current market prices; 2003): U.S.$2,084,631,000,000 (U.S.$25,250 per capita).

Structure of gross domestic product and labour force

	2001			
	in value €'000,000	% of total value	labour force	% of labour force
Agriculture	23,250	1.3	942,000	2.3
Public utilities	41,770	2.3	282,000	0.7
Mining			139,000	0.3
Manufacturing	442,000	23.8	8,609,000	21.2
Construction	90,960	4.9	2,904,000	7.2
Transp. and commun.	116,990	6.3	2,055,000	5.1
Trade, restaurants	225,720	12.2	6,476,000	16.0
Finance, real estate	575,370	31.0	4,351,000	10.7
Services			7,993,000	19.7
Pub. admin., defense	404,540	21.8	3,065,000	7.6
Other	−67,000[8]	−3.6[8]	3,734,000[9]	9.2[9]
TOTAL	1,853,600	100.0	40,550,000	100.0

Household income and expenditure. Average annual income per household (1998) DM 75,144 (U.S.$42,702); sources of take-home income (1997): wages 77.6%, self-employment 12.0%, transfer payments 10.4%; expenditure (2001): housing and energy 24.5%, transportation 14.2%, food and nonalcoholic beverages 12.3%, recreation and culture 9.7%, household furnishings 7.1%, clothing and footwear 6.4%, restaurants and hotels 4.9%.

Financial aggregates[10]

	1997	1998	1999	2000	2001	2002	2003
Exchange rate, DM per[11]:							
U.S. dollar	1.73	1.76	0.94	1.09	1.12	1.06	0.89
£	2.84	2.91	1.52	1.65	1.61	1.60	1.45
SDR	2.42	2.36	1.37	1.40	1.43	1.30	1.18
International reserves (U.S.$)							
Total (excl. gold; '000,000)	77,587	74,024	61,039	56,890	51,404	51,171	50,694
SDRs ('000,000)	1,788	1,868	1,959	1,763	1,793	1,980	1,942
Reserve pos. in IMF ('000,000)	5,946	8,023	6,419	5,460	5,901	6,695	7,656
Foreign exchange	69,853	64,133	52,661	49,667	43,710	42,495	41,095
Gold ('000,000 fine troy oz)	95.18	118.98	111.52	111.52	111.13	110.79	110.58
% world reserves	10.69	12.31	11.53	11.71	11.79	11.91	12.11
Interest and prices							
Central bank discount (%)	2.5	2.5	…	…	…	…	…
Govt. bond yield (%)	5.1	4.4	4.3	5.2	4.7	4.6	3.8
Industrial share prices (2000 = 100)[12]	60.4	77.3	80.1	100.0	76.2	57.6	45.5
Balance of payments (U.S.$'000,000,000)							
Balance of visible trade	+70.12	+76.91	+70.03	+57.45	+89.25	+128.21	+149.37
Imports, f.o.b.	439.90	465.71	472.69	492.38	481.28	489.30	600.95
Exports, f.o.b.	510.02	542.62	542.72	549.83	570.54	617.50	750.32
Balance of invisibles	−78.78	−88.56	−92.72	−82.67	−87.54	−84.77	−95.86
Balance of payments, current account	−8.66	−11.65	−22.69	−25.22	+1.71	+43.44	+53.51

Tourism (2002): receipts U.S.$19,158,000,000; expenditures U.S.$53,196,000,000.

Service enterprises (1991)

	no. of enter-prises	no. of employees	weekly wages as a % of all wages	annual turnover (DM '000,000)
Gas	151	37,000	…	42,228
Water	183	40,000	…	3,443
Electrical power	462	296,000	…	147,076
Transport				
air	133	57,390	…	20,270
buses	6,054	192,869	…	12,586
rail	1	416,199	…	14,697
shipping	1,449	9,076	…	…
Communications				
press	2,452	240,075	…	31,096
Postal services	…[13]	652,573	…	68,346
Hotels and restaurants	135,141	652,251	…	60,257
Wholesale trade	…[13]	1,214,000	…	1,015,984
Retail trade	152,629	2,241,000	…	605,755

Population economically active (2002): total 40,607,000; activity rate of total population 49.3% (participation rates: ages 15–64 [2001] 71.5%; female 44.3%; unemployed 10.0%).

Price and earnings indexes (2000 = 100)

	1997	1998	1999	2000	2001	2002	2003
Consumer price index	97.1	98.0	98.6	100.0	102.0	103.4	104.5
Hourly earnings index	…	…	97.8	100.0	102.5	104.8	107.6

Land use as % of total land area (2000): in temporary crops 33.8%, in permanent crops 0.6%, in pasture 14.5%; overall forest area 30.7%.

Foreign trade[13]

Balance of trade (current prices)

	1998	1999	2000	2001	2002	2003
€'000,000	+64,919	+65,211	+59,129	+95,494	+132,788	+129,643
% of total	7.1%	6.8%	5.2%	8.1%	11.4%	10.9%

Imports (2002): €522,062,000,000 (machinery and equipment 22.6%, of which televisions, telecommunications equipment, and electronic components 6.0%, office machinery and computers 5.3%; transport equipment 14.3%, of which road vehicles 10.2%; chemicals and chemical products 10.6%; crude petroleum and natural gas 6.0%; food products and beverages 5.0%; base metals 4.8%; wearing apparel 3.1%). *Major import sources:* France 9.5%; The Netherlands 8.3%; U.S. 7.7%; U.K. 6.4%; Italy 6.4%; Belgium 5.2%; Austria 4.1%; China 4.0%; Switzerland 3.7%; Japan 3.6%.

Exports (2002): €648,306,000,000 (machinery and equipment 26.3%, of which nonelectrical machinery 14.1%, televisions, telecommunications equipment, and electronic components 4.8%; transport equipment 23.4%, of which road vehicles 19.1%; chemicals and chemical products 11.8%; base metals 4.5%; medical and precision instruments and watches and clocks 4.0%). *Major export destinations:* France 10.8%; U.S. 10.3%; U.K. 8.4%; Italy 7.3%; The Netherlands 6.1%; Austria 5.1%; Belgium 4.8%; Spain 4.6%; Switzerland 4.1%; Poland 2.5%.

Transport and communications

Transport. Railroads (2001): length 53,222 mi, 85,653 km; (2002) passenger-mi 44,002,000,000, passenger-km 70,814,000,000; (2002) short ton-mi cargo 49,326,000,000, metric ton-km cargo 72,014,000,000. Roads (2002): total length 143,400 mi, 230,800 km (paved 99%). Vehicles (2002[3]): passenger cars 44,383,300; trucks and buses 2,735,600. Air transport (2003)[14]: passenger-km 112,089,000,000; metric ton-km cargo 7,088,600,000; airports (1997) 35.

Communications

Medium	date	unit	number	units per 1,000 persons
Daily newspapers	2000	circulation	25,100,000	305
Radio	2000	receivers	77,900,000	948
Television	2002	receivers	54,533,000	661
Telephones	2003	main lines	54,350,000	658
Cellular telephones	2003	subscribers	64,800,000	785
Personal computers	2002	units	35,921,000	435
Internet	2003	users	39,000,000	473

Education and health

Health: physicians (2001) 298,000 (1 per 276 persons); hospital beds (2001[3]) 552,680 (1 per 150 persons); infant mortality rate per 1,000 live births (2002) 4.2.

Education (2000–01)

	schools	teachers	students	student/ teacher ratio
Primary (age 6–10)	17,503[15]	164,664	3,394,700	20.6
Secondary (age 10–19)	19,897[15]	380,188	6,081,100	16.0
Voc., teacher tr.	9,580[15]	114,892	3,102,200	27.0
Higher	335[16]	422,067	1,799,300	4.3

Food (2001): daily per capita caloric intake 3,567 (vegetable products 71%, animal products 29%); 134% of FAO recommended minimum requirement.

Military

Total active duty personnel (2003): 284,500 (army 67.3%, navy 9.0%, air force 23.7%); German peacekeeping troops abroad (May 2004) 7,700; U.S. troops in Germany (August 2004) 75,600. *Military expenditure as percentage of GNP* (1999): 1.6% (world 2.4%); per capita expenditure U.S.$395.

[1]The Deutsche Mark (DM) was the former monetary unit; on Jan. 1, 2002, DM 1.96 = €1. [2]State names used in this table are English conventional. [3]January 1. [4]Detail does not add to total given because of rounding. [5]2000 estimate. [6]2002 city population estimate coextensive with urban agglomeration. [7]Part of the Rhine-Ruhr North urban agglomeration. [8]Less imputed bank service charges. [9]Unemployed. [10]End-of-period figures. [11]Beginning in 1999 exchange rates expressed in euros (€). [12]Period averages. [13]Imports c.i.f.; exports f.o.b. [14]Lufthansa Group, Condor, and Eurowings only. [15]1999–2000. [16]1995–96.

Internet resources for further information:

- **Federal Statistical Office of Germany (in English)** **http://www.destatis.de/e_home.htm**

Ghana

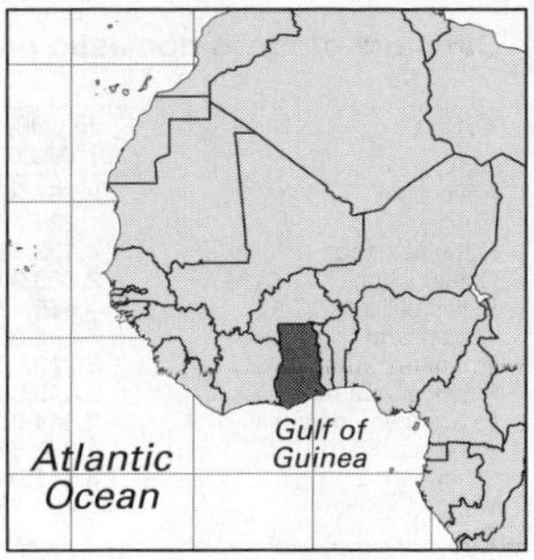

Official name: Republic of Ghana.
Form of government: unitary multiparty republic with one legislative house (House of Parliament [230]).
Head of state and government: President.
Capital: Accra.
Official language: English.
Official religion: none.
Monetary unit: 1 cedi (₵) = 100 pesewas; valuation (Sept. 1, 2004) 1 U.S.$ = ₵9,013; 1 £ = ₵16,213.

Area and population

		area		population
Regions	**Capitals**	sq mi	sq km	2000 census
Ashanti	Kumasi	9,417	24,389	3,600,358
Brong-Ahafo	Sunyani	15,273	39,557	1,798,058
Central	Cape Coast	3,794	9,826	1,593,888
Eastern	Koforidua	7,461	19,323	2,101,650
Greater Accra	Accra	1,253	3,245	2,903,753
Northern	Tamale	27,175	70,384	1,805,428
Upper East	Bolgatanga	3,414	8,842	919,549
Upper West	Wa	7,134	18,476	575,579
Volta	Ho	7,942	20,570	1,630,254
Western	Sekondi-Takoradi	9,236	23,921	1,916,748
TOTAL		92,098[1]	238,533	18,845,265[2]

Demography

Population (2004): 20,732,000.
Density (2004): persons per sq mi 225.1, persons per sq km 86.9.
Urban-rural (2003): urban 45.4%; rural 54.6%.
Sex distribution (2000): male 49.46%; female 50.54%.
Age breakdown (2000): under 15, 41.2%; 15–29, 28.3%; 30–44, 17.3%; 45–59, 7.9%; 60–74, 4.3%; 75 and over, 1.0%.
Population projection: (2010) 23,359,000; (2020) 27,625,000.
Doubling time: 46 years.
Ethnic composition (2000): Akan 41.6%; Mossi 23.0%; Ewe 10.0%; Ga-Adangme 7.2%; Gurma 3.4%; Nzima 1.8%; Yoruba 1.6%; other 11.4%.
Religious affiliation (2000): Christian 55.4%, of which Protestant 16.6%, African Christian 14.4%, Roman Catholic 9.5%; traditional beliefs 24.4%; Muslim 19.7%; other 0.5%.
Major cities (2002[3]): Accra 1,605,400; Kumasi 627,600; Tamale 269,200; Tema 237,700; Obuasi 122,600.

Vital statistics

Birth rate per 1,000 population (2003): 25.8 (world avg. 21.3).
Death rate per 1,000 population (2003): 10.5 (world avg. 9.1).
Natural increase rate per 1,000 population (2003): 15.3 (world avg. 12.2).
Total fertility rate (avg. births per childbearing woman; 2003): 3.3.
Life expectancy at birth (2003): male 55.7 years; female 57.4 years.
Major causes of death per 100,000 population: n.a.; however, principal infectious diseases as a percentage of outpatients (1989): malaria 43.8%, respiratory infections (including tuberculosis) 8.0%, diarrheal diseases 6.7%, intestinal worms 3.1%.

National economy

Budget (2000). Revenue: ₵5,385,000,000,000 (tax revenue 82.0%, of which indirect taxes 37.5%, direct taxes 26.2%, trade taxes 18.3%; grants 10.7%; nontax revenue 7.3%). Expenditures: ₵7,525,100,000,000 (current expenditure 66.9%, capital expenditure 33.1%).
Public debt (external, outstanding; 2002): U.S.$6,129,000,000.
Household income and expenditure. Average household size (1999) 4.3.
Gross national product (2003): U.S.$6,563,000,000 (U.S.$320 per capita).

Structure of gross domestic product and labour force

	2001		1999	
	in value ₵'000,000,000	% of total value	labour force[4]	% of labour force[5]
Agriculture	13,417	35.2	6,374,500	55.0
Mining	1,796	4.7	81,130	0.7
Manufacturing	3,428	9.0	1,356,030	11.7
Construction	3,347	8.8	162,260	1.4
Public utilities	1,029	2.7	23,180	0.2
Transp. and commun.	1,660	4.4	254,900	2.2
Trade, hotels	2,588	6.8	2,120,970	18.3
Finance	1,630	4.3	92,720	0.8
Pub. admin., defense	3,871	10.2	1,124,230	9.7
Services	1,353	3.5		
Other	3,953[6]	10.4[6]	—	—
TOTAL	38,071[1]	100.0	11,590,000	100.0

Production (metric tons except as noted). Agriculture, forestry, fishing (2002): roots and tubers 15,491,000 (of which cassava 9,731,000, yams 3,900,000, taro 1,860,000), bananas and plantains 2,291,000, cereals 2,162,000 (of which corn [maize] 1,407,000, sorghum 316,000, rice 280,000, millet 159,000), oil palm fruit 1,050,000, cacao 380,000, coconuts 315,000, oranges 300,000, tomatoes 200,000; livestock (number of live animals) 3,410,000 goats, 2,970,000 sheep, 1,430,000 cattle, 22,000,000 chickens; roundwood (2001) 21,979,000 cu m; fish catch (2001) 459,000. Mining and quarrying (2002): manganese (metal content) 363,000; bauxite 684,000; gold 2,241,000 troy oz; gem diamonds 770,000 carats. Manufacturing (value added in ₵; 1993): tobacco 71,474,700,000; footwear 60,350,600,000; chemical products 40,347,600,000; beverages 36,167,000,000; metal products 35,121,700,000; petroleum products 32,143,500,000; textiles 18,278,600,000; machinery and transport equipment 9,525,700,000. Energy production (consumption): electricity (kW-hr; 2001) 8,321,000,000 (8,029,000,000); coal (metric tons; 2000) none (3,000); crude petroleum (barrels; 2000) 87,000 (8,210,000); petroleum products (metric tons; 2000) 1,062,000 (1,567,000); natural gas, none (none).
Population economically active (1999)[4]: total 11,590,000; activity rate of total population 60.5% (participation rates: over age 15 [1984] 82.5%; female 51.1%; unemployed, n.a.).

Price and earnings indexes (2000 = 100)

	1997	1998	1999	2000	2001	2002	2003
Consumer price index	62.0	71.1	79.9	100.0	132.9	152.6	193.3
Monthly earnings index[7]	47.6	69.0	69.0	100.0	131.0	...	...

Tourism (2002): receipts U.S.$358,000,000; expenditures U.S.$120,000,000.
Land use as % of total land area (2000): in temporary crops 15.9%, in permanent crops 9.7%, in pasture 36.7%; overall forest area 27.8%.

Foreign trade[8]

Balance of trade (current prices)

	1995	1996	1997	1998	1999	2000
U.S.$'000,000	–257	–367	–638	–806	–1,073	–843
% of total	4.6%	10.5%	17.6%	16.2%	23.4%	18.2%

Imports (2000): U.S.$2,933,000,000 (crude and refined petroleum 18.9%, machinery and apparatus 18.8%, road vehicles 11.6%, food 10.9%). *Major import sources:* Nigeria 10.9%; U.K. 9.2%; U.S. 7.5%; Germany 7.1%; The Netherlands 6.3%; Italy 5.0%.
Exports (2000): U.S.$1,671,000,000 (gold 36.7%, cocoa beans 15.5%, aluminum 9.1%, sawn wood 4.9%). *Major export destinations:* Switzerland 23.5%; U.K. 18.9%; The Netherlands 11.2%; U.S. 5.9%; Germany 5.4%.

Transport and communications

Transport. Railroads (2000): route length 592 mi, 953 km; (1996) passenger-km 209,000,000; (1996) metric ton-km cargo 160,000,000. Roads (1996): total length 24,000 mi, 38,700 km (paved 40%). Vehicles (1999): passenger cars 90,400; trucks and buses 119,900. Air transport (2003)[9]: passenger-km 906,000,000, metric ton-km cargo 16,630,000; airports (1996) with scheduled flights 1.

Communications

Medium	date	unit	number	units per 1,000 persons
Daily newspapers	2000	circulation	273,000	14
Radio	2000	receivers	13,900,000	710
Television	2000	receivers	2,300,000	118
Telephones	2003	main lines	302,300	14
Cellular telephones	2003	subscribers	799,900	36
Personal computers	2002	units	82,000	3.8
Internet	2002	users	170,000	7.8

Education and health

Educational attainment (1984). Percentage of population age 25 and over having: no formal schooling 60.4%; primary education 7.1%; middle school 25.4%; secondary 3.5%; vocational and other postsecondary 2.9%; higher 0.6%. *Literacy* (2000): total population age 15 and over literate 8,070,000 (70.2%); males literate 4,520,000 (79.8%); females literate 3,550,000 (61.2%).

Education (1996–97)

	schools	teachers	students	student/teacher ratio
Primary (age 6–12)	13,014	71,330	2,333,347	32.7
Secondary (age 13–20)	6,384	51,875	932,833	18.0
Voc., teacher tr.[10]	957	422	13,232	31.4
Higher[11]	4	1,432	25,372	17.7

Health: physicians (1996) 1,058 (1 per 16,129 persons); hospital beds (1998) 26,991 (1 per 667 persons); infant mortality rate per 1,000 live births (2003) 53.0.
Food (2002): daily per capita caloric intake 2,667 (vegetable products 95%, animal products 5%); 116% of FAO recommended minimum requirement.

Military

Total active duty personnel (2003): 7,000 (army 71.4%, navy 14.3%, air force 14.3%). *Military expenditure as percentage of GNP* (1999): 0.8% (world 2.4%); per capita expenditure U.S.$3.

[1]Detail does not add to total given because of rounding. [2]Alternate census total is 18,912,079; unknown if this total is final or unadjusted. [3]January 1. [4]Projected (and estimated total) figures based on Ghana Living Standards Survey (GLSS) of 8,487 labourers. [5]Percentage breakdown of GLSS. [6]Indirect taxes. [7]Minimum wage, for December only. [8]Imports are f.o.b. in balance of trade and c.i.f. for commodities and trading partners. [9]Ghana Airways only. [10]1989–90. [11]1999–2000; universities only.

Internet resources for further information:

- **UNDP in Ghana http://www.undp-gha.org**
- **Bank of Ghana http://www.bog.gov.gh**

Greece

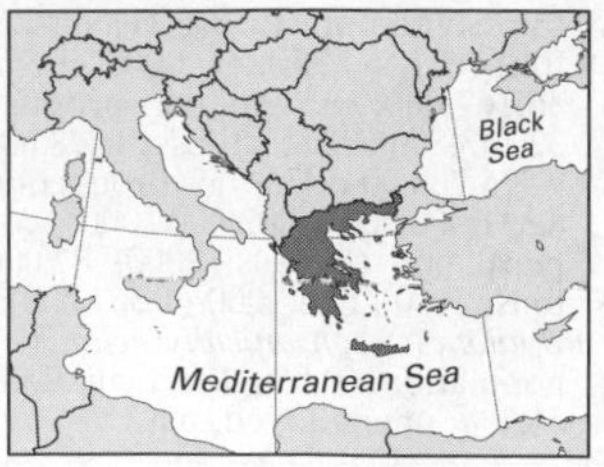

Official name: Ellinikí Dhimokratía (Hellenic Republic).
Form of government: unitary multiparty republic with one legislative house (Greek Chamber of Deputies [300]).
Chief of state: President.
Head of government: Prime Minister.
Capital: Athens.
Official language: Greek.
Official religion: Eastern Orthodox.
Monetary unit: 1 euro (€) = 100 cents; valuation (Sept. 1, 2004) 1 U.S.$ = €0.82; 1 £ = €1.48[1].

Area and population

		area		population
Regions[2]	**Principal cities**	sq mi	sq km	2001 census
Insular				
Aegean Islands	Mitilíni	3,519	9,113	508,807
Crete	Iráklion	3,218	8,336	601,131
Ionian Islands	Kérkira	891	2,307	212,984
Mainland				
Central Greece and Euboea[3]	Lamía	8,147	21,100	829,758
Epirus	Ioánnina	3,553	9,203	353,820
Greater Athens	Athens	1,470	3,808	3,761,810
Macedonia	Thessaloníki	13,195	34,174	2,424,765
Peloponnese	Pátrai	8,278	21,440	1,155,019
Thessaly	Lárisa	5,378	13,930	753,888
Thrace	Alexandroúpolis	3,312	8,578	362,038
TOTAL		50,949[4]	131,957[4]	10,964,020[5]

Demography

Population (2004): 11,015,000.
Density (2004): persons per sq mi 216.2, persons per sq km 83.5.
Urban-rural (2002): urban 60.3%; rural 39.7%.
Sex distribution (2001): male 49.49%; female 50.51%.
Age breakdown (2002): under 15, 15.2%; 15–29, 22.0%; 30–44, 22.3%; 45–59, 18.0%; 60–74, 16.5%; 75 and over, 6.0%.
Population projection: (2010) 11,031,000; (2020) 10,878,000.
Ethnic composition (2000)[6]: Greek 90.4%; Macedonian 1.8%; Albanian 1.5%; Turkish 1.4%; Pomak 0.9%; Roma (Gypsy) 0.8%; other 3.2%.
Religious affiliation (1995): Christian 95.2%, of which Eastern Orthodox 94.0%, Roman Catholic 0.5%; Muslim 1.3%; other 3.5%.
Major cities (2001): Athens 745,514 (urban agglomeration 3,120,000); Thessaloníki 363,987 (urban agglomeration [2000] 789,000); Piraeus (Piraiévs) 175,697[7]; Pátrai 163,446; Peristérion 137,918[7]; Iráklion 137,711.

Vital statistics

Birth rate per 1,000 population (2003): 9.7 (world avg. 21.3); (2001) legitimate 95.7%; illegitimate 4.3%.
Death rate per 1,000 population (2003): 10.0 (world avg. 9.1).
Natural increase rate per 1,000 population (2003): –0.3 (world avg. 12.2).
Total fertility rate (avg. births per childbearing woman; 2002): 1.3.
Marriage rate per 1,000 population (2001): 5.7.
Life expectancy at birth (2003): male 76.3 years; female 81.4 years.
Major causes of death per 100,000 population (1999): diseases of the circulatory system 480.0; malignant neoplasms (cancers) 216.0; ill-defined conditions 66.9; diseases of the respiratory system 66.7.

National economy

Budget (2001). Revenue: Dr 20,596,049,000,000 (indirect taxes 31.9%; direct taxes 22.5%; nontax revenue 28.9%; other 16.7%). Expenditures: Dr 20,596,049,000,000 (current expenditure 86.9%, of which health and social insurance 10.3%, education and culture 6.8%, defense 6.8%; capital expenditure 13.1%).
Public debt (2001): U.S.$116,870,000,000.
Production (metric tons except as noted). Agriculture, forestry, fishing (2002): sugar beets 2,780,000, wheat 2,033,000, corn (maize) 2,014,000, olives 2,000,000, tomatoes 1,700,000, seed cotton 1,180,000, oranges 1,170,000, grapes 1,150,000, peaches and nectarines 930,000, potatoes 875,000, barley 268,000, apples 230,000, tobacco 123,700; livestock (number of live animals) 9,205,000 sheep, 5,023,000 goats, 938,000 pigs; roundwood (2001) 1,915,930 cu m; fish catch (2001) 192,190. Mining and quarrying: bauxite (2001) 1,931,000; crude magnesite 483,000; marble 200,000 cu m. Manufacturing (value added in Dr '000,000,000; 1999): food 573; paints, soaps, varnishes, drugs, and medicines 371; electrical machinery 287; textiles 259; cement, bricks, and tiles 227; beverages 214. Energy production (consumption): electricity (kW-hr; 2000) 49,296,000,000 (49,285,000,000); hard coal (metric tons; 2000) none (1,121,000); lignite (metric tons; 2000) 63,887,000 (64,564,000); crude petroleum (barrels; 2000) 183,800 (138,800,000); petroleum products (metric tons; 2000) 20,265,000 (16,667,000); natural gas (cu m; 2000) 49,280,000 (2,030,900,000).
Land use as % of total land area (2000): in temporary crops 21.3%, in permanent crops 8.6%, in pasture 36.3%; overall forest area 27.9%.
Household income and expenditure. Average household size (2000) 3.0; income per family (1998–99) Dr 6,429,000 (U.S.$21,390); sources of income (1998–99): wages and salaries 35.7%, transfer payments 16.7%, self-employment 14.9%, other 32.7%; expenditure (1999): food and beverages 24.9%, transportation and communications 14.3%, cafe/hotel expenditures 9.4%, housing 8.1%, household furnishings 7.3%.
Gross national product (2003): U.S.$146,563,000,000 (U.S.$13,720 per capita).

Structure of gross domestic product and labour force

	2000		2002	
	in value Dr '000,000	% of total value	labour force	% of labour force
Agriculture	2,757,262	6.7	623,800	14.3
Mining	225,183	0.5	18,900	0.4
Manufacturing	4,192,932	10.1	540,800	12.4
Construction	2,583,398	6.2	293,900	6.7
Public utilities	665,420	1.6	33,700	0.8
Transp. and commun.	3,195,964	7.7	243,500	5.6
Trade, restaurants	8,123,638	19.6	947,300	21.7
Finance, real estate	8,446,838	20.4	324,300	7.4
Pub. admin., defense	2,644,010	6.4	922,700	21.1
Services	4,825,045	11.7		
Other	3,747,042[8]	9.1[8]	420,100[9]	9.6[9]
TOTAL	41,406,732	100.0	4,369,000	100.0

Population economically active (2001): total 4,362,300; activity rate of total population 42.1% (participation rates: ages 15–64, 56.9%; female 40.2%; unemployed 10.2%).

Price index (2000 = 100)

	1997	1998	1999	2000	2001	2002	2003
Consumer price index	90.2	94.5	96.9	100.0	103.7	107.7	111.4

Tourism (2002): receipts U.S.$9,741,000,000; expenditures U.S.$2,450,000,000.

Foreign trade[10]

Balance of trade (current prices)

	1998	1999	2000	2001	2002	2003
U.S.$'000,000	–18,656	–18,244	–18,852	–20,444	–20,849	–31,180
% of total	46.5%	46.5%	46.2%	51.9%	50.3%	54.2%

Imports (2000): U.S.$29,816,000,000 (machinery and apparatus 18.6%, chemicals and chemical products 11.5%, crude petroleum 10.1%, road vehicles 9.5%, food products 9.1%, ships and boats 5.2%). *Major import sources:* Italy 12.9%; Germany 12.8%; France 7.2%; The Netherlands 5.8%; U.K. 5.0%.
Exports (2000): U.S.$10,964,000,000 (food 14.6%, of which fruits and nuts 6.0%; clothing and apparel 12.8%; refined petroleum 12.5%; machinery and apparatus 9.8%; aluminum 4.2%). *Major export destinations:* Germany 12.3%; Italy 9.2%; U.K. 6.3%; U.S. 5.8%; Turkey 5.0%.

Transport and communications

Transport. Railroads (2000): route length 2,299 km; passenger-km 1,629,000,-000; metric ton-km cargo 427,000,000. Roads (1999): total length 117,000 km (paved 92%). Vehicles (2001): passenger cars 3,423,704; trucks and buses 1,112,926. Air transport (2003)[11]: passenger-km 6,240,000,000; metric ton-km cargo 55,800,000; airports (1997) 36.

Communications

Medium	date	unit	number	units per 1,000 persons
Daily newspapers	2000	circulation	1,530,000	140
Radio	2000	receivers	5,220,000	478
Television	2000	receivers	5,330,000	488
Telephones	2003	main lines	5,205,100	454
Cellular telephones	2003	subscribers	8,936,200	785
Personal computers	2002	units	900,000	82
Internet	2003	users	1,718,400	150

Education and health

Educational attainment (2001). Percentage of population age 25 and over having: no formal schooling/preprimary 12.7%; primary education 34.3%; lower secondary 8.5%; upper secondary 25.7%; postsecondary 3.4%; incomplete and complete higher 15.4%. *Literacy* (2000): total population age 15 and over literate 97.2%; males 98.6%; females 96.0%.

Education (2001–02)

	schools	teachers	students	student/ teacher ratio
Primary (age 6–12)	6,074	49,842	647,041	13.0
Secondary (age 12–18)	3,244	54,123	589,669	10.8
Voc., teacher tr.	591	13,245	154,400	11.7
Higher[12]	18	10,708	163,256	15.2

Health: physicians (2001) 46,325[13] (1 per 221 persons); hospital beds (2000) 49,804[13] (1 per 205 persons); infant mortality rate (2003) 5.7.
Food (2001): daily per capita caloric intake 3,754 (vegetable products 78%, animal products 22%); 150% of FAO recommended minimum requirement.

Military

Total active duty personnel (2003): 177,600 (army 70.7%, navy 10.7%, air force 18.6%). *Military expenditure as percentage of GNP* (1999): 4.7% (world 2.4%); per capita expenditure U.S.$573.

[1]The drachma (Dr) was the former monetary unit; on Jan. 1, 2002, Dr 340.75 = €1. [2]Created for planning and economic development; local administration is based on 50 departments, 4 prefectures, and 1 autonomous self-governing monastic region (Mount Athos). [3]Excluding Greater Athens. [4]Detail does not add to total given because of statistical discrepancy. [5]De facto figure; de jure total equals 10,215,539. [6]Government states there are no ethnic divisions in Greece. [7]Within Athens urban agglomeration. [8]Taxes less imputed bank service charges and subsidies. [9]Unemployed. [10]Imports c.i.f.; exports f.o.b. [11]Olympic Airways. [12]Universities only. [13]Derived figure based on pre-2001 census de jure population.

Internet resources for further information:
- **Bank of Greece http://www.bankofgreece.gr/en**

Greenland

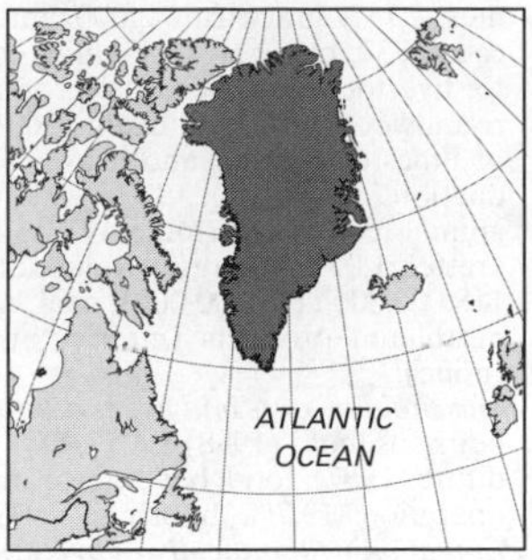

Official name: Kalaallit Nunaat (Greenlandic); Grønland (Danish) (Greenland).
Political status: integral part of the Danish realm with one legislative house (Parliament [31]).
Chief of state: Danish Monarch.
Heads of government: High Commissioner (for Denmark); Prime Minister (for Greenland).
Capital: Nuuk (Godthåb).
Official languages: Greenlandic; Danish.
Official religion: Evangelical Lutheran (Lutheran Church of Greenland).
Monetary unit: 1 Danish krone (Dkr) = 100 øre; valuation (Sept. 1, 2004) 1 U.S.$ = Dkr 6.12; 1 £ = Dkr 11.01.

Area and population

Counties / Communes	area sq mi	area sq km	population 2003[1] estimate
Avanersuaq (Nordgrønland)	...	...	
Qaanaaq (Thule)	...	...	859
Kitaa (Vestgrønland)	...	...	
Aasiaat (Egedesminde)	...	...	3,367
Ilulissat (Jakobshavn)	...	...	5,007
Ivittuut (Ivigtut)	...	...	178
Kangaatsiaq (Kangâtsiaq)	...	...	1,516
Maniitsoq (Sukkertoppen)	...	...	3,681
Nanortalik	...	...	2,468
Narsaq (Narssaq)	...	...	2,047
Nuuk (Godthåb)	...	...	14,265
Paamiut (Frederikshåb)	...	...	2,019
Qaqortoq (Julianehåb)	...	...	3,406
Qasigiannguit (Christianshåb)	...	...	1,422
Qeqertarsuaq (Godhavn)	...	...	1,059
Sisimiut (Holsteinsborg)	...	...	6,024
Upernavik	...	...	2,906
Uummannaq (Umanaq)	...	...	2,655
Tunu (Østgrønland)	...	...	
Illoqqortoormiit (Scoresbysund)	...	...	541
Ammassalik	...	...	3,007
TOTAL (ICE-FREE)	158,475	410,449	
PERMANENT ICE	677,855	1,755,637	
TOTAL	836,330	2,166,086	56,676[2]

Demography

Population (2004): 56,800.
Density[3] (2004): persons per sq mi 0.36, persons per sq km 0.14.
Urban-rural (2003[1]): urban (town) 82.2%; rural (settlement) 17.8%.
Sex distribution (2003[1]): male 53.37%; female 46.63%.
Age breakdown (2003[1]): under 15, 26.2%; 15–29, 19.7%; 30–44, 27.9%; 45–59, 17.4%; 60–74, 7.5%; 75 and over, 1.3%.
Population projection: (2010) 57,000; (2020) 57,000.
Doubling time: 82 years.
Ethnic composition (2000): Greenland Eskimo 79.1%; Danish 13.6%; other 7.3%.
Religious affiliation (2000): Protestant 69.2%, of which Evangelical Lutheran 64.2%, Pentecostal 2.8%; other Christian 27.4%; other/nonreligious 3.4%.
Major towns (2003[1]): Nuuk (Godthåb) 13,884; Sisimiut (Holsteinsborg) 5,263; Ilulissat (Jakobshavn) 4,525; Aasiaat (Egedesminde) 3,142; Qaqortoq (Julianehåb) 3,129.

Vital statistics

Birth rate per 1,000 population (2003): 16.1 (world avg. 21.3); (1993) legitimate 29.2%; illegitimate 70.8%.
Death rate per 1,000 population (2003): 7.7 (world avg. 9.1).
Natural increase rate per 1,000 population (2003): 8.4 (world avg. 12.2).
Total fertility rate (avg. births per childbearing woman; 2003): 2.4.
Marriage rate per 1,000 population (1993): 7.1.
Life expectancy at birth (2003): male 65.4 years; female 72.7 years.
Major causes of death per 100,000 population (1996–98): diseases of the circulatory system 187.5; malignant neoplasms (cancers) 181.5; violence 95.8; infectious and parasitic diseases 64.9; suicides 63.7; diseases of the respiratory system 51.8; accidents 46.4.

National economy

Budget (2001). Revenue: Dkr 7,648,000,000 (block grant from Danish government 37.9%; income tax 30.5%; import duties 8.8%). Expenditures (2001): Dkr 7,069,000,000 (current expenditure 92.1%, of which social welfare 24.1%, culture and education 21.1%, health 11.9%, defense 3.7%; capital [development] expenditure 7.9%).
Public debt (2000): U.S.$53,000,000.
Tourism (2002): number of overnight stays at hotels 179,349, of which visitors from within Greenland 94,552, from Denmark 55,602, from the U.S. 6,227.
Production (metric tons except as noted). Fishing, animal products: fish catch (2001) 292,000 (by local boats 143,000, of which prawn 85,800, halibut 20,700, crab 14,200; by foreign boats 149,000); livestock (number of live animals; 2002) 18,967 sheep, 3,100 reindeer; animal products (value of external sales in Dkr '000; 1998) sealskins 31,044, polar bear skins 579. Mining: [4]. Manufacturing: principally handicrafts and fish processing. Energy production (consumption): electricity (kW-hr; 2002) 311,000,000 ([2001] 284,000,000); coal, none (none); crude petroleum (barrels; 1999) none (1,307,000); petroleum products (metric tons; 2000) none (181,000); natural gas, none (none).
Gross national product (1998): U.S.$1,150,000,000 (U.S.$20,500 per capita).

Structure of gross domestic product and labour force

	1998 in value Dkr '000,000	1998 % of total value	2000 labour force	2000 % of labour force
Agriculture, fishing	...	...	2,039	7.0
Quarrying	...	...	18	0.1
Manufacturing	...	...	2,508	8.6
Public utilities	...	...	467	1.6
Construction	...	...	1,808	6.2
Transp. and commun.	...	...	2,195	7.5
Trade, restaurants	...	...	2,404	8.2
Finance, real estate	...	...	754	2.6
Public administration	...	...	12,588	43.1
Services	...	...	1,082	3.7
Other	...	...	3,356[5]	11.5[5]
TOTAL	7,719	100.0	29,219	100.0[6]

Population economically active (2002): total 31,506; activity rate of total population 55.7% (participation rates: ages 15–62, 82.9%; female [1987] 43.4%; unemployed [2002] 6.5%).

Price and earnings indexes (1999 = 100)

	1996	1997	1998	1999	2000	2001
Consumer price index	97.7	98.3	99.3	100.0	101.6	104.7
Monthly earnings index	99.5	100.6	100.1	100.0	...	...

Household income and expenditure. Average household size (1998): 2.6; income per person (1997): Dkr 144,700 (U.S.$17,700); sources of income: n.a.; expenditure (1994): food, beverages, and tobacco 41.6%, housing and energy 22.4%, transportation and communications 10.2%, recreation 6.4%.
Land use as % of total land area (2000): in temporary crops, negligible, in permanent crops, none, in pasture 0.6%; overall forest area, negligible.

Foreign trade

Balance of trade (current prices)

	1997	1998	1999	2000	2001	2002
Dkr '000,000	–688	–1,038	–924	–742	–460	–751
% of total	15.1%	23.4%	19.3%	14.4%	9.3%	14.9%

Imports (2002): Dkr 2,891,000,000 (goods for trades and industries 19.8%; food, beverages, and tobacco products 16.4%; goods for construction industry 14.8%; mineral fuels 8.9%; machinery 6.8%; transport equipment 3.1%). *Major import sources:* Denmark c. 70%; Norway c. 8%.
Exports (2002): Dkr 2,140,000,000 (marine products 88.4%, of which shrimp 55.7%, fish 20.6%, crab 10.1%). *Major export destinations:* Denmark c. 88%; U.S. c. 4%; U.K. c. 2%.

Transport and communications

Transport. Railroads: none. Roads (1998): total length 93 mi, 150 km (paved 60%). Vehicles (2001): passenger cars 2,485; trucks and buses 1,483. Air transport (2001)[7]: passenger-mi 131,100,000, passenger-km 211,000,000; short ton-mi cargo 16,400,000; metric ton-km cargo 24,000,000; airports (1998) with scheduled flights 18.

Communications

Medium	date	unit	number	units per 1,000 persons
Daily newspapers	1996	circulation	1,000	18
Radio	1997	receivers	27,000	482
Television	1997	receivers	22,000	393
Telephones	2002	main lines	25,300	447
Cellular telephones	2002	subscribers	17,700	313
Internet	2002	users	9,100	161

Education and health

Literacy (1999): total population age 15 and over literate: virtually 100%.

Education (2001–02)

	schools	teachers	students	student/ teacher ratio
Primary (age 6–15) / Secondary (age 15–19) / Voc., teacher tr.	87	1,191	11,368	9.5
Higher[8]	1	14	100	7.1

Health (2001): physicians 89 (1 per 634 persons); hospital beds 406 (1 per 139 persons); infant mortality rate per 1,000 live births (2003) 16.8.

Military

Total active duty personnel. Denmark is responsible for Greenland's defense. Greenlanders are not liable for military service.

[1]January 1. [2]Includes 249 people not distributed by county. [3]Population density calculated with reference to ice-free area only. [4]Greenland's first gold mine officially opened in August 2004. [5]Figure includes 2,245 people who are unemployed. [6]Detail does not add to total given because of rounding. [7]Air Greenland A/S only. [8]University of Greenland only.

Internet resources for further information:
- **Statistics Greenland http://www.statgreen.gl/english**
- **Danmarks Statistik http://www.dst.dk/yearbook**

Grenada

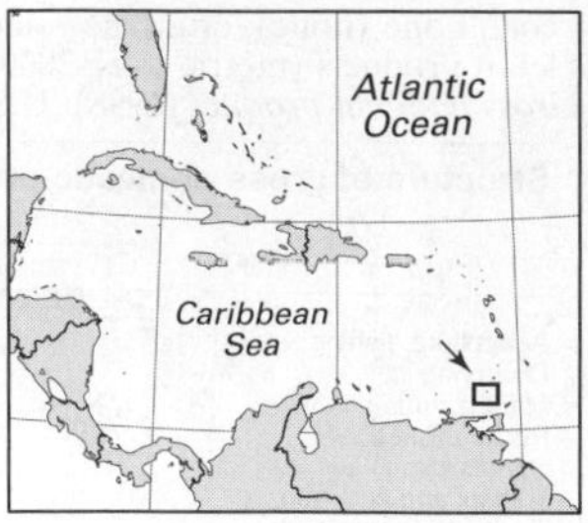

Official name: Grenada.
Form of government: constitutional monarchy with two legislative houses (Senate [13]; House of Representatives [15[1]]).
Chief of state: British Monarch represented by Governor-General.
Head of government: Prime Minister.
Capital: St. George's.
Official language: English.
Official religion: none.
Monetary unit: 1 East Caribbean dollar (EC$) = 100 cents; valuation (Sept. 1, 2004) 1 U.S.$ = EC$2.70; 1 £ = EC$4.86.

Area and population

		area		population
Local Councils	**Principal towns**	sq mi	sq km	2001[2] census
Carriacou	Hillsborough	10	26	6,063
Petite Martinique	...	3	8	
St. Andrew	Grenville	38	99	24,661
St. David	...	17	44	11,476
St. George	...	25[3]	65[3]	31,651
St. John	Gouyave	14	35	8,557
St. Mark	Victoria	10	25	3,955
St. Patrick	Sauteurs	16	42	10,624
Town				
St. George's	—	[3]	[3]	3,908
TOTAL		133	344	100,895

Demography

Population (2004): 103,000.
Density (2004): persons per sq mi 774.4, persons per sq km 299.4.
Urban-rural (2001)[4]: urban 38.4%; rural 61.6%.
Sex distribution (2001): male 49.55%; female 50.45%.
Age breakdown (2001): under 15, 35.1%; 15–29, 28.1%; 30–44, 17.6%; 45–59, 9.0%; 60 and over, 10.2%.
Population projection: (2010) 106,000; (2020) 112,000.
Doubling time: 46 years.
Ethnic composition (2000): black 51.7%; mixed 40.0%; Indo-Pakistani 4.0%; white 0.9%; other 3.4%.
Religious affiliation (1995): Roman Catholic 57.8%; Protestant 37.6%, of which Anglican 14.4%, Pentecostal 8.3%, Seventh-day Adventist 7.0%; other 4.6%, of which Rastafarian *c.* 3.0%.
Major localities (2001): St. George's 3,908 (urban agglomeration 35,559); Gouyave 3,100[5]; Grenville 2,300[5]; Victoria 2,100[5].

Vital statistics

Birth rate per 1,000 population (2003): 22.9 (world avg. 21.3).
Death rate per 1,000 population (2003): 7.5 (world avg. 9.1).
Natural increase rate per 1,000 population (2003): 15.4 (world avg. 12.2).
Total fertility rate (avg. births per childbearing woman; 2003): 2.5.
Marriage rate per 1,000 population (2001): 5.0.
Divorce rate per 1,000 population (2001): 1.1.
Life expectancy at birth (2003): male 62.7 years; female 66.3 years.
Major causes of death per 100,000 population (2000): diseases of the circulatory system 298; malignant neoplasms (cancers) 104; diseases of the respiratory system 65; accidents and violence 31.

National economy

Budget (2000). Revenue: EC$297,900,000 (tax revenue 89.1%, of which tax on international trade 51.3%, general sales taxes 17.1%, income taxes 17.5%; grants from abroad 10.9%). Expenditures: EC$365,700,000 (current expenditure 63.0%, of which wages 31.3%, transfers 13.2%, debt 11.3%; capital expenditure 37.0%).
Public debt (external, outstanding; 2002): U.S.$268,700,000.
Tourism (2002): receipts from visitors U.S.$84,000,000; expenditures by nationals abroad U.S.$8,000,000.
Gross national product (at current market prices; 2003): U.S.$396,000,000 (U.S.$3,790 per capita).

Structure of gross domestic product and labour force

	2000		1998	
	in value EC$'000,000[6]	% of total value[6]	labour force	% of labour force
Agriculture	70.0	7.7	4,794	11.7
Quarrying	4.4	0.5	58	0.1
Manufacturing	68.9	7.6	2,579	6.3
Construction	93.7	10.3	5,163	12.6
Public utilities	49.6	5.5	505	1.2
Transp. and commun.	211.3	23.4	2,043	5.0
Trade, restaurants	179.7	19.9	8,298	20.2
Finance, real estate	120.4	13.3	1,312	3.2
Pub. admin., defense	148.2	16.4	1,879	4.6
Services	29.4	3.2	6,837	16.7
Other	–70.7[7]	–7.8[7]	7,547[8]	18.4[8]
TOTAL	904.9	100.0	41,015	100.0

Production (metric tons except as noted). Agriculture, forestry, fishing (2002): sugarcane 7,200, coconuts 6,800, bananas 4,100, roots and tubers 3,200, nutmeg 2,747, grapefruit 2,000, mangoes 1,900, avocados 1,750, oranges 900, cacao 737, other crops include cotton, limes, cinnamon, cloves, and pimiento; livestock (number of live animals) 13,100 sheep, 7,100 goats, 5,850 pigs; roundwood, n.a.; fish catch (2001) 2,247. Mining and quarrying: excavation of limestone, sand, and gravel for local use. Manufacturing (value of production in EC$'000; 1997): wheat flour 13,390; soft drinks 9,798; beer 7,072; animal feed 5,852; rum 5,497; toilet paper 4,237; malt 4,192; stout 3,835; cigarettes 1,053. Energy production (consumption): electricity (kW-hr; 2000) 118,000,000 (118,000,000); coal, none (none); crude petroleum, none (none); petroleum products (metric tons; 2000) none (69,000); natural gas, none (none).
Household income and expenditure. Average household size (1991) 3.7; income per household (1988) EC$7,097 (U.S.$2,629); sources of income: n.a.; expenditure (1987): food, beverages, and tobacco 40.7%, household furnishings and operations 13.7%, housing 11.9%, transportation 9.1%.
Population economically active (1998): total 41,015; activity rate of total population *c.* 46% (participation rate: ages 15–64, *c.* 78%; female 43.5%; unemployed 15.2%).

Price index (2000 = 100)

	1997	1998	1999	2000	2001	2002
Consumer price index	96.0	97.3	97.9	100.0	101.7	102.8

Land use as % of total land area (2000): in temporary crops *c.* 3%, in permanent crops *c.* 29%, in pasture *c.* 3%; overall forest area *c.* 15%.

Foreign trade[9]

Balance of trade (current prices)

	1998	1999	2000	2001	2002
U.S.$'000,000	–136.7	–109.8	–135.9	–132.8	–144.7
% of total	59.8%	42.4%	44.6%	51.1%	52.9%

Imports (2002): U.S.$233,200,000 (machinery and transport equipment 27.4%; food 16.6%; chemicals and chemical products 11.1%; mineral fuels 9.8%). *Major import sources:* United States 45.8%; Caricom 25.6%; EU 12.5%, of which United Kingdom 6.0%; Venezuela 4.6%.
Exports (2002): U.S.$59,700,000 (domestic exports 92.1%, of which electronic components 39.2%, nutmeg 21.4%, fish 7.4%, paper products 2.5%, cocoa beans 2.3%; reexports 7.9%). *Major export destinations:* United States 38.9%; EU 34.5%, of which United Kingdom 1.2%; Caricom 22.2%.

Transport and communications

Transport. Railroads: none. Roads (1999): total length 646 mi, 1,040 km (paved 61%). Vehicles (1991)[10]: passenger cars 4,739; trucks and buses 3,068. Air transport (2001)[11]: passengers 331,000; cargo 2,747 metric tons; airports (1998) with scheduled flights 2.

Communications

Medium	date	unit	number	units per 1,000 persons
Radio	1997	receivers	57,000	615
Television	1997	receivers	33,000	353
Telephones	2002	main lines	33,500	317
Cellular telephones	2002	subscribers	7,600	71
Personal computers	2002	units	14,000	132
Internet	2002	users	15,000	142

Education and health

Educational attainment (1991). Percentage of population age 25 and over having: no formal schooling 1.8%; primary education 74.9%; secondary 15.5%; higher 4.7%, of which university 2.8%; other/unknown 3.1%. *Literacy* (1995): total population age 15 and over literate 50,000 (85.0%).

Education (1996–97)

	schools	teachers	students	student/ teacher ratio
Primary (age 5–11)[12]	58	879	23,449	26.7
Secondary (age 12–16)[12]	19[13]	381[13]	7,367	19.3
Vocational	...	...	...	...
Higher[13, 14]	1	66	651	9.9

Health (1999): physicians 81 (1 per 1,233 persons); hospital beds (2000) 623 (1 per 161 persons); infant mortality rate per 1,000 live births (2003) 14.6.
Food (2002): daily per capita caloric intake 2,932 (vegetable products 74%, animal products 26%); 121% of FAO recommended minimum requirement.

Military

Total active duty personnel (1997) [15]. *Military expenditure as percentage of GNP:* n.a.; per capita expenditure, n.a.

[1]Excludes the speaker, who may be elected from outside its elected membership. [2]Preliminary noninstitutional figures; another 2001 census total equals 101,306. [3]St. George local council includes St. George's town. [4]Urban defined as St. George's town and St. George local council. [5]1991. [6]At current prices. [7]Less imputed bank service charges. [8]Includes 1,321 activities not adequately defined and 6,226 unemployed. [9]Imports are f.o.b. in balance of trade and c.i.f. for commodities and trading partners. [10]Registered vehicles only. [11]Point Salines airport. [12]Excludes private schools. [13]1994–95. [14]Excludes Grenada Teachers' College. [15]A 730-member police force includes an 80-member paramilitary unit and a 30-member coast guard unit.

Internet resources for further information:
- **Eastern Caribbean Central Bank http://www.eccb-centralbank.org**
- **Caricom Statistics http://www.caricomstats.org**

Guadeloupe

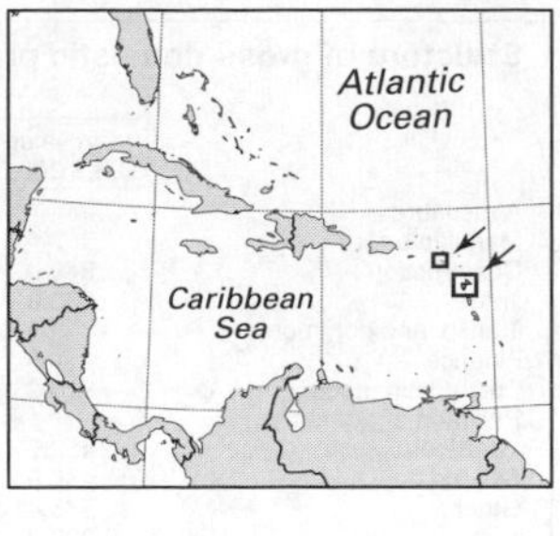

Official name: Département de la Guadeloupe (Department of Guadeloupe).
Political status: overseas department (France) with two legislative houses (General Council [42]; Regional Council [41]).
Chief of state: President of France.
Heads of government: Commissioner of the Republic (for France); President of the General Council (for Guadeloupe); President of the Regional Council (for Guadeloupe).
Capital: Basse-Terre.
Official language: French.
Official religion: none.
Monetary unit: 1 euro (€) = 100 centimes; valuation (Sept. 1, 2004) 1 U.S.$ = €0.82; 1 £ = €1.48[1].

Area and population

		area		population
Arrondissements	**Capitals**	sq mi	sq km	1999 census
Basse-Terre[2]	Basse-Terre	330	855	175,691
Pointe-à-Pitre[3]	Pointe-à-Pitre	299	775	210,875
Saint-Martin–Saint-Barthélemy[4, 5]	Marigot	29	74	35,930
TOTAL		658	1,705[6]	422,496

Demography

Population (2004): 443,000.
Density (2004): persons per sq mi 673.3, persons per sq km 259.8.
Urban-rural (2001): urban 99.6%; rural 0.4%.
Sex distribution (2002): male 47.93%; female 52.07%.
Age breakdown (1999): under 15, 23.6%; 15–29, 22.4%; 30–44, 24.3%; 45–59, 15.7%; 60–74, 9.3%; 75 and over, 4.7%.
Population projection: (2010) 460,000; (2020) 478,000.
Doubling time: 68 years.
Ethnic composition (2000): Creole (mulatto) 76.7%; black 10.0%; Guadeloupe mestizo (French–East Asian) 10.0%; white 2.0%; other 1.3%.
Religious affiliation (1995): Roman Catholic 81.1%; Jehovah's Witness 4.8%; Protestant 4.7%; other 9.4%.
Major communes (1999): Les Abymes 63,054[7]; Saint-Martin (Marigot) 29,078; Le Gosier 25,360[7]; Pointe-à-Pitre 20,948 (urban agglomeration 171,773); Basse-Terre 12,410 (urban agglomeration 54,076).

Vital statistics

Birth rate per 1,000 population (2003): 16.2 (world avg. 21.3); (1997) legitimate 37.0%; illegitimate 63.0%.
Death rate per 1,000 population (2003): 6.0 (world avg. 9.1).
Natural increase rate per 1,000 population (2003): 10.2 (world avg. 12.2).
Total fertility rate (avg. births per childbearing woman; 2003): 1.9.
Marriage rate per 1,000 population (2002): 4.1.
Divorce rate per 1,000 population (1997): 1.3.
Life expectancy at birth (2003): male 74.4 years; female 80.8 years.
Major causes of death per 100,000 population (1996): diseases of the circulatory system 183.7; malignant neoplasms (cancers) 134.8; accidents, violence, and poisoning 68.1; diseases of the respiratory system 32.1; diseases of the digestive system 31.4; endocrine and metabolic diseases 26.2; infectious and parasitic diseases 23.8.

National economy

Budget (1998). Revenue: F 4,227,000,000 (tax revenues 69.0%, of which direct taxes 42.5%, value-added taxes 25.1%; advances, loans, and transfers 26.8%). Expenditures: F 7,874,000,000 (current expenditures 70.6%, capital [development] expenditures 10.6%; advances and loans 18.8%).
Public debt: n.a.
Production (metric tons except as noted). Agriculture, forestry, fishing (2002): sugarcane 798,072, bananas 135,000, yams 10,032, plantains 9,158, pineapples 6,975, sweet potatoes 4,221, melons 4,072, tomatoes 3,071, eggplant 180; livestock (number of live animals) 85,000 cattle, 28,000 goats; roundwood (2001) 15,300 cu m; fish catch (2001) 10,114. Mining and quarrying (2000): pumice 210,000. Manufacturing (2002): cement 284,000; raw sugar 51,726; rum 67,151 hectolitres; other products include clothing, wooden furniture and posts, and metalware. Energy production (consumption): electricity (kW-hr; 2000) 1,220,000,000 (1,220,000,000); coal, none (none); crude petroleum, none (none); petroleum products (metric tons; 2000) none (497,000); natural gas, none (none).
Land use as % of total land area (2000): in temporary crops *c.* 11%, in permanent crops *c.* 4%, in pasture *c.* 14%; overall forest area *c.* 48%.
Population economically active (1999): total 191,362; activity rate of total population 45.3% (participation rates: ages 15–64 [1995] 73.2%; female 49.1%; unemployed [2003] 24.1%).

Price and earnings indexes (1998 = 100)

	1998	1999	2000	2001	2002	2003[8]	2004[8]
Consumer price index	100.0	100.4	100.4	103.0	106.6	108.4	109.4
Monthly earnings index	...	...	...	...	...	...	...

Gross national product (2000): U.S.$6,148,000,000 (U.S.$14,370 per capita).

Structure of gross domestic product and labour force

	1995		1998	
	in value F '000,000	% of total value	labour force	% of labour force
Agriculture	1,080.7	4.1	8,200	4.5
Mining, manufacturing	1,744.9	6.6	7,900	4.3
Construction	1,880.1	7.2	13,000	7.1
Public utilities	...	...	...	...
Transp. and commun.	2,156.2	8.2	4,200	2.3
Trade, hotels	6,121.6	23.4	20,700	11.4
Finance, real estate	1,043.2	4.0	3,500	1.9
Pub. admin., defense	9,926.7	37.9	43,400	23.8
Services	3,210.2	12.2	24,400	13.4
Other	–957.4[9]	–3.6[9]	56,900[10]	31.2[10]
TOTAL	26,206.2	100.0	182,200	100.0[6]

Household income and expenditure. Average household size (1999) 2.9; disposable income per household (1999) €26,938 (U.S.$25,284); sources of income (1988): wages and salaries 78.9%, self-employment 12.7%, transfer payments 8.4%; expenditure (1994–95): housing 26.2%, food and beverages 21.4%, transportation and communications 14.1%, household durables 6.0%, culture and leisure 4.2%.
Tourism (2000): receipts from visitors U.S.$418,000,000; expenditures, n.a.

Foreign trade

Balance of trade (current prices)

	1997	1998	1999	2000	2001	2002
€'000,000	–9,274[11]	–9,996[11]	–1,431	–1,666	–1,666	–1,635
% of total	86.3%	88.2%	83.4%	86.2%	83.1%	84.9%

Imports (2001): €1,835,000,000 (food and agriculture products 19.8%, consumer goods 18.6%, machinery and equipment 15.8%). *Major import sources* (1998): France 63.4%; Germany 4.4%; Italy 3.5%; Martinique 3.4%; U.S. 2.9%.
Exports (2001): €169,000,000 (food and agricultural products 58.4% [including bananas, sugar, rum, melons, eggplant, and flowers]). *Major export destinations* (1998): France 68.5%; Martinique 9.4%; Italy 4.8%; Belgium-Luxembourg 3.3%; French Guiana 3.0%.

Transport and communications

Transport. Railroads: none. Roads (1998): total length 1,988 mi, 3,415 km (paved [1986] 80%). Vehicles (1999): passenger cars 117,700; trucks and buses 31,400. Air transport (2002): passenger arrivals and departures 1,807,400; cargo handled 16,179 metric tons, cargo unloaded 5,204 metric tons; airports (1997) with scheduled flights 7.

Communications

Medium	date	unit	number	units per 1,000 persons
Daily newspapers	1995	circulation	35,000	81
Radio	1997	receivers	113,000	258
Television	1999	receivers	118,000	262
Telephones	2001	main lines	210,000	457
Cellular telephones	2002	subscribers	323,500	697
Personal computers	2001	units	100,000	217
Internet	2001	users	20,000	43

Education and health

Educational attainment (1990). Percentage of population age 25 and over having: incomplete primary, or no declaration 59.8%; primary education 14.5%; secondary 19.0%; higher 6.7%. *Literacy* (1992): total population age 15 and over literate 225,400 (90.1%); males literate 108,700 (89.7%); females literate 116,700 (90.5%).

Education (1998–99)

	schools	teachers	students	student/teacher ratio
Primary (age 6–10)	348	2,936	40,042	13.6
Secondary (age 11–17) / Vocational	85	3,392	51,491	15.2
Higher[12]	1	...	10,919	...

Health (2001): physicians 835 (1 per 515 persons); hospital beds 2,435 (1 per 177 persons); infant mortality rate per 1,000 live births (2003) 9.1.
Food (1995): daily per capita caloric intake 2,732 (vegetable products 75%, animal products 25%); 129% of FAO recommended minimum requirement.

Military

Total active duty personnel (2003): French troops in Antilles (Guadeloupe and Martinique) 4,100.

[1]French franc replaced by euro as of Jan. 1, 2002. [2]Comprises Basse-Terre 325 sq mi (842 sq km), pop. 172,693, and Îles des Saintes 5 sq mi (13 sq km), pop. 2,998. [3]Comprises Grande-Terre 230 sq mi (596 sq km), pop. 196,767; Marie-Galante 61 sq mi (158 sq km), pop. 12,488; La Désirade 8 sq mi (21 sq km), pop. 1,620; and the uninhabited Îles de la Petite-Terre. [4]Comprises the French part of Saint-Martin 21 sq mi (53 sq km), pop. 29,078; Saint-Barthélemy 8 sq mi (21 sq km), pop. 6,852; and the small, uninhabited island of Tintamarre. [5]The December 2003 referenda approving a new administrative status of Saint-Martin and Saint-Barthélemy separate from Guadeloupe was awaiting a French government decision in November 2004. [6]Detail does not add to total given because of rounding. [7]Within Pointe-à-Pitre urban agglomeration. [8]September. [9]Less imputed bank service charges. [10]Includes 55,900 unemployed. [11]In millions of French francs (F). [12]University of Antilles-French Guiana, Guadeloupe campus.

Internet resources for further information:
- **INSEE Guadeloupe**
http://www.insee.fr/fr/insee_regions/guadeloupe/home/home_page.asp

Guam

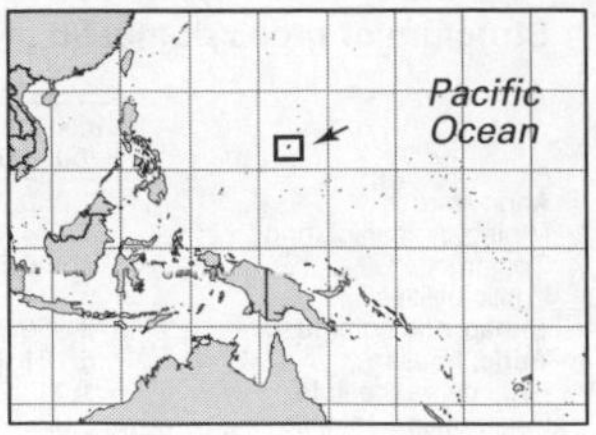

Official name: Teritorion Guam (Chamorro); Territory of Guam (English).
Political status: self-governing, organized, unincorporated territory of the United States with one legislative house (Guam Legislature [15]).
Chief of state: President of the United States.
Head of government: Governor.
Capital: Hagåtña (Agana).
Official languages: Chamorro; English.
Official religion: none.
Monetary unit: 1 United States dollar (U.S.$) = 100 cents; valuation (Sept. 1, 2004) 1 U.S.$ = £0.56.

Area and population

	land area		population[1]
Election Districts	sq mi	sq km	2000 census
Agat	11	29	5,656
Asan	6	16	2,090
Barrigada	9	23	8,652
Chalan Pago-Ordot	6	16	5,923
Dededo	30	78	42,980
Hagåtña (Agana)	1	3	1,100
Hagåtña Heights	1	3	3,940
Inarajan	19	49	3,052
Mangilao	10	26	13,313
Merizo	6	16	2,163
Mongmong-Toto-Maite	2	5	5,845
Piti	7	18	1,666
Santa Rita	16	42	7,500
Sinajana	1	3	2,853
Talofofo	17	44	3,215
Tamuning	6	16	18,012
Umatac	6	16	887
Yigo	35	91	19,474
Yona	20	52	6,484
TOTAL	209	541[2]	154,805

Demography

Population (2004): 165,000.
Density (2004)[3]: persons per sq mi 789.5, persons per sq km 305.0.
Urban-rural (2003): urban 93.7%; rural 6.3%.
Sex distribution (2000): male 51.15%; female 48.85%.
Age breakdown (2000): under 15, 30.5%; 15–29, 24.1%; 30–44, 23.3%; 45–59, 13.9%; 60–74, 6.7%; 75 and over, 1.5%.
Population projection: (2010) 180,000; (2020) 204,000.
Doubling time: 46 years.
Ethnic composition (2000): Pacific Islander 44.6%, of which Chamorro 37.0%; Asian 32.5%, of which Filipino 26.3%, Korean 2.5%; white 6.8%; black 1.0%; mixed 13.9%; other 1.2%.
Religious affiliation (1995): Roman Catholic 74.7%; Protestant 12.8%; other Christian 2.4%; other 10.1%.
Major populated places (2000): Tamuning 10,833; Mangilao 7,794; Yigo 6,391; Astumbo 5,207; Hagåtña 1,122.

Vital statistics

Birth rate per 1,000 population (2003): 19.7 (world avg. 21.3); (2000) legitimate 45.4%; illegitimate 54.6%.
Death rate per 1,000 population (2003): 4.3 (world avg. 9.1).
Natural increase rate per 1,000 population (2002): 15.4 (world avg. 12.2).
Total fertility rate (avg. births per childbearing woman; 2003): 2.6.
Marriage rate per 1,000 population (2000): 9.7.
Divorce rate per 1,000 population (2000): 4.0.
Life expectancy at birth (2003): male 74.8 years; female 81.0 years.
Major causes of death per 100,000 population (2002): diseases of the heart 130.4; malignant neoplasms (cancers) 77.0; cerebrovascular disease 32.3; accidents 22.3; suicide 13.7; pneumonia 13.7.

National economy

Budget (2001). Revenue: U.S.$662,994,000 (local taxes 63.6%, federal contributions 27.4%, other 9.0%). Expenditures: U.S.$518,433,000 (current expenditures 91.6%, capital expenditures 8.4%).
Production. Agriculture, forestry, fishing (value of production in U.S.$'000; 2000): long beans 234, cucumbers 166, watermelons 106, pineapples 65; livestock (number of live animals [2002]) 200,000 poultry, 5,000 pigs, 680 goats; fish catch (metric tons; 2001) 507, value of aquaculture production (1996) U.S.$1,442,000. Mining and quarrying: sand and gravel. Manufacturing (value of sales in U.S.$'000; 2002): food processing 26,733; printing and publishing 7,382; fabricated metal products 4,052. Construction (gross value of building and construction permits in U.S.$; 2001): residential 59,379,000; nonresidential 57,664,000. Energy production (consumption): electricity (kW-hr; 2000) 830,000,000 (830,000,000); petroleum products (metric tons; 2000) none (1,327,000).
Household income and expenditure. Average household size (2000) 3.9[4]; average annual income per household U.S.$38,983[4]; sources of income: n.a.; expenditure: n.a.
Gross domestic product (at current market prices; 2000): U.S.$3,419,920,000 (U.S.$22,120 per capita).

Structure of gross domestic product and labour force

	1995		2002	
	in value U.S.$'000,000	% of total value	labour force[5]	% of labour force[5]
Agriculture	[6]	[6]	290	0.5
Manufacturing	[6]	[6]	1,570	2.8
Construction	379.0	12.5	3,420	6.1
Trade	622.9	20.6	12,690	22.7
Transp. and commun.	[6]	[6]	4,590	8.2
Finance	[6]	[6]	2,450	4.4
Pub. admin. (local)	513.3	16.9	13,280	23.7
Pub. admin., defense (federal)	452.7	14.9	3,220	5.7
Services	486.9	16.1	14,510	25.9
Other	575.4[6]	19.0[6]	—	—
TOTAL	3,030.2	100.0	56,020	100.0

Population economically active (2001): total 64,800[7]; activity rate of total population *c.* 42% (participation rates: over age 15, 55.8%; female 45.1%; unemployed [September 2001] 13.5%).

Price and earnings indexes (2000 = 100)

	1997	1998	1999	2000	2001	2002	2003
Consumer price index	101.6	101.2	100.9	100.0	102.6	...	...
Weekly earnings index[8]	95.6	93.9	91.9	100.0	92.6	92.0	98.7

Tourism (1999): receipts from visitors U.S.$1,908,000,000.
Land use as % of total land area (2000): in temporary crops *c.* 9%, in permanent crops *c.* 16%, in pasture *c.* 15%; overall forest area *c.* 38%.

Foreign trade

Balance of trade (current prices)

	1996	1997[9]	1998[9]	1999[9]	2000	2001[9]
U.S.$'000,000	–600	–545	–480	–485	...	–442
% of total	88%	78%	73%	74%	...	78%

Imports (2001): *c.* U.S.$503,000,000[10, 11] (food products and nonalcoholic beverages *c.* 32%; leather products including footwear *c.* 20%; motor vehicles and parts *c.* 12%; clothing *c.* 8%). *Major import sources:* significantly U.S. and Japan.
Exports (2001): U.S.$60,800,000 (food products 52.2%, of which fish 51.4%; petroleum and natural gas products 6.2%; perfumes and colognes 6.0%; tobacco products 5.8%). *Major export destinations:* Japan 50.0%; Palau 9.4%; Federated States of Micronesia 9.1%; Hong Kong 7.4%; Taiwan 4.7%.

Transport and communications

Transport. Railroads: none. Roads (1999): total length 550 mi, 885 km (paved 76%). Vehicles (2001): passenger cars 64,018; trucks and buses 28,322. Air transport (2003)[12]: passenger-km 3,697,000,000; metric ton-km cargo 61,256,000; airports with scheduled flights 1.

Communications

Medium	date	unit	number	units per 1,000 persons
Daily newspapers	1996	circulation	28,000	178
Radio	1997	receivers	221,000	1,400
Television	1997	receivers	106,000	668
Telephones	2002	main lines	76,425	478
Cellular telephones	2001	subscribers	32,600	207
Internet	2002	users	50,000	313

Education and health

Educational attainment (2000). Percentage of population age 25 and over having: no formal schooling to some secondary education 23.7%; completed secondary 31.9%; some higher 24.5%; undergraduate 15.3%; advanced degree 4.6%. *Literacy:* virtually 100%.

Education (2000–01)

	schools	teachers	students	student/ teacher ratio
Primary (age 5–10)	24	1,063	17,001	16.0
Secondary (age 11–18)	11	1,010	18,217	18.0
Higher[13]	1	...	3,462	...

Health (1999): physicians 130[14] (1 per 1,169 persons); hospital beds 192[15] (1 per 792 persons); infant mortality rate per 1,000 live births (2003) 7.4.

Military

Total active duty U.S. personnel (2003): 3,293 (army 1.2%; navy 45.5%; air force 53.3%).

[1]Includes active-duty military personnel, U.S. Department of Defense employees, their dependents, and Guamanian nationals. [2]Detail does not add to total given because of rounding. [3]Based on land area; total area per most recent survey including area designated as inland water equals 217 sq mi (561 sq km). [4]Excludes U.S. military and dependents. [5]Per December 2001 survey; employed civilian labour force only, excludes proprietors, self-employed unpaid family workers, domestic servants, and military personnel. [6]Other includes Agriculture, Manufacturing, Transportation and communications, and Finance. [7]Per September survey; excludes nonimmigrant aliens and civilians living on military reservations. [8]Private sector only. [9]Estimated figures. [10]The estimated 1999 import total is based on a projection of summed figures for four months only (January, April, July, and October). [11]Excludes petroleum imports for transshipment. [12]Continental Micronesia only. [13]University of Guam only. [14]Members of Guam Medical Society only. [15]Guam Memorial Hospital only.

Internet resources for further information:
- **U.S. Office of Insular Affairs http://www.pacificweb.org**

Guatemala

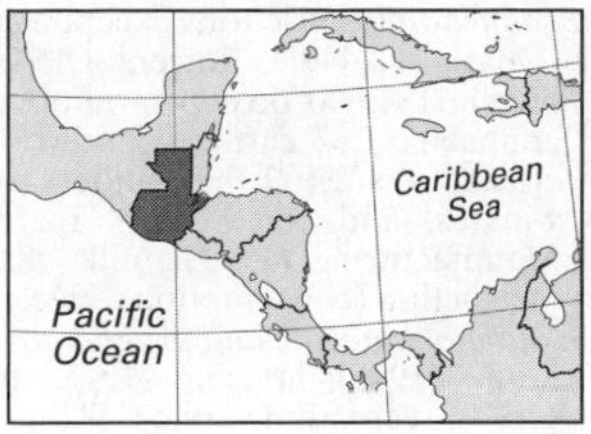

Official name: República de Guatemala (Republic of Guatemala).
Form of government: republic with one legislative house (Congress of the Republic [158]).
Head of state and government: President.
Capital: Guatemala City.
Official language: Spanish.
Official religion: none.
Monetary unit: 1 quetzal (Q) = 100 centavos; valuation (Sept. 1, 2004) 1 U.S.$ = Q 7.91; 1 £ = Q 14.23.

Area and population

Departments	Capitals	area sq mi	area sq km	population 2002 census[1]
Alta Verapaz	Cobán	3,695	9,569	776,246
Baja Verapaz	Salamá	1,198	3,104	215,915
Chimaltenango	Chimaltenango	757	1,960	446,133
Chiquimula	Chiquimula	912	2,361	302,485
El Progreso	Guastatoya (Progreso)	737	1,910	139,490
Escuintla	Escuintla	1,682	4,356	538,746
Guatemala	Guatemala City	856	2,218	2,541,581
Huehuetenango	Huehuetenango	2,813	7,285	846,544
Izabal	Puerto Barrios	3,468	8,981	314,306
Jalapa	Jalapa	792	2,050	242,926
Jutiapa	Jutiapa	1,235	3,199	389,085
Petén	Flores	12,987	33,635	366,735
Quetzaltenango	Quetzaltenango	810	2,098	624,716
Quiché	Santa Cruz del Quiché	3,927	10,172	655,510
Retalhuleu	Retalhuleu	712	1,844	241,411
Sacatepéquez	Antigua Guatemala	178	462	248,019
San Marcos	San Marcos	1,468	3,802	794,951
Santa Rosa	Cuilapa	1,134	2,936	301,370
Sololá	Sololá	405	1,050	307,661
Suchitepéquez	Mazatenango	930	2,409	403,945
Totonicapán	Totonicapán	403	1,043	339,254
Zacapa	Zacapa	1,032	2,673	200,167
TOTAL		42,130[2]	109,117	11,237,196

Demography

Population (2004): 12,661,000.
Density (2004): persons per sq mi 300.5, persons per sq km 116.0.
Urban-rural (2003): urban 46.3%; rural 53.7%.
Sex distribution (2003): male 50.67%; female 49.33%.
Age breakdown (2003): under 15, 42.9%; 15–29, 27.8%; 30–44, 15.6%; 45–59, 8.7%; 60–74, 4.0%; 75 and over, 1.0%.
Population projection: (2010) 14,584,000; (2020) 17,835,000.
Ethnic composition (2000): mestizo 63.7%, Amerindian 33.1%; black 2.0%; white 1.0%; other 0.2%.
Religious affiliation (1995): Roman Catholic 75.9%, of which Catholic/traditional syncretist 25.0%; Protestant 21.8%; other 2.3%.
Major cities (2002)[3]: Guatemala City 942,348 (urban agglomeration [2001] 3,366,000); Mixco 277,400[4]; Villa Nueva 187,700[4]; Quetzaltenango 106,700; Escuintla 65,400.

Vital statistics

Birth rate per 1,000 population (2003): 35.1 (world avg. 21.3).
Death rate per 1,000 population (2003): 6.8 (world avg. 9.1).
Natural increase rate per 1,000 population (2003): 28.3 (world avg. 12.2).
Total fertility rate (avg. births per childbearing woman; 2003): 4.7.
Marriage rate per 1,000 population (1999): 5.5.
Life expectancy at birth (2003): male 64.3 years; female 66.2 years.
Major causes of death per 100,000 population (1997): communicable diseases 197.7; diseases of the circulatory system 86.1; accidents and violence 78.1; malignant neoplasms (cancers) 47.5.

National economy

Budget (2000). Revenue: Q 15,554,320,000 (tax revenue 96.9%, of which VAT 45.2%, income tax 23.7%; grants 2.2%; nontax revenue 0.9%). Expenditures: Q 18,220,750,000 (current expenditures 80.6%; capital expenditures 19.4%).
Public debt (external, outstanding; 2002): U.S.$2,972,000,000.
Tourism (2002): receipts from visitors U.S.$612,000,000; expenditures by nationals abroad U.S.$267,000,000.
Production (metric tons except as noted). Agriculture, forestry, fishing (2003): sugarcane 17,500,000, corn (maize) 1,053,560, bananas 1,000,000, oil palm fruit 540,000, plantains 268,000, coffee 210,000; livestock (number of live animals) 2,540,000 cattle, 780,000 pigs, 27,000,000 chickens; roundwood (2001) 16,069,873 cu m; fish catch (2001) 14,300. Mining and quarrying (2001): gypsum 100,000; gold 4,500 kg; marble 3,800 cu m. Manufacturing (value added in Q '000,000; 1998[5]): food and beverage products 298; clothing and textiles 119; machinery and metal products 55. Energy production (consumption): electricity (kW-hr; 2000) 6,048,000,000 (5,344,000,000); crude petroleum (barrels; 2000) 7,500,000 (6,600,000); petroleum products (metric tons; 2000) 820,000 (2,859,000); natural gas (cu m; 2000) 11,020,000 (11,020,000).
Household income and expenditure. Average household size (2000) 4.5; income per household (1989) Q 4,306 (U.S.$1,529); sources of income: n.a.; expenditure (1981): food 64.4%, housing and energy 16.0%, transportation and communications 7.0%, household furnishings 5.0%, clothing 3.1%.
Gross national product (at current market prices; 2003): U.S.$23,486,000,000 (U.S.$1,910 per capita).

Structure of gross domestic product and labour force

	2000 in value Q '000,000[5]	2000 % of total value	1995 labour force	1995 % of labour force
Agriculture	1,159.1	23.0	1,798,227	58.1
Mining	27.3	0.5	3,095	0.1
Manufacturing	663.2	13.1	420,928	13.6
Construction	210.2	4.2	126,898	4.1
Public utilities	110.3	2.2	9,285	0.3
Transp. and commun.	473.2	9.4	77,377	2.5
Trade	1,239.9	24.6	225,940	7.3
Finance, real estate	499.9	9.9		
Pub. admin., defense	377.2	7.5	371,407	12.0
Services	287.7	5.7		
Other	—	—	61,901	2.0
TOTAL	5,048.0	100.0[2]	3,095,058	100.0

Population economically active (1998–99): total 4,207,946; activity rate of total population 38.9% (participation rates: ages 15–64, 53.4%; female 36.2%; unemployed [1995] 1.4%[6]).

Price and earnings indexes (2000 = 100)

	1997	1998	1999	2000	2001	2002	2003
Consumer price index	84.1	90.0	94.4	100.0	107.6	116.3	122.6
Monthly earnings index	73.2	81.7	103.5	100.0	...	...	...

Land use as % of total land area (2000): in temporary crops 12.5%, in permanent crops 5.0%, in pasture 24.0%; overall forest area 26.3%.

Foreign trade[7]

Balance of trade (current prices)

	1998	1999	2000	2001	2002	2003
U.S.$'000,000	–1,583	–1,613	–1,728	–2,768	–3,349	–3,474
% of total	23.5%	25.2%	24.3%	35.9%	42.9%	41.1%

Imports (2000): U.S.$4,882,000,000 (machinery and apparatus 22.1%, chemicals and chemical products 16.0%, crude and refined petroleum 11.0%, road vehicles 10.2%). *Major import sources:* United States 39.7%; Mexico 11.7%; El Salvador 6.4%; Venezuela 5.4%; Costa Rica 4.1%.
Exports (2000): U.S.$2,699,000,000 (agricultural products 52.1%, of which coffee 21.3%, sugar 7.1%, bananas 6.6%, spices 3.0%; crude petroleum 5.9%). *Major export destinations:* United States 36.1%; El Salvador 12.6%; Honduras 8.6%; Costa Rica 4.7%; Mexico 4.5%.

Transport and communications

Transport. Railroads (2003): route length 784 km[8]. Roads (1999): total length 14,118 km (paved 35%). Vehicles (1999): passenger cars 578,733; trucks and buses 53,236. Air transport (1998)[9]: passenger-km 480,000,000; metric ton-km cargo 50,000,000; airports (1996) 2.

Communications

Medium	date	unit	number	units per 1,000 persons
Daily newspapers	2000	circulation	377,000	33
Radio	2000	receivers	902,000	79
Television	2000	receivers	697,000	61
Telephones	2002	main lines	846,000	71
Cellular telephones	2002	subscribers	1,577,100	132
Personal computers	2002	units	173,000	14
Internet	2002	users	400,000	33

Education and health

Educational attainment (1994). Percentage of population age 25 and over having: no formal schooling 45.2%; incomplete primary education 20.8%; complete primary 18.0%; some secondary 4.8%; secondary 7.2%; higher 4.0%. *Literacy* (2002): total population age 15 and over literate 69.9%; males literate 77.3%; females literate 62.5%.

Education (1999)

	schools	teachers	students	student/ teacher ratio
Primary (age 7–12)	17,905	47,811	1,825,088	38.2
Secondary (age 13–18)	3,118	20,543	305,818	14.9
Higher	1,462	13,105	146,291	11.2

Health (2003): physicians 11,700 (1 per 1,053 persons); hospital beds (2002) 6,000 (1 per 2,000 persons); infant mortality rate per 1,000 live births 37.9.
Food (2001): daily per capita caloric intake 2,203 (vegetable products 91%, animal products 9%); 101% of FAO recommended minimum.

Military

Total active duty personnel (2003): 31,400 (army 93.0%, navy 4.8%, air force 2.2%). *Military expenditure as percentage of GNP* (1999): 0.7% (world 2.4%); per capita expenditure U.S.$10.

[1]Preliminary unadjusted results. [2]Detail does not add to total given because of rounding. [3]Urban populations of municipios. [4]Within Guatemala City urban agglomeration. [5]At prices of 1958. [6]Registered unemployed; majority of economically active population is estimated to be underemployed. [7]Import figures are f.o.b. in balance of trade and c.i.f. for commodities and trading partners. [8]Mostly inoperable in 2003; no passenger service is available. [9]Aviateca Airlines only.

Internet resources for further information:
- **Banco de Guatemala http://www.banguat.gob.gt**
- **Instituto Nacional de Estadistica http://www.segeplan.gob.gt/ine/index.htm**

Guernsey[1]

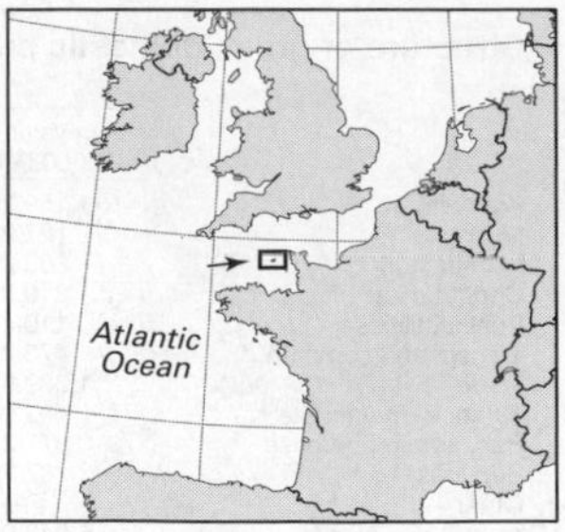

Official name: Bailiwick of Guernsey.
Political status: crown dependency (United Kingdom) with one legislative house (States of Deliberation [51[2, 3, 4]]).
Chief of state: British Monarch represented by Lieutenant Governor.
Head of government: [5].
Capital: St. Peter Port.
Official language: English.
Official religion: n.a.
Monetary unit: 1 Guernsey pound[6] = 100 pence; valuation (Sept. 1, 2004) 1 Guernsey pound = U.S.$1.80.

Area and population	area		population
			2001
	sq mi	sq km	census
Parishes of Guernsey			
Castel	3.9	10.1	8,975
Forest	1.6	4.1	1,549
St. Andrew	1.7	4.5	2,409
St. Martin	2.8	7.3	6,267
St. Peter (St. Pierre du Bois)	2.4	6.2	2,188
St. Peter Port	2.6	6.6	16,488
St. Sampson	2.3	6.0	8,592
St. Saviour	2.4	6.3	2,696
Torteval	1.2	3.1	973
Vale	3.4	8.8	9,573
Dependencies of Guernsey			
Alderney	3.1	7.9	2,294
Brechou	0.1	0.3	0
Herm[7]	0.5	1.3	95
Jethou[7]	0.1	0.2	2
Lihou	0.1	0.2	0
Little Sark	0.4	1.0	} 591
Sark (Great Sark)	1.6	4.2	
TOTAL	30.2	78.1	62,692

Demography

Population (2004)[8]: 63,300.
Density (2004)[8]: persons per sq mi 2,096.0, persons per sq km 810.5.
Urban-rural (2003)[9]: urban 30.5%; rural 69.5%.
Sex distribution (2001): male 48.72%; female 51.28%.
Age breakdown (2001): under 15, 17.2%; 15–29, 18.8%; 30–44, 23.2%; 45–59, 20.0%; 60–74, 13.4%; 75 and over, 7.4%.
Population projection[8]: (2010) 64,000; (2020) 65,000.
Population by place of birth (2001): Guernsey 64.3%; United Kingdom 27.4%; Portugal 1.9%; Jersey 0.7%; Ireland 0.7%; Alderney 0.2%; Sark 0.1%; other Europe 3.2%; other 1.5%.
Religious affiliation (*c.* 1990): Anglican 65.2%; other 34.8%.
Major cities (2001)[10]: St. Peter Port 16,488; Vale 9,573; Castel 8,975; St. Sampson 8,592; St. Martin 6,267.

Vital statistics

Birth rate per 1,000 population (2003): 9.4 (world avg. 21.3); (2000) legitimate 65.2%, illegitimate 34.8%.
Death rate per 1,000 population (2003): 9.8 (world avg. 9.1).
Natural increase rate per 1,000 population (2002): –0.4 (world avg. 12.2).
Total fertility rate (avg. births per childbearing woman; 2003): 1.4.
Marriage rate per 1,000 population (2000): 5.7.
Divorce rate per 1,000 population (2000): 2.9.
Life expectancy at birth (2003): male 77.0 years; female 83.1 years.
Major causes of death per 100,000 population (1993): diseases of the circulatory system 423.5; malignant neoplasms (cancers) 288.0; diseases of the respiratory system 133.8; endocrine and metabolic disorders 25.4; accidents, poisoning, and violence 22.0; diseases of the digestive system 11.8.

National economy

Budget (1999). Revenue: £306,991,000 (income tax 79.7%, customs duties and excise taxes 5.7%, document duties 2.7%, corporation taxes 2.1%, automobile taxes 1.9%). Expenditures: £244,418,000 (welfare 31.1%, health 26.2%, education 15.9%, administrative services 6.7%, law and order 4.9%, community services 4.1%).
Public debt: n.a.
Gross national product (at current market prices; 2002): U.S.$2,116,833,000 (U.S.$33,650 per capita).

Structure of gross domestic product and labour force	2000		2001	
	in value £'000	% of total value	labour force	% of labour force
Horticulture, fishing	24,377	1.9	1,476	4.6
Mining	—	—	—	—
Manufacturing	38,086	3.0	1,798	5.6
Construction	61,727	4.9	2,922	9.0
Public utilities	[11]	[11]	454	1.4
Transp. and commun.	[11]	[11]	1,228	3.8
Trade, real estate	[11]	[11]	5,737	17.8
Finance[12]	500,580	39.9	7,300	22.6
Pub. admin., defense	[11]	[11]	1,967	6.1
Services	629,591[11]	50.2[11]	9,411	29.1
TOTAL	1,254,361	100.0[13]	32,293	100.0

Production (metric tons except as noted). Agriculture, forestry, fishing (1999): tomatoes 2,449[14], flowers 1,154,000 boxes, of which roses 288,000 boxes, freesia 184,000 boxes, carnations 161,000 boxes; livestock (number of live animals) 3,262 cattle; roundwood, n.a.; fish catch (2001)[9]: 4,414, of which crustaceans 2,169 (sea spiders and crabs 1,988), mollusks 1,456 (abalones, winkles, and conch 523), marine fish 789. Mining and quarrying: n.a. Manufacturing (1999): milk 98,830 hectolitres. Construction: n.a. Energy production (consumption): electricity (kW-hr; 1999–2000), n.a. (273,013,000).
Household income and expenditure. Average household size (2001) 2.6; expenditure (1996): housing 21.6%, food 12.7%, household goods and services 11.2%, recreation services 9.2%, transportation 8.5%, clothing and footwear 5.6%, personal goods 4.9%, energy 4.1%.
Population economically active (2001): total 32,293; activity rate of total population 51.5% (participation rates: ages 15–64, 80.4%; female 45.3%; unemployed, n.a.).

Retail price and earnings indexes (1994 = 100)	1995	1996	1997	1998	1999	2000	2001
Consumer price index[15]	103.0	105.5	108.8	113.2	115.7	120.1	124.0
Earnings index	...	...	...	...	...	...	...

Tourism (1996): receipts U.S.$275,000,000.
Land use as % of total land area (1999): in temporary crops, n.a., in permanent crops, n.a., in pasture *c.* 37%; overall forest area *c.* 3%.

Foreign trade

Imports (1998): petroleum products are important. *Major import sources* (1998): mostly United Kingdom.
Exports (1998): £93,000,000[16] (manufactured goods *c.* 51%, of which electronic components *c.* 18%, printed products *c.* 10%; agricultural products *c.* 42%, of which flowers *c.* 25%, plants *c.* 10%; fish, crustaceans, and mollusks *c.* 7%). *Major export destinations* (1998): mostly United Kingdom.

Transport and communications

Transport. Railroads: n.a. Vehicles (2000): passenger cars 37,598; trucks and buses 7,338. Air transport (2001)[17]: passenger arrivals 429,076, passenger departures 430,254; cargo loaded 969 metric tons, cargo unloaded 3,557 metric tons; airports (1999) with scheduled flights 2[18].

Communications				units
				per 1,000
Medium	date	unit	number	persons
Daily newspapers	1998	circulation	15,784	260
Telephones	2001	main lines	55,000	877
Cellular telephones	2001	subscribers	31,500	502
Internet	2000	users	20,000	320

Education and health

Educational attainment: n.a. *Literacy* (2002): virtually 100%.

Education (2000)	schools	teachers	students	student/ teacher ratio
Primary (age 5–10)	22[19]	253	4,977	19.9
Secondary (age 11–16)	8[19]	295	3,900	13.2
Higher	1	...	211[20]	...

Health (1999): physicians 93 (1 per 654 persons); hospital beds, n.a.; infant mortality rate per 1,000 live births (2003) 4.9.
Food (2002)[21]: daily per capita caloric intake 3,412 (vegetable products 69%, animal products 31%); 135% of FAO recommended minimum requirement.

Military

Total active duty personnel: n.a.[22].

[1]Data excludes Alderney and Sark unless otherwise noted. [2]The States of Deliberation was reorganized in 2004. [3]Includes ex officio members and 2 representatives from Alderney. [4]Alderney and Sark have their own parliaments. The States of Alderney has 12 elected members; the parliament of Sark consists of 40 *tenants* or landowners and 12 elected deputies. [5]The government of Guernsey is conducted by committees appointed by the States of Deliberation. [6]Equivalent in value to pound sterling (£). [7]Populated islets that are directly administered by Guernsey. [8]Includes Alderney, Sark, and other dependencies. [9]Includes Jersey. [10]Parishes. [11]Services includes Trade, real estate, Public utilities, Transportation and communications, and Public administration, defense. [12]Mostly from 79 banks (located offshore) and 581 insurance companies (352 offshore and 217 domestic). [13]Detail does not add to total given because of rounding. [14]1998. [15]March. [16]Excluding administrative and financial services. [17]Guernsey airport. [18]Includes one airport on Alderney. [19]1992. [20]1999. [21]Data for the United Kingdom. [22]The United Kingdom is responsible for defense.

Internet resources for further information:
- **The States of Guernsey, Policy and Research Unit**
  http://www.gov.gg/esu/homepage.htm

Guinea

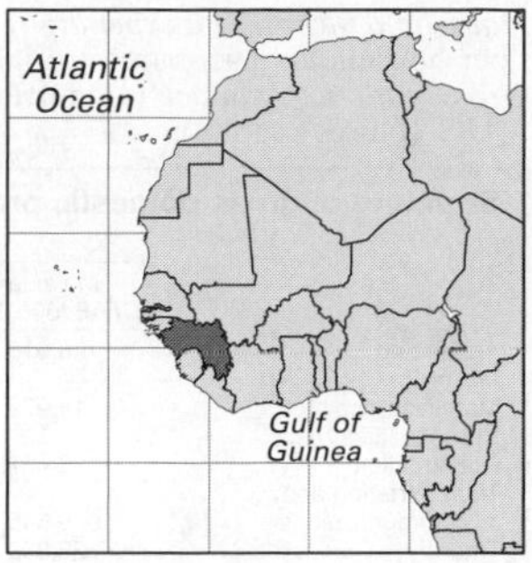

Official name: République de Guinée (Republic of Guinea).
Form of government: unitary multiparty republic with one legislative house (National Assembly [114 seats]).
Head of state and government: President assisted by the Prime Minister.
Capital: Conakry.
Official language: French.
Official religion: none.
Monetary unit: 1 Guinean franc (GF) = 100 cauris; valuation (Sept. 1, 2004) 1 U.S.$ = GF 2,560; 1 £ = GF 4,605.

Area and population

		area		population
Prefectures[1]	**Capitals**	sq mi	sq km	1996[2] census
Beyla	Beyla	5,256	13,612	169,730
Boffa	Boffa	1,950	5,050	156,558
Boké	Boké	4,295	11,124	293,917
Conakry	Conakry	174	450	1,092,936
Coyah	Coyah	492	1,275	85,148
Dabola	Dabola	2,452	6,350	111,363
Dalaba	Dalaba	1,285	3,328	136,656
Dinguiraye	Dinguiraye	3,075	7,965	137,380
Dubréka	…	1,680	4,350	131,337
Faranah	Faranah	5,006	12,966	147,347
Forécariah	Forécariah	1,693	4,384	195,836
Fria	Fria	778	2,016	81,790
Gaoual	Gaoual	2,995	7,758	137,624
Guéckédou	Guéckédou	1,834	4,750	347,541
Kankan	Kankan	7,626	19,750	262,350
Kérouané	Kérouané	2,710	7,020	154,861
Kindia	Kindia	3,725	9,648	287,611
Kissidougou	Kissidougou	3,205	8,300	206,755
Koubia	Koubia	1,438	3,725	91,882
Koundara	Koundara	2,022	5,238	90,230
Kouroussa	Kouroussa	5,425	14,050	150,059
Labé	Labé	866	2,242	251,702
Lélouma	Lélouma	1,651	4,275	137,273
Lola	Lola	1,810	4,688	134,326
Macenta	Macenta	2,724	7,056	278,789
Mali	Mali	3,398	8,802	204,041
Mamou	Mamou	3,517	9,108	236,326
Mandiana	Mandiana	4,952	12,825	173,150
Nzérékoré	Nzérékoré	1,402	3,632	283,413
Pita	Pita	1,791	4,638	239,236
Siguiri	Siguiri	7,143	18,500	271,224
Télimélé	Télimélé	3,558	9,216	228,380
Tougué	Tougué	1,477	3,825	114,647
Yomou	Yomou	1,514	3,920	134,988
TOTAL		94,919	245,836	7,156,406[3]

Demography

Population (2004): 8,620,000.
Density (2004): persons per sq mi 90.8, persons per sq km 35.1.
Urban-rural (2003): urban 34.9%; rural 65.1%.
Sex distribution (2003): male 49.95%; female 50.05%.
Age breakdown (2003): under 15, 44.5%; 15–29, 26.4%; 30–44, 15.4%; 45–59, 8.7%; 60–74, 4.1%; 75 and over, 0.9%.
Population projection: (2010) 9,990,000; (2020) 12,478,000.
Doubling time: 26 years.
Ethnic composition (1996): Fulani 38.6%; Malinke 23.2%; Susu 11.0%; Kissi 6.0%; Kpelle 4.6%; other 16.6%.
Religious affiliation (1996): Muslim 85.0%; Christian 10.0%; other 5.0%.
Major cities (2001): Conakry 1,565,200; Kankan 88,800; Labé 64,500; Kindia 56,000; Nzérékoré 55,000; Kissidougou 40,400.

Vital statistics

Birth rate per 1,000 population (2003): 42.5 (world avg. 21.3).
Death rate per 1,000 population (2003): 15.7 (world avg. 9.1).
Natural increase rate per 1,000 population (2003): 26.8 (world avg. 12.2).
Total fertility rate (avg. births per childbearing woman; 2003): 5.9.
Life expectancy at birth (2003): male 48.3 years; female 50.8 years.

National economy

Budget (2002). Revenue: GF 909,700,000,000 (tax revenue 76.2%, of which value-added tax 20.3%, mining sector 16.0%, tax on trade 15.3%, income tax 10.4%; grants 16.0%; nontax revenue 7.8%). Expenditures: GF 1,281,800,000 (current expenditure 61.5%, of which defense 14.4%, interest 8.2%; capital expenditure 38.5%).
Production (metric tons except as noted). Agriculture, forestry, fishing (2003): cassava 1,150,000, rice 845,000, oil palm fruit 830,000, plantains 430,000, sugarcane 270,000, corn (maize) 260,000, peanuts (groundnuts) 252,000, fresh vegetables 220,000, fresh citrus fruit 210,000, coffee 20,500; livestock (number of live animals) 3,285,000 cattle, 1,201,000 goats, 1,005,000 sheep, 13,500,000 chickens; roundwood 12,236,000 cu m; fish catch (2001) 90,000. Mining and quarrying (2001): bauxite 17,950,000; alumina 550,000; gold 13,000 kg; diamonds 370,000 carats. Manufacturing (2001): cement 300,000. Energy production (consumption): electricity (kW-hr; 2000) 569,000,000 (569,000,000); petroleum products (metric tons; 2000) none (373,000).
Household income and expenditure. Average household size (2000) 4.0; average annual income per capita, n.a.; expenditure (1985): food 61.5%, health 11.2%, clothing 7.9%, housing 7.3%.

Gross national product (2003): U.S.$3,372,000,000 (U.S.$430 per capita).

Structure of gross domestic product and labour force

	2001		1983	
	in value GF '000,000,000[4]	% of total value[4]	labour force	% of labour force
Agriculture, forestry, fishing	901.2	18.3	1,423,615	78.2
Mining	801.2	16.3	12,241	0.7
Manufacturing	201.1	4.1	11,215	0.6
Construction	501.2	10.2	9,115	0.5
Public utilities	29.1	0.6	3,205	0.2
Transp. and commun.	281.3	5.7	29,496	1.6
Trade, finance	1,247.8	25.3	40,865	2.2
Pub. admin., defense	257.0	5.2	137,600	7.5
Services	495.2	10.1		
Other	207.3[5]	4.2[5]	155,679	8.5
TOTAL	4,922.4	100.0	1,823,031	100.0

Public debt (external, outstanding; 2002): U.S.$2,972,000,000.
Population economically active (2000): total 4,047,000; activity rate of total population 49.9% (participation rates: n.a.; female, n.a.; unemployed, n.a.).

Price index (2000 = 100)

	1997	1998	1999	2000	2001	2002	2003
Consumer price index	87.4	89.1	93.6	100.0	105.4	108.6	120.8

Tourism (2002): receipts U.S.$43,000,000; expenditures U.S.$31,000,000.
Land use as % of total land area (2000): in temporary crops 3.6%, in permanent crops 2.4%, in pasture 43.5%; overall forest area 28.2%.

Foreign trade[6]

Balance of trade (current prices)

	1997	1998	1999	2000	2001	2002
U.S.$'000,000	+117.6	+121.0	+53.9	+79.3	+169.2	+50.8
% of total	10.3%	9.6%	4.4%	6.3%	13.1%	3.8%

Imports (2000): U.S.$612,400,000 (refined petroleum 24.8%, food 18.0%, machinery and apparatus 10.0%, road vehicles 8.7%). *Major import sources* (2000): Côte d'Ivoire 21.4%; France 19.8%; U.S. 7.9%; Belgium 7.7%; Japan 5.6%.
Exports (2002): U.S.$700,400,000 (bauxite 43.6%, gold 20.5%, alumina 18.3%, diamonds 4.9%, fish 4.0%, coffee 2.5%). *Major export destinations* (2002): Spain 10.5%; Belgium 10.1%; Cameroon 10.1%; United States 9.6%; France 7.4%; Germany 5.0%.

Transport and communications

Transport. Railroads (2000): route length of operational lines for cargo (mostly bauxite) transport 170 mi, 274 km; passenger-km, n.a.[7]; metric ton-km cargo (1993) 710,000,000. Roads (1999): total length 30,500 km (paved 16.5%). Vehicles (1996): passenger cars 14,100; trucks and buses 21,000. Air transport (1998): passenger-km 50,000,000; metric ton-km cargo 5,000,000; airports (2000) 1.

Communications

Medium	date	unit	number	units per 1,000 persons
Daily newspapers	1988	circulation	13,000	2.0
Radio	2000	receivers	422,000	52
Television	2000	receivers	357,000	44
Telephones	2003	main lines	26,200	3.4
Cellular telephones	2003	subscribers	111,500	14
Personal computers	2003	units	43,000	5.5
Internet	2003	users	40,000	5.2

Education and health

Educational attainment of those age 6 and over having attended school (1983): primary 55.2%; secondary 32.7%; vocational 3.4%; higher 8.7%. *Literacy* (2000): percentage of total population age 15 and over literate 41.0%; males literate 55.0%; females literate 27.0%.

Education (1997–98)

	schools	teachers	students	student/ teacher ratio
Primary (age 7–12)	3,723	13,883	674,732	48.6
Secondary (age 13–18)	239	4,958	143,245	28.9
Voc., teacher tr.[8]	55	1,268	8,569	6.8
Higher[9, 10]	2	947	8,151	8.6

Health: physicians (1995) 920 (1 per 7,693 persons); hospital beds (1990) 3,700 (1 per 1,667 persons); infant mortality rate (2003) 93.3.
Food (2001): daily per capita caloric intake 2,362 (vegetable products 96%, animal products 4%); 102% of FAO recommended minimum requirement.

Military

Total active duty personnel (2003): 9,700 (army 87.7%, navy 4.1%, air force 8.2%). *Military expenditure as percentage of GNP* (1999): 1.6% (world 2.4%); per capita expenditure U.S.$7.

[1]Prefectures represent second-level administration; Guinea is divided into 7 regions and 1 city (Conakry) at the first level of administration. [2]December 1. [3]1996 rounded census total equals 7,156,000. [4]1996 prices. [5]Indirect taxes. [6]Imports f.o.b. in balance of trade and c.i.f. for commodities and trading partners. [7]Passenger service has been limited and irregular since the late 1980s. [8]1995–96. [9]1996–97. [10]Universities only.

Internet resources for further information:
- **Official site of Guinea http://www.guinee.gov.gn**

Guinea-Bissau

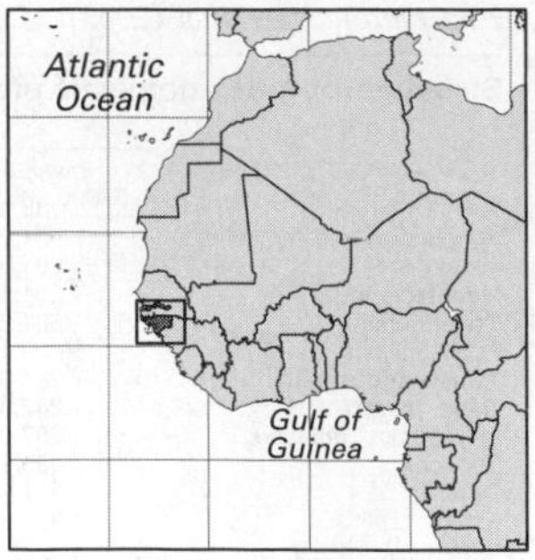

Official name: Républica da Guiné-Bissau (Republic of Guinea-Bissau).
Form of government: multiparty republic[1] with one legislative house (National People's Assembly [102]).
Head of state and government: President assisted by the Prime Minister.
Capital: Bissau.
Official language: Portuguese.
Official religion: none.
Monetary unit: 1 CFA franc[2] (CFAF) = 100 centimes; valuation (Sept. 1, 2004) 1 U.S.$ = CFAF 539.75; 1 £ = CFAF 970.98.

Area and population

Regions	Chief towns	area sq mi	area sq km	population 1991 census
Bafatá	Bafatá	2,309	5,981	143,377
Biombo	Quinhámel	324	840	60,420
Bolama	Bolama	1,013	2,624	26,691
Cacheu	Cacheu	1,998	5,175	146,980
Gabú	Gabú	3,533	9,150	134,971
Oio	Bissorã	2,086	5,403	156,084
Quinara	Fulacunda	1,212	3,138	44,793
Tombali	Catió	1,443	3,736	72,441
Autonomous sector				
Bissau	—	30	78	197,610
TOTAL		13,948[3]	36,125[3]	983,367

Demography

Population (2004): 1,388,000.
Density (2004)[4]: persons per sq mi 127.8, persons per sq km 49.4.
Urban-rural (2003): urban 34.0%; rural 66.0%.
Sex distribution (2003): male 48.52%; female 51.48%.
Age breakdown (2003): under 15, 41.9%; 15–29, 28.1%; 30–44, 15.9%; 45–59, 9.4%; 60–74, 4.0%; 75 and over, 0.7%.
Population projection: (2010) 1,566,000; (2020) 1,882,000.
Doubling time: 32 years.
Ethnic composition (1996): Balante 30%; Fulani 20%; Mandyako 14%; Malinke 13%; Pepel 7%; nonindigenous Cape Verdean mulatto 2%; other 14%.
Religious affiliation (2000): traditional beliefs 45.2%; Muslim 39.9%; Christian 13.2%, of which Roman Catholic 9.9%; other 1.7%.
Major cities (1997): Bissau 200,000 (urban agglomeration [2003] 336,000); Bafatá 15,000; Cacheu 14,000; Gabú 10,000.

Vital statistics

Birth rate per 1,000 population (2003): 38.4 (world avg. 21.3).
Death rate per 1,000 population (2003): 16.6 (world avg. 9.1).
Natural increase rate per 1,000 population (2003): 21.8 (world avg. 12.2).
Total fertility rate (avg. births per childbearing woman; 2003): 5.1.
Marriage rate per 1,000 population: n.a.
Divorce rate per 1,000 population: n.a.
Life expectancy at birth (2003): male 45.1 years; female 48.9 years.
Major causes of death per 100,000 population: n.a.; however, major diseases include tuberculosis of the respiratory system, whooping cough, typhoid fever, cholera, bacillary dysentery and amebiasis, malaria, pneumonia, and meningococcal infections; malnutrition is widespread.

National economy

Budget (2001). Revenue: CFAF 47,530,000,000 (foreign grants 40.0%; tax revenue 31.0%, of which taxes on international trade 13.6%, general sales tax 7.3%; nontax revenue 29.0%, of which fishing licenses 15.6%). Expenditures: CFAF 63,162,000,000 (current expenditures 65.7%, of which scheduled external interest payments 19.4%; capital expenditures 34.3%).
Public debt (external, outstanding; 2002): U.S.$662,100,000.
Production (metric tons except as noted). Agriculture, forestry, fishing (2002): cashew nuts 80,000, oil palm fruit 80,000, rice 79,900, roots and tubers 65,000, coconuts 46,000, plantains 38,000, millet 26,100, peanuts (groundnuts) 19,000, seed cotton 4,000; livestock (number of live animals) 515,000 cattle, 350,000 pigs, 325,000 goats, 285,000 sheep; roundwood (1999) 592,000 cu m; fish catch (2001) 5,000. Mining and quarrying: extraction of construction materials only. Manufacturing (2000): processed wood 11,200; wood products 4,400; dried and smoked fish 3,500; soap 2,500; vegetable oils 34,000 hectolitres; distilled liquor 11,000 hectolitres. Energy production (consumption): electricity (kW-hr; 2000) 58,000,000 (58,000,000); coal, none (none); crude petroleum, none (none); petroleum products (metric tons; 2000) none (88,000); natural gas, none (none).
Population economically active (1992): total 471,000; activity rate of total population 46.9% (participation rates [1991]: over age 10, 67.1%; female 40.5%; unemployed, n.a.).

Price and earnings indexes (2000 = 100)

	1997	1998	1999	2000	2001	2002	2003
Consumer price index	88.2	94.0	92.1	100.0	103.2	106.6	102.9
Monthly earnings index	…	…	…	…	…	…	…

Household income and expenditure. Average household size (1996) 6.9; income per household: n.a; sources of income: n.a.; expenditure: n.a.
Gross national product (at current market prices; 2003): U.S.$202,000,000 (U.S.$140 per capita).

Structure of gross domestic product and labour force

	2000 in value CFAF '000,000	2000 % of total value	1994 labour force	1994 % of labour force
Agriculture	88,015	57.4	365,000	77.2
Mining / Manufacturing / Public utilities	14,979	9.8	21,000	4.4
Construction	3,427	2.2		
Transportation and communications	5,545	3.6	87,000	18.4
Trade	23,332	15.2		
Finance, services	579	0.4		
Pub. admin., defense	13,835	9.0		
Other	3,702[5]	2.4[5]	…	…
TOTAL	153,413[6]	100.0	473,000	100.0

Tourism: n.a.
Land use as % of total land area (2000): in temporary crops 10.7%, in permanent crops 8.8%, in pasture 38.4%; overall forest area 60.5%.

Foreign trade[7]

Balance of trade (current prices)

	1997	1998	1999	2000	2001
U.S.$'000,000	–40.1	–38.9	–30.8	–41.7	–49.5
% of total	29.2%	42.9%	23.1%	25.1%	34.4%

Imports (2001): U.S.$96,700,000 (foodstuffs 18.7%, of which rice 6.6%; transport equipment 13.2%; equipment and machinery 7.7%; fuel and lubricants 6.2%; unspecified 39.3%). *Major import sources:* Portugal 30.9%; Senegal 28.3%; China 11.3%; The Netherlands 6.8%; Japan 5.8%.
Exports (2001): U.S.$47,200,000 (cashews 95.6%; cotton 2.3%; logs 1.5%). *Major export destinations:* India 85.6%; Portugal 3.8%; Senegal 2.5%; France 1.7%.

Transport and communications

Transport. Railroads: none. Roads (1999): total length 2,734 mi, 4,400 km (paved 10%). Vehicles (1996): passenger cars 7,120; trucks and buses 5,640. Air transport (1998): passenger-mi 6,200,000, passenger-km 10,000,000; short ton-mi cargo, n.a., metric ton-km cargo, n.a.; airports (1997) with scheduled flights 2.

Communications

Medium	date	unit	number	units per 1,000 persons
Daily newspapers	2000	circulation	6,390	5.0
Radio	2001	receivers	56,200	178
Television	1997	receivers	0	0
Telephones	2002	main lines	10,600	8.2
Cellular telephones	2003	subscribers	1,300	1.0
Internet	2003	users	19,000	15

Education and health

Educational attainment: n.a. *Literacy* (1995): total population age 15 and over literate 54.9%; males literate 68.0%; females literate 42.5%.

Education (1999)

	schools	teachers	students	student/ teacher ratio
Primary (age 7–13)	759	4,306	149,530	…
Secondary (age 13–18)	…	1,913	25,034[8]	…

Health: physicians (1996) 193 (1 per 6,024 persons); hospital beds (1998) 1,832 (1 per 667 persons); infant mortality rate per 1,000 live births (2003) 110.3.
Food (2002): daily per capita caloric intake 2,024 (vegetable products 93%, animal products 7%); 88% of FAO recommended minimum requirement.

Military

Total active duty personnel (2003): 9,250 (army 73.5%, navy 3.8%, air force 1.1%, paramilitary [gendarmerie] 21.6%). *Military expenditure as percentage of GNP* (1999): 2.7% (world 2.4%); per capita expenditure U.S.$4.

[1]Reestablished as of March 2004 legislative elections. [2]Formerly pegged to the French franc and since Jan. 1, 2002, to the euro at the rate of €1 = CFAF 655.96. [3]Includes water area of about 3,089 sq mi (8,000 sq km). [4]Based on land area of 10,859 sq mi (28,125 sq km). [5]Indirect taxes. [6]Detail does not add to total given because of rounding. [7]Imports c.i.f.; exports f.o.b. [8]UNESCO estimate.

Internet resources for further information:
- **Afristat http://www.afristat.org**
- **La Banque de France: La Zone Franc http://www.banque-france.fr/fr/zonefr/main.htm**

Guyana

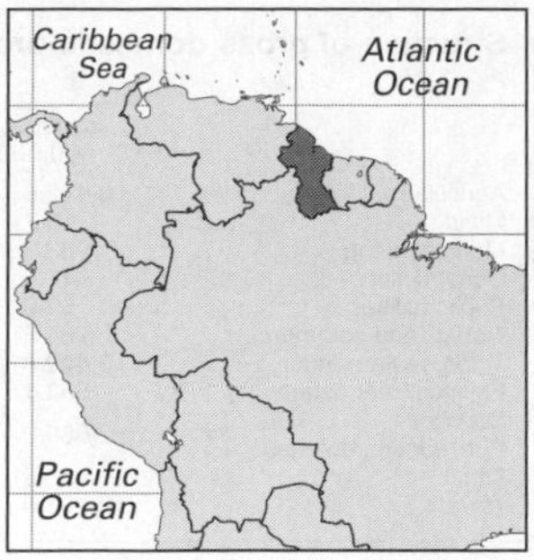

Official name: Co-operative Republic of Guyana.
Form of government: unitary multiparty republic with one legislative house (National Assembly [65[1]]).
Head of state and government: President.
Capital: Georgetown.
Official language: English.
Official religion: none.
Monetary unit: 1 Guyana dollar (G$) = 100 cents; valuation (Sept. 1, 2004) 1 U.S.$ = G$179.00; 1 £ = G$322.01.

Area and population

Administrative regions		Capitals	area sq mi	area sq km	population 2002 preliminary census
Region 1	(Barima-Waini)	Mabaruma	7,853	20,339	23,204
Region 2	(Pomeroon-Supenaam)	Anna Regina	2,392	6,195	48,411
Region 3	(Essequibo Islands–West Demerara)	Vreed en Hoop	1,450	3,755	101,920
Region 4	(Demerara-Mahaica)	Paradise	862	2,233	309,059
Region 5	(Mahaica-Berbice)	Fort Wellington	1,610	4,170	52,321
Region 6	(East Berbice–Corentyne)	New Amsterdam	13,998	36,255	122,849
Region 7	(Cuyuni-Mazaruni)	Bartica	18,229	47,213	15,935
Region 8	(Potaro-Siparuni)	Mahdia	7,742	20,052	9,211
Region 9	(Upper Takutu–Upper Essequibo)	Lethem	22,313	57,790	19,365
Region 10	(Upper Demerara–Berbice)	Linden	6,595	17,081	39,766
TOTAL			83,044[2]	215,083[2]	742,041

Demography

Population (2004): 752,000.
Density (2003)[3]: persons per sq mi 9.9, persons per sq km 3.8.
Urban-rural (2003): urban 37.6%; rural 62.4%.
Sex distribution (2002): male 49.30%; female 50.70%.
Age breakdown (2002): under 15, 27.6%; 15–29, 31.0%; 30–44, 21.3%; 45–59, 12.8%; 60–74, 5.4%; 75 and over, 1.9%.
Population projection: (2010) 755,000; (2020) 732,000.
Doubling time: 69 years.
Ethnic composition (1992–93): East Indian 49.4%; black (African Negro and Bush Negro) 35.6%; Amerindian 6.8%; Portuguese 0.7%; Chinese 0.4%; mixed 7.1%.
Religious affiliation (1995): Christian 40.9%, of which Protestant 27.5% (including Anglican 8.6%), Roman Catholic 11.5%, Ethiopian Orthodox 1.1%; Hindu 34.0%; Muslim 9.0%; other 16.1%.
Major cities (2002): Georgetown 137,330 (urban agglomeration [2003] 231,000); Linden 29,572; New Amsterdam (1997) 25,000; Corriverton (1997) 24,000.

Vital statistics

Birth rate per 1,000 population (2003): 18.7 (world avg. 21.3).
Death rate per 1,000 population (2003): 8.5 (world avg. 9.1).
Natural increase rate per 1,000 population (2003): 10.2 (world avg. 12.2).
Total fertility rate (avg. births per childbearing woman; 2003): 2.1.
Life expectancy at birth (2003): male 62.1 years; female 67.3 years.
Major causes of death per 100,000 population (1997): diseases of the circulatory system 238.2, of which cerebrovascular disease 86.9, ischemic heart diseases 69.2; communicable diseases 90.7; accidents and violence 73.9; malignant neoplasms 45.6; diabetes mellitus 32.5.

National economy

Budget (1999): Revenue: G$36,544,000,000 (tax revenue 91.6%, of which consumption taxes 32.0%, income taxes on companies 22.2%, personal income taxes 15.5%, import duties 11.4%; nontax revenue 8.2%). Expenditures: G$41,983,000,000 (current expenditure 71.2%, of which debt charges 13.8%; development expenditure 28.8%).
Production (metric tons except as noted). Agriculture, forestry, fishing (2002): rice 450,000, raw sugar (2001) 284,000, coconuts 45,000, cassava (manioc) 29,000, plantains 17,000, bananas 17,000, mangoes 12,000, oranges 5,000, pineapples 4,500; livestock (number of live animals) 130,000 sheep, 100,000 cattle, 12,500,000 chickens; roundwood (2001) 1,188,000 cu m; fish catch (2003) 56,307, of which shrimps and prawns 22,584. Mining and quarrying (2003): bauxite 1,716,000; gold 357,000 troy oz; diamonds 413,000 carats. Manufacturing (2002): flour 36,570; rum 145,900 hectolitres; beer and stout 108,500 hectolitres; soft drinks 4,251,000 cases; pharmaceuticals 9,042,000 tablets; garments 4,900,000 units. Construction: n.a. Energy production (consumption): electricity (kW-hr; 2000) 894,000,000 (894,000,000); coal, none (none); crude petroleum, none (none); petroleum products (metric tons; 2000) none (521,000); natural gas, none (none).
Population economically active (1997): total 263,807; activity rate of total population 33.9% (participation rates: ages 15–64 [1992] 59.5%; female 35.2%; unemployed 9.1%).

Price and earnings indexes (2000 = 100)

	1997	1998	1999	2000	2001	2002
Consumer price index	83.8	87.6	94.2	100.0	102.6	108.1
Earnings index	…	…	…	…	…	…

Gross national product (2003): U.S.$689,000,000 (U.S.$900 per capita).

Structure of gross domestic product and labour force

	1999 in value G$'000,000	1999 % of total value	1997 labour force	1997 % of labour force
Sugar	16,142[4]	13.4[4]		
Other agriculture	17,543[5]	14.5[5]	66,789	25.3
Fishing, forestry	8,851	7.3		
Mining	13,923	11.5	7,299	2.8
Manufacturing	3,681[6, 7]	3.1[6, 7]	27,869	10.6
Construction	4,771	4.0	16,545	6.3
Public utilities	[7]	[7]	2,547	0.9
Transp. and commun.	7,138	5.9	20,154	7.6
Trade	4,268	3.5	44,653	16.9
Finance, real estate	7,235	6.0	12,219	4.6
Pub. admin., defense	16,976	14.1	15,219	5.8
Services	1,570	1.3	26,553	10.1
Other	18,570[8]	15.4[8]	23,960[9]	9.1[9]
TOTAL	120,668	100.0	263,807	100.0

Public debt (external, outstanding; 2003): U.S.$1,084,000,000.
Household income and expenditure. Average household size (2002) 4.0.
Tourism (2002): receipts from visitors U.S.$49,000,000; expenditures by nationals abroad U.S.$38,000,000.
Land use as % of total land area (2000): in temporary crops 2.4%, in permanent crops 0.2%, in pasture 6.2%; overall forest area 78.5%.

Foreign trade[10]

Balance of trade (current prices)

	1997	1998	1999	2000	2001	2002
U.S.$'000,000	–48.2	–54.2	–25.2	–80.2	–93.8	–68.2
% of total	3.9%	4.7%	2.3%	7.4%	8.7%	6.4%

Imports (2002): U.S.$563,100,000 (consumer goods 28.0%, fuels and lubricants 22.3%, capital goods 20.1%). *Major import sources* (2001)[11]: U.S. 24%; Netherlands Antilles 17%; Chile 16%; Trinidad and Tobago 13%; U.K. 6%.
Exports (2002): U.S.$494,900,000 (gold 27.5%, sugar 24.1%, shrimp 10.6%, rice 9.2%, timber 7.2%, bauxite 7.1%). *Major export destinations* (2001)[11]: U.S. 22%; Canada 20%; U.K. 12%; Netherlands Antilles 12%; Belgium 5%.

Transport and communications

Transport. Railroads: [12]. Roads (1999): total length 4,952 mi, 7,970 km (paved 7%). Vehicles (1995): passenger cars 24,000; trucks and buses 9,000. Air transport (1999)[13]: passenger-mi 172,000,000, passenger-km 276,600,000; short ton-mi cargo 1,507,000, metric ton-km cargo 2,200,000; airports (2000) with scheduled flights 1[14].

Communications

Medium	date	unit	number	units per 1,000 persons
Daily newspapers	1996	circulation	42,000	54
Radio	1997	receivers	420,000	539
Television	1999	receivers	60,000	77
Telephones	2002	main lines	80,400	92
Cellular telephones	2002	subscribers	87,300	99
Personal computers	2002	units	24,000	27
Internet	2002	users	125,000	142

Education and health

Educational attainment (1980). Percentage of population age 25 and over having: no formal schooling 8.1%; primary education 72.8%; secondary 17.3%; higher 1.8%. *Literacy* (2002): total population age 15 and over literate 98.7%; males literate 99.0%; females literate 98.3%.

Education (1999–2000)

	schools	teachers	students	student/teacher ratio
Primary (age 6–11)	428	3,951	105,800	26.8
Secondary (age 12–17)	109	2,764	50,459	18.3
Voc., teacher tr.	7	512	6,266	12.2
Higher	1	371	7,496	20.2

Health: physicians (1999) 203 (1 per 3,846 persons); hospital beds (2002) 3,274 (1 per 229 persons); infant mortality rate per 1,000 live births (2003) 35.1.
Food (2002): daily per capita caloric intake 2,692 (vegetable products 84%, animal products 16%); 119% of FAO recommended minimum requirement.

Military

Total active duty personnel (2003): 1,600 (army 87.5%, navy 6.3%, air force 6.2%). *Military expenditure as percentage of GNP* (1999): 0.8% (world 2.4%), per capita expenditure U.S.$7.

[1]Includes 12 indirectly elected seats. [2]Includes inland water area equaling *c.* 7,000 sq mi (*c.* 18,000 sq km). [3]Based on land area only. [4]Includes sugar manufacturing. [5]Includes rice manufacturing. [6]Excludes sugar and rice manufacturing. [7]Manufacturing includes Public utilities. [8]Indirect taxes less subsidies. [9]Unemployed. [10]Imports are f.o.b. in balance of trade and commodities and c.i.f. for trading partners. [11]Estimated figures. [12]No public railways. [13]Scheduled traffic only. [14]International only; domestic air service is provided on a charter basis.

Internet resources for further information:
- **Bank of Guyana**
  http://www.bankofguyana.org.gy
- **UNDP Common Country Assessment**
  http://www.undp.org.gy/ccassess.pdf

Haiti

Official name: Repiblik Dayti (Haitian Creole); République d'Haïti (French) (Republic of Haiti).
Form of government: interim regime[1] with two legislative houses (Senate [27]; Chamber of Deputies [83]).
Chief of state: President.
Head of government: Prime Minister.
Capital: Port-au-Prince.
Official languages: Haitian Creole; French.
Official religions: [2].
Monetary unit: 1 gourde (G) = 100 centimes; valuation (Sept. 1, 2004) 1 U.S.$ = G 35.00; 1 £ = G 62.96.

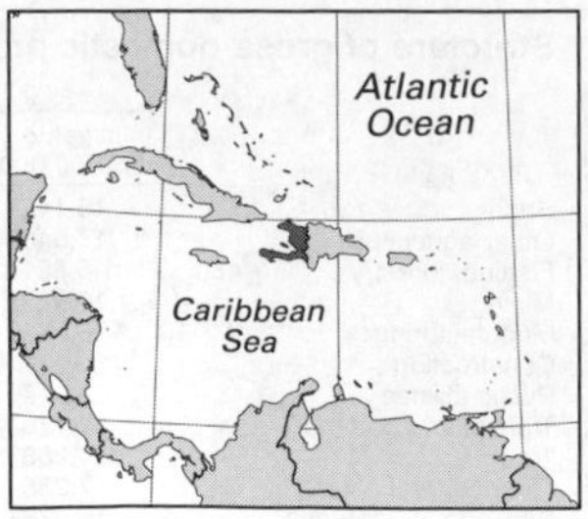

Area and population

Departements	Capitals	area sq mi	area sq km	population 2003 census[3]
Artibonite	Gonaïves	1,924	4,984	1,070,397
Centre	Hinche	1,419	3,675	565,043
Grand'Anse	Jérémie	1,278	3,310	603,894
Nord	Cap-Haïtien	813	2,106	773,546
Nord-Est	Fort-Liberté	697	1,805	300,493
Nord-Ouest	Port-de-Paix	840	2,176	445,080
Ouest	Port-au-Prince	1,864	4,827	3,093,699
Sud	Les Cayes	1,079	2,794	627,311
Sud-Est	Jacmel	781	2,023	449,585
TOTAL		10,695	27,700	7,929,048

Demography

Population (2004): 8,074,000[4].
Density (2004): persons per sq mi 754.9, persons per sq km 291.5.
Urban-rural (2003): urban 37.5%; rural 62.5%.
Sex distribution (2003): male 48.35%; female 51.65%.
Age breakdown (2003): under 15, 42.7%; 15–29, 29.3%; 30–44, 14.2%; 45–59, 8.2%; 60–74, 4.5%; 75 and over, 1.1%.
Population projection[4]: (2010) 8,740,000; (2020) 9,768,000.
Ethnic composition (2000): black 94.2%; mulatto 5.4%; other 0.4%.
Religious affiliation (1995): Roman Catholic 68.5%[5]; Protestant 24.1%, of which Baptist 5.9%, Pentecostal 5.3%, Seventh-day Adventist 4.6%; other 7.4%.
Major cities (1999): Port-au-Prince 990,558 (metropolitan area [2003] 1,977,036); Carrefour 336,222[6]; Delmas 284,079[6]; Cap-Haïtien 113,555; Pétion-Ville (1997) 76,155[6].

Vital statistics

Birth rate per 1,000 population (2003): 36.7 (world avg. 21.3).
Death rate per 1,000 population (2003): 12.7 (world avg. 9.1).
Natural increase rate per 1,000 population (2003): 24.0 (world avg. 12.2).
Total fertility rate (avg. births per childbearing woman; 2003): 5.2.
Life expectancy at birth (2003): male 51.0 years; female 53.7 years.
Adult population (ages 15–49) *living with HIV* (2004[7]): 5.6% (world avg. 1.1%).

National economy

Budget (2002)[8]. Revenue: G 7,721,700,000 (general sales tax 31.3%; customs duties 26.8%; individual taxes on income and profits 20.5%). Expenditures: G 10,376,700,000 (current expenditure 81.6%, of which wages 33.6%, transfers 4.8%, interest on public debt 1.2%; capital expenditure 18.4%).
Production (metric tons except as noted). Agriculture, forestry, fishing (2002): sugarcane 1,010,000, cassava (manioc) 335,000, bananas 295,000, plantains 285,000, mangoes 260,000, yams 198,000, corn (maize) 185,000, sweet potatoes 175,000, rice 104,000, coffee 30,000, sisal 5,700, cacao 4,500; livestock (number of live animals) 1,943,000 goats, 1,450,000 cattle, 1,001,000 pigs, 501,000 horses; roundwood (2001) 2,210,000 cu m; fish catch (2001) 5,000. Mining and quarrying (2001): sand 2,000,000 cu m. Manufacturing (value added in G '000,000; 2001[9]): food and beverages 467.1; textiles, wearing apparel, and footwear 202.4; chemical and rubber products 62.8; tobacco products 37.7. Energy production (consumption): electricity (kW-hr; 2000) 635,000,000 (635,000,000); petroleum products (metric tons; 2000) none (463,000).
Land use as % of total land area (2000): in temporary crops 28.3%, in permanent crops 11.6%, in pasture 17.8%; overall forest area 3.2%.
Population economically active (2002): total *c.* 4,100,000; activity rate of total population *c.* 55% (participation rates: ages 15–64 [1990] 64.8%; female [1996] 43.0%; unemployed unofficially [1996] *c.* 60%).

Price and earnings indexes (2000 = 100)

	1997	1998	1999	2000	2001	2002	2003
Consumer price index	73.1	80.9	87.9	100.0	114.2	125.4	174.7
Daily earnings index[10]	100.0	100.0	100.0	100.0	100.0	100.0	...

Household income and expenditure. Average household size (1982) 4.4; average annual income of urban wage earners (1984): G 1,545 (U.S.$309); expenditure (1996)[11]: food, beverages, and tobacco 49.4%, housing and energy 9.1%, transportation 8.7%, clothing and footwear 8.5%.
Public debt (external, outstanding; 2002): U.S.$1,063,000,000.
Gross national product (at current market prices; 2003): U.S.$3,214,000,000 (U.S.$380 per capita).

Structure of gross domestic product and labour force

	2001 in value G '000,000[9]	2001 % of total value	1990 labour force[12]	1990 % of labour force
Agriculture, forestry	3,445.6	26.5	1,535,444	57.3
Mining	13.7	0.1	24,012	0.9
Manufacturing	983.3	7.6	151,387	5.6
Construction	947.9	7.3	28,001	1.0
Public utilities	59.8	0.5	2,577	0.1
Transp. and commun.	764.6	5.9	20,691	0.8
Trade, restaurants	3,409.8	26.2	352,970	13.2
Finance, real estate	852.1	6.6	5,057	0.2
Services; Pub. admin., defense	2,089.0	16.1	155,347	5.8
Other	425.2[13]	3.2[13]	403,654[14]	15.1[14]
TOTAL	12,991.0	100.0	2,679,140	100.0

Tourism (2001): receipts from visitors U.S.$54,000,000; expenditures by nationals abroad (1998) U.S.$37,000,000.

Foreign trade[15, 16]

Balance of trade (current prices)

	1997	1998	1999	2000	2001	2002
U.S.$'000,000	–497.8	–522.7	–600.4	–698.0	–693.9	–705.8
% of total	54.8%	46.6%	46.9%	52.5%	54.2%	56.3%

Imports (2002): U.S.$1,054,200,000 (food and live animals 22.4%, basic manufactures 19.9%, machinery and transport equipment 15.2%, petroleum and derivatives 14.9%). *Major import sources* (1999)[17]: United States 60%; Dominican Republic 4%; Japan 3%; France 3%; Canada 3%.
Exports (2002): U.S.$274,400,000 (reexports to U.S. 80.8%, of which clothing and apparel 79.1%; mangoes 2.6%; cacao 2.0%; essential oils 1.5%; leather goods 1.1%). *Major export destinations* (1999)[17]: United States 90%; Canada 3%; Belgium 2%; France 2%.

Transport and communications

Transport. Railroad: none. Roads (1999): total length 2,585 mi, 4,160 km (paved 24%). Vehicles (1996): passenger cars 32,000; trucks and buses 21,000. Air transport (2000)[18]: passenger arrivals and departures 924,000; cargo unloaded and loaded 15,300 metric tons; airports (1997) with scheduled flights 2.

Communications

Medium	date	unit	number	units per 1,000 persons
Daily newspapers	2000	circulation	21,500	3.0
Radio	2000	receivers	395,000	55
Television	2000	receivers	35,900	5.0
Telephones	2002	main lines	130,000	16
Cellular telephones	2002	subscribers	140,000	17
Internet	2002	users	80,000	9.6

Education and health

Educational attainment (1986–87). Percentage of population age 25 and over having: no formal schooling 59.5%; primary education 30.5%; secondary 8.6%; vocational and teacher training 0.7%; higher 0.7%. *Literacy* (1995): total population age 15 and over literate 1,930,000 (45.0%); males literate 992,000 (48.0%); females literate 938,000 (42.2%).

Education (1994–95)

	schools	teachers	students	student/ teacher ratio
Primary (age 6–12)	10,071	30,205	1,110,398	36.8
Secondary (age 13–18); Voc., teacher tr.	1,038	...	195,418	...
Higher[19, 20]	2	899	12,348	13.7

Health: physicians (1999) 1,910 (1 per 4,000 persons); hospital beds (1996) 5,241 (1 per 1,242 persons); infant mortality rate per 1,000 live births (2003) 77.0.
Food (2002): daily per capita caloric intake 2,086 (vegetable products 93%, animal products 7%); 92% of FAO recommended minimum requirement.

Military

Total active duty personnel: [21, 22].

[1]From February 2004. [2]Roman Catholicism has special recognition per concordat with the Vatican; voodoo became officially sanctioned per governmental decree of April 2003. [3]Preliminary. [4]Estimate based on 2003 preliminary census total (7,929,048). [5]About 80% of all Roman Catholics also practice voodoo. [6]Within Port-au-Prince metropolitan area. [7]Beginning of year. [8]Does not include projects financed with loans and grants. [9]At prices of 1986–87. [10]Standard minimum wage rate. [11]Weights of consumer price index components. [12]The 2002 labour force equaled *c.* 4,100,000, of which formal sector equaled *c.* 110,000 (including 35,000 government employees). [13]Import duties less imputed bank service charges. [14]Includes 63,975 not adequately defined and 339,679 officially unemployed. [15]Includes reexports. [16]Import figures are f.o.b. in balance of trade and c.i.f. in commodities and trading partners. [17]Estimated percentages. [18]Port-au-Prince Airport only. [19]Port-au-Prince universities only. [20]2000–01. [21]The Haitian army was disbanded in 1995. The national police force had 5,300 personnel in 2003. [22]UN peacekeeping troops (October 2004) 3,092.

Internet resources for further information:
- **Embassy of Haiti (Washington, D.C.) http://www.haiti.org**
- **Banque de la République d'Haïti http://www.brh.net**

Honduras

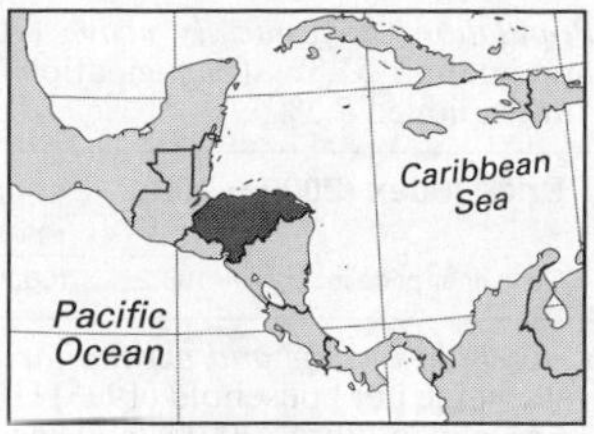

Official name: República de Honduras (Republic of Honduras).
Form of government: multiparty republic with one legislative house (National Assembly [128]).
Head of state and government: President.
Capital: Tegucigalpa.
Official language: Spanish.
Official religion: none.
Monetary unit: 1 Honduran lempira (L) = 100 centavos; valuation (Sept. 1, 2004) 1 U.S.$ = L 18.36; 1 £ = L 33.03.

Area and population

Departments	Administrative centres	area sq mi	area sq km	population 2001 census
Atlántida	La Ceiba	1,688	4,372	344,099
Choluteca	Choluteca	1,515	3,923	390,805
Colón	Trujillo	1,683	4,360	246,708
Comayagua	Comayagua	3,185	8,249	352,881
Copán	Santa Rosa de Copán	1,978	5,124	288,766
Cortés	San Pedro Sula	1,252	3,242	1,202,510
El Paraíso	Yuscarán	2,892	7,489	350,054
Francisco Morazán	Tegucigalpa	3,328	8,619	1,180,676
Gracias a Dios	Puerto Lempira	6,563	16,997	67,384
Intibucá	La Esperanza	1,206	3,123	179,862
Islas de la Bahía	Roatán	91	236	38,073
La Paz	La Paz	975	2,525	156,560
Lempira	Gracias	1,632	4,228	250,067
Ocotepeque	Nueva Ocotepeque	629	1,630	108,029
Olancho	Juticalpa	9,230	23,905	419,561
Santa Bárbara	Santa Bárbara	1,940	5,024	342,054
Valle	Nacaome	643	1,665	151,841
Yoro	Yoro	3,004	7,781	465,414
TOTAL		43,433[1]	112,492	6,535,344[2]

Demography

Population (2004): 6,948,000.
Density (2004): persons per sq mi 160.0, persons per sq km 61.8.
Urban-rural (2003): urban 47.5%; rural 52.5%.
Sex distribution (2002): male 50.09%; female 49.91%.
Age breakdown (2002): under 15, 41.9%; 15–29, 29.1%; 30–44, 15.3%; 45–59, 8.3%; 60–74, 4.1%; 75 and over, 1.3%.
Population projection: (2010) 7,884,000; (2020) 9,155,000.
Doubling time: 27 years.
Ethnic composition (2000): mestizo 86.6%; Amerindian 5.5%; black (including Black Carib) 4.3%; white 2.3%; other 1.3%.
Religious affiliation (1995): Roman Catholic 86.7%; Protestant 10.4%, of which Pentecostal 5.7%; other 2.9%.
Major cities (2001): Tegucigalpa 769,061; San Pedro Sula 439,086; La Ceiba 114,584; El Progreso 90,475; Choluteca 75,600.

Vital statistics

Birth rate per 1,000 population (2002): 32.3 (world avg. 21.3).
Death rate per 1,000 population (2002): 6.3 (world avg. 9.1).
Natural increase rate per 1,000 population (2002): 26.0 (world avg. 12.2).
Total fertility rate (avg. births per childbearing woman; 2002): 4.2.
Life expectancy at birth (2002): male 65.2 years; female 68.7 years.
Major causes of death (percent of total; 2000–02): diseases of the circulatory system 23.6%; accidents and violence 21.3%; malignant neoplasms (cancers) 12.2%; diseases of the respiratory system 10.9%.

National economy

Budget (1999). Revenue: L 14,621,500,000 (tax revenue 92.6%, of which indirect taxes 72.8%, direct taxes 19.8%; nontax revenue 5.1%; transfers 2.3%). Expenditures: L 18,197,700,000 (current expenditure 67.9%; capital expenditure 32.1%).
Public debt (external, outstanding; 2002): U.S.$4,211,000,000.
Production (metric tons except as noted). Agriculture, forestry, fishing (2002): sugarcane 4,300,000, bananas 965,066, oil palm fruit 735,802, corn (maize) 392,214, plantains 260,000, coffee 190,000, oranges 167,226, cantaloupes 131,298, pineapples 61,814; livestock (number of live animals) 1,859,737 cattle, 538,033 pigs, 18,648,000 chickens; roundwood (2001) 9,531,959 cu m; fish catch (2001) 16,451. Mining and quarrying (2001): gypsum 59,500; zinc (metal content) 48,485; silver 35,000 kg; gold 880 kg. Manufacturing (value added in L '000,000; 1996): food products 1,937; wearing apparel 1,266[3]; beverages 700; nonmetallic mineral products 504; wood products 326. Energy production (consumption): electricity (kW-hr; 2001) 4,191,600,000 (4,191,600,000); crude petroleum (barrels) none (n.a.); petroleum products (metric tons; 2000) none (1,382,000); natural gas (cu m) none (n.a.).
Tourism (2002): receipts from visitors U.S.$342,000,000; expenditures by nationals abroad U.S.$185,000,000.
Population economically active (2001): total 2,438,000; activity rate of total population 38.5% (participation rates: ages 15–64, 64.5%; female 35.7%; unemployed 4.2%).

Price index (2000 = 100)

	1997	1998	1999	2000	2001	2002	2003
Consumer price index	70.9	80.6	90.0	100.0	109.7	118.1	127.3

Gross national product (at current market prices; 2003): U.S.$6,760,000,000 (U.S.$970 per capita).

Structure of gross domestic product and labour force

	2003 in value L '000,000[4]	% of total value[4]	labour force	% of labour force
Agriculture	13,566	12.8	906,300	37.4
Mining	1,998	1.9	5,800	0.2
Manufacturing	21,980	20.7	381,200	15.7
Construction	4,922	4.6	122,800	5.1
Public utilities	5,052	4.7	9,600	0.4
Transp. and commun.	6,354	6.0	79,100	3.3
Trade	13,412	12.6	495,900	20.4
Finance, real estate	18,002	16.9	73,300	3.0
Public admin., defense	7,478	7.0	352,100	14.5
Services	13,577	12.8		
Other	—	—	...	...
TOTAL	106,341	100.0	2,426,100[5]	100.0[5]

Household income and expenditure. Average household size (2000) 5.1; sources of income (1985): wages and salaries 58.8%, transfer payments 1.8%, other 39.4%; expenditure (1986): food 44.4%, utilities and housing 22.4%, clothing and footwear 9.0%, household furnishings 8.3%.
Land use as % of total land area (2000): in temporary crops 9.5%, in permanent crops 3.2%, in pasture 13.5%; overall forest area 48.1%.

Foreign trade[6]

Balance of trade (current prices)

	1997	1998	1999	2000	2001	2002
U.S.$'000,000	–703	–1,002	–1,512	–1,485	–1,655	–1,585
% of total	19.6%	24.6%	39.4%	35.1%	38.4%	34.4%

Imports (2001): U.S.$2,984,000,000 (food products and live animals 18.3%, machinery and electrical equipment 15.1%, chemicals and chemical products 14.1%, mineral fuels and lubricants 13.2%). *Major import sources:* U.S. 46.2%; Guatemala 9.9%; El Salvador 6.2%; Mexico 4.7%; Costa Rica 3.5%.
Exports (2001): U.S.$1,329,000,000 (bananas 15.4%, shrimp 13.3%, coffee 12.1%, nontraditional exports [including African palm oil, decorative plants, and mangoes] 42.2%). *Major export destinations:* U.S. 45.7%; El Salvador 10.2%; Guatemala 9.7%; Belgium 4.7%; Germany 4.3%.

Transport and communications

Transport. Railroads (2000): serviceable lines *c.* 127 mi (*c.* 205 km); most tracks are out of use but not dismantled. Roads (2001): total length 8,452 mi, 13,603 km (paved 20%). Vehicles (1999): passenger cars 326,541; trucks and buses 59,322. Air transport (1995): passenger km 341,000,000; metric ton-km cargo 33,000,000; airports (1996) with scheduled flights 8.

Communications

Medium	date	unit	number	units per 1,000 persons
Daily newspapers	2000	circulation	349,000	55
Radio	2000	receivers	2,620,000	412
Television	2002	receivers	809,000	119
Telephones	2003	main lines	334,400	49
Cellular telephones	2002	subscribers	326,500	49
Personal computers	2002	units	91,000	14
Internet	2003	users	185,416	27

Education and health

Educational attainment (1988). Percentage of population age 10 and over having: no formal schooling 33.4%; primary education 50.1%; secondary education 13.4%; higher 3.1%. *Literacy* (2000): total population age 15 and over literate 74.6%; males literate 74.7%; females literate 74.5%.

Education (2001)

	schools	teachers	students	student/teacher ratio
Primary (age 7–13)	9,746	32,568	1,109,242	34.0
Secondary (age 14–19), Voc., teacher tr.	1,000	15,647	195,072	12.5
Higher	10	3,704	64,142	17.3

Health: physicians (2000) 5,287 (1 per 1,201 persons); hospital beds (2003) 5,069 (1 per 1,353 persons); infant mortality rate (2002) 30.9.
Food (2001): daily per capita caloric intake 2,405 (vegetable products 85%, animal products 15%); 106% of FAO recommended minimum.

Military

Total active duty personnel (2003): 12,000 (army 69.2%, navy 11.7%, air force 19.1%); U.S. troops (August 2003) 390. *Military expenditure as percentage of GNP* (1999): 0.7% (world 2.4%); per capita expenditure U.S.$6.

[1]Detail does not add to total given because of rounding. [2]Census population adjusted for underenumeration; unadjusted census figure is 6,071,200. [3]Important product of the maquiladora sector; garment assembly employed 110,000 in 2001. [4]At factor cost. [5]Does not include unemployed. [6]Imports c.i.f.; exports f.o.b.

Internet resources for further information:
- **Banco Central de Honduras http://www.bch.hn**
- **Instituto Nacional de Estadística http://www.ine-hn.org**

Hong Kong

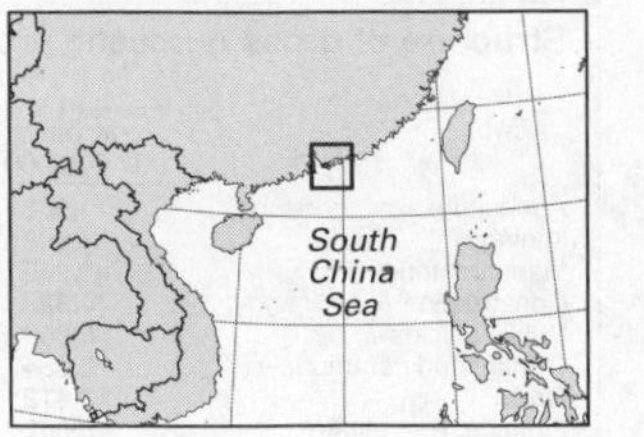

Official name: Xianggang Tebie Xingzhengqu (Chinese); Hong Kong Special Administrative Region (English).
Political status: special administrative region (People's Republic of China) with one legislative house (Legislative Council [60[1]]).
Chief of state: President of China.
Head of government: Chief Executive.
Government offices: Central & Western District (enclosing the historic capital area of Victoria), Hong Kong Island.
Official languages: Chinese; English.
Official religion: none.
Monetary unit: 1 Hong Kong dollar (HK$) = 100 cents; valuation (Sept. 1, 2004) 1 U.S.$ = HK$7.80; 1 £ = HK$14.03.

Area and population

Geographic areas	area sq mi	area sq km	population 2001 census
Hong Kong Island	31	81	1,335,469
Kowloon	18	47	2,023,979
New Territories (mainland)	288	747	3,256,379
New Territories (islands[2])	88	227	86,667
Marine	—	—	5,895
TOTAL	425	1,102	6,708,389

Demography

Population (2004): 6,848,000.
Density (2004): persons per sq mi 16,113, persons per sq km 6,214.
Urban-rural (2003): urban 100.0%.
Sex distribution (2003): male 48.42%; female 51.58%.
Age breakdown (2002): under 15, 16.1%; 15–29, 20.6%; 30–44, 28.9%; 45–59, 19.4%; 60–74, 10.4%; 75 and over, 4.6%.
Population projection: (2010) 7,083,000; (2020) 7,321,000.
Ethnic composition (2003): Chinese 95%; other 5%.
Religious affiliation (1994): Buddhist and Taoist 73.8%; Christian 8.4%, of which Protestant 4.3%, Roman Catholic 4.1%; New Religionist 3.2%; Muslim 0.8%; Hindu 0.2%; nonreligious/atheist 13.5%; other 0.1%.

Vital statistics

Birth rate per 1,000 population (2003): 6.8 (world avg. 21.3).
Death rate per 1,000 population (2003): 5.4 (world avg. 9.1).
Natural increase rate per 1,000 population (2003): 1.4 (world avg. 12.2).
Total fertility rate (avg. births per childbearing woman; 2003): 1.3.
Marriage rate per 1,000 population (2003): 5.2.
Life expectancy at birth (2003): male 78.6 years; female 84.3 years.
Major causes of death per 100,000 population (2003): malignant neoplasms (cancers) 175.0; diseases of the circulatory system 126.7; diseases of the respiratory system 87.1; accidents and violence 28.6.

National economy

Budget (2002–03). Revenue: HK$173,345,000,000 (earnings and profits taxes 41.2%; indirect taxes 22.6%, of which property taxes 5.1%; capital revenue 12.8%). Expenditures: HK$273,055,000,000 (education 14.7%; social welfare 11.9%; housing 10.6%; health 9.1%; police 7.5%; economic services 5.4%).
Gross domestic product (2003): U.S.$173,306,000,000 (U.S.$25,430 per capita).

Structure of gross domestic product and labour force

	2001 in value HK$'000,000	2001 % of total value	2002 labour force	2002 % of labour force
Agriculture	1,003	0.1	9,800	0.3
Mining	174	— }	289,900	8.3
Manufacturing	63,519	5.0		
Construction	58,971	4.7	286,700	8.2
Public utilities	40,126	3.2	15,900	0.5
Transp. and commun.	94,900	7.5	346,000	9.9
Trade	324,654	25.8	983,700	28.2
Finance, insurance, and real estate	274,030	21.8	474,700	13.6
Pub. admin., defense, and services	265,081	21.0	825,600	23.7
Other	137,342[3]	10.9[3]	255,500[4]	7.3[4]
TOTAL	1,259,800	100.0	3,487,800	100.0

Production (metric tons except as noted). Agriculture, forestry, fishing (2000): vegetables 42,500, fruits and nuts 2,022, field crops 508, eggs 3,710,000 units; livestock (2002; number of live animals) 100,000 pigs, 25,000 cattle, 3,000,000 chickens; fish catch (2001) 179,600. Manufacturing (value added in HK$'000,000; 2001): publishing and printed materials 12,309; electronic parts and components 9,945; textiles 6,874; food 5,589; wearing apparel 4,646; machinery and equipment 3,688; transport equipment 3,247; chemicals and chemical products 2,243; basic metals and fabricated metal products 2,194. Construction (2002)[5]: residential 1,411,000 sq m; nonresidential 549,000 sq m. Energy production (consumption): electricity (kW-hr; 2000) 31,329,000,000 (40,351,000,000); coal (metric tons; 2000) none (6,057,000); petroleum products (metric tons; 2000) none (5,070,000).

Population economically active (2003): total 3,487,800; activity rate of total population 51.3% (participation rates: over age 15, 61.1%; female 43.9%; unemployed 7.3%).

Price index (2000 = 100)

	1997	1998	1999	2000	2001	2002	2003
Consumer price index	105.2	108.2	103.9	100.0	98.4	95.4	92.9

Household income and expenditure. Average household size (2003) 3.1; annual income per household (1996) HK$210,000 (U.S.$27,600); sources of income: n.a.; expenditure (2001): housing and energy 22.2%, clothing and footwear 15.2%, food and nonalcoholic beverages 13.5%, household furnishings 12.6%, transportation 11.0%.
Tourism (2001): receipts U.S.$8,241,000,000; expenditures U.S.$12,494,000,000.
Land use as % of total land area (2000): in temporary and permanent crops 5.4%[6], in pasture 29.3%; overall forest area 18.0%.

Foreign trade[7]

Balance of trade (current prices)

	1998	1999	2000	2001	2002	2003
HK$'000,000	–81,443	–43,718	–85,273	–87,208	–58,902	–63,400
% of total	2.9%	1.6%	2.6%	2.9%	1.9%	1.8%

Imports (2003): HK$1,805,800,000,000 (consumer goods 31.9%, capital goods 26.7%, foodstuffs 3.2%, mineral fuels and lubricants 2.0%). *Major import sources:* China 43.5%; Japan 11.9%; Taiwan 6.9%; U.S. 5.5%; Singapore 5.0%.
Exports (2003): HK$1,742,400,000,000 (reexports 93.0%, of which consumer goods 35.4%, capital goods 26.0%; domestic exports 7.0%, of which clothing accessories and apparel 3.7%). *Major export destinations*[8]: China 42.6%; U.S. 18.6%; Japan 5.2%; U.K. 3.3%; Germany 3.2%.

Transport and communications

Transport. Railroads (2003): route length 40 mi, 64 km[9]; (2002) passenger-km 4,540,000,000[10]; metric ton-km cargo, n.a. Roads (2003): total length 1,196 mi, 1,924 km (paved 100%). Vehicles (2003): passenger cars 357,000; trucks and buses 137,000. Air transport (2003)[11]: passenger-km 46,523,000,000; metric ton-km cargo 6,057,000,000; airports (2003) with scheduled flights 1.

Communications

Medium	date	unit	number	units per 1,000 persons
Daily newspapers	2000	circulation	5,280,000	792
Radio	2000	receivers	4,560,000	684
Television	2000	receivers	3,290,000	493
Telephones	2003	main lines	3,820,000	561
Cellular telephones	2004	subscribers	7,625,700	1,114
Personal computers	2002	units	2,864,000	422
Internet	2003	users	3,212,800	469

Education and health

Educational attainment (2003). Percentage of population age 15 and over having: no formal schooling 6.9%; primary education 20.4%; secondary 46.2%; matriculation 5.3%; nondegree higher 7.8%; higher degree 13.4%.
Literacy (2000): total population age 15 and over literate 93.5%; males literate 96.5%; females literate 90.2%.

Education (2002–03)

	schools	teachers	students	student/ teacher ratio
Primary (age 6–11)	803	23,988	468,800	19.5
Secondary (age 12–18)	542	25,742	471,100	18.3
Vocational	1	1,008	59,400	58.9
Higher	9	5,620	86,900	14.9

Health (2003): physicians 10,884[12] (1 per 625 persons); hospital beds 35,378 (1 per 192 persons); infant mortality rate per 1,000 live births (2003) 2.3.
Food (2001): daily per capita caloric intake 3,104 (vegetable products 68%, animal products 32%); 136% of FAO recommended minimum requirement.

Military

Total active duty personnel (2003): 4,000 troops of Chinese army to intervene in local matters only at the request of the Hong Kong government; Chinese navy and air force, n.a.

[1]Thirty seats are directly elected by ordinary voters, and the remaining 30 are elected by special interest groups. [2]Primarily Lantau. [3]Ownership of premises, taxes on production and imports less adjustment for financial intermediation services. [4]Unemployed. [5]Usable floor area only. [6]Represents grassland that may not be grazed. [7]Imports are c.i.f., exports f.o.b. [8]Includes reexports and domestic exports. [9]Combined length of East Rail and West Rail; West Rail was inaugurated in December 2003. [10]East Rail only. [11]Cathay Pacific and Dragonair only. [12]Registered personnel; all may not be present and working in the country.

Internet resources for further information:
- **Census and Statistics Department http://www.info.gov.hk/censtatd**

Hungary

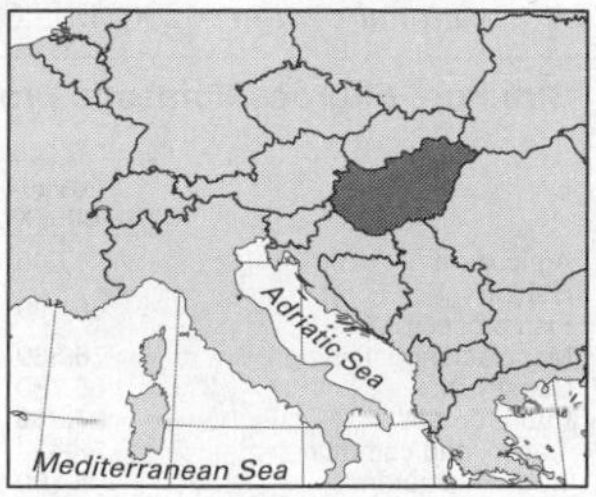

Official name: Magyar Köztársaság (Republic of Hungary).
Form of government: unitary multiparty republic with one legislative house (National Assembly [386]).
Chief of state: President.
Head of government: Prime Minister.
Capital: Budapest.
Official language: Hungarian.
Official religion: none.
Monetary unit: 1 forint (Ft) = 100 filler; valuation (Sept. 1, 2004) 1 U.S.$ = Ft 205.05; 1 £ = Ft 368.88.

Area and population

		area		population
Counties	Capitals	sq mi	sq km	2004[1] estimate
Bács-Kiskun	Kecskemét	3,261	8,445	542,000
Baranya	Pécs	1,710	4,430	402,000
Békés	Békéscsaba	2,174	5,631	393,000
Borsod-Abaúj-Zemplén	Miskolc	2,798	7,247	738,000
Csongrád	Szeged	1,646	4,263	426,000
Fejér	Székesfehérvár	1,683	4,359	428,000
Györ-Moson-Sopron	Györ	1,579	4,089	440,000
Hajdú-Bihar	Debrecen	2,398	6,211	550,000
Heves	Eger	1,404	3,637	324,000
Jász-Nagykun-Szolnok	Szolnok	2,155	5,582	413,000
Komárom-Esztergom	Tatabánya	875	2,265	316,000
Nógrád	Salgótarján	982	2,544	218,000
Pest	Budapest[1]	2,468	6,393	1,123,000
Somogy	Kaposvár	2,331	6,036	334,000
Szabolcs-Szatmár-Bereg	Nyíregyháza	2,292	5,937	583,000
Tolna	Szekszárd	1,430	3,703	247,000
Vas	Szombathely	1,288	3,336	267,000
Veszprém	Veszprém	1,781	4,613	368,000
Zala	Zalaegerszeg	1,461	3,784	297,000
Capital city				
Budapest[2]		203	525	1,708,000
TOTAL		35,919	93,030	10,117,000

Demography

Population (2004): 10,103,000.
Density (2004): persons per sq mi 281.3, persons per sq km 108.6.
Urban-rural (2004): urban 64.8%; rural 35.2%.
Sex distribution (2004): male 47.49%; female 52.51%.
Age breakdown (2004): under 15, 15.9%; 15–29, 21.9%; 30–44, 19.8%; 45–59, 21.4%; 60–74, 14.5%; 75 and over, 6.5%.
Population projection: (2010) 9,949,000; (2020) 9,669,000.
Ethnic composition (2000): Hungarian 84.4%; Rom (Gypsy) 5.3%; Ruthenian 2.9%; German 2.4%; Romanian 1.0%; Slovak 0.9%; Jewish 0.6%; other 2.5%.
Religious affiliation (1998): Roman Catholic 57.8%; Reformed 17.7%; Lutheran 3.9%; Jewish 0.2%; nonreligious 18.5%; other/unknown 1.9%.
Major cities (2004)[1]: Budapest 1,708,000; Debrecen 205,000; Miskolc 178,000; Szeged 163,000; Pécs 158,000; Györ 129,000.

Vital statistics

Birth rate per 1,000 population (2003): 9.3 (world avg. 21.3); (2002) legitimate 68.7%; illegitimate 31.3%.
Death rate per 1,000 population (2003): 13.4 (world avg. 9.1).
Natural increase rate per 1,000 population (2003): –4.1 (world avg. 12.2).
Total fertility rate (avg. births per childbearing woman; 2003): 1.3.
Marriage rate per 1,000 population (2003): 4.5.
Life expectancy at birth (2002): male 68.3 years; female 76.6 years.
Major causes of death per 100,000 population (2003): heart diseases *c.* 392; malignant neoplasms (cancers) *c.* 329; cerebrovascular diseases *c.* 183; arteriosclerosis *c.* 68; accidents *c.* 68; liver diseases *c.* 62.

National economy

Budget (2002). Revenue: Ft 6,338,100,000,000 (social contributions 34.1%, taxes on goods and services 32.1%, personal income taxes 15.1%). Expenditures: Ft 7,781,600,000,000 (social protection 30.2%, public debt 8.8%, transport 8.1%, health 5.8%, education 5.2%, defense 3.0%).
Production (metric tons except as noted). Agriculture, forestry, fishing (2003): corn (maize) 4,534,000, wheat 2,920,000, sugar beets 1,802,000, sunflower seeds 975,000, barley 813,000, apples 530,000, grapes 523,000; livestock (number of live animals) 4,658,000 pigs, 1,281,000 sheep, 714,000 cattle; roundwood (2002) 5,637,000 cu m; fish catch (2001) 19,694. Mining and quarrying (2002): bauxite 720,000. Manufacturing (value added in U.S.$'000,000; 2000): electrical machinery and apparatus 1,309; motor vehicles and parts 1,105; food products 1,001; chemicals and chemical products 870; nonelectrical machinery and apparatus 711; fabricated metal products 448. Energy production (consumption): electricity (kW-hr; 2003) 34,282,000,000 (43,188,000,000); hard coal (metric tons; 2003) 672,000 ([2000] 1,280,000); lignite (metric tons; 2003) 11,984,000 (14,619,000); crude petroleum (barrels; 2003) 7,586,000 ([2000] 45,853,000); petroleum products (metric tons; 2000) 6,202,000 (5,817,000); natural gas (cu m; 2003) 3,087,000,000 (14,558,000,000).
Public debt (external, outstanding; 2002): U.S.$13,551,000,000.
Population economically active (2003): total 4,166,400; activity rate of total population 41.1% (participation rates: ages 15–74, 53.8%; female [2002] 44.5%; unemployed 5.9%).

Price and earnings indexes (2000 = 100)

	1997	1998	1999	2000	2001	2002	2003
Consumer price index	72.5	82.8	91.1	100.0	109.2	115.0	120.3
Annual earnings index	67.7	79.1	88.7	100.0	113.2	130.2	146.8

Tourism (U.S.$'000,000; 2002): receipts 3,273; expenditures 1,722.
Gross national product (2003): U.S.$64,028,000,000 (U.S.$6,330 per capita).

Structure of gross domestic product and labour force

	2002		2003	
	in value Ft '000,000[3]	% of total value[3]	labour force	% of labour force
Agriculture, forestry	619,400	3.7	215,200	5.2
Mining	33,500	0.2	12,800	0.3
Manufacturing	3,632,700	21.7	925,500	22.2
Construction	887,200	5.3	299,400	7.2
Public utilities	502,200	3.0	68,200	1.6
Transp. and commun.	1,372,700	8.2	303,200	7.3
Trade, restaurants	2,209,700	13.2	692,500	16.6
Finance, real estate	3,582,400	21.4	338,700	8.1
Public administration, defense	1,573,600	9.4	295,400	7.1
Services	2,327,000	13.9	771,000	18.5
Other	—	—	244,500[4]	5.9[4]
TOTAL	16,740,400	100.0	4,166,400	100.0

Household income and expenditure. Average household size (2002) 2.5; income per household[5] (2001) Ft 2,898,000 (U.S.$10,300); sources of income (2001): wages 48.3%, transfers 25.7%, self-employment 16.3%; expenditure (2002): food products 28.8%, housing and energy 17.6%, transportation and communications 16.5%, recreation 7.0%.
Land use as % of total land area (2000): in temporary crops 50.0%, in permanent crops 2.2%, in pasture 11.4%; overall forest area 19.9%.

Foreign trade[6]

Balance of trade (current prices)

	1998	1999	2000	2001	2002	2003
Ft '000,000,000	–577	707	–1,121	–917	–830	–1,134
% of total	5.5%	5.6%	6.6%	5.0%	4.5%	5.6%

Imports (2002): Ft 9,704,000,000,000 (electrical machinery 17.0%, nonelectrical machinery 14.6%, road vehicles 8.1%, mineral fuels 7.0%, telecommunications equipment 6.2%). *Major import sources:* Germany 24.3%; Italy 7.5%; Austria 6.9%; Russia 6.1%; China 5.5%.
Exports (2002): Ft 8,874,000,000,000 (telecommunications equipment 15.5%, electrical machinery 11.2%, power-generating machinery 10.9%, road vehicles 8.7%, office machines and computers 7.1%). *Major export destinations:* Germany 35.5%; Austria 7.1%; Italy 5.8%; France 5.7%; U.K. 4.7%.

Transport and communications

Transport. Railroads (2003): route length 7,898 km; passenger-km (2002) 10,408,000,000; metric ton-km cargo 7,980,000,000. Roads (1999): total length 188,203 km (paved 43%). Vehicles (2003): passenger cars 2,777,000; trucks and buses 395,000. Air transport (2003): passenger-km 3,130,400,000; metric ton-km cargo 46,000,000; airports with scheduled flights 1.

Communications

Medium	date	unit	number	units per 1,000 persons
Daily newspapers	1996	circulation	1,895,000	186
Radio	2000	receivers	7,050,000	690
Television	2000	receivers	4,460,000	437
Telephones	2002	main lines	3,666,400	361
Cellular telephones	2002	subscribers	6,862,800	676
Personal computers	2002	units	1,100,000	108
Internet	2002	users	1,600,000	158

Education and health

Educational attainment (1990). Population age 25 and over having: no formal schooling 1.3%; primary education 57.9%; secondary 30.7%; higher 10.1%.

Education (2003–04)

	schools	teachers	students	student/ teacher ratio
Primary (age 6–13)	3,747	89,784	913,000	10.2
Secondary (age 14–17)	1,622	38,479	531,400	13.8
Vocational	622	9,716	134,800	13.9
Higher	68	22,663	409,075	18.1

Health (2002): physicians 32,452 (1 per 313 persons); hospital beds 80,340 (1 per 126 persons); infant mortality rate per 1,000 live births (2003) 7.3.
Food (2001): daily per capita caloric intake 3,520 (vegetable products 69%, animal products 31%); 134% of FAO recommended minimum requirement.

Military

Total active duty personnel (2003): 33,400 (army 70.7%, air force 23.1%, headquarters staff 6.2%). *Military expenditure as percentage of GNP* (1999): 1.7% (world 2.4%); per capita expenditures U.S.$185.

[1]January 1. [2]Budapest acts as the capital of Pest county even though it is administratively not part of Pest county. [3]Breakdown by sector is calculated based on percentage. [4]Unemployed. [5]Adjusted disposable income including government transfers. [6]Imports c.i.f.; exports f.o.b.

Internet resources for further information:
- **Hungarian Central Statistical Office http://portal.ksh.hu**

Iceland

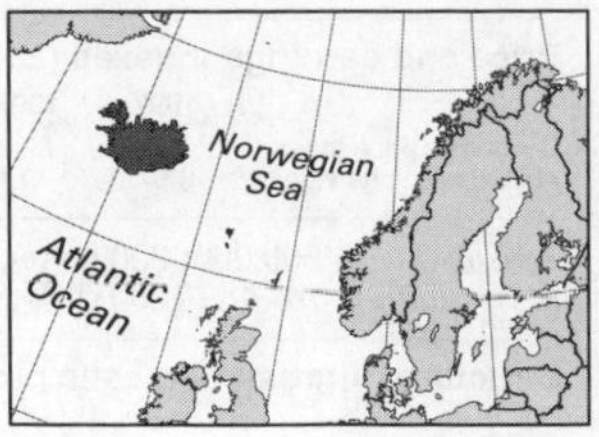

Official name: Lýdhveldidh Ísland (Republic of Iceland).
Form of government: unitary multiparty republic with one legislative house (Althingi [63]).
Chief of state: President.
Head of government: Prime Minister.
Capital: Reykjavík.
Official language: Icelandic.
Official religion: Evangelical Lutheran.
Monetary unit: 1 króna (ISK) = 100 aurar; valuation (Sept. 1, 2004) 1 U.S.$ = ISK 72.20; 1 £ = ISK 129.88.

Area and population

		area		population
				2003[2]
Constituencies[1]	Principal centres	sq mi	sq km	estimate
Austurland	Egilsstadhir	8,773	22,721	11,749
Höfudhborgarsvaedi[3]	Reykjavík	410	1,062	179,992
Nordhurland eystra	Akureyri	8,482	21,968	26,780
Nordhurland vestra	Saudhárkrókur	4,918	12,737	9,219
Sudhurland	Selfoss	9,469	24,526	21,498
Sudhurnes	Keflavík	320	829	16,802
Vestfirdhir	Ísafjördhur	3,633	9,409	7,915
Vesturland	Borgarnes	3,689	9,554	14,516
Unallocated area	—	47	122	0
TOTAL		39,741	102,928	288,471

Demography

Population (2004): 292,000.
Density (2004)[4]: persons per sq mi 31.8, persons per sq km 12.3.
Urban-rural (2003): urban 93.8%; rural 6.2%.
Sex distribution (2003): male 50.02%; female 49.98%.
Age breakdown (2003): under 15, 22.9%; 15–29, 22.1%; 30–44, 21.9%; 45–59, 17.8%; 60–74, 9.9%; 75 and over, 5.4%.
Population projection: (2010) 306,000; (2020) 327,000.
Doubling time: 90 years.
Ethnic composition (2003)[5]: Icelandic 96.5%; European 2.5%, of which Nordic 0.6%; Asian 0.6%; other 0.4%.
Religious affiliation (2001): Protestant 92.2%, of which Evangelical Lutheran 87.1%, other Lutheran 4.1%; Roman Catholic 1.7%; other and not specified 6.1%.
Major cities (2003): Reykjavík 112,554 (urban area 179,992); Kópavogur 25,016[6]; Hafnarfjördhur 20,720[6]; Akureyri 15,867; Gardabær 8,695[6].

Vital statistics

Birth rate per 1,000 population (2002): 14.1 (world avg. 21.3); (2001) legitimate 36.7%; illegitimate 63.3%.
Death rate per 1,000 population (2002): 6.3 (world avg. 9.1).
Natural increase rate per 1,000 population (2002): 7.8 (world avg. 12.2).
Total fertility rate (avg. births per childbearing woman; 2002): 1.9.
Marriage rate per 1,000 population (2002): 5.6.
Divorce rate per 1,000 population (2002): 1.8.
Life expectancy at birth (2001–02): male 78.4 years; female 82.6 years.
Major causes of death per 100,000 population (2001): diseases of the circulatory system 211.0, of which ischemic heart diseases 110.4, cerebrovascular disease 59.4; malignant neoplasms (cancers) 165.6; accidents and violence 44.2; diseases of the respiratory system 41.9; diseases of the nervous system 39.2.

National economy

Budget (2004). Revenue: ISK 279,425,000,000 (tax revenue 90.3%, of which value-added tax 30.8%, individual income tax 26.4%, social security contribution 10.4%; nontax revenue 9.7%). Expenditures: ISK 273,035,000,000 (social security and health 40.4%, education 11.8%, social affairs 8.4%, interest payment 5.5%).
Public debt (2003): U.S.$3,333,000,000.
Production (metric tons except as noted). Agriculture, forestry, fishing (2002): potatoes 8,800, cereals 4,400, tomatoes 948, hay 2,175,427 cu m; livestock (number of live animals) 469,657 sheep, 71,267 horses, 67,225 cattle; fish catch (value in ISK '000,000; 2002) 77,075, of which cod 28,655, redfish 5,918, herring 4,319, halibut 4,129, shrimp 4,110. Mining and quarrying (2002): diatomite 31,000. Manufacturing (value added in ISK '000,000; 1996): preserved and processed fish 18,114; other food products 10,848; printing and publishing 6,914; fabricated metal products 6,640; nonferrous metals 2,932; wood furniture 2,379. Energy production (consumption): electricity (kW-hr; 2002) 8,409,000,000 (8,409,000,000); coal (metric tons; 2000) none (101,000); crude petroleum, none (none); petroleum products (metric tons; 2000) none (560,000); natural gas (cu m) none (none).
Land use as % of total land area (2000): in temporary crops 0.07%, in permanent crops, none, in pasture 22.7%; overall forest area 0.3%.
Population economically active (2004): total 162,400; activity rate of total population 55.9% (participation rates: ages 16–74, 81.5%; female (2002) 46.9%; unemployed 2.6%).

Price and earnings indexes (2000 = 100)

	1997	1998	1999	2000	2001	2002	2003
Consumer price index	90.6	92.1	95.1	100.0	106.4	111.9	114.2
Hourly earnings index	...	...	...	100.0	108.9	116.6	...

Gross national product (2003): U.S.$8,813,000,000 (U.S.$30,810 per capita).

Structure of gross domestic product and labour force

	2002			
	in value ISK '000,000[7]	% of total value[7]	labour force	% of labour force
Agriculture	11,680	1.5	6,400	4.0
Fishing }	96,590	12.4	5,000	3.1
Fish processing }			6,000	3.7
Manufacturing, mining	76,330	9.8	16,400	10.1
Construction	60,760	7.8	12,200	7.5
Public utilities	27,260	3.5	1,500	0.9
Transp. and commun.	58,420	7.5	9,700	6.0
Trade, restaurants	105,160	13.5	26,900	16.6
Finance, real estate	8	8	19,400	12.0
Public administration	164,360	21.1 }	53,300	32.9
Services	178,400[8]	22.9[8] }		
Other	...	...	5,200	3.2
TOTAL	778,960	100.0	162,000	100.0

Household income and expenditure. Average household size (2002) 2.8; annual employment income per household (2002) ISK 2,330,000 (U.S.$28,900); sources of income (2001): wages and salaries 78.6%, pension 10.3%, self-employment 2.0%, other 9.1%; expenditure (2003): housing and energy 20.3%, food, beverages, and tobacco 19.9%, transportation and communications 18.7%, recreation and culture 13.9%, household goods 6.1%.
Tourism (2002): receipts U.S.$250,000,000; expenditures U.S.$365,000,000.

Foreign trade[9]

Balance of trade (current prices)

	1998	1999	2000	2001	2002	2003
ISK '000,000	–25,019	–22,382	–37,480	–5,936	+14,082	–15,901
% of total	8.4%	7.2%	11.2%	1.5%	3.6%	4.2%

Imports (2002): ISK 207,609,000,000 (machinery and apparatus 20.4%; transport equipment 11.9%; food products 9.5%; crude petroleum and petroleum products 7.9%; clothing and footwear 4.4%). *Major import sources:* U.S. 11.1%; Germany 10.7%; Denmark 8.5%; Norway 8.0%; U.K. 7.4%; The Netherlands 6.0%.
Exports (2002): ISK 203,394,000,000 (marine products 62.8%, of which cod 23.9%, shrimp 6.3%, redfish 5.3%, haddock 4.0%; aluminum 18.9%; medicinal products 3.0%). *Major export destinations:* Germany 18.5%; U.K. 17.6%; U.S. 10.8%; The Netherlands 10.8%; Spain 5.3%.

Transport and communications

Transport. Railroads: none. Roads (2002): total length 8,050 mi, 12,955 km (paved 33%). Vehicles (2003): passenger cars 161,721; trucks and buses 21,977. Air transport (2003)[10]: passenger-mi 1,869,400,000, passenger-km 2,999,800,000; short ton-mi cargo 65,345,000, metric ton-km cargo 95,500,000; airports (1996) with scheduled flights 24.

Communications

Medium	date	unit	number	units per 1,000 persons
Daily newspapers	2000	circulation	100,000	347
Radio	2000	receivers	270,000	960
Television	2000	receivers	143,000	509
Telephones	2003	main lines	190,700	660
Cellular telephones	2003	subscribers	279,100	966
Personal computers	2002	units	130,000	451
Internet	2003	users	195,000	675

Education and health

Educational attainment (2002): Percentage of population ages 25–64 having primary and some secondary education 34.4%; secondary 45.7%; higher 19.9%. *Literacy:* virtually 100%.

Education (2002)

	schools	teachers	students	student/ teacher ratio
Primary/lower secondary (age 7–15)	193	4,437	44,695	10.1
Upper secondary (age 16–19)	36	2,258	21,379	9.5
Higher	11	2,620	13,884	5.3

Health: physicians (2002) 1,029 (1 per 280 persons); hospital beds 2,432 (1 per 118 persons); infant mortality rate per 1,000 live births (2002) 2.2.
Food (2001): daily per capita caloric intake 3,313 (vegetable products 59%, animal products 41%); 121% of FAO recommended minimum requirement.

Military

Total active duty personnel (2003): 120 coast guard personnel; NATO-sponsored U.S.-manned Iceland Defense Force (August 2004): 1,800. *Military expenditure as percentage of GNP* (1999): none (world average 2.4%).

[1]Constituencies are electoral districts. Actual local administration is based on towns or rural districts. [2]January 1. [3]In English, Capital Region. [4]Population density calculated with reference to 9,191 sq mi (23,805 sq km) area free of glaciers (comprising 4,603 sq mi [11,922 sq km]), lava fields or wasteland (comprising 24,918 sq mi [64,538 sq km]), and lakes (comprising 1,064 sq mi [2,757 sq km]). [5]By citizenship. [6]Within Reykjavík urban area. [7]Breakdown value by sector is calculated based on percentage. [8]Services include Finance, real estate. [9]Imports f.o.b. in balance of trade and c.i.f. in commodities and trading partners. [10]Icelandair only.

Internet resources for further information:
- **Statistics Iceland http://www.statice.is**
- **Central Bank of Iceland http://www.sedlabanki.is**

India

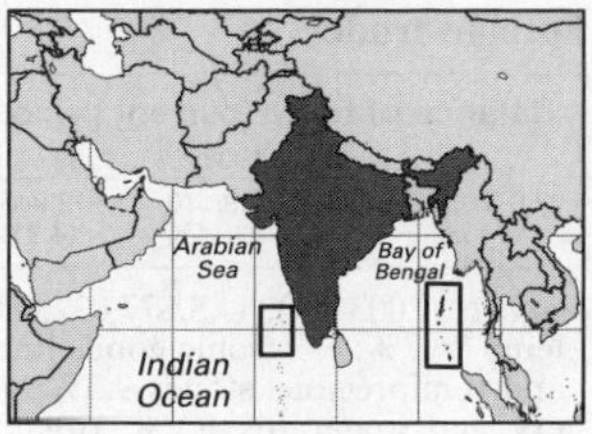

Official name: Bharat (Hindi); Republic of India (English).
Form of government: multiparty federal republic with two legislative houses (Council of States [245[1]]; House of the People [545[2]]).
Chief of state: President.
Head of government: Prime Minister.
Capital: New Delhi.
Official languages: Hindi; English.
Official religion: none.
Monetary unit: 1 Indian rupee (Re, plural Rs) = 100 paise; valuation (Sept. 1, 2004) 1 U.S.$ = Rs 46.35; 1 £ = Rs 83.37.

Area and population

States	Capitals	area sq mi	area sq km	population 2001 census
Andhra Pradesh	Hyderabad	106,204	275,068	76,210,007
Arunachal Pradesh	Itanagar	32,333	83,743	1,097,968
Assam	Dispur	30,285	78,438	26,655,528
Bihar	Patna	38,301	99,200	82,998,509
Chhattisgarh	Raipur	52,199	135,194	20,833,803
Goa	Panaji	1,429	3,702	1,347,668
Gujarat	Gandhinagar	75,685	196,024	50,671,017
Haryana	Chandigarh	17,070	44,212	21,144,564
Himachal Pradesh	Shimla	21,495	55,673	6,077,900
Jammu and Kashmir	Srinagar	39,146	101,387	10,143,700
Jharkhand	Ranchi	28,833	74,677	26,945,829
Karnataka	Bangalore	74,051	191,791	52,850,562
Kerala	Thiruvananthapuram (Trivandrum)	15,005	38,863	31,841,374
Madhya Pradesh	Bhopal	119,016	308,252	60,348,023
Maharashtra	Mumbai (Bombay)	118,800	307,690	96,878,627
Manipur	Imphal	8,621	22,327	2,166,788
Meghalaya	Shillong	8,660	22,429	2,318,822
Mizoram	Aizawl	8,139	21,081	888,573
Nagaland	Kohima	6,401	16,579	1,990,036
Orissa	Bhubaneshwar	60,119	155,707	36,804,660
Punjab	Chandigarh	19,445	50,362	24,358,999
Rajasthan	Jaipur	132,139	342,239	56,507,188
Sikkim	Gangtok	2,740	7,096	540,851
Tamil Nadu	Chennai (Madras)	50,216	130,058	62,405,679
Tripura	Agartala	4,049	10,486	3,199,203
Uttar Pradesh	Lucknow	93,933	243,286	166,197,921
Uttaranchal	Dehra Dun	19,739	51,125	8,489,349
West Bengal	Kolkata (Calcutta)	34,267	88,752	80,176,197
Union Territories				
Andaman and Nicobar Islands	Port Blair	3,185	8,249	356,152
Chandigarh	Chandigarh	44	114	900,635
Dadra and Nagar Haveli	Silvassa	190	491	220,490
Daman and Diu	Daman	43	112	158,204
Lakshadweep	Kavaratti	12	32	60,650
Pondicherry	Pondicherry	190	492	974,345
National Capital Territory				
Delhi[3]	Delhi	573	1,483	13,850,507
TOTAL		1,222,559[4, 5]	3,166,414[4]	1,028,610,328

Demography

Population (2004): 1,081,229,000.
Density (2004)[4]: persons per sq mi 884.4, persons per sq km 341.5.
Urban-rural (2001): urban 27.8%; rural 72.2%.
Sex distribution (2001): male 51.74%; female 48.26%.
Age breakdown (2001): under 15, 35.3%; 15–29, 26.6%; 30–44, 19.5%; 45–59, 10.9%; 60–74, 6.0%; 75 and over, 1.4%; unknown 0.3%.
Population projection: (2010) 1,173,806,000; (2020) 1,312,212,000.
Doubling time: 47 years.
Major cities (2001; *urban agglomerations,* 2001): Greater Mumbai (Greater Bombay) 11,914,398 (16,368,084); Delhi 9,817,439 (12,791,458); Kolkata (Calcutta) 4,580,544 (13,216,546); Bangalore 4,292,223 (5,686,844); Chennai (Madras) 4,216,268 (6,424,624); Ahmadabad 3,515,361 (4,519,278); Hyderabad 3,449,878 (5,533,640); Pune (Poona) 2,540,069 (3,755,525); Kanpur 2,532,138 (2,690,486); Surat 2,433,787 (2,811,466); Jaipur 2,324,319 (2,324,319); New Delhi[6] 294,783.

Other principal cities (2001)[7]

	population		population		population
Agra	1,259,979	Jodhpur	846,408	Shambajinagar (Aurangabad)	873,037
Allahabad (Prayag Raj)	990,298	Kalyan[8]	1,193,266		
		Kota	537,371	Sholapur (Solapur)	873,037
Amritsar	975,695	Lucknow	2,207,340	Srinagar	894,940
Bhopal	1,433,875	Ludhiana	1,395,053	Thane (Thana)[8]	1,261,517
Chandigarh	808,796	Madurai	922,913	Thiruvananthapuram (Trivandrum)	744,739
Coimbatore	923,085	Meerut	1,074,229		
Faridabad	1,054,981	Mysore	742,261		
Ghaziabad	968,521	Nagpur	2,051,320	Tiruchirappalli	746,062
Guwahati	808,021	Nashik (Nasik)	1,076,967	Vadodara (Baroda)	1,306,035
Gwalior	826,919	Patna	1,376,950	Varanasi (Benares)	1,100,748
Howrah (Haora)[9]	1,008,704	Pimpri-Chinchwad[10]	1,006,417	Vijayawada	825,436
Hubli-Dharwad	786,018				
Indore	1,597,441	Rajkot	966,642	Vishakhapatnam	969,608
Jabalpur	951,469	Ranchi	846,454		

Linguistic composition (1991)[11]: Hindi 27.58% (including associated languages and dialects, 38.58%); Bengali 8.22%; Telugu 7.80%; Marathi 7.38%; Tamil 6.26%; Urdu 5.13%; Gujarati 4.81%; Kannada 3.87%; Malayalam 3.59%; Oriya 3.32%; Punjabi 2.76%; Assamese 1.55%; Bhili/Bhilodi 0.66%; Santhali 0.62%; Kashmiri 0.47%[12]; Gondi 0.25%; Sindhi 0.25%; Nepali 0.25%; Konkani 0.21%; Tulu 0.18%; Kurukh 0.17%; Manipuri 0.15%; Bodo 0.14%; Khandeshi 0.12%; other 3.26%. Hindi (66.00%) and English (19.00%) are also spoken as lingua francas (second languages).
Religious affiliation (2000): Hindu 73.72%; Muslim 11.96%, of which Sunnī 8.97%, Shīʿī 2.99%; Christian 6.08%, of which Independent 2.99%, Protestant 1.47%, Roman Catholic 1.35%, Orthodox 0.27%; traditional beliefs 3.39%; Sikh 2.16%; Buddhist 0.71%; Jain 0.40%; Bahāʾī 0.12%; Zoroastrian (Parsi) 0.02%; other 1.44%.
Households (2001). Total number of households 191,963,935. Average household size 5.4. Type of household: permanent 51.8%; semipermanent 30.0%; temporary 18.2%. Average number of rooms per household 2.2; 1 room 38.4%, 2 rooms 30.0%, 3 rooms 14.3%, 4 rooms 7.5%, 5 rooms 2.9%, 6 or more rooms 3.7%, unspecified number of rooms 3.2%.

Vital statistics

Birth rate per 1,000 population (2003): 23.3 (world avg. 21.3).
Death rate per 1,000 population (2003): 8.5 (world avg. 9.1).
Natural increase rate per 1,000 population (2003): 14.8 (world avg. 12.2).
Total fertility rate (avg. births per childbearing woman; 2003): 2.9.
Life expectancy at birth (2003): male 62.9 years; female 64.4 years.
Major causes of death per 100,000 population (1987)[13]: diseases of the circulatory system 227; infectious and parasitic diseases 215; diseases of the respiratory system 108; certain conditions originating in the perinatal period 108; accidents, homicide, and other violence 102; diseases of the digestive system 48; diseases of the nervous system 43; malignant neoplasms 41.

Social indicators

Educational attainment (1991)[14, 15]. Percentage of population age 25 and over having: no formal schooling 57.5%; incomplete primary education 28.0%; complete primary or some secondary 7.2%; complete secondary or higher 7.3%.

Distribution of expenditure (1994)

percentage of household expenditure by decile/quintile

1	2	3	4	5	6	7	8	9	10 (highest)
4.1	5.1	—13.0—		—16.8—		—21.7—		14.3	25.0

Quality of working life. Average workweek (2001): *c.* 46 hours[16]. Rate of fatal injuries per 100,000 employees (2001) 36[16]. Agricultural workers in servitude to creditors (early 1990s) 10–20%.
Access to services (2001). Percentage of total (urban, rural) households having access to: electricity for lighting purposes 55.8% (87.6%, 43.5%); kerosene for lighting purposes 43.3% (11.6%, 55.6%), water closets 18.0% (46.1%, 7.1%), pit latrines 11.5% (14.6%, 10.3%), no latrines 63.6% (26.3%, 78.1%), closed drainage for waste water 12.5% (34.5%, 3.9%), open drainage for waste water 33.9% (43.4%, 30.3%), no drainage for waste water 53.6% (22.1%, 65.8%). Type of fuel used for cooking in households: firewood 52.5% (22.7%, 64.1%), LPG (liquefied petroleum gas) 17.5% (48.0%, 5.7%), kerosene 6.5% (19.2%, 1.6%), crop residue 10.0% (2.1%, 13.1%), cow dung 9.8% (2.0%, 12.8%), electricity 0.2% (0.3%, 0.1%). Source of drinking water: hand pump or tube well 41.3% (21.3%, 48.9%), piped water 36.7% (68.7%, 24.3%), well 18.2% (7.7%, 22.2%), river, canal, spring, public tank, pond, or lake 2.7% (0.7%, 3.5%).
Social participation. Eligible voters participating in April/May 2004 national election: 58.1%. Trade union membership (1998): *c.* 16,000,000 (primarily in the public sector).
Social deviance (1990)[17]. Offense rate per 100,000 population for: murder 4.1; dacoity (gang robbery) 1.3; theft and housebreaking 56.6; riots 12.0. Rate of suicide per 100,000 population (1991): 9.0.
Material well-being (2001). Total (urban, rural) households possessing: television receivers 31.6% (64.3%, 18.9%), telephones 9.1% (23.0%, 3.8%), scooters, motorcycles, or mopeds 11.7% (24.7%, 6.7%), cars, jeeps, or vans 2.5% (5.6%, 1.3%). Households availing banking services 35.5% (49.5%, 30.1%).

National economy

Gross national product (2003): U.S.$567,604,000,000 (U.S.$530 per capita).

Structure of gross domestic product and labour force

	2001–02 in value Rs '000,000,000[18]	2001–02 % of total value	1993–94 labour force	1993–94 % of labour force
Agriculture, forestry	5,225.9	25.0	240,700,000	64.7
Mining	462.6	2.2	2,600,000	0.7
Manufacturing	3,199.3	15.3	39,100,000	10.5
Construction	1,255.5	6.0	11,900,000	3.2
Public utilities	500.0	2.4	1,500,000	0.4
Transp. and commun.	1,544.6	7.4	10,400,000	2.8
Trade, restaurants	3,024.6	14.4	27,500,000	7.4
Finance, real estate	2,671.2	12.8	} 38,300,000	10.3
Pub. admin., defense	1,330.8	6.4		
Services	1,725.6	8.2		
TOTAL	20,940.1	100.0[5]	372,000,000	100.0

Budget (2002). Revenue[19]: Rs 3,088,200,000,000 (tax revenue 76.4%, of which excise taxes 29.5%, taxes on income and profits 29.4%; nontax revenue 23.1%; other 0.5%). Expenditures: Rs 4,239,100,000,000 (general public services 61.0%, of which public debt payments 26.8%; economic affairs 15.3%; defense 15.2%; education 2.5%; health 1.7%).
Public debt (external, outstanding; 2002): U.S.$88,271,000,000.
Production (in '000 metric tons except as noted). Agriculture, forestry, fishing (2002): cereals 491,174 (of which rice 116,580, wheat 71,814, corn [maize]

10,570, sorghum 7,060, millet 6,150), sugarcane 279,000, fruits 34,720 (of which bananas 16,450, mangoes 11,400, oranges 2,980, apples 1,420, lemons and limes 1,370, pineapples 1,100), oilseeds 16,750 (of which peanuts [groundnuts] 5,400, rapeseed 5,040, soybeans 4,270, sunflower seeds 870, castor beans 590, sesame 580), pulses 10,760 (of which chickpeas 5,320, dry beans 3,000, pigeon peas 2,440), coconuts 9,300, eggplants 8,800, seed cotton 5,580, jute 1,789, tea 826, natural rubber 650, tobacco 575, garlic 497, cashews 460, betel 330, coffee 317, ginger 275, pepper 51; livestock (number of live animals; 2002) 221,900,000 cattle, 124,000,000 goats, 95,100,000 water buffalo, 58,800,000 sheep, 18,000,000 pigs, 900,000 camels; roundwood 319,418,047 cu m, of which fuelwood 300,564,000 cu m, industrial roundwood 18,854,000; fish catch (metric tons; 2001) 5,965,230, of which freshwater fish 2,950,003, marine fish 2,301,609, crustaceans 498,827. Mining and quarrying (2002–03): limestone 136,224; iron ore 54,432[20]; bauxite 9,439; manganese 617[20]; chromium (2001–02) 543[20]; zinc 299[20]; lead 40.6[20]; copper 38[20]; gold 2,873 kg; gem diamonds (2002) 17,000 carats. Manufacturing (value added in U.S.$'000,000; 2000): industrial chemicals 4,274; food products 3,723; paints, soaps, varnishes, drugs, and medicines 3,500; textiles 3,498; iron and steel 2,989; nonelectrical machinery and apparatus 2,457; cements, bricks, and tiles 1,988; refined petroleum 1,870; motor vehicles and parts 1,744.

Manufacturing enterprises (1995–96)[21]

	no. of factories	no. of persons engaged	avg. wages as a % of avg. of all wages	annual value added (Rs '000,000)[22]
Chemicals and chemical products,	9,206	758,500	140.3	237,093
of which synthetic fibres	395	97,100	183.8	68,420
fertilizers/pesticides	753	104,500	217.4	59,521
drugs and medicine	2,542	204,600	129.3	40,050
Transport equipment,	6,120	838,600	142.7	120,207
of which motor vehicles	3,758	392,400	162.4	77,240
Textiles	16,228	1,579,400	80.2	99,855
Iron and steel	3,519	507,700	152.9	97,274
Nonelectrical machinery/apparatus	9,075	548,400	137.2	92,762
Food products,	22,878	1,285,900	60.4	92,163
of which refined sugar	1,285	341,000	92.0	28,125
Electrical machinery/apparatus,	5,472	443,700	149.4	84,320
of which industrial machinery	2,048	165,600	190.8	35,717
Refined petroleum	161	31,100	349.3	52,778
Bricks, cement, plaster products	10,067	394,500	70.3	49,413
Nonferrous basic metals	3,301	228,700	124.3	42,252
Fabricated metal products	7,984	277,700	98.6	32,565
Paper and paper products	2,742	175,200	99.5	26,380
Wearing apparel	3,463	263,700	55.0	23,485

Energy production (consumption): electricity (kW-hr; 2002) 529,692,000,000 (529,698,000,000); hard coal (metric tons; 2003) 348,432,000 ([2000] 315,583,000); lignite (metric tons; 2003) 26,004,000 ([2000] 22,704,000); crude petroleum (barrels; 2002) 248,520,000 ([2000] 579,300,000); petroleum products (metric tons; 2000) 75,409,000 (79,876,000); natural gas (cu m; 2002) 29,495,000,000 ([2000] 24,315,000,000).

Financial aggregates[23]

	1997	1998	1999	2000	2001	2002	2003
Exchange rate, Rs per:							
U.S. dollar	39.28	42.48	43.49	46.75	48.18	48.03	45.61
£	64.96	70.67	70.30	69.76	69.88	77.41	81.40
SDR	53.00	59.81	59.69	60.91	60.55	65.30	67.77
International reserves (U.S.$)							
Total (excl. gold; '000,000)	24,688	27,341	32,667	37,902	45,870	67,665	98,938
SDRs ('000,000)	77	83	4	2	5	7	3
Reserve pos. in IMF ('000,000)	287	300	671	637	614	665	1,318
Foreign exchange ('000,000)	24,324	26,958	31,992	37,264	45,251	66,994	97,617
Gold ('000,000 fine troy oz)	12.740	11.487	11.502	11.502	11.502	11.502	11.502
% world reserves	1.4	1.2	1.2	1.2	1.2	1.2	1.2
Interest and prices							
Central bank discount (%)	9.00	9.00	8.00	8.00	6.50	6.25	6.00
Advance (prime) rate (%)	13.8	13.5	12.5	12.3	12.1	11.9	11.5
Industrial share prices (2000 = 100)	82.4	72.4	89.9	100.0	75.5	70.7	117.6
Balance of payments (U.S.$'000,000)							
Balance of visible trade	–10,028	–10,752	–8,679	–12,193	–12,833	–12,416	…
Imports, f.o.b.	45,730	44,828	45,556	55,325	58,232	65,159	…
Exports, f.o.b.	35,702	34,076	36,877	43,132	45,399	52,743	…
Balance of invisibles	+7,063	+3,849	+5,451	+9,553	+14,594	+17,072	…
Balance of payments, current account	–2,965	–6,903	–3,228	–2,640	+1,761	+4,656	…

Land use as % of total land area (2000): in temporary crops 54.4%, in permanent crops 2.7%, in pasture 3.7%; overall forest area 21.6%.

Population economically active (2001): total 402,512,190; activity rate of total population 39.2% (participation rates: n.a.; female 36.5%; unemployed 10.4%).

Price and earnings indexes (2000 = 100)

	1997	1998	1999	2000	2001	2002	2003
Consumer price index	81.1	91.9	96.1	100.0	103.7	108.2	112.4
Monthly earnings index	…	…	…	…	…	…	…

Household income and expenditure. Average household size (2002) 5.4; sources of income (1984–85): salaries and wages 42.2%, self-employed 39.7%, interest 8.6%, profits and dividends 6.0%, rent 3.5%; expenditure (1998–99): food, beverages, and tobacco 52.1%, transportation and communications 13.7%, housing and energy 10.2%, clothing and footwear 5.2%, health 4.4%.

Service enterprises (net value added in Rs '000,000,000; 1998–99): wholesale and retail trade 1,562; finance, real estate, and insurance 1,310; transport and storage 804; community, social, and personal services 763; construction 545.

Tourism (2002): receipts from visitors U.S.$2,923,000,000; expenditures by nationals abroad U.S.$3,449,000,000.

Foreign trade[24]

Balance of trade (current prices)

	1998–99	1999–2000	2000–01	2001–02	2002–03	2003–04
U.S.$'000,000	–9,170	–12,848	–5,976	–7,587	–8,693	–13,578
% of total	12.1%	14.9%	6.3%	8.0%	7.6%	9.7%

Imports (2003–04): U.S.$77,032,000,000 (crude petroleum and refined petroleum 26.7%; electronic goods [including computer software] 10.2%; precious and semiprecious stones 9.3%; gold and silver 8.8%; nonelectrical machinery and apparatus 6.1%; organic and inorganic chemicals 5.2%). *Major import sources* (2002–03): U.S. 7.2%; Belgium 6.0%; U.K. 4.5%; China 4.5%; Germany 3.9%; Switzerland 3.8%; South Africa 3.4%; Japan 3.0%; Malaysia 2.4%; Singapore 2.2%.

Exports (2003–04): U.S.$63,454,000,000 (engineering goods 19.2%; cut and polished diamonds and jewelry 16.6%; chemicals and chemical products 14.5%; food and agricultural products 11.7%; cotton ready-made garments 9.6%; petroleum products 5.5%; cotton yarn, fabrics, and thread 5.2%). *Major export destinations* (2002–03): U.S. 20.7%; United Arab Emirates 6.3%; Hong Kong 5.0%; U.K. 4.7%; Germany 4.0%; China 3.7%; Japan 3.5%; Belgium 3.2%; Italy 2.5%; Bangladesh 2.2%.

Transport and communications

Transport. Railroads (2002): route length 89,879 mi, 144,647 km; passenger-mi 581,625,000,000[25], passenger-km 936,037,000,000[25]; short ton-mi cargo 370,711,000,000[26], metric ton-km cargo 541,783,000,000[26]. Roads (2002): total length 2,062,727 mi, 3,319,644 km (paved 46%). Vehicles (2001): passenger cars 7,058,000; trucks and buses 3,582,000. Air transport (2002–03): passenger-mi 17,747,500,000, passenger-km 28,561,922,000; short ton-mi cargo 388,152,000, metric ton-km cargo 567,272,000; airports (2002) with scheduled flights 96.

Communications

Medium	date	unit	number	units per 1,000 persons
Daily newspapers	2000	circulation	61,000,000	60
Radio	2000	receivers	123,000,000	121
Television	2000	receivers	79,000,000	78
Telephones	2003	main lines	48,917,000	46
Cellular telephones	2003	subscribers	26,154,400	24
Personal computers	2002	units	7,500,000	7.2
Internet	2003	users	18,481,000	17

Education and health

Literacy (2001): percentage of total population age 15 and over literate 64.8%; males literate 75.3%; females literate 53.7%.

Education (2001–02)

	schools	teachers	students	student/ teacher ratio
Primary (age 6–10)	664,041	1,928,075	113,883,060	59.0
Secondary (age 11–17)	311,061	2,486,715	64,882,221	26.1
Higher	42,057	758,706	10,453,229	13.8

Health (1999): physicians 519,000 (1 per 1,923 persons); hospital beds 918,000 (1 per 1,087 persons); infant mortality rate per 1,000 live births (2003) 59.6.

Food (2001): daily per capita caloric intake 2,487 (vegetable products 92%, animal products 8%); 113% of FAO recommended minimum requirement.

Military

Total active duty personnel (2003): 1,325,000 (army 83.0%, navy 4.2%, air force 12.8%); personnel in paramilitary forces 1,089,700. *Military expenditure as percentage of GNP* (1999): 2.5% (world 2.4%); per capita expenditure U.S.$11.

[1]Council of States can have a maximum of 250 members; a maximum of 12 of these members may be nominated by the President. [2]Includes 2 nonelective seats. [3]Bill changing the status of Delhi to full statehood introduced in the House of the People in August 2003. [4]Excludes 46,660 sq mi (120,849 sq km) of territory claimed by India as part of Jammu and Kashmir but occupied by Pakistan or China; inland water constitutes 9.6% of total area of India (including all of Indian-claimed Jammu and Kashmir). [5]Detail does not add to total given because of rounding. [6]Within Delhi urban agglomeration. [7]Preliminary figures. [8]Within Greater Mumbai urban agglomeration. [9]Within Kolkata urban agglomeration. [10]Within Pune urban agglomeration. [11]Mother tongue unless otherwise noted. [12]1981. [13]Projected rates based on about 3.5% of total deaths (317,392 registered deaths out of an estimated total of nearly 9,000,000 deaths). [14]Excludes Jammu and Kashmir. [15]No formal schooling (1991): males 43.3%, females 72.8%; complete secondary or higher education (1991): males 10.6%, females 3.7%. [16]Data apply to the workers employed in the "organized sector" only (27.8 million in 2001, of which 19.1 million were employed in the public sector and 8.7 million were employed in the private sector); few legal protections exist for the more than 370 million workers in the "unorganized sector." [17]Crimes reported to National Crime Records Bureau by police authorities of state governments. [18]At factor cost. [19]Central government only. [20]Approximate metal content of ore. [21]Establishments with at least 10 workers on any workday and all establishments employing 20 or more workers. [22]In factor values. [23]End-of-period. [24]Fiscal year beginning April 1. [25]Includes Indian Railways and 15 regional railways. [26]Includes Indian Railways and 9 regional railways.

Internet resources for further information:

- **India Image: Directory of Government Web Sites http://www.nic.in**
- **Census of India http://www.censusindia.net**
- **Reserve Bank of India http://www.rbi.org.in**
- **Union Budget and Economic Survey http://www.indiabudget.nic.in**

Indonesia

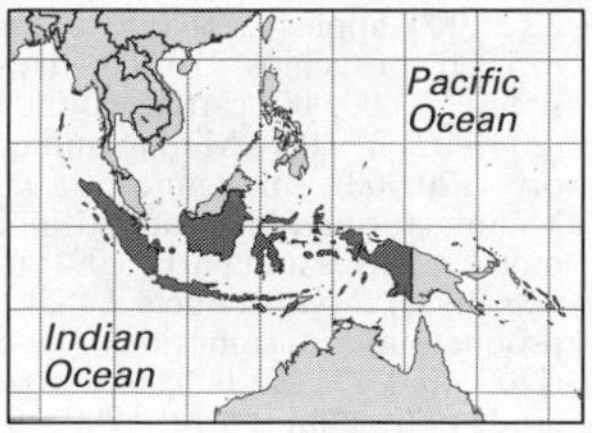

Official name: Republik Indonesia (Republic of Indonesia).
Form of government: unitary multiparty republic with two legislative houses (Regional Representatives Council [128]; House of Representatives [550]).
Head of state and government: President.
Capital: Jakarta.
Official language: Indonesian.
Official religion: monotheism.
Monetary unit: 1 Indonesian rupiah (Rp) = 100 sen; valuation (Sept. 1, 2004) 1 U.S.$ = Rp 9,375; 1 £ = Rp 16,865.

Area and population

Island(s) Provinces	area sq km	population 2000 census[1]
Bali and the Lesser Sunda Islands	73,137	11,112,702
Bali	5,633	3,151,162
East Nusa Tenggara	47,351	3,952,279
West Nusa Tenggara	20,153	4,009,261
Celebes (Sulawesi)[2]	191,671	14,946,488
Central Sulawesi	63,678	2,218,435
Gorontalo[3]	12,215	835,044
North Sulawesi	15,273	2,012,098
South Sulawesi[4]	38,140	8,059,627
Southeast Sulawesi	62,365	1,821,284
Java[2]	127,569	121,352,608
Banten[5]	8,651	8,098,780
Central Java	32,549	31,228,940
East Java	47,922	34,783,640
Jakarta[6]	664	8,389,443
West Java	34,597	35,729,537
Yogyakarta	3,186	3,122,268
Kalimantan[2, 7]	574,194	11,331,558
Central Kalimantan	153,564	1,857,000

Island(s) Provinces	area sq km	population 2000 census[1]
East Kalimantan	230,277	2,455,120
South Kalimantan	43,546	2,985,240
West Kalimantan	146,807	4,034,198
Maluku (Moluccas)	77,870	1,990,598
Maluku	46,975	1,205,539
North Maluku	30,895	785,059
Papua (Irian)[2, 8]	365,466	2,220,934
Sumatra[2]	480,847	43,309,707
Aceh[9]	51,937	3,930,905
Bangka-Belitung[3]	16,171	900,197
Bengkulu	19,789	1,567,432
Jambi	53,437	2,413,846
Lampung	35,384	6,741,439
North Sumatra	73,587	11,649,655
Riau[10] } Riau Islands[10] }	94,560	4,957,627
South Sumatra	93,083	6,899,675
West Sumatra	42,899	4,248,931
TOTAL	1,890,754	206,264,595

Demography

Population (2004): 222,611,000.
Density (2004): persons per sq mi 304.9, persons per sq km 117.7
Urban-rural (2003): urban 45.6%; rural 54.4%.
Sex distribution (2000): male 50.14%; female 49.86%.
Age breakdown (2000): under 15, 30.4%; 15–29, 29.3%; 30–44, 21.8%; 45–59, 11.3%; 60–74, 5.8%; 75 and over, 1.4%.
Population projection: (2010) 238,374,000; (2020) 261,053,000.
Ethnic composition (2000): Javanese 36.4%; Sundanese 13.7%; Malay 9.4%; Madurese 7.2%; Han Chinese 4.0%; Minangkabau 3.6%.
Religious affiliation (2000): Muslim 76.5%; Christian 13.1%, of which Protestant 5.7%, independent Christian 4.0%, Roman Catholic 2.7%; Hindu 3.4%; traditional beliefs 2.5%; nonreligious 1.9%; other 2.6%.
Major cities (2000): Jakarta 8,347,083 (urban agglomeration [2003] 12,300,000); Surabaya 2,599,796; Bandung 2,136,260; Medan 1,904,273; Bekasi 1,663,802; Palembang 1,451,419; Semarang 1,348,803; Tangerang 1,325,854.

Vital statistics

Birth rate per 1,000 population (2003): 21.5 (world avg. 21.3).
Death rate per 1,000 population (2003): 6.3 (world avg. 9.1).
Total fertility rate (avg. births per childbearing woman; 2003): 2.5.
Marriage rate per 1,000 population (2001): 8.7[11].
Life expectancy at birth (2003): male 66.5 years; female 71.5 years.

National economy

Budget (2002). Revenue: Rp 300,190,000,000,000 (tax revenue 70.3%, of which income tax 33.9%, VAT 21.9%; nontax revenue 29.7%, of which revenue from petroleum 15.9%). Expenditures: Rp 327,860,000,000,000 (current expenditure 57.7%; development expenditure 12.3%; expenditure 30.0%).
Public debt (external, outstanding; 2002): U.S.$70,011,000,000.
Population economically active (2001): total 98,812,448; activity rate 46.1% (participation rates: over age 15 [2000] 67.8%; unemployed 8.1%).

Price index (2000 = 100)

	1997	1998	1999	2000	2001	2002	2003
Consumer price index	48.2	76.0	91.5	100.0	112.5	123.8	130.1

Household income and expenditure. Average household size (2000) 3.9.
Production (metric tons except as noted). Agriculture, forestry, fishing (2002): rice 51,604,000, palm fruit oil 40,000,000, sugarcane 23,400,000, cassava 16,723,000, corn (maize) 9,277,000, natural rubber 1,600,000; livestock (number of live animals) 12,400,000 goats, 11,200,000 cattle, 7,350,000 sheep; roundwood (2001) 119,209,000 cu m; fish catch (2001) 5,068,000. Mining and quarrying (2002): bauxite 1,283,000; copper (metal content) 1,172,000; nickel (metal content) 123,000; silver 289,000 kg; gold 142,000 kg. Manufacturing (value added in Rp '000,000,000; 2000)[12]: machinery and transport equipment 57,296; food products 44,736; chemicals and plastics 39,168; textiles 38,471; wood products (including furniture) 14,976; paper and paper products 14,456. Energy production (consumption): electricity (kW-hr; 2000) 99,511,000,000 (99,511,000,000); coal (metric tons; 2001) 90,648,000 ([2000] 19,668,000); crude petroleum (barrels; 2003) 452,000,000 ([2000] 385,600,000); petroleum products (metric tons; 2000) 48,518,000 (50,136,000); natural gas (cu m; 2002) 86,400,000,000 ([2000] 21,500,000,000).
Gross national product (2003): U.S.$172,733,000,000 (U.S.$810 per capita).

Structure of gross domestic product and labour force

	2001			
	in value Rp '000,000,000	% of total value	labour force	% of labour force
Agriculture	244,381	16.4	39,743,908	40.2
Mining	202,680	13.6 }		
Manufacturing	389,321	26.1 }	13,177,242	13.3
Public utilities	17,286	1.2 }		
Construction	84,045	5.6	3,837,554	3.9
Transp. and commun.	79,825	5.3	4,448,279	4.5
Trade	239,959	16.1	17,469,129	17.7
Finance, real estate	92,459	6.2	1,127,823	1.2
Pub. admin., defense	81,851	5.5 }	11,003,482	11.1
Services	59,167	4.0 }		
Other	—	—	8,005,031[13]	8.1[13]
TOTAL	1,490,974	100.0	98,812,448	100.0

Tourism (2002): receipts U.S.$4,306,000,000; expenditures U.S.$3,368,000,000.
Land use as % of total land area (2000): in temporary crops 11.3%, in permanent crops 7.2%, in pasture 6.2%; overall forest area 58.0%.

Foreign trade[14]

Balance of trade (current prices)

	1998	1999	2000	2001	2002	2003
U.S.$'000,000	+21,510	+24,661	+28,609	+25,437	+26,831	–5,958
% of total	28.2%	33.9%	29.9%	29.1%	30.0%	7.7%

Imports (2000): U.S.$33,515,000,000 (machinery and apparatus 18.8%, refined petroleum 10.6%, food and live animals 8.3%, crude petroleum 7.8%, organic chemicals 7.3%). *Major import sources:* Japan 16.0%; Singapore 11.3%; U.S. 10.1%; South Korea 6.2%; China 6.0%.
Exports (2000): U.S.$62,124,000,000 (natural gas 10.7%, crude petroleum 9.8%, garments 7.7%, telecommunications equipment 5.6%, wood products 5.2%, computers and parts 4.9%). *Major export destinations:* Japan 23.2%; U.S. 13.7%; Singapore 10.6%; South Korea 7.0%; China 4.5%.

Transport and communications

Transport. Railroads (2000): route length 6,458 km; passenger-km 19,228,000,000; metric ton-km cargo 4,997,000,000. Roads (1999): length 355,951 km (paved 57%). Vehicles (2000): passenger cars 3,038,913; trucks and buses 2,373,414. Air transport (1999): passenger-km (2002) 19,690,000,000; metric ton-km cargo 340,932,000; airports (1996) 81.

Communications

Medium	date	unit	number	units per 1,000 persons
Daily newspapers	2000	circulation	4,870,000	23
Radio	2000	receivers	33,200,000	157
Television	2000	receivers	31,500,000	149
Telephones	2002	main lines	7,750,000	37
Cellular telephones	2002	subscribers	11,700,000	55
Personal computers	2002	units	2,519,000	12
Internet	2002	users	8,000,000	38

Education and health

Educational attainment (2000). Percentage of population age 15 and over having: no schooling or incomplete primary 23.9%; primary and some secondary 53.8%; complete secondary 17.9%; some higher 2.2%; complete higher 2.2%. *Literacy* (2000): total population age 15 and over literate 86.9%; males literate 91.8%; females literate 82.0%.

Education (1999–2000)

	schools	teachers	students	student/ teacher ratio
Primary (age 7–12)	150,612	1,141,168	25,614,836	22.4
Secondary (age 13–18)	28,766	656,850	10,496,957	16.0
Voc., teacher tr.	4,169	131,107	1,882,061	14.4
Higher	1,633	194,828	2,919,846	15.0

Health (1999): physicians 31,603 (1 per 6,605 persons); hospital beds 124,834 (1 per 1,671 persons); infant mortality rate per 1,000 live births (2003) 38.1.
Food (2002): daily per capita caloric intake 2,904 (vegetable products 96%, animal products 4%); 134% of FAO recommended minimum.

Military

Total active duty personnel (2003): 302,000 (army 76.2%, navy 14.9%, air force 8.9%). *Military expenditure as percentage of GNP* (1999): 1.1% (world 2.4%); per capita expenditure U.S.$7.

[1]Adjusted figure. [2]Includes area and population of nearby islands. [3]Formally established February 2001. [4]Creation of West Sulawesi province from part of South Sulawesi announced September 2004. [5]Formally established November 2000. [6]Formally a metropolitan district. [7]Kalimantan is the name of the Indonesian part of the island of Borneo. [8]Division of Papua into 3 provinces from January 2003 not fully implemented as of October 2004. [9]Formally an autonomous province. [10]Riau Islands formally separated from Riau in 2003. [11]Muslim population only. [12]Medium and large establishments only. [13]Unemployed. [14]Imports c.i.f.; exports f.o.b.

Internet resources for further information:
- **Central Bureau of Statistics http://www.bps.go.id**

Iran

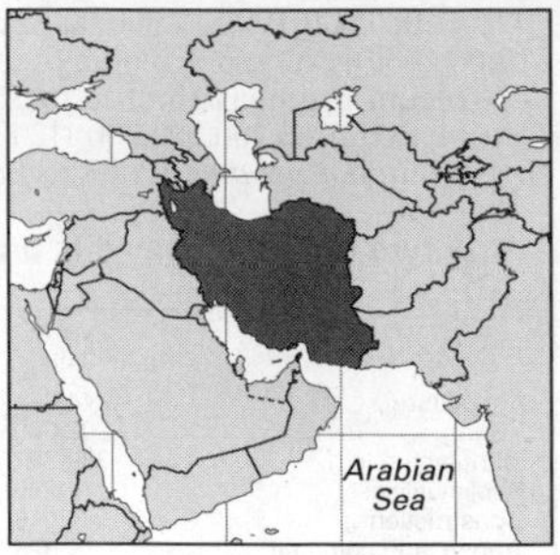

Official name: Jomhūrī-ye Eslāmī-ye Irān (Islamic Republic of Iran).
Form of government: unitary Islamic republic with one legislative house (Islamic Consultative Assembly [290]).
Supreme political/religious authority: Leader[1].
Head of state and government: President.
Capital: Tehrān.
Official language: Farsī (Persian).
Official religion: Islam.
Monetary unit: 1 rial (Rls); valuation (Sept. 1, 2004) 1 U.S.$ = Rls 8,738; 1 £ = Rls 15,719.

Area and population

	area	population		area	population
		2004[2]			2004[2]
Provinces	sq km	estimate	**Provinces**	sq km	estimate
Ardabīl	17,881	1,247,202	Khūzestān	63,213	4,277,998
Āzārbāyjān-e Gharbī	37,463	2,896,657	Kohgīlūyeh va Būyer Aḥmad	15,563	674,113
Āzārbāyjān-e Sharqī	45,481	3,482,672	Kordestān	28,817	1,546,256
Būshehr	23,168	808,482	Lorestān	28,392	1,739,644
Chahār Maḥāll va Bakhtīārī	16,201	832,945	Markazi	29,406	1,344,920
Eṣfahān	128,811	4,395,645	Māzandarān	23,833	2,796,120
Fārs	121,825	4,323,626	Qazvīn	15,491	1,133,547
Gilan	13,952	2,389,195	Qom	11,237	1,038,424
Golestān	20,893	1,613,691	Semnān	96,816	578,910
Hamadān	19,547	1,732,080	Sīstān va Balūchestān	178,431	2,219,393
Hormozgān	71,193	1,284,925	Tehrān	19,196	11,931,656
Ilām	20,150	538,877	Yazd	107,027	940,802
Kermān	181,714	2,380,682	Zanjān	21,841	963,434
Kermānshāh	24,641	1,921,284	TOTAL	1,629,807[3, 4]	67,477,500
Khorāsān	247,622	6,444,320			

Demography

Population: (2004): 67,503,000.
Density (2004)[5]: persons per sq mi 106.1, persons per sq km 41.0.
Urban-rural (2003): urban 66.7%; rural 33.3%.
Sex distribution (2003): male 50.99%; female 49.01%.
Age breakdown (2003): under 15, 29.4%; 15–29, 34.5%; 30–44, 19.4%; 45–59, 10.0%; 60–74, 5.1%; 75 and over, 1.6%.
Population projection: (2010) 71,861,000; (2020) 80,002,000.
Ethnic composition (2000): Persian 34.9%; Azerbaijani 15.9%; Kurd 13.0%; Lurī 7.2%; Gīlaki 5.1%; Mazāndarānī 5.1%; Afghan 2.8%; Arab 2.5%; other 13.5%.
Religious affiliation (2000): Muslim 95.6% (Shīʿī 90.1%, Sunnī 5.5%); Zoroastrian 2.8%; Christian 0.5%; other 1.1%.
Major cities (1996): Tehrān 6,758,845; Mashhad 1,887,405; Eṣfahān 1,266,072; Tabriz 1,191,043; Shīrāz 1,053,025; Karaj 940,968; Ahvāz 804,980.

Vital statistics

Birth rate per 1,000 population (2003): 17.2 (world avg. 21.3).
Death rate per 1,000 population (2003): 5.6 (world avg. 9.1).
Natural increase rate per 1,000 population (2003): 11.6 (world avg. 12.2).
Total fertility rate (avg. births per childbearing woman; 2003): 1.9.
Marriage rate per 1,000 population (2002–03): 9.9.
Life expectancy at birth (2003): male 68.0 years; female 70.7 years.
Major causes of death per 100,000 population (1990)[6]: diseases of the circulatory system 304; accidents and violence 108; malignant neoplasms (cancers) 61; diseases of the respiratory system 48; infectious diseases 34.

National economy

Budget (2001–02). Revenue: Rls 180,975,000,000,000 (petroleum and natural gas revenue 57.0%; taxes 23.0%, of which corporate 6.8%, import duties 6.5%; other 20.0%). Expenditures: Rls 168,992,000,000,000 (current expenditure 66.6%; development expenditures 15.1%; other 18.3%).
Public debt (external, outstanding; 2002): U.S.$6,578,000,000.
Tourism (2002): receipts U.S.$1,249,000,000; expenditures U.S.$2,514,000,000.
Gross national product (2003): U.S.$132,896,000,000 (U.S.$2,000 per capita).

Structure of gross domestic product and labour force

	2002–03		1996	
	in value Rls '000,000,000	% of total value	labour force	% of labour force
Agriculture, forestry	105,027.6	12.2	3,357,263	21.0
Petroleum, natural gas	169,264.2	19.7	119,884	0.7
Other mining	4,554.5	0.5		
Manufacturing	120,533.9	14.0	2,551,962	15.9
Construction	35,259.4	4.1	1,650,481	10.3
Public utilities	12,709.4	1.5	150,631	0.9
Transportation and communications	74,971.0	8.7	972,792	6.1
Trade, restaurants	116,256.1	13.5	1,927,067	12.0
Finance, real estate	130,179.7	15.1	301,962	1.9
Pub. admin., defense	123,556.5	14.4	1,618,100	10.1
Services	22,282.4	2.6	1,664,402	10.4
Other	–54,061.9[7]	–6.3[7]	1,712,028[8]	10.7[8]
TOTAL	860,532.8	100.0	16,026,572	100.0

Production (metric tons except as noted). Agriculture, forestry, fishing (2003): wheat 12,900,000, sugar beets 5,300,000, sugarcane 3,650,000, potatoes 3,550,000, rice 3,300,000, barley 3,100,000, tomatoes 3,005,000, grapes 2,525,000, apples 2,358,000, oranges 1,850,000, corn (maize) 1,800,000, dates 875,000, pistachios 310,000; livestock (number of live animals) 53,900,000 sheep, 9,000,000 cattle; roundwood (2003) 1,310,751 cu m; fish catch (2001–02) 399,000. Mining and quarrying (2001): iron ore 5,400,000[9]; copper ore 120,000[9]; manganese 105,000[9]; zinc 85,000[9]; chromium 10,000[9]. Manufacturing (value added in U.S.$'000,000; 2000): basic chemicals 5,871; motor vehicles and parts 5,091; iron and steel 4,199; refined petroleum products 3,997; food products 3,485; nonmetallic mineral products 3,443. Energy production (consumption): electricity (kW-hr; 2003–04) 146,923,000,000 ([2002–03] 136,231,000,000); coal (metric tons; 2000) 1,394,000 (2,094,000); crude petroleum (barrels; 2003–04) 1,364,000,000 ([2000] 470,000,000); petroleum products (metric tons; 2000) 68,687,000 (54,319,000); natural gas (cu m; 2001–02) 86,300,000,000 (66,600,000,000).
Population economically active (2002–03): total 19,819,000; activity rate 30.0% (participation rates: over age 15 [1996] 44.0%; female [1996] 12.7%; unemployed [2002–03] 15.7%).

Price and earnings indexes (2000–01 = 100)

	1998–99	1999–2000	2000–01	2001–02	2002–03	2003–04
Consumer price index	74.0	88.8	100.0	111.4	129.0	149.2
Daily earnings index[10]	79.6	90.3	100.0	109.7	129.3	159.7

Household income and expenditure. Average household size (2000) 4.6; annual average income per urban household (1998–99) Rls 15,151,894 (U.S.$8,644); sources of urban income (1998–99): wages 32.8%, self-employment 29.6%, other 37.6%; expenditure (1997–98): food, beverages, and tobacco 32.5%, housing and energy 27.0%, transportation 11.4%.
Land use as % of total land area (2000): in temporary crops 8.8%, in permanent crops 1.2%, in pasture 26.9%; overall forest area 4.5%.

Foreign trade[11]

Balance of trade (current prices)

	1998–99	1999–2000	2000–01	2001–02	2002–03	2003–04
U.S.$'000,000	–1,168	+7,597	+13,375	+5,775	+6,201	+4,993
% of total	4.3%	22.0%	30.7%	13.7%	12.3%	8.0%

Imports (2002): U.S.$20,336,000,000 (nonelectrical machinery and apparatus 22.1%, road vehicles 15.4%, chemicals and chemical products 11.1%, iron and steel 8.0%, food products 7.2%, gold 7.1%). *Major import sources* (2002): Germany 17.1%; Switzerland 9.3%; U.A.E. 9.0%; France 5.9%; Italy 5.8%.
Exports (2002): U.S.$28,356,000,000 (crude and refined petroleum 85.4%, carpets 1.9%, nuts 1.7%). *Major export destinations* (2003): Japan 23.0%; China 10.2%; Italy 6.6%; Taiwan 6.4%; South Korea 5.0%.

Transport and communications

Transport. Railroads (2002–03): route length 4,514 mi, 7,265 km; (2001–02) passenger-km 8,043,000,000; (2001–02) metric ton-km cargo 14,613,000,000. Roads (2001–02)[12]: length 50,157 mi, 80,720 km (paved 100%). Vehicles (2000–01): passenger cars 1,351,800; trucks and buses 384,900. Air transport (2003)[13]: passenger-km 7,658,000,000; metric ton-km cargo 99,050,000; airports (1996) 19.

Communications

Medium	date	unit	number	units per 1,000 persons
Daily newspapers	2000	circulation	1,780,000	28
Radio	2000	receivers	17,900,000	281
Television	2002	receivers	11,331,500	173
Telephones	2003	main lines	14,571,100	220
Cellular telephones	2003	subscribers	3,376,500	51
Personal computers	2002	units	4,900,000	75
Internet	2003	users	4,300,000	65

Education and health

Educational attainment: n.a. *Literacy* (2002): total population age 15 and over literate 77.1%; males literate 83.5%; females literate 70.4%.

Education (2000–01)

	schools	teachers	students	student/teacher ratio
Primary (age 7–11)	69,149	314,654	7,968,437	25.3
Secondary (age 12–18)	42,079	337,912	9,090,938	26.9
Higher	...	...	1,573,322	...

Health (2002–03): physicians 17,975[14] (1 per 3,726 persons); hospital beds 110,797 (1 per 604 persons); infant mortality rate (2003) 44.2.
Food (2001): daily per capita caloric intake 2,931 (vegetable products 90%, animal products 10%); 122% of FAO recommended minimum requirement.

Military

Total active duty personnel (2003): 540,000 (revolutionary guard corps 22.2%, army 64.9%, navy 3.3%, air force 9.6%). *Military expenditure as percentage of GNP* (1999): 2.9% (world 2.4%); per capita expenditure U.S.$106.

[1]Not required to be a supreme theological authority. [2]Official projection made in 2002; date within year unknown. [3]Land area only; estimated total area is 1,648,200 sq km. [4]Detail does not add to total given because of rounding. [5]Based on total area. [6]Projected rates based on about 20% of total deaths. [7]Less imputed bank service charge. [8]Includes 1,455,000 unemployed. [9]Metal content. [10]Construction sector only. [11]Imports f.o.b. in balance of trade and c.i.f. in commodities and trading partners. [12]Roads maintained by Ministry of Roads and Transportation only. [13]Iran Air. [14]Excludes private sector physicians.

Internet resources for further information:
- **Statistical Centre of Iran http://www.sci.org.ir/index.htm**
- **Central Bank of Iran http://www.cbi.ir**

Iraq

Official name: Al-Jumhūrīyah al-ʿIraqīyah (Republic of Iraq).
Form of government: transitional regime[1] with one legislative body (National Council [100[2]]).
Head of state and government: President assisted by Prime Minister.
Capital: Baghdad.
Official languages: Arabic; Kurdish.
Official religion: Islam.
Monetary unit[3]: 1 (new) Iraqi dinar (ID); valuation (Sept. 1, 2004) 1 U.S.$ = 1,462 (new) ID; 1 £ = 2,631 (new) ID.

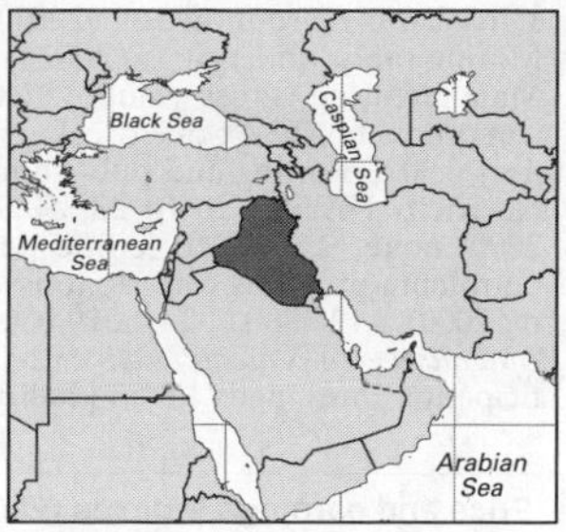

Area and population[4]

Governorates	Capitals	area sq mi	area sq km	population 1997 census
Al-Anbār	Ar-Ramādī	53,208	137,808	1,023,736
Bābil	Al-Ḥillah	2,163	5,603	1,181,751
Baghdād	Baghdad	1,572	4,071	5,423,964
Al-Baṣrah	Al-Baṣrah	7,363	19,070	1,556,445
Dhī Qār	An-Nāṣirīyah	4,981	12,900	1,184,796
Diyālā	Baʿqūbah	6,828	17,685	1,135,223
Karbalāʾ	Karbalāʾ	1,944	5,034	594,235
Maysān	Al-ʿAmārah	6,205	16,072	637,126
Al-Muthannā	As-Samāwah	19,977	51,740	436,825
An-Najaf	An-Najaf	11,129	28,824	775,042
Nīnawā	Mosul	14,410	37,323	2,042,852
Al-Qādisiyah	Ad-Dīwānīyah	3,148	8,153	751,331
Ṣalāḥ ad-Dīn	Tikrīt	9,407	24,363	904,432
At-Taʾmīm	Karkūk (Kirkūk)	3,737	9,679	753,171
Wāsiṭ	Al-Kūt	6,623	17,153	783,614
Kurdish Autonomous Region				
Dahūk	Dahūk	2,530	6,553	402,970
Irbīl	Irbīl	5,820	15,074	1,095,992
As-Sulaymānīyah	As-Sulaymānīyah	6,573	17,023	1,362,739
TOTAL		167,618	434,128	22,046,244

Demography

Population (2004): 25,375,000.
Density (2004): persons per sq mi 151.4, persons per sq km 58.5.
Urban-rural (2000): urban 67.5%; rural 32.5%.
Sex distribution (2001): male 50.57%; female 49.43%.
Age breakdown (2000): under 15, 42.1%; 15–29, 30.4%; 30–44, 15.6%; 45–59, 7.4%; 60–74, 3.5%; 75 and over, 1.0%.
Population projection: (2010) 29,672,000; (2020) 36,908,000.
Doubling time: 25 years.
Ethnic composition (2000): Arab 64.7%; Kurd 23.0%; Azerbaijani 5.6%; Turkmen 1.2%; Persian 1.1%; other 4.4%.
Religious affiliation (2000): Shīʿī Muslim 62.0%; Sunnī Muslim 34.0%; Christian (primarily Chaldean rite and Syrian rite Catholic and Nestorian) 3.2%; other (primarily Yazīdī syncretist) 0.8%.
Major cities (2003)[5]: Baghdad 5,750,000; Mosul 1,800,000; Al-Baṣrah 1,400,000; Irbīl 850,000; Karkūk 750,000.

Vital statistics

Birth rate per 1,000 population (2003): 33.7 (world avg. 21.3).
Death rate per 1,000 population (2003): 5.8 (world avg. 9.1).
Natural increase rate per 1,000 population (2003): 27.9 (world avg. 12.2).
Total fertility rate (avg. births per childbearing woman; 2003): 4.5.
Marriage rate per 1,000 population (2000): 7.3.
Divorce rate per 1,000 population (1997): 1.3.
Life expectancy at birth (2003): male 66.7 years; female 69.0 years.
Major causes of death per 100,000 population (1995): infectious and parasitic diseases 311.6, diseases of the circulatory system 130.2, malignant neoplasms (cancers) 111.5, diseases of the respiratory system 99.5, accidents and violence 65.3.

National economy

Budget (2003). Revenue: ID 4,596,000,000,000 (petroleum revenue 89%; other 11%). Expenditures: ID 9,233,000,000,000 (current expenditure 79.7%; development expenditure 20.3%).
Production (metric tons except as noted). Agriculture, forestry, fishing (2002): wheat 800,000, dates 650,000, potatoes 625,000, tomatoes 500,000, barley 500,000, watermelons 380,000, oranges 270,000, grapes 265,000, cucumbers 215,000; livestock (number of live animals) 6,200,000 sheep, 1,400,000 cattle; roundwood (2001) 111,294 cu m; fish catch (2001) 22,800. Mining and quarrying (2002): phosphate rock 100,000. Manufacturing (value added in U.S.$'000,000; 1995): refined petroleum 143; bricks, tiles, and cement 103; food products 59; industrial chemicals 52; metal products 27. Energy production (consumption): electricity (kW-hr; 2000) 30,521,000,000 (30,521,000,000); coal, none (none); crude petroleum (barrels; 2003) 485,400,000 ([2000] 180,793,000); petroleum products (metric tons; 2000) 20,589,000 (18,644,000); natural gas (cu m; 2002) 2,900,000,000 ([2000] 3,737,000,000).
Household income and expenditure (1988). Average household size 8.9; sources of income: self-employment 33.9%, wages and salaries 23.9%, transfers 23.0%, rent 18.6%; expenditure (1993)[6]: food *c.* 62%, housing *c.* 12%, clothing *c.* 10%.
Gross domestic product (2003): U.S.$19,110,000,000 (U.S.$770 per capita).

Structure of gross domestic product

	2001 in value ID '000,000[7]	2001 % of total value	2000 labour force	2000 % of labour force
Agriculture	1,962,510	24.6	...	...
Mining			...	...
Manufacturing	786,249	9.8	...	...
Public utilities			...	...
Construction	253,375	3.2	...	...
Transp. and commun.	1,241,586	15.5	...	...
Trade	2,083,053	26.1	...	...
Finance, real estate	914,625	11.5	...	...
Pub. admin., defense	921,570	11.5	...	...
Services			...	...
Other	–177,923[8]	–2.2[8]	...	...
TOTAL	7,985,045	100.0	6,339,000	100.0

Public debt (external, outstanding; 1999): U.S.$23,000,000,000.
Population economically active (1996): total 5,573,000; activity rate of total population 27.6% (participation rates: ages 15–64, 45.7%; female 25.0%).

Price index (December 2002 = 100)

	2002[9]	2003[9]	2004[10]
Consumer price index	100.0	146.9	150.0

Tourism (2001): receipts U.S.$14,500,000; expenditures U.S.$30,600,000.
Land use as % of total land area (2000): in temporary crops 12.5%, in permanent crops 0.8%, in pasture 9.1%; overall forest area 1.8%.

Foreign trade[11]

Balance of trade (current prices)

	1998	1999	2000	2001	2002	2003
U.S.$'000,000	+1,705	+2,491	+5,867	–248	+419	+153
% of total	13.0%	11.4%	18.6%	1.0%	2.1%	0.8%

Imports (2003): U.S.$9,933,000,000 (UN oil-for-food program 65.7%, capital goods 17.0%, consumer goods 11.4%). *Major import sources:* EU 36.4%; Asia (excluding Middle East) 25.7%; Arab countries 19.9%.
Exports (2003): U.S.$10,086,000,000 (crude petroleum 82.8%; food and live animals 5.0%). *Major export destinations:* Western Hemisphere (mostly U.S.) 71.2%; EU 13.3%; Arab countries 8.8%.

Transport and communications

Transport. Railroads (1999): route length 2,603 km; passenger-km 499,600,000; metric ton-km cargo 830,200,000. Roads (1999): total length 45,550 km (paved 84%). Vehicles (1998): passenger cars 735,521; trucks and buses 349,202. Air transport: [12].

Communications

Medium	date	unit	number	units per 1,000 persons
Daily newspapers	2000	circulation	431,000	19
Radio	2000	receivers	5,030,000	222
Television	2000	receivers	1,880,000	83
Telephones	2002	main lines	675,000	28
Cellular telephones	2002	subscribers	20,000	1.0
Internet	2002	users	25,000	1.0

Education and health

Educational attainment (1987). Percentage of population age 10 and over having: no formal schooling 52.8%; primary education 21.5%; secondary 11.6%; higher 4.1%; unknown 10.0%. *Literacy* (1995): total population age 15 and over literate 58.0%; males 70.7%; females 45.0%.

Education (1997–98)

	schools	teachers	students	student/ teacher ratio
Primary (age 6–11)	8,333	141,935	3,029,386	21.3
Secondary (age 12–17)	2,822	54,846	1,020,823	18.6
Voc., teacher tr.	303	8,838	102,004	11.5
Higher	11	12,101	266,505	22.0

Health: physicians (1998) 11,046 (1 per 1,937 persons); hospital beds (1999) 26,961 (1 per 817 persons); infant mortality rate per 1,000 live births (2003) 55.2.
Food (2000): daily per capita caloric intake 2,197 (vegetable products 96%, animal products 4%); 91% of FAO recommended minimum requirement.

Military

Total active duty personnel: n.a. U.S./allied coalition forces (November 2004): 138,000/24,000. *Military expenditure as percentage of GDP* (1999): 5.5% (world 2.4%); per capita expenditure U.S.$57.

[1]To be in place from the end of June 2004 to no later than the end of December 2005. [2]All seats are nonelected. [3]The (new) Iraqi dinar (ID) introduced on Oct. 15, 2003, replaced the (old) Iraqi dinar at a rate of 1 to 1. [4]Pre-April 2003 local government structure. [5]Unofficial estimate(s). [6]Weights of consumer price index components. [7]ESCWA estimate; in purchaser's value. [8]Imputed bank service charge. [9]December. [10]July. [11]Imports c.i.f.; exports f.o.b. [12]Iraqi Airways resumed international flights in September 2004 after 14 years of being grounded by war and sanctions.

Internet resources for further information:
- **Central Bank of Iraq**
  http://www.uruklink.net.cbi

Ireland

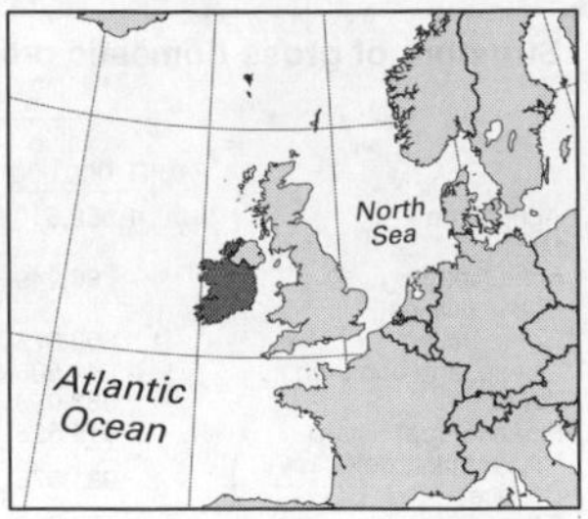

Official name: Éire (Irish); Ireland[1] (English).
Form of government: unitary multi-party republic with two legislative houses (Senate [60[2]]; House of Representatives [166]).
Chief of state: President.
Head of government: Prime Minister.
Capital: Dublin.
Official languages: Irish; English.
Official religion: none.
Monetary unit: 1 euro (€) = 100 cents; valuation (Sept. 1, 2004) 1 U.S.$ = €0.82; 1 £ = €1.48[3].

Area and population

Provinces Counties/County Boroughs (C.B.)	area sq km	population 2002 census	Provinces Counties/County Boroughs (C.B.)	area sq km	population 2002 census
Connacht	17,711	464,296	Westmeath	1,840	71,858
Galway	6,098	143,245	Wexford	2,367	116,596
Galway C.B.	51	65,832	Wicklow	2,027	114,676
Leitrim	1,590	25,799	Munster	24,674	1,100,614
Mayo	5,586	117,446	Clare	3,450	103,277
Roscommon	2,548	53,774	Cork	7,460	324,767
Sligo	1,838	58,200	Cork C.B.	40	123,062
Leinster	19,801[4]	2,105,579	Kerry	4,807	132,527
Carlow	897	46,014	Limerick	2,735	121,281
Dublin C.B.	118	495,781	Limerick C.B.	21	54,023
Dun Laoghaire-Rathdown	126	191,792	Tipperary North Riding	2,046	61,010
Fingal	455	196,413	Tipperary South Riding	2,258	79,121
Kildare	1,695	163,944	Waterford	1,816	56,952
Kilkenny	2,073	80,339	Waterford C.B.	41	44,594
Laoighis	1,720	58,774	Ulster (part of)	8,088	246,714
Longford	1,091	31,068	Cavan	1,932	56,546
Louth	826	101,821	Donegal	4,861	137,575
Meath	2,342	134,005	Monaghan	1,295	52,593
Offaly	2,001	63,663	TOTAL	70,273[4, 5]	3,917,203
South Dublin	224	238,835			

Demography

Population (2004): 4,024,000.
Density (2004): persons per sq mi 148.3, persons per sq km 57.3.
Urban-rural (2002): urban 59.6%; rural 40.4%.
Sex distribution (2003): male 49.68%; female 50.32%.
Age breakdown (2003): under 15, 21.0%; 15–29, 24.1%; 30–44, 22.3%; 45–59, 17.4%; 60–74, 10.3%; 75 and over, 4.9%.
Population projection: (2010) 4,240,000; (2020) 4,569,000.
Ethnic composition (2000): Irish 95.0%; British 1.7%, of which English 1.4%; Ulster Irish 1.0%; U.S. white 0.8%; other 1.5%.
Religious affiliation (2002): Roman Catholic 88.4%; Church of Ireland (Anglican) 3.0%; other Christian 1.6%; nonreligious 3.5%; other 3.5%.
Major cities (2002): Dublin 495,781 (urban agglomeration 1,004,600); Cork 123,062; Galway 65,832; Limerick 54,023; Waterford 44,594.

Vital statistics

Birth rate per 1,000 population (2003): 15.5 (world avg. 21.3).
Death rate per 1,000 population (2003): 7.2 (world avg. 9.1).
Natural increase rate per 1,000 population (2003): 8.3 (world avg. 12.2).
Marriage rate per 1,000 population (2003): 5.1.
Total fertility rate (avg. births per childbearing woman; 2003): 2.0.
Life expectancy at birth (2002): male 75.1 years; female 80.3 years.
Major causes of death per 100,000 population (2003): diseases of the circulatory system 275.3; malignant neoplasms (cancers) 189.7; diseases of the respiratory system 111.0; accidents and violence 34.0.

National economy

Budget (2000). Revenue: £Ir 21,741,000,000 (income taxes 33.0%, value-added tax 27.0%, excise taxes 15.4%). Expenditures: £Ir 19,297,000,000 (social welfare 27.9%, health 20.9%, education 14.9%, debt service 10.5%).
Total public debt (2001): U.S.$37,837,410,000.
Gross national product (2003): U.S.$105,160,000,000 (U.S.$26,960 per capita).

Structure of gross domestic product and labour force

	2001		2004[6]	
	in value €'000,000[7]	% of total value[7]	labour force	% of labour force
Agriculture	3,969	3.9	117,000	6.1
Mining, Manufacturing, Public utilities, Construction	42,734	41.7		
Mining, Manufacturing, Public utilities			300,600	15.6
Construction			206,000	10.7
Transp. and commun.	16,224	15.8	113,200	5.9
Trade, hotels			368,000	19.2
Pub. admin., defense	3,563	3.5	89,500	4.7
Services	40,162	39.2	404,900	21.1
Finance			237,000	12.3
Other	–4,257[8]	–4.2[8]	84,200[9]	4.4[9]
TOTAL	102,393[4]	100.0[4]	1,920,400	100.0

Tourism (2002): receipts U.S.$3,768,000,000; expenditures U.S.$3,741,000,000.
Production (metric tons except as noted). Agriculture, forestry, fishing (2002): sugar beets 1,313,000, barley 963,000, wheat 867,000, potatoes 519,000, oats 134,000; livestock (number of live animals) 6,408,000 cattle, 4,807,000 sheep, 1,763,000 pigs; roundwood (2001) 2,455,000 cu m; fish catch (2001) 417,244. Mining and quarrying (2002): zinc ore 252,700[10]; lead ore 32,500[10]. Manufacturing (gross value added in €'000,000; 2001): chemicals and chemical products 12,370; electrical and optical equipment 7,293; food and beverages 6,902; printing and publishing 3,250. Energy production (consumption): electricity (kW-hr; 2000) 23,750,000,000 (23,848,000,000); coal (metric tons; 2000) none (2,828,000); crude petroleum (barrels; 2000) none (24,540,000); petroleum products (metric tons; 2000) 3,197,000 (7,708,000); natural gas (cu m; 2000) 1,120,800,000 (4,019,000,000).
Population economically active (2002): total 1,827,100; activity rate 46.6% (participation rates: ages 15–64 [2000] *c.* 68%; female [2000] 40.3%; unemployed 4.3%).

Price and earnings indexes (2000 = 100)

	1997	1998	1999	2000	2001	2002	2003
Consumer price index	91.0	93.2	94.7	100.0	104.9	109.8	113.6
Weekly earnings index	63.0	75.5	86.6	100.0	110.2	118.8	126.3

Household income and expenditure. Average household size (2002) 2.9; income per household (1994–95): £Ir 16,224 (U.S.$25,100); expenditure (1996)[11]: food and beverages 35.4%, transportation 13.9%, rent/household goods 11.6%.
Land use as % of total land area (2000): in temporary crops 15.2%, in permanent crops 0.03%, in pasture 48.6%; overall forest area 9.6%.

Foreign trade[12]

Balance of trade (current prices)

	1997	1998	1999	2000	2001	2002
€'000,000	+12,004	+17,607	+22,629	+27,704	+35,306	+38,421
% of total	15.4%	18.1%	20.3%	20.2%	23.5%	25.8%

Imports (2000): €54,858,000,000 (machinery and apparatus 43.4%, of which computers and parts 20.5%, electronic microcircuits 5.1%; chemicals and chemical products 10.8%; road vehicles 7.3%; food 5.1%). *Major import sources:* U.K. 31.3%; U.S. 16.6%; Germany 5.8%; Japan 4.8%; France 4.7%.
Exports (2000): €82,562,000,000 (computers and parts 23.5%; organic chemicals 20.2%; food 7.1%; electronic microcircuits 5.3%; sound-recording devices 5.0%; telecommunications equipment 4.2%). *Major export destinations:* U.K. 21.8%; U.S. 17.2%; Germany 11.3%; France 7.6%; The Netherlands 5.6%.

Transport and communications

Transport. Railroads (2001): route length 1,947 km; passenger-km 1,515,303,000; metric ton-km cargo 515,754,000. Roads (1999): length 92,500 km (paved 94%). Vehicles (2000): passenger cars 1,269,245; trucks and buses 188,814. Air transport (2001)[13]: passenger-km 8,901,000,000; metric ton-km cargo 146,530,000; airports (1996) 9.

Communications

Medium	date	unit	number	units per 1,000 persons
Daily newspapers	2000	circulation	574,000	150
Radio	2000	receivers	2,660,000	695
Television	2002	receivers	2,707,000	694
Telephones	2003	main lines	1,955,000	486
Cellular telephones	2003	subscribers	3,400,000	845
Personal computers	2002	units	1,654,000	421
Internet	2003	users	1,260,000	313

Education and health

Educational attainment (1999). Percentage of population ages 25–64 and over having: no formal schooling through lower secondary 49%; upper secondary 30%; higher 21%, of which university 11%.

Education (1999–2000)

	schools	teachers	students	student/ teacher ratio
Primary (age 6–11)[14]	3,340	21,850	428,339	19.6
Secondary (age 12–18)	782	12,418	203,418	16.4
Voc., teacher tr.		8,683	150,442	17.3
Higher	56	5,644[15]	126,300	19.0[15]

Health: physicians (1998) 8,114 (1 per 457 persons); hospital beds (2002) 13,020[16] (1 per 306 persons); infant mortality rate per 1,000 live births (2000) 5.6.
Food (2001): daily per capita caloric intake 3,666 (vegetable products 69%, animal products 31%); 146% of FAO recommended minimum requirement.

Military

Total active duty personnel (2003): 10,460 (army 81.3%, navy 10.5%, air force 8.2%). *Military expenditure as percentage of GNP* (1999): 1.0% (world 2.4%); per capita expenditure U.S.$208.

[1]As provided by the constitution; the 1948 Republic of Ireland Act provides precedent for this longer formulation of the official name but, per official sources, "has not changed the usage *Ireland* as the name of the state in the English language." [2]Includes 11 nonelective seats. [3]The Irish pound was the former monetary unit; on Jan. 1, 2002, 1 £Ir = €1.27. [4]Detail does not add to total given because of rounding. [5]27,133 sq mi. [6]March–May. [7]At factor cost. [8]Less imputed bank service charges and statistical discrepancy. [9]Unemployed. [10]Metal content. [11]November. [12]Imports c.i.f.; exports f.o.b. [13]Aer Lingus only. [14]National schools only. [15]1998–99. [16]Publicly funded acute hospitals only.

Internet resources for further information:
- **Central Statistics Office (Ireland) http://www.cso.ie**
- **Central Bank of Ireland http://www.centralbank.ie**

Isle of Man

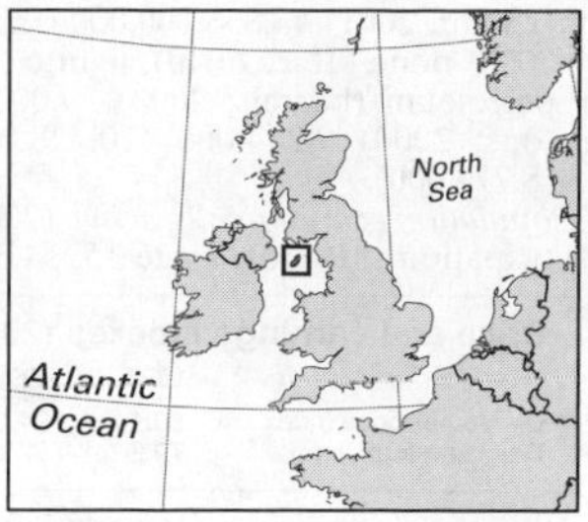

Official name: Isle of Man[1].
Political status: crown dependency (United Kingdom) with two legislative bodies[2] (Legislative Council [11[3]]; House of Keys [24]).
Chief of state: British Monarch represented by Lieutenant-Governor.
Head of government: Chief Minister assisted by the Council of Ministers.
Capital: Douglas.
Official language: English.
Official religion: none.
Monetary unit: 1 Manx pound (£M)[4] = 100 new pence; valuation (Sept. 1, 2004) 1 £M = U.S.$1.80.

Area and population

	area	population		area	population
	sq km	2001 census		sq km	2001 census
Towns			**Parishes** (cont.)		
Castletown	2.3	3,100	Ballaugh	23.6	868
Douglas	10.1	25,347	Braddan	42.6	2,665
Peel	1.7	3,785	Bride	21.7	408
Ramsey	3.7	7,322	German	45.3	1,010
			Jurby	17.7	677
Villages			Lezayre	62.3	1,134
Laxey	2.4	1,725	Lonan	35.2	1,393
Onchan	24.7	8,803	Malew	47.1	2,262
Port Erin	2.6	3,369	Marown	26.7	1,879
Port St. Mary	1.4	1,941	Maughold	34.5	941
			Michael	33.9	1,431
Parishes			Patrick	42.2	1,305
Andreas	31.1	1,152	Rushen	24.6	1,504
Arbory	17.7	1,714	Santon	16.9	580
			TOTAL	572.0[5]	76,315

Demography

Population (2004): 77,700.
Density (2004): persons per sq mi 351.6, persons per sq km 135.8.
Urban-rural (2001): urban 72.6%; rural 27.4%.
Sex distribution (2001): male 48.97%; female 51.03%.
Age breakdown (2001): under 15, 17.9%; 15–29, 17.5%; 30–44, 22.6%; 45–59, 20.1%; 60–74, 13.6%; 75 and over, 8.3%.
Population projection: (2010) 80,000; (2020) 84,000.
Population by place of birth (2001): Isle of Man 48.0%; United Kingdom 45.2%, of which England 38.2%, Scotland 3.5%, Northern Ireland 2.3%, Wales 1.2%; Ireland 2.3%; other Europe 1.0%; other 3.5%.
Religious affiliation (2000): Christian 63.7%, of which Anglican 40.5%, Methodist 9.9%, Roman Catholic 8.2%; other (mostly nonreligious) 36.3%.
Major towns (2001): Douglas 25,347; Onchan 8,803; Ramsey 7,322; Peel 3,785; Port Erin 3,369.

Vital statistics

Birth rate per 1,000 population (2003): 11.1 (world avg. 21.3); (2002) legitimate 64.6%; illegitimate 35.4%.
Death rate per 1,000 population (2003): 11.0 (world avg. 9.1).
Natural increase rate per 1,000 population (2003): 0.1 (world avg. 12.2).
Total fertility rate (avg. births per childbearing woman; 1999): 1.6.
Marriage rate per 1,000 population (2002): 5.6.
Divorce rate per 1,000 population (2000): 3.6.
Life expectancy at birth (1999): male 73.9 years; female 80.8 years.
Major causes of death per 100,000 population (2002): diseases of the circulatory system 495.6, of which ischemic heart diseases 264.1, cerebrovascular disease 132.7; neoplasms (cancers) 278.3; diseases of the respiratory system 106.7.

National economy

Budget (2001–02). Revenue: £466,177,000 (customs duties and excise taxes 64.3%; income taxes 34.8%, of which resident 30.5%, nonresident 4.3%; nontax revenue 0.9%). Expenditures: £360,499,000 (health and social security 39.8%; education 19.1%; transportation 6.8%; home affairs 6.0%; tourism and recreation 5.8%).
Public debt: n.a.
Production. Agriculture, forestry, fishing: main crops include hay, oats, barley, wheat, and orchard crops; livestock (number of live animals; 2002) 171,000 sheep, 34,000 cattle; fish catch (value of principal catch in £; 2001): 2,200,000, of which scallops 1,600,000, queen scallops 600,000. Mining and quarrying: sand and gravel. Manufacturing (value added in U.S.$; 1996–97): electrical and nonelectrical machinery/apparatus, textiles, other 103,700,000; food and beverages 18,600,000. Energy production (consumption): electricity (kW-hr; 2001–02), n.a. (345,000,000); crude petroleum, none (n.a.); petroleum products, n.a. (n.a.); natural gas, none (n.a.).
Household income and expenditure. Average household size (2001) 2.4; income per household (1981–82)[6, 7] £7,479 (U.S.$13,721); sources of income (1981–82)[6, 7]: wages and salaries 64.1%, transfer payments 16.9%, interest and dividends 11.2%, self-employment 6.6%; expenditure (1981–82)[6, 7]: food and beverages 31.0%, transportation 14.9%, energy 11.0%, housing 7.9%, clothing and footwear 7.0%.
Gross national product (at current market prices; 2001–02): U.S.$1,770,000,000 (U.S.$23,000 per capita).

Structure of gross domestic product and labour force

	2000–01		2001	
	in value £'000[8]	% of total value[8]	labour force	% of labour force
Agriculture, fishing	15,824	1.5	543	1.4
Mining Manufacturing	76,664	7.2	3,185	8.0
Construction	89,600	8.5	2,512	6.3
Public utilities	17,799	1.7	515	1.3
Transp. and commun.	72,256	6.8	2,970	7.5
Trade, hotels	83,452	7.9	7,171	18.1
Finance, real estate, insurance	505,382[9]	47.8[9]	8,959	22.6
Pub. admin., defense	53,566	5.1	3,105	7.8
Services	304,129[9]	28.7[9]	10,090	25.4
Other	–160,538[10]	–15.2[10]	635[11]	1.6[11]
TOTAL	1,058,134	100.0	39,685	100.0

Population economically active (2001): total 39,685; activity rate of total population 52.0% (participation rates: ages 16 and over 64.2%; female 45.4%; unemployed 1.6%).

Price and earnings indexes (2000 = 100)

	1997	1998	1999	2000	2001	2002	2003
Retail price index[12]	92.9	95.5	97.3	100.0	101.7	104.2	...
Weekly earnings index[12]	89.3	93.3	97.6	100.0	106.6	112.3	120.4

Tourism: receipts from visitors (1999) U.S.$90,600,000; expenditures by nationals abroad, n.a.; number of tourists (2001) 201,300.
Land use as % of total land area (2000): in temporary crops 8.1%, in permanent crops 0.7%, in pasture 71.5%; overall forest area, n.a.

Foreign trade[13]

Imports: n.a. *Major import sources:* mostly the United Kingdom.
Exports: traditional exports include scallops, herring, beef, lambs, and tweeds. *Major export destinations:* mostly the United Kingdom.

Transport and communications

Transport. Railroads (2001): route length 38 mi, 61 km[14]. Roads (2001): total length, more than 500 mi, more than 805 km (paved, n.a.). Vehicles (2001): passenger cars 45,195; trucks and buses 4,635. Merchant marine (2002): vessels (100 gross tons and over) 246; gross registered tonnage 5,835,174. Air transport (1998)[15]: passenger-mi 526,161,000, passenger-km 846,775,000; short ton-mi cargo 115,000, metric ton-km cargo 168,000; airports (2001) with scheduled flights 1.

Communications

Medium	date	unit	number	units per 1,000 persons
Daily newspapers	2001	circulation	—[16]	—
Television	2000	receivers	28,600	355
Telephones	2001	main lines	56,000	741
Cellular telephones	2001	subscribers	32,000	424

Education and health

Educational attainment: n.a. *Literacy:* n.a.

Education (2001)

	schools	teachers	students	student/ teacher ratio
Primary (age 5–10)	32	...	6,611	...
Secondary (age 11–16)	5	...	5,374	...
Higher	1	...	1,128[17]	...

Health: physicians (2003) 143 (1 per 540 persons); hospital beds (1998) 505 (1 per 143 persons); infant mortality rate per 1,000 live births (2002) 3.0.
Food (2002)[18]: daily per capita caloric intake 3,412 (vegetable products 69%, animal products 31%); 135% of FAO recommended minimum requirement.

Military

Total active duty personnel: [19].

[1]Ellan Vannin in Manx Gaelic. [2]Collective name is Tynwald. [3]Includes 3 nonelected seats. [4]Equivalent in value to pound sterling (£). [5]220.9 sq mi. [6]Fiscal year ending March 31st. [7]Based on survey of 259 households; "high income" and "pensioner" households are excluded. [8]At factor cost. [9]Most GDP in 2000–01 was derived from 60 banks (most of which are "offshore"), 80 investment businesses, and 183 insurance companies. [10]Ownership of dwellings less adjustments. [11]Unemployed. [12]June. [13]Because of the customs union between the Isle of Man and the U.K. since 1980, there are no customs controls on the movement of goods between the Isle of Man and the U.K. [14]Length of three tourist (novel) railways operating in summer. [15]Manx Airlines. [16]Isle of Man has 2 weekly newspapers and 1 biweekly newspaper. [17]Includes enrollees at Isle of Man College and students abroad in 1998–99. [18]Data for United Kingdom. [19]The United Kingdom is responsible for defense.

Internet resources for further information:
- **Isle of Man Government**
http://www.gov.im

Israel

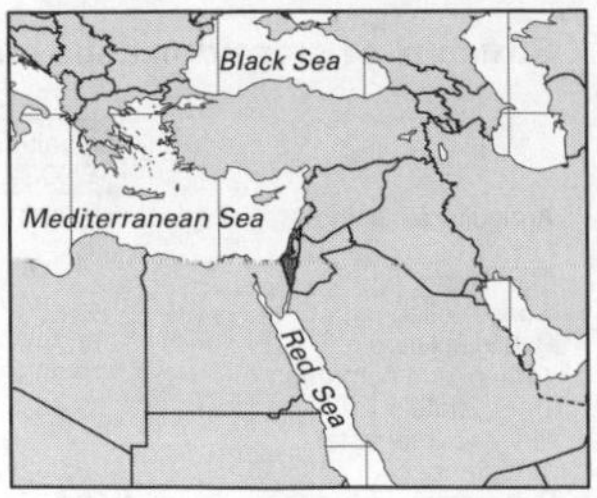

Official name: Medinat Yisra'el (Hebrew); Isrā'īl (Arabic) (State of Israel).
Form of government: multiparty republic with one legislative house (Knesset [120]).
Chief of state: President.
Head of government: Prime Minister.
Capital: Jerusalem is the proclaimed capital of Israel and the actual seat of government, but recognition of its status as capital by the international community has largely been withheld.
Official languages: Hebrew; Arabic.
Official religion: none.
Monetary unit: 1 New (Israeli) sheqel (NIS) = 100 agorot; valuation (Sept. 1, 2004) 1 U.S.$ = NIS 4.52; 1 £ = NIS 8.14.

Area and population

Districts	Capitals	area[1] sq mi	area[1] sq km	population 2004[2, 3] estimate
Central (Ha Merkaz)	Ramla	493	1,276	1,576,600
Haifa (Ḥefa)	Haifa	333	863	847,200
Jerusalem (Yerushalayim)	Jerusalem	252	652	810,900
Northern (Ha Ẕafon)	Tiberias	1,729	4,478	1,147,600
Southern (Ha Darom)	Beersheba	5,494	14,231	968,500
Tel Aviv	Tel Aviv–Yafo	66	171	1,167,500
TOTAL		8,367	21,671	6,518,300[3, 4]

Demography

Population (2004): 6,562,000.
Density (2004)[3]: persons per sq mi 784.3, persons per sq km 302.8.
Urban-rural (2002[2]): urban 91.6%; rural 8.4%.
Sex distribution (2000): male 49.33%; female 50.67%.
Age breakdown (2000): under 15, 28.6%; 15–29, 25.1%; 30–44, 18.7%; 45–59, 14.5%; 60–74, 8.8%; 75 and over, 4.3%.
Population projection: (2010) 7,240,000; (2020) 8,381,000.
Ethnic composition (2004[2]): Jewish 76.2%; Arab and other 23.8%.
Religious affiliation (2004[2]): Jewish 76.2%; Muslim (mostly Sunnī) 15.7%; Christian 2.1%; Druze 1.6%; other 4.4%.
Major cities (2003[2]): Jerusalem 680,400; Tel Aviv–Yafo 360,400; Haifa 270,800; Rishon LeẔiyyon 211,600; Ashdod 187,500; Beersheba 181,500.

Vital statistics

Birth rate per 1,000 population (2002): 21.0 (world avg. 21.3); (2000; Jewish population only) legitimate 97.2%; illegitimate 2.8%.
Death rate per 1,000 population (2002): 5.8 (world avg. 9.1).
Natural increase rate per 1,000 population (2002): 15.2 (world avg. 12.2).
Total fertility rate (avg. births per childbearing woman; 2002): 2.9.
Marriage rate per 1,000 population (2001): 5.9.
Divorce rate per 1,000 population (2001): 1.7.
Life expectancy at birth (2001): male 77.3 years; female 81.2 years.
Major causes of death per 100,000 population (1998): diseases of the circulatory system 222; malignant neoplasms (cancers) 149; accidents and violence 43; diseases of the respiratory system 40; diabetes mellitus 39.

National economy

Budget (2003). Revenue: NIS 205,703,000,000 (tax revenue 75.4%, of which income tax 35.4%, value-added tax 27.7%; nontax revenue 18.0%; grants 6.6%). Expenditures: NIS 220,903,000,000 (defense 21.2%; social security and welfare 19.5%; interest on loans 15.1%; education 14.6%; health 7.2%).
Public debt (2001): U.S.$111,658,000,000.
Gross national product (2003): U.S.$105,160,000,000 (U.S.$16,020 per capita).

Structure of net domestic product and labour force

	2001 in value NIS '000,000	2001 % of total value	2003 labour force	2003 % of labour force
Agriculture	7,351	1.5	41,900	1.6
Manufacturing, mining	72,727	14.8	381,800	14.7
Construction	21,321	4.3	129,500	5.0
Public utilities	8,170	1.7	18,400	0.7
Transp. and commun.	33,789	6.9	149,900	5.8
Trade, hotels	43,038	8.8	397,300	15.3
Finance, real estate	132,718	27.0	371,300	14.3
Public admin., defense	36,417	7.4	129,900	5.0
Services	82,454	16.8	682,200	26.2
Other	53,513[5]	10.9[5]	298,800[6]	11.5[6]
TOTAL	491,498	100.0[7]	2,601,000	100.0[7]

Production (metric tons except as noted). Agriculture, forestry, fishing (2002): potatoes 375,000, tomatoes 352,000, grapefruit and pomelos 255,000, oranges 198,000, wheat 175,000, grapes 114,000, apples 95,000, olives 60,000; livestock (number of live animals) 392,000 sheep, 390,000 cattle; roundwood (2002) 27,000 cu m; fish catch (2001) 25,100. Mining and quarrying (2001): phosphate rock 3,511,000, potash 1,774,000. Manufacturing (value added in U.S.$'000,000; 2000): electronic components 2,243; medical, measuring, and testing appliances 2,103; fabricated metals 1,686; food products 1,681; telecommunications equipment 1,615; transport equipment 956; chemicals and chemical products 914. Energy production (consumption): electricity (kW-hr; 2001) 43,838,000,000 ([2000] 41,459,000,000); hard coal (metric tons; 2000) none (10,257,000); lignite (metric tons; 2000) 888,000 (888,000); crude petroleum (barrels; 2000) 29,000 (75,800,000); petroleum products (metric tons; 2000) 9,244,000 (10,428,000); natural gas (cu m; 2000) 8,779,000 (8,779,000).
Population economically active (2003): total 2,601,000; activity rate 40.2% (participation rates: over age 15, 54.3%; female 46.0%; unemployed 10.7%).

Price and earnings indexes (2000 = 100)

	1997	1998	1999	2000	2001	2002	2003
Consumer price index	89.1	94.0	98.9	100.0	101.1	106.8	107.6
Daily earnings index	79.2	87.1	94.1	100.0	108.6	109.7	111.9

Household income and expenditure (2002). Average household size 3.4; net annual income per household (2001) NIS 136,332 (U.S.$28,285); sources of income (2000)[8]: salaries and wages 67.5%, self-employment 11.5%; expenditure (2001): housing 22.6%, transport and communications 20.1%, food and beverages 17.0%, education 13.4%, health 4.9%.
Tourism (2002): receipts U.S.$1,197,000,000; expenditures U.S.$2,547,000,000.
Land use as % of total land area (2000): in temporary crops 16.4%, in permanent crops 4.2%, in pasture 6.9%; overall forest area 6.4%.

Foreign trade[9]

Balance of trade (current prices)

	1998	1999	2000	2001	2002	2003
U.S.$'000,000	–3,051	–4,160	–3,034	–3,208	–3,894	–2,177
% of total	6.2%	7.4%	4.7%	5.5%	6.7%	3.5%

Imports (2002): U.S.$33,106,000,000 (machinery and apparatus 23.7%; diamonds 21.7%; chemicals and chemical products 9.6%; crude petroleum and refined petroleum 7.7%; road vehicles 5.7%). *Major import sources:* U.S. 18.5%; Belgium 9.1%; Germany 7.1%; U.K. 6.7%; Switzerland 6.3%.
Exports (2002): U.S.$29,511,000,000 (cut diamonds 28.2%; telecommunications equipment 9.2%; rough diamonds 6.5%; organic chemicals 3.9%; electronic microcircuits 3.6%; aircraft parts 3.6%; pharmaceuticals 3.1%). *Major export destinations:* U.S. 40.2%; Belgium 6.3%; Hong Kong 4.7%; U.K. 3.9%; Germany 3.5%.

Transport and communications

Transport. Railroads (2002): route length 678 km; passenger-km 1,116,000,000, metric ton-km cargo 1,102,000,000. Roads (2002): total length 16,903 km (paved 100%). Vehicles (2002): passenger cars 1,496,878; trucks and buses 347,566. Air transport (2003)[10]: passenger-km 12,126,000,000; metric ton-km cargo 1,091,342,000; airports (1999) with scheduled flights 7.

Communications

Medium	date	unit	number	units per 1,000 persons
Daily newspapers	2000	circulation	1,770,000	290
Radio	2000	receivers	3,210,000	526
Television	2000	receivers	2,040,000	335
Telephones	2002	main lines	3,006,000	453
Cellular telephones	2002	subscribers	6,334,000	954
Personal computers	2002	units	1,610,000	243
Internet	2002	users	2,000,000	301

Education and health

Educational attainment (2001). Percentage of population age 15 and over having: no formal schooling 3.1%; primary 1.7%; secondary 56.7%; postsecondary, vocational, and higher 38.5%. *Literacy* (2001): 96.9%.

Education (2002–03)

	schools	teachers	students	student/ teacher ratio
Primary (age 6–13)	2,178	60,600	758,798	12.5
Secondary (age 14–17)[11]	1,768	75,938	451,027	5.9
Vocational, teacher tr.	180	...	138,361	...
Higher	7	10,171	219,763	21.6

Health (2002): physicians 21,800[12] (1 per 291 persons); hospital beds 40,116 (1 per 158 persons); infant mortality rate per 1,000 live births 11.3.
Food (2001): daily per capita caloric intake 3,512 (vegetable products 81.1%, animal products 18.9%); 137% of FAO recommended minimum.

Military

Total active duty personnel (2003): 167,600 (army 74.6%, navy 4.5%, air force 20.9%). *Military expenditure as percentage of GNP* (1999): 8.8% (world 2.4%); per capita expenditure U.S.$1,510.

[1]Excludes the West Bank (2,278 sq mi [5,900 sq km]), the Gaza Strip (140 sq mi [363 sq km]), the Sea of Galilee (63 sq mi [164 sq km]), and the Dead Sea (120 sq mi [310 sq km]); includes the Golan Heights (446 sq mi [1,154 sq km]) and East Jerusalem (27 sq mi [70 sq km]). [2]January 1. [3]Includes the population of the Golan Heights (37,000) and East Jerusalem and excludes the Jewish population of the West Bank and the Gaza Strip (230,900). [4]Excludes 200,000–300,000 foreign workers. [5]Taxes on products less imputed bank service charges, subsidies, and statistical discrepancy. [6]Includes 20,500 not adequately classified and 278,300 unemployed. [7]Detail does not add to total given because of rounding. [8]Money income only. [9]Imports f.o.b. in balance of trade and c.i.f. in commodities and trading partners; balance of trade data excludes the Gaza Strip and the West Bank. [10]El Al only. [11]Includes intermediate schools. [12]Full-time doctors only.

Internet resources for further information:
- **Central Bureau of Statistics (Israel) http://www.cbs.gov.il/engindex.htm**
- **Bank of Israel http://www.bankisrael.gov.il/firsteng.htm**

Italy

Official name: Repubblica Italiana (Italian Republic).
Form of government: republic with two legislative houses (Senate [321[1]]; Chamber of Deputies [630]).
Chief of state: President.
Head of government: Prime Minister.
Capital: Rome.
Official language: Italian.
Official religion: none.
Monetary unit: 1 euro (€) = 100 cents; valuation (Sept. 1, 2004) 1 U.S.$ = €0.82; 1 £ = €1.48[2].

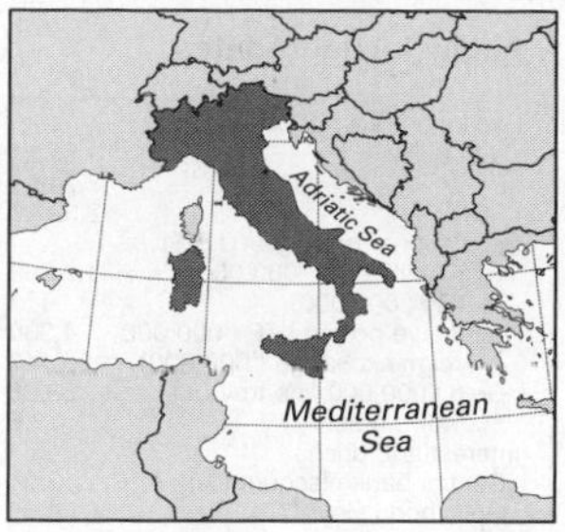

Area and population

Regions / Provinces	Capitals	area sq mi	area sq km	population 2003[3] estimate
Abruzzo	L'Aquila	4,168	10,794	1,273,284
Chieti	Chieti	999	2,587	383,058
L'Aquila	L'Aquila	1,944	5,034	298,082
Pescara	Pescara	473	1,225	302,983
Teramo	Teramo	752	1,948	289,161
Basilicata	Potenza	3,858	9,992	596,821
Matera	Matera	1,331	3,447	204,108
Potenza	Potenza	2,527	6,545	392,713
Calabria	Catanzaro	5,823	15,080	2,007,392
Catanzaro	Catanzaro	924	2,392	368,856
Cosenza	Cosenza	2,568	6,650	733,142
Crotone	Crotone	662	1,716	172,735
Reggio di Calabria	Reggio di Calabria	1,229	3,183	562,692
Vibo Valentia	Vibo Valentia	440	1,139	169,967
Campania	Naples	5,249	13,595	5,725,098
Avellino	Avellino	1,078	2,792	432,115
Benevento	Benevento	800	2,071	286,611
Caserta	Caserta	1,019	2,639	854,956
Napoli	Naples	452	1,171	3,075,660
Salerno	Salerno	1,900	4,922	1,075,756
Emilia-Romagna	Bologna	8,542	22,123	4,030,220
Bologna	Bologna	1,429	3,702	926,637
Ferrara	Ferrara	1,016	2,632	344,025
Forlì-Cesena	Forlì	969	2,510	362,245
Modena	Modena	1,039	2,690	643,043
Parma	Parma	1,332	3,449	396,782
Piacenza	Piacenza	1,000	2,589	267,274
Ravenna	Ravenna	718	1,859	351,193
Reggio nell'Emilia	Reggio nell'Emilia	885	2,292	462,637
Rimini	Rimini	154	400	276,384
Friuli-Venezia Giulia	Trieste	3,029	7,845	1,191,588
Gorizia	Gorizia	180	467	138,463
Pordenone	Pordenone	878	2,273	290,229
Trieste	Trieste	82	212	240,638
Udine	Udine	1,889	4,893	522,258
Lazio	Rome	6,642	17,203	5,145,805
Frosinone	Frosinone	1,251	3,239	485,041
Latina	Latina	869	2,251	497,415
Rieti	Rieti	1,061	2,749	148,547
Roma	Rome	2,066	5,352	3,723,649
Viterbo	Viterbo	1,395	3,612	291,153
Liguria	Genoa	2,092	5,418	1,572,107
Genova	Genoa	709	1,836	873,604
Imperia	Imperia	446	1,155	205,998
La Spezia	La Spezia	341	882	215,707
Savona	Savona	596	1,545	276,888
Lombardy	Milan	9,211	23,857	9,108,645
Bergamo	Bergamo	1,051	2,722	986,924
Brescia	Brescia	1,846	4,782	1,126,249
Como	Como	497	1,288	543,546
Cremona	Cremona	684	1,771	338,690
Lecco	Lecco	315	816	315,183
Lodi	Lodi	302	783	201,554
Mantova	Mantova	903	2,339	381,330
Milano	Milan	765	1,980	3,721,428
Pavia	Pavia	1,145	2,965	497,233
Sondrio	Sondrio	1,240	3,212	177,568
Varese	Varese	463	1,199	818,940
Marche	Ancona	3,743	9,693	1,484,601
Ancona	Ancona	749	1,940	452,175
Ascoli Piceno	Ascoli Piceno	806	2,087	372,407
Macerata	Macerata	1,071	2,774	305,080
Pesaro e Urbino	Pesaro	1,117	2,892	354,939
Molise	Campobasso	1,713	4,438	321,047
Campobasso	Campobasso	1,123	2,909	231,017
Isernia	Isernia	590	1,529	90,030
Piedmont	Turin	9,807[3]	25,399	4,231,334
Alessandria	Alessandria	1,375	3,560	418,203
Asti	Asti	583	1,511	209,116
Biella	Biella	352	913	187,962
Cuneo	Cuneo	2,665	6,903	561,729
Novara	Novara	530	1,373	345,952
Torino	Turin	2,637	6,830	2,172,226
Verbano-Cusio-Ossola	Verbania	858	2,221	159,636
Vercelli	Vercelli	806	2,088	176,510
Puglia	Bari	7,470	19,348	4,023,957
Bari	Bari	1,980	5,129	1,564,122
Brindisi	Brindisi	710	1,838	400,974
Foggia	Foggia	2,774	7,185	688,902
Lecce	Lecce	1,065	2,759	790,572
Taranto	Taranto	941	2,437	579,387
Sardinia	Cagliari	9,301	24,090	1,637,639
Cagliari	Cagliari	2,662	6,895	762,845
Nuoro	Nuoro	2,720	7,044	264,496
Oristano	Oristano	1,016	2,631	153,125
Sassari	Sassari	2,903	7,520	457,173
Sicily	Palermo	9,926	25,709	4,972,124
Agrigento	Agrigento	1,175	3,042	450,034
Caltanissetta	Caltanissetta	822	2,128	272,167
Catania	Catania	1,371	3,552	1,058,162
Enna	Enna	989	2,562	176,496
Messina	Messina	1,254	3,248	659,513
Palermo	Palermo	1,927	4,992	1,236,799
Ragusa	Ragusa	623	1,614	296,744
Siracusa	Siracusa	814	2,109	396,517
Trapani	Trapani	951	2,462	425,692
Trentino-Alto Adige	Bolzano	5,258	13,618	950,495
Bolzano-Bozen	Bolzano	2,857	7,400	467,338
Trento	Trento	2,401	6,218	483,157
Tuscany	Florence	8,877	22,992[3]	3,516,296
Arezzo	Arezzo	1,248	3,232	326,172
Firenze	Florence	1,365	3,536	935,883
Grosseto	Grosseto	1,739	4,504	212,001
Livorno	Livorno	468	1,213	327,472
Lucca	Lucca	684	1,773	373,820
Massa-Carrara	Massa-Carrara	447	1,157	197,562
Pisa	Pisa	945	2,448	386,466
Pistoia	Pistoia	373	965	271,443
Prato	Prato	133	344	231,207
Siena	Siena	1,475	3,821	254,270
Umbria	Perugia	3,265	8,456	834,210
Perugia	Perugia	2,446	6,334	613,004
Terni	Terni	819	2,122	221,206
Valle d'Aosta	Aosta	1,259	3,262	120,909
Veneto	Venice	7,090	18,364	4,577,408
Belluno	Belluno	1,420	3,678	210,503
Padova	Padova	827	2,142	857,660
Rovigo	Rovigo	691	1,789	242,608
Treviso	Treviso	956	2,477	808,076
Venezia	Venice	950	2,460	813,294
Verona	Verona	1,195	3,096	838,221
Vicenza	Vicenza	1,051	2,722	807,046
TOTAL		116,324[4, 5]	301,277[4, 5]	57,321,070

Demography

Population (2004): 57,537,000.
Density (2004): persons per sq mi 494.5, persons per sq km 190.9.
Urban-rural (2003): urban 67.4%; rural 32.6%.
Sex distribution (2003): male 48.44%; female 51.56%.
Age breakdown (2003): under 15, 14.2%; 15–29, 18.0%; 30–44, 23.5%; 45–59, 19.3%; 60–74, 16.3%; 75 and over, 8.7%.
Population projection: (2010) 57,569,000; (2020) 56,517,000.
Ethnolinguistic composition (2000): Italian 96.0%; North African Arab 0.9%; Italo-Albanian 0.8%; Albanian 0.5%; German 0.4%; Austrian 0.4%; other 1.0%.
Religious affiliation (2000): Roman Catholic 79.6%; nonreligious 13.2%; Muslim 1.2%; other 6.0%.
Major cities and urban agglomerations (2001/2000[6]): Rome 2,459,776 (2,649,000); Milan 1,182,693 (4,251,000); Naples 993,386 (3,012,000); Turin 857,433 (1,294,000); Palermo 652,640; Genoa 603,560 (890,000); Bologna 369,955; Florence 352,227 (778,000); Bari 312,452; Catania 306,464; Venice 266,181; Verona 243,474; Messina 236,621; Trieste 209,520.
National origin (1991): Italian 99.3%; foreign-born 0.7%, of which European 0.3%, African 0.2%, Asian 0.1%, other 0.1%.
Households. Average household size (2000) 2.6; composition of households: 1 person 23.3%, 2 persons 26.1%, 3 persons 23.0%, 4 persons 20.2%, 5 or more persons 7.4%. Family households (1991): 15,538,335 (73.8%); nonfamily 5,527,105 (26.2%), of which one-person 19.5%.
Immigration (1997): immigrants 162,857, from Europe 41.1%, of which EU countries 14.2%; Africa 25.5%; Asia 19.0%; Western Hemisphere 14.0%.

Vital statistics

Birth rate per 1,000 population (2003): 9.2 (world avg. 21.3); (2000) legitimate 89.8%; illegitimate 10.2%.
Death rate per 1,000 population (2003): 10.1 (world avg. 9.1).
Natural increase rate per 1,000 population (2003): –0.9 (world avg. 12.2).
Total fertility rate (avg. births per childbearing woman; 2002): 1.3.
Marriage rate per 1,000 population (2001): 4.7.
Divorce rate per 1,000 population (2000): 0.7.
Life expectancy at birth (2003): male 76.5 years; female 82.5 years.
Major causes of death per 100,000 population (1998): diseases of the circulatory system 432.5; malignant neoplasms 266.7; diseases of the respiratory system 68.6; diseases of the digestive system 45.1; accidents and violence 37.5.

Social indicators

Educational attainment (1995). Percentage of labour force age 15 and over having: basic literacy or primary education 40.4%; secondary 30.5%; post-secondary technical training 5.1%; some college 19.2%; college degree 4.3%.
Quality of working life. Average workweek (2001): 39.3 hours. Annual rate per 100,000 workers (2000) for: nonfatal injury 4,030; fatal injury 7. Percentage of labour force insured for damages or income loss (1992) resulting from: injury 100%; permanent disability 100%; death 100%. Number of working days lost to labour stoppages per 1,000 workers (1996): 97.
Material well-being. Rate per 1,000 of population possessing (1995): telephone 434; automobile 550; television 436.
Social participation. Eligible voters participating in last national election (May 13, 2001): 81.2%. Trade union membership in total workforce (2000): c. 35%.
Social deviance (2000). Offense rate per 100,000 population for: murder 1.3; rape 4.1; assault 210.4[7]; theft, including burglary and housebreaking 2,466; drug trafficking 61.1; suicide 6.3[8]
Access to services (2002). Nearly 100% of dwellings have access to electricity, a safe water supply, and toilet facilities.
Leisure (1998). Favourite leisure activities (as percentage of household spending on culture): cinema 21.8%; sporting events 14.6%; theatre 13.8%.

National economy

Gross national product (at current market prices; 2003): U.S.$1,242,978,000,000 (U.S.$21,560 per capita).

Structure of gross domestic product and labour force

	2001			
	in value €'000,000	% of total value	labour force	% of labour force
Agriculture	30,754	2.5	1,126,000	4.7
Mining	[9]	[9]	64,000	0.3
Manufacturing	228,533[9]	18.8[9]	4,907,000	20.5
Construction	55,584	4.6	1,707,000	7.1
Public utilities	30,783	2.5	162,000	0.7
Transportation and communications	81,089	6.7	1,180,000	4.9
Trade	191,246	15.7	4,296,000	18.0
Finance	298,950	24.6	2,209,000	9.2
Pub. admin., defense	60,896	5.0	1,987,000	8.3
Services	156,989	12.9	3,973,000	16.6
Other	81,868[10]	6.7[10]	2,287,000[11]	9.6[11]
TOTAL	1,216,694[3]	100.0	23,901,000[3]	100.0[3]

Budget (2000). Revenue: €444,502,000,000 (social security contributions 32.5%, individual income taxes 28.6%, taxes on goods and services 15.9%, corporate income tax 5.9%). Expenditures: €462,352,000,000 (social benefits 41.9%, interest payments 16.0%, grants to general government units 14.9%).
Tourism (2002): receipts U.S.$26,915,000,000; expenditures U.S.$16,935,000,000.

Manufacturing, mining, and construction enterprises (1995)

	no. of enterprises	no. of employees[12]	hourly wages as a % of avg. of all wages	annual value added (Lit '000,000,000)
Manufacturing				
Metal products	5,780	360,979	...	36,249
Machinery (nonelectrical)	4,503	379,027	...	35,221
Industrial chemicals	1,206	180,836	...	27,505
Electrical machinery	2,962	303,439	...	26,306
Food products	2,549	224,025	...	22,878
Transport equipment	1,122	275,077	...	22,642
Printing, publishing[13]	2,086	148,757	...	16,150
Pottery, ceramics, and glass	2,128	149,586	...	14,361
Textiles[14]	3,514	215,387	...	14,335
Rubber and plastic products	1,836	123,119	...	12,711
Wearing apparel	2,436	114,059	...	7,279
Paper and paper products[13]	...	...	...	...
Petroleum and gas	108	22,566	...	4,221
Mining and quarrying	340	20,013	...	5,991
Construction	6,228	1,564,100	...	94,887

Production (metric tons except as noted). Agriculture, forestry, fishing (2003): corn (maize) 8,978,000, sugar beets 8,300,000, grapes 7,484,000, tomatoes 6,634,000, wheat 6,243,000, olives 3,150,000, oranges 1,962,000, apples 1,945,000, potatoes 1,604,000, rice 1,360,000, peaches and nectarines 1,357,000, barley 1,026,000, lettuce 914,000, pears 822,000; livestock (number of live animals) 10,950,000 sheep, 9,111,000 pigs, 6,430,000 cattle, 100,000,000 chickens; roundwood (2002) 7,789,000 cu m; fish catch (2001) 528,666. Mining and quarrying (2001): loam rock 13,973,000; rock salt 3,281,300; feldspar 3,092,400; barite 10,800; lead 4,000. Manufacturing (value added in U.S.$'000,000; 2000): nonelectrical machinery and apparatus 25,935; fabricated metal products 22,934; food products 13,468; paints, soaps, pharmaceuticals 10,594; bricks, cement, ceramics 8,418; textiles 8,165; wearing apparel 7,524; motor vehicles and parts 7,254; plastic products 6,627; furniture 5,924; footwear and leather products 5,592; telecommunications equipment 5,374.

Service enterprises (1999)[15]

	no. of enterprises	no. of employees	hourly wage as a % of all wages	annual value added €'000,000
Public utilities	...	146,593	...	18,083
Transportation and communications	...	1,142,666	...	51,835
Real estate, research	...	1,828,536	...	66,887
Wholesale and retail trade	...	3,115,825	...	85,832
Health and social services	...	456,997	...	14,469
Hotels, restaurants	...	796,081	...	15,903

Energy production (consumption): electricity (kW-hr; 2003) 292,632,000,000 ([2000] 320,986,000,000); hard coal (metric tons; 2000) negligible (18,013,000); lignite (metric tons; 2000) 114,000 (130,000); crude petroleum (barrels; 2001) 27,714,000 ([2000] 599,600,000); petroleum products (metric tons; 2000) 84,900,000 (81,700,000); natural gas (cu m; 2003) 13,456,000,000 ([2000] 70,770,000,000).
Population economically active (2001): total 23,901,000; activity rate of total population 42.4% (participation rates: ages 15–64, 63.0%; female 38.7%; unemployed 9.6%).

Price and earnings indexes (2000 = 100)

	1997	1998	1999	2000	2001	2002	2003
Consumer price index	94.1	95.9	97.5	100.0	102.8	105.3	108.1
Earnings index	94.1	96.4	98.1	100.0	102.5	104.7	107.0

Household income and expenditure (2000). Average household size 2.6; average annual income per household: n.a.; sources of income (1996): salaries and wages 38.8%, property income and self-employment 38.5%, transfer payments 22.0%; expenditure (2001): housing 34.9%, food and beverages 18.9%, transportation and communications 16.7%, leisure 6.3%, other 16.2%.
Land use as % of total land area (2000): in temporary crops 28.2%, in permanent crops 9.7%, in pasture 15.1%; overall forest area 34.0%.

Financial aggregates

	1998	1999	2000	2001	2002	2003
Exchange rate, Lit per[16]:						
U.S. dollar	1,653.1	1.00	1.07	1.13	0.95	0.79
£	2,749.9	1.61	1.60	1.65	1.54	1.41
SDR	2,327.6	1.37	1.40	1.43	1.30	1.18
International reserves (U.S.$)						
Total (excl. gold; '000,000)	29,888	22,422	25,567	24,419	28,603	30,366
SDRs ('000,000)	111	168	238	297	108	156
Reserve pos. in IMF ('000,000)	4,330	3,546	2,906	3,217	3,907	4,154
Foreign exchange ('000,000)	25,447	18,623	22,423	20,905	24,588	26,056
Gold ('000,000 fine troy oz)	83.36	78.83	78.83	78.83	78.83	78.83
% world reserves	8.6	8.2	8.3	8.4	8.5	8.6
Interest and prices						
Central bank discount (%)	3.00	...	...	...	...	...
Govt. bond yield (%)	4.55	4.04	5.29	4.64	4.48	3.36
Industrial share prices (1995 = 100)	69.1	77.0	100.0	81.1	64.3	58.1
Balance of payments (U.S.$'000,000)						
Balance of visible trade	+35,361	+23,436	+9,548	+15,539	+16,533	+9,700
Imports, f.o.b.	–206,941	–212,420	–230,925	–229,392	–237,147	–283,565
Exports, f.o.b.	242,572	235,856	240,473	244,931	253,680	293,264
Balance of invisibles	–15,363	–15,326	–15,329	–16,191	–23,274	–31,642
Balance of payments, current account	+19,998	+8,110	–5,781	–652	–6,741	–21,942

Public debt (2002): U.S.$1,333,669,000,000.

Foreign trade[17]

Balance of trade (current prices)

	1996	1997	1998	1999	2000	2001
U.S.$'000,000	+43,983	+29,949	+26,512	+14,907	+1,781	+8,262
% of total	9.6%	6.7%	5.8%	3.3%	0.4%	1.7%

Imports (2000): U.S.$235,859,000,000 (machinery 20.5%, chemicals 12.0%, road vehicles 11.0%, crude petroleum 7.2%, food 6.9%, iron and steel 3.6%). *Major import sources:* Germany 17.5%; France 11.2%; The Netherlands 5.7%; U.K. 5.4%; U.S. 5.3%; Spain 4.1%; Belgium 4.0%; Switzerland 3.0%.
Exports (2000): U.S.$237,640,000,000 (machinery and apparatus 27.7%, chemicals and chemical products 9.1%, road vehicles 8.1%, apparel and clothing accessories 5.6%, textile yarn and fabrics 5.1%, food 4.3%). *Major export destinations:* Germany 15.0%; France 12.5%; U.S. 10.3%; U.K. 6.8%; Spain 6.2%; Switzerland 3.3%; Belgium 2.7%; The Netherlands 2.6%.

Transport and communications

Transport. Railroads: (2002) length 19,786 km; (2001) passenger-km 46,675,000,000; (2001) metric ton-km cargo 24,995,000,000. Roads (1997): total length 654,676 km (paved 100%). Vehicles (2001): passenger cars 33,129,300; trucks and buses 3,749,200. Air transport (2003)[18]: passenger-km 30,736,000,000; metric ton-km cargo 1,355,000,000; airports (1997) 34.

Communications

Medium	date	unit	number	units per 1,000 persons
Daily newspapers	2000	circulation	5,920,000	104
Radio	2000	receivers	50,000,000	878
Television	2000	receivers	28,100,000	494
Telephones	2003	main lines	26,596,000	453
Cellular telephones	2003	subscribers	55,918,000	1,018
Personal computers	2002	units	13,025,000	231
Internet	2003	users	18,500,000	337

Education and health

Literacy (2000): total population age 15 and over literate 48,100,000 (98.4%); males literate 23,800,000 (98.9%); females literate 24,300,000 (98.0%).

Education (2000–01)

	schools	teachers	students	student/ teacher ratio
Primary (age 6–10)	18,854	287,344	1,576,456	5.5
Secondary (age 11–18)	7,906	209,829	1,776,950	8.5
Voc., teacher tr.	6,637	307,279	2,565,029	8.3
Higher[19]	74	54,856	1,702,575	31.0

Health: physicians (2001) 348,862 (1 per 164 persons); hospital beds (2001) 254,663 (1 per 224 persons); infant mortality rate (2003) 6.2.
Food (2001): daily per capita caloric intake 3,680 (vegetable products 75%, animal products 25%); 146% of FAO recommended minimum requirement.

Military

Total active duty personnel (2003): 200,000 (army 58.0%, navy 18.0%, air force 24.0%); U.S. military forces (2004) 13,400. *Military expenditure as percentage of GNP* (1999): 2.0% (world 2.4%); per capita expenditure U.S.$412.

[1]Includes 6 nonelective seats in late 2004 (4 presidential appointees and 2 former presidents serving ex officio). [2]The Italian lira (Lit) was the former monetary unit; on Jan. 1, 2002, Lit 1,936 = €1. [3]January 1. [4]Detail does not add to total given because of rounding. [5]The total area for Italy, per 2001 survey, is 116,343 sq mi (301,328 sq km). [6]Major city populations are 2001 preliminary census figures; urban agglomeration populations are 2000 estimates by the UN. [7]1995. [8]1996. [9]Manufacturing includes Mining. [10]Other includes indirect import charges and building rental less imputed bank service charges. [11]Unemployed. [12]Total number of persons engaged. [13]Printing, publishing includes Paper and paper products. [14]1993. [15]Enterprises with 20 or more persons engaged. [16]Beginning in 1999 exchange rates in euros. [17]Imports c.i.f.; exports f.o.b. [18]Alitalia and Air One only. [19]2001–02.

Internet resources for further information:
- **National Statistical Institute http://www.istat.it/English**
- **Banca d'Italia http://www.bancaditalia.it**

Jamaica

Official name: Jamaica.
Form of government: constitutional monarchy[1] with two legislative houses (Senate [21]; House of Representatives [60]).
Chief of state: British Monarch represented by Governor-General.
Head of government: Prime Minister.
Capital: Kingston.
Official language: English.
Official religion: none.
Monetary unit: 1 Jamaica dollar (J$) = 100 cents; valuation (Sept. 1, 2004) 1 U.S.$ = J$61.20; 1 £ = J$110.10.

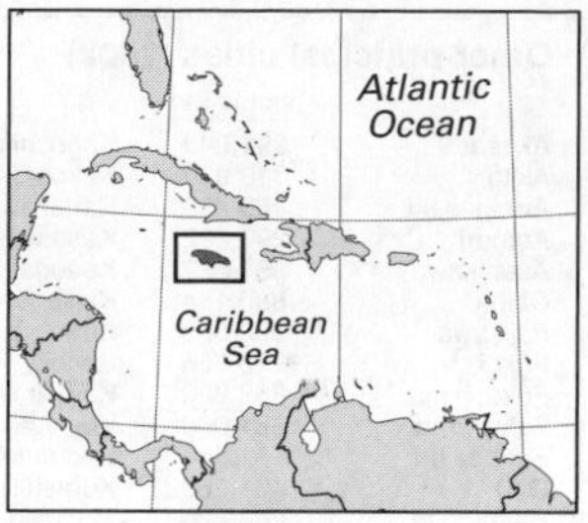

Area and population

Parishes	Capitals	area sq mi	area sq km	population 2001 census[2]
Clarendon	May Pen	462	1,196	237,025
Hanover	Lucea	174	450	67,037
Kingston	[3]	9	22	96,052
Manchester	Mandeville	320	830	185,801
Portland	Port Antonio	314	814	80,205
Saint Andrew	[3]	166	431	555,827
Saint Ann	Saint Ann's Bay	468	1,213	166,762
Saint Catherine	Spanish Town	460	1,192	482,308
Saint Elizabeth	Black River	468	1,212	146,404
Saint James	Montego Bay	230	595	175,127
Saint Mary	Port Maria	236	611	111,466
Saint Thomas	Morant Bay	287	743	91,604
Trelawny	Falmouth	338	875	73,066
Westmoreland	Savanna-la-Mar	312	807	138,947
TOTAL		4,244	10,991	2,607,631

Demography

Population (2004): 2,649,000.
Density (2004): persons per sq mi 624.2, persons per sq km 241.0.
Urban-rural (2001): urban 52.0%; rural 48.0%.
Sex distribution (2001): male 49.22%; female 50.78%.
Age breakdown (2002): under 15, 32.3%; 15–29, 25.9%; 30–44, 20.6%; 45–59, 11.0%; 60–74, 6.8%; 75 and over, 3.4%.
Population projection: (2010) 2,784,000; (2020) 3,053,000.
Doubling time: 55 years.
Ethnic composition (2001): black 91.6%; mixed race 6.2%; East Indian 0.9%; Chinese 0.2%; white 0.2%; other/unknown 0.9%.
Religious affiliation (2001): Protestant 61.2%, of which Church of God 23.8%[4], Seventh-day Adventist 10.8%, Pentecostal 9.5%; Roman Catholic 2.6%; other Christian 1.7%; Rastafarian 0.9%; nonreligious 20.9%; other/unknown 12.7%.
Major cities (2001): Kingston 96,052[5] (metro area 579,137); Portmore 161,658[6]; Spanish Town 131,515; Montego Bay 96,488; May Pen 57,334.

Vital statistics

Birth rate per 1,000 population (2003): 19.3 (world avg. 21.3).
Death rate per 1,000 population (2003): 6.4 (world avg. 9.1).
Natural increase rate per 1,000 population (2003): 12.9 (world avg. 12.2).
Total fertility rate (avg. births per childbearing woman; 2003): 2.0.
Marriage rate per 1,000 population (1999): 10.4.
Divorce rate per 1,000 population (1999): 0.4.
Life expectancy at birth (2003): male 73.8 years; female 78.0 years.
Major causes of death per 100,000 population (1991): circulatory diseases 189.4; malignant neoplasms 84.1; endocrine and metabolic disorders 51.3.

National economy

Budget (2000–01). Revenue J$101,018,000,000 (tax revenue 86.2%, of which income taxes 35.1%, consumption taxes 26.4%, custom duties 8.4%; nontax revenue 7.7%; bauxite levy 2.7%; capital revenue 1.7%; grants 1.7%). Expenditures: J$104,171,000,000 (current expenditure 91.0%, of which debt interest 41.2%, wages 33.8%; capital expenditure 9.0%).
Production (metric tons except as noted). Agriculture, forestry, fishing (2002): sugarcane 2,400,000, citrus fruits 221,000, vegetables and melons 197,000, coconuts 170,000, yams 158,000, bananas 130,000, plantains 29,000, tomatoes 24,000, cabbages 22,000, coffee 2,700; livestock (number of live animals) 440,000 goats, 400,000 cattle, 180,000 pigs; roundwood (2002) 867,000 cu m; fish catch (2001) 10,212. Mining and quarrying (2003): bauxite 13,443,000; alumina 3,844,000; gypsum 162,000. Manufacturing (2001): cement 595,000; animal feeds 385,000; sugar 205,000; flour 130,000; molasses 86,983; beer 622,000 hectolitres; rum [and other distilled spirits] 223,000 hectolitres; cigarettes 1,024,933,000 units. Energy production (consumption): electricity (kW-hr; 2000) 6,631,000,000 (6,631,000,000); coal (metric tons; 2000) none (72,000); crude petroleum (barrels; 2000) none (7,762,000); petroleum products (metric tons; 2000) 998,000 (3,326,000).
Population economically active (April 2001): total 1,105,800; activity rate of total population 42.4% (participation rates: ages 14 and over 63.0%; female 43.9%; unemployed 14.8%).

Price index (2000 = 100)

	1997	1998	1999	2000	2001	2002	2003
Consumer price index	80.3	87.3	92.4	100.0	107.0	114.6	126.4

Gross national product (2003): U.S.$7,285,000,000 (U.S.$2,760 per capita).

Structure of gross domestic product and labour force

	2001		2000	
	in value J$'000,000	% of total value	labour force	% of labour force
Agriculture	22,888	6.8	195,700	17.7
Mining	14,820	4.4	4,600	0.4
Manufacturing	46,554	13.9	69,600	6.3
Construction	34,763	10.4	81,500	7.4
Public utilities	14,125	4.2	6,300	0.6
Transp. and commun.	37,809	11.3	59,400	5.4
Trade	87,879	26.3	206,300	18.7
Pub. admin., defense	40,296	12.0	254,800	23.0
Finance, real estate	43,141	12.9	53,100	4.8
Services	9,673	2.9	2,300	0.2
Other	–17,249[7]	–5.1[7]	171,800[8]	15.5[8]
TOTAL	334,699	100.0	1,105,400	100.0

Public debt (external, outstanding; 2002): U.S.$4,592,000,000.
Household income and expenditure. Average household size (2001) 3.5; average annual income per household (1988) J$8,356 (U.S.$1,525); sources of income (1989): wages and salaries 66.1%, self-employment 19.3%, transfers 14.6%; expenditure (1988)[9]: food and beverages 55.6%, housing 7.9%, fuel and other household supplies 7.4%, health care 7.0%, transportation 6.4%.
Tourism: receipts (2002) U.S.$1,200,000,000; expenditures U.S.$258,000,000.
Land use as % of total land area (2000): in temporary crops 16.1%, in permanent crops 10.2%, in pasture 21.1%; overall forest area 30.0%.

Foreign trade[10]

Balance of trade (current prices)

	1996	1997	1998	1999	2000	2001
U.S.$'000,000	–1,567	–1,838	–1,714	–1,656	–1,907	–2,140
% of total	36.1%	41.6%	40.7%	39.9%	42.4%	46.6%

Imports (2001): U.S.$3,365,000,000 (consumer goods 29.4%, capital goods 16.8%, refined petroleum and other fuels and lubricants 12.4%, crude petroleum 5.0%). *Major import sources* (2001): U.S. 44.8%; Caricom 12.7%; Latin American countries 10.5%; EU 9.3%, of which U.K. 3.0%.
Exports (2001): U.S.$1,225,000,000 (alumina 52.5%, bauxite 7.7%, wearing apparel 7.2%, refined sugar 5.8%, coffee 2.5%, rum 2.4%). *Major export destinations:* U.S. 31.1%; Canada 15.6%; U.K. 12.8%; Norway 7.5%.

Transport and communications

Transport. Railroads (2003): route length 125 mi, 201 km[11]. Roads (1999): total length 11,620 mi, 18,700 km (paved 70%). Vehicles (2000–01): passenger cars 168,179, trucks and buses 62,634. Air transport (2003)[12]: passenger-km 5,005,000,000; metric ton-km cargo 48,859,000; airports (2000) with scheduled flights 4.

Communications

Medium	date	unit	number	units per 1,000 persons
Daily newspapers	2000	circulation	161,000	62
Radio	2000	receivers	2,030,000	784
Television	2000	receivers	502,000	194
Telephones	2002	main lines	444,400	169
Cellular telephones	2002	subscribers	1,400,000	533
Personal computers	2002	units	141,000	54
Internet	2002	users	600,000	228

Education and health

Educational attainment (2001). Percentage of population age 15 and over having: no formal schooling 0.9%; primary education 25.5%; secondary 55.5%; higher 12.3%, of which university 4.2%; other/unknown 5.8%. *Literacy* (2000): total population age 15 and over literate 88%; males 83%; females 91%.

Education (2000–01)

	schools	teachers	students	student/ teacher ratio
Primary (age 6–11)[14]	788[15]	10,215	334,735	32.8
Secondary (age 12–16)	135	9,077	174,094	19.2
Voc., teacher tr.	17	1,083	17,768	16.4
Higher[16]	1	418	8,191	19.6

Health (2000)[17]: physicians 435 (1 per 5,988 persons); hospital beds (2001) 3,795 (1 per 686 persons); infant mortality rate (2003) 13.3.
Food (2002): daily per capita caloric intake 2,685 (vegetable products 85%, animal products 15%); 120% of FAO recommended minimum requirement.

Military

Total active duty personnel (2003): 2,830 (army 88.3%, coast guard 6.7%, air force 5.0%). *Military expenditure as percentage of GNP* (1999): 0.8% (world 2.4%); per capita expenditure U.S.$19.

[1]Jamaica is to become a republic by 2007 per announcement of prime minister in September 2003. [2]Final adjusted figure. [3]The parishes of Kingston and Saint Andrew are jointly administered from the Half Way Tree section of Saint Andrew. [4]Includes numerous denominations. [5]City of Kingston is coextensive with Kingston parish. [6]Includes adjoining rural area of Hellshire per 2001 defined census boundaries. [7]Less imputed service charges. [8]Unemployed. [9]Weights of consumer price index components. [10]Imports c.i.f.; exports f.o.b. [11]Inoperable since 1992 except for 57-mi (92-km) section leased to a mining operator. [12]Air Jamaica only. [13]Includes lower-secondary students at all-age schools. [14]1991–92. [15]1996–97. [16]Public health only.

Internet resources for further information:
- **Statistical Institute of Jamaica http://www.statinja.com/stats.html**
- **Bank of Jamaica http://www.boj.org.jm**

Japan

Official name: Nihon (Japan).
Form of government: constitutional monarchy with a national Diet consisting of two legislative houses (House of Councillors [242]; House of Representatives [480]).
Symbol of state: Emperor.
Head of government: Prime Minister.
Capital: Tokyo.
Official language: Japanese.
Official religion: none.
Monetary unit: 1 yen (¥) = 100 sen; valuation (Sept. 1, 2004) 1 U.S.$ = ¥109.75; 1 £ = ¥197.43.

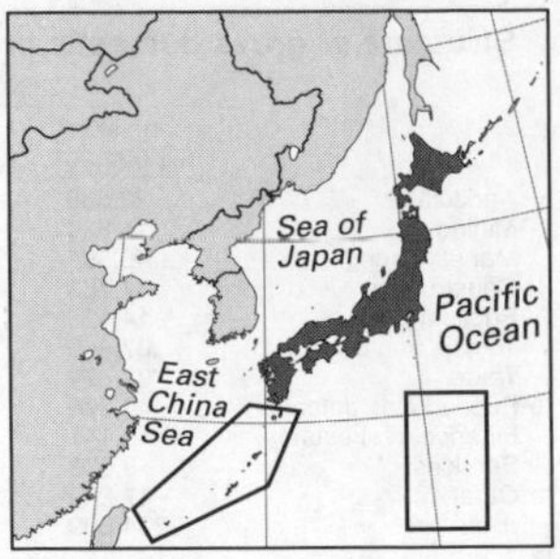

Area and population

Regions / Prefectures	Capitals	area sq mi	area sq km	population 2003 estimate
Chūbu		25,786	66,786	21,748,000
Aichi	Nagoya	1,991	5,156	7,158,000
Fukui	Fukui	1,617	4,189	827,000
Gifu	Gifu	4,092	10,598	2,111,000
Ishikawa	Kanazawa	1,616	4,185	1,180,000
Nagano	Nagano	5,245	13,585	2,215,000
Niigata	Niigata	4,858	12,582	2,460,000
Shizuoka	Shizuoka	3,003	7,779	3,793,000
Toyama	Toyama	1,640	4,247	1,117,000
Yamanashi	Kōfu	1,724	4,465	887,000
Chūgoku		12,322	31,913	7,707,000
Hiroshima	Hiroshima	3,273	8,477	2,878,000
Okayama	Okayama	2,746	7,112	1,953,000
Shimane	Matsue	2,590	6,707	753,000
Tottori	Tottori	1,354	3,507	611,000
Yamaguchi	Yamaguchi	2,359	6,110	1,512,000
Hokkaidō		32,221	83,453	5,659,000
Hokkaidō	Sapporo	32,221	83,453	5,659,000
Kantō		12,518	32,422	41,086,000
Chiba	Chiba	1,991	5,156	6,024,000
Gumma	Maebashi	2,457	6,363	2,034,000
Ibaraki	Mito	2,354	6,096	2,991,000
Kanagawa	Yokohama	932	2,415	8,687,000
Saitama	Saitama	1,466	3,797	7,029,000
Tochigi	Utsunomiya	2,474	6,408	2,011,000
Tokyo-to	Tokyo	844	2,187	12,310,000
Kinki		12,783	33,108	22,762,000
Hyōgo	Kōbe	3,240	8,392	5,585,000
Kyōto-fu	Kyōto	1,781	4,613	2,641,000
Mie	Tsu	2,230	5,776	1,862,000
Nara	Nara	1,425	3,691	1,436,000
Ōsaka-fu	Ōsaka	731	1893	8,816,000
Shiga	Ōtsu	1,551	4,017	1,366,000
Wakayama	Wakayama	1,825	4,726	1,056,000
Kyūshū		17,157	44,436	14,785,000
Fukuoka	Fukuoka	1,919	4,971	5,051,000
Kagoshima	Kagoshima	3,547	9,187	1,775,000
Kumamoto	Kumamoto	2,859	7,404	1,855,000
Miyazaki	Miyazaki	2,986	7,734	1,164,000
Nagasaki	Nagasaki	1,580	4,092	1,501,000
Ōita-ken	Ōita	2,447	6,338	1,218,000
Okinawa	Naha	877	2,271	1,349,000
Saga	Saga	942	2,439	872,000
Shikoku		7,259	18,802	4,127,000
Ehime	Matsuyama	2,192	5,676	1,483,000
Kagawa	Takamatsu	724	1,876	1,020,000
Kōchi	Kōchi	2,743	7,105	807,000
Tokushima	Tokushima	1,600	4,145	817,000
Tohoku		25,825	66,886	9,747,000
Akita	Akita	4,483	11,612	1,167,000
Aomori	Aomori	3,709	9,606	1,462,000
Fukushima	Fukushima	5,321	13,782	2,113,000
Iwate	Morioka	5,899	15,278	1,402,000
Miyagi	Sendai	2,813	7,285	2,373,000
Yamagata	Yamagata	3,600	9,323	1,230,000
TOTAL		145,898[1]	377,873[1]	127,619,000[2]

Demography

Population (2004): 127,757,000.
Density (2004): persons per sq mi 875.6, persons per sq km 338.1.
Urban-rural (2001): urban 78.9%; rural 21.1%.
Sex distribution (2003): male 48.85%; female 51.15%.
Age breakdown (2003): under 15, 14.1%; 15–29, 18.6%; 30–44, 20.3%; 45–59, 21.3%; 60–74, 17.4%; 75 and over, 8.3%.
Population projection: (2010) 127,485,000; (2020) 124,191,000.
Doubling time: not applicable; doubling time exceeds 100 years.
Composition by nationality (2002): Japanese 98.7%; Korean 0.5%; Chinese 0.3%; other 0.5%.
Immigration (2000): permanent immigrants/registered aliens admitted 1,686,444, from North and South Korea 37.7%, Taiwan, Hong Kong, and China 19.9%, Brazil 15.1%, Philippines 8.6%, Peru 2.7%, United States 2.6%, Thailand 1.7%, Indonesia 1.1%, United Kingdom 1.0%, Vietnam 0.6%, Canada 0.6%, India 0.6%, Pakistan 0.4%, other 7.4%.
Major cities (2002): Tokyo 8,025,538; Yokohama 3,433,612; Ōsaka 2,484,326; Nagoya 2,109,681; Sapporo 1,822,992; Kōbe 1,478,380; Kyōto 1,387,264; Fukuoka 1,302,454; Kawasaki 1,245,780; Hiroshima 1,113,786; Saitama[3] 1,029,327; Kita-Kyūshū 999,806; Sendai 986,713.

Other principal cities (2002)

	population		population		population
Akashi	291,649	Kagoshima	544,840	Nishinomiya	436,877
Akita	319,926	Kakogawa	265,393	Ōita	437,699
Amagasaki	463,256	Kanazawa	439,892	Okayama	621,809
Aomori	297,292	Kashiwa	326,097	Okazaki	336,169
Asahikawa	361,372	Kasugai	288,208	Ōtsu	291,322
Chiba	880,164	Kawagoe	325,373	Sagamihara	600,386
Fujisawa	382,038	Kawaguchi	463,879	Sakai	787,833
Fukui	249,656	Kōchi	326,490	Shimonoseki	246,924
Fukushima	288,926	Koriyama	330,776	Shizuoka	468,775
Fukuyama	381,098	Koshigaya	308,413	Suita	342,112
Funabashi	551,918	Kumamoto	653,835	Takamatsu	333,387
Gifu	401,269	Kurashiki	432,938	Takasaki	241,672
Hachinohe	243,880	Machida	384,572	Takatsuki	353,362
Hachiōji	521,359	Maebashi	283,005	Tokorozawa	330,020
Hakodate	284,690	Matsudo	464,224	Tokushima	262,286
Hamamatsu	573,504	Matsuyama	473,039	Toyama	321,049
Higashi-Ōsaka	496,747	Mito	246,095	Toyohashi	356,794
Himeji	475,892	Miyazaki	305,270	Toyonaka	387,869
Hirakata	401,753	Morioka	281,182	Toyota	342,835
Hiratsuka	252,982	Nagano	359,045	Utsunomiya	443,404
Ibaraki	257,577	Nagasaki	419,901	Wakayama	391,008
Ichihara	280,313	Naha	303,146	Yamagata	250,316
Ichikawa	447,686	Nara	364,411	Yao	268,012
Ichinomiya	277,473	Neyagawa	248,464	Yokkaichi	288,319
Iwaki	363,526	Niigata	514,678	Yokosuka	434,613

Religious affiliation (1995): Shintō and related religions 93.1%[4]; Buddhism 69.6%; Christian 1.2%; other 8.1%.
Households (2000). Total households 46,782,000; average household size 2.7; composition of households 1 person 27.6%, 2 persons 25.1%, 3 persons 18.8%, 4 persons 16.9%, 5 persons 6.8%, 6 or more persons 4.8%. Family households 33,769,000 (72.2%); nonfamily 13,013,000 (27.8%).

Type of household (1998)

Total number of occupied dwelling units: 43,922,000

	number of dwellings	percentage of total
by kind of dwelling		
exclusively for living	41,744,000	95.0
mixed use	124,000	0.3
combined with nondwelling	2,054,000	4.7
detached house	23,469,000	56.2
apartment building	16,420,000	39.3
tenement (substandard or overcrowded building)	1,735,000	4.2
other	120,000	0.3
by legal tenure of householder		
owned	26,468,000	60.3
rented	16,730,000	38.1
other	724,000	1.6
by kind of amenities		
flush toilet	36,461	83.0
bathroom	41,919	95.4
by year of construction		
prior to 1945	1,647,000	3.8
1945–70	8,077,000	18.9
1971–80	11,492,000	26.8
1981–90	11,973,000	28.0
1991–98 (Sept.)	9,650,000	22.5

Mobility (2002). Percentage of total population moving: within a prefecture 2.5%; between prefectures 2.1%.

Vital statistics

Birth rate per 1,000 population (2003): 8.9 (world avg. 21.3).
Death rate per 1,000 population (2003): 8.0 (world avg. 9.1).
Natural increase rate per 1,000 population (2003): 0.9 (world avg. 12.2).
Total fertility rate (avg. births per childbearing woman; 2003): 1.3.
Marriage rate per 1,000 population (2003): 5.9; average age at first marriage (2003) men 29.4 years, women 27.4 years.
Divorce rate per 1,000 population (2003): 2.3.
Life expectancy at birth (2003): male 78.4 years; female 85.3 years.
Major causes of death per 100,000 population (2001): circulatory diseases 329.2, of which cerebrovascular disease 103.6; malignant neoplasms (cancers) 236.2; pneumonia and bronchitis 78.8; accidents and adverse effects 63.8, of which suicide 23.1; nephritis, nephrotic syndrome, and nephrosis 13.9; cirrhosis of the liver 12.5; diabetes mellitus 9.5.

Social indicators

Educational attainment (1998). Percentage of population ages 25–64 having: no formal schooling through complete primary education 2.4%; incomplete through complete secondary 79.9%; postsecondary 17.7%.

Distribution of income (2000)

percentage of average household income by quintile

1	2	3	4	5 (highest)
11.2	15.3	18.7	23.0	31.7

Quality of working life. Average hours worked per month (2002): 153.1. Annual rate of industrial deaths per 100,000 workers (2001): 2.7. Proportion of labour force insured for damages or income loss resulting from injury, permanent disability, and death (2001): 65.4%. Average man-days lost to labour stoppages per 1,000,000 workdays (1998): 6.8. Average duration of journey to work (1996): 19.0 minutes. Rate per 1,000 workers of discouraged workers (unemployed no longer seeking work: 1997): 89.4.

Access to services (1989). Proportion of households having access to: gas supply 64.6%; safe public water supply 94.0%; public sewage collection 89.4%.
Social participation. Eligible voters participating in last national election (November 2003): 52%. Population 15 years and over participating in social-service activities on a voluntary basis (1991): 26.3%. Trade union membership in total workforce (2002): 20.2%.
Social deviance (2001). Offense rate per 100,000 population for: homicide 0.6; robbery 1.2; larceny and theft 14.2. Incidence in general population of: alcoholism per 100,000 population, n.a.; drug and substance abuse 0.1. Rate of suicide per 100,000 population: 23.1.

Leisure/use of personal time

Discretionary daily activities (1996)
(Population age 10 years and over)

	weekly average hrs./min.
Total discretionary daily time	6:12
of which	
Hobbies and amusements	0:36
Sports	0:13
Learning (except schoolwork)	0:12
Social activities	0:04
Associations	0:27
Radio, television, newspapers, and magazines	2:59
Rest and relaxation	1:15
Other activities	0:20

Major leisure activities (1996)
(Population age 15 years and over)

	percentage of participation		
	male	female	total
Sports	81.7	70.5	76.1
Light gymnastics	25.9	30.6	28.3
Swimming	24.6	20.9	22.8
Bowling	33.7	24.6	29.2
Learning (except schoolwork)	30.7	30.6	30.6
Travel (1991)			
Domestic	72.7	68.3	70.4
Foreign	10.4	7.6	9.0

Material well-being (2001). Households possessing: automobile 84.4%; telephone, virtually 100%; colour television receiver 99.3%; refrigerator 98.4%; air conditioner 87.2%; washing machine 99.3%; vacuum cleaner 98.2%; videocassette recorder 79.6%; camera 86.8%; microwave oven 96.2%; compact disc player 60.5%; personal computer 57.2%; cellular phone 78.6%.

National economy

Gross national product (at current market prices; 2003): U.S.$4,389,791,000,000 (U.S.$34,510 per capita).

Structure of gross domestic product and labour force

	2001		2002	
	in value ¥'000,000,000	% of total value	labour force	% of labour force
Agriculture, fishing	6,973.0	1.4	2,960,000	4.4
Mining	662.6	0.1	50,000	0.1
Manufacturing	104,230.8	20.5	12,220,000	18.3
Construction	35,762.3	7.0	6,180,000	9.2
Public utilities	14,494.8	2.9	340,000	0.5
Transportation and communications	32,161.5	6.3	4,010,000	6.0
Trade	70,524.6	13.9	14,380,000	21.5
Finance	101,020.7	19.9	2,410,000	3.6
Pub. admin., defense	47,122.2	9.3	20,750,000	31.0
Services	110,702.5	21.8		
Other	−16,199.6[5]	−3.2[5]	3,590,000[6]	5.4[6]
TOTAL	507,455.4	100.0[2]	66,890,000	100.0

Budget (2002–03). Revenue: ¥81,230,000,000,000 (government bonds 36.9%; income tax 19.5%; corporation tax 13.8%; value-added tax 12.1%; stamp and customs duties 3.9%). Expenditures: ¥81,230,000,000,000 (social security 22.5%; debt service 20.5%; public works 10.3%; national defense 6.1%).
Public debt (March 2004): U.S.$6,740,000,000,000.

Financial aggregates

	1997	1998	1999	2000	2001	2002	2003
Exchange rate[7], ¥ per:							
U.S. dollar	129.95	115.60	102.20	114.90	131.80	119.90	107.10
£	214.11	192.30	165.20	171.45	191.16	193.25	191.14
SDR	175.34	162.77	140.27	149.70	165.64	163.01	159.15
International reserves (U.S.$)							
Total (excl. gold; '000,000)	219,648	215,471	286,916	354,902	395,155	461,186	663,289
SDRs ('000,000)	2,638	2,663	2,656	2,437	2,377	2,524	2,766
Reserve pos. in IMF ('000,000)	9,144	9,593	6,552	5,253	5,051	7,203	7,733
Foreign exchange ('000,000)	207,866	203,215	277,708	347,212	387,727	451,458	652,790
Gold ('000,000 fine troy oz)	24.23	24.23	24.23	24.55	24.60	24.60	24.60
% world reserves	2.7	2.5	2.6	2.6	2.6	2.6	2.7
Interest and prices							
Central bank discount (%)[7]	0.50	0.50	0.50	0.50	0.10	0.10	0.10
Govt. bond yield (%)	1.69	1.10	1.77	1.75	1.33	1.25	1.01
Industrial share prices (2000 = 100)	90.2	76.2	89.6	100.0	77.3	62.7	59.4
Balance of payments (U.S.$'000,000,000)							
Balance of visible trade	+101.60	+122.39	+123.32	+116.72	+70.21	+93.83	+106.40
Imports, f.o.b.	307.64	251.66	280.37	342.80	313.38	301.75	342.72
Exports, f.o.b.	409.24	374.04	403.69	459.51	383.59	395.58	449.12
Balance of invisibles	−7.25	−1.69	−16.45	+0.16	+19.07	+18.62	+29.82
Balance of payments, current account	+94.35	+120.70	+106.87	+116.88	+89.28	+112.45	+136.22

Manufacturing and mining enterprises (2002)

	no. of establishments	avg. no. of persons engaged	annual wages as a % of avg. of all mfg. wages	annual value added (¥'000,000,000)
Electrical machinery	42,164	1,829,000	112.1	13,293
Food, beverages, and tobacco	66,507	1,488,000	70.1	7,888
Transport equipment	25,756	1,026,000	125.3	9,174
Chemical products	9,099	495,000	136.6	8,479
Nonelectrical machinery	73,782	1,168,000	112.9	7,176
Fabricated metal products	81,544	856,000	93.3	5,920
Printing and publishing	57,364	697,000	120.9	5,598
Ceramic, stone, and clay	28,148	413,000	104.6	2,702
Plastic products	28,120	472,000	90.7	4,265
Iron and steel	7,662	264,000	117.0	2,297
Paper and paper products	15,271	286,000	103.9	1,930
Apparel products	51,078	487,000	51.5	1,612
Precision instruments	11,793	250,000	103.4	2,426
Nonferrous metal products	5,830	181,000	111.6	1,380
Rubber products	7,798	161,000	85.1	1,560
Textiles	35,611	246,000	85.3	1,303
Furniture and fixtures	33,349	220,000	76.8	1,395
Lumber and wood products	22,055	192,000	82.7	900
Petroleum and coal products	1,379	38,000	161.9	883
Leather products	9,871	65,000	65.2	312
Mining and quarrying	3,764	47,000	101.3	839

Energy production (consumption): electricity (kW-hr; 2000) 1,091,499,000,000 (1,091,499,000,000); coal (metric tons; 2000) 3,127,000 (147,891,000); crude petroleum (barrels; 2000) 2,500,000 (1,535,900,000); petroleum products (metric tons; 2000) 182,429,000, of which (by volume [1998]) diesel 32.8%, heavy fuel oil 21.7%, gasoline 21.7%, kerosene and jet fuel 12.0% (190,196,000); natural gas (cu m; 2000) 2,452,600,000 (73,485,300,000). Composition of energy supply by source (1998): crude oil and petroleum products 50.9%, coal 17.0%, nuclear power 14.2%, natural gas 12.8%, hydroelectric power 4.1%, other 1.0%. Domestic energy demand by end use (1998): mining and manufacturing 46.3%, residential and commercial 26.3%, transportation 25.2%, other 2.2%.
Population economically active (2002): total 66,890,000; activity rate of total population 52.5% (participation rates: age 15 and over, 63.9%; female 40.9%; unemployed 5.4%).

Price and earnings indexes (2000 = 100)

	1997	1998	1999	2000	2001	2002	2003
Consumer price index	100.4	101.0	100.7	100.0	99.3	98.4	98.1
Monthly earnings index	99.8	99.5	99.8	100.0	99.5	97.9	97.9

Household income and expenditure (2002). Average household size 2.7; average annual income per household ¥6,338,000 (U.S.$51,400); sources of income (1994): wages and salaries 59.0%, transfer payments 20.5%, self-employment 12.8%, other 7.3%; expenditure (2002): food 23.3%, transportation and communications 12.0%, recreation 10.1%, fuel, light, and water charges 6.9%, housing 6.5%, clothing and footwear 4.7%, education 4.2%, medical care 3.8%, furniture and household utensils 3.4%.
Tourism (2002): receipts from visitors U.S.$3,499,000,000; expenditures by nationals abroad U.S.$26,681,000,000.

Retail and wholesale trade and services (2002)

	no. of establishments	avg. no. of employees	annual sales (¥'000,000,000)
Retail trade	1,300,043	7,974,000	135,125
Food and beverages	466,590	3,162,000	41,238
Grocery	36,469	755,000	15,080
Liquors	65,098	194,000	3,785
General merchandise	4,995	542,000	17,318
Department stores	2,029	523,000	16,938
Motor vehicles and bicycles	89,091	556,000	16,217
Furniture and home furnishings	120,743	535,000	11,884
Apparel and accessories	185,939	720,000	10,980
Gasoline service stations	65,261	425,000	11,137
Books and stationery	59,327	703,000	4,839
Wholesale trade	379,547	4,004,000	413,547
Machinery and equipment	97,730	1,167,000	146,500
Motor vehicles and parts	18,218	189,000	16,487
General machinery except electrical	34,970	334,000	24,277
General merchandise	1,156	40,000	48,129
Farm, livestock, and fishery products	38,300	413,000	40,267
Food and beverages	83,597	919,000	43,983
Minerals and metals	17,106	202,000	43,859
Building materials	86,803	767,000	91,132
Textiles, apparel, and accessories	31,281	328,000	20,889
Chemicals	16,006	168,000	21,266
Drugs and toilet goods	18,730	247,000	21,575

Production (metric tons except as noted). Agriculture, forestry, fishing (2002): rice 11,111,000, sugar beets 4,098,000, potatoes 2,980,000, cabbages 2,500,000, sugarcane 1,400,000, onions 1,270,000, sweet potatoes 1,030,000, apples 911,000, wheat 827,800, tomatoes 800,000, cucumbers 740,000, carrots 700,000, watermelons 570,000, lettuce 560,000, eggplant 450,000, pears 375,500, spinach 320,000, cantaloupes 305,000, soybeans 270,200, persimmons 269,300, grapes 231,700, pumpkins 220,000, taro 218,000, barley 217,000, strawberries 210,000, yams 200,000, peaches 175,100, peppers 171,000, cauliflower 115,000, plums 112,700; livestock (number of live animals) 9,612,000 pigs, 4,564,000 cattle, 283,102,000 chickens; roundwood (2001) 16,236,538 cu m; fish catch (2000) 5,752,178, of which squid 671,100, scallops 515,000, cod 398,900, crabs 42,000. Mining and quarrying (2001):

limestone 182,255,000; silica stone 14,213,000; dolomite 3,389,000; pyrophyllite 403,000; zinc 44,519; lead 4,997; copper 744; silver 80,397 kg; gold 7,815 kg. Manufacturing (2001): crude steel 102,866,000; steel products 78,927,000; pig iron 78,836,000; cement 76,550,000; sulfuric acid 6,727,000; plastic products 6,300,000; fertilizers 4,200,000; newsprint 3,210,000; cotton fabrics 710,000,000 sq m; synthetic fabrics 1,920,000 sq m; finished products (in number of units) 420,000,000 watches and clocks, 51,062,000 industrial robots, 46,072,000 cellular phones, 12,421,000 air conditioners, 11,350,000 computers, 9,777,000 passenger cars, 9,112,000 cameras, 8,993,000 video cameras, 5,446,000 vacuum cleaners, 4,184,000 bicycles, 4,059,000 automatic washing machines, 3,875,000 electric refrigerators, 3,130,000 colour television receivers, 2,675,000 microwave ovens, 2,398,000 photocopy machines, 2,328,000 motorcycles, 1,916,000 facsimile machines, 1,185,000 videocassette recorders. Construction (value in ¥'000,000; 2001): residential 42,700,000; nonresidential 28,271,000.

Land use as % of total land area (2000): in temporary crops 12.3%, in permanent crops 1.0%, in pasture 1.1%; overall forest area 64.0%.

Foreign trade[8]

Balance of trade (current prices)

	1997	1998	1999	2000	2001	2002
¥'000,000,000	+9,982	+13,991	+12,279	+10,716	+6,564	+9,931
% of total	10.9%	16.0%	14.8%	11.6%	7.2%	10.5%

Imports (2001): ¥42,415,500,000,000 (machinery and apparatus 28.5%, of which computers and office machinery 6.5%; crude and refined petroleum 13.3%; food products 12.4%, chemicals and chemical products 7.3%, apparel and clothing accessories 5.5%). *Major import sources:* U.S. 18.1%; China 16.6%; South Korea 4.9%; Indonesia 4.3%; Australia 4.1%; Taiwan 4.1%; Malaysia 3.7%; U.A.E. 3.7%; Germany 3.6%; Saudi Arabia 3.5%.

Exports (2001): ¥48,979,200,000,000 (machinery and apparatus 44.4%, of which electronic microcircuits 7.4%, computers and office machinery 5.8%; road vehicles and parts 18.6%; base and fabricated metals 5.9%; precision instruments 5.4%). *Major export destinations:* U.S. 30.0%; China 7.7%; South Korea 6.3%; Taiwan 6.0%; Hong Kong 5.8%; Germany 3.9%; Singapore 3.6%; U.K. 3.0%; Thailand 2.9%; The Netherlands 2.8%.

Trade by commodity group (2001)

	imports		exports	
SITC group	U.S.$'000,000	%	U.S.$'000,000	%
00 Food and live animals	38,583	11.0	2,608	0.6
01 Beverages and tobacco	4,479	1.3		
02 Crude materials, excluding fuels	22,485[9]	6.4[9]	3,349[9]	0.8[9]
03 Mineral fuels, lubricants, and related materials	70,424	20.2	...	...
04 Animal and vegetable oils, fats, and waxes	9	9	9	9
05 Chemicals and related products, n.e.s.	24,961	7.2	29,662	7.4
06 Basic manufactures	25,872	7.4	44,825	11.1
07 Machinery and transport equipment	95,143	27.2	269,888	66.9
08 Miscellaneous manufactured articles	54,905	15.7	36,226	9.0
09 Goods not classified by kind	12,448	3.6	16,806	4.2
TOTAL	349,300	100.0	403,364	100.0

Direction of trade (2001)

	imports		exports	
	U.S.$'000,000	%	U.S.$'000,000	%
Africa	4,931	1.4	4,311	1.1
Asia	192,798	55.2	174,136	43.2
South America	9,119	2.6	4,891	1.2
North America and Central America	71,584	20.5	140,641	34.9
United States	63,758	18.3	122,549	30.4
other North and Central America	7,826	2.2	18,092	4.5
Europe	53,659	15.4	69,037	17.1
EU	44,594	12.8	64,469	16.0
Russia	4,062	1.2	1,439	0.4
other Europe	5,003	1.4	3,129	0.7
Oceania	17,209	4.9	10,348	2.6
TOTAL	349,300	100.0	403,364	100.0[2]

Transport and communications

Transport. Railroads (2001): length 14,698 mi, 23,654 km; rolling stock—(1995) locomotives 1,787, (1995) passenger cars 25,973, (1995) freight cars 12,688; passengers carried 21,700,000,000; passenger-mi 239,489,000,000, passenger-km 385,421,000,000; short ton-mi cargo 15,200,000,000, metric ton-km cargo 22,193,000,000. Roads (2002): total length 765,600 mi, 1,232,000 km (paved 82%). Vehicles (2002): passenger cars 42,655,000; trucks and buses 18,200,000. Merchant marine (2001): vessels (100 gross tons and over) 7,924; total deadweight tonnage 16,653,000. Air transport (2000): passengers carried 205,106,000; passenger-mi 159,337,000,000, passenger-km 256,428,000,000; short ton-mi cargo 6,712,000,000, metric ton-km cargo 9,800,000,000; airports (1996) with scheduled flights 73.

Urban transport (2000)[10]: passengers carried 57,719,000, of which by rail 34,020,000, by road 19,466,000, by subway 4,233,000.

Distribution of traffic (2001)

	cargo carried ('000,000 tons)	% of national total	passengers carried ('000,000)	% of national total
Road	5,578	90.6	64,590	74.7
Rail (intercity)	59	1.0	21,720	25.1
Inland water	520	8.4	112	0.1
Air	1	0.0	95	0.1
TOTAL	6,158	100.0	86,517	100.0

Communications

Medium	date	unit	number	units per 1,000 persons
Daily newspapers	2000	circulation	73,300,000	578
Radio	2000	receivers	121,000,000	956
Television	2002	receivers	99,852,000	785
Telephones	2002	main lines	71,149,000	558
Cellular telephones	2003	subscribers	86,659,000	680
Personal computers	2002	units	48,700,000	383
Internet	2002	users	57,200,000	449

Radio and television broadcasting (2001): total radio stations 1,586, of which commercial 707; total television stations 15,088, of which commercial 8,299. Commercial broadcasting hours (by percentage of programs; 2001): reports—radio 12.6%, television 21.4%; education—radio 2.4%, television 12.1%; culture—radio 13.5%, television 24.8%; entertainment—radio 69.0%, television 39.2%. Advertisements (daily average; 2001): radio 158, television 431.

Other communications media (2001)

	titles
Print	
Books (new)	71,073
of which	
Social sciences	14,648
Fiction	12,119
Arts	10,199
Engineering	7,709
Natural sciences	5,385
History	5,148
Philosophy	2,967
Magazines/journals	4,447
Weekly	145
Monthly	2,793

	titles
Cinema	
Feature films	640
Domestic	293
Foreign	347
	traffic ('000)
Post	
Postal offices	24,773
Mail	26,216,000
Domestic	25,578,000
International	638,000
Parcels	411,000,000
Domestic	387,000,000
International	24,000,000

Education and health

Literacy: total population age 15 and over literate, virtually 100%.

Education (2002)

	schools	teachers	students	student/ teacher ratio
Primary (age 6–11)	23,316	410,505	7,239,000	17.6
Secondary (age 12–17)	16,427	516,325	7,792,000	15.1
Higher	1,289	174,006	3,110,349	17.9

Health (2002): physicians 260,500 (1 per 489 persons); dentists 91,783 (1 per 1,388 persons); nurses 1,096,967 (1 per 116 persons); pharmacists 212,720 (1 per 583 persons); midwives (2000) 24,511 (1 per 5,176 persons); hospital beds 1,642,593 (1 per 78 persons); infant mortality rate per 1,000 live births (2003) 3.0.

Food (2001): daily per capita caloric intake 2,768 (vegetable products 79%, animal products 21%); 118% of FAO recommended minimum requirement.

Military

Total active duty personnel (2003): 239,900 (army 61.8%, navy 18.5%, air force 19.0%); U.S. troops (August 2004) 40,000. *Military expenditure as percentage of GNP* (1999): 1.0% (world 2.4%); per capita expenditure U.S.$342.

[1]Regional prefecture areas do not sum to total given because of particular excluded inland water areas; total area per more recent 2002 survey equals 145,903 sq mi (377,887 sq km). [2]Detail does not add to total given because of rounding. [3]Saitama was created in 2001 with the merger of the cities of Urawa, Omiya, and Yono. [4]Many Japanese practice both Shintōism and Buddhism. [5]Import duties and statistical discrepancy less imputed bank service charge. [6]Unemployed. [7]End of period. [8]Imports c.i.f.; exports f.o.b. [9]Crude materials includes Animal and vegetable oils, fats, and waxes. [10]Tokyo, Nagoya, and Ōsaka metropolis traffic range only.

Internet resources for further information:

- **Bank of Japan http://www.boj.or.jp/en/index.htm**
- **Statistics Bureau and Statistics Center (Japan) http://www.stat.go.jp/english/index.htm**

Jersey

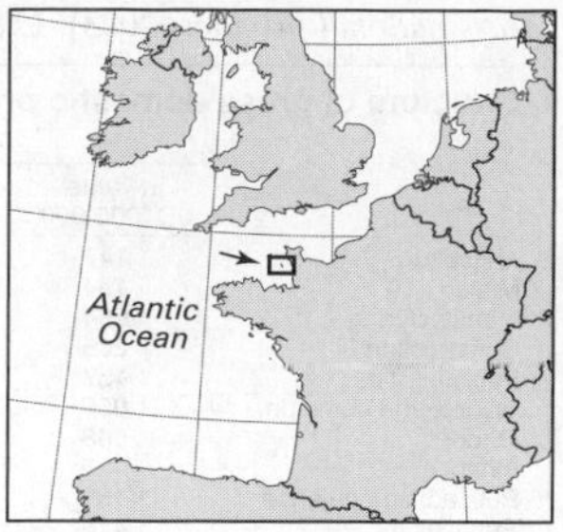

Official name: Bailiwick of Jersey.
Political status: crown dependency (United Kingdom) with one legislative house (States of Jersey [58][1]).
Chief of state: British Monarch represented by Lieutenant Governor.
Head of government: [2].
Capital: Saint Helier.
Official language: English[3].
Official religion: none.
Monetary unit: 1 Jersey pound (£J) = 100 pence; valuation (Sept. 1, 2004) 1 Jersey pound = U.S.$1.80; at par with the British pound.

Area and population

Parishes	area sq mi	area sq km	population 2001 census
Grouville	3.0	7.8	4,702
St. Brelade	4.9	12.8	10,134
St. Clement	1.6	4.2	8,196
St. Helier	4.1	10.6	28,310
St. John	3.4	8.7	2,618
St. Lawrence	3.7	9.5	4,702
St. Martin	3.8	9.9	3,628
St. Mary	2.5	6.5	1,591
St. Ouen	5.8	15.0	3,803
St. Peter	4.5	11.6	4,293
St. Saviour	3.6	9.3	12,491
Trinity	4.7	12.3	2,718
TOTAL	45.6	118.2	87,186

Demography

Population (2004): 87,900.
Density (2004): persons per sq mi 1,927.6, persons per sq km 743.7.
Urban-rural (2001)[4]: urban 28.9%, rural 71.1%.
Sex distribution (2001): male 48.73%; female 51.27%.
Age breakdown (2001): under 15, 16.9%; 15–29, 18.4%; 30–44, 25.9%; 45–59, 19.7%; 60–74, 12.6%; 75 and over, 6.5%.
Population projection: (2010) 89,000; (2020) 89,000.
Population by place of birth (2001): Jersey 52.6%; United Kingdom, Guernsey, or Isle of Man 35.8%; Portugal 5.9%; France 1.2%; other 4.5%.
Religious affiliation (2000)[4]: Christian 86.0%, of which Anglican 44.1%, Roman Catholic 14.6%, other Protestant 6.9%, unaffiliated Christian 20.1%; nonreligious/atheist 13.4%; other 0.6%.
Major cities (2001)[5]: St. Helier 28,310; St. Saviour 12,491; St. Brelade 10,134.

Vital statistics

Birth rate per 1,000 population (2003): 10.4 (world avg. 21.3).
Death rate per 1,000 population (2003): 9.2 (world avg. 9.1).
Natural increase rate per 1,000 population (2003): 1.2 (world avg. 12.2).
Total fertility rate (avg. births per childbearing woman; 2003): 1.6.
Marriage rate per 1,000 population (2001): 7.6.
Divorce rate per 1,000 population (2001): 3.2.
Life expectancy at birth (2003): male 76.5 years; female 81.6 years.
Major causes of death per 100,000 population (2000): diseases of the circulatory system *c.* 328, malignant neoplasms (cancers) *c.* 255, diseases of the respiratory system *c.* 136, accidents and violence *c.* 35, diseases of the digestive system *c.* 35.

National economy

Budget (2001). Revenue: £400,085,000 (income tax 86.8%, import duties 8.7%, interest payment 1.5%, other 3.0%). Expenditures: £369,138,000 (current expenditure 79.3%, of which health 25.7%, education 19.0%, social security 18.2%, public services 5.1%; capital expenditure 20.7%).
Production. Agriculture, forestry, fishing: fruits and vegetables, mostly potatoes and greenhouse tomatoes; greenhouse flowers are important export crops; livestock (number of live animals; 2001) 4,552 mature dairy cattle; roundwood, none; fish catch (value of catch in £'000; 2002): 6,053, of which crustaceans (including lobsters and crabs) 3,695, scallops 758, marine fish 713, oysters 607. Mining and quarrying: n.a. Manufacturing: light industry, mainly electrical goods, textiles and clothing. Energy production (consumption): electricity (kW-hr; 2001) 153,000,000 (567,000,000); crude petroleum, none (n.a.); petroleum products, n.a. (n.a.); natural gas, none (n.a.).
Gross national product (at current market prices; 2003): U.S.$4,805,000,000 (U.S.$54,810 per capita).

Structure of gross domestic product and labour force

	2003 in value £J '000,000	% of total value	labour force	% of labour force
Agriculture, fishing	49	1.6	2,140	4.6
Mining	...	... }	4,690	10.1
Construction	163	5.2 }		
Manufacturing	66	2.1	2,120	4.5
Public utilities	36	1.1	540	1.2
Transp. and commun.	130	4.2	1,450	3.1
Trade, hotels, restaurants	321	10.3	14,690	31.5
Finance, real estate[6]	2,143	68.4	12,090	25.9
Pub. admin., defense	222	7.1 }	8,900	19.2
Services	...	... }		
TOTAL	3,131[7, 8]	100.0	46,620	100.0[7]

Household income and expenditure. Average household size (2001) 2.4; average annual income of workers (2001) £22,700 (U.S.$35,200); sources of income: n.a.; expenditure (1998–99)[9]: housing 20.1%, recreation 16.5%, transportation 12.8%, household furnishings 11.6%, food 11.5%, alcoholic beverages 6.0%, clothing and footwear 5.5%.
Population economically active (2003): total 46,620; activity rate of total population 53.2% (participation rates [2001]: ages 15–64, 81.7%; female 45.5%; unemployed [June 2004] 0.9%).

Price index (2000 = 100)[10]

	1998	1999	2000	2001	2002	2003	2004
Consumer price index	92.9	96.2	100.0	103.9	108.3	112.9	118.3

Public debt: none.
Tourism (1996): receipts U.S.$429,000,000; expenditures by nationals abroad, n.a.; number of visitors for at least one night (2001) 470,000.
Land use as % of total land area (1997): in temporary and permanent crops *c.* 29%, in pasture *c.* 22%; overall forest area *c.* 6%.

Foreign trade

Imports: [11]. *Major import sources* (2001): mostly the United Kingdom.
Exports: [11]; agricultural and marine exports (2001): £40,626,000 (potatoes 67.4%, greenhouse tomatoes 19.1%, flowers 3.3%, zucchini 3.0%, crustaceans 2.0%, mollusks 2.0%). *Major export destinations:* mostly the United Kingdom.

Transport and communications

Transport. Railroads: none. Roads (1995): total length 346 mi, 557 km (paved 100%). Vehicles (2002): passenger cars 74,007; trucks and buses 12,957. Air transport (1999)[12]: passenger-mi 553,291,000, passenger-km 890,438,000; short ton-mi cargo 632,000, metric ton-km cargo 923,000; airports (2002) with scheduled flights 1.

Communications

Medium	date	unit	number	units per 1,000 persons
Daily newspapers	2002	circulation	22,897	262
Telephones	2002	main lines	74,300	851
Cellular telephones	2002	subscribers	72,000	824
Internet	2001	users	8,000	92

Education and health

Educational attainment (2001). Percentage of male population (16–64), female population (16–59) having: no formal degree 34.1%; primary education, n.a.; secondary, n.a.; undergraduate 7.1%; graduate (advanced degree) 4.1%.
Literacy (2002): 100.0%.

Education (2002)

	schools	teachers	students	student/ teacher ratio
Primary (age 5–10)	21	...	7,386	...
Secondary (age 11–16)	10	...	5,715	...
Voc., teacher tr.	...	...	...	...
Higher[13]	1	...	582	...

Health: physicians (2001) 174 (1 per 500 persons); hospital beds (1995) 651 (1 per 130 persons); infant mortality rate per 1,000 live births (2003) 5.4.
Food: daily per capita caloric intake, n.a.

Military

Total active duty personnel (2003): none; defense is the responsibility of the United Kingdom.

[1]Includes 53 elected officials and 5 ex officio members with limited legislative rights. [2]Executive committees appointed by the States of Jersey (alternately called States Assembly). [3]Until the 1960s French was an official language of Jersey and is still used by the court and legal professions; Jerriais, a Norman-French dialect, is spoken by a small number of residents. [4]Includes Guernsey. [5]Population of parishes. [6]Jersey is an international finance centre with 59 banks in 2002 and 2,829 registered companies; more than U.S.$209,000,000,000 is deposited in the island. [7]Detail does not add to total given because of rounding. [8]A second measurement of GDP for 2003 equals £J 2,610,000,000. [9]Weights of retail price index components. [10]June. [11]Customs ceased recording imports and exports as of 1980. [12]Jersey European Airways. [13]2001; Highlands College.

Internet resources for further information:
- **States of Jersey**
  http://www.gov.je

Jordan

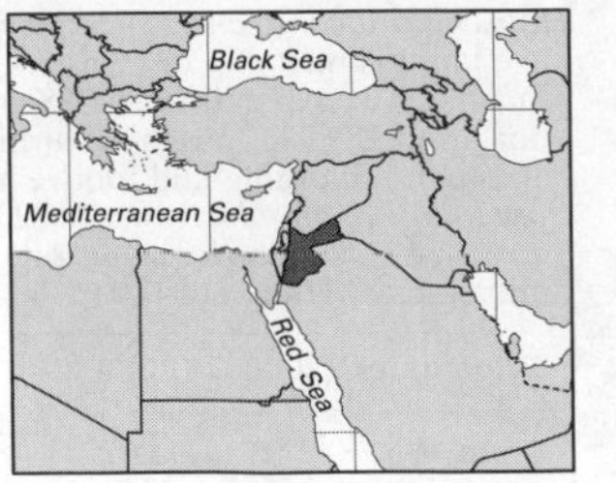

Official name: Al-Mamlakah al-Urdunnīyah al-Hāshimīyah (Al-Urdun) (Hashemite Kingdom of Jordan).
Form of government: constitutional monarchy with two legislative houses (Senate [55[1]]; House of Representatives [110]).
Head of state and government: King assisted by Prime Minister.
Capital: Amman.
Official language: Arabic.
Official religion: Islam.
Monetary unit: 1 Jordan dinar (JD) = 1,000 fils; valuation (Sept. 1, 2004) JD 1.00 = U.S.$1.41 = £0.78.

Area and population

		area		population
Governorates	**Capitals**	sq mi	sq km	2004[2] estimate
ʿAjlūn	ʿAjlūn	159	412	121,700
ʿAmman	Amman	3,178	8,231	2,085,100
Al-ʿAqabah	Al-ʿAqabah	2,542	6,583	110,200
Al-Balqāʾ	Aṣ-Ṣalt	415	1,076	359,500
Irbid	Irbid	626	1,621	977,600
Jarash	Jarash	155	402	161,100
Al-Karak	Al-Karak	1,242	3,217	220,300
Maʿān	Maʿān	12,804	33,163	106,700
Mādabā	Mādabā	775	2,008	139,700
Al-Mafraq	Al-Mafraq	10,207	26,435	252,600
Aṭ-Ṭafīlah	Aṭ-Ṭafīlah	816	2,114	83,300
Az-Zarqāʾ	Az-Zarqāʾ	1,575	4,080	862,000
TOTAL		34,495[3]	89,342	5,479,800

Demography

Population (2004): 5,543,000.
Density (2004): persons per sq mi 160.7, persons per sq km 62.0.
Urban-rural (2003): urban 78.7%; rural 21.3%.
Sex distribution (2003): male 52.30%; female 47.70%.
Age breakdown (2002): under 15, 36.6%; 15–29, 30.4%; 30–44, 19.8%; 45–59, 8.0%; 60–74, 4.3%; 75 and over, 0.9%.
Population projection: (2010) 6,304,000; (2020) 7,464,000.
Doubling time: 29 years.
Ethnic composition (2000): Arab 97.8%, of which Jordanian 32.4%, Palestinian 32.2%, Iraqi 14.0%, Bedouin 12.8%; Circassian 1.2%; other 1.0%.
Religious affiliation (2000): Sunnī Muslim 93.5%; Christian 4.1%; other 2.4%.
Major cities (1994): Amman 969,598; Az-Zarqāʾ 350,849; Irbid 208,329; Ar-Ruṣayfah 137,247; Wādi Essier 89,104; Al-ʿAqabah 62,773.

Vital statistics

Birth rate per 1,000 population (2003): 27.4 (world avg. 21.3).
Death rate per 1,000 population (2003): 3.1 (world avg. 9.1).
Natural increase rate per 1,000 population (2003): 24.3 (world avg. 12.2).
Total fertility rate (avg. births per childbearing woman; 2003): 3.7.
Marriage rate per 1,000 population (2003): 9.0.
Divorce rate per 1,000 population (2003): 1.7.
Life expectancy at birth (2003): male 70.6 years; female 72.4 years.
Major causes of death per 100,000 population: n.a.

National economy

Budget (2003). Revenue: JD 2,511,000,000 (tax revenue 43.1%, of which sales tax 23.7%, custom duties 8.0%, income and profits taxes 7.8%; nontax revenue 32.9%, of which licenses and fees 11.2%; foreign grants 24.0%). Expenditures: JD 2,678,000,000 (current expenditure 76.8%, of which defense 23.5%, social security and other transfers 21.7%, wages 15.6%, interest payments 10.1%; capital expenditure 23.2%).
Public debt (external, outstanding; 2002): U.S.$7,076,000,000.
Production (metric tons except as noted). Agriculture, forestry, fishing (2002): tomatoes 359,830, olives 180,900, cucumbers 150,000, citrus fruits 121,900, potatoes 105,330, watermelons 71,780, zucchini (2001) 57,500, barley 56,700, bananas 47,400, apples 39,230, grapes 34,770; livestock (number of live animals) 1,457,910 sheep, 557,260 goats; roundwood (2001) 233,544 cu m; fish catch (2001) 1,060. Mining and quarrying (2002): phosphate ore 7,107,200; potash 1,956,200. Manufacturing (value added in U.S.$'000,000; 2000): chemicals and chemical products 236; tobacco products 184; bricks, cement, ceramics 168; food products 132; refined petroleum 90; beverages 82. Energy production (consumption): electricity (kW-hr; 2003) 7,341,000,000 (7,341,-000,000); crude petroleum (barrels; 2002) 14,600 ([2000] 27,789,000); petroleum products (metric tons; 2002) 3,627,000 ([2000] 4,481,000); natural gas (cu m; 2002) 269,000,000 ([2000] 283,000,000).
Land use as % of total land area (2000): in temporary crops 2.7%, in permanent crops 1.8%, in pasture 8.9%; overall forest area 1.0%.
Tourism (2002): receipts U.S.$786,000,000; expenditures U.S.$416,000,000.
Population economically active (2001): total 1,293,000; activity rate of total population 23.6% (participation rates: over age 15, 40.2%; female 14.9%; unemployed 14.5%).

Price and earnings indexes (2000 = 100)

	1997	1998	1999	2000	2001	2002	2003
Consumer price index	95.8	98.7	99.3	100.0	101.8	103.6	106.1
Daily earnings index	...	...	...	...	...	...	...

Gross national product (2003): U.S.$9,800,000,000 (U.S.$1,850 per capita).

Structure of gross domestic product and labour force

	2003		2001	
	in value JD '000,000	% of total value	labour force	% of labour force
Agriculture	147	2.1	53,000	4.1
Mining	194	2.8	182,000 (Mining and Manufacturing)	14.1
Manufacturing	954	13.6		
Construction	265	3.8	88,000	6.8
Public utilities	157	2.2	19,000	1.5
Transp. and commun.	1,050	15.0	129,000	10.0
Trade[4]	668	9.6	265,000	20.5
Finance	[5]	[5]	75,000	5.8
Pub. admin., defense	1,161	16.6	482,000 (Pub. admin., defense; Services; Other)	37.2
Services	1,478[5]	21.1[5]		
Other	917[6]	13.1[6]		
TOTAL	6,991	100.0[3]	1,293,000	100.0

Household income and expenditure. Average household size (2003) 5.7; income per household (1997) JD 5,464 (U.S.$7,700); sources of income (1997): wages and salaries 52.4%, rent and property income 24.5%, transfer payments 12.8%, self-employment 10.3%; expenditure (1997): food and beverages 44.3%, housing and energy 23.5%, transportation 8.2%, clothing and footwear 6.2%, education 4.5%, health care 2.5%.

Foreign trade[7]

Balance of trade (current prices)

	1998	1999	2000	2001	2002	2003
JD '000,000	–1,436	–1,336	–1,913	–1,827	–1,635	–1,887
% of total	36.0%	34.0%	41.5%	36.0%	29.4%	30.2%

Imports (2003): JD 4,072,000,000 (food products 15.5%; machinery and apparatus 13.4%; crude petroleum 11.5%; chemicals and chemical products 10.9%; transport equipment 9.2%). *Major import sources:* Saudi Arabia 11.3%; Germany 7.9%; China 7.9%; United States 6.8%; Iraq 6.5%.
Exports (2003): JD 2,185,000,000 (domestic exports 76.7%, of which clothing 20.5%, chemicals and chemical products 17.8% [including medicines and pharmaceuticals 6.0%], potash 6.6%, vegetables 4.6%, phosphates 4.2%; reexports 23.3%). *Major export destinations*[8]: United States 29.0%; Iraq 13.4%; India 8.4%; Saudi Arabia 6.5%; Israel 4.1%.

Transport and communications

Transport. Railroads (2003): length 788 km; passenger-km 2,100,000; metric ton-km cargo 348,000,000. Roads (2000): total length 7,245 km (paved 69%). Vehicles (2001): passenger cars 245,357; trucks and buses 110,920. Air transport (2003)[9]: passenger-km 4,553,000,000; metric ton-km cargo 200,728,000; airports (1999) 3.

Communications

Medium	date	unit	number	units per 1,000 persons
Daily newspapers	2000	circulation	383,000	77
Radio	2000	receivers	1,850,000	372
Television	2002	receivers	138,900	177
Telephones	2003	main lines	622,600	113
Cellular telephones	2003	subscribers	1,325,300	242
Personal computers	2002	units	200,000	38
Internet	2003	users	457,000	45

Education and health

Educational attainment (2003). Percentage of population age 15 and over having: no formal schooling 9.9%; primary education 54.8%; secondary 17.8%; postsecondary and vocational 8.1%; higher 9.4%. *Literacy* (2003): percentage of population age 15 and over literate 90.1%; males literate 94.9%; females literate 85.1%.

Education (2002–03)

	schools[10]	teachers	students	student/ teacher ratio
Primary (age 6–14)	2,708	55,900	1,222,400	21.9
Secondary (age 15–17)	912	15,200	179,800	11.8
Voc., teacher tr.[10]	214	3,026	43,861	14.5
Higher[10]	22	6,036	153,965	25.5

Health: physicians (2000) 9,493 (1 per 523 persons); hospital beds (2001) 8,982 (1 per 577 persons); infant mortality rate per 1,000 live births (2003) 22.0.
Food (2001): daily per capita caloric intake 2,769 (vegetable products 89%, animal products 11%); 113% of FAO recommended minimum requirement.

Military

Total active duty personnel (2003): 100,500 (army 84.6%, navy 0.5%, air force 14.9%). *Military expenditure as percentage of GDP* (1999): 9.2% (world 2.4%); per capita expenditure U.S.$150.

[1]Appointed by king. [2]January 1. [3]Detail does not add to total given because of rounding. [4]Includes hotels. [5]Services includes Finance, real estate, and business services. [6]Net taxes on products less imputed bank service charges. [7]Imports c.i.f.; exports f.o.b. [8]Domestic exports only. [9]Royal Jordanian airlines only. [10]2001.

Internet resources for further information:
- **Dept. of Statistics http://www.dos.gov.jo**
- **Central Bank of Jordan http://www.cbj.gov.jo**

Kazakhstan

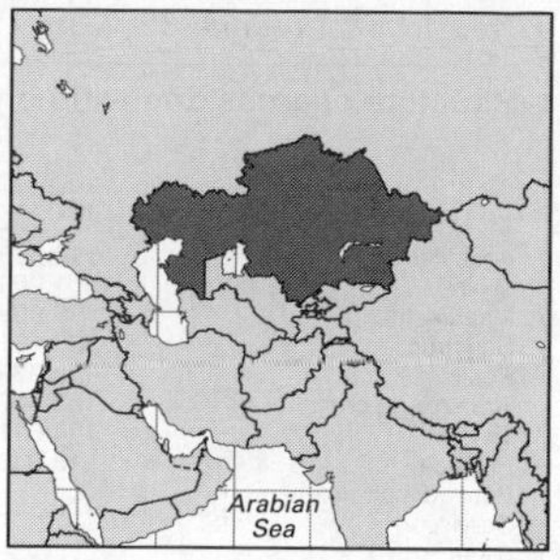

Official name: Qazaqstan Respūblīkasy (Republic of Kazakhstan).
Form of government: unitary republic with a Parliament consisting of two chambers (Senate [39[1]] and Assembly [77]).
Head of state and government: President assisted by Prime Minister.
Capital: Astana[2].
Official language: Kazakh[3].
Official religion: none.
Monetary unit: 1 tenge (T) = 100 tiyn; valuation (Sept. 1, 2004) 1 U.S.$ = 136.26 tenge; 1 £ = 245.12 tenge.

Area and population

		area		population
Provinces	**Capitals**	sq mi	sq km	2001[4] estimate
Almaty	Taldykorgan	86,450	223,900	1,561,800
Aqmola	Kokshetau	56,450	146,200	810,300
Aqtöbe	Aqtöbe	116,050	300,600	672,600
Atyraū	Atyraū	45,800	118,600	447,100
Batys Qazaqstan	Oral	58,400	151,300	604,400
Mangghystaū	Aqtaū	63,950	165,600	323,700
Ongtüstik Qazaqstan	Shymkent	45,300	117,300	2,025,400
Pavlodar	Pavlodar	48,200	124,800	776,800
Qaraghandy	Qaraghandy	165,250	428,000	1,381,600
Qostanay	Qostanay	75,700	196,000	972,300
Qyzylorda[5]	Qyzylorda	87,250	226,000	605,500
Shyghys Qazaqstan	Öskemen	109,400	283,300	1,504,300
Soltüstik Qazaqstan	Petropavlovsk	37,850	98,000	706,400
Zhambyl	Taraz	55,700	144,300	985,700
Cities				
Almaty[6]	—	100	300	1,139,900
Astana[2]	—	250	700	324,100
TOTAL		1,052,100	2,724,900	14,841,900

Demography

Population (2004): 15,144,000.
Density (2004): persons per sq mi 14.4, persons per sq km 5.6.
Urban-rural (2001): urban 55.8%; rural 44.2%.
Sex distribution (2003): male 48.35%; female 51.65%.
Age breakdown (2003): under 15, 25.3%; 15–29, 27.8%; 30–44, 21.3%; 45–59, 14.4%; 60–74, 8.9%; 75 and over, 2.3%.
Population projection: (2010) 15,460,000; (2020) 15,977,000.
Ethnic composition (1999): Kazakh 53.4%; Russian 30.0%; Ukrainian 3.7%; Uzbek 2.5%; German 2.4%; Tatar 1.7%; other 6.3%.
Religious affiliation (1995): Muslim (mostly Sunnī) 47.0%; Russian Orthodox 8.2%; Protestant 2.1%; other (mostly nonreligious) 42.7%.
Major cities (1999): Almaty[6] 1,130,068; Qaraghandy (Karaganda) 436,900; Shymkent (Chimkent) 360,100; Taraz 330,100; Astana 319,318[2].

Vital statistics

Birth rate per 1,000 population (2003): 15.3 (world avg. 21.3); (2000) legitimate 76.1%, illegitimate 23.9%.
Death rate per 1,000 population (2003): 9.7 (world avg. 9.1).
Natural increase rate per 1,000 population (2003): 5.6 (world avg. 12.2).
Total fertility rate (avg. births per childbearing woman; 2003): 1.9.
Life expectancy at birth (2003): male 65.6 years; female 71.3 years.
Major causes of death per 100,000 population (2000): diseases of the circulatory system 500.5; accidents, poisoning, and violence 140.7; malignant neoplasms (cancers) 129.1; diseases of the respiratory system 71.1.

National economy

Budget (2001). Revenue: 743,550,000,000 tenge (tax revenue 91.1%, of which income and profits taxes 34.8%, sales tax 29.3%, social security 17.5%; nontax revenue 8.9%). Expenditures: 749,092,000,000 tenge (social security 24.9%; education 14.0%; health 8.3%; debt 6.7%; defense 4.3%).
Population economically active (2001): total 7,479,100; activity rate of total population 50.4% (participation rates: ages 16–59 [male], 16–54 [female] 73.6%; female 46.0%; unemployed 12.8%).

Price and earnings indexes (2000 = 100)

	1997	1998	1999	2000	2001	2002	2003
Consumer price index	76.1	81.6	88.4	100.0	108.4	114.7	122.1
Monthly earnings index	61.9	70.1	80.7	100.0	125.6	147.5	168.8

Production (metric tons except as noted). Agriculture, forestry, fishing (2003): wheat 11,519,000, potatoes 2,320,000, barley 2,220,000, tomatoes 468,000, corn (maize) 438,000, sugar beets 424,000, cotton 387,000; livestock (number of live animals) 9,920,200 sheep, 4,559,500 cattle, 23,600,000 chickens; roundwood, n.a.; fish catch (2001) 31,071. Mining and quarrying (2000): iron ore 13,828,000; bauxite 3,730,000; chromite 2,607,000; copper (metal content) 430,200; zinc (metal content) 322,100; gold 28,171 kg. Manufacturing (value of production in '000,000 tenge; 2002): metallurgy 396,000; food 307,000; oil and nuclear energy 149,000; machinery 69,000; textiles 44,000. Energy production (consumption): electricity (kW-hr; 2002) 58,464,000,000 ([2000] 54,616,000,000); hard coal (metric tons; 2002) 70,608,000 ([2000] 45,503,000); lignite (metric tons; 2002) 2,616,000 ([2000] 2,235,000); crude petroleum (barrels; 2002) 348,224,000 ([2000] 18,800,000); petroleum products (metric tons; 2000) 5,961,000 (5,592,000); natural gas (cu m; 2002) 9,112,000,000 ([2000] 11,001,800,000).

Gross national product (2003): U.S.$26,535,000,000 (U.S.$1,780 per capita).

Structure of gross domestic product and labour force

	2002			
	in value '000,000 tenge	% of total value	labour force[7]	% of labour force[7]
Agriculture	298,000	8.0	2,381,000	35.5
Manufacturing, mining, public utilities	1,099,000	29.3	824,000	12.3
Construction	230,000	0.1	268,000	4.0
Transp. and commun.	430,000	11.5	504,000	7.5
Trade	450,000	12.0	1,064,000	15.8
Finance	496,000	13.2	253,000	3.8
Pub. admin., defense }	744,000	19.9	281,000	4.2
Services }			1,134,000	16.9
Other	—	—	...	...
TOTAL	3,747,000	100.0	6,709,000	100.0

Public debt (external, outstanding; 2002): U.S.$3,209,000,000.
Household income and expenditure. Average household size (1999) 3.6; sources of income (2001): salaries and wages 72.1%, social benefits 9.2%; expenditure (2001): food and beverages 56.0%, housing 11.7%.
Land use as % of total land area (2000): in temporary crops 8.0%, in permanent crops 0.05%, in pasture 68.6%; overall forest area 4.5%.
Tourism (2002): receipts U.S.$621,000,000; expenditures U.S.$756,000,000.

Foreign trade[8]

Balance of trade (current prices)

	1997	1998	1999	2000	2001	2002[9]
U.S.$'000,000	+2,196	+1,086	+1,912	+4,087	+2,284	+2,855
% of total	20.3%	11.1%	20.6%	28.8%	15.2%	19.8%

Imports (2000): U.S.$5,052,000,000 (machinery and apparatus 27.4%; mineral fuels and lubricants 11.5%; chemicals and chemical products 11.4%; transport equipment 11.1%). *Major import sources:* Russia 48.7%; Germany 6.6%; U.S. 5.5%; U.K. 4.3%; Italy 3.1%.
Exports (2000): U.S.$9,139,000,000 (crude petroleum 49.4%; nonferrous metals 13.7%, of which copper 7.5%; iron and steel 12.0%; cereals 6.0%). *Major export destinations:* Russia 19.5%; Bermuda 14.9%; British Virgin Islands 11.6%; Italy 9.8%; China 7.3%.

Transport and communications

Transport. Railroads (2001): route length 13,500 km; passenger-km 10,384,000,000; metric ton-km cargo 135,653,000,000. Roads (1999): total length 109,445 km (paved 90%). Vehicles (2001): passenger cars 1,000,298; trucks and buses 278,711. Air transport (2001): passenger-km 1,901,100,000; metric ton-km cargo 44,000,000; airports (1999) with scheduled flights 20.

Communications

Medium	date	unit	number	units per 1,000 persons
Radio	2000	receivers	6,270,000	422
Television	2000	receivers	3,580,000	241
Telephones	2002	main lines	2,081,900	130
Cellular telephones	2002	subscribers	1,027,000	64
Internet	2002	users	250,000	16

Education and health

Educational attainment (1999). Population age 25 and over having: no formal schooling or some primary education 9.1%; primary education 23.1%; secondary and some postsecondary 57.8%; higher 10.0%. *Literacy* (2002): percentage of total population age 15 and over literate 99.4%; males literate 99.7%; females literate 99.2%.

Education (1999–2000)

	schools	teachers	students	student/ teacher ratio
Primary (age 7–13)	1,447	62,700	1,208,300	19.3
Secondary (age 14–17)	8,309	176,900	1,913,100	10.8
Voc., teacher tr.	293	...	89,900	...
Higher	170	39,187[10]	440,700	...

Health (2002): physicians 55,800 (1 per 277 persons); hospital beds 108,300 (1 per 143 persons); infant mortality rate per 1,000 live births (2003) 31.9.
Food (2001): daily per capita caloric intake 2,477 (vegetable products 73%, animal products 27%); 97% of FAO minimum requirement.

Military

Total active duty personnel (2003): 65,800 (army 71.1%, air force 28.9%). *Military expenditure as percentage of GNP* (1999): 0.9% (world avg. 2.4%); per capita expenditure U.S.$40.

[1]Includes 7 nonelective seats. [2]City of Akmola (Kazakh: Aqmola; capital replacing Almaty) was renamed Astana on May 6, 1998. [3]Russian has equal status with Kazakh at state-owned organizations and bodies of local government per a law effective July 16, 1997. [4]January 1. [5]Includes an area of 6,000 sq km enclosing the Bayqongyr (Baykonur) space launch facilities and the city of Bayqongyr (formerly Leninsk) leased to Russia in 1995 for a period of 20 years. [6]Formerly known as Alma-Ata. [7]Employed only. [8]Imports c.i.f.; exports f.o.b. [9]Excludes December. [10]1995–96.

Internet resources for further information:
- **National Bank of Kazakhstan http://www.nationalbank.kz**
- **Agency on Statistics of Kazakhstan http://www.stat.kz/en/releases**

Kenya

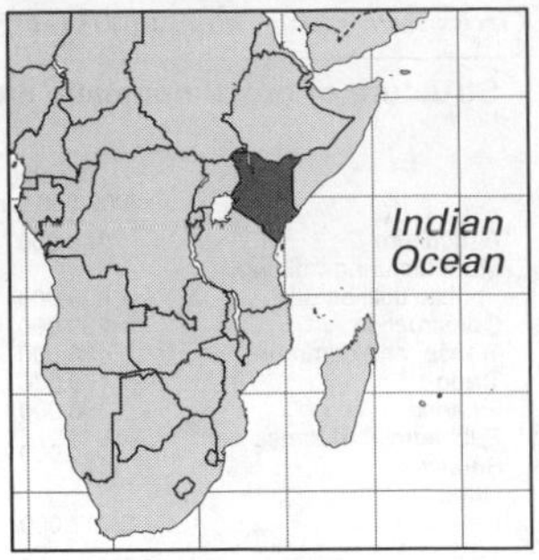

Official name: Jamhuri ya Kenya (Swahili); Republic of Kenya (English).
Form of government: unitary multiparty republic with one legislative house (National Assembly [224[1]]).
Head of state and government: President.
Capital: Nairobi.
Official languages: Swahili; English.
Official religion: none.
Monetary unit: 1 Kenya shilling[2] (K Sh) = 100 cents; valuation (Sept. 1, 2004) 1 U.S.$ = K Sh 79.85; 1 £ = K Sh 143.65.

Area and population		area		population
				1999
Provinces	**Provincial headquarters**	sq mi	sq km	census[3]
Central	Nyeri	5,087	13,176	3,724,159
Coast	Mombasa	32,279	83,603	2,487,264
Eastern	Embu	61,734	159,891	4,631,779
North Eastern	Garissa	48,997	126,902	962,143
Nyanza	Kisumu	6,240	16,162	4,392,196
Rift Valley	Nakuru	67,131	173,868	6,987,036
Western	Kakamega	3,228	8,360	3,358,776
Special area				
Nairobi	—	264	684	2,143,254
TOTAL		224,961[4, 5]	582,646[5]	28,686,607

Demography

Population (2004): 32,022,000.
Density (2004): persons per sq mi 142.3, persons per sq km 55.0.
Urban-rural (2003): urban 39.4%; rural 60.6%.
Sex distribution (2003): male 50.11%; female 49.89%.
Age breakdown (2003): under 15, 42.4%; 15–29, 31.5%; 30–44, 15.1%; 45–59, 7.3%; 60–74, 3.0%; 75 and over, 0.7%.
Population projection: (2010) 33,654,000; (2020) 34,848,000.
Doubling time: 28 years.
Ethnic composition (1989): Kikuyu 17.7%; Luhya 12.4%; Luo 10.6%; Kalenjin 9.8%; Kamba 9.8%; other 39.7%.
Religious affiliation (2000): Christian 79.3%, of which Roman Catholic 22.0%, African Christian 20.8%, Protestant 20.1%; Muslim 7.3%; other 13.4%.
Major cities (1999)[6]: Nairobi 2,143,354; Mombasa 665,018; Kisumu 322,734; Nakuru 219,366; Eldoret 167,016; Machacos 144,109.

Vital statistics

Birth rate per 1,000 population (2003): 40.2 (world avg. 21.3).
Death rate per 1,000 population (2003): 15.6 (world avg. 9.1).
Natural increase rate per 1,000 population (2003): 24.6 (world avg. 12.2).
Total fertility rate (avg. births per childbearing woman; 2003): 5.0.
Life expectancy at birth (2003): male 47.4 years; female 45.7 years.
Adult population (ages 15–49) *living with HIV* (2004[7]): 6.7% (world avg. 1.1%).

National economy

Budget (2001–02). Revenue: K Sh 206,665,600,000 (tax revenue 86.6%, of which income and profit taxes 29.0%, value-added tax 27.2%, import duties 15.3%; nontax revenue 13.4%). Expenditures: K Sh 235,832,000,000 (recurrent expenditure 80.4%, of which administration 29.7%, education 22.2%, defense 6.1%, health 6.0%; development expenditure 19.6%).
Public debt (external, outstanding; 2002): U.S.$5,139,000,000.
Production (metric tons except as noted). Agriculture, forestry, fishing (2003): sugarcane 4,500,000, corn (maize) 2,300,000, potatoes 900,000, plantains 830,000, cassava 600,000, pineapples 600,000, fresh vegetables 570,000, sweet potatoes 520,000, tea 290,000, cabbages 270,000, tomatoes 260,000, dry beans 255,000, wheat 210,000, bananas 210,000, mangoes 118,000, sorghum 110,000, fresh fruit 90,000, coffee 65,000, coconuts 60,000, onions 58,000, peas 55,000, rice 50,000, barley 47,000, millet 45,000; livestock (number of live animals) 11,500,000 cattle, 11,000,000 goats, 7,700,000 sheep; roundwood (2002) 1,704,250 cu m; fish catch (2001) 165,160, of which freshwater fish 95.5%. Mining and quarrying (2000): soda ash 238,200; fluorite 100,100; salt 16,400. Manufacturing (value added in K£'000[2]; 1995): food products 847,000; beverages and tobacco 249,000; machinery and transport equipment 226,000; chemical products 181,000; metal products 131,000; textiles 94,000; paper and paper products 86,000; plastic products 75,000; clothing and footwear 58,000. Energy production (consumption): electricity (kW-hr; 2001) 4,338,400,000 (3,654,800,000); coal (metric tons; 2000) none (98,000); crude petroleum (barrels; 2000) none (18,000,000); petroleum products (metric tons; 2001) 1,695,600 (2,385,200); natural gas, none (none).
Household income and expenditure. Average household size (1998) 3.4; average annual income per household: n.a.; sources of income: n.a.; expenditure (1993–94): food 42.4%, housing and energy 24.1%, clothing and footwear 9.1%, transportation 6.4%, other 18.0%.
Population economically active (2001): total 12,952,000; activity rate of total population 42.1% (participation rates [1985]: ages 15–64, 76.2%; female [1997] 46.1%; unemployed, n.a.).

Price index (2000 = 100)	1997	1998	1999	2000	2001	2002	2003
Consumer price index	80.6	86.0	90.9	100.0	105.7	107.8	118.4

Gross national product (2003): U.S.$12,604,000,000 (U.S.$390 per capita).

Structure of gross domestic product and labour force	2001			
	in value K Sh '000,000	% of total value	labour force	% of labour force
Agriculture	146,639	19.0	312,500[8]	2.4[8]
Mining	1,260	0.2	5,200[8]	—[8]
Manufacturing	96,969	12.5	216,600[8]	1.7[8]
Construction	33,161	4.3	76,800[8]	0.6[8]
Public utilities	8,937	1.2	21,400[8]	0.2[8]
Transp. and commun.	53,107	6.9	84,300[8]	0.7[8]
Trade	194,611	25.2	156,900[8]	1.2[8]
Finance	115,046	14.9	83,800[8]	0.6[8]
Pub. admin., defense; Services	123,163	15.8	719,600[8]	5.6[8]
Other	—	—	11,274,900[9]	87.0[9]
TOTAL	772,893	100.0	12,952,000	100.0

Tourism (2002): receipts from visitors U.S.$297,000,000; expenditures by nationals abroad (2001) U.S.$143,000,000.
Land use as % of total land area (2000): in temporary crops 7.9%, in permanent crops 1.0%, in pasture 37.4%; overall forest area 30.0%.

Foreign trade[10]

Balance of trade (current prices)	1997	1998	1999	2000	2001	2002
K Sh '000,000	–70,714	–71,780	–76,246	–104,430	–98,070	–118,675
% of total	22.8%	22.8%	23.8%	28.3%	24.3%	27.2%

Imports (2002): K Sh 277,275,000,000 (crude petroleum and petroleum products 22.8%, machinery and transport equipment 19.3%, chemicals and chemical products 14.1%). *Major import sources* (2001): U.S. 16.4%; U.A.E. 10.7%; Saudi Arabia 7.8%; South Africa 7.1%; U.K. 7.1%.
Exports (2002): K Sh 158,600,000,000 (tea 21.4%, horticultural products [mostly cut flowers] 13.8%, petroleum products 7.6%, coffee 4.1%, other [including nontraditional fruits and vegetables, iron and steel, and fish] 53.1%). *Major export destinations* (2001): Uganda 17.4%; U.K. 12.5%; The Netherlands 6.5%; Pakistan 6.1%; U.S. 5.6%.

Transport and communications

Transport. Railroads (2000): route length 1,678 mi, 2,700 km; passenger-mi 187,600,000; passenger-km 302,000,000; short ton-mi cargo 967,000,000, metric ton-km cargo 1,557,000,000. Roads (1999): total length 39,600 mi, 63,800 km (paved 14%). Vehicles (2000): passenger cars 244,836; trucks and buses 96,726. Air transport (1998): passenger-mi 1,299,000,000, passenger-km 2,091,000,000; short ton-mi cargo 151,000,000, metric ton-km cargo 243,000,000; airports (1997) with scheduled flights 11.

Communications Medium	date	unit	number	units per 1,000 persons
Daily newspapers	2000	circulation	303,000	10
Radio	2001	receivers	6,801,000	221
Television	2000	receivers	758,000	25
Telephones	2003	main lines	328,400	10
Cellular telephones	2003	subscribers	1,590,800	50
Personal computers	2002	units	204,000	6.5
Internet	2002	users	400,000	13

Education and health

Educational attainment: n.a. *Literacy* (2002): total population over age 15 literate 84.3%; males literate 90.0%; females literate 78.5%.

Education (2001)	schools[11]	teachers	students	student/ teacher ratio
Primary (age 5–11)	15,906	185,720	6,314,500	34.0
Secondary (age 12–17)	2,878	48,129	818,200	17.0
Voc., teacher tr.	62	...	44,700	...
Higher[12]	14	4,392[11]	62,100	...

Health (2002): physicians 4,740 (1 per 6,623 persons); hospital beds 60,657 (1 per 515 persons); infant mortality rate per 1,000 live births (2003): 65.6.
Food (2001): daily per capita caloric intake 2,058 (vegetable products 88%, animal products 12%); 89% of FAO recommended minimum requirement.

Military

Total active duty personnel (2003): 24,120 (army 82.9%, navy 6.7%, air force 10.4%). *Military expenditure as percentage of GNP* (1999): 1.9% (world 2.4%); per capita expenditure U.S.$7.

[1]Includes 14 nonelective seats. [2]Kenya pound (K£) as a unit of account equals 20 K Sh. [3]Preliminary. [4]Detail does not add to total given because of rounding. [5]Includes water area of 4,336 sq mi (11,230 sq km). [6]Population of urban core(s). [7]January 1. [8]Formally employed only. [9]Includes informally employed, small-scale farmers and pastoralists, unemployed, self-employed, and unpaid family workers. [10]Import figures are c.i.f. [11]1993. [12]Universities only.

Internet resources for further information:
- **Central Bank of Kenya http://www.centralbank.go.ke**
- **Central Bureau of Statistics http://www.cbs.go.ke**

Kiribati

Official name: Republic of Kiribati.
Form of government: unitary republic with a unicameral legislature (House of Assembly [42[1]]).
Head of state and government: President.
Capital: Bairiki, on Tarawa Atoll.
Official language: English.
Official religion: none.
Monetary unit: 1 Australian dollar ($A) = 100 cents; valuation (Sept. 1, 2004) 1 U.S.$ = $A 1.42; 1 £ = $A 2.55.

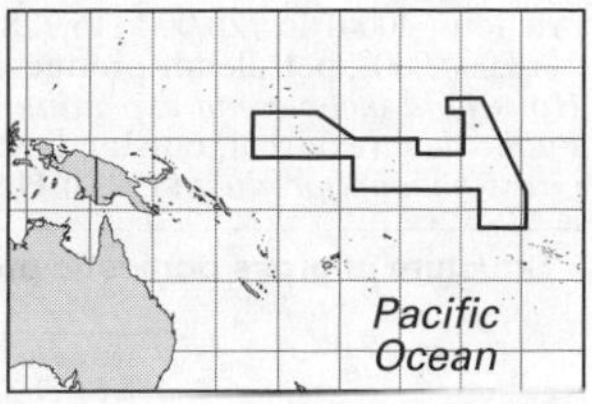

Area and population

Island Groups / Islands	Capitals	area[2] sq mi	area[2] sq km	population 2000 census
Gilberts Group		110.2[3]	285.5[3]	78,158
Abaiang	Tuarabu	6.8	17.5	5,794
Abemama	Kariatebike	10.6	27.4	3,142
Aranuka	Takaeang	4.5	11.6	966
Arorae	Roreti	3.7	9.5	1,225
Banaba	Anteeren	2.4	6.3	276
Beru	Taubukinberu	6.8	17.7	2,732
Butaritari	Butaritari	5.2	13.5	3,464
Kuria	Tabontebike	6.0	15.5	961
Maiana	Tebangetua	6.4	16.7	2,048
Makin	Makin	3.1	7.9	1,691
Marakei	Rawannawi	5.4	14.1	2,544
Nikunau	Rungata	7.4	19.1	1,733
Nonouti	Teuabu	7.7	19.9	3,176
Onotoa	Buariki	6.0	15.6	1,668
Tabiteuea, North	Utiroa	10.0	25.8	3,365
Tabiteuea, South	Buariki	4.6	11.9	1,217
Tamana	Bakaka	1.8	4.7	962
Tarawa, North	Abaokoro	5.9	15.3	4,477
Tarawa, South	Bairiki	6.1	15.8	36,717
Line and Phoenix Group		202.7[3]	525.0[3]	6,336
Northern Line		166.7	431.7	6,275
Kiritimati (Christmas)	London	150.0	388.4	3,431
Tabuaeran (Fanning)	Paelau	13.0	33.7	1,757
Teraina (Washington)	Washington	3.7	9.6	1,087
Southern Line and Phoenix Group		36.1	93.4	61
Kanton (Canton) in Phoenix Group	Kanton	3.6	9.2	61
TOTAL		312.9	810.5	84,494

Demography

Population (2004): 89,100.
Density (2004)[4]: persons per sq mi 318.2, persons per sq km 122.7.
Urban-rural (2003): urban 47.3%; rural 52.7%.
Sex distribution (2003): male 49.65%; female 50.35%.
Age breakdown (2003): under 15, 39.7%; 15–29, 26.3%; 30–44, 18.8%; 45–59, 10.1%; 60–74, 4.3%; 75 and over, 0.9%.
Population projection: (2010) 95,000; (2020) 107,000.
Doubling time: 26 years.
Ethnic composition (2000): Micronesian 98.8%; Polynesian 0.7%; European 0.2%; other 0.3%.
Religious affiliation (2000): Roman Catholic 54.6%; Kiribati Protestant (Congregational) 37.0%; Mormon 2.7%; Bahā'ī 2.4%; other Protestant 2.3%; other/nonreligious 1.0%.
Major city (2000): Tarawa (urban area) 36,717.

Vital statistics

Birth rate per 1,000 population (2003): 31.2 (world avg. 21.3).
Death rate per 1,000 population (2003): 8.6 (world avg. 9.1).
Total fertility rate (avg. births per childbearing woman; 2003): 4.3.
Natural increase rate per 1,000 population (2003): 22.6 (world avg. 12.2).
Marriage rate per 1,000 population (1988): 5.2.
Life expectancy at birth (2003): male 58.0 years; female 64.0 years.
Major causes of death per 100,000 population (1993): senility without mention of psychosis 61.2; stroke 39.1; diarrhea 37.8; hepatitis 32.5; diabetes mellitus 28.6; malnutrition 23.4; meningitis 18.2.

National economy

Budget (2000). Revenue: $A 107,800,000 (nontax revenue 59.5%, tax revenue 22.9%, grants 17.6%). Expenditures: $A 90,000,000 (current expenditures 87.2%, capital expenditures 12.8%).
Public debt (external, outstanding; 1999): U.S.$9,500,000.
Tourism: receipts from visitors (2001) U.S.$3,200,000; expenditures by nationals abroad (1999) U.S.$2,000,000.
Land use as % of total land area (2000): in temporary crops *c.* 3%, in permanent crops *c.* 51%, in pasture, none; overall forest area *c.* 38%.
Production (metric tons except as noted). Agriculture, forestry, fishing (2003): coconuts 99,000, roots and tubers 7,300 (of which taro 1,900), fresh vegetables 5,800, bananas 4,800, tropical fruit 1,300; livestock (number of live animals) 12,000 pigs, 450,000 chickens; fish catch (2001) 32,393. Mining and quarrying: none. Manufacturing (1996): processed copra 9,321; other important products are processed fish, baked goods, clothing, and handicrafts. Energy production (consumption): electricity (kW-hr; 2000) 7,000,000 (7,000,000); petroleum products (metric tons; 2000) none (8,000).
Gross national product (2003): U.S.$84,000,000 (U.S.$880 per capita).

Structure of gross domestic product and labour force

	2001 in value $A '000	2001 % of total value	2000 labour force	2000 % of labour force
Agriculture, fishing	4,592	7.1	30,966[5]	71.7[5]
Mining	—	—	—	—
Manufacturing	717	1.1	150	0.4
Construction	3,714	5.7	346	0.8
Public utilities	988	1.5	187	0.4
Transp. and commun.	7,734	11.9	944	2.2
Trade	11,167	17.2	1,181	2.7
Finance	4,795	7.4	317	0.7
Pub. admin., defense	30,213	46.6	5,821	13.5
Services } Other }	904[6]	1.5[6]	2,649	6.1
			644[7]	1.5[7]
TOTAL	64,824	100.0	43,205	100.0

Population economically active (1995): total 38,407; activity rate of total population 49.5% (participation rates: over age 15, 84.0%; female 47.8%; unemployed [2000] 1.5%).

Price index (2000 = 100)

	1997	1998	1999	2000	2001	2002	2003
Consumer price index	91.1	94.5	96.2	100.0	106.0	109.4	110.9

Household income and expenditure. Average household size (1995) 6.5; expenditure (1996)[8]: food 45.0%, nonalcoholic beverages 10.0%, transportation 8.0%, energy 8.0%, education 8.0%.

Foreign trade

Balance of trade (current prices)

	1995	1996	1997	1998	1999	2000
$A '000,000	–37.5	–41.8	–44.1	–42.6	–49.7	–57.2
% of total	65.2%	75.4%	72.3%	69.6%	63.8%	72.8%

Imports (1999): $A 63,700,000 (food and live animals 28.3%; machinery and transport equipment 22.6%; mineral fuels 10.3%; beverages and tobacco products 7.7%). *Major import sources* (2001): Australia 26.5%; Poland 15.7%; Fiji 14.8%; United States 9.5%; Japan 8.0%.
Exports (1999): $A 14,000,000 (domestic exports 92.6%, of which copra 63.9%, seaweed 5.1%, other [including fish for food and pet fish] 23.6%; reexports 7.4%). *Major export destinations* (2001): Japan 45.8%; Thailand 24.8%; South Korea 10.7%; Bangladesh 5.5%; Brazil 3.0%.

Transport and communications

Transport. Roads (1996): total length 416 mi, 670 km (paved 5%). Vehicles (2000)[9]: passenger cars 477; trucks and buses 277. Air transport (1996): passenger-mi 4,350,000, passenger-km 7,000,000; short ton-mi cargo 621,000, metric ton-km cargo 1,000,000; airports 9.

Communications

Medium	date	unit	number	units per 1,000 persons
Radio	2000	receivers	32,600	386
Television	2000	receivers	3,030	36
Telephones	2002	main lines	4,500	51
Cellular telephones	2002	subscribers	500	5.7
Personal computers	2001	units	2,000	25
Internet	2002	users	2,000	23

Education and health

Educational attainment (1995). Percentage of population age 25 and over having: no schooling 7.8%; primary education 68.5%; secondary or higher 23.7%.
Literacy (1998): population age 15 and over literate 92%; males literate 94%; females literate 91%.

Education (2001)

	schools	teachers	students	student/ teacher ratio
Primary (age 6–13)	88	627	16,096	25.7
Secondary (age 14–18)	19	324	5,743	17.7
Voc., teacher tr.	2	39	1,501	38.5
Higher[10]	—	—	—	—

Health: physicians (1998) 26 (1 per 3,378 persons); hospital beds (1990) 306 (1 per 233 persons); infant mortality rate per 1,000 live births (2003) 51.3.
Food (2001): daily per capita caloric intake 2,922 (vegetable products 88%, animal products 12%); 128% of FAO recommended minimum requirement.

[1]Includes two nonelective members. [2]Includes uninhabited islands. [3]Detail does not add to total given because of rounding. [4]Based on inhabited island areas (280 sq mi [726 sq km]) only. [5]Includes 30,712 persons engaged in "village work" (subsistence agriculture or fishing). [6]Indirect taxes less subsidies and imputed bank service charge and unknown. [7]Unemployed. [8]Weights of consumer price index components. [9]Registered vehicles in South Tarawa only. [10]129 students overseas in 2001.

Internet resources for further information:
- **Key Indicators of Developing Asian and Pacific Countries http://www.adb.org/Documents/Books/Key_Indicators/2003**
- **Kiribati Statistics Office http://www.spc.org.nc/prism/Country/KI/Stats/index.html**

Korea, North

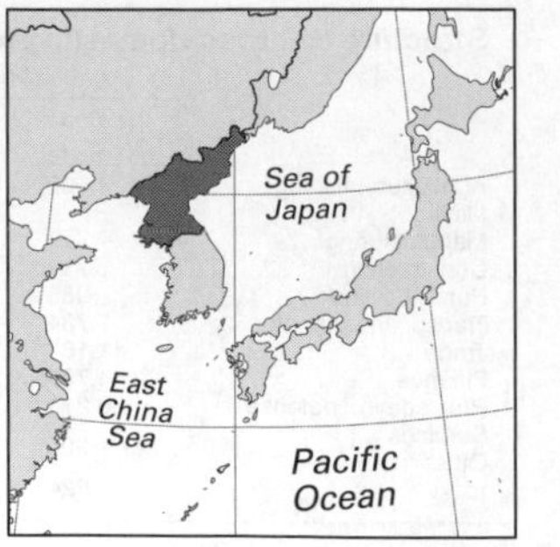

Official name: Chosŏn Minjujuŭi In'min Konghwaguk (Democratic People's Republic of Korea).
Form of government: unitary single-party republic with one legislative house (Supreme People's Assembly [687]).
Head of state and government: Chairman of the National Defense Commission[1].
Capital: P'yŏngyang.
Official language: Korean.
Official religion: none.
Monetary unit: 1 won = 100 chŏn; valuation (Sept. 1, 2004) 1 U.S.$ = 900 won; 1 £ = 1,619 won.

Area and population

		area		population
Provinces	**Capitals**	sq mi	sq km	1993 census
Chagang-do	Kanggye	6,551	16,968	1,152,733
Kangwŏn-do	Wŏnsan	4,306	11,152	1,304,481
North Hamgyŏng (Hamgyŏng-pukto)	Ch'ŏngjin	6,784[2]	17,570[2]	2,060,725[2]
North Hwanghae (Hwanghae-pukto)	Sariwŏn	3,091	8,007	1,512,060
North P'yŏngan (P'yŏngan-pukto)	Sinŭiju	4,656[3]	12,059[3]	2,404,490[4]
South Hamgyŏng (Hamgyŏng-namdo)	Hamhŭng	7,324	18,970	2,732,232
South Hwanghae (Hwanghae-namdo)	Haeju	3,090	8,002	2,010,953
South P'yŏngan (P'yŏngan-namdo)	P'yŏngsan	4,470	11,577	2,866,109
Yanggang-do	Hyesan	5,528	14,317	638,474
Special administrative region[5]				
Sinŭiju	—	51	132	[4]
Special cities				
Kaesŏng	—	485	1,255	334,433
Najin Sŏnbong	—	[2]	[2]	[2]
Namp'o	—	291	753	731,448
P'yŏngyang	—	772	2,000	2,741,260
Special district				
Hyangsan-chigu	—	[3]	[3]	32,952
TOTAL		47,399	122,762	20,522,350

Demography

Population (2004): 22,698,000.
Density (2004): persons per sq mi 478.9, persons per sq km 184.9.
Urban-rural (2003): urban 61.1%; rural 38.9%.
Sex distribution (2000): male 48.48%; female 51.52%.
Age breakdown (2000): under 15, 25.6%; 15–29, 24.5%; 30–44, 24.7%; 45–59, 14.4%; 60–74, 9.0%; 75 and over, 1.8%.
Population projection: (2010) 23,802,000; (2020) 25,210,000.
Doubling time: 65 years.
Ethnic composition (1999): Korean 99.8%; Chinese 0.2%.
Religious affiliation (2000): nonreligious 55.6%; atheist 15.6%; Ch'ŏndogyo 12.9%; traditional beliefs 12.3%; Christian 2.1%; Buddhist 1.5%.
Major cities (1993): P'yŏngyang (2001) 3,164,000[6]; Namp'o (2000) 1,022,000[6]; Hamhŭng 709,730; Ch'ŏngjin 582,480; Kaesŏng 334,433; Sinŭiju 326,011.

Vital statistics

Birth rate per 1,000 population (2003): 17.6 (world avg. 21.3).
Death rate per 1,000 population (2003): 6.9 (world avg. 9.1).
Natural increase rate per 1,000 population (2003): 10.7 (world avg. 12.2).
Total fertility rate (avg. births per childbearing woman; 2003): 2.3.
Marriage rate per 1,000 population (1987): 9.3.
Divorce rate per 1,000 population (1987): 0.2.
Life expectancy at birth (2003): male 68.1 years; female 73.6 years.
Major causes of death per 100,000 population (1986): diseases of the circulatory system 224.9; malignant neoplasms (cancers) 69.0; diseases of the digestive system 51.6; diseases of the respiratory system 46.7.

National economy

Budget (1999). Revenue: 19,801,000,000 won (turnover tax and profits from state enterprises). Expenditures: 20,018,200,000 won (1994; national economy 67.8%, social and cultural affairs 19.0%, defense 11.6%).
Population economically active (1997)[7]: total 11,898,000; activity rate of total population 55.8% (participation rates [1988–93]: ages 15–64, 49.5%; female 46.0%; unemployed, n.a.).
Production (metric tons except as noted). Agriculture, forestry, fishing (2002): rice 2,190,000, potatoes 1,884,000, corn (maize) 1,651,000, cabbages 680,000, apples 660,000, soybeans 360,000, sweet potatoes 340,000, wheat 130,000, pears 130,000, peaches and nectarines 115,000, watermelons 105,000, tomatoes 70,000, barley 69,000, cucumbers and gherkins 65,000, tobacco leaves 63,000, millet 45,000, oats 11,000; livestock (number of live animals) 3,152,000 pigs, 2,693,000 goats, 575,000 cattle, 170,000 sheep; roundwood (2000) 4,900,000 cu m; fish catch (2001): 264,000. Mining and quarrying (2002): iron ore (metal content) 1,150,000; magnesite 1,000,000; phosphate rock 300,000; zinc (metal content) 100,000; lead (metal content) 60,000; sulfur 42,000; copper (metal content) 13,000; silver 40; gold 2,000 kg. Manufacturing (1999): cement 16,000,000; crude steel 8,100,000; pig iron 6,600,000; coke 3,400,000; steel semimanufactures 2,700,000[8]; chemical fertilizers 2,500,000[8]; meat 259,200[8]; gasoline 8,600,000[9] barrels; textile fabrics 350,000,000 sq m[8]. Energy production (consumption): electricity (kW-hr; 2000) 32,815,000,000 (32,815,000,000); hard coal (metric tons; 2000) 53,873,000 (55,540,000); lignite (metric tons; 2000) 15,728,000 (15,728,000); crude petroleum (barrels; 2000) none (18,000,000); petroleum products (metric tons; 2000) 2,654,000 (4,063,000).
Household income and expenditure. Average household size (1999) 4.6.
Public debt (external, outstanding; 1999): U.S.$12,000,000,000.
Gross national product (1999): U.S.$9,912,000,000 (U.S.$457 per capita).

Structure of gross domestic product and labour force

	1999		1997	
	in value U.S.$'000,000	% of total value	labour force	% of labour force
Agriculture	...	25.0	3,853,000	32.4
Mining and manufacturing				
Construction				
Public utilities	...	60.0		
Transp. and commun.				
Trade			8,045,000	67.6
Finance	...	...		
Pub. admin., defense				
Services	...	15.0		
Other				
TOTAL	22,600	100.0	11,898,000	100.0

Land use as % of total land area (2000): in temporary crops 20.8%, in permanent crops 2.5%, in pasture 0.4%; overall forest area 68.2%.

Foreign trade

Balance of trade (current prices)

	1996	1997	1998	1999	2000	2001
U.S.$'000,000	–1,050	–390	–320	–540	–961	–1,021
% of total	36.3%	18.1%	22.2%	29.8%	40.1%	38.2%

Imports (2001): U.S.$1,847,000,000 ([10]food, beverages, and other agricultural products 23.7%, machinery and apparatus 15.0%, mineral fuels and lubricants 14.3%, textiles and clothing 12.6%). *Major import sources:* China 31.0%; Japan 13.5%; South Korea 12.3%; India 8.4%; Singapore 6.1%.
Exports (2001): U.S.$826,000,000 ([10]live animals and agricultural products 30.2%, textiles and wearing apparel 21.6%, machinery and apparatus 15.1%, base and fabricated metals 9.3%). *Major export destinations:* Japan 27.3%; South Korea 21.3%; China 20.2%; Hong Kong 4.6%; Thailand 3.0%.

Transport and communications

Transport. Railroads (1999): length 8,533 km. Roads (1998): total length 14,544 mi, 23,407 km (paved 8%). Vehicles (1990): passenger cars 248,000. Air transport (1997): passenger-mi 177,712,000, passenger-km 286,000,000; short ton-mi cargo 18,600,000; metric ton-km cargo 30,000,000; airports (2001) with scheduled flights 1.

Communications

Medium	date	unit	number	units per 1,000 persons
Daily newspapers	2000	circulation	4,500,000	208
Radio	2000	receivers	3,330,000	154
Television	2000	receivers	1,170,000	54
Telephones	1999	main lines	1,100,000	46

Education and health

Educational attainment (1987–88). Percentage of population age 16 and over having attended or graduated from postsecondary-level school: 13.7%.
Literacy (1997): 95%.

Education (1988)

	schools	teachers	students	student/ teacher ratio
Primary (age 6–9)	4,810	59,000	1,543,000	26.2
Secondary (age 10–15)	4,840	111,000	2,468,000	22.2
Voc., teacher tr.	...	...	...	...
Higher	46	23,000	325,000	14.1

Health (1995): physicians 64,039 (1 per 337 persons); hospital beds 293,457 (1 per 73 persons); infant mortality rate (2003) 25.7.
Food (2002): daily per capita caloric intake 2,142 (vegetable products 94%, animal products 6%); 92% of FAO recommended minimum requirement.

Military

Total active duty personnel (2003): 1,082,000 (army 87.8%, navy 4.3%, air force 7.9%). *Military expenditure as percentage of GNP* (1999): 18.8% (world 2.4%); per capita expenditure U.S.$199.

[1]Position in effect from Sept. 5, 1998, is the declared "highest office of state." It is defined as an enhanced military post with revised constitutional powers. [2]North Hamgyŏng includes Najin Sŏnbong special city created in 2001. [3]North P'yŏngan includes special district of Hyangsan-chigu. [4]North P'yŏngan includes Sinŭiju. [5]Economic trade zone formally established September 2002. [6]Urban agglomeration. [7]The Democratic People's Republic of Korea categorizes economically active as including students in higher education, retirees, and heads of households, as well as those in the civilian labour force. [8]1994. [9]1996. [10]Data for commodities exclude trade with South Korea.

Internet resources for further information:

- **Digital KOTRA: North Korean Economy**
  http://crm.kotra.or.kr/eng/index.php3
- **United States Department of Energy**
  http://www.eia.doe.gov/emeu/cabs/nkorea.html

Korea, South

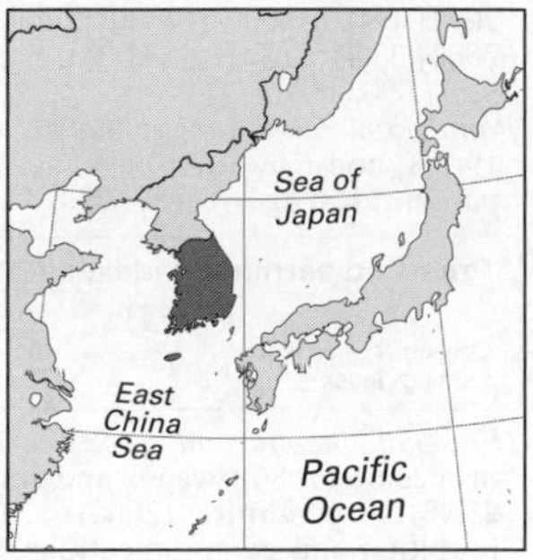

Official name: Taehan Min'guk (Republic of Korea).
Form of government: unitary multiparty republic with one legislative house (National Assembly [299]).
Head of state and government: President, assisted by Prime Minister.
Capital: Seoul.
Official language: Korean.
Official religion: none.
Monetary unit: 1 won (W) = 100 chon; valuation (Sept. 1, 2004) 1 U.S.$ = W 1,152; 1 £ = W 2,072.

Area and population

Provinces	Capitals	area sq mi	area sq km	population 2000 census
Cheju	Cheju	713	1,847	513,260
Kangwŏn	Ch'unch'ŏn'	6,515	16,873	1,487,011
Kyŏnggi	Suwŏn	3,931	10,181	8,984,134
North Chŏlla	Chŏnju	3,108	8,051	1,890,669
North Ch'ungch'ŏng	Ch'ŏngju	2,869	7,432	1,466,567
North Kyŏngsang	Taegu	7,346	19,025	2,724,931
South Chŏlla	Kwangju	4,648	12,037	1,996,456
South Ch'ungch'ŏng	Taejŏn	3,320	8,598	1,845,321
South Kyŏngsang	Ch'angwŏn	4,061	10,518	2,978,502
Metropolitan cities				
Inch'ŏn	Inch'ŏn	381	986	2,475,139
Kwangju	Kwangju	193	501	1,352,797
Pusan	Pusan	295	763	3,662,884
Sŏul (Seoul)	Seoul	234	606	9,895,217
Taegu	Taegu	342	886	2,480,578
Taejŏn	Taejŏn	208	540	1,368,207
Ulsan	Ulsan	408	1,056	1,014,428
TOTAL		38,572	99,900	46,136,101

Demography

Population (2004): 48,199,000.
Density (2004): persons per sq mi 1,249.6, persons per sq km 482.5.
Urban-rural (2003): urban 80.3%; rural 19.7%.
Sex distribution (2003): male 50.30%; female 49.70%.
Age breakdown (2003): under 15, 20.2%; 15–29, 23.6%; 30–44, 26.8%; 45–59, 17.5%; 60–74, 9.4%; 75 and over, 2.5%.
Population projection: (2010) 49,335,000; (2020) 50,285,000.
Ethnic composition (2000): Korean 97.7%; Japanese 2.0%; U.S. white 0.1%; Han Chinese 0.1%; other 0.1%.
Religious affiliation (1995): religious 50.7%, of which Buddhist 23.2%, Protestant 19.7%, Roman Catholic 6.6%, Confucian 0.5%, Wonbulgyo 0.2%, Ch'ŏndogyo 0.1%, other 0.4%; nonreligious 49.3%.
Major cities (2003): Seoul 10,280,523; Pusan 3,747,369; Inch'ŏn 2,596,102; Taegu 2,540,647; Taejŏn 1,424,844.

Vital statistics

Birth rate per 1,000 population (2003): 10.3 (world avg. 21.3).
Death rate per 1,000 population (2003): 6.0 (world avg. 9.1).
Natural increase rate per 1,000 population (2003): 4.3 (world avg. 12.2).
Total fertility rate (avg. births per childbearing woman; 2003): 1.2.
Marriage rate per 1,000 population (2002): 6.3.
Divorce rate per 1,000 population (2002): 3.0.
Life expectancy at birth (2003): male 71.7 years; female 79.3 years.
Major causes of death per 100,000 population (2000): malignant neoplasms (cancers) 125.6; diseases of the circulatory system 124.6; accidents, poisoning, and violence 61.4; diseases of the respiratory system 34.3.

National economy

Budget (2002). Revenue: W 105,876,700,000,000 (tax revenue 88.6%, of which income and profits taxes 34.3%, value-added tax 30.2%; nontax revenue 11.4%). Expenditures: W 105,876,700,000,000 (economic services 25.9%, education 17.4%, defense 16.2%, social services 13.1%).
Public debt (external, outstanding; 2001): U.S.$33,742,000,000.
Production (metric tons except as noted). Agriculture, forestry, fishing (2003): rice 6,068,000, cabbages 2,576,000, onions 933,000, potatoes 666,000, tangerines, mandarins, etc. 666,000, cucumbers and gherkins 464,000, apples 433,000, grapes 422,000; livestock (number of live animals) 8,912,000 pigs, 1,935,000 cattle, 98,000,000 chickens; roundwood (2002) 4,062,638 cu m; fish catch (2001) 2,282,486. Mining and quarrying (2001): iron ore 195,000. Manufacturing (units; 2001): transistors 21,126,000,000; mobile phones 89,834,000; colour television receivers 15,914,000; room air conditioners 5,955,659; computer mainframes 3,920,832; rice cookers 2,998,000; passenger cars 2,155,000; cement 53,062,000 metric tons. Energy production (consumption): electricity (kW-hr; 2000) 295,156,000,000 (295,156,000,000); coal (metric tons; 2000) 4,150,000 (66,525,000); crude petroleum (barrels; 2000) none (891,500,000); petroleum products (metric tons; 2000) 97,275,000 (63,447,000); natural gas (cu m; 2000) none (19,833,700,000).
Household income and expenditure (2001). Average household size 3.5; annual income per household W 31,501,200 (U.S.$24,400); sources of income: wages 84.2%, other 15.8%; expenditure: food and beverages 26.3%, transportation and communications 16.3%, education 11.3%.
Gross national product (at current market prices; 2003): U.S.$576,426,000,000 (U.S.$12,030 per capita).

Structure of gross domestic product and labour force

	2000 in value W '000,000,000[1]	2000 % of total value[1]	2000 labour force	2000 % of labour force
Agriculture	24,859.8	6.0	2,288,000	10.4
Mining	1,439.4	0.3	18,000	0.1
Manufacturing	163,014.5	39.6	4,244,000	19.3
Construction	36,881.8	9.0	1,583,000	7.2
Public utilities	12,265.2	3.0	63,000	0.3
Transp. and commun.	41,276.1	10.0	1,260,000	5.7
Trade	58,469.5	14.2	5,943,000	27.1
Finance	83,860.0	20.4	2,089,000	9.5
Pub. admin., defense	29,171.7	7.1	753,000	3.4
Services	30,396.9	7.4	2,798,000	12.8
Other	–69,946.4[2]	–17.0[2]	911,000[3]	4.2[3]
TOTAL	411,688.5	100.0	21,950,000	100.0

Population economically active (2001): total 22,181,000; activity rate 46.9% (participation rates: ages 15–64, 64.6%; female 41.3%; unemployed [2002] 3.1%).

Price and earnings indexes (2000 = 100)

	1997	1998	1999	2000	2001	2002	2003
Consumer price index	90.2	97.0	97.8	100.0	104.1	106.9	110.7
Monthly earnings index	86.1	87.4	92.2	100.0	106.0	116.7	125.7

Tourism (2002): receipts U.S.$5,919,000,000; expenditures U.S.$9,036,000,000.
Land use as % of total land area (2000): in temporary crops 17.4%, in permanent crops 2.0%, in pasture 0.5%; overall forest area 63.3%.

Foreign trade[4]

Balance of trade (current prices)

	1997	1998	1999	2000	2001	2002
U.S.$'000,000	–8,452	+39,031	+23,934	+11,787	+9,341	+10,812
% of total	3.0%	17.3%	9.1%	3.5%	3.2%	3.4%

Imports (2001): U.S.$141,098,000,000 (electric and electronic products 19.4%, crude petroleum 15.1%, nonelectrical machinery and transport equipment 14.5%, chemicals and chemical products 9.2%, food and live animals 4.8%). *Major import sources:* Japan 18.9%; U.S. 15.9%; China 9.4%; Saudi Arabia 5.7%; Australia 3.9%.
Exports (2001): U.S.$150,439,000,000 (electric and electronic products 25.0%, transport equipment 17.0%, nonelectrical machinery and apparatus 15.6%, chemicals and chemical products 8.3%). *Major export destinations:* U.S. 20.7%; China 12.1%; Japan 11.0%; Hong Kong 6.3%; Taiwan 3.9%.

Transport and communications

Transport. Railroads (2001): length 6,819 km; passenger-km 29,172,000,000; metric ton-km cargo 10,492,000,000. Roads (2001): total length 91,396 km (paved 77%). Vehicles (2001): passenger cars 8,889,000; trucks and buses 3,768,000. Air transport (2002)[5]: passenger-km 48,325,000,000; metric ton-km cargo 4,590,000,000; airports (1996) with scheduled flights 14.

Communications

Medium	date	unit	number	units per 1,000 persons
Daily newspapers	2000	circulation	18,500,000	393
Radio	2000	receivers	48,600,000	1,033
Television	2000	receivers	17,100,000	364
Telephones	2003	main lines	22,877,000	472
Cellular telephones	2003	subscribers	33,592,000	694
Personal computers	2003	units	26,700,000	551
Internet	2003	users	29,220,000	603

Education and health

Educational attainment (1995). Percentage of population age 25 and over having: no formal schooling 8.5%; primary education or less 17.7%; some secondary and secondary 53.1%; postsecondary 20.6%. *Literacy* (2001): total population age 15 and over literate 97.9%; males 99.2%; females 96.6%.

Education (2001)

	schools	teachers	students	student/ teacher ratio
Primary (age 6–13)	13,739	171,690	4,634,571	27.0
Secondary (age 14–19)	4,739	197,699	3,742,325	18.9
Voc., teacher tr.	169	12,607	974,067	77.3
Higher[6]	162	43,309	1,729,638	39.9

Health (2002): physicians 78,592 (1 per 606 persons); hospital beds 316,015 (1 per 151 persons); infant mortality rate (2003) 7.3.
Food (2001): daily per capita caloric intake 3,055 (vegetable products 85%, animal products 15%); 130% of FAO recommended minimum.

Military

Total active duty personnel (2003): 686,000 (army 81.6%, navy 9.2%, air force 9.2%); U.S. military forces (2004): 40,258. *Military expenditure as percentage of GNP* (1999): 2.9% (world 2.4%); per capita expenditure U.S.$246.

[1]At 1995 constant prices. [2]Import duties less imputed bank service charges. [3]Includes 22,000 inadequately defined and 889,000 unemployed. [4]Imports c.i.f.; exports f.o.b. [5]Scheduled flights of Asiana and Korean Air only. [6]Excludes graduate schools.

Internet resources for further information:
- **National Statistical Office http://www.nso.go.kr/eng**

Kuwait

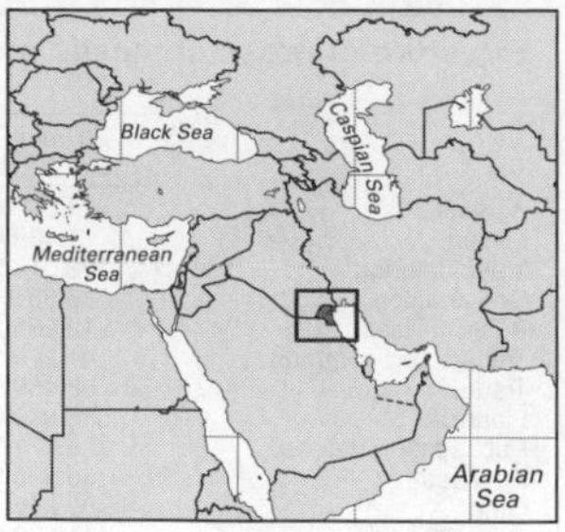

Official name: Dawlat al-Kuwayt (State of Kuwait).
Form of government: constitutional monarchy with one legislative body (National Assembly [50[1]]).
Head of state and government: Emir assisted by the Prime Minister[2].
Capital: Kuwait (city)[3].
Official language: Arabic.
Official religion: Islam.
Monetary unit: 1 Kuwaiti dinar (KD) = 1,000 fils; valuation (Sept. 1, 2004) 1 KD = U.S.$3.39 = £1.89.

Area and population

		area		population
Governorates	Capitals	sq mi	sq km	2001 estimate
Al-Aḥmadī	Al-Aḥmadī	1,977	5,120	364,484
Al-ʿAṣimah	Kuwait (city)	77	200	388,532
Al-Farwānīyah	Al-Farwānīyah	73	190	572,252
Al-Jahrāʾ	Al-Jahrāʾ	4,336	11,230	282,353
Ḥawallī	Ḥawallī }	69	178	488,294
Mubārak al-Kabīr	... }			144,981
Islands[4]	—	347	900	...
TOTAL		6,880[5]	17,818	2,240,896[6]

Demography

Population (2004): 2,586,000.
Density (2004): persons per sq mi 375.9, persons per sq km 145.1.
Urban-rural (2001): urban 96.1%; rural 3.9%.
Sex distribution (2003): male 60.31%; female 39.69%.
Age breakdown (2003): under 15, 27.9%; 15–29, 31.8%; 30–44, 23.9%; 45–59, 12.1%; 60–74, 3.7%; 75 and over, 0.6%.
Population projection: (2010) 3,032,000; (2020) 3,634,000.
Doubling time: 36 years.
Ethnic composition (2000): Arab 74%, of which Kuwaiti 30%, Palestinian 17%, Jordanian 10%, Bedouin 9%; Kurd 10%; Indo-Pakistani 8%; Persian 4%; other 4%.
Religious affiliation (1995): Muslim 85%, of which Sunnī 45%, Shīʿī 30%, other Muslim 10%; other (mostly Christian and Hindu) 15%.
Major cities (1995): As-Sālimīyah 130,215; Qalīb ash-Shuyūkh 102,178; Ḥawallī 82,238; Kuwait (city) 28,859 (urban agglomeration [2003] 1,222,000).

Vital statistics

Birth rate per 1,000 population (2003): 21.8 (world avg. 21.3).
Death rate per 1,000 population (2003): 2.5 (world avg. 9.1).
Natural increase rate per 1,000 population (2003): 19.3 (world avg. 12.2).
Total fertility rate (avg. births per childbearing woman; 2003): 3.1.
Marriage rate per 1,000 population (2000): 4.9.
Divorce rate per 1,000 population (2000): 1.7.
Life expectancy at birth (2003): male 75.7 years; female 77.6 years.
Major causes of death per 100,000 population (2000): circulatory diseases 75.5; accidents and violence 24.6; cancers 22.3; congenital anomalies 13.2; endocrine and metabolic diseases 10.9; respiratory diseases 9.1.

National economy

Budget[7] (2003–04). Revenue: KD 3,397,000,000 (oil revenue 87.5%). Expenditures: KD 5,666,000,000 (wages 32.4%, defense 18.5%, social security and welfare 14.8%, health 14.8%, economic development 8.5%, education 6.0%).
Tourism (2002): receipts from visitors U.S.$119,000,000; expenditures by nationals abroad U.S.$3,021,000,000.
Gross national product (2003): U.S.$38,037,000,000 (U.S.$16,340 per capita).

Structure of gross domestic product and labour force

	2003		2002	
	in value KD '000,000	% of total value	labour force	% of labour force
Agriculture	65.8	0.5	22,000	1.6
Mining (petroleum sector)	5,794.0[8]	46.6[8]	7,500	0.5
Manufacturing	897.3[8]	7.2[8]	83,600	6.1
Construction	285.3	2.3	108,300	7.9
Public utilities	300.8	2.4	8,700	0.6
Transp. and commun.	633.0	5.1	43,000	3.2
Trade, hotels	791.5	6.4	220,000	16.1
Finance and business services	1,385.8	11.1	59,100	4.3
Pub. admin., defense } Services }	2,744.1	22.1	720,500	52.8
Other	–456.3[9]	–3.7[9]	91,600[10]	6.7[10]
TOTAL	12,441.3	100.0	1,364,300	100.0[5]

Production (metric tons except as noted). Agriculture, forestry, fishing (2002): tomatoes 35,127, cucumbers and gherkins 33,004, eggplants 12,002, onions 3,327, garlic 448; livestock (number of live animals) 800,000 sheep, 130,000 goats, 18,000 cattle, 9,000 camels; fish catch (2001) 6,041. Mining and quarrying (2001): sulfur 524,000; lime 40,000. Manufacturing (value added in U.S.$'000,000; 1999): refined petroleum products 2,481; food products 170; nonmetallic mineral products 158; clothing and apparel 116; fabricated metal products 109. Construction (number of construction permits; 2001): residential 11,183; nonresidential 1,148. Energy production (consumption): electricity (kW-hr; 2000) 32,853,000,000 (32,853,000,000); crude petroleum (barrels; 2002) 680,000,000 ([2000] 274,129,000); petroleum products (metric tons; 2000) 33,410,000 (8,583,000); natural gas (cu m; 2002) 8,297,000,000 ([2000] 9,177,000,000).
Population economically active (2003): total 1,466,092, of which Kuwaiti 19.1%, non-Kuwaiti 80.9%; activity rate of total population 57.6% (participation rates: ages 15–59, 73.8%; female [1995] 26.1%; unemployed 1.2%).

Price and earnings indexes (2000 = 100)

	1997	1998	1999	2000	2001	2002
Consumer price index	95.2	95.4	98.2	100.0	101.7	103.1
Earnings index	...	...	...	...	...	...

Household income and expenditure. Average household size (2002) 5.0; sources of income (1986): wages and salaries 53.8%, self-employment 20.8%, other 25.4%; expenditure (2000)[11]: housing energy 26.7%, food 18.3%, transportation and communications 16.1%, household furnishings 14.7%, clothing and footwear 8.9%.
Land use as % of total land area (2000): in temporary crops 0.6%, in permanent crops 0.1%, in pasture 7.6%; overall forest area 0.3%.

Foreign trade[12]

Balance of trade (current prices)

	1998	1999	2000	2001	2002	2003
KD '000,000	+285	+1,384	+3,767	+2,556	+1,930	+2,945
% of total	5.2%	23.0%	46.2%	34.6%	26.1%	31.4%

Imports (2003): KD 3,217,000,000 (machinery and apparatus 24.0%, transport equipment 20.5%, food 14.0%, chemicals and chemical products 8.7%). *Major import sources:* U.S. 11.1%; Japan 10.7%; Germany 9.5%; Saudi Arabia 6.6%; Italy 5.5%, China 5.3%.
Exports (2003): KD 6,162,000,000 (crude petroleum and petroleum products 91.9%, ethylene products 3.0%, reexports 2.5%). *Major export destinations:* Japan 22.1%; South Korea 13.1%; U.S. 12.0%; Taiwan 10.7%; Singapore 10.2%.

Transport and communications

Transport. Railroads: none. Roads (1999): total length 2,765 mi, 4,450 km (paved 81%). Vehicles (2001): passenger cars 715,000; trucks and buses 226,000. Air transport (2003): passenger-mi 4,172,308,000, passenger-km 6,714,693,000; short ton-mi cargo 150,142,000, metric ton-km cargo 219,428,000; airports (2003) with scheduled flights 1.

Communications

Medium	date	unit	number	units per 1,000 persons
Daily newspapers	2000	circulation	836,000	374
Radio	2000	receivers	1,400,000	624
Television	2000	receivers	1,090,000	486
Telephones	2003	main lines	486,900	198
Cellular telephones	2003	subscribers	1,420,000	578
Personal computers	2002	units	285,000	121
Internet	2003	users	567,000	231

Education and health

Educational attainment (1988). Percentage of population age 25 and over having: no formal schooling 44.8%; primary education 8.6%; some secondary 15.1%; complete secondary 15.1%; higher 16.4%. *Literacy* (2001): total population age 15 and over literate 82.4%; males literate 84.3%; females literate 80.3%.

Education (2000–01)

	schools	teachers	students	student/ teacher ratio
Primary (age 6–9)[13, 14]	349	17,385	193,582	11.1
Secondary (age 10–17)[13]	117	9,234	76,221	8.3
Voc., teacher tr.[13]	40	1,107	2,997	2.7
Higher[15]	1	918	17,447	19.0

Health (2002): physicians 3,780 (1 per 625 persons); hospital beds 5,200 (1 per 455 persons); infant mortality rate per 1,000 live births (2003) 10.7.
Food (2001): daily per capita caloric intake 3,170 (vegetable products 78%, animal products 22%); 131% of FAO recommended minimum requirement.

Military

Total active duty personnel (2003): 15,500 (army [including central staff] 71.0%, navy 12.9%, air force 16.1%); U.S. and coalition troops (March 2004) 26,000. *Military expenditure as percentage of GNP* (1999): 7.7% (world 2.4%); per capita expenditure U.S.$1,410.

[1]Excludes cabinet ministers not elected to National Assembly serving ex officio. [2]As of July 13, 2003, the office of prime minister became separated from the role of emir for the first time since independence in 1961. [3]Officially Al-Kuwayt; Kuwait is variant. [4]Būbiyān Island 333 sq mi (863 sq km) and Warbah Island 14 sq mi (37 sq km). [5]Detail does not add to total given because of rounding. [6]Sum of governorate populations. Actual mid-year est. pop. is 2,243,080. [7]Preliminary. [8]Manufacturing includes petroleum products; Mining (petroleum sector) excludes petroleum products. [9]Includes import duties less imputed bank service charges. [10]Unclassified. [11]Weights of consumer price index components. [12]Imports c.i.f.; exports f.o.b. [13]Government schools only; private education: 112 schools, 7,324 teachers, 128,204 students. [14]Includes intermediate. [15]University only.

Internet resources for further information:
- **Central Bank of Kuwait http://www.cbk.gov.kw**
- **Ministry of Planning http://www.mop.gov.kw/MopWebSite/english/default.asp**

Kyrgyzstan

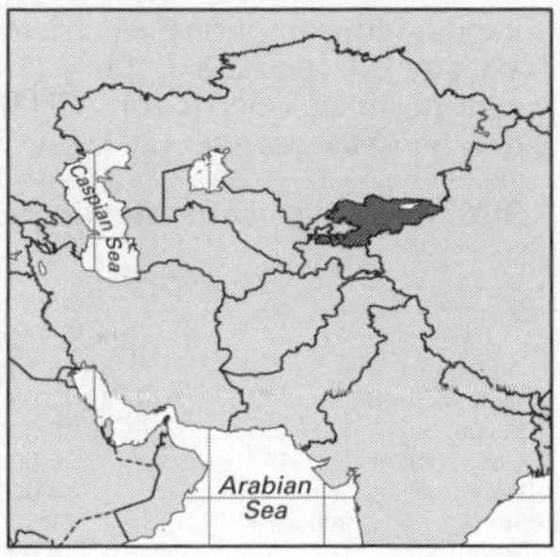

Official name: Respublika Kirgizstan (Kyrgyz); Kyrgyz Respublikasy (Russian) (Kyrgyz Republic).
Form of government: unitary multiparty republic with two legislative houses (Assembly of People's Representatives [45]; Legislative Assembly [60]).
Head of state and government: President assisted by Prime Minister.
Capital: Bishkek.
Official languages: Kyrgyz; Russian.
Official religion: none.
Monetary unit: 1 som (K.S.) = 100 tyiyn; valuation (Sept. 1, 2004) 1 U.S.$ = K.S. 42.22; 1 £ = K.S. 75.95.

Area and population

		area		population
Provinces	Capitals	sq mi	sq km	1999 census
Batken	Batken	6,573	17,024	382,426
Chüy (Chu)	Tokmok[1]	7,214	18,684	770,811
Jalal-Abad (Dzhalal-Abad)	Jalal-Abad (Dzhalal-Abad)	12,992	33,648	869,259
Naryn	Naryn	18,035	46,710	249,115
Osh	Osh	11,261	29,165	1,175,998
Talas	Talas	4,419	11,446	199,872
Ysyk-Köl (Issyk-Kul)	Ysyk-Köl (Issyk-Kul)	16,646	43,114	413,149
City				
Bishkek (Frunze)	—	49	127	762,308
TOTAL		77,199[2, 3]	199,945[2, 3]	4,822,938

Demography

Population (2004): 5,081,000.
Density (2004): persons per sq mi 65.8, persons per sq km 25.4.
Urban-rural (2003): urban 33.9%; rural 66.1%.
Sex distribution (2001): male 48.84%; female 51.16%.
Age breakdown (2001): under 15, 35.0%; 15–29, 28.1%; 30–44, 18.6%; 45–59, 9.2%; 60–74, 7.0%; 75 and over, 2.1%.
Population projection: (2010) 5,509,000; (2020) 6,314,000.
Doubling time: 48 years.
Ethnic composition (1999): Kyrgyz 64.9%; Uzbek 13.8%; Russian 12.5%; Hui 1.1%; Ukrainian 1.0%; Uighur 1.0%; other 5.7%.
Religious affiliation (1997): Muslim (mostly Sunnī) 75.0%; Christian 6.7%, of which Russian Orthodox 5.6%; other (mostly nonreligious) 18.3%.
Major cities (1999): Bishkek (Frunze) 750,327; Osh 208,520; Jalal-Abad 70,401; Tokmok 59,409; Kara-Köl 47,159.

Vital statistics

Birth rate per 1,000 population (2003): 21.9 (world avg. 21.3); (1994) legitimate 83.2%; illegitimate 16.8%.
Death rate per 1,000 population (2003): 7.3 (world avg. 9.1).
Natural increase rate per 1,000 population (2003): 14.6 (world avg. 12.2).
Total fertility rate (avg. births per childbearing woman; 2001): 2.5.
Marriage rate per 1,000 population (1999): 5.6.
Divorce rate per 1,000 population (1999): 4.6.
Life expectancy at birth (2003): male 63.5 years; female 71.7 years.
Major causes of death per 100,000 population (1999): diseases of the circulatory system 285.6; diseases of the respiratory system 84.2; malignant neoplasms (cancers) 59.9; accidents, poisoning, and violence 45.4.

National economy

Budget (2001). Revenue: K.S. 12,544,000,000 (tax revenue 73.2%, of which VAT 33.6%, taxes on income 16.0%, excise taxes 8.8%, other taxes 14.8%; nontax revenue 21.3%; grants 5.5%). Expenditures: K.S. 13,133,000,000 (education 21.7%; general public services 16.0%; social security 10.8%; health 10.5%; defense 7.5%).
Public debt (external, outstanding; 2002): U.S.$1,394,000,000.
Land use as % of total land area (2000): in temporary crops 7.1%, in permanent crops 0.3%, in pasture 48.4%; overall forest area 5.2%.
Population economically active (2001): total 1,939,000; activity rate of total population 39.2% (participation rates [2000]: ages 16–59 [male], 16–54 [female] 62.0%; female (1999) 44.9%; unemployed [2001] 7.8%).

Price and earnings indexes (2000 = 100)

	1997	1998	1999	2000	2001	2002	2003
Consumer price index	56.1	62.0	84.3	100.0	106.9	109.2	113.0
Average earnings index	57.8	71.4	89.2	100.0	118.4	137.5	...

Production (metric tons except as noted). Agriculture, forestry, fishing (2002): mixed grasses and legumes 2,900,000, wheat 1,306,000, potatoes 1,244,000, sugarbeets 525,000, corn (maize) 428,000, seed cotton 98,000, tobacco leaves 8,183; livestock (number of live animals) 3,104,000 sheep, 988,000 cattle, 350,000 horses; roundwood (2001) 26,000 cu m; fish catch (2001) 201. Mining and quarrying (2002): mercury 300; antimony 200; gold (2001) 24,600 kg. Manufacturing (value of production in '000,000 som; 2001): ferrous metals 21,268; nonferrous metals 21,243; flour 3,914; nonelectrical machinery 2,518; textiles 2,216; tobacco products 1,375. Energy production (consumption): electricity (kW-hr; 2001) 13,667,000,000 (11,503,000,000); hard coal (metric tons; 1999) 97,000 (878,000); lignite (metric tons; 2000) 321,000 (339,000); crude petroleum (barrels; 2001) 553,000 (553,000); petroleum products (metric tons; 2001) 131,000 (387,000); natural gas (cu m; 2001) 32,800,000 (655,700,000).
Household income and expenditure. Average household size (1999) 4.3; income per household (1994) 4,359 som (U.S.$325); sources of income (1999): wages and salaries 29.2%, self-employment 25.6%, other 45.2%; expenditure (1990): food and clothing 48.0%, health care 13.1%, housing 5.9%.
Gross national product (2003): U.S.$1,649,000,000 (U.S.$330 per capita).

Structure of gross domestic product and labour force

	2001		1999	
	in value K.S. '000,000	% of total value	labour force	% of labour force
Agriculture	25,554.6	34.6	924,300	48.6
Mining	16,596.4	22.5	9,500	0.5
Manufacturing			127,000	6.7
Public utilities			22,100	1.2
Construction	2,793.8	3.8	45,200	2.4
Transp. and commun.	3,230.5	4.4	65,800	3.4
Trade	9,343.9	12.6	195,200	10.3
Finance	866.7	1.2	35,800	1.9
Public admin., defense	3,729.1	5.0	65,700	3.4
Services	6,412.0	8.7	273,700	14.4
Other	5,356.3[4]	7.2[4]	136,800[5]	7.2[5]
TOTAL	73,883.3	100.0	1,901,100	100.0

Tourism (2002): receipts from visitors, U.S.$36,000,000; expenditures by nationals abroad, U.S.$10,000,000.

Foreign trade[6]

Balance of trade (current prices)

	1996	1997	1998	1999	2000	2001
U.S.$'000,000	–251.7	–15.2	–220.7	–88.6	+4.0	+39.9
% of total	19.2%	1.2%	17.1%	8.7%	0.4%	4.3%

Imports (2001): U.S.$467,200,000 (petroleum and natural gas 22.6%, machinery and apparatus 21.0%, food products 11.7%, chemicals and chemical products 9.5%). *Major import sources:* Russia 18.2%; Kazakhstan 17.5%; Uzbekistan 14.3%; China 10.4%; United States 5.7%.
Exports (2001): U.S.$476,200,000 (nonferrous metals [significantly gold] 51.7%, machinery and apparatus 12.0%, electricity 9.8%, agricultural products [significantly tobacco] 9.5%). *Major export destinations:* Switzerland 26.1%; Germany 19.8%; Russia 13.5%; Uzbekistan 10.1%; Kazakhstan 8.2%.

Transport and communications

Transport. Railroads (2000): length 424 km; passenger km 44,000,000; metric ton-km cargo 348,000,000. Roads (1999): total length 18,500 km (paved 91%). Vehicles (2000): passenger cars 187,322; trucks and buses, n.a. Air transport (1999): passenger-km 532,000,000; metric ton-km cargo 56,000,000; airports with scheduled flights 2.

Communications

Medium	date	unit	number	units per 1,000 persons
Daily newspapers	2000	circulation	73,000	15
Radio	2000	receivers	542,000	111
Television	2000	receivers	239,000	49
Telephones	2002	main lines	394,800	79
Cellular phones	2002	subscribers	53,100	10
Personal computers	2002	units	65,000	13
Internet	2002	users	152,000	30

Education and health

Educational attainment (1999). Percentage of population age 15 and over having: primary education 6.3%; some secondary 18.3%; completed secondary 50.0%; some postsecondary 14.9%; higher 10.5%. *Literacy* (1999): total population age 15 and over literate 97.5%; males 98.5%; females 96.5%.

Education (1999–2000)

	schools	teachers	students	student/ teacher ratio
Primary (age 6–13)	1,985	19,200	466,200	24.3
Secondary (age 14–17)	1,474[7]	36,600	633,900	17.3
Voc., teacher tr.	53[7]	5,100	52,200	10.2
Higher	23	8,400	159,200	19.0

Health (1997): physicians 15,100 (1 per 307 persons); hospital beds 40,700 (1 per 114 persons); infant mortality rate per 1,000 live births (2003) 38.0.
Food (2001): daily per capita caloric intake 2,882 (vegetable products 81%, animal products 19%); 111% of FAO recommended minimum.

Military

Total active duty personnel (2003): 10,900 (army 78.0%, air force 22.0%)[8]. *Military expenditure as percentage of GNP* (1999): 2.4% (world 2.4%); per capita expenditure U.S.$62.

[1]As of March 2003. [2]Area of Kyrgyzstan prior to border demarcation agreement signed with China in September 2004. [3]Detail does not add to total given because of statistical discrepancy. [4]Taxes on products less imputed bank service charge. [5]Unemployed. [6]Imports are f.o.b. in balance of trade and c.i.f. for commodities and trading partners. [7]1993–94. [8]U.S. troops (July 2004) 1,200. A Russian air base opened in Kyrgyzstan in October 2003.

Internet resources for further information:
- **National Statistical Committee of the Kyrgyz Republic http://nsc.bishkek.su/English/index.html**
- **National Bank of Kyrgyz Republic http://www.nbkr.kg/web/interfeis.builder_frame?language=ENG**

Laos

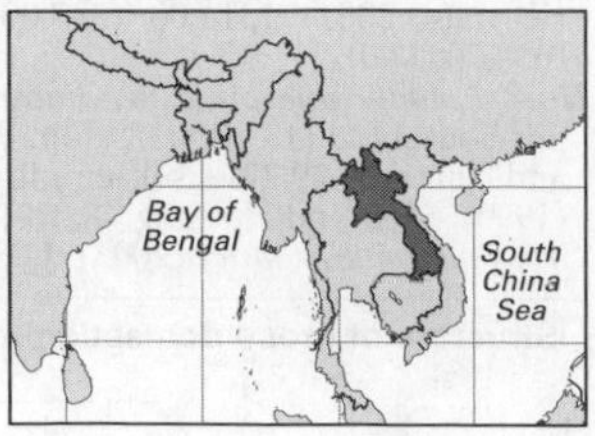

Official name: Sathalanalat Paxathipatai Paxaxôn Lao (Lao People's Democratic Republic).
Form of government: unitary single-party people's republic with one legislative house (National Assembly [109]).
Chief of state: President.
Head of government: Prime Minister.
Capital: Vientiane (Viangchan).
Official language: Lao.
Official religion: none.
Monetary unit: 1 kip (KN) = 100 at; valuation (Sept. 1, 2004) 1 U.S.$ = KN 7,841; 1 £ = KN 14,106.

Area and population

Provinces	Capitals	area sq mi	area sq km	population 1996 estimate
Attapu	Attapu	3,985	10,320	87,700
Bokèo	Houayxay	2,392	6,196	114,900
Bolikhamxai	Pakxan	5,739	14,863	164,900
Champasak	Pakxé	5,952	15,415	503,300
Houaphan	Xam Nua	6,371	16,500	247,300
Khammouan	Thakhek	6,299	16,315	275,400
Louangnamtha	Louangnamtha	3,600	9,325	115,200
Louangphrabang	Louangphrabang	6,515	16,875	367,200
Oudomxay	Xay	5,934	15,370	211,300
Phôngsali	Phôngsali	6,282	16,270	153,400
Salavan	Salavan	4,128	10,691	258,300
Savannakhét	Savannakhét	8,407	21,774	674,900
Special Region	...	2,743	7,105	54,200
Viangchan	Muang Phôn-Hông	6,149	15,927	286,800
Xaignabouli	Xaignabouli	6,328	16,389	293,300
Xékong	Thong	2,959	7,665	64,200
Xiangkhoang	Phônsavan	6,131	15,880	201,200
Municipalities				
Viangchan	Vientiane (Viangchan)	1,514	3,920	531,800
TOTAL		91,429[1]	236,800	4,605,300

Demography

Population (2004): 5,787,000.
Density (2004): persons per sq mi 63.3, persons per sq km 24.4.
Urban-rural (2002): urban 25.0%; rural 75.0%.
Sex distribution (2002): male 49.97%; female 50.03%.
Age breakdown (2000): under 15, 42.8%; 15–29, 27.0%; 30–44, 16.3%; 45–59, 8.3%; 60–74, 4.6%; 75 and over, 1.0%.
Population projection: (2010) 6,592,000; (2020) 7,967,000.
Doubling time: 28 years.
Ethnic composition (2000): Lao-Lum (Lao) 53.0%; Lao-Theung (Mon-Khmer) 23.0%; Lao-Tai (Tai) 13.0%; Lao-Soung (Miao [Hmong] and Man [Yao]) 10.0%; other (ethnic Chinese or Vietnamese) 1.0%.
Religious affiliation (2000): Buddhist 48.8%; traditional beliefs 41.7%; nonreligious 4.3%; Christian 2.1%; other 3.1%.
Major cities (2003): Vientiane 194,200 (urban agglomeration [2001] 663,000); Savannakhét 58,200; Pakxé 50,100; Xam Nua 40,700; Muang Khammouan 27,300; Louangphrabang 26,400.

Vital statistics

Birth rate per 1,000 population (2003): 36.9 (world avg. 21.3).
Death rate per 1,000 population (2004): 12.4 (world avg. 9.1).
Natural increase rate per 1,000 population (2003): 24.5 (world avg. 12.2).
Total fertility rate (avg. births per childbearing woman; 2003): 4.9.
Life expectancy at birth (2003): male 52.3 years; female 56.3 years.
Major causes of death per 100,000 population (incomplete, 1990): malaria 7.6; pneumonia 3.0; meningitis 1.5; diarrhea 1.2; tuberculosis 0.8.

National economy

Budget (2001–02). Revenue: KN 2,481,000,000,000 (tax revenue 82.3%; nontax revenue 17.7%). Expenditures: KN 3,614,000,000,000 (capital expenditure 59.9%, of which foreign-financed 34.8%; current expenditure 40.1%).
Public debt (external, outstanding; 2002): U.S.$2,620,000,000.
Tourism (2002): receipts from visitors U.S.$113,000,000; expenditures by nationals abroad (2000) U.S.$8,000,000.
Population economically active (2000): total 2,625,000; activity rate of total population *c.* 50% (participation rates: ages 15–64, n.a.; female *c.* 47%; unemployed [1994] 2.6%).

Price index (2000 = 100)

	1999	2000	2001	2002	2003
Consumer price index	79.9	100.0	107.8	119.3	137.7

Production (metric tons except as noted). Agriculture, forestry, fishing (2002): rice 2,410,000, sugarcane 210,000, corn (maize) 113,000, sweet potatoes 102,000, cassava 70,000, pineapples 35,000, potatoes 35,000, oranges 28,000, bananas 23,500, coffee 18,000, seed cotton 10,145; livestock (number of live animals) 1,425,900 pigs, 1,150,000 cattle, 1,060,000 water buffalo, 15,000,000 chickens; roundwood (2001) 6,455,000 cu m; fish catch (2001) 80,000. Mining and quarrying (2002): gypsum 130,000; tin (metal content) 350; gold (2003) 115,000 troy oz[2]. Manufacturing (1998): plastic products 3,225; tobacco 1,000; detergent 912; nails 624; clothing 23,000,000 pieces; cigarettes 55,000,000 packs; beer 332,000 hectolitres; soft drinks 125,000 hectolitres. Energy production (consumption): electricity (kW-hr; 2000) 1,225,000,000 (497,000,000); coal (metric tons; 2000) 1,000 (1,000); crude petroleum, none (none); petroleum products (metric tons; 2000) none (119,000); natural gas, none (none).
Gross national product (2003): U.S.$1,821,000,000 (U.S.$320 per capita).

Structure of gross domestic product and labour force

	2001 in value KN '000,000[3]	2001 % of total value	2000 labour force	2000 % of labour force
Agriculture	606,000	50.9	2,007,000	76.5
Manufacturing	211,000	17.7		
Mining	6,000	0.5		
Construction	29,000	2.4		
Public utilities	34,000	2.8		
Transp. and commun.	71,000	6.0	618,000	23.5
Trade	114,000	9.6		
Finance	44,000	3.7		
Pub. admin., defense	34,000	2.8		
Services	33,000	2.8		
Other	9,000	0.8		
TOTAL	1,191,000	100.0	2,625,000	100.0

Household income and expenditure. Average household size (1995) 6.1; average annual income per household KN 3,710 (U.S.$371); sources of income: n.a.; expenditure: n.a.
Land use as % of total land area (2000): in temporary crops 3.8%, in permanent crops 0.4%, in pasture 3.8%; overall forest area 54.4%.

Foreign trade[4]

Balance of trade (current prices)

	1997	1998	1999	2000	2001	2002
U.S.$'000,000	–347	–183	–214	–218	–197	–133
% of total	32.6%	19.9%	25.6%	23.7%	22.9%	18.3%

Imports (2000): U.S.$569,000,000 (consumption goods 50.6%, mineral fuels 13.9%, materials for garment assembly 10.6%, construction and electrical equipment 7.6%). *Major import sources* (2001): Thailand 52.0%; Vietnam 26.5%; China 5.7%; Singapore 3.3%; Japan 1.5%.
Exports (2000): U.S.$351,000,000 (electricity 32.0%, garments 26.1%, wood products [mostly logs and timber] 24.8%, motorcycles 6.3%). *Major export destinations* (2001): Vietnam 41.5%; Thailand 14.8%; France 6.1%; Germany 4.6%; Belgium 2.2%.

Transport and communications

Transport. Railroads: none. Roads (1999): total length 13,494 mi, 21,716 km (paved [1995] 45%). Vehicles (1996): passenger cars 16,320; trucks and buses 4,200. Air transport (1997): passenger-mi 29,000,000, passenger-km 48,000,000; short ton-mi cargo 3,000,000, metric ton-km cargo 5,000,000; airports (1996) with scheduled flights 11.

Communications

Medium	date	unit	number	units per 1,000 persons
Daily newspapers	2000	circulation	21,100	4.0
Radio	2000	receivers	781,000	148
Television	2000	receivers	52,800	10
Telephones	2002	main lines	61,900	11
Cellular telephones	2002	subscribers	55,200	10
Personal computers	2002	units	15,000	2.7
Internet	2002	users	18,000	3.3

Education and health

Educational attainment (1985). Percentage of population age 6 and over having: no schooling 49.3%; primary 41.2%; secondary 9.1%; higher 0.4%. *Literacy* (1995): total population age 15 and over literate 56.6%; males literate 69.4%; females literate 44.4%.

Education (1996–97)

	schools	teachers	students	student/ teacher ratio
Primary (age 6–10)	7,896	25,831	786,335	30.4
Secondary (age 11–16)	...	10,717	180,160	16.8
Voc., teacher tr.	...	1,600[5]	9,400[5]	5.9[5]
Higher	...	1,369	12,732	9.3

Health: physicians (1996) 1,167 (1 per 4,115 persons); hospital beds (1990) 10,364 (1 per 402 persons); infant mortality rate (2003) 88.9.
Food (2001): daily per capita caloric intake 2,309 (vegetable products 93%, animal products 7%); (2001) 108% of FAO recommended minimum requirement.

Military

Total active duty personnel (2003): 29,100 (army 88.0%, air force 12.0%). *Military expenditure as percentage of GNP* (1999): 2.0% (world 2.4%); per capita expenditure U.S.$5.

[1]Detail does not add to total given because of rounding. [2]Gold production began February 2003; production figure is through mid-September 2003 only. [3]At constant 1990 prices. [4]Imports c.i.f.; exports f.o.b. [5]1995–96.

Internet resources for further information:
- **Asian Development Bank: Key Indicators 2004 http://www.adb.org**

Latvia

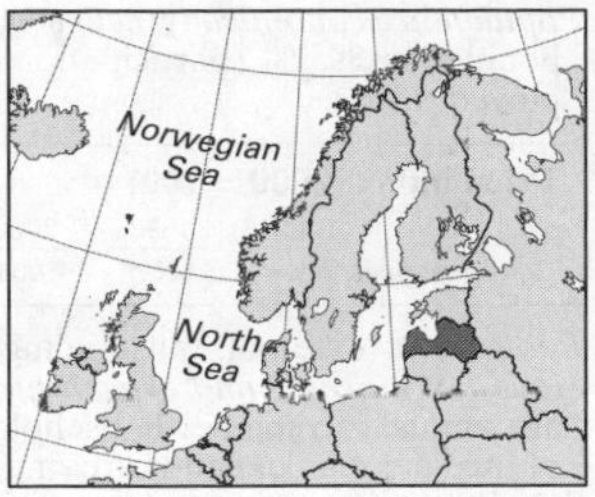

Official name: Latvijas Republika (Republic of Latvia).
Form of government: unitary multiparty republic with a single legislative body (Parliament, or Saeima [100]).
Chief of state: President.
Head of government: Prime Minister.
Capital: Riga.
Official language: Latvian.
Official religion: none.
Monetary unit: 1 lats (Ls; plural lati) = 100 santimi; valuation (Sept. 1, 2004) 1 U.S.$ = 0.54 lats; 1 £ = 0.97 lats.

Area and population

	area	population		area	population
Cities	sq km	2002[1] estimate	**Districts**	sq km	2002[1] estimate
Daugavpils	72	113,409	Jelgava	1,604	37,086
Jelgava	60	65,927	Krāslava	2,285	36,203
Jūrmala	100	55,328	Kuldīga	2,502	37,584
Liepāja	60	87,505	Liepāja	3,594	46,170
Rēzekne	17	38,054	Limbaži	2,602	39,920
Riga	307	747,157	Ludza	2,569	34,380
Ventspils	46	44,004	Madona	3,346	45,717
			Ogre	1,840	63,028
Districts			Preiļi	2,041	41,041
Aizkraukle	2,565	41,546	Rēzekne	2,655	43,012
Alūksne	2,243	26,020	Rīga (Riga)	3,059	145,261
Balvi	2,386	29,843	Saldus	2,182	38,311
Bauska	1,882	52,517	Talsi	2,751	48,959
Cēsis	3,067	59,914	Tukums	2,447	55,050
Daugavpils	2,525	42,193	Valka	2,437	33,597
Dobele	1,633	39,791	Valmiera	2,365	59,593
Gulbene	1,877	27,937	Ventspils	2,472	14,529
Jēkabpils	2,998	55,182	TOTAL	64,589	2,345,768

Demography

Population (2004): 2,312,000.
Density (2004): persons per sq mi 92.7, persons per sq km 35.8.
Urban-rural (2002): urban 67.8%; rural 32.2%.
Sex distribution (2002): male 46.03%; female 53.97%.
Age breakdown (2000): under 15, 18.1%; 15–29, 21.2%; 30–44, 21.4%; 45–59, 18.3%; 60–74, 15.7%; 75 and over, 5.3%.
Population projection: (2010) 2,224,000; (2020) 2,083,000.
Ethnic composition (2002): Latvian 58.2%; Russian 29.2%; Belarusian 4.0%; Ukrainian 2.6%; Polish 2.5%; Lithuanian 1.4%; other 2.1%.
Religious affiliation (1995): Christian 39.6%, of which Protestant 16.7% (of which Lutheran 14.6%), Roman Catholic 14.9%, Orthodox 8.0%; Jewish 0.6%; other (mostly nonreligious) 59.8%.
Major cities (2002[1]): Riga 747,157; Daugavpils 113,409; Liepāja 87,505; Jelgava 65,927; Jūrmala 55,328.

Vital statistics

Birth rate per 1,000 population (2002): 8.6 (world avg. 21.3); (1998) legitimate 62.9%; illegitimate 37.1%.
Death rate per 1,000 population (2002): 13.9 (world avg. 9.1).
Natural increase rate per 1,000 population (2002): –5.3 (world avg. 12.2).
Total fertility rate (avg. births per childbearing woman; 2002): 1.2.
Marriage rate per 1,000 population (2002): 4.2.
Divorce rate per 1,000 population (2002): 2.5.
Life expectancy at birth (2002): male 65.4 years; female 76.8 years.
Major causes of death per 100,000 population (2002): diseases of the circulatory system 777.8; malignant neoplasms (cancers) 245.0; accidents, poisoning, and violence 156.8, of which suicide 28.7; diseases of the digestive system 43.1.

National economy

Budget (2001). Revenue: Ls 1,244,100,000 (social security contributions 35.3%, value-added taxes 28.2%, income taxes 14.3%, excises 13.0%, nontax revenue 9.2%). Expenditures: Ls 1,399,800,000 (social security and welfare 40.7%, health 11.0%, police 7.0%, education 6.3%, defense 3.1%).
Public debt (external, outstanding; 2002): U.S.$1,124,000,000.
Production (metric tons except as noted). Agriculture, forestry, fishing (2002): grasses for forage and silage 14,000,000, potatoes 768,000, sugar beets 622,000, wheat 520,000, barley 262,000, rye 102,000; livestock (number of live animals) 453,000 pigs, 388,000 cattle; roundwood (2001) 14,037,000 cu m; fish catch (2002) 105,000. Mining and quarrying (2001): peat 555,000. Manufacturing (value added in Ls '000,000; 1998): alcoholic beverages 79.4; sawn wood 64.4; veneer/plywood 37.6; dairy products 30.5; wearing apparel 30.4; bakery products 29.8; fish processing 24.2. Energy production (consumption): electricity (kW-hr; 2001) 4,236,000,000 ([2002] 6,323,000,000); coal (2002) none (102,000); crude petroleum[2], none (none); petroleum products[2] (2002) none (1,084,000); natural gas (cu m; 2002) none (1,610,000,000).
Household income and expenditure. Average household size (2000) 2.7; annual disposable income per household (2002) Ls 2,076 (U.S.$3,460); sources of income (1998): wages and salaries 55.8%, pensions and transfers 25.7%; expenditure (2001–02): food, beverages, and tobacco 40.0%, transportation and communications 15.0%, housing and energy 14.0%.
Tourism (in U.S.$'000,000; 2002): receipts 161; expenditures 230.
Gross national product (2003): U.S.$9,441,000,000 (U.S.$4,070 per capita).

Structure of gross domestic product and labour force

	2001		2002	
	in value Ls '000,000	% of total value	labour force	% of labour force
Agriculture, forestry	174.3	3.7	153,000	13.6
Mining and quarrying	5.6	0.1	} 193,000	} 17.2
Manufacturing	624.9	13.2		
Public utilities	158.7	3.3		
Construction	259.7	5.5	60,000	5.3
Transp. and commun.	645.4	13.6	86,000	7.7
Trade, restaurants	845.2	17.8	172,000	15.3
Finance, real estate	674.5	14.2	52,000	4.6
Pub. admin., defense	271.1	5.7	68,000	6.1
Services	544.8	11.5	204,000	18.2
Other	536.6[3]	11.3[3]	135,000[4]	12.0[4]
TOTAL	4,740.8	100.0[5]	1,123,000	100.0

Population economically active (2002): total 1,123,000; activity rate of total population 48.1% (participation rates: ages 15–64 [2000] 67.5%; female [2000] 48.5%; unemployed 12.0%).

Price and earnings indexes (2000 = 100)

	1997	1998	1999	2000	2001	2002	2003
Consumer price index	90.9	95.2	97.4	100.0	102.5	104.5	107.5
Annual earnings index	80.8	89.2	94.3	100.0	106.1	114.1	...

Land use as % of total land area (2000): in temporary crops 29.7%, in permanent crops 0.5%, in pasture 9.8%; overall forest area 47.1%.

Foreign trade[6]

Balance of trade (current prices)

	1997	1998	1999	2000	2001	2002
Ls '000,000	–610	–812	–716	–803	–945	–1,088
% of total	23.9%	27.5%	26.2%	26.2%	27.4%	27.9%

Imports (2002): Ls 2,497,000,000 (machinery and apparatus 21.3%, chemicals and chemical products 10.5%, transport vehicles 9.8%, mineral fuels 9.7%). *Major import sources:* Germany 17.2%; Lithuania 9.8%; Russia 8.8%; Finland 8.0%; Sweden 6.4%.
Exports (2002): Ls 1,409,000,000 (wood and wood products [mostly sawn wood] 33.6%, base and fabricated metals [mostly iron and steel] 13.2%, textiles and clothing 12.8%). *Major export destinations:* Germany 15.5%; U.K. 14.6%; Sweden 10.5%; Lithuania 8.4%; Estonia 6.0%.

Transport and communications

Transport. Railroads (2002): length 2,270 km; passenger-km (2000) 715,000,000; metric-km cargo 15,020,000,000. Roads (1999): total length 73,227 km (paved 39%). Vehicles (2002): passenger cars 552,200; trucks and buses 113,900. Air transport (1999): passenger-km 238,000,000; metric ton km cargo 10,000,000; airports with scheduled flights (2001) 2.

Communications

Medium	date	unit	number	units per 1,000 persons
Daily newspapers	2000	circulation	586,000	247
Radio	2000	receivers	1,650,000	695
Television	2002	receivers	1,955,000	850
Telephones	2003	main lines	653,900	283
Cellular telephones	2003	subscribers	1,219,600	529
Personal computers	2002	units	400,000	171
Internet	2003	users	936,000	406

Education and health

Educational attainment (2000). Percentage of population age 15 and over having: some and complete primary education 8.5%; lower secondary 26.5%; upper secondary 51.1%; higher 13.9%. *Literacy* (2000): 99.8%.

Education (2000–01)

	schools	teachers	students	student/ teacher ratio
Primary } Secondary }	1,074	25,795	359,818	13.9
Vocational	...	5,439	48,625	8.9
Higher	33	4,486[7]	101,270	...

Health (2002): physicians 7,900 (1 per 295 persons); hospital beds 18,200 (1 per 128 persons); infant mortality rate per 1,000 live births (2002) 9.9.
Food (2001): daily per capita caloric intake 2,809 (vegetable products 72%, animal products 28%); 110% of FAO recommended minimum requirement.

Military

Total active duty personnel (2003): 4,880[8] (army 82.0%, navy 12.7%, air force 5.3%). *Military expenditure as percentage of GNP* (1999): 0.9% (world 2.4%); per capita expenditure U.S.$59.

[1]January 1. [2]In late 2002 shipments of Russian crude and refined petroleum through Latvia were halted by the Russian government. These shipments had not resumed by November 2004. [3]Indirect taxes less subsidies. [4]Unemployed. [5]Detail does not add to total given because of rounding. [6]Imports c.i.f.; exports f.o.b. [7]1996–97. [8]Excludes 3,200 border guards classified as paramilitary.

Internet resources for further information:
- **Bank of Latvia http://www.bank.lv/eng/info/jaunzin**
- **Central Statistical Bureau of Latvia http://www.csb.lv/avidus.cfm**

Lebanon

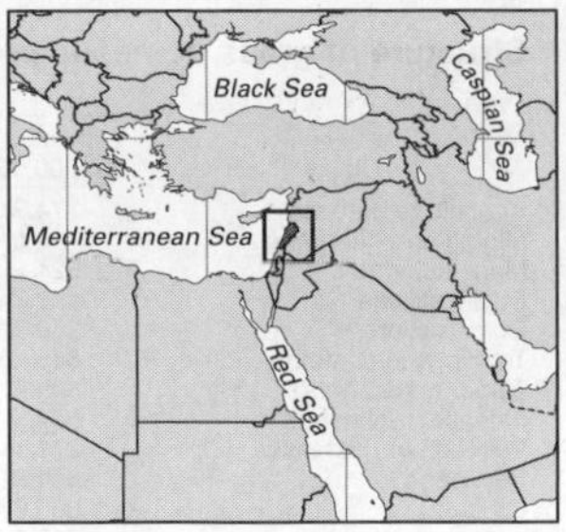

Official name: Al-Jumhūrīyah al-Lubnānīyah (Lebanese Republic).
Form of government: unitary multiparty republic with one legislative house (National Assembly [128])[1].
Chief of state: President.
Head of government: Prime Minister.
Capital: Beirut.
Official language: Arabic.
Official religion: none.
Monetary unit: 1 Lebanese pound (£L) = 100 piastres; valuation (Sept. 1, 2004) 1 U.S.$ = £L 1,508; 1 £ = £L 2,713.

Area and population

		area		population
Governorates	**Capitals**	sq mi	sq km	1996 estimate
Al-Biqāʿ	Zaḥlah	1,653	4,280	399,890
Al-Janūb	Sidon (Ṣaydā)	364	943	283,056
An-Nabaṭīyah	An-Nabaṭīyah	408	1,058	205,412
Ash-Shamāl	Tripoli (Ṭarābulus)	765	1,981	670,609
Bayrūt	Beirut (Bayrūt)	7	18	407,403
Jabal Lubnān	Bʿabdā	753	1,950	1,145,458
TOTAL		4,016[2]	10,400[2]	3,111,828

Demography

Population (2004): 3,777,000[3].
Density (2004): persons per sq mi 940.5, persons per sq km 363.2.
Urban-rural (2001): urban 90.1%; rural 9.9%.
Sex distribution (2002): male 48.48%; female 51.52%.
Age breakdown (2002): under 15, 27.4%; 15–29, 32.2%; 30–44, 21.0%; 45–59, 10.1%; 60–74, 7.1%; 75 and over, 2.2%.
Population projection: (2010) 4,056,000; (2020) 4,417,000.
Doubling time: 53 years.
Ethnic composition (2000): Arab 84.5%, of which Lebanese 71.2%, Palestinian 12.1%; Armenian 6.8%; Kurd 6.1%; other 2.6%.
Religious affiliation (1995): Muslim 55.3%, of which Shīʿī 34.0%, Sunnī 21.3%; Christian 37.6%, of which Catholic 25.1% (Maronite 19.0%, Greek Catholic or Melchite 4.6%), Orthodox 11.7% (Greek Orthodox 6.0%, Armenian Apostolic 5.2%), Protestant 0.5%; Druze 7.1%.
Major cities (1998): Beirut 1,100,000 (urban agglomeration 2,115,000[4]); Tripoli 200,000; Sidon 140,000; Tyre (Ṣūr) 110,000; An-Nabaṭīyah 84,000; Jūniyah 75,000.

Vital statistics

Birth rate per 1,000 population (2003): 19.7 (world avg. 21.3).
Death rate per 1,000 population (2003): 6.3 (world avg. 9.1).
Natural increase rate per 1,000 population (2003): 13.4 (world avg. 12.2).
Total fertility rate (avg. births per childbearing woman; 2003): 1.9.
Life expectancy at birth (2003): male 69.6 years; female 74.6 years.
Major causes of death: n.a.

National economy

Budget (2000). Revenue: £L 4,091,435,000,000 (1998; tax revenue 74.6%, of which customs revenues 44.1%, income tax 9.0%, taxes on goods and services 8.4%, property tax 8.4%, miscellaneous taxes and fees 2.1%; nontax revenue 25.4%). Expenditures: £L 8,190,034,000,000 (current expenditures 81.1%, of which debt service 40.0%, public services 13.3%, defense 9.7%, education 8.3%, social security 6.4%, health 2.6%; capital expenditures 18.9%).
Production (metric tons except as noted). Agriculture, forestry, fishing (2002): potatoes 257,000, tomatoes 247,000, cucumbers and gherkins 161,000, oranges 155,800, onions 144,200, wheat 139,500, grapes 116,200, apples 112,000, lemons and limes 103,100, olives 85,800; livestock (number of live animals) 385,000 goats, 350,000 sheep, 79,000 cattle, 33,000,000 chickens; roundwood (2001) 89,426 cu m; fish catch (2001) 3,970. Mining and quarrying (1996): lime 16,000; salt 4,000; gypsum 2,000. Manufacturing (2001): cement 2,727,000; flour 420,000; olive oil 7,000. Construction (2001): 6,923,000 sq m[5]. Energy production (consumption): electricity (kW-hr; 2001) 10,452,000,000 ([2000] 10,633,000,000); coal, n.a. (117,000); crude petroleum (barrels; 1998) none (1,358,000); petroleum products (metric tons; 2001) none (4,784,000).
Gross national product (2003): U.S.$18,187,000,000 (U.S.$4,040 per capita).

Structure of gross domestic product and labour force

	1995			
	in value U.S.$'000,000	% of total value	labour force	% of labour force
Agriculture	380	4.0	143,900	14.0
Mining	—	—		
Manufacturing	1,235	13.0	277,600	27.0
Construction	950	10.0		
Public utilities Transp. and commun.	2,375[6]	25.0[6]		
Trade	2,660	28.0	606,500	59.0
Finance Real estate and business services Services	1,900	20.0		
Pub. admin., defense	[6]	[6]		
TOTAL	9,500	100.0	1,028,000	100.0

Population economically active (1997): total 1,362,000; activity rate of total population 39.7% (participation rates: over age 15, n.a.; female, n.a.; unemployed 8.5%).

Price index (2000 = 100)

	1999	2000	2001	2002	2003
Consumer price index	100.1	100.0	99.5	98.9	98.9

Public debt (external, outstanding; 2002): U.S.$13,829,000,000.
Household income and expenditure. Average household size (2000) 4.5; average annual income per household (1994)[7] £L 2,400,000 (U.S.$1,430); sources of income: n.a.; expenditure: n.a.
Tourism (2002): receipts from visitors U.S.$956,000,000.
Land use as % of total land area (2000): in temporary crops 18.6%, in permanent crops 13.9%, in pasture 1.6%; overall forest area 3.5%.

Foreign trade[8]

Balance of trade (current prices)

	1997	1998	1999	2000	2001	2002
U.S.$'000,000	–6,824	–6,408	–5,530	–5,514	–6,423	–5,399
% of total	84.1%	82.9%	80.3%	79.4%	78.7%	72.1%

Imports (2002): U.S.$6,445,000,000 (mineral products 15.1%, machinery and apparatus 13.4%, food and live animals 13.3%, chemicals and chemical products 9.8%). *Major import sources:* Italy 10.8%; Germany 9.0%; France 8.0%; U.S. 7.2%; China 6.7%.
Exports (2002): U.S.$1,046,000,000 (precious metal [significantly gold] jewelry 20.5%, machinery and apparatus 11.4%, chemicals and chemical products 10.3%, food and beverages 9.8%, paper and paper products 9.4%). *Major export destinations:* Switzerland 12.6%; Saudi Arabia 9.2%; U.A.E. 9.1%; Syria 7.2%; Iraq 6.8%.

Transport and communications

Transport. Railroads: [9]. Roads (1996): total length 6,350 km (paved 95%). Vehicles (1997): passenger cars 1,299,398; trucks and buses 85,242. Merchant marine (1992): vessels (100 gross tons and over) 163; total deadweight tonnage 438,165. Air transport (2001)[10]: passenger-km 1,661,000,000; metric ton-km cargo 216,700,000; airports (1999) 1.

Communications

Medium	date	unit	number	units per 1,000 persons
Daily newspapers	2000	circulation	383,000	107
Radio	2000	receivers	2,460,000	687
Television	2000	receivers	1,200,000	335
Telephones	2002	main lines	678,800	198
Cellular telephones	2002	subscribers	775,100	227
Personal computers	2002	units	275,000	81
Internet	2002	users	400,000	117

Education and health

Educational attainment: n.a. *Literacy* (2000): total population age 15 and over literate 87.4%; males literate 93.1%; females literate 82.2%.

Education (1996–97)

	schools	teachers	students	student/ teacher ratio
Primary (age 5–9)	2,160	...	382,309	...
Secondary (age 10–16)	...	...	292,002	...
Voc., teacher tr.	275[11]	7,745	55,848	7.2
Higher	20	10,444[12]	81,588[12]	7.8[12]

Health (1997): physicians 7,203 (1 per 476 persons); hospital beds (1995) 11,596 (1 per 319 persons); infant mortality rate per 1,000 live births (2003) 26.4.
Food (2001): daily per capita caloric intake 3,184 (vegetable products 85%, animal products 15%); 128% of FAO recommended minimum.

Military

Total active duty personnel (2003): Lebanese national armed forces 72,100 (army 97.1%, navy 1.5%, air force 1.4%). External regular military forces include: UN peacekeeping force in Lebanon (August 2004) 2,000; Syrian army (September 2004) 14,000. *Military expenditure as percentage of GNP* (1999): 4.0% (world 2.4%); per capita expenditure: U.S.$185.

[1]The current legislature was elected between August and September 2000; one-half of its membership is Christian and one-half Muslim/Druze. [2]Includes water area of 66 sq mi (170 sq km) not distributed by governorate. [3]Excludes about 300,000 unnaturalized Palestinian refugees. [4]2001. [5]Permits authorized. [6]Public utilities and Transportation and communications includes Public administration, defense. [7]ESCWA estimate for Beirut only. [8]Imports are c.i.f. [9]Apart from a 14-mi (23-km) section delivering oil from the Zahrani refinery to a thermal power station serving Beirut, no passenger or general cargo track was in use in 2001. [10]For Middle East Airlines and Trans-Mediterranean Airways. [11]1994–95. [12]1995–96.

Internet resources for further information:
- **Central Administration for Statistics http://www.cas.gov.lb**
- **Central Bank of Lebanon http://www.bdl.gov.lb**

Lesotho

Official name: Lesotho (Sotho); Kingdom of Lesotho (English).
Form of government: constitutional monarchy with 2 legislative houses (Senate [33[1]]; National Assembly [120]).
Chief of state: King.
Head of government: Prime Minister.
Capital: Maseru.
Official languages: Sotho; English.
Official religion: Christianity.
Monetary unit: 1 loti (plural maloti [M]) = 100 lisente; valuation (Sept. 1, 2004) 1 U.S.$ = M 6.66; 1 £ = M 11.97.

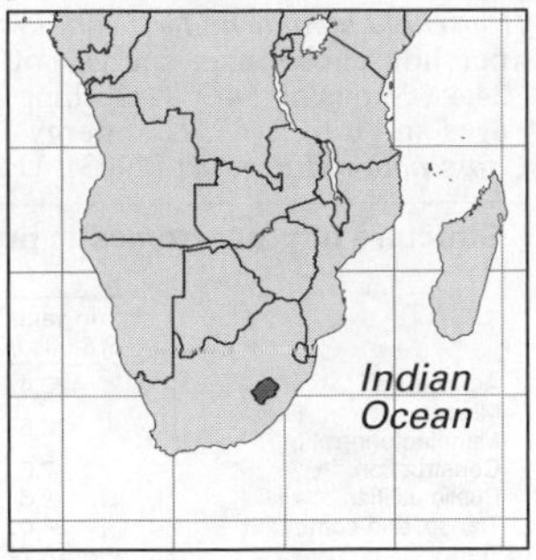

Area and population

		area		population
Districts	Capitals	sq mi	sq km	2002 census[2]
Berea	Teyateyaneng	858	2,222	300,557
Butha-Buthe	Butha-Buthe	682	1,767	126,907
Leribe	Hlotse	1,092	2,828	362,339
Mafeteng	Mafeteng	818	2,119	238,946
Maseru	Maseru	1,652	4,279	477,599
Mohale's Hoek	Mohale's Hoek	1,363	3,530	206,842
Mokhotlong	Mokhotlong	1,573	4,075	89,705
Qacha's Nek	Qacha's Nek	907	2,349	80,323
Quthing	Quthing	1,126	2,916	140,641
Thaba-Tseka	Thaba-Tseka	1,649	4,270	133,680
TOTAL		11,720	30,355	2,157,539

Demography

Population (2004): 1,800,000[3].
Density (2004): persons per sq mi 153.6, persons per sq km 59.3.
Urban-rural (2001)[2]: urban 13.4%; rural 86.6%.
Sex distribution (2001)[2]: male 50.62%; female 49.38%.
Age breakdown (2001)[2]: under 15, 35.3%; 15–29, 31.4%; 30–44, 14.8%; 45–59, 10.0%; 60–74, 5.9%; 75 and over, 2.6%.
Population projection[3]: (2010) 1,757,000; (2020) 1,663,000.
Doubling time: 50 years.
Ethnic composition (2000): Sotho 80.3%; Zulu 14.4%; other 5.3%.
Religious affiliation (2000): Christian 91.0%, of which Roman Catholic 37.5%, Protestant (mostly Presbyterian) 13.0%, African Christian 11.8%; other (mostly traditional beliefs) 9.0%.
Major urban centres (1996): Maseru 137,837 (urban agglomeration [2001] 271,000); Teyateyaneng 48,869; Maputsoe 27,951; Hlotse 23,122; Mafeteng 20,804.

Vital statistics

Birth rate per 1,000 population (2003): 27.3 (world avg. 21.3).
Death rate per 1,000 population (2003): 24.6 (world avg. 9.1).
Natural increase rate per 1,000 population (2003): 2.7 (world avg. 12.2).
Total fertility rate (avg. births per childbearing woman; 2003): 3.5.
Life expectancy at birth (2003): male 36.8 years; female 37.1 years.
Adult population (ages 15–49) *living with HIV* (2004[4]): 28.9% (world avg. 1.1%).

National economy

Budget (2000–01). Revenue: M 2,752,200,000 (customs receipts 40.9%, grants and nontax revenue 29.4%, income tax 11.4%, sales tax 10.2%). Expenditures: M 2,897,900,000 (personal emoluments 31.8%, capital expenditure 17.8%, subsidies and transfers 9.6%, interest payments 9.0%).
Public debt (external, outstanding; 2002): U.S.$611,000,000.
Production (metric tons except as noted). Agriculture, forestry, fishing (2002): corn (maize) 300,000, potatoes 90,000, wheat 51,000, sorghum 46,000, vegetables 18,000, fruit 13,000, dry beans 8,000; livestock (number of live animals) 850,000 sheep, 650,000 goats, 540,000 cattle, 154,000 asses, 100,000 horses; roundwood (2001) 2,028,134 cu m; fish catch (2001) 32. Mining and quarrying (2001): diamonds 1,140 carats. Manufacturing (value added in U.S.$'000,000; 1995): food products 58; beverages 38; textiles 14; chemical products 9; metal products 4; wearing apparel 4. Energy production (consumption): electricity, data for Lesotho included with South Africa; coal, none (none); petroleum, none (n.a.); natural gas, none (none).
Tourism (2002): receipts from visitors U.S.$20,000,000; expenditures by nationals abroad U.S.$14,000,000.
Population economically active (1993): total 617,871; activity rate of total population 45.1% (participation rates: ages 15–64 [1986] 79.8%; female 23.7%; unemployed [2001] *c.* 40%).

Price index (2000 = 100)

	1997	1998	1999	2000	2001	2002	2003
Consumer price index	...	...	94.2	100.0	90.4	120.9	129.0

Household income and expenditure. Average household size (2000) 5.0; average annual income per household: n.a.; sources of income: n.a.; expenditure (1989): food 48.0%, clothing 16.4%, household durable goods 11.9%, housing and energy 10.1%, transportation 4.7%.
Gross national product (at current market prices; 2003): U.S.$1,049,000,000 (U.S.$590 per capita).

Structure of gross domestic product and labour force

	2002		2001	
	in value M '000,000	% of total value	labour force	% of labour force
Agriculture	1,178.1	15.7	329,000	37.6
Mining	10.0	0.1		
Manufacturing	1,353.0	18.0		
Construction	1,220.4	16.2		
Public utilities	348.9	4.6		
Transp. and commun.	256.8	3.4		
Trade	738.8	9.8	545,000[5]	62.4
Finance	1,033.8	13.7		
Pub. admin., defense	511.7	6.8		
Services	772.7	10.3		
Other	106.4[6]	1.4[6]		
TOTAL	7,530.6	100.0	874,000	100.0

Land use as % of total land area (2000): in temporary crops 10.9%, in permanent crops 0.1%, in pasture 65.9%; overall forest area 0.5%.

Foreign trade[7]

Balance of trade (current prices)

	1996	1997	1998	1999	2000	2001
M '000,000	–3,491	–3,818	–3,590	–3,707	–3,582	–3,398
% of total	68.3%	67.9%	61.8%	63.7%	55.0%	41.2%

Imports (2001): M 5,824,000,000 (1999; food products 15.3%, unspecified commodities 84.7%). *Major import sources* (2001): Customs Union of Southern Africa (mostly South Africa) 82.8%; Asian countries 14.9%.
Exports (2001): M 2,426,000,000 (manufactured goods [mostly clothing] 74.7%, machinery and transport equipment 10.5%, beverages 3.6%, wool 2.5%). *Major export destinations:* North America (mostly the United States) 62.8%; Customs Union of Southern Africa (mostly South Africa) 37.0%.

Transport and communications

Transport. Railroads (2001): length 1.6 mi, 2.6 km. Roads (1999): total length 3,691 mi, 5,940 km (paved 18%). Vehicles (1996): passenger cars 12,610; trucks and buses 25,000. Air transport (1999): passenger-km, negligible (less than 500,000); metric ton-km cargo, negligible; airports (1997) with scheduled flights 1.

Communications

Medium	date	unit	number	units per 1,000 persons
Daily newspapers	2000	circulation	14,300	8
Radio	2000	receivers	94,600	53
Television	2002	receivers	63,000	35
Telephones	2002	main lines	28,600	13
Cellular telephones	2002	subscribers	96,800	45
Internet	2002	users	21,000	9.7

Education and health

Educational attainment (1986–87). Percentage of population age 10 and over having: no formal education 22.9%; primary 52.8%; secondary 23.2%; higher 0.6%. *Literacy* (2000–04): total population age 15 and over literate 81.4%; males literate 73.7%; females literate 90.3%.

Education (2002)

	schools	teachers	students	student/ teacher ratio
Primary (age 6–12)	1,333	8,908	418,668	47.0
Secondary (age 13–17)	224	3,384	81,130	24.0
Vocational	8	172	1,859	10.8
Higher	1	436[8]	6,273	8.0

Health: physicians (1995) 105 (1 per 18,527 persons); hospital beds (1992) 2,400 (1 per 765 persons); infant mortality rate per 1,000 live births (2003) 86.2.
Food (2001): daily per capita caloric intake 2,320 (vegetable products 97%, animal products 3%); 102% of FAO recommended minimum requirement.

Military

Total active duty personnel (2003): 2,000[9]. *Military expenditure as percentage of GNP* (1999): 2.6% (world 2.4%); per capita expenditure U.S.$14.

[1]All seats are nonelective. [2]De jure figure including absentee miners working in South Africa. [3]De facto figure(s). [4]January 1. [5]Includes 61,400 mine workers in South Africa. [6]Indirect taxes less imputed bank service charges. [7]Import figures are f.o.b. in balance of trade and c.i.f. in commodities and trading partners. [8]1998. [9]Royal Lesotho Defence Force.

Internet resources for further information:
- **Central Bank of Lesotho http://www.centralbank.org.ls**

Liberia

Official name: Republic of Liberia.
Form of government: transitional regime[1].
Head of state and government: Chairman[1].
Capital: Monrovia.
Official language: English.
Official religion: none.
Monetary unit: 1 Liberian dollar (L$) = 100 cents; valuation (Sept. 1, 2004) 1 U.S.$ = L$56.00; 1 £ = L$100.74.

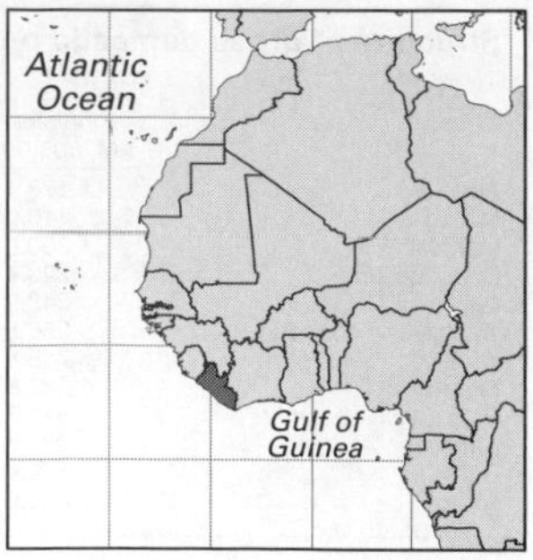

Area and population		area		population
				1999
Counties	**Capitals**	sq mi	sq km	estimate
Bomi	Tubmanburg	755	1,955	114,316
Bong	Gbarnga	3,127	8,099	299,825
Gbarpolu	Bopulu	2,982	7,723	[2]
Grand Bassa	Buchanan	3,382	8,759	215,338
Grand Cape Mount	Robertsport	2,250	5,827	120,141
Grand Gedeh	Zwedru	6,575[3]	17,029[3]	94,497[3]
Grand Kru	Barclayville	[4]	[4]	39,062
Lofa	Voinjama	4,493	11,367	351,492[2]
Margibi	Kakata	1,260	3,263	219,417
Maryland	Harper	2,066[4]	5,351[4]	71,977
Montserrado	Bensonville	1,058	2,740	843,783
Nimba	Sanniquellie	4,650	12,043	338,887
River Gee	Fish Town	[3]	[3]	[3]
Rivercess	Rivercess City	1,693	4,385	38,167
Sinoe	Greenville	3,959	10,254	79,241
TOTAL		38,250[5]	99,067[5, 6]	2,826,143

Demography

Population (2004): 3,391,000.
Density (2004)[5]: persons per sq mi 89.8, persons per sq km 34.7.
Urban-rural (2001): urban 45.5%; rural 54.5%.
Sex distribution (2002): male 49.47%; female 50.53%.
Age breakdown (2001): under 15, 43.2%; 15–29, 27.0%; 30–44, 15.1%; 45–59, 9.4%; 60–74, 4.2%; 75 and over, 1.1%.
Population projection: (2010) 3,935,000; (2020) 4,900,000.
Doubling time: 25 years.
Ethnic composition (2000): Kpelle 18.9%; Bassa 13.1%; Grebo 10.3%; Gio (Dan) 7.4%; Kru 6.9%; Mano 6.1%; Loma 5.3%; Kissi 3.8%; Krahn 3.7%; Americo-Liberians 2.4%[7]; other 22.1%.
Religious affiliation (1995): traditional beliefs 63.0%; Christian 21.0%, of which Protestant 13.5%, African Christian 5.1%, Roman Catholic 2.4%; Muslim 16.0%.
Major cities (2002): Monrovia 543,000; Zwedru 33,800; Buchanan 27,000; Yekepa 22,500; Harper 19,600.

Vital statistics

Birth rate per 1,000 population (2003): 45.3 (world avg. 21.3).
Death rate per 1,000 population (2003): 17.8 (world avg. 9.1).
Natural increase rate per 1,000 population (2003): 27.5 (world avg. 12.2).
Total fertility rate (avg. births per childbearing woman; 2003): 6.2.
Marriage rate per 1,000 population: n.a.
Divorce rate per 1,000 population: n.a.
Life expectancy at birth (2003): male 47.0 years; female 49.3 years.
Adult population (ages 15–49) *living with HIV* (2004[8]): 5.9% (world avg. 1.1%).

National economy

Budget (2002). Revenue: U.S.$72,700,000 (tax revenue 96.7%, of which import duties 23.1%, income and profit taxes 19.8%, maritime revenue 18.4%, stamps and land rental 17.9%, petroleum sales tax 8.3%; nontax revenue 3.3%). Expenditures: U.S.$80,100,000 (development expenditures [including national security] 67.5%; current expenditures 32.5%, of which wages 16.7%, interest on debt 7.9%, goods and services 7.4%).
Population economically active (1997): total 1,183,000; activity rate 51.4% (participation rates: ages 10–64 [1994] 64.0%; female 39.5%; unemployed [1996] 95%).

Price and earnings indexes (2000 = 100)					
	1998	1999	2000	2001	2002
Consumer price index	90.0	95.0	100.0	112.2	128.1
Earnings index	...	...	...	...	...

Production (metric tons except as noted). Agriculture, forestry, fishing (2002): cassava 445,000, natural rubber 220,000, rice 187,000, oil palm fruit 174,000, bananas 110,000, plantains 39,500, yams 20,000, cacao beans 626, coffee 439; livestock (number of live animals) 220,000 goats, 210,000 sheep, 130,000 pigs, 5,000,000 chickens; roundwood (2001) 5,261,930 cu m; fish catch 11,514. Mining and quarrying (2001): diamonds 170,000 carats; gold 1,000 kg. Manufacturing (2000): palm oil 42,000; cement 15,000; cigarettes 22,000,000 units[9]. International maritime licensing (fees earned; 2002): more than U.S.$13,000,000. Energy production (consumption): electricity (kW-hr; 2000) 524,000,000 (524,000,000); coal, none (none); crude petroleum, none (none); petroleum products (metric tons; 2000) none (128,000); natural gas, none (none).
Public debt (external, outstanding; 2002): U.S.$1,065,000,000.

Household income and expenditure. Average household size (1983) 4.3; income per household: n.a.; sources of income: n.a.; expenditure (1998)[10]: food 34.4%, housing 14.9%, clothing 13.8%, household furnishings 6.1%, beverages and tobacco 5.7%, energy 5.0%.
Gross national product (2003): U.S.$445,000,000 (U.S.$130 per capita).

Structure of gross domestic product and labour force	2002		2000	
	in value U.S.$'000,000[11]	% of total value	labour force	% of labour force
Agriculture	420.4	78.5	829,000	67.0
Mining / Manufacturing	23.5	4.4	408,000	33.0
Construction	7.6	1.4		
Public utilities	2.6	0.5		
Transp. and commun.	26.0	4.9		
Trade	18.7	3.5		
Finance	12.8	2.3		
Pub. admin., defense	11.3	2.1		
Services	12.6	2.4		
Other	...	...	...	...
TOTAL	535.5	100.0	1,237,000	100.0

Land use as % of total land area (2000): in temporary crops 3.9%, in permanent crops 2.2%, in pasture 20.8%; overall forest area 31.3%.

Foreign trade

Balance of trade (current prices)					
	1997	1998	1999	2000	2001
U.S.$'000,000	–217.9	–118.5	–150.7	–64.9	–69.0
% of total	81.1%	58.1%	56.1%	21.2%	21.2%

Imports (2001): U.S.$196,900,000 (food and live animals 31.1%, of which rice 14.0%; petroleum and petroleum products 20.7%; machinery and transport equipment 18.0%). *Major import sources* (1999): South Korea *c.* 27%; Japan *c.* 25%; Germany *c.* 14%; Singapore *c.* 7%; Croatia *c.* 5%.
Exports (2001): U.S.$127,900,000 (logs and timber 54.1%, rubber 42.2%). *Major export destinations* (2001): Norway *c.* 24%; Germany *c.* 11%; United States *c.* 9%; France *c.* 8%; Singapore *c.* 7%.

Transport and communications

Transport. Railroads (2001): route length 304 mi, 490 km; (1998) short ton-mi cargo 534,000,000, metric ton-km cargo 860,000,000. Roads (1999): total length 6,600 mi, 10,600 km (paved 6%). Vehicles (1996): passenger cars 9,400; trucks and buses 25,000. Air transport (1992): passenger-mi 4,300,000, passenger-km 7,000,000; short ton-mi cargo 621,000, metric ton-km cargo 1,000,000; airports (2000) with scheduled flights 2.

Communications				units
Medium	date	unit	number	per 1,000 persons
Daily newspapers	2000	circulation	37,800	12
Radio	2000	receivers	863,000	274
Television	2000	receivers	78,700	25
Telephones	1999	main lines	6,600	2.2

Education and health

Educational attainment, n.a. *Literacy* (2000): total population age 15 and over literate 54.0%.

Education (1998)	schools	teachers	students	student/ teacher ratio
Primary (age 6–12)	...	10,047	395,611	39.4
Secondary (age 13–18)	...	6,621	113,878	17.2
Higher	...	633	20,804	32.9

Health: physicians (1992) 257 (1 per 8,333 persons); hospital beds, n.a.; infant mortality rate per 1,000 live births (2002) 133.8.
Food (2001): daily per capita caloric intake 1,946 (vegetable products 97%, animal products 3%); 84% of FAO recommended minimum requirement.

Military

Total active duty personnel: UN peacekeeping troops (September 2004) 14,700; 18,000 of 40,000 former combatants were disarmed by April 2004. *Military expenditure as percentage of GNP* (1999): 1.2% (world 2.4%); per capita expenditure U.S.$2.

[1]Transitional government established in October 2003 to be in place until 2005. [2]Gbarpolu (created late 2000) included with Lofa. [3]River Gee (created mid-2000) included with Grand Gedeh. [4]Grand Kru included with Maryland. [5]Total area per more recent survey is 37,743 sq mi (97,754 sq km). [6]Detail does not add to total given because of rounding. [7]Descendants of freed U.S. slaves. [8]January 1. [9]1992. [10]Weights of consumer price index components. [11]At constant prices of 1992.

Libya

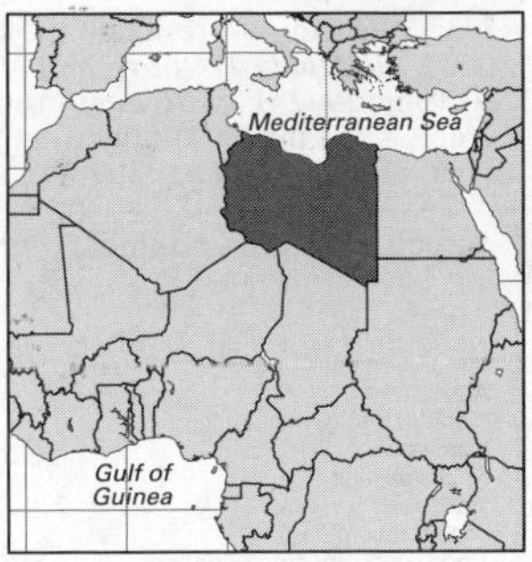

Official name: Al-Jamāhīrīyah al-ʿArabīyah al-Lībīyah ash-Shaʿbīyah al-Ishtirākīyah al-ʿUẓmā (Socialist People's Libyan Arab Jamahiriya).
Form of government: socialist state with one policy-making body (General People's Congress [760]).
Chief of state: Muammar al-Qaddafi (de facto)[1]; Secretary of General People's Congress (de jure).
Head of government: Secretary of the General People's Committee (prime minister).
Capital: Tripoli[2].
Official language: Arabic.
Official religion: Islam.
Monetary unit: 1 Libyan dinar (LD) = 1,000 dirhams; valuation (Sept. 1, 2004) 1 U.S.$ = LD 1.31; 1 £ = LD 2.36.

Area and population

		area		population
Administrative regions[3]	Capitals	sq mi	sq km	1995 census[4]
Banghāzī	Banghāzī	...	...	665,615
Al-Bāṭin	...	...	...	151,240
Fazzān	...	...	...	314,029
Al-Jabal al-Akhḍar	Al-Bayḍā'	...	...	381,165
Al-Jabal al-Gharbī	Gharyān	...	...	316,970
Al-Jufrah	...	...	...	39,335
Miṣrātah (Misurata)	...	...	...	488,573
Najghaza	...	...	...	244,553
Sofuljin	...	...	...	76,401
Ṭarābulus	Tripoli (Ṭarābulus)	...	...	1,313,996
Al Wāḥah	...	...	...	62,056
Al-Wasṭa	...	...	...	240,574
Az-Zāwiyah	Az-Zāwiyah	...	...	517,395
TOTAL		679,362	1,759,540	4,811,902

Demography

Population (2004): 5,659,000.
Density (2004): persons per sq mi 8.3, persons per sq km 3.2.
Urban-rural (2001): urban 88.0%; rural 12.0%.
Sex distribution (2001): male 51.41%; female 48.59%.
Age breakdown (2001): under 15, 35.4%; 15–29, 31.7%; 30–44, 19.1%; 45–59, 8.0%; 60–74, 4.5%; 75 and over, 1.3%.
Population projection: (2010) 6,332,000; (2020) 7,378,000.
Doubling time: 29 years.
Ethnic composition (2000): Arab 87.1%, of which Libyan 57.2%, Bedouin 13.8%, Egyptian 7.7%, Sudanese 3.5%, Tunisian 2.9%; Berber 6.8%, of which Arabized 4.2%; other 6.1%.
Religious affiliation (1995): Sunnī Muslim 96.1%; other 3.9%.
Major cities (1995): Tripoli 1,140,000 (urban agglomeration [2001] 1,776,000); Banghāzī 650,000 (urban agglomeration [2000] 829,000); Miṣrātah 280,000; Surt 150,000.

Vital statistics

Birth rate per 1,000 population (2003): 27.4 (world avg. 21.3).
Death rate per 1,000 population (2003): 3.5 (world avg. 9.1).
Natural increase rate per 1,000 population (2003): 23.9 (world avg. 12.2).
Total fertility rate (avg. births per childbearing woman; 2003): 3.5.
Life expectancy at birth (2003): male 73.9 years; female 78.3 years.
Major causes of death per 100,000 population: n.a.; however, the main causes of hospital mortality in 1987 were injuries and poisoning 15.5%, diseases of the circulatory system 11.6%, conditions originating in the perinatal period 11.4%, diseases of the respiratory system 7.0%, neoplasms (cancers) 4.4%.

National economy

Budget (2001). Revenue: LD 5,998,800,000 (oil revenues 60.1%, other 39.9%). Expenditures: LD 5,625,600,000 (current expenditures 63.9%, development expenditures 27.3%, extraordinary expenditures 8.8%).
Public debt (2001): U.S.$2,359,000,000.
Production (metric tons except as noted). Agriculture, forestry, fishing (2002): watermelons 218,000, potatoes 195,000, dry onions 182,000, olives 170,000, tomatoes 160,000, dates 133,500, wheat 130,000, barley 80,000; livestock (number of live animals; 2001) 4,130,000 sheep, 1,265,000 goats, 220,000 cattle, 72,000 camels, 25,000,000 chickens; roundwood (2001) 652,000 cu m; fish catch (2001) 33,339. Mining and quarrying (2001): lime 250,000; gypsum 150,000; salt 40,000. Manufacturing (value of production in LD '000,000; 1996): base metals 212, electrical equipment 208, petrochemicals 175, food products 79, cement and other building materials 68. Energy production (consumption): electricity (kW-hr; 2001) 20,180,000,000 (18,770,000,000); coal (metric tons; 2000) none (5,000); crude petroleum (barrels; 2002) 482,000,000 ([2000] 157,000,000); petroleum products (metric tons; 2001) 15,070,700 (6,629,200); natural gas (cu m; 2001) 6,174,000,000 (4,265,100,000).
Household income and expenditure. Average household size (2000) 6.3; income per household: n.a.; sources of income: n.a.; expenditure: n.a.
Tourism (2002): receipts U.S.$75,000,000; expenditures U.S.$548,000,000.
Population economically active (1996): total 1,224,000; activity rate of total population 26.1% (participation rates [1993]: ages 10 and over, 35.2%; female 9.8%; unemployed [2000] 30.0%).

Price index (2000 = 100)

	1997	1998	1999	2000	2001	2002	2003
Consumer price index	96.8	100.4	103.0	100.0	91.2	82.2	80.4

Gross domestic product (2000): U.S.$38,000,000,000 (U.S.$6,200 per capita).

Structure of gross domestic product and labour force

	2001		1996	
	in value LD '000,000[5]	% of total value	labour force	% of labour force
Agriculture	1,512.5	8.6	219,500	17.9
Oil and natural gas	6,009.0	34.1	31,000	2.5
Other mining	340.0	1.9		
Manufacturing	1,040.0	5.9	128,500	10.5
Construction	1,185.0	6.7	171,000	14.0
Public utilities	309.5	1.8	35,500	2.9
Transp. and commun.	1,315.5	7.5	104,000	8.5
Trade	1,803.5	10.3	73,000	6.0
Finance, insurance	881.0	5.0	22,000	1.8
Pub. admin., defense Services	3,208.5	18.2	439,500	35.9
TOTAL	17,604.5	100.0	1,224,000	100.0

Land use as % of total land area (2000): in temporary crops 1.0%, in permanent crops 0.2%, in pasture 7.6%; overall forest area 0.2%.

Foreign trade

Balance of trade (current prices)

	1997	1998	1999	2000	2001[6]	2002[6]
U.S.$'000,000	+2,716	+471	+2,974	...	+2,950	+3,100
% of total	15.9%	3.9%	25.7%	...	14%	24%

Imports (2001): U.S.$8,700,000,000 (1997; machinery 25.9%, food products 20.0%, road vehicles 10.1%, chemical products 7.5%). *Major import sources* (2001): Italy 28.5%; Germany 12.1%; U.K. 6.6%; Tunisia 6.0%; France 5.9%.
Exports (2001): U.S.$7,500,000,000 (crude petroleum *c.* 85%, refined petroleum *c.* 11%, natural gas *c.* 2%). *Major export destinations:* Italy 39.8%; Germany 15.6%; Spain 14.1%; Turkey 6.4%; France 5.5%.

Transport and communications

Transport. Railroads: none. Roads (1999): total length 83,200 km (paved 57%). Vehicles (1996): passenger cars 809,514; trucks and buses 357,528. Air transport (2001): passenger-km 410,000,000; metric ton-km cargo 259,000; airports with scheduled flights, n.a.

Communications

Medium	date	unit	number	units per 1,000 persons
Daily newspapers	2000	circulation	78,600	14
Radio	2000	receivers	1,430,000	259
Television	2000	receivers	717,000	133
Telephones	2003	main lines	750,000	136
Cellular telephones	2003	subscribers	100,000	18
Personal computers	2002	units	130,000	23
Internet	2003	users	160,000	29

Education and health

Educational attainment (1984). Percentage of population age 25 and over having: no formal schooling (illiterate) 59.7%; incomplete primary education 15.4%; complete primary 8.5%; some secondary 5.2%; secondary 8.5%; higher 2.7%. *Literacy* (1998): percentage of total population age 15 and over literate 78.1%; males literate 89.6%; females literate 65.4%.

Education (1995–96)

	schools	teachers	students	student/ teacher ratio
Primary (age 6–12)	2,733[7]	122,020	1,333,679	10.9
Secondary (age 13–18)	...	17,668	189,202[8]	...
Voc., teacher tr.	480	...	147,689[9]	...
Higher	13	...	126,348	...

Health: physicians (1997) 6,092 (1 per 781 persons); hospital beds (1998) 18,100[10] (1 per 312 persons); infant mortality rate per 1,000 live births (2003) 26.8.
Food (2001): daily per capita caloric intake 3,333 (vegetable products 89%, animal products 11%); 141% of FAO recommended minimum requirement.

Military

Total active duty personnel (2003): 76,000 (army 59.2%, navy 10.5%, air force 30.3%). *Military expenditure as percentage of GNP* (1995): 6.1% (world 2.4%); per capita expenditure U.S.$342.

[1]No formal titled office exists. [2]Policy-making body (General People's Congress) may meet in Surt or Tripoli. [3]Libya was divided into 34 administrative entities as of 2001; area and population details are unavailable. [4]Preliminary. [5]At factor cost. [6]Estimated figures. [7]1994–95. [8]1992–93. [9]1993–94. [10]Includes beds in clinics.

Internet resources for further information:
- **Central Bank of Libya**
http://www.cbl-ly.com/eng/about.html

Liechtenstein

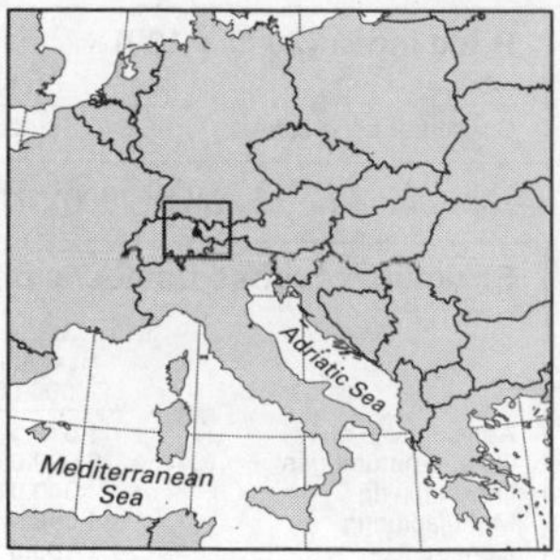

Official name: Fürstentum Liechtenstein (Principality of Liechtenstein).
Form of government: constitutional monarchy with one legislative house (Diet [25]).
Chief of state: Prince.
Head of government: Prime Minister.
Capital: Vaduz.
Official language: German.
Official religion: none.
Monetary unit: 1 Swiss franc (Sw F) = 100 centimes; valuation (Sept. 1, 2004) 1 U.S.$ = Sw F 1.27; 1 £ = Sw F 2.28.

Area and population

Regions / Communes	area sq mi	area sq km	population 2003[1] estimate
Oberland (Upland)	48.3	125.2	22,454
Balzers	7.6	19.6	4,312
Planken	2.0	5.3	366
Schaan	10.3	26.8	5,573
Triesen	10.2	26.4	4,558
Triesenberg	11.5	29.8	2,607
Vaduz	6.7	17.3	5,038
Unterland (Lowland)	13.4[2]	34.8	11,409
Eschen	4.0	10.3	3,886
Gamprin	2.4	6.1	1,229
Mauren	2.9	7.5	3,516
Ruggell	2.9	7.4	1,805
Schellenberg	1.4	3.5	973
TOTAL	61.8[2]	160.0	33,863

Demography

Population (2004): 34,500.
Density (2003): persons per sq mi 556.5, persons per sq km 215.6.
Urban-rural (2003): urban 21.6%; rural 78.4%.
Sex distribution (2003[1]): male 49.11%; female 50.89%.
Age breakdown (2003[1]): under 15, 17.0%; 15–29, 20.2%; 30–44, 25.9%; 45–59, 21.2%; 60–74, 10.8%; 75 and over, 4.9%.
Population projection: (2010) 36,000; (2020) 38,000.
Ethnic composition (2002): Liechtensteiner 65.8%; Swiss 10.9%; Austrian 5.9%; German 3.4%; Italian 3.3%; other 10.7%.
Religious affiliation (1998): Roman Catholic 80.0%; Protestant 7.5%; Muslim 3.3%; Eastern Orthodox 0.7%; atheist 0.6%; other 7.9%.
Major cities (2002): Schaan 5,556; Vaduz 4,949.

Vital statistics

Birth rate per 1,000 population (2003): 10.9 (world avg. 21.3); (1997) legitimate 86.0%; illegitimate 14.0%.
Death rate per 1,000 population (2003): 6.8 (world avg. 9.1).
Natural increase rate per 1,000 population (2003): 4.1 (world avg. 12.2).
Total fertility rate (avg. births per childbearing woman; 2002): 1.5.
Marriage rate per 1,000 population (2001): 11.5.
Divorce rate per 1,000 population (1994): 1.4.
Life expectancy at birth (2003): male 75.6 years; female 82.9 years.
Major causes of death per 100,000 population (2001): diseases of the circulatory system 232.0; malignant neoplasms (cancers) 147.6; old age 75.3; accidents, poisonings, and acts of violence 51.2; diseases of the respiratory system 36.2; diseases of the digestive tract 21.1.

National economy

Budget (2001). Revenue: Sw F 804,100,000 (taxes and duties 85.8%, investment income 5.5%, charges and fees 5.0%, real estate capital-gains taxes and death and estate taxes 3.7%). Expenditures: Sw F 751,400,000 (financial affairs 34.8%, social welfare 19.5%, education 14.1%, general administration 10.2%, public safety 5.5%, transportation 4.8%).
Public debt: none.
Tourism (2001): 123,273 tourist overnight stays; receipts from visitors, n.a.; expenditures by nationals abroad, n.a.
Population economically active (2002[2]): total 17,011; activity rate of total population 50.7% (participation rates: ages 15–64, 71.4%; female 40.4%; unemployed 2.1%).

Price and earnings indexes (2000 = 100)

	1995	1996	1997	1998	1999	2000	2001
Consumer price index	96.3	97.1	97.6	97.6	98.5	100.0	101.2
Earnings index	...	...	...	...	...	...	...

Household income and expenditure. Average household size (1990) 2.7; income per household: n.a.; sources of income: n.a.; expenditure: n.a.
Production (metric tons except as noted). Agriculture, forestry, fishing (2002): significantly market gardening, other crops include cereals and apples; livestock (number of live animals) 6,000 cattle, 3,000 pigs, 2,900 sheep; commercial timber (1999) 22,000 cu m; fish catch, n.a. Mining and quarrying: n.a. Manufacturing (2000): small-scale precision manufacturing includes optical lenses, electron microscopes, electronic equipment, and high-vacuum pumps; metal manufacturing, construction machinery, and ceramics are important; dairy products and wine are also produced. Construction (2000): residential 273,935 cu m; nonresidential 592,737 cu m. Energy production (consumption): electricity (kW-hr; 2001) 93,282,000 (313,450,000); coal (metric tons; 2000) none (24); petroleum products (metric tons; 2000) none (47,100); natural gas (cu m; 2000) none (n.a.).
Gross national product (1999): U.S.$2,664,000,000 (U.S.$63,550 per capita[3]).

Structure of gross domestic product and labour force

	1999 in value Sw F '000,000	1999 % of total value	2002[1] labour force	2002[1] % of labour force
Agriculture	...	...	322	1.9
Manufacturing, mining	1,600[4]	40.0[4]	4,386	25.8
Construction	...	...	1,648	9.7
Public utilities	...	...	154	0.9
Transportation and communications	...	...	585	3.4
Trade, public accommodation	...	...	2,291	13.5
Finance, insurance, real estate	1,200	30.0	1,280	7.5
Pub. admin., defense	960	24.0	1,269	7.5
Services			4,722	27.8
Other	240	6.0	354[5]	2.1[5]
TOTAL	4,000	100.0	17,011[6]	100.0[2]

Land use as % of total land area (2000): in temporary crops *c.* 25%, in permanent crops *c.* 1%, in pasture *c.* 31%; overall forest area *c.* 47%.

Foreign trade[7, 8]

Balance of trade (current prices)

	1995	1996	1997	1998	1999	2000
Sw F '000,000	+1,078	+1,165	+1,515	+2,394	+1,632	+1,576
% of total	33.5%	34.0%	39.1%	49.1%	39.5%	35.1%

Imports (2000): Sw F 1,456,000,000 (machinery and apparatus 30.4%, glass [all forms] and ceramics 11.0%, fabricated metals 10.0%, iron and steel 5.7%, transport equipment 5.7%). *Major import sources:* Germany 34.6%; Austria 31.8%; Italy 7.9%; U.S. 6.1%; France 3.5%.
Exports (2000): Sw F 3,032,000,000 (machinery and apparatus [mostly electronic products and precision tools] 35.1%, fabricated metals 15.2%, glass and ceramic products [including lead crystal and specialized dental products] 9.9%, food products 5.3%). *Major export destinations:* Germany 25.8%; U.S. 20.0%; Austria 8.4%; France 7.8%; Italy 6.5%.

Transport and communications

Transport. Railroads (1998): length 11.5 mi, 18.5 km; passenger and cargo traffic, n.a. Roads (1999): total length 201 mi, 323 km. Vehicles (2002): passenger cars 23,265; trucks and buses 2,824. Merchant marine: none. Air transport: the nearest scheduled airport service is through Zürich, Switzerland.

Communications

Medium	date	unit	number	units per 1,000 persons
Daily newspapers	1998	circulation	17,900	565
Radio	1997	receivers	21,000	658
Television	1997	receivers	12,000	364
Telephones	2002	main lines	19,900	583
Cellular telephones	2002	subscribers	11,400	333
Internet	2002	users	20,000	585

Education and health

Educational attainment (1990). Percentage of population not of preschool age or in compulsory education having: no formal schooling 0.3%; primary and lower secondary education 39.3%; higher secondary and vocational 47.6%; some postsecondary 7.4%; university 4.2%; other and unknown 1.1%.
Literacy: virtually 100%.

Education (1998–99)

	schools	teachers	students	student/ teacher ratio
Primary (age 7–12)	14	151	2,048	13.6
Secondary (age 13–19)	9	162	1,859	11.5
Vocational[9]	2	309	2,307	7.5

Health: physicians (2000) 46 (1 per 714 persons); hospital beds (1997) 108 (1 per 288 persons); infant mortality rate per 1,000 live births (2003) 4.9.
Food (1999)[10]: daily per capita caloric intake 3,600 (vegetable products 65%, animal products 35%); 134% of FAO recommended minimum requirement.

Military

Total active duty personnel: none; Liechtenstein has had no standing army since 1868. *Military expenditure as percentage of GNP:* none.

[1]January 1. [2]Detail does not add to total given because of rounding. [3]Includes 9,700 foreign workers domiciled abroad. [4]Includes other undefined economic sectors. [5]Unemployed. [6]Excludes 11,772 foreign employees. [7]Excludes trade with Switzerland and transshipments through Switzerland. [8]Liechtenstein has formed a customs union with Switzerland since 1923. [9]1997–98. [10]Figures are derived from statistics for Switzerland and Austria.

Internet resources for further information:
- **Liechtenstein Government Portal**
  http://www.llv.li/en/amtsstellen/llv-avw-home.htm

Lithuania

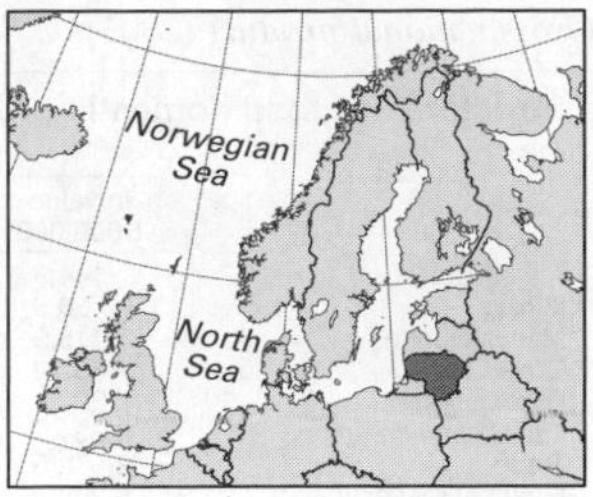

Official name: Lietuvos Respublika (Republic of Lithuania).
Form of government: unitary multiparty republic with a single legislative body, the Seimas (141).
Head of state: President.
Head of government: Prime Minister.
Capital: Vilnius.
Official language: Lithuanian.
Official religion: none.
Monetary unit: 1 litas (LTL) = 100 centai; valuation (Sept. 1, 2004) 1 U.S.$ = LTL 2.84; 1 £ = LTL 5.11[1].

Area and population

		area		population
Provinces	Capitals	sq mi	sq km	2004[2] estimate
Alytus	Alytus	2,095	5,425	184,804
Kaunas	Kaunas	3,112	8,060	691,459
Klaipėda	Klaipėda	2,011	5,209	383,201
Marijampolė	Marijampolė	1,723	4,463	186,726
Panevėžys	Panevėžys	3,043	7,881	295,178
Šiauliai	Šiauliai	3,297	8,540	364,083
Tauragė	Tauragė	1,703	4,411	132,751
Telšiai	Telšiai	1,680	4,350	178,135
Utena	Utena	2,780	7,201	181,119
Vilnius	Vilnius	3,768	9,760	848,281
TOTAL		25,212	65,300	3,445,737

Demography

Population (2004): 3,439,000.
Density (2004): persons per sq mi 136.4, persons per sq km 52.7.
Urban-rural (2003): urban 66.8%; rural 33.2%.
Sex distribution (2003): male 46.70%; female 53.30%.
Age breakdown (2004[2]): under 15, 17.7%; 15–29, 21.9%; 30–44, 22.4%; 45–59, 17.8%; 60–74, 14.2%; 75 and over, 6.0%.
Population projection: (2010) 3,379,000; (2020) 3,274,000.
Ethnic composition (2001): Lithuanian 83.5%; Polish 6.7%; Russian 6.3%; Belarusian 1.2%; Ukrainian 0.7%; other 1.6%.
Religious affiliation (2001): Roman Catholic 79.0%; nonreligious 9.5%; Orthodox 4.8%, of which Old Believers 0.8%; Protestant 1.0%; unknown 5.4%; other 0.3%.
Major cities (2004[2]): Vilnius 553,038; Kaunas 368,917; Klaipėda 190,098; Šiauliai 131,184; Panevėžys 117,606; Alytus 70,774.

Vital statistics

Birth rate per 1,000 population (2003): 8.9 (world avg. 21.3); (2001) legitimate 74.6%; illegitimate 25.4%.
Death rate per 1,000 population (2003): 11.9 (world avg. 9.1).
Natural increase rate per 1,000 population (2003): –3.0 (world avg. 12.2).
Total fertility rate (avg. births per childbearing woman; 2003): 1.3.
Marriage rate per 1,000 population (2003): 4.9.
Divorce rate per 1,000 population (2003): 3.1.
Life expectancy at birth (2003): male 66.5 years; female 77.9 years.
Major causes of death per 100,000 population (2001): diseases of the circulatory system 628.2; malignant neoplasms (cancers) 223.9; accidents, injury, homicide 145.8, of which suicide 46.6.

National economy

Budget (2002). Revenue: LTL 15,112,000,000 (tax revenue 92.5%, of which value-added tax 25.2%, individual income tax 23.6%, social security tax 22.7%, excise tax 10.6%; nontax revenue 7.5%). Expenditures: LTL 15,907,000,000 (current expenditure 90.0%, of which social security and welfare 28.0%, wages 23.2%; capital expenditure 10.0%).
Gross national product (2003): U.S.$15,509,000,000 (U.S.$4,490 per capita).

Structure of gross national product and labour force

	2002		2001	
	in value LTL '000,000	% of total value	labour force	% of labour force
Agriculture, forestry	3,219	6.4	271,700	15.6
Mining	288	0.6	3,300	0.2
Manufacturing	8,867	17.5	272,500	15.6
Construction	2,964	5.8	94,400	5.4
Public utilities	1,911	3.8	34,500	2.0
Transp. and commun.	6,241	12.3	92,000	5.3
Trade, restaurants	8,972	17.7	261,800	15.0
Finance, real estate	4,776	9.4	70,400	4.0
Pub. admin., defense	2,497	4.9	77,100	4.4
Services	5,241	10.3	346,100	19.8
Other	5,703[3]	11.3[3]	221,500[4]	12.7[4]
TOTAL	50,679	100.0	1,745,300	100.0

Production (metric tons except as noted). Agriculture, forestry, fishing (2002): hay 2,500,000, potatoes 1,531,300, wheat 1,165,100, sugar beets 1,052,000, barley 800,000, rye 360,000, apples 145,000, cabbages 112,000, rapeseed 105,600, oats 104,000; livestock (number of live animals) 1,010,800 pigs, 751,500 cattle; roundwood (2001) 5,700,000 cu m; fish catch (2001) 153,932. Mining and quarrying (2002): limestone 857,500; peat 262,700. Manufacturing (value of production in LTL '000,000; 2000): food and beverages 4,952; refined petroleum products 4,303; wearing apparel 2,034; textiles 1,248; chemicals and chemical products 1,231; wood and wood products (excluding furniture) 1,164. Energy production (consumption): electricity (kW-hr; 2000) 11,424,000,000 (10,088,000,000); coal (metric tons; 2000) none (131,000); crude petroleum (barrels; 2000) 2,316,000 (34,766,000); petroleum products (metric tons; 2002) 6,543,500 (2,756,000); natural gas (cu m; 2000) none (2,462,000,000).
Public debt (external outstanding; 2002): U.S.$2,486,000,000.
Population economically active (2001): total 1,745,300; activity rate of total population 50.2% (participation rates: ages 15–64, 69.3%; female 49.8%; registered unemployed 12.7%).

Price and earnings indexes (2000 = 100)

	1997	1998	1999	2000	2001	2002	2003
Consumer price index	93.5	98.3	99.0	100.0	101.3	101.6	100.4
Annual earnings index	84.5	95.2	100.7	100.0	100.9	103.0	106.5

Household income and expenditure. Average household size (2000) 2.7; average annual household disposable income (1997): LTL 12,914 (U.S.$3,228); sources of income (2001): wages and salaries 53.6%, transfers 24.2%, self-employment 11.3%; expenditure (2001): food and beverages 42.4%, housing and energy 13.6%, transportation and communications 11.8%, clothing and footwear 6.5%.
Land use as % of total land area (2000): in temporary crops 45.3%, in permanent crops 0.9%, in pasture 7.7%; overall forest area 31.9%.
Tourism (2001): receipts from visitors U.S.$513,000,000; expenditures by nationals abroad U.S.$341,000,000.

Foreign trade[5]

Balance of trade (current prices)

	1998	1999	2000	2001	2002	2003
LTL '000,000	–8,332	–7,323	–6,588	–7,081	–7,940	–8,124
% of total	21.9%	23.4%	17.8%	16.2%	16.4%	15.5%

Imports (2002): LTL 28,220,000,000 (mineral fuels [mostly crude petroleum] 17.8%, machinery and apparatus 17.5%, transport equipment 16.4%, chemicals and chemical products 8.7%, textiles and clothing 7.9%). *Major import sources:* Russia 21.4%; Germany 17.2%; Italy 4.9%; Poland 4.8%; France 3.9%.
Exports (2002): LTL 20,280,000,000 (mineral fuels [mostly refined petroleum] 19.0%, transport equipment [mostly auto components] 15.9%, textiles and clothing 15.0%, agricultural and food products 10.8%, machinery and apparatus 9.9%). *Major export destinations:* United Kingdom 13.5%; Russia 12.1%; Germany 10.3%; Latvia 9.6%; Denmark 5.0%.

Transport and communications

Transport. Railroads (2001): route length 1,054 mi, 1,696 km; passenger-mi 331,000,000, passenger-km 533,000,000; short ton-mi cargo 5,302,000,000, metric ton-km cargo 7,741,000,000. Roads (2002): total length 47,580 mi, 76,573 km (paved 91%). Vehicles (2002): passenger cars 1,133,477; trucks and buses 104,544. Air transport (2001): passenger-mi 301,000,000; passenger-km 484,000,000; short ton-mi cargo 2,055,000, metric ton-km cargo 3,000,000; airports with scheduled flights (2001) 3.

Communications

Medium	date	unit	number	units per 1,000 persons
Daily newspapers	1996	circulation	344,000	93
Radio	2000	receivers	1,750,000	500
Television	2002	receivers	1,704,500	487
Telephones	2003	main lines	824,200	253
Cellular telephones	2003	subscribers	2,169,900	666
Personal computers	2003	units	380,000	110
Internet	2003	users	695,700	213

Education and health

Educational attainment (2001). Percentage of population age 10 and over having: no schooling and incomplete primary education 5.1%; complete primary 20.8%; incomplete and complete secondary 42.2%; postsecondary 31.9%, of which university 12.6%. *Literacy* (2000): total population age 15 and over literate 99.6%.

Education (2002–03)

	schools	teachers	students	student/teacher ratio
Primary (age 7–10)[6] Secondary (age 11–18)	2,172	50,200	594,300	11.8
Voc., teacher tr.	82	4,700	44,400	9.4
Higher	70	14,200	168,200	11.8

Health (2004[2]): physicians 13,682 (1 per 252 persons); hospital beds 29,990 (1 per 115 persons); infant mortality rate per 1,000 live births (2003) 6.7.
Food (2001): daily per capita caloric intake 3,384 (vegetable products 76%, animal products 24%); 132% of FAO recommended minimum requirement.

Military

Total active duty personnel (2003): 12,700[7] (army 62.6%, navy 5.1%, air force 9.1%, volunteer national defense force 13.5%, centrally controlled staff 9.7%). *Military expenditure as percentage of GNP* (1999): 1.3% (world 2.4%); per capita expenditure U.S.$87.

[1]Pegged to the euro from Feb. 2, 2002, at the rate of 1€ = LTL 3.45. [2]January 1. [3]Taxes less imputed bank service charges and subsidies. [4]Unemployed. [5]Imports c.i.f.; exports f.o.b. [6]Excludes special education. [7]Excludes 13,850 in paramilitary.

Internet resources for further information:
- **Lithuanian Department of Statistics http://www.std.lt**
- **Bank of Lithuania http://www.lbank.lt/eng/default.htm**

Luxembourg

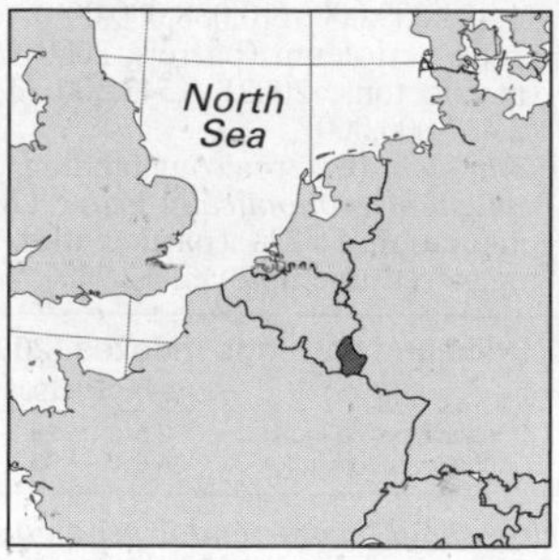

Official name: Groussherzogtum Lëtzebuerg (Luxemburgian); Grand-Duché de Luxembourg (French); Grossherzogtum Luxemburg (German) (Grand Duchy of Luxembourg).
Form of government: constitutional monarchy with two legislative houses (Council of State [21][1]; Chamber of Deputies [60]).
Chief of state: Grand Duke.
Head of government: Prime Minister.
Capital: Luxembourg.
Official language: none; Luxemburgian (national); French (used for most official purposes); German (lingua franca).
Official religion: none.
Monetary unit: 1 € (euro) = 100 cents; valuation (Sept. 1, 2004) 1 U.S.$ = €0.82; 1 £ = €1.48[2].

Area and population

Districts / Cantons	area sq mi	area sq km	population 2001 preliminary census
Diekirch	447	1,157	67,487
Clervaux	128	332	12,411
Diekirch	92	239	26,748
Redange	103	267	13,689
Vianden	21	54	2,920
Wiltz	103	265	11,719
Grevenmacher	203	525	51,960
Echternach	72	186	14,141
Grevenmacher	82	211	21,664
Remich	49	128	16,155
Luxembourg	349	904	320,317
Capellen	77	199	30,523
Esch	94	243	134,846
Luxembourg (Ville et Campagne)	92	238	131,652
Mersch	86	224	23,296
TOTAL	999	2,586	439,764

Demography

Population (2004): 454,000.
Density (2004): persons per sq mi 454.5, persons per sq km 175.6.
Urban-rural (2003): urban 91.9%; rural 8.1%.
Sex distribution (2003): male 49.30%; female 50.70%.
Age breakdown (2003): under 15, 18.9%; 15–29, 18.6%; 30–44, 25.5%; 45–59, 18.4%; 60–74, 12.9%; 75 and over, 5.7%.
Population projection: (2010) 474,000; (2020) 504,000.
Ethnic composition (nationality; 2003): Luxemburger 61.9%; Portuguese 13.5%; French 4.8%; Italian 4.2%; Belgian 3.5%; German 2.3%; English 1.0%; other 8.8%.
Religious affiliation (2000): Roman Catholic 90.6%; Protestant 2.1%; other Christian 1.1%; Muslim 1.0%; nonreligious 3.7%; other 1.5%.
Major cities (2001)[3]: Luxembourg 76,688; Esch-sur-Alzette 27,146; Dudelange 17,320; Schifflange 7,849; Bettembourg 7,157.

Vital statistics

Birth rate per 1,000 population (2003): 11.8 (world avg. 21.3); (2002) legitimate 76.8%; illegitimate 23.2%.
Death rate per 1,000 population (2003): 9.0 (world avg. 9.1).
Natural increase rate per 1,000 population (2003): 2.8 (world avg. 12.2).
Total fertility rate (avg. births per childbearing woman; 2003): 1.6.
Marriage rate per 1,000 population (2003): 4.5.
Divorce rate per 1,000 population (2003): 2.3.
Life expectancy at birth (2000–02): male 74.9 years; female 81.0 years.
Major causes of death per 100,000 population (2003): diseases of the circulatory system 350.0; malignant neoplasms (cancers) 218.9.

National economy

Budget (2002). Revenue: €5,977,200,000 (direct taxes 47.4%, indirect taxes 38.5%, other 14.1%). Expenditures: €5,976,100,000 (current expenditure 85.7%, development expenditure 14.3%).
Public debt (2001): U.S.$1,080,000,000.
Production (metric tons except as noted). Agriculture, forestry, fishing (2002): corn (maize) 139,000, wheat 67,126, barley 65,000, potatoes 20,105, apples 13,000, grapes (2001) 1,298 ha (3,208 acres); livestock (number of live animals; 2000) 205,000 cattle, 80,141 pigs; roundwood (2001) 142,000 cu m. Mining and quarrying (2002): limited quantities of limestone and slate. Manufacturing (2002): rolled steel 4,467,000; crude steel 2,736,000; cement 800,000; wine 154,000 hectolitres. Energy production (consumption): electricity (kW-hr; 2000) 1,228,000,000 (6,950,000,000); coal (metric tons; 2000) none (171,000); crude petroleum, none (none); petroleum products (metric tons; 2000) none (1,906,000); natural gas (cu m; 2000) none (782,000,000).
Land use as % of total land area (2000): in temporary crops 23.6%, in permanent crops 0.5%, in pasture 25.2%; overall forest area 34.3%.
Tourism (2002): receipts from visitors U.S.$2,186,000,000; expenditures U.S.$1,896,000,000.

Gross national product (2003): U.S.$15,509,000,000 (U.S.$43,940 per capita).

Structure of gross domestic product and labour force

	2001 in value €'000,000	2001 % of total value	2002 labour force	2002 % of labour force
Agriculture	144.9	0.7	3,600	1.3
Mining	30.5	0.1	34,300	12.0
Manufacturing	2,415.9	11.4		
Construction	1,332.2	6.3	28,100	9.8
Public utilities	227.1	1.1	1,600	0.6
Transp. and commun.	2,331.1	11.0	23,100	8.1
Trade	2,572.5	12.1	53,400	18.7
Finance, real estate	8,299.3	39.1	79,300	27.7
Pub. admin., defense	1,230.2	5.8	14,900	5.2
Services	2,248.8	10.6	47,400	16.6
Other	391.0[4]	1.8[4]	—	—
TOTAL	21,223.5	100.0	285,700	100.0

Population economically active (2002): total 285,700; activity rate of total population 63.9% (participation rates: ages 15–64 [2001] 64.4%; female [2001] 40.2%; unemployed [2002] 3.0%).

Price and earnings indexes (2000 = 100)

	1997	1998	1999	2000	2001	2002	2003
Consumer price index	95.1	96.0	96.9	100.0	102.7	104.8	106.9
Hourly earnings index[5]	...	...	97.4	100.0	100.6	104.8	...

Household income and expenditure. Average household size (2000) 2.5; income per household (2002) €61,800 (U.S.$55,600); sources of income (1992): wages and salaries 67.1%, transfer payments 28.1%, self-employment 4.8%; expenditure (2002): food, beverages, and tobacco 21.0%, housing 20.7%, transportation and communications 19.3%, entertainment and education 8.6%, household goods and furniture 8.3%, clothing and footwear 5.3%.

Foreign trade[6]

Balance of trade (current prices)

	1997	1998	1999	2000	2001	2002
€'000,000	–2,283	–2,513	–2,967	–3,032	–3,253	–3,170
% of total	15.4%	14.8%	16.7%	15.0%	15.2%	15.0%

Imports (2001): €12,335,000,000 (machinery and apparatus 21.5%, transport equipment 15.2%, base and fabricated metals 11.3%, chemicals and chemical products 10.1%). *Major import sources:* Belgium 34.3%; Germany 25.1%; France 12.8%; The Netherlands 5.8%; U.S. 5.1%.
Exports (2001): €9,082,000,000 (base and fabricated metals [mostly iron and steel] 28.1%, machinery and apparatus 24.0%, chemicals and chemical products 6.3%, transport equipment 4.3%, food products 4.2%). *Major export destinations:* Germany 24.6%; France 19.6%; Belgium 12.3%; U.K. 8.2%; Italy 6.2%.

Transport and communications

Transport. Railroads (2002): route length 170 mi, 274 km; passenger-mi 166,500,000, passenger-km 268,000,000; short ton-mi cargo 420,000,000, metric ton-km cargo 613,000,000. Roads (1999): total length 3,209 mi, 5,166 km (paved 100%). Vehicles (2003): passenger cars 287,245; trucks and buses 22,691. Air transport (2002): passengers carried 1,517,000; cargo 578,944 metric tons; airports with scheduled flights 1.

Communications

Medium	date	unit	number	units per 1,000 persons
Daily newspapers	1996	circulation	135,000	325
Radio	2000	receivers	300,000	685
Television	2000	receivers	170,000	391
Telephones	2002	main lines	355,400	797
Cellular telephones	2002	subscribers	473,000	1,061
Personal computers	2002	units	265,000	594
Internet	2002	users	165,000	370

Education and health

Educational attainment: n.a. *Literacy* (2001): virtually 100% literate.

Education (2000–01)

	schools	teachers	students	student/ teacher ratio
Primary (age 6–11)[7]	...	2,135	31,278	14.7
Secondary (age 12–18)	...	3,125	9,859	...
Voc., teacher tr.	...		21,359	...
Higher	5	...	2,533	...

Health (2002): physicians 1,137 (1 per 393 persons); hospital beds 3,035 (1 per 147 persons); infant mortality rate per 1,000 live births (2003) 5.0.
Food (1995): daily per capita caloric intake 3,530 (vegetable products 68%, animal products 32%); 134% of FAO recommended minimum.

Military

Total active duty personnel (2003): 900 (army 100.0%). *Military expenditure as percentage of GNP* (1999): 0.8% (world 2.4%); per capita expenditure U.S.$326.

[1]Has limited legislative authority. [2]The Luxembourg franc was the former monetary unit; on Jan. 1, 2002, Lux F 40.34 = €1. [3]Populations of localities (comparable to cities proper or towns proper). [4]Imputed bank service charges. [5]Manufacturing only. [6]Imports c.i.f.; exports f.o.b. [7]Public schools only.

Internet resources for further information:

- **STATEC: Luxembourg in Figures http://statec.gouvernement.lu/html_en**

Macau

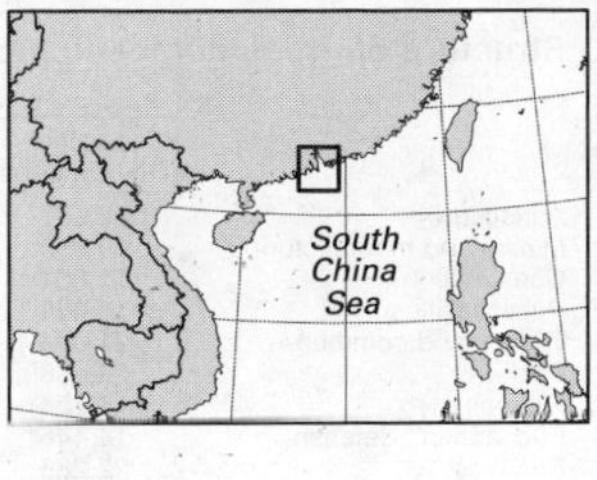

Official name: Aomen Tebie Xingzhengqu (Chinese); Região Administrativa Especial de Macau (Portuguese) (Macau Special Administrative Region).
Political status: special administrative region (China[1]) with one legislative house (Legislative Council [27[2]]).
Chief of state: President of China.
Head of government: Chief Executive.
Capital: Macau.
Official languages: Chinese; Portuguese.
Official religion: none.
Monetary unit: 1 pataca (MOP) = 100 avos; valuation (Sept. 1, 2004) 1 U.S.$ = MOP 8.03; 1 £ = MOP 14.45.

Area and population

Geographic areas	area sq mi	area sq km	population 2001 census
Macau peninsula	3.4	8.7	388,647
Islands	5.3	13.9	44,690
Coloane	2.9	7.6	2,904
Taipa	2.4	6.3	41,786
Marine	—	—	1,898
Embankment[3]	1.8	4.7	—
TOTAL	10.5	27.3	435,235

Demography

Population (2004): 451,000.
Density (2004): persons per sq mi 42,952, persons per sq km 16,520.
Urban-rural (2004): urban, virtually 100%[4].
Sex distribution (2003): male 48.07%; female 51.93%.
Age breakdown (2003): under 15, 18.7%; 15–29, 22.8%; 30–44, 27.3%; 45–59, 21.0%; 60–74, 6.7%; 75 and over, 3.5%.
Population projection: (2010) 454,000; (2020) 512,000.
Doubling time: over 100 years.
Nationality (2001)[5]: Chinese 95.2%; Portuguese 2.0%; Filipino 1.2%; other 1.6%.
Religious affiliation (1998): nonreligious 60.8%; Buddhist 16.7%; other 22.5%.
Major city (2000 est.): Macau 437,900.

Vital statistics

Birth rate per 1,000 population (2003): 7.2 (world avg. 21.3).
Death rate per 1,000 population (2003): 3.3 (world avg. 9.1).
Natural increase rate per 1,000 population (2003): 3.9 (world avg. 12.2).
Total fertility rate (avg. births per childbearing woman; 2002): 1.1.
Marriage rate per 1,000 population (2003): 2.9.
Divorce rate per 1,000 population (2003): 1.0.
Life expectancy at birth (2002): male 77.0 years; female 82.0 years.
Major causes of death per 100,000 population (1999): diseases of the circulatory system 107.9; malignant neoplasms (cancers) 83.7; diseases of the respiratory system 38.4; accidents, poisoning, and violence 26.3; diseases of the digestive system 12.1; diseases of the genitourinary system 9.4; infectious and parasitic diseases 7.5; endocrine and metabolic disorders 6.4; diseases of the nervous system 2.9.

National economy

Budget (1998). Revenue: MOP 14,831,099,000 (recurrent receipts 69.1%, autonomous agency receipts 21.4%, capital receipts 2.2%). Expenditures: MOP 14,831,099,000 (recurrent payments 61.1%, autonomous agency expenditures 21.4%, capital payments 17.5%).
Tourism: receipts from visitors (2002) U.S.$4,415,000,000; expenditures by nationals abroad (1999) U.S.$131,000,000.
Land use as % of total land area (2000): "green area" 22.4%.
Gross domestic product (at current market prices; 2002): U.S.$6,731,246,000 (U.S.$15,320 per capita).

Structure of gross domestic product and labour force

	2001		2002	
	in value MOP '000,000	% of total value	labour force	% of labour force
Agriculture and mining	[6]	[6]	[6]	[6]
Manufacturing	4,238.3	8.5	40,900	19.2
Construction	997.2	2.0	15,000	7.0
Public utilities	1,545.7	3.1	…	…
Transportation and communications	3,340.8	6.7	12,800	6.0
Trade	5,883.7	11.8	54,000	25.3
Finance	10,919.8	21.9	17,100	8.0
Public administration / Services[7]	25,778.8	51.7	59,000	27.7
Other	–2,842.1[8]	–5.7[8]	14,400[9]	6.8[9]
TOTAL	49,862.2	100.0	213,200	100.0

Production (metric tons except as noted). Agriculture, forestry, fishing (1999): eggs 650; livestock (number of live animals) 500,000 chickens; fish catch (2000) 1,500. Quarrying (value added in MOP '000,000; 1997): 13. Manufacturing (value added in MOP '000,000; 2001): wearing apparel 2,090; textiles 522; printing and publishing 95; food products 93; chemicals 73; footwear 70. Construction (2002): residential 36,387 sq m; nonresidential 66,162 sq m. Energy production (consumption): electricity (kW-hr; 2000) 1,571,000,000 (1,766,000,000); petroleum products (metric tons; 2000) none (500,000).
Public debt (long-term, external; 1999): U.S.$706,000,000.
Population economically active (2001): total 231,266; activity rate of total population 53.1% (participation rates: over age 14, 66.1%; female 46.5%; unemployed 7.0%).

Price and earnings indexes (2000 = 100)

	1998	1999	2000	2001	2002	2003
Consumer price index[10]	105.0	101.6	100.0	98.0	95.4	93.9
Earnings index	…	…	…	…	…	…

Household income and expenditure. Average household size (2001) 3.1; annual income per household MOP 181,884 (U.S.$22,764); sources of income: n.a.; expenditure (1987–88): food 38.3%, housing 19.7%, education, health, and other services 12.1%, transportation 7.4%, clothing and footwear 6.8%, energy 4.0%, household durable goods 3.7%, other goods 8.0%.

Foreign trade[11]

Balance of trade (current prices)

	1997	1998	1999	2000	2001	2002
MOP '000,000	+526	+1,487	+1,280	+2,283	–697	–1,398
% of total	1.6%	4.6%	3.8%	5.9%	1.9%	3.6%

Imports (2002): MOP 20,323,000,000 (textile materials 32.3%; capital goods 13.8%; clothing and footwear 13.3%; food, beverages, and tobacco 11.4%). *Major import sources:* China 41.7%; Hong Kong 14.5%; Taiwan 6.7%; Japan 6.7%; France 4.3%.
Exports (2002): MOP 18,925,000,000 (domestic exports 78.1%, of which machine-knitted clothing 42.1%, machine-woven clothing 27.4%, footwear 3.6%; reexports 21.9%). *Major export destinations:* United States 48.4%; China 15.6%; Germany 7.5%; Hong Kong 5.8%; United Kingdom 5.4%.

Transport and communications

Transport. Railroads: none. Roads (2003): total length 214 mi, 345 km (paved 100%). Vehicles (1999): passenger cars 47,776; trucks and buses 5,812. Air transport (2001)[12]: passenger-mi 1,185,567,000, passenger-km 1,907,988,000; short ton-mi cargo 15,491,000, metric ton-km cargo 22,616,000.

Communications

Medium	date	unit	number	units per 1,000 persons
Daily newspapers	2000	circulation	210,100	488
Radio	2000	receivers	215,300	500
Television	2000	receivers	123,100	286
Telephones	2003	main lines	174,600	391
Cellular telephones	2003	subscribers	364,000	815
Personal computers	2002	units	92,000	208
Internet	2003	users	120,000	269

Education and health

Educational attainment (2001). Population age 25 and over having: no formal schooling 7.6%; incomplete primary education 13.6%; completed primary 26.6%; some secondary 23.9%; completed secondary and post-secondary 28.3%. *Literacy* (2001): percentage of population age 15 and over literate 91.3%; males literate 95.3%; females literate 87.8%.

Education (2001–02)

	schools	teachers[13]	students	student/ teacher ratio[13]
Primary (age 6–11)	80	1,744	43,709	27.1
Secondary (age 12–18)	54	1,577	38,751	17.9
Voc., teacher tr.	4	47	2,381	14.9
Higher	11	818	8,520	9.4

Health (2002): physicians 915 (1 per 480 persons); hospital beds 990 (1 per 444 persons); infant mortality rate per 1,000 live births (2003) 0.6.
Food (1998): daily per capita caloric intake 2,471 (vegetable products 76%, animal products 24%); 108% of FAO recommended minimum requirement.

Military

Total active duty personnel: Chinese troops (2001) 500.

[1]Macau reverted to Chinese sovereignty on Dec. 20, 1999. [2]Includes 10 directly elected seats, 7 seats appointed by the chief executive, and 10 seats appointed by special-interest groups. [3]Landfill linking Coloane and Taipa. [4]About 0.5% of Macau's population live on sampans and other vessels. [5]Resident population. [6]Negligible. [7]Includes gambling. [8]Imputed bank service charge. [9]Includes 1,800 in activities undefined and 12,600 unemployed. [10]Excluding rent; base year is July 1995–June 1996. [11]Includes reexports. [12]Air Macau only. [13]1997–98.

Internet resources for further information:
- **Government of Macau Special Administrative Region, P.R.C.**
  http://www.macau.gov.mo/index_en.html
- **Macau Census and Statistics Service**
  http://www.dsec.gov.mo/e_index.html

Macedonia

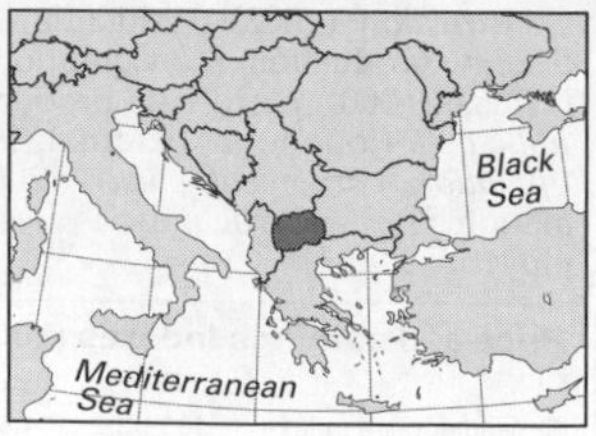

Official name[1]: Republika Makedonija (Macedonian); Republika e Maqedonisë (Albanian) (Republic of Macedonia).
Form of government: unitary multiparty republic with a unicameral legislative (Assembly [120]).
Head of state: President.
Head of government: Prime Minister.
Capital: Skopje.
Official languages[2]: Macedonian; Albanian.
Official religion: none.
Monetary unit: denar (MKD); valuation (Sept. 1, 2004) 1 U.S.$ = MKD 51.25; 1 £ = MKD 92.20.

Area and population

Former administrative districts[3]	area sq km	population 1994 census	Former administrative districts[3]	area sq km	population 1994 census
Berovo	806	19,737	Negotino	734	23,094
Bitola	1,798	106,012	Ohrid	1,069	60,841
Brod	924	10,912	Prilep	1,675	93,248
Debar	274	26,449	Probištip	326	16,373
Delčevo	589	25,052	Radoviš	735	30,378
Demir Hisar	443	10,321	Resen	739	17,467
Gevgelija	757	34,767	Skopje	1,818	541,280
Gostivar	1,341	108,189	Štip	815	50,531
Kavadarci	1,132	41,801	Struga	507	62,305
Kičevo	854	53,044	Strumica	952	89,759
Kočani	570	48,105	Sveti Nikole	649	21,391
Kratovo	376	10,855	Tetovo	1,080	174,748
Kriva Palanka	720	25,112	Titov Veles	1,536	65,523
Kruševo	239	11,981	Valandovo	331	12,049
Kumanovo	1,212	126,543	Vinica	432	19,010
			TOTAL	25,713[4]	1,936,877[5]

Demography

Population (2004): 2,035,000.
Density (2004): persons per sq mi 205.0, persons per sq km 79.1.
Urban-rural (2003): urban 59.5%; rural 40.5%.
Sex distribution (2002): male 50.20%; female 49.80%.
Age breakdown (2002): under 15, 21.1%; 15–29, 23.8%; 30–44, 22.0%; 45–59, 18.1%; 60–64, 11.2%; 65 and over, 3.3%.
Population projection: (2010) 2,079,000; (2020) 2,134,000.
Ethnic composition (2002): Macedonian 64.2%; Albanian 25.2%; Turkish 3.9%; Rom (Gypsy) 2.7%; Serbian 1.8%; Bosniac 0.8%; other 1.5%.
Religious affiliation (2000): Orthodox 59.3%; Sunnī Muslim 28.3%; Roman Catholic 3.5%; nonreligious 6.6%; other 2.3%.
Major cities (1994): Skopje 440,577; Bitola 75,386; Prilep 67,371; Kumanovo 66,237; Tetovo 50,376.

Vital statistics

Birth rate per 1,000 population (2003): 11.9 (world avg. 21.3); (2000) legitimate 90.2%; illegitimate 9.8%.
Death rate per 1,000 population (2003): 8.8 (world avg. 9.1).
Natural increase rate per 1,000 population (2003): 3.1 (world avg. 12.2).
Total fertility rate (avg. births per childbearing woman; 2003): 1.6.
Marriage rate per 1,000 population (2000): 7.0.
Life expectancy at birth (2003): male 70.8 years; female 75.8 years.
Major causes of death per 100,000 population (2000): diseases of the circulatory system 582.2; malignant neoplasms 163.3; accidents, violence, and poisoning 37.9; diseases of the respiratory system 36.8; diabetes mellitus 30.2.

National economy

Budget (2002). Revenue: 53,089,000,000 denar (tax revenue 94.2%, of which value-added tax 33.7%, excise taxes 20.6%, income and profit tax 19.6%, import duties 10.0%; nontax revenue 5.8%). Expenditure: 59,979,000,000 denar (wages and salaries 29.5%, pensions 26.1%, goods and services 20.0%, interest 6.1%).
External debt (2002): U.S.$1,262,000,000.
Production (metric tons except as noted). Agriculture, forestry, fishing (2002): wheat 267,100, potatoes 183,000, corn (maize) 140,200, grapes 119,000, tomatoes 109,500, tobacco leaves 22,044; livestock (number of live animals) 1,233,800 sheep, 259,000 cattle; roundwood (2001) 740,000 cu m; fish catch (2001) 1,181. Mining and quarrying (2001)[6]: lead 11,000; copper 7,000; silver 15,000 kg. Manufacturing (1998): cement 461,195; steel sheets 276,464; detergents 21,990; wool yarn 3,252; refrigerators 4,007 units; freezers 3,488 units; leather footwear 1,382,000 pairs; cotton fabric 13,700,000 sq m; cigarettes 7,009,000 units. Energy production (consumption): electricity (kW-hr; 2000) 6,811,000,000 (6,923,000,000); hard coal (metric tons; 2000) none (155,000); lignite (metric tons; 2000) 7,516,000 (7,702,000); crude petroleum (barrels; 2000) none (5,886,000); petroleum products (metric tons; 2000) 775,000 (838,000); natural gas (cu m; 2000) none (64,503,000).
Household income and expenditure. Average household size (2002) 3.6; income per household (2000) U.S.$3,798; sources of income (2000): wages and salaries 54.2%, transfer payments 22.6%, savings 3.2%, other 20.0%; expenditure: food 38.4%, transportation and communications 9.7%, fuel and lighting 8.2%, beverages and tobacco 7.6%.
Gross national product (at current market prices; 2003): U.S.$4,058,000,000 (U.S.$1,980 per capita).

Structure of gross domestic product and labour force

	2001 in value '000,000 denar	2001 % of total value	2000 labour force	2000 % of labour force
Agriculture	22,957	9.8	123,038	15.2
Mining and manufacturing	40,899	17.5	148,633	18.3
Construction	11,801	5.0	35,712	4.4
Public utilities	10,041	4.3	10,627	1.3
Transp. and commun.	21,694	9.3	27,486	3.4
Trade	29,486	12.7	68,732	8.5
Finance	15,724	6.8	15,667	1.9
Pub. admin., defense	14,445	6.2	32,508	4.0
Services	22,286	9.5	118,419	14.6
Other	44,508	18.9	230,178[7]	28.4[7]
TOTAL	233,841	100.0	811,000	100.0

Population economically active (2000): total 811,000; activity rate 39.9% (participation rates: ages 15–64, 52.9%; female 38.5%; unemployed [2002] 31.9%).

Price and earnings indexes (2000 = 100)

	1997	1998	1999	2000	2001	2002	2003
Consumer price index	100.0	100.6	99.3	100.0	99.3	99.3	99.4
Annual earnings index	88.9	92.1	94.7	100.0	103.6	110.7	116.0

Land use as % of total land area (2000): in temporary crops 21.8%, in permanent crops 1.7%, in pasture 25.0%; overall forest area 35.6%.
Tourism (2002): receipts from visitors U.S.$39,000,000; expenditures by nationals abroad U.S.$45,000,000.

Foreign trade[8]

Balance of trade (current prices)

	1997	1998	1999	2000	2001	2002
U.S.$'000,000	–542	–604	–604	–766	–533	–809
% of total	18.0%	18.7%	20.2%	22.5%	18.7%	26.7%

Imports (2001): U.S.$1,688,000,000 (mineral fuels 13.9%, machinery and apparatus 13.0%, food and live animals 11.5%, chemicals and chemical products 10.2%). *Major import sources* (2002): Germany 14.3%; Greece 12.1%; Yugoslavia 9.4%; Slovenia 6.6%; Bulgaria 6.5%; Italy 6.0%.
Exports (2001): U.S.$1,155,000,000 (clothing 27.7%, iron and steel 16.9%, tobacco [all forms] 6.5%, nonferrous base metals 6.4%, beverages 4.0%). *Major export destinations* (2002): Yugoslavia 22.1%; Germany 21.0%; Greece 10.4%; Italy 7.1%; United States 7.0%.

Transport and communications

Transport. Railroads (2002): route length 434 mi, 699 km; passenger-km 98,000,000; metric ton-km cargo 334,000,000. Roads (2000): length 7,782 mi, 12,522 km (paved 58%). Vehicles (2002): passenger cars 307,600; trucks and buses 33,000. Air transport (2003)[9]: passenger-km 294,000,000; metric ton-km cargo 141,000; airports (2002) with scheduled flights 2.

Communications

Medium	date	unit	number	units per 1,000 persons
Daily newspapers	2000	circulation	89,400	44
Radio	2000	receivers	415,000	205
Television	2000	receivers	571,000	282
Telephones	2002	main lines	560,000	271
Cellular telephones	2002	subscribers	365,300	177
Internet	2002	users	100,000	48

Education and health

Educational attainment (1994). Percentage of population age 15 and over having: less than full primary education 25.0%; primary 33.4%; secondary 32.3%; postsecondary and higher 8.7%; unknown 0.6%. *Literacy* (1998): 94.6%.

Education (1999–2000)

	schools	teachers	students	student/ teacher ratio
Primary (age 7–14)	1,036	13,782	252,212	18.3
Secondary (age 15–18)	96	5,557	89,775	16.2
Higher[10]	31	1,495	40,246	26.9

Health (2000): physicians 4,455 (1 per 454 persons); hospital beds 10,248 (1 per 198 persons); infant mortality rate per 1,000 live births (2003) 10.7.
Food (2001): daily per capita caloric intake 2,552 (vegetable products 80%, animal products 20%); 100% of FAO recommended minimum requirement.

Military

Total active duty personnel (2003): 12,850 (army 90.7%, headquarters staff 9.3%). *Military expenditure as percentage of GNP* (1999): 2.5% (world 2.4%); per capita expenditure U.S.$112.

[1]Member of the United Nations under the name The Former Yugoslav Republic of Macedonia (FYROM). [2]Albanian was made an official language in June 2002. [3]Local government was reorganized into 123 municipalities in 1996. [4]Total includes 280 sq km of inland water not distributed by district. [5]2002 census population: 2,022,547. [6]Contained metal of ore. [7]Unemployed. [8]Imports c.i.f.; exports f.o.b. [9]Macedonian Airline. [10]2000–01.

Internet resources for further information:
- **National Bank of the Republic of Macedonia http://www.nbrm.gov.mk**
- **State Statistical Office http://www.stat.gov.mk/english/glauna_eng.asp**

Madagascar

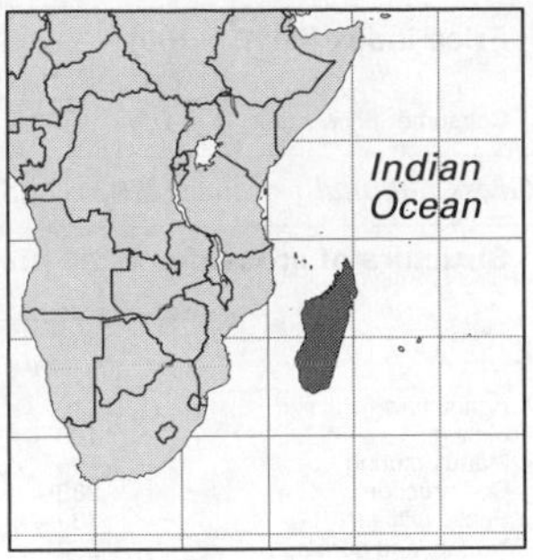

Official name: Repoblikan'i Madagasikara (Malagasy); République de Madagascar (French) (Republic of Madagascar).
Form of government: federal[1] multiparty republic with two legislative houses (Senate [90]; National Assembly [160]).
Heads of state and government: President assisted by Prime Minister.
Capital: Antananarivo.
Official languages: [2].
Official religion: none.
Monetary unit: 1 ariary[3] (MGA) = 5 iraimbilanja; valuation (Sept. 1, 2004) 1 U.S.$ = MGA 2,015; 1 £ = MGA 3,625.

Area and population

Autonomous provinces[1]	Capitals	area sq mi	area sq km	population 2001 estimate
Antananarivo	Antananarivo	22,503	58,283	4,580,788
Antsirañana	Antsirañana	16,620	43,046	1,188,425
Fianarantsoa	Fianarantsoa	39,527	102,373	3,366,291
Mahajanga	Mahajanga	57,924	150,023	1,733,917
Toamasina	Toamasina	27,765	71,911	2,593,063
Toliary	Toliary	62,319	161,405	2,229,550
TOTAL		226,658	587,041	15,692,034

Demography

Population (2004): 17,082,000.
Density (2004): persons per sq mi 75.4, persons per sq km 29.1.
Urban-rural (2001): urban 30.1%; rural 69.9%.
Sex distribution (2000): male 49.70%; female 50.30%.
Age breakdown (2000): under 15, 45.0%; 15–29, 26.5%; 30–44, 15.8%; 45–59, 7.9%; 60–74, 3.8%; 75 and over, 1.0%.
Population projection: (2010) 20,134,000; (2020) 25,847,000.
Doubling time: 23 years.
Ethnic composition (2000): Malagasy 95.9%, of which Merina 24.0%, Betsimisaraka 13.4%, Betsileo 11.3%, Tsimihety 7.0%, Sakalava 5.9%; Makua 1.1%; French 0.6%; Comorian 0.5%; Reunionese 0.4%; other 1.5%.
Religious affiliation (2000): Christian 49.5%, of which Protestant 22.7%, Roman Catholic 20.3%; traditional beliefs 48.0%; Muslim 1.9%; other 0.6%.
Major cities (2001): Antananarivo 1,403,449; Toamasina 179,045; Antsirabe 160,356; Fianarantsoa 144,225; Mahajanga 135,660.

Vital statistics

Birth rate per 1,000 population (2003): 42.2 (world avg. 21.3).
Death rate per 1,000 population (2003): 11.9 (world avg. 9.1).
Natural increase rate per 1,000 population (2003): 30.3 (world avg. 12.2).
Total fertility rate (avg. births per childbearing woman; 2003): 5.7.
Life expectancy at birth (2003): male 53.8 years; female 58.5 years.
Major causes of death per 100,000 population: n.a.; however, major causes of death in the 1990s included maternal and perinatal diseases, malaria, infectious and parasitic diseases, malnutrition, diarrhea, and respiratory diseases.

National economy

Budget (2000). Revenue: FMG 3,068,000,000,000 (taxes 96.9%, of which duties on trade 51.9%, value-added tax 16.7%, income tax 15.2%; nontax receipts 3.1%). Expenditures: FMG 4,168,600,000,000 (current expenditure 57.6%, of which general administration 21.1%, debt service 14.7%, education 13.3%, defense 7.7%, health 4.4%, agriculture 2.0%; capital expenditure 42.4%).
Public debt (external, outstanding; 2002): U.S.$4,137,000,000.
Production (metric tons except as noted). Agriculture, forestry, fishing (2002): paddy rice 2,671,000, cassava 2,510,000, sugarcane 2,223,000, sweet potatoes 526,000, potatoes 296,000, bananas 290,000, mangoes 210,000, taro 200,000, corn (maize) 181,000, dry beans 84,000, oranges 83,000, coffee 64,600, pineapples 51,000, seed cotton 28,000, cloves (whole and stem) 15,500, vanilla 1,518; livestock (number of live animals) 11,000,000 cattle, 1,600,000 pigs, 1,350,000 goats; roundwood (2001) 10,012,542 cu m; fish catch (2001) 143,000, of which crustaceans (2001) 18,881. Mining and quarrying (2002): chromite ore 15,600; graphite 1,300; gold, none (illegally smuggled, *c.* 3,500 kg); sapphires 5,600 kg. Manufacturing (2000): refined sugar 62,487; cement 50,938; soap 15,385; cigarettes 3,633[4]; beer 645,000 hectolitres; fuel oil 226,000 cu m; gas oil 150,000 cu m; gasoline 123,000 cu m; kerosene 65,200 cu m; shoes 873,000 pairs. Energy production (consumption): electricity (kW-hr; 2000) 807,000,000 (807,000,000); coal (metric tons; 2000) none (10,000); crude petroleum (barrels; 2000) none (3,379,000); petroleum products (metric tons; 2000) 311,000 (568,000); natural gas, none (n.a.).
Population economically active (1993): total 5,914,000; activity rate of total population 48.9% (participation rates [1995]: over age 10, 59.4%; female 38.4%; unemployed, n.a.).

Price and earnings indexes (2000 = 100)

	1997	1998	1999	2000	2001	2002	2003
Consumer price index[5]	76.5	81.2	89.3	100.0	106.9	124.0	122.5
Annual earnings index	...	...	...	...	...	...	...

Gross national product (at current market prices; 2003): U.S.$4,848,000,000 (U.S.$290 per capita).

Structure of gross domestic product and labour force

	2000 in value FMG '000,000[6]	2000 % of total value[6]	1993 labour force	1993 % of labour force
Agriculture	6,858	29.1	5,100,000	86.2
Manufacturing } Mining	3,412	14.4	86,000	1.5
Public utilities } Construction	396	1.7	46,000	0.8
Transp. and commun.	4,501	19.1	42,000	0.7
Trade	2,927	12.4	} 149,000	2.5
Finance	7	7		
Services	4,404[7]	18.7[7]	243,000	4.1
Pub. admin., defense	1,412	6.0	208,000	3.5
Other	–327[8]	–1.4[8]	40,000	0.7
TOTAL	23,583	100.0	5,914,000	100.0

Household income and expenditure. Average household size (1993) 4.6[9]; expenditure (1983)[5, 10]: food 60.4%, fuel and light 9.1%, clothing and footwear 8.6%, household goods and utensils 2.4%.
Land use as % of total land area (2000): in temporary crops 5.0%, in permanent crops 1.0%, in pasture 41.3%; overall forest area 20.2%.
Tourism (2002): receipts from visitors U.S.$36,000,000; expenditures by nationals abroad U.S.$91,000,000.

Foreign trade[11]

Balance of trade

	1997	1998	1999	2000	2001
FMG '000,000,000	–892	–815	–995	–702	+97
% of total	14.7%	12.5%	11.9%	5.9%	0.8%

Imports (2001): FMG 7,363,000,000,000 (petroleum [all forms] 15.0%, machinery and apparatus 14.7%, consumer goods 11.8%, other [mostly imports for EPZ[12]] 39.3%). *Major import sources:* France 21.5%; China 9.1%; South Africa 5.5%; Japan 4.4%; U.S. 4.2%.
Exports (2001): FMG 6,356,000,000,000 (EPZ[12] exports [mostly textiles and clothing] 35.3%, vanilla 17.0%, cloves 9.9%, shellfish 9.6%). *Major export destinations:* France 29.7%; U.S. 13.9%; Mauritius 2.6%; unspecified countries 34.7%.

Transport and communications

Transport. Railroads: route length (2003) 560 mi, 901 km[13]; (2000) passenger-mi 15,209,000, passenger-km 24,471,000; (2000) short ton-mi cargo 18,630,000, metric ton-km cargo 27,200,000. Roads (1999): total length 30,968 mi, 49,827 km (paved 12%). Vehicles (1998): passenger cars 64,000; trucks and buses 9,100. Air transport (2003)[14]: passenger-km 715,920,000; metric ton-km cargo 9,740,000; airports (1994) with scheduled flights 44.

Communications

Medium	date	unit	number	units per 1,000 persons
Daily newspapers	2000	circulation	77,500	5.0
Radio	2000	receivers	3,350,000	216
Television	2002	receivers	410,000	25
Telephones	2003	main lines	59,600	3.6
Cellular telephones	2003	subscribers	279,500	17
Personal computers	2003	users	80,000	4.9
Internet	2003	users	70,500	4.3

Education and health

Educational attainment: n.a. *Literacy* (2000): percentage of total population age 15 and over literate 66.5%; males literate 73.6%; females literate 59.7%.

Education (1998–99)

	schools	teachers	students	student/ teacher ratio
Primary (age 6–13)	14,438	42,678	2,012,416	47.2
Secondary (age 14–18)	...	18,987	334,250	17.6
Voc., teacher tr.[15]	...	1,150	8,479	7.3
Higher	6	1,471	31,013	21.1

Health (2000): physicians 1,428 (1 per 10,859 persons); hospital beds 7,043[16] (1 per 2,202 persons); infant mortality rate (2002) 81.9.
Food (2001): daily per capita caloric intake 2,072 (vegetable products 91%, animal products 9%); 91% of FAO recommended minimum requirement.

Military

Total active duty personnel (2003): 13,500 (army 92.6%, navy 3.7%, air force 3.7%). *Military expenditure as percentage of GNP* (1999): 1.2% (world 2.4%); per capita expenditure U.S.$3.

[1]Each of the six autonomous provinces is adopting its own statutory laws per article 2 of the 1998 constitution. [2]The 1998 constitution identifies Malagasy as the "national" language, although neither Malagasy nor French, the languages of the two official texts of the constitution, is itself "official." [3]The ariary (MGA), the precolonial currency of Madagascar, officially replaced the Malagasy franc (FMG) in August 2003 at a rate of 1 MGA = FMG 5; both currencies were to circulate through the end of 2004. [4]1999. [5]Antananarivo only. [6]At factor cost. [7]Services includes Finance. [8]Less imputed bank charges. [9]Malagasy households only. [10]Weights of consumer price index components; excludes housing. [11]Imports are f.o.b. in balance of trade and c.i.f. for commodities and trading partners. [12]Export-processing zones. [13]Railroad infrastructure was either inoperable or in poor condition in June 2003. [14]Air Madagascar. [15]1995–96. [16]Total number of regional and provincial hospital beds.

Internet resources for further information:
- **Institut National de la Statistique**
http://www.cite.mg/instat/Prod/Annuaire/tab_jas.htm

Malawi

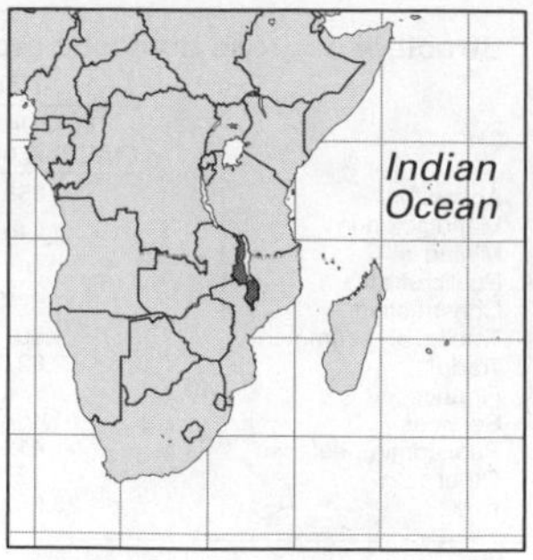

Official name: Republic of Malawi.
Form of government: multiparty republic with one legislative house (National Assembly [193]).
Head of state and government: President.
Capital: Lilongwe[1].
Official language: none.
Official religion: none.
Monetary unit: 1 Malawi kwacha (MK) = 100 tambala; valuation (Sept. 1, 2004) 1 U.S.$ = MK 109.00; 1 £ = MK 196.09.

Area and population

Regions / Districts	Capitals	area sq mi	area sq km	population 1998 census
Central	Lilongwe	13,742	35,592	4,066,340
Dedza	Dedza	1,399	3,624	486,682
Dowa	Dowa	1,174	3,041	411,387
Kasungu	Kasungu	3,042	7,878	480,659
Lilongwe	Lilongwe	2,378	6,159	1,346,360
Mchinji	Mchinji	1,296	3,356	324,941
Nkhotakota	Nkhotakota	1,644	4,259	229,460
Ntcheu	Ntcheu	1,322	3,424	370,757
Ntchisi	Ntchisi	639	1,655	167,880
Salima	Salima	848	2,196	248,214
Northern	Mzuzu	10,398	26,931	1,233,560
Chitipa	Chitipa	1,656	4,288	126,799
Karonga	Karonga	1,295	3,355	194,572
Likoma	Likoma	7	18	8,074
Mzimba	Mzimba	4,027	10,430	610,994
Nkhata Bay	Nkhata Bay	1,572	4,071	164,761
Rumphi	Rumphi	1,841	4,769	128,360
Southern	Blantyre	12,260	31,753	4,633,968
Balaka	Balaka	847	2,193	253,098
Blantyre	Blantyre	777	2,012	809,397
Chikwawa	Chikwawa	1,836	4,755	356,682
Chiradzulu	Chiradzulu	296	767	236,050
Machinga	Machinga	1,456	3,771	369,614
Mangochi	Mangochi	2,422	6,273	610,239
Mulanje	Mulanje	794	2,056	428,322
Mwanza	Mwanza	886	2,295	138,015
Nsanje	Nsanje	750	1,942	194,924
Phalombe	Phalombe	538	1,394	231,990
Thyolo	Thyolo	662	1,715	458,976
Zomba	Zomba	996	2,580	546,661
TOTAL LAND AREA		36,400	94,276	
INLAND WATER		9,347	24,208	
TOTAL		45,747	118,484	9,933,868

Demography

Population (2004): 11,907,000.
Density (2004)[2]: persons per sq mi 327.1, persons per sq km 126.3.
Urban-rural (2002): urban 15.1%; rural 84.9%.
Sex distribution (2001): male 49.39%; female 50.61%.
Age breakdown (2001): under 15, 44.4%; 15–29, 30.4%; 30–44, 13.5%; 45–59, 7.2%; 60–74, 3.7%; 75 and over, 0.8%.
Population projection: (2010) 13,416,000; (2020) 16,150,000.
Ethnic composition (2000): Chewa 34.7%; Maravi 12.2%; Ngoni 9.0%; Yao 7.9%; Tumbuka 7.9%; Lomwe 7.7%; Ngonde 3.5%; other 17.1%.
Religious affiliation (2000): Protestant 38.5%; Roman Catholic 24.7%; Muslim 14.8%; traditional beliefs 7.8%; other 14.2%.
Major cities (1998): Blantyre 502,053; Lilongwe 440,471; Mzuzu 86,980; Zomba 65,915; Karonga 27,811.

Vital statistics

Birth rate per 1,000 population (2003): 44.7 (world avg. 21.3).
Death rate per 1,000 population (2003): 22.6 (world avg. 9.1).
Natural increase rate per 1,000 population (2003): 22.1 (world avg. 12.2).
Total fertility rate (avg. births per childbearing woman; 2003): 6.1.
Life expectancy at birth (2003): male 37.6 years; female 38.4 years.
Adult population (ages 15–49) *living with HIV* (2004[3]): 14.2% (world avg. 1.1%).

National economy

Budget (2001–02). Revenue: MK 22,853,200,000 (tax revenue 72.5%, of which surtax 21.5%, income and profit tax 17.1%, import tax 8.4%; grants 19.8%; nontax revenue 7.7%). Expenditures: MK 30,476,300,000 (current expenditure 86.7%; capital expenditure 9.9%; other 3.4%).
Public debt (external, outstanding; 2002): U.S.$2,688,000,000.
Production (metric tons except as noted). Agriculture (2002): sugarcane 1,900,000, corn (maize) 1,603,000, cassava 1,540,000, potatoes 1,082,000, plantains 200,000, peanuts (groundnuts) 158,000, tobacco leaves 69,401, tea 38,000, coffee 3,600; livestock (number of live animals) 1,700,000 goats, 750,000 cattle, 456,000 pigs; roundwood (2001) 5,515,659 cu m; fish catch (2001) 41,187. Mining and quarrying (2002): limestone 175,000; gemstones 16,500 kg. Manufacturing (value added in U.S.$'000,000; 2001): food products 62; beverages 28; chemicals and chemical products 11; wearing apparel 7. Energy production (consumption): electricity (kW-hr; 2002) 1,156,000,000 ([2000] 884,000,000); hard coal (metric tons; 2002) 41,900 ([2000] 17,000); petroleum products (metric tons; 2000) none (209,000).
Land use as % of total land area (2000): in temporary crops 22.3%, in permanent crops 1.5%, in pasture 19.7%; overall forest area 27.2%.
Population economically active (1998): total 4,509,290; activity rate 45.4% (participation rates: ages 10 and over 66.9%; female 50.2%).

Price index (2000 = 100)

	1997	1998	1999	2000	2001	2002	2003
Consumer price index	41.1	53.3	77.2	100.0	122.7	140.8	154.3

Gross national product (2003): U.S.$1,832,000,000 (U.S.$170 per capita).

Structure of gross domestic product and labour force

	2000 in value MK '000,000[4]	2000 % of total value[4]	1998 labour force	1998 % of labour force
Agriculture	5,210	39.2	3,765,827	83.6
Mining	188	1.4	2,499	0.1
Manufacturing	1,705	12.8	118,483	2.6
Construction	288	2.2	73,402	1.6
Public utilities	189	1.4	7,319	0.2
Transp. and commun.	552	4.2	32,623	0.7
Trade	2,760	20.8	257,389	5.7
Finance	1,242	9.3	13,957	0.3
Public administration	1,282	9.6	101,433	2.2
Services	271	2.0	85,996	1.9
Other	−387[5]	−2.9[5]	50,362[6]	1.1[6]
TOTAL	13,300	100.0	4,509,290	100.0

Household income and expenditure. Average household size (1998) 4.3; income per household: n.a.; sources of income: n.a.; expenditure (2001)[7]: food 55.5%, clothing and footwear 11.7%, housing 9.6%, household goods 8.4%.
Tourism: receipts (2002) U.S.$125,000,000; expenditures (1994) U.S.$78,000,000.

Foreign trade[8]

Balance of trade (current prices)

	1997	1998	1999	2000	2001	2002
MK '000,000	−4,168	−3,361	−9,788	−8,658	−7,663	−22,240
% of total	19.0%	9.3%	19.7%	15.5%	10.7%	26.1%

Imports (2001): MK 39,480,000,000 (1998; food 16.4%, of which cereals 13.1%; machinery and apparatus 15.3%; chemicals and chemical products 13.2%; road vehicles 11.6%; mineral fuels 9.6%). *Major import sources* (2001): South Africa 39.7%; Zimbabwe 16.0%; Zambia 10.9%; India 3.2%; Germany 2.7%.
Exports (2001): MK 31,816,000,000 (tobacco 57.7%; sugar 12.5%; tea 7.7%; apparel 1.7%; coffee 1.4%). *Major export destinations:* South Africa 19.1%; U.S. 15.4%; Germany 11.2%; Japan 7.6%; The Netherlands 5.4%.

Transport and communications

Transport. Railroads (1999–2000): route length 495 mi, 797 km; passenger-km 19,000,000; metric ton-km cargo 62,000,000. Roads (1998): total length 10,222 mi, 16,451 km (paved 19%). Vehicles (2001): passenger cars 22,500; trucks and buses 57,600. Air transport (2003)[9]: passenger-km 146,900,000; metric ton-km cargo 1,176,000; airports (1998) 5.

Communications

Medium	date	unit	number	units per 1,000 persons
Daily newspapers	1996	circulation	22,000[10]	2.3[10]
Radio	2000	receivers	5,426,000	499
Television	2000	receivers	32,600	3.0
Telephones	2003	main lines	85,000	8.1
Cellular telephones	2003	subscribers	135,100	13
Personal computers	2003	units	16,000	1.5
Internet	2003	users	36,000	3.4

Education and health

Educational attainment (1998). Percentage of population age 25 and over having: no formal education 40.9%; primary education 48.7%; secondary 9.7%; university 0.7%. *Literacy* (2000): total population age 15 and over literate 60.1%; males literate 74.5%; females literate 46.5%.

Education (1995–96)

	schools	teachers	students	student/ teacher ratio
Primary (age 6–13)	3,706	49,138	2,887,107	58.8
Secondary (age 14–18)	...	2,948	139,386	47.3
Voc., teacher tr.	...	224	2,525	11.3
Higher	6[11]	329	3,872	11.8

Health: physicians (1989) 186 (1 per 47,634 persons); hospital beds (1998) 14,200 (1 per 746 persons); infant mortality rate (2003) 105.2.
Food (2001): daily per capita caloric intake 2,168 (vegetable products 97%, animal products 3%); 93% of FAO recommended minimum requirement.

Military

Total active duty personnel (2003): 5,300 (army 100%; navy, none; air force, none). *Military expenditure as percentage of GNP* (1999): 0.6% (world 2.4%); per capita expenditure U.S.$1.

[1]Judiciary meets in Blantyre. [2]Based on land area. [3]Beginning of year. [4]At constant prices of 1994. [5]Less imputed bank service charges. [6]Unemployed. [7]Weights of consumer price index components. [8]Imports c.i.f.; exports f.o.b. [9]Air Malawi only. [10]Circulation for one newspaper only. [11]Universities only.

Internet resources for further information:

- **National Statistical Office of Malawi http://www.nso.malawi.net**
- **Reserve Bank of Malawi http://www.rbm.malawi.net**

Malaysia

Official name: Malaysia.
Form of government: federal constitutional monarchy with two legislative houses (Senate [70[1]]; House of Representatives [219]).
Chief of state: Yang di-Pertuan Agong (Paramount Ruler).
Head of government: Prime Minister.
Capitals: Kuala Lumpur/Putrajaya[2].
Official language: Malay.
Official religion: Islam.
Monetary unit: 1 ringgit, or Malaysian dollar (RM) = 100 cents; valuation[3] (Sept. 1, 2004) 1 U.S.$ = RM 3.80; 1 £ = RM 6.84.

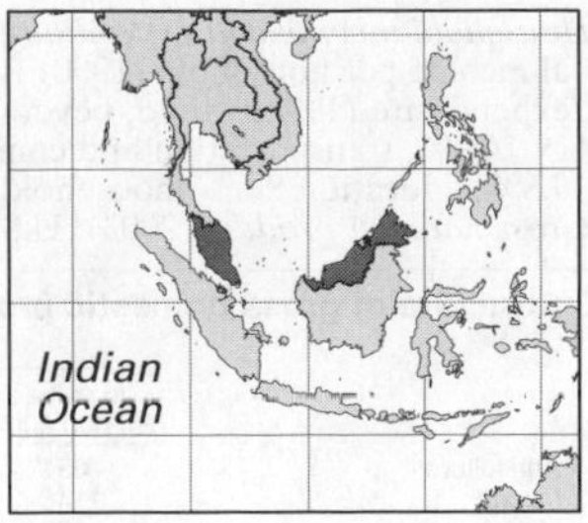

Area and population

Regions States	Capitals	area sq mi	area sq km	population 2000 census
East Malaysia				
Sabah	Kota Kinabalu	28,425	73,619	2,603,485
Sarawak	Kuching	48,050	124,450	2,071,506
West Malaysia (Peninsular Malaysia)				
Johor	Johor Bahru	7,331	18,987	2,740,625
Kedah	Alor Setar	3,639	9,425	1,649,756
Kelantan	Kota Baharu	5,801	15,024	1,313,014
Melaka	Melaka	638	1,652	635,791
Negeri Sembilan	Seremban	2,565	6,644	859,924
Pahang	Kuantan	13,886	35,965	1,288,376
Perak	Ipoh	8,110	21,005	2,051,236
Perlis	Kangar	307	795	204,450
Pulau Pinang	George Town	398	1,031	1,313,449
Selangor	Shah Alam	3,054	7,910	4,188,876[4]
Terengganu	Kuala Terengganu	5,002	12,955	898,825
Federal Territories				
Kuala Lumpur	—	94	243	1,379,310
Labuan	—	36	92	76,067
Putrajaya	—	19	50	[4]
TOTAL		127,355	329,847	23,274,690

Demography

Population (2004): 25,584,000.
Density (2004): persons per sq mi 200.9, persons per sq km 77.6.
Urban-rural (2002): urban 59.0%; rural 41.0%.
Sex distribution (2000): male 50.93%; female 49.07%.
Age breakdown (2000): under 15, 33.0%; 15–29, 28.3%; 30–44, 21.0%; 45–59, 11.6%; 60–74, 4.9%; 75 and over, 1.2%.
Population projection: (2010) 28,332,000; (2020) 32,520,000.
Ethnic composition (2000): Malay and other indigenous 61.3%; Chinese 24.5%; Indian 7.2%; other nonindigenous 1.1%; noncitizen 5.9%.
Religious affiliation (2000): Muslim 60.4%; Buddhist 19.2%; Christian 9.1%; Hindu 6.3%; Chinese folk religionist 2.6%; other 2.4%.
Major cities (2000[5]): Kuala Lumpur 1,297,526; Ipoh 566,211; Klang 563,173; Petaling Jaya 438,084; Johor Bahru 384,613.

Vital statistics

Birth rate per 1,000 population (2003): 21.9 (world avg. 21.3).
Death rate per 1,000 population (2003): 4.7 (world avg. 9.1).
Natural increase rate per 1,000 population (2003): 17.2 (world avg. 12.2).
Total fertility rate (avg. births per childbearing woman; 2003): 3.1.
Life expectancy at birth (2003): male 71.0 years; female 75.5 years.
Major causes of death per 100,000 population (1998): diseases of the circulatory system 37.7; malignant neoplasms (cancers) 20.7; infectious and parasitic diseases 16.1; accidents and violence 12.8; respiratory diseases 10.5.

National economy

Budget (2001). Revenue: RM 79,567,000,000 (income tax 52.9%, nontax revenue 25.1%, taxes on goods and services 16.9%, taxes on international trade 5.1%). Expenditures: RM 63,757,000,000 (education 22.6%, interest payments 15.1%, defense and internal security 13.0%, social security 8.7%, health 7.3%, transport 2.1%, agriculture 2.1%).
Population economically active (1999): total 9,010,000; activity rate 39.7% (participation rates: ages 15–64, 60.6%; female [2000] 34.7%; unemployed 3.0%).

Price index (2000 = 100)

	1997	1998	1999	2000	2001	2002	2003
Consumer price index	91.1	95.9	98.5	100.0	101.4	103.3	104.3

Production (metric tons except as noted). Agriculture, forestry, fishing (2002): palm fruit oil 67,400,000, rice 2,091,000, coconuts 700,000, rubber 589,000, bananas 500,000, pepper 28,600; livestock (number of live animals) 1,824,000 pigs, 748,000 cattle; roundwood (2001) 16,347,000 cu m; fish catch (2001) 1,393,000. Mining and quarrying (2001): iron ore 376,000; struverite 9,657; tin (metal content) 4,973; gold 3,965 kg. Manufacturing (value added in U.S.$'000,000; 2000): electronic products 4,962; refined petroleum products 2,492; telecommunications equipment 2,062; food products 1,982; basic chemicals 1,602; computers/office equipment 1,488. Energy production (consumption): electricity (kW-hr; 2003) 84,024,000,000[6] ([2000] 69,268,000,000); coal (metric tons; 2003) 168,000 ([2000] 3,761,000,000); crude petroleum (barrels; 2003) 268,300,000[7] ([2000] 155,548,000); petroleum products (metric tons; 2000) 19,386,000 (20,495,000); natural gas (cu m; 2003) 51,808,000,000 ([2000] 29,454,000,000).

Gross national product (2003): U.S.$93,683,000,000 (U.S.$3,780 per capita).

Structure of gross domestic product and labour force

	2000			
	in value RM '000,000	% of total value	labour force	% of labour force
Agriculture	17,687	8.4	1,408,000	14.7
Mining	14,416	6.9	41,000	0.4
Manufacturing	69,867	33.4	2,559,000	26.7
Construction	6,996	3.3	755,000	7.9
Public utilities	7,880	3.8	75,000	0.8
Transp. and commun.	16,694	8.0	462,000	4.8
Trade	30,949	14.8	1,584,000	16.5
Finance	26,161	12.5	509,000	5.3
Pub. admin., defense }	30,057	14.4	981,000	10.3
Services			899,000	9.4
Other	–11,348[8]	–5.5[8]	302,000	3.2
TOTAL	209,365	100.0	9,575,000	100.0

Public debt (external, outstanding; 2002): U.S.$26,200,000,000.
Household income and expenditure. Average household size (2000) 4.5; annual income per household (1999) RM 32,784 (U.S.$8,627); sources of income: n.a.; expenditure (1998–99): food at home 22.2%, housing and energy *c.* 21%, food away from home 10.9%.
Tourism (2002): receipts U.S.$6,785,000,000; expenditures U.S.$2,618,000,000.
Land use as % of total land area (2000): in temporary crops 5.5%, in permanent crops 17.6%, in pasture 0.9%; overall forest area 58.7%.

Foreign trade[9]

Balance of trade (current prices)

	1997	1998	1999	2000	2001	2002
RM '000,000	–50	+58,440	+73,080	+61,810	+54,050	+50,970
% of total	0.0%	11.4%	12.8%	9.0%	8.8%	7.7%

Imports (2002): RM 303,510,000,000 (microcircuits, transistors, and valves 29.2%; computers/office machines 6.9%; telecommunications equipment 4.3%; other electrical machinery 6.6%). *Major import sources:* Japan 17.8%; U.S. 16.4%; Singapore 12.0%; China 7.8%; Taiwan 5.6%.
Exports (2002): RM 354,480,000,000 (microcircuits, transistors, and valves 20.5%; computers/office machines 18.4%; telecommunications equipment 5.4%; fixed vegetable oils 3.9%; crude petroleum 3.3%). *Major export destinations:* U.S. 20.2%; Singapore 17.1%; Japan 11.2%; Hong Kong 5.7%; China 5.6%.

Transport and communications

Transport. Railroads (2000): route length 2,227 km; passenger-km 1,241,000,000[10]; metric ton-km cargo 918,000,000[10]. Roads (2000): total length 66,445 km (paved 76%). Vehicles (2000): passenger cars 4,212,567; trucks and buses 713,946. Air transport (2003)[11]: passenger-km 36,797,000,000; metric ton-km cargo 2,176,000,000; airports (1997) 39.

Communications

Medium	date	unit	number	units per 1,000 persons
Daily newspapers	2000	circulation	3,672,000	158
Radio	2000	receivers	9,762,000	420
Television	2002	receivers	5,103,000	210
Telephones	2003	main lines	4,571,600	182
Cellular telephones	2003	subscribers	11,124,100	442
Personal computers	2002	units	3,600,000	147
Internet	2003	users	8,692,100	345

Education and health

Educational attainment (1996). Percentage of population age 25 and over having: no formal schooling 16.7%; primary education 33.7%; secondary 42.8%; higher 6.8%. *Literacy* (2000): total population age 15 and over literate 87.5%; males literate 91.4%; females literate 83.4%.

Education (2000)

	schools	teachers	students	student/ teacher ratio
Primary (age 7–12)	7,231	154,509	2,934,000	19.0
Secondary (age 13–19)	1,561	107,598	1,938,000	18.0
Voc., teacher tr.[12]	80	5,111	51,000	10.0
Higher	55	19,702	344,000	17.5

Health (2002): physicians 17,442 (1 per 1,406 persons); hospital beds (2001) 41,927 (1 per 570 persons); infant mortality rate per 1,000 live births 7.9.
Food (2001): daily per capita caloric intake 2,927 (vegetable products 82%, animal products 18%); 131% of FAO recommended minimum.

Military

Total active duty personnel (2003): 104,000 (army 77.0%, navy 13.5%, air force 9.5%). *Military expenditure as percentage of GDP* (1999): 2.3% (world 2.4%); per capita expenditure U.S.$78.

[1]Includes 44 appointees of the Paramount Ruler; the remaining 26 are indirectly elected. [2]The transfer of government offices to the new federal administrative centre at Putrajaya is occurring between 1999 and 2012. [3]Pegged to the U.S. dollar at RM 3.80 = 1 U.S.$ from October 2000. [4]Selangor includes population data for Putrajaya. [5]Preliminary. [6]Excludes Sabah and Sarawak. [7]Sabah and Sarawak only. [8]Net bank service charges. [9]Imports c.i.f.; exports f.o.b. [10]Peninsular Malaysia and Singapore. [11]Malaysian airline only. [12]1999.

Internet resources for further information:
- **Department of Statistics http://www.statistics.gov.my**
- **Central Bank of Malaysia http://www.bnm.gov.my/**

Maldives

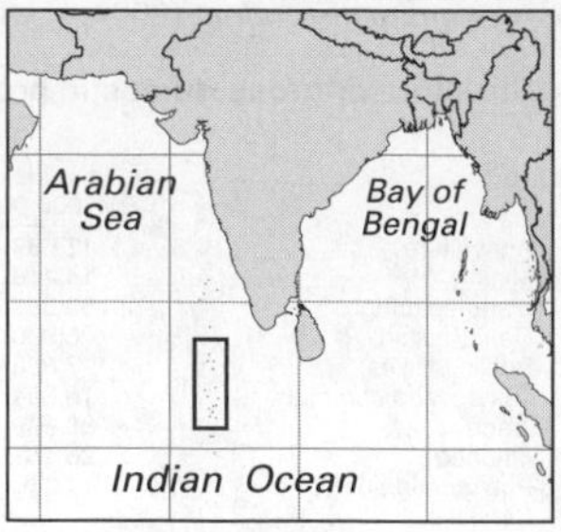

Official name: Divehi Jumhuriyya (Republic of Maldives).
Form of government: republic with one legislative house (Majlis[1] [42[2]]).
Head of state and government: President.
Capital: Male.
Official language: Divehi.
Official religion: Islam.
Monetary unit: 1 Maldivian rufiyaa (Rf) = 100 laari; valuation (Sept. 1, 2004) 1 U.S.$ = Rf 12.80; 1 £ = Rf 23.03.

Area and population[3]

		area		population
Administrative atolls	Capitals	sq mi	sq km	2000 census
North Thiladhunmathi (Haa-Alifu)	Dhidhdhoo	...	...	14,161
South Thiladhunmathi (Haa-Dhaalu)	Nolhivaranfaru	...	...	16,956
North Miladhunmadulu (Shaviyani)	Farukolhu-funadhoo	...	...	11,406
South Miladhunmadulu (Noonu)	Manadhoo	...	...	10,429
North Maalhosmadulu (Raa)	Ugoofaaru	...	...	14,486
South Maalhosmadulu (Baa)	Eydhafushi	...	...	9,612
Faadhippolhu (Lhaviyani)	Naifaru	...	...	9,385
Male (Kaafu)	Thulusdhoo	...	...	13,474
Ari Atoll Uthuru Gofi (Alifu)	Rasdhoo	...	...	5,518
Ari Atoll Dhekunu Gofi (Alifu)	Mahibadhoo	...	...	7,803
Felidhu Atoll (Vaavu)	Felidhoo	...	...	1,753
Mulakatholhu (Meemu)	Muli	...	...	5,084
North Nilandhe Atoll (Faafu)	Magoodhoo	...	...	3,827
South Nilandhe Atoll (Dhaalu)	Kudahuvadhoo	...	...	5,067
Kolhumadulu (Thaa)	Veymandoo	...	...	9,305
Hadhdhunmathi (Laamu)	Hithadhoo	...	...	11,588
North Huvadhu Atoll (Gaafu-Alifu)	Viligili	...	...	8,249
South Huvadhu Atoll (Gaafu-Dhaalu)	Thinadhoo	...	...	11,886
Foammulah (Gnyaviyani)	Foahmulah	...	...	7,528
Addu Atoll (Seenu)	Hithadhoo	...	...	18,515
Capital island				
Male (Maale)		...	...	74,069
TOTAL		115	298	270,101

Demography

Population (2004): 289,000.
Density (2004): persons per sq mi 2,513, persons per sq km 969.8.
Urban-rural (2002): urban 27.0%; rural 73.0%.
Sex distribution (2003): male 50.73%; female 49.27%.
Age breakdown (2003): under 15, 36.1%; 15–29, 31.7%; 30–44, 18.0%; 45–59, 7.9%; 60–74, 5.2%; 75 and over, 1.1%.
Population projection: (2010) 318,000; (2020) 372,000.
Doubling time: 23 years.
Ethnic composition (2000): Maldivian 98.5%; Sinhalese 0.7%; other 0.8%.
Religious affiliation: virtually 100% Sunnī Muslim.
Major city (2000): Male 74,069.

Vital statistics

Birth rate per 1,000 population (2003): 35.7 (world avg. 21.3).
Death rate per 1,000 population (2003): 6.0 (world avg. 9.1).
Natural increase rate per 1,000 population (2003): 29.7 (world avg. 12.2).
Total fertility rate (avg. births per childbearing woman; 2003): 5.3.
Marriage rate per 1,000 population (2001): 11.6.
Divorce rate per 1,000 population (2001): 5.5.
Life expectancy at birth (2003): male 62.0 years; female 64.6 years.
Major causes of death per 100,000 population (1988): rheumatic fever 106.0; ischemic heart diseases 65.0; bronchitis, emphysema, and asthma 61.0; tetanus 23.5; tuberculosis 13.0; accidents and suicide 10.0.

National economy

Budget (2001). Revenue: Rf 2,513,200,000 (nontax revenue 50.8%; taxation 41.4%; foreign aid 7.3%). Expenditures: Rf 2,886,200,000 (general public services 42.1%, of which defense 15.2%; education 18.5%; health 10.4%; transportation and communications 8.9%; transfer payments 2.3%).
Public debt (external, outstanding; 2002): U.S.$221,700,000.
Production (metric tons except as noted). Agriculture, forestry, fishing (2001): vegetables and melons 28,000, coconuts 15,000, fruits (excluding melons) 9,000, roots and tubers (including cassava, sweet potatoes, and yams) 8,000; fish catch 125,814. Mining and quarrying: coral for construction materials. Manufacturing: details, n.a.; however, major industries include boat building and repairing, coir yarn and mat weaving, coconut and fish processing, lacquerwork, garment manufacturing, and handicrafts. Energy production (consumption): electricity (kW-hr; 2000) 104,000,000 (104,000,000); petroleum products (metric tons; 2000) none (163,000).
Tourism (2002): receipts from visitors U.S.$318,000,000; expenditures by nationals abroad U.S.$46,000,000.
Population economically active (2000): total 87,987; activity rate of total population 32.6% (participation rates: ages 15–64, 58.5%; female 33.8%; unemployed 2.0%).

Price index (2000 = 100)

	1997	1998	1999	2000	2001	2002	2003
Consumer price index	99.7	98.3	101.2	100.0	100.7	101.6	98.7

Household income and expenditure. Average household size (2000) 6.8; annual income per household (1990) Rf 2,616 (U.S.$274); sources of income: n.a.; expenditure (1995)[4]: food, beverages and tobacco 36.9%, housing and energy 14.9%, transportation and communications 11.1%, clothing and footwear 9.8%, education 8.6%, household furnishings 8.3%.
Gross national product (2003): U.S.$674,000,000 (U.S.$2,300 per capita).

Structure of gross domestic product and labour force

	2003		2000	
	in value Rf '000,000[5]	% of total value	labour force	% of labour force
Agriculture[6]	694	8.3	11,789	13.4
Mining	46	0.5	473	0.5
Manufacturing	630	7.5	11,081	12.6
Public utilities	273	3.3	1,132	1.3
Construction	275	3.3	3,691	4.2
Transp. and commun.	1,079	12.9	7,873	9.0
Trade	308	3.7	15,606	17.7
Tourism (resorts)	2,482	29.6	...	...
Finance, real estate	1,048	12.5	1,690	1.9
Pub. admin., defense	907	10.8	} 18,089	} 20.6
Services	144	1.7		
Other	496	5.9	16,563	18.8
TOTAL	8,382	100.0	87,987	100.0

Land use as % of total land area (2000): in temporary crops *c.* 13%, in permanent crops *c.* 17%, in pasture *c.* 3%; overall forest area *c.* 3%.

Foreign trade[7, 8]

Balance of trade (current prices)

	1997	1998	1999	2000	2001	2002
U.S.$'000,000	–255.8	–258.4	–310.7	–279.9	–285.2	–258.0
% of total	57.9%	57.5%	62.9%	56.3%	56.4%	49.1%

Imports (2001): U.S.$395,400,000 (food products 36.9%; petroleum products 12.1%; transport equipment 10.5%; construction-related goods 10.2%). *Major import sources:* Asian countries 69%, of which Singapore 25%, Sri Lanka 13%, India 10%, Malaysia 9%; European countries 14%.
Exports (2001): U.S.$110,200,000 (domestic exports 69.1%, of which fish 32.5%, garments 29.3%, live tropical fish 2.8%; reexports 30.9%, of which jet fuel 25.6%). *Major export destinations:* United States 39%; Sri Lanka 21%; European countries 15%.

Transport and communications

Transport. Railroads: none. Roads: total length, n.a. Vehicles (2002): passenger cars 2,594; trucks and buses 644. Air transport (2001): passenger-km 385,000,000; airports (1997) with scheduled flights 5.

Communications

Medium	date	unit	number	units per 1,000 persons
Daily newspapers	1996	circulation	5,000	19
Radio	1997	receivers	34,000	129
Television	2000	receivers	10,900	40
Telephones	2002	main lines	28,700	102
Cellular telephones	2002	subscribers	41,900	149
Personal computers	2002	units	20,000	71
Internet	2002	users	15,000	53

Education and health

Educational attainment (2000). Population age 25 and over 71,937; percentage with university education 0.4%. *Literacy* (1995): total population age 15 and over literate 93.2%; males literate 93.0%; females literate 93.3%.

Education (1998)

	schools	teachers	students	student/ teacher ratio
Primary (age 6–11)	228	1,992	48,895	24.5
Secondary (age 11–18)	...	...	15,933[9]	...
Voc., teacher tr.	...	...	452[9]	...
Higher	—	—	—	—

Health (2003): physicians 314 (1 per 905 persons); hospital beds 643 (1 per 443 persons); infant mortality rate per 1,000 live births (2002) 38.0.
Food (2001): daily per capita caloric intake 2,587 (vegetable products 75%, animal products 25%); 117% of FAO recommended minimum requirement.

Military

Total active duty personnel: combined army/police force *c.* 700–1,000. *Military expenditure as percentage of GDP* (2002): 6.2% (world, n.a.); per capita expenditure U.S.$103.

[1]Also known or translated as People's Majlis, Citizens' Council, or Citizens' Assembly. [2]Excludes eight nonelective seats. [3]Maldives is divided into 20 administrative districts corresponding to atoll groups; arrangement shown here is from north to south. Total area excludes 34,634 sq mi (89,702 sq km) of tidal waters. [4]Weights of consumer price index components. [5]At 1995 prices. [6]Primarily fishing. [7]Imports c.i.f.; exports f.o.b. [8]Exports include reexports. [9]1992.

Internet resources for further information:
- **Ministry of Planning and National Development http://www.planning.gov.mv/index2.htm**
- **Maldives Monetary Authority http://www.mma.gov.mv**

Mali

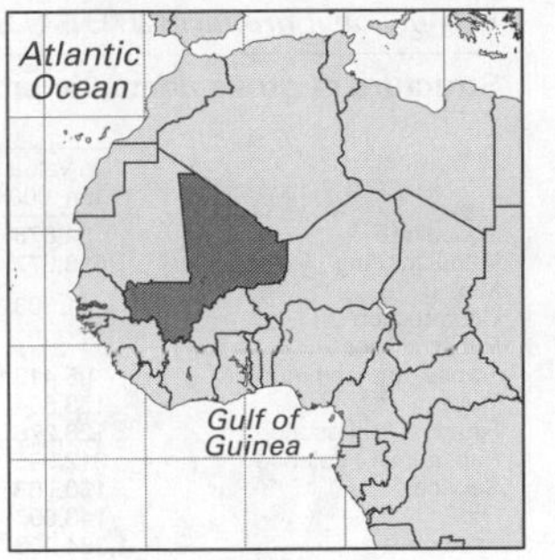

Official name: République du Mali (Republic of Mali).
Form of government: multiparty republic with one legislative house (National Assembly [147]).
Chief of state: President.
Head of government: Prime Minister.
Capital: Bamako.
Official language: French.
Official religion: none.
Monetary unit: 1 CFA franc (CFAF) = 100 centimes; valuation (Sept. 1, 2004) 1 U.S.$ = CFAF 539.75; 1 £ = CFAF 970.98[1].

Area and population

		area		population
Regions	**Capitals**	sq mi	sq km	1998 census
Gao	Gao	65,858	170,572	495,178
Kayes	Kayes	46,233	119,743	1,424,657
Kidal	Kidal	58,467	151,430	65,524
Koulikoro	Koulikoro	37,007	95,848	1,620,811
Mopti	Mopti	30,509	79,017	1,405,370
Ségou	Ségou	25,028	64,821	1,652,594
Sikasso	Sikasso	27,135	70,280	1,839,747
Tombouctou	Tombouctou (Timbuktu)	191,743	496,611	496,312
District				
Bamako	Bamako	97	252	1,178,977
TOTAL		482,077	1,248,574	10,179,170[2]

Demography

Population (2004): 11,957,000.
Density (2004): persons per sq mi 24.8, persons per sq km 9.6.
Urban-rural (1998): urban 28.7%; rural 71.3%.
Sex distribution (2001): male 48.9%; female 51.1%.
Age breakdown (2001): under 15, 47.2%; 15–29, 26.8%; 30–44, 13.3%; 45–59, 7.9%; 60–74, 4.0%; 75 and over, 0.8%.
Population projection: (2010) 14,012,000; (2020) 17,847,000.
Doubling time: 24 years.
Ethnic composition (2000): Bambara 30.6%; Senufo 10.5%; Fula Macina (Niafunke) 9.6%; Soninke 7.4%; Tuareg 7.0%, Maninka 6.6%; Songhai 6.3%; Dogon 4.3%; Bobo 3.5%; other 14.2%.
Religious affiliation (2000): Muslim *c.* 82%; traditional beliefs *c.* 16%; Christian *c.* 2%.
Major cities (1998): Bamako 1,016,167; Sikasso 113,803; Ségou 90,898; Mopti 79,840, Gao 54,903.

Vital statistics

Birth rate per 1,000 population (2003): 47.8 (world avg. 21.3).
Death rate per 1,000 population (2003): 19.2 (world avg. 9.1).
Natural increase rate per 1,000 population (2003): 28.6 (world avg. 12.2).
Total fertility rate (avg. births per childbearing woman; 2003): 6.7.
Life expectancy at birth (2003): male 44.7 years; female 46.2 years.
Major causes of death per 100,000 population: n.a.; morbidity ([notified cases of illness] by cause as a percentage of all reported infectious disease; 1985): malaria 62.1%; measles 10.3%; amebiasis 10.3%; syphilis and gonococcal infections 6.0%; influenza 4.9%.

National economy

Budget (2002). Revenue: CFAF 379,400,000,000 (tax revenue 82.7%, nontax revenue 17.3%). Expenditures: CFAF 601,500,000,000 (current expenditure 46.7%, of which wages and salaries 14.9%, education 4.9%, interest on public debt 3.5%; capital expenditure 53.3%).
Public debt (external, outstanding; 2002): U.S.$2,487,000,000.
Tourism (2000): receipts from visitors U.S.$71,000,000; expenditures by nationals abroad U.S.$41,000,000.
Population economically active (2001): total 5,895,000; activity rate of total population 53.7% (participation rates: ages 15–64, n.a.; female, n.a.; unemployed, n.a.).

Price index (2000 = 100)

	1998	1999	2000	2001	2002	2003
Consumer price index	101.9	100.7	100.0	105.2	110.5	109.0

Production (metric tons except as noted). Agriculture, forestry, fishing (2002): millet 1,034,211, sorghum 951,417, rice 926,497, seed cotton 611,938, corn (maize) 320,502, sugarcane 300,000, peanuts (groundnuts) 257,108, sweet potatoes 74,483; livestock (number of live animals) 15,000,000 goats and sheep, 6,818,000 cattle, 700,000 asses, 470,000 camels, 170,000 horses, 85,000 pigs; roundwood (2001) 5,200,428 cu m; fish catch (2001) 100,035. Mining and quarrying (2002): limestone 20,000[3]; phosphate 3,000[3]; iron oxide 708[3]; gypsum 500; gold 63,000 kg; silver 1,000 kg. Manufacturing (2000): cement 40,000; sugar 28,000; soap 10,097[4]; soft drinks 68,609 hectolitres[4]; beer 41,690 hectolitres[4]; shoes 111,000 pairs[4]; cigarettes 51,400 cartons. Construction: n.a. Energy production (consumption): electricity (kW-hr; 2000) 412,000,000 (412,000,000); coal, none (n.a.); crude petroleum, none (n.a.); petroleum products (metric tons; 2000) none (161,000); natural gas, none (n.a.).
Gross national product (2003): U.S.$3,428,000,000 (U.S.$290 per capita).

Structure of gross domestic product and labour force

	2001			
	in value CFAF '000,000	% of total value	labour force	% of labour force
Agriculture	986,800	47.6	4,580,000	77.7
Mining	169,900	8.2		
Manufacturing	88,900	4.2		
Construction	114,100	5.5		
Public utilities	29,800	1.4		
Transp. and commun.	85,700	4.1	1,315,000	22.3
Trade Finance	268,900	13.0		
Pub. admin., defense	129,500	6.3		
Services	71,600	3.5	...	...
Other	128,400[5]	6.2[5]	...	...
TOTAL	2,073,600	100.0	5,895,000	100.0

Household income and expenditure. Average household size (2000) 5.6; average annual income per household: n.a.; sources of income: n.a.; expenditure: n.a.
Land use as % of total land area (2000): in temporary crops 3.8%, in permanent crops, negligible, in pasture 24.6%; overall forest area 10.8%.

Foreign trade

Balance of trade (current prices)

	1996	1997	1998	1999	2000	2001
CFAF '000,000,000	–60.7	+9.2	–1.2	–21.2	–33.4	–2.4
% of total	12.1%	1.4%	0.2%	2.9%	4.1%	0.2%

Imports (2001): CFAF 532,900,000,000 (machinery and apparatus 46.0%, petroleum products 25.9%, food products 13.0%). *Major import sources* (1999)[6]: African countries *c.* 51%, of which Côte d'Ivoire *c.* 20%; France *c.* 18%; Germany *c.* 3%; Hong Kong *c.* 3%.
Exports (2001): CFAF 530,500,000,000 (gold 66.7%, raw cotton and cotton products 15.7%, live animals 8.5%). *Major export destinations* (1999)[6]: Italy *c.* 12%; Taiwan *c.* 10%; Thailand *c.* 10%; South Korea *c.* 9%; Canada *c.* 8%; Portugal *c.* 5%.

Transport and communications

Transport. Railroads (1999): route length 453 mi, 729 km; passenger-mi 130,000,000, passenger-km 210,000,000; short ton-mi cargo 165,000,000, metric ton-km cargo 241,000,000. Roads (1996): total length 9,383 mi, 15,100 km (paved 12%). Vehicles (1996): passenger cars 26,190; trucks and buses 18,240. Merchant marine: vessels (100 gross tons and over) none. Air transport (1999)[7]: passenger-mi 146,000,000, passenger-km 235,000,000; short ton-mi cargo 25,000,000, metric ton-km cargo 36,000,000; airports (1999) 9.

Communications

Medium	date	unit	number	units per 1,000 persons
Daily newspapers	1997	circulation	45,000	4.6
Radio	2001	receivers	1,976,000	180
Television	2002	receivers	376,200	33
Telephones	2002	main lines	56,600	5.3
Cellular phones	2002	subscribers	250,000	23
Personal computers	2002	units	15,000	1.5
Internet	2002	users	25,000	2.3

Education and health

Educational attainment: n.a. *Literacy* (2000): percentage of total population age 15 and over literate 41.5%; males literate 48.9%; females literate 34.4%.

Education (2000–01)

	schools	teachers	students	student/ teacher ratio
Primary (age 6–14)	2,871	14,962	1,115,563	74.5
Secondary (age 15–17)	...	...	257,574	...
Vocational	...	...	47,883	...
Higher	...	1,312	28,000	21.3

Health: physicians (1993) 483 (1 per 18,376 persons); hospital beds (1998) 2,412 (1 per 4,168 persons); infant mortality rate per 1,000 live births (2003) 119.2.
Food (2001): daily per capita caloric intake 2,376 (vegetable products 91%, animal products 9%); 101% of FAO recommended minimum requirement.

Military

Total active duty personnel (2003): 7,350 (army 100.0%). *Military expenditure as percentage of GNP* (1999): 2.3% (world 2.4%); per capita expenditure U.S.$6.

[1]Formerly pegged to the French franc, and since Jan. 1, 2002, to the euro at the rate of €1 = CFAF 655.96. [2]Excludes 772,006 Malians living abroad. [3]1997. [4]1995. [5]Import taxes. [6]Estimated figures. [7]Represents 1/11 of the traffic of Air Afrique, which was operated by 11 West African states and was declared bankrupt in February 2002.

Internet resources for further information:
- **La Banque de France: La Zone Franc**
  http://www.banque-france.fr/fr/zonefr/main.htm
- **Le Ministère de la Culture du Mali**
  http://w3.culture.gov.ml

Malta

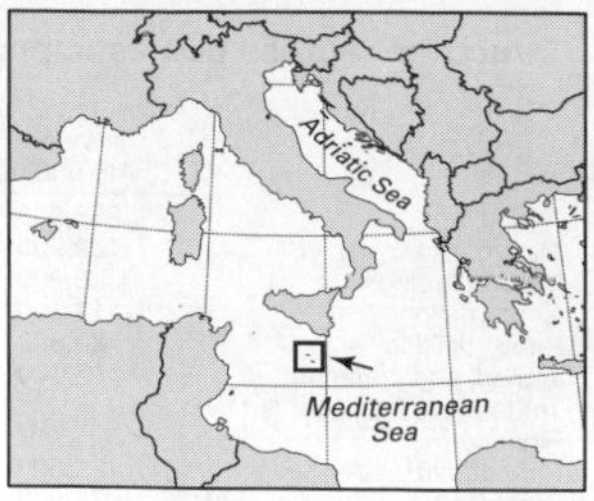

Official name: Repubblikka ta' Malta (Maltese); Republic of Malta (English).
Form of government: unitary multiparty republic with one legislative house (House of Representatives [65]).
Chief of state: President.
Head of government: Prime Minister.
Capital: Valletta.
Official languages: Maltese; English.
Official religion: Roman Catholicism.
Monetary unit: 1 Maltese lira (Lm) = 100 cents = 1,000 mils; valuation (Sept. 1, 2004) 1 U.S.$ = Lm 0.35; 1 £ = Lm 0.63.

Area and population

Islands/statistical districts[2]	area sq mi	area sq km	population 2004[1] estimate
Comino	1.4	3.5	4
Gozo	25.2	65.2	31,613
Malta	95.1[3]	246.4	368,250
Northern District	28.5	73.7	49,395
Northern Harbour	9.3	24.1	122,913
South Eastern District	19.2	49.7	55,199
Southern Harbour	10.1	26.1	85,629
Western District	28.1	72.8	55,114
TOTAL	121.7	315.1	399,867[4]

Demography

Population (2004): 401,000.
Density (2004): persons per sq mi 3,287, persons per sq km 1,273.
Urban-rural (2000): urban 90.5%; rural 9.5%.
Sex distribution (2004)[1]: male 49.54%; female 50.46%.
Age breakdown (2004)[1]: under 15, 18.2%; 15–29, 22.1%; 30–44, 20.0%; 45–59, 22.3%; 60–74, 12.1%; 75 and over, 5.3%.
Population projection: (2010) 411,000; (2020) 424,000.
Ethnic composition (2000): Maltese 93.8%; British 2.1%; Arab 2.0%; Italian 1.5%; other 0.6%.
Religious affiliation (2000): Roman Catholic 94.5%; unaffiliated Christian 2.7%; Protestant 0.8%; Muslim 0.5%; nonreligious 1.0%; other 0.5%.
Major localities (2004[1]): Birkirkara 22,435; Qormi 18,547; Mosta 18,070; Zabbar 15,134; Valletta 7,137 (urban agglomeration [2003] 83,000).

Vital statistics

Birth rate per 1,000 population (2003): 10.1 (world avg. 21.3); legitimate 83.2%; illegitimate 16.8%.
Death rate per 1,000 population (2003): 7.9 (world avg. 9.1).
Natural increase rate per 1,000 population (2003): 2.2 (world avg. 12.2).
Total fertility rate (avg. births per childbearing woman; 2003): 1.5.
Marriage rate per 1,000 population (2003): 6.1.
Life expectancy at birth (2003): male 76.3 years; female 80.8 years.
Major causes of death per 100,000 population (2002): diseases of the circulatory system 335.4; malignant neoplasms (cancers) 185.6; diseases of the respiratory system 88.0; accidents, poisonings, and violence 31.4; endocrine and metabolic diseases 26.3; diseases of the digestive system 26.3.

National economy

Budget (2001). Revenue: Lm 797,400,000 (social security 22.5%; income tax 20.9%; value-added tax 14.4%; grants and loans 13.6%). Expenditures: Lm 766,700,000 (recurrent expenditures 80.2%, of which social security 24.1%, education 6.1%; capital expenditure 10.5%; public debt service 9.3%).
Public debt (2001): U.S.$616,000,000.
Production (metric tons except where noted). Agriculture, forestry, fishing (2002): vegetables 49,200 (of which melons 12,800, tomatoes 7,400, onions 4,392, cabbage 3,900, garlic 551), potatoes 27,500, wheat 9,600, barley 2,200; livestock (number of live animals; 2002) 79,300 pigs, 18,000 cattle, 6,600 sheep; fish catch (2003) 1,070. Quarrying (2002): small quantities of limestone and salt. Manufacturing (value added in U.S.$'000,000; 1998): telecommunications equipment and electronics 149; food products 69; wearing apparel 63; beverages 55; printing and publishing 52. Energy production (consumption): electricity (kW-hr; 2000) 1,875,000,000 (1,875,000,000); coal (metric tons; 2000) none (325,000); crude petroleum, none (none); petroleum products (metric tons; 2000) none (677,000).
Population economically active (1998): total 144,824; activity rate of total population 38.4% (participation rates: ages 15–64 [1985] 45.9%; female 27.6%; unemployed [2001] 6.1%).

Price and earnings indexes (2000 = 100)

	1997	1998	1999	2000	2001	2002	2003
Consumer price index	93.4	95.6	97.7	100.0	102.9	105.1	106.6
Earnings index	86.1	92.2	95.8	100.0	104.5	111.1	121.3

Household income and expenditure. Average household size (2001) 3.1; average annual income per household (1982) Lm 4,736 (U.S.$11,399); sources of income (1993): wages and salaries 63.8%, professional and unincorporated enterprises 19.3%, rents, dividends, and interest 16.9%; expenditure (2000): food and beverages 36.6%, transportation and communications 23.4%, recreation, entertainment, and education 9.4%, household furnishings and operations 7.6%.
Tourism (2002): receipts from visitors U.S.$568,000,000; expenditures by nationals abroad U.S.$153,000,000.

Gross national product (2003): U.S.$3,678,000,000 (U.S.$9,260 per capita).

Structure of gross domestic product and labour force

	2001 in value Lm '000	2001 % of total value	2001 labour force	2001 % of labour force
Agriculture	32,678	2.3	2,956	1.9
Manufacturing	318,677	23.0	32,532	21.0
Mining }	41,303	3.0	1,015	0.7
Construction }			10,075	6.5
Public utilities	5	5	3,352	2.2
Transp. and commun.	95,413	6.9	10,485	6.8
Trade	153,504	11.1	32,881	21.3
Finance, real estate	126,278	9.1	12,377	8.0
Pub. admin., defense	312,595[5]	22.6[5]	12,804	8.3
Services	160,763	11.6	26,499	17.1
Other	143,695	10.4	9,638[6]	6.2[6]
TOTAL	1,384,906	100.0	154,614	100.0

Land use as % of total land area (2000): in temporary crops *c.* 25%, in permanent crops *c.* 3%, in pasture, n.a.; overall forest area, negligible.

Foreign trade[7]

Balance of trade (current prices)

	1996	1997	1998	1999	2000	2001
Lm '000,000	–383.7	–355.3	–322.9	–345.1	–420.0	–345.7
% of total	23.5%	22.0%	18.5%	17.9%	16.4%	16.4%

Imports (2000): Lm 1,492,400,000 (electronic microcircuits 37.3%, refined petroleum 7.0%, chemicals and chemical products 6.9%, food 6.0%). *Major import sources* (2001): Italy 17.3%; France 10.3%; Singapore 8.3%; Japan 7.6%; U.K. 7.5%.
Exports (2000): Lm 1,072,400,000 (electronic microcircuits 62.1%, apparel and clothing accessories 5.9%, refined petroleum 4.4%, children's toys and games 4.3%). *Major export destinations* (2001): U.S. 15.2%; Germany 13.4%; Singapore 11.6%; France 8.9%; U.K. 8.7%.

Transport and communications

Transport. Railroads: none. Roads (1997): total length 1,219 mi, 1,961 km (paved 94%). Vehicles (2000): passenger cars 202,883; trucks and buses 52,604. Air transport (2001): passenger-mi 1,469,000,000, passenger km 2,364,000,000; (2000) short ton-mi cargo 9,789,000; metric ton-km cargo 14,292,000; airports (1999) with scheduled flights 1.

Communications

Medium	date	unit	number	units per 1,000 persons
Daily newspapers	1996	circulation	54,000	145
Radio	1997	receivers	255,000	680
Television	2000	receivers	217,000	556
Telephones	2003	main lines	208,300	521
Cellular telephones	2003	subscribers	290,000	725
Personal computers	2002	units	101,000	255
Internet	2002	users	120,000	303

Education and health

Educational attainment (2001). Percentage of population age 15 and over having: no formal schooling 4.3%; primary education 34.4%; general secondary 37.6%; vocational secondary 5.7%; some postsecondary 11.8%; undergraduate 5.4%; graduate 0.8%. *Literacy* (2000): total population age 15 and over literate 279,000 (92.1%).

Education (1995–96)

	schools	teachers	students	student/ teacher ratio
Primary (age 5–10)	111	1,990	33,530[8]	17.8
Secondary (age 11–17)	59	2,679	27,647[8]	20.9
Voc., teacher tr.	22	541	4,539	8.4
Higher[9]	1	522	6,420	12.3

Health (1996): physicians 925 (1 per 403 persons); hospital beds 2,140 (1 per 174 persons); infant mortality rate per 1,000 live births (2003) 4.0.
Food (2001): daily per capita caloric intake 3,495 (vegetable products 73%, animal products 27%); 141% of FAO recommended minimum requirement.

Military

Total active duty personnel (2003): 2,140 (army 100%). *Military expenditure as percentage of GNP* (1999): 0.8% (world 2.4%); per capita expenditure U.S.$73.

[1]January 1. [2]Actual local administration in 2003 was based on 3 regions divided into 68 local councils. [3]Detail does not add to total given because of rounding. [4]Includes foreign workers and foreign residents (11,000 persons as of Jan. 1, 2004). [5]Pub. admin., defense includes Public utilities. [6]Includes 9,432 unemployed. [7]Imports c.i.f.; exports f.o.b. [8]2000–01. [9]University of Malta only; full-time faculty and students in 2000–01.

Internet resources for further information:
- **National Statistics Office http://www.nso.gov.mt**
- **Central Bank of Malta http://www.centralbankmalta.com**

Marshall Islands

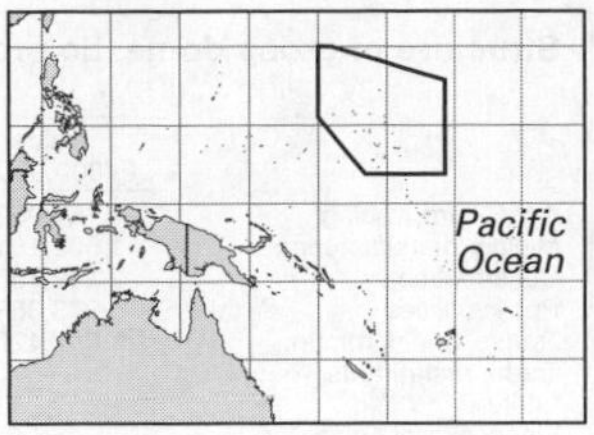

Official name: Majōl (Marshallese); Republic of the Marshall Islands (English).
Form of government: unitary republic with two legislative houses (Council of Iroij [12][1]; Nitijela [33]).
Head of state and government: President.
Capital: Majuro[2].
Official languages: Marshallese (Kajin-Majōl); English.
Official religion: none.
Monetary unit: 1 U.S. dollar (U.S.$) = 100 cents; valuation (Sept. 1, 2004) 1 U.S.$ = £0.56.

Area and population

Atolls/Islands[3]	area sq mi	area sq km	population 1999 census
Ailinglaplap	5.67	14.69	1,959
Ailuk	2.07	5.36	514
Arno	5.00	12.95	2,069
Aur	2.17	5.62	537
Bikini	2.32	6.01	13
Ebon	2.22	5.75	902
Enewetak	2.26	5.85	853
Jabat	0.22	0.57	95
Jaluit	4.38	11.34	1,669
Kili	0.36	0.93	774
Kwajalein	6.33	16.39	10,903
Lae	0.56	1.45	322
Lib	0.36	0.93	147
Likiep	3.96	10.26	527
Majuro	3.75	9.71	23,682
Maloelap	3.79	9.82	856
Mejit	0.72	1.86	416
Mili	6.15	15.93	1,032
Namorik	1.07	2.77	772
Namu	2.42	6.27	903
Rongelap	3.07	7.95	19
Ujae	0.72	1.86	440
Ujelang	0.67	1.74	0
Utirik	0.94	2.43	433
Wotho	1.67	4.33	145
Wotje	3.16	8.18	866
Other atolls	4.04	10.46	0
TOTAL	70.05[4]	181.43[4, 5]	50,848

Demography

Population (2004): 54,600.
Density (2004): persons per sq mi 780.0, persons per sq km 301.7.
Urban-rural (2004): urban 65.0%; rural 35.0%.
Sex distribution (2003): male 51.07%; female 48.93%.
Age breakdown (2003): under 15, 39.2%; 15–29, 30.7%; 30–44, 16.4%; 45–59, 9.6%; 60–74, 3.1%; 75 and over, 1.0%.
Population projection: (2010) 59,000; (2020) 68,000.
Doubling time: 24 years.
Ethnic composition (nationality; 2000): Marshallese 88.5%; U.S. white 6.5%; other Pacific islanders and East Asians 5.0%.
Religious affiliation (1995): Protestant 62.8%; Roman Catholic 7.1%; Mormon 3.1%; Jehovah's Witness 1.0%; other 26.0%.
Major towns (1999): Majuro[2] 19,300; Ebeye 9,300; Laura 2,300; Ajeltake 1,200; Enewetak 820.

Vital statistics

Birth rate per 1,000 population (2003): 34.2 (world avg. 21.3).
Death rate per 1,000 population (2003): 5.0 (world avg. 9.1).
Natural increase rate per 1,000 population (2003): 29.2 (world avg. 12.2).
Total fertility rate (avg. births per childbearing woman; 2003): 4.1.
Life expectancy at birth (2003): male 67.4 years; female 71.4 years.
Major causes of death per 100,000 population (1990–93; registered deaths only): infectious and parasitic diseases 169.9; circulatory diseases 155.1; respiratory diseases 105.1; malignant neoplasms (cancers) 68.4; digestive diseases 63.3.

National economy

Budget (2002). Revenue: U.S.$83,600,000 (U.S. government grants 70.3%, tax revenue 22.2%, nontax revenue 7.5%). Expenditures: U.S.$74,000,000 (current expenditure 79.3%, capital expenditure 20.7%).
Public debt (external, outstanding; 1996–97): U.S.$124,900,000.
Production (metric tons except as noted). Agriculture, forestry, fishing (value of production for household consumption in U.S.$'000; 1999): fish 3,920; pork 1,496; breadfruit 646; chickens 591; coconuts 434; taro 166; bananas 108; fish catch (2002) 38,242, of which skipjack 37,057. Mining and quarrying: for local construction only. Manufacturing (2002): copra 2,653; coconut oil and processed (chilled or frozen) fish are important products; the manufacture of handicrafts and personal items (clothing, mats, boats, etc.) by individuals is also significant. Energy production (consumption): electricity (kW-hr; 2002) 79,764,000 (79,764,000); coal, none (none); petroleum products, n.a. (n.a.).
Household income and expenditure. Average household size (2000) 7.8; annual median income per household (1999) U.S.$6,840; sources of income: n.a.; expenditure (2003)[6]: food 35.9%, housing and energy 17.1%, transportation 13.7%, education and communication 6.6%, clothing 4.3%.
Gross national product (2003): U.S.$143,000,000 (U.S.$2,710 per capita).

Structure of gross domestic product and labour force

	2001 in value U.S.$'000	2001 % of total value	1999 labour force	1999 % of labour force
Agriculture	10,296.0	10.5	2,114	14.4
Mining	291.4	0.3	—	—
Manufacturing	4,489.5	4.6	761	5.2
Public utilities	3,402.2	3.5	258	1.8
Construction	11,314.1	11.5	848	5.8
Transp. and commun.	5,044.8	5.1	763	5.2
Trade, restaurants, hotels	16,937.3	17.2	788	5.4
Finance, insurance, real estate	15,458.2	15.7	559	3.8
Public administration, services }	31,043.6	31.6	3,803	25.9
Other }			4,783[7]	32.6[7]
TOTAL	98,277.1	100.0	14,677	100.0[5]

Population economically active (1999): total 14,677; activity rate of total population 28.9% (participation rates: over age 15, 51.1%; female 34.1%; unemployed 30.9%).

Price index (2000 = 100)

	1994	1995	1996	1997	1998	1999	2000
Consumer price index[8]	78.9	85.4	93.6	98.1	100.2	102.0	100.0

Tourism (2002): receipts U.S.$4,000,000; expenditures, n.a.
Land use as % of total land area (2000): in temporary crops *c.* 17%, in permanent crops *c.* 39%, in pasture *c.* 22%; overall forest area, n.a.

Foreign trade[9]

Balance of trade (current prices)

	1995	1996	1997	1998	1999	2000
U.S.$'000,000	–52.0	–53.6	–45.2	–61.5	–61.2	–60.9
% of total	53.0%	58.6%	58.0%	84.1%	79.9%	80.8%

Imports (2000): U.S.$68,200,000 (mineral fuels and lubricants 43.6%; machinery and transport equipment 16.9%; food, beverages, and tobacco 10.9%). *Major import sources:* U.S. 61.4%; Japan 5.1%; Australia 2.0%; Hong Kong 1.9%; Taiwan 1.3%.
Exports (2000): U.S.$7,300,000 (chilled and frozen fish, n.a.; copra cake 16.2%; crude coconut oil 14.7%; aquarium fish 6.2%). *Major export destinations:* U.S. *c.* 71%; other *c.* 29%.

Transport and communications

Transport. Roads: only Majuro and Kwajalein have paved roads. Vehicles (2002): passenger cars 1,910; trucks and buses 193. Air transport (2001)[10]: passenger-km 24,972,000; metric ton-km cargo 183,000; airports (2002) 32.

Communications

Medium	date	unit	number	units per 1,000 persons
Telephones	2003	main lines	4,500	83
Cellular telephones	2003	subscribers	600	11
Personal computers	2002	units	3,000	56
Internet	2003	users	1,400	26

Education and health

Educational attainment (1999). Percentage of population age 25 and over having: no formal schooling 3.1%; elementary education 35.5%; secondary 46.5%; some higher 12.3%; undergraduate degree 1.7%; advanced degree 0.9%. *Literacy* (latest): total population age 15 and over literate 19,377 (91.2%); males literate 9,993 (92.4%); females literate 9,384 (90.0%).

Education (2002–03)

	schools	teachers	students	student/ teacher ratio
Primary (age 6–14)	100	703	10,957	15.6
Secondary (age 15–18)	16	202	3,147	15.6
Higher	1	...	3,131	...

Health: physicians (1997) 34 (1 per 1,452 persons); hospital beds (2002) 140 (1 per 380 persons); infant mortality rate per 1,000 live births (2003) 31.6.

Military

The United States provides for the defense of the Republic of the Marshall Islands under the 1984 and 2003 compacts of free association.

[1]Council of Iroij is an advisory body only. [2]Local name of town (not atoll) is Rita. [3]Four districts centred at Majuro, Ebeye, Wotje, and Jaluit make up the local government structure. [4]Land area only; excludes lagoon area of 4,507 sq mi (11,673 sq km). [5]Detail does not add to total given because of rounding. [6]Weights of consumer price index components. [7]Includes 4,536 unemployed and 247 undistributed employees. [8]Majuro only. [9]Imports c.i.f.; exports f.o.b. [10]Air Marshall Islands only.

Internet resources for further information:
- **Secretariat of the Pacific Community: PRISM http://www.spc.org.nc/prism/country/country.html**
- **U.S. Office of Insular Affairs http://www.pacificweb.org**

Martinique

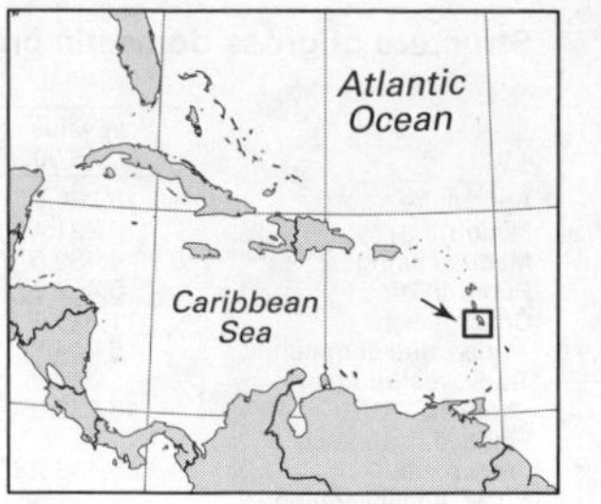

Official name: Département de la Martinique (Department of Martinique).
Political status: overseas department (France) with two legislative houses (General Council [45]; Regional Council [41]).
Chief of state: President of France.
Heads of government: Prefect (for France); President of the General Council (for Martinique); President of the Regional Council (for Martinique).
Capital: Fort-de-France.
Official language: French.
Official religion: none.
Monetary unit: 1 euro (€) = 100 cents; valuation (Sept. 1, 2004)
1 U.S.$ = €0.82; 1 £ = €1.48[1].

Area and population

		area		population
Arrondissements	Capitals	sq mi	sq km	1999 census
Fort-de-France	Fort-de-France	66	171	166,139
La Trinité	La Trinité	131	338	85,006
Le Marin	Le Marin	158	409	106,818
Saint-Pierre	Saint-Pierre	81	210	23,464
TOTAL		436	1,128	381,427

Demography

Population (2004): 395,000.
Density (2004): persons per sq mi 906.0, persons per sq km 350.2.
Urban-rural (2001): urban 95.2%; rural 4.8%.
Sex distribution (2001): male 49.47%; female 50.53%.
Age breakdown (2001): under 15, 23.1%; 15–29, 23.3%; 30–44, 26.3%; 45–59, 13.8%; 60–74, 9.1%; 75 and over, 4.4%.
Population projection: (2010) 404,000; (2020) 419,000.
Doubling time: 81 years.
Ethnic composition (2000): mixed race (black/white/Asian) 93.4%; French (metropolitan and Martinique white) 3.0%; East Indian 1.9%; other 1.7%.
Religious affiliation (1995): Roman Catholic 86.5%; Protestant 8.0% (mostly Seventh-day Adventist); Jehovah's Witness 1.6%; other 3.9%, including Hindu, syncretist, and nonreligious.
Major communes (1999): Fort-de-France 94,049; Le Lamentin 35,460; Le Robert 21,201; Schoelcher 20,845; Sainte-Marie 20,058.

Vital statistics

Birth rate per 1,000 population (2003): 15.0 (world avg. 21.3); (1997) legitimate 31.8%; illegitimate 68.2%.
Death rate per 1,000 population (2003): 6.4 (world avg. 9.1).
Natural increase rate per 1,000 population (2003): 8.6 (world avg. 12.2).
Total fertility rate (avg. births per childbearing woman; 2003): 1.8.
Marriage rate per 1,000 population (1999): 4.2.
Divorce rate per 1,000 population (1999): 0.9.
Life expectancy at birth (2003): male 79.3 years; female 78.2 years.
Major causes of death per 100,000 population (1996): diseases of the circulatory system 206.8; malignant neoplasms (cancers) 150.3; accidents, poisoning, and violence 47.2; diseases of the respiratory system 36.3; endocrine and metabolic disorders 27.8; diseases of the digestive system 27.2.

National economy

Budget (1999). Revenue: F 1,298,000,000 (general receipts from French central government and local administrative bodies 45.0%; tax receipts 34.0%, of which indirect taxes 19.5%, direct taxes 14.5%). Expenditures: F 1,298,000,000 (health and social assistance 42.0%; wages and salaries 16.7%; other administrative services 7.2%; debt amortization 5.0%).
Public debt (1994): U.S.$186,700,000.
Production (metric tons except as noted). Agriculture, forestry, fishing (2002): bananas 303,800, sugarcane 207,000, pineapples 18,000, plantains 16,000, roots and tubers 13,250, lettuce 7,800, yams 7,500, tomatoes 6,100, cucumbers and gherkins 4,000, melons 2,240, sweet potatoes 1,170, coconuts 1,150; livestock (number of live animals) 35,000 pigs, 34,000 sheep, 25,000 cattle, 17,000 goats; roundwood (2001) 12,000 cu m; fish catch (2001) 6,251. Mining and quarrying (2001): salt 200,000, pumice 130,000. Manufacturing (2002): cement (2001) 220,000; sugar 5,340; rum 91,629 hectolitres; other products include clothing, fabricated metals, and yawls and sails. Energy production (consumption): electricity (kW-hr; 2000) 1,085,000,000 (1,085,000,000); coal, none (none); crude petroleum (barrels; 2000) none (6,000,000); petroleum products (metric tons; 2000) 751,000 (575,000); natural gas, none (none).
Household income and expenditure. Average household size (1999) 3.0; annual net income per household (1997) €29,516 (U.S.$33,174); sources of income (1997): wages and salaries 49.0%, inheritance or endowment 16.4%, self-employment 14.7%, other 19.9%; expenditure (1993): food and beverages 32.1%, transportation and communications 20.7%, housing and energy 10.6%, household durable goods 9.4%, clothing and footwear 8.0%.
Tourism (2001): receipts from visitors U.S.$237,000,000; number of visitors 654,000.
Gross domestic product (2000): U.S.$5,064,000,000 (U.S.$13,160 per capita).

Structure of gross domestic product and labour force

	1995		1998	
	in value F '000,000	% of total value	labour force	% of labour force
Agriculture, fishing	1,151,952	4.1	7,650	4.6
Mining, manufacturing	1,502,161	5.3	7,103	4.3
Construction	2,249,756	7.9	10,405	6.3
Public utilities	973,068	3.4		
Transp. and commun.	1,797,425	6.3	4,383	2.6
Trade, restaurants, hotels	5,660,282	20.0	16,196	9.8
Finance, real estate, insurance	1,180,409	4.2	25,909	15.6
Pub. admin., defense	13,159,431	46.4	18,742	11.3
Services			25,667	15.5
Other	693,355[2]	2.4[2]	49,845[3]	30.0[3]
TOTAL	28,367,839	100.0	165,900	100.0

Population economically active (1998): total 165,900; activity rate of total population 43.7% (participation rates: ages 15–64, 70.7%; female 45.9%; unemployed [March 2003] 22.2%).

Price and earnings indexes (2000 = 100)

	1997	1998	1999	2000	2001	2002	2003
Consumer price index	97.4	98.6	99.0	100.0	102.1	104.3	106.4
Monthly earnings index[4]	98.2	99.5	99.5	100.0	...	...	...

Land use as % of total land area (2000): in temporary crops *c.* 10%, in permanent crops *c.* 9%, in pasture *c.* 11%; overall forest area *c.* 44%.

Foreign trade[5]

Balance of trade (current prices)

	1998	1999	2000	2001
€'000,000	–1,266	–1,355	–1,438	–1,604
% of total	71.0%	72.2%	71.0%	74.5%

Imports (2001): €1,878,000,000 (consumer goods *c.* 20%, processed foods, beverages, and tobacco *c.* 18%, automobiles *c.* 12%). *Major import sources* (2000): France 63.5%; Venezuela 5.8%; Germany 3.9%; Italy 3.1%; Netherlands Antilles 2.3%.
Exports (2001): €274,000,000 (bananas *c.* 35%, processed foods and beverages [significantly rum] *c.* 21%, machinery and apparatus *c.* 15%, refined petroleum *c.* 9%). *Major export destinations* (2000): France 57.8%; Guadeloupe 21.4%; French Guiana 3.7%; U.K. 3.4%; Belgium 2.7%.

Transport and communications

Transport. Railroads: none. Roads (1994): total length 1,291 mi, 2,077 km (paved [1988] 75%). Vehicles (1998): passenger cars 147,589; trucks and buses 35,615. Air transport (2001): passenger arrivals 706,929, passenger departures 701,597; cargo loaded 5,656 metric tons; cargo unloaded 9,303 metric tons; airports (2000) 1.

Communications

Medium	date	unit	number	units per 1,000 persons
Daily newspapers	1996	circulation	32,000	83
Radio	1997	receivers	82,000	213
Television	1999	receivers	66,000	168
Telephones	2001	main lines	172,192	417
Cellular telephones	2002	subscribers	319,900	790
Personal computers	2001	units	52,000	130
Internet	2001	users	40,000	100

Education and health

Educational attainment (1990). Percentage of population age 25 and over having: incomplete primary, or no declaration 54.3%; primary education 18.0%; secondary 20.0%; higher 7.7%. *Literacy:* n.a.

Education (2001–02)

	schools	teachers	students	student/ teacher ratio
Primary (age 6–11)	273	3,260	53,347	16.4
Secondary (age 12–18)	78	4,257	51,057	12.0
Vocational[6]	15	896[7]	7,661	...
Higher	1	...	11,755[8]	...

Health (2000): physicians 762 (1 per 507 persons); hospital beds 2,674 (1 per 144 persons); infant mortality rate per 1,000 live births (2003) 7.4.
Food (1998): daily per capita caloric intake 2,865 (vegetable products 75%, animal products 25%); 118% of FAO recommended minimum requirement.

Military

Total active duty personnel (2004): 4,100 French troops.

[1]The French franc was the former monetary unit; on Jan. 1, 2002, F 6.56 = €1. [2]Statistical discrepancy. [3]Unemployed. [4]Based on minimum-level wage of public employees. [5]Imports c.i.f.; exports f.o.b. [6]1998–99. [7]1995–96. [8]Total enrollment of the University of the Antilles and French Guiana at 7 sites.

Internet resources for further information:
- **INSEE: Martinique http://www.insee.fr/fr/insee_regions/Martinique**
- **Martinique Chamber of Commerce and Industry http://www.martinique.cci.fr**

Mauritania

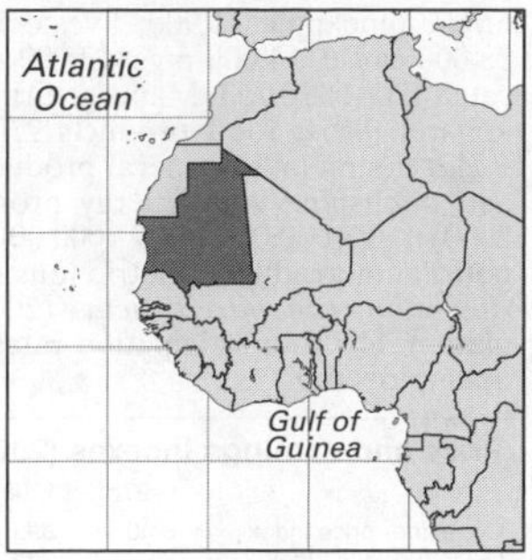

Official name: Al-Jumhūrīyah al-Islāmīyah al-Mūrītānīyah (Arabic) (Islamic Republic of Mauritania).
Form of government: unitary multiparty republic with two legislative houses (Senate [56]; National Assembly [81]).
Head of state and government: President assisted by the Prime Minister.
Capital: Nouakchott.
Official language: Arabic[1].
Official religion: Islam.
Monetary unit: 1 ouguiya (UM) = 5 khoums; valuation (Sept. 1, 2004) 1 U.S.$ = UM 266.00; 1 £ = UM 478.52.

Area and population

Regions	Capitals	area sq mi	area sq km	population 2000 census
El-ʾAçâba	Kiffa	14,100	36,600	242,265
Adrar	Atar	83,100	215,300	69,542
Brakna	Aleg	13,000	33,800	247,006
Dakhlet Nouadhibou	Nouadhibou	8,600	22,300	79,516
Gorgol	Kaédi	5,300	13,600	242,711
Guidimaka	Sélibaby	4,000	10,300	177,707
Hodh ech-Chargui	Néma	70,600	182,700	281,600
Hodh el-Gharbi	ʿAyoûn el-ʿAtroûs	20,600	53,400	212,156
Inchiri	Akjoujt	18,100	46,800	11,500
Tagant	Tidjikdja	36,800	95,200	76,620
Tiris Zemmour	Zouérate	97,600	252,900	41,121
Trarza	Rosso	25,800	66,800	268,220
Capital District				
Nouakchott	Nouakchott	400	1,000	558,195
TOTAL		398,000	1,030,700	2,508,159

Demography

Population (2004): 2,774,000.
Density (2004): persons per sq mi 7.0, persons per sq km 2.7.
Urban-rural (2000): urban 57.7%; rural 42.3%.
Sex distribution (2000): male 49.51%; female 50.49%.
Age breakdown (2000): under 15, 43.9%; 15–29, 27.0%; 30–44, 15.9%; 45–59, 7.7%; 60–74, 4.3%; 75 and over, 1.2%.
Population projection: (2010) 3,290,000; (2020) 4,181,000.
Doubling time: 24 years.
Ethnic composition (1993)[2]: Moor 70% (of which about 40% "black" Moor [Ḥarāṭīn, or African Sudanic] and about 30% "white" Moor [Bidan, or Arab-Berber]); other black African 30% (mostly Wolof, Tukulor, Soninke, and Fulani).
Religious affiliation (2000): Sunnī Muslim 99.1%; traditional beliefs 0.5%; Christian 0.3%; other 0.1%.
Major cities (2000): Nouakchott 558,195[3]; Nouadhibou 72,337; Rosso 48,922; Boghé 37,531; Adel Bagrou 36,007.

Vital statistics

Birth rate per 1,000 population (2003): 42.1 (world avg. 21.3).
Death rate per 1,000 population (2003): 13.0 (world avg. 9.1).
Natural increase rate per 1,000 population (2003): 29.1 (world avg. 12.2).
Total fertility rate (avg. births per childbearing woman; 2003): 6.1.
Life expectancy at birth (2003): male 49.7 years; female 54.1 years.

National economy

Budget (2002). Revenue: UM 101,000,000,000 (fishing royalties 51.2%; tax revenue 38.7%, of which taxes on goods and services 19.3%, income taxes 12.0%, import taxes 6.2%; revenue from public enterprises 4.8%; capital revenue 2.3%; other 3.0%). Expenditures: UM 84,400,000,000 (current expenditure 62.1%, of which goods and services 25.6%, wages and salaries 15.4%, interest on public debt 9.8%, defense 5.8%; capital expenditure 37.9%).
Land use as % of total land area (2000): in temporary crops 0.5%, in permanent crops 0.01%, in pasture 38.3%; overall forest area 0.3%.
Production (metric tons except as noted). Agriculture, forestry, fishing (2002): rice 67,900, millet 51,500, sorghum 25,405, cow peas 24,000, dates 20,000, pulses 16,000; livestock (number of live animals) 7,600,000 sheep, 5,100,000 goats, 1,500,000 cattle, 1,230,000 camels; roundwood (2001) 1,470,448 cu m; fish catch (metric tons; 2001) 83,596, of which octopuses 20,308[4]. Mining and quarrying (gross weight; 2002): iron ore 9,553,000; gypsum 100,000. Manufacturing (value added in U.S.$'000,000; 1997): food, beverages, and tobacco products 5.2; machinery, transport equipment, and fabricated metals 3.8; bricks, tiles, and cement 1.6. Energy production (consumption): electricity (kW-hr; 2002) 263,972,000 (191,893,000); coal (metric tons; 2000) none (6,000); crude petroleum (barrels; 2000) none (7,147,000); petroleum products (metric tons; 2000) 860,000 (961,000); natural gas, none (none).
Population economically active (2001): total 786,000; activity rate of total population 30.9% (participation rates: over age 10 [1991] 45.5%; female [1994] 22.9%; unemployed [1999] 21.0%).

Price and earnings indexes (2000 = 100)

	1998	1999	2000	2001	2002	2003	2004[5]
Consumer price index[6]	93.1	96.8	100.0	104.7	108.8	114.4	116.3
Hourly earnings index[7]	100.0	100.0	100.0	100.0	100.0	...	...

Household income and expenditure. Average household size (2000): 5.3; expenditure (1990): food and beverages 73.1%, clothing and footwear 8.1%, energy and water 7.7%, transportation and communications 2.0%.
Gross national product (2003): U.S.$1,163,000,000 (U.S.$430 per capita).

Structure of gross domestic product and labour force

	2002 in value UM '000,000	2002 % of total value	2001 labour force[8]	2001 % of labour force
Agriculture, livestock	50,436	18.7	310,000	39.0
Mining	29,521	11.0		
Manufacturing	21,490	8.0	62,000	8.0
Public utilities	9	9		
Construction	20,253	7.5		
Transp. and commun.	29,233	10.9		
Trade and finance	47,965	17.8	248,000	32.0
Services	14,340[9]	5.3[9]		
Pub. admin., defense	29,465	11.0		
Other	26,353[10]	9.8[10]	166,000[11]	21.0[11]
TOTAL	269,056	100.0	786,000	100.0

Public debt (external, outstanding; 2002): U.S.$1,984,000,000.
Tourism (1999): receipts U.S.$28,000,000; expenditures U.S.$55,000,000.

Foreign trade

Balance of trade (current prices)

	1998	1999	2000	2001	2002
U.S.$'000,000	+1.9	+22.6	+8.5	–33.7	–87.7
% of total	0.3%	3.5%	1.2%	4.7%	11.7%

Imports (2002): U.S.$418,000,000 (capital goods 26.0%; petroleum products 25.8%; food products 12.8%; vehicles and parts 9.3%; construction materials 9.1%). *Major import sources:* France 20.8%; Belgium-Luxembourg 8.8%; Spain 6.7%; Germany 5.6%; Italy 4.2%.
Exports (2002): U.S.$330,300,000 (iron ore 55.6%; fish 43.4%, of which cephalopods 29.0%). *Major export destinations:* Italy 14.8%; France 14.4%; Spain 12.1%; Germany 10.8%; Belgium-Luxembourg 10.3%; Japan 6.4%.

Transport and communications

Transport. Railroads (2000): route length 446 mi, 717 km; passenger-km, negligible; (2000) metric ton-km cargo 7,766,000,000. Roads (1999): total length 4,900 mi, 7,891 km (paved 26%). Vehicles (1999): passenger cars 9,900; trucks and buses 17,300. Air transport (1999)[12]: passenger-km 290,000,000; metric ton-km cargo (1998) 13,524,000; airports (1997) with scheduled flights 9.

Communications

Medium	date	unit	number	units per 1,000 persons
Daily newspapers	1996	circulation	1,000	0.4
Radio	1997	receivers	360,000	147
Television	1999	receivers	247,000	100
Telephones	2002	main lines	31,500	12
Cellular telephones	2003	subscribers	300,000	109
Personal computers	2002	units	29,000	11
Internet	2002	users	10,000	3.7

Education and health

Educational attainment (2000). Percentage of population age 6 and over having: no formal schooling 43.9%; no formal schooling but literate 2.5%; Islamic schooling 18.4%; primary education 23.2%; lower secondary 5.3%; upper secondary 4.6%; higher technical 0.4%; higher 1.7%. *Literacy* (2000): percentage of total population age 10 and over literate 52.5%; males literate 60.1%; females literate 45.3%.

Education (1998–99)

	schools	teachers	students	student/teacher ratio
Primary (age 6–11)	2,676	7,366	355,822[13]	...
Secondary (age 12–17)	...	2,185	63,735[13]	...
Voc., teacher tr.[14]	...		2,812	...
Higher	...	270[15]	12,912	...

Health: physicians (1994) *c.* 200 (1 per 11,085 persons); hospital beds (1988) 1,556 (1 per 1,217 persons); infant mortality rate per 1,000 live births (2003) 73.8.
Food (2001): daily per capita caloric intake 2,764 (vegetable products 84%, animal products 16%); 120% of FAO recommended minimum requirement.

Military

Total active duty personnel (2003): 15,750 (army 95.2%, navy 3.2%, air force 1.6%). *Military expenditure as percentage of GNP* (1999): 4.0% (world 2.4%); per capita expenditure U.S.$14.

[1]The 1991 constitution names Arabic as the official language and the following as national languages: Arabic, Fulani, Soninke, and Wolof. [2]Estimated figures. [3]Limits are coextensive with the capital district. [4]Fish catch (2002) including foreign fishing vessels equals 672,643 metric tons. [5]January. [6]Nouakchott only. [7]Minimum wage. [8]Estimate based on percentage. [9]Public utilities included with Services. [10]Indirect taxes. [11]Unemployed. [12]Data represent 1/11 of the total scheduled traffic of Air Afrique; Air Afrique was declared bankrupt in February 2002. [13]1999–2000. [14]1995–96. [15]Excludes health-related programs.

Internet resources for further information:
- **Office National de la Statistique**
  http://www.ons.mr

Mauritius

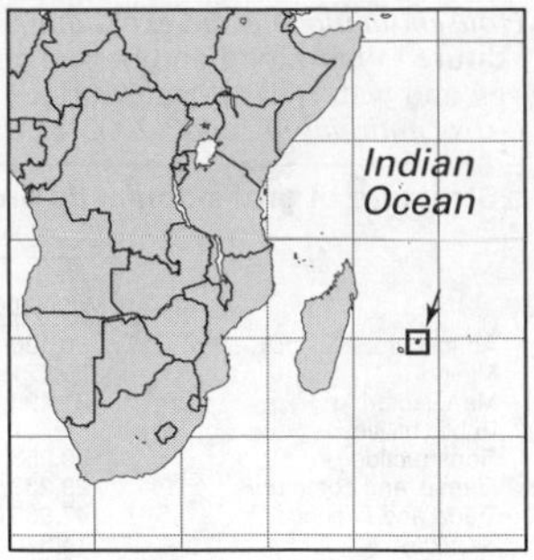

Official name: Republic of Mauritius.
Form of government: republic with one legislative house (National Assembly [70[1]]).
Chief of state: President.
Head of government: Prime Minister.
Capital: Port Louis.
Official language: English.
Official religion: none.
Monetary unit: 1 Mauritian rupee (Mau Re; plural Mau Rs) = 100 cents; valuation (Sept. 1, 2004) 1 U.S.$ = Mau Rs 28.48; 1 £ = Mau Rs 51.23.

Area and population

Islands Districts/Dependencies	Administrative Centres	area sq mi	area sq km	population 2003 estimate
Mauritius		720	1,865[2]	1,186,400
Black River	Tamarin	100	259	65,700
Flacq	Centre de Flacq	115	298	132,400
Grand Port	Mahébourg	100	260	110,600
Moka	Moka	89	231	77,900
Pamplemousses	Pamplemousses	69	179	128,100
Plaines Wilhems	Rose Hill	78	203	370,100
Port Louis	Port Louis	17	43	130,200
Rivière du Rempart	Poudre d'Or	57	148	103,100
Savanne	Souillac	95	245	68,300
Mauritian dependencies				
Agalega[3]	...	27	70	300
Cargados Carajos Shoals (Saint Brandon)[3]	—	0.4	1	0
Rodrigues[4]	Port Mathurin	40	104	36,400
TOTAL		788[2]	2,040	1,223,100

Demography

Population (2004): 1,233,000.
Density (2004): persons per sq mi 1,565, persons per sq km 604.4.
Urban-rural (2002): urban 42.5%; rural 57.5%.
Sex distribution (2003): male 49.49%; female 50.51%.
Age breakdown (2000): under 15, 25.2%; 15–29, 26.0%; 30–44, 24.8%; 45–59, 14.9%; 60–74, 6.8%; 75 and over, 2.3%.
Population projection: (2010) 1,296,000; (2020) 1,384,000.
Doubling time: 73 years.
Ethnic composition (2000): Indo-Pakistani 67.0%; Creole (mixed Caucasian, Indo-Pakistani, and African) 27.4%; Chinese 3.0%; other 2.6%.
Religious affiliation (2000)[5]: Hindu 49.6%; Christian 32.2%, of which Roman Catholic 23.6%; Muslim 16.6%; Buddhist 0.4%; other 1.2%.
Major urban areas (2000)[5]: Port Louis 144,303; Beau Bassin-Rose Hill 103,872; Vacoas-Phoenix 100,066; Curepipe 78,920; Quatre Bornes 75,884.

Vital statistics

Birth rate per 1,000 population (2003): 16.3[6] (world avg. 21.3).
Death rate per 1,000 population (2003): 6.7[6] (world avg. 9.1).
Natural increase rate per 1,000 population (2003): 9.6[6] (world avg. 12.2).
Total fertility rate (avg. births per childbearing woman; 2003): 1.9[6].
Marriage rate per 1,000 population (2003): 8.5[6].
Divorce rate per 1,000 population (2003): 0.9[6].
Life expectancy at birth (2003)[6]: male 68.6 years; female 75.5 years.
Major causes of death per 100,000 population (2002)[6]: diseases of the circulatory system 351.3; malignant neoplasms (cancers) 72.7; diseases of the respiratory system 57.1; homicide, suicide, and accidents 44.1.

National economy

Budget (2001–02). Revenue: Mau Rs 28,319,500,000 (tax revenue 82.2%, of which taxes on goods and services 39.2%, import duties 20.8%, income tax 12.6%; nontax revenue 16.2%; grants 1.1%). Expenditures: Mau Rs 33,385,800,000 (social security 21.8%; government services 18.1%; education 15.4%; economic services 12.3%; interest on debt 10.6%; health 8.7%).
Tourism (2001): receipts from visitors U.S.$612,000,000; expenditures by nationals abroad U.S.$204,000,000.
Public debt (external, outstanding; 2002): U.S.$832,000,000.
Gross national product (2003): U.S.$5,012,000,000 (U.S.$4,090 per capita).

Structure of gross domestic product and labour force

	2002 in value Mau Rs '000,000	% of total value	labour force[7]	% of labour force[7]
Agriculture	8,810	5.6	25,258	8.5
Mining	80	0.1	170	0.1
Manufacturing	30,330	19.3	111,017	37.5
Construction	8,035	5.1	13,027	4.4
Public utilities	3,150	2.0	3,041	1.0
Transp. and commun.	19,350	12.3	17,521	5.9
Trade	23,510	14.9	34,051	11.5
Finance	25,965	16.5	15,745	5.3
Pub. admin., defense	19,215	12.2	67,670	22.9
Services	5,790	3.7	7,103	2.4
Other	13,070[8]	8.3[8]	1,597	0.5
TOTAL	157,305	100.0	296,200[9]	100.0[9]

Production (metric tons except as noted). Agriculture, forestry, fishing (2002): sugarcane 4,874,000, vegetables 21,000, roots and tubers 15,000, potatoes 14,000, tomatoes 12,000, carrots 8,700, cabbages 8,300, onions 7,200, bananas 6,700, pineapples 1,900; livestock (number of live animals) 93,000 goats, 28,000 cattle, 14,000 pigs, 12,000 sheep; roundwood (2001) 17,000 cu m; fish catch (2001) 10,753. Manufacturing (value added in Mau Rs '000,000; 2001): apparel 9,651; food products 2,757; beverages and tobacco 1,717; textiles 1,712; nonmetallic mineral products 1,269; chemical products 1,109; printing and publishing 906. Energy production (consumption): electricity (kW-hr; 2000) 1,777,000,000 (1,777,000,000); coal (metric tons; 2000) none (254,000); petroleum products (metric tons; 2000) none (724,000).
Population economically active (2002): total 541,100; activity rate of total population 44.7% (participation rates: ages 15 and over, 59.8%; female 34.6%; unemployed 9.7%).

Price and earnings indexes (2000 = 100)

	1997	1998	1999	2000	2001	2002	2003
Consumer price index	84.0	89.8	96.0	100.0	105.4	112.5	117.2
Daily earnings index[10]	85.3	92.6	95.2	100.0	...	...	...

Household income and expenditure. Average household size (2000) 4.2; annual income per household (2001–02) Mau Rs 170,784 (U.S.$5,780); sources of income (1990): salaries and wages 48.4%, entrepreneurial income 41.2%, transfer payments 10.4%; expenditure (2001–02): food and nonalcoholic beverages 31.9%, transportation 12.7%, housing and energy 9.4%, alcoholic beverages and tobacco products 9.1%, clothing and footwear 6.4%.
Land use as % of total land area (2000): in temporary crops *c.* 49%, in permanent crops *c.* 3%, in pasture *c.* 3%; overall forest area *c.* 8%.

Foreign trade[11]

Balance of trade (current prices)

	1998	1999	2000	2001	2002	2003
Mau Rs '000,000	–9,691	–16,604	–14,046	–10,429	–10,995	–12,265
% of total	11.7%	17.2%	14.7%	9.9%	9.3%	10.2%

Imports (2001): Mau Rs 57,940,000,000 (fabrics and yarn 18.3%; food and live animals 14.3%; machinery and apparatus 14.3%; refined petroleum 9.5%; transport equipment 8.1%). *Major import sources:* South Africa 13.9%; France 9.3%; India 7.9%; China 7.1%; Germany 5.4%.
Exports (2001): Mau Rs 47,511,000,000 (domestic exports 91.8%, of which clothing 54.4%, sugar 18.0%, fabric, yarn, and made-up articles 4.7%; reexports 4.1%; ships' stores and bunkers 4.1%). *Major export destinations:* U.K. 31.3%; U.S. 20.3%; France 18.7%; Madagascar 6.1%; Italy 3.8%.

Transport and communications

Transport. Railroads: none. Roads (1998): total length 1,184 mi, 1,905 km (paved 93%). Vehicles (2002): passenger cars 61,885; trucks and buses 13,892. Air transport (2003)[12]: passenger-km 5,213,000,000; metric ton-km cargo 194,510,000; airports (1998) with scheduled flights 1.

Communications

Medium	date	unit	number	units per 1,000 persons
Daily newspapers	2000	circulation	84,300	71
Radio	2000	receivers	450,000	379
Television	2000	receivers	318,000	268
Telephones	2003	main lines	348,200	285
Cellular telephones	2003	subscribers	462,400	379
Personal computers	2002	units	180,000	149
Internet	2003	users	150,000	123

Education and health

Educational attainment (2000). Percentage of population age 25 and over having: no formal education 12.3%; primary 44.1%; lower secondary 23.2%; upper secondary/some higher 17.3%; complete higher 2.6%; unknown 0.5%. *Literacy* (2000): percentage of total population age 12 and over literate 85.1%; males literate 88.7%; females literate 81.6%.

Education (2002)

	schools	teachers	students	student/ teacher ratio
Primary (age 5–12)	290	5,256	132,432	25.2
Secondary (age 12–20)	143	5,553	99,687	18.0
Voc., teacher tr.	13	380	5,966	15.7
Higher[13]	3	461	6,429	13.9

Health (2003): physicians 1,172 (1 per 1,043 persons); hospital beds 3,827 (1 per 320 persons); infant mortality rate per 1,000 live births 13.2[6].
Food (2001): daily per capita caloric intake 2,995 (vegetable products 86%, animal products 14%); 132% of FAO recommended minimum requirement.

Military

Total active duty personnel (2003): none; however, a special 2,000-person paramilitary force ensures internal security. *Military expenditure as percentage of GNP* (1999): 0.2% (world 2.4%); per capita expenditure U.S.$7.

[1]Includes 8 "bonus" seats allocated to minor parties. [2]Detail does not add to total given because of rounding. [3]Administered directly from Port Louis. [4]Local autonomy status granted by Mauritius in November 2001. [5]Based on census. [6]Excludes Agalega. [7]Employed persons in large establishments only. [8]Indirect taxes less imputed bank service charges. [9]Total labour force equals 541,100 and includes 193,800 employees of small businesses or self-employed and 51,100 unemployed. [10]Manufacturing sector; March data only. [11]Imports c.i.f.; exports f.o.b. [12]Air Mauritius only. [13]1998.

Internet resources for further information:
- **Central Statistical Office http://statsmauritius.gov.mu**
- **Bank of Mauritius http://bom.intnet.mu**

Mayotte

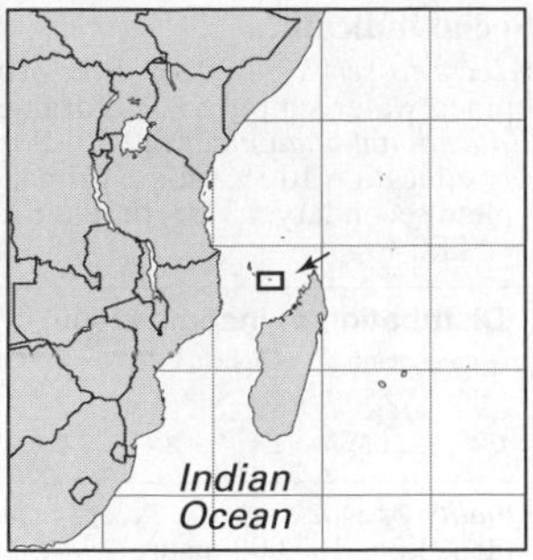

Official name: Collectivité Départementale de Mayotte[1] (Departmental Collectivity of Mayotte).
Political status: overseas dependency of France[2] with one legislative house (General Council [19]).
Chief of state: President of France.
Head of government: President of the General Council[3].
Capital: Mamoudzou.
Official language: French.
Official religion: none.
Monetary unit: 1 euro (€) = 100 cents; valuation (Sept. 1, 2004) 1 U.S.$ = €0.82; 1 £ = €1.48[4].

Area and population

Islands / Communes	Capitals	area sq mi	area sq km	population 2002 census
Grande Terre				
Acoua	Acoua	4.9	12.6	4,605
Bandraboua	Bandraboua	12.5	32.4	7,501
Bandrele	Bandrele	14.1	36.5	5,537
Boueni	Boueni	5.4	14.1	5,151
Chiconi	Chiconi	3.2	8.3	6,167
Chirongui	Chirongui	10.9	28.3	5,696
Dembeni	Dembeni	15.0	38.8	7,825
Kani-Keli	Kani-Keli	7.9	20.5	4,336
Koungou	Koungou	11.0	28.4	15,383
Mamoudzou	Mamoudzou	16.2	41.9	45,485
M'tsangamouji	M'tsangamouji	8.4	21.8	5,382
M'tzamboro	M'tzamboro	5.3	13.7	7,068
Ouangani	Ouangani	7.3	19.0	5,569
Sada	Sada	4.3	11.2	6,963
Tsingoni	Tsingoni	13.4	34.8	7,779
Petite Terre				
Dzaoudzi-Labattoir	Dzaoudzi	2.6	6.7	12,308
Pamandzi	Pamandzi	1.7	4.3	7,510
TOTAL		144.1[5]	373.3[5]	160,265[6]

Demography

Population (2004): 172,000.
Density (2004): persons per sq mi 1,194, persons per sq km 459.9.
Urban-rural: n.a.
Sex distribution (2002): male 50.10%; female 49.90%.
Age breakdown (2002): under 15, 42.0%; 15–29, 29.0%; 30–44, 17.0%; 45–59, 7.0%; 60 and over, 5.0%.
Population projection: (2010) 216,000; (2020) 292,000.
Doubling time: 21 years.
Place of birth (2002): Mayotte (including 2–4% for metropolitan France) 65.6%[7]; nearby islands of the Comoros 33.1%[7]; other 1.3%.
Ethnic composition (2000): Comorian (Mauri, Mahorais) 92.3%; Swahili 3.2%; white (French) 1.8%; Makua 1.0%; other 1.7%.
Religious affiliation (2000): Sunnī Muslim 96.5%; Christian, principally Roman Catholic, 2.2%; other 1.3%.
Major communes (2002): Mamoudzou 45,485; Koungou 15,383; Dzaoudzi 12,308.

Vital statistics

Birth rate per 1,000 population (2003): 42.9 (world avg. 21.3).
Death rate per 1,000 population (2003): 8.3 (world avg. 9.1).
Natural increase rate per 1,000 population (2003): 34.6 (world avg. 12.2).
Total fertility rate (avg. births per childbearing woman; 2003): 6.1.
Marriage rate per 1,000 population: n.a.
Divorce rate per 1,000 population: n.a.
Life expectancy at birth (2003): male 58.5; female 62.8.

National economy

Budget (1997). Revenue: F 1,022,400,000 (1993; current revenue 68.8%, of which subsidies 40.0%, indirect taxes 16.8%, direct taxes 4.9%; development revenue 31.2%, of which loans 11.6%, subsidies 7.9%). Expenditures: F 964,200,000 (current expenditure 75.2%; development expenditure 24.8%).
Production (metric tons except as noted). Agriculture, forestry, fishing (1997): bananas 30,200, cassava 10,000, cinnamon 27,533 kg, ylang-ylang 14,300 kg, vanilla 4,417 kg; livestock (number of live animals; 1997) 25,000 goats, 17,000 cattle, 2,000 sheep; roundwood, n.a.; fish catch (1999) 1,502. Mining and quarrying: negligible. Manufacturing: mostly processing of agricultural products and materials used in housing construction (including siding and roofing materials, joinery, and latticework). Energy production (consumption): electricity (kW-hr; 2002) 107,056,000 (107,056,000); coal, none (none); crude petroleum, none (none); petroleum products, none (n.a.); natural gas, none (none).
Tourism (number of visitors; 2001): 35,000; receipts (1999) U.S.$10,000,000.
Population economically active (1997): total 42,896; activity rate of total population 32.7% (participation rates: ages 15–64, 58.6%; female 43.4%; unemployed 41.5%).

Price index (2000 = 100)

	1997	1998	1999	2000	2001	2002	2003
Consumer price index	97.9	99.5	100.4	100.0	100.3	103.2	104.7[8]

Gross national product (2000): U.S.$398,000,000 (U.S.$2,700 per capita).

Structure of gross domestic product and labour force

	1997 in value U.S.$'000	% of total value	labour force	% of labour force
Agriculture, forestry, and fishing	...	...	4,824	11.2
Mining	...	...	80	0.2
Manufacturing	...	...	1,083	2.5
Construction	...	...	3,840	9.0
Public utilities	...	...	399	0.9
Transp. and commun.	...	...	1,563	3.6
Trade	...	...	3,057	7.1
Finance, insurance, real estate	...	...	647	1.5
Pub. admin., defense	...	...	4,526	10.6
Services	...	...	5,074	11.8
Other	...	...	17,803[9]	41.6[9]
TOTAL	154,900	100.0	42,896	100.0

Household income and expenditure. Average household size (1997) 4.6; expenditure (1991)[10]: food 42.2%, clothing and footwear 31.5%, household furnishings 8.8%, energy and water 6.8%, transportation 5.1%.
Land use as % of total land area (2000): in temporary crops, n.a., in permanent crops, n.a., in pasture, n.a.; overall forest area, n.a.

Foreign trade

Balance of trade (current prices)

	1998	1999	2000	2001	2002
€'000,000	–136.5	–126.7	–147.8	–171.5	–175.5
% of total	95.9%	96.2%	96.2%	95.7%	93.3%

Imports (2002): €181,800,000 (food products 27.0%; machinery and apparatus 18.9%; transport equipment 16.1%; chemicals 8.7%; metals and metal products 7.4%). *Major import sources* (1997): France 66.0%; South Africa 14.0%; Asia 11.0%.
Exports (2002): €6,300,000 (ylang-ylang 11.1%; vanilla 3.2%; unspecified commodities 85.7%). *Major export destinations* (1997): France 80.0%; Comoros 15.0%.

Transport and communications

Transport. Railroads: none. Roads (1998): total length 145 mi, 233 km (paved 77%). Vehicles (1998): 8,213. Air transport (2002): passenger arrivals and departures 133,686; cargo unloaded and loaded 1,048 metric tons; airports (2002) with scheduled flights 1.

Communications

Medium	date	unit	number	units per 1,000 persons
Daily newspapers[11]	1998	circulation	...	...
Radio	1996	receivers	50,000	427
Television	1999	receivers	3,500	30
Telephones	2001	main lines	10,000	70
Cellular telephones	2002	subscribers	21,700	147

Education and health

Educational attainment (2002). Percentage of population age 15 and over having: no formal education *c.* 46%; primary education *c.* 25%; lower secondary *c.* 16%; upper secondary *c.* 8%; higher *c.* 5%. *Literacy* (1997): total population age 15 and over literate 63,053 (86.1%).

Education (2001–02)

	schools	teachers	students	student/ teacher ratio
Primary (age 6–11)	112	555[12]	28,591	38.9[12]
Secondary (age 12–18)	14	246[12]	15,626	16.2[12]
Voc., teacher tr.	2[13]	...	1,733	...
Higher	—	—	—	—

Health: physicians (1997) 57 (1 per 2,304 persons); hospital beds 186 (1 per 706 persons); infant mortality rate per 1,000 live births (2003) 65.9.

Military

Total active duty personnel (2003): 3,600 French troops are assigned to Mayotte and Réunion.

[1]Mahoré or Maore in Shimaoré, the local Swahili-based language. [2]Final status of Mayotte has not yet been determined; it is claimed by Comoros as an integral part of that country. [3]From April 2004 executive authority in Mayotte is with the President of the General Council; the position of prefect (France's representative in Mayotte) is to be phased out by 2007. [4]The French franc was the former monetary unit; on Jan. 1, 2002, F 6.56 = €1. [5]Revised area as of 2002 census equals 144.5 sq mi (374.2 sq km). [6]Including about 45,000 illegal residents, of which nearly all are Comorians from adjacent islands. [7]Nearly all ethnic Comorian (a mixture of Bantu, Arab, and Malagasy peoples). [8]June. [9]Unemployed. [10]Weights of consumer price index components. [11]One weekly newspaper has a total circulation of 15,000. [12]1992–93. [13]1997.

Internet resources for further information:
- **Ministère de l'Outre-Mer http://www.outre-mer.gouv.fr**
- **INSEE: Mayotte http://www.insee.fr/fr/insee_regions/reunion/zoom/Mayotte**

Mexico

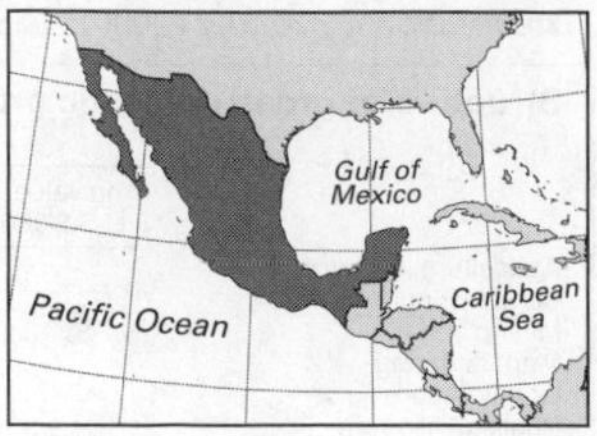

Official name: Estados Unidos Mexicanos (United Mexican States).
Form of government: federal republic with two legislative houses (Senate [128]; Chamber of Deputies [500]).
Head of state and government: President.
Capital: Mexico City.
Official language: Spanish.
Official religion: none.
Monetary unit: 1 Mexican peso (Mex$) = 100 centavos; valuation (Sept. 1, 2004) 1 U.S.$ = Mex$11.39; 1 £ = Mex$20.48.

Area and population

States	Capitals	area sq mi	area sq km	population 2000 census
Aguascalientes	Aguascalientes	2,112	5,471	944,285
Baja California	Mexicali	26,997	69,921	2,487,367
Baja California Sur	La Paz	28,369	73,475	424,041
Campeche	Campeche	19,619	50,812	690,689
Chiapas	Tuxtla Gutiérrez	28,653	74,211	3,920,892
Chihuahua	Chihuahua	94,571	244,938	3,052,907
Coahuila de Zaragoza	Saltillo	57,908	149,982	2,298,070
Colima	Colima	2,004	5,191	542,627
Durango	Durango	47,560	123,181	1,448,661
Guanajuato	Guanajuato	11,773	30,491	4,663,032
Guerrero	Chilpancingo	24,819	64,281	3,079,649
Hidalgo	Pachuca	8,036	20,813	2,235,591
Jalisco	Guadalajara	31,211	80,836	6,322,002
México	Toluca	8,245	21,355	13,096,686
Michoacán de Ocampo	Morelia	23,138	59,928	3,985,667
Morelos	Cuernavaca	1,911	4,950	1,555,296
Nayarit	Tepic	10,417	26,979	920,185
Nuevo León	Monterrey	25,067	64,924	3,834,141
Oaxaca	Oaxaca	36,275	93,952	3,438,765
Puebla	Puebla	13,090	33,902	5,076,686
Querétaro de Arteaga	Querétaro	4,420	11,449	1,404,306
Quintana Roo	Chetumal	19,387	50,212	874,963
San Luis Potosí	San Luis Potosí	24,351	63,068	2,299,360
Sinaloa	Culiacán	22,521	58,328	2,536,844
Sonora	Hermosillo	70,291	182,052	2,216,969
Tabasco	Villahermosa	9,756	25,267	1,891,829
Tamaulipas	Ciudad Victoria	30,650	79,384	2,753,222
Tlaxcala	Tlaxcala	1,551	4,016	962,646
Veracruz–Llare	Xalapa (Jalapa)	27,683	71,699	6,908,975
Yucatán	Mérida	14,827	38,402	1,658,210
Zacatecas	Zacatecas	28,283	73,252	1,353,610
Federal District				
Distrito Federal	—	571	1,479	8,605,239
CONTINENTAL AREA		756,066[1]	1,958,201[1]	
LAND		736,949	1,908,690	
WATER		19,116	49,511	
INSULAR AREA[2]		1,980	5,127	
TOTAL		758,449[3]	1,964,375[3]	97,483,412

Demography

Population (2004): 105,447,000.
Density (2004): persons per sq mi 139.0, persons per sq km 53.7.
Urban-rural (2002): urban 74.6%; rural 25.4%.
Sex distribution (2002): male 48.82%; female 51.18%.
Age breakdown (2000): under 15, 34.3%; 15–29, 28.5%; 30–44, 19.5%; 45–59, 10.5%; 60–74, 5.3%; 75 and over, 1.9%.
Population projection: (2010) 112,991,000; (2020) 125,232,000.
Doubling time: 41 years.
Ethnic composition (2000): mestizo 64.3%; Amerindian 18.0%, of which detribalized 10.5%; Mexican white 15.0%; Arab 1.0%; Mexican black 0.5%; Spaniard 0.3%; U.S. white 0.2%; other 0.7%.
Religious affiliation (2000): Roman Catholic 90.4%; Protestant (including Evangelical) 3.8%; other 5.8%.
Major cities (2000): Mexico City 8,605,239 (urban agglomeration [2001] 18,268,000); Guadalajara 1,646,183 (urban agglomeration 3,697,000); Puebla 1,271,673 (urban agglomeration 1,888,000); Ciudad Netzahualcóyotl 1,225,-083; Juárez 1,187,275; Tijuana 1,148,681; Monterrey 1,110,909 (urban agglomeration 3,267,000); León 1,020,818; Mérida 662,530; Chihuahua 657,876.
Place of birth (1990): 93.1% native-born; 6.9% foreign-born and unknown.
Households. Total households (2000) 21,954,733; distribution by size (2000): 1 person 6.0%, 2 persons 12.3%, 3 persons 17.2%, 4 persons 21.8%, 5 persons 17.7%, 6 persons 10.9%, 7 or more persons 14.1%.
Emigration (2000): legal immigrants into the United States 173,900.

Vital statistics

Birth rate per 1,000 population (2003): 21.9 (world avg. 21.3).
Death rate per 1,000 population (2003): 4.7 (world avg. 9.1).
Natural increase rate per 1,000 population (2003): 17.2 (world avg. 12.2).
Total fertility rate (avg. births per childbearing woman; 2002): 2.3.
Marriage rate per 1,000 population (2001): 6.6.
Divorce rate per 1,000 population (2001): 0.6.
Life expectancy at birth (2003): male 71.9 years; female 77.6 years.
Major causes of death per 100,000 population (2001): diseases of the circulatory system 98.5; diabetes mellitus 62.2; malignant neoplasms (cancers) 58.3; accidents and violence 51.3; diseases of the digestive system 42.3; diseases of the respiratory system 36.9.

Social indicators

Access to services (2000). Proportion of dwellings having: electricity 94.8%; piped water supply 83.3%; drained sewage 76.2%.
Educational attainment (2000). Population age 15 and over having: no primary education 10.3%; some primary 18.1%; completed primary 19.4%; incomplete secondary 5.3%; complete secondary 19.1%; some higher 16.8%; higher 11.0%.

Distribution of income (2000)

percentage of household income by decile

1	2	3	4	5	6	7	8	9	10 (highest)
0.4	1.5	2.4	3.4	4.7	6.2	8.1	11.0	16.7	45.6

Quality of working life. Average workweek (1999): 44.4 hours[4]. Annual rate (1992) per 100,000 insured workers for: temporary disability 6,426; indemnification for permanent injury 239; death 18. Labour stoppages (2001): 35, involving 23,234 workers.
Social participation. Eligible voters participating in last national election (July 2003): 41.7%. Trade union membership in total workforce: n.a. Practicing religious population in total affiliated population: national average of weekly attendance (1993) 11%.
Social deviance (1991). Criminal cases tried by local authorities per 100,000 population for: murder 60.3; rape 22.4; other assault 301.0; theft 703.8. Incidence per 100,000 in general population of: alcoholism (2000) 7.6; drug and substance abuse 26.6; suicide (2001) 3.1.

National economy

Gross national product (2003): U.S.$637,159,000,000 (U.S.$6,230 per capita).

Structure of gross domestic product and labour force

	2001 in value Mex$'000,000[5]	% of total value	labour force	% of labour force
Agriculture	218,770	3.8	7,074,400	17.8
Mining	72,144	1.2	127,200	0.3
Manufacturing	1,037,134	17.8	7,373,000	18.6
Construction	262,631	4.5	2,396,900	6.0
Public utilities	62,526	1.1	194,900	0.5
Transp. and commun.	595,607	10.2	1,776,700	4.5
Trade	1,105,047	19.0	10,821,400	27.3
Finance	642,115	11.0	1,504,600	3.8
Pub. admin., defense } Services }	1,380,406	23.7	1,682,100 6,054,000	4.2 15.3
Other	452,211[6]	7.7[6]	677,600[7]	1.7[7]
TOTAL	5,828,591	100.0	39,682,800	100.0

Budget (2001). Revenue: Mex$939,114,500,000 (income tax 30.4%, VAT 22.2%, royalties 21.7%, excise tax 11.8%, import duties 3.1%, other 10.8%). Expenditures: Mex$996,950,600,000 (current expenditure 63.4%, of which social security and welfare 41.8%, interest on public debt 16.7%; capital expenditure 36.6%).
Public debt (external, outstanding; 2002): U.S.$76,327,000,000.
Tourism (2002): receipts from visitors U.S.$8,858,000,000; expenditures by nationals abroad U.S.$6,060,000,000.

Manufacturing (2000)

	no. of enterprises[8]	no. of employees ('000)	yearly wages as a % of avg. of all wages	value added (U.S.$'000,000)
Manufacturing	266,033	1,476,309	100.0	60,760
Transport equipment	...	105,429	105.4	9,439
Food	91,894	247,869	91.5	8,883
Chemicals	7,321	131,530	165.7	8,726
Beverages	...	110,074	92.9	5,422
Nonmetallic mineral products	24,397	46,520	99.4	3,580
Electrical machinery	...	132,335	93.0	3,484
Iron and steel	401	34,591	135.3	2,891
Nonelectrical machinery	...	49,374	105.1	2,254
Paper and paper products	15,022	51,860	91.9	2,243
Rubber and plastic	...	85,470	103.8	2,031
Metal products	...	60,180	83.2	1,691
Automobile parts	...	49,737	102.4	1,585
Tobacco	...	4,337	169.3	1,104
Nonferrous metals	...	19,627	95.1	1,093

Production (metric tons except as noted). Agriculture, forestry, fishing (2002): sugarcane 46,000,000, corn (maize) 17,500,000, sorghum 5,800,000, oranges 3,844,000, wheat 3,273,000, tomatoes 2,084,000, bananas 2,077,000, chilies and green peppers 1,756,000, lemons and limes 1,680,000, dry beans 1,648,000, mangoes 1,413,000, watermelons 1,226,000, coconuts 959,000, avocados 897,000, barley 839,000, papayas 689,000, pineapples 585,000, grapes 446,000, carrots 379,000, coffee (green) 320,000, cauliflower 200,000; livestock (number of live animals) 30,600,000 cattle, 17,000,000 pigs, 9,400,000 goats, 8,100,000 ducks, 6,700,000 sheep, 6,255,000 horses, 5,850,000 turkeys, 3,280,000 mules, 3,260,000 asses, 520,800,000 chickens; roundwood (2001) 45,156,000 cu m; fish catch (2001) 1,475,000. Mining and quarrying (2002): bismuth 1,126[9] [world rank: 1]; celestite 94,015 [world rank: 1]; silver 2,747,000 kg[9] [world rank: 1]; fluorite 622,000 [world rank: 2]; cadmium 1,609[9] [world rank: 4]; lead 138,700[9] [world rank: 5]; gypsum 6,740,000 [world rank: 6]; zinc 446,100[9] [world rank: 6]; sulfur 1,460,000 [world rank: 9]; copper 329,900[9] [world rank: 12]; gold 21,324 kg [world rank: 19]; iron ore 5,965,000[9]. Manufacturing (value added in U.S.$'000,000; 2000): motor vehicles and parts 10,718; food products 8,883; paints, soaps, pharmaceuticals 7,044; beverages 5,422; bricks, cement, ceramics 3,580; iron and steel 2,891; paper and paper products 2,243; basic chemicals 1,682; fabricated metal products 1,518.
Household income and expenditure. Average household size (2000) 4.4; income per household (2000) Mex$15,762 (U.S.$1,667); sources of income (2000):

wages and salaries 63.4%, property and entrepreneurship 23.6%, transfer payments 10.0%, other 2.9%; expenditure (2000): food, beverages, and tobacco 29.9%, transportation and communications 17.8%, education 17.3%, housing (includes household furnishings) 16.5%, clothing and footwear 5.8%.

Trade and service enterprises (1998)

	no. of establish-ments	no. of employees	yearly wage as a % of avg. of all wages	annual income (Mex$'000,000)[8]
Trade	1,497,828	3,790,764	...	565,728,373
Wholesale	110,180	864,569	...	249,597,035
Retail	1,387,648	2,926,195	...	316,131,338
Boutiques (excluding food products)	536,900	1,192,597	...	108,507,889
Food and tobacco speciality stores	768,799	1,234,656	...	65,305,180
Automobile, tire, and auto parts dealers	41,236	164,493	...	47,888,576
Supermarkets and grocery stores	24,697	254,497	...	48,769,283
Gasoline stations	4,345	53,610	...	32,517,091
Other	11,671	26,342	...	13,143,319
Services[8]	711,843	2,766,750	...	200,001,682
Professional services	130,475	652,148	...	53,533,318
Food and beverage services	677	11,258	...	1,012,369
Transp. and travel agencies	9,967	62,767	...	11,858,406
Lodging	9,913	151,445	...	8,960,922
Automotive repair	112,293	252,950	...	7,263,560
Educational services (private)	20,622	247,086	...	10,815,238
Medical and social assistance	79,748	203,348	...	7,497,794
Amusement services (cinemas and theatres)	4,855	65,608	...	9,845,129
Recreation[8]	20,973	65,936	...	3,065,672
Other repair[8]	72,129	104,478	...	2,625,370
Commercial and professional organizations[8]	1,946	11,946	...	264,770
Other[8]	248,245	937,780	...	83,259,134

Energy production (consumption): electricity (kW-hr; 2003) 263,488,000,000 ([2000] 229,747,000,000); hard coal (metric tons; 2000) 2,214,000 (2,724,000); lignite (metric tons; 2000) 9,130,000 (9,570,000); crude petroleum (barrels; 2003) 1,244,000,000 ([2000] 467,393,000); petroleum products (metric tons; 2000) 73,045,000 (87,048,000); natural gas (cu m; 2003) 47,377,000,000 ([2000] 36,953,000,000).

Population economically active (2001): total 39,682,800; activity rate of total population 39.9% (participation rates: ages 15–64 [1999] 63.4%; female 29.9%; unemployed [2002] 4.4%).

Price and earnings indexes (2000 = 100)

	1997	1998	1999	2000	2001	2002	2003
Consumer price index	67.6	78.3	91.3	100.0	106.4	111.7	116.8
Monthly earnings index	90.4	93.0	94.4	100.0	106.7	108.7	110.0

Financial aggregates

	1997	1998	1999	2000	2001	2002	2003
Exchange rate[10], Mex$ per:							
U.S. dollar	8.08	9.87	9.51	9.57	9.14	10.31	11.24
£	13.37	16.41	15.38	14.28	13.26	16.62	20.05
SDR	10.91	13.89	13.06	12.47	11.49	14.02	16.70
International reserves (U.S.$)							
Total (excl. gold; '000,000)	28,797	31,799	31,782	35,509	44,741	50,594	58,956
SDRs ('000,000)	661	337	790	366	356	392	433
Reserve pos. in IMF ('000,000)	—	—	—	—	—	308	782
Foreign exchange	28,136	31,461	30,992	35,142	44,384	49,895	57,740
Gold ('000,000 fine troy oz)	0.19	0.22	0.16	0.25	0.23	0.23	0.17
% world reserves	0.02	0.03	0.02	0.02	0.02	0.02	0.02
Interest and prices							
Treasury bill rate	19.80	24.76	21.41	15.24	11.31	7.09	6.23
Balance of payments (U.S.$'000,000)							
Balance of visible trade, of which:	+623	–7,914	–5,584	–8,003	–9,954	–7,916	–5,624
Imports, f.o.b.	–109,808	–125,373	–141,975	–174,458	–168,397	–168,679	–170,546
Exports, f.o.b.	110,431	117,459	136,391	166,455	158,443	160,763	164,922
Balance of invisibles	–8,319	–8,183	–8,454	–10,209	–8,264	–6,183	–3,623
Balance of payments, current account	–7,696	–16,097	–14,038	–18,212	–18,218	–14,099	–9,247

Land use as % of total land area (2000): in temporary crops 13.0%, in permanent crops 1.3%, in pasture 41.9%; overall forest area 28.9%.

Foreign trade

Balance of trade (current prices)

	1998	1999	2000	2001	2002	2003
U.S.$'000,000	–7,914	–5,584	–8,003	–9,954	–7,997	–5,624
% of total	3.3%	2.0%	2.3%	3.0%	2.4%	1.7%

Imports (2002): U.S.$168,679,000,000 (non-maquiladora sector 64.8%, of which machinery and apparatus 18.9%, transport and communications equipment 13.0%, chemicals and chemical products 7.4%, processed food, beverages, and tobacco 3.7%; maquiladora sector 35.2%, of which electrical machinery, apparatus, and electronics 15.9%, nonelectrical machinery and apparatus 5.4%, textiles and clothing 3.3%, rubber and plastic products 3.0%). *Major import sources:* U.S. 63.2%; Japan 5.5%; China 3.7%; Germany 3.6%; Canada 2.7%; Taiwan 2.5%; South Korea 2.3%.

Exports (2002): U.S.$160,682,000,000 (non-maquiladora sector 51.4%, of which road vehicles and parts 16.0%, machinery and apparatus 8.9%, crude petroleum 8.2%; maquiladora sector 48.6%, of which electrical machinery, apparatus, and electronics 24.2%, nonelectrical machinery and apparatus 10.2%, textiles and clothing 4.3%). *Major export destinations:* U.S. 89.0%; Canada 1.7%; South America 1.5%; Caribbean countries 1.4%; Central America 1.1%; Germany 0.9%; Spain 0.8%.

Trade by commodity group (2002)

	imports		exports	
SITC group	U.S.$'000,000	%	U.S.$'000,000	%
00 Food and live animals	8,132	4.8	6,015	3.7
01 Beverages and tobacco	[11]	[11]	1,974	1.2
02 Crude materials, excluding fuels	4,667	2.8	1,594	1.0
03 Mineral fuels, lubricants, and related materials	4,564	2.7	14,318	8.9
04 Animal and vegetable oils, fats, and waxes	[11]	[11]	[12]	[12]
05 Chemicals and related products, n.e.s.	15,342	9.1	5,512	3.4
06 Basic manufactures	27,360	16.2	13,230	8.2
07 Machinery and transport equipment	86,094	51.0	94,740	59.0
08 Miscellaneous manufactured articles	20,138	11.9	23,058	14.4
09 Goods not classified by kind	1,475	0.9	[12]	[12]
TOTAL	168,650	100.0	160,670	100.0

Direction of trade (2002)

	imports		exports	
	U.S.$'000,000	%	U.S.$'000,000	%
Western Hemisphere	117,721	69.8	152,268	94.8
United States	106,901	63.4	143,151	89.1
Latin America and the Caribbean	6,340	3.8	6,308	3.9
Canada	4,480	2.6	2,809	1.8
Europe	17,914	10.6	5,729	3.6
EU	16,443	9.7	5,216	3.3
Other Europe	1,471	0.9	513	0.3
Asia	31,479	18.7	2,443	1.5
Japan	9,349	5.6	469	0.3
China	6,274	3.7	456	0.3
Other Asia	15,856	9.4	1,518	0.9
Africa	388	0.2	53	—
Other	1,149	0.7	177	0.1
TOTAL	168,651	100.0	160,670	100.0

Transport and communications

Transport. Railroads (2003): route length 16,563 mi, 26,655 km; passenger-km 67,000,000; metric ton-km cargo 54,813,000,000. Roads (2003): total length 216,565 mi, 348,529 km (paved 33%). Vehicles (1999): passenger cars 9,842,006; trucks and buses 4,749,789. Air transport (2003)[13]: passenger-km 25,409,000,000; metric ton-km cargo 145,351,000,000; airports (2001) 85.

Communications

Medium	date	unit	number	units per 1,000 persons
Daily newspapers	2000	circulation	9,580,000	98
Radio	2000	receivers	32,300,000	330
Television	2000	receivers	27,700,000	283
Telephones	2002	main lines	14,941,600	147
Cellular telephones	2002	subscribers	25,928,000	254
Personal computers	2002	units	8,353,000	83
Internet	2002	users	10,033,000	98

Education and health

Literacy (2000): total population age 15 and over literate 91.4%; males literate 93.4%; females literate 89.5%.

Education (2001–02)

	schools	teachers	students	student/teacher ratio
Primary (age 6–12)	99,230	609,654	14,843,400	24.3
Secondary (age 12–18)	39,691	536,579	8,600,700	16.0
Voc., teacher tr.[14]	6,610	63,674	883,000	13.9
Higher	4,183	216,804	2,147,100	9.9

Health (2002): physicians 140,286 (1 per 734 persons); hospital beds 76,529 (1 per 1,346 persons); infant mortality rate per 1,000 live births (2002) 17.4.

Food (2001): daily per capita caloric intake 3,160 (vegetable products 82%, animal products 18%); 136% of FAO recommended minimum requirement.

Military

Total active duty personnel (2003): 192,770 (army 74.7%, navy 19.2%, air force 6.1%). *Military expenditure as percentage of GNP* (1999): 0.6% (world 2.4%); per capita expenditure U.S.$27.

[1]Continental area per more recent survey equals 756,470 sq mi (1,959,248 sq km). [2]Uninhabited (nearly all Pacific) islands directly administered by federal government. [3]Total area based on more recent survey figure for continental area. [4]Manufacturing only. [5]At factor cost. [6]Imputed bank service charge. [7]Unemployed. [8]1993. [9]Metal content. [10]End of year. [11]Together categories 01 and 04 equal U.S.$878,000,000 and 0.6%. [12]Together categories 04 and 09 equal U.S.$221,000,000 and 0.2%. [13]AeroMexico and Mexicana only. [14]1996–97.

Internet resources for further information:

- **National Institute of Statistics, Geography, and Informatics**
  http://www.inegi.gob.mx/difusion/ingles/portadai.html
- **Banco de México**
  http://www.banxico.org.mx/siteBanxicoINGLES/index.html

Micronesia

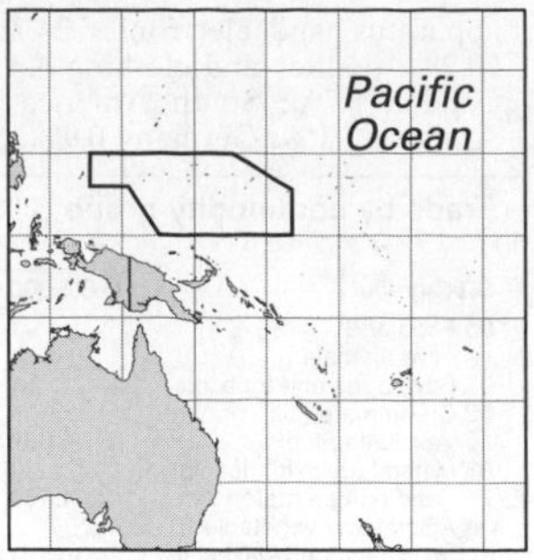

Official name: Federated States of Micronesia.
Form of government: federal nonparty republic in free association with the United States with one legislative house (Congress [14])[1].
Head of state and government: President.
Capital: Palikir, on Pohnpei.
Official language: none.
Official religion: none.
Monetary unit: 1 U.S. dollar (U.S.$) = 100 cents; valuation (Sept. 1, 2004) 1 U.S.$ = £0.56.

Area and population

States Major Islands	Capitals	area sq mi	 sq km	population 2000 census
Chuuk (Truk)	Weno (Moen)	49.1	127.2	53,595
Chuuk Islands		...	...	40,465
Kosrae	Lelu	42.3	109.6	7,686
Kosrae Island		42.3	109.6	7,686
Pohnpei (Ponape)	Kolonia	133.3	345.2	34,486
Pohnpei Island		129.0	334.1	32,178
Yap	Colonia	45.9	118.9	11,241
Yap Island		38.7	100.2	7,391
TOTAL		270.8[2]	701.4[2]	107,008

Demography

Population (2004): 114,000.
Density (2004): persons per sq mi 420.7, persons per sq km 162.6.
Urban-rural (2000): urban 28.5%; rural 71.5%.
Sex distribution (2000): male 50.64%; female 49.36%.
Age breakdown (2000): under 15, 40.3%; 15–29, 28.4%; 30–44, 16.9%; 45–59, 9.1%; 60–74, 3.9%; 75 and over, 1.4%.
Population projection: (2010) 120,000; (2020) 126,000.
Doubling time: 33 years.
Ethnic composition (2000): Chuukese/Mortlockese 33.6%; Pohnpeian 24.9%; Yapese 10.6%; Kosraean 5.2%; U.S. white 4.5%; Asian 1.3%; other 19.9%.
Religious affiliation (2000): Roman Catholic 52.7%; Protestant 41.7%, of which Congregational 40.1%; Mormon 1.0%; other/unknown 4.6%.
Major towns (2000): Weno, in Chuuk state 13,900; Tol, in Chuuk state 9,500; Palikir, on Pohnpei 6,227; Kolonia, on Pohnpei 5,681; Colonia, on Yap 3,350.

Vital statistics

Birth rate per 1,000 population (2003): 26.5 (world avg. 21.3).
Death rate per 1,000 population (2003): 5.1 (world avg. 9.1).
Natural increase rate per 1,000 population (2003): 21.4 (world avg. 12.2).
Total fertility rate (avg. births per childbearing woman; 2003): 3.5.
Life expectancy at birth (2003): male 67.4 years; female 71.0 years.
Major causes of death per 100,000 population (1998)[3]: diseases of the circulatory system 89.7; malignant neoplasms (cancers) 50.5; homicide, suicide, and accidents 48.6; diseases of the respiratory system 47.7; infectious and parasitic diseases 38.3; endocrine and metabolic diseases 33.6.

National economy

Budget (2001–02). Revenue: U.S.$160,400,000 (external grants 71.2%, tax revenue 17.7%, nontax revenue [including fishing rights fees] 11.1%). Expenditures: U.S.$154,800,000 (current expenditures 83.4%, capital expenditure 16.6%).
Public debt (external, outstanding; 2000): U.S.$85,700,000.
Population economically active (2000): total 37,414; activity rate of total population 35.0% (participation rates: ages 15–64, 61.7%; female 42.9%; unemployed 22.0%).

Price index (2000 = 100)

	1999	2000	2001	2002	2003
Price index	98.0	100.0	101.3	101.1	100.9

Production (metric tons except as noted). Agriculture, forestry, fishing (2002): coconuts 140,000, cassava 11,800, sweet potatoes 3,000, bananas 2,000; livestock (number of live animals) 32,000 pigs, 13,900 cattle, 4,000 goats; fish catch (2001) 18,100, of which skipjack tuna 10,300, yellowfin tuna 5,300. Mining and quarrying: quarrying of sand and aggregate for local construction only. Manufacturing: n.a.; however, copra and coconut oil, traditionally important products, are being displaced by garment production; the manufacture of handicrafts and personal items (clothing, mats, boats, etc.) by individuals is also important. Energy production (consumption): electricity (kW-hr; 1997) 100,333,000 (100,333,000); coal, none (none); crude petroleum, none (none); petroleum products (metric tons; 1992) none (77,000); natural gas, none (none).
Household income and expenditure. Average household size (2000) 6.7; annual income per household U.S.$8,944 (median income: U.S.$4,618); sources of income (1994): wages and salaries 51.8%, operating surplus 23.0%, social security 2.1%; expenditure (1985): food and beverages 73.5%.
Land use as % of total land area (2000): in temporary crops *c.* 6%, in permanent crops *c.* 46%, in pasture *c.* 16%; overall forest area *c.* 22%.
Gross national product (at current market prices; 2003): U.S.$261,000,000 (U.S.$2,090 per capita).

Structure of gross domestic product and labour force

	1996 in value U.S.$'000,000	 % of total value	2000 labour force	 % of labour force
Agriculture and fishing[4]	34.7	19.1	15,216	40.7
Mining	0.7	0.4	1,164	3.1
Manufacturing	2.6	1.4		
Construction	1.9	1.0	781	2.1
Public utilities	2.0	1.1	360	1.0
Transp. and commun.	8.5	4.7	806	2.2
Finance	4.2	2.3	726	1.9
Services	3.1	1.7	1,445	3.9
Trade, hotels	43.6	24.0	2,540	6.8
Public administration	80.4	44.3	6,137	16.4
Other	...	...	8,239[5]	22.0[5]
TOTAL	181.6[2]	100.0	37,414	100.0[2]

Tourism (2001): receipts from visitors U.S.$13,000,000.

Foreign trade

Balance of trade (current prices)

	1994	1995	1996	1997	1998	1999
U.S.$'000,000	–50.5	–60.3	–73.4	–67.2	–46.1	–10.2
% of total	24.4%	43.4%	77.4%	80.7%	87.4%	70.6%

Imports (1999): U.S.$12,328,000 (food and live animals 24.8%, mineral fuels 20.3%, machinery and transport equipment 19.5%, beverages and tobacco products 6.0%). *Major import sources* (2000): United States 43.9%; Australia 19.8%; Japan 12.5%.
Exports (1999): U.S.$2,128,000 (fish 92.0%, bananas 1.2%). *Major export destinations* (1996): Japan 79.0%; United States 18.3%.

Transport and communications

Transport. Railroads: none. Roads (1990): total length 140 mi, 226 km (paved 17%). Vehicles (1998): passenger cars 2,044; trucks and buses 354. Air transport: n.a.; airports (1997) with scheduled flights 4.

Communications

Medium	date	unit	number	units per 1,000 persons
Radio	1996	receivers	70,000	667
Television	1999	receivers	2,400	21
Telephones	2001	main lines	10,000	93
Cellular telephones	2002	subscribers	1,800	150
Internet	2000	users	6,000	51

Education and health

Educational attainment (2000). Percentage of population age 25 and over having: no formal schooling 12.3%; primary education 37.0%; some secondary 18.3%; secondary 12.9%; some college 18.4%. *Literacy* (2000): total population age 10 and over literate 72,140 (92.4%); males literate 36,528 (92.9%); females literate 35,612 (91.9%).

Education (1997–98)

	schools	teachers	students	student/ teacher ratio
Elementary (age 6–12)	171	1,486	25,915	18.6
Secondary (age 13–18)	24	418	6,809	16.2
College	1	71	1,884	26.5

Health (1998): physicians 68 (1 per 1,677 persons); hospital beds (1997) 260 (1 per 447 persons); infant mortality rate per 1,000 live births (2003) 32.4.
Food: daily per capita caloric intake, n.a.

Military

External security is provided by the United States.

[1]The compact of free association (from 1986) between the United States and the Federated States of Micronesia (FSM) was renewed in 2003 for another 20 years. Terms of the new compact included a cut in U.S. grants after 2004. [2]Detail does not add to total given because of rounding. [3]Based on registered deaths only. [4]Includes subsistence farming and fishing. [5]Unemployed.

Internet resources for further information:
- **General Information on The FSM**
  http://www.boh.com/econ/pacific
- **U.S. Office on Insular Affairs**
  http://www.pacificweb.org

Moldova

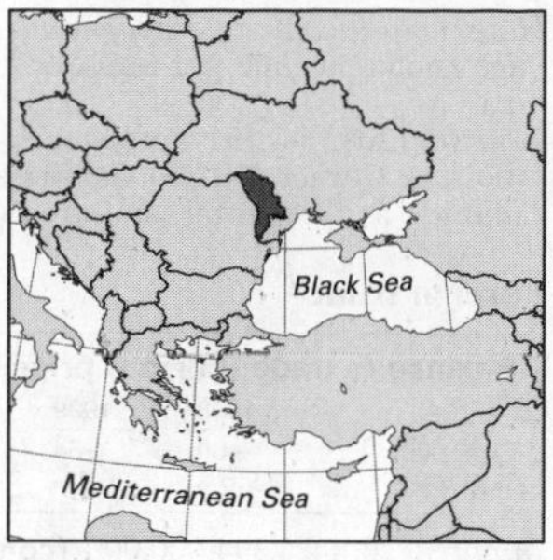

Official name: Republica Moldova (Republic of Moldova).
Form of government: unitary parliamentary republic with a single legislative body (Parliament [101]).
Head of state: President.
Head of government: Prime Minister.
Capital: Chişinău.
Official language: Romanian[1].
Official religion: none.
Monetary unit: 1 Moldovan leu (plural lei) = 100 bani; valuation (Sept. 1, 2004) 1 U.S.$ = 12.02 Moldovan lei; 1 £ = 21.62 Moldovan lei.

Area and population[2]

		area		population
Counties	**Capitals**	sq mi	sq km	2003[3] estimate
Bălţi	Bălţi	1,576	4,081	500,900
Cahul	Cahul	941	2,438	190,800
Chişinău	Chişinău	1,073	2,780	382,400
Edinet	Edinet	1,231	3,187	279,100
Lăpuşna	Lăpuşna	1,327	3,436	276,300
Orhei	Orhei	1,100	2,850	300,400
Soroca	Soroca	1,221	3,162	274,600
Taraclia	Taraclia	395	1,022	45,600
Tighina	Tighina	1,119	2,899	169,000
Ungheni	Ungheni	971	2,516	260,300
City District				
Chişinău	—	189	490	779,400
Autonomous Region				
Găgăuzia	Comrat	580	1,503	158,900
Disputed Territory[4]				
Transnistria (Stonga Nistrului)[5]	Tiraspol	1,343	3,479	611,200
TOTAL		13,068[6]	33,845[6]	4,228,900

Demography

Population (2004): 4,216,000[7].
Density (2004): persons per sq mi 322.6, persons per sq km 124.6.
Urban-rural (2002): urban 45.3%; rural 54.7%.
Sex distribution (2002): male 47.84%; female 52.16%.
Age breakdown (2001): under 15, 22.4%; 15–29, 25.5%, 30–44, 21.1%, 45–59, 16.6%; 60–74, 11.0%; 75 and over, 3.4%.
Population projection: (2010) 4,184,000; (2020) 4,118,000.
Ethnic composition (2000): Moldovan 48.2%; Ukrainian 13.8%; Russian 12.9%; Bulgarian 8.2%; Rom (Gypsy) 6.2%; Gagauz 4.2%; other 6.5%.
Religious affiliation (1995): Orthodox 46.0%, of which Romanian Orthodox 35.0%, Russian Orthodox 9.5%; Muslim 5.5%; Catholic 1.8%, of which Roman Catholic 0.6%; Protestant 1.7%; Jewish 0.9%; other (mostly nonreligious) 44.1%.
Major cities (2003)[7]: Chişinău 662,400; Tiraspol 185,000; Bălţi 145,900; Tighina 125,000; Râbniţa 62,000.

Vital statistics

Birth rate per 1,000 population (2002): 9.9 (world avg. 21.3); (1995) legitimate 87.7%; illegitimate 12.3%.
Death rate per 1,000 population (2002): 11.5 (world avg. 9.1).
Natural increase rate per 1,000 population (2002): –1.6 (world avg. 12.2).
Total fertility rate (avg. births per childbearing woman; 2002): 1.7.
Marriage rate per 1,000 population (2002): 6.0.
Life expectancy at birth (2002): male 60.6 years; female 69.4 years.
Major causes of death per 100,000 population (1994): circulatory diseases 500.7; cancers 136.1; accidents and violence 113.3; digestive system diseases 110.4.

National economy

Budget (2002). Revenue: 6,611,000,000 lei (value-added tax 30.8%; social fund contributions 24.9%; excise taxes 9.9%; personal income tax 7.1%; profits tax 6.5%; duties and customs taxes 5.0%). Expenditures: 7,057,000,000 lei (current expenditures 95.3%, of which social fund expenditures 26.9%, education 17.6%, interest payments 6.9%, health care 11.2%; capital expenditure 4.7%).
Production (metric tons except as noted). Agriculture, forestry, fishing (2002): corn (maize) 1,192,770, wheat 1,122,270, sugar beets 1,116,034, grapes 660,218, potatoes 324,938, sunflower seeds 320,101, apples 271,000, tobacco leaves 11,567; livestock (number of live animals) 834,870 sheep, 448,898 pigs, 404,845 cattle; roundwood (2001) 56,800 cu m; fish catch (2001) 1,576. Mining and quarrying (2000): sand and gravel 277,000; gypsum 32,100. Manufacturing (value of production in U.S.$'000,000; 1998)[8]: food products 299; beverages 194; tobacco products 44; nonelectrical machinery 39. Energy production (consumption): electricity (kW-hr; 2000) 3,110,000,000 (5,095,000,000); coal (metric tons; 2000) none (180,000); crude petroleum (barrels) none (none); petroleum products (metric tons; 2000) none (409,000); natural gas (cu m; 2000) none (2,519,000,000).
Population economically active (2003): total 1,473,580; activity rate of total population 34.8% (participation rates: ages 15–64, n.a.; female [2001] 50.1%; unemployed 7.9%).

Price and earnings indexes (2000 = 100)

	1997	1998	1999	2000	2001	2002	2003
Consumer price index	48.9	52.2	76.2	100.0	109.8	115.6	129.2
Earnings index	...	...	...	100.0	133.3	169.6	...

Gross national product (2003): U.S.$2,137,000,000 (U.S.$590 per capita).

Structure of gross domestic product and labour force

	2002		2001	
	in value '000,000 lei[8]	% of total value[8]	labour force	% of labour force
Agriculture	4,630	21.0	764,800	47.3
Manufacturing, mining	3,337	15.1	138,800	8.6
Public utilities	713	3.2	26,400	1.6
Construction	642	2.9	43,200	2.7
Transp. and commun.	2,252	10.2	64,300	4.0
Trade[9]	2,537	11.5	163,800	10.1
Finance	984	4.5	28,700	1.8
Pub. admin., defense	4,098	18.6	65,800	4.1
Services			203,200	12.6
Other	2,847[10]	12.9[10]	117,700[11]	7.3[11]
TOTAL	22,040	100.0[6]	1,616,700	100.0[6]

Public debt (external, outstanding; 2002): U.S.$846,000,000.
Tourism (2002): receipts from visitors U.S.$47,000,000; expenditures by nationals abroad U.S.$86,000,000.
Household income and expenditure. Average household size (2002) 3.3; annual average income per household (2002) U.S.$1,200; sources of income (1994): wages and salaries 41.2%, social benefits 15.3%, agricultural income 10.4%, other 33.1%; expenditure (2001): food and drink 40.4%, housing 13.5%, utilities 10.5%, transportation 8.9%, clothing 7.6%, health 3.9%.
Land use as % of total land area (2000): in temporary crops 55.1%, in permanent crops 10.7%, in pasture 11.7%; overall forest area 9.9%.

Foreign trade

Balance of trade (current prices)

	1997	1998	1999	2000	2001	2002
U.S.$'000,000	–297	–392	–122	–306	–327	–393
% of total	14.5%	23.7%	11.7%	24.5%	22.3%	21.6%

Imports (2002): U.S.$1,103,000,000 (mineral products 21.7%; machinery and apparatus 14.0%; chemicals and chemical products 10.7%; textiles 10.0%). *Major import sources:* Ukraine 20.4%; Russia 15.3%; Romania 11.4%; Germany 9.2%; Italy 7.5%.
Exports (2002): U.S.$710,000,000 (processed food, beverages [significantly wine], and tobacco products 37.8%; textiles and wearing apparel 16.7%; vegetables, fruits, seeds, and nuts 15.0%). *Major export destinations:* Russia 35.4%; Ukraine 9.1%; Italy 9.1%; Romania 8.4%; Germany 7.4%.

Transport and communications

Transport. Railroads (2000): length 2,710 km; passenger-km 315,000,000; metric ton-km cargo 1,513,000,000. Roads (2000): total length 12,691 km (paved 86%). Vehicles (2001): passenger cars 256,500; trucks and buses, n.a. Air transport (2003)[12]: passenger-km 238,000,000; metric ton-km cargo 540,000; airports (2001) 1.

Communications

Medium	date	unit	number	units per 1,000 persons
Daily newspapers	2000	circulation	660,000	154
Radio	2000	receivers	3,250,000	758
Television	2000	receivers	1,270,000	297
Telephones	2002	main lines	706,900	161
Cellular telephones	2002	subscribers	338,200	77
Personal computers	2002	units	77,000	18
Internet	2002	users	150,000	34

Education and health

Educational attainment: n.a. *Literacy* (2000): total population age 15 and over literate 98.9%; males 99.5%; females 98.3%.

Education (2002–03)

	schools	teachers	students	student/ teacher ratio
Primary (age 7–13) Secondary (age 14–17)	1,580	42,300	542,600	12.8
Voc., teacher tr.	83	2,300	22,600	9.8
Higher[13]	45	5,300	95,039	17.9

Health (2001): physicians 12,800 (1 per 334 persons); hospital beds 25,000 (1 per 171 persons); infant mortality rate per 1,000 live births (2002) 41.6.
Food (2001): daily per capita caloric intake 2,766 (vegetable products 86%, animal products 14%); 108% of FAO recommended minimum requirement.

Military

Total active duty personnel (2003): 6,910 (army 84.1%, air force 15.9%). Opposition forces in Transnistria (excluding militia; 2003) *c.* 9,500. *Military expenditure as percentage of GNP* (1999): 1.6% (world 2.4%); per capita expenditure U.S.$10.

[1]Officially designated Moldovan per constitution. [2]Effective implementation of 2003 administrative reorganization unknown in July 2004; 32 districts (including Stonga Nistruli), 2 cities (Chişinău and Bălţi), and Găgăuzia autonomous region are part of the reorganization. [3]January 1. [4]Breakaway area from 1991. [5]Also known as Transdniester or Dubăsari. [6]Detail does not add to total given because of rounding. [7]De jure figure including Moldovans working abroad (particularly in Western Europe). [8]Excludes Transnistria (Stonga Nistruli). [9]Includes hotels. [10]Import and production taxes less subsidies. [11]Includes unemployed. [12]Air Moldova only. [13]Universities only.

Internet resources for further information:
- **Department for Statistics and Sociology http://www.statistica.md**
- **Moldovan Economic Trends http://www.met.dnt.md**

Monaco

Official name: Principauté de Monaco (Principality of Monaco).
Form of government: constitutional monarchy with one legislative body (National Council [24]).
Chief of state: Prince.
Head of government[1]: Minister of State assisted by the Council of Government.
Capital: [2].
Official language: French.
Official religion: Roman Catholicism.
Monetary unit: 1 euro[3] (€) = 100 centimes; valuation (Sept. 1, 2004) 1 U.S.$ = €0.82; 1 £ = €1.48.

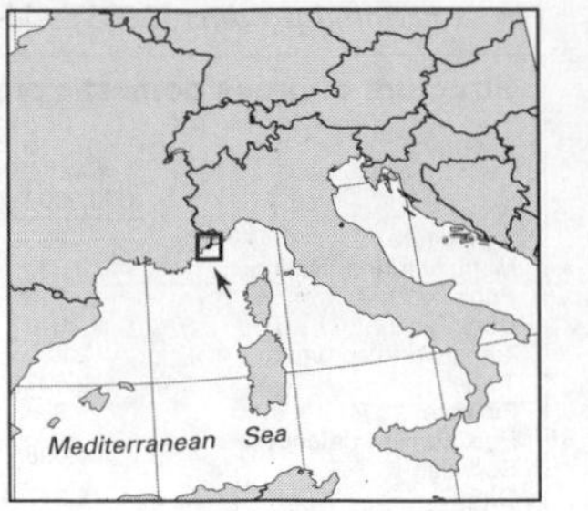

Area and population		area		population
				2000
Quarters	Capitals[2]	sq mi	sq km	census
Fontvieille	—	0.13	0.33	3,292
La Condamine	—	0.23	0.61	12,187
Monaco-Ville	—	0.07	0.19	1,034
Monte-Carlo	—	0.32	0.82	15,507
TOTAL		0.75	1.95	32,020

Demography

Population (2004): 32,600.
Density (2004): persons per sq mi 43,467, persons per sq km 16,718.
Urban-rural (2000): urban 100%; rural 0%.
Sex distribution (2000): male 48.54%; female 51.4%.
Age breakdown (2000): under 15, 13.2%; 15–29, 13.4%; 30–44, 22.1%; 45–59, 22.4%; 60–74, 17.4%; 75 and over, 11.5%.
Population projection: (2010) 33,000; (2020) 35,000.
Doubling time: not applicable.
Ethnic composition (2000): French 45.8%; Ligurian (Genoan) 17.2%; Monegasque 16.9%; British 4.5%; Jewish 1.7%; other 13.9%.
Religious affiliation (2000): Christian 93.2%, of which Roman Catholic 89.3%; Jewish 1.7%; nonreligious and other 5.1%.

Vital statistics

Birth rate per 1,000 population (2003): 9.5 (world avg. 21.3).
Death rate per 1,000 population (2003): 12.8 (world avg. 9.1).
Natural increase rate per 1,000 population (2003): –3.3 (world avg. 12.2).
Total fertility rate (avg. births per childbearing woman; 2003): 1.8.
Marriage rate per 1,000 population (2002): 5.4.
Divorce rate per 1,000 population (2002): 2.1.
Life expectancy at birth (2003): male 75.4 years; female 83.4 years.
Major causes of death per 100,000 population: n.a.; however, principal causes are those of a developed country with an older population.

National economy

Budget (2001). Revenue: €624,254,804 (value-added taxes *c.* 50%[4], state-run monopolies *c.* 20%). Expenditures: €621,041,725 (current expenditure 65.5%, capital expenditure 34.5%).
Public debt: n.a.
Production. Agriculture, forestry, fishing: some horticulture and greenhouse cultivation; no agriculture as such. Mining and quarrying: none. Manufacturing (value of export sales in €'000,000; 2001): chemicals, cosmetics, perfumery, and pharmaceuticals 347; plastic products 179; light electronics and precision instruments 81; paper and card manufactures 45; textiles 26. Energy production (consumption): electricity (kW-hr; 2001), n.a. (475,000,000 [imported from France]); coal, none (n.a.); crude petroleum, none (n.a.); natural gas, none (n.a.).
Gross national product (2002): U.S.$849,000,000 (U.S.$26,300 per capita).

Distribution of value of sales and labour force	1992		2001	
	in value F '000,000	% of total value	labour force	% of labour force
Agriculture	...	...	6,920	17.5
Manufacturing	3,650	11.3		
Construction	[5]	[5]		
Public utilities				
Hotels, restaurants	1,140	3.5	32,623	82.5
Transp. and commun.	...	...		
Finance, real estate	3,780[5]	11.6[5]		
Services	23,870	73.6		
Pub. admin., defense	...	...		
Other	—	—		
TOTAL	32,440	100.0	39,543[6]	100.0[6]

Population economically active (2001): total 39,543, of which Monegasque 3,471, foreign workers 36,072; female participation in labour force 42.4%; unemployed, n.a.

Price and earnings indexes (2000 = 100)	1997	1998	1999	2000	2001	2002	2003
Consumer price index[7]	97.2	97.8	98.3	100.0	101.6	103.6	105.8
Earnings index[7]	91.0	93.6	95.7	100.0	104.5	108.4	112.4

Household income and expenditure. Average household size (1998) 2.2; average annual income per household: n.a.; sources of income: n.a.; expenditure: n.a.
Tourism (2002): 2,191 hotel rooms; 263,000 overnight stays; 3 casinos run by the state attract 400,000 visitors annually.
Land use as % of total land area (2000): public gardens *c.* 20%.

Foreign trade[8]

Balance of trade (current prices)	1998	1999	2000	2001
€'000,000	–69	–54	+20	+9
% of total	9.6%	6.4%	2.1%	1.1%

Imports (2001): €394,000,000 (consumer goods and parts for industrial production [including pharmaceuticals, perfumes, clothing, publishing] 23.8%, food products 22.6%, transport equipment and parts 20.0%). *Major import sources:* EEC 64.0%; U.S., Japan, Switzerland, and Norway 11.6%; African countries 8.8%.
Exports (2001): €403,000,000 (rubber and plastic products, glass, construction materials, organic chemicals, and paper and paper products 31.4%, products of automobile industry 21.4%, consumer goods 17.0%). *Major export destinations:* EEC 63.5%; U.S., Japan, Switzerland, and Norway 10.6%; African countries 8.6%.

Transport and communications

Transport. Railroads (2001): length 1.1 mi, 1.7 km; passengers 2,171,100; cargo 3,357 tons. Roads (2001): total length 31 mi, 50 km (paved 100%). Vehicles (1997): passenger cars 21,120; trucks and buses 2,770. Air transport: airports with scheduled flights, none[9].

Communications				units per 1,000
Medium	date	unit	number	persons
Daily newspapers	1999	circulation	10,000	300
Radio	1997	receivers	34,000	1,030
Television	1997	receivers	25,000	758
Telephones	2002	main lines	33,700	1,040
Cellular telephones	2002	subscribers	19,300	596
Internet	2002	users	16,000	494

Education and health

Education (2002–03)	schools	teachers	students	student/ teacher ratio
Primary (age 6–10)	7	...	1,899	...
Secondary (age 11–17)	4	...	3,140	...
Higher	1	53	650	12.3

Literacy: virtually 100%.
Health (2002): physicians 156 (1 per 207 persons); hospital beds 521 (1 per 62 persons); infant mortality rate per 1,000 live births (2003) 5.6.
Food: daily per capita caloric intake, n.a.; assuming consumption patterns similar to France (2000) 3,591 (vegetable products 62%, animal products 38%); 143% of FAO recommended minimum requirement.

Military

Defense responsibility lies with France according to the terms of the Versailles Treaty of 1919.

[1]Under the authority of the prince. [2]The principality is a single administrative unit, and no separate area within it is distinguished as capital. [3]French franc (F) replaced by euro on Jan. 1, 2002. [4]On hotels, banks, and the industrial sector. [5]Finance, real estate includes Construction and Public utilities. [6]Includes 36,072 foreigners. [7]The index is for France. [8]Excludes trade with France; Monaco has participated in a customs union with France since 1963. [9]Fixed-wing service is provided at Nice, France; helicopter service is available at Fontvieille.

Internet resources for further information:
- **La Principauté de Monaco http://www.monaco.gouv.mc**
- **Monaco—Monte-Carlo http://www.monte-carlo.mc**

Mongolia

Official name: Mongol Uls (Mongolia).
Form of government: unitary multiparty republic with one legislative house (State Great Hural [76]).
Chief of state: President.
Head of government: Prime Minister.
Capital: Ulaanbaatar (Ulan Bator).
Official language: Khalkha Mongolian.
Official religion: none.
Monetary unit: 1 tugrik (Tug) = 100 möngö; valuation (Sept. 1, 2004) 1 U.S.$ = Tug 1,193; 1 £ = Tug 2,146.

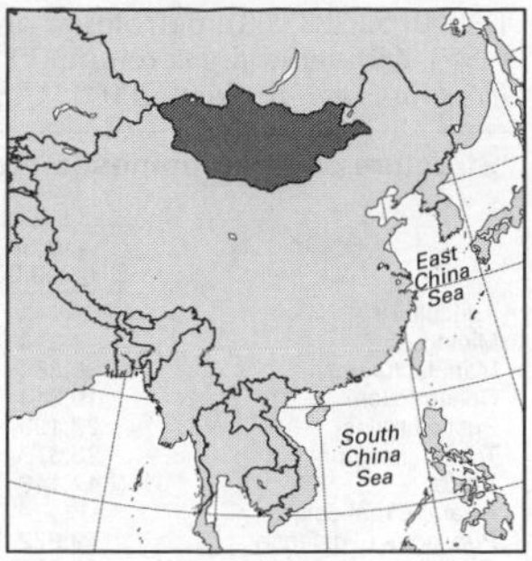

Area and population

		area[1]		population
Provinces	Capitals	sq mi	sq km	2002[2] estimate
Arhangay	Tsetserleg	21,400	55,300	98,300
Bayan-Ölgiy	Ölgiy	17,600	45,700	96,900
Bayanhongor	Bayanhongor	44,800	116,000	85,700
Bulgan	Bulgan	18,800	48,700	63,300
Darhan-Uul	Darhan	1,270	3,280	86,000
Dornod	Choybalsan	47,700	123,600	74,500
Dornogovĭ	Saynshand	42,300	109,500	51,500
Dundgovĭ	Manalgovi	28,800	74,700	51,300
Dzavhan	Uliastay	31,900	82,500	86,800
Govĭ-Altay	Altay	54,600	141,400	64,200
Govĭ-Sümber	Choyr	2,140	5,540	12,400
Hentiy	Öndörhaan	31,000	80,300	71,900
Hovd	Hovd	29,400	76,100	88,700
Hövsgöl	Mörön	38,800	100,600	120,900
Ömnögovĭ	Dalandzadgad	63,900	165,400	47,300
Orhon	Erdenet	320	840	76,500
Övörhangay	Arvayheer	24,300	62,900	114,000
Selenge	Sühbaatar	15,900	41,200	101,700
Sühbaatar	Baruun-Urt	31,800	82,300	56,000
Töv	Dzüünmod	28,600	74,000	96,300
Uvs	Ulaangom	26,900	69,600	85,800
Autonomous municipality				
Ulaanbaatar	—	1,800	4,700	812,500
TOTAL	...	603,930[3]	1,564,160	2,442,500

Demography

Population (2004): 2,519,000.
Density (2004): persons per sq mi 4.2, persons per sq km 1.6.
Urban-rural (2002): urban 56.4%; rural 43.6%.
Sex distribution (2002): male 49.53%; female 50.47%.
Age breakdown (2002): under 15, 32.7%; 15–29, 31.4%; 30–44, 21.2%; 45–59, 9.2%; 60–69, 3.4%; 70 and over, 2.1%.
Population projection: (2010) 2,740,000; (2020) 3,088,000.
Doubling time: 50 years.
Ethnic composition (2000): Khalkha Mongol 81.5%; Kazakh 4.3%; Dörbed Mongol 2.8%; Bayad 2.1%; Buryat Mongol 1.7%; Dariganga Mongol 1.3%; Zakhchin 1.3%; Tuvan (Uriankhai) 1.1%; other 3.9%.
Religious affiliation (1995): Tantric Buddhist (Lamaism) 96.0%; Muslim 4.0%.
Major cities (2000): Ulaanbaatar (Ulan Bator) 760,077; Erdenet 68,310; Darhan 65,791; Choybalsan 41,714; Ulaangom 26,319.

Vital statistics

Birth rate per 1,000 population (2003): 21.4 (world avg. 21.3); legitimate 82.2%; illegitimate 17.8%.
Death rate per 1,000 population (2003): 7.2 (world avg. 9.1).
Natural increase rate per 1,000 population (2003): 14.2 (world avg. 12.2).
Total fertility rate (avg. births per childbearing woman; 2003): 2.3.
Marriage rate per 1,000 population (2001): 5.1.
Divorce rate per 1,000 population (2001): 1.5.
Life expectancy at birth (2003): male 61.6 years; female 66.1 years.
Major causes of death per 100,000 population (2001): diseases of the circulatory system 103.7; malignant neoplasms (cancers) 56.2; diseases of the digestive system 22.0; diseases of the respiratory system 21.0; accidents 15.8.

National economy

Budget (2002). Revenue: Tug 466,527,000,000 (taxes 76.4%, of which VAT 25.2%, income tax 15.2%, social security contributions 11.4%, customs duties 11.2%; nontax revenue 23.6%). Expenditures: Tug 536,549,300,000 (education, health, social services 52.3%; wages 19.6%; capital investment 11.9%; interest 3.3%; other 12.9%).
Public debt (external; 2002): U.S.$950,400,000.
Tourism (2002): receipts U.S.$167,000,000; expenditures U.S.$119,000,000.
Population economically active (2002[2]): total 872,600; activity rate of total population 35.7% (participation rates: ages 15 and over 62.2%; female 49.8%; unemployed 4.6%).

Price index (2000 = 100)

	1997	1998	1999	2000	2001	2002	2003
Consumer price index	79.3	84.1	92.5	100.0	108.0	109.7	114.9

Production (metric tons except as noted). Agriculture, forestry, fishing (2002): wheat 149,336, potatoes 65,560, vegetables and melons 45,000; livestock (number of live animals) 11,937,300 sheep, 8,858,000 goats, 3,100,000 horses, 2,053,700 cattle, 352,000 camels, 15,000 pigs; roundwood (2001) 631,000 cu m; fish catch (2001) 117. Mining and quarrying (2002): copper 376,300; fluorspar concentrate 159,800; molybdenum 3,384; gold 12,097 kg. Manufacturing (value added by manufacturing in Tug '000,000; 2001): textiles 82,486; food and beverages 81,319; clothing and apparel 23,007; printing 6,380; nonmetallic mineral products 6,088; chemicals 4,849; wood products 2,694; leather and footwear 1,573. Energy production (consumption): electricity (kW-hr; 2001) 3,017,000,000 (3,213,000,000); hard coal (metric tons; 2000) 833,000 (876,000); lignite (metric tons; 2000) 4,178,000 (4,177,000); petroleum products (metric tons; 2000) none (420,000).
Gross national product (2003): U.S.$1,188,000,000 (U.S.$480 per capita).

Structure of gross domcstic product and labour force

	2001		2002[2]	
	in value Tug '000,000	% of total value	labour force	% of labour force
Agriculture	300,644.7	26.0	402,400	46.1
Mining	135,418.1	11.7	19,900	2.3
Manufacturing	83,484.7	7.2	55,600	6.4
Construction	23,702.3	2.0	20,400	2.3
Public utilities	27,386.1	2.4	17,800	2.0
Transp. and commun.	135,759.8	11.7	35,100	4.0
Trade	284,465.7	24.6	106,800	12.2
Finance, real estate	40,459.3	3.5	14,200	1.6
Public admin., defense	52,244.2	4.5	41,000	4.7
Services	107,627.5	9.3	119,200	13.7
Other	–32,984.3[4]	–2.8[4]	40,200[5]	4.6[5]
TOTAL	1,158,208.1	100.0[3]	872,600	100.0[3]

Household income and expenditure (2001): Average household size 4.4; annual income per household (2001) Tug 1,226,000 (U.S.$1,100); sources of income (2001): wages 29.2%, self-employment 28.6%, transfer payments 8.0%, other 34.2%; expenditure (2001): food 42.5%, clothing 16.2%, transportation and communications 7.8%, education 7.1%, housing 6.8%, health care 1.7%.
Land use as % of total land area (2000): in temporary crops 0.7%, in permanent crops, negligible, in pasture 82.5%; overall forest area 6.8%.

Foreign trade

Balance of trade (current prices)

	1998	1999	2000	2001	2002
U.S.$'000,000	–41.0	–58.6	–78.7	–116.2	–158.1
% of total	4.2%	6.1%	6.8%	10.0%	13.6%

Imports (2002): U.S.$659,000,000 (machinery and apparatus 19.5%, food and agricultural products 19.0%, mineral fuels 18.6%, textiles and clothing 12.7%). *Major import sources:* Russia 34.1%; China 24.4%; South Korea 12.2%; Japan 6.2%; Germany 4.5%.
Exports (2002): U.S.$500,900,000 (2001; copper concentrate 28.1%, gold 14.3%, cashmere [all forms] 13.4%, fluorspar 3.8%). *Major export destinations* (2002): China 42.4%; United States 31.6%; Russia 8.6%; South Korea 4.4%; Australia 3.5%.

Transport and communications

Transport. Railroads (2001): length 1,815 km; passenger-km (2001): 1,062,200,000; metric ton-km cargo 5,287,900,000. Roads (2001): total length 49,250 km (paved 4%). Vehicles (2001): passenger cars 53,200; trucks and buses 36,600. Air transport (2001): passenger-km 538,900,000; metric ton-km cargo 9,500,000; airports (2001) with scheduled flights 1.

Communications

Medium	date	unit	number	units per 1,000 persons
Daily newspapers	1996	circulation	68,000	27
Radio	2000	receivers	368,000	154
Television	2002	receivers	189,600	79
Telephones	2002	main lines	128,000	53
Cellular telephones	2002	subscribers	216,000	89
Personal computers	2002	units	69,000	21
Internet	2002	users	50,000	28

Education and health

Educational attainment (2000). Percentage of population age 10 and over having: no formal education 11.6%; primary education 23.5%; secondary 46.1%; vocational secondary 11.2%; higher 7.6%. *Literacy* (2000): percentage of total population age 15 and over literate 98.9%; males 99.1%; females 98.8%.

Education (2001–02)

	schools	teachers	students	student/ teacher ratio
Primary (age 6–12) } Secondary (age 13–16) }	700	20,076	510,300	25.4
Vocational (age 16–18)	32	985	15,000	15.2
Higher	178	5,400	92,300	17.1

Health (2001): physicians 6,639 (1 per 365 persons); hospital beds 18,100 (1 per 135 persons); infant mortality rate per 1,000 live births (2003) 23.8.
Food (2001): daily per capita caloric intake 1,974 (vegetable products 60%, animal products 40%); 81% of FAO recommended minimum.

Military

Total active duty personnel (2003): 8,600 (army 87.2%, air force 12.8%). *Military expenditure as percentage of GNP* (1999): 2.1% (world 2.4%); per capita expenditure U.S.$5.

[1]Rounded figures. [2]January 1. [3]Detail does not add to total given because of rounding. [4]Imputed bank service charges. [5]Unemployed.

Internet resources for further information:
- **National Statistical Office of Mongolia http://www.nso.mn/eng/index.php**
- **Bank of Mongolia http://www.mongolbank.mn**

Morocco

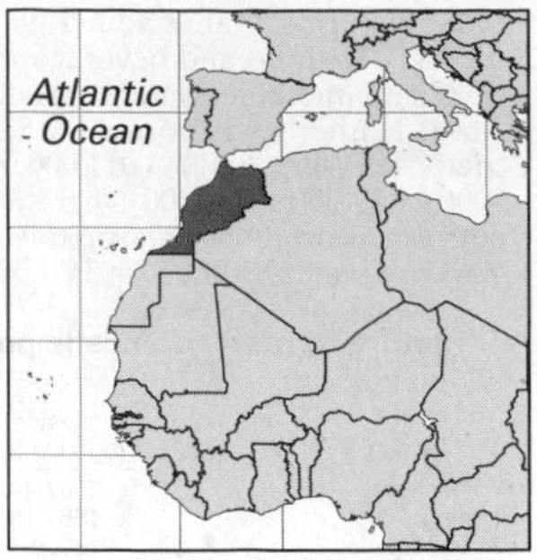

Official name: Al-Mamlakah al-Maghribīyah (Kingdom of Morocco).
Form of government: constitutional monarchy with two legislative houses (House of Councillors [270[1]]; House of Representatives [325]).
Chief of state and head of government: King assisted by Prime Minister.
Capital: Rabat.
Official language: Arabic.
Official religion: Islam.
Monetary unit: 1 Moroccan dirham (DH) = 100 Moroccan francs; valuation (Sept. 1, 2004) 1 U.S.$ = DH 9.04; 1 £ = DH 16.26.

Population[2]

Provinces	Administrative centres	population 2002 estimate
Chaouia-Ouardigha	Settat	1,663,000
Doukkala-Abda	Safi	1,984,000
Fès-Boulemane	Fès	1,586,000
Gharb-Chrarda-Béni Hsen	Kénitra	1,868,000
Grand Casablanca	Casablanca	3,546,000
Guelmim-Es Semara	Guelmim	436,000
Laâyoune-Bojador-Sakia El-Hamra	Laâyoune	217,000
Marrakech-Tensift-El Haouz	Marrakech	3,027,000
Meknès-Tafilalt	Meknès	2,119,000
Oriental	Oujda	1,914,000
Oued Eddahab-Lagouira[3]	Dakhla	52,000
Rabat-Salé-Zemmour-Zaër	Rabat	2,389,000
Sous-Massa-Draâ	Agadir	3,081,000
Tadla-Azilal	Béni Mellal	1,474,000
Tangier-Tetouan	Tangier	2,430,000
Taza-Al Hoceïma-Taounate	Al-Hoceïma	1,845,000
TOTAL		29,631,000

Demography

Area[2]: 274,461 sq mi, 710,850 sq km.
Population (2004)[2]: 30,569,000.
Density (2004)[2]: persons per sq mi 111.4, persons per sq km 43.0.
Urban-rural (2002): urban 56.6%; rural 43.4%.
Sex distribution (2002): male 49.75%; female 50.25%.
Age breakdown (2002): under 15, 30.9%; 15–29, 30.3%; 30–44, 20.4%; 45–59, 10.9%; 60–74, 5.9%; 75 and over, 1.6%.
Population projection[2]: (2010) 33,562,000; (2020) 38,281,000.
Doubling time: 46 years.
Ethnic composition (2000): Berber *c.* 45%, of which Arabized *c.* 24%; Arab *c.* 44%; Moors originally from Mauritania *c.* 10%; other *c.* 1%.
Religious affiliation (2000): Muslim (mostly Sunnī) 98.3%; Christian 0.6%; other 1.1%.
Major urban areas (2003): Casablanca 3,353,000; Rabat-Salé (2000) 1,616,000; Fès 1,053,000; Marrakech (2000) 822,000; Tangier 681,444; Agadir 550,200.

Vital statistics

Birth rate per 1,000 population (2002): 21.0 (world avg. 21.3).
Death rate per 1,000 population (2002): 5.6 (world avg. 9.1).
Natural increase rate per 1,000 population (2002): 15.4 (world avg. 12.2).
Total fertility rate (avg. birth per childbearing woman; 2002): 3.0.
Life expectancy at birth (2002): male 67.5 years; female 72.1 years.
Major causes of death (1995) as percentage of total: diseases of the perinatal period *c.* 22%; diseases of the circulatory system *c.* 19%; malignant neoplasms (cancers) *c.* 7%; endocrine, nutritional, and metabolic disorders *c.* 6%.

National economy

Budget. Revenue (2003): DH 102,482,000,000 (value-added tax 25.5%; individual income tax 17.2%; excise taxes 15.2%; corporate taxes 14.2%; international trade 12.2%; stamp tax 5.2%). Expenditures (2003): DH 128,113,000,000 (current expenditure 76.8%, of which wages 42.1%, debt payment 13.5%; capital expenditure 17.1%; transfers to local governments 6.1%).
Public debt (external, outstanding; 2002): U.S.$15,001,000,000.
Population economically active (2001): total 10,230,000; activity rate 35.4% (participation rates: ages 15–64, n.a.; female, n.a.; unemployed [2002] 11.6%).

Price index (2000 = 100)

	1997	1998	1999	2000	2001	2002	2003
Consumer price index	94.9	97.5	98.1	100.0	100.6	103.4	104.8

Production (metric tons except as noted). Agriculture, forestry, fishing (2002): wheat 3,356,000, sugar beets 2,985,900, barley 1,669,000, potatoes 1,334,000, tomatoes 991,000, oranges 723,100, olives 420,000; livestock (number of live animals) 16,335,000 sheep, 5,090,000 goats, 2,669,000 cattle, 1,000,000 asses; roundwood (2001) 971,000 cu m; fish catch (2001) 1,083,000, of which sardines 763,000, octopuses 113,000. Mining and quarrying (2002): phosphate rock 21,808,000; barite 469,900; zinc (metal content) 178,400; lead (metal content) 87,400; silver 276,800 kg[4]. Manufacturing (value added in U.S.$'000,000; 2001): food products 778; tobacco products 635; wearing apparel 565; bricks, pottery, and cement 456; basic chemicals 358. Energy production (consumption): electricity (kW-hr; 2002) 15,539,300,000 (14,085,000,000); coal (metric tons; 2001) 135,000 ([2000] 4,029,000); crude petroleum (barrels; 2002) 97,000 ([2000] 52,288,000); petroleum products (metric tons; 2002) 6,339,500 ([2000] 6,553,000); natural gas (cu m; 2002) 48,700,000 ([2000] 49,900,000).
Gross national product (2003): U.S.$39,661,000,000 (U.S.$1,320 per capita).

Structure of gross domestic product and labour force

	2002		2001	
	in value DH '000,000	% of total value	labour force	% of labour force
Agriculture	64,141	16.1	3,900,000	38.1
Mining	7,314	1.8	1,169,000	11.4
Manufacturing	66,864	16.8		
Construction	19,314	4.9	598,000	5.9
Public utilities	27,129	6.8		
Transp. and commun.	28,673	7.2	317,000	3.1
Trade	47,149	11.9	1,155,000	11.3
Finance, real estate	[5]	[5]	835,000	8.2
Pub. admin., defense	59,972	15.1	976,000	9.5
Services	48,667[5]	12.2[5]		
Other	28,559	7.2	1,280,000[6]	12.5[6]
TOTAL	397,782	100.0	10,230,000	100.0

Tourism (2002): receipts U.S.$2,046,000,000; expenditures U.S.$444,000,000.
Household income and expenditure. Average household size (2002) 5.5; expenditure (1994)[7]: food 45.2%, housing 12.5%, transportation 7.6%.
Land use as % of total land area (2000): in temporary crops 19.6%, in permanent crops 2.2%, in pasture 47.1%; overall forest area 6.8%.

Foreign trade[8]

Balance of trade (current prices)

	1997	1998	1999	2000	2001	2002
DH '000,000	–30,467	–30,068	–32,314	–43,700	–43,641	–43,693
% of total	25.5%	18.0%	18.0%	21.7%	21.3%	20.3%

Imports (2002): DH 129,346,000,000 (machinery and apparatus 19.3%; mineral fuels 15.6%, of which crude petroleum 10.0%; food, beverages, and tobacco 11.8%; cotton fabric and fibres 6.4%). *Major import sources* (2001): France 24.1%; Spain 10.3%; U.K. 6.2%; Italy 5.0%; Germany 5.0%.
Exports (2002)[9]: DH 85,653,000,000 (garments 21.4%; food, beverages, and tobacco 20.5%, of which crustaceans and mollusks 6.6%; knitwear 10.4%; phosphoric acid 6.8%; machinery and apparatus 6.6%; phosphates 5.2%). *Major export destinations* (2001): France 32.8%; Spain 15.3%; U.K. 8.6%; Italy 5.7%; Germany 4.2%.

Transport and communications

Transport. Railroads (2002): route length 1,907 km; passenger-km 2,145,000,000; metric ton-km cargo 4,974,000,000. Roads (2001): total length 57,226 km (paved 56%). Vehicles (2000): passenger cars 1,211,100; trucks and buses 415,700. Air transport (2002)[10]: passenger-km 6,044,800,000; metric ton-km cargo 51,285,000; airports (2002) 15.

Communications

Medium	date	unit	number	units per 1,000 persons
Daily newspapers	2000	circulation	740,000	26
Radio	2000	receivers	6,920,000	243
Television	2000	receivers	4,720,000	166
Telephones	2003	main lines	1,219,200	41
Cellular telephones	2003	subscribers	7,332,800	243
Personal computers	2003	units	600,000	20
Internet	2003	users	800,000	27

Education and health

Educational attainment: n.a. *Literacy* (2000): total population over age 15 literate 48.9%; males literate 61.1%; females literate 35.1%.

Education (2002–03)

	schools[11]	teachers	students	student/ teacher ratio
Primary (age 7–12)	6,565	135,199	4,101,157	30.3
Secondary (age 13–17)	1,664	87,887	1,679,077	19.1
Vocational	69	...	143,692	...
Higher	68	10,064	276,018	27.4

Health (2002): physicians 13,955 (1 per 2,123 persons); hospital beds (1998) 26,153 (1 per 1,062 persons); infant mortality rate (2002) 44.0.
Food (2001): daily per capita caloric intake 3,046 (vegetable products 93%, animal products 7%); 126% of FAO recommended minimum requirement.

Military

Total active duty personnel (2003): 196,300 (army 89.1%, navy 4.0%, air force 6.9%). *Military expenditure as percentage of GNP* (1999): 4.3% (world 2.4%); per capita expenditure U.S.$49.

[1]All seats indirectly elected: 162 by regional councils; 108 by industry, agriculture, and trade unions. [2]Includes Western Sahara, annexure of Morocco whose unresolved political status (from 1991) is to be eventually decided by an internationally sponsored referendum; Western Sahara area: 97,344 sq mi, 252,120 sq km; Western Sahara population (2004 est.) 267,000. [3]Includes Aousserd province created in late 1990s. [4]Includes smelter bullion. [5]Services include Finance, real estate. [6]Includes 1,275,000 unemployed. [7]Weights of consumer price index components. [8]Imports c.i.f.; exports f.o.b. [9]Cannabis is an important illegal export. [10]Royal Air Maroc only. [11]1999–2000.

Internet resources for further information:
- **Moroccan Central Statistical Office http://www.statistic.gov.ma**
- **Bank al-Maghrib http://www.bkam.ma**

Mozambique

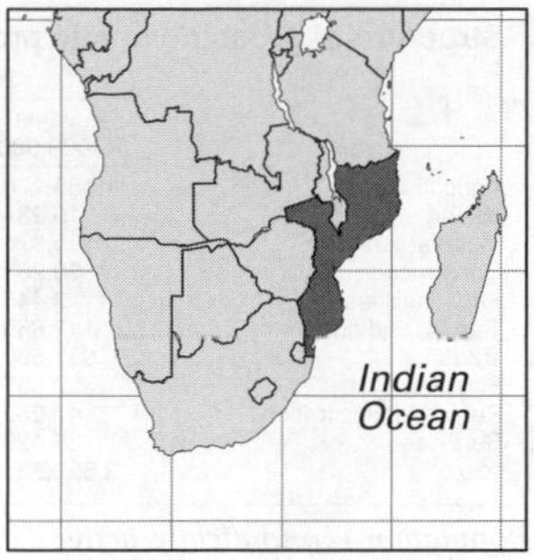

Official name: República de Moçambique (Republic of Mozambique).
Form of government: multiparty republic with a single legislative house (Assembly of the Republic [250]).
Head of state and government: President.
Capital: Maputo.
Official language: Portuguese.
Official religion: none.
Monetary unit: 1 metical (Mt; plural meticais) = 100 centavos; valuation (Sept. 1, 2004) 1 U.S.$ = Mt 22,082; 1 £ = Mt 39,725.

Area and population

		area		population
Provinces	**Capitals**	sq mi	sq km	2002 estimate
Cabo Delgado	Pemba	31,902	82,625	1,525,634
Gaza	Xai-Xai	29,231	75,709	1,266,431
Inhambane	Inhambane	26,492	68,615	1,326,848
Manica	Chimoio	23,807	61,661	1,207,332
Maputo	Maputo	9,944	25,756	1,003,992
Nampula	Nampula	31,508	81,606	3,410,141
Niassa	Lichinga	49,828	129,055	916,672
Sofala	Beira	26,262	68,018	1,516,166
Tete	Tete	38,890	100,724	1,388,205
Zambézia	Quelimane	40,544	105,008	3,476,484
City				
Maputo	—	232	602	1,044,618
TOTAL LAND AREA		308,642[1]	799,379	
INLAND WATER		5,019	13,000	
TOTAL		313,661	812,379	18,082,523

Demography

Population (2004): 18,812,000.
Density (2004): persons per sq mi 60.0, persons per sq km 23.2.
Urban-rural (2001): urban 33.3%; rural 66.7%.
Sex distribution (2003): male 49.27%; female 50.73%.
Age breakdown (2003): under 15, 43.8%; 15–29, 26.5%; 30–44, 16.2%; 45–59, 8.9%; 60–74, 3.8%; 75 and over, 0.7%.
Population projection: (2010) 19,721,000; (2020) 20,547,000.
Doubling time: 50 years.
Ethnic composition (2000): Makuana 15.3%; Makua 14.5%; Tsonga 8.6%; Sena 8.0%; Lomwe 7.1%; Tswa 5.7%; Chwabo 5.5%; other 35.3%.
Linguistic composition (1997): Makua 26.3%; Tsonga 11.4%; Lomwe 7.6%; Sena 7.0%; Portuguese 6.5%; Chuaba 6.3%; other Bantu languages 33.0%; other 1.9%.
Religious affiliation (2000): traditional beliefs 50.4%; Christian 38.4%, of which Roman Catholic 15.8%, Protestant 8.9%; Muslim 10.5%.
Major cities (1997): Maputo 989,386; Matola 440,927; Beira 412,588; Nampula 314,965; Chimoio 177,608.

Vital statistics

Birth rate per 1,000 population (2003): 36.9 (world avg. 21.3).
Death rate per 1,000 population (2003): 23.0 (world avg. 9.1).
Natural increase rate per 1,000 population (2003): 13.9 (world avg. 12.2).
Total fertility rate (avg. births per childbearing woman; 2003): 5.0.
Life expectancy at birth (2003): male 38.9 years; female 37.4 years.
Adult population (ages 15–49) *living with HIV* (2004[2]): 12.2% (world avg. 1.1%).

National economy

Budget (2002). Revenue: Mt 22,077,000,000,000 (tax revenue 48.1%, of which VAT 20.8%, taxes on international trade 8.4%, personal income tax 5.9%; grants 45.1%; nontax revenue 6.8%). Expenditures: Mt 29,032,000,000,000 (current expenditures 46.4%; capital expenditures 41.8%; net lending 11.8%).
Public debt (external, outstanding; 2002): U.S.$2,526,000,000.
Production (metric tons except as noted). Agriculture, forestry, fishing (2003): cassava 6,149,897, corn (maize) 1,248,000, sugarcane 400,000, sorghum 314,000, coconuts 265,000, rice 200,439, peanuts (groundnuts) 109,915, bananas 90,000, cashews 58,000; livestock (number of live animals) 1,320,000 cattle, 392,000 goats, 28,000,000 chickens; roundwood (2002) 18,043,000 cu m; fish catch (2001) 32,512. Mining and quarrying (2002): tantalite 46,900 kg; gold 17 kg[3]. Manufacturing (value added in Mt '000,000,000; 2002): aluminum 13,547; beverages 2,130; food products 1,789; paper and paper products 1,449; textiles 596. Energy production (consumption): electricity (kW-hr; 2000) 6,974,000,000 (1,562,000,000); coal (metric tons; 2001) 17,700 (n.a.); crude petroleum, none (none); petroleum products (metric tons; 2000) none (334,000); natural gas (cu m; 2000) 563,800 (563,800).
Household income and expenditure. Average family size (1997) 4.1; income per household: n.a.; source of income (1992–93)[4]: wages and salaries 51.6%, self-employment 12.5%, barter 11.5%, private farming 7.7%; expenditure (1992–93)[4]: food, beverages, and tobacco 74.6%, housing and energy 11.7%, transportation and communications 4.7%, clothing and footwear 3.7%, education and recreation 1.4%, health 0.8%.
Tourism (2002): receipts from visitors U.S.$144,000,000; expenditures by nationals abroad U.S.$298,000,000.
Population economically active (2002): total 9,696,000; activity rate 55.3% (participation rates: over age 15, n.a.; female, n.a.; unemployed, n.a.).

Price index (2000 = 100)

	1997	1998	1999	2000	2001	2002	2003
Consumer price index	85.0	86.2	88.7	100.0	109.1	127.4	144.4

Gross national product (2003): U.S.$3,897,000,000 (U.S.$210 per capita).

Structure of gross domestic product and labour force

	2002			
	in value Mt '000,000,000	% of total value	labour force	% of labour force
Agriculture	18,011	21.1	7,837,000	80.8
Mining } Manufacturing }	9,903	11.6	1,859,000	19.2
Construction	13,553	15.9		
Public utilities	2,640	3.1		
Transp. and commun.	9,468	11.1		
Finance	4,247	5.0		
Trade	16,140	18.9		
Pub. admin., defense	5,394	6.3		
Services	5,850	6.9		
Other	...	...	...	...
TOTAL	85,206	100.0[1]	9,696,000	100.0

Land use as % of total land area (2000): in temporary crops 5.0%, in permanent crops 0.3%, in pasture 56.1%; overall forest area 39.0%.

Foreign trade[5]

Balance of trade (current prices)

	1998	1999	2000	2001	2002	2003
U.S.$'000,000	–491	–806	–682	–271	–536	–348
% of total	50.1%	58.7%	48.4%	15.7%	28.3%	16.5%

Imports (2001): U.S.$1,063,000,000 (machinery and apparatus 14.9%; refined petroleum 12.5%; food products 11.8%, of which cereals 8.0%; transport equipment 7.0%; unspecified commodities 21.9%). *Major import sources:* South Africa *c.* 42%; Australia *c.* 7%; Spain *c.* 4%; unspecified *c.* 23%.
Exports (2001): U.S.$703,000,000 (aluminum 54.5%; food products 20.1%, of which crustaceans and mollusks 13.4%; electricity 8.1%; cotton 2.3%). *Major export destinations:* Belgium *c.* 35%; Zimbabwe *c.* 10%; Germany *c.* 7%; The Netherlands *c.* 7%; Spain *c.* 5%.

Transport and communications

Transport. Railroads (2002): route length 1,940 mi, 3,123 km; (2001) passenger-km 142,000,000; (2001) metric ton-km cargo 774,500,000. Roads (1996): total length 18,890 mi, 30,400 km (paved 19%). Vehicles (1999): passenger cars 78,600; trucks and buses 46,900. Air transport: (2001) passenger-km 272,400,000; metric ton-km cargo 6,700,000; airports (1997) with scheduled flights 7.

Communications

Medium	date	unit	number	units per 1,000 persons
Daily newspapers	2000	circulation	53,000	3.0
Radio	2000	receivers	778,000	44
Television	2002	receivers	257,600	14
Telephones	2002	main lines	83,700	4.6
Cellular telephones	2003	subscribers	428,900	23
Personal computers	2002	units	82,000	4.5
Internet	2002	users	50,000	2.8

Education and health

Educational attainment (1997). Percentage of population 15 and over having: no formal schooling 78.4%; primary education 18.4%; secondary 2.0%; technical 0.4%; higher 0.2%; other/unknown 0.6%. *Literacy* (2000): percentage of total population age 15 and over literate 43.8%; males literate 59.9%; females literate 28.4%.

Education (1998)

	schools	teachers	students	student/ teacher ratio
Primary (age 7–12)	6,263	31,512	1,918,400	60.9
Secondary (age 13–18)	75[6]	8,073	254,540	31.5
Voc., teacher tr.[6]	25	565	12,001	21.2
Higher[6]	3	954	7,156	7.5

Health: physicians (2003) *c.* 500 (1 per *c.* 37,000 persons); hospital beds (1997) 12,630 (1 per 1,210 persons); infant mortality rate per 1,000 live births (2003) 137.8.
Food (2001): daily per capita caloric intake 1,980 (vegetable products 98%, animal products 2%); 85% of FAO recommended minimum requirement.

Military

Total active duty personnel (2003): 8,200 (army 85.4%, navy 2.4%, air force 12.2%). *Military expenditure as percentage of GNP* (1999): 2.5% (world 2.4%); per capita expenditure U.S.$5.

[1]Detail does not add to total given because of rounding. [2]Beginning of year. [3]Official figures; unofficial artisanal production is 360–480 kg per year. [4]City of Maputo only. [5]Imports are f.o.b. in balance of trade and c.i.f. for commodities and trading partners. [6]1997.

Internet resources for further information:
- **Instituto Nacional de Estatística http://www.ine.gov.mz**
- **Banco de Moçambique http://www.bancomoc.mz**

Myanmar (Burma)

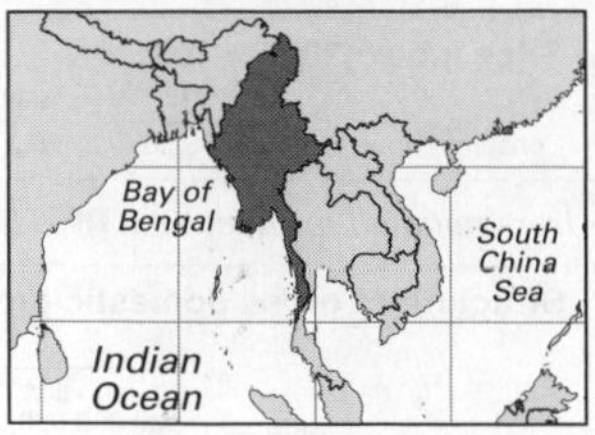

Official name: Pyidaungzu Myanma Naingngandaw (Union of Myanmar).
Form of government: military regime.
Head of state and government: Chairman of the State Peace and Development Council, assisted by Prime Minister.
Capital: Yangôn (Rangoon).
Official language: Burmese.
Official religion: none.
Monetary unit: 1 Myanmar kyat (K) = 100 pyas; valuation[1] (Sept. 1, 2004) 1 U.S.$ = K 6.42; 1 £ = K 11.55.

Area and population

Divisions	Capitals	area sq mi	area sq km	population 1994 estimate
Irrawaddy (Ayeyarwady)	Bassein (Pathein)	13,567	35,138	6,107,000
Magwe (Magway)	Magwe (Magway)	17,305	44,820	4,067,000
Mandalay	Mandalay	14,295	37,024	5,823,000
Pegu (Bago)	Pegu (Bago)	15,214	39,404	4,607,000
Sagaing	Sagaing	36,535	94,625	4,889,000
Tenasserim (Tanintharyi)	Tavoy (Dawei)	16,735	43,343	1,187,000
Yangôn	Yangôn (Rangoon)	3,927	10,171	5,037,000
States				
Chin	Hakha	13,907	36,019	438,000
Kachin	Myitkyinā	34,379	89,041	1,135,000
Karen	Pa-an (Hpa-an)	11,731	30,383	1,323,000
Kayah	Loi-kaw	4,530	11,733	228,000
Mon	Moulmein (Mawlamyine)	4,748	12,297	2,183,000
Rakhine (Arakan)	Sittwe (Akyab)	14,200	36,778	2,482,000
Shan	Taunggyi	60,155	155,801	4,416,000
TOTAL		261,228	676,577	43,922,000

Demography

Population (2004): 42,720,000.
Density (2004): persons per sq mi 163.5, persons per sq km 63.1.
Urban-rural (2002): urban 29.0%; rural 71.0%.
Sex distribution (2002): male 49.81%; female 50.19%.
Age breakdown (2002): under 15, 28.5%; 15–29, 30.8%; 30–44, 22.0%; 45–59, 11.4%; 60 and over, 5.7%.
Population projection: (2010) 43,721,000; (2020) 44,825,000.
Doubling time: 56 years.
Ethnic composition (2000): Burman 55.9%; Karen 9.5%; Shan 6.5%; Han Chinese 2.5%; Mon 2.3%; Yangbye 2.2%; Kachin 1.5%; other 19.6%.
Religious affiliation (2000): Buddhist 72.7%; Christian 8.3%; Muslim 2.4%; Hindu 2.0%; traditional beliefs 12.6%; other 2.0%.
Major cities (2004 est.): Yangôn (Rangoon) 4,455,500; Mandalay 1,176,900; Moulmein (Mawlamyine) 405,800; Bassein (Pathein) 215,600; Pegu (Bago) 200,900.

Vital statistics

Birth rate per 1,000 population (2003): 23.7 (world avg. 21.3).
Death rate per 1,000 population (2003): 11.2 (world avg. 9.1).
Natural increase rate per 1,000 population (2003): 12.5 (world avg. 12.2).
Total fertility rate (avg. births per childbearing woman; 2003): 2.2.
Life expectancy at birth (2002): male 54.1 years; female 57.6 years.
Major causes of death per 100,000 population (1994): infectious and parasitic diseases 27.7; circulatory diseases 17.4; respiratory diseases 15.1; malignant neoplasms (cancers) 7.6; malnutrition 3.2.

National economy

Budget (2000–01). Revenue: K 134,550,000,000 (revenue from taxes 56.4%, of which taxes on goods and services 32.8%, taxes on income 19.4%; nontax revenue 43.4%; foreign grants 0.2%). Expenditures: K 221,255,000,000 (defense 28.7%; agriculture and forestry 17.4%; education 14.2%; public works and housing 9.2%).
Public debt (external, outstanding; 2002): U.S.$5,391,000,000.
Tourism (2001): receipts from visitors U.S.$45,000,000; expenditures by nationals abroad U.S.$27,000,000.
Production (metric tons except as noted). Agriculture, forestry, fishing (2002): rice 21,900,000, sugarcane 6,333,000, dry beans 1,467,330, peanuts (groundnuts) 700,000, corn (maize) 660,000, plantains 400,000, sesame seeds 225,000, seed cotton 152,694, natural rubber 35,662, opium poppy (2000) 1,085; livestock (number of live animals) 11,551,000 cattle, 4,498,680 pigs, 2,252,020 buffalo; roundwood (2001) 39,365,000 cu m; fish catch (2001) 1,288,134. Mining and quarrying (2001): copper (metal content) 26,300; jade 1,700,000 kg; rubies, sapphires, and spinel 8,630,000 carats. Manufacturing (2001): cement 384,000; refined sugar 101,000; fertilizers 60,100; paper 20,600; cotton yarn 5,500; plywood 28,000 cu m; cigarettes 1,991,000,000 units[2]; clay bricks 68,000,000 units[2]. Energy production (consumption): electricity (kW-hr; 2000) 5,076,000,000 (5,076,000,000); hard coal (metric tons; 2000) 51,000 (43,000); lignite (metric tons; 2000) 524,000 (524,000); crude petroleum (barrels; 2001) 3,300,000 ([2000] 7,339,000); petroleum products (metric tons; 2000) 820,000 (1,625,000); natural gas (cu m; 2001) 6,800,300,000 ([2000] 1,427,000,000).
Household income and expenditure. Average household size (2000) 4.8; average annual income per household: n.a.; sources of income: n.a.; expenditure (1994)[3]: food and beverages 67.1%, fuel and lighting 6.6%, transportation 4.0%, charitable contributions 3.1%, medical care 3.1%.
Gross national product (1996): U.S.$119,334,000,000 (U.S.$2,610 per capita).

Structure of gross domestic product and labour force

	2000–01 in value K '000,000	2000–01 % of total value	1997–98 labour force[4]	1997–98 % of labour force[4]
Agriculture	1,458,270	57.1	12,093,000	65.9
Mining	15,234	0.5	121,000	0.7
Manufacturing	195,876	7.7	1,666,000	9.1
Construction	50,263	2.0	400,000	2.2
Public utilities	3,445	0.1	26,000	0.1
Transp. and commun.	149,669	5.9	495,000	2.7
Trade	601,690	23.6	1,781,000	9.7
Finance	2,587	0.1	1,485,000	8.1
Public administration	40,260	1.6		
Services	35,429	1.4	270,000	1.5
TOTAL	2,552,723	100.0	18,337,000	100.0

Population economically active (1999): total 23,700,000; activity rate of total population 57.1% (participation rates: ages 15–64, n.a.; female, n.a.; unemployed 4.1%).

Price index (2000 = 100)

	1997	1998	1999	2000	2001	2002	2003
Consumer price index	55.8	84.6	100.1	100.0	121.1	190.2	259.8

Land use as % of total land area (2000): in temporary crops 15.1%, in permanent crops 0.9%, in pasture 0.5%; overall forest area 52.3%.

Foreign trade[5]

Balance of trade (current prices)[6]

	1996–97	1997–98	1998–99	1999–2000	2000–01	2001–02
K '000,000	–6,291	–7,919	–10,116	–7,318	–2,638	–1,346
% of total	36.4%	38.0%	42.8%	29.0%	9.7%	3.5%

Imports (2000–01[6]): K 14,900,000,000 (machinery and transport equipment 25.2%, chemicals and chemical products 12.9%, mineral fuels 7.7%, food and live animals 3.9%). *Major import sources* (2001): China 21.8%; Singapore 16.6%; Thailand 13.9%; South Korea 9.1%; Malaysia 8.0%; Japan 7.1%.
Exports (2000–01[6]): K 12,262,000,000 (domestic exports 68.6%, of which food 26.1% [including pulses 13.5%], mineral fuels [significantly natural gas] 9.6%, teak and other hardwood 6.5%; reexports [significantly garments] 31.4%). *Major export destinations* (2001): Thailand 26.0%; United States 16.2%; India 10.2%; China 5.0%; Singapore 3.6%.

Transport and communications

Transport. Railroads (2000): route length 3,955 km; passenger-km 4,451,000,000; metric ton-km cargo 1,222,000,000. Roads (1996): total length 28,200 km (paved 12%). Vehicles (1999): passenger cars 171,300; trucks and buses 83,400. Air transport (1999): passenger-km 355,000,000; metric ton-km cargo 40,000,000; airports (1996) 19.

Communications

Medium	date	unit	number	units per 1,000 persons
Daily newspapers	2000	circulation	376,000	9.0
Radio	2001	receivers	2,772,000	66
Television	2002	receivers	390,400	8.0
Telephones	2003	main lines	357,300	7.2
Cellular telephones	2003	subscribers	66,500	1.3
Personal computers	2002	units	250,000	5.1
Internet	2003	users	28,000	0.5

Education and health

Educational attainment: n.a. *Literacy* (2000): total population age 15 and over literate 84.7%; males literate 89.0%; females literate 80.5%.

Education (1997–98)

	schools	teachers	students	student/ teacher ratio
Primary (age 5–9)	35,877	167,134	5,145,400	30.8
Secondary (age 10–15)	2,091	56,955	1,545,600	27.1
Voc., teacher tr.[7]	103	2,462	25,374	10.3
Higher	923	17,089	385,300	22.5

Health (1999): physicians 14,622 (1 per 2,838 persons); hospital beds (1997) 28,943 (1 per 1,433 persons); infant mortality rate per 1,000 live births (2003) 83.0.
Food (2001): daily per capita caloric intake 2,822 (vegetable products 96%, animal products 4%); 132% of FAO recommended minimum requirement.

Military

Total active duty personnel (2003): 488,000 (army 93.6%, navy 3.3%, air force 3.1%). *Military expenditure as percentage of GNP* (1999): 7.8% (world 2.4%); per capita expenditure U.S.$112.

[1]The kyat is pegged to the Special Drawing Right of the International Monetary Fund at 1 SDR = K 8.51; the illegal black market rate in August 2004 was about 1 U.S.$ = K 935. [2]1999. [3]Yangôn only. [4]Employed only. [5]Imports c.i.f.; exports f.o.b. [6]Fiscal year beginning April 1. [7]1994–95.

Internet resources for further information:
- **Key Indicators of Developing Asian and Pacific Countries http://www.adb.org/Documents/Books/Key_Indicators/default.asp**

Namibia

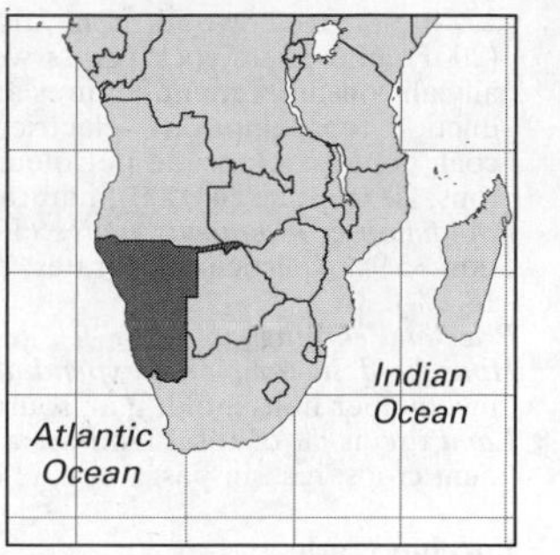

Official name: Republic of Namibia.
Form of government: republic with two legislative houses (National Council [26]; National Assembly [72[1]]).
Head of state and government: President.
Capital: Windhoek.
Official language: English.
Official religion: none.
Monetary unit: 1 Namibian dollar (N$) = 100 cents; valuation (Sept. 1, 2004) 1 U.S.$ = N$6.66; 1 £ = N$11.97.

Area and population

Regions	Largest towns	area sq mi	area sq km	population 2001 census
Erongo	Walvis Bay	24,602	63,719	107,629
Hardap	Rehoboth	42,428	109,888	67,998
Karas	Keetmanshoop	62,288	161,324	69,677
Khomas	Windhoek	14,210	36,804	250,305
Kunene	Khorixas	55,697	144,254	68,224
Liambezi (Caprivi)	Katima Mulilo	7,541	19,532	79,852
Ohangwena	Oshikango	4,086	10,582	227,728
Okavango	Rundu	16,763	43,417	201,093
Omaheke	Gobabis	32,715	84,731	67,496
Omusati	Ongandjera	5,265	13,637	228,364
Oshana	Oshakati	2,042	5,290	161,977
Oshikoto	Tsumeb	10,273	26,607	160,788
Otjozondjupa	Otjiwarongo	40,667	105,327	135,723
TOTAL		318,580[2]	825,118[2]	1,826,854

Demography

Population (2004): 1,954,000.
Density (2004): persons per sq mi 6.2, persons per sq km 2.4.
Urban-rural (2001): urban 31.4%; rural 68.6%.
Sex distribution (2001): male 48.73%; female 51.27%.
Age breakdown (1999): under 15, 43.2%; 15–29, 28.6%; 30–44, 15.1%; 45–59, 7.7%; 60–74, 4.0%; 75 and over, 1.4%.
Population projection: (2010) 2,036,000; (2020) 2,081,000.
Doubling time: 66 years.
Ethnic composition (2000): Ovambo 34.4%; mixed race (black/white) 14.5%; Kavango 9.1%; Afrikaner 8.1%; San (Bushmen) and Bergdama 7.0%; Herero 5.5%; Nama 4.4%; Kwambi 3.7%; German 2.8%; other 10.5%.
Religious affiliation (2000): Protestant (mostly Lutheran) 47.5%; Roman Catholic 17.7%; African Christian 10.8%; traditional beliefs 6.0%; other 18.0%.
Major cities (2001): Windhoek 216,000[3]; Walvis Bay 40,849; Swakopmund 25,442[4]; Rehoboth 21,782; Rundu 19,597.

Vital statistics

Birth rate per 1,000 population (2003): 27.4 (world avg. 21.3).
Death rate per 1,000 population (2003): 16.7 (world avg. 9.1).
Natural increase rate per 1,000 population (2003): 10.7 (world avg. 12.2).
Total fertility rate (avg. births per childbearing woman; 2003): 3.5.
Life expectancy at birth (2003): male 46.0 years; female 46.1 years.
Adult population (ages 15–49) *living with HIV* (2004[5]): 21.3% (world avg. 1.1%).

National economy

Budget (2002–03). Revenue: N$10,256,000,000 (taxes on income and profits 38.5%; taxes on international trade 25.3%; taxes on goods and services 23.6%; nontax revenue 9.7%). Expenditures: N$12,257,000,000 (current expenditure 84.3%; development expenditure 15.7%).
Public debt (external, outstanding 1998): U.S.$747,700,000.
Production (metric tons except as noted). Agriculture, forestry, fishing (2002): roots and tubers 270,000, millet 65,000, corn (maize) 27,700, fruits 11,000, vegetables 11,000, pulses 8,500, sorghum 8,100, wheat 6,100; livestock (number of live animals) 2,509,000 cattle, 2,370,000 sheep, 1,769,000 goats; fish catch (2001) 547,542. Mining and quarrying (2001): gem diamonds (2002) 1,550,000 carats; fluorite 81,200; zinc (metal content) 31,803; marble 20,000; copper (metal content) 12,392; uranium oxide 2,640; silver 407,639 troy oz; gold 91,662 troy oz. Manufacturing: n.a.; products include cut gems (primarily diamonds), fur products (from Karakul sheep), processed foods (fish, meats, and dairy products), textiles, carved wood products, refined metals (copper and lead). Energy production (consumption): electricity (kW-hr; 2001) 27,000,000 (603,000,000); coal (metric tons; 2000) none (3,000); petroleum products (metric tons; 2001) none (n.a.).
Household income and expenditure. Average household size (2001) 5.1; average annual income per household, n.a.; sources of income (1992): wages and salaries 69.0%, income from property 25.6%, transfer payments 5.4%; expenditure: n.a.
Population economically active: total (1991) 493,580; activity rate of total population, 34.9% (participation rates: ages 15–64, 61.3%; female 43.5%; unemployed 20.1%).

Price index (2000 = 100)

	1997	1998	1999	2000	2001	2002	2003
Consumer price index	79.5	84.5	91.7	100.0	109.5	122.0	130.7

Gross national product (2003): U.S.$3,771,000,000 (U.S.$1,870 per capita).

Structure of gross domestic product and labour force

	2001 in value N$'000,000	2001 % of total value	1991 labour force[6]	1991 % of labour force[6]
Agriculture	2,431	8.9	189,929	38.5
Mining	3,489	12.8	14,686	3.0
Manufacturing	2,638	9.7	22,884	4.6
Construction	773	2.8	18,638	3.8
Public utilities	652	2.4	2,974	0.6
Transp. and commun.	1,405	5.0	9,322	1.9
Trade, hotels	3,481	12.8	37,820	7.7
Finance, real estate			8,547	1.7
Services	12,332	45.3		
Public administration and defense			89,541	18.1
Other			99,239[7]	20.1[7]
TOTAL	27,231	100.0	493,580	100.0

Tourism (2002): receipts U.S.$219,000,000; expenditures (1998) U.S.$56,000,000.
Land use as % of total land area (2000): in temporary crops 1.0%, in permanent crops, negligible, in pasture 46.2%; overall forest area 9.8%.

Foreign trade[8]

Balance of trade (current prices)

	1996	1997	1998	1999	2000	2001
N$'000,000	–396	–1,232	–1,562	–1,453	–1,099	–1,572
% of total	3.9%	9.1%	10.3%	8.8%	6.5%	8.1%

Imports (1997): N$7,718,000,000 (food, beverages, and tobacco 24.1%; machinery and apparatus 15.0%; transport equipment 14.7%; base and fabricated metals 7.5%). *Major import sources* (2000): South Africa 86.4%; Germany 2.0%; U.K. 2.0%; U.S. 1.3%.
Exports (2001): N$8,901,000,000 (diamonds 45.4%; metals 18.6%, of which gold 2.3%, zinc 1.5%, other [mostly uranium and copper] 14.8%; fish 10.4%; meat [mostly beef] 7.0%). *Major export destinations* (1998): U.K. *c.* 43%; South Africa *c.* 26%; Spain *c.* 14%; France *c.* 8%.

Transport and communications

Transport. Railroads: route length (1999) 1,480 mi, 2,382 km; (1995–96) passenger-km 48,300,000; (1995–96) metric ton-km 1,082,000,000. Roads (2000): total length 41,301 mi, 66,467 km (paved 7%). Vehicles (1996): passenger cars 74,875; trucks and buses 66,500[9]. Air transport (2001)[10]: passenger-km 624,000,000; metric ton-km cargo 72,575,000; airports (1997) 11.

Communications

Medium	date	unit	number	units per 1,000 persons
Daily newspapers	2000	circulation	34,700	19
Radio	2000	receivers	258,000	141
Television	2000	receivers	69,400	38
Telephones	2003	main lines	127,400	66
Cellular telephones	2003	subscribers	223,700	116
Personal computers	2003	units	191,000	99
Internet	2003	users	65,000	34

Education and health

Educational attainment (1991). Percentage of population age 25 and over having: no formal schooling 35.1%; primary education 31.9%; secondary 28.5%; higher 4.5%. *Literacy* (2000): total population age 15 and over literate 830,200 (82.1%); males literate 416,000 (82.9%); females literate 414,200 (81.2%).

Education (1998)

	schools	teachers	students	student/ teacher ratio
Primary (age 6–12)	1,362	11,992	386,647	32.2
Secondary (age 13–19)	114[11]	5,093	110,076	21.6
Higher	24[11]	619	12,787	20.7

Health (2000): physicians 244[12] (1 per 7,500 persons); hospital beds 6,739[12] (1 per 271 persons); infant mortality rate per 1,000 live births (2003) 50.7.
Food (2001): daily per capita caloric intake 2,745 (vegetable products 85%, animal products 15%); 120% of FAO recommended minimum requirement.

Military

Total active duty personnel (2003): 9,000 (army 100.0%). *Military expenditure as percentage of GNP* (1999): 2.9% (world 2.4%); per capita expenditure U.S.$53.

[1]72 elected and up to 6 appointed members. [2]Detail does not add to total given because of rounding. [3]Urban agglomeration. [4]Population of constituency (second-order administrative subdivision). [5]Beginning of year. [6]Includes more than 140,000 nonwage (informal) workers. [7]Unemployed. [8]Imports are f.o.b. in balance of trade and c.i.f. for commodities and trading partners. [9]1995. [10]Air Namibia only. [11]1994. [12]Public sector only.

Internet resources for further information:
- **Bank of Namibia http://www.bon.com.na**

Nauru

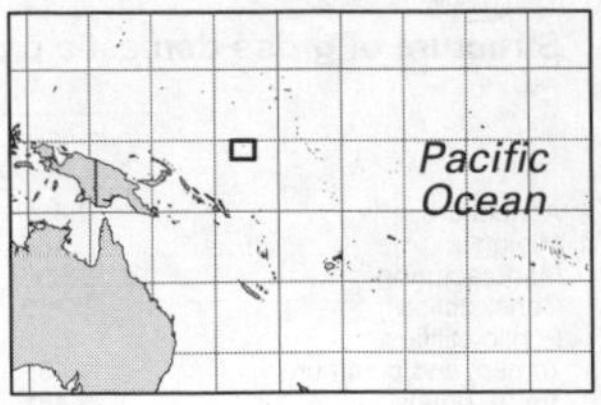

Official name: Naoero (Nauruan[1]); (Republic of Nauru).
Form of government: republic with one legislative house (Parliament [18]).
Head of state and government: President.
Capital: [2].
Official language: none[1].
Official religion: none.
Monetary unit: 1 Australian dollar ($A) = 100 cents; valuation (Sept. 1, 2004) 1 U.S.$ = $A 1.42; 1 £ = $A 2.55.

Area and population

	area		population
Districts	sq mi	sq km	1992 census[3]
Aiwo	0.4	1.1	1,072
Anabar	0.6	1.5	320
Anetan	0.4	1.0	427
Anibare	1.2	3.1	165
Baitsi	0.5	1.2	450
Boe	0.2	0.5	750
Buada	1.0	2.6	661
Denigomodu	0.3	0.9	2,548
Ewa	0.5	1.2	355
Ijuw	0.4	1.1	206
Meneng	1.2	3.1	1,269
Nibok	0.6	1.6	577
Uaboe	0.3	0.8	447
Yaren	0.6	1.5	672
TOTAL	8.2	21.2	9,919

Demography

Population (2004): 10,100.
Density (2004): persons per sq mi 1,232, persons per sq km 476.4.
Urban-rural (2001): urban 100%.
Sex distribution (2001): male 50.50%; female 49.50%.
Age breakdown (2001): under 15, 40.3%; 15–29, 26.8%; 30–44, 19.0%; 45–59, 10.7%; 60–74, 3.0%; 75 and over, 0.2%.
Population projection: (2010) 11,000; (2020) 12,000.
Doubling time: 35 years.
Ethnic composition (1992): Nauruan 68.9%; other Pacific Islander 23.7%, of which Kiribati 12.8%, Tuvaluan 8.7%; Asian 5.9%, of which Filipino 2.5%, Chinese 2.3%; other 1.5%.
Religious affiliation (1995): Protestant 53.5%, of which Congregational 35.3%, Pentecostal 4.8%; Roman Catholic 27.5%; other 19.0%.
Major cities: none; population of Yaren district (1996) 700.

Vital statistics

Birth rate per 1,000 population (2002): 21.8 (world avg. 21.3); legitimate, n.a.; illegitimate, n.a.
Death rate per 1,000 population (2002): 7.5 (world avg. 9.1).
Natural increase rate per 1,000 population (2002): 14.3 (world avg. 12.2).
Total fertility rate (avg. births per childbearing woman; 2003): 3.4.
Marriage rate per 1,000 population (1995): 5.3.
Divorce rate per 1,000 population: n.a.
Life expectancy at birth (2003): male 58.4 years; female 65.7 years.
Major causes of death per 100,000 population (2003): diabetes mellitus 159.0; diseases of the respiratory system 149.0; diseases of the circulatory system 119.2; neoplasms 79.5; accidents 79.5.

National economy

Budget (1999). Revenue: $A 38,700,000[4]. Expenditures: $A 37,200,000.
Public debt (external, outstanding; beginning of 1996): *c.* U.S.$150,000,000.
Tourism: receipts from visitors, virtually none; expenditures by nationals abroad, n.a.
Gross national product (at current market prices; 1997): U.S.$128,000,000 (U.S.$11,538 per capita).

Distribution of gross domestic product and labour force

	1997			
	in value U.S.$'000,000	% of total value	labour force[5, 6, 7]	% of labour force
Agriculture	...	...	...	...
Mining (phosphate)	...	...	528	24.7
Manufacturing	...	...	...	...
Construction	...	...	...	...
Public utilities	...	...	...	...
Transportation and communications	...	...	...	...
Hotels	...	...	137	6.4
Finance[8]	...	...	33	1.6
Services	...	...	...	...
Pub. admin.	...	...	1,238	58.0
Other	...	...	198	9.3
TOTAL	540	100.0	2,134	100.0

Production (metric tons except as noted). Agriculture, forestry, fishing (2002): coconuts 1,600, vegetables 450, tropical fruit (including mangoes) 275; almonds, figs, and pandanus are also cultivated, but most foodstuffs and beverages (including water) are imported; livestock (number of live animals) 2,800 pigs; roundwood, none; fish catch (2001) 400. Mining and quarrying (2001): phosphate rock (gross weight) 400,000. Manufacturing: none; virtually all consumer manufactures are imported. Construction: n.a. Energy production (consumption): electricity (kW-hr; 2000) 33,000,000 (33,000,000); coal, none (n.a.); crude petroleum, none (n.a.); petroleum products (metric tons; 2000) none (44,000); natural gas, none (n.a.).
Population economically active (1992): 2,453[6, 9]; activity rate of total population 35.9% (participation rates: over age 15, n.a.; female, n.a.; unemployed, 18.2%).
Price and earnings indexes: [10].
Household income and expenditure. Average household size (1992) 10.0[5]; income per household: n.a.; sources of income: n.a.; expenditure: n.a.
Land use as % of total land area (2000): in temporary crops, n.a., in permanent crops, n.a., in pasture, n.a.; overall forest area, n.a.

Foreign trade

Balance of trade (current prices)

	1994	1995	1996	1997	1998	1999
U.S.$'000,000	+20.0	+0.2	+3.3	+10.1	+20.0	+20.0
% of total	33.3%	0.4%	4.6%	24.9%	33.3%	33.3%

Imports (1999): U.S.$20,000,000 (agricultural products 65.0%, of which food 45.0%; remainder 35.0%). *Major import sources* (2001): Australia 49.4%; United States 16.9%; Indonesia 7.9%; India 4.8%; United Kingdom 4.6%.
Exports (1999): U.S.$40,000,000 (phosphate, virtually 100%). *Major export destinations* (2001): New Zealand 28.6%; Australia 23.6%; Thailand 14.7%; South Korea 11.5%; Japan 9.6%.

Transport and communications

Transport. Railroads (2001): length 3 mi, 5 km; passenger traffic, n.a.; metric ton-km cargo, n.a. Roads (2001): total length 19 mi, 30 km (paved 79%). Vehicles (1989): passenger cars, trucks, and buses 1,448. Merchant marine (1992): vessels 2, total deadweight tonnage 5,791. Air transport (1996): passenger-mi 151,000,000, passenger-km 243,000,000; short ton-mi cargo 15,000,000, metric ton-km cargo 24,000,000; airports (2001) with scheduled flights 1.

Communications

Medium	date	unit	number	units per 1,000 persons
Daily newspapers	—	circulation	—	—
Radio	1997	receivers	7,000	609
Television	1997	receivers	500	48
Telephones	2001	main lines	1,900	160
Cellular telephones	2001	subscribers	1,500	130
Internet	2001	users	300	26

Education and health

Educational attainment (1992)[6]. Percentage of population age 5 and over having: primary education or less 77.4%; secondary education 12.9%; higher 4.1%; not stated 5.6%. *Literacy* (1999): total population age 15 and over literate 99%.

Education (2002)[6]

	schools	teachers	students	student/ teacher ratio
Primary (age 6–13)	5	64[11]	1,566	...
Secondary (age 14–17)	4	53[11]	609	...

Health (2003): physicians 5 (1 per 2,016 persons); hospital beds 60 (1 per 168 persons); infant mortality rate per 1,000 live births 10.3.
Food (2002)[12]: daily per capita caloric intake 2,952 (vegetable products 70%, animal products 30%); 129% of FAO recommended minimum requirement.

Military

Total active duty personnel (2003): Nauru does not have any military establishment. The defense is assured by Australia, but no formal agreement exists.

[1]Nauruan is the national language; English is the language of business and government. [2]Government offices are located in Yaren district. [3]Preliminary. [4]Largely from phosphate exports. [5]Employed only. [6]Nauruan only. [7]Most non-Nauruans are phosphate industry contract workers. [8]400 offshore banks were registered in Nauru in mid-2001. [9]Excludes activity not stated. [10]Minimum wage remained constant between November 1992 and the end of 1997. [11]1997. [12]Data for Oceania.

Internet resources for further information:
- **Secretariat of the Pacific Community**
  http://www.spc.org.nc/prism/country/country.html

Nepal

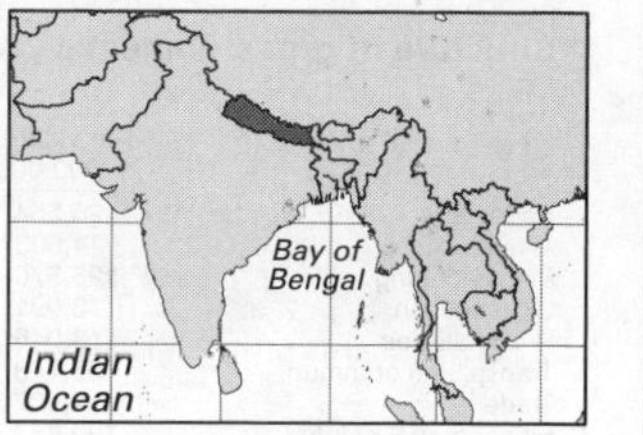

Official name: Nepal Adhirajya (Kingdom of Nepal).
Form of government: constitutional monarchy[1].
Chief of state: King.
Head of government: Prime Minister.
Capital: Kathmandu.
Official language: Nepali.
Official religion: Hinduism.
Monetary unit: 1 Nepalese rupee (NRs) = 100 paisa (pice); valuation (Sept. 1, 2004) 1 U.S.$ = NRs 74.15; 1 £ = NRs 133.40.

Area and population

Development regions	Capitals	area sq mi	area sq km	population 2001 census[2]
Eastern	Dhankuta	10,987	28,456	5,344,476
Central	Kathmandu	10,583	27,410	8,031,629
Western	Pokhara	11,351	29,398	4,571,013
Mid-western	Surkhet	16,362	42,378	3,012,975
Far-western	Dipayal	7,544	19,539	2,191,330
TOTAL		56,827	147,181	23,151,423

Demography

Population (2004): 24,692,000.
Density (2004): persons per sq mi 434.5, persons per sq km 167.8.
Urban-rural (2002): urban 13.0%; rural 87.0%.
Sex distribution (2001): male 49.95%; female 50.05%.
Age breakdown (2001): under 15, 39.3%; 15–29, 27.0%; 30–44, 17.1%; 45–59, 10.1%; 60–74, 5.2%; 75 and over, 1.3%.
Population projection: (2010) 28,061,000; (2020) 33,600,000.
Doubling time: 29 years.
Ethnic composition (2000): Nepalese 55.8%; Maithili 10.8%; Bhojpuri 7.9%; Tharu 4.4%; Tamang 3.6%; Newar 3.0%; Awadhi 2.7%; Magar 2.5%; Gurkha 1.7%; other 7.6%.
Religious affiliation (2001): Hindu 80.6%; Buddhist 10.7%; Muslim 4.2%; Kirat (local traditional belief) 3.6%; Christian 0.5%; other 0.4%.
Major cities (2001): Kathmandu 671,846; Biratnagar 166,674; Lalitpur 162,991; Pokhara 156,312; Birganj 112,484.

Vital statistics

Birth rate per 1,000 population (2003): 32.5 (world avg. 21.3).
Death rate per 1,000 population (2003): 9.8 (world avg. 9.1).
Natural increase rate per 1,000 population (2002): 22.7 (world avg. 12.2).
Total fertility rate (avg. births per childbearing woman; 2003): 4.4.
Life expectancy at birth (2003): male 59.4 years; female 58.6 years.
Major causes of death per 100,000 population: n.a.; however, the leading causes of mortality are infectious and parasitic diseases, diseases of the respiratory system, and diseases of the nervous system.

National economy

Budget (2001). Revenue: NRs 48,596,000,000 (taxes on goods and services 34.1%, taxes on international trade 28.1%, income taxes 19.0%, state property revenues 1.9%, other 16.9%). Expenditures: NRs 74,289,000,000 (current expenditure 59.3%, of which education 14.0%, defense 7.8%, health 2.8%; development expenditure 40.7%, of which economic services 25.7%).
Public debt (external, outstanding; 2002): U.S.$2,913,000,000.
Production (metric tons except as noted). Agriculture, forestry, fishing (2002): rice 4,130,000, sugarcane 2,248,000, corn (maize) 1,511,000, potatoes 1,473,000, wheat 1,258,000, millet 282,000; livestock (number of live animals) 6,979,000 cattle, 6,607,000 goats, 3,701,000 buffalo, 934,000 pigs, 840,000 sheep; roundwood (2002) 13,988,000 cu m; fish catch (2002) 33,270. Mining and quarrying (2001): limestone 280,000; talc 6,000; salt 2,000. Manufacturing (value added in U.S.$'000,000; 1996): textiles 99; tobacco products 46; beverages 35; food products 30; wearing apparel 24. Energy production (consumption): electricity (kW-hr; 2000) 1,425,000,000 (1,525,000,000); coal (metric tons; 2000) 18,000 (435,000); petroleum products (metric tons; 2000) none (684,000).
Tourism (2002): receipts from visitors U.S.$107,000,000; expenditures by nationals abroad (2001) U.S.$80,000,000.
Population economically active (2001): total 11,138,000; activity rate of total population *c.* 48% (participation rates: ages 10 years and over, 58.2%[3]; female [1991] 45.5%; unemployed 5.1%).

Price and earnings indexes (2000 = 100)

	1997	1998	1999	2000	2001	2002	2003
Consumer price index	81.6	90.8	97.6	100.0	102.7	105.8	111.8
Monthly earnings index[4]	68.5	85.1	85.1	100.0	100.0	100.0	...

Household income and expenditure (1984–85). Average household size (2001) 5.4; income per household NRs 14,796 (U.S.$853); sources of income: self-employment 63.4%, wages and salaries 25.1%, rent 7.5%, other 4.0%; expenditure: food and beverages 61.2%, housing 17.3%, clothing 11.7%, health care 3.7%, education and recreation 2.9%, transportation and communications 1.2%.
Gross national product (at current market prices; 2003): U.S.$5,824,000,000 (U.S.$240 per capita).

Structure of gross domestic product and labour force

	2000–01 in value NRs '000,000	2000–01 % of total value	1999 labour force[5]	1999 % of labour force[5]
Agriculture	149,040	36.3	7,203,000	76.1
Mining	1,981	0.5	8,000	0.1
Manufacturing	35,566	8.7	552,000	5.8
Construction	39,571	9.6	344,000	3.7
Public utilities	6,989	1.7	26,000	0.3
Transp. and commun.	33,050	8.1	135,000	1.4
Trade	45,381	11.0	522,000	5.5
Finance	41,835	10.2	51,000	0.5
Services	40,060	9.8	614,000	6.5
Other	16,721[6]	4.1[6]	8,000	0.1
TOTAL	410,194	100.0	9,463,000	100.0

Land use as % of total land area (2000): in temporary crops 21.3%, in permanent crops 0.6%, in pasture 12.3%; overall forest area 27.3%.

Foreign trade[7]

Balance of trade (current prices)

	1997	1998	1999	2000	2001	2002
NRs '000,000	–74,419	–50,613	–55,969	–54,569	–55,141	–66,368
% of total	61.2%	44.7%	40.5%	32.3%	33.3%	42.9%

Imports (2000–01): NRs 115,687,000,000 (basic manufactures [including fabrics, yarns, and made-up articles] 35.6%, machinery and transport equipment 19.9%, chemicals and chemical products 11.2%, mineral fuels [mostly refined petroleum] 9.7%). *Major import sources* (2001): India 36.7%; Argentina 15.5%; China 15.3%; U.A.E. 5.8%; Singapore 5.1%.
Exports (2000–01): NRs 55,654,000,000 (ready-made garments 23.6%, carpets 15.4%, pashminas[8] 12.4%, vegetable ghee 6.4%). *Major export destinations* (2001): U.S. 30.7%; India 30.2%; Germany 11.6%; Argentina 7.4%; Japan 2.3%.

Transport and communications

Transport. Railroads (2002): route length 59 km; passengers carried 1,600,000; freight handled 22,000 metric tons. Roads (1997): total length 7,700 km (paved 42%). Vehicles (2000): passenger cars 53,073; trucks and buses 32,065. Air transport (2000): passenger-km 1,023,000,000; metric ton-km cargo 108,000,000; airports (1996) with scheduled flights 24.

Communications

Medium	date	unit	number	units per 1,000 persons
Daily newspapers	1996	circulation	250,000	11
Radio	2000	receivers	883,000	39
Television	2000	receivers	159,000	7.0
Telephones	2003	main lines	371,800	16
Cellular telephones	2003	subscribers	50,400	2.1
Personal computers	2002	units	85,000	3.7
Internet	2002	users	80,000	3.4

Education and health

Educational attainment (2001). Percentage of population age 6 and over having: no formal schooling 8.7%; primary education 41.9%; incomplete secondary 30.6%; complete secondary and higher 17.6%; unknown 1.2%. *Literacy* (2001): total population age 15 and over literate *c.* 53%; males literate *c.* 60%; females literate *c.* 43%.

Education (2000)

	schools	teachers	students	student/ teacher ratio
Primary (age 6–10)	25,927	97,879	3,623,150	37.0
Secondary (age 11–15) Vocational	11,639	44,873	1,330,360	29.6
Higher	2	6,313	149,060	23.6

Health (1999): physicians 1,259 (1 per 17,589 persons); hospital beds 5,190 (1 per 4,267 persons); infant mortality rate per 1,000 live births (2003) 70.6.
Food (2001): daily per capita caloric intake 2,459 (vegetable products 94%, animal products 6%); 112% of FAO recommended minimum.

Military

Total active duty personnel (2003): 63,000 (army 100.0%). *Military expenditure as percentage of GNP* (1999): 0.8% (world 2.4%); per capita expenditure U.S.$2.

[1]Bicameral parliament dissolved by the monarch from May 2002 through early October 2004. [2]Final figures adjusted for undercount. [3]Usually economically active. [4]Ending fiscal year; minimum monthly wage rates for unskilled industrial workers. [5]Employed only. [6]Includes indirect taxes less imputed bank service charges. [7]Imports c.i.f.; exports f.o.b. [8]Fine shawls made of cashmere or cashmere-silk blend.

Internet resources for further information:
- **Central Bank of Nepal http://www.nrb.org.np**
- **National Planning Commission http://npc.gov.np:8080**

Netherlands, The

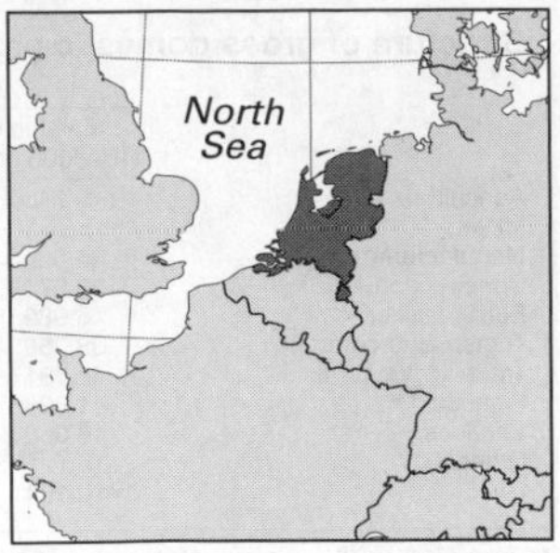

Official name: Koninkrijk der Nederlanden (Kingdom of The Netherlands).
Form of government: constitutional monarchy with a parliament (States General) comprising two legislative houses (First Chamber [75]; Second Chamber [150]).
Chief of state: Monarch.
Head of government: Prime Minister.
Seat of government: The Hague.
Capital: Amsterdam.
Official language: Dutch.
Official religion: none.
Monetary unit: 1 euro (€) = 100 cents; valuation (Sept. 1, 2004) 1 U.S.$ = €0.82; 1 £ = €1.48[1].

Area and population

		area		population
Provinces	Capitals	sq mi	sq km	2003[2] estimate
Drenthe	Assen	1,035	2,680	481,472
Flevoland	Lelystad	931	2,412	351,558
Friesland	Leeuwarden	2,217	5,741	640,060
Gelderland	Arnhem	1,983	5,137	1,960,384
Groningen	Groningen	1,146	2,968	573,225
Limburg	Maastricht	853	2,209	1,142,017
Noord-Brabant	's-Hertogenbosch	1,962	5,082	2,400,164
Noord-Holland	Haarlem	1,567	4,059	2,572,809
Overijssel	Zwolle	1,321	3,421	1,100,741
Utrecht	Utrecht	556	1,439	1,152,357
Zeeland	Middelburg	1,133	2,934	378,142
Zuid-Holland	The Hague	1,331	3,446	3,439,913
TOTAL		16,034[3, 4]	41,528[4]	16,192,842

Demography

Population (2004): 16,275,000.
Density (2004)[5]: persons per sq mi 1,248, persons per sq km 481.8.
Urban-rural (2001): urban 89.6%; rural 10.4%.
Sex distribution (2003[2]): male 49.50%; female 50.50%.
Age breakdown (2000[2]): under 15, 18.6%; 15–29, 19.3%; 30–44, 24.2%; 45–59, 19.8%; 60–74, 12.1%; 75 and over, 6.0%.
Population projection: (2010) 16,667,000; (2020) 17,212,000.
Ethnic composition (by place of origin [including 2nd generation]; 2002[2]): Netherlander 81.6%; Indonesian 2.5%; German 2.5%; Turkish 2.1%; Surinamese 2.0%; Moroccan 1.8%; Netherlands Antillean/Aruban 0.8%; other 6.7%[6].
Religious affiliation (1999[2]): Roman Catholic 31.0%; Reformed (NHK) 14.0%; other Reformed 7.0%; Muslim 4.5%; Hindu 0.5%; nonreligious and other 43.0%.
Major urban agglomerations (2000[2]): Amsterdam 1,002,868; Rotterdam 989,956; The Hague 610,245; Utrecht 366,186; Eindhoven 302,274.

Vital statistics

Birth rate per 1,000 population (2003): 12.4 (world avg. 21.3); legitimate 72.8%; illegitimate 27.2%.
Death rate per 1,000 population (2003): 8.7 (world avg. 9.1).
Natural increase rate per 1,000 population (2003): 3.0 (world avg. 12.2).
Total fertility rate (avg. births per childbearing woman; 2003): 1.7.
Marriage rate per 1,000 population (2000): 5.3.
Life expectancy at birth (2003): male 76.2 years; female 80.9 years.
Major causes of death per 100,000 population (2000): diseases of the circulatory system 310.1; malignant neoplasms (cancers) 237.9; diseases of the respiratory system 92.5; accidents and violence 32.6.

National economy

Budget (1997). Revenue: f. 324,360,000,000 (social security taxes 41.1%, income and corporate taxes 24.8%, value-added and excise taxes 22.7%, property taxes 3.0%). Expenditures: f. 337,620,000,000 (social security and welfare 37.4%, health 14.8%, education 10.0%, interest payments 9.1%, defense 3.9%, transportation 3.5%).
Public debt (2002): U.S.$240,951,000,000.
Production (metric tons except as noted). Agriculture, forestry, fishing (2002): potatoes 7,363,000, sugar beets 6,250,000, wheat 1,057,000, onions 882,000, tomatoes 580,000, carrots 375,000, apples 333,000, barley 315,000, flowering bulbs and tubers 59,800 acres (24,200 hectares), of which tulips 26,200 acres (10,600 hectares), cut flowers/plants under glass 14,392 acres (5,823 hectares); livestock (number of live animals; 2002) 11,648,000 pigs, 3,858,000 cattle, 1,186,000 sheep; roundwood (2002) 839,000 cu m; fish catch (2001) 570,226. Manufacturing (value added in €'000,000; 2000): food, beverages, and tobacco 11,625; chemicals and chemical products 8,314; electric/electronic machinery 6,429; printing and publishing 5,699. Energy production (consumption): electricity (kW-hr; 2000) 92,110,000,000 (111,025,000,000); coal (metric tons; 2000) negligible (12,972,000); crude petroleum (barrels; 2000) 9,889,000 (377,450,000); petroleum products (metric tons; 2000) 63,322,000 (34,027,000); natural gas (cu m; 2000) 76,741,000,000 (51,469,000,000).
Household income and expenditure. Average household size (2003) 2.3; disposable income per household (2000) €26,653 (U.S.$24,521); sources of income (1996): wages 48.4%, transfers 28.5%, self-employment 11.3%; expenditure (2000): housing and energy 23.2%, food and beverages 14.2%, transportation and communications 11.7%, textiles and clothing 6.4%.
Gross national product (2003): U.S.$426,641,000,000 (U.S.$26,310 per capita).

Structure of gross domestic product and labour force

	1999		2001	
	in value f. '000,000	% of total value	labour force	% of labour force
Agriculture	20,554	2.5	224,000	2.8
Mining	14,503	1.8	9,000	0.1
Manufacturing	125,570	15.2	1,115,000	13.8
Construction	43,091	5.2	508,000	6.3
Public utilities	13,046	1.6	34,000	0.4
Transp. and commun.	55,723	6.8	486,000	6.0
Trade	112,907	13.7	1,545,000	19.1
Finance, real estate	199,652	24.2	1,251,000	15.5
Pub. admin., defense	87,044	10.6	541,000	6.7
Services	84,717	10.3	1,613,000	19.9
Other	67,176[7]	8.1[7]	756,000[8]	9.4[8]
TOTAL	823,983	100.0	8,086,000[3]	100.0

Population economically active (1998): total 7,735,000; activity rate of total population 49.3% (participation rates: ages 15–64, 72.9%; female 42.5%; unemployed [February 2001–January 2002] 2.0%).

Price and earnings indexes (2000 = 100)

	1997	1998	1999	2000	2001	2002	2003
Consumer price index	93.5	95.4	97.5	100.0	104.5	108.2	110.4
Hourly earnings index	90.8	93.7	96.4	100.0	104.2	108.0	110.8

Tourism (2002): receipts U.S.$7,706,000,000; expenditures U.S.$12,919,000,000.
Land use as % of total land area (2000): in temporary crops 26.9%, in permanent crops 1.0%, in pasture 29.9%; overall forest area 11.1%.

Foreign trade[9]

Balance of trade (current prices)

	1997	1998	1999	2000	2001	2002
€'000,000	+32,732[10]	+26,926[10]	+9,325	+12,367	+23,682	+31,053
% of total	4.4%	4.5%	2.5%	2.8%	5.2%	7.1%

Imports (2001): €217,151,000,000 (computers and related equipment 11.9%, chemicals and chemical products 11.4%, mineral fuels 10.1%, food 8.2%, road vehicles 7.0%). *Major import sources:* Germany 18.5%; U.S. 9.8%; Belgium Luxembourg 9.3%; U.K. 8.9%; France 5.7%.
Exports (2001): €240,833,000,000 (chemicals and chemical products 15.4%, food 12.3%, computers and related equipment 11.7%, mineral fuels 9.2%). *Major export destinations:* Germany 25.6%; Belgium-Luxembourg 11.9%; U.K. 11.2%; France 10.3%; Italy 6.2%.

Transport and communications

Transport. Railroads (2001): length 2,809 km; passenger-km 14,392,000,000; metric ton-km cargo 4,293,000,000. Roads (1999): total length 116,500 km (paved 90%). Vehicles (2002): passenger cars 6,711,000; trucks and buses 997,000. Air transport (2001)[11]: passenger-km 57,848,000,000; metric ton-km cargo 4,464,000,000; airports (1996) 6.

Communications

Medium	date	unit	number	units per 1,000 persons
Daily newspapers	2000	circulation	4,870,000	306
Radio	2000	receivers	15,600,000	980
Television	2000	receivers	8,570,000	538
Telephones	2003	main lines	10,004,000	614
Cellular telephones	2003	subscribers	12,500,000	768
Personal computers	2002	units	7,557,000	467
Internet	2003	users	8,500,000	822

Education and health

Educational attainment (2001). Percentage of population ages 15–64 having: primary education 14.1%; lower secondary 9.3%; upper secondary/vocational 54.3%; tertiary vocational 15.1%; university 6.9%; unknown 0.3%.

Education (2001–02)[12]

	schools	teachers	students	student/ teacher ratio
Primary (age 6–12)	7,397	...	1,604,000	...
Secondary (age 12–18)	795	...	904,000	...
Vocational[13]	64	...	258,000	...
Higher[14]	13	...	159,000	...

Health (2000): physicians 27,161 (1 per 586 persons); hospital beds 90,747 (1 per 175 persons); infant mortality rate per 1,000 live births (2003) 5.2.
Food (2001): daily per capita caloric intake 3,282 (vegetable products 64%, animal products 36%); 117% of FAO recommended minimum requirement.

Military

Total active duty personnel (2003): 53,130 (army 43.6%, navy 22.8%, air force 20.8%, paramilitary 12.8%). *Military expenditure as percentage of GNP* (1999): 1.8% (world 2.4%); per capita expenditure U.S.$445.

[1]The Netherlands guilder (f.) was the former monetary unit; on Jan. 1, 2002, f. 2.20 = €1. [2]January 1. [3]Detail does not add to total given because of rounding. [4]Includes inland water area totaling 1,380 sq mi (3,574 sq km) and coastal water totaling 1,610 sq mi (4,171 sq km). [5]Based on land area only (13,044 sq mi [33,783 sq km]). [6]Includes Netherlander-EU country 4.7%. [7]Imputed value-added tax less subsidies and bank service charges. [8]Includes 220,000 registered unemployed. [9]Imports c.i.f.; exports f.o.b. [10]In guilders. [11]KLM only. [12]Public schools only. [13]Colleges only. [14]Universities.

Internet resources for further information:
- **Statistics Netherlands http://www.cbs.nl/en**

Netherlands Antilles

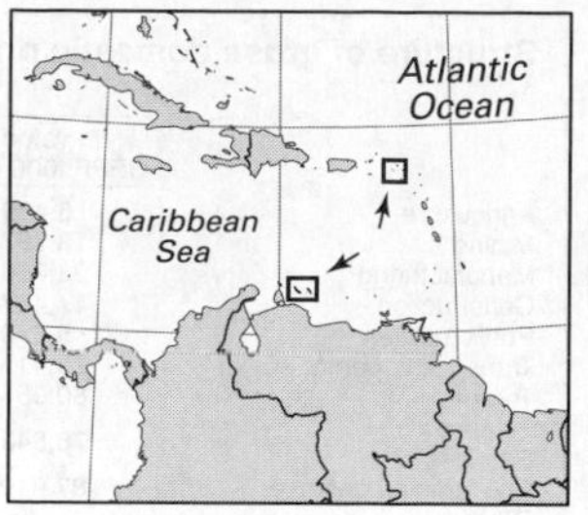

Official name: Nederlandse Antillen (Netherlands Antilles).
Political status: nonmetropolitan territory of The Netherlands with one legislative house (States of the Netherlands Antilles [22]).
Chief of state: Dutch Monarch represented by Governor.
Head of government: Prime Minister.
Capital: Willemstad.
Official language: Dutch.
Official religion: none.
Monetary unit: 1 Netherlands Antillean guilder (NA f.) = 100 cents; valuation (Sept. 1, 2004) 1 U.S.$ = NA f. 1.79; 1 £ = NA f. 3.22.

Area and population

		area		population
Island councils	Capitals	sq mi	sq km	2001 census
Leeward Islands				
Bonaire	Kralendijk	111	288	10,791
Curaçao	Willemstad	171	444	130,627
Windward Islands				
Saba	The Bottom	5	13	1,349
Sint Eustatius, or Statia	Oranjestad	8	21	2,292
Sint Maarten (Dutch part only)	Philipsburg	13	34	30,594
TOTAL		308	800	175,653

Demography

Population (2004): 179,000.
Density (2004): persons per sq mi 581.1, persons per sq km 223.7.
Urban-rural (2001): urban 69.6%; rural 30.4%.
Sex distribution (2003): male 46.81%; female 53.19%.
Age breakdown (2001): under 15, 24.2%; 15–29, 18.2%; 30–44, 25.5%; 45–59, 19.0%; 60–74, 9.4%; 75 and over, 3.7%.
Population projection: (2010) 179,000; (2020) 179,000.
Ethnic composition (2000): local black-other (Antillean Creole) 81.1%; Dutch 5.3%; Surinamese 2.9%; other (significantly West Indian black) 10.7%.
Religious affiliation (2001): Roman Catholic 72.0%; Protestant 16.0%; Spiritist 0.9%; Buddhist 0.5%; Jewish 0.4%; Bahā'ī 0.3%; Hindu 0.2%; Muslim 0.2%; other/unknown 9.5%.
Major cities (2001): Willemstad (urban agglomeration) 125,000; Kralendijk 7,900; Philipsburg 6,300.

Vital statistics

Birth rate per 1,000 population (2001): 13.6 (world avg. 21.3); (1988)[1] legitimate 51.6%; illegitimate 48.4%.
Death rate per 1,000 population (2001): 6.4 (world avg. 9.1).
Natural increase rate per 1,000 population (2001): 7.2 (world avg. 12.2).
Total fertility rate (avg. births per childbearing woman; 2003): 2.0.
Marriage rate per 1,000 population (2003): 4.2.
Divorce rate per 1,000 population (1999): 2.6.
Life expectancy at birth (2003): male 73.2 years; female 77.7 years.
Major causes of death per 100,000 population (1993): infectious and parasitic diseases/diseases of the respiratory system 209.0; diseases of the circulatory system 180.2; malignant neoplasms (cancers) 117.7.

National economy

Budget (2002). Revenue: NA f. 616,500,000 (tax revenue 86.5%, of which sales tax 40.6%, import duties 20.6%, excise on gasoline 12.7%; nontax revenue 11.7%; grants 1.8%). Expenditures: NA f. 669,000,000 (current expenditures 94.7%, of which transfers 32.0%, wages 31.1%, interest payments 16.1%, goods and services 12.9%; development expenditures 5.3%).
Production (metric tons except as noted). Agriculture, forestry, fishing: [2]; livestock (number of live animals; 2002) 13,000 goats, 7,300 sheep, 2,600 asses, 135,000 chickens; roundwood, n.a.; fish catch (2001) 955. Mining and quarrying (2001): salt 500,000, sulfur by-product 30,000. Manufacturing (2000): residual fuel oil 5,112,000; gas-diesel oils 2,525,000; other manufactures include electronic parts, cigarettes, textiles, rum, and Curaçao liqueur. Energy production (consumption): electricity (kW-hr; 2000) 1,120,500,000 (1,120,000,000); coal, none (none); crude petroleum (barrels; 2000) none (107,000,000); petroleum products (metric tons; 2000) 10,459,000 (2,052,000); natural gas, none (none).
Land use as % of total land area (2000): in temporary crops 10.0%, in permanent crops, n.a., in pasture, n.a.; overall forest area *c.* 1%.
Tourism (2001): receipts from visitors U.S.$746,000,000; expenditures by nationals abroad (2000) U.S.$339,000,000.
Household income and expenditure. Average household size (2001) 2.9; income per household: n.a.; sources of income: n.a.; expenditure (1996)[3, 4]: housing 26.5%, transportation and communications 19.9%, food 14.7%, household furnishings 8.8%, recreation and education 8.2%, clothing and footwear 7.5%.
Gross domestic product (at current market prices; 2001): U.S.$2,546,000,000 (U.S.$14,720 per capita).

Structure of gross domestic product and labour force

	1999		2001	
	in value NA f. '000,000	% of total value	labour force	% of labour force
Agriculture, forestry / Mining	40.6	0.8	441 / 131	0.5 / 0.2
Manufacturing	231.0	4.8	4,619	5.7
Construction	185.5	3.9	5,335	6.5
Public utilities	180.5	3.7	1,131	1.4
Transp. and commun.	401.1	8.3	5,410	6.6
Trade, hotels, restaurants	785.9	16.3	19,002	23.3
Finance, real estate, insurance	1,059.9	22.0	10,103	12.4
Pub. admin., defense	779.6	16.2	5,997	7.3
Services	756.1	15.7	15,961	19.6
Other	399.1[5]	8.3[5]	13,428[6]	16.5[6]
TOTAL	4,819.3	100.0	81,558	100.0

Population economically active (2001): total 81,558; activity rate of total population 46.4% (participation rates: ages 15–64, 68.7%; female 49.0%; unemployed [2002] 14.2%).

Price and earnings indexes (2000 = 100)

	1997	1998	1999	2000	2001	2002	2003
Consumer price index	93.1	94.2	94.5	100.0	101.8	102.2	104.3
Monthly earnings index[7]	100.0	100.0	...	...	...	...	...

Public debt (2003): U.S.$2,458,000,000.

Foreign trade

Balance of trade (current prices)

	1997	1998	1999	2000	2001	2002[8]
NA f. '000,000	–1,723	–1,616	–1,709	–1,764	–1,866	–1,309
% of total	52.6%	50.4%	53.3%	46.3%	48.7%	49.2%

Imports (2001): NA f. 2,850,000,000 (nonpetroleum domestic imports 67.8%, crude petroleum and petroleum products 17.6%, imports of Curaçao free zone 14.6%). *Major import sources* (2000): United States 25.8%; Mexico 20.7%; Gabon 6.6%; Italy 5.8%; The Netherlands 5.5%.
Exports (2001): NA f. 984,000,000 (goods procured in ports for ships' bunkers 37.7%, reexports of Curaçao free zone 30.9%, nonpetroleum domestic exports 18.3%). *Major export destinations* (2000): United States 35.9%; Guatemala 9.4%; Venezuela 8.7%; France 5.4%; Singapore 2.8%.

Transport and communications

Transport. Railroads: none. Roads (1992): total length 367 mi, 590 km (paved 51%). Vehicles (1999): passenger cars 74,840; trucks and buses 17,415. Air transport (2001)[9]: passenger arrivals and departures 2,131,000; freight loaded and unloaded 18,900 metric tons; airports (2000) with scheduled flights 5.

Communications

Medium	date	unit	number	units per 1,000 persons
Daily newspapers	1996	circulation	70,000	341
Radio	1997	receivers	217,000	1,039
Television	1997	receivers	69,000	330
Telephones	2001	main lines	81,000	372
Cellular telephones	1998	subscribers	16,000	77
Internet	1999	users	2,000	9.3

Education and health

Educational attainment (2001). Percentage of population 25 and over having: no formal schooling 0.8%; primary education 24.2%; lower secondary 42.8%; upper secondary 16.8%; higher 11.4%; unknown 4.0%. *Literacy* (1995): total population age 15 and over literate 194,900 (96.6%); males literate 93,300 (96.6%); females literate 101,600 (96.6%).

Education (1999–2000)

	schools	teachers	students	student/ teacher ratio
Primary (age 6–12)	90	1,139[10]	23,205	21.1[10]
Secondary (age 12–17)	22	461[10]	8,112	18.2[10]
Voc., teacher tr.	32	853[10]	7,576	9.7[10]
Higher	2	123	825	6.7

Health (2001): physicians 333 (1 per 520 persons); hospital beds 1,343 (1 per 129 persons); infant mortality rate per 1,000 live births (2003) 10.7.
Food (2001): daily per capita caloric intake 2,565 (vegetable products 72%, animal products 28%); 106% of FAO recommended minimum requirement.

Military

Total active duty personnel (2004): 1,000 Dutch naval personnel in Netherlands Antilles and Aruba.

[1]Excludes Sint Eustatius. [2]Mostly tomatoes, beans, cucumbers, gherkins, melons, and lettuce grown on hydroponic farms; aloes grown for export, divi-divi pods, and sour orange fruit are nonhydroponic crops. [3]Curaçao only. [4]Weights of consumer price index components. [5]Taxes less subsidies. [6]Includes 11,876 unemployed. [7]Minimum wages only. [8]Excludes fourth quarter. [9]Curaçao and Sint Maarten airports. [10]1996–97.

Internet resources for further information:
- **Central Bank of the Netherlands Antilles**
  http://www.centralbank.an
- **Central Bureau of Statistics**
  http://central-bureau-of-statistics.an

New Caledonia

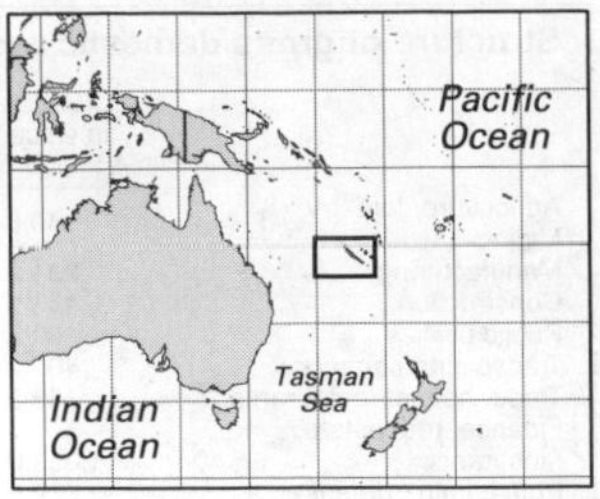

Official name: Nouvelle-Calédonie (New Caledonia).
Political status[1]: overseas collectivity (France) with one legislative house (Congress[2] [54]).
Chief of state: President of France represented by High Commissioner.
Head of government: President.
Capital: Nouméa.
Official language: none[3].
Official religion: none.
Monetary unit: 1 franc of the Comptoirs français du Pacifique (CFPF) = 100 centimes; valuation (Sept. 1, 2004)[4] 1 U.S.$ = CFPF 98.12; 1 £ = CFPF 176.52.

Area and population

Provinces Island(s)	Capitals	area sq mi	area sq km	population 2001 estimate
Loyauté (Loyalty)	Wé	765	1,981	23,297
Lifou		466	1,207	11,131
Maré		248	642	7,758
Ouvéa		51	132	4,408
Nord (Northern)	Koné	3,305	8,561	45,434
Belep		27	70	1,032
New Caledonia (part)		3,278	8,491	44,402
Sud (Southern)	Nouméa	3,102	8,033	147,158
New Caledonia (part)		3,043	7,881	145,297
Pins		59	152	1,861
TOTAL		7,172	18,575	215,889

Demography

Population (2004): 224,000.
Density (2004): persons per sq mi 31.2, persons per sq km 12.0.
Urban-rural (2002): urban 79.0%; rural 21.0%.
Sex distribution (2003): male 50.33%; female 49.67%.
Age breakdown (2003): under 15, 29.7%; 15–29, 25.4%; 30–44, 21.6%; 45–59, 13.9%; 60–74, 7.5%; 75 and over, 1.9%.
Population projection: (2010) 241,000; (2020) 265,000.
Doubling time: 52 years.
Ethnic composition (1996): Melanesian 45.3%, of which local (Kanak) 44.1%, Vanuatuan 1.2%; European 34.1%; Wallisian or Futunan 9.0%; Indonesian 2.6%; Tahitian 2.6%; Vietnamese 1.4%; other 5.0%.
Religious affiliation (2000): Roman Catholic 54.2%; Protestant 14.0%; Muslim 2.7%; other Christian 2.1%; other 27.0%.
Major cities (1996): Nouméa 76,293 (urban agglomeration 118,823); Mont-Dore 20,780[5]; Dumbéa 13,888[5].

Vital statistics

Birth rate per 1,000 population (2003): 18.6 (world avg. 21.3); (1996) legitimate 36.4%; illegitimate 63.6%.
Death rate per 1,000 population (2003): 5.1 (world avg. 9.1).
Natural increase rate per 1,000 population (2003): 13.5 (world avg. 12.2).
Total fertility rate (avg. births per childbearing woman; 2003): 2.4.
Marriage rate per 1,000 population (2001): 4.3.
Divorce rate per 1,000 population (1999): 0.8.
Life expectancy at birth (2003): male 70.6 years; female 76.6 years.
Major causes of death per 100,000 population (1999): diseases of the circulatory system 143.5; malignant neoplasms (cancers) 119.9; accidents, poisonings, and violence 95.4; diseases of the respiratory system 52.0.

National economy

Budget (2001). Revenue: $A 1,184,000,000 (tax revenue 74.7%, nontax revenue 25.3%). Expenditures: $A 1,156,000,000 (current expenditure 90.1%, development expenditure 9.9%).
Production (metric tons except as noted). Agriculture, forestry, fishing (2003): coconuts 16,000, yams 11,222, vegetables 3,900, sweet potatoes 3,000, fruit 2,968, corn (maize) 2,500; livestock (number of live animals) 110,000 cattle, 25,500 pigs, 510,000 poultry; roundwood (2002) 4,800 cu m; fish catch (2001) 5,197, of which shrimp 1,870, tuna 1,008, sea cucumbers 489. Mining and quarrying (metric tons): nickel ore (2003) 6,625,000, of which nickel content (2002) 59,867; cobalt (2002) 900 (recovered). Manufacturing (metric tons; 2003): cement (2002) 100,080; ferronickel (metal content) 50,666; nickel matte (metal content) 10,857; other manufactures include beer, copra cake, and soap. Energy production (consumption): electricity (kW-hr; 2002) 1,758,000,000 (1,758,000,000); coal (metric tons; 2000) none (160,000); crude petroleum, none (none); petroleum products (metric tons; 2000) none (405,000); natural gas, none (none).
Population economically active (1996): total 80,589; activity rate of total population 40.9% (participation rates: over age 14, 57.3%; female 39.7%; unemployed 18.6%).

Price and earnings indexes (2000 = 100)[6]

	1997	1998	1999	2000	2001	2002	2003
Consumer price index	97.4	97.7	97.8	100.0	102.3	103.8	104.9
Earnings index[7]	97.2	98.4	98.9	100.0	127.5	127.5	131.9

Public debt (external, outstanding; 1999): U.S.$746,000,000.
Gross national product (at current market prices; 2001): U.S.$3,200,000,000 (U.S.$15,060 per capita).

Structure of gross domestic product and labour force

	1997 in value CFPF '000,000	1997 % of total value	2001 labour force[8]	2001 % of labour force[8]
Agriculture	6,439	1.9	2,490	4.0
Mining	13,307	3.8	1,772	2.9
Manufacturing	38,766	11.1	5,720[9]	9.3[9]
Construction	17,447	5.0	7,031	11.4
Public utilities	5,370	1.5	[9]	[9]
Transp. and commun.	23,415	6.7	2,861	4.6
Trade	80,054	22.9	9,799	15.9
Finance }	76,543	21.9	5,461	8.9
Services }			11,165	18.1
Pub. admin., defense	87,919	25.2	…	…
Other	—	—	15,348[10]	24.9[10]
TOTAL	349,260	100.0	61,647	100.0

Household income and expenditure. Average household size (2002) 3.9; average annual income per household (1991) CFPF 3,361,233 (U.S.$32,879)[11]; sources of income (1991): wages and salaries 68.2%, transfer payments 13.7%, other 18.1%; expenditure (1991): food and beverages 25.9%, housing 20.4%, transportation and communications 16.1%, recreation 4.8%.
Tourism: receipts from visitors (2001) U.S.$93,000,000.
Land use as % of total land area (2000): in temporary crops 0.4%, in permanent crops 0.3%, in pasture 11.8%; overall forest area 20.4%.

Foreign trade[12]

Balance of trade (current prices)

	1997	1998	1999	2000	2001	2002
CFPF '000,000	–40,949	–58,910	–60,521	–41,312	–63,824	–68,022
% of total	26.2%	42.0%	36.6%	20.8%	34.6%	36.5%

Imports (2002): CFPF 127,123,000,000 (machinery and apparatus 18.2%, food 15.6%, transportation equipment 15.2%, mineral products [mostly coal and refined petroleum] 13.4%, chemicals and chemical products 8.4%). *Major import sources* (2003): France 50.0%; Singapore 10.4%; Australia 10.2%; New Zealand 4.1%; Germany 3.8%.
Exports (2002): CFPF 59,101,000,000 (ferronickel 64.2%, nickel matte 13.0%, nickel ore 12.3%, shrimp 2.3%). *Major export destinations* (2003): France 26.0%; Japan 21.4%; Taiwan 16.6%; Spain 8.8%; Australia 6.4%.

Transport and communications

Transport. Railroads: none. Roads (2000): total length 3,375 mi, 5,432 km (paved [1993] 52%). Vehicles: passenger cars (2001) 85,500; trucks and buses (1997) 23,000. Air transport (2003)[13]: passenger-km 46,000,000, metric ton-km cargo 4,115,000; airports (2004) with scheduled flights 11.

Communications

Medium	date	unit	number	units per 1,000 persons
Daily newspapers	1996	circulation	24,000	121
Radio	1997	receivers	107,000	533
Television	1999	receivers	101,000	480
Telephones	2002	main lines	52,000	232
Cellular telephones	2002	subscribers	80,000	357
Internet	2003	users	60,000	262

Education and health

Educational attainment (1996). Percentage of population age 14 and over having: no formal schooling 5.7%; primary education 28.9%; lower secondary 30.2%; upper secondary 24.6%; higher 10.5%. *Literacy:* n.a.

Education (2001)

	schools	teachers	students	student/ teacher ratio
Primary (age 6–10)	289	1,837	36,996	20.1
Secondary (age 11–17) } Vocational }	64	2,371	29,036	12.2
Higher	4[14]	55[15]	2,069[15]	37.6[15]

Health (1999): physicians 418 (1 per 497 persons); hospital beds 838 (1 per 248 persons); infant mortality rate per 1,000 live births (2003) 8.1.
Food (2001): daily per capita caloric intake 2,770 (vegetable products 76%, animal products 24%); 120% of FAO recommended minimum requirement.

Military

Total active duty personnel (2003): 2,700 French troops. *Military expenditure as percentage of GNP:* n.a.

[1]The Nouméa Accord granting New Caledonia limited autonomy (with likely independence by 2013) was formally signed on May 5, 1998. New Caledonia became an overseas collectivity per March 2003 amendments to the French constitution. [2]Operates in association with 3 provincial assemblies. [3]Kanak languages and French have special recognition per Nouméa Accord. [4]Pegged to the euro on January 1, 2002, at €1 = CFPF 119.25. [5]Within Nouméa urban agglomeration. [6]All figures are end-of-year. [7]Based on minimum hourly wage. [8]Excludes civil servants and self-employed. [9]Manufacturing includes Public utilities. [10]Includes 5,488 not adequately defined and 9,860 unemployed. [11]Includes both monetary (92%) and nonmonetary income (8%). [12]Imports c.i.f.; exports f.o.b. [13]Air Calédonie only. [14]1996. [15]2000.

Internet resources for further information:

- **Ministère de l'Outre-Mer http://www.outre-mer.gouv.fr**
- **Institut de la statistique et des études économiques Nouvelle-Calédonie http://www.isee.nc**

New Zealand

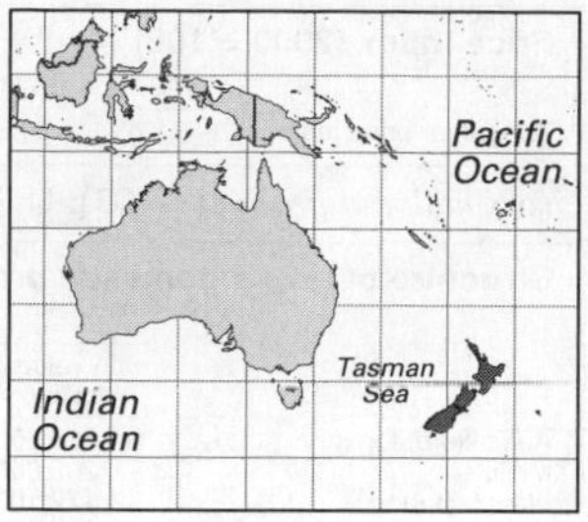

Official name: New Zealand (English); Aotearoa (Māori).
Form of government: constitutional monarchy with one legislative house (House of Representatives [120[1]]).
Chief of state: British Monarch, represented by Governor-General.
Head of government: Prime Minister.
Capital: Wellington.
Official languages: English; Māori.
Official religion: none.
Monetary unit: 1 New Zealand dollar ($NZ) = 100 cents; valuation (Sept. 1, 2004) 1 U.S.$ = $NZ 1.52; 1 £ = $NZ 2.74.

Area and population

Islands / Regional Councils	area sq mi	area sq km	population 2001 census
North Island	44,702	115,777	2,870,688
Auckland	...	...	1,173,639
Bay of Plenty	...	...	245,100
Gisborne[2]	...	...	44,142
Hawkes Bay	...	...	146,109
Manawatu-Wanganui	...	...	222,123
Northland	...	...	144,363
Taranaki	...	...	102,684
Waikato	...	...	364,986
Wellington	...	...	427,542
South Island	58,384	151,215	949,242
Canterbury	...	...	494,952
Marlborough[2]	...	...	42,528
Nelson[2]	...	...	43,560
Otago	...	...	194,487
Southland	...	...	94,371
Tasman[2]	...	...	44,880
West Coast	...	...	34,464
Offshore islands	1,368	3,542	819
TOTAL	104,454	270,534	3,820,749

Demography

Population (2004): 4,060,000[3].
Density (2004): persons per sq mi 38.9, persons per sq km 15.0.
Urban-rural (2002): urban 86.0%; rural 14.0%.
Sex distribution (2001): male 49.07%; female 50.93%.
Age breakdown (2001): under 15, 22.5%; 15–29, 20.4%; 30–44, 23.0%; 45–59, 18.0%; 60–74, 10.7%; 75 and over, 5.4%.
Population projection: (2010) 4,298,000; (2020) 4,621,000.
Ethnic composition (2001): European 73.8%; Māori (local Polynesian) 13.5%; Asian 6.1%; other Pacific Peoples (mostly other Polynesian) 6.0%; other 0.6%.
Religious affiliation (2001): Christian 55.2%, of which Anglican 15.3%, Roman Catholic 12.7%, Presbyterian 11.3%; nonreligious 26.9%; Buddhist 1.1%; Hindu 1.0%; other religions/not specified 15.8%.
Major urban areas (2001): Auckland 1,074,513; Wellington 339,750; Christchurch 334,107; Hamilton 166,128; Dunedin 107,088.

Vital statistics

Birth rate per 1,000 population (2003): 14.1 (world avg. 21.3); (2001) legitimate 56.3%; illegitimate 43.7%.
Death rate per 1,000 population (2003): 7.5 (world avg. 9.1).
Natural increase rate per 1,000 population (2003): 6.6 (world avg. 12.2).
Total fertility rate (avg. births per childbearing woman; 2003): 1.8.
Marriage rate per 1,000 population (2001): 5.1.
Life expectancy at birth (2003): male 75.3 years; female 81.4 years.
Major causes of death per 100,000 population (2001): diseases of the circulatory system 273.5; malignant neoplasms (cancers) 201.0; diseases of the respiratory system 52.4; accidents, suicide, homicide, and other violence 35.4.

National economy

Budget (2000–01). Revenue: $NZ 37,156,000,000 (income taxes 59.4%, taxes on goods and services 34.4%, nontax revenue 6.2%). Expenditures: $NZ 37,019,000,000 (social welfare 37.0%, health 19.0%, education 17.6%).
Production (metric tons except as noted). Agriculture, forestry, fishing (2002): apples 537,000, barley 406,000, wheat 355,000, corn (maize) 157,000; livestock (number of live animals) 43,142,000 sheep, 9,633,000 cattle, 358,000 pigs; roundwood (2000) 20,523,000 cu m; fish catch (2001) 637,000. Mining and quarrying (2001): limestone 4,746,000; iron ore and sand concentrate 1,636,000; gold 9,850 kg. Manufacturing (1999): wood pulp 1,572,000; chemical fertilizers 1,365,000; wool yarn 23,500; wine 602,000 hectolitres; carpets 9,980,000 sq m[4]. Energy production (consumption): electricity (kW-hr; 2000) 39,010,000,000 (39,010,000,000); hard coal (metric tons; 2000) 3,355,000 (1,755,000); lignite (metric tons; 2000) 213,000 (261,000); crude petroleum (barrels; 2000) 13,068,000 (40,001,000); petroleum products (metric tons; 2000) 5,038,000 (5,365,000); natural gas (cu m; 2000) 5,445,000,000 (5,444,000,000).
Household income and expenditure. Average household size (1998) 2.8; annual income per household[5] (2000–01) $NZ 53,076 (U.S.$24,403); sources of income (1998): wages and salaries 65.8%, transfer payments 15.2%, self-employment 9.8%, other 9.2%; expenditure (2000–01): housing 23.9%, food 16.5%, transportation 15.9%, household goods 12.8%, clothing 3.2%.
Tourism (2002): receipts U.S.$2,918,000,000; expenditures U.S.$1,480,000,000.
Gross national product (2003): U.S.$63,608,000,000 (U.S.$15,870 per capita).

Structure of gross domestic product and labour force

	2001–02 in value $NZ '000,000[6]	2001–02 % of total value	2001 labour force	2001 % of labour force
Agriculture	8,991 (Agriculture and Mining)	8.3 (Agriculture and Mining)	166,100	8.6
Mining			3,700	0.2
Manufacturing	16,886	15.6	288,900	15.0
Construction	3,872	3.6	112,200	5.8
Public utilities	2,041	1.9	10,100	0.5
Transp. and commun.	11,164	10.3	112,400	5.8
Trade	16,699	15.4	393,600	20.5
Finance	26,878	24.8	232,000	12.1
Pub. admin., defense	4,349	4.0	499,600 (Pub. admin., defense and Services)	25.9 (Pub. admin., defense and Services)
Services	13,328	12.3		
Other	4,152	3.8	107,100[7]	5.6[7]
TOTAL	108,360	100.0	1,925,700	100.0

Population economically active (2000): total 1,923,700; activity rate 50.1% (participation rates: over age 15, 66.2%; female 45.3%; unemployed 5.7%).

Price and earnings indexes (2000 = 100)

	1997	1998	1999	2000	2001	2002	2003
Consumer price index	96.3	97.6	97.4	100.0	102.6	105.4	107.2
Weekly earnings index[8]	93.4	95.4	98.4	100.0	102.7	...	...

Land use as % of total land area (2000): in temporary crops 5.6%, in permanent crops 6.9%, in pasture 51.7%; overall forest area 29.7%.

Foreign trade[9]

Balance of trade (current prices)

	1997	1998	1999	2000	2001	2002[10]
$NZ '000,000	+1,007	+812.0	–1,896	+347	+2,987	+760
% of total	2.4%	1.8%	3.9%	0.6%	4.8%	1.3%

Imports (2001–02[11]): $NZ 32,165,000,000 (machinery and apparatus 21.4%, crude and refined petroleum 13.7%, vehicles 13.4%, plastics 3.7%). *Major import sources:* Australia 21.4%; U.S. 13.7%; Japan 10.8%; China 7.2%; Germany 4.7%.
Exports (2001–02[11]): $NZ 31,676,000,000 (domestic exports 96.2%, of which dairy products 20.6%, beef and sheep meat 12.7%, wood and paper products 10.8%, machinery and apparatus 6.1%, fruits and nuts 3.7%; reexports 3.8%). *Major export destinations:* Australia 19.9%; U.S. 15.3%; Japan 11.5%; U.K. 4.9%; South Korea 4.5%; China 4.5%.

Transport and communications

Transport. Railroads (1999): route length 3,912 km; passengers carried (2001–02) 14,330,000; metric ton-km cargo (1998) 3,960,000,000. Roads (1999): total length 92,075 km (paved 62%). Vehicles (2002): passenger cars 1,960,503; trucks and buses 374,005. Air transport[12] (1999): passenger km 19,879,000,000; metric ton-km cargo 851,744,000; airports (1997) 36.

Communications

Medium	date	unit	number	units per 1,000 persons
Daily newspapers	2000	circulation	799,000	207
Radio	2000	receivers	3,850,000	997
Television	2000	receivers	2,010,000	522
Telephones	2002	main lines	1,765,000	448
Cellular telephones	2003	subscribers	2,599,000	648
Personal computers	2002	units	1,630,000	414
Internet	2003	users	2,110,000	526

Education and health

Educational attainment (2001). Percentage of population ages 25–64 having: no formal schooling to incomplete secondary 26%; secondary 36%; vocational and some undergraduate 24%; completed undergraduate 14%.
Literacy: virtually 100.0%.

Education (1999)

	schools	teachers	students	student/ teacher ratio
Primary (age 5–12)[13]	2,366	25,832	478,065	18.5
Secondary (age 13–17)	335	15,401	226,164	14.7
Voc., teacher tr.	29	5,428	111,855	20.6
Higher[14]	7	5,008	105,996	21.2

Health (2002): physicians 8,403 (1 per 469 persons); hospital beds 23,825 (1 per 165 persons); infant mortality rate per 1,000 live births (2003) 6.1.
Food (2001): daily per capita caloric intake 3,235 (vegetable products 67%, animal products 33%); 123% of FAO recommended minimum requirement.

Military

Total active duty personnel (2003): 8,610 (army 51.5%, air force 23.0%, navy 25.6%). *Military expenditure as percentage of GNP* (1999): 1.2% (world 2.4%); per capita expenditure U.S.$156.

[1]Includes seven elected seats allocated to Māoris. [2]Reorganized as a unitary authority that is administered by a district council with regional powers. [3]Adjusted for undercount of the 2001 census including New Zealand residents temporarily overseas. [4]1996–97. [5]Gross income. [6]Constant 1995–96 prices. [7]Mostly unemployed. [8]Excluding overtime. [9]Import figures are f.o.b. in balance of trade and c.i.f. in commodities and trading partners. [10]Excludes December. [11]Beginning October 1. [12]Air New Zealand only. [13]Includes composite schools that provide both primary and secondary education. [14]Universities only.

Internet resources for further information:

- **Statistics New Zealand/Te Tari Tatau http://www.stats.govt.nz**
- **Reserve Bank of New Zealand http://www.rbnz.govt.nz**

Nicaragua

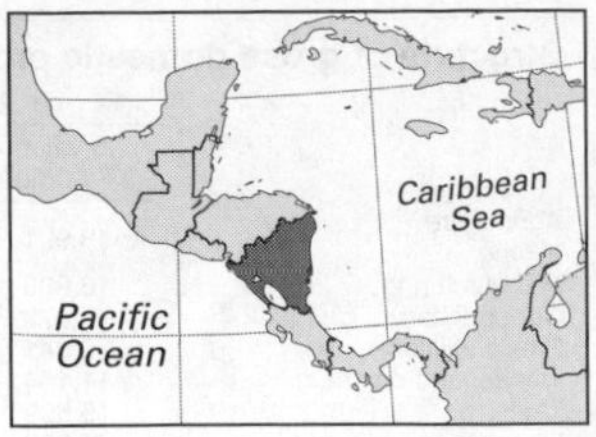

Official name: República de Nicaragua (Republic of Nicaragua).
Form of government: unitary multiparty republic with one legislative house (National Assembly [92[1]]).
Head of state and government: President.
Capital: Managua.
Official language: Spanish.
Official religion: none.
Monetary unit: 1 córdoba oro (C$) = 100 centavos; valuation (Sept. 1, 2004) 1 U.S.$ = C$15.94; 1 £ = C$28.68.

Area and population

		area[2]		population
Departments	Capitals	sq mi	sq km	2004 estimate[3]
Boaco	Boaco	1,613	4,177	173,444
Carazo	Jinotepe	417	1,081	182,640
Chinandega	Chinandega	1,862	4,822	452,190
Chontales	Juigalpa	2,502	6,481	186,672
Estelí	Estelí	861	2,230	220,521
Granada	Granada	402	1,040	196,275
Jinotega	Jinotega	3,714	9,620	305,818
León	León	2,107	5,457	402,710
Madriz	Somoto	659	1,708	137,111
Managua	Managua	1,338	3,465	1,413,257
Masaya	Masaya	236	611	324,855
Matagalpa	Matagalpa	2,627	6,804	497,931
Nueva Segovia	Ocotal	1,194	3,093	217,444
Río San Juan	San Carlos	2,912	7,541	97,825
Rivas	Rivas	835	2,162	172,119
Autonomous regions				
North Atlantic	Puerto Cabezas	12,549	32,501	256,440
South Atlantic	Bluefields	10,636	27,546	389,240
TOTAL LAND AREA		46,464	120,340[4]	
INLAND WATER		3,874	10,034	
TOTAL		50,337[4]	130,373[4]	5,626,492

Demography

Population (2004): 5,360,000[5].
Density (2004)[6]: persons per sq mi 115.4, persons per sq km 44.5.
Urban-rural (2001): urban 56.5%; rural 43.5%.
Sex distribution (2003): male 50.01%; female 49.99%.
Age breakdown (2003): under 15, 38.8%; 15–29, 30.4%; 30–44, 17.5%; 45–59, 8.6%; 60–74, 3.7%; 75 and over, 0.9%.
Population projection: (2010) 5,990,000; (2020) 7,020,000.
Doubling time: 32 years.
Ethnic composition (2000): mestizo (Spanish/Indian) 63.1%; white 14.0%; black 8.0%; multiple ethnicities 5.0%; other 9.9%.
Religious affiliation (1995): Roman Catholic 85.1%; Protestant 11.6%, of which Evangelical 8.8%; nonreligious 1.3%; other 2.0%.
Major cities (1995): Managua (urban agglomeration, 2003) 1,098,000; León 123,865; Chinandega 97,387; Masaya 88,971; Granada 71,783; Estelí 71,550.

Vital statistics

Birth rate per 1,000 population (2003): 26.1 (world avg. 21.3).
Death rate per 1,000 population (2003): 4.6 (world avg. 9.1).
Natural increase rate per 1,000 population (2003): 21.5 (world avg. 12.2).
Total fertility rate (avg. births per childbearing woman; 2003): 3.0.
Life expectancy at birth (2003): male 67.7 years; female 71.8 years.
Major causes of death per 100,000 population (2000)[7]: diseases of the circulatory system 63; malignant neoplasms 30; accidents, injuries, and violence 20; diseases of the respiratory system 18; infectious and parasitic diseases 15.

National economy

Budget (2002). Revenue: C$8,592,400,000 (tax revenue 94.7%, of which sales tax 42.2%, import duties 29.2%, tax on income and profits 18.8%; nontax revenue 5.3%). Expenditures: C$11,905,000,000 (current expenditure 67.2%, development expenditure 32.8%).
Public debt (external, outstanding; 2002): U.S.$5,576,000,000.
Production (metric tons except as noted). Agriculture, forestry, fishing (2002): sugarcane 3,389,000, corn (maize) 483,330, rice 264,000, dry beans 183,000, sorghum 90,000, oranges 73,000, bananas 54,000, cassava 52,000, coffee 48,000, soybeans 3,400; livestock (number of live animals) 3,350,000 cattle, 420,000 pigs; roundwood 5,920,000 cu m; fish catch (2001) 28,520, of which crustaceans 15,486. Mining and quarrying (2001): gold 117,350 troy oz. Manufacturing (value added in C$'000,000; 2002[8]): food 1,975; beverages 1,349; cement, bricks, tiles 576; refined petroleum 222; chemical products 206. Energy production (consumption): electricity (kW-hr; 2002) 2,620,000,000 ([2000] 2,403,000,000); coal, none (none); crude petroleum (barrels; 2000) none (6,069,000); petroleum products (metric tons; 2000) 785,000 (1,138,000); natural gas, none (none).
Tourism (2002): receipts from visitors U.S.$110,000,000; expenditures by nationals abroad U.S.$69,000,000.
Land use as % of total land area (2000): in temporary crops 15.9%, in permanent crops 1.9%, in pasture 39.7%; overall forest area 27.0%.
Population economically active (2001): total 1,900,400; activity rate of total population 37.7% (participation rates: ages 15–64 [2000] 64.1%; female [2000] 29.5%; unemployed 10.5%).

Price index (2000 = 100)

	1997	1998	1999	2000	2001	2002	2003
Consumer price index	71.3	80.6	89.6	100.0	107.4	111.6	117.4

Gross national product (2003): U.S.$3,989,000,000 (U.S.$730 per capita).

Structure of gross domestic product and labour force

	2002		2001	
	in value C$'000	% of total value	labour force	% of labour force
Agriculture, forestry	11,339,600	31.6	728,000	38.3
Mining	290,800	0.8	10,800	0.6
Manufacturing	5,172,100	14.4	132,300	7.0
Construction	2,265,400	6.3	105,200	5.5
Public utilities	399,800	1.1	6,100	0.3
Transp. and commun.	1,230,500	3.4	52,600	2.8
Trade, restaurants	8,266,000	23.0	278,000	14.6
Finance, real estate	1,879,700	5.2	22,500	1.2
Pub. admin., defense	3,085,600	8.6	65,000	3.4
Services	2,007,500	5.6	303,300	16.0
Other	—	—	202,800[9]	10.7[9]
TOTAL	35,937,000	100.0	1,900,400[4]	100.0[4]

Household income and expenditure. Average household size (2002) 5.6; expenditure (1999)[10]: food and beverages 41.8%, education 9.8%, housing 9.8%, transportation 8.5%.

Foreign trade[11]

Balance of trade (current prices)

	1998	1999	2000	2001	2002	2003
U.S.$'000,000	–824	–1,154	–1,008	–1,015	–1,057	–1,116
% of total	41.8%	51.4%	43.9%	45.6%	48.5%	48.0%

Imports (2003): U.S.$1,887,000,000 (nondurable consumer goods 25.9%; mineral fuels 17.4%; capital goods for industry 11.8%; durable consumer goods 7.5%). *Major import sources:* U.S. 24.7%; Venezuela 9.7%; Costa Rica 9.0%; Mexico 8.4%; Guatemala 7.3%.
Exports (2003): U.S.$605,000,000 (non-marine food products 44.6%, of which coffee 14.1%, meat 13.5%; lobster 6.0%; gold 5.8%; shrimp 5.5%). *Major export destinations:* U.S. 33.4%; El Salvador 17.3%; Costa Rica 8.1%; Honduras 7.2%; Mexico 4.6%.

Transport and communications

Transport. Railroads: [12]. Roads (2002): total length 18,709 km (paved 11%). Vehicles (2002): passenger cars 83,168; trucks and buses 121,796. Air transport (2000): passenger-km 72,000,000; metric ton-km cargo 600,000; airports (1997) with scheduled flights 10.

Communications

Medium	date	unit	number	units per 1,000 persons
Daily newspapers	2000	circulation	152,000	30
Radio	2000	receivers	1,370,000	270
Television	2000	receivers	350,000	69
Telephones	2002	main lines	171,600	32
Cellular telephones	2002	subscribers	202,800	38
Personal computers	2002	units	90,000	17
Internet	2002	users	150,000	28

Education and health

Educational attainment (1995). Percentage of population age 25 and over having: no formal schooling 30.6%; no formal schooling (literate) 3.9%; primary education 39.2%; secondary 17.0%; technical 3.1%; incomplete undergraduate 2.2%; complete undergraduate 4.0%. *Literacy* (2000): total population age 15 and over literate 66.5%; males literate 66.3%; females literate 66.8%.

Education (2002)

	schools	teachers	students	student/ teacher ratio
Primary (age 7–12)	8,251	21,020[13]	923,391	...
Secondary (age 13–18)	1,249	5,970[13]	364,012	...
Higher	108[14]	3,840[14]	...	14.6[14]

Health: physicians (2002) 2,066 (1 per 2,491 persons); hospital beds 5,031 (1 per 1,023 persons); infant mortality rate (2003) 31.2.
Food (2001): daily per capita caloric intake 2,256 (vegetable products 92%, animal products 8%); 99% of FAO recommended minimum requirement.

Military

Total active duty personnel (2003): 14,000 (army 85.7%, navy 5.7%, air force 8.6%). *Military expenditure as percentage of GNP* (1999): 1.2% (world 2.4%); per capita expenditure U.S.$5.

[1]Includes 2 unsuccessful 2001 presidential candidates meeting special conditions. [2]Lakes and lagoons are excluded from the areas of departments and autonomous regions. [3]Official projection based on 1995 census. [4]Detail does not add to total given because of rounding. [5]Estimate of U.S. Bureau of the Census International Database (2004 revision). [6]Based on land area. [7]Estimates. [8]At prices of 1980. [9]Represents unemployed. [10]Weights of consumer price index components. [11]Imports f.o.b. in balance of trade and c.i.f. in commodities and trading partners. [12]Public railroad service ended in January 1994; private rail service (2000) 4 mi (6 km). [13]1996. [14]2000.

Internet resources for further information:
- **Central Bank of Nicaragua http://www.bcn.gob.ni/english**
- **Instituto Nacional de Estadísticas y Censos http://www.inec.gob.ni**

Niger

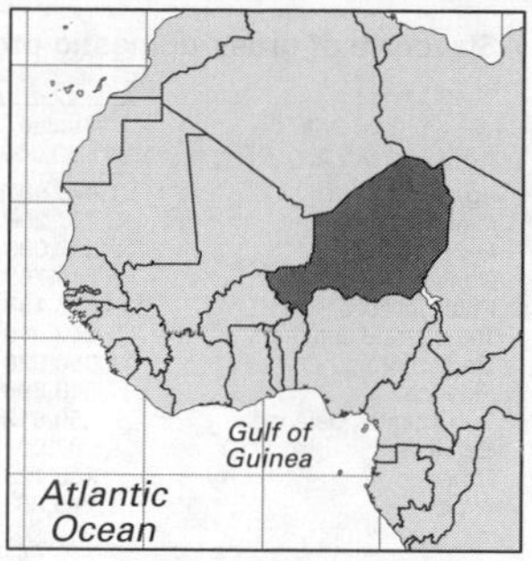

Official name: République du Niger (Republic of Niger).
Form of government: multiparty republic with one legislative house (National Assembly [113]).
Head of state and government: President, assisted by Prime Minister.
Capital: Niamey.
Official language: French.
Official religion: none.
Monetary unit: 1 CFA franc (CFAF) = 100 centimes; valuation (Sept. 1, 2004) 1 U.S.$ = CFAF 539.75; 1 £ = CFAF 970.98[1].

Area and population

		area		population
				2001
Departments	Capitals	sq mi	sq km	census
Agadez	Agadez	242,117	627,080	313,274
Diffa	Diffa	56,764	147,017	329,658
Dosso	Dosso	12,255	31,740	1,479,095
Maradi	Maradi	15,143	39,219	2,202,035
Tahoua	Tahoua	41,080	106,397	1,908,100
Tillabéri	Tillabéri	35,336	91,521	1,858,342
Zinder	Zinder	56,437	146,170	2,024,898
City				
Niamey	Niamey	155	402	674,950
TOTAL		459,286[2]	1,189,546	10,790,352

Demography

Population (2004): 11,679,000.
Density (2004): persons per sq mi 25.4, persons per sq km 9.8.
Urban-rural (2001): urban 16.2%; rural 83.8%.
Sex distribution (2001): male 49.86%; female 50.14%.
Age breakdown (2001): under 15, 48.0%; 15–29, 26.3%; 30–44, 14.1%; 45–59, 7.8%; 60–74, 3.2%; 75 and over, 0.6%.
Population projection: (2010) 13,647,000; (2020) 17,112,000.
Doubling time: 25 years.
Ethnolinguistic composition (2000): Zerma- (Djerma-) Songhai 25.7%; Tazarawa 14.9%; Fulani (Peul) 11.1%; Hausa 6.6%; other 41.7%.
Religious affiliation (2000): Sunnī Muslim 90.7%; traditional beliefs 8.7%; Christian 0.5%; other 0.1%.
Major cities (2001): Niamey 674,950 (urban agglomeration [2003] 890,000); Zinder 170,574; Maradi 147,038; Agadez 76,957; Tahoua 72,446; Arlit 67,398.

Vital statistics

Birth rate per 1,000 population (2003): 49.5 (world avg. 21.3).
Death rate per 1,000 population (2003): 21.7 (world avg. 9.1).
Natural increase rate per 1,000 population (2003): 27.8 (world avg. 12.2).
Total fertility rate (avg. births per childbearing woman; 2003): 6.9.
Marriage rate per 1,000 population: n.a.
Divorce rate per 1,000 population: n.a.
Life expectancy at birth (2003): male 42.3 years; female 42.1 years.
Major causes of death: n.a.; however, among selected major causes of infectious disease registered at medical facilities were malaria, measles, diarrhea, meningitis, pneumonia, diphtheria, tetanus, viral hepatitis, and poliomyelitis; malnutrition and shortages of trained medical personnel are widespread.

National economy

Budget (2003). Revenue: CFAF 221,281,000,000 (taxes 69.3%, external aid and gifts 29.2%, nontax revenue 1.5%). Expenditures: CFAF 272,200,000,000 (current expenditures 57.6%, of which education 10.9%, defense and public order 8.4%, interest 6.4%, health 3.8%; development expenditures 42.4%).
Public debt (external, outstanding; 2002): U.S.$1,604,000,000.
Tourism (2002): receipts from visitors U.S.$28,000,000; expenditures by nationals abroad U.S.$16,000,000.
Gross national product (2003): U.S.$2,361,000,000 (U.S.$200 per capita).

Structure of gross domestic product and labour force

	2003		1988	
	in value CFAF '000,000	% of total value	labour force[3]	% of labour force[3]
Agriculture	632,800	39.9	1,764,049	76.2
Mining	96,500	6.1	5,295	0.2
Manufacturing	104,200	6.6	65,793	2.8
Construction	30,900	1.9	13,742	0.6
Public utilities	34,500	2.2	1,778	0.1
Transp. and commun.	77,900	4.9	14,764	0.6
Trade and finance	294,000	18.5	210,354	9.1
Pub. admin., defense	121,000	7.6	59,271	2.6
Services	156,600	9.9	63,991	2.8
Other	39,300[4]	2.5[4]	116,657	5.0
TOTAL	1,587,500[2]	100.0[2]	2,315,694	100.0

Production (metric tons except as noted). Agriculture, forestry, fishing (2003): millet 2,567,200, sorghum 669,700, cowpeas 654,200, onions 320,500, sugarcane 220,000, peanuts (groundnuts) 153,700, cassava 105,000, tomatoes 100,000, rice 79,900, tobacco leaf 1,000; livestock (number of live animals) 6,900,000 goats, 4,500,000 sheep, 2,260,000 cattle, 580,000 asses, 420,000 camels, 106,000 horses; roundwood (2002) 8,601,400 cu m; fish catch (2001) 20,821. Mining and quarrying (2003): uranium 3,143; salt 3,000. Manufacturing (value added in CFAF '000,000; 1998): paper and products 3,171; food 1,697; soaps and other chemical products 1,547; textiles 784. Energy production (consumption): electricity (kW-hr; 2000) 238,000,000 (451,000,000); coal (metric tons; 2000) 175,000 (175,000); crude petroleum, none (none); petroleum products (metric tons; 2001) none (138,300); natural gas, none (none).
Population economically active (1988)[3]: total 2,315,694; activity rate of total population 31.9% (participation rates: ages 15–64, 55.2%; female 20.4%).

Price index (2000 = 100)

	1997	1998	1999	2000	2001	2002	2003
Consumer price index	108.4	113.3	110.7	100.0	104.0	106.7	105.0

Household income and expenditure. Average household size (2002) 6.4; income per household: n.a.; expenditure (1996)[5]: food, beverages, and tobacco products 45.1%, housing and energy 13.9%, transportation 12.1%, household furnishings 7.7%, clothing and footwear 5.8%.
Land use as % of total land area (2000): in temporary crops 3.5%, in permanent crops 0.01%, in pasture 9.5%; overall forest area 1.0%.

Foreign trade

Balance of trade (current prices)

	1998	1999	2000	2001	2002	2003
CFAF '000,000	–35,500	–26,200	–33,900	–43,300	–63,800	–72,400
% of total	8.3%	6.9%	7.8%	9.8%	14.1%	15.1%

Imports (2003): CFAF 275,700,000,000 (food products 28.6%, capital goods 26.3%, petroleum products 11.5%, intermediate goods 6.7%). *Major import sources:* France 17.1%; Côte d'Ivoire 15.0%; Nigeria 8.1%; Japan 4.6%.
Exports (2003): CFAF 203,300,000,000 (uranium 32.2%, reexports 17.9%, cattle 17.5%, onions 7.7%, cowpeas 5.3%). *Major export destinations:* France 37.1%; Nigeria 33.6%; Japan 17.2%; Spain 3.8%.

Transport and communications

Transport. Railroads: none. Roads (2000): total length 8,700 mi, 14,000 km (paved 26%). Vehicles (1999): passenger cars 26,000, trucks and buses 35,600. Air transport (2000)[6]: passenger-km 216,000,000; metric ton-km cargo, n.a.; airports (1999) with scheduled flights 6.

Communications

Medium	date	unit	number	units per 1,000 persons
Daily newspapers	1996	circulation	2,000	0.2
Radio	2000	receivers	1,270,000	121
Television	2000	receivers	388,000	37
Telephones	2002	main lines	22,400	1.9
Cellular telephones	2003	subscribers	24,000	2.0
Personal computers	2002	units	7,000	0.6
Internet	2002	users	15,000	1.3

Education and health

Educational attainment (1988). Percentage of population age 25 and over having: no formal schooling 85.0%; Koranic education 11.2%; primary education 2.5%; secondary 1.1%; higher 0.2%. *Literacy* (2001): total population age 15 and over literate 16.5%; males literate 24.4%; females literate 8.9%.

Education (2001–02)

	schools	teachers	students	student/ teacher ratio
Primary (age 7–12)	5,970	18,441	760,087	41.3
Secondary (age 13–19)	242	3,634	100,140	27.6
Voc., teacher tr.[7]	...	215	2,145	10.0
Higher[8]	2	355	5,569	15.7

Health: physicians (1997) 324 (1 per 28,171 persons); hospital beds, n.a.; infant mortality rate per 1,000 live births (2003) 123.6.
Food (2001): daily per capita caloric intake 2,118 (vegetable products 94%, animal products 6%); 90% of FAO recommended minimum requirement.

Military

Total active duty personnel (2003): 5,300 (army 98.1%, air force 1.9%). *Military expenditure as percentage of GNP* (1999): 1.2% (world 2.4%); per capita expenditure U.S.$2.

[1]Formerly pegged to the French franc and since Jan. 1, 2002, to the euro at the rate of 1€ = CFAF 655.96. [2]Detail does not add to total given because of rounding. [3]Excluding nomadic population. [4]Import taxes and duties. [5]Weights of consumer price index components. [6]Represents 1/11 of the traffic of Air Afrique, which is operated by 11 West African states. [7]1996–97. [8]Université de Niamey and École Nationale d'Administration du Niger only; 1997–98.

Internet resources for further information:
- **Niger Profile**
  http://www.nigerembassyusa.org/profile.html
- **Investir en zone franc**
  http://www.izf.net/izf/Index.htm

Nigeria

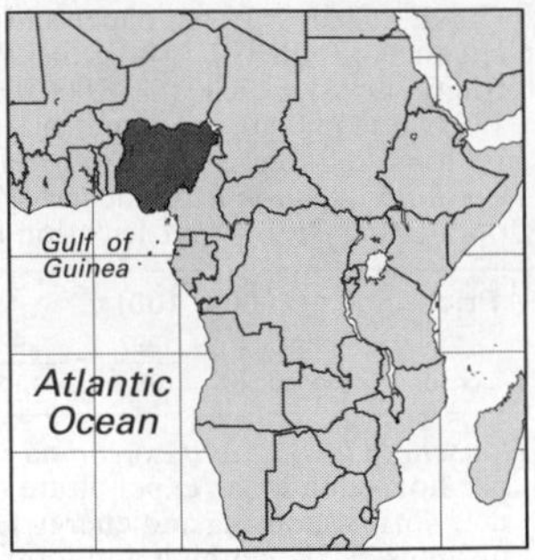

Official name: Federal Republic of Nigeria.
Form of government: federal republic with two legislative bodies (Senate [109]; House of Representatives [360]).
Head of state and government: President.
Capital: Abuja.
Official language: English.
Official religion: none.
Monetary unit: 1 Nigerian naira (₦) = 100 kobo; valuation (Sept. 1, 2004) 1 U.S.$ = ₦133.20; 1 £ = ₦239.62.

Area and population

	area	population		area	population
States[1]	sq km	1995 estimate	**States**[1]	sq km	1995 estimate
Abia	6,320	2,569,362[2]	Kebbi	36,800	2,305,768
Adamawa	36,917	2,374,892	Kogi	29,833	2,346,936
Akwa Ibom	7,081	2,638,413	Kwara	36,825	1,751,464
Anambra	4,844	3,094,783	Lagos	3,345	6,357,253
Bauchi	45,837	4,801,569[3]	Nassarawa	27,117	[6]
Bayelsa	10,773	[4]	Niger	76,363	2,775,526
Benue	34,059	3,108,754	Ogun	16,762	2,614,747
Borno	70,898	2,903,238	Ondo	14,606	4,343,230[5]
Cross River	20,156	2,085,926	Osun	9,251	2,463,185
Delta	17,698	2,873,711	Oyo	28,454	3,900,803
Ebonyi	5,670	[2]	Plateau	30,913	3,671,498[6]
Edo	17,802	2,414,919	Rivers	11,077	4,454,337[4]
Ekiti	6,353	[5]	Sokoto	25,973	4,911,118[7]
Enugu	7,161	3,534,633[2]	Taraba	54,473	1,655,443
Gombe	18,768	[3]	Yobe	45,502	1,578,172
Imo	5,530	2,779,028	Zamfara	39,762	[7]
Jigawa	23,154	3,164,134			
Kaduna	46,053	4,438,007	**Federal Capital Territory**		
Kano	20,131	6,297,165			
Katsina	24,192	4,336,363	Abuja	7,315	423,391
			TOTAL	923,768	98,967,768

Demography

Population (2004): 128,254,000.
Density (2004): persons per sq mi 359.6, persons per sq km 138.8.
Urban-rural (2002): urban 44.9%; rural 55.1%.
Sex distribution (2003): male 50.59%; female 49.41%.
Age breakdown (2003): under 15, 43.6%; 15–29, 27.9%; 30–44, 15.4%; 45–59, 8.5%; 60–74, 3.9%; 75 and over, 0.7%.
Population projection: (2010) 147,677,000; (2020) 179,288,000.
Doubling time: 25 years.
Ethnic composition (2000): Yoruba 17.5%; Hausa 17.2%; Igbo (Ibo) 13.3%; Fulani 10.7%; Ibibio 4.1%; Kanuri 3.6%; Egba 2.9%; Tiv 2.6%; Bura 1.1%; Nupe 1.0%; Edo 1.0%; other 25.0%.
Religious affiliation (2000): Christian 45.9%, of which independent Christian 15.0%, Anglican 13.0%, other Protestant 9.0%, Roman Catholic 8.0%; Muslim 43.9%; African indigenous 9.8%; other 0.4%.
Major cities (2002): Lagos 8,030,000; Kano 3,250,000; Ibadan 3,080,000; Kaduna 1,460,000; Benin City 1,050,000; Port Harcourt 1,050,000; Maiduguri 971,700; Zaria 898,900; Aba 784,500; Ilorin 756,400; Jos 742,100.

Vital statistics

Birth rate per 1,000 population (2003): 38.8 (world avg. 21.3).
Death rate per 1,000 population (2003): 13.8 (world avg. 9.1).
Natural increase rate per 1,000 population (2003): 25.0 (world avg. 12.2).
Total fertility rate (avg. births per childbearing woman; 2003): 5.4.
Life expectancy at birth (2003): male 50.9 years; female 51.1 years.
Adult population (ages 15–49) *living with HIV* (2004[8]): 5.4% (world avg. 1.1%).

National economy

Budget (2003). Revenue: ₦2,752,107,000,000 (nontax revenue 62.6%, of which crude oil export proceeds 35.1%, crude oil sales to domestic refineries 14.0%; tax revenue 37.4%, of which oil profits tax 15.9%, tax on international trade 8.5%). Expenditures: ₦2,853,918,000,000 (state and local governments 40.5%, current expenditure 32.0%, Nigerian National Petroleum Corporation [NNPC] 15.8%, capital expenditure 8.8%).
Production (metric tons except as noted). Agriculture, forestry, fishing (2003): cassava 40,927,000, yams 30,439,000, millet 9,974,000, sorghum 7,377,000, corn (maize) 6,806,000, rice 4,183,000, taro 3,500,000, peanuts (groundnuts) 2,379,000, cow peas 2,200,000, sweet potatoes 2,150,000, plantains 2,110,000, cocoa beans 380,000; livestock 27,000,000 goats, 22,500,000 sheep, 15,163,700 cattle, 6,356,297 pigs; roundwood (2002) 69,482,328 cu m; fish catch (2001) 476,544. Mining and quarrying (2002): limestone 3,400,000; marble 130,000. Manufacturing (value added in ₦'000,000; 1995): food and beverages 25,415; textiles 16,193; chemical products 11,181; machinery and transport equipment 5,639; paper products 2,828. Energy production (consumption): electricity (kW-hr; 2000) 17,757,000,000 (17,757,000,000); coal (metric tons; 2000) 61,000 (61,000); crude petroleum (barrels; 2003) 899,300,000 ([2001] 106,580,000); petroleum products (metric tons; 2000) 4,500,000 (10,199,000); natural gas (cu m; 2000) 12,539,000 (7,123,000).
Household income and expenditure. Avg. household size (2002) 4.9; annual income per household (1992–93) ₦15,000 (U.S.$760); sources of income: n.a.; expenditures: n.a.
Gross national product (2003): U.S.$42,984,000,000 (U.S.$320 per capita).

Structure of gross domestic product and labour force

	2003		1986	
	in value ₦'000,000	% of total value	labour force	% of labour force
Agriculture	1,940,587	25.7	13,259,000	43.1
Mining[9]	3,297,206	43.7	6,800	0.1
Manufacturing	293,083	3.9	1,263,700	4.1
Construction	44,753	0.6	545,600	1.8
Public utilities	5,153	0.1	130,400	0.4
Transp. and commun.	243,015	3.2	1,111,900	3.6
Trade, hotels	1,050,928	13.9	7,417,400	24.1
Finance	346,696	4.6	120,100	0.4
Pub. admin., defense	50,812	0.7	4,902,100	15.9
Services	87,907	1.2		
Other	185,123[10]	2.4[10]	2,008,500[11]	6.5[11]
TOTAL	7,545,263	100.0	30,765,500	100.0

Public debt (external, outstanding; 2002): U.S.$28,057,000,000.
Population economically active (1993–94): total 29,000,000; activity rate 31.0% (participation rates: ages 15–59, 64.4%; female 44.0%).

Price index (2000 = 100)

	1997	1998	1999	2000	2001	2002	2003
Consumer price index	75.5	83.3	87.3	100.0	113.0	127.5	145.4

Tourism (2002): receipts U.S.$263,000,000; expenditures U.S.$950,000,000.
Land use as % of total land area (2000): in temporary crops 31.0%, in permanent crops 2.9%, in pasture 43.0%; overall forest area 14.8%.

Foreign trade[12]

Balance of trade (current prices)

	1998	1999	2000	2001	2002	2003
U.S.$'000,000	+644	+5,268	+12,254	+5,675	+7,560	+9,034
% of total	3.4%	23.5%	41.3%	19.7%	33.4%	29.4%

Imports (2003): U.S.$10,853,000,000 ([2000] machinery and apparatus 21.1%; chemicals and chemical products 20.1%; food 18.9%, of which cereals 7.1%; road vehicles 10.4%; iron and steel 6.2%). *Major import sources* (2003): China 13.6%; U.K. 9.3%; France 8.0%; U.S. 7.8%; The Netherlands 6.5%; Germany 5.9%; South Korea 5.8%.
Exports (2003): U.S.$19,887,000,000 (crude petroleum 99.7%, remainder 0.3%). *Major export destinations* (2003): U.S. 40.2%; Spain 8.3%; Brazil 5.3%; France 5.0%; Indonesia 4.6%; Japan 4.1%; India 4.0%.

Transport and communications

Transport. Railroads (2000): length 3,505 km; passenger-km 179,000,000[13]; metric ton-km cargo 120,000,000[13]. Roads (1999): total length 62,598 km (paved 19%). Vehicles (1996): passenger cars 773,000; trucks and buses, n.a. Air transport[14] (2002): passenger-km 892,720,000; metric ton-km cargo 10,783,000; airports (1998) 12.

Communications

Medium	date	unit	number	units per 1,000 persons
Daily newspapers	2000	circulation	2,770,000	24
Radio	2000	receivers	23,000,000	200
Television	2000	receivers	7,840,000	68
Telephones	2003	main lines	853,100	6.9
Cellular telephones	2003	subscribers	3,149,500	26
Personal computers	2002	units	853,000	7.1
Internet	2003	users	750,000	6.1

Education and health

Literacy (2002): total population age 15 and over literate 40,700,000 (64.1%); males literate 22,600,000 (62.3%); females literate 18,100,000 (56.2%).

Education (2002)

	schools	teachers	students	student/ teacher ratio
Primary (age 6–12)	49,343	537,741	29,575,790	55.0
Secondary (age 12–17)	10,000	187,126	7,485,072	40.0
Higher	158	...	1,249,776	...

Health (2002): physicians 25,914 (1 per 4,722 persons); hospital beds 54,872 (1 per 2,230 persons); infant mortality rate per 1,000 live births (2003) 71.3.
Food (2001): daily per capita caloric intake 2,747 (vegetable products 97%, animal products 3%); 116% of FAO recommended minimum requirement.

Military

Total active duty personnel (2003): 78,500 (army 79.0%, navy 8.9%, air force 12.1%). *Military expenditure as percentage of GNP* (1999): 1.7% (world 2.4%); per capita expenditure U.S.$13.

[1]In October 1996 six new states were created: Bayelsa, Ebonyi, Ekiti, Gombe, Nassarawa, and Zamfara. [2]Ebonyi is included partly in Abia and partly in Enugu. [3]Bauchi includes Gombe. [4]Rivers includes Bayelsa. [5]Ondo includes Ekiti. [6]Plateau includes Nassarawa. [7]Sokoto includes Zamfara. [8]January 1. [9]Includes ₦3,291,115 (43.6%) from petroleum and natural gas. [10]Indirect taxes less subsidies. [11]Includes 1,263,000 unemployed. [12]Imports c.i.f.; exports f.o.b. [13]1997. [14]Nigeria Airways only.

Internet resources for further information:
- **Information on corporate Nigeria http://www.nigeriabusinessinfo.com**
- **Central Bank of Nigeria http://www.cenbank.org**

Northern Mariana Islands

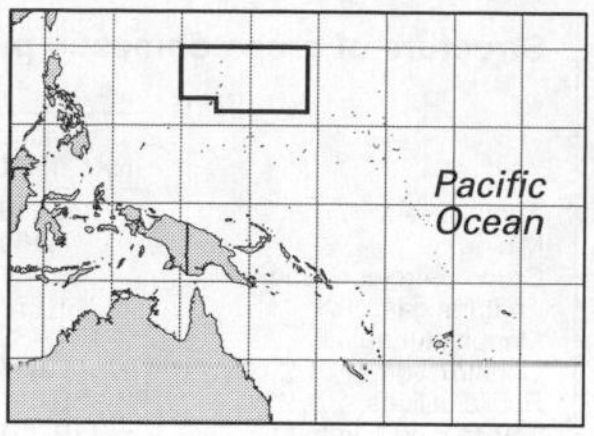

Official name: Commonwealth of the Northern Mariana Islands.
Political status: self-governing commonwealth in association with the United States, having two legislative houses (Senate [9]; House of Representatives [18])[1]
Chief of state: President of the United States.
Head of government: Governor.
Seat of government: on Saipan[2].
Official languages: Chamorro, Carolinian, and English.
Official religion: none.
Monetary unit: 1 dollar (U.S.$) = 100 cents; valuation (Sept. 1, 2004) 1 U.S.$ = £0.56.

Area and population

		area		population
Municipal councils	Major villages	sq mi	sq km	2000 census
Northern Islands[3]	...	55.3	143.2	6
Rota (island)	Songsong	32.8	85.0	3,283
Saipan (island)	San Antonio	46.5	120.4	62,392
Tinian[4]	San Jose	41.9	108.5	3,540
TOTAL		176.5[5]	457.1[5]	69,221

Demography

Population (2004): 78,000.
Density (2004): persons per sq mi 443.2, persons per sq km 170.7.
Urban-rural (2002)[6]: urban 90.0%; rural 10.0%.
Sex distribution (2000): male 46.21%; female 53.79%.
Age breakdown (2000): under 15, 22.5%; 15–29, 31.8%; 30–44, 32.3%; 45–59, 10.7%; 60–74, 2.3%; 75 and over, 0.4%.
Population projection: (2010) 78,000; (2020) 78,000.
Doubling time: 40 years.
Ethnic composition (2000)[7]: Filipino 26.2%; Chinese 22.1%; Chamorro 21.3%; Carolinian 3.8%; other Asian 7.5%; other Pacific Islander 6.6%; white 1.8%; multiethnic and other 10.7%.
Religious affiliation (1995)[8]: Roman Catholic 59.6%; Protestant 18.7%; other Christian 1.4%; other 20.3%.
Major villages (2000)[6, 9]: San Antonio 4,741; Garapan 3,588; Susupe 2,083; Capital Hill 1,498; Songsong (on Rota) 1,411; San Jose (on Tinian) 1,361.

Vital statistics

Birth rate per 1,000 population (2002): 20.0 (world avg. 21.3).
Death rate per 1,000 population (2002): 2.4 (world avg. 9.1).
Natural increase rate per 1,000 population (2002): 17.6 (world avg. 12.2).
Total fertility rate (avg. births per childbearing woman; 2002): 1.4.
Life expectancy at birth (2002): male 72.9 years; female 79.2 years.
Major causes of death per 100,000 population (1998): heart diseases 51; malignant neoplasms (cancers) 40; cerebrovascular disease 22; perinatal conditions 20; accidents 18.

National economy

Budget (2002). Revenue: U.S.$199,713,000 (tax revenue 83.5%, of which income tax 28.5%, corporate tax 24.3%, excise tax 9.4%; nontax revenue 16.5%). Expenditures: U.S.$212,089,000 (2001; health 20.4%, education 20.1%, general government 15.0%, social services 12.0%, public safety 9.3%).
Public debt (external, outstanding; 1999): U.S.$146,000,000.
Gross national product (1999): U.S.$664,600,000 (U.S.$9,600 per capita).

Structure of labour force

	2000	
	labour force	% of labour force
Agriculture, forestry, and fishing	623	1.4
Mining and quarrying	—	—
Manufacturing	17,398	39.1
Public utilities	2,117	4.8
Construction	2,785	6.2
Transp. and commun.	1,449	3.3
Trade	3,736	8.4
Finance, insurance, and real estate	1,013	2.3
Pub. admin., defense	2,583	5.8
Services	10,446	23.5
Other	2,321	5.2
TOTAL	44,471	100.0

Production (metric tons except as noted). Agriculture, forestry, fishing (1998): cucumbers 175, bananas 174, watermelons 134, radishes 99, onions 81, eggplant 76; livestock (number of live animals; 1998) 1,789 cattle, 831 pigs, 29,409 chickens; roundwood, n.a.; fish catch (2001) 197. Mining and quarrying: negligible amount of quarrying for building material. Manufacturing (value of sales in U.S.$'000,000; 2002): garments 639; bricks, tiles, and cement 12; printing and related activities 5; food products 3. Construction (new permits in U.S.$'000,000; 2002): 11.9. Energy production (consumption): electricity (kW-hr) n.a.[10]; coal, none (none); crude petroleum, none (none); petroleum products, none (none); natural gas, none (none).
Tourism (1998): receipts from visitors U.S.$394,000,000; expenditures by nationals abroad, n.a.

Population economically active (2000): total 44,471; activity rate of total population 64.2% (participation rates: ages 16 and over, 84.1%; female 49.9%; unemployed 3.9%).

Price index (2000 = 100)

	1998	1999	2000	2001	2002
Consumer price index	96.9	98.0	100.0	99.2	99.3

Household income and expenditure. Average household size (2000) 3.7; average income per household (2000) U.S.$37,015; sources of income (1994): wages 83.9%, interest and rental 7.2%, self-employment 7.2%, transfer payments 1.7%.
Land use as % of total land area (2000): in temporary crops *c.* 13%, in permanent crops *c.* 4%, in pasture *c.* 11%; overall forest area *c.* 30%.

Foreign trade

Balance of trade (current prices)

	1989	1990	1991
U.S.$'000,000	–162	–138	–129
% of total	34.7%	25.3%	19.7%

Imports (1997): U.S.$836,200,000 (clothing and accessories 37.0%, foodstuffs 9.6%, petroleum and petroleum products 8.2%, transport equipment and parts 5.0%, construction materials 4.2%). *Major import sources:* Guam 35.6%, Hong Kong 24.0%, Japan 14.1%, South Korea 9.6%, United States 7.6%.
Exports (2002): U.S.$817,000,000[11] (garments and accessories 99.8%, of which cotton garments 69.8%; remainder 0.2%). *Major export destinations:* nearly all to the United States.

Transport and communications

Transport. Railroads: none. Roads (1998): total length *c.* 225 mi, *c.* 360 km (paved, nearly 100%). Vehicles (2001): passenger cars 11,019; trucks and buses 4,928. Air transport (1999)[12]: aircraft landings 23,853; boarding passengers 562,364; airports (2002) with scheduled flights 2[13].

Communications

Medium	date	unit	number	units per 1,000 persons
Radio	1999	receivers	10,500	152
Television	1999	receivers	4,100	59
Telephones	2000	main lines	20,990	309
Cellular telephones	2000	subscribers	3,000	57
Personal computers	...	units	...	...
Internet	...	users	...	...

Education and health

Educational attainment (2000). Percentage of population age 25 and over having: primary education 14.1%; some secondary 17.5%; completed secondary 35.8%; some postsecondary 12.0%; completed undergraduate or higher 20.6%. *Literacy* (2000): *c.* 100%.

Education (2001–02)

	schools	teachers	students	student/ teacher ratio
Primary (age 6–11) } Secondary (age 12–17) }	37	728	13,323	18.3
Higher[14]	1	504	2,383	4.7

Health: physicians (1999) 31 (1 per 2,170 persons); hospital beds (1998) 74 (1 per 877 persons); infant mortality rate per 1,000 live births (2002): 7.5.
Food: n.a.

Military

The United States is responsible for military defense; headquarters of the U.S. Pacific Command are in Hawaii.

[1]Residents elect a nonvoting representative to U.S. Congress. [2]Executive and legislative branches meet at Capital Hill; the judiciary meets at Susupe. [3]Comprises the islands of Agrihan, Pagan, and Alamagan, as well as seven other uninhabited islands. [4]Comprises Tinian island and Aguijan island. [5]Area measured at high tide; at low tide, total dry land area is 184.0 square miles (476.6 square km). [6]All of Saipan was designated an urban area in 2002. [7]Includes aliens. [8]Unofficial estimate. [9]All villages are unincorporated census designated places. [10]The installed electrical capacity in 1992 was 114,020 kilowatts. [11]To U.S. only. [12]Saipan International Airport only. [13]International flights are regularly scheduled at Saipan and at Rota; Tinian has nonscheduled domestic service. Additional domestic airports mainly handle charter flights. [14]Northern Marianas College; 2000–01.

Internet resources for further information:

- **Bank of Hawaii: Economics Research Center http://www.boh.com/econ/pacific**
- **CNMI: Central Statistics Division http://www.commerce.gov.mp/csdhome.htm**

Norway

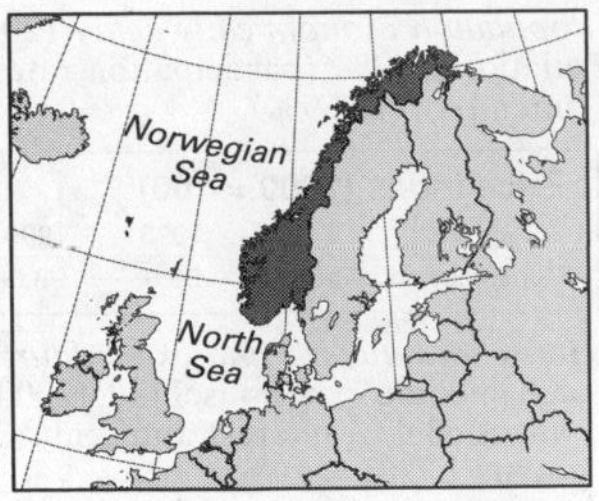

Official name: Kongeriket Norge (Kingdom of Norway).
Form of government: constitutional monarchy with one legislative house (Parliament [165]).
Chief of state: King.
Head of government: Prime Minister.
Capital: Oslo.
Official language: Norwegian.
Official religion: Evangelical Lutheran.
Monetary unit: 1 Norwegian krone (NKr) = 100 øre; valuation (Sept. 1, 2004) 1 U.S.$ = NKr 6.91; 1 £ = NKr 12.43.

Area and population

Counties	Capitals	area[1] sq mi	area[1] sq km	population 2003[2] estimate
Akershus	Oslo	1,898	4,917	483,283
Aust-Agder	Arendal	3,557	9,212	103,195
Buskerud	Drammen	5,763	14,927	241,371
Finnmark	Vadsø	18,779	48,637	73,514
Hedmark	Hamar	10,575	27,388	188,281
Hordaland	Bergen	5,965	15,449	441,660
Møre og Romsdal	Molde	5,832	15,104	244,309
Nordland	Bodø	14,851	38,463	236,950
Nord-Trøndelag	Steinkjer	8,647	22,396	127,610
Oppland	Lillehammer	9,726	25,191	183,582
Oslo	Oslo	175	454	517,401
Østfold	Moss	1,615	4,183	255,122
Rogaland	Stavanger	3,601	9,326	385,020
Sogn og Fjordane	Leikanger	7,189	18,619	107,274
Sør-Trøndelag	Trondheim	7,271	18,832	268,188
Telemark	Skien	5,913	15,315	165,855
Troms	Tromsø	9,980	25,848	152,247
Vest-Agder	Kristiansand	2,811	7,281	159,219
Vestfold	Tønsberg	856	2,216	218,171
TOTAL		125,004	323,758	4,552,252[3]

Demography

Population (2004): 4,591,000.
Density (2004): persons per sq mi 36.7, persons per sq km 14.2.
Urban-rural (2003): urban 78.6%; rural 21.4%.
Sex distribution (2003[2]): male 49.56%; female 50.44%.
Age breakdown (2003[2]): under 15, 20.0%; 15–29, 18.7%; 30–44, 22.4%; 45–59, 19.7%; 60–74, 11.4%; 75 and over, 7.8%.
Population projection: (2010) 4,731,000; (2020) 4,983,000.
Ethnic composition (2000): Norwegian 93.8%; Vietnamese 2.4%; Swedish 0.5%; Punjabi 0.4%; Urdu 0.3%; U.S. white 0.3%; Lapp 0.3%; Danish 0.3%; other 1.7%.
Major cities (2003)[2, 4]: Oslo 517,401 (urban agglomeration [2003] 795,000); Bergen 235,423; Trondheim 152,699; Stavanger 111,007; Bærum 102,529.

Vital statistics

Birth rate per 1,000 population (2003): 12.4 (world avg. 21.3); legitimate 50.0%; illegitimate 50.0%.
Death rate per 1,000 population (2003): 9.3 (world avg. 9.1).
Natural increase rate per 1,000 population (2003): 3.1 (world avg. 12.2).
Total fertility rate (avg. births per childbearing woman; 2003): 1.8.
Marriage rate per 1,000 population (2001): 5.1.
Divorce rate per 1,000 population (2001): 2.3.
Life expectancy at birth (2003): male 77.0 years; female 81.9 years.
Major causes of death per 100,000 population (2000): circulatory diseases 405.4; malignant neoplasms (cancers) 238.7; respiratory diseases 97.7; violence 52.8.

National economy

Budget (2001). Revenue: NKr 829,345,000,000 (value-added taxes 30.7%, tax on income 28.6%, social security taxes 20.2%). Expenditures: NKr 617,372,000,000 (social security and welfare 37.8%, health 15.9%, education 13.6%, debt service 4.6%).
Public debt (December 2002): U.S.$60,900,000,000.
Production (metric tons except as noted). Agriculture, forestry, fishing (2002): barley 601,000, potatoes 389,000, oats 312,000, wheat 268,000; livestock (number of live animals) 2,396,000 sheep, 967,200 cattle; roundwood (2002) 8,649,000 cu m; fish catch (2003) 2,544,692, of which herring 561,858, capelin 249,124, cod 217,462[5], pollock 212,209. Mining and quarrying (2001): ilmenite concentrate 600,000, iron ore (metal content) 340,000, cobalt 3,134. Manufacturing (value added in U.S.$'000,000; 2001): food products 2,353; ship/boat construction and repair 1,543; nonelectrical machinery 1,257; publishing 1,092; base nonferrous metals 940; fabricated metal products 898; paper and paper products 788. Energy production (consumption): electricity (kW-hr; 2003) 107,268,000,000 ([2000] 123,985,000,000); coal (metric tons; 2000) 632,000 (1,035,000); crude petroleum (barrels; 2001) 1,275,000,000 ([2000] 119,000,000); petroleum products (metric tons; 2000) 17,338,000 (11,321,000); natural gas (cu m; 2001) 57,848,000,000 ([2000] 4,167,500).
Household income and expenditure. Average household size (2001) 2.3; annual income (excluding taxes) per household (2002) NKr 333,500 (U.S.$41,772); expenditure (2001–03): housing 20.1%, transportation 17.3%, recreation and culture 12.6%, food 10.3%, household furnishings 7.0%.
Land use as % of total land area (2000): in temporary crops 2.9%, in permanent crops, n.a., in pasture 0.5%; overall forest area 28.9%.
Gross national product (2003): U.S.$197,658,000,000 (U.S.$43,350 per capita).

Structure of gross domestic product and labour force

	2001 in value NKr '000,000	% of total value	labour force	% of labour force
Agriculture	25,010	1.7	89,000	3.8
Mining	2,769	0.2	[6]	[6]
Crude petroleum and natural gas	311,274	20.6	32,000	1.4
Manufacturing	131,432	8.7	290,000[7]	12.3[7]
Construction	56,654	3.7	152,000	6.4
Public utilities	30,844	2.0	18,000	0.8
Transp. and commun.	119,351	7.9	169,000	7.1
Trade	141,378[7]	9.4[7]	398,000	16.9
Finance	247,619	16.4	273,000	11.6
Pub. admin., defense	233,950	15.5 }	855,000	36.2
Services	68,652	4.5 }		
Other	141,935	9.4	84,000[8]	3.5[8]
TOTAL	1,510,866[9]	100.0	2,362,000[9]	100.0

Population economically active (2001): total 2,362,000; activity rate of total population 52.3% (participation rates: ages 15–64, 80.3%; female 46.6%; unemployed [2003] 3.9%).

Price and earnings indexes (2000 = 100)

	1997	1998	1999	2000	2001	2002	2003
Consumer price index	92.7	94.8	97.0	100.0	103.0	104.3	106.9
Hourly earnings index	...	91.3	96.1	100.0	104.5	110.0	115.2

Tourism (2002): receipts U.S.$2,738,000,000; expenditures U.S.$5,814,000,000.

Foreign trade[10]

Balance of trade (current prices)

	1997	1998	1999	2000	2001	2002
NKr '000,000	+90,189	+25,998	+84,886	+219,605	+233,805	+208,365
% of total	15.1%	4.5%	13.8%	27.6%	28.3%	27.4%

Imports (2001): NKr 296,161,000,000 (machinery and transport equipment 42.1%, of which road vehicles 8.7%; ships 3.4%; chemicals and chemical products 9.5%; metals and metal products 7.7%; food products 6.7%; petroleum products 3.0%). *Major import sources:* Sweden 15.2%; Germany 12.6%; U.K. 7.9%; Denmark 7.1%; U.S. 7.1%.
Exports (2001): NKr 529,966,000,000 (crude petroleum 44.3%; natural gas 11.5%; machinery and transport equipment 11.4%; metals and metal products 7.9%; fish 5.6%). *Major export destinations:* U.K. 19.6%; Germany 12.2%; The Netherlands 10.4%; France 9.4%; Sweden 8.0%.

Transport and communications

Transport. Railroads (2001): route length 4,178 km; passenger-km 2,536,000,000; metric ton-km cargo 2,451,000,000. Roads (2002): total length 91,545 km (paved [1998] 74%). Vehicles (2001): passenger cars 1,872,862; trucks and buses 444,626. Air transport (2002)[11]: passenger-km 11,549,000,000; metric ton-km cargo 190,500,000; airports (1996) 50.

Communications

Medium	date	unit	number	units per 1,000 persons
Daily newspapers	2000	circulation	2,620,000	585
Radio	2000	receivers	4,110,000	915
Television	2000	receivers	3,000,000	669
Telephones	2002	main lines	3,343,000	734
Cellular telephones	2003	subscribers	4,163,400	909
Personal computers	2002	units	2,405,000	528
Internet	2002	users	2,288,000	503

Education and health

Educational attainment (2000). Percentage of population age 16 and over having: primary and lower secondary education 21.5%; higher secondary 55.0%; higher 21.3%; unknown 2.2%. *Literacy* (2000): virtually 100% literate.

Education (2000–01)

	schools	teachers	students	student/ teacher ratio
Primary (age 7–12)	3,260	45,247	590,471	13.0
Secondary (age 13–18) and vocational	696	20,567	220,328	10.7
Higher	70	12,071	191,454	15.9

Health: physicians (2003) 12,322 (1 per 370 persons); hospital beds (2003[2]) 22,662 (1 per 201 persons); infant mortality rate (2003) 3.4.
Food (2001): daily per capita caloric intake 3,382 (vegetable products 67%, animal products 33%); 126% of FAO recommended minimum requirement.

Military

Total active duty personnel (2003): 26,600 (army 58.3%, navy 22.9%, air force 18.8%). *Military expenditure as percentage of GNP* (1999): 2.2% (world avg. 2.4%); per capita expenditure U.S.$742.

[1]Excludes Svalbard (23,560 sq mi [61,020 sq km]) and Jan Mayen (146 sq mi [377 sq km]). [2]January 1. [3]Includes Norwegian population of Svalbard and Jan Mayen, registered as residents on the mainland. [4]Population of municipalities. [5]Norwegian catches on quotas bought from other countries are included. [6]Manufacturing includes mining. [7]Includes hotels. [8]Unemployed. [9]Detail does not add to total given because of rounding. [10]Imports c.i.f.; exports f.o.b. [11]Principally SAS and Braathens ASA.

Internet resources for further information:
- **Statistics Norway http://www.ssb.no/www-open/english**

Oman

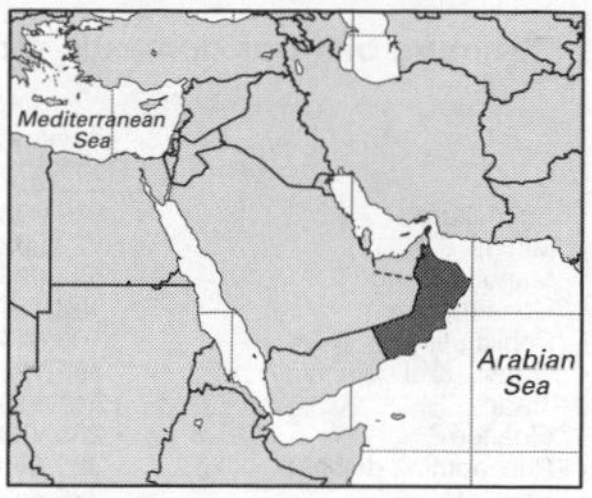

Official name: Salṭanat ʿUmān (Sultanate of Oman).
Form of government: monarchy with two advisory bodies (Council of State [57[1]]; Consultative Council [83]).
Head of state and government: Sultan.
Capital: Muscat.
Official language: Arabic.
Official religion: Islam.
Monetary unit: 1 rial Omani (RO) = 1,000 baizas; valuation (Sept. 1, 2004) 1 RO = U.S.$2.60 = £1.44.

Area and population

		area[2]		population
Regions	Capitals	sq mi	sq km	2003 census[3]
Al-Bāṭinah	Ar-Rustāq; Ṣuḥār	4,850	12,500	652,667
Ad-Dākhilīyah	Nizwā; Samāʾil	12,300	31,900	265,083
Ash-Sharqīyah	Ibrā; Ṣūr	14,200	36,800	312,708
Al-Wusṭa	Haymāʾ	30,750	79,700	23,058
Az-Zāhirah	Al-Buraymī; ʿIbrī	17,000	44,000	204,250
Governorates				
Masqaṭ	Muscat (Masqaṭ)	1,350	3,500	631,031
Musandam	Khaṣab	700	1,800	28,263
Ẓufār (Dhofar)	Salālah	38,350	99,300	214,331
TOTAL		119,500	309,500	2,331,391

Demography

Population (2004): 2,350,000.
Density (2004): persons per sq mi 19.7, persons per sq km 7.6.
Urban-rural (2001): urban 76.5%; rural 23.5%.
Sex distribution (2002): male 56.9%; female 43.1%.
Age breakdown (2002): under 15, 33.7%; 15–29, 32.3%; 30–44, 22.5%; 45–59, 7.7%; 60–74, 3.0%; 75 and over 0.8%.
Population projection: (2010) 2,770,000; (2020) 3,483,000.
Doubling time: 21 years.
Ethnic composition (2000): Omani Arab 48.1%; Indo-Pakistani 31.7%, of which Balochi 15.0%, Bengali 4.4%, Tamil 2.5%; other Arab 7.2%; Persian 2.8%; Zanzibari (blacks originally from Zanzibar) 2.5%; other 7.7%.
Religious affiliation (2000): Muslim 87.4%, of which Ibāḍiyah Muslim *c.* 75% (principal minorities are Sunni Muslim and Shiʿi Muslim); Hindu 5.7%; Christian 4.9%; Buddhist 0.8%; other 1.2%.
Major cities (2003): As-Sīb 223,267[4]; Salālah 156,587; Maṭraḥ 154,316[4]; Bawshar 149,506[4]; Ṣuḥār 104,057; Muscat 24,769 (urban agglomeration [2003] 638,000).

Vital statistics

Birth rate per 1,000 population (2003): 37.5 (world avg. 21.3).
Death rate per 1,000 population (2003): 4.0 (world avg. 9.1).
Natural increase rate per 1,000 population (2003): 33.5 (world avg. 12.2).
Total fertility rate (avg. births per childbearing woman; 2003): 5.9.
Life expectancy at birth (2003): male 70.4 years; female 74.9 years.
Major causes of death per 100,000 population: n.a.; however, the main causes of hospital deaths in 1995 were diseases of the circulatory system 34.1%, infectious diseases 11.1%, malignant neoplasms (cancers) 9.4%, perinatal problems 7.2%, diseases of the respiratory system 6.3%.

National economy

Budget (2004). Revenue: RO 2,925,000,000 (oil revenue 72.8%; other 27.2%). Expenditures: RO 3,425,000,000 (current expenditure 71.3%, of which civil ministries 36.7%, defense 28.4%, interest paid on loans 2.3%; capital expenditure 26.6%; other 2.1%).
Public debt (external, outstanding; 2002): U.S.$1,979,000,000.
Gross national product (2003): U.S.$19,877,000,000 (U.S.$7,830 per capita).

Structure of gross national product and labour force

	2003			
	in value RO '000,000	% of total value	labour force[5]	% of labour force[5]
Agriculture, fishing	164.9	2.0	68,839	9.8
Oil and natural gas	3,470.2[6]	41.8[6]	7,395	1.1
Other mining	14.2	0.2		
Manufacturing	685.1[6]	8.2[6]	72,796	10.4
Construction	189.0	2.3	148,115	21.1
Public utilities	105.5	1.3	1,561	0.2
Transp. and commun.	582.1	7.0	4,873	0.7
Trade, restaurants, hotels	1,038.2	12.5	175,360	25.0
Finance, real estate	673.8	8.1	6,582	0.9
Pub. admin., defense	803.1	9.7	123,045	17.5
Services	750.8	9.0	93,086	13.2
Other	–174.5[7]	–2.1[7]	1,036	0.1
TOTAL	8,302.4	100.0	702,688	100.0

Tourism (2002): receipts U.S.$242,000,000; expenditures U.S.$771,000,000.
Household income and expenditure. Average household size (2002) 6.7; expenditure (1995): housing and utilities 27.9%, food, beverages, and tobacco 26.4%, transportation 19.8%, clothing and shoes 7.9%, household goods and furniture 6.2%, education, health services, entertainment, and other 11.8%.
Production (metric tons except as noted). Agriculture, forestry, fishing (2002): dates 248,458, bananas 33,680, watermelons 29,914, dry onions 17,360, potatoes 12,688, mangoes 10,945, papayas 2,360, tobacco leaves 1,270; livestock (number of live animals) 998,000 goats, 354,000 sheep, 314,000 cattle, 122,700 camels; fish catch (2001) 128,544. Mining and quarrying (2002): marble 136,000; chromite (gross weight) 23,975; gold 301 kg. Manufacturing (value added in U.S.$'000,000; 2001): petroleum products 1,012; nonmetallic mineral products 124; food products 106; chemicals and chemical products 45; fabricated metals 40; furniture 36. Energy production (consumption): electricity (kW-hr; 2002) 10,331,000,000 (10,331,000,000); crude petroleum (barrels; 2003) 299,000,000 (20,000,000); petroleum products (metric tons; 2000) 4,134,000 (3,176,000); natural gas (cu m; 2001) 9,100,000,000 (6,300,000,000).
Population economically active (2003)[5]: total 702,688; activity rate of total population 30.1% (participation rates: over age 15, 60.9%; female 9.7%; unemployed [1996] *c.* 20%).

Price index (2000 = 100)

	1997	1998	1999	2000	2001	2002	2003
Consumer price index	101.6	100.7	101.2	100.0	98.9	98.3	97.9

Land use as % of total land area (2000): in temporary crops 0.1%, in permanent crops 0.1%, in pasture 3.2%; overall forest area, negligible.

Foreign trade[8]

Balance of trade (current prices)

	1997	1998	1999	2000	2001	2002
RO '000,000	+1,158	+118	+1,130	+2,586	+2,216	+2,129
% of total	24.5%	2.9%	25.5%	42.3%	35.2%	33.0%

Imports (2003): RO 2,527,000,000 (machinery and apparatus 28.4%; manufactured goods 15.4%; motor vehicles and parts 13.4%; food and live animals 11.4%; chemicals and chemical products 7.5%). *Major import sources:* United Arab Emirates 21.6%; Japan 17.1%; United States 6.2%; United Kingdom 5.7%; Germany 4.4%; India 4.4%.
Exports (2003): RO 4,487,000,000 (domestic exports 86.6%, of which crude and refined petroleum 66.5%, natural gas 13.3%, live animals and animal products 1.4%, base and fabricated [mostly copper] metals 0.9%; reexports 13.4%, of which motor vehicles and parts 7.5%, beverages and tobacco products 1.8%). *Major export destinations*[9]: United Arab Emirates 32.7%; Iran 18.3%; Saudi Arabia 8.4%; United States 3.6%; Yemen 2.6%.

Transport and communications

Transport. Railroads: none. Roads (1999): total length 20,518 mi, 33,020 km (paved 24%). Vehicles (2001): passenger cars 309,217; trucks and buses 132,290. Air transport (2002)[10]: passenger-mi 739,000,000, passenger-km 1,189,300,000; short ton-mi cargo 6,316,000, metric ton-km cargo 9,230,000; airports (1999) with scheduled flights 6.

Communications

Medium	date	unit	number	units per 1,000 persons
Daily newspapers	1996	circulation	63,000	28
Radio	2000	receivers	1,490,000	621
Television	2002	receivers	1,382,500	553
Telephones	2002	main lines	233,900	92
Cellular telephones	2002	subscribers	464,900	183
Personal computers	2002	units	95,000	37
Internet	2002	users	180,000	71

Education and health

Educational attainment (1993). Percentage of population age 15 and over having: no formal schooling (illiterate) 41.2%; no formal schooling (literate) 14.9%; primary 18.9%; secondary 21.1%; higher technical 2.0%; higher undergraduate 1.5%; higher graduate 0.1%; other 0.3%. *Literacy* (2003): percentage of total population age 15 and over literate 75.8%; males literate 83.0%; females literate 67.2%.

Education (2001–02)

	schools	teachers	students	student/ teacher ratio
Primary (age 6–14)	294[11]	8,417	236,904	28.1
Secondary (age 15–17)[12]	674[13]	13,096	266,923	20.4
Voc., teacher tr.	15	1,072	16,472	15.4
Higher[14]	1	918	11,834	12.9

Health (2002): physicians 3,536 (1 per 713 persons); hospital beds 5,168 (1 per 488 persons); infant mortality rate per 1,000 live births (2003) 21.0.

Military

Total active duty personnel (2003): 41,700 (army 60.0%, navy 10.1%, air force 9.8%, royal household 20.1%). *Military expenditure as percentage of GNP* (1999): 15.3% (world 2.4%); per capita expenditure U.S.$726.

[1]All seats are nonelected. [2]Approximate; no comprehensive survey of surface area has ever been carried out in Oman. [3]Preliminary. [4]Within Muscat urban agglomeration. [5]Employed only; includes 579,643 expatriate workers in private sector and 123,045 government employees, of which 80.5% are Omani. [6]Manufacturing includes petroleum products; Oil and natural gas excludes petroleum products. [7]Includes import taxes less bank service charges. [8]Imports are f.o.b. in balance of trade and c.i.f. for commodities and trading partners. [9]Excludes petroleum and natural gas; includes reexports. [10]Oman Air only. [11]2000–01. [12]Includes preparatory. [13]1998–99. [14]University only.

Internet resources for further information:

- **Ministry of National Economy**
  http://www.moneoman.gov.om/english.htm
- **Central Bank of Oman**
  http://www.cbo-oman.org/pub_annual.htm

Pakistan

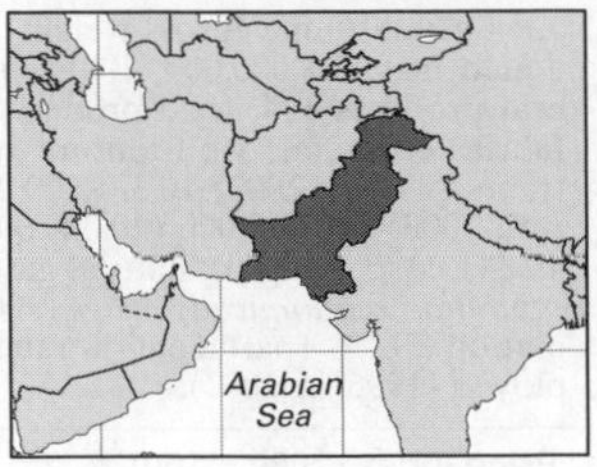

Official name: Islam-i Jamhuriya-e Pakistan (Islamic Republic of Pakistan).
Form of government: military-backed constitutional regime with two legislative houses (Senate [100]; National Assembly [342]).
Chiefs of state and government: President[1] assisted by Prime Minister.
Capital: Islamabad.
Official language: Urdu.
Official religion: Islam.
Monetary unit: 1 Pakistan rupee (PRs) = 100 paisa; valuation (Sept. 1, 2004) 1 U.S.$ = PRs 58.75; 1 £ = PRs 105.69.

Area and population

		area[2]		population
Provinces	Capitals	sq mi	sq km	2003 estimate[3]
Balochistan	Quetta	134,051	347,190	7,450,000
North-West Frontier	Peshawar	28,773	74,521	20,170,000
Punjab	Lahore	79,284	205,345	82,710,000
Sindh	Karachi	54,407	140,914	34,240,000
Federally Administered Tribal Areas	...	10,509	27,220	3,420,000
Federal Capital Area				
Islamabad	...	350	906	1,040,000
TOTAL		307,374	796,096	149,030,000

Demography

Population (2004)[3]: 151,600,000.
Density (2003)[2, 3]: persons per sq mi 493.2, persons per sq km 190.4.
Urban-rural (2002)[3, 4]: urban 38.0%; rural 62.0%.
Sex distribution (2002)[3, 4]: male 51.92%; female 48.08%.
Age breakdown (1998)[3, 4]: under 15, 43.2%; 15–29, 26.9%; 30–44, 15.6%; 45–59, 8.8%; 60–74, 4.3%; 75 and over, 1.2%.
Population projection[3]: (2010) 171,023,000; (2020) 202,767,000.
Doubling time: 30 years.
Ethnic composition (2000): Punjabi 52.6%; Pashtun 13.2%; Sindhi 11.7%; Urdu-speaking muhajirs 7.5%; Balochi 4.3%; other 10.7%.
Religious affiliation (2000): Muslim 96.1%[5]; Christian 2.5%; Hindu 1.2%; others (including Ahmadiyah) 0.2%.
Major cities (1998): Karachi 9,269,000; Lahore 5,063,000; Faisalabad 1,977,000; Rawalpindi 1,406,000; Multan 1,182,000; Islamabad 525,000.

Vital statistics

Birth rate per 1,000 population (2003): 32.0 (world avg. 21.3).
Death rate per 1,000 population (2003): 8.9 (world avg. 9.1).
Natural increase rate per 1,000 population (2003): 23.1 (world avg. 12.2).
Total fertility rate (avg. births per childbearing woman; 2003): 4.4.
Life expectancy at birth (2003): male 61.3 years; female 63.1 years.
Major cause of death (percentage of total deaths; 1987): malaria 18.2%; childhood diseases 12.1%; diseases of digestive system 9.8%; diseases of respiratory system 9.2%; infection of intestinal tract 7.7%.

National economy

Budget (2001–02). Revenue: PRs 632,799,000,000 (sales tax 26.9%, nontax receipts 26.0%, income taxes 22.4%, customs duties 8.0%, excise taxes 7.4%). Expenditures: PRs 773,289,000,000 (public-debt service 41.4%, defense 19.6%, development 16.1%, general administration 6.6%, grants and subsidies 3.3%).
Public debt (external, outstanding; 2002): U.S.$28,102,000,000.
Production (metric tons except as noted). Agriculture, forestry, fishing (2002): sugarcane 48,041,600, wheat 18,226,100, rice 6,343,000, seed cotton 5,040,000, potatoes 1,721,600, corn (maize) 1,689,000, chickpeas 362,100, rapeseed 230,000; livestock (number of live animals) 50,900,000 goats, 24,398,000 sheep, 24,000,000 buffalo, 22,857,000 cattle, 153,000,000 chickens; roundwood (2002) 27,691,679 cu m; fish catch (2001) 623,425. Mining and quarrying (2001–02): limestone 9,805,000; rock salt 1,359,000; gypsum 328,000; silica sand 157,000; chromite 15,984. Manufacturing (2001–02): cement 9,935,000; urea 4,216,200; refined sugar 3,246,600; cotton yarn 1,808,600; vegetable ghee 774,000; jute textiles 82,000; cotton textiles 568,400,000 sq m; cigarettes 55,320,000,000 units; motor-vehicle tires 1,463,000 units; bicycles 553,400 units; (2000–01) sewing machines 26,900 units. Energy production (consumption): electricity (kW-hr; 2001) 67,704,000,000 (67,704,000,000); coal (metric tons; 2000) 3,168,000 (4,125,000); crude petroleum (barrels; 2000–01) 21,100,000 ([2000] 51,188,000); petroleum products (metric tons; 2000) 6,123,000 (17,856,000); natural gas (cu m; 2000–01) 24,800,000,000 ([2000] 21,036,000,000).
Population economically active (2002): total 41,540,000; activity rate of total population 28.5% (participation rates: ages 15–64 [1999] 43.1%; female [1996–97] 14.4%; unemployed 7.8%).

Price index (2000 = 100)

	1997	1998	1999	2000	2001	2002	2003
Consumer price index	86.6	92.0	95.8	100.0	103.1	106.5	109.6

Gross national product (2003): U.S.$69,236,000,000 (U.S.$470 per capita).

Structure of gross domestic product and labour force

	2001–02		2001	
	in value PRs '000,000	% of total value	labour force	% of labour force
Agriculture	829,398	22.3	18,160,000	44.6
Mining	22,803	0.6	4,330,000	10.7
Manufacturing	537,035	14.4		
Construction	103,157	2.8	2,170,000	5.3
Public utilities	106,614	2.9	260,000	0.6
Transp. and commun.	393,799	10.6	1,890,000	4.7
Trade	511,819	13.7	5,060,000	12.4
Finance	265,760	7.1		
Pub. admin., defense	321,090	8.6	5,630,000	13.8
Services	336,843	9.0		
Other	298,293	8.0	3,190,000[6]	7.9[6]
TOTAL	3,726,611	100.0	40,690,000	100.0

Household income and expenditure (1998–99). Average household size 6.8; income per household PRs 81,444 (U.S.$441); sources of income: self-employment 40.9%, wages and salaries 32.3%, transfer payments 11.3%, other 15.5%; expenditure: food 49.1%, housing 20.9%, clothing and footwear 7.8%, education 3.6%, transportation and communications 3.3%, recreation 0.2%.
Tourism (2002): receipts U.S.$105,000,000; expenditures U.S.$179,000,000.
Land use as % of total land area (2000): in temporary crops 27.6%, in permanent crops 0.9%, in pasture 6.5%; overall forest area 3.1%.

Foreign trade[7]

Balance of trade (current prices)

	1996–97	1997–98	1998–99	1999–2000	2000–01	2001–02
U.S.$'000,000	–3,145	–1,868	–2,085	–1,412	–1,269	–360
% of total	16.3%	10.0%	12.2%	7.9%	6.6%	1.9%

Imports (2001–02): U.S.$10,339,000,000 (machinery and apparatus 15.6%; refined petroleum 15.2%; chemicals and chemical products 14.4%; crude petroleum 11.9%; food 8.0%; transport equipment 4.8%). *Major import sources* (2000–01): U.A.E. 12.5%; Saudi Arabia 11.7%; Kuwait 8.9%; Japan 5.4%; U.S. 5.2%; China 4.9%.
Exports (2001–02): U.S.$9,135,000,000 (textiles 63.6%, of which cotton yarn and fabric 22.6%, bedding 10.1%, ready-made garments 9.6%, knitwear 9.3%; leather and leather products 7.1%; rice 4.9%; sporting goods 3.3%; carpets 2.7%). *Major export destinations:* EU 27.4%, of which U.K. 7.2%, Germany 4.9%; U.S. 24.7%; U.A.E. 7.9%; Hong Kong 4.8%.

Transport and communications

Transport. Railroads (2000–01): route length 7,791 km; passenger-km 19,590,000,000; metric ton-km cargo 4,520,000,000. Roads (2001–02): total length 156,375 mi, 251,661 km (paved 59%). Vehicles (2001): passenger cars 758,600; trucks and buses 253,100. Air transport (2000–01): passenger-km 9,739,000,000; (1999) metric ton-km cargo 329,832,000; airports (1997) 35.

Communications

Medium	date	unit	number	units per 1,000 persons
Daily newspapers	2000	circulation	4,190,000	30
Radio	2000	receivers	14,700,000	121
Television	2000	receivers	18,300,000	131
Telephones	2003	main lines	3,982,800	27
Cellular telephones	2003	subscribers	2,624,800	18
Personal computers	2001	units	600,000	4.1
Internet	2002	users	1,500,000	10

Education and health

Educational attainment (1990). Percentage of population age 25 and over having: no formal schooling 73.8%; some primary education 9.7%; secondary 14.0%; postsecondary 2.5%. *Literacy* (2000): total population age 15 and over literate 43.2%; males literate 57.5%; females literate 27.9%.

Education (2000–01)

	schools	teachers	students	student/ teacher ratio
Primary (age 5–9)	165,700	373,900	20,999,000	56.2
Secondary (age 10–14)	31,600	320,100	6,576,000	20.5
Voc., teacher tr.	580	7,062	75,000	10.6
Higher	1,187	41,673	1,067,999	25.6

Health (2001): physicians 96,248 (1 per 1,516 persons); hospital beds 97,945 (1 per 1,490 persons); infant mortality rate per 1,000 live births (2003) 76.6.
Food (2001): daily per capita caloric intake 2,457 (vegetable products 81%, animal products 19%); 106% of FAO recommended minimum.

Military

Total active duty personnel (2003): 620,000 (army 88.7%, navy 4.0%, air force 7.3%). *Military expenditure as percentage of GNP* (1999): 5.9% (world 2.4%); per capita expenditure U.S.$25.

[1]Military leader (from October 1999) who was sworn in as president in June 2001. [2]Excludes 32,494-sq-mi (84,159-sq-km) area of Pakistani-administered Jammu and Kashmir (comprising both Azad Kashmir [AK] and the Northern Areas [NA]). [3]Excludes Afghan refugees (2004; 1,100,000) and the 2004 populations of AK (3,175,000) and NA (1,075,000). [4]Excludes Federally Administered Tribal Areas. [5]Mostly Sunnī, with Shīʿī comprising about 17% of total population. [6]Unemployed. [7]Import figures are f.o.b. in balance of trade and c.i.f. for commodities and trading partners.

Internet resources for further information:
- **Economic Survey, Ministry of Finance http://www.finance.gov.pk**
- **Statistics Division: Government of Pakistan http://www.statpak.gov.pk**

Palau

Official name: Belu'u er a Belau (Palauan); Republic of Palau (English).
Form of government: unitary republic with a national congress composed of two legislative houses (Senate [9]; House of Delegates [16]).
Head of state and government: President.
Capital: Koror (acting)[1].
Official languages[2]: Palauan; English.
Official religion: none.
Monetary unit: 1 U.S. dollar (U.S.$) = 100 cents; valuation (Sept. 1, 2004) 1 U.S.$ = £0.56.

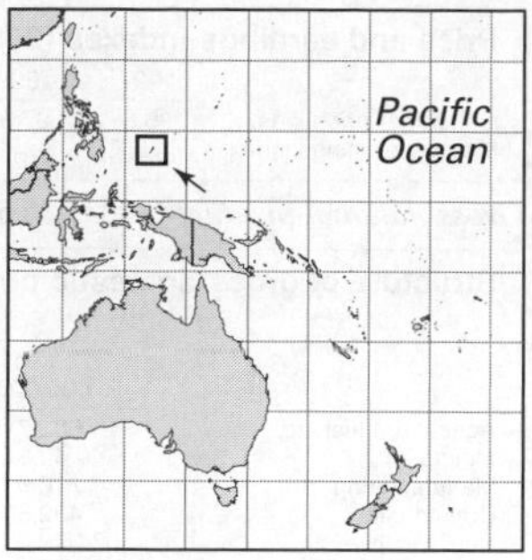

Area and population

States	area sq mi	area sq km	population 2000 census
Aimeliik	20	52	272
Airai	17	44	2,104
Angaur	3	8	188
Hatobohel	1	3	23
Kayangel	1	3	138
Koror	7	18	13,303
Melekeok	11	28	239
Ngaraard	14	36	638
Ngarchelong	4	10	267
Ngardmau	18	47	286
Ngatpang	18	47	367
Ngchesar	16	41	280
Ngeremlengui	25	65	221
Ngiwal	10	26	193
Peleliu	5	13	571
Sonsorol	1	3	39
Other			
Rock Islands	18	47	—
TOTAL	188[3]	488[3]	19,129

Demography

Population (2004): 20,700.
Density (2004): persons per sq mi 110.1, persons per sq km 42.4.
Urban-rural (2002): urban 73.0%; rural 27.0%.
Sex distribution (2000): male 54.63%; female 45.37%.
Age breakdown (2000): under 15, 23.9%; 15–29, 24.2%; 30–44, 29.9%; 45–59, 14.2%; 60–74, 5.5%; 75 and over 2.3%.
Population projection: (2010) 22,000; (2020) 23,000.
Doubling time: 58 years.
Ethnic composition (2000): Palauan 69.9%; Asian 25.5%; other Micronesian 2.5%; other 2.1%.
Religious affiliation (2000): Roman Catholic 41.6%; Protestant 23.3%; Modekngei (marginal Christian sect) 8.8%; other Christian 6.8%; other 19.5%.
Major city (2000): Koror 13,303.

Vital statistics

Birth rate per 1,000 population (2003): 19.0 (world avg. 21.3).
Death rate per 1,000 population (2003): 7.0 (world avg. 9.1).
Natural increase rate per 1,000 population (2003): 12.0 (world avg. 12.2).
Total fertility rate (avg. births per childbearing woman; 2003): 2.5.
Life expectancy at birth (2003): male 66.4 years; female 72.8 years.
Major causes of death per 100,000 population (1999): diseases of the circulatory system 227.4; malignant and benign neoplasms (cancers) 119.1; accidents, poisoning, and violence 92.1; endocrine, nutritional, metabolic, and immunity disorders 59.6; diseases of the respiratory system 43.3; diseases of the digestive system 21.7; diseases of the genitourinary system 21.7; infectious and parasitic diseases 16.2.

National economy

Budget (2002). Revenue: U.S.$70,058,000 (grants from the U.S. 49.4%; tax revenue 36.0%; nontax revenue 14.6%). Expenditures: U.S.$79,691,000 (current expenditure 74.6%, of which wages and salaries 38.1%; capital expenditure 25.4%).
Public debt (external, outstanding; 2000): U.S.$20,000,000.
Production (metric tons except as noted). Agriculture, forestry, fishing (value of sales in U.S.$; 1998): eggs (1999) 609,626, fruit and vegetables 97,225, root crops (taro, cassava, sweet potatoes) 6,566, betel nuts 4,291; livestock (number of live animals; 2001) 702 pigs, 21,189 poultry; roundwood, n.a.; fish catch (2001; pounds) 593,473, of which sturgeon and unicorn fish 101,613, parrot fish 57,516, rabbit fish 25,613, groupers 23,835, emperor fish 20,586, crabs 17,347, wrasses 14,315, tuna and mackerel 13,366. Mining and quarrying: n.a. Manufacturing: includes handicrafts and small items. Construction: n.a. Energy production (consumption): electricity (kW-hr; 2000) 210,000,000 (210,000,000); coal, none (n.a.); crude petroleum, none (n.a.); petroleum products (metric tons; 2000), none (79,000); natural gas, none (n.a.).
Tourism (2002): receipts from visitors U.S.$59,000,000.
Land use as % of total land area (2000): in temporary crops *c.* 9%, in permanent crops *c.* 4%, in pasture *c.* 7%; overall forest area *c.* 76%.
Population economically active (2000): total 9,845; activity rate of total population 51.5% (participation rates: over age 15, 67.6%; female [1995] 39.6%; unemployed 2.3%).

Price index (2000 = 100)

	2000	2001	2002	2003
Consumer price index	100.0	99.4	99.4	100.8

Gross national product (at current market prices; 2003): U.S.$150,000,000 (U.S.$7,500 per capita).

Structure of gross domestic product and labour force

	2001 in value U.S.$'000	2001 % of total value	2000 labour force	2000 % of labour force
Agriculture, fisheries	4,771	4.0	215	2.2
Mining	240	0.2		
Manufacturing	1,774	1.5	345	3.5
Public utilities	3,741	3.1	[4]	[4]
Construction	9,181	7.6	1,112	11.3
Transportation and communications	10,855	9.0	765[4]	7.8[4]
Trade	36,756	30.4	2,619	26.6
Finance	9,683	8.0	116	1.2
Public administration, defense	30,860	25.5	3,203	32.5
Services	10,381	8.6	1,246	12.6
Other	2,592[5]	2.1[5]	224[6]	2.3[6]
TOTAL	120,834	100.0	9,845	100.0

Household income and expenditure. Average household size (2000) 5.7; income per household (1989) U.S.$8,882; sources of income (1989): wages 63.7%, social security 12.0%, self-employment 7.4%, retirement 5.5%, interest, dividend, or net rental 4.3%, remittance 4.1%, public assistance 1.0%, other 2.0%; expenditure (1997): food 42.2%, beverages and tobacco 14.8%, entertainment 13.1%, transportation 6.4%, clothing 5.7%, household goods 2.7%, other 15.1%.

Foreign trade

Balance of trade (current prices)

	1997	1998	1999	2000	2001	2002
U.S.$'000	–57,500	–54,800	–92,400	–111,500	–86,700	–77,200
% of total	70.9%	71.2%	79.8%	82.0%	82.8%	81.1%

Imports (2001): U.S.$95,700,000 (machinery and transport equipment 24.2%; food and live animals 15.2%; mineral fuels and lubricants 10.4%; beverages and tobacco products 8.3%; chemicals and chemical products 7.4%). *Major import sources:* United States 39.3%; Guam 14.0%; Japan 10.2%; Singapore 7.7%; South Korea 6.4%; Taiwan 5.3.
Exports (2001): U.S.$9,000,000 (mostly high-grade tuna and garments). *Major export destinations:* mostly U.S., Japan, and Taiwan.

Transport and communications

Transport. Railroads: none. Roads (1993): total length 40 mi, 64 km (paved 59%). Vehicles (2001): passenger cars and trucks 4,452. Merchant marine (1991): vessels (100 gross tons and over) 4; total deadweight tonnage, n.a. Air transport (2001): passenger arrivals 64,143, passenger departures 61,472; airports (1997) with scheduled flights 1.

Communications

Medium	date	unit	number	units per 1,000 persons
Radio	1997	receivers	12,000	663.0
Television	1997	receivers	11,000	606.0
Telephones	1994	main lines	2,615	160.0

Education and health

Educational attainment (2000). Percentage of population age 25 and over having: no formal schooling 3.1%; completed primary 11.5%; some secondary 7.9%; completed secondary 48.9%; some postsecondary 18.6%; higher 10.0%. *Literacy* (1997): total population age 15 and over literate 99.9%.

Education (2001–02)

	schools	teachers	students	student/ teacher ratio
Primary (age 6–13)	23	235	3,033	12.9
Secondary (age 14–18)	6	132	1,168	8.8
Higher[7]	1	25	598	23.9

Health: physicians (1998) 20 (1 per 906 persons); hospital beds (1990) 70 (1 per 200 persons); infant mortality rate per 1,000 live births (2003) 6.4.
Food: daily per capita caloric intake, n.a.

Military

The United States is responsible for the external security of Palau, as specified in the Compact of Free Association of Oct. 1, 1994.

[1]New capital buildings at Melekeok on Babelthuap were not completed as of July 2004. [2]Sonsorolese-Tobian is also, according to official sources, considered an official language. [3]Detail does not add to total given because of rounding. [4]Transportation and communications includes Public utilities. [5]Includes import duties and imputed bank service charge. [6]Unemployed. [7]Palau Community College.

Internet resources for further information:
- **Department of the Interior: Office of Insular Affairs http://www.pacificweb.org**
- **Palau Office of Planning and Statistics http://www.palaugov.net/stats**

Panama

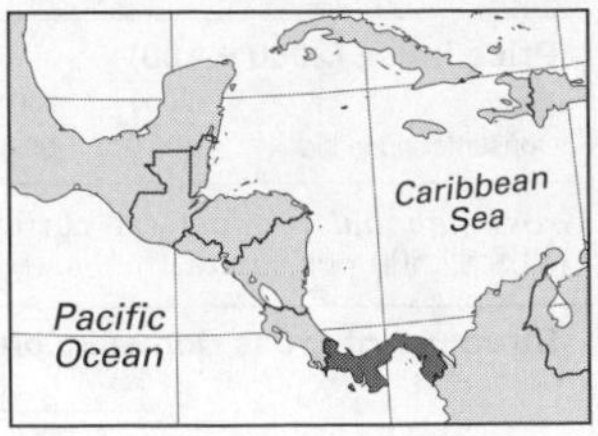

Official name: República de Panamá (Republic of Panama).
Form of government: multiparty republic with one legislative house (Legislative Assembly [78]).
Head of state and government: President assisted by Vice Presidents.
Capital: Panama City.
Official language: Spanish.
Official religion: none.
Monetary unit: 1 balboa (B) = 100 cents; valuation (Sept. 1, 2004) 1 U.S.$ = B 1.00; 1 £ = B 1.80.

Area and population

		area		population
				2000
Provinces	Capitals	sq mi	sq km	census
Bocas del Toro	Bocas del Toro	1,793	4,644	89,269
Chiriquí	David	2,528	6,547	368,790
Coclé	Penonomé	1,911	4,950	202,461
Colón	Colón	1,880	4,868	204,208
Darién	La Palma	4,593	11,897	40,284
Herrera	Chitré	902	2,336	102,465
Los Santos	Las Tablas	1,469	3,805	83,495
Panamá	Panama City	4,506	11,671	1,388,357
Veraguas	Santiago	4,104	10,630	209,076
Indigenous districts[1]				
Emberá	Unión Chocó	1,693	4,384	8,246
Kuna Yala (San Blas)	El Porvenir	904	2,341	32,446
Ngöbe Buglé	Quebrada Guabo	2,690	6,968	110,080
TOTAL		28,973	75,040[2]	2,839,177[3]

Demography

Population (2004): 3,172,000.
Density (2004): persons per sq mi 109.5, persons per sq km 42.3.
Urban-rural (2000): urban 56.3%; rural 43.7%.
Sex distribution (2002): male 50.48%; female 49.52%.
Age breakdown (2002): under 15, 31.3%; 15–29, 26.9%; 30–44, 21.4%; 45–59, 12.2%; 60–74, 6.1%; 75 and over, 2.1%.
Population projection: (2010) 3,504,000; (2020) 4,011,000.
Doubling time: 46 years.
Ethnic composition (2000): mestizo 58.1%; black and mulatto 14.0%; white 8.6%; Amerindian 6.7%; Asian 5.5%; other 7.1%.
Religious affiliation (1995): Roman Catholic 82.2%; unaffiliated Christian 12.9%; other (mostly ethnoreligionist) 4.9%.
Major cities (2000): Panama City 415,964 (urban agglomeration [2001] 1,202,000); San Miguelito 293,745[4]; David 77,734[5]; Arraiján 63,753[5]; La Chorrera 55,871.

Vital statistics

Birth rate per 1,000 population (2003): 19.5 (world avg. 21.3); legitimate 19.7%; illegitimate 80.3%.
Death rate per 1,000 population (2003): 6.3 (world avg. 9.1).
Natural increase rate per 1,000 population (2003): 13.2 (world avg. 12.2).
Total fertility rate (avg. births per childbearing woman; 2003): 2.5.
Marriage rate per 1,000 population (2001): 3.6.
Divorce rate per 1,000 population (2001): 0.9.
Life expectancy at birth (2003): male 70.0 years; female 74.8 years.
Major causes of death per 100,000 population (2002): diseases of the circulatory system 108.8; malignant neoplasms (cancers) 64.5; accidents and violence 39.3; diseases of the respiratory system 34.9; infectious and parasitic diseases 31.0.

National economy

Budget (2000). Revenue: B 2,688,400,000 (tax revenue 62.6%, of which income taxes 12.6%, social security contributions 18.5%, corporate tax 5.8%; nontax revenue 37.4%, of which entrepreneurial and property income 21.1%). Expenditures: B 2,803,900,000 (social security and welfare 20.9%; health 17.2%; education 16.6%; defense 7.1%; economic affairs 7.0%).
Public debt (external, outstanding; 2002): U.S.$6,408,000,000.
Production (metric tons except as noted). Agriculture, forestry, fishing (2002): sugarcane 1,441,000, bananas 600,000, rice 320,000, plantains 105,000, corn (maize) 94,500, oranges 46,600, yams 16,720, coffee 13,900, tobacco 2,130; livestock (number of live animals) 1,533,000 cattle, 280,000 pigs, 170,000 horses; roundwood 1,321,000 cu m; fish catch (2001) 237,394. Mining and quarrying (2001): limestone 270,000; gold 48,600 troy oz. Manufacturing (value of production in B '000,000; 1998): food products 1,203, of which meat 341, dairy products 144; refined petroleum 299; beverages 176; cement, bricks, and tiles 154. Energy production (consumption): electricity (kW-hr; 2001) 4,858,000,000 ([2000] 4,953,000,000); coal (metric tons; 2000) none (70,000); crude petroleum (barrels; 2000) none (16,251,000); petroleum products (metric tons; 2000) 2,066,000 (2,258,000); natural gas (cu m; 2000) none (61,505,000).
Tourism (2002): receipts from visitors U.S.$679,000,000; expenditures by nationals abroad U.S.$178,000,000.
Household income and expenditure. Average household size (2000) 4.2; average annual income per household (1990) B 5,450 (U.S.$5,450); expenditure, n.a.
Population economically active (1998)[6]: total 1,083,580; activity rate of total population 42.2%[7] (participation rates: ages 15–69 [1997] 64.3%, female [1997] 35.6%, unemployed 13.6%).

Price and earnings indexes (2000 = 100)

	1997	1998	1999	2000	2001	2002	2003
Consumer price index	96.8	97.3	98.5	100.0	100.3	101.3	102.7
Monthly earnings index	...	...	...	...	...	...	...

Gross national product (2003): U.S.$12,681,000,000 (U.S.$4,250 per capita).

Structure of gross domestic product and labour force

	2000		2001	
	in value B '000,000	% of total value	labour force[6]	% of labour force[6]
Agriculture, fishing	682.7	6.8	220,700	18.7
Mining	42.8	0.4	2,200	0.2
Manufacturing	712.9	7.1	91,300	7.7
Construction	492.8	4.9	67,800	5.8
Public utilities	399.0	4.0	9,900	0.8
Transp. and commun.	1,727.5	17.2	77,700	6.6
Trade, restaurants	1,758.8	17.6	220,000	18.7
Finance, real estate	2,659.6	26.6	55,500	4.7
Pub. admin.	1,716.2	17.1	66,600	5.7
Services			204,100	17.3
Other	−173.3[8]	−1.7[8]	163,100[9]	13.8[9]
TOTAL	10,019.0	100.0	1,178,900	100.0

Land use as % of total land area (2000): in temporary crops 7.3%, in permanent crops 2.0%, in pasture 20.2%; overall forest area 38.6%.

Foreign trade[10, 11]

Balance of trade (current prices)

	1996	1997	1998	1999	2000	2001
B '000,000	−2,215	−2,358	−2,714	−2,781	−2,626	−2,155
% of total	66.2%	64.5%	65.8%	66.2%	62.8%	57.1%

Imports (2001): B 2,964,000,000 (mineral fuels 21.0%, of which crude petroleum 14.4%; machinery and apparatus 19.1%; chemicals and chemical products 11.2%; transport equipment 8.7%). *Major import sources:* U.S. 32.5%; Colón Free Zone 11.9%; Ecuador 8.0%; Colombia 5.7%; Venezuela 5.2%.
Exports (2001): B 809,000,000 (bananas 15.1%; fish 11.9%; shrimps 8.7%; petroleum products 7.1%; unspecified 38.6%). *Major export destinations:* U.S. 48.1%; Nicaragua 5.1%; Costa Rica 4.8%; Belgium 4.5%; Sweden 3.7%.

Transport and communications

Transport. Railroads (2000): route length 220 mi, 354 km. Roads (1997): total length 7,022 mi, 11,301 km (paved 33%). Vehicles: passenger cars (1998) 228,722; trucks and buses 84,020. Panama Canal traffic (2000–01): oceangoing transits 12,197; cargo 196,242,000 metric tons. Air transport (2001)[12]: passenger-km 3,004,000,000; metric ton-km cargo 25,235,000; airports (1996) 10.

Communications

Medium	date	unit	number	units per 1,000 persons
Daily newspapers	2000	circulation	183,000	62
Radio	2000	receivers	884,000	300
Television	2002	receivers	553,900	191
Telephones	2002	main lines	386,900	129
Cellular telephones	2003	subscribers	834,000	268
Personal computers	2002	units	115,000	38
Internet	2001	users	120,000	41

Education and health

Educational attainment (1990). Percentage of population age 25 and over having: no formal schooling 11.6%; primary 41.6%; secondary 28.7%; undergraduate 12.4%; graduate 0.7%; other/unknown 5.0%. *Literacy* (2000): total population age 15 and over literate 91.3%; males 92.5%; females 91.3%.

Education (1997)

	schools	teachers	students	student/ teacher ratio
Primary (age 6–11)	2,866	15,058	377,898	25.1
Secondary (age 12–17) Voc., teacher tr.	417	12,450	223,155	17.9
Higher	14	6,409	95,341	14.9

Health (2000): physicians 3,798 (1 per 776 persons); hospital beds 7,553 (1 per 390 persons); infant mortality rate per 1,000 live births (2003) 21.4.
Food (2001): daily per capita caloric intake 2,386 (vegetable products 76%, animal products 24%); 103% of FAO recommended minimum requirement.

Military

Total active duty personnel (2003): none; Panama has an 11,800-member national police force. *Military expenditure as percentage of GNP* (1999): 1.4% (world avg. 2.4%); per capita expenditure U.S.$45.

[1]Province-level indigenous districts only. [2]Detail does not add to total given because of rounding. [3]Census adjusted for undercount equals 2,938,548. [4]District adjacent to Panama City within Panama City urban agglomeration. [5]Population of *cabecera*. [6]Excludes indigenous population. [7]Estimated figure. [8]Imputed finance service charges less import duties. [9]Includes 161,400 unemployed. [10]Imports c.i.f.; exports f.o.b. [11]Excludes Colón Free Zone (2001 imports c.i.f. B 4,760,000,000; 2001 reexports f.o.b. B 5,406,000,000, of which textiles and clothing 25.9%, machinery and apparatus 23.7%). [12]COPA only.

Internet resources for further information:
- **Contraloría General de la República Panamá http://www.contraloria.gob.pa/index.htm**

Papua New Guinea

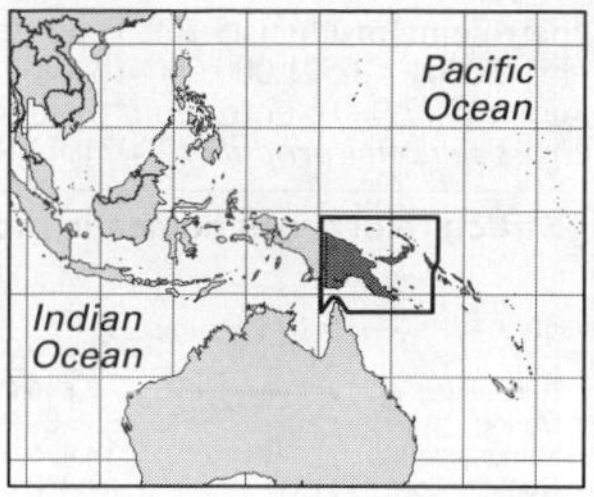

Official name: Independent State of Papua New Guinea.
Form of government: constitutional monarchy with one legislative house (National Parliament [109]).
Chief of state: British Monarch represented by Governor-General.
Head of government: Prime Minister.
Capital: Port Moresby.
Official language: English[1].
Official religion: none.
Monetary unit: 1 Papua New Guinea kina (K) = 100 toea; valuation (Sept. 1, 2004) 1 U.S.$ = K 3.04; 1 £ = K 5.47.

Area and population

		area		population
Provinces	**Administrative centres**	sq mi	sq km	2000 census
Central	Port Moresby	11,400	29,500	183,983
East New Britain	Rabaul	6,000	15,500	220,133
East Sepik	Wewak	16,550	42,800	343,181
Eastern Highlands	Goroka	4,300	11,200	432,972
Enga	Wabag	4,950	12,800	295,031
Gulf	Kerema	13,300	34,500	106,898
Madang	Madang	11,200	29,000	365,106
Manus	Lorengau	800	2,100	43,387
Milne Bay	Alotau	5,400	14,000	210,412
Morobe	Lae	13,300	34,500	539,404
National Capital District	Port Moresby	100	240	254,158
New Ireland	Kavieng	3,700	9,600	118,350
Oro (Northern)	Popondetta	8,800	22,800	133,065
Sandaun (West Sepik)	Vanimo	14,000	36,300	185,741
Simbu (Chimbu)	Kundiawa	2,350	6,100	259,703
Southern Highlands	Mendi	9,200	23,800	546,265
West New Britain	Kimbe	8,100	21,000	184,508
Western	Daru	38,350	99,300	153,304
Western Highlands	Mount Hagen	3,300	8,500	440,025
Autonomous region (pending)				
Bougainville[2]	Buka	3,600	9,300	175,160
TOTAL		178,704[3]	462,840	5,190,786

Demography

Population (2004): 5,695,000.
Density (2004): persons per sq mi 31.9, persons per sq km 12.3.
Urban-rural (2001): urban 17.6%; rural 82.4%.
Sex distribution (2000): male 51.87%; female 48.13%.
Age breakdown (2000): under 15, 38.8%; 15–29, 28.7%; 30–44, 17.1%; 45–59, 9.7%; 60–74, 4.7%; 75 and over, 1.0%.
Population projection: (2010) 6,407,000; (2020) 7,609,000.
Ethnic composition (1983)[4]: New Guinea Papuan 84.0%; New Guinea Melanesian 15.0%; other 1.0%.
Religious affiliation (2000): Christian 95.1%, of which non-Anglican Protestant 56.6%, Roman Catholic 30.0%, Anglican 6.7%; traditional beliefs 3.6%; Bahā'ī 0.8%; other 0.5%.
Major cities (2000): Port Moresby 254,158; Lae 78,038; Madang 27,394; Wewak 19,724; Goroka 18,618.

Vital statistics

Birth rate per 1,000 population (2003): 31.1 (world avg. 21.3).
Death rate per 1,000 population (2003): 7.6 (world avg. 9.1).
Natural increase rate per 1,000 population (2003): 23.5 (world avg. 12.2).
Total fertility rate (avg. births per childbearing woman; 2003): 4.1.
Life expectancy at birth (2003): male 62.1 years; female 66.4 years.
Major causes of death per 100,000 population (1993): acute respiratory infections 34.6; pneumonia 27.8; meningitis 7.6; conditions originating from perinatal period 6.2; malaria 3.8.

National economy

Budget (2001). Revenue: K 2,859,000,000 (tax revenue 86.6%, of which value-added tax 27.0%, corporate tax 24.2%, income tax 22.7%, excise tax 6.5%; nontax revenue 13.4%). Expenditures (2000): K 3,081,800,000 (current expenditure 70.8%, of which transfer to provincial governments 16.8%, interest payments 12.4%; development expenditure 29.2%).
Public debt (external, outstanding; 2002): U.S.$1,488,000,000.
Production (metric tons except as noted). Agriculture, forestry, fishing (2002): oil palm fruit 1,250,000, bananas 725,000, coconuts 513,000, sweet potatoes 490,000, sugarcane 425,000, yams 232,000, taro 174,000, cassava 125,000, coffee 62,500, cacao 45,000, tea 9,000, natural rubber 7,300; livestock (number of live animals) 1,650,000 pigs, 3,800,000 chickens; roundwood (2002) 8,597,000 cu m; fish catch (2001) 53,763. Mining and quarrying (2000): copper (metal content) 200,900; gold 74,300 kg; silver 73,200 kg. Manufacturing (1998): palm oil 241,485; copra 124,349; wood products (excluding furniture) 3,054,000 cu m. Energy production (consumption): electricity (kW-hr; 2000) 2,180,000,000 (2,180,000,000); coal (metric tons; 2000) none (1,000); crude petroleum (barrels; 2000) 28,807,000 (513,100); natural gas (cu m; 2000) 83,544,000 (83,544,000); petroleum products (metric tons; 2000) 49,000 (717,000).
Land use as % of total land area (2000): in temporary crops 0.5%, in permanent crops 1.4%, in pasture 0.4%; overall forest area 67.6%.
Gross national product (2003): U.S.$2,823,000,000 (U.S.$510 per capita).

Structure of gross domestic product and labour force

	2001		1980	
	in value K '000,000	% of total value	labour force[5]	% of labour force[5]
Agriculture	2,848	28.3	564,500	77.0
Mining	2,745	27.2	4,300	0.6
Manufacturing	859	8.5	14,000	1.9
Construction	349	3.5	21,600	2.9
Public utilities	132	1.3	2,800	0.4
Transp. and commun.	431	4.3	17,400	2.4
Trade	866	8.6	25,100	3.4
Finance	358	3.5	4,500	0.6
Pub. admin., defense } Services	1,253	12.4	77,100	10.5
Other	238[6]	2.4[6]	1,500	0.2
TOTAL	10,079	100.0	732,800	100.0[3]

Population economically active (1990)[5]: total 1,715,330; activity rate 36.9% (participation rates: over age 10, n.a.; female 41.5%; unemployed 7.7%).

Price and earnings indexes (2000 = 100)

	1997	1998	1999	2000	2001	2002	2003
Consumer price index	66.3	75.3	86.5	100.0	109.3	122.2	140.2
Weekly earnings index[7]	93.0	100.0	100.0	100.0	100.0	100.0	100.0

Tourism (2001): receipts U.S.$101,000,000; expenditures U.S.$38,000,000.

Foreign trade[8]

Balance of trade (current prices)

	1997	1998	1999	2000	2001
U.S.$'000,000	+213	+424	+494	...	+609
% of total	5.2%	12.9%	13.9%	...	19.3%

Imports (2000): U.S.$1,035,000,000 (petroleum products *c.* 22%; food *c.* 16%; transport equipment *c.* 14%; nonelectrical machinery *c.* 12%; chemicals and chemical products *c.* 7%). *Major import sources* (2000): Australia 55.8%; Japan 11.3%; U.S. 6.5%; Singapore 5.4%; New Zealand 3.5%.
Exports (2002): U.S.$1,638,000,000 (gold 36.0%; crude petroleum 22.5%; copper 16.0%; logs 5.7%; palm oil 5.1%). *Major export destinations* (2002): Australia 49.3%; Singapore 18.8%; New Zealand 4.4%; Japan 4.2%; Malaysia 2.8%.

Transport and communications

Transport. Railroads: none. Roads (1996): total length 19,600 km (paved 4%). Vehicles (1998): passenger cars 21,700; trucks and buses 89,700. Air transport (1999): passenger-km 641,000,000; metric ton-km cargo 80,000,000; airports (1999) with scheduled flights 42.

Communications

Medium	date	unit	number	units per 1,000 persons
Daily newspapers	2000	circulation	72,600	14
Radio	2000	receivers	446,000	86
Television	2000	receivers	88,200	17
Telephones	2002	main lines	62,000	11
Cellular telephones	2002	subscribers	15,000	2.7
Personal computers	2002	units	321,000	59
Internet	2002	users	75,000	14

Education and health

Educational attainment (1990). Percentage of population age 25 and over having: no formal schooling 82.6%; some primary education 8.2%; completed primary 5.0%; some secondary 4.2%. *Literacy* (2000): total population age 15 and over literate 63.9%; males literate 70.6%; females literate 56.8%.

Education (1997)

	schools	teachers	students	student/ teacher ratio
Primary (age 7–12)	3,518	13,457[9]	587,788	...
Secondary (age 13–16)	159	2,415[10]	74,873	...
Voc., teacher tr.	128	878[10]	15,422	...
Higher	3	957[9]	9,220	...

Health: physicians (1998) 342 (1 per 13,708 persons); hospital beds (1993) 14,119 (1 per 294 persons); infant mortality rate (2003) 54.8.
Food (2001): daily per capita caloric intake 2,193 (vegetable products 91%, animal products 9%); 96% of FAO recommended minimum.

Military

Total active duty personnel (2004): 3,100 (army 80.6%, navy 12.9%, air force 6.5%). *Military expenditure as percentage of GNP* (1999): 1.1% (world 2.4%); per capita expenditure U.S.$7.

[1]The national languages are English, Tok Pisin (English Creole), and Motu. [2]Formal peace agreement signed on Aug. 30, 2001, ended nine years of civil war and promised Bougainville autonomy; internationally supported autonomy process under way through October 2004. [3]Detail does not add to total given because of rounding. [4]Papua New Guinea has several thousand separate communities, most with only a few hundred people. [5]Citizens of Papua New Guinea over age 10 involved in "money-raising activities" only. [6]Import duties. [7]Minimum wage only. [8]Imports c.i.f.; exports f.o.b. [9]1995. [10]1992.

Internet resources for further information:
- **Bank of Papua New Guinea http://www.bankpng.gov.pg**
- **Papua New Guinea Embassy, U.S. http://www.pngembassy.org/statistics.html**

Paraguay

Official name: República del Paraguay (Spanish); Tetä Paraguáype (Guaraní) (Republic of Paraguay).
Form of government: multiparty republic with two legislative houses (Senate [45]; Chamber of Deputies [80]).
Head of state and government: President.
Capital: Asunción.
Official languages: Spanish; Guaraní.
Official religion: none[1].
Monetary unit: 1 Paraguayan Guaraní (₲) = 100 céntimos; valuation (Sept. 1, 2004) 1 U.S.$ = ₲5,915; 1 £ = ₲10,641.

Area and population

Regions / Departments	Capitals	area sq mi	area sq km	population 2002 census
Occidental		95,338	246,925	142,501
Alto Paraguay	Fuerte Olimpo	31,795	82,349	15,008
Boquerón	Filadelfia	35,393	91,669	45,617
Presidente Hayes	Pozo Colorado	28,150	72,907	81,876
Oriental		61,710	159,827	5,063,600
Alto Paraná	Ciudad del Este	5,751	14,895	563,042
Amambay	Pedro Juan Caballero	4,994	12,933	113,888
Asunción[2]	—	45	117	513,399
Caaguazú	Coronel Oviedo	4,430	11,474	448,983
Caazapá	Caazapá	3,666	9,496	139,241
Canindeyú	Salto del Guairá	5,663	14,667	140,551
Central	Asunción	952	2,465	1,363,399
Concepción	Concepción	6,970	18,051	180,277
Cordillera	Caacupé	1,910	4,948	234,805
Guairá	Villarrica	1,485	3,846	176,933
Itapúa	Encarnación	6,380	16,525	463,410
Misiones	San Juan Bautista	3,690	9,556	103,633
Ñeembucú	Pilar	4,690	12,147	76,738
Paraguarí	Paraguarí	3,361	8,705	226,514
San Pedro	San Pedro	7,723	20,002	318,787
TOTAL		157,048	406,752	5,206,101[3]

Demography

Population (2004): 5,773,000.
Density (2004): persons per sq mi 36.8, persons per sq km 14.2.
Urban-rural (2002): urban 56.7%; rural 43.3%.
Sex distribution (2002): male 50.70%; female 49.30%.
Age breakdown (2003): under 15, 38.4%; 15–29, 26.1%; 30–44, 17.8%; 45–59, 10.8%; 60–74, 5.2%; 75 and over, 1.7%.
Population projection: (2010) 6,622,000; (2020) 8,082,000.
Ethnic composition (2000): mixed (white/Amerindian) 85.6%; white 9.3%, of which German 4.4%, Latin American 3.4%; Amerindian 1.8%; other 3.3%.
Religious affiliation (2000): Roman Catholic 90.1%; Protestant 5.2%; nonreligious/atheist 1.3%; other 3.4%.
Major urban areas (2002): Asunción 513,399[4]; Ciudad del Este 223,350; Encarnación 69,769; Pedro Juan Caballero 64,153; Caaguazú 50,329.

Vital statistics

Birth rate per 1,000 population (2003): 30.1 (world avg. 21.3).
Death rate per 1,000 population (2003): 4.6 (world avg. 9.1).
Natural increase rate per 1,000 population (2003): 25.5 (world avg. 12.2).
Total fertility rate (avg. births per childbearing woman; 2002): 4.1.
Marriage rate per 1,000 population (2002): 3.0[5].
Life expectancy at birth (2003): male 71.9 years; female 77.0 years.
Major causes of death per 100,000 population (2001)[6]: diseases of the circulatory system 114; malignant neoplasms (cancers) 67; accidents 55; diseases of the respiratory system 32; infectious and parasitic diseases 22.

National economy

Budget (2002): Revenue: ₲5,048,300,000,000 (tax revenue 64.2%, of which taxes on goods and services 38.9%, customs duties 10.3%, income taxes 8.9%, social security 6.1%; nontax revenue including grants 35.8%). Expenditures: ₲6,072,900,000,000 (current expenditure 78.6%; capital expenditure 21.4%).
Public debt (external, outstanding; 2002): U.S.$2,064,000,000.
Population economically active (2000): total 2,560,608; activity rate 48.5% (participation rates: ages 15 and over, 81.0%; female 38.6%; unemployed [2001] 15.3%).

Price index (2000 = 100)

	1997	1998	1999	2000	2001	2002	2003
Consumer price index	77.1	86.0	91.8	100.0	107.3	118.5	135.4

Production (metric tons except as noted). Agriculture, forestry, fishing (2002): cassava 4,142,000, soybeans 3,276,000, sugarcane 3,210,000, corn (maize) 783,000, wheat 355,000, oranges 210,000, seed cotton 153,000, sweet potatoes 132,000, bananas 65,000; livestock (number of live animals) 9,900,000 cattle, 2,750,000 pigs, 15,500,000 chickens; roundwood 9,787,000 cu m; fish catch (2001) 25,000. Mining and quarrying (2002): hydraulic cement 650,000; kaolin 66,700; gypsum 4,300. Manufacturing (value added in constant prices of 1982, ₲'000,000; 2001): food products 61,056; wood products (excluding furniture) 21,695; beverages 18,589; handicrafts 10,440; textiles 8,412; printing and publishing 8,387; leather and hides 8,249; nonmetal products 5,391; plastics 4,428; petroleum products 3,208. Energy production (consumption): electricity (kW-hr; 2000) 53,521,000,000 (6,136,000,000); crude petroleum (barrels; 2000) none (777,000); petroleum products (metric tons; 2000) 102,000 (1,076,000).
Gross national product (2003): U.S.$6,213,000,000 (U.S.$1,100 per capita).

Structure of gross domestic product and labour force

	2002 in value ₲'000,000,000	2002 % of total value	2000 labour force	2000 % of labour force
Agriculture	7,546.6	23.6	902,322	35.2
Mining	87.9	0.3	2,500	0.1
Manufacturing	4,475.0	14.0	286,186	11.2
Construction	1,432.8	4.5	107,340	4.2
Public utilities	2,041.8	6.4	13,732	0.5
Transp. and commun.	1,679.6	5.2	74,249	2.9
Trade	8,189.4	25.6	587,967	23.0
Finance, real estate	7	7	84,786	3.3
Pub. admin., defense	1,570.9	4.9		
Services	7	7	501,526	19.6
Other	4,952.9[7]	15.5[7]		
TOTAL	31,976.9	100.0	2,560,608	100.0

Household income and expenditure. Average household size (2000) 4.4.
Tourism (2002): receipts U.S.$62,000,000; expenditures U.S.$65,000,000.
Land use as % of total land area (2000): in temporary crops 7.2%, in permanent crops 0.2%, in pasture 54.6%; overall forest area 58.8%.

Foreign trade[8]

Balance of trade (current prices)

	1997	1998	1999	2000	2001	2002
U.S.$'000,000	–1,956	–1,457	–984	–1,181	–999	–560
% of total	46.1%	41.8%	39.9%	40.4%	33.5%	22.8%

Imports (2002): U.S.$1,672,000,000 (machinery and apparatus 21.6%, chemicals and chemical products 17.4%, refined petroleum 14.3%, transport equipment 6.0%, food products 5.6%). *Major import sources:* Brazil 30.6%; Argentina 20.6%; China 12.6%; U.S. 5.0%; Japan 4.0%.
Exports (2002): U.S.$951,000,000[9] (soybeans 35.8%, processed meats 7.6%, soybean oil 7.5%, leather and leather products 6.1%, wood manufactures 5.9%). *Major export destinations:* Brazil 37.1%; Uruguay 17.4%; Cayman Islands 8.2%; Chile 5.2%; U.S. 3.9%.

Transport and communications

Transport. Railroads (1998): route length 441 km; passenger-km 3,000,000; metric ton-km cargo 5,500,000. Roads (1999): total length 29,500 km (paved 51%). Vehicles (2002): passenger cars 274,186; trucks 189,115. Air transport (2000): passenger-km 270,503,000; metric ton-km cargo 24,346,000; airports (1998) 5.

Communications

Medium	date	unit	number	units per 1,000 persons
Daily newspapers	2000	circulation	227,000	43
Radio	2000	receivers	961,000	182
Television	2000	receivers	1,150,000	218
Telephones	2003	main lines	273,200	46
Cellular telephones	2003	subscribers	1,770,300	299
Personal computers	2002	units	200,000	35
Internet	2003	users	120,000	20

Education and health

Educational attainment (2002). Percentage of population age 15 and over having: no formal schooling 5.0%; primary education 55.0%; secondary 33.5%; higher 5.3%; not stated 1.2%. *Literacy* (2002): percentage of total population age 15 and over literate 92.9%; males 93.9%; females 91.9%.

Education (1999)

	schools	teachers	students	student/teacher ratio
Primary (age 7–12)	7,456	59,423[10]	1,036,700	15.7[10]
Secondary (age 13–18)[11]	1,844	21,052	260,500	12.3
Higher	111	1,135	57,292	...

Health: physicians (1995) 3,730 (1 per 1,294 persons); hospital beds (2002) 5,834 (1 per 945 persons); infant mortality rate per 1,000 live births (2003) 27.7.
Food (2001): daily per capita caloric intake 2,576 (vegetable products 78%, animal products 22%); 112% of FAO recommended minimum requirement.

Military

Total active duty personnel (2003): 18,600 (army 80.1%, navy 10.8%, air force 9.1%). *Military expenditure as percentage of GNP* (1999): 1.1% (world 2.4%); per capita expenditure U.S.$15.

[1]Roman Catholicism, although not official, enjoys special recognition in the 1992 constitution. [2]Asunción is the capital city, not a department. [3]Preliminary figure; adjusted preliminary total equals 5,534,378. [4]2003 urban agglomeration population equals 1,639,000. [5]Civil Registry records only. [6]Projected rates based on about 71% of total deaths. [7]Other includes Services and Finance, real estate. [8]Imports f.o.b. in balance of trade and c.i.f. in commodities and trading partners. [9]Excludes value of hydroelectricity exports to Brazil and Argentina. [10]1998. [11]Includes vocational and teacher training.

Internet resources for further information:
- **Banco Central del Paraguay http://www.bcp.gov.py**
- **Dirección General Estadística, Encuestas y Censos http://www.dgeec.gov.py/index.htm**

Peru

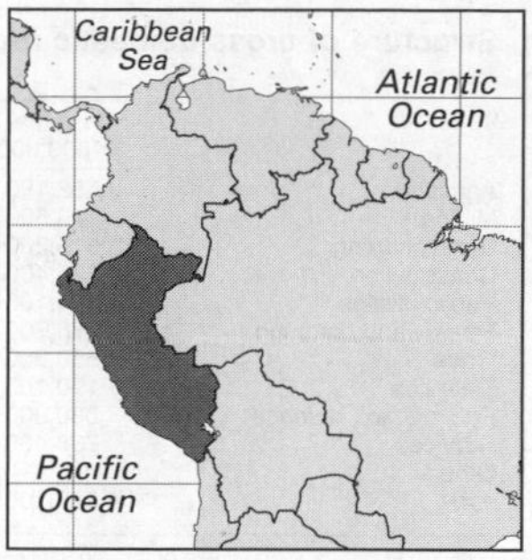

Official name: República del Perú (Spanish) (Republic of Peru).
Form of government: unitary multiparty republic with one legislative house (Congress [120]).
Head of state and government: President, assisted by Prime Minister.
Capital: Lima.
Official languages: Spanish; Quechua; Aymara.
Official religion: Roman Catholicism.
Monetary unit: 1 nuevo sol (S/.) = 100 céntimos; valuation (Sept. 1, 2004) 1 U.S.$ = S/. 3.35; 1 £ = S/. 6.03.

Area and population

Regions[1]	area sq km	population 2002 estimate	Regions[1]	area sq km	population 2002 estimate
Amazonas	39,249	428,095	Lambayeque	14,231	1,121,358
Ancash	35,877	1,107,828	Lima	34,802	7,748,528
Apurímac	20,896	463,131	Loreto	368,852	907,341
Arequipa	63,345	1,101,005	Madre de Dios	85,183	99,452
Ayacucho	43,815	550,751	Moquegua	15,734	156,750
Cajamarca	33,318	1,498,567	Pasco	25,320	264,702
Callao	147	787,154	Piura	35,892	1,636,047
Cusco	72,104	1,208,689	Puno	71,999[2]	1,263,995
Huancavelica	22,131	443,213	San Martin	51,253	757,740
Huánuco	36,887	811,865	Tacna	16,076	294,214
Ica	21,328	687,334	Tumbes	4,669	202,088
Junín	44,197	1,246,663	Ucayali	102,411	456,340
La Libertad	25,500	1,506,122	TOTAL	1,285,216[2]	26,748,972

Demography

Population (2004): 27,544,000.
Density (2004): persons per sq mi 55.5, persons per sq km 21.4.
Urban-rural (2003): urban 73.5%; rural 26.5%.
Sex distribution (2003): male 50.35%; female 49.65%.
Age breakdown (2003): under 15, 32.6%; 15–29, 27.2%; 30–44, 20.8%; 45–59, 11.9%; 60–74, 6.0%; 75 and over, 1.5%.
Population projection: (2010) 29,758,000; (2020) 33,040,000.
Doubling time: 44 years.
Ethnic composition (2000): Quechua 47.0%; mestizo 31.9%; white 12.0%; Aymara 5.4%; Japanese 0.5%; other 3.2%.
Religious affiliation (2000): Roman Catholic 95.7%; other (of which mostly Protestant) 4.3%.
Major cities (2000): metropolitan Lima 7,496,831; Arequipa 762,000; Trujillo 652,000; Chiclayo 517,000; Iquitos 367,000.

Vital statistics

Birth rate per 1,000 population (2003): 22.6 (world avg. 21.3).
Death rate per 1,000 population (2003): 6.2 (world avg. 9.1).
Natural increase rate per 1,000 population (2003): 16.4 (world avg. 12.2).
Total fertility rate (avg. births per childbearing woman; 2003): 2.7.
Life expectancy at birth (2003): male 67.2 years; female 70.7 years.
Major causes of death per 100,000 population (2000): diseases of the circulatory system 536.0; malignant neoplasms (cancers) 522.6; respiratory diseases 453.5; accidents, poisoning, and violence 274.0; infectious diseases 243.2.

National economy

Budget (2001). Revenue: S/. 27,039,000,000 (VAT 43.7%, income taxes 20.8%, nontax revenue 15.1%, import duties 10.1%, payroll tax 3.1%), other taxes 7.2%. Expenditures: S/. 32,378,000,000 (current expenditure 73.7%, capital expenditure 13.8%, interest payments 12.5%).
Public debt (external, outstanding; 2002): U.S.$20,477,000,000.
Tourism (2002): receipts U.S.$801,000,000; expenditures U.S.$616,000,000.
Production (metric tons except as noted). Agriculture, forestry, fishing (2002): sugarcane 8,422,000, potatoes 3,299,000, rice 2,124,000, corn (maize) 2,099,000, plantains 1,560,000, cassava 887,000; livestock (number of live animals) 14,300,000 sheep, 4,950,000 cattle, 2,800,000 pigs, 2,010,000 goats, 90,000,000 chickens; roundwood 9,928,385 cu m; fish catch (2001) 7,995,500. Mining and quarrying (2003): iron ore 3,540,700[3]; zinc 1,171,000[3]; copper 625,300[3]; lead 283,200[3]; silver 2,611[3]; gold 172,900 kg. Manufacturing (value in S/. '000,000[4]; 1996): processed foods 275.1; base metal products 188.6; textiles and leather products 129.5; industrial chemicals 112.3; wood products 80.0. Energy production (consumption): electricity (kW-hr; 2000) 19,912,000,000 (19,912,000,000); coal (metric tons; 2000) 12,000 (528,000); crude petroleum (barrels; 2002) 35,661,000 ([2001] 70,800,000); petroleum products (metric tons; 2000) 7,503,000 (7,620,000); natural gas (cu m; 2000) 820,932,000 (820,932,000).
Population economically active (1998): total 7,407,280; activity rate of total population 45.7% (participation rates: over age 15, 66.9%; female 43.8%; urban unemployed [2001] 7.9%).

Price and earnings indexes (2000 = 100)

	1997	1998	1999	2000	2001	2002	2003
Consumer price index	86.9	93.1	96.4	100.0	102.0	102.2	104.5
Monthly earnings index[5]	90.1	94.6	95.8	100.0	100.8	...	...

Gross national product (at current market prices; 2003): U.S.$58,458,000,000 (U.S.$2,150 per capita).

Structure of gross domestic product and labour force

	2002		2001	
	in value S/. '000	% of total value	labour force	% of labour force
Agriculture	14,323,400	7.2	667,800	8.1
Mining	11,272,500	5.7	45,900	0.6
Manufacturing	28,658,000	14.4	956,400	11.6
Construction	10,515,800	5.3	341,300	4.1
Public utilities	4,327,600	2.2	20,400	0.2
Transp. and commun.	15,700,900	7.9	641,000	7.7
Trade	35,787,500	18.0	2,718,300	32.9
Finance, real estate	6	6	390,500	4.7
Pub. admin., defense	14,585,200	7.4	298,100	3.6
Services	46,368,200[6]	23.4[6]	1,540,200	18.6
Other	16,829,800[7]	8.5[7]	651,500[8]	7.9[8]
TOTAL	198,436,900	100.0	8,271,400	100.0

Household income and expenditure. Average household size (2001) 4.5; income per household (1988) U.S.$2,173; sources of income (1991): self-employment 67.1%, wages 23.3%, transfers 7.6%; expenditure (1990): food 29.4%, recreation and education 13.2%, household durables 10.1%.
Land use as % of total land area (2000): in temporary crops 2.9%, in permanent crops 0.4%, in pasture 21.2%; overall forest area 50.9%.

Foreign trade[9]

Balance of trade (current prices)

	1998	1999	2000	2001	2002	2003
U.S.$'000,000	–2,505	–706	–456	–267	+207	+735
% of total	17.8%	5.5%	3.2%	1.9%	1.4%	4.3%

Imports (2001): U.S.$7,316,000,000 (machinery and apparatus 25.0%, chemicals and chemical products 16.1%, crude and refined petroleum 11.9%, food 11.0%). *Major import sources:* U.S. 23.1%; Argentina 6.2%; Japan 5.9%; Chile 5.9%; Colombia 5.2%.
Exports (2001): U.S.$6,826,000,000 (gold 17.1%, fish foodstuffs for animals 12.3%, refined copper and copper products 11.7%, apparel and clothing accessories 7.4%, crude and refined petroleum 6.1%, zinc ores and concentrates 5.2%). *Major export destinations:* U.S. 24.8%; U.K. 13.5%; China 6.2%; Japan 5.6%; Switzerland 4.5%.

Transport and communications

Transport. Railroads (2000): route length 1,608 km; (1999) passenger-km 144,000,000; metric ton-km cargo 891,000,000. Roads (1999): total length 78,128 km (paved 13%). Vehicles (1999): passenger cars 684,533; trucks and buses 403,652. Air transport (2002)[10]: passenger-km 2,214,000,000; metric ton-km cargo 99,000,000; airports (1996) 27.

Communications

Medium	date	unit	number	units per 1,000 persons
Daily newspapers	1996	circulation	2,000,000	84
Radio	1997	receivers	7,080,000	273
Television	2002	receivers	4,592,400	172
Telephones	2003	main lines	1,839,200	67
Cellular telephones	2003	subscribers	2,908,800	106
Personal computers	2002	units	1,149,000	43
Internet	2003	users	2,850,000	104

Education and health

Educational attainment (1993). Percentage of population age 15 and over having: no formal schooling 12.3%; less than primary education 0.3%; primary 31.5%; secondary 35.5%; higher 20.4%. *Literacy* (2000): total population age 15 and over literate 89.9%; males 94.7%; females 85.3%.

Education (2002)

	schools	teachers	students	student/ teacher ratio
Primary (age 6–11)	33,734	177,257	4,219,800	23.8
Secondary (age 12–16)	9,168	139,349	2,302,099	16.5
Higher[11]	2,161	57,874	1,495,957	25.8

Health (2002): physicians 32,619 (1 per 821 persons); hospital beds 43,074 (1 per 621 persons); infant mortality rate per 1,000 live births (2003) 34.0.
Food (2001): daily per capita caloric intake 2,610 (vegetable products 87%, animal products 13%); 111% of FAO recommended minimum requirement.

Military

Total active duty personnel (2003): 100,000 (army 60.0%, navy 25.0%, air force 15.0%). *Military expenditure as percentage of GNP* (1999): 2.4% (world 2.4%); per capita expenditure U.S.$45.

[1]Elections to newly decentralized regions held in November 2002. [2]Includes the 4,996 sq km area of the Peruvian part of Lake Titicaca. [3]Metal content. [4]At market prices. [5]Private sector only, Lima metropolitan area. [6]Services includes Finance, real estate. [7]Other includes import duties and other taxes on products. [8]Unemployed. [9]Imports are f.o.b. in balance of trade and c.i.f. in commodities and trading partners. [10]Total for 5 national airlines. [11]2000.

Internet resources for further information:
- **Instituto Nacional de Estadística e Informática (Spanish) http://www.inei.gob.pe**
- **Banco Central de Reserva del Peru http://www.bcrp.gob.pe**

Philippines

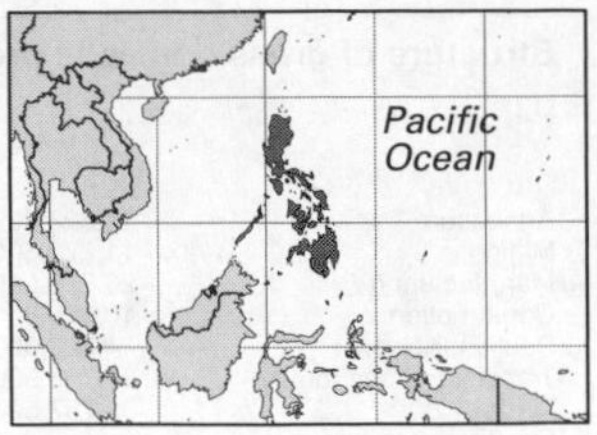

Official name: Republika ng Pilipinas (Pilipino); Republic of the Philippines (English).
Form of government: unitary republic with two legislative houses (Senate [24]; House of Representatives [236]).
Chief of state and head of government: President.
Capital: Quezon City/Manila[1].
Official languages: Pilipino; English.
Official religion: none.
Monetary unit: 1 Philippine peso (₱) = 100 centavos; valuation (Sept. 1, 2004) 1 U.S.$ = ₱ 56.18; 1 £ = ₱ 101.06.

Area and population

Regions	Capitals	area sq mi	area sq km	population 2000 census
Bicol	Legaspi	6,963	18,035	4,674,855
Cagayan Valley	Tuguegarao	11,641	30,149	2,813,159
Calabarzon[2]	Quezon City[3]	6,198	16,052	9,320,629
Caraga	Butuan	7,461	19,324	2,095,367
Central Luzon	San Fernando	7,559	19,579	8,204,742
Central Mindanao	Cotabato	6,135	15,890	2,598,210
Central Visayas	Cebu	6,016	15,582	5,701,064
Cordillera Administrative	Baguio	6,465	16,745	1,365,220
Eastern Visayas	Tacloban	8,490	21,988	3,610,355
Ilocos	San Fernando	4,950	12,821	4,200,478
Mimaropa[2]	...	11,274	29,199	2,299,229
National Capital	Manila	244	633	9,932,560
Northern Mindanao	Cagayan de Oro	6,030	15,617	2,747,585
Southern Mindanao	Davao	10,491	27,172	5,189,335
Western Mindanao	Zamboanga	7,009	18,154	3,091,208
Western Visayas	Iloilo	7,783	20,158	6,208,733
Autonomous region				
Muslim Mindanao	Sultan Kudarat	7,412	19,196	2,412,159
TOTAL		122,121	316,294[4]	76,498,735[5]

Demography

Population (2004): 82,670,000.
Density (2004): persons per sq mi 677.0, persons per sq km 261.4.
Urban-rural (2003): urban 61.0%; rural 39.0%.
Sex distribution (2002): male 50.37%; female 49.63%.
Age breakdown (2002): under 15, 35.1%; 15–29, 28.1%; 30–44, 19.3%; 45–59, 11.2%; 60–74, 5.0%; 75 and over, 1.3%.
Population projection: (2010) 92,330,000; (2020) 107,235,000.
Ethnolinguistic composition (by mother tongue of households; 1995): Pilipino (Tagalog) 29.3%; Cebuano 23.3%; Ilocano 9.3%; Hiligaynon Ilongo 9.1%; Bicol 5.7%; Waray 3.8%; Pampango 3.0%; Pangasinan 1.8%; other 14.7%.
Religious affiliation (2000): Roman Catholic 81.0%; Protestant 6.6%; Muslim 5.1%; indigenous Christian 4.3%; other Christian 0.7%; traditional beliefs 0.2%; other/unknown 2.1%.
Major cities (2000): Quezon City 2,173,831; Manila 1,581,082 (Metro Manila, 9,932,560); Caloocan 1,177,604; Davao 1,147,116; Cebu 718,821.

Vital statistics

Birth rate per 1,000 population (2003): 25.1 (world avg. 21.3).
Death rate per 1,000 population (2003): 5.1 (world avg. 9.1).
Natural increase rate per 1,000 population (2003): 20.0 (world avg. 12.2).
Total fertility rate (avg. births per childbearing woman; 2003); 3.1.
Life expectancy at birth (2003): male 67.2 years; female 72.5 years.
Major causes of death per 100,000 population (1998): circulatory diseases 132.9; respiratory diseases 75.9; malignant neoplasms (cancers) 43.9; accidents 40.8; tuberculosis 38.3; diabetes mellitus 12.1.

National economy

Budget (2001). Revenue: ₱ 563,732,000,000 (income taxes 39.6%, international duties 17.1%, sales tax 15.4%, nontax revenues 12.8%). Expenditures: ₱ 706,327,000,000 (debt service 24.6%, education 17.2%, economic affairs 12.9%, public order 6.8%, defense 4.6%).
Public debt (external, outstanding; 2002): U.S.$32,967,000,000.
Production (metric tons except as noted). Agriculture, forestry, fishing (2002): sugarcane 25,835,000, coconuts 13,682,560, rice 13,270,653, bananas 5,264,470, corn (maize) 4,319,262, pineapples 1,635,930; livestock (number of live animals) 11,652,700 pigs, 6,250,000 goats, 3,122,026 buffalo, 125,730,000 chickens; roundwood (2001) 16,013,084 cu m; fish catch (2001) 2,280,512. Mining and quarrying (2002): nickel 26,532[6]; copper 18,364[6]; chromite 2,000; gold 65,200 kg. Manufacturing (gross value added in ₱ '000,000; 2001): food products 361,217; electrical machinery 95,592; petroleum and coal products 73,280; chemicals 58,487; beverages and tobacco 49,933. Energy production (consumption): electricity (kW-hr; 2002) 48,180,000,000 ([2001] 47,049,000,000); hard coal (metric tons; 2002) 1,644,000 ([2000] 8,599,000); crude petroleum (barrels; 2000) 401,000 (117,700,000); petroleum products (metric tons; 2000) 13,913,000 (15,003,000); natural gas (cu m; 2000) 10,276,000 (10,276,000).
Household income and expenditure (2000). Average household size (2002) 5.0; income per family ₱ 144,506 (U.S.$3,150); sources of income: wages 52.1%, entrepreneurial income 25.1%, receipts from abroad 11.1%; expenditure: food, beverages, and tobacco 45.4%, housing 14.2%, transportation 6.8%.
Gross national product (at current market prices; 2003): U.S.$87,771,000,000 (U.S.$1,080 per capita).

Structure of gross domestic product and labour force

	2002 in value ₱ '000,000	% of total value	labour force	% of labour force
Agriculture	592,100	14.7	11,145,000	31.5
Mining	33,500	0.8	122,000	0.3
Manufacturing	915,200	22.7	3,107,000	8.8
Construction	235,400	5.9	1,709,000	4.8
Public utilities	124,100	3.1	110,000	0.3
Transp. and commun.	276,700	6.9	2,433,000	6.9
Trade	556,300	13.8	6,667,000	18.8
Finances	170,100	4.2	1,023,000	2.9
Pub. admin., defense	380,900	9.5	1,475,000	4.2
Services	738,400	18.4	3,731,000	10.5
Others	—	—	3,899,000[7]	11.0[7]
TOTAL	4,022,700	100.0	35,421,000	100.0

Population economically active (2002): total 35,421,000; activity rate 42.8% (participation rates: ages 15 and over [2003] 67.1%; female [2001] 38.6%; unemployed [2003] 11.4%).

Price index (2000 = 100)

	1997	1998	1999	2000	2001	2002	2003
Consumer price index	81.8	89.8	95.8	100.0	106.1	109.3	112.5

Tourism (2002): receipts U.S.$1,741,000,000; expenditures U.S.$871,000,000.
Land use as % of total land area (2000): in temporary crops 18.9%, in permanent crops 16.8%, in pasture 4.3%; overall forest area 19.4%.

Foreign trade[8]

Balance of trade (current prices)

	1998	1999	2000	2001	2002
U.S.$'000,000	–2,034	+1,230	+6,720	+2,599	–218
% of total	3.3%	1.8%	9.7%	4.2%	0.3%

Imports (2001): U.S.$29,551,000,000 (electronic components 16.0%, computer parts 9.3%, crude petroleum 9.0%, chemicals and chemical products 8.5%, food 7.4%, telecommunications equipment 5.8%). *Major import sources:* Japan 20.6%; United States 16.9%; South Korea 6.6%; Singapore 6.1%; Taiwan 5.4%; Hong Kong 4.3%.
Exports (2001): U.S.$32,150,000,000 (electronic microcircuits 34.4%, computers and computer parts 21.9%, apparel and clothing accessories 7.5%, food 4.0%). *Major export destinations:* United States 27.5%; Japan 15.7%; The Netherlands 9.3%; Singapore 7.2%; Taiwan 6.6%; Hong Kong 4.9%.

Transport and communications

Transport. Railroads (2000): route length 897 km; passenger-km 12,000,000; metric ton-km cargo 660,000,000. Roads (2000): total length 201,994 km (paved 39%). Vehicles (2001): passenger cars 729,350; trucks and buses 285,282. Air transport (2002)[9]: passenger-km 13,956,270,000; metric ton-km cargo 266,913,000; airports (1996) with scheduled flights 21.

Communications

Medium	date	unit	number	units per 1,000 persons
Daily newspapers	2000	circulation	6,300,000	82
Radio	2000	receivers	12,400,000	161
Television	2002	receivers	14,542,000	182
Telephones	2002	main lines	3,310,900	42
Cellular telephones	2002	subscribers	15,201,000	191
Personal computers	2002	units	2,200,000	28
Internet	2002	users	3,500,000	44

Education and health

Educational attainment (2000). Percentage of population age 25 and over having: no formal schooling 3.8%; primary education 38.5%; incomplete secondary 12.5%; complete secondary 17.2%; technical 5.9%; incomplete undergraduate 11.8%; complete undergraduate 7.3%; graduate 0.7%; unknown 2.3%. *Literacy* (2001): total population age 15 and over literate 95.1%.

Education (2001–02)

	schools	teachers	students	student/ teacher ratio
Primary (age 7–12)	40,761	331,448	12,826,218	38.7
Secondary (age 13–16)	7,683	112,210	5,813,879	51.8
Higher	1,603	66,876[10]	2,373,486	30.2[10]

Health (2002): physicians 91,408 (1 per 872 persons); hospital beds 85,166 (1 per 936 persons); infant mortality rate per 1,000 live births (2003) 25.0.
Food (2001): daily per capita caloric intake 2,372 (vegetable products 85%, animal products 15%); 105% of FAO recommended minimum.

Military

Total active duty personnel (2003): 106,000 (army 62.3%, navy 22.6%, air force 15.1%). *Military expenditure as percentage of GNP* (1999): 1.4% (world 2.4%); per capita expenditure U.S.$14.

[1]Additional offices/ministries are located in other suburbs of Metro Manila. [2]Created 2002. [3]Located outside of Calabarzon. [4]Sum of regional areas; actual total may be different. [5]Includes foreign-service employees stationed abroad. [6]Metal content. [7]Unemployed. [8]Imports c.i.f.; exports f.o.b. [9]Philippines Airlines only. [10]1995–96.

Internet resources for further information:
- **National Statistics Office http://www.census.gov.ph**

Poland

Official name: Rzeczpospolita Polska (Republic of Poland).
Form of government: unitary multiparty republic with two legislative houses (Senate [100]; Diet [460]).
Chief of state: President.
Head of government: Prime Minister.
Capital: Warsaw.
Official language: Polish.
Official religion: none[1].
Monetary unit: 1 zloty (Zł) = 100 groszy; valuation (Sept. 1, 2004) 1 U.S.$ = Zł 3.66; 1 £ = Zł 6.58.

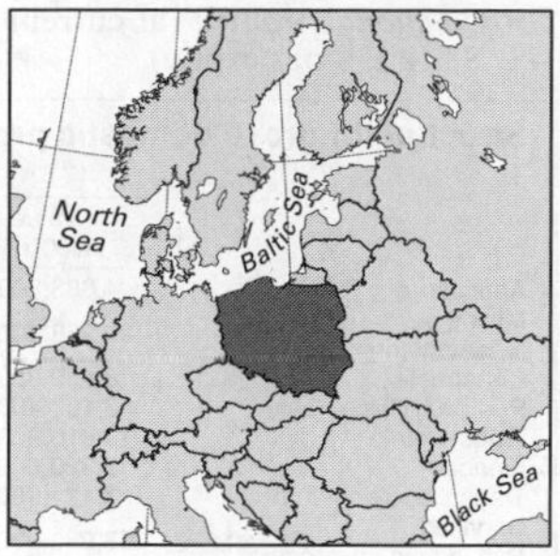

Area and population

Provinces[3]	Capitals	area sq mi	area sq km	population 2003[2] estimate
Dolnośląskie	Wrocław	7,702	19,948	2,902,400
Kujawsko-pomorskie	Bydgoszcz/Toruń	6,938	17,970	2,068,400
Łódzkie	Łódź	7,034	18,219	2,603,700
Lubelskie	Lublin	9,697	25,114	2,194,900
Lubuskie	Gorzów Wielkopolski/ Zielona Góra	5,399	13,984	1,008,000
Małopolskie	Kraków	5,847	15,144	3,245,900
Mazowieckie	Warsaw (Warszawa)	13,744	35,598	5,128,400
Opolskie	Opole	3,634	9,412	1,059,400
Podkarpackie	Rzeszów	6,921	17,926	2,096,100
Podlaskie	Białystok	7,792	20,180	1,206,700
Pomorskie	Gdańsk	7,063	18,293	2,184,400
Śląskie	Katowice	4,747	12,294	4,726,000
Świętokrzyskie	Kielce	4,507	11,672	1,294,200
Warmińsko-Mazurskie	Olsztyn	9,345	24,203	1,428,200
Wielkopolskie	Poznań	11,516	29,826	3,355,200
Zachodniopomorskie	Szczecin	8,843	22,902	1,697,200
TOTAL		120,728[4]	312,685	38,199,100

Demography

Population (2004): 38,176,000.
Density (2004): persons per sq mi 316.2, persons per sq km 122.1.
Urban-rural (2002): urban 61.8%; rural 38.2%.
Sex distribution (2002): male 48.43%; female 51.57%.
Age breakdown (2002): under 15, 18.3%; 15–29, 24.6%; 30–44, 20.6%; 45–59, 20.1%; 60–74, 11.5%; 75 and over, 4.5%.
Population projection: (2010) 38,240,000; (2020) 38,006,000.
Ethnolinguistic composition (1997): Polish 94.2%; Ukrainian 3.9%; German 1.3%; Belarusian 0.6%.
Religious affiliation (1995): Roman Catholic 90.7%; Ukrainian Catholic 1.4%; Polish Orthodox 1.4%; Protestant 0.5%; Jehovah's Witness 0.5%; other (mostly nonreligious) 5.5%.
Major cities (2002): Warsaw 1,671,670 (urban agglomeration; 2001) 2,282,000; Łódź 789,318; Kraków 758,544; Wrocław 640,367; Poznań 578,886; Gdańsk 461,334.

Vital statistics

Birth rate per 1,000 population (2003): 10.5 (world avg. 21.3); (2000) legitimate 87.9%; illegitimate 12.1%.
Death rate per 1,000 population (2003): 10.0 (world avg. 9.1).
Natural increase rate per 1,000 population (2003): 0.5 (world avg. 12.2).
Total fertility rate (avg. births per childbearing woman; 2003): 1.4.
Marriage rate per 1,000 population (2002): 5.0.
Divorce rate per 1,000 population (2002): 1.2.
Life expectancy at birth (2003): male 69.8 years; female 78.3 years.
Major causes of death per 100,000 population (2001): diseases of the circulatory system 449.8; malignant neoplasms (cancers) 228.3; accidents, poisoning, and violence 64.8; diseases of the respiratory system 40.8.

National economy

Budget (2002). Revenue: Zł 143,022,000,000 (value-added tax 40.0%, income tax 27.3%, excise tax 21.9%, nontax revenue 10.8%). Expenditures: Zł 182,922,000,000 (social security and welfare 25.2%, public debt 13.1%, education 12.2%, defense 5.1%).
Gross national product (2003): U.S.$201,389,000,000 (U.S.$5,270 per capita).

Structure of gross domestic product and labour force

	2001		2002[5]	
	in value Zł '000,000	% of total value	labour force	% of labour force
Agriculture	24,731.9	3.2	4,296,800	24.2
Mining	15,283.4	2.0	216,500	1.2
Manufacturing	118,590.1	15.6	2,501,500	14.1
Public utilities	24,213.6	3.2	245,600	1.4
Construction	48,194.5	6.3	737,100	4.1
Transp. and commun.	48,191.9	6.3	714,400	4.0
Trade, restaurants	142,645.0	18.7	2,186,400	12.3
Finance, real estate	100,687.2	13.2	1,128,700	6.3
Pub. admin., defense	45,155.9	5.9	525,700	3.0
Services	88,401.2	11.6	2,117,900	11.9
Other	105,261.5[6]	13.8[6]	3,115,100[7]	17.5[7]
TOTAL	761,356.2	100.0[4]	17,785,700	100.0

Production (metric tons except as noted). Agriculture, forestry, fishing (1999): (gross value of production in Zł '000,000) potatoes 4,066, wheat 3,747, fruit 3,578, vegetables 3,484, rye 1,420, sugar beets 1,254; livestock (number of live animals) 18,538,000 pigs, 6,555,000 cattle; roundwood (2001) 21,170,000 cu m; fish catch (2001) 261,376. Mining and quarrying (2000): sulfur 1,369,000; copper ore (metal content) 390,700; silver (recoverable metal content) 1,144. Manufacturing (value added in Zł '000,000; 1999): food products 13,764; beverages 13,582; transport equipment 10,596; nonelectrical machinery 7,542; electrical machinery 7,506. Energy production (consumption): electricity ('000,000 kW-hr; 2002) 140,880 ([2000] 138,810); hard coal ('000 metric tons; 2002) 104,112 ([2000] 83,390); lignite ('000 metric tons; 2002) 58,212 ([2000] 59,500); crude petroleum (barrels; 2000) 4,844,000 (134,125,000); petroleum products (metric tons; 2000) 16,417,000 (16,668,000); natural gas (cu m; 2002) 5,255,000,000 ([2000] 14,760,000,000).
Public debt (external, outstanding; 2002): U.S.$29,374,000,000.
Population economically active (2002[5]): total 17,785,700; activity rate of total population 46.0% (participation rates: 15 and over, 55.0%; female 45.7%; unemployed 17.5%).

Price and earnings indexes (2000 = 100)

	1997	1998	1999	2000	2001	2002	2003
Consumer price index	75.7	84.6	90.8	100.0	105.5	107.5	108.3
Annual earnings index	72.3	83.1	90.6	100.0	106.9	111.0	114.2

Household income and expenditure. Average household size (2002) 2.9; average annual income (2002) Zł 25,600 (U.S.$6,400); sources of income (2001): wages 46.7%, transfers 33.8%, self-employment 13.9%; expenditure (2001): food, beverages, and tobacco 28.0%, housing and energy 25.6%, transportation and communications 14.6%, recreation 6.6%.
Tourism (2002): receipts U.S.$4,500,000,000; expenditures U.S.$3,200,000,000.
Land use as % of total land area (2000): in temporary crops 46.0%, in permanent crops 1.1%, in pasture 13.4%; overall forest area 29.7%.

Foreign trade[8]

Balance of trade (current prices)

	1997	1998	1999	2000	2001	2002
Zł '000,000	−54,418	−67,443	−73,656	−75,163	−58,138	−57,478
% of total	24.4%	26.2%	25.3%	21.4%	16.4%	14.7%

Imports (2001): Zł 206,253,000,000 (machinery and apparatus 26.1%, chemicals and chemical products 13.9%, road vehicles 7.8%, crude petroleum 5.7%, food 5.3%, textile yarn and fabrics 5.2%). *Major import sources:* Germany 24.0%; Russia 8.8%; Italy 8.3%; France 6.8%; U.K. 4.2%.
Exports (2001): Zł 148,115,000,000 (machinery and apparatus 20.4%, road vehicles 8.9%, food 7.1%, furniture and furniture parts 6.9%, chemicals and chemical products 5.9%, apparel and clothing accessories 5.4%, ships and boats 5.2%). *Major export destinations:* Germany 34.4%; Italy 5.4%; France 5.4%; U.K. 5.0%; The Netherlands 4.7%.

Transport and communications

Transport. Railroads (2002): length 22,981 km; passenger-km 20,809,000,000; metric ton-km cargo 47,756,000. Roads (1999): total length 381,046 km (paved 66%). Vehicles (2001[5]): passenger cars 9,991,260; trucks and buses 1,783,008. Air transport (2002)[9]: passenger-km 6,672,000,000; metric ton-km cargo 80,000,000; airports (1997) 8.

Communications

Medium	date	unit	number	units per 1,000 persons
Daily newspapers	2000	circulation	4,170,000	108
Radio	2000	receivers	20,200,000	523
Television	2000	receivers	15,500,000	400
Telephones	2003	main lines	12,300,000	319
Cellular telephones	2003	subscribers	17,400,000	451
Personal computers	2002	units	4,079,000	106
Internet	2003	users	8,970,000	232

Education and health

Educational attainment (2002). Percentage of population age 13 and over having: no formal schooling/incomplete primary education 5.6%; complete primary 29.8%; secondary/vocational 51.5%; postsecondary 3.2%; university 9.9%, of which doctorate 0.3%. *Literacy* (2000): 99.8%.

Education (2000–01)

	schools	teachers	students	student/ teacher ratio
Primary (age 7–12)	16,766	226,400	3,220,600	14.2
Secondary (age 13–18)	8,587	115,700	2,114,100	18.3
Voc., teacher tr.	8,251	89,700	1,527,900	17.0
Higher	310	79,900	1,584,800	19.8

Health (2002[5]): physicians 86,608 (1 per 446 persons); hospital beds 188,038 (1 per 205 persons); infant mortality rate per 1,000 live births (2003) 9.0.
Food (2001): daily per capita caloric intake 3,397 (vegetable products 75%, animal products 25%); 130% of FAO recommended minimum requirement.

Military

Total active duty personnel (2003): 163,000 (army 63.8%, navy 8.8%, air force 22.4%, other 5.0%). *Military expenditure as percentage of GNP* (1999): 2.1% (world 2.4%); per capita expenditure U.S.$173.

[1]Roman Catholicism has special recognition per 1997 concordat with Vatican City. [2]March 31. [3]Administrative organization effective from Jan. 1, 1999. [4]Detail does not add to total given because of rounding. [5]January 1. [6]Taxes less subsidies. [7]Unemployed. [8]Imports c.i.f.; exports f.o.b. [9]LOT only.

Internet resources for further information:
- **Polish Official Statistics**
  http://www.stat.gov.pl/english/index.htm

Portugal

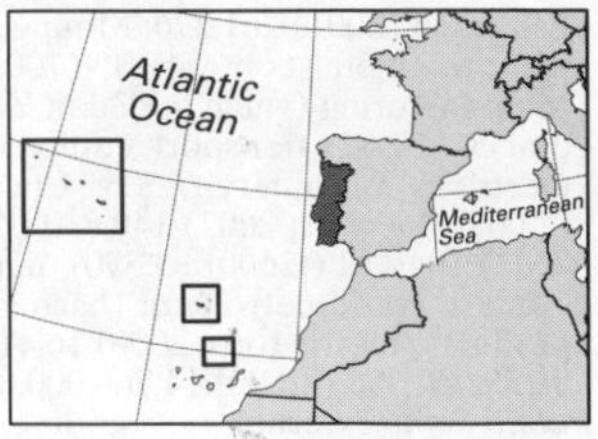

Official name: República Portuguesa (Portuguese Republic).
Form of government: republic with one legislative house (Assembly of the Republic [230]).
Chief of state: President.
Head of government: Prime Minister.
Capital: Lisbon.
Official language: Portuguese.
Official religion: none.
Monetary unit: 1 euro (€) = 100 cents; valuation (Sept. 1, 2004) 1 U.S.$ = €0.82; 1 £ = €1.48[1].

Area and population

		area[2, 3]		population
Continental Portugal		sq mi	sq km	2001 census
Regions	**Principal cities**			9,656,471
Alentejo	Évora	12,080	31,280	760,896
Algarve	Faro	1,920	4,970	420,166
Centre (Centro)	Coimbra	11,030	28,570	2,303,579
Lisbon and Tagus Valley (Lisboa e Vale do Tejo)	Lisbon	1,140	2,950	2,576,823
North (Norte)	Porto	8,220	21,280	3,595,007
Insular Portugal				
Autonomous regions				491,788
Azores (Açores)	Ponta Delgado	897	2,322	240,565
Madeira	Funchal	303	785	251,223
TOTAL		35,580[4]	92,152[4]	10,148,259[5]

Demography

Population (2004): 10,524,000[6].
Density (2004): persons per sq mi 295.8, persons per sq km 114.2.
Urban-rural (2001): urban 65.8%; rural 34.2%.
Sex distribution (2001): male 48.34%; female 51.66%.
Age breakdown (2000): under 15, 17.1%; 15–29, 23.0%; 30–44, 21.5%; 45–59, 17.8%; 60–74, 14.5%; 75 and over, 6.1%.
Population projection[6]: (2010) 10,736,000; (2020) 10,842,000.
Ethnic composition (2000): Portuguese 91.9%; mixed race people from Angola, Mozambique, and Cape Verde 1.6%; Brazilian 1.4%; Marrano 1.2%; other European 1.2%; Han Chinese 0.9%; other 1.8%.
Religious affiliation (2000): Christian 92.4%, of which Roman Catholic 87.4%, independent Christian 2.7%, Protestant 1.3%, other Christian 1.0%; nonreligious/atheist 6.5%; Buddhist 0.6%; other 0.5%.
Major cities (2001)[6]: Lisbon 564,657 (urban agglomeration 3,447,173); Porto 263,131; Amadora 175,872; Braga 164,192; Coimbra 148,443; Funchal 103,961.

Vital statistics

Birth rate per 1,000 population (2003): 11.0 (world avg. 21.3).
Death rate per 1,000 population (2003): 10.3 (world avg. 9.1).
Natural increase rate per 1,000 population (2003): 0.7 (world avg. 12.2).
Total fertility rate (avg. births per childbearing woman; 2003): 1.5.
Marriage rate per 1,000 population (2002): 5.4.
Divorce rate per 1,000 population (2001): 1.8.
Life expectancy at birth (2003): male 73.9 years; females 80.7 years.
Major causes of death per 100,000 population (2000): circulatory diseases 396.6; malignant neoplasms (cancers) 207.6; respiratory diseases 99.5; accidents and violence 46.1.

National economy

Budget (2001). Revenue: Esc 5,793,400,000,000 (taxes on goods and services 52.0%, income taxes 39.5%). Expenditures: Esc 6,616,800,000,000 (current expenditure 89.2%, development expenditure 10.8%).
Public debt (2001): U.S.$61,224,180,000.
Production (metric tons except as noted). Agriculture, forestry, fishing (2002): potatoes 1,200,000, tomatoes 994,000, grapes 900,000, corn (maize) 851,000, sugar beets 600,000, wheat 387,000, olives 320,000, apples 240,000, oranges 220,000, cork (1998) 163,000; livestock (number of live animals) 5,478,000 sheep, 2,389,000 pigs, 1,399,000 cattle; roundwood (2002) 8,742,000 cu m; fish catch (2001) 199,000. Mining and quarrying (2001): marble 1,000,000; copper (metal content) 83,000; tin (metal content) 1,200; silver 23,100 kg. Manufacturing (value added in Esc '000,000; 1998): machinery and transport equipment 606,000, of which transport equipment 232,000; petroleum refining 517,000; wearing apparel and footwear 307,000; food and beverages 290,000; textiles 283,000; tobacco 187,000; printing and publishing 165,000. Energy production (consumption): electricity (kW-hr; 2000) 47,459,000,000 (48,390,000,000); coal (metric tons; 2000) negligible (6,154,000); crude petroleum (barrels; 2000) none (85,200,000); petroleum products (metric tons; 2000) 10,170,000 (12,200,000); natural gas (cu m; 2000) none (2,424,600,000).
Tourism (2002): receipts U.S.$5,919,000,000; expenditures U.S.$2,276,000,000.
Population economically active (2001): total 5,211,300; activity rate of total population 51.3% (participation rates: ages 15–64 [1997], 68.5%; female 45.6%; unemployed 4.1%).

Price and earnings indexes (2000 = 100)

	1997	1998	1999	2000	2001	2002	2003
Consumer price index	92.5	95.0	97.2	100.0	104.4	108.1	111.6
Annual earnings index	...	...	...	...	...	...	...

Gross national product (at current market prices; 2003): U.S.$123,664,000,000 (U.S.$12,130 per capita).

Structure of gross domestic product and labour force

	2002		2001	
	in value €'000	% of total value	labour force	% of labour force
Agriculture	4,083,800	3.2	628,700	12.1
Mining }	20,958,200	16.2	16,200	0.3
Manufacturing }			1,081,900	20.8
Construction	8,450,800	6.5	581,200	11.1
Public utilities	3,151,400	2.4	36,200	0.7
Trade, hotels	19,816,900	15.3	1,007,200	19.3
Finance	13,920,600	10.8	311,200	6.0
Transp. and commun.	7,171,900	5.5	194,200	3.7
Services }	38,982,000	30.1	678,300	13.0
Pub. admin., defense }			321,500	6.2
Other	12,864,200[7]	9.9[7]	354,700[8]	6.8[8]
TOTAL	129,399,800	100.0[4]	5,211,300	100.0

Household income and expenditure. Average household size (1999) 3.1; sources of income (1995): wages and salaries 44.4%, self-employment 23.4%, transfers 22.2%; expenditure (1994–95): food 23.9%, housing 20.6%, transportation and communications 18.9%.
Land use as % of total land area (2000): in temporary crops 21.7%, in permanent crops 7.8%, in pasture 15.7%; overall forest area 40.1%.

Foreign trade[9]

Balance of trade (current prices)

	1997	1998	1999	2000	2001	2002
€'000,000	–1,945[10]	–2,454[10]	–13,790	–16,912	–15,667	–13,568
% of total	18.8%	21.6%	22.5%	24.2%	22.7%	20.0%

Imports (2000): €43,358,000,000 (road vehicles 14.1%; nonelectrical machinery and apparatus 11.4%; mineral fuels and lubricants 10.3%; electrical machinery and telecommunications equipment 9.9%; food products 9.3%; chemicals and chemical products 9.1%). *Major import sources* (2001): Spain 26.5%; Germany 13.9%; France 10.3%; Italy 6.7%; U.K. 5.0%.
Exports (2000): €26,446,000,000 (machinery and apparatus 19.7%, of which telecommunications equipment 4.2%; road vehicles 13.5%; apparel and clothing accessories 11.6%; footwear 5.7%; chemicals and chemical products 5.5%; fabrics 4.7%). *Major export destinations* (2001): Germany 19.2%; Spain 18.6%; France 12.6%; U.K. 10.3%; U.S. 5.8%.

Transport and communications

Transport. Railroads (1999): route length 3,579 km; passenger-km 4,380,000,000; metric ton-km cargo 2,560,000,000. Roads (1999): total length 68,732 km (paved 86%). Vehicles (1998): passenger cars 3,200,000; trucks and buses 1,097,000. Air transport (2001): passenger-km 10,457,000,000; metric ton-km cargo 53,865,000; airports (2000) 16.

Communications

Medium	date	unit	number	units per 1,000 persons
Daily newspapers	2000	circulation	324,000	32
Radio	2000	receivers	3,080,000	304
Television	2000	receivers	6,380,000	630
Telephones	2003	main lines	4,279,000	414
Cellular telephones	2003	subscribers	9,341,000	904
Personal computers	2002	units	1,394,000	134
Internet	2002	users	2,000,000	194

Education and health

Educational attainment (1991). Percentage of population age 25 and over having: no formal schooling 16.1%; some primary education 61.5%; some secondary 10.6%; postsecondary 3.5%. *Literacy* (2000): total population age 15 and over literate 92.2%; males literate 94.8%; females literate 90.0%.

Education (1998–99)

	schools	teachers	students	student/ teacher ratio
Primary (age 5–11) }	12,635	145,513	1,563,700	10.7
Secondary (age 12–19) }				
Vocational	215	6,895	80,130[11]	...
Higher	282	16,192[11]	346,034	...

Health (2001): physicians 33,536 (1 per 310 persons); hospital beds 38,802 (1 per 268 persons); infant mortality rate per 1,000 live births (2003) 5.2.
Food (2002): daily per capita caloric intake 3,741 (vegetable products 71%, animal products 29%); 153% of FAO recommended minimum requirement.

Military

Total active duty personnel (2003): 44,900 (army 59.5%, navy 24.4%, air force 16.1%). *Military expenditure as percentage of GNP* (1999): 2.1% (world 2.4%); per capita expenditure U.S.$240.

[1]The escudo was the former monetary unit; on Jan. 1, 2002, Esc 200.48 = €1. [2]Includes new areas based on regional boundaries changed in *c.* 2001. [3]Regional figures are rounded. [4]Detail does not add to total given because of rounding. [5]Final de facto figure; final de jure figure equals 10,356,117. [6]De jure figures. [7]Includes imputed bank service charges. [8]Includes 143,200 inadequately defined and 211,500 unemployed. [9]Imports c.i.f.; exports f.o.b. [10]In billions of escudos. [11]1996–97.

Internet resources for further information:
- **Instituto Nacional de Estatística http://www.ine.pt/index_eng.htm**
- **Banco de Portugal http://www.bportugal.pt/default_e.htm**

Puerto Rico

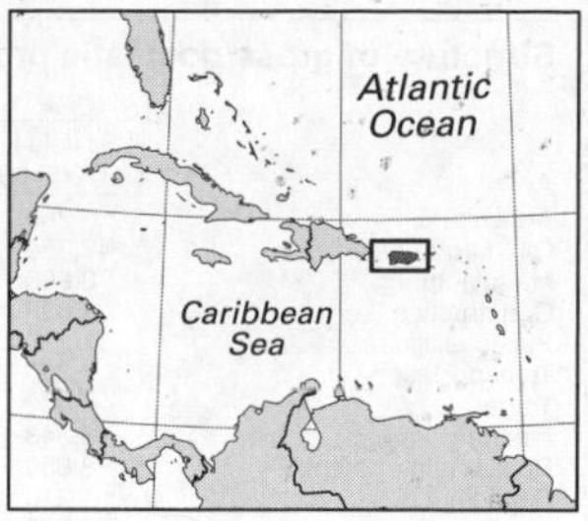

Official name: Estado Libre Asociado de Puerto Rico; Commonwealth of Puerto Rico.
Political status: self-governing commonwealth in association with the United States, having two legislative houses (Senate [27[1]]; House of Representatives [51[1]]).
Chief of state: President of the United States.
Head of government: Governor.
Capital: San Juan.
Official languages: Spanish; English.
Monetary unit: 1 U.S. dollar (U.S.$) = 100 cents; valuation (Sept. 1, 2004) 1 £ = U.S.$1.80.

Population (2002 estimate)

Municipios	population	Municipios	population	Municipios	population
Adjuntas	19,056	Fajardo	41,377	Naguabo	23,944
Aguada	43,143	Florida	13,105	Naranjito	30,014
Aguadilla	65,607	Guánica	22,217	Orocovis	24,316
Agunas Buenas	29,671	Guayama	44,762	Patillas	20,238
Aibonito	26,751	Guayanilla	23,326	Peñuelas	27,480
Añasco	28,894	Guaynabo	101,280	Ponce	186,112
Arecibo	101,283	Gurabo	38,256	Quebradillas	26,179
Arroyo	19,151	Hatillo	40,053	Rincón	15,234
Barceloneta	22,556	Hormigueros	16,856	Río Grande	53,554
Barranquitas	29,490	Humacao	59,688	Sabana Grande	26,481
Bayamón	224,670	Isabela	45,379	Salinas	31,594
Cabo Rojo	48,453	Jayuya	17,631	San Germán	37,469
Caguas	141,693	Juana Díaz	51,464	San Juan	433,412
Camuy	36,407	Juncos	37,511	San Lorenzo	42,042
Canóvanas	44,510	Lajas	26,787	San Sebastián	45,160
Carolina	187,468	Lares	35,392	Santa Isabel	22,076
Cataño	28,888	Las Marías	11,379	Toa Alta	67,950
Cayey	47,505	Las Piedras	35,706	Toa Baja	94,867
Ceiba	18,149	Loíza	33,100	Trujillo Alto	78,439
Ciales	20,110	Luquillo	20,114	Utuado	35,395
Cidra	44,057	Manatí	46,617	Vega Alta	38,490
Coamo	38,252	Maricao	6,490	Vega Baja	62,960
Comerío	19,927	Maunabo	12,807	Vieques	9,191
Corozal	37,525	Mayagüez	97,886	Villalba	28,700
Culebra	1,928	Moca	40,934	Yabucoa	39,719
Dorado	34,583	Morovis	30,811	Yauco	47,135
				TOTAL	3,858,806

Demography

Area: 3,515 sq mi, 9,104 sq km.
Population (2004): 3,898,000.
Density (2004): persons per sq mi 1,109, persons per sq km 428.2.
Urban-rural (2001): urban 75.6%; rural 24.4%.
Sex distribution (2002): male 48.09%; female 51.91%.
Age breakdown (2000): under 15, 23.8%; 15–29, 23.3%; 30–44, 20.4%; 45–59, 17.1%; 60–74, 10.6%; 75 and over, 4.8%.
Population projection: (2010) 4,001,000; (2020) 4,109,000.
Ethnic composition (2000): local white 72.1%; black 15.0%; mulatto 10.0%; U.S. white 2.2%; other 0.7%.
Religious affiliation (2000): Roman Catholic 75.0%; Protestant 19.5%; other 5.5%.
Major metropolitan areas (2002): San Juan 2,541,914; Aguadilla 319,743; Ponce 266,276; San Germán 139,190; Yauco 120,158.

Vital statistics

Birth rate per 1,000 population (2003): 14.3 (world avg. 21.3).
Death rate per 1,000 population (2003): 7.7 (world avg. 9.1).
Natural increase rate per 1,000 population (2003): 6.6 (world avg. 12.2).
Total fertility rate (avg. births per childbearing woman; 2003): 1.9.
Marriage rate per 1,000 population (2001): 6.9.
Divorce rate per 1,000 population (2001): 3.8.
Life expectancy at birth (2003): male 73.3 years; female 81.6 years.
Major causes of death per 100,000 population (2002): malignant neoplasms (cancers) 124.2; heart disease 110.5; communicable diseases 70.9; diabetes mellitus 63.6; cerebrovascular disease 43.7; accidents 34.7; violence and suicide 26.6.

National economy

Budget. Revenue (2002): U.S.$10,556,400,000 (tax revenue 62.6%, of which income taxes 46.5%, excise taxes 14.1%; federal grants 19.0%; nontax revenue 18.4%). Expenditures: U.S.$10,556,400,000 (2001; welfare 22.3%; education 22.3%; public safety and protection 15.7%; debt service 9.8%; health 9.2%).
Public debt (outstanding; 1999): U.S.$22,678,200,000.
Tourism (2002): receipts U.S.$2,486,000,000; expenditures U.S.$928,000,000.
Production (in metric tons except as noted). Agriculture, forestry, fishing (2002): sugarcane 320,000, plantains 82,000, bananas 50,000, oranges 25,712, mangoes 17,375, pineapples 15,000, coffee 12,800, pumpkins, squash, and gourds 11,000; livestock (number of live animals) 390,000 cattle, 118,000 pigs; roundwood, n.a.; fish catch (2001) 3,952 metric tons. Mining (value of production in U.S.$'000; 2002): crushed stone 38. Manufacturing (value added in U.S.$'000,000; 2001): chemicals, pharmaceuticals, and allied products 17,365; nonelectrical machinery 3,320; professional and scientific equipment 1,874; electrical machinery 1,739; beverages 1,455. Energy production (consumption): electricity (kW-hr; 2003) 23,700,000,000 (23,700,000,000); coal (metric tons; 2001) none (172,000); crude petroleum (barrels; 2001) none (58,400,000); petroleum products (metric tons; 2000) 2,478,000 (4,641,000).
Gross national product (2003): U.S.$47,400,000,000 (U.S.$12,240 per capita).

Structure of gross domestic product and labour force

	2002–03		2002	
	in value U.S.$'000,000	% of total value	labour force	% of labour force
Agriculture	203,000	0.3	23,000	1.7
Manufacturing	31,297,300	42.1	136,000	10.0
Mining }	1,759,800	2.4	2,000	0.1
Construction }			85,000	6.3
Public utilities }	5,145,000	6.9	14,000	1.0
Transp. and commun. }			42,000	3.1
Trade	8,622,500	11.6	250,000	18.4
Finance, real estate	12,731,600	17.1	44,000	3.2
Pub. admin., defense	7,146,800	9.6 }	595,000	43.9
Services	7,390,800	9.9 }		
Other	65,600[2]	–0.1[2]	166,000[3]	12.2[3]
TOTAL	74,362,400	100.0[4]	1,356,000[4]	100.0[4]

Population economically active (July 2004): total 1,400,400; activity rate 35.9% (participation rates: ages 16 and over, 46.3%; female (2002) 40.1%; unemployed 12.2%).

Price index (2000 = 100)

	1997	1998	1999	2000	2001	2002	2003
Consumer price index	85.1	89.9	94.6	100.0	107.0	113.6	122.4

Household income and expenditure (2002). Average family size 3.6; income per family U.S.$27,017; sources of income: wages and salaries 56.3%, transfers 29.5%, self-employment 6.4%, rent 5.2%, other 2.6%; expenditure (1999): food and beverages 18.8%, health care 17.8%, transportation 12.8%, housing 12.1%, household furnishings 11.6%, clothing 7.9%, recreation 7.7%.
Land use as % of total land area (2000): in temporary crops 3.9%, in permanent crops 5.5%, in pasture 23.7%; overall forest area 25.8%.

Foreign trade

Balance of trade (current prices)[5]

	1998	1999	2000	2001	2002	2003
U.S.$'000,000	+8,500	+9,600	+11,500	+17,800	+17,200	+21,400
% of total	16.3%	15.9%	17.6%	23.4%	22.3%	24.1%

Imports (2002–03): U.S.$33,800,000,000 (chemicals 44.8%, electronics 10.2%, transport equipment 7.0%, food and beverages 6.7%, refined petroleum 6.0%). *Major import sources:* U.S. 48.9%; Ireland 20.7%; Japan 3.9%.
Exports (2002–03): U.S.$55,200,000,000 (pharmaceutical and chemical products 71.8%, electronic and electrical products 12.5%). *Major export destinations:* U.S. 86.4%; The Netherlands 2.1%; Belgium 2.0%.

Transport and communications

Transport. Railroads (2002)[6]: length 59 mi, 96 km. Roads (2003): total length 15,181 mi, 24,431 km (paved 94%). Vehicles: passenger cars (2001) 2,064,100; trucks and buses (1999) 306,600. Air transport (1998): passenger arrivals and departures 9,285,000; cargo loaded and unloaded 275,500 metric tons[7]; airports (1998) with scheduled flights 7.

Communications

Medium	date	unit	number	units per 1,000 persons
Daily newspapers	2000	circulation	481,000	126
Radio	2000	receivers	2,830,000	742
Television	2000	receivers	1,260,000	330
Telephones	2001	main lines	1,330,000	336
Cellular telephones	2001	subscribers	1,211,000	307
Internet	2001	users	600,000	152

Education and health

Educational attainment (2000). Percentage of population age 25 and over having: no formal schooling to secondary education 25.4%; some upper secondary to some higher 56.3%; undergraduate or graduate degree 18.3%.
Literacy (2001): total population age 15 and over literate 93.8%.

Education (1985–86)

	schools	teachers	students	student/teacher ratio
Primary (age 5–12)	1,542	18,359	427,582	23.3
Secondary (age 13–18)	395	13,612	334,661	24.6
Voc., teacher tr.	52	...	149,191	...
Higher	45	9,045	156,818	17.3

Health: physicians (1999) 6,650 (1 per 571 persons); hospital beds (2001) 12,669 (1 per 303 persons); infant mortality rate (2003) 8.5.

Military

Total active duty personnel (2004): [8].

[1]Number of members per constitution. Excludes additional seats allotted to either the Senate or House of Representatives to meet 1/3 total representation requirements for minority parties per constitution. [2]Statistical discrepancy. [3]Unemployed. [4]Detail does not add to total given because of rounding. [5]For fiscal year ending June 30. [6]Privately owned railway for sugarcane transport only. [7]Handled by the Luis Muñoz Marín International Airport only. [8]The U.S. naval base at Ceiba was closed in March 2004.

Internet resources for further information:
- **Junta de Planificación http://www.jp.gobierno.pr**
- **Global Development Bank http://www.gdb-pur.com**

Qatar

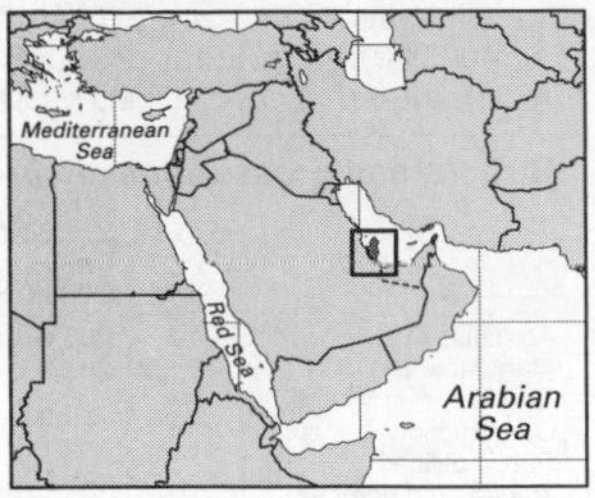

Official name: Dawlat Qaṭar (State of Qatar).
Form of government: constitutional emirate[1].
Heads of state and government: Emir assisted by Prime Minister.
Capital: Doha.
Official language: Arabic.
Official religion: Islam.
Monetary unit: 1 riyal (QR) = 100 dirhams; valuation (Sept. 1, 2004) 1 U.S.$ = QR 3.64; 1 £ = QR 6.55.

Area and population

Municipalities	Capitals	area sq mi	area sq km	population 1997 census
Ad-Dawḥah (Doha)	—	51	132	264,009
Al-Ghuwayrīyah	Al-Ghuwayrīyah	240	622	1,716
Jarayān al-Bāṭinah	Jarayān al-Bāṭinah	1,434[2]	3,715[2]	4,742[2]
Al-Jumaylīyah	Al-Jumaylīyah	991[3]	2,565[3]	9,836
Al-Khawr	Al-Khawr	385	996	17,793
Ar-Rayyān	Ar-Rayyān	343	889	169,774
Ash-Shamāl	Madinat ash-Shamāl	348	901	4,059
Umm Sa'īd	Umm Sa'īd	[2]	[2]	[2]
Umm Ṣalāl	Umm Ṣalāl Muḥammad	190	493	18,392
Al-Wakrah	Al-Wakrah	430[2]	1,114[2]	31,702[2]
TOTAL		4,412	11,427	522,023

Demography

Population (2004): 754,000.
Density (2004): persons per sq mi 170.9, persons per sq km 66.0.
Urban-rural (2001): urban 92.9%; rural 7.1%.
Sex distribution (2003): male 65.5%; female 34.5%.
Age breakdown (2003): under 15, 24.7%; 15–29, 23.5%; 30–44, 24.3%; 45–59, 21.8%; 60–74, 5.1%; 75 and over, 0.6%.
Population projection: (2010) 870,000; (2020) 1,002,000.
Doubling time: 63 years.
Ethnic composition (2000): Arab 52.5%, of which Palestinian 13.4%, Qatari 13.3%, Lebanese 10.4%, Syrian 9.4%; Persian 16.5%; Indo-Pakistani 15.2%; black African 9.5%; other 6.3%.
Religious affiliation (2000): Muslim (mostly Sunnī) 82.7%; Christian 10.4%; Hindu 2.5%; other 4.4%.
Major cities (2004): Ad-Dawḥah (Doha) 338,760; Ar-Rayyān 272,583; Al-Wakrah 20,205[4]; Umm Ṣalāl 15,935[4].

Vital statistics

Birth rate per 1,000 population (2004): 15.6 (world avg. 21.3).
Death rate per 1,000 population (2004): 4.5 (world avg. 9.1).
Natural increase rate per 1,000 population (2004): 11.1 (world avg. 12.2).
Total fertility rate (avg. births per childbearing woman; 2003): 3.1.
Marriage rate per 1,000 population (2002): 3.9.
Divorce rate per 1,000 population (2002): 1.2.
Life expectancy at birth (2003): male 70.7 years; female 75.8 years.
Major causes of death per 100,000 population (2002)[5]: diseases of the circulatory system 95; accidents and violence 74; malignant neoplasms (cancers) 45; endocrine, metabolic, and nutritional disorders 32; diseases of the respiratory system 21; ill-defined conditions 73.

National economy

Budget (2003–04). Revenue: QR 29,155,000,000 (oil and natural gas revenue 67.5%, investment income 23.5%, other 9.0%). Expenditures: QR 23,212,000,000 (current expenditure 73.6%, of which wages and salaries 26.0%; capital expenditure 26.4%).
Production (metric tons except as noted). Agriculture, forestry, fishing (2002): dates 16,500, tomatoes 11,000, pumpkin and squash 8,500, barley 4,650, dry onions 4,000, melons 3,450, watermelons 1,400; livestock (number of live animals; 2002) 200,000 sheep, 179,000 goats, 50,000 camels, 15,000 cattle; fish catch (2001) 7,142. Mining and quarrying (2002): limestone 900,000; sulfur 221,000; gypsum, sand and gravel, and clay are also produced. Manufacturing (value added in U.S.$'000,000; 2000): iron and steel 210; refined petroleum 144; industrial chemicals 133; wearing apparel 71; metal products 42; publishing 23. Construction (value in QR '000, 2002): 2,869,243. Energy production (consumption): electricity (kW-hr; 2001) 9,951,100,000 (9,951,100,000); coal, none (n.a.); crude petroleum (barrels; 2001) 243,788,000 ([2000] 27,200,000); petroleum products (metric tons; 2000) 8,265,000 (1,974,000); natural gas (cu m; 2000) 29,558,000,000 (15,993,000,000).
Tourism (2002): receipts and expenditures, n.a.; total number of tourists staying in hotels 586,645.
Population economically active (2001): total 317,000; activity rate of total population 53.1% (participation rates [1997]: ages 15–64, 59.7%; female 21.0%; unemployed, n.a.).

Price index (2000 = 100)

	1997	1998	1999	2000	2001	2002	2003
Consumer price index	93.8	96.3	98.3	100.0	101.4	101.7	104.0

Gross national product (2001): U.S.$7,200,000,000 (U.S.$12,000 per capita).

Structure of gross domestic product and labour force

	2003 in value QR '000,000	2003 % of total value	2002 labour force	2002 % of labour force
Agriculture	260	0.4	4,000	1.2
Oil, natural gas	42,350	59.8	327,000	98.8
Manufacturing	3,960	5.6		
Construction	2,850	4.0		
Public utilities	980	1.4		
Transportation	2,360	3.3		
Trade	4,030	5.7		
Finance	5,348	7.6		
Pub. admin., defense	8,850	12.5		
Services	1,210	1.7		
TOTAL	70,828	100.0	331,000	100.0

Household income and expenditure. Average household size (2002) 7.1; income per household: n.a.; sources of income, n.a.; expenditure (2001): housing 17.8%, food 16.5%, transportation 15.8%, household furnishings 8.6%, clothing and footwear 7.1%, education 5.5%, communications 5.5%.
Land use as % of total land area (2000): in temporary crops 1.6%, in permanent crops 0.3%, in pasture 4.5%; overall forest area 0.1%.

Foreign trade[6]

Balance of trade (current prices)

	1998	1999	2000	2001	2002
U.S.$'000,000	+1,622	+4,712	+5,595	+6,948	+4,179
% of total	19.2%	48.5%	46.2%	48.0%	34.0%

Imports (2002): U.S.$4,052,000,000 (machinery and apparatus 30.7%, of which general industrial machinery 9.0%, specialized machinery 6.4%; road vehicles 13.3%; food and live animals 10.4%; chemicals and chemical products 6.8%). *Major import sources:* U.S. 13.0%; Japan 10.5%; Italy 9.0%; U.K. 7.6%; Germany 7.0%; United Arab Emirates 7.0%; Saudi Arabia 6.2%.
Exports (2002): U.S.$8,231,000,000 (liquefied natural gas 42.6%; crude petroleum 35.0%; refined petroleum 6.7%; iron and steel 2.8%). *Major export destinations:* Japan 28.9%; South Korea 21.1%; Singapore 12.4%; United Arab Emirates 5.3%; Thailand 4.6%.

Transport and communications

Transport. Railroads: none. Roads (1996): total length 764 mi, 1,230 km (paved 90%). Vehicles (2000): passenger cars 199,600; trucks and buses 92,900. Air transport (2002)[7]: passenger-mi 3,519,626,000, passenger-km 5,664,301,000; short ton-mi cargo 122,281,000, metric ton-km cargo 178,710,000; airports (2002) with scheduled flights 1.

Communications

Medium	date	unit	number	units per 1,000 persons
Daily newspapers	1995	circulation	90,000	161
Radio	1997	receivers	250,000	432
Television	1998	receivers	490,000	846
Telephones	2003	main lines	184,500	289
Cellular telephones	2003	subscribers	376,500	590
Personal computers	2002	units	110,000	178
Internet	2003	users	126,000	197

Education and health

Educational attainment (1986). Percentage of population age 25 and over having: no formal education 53.3%, of which illiterate 24.3%; primary 9.8%; preparatory (lower secondary) 10.1%; secondary 13.3%; postsecondary 13.3%; other 0.2%. *Literacy* (2001): total population age 15 and over literate 81.7%; males literate 80.8%; females literate 83.7%.

Education (2001)[8]

	schools	teachers	students	student/teacher ratio
Primary (age 6–11)	113	3,445	37,923	11.0
Secondary (age 12–17)	102	3,296	32,624	9.9
Vocational	5	109	778	7.1
Higher	1	669	9,915	14.8

Health (2002): physicians 1,518 (1 per 399 persons); hospital beds 1,357 (1 per 447 persons); infant mortality rate per 1,000 live births (2002) 20.3.

Military

Total active duty personnel (2003): 12,400 (army 68.5%, navy 14.5%, air force 16.9%); U.S. troops (August 2004) 3,400. *Military expenditure as percentage of GNP* (1999): 10.0% (world 2.4%); per capita expenditure U.S.$1,470.

[1]Constitution approved by emir on June 8, 2004, is expected to become fully effective in 2005 when published in the official gazette. [2]Umm Sa'īd municipality created in 2004 from parts of Jarayān al-Bāṭinah and Al-Wakrah municipalities. [3]Includes the area of the unpopulated and formerly disputed (with Bahrain) Hawar Islands. The International Court of Justice awarded Hawar to Bahrain in 2001. Qatar was awarded jurisdiction over some nearby islets. [4]1997. [5]Projected rates based on about 42% of total deaths. [6]Imports c.i.f., exports f.o.b. [7]Qatar Airways. [8]Public schools only; number of students in private schools (2001–02) 41,344, of which primary 26,456, preparatory 9,072, secondary 5,816.

Internet resources for further information:
- **Qatar: The Planning Council http://www.planning.gov.qa**

Réunion

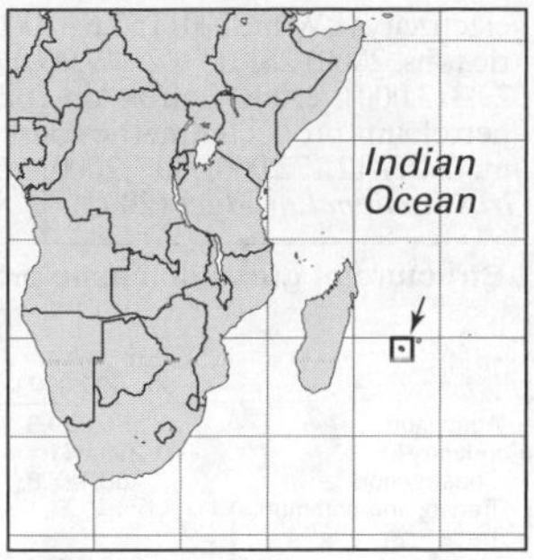

Official name: Département de la Réunion (Department of Réunion).
Political status: overseas department (France) with two legislative houses (General Council [49]; Regional Council [45]).
Chief of state: President of France.
Heads of government: Prefect (for France); President of General Council (for Réunion); President of Regional Council (for Réunion).
Capital: Saint-Denis.
Official language: French.
Official religion: none.
Monetary unit: 1 euro (€) = 100 cents; valuation (Sept. 1, 2004) 1 U.S.$ = €0.82; 1 £ = €1.48[1].

Area and population

		area		population
				1999
Arrondissements	Capitals	sq mi	sq km	census
Saint-Benoît	Saint-Benoît	285	737	101,804
Saint-Denis	Saint-Denis	163	421	236,599
Saint-Paul	Saint-Paul	180	467	138,551
Saint-Pierre	Saint-Pierre	341	883	229,346
TOTAL		968[2, 3]	2,507[2, 3]	706,300

Demography

Population (2004): 773,000.
Density (2004): persons per sq mi 798.6, persons per sq km 308.3.
Urban-rural (1999): urban 82.7%; rural 17.3%[4].
Sex distribution (1999): male 49.15%; female 50.85%.
Age breakdown (1999): under 15, 27.0%; 15–29, 24.8%; 30–44, 24.4%; 45–59, 13.8%; 60–74, 7.2%; 75 and over, 2.8%.
Population projection: (2010) 836,000; (2020) 940,000.
Doubling time: 48 years.
Ethnic composition (2000): mixed race (black-white-South Asian) 42.6%; local white 25.6%; South Asian 23.0%, of which Tamil 20.0%; Chinese 3.4%; East African 3.4%; Malagasy 1.4%; other 0.6%.
Religious affiliation (1995): Roman Catholic 89.4%; Pentecostal 2.7%; other Christian 1.8%; other (mostly Muslim) 6.1%.
Major cities (1999): Saint-Denis 131,557[5] (agglomeration 158,139); Saint-Paul 87,712[5]; Saint-Pierre 68,915[5] (agglomeration 129,238); Le Tampon 60,323[5, 6]; Saint-Louis 43,519[5].

Vital statistics

Birth rate per 1,000 population (2003): 20.2 (world avg. 21.3); (1997) legitimate 41.5%; illegitimate 58.5%.
Death rate per 1,000 population (2003): 5.5 (world avg. 9.1).
Natural increase rate per 1,000 population (2003): 14.7 (world avg. 12.2).
Total fertility rate (avg. births per childbearing woman; 2003): 2.5.
Marriage rate per 1,000 population (1998): 4.8.
Divorce rate per 1,000 population (1997): 1.3.
Life expectancy at birth (2003): male 70.0 years; female 77.0 years.
Major causes of death per 100,000 population (1996): diseases of the circulatory system 170.7; malignant neoplasms (cancers) 98.0; accidents, suicide, and violence 53.0; diseases of the respiratory system 48.5.

National economy

Budget (1998). Revenue: F 4,624,000,000 (receipts from the French central government and local administrative bodies 52.7%, tax receipts 20.2%, loans 8.9%). Expenditures: F 4,300,000,000 (current expenditures 68.7%, development expenditures 31.3%).
Public debt (external, outstanding): n.a.
Tourism (2002): receipts U.S.$284,000,000; expenditures, n.a.
Gross national product (1998): U.S.$5,070,000,000 (U.S.$7,270 per capita).

Structure of gross domestic product and labour force

	1996		1999	
	in value €'000,000	% of total value	labour force	% of labour force
Agriculture, fishing	219	3.2	9,562	3.2
Manufacturing, mining; Public utilities	451	6.7	13,424	4.5
Construction	396	5.9	11,003	3.7
Transp. and commun.	339	5.0	5,494	1.8
Trade, restaurants	832	12.3	24,658	8.2
Finance, real estate, business services	1,114	16.5	16,076	5.4
Pub. admin., defense	3,063	45.4	40,019	13.4
Services			54,408	18.2
Other	339[7]	5.0[7]	124,203[8]	41.6[8]
TOTAL	6,753	100.0	298,847	100.0

Production (metric tons except as noted). Agriculture, forestry, fishing (2001): sugarcane 1,850,000, corn (maize) 17,000, bananas 10,200, pineapples 10,000, cabbages 8,500, tomatoes 5,400, lettuce 4,500, potatoes 4,000, carrots 3,800, eggplants 3,200, pimento 800, ginger 200, vanilla 35, tobacco 20, geranium essence (1998) 6.3; livestock (number of live animals) 78,000 pigs, 37,000 goats, 30,000 cattle; roundwood (2002) 36,100 cu m; fish catch (2002) 3,635. Mining and quarrying: gravel and sand for local use. Manufacturing (value added in F '000,000; 1997): food and beverages 1,019, of which meat and milk products 268; construction materials (mostly cement) 394; fabricated metals 258; printing and publishing 192. Energy production (consumption): electricity (kW-hr; 2000) 1,575,000,000 (1,575,000,000); petroleum products (metric tons; 2000) none (741,000).
Population economically active (1998): total 288,760; activity rate of total population 41.2% (participation rates: ages 15–64, 57.5%; female 44.3%; unemployed [2000] 36.5%).

Price and earnings indexes (2000 = 100)[9]

	1997	1998	1999	2000	2001	2002	2003
Consumer price index	96.0	97.5	98.3	100.0	101.3	104.0	105.0
Monthly earnings index[10]	95.3	97.5	98.8	100.0	101.0	102.4	103.1

Household income and expenditure. Average household size (1999) 3.3; average annual income per household (1997) F 136,800 (U.S.$23,438); sources of income (1997): wages and salaries and self-employment 41.8%, transfer payments 41.3%, other 16.9%; expenditure (1994–95): food and beverages 22.0%, transportation and communications 19.0%, housing and energy 10.0%, household furnishings 8.0%, recreation 6.0%.
Land use as % of total land area (2000): in temporary crops *c.* 14%, in permanent crops *c.* 2%, in pasture *c.* 5%; overall forest area *c.* 28%.

Foreign trade

Balance of trade (current prices)

	1997[11]	1998	1999	2000	2001	2002
€'000,000	–13,011	–2,155	–2,226	–2,503	–2,556	–2,746
% of total	83.9%	85.3%	84.6%	84.7%	84.8%	86.2%

Imports (2002): €2,966,000,000 (food and agricultural products 18.2%, automobiles 12.9%, electrical machinery and electronics 9.0%, pharmaceuticals and medicines 8.4%, clothing and footwear 7.9%). *Major import sources* (1998): France 66.0%; EC 14.0%.
Exports (1998): €185,700,000 (sugar 58.9%, machinery, apparatus, and transport equipment 17.5%, rum 2.5%, lobster 1.7%). *Major export destinations* (1998): France 70.0%; EC 9.0%; Madagascar 4.5%; Mauritius 2.3%.

Transport and communications

Transport. Railroads: [12]. Roads (1994): total length 1,711 mi, 2,754 km (paved [1991] 79%). Vehicles (1999): passenger cars 190,300; trucks and buses 44,300. Air transport (2001)[13]: passenger arrivals 747,044, passenger departures 744,788; cargo unloaded 17,945 metric tons, cargo loaded 8,881 metric tons; airports (2001) with scheduled flights 2.

Communications

Medium	date	unit	number	units per 1,000 persons
Daily newspapers	1996	circulation	83,000	123
Radio	1997	receivers	173,000	252
Television	1998	receivers	130,000	186
Telephones	2001	main lines	300,000	410
Cellular telephones	2002	subscribers	489,800	659
Personal computers	1999	units	32,000	45
Internet	2002	users	150,000	202

Education and health

Educational attainment (1986–87). Percentage of population age 25 and over having: no formal schooling 18.8%; primary education 44.3%; lower secondary 21.6%; upper secondary 11.0%; higher 4.3%. *Literacy* (1996): total population age 16–66 literate 373,487 (91.3%); males literate 179,154 (89.9%); females literate 194,333 (92.7%).

Education (2001–02)

	schools	teachers	students	student/ teacher ratio
Primary (age 6–10)	354[14]	...	77,792	...
Secondary (age 11–17)	118	7,868	98,848	12.6
Higher[15]	1	343	10,637	31.0

Health (2002): physicians 1,137 (1 per 449 persons); hospital beds (2000) 2,124 (1 per 337 persons); infant mortality rate per 1,000 live births (2003) 8.3.
Food (2001): daily per capita caloric intake, n.a.

Military

Total active duty personnel (2003): 3,600 French troops[16].

[1]The French franc (F) was the former monetary unit; on Jan. 1, 2002, F 6.56 = €1. [2]Detail does not add to total given because of rounding. [3]Indian Ocean islets administered by France from Réunion are excluded from total. Islets between Africa and Réunion, which have no permanent population, are: Îles Glorieuses 1.9 sq mi (5.0 sq km), Île Juan de Nova 1.7 sq mi (4.4 sq km), Île Tromelin 0.4 sq mi (1.0 sq km), Bassas da India 0.1 sq mi (0.2 sq km), and Île Europa 7.8 sq mi (20.2 sq km). The French overseas territory of French Southern and Antarctic Territories has been administered from Réunion since April 2000. It comprises 2 archipelagos and 2 islands in the South Indian Ocean as well as the French-claimed part of Antarctica. Non-Antarctic scientific population in summer (2000) 172; non-Antarctic area 4,844 sq mi (7,796 sq km). [4]Includes semi-urban. [5]Population of commune. [6]Within Saint-Pierre agglomeration. [7]Less imputed bank service charges. [8]Unemployed. [9]Indexes refer to December. [10]Minimum salary in public administration. [11]In F '000,000. [12]No public railways; railways in use are for sugar industry. [13]Saint-Denis airport only. [14]2000–01. [15]University only. [16]Includes troops stationed on Mayotte.

Internet resources for further information:
- **INSEE: Réunion http://www.insee.fr/fr/insee_regions/reunion/home/home_page.asp**
- **Ministère de l'Outre-mer (Paris) http://www.outre-mer.gouv.fr**

Romania

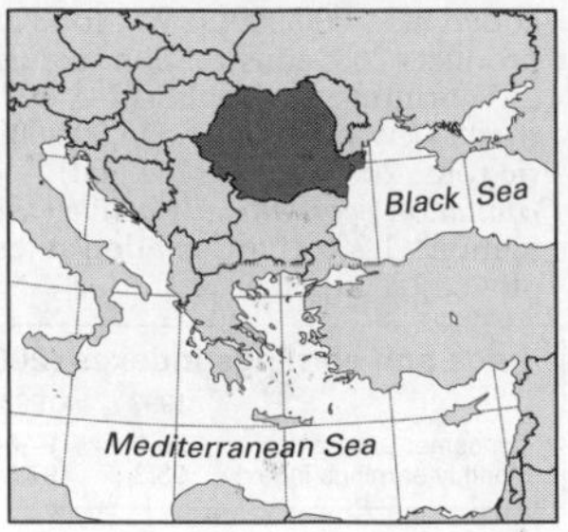

Official name: România (Romania).
Form of government: unitary republic with two legislative houses (Senate [137]; Assembly of Deputies [332[1]]).
Chief of state: President.
Head of government: Prime Minister.
Capital: Bucharest.
Official language: Romanian.
Official religion: none.
Monetary unit: 1 Romanian leu (plural lei) = 100 bani; valuation (Sept. 1, 2004) 1 U.S.$ = 33,745 lei; 1 £ = 60,705 lei.

Area and population

Counties	area sq km	population 2002[2] census	Counties	area sq km	population 2002[2] census
Alba	6,242	382,747	Iaşi	5,476	816,910
Arad	7,754	461,791	Ilfov	1,583	300,123
Argeş	6,826	652,625	Maramureş	6,304	510,110
Bacău	6,621	706,623	Mehedinţi	4,933	306,732
Bihor	7,544	600,246	Mureş	6,714	580,851
Bistriţa-Năsăud	5,355	311,657	Neamţ	5,896	554,516
Botoşani	4,986	452,834	Olt	5,498	489,274
Brăila	4,766	373,174	Prahova	4,716	829,945
Braşov	5,363	589,028	Sălaj	3,864	248,015
Buzău	6,103	496,214	Satu Mare	4,418	367,281
Călăraşi	5,088	324,617	Sibiu	5,432	421,724
Caraş-Severin	8,520	333,219	Suceava	8,553	688,435
Cluj	6,674	702,755	Teleorman	5,790	436,025
Constanţa	7,071	715,151	Timiş	8,697	677,926
Covasna	3,710	222,449	Tulcea	8,499	256,492
Dâmboviţa	4,054	541,763	Vâlcea	5,765	413,247
Dolj	7,414	734,231	Vaslui	5,318	455,049
Galaţi	4,466	619,556	Vrancea	4,857	387,632
Giurgiu	3,526	297,859			
Gorj	5,602	387,308	**Municipality**		
Harghita	6,639	326,222	Bucharest	238	1,926,334
Hunedoara	7,063	485,712	TOTAL	238,391	21,680,974
Ialomiţa	4,453	296,572			

Demography

Population (2004): 21,549,000.
Density (2004): persons per sq mi 234.1, persons per sq km 90.4.
Urban-rural (2002): urban 52.7%; rural 47.3%.
Sex distribution (2002): male 48.75%; female 51.25%.
Age breakdown (2002): under 15, 17.6%; 15–29, 23.4%; 30–44, 21.0%; 45–59, 18.7%; 60–74, 14.4%; 75 and over, 4.9%.
Population projection: (2010) 21,249,000; (2020) 20,555,000.
Ethnic composition (2002): Romanian 89.5%; Hungarian 6.6%; Roma (Gypsy) 2.5%; other 1.4%.
Religious affiliation (2002): Romanian Orthodox 86.7%; Protestant 6.4%; Roman Catholic 4.7%; Greek Orthodox 0.9%; Muslim 0.3%; other 1.0%.
Major cities (2002): Bucharest 1,921,751; Iaşi 321,580; Cluj-Napoca 318,027; Timişoara 317,651; Constanţa 310,526; Craiova 302,622.

Vital statistics

Birth rate per 1,000 population (2002): 9.7 (world avg. 21.3).
Death rate per 1,000 population (2002): 12.4 (world avg. 9.1).
Natural increase rate per 1,000 population (2002): –2.7 (world avg. 12.2).
Total fertility rate (avg. births per childbearing woman; 2002): 1.3.
Marriage rate per 1,000 population (1995): 6.8.
Life expectancy at birth (2002): male 67.4 years; female 74.8 years.
Major causes of death per 100,000 population (2000): circulatory disease 1,439.9; malignant neoplasms (cancers) 187.2; respiratory disease 67.7; diseases of the digestive system 65.6.

National economy

Budget ('000,000 lei; 2000). Revenue: 119,763,500 (value-added tax 42.1%, excise tax 17.2%, personal income tax 16.6%, nontax revenue 4.5%). Expenditures: 105,923,100 (economic affairs 23.0%, education 19.0%, defense 13.3%, public order 13.2%).
Public debt (external, outstanding; 2002): U.S.$8,112,000,000.
Population economically active (2001): total 11,446,900; activity rate 52.6% (participation rates: ages 15–64, 74.5%; female 46.2%; unemployed 6.6%).

Price and earnings indexes (2000 = 100)

	1997	1998	1999	2000	2001	2002	2003
Consumer price index	29.6	47.1	68.6	100.0	134.5	164.8	190.0
Annual earnings index	29.1	48.0	71.5	100.0	138.9	178.6	224.0

Household income and expenditure. Average household size (2000) 3.1.
Production (metric tons). Agriculture (2002): corn (maize) 8,500,000, wheat 4,380,000, potatoes 4,000,000, grapes 895,000, sugar beets 870,000, plums 530,000; livestock (number of live animals) 7,251,000 sheep, 4,446,800 pigs, 2,799,800 cattle; roundwood (2002) 15,154,000 cu m; fish catch (2001) 18,455. Mining (2000): iron (metal content) 55,000; bauxite 135,000; zinc (metal content of concentrate) 27,455; lead (metal content of concentrate) 18,744; copper (metal content of concentrate) 16,079. Manufacturing (value-added in '000,000,000,000 lei; 1996): food products 5.8; beverages 3.0; iron and steel 1.6; glass products 1.5; textiles 1.4; motor vehicles 1.3; electrical machinery 0.9. Construction (1995): 9,300 dwelling units. Energy production (consumption): electricity (kW-hr; 2001) 53,640,000,000 ([2000] 51,241,000,000); hard coal (metric tons; 2000) 281,000 (2,649,000); lignite (metric tons; 2001) 29,431,000 ([2000] 29,313,000); crude petroleum (barrels; 2001) 45,164,000 ([2000] 80,419,000); petroleum products (metric tons; 2000) 9,192,000 (8,230,000); natural gas (cu m; 2001) 12,172,000,000 ([2000] 16,000,000,000).
Gross national product (2003): U.S.$51,194,000,000 (U.S.$2,310 per capita).

Structure of gross domestic product and labour force

	2000 in value '000,000,000 lei	2000 % of total value	2001 labour force	2001 % of labour force
Agriculture	90,929.3	11.4	4,526,800	39.5
Industry[3]	219,861.1	27.6	2,373,700	20.7
Construction	38,127.3	4.8	430,000	3.8
Transp. and commun.			519,400	4.5
Trade			1,082,800	9.5
Finance	370,916.4	46.5	200,000	1.7
Pub. admin.			581,400	5.1
Services			982,800	8.6
Other	78,699.6[4]	9.9[4]	750,000[5]	6.6[5]
TOTAL	796,533.7	100.0[6]	11,446,900	100.0

Tourism (2002): receipts U.S.$612,000,000; expenditures U.S.$396,000,000.
Land use as % of total land area (2000): in temporary crops 40.7%, in permanent crops 2.3%, in pasture 21.5%; overall forest area 28.0%.

Foreign trade[7]

Balance of trade (current prices)

	1997	1998	1999	2000	2001	2002
U.S.$'000,000	–1,980	–2,611	–1,087	–1,683	–2,973	–2,611
% of total	10.5%	13.6%	6.0%	7.5%	11.5%	8.6%

Imports (2001): U.S.$15,552,000,000 (nonelectrical machinery and apparatus 11.9%, fabrics 11.6%, electrical machinery and telecommunications equipment 10.9%, chemicals and chemical products 9.3%, crude and refined petroleum 8.7%). *Major import sources:* Italy 20.0%; Germany 15.2%; Russia 7.6%; France 6.3%; Hungary 3.9%.
Exports (2001): U.S.$11,385,000,000 (apparel and clothing accessories 24.4%, electrical machinery and telecommunications equipment 8.0%, iron and steel 7.2%, nonelectrical machinery and apparatus 6.7%, footwear 5.6%, refined petroleum 5.3%). *Major export destinations:* Italy 25.1%; Germany 15.6%; France 8.1%; U.K. 5.2%; Turkey 4.0%.

Transport and communications

Transport. Railroads (2000): length 11,385 km; passenger-km 11,632,000,000; metric ton-km cargo 17,982,000,000. Roads (2001): length 198,603 km (paved 64%). Vehicles (2000): cars 3,128,782; trucks and buses 461,635. Air transport (2002): passenger-km 1,908,000,000; metric ton-km cargo 8,664,000; airports (2001) 8.

Communications

Medium	date	unit	number	units per 1,000 persons
Daily newspapers	2000	circulation	6,560,000	300
Radio	2000	receivers	7,310,000	334
Television	2000	receivers	8,340,000	381
Telephones	2003	main lines	4,300,000	205
Cellular telephones	2003	subscribers	6,900,000	329
Personal computers	2002	units	1,800,000	83
Internet	2003	users	4,000,000	191

Education and health

Educational attainment (1992). Percentage of population age 25 and over having: no schooling 5.4%; some primary education 24.4%; some secondary 63.2%; postsecondary 6.9%. *Literacy* (2000): total population age 15 and over literate 98.1%; males 99.0%; females 97.3%.

Education (2000–01)

	schools	teachers	students	student/ teacher ratio
Primary (age 6–9)	12,709	162,606	2,411,505	14.8
Secondary (age 10–17)	1,367	64,018	687,919	10.7
Voc., teacher tr.	201	6,387	330,655	51.8
Higher	126	27,959	533,152	19.1

Health: physicians (2002) 41,300 (1 per 525 persons); hospital beds (2002) 161,500 (1 per 135 persons); infant mortality rate (2002) 17.3.
Food (2001): daily per capita caloric intake 3,407 (vegetable products 80%, animal products 20%); 125% of FAO recommended minimum requirement.

Military

Total active duty personnel (2004): 97,200 (army 67.9%, navy 7.4%, air force 14.4%, other 10.3%). *Military expenditure as percentage of GNP* (2001): 1.6% (world 2.4%); per capita expenditure U.S.$97.

[1]Includes 18 elective seats for minority parties. [2]March 18. [3]Mining, manufacturing, and public utilities. [4]Taxes less imputed bank charges. [5]Unemployed. [6]Detail does not add to total given because of rounding. [7]Imports f.o.b. in balance of trade and c.i.f. in commodities and trading partners.

Internet resources for further information:
- **Embassy of Romania (Washington, D.C.) http://www.roembus.org**
- **National Institute of Statistics http://www.insse.ro**
- **National Bank of Romania http://www.bnro.ro/def_en.htm**

Russia

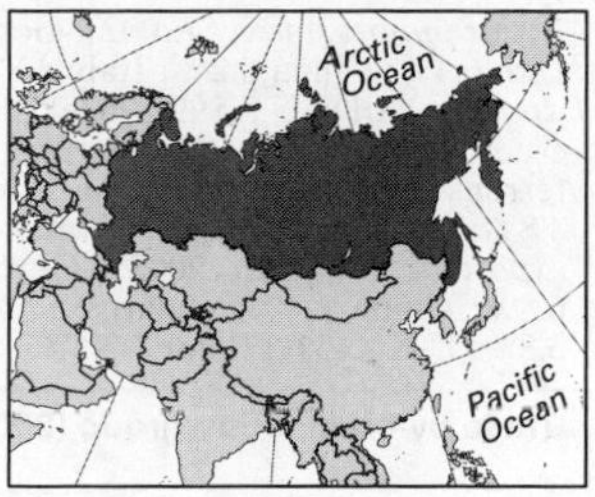

Official name: Rossiyskaya Federatsiya (Russian Federation).
Form of government: federal multiparty republic with a bicameral legislative body (Federal Assembly comprising the Federation Council [178] and the State Duma [450]).
Head of state: President.
Head of government: Prime Minister.
Capital: Moscow.
Official language: Russian.
Official religion: none.
Monetary unit: 1 ruble (Rub) = 100 kopecks; valuation (Sept. 1, 2004) 1 U.S.$ = Rub 29.26; 1 £ = Rub 52.64.

Area and population

		area		population
Federal districts[1]	Capitals	sq mi	sq km	2002 census
Central	Moscow (Moskva)	251,200	650,700	38,000,651
Belgorod (region)	Belgorod	10,500	27,100	1,511,620
Bryansk (region)	Bryansk	13,500	34,900	1,378,941
Ivanovo (region)	Ivanovo	8,400	21,800	1,148,329
Kaluga (region)	Kaluga	11,500	29,900	1,041,641
Kostroma (region)	Kostroma	23,200	60,100	736,641
Kursk (region)	Kursk	11,500	29,800	1,235,091
Lipetsk (region)	Lipetsk	9,300	24,100	1,213,499
Moscow (city)		[2]	[2]	10,382,754
Moskva (Moscow; region)	Moscow (Moskva)	18,200[2]	47,000[2]	6,618,538
Oryol (region)	Oryol	9,500	24,700	860,262
Ryazan (region)	Ryazan	15,300	39,600	1,227,910
Smolensk (region)	Smolensk	19,200	49,800	1,049,574
Tambov (region)	Tambov	13,200	34,300	1,178,443
Tula (region)	Tula	9,900	25,700	1,675,758
Tver (region)	Tver	32,500	84,100	1,471,459
Vladimir (region)	Vladimir	11,200	29,000	1,523,990
Voronezh (region)	Voronezh	20,200	52,400	2,378,803
Yaroslavl (region)	Yaroslavl	14,100	36,400	1,367,398
Far Eastern	Khabarovsk	2,400,000	6,215,900	6,692,865
Amur (region)	Blagoveshchensk	140,400	363,700	902,844
Chukot (autonomous district)	Anadyr	284,800	737,700	53,824
Kamchatka (region)	Petropavlovsk-Kamchatsky	66,000	170,800	333,644
Khabarovsk (territory)	Khabarovsk	304,500	788,600	1,436,570
Koryak (autonomous district)	Palana	116,400	301,500	25,157
Magadan (region)	Magadan	178,100	461,400	182,726
Primorye (territory)	Vladivostok	64,100	165,900	2,071,210
Sakha (republic)	Yakutsk	1,198,200	3,103,200	949,280
Sakhalin (region)	Yuzhno-Sakhalinsk	33,600	87,100	546,695
Yevreyskaya (autonomous region)	Birobidzhan	13,900	36,000	190,915
Northwest	St. Petersburg	648,000	1,677,900	13,974,466
Arkhangelsk (region)	Arkhangelsk	158,700	411,000	1,294,993
Kaliningrad (region)	Kaliningrad	5,800	15,100	955,281
Kareliya (republic)	Petrozavodsk	66,600	172,400	716,281
Komi (republic)	Syktyukar	160,600	415,900	1,018,674
Leningrad (region)	St. Petersburg	33,200[3]	85,900[3]	1,669,205
Murmansk (region)	Murmansk	55,900	144,900	892,534
Nenets (autonomous district)	Naryan-Mar	68,100	176,400	41,546
Novgorod (region)	Novgorod	21,400	55,300	694,355
Pskov (region)	Pskov	21,400	55,300	760,810
St. Petersburg (city)		[3]	[3]	4,661,219
Vologda (region)	Vologda	56,300	145,700	1,269,568
Siberia	Novosibirsk	1,974,800	5,114,800	20,062,938
Agin Buryat (autonomous district)	Aginskoye	7,300	19,000	72,213
Altay (republic)	Gorno-Altaysk	35,700	92,600	202,947
Altay (territory)	Barnaul	65,300	169,100	2,607,426
Buryatiya (republic)	Ulan-Ude	135,600	351,300	981,238
Chita (region)	Chita	159,300	412,500	1,083,133
Evenk (autonomous district)	Tyra	296,400	767,600	17,697
Irkutsk (region)	Irkutsk	287,900	745,500	2,446,378
Kemerovo (region)	Kemerovo	36,900	95,500	2,899,142
Khakassia (republic)	Abakan	23,900	61,900	546,072
Krasnoyarsk (territory)	Krasnoyarsk	274,100	710,000	2,908,559
Novosibirsk (region)	Novosibirsk	68,800	178,200	2,692,251
Omsk (region)	Omsk	53,900	139,700	2,079,220
Taymyr (Dolgano-Nenets) (autonomous district)	Dudinka	332,900	862,100	39,786
Tomsk (region)	Tomsk	122,400	316,900	1,046,039
Tuva (republic)	Kyzyl-Orda	65,800	170,500	305,510
Ust-Ordyn Buryat	Ust-Ordinsky	8,600	22,400	135,327
Southern	Rostov-na-Donu	227,300	589,200	22,907,141
Adygeya (republic)	Maykop	2,900	7,600	447,109
Astrakhan (region)	Astrakhan	17,000	44,100	1,005,276
Chechnia (republic)	Grozny	6,010	15,700	1,103,686
Dagestan (republic)	Makhachkala	19,400	50,300	2,576,531
Ingushetiya (republic)	Magas	1,390	3,600	467,294
Kabardino-Balkariya (republic)	Nalchik	4,800	12,500	901,494
Kalmykiya (republic)	Elista	29,400	76,100	292,410
Karachayevo-Cherkessia (republic)	Cherkessk	5,400	14,100	439,470
Krasnodar (territory)	Krasnodar	29,300	76,000	5,125,221
Rostov (region)	Rostov-na-Donu	38,900	100,800	4,404,013
Severnaya Osetiya–Alania (republic)	Vladikavkaz	3,100	8,000	710,275
Stavropol (territory)	Stavropol	25,700	66,500	2,735,139
Volgograd (region)	Volgograd	44,000	113,900	2,699,223
Urals	Yekaterinburg	690,600	1,788,900	12,373,926
Chelyabinsk (region)	Chelyabinsk	33,900	87,900	3,603,339
Khanty-Mansi (autonomous district)	Khanty-Mansiysk	202,000	523,100	1,432,817
Kurgan (region)	Kurgan	27,400	71,000	1,019,532
Sverdlovsk (region)	Sverdlovsk	75,200	194,800	4,486,214
Tyumen (region)	Tyumen	62,400	161,800	1,325,018
Yamalo-Nenets (autonomous district)	Salekhard	289,700	750,300	507,006

Area and population (continued)

Volga	Nizhny Novgorod	400,900	1,038,300[4]	31,154,744
Bashkortostan (republic)	Ufa	55,400	143,600	4,104,336
Chuvashiya (republic)	Cheboksary	7,100	18,300	1,313,754
Kirov (region)	Kirov	46,600	120,800	1,503,529
Komi-Permyak (autonomous district)	Kudymkar	12,700	32,900	136,076
Mari-El (republic)	Toshkar-Ola	9,000	23,200	727,979
Mordoviya (republic)	Saransk	10,100	26,200	888,766
Nizhny Novgorod (region)	Nizhny Novgorod	29,700	76,900	3,524,028
Orenburg (region)	Orenburg	47,900	124,000	2,179,551
Penza (region)	Penza	16,700	43,200	1,452,941
Perm (region)	Perm	49,300	127,700	2,683,345
Samara (region)	Samara	20,700	53,600	3,239,737
Saratov (region)	Saratov	38,700	100,200	2,668,310
Tatarstan (republic)	Kazan	26,300	68,000	3,779,265
Udmurtia (republic)	Izhevsk	16,300	42,100	1,570,316
Ulyanovsk (Simbirsk; region)	Simbirsk	14,400	37,300	1,382,811
TOTAL		6,592,800	17,075,400[4]	145,166,731

Demography

Population (2004): 144,315,000.
Density (2004): persons per sq mi 21.9, persons per sq km 8.5.
Urban-rural (2003): urban 73.3%; rural 26.7%.
Sex distribution (2002): male 46.60%; female 53.40%.
Age breakdown (2002): under 15, 16.7%; 15–29, 23.4%; 30–44, 22.4%; 45–59, 18.7%; 60–74, 14.0%; 75 and over, 4.8%.
Population projection: (2010) 140,990,000; (2020) 136,062,000.
Ethnic composition (2002): Russian 79.82%; Tatar 3.83%; Ukrainian 2.03%; Bashkir 1.15%; Chuvash 1.13%; Chechen 0.94%; Armenian 0.78%; Mordvin 0.58%; Belarusian 0.56%; Avar 0.52%; Kazakh 0.45%; Udmurt 0.44%; Azerbaijani 0.43%; Mari 0.42%; German 0.41%; Kabardinian 0.36%; Ossetian 0.35%; other 5.80%.
Religious affiliation (2000): Christian 57.4%, of which Orthodox 49.7%, Protestant 6.2%, Roman Catholic 1.0%, other Christian 0.5%; Muslim 7.6%; traditional beliefs 0.8%; Jewish 0.7%; Hindu 0.5%; Buddhist 0.4%; nonreligious 27.4%; atheist 5.2%.
Major cities (2002): Moscow 10,101,500; St. Petersburg 4,669,400; Novosibirsk 1,425,600; Nizhny Novgorod 1,311,200; Yekaterinburg 1,293,000; Samara 1,158,100; Omsk 1,133,900; Kazan 1,105,300; Chelyabinsk 1,078,300; Rostov-na-Donu 1,070,200; Ufa 1,042,400; Volgograd 1,012,800.

Other principal cities (2002)

	population		population		population
Astrakhan	506,400	Lipetsk	506,900	Simbirsk (Ulyanovsk)	635,600
Barnaul	603,500	Naberezhnye Chelny	510,000	Tolyatti	701,900
Irkutsk	593,400	Novokuznetsk	550,100	Tomsk	487,700
Izhevsk	632,100	Orenburg	548,800	Tula	472,300
Kemerovo	485,000	Penza	518,200	Tyumen	510,700
Khabarovsk	582,700	Perm	1,000,100	Vladivostok	591,800
Krasnodar	644,800	Ryazan	521,700	Voronezh	848,700
Krasnoyarsk	911,700	Saratov	873,500	Yaroslavl	613,200

Migration (2002): immigrants 184,612; emigrants 106,685.
Refugees (2002): 828,784, of which from Kazakhstan 301,137, Uzbekistan 106,299, Tajikistan 86,041, Georgia 62,868.
Households (1999). Total households 52,116,000; average household size 2.8; distribution by size (1995): 1 person 19.2%; 2 persons 26.2%; 3 persons 22.6%; 4 persons 20.5%; 5 persons or more 11.5%.

Vital statistics

Birth rate per 1,000 population (2002): 9.6 (world avg. 21.3); (2001) legitimate 70.5%; illegitimate 29.5%.
Death rate per 1,000 population (2002): 16.3 (world avg. 9.1).
Natural increase rate per 1,000 population (2002): –6.5 (world avg. 12.2).
Total fertility rate (avg. births per childbearing woman; 2002): 1.3.
Marriage rate per 1,000 population (2002): 7.1.
Divorce rate per 1,000 population (2002): 6.0.
Life expectancy at birth (2002): male 58.5 years; female 71.9 years.
Major causes of death per 100,000 population (2002): circulatory diseases 909; accidents, poisoning, and violence 230, of which suicide 39, murder 31, alcohol poisoning 28; malignant neoplasms (cancers) 204; respiratory diseases 70; digestive diseases 52; infectious and parasitic diseases 25.0.

Social indicators

Educational attainment (2002). Percentage of population age 15 and over having: no formal schooling 2.1%; primary education 7.7%; some secondary 18.1%; complete secondary/basic vocational 53.0%; incomplete higher 3.1%; complete higher 16.0%, of which advanced degrees 0.3%.
Quality of working life (2002). Average workweek: 40 hours. Annual rate per 100,000 workers of: injury or accident 460; industrial illness 22.2; death 13.8. Average days lost to labour strikes per 1,000 employees (1999): 35.7.
Social participation. Eligible voters participating in last national election (2003): n.a. Trade union membership in total workforce (2000[5]): 100%.
Social deviance. Offense rate per 100,000 population (2002) for: murder 22.5; rape 5.6; serious injury 40.7; larceny-theft 761.5. Incidence per 100,000 population (2000) of: alcoholism (1992) 1,727.5; substance abuse 25.6; suicide 39.2.
Material well-being (2002). Durable goods possessed per 100 households: automobiles 27; personal computers 7; television receivers 126; refrigerators and freezers 113; washing machines 93; VCRs 50; motorcycles 26; bicycles 71.

National economy

Public debt (external, outstanding: 2002): U.S.$96,223,000,000.
Budget (2001). Revenue: Rub 2,438,105,000,000 (tax revenue 83.3%, of which value-added tax 26.2%, social security tax 25.4%, individual income tax 9.0%, excise tax 8.5%; nontax revenue 16.7%). Expenditures: Rub 2,202,868,000,000 (current expenditure 91.3%, of which social security

33.7%, defense 12.6%, public services 8.2%, law enforcement 5.9%; capital expenditure 8.7%).
Gross national product (2003): U.S.$374,937,000,000 (U.S.$2,160 per capita).

Structure of gross domestic product and labour force

	2002			
	in value Rub '000,000	% of total value	labour force	% of labour force
Agriculture	666,000	6.1	7,933,000	11.0
Mining				
Manufacturing	2,882,000	26.5	14,768,000	20.5
Public utilities			3,295,000	4.6
Construction	797,000	7.3	5,140,000	7.1
Transp. and commun.	1,089,000	10.0	5,141,000	7.1
Trade	2,480,000	22.8	10,463,000	14.5
Finance	1,577,000	14.5	818,000	1.1
Services	881,000	8.1	15,272,500	21.2
Pub. admin., defense	491,000	4.5	2,935,000	4.1
Other	—	—	6,153,500[6]	8.6[6]
TOTAL	10,863,000	100.0[7]	71,919,000	100.0[7]

Production (metric tons except as noted). Agriculture, forestry, fishing (2002): wheat 50,557,000, potatoes 31,900,000, barley 18,688,000, sugar beets 15,500,000, vegetables (other than potatoes) 13,800,000, rye 7,139,000, oats 5,700,000, sunflower seeds 3,600,000, apples 1,800,000, peas 1,578,000, corn (maize) 1,541,000, rice 483,000, buckwheat 304,000; livestock (number of live animals) 27,106,000 cattle, 16,048,000 pigs, 13,035,000 sheep; roundwood (2002) 176,900,000 cu m; fish catch (2001) 3,718,000. Mining and quarrying (2001): iron ore 82,800,000; copper (metal content) 600,000; nickel (metal content) 325,000; zinc (metal content) 124,000; chrome ore (marketable) 69,926; platinum 35,000; vanadium 9,000; antimony (metal content) 4,500; molybdenum 2,600; silver 380,000 kg; gold 152,500 kg; gem diamonds 11,600,000 carats. Manufacturing (value added in U.S.$'000,000; 2001): food products 5,090; nonferrous base metals 4,282; iron and steel 3,083; motor vehicles and parts 2,547; bricks, cement, ceramics 2,254; special purpose machinery 2,213; basic chemicals 2,037; general purpose machinery 2,024; fabricated metal products 1,794; beverages 1,780; refined petroleum products 1,761; paper and paper products 1,294; paints, soaps, pharmaceuticals 1,252; tobacco products 754; wood and wood products (excluding furniture) 753; electricity distribution and control apparatus 561.

Financial aggregates

	1998	1999	2000	2001	2002	2003
Exchange rate[8], Rub per:						
U.S. dollar	20.65	27.00	28.16	30.14	31.78	29.45
£	34.35	43.64	42.02	43.72	51.22	52.56
SDR	29.08	37.06	36.69	37.88	43.21	43.77
International reserves (U.S.$)						
Total (excl. gold; '000,000)	7,801	8,457	24,264	32,542	44,054	73,175
SDRs ('000,000)	0.1	0.6	0.5	2.9	1.2	0.7
Reserve pos. in IMF ('000,000)	1.3	1.3	1.2	1.4	1.6	2.1
Foreign exchange ('000,000)	7,800	8,455	24,263	32,538	44,051	73,175
Gold ('000,000 fine troy oz)	14.74	13.33	12.36	13.60	12.46	12.55
% world reserves	1.5	1.4	1.3	1.4	1.3	1.4
Balance of payments (U.S.$'000,000)						
Balance of visible trade	+16,429	+36,012	+60,172	+48,121	+46,335	+60,493
Imports, f.o.b.	–58,014	–39,537	–44,862	–53,764	–60,966	–75,436
Exports, f.o.b.	74,443	75,549	105,034	101,884	107,301	135,929
Balance of invisibles	–16,213	–11,401	–13,332	–14,326	–17,219	–24,648
Balance of payments, current account	+216	+24,611	+46,840	+33,795	+29,116	+35,845

Energy production (consumption): electricity (kW-hr; 2003) 913,900,000,000 ([2000] 863,700,000,000); hard coal (metric tons; 2003) 195,900,000 ([2000] 142,224,000); lignite (metric tons; 2003) 79,000,000 ([2000] 91,700,000); crude petroleum (barrels; 2003) 3,019,000,000 ([2000] 1,312,000,000); petroleum products (metric tons; 2000) 159,281,000 (96,990,000); natural gas (cu m; 2003) 526,000,000,000 ([2000] 318,000,000,000).
Population economically active (2002): total 71,919,000; activity rate of total population 50.0% (participation rates: ages over 15, 82.6%; female 48.6%; unemployed 8.6%).

Price and earnings indexes (2000 = 100)

	1997	1998	1999	2000	2001	2002	2003
Consumer price index	34.9	44.6	82.8	100.0	121.5	140.6	159.9
Monthly earnings index	36.7	42.4	65.6	100.0	143.3	182.4	230.0

Land use as % of total land area (2000): in temporary crops 7.4%, in permanent crops 0.1%, in pasture 5.4%; overall forest area 50.4%.
Household income and expenditure. Average household size (2002) 2.8; income per household: Rub 52,400 (U.S.$1,692); sources of income (2002): wages 66.2%, pensions and stipends 14.9%, income from entrepreneurial activities 12.0%, property income 4.9%, other 2.0%; expenditure (2002): food 41.7%, clothing 13.3%, housing 6.2%, furniture and household appliances 5.7%, alcohol and tobacco 3.2%, transportation 2.7%.
Tourism (2002): receipts U.S.$4,188,000,000; expenditures U.S.$12,005,000,000.

Foreign trade[9]

Balance of trade (current prices)

	1998	1999	2000	2001	2002	2003
U.S.$'000,000	+11,067	+32,077	+55,440	+57,670	+40,867	+52,723
% of total	8.0%	26.9%	36.5%	41.0%	23.6%	24.4%

Imports (2001): U.S.$41,528,000,000 (machinery and apparatus 21.8%, of which general industrial machinery 5.9%; food and live animals 16.1%; chemicals and chemical products 12.1%; road vehicles 4.5%; iron and steel 3.5%). *Major import sources* (2002): Germany 14.3%; Belarus 8.8%; Ukraine 7.0%; U.S. 6.4%; China 5.2%; Italy 4.8%; Kazakhstan 4.2%; France 4.1%.
Exports (2001): U.S.$99,198,000,000 (fuels and lubricants 53.9%, of which crude petroleum 24.8%, natural gas 18.0%, refined petroleum 9.5%; nonferrous metals 6.8%; iron and steel 5.6%; chemicals and chemical products 4.8%; machinery and apparatus 4.6%; special transactions 11.6%). *Major export destinations* (2002): Germany 7.6%; Italy 7.0%; The Netherlands 6.8%; China 6.4%; Belarus 5.5%; Ukraine 5.5%; Switzerland 5.1%; U.S. 3.8%; U.K. 3.6%; Poland 3.5%.

Trade by commodity group (2001)[10]

	imports		exports	
SITC group	U.S.$'000,000	%	U.S.$'000,000	%
0 Food and live animals	6,705	16.1	1,212	1.2
3 Mineral fuels, lubricants	1,013	2.4	53,478	53.9
5 Chemicals, related products	5,023	12.1	4,802	4.8
67 Iron and steel	1,471	3.5	5,582	5.6
68 Nonferrous metals	372	0.9	6,765	6.8
74 General industrial machinery	2,467	5.9	1,283	1.3
76 Telecommunications, incl. parts	1,433	3.5	—	—
78 Road vehicles	1,869	4.5	826	0.8
TOTAL (all groups)	41,528		99,197	

Direction of trade (2001)

	imports		exports	
	U.S.$'000,000	%	U.S.$'000,000	%
Africa	405	1.0	942	0.9
Americas	5,433	13.1	6,875	6.9
United States	3,208	7.7	2,876	2.9
Asia (excl. former U.S.S.R.)	5,401	13.0	15,772	15.9
China	1,617	3.9	3,878	3.9
Asia (former U.S.S.R. only)	2,833	6.8	47,449	4.8
Europe	23,058	55.5	58,598	59.1
EU	15,282	36.8	33,295	33.6
Eastern Europe	2,218	5.3	11,279	11.4
Europe (former U.S.S.R. only)	4,552	11.0	11,150	11.2
Oceania	177	0.4	20	—
TOTAL	41,528[11]		99,198[11]	

Transport and communications

Transport. Railroads (2002): length 139,000 km; passenger-km 152,900,000,000; metric ton-km cargo 1,510,000,000. Roads (2002): total length 593,000 km (paved 91%). Vehicles (2000): passenger cars 20,247,800; trucks and buses (1999) 5,021,000. Air transport (2002): passenger-km 64,700,000,000; metric ton-km cargo 2,700,000,000; airports (1998) 75.

Distribution of traffic (2000)

	cargo carried ('000,000 tons)	% of national total	passengers carried ('000,000)	% of national total
Intercity transport			23,502	54.5
Road	550	21.5	22,033	51.1
Rail	1,046	40.9	1,419	3.3
Sea and river	134	5.2	27	0.1
Air	0.8	...	23	...
Pipeline	829	32.4	—	—
Urban transport	—	—	19,628	45.5
TOTAL	2,559.8	100.0	43,130	100.0

Communications

Medium	date	unit	number	units per 1,000 persons
Daily newspapers	2000	circulation	15,300,000	105
Radio	2000	receivers	61,100,000	418
Television	2000	receivers	61,500,000	421
Telephones	2002	main lines	35,500,000	242
Cellular telephones	2002	subscribers	17,608,800	120
Personal computers	2002	units	13,000,000	89
Internet	2002	users	6,000,000	41

Education and health

Education (2002–03)

	schools	teachers	students	student/teacher ratio
Primary (age 6–13) / Secondary (age 14–17)	67,431	1,719,000	18,918,000	11.0
Voc., teacher tr.	2,626	134,200	2,489,000	18.5
Higher	1,039	291,800	5,948,000	20.4

Health (2002): physicians 678,000 (1 per 212 persons); hospital beds 1,653,000 (1 per 87 persons); infant mortality rate per 1,000 live births (2002) 13.3.
Food (2001): daily per capita caloric intake 3,014 (vegetable products 78%, animal products 22%); 115% of FAO recommended minimum requirement.

Military

Total active duty personnel (2004): 1,212,700 (army 29.7%, navy 12.8%, air force 15.2%, strategic deterrent forces 8.2%, paramilitary 34.1%[12]). *Military expenditure as percentage of GNP* (1999): 5.6% (world 2.4%); per capita expenditure U.S.$239.

[1]Federal districts were formally established in May 2000. [2]Moskva (Moscow; region) includes Moscow (city). [3]Leningrad region includes the city of St. Petersburg. [4]Detail does not add to total given because of statistical discrepancy. [5]State enterprises only. [6]Unemployed. [7]Detail does not add to total given because of rounding. [8]End of period. [9]Imports c.i.f.; exports f.o.b. [10]Selected commodities only. [11]Includes unspecified. [12]Includes railway troops, special construction troops, federal border guards, interior troops, and other federal guard units.

Internet resources for further information:
- **Russian Statistical Agency http://www.gks.ru/eng/default.asp**

Rwanda

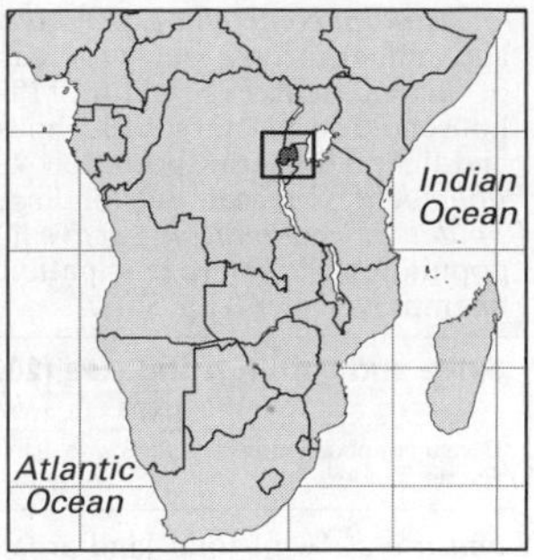

Official name: Repubulika y'u Rwanda (Rwanda); République Rwandaise (French); Republic of Rwanda (English).
Form of government: multiparty republic with two legislative bodies (Senate [26]; Chamber of Deputies [80])[1].
Head of state and government: President assisted by Prime Minister.
Capital: Kigali.
Official languages: Rwanda; French; English.
Official religion: none.
Monetary unit: 1 Rwanda franc (RF); valuation (Sept. 1, 2004) 1 U.S.$ = RF 563.90; 1 £ = RF 1,014.

Area and population

Provinces	Capitals	area sq mi	area sq km	population 2002 preliminary census
Butare	Butare	709	1,837	722,616
Byumba[2]	Byumba	1,838	4,761	712,372
Cyangugu	Cyangugu	713	1,847	609,504
Gikongoro	Gikongoro	794	2,057	492,607
Gisenyi	Gisenyi	791	2,050	867,225
Gitarama	Gitarama	845	2,189	864,594
Kibungo[2]	Kibungo	1,562	4,046	707,548
Kibuye	Kibuye	658	1,705	467,745
Kigali (city)	—	1,204	3,118	608,141
Kigali Ngali	Kigali (city)			792,542
Ruhengeri	Ruhengeri	642	1,663	894,179
Umutara[2]	Nyagatare	…	…	423,642
TOTAL LAND AREA		9,758[3]	25,273	
LAKE KIVU (Rwandan part)		411	1,065	
TOTAL		10,169	26,338	8,162,715[4]

Demography

Population (2004): 8,380,000.
Density (2004)[5]: persons per sq mi 858.7, persons per sq km 331.6.
Urban-rural (2002): urban 16.7%; rural 83.3%.
Sex distribution (2002): male 47.71%; female 52.29%.
Age breakdown (2002): under 15, 42.7%; 15–29, 30.7%; 30–44, 14.9%; 45–59, 7.6%; 60–74, 3.3%; 75 and over, 0.8%.
Population projection: (2010) 9,374,000; (2020) 11,333,000.
Doubling time: 29 years.
Ethnic composition (2002): Hutu 85%; Tutsi 14%; Twa 1%.
Religious affiliation (2000): Roman Catholic 51.0%; Protestant 28.8%; traditional beliefs 9.0%; Muslim 7.9%; independent Christian 2.1%; other 1.2%.
Major cities (2002): Kigali 608,141; Gitarama 84,669; Butare 77,449; Ruhengeri 70,525; Gisenyi 67,192.

Vital statistics

Birth rate per 1,000 population (2003): 40.8 (world avg. 21.3).
Death rate per 1,000 population (2003): 16.8 (world avg. 9.1).
Natural increase rate per 1,000 population (2003): 24.0 (world avg. 12.2).
Total fertility rate (avg. births per childbearing woman; 2003): 5.6.
Life expectancy at birth (2003): male 45.3 years; female 47.4 years.
Adult population (ages 15–49) *living with HIV* (2004[6]): 5.1% (world avg. 1.1%).

National economy

Budget (2001). Revenue: RF 149,500,000,000 (grants 42.3%; taxes on goods and services 27.4%; income tax 16.0%; import and export duties 7.4%; nontax revenue 6.9%). Expenditures: RF 189,200,000,000 (current expenditures 56.8%, of which wages 28.4%, education 15.8%, defense 15.1%, health 2.7%, debt payment 1.5%; capital expenditure 43.2%).
Production (metric tons except as noted). Agriculture, forestry, fishing (2002): plantains 2,784,870, sweet potatoes 1,292,361, potatoes 1,038,931, cassava 1,031,077, sorghum 194,351, corn (maize) 91,686, coffee 19,400, tea 14,900; livestock (number of live animals) 815,000 cattle, 760,000 goats, 260,000 sheep, 180,000 pigs; roundwood (2002) 7,836,000 cu m; fish catch (2001) 7,263. Mining and quarrying (2002): cassiterite (tin content) 197; niobium 43; tantalum 24; gold 10 kg. Manufacturing (value added in RF '000,000; 2000): food and nonalcoholic beverages 37,981; nonmetallic products 3,109; metal products 1,087; chemicals 965; textiles 791; paper 615. Energy production (consumption): electricity (kW-hr; 2000) 169,000,000 (182,000,000); petroleum products (metric tons; 2000) none (174,000); natural gas (cu m; 2000) 250,300 (250,300).
Population economically active (1996): total 3,021,000; activity rate of total population 50.8% (participation rates: ages 14 and over, 86.0%; female 49.0%; unemployed, n.a.).

Price index (2000 = 100)

	1997	1998	1999	2000	2001	2002	2003
Consumer price index	92.5	98.2	95.9	100.0	103.0	105.5	112.8

Land use as % of total land area (2000): in temporary crops 36.5%, in permanent crops 10.1%, in pasture 22.1%; overall forest area 12.4%.
Household income and expenditure. Average household size (1991) 4.7; average annual income per household, n.a.; sources of income: n.a.; expenditure: n.a.

Gross national product (2002): U.S.$1,826,000,000 (U.S.$220 per capita).

Structure of gross domestic product and labour force

	2002 in value RF '000,000	2002 % of total value	2001 labour force	2001 % of labour force
Agriculture	342,352	43.1	3,897,000	90.2
Mining	3,918	0.5	424,000	9.8
Manufacturing	75,904	9.6		
Construction	64,443	8.1		
Public utilities	3,552	0.4		
Transp. and commun.	59,634	7.5		
Trade	79,371	10.0		
Finance	25,581	3.2		
Pub. admin., defense	55,813	7.0		
Services	84,410	10.6		
Other	20[7]	—[7]		
TOTAL	794,998	100.0	4,321,000	100.0

Public debt (external, outstanding; 2002): U.S.$1,305,000,000.
Tourism: receipts (2002) U.S.$31,000,000; expenditures U.S.$24,000,000.

Foreign trade

Balance of trade (current prices)

	1996	1997	1998	1999	2000	2001
U.S.$'000,000	–156.9	–184.5	–168.5	–186.7	–168.6	–147.4
% of total	56.0%	52.5%	56.8%	60.0%	55.0%	44.9%

Imports (2000): U.S.$239,800,000 (capital goods 22.1%, food 19.4%, energy products 18.7%, intermediate goods 18.1%). *Major import sources* (2002): Kenya 21.9%; Germany 8.4%; Belgium 7.9%; Israel 4.3%; U.S. 3.5%.
Exports (2001): U.S.$90,400,000 (niobium and tantalum 45.2%, tea 25.6%, coffee 20.1%). *Major export destinations* (2002): Indonesia 30.8%; Germany 14.6%; Hong Kong 8.9%; South Africa 5.5%.

Transport and communications

Transport. Railroads: none. Roads (1999): total length 7,460 mi, 12,000 km (paved 8%). Vehicles (1996): passenger cars 13,000; trucks 17,100. Air transport (2000)[7]: passengers embarked and disembarked 101,000; cargo loaded and unloaded 4,300 metric tons; airports (2002) with scheduled flights 2.

Communications

Medium	date	unit	number	units per 1,000 persons
Daily newspapers	1995	circulation	500	0.1
Radio	1997	receivers	601,000	101
Telephones	2002	main lines	23,200	2.8
Cellular telephones	2003	subscribers	134,000	16
Internet	2002	users	25,000	3.0

Education and health

Educational attainment: n.a. *Literacy* (2000): percentage of total population age 15 and over literate 66.8%; males literate 73.7%; females literate 60.2%.

Education (1998)

	schools	teachers	students	student/ teacher ratio
Primary (age 7–15)	1,710[9]	23,730	1,288,669	54.3
Secondary (age 16–19)[10]	…	3,413[9]	91,219	…
Higher	…	646[9]	5,678	…

Health: physicians (1992) 150 (1 per 50,000 persons); hospital beds (1990) 12,152 (1 per 588 persons); infant mortality rate (2003) 94.3.
Food (2001): daily per capita caloric intake 2,086 (vegetable products 97%, animal products 3%); 90% of FAO recommended minimum requirement.

Military

Total active duty personnel (2003): 51,000 (army 78.4%, navy 2.0%, national police 19.6%). *Military expenditure as percentage of GNP* (1999): 4.5% (world 2.4%); per capita expenditure U.S.$12.

[1]Referendum on new draft constitution approved May 26, 2003. Executive and legislative elections in August/September 2003 ended 9 years of transitional rule. [2]Umutara prefecture created in 1996 from parts of Byumba and Kibungo prefectures. [3]Detail does not add to total given because of rounding. [4]The 2002 final census total was 8,128,553. [5]Based on land area. [6]Beginning of year. [7]Import taxes less banking services. [8]Kigali airport only. [9]1991–92. [10]Includes vocational and teacher training.

Internet resources for further information:
- **Republic of Rwanda (official Web site) http://www.rwanda1.com**
- **Banque Nationale du Rwanda http://www.bnr.rw**

Saint Kitts and Nevis

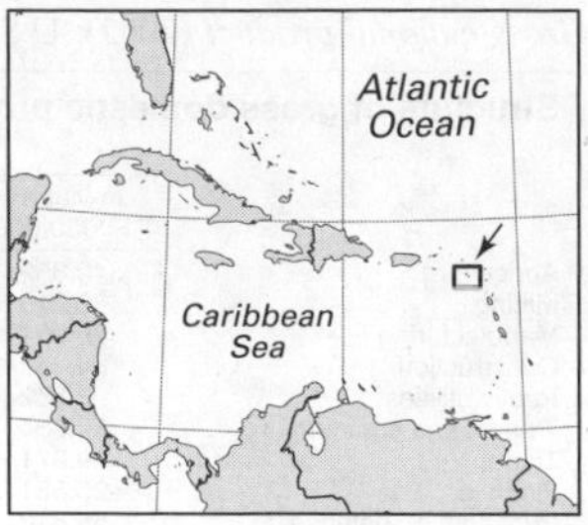

Official name: Federation of Saint Kitts and Nevis[1].
Form of government: constitutional monarchy with one legislative house (National Assembly [15[2]]).
Chief of state: British Monarch represented by Governor-General.
Head of government: Prime Minister.
Capital: Basseterre.
Official language: English.
Official religion: none.
Monetary unit: 1 Eastern Caribbean dollar (EC$) = 100 cents; valuation (Sept. 1, 2004) 1 U.S.$ = EC$2.70; 1 £ = EC$4.86.

Area and population		area		population
				2001
Islands	**Capitals**	sq mi	sq km	census[3]
Nevis[4]	Charlestown	36.0	93.2	11,181
St. Kitts	Basseterre	68.0	176.2	34,703
TOTAL		104.0	269.4	45,884

Demography

Population (2004): 46,300.
Density (2004): persons per sq mi 445.2, persons per sq km 172.1.
Urban-rural (2000): urban 34.2%; rural 65.8%.
Sex distribution (2001): male 49.70%; female 50.30%.
Age breakdown (2000): under 15, 30.3%; 15–29, 24.9%; 30–44, 22.2%; 45–59, 11.2%; 60–74, 7.1%; 75 and over, 4.3%.
Population projection: (2010) 48,000; (2020) 53,000.
Doubling time: 72 years.
Ethnic composition (2000): black 90.4%; mulatto 5.0%; Indo-Pakistani 3.0%; white 1.0%; other/unspecified 0.6%.
Religious affiliation (1995): Protestant 84.6%, of which Anglican 25.2%, Methodist 25.2%, Pentecostal 8.4%, Moravian 7.6%; Roman Catholic 6.7%; Hindu 1.5%; other 7.2%.
Major towns (2001): Basseterre 13,033; Charlestown (1994) 1,411.

Vital statistics

Birth rate per 1,000 population (2003): 18.5 (world avg. 21.3); (1983) legitimate 19.2%; illegitimate 80.8%.
Death rate per 1,000 population (2003): 8.9 (world avg. 9.1).
Natural increase rate per 1,000 population (2001): 9.6 (world avg. 12.2).
Total fertility rate (avg. births per childbearing woman; 2003): 2.4.
Marriage rate per 1,000 population (2001): 7.1.
Divorce rate per 1,000 population (2002): 0.5.
Life expectancy at birth (2003): male 68.8 years; female 74.6 years.
Major causes of death per 100,000 population (1985): diseases of the circulatory system 443.2, of which cerebrovascular disease 220.5, diseases of pulmonary circulation and other heart disease 122.7; malignant neoplasms (cancers) 95.5.

National economy

Budget (2001). Revenue: EC$270,100,000 (tax revenue 72.8%, of which import duties 34.0%, taxes on income and profits 21.4%, taxes on domestic goods and services 14.1%; nontax revenue 27.2%). Expenditures: EC$406,000,000 (current expenditure 75.6%; development expenditure 24.4%).
Production (metric tons except as noted). Agriculture, forestry, fishing (2002): sugarcane 191,400, tropical fruit 1,300, coconuts 1,000, roots and tubers 700, pulses 210, potatoes 160, sweet potatoes 150, tomatoes 100, cabbages 60, onions 60; sea island cotton is grown on Nevis; livestock (number of live animals) 14,400 goats, 14,000 sheep, 4,300 cattle, 4,000 pigs; roundwood, n.a.; fish catch (2001) 291. Mining and quarrying: excavation of sand for local use. Manufacturing (2001): raw sugar 20,193; carbonated beverages 45,000 hectolitres[5]; beer 20,000 hectolitres[5]; other manufactures include electronic components, garments, footwear, and batik. Construction (value added; 1994): EC$57,000,000. Energy production (consumption): electricity (kW-hr; 2000) 100,000,000 (100,000,000); coal, none (none); crude petroleum, none (none); petroleum products (metric tons; 2000) none (33,000); natural gas, none (none).
Gross national product (2003): U.S.$321,000,000 (U.S.$6,880 per capita).

Structure of gross domestic product and labour force	2002		1994	
	in value EC$'000,000	% of total value	labour force[6]	% of labour force[6]
Sugarcane	6.3	0.8	1,525[7]	9.2[7]
Other agriculture, forestry, fisheries	20.2	2.5	914	5.5
Mining	2.6	0.3	29	0.2
Manufacturing	78.2	9.7	1,290[8]	7.8[8]
Construction	137.0	16.9	1,745	10.5
Public utilities	22.0	2.7	416	2.5
Transp. and commun.	116.1	14.4	534	3.2
Trade, restaurants	142.4	17.6	3,367	20.3
Finance, real estate	146.9	18.2	3,708[9]	22.3[9]
Pub. admin., defense	156.2	19.3	2,738	16.5
Services	34.2	4.2	[9]	[9]
Other	–53.6[10]	–6.6[10]	342	2.1
TOTAL	808.5	100.0	16,608	100.0[11]

Household income and expenditure. Average household size (2001) 2.9; average annual income per wage earner (1994) EC$9,940 (U.S.$3,681); sources of income: n.a.; expenditure (1978)[12]: food, beverages, and tobacco 55.6%, household furnishings 9.4%, housing 7.6%, clothing and footwear 7.5%, fuel and light 6.6%, transportation 4.3%, other 9.0%.
Public debt (external, outstanding; 2002): U.S.$252,200,000.
Population economically active (1980): total 17,125; activity rate of total population 39.5% (participation rates: ages 15–64, 69.5%; female 41.0%; unemployed [1997] 4.5%).

Price and earnings indexes (2000 = 100)	1996	1997	1998	1999	2000	2001	2002
Consumer price index	83.6	91.1	94.3	97.9	100.0	101.5	103.6
Earnings index	...	...	...	...	...	...	...

Land use as % of total land area (2000): in temporary crops *c.* 19%, in permanent crops *c.* 3%, in pasture *c.* 6%; overall forest area *c.* 11%.
Tourism: receipts from visitors (2002) U.S.$57,000,000; expenditures by nationals abroad (2001) U.S.$8,000,000.

Foreign trade[13]

Balance of trade (current prices)	1997	1998	1999	2000	2001
U.S.$'000,000	–106.1	...	–124.9	–163.1	–158.2
% of total	56.3%	...	69.1%	71.4%	71.9%

Imports (2001): U.S.$189,200,000 (machinery and apparatus 22.4%; food 14.4%; fabricated metals 7.9%; chemicals and chemical products 6.9%; refined petroleum 6.4%). *Major import sources* (2002): United States 41.5%; Trinidad and Tobago 16.2%; Canada 9.8%; United Kingdom 6.9%; Japan 4.0%.
Exports (2001): U.S.$31,000,000 (electrical switches, relays, and fuses 56.1%; raw sugar 21.0%; telecommunications equipment [parts] 3.2%). *Major export destinations* (2002): United States 66.6%; United Kingdom 7.6%; Canada 6.8%; Portugal 6.0%; Germany 2.9%.

Transport and communications

Transport. Railroads (2000)[14]: length 36 mi, 58 km. Roads (2001): total length 197 mi, 318 km (paved 44%). Vehicles (2001): passenger cars 5,826; trucks and buses 2,989. Merchant marine (1992): vessels (100 gross tons and over) 1; total deadweight tonnage 550. Air transport (2001)[15]: passenger arrivals 135,237; passenger departures 134,937; cargo handled 1,802; airports (1998) with scheduled flights 2.

Communications				units per 1,000
Medium	date	unit	number	persons
Radio	1997	receivers	28,000	701
Television	1997	receivers	10,000	264
Telephones	2002	main lines	23,500	500
Cellular telephones	2002	units	5,000	106
Personal computers	2002	units	9,000	191
Internet	2002	users	10,000	213

Education and health

Educational attainment (1991). Percentage of population age 25 and over having: no formal schooling 1.6%; primary education 45.9%; secondary 38.4%; higher 8.9%; other or not stated 5.2%. *Literacy* (1990): total population age 15 and over literate 25,500 (90.0%); males literate 13,100 (90.0%); females literate 12,400 (90.0%).

Education (2001–02)	schools	teachers	students	student/ teacher ratio
Primary (age 5–12)[16]	24	301	5,608	18.6
Secondary (age 13–17)[16]	7	389	4,445	11.4
Higher[17]	1	51	394	7.7

Health (2001): physicians 49 (1 per 936 persons); hospital beds 178 (1 per 258 persons); infant mortality rate per 1,000 live births (2003) 15.4.
Food (2001): daily per capita caloric intake 2,997 (vegetable products 74%, animal products 26%); 124% of FAO recommended minimum requirement.

Military

Total active duty personnel: in July 1997 the National Assembly approved a bill creating a 50-member army. *Military expenditure as percentage of GNP* (1998): 3.5%[18] (world, n.a.); per capita expenditure U.S.$226[18].

[1]Both Saint Christopher and Nevis and the Federation of Saint Christopher and Nevis are officially acceptable, variant, short- and long-form names of the country. [2]Includes 4 nonelective seats. [3]Preliminary figures. [4]Nevis has full internal self-government. The Nevis legislature is subordinate to the National Assembly only with regard to external affairs and defense. [5]1995. [6]Employed persons only. [7]Includes sugar manufacturing. [8]Excludes sugar manufacturing. [9]Finance, real estate includes Services. [10]Imputed service charge. [11]Detail does not add to total given because of rounding. [12]Weights of consumer price index components. [13]Imports c.i.f.; exports f.o.b. [14]Light railway serving the sugar industry on Saint Kitts. [15]Saint Kitts airport only. [16]Public schools only. [17]1992–93. [18]Includes expenditure for police.

Internet resources for further information:
- **Official Web site of the Government of St. Kitts & Nevis**
http://www.stkittsnevis.net
- **Eastern Caribbean Central Bank**
http://www.eccb-centralbank.org

Saint Lucia

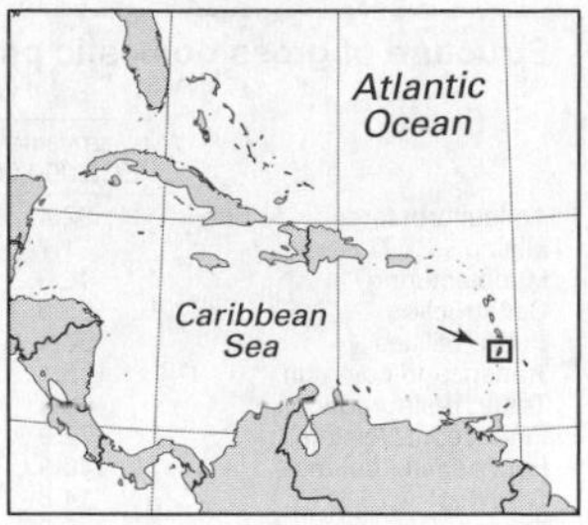

Official name: Saint Lucia.
Form of government: constitutional monarchy with a Parliament consisting of two legislative chambers (Senate [11]; House of Assembly [17[1]]).
Chief of state: British Monarch represented by Governor-General.
Head of government: Prime Minister.
Capital: Castries.
Official language: English.
Official religion: none.
Monetary unit: 1 Eastern Caribbean dollar (EC$) = 100 cents; valuation (Sept. 1, 2004) 1 U.S.$ = EC$2.70; 1 £ = EC$4.86.

Area and population

Districts	Capitals	area sq mi	area sq km	population 2001 census[2]
Anse-la-Raye	Anse-la-Raye	18	47	6,060
Canaries	Canaries			1,788
Castries	Castries	31	79	64,344
Choiseul	Choiseul	12	31	6,128
Dennery	Dennery	27	70	12,767
Gros Islet	Gros Islet	39	101	20,872
Laborie	Laborie	15	38	7,363
Micoud	Micoud	30	78	16,041
Soufrière	Soufrière	19	51	7,656
Vieux Fort	Vieux Fort	17	44	14,754
TOTAL		238[3]	617[3]	157,773[4]

Demography

Population (2004): 164,000.
Density (2004): persons per sq mi 689.1, persons per sq km 265.8.
Urban-rural (2001): urban 38.0%; rural 62.0%.
Sex distribution (2001): male 48.92%; female 51.08%.
Age breakdown (2001): under 15, 31.2%; 15–29, 27.4%; 30–44, 20.6%; 45–59, 10.7%; 60 and over, 10.1%.
Population projection: (2010) 177,000; (2020) 199,000.
Doubling time: 45 years.
Ethnic composition (2000): black 50%; mulatto 44%; East Indian 3%; white 1%; other 2%.
Religious affiliation (2001): Roman Catholic 67.5%; Protestant 22.0%, of which Seventh-day Adventist 8.4%, Pentecostal 5.6%; Rastafarian 2.1%; nonreligious 4.5%; other/unknown 3.9%.
Major urban area (2001): Castries 37,549.

Vital statistics

Birth rate per 1,000 population (2003): 20.9 (world avg. 21.3); (2000) legitimate 14.3%; illegitimate 85.7%.
Death rate per 1,000 population (2003): 5.2 (world avg. 9.1).
Natural increase rate per 1,000 population (2003): 15.7 (world avg. 12.2).
Total fertility rate (avg. births per childbearing woman; 2003): 2.3.
Marriage rate per 1,000 population (2001): 2.8.
Divorce rate per 1,000 population (2001): 0.4.
Life expectancy at birth (2003): male 69.5 years; female 76.9 years.
Major causes of death per 100,000 population (2002): diseases of the circulatory system 192.7, of which cerebrovascular diseases 75.9; malignant neoplasms (cancers) 101.8; diabetes mellitus 77.4; communicable diseases 39.4.

National economy

Budget (2002). Revenue: EC$505,700,000 (tax revenue 81.6%, of which consumption duties on imported goods 42.5%, taxes on income and profits 21.3%, goods and services 16.5%; nontax revenue 12.7%; grants 5.7%). Expenditures: EC$543,600,000 (current expenditures 74.6%; development expenditures and net lending 25.4%).
Public debt (external, outstanding; 2002): U.S.$210,700,000.
Production (metric tons except as noted). Agriculture, forestry, fishing (2002): bananas 92,000, mangoes 28,000, coconuts 14,000, yams 4,500, grapefruit 2,973, tropical fruit 2,800, plantains 1,300, cassava 1,000, vegetables 1,000, oranges 602; livestock (number of live animals) 14,950 pigs, 12,500 sheep, 12,400 cattle, 9,800 goats; roundwood, n.a.; fish catch (2001) 1,984. Mining and quarrying: excavation of sand for local construction and pumice. Manufacturing (value of production in EC$'000; 1998): alcoholic beverages and tobacco 31,120; paper products and cardboard boxes 28,747; electrical and electronic components 16,245; food 9,535; garments 6,563; textiles 3,999; refined coconut oil 2,330; copra 1,330. Energy production (consumption): electricity (kW-hr; 2000) 375,000,000 (375,000,000); coal, none (none); crude petroleum, none (none); petroleum products (metric tons; 2000) none (110,000); natural gas, none (none).
Population economically active (2002): total 74,949; activity rate of total population 47.0% (participation rates: ages 15 and over, 66.8%; female [2000] 47.2%; unemployed 16.2%).

Price index (2000 = 100)

	1997	1998	1999	2000	2001	2002	2003
Consumer price index	90.3	93.2	96.3	100.0	100.1	101.7	102.7

Gross national product (at current market prices; 2003): U.S.$650,000,000 (U.S.$4,050 per capita).

Structure of gross domestic product and labour force

	2002 in value EC$'000,000[5]	2002 % of total value[5]	2000 labour force	2000 % of labour force
Agriculture	97.62	6.5	12,560	16.1
Mining	6.05	0.4	—	—
Manufacturing	73.34	4.8	6,610	8.4
Construction	118.77	7.9	6,460	8.3
Public utilities	76.38	5.0	530	0.7
Transportation and communications	326.15	21.6	4,540	5.8
Trade, restaurants	367.21	24.3	17,230	22.1
Finance, real estate	259.36	17.1	2,320	3.0
Pub. admin., defense	234.17	15.5	8,180	10.5
Services	80.31	5.3	4,360	5.6
Other	–126.78[6]	–8.4[6]	15,210[7]	19.5[7]
TOTAL	1,512.58	100.0	78,000	100.0

Household income and expenditure. Average household size (2001) 3.2; income per household: n.a.; sources of income: n.a.; expenditure: n.a.
Land use as % of total land area (2000): in temporary crops *c.* 7%, in permanent crops *c.* 23%, in pasture *c.* 3%; overall forest area *c.* 15%.
Tourism: receipts from visitors (2002) U.S.$218,000,000; expenditures by nationals abroad (2001) U.S.$32,000,000.

Foreign trade

Balance of trade (current prices)

	1997	1998	1999	2000	2001	2002
U.S.$'000,000	–222.1	–224.7	–251.1	–249.4	–206.9	–222.2
% of total	61.2%	61.5%	67.3%	66.4%	66.6%	66.9%

Imports (2002): U.S.$277,100,000 (food and beverages 26.2%; machinery and apparatus 23.5%; manufactured goods 17.3%; chemicals and chemical products 9.0%; refined petroleum 8.7%). *Major import sources:* United States 38.0%; Trinidad and Tobago 14.6%; United Kingdom 9.5%; Japan 3.3%; Canada 3.1%.
Exports (2002): U.S.$54,900,000 (bananas 49.9%; beer and ale 15.9%; clothing 3.2%; electrical and electronic components 3.2%). *Major export destinations:* United Kingdom 37.6%; United States 20.3%; Trinidad and Tobago 11.8%; Barbados 9.7%; Dominica 5.3%.

Transport and communications

Transport. Railroads: none. Roads (1999): total length 750 mi, 1,210 km (paved 5%). Vehicles (2001): passenger cars 22,453; trucks and buses 8,972. Air transport (2001)[8]: passenger arrivals and departures 679,000; cargo unloaded and loaded 3,500 metric tons; airports (2000) with scheduled flights 2.

Communications

Medium	date	unit	number	units per 1,000 persons
Radio	1997	receivers	100,000	668
Television	1997	receivers	40,000	267
Telephones	2002	main lines	51,100	320
Cellular telephones	2002	subscribers	14,300	90
Personal computers	2002	units	24,000	150
Internet	2001	users	13,000	82

Education and health

Educational attainment (2000). Percentage of population age 15 and over having: no formal schooling 6.5%; primary education 56.2%; secondary 27.5%; higher vocational 4.5%; university 2.7%; other/unknown 2.6%. *Literacy* (2000): 90.2%.

Education (2000–01)

	schools	teachers	students	student/ teacher ratio
Primary (age 5–11)	82	1,052	28,618	27.2
Secondary (age 12–16)	18	678	12,865	19.0
Higher	...	127	1,403	11.0

Health (2002): physicians 92 (1 per 1,740 persons); hospital beds 285 (1 per 562 persons); infant mortality rate per 1,000 live births (2003) 15.4.
Food (2001): daily per capita caloric intake 2,849 (vegetable products 72%, animal products 28%); 118% of FAO recommended minimum requirement.

Military

Total active duty personnel (2000): [9].

[1]Represents elected seats only. Attorney general and speaker serve ex officio. [2]Preliminary. [3]Total includes the uninhabited 30 sq mi (78 sq km) Central Forest Reserve. [4]Total adjusted pop. (including institutionalized individuals but excluding visitors) equals 158,361. [5]At factor cost in current prices. [6]Less imputed bank service charges. [7]Includes 13,630 unemployed. [8]Combined data for both Castries and Vieux Fort airports. [9]The 300-member police force includes a specially trained paramilitary unit and a coast guard unit.

Internet resources for further information:
- **Saint Lucian Government Statistics Department http://www.stats.gov.lc**
- **Eastern Caribbean Central Bank http://www.eccb-centralbank.org**

Saint Vincent and the Grenadines

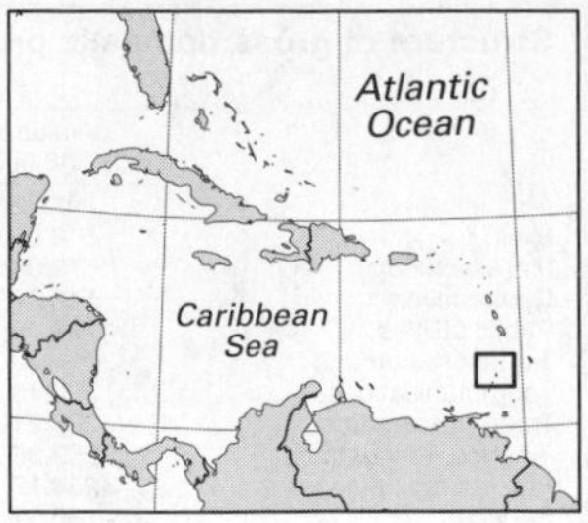

Official name: Saint Vincent and the Grenadines.
Form of government: constitutional monarchy with one legislative house (House of Assembly [21[1]]).
Chief of state: British Monarch represented by Governor-General.
Head of government: Prime Minister.
Capital: Kingstown.
Official language: English.
Official religion: none.
Monetary unit: 1 Eastern Caribbean dollar (EC$) = 100 cents; valuation (Sept. 1, 2004) 1 U.S.$ = EC$2.70; 1 £ = EC$4.86.

Area and population

Census Divisions[3]	area sq mi	area sq km	population 2003[2] estimate
Island of Saint Vincent			
Barrouallie	14.2	36.8	5,313
Bridgetown	7.2	18.6	6,593
Calliaqua	11.8	30.6	22,084
Chateaubelair	30.9	80.0	5,915
Colonarie	13.4	34.7	7,286
Georgetown	22.2	57.5	6,794
Kingstown (city)	1.9	4.9	13,477
Kingstown (suburbs)	6.4	16.6	12,670
Layou	11.1	28.7	6,164
Marriaqua	9.4	24.3	8,028
Sandy Bay	5.3	13.7	2,728
Saint Vincent Grenadines			
Northern Grenadines	9.0	23.3	5,492
Southern Grenadines	7.5	19.4	3,491
TOTAL	150.3	389.3[4]	106,035

Demography

Population (2004): 113,000.
Density (2004): persons per sq mi 753.3, persons per sq km 290.5.
Urban-rural (2000): urban 54.4%; rural 45.6%.
Sex distribution (2000): male 49.90%; female 50.10%.
Age breakdown (1999): under 15, 31.3%; 15–29, 31.2%; 30–44, 19.6%; 45–59, 9.4%; 60–74, 5.9%; 75 and over, 2.6%.
Population projection: (2010) 115,000; (2020) 115,000.
Doubling time: 61 years.
Ethnic composition (1999): black 65.5%; mulatto 23.5%; Indo-Pakistani 5.5%; white 3.5%; black-Amerindian 2.0%.
Religious affiliation (1995): Protestant 57.6%; unaffiliated Christian 20.6%; Roman Catholic 10.7%; Hindu 3.3%; Muslim 1.5%; other/nonreligious 6.3%.
Major city (2000[2]): Kingstown 16,209.

Vital statistics

Birth rate per 1,000 population (2002): 17.6 (world avg. 21.3); (1999) legitimate 17.9%; illegitimate 82.1%.
Death rate per 1,000 population (2002): 6.9 (world avg. 9.1).
Natural increase rate per 1,000 population (2002): 10.7 (world avg. 12.2).
Total fertility rate (avg. births per childbearing woman; 2003): 2.0.
Marriage rate per 1,000 population (2002): 4.5.
Divorce rate per 1,000 population (2002): 0.4.
Life expectancy at birth (2003): male 71.3 years; female 74.9 years.
Major causes of death per 100,000 population (2002): diseases of the circulatory system 229.9; malignant neoplasms (cancers) 106.9; diabetes mellitus 82.0; diseases of the respiratory system 57.0; infectious and parasitic diseases 54.4.

National economy

Budget (2002). Revenue: EC$312,000,000 (current revenue 80.8%, of which taxes on international trade and transactions 38.8%, income tax 25.6%, taxes on goods and services 15.7%; grants 5.1%; nontax revenue 13.8%; capital revenue 0.3%). Expenditures: EC$348,000,000 (current expenditure 81.3%, development expenditure 18.7%).
Public debt (external, outstanding; 2002): U.S.$173,700,000.
Production (metric tons except as noted). Agriculture, forestry, fishing (2000): bananas 45,951, coconuts 23,700, eddoes and dasheens[5] 4,400, plantains 2,048, corn (maize) 2,000, sweet potatoes 1,850, oranges 960, ginger 528, arrowroot starch 209, nutmegs 195; soursops, guavas, mangoes, and papayas are also grown; livestock (number of live animals) 13,000 sheep, 9,500 pigs, 6,200 cattle; roundwood, n.a.; fish catch (2002) 643. Mining and quarrying: sand and gravel for local use. Manufacturing (value added in EC$'000,000; 2000): beverages and tobacco products 17.4; food 15.6; paper products and publishing 3.6; textiles, clothing, and footwear 3.3. Energy production (consumption): electricity (kW-hr; 2000) 85,000,000 (85,000,000); coal, none (none); crude petroleum, none (none); petroleum products (metric tons; 2000) none (53,000); natural gas, none (none).
Tourism: receipts from visitors (2002) U.S.$81,000,000; expenditures by nationals abroad (2001) U.S.$10,000,000.
Land use as % of total land area (2000): in temporary crops *c.* 18%, in permanent crops *c.* 18%, in pasture *c.* 5%; overall forest area *c.* 15%.
Gross national product (2003): U.S.$361,000,000 (U.S.$3,300 per capita).

Structure of gross domestic product and labour force

	2000 in value EC$'000,000	2000 % of total value	1991 labour force	1991 % of labour force
Agriculture, forestry, fishing	82.4	10.8	8,377	20.1
Mining	1.7	0.2	98	0.2
Manufacturing	46.0	6.0	2,822	6.8
Construction	85.9	11.3	3,535	8.5
Public utilities	50.1	6.6	586	1.4
Transp. and commun.	155.1	20.3	2,279	5.5
Trade, restaurants	156.4	20.5	6,544	15.7
Finance, real estate	78.9	10.3	1,418	3.4
Pub. admin., defense	140.9	18.5	7,696	18.5
Services	14.8	1.9		
Other	–49.3[6]	–6.4[6]	8,327[7]	20.0[7]
TOTAL	762.9	100.0	41,682	100.0[4]

Population economically active (1991): total 41,682; activity rate of total population 39.1% (participation rates: ages 15–64, 67.5%; female 35.9%; unemployed [1996] more than 30%).

Price and earnings indexes (2000 = 100)

	1997	1998	1999	2000	2001	2002	2003
Consumer price index	96.7	98.8	99.8	100.0	100.8	101.6	101.9
Daily earnings index	...	...	...	...	...	...	...

Household income and expenditure. Average household size (1991) 3.9; income per household (1988) EC$4,579 (U.S.$1,696); sources of income: n.a.; expenditure: n.a.

Foreign trade[8]

Balance of trade (current prices)

	1997	1998	1999	2000	2001	2002
U.S.$'000,000	–127.2	–151.2	–161.1	–111.5	–140.8	–136.3
% of total	58.2%	60.1%	61.9%	51.8%	60.6%	64.1%

Imports (2001): U.S.$186,500,000 (food products 20.4%; machinery and transport equipment 19.0%; chemicals and chemical products 9.8%; fuels 9.0%). *Major import sources:* U.S. 34.5%; Caricom countries 31.2%, of which Trinidad and Tobago 19.9%; U.K. 9.8%; Japan 3.5%.
Exports (2001): U.S.$45,700,000 (domestic exports 86.9%, of which bananas 28.4%, packaged flour 13.2%, packaged rice 9.2%, eddoes and dasheens[5] 3.4%; reexports 13.1%). *Major export destinations:* Caricom countries 53.7%, of which Trinidad and Tobago 17.0%, Barbados 9.8%, St. Lucia 7.9%; U.K. 36.8%.

Transport and communications

Transport. Railroads: none. Roads (1999): total length 646 mi, 1,040 km (paved 31%). Vehicles (1999): passenger cars 7,989; trucks and buses 3,920. Merchant marine (1997): vessels (100 gross tons and over) 946; total deadweight tonnage 1,253,000. Air transport (2000): passenger arrivals 132,445; passenger departures 134,012; airports (1998) with scheduled flights 5.

Communications

Medium	date	unit	number	units per 1,000 persons
Radio	1995	receivers	65,000	591
Television	1995	receivers	17,700	161
Telephones	2002	main lines	27,300	234
Cellular telephones	2002	subscribers	10,000	85
Personal computers	2002	units	14,000	192
Internet	2002	users	7,000	60

Education and health

Educational attainment (1980). Percentage of population age 25 and over having: no formal schooling 2.4%; primary education 88.0%; secondary 8.2%; higher 1.4%. *Literacy* (1991): total population age 15 and over literate 64,000 (96.0%).

Education (2000)

	schools	teachers	students	student/ teacher ratio
Primary (age 5–11)	60	987	20,530	20.8
Secondary (age 12–18)	21	406	7,939	19.6
Voc., teacher tr.	4	48	904	18.8

Health (1998): physicians 59 (1 per 1,883 persons); hospital beds (2000) 209 (1 per 535 persons); infant mortality rate per 1,000 live births (2002) 18.1.
Food (2001): daily per capita caloric intake 2,609 (vegetable products 83%, animal products 17%); 108% of FAO recommended minimum requirement.

Military

Total active duty personnel (1992): 634-member police force includes a coast guard and paramilitary unit.

[1]Includes 6 nonelective seats; excludes speaker who may be elected from within or from outside of the House of Assembly membership. [2]January 1. [3]For statistical purposes and the election of legislative representatives only. [4]Detail does not add to total given because of rounding. [5]Varieties of taro roots. [6]Net of indirect taxes less imputed bank service charges. [7]Unemployed. [8]Imports c.i.f.; exports f.o.b.

Internet resources for further information:
- **Eastern Caribbean Central Bank http://www.eccb-centralbank.org**

Samoa[1]

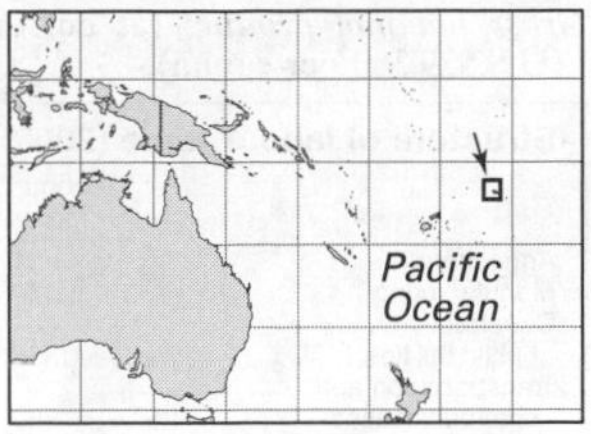

Official name: Malo Sa'oloto Tuto'atasi o Samoa (Samoan); Independent State of Samoa (English).
Form of government: constitutional monarchy[2] with one legislative house (Legislative Assembly [49]).
Chief of state: Head of State.
Head of government: Prime Minister.
Capital: Apia.
Official languages: Samoan; English.
Official religion: none.
Monetary unit: 1 tala (SA$[3], plural tala) = 100 sene; valuation (Sept. 1, 2004) 1 U.S.$ = SA$2.82; 1 £ = SA$5.08.

Area and population

Islands / Districts	Largest towns	area sq mi	area sq km	population 2001 census
Savai'i	Matavai	649[4]	1,682	46,010
Fa'aseleleaga		103	266	12,949
Gaga'emauga		86	223	7,108
Gaga'ifomauga		141	365	4,770
Palauli		202	523	8,984
Satupa'itea		49	127	5,556
Vaisigano		69	178	6,643
Upolu[5]	Apia	444	1,150	130,700
A'ana[5]		75	193	20,167
Aiga-i-le-Tai		10	27	4,508
Atua[5]		159	413	21,168
Tuamasaga		185	479	83,191
Vaa-o-Fonoti		15	38	1,666
TOTAL		1,093	2,831[4]	176,710

Demography

Population (2004): 183,000.
Density (2004): persons per sq mi 167.4, persons per sq km 64.6.
Urban-rural (2002): urban 22.0%; rural 78.0%.
Sex distribution (2001): male 52.09%; female 47.91%.
Age breakdown (2001): under 15, 40.8%; 15–29, 25.6%; 30–44, 17.9%; 45–59, 9.2%; 60–74, 5.0%; 75 and over, 1.5%.
Population projection: (2010) 195,000; (2020) 217,000.
Doubling time: 31 years.
Ethnic composition (1997): Samoan (Polynesian) 92.6%; Euronesian (European and Polynesian) 7.0%; European 0.4%.
Religious affiliation (1995): Mormon 25.8%; Congregational 24.6%; Roman Catholic 21.3%; Methodist 12.2%; Pentecostal 8.0%; Seventh-day Adventist 3.9%; other Christian 1.7%; other 2.5%.
Major towns (2001): Apia 38,836 (urban agglomeration 60,734); Vaitele 5,200[6]; Faleasi'u 3,209; Vailele 3,175[6]; Le'auva'a 2,828.

Vital statistics

Birth rate per 1,000 population (2003): 28.6 (world avg. 21.3).
Death rate per 1,000 population (2003): 5.5 (world avg. 9.1).
Natural increase rate per 1,000 population (2003): 23.1 (world avg. 12.2).
Total fertility rate (avg. births per childbearing woman; 2003): 4.1.
Marriage rate per 1,000 population: n.a.
Divorce rate per 1,000 population: n.a.
Life expectancy at birth (2003): male 67.4 years; female 73.0 years.
Major causes of death per 100,000 population (2002): cerebrovascular diseases 24.3; septicemia 19.2; congestive heart failure 15.8; pneumonia 15.8; myocardial infarction 13.6.

National economy

Budget (2000–01). Revenue: SA$262,400,000 (tax revenue 66.6%, grants 24.8%, nontax revenue 8.6%). Expenditures: SA$281,700,000 (current expenditure 58.4%, development expenditure 36.6%, net lending 5.0%).
Public debt (external, outstanding; 2002): U.S.$156,800,000.
Production (metric tons except as noted). Agriculture, forestry, fishing (2002): coconuts 140,000, bananas 21,500, taro 17,000, pineapples 4,600, papayas 3,600, mangoes 2,500, avocados 1,000, cacao beans 500; livestock (number of live animals) 201,000 pigs, 28,000 cattle, 450,000 chickens; roundwood (2001) 131,000 cu m; fish catch (2001) 12,966. Mining and quarrying: n.a. Manufacturing (in WS$'000; 1990): beer 8,708; cigarettes 6,551; coconut cream 5,576; sawn wood 3,662; coconut oil 3,442; corned meat 2,905; soap 1,487; paints 1,457. Construction (permits issued in WS$; 1995): residential 7,749,000; commercial, industrial, and other 30,867,000. Energy production (consumption): electricity (kW-hr; 2000) 66,000,000 (66,000,000); coal, none (n.a.); crude petroleum, none (n.a.); petroleum products (metric tons; 2000) none (45,000).
Household income and expenditure. Average household size (2001) 7.7; income per household: n.a.; sources of income: n.a.; expenditure: n.a.
Population economically active (2001): total 50,000; activity rate of total population 28.3% (participation rates: ages 15–64, n.a.; female [1991] 32.0%).

Price and earnings indexes (2000 = 100)

	1997	1998	1999	2000	2001	2002	2003
Consumer price index	96.6	98.8	99.0	100.0	103.8	112.2	112.3
Earnings index	...	...	...	...	...	...	...

Gross national product (at current market prices; 2003): U.S.$284,000,000 (U.S.$1,600 per capita).

Structure of gross domestic product and labour force

	2001 in value SA$'000	% of total value	labour force	% of labour force
Agriculture	121,500	14.3	20,600	41.2
Mining	...	...		
Manufacturing	137,000	16.1		
Construction	59,500	7.0		
Public utilities	25,500	3.0		
Transp. and commun.	116,800	13.7	29,400	58.8
Trade	175,800	20.6		
Finance	59,300	7.0		
Pub. admin., defense	69,500	8.2		
Services	92,400	10.9		
Other	–5,800[7]	–0.7[7]		
TOTAL	851,500	100.0[4]	50,000	100.0

Tourism: receipts from visitors (2002) U.S.$46,000,000; expenditures by nationals abroad (1999) U.S.$4,000,000.
Land use as % of total land area (2000): in temporary crops 20.8%, in permanent crops 24.0%, in pasture 0.7%; overall forest area 37.2%.

Foreign trade[8]

Balance of trade (current prices)

	1997	1998	1999	2000	2001	2002
SA$'000,000	–218.8	–230.1	–293.6	–303.9	–396.2	–407.9
% of total	74.5%	67.5%	72.9%	77.2%	79.0%	81.5%

Imports (2001–02): SA$465,000,000 (petroleum products 10.2%, imports for government 5.2%, unspecified 84.6%). *Major import sources:* New Zealand 34.4%; Australia 26.6%; United States 11.8%; Fiji 8.7%; Japan 6.6%.
Exports (2001–02): SA$49,500,000 (fresh fish 66.9%, garments 11.5%, beer 6.7%, coconut cream 6.6%). *Major export destinations:* American Samoa 52.3%; United States 32.2%; New Zealand 6.8%; Germany 3.4%; Australia 2.7%.

Transport and communications

Transport. Railroads: none. Roads (1996): total length 491 mi, 790 km (paved 42%). Vehicles (1995): passenger cars 1,068; trucks and buses 1,169. Merchant marine (2001): vessels (100 gross tons and over) 7; total deadweight tonnage (1992) 6,501. Air transport (1999): passenger-km 244,000,000; metric ton-km cargo 23,000,000; airports (1997) with scheduled flights 3.

Communications

Medium	date	unit	number	units per 1,000 persons
Radio	1997	receivers	178,000	1,035
Television	1998	receivers	9,000	52
Telephones	2002	main lines	11,800	65
Cellular telephones	2002	subscribers	2,700	15
Personal computers	2002	units	1,000	6.7
Internet	2002	users	4,000	22

Education and health

Educational attainment: n.a. *Literacy* (2000): total population over age 15 literate 80.2%; males literate 81.2%; females literate 79.0%.

Education (1998)

	schools	teachers	students	student/ teacher ratio
Primary (age 5–11)	155[9]	1,233[10]	35,749[10]	23.9[10]
Secondary (age 12–18)	...	665[9]	12,672[9]	19.1[9]
Higher[11]	1	28	328	11.7

Health: physicians (1996) 62 (1 per 2,919 persons); hospital beds (1991) 863 (1 per 255 persons); infant mortality rate per 1,000 live births (2003) 26.0.
Food (1992): daily per capita caloric intake 2,828 (vegetable products 74%, animal products 26%); 124% of FAO recommended minimum requirement.

Military

No military forces are maintained; New Zealand is responsible for defense.

[1]In July 1997 the short-form name of the country was officially changed from Western Samoa to Samoa. [2]According to the constitution, the current Head of State, paramount chief HH Malietoa Tanumafili II, will hold office for life. Upon his death, the monarchy will functionally cease, and future Heads of State will be elected by the Legislative Assembly. [3]Symbol of the monetary unit changed from WS$ to SA$ as of July 1997. [4]Detail does not add to total given because of rounding. [5]Includes area and any population of offshore islets. [6]Within Apia urban agglomeration. [7]Less imputed bank service charges. [8]Imports c.i.f.; exports f.o.b. [9]1996. [10]1999. [11]National University of Samoa only.

Internet resources for further information:
- **Central Bank of Samoa http://www.cbs.gov.ws**
- **Samoa Statistical Services Division http://www.spc.org.nc/prism/Country/WS/stats/index.html**

San Marino

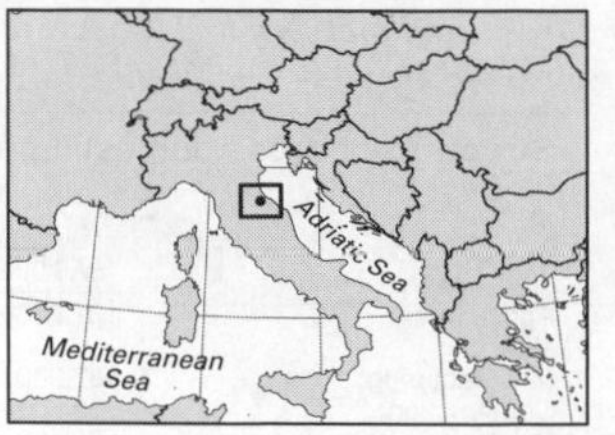

Official name: Serenissima Repubblica di San Marino (Most Serene Republic of San Marino).
Form of government: unitary multiparty republic with one legislative house (Great and General Council [60]).
Head of state and government: Captains-Regent (2).
Capital: San Marino.
Official language: Italian.
Official religion: none.
Monetary unit: 1 euro (€) = 100 cents; valuation (Sept. 1, 2004) 1 U.S.$ = €0.82; 1 £ = €1.48[1].

Area and population

		area		population
Castles	Capitals	sq mi	sq km	2003[2] estimate
Acquaviva	Acquaviva	1.88	4.86	1,602
Borgo Maggiore	Borgo Maggiore	3.48	9.01	5,916
Chiesanuova	Chiesanuova	2.11	5.46	969
Città	San Marino	2.74	7.09	4,483
Domagnano	Domagnano	2.56	6.62	2,651
Faetano	Faetano	2.99	7.75	1,050
Fiorentino	Fiorentino	2.53	6.57	2,031
Montegiardino	Montegiardino	1.28	3.31	786
Serravalle/Dogano	Serravalle	4.07	10.53	9,265
TOTAL		23.63[3]	61.20	28,753

Demography

Population (2004): 29,400.
Density (2004): persons per sq mi 1,225, persons per sq km 482.0.
Urban-rural (2003): urban 88.7%; rural 11.3%.
Sex distribution (2003[2]): male 48.94%; female 51.06%.
Age breakdown (2003[2]): under 15, 14.1%; 15–29, 16.6%; 30–44, 27.3%; 45–59, 19.7%; 60–74, 14.2%; 75 and over, 8.1%.
Population projection: (2010) 32,000; (2020) 35,000.
Ethnic composition (2003[2]): Sammarinesi 85.7%; Italian 13.0%; other 1.3%.
Religious affiliation (2000): Roman Catholic 88.7%; Pentecostal 1.8%; other 9.5%.
Major cities (2000): Serravalle/Dogano 8,547; San Marino 4,439; Borgo Maggiore 2,394[4]; Murata 1,549[4]; Domagnano 1,048[4].

Vital statistics

Birth rate per 1,000 population (2002): 10.4 (world avg. 21.3).
Death rate per 1,000 population (2002): 7.1 (world avg. 9.1).
Natural increase rate per 1,000 population (2002): 3.3 (world avg. 12.2).
Total fertility rate (avg. births per childbearing woman; 2002): 1.3.
Marriage rate per 1,000 population (2002): 7.3.
Divorce rate per 1,000 population (1998–2000): 1.6.
Life expectancy at birth (2000): male 77.6 years; female 85.0 years.
Major causes of death per 100,000 population (1994–98): disease of the circulatory system 338.3; malignant neoplasms (cancers) 224.5; accidents, violence, and suicide 60.9; diseases of the respiratory system 9.5.

National economy

Budget (2003). Revenue: €288,000,000 (direct taxes 34.7%; import taxes 33.0%; nontax revenue 22.0%). Expenditures: €272,400,000 (current expenditures 92.0%; capital expenditures 8.0%).
Public debt (2003): U.S.$52,900,000.
Tourism: number of tourist arrivals (2002) 3,102,453; receipts from visitors (1994) U.S.$252,500,000; expenditures by nationals abroad, n.a.
Population economically active (2003): total 20,236; activity rate of total population 69.3% (participation rates: ages 15–64 [2002] 72.1%; female 41.5%; unemployed [2004[2]] 3.9%).

Price and earnings indexes (1995 = 100)

	1993	1994	1995	1996	1997	1998	1999
Consumer price index	91.6	95.3	100.0	104.1	106.2	108.6	112.1
Annual earnings index	87.9	93.9	100.0	110.9	118.4	…	…

Household income and expenditure. Total number of households (2003[2]) 11,723; average household size (2003[2]) 2.5; income per household: n.a.; sources of income: n.a.; expenditure (1991)[5]: food, beverages, and tobacco 22.1%, housing, fuel, and electrical energy 20.9%, transportation and communications 17.6%, clothing and footwear 8.0%, furniture, appliances, and goods and services for the home 7.2%, education 7.1%, health and sanitary services 2.6%, other goods and services 14.5%.
Production (metric tons except as noted). Agriculture, forestry, fishing[6]: wheat *c.* 4,400, grapes *c.* 700, barley *c.* 500; livestock (number of live animals; 1998) 831 cattle, 748 pigs. Manufacturing (1998): processed meats 324,073 kg, of which beef 226,570 kg, pork 87,764 kg, veal 7,803 kg; cheese 61,563 kg; butter 12,658 kg; milk 1,167,620 litres; yogurt 5,131 litres; other major products include electrical appliances, musical instruments, printing ink, paint, cosmetics, furniture, floor tiles, gold and silver jewelry, clothing, and postage stamps. Construction (new units completed; 1998): residential 69; nonresidential 165. Energy production (consumption): all electrical power is imported via electrical grid from Italy (consumption [2001] 193,371,696); coal, none (n.a.); crude petroleum, none (n.a.); petroleum products, none (n.a.); natural gas, none ([2001] 50,641,790).

Gross national product (at current market prices; 2002): U.S.$836,000,000 (U.S.$29,360 per capita).

Structure of labour force (2003)

	labour force	% of labour force
Agriculture	31	0.2
Manufacturing	6,070	29.9
Construction and public utilities	1,363	6.7
Transportation and communications	380	1.9
Trade	2,650	13.1
Finance and insurance	660	3.3
Services	2,059	10.2
Public administration and defense	4,136	20.4
Other	2,887[7]	14.3[7]
TOTAL	20,236	100.0

Land use as % of total land area (2000): in temporary crops, permanent crops, pasture, or forest *c.* 65%[8].

Foreign trade[9]

Balance of trade (current prices)

	1997	1998	1999	2000	2001	2002
U.S.$'000,000	–34.0	–17.9	–28.0	–53.3	–54.4	–91.0
% of total	1.0%	0.5%	0.8%	1.5%	1.8%	2.8%

Imports (2002): U.S.$1,657,000,000 (manufactured goods of all kinds, petroleum products, electricity, and gold). *Major import source:* Italy[9].
Exports (2002): U.S.$1,566,000,000 (goods include electronics, postage stamps, leather products, ceramics, wine, wood products, and building stone). *Major export destination:* Italy[10].

Transport and communications

Transport. Railroads: none (nearest rail terminal is at Rimini, Italy, 17 mi [27 km] northeast). Roads (2001): total length 156 mi, 252 km. Vehicles (2002): passenger cars 28,470; trucks and buses 2,748. Air transport: airports with scheduled flights, none; there is, however, a heliport that provides passenger and cargo service between San Marino and Rimini, Italy, during the summer months.

Communications

Medium	date	unit	number	units per 1,000 persons
Daily newspapers	1996	circulation	2,000	72
Radio	1998	receivers	16,000	610
Television	1998	receivers	9,055	358
Telephones	2002	main lines	20,601	716
Cellular telephones	2002	subscribers	16,759	583
Internet	2002	users	14,300	531

Education and health

Educational attainment (2003[2]). Percentage of population age 14 and over having: basic literacy or primary education 41.0%; some secondary 25.0%; secondary 27.0%; higher degree 7.0%. *Literacy* (2001): total population age 15 and over literate 98.7%; males literate 98.9%; females literate 98.4%.

Education (2002–03)

	schools	teachers	students	student/ teacher ratio
Primary (age 6–10)	14	242	1,343	5.4
Secondary (age 11–18)[11]	7	227	2,162	8.7
Higher	1	27	950	35.6

Health (2002): physicians 117 (1 per 230 persons); hospital beds 134 (1 per 191 persons); infant mortality rate per 1,000 live births (2002) 6.8.
Food (2000)[12]: daily per capita caloric intake 3,661 (vegetable products 74%, animal products 26%); 146% of FAO recommended minimum requirement.

Military

Total active duty personnel (2003): none[13]. *Military expenditure as percentage of national budget* (1992): 1.0% (world 3.6%); per capita expenditure (1987) U.S.$155.

[1]Italian lira replaced by euro (€) from Jan. 1, 2002. [2]January 1. [3]Detail does not add to total given because of rounding. [4]1997. [5]Weighting coefficients for component expenditures are those of the 1991 official Italian consumer price index for the North-Central region of Italy. [6]Early 1980s. [7]Includes 619 unemployed and 2,268 self-employed. [8]Includes rock outcrops. [9]A customs union with Italy has existed since 1862. [10]In the late 1990s Italy accounted for 87% of all foreign trade. [11]Includes vocational schools. [12]Figures are for Italy. [13]Defense is provided by a public security force of about 50.

Internet resources for further information:
- **San Marino http://www.esteri.sm/eindex.htm**

São Tomé and Príncipe

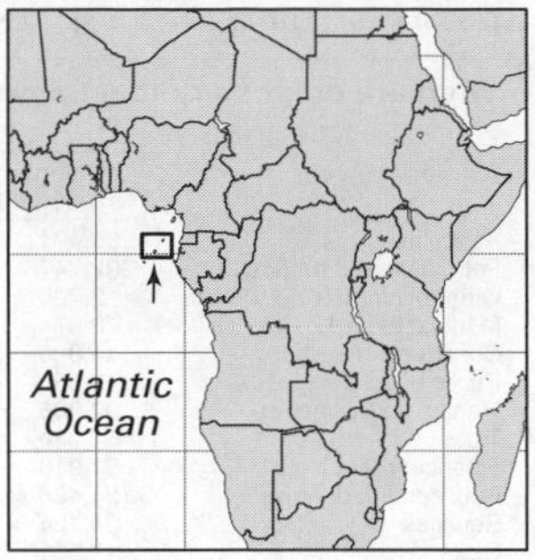

Official name: República democrática de São Tomé e Príncipe (Democratic Republic of São Tomé and Príncipe).
Form of government: multiparty republic with one legislative house (National Assembly [55]).
Chief of state: President.
Head of government: Prime Minister.
Capital: São Tomé.
Official language: Portuguese.
Official religion: none.
Monetary unit: 1 dobra (Db) = 100 cêntimos; valuation (Sept. 1, 2004) 1 U.S.$ = Db 8,818; 1 £ = Db 15,863.

Area and population

Islands / Districts	Capitals	area sq mi	area sq km	population 2001 census
São Tomé		332	859	131,633
Aqua Grande	São Tomé	7	17	51,886
Cantagalo	Santana	46	119	13,258
Caué	São João Angolares	103	267	5,501
Lemba	Neves	88	229	10,696
Lobata	Guadalupe	41	105	15,187
Mé-Zóchi	Trindade	47	122	35,105
Autonomous Island				
Príncipe (Paguê)	Santo António	55	142	5,966
TOTAL		386[1]	1,001	137,599

Demography

Population (2004): 144,000.
Density (2004): persons per sq mi 373.1, persons per sq km 143.9.
Urban-rural (2001): urban 47.7%; rural 52.3%.
Sex distribution (2001): male 49.59%, female 50.41%.
Age breakdown (2001): under 15, 47.7%; 15–29, 27.5%; 30–44, 12.6%; 45–59, 6.3%; 60–74, 4.5%; 75 and over, 1.4%.
Population projection: (2010) 158,200; (2020) 185,000.
Doubling time: 20 years.
Ethnic composition (2000): black-white admixture 79.5%; Fang 10.0%; angolares (descendants of former Angolan slaves) 7.6%; Portuguese 1.9%; other 1.0%.
Religious affiliation (1995): Roman Catholic, about 89.5%; remainder mostly Protestant, predominantly Seventh-day Adventist and an indigenous Evangelical Church.
Major cities (2001): São Tomé 51,886; Neves 6,700[2]; Santana 6,300[2]; Trindade 6,000[2]; Santo António 1,040[2].

Vital statistics

Birth rate per 1,000 population (2003): 41.9 (world avg. 21.3).
Death rate per 1,000 population (2003): 7.1 (world avg. 9.1).
Natural increase rate per 1,000 population (2003): 34.8 (world avg. 12.2).
Total fertility rate (avg. births per childbearing woman; 2003): 5.8.
Marriage rate per 1,000 population: n.a.
Divorce rate per 1,000 population: n.a.
Life expectancy at birth (2003): male 64.8 years; female 67.8 years.
Major causes of death per 100,000 population (1987): malaria 160.6; direct obstetric causes 76.7; pneumonia 74.0; influenza 61.5; anemias 47.3; hypertensive disease 32.1.

National economy

Budget (2000). Revenue: Db 183,400,000,000 (grants 56.4%; taxes 32.4%, of which sales taxes 10.9%, import taxes 9.8%, income and profit taxes 9.1%; nontax revenue 11.2%). Expenditures: Db 244,400,000,000 (capital expenditure 63.3%; recurrent expenditure 36.7%, of which personnel costs 11.8%, debt service 10.0%, goods and services 6.2%, transfers 3.0%, defense 0.5%).
Public debt (external, outstanding; 2002): U.S.$307,900,000.
Production (metric tons except as noted). Agriculture, forestry, fishing (2002): oil palm fruit 40,000, bananas 35,000, coconuts 26,600, taro 25,000, vegetables 6,200, cassava 5,500, cacao 4,000, fruits (other than melon) 2,500, corn (maize) 2,500, cinnamon 30, coffee 20; livestock (number of live animals) 4,800 goats, 4,100 cattle, 2,600 sheep, 2,100 pigs; roundwood (2001) 9,000 cu m; fish catch (2001) 3,500, principally marine fish and shellfish. Mining and quarrying: some quarrying to support local construction industry. Manufacturing (value in Db; 1995): beer 880,000; clothing 679,000; lumber 369,000; bakery products 350,000; palm oil 228,000; soap 133,000; ceramics 87,000. Energy production (consumption): electricity (kW-hr; 2000) 18,000,000 (18,000,000); coal, none (n.a.); crude petroleum, none (n.a.); petroleum products (metric tons; 2000) none (29,000); natural gas, none (n.a.).
Household income and expenditure. Average household size (1981) 4.0; income per household: n.a.; sources of income: n.a.; expenditure (1995)[3]: food 71.9%, housing and energy 10.2%, transportation and communications 6.4%, clothing and other items 5.3%, household durable goods 2.8%, education and health 1.7%.
Tourism (2002): receipts from visitors U.S.$10,000,000; expenditures by nationals abroad U.S.$1,000,000.
Population economically active (1994): total 51,789; activity rate of total population 40.8% (participation rates: ages 15–64 [1981] 61.1%; female [1991] 32.4%; unemployed [1994] 29.0%).

Price index (2000 = 100)

	1997	1998	1999	2000	2001	2002	2003
Consumer price index	55.9	79.1	89.1	100.0	109.2	120.2	132.1

Gross national product (2003): U.S.$50,000,000 (U.S.$320 per capita).

Structure of gross domestic product and labour force

	2000		1998	
	in value Db '000,000	% of total value	labour force[4]	% of labour force[4]
Agriculture	74,300	20.1	16,004	41.5
Mining	...	...	...	...
Manufacturing / Public utilities	20,300	5.5	2,420	6.2
Construction	43,700	11.8	3,515	9.1
Transp. and commun. / Trade	85,700	23.2	2,819 / 5,350	7.3 / 13.9
Finance	32,100	8.7	215	0.6
Pub. admin., defense	84,800	22.9	3,338	8.7
Services	28,800	7.8	...	...
Other	...	...	4,921	12.8
TOTAL	369,700	100.0	38,582	100.0[1]

Land use as % of total land area (2000): in temporary crops 6.3%, in permanent crops 46.9%, in pasture 1.0%; overall forest area 28.3%.

Foreign trade

Balance of trade (current prices)

	1997	1998	1999	2000	2001	2002
U.S.$'000,000	–13.9	–12.1	–18.0	–19.1	–21.2	–19.3
% of total	56.7%	56.3%	69.8%	74.9%	76.3%	63.7%

Imports (2002): U.S.$24,800,000 ([5]investment goods 52.9%, food and other agricultural products 20.2%, petroleum products 17.9%). *Major import sources:* Portugal 38.9%; U.S. 22.2%; U.K. 9.3%.
Exports (2002): U.S.$5,500,000 (cocoa beans 80.0%; other exports include copra, coffee, and palm oil). *Major export destinations:* The Netherlands 27.3%; Portugal 18.2%; Canada 9.1%.

Transport and communications

Transport. Railroads: none. Roads (1999): total length 199 mi, 320 km (paved 68%). Vehicles (1996): passenger cars 4,040; trucks and buses 1,540. Merchant marine (2000): vessels (100 gross tons and over) 39; total deadweight tonnage 149,048. Air transport (1998): passenger-mi 6,000,000, passenger-km 9,000,000; short ton-mi cargo 700,000, short ton-km cargo 1,000,000; airports (2000) 2.

Communications

Medium	date	unit	number	units per 1,000 persons
Radio	1997	receivers	38,000	272
Television	1997	receivers	23,000	163
Telephones	2003	main lines	7,000	46
Cellular telephones	2003	subscribers	4,800	32
Internet	2003	users	15,000	97

Education and health

Educational attainment: n.a. *Literacy* (1991): total population age 15 and over literate 73.0%; males literate 85.0%; females literate 62.0%.

Education (1998)

	schools	teachers[6]	students	student/ teacher ratio
Primary (age 6–13)	71	638	20,287	34.1[6]
Secondary (age 14–18)[7]	11	415	11,814	29.6[6]
Voc., teacher tr.	...	...	...	...
Higher	...	...	...	...

Health: physicians (1996) 61 (1 per 2,147 persons); hospital beds (1983) 640 (1 per 158 persons); infant mortality rate per 1,000 live births (2003) 46.0.
Food (2001): daily per capita caloric intake 2,567 (vegetable products 96%, animal products 4%); 109% of FAO recommended minimum requirement.

Military

Total active duty personnel (1995): 600[8]. *Military expenditure as percentage of GNP* (1999): 1.0% (world 2.4%); per capita expenditure U.S.$3.

[1]Detail does not add to total given because of rounding. [2]August 25. [3]Weights based on CPI components. [4]Employed only. [5]Based on imports for 2000 equaling U.S.$22,300,000. [6]1997. [7]Includes vocational. [8]A 5-member crew of the Portuguese air force is stationed in São Tomé and Príncipe to provide humanitarian assistance.

Internet resources for further information:
- **UN Development Programme: Human Development Indicators (2003) http://www.undp.org/hdr2003/indicator/cty_f_STP.html**

Saudi Arabia

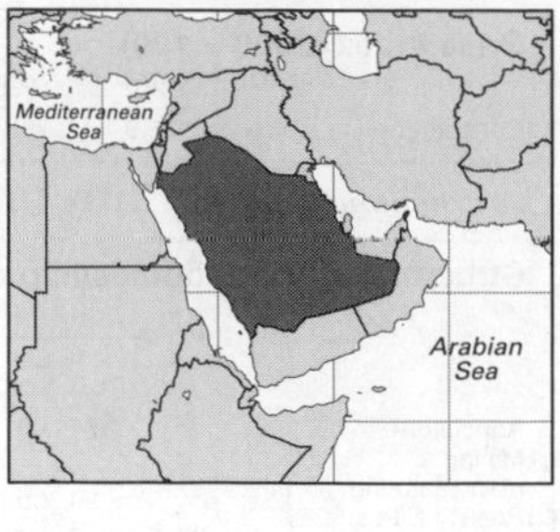

Official name: Al-Mamlakah al-ʿArabīyah as-Saʿūdīyah (Kingdom of Saudi Arabia).
Form of government: monarchy[1].
Heads of state and government: King assisted by Crown Prince.
Capital: Riyadh.
Official language: Arabic.
Official religion: Islam.
Monetary unit: 1 Saudi riyal (SRls) = 100 halalah; valuation (Sept. 1, 2004) 1 U.S.$ = SRls 3.75; 1 £ = SRls 6.75.

Area and population

Geographic Regions / Administrative Regions	Capitals	area sq mi	area sq km	population 2000 estimate
Al-Gharbīyah (Western)		121,637	315,039	7,304,025
Al-Bāḥah	Al-Bāḥah	3,830	9,921	476,382
Al-Madīnah al-Munawwarah	Medina (Al-Madīnah)	58,684	151,990	1,378,870
Makkah al-Mukarramah	Mecca (Makkah)	59,123	153,128	5,448,773
Al-Janūbīyah (Southern)		91,844	237,875	3,106,074
ʿAsīr	Abha	29,611	76,693	1,637,464
Jīzān	Jīzān	4,506	11,671	1,083,022
Najrān	Najrān	57,727	149,511	385,588
Ash-Shamālīyah (Northern)		138,256	358,081	1,197,700
Al-Ḥudūd ash-Shamālīyah (Northern Borders)	ʿArʿar	43,165	111,797	249,544
Al-Jawf	Sakākah	38,692	100,212	354,450
Tabūk	Tabūk	56,399	146,072	593,706
Ash-Sharqīyah (Eastern)		259,662	672,522	3,008,913[2]
Ash-Sharqīyah (Eastern)	Ad-Dammām	259,662	672,522	3,008,913[2]
Al-Wūsṭā (Central)		218,601	566,173	6,230,172
Ḥā'il	Ḥā'il	40,111	103,887	519,984
Al-Qaṣīm	Buraydah	22,412	58,046	979,858
Ar-Riyāḍ	Riyadh (Ar-Riyāḍ)	156,078	404,240	4,730,330
TOTAL		830,000	2,149,690	20,846,884

Demography

Population (2004): 24,580,000[3].
Density (2004): persons per sq mi 29.6, persons per sq km 11.4.
Urban-rural (2001): urban 86.7%; rural 13.3%.
Sex distribution (2003): male 54.90%; female 45.10%.
Age breakdown (2003): under 15, 39.7%; 15–29, 26.9%; 30–44, 21.7%; 45–59, 8.0%; 60–74, 2.9%; 75 and over, 0.8%.
Population projection: (2010) 27,948,000; (2020) 32,114,000.
Doubling time: 22 years.
Ethnic composition (2000): Arab 88.1%, of which Saudi Arab 74.2%, Bedouin 3.9%, Gulf Arab 3.0%; Indo-Pakistani 5.5%; African black 1.5%; Filipino 1.0%; other 3.9%.
Religious affiliation (2000): Muslim *c.* 94%, of which Sunnī *c.* 84%, Shīʿī *c.* 10%; Christian *c.* 3.5%, of which Roman Catholic *c.* 3%; Hindu *c.* 1%; nonreligious/other *c.* 1.5%.
Major urban agglomerations (2000): Riyadh 4,549,000; Jiddah 3,192,000; Mecca 1,335,000; Medina 891,000; Ad-Dammām 764,000.

Vital statistics

Birth rate per 1,000 population (2002): 37.3 (world avg. 21.3).
Death rate per 1,000 population (2002): 5.9 (world avg. 9.1).
Natural increase rate per 1,000 population (2002): 31.4 (world avg. 12.2).
Total fertility rate (avg. births per childbearing woman; 2002): 6.2.
Life expectancy at birth (2002): male 66.7 years; female 70.2 years.
Major causes of death per 100,000 population: n.a.

National economy

Budget (2002). Revenue: SRls 157,000,000,000 (oil revenues 78.9%). Expenditures: SRls 202,000,000,000 (defense and security 34.3%, human resource development 23.3%, public administration, municipal transfers, and subsidies 22.4%, health and social development 9.4%).
Production (metric tons except as noted). Agriculture, forestry, fishing (2002): alfalfa 2,000,000, wheat 1,800,000, dates 783,000, potatoes 400,000, tomatoes 310,000, watermelons 275,000, sorghum 200,000, grapes 117,000, cantaloupes 105,000, barley 100,000, dry onions 97,000; livestock (number of live animals) 8,000,000 sheep, 4,650,000 goats, 415,000 camels, 330,000 cattle; fish catch (2001) 57,385. Mining and quarrying (2002): gypsum 450,000; silver 14,000 kg; gold 5,000 kg. Manufacturing (value added in U.S.$'000,000; 1998): industrial chemicals 3,349; refined petroleum 1,806; cement, bricks, and tiles 1,505; fabricated metal products 1,129; food products 990; iron and steel 615. Energy production (consumption): electricity (kW-hr; 2002) 138,200,000,000 ([2000] 126,441,000,000); coal, none (none); crude petroleum (barrels; 2002) 2,589,000,000 ([2000] 658,800,000); petroleum products (metric tons; 2000) 100,994,000 (52,045,000); natural gas (cu m; 2002) 62,014,000,000 ([2000] 49,808,300,000).
Population economically active (2003): total 7,437,400, of which 3,833,000 foreign workers and 3,604,400 Saudi nationals; activity rate of total population 31.0% (participation rates: ages 15–64, 56.2%; female, n.a.; unemployed [2002] 11.0%).

Price and earnings indexes (2000 = 100)

	1997	1998	1999	2000	2001	2002	2003
Consumer price index	102.9	102.5	101.1	100.0	98.9	99.1	99.7
Earnings index	...	...	...	...	...	...	...

Gross national product (2003): U.S.$186,776,000,000 (U.S.$8,530 per capita).

Structure of gross domestic product and labour force

	2002		2003	
	in value SRls '000,000	% of total value	labour force	% of labour force
Agriculture	36,101	5.1	577,300	7.8
Petroleum and natural gas	232,747	33.0	100,100	1.3
Other mining	2,720	0.4	14,400	0.2
Manufacturing[4]	72,874	10.3	645,900	8.7
Construction	44,890	6.4	1,084,300	14.6
Public utilities	9,385	1.3	99,900	1.3
Transp. and commun.	32,035	4.5	307,900	4.1
Trade	51,934	7.4	1,064,200	14.3
Finance, real estate[5]	81,919	11.6	366,800	4.9
Pub. admin., defense	124,486	17.6	929,100	12.5
Services	24,124	3.4	2,247,500	30.2
Other	–7,361[6]	–1.0[6]		
TOTAL	705,854	100.0	7,437,400[7]	100.0[7, 8]

Household income and expenditure. Average household size (2002) 6.1; income per household: n.a.; sources of income: n.a.; expenditure (1998–99): food and nonalcoholic beverages 37.3%, transportation 18.9%, housing and energy 15.7%, household furnishings 9.7%.
Tourism (in U.S.$'000,000; 2002): receipts 3,420; expenditures 7,356.
Land use as % of total land area (2000): in temporary crops 1.7%, in permanent crops 0.1%, in pasture 79.1%; overall forest area 0.7%.

Foreign trade[9]

Balance of trade (current prices)

	1997	1998	1999	2000	2001	2002
SRls '000,000,000	+119.8	+33.0	+85.1	+177.1	+157.2	+150.7
% of total	35.8%	12.8%	28.9%	43.8%	40.2%	38.4%

Imports (2001): SRls 116,930,000,000 (transport equipment 21.3%, of which road vehicles 16.5%; machinery and apparatus 20.6%, of which general industrial machinery 5.7%; food and live animals 13.5%; chemicals and chemical products 9.6%; iron and steel 4.0%). *Major import sources* (2003): U.S. 15.0%; Japan 10.3%; Germany 8.9%; U.K. 5.9%; China 5.9%.
Exports (2001): SRls 274,085,000,000 (crude petroleum 72.8%; refined petroleum 16.0%; organic chemicals 3.6%; polyethylene 1.6%). *Major export destinations* (2002): U.S. 19.7%; Japan 14.3%; South Korea 9.5%; Singapore 5.4%; India 5.1%.

Transport and communications

Transport. Railroads (2003): route length 1,392 km; (2001) passenger-km 222,000,000; (2001) metric ton-km cargo 856,000,000. Roads (2003): total length 167,857 km (paved 100%). Vehicles (1996): passenger cars 1,744,000; trucks and buses 1,192,000. Air transport (2003): passenger-km 23,372,000,000[10]; metric ton-km cargo 85,451,000[10]; airports (2002) with scheduled flights 25.

Communications

Medium	date	unit	number	units per 1,000 persons
Daily newspapers	1996	circulation	1,105,000	59
Radio	2000	receivers	7,180,000	326
Television	2002	receivers	5,803,500	265
Telephones	2003	main lines	3,502,600	155
Cellular telephones	2003	subscribers	7,238,200	321
Personal computers	2002	units	3,003,000	137
Internet	2003	users	1,500,000	67

Education and health

Educational attainment (2000). Percentage of Saudi (non-Saudi) population age 10 and over who: are illiterate 19.9% (12.1%), are literate/have primary education 39.5% (40.6%), have some/completed secondary education 34.2% (36.0%), have at least begun university education 6.4% (11.3%).

Education (2002)

	schools	teachers	students	student/ teacher ratio
Primary (age 6–12)	12,815	199,741	2,316,166	11.6
Secondary (age 13–18)	10,270	161,702	1,955,424	12.1
Voc., teacher tr.[11]	95	7,028	81,177	11.6
Higher	92	10,790	191,206	17.7

Health (2001): physicians 31,983 (1 per 709 persons); hospital beds 46,622 (1 per 485 persons); infant mortality rate per 1,000 live births (2002) 49.6.
Food (2001): daily per capita caloric intake 2,841 (vegetable products 85%, animal products 15%); 119% of FAO recommended minimum requirement.

Military

Total active duty personnel (2003): 124,500 (army 60.2%, navy 12.4%, air force 27.4%); most U.S. military withdrew in 2003. *Military expenditure as percentage of GNP* (1999): 14.9% (world 2.4%); per capita expenditure U.S.$996.

[1]Assisted by the Consultative Council consisting of 120 appointed members. [2]Geographic and administrative regions are coextensive. [3]Expatriates comprise 25% of total population. [4]Includes refined petroleum. [5]Includes business services. [6]Other equals import duties less imputed bank services charge. [7]Includes 3,833,000 (51.5%) foreign workers in the private sector. [8]Detail does not add to total given because of rounding. [9]Imports c.i.f., exports f.o.b. [10]Saudi Arabian Airlines only. [11]2000–01.

Internet resources for further information:
- **Ministry of Information http://www.saudinf.com**

Senegal

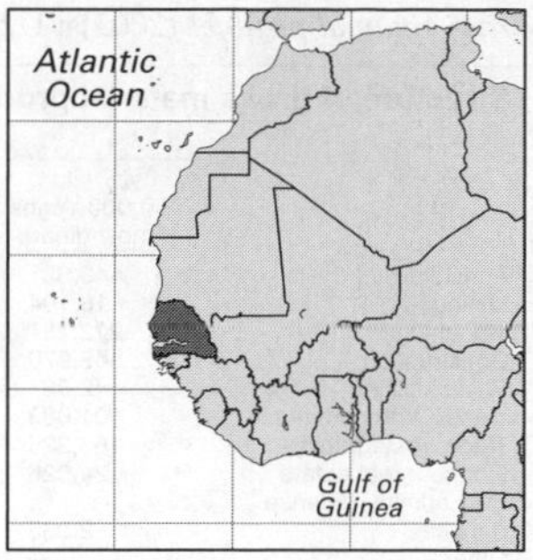

Official name: République du Sénégal (Republic of Senegal).
Form of government: multiparty republic with one legislative house (National Assembly [120]).
Head of state and government: President assisted by Prime Minister.
Capital: Dakar[1].
Official language: French.
Official religion: none.
Monetary unit: 1 CFA franc (CFAF) = 100 centimes; valuation (Sept. 1, 2004) 1 U.S.$ = CFAF 539.75; 1 £ = CFAF 970.98[2].

Area and population

		area		population
				2002
Regions	Capitals	sq mi	sq km	census[3]
Dakar	Dakar	212	550	2,267,356
Diourbel	Diourbel	1,683	4,359	1,049,954
Fatick	Fatick	3,064	7,935	613,000
Kaolack	Kaolack	6,181	16,010	1,066,375
Kolda	Kolda	8,112	21,011	847,243
Louga	Louga	11,270	29,188	677,533
Matam	Matam	9,685	25,083	423,041
Saint-Louis	Saint-Louis	7,353	19,044	688,767
Tambacounda	Tambacounda	23,012	59,602	605,695
Thiès	Thiès	2,549	6,601	1,290,265
Ziguinchor	Ziguinchor	2,834	7,339	437,986
TOTAL		75,955	196,722	9,967,215

Demography

Population (2004): 10,339,000.
Density (2004): persons per sq mi 136.1, persons per sq km 52.6.
Urban-rural (2000): urban 47.4%; rural 52.6%.
Sex distribution (2003): male 49.09%; female 50.91%.
Age breakdown (2003): under 15, 43.7%; 15–29, 28.1%; 30–44, 15.7%; 45–59, 8.0%; 60–74, 3.6%; 75 and over, 0.9%.
Population projection: (2010) 11,869,000; (2020) 14,422,000.
Doubling time: 28 years.
Ethnic composition (2000): Wolof 34.6%; Peul (Fulani) and Tukulor 27.1%; Serer 12.0%; Malinke (Mandingo) 9.7%; other 16.6%.
Religious affiliation (2000): Muslim 87.6%; traditional beliefs 6.2%; Christian 5.5%, of which Roman Catholic 4.7%; other 0.7%.
Major cities (2002)[3]: Dakar 1,983,093[4]; Thiès 237,849; Kaolack 172,305; Saint-Louis 154,555; Mbour 153,503; Ziguinchor 153,269.

Vital statistics

Birth rate per 1,000 population (2003): 36.2 (world avg. 21.3).
Death rate per 1,000 population (2003): 11.0 (world avg. 9.1).
Natural increase rate per 1,000 population (2003): 25.2 (world avg. 12.2).
Total fertility rate (avg. births per childbearing woman; 2003): 4.9.
Life expectancy at birth (2003): male 54.8 years; female 58.0 years.
Major causes of death: n.a.; major diseases are malaria, tetanus, meningitis, and tuberculosis.

National economy

Budget (2002). Revenue: CFAF 713,900,000,000 (tax revenue 85.7%; grants 9.6%; nontax revenue 4.7%). Expenditures: CFAF 738,100,000,000 (current expenditures 62.6%, of which wages 27.0%, education 21.2%, health 5.7%, interest payment 3.8%; development expenditure 37.4%).
Public debt (external, outstanding; 2002): U.S.$3,339,000,000.
Production (metric tons except as noted). Agriculture, forestry, fishing (2002): sugarcane 890,000, peanuts (groundnuts) 501,298, millet 414,687, watermelons 224,064, paddy rice 177,756, sorghum 143,892, cassava 110,617, corn (maize) 97,858, oil palm fruit 65,000; livestock (number of live animals) 4,900,000 sheep, 4,000,000 goats, 3,230,000 cattle, 492,000 horses; roundwood (2002) 5,971,559 cu m; fish catch (2001) 405,409, of which crustaceans and mollusks 22,288. Mining and quarrying (2003): phosphate 1,918,900; salt (2002) 141,000. Manufacturing (U.S.$'000,000; 2000): food products 81; transport equipment 74, of which ships and boats 39; printing and publishing 63; textiles 53; chemicals 47; special purpose machinery 40. Energy production (consumption): electricity (kW-hr; 2001) 1,651,200,000 (1,651,200,000); coal, none (none); crude petroleum (barrels; 2000) none (6,707,000); petroleum products (metric tons; 2000) 979,000 (1,243,000); natural gas (cu m; 2000) 538,000 (538,000).
Population economically active (2001): total 4,294,000; activity rate of total population 44.6% (participation rates: n.a.; female, n.a.; unemployed, n.a.).

Price and earnings indexes (2000 = 100)

	1997	1998	1999	2000	2001	2002	2003
Consumer price index	97.3	98.5	99.3	100.0	103.1	105.4	105.3
Hourly earnings index	...	...	...	...	...	...	...

Household income and expenditure. Average household size (2002) 8.7.
Tourism (2000): receipts U.S.$140,000,000; expenditures (1999) U.S.$54,000,000.
Gross national product (at current market prices; 2003): U.S.$5,563,000,000 (U.S.$550 per capita).

Structure of gross domestic product and labour force

	2002		1991	
	in value CFAF '000,000,000	% of total value	labour force	% of labour force
Agriculture	579.9	16.3	1,789,467	65.3
Mining }	526.0	14.8	1,998	0.1
Manufacturing }			161,124	5.9
Public utilities	83.3	2.4	...	...
Construction	169.9	4.8	60,935	2.2
Transp. and commun.	448.8	12.6	58,081	2.1
Trade, hotels	948.1	26.7	378,241	13.8
Finance }	477.2	13.4	4,623	0.2
Services }			...	...
Pub. admin., defense	318.6	9.0	268,721	9.8
Other	—	—	16,286	0.6
TOTAL	3,551.8	100.0	2,739,476	100.0

Land use as % of total land area (2000): in temporary crops 12.3%, in permanent crops 0.2%, in pasture 29.3%; overall forest area 32.2%.

Foreign trade[5]

Balance of trade (current prices)

	1998	1999	2000	2001	2002	2003
U.S.$'000,000	–293	–326	–416	–425	–537	–714
% of total	12.9%	13.5%	18.5%	17.5%	20.1%	21.4%

Imports (2001): U.S.$1,730,000,000 (food and live animals 22.3%, of which cereals 13.2%, rice 8.2%; mineral fuels and lubricants 16.8%, of which crude petroleum 9.8%; machinery and apparatus 15.1%; chemicals and chemical products 11.1%). *Major import sources:* France 27.8%; Nigeria 9.8%; Thailand 7.7%; Germany 4.8%; United States 4.2%.
Exports (2001): U.S.$785,000,000 (fresh fish 16.1%; refined petroleum 15.5%; fresh crustaceans and mollusks 12.0%; bunkers and ships' stores 12.0%; phosphorous pentoxide and phosphoric acids 9.5%; peanut [groundnut] oil 9.1%). *Major export destinations:* France 16.7%; India 12.4%; Greece 7.3%; Mali 6.9%; Italy 6.0%.

Transport and communications

Transport. Railroads (2002): route length 563 mi, 906 km; passenger-km 105,000,000; metric ton-km cargo 345,000,000. Roads (1999): total length 9,057 mi, 14,576 km (paved 29%). Vehicles (2001): passenger cars 193,000; trucks and buses 79,000. Air transport (2001)[6]: passenger-km 304,000,000; metric ton-km cargo, n.a.; airports (1996) with scheduled flights 7.

Communications

Medium	date	unit	number	units per 1,000 persons
Daily newspapers	2000	circulation	47,000	5.0
Radio	2001	receivers	1,254,400	128
Television	2000	receivers	376,000	40
Telephones	2003	main lines	228,800	22
Cellular telephones	2003	subscribers	575,900	56
Personal computers	2003	units	220,000	21
Internet	2003	users	225,000	22

Education and health

Educational attainment: n.a. *Literacy* (2000): percentage of total population age 15 and over literate 38.3%; males literate 48.1%; females literate 28.7%.

Education (2002–03)

	schools	teachers	students	student/ teacher ratio
Primary (age 6–12)	5,670	29,216	1,287,093	44.1
Secondary (age 13–18)	579	7,601	306,026	40.3
Vocational[7]	12	384	4,425	11.5
Higher[8]	2	963	22,157	23.0

Health: physicians (1996) 649 (1 per 13,162 persons); hospital beds (1998) 3,582 (1 per 2,500 persons); infant mortality rate per 1,000 live births (2003): 57.6.
Food (2001): daily per capita caloric intake 2,277 (vegetable products 91%, animal products 9%); 95% of FAO recommended minimum requirement.

Military

Total active duty personnel (2004): 13,620 (army 87.4%, navy 7.0%, air force 5.6%); French troops (August 2004) 1,100. *Military expenditure as percentage of GNP* (1999): 1.7% (world 2.4%); per capita expenditure U.S.$8.

[1]A new capital is to be built at Mekhé, 120 km (75 mi) northeast of Dakar, per announcement of December 2002. [2]Formerly pegged to the French franc and since Jan. 1, 2002, to the euro at the rate of 1€ = CFAF 656.96. [3]Preliminary. [4]Includes urban departments of Pikine (pop. 768,826) and Guédiawaye (pop. 258,370), adjacent to Dakar department (pop. 955,897). [5]Imports f.o.b. in balance of trade and c.i.f. in commodities and trading partners. [6]Air Afrique, an airline jointly owned by 11 African countries (including Senegal), was declared bankrupt in February 2002. [7]1999–2000. [8]Universities only; 2000–01.

Internet resources for further information:
- **République du Sénégal: Site officiel du Gouvernement http://www.gouv.sn**
- **La Banque de France: La Zone Franc http://www.banque-france.fr/fr/zonefr/main.htm**

Serbia and Montenegro

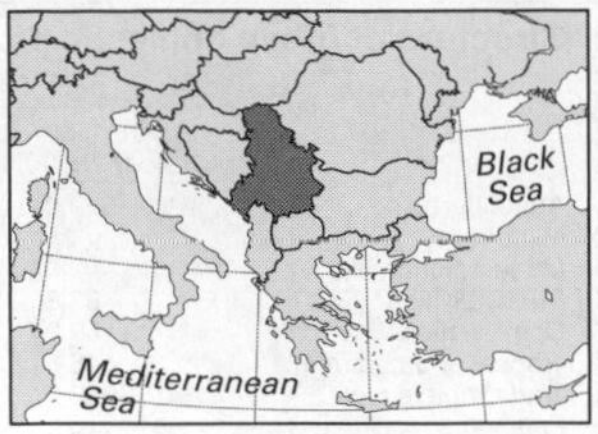

Official name: Srbija i Crna Gora (Serbia and Montenegro[1]).
Form of government: state union ("loose confederation") with one legislative house (Parliament [126]).
Head of state and government: President assisted by Council of Ministers.
Administrative centre: Belgrade[2].
Official language: none.
Official religion: none.
Monetary unit: 1 Serbian dinar[3] = 100 paras; valuation (Sept. 1, 2004) 1 U.S.$ = 53.50 Serbian dinars; 1 £ = 99.00 Serbian dinars.

Area and population

		area		population
Republics	**Major cities**	sq mi	sq km	2002–03 data[4]
Montenegro (Crna Gora)	Podgorica	5,333	13,812	672,656[4]
Serbia (Srbija)	Belgrade	29,913	77,474	7,479,437[4]
Central Serbia	Belgrade	21,609	55,968	5,454,950
Vojvodina	Novi Sad	8,304	21,506	2,024,487
UN interim-admin. province				
Kosovo (Kosova)[5]	Priština	4,203	10,887	1,900,000[4]
TOTAL		39,449	102,173	10,052,093[4]

Demography

Population (2004): 10,826,000.
Density (2004): persons per sq mi 274.4, persons per sq km 106.0.
Urban-rural (2002): urban 51.7%; rural 48.3%.
Sex distribution (2003): male 49.19%; female 50.81%.
Age breakdown (2003): under 15, 18.6%; 15–29, 22.5%; 30–44, 20.5%; 45–59, 19.0%; 60–74, 13.9%; 75 and over, 5.5%.
Population projection: (2010) 10,839,000; (2020) 10,750,000.
Ethnic composition (2000): Serb 62.1%; Albanian 17.1%; Montenegrin 4.3%; Hungarian 4.3%; Croat 3.1%; Bosniac 1.8%; Rom (Gypsy) 1.4%; Slovak 0.9%; Romanian 0.8%; other 4.2%.
Religious affiliation (1995): Serbian Orthodox 62.6%; Muslim 19.0%; Roman Catholic 5.8%; other, mostly nonreligious 12.6%.
Major cities (2002): Belgrade 1,120,092; Novi Sad 191,405; Niš 173,724; Priština 165,844[6]; Kragujevac 146,373; Podgorica 139,724[6].

Vital statistics

Birth rate per 1,000 population (2003): 12.1 (world avg. 21.3).
Death rate per 1,000 population (2003): 10.6 (world avg. 9.1).
Natural increase rate per 1,000 population (2003): 1.5 (world avg. 12.2).
Total fertility rate (avg. births per childbearing woman; 2003): 1.7.
Life expectancy at birth (2003): male 71.6 years; female 76.7 years.
Major causes of death per 100,000 population (2000): diseases of the circulatory system 570.3; malignant neoplasms (cancers) 170.8; diseases of the respiratory system 45.4; accidents, violence, and poisoning 41.9.

National economy

Budget (2001)[7]. Revenue: 421,000,000,000 Yugoslav new dinars (tax revenue 91.5%, of which social security tax 26.8%, VAT 26.2%, income tax 12.5%, excise tax 11.9%; nontax revenue 8.5%). Expenditure: 477,000,000,000 Yugoslav new dinars (transfers 50.1%, wages 20.7%, other 29.2%).
Public debt (external, outstanding; 2002): U.S.$8,514,000,000.
Production[8] (metric tons except as noted). Agriculture, forestry, fishing (2002): corn (maize) 5,597,207, wheat 2,245,030, sugar beets 2,098,080, potatoes 1,030,022, grapes 429,765, cabbages 354,686, plums 205,371, raspberries 94,400; livestock (number of live animals) 3,608,000 pigs, 1,691,000 sheep, 1,355,000 cattle; roundwood (2003) 3,155,000 cu m; fish catch (2001) 3,557. Mining and quarrying (2001): bauxite 610,000; copper (metal content of ore) 28,000; lead (metal content of ore) 19,000. Manufacturing (2000): cement 2,117,000; wheat flour 840,000; crude steel 682,000; pig iron 563,000; sulfuric acid 211,000[9]; nitric acid 185,000[9]; electrolytic copper 94,000[9]; welded pipes 43,000[9]; rolled copper 27,055[9]; refined lead 22,900; medicines 22,871[9]. Energy production (consumption): electricity (kW-hr; 2001) 34,594,000,000 (34,594,000,000); hard coal (metric tons; 2002) 70,000 ([2000] 137,000); lignite (metric tons; 2002) 31,789,000 ([2000] 34,343,000); crude petroleum (barrels; 2002) 5,534,000,000 ([2001] 5,534,000,000); petroleum products (metric tons; 2000) 934,000 (2,538,000); natural gas (cu m; 2002) 111,000,000 ([2000] 2,085,200,000).
Population economically active (2001)[8]: total 3,092,000; activity rate 37.1% (participation rates: over age 15 [1998] 58.3%; female [1995] 43.7%; [2003] unemployed 15.2%[8]).

Price and earnings indexes (2000 = 100)

	1997	1998	1999	2000	2001	2002	2003
Consumer price index	28.6	37.2	53.9	100.0	188.9	220.4	242.6
Monthly earnings index[10]	...	36.9	47.2	100.0	214.6	...	...

Household income and expenditure[8]. Average household size (2002) 2.9[8]; income per household (2002) 206,267 Yugoslav new dinars (U.S.$3,370); sources of income (2002): wages and salaries 50.4%, transfers 27.3%, self-employment 8.8%; expenditure (2002): food 46.2%, housing, n.a., energy 11.9%, clothing and footwear 8.3%, transportation and communications 8.2%.

Gross national product (2003)[8]: U.S.$15,512,000,000 (U.S.$1,910 per capita).

Structure of gross material product and labour force

	2002[8]			
	in value '000,000 Yugoslav new dinars	% of total value	labour force	% of labour force
Agriculture	143,621	18.8	87,000	2.8
Mining	18,104	2.4	40,000	1.3
Manufacturing	222,187	29.2	591,000	18.9
Construction	43,970	5.8	97,000	3.1
Public utilities	42,067	5.5	58,000	1.9
Transp. and commun.	101,009	13.2	138,000	4.4
Trade, restaurants	163,225	21.4	267,000	8.5
Finance, real estate	24,926	3.3	87,000	2.8
Pub. admin., defense	...	...	72,000	2.3
Services	2,933	0.4	764,000	24.4
Other	—	—	924,000[11]	29.6[11]
TOTAL	762,042	100.0	3,125,000	100.0

Land use as % of total land area (2000): in temporary crops 33.4%, in permanent crops 3.2%, in pasture 18.1%; overall forest area 28.3%.
Tourism (2002): receipts from visitors U.S.$77,000,000; expenditures, n.a.

Foreign trade

Balance of trade (current prices)

	1997	1998	1999	2000	2001	2002
U.S.$'000,000	–2,431	–1,991	–1,798	–1,988	–2,934	–4,045
% of total	33.9%	25.8%	37.5%	36.6%	43.5%	47.1%

Imports (2002): U.S.$6,320,000,000 (machinery and transport equipment 25.8%; mineral fuels 16.9%, of which crude petroleum 7.6%; chemical products 11.0%; food 7.0%). *Major import sources:* Germany 13.1%; Russia 12.5%; Italy 10.3%; Hungary 4.4%; Slovenia 3.8%.
Exports (2002): U.S.$2,275,000,000 (food 21.2%, of which refined sugar 4.0%; machinery and transport equipment 11.2%; chemical products 7.4%; aluminum 6.9%). *Major export destinations:* Bosnia and Herzegovina 14.6%; Italy 14.5%; Germany 10.7%; Macedonia 9.1%; Switzerland 7.5%.

Transport and communications

Transport. Railroads (2002): length *c.* 4,130 km; passenger-km (2001) 1,262,000,000[8]; metric ton-km cargo (2001) 2,040,000,000[8]. Roads (2000): total length 44,777 km (paved 63%). Vehicles (2001): passenger cars 1,481,400; trucks and buses 330,500. Air transport (2001)[8]: passenger-km 1,003,000,000; metric ton-km cargo 4,332,000; airports (2000) 5.

Communications

Medium	date	unit	number	units per 1,000 persons
Daily newspapers	2000	circulation	1,130,000	107
Radio	2000	receivers	3,130,000	297
Television	2000	receivers	2,980,000	282
Telephones	2003	main lines	2,611,700	243
Cellular telephones	2003	subscribers	3,634,600	338
Personal computers	2002	units	290,000	27
Internet	2003	users	847,000	79

Education and health

Educational attainment (1991). Percentage of population age 15 and over having: less than full primary education 33.5%; primary 25.0%; secondary 32.2%; postsecondary and higher 9.3%. *Literacy* (1991): total population age 10 and over literate 93.0%; males literate 97.2%; females literate 88.9%.

Education (2000–01)

	schools	teachers	students	student/ teacher ratio
Primary (age 7–14)	4,087	48,868	787,423	16.1
Secondary (age 15–18)	518	26,740	355,424	13.3
Higher	51	1,612	50,901	31.6

Health (2001): physicians 27,769[8] (1 per 300 persons); hospital beds 51,785[8] (1 per 161 persons); infant mortality rate per 1,000 live births (2003) 14.0.
Food (2001): daily per capita caloric intake 2,778 (vegetable products 65%, animal products 35%); 109% of FAO recommended minimum.

Military

Total active duty personnel (2003)[12]: 74,200 (army 84.1%, air force 10.8%, navy 5.1%). *Military expenditure as percentage of government expenditure* (1991): 3.9% (world 4.0%); per capita expenditure U.S.$176.

[1]Replaced Yugoslavia per effective date of new constitution (Feb. 4, 2003). [2]Principal executive and legislative bodies meet in Belgrade; the principal judicial body meets in Podgorica. [3]Replaced Yugoslav new dinar on Feb. 4, 2003, at rate of 1 to 1. Montenegro and Kosovo (Kosova) use the euro adopted on Jan. 1, 2002. [4]Summed total for 2003 census (for Montenegro), 2002 census (for Serbia), and 2002 estimate (for Kosovo [Kosova]). [5]Region under interim UN administration from June 1999. [6]2003. [7]Consolidated general government. [8]Excludes Kosovo. [9]1998. [10]Public sector only. [11]Unemployed. [12]About 19,000 troops from many NATO and non-NATO countries were deployed in Kosovo in October 2004.

Internet resources for further information:
- **Serbia and Montenegro Statistical Office http://www.szs.sv.gov.yu/english.htm**
- **National Bank of Serbia http://www.nbs.yu/english/index.htm**
- **Central Bank of Montenegro http://www.cb-mn.org/lijevoE.htm**
- **Statistical Office of Kosovo http://www.sok-kosovo.org**

Seychelles

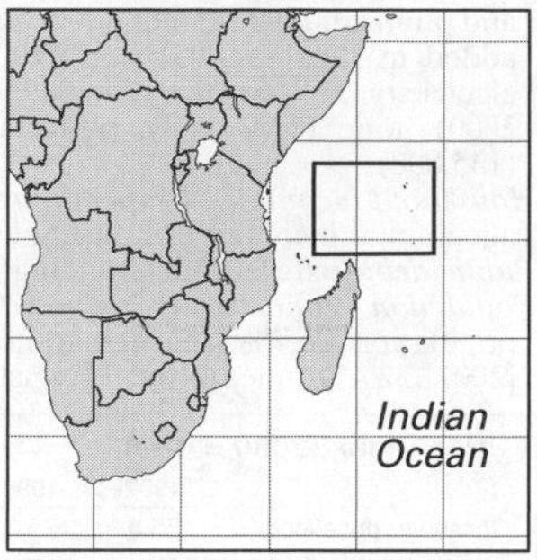

Official name: Repiblik Sesel (Creole); Republic of Seychelles (English); République des Seychelles (French).
Form of government: multiparty republic with one legislative house (National Assembly [34]).
Head of state and government: President.
Capital: Victoria.
Official languages: none[1].
Official religion: none.
Monetary unit: 1 Seychelles rupee (SR) = 100 cents; valuation (Sept. 1, 2004) 1 U.S.$ = SR 5.52; 1 £ = SR 9.93.

Area and population

Island Groups[2]	Capital	area sq mi	area sq km	population 2001 estimate
Central (Granitic) group				
La Digue and satellites	—	6	15	2,100
Mahé and satellites	Victoria	59	153	72,100
Praslin and satellites	—	15	40	6,500
Silhouette	—	8	20	500
Other islands	—	2	4	0
Outer (Coralline) islands	—	86	223	0
TOTAL		176	455	81,200[3]

Demography

Population (2004): 81,800.
Density (2004): persons per sq mi 464.8, persons per sq km 179.8.
Urban-rural (2002): urban 64.6%; rural 35.4%.
Sex distribution (2002): male 49.81%; female 50.19%.
Age breakdown (2003): under 15, 27.3%; 15–29, 28.2%; 30–44, 26.4%; 45–59, 9.9%; 60–74, 5.5%; 75 and over, 2.7%.
Population projection: (2010) 84,000; (2020) 88,000.
Doubling time: 68 years.
Ethnic composition (2000): Seychellois Creole (mixture of Asian, African, and European) 93.2%; British 3.0%; French 1.8%; Chinese 0.5%; Indian 0.3%; other unspecified 1.2%.
Religious affiliation (2000): Roman Catholic 90.4%; Anglican 6.7%; Hindu 0.6%; other (mostly nonreligious) 2.3%.
Major city (2004): Victoria 25,500.

Vital statistics

Birth rate per 1,000 population (2002): 18.3 (world avg. 21.3), (1998) legitimate 24.7%; illegitimate 75.3%.
Death rate per 1,000 population (2002): 8.0 (world avg. 9.1).
Natural increase rate per 1,000 population (2002): 10.3 (world avg. 12.2).
Total fertility rate (avg. births per childbearing woman; 2002): 2.0.
Marriage rate per 1,000 population (2002): 5.3.
Divorce rate per 1,000 population (2002): 1.4.
Life expectancy at birth (2002): male 66.6 years; female 75.8 years.
Major causes of death per 100,000 population (2002): diseases of the circulatory system 306.7; malignant neoplasms (cancers) 122.0; diseases of the respiratory system 66.5; diseases of the digestive system 37.0.

National economy

Budget (2002). Revenue: SR 1,487,000,000 (tax revenue 70.0%, of which customs taxes and duties 23.7%, sales tax 18.9%, tax on income and profit 16.9%; nontax revenue 28.3%; grants 1.7%). Expenditures: SR 2,061,000,000 (current expenditure 82.0%, of which debt service 15.4%, education 7.6%, health 6.7%; capital expenditure 16.0%; net lending 2.0%).
Tourism (2002): receipts from visitors U.S.$130,000,000; expenditures by nationals abroad U.S.$32,000,000.
Land use as % of total land area (2000): in temporary crops *c.* 2%, in permanent crops *c.* 13%, in pasture, n.a.; overall forest area *c.* 67%.
Gross national product (2003): U.S.$626,000,000 (U.S.$7,480 per capita).

Structure of gross domestic product and labour force

	2002 in value SR '000,000	% of total value	labour force[4]	% of labour force[4]
Agriculture	110.3	2.9	2,122	6.2
Manufacturing	698.0	18.2	3,656	10.7
Construction, mining	384.2	10.0	2,778	8.2
Public utilities	66.6	1.7	1,034	3.0
Trade	870.1	22.7	7,406	21.8
Transportation and communications	620.8	16.2	3,693	10.9
Pub. admin., defense	458.0	12.0	13,328	39.2
Finance / Services	510.5	13.3		
Other	111.4[5]	2.9[5]	…	…
TOTAL	3,829.9	100.0[6]	34,017	100.0

Production (metric tons except as noted). Agriculture, forestry, fishing (2003): coconuts 3,200, bananas 1,970, cinnamon 230, tea 225; livestock (number of live animals) 18,500 pigs, 5,150 goats, 1,400 cattle, 520,000 chickens; fish catch (2002) 48,960. Mining and quarrying (1998): guano 5,000. Manufacturing (2002): canned tuna 34,503; animal feed 18,565; copra 262; tea 222; soft drinks 94,210 hectolitres; beer and stout 76,000 hectolitres; fruit juices 31,300 hectolitres; cigarettes 24,000,000 units. Energy production (consumption): electricity (kW-hr; 2002) 218,800,000 (182,400,000,000); coal, none (n.a.); crude petroleum, none (n.a.); petroleum products (metric tons; 2000) none (74,000); natural gas, none (n.a.).
Population economically active (2002): total 34,017[4]; activity rate of total population 41.9% (participation rates [2000]: ages 15–64, 81.5%; female [2000] 43.0%; unemployed [1999] 11.5%).

Price index (2000 = 100)

	1997	1998	1999	2000	2001	2002	2003
Consumer price index	86.3	88.5	94.1	100.0	106.0	106.2	109.7

Public debt (external, outstanding; 2002): U.S.$149,300,000.
Household income and expenditure. Average household size (2002) 4.0; average annual income per household, n.a.; sources of income (1997): wages and salaries 77.2%, self-employment 3.8%, transfer payments 3.2%; expenditure (2001)[7]: food 25.5%, housing and energy 14.8%, beverages 13.3% (of which alcoholic 10.7%), clothing and footwear 6.7%, transportation 5.8%, recreation 5.5%.

Foreign trade[8]

Balance of trade (current prices)

	1998	1999	2000	2001	2002	2003
SR '000,000	–1,372	–1,542	–841	–1,513	–1,046	–747
% of total	51.6%	49.9%	27.5%	37.5%	29.5%	20.1%

Imports (2003): SR 2,231,000,000 (food and beverages 31.0%, of which fish, crustaceans, and mollusks 16.1%; mineral fuels 16.1%; machinery 12.3%; base and fabricated metals 8.1%; transport equipment 5.7%). *Major import sources:* Saudi Arabia 15.7%; South Africa 12.6%; Italy 10.6%; France 10.4%; Spain 10.4%; U.K. 7.7%.
Exports (2003): SR 1,484,000,000 (domestic exports 76.9%, of which canned tuna 69.0%, other processed fish 1.8%, fresh and frozen fish 1.9%; reexports 23.1%, of which petroleum products 19.8%). *Major export destinations* (2002)[9]: United Kingdom 39.2%; France 32.0%; Italy 14.5%; Germany 7.5%.

Transport and communications

Transport. Railroads: none. Roads (2002): total length 283 mi, 456 km (paved 96%). Vehicles (2002): passenger cars 6,923; trucks and buses 2,551. Air transport (2002)[10]: passenger-km 1,397,000,000; metric ton-km cargo 28,000,000; airports (2002) with scheduled flights 2.

Communications

Medium	date	unit	number	units per 1,000 persons
Daily newspapers	1996	circulation	3,000	46
Radio	1997	receivers	42,000	560
Television	2000	receivers	16,000	200
Telephones	2002	main lines	21,700	269
Cellular telephones	2003	subscribers	54,500	682
Personal computers	2002	units	13,000	157
Internet	2002	users	11,700	145

Education and health

Educational attainment (2003). Percentage of population age 12 and over having: less than primary or primary education 23.2%; secondary 73.4%; higher 3.4%. *Literacy* (2002): total population age 12 and over literate 91.0%; males literate 90.0%; females literate 92.0%.

Education (2003)

	schools	teachers	students	student/ teacher ratio
Primary (age 6–15)	26	675	9,477	14.0
Secondary (age 16–18)	12	552	7,551	13.7
Voc., teacher tr.	11	193	1,652	8.6

Health (2002): physicians 103 (1 per 792 persons); hospital beds 438 (1 per 185 persons); infant mortality rate per 1,000 live births (2002) 17.6.
Food (2001): daily per capita caloric intake 2,461 (vegetable products 81%, animal products 19%); 105% of FAO recommended minimum requirement.

Military

Total active duty personnel (2003): 450[11]. *Military expenditure as percentage of GNP* (1997): 3.8% (world 2.6%); per capita expenditure U.S.$194.

[1]Creole, English, and French are all national languages per 1993 constitution. [2]The Seychelles are administratively divided into 25 districts. [3]2002 preliminary census total equals 81,177. [4]Excludes unemployed, self-employed, and domestic workers. [5]Import duties less bank service charges. [6]Detail does not add to total given because of rounding. [7]Weights of consumer price index components. [8]Imports c.i.f.; exports f.o.b. [9]Domestic exports only. [10]Air Seychelles only. [11]All services form part of the army.

Internet resources for further information:
- **Seychelles in Figures http://www.seychelles.net/misdstat**
- **Central Bank of Seychelles http://www.cbs.sc**

Sierra Leone

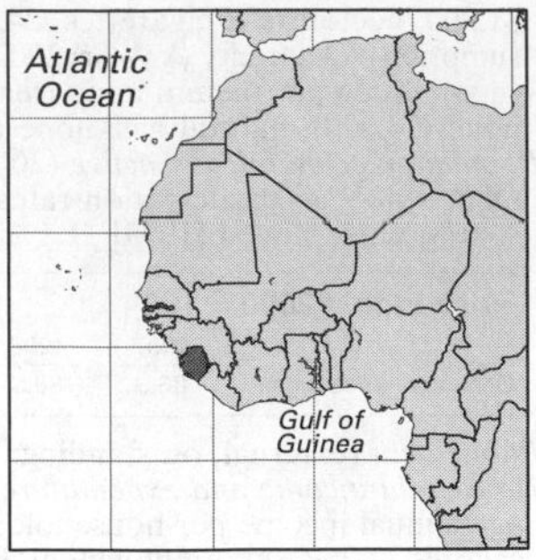

Official name: Republic of Sierra Leone.
Form of government: republic with one legislative body (Parliament [124[1]]).
Head of state and government: President.
Capital: Freetown.
Official language: English.
Official religion: none.
Monetary unit: 1 leone (Le) = 100 cents; valuation (Sept. 1, 2004) 1 U.S.$ = Le 2,455; 1 £ = Le 4,416.

Area and population

Provinces / Districts	Capitals	area sq mi	area sq km	population 1985 census[2]
Eastern Province	Kenema	6,005	15,553	960,551
Kailahun	Kailahun	1,490	3,859	233,839
Kenema	Kenema	2,337	6,053	337,055
Kono	Sefadu	2,178	5,641	389,657
Northern Province	Makeni	13,875	35,936	1,259,641
Bombali	Makeni	3,083	7,985	317,729
Kambia	Kambia	1,200	3,108	186,231
Koinaduga	Kabala	4,680	12,121	183,286
Port Loko	Port Loko	2,208	5,719	329,344
Tonkolili	Magburaka	2,704	7,003	243,051
Southern Province	Bo	7,604	19,694	741,377
Bo	Bo	2,015	5,219	268,671
Bonthe (incl. Sherbro)	Bonthe	1,339	3,468	105,007
Moyamba	Moyamba	2,665	6,902	250,514
Pujehun	Pujehun	1,585	4,105	117,185
Western Area[3]	Freetown	215	557	554,243
TOTAL		27,699	71,740	3,515,812

Demography

Population (2004): 5,168,000.
Density (2004): persons per sq mi 186.6, persons per sq km 72.0.
Urban-rural (2000): urban 36.6%; rural 63.4%.
Sex distribution (2003): male 48.31%; female 51.69%.
Age breakdown (2003): under 15, 44.8%; 15–29, 26.1%; 30–44, 15.3%; 45–59, 8.5%; 60–74, 4.4%; 75 and over, 0.8%.
Population projection: (2010) 5,859,000; (2020) 6,979,000.
Doubling time: 30 years.
Ethnic composition (2000): Mende 26.0%; Temne 24.6%; Limba 7.1%; Kuranko 5.5%; Kono 4.2%; Fulani 3.8%; Bullom-Sherbro 3.5%; other 25.3%.
Religious affiliation (2000): Sunnī Muslim 45.9%; traditional beliefs 40.4%; Christian 11.4%; other 2.3%.
Major cities (2003): Freetown (urban agglomeration; 2001) 837,000; Koidu 113,700; Makeni 110,700; Bo 82,400; Kenema 72,400.

Vital statistics

Birth rate per 1,000 population (2003): 43.9 (world avg. 21.3).
Death rate per 1,000 population (2003): 20.7 (world avg. 9.1).
Natural increase rate per 1,000 population (2003): 23.2 (world avg. 12.2).
Total fertility rate (avg. births per childbearing woman; 2003): 5.9.
Life expectancy at birth (2003): male 40.3 years; female 45.4 years.
Major causes of death per 100,000 population: n.a.; however, the major diseases are malaria, tuberculosis, leprosy, measles, tetanus, and diarrhea.

National economy

Budget (2002). Revenue: Le 239,425,000,000 (customs duties and excise taxes 64.0%, income tax 25.1%, other 10.9%). Expenditures: Le 701,834,000,000 (recurrent expenditures 65.1%, of which wages and salaries 18.8%, goods and services 12.9%, defense and security 12.9%, debt service 9.4%; capital expenditures 34.9%).
Gross national product (2003): U.S.$808,000,000 (U.S.$150 per capita).

Structure of gross domestic product and labour force

	2000 in value Le '000,000	2000 % of total value	2002 labour force	2002 % of labour force
Agriculture	731,865	55.0	1,083,000	61.2
Mining	275,891	20.7		
Manufacturing	44,509	3.3		
Construction	30,540	2.3		
Public utilities	5,042	0.4		
Transp. and commun.	27,345	2.1	688,000	38.8
Trade[4]	67,156	5.0		
Finance	31,182	2.3		
Pub. admin., defense	37,966	2.9		
Services	22,833	1.7		
Other	55,989[5]	4.2[5]		
TOTAL	1,330,318	100.0[6]	1,771,000	100.0

Production (metric tons except as noted). Agriculture, forestry, fishing (2002): cassava 260,000, rice 250,000, oil palm fruit 180,000, pulses 53,000, sweet potatoes 30,000, plantains 30,000, sugarcane 24,000, coffee 17,000, peanuts (groundnuts) 16,000, tomatoes 13,500, cacao beans 10,920, sorghum 9,000, mangoes 6,500, millet 4,500; livestock (number of live animals) 400,000 cattle, 370,000 sheep, 220,000 goats, 55,000 pigs; roundwood (2002) 5,497,220 cu m; fish catch (2003) 82,923. Mining and quarrying (2002): rutile, none[7]; diamonds 351,860[8] carats; gold 30 kg. Manufacturing (value added in Le '000,000; 1993): food 36,117; chemicals 10,560; earthenware 1,844; printing and publishing 1,171; metal products 1,073; furniture 647. Construction (value added in Le; 1994–95): 15,788,200,000. Energy production (consumption): electricity (kW-hr; 2000) 246,000,000 (246,000,000); crude petroleum (barrels; 2000) none (1,796,000); petroleum products (metric tons; 2000) 183,000 (145,000).
Household income and expenditure. Average household size (2002) 6.6; average annual income per household, n.a.
Public debt (external, outstanding; 2002): U.S.$1,262,000,000.
Population economically active (2002): total 1,771,000; activity rate of total population 36.7% (participation rates [1991]: ages 10–64, 53.3%; female [2001] 32.4%; unemployed [registered; 1992] 10.6%).

Price index (2000 = 100)

	1997	1998	1999	2000	2001	2002	2003
Consumer price index	55.5	75.2	100.8	100.0	102.1	98.7	106.2

Tourism (1999): receipts U.S.$8,000,000; expenditures U.S.$4,000,000.
Land use as % of total land area (2000): in temporary crops 6.8%, in permanent crops 0.8%, in pasture 30.7%; overall forest area 14.7%.

Foreign trade[9]

Balance of trade (current prices)

	1998	1999	2000	2001	2002	2003
Le '000,000	−137,744	−142,509	−287,868	−313,608	−452,826	−490,166
% of total	86.8%	86.3%	84.3%	73.0%	68.9%	53.0%

Imports (2002): Le 554,837,500,000 (food and live animals 26.7%; fuels 19.6%; machinery and transport equipment 18.9%; chemicals and chemical products 6.9%). *Major import sources* (2001): U.K. 25.3%; The Netherlands 10.1%; U.S. 7.9%; Germany 6.3%; Italy 5.6%.
Exports (2002): Le 102,011,900,000 (diamonds 85.7%; cacao 2.5%; rutile, none[7]; reexports 4.8%). *Major export destinations* (2001): Belgium 40.6%; U.S. 9.1%; U.K. 8.5%; Germany 7.8%; Japan 5.6%.

Transport and communications

Transport. Railroads (2002)[10]: length 52 mi, 84 km. Roads (1999): total length 7,270 mi, 11,700 km (paved 11%). Vehicles (2003): passenger cars 17,439; trucks and buses 12,428. Air transport (2000): passenger-km 93,000,000; metric ton-km cargo, n.a.; airports (2003) with scheduled flights 1.

Communications

Medium	date	unit	number	units per 1,000 persons
Daily newspapers	2000	circulation	17,700	4.0
Radio	2000	receivers	1,140,000	259
Television	2000	receivers	57,400	13
Telephones	2002	main lines	24,000	4.8
Cellular telephones	2002	subscribers	67,000	14
Personal computers	1999	units	100	—
Internet	2002	users	8,000	1.6

Education and health

Educational attainment (1985). Percentage of population age 5 and over having: no formal schooling 64.1%; primary education 18.7%; secondary 9.7%; higher 1.5%. *Literacy* (1995): total population age 15 and over literate 791,000 (31.4%); males 555,000 (45.4%); females 236,000 (18.2%).

Education (2000–01)

	schools	teachers	students	student/teacher ratio
Primary (age 5–11)	2,704	14,932	554,308	37.1
Secondary (age 12–18)	495	5,264	70,900[11]	16.4[11]
Voc., teacher tr.	44[11]	1,321	9,660	7.3
Higher[12]	2	257	2,571	10.0

Health: physicians (1996) 339 (1 per 13,696 persons); hospital beds (1998) 3,364 (1 per 1,250 persons); infant mortality rate per 1,000 live births (2003) 146.9.
Food (2001): daily per capita caloric intake 1,874 (vegetable products 97%, animal products 3%); 81% of FAO recommended minimum requirement.

Military

Total active duty personnel (2003): 14,000 (army 98.6%, navy 1.4%, air force, none); UN peacekeeping troops (September 2004) 8,500. *Military expenditure as percentage of GNP* (1999): 3.0% (world 2.4%); per capita expenditure U.S.$4.

[1]Includes 12 paramount chiefs elected to represent each of the provincial districts. [2]Preliminary figures exclude adjustment for underenumeration; adjusted total is 3,760,000. [3]Not officially a province; the administration of the Western Area is split among Greater Freetown (the city and its suburbs) and other administrative bodies. [4]Includes hotels. [5]Import duties less imputed bank service charges. [6]Detail does not add to total given because of rounding. [7]Production at world's richest deposit was halted between 1995 and August 2004 because of the civil war and its lasting effects. [8]Does not include smuggled artisanal production, which was estimated to be 600,000 carats between 1999 and 2001. [9]Imports c.i.f.; exports f.o.b. [10]Marampa Mineral Railway; there are no passenger railways. [11]1992–93. [12]1990–91.

Internet resources for further information:
- **Sierra Leone Annual Statistical Digest, 2004 http://www.statistics-sierra-leone.org/annual_statistical_digests.htm**
- **Bank of Sierra Leone http://www.bankofsierraleone-centralbank.org**

Singapore

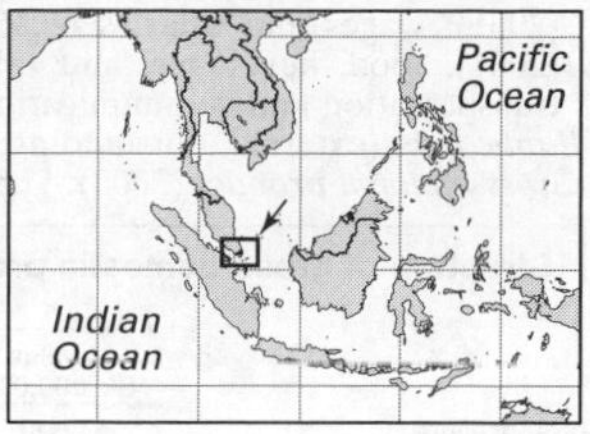

Official name: Hsin-chia-p'o Kung-ho-kuo (Mandarin Chinese); Republik Singapura (Malay); Singapore Kudiyarasu (Tamil); Republic of Singapore (English).
Form of government: unitary multiparty republic with one legislative house (Parliament [90[1]]).
Chief of state: President[2].
Head of state government: Prime Minister[3].
Capital: Singapore.
Official languages: Chinese; Malay; Tamil; English.
Official religion: none.
Monetary unit: 1 Singapore dollar (S$) = 100 cents; valuation (Sept. 1, 2004) 1 U.S.$ = S$1.71; 1 £ = S$3.08.

Population (2003 estimate)

De facto population	4,185,200[4]
De jure population	3,437,300[5]

Demography

Area: 269.2 sq mi, 697.1 sq km.
Population (2004): 4,229,000.
Density (2004): persons per sq mi 15,710, persons per sq km 6,067.
Urban-rural: urban 100.0%.
Sex distribution (2003)[6]: male 49.75%; female 50.25%.
Age breakdown (2003)[6]: under 15, 20.8%; 15–29, 20.2%; 30–44, 27.4%; 45–59, 20.4%; 60–74, 8.5%; 75 and over, 2.7%.
Population projection: (2010) 4,501,000; (2020) 4,735,000.
Ethnic composition (2003)[6]: Chinese 76.3%; Malay 13.8%; Indian 8.3%; other 1.6%.
Religious affiliation (2000)[6]: Buddhist 42.5%; Muslim 14.9%; Christian 14.6%; Taoist 8.5%; Hindu 4.0%; traditional beliefs 0.6%; nonreligious 14.9%.

Vital statistics

Birth rate per 1,000 population (2003)[6]: 10.4 (world avg. 21.3).
Death rate per 1,000 population (2003)[6]: 4.4 (world avg. 9.1).
Natural increase rate per 1,000 population (2003)[6]: 6.0 (world avg. 12.2).
Total fertility rate (avg. births per childbearing woman; 2003)[6]: 1.3.
Marriage rate per 1,000 population (2003)[6]: 6.4.
Life expectancy at birth (2003)[6]: male 76.9 years; female 80.9 years.
Major causes of death per 100,000 population (2003)[6]: malignant neoplasms (cancers) 120.8; heart diseases 116.9; pneumonia 68.1; cerebrovascular diseases 45.2; accidents and violence 30.8.

National economy

Budget (2003). Revenue: S$24,659,200,000 (income tax 42.2%, nontax revenue 14.6%, goods and services tax 11.0%, customs and excise duties 7.3%, motor vehicle taxes 5.3%). Expenditures: S$27,189,300,000 (security 34.0%, development expenditure 29.3%, education 17.9%, health 6.1%, trade and industry 1.9%).
Production (metric tons except as noted). Agriculture, forestry, fishing (2003): vegetables and fruits 5,010; livestock (number of live animals) 250,000 pigs, 2,000,000 chickens; fish catch (2001) 8,704. Mining and quarrying (value of output in S$; 1994): granite 75,800,000. Manufacturing (value added in U.S.$'000,000; 2001): office, accounting, and computer equipment 5,576; electronic valves and tubes 4,829; chemicals and chemical products 4,209; refined petroleum products 1,165; special purpose machinery 1,029; aircraft and spacecraft 1,007; fabricated metal products 910. Energy production (consumption): electricity (kW-hr; 2000) 31,665,000,000 (31,665,000,000); crude petroleum (barrels; 2000) none (306,629,000); petroleum products (metric tons; 2000) 27,613,000 (10,790,000); natural gas (cu m; 2000) none (1,411,000,000).
Household income and expenditure. Average household size (2002) 4.2; income per household (2000) S$59,316 (U.S.$34,406); sources of income: n.a.; expenditure (1998): food 23.7%, transportation and communications 22.8%, housing costs and furnishings 21.6%, education 6.9%, clothing and footwear 4.1%, health 3.3%, other 17.6%.
Tourism (2002). receipts from visitors U.S.$4,932,000,000; expenditures by nationals abroad U.S.$5,213,000,000.
Gross national product (2003): U.S.$90,228,000,000 (U.S.$21,230 per capita).

Structure of gross domestic product and labour force

	2003		2002	
	in value S$'000,000	% of total value	labour force	% of labour force
Agriculture, Quarrying	163.5	0.1	6,100	0.3
Manufacturing	41,601.2	26.1	368,600	17.3
Construction	7,833.9	4.9	119,100	5.6
Public utilities	2,621.9	1.6	9,000	0.4
Transp. and commun.	17,571.3	11.0	218,800	10.3
Trade	23,604.2	14.9	429,700	20.2
Finance	45,030.2	28.3	326,700	15.3
Services	19,427.3	12.2	539,400	25.3
Other	1,201.5[7]	0.8[7]	111,200[8]	5.2[8]
TOTAL	159,135.0	100.0[9]	2,128,600	100.0[9]

Population economically active (2003): total 2,150,100[6]; activity rate of total population 62.6% (participation rates: ages 15 and over, 64.2%; female 53.9%; unemployed 4.6%).

Price and earnings indexes (2000 = 100)

	1997	1998	1999	2000	2001	2002	2003
Consumer price index	98.9	98.6	98.7	100.0	101.0	100.6	101.1
Monthly earnings index	87.1	89.5	91.9	100.0	102.3	...	...

Land use as % of total land area (2000): in temporary and permanent crops 1.4%, in pasture, n.a.; overall forest area 3.3%.

Foreign trade[10]

Balance of trade (current prices)

	1998	1999	2000	2001	2002	2003
S$'000,000	+8,896	+6,147	+5,651	+10,335	+15,590	+28,285
% of total	2.5%	1.6%	1.2%	2.4%	5.8%	6.0%

Imports (2003): S$222,811,000,000 (electronic valves [including integrated circuits and semiconductors] 21.7%; crude and refined petroleum 13.5%; computers and related parts 11.2%; chemicals and chemical products 6.7%; telecommunications equipment 4.0%). *Major import sources:* Malaysia 16.8%; U.S. 13.9%; Japan 12.0%; China 8.7%; Taiwan 5.1%; Thailand 4.3%.
Exports (2003): S$251,096,000,000 (electronic valves 20.9%; computers and related parts 17.9%; chemicals and chemical products 11.8%, of which organic chemicals 6.4%; crude and refined petroleum 10.9%; telecommunications equipment 4.6%). *Major export destinations:* Malaysia 15.8%; U.S. 13.3%; Hong Kong 10.0%; China 7.0%; Japan 6.7%; Taiwan 4.8%; Thailand 4.3%.

Transport and communications

Transport. Railroads (2003): length 131 km. Roads (2003): total length 3,144 km (paved 99%). Vehicles (2003): passenger cars 424,712; trucks and buses 138,538. Air transport (2003): passenger-km 65,376,000,000; metric ton-km cargo 6,683,000,000; airports (2003) 1.

Communications

Medium	date	unit	number	units per 1,000 persons
Daily newspapers	2000	circulation	1,197,301	298
Radio	2000	receivers	2,700,000	672
Television	2000	receivers	1,220,000	304
Telephones	2002	main lines	1,927,200	463
Cellular telephones	2002	subscribers	3,312,600	795
Personal computers	2002	units	2,590,000	622
Internet	2002	users	2,100,000	504

Education and health

Educational attainment (2000)[6]. Percentage of population age 15 and over having: no schooling 19.6%; primary education 23.1%; secondary 39.5%; post-secondary 17.8%. *Literacy* (2003)[6]: total population age 15 and over literate 94.2%.

Education (2003)

	schools[11]	teachers	students	student/ teacher ratio
Primary (age 6–11)	201	12,025	299,939	24.9
Secondary (age 12–18)	180	10,830	206,426	19.1
Voc., teacher tr.	10	1,956	23,708	12.1
Higher[11]	8	7,318	111,538	15.2

Health (2003): physicians 6,292 (1 per 670[6] persons); hospital beds 11,855 (1 per 290[6] persons); infant mortality rate per 1,000 live births 2.2.
Food (1988–90): daily per capita caloric intake 3,121 (vegetable products 76%, animal products 24%); 136% of FAO recommended minimum requirement.

Military

Total active duty personnel (2003): 72,500 (army 69.0%, navy 12.4%, air force 18.6%). *Military expenditure as percentage of GNP* (1999): 4.8% (world 2.4%); per capita expenditure U.S.$1,100.

[1]Includes 6 nonelective seats. [2]Title per constitution is Head of State. [3]Has principal executive authority per constitution. [4]The de facto population figure (as of the 2000 census) includes citizens (2,973,091), noncitizens with permanent residency status (290,118), and temporary residents (754,524). [5]The de jure population figure excludes temporary residents. [6]Based on de jure population. [7]Imputed bank service charges. [8]Unemployed. [9]Detail does not add to total given because of rounding. [10]Imports c.i.f., exports f.o.b. [11]2000.

Internet resources for further information:
- **Statistics Singapore http://www.singstat.gov.sg**
- **Monetary Authority of Singapore http://www.mas.gov.sg/masmcm/bin/pt1home.htm**

Slovakia

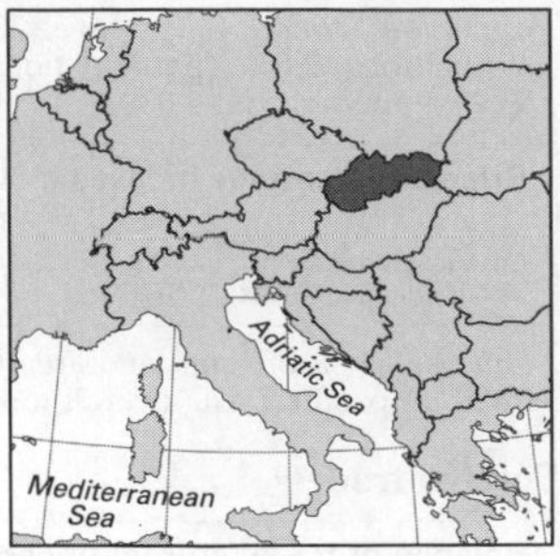

Official name: Slovenská Republika (Slovak Republic).
Form of government: unitary multiparty republic with one legislative house (National Council [150]).
Chief of state: President.
Head of government: Prime Minister.
Capital: Bratislava.
Official language: Slovak.
Official religion: none.
Monetary unit: 1 Slovak koruna (Sk) = 100 halura; valuation (Sept. 1, 2004) 1 U.S.$ = Sk 33.12; 1 £ = Sk 59.57.

Area and population

		area		population
				2001
Regions	Capitals	sq mi	sq km	census
Banská Bystrica	Banská Bystrica	3,651	9,455	662,121
Bratislava	Bratislava	793	2,053	599,015
Košice	Košice	2,607	6,753	766,012
Nitra	Nitra	2,449	6,343	713,422
Prešov	Prešov	3,472	8,993	789,968
Trenčín	Trenčín	1,738	4,501	605,582
Trnava	Trnava	1,602	4,148	551,003
Žilina	Žilina	2,621	6,788	692,332
TOTAL		18,933	49,035[1]	5,379,455[2]

Demography

Population (2004): 5,383,000.
Density (2004): persons per sq mi 284.3, persons per sq km 109.8.
Urban-rural (2002): urban 57.6%; rural 42.4%.
Sex distribution (2004[3]): male 48.53%; female 51.47%.
Age breakdown (2001): under 15, 18.9%; 15–29, 25.1%; 30–44, 21.5%; 45–59, 18.9%; 60–74, 11.0%; 75 and over, 4.6%.
Population projection: (2010) 5,411,000; (2020) 5,405,000.
Ethnic composition (2001): Slovak 85.8%; Hungarian 9.7%; Rom (Gypsy) 1.7%; Czech 0.8%; Ruthenian and Ukrainian 0.7%; other 1.3%.
Religious affiliation (2001): Roman Catholic 68.9%; Protestant 9.2%, of which Slovak Evangelical 6.9%, Reformed Christian 2.0%; Greek Catholic 4.1%; Eastern Orthodox 0.9%; nonreligious and other 16.9%.
Major cities (2001): Bratislava 428,672; Košice 236,093; Prešov 92,786; Nitra 87,285; Žilina 85,400; Banská Bystrica 83,056.

Vital statistics

Birth rate per 1,000 population (2003): 9.6 (world avg. 21.3); (2001) legitimate 80.2%; illegitimate 19.8%.
Death rate per 1,000 population (2003): 9.7 (world avg. 9.1).
Natural increase rate per 1,000 population (2003): –0.1 (world avg. 12.2).
Total fertility rate (avg. births per childbearing woman; 2002): 1.3.
Marriage rate per 1,000 population (2003): 4.8.
Divorce rate per 1,000 population (2003): 2.0.
Life expectancy at birth (2002): male 69.6 years; female 77.7 years.
Major causes of death per 100,000 population (2001): diseases of the circulatory system 533.4; malignant neoplasms (cancers) 220.6; accidents and violence 56.5; diseases of the respiratory system 50.7; diseases of the digestive system 48.4.

National economy

Budget (2002). Revenue: Sk 391,800,000,000 (tax revenue 88.1%, of which social security contribution 35.6%, value-added tax 21.0%, income tax 11.9%; nontax revenue 11.9%). Expenditures: Sk 459,300,000,000 (current expenditures 88.9%, of which social welfare 26.5%, wages 14.4%, health 11.7%, debt service 8.3%; investment 11.1%).
Production (metric tons except as noted). Agriculture, forestry, fishing (2002): wheat 1,554,000, sugar beets 1,340,000, corn [maize] 754,000, barley 695,000, potatoes 484,000, rapeseed 257,000, sunflower seeds 117,000, rye 96,000; livestock (number of live animals) 1,554,000 pigs, 608,000 cattle, 316,000 sheep; roundwood (2002) 5,765,400 cu m; fish catch (2001) 3,142. Mining and quarrying (2001): iron ore (metal content) 300,000; gold 157 kg. Manufacturing (value added in U.S.$'000,000; 1998)[4]: food products 289; nonelectrical machinery 280; iron and steel 232; motor vehicles 192; paper and paper products 180; refined petroleum 180; fabricated metal products 165. Energy production (consumption): electricity (kW-hr; 2002) 32,436,000,000 ([2000] 29,297,000,000); hard coal (metric tons; 2000) none (4,656,000); lignite (metric tons; 2001) 3,424,000 ([2000] 4,213,000); crude petroleum (barrels; 2001) 400,000 ([2000] 42,822,000); petroleum products (metric tons; 2000) 4,181,000 (1,777,000); natural gas (cu m; 2001) 212,000,000 ([2000] 6,886,000,000).
Population economically active (2001): total 2,665,837; activity rate of total population 49.6% (participation rates: ages 15–64, 79.6%; female 47.7%; unemployed 18.0%).

Price and earnings indexes (2000 = 100)

	1997	1998	1999	2000	2001	2002	2003
Consumer price index	75.7	80.7	89.3	100.0	107.3	110.9	120.4
Annual earnings index	80.7	87.5	93.9	100.0	108.2	118.2	125.7

Household income and expenditure. Average household size (2002) 3.2; gross income per household (2001) Sk 89,352 (U.S.$1,848); sources of income (2001): wages and salaries 67.1%, transfer payments 15.8%; expenditure (2001): food, beverages, and tobacco 27.4%, housing and energy 17.2%, transportation and communications 13.7%, clothing and footwear 8.6%.
Public debt (external, outstanding; 2002): U.S.$4,295,000,000.
Gross national product (2003): U.S.$26,483,000,000 (U.S.$4,920 per capita).

Structure of gross domestic product and labour force

	2002			
	in value Sk '000,000	% of total value	labour force	% of labour force
Agriculture	44,600	4.2	131,400	6.2
Mining	6,800	0.6	640,900[5]	30.1[5]
Manufacturing	220,100	20.5		
Construction	53,100	4.9	176,000	8.3
Public utilities	33,300	3.1	[5]	[5]
Transp. and commun.	109,300	10.2	154,400	7.3
Trade	154,700	14.4	340,000	16.0
Finance	362,400	33.8	143,100	6.7
Pub. admin., defense			149,700	7.0
Services			391,300	18.4
Other	89,300[6]	8.3[6]	600	—
TOTAL	1,073,600	100.0	2,127,000[1, 7]	100.0

Tourism: receipts from visitors (2002) U.S.$724,000,000; expenditure by nationals abroad U.S.$442,000,000.
Land use as % of total land area (2000): in temporary crops 30.2%, in permanent crops 2.6%, in pasture 18.0%; overall forest area 45.3%.

Foreign trade

Balance of trade (current prices)

	1998	1999	2000	2001	2002	2003
U.S.$'000,000	–2,353	–1,093	–904	–2,135	–2,117	–635
% of total	9.9%	5.1%	3.7%	7.8%	6.9%	1.4%

Imports (2002): U.S.$16,502,000,000 (machinery and apparatus 25.6%, mineral fuels 14.6%, transport equipment 12.8%, base and fabricated metals 8.9%). *Major import sources:* Germany 22.6%; Czech Republic 15.2%; Russia 12.5%; Italy 6.9%; France 4.4%.
Exports (2002): U.S.$14,385,000,000 (transport equipment [mostly road vehicles] 21.2%, machinery and apparatus 18.8%, base and fabricated metals [mostly iron and steel] 14.3%, mineral fuels 7.2%). *Major export destinations:* Germany 26.0%; Czech Republic 15.2%; Italy 10.7%; Austria 7.7%; Hungary 5.5%; Poland 5.3%.

Transport and communications

Transport. Railroads (2001): length 3,665 km; passenger-km 2,805,000,000; metric ton-km cargo 10,929,000,000. Roads (2001): total length 17,735 km (paved, n.a.). Vehicles (2003): passenger cars 1,327,000; trucks and buses 141,000. Air transport (2003)[8]: passenger-km 41,003,000; metric ton-km cargo 308,000; airports (2002) with scheduled flights 2.

Communications

Medium	date	unit	number	units per 1,000 persons
Daily newspapers	2000	circulation	938,000	174
Radio	2000	receivers	5,200,000	965
Television	2000	receivers	2,190,000	407
Telephones	2002	main lines	1,294,700	241
Cellular telephones	2003	subscribers	3,678,800	684
Personal computers	2002	units	970,000	180
Internet	2003	users	1,375,800	256

Education and health

Educational attainment (1991). Percentage of adult population having: incomplete primary education 0.7%; primary and incomplete secondary 37.9%; complete secondary 50.9%; higher 9.5%; unknown 1.0%. *Literacy* (2001): total population age 15 and over literate 100%.

Education (2002)

	schools	teachers[9]	students	student/ teacher ratio[9]
Primary (age 6–14)	2,396	39,745	602,360	16.4
Secondary (age 15–18)	220	6,259	93,283	13.1
Voc., teacher tr.	299	11,255	93,034	9.9
Higher	20	9,047	139,036	13.9

Health (2001): physicians 20,430 (1 per 263 persons); hospital beds 54,759 (1 per 98 persons); infant mortality rate per 1,000 live births (2002) 8.1.
Food (2000): daily per capita caloric intake 3,133 (vegetable products 75%, animal products 25%); 127% of FAO recommended minimum requirement.

Military

Total active duty personnel (2003): 22,000 (army 62.3%, air force 31.8%, headquarters staff 5.9%). *Military expenditure as percentage of GNP* (1999): 1.8% (world 2.4%); per capita expenditure U.S.$187.

[1]Detail does not add to total given because of rounding. [2]De jure figure; 2001 de facto census total equals 5,193,376. [3]January 1. [4]Establishments employing 20 or more persons only. [5]Manufacturing includes Public utilities. [6]Bank service charges and indirect taxes. [7]Excludes unemployed, women on maternity and additional leave, and armed forces. [8]Slovak Airlines only. [9]2000–01.

Internet resources for further information:

- **National Bank of Slovakia http://www.nbs.sk**
- **Statistical Office of the Slovak Republic http://www.statistics.sk/webdata/english/index2_a.htm**

Slovenia

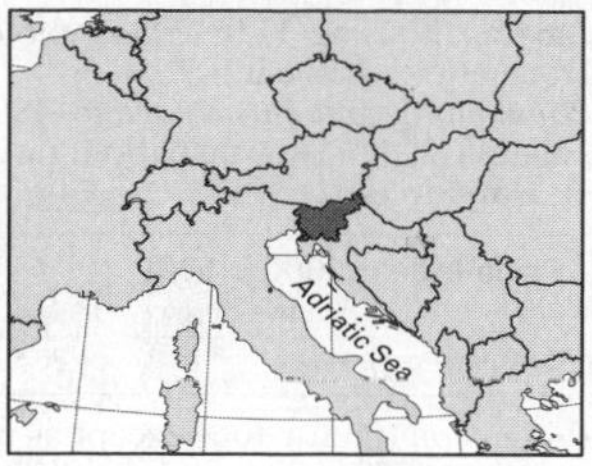

Official name: Republika Slovenija (Republic of Slovenia).
Form of government: unitary multiparty republic with two legislative houses (National Council [40]; National Assembly [90]).
Head of state: President.
Head of government: Prime Minister.
Capital: Ljubljana.
Official language: Slovene.
Official religion: none.
Monetary unit: 1 Slovene tolar (SIT; plural tolarjev) = 100 stotin; valuation (Sept. 1, 2004) 1 U.S.$ = SIT 197.48; 1 £ = SIT 355.26.

Area and population

		area		population
Statistical regions[1]	**Principal cities**	sq mi	sq km	2002 census
Gorenjska	Kranj	825	2,137	195,885
Goriška	Nova Gorica	898	2,325	118,511
Jugovzhodna Slovenija	Novo Mesto	653	1,690	136,474
Koroška	Ravne na Koroškem	401	1,041	73,296
Notranjsko-kraška	Postojna	562	1,456	50,243
Obalno Kraško	Koper	403	1,044	102,070
Osrednjeslovenska	Ljubljana	1,367	3,540	488,364
Podravska	Maribor	838	2,170	310,743
Pomurska	Murska Sobota	516	1,337	120,875
Savinjska	Celje	920	2,384	253,574
Spodnjeposavska	Krško	342	885	68,565
Zasavska	Trbovlje	102	264	45,436
TOTAL		7,827	20,273	1,964,036

Demography

Population (2004): 1,997,000.
Density (2004): persons per sq mi 255.1, persons per sq km 98.5.
Urban-rural (2002): urban 50.8%; rural 49.2%.
Sex distribution (2003): male 48.95%; female 51.05%.
Age breakdown (2002): under 15, 15.3%; 15–29, 21.5%; 30–44, 22.7%; 45–59, 20.5%; 60–74, 14.4%; 75 and over, 5.6%.
Population projection: (2010) 1,988,000; (2020) 1,937,000.
Ethnic composition (2002)[2]: Slovene 91.2%; Serb 2.2%; Croat 2.0%; Bosniac (ethnic Muslim) 1.8%; other 2.8%.
Religious affiliation (2000): Christian 92.1%, of which Roman Catholic 83.5%, unaffiliated Christian 4.7%, Protestant 1.6%, Orthodox 0.6%; nonreligious/atheist 7.8%; other 0.1%.
Major cities (2002): Ljubljana 258,873; Maribor 93,847; Celje 37,834; Kranj 35,587; Velenje 26,742.

Vital statistics

Birth rate per 1,000 population (2002): 8.8 (world avg. 21.3); legitimate 59.8%; illegitimate 40.2%.
Death rate per 1,000 population (2002): 9.4 (world avg. 9.1).
Natural increase rate per 1,000 population (2002): –0.6 (world avg. 12.2).
Total fertility rate (avg. births per childbearing woman; 2002): 1.2.
Marriage rate per 1,000 population (2002): 3.5.
Divorce rate per 1,000 population (2002): 1.2.
Life expectancy at birth (2002): male 72.3 years; female 79.9 years.
Major causes of death per 100,000 population (2002): diseases of the circulatory system 359.2; malignant neoplasms (cancers) 253.7; accidents and violence 74.6; diseases of the respiratory system 70.5.

National economy

Budget (2003). Revenue: SIT 2,376,000,000,000 (2002; tax revenue 91.7%, of which social security contributions 32.7%, taxes on goods and services 32.3%, personal income tax 19.0%; nontax revenue 8.3%). Expenditures: SIT 2,454,000,000,000 (2002; current expenditures 90.8%, of which wages 45.9%, transfers 44.9%; development expenditures 9.2%).
Public debt (external, outstanding; 2001): U.S.$2,700,000,000.
Production (metric tons except as noted). Agriculture, forestry, fishing (2002): silage 1,085,000, corn (maize) 255,000, sugar beets 190,000, wheat 175,000, potatoes 150,000, grapes 126,800, apples 75,000; livestock (number of live animals) 599,895 pigs, 477,075 cattle; roundwood (2001) 2,283,000 cu m; fish catch (2001) 3,040. Mining and quarrying (2002): dimension stone 105,000. Manufacturing (value added in U.S.$'000,000; 2001): base and fabricated metals 771; nonelectrical machinery and professional equipment 573; chemicals and chemical products 473; food, beverages, and tobacco products 457; electrical machinery 424. Energy production (consumption): electricity (kW-hr; 2003) 13,064,000,000 (12,588,000,000); hard coal (metric tons; 2000) none (446,000); lignite (metric tons; 2003) 4,854,000 (5,358,000); crude petroleum (barrels; 2000) 7,330 (1,165,000); petroleum products (metric tons; 2000) 133,000 (2,214,000); natural gas (cu m; 2003) 4,900,000 (1,114,000,000).
Land use as % of total land area (2000): in temporary crops 8.6%, in permanent crops 1.5%, in pasture 15.6%; overall forest area 55.0%.
Household income and expenditure (2001). Average household size (2002) 2.8; income per household SIT 3,090,000 (U.S.$12,800); sources of income: wages 60.0%, transfers 26.6%; expenditure: transportation and communications 25.8%, food and beverages 17.8%, housing 10.4%, recreation 9.3%.
Gross national product (at current market prices; 2003): U.S.$23,229,000,000 (U.S.$11,830 per capita).

Structure of gross domestic product and labour force

	2002			
	in value SIT '000,000	% of total value	labour force[3]	% of labour force[3]
Agriculture, forestry	147,785	3.2	89,000	9.1
Mining	24,284	0.5	4,000	0.4
Manufacturing	1,231,154	27.0	287,000	29.3
Construction	260,712	5.7	54,000	5.5
Public utilities	132,555	2.9	11,000	1.1
Transp. and commun.	337,472	7.4	55,000	5.6
Trade, restaurants	656,800	14.4	156,000	15.9
Finance, real estate	936,403	20.5	67,000	6.8
Pub. admin., defense	306,092	6.7	50,000	5.1
Services	397,913	8.7	145,000	14.8
Other	128,748[4]	2.8[4]	63,000[5]	6.4[5]
TOTAL	4,559,918	100.0[6]	981,000	100.0

Population economically active (2003): total 959,000; activity rate 48.0% (participation rates: ages 15 and over 56.5%; female 45.9%; unemployed 10.9%).

Price and earnings indexes (2000 = 100)

	1997	1998	1999	2000	2001	2002	2003
Consumer price index	80.2	86.6	91.9	100.0	108.4	116.5	123.0
Annual earnings index	75.3	82.5	90.4	100.0	111.9	122.9	132.1

Tourism (2002): receipts from visitors U.S.$1,083,000,000; expenditures by nationals abroad U.S.$614,000,000.

Foreign trade[7]

Balance of trade (current prices)

	2000	2001	2002	2003
€'000,000	–1,492	–998	–612	–952
% of total	7.3%	4.6%	2.7%	4.0%

Imports (2003): €12,237,000,000 (machinery and transport equipment 34.4%, of which road vehicles 11.1%; chemicals and chemical products 13.3%; mineral fuels 7.7%; food products 5.1%). *Major import sources:* Germany 19.3%; Italy 18.3%; France 10.1%; Austria 8.6%; Croatia 3.6%.
Exports (2003): €11,285,000,000 (machinery and transport equipment 36.5%, of which electrical machinery and apparatus 11.6%, road vehicles 11.4%; chemicals and chemical products 13.8%, of which medicines and pharmaceuticals 7.0%; furniture and parts 6.9%). *Major export destinations:* Germany 23.1%; Italy 13.1%; Croatia 8.9%; Austria 7.3%; France 5.7%.

Transport and communications

Transport. Railroads (2003): length 764 mi, 1,229 km; passenger-km 778,000,000; metric ton-km cargo 3,274,000,000. Roads (2003): total length 12,524 mi, 20,155 km (paved 81%). Vehicles: passenger cars (2003) 889,580; trucks and buses 69,363. Air transport (2003): passenger-km 837,000,000; metric ton-km cargo 3,538,000; airports (2003) with scheduled flights 3.

Communications

Medium	date	unit	number	units per 1,000 persons
Daily newspapers	2000	circulation	334,000	171
Radio	2000	receivers	792,000	405
Television	2002	receivers	732,000	366
Telephones	2003	main lines	812,300	407
Cellular telephones	2003	subscribers	1,739,100	871
Personal computers	2002	units	600,000	301
Internet	2002	users	750,000	376

Education and health

Educational attainment (2002). Percentage of population age 15 and over having: no formal schooling 0.7%; incomplete and complete primary education 32.2%; secondary 54.1%; some higher 5.1%; undergraduate 6.9%; advanced degree 1.0%. *Literacy* (2001): 99.6%.

Education (2002–03)

	schools	teachers	students	student/teacher ratio
Primary (age 7–14)	811	15,625	175,211	11.2
Secondary (age 15–18)	143	8,482	103,538	12.2
Higher	49	3,056[8]	87,205	18.9[8]

Health (2002): physicians 4,636 (1 per 430 persons); hospital beds 10,147 (1 per 197 persons); infant mortality rate per 1,000 live births 3.8.

Military

Total active duty personnel (2003): 6,550 (army 100%). *Military expenditure as percentage of GNP* (1999): 1.4% (world 2.4%); per capita expenditure U.S.$227.

[1]Actual first-order administration is based on 192 municipalities. [2]Prorating 8.9% of population not responding to census questionnaire. [3]May. [4]Import taxes less imputed bank service charges. [5]Includes 58,000 unemployed and 5,000 not distributed. [6]Detail does not add to total given because of rounding. [7]Imports c.i.f.; exports f.o.b. [8]2001–02.

Internet resources for further information:
- **Statistical Office of the Republic of Slovenia http://www.sigov.si/zrs/eng/index.html**
- **Bank of Slovenia http://www.bsi.si**

Solomon Islands

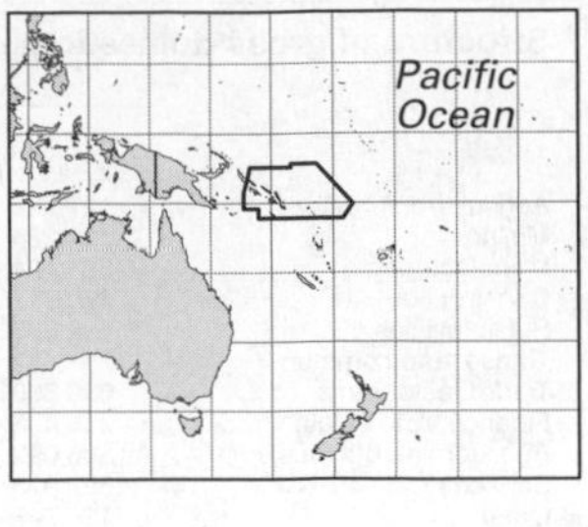

Official name: Solomon Islands.
Form of government: constitutional monarchy[1] with one legislative house (National Parliament [50]).
Chief of state: British Monarch represented by Governor-General.
Head of government: Prime Minister.
Capital: Honiara.
Official language: English.
Official religion: none.
Monetary unit: 1 Solomon Islands dollar (SI$) = 100 cents; valuation (Sept. 1, 2004) 1 U.S.$ = SI$7.49; 1 £ = SI$13.48.

Area and population

		area		population
				1999
Provinces	**Capitals**	sq mi	sq km	census
Central Islands	Tulagi	237	615	21,577
Choiseul	Taro	1,481	3,837	20,008
Guadalcanal	Honiara	2,060	5,336	60,275
Isabel	Buala	1,597	4,136	20,421
Makira-Ulawa	Kira Kira	1,231	3,188	31,006
Malaita	Auki	1,631	4,225	122,620
Rennell and Bellona	Tigoa	259	671	2,377
Temotu	Santa Cruz	334	865	18,912
Western	Gizo	2,114	5,475	62,739
Capital Territory				
Honiara	—	8	22	49,107
TOTAL		10,954[2]	28,370	409,042

Demography

Population (2004): 461,000.
Density (2004): persons per sq mi 42.1, persons per sq km 16.2.
Urban-rural (2002): urban 21.0%; rural 79.0%.
Sex distribution (2004): male 51.64%; female 48.36%.
Age breakdown (2003): under 15, 42.9%; 15–29, 29.2%; 30–44, 15.5%; 45–59, 7.6%; 60–74, 3.8%; 75 and over, 1.0%.
Population projection: (2010) 539,000; (2020) 670,000.
Doubling time: 25 years.
Ethnic composition (2002): Melanesian 93.0%; Polynesian 4.0%; Micronesian 1.5%; other 1.5%.
Religious affiliation (2000): Christian 90.8%, of which Protestant 74.0% (including Church of Melanesia [Anglican] 38.2%), Roman Catholic 10.8%; traditional beliefs 3.1%; other 6.1%.
Major cities (1999): Honiara 49,107 (urban agglomeration [2001] 78,000); Noro 3,482; Gizo 2,960; Auki 1,606; Tulagi 1,333.

Vital statistics

Birth rate per 1,000 population (2003): 32.5 (world avg. 21.3).
Death rate per 1,000 population (2003): 4.1 (world avg. 9.1).
Natural increase rate per 1,000 population (2003): 28.4 (world avg. 12.2).
Total fertility rate (avg. births per childbearing woman; 2003): 4.5.
Marriage rate per 1,000 population: n.a.
Life expectancy at birth (2003): male 69.6 years; female 74.7 years.
Major causes of death per 100,000 population (2004): about 20% of the population has malaria, one of the world's highest rates.

National economy

Budget (2003). Revenue: SI$681,300,000 (tax revenue 48.9%, of which international trade tax 19.3%, sales tax 16.4%, income tax 13.2%; grants 45.4%; nontax revenue 5.7%). Expenditures: SI$670,900,000 (current expenditure 60.2%, of which wages 24.4%, goods and services 13.2%, interest 7.4%; capital expenditure 39.8%).
Tourism (2002): receipts from visitors U.S.$1,000,000; expenditures by nationals abroad U.S.$6,000,000.
Land use as % of total land area (2000): in temporary crops 0.6%, in permanent crops 2.0%, in pasture 1.4%; overall forest area 88.8%.
Gross national product (at current market prices; 2003): U.S.$273,000,000 (U.S.$600 per capita).

Structure of gross domestic product and labour force

	2003		1993	
	in value SI$'000[3]	% of total value[3]	labour force[4]	% of labour force[4]
Agriculture	123,500	31.9	7,426	21.8
Mining	—	—	4,348	12.8
Manufacturing	16,100	4.2		
Construction	3,200	0.8	1,187	3.5
Public utilities	15,800	4.1	387	1.1
Transportation and communications	11,800	3.0	1,878	5.5
Trade	68,100	17.6	4,641	13.6
Finance	29,100	7.5	1,183	3.5
Pub. admin., defense	119,700	30.9	4,261	12.5
Services			8,750	25.7
Other	...	...	...	...
TOTAL	387,300	100.0	34,061	100.0

Household income and expenditure. Average household size (2002) 6.6; average annual income per household[5] (1991) U.S.$2,387; sources of income (1983): wages and salaries 74.1%, other 25.9%; expenditure (1992)[6]: food 46.8%, housing 11.0%, household operations 10.9%, transportation 9.9%, recreation and health 7.9%.
Population economically active (1999)[7]: total 85,124; activity rate of total population 21.0% (participation rates: ages 14 and over, n.a.; female 32.2%; unemployed 32.5%).

Price index (2000 = 100)

	1997	1998	1999	2000	2001	2002	2003
Consumer price index	76.9	86.5	93.4	100.0	106.9	117.7	129.5

Production (metric tons except as noted). Agriculture, forestry, fishing (2002): coconuts 330,000, palm oil fruit 140,000, sweet potatoes 84,000, taro 36,000, yams 31,500, vegetables 5,700, cacao beans 3,000; livestock (number of live animals) 68,000 pigs, 13,000 cattle, 220,000 chickens; roundwood (2002) 692,000 cu m; fish catch (2001) 30,075. Mining and quarrying (1999): gold 3,456 kg[8]. Manufacturing (2002): vegetable oils and fats 50,000, palm oil 35,000, coconut oil 15,000, dried coconut 8,100. Energy production (consumption): electricity (kW-hr; 2002) 57,061,000 (57,061,000); coal, none (n.a.); petroleum products (metric tons; 2000) none (54,000); natural gas, none (n.a.).
Public debt (external, outstanding; 2002): U.S.$150,200,000.

Foreign trade[9]

Balance of trade (current prices)

	1998	1999	2000	2001	2002	2003
SI$'000,000	−7.1	+69.0	−167.7	−229.5	−27.1	−82.5
% of total	0.6%	6.0%	19.3%	31.6%	3.3%	6.9%

Imports (2003): SI$639,500,000 (food, beverages, and tobacco 23.6%, crude petroleum 17.3%, machinery and transport equipment 12.7%, construction materials 10.7%, unspecified 32.9%). *Major import sources:* Australia 28.0%; Singapore 23.2%; New Zealand 5.2%; Fiji 4.6%; Papua New Guinea 4.4%.
Exports (2003): SI$557,000,000 (timber 66.6%, fish products 16.7%, cacao beans 9.6%). *Major export destinations:* China 25.8%; Japan 17.9%; South Korea 15.2%; Philippines 9.9%; Thailand 6.2%; Singapore 5.6%.

Transport and communications

Transport. Railroads: none. Roads (1996): total length 1,360 km (paved 2.5%). Vehicles (1993): passenger cars 2,052; trucks and buses 2,574. Air transport (1999): passenger-km 47,278,000; metric ton-km cargo 1,250,000; airports (1997) with scheduled flights 21.

Communications

Medium	date	unit	number	units per 1,000 persons
Radio	1997	receivers	57,000	141
Television	2000	receivers	9,570	23
Telephones	2002	main lines	6,600	15
Cellular telephones	2002	subscribers	1,000	2.2
Personal computers	2002	units	18,000	41
Internet	2002	users	2,200	5.0

Education and health

Educational attainment (1986)[10]. Percentage of population age 25 and over having: no schooling 44.4%; primary education 46.2%; secondary 6.8%; higher 2.6%. *Literacy* (1999): total population age 15 and over literate 181,000 (76%); males 102,500 (83%); females 78,500 (68%).

Education (2002)

	schools	teachers	students	student/teacher ratio
Primary (age 6–11)	520[11]	2,510[11]	82,330	...
Secondary (age 12–16)	23[11]	618[11]	21,700	...
Voc., teacher tr.[12] / Higher[12]	1	...	9,560	...

Health: physicians (2003) 53 (1 per 8,491 persons); hospital beds (1999) 881 (1 per 459 persons); infant mortality rate per 1,000 live births (2003) 22.9.
Food (2001): daily per capita caloric intake 2,272 (vegetable products 92%, animal products 8%); 100% of FAO recommended minimum requirement.

Military

Total active duty personnel (2003): none; multinational regional intervention force (from mid-2003; primarily Australian) for combating violence and lawlessness withdrew in 2004 except for police forces.

[1]New constitution implementing a federal structure was being drafted in November 2003. [2]Detail does not add to total given because of rounding. [3]At 1992 factor cost. [4]Persons employed in the monetary sector only. [5]Public-service earnings. [6]Retail price index components. [7]Total includes 57,472 employed in the monetary sector and 27,652 unemployed; activity rate, female participation, and unemployment rates are based on this total. [8]Production at the country's only gold mine was suspended from 2000 through mid-2004 because of civil unrest. [9]Imports c.i.f.; exports f.o.b. [10]Indigenous population only. [11]1994. [12]Vocational and teacher training are carried out at the College of Higher Education.

Internet resources for further information:
- **Solomon Islands Government Ministries**
  http://www.commerce.gov.sb
- **Central Bank of Solomon Islands**
  http://www.cbsi.com.sb

Somalia[1]

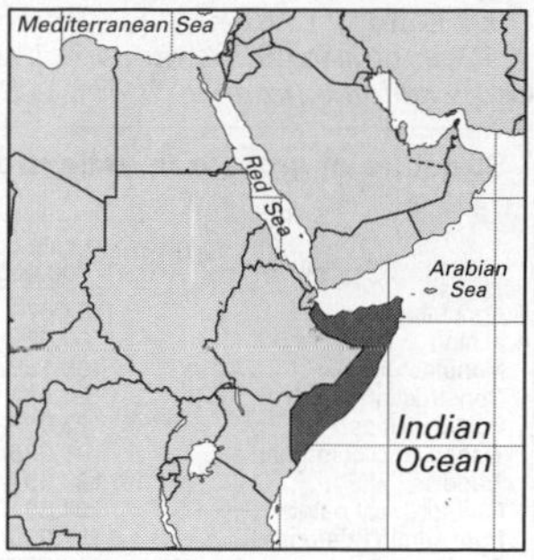

Official name: Soomaaliya (Somali) (Somalia).
Form of government: transitional regime[2] with one legislative body (Transitional Federal Assembly [216[3]]).
Head of state and government: President assisted by Prime Minister[2].
Capital: Mogadishu.
Official languages: Somali; Arabic.
Official religion: Islam.
Monetary unit: 1 Somali shilling (So.Sh.) = 100 cents; valuation (Sept. 1, 2004) 1 U.S.$ = So.Sh. 2,728[4]; 1 £ = So.Sh. 4,908.

Area and population

Regions	Principal cities	area sq mi	area sq km	population 1980 estimate
Bakool[5]	Xuddur	10,000	27,000	148,700
Banaadir	Mogadishu (Muqdisho)	400	1,000	520,100
Bari[6]	Boosaaso	27,000	70,000	222,300
Bay[5]	Baydhabo	15,000	39,000	451,000
Galguduud	Dhuusamarreeb	17,000	43,000	255,900
Gedo[5]	Garbahaarrey	12,000	32,000	235,000
Hiiraan	Beledweyne	13,000	34,000	219,300
Jubbada Dhexe[5]	Bu'aale	9,000	23,000	147,800
Jubbada Hoose[5]	Kismaayo	24,000	61,000	272,400
Mudug[6]	Gaalkacyo	27,000	70,000	311,200
Nugaal[6]	Garoowe	19,000	50,000	112,200
Sanaag[7]	Ceerigaabo	21,000	54,000	216,500
Shabeellaha Dhexe	Jawhar	8,000	22,000	352,000
Shabeellaha Hoose[5]	Marka	10,000	25,000	570,700
Togdheer[7]	Burao	16,000	41,000	383,900
Woqooyi Galbeed[7]	Hargeysa	17,000	45,000	655,000
TOTAL		246,000[8]	637,000	5,074,000

Demography

Population (2004): 8,305,000[9].
Density (2004): persons per sq mi 33.8, persons per sq km 13.0.
Urban-rural (2002): urban 34%; rural 66%.
Sex distribution (2002): male 51.47%; female 48.53%.
Age breakdown (2002): under 15, 46.4%; 15–29, 26.4%; 30–44, 16.3%; 45–59, 8.1%; 60–74, 2.4%; 75 and over, 0.4%.
Population projection: (2010) 9,922,000; (2020) 13,023,000.
Doubling time: 24 years.
Ethnic composition (2000): Somali 92.4%[9]; Arab 2.2%; Afar 1.3%; other 4.1%.
Religious affiliation (1995): Sunnī Muslim 99.9%; other 0.1%.
Major cities (1990): Mogadishu 1,212,000[10]; Hargeysa 90,000; Kismaayo 90,000; Berbera 70,000; Marka 62,000.

Vital statistics

Birth rate per 1,000 population (2003): 46.4 (world avg. 21.3).
Death rate per 1,000 population (2003): 17.6 (world avg. 9.1).
Natural increase rate per 1,000 population (2003): 28.8 (world avg. 12.2).
Total fertility rate (avg. births per childbearing woman; 2003): 7.0.
Life expectancy at birth (2003): male 45.7 years; female 49.1 years.
Major causes of death as percentage of all deaths (2002): sickness 61.1%; old age 19.0%; accidents 11.0%, of which land mines 3.6%; war-related 4.3%; pregnancy/childbirth-related 4.0%.

National economy

Budget (1991). Revenue: So.Sh. 151,453,000,000 (domestic revenue sources, principally indirect taxes and import duties 60.4%; external grants and transfers 39.6%). Expenditures: So.Sh. 141,141,000,000 (general services 46.9%; economic and social services 31.2%; debt service 7.0%).
Production (metric tons except as noted). Agriculture, forestry, fishing (2002): fruits (excluding melons) 220,000, sugarcane 210,000, corn (maize) 210,000, sorghum 90,000, cassava 85,000, bananas 60,000, sesame seed 25,000, beans 16,500, dates 11,000, seed cotton 6,000, other forest products include khat, frankincense, and myrrh; livestock (number of live animals) 13,100,000 sheep, 12,700,000 goats, 6,200,000 camels, 5,300,000 cattle; roundwood (2001) 9,936,520 cu m; fish catch (2001) 20,000. Mining and quarrying (2001): gypsum 1,500; salt 1,000. Manufacturing (value added in So.Sh. '000,000; 1988): food 794; cigarettes and matches 562; hides and skins 420; paper and printing 328; plastics 320; chemicals 202; beverages 144. Energy production (consumption): electricity (kW-hr; 2000) 282,000,000 (282,000,000); coal, none (none); crude petroleum (barrels; 1991) none (806,000); petroleum products (metric tons; 1991) none (59,000); natural gas, none (none).
Household income and expenditure. Average household size (2002) 5.2; income per household (2002): U.S.$226; sources of income (2002): self-employment 50%, remittances 22.5%, wages 14%, rent/aid 13.5%; expenditure (1983)[11]: food and tobacco 62.3%, housing 15.3%, clothing 5.6%, energy 4.3%, other 12.5%.
Population economically active (2001): total 3,906,000; activity rate of total population 52.2% (participation rates: ages 15–64 [2002] 56.4%; female, n.a.; unemployed [2002] 47.5%).

Price index (1989 = 100)

	1989	1990	1991	1992	1993	1994	1995
Consumer price index[12]	100.0	240.0	372.2	507.4	630.7	749.8	872.1

Gross domestic product (2001)[13]: U.S.$1,000,000,000 (U.S.$110 per capita).

Structure of gross domestic product and labour force

	2001 in value U.S.$'000,000[13]	% of total value	labour force	% of labour force
Agriculture	630	63.0	2,762,000	70.7
Mining, public utilities	10	1.0		
Manufacturing	30	3.0		
Construction	50	5.0		
Transp. and commun.	90	9.0		
Trade, restaurants	100	10.0	1,144,000	29.3
Finance, Pub. admin., defense, Services, Other	90	9.0		
TOTAL	1,000	100.0	3,906,000	100.0

Public debt (external, outstanding; 2002): U.S.$1,860,000,000.
Tourism: n.a.
Land use as % of total land area (2000): in temporary crops 1.7%, in permanent crops 0.04%, in pasture 68.5%; overall forest area 12.0%.

Foreign trade[14]

Balance of trade (current prices)

	1997	1998	1999	2000	2001	2002
U.S.$'000,000	–132	–118	–179	–254	–267	–257
% of total	29.6%	31.6%	43.5%	60.8%	60.3%	57.0%

Imports (2002): U.S.$354,000,000 (agricultural products 32.9%, of which raw sugar 20.0%, cereals 5.1%; unspecified 67.1%). *Major import sources* (2003): Djibouti 32%; Kenya 15%; Brazil 11%; United Arab Emirates 5%; Thailand 4%.
Exports (2002): U.S.$97,000,000 (agricultural products 85.4%, of which goats and sheep 56.9%, bovines 17.5%, camels 10.0%; unspecified 14.6%). *Major export destinations* (2003): United Arab Emirates 39%; Yemen 24%; Oman 11%; China 6%; Kuwait 4%.

Transport and communications

Transport. Railroads: none. Roads (1999): total length 13,700 mi, 22,100 km (paved 12%). Vehicles (1996): passenger cars 1,020; trucks and buses 6,440. Air transport (1991): passenger-mi 81,000,000, passenger-km 131,000,000; short ton-mi cargo 3,000,000, metric ton-km cargo 5,000,000; airports (2002) with scheduled flights 1.

Communications

Medium	date	unit	number	units per 1,000 persons
Daily newspapers	2000	circulation	7,250	1.0
Radio	2002	receivers	760,000	98
Television	2002	receivers	28,700	3.7
Telephones[15]	2002	main lines	116,000	15
Personal computers	2002	units	6,200	0.8

Education and health

Educational attainment: n.a. *Literacy* (2002): percentage of total population age 15 and over literate 19.2%; males literate 25.1%; females literate 13.1%.

Education (1989–90)

	schools	teachers	students	student/ teacher ratio
Primary (age 6–14)	1,125	8,208	377,000	20.9
Secondary (age 15–18)	82	2,109	44,000	20.3
Voc., teacher tr.	21	498	10,400	9.7
Higher	1	549	4,640	...

Health (1997): physicians 265 (1 per 25,032 persons); hospital beds 2,786 (1 per 2,381 persons); infant mortality rate per 1,000 live births (2003) 120.3.
Food (2000): daily per capita caloric intake 1,628 (vegetable products 62%, animal products 38%); 70% of FAO recommended minimum requirement.

Military

Total active duty personnel: no national army from 1991. *Military expenditure as percentage of GNP* (1990): 0.9% (world 4.3%); per capita expenditure U.S.$1.

[1]Proclamation of the "Republic of Somaliland" in May 1991 on territory corresponding to the former British Somaliland (which unified with the former Italian Trust Territory of Somalia to form Somalia in 1960) had not received international recognition as of November 2004. This entity represented about a quarter of Somalia's territory. [2] "New transitional government" from October 2004 lacked effective control in December 2004. [3]Planned number in August 2004; number sworn in on Aug. 22, 2004, was 194. [4]1 U.S.$ equaled about 18,000 So.Sh. on the black market in September 2003. [5]Part of "autonomous region" of Southwestern Somalia from April 2002. [6]Part of "autonomous region" of Puntland from 1998. [7]Part of "Republic of Somaliland" from 1991. [8]Detail does not add to total given because of rounding. [9]Estimate of U.S. Bureau of the Census International Database. [10]Estimated urban agglomeration, 2003. [11]Mogadishu only. [12]Reported inflation rate. [13]Estimated figure(s). [14]Imports c.i.f.; exports f.o.b. [15]Includes cellular telephones.

Internet resources for further information:
- **World Bank and UNDP Survey on Somalia http://www.so.undp.org/socecon.htm**

South Africa

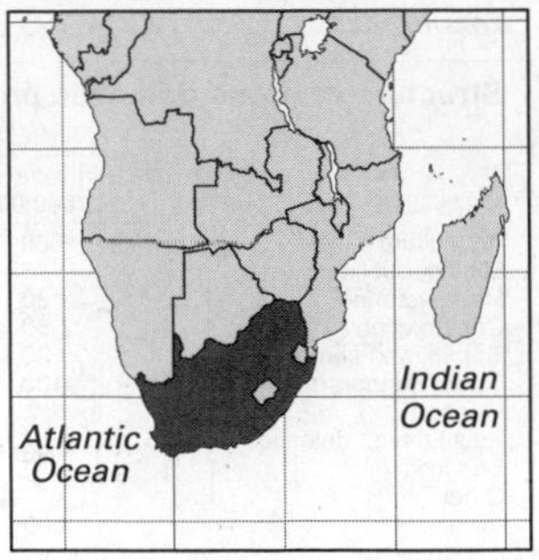

Official name: Republic of South Africa (English).
Form of government: multiparty republic with two legislative houses (National Council of Provinces [90]; National Assembly [400]).
Head of state and government: President.
Capitals (de facto): Pretoria/Tshwane[1] (executive); Bloemfontein/Mangaung[1] (judicial); Cape Town (legislative).
Official languages: [2].
Official religion: none.
Monetary unit: 1 rand (R) = 100 cents; valuation (Sept. 1, 2004) 1 U.S.$ = R 6.66; 1 £ = R 11.97.

Area and population

		area		population
				2001
Provinces	**Capitals**	sq mi	sq km	census
Eastern Cape	Bisho	65,475	169,580	6,436,763
Free State	Bloemfontein	49,993	129,480	2,706,775
Gauteng	Johannesburg	6,568	17,010	8,837,178
KwaZulu–Natal	Pietermaritzburg	35,560	92,100	9,426,017
Limpopo	Polokwane	47,842	123,910	5,273,642
Mpumalanga	Nelspruit	30,691	79,490	3,122,990
North West	Mafikeng/Mmabatho	44,911	116,320	3,669,349
Northern Cape	Kimberley	139,703	361,830	822,727
Western Cape	Cape Town	49,950	129,370	4,524,335
TOTAL		470,693	1,219,090	44,819,778[3]

Demography

Population (2004): 46,587,000.
Density (2004): persons per sq mi 99.0, persons per sq km 38.2.
Urban-rural (2002): urban 57.7%; rural 42.3%.
Sex distribution (2001): male 47.82%; female 52.18%.
Age breakdown (2001): under 15, 32.0%; 15–29, 29.5%; 30–44, 20.2%; 45–59, 11.0%; 60–74, 5.5%; 75 and over, 1.8%.
Population projection: (2010) 46,303,000; (2020) 45,009,000.
Ethnic composition (2001): black 78.4%, of which Zulu 23.8%, Xhosa 17.6%, Pedi 9.4%, Tswana 8.2%, Sotho 7.9%, Tsonga 4.4%, Swazi 2.7%, other black 4.4%; white 9.6%; Coloured 8.9%; Asian 2.5%; other 0.6%.
Religious affiliation (2000): Christian 83.1%, of which black independent churches 39.1%, Protestant 31.8%, Roman Catholic 7.1%; traditional beliefs 8.4%; Hindu 2.4%; Muslim 2.4%; nonreligious 2.4%; other 1.3%.
Major cities (2003): Cape Town 2,733,000; Durban 2,396,100[4]; Johannesburg 1,675,200[4]; Pretoria 1,249,700; Port Elizabeth 848,400.

Vital statistics

Birth rate per 1,000 population (2003): 19.7[5] (world avg. 21.3).
Death rate per 1,000 population (2003): 19.3[5] (world avg. 9.1).
Natural increase rate per 1,000 population (2003): 0.4[5] (world avg. 12.2).
Marriage rate per 1,000 population (2000): 3.2.
Divorce rate per 1,000 population (2000): 0.8.
Total fertility rate (avg. births per childbearing woman; 2003): 2.4[5].
Life expectancy at birth (2003): male 44.6[5] years; female 46.0[5] years.
Adult population (ages 15–49) *living with HIV* (2004[6]): 21.5% (world avg. 1.1%).

National economy

Budget (2001–02). Revenue: R 248,447,200,000 (personal income taxes 36.6%, value-added taxes 23.6%, company income taxes 17.7%, other 22.1%). Expenditures: R 262,589,800,000 (transfer to provinces 46.2%, interest on public debt 18.1%, police and prisons 9.2%, defense 6.1%).
Public debt (external, outstanding; 2002): U.S.$9,427,000,000.
Production (in R '000,000 except as noted). Agriculture, forestry, fishing (in value of production; 2000): poultry 8,270, corn (maize) 5,654, beef 3,904, temperate fruits 2,975, sugarcane 2,530, vegetables 2,516, milk 2,229, wheat 2,100, citrus fruits 1,835, potatoes 1,599, sheep and goat meat 1,322; roundwood (2001) 30,616,000 cu m; fish catch (2001) 760,000 metric tons. Mining and quarrying (in value of sales; 2002): gold 41,386; platinum-group metals 34,829; coal 31,140; iron ore 5,109; nickel 2,639; copper 2,143; manganese 1,627; rough diamonds 10,883,000 carats. Manufacturing (value added in U.S.$'000,000; 1999): food products 2,225; iron and steel 2,225; transport equipment 2,100; fabricated metals 1,400; electrical machinery 1,325; refined petroleum 1,325; nonferrous base metals 1,200. Energy production (consumption): electricity (kW-hr; 2002) 217,704,000,000 ([2001] 182,565,000,000); coal (metric tons; 2002) 222,456,000 ([2000] 156,248,000); crude petroleum (barrels; 2000) 6,027,000 (193,255,000[7]); petroleum products (metric tons; 2000) 24,653,000[7] (17,645,000[7]); natural gas (cu m; 2000) 1,666,000,000 (1,666,000,000).
Population economically active (2001): total 15,358,000; activity rate of total population 34.5% (participation rates: over age 15, 50.7%; female 46.7%; unemployed [2001] 29.5%).

Price and earnings indexes (2000 = 100)

	1997	1998	1999	2000	2001	2002	2003
Consumer price index	84.4	90.3	94.9	100.0	105.7	115.4	122.1
Monthly earnings index[8]	...	87.9	92.9	100.0	108.6	...	...

Household income and expenditure. Average household size (2001) 3.8; average annual disposable income per household (1996)[9] R 47,600 (U.S.$11,070); expenditure (1998): food, beverages, and tobacco 31.3%; transportation 14.3%; housing 9.3%; household furnishings and operation 8.9%.
Gross national product (2003): U.S.$125,971,000,000 (U.S.$2,780 per capita).

Structure of gross domestic product and labour force

	2002		2001	
	in value R '000,000	% of total value	labour force	% of labour force
Agriculture	37,674	3.4	1,051,000	6.8
Mining	80,586	7.3	487,000	3.2
Manufacturing	188,182	17.1	1,605,000	10.5
Construction	27,545	2.5	594,000	3.9
Public utilities	23,965	2.2	95,000	0.6
Transp. and commun.	96,086	8.7	543,000	3.5
Trade	132,691	12.1	2,397,000	15.6
Finance, real estate	194,591	17.7	975,000	6.3
Pub. admin., defense	157,936	14.4	3,043,000	19.8
Services	59,659	5.4		
Other	99,799[10]	9.1[10]	4,568,000[11]	29.7[11]
TOTAL	1,098,714	100.0[12]	15,358,000	100.0[12]

Tourism (2002): receipts U.S.$2,728,000,000; expenditures U.S.$1,804,000,000.
Land use as % of total land area (2000): in temporary crops 12.1%, in permanent crops 0.8%, in pasture 68.7%; overall forest area 7.3%.

Foreign trade

Balance of trade (current prices)

	1997	1998	1999	2000	2001	2002
U.S.$'000,000	+2,324	+2,056	+4,073	+4,316	+4,860	+4,372
% of total	3.9%	3.6%	7.7%	7.3%	8.6%	7.6%

Imports (2001): U.S.$24,188,000,000 (nonelectrical machinery 18.0%, crude petroleum 12.9%, chemicals and chemical products 11.9%, electrical machinery 11.5%). *Major import sources* (2001): U.S. 11.0%; Germany 10.5%; U.K. 7.4%; Japan 5.5%; China 4.4%; unspecified 17.1%.
Exports (2001): U.S.$27,928,000,000 (diamonds 18.6%, gold 12.6%, iron and steel 7.8%, food 6.5%, nonelectrical machinery 6.3%, industrial chemicals 6.2%, road vehicles 5.6%, coal 5.2%). *Major export destinations* (2002): U.K. 12.9%; U.S. 12.8%; Germany 9.1%; Japan 8.9%; Italy 5.8%.

Transport and communications

Transport. Railroads: route length (2001) 20,384 km; passenger-km 3,930,000,000; metric ton-km cargo 106,786,000,000. Roads (1999): length 331,265 km (paved 41%). Vehicles (2002): passenger cars 4,135,037; trucks and buses 2,202,032. Air transport (2000)[13]: passenger-km 19,320,000,000; metric ton-km cargo 677,048,000; airport (1996) 24.

Communications

Medium	date	unit	number	units per 1,000 persons
Daily newspapers	2000	circulation	1,590,000	32
Radio	2000	receivers	16,800,000	338
Television	2002	receivers	8,018,000	177
Telephones	2002	main lines	4,844,000	107
Cellular telephones	2003	subscribers	16,860,000	364
Personal computers	2002	units	3,300,000	73
Internet	2002	users	3,100,000	68

Education and health

Educational attainment (2000). Percentage of population age 20 and over having: no formal schooling 17.9%; some primary education 16.0%; complete primary/some secondary 37.2%; complete secondary 20.4%; higher 8.5%.
Literacy (2000): total population age 15 and over literate 85.3%; males 86.0%; females 84.6%.

Education (2000)

	schools	teachers	students	student/ teacher ratio
Primary (age 6–12)	17,213	183,639	6,266,223	34.1
Secondary (age 13–17)[14]	10,547	177,084	5,588,866	31.6
Higher[15]	21	...	169,604	...

Health: physicians (2000) 29,788 (1 per 1,453 persons); hospital beds (1998) 144,363 (1 per 290 persons); infant mortality rate (2003) 63.7[5].
Food (2001): daily per capita caloric intake 2,889 (vegetable products 87%, animal products 13%); 114% of FAO recommended minimum.

Military

Total active duty personnel (2003): 55,750 (army 64.6%, navy 8.1%, air force 16.6%, intraservice medical service 10.7%). *Military expenditure as percentage of GNP* (1999): 1.5% (world 2.4%); per capita expenditure U.S.$45.

[1]Renamed within larger municipality in December 2000. [2]Afrikaans; English; Ndebele; Pedi (North Sotho); Sotho (South Sotho); Swazi; Tsonga; Tswana (West Sotho); Venda; Xhosa; Zulu. [3]Reported total; summation equals 44,819,776. [4]Name change pending. [5]Estimate from the U.S. Bureau of the Census, International Database. [6]January 1. [7]Includes Botswana, Lesotho, Namibia, and Swaziland. [8]Manufacturing sector only. [9]Estimated figures. [10]Taxes on products less subsidies on products. [11]Includes 43,000 not adequately defined and 4,525,000 unemployed. [12]Detail does not add to total given because of rounding. [13]SAA only. [14]Includes combined and intermediate. [15]Universities only.

Internet resources for further information:
- **South African Reserve Bank http://www.reservebank.co.za**
- **Statistics South Africa http://www.statssa.gov.za**

Spain

Official name: Reino de España (Kingdom of Spain).
Form of government: constitutional monarchy with two legislative houses (Senate [259[1]]; Congress of Deputies [350]).
Chief of state: King.
Head of government: Prime Minister.
Capital: Madrid.
Official languages: Castilian Spanish[2].
Official religion: none.
Monetary unit: 1 euro (€) = 100 céntimos; valuation (Sept. 1, 2004) 1 U.S.$ = €0.82; 1 £ = €1.48[3].

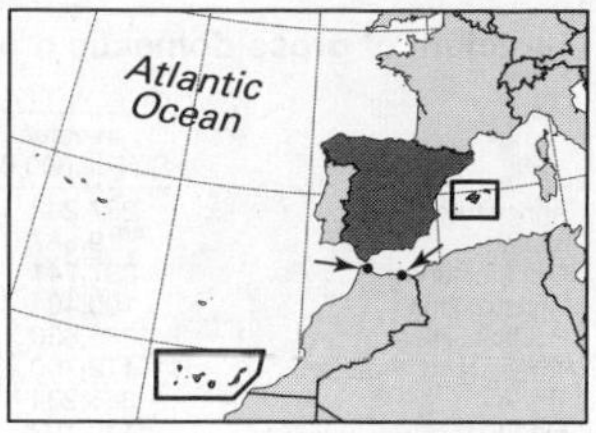

Area and population

Autonomous communities	Capitals	area sq mi	area sq km	population 2001 census
Andalucía	Seville	33,821	87,597	7,357,558
Aragón	Zaragoza	18,425	47,720	1,204,215
Asturias	Oviedo	4,094	10,604	1,062,998
Baleares (Balearic Islands)	Palma de Mallorca	1,927	4,992	841,669
Canarias (Canary Islands)	Santa Cruz de Tenerife	2,876	7,447	1,694,477
Cantabria	Santander	2,054	5,321	535,131
Castilla-La Mancha	Toledo	30,681	79,463	1,760,516
Castilla y León	Valladolid	36,380	94,223	2,456,474
Cataluña	Barcelona	12,399	32,114	6,343,110
Extremadura	Mérida	16,075	41,634	1,058,503
Galicia	Santiago	11,419	29,574	2,695,880
La Rioja	Logroño	1,948	5,045	276,702
Madrid	Madrid	3,100	8,028	5,423,384
Murcia	Murcia	4,368	11,313	1,197,646
Navarra	Pamplona	4,012	10,391	555,829
País Vasco	Vitoria (Gasteiz)	2,793	7,234	2,082,587
Valenciana	Valencia	8,979	23,255	4,162,776
Autonomous cities				
Ceuta	—	7	19	71,505
Melilla	—	5	13	66,411
TOTAL		195,363	505,988[4]	40,847,371[5]

Demography

Population (2004): 43,768,000.
Density (2004): persons per sq mi 224.0, persons per sq km 86.5.
Urban-rural (2002): urban 77.8%; rural 22.2%.
Sex distribution (2002): male 48.95%; female 51.05%.
Age breakdown (2002): under 15, 14.6%; 15–29, 21.7%; 30–44, 24.0%; 45–59, 18.0%; 60–74, 14.2%; 75 and over, 7.5%.
Population projection: (2010) 45,530,000; (2020) 48,626,000.
Ethnic composition (2000): Spaniard 44.9%; Catalonian 28.0%; Galician 8.2%; Basque 5.5%; Aragonese 5.0%; Rom (Gypsy) 2.0%; other 6.4%.
Religious affiliation (2000): Roman Catholic 92.0%; Muslim 0.5%; Protestant 0.3%; other 7.2%.
Major cities (2001): Madrid 2,938,723; Barcelona 1,503,884; Valencia 738,441; Seville 684,633; Zaragoza 614,905.

Vital statistics

Birth rate per 1,000 population (2003): 10.1 (world avg. 21.3).
Death rate per 1,000 population (2003): 8.8 (world avg. 9.1).
Total fertility rate (avg. births per childbearing woman; 2003): 1.3.
Life expectancy at birth (2002): male 75.7 years; female 83.1 years.
Major causes of death per 100,000 population (2001): circulatory diseases 191.0; malignant neoplasms (cancers) 171.4; respiratory diseases 56.0; diseases of the nervous system 34.4; accidents, poisonings, violence 33.7.

National economy

Budget (2002). Revenue: €108,824,300,000 (direct taxes 46.6%, of which income tax 27.2%; indirect taxes 41.8%, of which value-added tax on products 27.8%; other taxes 11.6%). Expenditures: €112,586,900,000 (public debt 15.7%; health 9.8%; pensions 5.7%; defense 5.6%; public works 4.4%).
Tourism (2002): receipts U.S.$33,609,000,000; expenditures U.S.$6,638,000,000.
Gross national product (2003): U.S.$698,208,000,000 (U.S.$16,990 per capita).

Structure of gross domestic product and labour force

2001	in value €'000,000	% of total value	labour force	% of labour force
Agriculture	21,001	3.2	1,019,200	5.7
Mining	103,511	15.9	63,300	0.4
Manufacturing			3,005,600	16.9
Public utilities	19,221	2.9	98,800	0.6
Construction	53,673	8.2	1,850,200	10.4
Transp. and commun.	...	...	965,200	5.4
Trade and hotels	418,235	64.2	3,526,200	19.8
Finance			1,630,400	9.2
Services			2,778,600	15.6
Pub. admin., defense			1,008,100	5.6
Other	35,999[6]	5.5[6]	1,869,000[7]	10.5[7]
TOTAL	651,641[8]	100.0[8]	17,814,600	100.0[8]

Land use as % of total land area (2000): in temporary crops 26.5%, in permanent crops 9.9%, in pasture 22.9%; overall forest area 28.8%.
Production (metric tons except as noted). Agriculture, forestry, fishing (2002): barley 8,332,900, sugar beets 7,877,000, wheat 6,782,000, grapes 5,609,300, corn (maize) 4,394,500, olives 4,303,700, tomatoes 3,878,400, potatoes 3,103,000; livestock (number of live animals) 24,300,624 sheep, 23,857,776 pigs, 6,411,000 cattle; roundwood (2001) 15,839,000 cu m; fish catch (2001) 1,289,081. Mining and quarrying (metal content in metric tons; 2001): zinc 164,900; lead 49,500. Manufacturing (value added in €'000,000; 2001): transport equipment 35,774; petroleum products 26,242; food products 14,771; chemical products 14,137; plastics 11,893; pharmaceutical products 10,050; furniture 9,653; alcoholic beverages 9,195. Energy production (consumption): electricity (kW-hr; 2002) 229,000,000,000 (218,400,000,000); hard coal (metric tons; 2001) 10,491,000 ([2000] 32,804,000); lignite (metric tons; 2000) 12,154,000 (12,850,000); crude petroleum (barrels; 2003) 2,701,000 ([2000] 429,000,000); petroleum products (metric tons; 2000) 50,071,000 (50,840,000); natural gas (cu m; 2002) 509,700,000 ([2000] 17,752,000,000).
Public debt (2001): U.S.$334,240,000,000.
Population economically active (2001): total 17,814,600; activity rate of total population 43.7% (participation rates: ages [1995] 16–64, 60.7%; female 39.2%; unemployed 10.5%).

Price and earnings indexes (2000 = 100)

	1997	1998	1999	2000	2001	2002	2003
Consumer price index	92.8	94.5	96.7	100.0	103.6	106.8	110.0
Earnings index	92.7	95.3	97.7	100.0	103.8	108.1	112.7

Household income and expenditure. Average household size (2000) 3.2; income per household (2000) Ptas 3,205,693 (U.S.$18,470); expenditure (1995): housing 26.0%, food 24.0%, transportation 12.8%, clothing/footwear 7.4%.

Foreign trade[9]

Balance of trade (current prices)

	1997	1998	1999	2000	2001	2002
U.S.$'000,000	−13,407	−20,758	−30,339	−34,820	−32,539	−33,098
% of total	5.9%	8.5%	11.9%	13.0%	12.1%	11.6%

Imports (2001): U.S.$154,993,000,000 (road vehicles 15.6%, nonelectrical machinery 13.3%, chemicals and chemical products 11.2%, electrical machinery 8.7%, crude and refined petroleum 8.6%). *Major import sources* (2002): France 16.9%; Germany 16.5%; Italy 8.6%; U.K. 6.4%; Netherlands 4.8%.
Exports (2001): U.S.$116,149,000,000 (road vehicles 23.0%; machinery 16.0%; food 12.0%, of which fruits and vegetables 6.3%; chemicals and chemical products 9.7%). *Major export destinations* (2002): France 18.9%; Germany 11.4%; Portugal 9.5%; U.K. 9.5%; Italy 9.3%.

Transport and communications

Transport. Railroads (2001): route length 13,832 km; passenger-km 19,190,000,000; metric ton-km cargo 12,216,000,000. Roads (1999): length 346,548 km (paved 99%). Vehicles (2001): cars 18,151,000; trucks and buses 4,005,000. Air transport (2003)[10]: passenger-km 61,674,000,000; metric ton-km cargo 820,963,000; airports (1997) with scheduled flights 25.

Communications

Medium	date	unit	number	units per 1,000 persons
Daily newspapers	2000	circulation	4,060,000	100
Radio	2000	receivers	13,500,000	333
Television	2000	receivers	24,000,000	591
Telephones	2003	main lines	17,507,500	429
Cellular telephones	2003	subscribers	37,507,000	916
Personal computers	2002	units	7,972,000	196
Internet	2003	users	9,789,000	239

Education and health

Educational attainment (2001). Percentage of population age 16 and over having: no formal schooling 15.4%; primary education 23.1%; secondary 48.0%; undergraduate degree 6.6%; graduate degree 6.9%. *Literacy* (2001): total population age 15 and over literate 97.7%; males 96.9%; females 98.6%.

Education (2001–02)

	schools	teachers	students	student/teacher ratio
Primary (age 6–11)	8,547	170,691	2,475,027	14.5
Secondary (age 12–18)[11]	4,319	264,464	3,116,895	11.8
Higher	1,774	98,567	1,508,116	15.3

Health: physicians (2000) 179,033 (1 per 227 persons); hospital beds (2001) 160,815 (1 per 254 persons); infant mortality rate (2003) 3.6.
Food (2000): daily per capita caloric intake 3,352 (vegetable products 73%, animal products 27%); 136% of FAO recommended minimum requirement.

Military

Total active duty personnel (2003): 150,700 (army 63.4%, navy 15.2%, air force 15.1%, other 6.3%). *Military expenditure as percentage of GNP* (1999): 1.3% (world 2.4%); per capita expenditure U.S.$192.

[1]Includes 51 indirectly elected seats. [2]The constitution states that "Castilian is the Spanish official language of the State," but that "all other Spanish languages (including Euskera [Basque], Catalan, and Galician) will also be official in the corresponding Autonomous Communities." [3]The peseta (Pta) was the former monetary unit; on Jan. 1, 2002, Ptas 166.33 = €1. [4]Detail does not add to total given due to North African islets not listed equaling 0.66 sq km in area. [5]Census figure including temporary residents and guests equals 52,467,572. [6]Import taxes and value-added tax on products. [7]Unemployed. [8]Detail does not add to total given because of rounding. [9]Imports are f.o.b. in balance of trade. [10]Combined total of Iberia, Air Europa, Air Nostrum, Binter Canarias, and Spanair. [11]Includes vocational.

Internet resources for further information:
- **Banco de España http://www.bde.es**
- **National Institute of Statistics http://www.ine.es/en/welcome_en.htm**

Sri Lanka

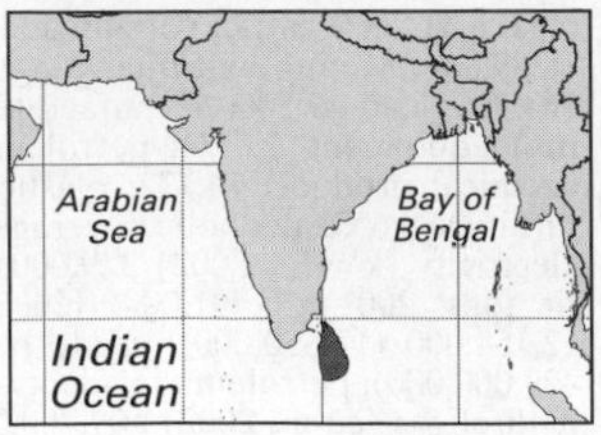

Official name: Śri Lanka Prajatantrika Samajavadi Janarajaya (Sinhala); Ilangai Jananayaka Socialisa Kudiarasu (Tamil) (Democratic Socialist Republic of Sri Lanka).
Form of government: unitary multiparty republic with one legislative house (Parliament [225]).
Head of state and government: President assisted by Prime Minister.
Capitals: Colombo (executive); Sri Jayewardenepura Kotte (Colombo suburb; legislative and judicial).
Official languages: Sinhala; Tamil.
Official religion: none.
Monetary unit: 1 Sri Lanka rupee (SL Rs) = 100 cents; valuation (Sept. 1, 2004) 1 U.S.$ = SL Rs 103.13; 1 £ = SL Rs 185.52.

Area and population

Districts	Capitals	area sq mi	area sq km	population 2001 census[1]
Amparai	Amparai	1,705	4,415	589,344
Anuradhapura	Anuradhapura	2,772	7,179	746,466
Badulla	Badulla	1,105	2,861	774,555
Batticaloa	Batticaloa	1,102	2,854	486,447[2]
Colombo	Colombo	270	699	2,234,289
Galle	Galle	638	1,652	990,539
Gampaha	Gampaha	536	1,387	2,066,096
Hambantota	Hambantota	1,007	2,609	525,370
Jaffna	Jaffna	396	1,025	490,621[2]
Kalutara	Kalutara	617	1,598	1,060,800
Kandy	Kandy	749	1,940	1,272,463
Kegalle	Kegalle	654	1,693	779,774
Kilinochchi	Kilinochchi	494	1,279	127,263[2]
Kurunegala	Kurunegala	1,859	4,816	1,452,369
Mannar	Mannar	771	1,996	151,577[2]
Matale	Matale	770	1,993	442,427
Matara	Matara	495	1,283	761,236
Monaragala	Monaragala	2,177	5,639	396,173
Mullaitivu	Mullaitivu	1,010	2,617	121,667[2]
Nuwara Eliya	Nuwara Eliya	672	1,741	700,083
Polonnaruwa	Polonnaruwa	1,271	3,293	359,197
Puttalam	Puttalam	1,186	3,072	705,342
Ratnapura	Ratnapura	1,264	3,275	1,008,164
Trincomalee	Trincomalee	1,053	2,727	340,158[2]
Vavuniya	Vavuniya	759	1,967	149,835[2]
TOTAL		25,332	65,610	18,732,255

Demography

Population (2004): 19,218,000.
Density (2004): persons per sq mi 758.6, persons per sq km 292.9.
Urban-rural (2002): urban 25.0%; rural 75.0%.
Sex distribution (2001): male 49.47%; female 50.53%.
Age breakdown (2001): under 15, 27.9%; 15–29, 27.1%; 30–44, 22.7%; 45–59, 13.6%; 60–74, 7.0%; 75 and over, 1.7%.
Population projection: (2010) 20,046,000; (2020) 21,121,000.
Ethnic composition (2000): Sinhalese 72.4%; Tamil 17.8%; Sri Lankan Moor 7.4%; other 2.4%.
Religious affiliation (2001): Buddhist 76.7%; Muslim 8.5%; Hindu 7.9%; Christian 6.8%; other 0.1%.
Major cities (2001)[1]: Colombo 642,163; Dehiwala–Mount Lavinia 209,787; Moratuwa 177,190; Negombo 121,933; Sri Jayewardenepura Kotte 115,826.

Vital statistics

Birth rate per 1,000 population (2003): 16.1 (world avg. 21.3).
Death rate per 1,000 population (2003): 6.5 (world avg. 9.1).
Natural increase rate per 1,000 population (2003): 11.1 (world avg. 12.2).
Total fertility rate (avg. births per childbearing woman; 2003): 1.9.
Marriage rate per 1,000 population (1997): 8.9.
Life expectancy at birth (2003): male 70.1 years; female 75.3 years.
Major causes of death per 100,000 population (1996): violence 127.5; diseases of the circulatory system 123.8; diseases of the respiratory system 35.1; diseases of the nervous system 32.4; malignant neoplasms (cancers) 17.2.

National economy

Budget (2001). Revenue: SL Rs 231,463,000,000 (sales tax 19.7%, excise taxes 19.4%, income taxes 15.0%, nontax revenue 11.6%). Expenditures: SL Rs 383,686,000,000 (interest payments 24.6%, defense 17.8%, social welfare 13.4%).
Public debt (external, outstanding; 2002): U.S.$8,455,000,000.
Production (metric tons except as noted). Agriculture, forestry, fishing (2002): rice 2,794,000, coconuts 1,900,000, sugarcane 1,050,000, plantains 610,000, tea 310,000, natural rubber 87,000; livestock (number of live animals) 1,565,000 cattle, 661,200 buffalo; roundwood (2001) 6,468,369 cu m; fish catch (2001) 288,010. Mining and quarrying (2001): graphite 6,585; sapphires 453,800 carats; diamonds, n.a. Manufacturing (value added, in U.S.$'000,000; 1995): food, beverages, and tobacco 601; textiles and apparel 391; petrochemicals 116. Energy production (consumption): electricity (kW-hr; 2001) 6,520,000,000 (6,520,000,000); coal (metric tons; 2000) none (negligible); crude petroleum (barrels; 2000) none (16,712,000); petroleum products (metric tons; 2000) 2,062,000 (3,215,000).
Gross national product (2003): U.S.$17,846,000,000 (U.S.$930 per capita).

Structure of gross domestic product and labour force

	2002 in value SL Rs '000,000	2002 % of total value	2000 labour force[3]	2000 % of labour force[3]
Agriculture	237,282	15.1	2,290,000	33.5
Mining	19,887	1.3	77,800	1.1
Manufacturing	297,741	19.0	1,013,200	14.8
Construction	100,404	6.4	320,600	4.7
Public utilities	36,850	2.3	25,000	0.4
Transp. and commun.	172,700	11.0	278,100	4.1
Trade	386,234	24.6	767,700	11.2
Finance	140,102	8.9	122,600	1.8
Pub. admin., defense	140,474	8.9	1,153,700	16.9
Services	38,586	2.5		
Other	…	…	778,600[5]	11.5[5]
TOTAL	1,570,260	100.0	6,827,300	100.0

Land use as % of total land area (2000): in temporary crops 13.8%, in permanent crops 15.7%, in pasture 6.8%; overall forest area 30.0%.
Population economically active: total (2001) 6,729,700[3]; activity rate *c.* 40% (participation rates: ages 10 and over, 48.3%; female 33.3%; unemployed 7.8%).

Price and earnings indexes (2000 = 100)

	1997	1998	1999	2000	2001	2002	2003
Consumer price index	79.9	94.6	98.5	100.0	112.0	123.4	126.6
Minimum wage index	84.9	95.3	97.7	100.0	104.9	112.6	…

Household income and expenditure (1992). Average household size (2000) 4.6[3]; income per household SL Rs 116,100 (U.S.$2,600); sources of income: wages 48.5%, property income and self-employment 41.8%, transfers 9.7%; expenditure: food 58.6%, transportation 16.0%, clothing 8.4%.
Tourism (2002): receipts U.S.$253,000,000; expenditures U.S.$253,000,000.

Foreign trade[6]

Balance of trade (current prices)

	1997	1998	1999	2000	2001	2002
SL Rs '000,000	–71,833	–69,740	–96,717	–134,176	–102,591	–134,641
% of total	11.6%	10.1%	12.9%	13.8%	10.6%	13.0%

Imports (2002): SL Rs 584,491,000,000 (textiles [mostly yarns and fabrics] 21.6%; petroleum and natural gas 12.9%; foods 11.4%; machinery and equipment 10.5%). *Major import sources:* India 13.9%; Hong Kong 8.2%; Singapore 7.2%; Japan 5.9%; South Korea 5.0%; Taiwan 4.8%.
Exports (2002): SL Rs 449,850,000,000 (clothing and accessories 51.6%; tea 13.5%; precious and semiprecious stones 5.9%; rubber products 3.9%). *Major export destinations:* U.S. 38.9%; U.K. 13.0%; Belgium-Luxembourg 5.7%; Germany 4.4%; India 3.8%.

Transport and communications

Transport. Railroads (2001): route length 1,449 km; (1998) passenger-km 3,264,000,000; (1998) metric ton-km cargo 132,000,000. Roads (1996): total length 99,200 km (paved 40%). Vehicles (2001): passenger cars 353,701; trucks and buses 244,166. Air transport (2001): passenger-km 4,126,000,000; metric ton-km cargo 224,000,000; airports (2001) 1.

Communications

Medium	date	unit	number	units per 1,000 persons
Daily newspapers	2000	circulation	539,000	29
Radio	2000	receivers	3,870,000	208
Television	2000	receivers	2,060,000	111
Telephones	2002	main lines	881,400	47
Cellular telephones	2002	subscribers	931,600	49
Personal computers	2002	units	250,000	13
Internet	2002	users	200,000	11

Education and health

Educational attainment: n.a. *Literacy* (2000): percentage of population age 15 and over literate 91.6%; males literate 94.4%; females literate 89.0%.

Education (2000–01)

	schools	teachers	students	student/teacher ratio
Primary (age 5–10) / Secondary (age 11–17)	10,977	199,948	4,337,161	21.7
Voc., teacher tr.	36	574	11,270	19.6
Higher	12	2,999	48,899	16.3

Health (1999): physicians 6,938 (1 per 2,740 persons); hospital beds (2001) 57,946 (1 per 324 persons); infant mortality rate (2003) 15.2.
Food (2001): daily per capita caloric intake 2,274 (vegetable products 93%, animal products 7%); 102% of FAO recommended minimum.

Military

Total active duty personnel (2003): 152,300 (army 77.5%, navy 9.8%, air force 12.7%). *Military expenditure as percentage of GNP* (1999): 4.7% (world 2.4%); per capita expenditure U.S.$38.

[1]Provisional figures (except for 7 districts experiencing civil war). [2]Registrar-general estimates. [3]Excludes 7 districts experiencing civil war. [4]Import duties. [5]Mainly unemployed. [6]Imports c.i.f.; exports f.o.b.

Internet resources for further information:
- **Central Bank of Sri Lanka http://www.centralbanklanka.org**
- **Department of Census and Statistics http://www.statistics.gov.lk**

Sudan, The

Official name: Jumhūrīyat as-Sūdān (Republic of the Sudan).
Form of government: military regime[1] with one legislative body (National Assembly [360[2]]).
Head of state and government: President.
Capitals: Khartoum (executive); Omdurman (legislative).
Official language: Arabic[3].
Official religion: [4].
Monetary unit: 1 Sudanese dinar (Sd)[5]; valuation (Sept. 1, 2004) 1 U.S.$ = Sd 259.03; 1 £ = Sd 465.97.

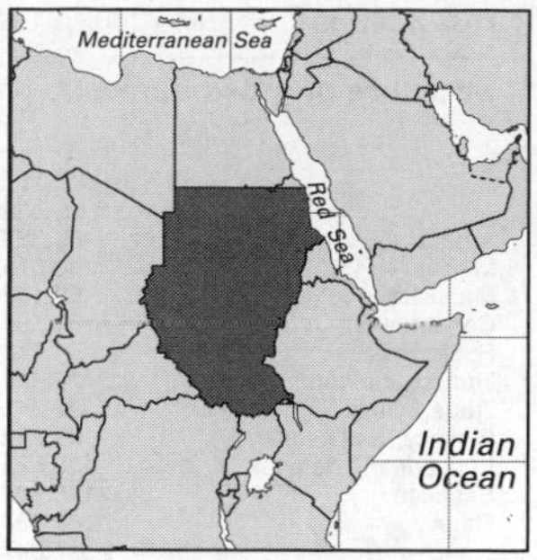

Area and population

States[6]	area sq km	population 2000 estimate	States[6]	area sq km	population 2000 estimate
Bahr el-Ghazal[7]	...	2,256,942	Red Sea	...	709,637
Blue Nile	...	633,129	River Nile	...	895,893
Equatoria	...	1,234,486	Sinnar	...	1,132,758
Gedaref	...	1,414,531	Southern Darfur	...	2,708,007
Gezira	...	3,310,928	Southern Kordofan	...	1,066,117
Kassalā	...	1,433,730	Upper Nile	...	1,342,943
Khartoum	...	4,740,290	Western Darfur	...	1,531,682
Northern	...	578,376	Western Kordofan	...	1,078,330
Northern Darfur	...	1,409,894	White Nile	...	1,431,701
Northern Kordofan	...	1,439,930	TOTAL	2,503,890[8]	30,349,304[9, 10]

Demography

Population (2004): 39,148,000.
Density (2004): persons per sq mi 40.5, persons per sq km 15.6.
Urban-rural (2002): urban 37.1%; rural 62.9%.
Sex distribution (2001): male 50.64%; female 49.36%.
Age breakdown (2001): under 15, 44.6%; 15–29, 27.6%; 30–44, 15.6%; 45–59, 8.4%; 60–74, 3.3%; 75 and over, 0.5%.
Population projection: (2010) 45,485,000; (2020) 56,162,000.
Doubling time: 25 years.
Ethnic composition (1983): Sudanese Arab 49.1%; Dinka 11.5%; Nuba 8.1%; Beja 6.4%, Nuer 4.9%; Zande 2.7%; Bari 2.5%; Fur 2.1%; other 12.7%.
Religious affiliation (2000): Sunnī Muslim 70.3%; Christian 16.7%, of which Roman Catholic *c.* 8%, Anglican *c.* 6%; traditional beliefs 11.9%; other 1.1%.
Major cities (1993): Omdurman 1,271,403; Khartoum 947,483; Khartoum North 700,887; Port Sudan 308,195; Kassalā 234,622.

Vital statistics

Birth rate per 1,000 population (2003): 36.5 (world avg. 21.3).
Death rate per 1,000 population (2003): 9.6 (world avg. 9.1).
Natural increase rate per 1,000 population (2003): 26.9 (world avg. 12.2).
Total fertility rate (avg. births per childbearing woman; 2003): 5.1.
Life expectancy at birth (2003): male 56.6 years; female 58.9 years.
Major causes of death per 100,000 population: n.a.

National economy

Budget (2001). Revenue: Sd 365,200,000,000[5] (tax revenue 51.5%, of which customs duties 21.3%, VAT 10.3%; nontax revenue 48.5%). Expenditures: Sd 418,800,000,000[5] (current expenditure 81.9%, of which wages 31.4%; development expenditure 18.1%).
Public debt (external, outstanding; 2002): U.S.$9,043,000,000.
Production (metric tons except as noted). Agriculture, forestry, fishing (2002): sugarcane 5,000,000, sorghum 2,800,000, peanuts (groundnuts) 945,000, millet 618,000, sesame seeds 274,000, wheat 247,000, seed cotton 193,000, dates 177,000, tea 173,000, gum arabic 15,700; livestock (number of live animals) 47,043,000 sheep, 40,000,000 goats, 38,325,000 cattle, 3,203,000 camels; roundwood (2002) 19,241,332 cu m; fish catch (2001) 59,000. Mining and quarrying (2001): salt 120,000; gold 6,800 kg. Manufacturing (2000): raw sugar 689,000[11]; flour 600,000; cement 190,000[11]; vegetable oils 120,000; cattle hides and horsehides 8,500,000 units; shoes 50,000,000 pairs. Energy production (consumption): electricity (kW-hr; 2000) 2,264,000,000 (2,264,000,000); coal, none (none); crude petroleum (barrels; 2001) 145,100,000 ([2000] 14,609,000); petroleum products (metric tons; 2001) 2,674,700 ([2000] 1,876,000); natural gas, none (none).
Gross national product (2003): U.S.$15,372,000,000 (U.S.$460 per capita).

Structure of gross domestic product and labour force

	2001 in value Sd '000,000,000	2001 % of total value	2000 labour force[12]	2000 % of labour force[12]
Agriculture	1,543.0	45.6	7,454,000	61.1
Mining	293.2	8.7		
Manufacturing	265.8	7.9		
Construction	153.4	4.5		
Public utilities	57.5	1.7		
Transportation and communications				
Trade, hotels	864.9	25.6	4,753,000	38.9
Finance				
Services				
Pub. admin., defense	202.8	6.0		
Other	—	—		
TOTAL	3,380.6	100.0	12,207,000	100.0

Population economically active (2000): total 12,207,000; activity rate of total population 37.8% (participation rates: n.a.; female 29.9%; unemployed, n.a.).

Price and earnings indexes (2000 = 100)

	1997	1998	1999	2000	2001
Consumer price index	69.7	81.6	94.6	100.0	105.8
Earnings index	...	...	...	...	...

Household income and expenditure. Average household size (2000): 6.1; income per household: n.a.; expenditure: n.a.
Tourism (2002): receipts from visitors U.S.$62,000,000; expenditures by nationals abroad U.S.$91,000,000.
Land use as % of total land area (2000): in temporary crops 6.8%, in permanent crops 0.2%, in pasture 49.3%; overall forest area 25.9%.

Foreign trade[13]

Balance of trade (current prices)

	1996	1997	1998	1999	2000	2001
U.S.$'000,000	–884	–985	–1,329	–635	+254	+113
% of total	41.6%	45.2%	52.7%	28.8%	7.6%	3.4%

Imports (2001): U.S.$1,586,000,000 (machinery and equipment 27.9%; foodstuffs 16.4%, of which wheat and wheat flour 8.7%; transport equipment 12.8%; chemicals and chemical products 7.8%). *Major import sources* (2002): China 19.8%; Saudi Arabia 6.9%; India 5.5%; Germany 5.5%; U.K. 5.4%.
Exports (2001): U.S.$1,699,000,000 (crude petroleum 74.7%; refined petroleum 6.3%; sesame seeds 6.2%; gold 2.6%; cotton 2.6%). *Major export destinations* (2002): China 55.3%; Japan 13.9%; Saudi Arabia 5.4%; South Korea 3.8%; Egypt 3.3%.

Transport and communications

Transport. Railroads: route length (2000) 5,901 km; (2001) passenger-km 78,000,000; metric ton-km cargo 1,250,000,000. Roads (1999): total length 11,900 km (paved 36%). Vehicles (1996): passenger cars 285,000; trucks and buses 53,000. Air transport (2001): passenger-km 803,000,000; metric ton-km cargo 54,542,000; airports (1997) with scheduled flights 3.

Communications

Medium	date	unit	number	units per 1,000 persons
Daily newspapers	2000	circulation	912,000	26
Radio	2001	receivers	16,642,000	461
Television	2002	receivers	12,661,000	386
Telephones	2003	main lines	900,000	27
Cellular telephones	2003	subscribers	650,000	20
Personal computers	2002	units	200,000	6.1
Internet	2003	users	300,000	2.6

Education and health

Educational attainment: n.a. *Literacy* (2000): total population age 15 and over literate 55.8%; males 69.5%; females 46.3%.

Education (1999–2000)

	schools	teachers	students	student/ teacher ratio
Primary (age 7–12)	11,923	117,151	3,137,494	26.8
Secondary (age 13–18)	1,694	21,114	401,424	19.0
Vocational[14]	...	761	26,421	34.7
Higher[15]	19	1,417[14]	200,538	...

Health: physicians (1997) 3,423 (1 per 9,395 persons); hospital beds (1998) 36,419 (1 per 909 persons); infant mortality rate (2003) 65.6.
Food (2001): daily per capita caloric intake 2,288 (vegetable products 80%, animal products 20%); 97% of FAO recommended minimum.

Military

Total active duty personnel (2004): 104,800 (army 95.4%, navy 1.7%, air force 2.9%); main opposition force in southern Sudan (Sudanese People's Liberation Army) between 20,000 and 30,000[16]. African Union peacekeeping troops in Darfur (October 2004): 400; authorized 3,300. *Military expenditure as percentage of GNP* (1999): 4.8% (world 2.4%); per capita expenditure U.S.$33.

[1]A state of emergency introduced Dec. 12, 1999, was still in effect in September 2004. [2]Includes 90 indirectly elected or appointed seats. [3]English has been designated the "principal" language in southern Sudan. [4]Islamic law and custom are sources of national law per 1998 constitution. [5]The Sudanese dinar (Sd), introduced May 1992 at a value equal to 10 Sudanese pounds (LSd), officially replaced the Sudanese pound on March 1, 1999. [6]Local administrative reorganization into 26 new states was announced in February 1994 and confirmed in June 1998. Names listed below are English-language variants; six southern states are excluded. [7]Includes Western Bahr el-Ghazal and Northern Bahr el-Ghazal. [8]Including *c.* 130,000 sq km of inland water area. [9]Summary total; actual total per official source is 31,081,000. [10]Population estimates are unavailable for six states in southern Sudan experiencing civil war since 1983. [11]2001. [12]FAO estimate. [13]Imports c.i.f.; exports f.o.b. [14]1996–97. [15]Universities only. [16]A permanent cease-fire between the central government and the main opposition force in southern Sudan was signed on Dec. 31, 2004; a comprehensive peace plan was to be implemented in January 2005.

Internet resources for further information:
- **Bank of Sudan**
  http://www.bankofsudan.org

Suriname

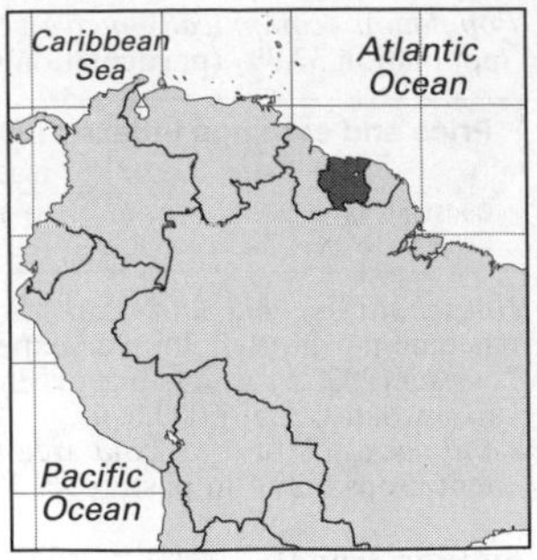

Official name: Republiek Suriname (Republic of Suriname).
Form of government: multiparty republic with one legislative house (National Assembly [51]).
Head of state and government: President.
Capital: Paramaribo.
Official language: Dutch.
Official religion: none.
Monetary unit: 1 Suriname dollar (SRD)[1] = 100 cents; valuation (Sept. 1, 2004) 1 U.S.$ = SRD 2.74; 1 £ = SRD 5.17.

Area and population

		area		population
Districts	Capitals	sq mi	sq km	1996 estimate
Brokopondo	Brokopondo	2,843	7,364	7,200
Commewijne	Nieuw Amsterdam	908	2,353	20,900
Coronie	Totness	1,507	3,902	2,900
Marowijne	Albina	1,786	4,627	12,600
Nickerie	Nieuw Nickerie	2,067	5,353	33,600
Para	Onverwacht	2,082	5,393	14,400
Saramacca	Groningen	1,404	3,636	13,000
Sipaliwini	[2]	50,412	130,566	23,500
Wanica	Lelydorp	171	443	72,400
Town district				
Paramaribo	Paramaribo	71	183	222,800
TOTAL		63,251[3]	163,820[3]	423,400[4]

Demography

Population (2004): 437,000.
Density (2004): persons per sq mi 6.9, persons per sq km 2.7.
Urban-rural (2001): urban 74.8%; rural 25.2%.
Sex distribution (2000): male 50.77%; female 49.23%.
Age breakdown (2000): under 15, 32.1%; 15–29, 27.2%; 30–44, 22.7%; 45–59, 9.9%; 60–74, 6.4%; 75 and over, 1.7%.
Population projection: (2010) 441,000; (2020) 439,000.
Doubling time: 56 years.
Ethnic composition (1999): Indo-Pakistani 37.0%; Suriname Creole 31.0%; Javanese 15.0%; Bush Negro 10.0%; Amerindian 2.5%; Chinese 2.0%; white 1.0%; other 1.5%.
Religious affiliation (2000): Christian 50.4%, of which Roman Catholic 22.3%, Protestant (mostly Moravian) 17.1%, unaffiliated/other Christian 11.0%; Hindu 17.8%; Muslim 13.9%; nonreligious 4.8%; Spiritists (including followers of Voodoo) 3.5%; traditional beliefs 1.9%; other 7.7%.
Major cities (1996/1997): Paramaribo 222,800 (urban agglomeration 289,000); Lelydorp 15,600; Nieuw Nickerie 11,100; Mungo (Moengo) 6,800; Meerzorg 6,600.

Vital statistics

Birth rate per 1,000 population (2003): 19.4 (world avg. 21.3).
Death rate per 1,000 population (2003): 6.8 (world avg. 9.1).
Natural increase rate per 1,000 population (2003): 12.6 (world avg. 12.2).
Total fertility rate (avg. births per childbearing woman; 2003): 2.4.
Marriage rate per 1,000 population (2000): 5.3.
Divorce rate per 1,000 population (2000): 0.9.
Life expectancy at birth (2003): male 66.8 years; female 71.8 years.
Major causes of death per 100,000 population (1992): noncommunicable diseases 769.0; external and other causes 608.1; communicable and perinatal diseases 232.8; ill-defined diseases 279.0.

National economy

Budget (1998). Revenue: Sf 137,200,000,000 (indirect taxes 40.4%; direct taxes 36.2%; bauxite levy 10.9%; grants 12.5%). Expenditures: Sf 188,000,000,000 (current expenditures 90.2%, of which wages and salaries 39.1%, transfers 11.7%, debt service 1.3%; capital expenditures 9.8%).
Public debt (external, outstanding; 1996): U.S.$216,500,000.
Production (metric tons except as noted). Agriculture, forestry, fishing (2002): rice 192,000, sugarcane 120,000, bananas 43,000, plantains 11,000, oranges 10,300, coconuts 8,000, cassava 5,235; livestock (number of live animals) 136,000 cattle, 24,000 pigs, 2,200,000 chickens; roundwood (2002) 200,000 cu m; fish catch (2001) 18,915, of which shrimp 7,390. Mining and quarrying (2001): bauxite 4,512,000; alumina 1,900,000; gold 300 kg[5]. Manufacturing (value of production at factor cost in Sf; 1993): food products 992,000,000; beverages 558,000,000; tobacco 369,000,000; chemical products 291,000,000; pottery and earthenware 258,000,000; wood products 180,000,000. Energy production (consumption): electricity (kW-hr; 2000) 1,648,000,000 (1,648,000,000); hard coal (metric tons) none (none); crude petroleum (barrels; 2001) 5,000,000 ([2000] 3,000,000); petroleum products (metric tons; 2000) none[6] (478,000); natural gas, none (none).
Population economically active (1999): total 84,646[7]; activity rate of total population 19.8%[7] (participation rates[8]: [1992] ages 15–64, 56.0%; female 34.4%; unemployed 14.0%).

Price and earnings indexes (2000 = 100)

	1997	1998	1999	2000	2001	2002	2003
Consumer price index	26.5	31.5	62.7	100.0	138.6	160.1	196.9
Earnings index	…	…	…	…	…	…	…

Gross national product (2003): U.S.$841,000,000 (U.S.$1,940 per capita).

Structure of gross domestic product and labour force

	2001		1999	
	in value Sf '000,000	% of total value	labour force[7]	% of labour force[7]
Agriculture, forestry	165,227	10.3	4,456	5.3
Mining	298,318	18.7	1,127	2.0
Manufacturing	89,102	5.6	2,863	3.4
Construction	51,598	3.2	4,953	5.9
Public utilities	54,273	3.4	1,000	1.2
Transp. and commun.	124,630	7.8	5,817	6.9
Trade, hotels	192,341	12.0	17,262	20.4
Finance, real estate	199,232	12.5	4,544	5.4
Pub. admin., defense	123,529	7.7	27,305	32.3
Services	116,202	7.3		
Other	182,897[9]	11.5[9]	14,720[10]	17.4[10]
TOTAL	1,597,347[4]	100.0	84,646[4]	100.0[4]

Household income and expenditure. Average household size (1998) 4.8; income per household: n.a.; sources of income: n.a.; expenditure: n.a.
Tourism (2002): receipts from visitors U.S.$3,000,000; expenditures by nationals abroad U.S.$10,000,000.
Land use as % of total land area (2000): in temporary crops 0.4%, in permanent crops 0.06%, in pasture 0.1%; overall forest area 90.5%.

Foreign trade[11]

Balance of trade (current prices)

	1996	1997	1998	1999	2000
U.S.$'000,000	–29.2	–83.8	–60.3	…	–12.5
% of total	3.3%	7.4%	5.9%	…	1.2%

Imports (2000): U.S.$526,500,000 (nonelectrical machinery 22.5%, food products 13.4%, road vehicles 13.2%, chemicals and chemical products 10.2%, refined petroleum 5.8%). *Major import sources* (2001): U.S. *c.* 34%; The Netherlands *c.* 17%; Trinidad and Tobago *c.* 13%; Netherlands Antilles *c.* 8%; Japan *c.* 5%.
Exports (2000): U.S.$514,000,000 (alumina 62.1%, gold 11.4%, crustaceans and mollusks 7.0%, crude petroleum 4.3%, refined petroleum 2.3%, rice 2.2%). *Major export destinations* (2001): U.S. *c.* 26%; Norway *c.* 16%; France *c.* 10%; The Netherlands *c.* 9%; Canada *c.* 7%.

Transport and communications

Transport. Railroads (1997)[12]: length 187 mi, 301 km; passengers, not applicable; cargo, n.a. Roads (1996): total length 2,815 mi, 4,530 km (paved 26%). Vehicles (2000): passenger cars 61,365; trucks and buses 23,220. Air transport (1998): passenger-mi 666,109,000, passenger-km 1,072,000,000; short ton-mi cargo 86,988,000, metric ton-km cargo 127,000,000; airports with scheduled flights 1.

Communications

Medium	date	unit	number	units per 1,000 persons
Daily newspapers	1996	circulation	50,000	122
Radio	1997	receivers	300,000	728
Television	2000	receivers	109,000	253
Telephones	2003	main lines	79,800	152
Cellular telephones	2003	subscribers	168,100	320
Personal computers	2001	units	20,000	45
Internet	2002	users	20,000	42

Education and health

Educational attainment: n.a. *Literacy* (2001): total population age 15 and over literate 92.2%; males literate 93.6%; females literate 90.7%.

Education (1995–96)

	schools	teachers	students	student/ teacher ratio
Primary (age 6–11)	304	3,611	75,585	20.9
Secondary (age 12–18)	104	2,286	31,918	13.9
Teacher training	1	…	1,462	…
Higher[13]	1	286	3,081	10.8

Health: physicians (1999) 213 (1 per 2,000 persons); hospital beds (1998) 1,449 (1 per 288 persons); infant mortality rate per 1,000 live births (2003) 24.7.
Food (2001): daily per capita caloric intake 2,643 (vegetable products 86%, animal products 14%); 117% of FAO recommended minimum requirement.

Military

Total active duty personnel (2003): 1,840[14] (army 76.1%, navy 13.0%, air force 10.9%). *Military expenditure as percentage of GNP* (1999): 1.8% (world 2.4%); per capita expenditure U.S.$33.

[1]The Suriname dollar (SRD) replaced the Suriname guilder (Sf) on Jan. 1, 2004, at a rate of 1 SRD = Sf1,000. [2]No capital; administered from Paramaribo. [3]Area excludes 6,809 sq mi (17,635 sq km) of territory disputed with Guyana. [4]Detail does not add to total given because of rounding. [5]Recorded production; unrecorded production may be as high as 30,000 kg. [6]Production of petroleum products began in 2000; data not available. [7]Based on sample survey. [8]Districts of Wanica and Paramaribo only. [9]Taxes on products less imputed bank service charges. [10]Includes 11,812 unemployed. [11]Imports c.i.f.; exports f.o.b. [12]There are no public railways operating in Suriname. [13]Anton de Kom University of Suriname; 2001–02. [14]All services are part of the army.

Internet resources for further information:
- **Suriname Statistical Yearbook**
  http://www.suriname.nu/101alg/statis01.html
- **Caricom Statistics**
  http://www.caricomstats.org

Swaziland

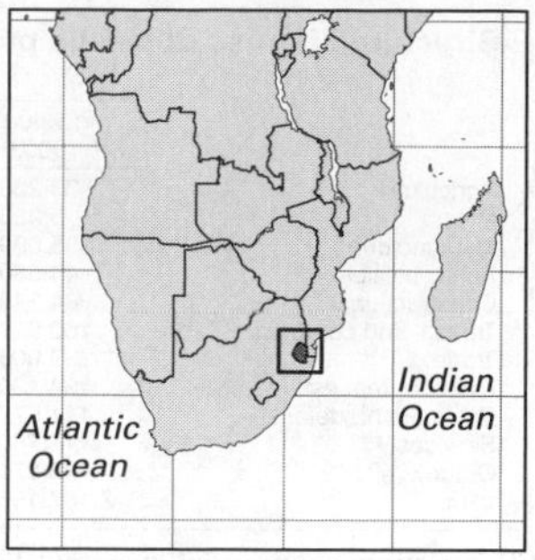

Official name: Umbuso weSwatini (Swazi); Kingdom of Swaziland (English).
Form of government: monarchy[1] with two legislative houses (Senate [30[2]]; House of Assembly [65[3]]).
Head of state and government: King, assisted by Prime Minister.
Capitals: Mbabane (administrative and judicial); Lozitha and Ludzidzini (royal); Lobamba (legislative).
Official languages: Swati (Swazi); English.
Official religion: none.
Monetary unit: 1 lilangeni[4] (plural emalangeni [E]) = 100 cents; valuation (Sept. 1, 2004) 1 U.S.$ = E 6.66; 1 £ = E 11.97.

Area and population		area		population
				1997
Districts	Capitals	sq mi	sq km	census
Hhohho	Mbabane	1,378	3,569	269,826
Lubombo	Siteki	2,296	5,947	201,696
Manzini	Manzini	1,571	4,068	292,100
Shiselweni	Nhlangano	1,459	3,780	217,100
TOTAL		6,704	17,364	980,722[5]

Demography

Population (2004): 1,083,000.
Density (2004): persons per sq mi 161.5; persons per sq km 62.4.
Urban-rural (2003): urban 23.5%; rural 76.5%.
Sex distribution (2003): male 49.80%; female 50.20%.
Age breakdown (2003): under 15, 41.4%; 15–29, 30.7%; 30–44, 14.7%; 45–59, 7.9%; 60–74, 4.3%; 75 and over, 1.0%.
Population projection: (2010) 1,084,000; (2020) 1,062,000.
Ethnic composition (2000): Swazi 82.3%; Zulu 9.6%; Tsonga 2.3%; Afrikaner 1.4%; mixed (black-white) 1.0%; other 3.4%.
Religious affiliation (2000): Christian 67.5%, of which African indigenous 45.6%, Protestant 15.2%, Roman Catholic 5.4%; traditional beliefs 12.2%; other (mostly unaffiliated Christian) 20.3%.
Major cities (1997): Mbabane 57,992; Manzini 25,571 (urban agglomeration 78,734); Big Bend 9,374; Mhlume 7,661; Malkerns 7,400.

Vital statistics

Birth rate per 1,000 population (2003): 28.6 (world avg. 21.3).
Death rate per 1,000 population (2003): 23.1 (world avg. 9.1).
Natural increase rate per 1,000 population (2003): 5.5 (world avg. 12.2).
Total fertility rate (avg. births per childbearing woman; 2003): 3.8.
Life expectancy at birth (2003): male 41.0 years; female 38.9 years.
Adult population (ages 15–49) *living with HIV* (2004[6]): 38.8% (world avg. 1.1%).

National economy

Budget (2001–02). Revenue: E 3,094,000,000 (receipts from Customs Union of Southern Africa 48.6%; tax on income and profits 23.4%; sales tax 13.2%; foreign-aid grants 3.9%). Expenditures: E 3,409,000,000 (current expenditure 74.4%; development expenditure 25.4%; net lending 0.2%).
Gross national product (2003): U.S.$1,492,000,000 (U.S.$1,350 per capita).

Structure of gross domestic product and labour force	2001			
	in value E '000	% of total value	labour force[7]	% of labour force[7]
Agriculture	1,055,100	9.6	195,098[8]	49.8[8]
Mining	24,900	0.2	620	0.1
Manufacturing	2,757,100	25.1	19,898	5.1
Construction	452,000	4.1	5,779	1.5
Public utilities	111,700	1.0	1,409	0.3
Transp. and commun.	391,300	3.6	12,509	3.2
Trade	689,200	6.3		
Finance	326,200	3.0	7,492	1.9
Pub. admin., defense	1,367,900	12.5	25,323	6.5
Services	82,600	0.8		
Other	3,713,000[9]	33.8[9]	123,872[10]	31.6[10]
TOTAL	10,971,000	100.0	392,000	100.0

Population economically active (2001): total 392,000; activity rate of total population 39.3% (participation rates: ages 15 and over, n.a.; female n.a.; unemployed 31.6%).

Price and earnings indexes (2000 = 100)	1997	1998	1999	2000	2001	2002	2003
Consumer price index	98.9	98.7	99.1	100.0	102.4	104.6	106.6
Weekly earnings index	91.7	95.0	96.7	100.0	102.9	106.4	109.4

Public debt (external, outstanding; 2002): U.S.$273,700,000.
Land use as % of total land area (2000): in temporary crops 10.3%, in permanent crops 0.7%, in pasture 69.8%; overall forest area 30.3%.
Production (metric tons except as noted). Agriculture, forestry, fishing (2002): sugarcane 4,000,000, corn (maize) 85,000, grapefruit and pomelo 37,000, oranges 36,000, seed cotton 22,500, pineapples 19,700; livestock (number of live animals) 615,000 cattle, 422,000 goats; roundwood (2002) 890,000 cu m; fish catch (2001) 142. Mining and quarrying (2001): stone 350,000 cu m. Manufacturing (value added in U.S.$'000; 1994): food and beverages 244,000, of which beverage processing 153,000; paper and paper products 35,000; textiles 19,000; printing and publishing products 18,000; clothing 7,000; metal and metal products 7,000. Energy production (consumption): electricity (kW-hr; 2000) 265,000,000 (702,000,000); coal (metric tons; 2001) 380,000 (n.a.); crude petroleum, n.a. (n.a.).
Household income and expenditure. Average household size (1986) 5.7; annual income per household (1985) E 332 (U.S.$151); sources of income (1985): wages and salaries 44.4%, self-employment 22.2%, transfers 12.2%, other 21.2%; expenditure (1985): food and beverages 33.5%, rent and fuel 13.4%, household durable goods 12.8%, transportation and communications 8.8%, clothing and footwear 6.0%, recreation 3.3%.
Tourism (2002): receipts U.S.$26,000,000; expenditures U.S.$33,000,000.

Foreign trade[11]

Balance of trade (current prices)	1996	1997	1998	1999	2000	2001
U.S.$'000,000	−204	−104	−106	−131	−136	−73
% of total	10.7%	5.1%	5.2%	6.5%	7.0%	4.3%

Imports (2001): U.S.$832,000,000 (food and live animals 15.6%; machinery and apparatus 13.6%; chemicals and chemical products 13.2%; road vehicles 9.5%; refined petroleum 9.2%). *Major import sources:* South Africa 94.5%; Hong Kong 1.0%; Japan 0.9%.
Exports (2001): U.S.$678,000,000 (soft drink [including sugar and fruit juice] concentrates *c.* 38%; sugar *c.* 14%; apparel and clothing accessories *c.* 12%; wood pulp *c.* 9%). *Major export destinations:* South Africa 78.0%; Mozambique 4.6%; U.S. 4.0%.

Transport and communications

Transport. Railroads (2001): route length 187 mi, 301 km; passenger-km, n.a.[12]; metric ton-km cargo 700,000,000. Roads (1996): total length 2,367 mi, 3,810 km (paved 29%). Vehicles (1998): passenger cars 34,064; trucks and buses 35,030. Air transport: (1998) passenger-mi 26,718,910, passenger-km 43,000,000; (1995) short ton-mi cargo 87,000, metric ton-km cargo 127,000; airports (1997) with scheduled flights 1.

Communications				units
Medium	date	unit	number	per 1,000 persons
Daily newspapers	2000	circulation	27,100	26
Radio	2000	receivers	169,000	162
Television	2000	receivers	124,000	110
Telephones	2003	main lines	46,200	44
Cellular telephones	2003	subscribers	88,000	84
Personal computers	2003	units	30,000	29
Internet	2003	users	27,000	26

Education and health

Educational attainment (1986). Percentage of population age 25 and over having: no formal schooling 42.1%; some primary education 23.9%; complete primary 10.5%; some secondary 19.2%; complete secondary and higher 4.3%.
Literacy (2000): total population age 15 and over literate 79.6%; males literate 80.8%; females literate 78.6%.

Education (2001)	schools	teachers	students	student/ teacher ratio
Primary (age 6–13)	541	6,594	212,064	32.2
Secondary (age 14–18)	182	3,647	61,335	16.8
Voc., teacher tr.	5	...	1,822	...
Higher	1	...	3,692	...

Health: physicians (1996) 148 (1 per 6,663 persons); hospital beds (2000) 1,570[13] (1 per 665 persons); infant mortality rate per 1,000 live births (2003) 67.4.
Food (2001): daily per capita caloric intake 2,593 (vegetable products 85%, animal products 15%); 112% of FAO recommended minimum requirement.

Military

Total active duty personnel (2003): *c.* 3,500 troops. *Military expenditure as percentage of GNP* (1999): 1.5% (world 2.4%); per capita expenditure U.S.$20.

[1]Constitution accepted by the King in November 2003 had not become effective by September 2004. [2]Includes 20 nonelective seats. [3]Includes 10 nonelective seats. [4]The lilangeni is at par with the South African rand. [5]Final results, includes 51,005 residents abroad. [6]January 1. [7]Formally employed only (except for Agriculture and Other). [8]Includes informally employed (mostly in Agriculture). [9]Includes indirect taxes less imputed bank service charges and subsidies. [10]Unemployed. [11]Imports f.o.b. in balance of trade and c.i.f. in commodities and trading partners. [12]Scheduled passenger train service was terminated in January 2001. [13]Excludes National Psychiatric Hospital.

Internet resources for further information:
- **Central Bank of Swaziland http://www.centralbank.org.sz**
- **Swaziland Government http://www.gov.sz/home.asp**

Sweden

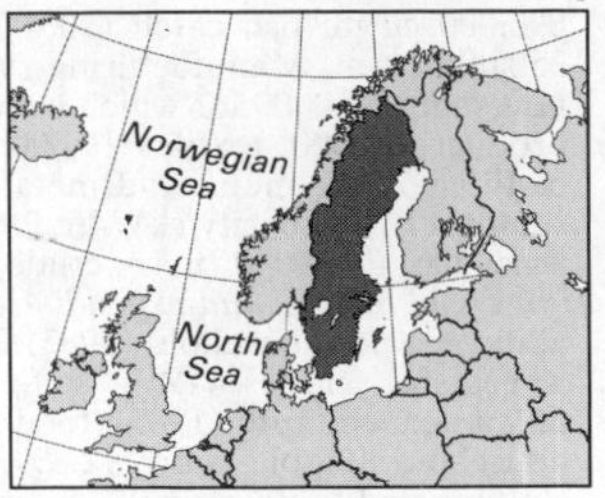

Official name: Konungariket Sverige (Kingdom of Sweden).
Form of government: constitutional monarchy and parliamentary state with one legislative house (Parliament [349]).
Chief of state: King.
Head of government: Prime Minister.
Capital: Stockholm.
Official language: Swedish.
Official religion: none.
Monetary unit: 1 Swedish krona (SKr) = 100 ore; valuation (Sept. 1, 2004) 1 U.S.$ = SKr 7.51; 1 £ = SKr 13.52.

Area and population

Counties	area sq km	population 2002[1] estimate	Counties	area sq km	population 2002[1] estimate
Blekinge	3,055	150,036	Södermanland	6,607	258,389
Dalarna	30,404	276,765	Stockholm	6,789	1,849,206
Gävleborg	19,756	277,171	Uppsala	7,206	298,556
Gotland	3,184	57,458	Värmland	19,388	273,716
Halland	5,719	278,236	Västerbotten	59,284	254,936
Jämtland	54,100	127,953	Västernorrland	23,107	244,734
Jönköping	11,253	327,917	Västmanland	6,614	258,855
Kalmar	11,694	234,776	Västra Götaland	25,389	1,507,182
Kronoberg	9,429	176,955	TOTAL LAND AND SMALL LAKES AREA	441,348[2]	
Norrbotten	106,012	253,945	4 LARGE LAKES	8,926[2]	
Örebro	9,343	273,419	OTHER UNDISTRIBUTED	21	
Östergötland	11,646	413,401	TOTAL	450,295	8,937,119
Skåne	11,369	1,143,513			

Demography

Population (2004): 8,991,000.
Density (2004)[3]: persons per sq mi 53.7, persons per sq km 20.4.
Urban-rural (2001[4]): urban 81.2%; rural 18.8%.
Sex distribution (2002): male 49.52%; female 50.48%.
Age breakdown (2002[4]): under 15, 18.2%; 15–29, 18.1%; 30–44, 20.8%; 45–59, 20.6%; 60–74, 13.4%; 75 and over, 8.9%.
Population projection: (2010) 9,241,000; (2020) 9,692,000.
Ethnic composition (2002[4])[5]: Swedish 88.5%; other European 6.9%, of which Finnish 2.2%, Serb/Montenegrin 0.8%, Bosniac 0.6%; Asian 3.0%, of which Iranian 0.6%; African 0.6%; other 1.0%.
Religious affiliation (1999): Church of Sweden 86.5% (about 30% nonpracticing); Muslim 2.3%; Roman Catholic 1.8%; Pentecostal 1.1%; other 8.3%.
Major cities (2003): Stockholm 758,148; Göteborg 474,921; Malmö 265,481; Uppsala 179,673; Linköping 135,066; Västerås 128,902.

Vital statistics

Birth rate per 1,000 population (2002): 10.7 (world avg. 21.3); legitimate (2001) 44.5%; illegitimate 55.5%.
Death rate per 1,000 population (2002): 10.6 (world avg. 9.1).
Natural increase rate per 1,000 population (2002): 0.1 (world avg. 12.2).
Total fertility rate (avg. births per childbearing woman; 2002): 1.6.
Marriage rate per 1,000 population (2002): 4.3.
Divorce rate per 1,000 population (2002): 2.4.
Life expectancy at birth (2003): male 78.1 years; female 82.5 years.
Major causes of death per 100,000 population (1999): heart disease 503.0; malignant neoplasms (cancers) 238.3; cerebrovascular disease 116.4.

National economy

Budget (2001). Revenue: SKr 755,126,000,000 (value-added and excise taxes 36.0%, social security 31.6%, income and capital gains taxes 17.9%, property taxes 5.3%). Expenditures: SKr 716,379,000,000 (health and social affairs 30.6%, debt service 11.3%, defense 6.3%, education 5.7%).
Public debt (2004[4]): U.S.$170,915,000,000.
Production (metric tons except as noted). Agriculture, forestry, fishing (2002): sugar beets 2,800,000, wheat 2,117,000, barley 1,778,500, oats 1,186,000, potatoes 907,000, rapeseed 159,900; livestock (number of live animals) 1,882,000 pigs, 1,637,000 cattle, 427,000 sheep; roundwood (2002) 67,500,000 cu m; fish catch (2001) 318,600. Mining and quarrying (2001): iron ore 19,486,000; zinc (metal content) 156,300; copper (metal content) 74,300; silver (metal content) 306,000 kg. Manufacturing (value added, in U.S.$'000,000; 1999): telecommunications equipment, electronics 9,200; nonelectrical machinery and apparatus 6,100; road vehicles 6,000; paper and paper products 5,950; fabricated metals 4,050; printing and publishing 3,500; food products 3,450. Energy production (consumption): electricity (kW-hr; 2002) 143,136,000,000 ([2000] 152,193,000,000); coal (metric tons; 2000) none (3,057,000); crude petroleum (barrels; 2000) none (149,000,000); petroleum products (metric tons; 2000) 18,985,000 (12,227,000); natural gas (cu m; 2000) none (833,083,000).
Household income and expenditure. Average household size (2000) 2.2; average annual disposable income per household (2000) SKr 239,000 (U.S.$26,091); sources of income (1996): wages and salaries 59.2%, transfer payments 26.1%, other 14.7%; expenditure (1996): housing 27.6%, transportation and communications 17.1%, food and beverages 16.5%, recreation 9.1%, energy 5.8%.
Tourism (2002): receipts U.S.$4,233,000,000; expenditures U.S.$6,816,000,000.
Gross national product (at current market prices; 2003): U.S.$258,319,000,000 (U.S.$28,840 per capita).

Structure of gross domestic product and labour force

	2001 in value SKr '000,000	% of total value	labour force	% of labour force
Agriculture	33,236	1.5	96,000	2.1
Mining	5,266	0.2		
Manufacturing	395,099	18.2	777,000	17.6
Public utilities	44,580	2.1		
Construction	84,349	3.9	232,000	5.3
Transp. and commun.	160,013	7.4	804,000	18.2
Trade	239,003	11.0		
Finance, real estate	494,130	22.8	601,000	13.6
Pub. admin., defense	411,577	19.0	232,000	5.3
Services	114,769	5.3	1,491,000	33.8
Other	185,174[6]	8.5[6]	181,000[7]	4.1[7]
TOTAL	2,167,196	100.0[8]	4,414,000	100.0

Population economically active (2001): total 4,414,000; activity rate of total population 49.5% (participation rates: ages 16–64 [2000] 77.9%; female 47.8%; unemployed 4.0%).

Price and earnings indexes (2000 = 100)

	1997	1998	1999	2000	2001	2002	2003
Consumer price index	98.7	98.6	99.0	100.0	102.5	104.6	106.7
Hourly earnings index	91.7	95.0	96.7	100.0	102.9	106.4	109.4

Land use as % of total land area (2000): in temporary crops 6.6%, in permanent crops 0.01%, in pasture 10.9%; overall forest area 65.9%.

Foreign trade[9]

Balance of trade (current prices)

	1997	1998	1999	2000	2001	2002
SKr '000,000	+131,400	+130,200	+133,000	+129,700	+127,300	+146,600
% of total	11.6%	10.7%	10.5%	16.3%	9.8%	10.3%

Imports (2001): SKr 656,200,000,000 (nonelectrical machinery and apparatus 16.6%; electrical machinery and apparatus 14.0%; chemicals and chemical products 10.8%; road vehicles 9.3%; crude and refined petroleum 7.8%). *Major import sources* (2002): Germany 18.5%; Denmark 8.8%; U.K. 8.6%; Norway 8.2%; The Netherlands 6.7%.
Exports (2001): SKr 783,500,000,000 (nonelectrical machinery and apparatus 16.9%; road vehicles 12.1%; telecommunications equipment, electronics 9.3%; paper and paper products 8.5%; medicines and pharmaceuticals 5.5%; iron and steel 5.0%). *Major export destinations* (2002): U.S. 11.6%; Germany 10.1%; Norway 9.0%; U.K. 8.2%; Denmark 5.9%.

Transport and communications

Transport. Railroads (2001): length 6,994 mi, 11,255 km; (2000) passenger-km 8,251,000,000; metric ton-km cargo 20,088,000,000. Roads (2002[4]): total length 262,200 mi, 422,000 km (public 50.2%). Vehicles (2001[4]): passenger cars 4,019,000; trucks and buses 410,000. Air transport (2002)[10]: passenger-km 10,896,000; metric ton-km cargo 266,676,000; airports (2001) 49.

Communications

Medium	date	unit	number	units per 1,000 persons
Daily newspapers	2000	circulation	3,830,000	432
Radio	2000	receivers	8,270,000	932
Television	2000	receivers	5,090,000	574
Telephones	2002	main lines	6,579,000	736
Cellular telephones	2002	subscribers	7,949,000	889
Personal computers	2002	units	5,556,000	621
Internet	2002	users	5,125,000	573

Education and health

Educational attainment (2002[4]). Percentage of population age 16–74 having: lower secondary education 27%; incomplete or complete upper secondary education 45%; up to 3 years postsecondary 12%; 3 years or more postsecondary 14%; unknown 2%. *Literacy* (2002): virtually 100%.

Education (1999–2000)

	schools	teachers	students	student/teacher ratio
Primary (age 7–12)	5,048	100,827	1,034,881	10.3
Secondary (age 13–18)		30,295	312,936	10.3
Higher	64	...	372,108	...

Health (2001): physicians 25,200 (1 per 354 persons); hospital beds 29,122 (1 per 306 persons); infant mortality rate per 1,000 live births (2002) 3.3.
Food (2001): daily per capita caloric intake 3,164 (vegetable 70%, animal 30%); 118% of FAO recommended minimum requirement.

Military

Total active duty personnel (2003): 27,600 (army 50.0%, navy 28.6%, air force 21.4%). *Military expenditure as percentage of GNP* (1999): 2.3% (world 2.4%); per capita expenditure U.S.$601.

[1]September 30. [2]Area of small lakes equals 31,034 sq km; total inland water area including 4 large lakes equals 39,960 sq km. [3]Density based on land area only (410,335 sq km). [4]January 1. [5]By place of birth. [6]Taxes less subsidies and imputed bank service charges. [7]Includes 175,000 unemployed. [8]Detail does not add to total given because of rounding. [9]Imports c.i.f.; exports f.o.b. [10]Includes SAS international and domestic traffic applicable to Sweden.

Internet resources for further information:
- **Statistics Sweden http://www.scb.se/indexeng.asp**

Switzerland

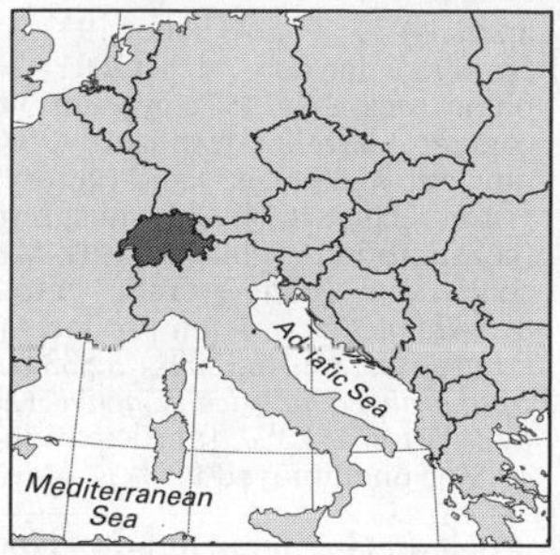

Official name: Confédération Suisse (French); Schweizerische Eidgenossenschaft (German); Confederazione Svizzera (Italian) (Swiss Confederation)[1].
Form of government: federal state with two legislative houses (Council of States [46]; National Council [200]).
Head of state and government: President of the Federal Council.
Capitals: Bern (administrative); Lausanne (judicial).
Official languages: French; German; Italian; Romansh (locally).
Official religion: none.
Monetary unit: 1 Swiss Franc (Sw F) = 100 centimes; valuation (Sept. 1, 2004) 1 U.S.$ = Sw F 1.27; 1 £ = Sw F 2.28.

Area and population

Cantons	Capitals	area sq mi	area sq km	population 2003[2] estimate
Aargau	Aarau	542	1,404	556,229
Appenzell Ausser-Rhoden[3]	Herisau	94	243	53,189
Appenzell Inner-Rhoden[3]	Appenzell	66	172	14,995
Basel-Landschaft[3]	Liestal	200	518	263,194
Basel-Stadt[3]	Basel	14	37	186,871
Bern	Bern	2,301	5,959	950,209
Fribourg	Fribourg	645	1,671	242,679
Genève	Geneva	109	282	419,254
Glarus	Glarus	264	685	38,380
Graubünden	Chur	2,743	7,105	186,105
Jura	Delémont	324	838	69,190
Luzern	Luzern	576	1,493	352,311
Neuchâtel	Neuchâtel	310	803	166,949
Nidwalden[3]	Stans	107	276	38,897
Obwalden[3]	Sarnen	190	491	32,999
Sankt Gallen	Sankt Gallen	782	2,026	455,193
Schaffhausen	Schaffhausen	115	298	73,916
Schwyz	Schwyz	351	908	133,358
Solothurn	Solothurn	305	791	246,504
Thurgau	Frauenfeld	383	991	229,882
Ticino	Bellinzona	1,086	2,812	314,563
Uri	Altdorf	416	1,077	35,246
Valais	Sion	2,017	5,224	281,020
Vaud	Lausanne	1,240	3,212	631,999
Zug	Zug	92	239	102,247
Zürich	Zürich	668	1,729	1,242,488
TOTAL		15,940	41,284	7,317,873[4]

Demography

Population (2004): 7,392,000.
Density (2004): persons per sq mi 463.7, persons per sq km 179.1.
Urban-rural (2002): urban 67.8%; rural 32.2%.
Sex distribution (2003[2]): male 48.90%; female 51.10%.
Age breakdown (2003[2]): under 15, 16.9%; 15–29, 18.0%; 30–44, 24.2%; 45–59, 20.2%; 60–74, 13.3%; 75 and over, 7.4%.
Population projection: (2010) 7,563,000; (2020) 7,689,000.
National composition (2001[2]): Swiss 80.2%; Yugoslav 4.8%; Italian 4.5%; Portuguese 1.9%; German 1.5%; Spanish 1.2%; other 5.9%.
Religious affiliation (2000): Roman Catholic 41.8%; Protestant 35.2%; Muslim 4.3%; Orthodox 1.8%; Jewish 0.2%; nonreligious 11.1%; other 5.6%.
Major urban agglomerations (2003[2]): Zürich 978,300; Geneva 476,100; Basel 403,800; Bern 321,600; Lausanne 294,500; Luzern 185,700.

Vital statistics

Birth rate per 1,000 population (2003): 9.8 (world avg. 21.3); legitimate 87.6%; illegitimate 12.4%.
Death rate per 1,000 population (2003): 8.6 (world avg. 9.1).
Natural increase rate per 1,000 population (2003): 1.2 (world avg. 12.2).
Total fertility rate (avg. births per childbearing woman; 2002): 1.4.
Marriage rate per 1,000 population (2003): 5.5.
Divorce rate per 1,000 population (2003): 2.2.
Life expectancy at birth (2003): male 77.7 years; female 83.0 years.
Major causes of death per 100,000 population (1998): diseases of the circulatory system 357.2; malignant neoplasms (cancers) 212.2; diseases of the respiratory system 63.8; accidents, suicide, violence 50.0.

National economy

Budget (2002)[5]. Revenue: Sw F 130,595,000,000 (1999; taxes on income and profits 51.1%, taxes on goods and services 20.1%, property taxes 1.5%). Expenditures: Sw F 132,989,000,000 (1999; social security 19.4%, education 18.4%, economic affairs 14.0%, health 12.6%, interest 8.4%, defense 4.5%).
National debt (end of year; 2002): Sw F 122,366,000,000.
Tourism (2002): receipts from visitors U.S.$7,628,000,000; expenditures by nationals abroad U.S.$6,427,000,000.
Production (metric tons except as noted). Agriculture, forestry, fishing (2002): sugar beets 1,100,000, cow's milk (2001) 626,000, wheat 584,000, potatoes 515,000, barley 265,800, apples 170,000, grapes 153,000; livestock (number of live animals) 1,593,000 cattle, 1,536,000 pigs; roundwood (2002) 4,344,000 cu m; fish catch (2001) 2,850. Mining (2003): salt 300,000.[6] Manufacturing (value added in U.S.$'000,000; 2001): chemicals and chemical products 7,363; nonelectrical machinery 7,067; professional and scientific equipment 6,233; fabricated metal products 5,034; food products 3,572. Energy production (consumption): electricity (kW-hr; 2002) 65,011,000,000 (60,503,000,000); coal (metric tons; 2000) none (156,000); crude petroleum (barrels; 2000) none (33,900,000); petroleum products (metric tons; 2000) 4,861,000 (10,181,000); natural gas (cu m; 2000) negligible (2,971,000,000).
Gross national product (2003): U.S.$292,892,000,000 (U.S.$39,880 per capita).

Structure of gross domestic product and labour force

	2001[7] in value Sw F '000,000	2001[7] % of total value	2002 labour force	2002 % of labour force
Agriculture	7,142	2.0	176,000	4.2
Manufacturing	72,471	20.8	716,000	17.1
Mining	636	0.2	6,000	0.1
Public utilities	8,542	2.4	22,000	0.5
Construction	20,192	5.8	308,000	7.4
Transp. and commun.	26,545	7.6	257,000	6.2
Trade, restaurants	50,911	14.6	922,000	22.1
Finance, insurance	87,521	25.1	660,000	15.8
Pub. admin., defense	45,619	13.1	157,000	3.8
Services	25,776	7.4	953,000	22.8
Other	3,628[8]	1.0[8]		
TOTAL	348,983	100.0	4,177,000[9]	100.0

Population economically active (2002): total 4,177,000[9]; activity rate of total population 56.2% (participation rates: ages 15 and over, 68.7%; female 44.5%; unemployed 2.5%).

Price and earnings indexes (2000 = 100)

	1997	1998	1999	2000	2001	2002	2003
Consumer price index	97.7	97.7	98.5	100.0	101.0	101.6	102.3
Annual earnings index	99.4	99.4	99.6	100.0	102.4	...	...

Household income and expenditure (2000). Average household size 2.4; average gross income per household Sw F 104,352 (U.S.$64,400); sources of income (2000): work 72.4%, transfers 22.3%; expenditure (2001): housing and energy 27.5%, food and nonalcoholic beverages 13.5%, transportation 11.0%, recreation 10.5%, hotels and cafes 10.0%.
Land use as % of total land area (2000): in temporary crops 10.4%, in permanent crops 0.6%, in pasture 28.9%; overall forest area 30.3%.

Foreign trade[10]

Balance of trade (current prices)

	1998	1999	2000	2001	2002	2003
Sw F '000,000	+2,247	+1,030	−2,000	+1,005	+7,255	+6,900
% of total	1.0%	0.5%	0.8%	0.6%	2.9%	2.7%

Imports (2002): Sw F 123,125,000,000 (chemical products 22.1%, machinery 21.1%, vehicles 10.4%, food products 8.0%). *Major import sources* (2003): Germany 33.3%; Italy 11.1%; France 11.1%; U.S. 4.4%; U.K. 4.0%.
Exports (2002): Sw F 130,380,000,000 (chemicals and chemical products 34.4%, machinery 24.3%, precision instruments, watches, jewelry 17.3%, fabricated metals 7.5%). *Major export destinations* (2003): Germany 21.2%; U.S. 10.6%; France 8.8%; Italy 8.4%; U.K. 4.8%; Japan 3.9%.

Transport and communications

Transport. Railroads: length (2000) 3,145 mi, 5,062 km; passenger-km 14,665,000,000; metric ton-km cargo 9,112,000,000. Roads (2002): total length 44,237 mi, 71,192 km. Vehicles (2003): passenger cars 3,753,890; trucks and buses 292,329. Air transport (2003)[11]: passenger-km 24,083,000,000; metric ton-km cargo 1,305,000,000; airports (1996) with scheduled flights 5.

Communications

Medium	date	unit	number	units per 1,000 persons
Daily newspapers	2000	circulation	2,650,000	369
Radio	2000	receivers	7,200,000	1,002
Television	2000	receivers	3,940,000	548
Telephones	2002	main lines	5,419,000	744
Cellular telephones	2003	subscribers	6,172,000	843
Personal computers	2002	units	5,160,000	709
Internet	2002	users	2,556,000	351

Education and health

Educational attainment (2000). Percentage of resident Swiss and resident alien population age 25–64 having: compulsory education 19.0%; secondary 56.8%; higher 24.2%.
Health (2002): physicians 25,921 (1 per 281 persons); hospital beds (2001) 44,316 (1 per 163 persons); infant mortality rate per 1,000 live births 4.5.
Food (2001): daily per capita caloric intake 3,440 (vegetable products 66%, animal products 34%); 129% of FAO recommended minimum.

Military

Total active duty personnel (2003): 3,300[12]. *Military expenditure as percentage of GNP* (1999): 1.2% (world 2.4%); per capita expenditure U.S.$469.

[1]Long-form name in Romansh is Confederaziun Svizra. [2]January 1. [3]Demicanton; functions as a full canton. [4]Includes 1,484,800 resident aliens. [5]Consolidated central government. [6]Cut and polished diamond exports (1998): U.S.$1,340,000,000. [7]1990 prices. [8]Import duties less imputed bank charges. [9]Includes 1,058,000 foreign workers. [10]Imports c.i.f.; exports f.o.b. [11]Swiss airlines only. [12]Excludes 351,000 reservists.

Internet resources for further information:
- **Embassy of Switzerland (Washington, D.C.) http://www.swissemb.org**
- **Swiss Federal Statistical Office http://www.statistik.admin.ch**

Syria

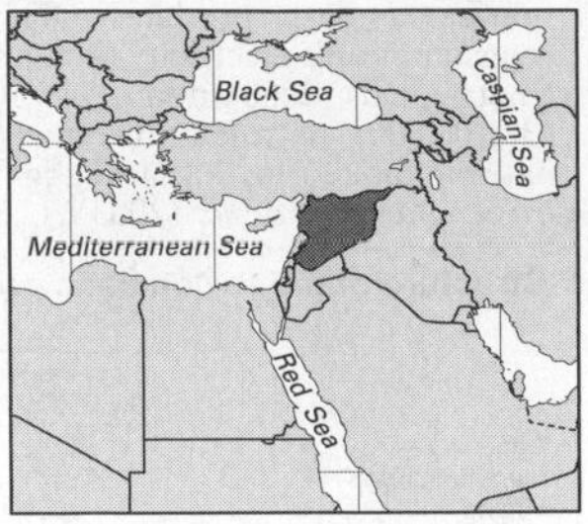

Official name: Al-Jumhūrīyah al-ʿArabīyah as-Sūrīyah (Syrian Arab Republic).
Form of government: unitary multiparty republic with one legislative house (People's Council [250[1]]).
Head of state and government: President.
Capital: Damascus.
Official language: Arabic.
Official religion: none[2].
Monetary unit: 1 Syrian pound (LS) = 100 piastres; valuation (Sept. 1, 2004) 1 U.S.$ = LS 51.69; 1 £ = LS 92.99.

Area and population

		area		population
Governorates	Capitals	sq mi	sq km	2002 estimate
Darʿā	Darʿā	1,440	3,730	780,000
Dayr az-Zawr	Dayr az-Zawr	12,765	33,060	919,000
Dimashq	Damascus	6,962	18,032	2,235,000
Ḥalab	Aleppo	7,143	18,500	3,719,000
Ḥamāh	Ḥamāh	3,430	8,883	1,335,000
Al-Ḥasakah	Al-Ḥasakah	9,009	23,334	1,265,000
Ḥimṣ	Homs (Ḥimṣ)	16,302	42,223	1,490,000
Idlib	Idlib	2,354	6,097	1,120,000
Al-Lādhiqīyah	Latakia	887	2,297	876,000
Al-Qunayṭirah	Al-Qunayṭirah (abandoned)	719[3]	1,861[3]	66,000
Ar-Raqqah	Ar-Raqqah	7,574	19,616	691,000
As-Suwaydāʾ	As-Suwaydāʾ	2,143	5,550	307,000
Ṭarṭūs	Ṭarṭūs	730	1,892	674,000
Municipality				
Damascus	—	41	105	1,653,000
TOTAL		71,498[3, 4]	185,180[3]	17,130,000

Demography

Population (2004): 18,017,000.
Density (2004): persons per sq mi 252.0, persons per sq km 97.3.
Urban-rural (2001): urban 51.8%; rural 48.2%.
Sex distribution (2001): male 51.15%; female 48.85%.
Age breakdown (2001): under 15, 40.4%; 15–29, 30.1%; 30–44, 15.6%; 45–59, 8.8%; 60 and over, 5.1%.
Population projection: (2010) 20,606,000; (2020) 24,676,000.
Doubling time: 28 years.
Ethnic composition (2000): Syrian Arab 74.9%; Bedouin Arab 7.4%; Kurd 7.3%; Palestinian Arab 3.9%; Armenian 2.7%; other 3.8%.
Religious affiliation (1992): Muslim 86.0%, of which Sunnī 74.0%, ʿAlawite (Shīʿī) 12.0%; Christian 5.5%; Druze 3.0%; other 5.5%.
Major cities: Aleppo (2000) 2,229,000[5]; Damascus (2001) 2,195,000[5]; Homs (Ḥimṣ) (2000) 811,000[5]; Latakia (1994) 306,535; Ḥamāh (1994) 229,000.

Vital statistics

Birth rate per 1,000 population (2003): 29.5 (world avg. 21.3).
Death rate per 1,000 population (2003): 5.0 (world avg. 9.1).
Natural increase rate per 1,000 population (2003): 24.5 (world avg. 12.2).
Total fertility rate (avg. births per childbearing woman; 2003): 3.7.
Marriage rate per 1,000 population (2000)[6]: 8.6.
Divorce rate per 1,000 population (2000)[6]: 0.7.
Life expectancy at birth (2003): male 68.2 years; female 70.7 years.
Major causes of death per 100,000 population (1989): n.a.; however, the leading causes of mortality among the total population were diseases of the circulatory system 39.6%, injuries and poisoning 9.1%, diseases of the nervous system 7.4%, diseases of the respiratory system 7.4%.

National economy

Budget (2000). Revenue: LS 275,400,000,000 (taxes 31.2%, revenue from loans 13.4%, transit duties 8.0%, other 47.4%). Expenditures: LS 275,400,000,000 (current expenditures 52.1%, capital [development] expenditures 47.9%).
Public debt (external, outstanding; 2002): U.S.$15,849,000,000.
Gross national product (2003): U.S.$20,211,000,000 (U.S.$1,160 per capita).

Structure of gross domestic product and labour force

	2000			
	in value LS '000,000	% of total value	labour force	% of labour force
Agriculture	229,452	25.6	1,430,000	29.0
Mining / Manufacturing / Public utilities	267,568	29.8	585,000	11.8
Construction	28,795	3.2	554,000	11.2
Transp. and commun.	113,615	12.7	237,000	4.8
Trade	134,239	15.0	648,000	13.1
Finance	32,402	3.6		
Pub. admin.	68,982	7.7	1,014,000	20.5
Services	21,581	2.4		
Other	...	...	469,000[7]	9.5[7]
TOTAL	896,634	100.0	4,937,000	100.0[4]

Production (metric tons except as noted). Agriculture, forestry, fishing (2002): wheat 4,755,000, sugar beets 1,481,000, olives 999,000, seed cotton 802,000, tomatoes 546,000, potatoes 515,000, watermelons 480,000, oranges 427,000, grapes 369,000, apples 216,000, eggplants 120,000; livestock (number of live animals) 13,497,000 sheep, 932,000 goats, 867,000 cattle; roundwood (2001) 50,400 cu m; fish catch (2001) 14,171. Mining and quarrying (2001): phosphate rock 2,043,000; gypsum 345,000; salt 106,000. Manufacturing (2000): cement 4,631,000; fertilizers 453,000; cottonseed cake 288,000; soap 88,863; olive oil 80,000; glass and pottery products 59,862; vegetable oil 45,087; television receivers 169,000 units; refrigerators 130,000 units. Energy production (consumption): electricity (kW-hr; 2000) 22,626,000,000 (23,946,000,000); coal, none (none); crude petroleum (barrels; 2002) 191,900,000 ([2000] 88,342,000); petroleum products (metric tons; 2000) 11,351,000 (11,020,000); natural gas (cu m; 2001) 5,833,000,000 (5,833,000,000).
Population economically active (2000): total 4,937,000; activity rate of total population 30.3% (participation rates: ages 15 and over, 50.9%; female 19.8%; unemployed 9.5%).

Price and earnings indexes (2000 = 100)

	1996	1997	1998	1999	2000	2001	2002
Consumer price index	...	108.9	108.0	104.0	100.0	103.0	104.0
Earnings index[8]	84.0	85.7	90.7	91.8	100.0	...	...

Average household size (2000): 6.0; income per household: n.a.; sources of income: n.a.; expenditure: n.a.
Tourism (2002): receipts U.S.$1,366,000,000; expenditures (2001) U.S.$610,000,000.
Land use as % of total land area (2000): in temporary crops 24.7%, in permanent crops 4.4%, in pasture 45.5%; overall forest area 2.5%.

Foreign trade[9]

Balance of trade (current prices)

	1996	1997	1998	1999	2000	2001
U.S.$'000,000	+82	+129	–890	–222	+819	+492
% of total	1.0%	1.7%	13.7%	3.2%	9.7%	5.0%

Imports (2000): U.S.$3,815,000,000 (food 14.6%, of which cereals 4.9%; chemicals and chemical products 12.9%; nonelectrical machinery and equipment 10.9%; iron and steel 10.7%; textile yarn 7.5%). *Major import sources:* Germany 6.8%; U.S. 6.8%; Italy 6.2%; Ukraine 6.2%; China 5.3%; Turkey 5.0%; South Korea 5.0%.
Exports (2000): U.S.$4,634,000,000 (crude petroleum 69.1%; refined petroleum 7.0%; raw cotton 4.1%; vegetables 2.9%; apparel and clothing accessories 2.8%). *Major export destinations:* Italy 32.0%; France 22.5%; Turkey 10.4%; Saudi Arabia 5.9%; Lebanon 4.1%.

Transport and communications

Transport. Railroads (2001)[10]: route length 2,676 km; passenger-km 304,000,000; metric ton-km cargo 1,491,000,000. Roads (2000): total length 44,575 km (paved 21%). Vehicles (2000): passenger cars 138,823; trucks and buses (1998) 282,664. Air transport (2001): passenger-km 1,626,950; metric ton-km cargo 15,357,000; airports with scheduled flights 5.

Communications

Medium	date	unit	number	units per 1,000 persons
Daily newspapers	2000	circulation	326,000	20
Radio	2000	receivers	4,500,000	276
Television	2002	receivers	3,094,000	182
Telephones	2002	main lines	2,099,300	123
Cellular telephones	2002	units	400,000	24
Personal computers	2002	units	330,000	19
Internet	2002	users	220,000	13

Education and health

Educational attainment: n.a. *Literacy* (2000): percentage of population age 15 and over literate 74.4%; males literate 88.3%; females literate 60.5%.

Education (2000)

	schools	teachers	students	student/ teacher ratio
Primary (age 6–11)	11,482	121,880	2,774,922	22.8
Secondary (age 12–18)	2,911	63,889	955,290	15.0
Voc., teacher tr.	587	15,103	134,473	8.9
Higher[11]	4	5,664	155,137	27.4

Health (2003): physicians 25,147 (1 per 699 persons); hospital beds 26,202 (1 per 671 persons); infant mortality rate (2003) 31.7.
Food (2001): daily per capita caloric intake 3,038 (vegetable products 88%, animal products 12%); 123% of FAO recommended minimum.

Military

Total active duty personnel (2003): 319,000 (army 67.4%, navy 1.3%, air force 12.5%, air defense 18.8%); troops stationed in Lebanon (October 2003) 20,000. *Military expenditure as percentage of GNP* (1999): 7.0% (world 2.4%); per capita expenditure U.S.$280.

[1]Elections held March 2003. [2]Islam is required to be the religion of the head of state and is the basis of the legal system. [3]Includes territory in the Golan Heights recognized internationally as part of Syria. [4]Detail does not add to total given because of rounding. [5]Population of urban agglomeration. [6]Syrian Arabs only. [7]Unemployed. [8]Manufacturing sector only. [9]Imports c.i.f.; exports f.o.b. [10]Excludes length of Syrian part of railway opened in August 2000 linking Aleppo, Syria, and Mosul, Iraq. [11]University-level institutions only.

Internet resources for further information:
- **Ministry of Economy and Foreign Trade**
http://www.syrecon.org/right_frame1.html

Taiwan

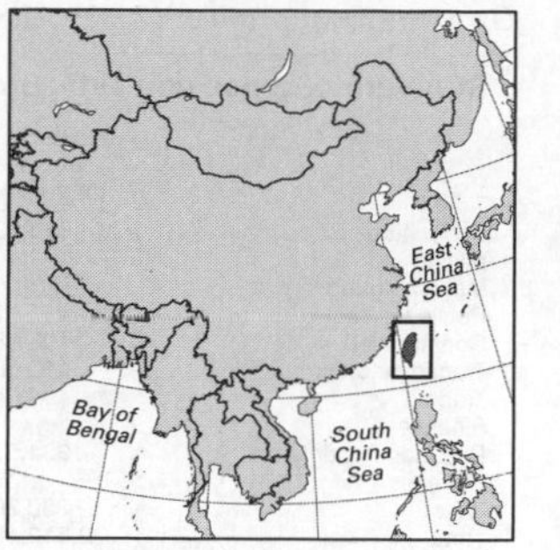

Official name: Chung-hua Min-kuo (Republic of China).
Form of government: multiparty republic with a Legislature (Legislative Yuan [225])[1].
Chief of state: President.
Head of government: Premier.
Capital: Taipei.
Official language: Mandarin Chinese.
Official religion: none.
Monetary unit: 1 New Taiwan dollar (NT$) = 100 cents; valuation (Sept. 1, 2004) 1 U.S.$ = NT$34.04; 1 £ = NT$61.24.

Area and population

Taiwan area Counties	area sq km	population 2003 estimate	Municipalities	area sq km	population 2003 estimate
Chang-hua	1,074	1,316,256	Chia-i	60	268,263
Chia-i	1,902	561,747	Chi-lung	133	391,657
Hsin-chu	1,428	453,906	Hsin-chu	104	379,938
Hua-lien	4,629	351,631	Kao-hsiung	154	1,508,917
I-lan	2,137	463,954	T'ai-chung	163	999,476
Kao-hsiung	2,793	1,235,203	T'ai-nan	176	746,287
Miao-li	1,820	560,581	Taipei	272	2,638,065
Nan-t'ou	4,106	541,222			
P'eng-hu	127	92,366	**Non-Taiwan area Counties**		
P'ing-tung	2,776	905,660	Kinmen (Quemoy)	}	
T'ai-chung	2,051	1,513,537	Lienchiang (Matsu)	179	68,274
T'ai-nan	2,016	1,106,919			
T'ai-pei	2,052	3,651,248			
T'ai-tung	3,515	243,581			
T'ao-yüan	1,221	1,799,061	TOTAL	36,179[2]	22,540,155
Yün-lin	1,291	742,406			

Demography

Population (2004)[3]: 22,640,000.
Density (2004)[2, 3]: persons per sq mi 1,620.4, persons per sq km 625.6.
Urban-rural (1991)[4]: urban 74.7%; rural 25.3%.
Sex distribution (2003)[3]: male 50.98%; female 49.02%.
Age breakdown (2002)[3]: under 15, 20.8%; 15–29, 24.9%; 30–44, 25.3%; 45–59, 16.7%; 60–74, 9.1%; 75 and over, 3.2%.
Population projection: (2010) 23,338,000; (2020) 24,140,000.
Ethnic composition (1997): Han Chinese, Chinese mainland minorities, and others 98.2%; indigenous tribal peoples 1.8%, of which Ami 0.6%.
Religious affiliation (1997)[5, 6]: Buddhism 22.4%; Taoism 20.7%; I-kuan Tao 4.3%; Protestant 1.6%; Roman Catholic 1.4%; other Christian 0.3%; Muslim 0.2%; Bahāʾī 0.1%; other (mostly Christian folk-religionists) 49.0%.
Major cities (2003): Taipei 2,638,065; Kao-hsiung 1,508,917; T'ai-chung 999,476; T'ai-nan 746,287; Chi-lung 391,657; Chung-ho (1998) 388,174.

Vital statistics

Birth rate per 1,000 population (2003): 10.1 (world avg. 21.3).
Death rate per 1,000 population (2003): 5.8 (world avg. 9.1).
Natural increase rate per 1,000 population (2003): 4.3 (world avg. 12.2).
Total fertility rate (avg. births per childbearing woman; 2003): 1.2.
Marriage rate per 1,000 population (2003): 7.6.
Divorce rate per 1,000 population (2003): 2.9.
Life expectancy at birth (2003): male 73.4 years; female 79.1 years.
Major causes of death per 100,000 population (2001)[4]: malignant neoplasms 147.6; cerebrovascular diseases 58.8; heart disease 49.2; accidents and suicide 42.6; diabetes 40.8; liver diseases 23.5; kidney diseases 18.2; pneumonia 16.8.

National economy

Budget (1999[7]). Revenue: NT$3,391,948,000,000 (income taxes 18.0%, business tax 9.1%, commodity tax 6.5%, land tax 6.4%, customs duties 4.6%). Expenditures: NT$3,371,702,000,000 (administration and defense 24.5%, education 19.4%).
Population economically active (May 2003): total 10,022,000; activity rate of total population 44.4% (participation rates: over age 15 [December 2002], c. 57%; female [May 2003] 40.4%; unemployed [May 2003] 5.0%).

Price and earnings indexes (2000 = 100)

	1997	1998	1999	2000	2001	2002	2003
Consumer price index	97.0	98.6	98.8	100.0	100.0	99.8	99.5
Monthly earnings index[8]	90.8	93.5	96.9	100.0	98.7	98.7	101.3

Production (metric tons except as noted). Agriculture, forestry, fishing (2000): sugarcane 2,894,000, rice 1,559,000, citrus fruits 440,382, pineapples 357,535, bananas 198,454, sweet potatoes 198,000; livestock (number of live animals) 7,494,954 pigs, 202,491 goats, 161,700 cattle; timber 21,134 cu m; fish catch (2003) 1,498,983. Mining and quarrying (2000): marble 17,800,000. Manufacturing (2002): cement 19,228,026; steel ingots 18,240,256; paperboard 3,274,932; fertilizers (2000) 1,706,861; polyester filament 1,603,096; polyvinyl chloride plastics 1,483,947; telephones 4,722,353 units; televisions 1,014,755 units. Energy production (consumption): electricity (kW-hr; 2002) 165,901,000,000 (151,193,000,000); coal (metric tons; 2001)[9] (48,000,000); crude petroleum (barrels; 2002) 349,000 (360,000,000); natural gas (cu m; 2001) 918,000,000 (8,264,000,000).
Tourism (2002): receipts from visitors U.S.$4,584,000,000; expenditures by nationals abroad U.S.$6,956,000,000.

Gross national product (2002): U.S.$283,375,000,000 (U.S.$12,570 per capita).

Structure of gross domestic product and labour force[4]

	2002			
	in value NT$'000,000	% of total value	labour force[10]	% of labour force[10]
Agriculture	180,857	1.8	709,000	7.1
Mining	42,024	0.4	9,000	0.1
Manufacturing	2,505,856	25.7	2,563,000	25.7
Construction	252,950	2.6	725,000	7.3
Public utilities	219,975	2.3	35,000	0.3
Transp. and commun.	677,728	7.0	477,000	4.8
Trade	1,883,665	19.4	1,693,000	17.0
Finance	2,294,642	23.6	953,000	9.5
Pub. admin., defense	1,023,175	10.5	}	
Services	1,005,747	10.3	2,290,000	23.0
Other	–352,268[11]	–3.6[11]	515,000[12]	5.2[12]
TOTAL	9,734,351	100.0	9,969,000	100.0

Household income and expenditure (1999). Average household size (2003) 3.2; income per household NT$1,181,082 (U.S.$37,153); expenditure: food, beverages, and tobacco 25.1%, rent, fuel, and power 24.9%, education and recreation 13.0%, transportation 11.1%, health care 11.0%, clothing 4.1%.
Land use as % of total land area (2001): in temporary crops 16.1%, in permanent crops 6.6%, in pasture 0.3%; overall forest area 58.1%.

Foreign trade[13]

Balance of trade (current prices)

	1997	1998	1999	2000	2001	2002
U.S.$'000,000	+7,656	+5,917	+10,901	+8,310	+15,629	+18,050
% of total	3.2%	2.7%	4.7%	2.8%	6.8%	7.4%

Imports (2002): U.S.$112,591,000,000 (electronic machinery 28.5%, nonelectrical machinery 16.0%, minerals 11.2%, chemicals 10.1%, metals and metal products 8.2%, precision instruments, clocks, watches, and musical instruments 5.8%). *Major import sources:* Japan 24.2%; U.S. 16.1%; South Korea 6.8%; Germany 3.9%; Malaysia 3.7%.
Exports (2002): U.S.$130,641,000,000 (nonelectrical machinery, electrical machinery, and electronics 57.4%, textile products 10.0%, plastic articles 5.9%, transportation equipment 3.7%). *Major export destinations:* Hong Kong 23.6%; U.S. 20.5%; Japan 9.2%; Singapore 3.2%; Germany 2.9%.

Transport and communications

Transport. Railroads (2002)[14]: route length 1,119 km; passenger-km 9,666,000,000, metric ton-km cargo 919,000,000. Roads (2002): total length 20,816 km[15] (paved, n.a.). Vehicles (2002): passenger cars 4,989,000; trucks and buses 882,000. Air transport (1998): passenger-km 39,218,000,000; metric ton-km cargo 4,129,300,000; airports (1996) 13.

Communications

Medium	date	unit	number	units per 1,000 persons
Radio	1996	receivers	8,620,000	402
Television	1999	receivers	9,200,000	418
Telephones	2003	main lines	13,355,000	590
Cellular telephones	2003	subscribers	25,089,600	1,108
Personal computers	2002	units	8,887,000	396
Internet	2003	users	8,830,000	390

Education and health

Educational attainment (1999). Percentage of population age 25 and over having: no formal schooling 7.0%; less than complete primary education 6.3%; primary 21.3%; incomplete secondary 25.7%; secondary 21.8%; some college 10.4%; higher 7.5%. *Literacy* (1999): population age 15 and over literate 16,414,896 (94.6%); males 8,641,549 (97.6%); females 7,773,347 (91.4%).

Education (2002–03)

	schools	teachers	students	student/teacher ratio
Primary (age 6–12)	2,627	104,300	1,918,034	18.4
Secondary (age 13–18) } Vocational	1,188	97,710	1,679,959	17.2
Higher	154	46,042	1,240,330	26.9

Health (2001): physicians 30,562 (1 per 731 persons); hospital beds 127,676 (1 per 175 persons); infant mortality rate per 1,000 live births (2003) 5.3.

Military

Total active duty personnel (2002): 290,000 (army 69.0%, navy 15.5%, air force 15.5%). *Military expenditure as percentage of GNP* (1999): 5.2% (world 2.4%); per capita expenditure U.S.$690.

[1]The National Assembly became a nonstanding body with limited specialized authority per April 2000 amendment; the Legislature is the formal lawmaking body. [2]Total area per more recent survey is 36,188 sq km (13,972 sq mi). [3]Includes Quemoy and Matsu groups. [4]For Taiwan area only, excluding Quemoy and Matsu groups. [5]Formal subscribers to religious beliefs. [6]Almost all Taiwanese adults engage in religious practices stemming from one or a combination of traditional folk religions. [7]General government. [8]In manufacturing. [9]Coal production ceased in 2000. [10]Civilian persons only. [11]Import duties less imputed bank service charge. [12]Unemployed. [13]Imports c.i.f.; exports f.o.b. [14]Taiwan Railway Administration only. [15]Excludes urban.

Internet resources for further information:

- **Directorate-General of Budget, Accounting and Statistics (Taiwan) http://www.dgbasey.gov.tw/english/dgbas_e0.htm**
- **Taiwan Yearbook 2004 http://www.stat.gov.tw/bs2/2004YearBook.pdf**

Tajikistan

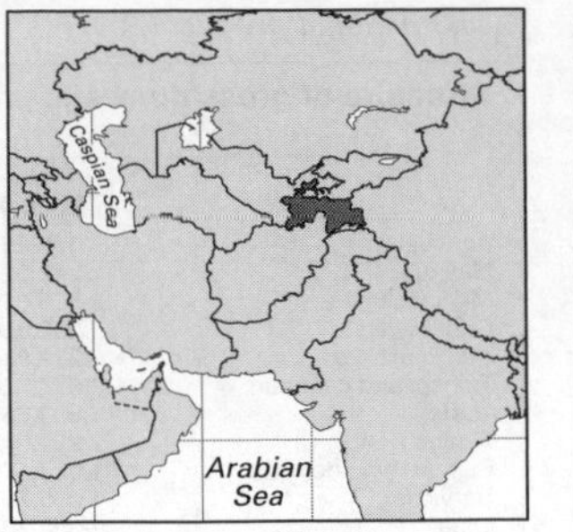

Official name: Jumhurii Tojikiston (Republic of Tajikistan).
Form of government: parliamentary republic with two legislative houses (National Assembly [33[1]]; Assembly of Representatives [63]).
Chief of state: President.
Head of government: Prime Minister.
Capital: Dushanbe.
Official language: Tajik (Tojik).
Official religion: none.
Monetary unit: 1 somoni[2] = 100 dinars; valuation (July 31, 2004) 1 U.S.$ = 3.01 somoni; 1 £ = 5.48 somoni.

Area and population

		area		population
Oblasts	**Capitals**	sq mi	sq km	2000 census
Khatlon (Qŭrghonteppa)	Qŭrghonteppa	9,500	24,600	2,151,000
Sughd	Khujand	10,100	26,100	1,870,000
Autonomous oblast				
Kŭhistoni Badakhshon (Gorno-Badakhshan)	Khorugh	24,600	63,700	206,000
City				
Dushanbe	—	100	300	562,000
Other[3]	—	11,000	28,400	1,338,000
TOTAL		55,300[4]	143,100[4]	6,127,000

Demography

Population (2004): 6,606,000.
Density (2004): persons per sq mi 119.5, persons per sq km 46.2.
Urban-rural (2000): urban 26.6%; rural 73.4%.
Sex distribution (2000): male 50.30%; female 49.70%.
Age breakdown (2000): under 15, 39.4%; 15–29, 27.7%; 30–44, 18.4%; 45–59, 7.6%; 60–74, 5.4%; 75 and over, 1.5%.
Population projection: (2010) 7,046,000; (2020) 8,105,000.
Doubling time: 39 years.
Ethnic composition (2000): Tajik 80.0%; Uzbek 15.3%; Russian 1.1%; Tatar 0.3%; other 3.3%.
Religious affiliation (1995): Sunnī Muslim 80.0%; Shīʿī Muslim 5.0%; Russian Orthodox 1.5%; Jewish 0.1%; other (mostly nonreligious) 13.4%.
Major cities (2002): Dushanbe 575,900; Khujand 147,400; Kulyab 79,500; Kurgan-Tyube 61,200; Ura-Tyube 51,700.

Vital statistics

Birth rate per 1,000 population (2003): 24.3 (world avg. 21.3); (1994) legitimate 90.8%; illegitimate 9.2%.
Death rate per 1,000 population (2003): 6.0 (world avg. 9.1).
Natural increase rate per 1,000 population (2003): 18.3 (world avg. 12.2).
Total fertility rate (avg. births per childbearing woman; 2003): 3.0.
Marriage rate per 1,000 population (2001): 4.6.
Divorce rate per 1,000 population (1994): 0.8.
Life expectancy at birth (2003): male 61.4 years; female 67.5 years.
Major causes of death per 100,000 population (1999): diseases of the circulatory system 211.5; diseases of the respiratory system 56.3; infectious and parasitic diseases 31.6; violence, poisoning, and accidents 28.3; malignant neoplasms (cancers) 27.9; diseases of the digestive system 19.0.

National economy

Budget (2001). Revenue: 342,316,000 somoni (tax revenue 91.6%, of which value-added tax 25.1%, taxes on aluminum and cotton 18.3%, customs duties 15.1%, income and profit taxes 13.8%, excise taxes 4.5%; nontax revenue 8.4%). Expenditures: 338,418,000 somoni (current expenditures 77.5%, of which state authorities 19.7%, education 18.9%, state bodies and administration 11.7%, defense 8.7%, health 7.3%, law enforcement 4.1%, debt payment 4.1%; capital expenditures 22.5%).
Production (metric tons except as noted). Agriculture, forestry, fishing (2002): raw seed cotton 515,000, potatoes 400,000, wheat 361,000, tomatoes 170,000, grapes 100,000; livestock (number of live animals) 1,490,000 sheep, 1,091,000 cattle, 779,000 goats; roundwood, n.a.; fish catch (2001) 236. Mining and quarrying (2000): antimony (metal content) 2,000; gold 2,700 kg. Manufacturing (value of production in '000,000 somoni[5]; 2001): nonferrous metals 442,000[6]; food 138,000; textiles 104,000; grain mill products 51,000; basic chemicals 10,000. Energy production (consumption): electricity (kW-hr; 2001) 14,400,000,000 (13,500,000,000); coal (metric tons; 2001) 24,900 (122,000); crude petroleum (barrels; 2000) 132,000 (95,000); petroleum products (metric tons; 2000) none (753,000); natural gas (cu m; 2000) 38,594,000 (748,500,000).
Tourism (2002): receipts from visitors U.S.$2,000,000; expenditures by nationals abroad U.S.$2,000,000.
Population economically active (2002): total 1,829,000; activity rate of total population 29.6% (participation rates: ages 15–59 [male], 15–54 [female] 55.1%; female [1996] 46.5%; unemployed 2.3%).

Price and earnings indexes (2000 = 100)

	1997	1998	1999	2000	2001	2002	2003
Consumer price index	44.8	64.0	80.6	100.0	137.0	150.7	176.3
Monthly earnings index	31.9	58.9	74.6	100.0	150.9	...	...

Gross national product (2003): U.S.$1,221,000,000 (U.S.$190 per capita).

Structure of gross domestic product and labour force

	2001			
	in value '000 somoni	% of total value	labour force	% of labour force
Agriculture	670,027	26.7	1,167,000	62.3
Mining; Manufacturing	566,822	22.6	131,000	7.0
Public utilities	...	...	...	...
Construction	103,682	4.1	31,000	1.7
Transp. and commun.	112,588	4.5	43,000	2.3
Trade	494,642	19.7	140,000	7.5
Finance; Pub. admin., defense; Services	334,034	13.3	26,000	1.4
Services			291,000	15.5
Other	230,305[7]	9.2[7]	43,000[8]	2.3[8]
TOTAL	2,512,100	100.0[9]	1,872,000	100.0

Public debt (external, outstanding; 2002): U.S.$912,000,000.
Land use as % of total land area (2000): in temporary crops 6.6%, in permanent crops 0.9%, in pasture 24.9%; overall forest area 2.8%.
Household income and expenditure. Average household size (2000) 5.9; (1995) income per household 18,744 Tajik rubles[2] (U.S.$114); sources of income (1995): wages and salaries 34.5%, self-employment 34.0%, borrowing 2.4%, pension 2.0%, other 27.1%; expenditure: food 81.5%, clothing 10.2%, transport 2.5%, fuel 2.1%, other 3.7%.

Foreign trade

Balance of trade (current prices)

	1997	1998	1999	2000	2001	2002
U.S.$'000,000	–61	–139	–27	–46	–121	–124
% of total	3.9%	10.6%	2.0%	2.8%	12.4%	8.1%

Imports (2001): U.S.$773,000,000 (alumina 23.9%, petroleum products and natural gas 12.9%, electricity 12.7%, grain and flour 8.0%). *Major import sources* (2000): Uzbekistan 28.8%; Russia 16.1%; Ukraine 13.1%; Kazakhstan 12.8%; Azerbaijan 9.8%.
Exports (2001): U.S.$652,000,000 (aluminum 61.0%, electricity 12.1%, cotton fibre 10.9%). *Major export destinations* (2000): Russia 37.4%; The Netherlands 25.7%; Uzbekistan 14.1%; Switzerland 10.4%; Italy 2.8%.

Transport and communications

Transport. Railroads (2001): length 299 mi, 482 km; passenger-mi 20,000,000, passenger-km 32,000,000; short ton-mi cargo 855,000,000, metric ton-km cargo 1,248,000,000. Roads (1996): total length 8,500 mi, 13,747 km (paved 83%). Vehicles (1996): passenger cars 680,000; trucks and buses 8,190. Air transport (2001)[10]: passenger-mi 376,000,000, passenger-km 605,000,000; short ton-mi cargo 3,316,000, metric ton-km cargo 4,841,000; airports (2002) 2.

Communications

Medium	date	unit	number	units per 1,000 persons
Daily newspapers	2000	circulation	123,000	20
Radio	2000	receivers	870,000	141
Television	2000	receivers	2,010,000	326
Telephones	2003	main lines	242,100	37
Cellular phones	2003	subscribers	47,600	7.3
Personal computers	...	units	...	...
Internet	2003	users	4,100	0.6

Education and health

Educational attainment (1989). Percentage of population age 25 and over having: primary education or no formal schooling 16.3%; some secondary 21.1%; completed secondary and some postsecondary 55.1%; higher 7.5%. *Literacy* (2001): percentage of total population age 15 and over literate 99.3%; males literate 98.9%; females literate 99.6%.

Education (2001–02)

	schools	teachers	students	student/teacher ratio
Primary (age 6–13)	660	100,200	1,520,000	15.2
Secondary (age 14–17)[11]	2,861			
Voc., teacher tr.	55	...	29,842[12]	...
Higher	31	6,100	84,400	13.8

Health (2002): physicians 13,393 (1 per 472 persons); hospital beds 40,387 (1 per 157 persons); infant mortality rate per 1,000 live births (2003) 50.0.
Food (2001): daily per capita caloric intake 1,662 (vegetable products 92%, animal products 8%); 65% of FAO recommended minimum requirement.

Military

Total active duty personnel (2003): 6,000 (army 100%); Russian troops (2004) 20,000 including 9,000 along the Tajik-Afghan border; U.S. troops (2004) 3,000. *Military expenditure as percentage of GNP* (1999): 1.3% (world 2.4%); per capita expenditure U.S.$13.

[1]Eight members are appointed by the President. [2]The somoni (equal to 1,000 Tajik rubles) was introduced on Oct. 30, 2000. [3]No oblast-level administration. [4]Includes *c.* 400 sq mi (*c.* 1,035 sq km) ceded to China in May 2002. [5]At 1998 constant prices. [6]Aluminum production by weight in 2001 equaled 289,100 metric tons. [7]Indirect taxes. [8]Unemployed. [9]Detail does not add to total given because of rounding. [10]Tajikistan Airlines only. [11]Excludes special education. [12]1994–95.

Internet resources for further information:
- **Key Indicators of Developing Asian and Pacific Countries http://www.adb.org/Documents/Books/Key_Indicators/default.asp**

Tanzania

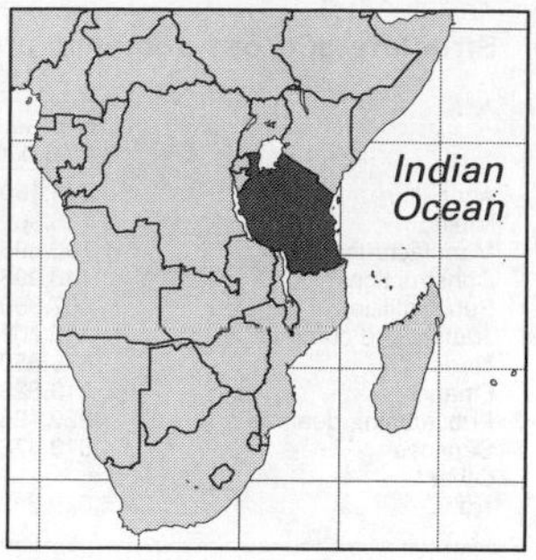

Official name: Jamhuri ya Muungano wa Tanzania (Swahili); United Republic of Tanzania (English).
Form of government: unitary multiparty republic with one legislative house (National Assembly [274]).
Head of state and government: President.
Capital: Dar es Salaam (acting)[1].
Official languages: Swahili; English.
Official religion: none.
Monetary unit: 1 Tanzania shilling (T Sh) = 100 cents; valuation (Sept. 1, 2004) 1 U.S.$ = T Sh 1,080; 1 £ = T Sh 1,942.

Area and population

Administrative regions	area sq km	population 2002 census
Mainland Tanzania (Tanganyika)		
Arusha	36,486	1,292,973
Dar es Salaam	1,393	2,497,940
Dodoma	41,311	1,698,996
Iringa	56,864	1,495,333
Kagera	28,388	2,033,888
Kigoma	37,037	1,679,109
Kilimanjaro	13,309	1,381,149
Lindi	66,046	791,306
Manyara	45,820	1,040,461
Mara	19,566	1,368,602
Mbeya	60,350	2,070,046
Morogoro	70,799	1,759,809
Mtwara	16,707	1,128,523
Mwanza	19,592	2,942,148
Pwani (Coast)	32,407	889,154
Rukwa	68,635	1,141,743
Ruvuma	63,498	1,117,166
Shinyanga	50,781	2,805,580
Singida	49,341	1,090,758
Tabora	76,151	1,717,908
Tanga	26,808	1,642,015
Autonomous territory		
Zanzibar and Pemba[2]		
Pemba	906	362,166
Zanzibar	1,554	622,459
TOTAL LAND AREA	883,749	
INLAND WATER	59,050	
TOTAL	942,799[3]	34,569,232

Demography

Population (2004): 35,782,000.
Density (2004)[4]: persons per sq mi 104.9, persons per sq km 40.5.
Urban-rural (2002): urban 23.0%; rural 77.0%.
Sex distribution (2002): male 48.92%; female 51.08%.
Age breakdown (2002): under 15, 44.3%; 15–29, 27.7%; 30–44, 15.3%; 45–59, 7.1%; 60–74, 4.1%; 75 and over, 1.5%.
Population projection: (2010) 40,176,000; (2020) 47,682,000.
Doubling time: 32 years.
Ethnolinguistic composition (2000): Sukuma 9.5%; Hehet and Bena 4.5%; Gogo 4.4%; Haya 4.2%; Nyamwezi 3.6%; Makonde 3.3%; Chagga 3.0%; Ha 2.9%; other 64.6%.
Religious affiliation (2000): Christian 46.9%; Muslim 31.8%; ethnoreligionist 16.1%.
Major urban areas (2002): Dar es Salaam 2,336,055; Arusha 270,485; Mbeya 230,318; Mwanza 209,806; Morogoro 206,868; Zanzibar 205,870.

Vital statistics

Birth rate per 1,000 population (2003): 39.5 (world avg. 21.3).
Death rate per 1,000 population (2003): 17.4 (world avg. 9.1).
Natural increase rate per 1,000 population (2003): 22.1 (world avg. 12.2).
Total fertility rate (avg. births per childbearing woman; 2003): 5.3.
Life expectancy at birth (2003): male 43.3 years; female 45.8 years.
Adult population (ages 15–49) *living with HIV* (2004[5]): 8.8% (world avg. 1.1%).

National economy

Budget (2003–04). Revenue: T Sh 1,447,500,000,000 (VAT 34.2%, income tax 24.9%, excise tax 15.0%, import duties 9.0%). Expenditures: T Sh 2,531,-500,000 (current expenditure 74.5%, of which wages 18.3%, education 17.7%, health 8.4%, interest payments on debt 4.8%; capital expenditure 25.5%).
Tourism (2002): receipts from visitors U.S.$694,000,000; expenditures by nationals abroad U.S.$337,000,000.
Land use as % of total land area (2000): in temporary crops 4.5%, in permanent crops 1.1%, in pasture 39.6%; overall forest area 43.9%.
Gross national product (2002)[6]: U.S.$10,201,000,000 (U.S.$290 per capita).

Structure of gross domestic product and labour force

	2003		2002	
	in value T Sh '000,000	% of total value	labour force	% of labour force
Agriculture	4,417,900	41.3	14,745,000	79.6
Mining	191,200	1.8	3,780,000	20.4
Manufacturing	711,000	6.6		
Construction	546,200	5.1		
Public utilities	157,000	1.5		
Transp. and commun.	454,000	4.2		
Trade	1,153,300	10.8		
Finance	564,300	5.3		
Pub. admin., defense	869,300	8.1		
Services	929,800	8.7		
Other	698,400[7]	6.5[7]		
TOTAL	10,692,400	100.0[8]	18,525,000	100.0

Public debt (external, outstanding; 2002): U.S.$6,201,000,000.
Production (metric tons except as noted). Agriculture (2002): cassava 6,880,000, corn (maize) 2,700,500, sweet potatoes 950,100, sorghum 650,000, rice 514,000, seed cotton 243,000, bananas 150,400, cashew nuts 121,900, coffee 58,100, tea 25,500, tobacco leaves 24,470; livestock (number of live animals) 17,700,000 cattle, 11,650,000 goats, 3,550,000 sheep; roundwood 23,438,758 cu m; fish catch (2001) 336,200. Mining and quarrying (2002): gold 37,000 kg; garnets 23,000 kg; tanzanites 4,800 kg; sapphires 4,200 kg; diamonds 213,491 carats. Manufacturing (value added in U.S.$'000,000; 1999): beverages 39; food products 33; tobacco products 28; paper and paper products 22; bricks, tiles, and cement 22. Energy production (consumption): electricity (kW-hr; 2000) 2,603,000,000 (2,548,000,000); coal (metric tons; 2000) 79,000 (79,000); crude petroleum (barrels; 2000) none (3,738,000); petroleum products (metric tons; 2000) 475,000 (1,170,000); natural gas, none (none).
Population economically active (2002): total 18,525,000; activity rate 53.8% (participation rates [1991]: over age 10, 87.8%; female [1991] 40.0%).

Price index (2000 = 100)

	1997	1998	1999	2000	2001	2002
Consumer price index	77.6	87.5	94.4	100.0	105.1	109.9

Household income and expenditure. Average household size (2002) 4.9; income per household: n.a.; sources of income: n.a.; expenditure (1994): food 64.2%, clothing 9.9%, housing 8.3%, energy 7.6%, transportation 4.1%.

Foreign trade[9]

Balance of trade (current prices)

	1997	1998	1999	2000	2001	2002
T Sh '000,000,000	–244	–516	–649	–537	–626	–547
% of total	20.9%	39.7%	44.1%	33.6%	31.5%	24.4%

Imports (2002): T Sh 1,601,000,000,000 (consumer goods 31.0%, of which food products 8.8%; machinery and apparatus 22.2%; transport equipment 13.2%; crude and refined petroleum 11.8%). *Major import sources:* South Africa 11.4%; Japan 8.4%; India 6.5%; Russia 6.1%; U.A.E. 5.9%; U.K. 5.7%; Kenya 5.7%.
Exports (2002): T Sh 846,000,000,000 (minerals [mostly gold, significantly diamonds and other gemstones] 42.4%; cashews 5.8%; tobacco 5.6%; coffee 4.0%; tea 3.4%; other [significantly fish products] 38.8%). *Major export destinations:* U.K. 18.5%; France 17.4%; Japan 11.0%; India 7.3%; The Netherlands 6.2%.

Transport and communications

Transport. Railroads (2001): length 3,690 km; passenger-km 471,000,000[10]; metric ton-km cargo 1,380,000,000[10]. Roads (1999): length 88,200 km (paved 4.2%). Vehicles (1999): passenger cars 33,900; trucks and buses 98,800. Air transport (2003)[11]: passenger-km 151,332,000; metric ton-km 1,796,000; airports (1999) with scheduled flights 11.

Communications

Medium	date	unit	number	units per 1,000 persons
Daily newspapers	2000	circulation	130,000	4.0
Radio	2000	receivers	9,130,000	281
Television	2000	receivers	650,000	20
Telephones	2003	main lines	149,100	4.2
Cellular telephones	2003	subscribers	891,200	25
Personal computers	2003	units	200,000	5.7
Internet	2003	users	250,000	7.1

Education and health

Educational attainment: n.a. *Literacy* (2001): percentage of population age 15 and over literate 76.0%; males 84.5%; females 67.9%.

Education (1998)[6]

	schools	teachers	students	student/ teacher ratio
Primary (age 7–13)	11,339	106,329	4,042,568	38.0
Secondary (age 14–19)	491[12]	11,691	226,903	19.4
Teacher training	40[12]	1,062	9,136	8.6
Higher	...	2,064	18,867	9.1

Health: physicians (1995) 1,277 (1 per 22,030 persons); hospital beds (1993) 26,820 (1 per 1,000 persons); infant mortality rate (2003) 103.7.
Food (2001): daily per capita caloric intake 1,997 (vegetable products 94%, animal products 6%); 86% of FAO recommended minimum requirement.

Military

Total active duty personnel (2003): 27,000 (army 85.2%, navy 3.7%, air force 11.1%). *Military expenditure as percentage of GNP* (1999): 1.4% (world 2.4%); per capita expenditure U.S.$4.

[1]Dodoma is the longtime planned capital. [2]Has local internal government structure; Zanzibar has 3 administrative regions, Pemba has 2. [3]A recent survey indicates a total area of 945,090 sq km (364,901 sq mi). [4]Based on land area only. [5]January 1. [6]Mainland Tanzania only. [7]Net taxes less imputed bank service charge. [8]Detail does not add to total given because of rounding. [9]Imports f.o.b. in balance of trade and c.i.f. in commodities and trading partners. [10]Tanzanian Railways only. [11]Air Tanzania only. [12]1994.

Internet resources for further information:
- **Bank of Tanzania http://www.bot-tz.org**

Thailand

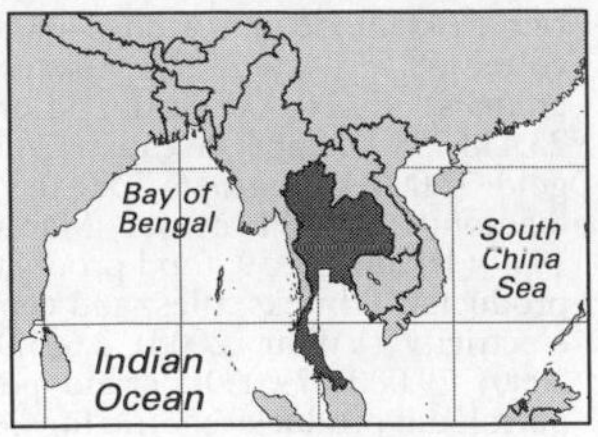

Official name: Muang Thai, or Prathet Thai (Kingdom of Thailand).
Form of government: constitutional monarchy with two legislative houses (Senate [200]; House of Representatives [500]).
Chief of state: King.
Head of government: Prime Minister.
Capital: Bangkok.
Official language: Thai.
Official religion: Buddhism.
Monetary unit: 1 Thai baht (B) = 100 stangs; valuation (Sept. 1, 2004) 1 U.S.$ = B 41.65; 1 £ = B 74.93.

Area and population	area		population
			2002
Regions[1]	sq mi	sq km	estimate
Bangkok and vicinities	2,997	7,762	9,668,854
Eastern	14,094	36,503	4,300,513
Northeastern	65,195	168,855	21,609,185
Northern	65,500	169,644	12,152,502
Southern	27,303	70,715	8,415,908
Sub-central	6,407	16,594	3,002,544
Western	16,621	43,047	3,650,366
TOTAL	198,117	513,120	62,799,872

Demography

Population (2004): 64,485,000.
Density (2004): persons per sq mi 325.5, persons per sq km 125.7.
Urban-rural (2001): urban 28.6%; rural 71.4%.
Sex distribution (2000): male 49.24%; female 50.76%.
Age breakdown (2003): under 15, 24.5%; 15–29, 26.5%; 30–44, 23.7%; 45–59, 15.7%; 60–74, 7.8%; 75 and over, 1.8%.
Population projection: (2010) 67,734,000; (2020) 71,551,000.
Doubling time: 87 years.
Ethnic composition (2000): Tai peoples 81.4%, of which Thai (Siamese) 34.9%, Lao 26.5%; Han Chinese 10.6%; Malay 3.7%; Khmer 1.9%; other 2.4%.
Religious affiliation (2000): Buddhist 94.2%; Muslim 4.6%; Christian and other 1.2%.
Major cities (2000)[2]: Bangkok 6,320,174; Samut Prakan 378,694; Nonthaburi 291,307; Udon Thani 220,493; Nakhon Ratchasima 204,391.

Vital statistics

Birth rate per 1,000 population (2002): 14.0 (world avg. 21.3).
Death rate per 1,000 population (2002): 6.0 (world avg. 9.1).
Natural increase rate per 1,000 population (2002): 8.0 (world avg. 12.2).
Total fertility rate (avg. births per childbearing woman; 2002): 1.8.
Marriage rate per 1,000 population (2000): 5.4.
Divorce rate per 1,000 population (2000): 1.1.
Life expectancy at birth (2002): male 69.9 years; female 74.9 years.
Major causes of death per 100,000 population (1998): diseases of the circulatory system 75.9; accidents, homicide, and poisonings 51.0; malignant neoplasms (cancers) 49.2.

National economy

Budget (2001–02). Revenue: B 903,550,000,000 (tax revenue 90.3%, of which income taxes 28.7%, VAT 26.1%, taxes on international trade 11.5%, consumption tax 10.8%; nontax revenue 9.7%). Expenditures: B 1,023,000,000,000 (education 21.8%; defense 7.5%; agriculture 7.4%; health 7.1%; social security 6.9%; public order 5.5%).
Public debt (external, outstanding; 2002): U.S.$22,628,000,000.
Production (metric tons except as noted). Agriculture, forestry, fishing (2002): sugarcane 62,350,000, rice 25,945,000, cassava 16,870,000, corn (maize) 4,170,000, natural rubber 2,460,000, pineapples 1,978,822, bananas 1,750,000, mangoes 1,700,000, coconuts 1,396,000, tobacco 73,000; livestock (number of live animals) 6,688,904 pigs, 4,640,355 cattle, 1,800,000 buffalo, 121,000,000 chickens; roundwood (2001) 27,351,000 cu m; fish catch (2001) 3,605,544, of which mollusks 224,222. Mining and quarrying (2001): gypsum 6,191,000; dolomite 871,300; feldspar 710,500; zinc [metal content] 24,000; gemstones (significantly rubies and sapphires) 1,071,000 carats. Manufacturing (2001): cement 27,913,000; refined sugar 4,865,000; crude steel 2,127,000; paper products 917,000; tin plate (2002) 233,000; beer 12,380,000 hectolitres. Energy production (consumption): electricity (kW-hr; 2002) 108,418,000,000 (105,182,000,000); hard coal (metric tons; 2000) negligible (4,098,000); lignite (metric tons; 2001) 19,619,000 ([2000] 17,586,000); crude petroleum (barrels; 2001) 22,600,000 ([2000] 252,000,000); petroleum products (metric tons; 2000) 34,968,000 (30,468,000); natural gas (cu m; 2001) 20,633,000,000 ([2000] 19,338,400,000).
Tourism (2002): receipts from visitors U.S.$7,902,000,000; expenditures by nationals abroad U.S.$3,303,000,000.
Population economically active (2001): total 33,920,000; activity rate of total population 53.9% (participation rates: over age 14, 72.1%; female [2000] 45.0%; unemployed 3.2%).

Price and earnings indexes (2000 = 100)	1997	1998	1999	2000	2001	2002	2003
Consumer price index	90.8	98.2	98.5	100.0	101.6	102.3	104.2
Average earnings index	89.0	99.6	99.8	100.0	101.0	100.2	102.5

Gross national product (2001): U.S.$136,063,000,000 (U.S.$2,190 per capita).

Structure of gross domestic product and labour force	2001			
	in value B '000,000	% of total value	labour force	% of labour force
Agriculture	436,160	8.5	13,590,000	40.1
Mining	125,869	2.5	470,000	1.4
Manufacturing	1,706,695	33.5	5,680,000	16.7
Construction	148,996	2.9	1,580,000	4.7
Public utilities	167,850	3.3	170,000	0.5
Transp. and commun.	410,701	8.0	1,020,000	3.0
Trade	875,850	17.2	4,490,000	13.2
Finance	319,623	6.3		
Pub. admin., defense	229,425	4.5	5,600,000	16.5
Services	678,473	13.3		
Other	—	—	1,320,000[3]	3.9[3]
TOTAL	5,099,642	100.0	33,920,000	100.0

Household income and expenditure (1998). Average household size (2000) 3.9; average annual income per household B 149,904 (U.S.$3,624); sources of income: wages and salaries 40.1%, self-employment 29.8%, transfer payments 7.9%, other 22.2%; expenditure: food, tobacco, and beverages 37.7%, housing 21.4%, transportation and communications 13.3%, medical and personal care 5.1%, clothing 3.5%, education 2.3%.
Land use as % of total land area (2000): in temporary crops 29.4%, in permanent crops 6.5%, in pasture 1.6%; overall forest area 28.9%.

Foreign trade[4]

Balance of trade (current prices)	1997	1998	1999	2000	2001	2002
U.S.$'000,000	+1,572	+16,238	+14,013	+11,700	+8,582	+9,775
% of total	1.4%	18.2%	14.1%	9.4%	7.3%	7.9%

Imports (2001): U.S.$62,057,000,000 (electrical machinery 22.1%, of which electronic components and parts 10.9%; nonelectrical machinery 17.4%, of which computers and parts 6.3%; chemicals and chemical products 10.3%; crude petroleum 9.3%). *Major import sources* (2002): Japan 23.0%; U.S. 9.6%; China 7.6%; Malaysia 5.6%; Singapore 4.5%.
Exports (2001): U.S.$65,113,000,000 (food products 14.9%, of which fish, crustaceans, and mollusks 6.2%; computers and parts 12.3%; microcircuits and other electronics 7.2%; chemicals and chemical products 5.7%; garments and clothing accessories 5.6%). *Major export destinations* (2002): U.S. 19.6%; Japan 14.5%; Singapore 8.1%; Hong Kong 5.4%; China 5.2%.

Transport and communications

Transport. Railroads (2000): route length 4,041 km; passenger-km 10,040,000,000; metric ton-km cargo 3,347,000,000. Roads (2001): total length 53,436 km (paved 98%). Vehicles (2002): passenger cars 2,281,000; trucks and buses 4,145,000. Air transport (1999): passenger-km 38,345,195,000; metric ton-km cargo 1,670,717,000; airports (1996) 25.

Communications Medium	date	unit	number	units per 1,000 persons
Daily newspapers	2000	circulation	3,990,000	64
Radio	2000	receivers	14,700,000	235
Television	2000	receivers	17,700,000	284
Telephones	2003	main lines	6,600,000	106
Cellular telephones	2002	subscribers	16,117,000	260
Personal computers	2002	units	2,461,000	40
Internet	2003	users	6,031,300	96

Education and health

Educational attainment (2000). Percentage of population age 6 and over having: no formal schooling 8.5%; primary education 59.0%; lower secondary 12.5%; upper secondary 11.2%; some higher 2.2%; undergraduate 5.2%; advanced degree 0.4%; other/unknown 1.0%. *Literacy* (2000): 95.5%.

Education (1997–98)	schools	teachers	students	student/ teacher ratio
Primary (age 7–12)	34,001[5]	445,542[6]	5,927,902	19.3[6]
Secondary (age 13–18)	2,318[6]	107,025[6]	3,358,470	19.8[6]
Voc., teacher tr.	679[6]	40,116[6]	738,861	19.8[6]
Higher	102[6]	38,423[5]	1,522,142	31.8[5]

Health (2001): physicians 18,531 (1 per 3,395 persons); hospital beds 141,380 (1 per 445 persons); infant mortality rate (2002) 20.0.
Food (2001): daily per capita caloric intake 2,486 (vegetable products 88%, animal products 12%); 112% of FAO recommended minimum requirement.

Military

Total active duty personnel (2003): 314,200 (army 60.5%, navy 25.2%, air force 14.3%). *Military expenditure as percentage of GNP* (1999): 1.7% (world 2.4%); per capita expenditure U.S.$34.

[1]Actual local administration is based on 76 provinces. [2]Preliminary census figures. [3]Unemployed. [4]Import figures are f.o.b. in balance of trade and c.i.f. for commodities and trading partners. [5]1995–96. [6]1993.

Internet resources for further information:
- **National Statistical Office Thailand**
  http://www.nso.go.th
- **Bank of Thailand**
  http://www.bot.or.th

Togo

Official name: République Togolaise (Togolese Republic).
Form of government: multiparty republic[1] with one legislative body (National Assembly [81]).
Chief of state: President[1].
Head of government: Prime Minister.
Capital: Lomé.
Official language: French.
Official religion: none.
Monetary unit: 1 CFA franc (CFAF) = 100 centimes; valuation (Sept. 1, 2004) 1 U.S.$ = CFAF 539.75; 1 £ = CFAF 970.98[2].

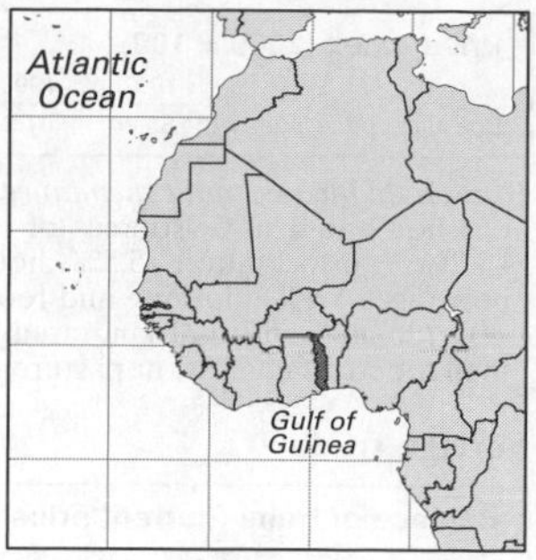

Population

Regions Prefectures	population 1998 estimate	Regions Prefectures	population 1998 estimate
Centrale	449,000	Kloto	161,000
Blitta	99,000	Moyen-Mono	62,000
Sotouboua	124,000	Ogou	220,000
Tchamba	74,000	Wawa	143,000
Tchaoudjo	152,000	Des Savanes	542,000
De la Kara	580,000	Kpendjal	104,000
Assoli	45,000	Oti	119,000
Bassar	92,000	Tandjouaré	80,000
Binah	58,000	Tône	239,000
Dankpen	65,000	Maritime	1,828,000
Doufelgou	73,000	Avé	80,000
Kéran	62,000	Golfe	294,000
Kozah	185,000	Lacs	211,000
Des Plateaux	1,007,000	Lomé[3]	673,000
Agou	76,000	Vo	204,000
Amou	76,000	Yoto	138,000
Danyi	37,000	Zio	228,000
Est-Mono	67,000	TOTAL	4,406,000
Haho	165,000		

Demography

Area: 21,925 sq mi, 56,785 sq km.
Population (2004): 5,557,000.
Density (2004): persons per sq mi 253.5, persons per sq km 97.9.
Urban-rural (2002): urban 33.9%; rural 66.1%.
Sex distribution (2004): male 49.55%; female 50.45%.
Age breakdown (2001): under 15, 45.6%; 15–29, 28.1%; 30–44, 14.8%; 45–59, 7.5%; 60–74, 3.3%; 75 and over, 0.7%.
Population projection: (2010) 6,256,000; (2020) 7,195,000.
Doubling time: 29 years.
Ethnic composition (2000): Ewe 22.2%; Kabre 13.4%; Wachi 10.0%; Mina 5.6%; Kotokoli 5.6%; Bimoba 5.2%; Losso 4.0%; Gurma 3.4%; Lamba 3.2%; Adja 3.0%; other 24.4%.
Religious affiliation (2000): Christian 37.8%, of which Roman Catholic 24.3%; traditional beliefs 37.7%; Muslim 18.9%; other 5.6%.
Major cities (2003): Lomé 676,400 (urban agglomeration 749,700); Sokodé 84,200; Kpalimé 75,200; Atakpamé 64,300; Kara 49,800.

Vital statistics

Birth rate per 1,000 population (2003): 35.2 (world avg. 21.3).
Death rate per 1,000 population (2003): 11.5 (world avg. 9.1).
Natural increase rate per 1,000 population (2003): 23.7 (world avg. 12.2).
Total fertility rate (avg. births per childbearing woman; 2003): 5.0.
Life expectancy at birth (2003): male 52.0 years; female 54.0 years.
Adult population (ages 15–49) *living with HIV* (2004[4]): 4.1% (world avg. 1.1%).

National economy

Budget (2002). Revenue: CFAF 128,300,000,000 (tax revenue 92.5%, nontax revenue 4.8%, grants 2.7%). Expenditures: CFAF 135,300,000,000 (current expenditure 89.4%, capital expenditure 10.6%).
Public debt (external, outstanding; 2002): U.S.$1,337,000,000.
Production (metric tons except as noted). Agriculture, forestry, fishing (2002): cassava 651,530, yams 549,070, corn (maize) 463,930, seed cotton 175,000, sorghum 141,723, vegetables 130,000, oil palm fruit 130,000, rice 63,693, coffee 17,000, cacao beans 8,000; livestock (number of live animals) 1,700,000 sheep, 1,460,000 goats, 300,000 pigs, 278,500 cattle; roundwood 5,835,447 cu m; fish catch (2001) 23,283. Mining and quarrying: limestone (2001) 2,400,000; phosphate rock (2002) 1,380,000. Manufacturing (value added in CFAF '000,000; 1998): food products, beverages, and tobacco manufactures 41,400; metallic goods 12,000; nonmetallic manufactures 8,500; textiles, clothing, and leather 4,900; wood products 4,700; paper, printing, and publishing 4,600; chemicals 3,600. Energy production (consumption): electricity (kW-hr; 2000) 68,000,000 (580,000,000); petroleum products (metric tons; 2000) none (471,000).
Population economically active (2000): total 1,913,000; activity rate of total population 38.1% (participation rates: over age 15, 70.7%; female 39.9%; unemployed [1994] 16–18%).

Price index (2000 = 100)

	1997	1998	1999	2000	2001	2002	2003
Consumer price index	97.3	98.2	98.1	100.0	103.9	107.1	106.1

Gross national product (at current market prices; 2003): U.S.$1,492,000,000 (U.S.$310 per capita).

Structure of gross domestic product and labour force

	1999 in value CFAF '000,000,000	1999 % of total value	2000 labour force	2000 % of labour force
Agriculture	366.3	41.8	1,142,000	59.7
Mining	44.9	5.1		
Manufacturing	80.6	9.2		
Construction	32.3	3.7		
Public utilities	27.8	3.2		
Transp. and commun.	47.5	5.4	771,000	40.3
Trade and finance	150.7	17.2		
Pub. admin., defense	60.9	6.9		
Services	66.1	7.5		
TOTAL	877.1	100.0	1,913,000	100.0

Household income and expenditure. Average household size (1999) 6.0; expenditure (1987): food and beverages 45.9%, services 20.5%, household durable goods 13.9%, clothing 11.4%, housing 5.9%.
Land use as % of total land area (2000): in temporary crops 46.1%, in permanent crops 2.2%, in pasture 18.4%; overall forest area 9.4%.
Tourism (2002): receipts U.S.$9,000,000; expenditures U.S.$4,000,000.

Foreign trade[5]

Balance of trade (current prices)

	1997	1998	1999	2000	2001	2002
U.S.$'000,000	−283.5	−293.5	−307.9	−131.9	−134.8	−172.7
% of total	28.9%	27.2%	29.9%	25.6%	23.4%	17.0%

Imports (2001): U.S.$355,000,000 (food 18.2%, of which cereals 9.4%; refined petroleum 15.7%; chemicals and chemical products 10.4%; machinery and apparatus 9.8%; cement 8.8%; iron and steel 8.8%). *Major import sources:* France 19.1%; Canada 6.5%; Italy 6.1%; Côte d'Ivoire 5.7%; Germany 4.5%.
Exports (2001): U.S.$220,200,000 (cement 29.4%, phosphates 20.3%, cotton 10.1%, iron and steel 8.6%). *Major export destinations:* Ghana 22.4%; Benin 16.9%; Burkina Faso 10.4%; Philippines 6.3%; Niger 4.5%.

Transport and communications

Transport. Railroads (1999): route length 395 km; (1998) passenger-km 35,200,000; metric ton-km cargo 758,700,000. Roads (1999): total length 7,520 km (paved 32%). Vehicles (1996): passenger cars 79,200; trucks and buses 34,240. Air transport[6]: airports (1998) 2.

Communications

Medium	date	unit	number	units per 1,000 persons
Daily newspapers	2000	circulation	20,100	4.0
Radio	2000	receivers	1,330,000	265
Television	2002	receivers	590,000	123
Telephones	2003	main lines	60,600	12
Cellular telephones	2003	subscribers	220,000	44
Personal computers	2003	units	160,000	32
Internet	2003	users	210,000	42

Education and health

Educational attainment (1981). Percentage of population age 25 and over having: no formal schooling 76.5%; primary education 13.5%; secondary 8.7%; higher 1.3%. *Literacy* (2000): total population age 15 and over literate 57.1%; males 72.4%; females 42.5%.

Education (1996–97)

	schools	teachers	students	student/ teacher ratio
Primary (age 6–11)	3,283[7]	18,535	859,574	46.4
Secondary (age 12–18)	314[8]	4,736[8]	169,178	...
Vocational	...	653	9,076	13.9
Higher[9]	1	443	11,639	26.3

Health: physicians (1995) 320 (1 per 13,158 persons); hospital beds (1990) 5,307 (1 per 694 persons); infant mortality rate (2003) 80.0.
Food (2001): daily per capita caloric intake 2,287 (vegetable products 97%, animal products 3%); 99% of FAO recommended minimum requirement.

Military

Total active duty personnel (2003): 8,550 (army 94.7%, navy 2.3%, air force 3.0%). *Military expenditure as percentage of GNP* (1999): 1.8% (world 2.4%); per capita expenditure U.S.$5.

[1]Personal military-supported rule from 1967 continues under constitution approved by referendum in September 1992. [2]Formerly pegged to the French franc and since Jan. 1, 2002, to the euro at the rate of €1 = CFAF 655.96. [3]Commune. [4]January 1. [5]Import figures are c.i.f. (except in 2002 balance of trade). [6]Air Afrique, an airline jointly owned by 11 African countries (including Togo), was declared bankrupt in February 2002. [7]1995–96. [8]1990. [9]University only.

Internet resources for further information:
- **AFRISTAT http://www.afristat.org**
- **La Banque de France: La Zone Franc http://www.banque-france.fr/fr/zonefr/main.htm**

Tonga

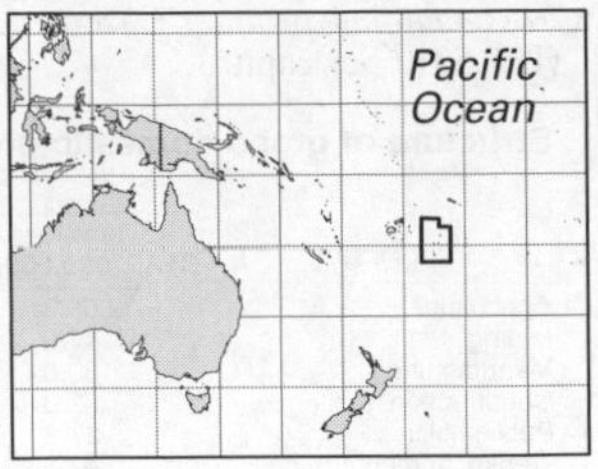

Official name: Pule'anga Fakatu'i 'o Tonga (Tongan); Kingdom of Tonga (English).
Form of government: constitutional monarchy with one legislative house (Legislative Assembly [30[1]]).
Head of state and government: King assisted by Privy Council.
Capital: Nuku'alofa.
Official languages: Tongan; English.
Official religion: none.
Monetary unit: 1 pa'anga (T$) = 100 seniti; valuation (Sept. 1, 2004) 1 U.S.$ = T$2.00; 1 £ = T$3.59.

Area and population

Divisions	Capitals	area sq mi	area sq km	population 1996 census[2]
'Eua[3]	'Ohonua	33.7	87.4	4,934
Ha'apai[4]	Pangai	42.5	110.0	8,138
Niuas[5]	Hihifo	27.7	71.7	2,018
Tongatapu[3]	Nuku'alofa	100.6	260.5	66,979
Vava'u[4]	Neiafu	46.0	119.2	15,715
TOTAL LAND AREA		278.1[6]	720.3[6]	
INLAND WATER		11.4	29.6	
TOTAL		289.5	749.9	97,784

Demography

Population (2004): 98,400.
Density (2004)[7]: persons per sq mi 353.8, persons per sq km 136.6.
Urban-rural (2002): urban 39.0%; rural 61.0%.
Sex distribution (2002): male 50.93%; female 49.07%.
Age breakdown (1996): under 15, 39.1%; 15–29, 28.0%; 30–44, 15.1%; 45–59, 10.0%; 60–74, 6.0%; 75 and over, 1.8%.
Population projection: (2010) 103,000; (2020) 111,000.
Doubling time: 37 years.
Ethnic composition (1996): Tongan and part Tongan 98.2%; other 1.8%.
Religious affiliation (1998): Free Wesleyan 41.2%; Roman Catholic 15.8%; Mormon 13.6%; other (mostly other Protestant) 29.4%.
Major cities (1986): Nuku'alofa (1996) 22,400[8]; Neiafu 3,879; Haveluloto 3,070.

Vital statistics

Birth rate per 1,000 population (2003): 24.5 (world avg. 21.3).
Death rate per 1,000 population (2003): 5.5 (world avg. 9.1).
Natural increase rate per 1,000 population (2003): 19.0 (world avg. 12.2).
Total fertility rate (avg. births per childbearing woman; 2003): 3.0.
Marriage rate per 1,000 population (1994): 7.7.
Divorce rate per 1,000 population (1994): 0.8.
Life expectancy at birth (2003): male 66.4 years; female 71.4 years.
Major causes of death per 100,000 population (2002): circulatory diseases 190.1; malignant neoplasms (cancers) 77.2; respiratory diseases 49.5; endocrine, nutritional, and metabolic disorders 43.6.

National economy

Budget (2002). Revenue: T$93,200,000 (foreign-trade taxes 52.0%, government services revenue 13.7%, income tax 16.7%, sales taxes 8.2%). Expenditures: T$99,400,000 (2001; general administration 20.9%, education 14.0%, health 10.2%, social security 6.7%, agriculture 6.5%, law and order 5.7%, defense 4.6%).
Public debt (external, outstanding; 2002): U.S.$72,600,000.
Production (metric tons except as noted). Agriculture, forestry, fishing (2002): coconuts 57,700, pumpkins, squash, and gourds 17,000, cassava 9,000, vegetables 5,500, sweet potatoes 5,500, yams 4,400, vanilla 14; livestock (number of live animals) 80,853 pigs, 12,500 goats, 11,400 horses, 11,250 cattle, 300,000 chickens; roundwood 2,100 cu m; fish catch (2001) 4,673. Mining and quarrying: coral and sand for local use. Manufacturing (output in T$'000,000; 1996): food products and beverages 8,203; paper products 1,055; chemical products 964; metal products 889; textile and wearing apparel 742; nonmetallic products 715. Energy production (consumption): electricity (kW-hr; 2002) 36,176,000 (36,176,000); crude petroleum, none (none); petroleum products (metric tons; 2000) n.a. (39,000).
Tourism: receipts (2002) U.S.$9,000,000; expenditures (2001) U.S.$3,000,000.
Gross national product (2003): U.S.$152,000,000 (U.S.$1,490 per capita).

Structure of gross domestic product and labour force

	2001–02 in value T$'000,000	2001–02 % of total value	1996 labour force	1996 % of labour force
Agriculture	70.2	23.7	9,953	29.3
Mining	1.1	0.4	43	0.1
Manufacturing	13.7	4.6	6,710	19.8
Construction	16.9	5.7	500	1.5
Public utilities	5.5	1.9	504	1.5
Transp. and commun.	19.7	6.6	1,209	3.6
Trade	33.8	11.4	2,506	7.4
Finance	35.9	12.1	657	1.9
Pub. admin., defense	47.8	16.1	3,701	10.9
Services	14.6	4.9	3,623	10.7
Other	37.3	12.6	4,502	13.3
TOTAL	296.5	100.0	33,908	100.0

Population economically active (1996): total 33,908; activity rate 34.7% (participation rates: ages 15 and over 57.0%; female 36.0%; unemployed 13.3%).

Price index (2000 = 100)

	1997	1998	1999	2000	2001	2002	2003
Consumer price index	85.2	87.8	93.3	100.0	110.7	123.9	138.5

Household income and expenditure. Average household size (1996) 6.0; income per household: n.a.; sources of income: n.a.; expenditure (1991–92)[9]: food 43.2%, transportation 15.5%, household 14.2%, housing 6.4%, tobacco and beverages 5.4%, clothing and footwear 4.2%.
Land use as % of total land area (2000): in temporary crops *c.* 24%, in permanent crops *c.* 43%, in pasture *c.* 6%; overall forest area *c.* 5%.

Foreign trade[10]

Balance of trade (current prices)

	1996–97	1997–98	1998–99	1999–2000	2000–01	2001–02
U.S.$'000,000	–47.0	–66.2	–43.5	–43.0	–49.9	–44.0
% of total	64.0%	73.6%	64.3%	65.5%	67.6%	55.1%

Imports (2000–01): U.S.$70,100,000 (food and live animals 32.3%, mineral fuels and chemical products 25.6%, machinery and transport equipment 11.2%). *Major import sources* (2002): New Zealand 30.8%; Fiji 20.7%; U.S. 14.3%; Australia 13.2%; China 6.2%.
Exports (2000–01): U.S.$6,700,000 (squash 40.8%, fish 27.7%, root crops 15.4%, kava 2.3%, vanilla beans 2.3%). *Major export destinations* (2002): Japan 43.3%; U.S. 41.0%; Greece 3.8%; New Zealand 3.6%; Taiwan 2.7%.

Transport and communications

Transport. Railroads: none. Roads (1996): total length 680 km (paved 27%). Vehicles (1998): passenger cars 6,419, commercial vehicles 9,189. Air transport (1999): passenger-km 19,000,000; metric ton-km cargo 2,000,000; airports (1996) with scheduled flights 6.

Communications

Medium	date	unit	number	units per 1,000 persons
Daily newspapers	2000	circulation	12,300	123
Radio	1997	receivers	61,000	619
Television	1997	receivers	2,000	21
Telephones	2002	main lines	11,200	113
Cellular telephones	2002	subscribers	3,400	34
Personal computers	2002	units	2,000	20
Internet	2002	users	2,900	29

Education and health

Educational attainment (1996). Percentage of population age 25 and over having: primary education 26%; lower secondary 58%; upper secondary 8%; higher 6%; not stated 2%. *Literacy* (1996): 98.5%.

Education (1999)

	schools	teachers	students	student/ teacher ratio
Primary (age 6–11)	117	745	16,206	21.8
Secondary (age 12–18)	39	961	13,987	14.6
Voc., teacher tr.	5	67	755	11.3
Higher[11]	1	19	226	11.9

Health: physicians (2002) 32[12] (1 per 3,057 persons); hospital beds (1992) 307 (1 per 320 persons); infant mortality rate per 1,000 live births (2003) 13.4.
Food (1992): daily per capita caloric intake 2,946 (vegetable products 82%, animal products 18%); 129% of FAO recommended minimum requirement.

Military

Total active duty personnel (1999): 125-member naval force; an air force was created in 1996. *Military expenditure as percentage of GNP:* n.a.

[1]Includes 12 nonelective seats and 9 nobles elected by the 33 hereditary nobles of Tonga. [2]Final figures. [3]'Eua and Tongatapu together comprise Tongatapu island group. [4]Also the name of an island group. [5]Also known as Niuatoputapu island group. [6]Total includes 27.6 sq mi (71.5 sq km) of uninhabited islands. [7]Based on land area. [8]Population of urban agglomeration (2001) is 33,000. [9]Weight of consumer price index components. [10]Imports f.o.b. in balance of trade and c.i.f. in commodities and trading partners. [11]1992. [12]Government only.

Internet resources for further information:

- **Secretariat of the Pacific Community http://www.spc.org.nc**
- **National Reserve Bank of Tonga http://www.reservebank.to**

Trinidad and Tobago

Official name: Republic of Trinidad and Tobago.
Form of government: multiparty republic with two legislative houses (Senate [31]; House of Representatives [36[1]]).
Chief of state: President.
Head of government: Prime Minister.
Capital: Port of Spain.
Official language: English.
Official religion: none.
Monetary unit: 1 Trinidad and Tobago dollar (TT$) = 100 cents; valuation (Sept. 1, 2004) 1 U.S.$ = TT$6.23; 1 £ = TT$11.20.

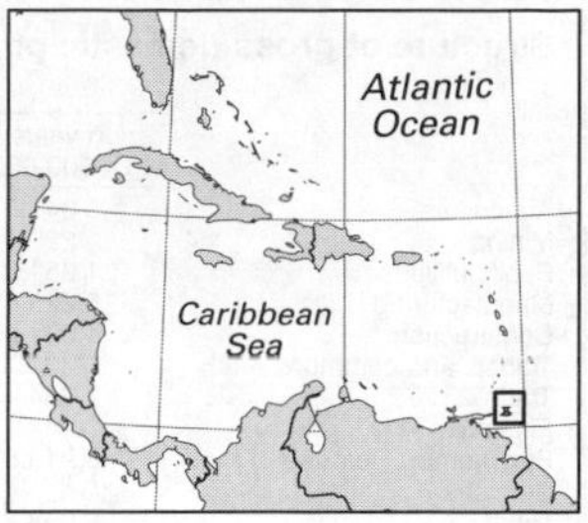

Area and population

	area[2] sq km	population 2000 census		area[2] sq km	population 2000 census
Trinidad	4,827	1,208,282	**Cities**		
Counties			Port of Spain	12	49,031
Couva/Tabaquite/Talparo	723	162,779	San Fernando	19	55,419
Diego Martin	126	105,720	**Boroughs**		
Mayaro/Rio Claro	814	33,480	Arima	12	32,278
Penal/Debe	246	83,609	Chaguanas	59	67,433
Princes Town	620	91,947	Point Fortin	25	19,056
San Juan/Laventille	239	157,295	**Tobago**[3]	300	54,084
Sangre Grande	927	64,343	TOTAL	5,127	1,262,366
Siparia	495	81,917			
Tunapuna/Piarco	510	203,975			

Demography

Population (2004): 1,286,000.
Density (2004): persons per sq mi 649.5, persons per sq km 250.8.
Urban-rural (2002): urban 74.5%; rural 25.5%.
Sex distribution (2001): male 51.22%; female 48.78%.
Age breakdown (2001): under 15, 24.3%; 15–29, 27.1%; 30–44, 22.5%; 45–59, 15.5%; 60–74, 7.7%; 75 and over, 2.9%.
Population projection: (2010) 1,310,000; (2020) 1,325,000.
Ethnic composition (2000): black 39.2%; East Indian 38.6%; mixed 16.3%; Chinese 1.6%; white 1.0%; other/not stated 3.3%.
Religious affiliation (1990): six largest Protestant bodies 29.7%; Roman Catholic 29.4%; Hindu 23.7%; Muslim 5.9%; other 11.3%.
Major cities (2000): Chaguanas 67,433; San Fernando 55,149; Port of Spain 49,031; Arima 32,278; Point Fortin 19,056.

Vital statistics

Birth rate per 1,000 population (2003): 12.7 (world avg. 21.3).
Death rate per 1,000 population (2003): 8.7 (world avg. 9.1).
Natural increase rate per 1,000 population (2003): 4.0 (world avg. 12.2).
Total fertility rate (avg. births per childbearing woman; 2003): 1.8.
Marriage rate per 1,000 population (1998): 6.2.
Divorce rate per 1,000 population (1998): 1.1.
Life expectancy at birth (2003): male 67.1 years; female 72.2 years.
Major causes of death per 100,000 population (1997): diseases of the circulatory system 289.7; malignant neoplasms (cancers) 102.0; accidents, violence, and homicide 49.8; communicable diseases 42.5.

National economy

Budget (2001–02). Revenue: TT$14,672,000,000 (income taxes 31.5%; petroleum sector 29.0%; sales tax 23.7%; taxes on international trade 5.7%; other 10.1%). Expenditures: TT$13,861,000,000 (current expenditures 90.4%, of which transfers and subsidies 33.9%, wages 30.9%, interest payment 16.8%, other 8.8%; development expenditures 9.6%).
Production (metric tons except as noted). Agriculture, forestry, fishing (2002): sugarcane 1,050,000, coconuts 24,000, oranges 4,987, rice 3,882, pigeon peas 2,780, cocoa 1,218, coffee 243, nutmeg 140; livestock (number of live animals) 60,500 goats, 31,600 cattle, 25,000,000 chickens; roundwood (2000) 116,500 cu m; fish catch (2001) 11,415. Mining and quarrying (2000): natural asphalt 9,900. Manufacturing (2000): anhydrous ammonia and urea 3,719,000, methanol 2,480,000; steel billets 744,000; cement 743,000; steel wire rods 631,000; refined sugar 52,000; beer and stout 524,000 hectolitres; rum 146,000 hectolitres. Energy production (consumption): electricity (kW-hr; 2000) 5,460,000,000 (5,460,000,000); crude petroleum (barrels; 2000) 43,786,000 (59,102,000); petroleum products (metric tons; 2000) 8,037,000 (1,055,000); natural gas (cu m; 2000) 10,448,000,000 (10,448,000,000).
Household income and expenditure. Average household size (2000) 3.7; average income per household, n.a.; expenditure (1993): food, beverages, and tobacco 25.5%, housing 21.6%, transportation 15.2%, household furnishings 14.3%, clothing and footwear 10.4%.
Tourism (2002): receipts from visitors U.S.$224,000,000; expenditures by nationals abroad (2001) U.S.$151,000,000.
Land use as % of total land area (2000): in temporary crops 14.6%, in permanent crops 9.2%, in pasture 2.1%; overall forest area 50.5%.
Gross national product (at current market prices; 2003): U.S.$9,538,000,000 (U.S.$7,260 per capita).

Structure of gross domestic product and labour force

	2002		2001	
	in value TT$'000,000	% of total value	labour force	% of labour force
Agriculture	800	0.9	40,300	7.0
Petroleum	11,693	13.7	16,600	2.9
Manufacturing[4]	15,812	18.5	52,700	9.1
Construction	5,952	7.0	71,200	12.3
Public utilities	} 12,377	} 14.5	7,500	1.3
Transp. and commun.			38,900	6.7
Trade	19,248	22.5	89,900	15.6
Finance, real estate	14,437	16.9	41,000	7.1
Pub. admin., defense	} 7,187	} 8.4	} 156,100	} 27.1
Services				
Other	–2,001[5]	–2.3[5]	62,700[6]	10.9[6]
TOTAL	85,503[7]	100.0[7]	576,900	100.0

Population economically active (2001): total 576,900; activity rate of total population 45.5% (participation rates: ages 15 and over 60.7%; female 36.6%; unemployed 10.9%).

Price and earnings indexes (2000 = 100)

	1997	1998	1999	2000	2001	2002	2003
Consumer price index	88.4	93.4	96.6	100.0	105.5	109.9	114.1
Weekly earnings index[8]	74.0	77.7	80.2	100.0	99.2	...	...

Public debt (external, outstanding; 2002): U.S.$1,697,000,000.

Foreign trade[9]

Balance of trade (current prices)

	1997	1998	1999	2000	2001	2002
TT$'000,000	–2,818	–4,666	+398	+6,082	+7,363	+1,470
% of total	8.1%	14.1%	1.1%	12.7%	13.1%	3.1%

Imports (2001): TT$24,510,000,000 (crude petroleum 19.3%, general industrial machinery 16.1%, floating docks 9.3%, food products 7.5%, refined petroleum 4.1%). *Major import sources:* United States 34.4%; Venezuela 11.1%; Brazil 5.1%; United Kingdom 4.9%; Panama 4.6%.
Exports (2001): TT$31,873,000,000 (refined petroleum 29.4%, floating docks 12.6%, crude petroleum 9.3%, anhydrous ammonia 8.5%, iron and steel 5.7%, methanol 5.0%). *Major export destinations:* United States 42.3%; Mexico 7.4%; Jamaica 7.0%; Barbados 5.5%; France 3.9%.

Transport and communications

Transport. Railroads: none. Roads (1999): total length 7,900 km (paved 51%). Vehicles (1996): passenger cars 122,000; trucks and buses 24,000. Air transport (2001)[10]: passenger-km 2,496,000,000; metric ton-km cargo 56,236,000; airports (2000) with scheduled flights 2.

Communications

Medium	date	unit	number	units per 1,000 persons
Daily newspapers	2000	circulation	155,000	123
Radio	2000	receivers	672,000	532
Television	2000	receivers	429,000	340
Telephones	2002	main lines	325,100	250
Cellular telephones	2002	subscribers	361,900	278
Personal computers	2002	units	104,000	80
Internet	2002	users	138,000	106

Education and health

Educational attainment (1990). Percentage of population age 25 and over having: no formal schooling 4.5%; primary education 56.4%; secondary 32.1%; higher 3.4%; other/not stated 3.6%. *Literacy* (2000): total population age 15 and over literate 93.8%; males 95.5%; females 92.1%.

Education (1999–2000)

	schools	teachers	students	student/teacher ratio
Primary (age 5–11)	481	7,311[11]	162,736	24.8[11]
Secondary (age 12–16)	...	5,070[11]	105,500	20.6[11]
Higher[12]	1	477	7,585	15.9

Health: physicians (1999) 1,171 (1 per 1,076 persons); hospital beds 4,384 (1 per 287 persons); infant mortality rate (2003) 25.0.
Food (2001): daily per capita caloric intake 2,756 (vegetable products 84%, animal products 16%); 114% of FAO recommended minimum requirement.

Military

Total active duty personnel (2003): 2,700 (army 74.1%, coast guard 25.9%). *Military expenditure as percentage of GNP* (1999): 1.4% (world 2.4%); per capita expenditure U.S.$78.

[1]Excludes speaker, who may be elected from outside the House of Representatives. [2]Area figures for counties are estimated. [3]Semiautonomous island. [4]Includes petroleum refining and petrochemicals. [5]Net of value-added taxes less imputed bank service charges. [6]Unemployed. [7]Detail does not add to total given because of rounding. [8]Manufacturing only. [9]Imports c.i.f.; exports f.o.b. [10]BWIA only. [11]1996–97. [12]University of the West Indies.

Internet resources for further information:
- **Central Bank of Trinidad and Tobago** **http://www.central-bank.org.tt**
- **Central Statistical Office** **http://www.cso.gov.tt**

Tunisia

Official name: Al-Jumhūrīyah at-Tūnisīyah (Republic of Tunisia).
Form of government: multiparty republic[1] with one legislative house (Chamber of Deputies [189]).
Chief of state: President.
Head of government: Prime Minister.
Capital: Tunis.
Official language: Arabic.
Official religion: Islam.
Monetary unit: 1 dinar (D) = 1,000 millimes; valuation (Sept. 1, 2004) 1 U.S.$ = D 1.27; 1 £ = D 2.28.

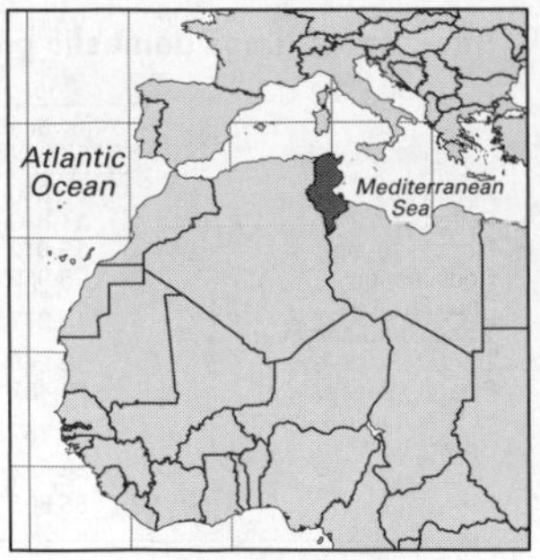

Area and population

Governorates	Capitals	area sq mi	area sq km	population 2002 estimate
Al-Ariānah	Al-Ariānah	192	498	382,600
Bājah	Bājah	1,374	3,558	320,200
Banzart	Bizerte (Banzart)	1,423	3,685	527,600
Bin ʿArūs	Bin ʿArūs	294	761	467,200
Jundūbah	Jundūbah	1,198	3,102	430,100
Al-Kāf	Al-Kāf	1,917	4,965	281,900
Madanīn	Madanīn	3,316	8,588	432,000
Al-Mahdīyah	Al-Mahdīyah	1,145	2,966	376,400
Manūbah	Manūbah	409	1,060	327,000
Al-Munastīr	Al-Munastīr	393	1,019	429,100
Nābul	Nābul	1,076	2,788	649,900
Qābis	Qābis	2,770	7,175	337,000
Qafṣah	Qafṣah	3,471	8,990	333,400
Al-Qaṣrayn	Al-Qaṣrayn	3,114	8,066	424,800
Al-Qayrawān	Al-Qayrawān	2,592	6,712	571,000
Qibilī	Qibilī	8,527	22,084	144,200
Ṣafāqis	Ṣafāqis	2,913	7,545	832,500
Sīdī Bū Zayd	Sīdī Bū Zayd	2,700	6,994	404,100
Siliānah	Siliānah	1,788	4,631	258,100
Sūsah	Sūsah	1,012	2,621	510,000
Tatāuīn	Tatāuīn	15,015	38,889	150,500
Tawzar	Tawzar	1,822	4,719	98,500
Tūnis	Tunis (Tūnis)	134	346	933,700
Zaghwān	Zaghwān	1,069	2,768	157,300
TOTAL		63,170[2]	163,610[2]	9,779,100

Demography

Population (2004): 9,975,000.
Density (2004): persons per sq mi 157.9, persons per sq km 61.0.
Urban-rural (2002): urban 63.4%; rural 36.6%.
Sex distribution (2002): male 50.30%; female 49.70%.
Age breakdown (2002): under 15, 27.9%; 15–29, 30.6%; 30–44, 21.6%; 45–59, 10.8%; 60–74, 7.8%; 75 and over, 1.3%.
Population projection: (2010) 10,583,000; (2020) 11,552,000.
Doubling time: 58 years.
Ethnic composition (2000): Tunisian Arab 67.2%; Bedouin Arab 26.6%; Algerian Arab 2.4%; Berber 1.4%; other 2.4%.
Religious affiliation (2000): Sunnī Muslim 98.9%; Christian 0.5%; other 0.6%.
Major cities (2003): Tunis 699,700 (urban agglomeration [2001] 1,927,000); Ṣafāqis 270,700; Al-Ariānah 217,100[3]; Ettadhamen 188,700[3]; Sūsah 155,900.

Vital statistics

Birth rate per 1,000 population (2003): 16.0 (world avg. 21.3).
Death rate per 1,000 population (2003): 5.0 (world avg. 9.1).
Natural increase rate per 1,000 population (2003): 11.0 (world avg. 12.2).
Total fertility rate (avg. births per childbearing woman; 2003): 1.8.
Marriage rate per 1,000 population (2001): 6.4.
Divorce rate per 1,000 population (1999): 0.1.
Life expectancy at birth (2003): male 72.8 years; female 76.2 years.
Major causes of death: n.a.

National economy

Budget (2002). Revenue: D 11,533,000,000 (tax revenue 91.5%, of which goods and services 34.4%, income tax 22.1%, social security 18.9%, import duties 9.9%; nontax revenue 8.5%). Expenditures: D 11,533,000,000 (current expenditure 79.8%, of which interest on public debt 8.5%; development expenditure 20.2%).
Public debt (external, outstanding; 2002): U.S.$10,641,000,000.
Production (metric tons except as noted). Agriculture, forestry, fishing (2002): olives 1,500,000, tomatoes 810,000, cereals 538,000, watermelons 400,000, potatoes 300,000, dates 110,000, oranges 106,000, apples 100,000; livestock (live animals) 6,850,000 sheep, 1,450,000 goats, 760,000 cattle; roundwood (2002) 2,329,000 cu m; fish catch (2001) 100,000. Mining and quarrying (2002): phosphate rock 8,144,000; iron ore 198,000; zinc (metal content) 35,692. Manufacturing (2002): cement 6,022,000; phosphoric acid 1,219,000; lime 471,000; crude steel 220,000; pig iron 152,000. Energy production (consumption): electricity (kW-hr; 2001) 9,787,000,000 ([2000] 9,944,000,000); coal (metric tons; 2000) none (1,000); crude petroleum (barrels; 2001) 25,712,000 (13,625,000); petroleum products (metric tons; 2000) 1,889,000 (3,649,000); natural gas (cu m; 2001) 2,143,100,000 ([2000] 1,923,000,000).
Household income and expenditure. Average household size (2000) 4.7; income per household D 6,450 (U.S.$4,640); expenditure (2000): food and beverages 38.0%, housing and energy 21.5%, household durables 11.1%, health and personal care 10.0%, transportation 9.7%, recreation 8.7%, other 1.0%.
Gross national product (2003): U.S.$22,211,000,000 (U.S.$2,240 per capita).

Structure of gross domestic product and labour force

	2001		2002	
	in value D '000,000	% of total value	labour force	% of labour force
Agriculture	3,347.0	11.6	709,000	21.0
Mining	220.1	0.8	1,144,400	33.9
Public utilities	1,351.9	4.7		
Manufacturing	5,325.6	18.5		
Construction	1,391.2	4.8		
Transp. and commun.	2,390.7	8.3	1,522,300	45.1
Trade	7,784.4	27.0		
Finance; Pub. admin., defense; Services	3,913.5	13.6		
Other	3,068.7[4]	10.7[4]	...	...
TOTAL	28,793.1	100.0	3,375,700	100.0

Population economically active (2002): total 3,375,700; activity rate of total population 34.5% (participation rates: age 15 and over 48.0%; female 24.3%; unemployed 14.9%).

Price and earnings indexes (2000 = 100)

	1997	1998	1999	2000	2001	2002	2003
Consumer price index	91.7	94.6	97.2	100.0	102.0	104.8	107.6
Hourly earnings index	...	...	...	...	...	...	...

Tourism (2002): receipts U.S.$1,422,000,000; expenditures U.S.$260,000,000.
Land use as % of total land area (2000): in temporary crops 18.4%, in permanent crops 13.7%, in pasture 26.3%; overall forest area 3.1%.

Foreign trade[5]

Balance of trade (current prices)

	1997	1998	1999	2000	2001	2002
D '000,000	–2,645	–2,971	–3,103	–3,733	–4,193	–3,762
% of total	17.7%	18.6%	18.2%	18.9%	18.1%	16.2%

Imports (2002): D 13,511,000,000 (nonelectrical machinery and equipment 19.6%, fabric 12.7%, food products 10.5%, electrical machinery and equipment 10.0%, crude and refined petroleum 8.3%). *Major import sources:* France 25.6%; Italy 19.5%; Germany 8.9%; Spain 5.0%; U.S. 3.2%.
Exports (2002): D 9,749,000,000 (clothing 30.4%, knitwear 8.4%, crude petroleum 7.3%, phosphates and phosphate derivatives 6.8%, electrical cable and wire 4.7%). *Major export destinations:* France 31.3%; Italy 21.6%; Germany 11.5%; Spain 4.8%; Libya 4.6%.

Transport and communications

Transport. Railroads (2001): route length 2,169 km; passenger-km 1,283,500,-000; metric ton-km cargo 2,286,100,000. Roads (1997): total length 23,100 km (paved 79%). Vehicles (2000): passenger cars 482,700; trucks and buses 250,300. Air transport (2001)[6]: passenger-km 2,696,313,000; metric ton-km cargo 20,104,000; airports (1998) 5.

Communications

Medium	date	unit	number	units per 1,000 persons
Daily newspapers	1996	circulation	280,000	31
Radio	1997	receivers	2,060,000	224
Television	1999	receivers	1,800,000	190
Telephones	2003	main lines	1,163,800	118
Cellular telephones	2003	subscribers	1,899,900	192
Personal computers	2003	units	400,000	41
Internet	2003	users	630,000	64

Education and health

Educational attainment: n.a. *Literacy* (2000): total population age 10 and over literate 74.4%; males literate 83.5%; females literate 65.3%.

Education (2001–02)

	schools	teachers	students	student/ teacher ratio
Primary (age 6–11)	4,518	60,566	1,325,707	21.9
Secondary (age 12–18)	1,356	57,821	1,074,391	18.6
Higher	128	11,412	226,102	19.8

Health (2002): physicians 8,463 (1 per 1,156 persons); hospital beds 16,682 (1 per 586 persons); infant mortality rate per 1,000 live births (2003) 26.8.
Food (2001): daily per capita caloric intake 3,293 (vegetable products 89%, animal products 11%); 138% of FAO recommended minimum requirement.

Military

Total active duty personnel (2003): 35,000 (army 77.1%, navy 12.9%, air force 10.0%). *Military expenditure as percentage of GNP* (1999): 1.8% (world 2.4%); per capita expenditure U.S.$38.

[1]A single party dominates the political system in practice. [2]Total includes 3,506 sq mi- (9,080 sq km-) area of saline lakes that are not distributed by governorate. [3]Within Tunis urban agglomeration. [4]Indirect taxes less subsidies. [5]Imports c.i.f.; exports f.o.b. [6]Tunis Air only.

Internet resources for further information:
- **Central Bank of Tunisia http://www.bct.gov.tn/english/index.html**
- **National Statistics Institute (French only) http://www.ins.nat.tn**

Turkey

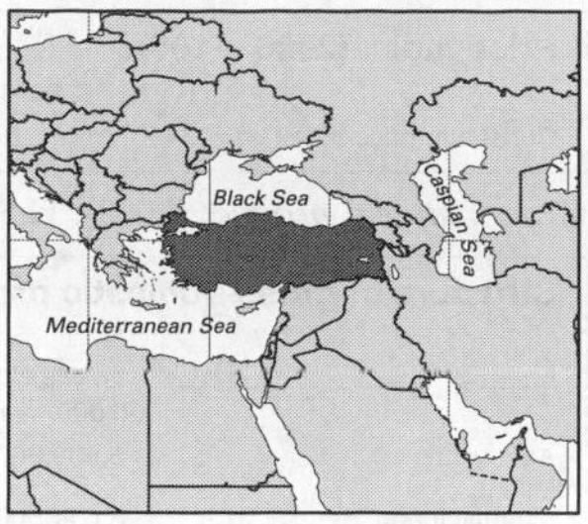

Official name: Türkiye Cumhuriyeti (Republic of Turkey).
Form of government: multiparty republic with one legislative house (Turkish Grand National Assembly [550]).
Chief of state: President.
Head of government: Prime Minister.
Capital: Ankara.
Official language: Turkish.
Official religion: none.
Monetary unit: 1 Turkish lira (TL) = 100 kurush; valuation (Sept. 1, 2004) 1 U.S.$ = TL 1,504,000; 1 £ = TL 2,705,000[1].

Area and population

		area[2]		population
				2000
Geographic regions[3]	Largest cities	sq mi	sq km	census
Aegean	İzmir	34,920	90,442	8,938,781
Black Sea	Samsun	32,080	83,088	7,120,747
Central Anatolia	Ankara	97,218	251,793	16,073,370
East Anatolia	Diyarbakir	67,916	175,901	8,004,382
Marmara	Istanbul	24,539	63,556	16,414,533
Mediterranean	Adana	28,485	73,775	7,703,621
South Eastern Anatolia	Gaziantep	13,521	35,020	3,548,493
TOTAL		299,158[4]	774,815[4]	67,803,927

Demography

Population (2004): 71,617,000.
Density (2004): persons per sq mi 239.4, persons per sq km 92.4.
Urban-rural (2004): urban 61.2%; rural 38.8%.
Sex distribution (2000): male 50.57%; female 49.43%.
Age breakdown (2000): under 15, 29.1%; 15–29, 28.8%; 30–44, 21.5%; 45–59, 11.8%; 60–74, 6.8%; 75 and over, 2.0%.
Population projection: (2010) 77,297,000; (2020) 84,971,000.
Doubling time: 50 years.
Ethnic composition (2000)[5]: Turk 65.1%; Kurd 18.9%; Crimean Tatar 7.2%; Arab 1.8%; Azerbaijani 1.0%; Yoruk 1.0%; other 5.0%.
Religious affiliation (2000): Muslim 97.2%, of which Sunnī *c.* 67%, Shīʿī *c.* 30% (including nonorthodox Alevi *c.* 26%); Christian (mostly Eastern Orthodox) 0.6%; other 2.2%.
Major urban agglomerations (2001): Istanbul 10,243,000; Ankara 4,611,000; İzmir 3,437,000; Bursa (2000) 1,166,000; Adana (2000) 1,091,000.

Vital statistics

Birth rate per 1,000 population (2003): 20.9 (world avg. 21.3).
Death rate per 1,000 population (2003): 7.0 (world avg. 9.1).
Natural increase rate per 1,000 population (2003): 13.9 (world avg. 12.2).
Total fertility rate (avg. births per childbearing woman; 2003): 2.4.
Marriage rate per 1,000 population (2000): 7.1.
Divorce rate per 1,000 population (2000): 0.5.
Life expectancy at birth (2003): male 66.4 years; female 71.0 years.
Major causes of death per 100,000 population (1995)[6]: diseases of the circulatory system 322; malignant neoplasms (cancers) 71; accidents and violence 32; infectious and parasitic diseases 20; ill-defined conditions 129.

National economy

Budget (2003). Revenue: TL 100,238,122,000,000,000 (tax revenue 84.1%, of which tax on income 27.7%; nontax revenue 14.0%; grants 1.9%). Expenditures: TL 140,053,981,000,000,000 (interest payments 41.8%; personnel 21.6%; investments 5.1%).
Public debt (external, outstanding; 2002): U.S.$61,823,000,000.
Production (in '000 metric tons except as noted). Agriculture, forestry, fishing (2003): wheat 19,000, sugar beets 13,090, tomatoes 9,750, barley 8,100, potatoes 5,300, watermelons 4,250, grapes 3,650, corn (maize) 2,800, apples 2,500, seed cotton 2,489, oranges 1,215, sunflower seeds 800, olives 700, lentils 548, hazelnuts 490, peaches 460, apricots 440, figs 280, tobacco 152, tea 131, garlic 117, attar of roses (1993) 800 kg; livestock (number of live animals) 27,000,000 sheep, 10,400,000 cattle, (2000) 373,000 angora goats; roundwood (2002) 18,465,000 cu m; fish catch (2001) 595,000. Mining (2002): refined borates 436,000; chromite 313,637; copper ore (metal content) 48,253. Manufacturing (value added in U.S.$'000,000; 2000): textiles 16,289; refined petroleum 4,839; food products 4,111; chemicals and chemical products 3,805; motor vehicles 2,177; nonelectrical machinery 2,020. Energy production (consumption): electricity (kW-hr; 2003) 139,700,000,000 ([2000] 117,709,000,000); hard coal (metric tons; 2003) 2,996,000 ([2000] 15,393,000); lignite (metric tons; 2003) 43,536,000 ([2000] 64,406,000); crude petroleum (barrels; 2003) 16,988,000 ([2000] 172,115,000); petroleum products (metric tons; 2000) 19,723,000 (26,108,000); natural gas (cu m; 2000) 630,102,000 (15,762,000,000).
Tourism (2002): receipts from visitors U.S.$11,901,000,000; expenditures by nationals abroad U.S.$1,880,000,000.
Population economically active (2004)[7]: total 24,457,000; activity rate of total population 34.1% (participation rates: over age 14, 49.2%; female 26.6%; unemployed 9.3%).

Price and earnings indexes (2000 = 100)

	1997	1998	1999	2000	2001	2002	2003
Consumer price index	21.2	39.2	64.6	100.0	154.4	223.8	280.4
Annual earnings index	...	...	...	100.0	...	...	...

Gross national product (2003): U.S.$197,220,000,000 (U.S.$2,790 per capita).

Structure of gross domestic product and labour force

	2002			
	in value TL '000,000,000	% of total value	labour force	% of labour force
Agriculture	32,933,706	11.9	6,745,000	29.7
Mining	2,914,077	1.0	114,000	0.5
Manufacturing	55,764,399	20.2	3,675,000	16.2
Construction	11,495,788	4.2	931,000	4.1
Public utilities	11,355,859	4.1	99,000	0.4
Transp. and commun.	41,591,326	15.1	973,000	4.3
Trade	56,111,341	20.3	3,898,000	17.2
Finance, real estate	24,498,802	8.9	679,000	3.0
Pub. admin., defense	27,838,383	10.1	1,096,000	4.8
Services	11,440,615	4.1	2,076,000	9.1
Other	59,692[8]	0.0[8]	2,412,000[9]	10.6[9]
TOTAL	276,002,988	100.0[4]	22,698,000	100.0[4]

Household income and expenditure (1994). Average household size (2002) 4.5; income per household TL 165,089,000 (U.S.$5,576); expenditure: food, tobacco, and café expenditures 38.5%, housing 22.8%, clothing 9.0%.
Land use as % of total land area (2000): in temporary crops 31.4%, in permanent crops 3.3%, in pasture 16.1%; overall forest area 13.3%.

Foreign trade[10]

Balance of trade (current prices)

	1998	1999	2000	2001	2002	2003
U.S.$'000,000	–18,947	–14,084	–26,782	–10,065	–15,450	–21,856
% of total	26.0%	20.9%	32.5%	13.8%	17.8%	18.9%

Imports (2003): U.S.$68,734,000,000 (chemicals and chemical products 16.2%; nonelectrical machinery 11.9%; crude petroleum and natural gas 11.3%; motor vehicles 9.3%; electrical machinery 9.1%; iron and steel 6.8%). *Major import sources:* Germany 13.7%; Italy 7.9%; Russia 7.9%; France 6.0%; U.S. 5.0%; U.K. 5.0%.
Exports (2003): U.S.$46,878,000,000 (textiles, apparel, and clothing accessories 20.3%; vehicles 11.2%; electrical and electronic machinery 7.4%; nonelectrical machinery 6.3%; iron and steel 6.2%; raw and prepared fruits and vegetables 5.3%). *Major export destinations:* Germany 15.9%; U.S. 8.0%; U.K. 7.8%; Italy 6.8%; France 6.0%.

Transport and communications

Transport. Railroads (2003): length 5,388 mi, 8,671 km; passenger-km 5,893,000,000; metric ton-km cargo 8,271,000,000. Roads (2000): total length 238,379 mi, 383,636 km (paved [1997] 25%). Vehicles (2003): passenger cars 4,677,765; trucks and buses 1,713,605. Air transport (2003)[11]: passenger-km 16,113,000; metric ton-km cargo 369,199,000; airports (1996) 26.

Communications

Medium	date	unit	number	units per 1,000 persons
Daily newspapers	2000	circulation	7,480,000	111
Radio	2001	receivers	32,195,000	470
Television	2002	receivers	29,440,000	423
Telephones	2003	main lines	18,916,700	277
Cellular telephones	2003	subscribers	27,887,500	408
Personal computers	2002	units	3,000,000	45
Internet	2003	users	5,500,000	81

Education and health

Educational attainment (1993). Percentage of population age 25 and over having: no formal schooling 30.5%; incomplete primary education 6.6%; complete primary 40.4%; incomplete secondary 3.1%; complete secondary or higher 19.1%; unknown 0.3%. *Literacy* (2003): total population age 15 and over literate 88.3%; males literate 95.3%; females literate 79.9%.

Education (2000)

	schools	teachers	students	student/ teacher ratio
Primary (age 6–10)	36,072	345,015	10,480,700	30.4
Secondary (age 11–16)	2,747	73,418	1,487,400	20.3
Voc., teacher tr.	3,544	71,665	875,200	12.2
Higher	1,273	67,880	1,607,400	23.7

Health: physicians (2001) 82,920 (1 per 826 persons); hospital beds (2000) 156,549 (1 per 431 persons); infant mortality rate (2003) 38.3.
Food (2000): daily per capita caloric intake 3,343 (vegetable products 90%, animal products 10%); 133% of FAO recommended minimum requirement.

Military

Total active duty personnel (2003): 514,850 (army 78.1%, navy 10.2%, air force 11.7%). *Military expenditure as percentage of GNP* (1999): 5.3% (world 2.4%); per capita expenditure U.S.$154.

[1]New Turkish lira (YTL) to be introduced Jan. 1, 2005; 1 YTL = TL 1,000,000. [2]Estimated figures. [3]Administratively divided into 81 provinces as of 2004. [4]Detail does not add to total given because of rounding. [5]Per unofficial source. [6]Projected rates based on about 42% of total deaths. [7]Second quarter; civilian population only. [8]Import duties less imputed bank charges. [9]Unemployed. [10]Imports c.i.f.; exports f.o.b. [11]Turkish Airlines only.

Internet resources for further information:
- **Ministry of Foreign Affairs http://www.mfa.gov.tr**
- **Central Bank of Turkey http://www.tcmb.gov.tr**
- **State Institute of Statistics http://www.die.gov.tr**

Turkmenistan

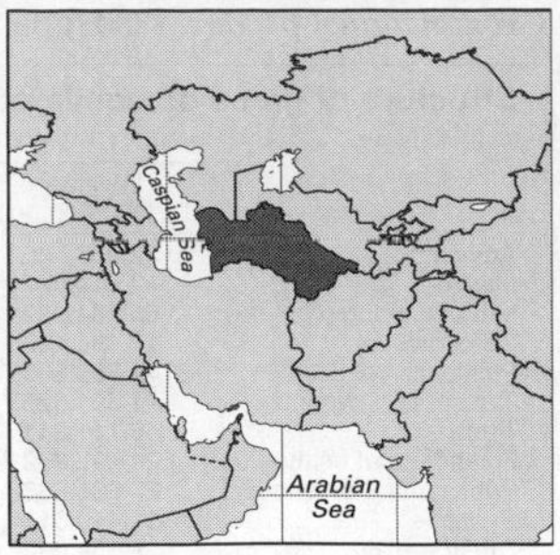

Official name: Türkmenistan (Turkmenistan).
Form of government: unitary republic with one legislative body (Majlis [Parliament; 50]).
Head of state and government: President assisted by the People's Council[1].
Capital: Ashgabat (formerly Ashkhabad).
Official language: Turkmen.
Official religion: none.
Monetary unit: manat; valuation (July 31, 2004) 1 U.S.$ = 5,200 manat; 1 £ = 9,468 manat.

Area and population

Provinces	Capitals	area sq mi	area sq km	population 2001 estimate
Ahal	Ashgabat	37,500[2]	97,100[2]	767,700
Balkan	Balkanabat	53,500	138,600	468,900
Daşoguz	Daşoguz	28,100	72,700	1,165,000
Lebap	Türkmenabat (Chärjew)	36,000	93,200	1,130,700
Mary	Mary	33,400	86,400	1,251,300
City				
Ashgabat	—	[2]	[2]	695,300
TOTAL		188,500	488,100[3]	5,478,900

Demography

Population (2004): 4,940,000[4].
Density (2004): persons per sq mi 26.2, persons per sq km 10.1.
Urban-rural (2002): urban 44.9%; rural 55.1%.
Sex distribution (2001): male 49.44%; female 50.56%.
Age breakdown (2001): under 15, 37.9%; 15–29, 27.9%; 30–44, 23.7%; 45–59, 6.5%; 60–74, 3.5%; 75 and over, 0.5%.
Population projection[4]: (2010) 5,412,000; (2020) 6,211,000.
Doubling time: 37 years.
Ethnic composition (1997): Turkmen 77.0%; Uzbek 9.2%; Russian 6.7%; Kazakh 2.0%; Tatar 0.8%; other 4.3%.
Religious affiliation (1995): Muslim (mostly Sunnī) 87.0%; Russian Orthodox 2.4%; other (mostly nonreligious) 10.6%.
Major cities (1999): Ashgabat (2002) 743,000; Türkmenabat 203,000; Daşoguz 165,000; Mary 123,000; Balkanabat 108,000.

Vital statistics

Birth rate per 1,000 population (2003): 28.0 (world avg. 21.3); (1998) legitimate 96.2%; illegitimate 3.8%.
Death rate per 1,000 population (2003): 8.9 (world avg. 9.1).
Natural increase rate per 1,000 population (2003): 19.1 (world avg. 12.2).
Total fertility rate (avg. births per childbearing woman; 2003): 3.5.
Marriage rate per 1,000 population (1998): 5.4.
Divorce rate per 1,000 population (1994): 1.5.
Life expectancy at birth (2003): male 57.7 years; female 64.8 years.
Major causes of death per 100,000 population (1998): diseases of the circulatory system 314.6; diseases of the respiratory system 101.1; infectious and parasitic diseases 99.1; accidents, poisoning, and violence 59.3; malignant neoplasms (cancers) 43.9; diseases of the digestive system 30.2.

National economy

Budget (1999). Revenue: 3,693,100,000,000 manat (value-added tax 25.6%, pension and social security fund 22.5%, repayments of scheduled gas 13.0%, excise tax 10.2%, personal income tax 6.1%). Expenditures: 3,894,300,000,000 manat (education 26.9%, pension and social security 15.6%, defense and security 14.9%, health 14.1%, agriculture 5.7%).
Public debt (external, outstanding; 2000): U.S.$1,731,000,000.
Production (metric tons except as noted). Agriculture, forestry, fishing (2002): wheat 2,033,000, seed cotton 600,000, vegetables and melons 327,000, watermelons 230,000, fruit excluding watermelons 185,000; livestock (number of live animals) 6,375,000 sheep and goats, 860,000 cattle, 4,800,000 poultry; roundwood (2000) 2,000,000 cu m; fish catch (2001) 12,792. Mining and quarrying (2000): gypsum 100,000, sodium sulfate 60,000, sulfur 9,000, iodine 355. Manufacturing (value of production in '000,000 manat; 1994): ferrous and nonferrous metals 278; machinery and metalworks 223; food products 129; chemical products 90; construction materials 52; wood products 31. Construction (1994): 1,700,000 sq m. Energy production (consumption): electricity (kW-hr; 2000) 9,845,000,000 (8,777,000,000); crude petroleum (barrels; 2001) 58,000,000 (19,000,000); petroleum products (metric tons; 2000) 6,113,000 (2,354,000); natural gas (cu m; 2001) 46,439,000,000 (7,362,000,000).
Household income and expenditure. Average household size (2000) 4.7; income per household: n.a.; sources of income (1998): wages and salaries 70.6%, pensions and grants 20.9%, self-employment (mainly agricultural income) 2.3%, nonwage income of workers 1.1%; expenditure (1998): food 45.2%, clothing and footwear 16.8%, furniture 13.3%, transportation 7.6%, health 7.0%.
Population economically active (2000): total 1,950,000; activity rate of total population 42.0% (participation rates [1996]: ages 16–59 [male], 16–54 [female] 73.0%; female 42.7%; unemployed, n.a.).

Price index (2000 = 100)

	1997	1998	1999	2000	2001	2002	2003
Consumer price index	64.2	75.0	92.6	100.0	111.6	121.4	128.2

Gross national product (2003): U.S.$5,400,000,000 (U.S.$1,120 per capita).

Structure of gross domestic product and labour force

	2000 in value '000,000 manat	2000 % of total value	1998 labour force	1998 % of labour force
Agriculture	5,903,300	25.8	892,400	48.5
Mining, Manufacturing, Public utilities	8,644,500	37.8		
Mining, Manufacturing			226,800	12.3
Public utilities			48,300	2.6
Construction	2,244,000	9.8	108,200	5.9
Transp. and commun.	1,043,700	4.6	90,700	4.9
Trade	1,008,100	4.4	115,800	6.4
Finance, Public administration, defense, Services, Other	4,051,000	17.7		
Finance			12,600	0.7
Public administration, defense			28,800	1.6
Services			284,900	15.5
Other			30,200	1.6
TOTAL	22,894,600	100.0[3]	1,838,700	100.0

Tourism: receipts from visitors (1998) U.S.$192,000,000; expenditures (1997) U.S.$125,000,000.
Land use as % of total land area (2000): in temporary crops 3.7%, in permanent crops 0.1%, in pasture 65.3%; overall forest area 8.0%.

Foreign trade[5]

Balance of trade (current prices)

	1997	1998	1999	2000	2001	2002
U.S.$'000,000	−231	−414	−291	+721	+271	+737
% of total	13.0%	25.8%	10.9%	16.8%	5.5%	14.8%

Imports (2002): U.S.$2,119,000,000 (machinery and transport equipment 40.5%, basic manufactures 18.6%, chemicals and chemical products 9.9%, food products 5.4%). *Major import sources* (2002): Ukraine 17.9%; Germany 12.1%; U.A.E. 11.7%; Russia 10.6%; Turkey 8.8%; Iran 7.3%.
Exports (2002): U.S.$2,856,000,000 (natural gas 57.5%, petrochemicals 14.2%, crude petroleum 11.9%, cotton yarn and fabrics 2.8%, raw cotton 1.7%). *Major export destinations* (2000): Russia 41.1%; Germany 16.2%; Iran 9.7%; Turkey 7.4%; Ukraine 6.6%.

Transport and communications

Transport. Railroads (1999): length 1,437 mi, 2,313 km; passenger-km 701,000,000; metric ton-km cargo 7,337,000,000. Roads (1999): total length 24,000 km (paved 81%). Vehicles (1995): passenger cars 220,000; trucks and buses 58,200. Air transport (2001)[6]: passenger-km 1,631,000,000; metric ton-km cargo 35,000,000; airports (2002) with scheduled flights 1.

Communications

Medium	date	unit	number	units per 1,000 persons
Radio	2000	receivers	1,190,000	256
Television	2000	receivers	911,000	196
Telephones	2002	main lines	374,000	77
Cellular phones	2002	subscribers	8,200	1.7
Internet	2001	users	8,000	1.6

Education and health

Educational attainment: n.a. *Literacy* (1999): total population age 15 and over literate 98.0%.

Education (1994–95)

	schools	teachers	students	student/ teacher ratio
Primary (age 6–13), Secondary (age 14–17)	1,900	72,900	940,600	12.9
Voc., teacher tr.	78	...	26,000	...
Higher	15	...	29,435[7]	...

Health (1995): physicians 13,500 (1 per 330 persons); hospital beds 46,000 (1 per 97 persons); infant mortality rate per 1,000 live births (2003) 73.2.
Food (2001): daily per capita caloric intake 2,738 (vegetable products 97%, animal products 3%); 107% of FAO recommended minimum requirement.

Military

Total active duty personnel (2003): 29,000 (army 86.3%, navy 3.4%, air force 10.3%). *Military expenditure as percentage of GNP* (1999): 3.4% (world 2.4%); per capita expenditure U.S.$122.

[1]Hybrid body that is a branch of state power per August 2003 constitutional amendment. [2]Ahal includes Ashgabat. [3]Detail does not add to total given because of rounding. [4]UN estimate; official Turkmen estimates are significantly higher. [5]Import data in balance of trade is c.i.f. [6]Turkmenavia only. [7]1995–96.

Internet resources for further information:
- **Interstate Statistical Committee of the Commonwealth of Independent States http://www.cisstat.com/eng/macro0.htm**
- **Asia Development Bank: Turkmenistan http://www.adb.org/Turkmenistan/default.asp**

Tuvalu

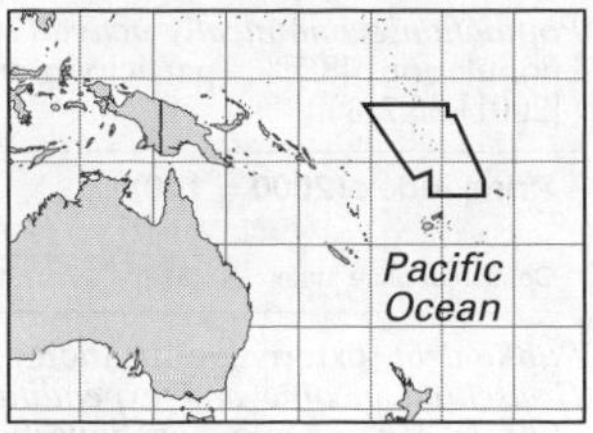

Official name: Tuvalu.
Form of government: constitutional monarchy with one legislative house (Parliament [12]).
Chief of state: British Monarch, represented by Governor-General.
Head of government: Prime Minister.
Capital: government offices are at Vaiaku, Fongafale islet, of Funafuti atoll.
Official language: none.
Official religion: none.
Monetary units[1]: 1 Tuvalu dollar = 1 Australian dollar ($T = $A) = 100 Tuvalu and Australian cents; valuation (Sept. 1, 2004) 1 U.S.$ = $A 1.42; 1 £ = $A 2.55.

Area and population

		area		population
				2002
Islands[2]	**Capitals**	sq mi	sq km	census
Funafuti	Fongafale	1.08	2.79	4,492
Nanumaga	Tonga	1.07	2.78	589
Nanumea	Lolua	1.49	3.87	664
Niulakita	—	0.16	0.42	35
Niutao	Kua	0.98	2.53	663
Nui	Tanrake	1.09	2.83	548
Nukufetau	Savave	1.15	2.99	586
Nukulaelae	Fangaua	0.70	1.82	393
Vaitupu	Asau	2.16	5.60	1,591
TOTAL		9.90[3, 4]	25.63[3]	9,561

Demography

Population (2004): 9,600.
Density (2004): persons per sq mi 969.7, persons per sq km 374.6.
Urban-rural (2002): urban 47.0%; rural 53.0%.
Sex distribution (2002): male 49.46%; female 50.54%.
Age breakdown (2002): under 15, 36.2%; 15–29, 21.2%; 30–44, 20.2%; 45–59, 13.8%; 60–74, 6.8%; 75 and over, 1.8%.
Population projection: (2010) 11,000; (2020) 12,000.
Doubling time: 41 years.
Ethnic composition (2000): Tuvaluan (Polynesian) 96.3%; mixed (Pacific Islander/European/Asian) 1.0%; Micronesian 1.0%; European 0.5%; other 1.2%.
Religious affiliation (1995): Church of Tuvalu (Congregational) 85.4%; Seventh-day Adventist 3.6%; Roman Catholic 1.4%; Jehovah's Witness 1.1%; Bahā'ī 1.0%; other 7.5%.
Major locality (2002): Fongafale, on Funafuti atoll, 4,492.

Vital statistics

Birth rate per 1,000 population (2002): 27.1 (world avg. 21.3).
Death rate per 1,000 population (2002): 9.9 (world avg. 9.1).
Natural increase rate per 1,000 population (2002): 17.2 (world avg. 12.2).
Total fertility rate (avg. births per childbearing woman; 2002): 3.7.
Life expectancy at birth (2002): male 61.7 years; female 65.1 years.
Major causes of death per 100,000 population (1985): diseases of the digestive system 170.0; diseases of the circulatory system 150.0; diseases of the respiratory system 120.0; diseases of the nervous system 120.0; malignant neoplasms (cancers) 70.0; infectious and parasitic diseases 40.0; endocrine and metabolic disorders 20.0; ill-defined conditions 430.0.

National economy

Budget (2001). Revenue: $A 33,519,000. Expenditures: $A 24,091,000.
Public debt (external; 2003): n.a.
Gross national product (1998): U.S.$14,700,000 (U.S.$1,400 per capita).

Structure of gross domestic product and labour force

	1998		1991	
	in value $A '000[5]	% of total value[5]	labour force	% of labour force
Agriculture, fishing, forestry	3,484	15.8	4,020	68.0
Mining	638	2.9	—	—
Manufacturing[6]	881	4.0	60	1.0
Construction	2,951	13.4	240	4.0
Public utilities	574	2.6	—	—
Transp. and commun.	1,380	6.2	60	1.0
Trade, hotels, and restaurants	2,972	13.5	240	4.0
Finance	2,376	10.8	—	—
Pub. admin., defense Services	4,806	21.8	1,290	22.0
Other	1,983	9.0	...	...
TOTAL	22,045	100.0	5,910	100.0

Production (metric tons except as noted). Agriculture[7], forestry, fishing (2002): coconuts 1,000, tropical fruit 400, vegetables 380, bananas 250, roots and tubers 120, other agricultural products include breadfruit, pulaka (taro), pandanus fruit, sweet potatoes, and pawpaws; livestock (number of live animals) 13,200 pigs, 10,000 ducks, 40,000 chickens; forestry, n.a.; fish catch (2001) 500. Mining and quarrying[8]: n.a. Manufacturing: tiny amounts of copra, handicrafts, and garments. Overseas employment (2000) of Tuvaluan seafarers contributes about U.S.$5,000,000 annually to the Tuvalu economy.
Energy production (consumption): electricity (kW-hr; 1992) 1,300,000 (1,300,000); coal, none (none); crude petroleum, none (n.a.); petroleum products, none (n.a.); natural gas, none (none).
Tourism (1998): receipts from visitors U.S.$200,000; expenditures by nationals abroad, n.a.
Population economically active (1991): total 5,910; activity rate of total population 65.3% (participation rates: ages 15–64, 85.5%; female [1979] 51.3%; unemployed [1979] 4.0%).

Price index (2000 = 100)

	1997	1998	1999	2000	2001	2002	2003
Consumer price index	111.5	112.4	96.2	100.0	101.4	106.6	110.1

Household income and expenditure. Average household size (1994): Funafuti 7.0, other islands 5.8; average annual gross income per household (1994): Funafuti $A 12,012 (U.S.$8,789), other islands $A 3,536 (U.S.$2,587); sources of income (1987): agriculture and other 45.0%, cash economy only 38.0%, overseas remittances 17.0%; expenditure (1992)[9]: food 45.5%, housing and household operations 11.5%, transportation 10.5%, alcohol and tobacco 10.5%, clothing 7.5%, other 14.5%.
Land use as % of total land area (2000): in temporary crops, n.a., in permanent crops, n.a., in pasture, n.a.; overall forest area, n.a.[10].

Foreign trade

Balance of trade (current prices)

	1997	1998	1999	2000	2001	2002
$A '000	–10,028	–15,495	–12,289	–8,866	–6,737	–20,110
% of total	96.9%	96.8%	97.2%	99.6%	99.1%	97.6%

Imports (2002): $A 20,362,000 (food products including live animals 23.5%, mineral fuels 13.8%, machinery and apparatus 12.4%, base and fabricated metals 8.8%, transport equipment 7.3%). *Major import sources:* Australia 34.7%; Fiji 29.4%; New Zealand 13.9%; Japan 10.3%; China 3.7%.
Exports (2002): $A 252,000 (primarily copra, stamps, and handicrafts). *Major export destinations:* Fiji 58.9%; Australia 22.3%; New Zealand 11.4%; Japan 5.7%.

Transport and communications

Transport. Railroads: none. Roads (2000): total length 28 km (paved, none). Vehicles[11]: n.a. Merchant marine (1992): vessels (100 gross tons and over) 6; total deadweight tonnage 16,005. Air transport: n.a.; airports (2001) 1.

Communications

Medium	date	unit	number	units per 1,000 persons
Radio	1997	receivers	4,000	384
Television	1996	receivers	100	13
Telephones	2002	main lines	1,300	125

Education and health

Educational attainment (mid-1990s). Percentage of population age 15 and over (on Funafuti) having: no formal schooling through completed primary education 31.9%; some secondary 46.6%; completed secondary to some higher 18.6%; completed higher 2.9%. *Literacy* (1990): total population literate in Tuvaluan 8,593 (95.0%); literacy in English estimated at 45.0%.

Education (2000)

	schools	teachers	students	student/ teacher ratio
Primary (age 5–11)	12[12]	91[13]	1,811[13]	19.9[13]
Secondary (age 12–18)	1	31	345	11.1
Vocational[14]	1	10	58	...
Higher	—	—	—	—

Health (1999): physicians 8 (1 per 1,375 persons); hospital beds (1990) 30 (1 per 302 persons); infant mortality rate per 1,000 live births (2002): 35.0.

Military

Total active duty personnel: none; Tuvalu relies on Australian-trained volunteers from Fiji and Papua New Guinea.

[1]The value of the Tuvalu dollar is pegged to the value of the Australian dollar, which is also legal currency in Tuvalu. [2]Local government councils have been established on all islands except Niulakita. [3]Another survey puts the area at 9.4 sq mi (24.4 sq km). [4]Detail does not add to total given because of rounding. [5]In purchasers' values. [6]Including cottage industry. [7]Because of poor soil quality, only limited subsistence agriculture is possible on the islands. [8]Research into the mineral potential of Tuvalu's maritime exclusive economic zone (289,500 sq mi [750,000 sq km] of the Pacific Ocean) is currently being conducted by the South Pacific Geo-Science Commission. [9]Weights of consumer price index components. [10]Coconut trees occupy *c.* 77% of land area. [11]There are several cars, tractors, trailers, and light trucks on Funafuti; a few motorcycles are in use on most islands. [12]1998. [13]1994. [14]1991.

Internet resources for further information:
- **United Nations Development Programme, Common Country Assessments http://www.undp.org.fj/CCAs.htm**
- **Secretariat of Pacific Community http://www.spc.int/prism/country/tv/tv_index.html**

Uganda

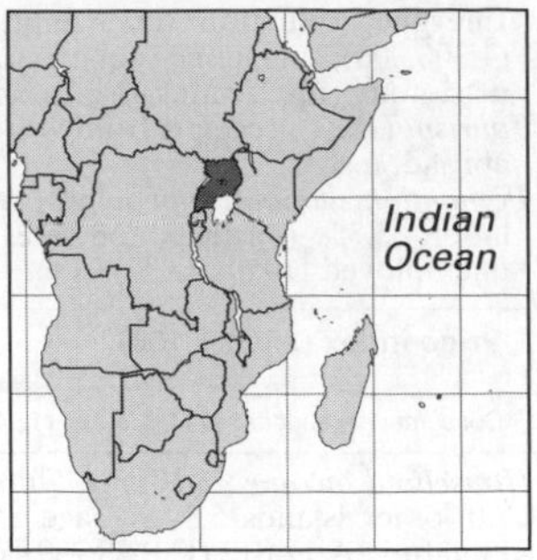

Official name: Republic of Uganda.
Form of government: nonparty republic with one legislative house (Parliament [305[1]]).
Head of state and government: President.
Capital: Kampala.
Official language: English[2].
Official religion: none.
Monetary unit: 1 Uganda shilling (U Sh) = 100 cents; valuation (Sept. 1, 2004) 1 U.S.$ = U Sh 1,714; 1 £ = U Sh 3,084.

Area and population

Geographic regions[3]	Principal cities	area sq mi	area sq km	population 2002 census[4]
Central	Kampala	23,749	61,510	6,683,887
Eastern	Jinja	15,426	39,953	6,301,677
Northern	Gulu	32,687	84,658	5,345,964
Western	Mbarara	21,204	54,917	6,417,449
TOTAL		93,065[5, 6]	241,038[5]	24,748,977

Demography

Population (2004): 26,335,000.
Density (2004)[7]: persons per sq mi 346.1, persons per sq km 133.6.
Urban-rural (2002): urban 12.2%; rural 87.8%.
Sex distribution (2002): male 48.99%; female 51.01%.
Age breakdown (2002): under 15, 50.9%; 15–29, 26.4%; 30–44, 13.4%; 45–59, 5.6%; 60–74, 3.0%; 75 and over, 0.7%.
Population projection: (2010) 32,424,000; (2020) 45,826,000.
Doubling time: 23 years.
Ethnolinguistic composition (1991): Ganda 18.1%; Nkole 10.7%; Kiga 8.4%; Soga 8.2%; Lango 5.9%; Lugbara 4.7%; Gisu 4.5%; Acholi 4.4%.
Religious affiliation (1995): Christian 66%, of which Roman Catholic 33%, Protestant 33% (of which mostly Anglican); traditional beliefs 18%; Muslim 16%.
Major cities (2002): Kampala 1,208,544[8]; Gulu 113,144; Lira 89,871; Jinja 86,520; Mbale 70,437.

Vital statistics

Birth rate per 1,000 population (2003): 46.6 (world avg. 21.3).
Death rate per 1,000 population (2003): 17.0 (world avg. 9.1).
Natural increase rate per 1,000 population (2003): 29.6 (world avg. 12.2).
Total fertility rate (avg. births per childbearing woman; 2003): 6.7.
Life expectancy at birth (2003): male 43.4 years; female 46.4 years.
Adult population (ages 15–49) *living with HIV* (2004[9]): 4.1% (world avg. 1.1%).

National economy

Budget (2001–02). Revenue: U Sh 1,977,500,000,000 (tax revenue 58.4%, of which VAT 19.9%, excise taxes 18.3%, income taxes 14.4%, tax on international trade 5.9%; grants 36.6%; nontax revenue 5.0%). Expenditures: U Sh 2,565,000,000,000 (current expenditures 55.8%, of which public administration 14.3%, education 14.1%, defense 8.2%, health 6.4%, public order 4.5%; capital expenditures 44.2%).
Production (metric tons except as noted). Agriculture, forestry, fishing (2002): plantains 9,600,000, cassava 5,300,000, sweet potatoes 2,515,000, sugarcane 1,600,000, corn (maize) 1,174,000, millet 590,000, potatoes 510,000, sorghum 430,000, coffee 198,000, peanuts (groundnuts) 148,000, rice 114,000; livestock (number of live animals) 5,900,000 cattle, 5,600,000 goats, 1,550,000 pigs, 1,200,000 sheep, 25,500,000 chickens; roundwood 38,316,824 cu m; fish catch (2001) 356,032. Mining and quarrying (2002): cobalt 450; columbite-tantalite (ore and concentrate) 6,463 kg. Manufacturing (2001): cement 431,084; sugar 130,326; soap 90,807; metal products 77,049; footwear 1,979,000 pairs; beer 1,079,000 hectolitres; soft drinks 816,860 hectolitres. Energy production (consumption): electricity (kW-hr; 2001) 1,534,700,000 (1,534,700,000); coal (metric tons) none (none); crude petroleum (barrels) none (none); petroleum products (metric tons; 2000) none (436,000); natural gas (cu m) none (none).
Tourism (2002): receipts from visitors U.S.$185,000,000; expenditures by nationals abroad (1999) U.S.$141,000,000.
Gross national product (2003): U.S.$6,173,000,000 (U.S.$240 per capita).

Structure of gross domestic product and labour force

	2001–02 in value U Sh '000,000	2001–02 % of total value	2002 labour force	2002 % of labour force
Agriculture	2,956,000	28.7	9,493,000	79.1
Mining	82,000	0.8		
Manufacturing	957,000	9.3		
Construction	858,000	8.3		
Public utilities	240,000	2.3		
Transp. and commun.	522,000	5.1	2,502,000	20.9
Trade	1,240,000	12.0		
Finance	390,000	3.8		
Pub. admin., defense	491,000	4.8		
Services	1,684,000	16.4		
Other	872,000[10]	8.5[10]		
TOTAL	10,292,000	100.0	11,995,000	100.0

Population economically active (2002): total 11,995,000; activity rate of total population 48.5% (participation rates [2001]: ages 15–64, 78.9%; female [2001] 35.2%).

Price index (2000 = 100)

	1997	1998	1999	2000	2001	2002	2003
Consumer price index	91.5	91.4	97.3	100.0	102.0	101.7	109.6

Public debt (external, outstanding; 2002): U.S.$3,690,000,000.
Household income and expenditure (1999–2000)[11]. Average household size (2002) 4.7; income per household U Sh 141,000 (U.S.$91[12]); sources of income: wages and self-employment 78.0%, transfers 13.0%, rent 9.0%; expenditure: food and beverages 51.0%, rent, energy, and services 17.0%, education 7.0%, household durable goods 6.0%, transportation 5.0%, health 4.0%.
Land use as % of total land area (2000): in temporary crops 25.7%, in permanent crops 10.7%, in pasture 25.9%; overall forest area 21.0%.

Foreign trade[13]

Balance of trade (current prices)

	1997–98	1998–99	1999–2000	2000–01	2001–02
U.S.$'000,000	–506.7	–490.3	–525.1	–527.7	–609.4
% of total	35.5%	30.9%	36.7%	37.2%	39.5%

Imports (2001–02): U.S.$1,084,900,000 (machinery and apparatus 28.3%, refined petroleum 16.1%, food and live animals 15.9%, road vehicles 15.8%, pharmaceuticals 4.9%). *Major import sources* (2002): Kenya 45.1%; South Africa 6.7%; India 5.6%; U.K. 5.5%; France 3.4%.
Exports (2001–02): U.S.$475,500,000 (unroasted coffee 21.6%, fish products 17.0%, tea 5.7%, cereal 2.8%, cotton 2.8%). *Major export destinations* (2002): Belgium 16.2%; The Netherlands 13.7%; Germany 7.5%; Spain 5.5%; Hong Kong 4.9%.

Transport and communications

Transport. Railroads (2000): route length 1,241 km; passenger-km[14]; metric ton-km cargo (2001) 220,000,000. Roads (1996): total length 26,800 km (paved 7.7%). Vehicles (2000): passenger cars 49,016; trucks and buses 55,683. Air transport (2000): passenger-km 215,000,000; metric ton-km cargo, n.a.; airports (2002) 1.

Communications

Medium	date	unit	number	units per 1,000 persons
Daily newspapers	2000	circulation	45,900	2.0
Radio	2000	receivers	2,920,000	127
Television	2002	receivers	442,800	18
Telephones	2003	main lines	61,000	2.4
Cellular telephones	2003	subscribers	776,200	30
Personal computers	2003	units	103,000	4.0
Internet	2003	users	125,000	4.9

Education and health

Educational attainment (1991). Percentage of population age 25 and over having: no formal schooling or less than one full year 46.9%; primary education 42.1%; secondary 10.5%; higher 0.5%. *Literacy* (2001): population age 10 and over literate 68.0%; males literate 78.1%; females literate 58.0%.

Education (2001)

	schools	teachers	students	student/teacher ratio
Primary (age 5–11)	12,280	127,038	6,900,916	54.3
Secondary (age 12–15)	2,400	30,425	539,786	17.7
Voc., teacher tr.[15, 16]	...	2,094	38,500	18.4
Higher[17]	2	1,134[18]	30,243	12.6[18]

Health: physicians (1993) 840 (1 per 22,399 persons); hospital beds (1996) 22,788 (1 per 880 persons); infant mortality rate (2003) 87.9.
Food (2001): daily per capita caloric intake 2,398 (vegetable products 94%, animal products 6%); 103% of FAO recommended minimum requirement.

Military

Total active duty personnel (2003): 60,000 (army 100%). *Military expenditure as percentage of GNP* (1999): 2.3% (world 2.4%); per capita expenditure U.S.$6.

[1]Includes 10 ex officio members (ministers who are not elected to Parliament). [2]The constitution was translated into six local languages in 1999 including Ganda (Luganda), Acholi, Teso (Ateso), Lugbara, and two others. [3]The 39 administrative districts in Uganda as of 1994 were increased to 45 administrative districts in 1997. Eight additional administrative districts were announced in November 2000 and 3 more in July 2001, for a total of 56 administrative districts. [4]Revised preliminary. [5]Includes water area of 16,984 sq mi (43,989 sq km); Uganda's portion of Lake Victoria comprises 11,954 sq mi (30,960 sq km). [6]Detail does not add to total given because of rounding. [7]Based on land area only. [8]Urban agglomeration. [9]Beginning of year. [10]Indirect taxes. [11]Based on nationally representative household survey. [12]The household income for urban areas is U Sh 302,900 (U.S.$195). [13]Imports c.i.f.; exports f.o.b. [14]Uganda has had no railway passenger service from 1997 through mid-2004. [15]Public sector only. [16]1998. [17]State universities only. [18]1999.

Internet resources for further information:
- **Uganda Bureau of Statistics http://www.ubos.org**
- **Bank of Uganda http://www.bou.or.ug**

Ukraine

Official name: Ukrayina (Ukraine).
Form of government: unitary multiparty republic with a single legislative body (Supreme Council [450]).
Head of state: President.
Head of government: Prime Minister.
Capital: Kiev (Kyyiv).
Official language: Ukrainian.
Official religion: none.
Monetary unit: hryvnya (pl. hryvnyas); (Sept. 1, 2004) 1 U.S.$ = 5.32 hryvnyas; 1 £ = 9.56 hryvnyas.

Area and population

	area	population		area	population
Provinces	sq km	2004[1] estimate	Provinces	sq km	2004[1] estimate
Cherkasy	20,900	1,365,464	Rivne	20,047	1,162,422
Chernihiv	31,865	1,197,075	Sumy	23,834	1,252,255
Chernivtsi	8,097	912,856	Ternopil	13,823	1,122,847
Dnipropetrovsk	31,974	3,486,927	Vinnytsya	26,513	1,728,166
Donetsk	26,517	4,693,197	Volyn	20,144	1,047,122
Ivano-Frankivsk	13,928	1,395,423	Zakarpatska	12,777	1,249,608
Kharkiv	31,415	2,851,078	Zaporizhzhya	27,180	1,884,243
Kherson	28,461	1,144,103	Zhytomyr	29,832	1,352,788
Khmelnytsky	20,645	1,394,890	**Autonomous republic**		
Kirovohrad	24,588	1,091,767			
Kyyiv (Kiev)	28,131	1,786,450	Crimea (Krym)	26,081	1,999,118
Luhansk	26,684	2,454,963			
Lviv	21,833	2,591,602	**Cities**		
Mykolayiv	24,598	1,234,785	Kiev	839	2,644,419
Odessa	33,310	2,420,272	Sevastopol	864	378,152
Poltava	28,748	1,581,038	TOTAL	603,628	47,423,030

Demography

Population (2004): 47,470,000.
Density (2004): persons per sq mi 203.7, persons per sq km 78.6.
Urban-rural (2004): urban 67.6%; rural 32.4%.
Sex distribution (2004): male 46.22%; female 53.78%.
Age breakdown (2003): under 15, 16.3%; 15–29, 22.6%; 30–44, 21.7%; 45–59, 18.7%; 60–74, 15.0%; 75 and over, 5.7%.
Population projection: (2010) 45,889,000; (2020) 44,070,000.
Ethnic composition (2001): Ukrainian 77.8%; Russian 17.3%; Belarusian 0.6%; Moldovan 0.5%; Crimean Tatar 0.5%; other 3.3%.
Religious affiliation (1995): Ukrainian Orthodox (Russian patriarchy) 19.5%; Ukrainian Orthodox (Kiev patriarchy) 9.7%; Ukrainian Catholic (Uniate) 7.0%; Protestant 3.6%; other Orthodox 1.6%; Roman Catholic 1.2%; Jewish 0.9%; other (mostly nonreligious) 56.5%.
Major cities (2001): Kiev 2,621,700[2]; Kharkiv 1,470,000; Dnipropetrovsk 1,064,000; Odessa 1,029,000; Donetsk 1,016,000; Zaporizhzhya 814,000.

Vital statistics

Birth rate per 1,000 population (2003): 8.6 (world avg. 21.3); legitimate 80.1%; illegitimate 19.9%.
Death rate per 1,000 population (2003): 16.1 (world avg. 9.1).
Natural increase rate per 1,000 population (2003): –7.5 (world avg. 12.2).
Total fertility rate (avg. births per childbearing woman; 2003): 1.3.
Life expectancy at birth (2003): male 61.1 years; female 72.2 years.
Major causes of death per 100,000 population (2002): diseases of the circulatory system 799.7, of which ischemic heart disease 517.0, cerebrovascular disease 184.6; malignant neoplasms (cancers) 166.9; accidents and violence 153.5; diseases of the respiratory system 56.7.

National economy

Budget (2003). Revenue: 54,986,700,000 hryvnyas (tax revenue 64.9%, of which tax on profits of enterprises 23.8%, VAT 22.9%, excise tax 9.3%; nontax revenue 28.6%; other 6.5%). Expenditures: 56,010,900,000 hryvnyas (2001; social security 43.2%; economy 8.2%; debt payment 6.7%; education 6.2%; public order 6.1%; defense 5.8%; health 1.9%).
Production (metric tons except as noted). Agriculture, forestry, fishing (2002): wheat 20,550,000, potatoes 16,100,000, sugar beets 14,400,000, barley 10,358,000, corn (maize) 4,171,000, rye 1,500,000, oats 942,000; livestock (number of live animals) 9,421,000 cattle, 8,370,000 pigs, 1,875,000 sheep and goats; roundwood (2002) 9,859,300 cu m; fish catch (2001) 382,300. Mining and quarrying (2001): iron ore (2003) 62,952,000; manganese (metal content) 930,000; ilmenite concentrate 600,000. Manufacturing (value of production in '000,000 hryvnyas; 1998): iron and steel 14,525; food and beverages 12,974; nonelectrical machinery 3,838; fabricated metal products 2,919; industrial chemicals 2,741. Energy production (consumption): electricity (kW-hr; 2002) 172,800,000,000 ([2000] 167,596,000,000); hard coal (2003) 75,792,000 ([2000] 84,209,000); lignite (2003) 648,000 ([2000] 1,058,000); crude petroleum (barrels; 2003) 29,027,000 ([2000] 70,265,000); petroleum products (barrels; 2000) 8,822,000 (9,999,000); natural gas (cu m; 2003) 16,346,000,000 (76,089,500,000).
Population economically active (2002): total 22,701,700; activity rate of total population 47.2% (participation rates: ages 16–59 [male], 15–64 [female] 56.6%; female 48.9%; unemployed 10.1% [registered 5.8%]).

Price and earnings indexes (2000 = 100)

	1998	1999	2000	2001	2002	2003
Consumer price index	68.7	78.0	100.0	113.1	114.0	126.6
Monthly earnings index	66.7	77.1	100.0	...	...	...

Public debt (external; 2002): U.S.$8,349,000,000.
Gross national product (2003): U.S.$46,739,000,000 (U.S.$970 per capita).

Structure of gross domestic product and labour force

	2002			
	in value '000,000 hryvnyas	% of total value	labour force	% of labour force
Agriculture	29,632	13.4	4,049,300	17.8
Mining			797,600	3.5
Manufacturing	67,238	30.5	3,702,700	16.7
Public utilities			741,100	3.3
Construction	7,504	3.4	966,400	4.3
Transp. and commun.	25,291	11.5	1,428,500	6.3
Trade	21,773	9.9	2,859,400	12.6
Finance			828,000	3.6
Pub. admin., defense	40,392	18.3	1,113,500	4.9
Services			3,834,200	16.9
Other	28,726[3]	13.0[3]	2,301,000[4]	10.1[4]
TOTAL	220,556	100.0	22,701,700	100.0

Tourism (2002): receipts U.S.$2,992,000,000; expenditures U.S.$2,087,000,000.
Household income and expenditure. Average household size (2002): 2.7; income per household (2003) 8,800 hryvnyas (U.S.$1,640); sources of income (2003): wages and salaries 43.4%, subsidies and pensions 35.2%, profit and mixed income 16.4%, property income 5.0%; expenditures (2003): food and beverages 62.7%, consumer goods 30.6%, housing 6.7%.
Land use as % of total land area (2000): in temporary crops 56.2%, in permanent crops 1.6%, in pasture 13.7%; overall forest area 16.5%.

Foreign trade

Balance of trade (current prices)

	1998	1999	2000	2001	2002	2003
U.S.$'000,000	–2,584	+244	+829	+198	+710	+269
% of total	8.6%	0.9%	2.7%	0.6%	1.9%	0.6%

Imports (2002): U.S.$17,959,000,000 (machinery 22.4%, natural gas 19.6%, crude petroleum 13.5%, chemicals and chemical products 13.1%, food and raw materials 6.6%). *Major import sources* (2003): Russia 32.9%; Germany 13.5%; Turkmenistan 9.6%; Italy 4.6%; China 4.3%.
Exports (2002): U.S.$18,669,000,000 (ferrous and nonferrous metals 39.3%, wood and wood products 14.5%, food and raw materials 13.2%, machinery 11.5%, chemicals and chemical products 10.0%). *Major export destinations* (2003): Russia 17.6%; Turkey 7.3%; Italy 6.0%; China 5.3%; Germany 3.6%.

Transport and communications

Transport. Railroads (2001): length 22,218 km; passenger-km 52,661,000,000; metric ton-km cargo 177,465,000,000. Roads (2003): total length 169,739 km (paved 97%). Vehicles (2001): passenger cars 5,313,000. Air transport (2003): passenger-km 2,352,000,000; metric ton-km cargo 13,536,000; airports (1999) with scheduled flights 12.

Communications

Medium	date	unit	number	units per 1,000 persons
Daily newspapers	2000	circulation	4,970,000	101
Radio	2000	receivers	43,800,000	889
Television	2000	receivers	22,500,000	456
Telephones	2002	main lines	10,833,200	216
Cellular telephones	2002	subscribers	4,200,000	84
Personal computers	2002	units	951,000	19
Internet	2002	users	900,000	18

Education and health

Educational attainment: n.a. *Literacy* (1999): percentage of total population age 15 and over literate 99.6%; males literate 99.7%; females literate 99.5%.

Education (2002–03)

	schools	teachers	students	student/ teacher ratio
Primary (age 6–13) / Secondary (age 14–17)	22,100	561,000	6,350,000	11.3
Voc., teacher tr.	962	...	501,900	...
Higher	997	...	2,270,000	...

Health (2003): physicians 223,000 (1 per 214 persons); hospital beds 458,000 (1 per 104 persons); infant mortality rate per 1,000 live births (2003) 20.8.
Food (2001): daily per capita caloric intake 3,008 (vegetable products 80%, animal products 20%); 118% of FAO recommended minimum requirement.

Military

Total active duty personnel (2003): 295,500 (army 50.1%, air force 16.6%, navy 4.6%, headquarters 14.2%, paramilitary 14.5%). *Military expenditure as percentage of GNP* (1999): 3.0% (world 2.4%); per capita expenditure U.S.$103.

[1]August 1. [2]2003. [3]Less imputed bank service charges, net indirect taxes, and taxes on production. [4]Unemployed.

Internet resources for further information:
- **National Bank of Ukraine**
  http://www.bank.gov.ua/ENGL/Of_publ/index.htm
- **The State Statistics Committee of Ukraine**
  http://www.ukrstat.gov.ua

United Arab Emirates

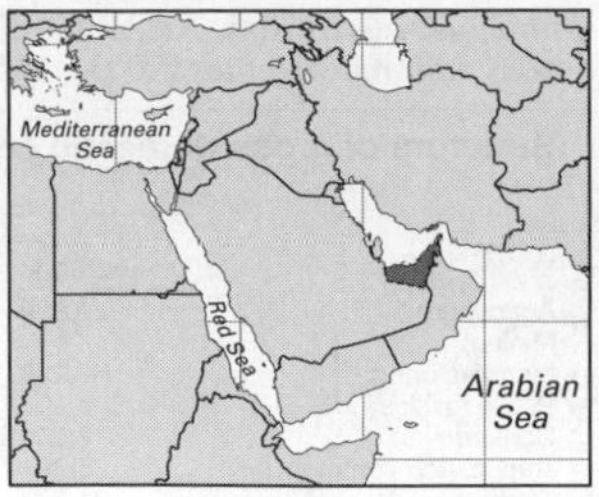

Official name: Al-Imārāt al-ʿArabīyah al-Muttaḥidah (United Arab Emirates).
Form of government: federation of seven emirates with one appointive advisory body (Federal National Council [40[1]]).
Chief of state: President.
Head of government: Prime Minister.
Capital: Abu Dhabi.
Official language: Arabic.
Official religion: Islam.
Monetary unit: 1 U.A.E. dirham (Dh) = 100 fils; valuation (Sept. 1, 2004) 1 U.S.$ = Dh 3.67; 1 £ = Dh 6.61.

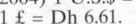

Area and population

Emirates	Capitals	area[2] sq mi	area[2] sq km	population 2003 estimate
Abū Ẓaby (Abu Dhabi)	Abu Dhabi	28,210	73,060	1,591,000
ʿAjmān (Ajman)	ʿAjmān	100	260	235,000
Dubayy (Dubai)	Dubai	1,510	3,900	1,204,000
Al-Fujayrah (Fujairah)	Al-Fujayrah	500	1,300	118,000
Ra's al-Khaymah (Ras al-Khaimah)	Ra's al-Khaymah	660	1,700	195,000
Ash-Shāriqah (Sharjah)	Sharjah	1,000	2,600	636,000
Umm al-Qaywayn (Umm al-Qaiwain)	Umm al-Qaywayn	300	780	62,000
TOTAL		32,280	83,600	4,041,000

Demography

Population (2004): 4,298,000.
Density (2004): persons per sq mi 133.1, persons per sq km 51.4.
Urban-rural (2001): urban 87.2%; rural 12.8%.
Sex distribution (2001): male 67.63%; female 32.37%.
Age breakdown (2001): under 15, 26.2%; 15–29, 29.2%; 30–44, 33.4%; 45–59, 9.6%; 60–74, 1.4%; 75 and over, 0.2%.
Population projection: (2010) 4,738,000; (2020) 5,333,000.
Doubling time: 51 years.
Ethnic composition (2000): Arab 48.1%, of which U.A.E. Arab 12.2%, U.A.E Bedouin 9.4%, Egyptian Arab 6.2%, Omani Arab 4.1%, Saudi Arab 4.0%; South Asian 35.7%, of which Pashtun 7.1%, Balochi 7.1%, Malayali 7.1%; Persian 5.0%; Filipino 3.4%; white 2.4%; other 5.4%.
Religious affiliation (1995): Muslim 96.0% (Sunnī 80.0%, Shīʿī 16.0%); other (mostly Christian and Hindu) 4.0%.
Major cities (2003): Dubai 1,171,000; Abu Dhabi 552,000; Sharjah 519,000; Al-ʿAyn 348,000; ʿAjmān 225,000; Ra's al-Khaymah 102,000.

Vital statistics

Birth rate per 1,000 population (2003): 15.1 (world avg. 21.3).
Death rate per 1,000 population (2003): 1.5 (world avg. 9.1).
Natural increase rate per 1,000 population (2003): 13.6 (world avg. 12.2).
Total fertility rate (avg. births per childbearing woman; 2003): 2.5.
Marriage rate per 1,000 population (2003): 3.0.
Divorce rate per 1,000 population (2003): 0.8.
Life expectancy at birth (2003): male 72.3 years; female 77.4 years.
Major causes of death per 100,000 population (1998): cardiovascular diseases 44.1; accidents and poisoning 31.1; malignant neoplasms (cancers) 15.3; congenital anomalies 9.4.

National economy

Budget (2001). Revenue: Dh 82,480,000,000 (oil revenue 58.5%, non-oil revenue 41.5%). Expenditures: Dh 96,083,000,000 (current expenditures 80.5%, capital [development] expenditure 19.5%).
Gross national product (2001): U.S.$69,568,000,000 (U.S.$19,945 per capita).

Structure of gross domestic product and labour force

	2002		2001	
	in value Dh '000,000[3]	% of total value[3]	labour force	% of labour force
Agriculture	9,499	3.6	128,000	6.9
Crude petroleum production / Mining and quarrying	72,146	27.7	26,000	1.4
Manufacturing	37,398	14.3	246,000	13.3
Construction	17,988	6.9	302,000	16.3
Public utilities	5,125	2.0	31,000	1.7
Transp. and commun.	20,177	7.7	109,000	5.9
Trade	30,095	11.5	448,000	24.2
Finance, real estate	38,323	14.7	71,000	3.8
Pub. admin., defense	28,756	11.0	214,000	11.5
Services	6,573	2.5	278,000	15.0
Other	–5,432[4]	–2.0[4]	—	—
TOTAL	260,648	100.0[5]	1,853,000[6]	100.0[6]

Public debt: n.a.
Tourism (2002): receipts U.S.$1,328,000,000.
Production (metric tons except as noted). Agriculture, forestry, fishing (2002): dates 760,000, spinach 620,000, tomatoes 400,000, cabbages 290,000, cantaloupes and watermelons 175,631, eggplants 140,000, onions 84,000, pumpkins and squash 41,500, cucumbers and gherkins 37,000, lemons and limes 16,195, mangoes 9,137; livestock (number of live animals) 1,300,000 goats, 510,000 sheep, 220,000 camels, 100,000 cattle, 17,000,000 chickens; fish catch (2001) 117,607. Mining and quarrying (2001): aluminum 500,000; gypsum 90,000; lime 50,000; chromite 10,000. Manufacturing (value of production in Dh '000,000; 1998): chemical products (including refined petroleum) 10,096; textiles and wearing apparel 2,397; fabricated metal products 1,999; food, beverages, and tobacco 1,510; cement, bricks, and ceramics 1,409. Energy production (consumption): electricity (kW-hr; 2000) 31,890,000,000 (31,890,000,000); crude petroleum (barrels; 2001) 740,000,000 ([2000] 152,801,000); petroleum products (metric tons; 2000) 26,137,000 (6,028,000); natural gas (cu m; 2001) 41,300,000,000 ([2000] 16,469,000,000).
Population economically active (2001): total 1,853,000; activity rate of total population 53.1% (participation rates [1995]: over age 15, 55.4%; female 11.7%; unemployed [2001] 1.8%).

Price and earnings indexes (2000 = 100)

	1997	1998	1999	2000	2001	2002	2003
Consumer price index	94.5	96.5	98.4	100.0	102.2	105.7	108.9
Wages and services index	...	...	...	100.0	117.0	125.2	130.9

Household income and expenditure. Average household size (2000) 5.0; income per household: n.a.; sources of income: n.a.; expenditure (1996): rent, fuel, and light 36.1%, transportation and communications 14.9%, food 14.4%, education, recreation, and entertainment 10.3%, durable household goods 7.4%, clothing 6.7%.
Land use as % of total land area (2000): in temporary crops 0.7%, in permanent crops 2.2%, in pasture 3.6%; overall forest area 3.8%.

Foreign trade

Balance of trade (current prices)[7]

	1997	1998	1999	2000	2001	2002
Dh '000,000,000	+23.2	+4.6	+17.5	+54.5	+42.2	+38.4
% of total	8.5%	1.9%	7.0%	17.5%	13.3%	11.8%

Imports (2001): Dh 120,600,000,000[8] (machinery and transport equipment 37.6%, food 23.2%, textiles 13.9%, basic manufactures 8.4%, chemicals 6.3%, optical and medical equipment 2.8%). *Major import sources:* Japan 10.2%; United States 9.6%; United Kingdom 8.8%; China 8.6%; Germany 6.7%; India 6.7%; Italy 6.2%; South Korea 5.3%.
Exports (2001): Dh 176,900,000,000 (domestic exports 71.1%, of which crude petroleum 36.7%, natural gas 7.1%, refined petroleum products 4.6%, nonmonetary gold 4.4%; reexports 28.9%). *Major export destinations:* Japan 36.4%; India 7.5%; South Korea 7.1%; Singapore 6.3%; Iran 3.8%; Oman 3.4%.

Transport and communications

Transport. Railroads: none. Roads (1999): total length 2,355 mi, 3,791 km (paved 100%). Vehicles (1996): passenger cars 201,000; trucks and buses 56,950. Air transport (2002)[9]: passenger-mi 18,747,000,000, passenger-km 30,170,000,000; short ton-mi cargo 1,343,000,000, metric ton-km cargo 1,960,764,000; airports (2001) with scheduled flights 6.

Communications

Medium	date	unit	number	units per 1,000 persons
Daily newspapers	2000	circulation	507,000	156
Radio	2000	receivers	1,030,000	318
Television	2000	receivers	948,000	292
Telephones	2003	main lines	1,135,800	281
Cellular telephones	2003	subscribers	2,972,300	736
Personal computers	2002	units	450,000	141
Internet	2003	users	1,110,200	275

Education and health

Educational attainment (1995). Percentage of population age 10 and over having: no formal schooling 47.6%; primary education 27.8%; secondary 16.0%; higher 8.6%. *Literacy* (2000): total population age 15 and over literate 76.3%; males literate 75.0%; females literate 79.3%.

Education (1998–99)

	schools	teachers	students	student/teacher ratio
Primary (age 6–11)	...	16,148[10]	270,486	16.1[10]
Secondary (age 12–18)	...	12,388[11]	198,439	12.0[11]
Vocational	...	249[10]	3,113	7.7[10]
Higher	4[10]	510[11]	17,950[10]	19.2[11]

Health (1999): physicians 6,059 (1 per 485 persons); hospital beds 7,448 (1 per 394 persons); infant mortality rate per 1,000 live births (2003) 8.0.
Food (2001): daily per capita caloric intake 3,192 (vegetable products 75%, animal products 25%); 132% of FAO recommended minimum requirement.

Military

Total active duty personnel (2003): 50,500 (army 87.1%, navy 5.0%, air force 7.9%). *Military expenditure as percentage of GDP* (1999): 4.1% (world 2.4%); per capita expenditure U.S.$935.

[1]All appointed seats. [2]Approximate figures. [3]At factor cost. [4]Imputed bank service charges. [5]Detail does not add to total given because of rounding. [6]Excludes defense personnel. [7]For all Emirates. [8]For Emirates of Abu Dhabi, Dubai, and Sharjah only. [9]Emirates Air only. [10]1996–97. [11]1994–95.

Internet resources for further information:
- **Government of United Arab Emirates http://www.uae.gov.ae**
- **Central Bank of the United Arab Emirates http://www.cbuae.gov.ae**

United Kingdom

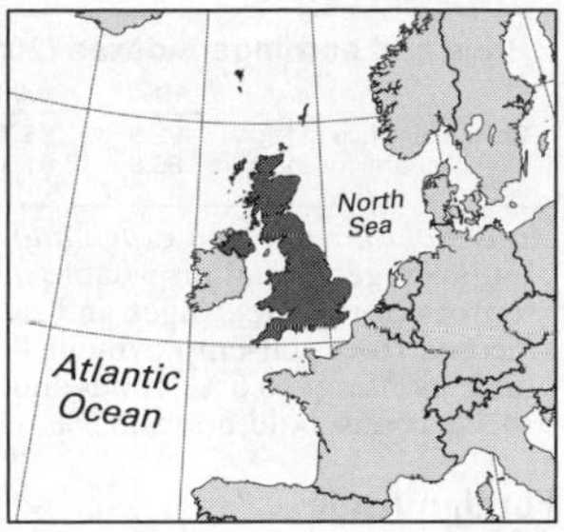

Official name: United Kingdom of Great Britain and Northern Ireland.
Form of government: constitutional monarchy with two legislative houses (House of Lords [688]; House of Commons [659]).
Chief of state: Sovereign.
Head of government: Prime Minister.
Capital: London.
Official language: English.
Official religion: Churches of England and Scotland "established" (protected by the state, but not "official") in their respective countries; no established church in Northern Ireland or Wales.
Monetary unit: 1 pound sterling (£) = 100 new pence; valuation (Sept. 1, 2004) 1 £ = U.S.$1.80; 1 U.S.$ = £0.56.

Population (2001 census[1])

Countries[2]	population		population		population
England	49,138,831	Nottingham	266,988	Scotland	5,062,011
Counties		Peterborough	156,061	**Unitary Districts**	
Bedfordshire	381,572	Plymouth	240,720	Aberdeen City	212,125
Buckinghamshire	479,026	Poole	138,288	Aberdeenshire	226,871
Cambridgeshire	552,658	Portsmouth	186,701	Angus	108,400
Cheshire	673,788	Reading	143,096	Argyll and Bute	91,306
Cornwall (incl.		Redcar and		City of Edinburgh	448,624
Isles of Scilly)	501,267	Cleveland	139,132	Clackmannanshire	48,077
Cumbria	487,607	Rutland	34,563	Dumfries and	
Derbyshire	734,585	Slough	119,067	Galloway	147,765
Devon	704,493	South		Dundee City	145,663
Dorset	390,980	Gloucestershire	245,641	East Ayrshire	120,235
Durham	493,470	Southampton	217,445	East Dumbarton-	
East Sussex	492,324	Southend-on-Sea	160,257	shire	108,243
Essex	1,310,835	Stockton-on-Tees	178,408	East Lothian	90,088
Gloucestershire	564,559	Stoke-on-Trent	240,636	East Renfrewshire	89,311
Hampshire	1,240,103	Swindon	180,051	Eilean Siar[5]	26,502
Hertfordshire	1,033,977	Telford and		Falkirk	145,191
Isle of Wight[3]	132,731	Wrekin	158,325	Fife	349,429
Kent	1,329,718	Thurrock	143,128	Glasgow City	577,869
Lancashire	1,134,974	Torbay	129,706	Highland	208,914
Leicestershire	609,578	Warrington	191,080	Inverclyde	84,203
Lincolnshire	646,645	West Berkshire	144,483	Midlothian	80,941
Norfolk	796,728	Windsor and		Moray	86,940
North Yorkshire	569,660	Maidenhead	133,626	North Ayrshire	135,817
Northamptonshire	629,676	Wokingham	150,229	North Lanarkshire	321,067
Northumberland	307,190	York	181,094	Orkney Islands	19,245
Nottinghamshire	748,510	**Metropolitan**		Perth and Kinross	134,949
Oxfordshire	605,488	**Counties/Greater**		Renfrewshire	172,867
Shropshire	283,173	**London**		Scottish Borders	106,764
Somerset	498,093	Greater London[4]	7,172,091	Shetland Islands	21,988
Staffordshire	806,744	Greater		South Ayrshire	112,097
Suffolk	668,553	Manchester	2,482,328	South Lanarkshire	302,216
Surrey	1,059,015	Merseyside	1,362,026	Stirling	86,212
Warwickshire	505,860	South Yorkshire	1,266,338	West Dumbarton-	
West Sussex	753,614	Tyne and Wear	1,075,938	shire	93,378
Wiltshire	432,973	West Midlands	2,555,592	West Lothian	158,714
Worcestershire	542,107	West Yorkshire	2,079,211		
Unitary Districts				Northern Ireland	1,685,267
Bath and		Wales	2,903,085	**Districts**	
NE Somerset	169,040	**Unitary Districts**		Antrim	48,366
Blackburn with		Blaenau Gwent	70,064	Ards	73,244
Darwen	137,470	Bridgend	128,645	Armagh	54,263
Blackpool	142,283	Caerphilly	169,519	Ballymena	58,610
Bournemouth	163,444	Cardiff	305,353	Ballymoney	26,894
Bracknell Forest	109,617	Carmarthenshire	172,842	Banbridge	41,392
Brighton and		Ceredigion	74,941	Belfast	277,391
Hove	247,817	Conwy	109,596	Carrickfergus	37,659
Bristol	380,615	Denbighshire	93,065	Castlereagh	66,488
Darlington	97,838	Flintshire	148,594	Coleraine	56,315
Derby	221,708	Gwynedd	116,843	Cookstown	32,581
East Riding of		Isle of Anglesey	66,829	Craigavon	80,671
Yorkshire	314,113	Merthyr Tydfil	55,981	Derry	105,066
Halton	118,208	Monmouthshire	84,885	Down	63,828
Hartlepool	88,611	Neath and		Dungannon	47,735
Herefordshire	174,871	Port Talbot	134,468	Fermanagh	57,527
Kingston upon		Newport	137,011	Larne	30,832
Hull	243,589	Pembrokeshire	114,131	Limvady	32,422
Leicester	279,921	Powys	126,354	Lisburn	108,694
Luton	184,371	Rhondda, Cynon,		Magherafelt	39,780
Medway	249,488	Taff	231,946	Moyle	15,933
Middlesborough	134,855	Swansea	223,301	Newry and Mourne	87,058
Milton Keynes	207,057	Torfaen	90,949	Newtownabbey	79,995
NE Lincolnshire	157,979	The Vale of		North Down	76,323
North Lincolnshire	152,849	Glamorgan	119,292	Omagh	47,952
North Somerset	188,564	Wrexham	128,476	Strabane	38,248
				TOTAL	58,789,194

Demography

Population (2004): 59,561,000.
Area: 93,788 sq mi, 242,910 sq km, of which England 50,356 sq mi, 130,422 sq km; Wales 8,023 sq mi, 20,779 sq km; Scotland 30,167 sq mi, 78,133 sq km; Northern Ireland 5,242 sq mi, 13,576 sq km.
Density (2004): persons per sq mi 635.1, persons per sq km 245.2.
Urban-rural (2003): urban 89.1%; rural 10.9%.
Age breakdown (2001): under 15, 18.9%; 15–29, 18.8%; 30–44, 22.6%; 45–59, 18.9%; 60–74, 13.3%; 75 and over, 7.5%.
Ethnic composition (2001): white 92.1%; black 2.0%, of which Caribbean origin 1.0%, African origin 0.8%; Asian Indian 1.8%; Pakistani 1.3%; Bangladeshi 0.5%; Chinese 0.4%; other and not stated 1.9%.
Population projection: (2010) 60,560,000; (2020) 62,447,000.
Sex distribution (2001): male 48.62%; female 51.38%.
Religious affiliation (2001): Christian 71.6%, of which Anglican 29.0%, Roman Catholic 11.0%; Muslim 2.7%; Hindu 1.0%; Sikh 0.6%; Jewish 0.5%; nonreligious 15.5%; other 8.1%.
Major cities (2001; urban agglomeration [2000]): Greater London 7,172,091; Manchester 392,819 ([2001] 2,482,328); Birmingham 977,087 (2,272,000); Leeds 715,402 (1,433,000); Newcastle 259,536 (1,026,000); Liverpool 439,473 (951,000); Glasgow 629,501; Sheffield 513,234; Bradford 467,665; Edinburgh 452,194; Bristol 380,615; Wakefield 315,172; Cardiff 305,353; Coventry 300,848; Doncaster 286,865; Sunderland 280,807; Belfast 277,391.
Mobility (1991)[6]. Population living in the same residence as 1990: 90.1%; different residence, same country (of Great Britain) 8.1%; different residence, different country of Great Britain 1.2%; from outside Great Britain 0.6%.
Households (2002)[6]. Average household size 2.4; 1 person 29%, couple 29%, couple with 1–2 children 19%, couple with 3 or more children 10%, single parent with children 9%, other 4%.
Immigration (2001): permanent residents 372,000, from Australia 13.4%, Bangladesh, India, and Sri Lanka 6.2%, South Africa 4.8%, New Zealand 4.3%, Pakistan 3.5%, United States 3.2%, Canada 1.6%, other 63.0%, of which EU 22.3%.

Vital statistics

Birth rate per 1,000 population (2003): 11.7 (world avg. 21.3); (2002) legitimate[7] 59.4%; illegitimate[7] 40.6%.
Death rate per 1,000 population (2003): 10.3 (world avg. 9.1).
Natural increase rate per 1,000 population (2003): 1.4 (world avg. 12.2).
Total fertility rate (avg. births per childbearing woman; 2003): 1.7.
Marriage rate per 1,000 population (2001): 4.9.
Divorce rate per 1,000 population (2002): 2.7.
Life expectancy at birth (2002): male 75.7 years; female 80.4 years.
Major causes of death per 100,000 population (2003)[7]: diseases of the circulatory system 346.2, of which ischemic heart disease 168.2, cerebrovascular disease 97.4; malignant neoplasms (cancers) 229.0; diseases of the respiratory system 126.2, of which pneumonia 57.8; diseases of the digestive system 42.0; diseases of the genitourinary system 15.4; diseases of the endocrine system 13.5, of which diabetes mellitus 10.6; suicide 5.5.

Social indicators

Educational attainment (1999). Percentage of population age 25–64 having: up to lower secondary education only 38%; completed secondary 37%; higher 25%, of which at least some university 17%.

Distribution of disposable income (2000–01)

percentage of household income by quintile

1	2	3	4	5 (highest)
8.8	12.0	17.4	26.1	35.7

Quality of working life (2002). Average full-time workweek (hours): male 39.6, female 34.4. Annual rate per 100,000 workers for (2000–01)[6]: injury or accident 2,778.6; death 5.0. Proportion of labour force (employed persons) insured for damages or income loss resulting from: injury 100%; permanent disability 100%; death 100%. Average days lost to labour stoppages per 1,000 employee workdays (2001): 20.
Access to services (2000). Proportion of households having access to: bath or shower 100%; toilet 100%.
Social participation. Eligible voters participating in last national election (June 2001): 59.4%. Population age 16 and over participating in voluntary work (2001)[6]: 39%. Trade union membership in total workforce (2001) 29.1%.
Social deviance (2001–02)[7]. Offense rate per 100,000 population for: theft and handling stolen goods 3,856.2; vandalism 1,809.9; burglary 1,296.2; violence against the person 1,105.6; fraud and forgery 539.2; robbery 205.8; sexual offense 69.7.
Leisure (1994). Favourite leisure activities (hours weekly): watching television 17.1; listening to radio 10.3; reading 8.8, of which books 3.8, newspapers 3.3; gardening 2.1.
Material well-being (2001). Households possessing: automobile 74.0%, telephone 94.0%, television receiver (2000) 98.3%, refrigerator/freezer 95.0%, washing machine 93.0%, central heating 92.0%, video recorder 90.0%.

National economy

Budget (2001–02). Revenue: £388,357,000,000 (production and import taxes 35.5%, income tax 28.1%, social security contributions 16.3%). Expenditures: £380,867,000,000 (social protection 41.8%, health 16.1%, education 12.3%, defense 7.3%).
Gross national product (2003): U.S.$1,680,300,000,000 (U.S.$28,350 per capita).

Structure of gross domestic product and labour force

	2001		2002	
	in value £'000,000	% of total value	labour force	% of labour force
Agriculture	8,241	0.8	255,000	0.9
Mining[8]	25,665	2.6	75,000	0.3
Manufacturing	153,132	15.5	3,668,000	12.6
Construction	47,327	4.8	1,186,000	4.1
Public utilities	15,713	1.6	177,000	0.6
Transp. and commun.	70,252	7.1	1,524,000	5.2
Trade[9]	136,125	13.7	6,162,000	21.1
Finance	255,871	25.9	4,969,000	17.0
Pub. admin., defense	42,096	4.3	1,382,000	4.7
Services	159,170	16.1	6,277,000	21.5
Other	75,422[10]	7.6[10]	3,508,000[11]	12.0[11]
TOTAL	989,014	100.0	29,183,000	100.0

Total national debt (March 31, 2000): £426,239,200,000 (U.S.$679,894,200,000).
Land use as % of total land area (2000): in temporary crops 24.4%, in permanent crops 0.2%, in pasture 45.8%; overall forest area 11.6%.
Tourism (2002): receipts from visitors U.S.$17,591,000,000; expenditures by nationals abroad U.S.$40,409,000,000.
Production (value of production in £'000,000). Agriculture, forestry, fishing (2001): wheat 1,322, vegetables 970, barley 726, potatoes 600, rapeseed 275, sugar beets 255, fruit 243, oats 64; livestock (number of live animals) 36,716,000 sheep, 10,602,000 cattle, 5,845,000 pigs; roundwood (2002) 7,577,000 cu m; fish catch (2001) 530,000 tons. Mining and quarrying (2000): limestone and dolomite 662; sand and gravel 619; china clay (kaolin) 234. Manufacturing (value added in £'000,000; 2000): electrical and optical equipment 21,137; food and beverages 20,628; paper, printing, and publishing 19,575; metal manufacturing 16,275; transport equipment 15,968; chemicals and chemical products 14,918; machinery and equipment 12,319; textiles and leather products 7,159. Construction (value in £; 2001)[6]: residential 8,796,000,000; nonresidential 1,437,000,000.

Financial aggregates

	1997	1998	1999	2000	2001	2002	2003
Exchange rate (end of year)							
U.S. dollar per £	1.65	1.66	1.62	1.49	1.45	1.61	1.78
SDRs per £	1.23	1.18	1.18	1.15	1.15	1.19	1.20
International reserves (U.S.$)							
Total (excl. gold; '000,000,000)	32.32	32.21	35.87	43.89	37.28	39.36	41.85
SDRs ('000,000,000)	0.47	0.47	0.51	0.33	0.29	0.36	0.38
Reserve pos. in IMF ('000,000)	2.97	4.38	5.28	4.28	5.05	6.21	6.32
Foreign exchange	28.88	27.36	30.08	39.28	31.94	32.79	35.15
Gold ('000,000 fine troy oz)	18.42	23.00	20.55	15.67	11.42	10.09	10.07
% world reserves	2.1	2.4	2.1	1.6	1.2	1.1	1.1
Interest and prices							
Central bank discount (%)	...	...	...	...	...	...	...
Govt. bond yield (%) long term	7.09	5.45	4.70	4.68	4.78	4.83	4.64
Industrial share prices (1995 = 100)	128.3	150.5	...	...	...	...	...
Balance of payments (U.S.$'000,000,000,000)							
Balance of visible trade	–20.20	–36.13	–47.02	–49.85	–58.48	–70.21	–77.30
Imports, f.o.b.	–301.74	–307.85	–315.90	–334.23	–332.14	–350.07	–384.30
Exports, f.o.b.	281.54	271.72	268.88	284.38	273.66	279.86	307.00
Balance of invisibles	+18.64	+29.57	+7.47	+13.63	+26.34	+43.15	+43.84
Balance of payments, current account	–1.56	–6.56	–39.55	–36.22	–32.14	–27.06	–33.46

Manufacturing, mining, and construction enterprises (2001)

	no. of enterprises	no. of employees	annual costs as a % of avg. of employment costs[12]	annual value added (£'000,000)
Manufacturing				
Food, beverages, and tobacco	7,706	515,000	86.6	20,370
Paper and paper products; printing and publishing	32,493	475,000	101.5	19,444
Chemical products	3,864	251,000	138.8	14,850
Metal manufacturing	31,629	487,000	92.3	15,269
Machinery and equipment	13,650	355,000	104.3	11,696
Mineral products (nonmetallic)	5,439	134,000	93.7	4,852
Electrical and optical equipment	16,141	475,000	118.3	16,070
Transport equipment	5,665	390,000	120.0	17,411
Rubber and plastics	7,021	233,000	92.3	7,632
Textiles	11,310	210,000	66.5	5,147
Wood and wood products	8,444	89,000	68.2	2,345
Other manufacturing	20,155	229,000	76.8	6,452
Mining				
Extraction of coal, mineral oil, and natural gas	444	39,000	...	20,629
Extraction of minerals other than fuels	1,224	33,000	...	1,798
Construction	192,000	1,367,000	...	47,969

Retail trade and service enterprises (2001)

	no. of-enterprises	no. of employees	weekly wage as a % of all wages	annual turnover (£'000,000)
Food, beverages, and tobacco	27,074	993,000	...	85,534
of which meats	8,485	46,000	...	2,216
Household goods,	23,553	319,000	...	29,151
of which electronics, appliances	7,157	101,000	...	10,821
furniture	10,592	119,000	...	8,784
Clothing and footwear	17,869	446,000	...	25,963
Pharmaceuticals and cosmetics	6,915	110,000	...	9,543
Business services,	534,956	4,273,000	...	265,631
of which real estate	30,779	79,000	...	32,779
Transp. and commun.	81,154	1,621,000	...	181,669
Hotels, restaurants	118,988	1,792,000	...	49,902
Social services,	35,622	1,026	...	16,233
of which health	9,683	453,000	...	7,575

Energy production (consumption): electricity (kW-hr; 2001) 352,985,000,000 ([2000] 391,093,000,000); hard coal (metric tons; 2000) 30,600,000 (58,440,-000); crude petroleum (barrels; 2000) 880,107,000 (605,657,000); petroleum products (metric tons; 2000) 80,410,000 (72,458,000); natural gas (cu m; 2000) 127,197,000,000 (113,807,600,000).
Population economically active (2002): total 29,183,000; activity rate of total population 59.6% (participation rates: ages 16–64, 74.4%; female 45.9%; unemployed 5.2%).

Price and earnings indexes (2000 = 100)

	1997	1998	1999	2000	2001	2002	2003
Consumer price index	92.5	95.7	97.2	100.0	101.8	103.5	106.5
Monthly earnings index	86.8	91.3	95.7	100.0	104.4	108.1	...

Household income and expenditure (2000–01). Average household size (2002) 2.4; average annual disposable income per household £21,242 (U.S.$31,395); sources of income: wages and salaries 67.0%, social security benefits 12.0%, income from self-employment 8.9%, dividends and interest 4.0%; expenditure: housing 16.6%, food and beverages 16.0%, transport and vehicles 14.3%, household goods 8.5%, clothing 5.7%.

Foreign trade

Balance of trade (current prices)

	1997	1998	1999	2000	2001	2002
£'000,000	–12,342	–21,813	–27,372	–30,326	–33,510	–34,394
% of total	3.5%	6.2%	7.6%	7.5%	8.1%	8.5%

Imports (2002): £220,242,000,000 (machinery and apparatus 27.3%, of which radios, televisions, and electronics 6.7%, computers 6.1%; transport equipment 19.8%, of which motor vehicles and parts 13.7%, aircraft 5.4%; chemicals and chemical products 10.7%, of which pharmaceuticals 3.9%, basic chemicals 3.8%; food products 5.1%; wearing apparel 3.5%). *Major import sources:* Germany 13.7%; U.S. 11.3%; France 8.5%; The Netherlands 6.8%; Belgium-Luxembourg 5.9%; Italy 4.7%; Ireland 4.2%; Japan 3.7%; Spain 3.7%; China 3.0%.
Exports (2002): £185,848,000,000 (machinery and apparatus 32.5%, of which radios, televisions, and electronics 10.6%, nonelectrical machinery 8.5%, computers 5.6%; transport equipment 16.8%, of which motor vehicles and parts 10.1%, aircraft 6.2%; chemicals and chemical products 15.4%, of which pharmaceuticals 5.7%; crude petroleum and natural gas 5.8%; base metals 3.5%). *Major export destinations:* U.S. 15.1%; Germany 11.8%; France 10.0%; Ireland 8.3%; The Netherlands 7.5%; Belgium-Luxembourg 5.7%; Italy 4.6%; Spain 4.5%; Sweden 2.1%; Japan 1.9%.

Transport and communications

Transport. Railroads (2001–02)[6]: length 19,883 mi[13], 32,000 km[13]; passenger-mi 24,298,000,000, passenger-km 39,104,000,000; ton-mi cargo 13,493,000,000, metric ton-km cargo 19,700,000,000. Roads (2001): total length 243,831 mi, 392,408 km (paved 100%). Vehicles (2001): passenger cars 23,899,000, trucks and buses 2,544,000. Merchant marine (2001): vessels (over 100 gross tons) 594; total deadweight tonnage 12,100,000. Air transport (2001): passenger-mi 154,700,000,000, passenger-km 249,000,000,000; short ton-mi cargo 3,559,000,000, metric ton-km cargo 5,196,000,000; airports (2001) 150[13].

Communications

Medium	date	unit	number	units per 1,000 persons
Daily newspapers	2000	circulation	19,300,000	329
Radio	2000	receivers	84,500,000	1,432
Television	1999	receivers	38,800,000	652
Telephones	2002	main lines	34,898,000	591
Cellular telephones	2002	subscribers	49,677,000	841
Personal computers	2002	units	23,972,000	406
Internet	2002	users	25,000,000	423

Education and health

Literacy (2002): total population literate, virtually 100%.

Education (2002)[14]

	schools	teachers	students	student/ teacher ratio
Primary (age 5–10)	22,800	231,400	5,083,400	25.9
Secondary (age 11–19)	4,306	241,000	3,948,000	16.4
Voc., teacher tr.	...	...	586,000[15]	...
Higher[16]	89	*c.* 48,000[17]	*c.* 810,000[17]	*c.* 17.0[17]

Health: physicians (2001) 71,107[6] (1 per 826 persons); hospital beds (2000) 242,671 (1 per 246 persons); infant mortality rate per 1,000 live births (2003) 4.7.
Food (2001): daily per capita caloric intake 3,368 (vegetable products 70%, animal products 30%); 134% of FAO recommended minimum requirement.

Military

Total active duty personnel (2003): 212,660 (army 54.9%, navy 19.9%, air force 25.2%); U.S. troops (2004) 11,800. *Military expenditure as percentage of GNP* (1999): 2.5% (world 2.4%); per capita expenditure U.S.$615.

[1]Preliminary. [2]The reorganization of first-order administrative units was completed in 1999: England's former 46 counties (including 7 metropolitan counties) reorganized into 35 counties, 45 unitary districts, 6 metropolitan counties, and Greater London; Wales's former 8 counties reorganized into 22 unitary districts; Scotland's former 9 regions and 3 island councils reorganized into 32 unitary districts; Northern Ireland did not change. [3]Only unitary district with county status. [4]Has administrative authority from July 2000. [5]Formerly Western Isles. [6]Great Britain only. [7]England and Wales only. [8]Includes petroleum extraction. [9]Includes hotels and restaurants. [10]Plus rent and value-added taxes; less imputed bank service charges. [11]Includes 1,524,000 unemployed. [12]Wages in manufacturing account for *c.* 90% of employment costs. [13]Estimate. [14]Public sector only. [15]1992–93. [16]Universities only. [17]1994–95.

Internet resources for further information:
- **Office for National Statistics http://www.statistics.gov.uk**

United States

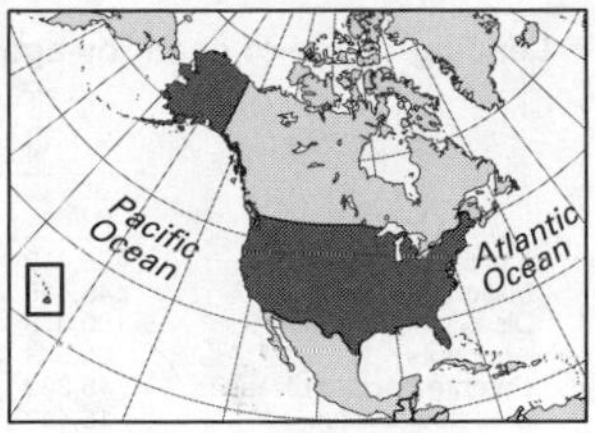

Official name: United States of America.
Form of government: federal republic with two legislative houses (Senate [100]; House of Representatives [435[1]]).
Head of state and government: President.
Capital: Washington, D.C.
Official language: none.
Official religion: none.
Monetary unit: 1 dollar (U.S.$) = 100 cents; valuation (Sept. 1, 2004) 1 U.S.$ = €0.82; 1 U.S.$ = £0.56.

Area and population

		area		population
States	Capitals	sq mi	sq km	2003 estimate
Alabama	Montgomery	51,700	133,902	4,500,752
Alaska	Juneau	589,194	1,526,005	648,818
Arizona	Phoenix	113,999	295,256	5,580,811
Arkansas	Little Rock	53,178	137,730	2,725,714
California	Sacramento	158,633	410,858	35,484,453
Colorado	Denver	104,094	269,602	4,550,688
Connecticut	Hartford	5,006	12,966	3,483,372
Delaware	Dover	2,026	5,247	817,491
Florida	Tallahassee	58,599	151,771	17,019,068
Georgia	Atlanta	58,922	152,607	8,684,715
Hawaii	Honolulu	6,461	16,734	1,257,608
Idaho	Boise	83,570	216,445	1,366,332
Illinois	Springfield	57,915	149,999	12,653,544
Indiana	Indianapolis	36,418	94,322	6,195,643
Iowa	Des Moines	56,271	145,741	2,944,062
Kansas	Topeka	82,277	213,096	2,723,507
Kentucky	Frankfort	40,409	104,659	4,117,827
Louisiana	Baton Rouge	47,716	123,584	4,496,334
Maine	Augusta	33,126	85,795	1,305,728
Maryland	Annapolis	10,454	27,076	5,508,909
Massachusetts	Boston	8,263	21,401	6,433,422
Michigan	Lansing	96,716	250,493	10,079,985
Minnesota	St. Paul	86,939	225,171	5,059,375
Mississippi	Jackson	47,692	123,522	2,881,281
Missouri	Jefferson City	69,704	180,533	5,704,484
Montana	Helena	147,042	380,837	917,621
Nebraska	Lincoln	77,353	200,343	1,739,291
Nevada	Carson City	110,561	286,352	2,241,154
New Hampshire	Concord	9,282	24,040	1,287,687
New Jersey	Trenton	7,813	20,236	8,638,396
New Mexico	Santa Fe	121,590	314,917	1,874,614
New York	Albany	53,097	137,521	19,190,115
North Carolina	Raleigh	52,671	136,417	8,407,248
North Dakota	Bismarck	70,700	183,112	633,837
Ohio	Columbus	44,825	116,096	11,435,798
Oklahoma	Oklahoma City	69,898	181,035	3,511,532
Oregon	Salem	97,047	251,351	3,559,596
Pennsylvania	Harrisburg	46,056	119,284	12,365,455
Rhode Island	Providence	1,223	3,168	1,076,164
South Carolina	Columbia	31,118	80,595	4,147,152
South Dakota	Pierre	77,117	199,732	764,309
Tennessee	Nashville	42,143	109,150	5,841,748
Texas	Austin	266,853	691,146	22,118,509
Utah	Salt Lake City	84,899	219,887	2,351,467
Vermont	Montpelier	9,615	24,903	619,107
Virginia	Richmond	40,600	105,154	7,386,330
Washington	Olympia	68,097	176,370	6,131,445
West Virginia	Charleston	24,230	62,755	1,810,354
Wisconsin	Madison	65,498	169,639	5,472,299
Wyoming	Cheyenne	97,813	253,334	501,242
District				
District of Columbia	—	68	176	563,384
TOTAL		3,676,487[2, 3]	9,522,058[2, 3]	290,809,777[4]

Demography

Population (2004): 293,850,000.
Density (2004)[5]: persons per sq mi 83.1, persons per sq km 32.1.
Urban-rural (2000): urban 79.0%; rural 21.0%.
Sex distribution (2003): male 49.19%; female 50.81%.
Age breakdown (2003): under 15, 20.9%; 15–29, 20.8%; 30–44, 22.4%; 45–59, 19.4%; 60–74, 10.5%; 75 and over, 6.0%.
Population projection: (2010) 309,181,000; (2020) 336,081,000.
Doubling time: not applicable; doubling time exceeds 100 years.
Population by race and Hispanic[6] origin (2002): non-Hispanic white 68.5%; Hispanic 13.5%; non-Hispanic black 12.8%; Asian and Pacific Islander 4.2%; American Indian and Eskimo 1.0%.
Religious affiliation (2000): Christian 84.7%, of which Protestant 45.7%, Roman Catholic 18.2%, unaffiliated Christian 15.8%, Orthodox 1.8%, other Christian (primarily Mormon and Jehovah's Witness) 3.2%; Jewish 2.0%; Muslim 1.5%; Buddhist 0.9%; Hindu 0.4%; nonreligious 9.0%; atheist 0.8%; other 0.7%.
Mobility (2000). Population living in the same residence as in 1999: 84.0%; different residence, same county 9.0%; different county, same state 3.0%; different state 3.0%; moved from abroad 1.0%.
Households (2002). Total households 109,297,000 (married-couple families 56,747,000 [51.9%]). Average household size (2002) 2.6; 1 person 26.4%, 2 persons 33.1%, 3 persons 16.2%, 4 persons 14.5%, 5 or more persons 9.8%. Family households: 74,329,000 (68.0%); nonfamily 34,968,000 (32.0%), of which 1-person 82.3%.
Place of birth (2000): native-born 245,708,000 (89.6%); foreign born 28,379,000 (10.4%), of which Mexico 7,841,000, the Philippines 1,222,000, China and Hong Kong 1,067,000, India 1,007,000, Cuba 952,000, Vietnam 863,000, El Salvador 765,000, South Korea 701,000.

Components of population change (2000–02)[7]

States	Net change in population	Percentage change	Births	Deaths	Net domestic/ international migration
Alabama	39,408	0.9	141,164	101,209	404
Alaska	16,855	2.7	23,050	6,853	535
Arizona	325,821	6.4	189,903	92,575	227,283
Arkansas	36,681	1.4	84,467	62,903	15,275
California	1,244,385	3.7	1,189,741	517,484	570,240
Colorado	205,211	4.8	147,649	64,037	119,836
Connecticut	54,938	1.6	96,005	68,197	28,832
Delaware	23,785	3.0	24,661	15,966	15,371
Florida	730,749	4.6	467,910	375,504	633,076
Georgia	373,824	4.6	308,097	145,605	206,296
Hawaii	33,361	2.8	42,549	17,398	8,533
Idaho	47,178	3.6	45,257	22,094	23,623
Illinois	181,324	1.5	418,059	240,356	2,279
Indiana	78,583	1.3	192,533	125,353	12,515
Iowa	10,433	0.4	83,324	62,976	–8,902
Kansas	27,466	1.0	86,942	56,170	–3,210
Kentucky	50,862	1.3	122,338	89,612	18,816
Louisiana	13,667	0.3	154,863	93,883	–47,039
Maine	19,541	1.5	30,046	28,113	17,956
Maryland	161,654	3.1	170,930	99,368	86,182
Massachusetts	78,704	1.2	182,496	128,614	26,382
Michigan	112,002	1.1	303,264	196,770	7,989
Minnesota	100,241	2.0	144,014	83,933	39,992
Mississippi	27,124	1.0	100,709	63,695	–9,802
Missouri	77,368	1.4	169,965	123,559	31,789
Montana	7,258	0.8	24,461	18,760	1,576
Nebraska	17,917	1.0	54,972	34,242	–2,404
Nevada	175,234	8.8	69,597	34,967	138,214
New Hampshire	39,270	3.2	32,274	22,192	29,240
New Jersey	175,950	2.1	255,719	165,004	87,009
New Mexico	36,013	2.0	60,864	31,585	6,801
New York	181,075	1.0	581,993	357,231	–43,202
North Carolina	270,672	3.4	271,428	160,019	159,599
North Dakota	–8,090	–1.3	17,073	13,609	–11,621
Ohio	68,259	0.6	353,686	245,913	–36,827
Oklahoma	43,058	1.2	110,488	76,462	9,717
Oregon	100,110	2.9	101,142	68,344	68,158
Pennsylvania	54,037	0.4	323,841	289,003	24,621
Rhode Island	21,406	2.0	27,544	21,993	16,365
South Carolina	95,173	2.4	128,984	82,702	50,137
South Dakota	6,219	0.8	23,522	15,809	–1,448
Tennessee	108,012	1.9	178,486	126,612	56,861
Texas	928,081	4.5	792,093	325,428	457,274
Utah	83,087	3.7	105,187	28,654	6,580
Vermont	7,765	1.3	14,086	11,792	5,722
Virginia	215,043	3.0	225,928	126,184	113,418
Washington	174,877	3.0	179,174	101,004	97,278
West Virginia	–6,477	–0.4	42,589	45,442	–3,265
Wisconsin	77,106	1.4	153,729	106,386	31,922
Wyoming	4,921	1.0	13,539	9,175	576
District					
District of Columbia	–1,161	–0.2	18,409	12,886	–6,682
TOTAL/RATE	6,946,189	2.5	9,080,744	5,413,795	3,279,240

Major cities (2003): New York 8,085,742; Los Angeles 3,819,951; Chicago 2,869,121; Houston 2,009,690; Philadelphia 1,479,339; Phoenix 1,388,416; San Diego 1,266,753; San Antonio 1,214,725; Dallas 1,208,318; Detroit 911,402.

Other principal cities (2003)

	population		population		population
Akron	212,215	Garland (Tex.)	218,027	Norfolk	241,727
Albuquerque	471,856	Glendale (Ariz.)	232,838	Oakland	398,844
Anaheim	332,361	Glendale (Calif.)	200,499	Oklahoma City	523,303
Anchorage	270,951	Greensboro	229,110	Omaha	404,267
Arlington (Tex.)	355,007	Hialeah (Fla.)	226,401	Pittsburgh	325,337
Atlanta	423,019	Honolulu	380,149	Plano (Tex.)	241,991
Austin	672,011	Indianapolis	783,438	Portland (Ore.)	538,544
Bakersfield	271,035	Jacksonville	773,781	Raleigh	316,802
Baltimore	628,670	Jersey City	239,097	Riverside	281,514
Baton Rouge	225,090	Kansas City (Mo.)	442,768	Rochester	215,093
Birmingham	236,620	Las Vegas	517,017	Sacramento	445,335
Boston	581,616	Lexington (Ky.)	266,798	St. Louis	332,223
Buffalo	285,018	Lincoln	235,594	St. Paul	280,404
Chandler (Ariz.)	211,299	Long Beach	475,460	St. Petersburg	247,610
Charlotte	584,658	Louisville	248,762	San Francisco	751,682
Chesapeake (Va.)	210,834	Lubbock	206,481	San Jose	898,349
Cincinnati	317,361	Madison	218,432	Santa Ana	342,510
Cleveland	461,324	Memphis	645,978	Scottsdale	217,989
Colorado Springs	370,448	Mesa (Ariz.)	432,376	Seattle	569,101
Columbus	728,432	Miami	376,815	Stockton	271,466
Corpus Christi	279,208	Milwaukee	586,941	Tampa	317,647
Denver	557,478	Minneapolis	373,188	Toledo	308,973
El Paso	584,113	Modesto	206,872	Tucson	507,658
Fort Wayne	219,495	Montgomery	200,123	Tulsa	387,807
Fort Worth	585,122	Nashville	544,765	Virginia Beach	439,467
Fremont (Calif.)	204,525	New Orleans	469,032	Washington, D.C.	563,384
Fresno	451,455	Newark	277,911	Wichita	354,617

Immigration (2001): permanent immigrants admitted 1,064,318, from Mexico 19.2%, India 6.2%, former U.S.S.R. 5.2%, China 4.8%, the Philippines 4.8%, Africa 4.7%, Vietnam 3.3%, El Salvador 2.9%, Canada 2.8%, Cuba 2.4%, Haiti 2.1%, Dominican Republic 2.0%, South Korea 1.9%, Jamaica 1.4%, other 36.3%. Refugees (end of 2003) 452,548. Asylum seekers (end of 2000): 386,330.

Vital statistics

Birth rate per 1,000 population (2001): 14.5 (world avg. 21.3); legitimate 66.5%; illegitimate 33.5%.
Death rate per 1,000 population (2001): 8.5 (world avg. 9.1).
Natural increase rate per 1,000 population (2001): 6.0 (world avg. 12.2).
Marriage rate per 1,000 population (2001): 8.4; median age at first marriage (1991): men 26.3 years, women 24.1 years.

Divorce rate per 1,000 population (2001): 4.0.
Total fertility rate (avg. births per childbearing woman; 2001): 2.1.
Life expectancy at birth (2001): white male 75.0 years, black and other male (1996) 68.9 years; white female 80.2 years, black and other female 76.1 (1996) years.

Vital statistics (2001)

States	Live births	Birth rate per 1,000 population	Death rate per 1,000 population	Infant mortality rate per 1,000 live births	Abortion rate per 1,000 live births[8]	Life expectancy[9]
Alabama	60,454	13.7	10.1	9.4	221.2	73.6
Alaska	10,003	16.0	4.7	8.1	200.5	...
Arizona	85,597	17.1	7.7	6.9	211.1	76.1
Arkansas	37,010	14.3	10.3	8.3	158.8	74.3
California	527,759	15.5	6.8	5.4	443.6	75.9
Colorado	67,007	15.9	6.4	5.8	244.5	77.0
Connecticut	42,648	12.9	8.7	6.1	348.6	76.9
Delaware	10,749	13.9	8.9	10.7	452.4	74.8
Florida	205,793	13.2	10.2	7.3	504.6	75.8
Georgia	133,526	16.5	7.7	8.6	241.2	73.6
Hawaii	17,072	14.5	6.8	6.2	341.9	78.2
Idaho	20,688	16.0	7.4	6.2	98.2	76.9
Illinois	184,064	15.0	8.4	7.7	345.9	74.9
Indiana	86,459	14.4	9.0	7.5	136.8	75.4
Iowa	37,619	13.0	9.5	5.6	156.8	77.3
Kansas	38,869	14.5	9.1	7.4	302.5	76.8
Kentucky	54,658	13.6	9.8	5.9	89.2	74.4
Louisiana	65,352	14.9	9.3	9.8	191.5	73.0
Maine	13,759	10.9	9.7	6.1	220.5	73.1
Maryland	73,218	13.9	8.1	8.1	471.0	76.4
Massachusetts	81,077	13.0	8.9	5.0	367.6	74.8
Michigan	133,427	13.4	8.6	8.0	337.8	75.0
Minnesota	67,562	13.8	7.6	5.3	221.9	77.8
Mississippi	42,282	15.1	9.9	10.5	90.8	73.0
Missouri	75,464	13.6	9.8	7.4	104.6	75.3
Montana	10,970	12.3	9.1	6.7	273.8	76.2
Nebraska	24,820	14.8	8.8	6.8	162.3	76.9
Nevada	31,382	16.1	7.8	5.7	454.1	74.2
New Hampshire	14,656	11.9	7.8	3.8	205.4	76.7
New Jersey	115,795	14.0	8.8	6.5	570.8	75.4
New Mexico	27,128	15.4	7.7	6.4	220.4	75.7
New York	254,026	13.9	8.3	5.8	637.7	74.7
North Carolina	118,185	15.1	8.6	8.5	315.8	74.5
North Dakota	7,629	12.2	9.5	8.8	130.3	77.6
Ohio	151,570	13.4	9.5	7.7	257.3	75.3
Oklahoma	50,118	14.8	10.0	7.3	140.6	75.1
Oregon	45,322	13.5	8.7	5.4	371.1	76.4
Pennsylvania	143,495	12.0	10.5	7.2	252.9	75.4
Rhode Island	12,713	12.7	9.5	6.8	479.8	76.5
South Carolina	55,756	14.1	9.0	8.9	142.6	73.5
South Dakota	10,483	14.1	9.1	7.4	96.7	76.9
Tennessee	78,340	14.0	9.6	8.7	238.7	74.3
Texas	365,410	17.6	7.1	5.9	244.9	75.1
Utah	47,959	21.8	5.6	4.8	84.5	77.7
Vermont	6,366	10.6	8.5	5.5	307.7	76.5
Virginia	98,884	14.0	7.8	7.6	293.1	75.2
Washington	79,570	13.6	7.4	5.8	320.8	76.8
West Virginia	20,428	11.4	11.6	7.2	143.8	74.3
Wisconsin	69,072	12.9	8.6	7.1	158.7	76.9
Wyoming	6,115	12.7	8.2	5.9	...	76.2
District						
District of Columbia	7,625	14.8	10.4	10.6	1,304.4	68.0
TOTAL/RATE	4,025,933	14.5	8.5	6.8	343.5	75.8

Major causes of death per 100,000 population (2002): cardiovascular diseases 318.3, of which ischemic heart disease 171.1, cerebrovascular diseases 56.5, atherosclerosis 4.8; malignant neoplasms (cancers) 193.8; diseases of the respiratory system 81.8, of which pneumonia 22.6; accidents and adverse effects 35.5, of which motor-vehicle accidents 15.5; diabetes mellitus 25.4; suicide 10.6; chronic liver disease and cirrhosis 9.4; AIDS 4.9.
Morbidity rates of infectious diseases per 100,000 population (2002): chlamydia 296.6; gonorrhea 125.0; salmonellosis 15.7; AIDS 15.3; syphilis 11.7; chicken pox 10.3; shigellosis 8.4; lyme disease 8.4; pertussis 3.5; hepatitis A (infectious) 3.1; hepatitis B (serum) 2.8.

Leading cause of death by age group (2002)

	Number of deaths			Total death rate per 100,000 population	Percentage of all deaths
	Total	Male[10]	Female[10]		
All ages[11]	2,447,862	1,201,009	1,246,853	848.9	100.0
1 to 4 years	4,838	2,920	2,331	31.1	0.20
Accidents	1,609	1,155	780	10.3	0.07
Congenital anomalies	521	287	277	3.3	0.02
Malignant neoplasms	401	189	176	2.6	0.02
Homicide	384	223	175	2.5	0.02
Diseases of the heart	164	...	...	1.1	0.01
5 to 14 years	7,152	4,686	3,105	17.4	0.29
Accidents	2,692	2,086	1,158	6.6	0.11
Malignant neoplasms	1,061	582	431	2.6	0.04
Congenital anomalies	395	...	...	1.0	0.02
Homicide	342	257	203	0.8	0.01
Suicide	259	241	83	0.6	0.01
15 to 24 years	33,009	22,717	7,910	81.3	1.35
Accidents	15,026	9,887	3,462	37.0	0.61
Homicide	5,070	4,720	785	12.5	0.21
Suicide	3,932	3,532	603	9.7	0.16
Malignant neoplasms	1,728	1,029	670	4.3	0.07
Diseases of the heart	948	...	...	2.3	0.04
25 to 44 years	132,052	86,354	45,028	155.6	5.39
Accidents	27,454	20,232	6,940	32.4	1.12
Malignant neoplasms	20,008	9,684	11,723	23.6	0.82
Diseases of the heart	16,155	...	...	19.0	0.66
Suicide	11,501	9,700	2,502	13.6	0.47
HIV infection	7,531	6,509	2,149	8.9	0.31
45 to 64 years	425,412	231,861	146,342	637.9	17.38
Malignant neoplasms	143,416	70,736	62,035	215.1	5.86
Diseases of the heart	100,378	70,138	29,986	150.5	4.10
Accidents	21,578	12,971	5,315	32.4	0.88
Cerebrovascular diseases	15,869	...	...	23.8	0.65
Diabetes mellitus	15,452	7,139	5,952	23.2	0.63
65 and over	1,817,095	792,612	960,608	5,103.9	74.2
Diseases of the heart	577,353	270,637	335,036	1,621.7	23.59
Malignant neoplasms	392,145	199,794	184,392	1,101.5	16.02
Cerebrovascular diseases	143,780	...	...	403.9	5.87
Lower respiratory diseases	109,158	...	...	306.6	4.46
Pneumonia and influenza	59,235	35,790	47,199	166.4	2.42

Incidence of chronic health conditions per 1,000 population (1996): arthritis 126.8; chronic sinusitis 125.0; deformities or orthopedic impairments 111.2; hypertension 106.8; hay fever 89.4; hearing impairment 83.1; heart conditions 77.9; asthma 55.0; chronic bronchitis 53.4; migraine 43.5.

Social indicators

Educational attainment (2000). Percentage of population age 25 and over having: primary and incomplete secondary 15.9%; secondary 33.1%; some post-secondary 25.4%; 4-year higher degree 17.0%; advanced degree 8.6%. Number of earned degrees (2000): bachelor's degree 1,237,875; master's degree 457,056; doctor's degree 44,808; first-professional degrees (in fields such as medicine, theology, and law) 80,057.

Distribution of income (2003)

percentage of disposable family income by quintile

1	2	3	4	5 (highest)
3.4	8.7	14.7	23.4	49.8

Quality of working life (2001). Average workweek: 39.2 hours. Annual death rate per 100,000 workers (2000): 4.5; leading causes of occupational deaths (1999): transportation incidents 43.4%, contact with objects/equipment 17.1%, assaults/violent acts 14.8%. Average days per 1,000 workdays lost to labour stoppages (2000): 1.8. Average duration of journey to work (2000): 20.7 minutes (private automobile 87.9%, of which drive alone 75.7%, carpool 12.2%; take public transportation 4.7%; walk 2.9%; work at home 3.3%; other 1.2%). Rate per 1,000 employed workers of discouraged workers (unemployed no longer seeking work; 2000): 1.8.
Access to services (1995). Proportion of occupied dwellings having access to: electricity, virtually 100.0%; safe public water supply 99.4% (12.6% from wells); public sewage collection 77.0%; septic tanks 22.8%.
Social participation. Eligible voters participating in last presidential election (2004): 60.7%. Population age 18 and over participating in voluntary work (1999): 66.0%. Trade-union membership in total workforce (2000): 14.9%.
Social deviance (2002). Offense rate per 100,000 population for: murder 6.0; rape 33.9; robbery 158.6; aggravated assault 326.4; motor-vehicle theft 464.3; burglary and housebreaking 774.7; larceny-theft 2,540.1; drug-abuse violation 587.1; drunkenness 149.1. Estimated drug and substance users (population age 12 and over; 1999)[12]: cigarettes 57,296,000; binge alcohol[13] 44,486,000; marijuana 11,476,000; other illicit drugs 6,645,000. Rate per 100,000 population of suicide (1999): 10.7.
Leisure (2002). Favourite leisure activities (percentage of total population age 18 and over that undertook activity at least once in the previous year): movie 60.0%, exercise program 55.0%, gardening 47.0%, home improvement 42.0%, amusement park 42.0%, sports events 35.0%, playing sports 30.0%, charity work 29.0%.
Material well-being (2001). Occupied dwellings with householder possessing: automobile 95.6%; telephone 94.6%; radio receiver 99.0%; television receiver 98.9%; videocassette recorder and DVD players 89.8%; washing machine 78.6%; air conditioner 75.5%; clothers dryer 73.6%; cable television 68.0%.
Recreational expenditures (2001): U.S.$593,900,000,000 (television and radio receivers, computers, and video equipment 17.8%; golfing, bowling, and other participatory activities 12.3%; nondurable toys and sports equipment 11.2%; sports supplies 10.2%; magazines and newspapers 5.9%; books and maps 5.9%; spectator amusements 4.9%, of which theatre and opera 1.7%, spectator sports 1.7%, movies 1.5%; flowers, seeds, and potted plants 3.1%; other 28.7%).

National economy

Budget (2001). Revenue: U.S.$2,136,900,000,000 (individual income tax 48.8%, social-insurance taxes and contributions 36.4%, corporation income tax 10.4%, excise taxes 3.4%, customs duties 1.0%). Expenditures: U.S.$1,856,200,000,000 (social security and medicare 37.5%, defense 16.1%, interest on debt 11.1%, other 35.3%).
Total outstanding national debt (mid-Nov. 2004): U.S.$7,443,900,000,000.

Manufacturing, mining, and construction enterprises (2000)

	no. of enterprises	no. of employees	hourly wages as a % of all wages	value added (U.S.$'000,000)
Manufacturing				
Chemical and related products	13,426	886,000	131.0	191,100
Transportation equipment	12,766	1,873,000	137.2	182,900
Electric and electronic machinery, and computers	24,189	2,146,000	100.9	181,200
Machinery, except electrical	29,442	1,378,000	113.2	167,600
Food and related products	26,401	1,468,000	90.1	137,000

Manufacturing, mining, and construction enterprises (2000) (continued)

	no. of enter- prises	no. of employees	hourly wages as a % of all wages	value added (U.S.$'000,000)
Manufacturing (continued)				
Fabricated metal products	61,144	1,791,000	100.4	108,700
Printing and publishing	39,035	813,000	104.0	105,500
Rubber and plastic products	16,292	1,057,000	92.2	60,200
Paper and related products	5,790	554,000	118.0	59,900
Primary metals	6,300	602,000	119.9	52,900
Lumber and wood	17,328	598,000	85.4	44,400
Stone, clay, and glass products	16,537	524,000	102.9	43,900
Petroleum and coal products	2,210	109,000	162.1	36,500
Furniture and fixtures	19,848	640,000	84.6	26,700
Textile-mill products	6,881	216,000	79.8	24,700
Apparel and related products	16,505	510,000	66.3	23,600
Beverages and tobacco products	2,869	169,000	127.4	22,300
Leather and leather products	1,783	69,000	72.6	4,000
Miscellaneous manufacturing industries	31,303	732,000	85.1	29,100
Mining[14]				
Oil and gas extraction	8,312	110,881	124.1	82,350
Coal mining	1,511	87,965	142.7	15,567
Nonmetallic, except fuels	5,344	95,887	112.0	12,253
Metal mining	493	45,467	126.2	7,387
Construction[14]				
Special trade contractors	414,602	3,441	130.4	307,743
General contractors and operative builders	199,289	1,342,953	124.3	198,827
Heavy construction contractors	42,557	880,400	121.5	105,639

Gross national product (2003): U.S.$10,945,792,000,000 (U.S.$37,610 per capita).

Structure of gross domestic product and labour force

	2001		2000	
	in value U.S.$'000,000,000	% of total value	labour force[15]	% of labour force[15]
Agriculture	140.6	1.4	3,457,000	2.5
Mining	139.0	1.4	521,000	0.4
Manufacturing	1,423.0	14.1	19,940,000	14.2
Construction	480.0	4.8	9,433,000	6.7
Public utilities	221.9	2.2	1,447,000	1.0
Transp. and commun.	597.6	5.9	9,433,000	6.7
Trade, hotels	1,700.9	16.9	27,832,000	19.8
Finance, real estate	2,076.9	20.6	8,294,000	5.9
Public administration, defense	1,281.3	12.7	7,082,000	5.0
Services	2,138.2	21.2	47,770,000	33.9
Other	–117.2[10]	–1.2[16]	6,661,000[17]	4.0[17]
TOTAL	10,082.2	100.0	140,863,000	100.0[3]

Gross domestic product

(In U.S.$'000,000,000)

	1998	1999	2000	2001	2002
Gross domestic product	8,751.5	9,274.3	9,824.6	10,082.2	10,446.2
By type of expenditure					
Personal consumption expenditures	5,856.0	6,246.5	6,683.7	6,987.0	7,303.7
Durable goods	693.2	755.9	803.9	835.9	871.9
Nondurable goods	1,708.5	1,830.1	1,972.9	2,041.3	2,115.0
Services	3,454.3	3,660.5	3,906.9	4,109.9	4,316.8
Gross private domestic investment	1,538.7	1,636.7	1,755.4	1,586.0	1,593.2
Fixed investment	1,465.6	1,577.2	1,691.8	1,646.3	1,589.3
Changes in business inventories	73.1	59.5	63.6	–60.3	3.9
Net exports of goods and services	–151.7	–249.9	–365.5	–348.9	–423.6
Exports	964.9	989.3	1,101.1	1,034.1	1,014.9
Imports	1,116.7	1,239.2	1,466.6	1,383.0	1,438.5
Government purchases of goods and services	1,538.5	1,641.0	1,751.0	1,858.0	1,972.9
Federal	539.2	565.0	589.2	628.1	693.7
State and local	999.3	1,076.0	1,161.8	1,229.9	1,279.2
By major type of product					
Goods output	3,305.4	3,473.4	3,651.0	3,593.7	3,694.1
Durable goods	1,569.0	1,649.6	1,735.0	1,611.4	1,644.8
Nondurable goods	1,736.4	1,823.8	1,915.9	1,982.3	2,049.3
Services	4,678.6	4,947.1	5,259.2	5,535.1	5,814.7
Structures	797.5	853.8	914.5	953.3	937.5
National income (incl. capital consumption adjustment)	...	...	...	8,979.8	9,225.4
By type of income					
Compensation of employees	...	...	...	5,942.1	6,069.5
Proprietors' income	...	...	...	771.9	769.6
Rental income of persons	...	...	...	167.4	170.9
Corporate profits	...	...	...	767.3	874.6
Net interest	...	...	...	566.3	532.9
By industry division (incl. capital consumption adjustment)					
Agriculture, forestry, fishing	102.4	93.8	98	103	98.6
Mining and construction	449.2	492	557.2	578.2	570.5
Manufacturing	1,343.90	1,373.10	1,426.20	1,346.00	1,351.60
Durable	806.9	820.4	865.3	788	786.1
Nondurable	537	552.7	560.9	558	565.5
Transportation	273.7	287.4	301.6	295.1	294.9
Communications	381.6	439.3	458.3	474.8	484
Public utilities	180.8	185.4	189.3	195.1	201.6
Wholesale and retail trade	1,141.5	1,213.2	1,254.1	1,290.7	1,388.7
Finance, insurance, real estate	1,684.60	1,798.40	1,931.00	2,028.00	2,125.70
Services	2,094.8	2,244.6	2,398.4	2,530.3	2,638.5
Government and government enterprise	1,094.50	1,141.20	1,202.70	1,259.60	1,326.70

Business activity (1997): number of businesses 23,645,000 (sole proprietorships 72.6%, active corporations 19.9%, active partnerships 7.5%), of which services 10,114,000, wholesaling and retailing 4,455,000; business receipts U.S.$18,057,000,000,000 (active corporations 88.0%, sole proprietorships 4.8%, active partnerships 7.2%), of which wholesaling and retailing U.S.$5,136,000,000,000, services U.S.$2,130,000,000,000; net profit U.S.$1,270,000,000,000 (active corporations 72.0%, sole proprietorships 14.7%, partnerships 13.3%), of which services U.S.$203,000,000,000, wholesaling and retailing U.S.$10,000,000,000. New business starts and business failures (1995): total number of new business starts 168,158; total failures 71,194, of which commercial service 21,850, retail trade 12,952; failure rate per 10,000 concerns 90.0; current liabilities of failed concerns U.S.$37,507,000,000; average liability U.S.$526,830. Business expenditures for new plant and equipment (1995): total U.S.$594,465,000,000, of which trade, services, and communications U.S.$244,829,000,000, manufacturing businesses U.S.$172,308,000,000 (durable goods 53.0%, nondurable goods 47.0%), public utilities U.S.$42,816,000,000, transportation U.S.$37,021,000,000, mining and construction U.S.$35,985,000.

Components of gross domestic product (2001)

States	Gross state product (U.S.$'000,000,000)	Personal income (U.S.$'000,000,000)	Disposable personal income (U.S.$'000,000,000)	Per capita disposable personal income (U.S.$)
Alabama	119.9	109.0	95.9	21,481
Alaska	27.7	19.7	17.2	27,131
Arizona	156.3	135.2	116.5	21,942
Arkansas	67.7	61.7	54.2	20,151
California	1,344.6	1,127.4	929.7	26,947
Colorado	167.9	145.6	122.3	27,683
Connecticut	159.3	143.6	115.6	33,765
Delaware	36.3	25.6	21.7	27,237
Florida	472.1	467.2	402.6	24,554
Georgia	296.1	238.4	203.7	24,296
Hawaii	42.4	35.0	30.4	24,810
Idaho	37.0	32.0	27.7	20,967
Illinois	457.3	408.9	345.9	27,711
Indiana	192.2	168.3	145.5	23,801
Iowa	89.6	79.7	69.4	23,754
Kansas	85.1	76.8	66.0	24,506
Kentucky	118.5	101.9	87.9	21,631
Louisiana	137.7	107.5	95.1	21,286
Maine	36.0	33.9	29.2	22,663
Maryland	186.1	187.9	156.9	29,197
Massachusetts	284.9	247.8	202.2	31,694
Michigan	325.4	295.1	251.3	25,158
Minnesota	184.8	163.0	137.3	27,622
Mississippi	67.3	61.9	55.4	19,401
Missouri	178.8	157.8	136.3	24,217
Montana	21.7	21.3	18.6	20,544
Nebraska	56.1	48.0	42.3	24,707
Nevada	42.4	62.9	54.0	25,637
New Hampshire	47.7	42.7	36.8	29,259
New Jersey	363.1	323.7	268.9	31,693
New Mexico	54.4	42.4	37.2	20,340
New York	799.2	682.2	559.0	29,402
North Carolina	281.7	224.4	192.9	23,567
North Dakota	18.3	16.2	14.4	22,691
Ohio	372.6	325.5	277.7	24,420
Oklahoma	91.8	85.8	74.8	21,613
Oregon	118.6	97.2	82.1	23,650
Pennsylvania	404.0	376.2	322.0	26,203
Rhode Island	36.5	31.8	27.3	25,769
South Carolina	113.4	99.9	87.0	21,420
South Dakota	23.2	19.9	17.7	23,454
Tennessee	178.4	153.6	136.7	23,819
Texas	742.3	607.5	533.4	25,015
Utah	68.5	54.9	47.2	20,803
Vermont	18.4	17.2	14.8	24,064
Virginia	261.4	232.1	193.9	26,972
Washington	219.9	189.1	160.3	26,773
West Virginia	42.3	40.9	36.2	20,068
Wisconsin	173.5	156.2	133.5	24,710
Wyoming	19.3	14.2	12.2	24,575
District				
District of Columbia	59.4	23.2	18.9	33,031
TOTAL/AVERAGE	9,899.1	8,620.8	7,315.7	25,688

Retail and wholesale trade and services (2000)

	no. of establish- ments	no. of employees	hourly wage as a % of all wages	annual sales or receipts (U.S.$'000,000)
Retail trade	1,113,600	14,841,000	68.7	3,105,585
Automotive dealers	124,500	1,866,000	93.5	927,141
Food stores	154,500	3,004,000	68.8	464,288
General merchandise group stores	39,600	2,526,000	74.7	417,852
Eating and drinking places	483,000	8,113,000	50.0[18, 19]	303,905
Building materials, hardware, garden supply, and mobile home dealers	91,900	1,235,000	74.2	298,604
Gasoline service stations	119,600	937,000	93.5	199,420
Apparel and accessory stores	150,900	1,369,000	67.8	169,815
Drugstores and proprietary stores	81,200	914,000	79.8	152,780
Furniture, home furnishings, equipment stores	64,800	549,000	92.2	90,503
Electronics and appliances	45,600	407,000	75.1	88,678
Sporting goods, book and music stores	65,000	616,000	92.1	74,080
Liquor stores	28,500	134,000	...	23,400
Wholesale trade	446,200	6,112,000	110.1	2,755,500
Durable goods	288,600	3,627,000	114.9	1,435,100
Professional and commercial equipment	44,400	763,000	136.6	279,300
Machinery, equipment, and supplies	73,700	796,000	115.9	257,900
Electrical goods	38,300	535,000	117.5	239,500
Motor vehicles, automotive equipment	28,400	402,000	101.8	195,700
Computers and software	...	...	...	164,700

Retail and wholesale trade and services (2000) (continued)

	no. of establish-ments	no. of employees	hourly wage as a % of all wages	annual sales or receipts (U.S.$'000,000)
Metals and minerals, except petroleum	12,100	173,000	109.1	103,300
Lumber and other construction materials	15,100	184,000	101.8	71,500
Hardware, plumbing, heating equipment and supplies	21,400	249,000	106.4	65,500
Furniture and home furnishings	14,900	167,000	100.8	46,500
Miscellaneous durable goods	40,200	355,000	89.6	175,900
Nondurable goods	157,700	2,487,000	97.3	1,320,500
Groceries and related products	39,700	875,000	101.5	387,900
Petroleum and products	10,700	132,000	93.8	171,900
Drugs, drug proprietaries, and druggists' sundries	7,400	210,000	142.6	166,300
Farm-products raw materials	9,500	92,000	79.2	106,200
Apparel and accessories	20,000	214,000	97.6	94,200
Paper and paper products	14,900	232,000	104.9	79,000
Beer, wine, and distilled alcoholic beverages	4,600	153,000	115.0	71,700
Chemicals and allied products	15,300	166,000	119.7	60,000
Miscellaneous nondurable goods	35,400	409,000	84.0	184,300
Services	3,842,000	61,662,000	101.6	1,843,800[14]
Health	659,000	14,109,000	107.1	398,500[14]
Business, except computer services	623,000	5,645,000	100.9	304,400[14]
Computer and data-processing services	100,000	1,171,000	168.4	224,100[14]
Legal services	177,000	1,089,000	145.3	122,600[14]
Automotive repair, services, garages	164,000	856,000	86.7	99,600[14]
Management and public relations	47,000	2,874,000	139.6	101,300[14]
Hotels and motels	60,000	1,768,000	70.1	97,900[14]
Amusement and recreation	64,000	1,279,000	76.4	67,900[14]
Engineering services	102,000	1,213,000	139.5	108,600[14]
Personal services	199,000	1,293,000	72.2	53,100[14]
Motion pictures	23,000	304,000	111.4	67,900[14]

Production. Agriculture, forestry, fishing (value of production/catch in U.S.$'000,000 except as noted; 2002): corn (maize) 21,213, soybeans 14,755, wheat 5,863, cotton lint 3,394, potatoes 3,151, grapes 2,853, oranges 1,834, tobacco 1,726, apples 1,571, head lettuce 1,456, tomatoes 1,171, almonds 1,049, sorghum 884, rice 841, onions 716, cottonseed 638, barley 597, peanuts (groundnuts) 594, broccoli 551, carrots 551, sweet corn 531, dry beans 519, peaches 507, bell peppers 499, cantaloupes 404, avocados 362, lemons 341, watermelons 329, sunflower seeds 317, cabbage 301, pears 297, grapefruit 286, sweet cherries 274, cauliflower 241, pecans 169, strawberries 121; livestock (number of live animals) 97,277,000 cattle, 58,943,000 pigs, 6,685,000 sheep, 5,300,000 horses, 1,940,000 chickens; roundwood 500,434,000 cu m; fish and shellfish catch 3,467, of which fish 1,558 (including salmon 359, Alaska pollack 163), shellfish 1,909 (including shrimp 560, crabs 521). Mining (metal content in metric tons except as noted; 2001): iron 37,800,000; copper 1,340,000; zinc 830,000; lead 420,000; molybdenum 38,300; vanadium 2,700; mercury 550; silver 1,800,000 kg; gold 350,000 kg; helium 101,000,000 cu m. Quarrying (metric tons; 2000): crushed stone 1,300,000,000; sand and gravel 1,139,000,000; cement 75,000,000; common salt 45,000,000; clay 40,700,000; phosphate rock 34,200,000; lime 20,000,000; gypsum 18,800,000. Manufacturing (value added in U.S.$'000,000; 1999): transportation equipment 268,511, of which motor vehicle parts 86,310, motor vehicles 80,134, aerospace products and parts 73,897; computers and electronic products 265,442, of which semiconductors and related components 102,003; chemicals and chemical products 229,284, of which pharmaceuticals and medicine 74,108; food 177,659; fabricated metal products 142,451; nonelectrical machinery 138,798; paper and paper products 74,602; plastics 72,183; base metals 66,733; printing 62,428; electrical machinery 60,458. Construction (completed; 2000): private U.S.$640,654,000,000, of which residential U.S.$374,274,000,000, nonresidential U.S.$210,140,000,000; public U.S.$174,860,000,000.

Energy production (consumption): electricity (kW-hr; 2001) 3,778,500,000,000 ([2000] 4,159,039,000); hard coal (metric tons; 2000) 895,189,000 (893,343,-000); lignite (metric tons; 2000) 80,505,000 (77,151,000); crude petroleum (barrels; 2001) 2,163,000,000 ([2000] 5,664,000,000); petroleum products (metric tons; 2000) 767,065,000 (767,031,000); natural gas (cu m; 2001) 549,557,000,000 ([2000] 660,039,000,000). Domestic production of energy by source (2001): coal 32.7%, natural gas 27.7%, crude petroleum 17.3%, nuclear power 11.2%, renewable energy 7.7%, other 3.4%.

Energy consumption by source (2000): petroleum and petroleum products 40.5%, natural gas 24.2%, coal 23.8%, nuclear electric power 8.3%, hydroelectric and thermal 3.2%; by end use: industrial 38.9%, residential and commercial 33.7%, transportation 27.4%.

Energy consumption by source and by state (2000)

('000,000,000,000 Btu)

States	Petroleum	Natural gas[20]	Coal	Hydroelectric power	Nuclear electric power
Alabama	581	351	900	59	327
Alaska	260	334	22	10	0.0
Arizona	506	207	433	89	317
Arkansas	394	259	268	24	122
California	3,558	2,273	70	436	367
Colorado	455	349	388	15	0.0
Connecticut	376	130	36	16	171
Delaware	139	54	50	0.0	0.0
Florida	1,971	561	761	1	337
Georgia	1,040	408	820	24	339
Hawaii	222	3	18	1	0.0
Idaho	175	73	14	113	0.0
Illinois	1,327	1,043	1,027	2	933

Energy consumption by source and by state (2000) (continued)

('000,000,000,000 Btu)

States	Petroleum	Natural gas[20]	Coal	Hydroelectric power	Nuclear electric power
Indiana	910	591	1,495	6	0.0
Iowa	417	234	446	9	46
Kansas	407	324	363	0.0	95
Kentucky	713	234	1,002	24	0.0
Louisiana	1,681	1,605	253	5	165
Maine	251	9	10	78	0.0
Maryland	553	217	312	18	144
Massachusetts	677	349	115	15	58
Michigan	1,062	950	779	13	197
Minnesota	680	360	374	64	135
Mississippi	469	294	148	0.0	112
Missouri	693	290	689	4	104
Montana	168	68	177	98	0.0
Nebraska	226	125	207	15	90
Nevada	230	188	199	25	0.0
New Hampshire	181	22	44	25	83
New Jersey	1,262	614	115	–1[21]	298
New Mexico	251	227	306	2	0.0
New York	1,699	1,292	331	315	329
North Carolina	976	236	786	33	408
North Dakota	120	59	425	23	0.0
Ohio	1,331	917	1,438	6	175
Oklahoma	522	539	381	22	0.0
Oregon	378	231	39	390	0.0
Pennsylvania	1,416	728	1,507	19	769
Rhode Island	97	81	[22]	10	0.0
South Carolina	481	160	432	5	531
South Dakota	119	40	51	59	0.0
Tennessee	720	276	705	58	269
Texas	5,501	4,253	1,548	12	392
Utah	275	173	403	8	0.0
Vermont	88	11	[22]	38	47
Virginia	904	282	505	–6[21]	295
Washington	868	297	106	795	90
West Virginia	218	154	980	12	0.0
Wisconsin	666	396	499	23	120
Wyoming	158	102	506	10	0.0
District					
District of Columbia	34	34	[22]	0.0	0.0
TOTAL	38,406	23,007	22,483	3,022	7,865

Household income[23] level by selected characteristics (2000)

Characteristics	Number of households ('000)	Under $15,000	$15,000–$34,999	$35,000–$74,999	$75,000 and over	Median income ($)
		Number ('000)				
Total/Average	106,418	16,952	27,584	36,570	25,313	42,151
Age of householder						
15 to 24 years	6,393	1,506	2,445	1,922	520	27,711
25 to 34 years	18,554	2,098	4,881	7,722	3,853	44,477
35 to 44 years	23,904	2,163	4,921	9,561	7,259	53,243
45 to 54 years	21,797	2,082	3,918	7,823	7,975	58,217
55 to 64 years	13,944	2,220	3,221	4,773	3,728	44,993
65 years and over	21,826	6,883	8,198	4,769	1,978	23,047
Size of household						
One person	27,820	10,112	9,524	6,362	1,820	21,468
Two persons	35,388	3,716	9,987	13,028	8,657	44,530
Three persons	17,259	1,530	3,425	6,922	5,382	54,196
Four persons	15,430	904	2,614	6,073	5,840	61,847
Five persons	6,686	425	1,239	2,597	2,424	60,295
Six persons	2,396	154	502	1,000	740	54,841
Seven or more persons	1,439	108	293	589	449	54,663
Educational attainment of householder						
Total[24]	100,025	15,446	25,139	34,646	24,795	43,556
Less than 9th grade	6,753	2,898	2,302	1,244	308	17,557
Some high school	9,111	3,023	3,224	2,276	587	22,753
High school graduate	30,785	5,248	9,363	11,410	4,765	36,722
Some college, no degree	18,165	2,155	4,834	7,087	4,089	44,449
Associate degree	8,214	730	1,888	3,351	2,246	50,356
Bachelor's degree	17,521	1,006	2,607	6,462	7,446	65,922
Master's degree	6,435	265	685	2,076	3,410	77,935
Professional degree	1,641	70	145	342	1,085	100,000
Doctorate degree	1,400	51	91	398	859	93,361

Household income and expenditure. Average household size (2002) 2.6; median annual income per household (2001) U.S.$42,228, of which median Asian and Pacific Islander household U.S.$53,635, median white household U.S.$44,517, median non-Hispanic household U.S.$46,305, median Hispanic[6] household U.S.$33,565, median black (including Hispanic) household U.S.$29,470; sources of personal income (2000): wages and salaries 57.6%, self-employment 8.6%, transfer payments 8.5%, other 25.3%; expenditure (1999): transportation 18.9%, housing 18.9%, food at home 7.9%, household furnishings 7.2%, fuel and utilities 6.4%, food away from home 5.7%, recreation 5.5%, health 5.3%, wearing apparel 4.7%, education 1.7%, other 17.8%.

Financial aggregates

	1998	1999	2000	2001	2002	2003	2004[25]
Exchange rate, U.S.$ per:							
£[26]	1.66	1.62	1.52	1.44	1.50	1.63	1.79
SDR[26]	1.36	1.37	1.32	1.27	1.29	1.40	1.46
International reserves (U.S.$)[27]							
Total (excl. gold; '000,000,000)	70.71	60.50	56.60	57.63	67.96	74.89	71.53
SDRs ('000,000,000)	10.60	10.35	10.54	10.78	12.17	12.64	12.78
Reserve pos. in IMF ('000,000,000)	24.11	17.97	14.82	17.87	21.98	22.53	19.44
Foreign exchange ('000,000,000)	36.00	32.18	31.24	29.98	33.82	39.72	39.31

Financial aggregates (continued)

	1998	1999	2000	2001	2002	2003	2004[25]
Gold ('000,000 fine troy oz)	261.78	261.67	261.61	262.00	262.00	261.55	261.55
% world reserves	27.09	27.13	27.52	27.83	28.16	28.60	...
Interest and prices							
Central bank discount (%)[27]	4.50	5.00	6.00	1.25	0.75	2.00	2.58
Govt. bond yield (%)[26]	5.26	5.64	6.03	5.02	4.61	4.02	4.13
Industrial share prices[26] (2000 = 100)	72.8	92.1	100.0	78.9	65.3	62.9	72.4
Balance of payments (U.S.$'000,000,000)							
Balance of visible trade	–244.74	–343.72	–449.79	–424.09	–479.41	–544.30	...
Imports, f.o.b.	–917.12	–1,029.99	–1,224.43	–1,145.93	–1,164.75	–1,260.71	...
Exports, f.o.b.	672.38	686.27	774.63	721.84	685.34	716.41	...
Balance of invisibles	+35.21	+46.87	+36.46	+38.39	+5.47	+13.64	...
Balance of payments, current account	–209.53	–296.85	–413.44	–385.70	–473.94	–530.66	...

Average employee earnings

	average hourly earnings in U.S.$		average weekly earnings in U.S.$	
	Feb. 1999	Feb. 2000	Feb. 1999	Feb. 2000
Manufacturing				
Durable goods	13.66	14.19	564.16	588.89
Lumber and wood products	11.26	11.61	453.78	469.04
Furniture and fixtures	11.06	11.50	440.17	457.70
Stone, clay, and glass products	13.64	13.99	576.96	593.18
Primary metal industries	15.41	16.29	673.42	723.28
Fabricated metal products	13.29	13.65	555.52	576.03
Machinery, except electrical	14.72	15.39	619.71	652.54
Electrical and electronic equipment	13.25	13.71	544.58	567.59
Transportation equipment	17.50	18.65	768.25	818.74
Instruments and related products	13.94	14.41	578.51	595.13
Miscellaneous manufacturing	11.17	11.56	442.33	455.46
Nondurable goods	12.97	13.38	525.29	543.23
Food and kindred products	11.91	12.25	489.50	501.03
Tobacco manufactures	17.80	17.32	662.16	680.68
Textile mill products	10.60	10.84	426.12	447.69
Apparel and other textile products	8.65	9.01	322.65	338.78
Paper and allied products	15.70	16.03	675.10	689.29
Printing and publishing	13.67	14.13	515.36	536.53
Chemicals and allied products	17.20	17.80	734.44	756.50
Petroleum and coal products	21.43	22.03	927.92	962.71
Rubber and miscellaneous plastics products	12.16	12.53	503.42	518.74
Leather and leather products	9.56	9.87	355.63	370.13
Nonmanufacturing				
Metal mining	18.16	18.63	793.59	815.99
Coal mining	19.11	19.40	865.68	873.00
Oil and gas extraction	16.98	16.68	696.18	738.47
Nonmetallic minerals, except fuels	14.81	15.22	662.00	672.02
Construction	16.00	17.37	633.08	672.09
Transportation and public utilities	15.56	16.06	606.84	613.49
Wholesale trade	14.38	14.96	550.75	571.47
Retail trade	8.98	9.34	256.83	266.19
Finance, insurance, and real estate	14.55	14.91	528.17	536.76
Hotels, motels, and tourist courts	9.20	9.53	280.60	289.71
Health services	14.06	14.55	462.57	480.15
Legal services	18.74	19.75	652.15	693.23
Miscellaneous services	18.38	18.67	637.79	681.46

Median household income[28]

(in current 2003 U.S.$)

States	1999	2000	2001	2002	2003
Alabama	36,251	35,424	35,160	37,603	37,225
Alaska	51,396	52,847	57,363	52,774	51,837
Arizona	36,995	39,783	42,704	39,734	41,166
Arkansas	29,682	29,697	33,339	32,387	32,002
California	43,629	46,816	47,262	47,437	49,300
Colorado	48,177	48,240	49,397	48,294	49,940
Connecticut	50,593	50,172	53,347	53,387	54,965
Delaware	46,628	50,365	49,602	49,650	49,019
Florida	35,831	38,856	36,421	38,024	38,972
Georgia	39,425	41,901	42,576	42,939	42,438
Hawaii	44,504	51,546	47,439	47,303	51,834
Idaho	35,800	37,611	38,241	37,715	42,372
Illinois	46,330	46,064	46,171	42,710	45,153
Indiana	40,838	40,865	40,379	41,047	42,425
Iowa	41,098	40,991	40,976	41,049	41,384
Kansas	37,348	41,059	41,415	42,619	44,232
Kentucky	33,738	36,265	38,437	36,762	36,936
Louisiana	32,654	30,718	33,322	34,008	33,507
Maine	38,862	37,266	36,612	36,853	37,113
Maryland	52,205	54,535	53,530	56,407	52,314
Massachusetts	44,005	46,753	52,253	49,855	50,955
Michigan	46,089	45,512	45,047	42,715	45,022
Minnesota	47,038	54,251	52,681	54,622	52,823
Mississippi	32,478	34,299	30,161	30,882	32,728
Missouri	41,383	45,097	41,339	42,776	43,762
Montana	31,038	32,777	32,126	34,835	34,108
Nebraska	38,626	41,750	43,611	42,796	43,974
Nevada	41,461	45,758	45,403	44,958	45,184
New Hampshire	46,055	50,926	51,331	55,321	55,567
New Jersey	49,734	50,405	51,771	54,568	56,045
New Mexico	32,574	35,093	33,124	35,457	35,105
New York	39,989	40,744	42,114	41,900	42,788
North Carolina	37,254	38,317	38,162	36,515	37,279
North Dakota	32,663	35,996	35,793	36,200	40,410
Ohio	39,489	42,962	41,785	42,684	43,520
Oklahoma	32,683	32,432	35,609	36,458	35,902

Median household income[28] (continued)

(in current 2003 U.S.$)

States	1999	2000	2001	2002	2003
Oregon	40,619	42,499	41,273	41,802	41,638
Pennsylvania	37,758	42,176	43,499	42,498	42,933
Rhode Island	42,719	42,197	45,723	42,417	44,711
South Carolina	36,462	37,570	37,736	37,812	38,479
South Dakota	35,828	36,475	39,671	37,873	39,522
Tennessee	36,522	34,096	35,783	37,030	37,523
Texas	38,688	38,609	40,860	40,149	39,271
Utah	46,050	47,550	47,342	47,861	49,275
Vermont	41,584	39,594	40,794	42,999	43,261
Virginia	45,693	47,163	50,241	49,631	54,783
Washington	45,473	42,525	42,490	45,183	47,508
West Virginia	29,297	29,411	29,673	29,359	32,763
Wisconsin	45,667	45,088	45,346	45,903	46,269
Wyoming	37,248	39,629	39,719	39,763	42,555
District					
District of Columbia	38,670	41,222	41,169	39,070	45,044
U.S. AVERAGE	40,696	41,990	42,228	42,409	43,318

Average annual expenditure of "consumer units" (households, plus individuals sharing households or budgets; 2001): total U.S.$39,518, of which housing U.S.$13,011, transportation U.S.$7,633, food U.S.$5,321, pensions and social security U.S.$3,326, health care U.S.$2,182, clothing U.S.$1,743, other U.S.$6,302.

Selected household characteristics (2002). Total number of households 109,297,000, of which (family households by race) white 83.0%, black 12.2%, other 4.8%; in central cities 31.4%[29], in suburbs 46.3%[29], outside metropolitan areas 22.3%[29]; (by tenure[29]) owned 74,399,000 (68.1%), rented 34,897,000 (31.9%); family households 74,329,000, of which married couple 76.4%, female head with own children[30] under age 18, 10.8%, female head without own children[30] under 18, 6.9%; nonfamily households 34,969,000, of which female living alone 48.0%, male living alone 34.3%, other 17.7%.

Population economically active (2002): total 144,863,000[15]; activity rate of total population 50.1% (participation rates: age 16 and over 66.6%; female 46.5%; unemployed [October 2004] 5.5%).

Price and earnings indexes (2000 = 100)

	1997	1998	1999	2000	2001	2002	2003
Consumer price index	93.2	94.7	96.7	100.0	102.8	104.5	106.8
Hourly earnings index	91.7	93.9	96.7	100.0	103.1	106.8	109.9

Tourism (2002): receipts from visitors U.S.$66,547,000,000; expenditures by nationals abroad U.S.$58,044,000,000; number of foreign visitors 41,892,000,000 ([2000] 14,594,000 from Canada, 10,322,000 from Mexico, 11,597,000 from Europe); number of nationals traveling abroad 56,359,000 ([2000] 18,849,000 to Mexico, 15,114,000 to Canada).

Land use as % of total land area (2000): in temporary crops 19.3%, in permanent crops 0.2%, in pasture 25.5%; overall forest area 24.7%.

Foreign trade

Balance of trade (current prices)

	1998	1999	2000	2001	2002	2003
U.S.$'000,000,000	–229.8	–328.8	–436.1	–411.9	–468.3	–549.4
% of total	14.4%	19.1%	21.8%	22.0%	25.3%	27.8%

Imports (2002): U.S.$1,161,400,000,000 (motor vehicles and parts 14.5%, electrical machinery [excluding televisions and electronic components] 7.0%, crude petroleum 6.8%, computers and office equipment 6.6%, chemicals and chemical products 6.5%, televisions and electronic components 5.7%, wearing apparel 5.5%, general industrial machinery 3.0%, power generating machinery 2.9%). *Major import sources:* Canada 18.0%; Mexico 11.6%; China 10.8%; Japan 10.5%; Germany 5.4%; United Kingdom 3.5%; South Korea 3.1%; Taiwan 2.8%; France 2.4%; Italy 2.1%; Malaysia 2.1%; Ireland 1.9%.

Exports (2002): U.S.$693,100,000,000 (electrical machinery [excluding televisions and electronic components] 9.7%, chemicals and related products 8.9%, motor vehicles 8.3%, agricultural commodities 7.7%, power generating machinery 4.7%, computers and office equipment 4.4%, general industrial machinery 4.3%, airplanes 3.9%, scientific and precision equipment 3.9%, specialized industrial machinery 3.4%). *Major export destinations:* Canada 23.2%; Mexico 14.1%; Japan 7.4%; United Kingdom 4.8%; Germany 3.8%; South Korea 3.3%; China 3.2%; Taiwan 2.7%; France 2.7%; The Netherlands 2.6%; Singapore 2.3%; Belgium 1.9%.

Trade by commodity group (2001)[31]

	imports		exports	
SITC Group	U.S.$'000,000	%	U.S.$'000,000	%
00 Food and live animals	39,992	3.4	41,136	5.6
01 Beverages and tobacco	10,253	0.9	5,645	0.8
02 Crude materials, excluding fuels	21,919	1.9	28,057	3.8
03 Mineral fuels, lubricants, and related materials	129,087	10.9	13,298	1.8
04 Animal and vegetable oils, fat, and waxes	1,276[32]	0.1[32]	1,326[32]	0.2[32]
05 Chemicals and related products, n.e.s.	79,948	6.8	80,008	11.0
06 Basic manufactures	130,951	11.1	67,994	9.3
07 Machinery and transport equipment	508,043	43.0	374,355	51.2
08 Miscellaneous manufactured articles	206,825	17.5	87,281	11.9
09 Goods not classified by kind	51,780	4.4	31,906	4.4
TOTAL	1,180,074	100.0	731,006	100.0

Direction of trade (2001)[31]

	imports		exports	
	U.S.$'000,000	%	U.S.$'000,000	%
Africa	26,778	2.3	12,367	1.7
Nigeria	9,180	0.8	955	0.1
South Africa	2,090	0.2	2,659	0.4
Americas	424,701	36.0	323,418	44.3
Brazil	15,259	1.3	15,929	2.2
Canada	220,104	18.7	163,722	22.4
Caribbean countries	9,796	0.8	10,692	1.5
Central America	11,653	1.0	9,022	1.2
Mexico	132,775	11.3	101,508	13.9
Venezuela	16,141	1.4	5,684	0.8
Asia	461,201	39.1	202,715	27.7
China	109,381	9.3	19,234	2.6
Israel	12,158	1.0	7,482	1.0
Japan	129,708	11.0	57,637	7.9
Saudi Arabia	14,414	1.2	5,971	0.8
Singapore	15,261	1.3	17,691	2.4
South Korea	36,491	3.1	22,197	3.0
Europe	249,155	21.1	174,722	23.9
France	30,980	2.6	20,125	2.8
Germany	60,491	5.1	30,113	4.1
Italy	24,953	2.1	9,923	1.4
Russia	6,531	0.6	3,208	0.4
United Kingdom	42,347	3.6	40,796	5.6
Oceania	9,575	0.8	13,418	1.8
Australia	6,803	0.6	10,945	1.5
Unallocated	8,664	0.7	4,366	0.6
TOTAL	1,180,074	100.0	731,006	100.0

Transport and communications

Transport. Railroads (1998): length 132,000 mi, 212,433 km; (1999) passenger-mi 13,402,000,000, passenger-km 21,568,000,000; short ton-mi cargo (1997) 1,421,000,000,000, metric ton-km cargo (1997) 2,075,000,000. Roads (2001): total length 3,948,335 mi, 6,354,231 km (paved 91%). Vehicles (2001): passenger cars 137,633,000; trucks and buses 92,795,000. Merchant marine (1999): vessels (1,000 gross tons and over) 579; total deadweight tonnage 16,747,000. Air transport (2002): passenger-mi 992,849,000,000, passenger-km 1,598,000,000,000; short ton-mi cargo 54,302,000,000, metric ton-km cargo 87,390,000,000; localities (1996) with scheduled flights 834[33]. Certified route passenger/cargo air carriers (1992) 77; operating revenue (U.S.$'000,000; 1991) 74,942, of which domestic 56,119, international 18,823; operating expenses 76,669, of which domestic 56,596, international 20,073.

Intercity passenger and freight traffic by mode of transportation (1999)

	cargo traffic ('000,000,000 ton-mi)	% of nat'l total	passenger traffic ('000,000,000 passenger-mi)	% of nat'l total
Rail	1,499	40.3	14	0.6
Road	1,093	29.4	1,885	78.5
Inland water	486	13.1	—	—
Air	14	0.4	501	20.9
Petroleum pipeline	623	16.8	—	—
TOTAL	3,715	100.0	2,400	100.0

Communications

Medium	date	unit	number	units per 1,000 persons
Daily newspapers	2000	circulation	55,773,000	198
Radio	2000	receivers	598,000,000	2,118
Television	2000	receivers	241,000,000	854
Telephones	2003	main lines	181,599,900	621
Cellular telephones	2003	subscribers	158,722,000	543
Personal computers	2002	units	190,000,000	659
Internet	2002	users	159,000,000	551

Other communications media (2000)

	titles		titles
Print		Engineering	265
Books (new)	123,108	Fine and applied arts	145
of which		General interest	181
Agriculture	1,073	History	151
Art	5,980	Home economics	90
Biography	3,899	Industrial arts	106
Business	4,068	Journalism and commun.	90
Education	3,378	Labour and industrial relations	70
Fiction	14,617	Law	273
General works	1,318	Library and information sciences	118
History	7,931	Literature and language	158
Home economics	2,513	Mathematics and science	238
Juvenile	8,690	Medicine	182
Language	2,536	Philosophy and religion	130
Law	3,070	Physical education and recreation	151
Literature	3,371	Political science	136
Medicine	6,234	Psychology	138
Music	1,582	Sociology and anthropology	149
Philosophy, psychology	5,556	Zoology	94
Poetry, drama	2,479		
Religion	6,206	**Cinema**	
Science	8,464	Feature films	478
Sociology, economics	14,908		
Sports, recreation	3,483		(pieces of mail)
Technology	8,582	**Post**	
Travel	3,170	Mail	207,483,000,000
Periodicals[18]	3,731	Domestic	206,381,000,000
of which		International	1,102,000,000
Agriculture	153		
Business and economics	262		
Chemistry and physics	170		
Children's periodicals	78		
Education	203		

Education and health

Literacy: n.a.

Education (2001–02)

	schools	teachers	students	student/ teacher ratio
Primary (age 5–13)[34]	...	2,206,000	38,163,000	17.3
Secondary and vocational (age 14–17)	...	1,341,000	14,902,000	11.1
Higher, including teacher-training colleges	4,064[18]	1,012,000	15,300,000	15.1

Food (2001): daily per capita caloric intake 3,776 (vegetable products 73%, animal products 27%); 143% of FAO recommended minimum requirement. Per capita consumption of major food groups (kilograms annually; 2001): milk 256.6; fresh vegetables 124.5; cereal products 116.9; fresh fruits 113.4; red meat 72.5; potatoes 64.4; poultry products 47.8; sugar 32.6; fats and oils 32.5; fish and shellfish 21.2.

Health: doctors of medicine (2001) 836,200[35] (1 per 346 persons), of which office-based practice 514,000 (including specialties in internal medicine 18.4%, general and family practice 13.6%, pediatrics 8.7%, other specialty 8.6%, obstetrics and gynecology 6.3%, anesthesiology 5.6%, psychiatry 5.0%, general surgery 5.0%, orthopedic surgery 3.5%, cardiovascular diseases 3.3%, ophthalmology 3.1%, emergency medicine 3.1%, diagnostic radiology 3.0%); doctors of osteopathy 47,000; nurses (2002) 2,311,000 (1 per 125 persons); dentists (2002) 180,000 (1 per 1,603 persons); hospital beds (2001) 987,000 (1 per 289 persons), of which nonfederal 94.7% (community hospitals 83.7%, psychiatric 9.0%, long-term general and special 1.9%), federal 5.3%; infant mortality rate per 1,000 live births (2001) 7.0.

Military

Total active duty personnel (2003): 1,427,000 (army 34.0%, navy 28.0%, air force 25.8%, marines 12.2%). *Military expenditure as percentage of GNP* (1999): 3.0% (world 2.4%); per capita expenditure U.S.$1,030. *Security assistance to the world* (2002): U.S.$7,209,000,000, for underwriting the purchase of U.S. weapons 50.6%, of which Israel 28.3%, Egypt 18.0%, Jordan 1.0%; for economic support 30.5%, of which Israel 10.0%, Egypt 9.1%, Jordan 2.1%; for the Andean Counterdrug Initiative 9.2%; for nonproliferation, antiterrorism, and de-mining 4.3%; for international narcotics and law enforcement 3.0%; for peacekeeping operations 1.9%.

[1]Excludes 4 nonvoting delegates from the District of Columbia, the U.S. Virgin Islands, American Samoa, and Guam; a nonvoting resident commissioner from Puerto Rico; and a nonvoting resident representative from the Northern Mariana Islands. [2]Total area per 2000 computer-based survey (excluding 42,225 sq mi [109,362 sq km] of coastal water and 75,372 sq mi [195,213 sq km] of territorial water) equals 3,676,487 sq mi (9,522,058 sq km), of which land area equals 3,537,439 sq mi (9,161,926 sq km), inland water area equals 78,797 sq mi (204,083 sq km), and Great Lakes water area equals 60,251 sq mi (156,049 sq km). [3]Detail does not add to total given because of rounding. [4]Excludes 239,369 military personnel overseas; adjusted 2000 census total announced December 2002 equaled 284,683,782. [5]Based on land area only. [6]Persons of Hispanic origin may be of any race. [7]April 1, 2000, to July 1, 2002. [8]2000. [9]1989–91. [10]Age breakdown by causes is for 1998. [11]Includes deaths with age not known. [12]Individuals who used drugs at least once within month prior to survey. [13]Drinking 5 or more drinks on the same occasion on at least one day in the past 30 days per survey. [14]1997. [15]Excludes military personnel overseas. [16]Statistical discrepancy. [17]Unemployed. [18]1999. [19]Excludes tips. [20]Includes supplemental gaseous fuels. [21]Minus sign indicates when amount of energy expended exceeds amount consumed. [22]Less than 0.5 trillion Btu. [23]Gross income from all sources, including transfer payments to individuals. [24]Householder 25 years old or older. [25]September. [26]Period average. [27]End-of-period. [28]In 2003 current dollars in conjunction with annually revised U.S. Bureau of Labor Statistics experimental Consumer Price Index (or CPI-U-RS deflator). [29]1994. [30]"Own children" includes adopted children and stepchildren. [31]Includes Puerto Rico and U.S. Virgin Islands. [32]Figure(s) represent remainder; specific data for 04 category unavailable. [33]Includes 292 localities in Alaska. [34]Primary includes kindergarten. [35]751,700 professionally active.

Internet resources for further information:

- **U.S. Census Bureau**
  http://www.census.gov
- **Statistical Abstract of the United States**
  http://www.census.gov/prod/www/statistical-abstract-us.html

Uruguay

Official name: República Oriental del Uruguay (Oriental Republic of Uruguay).
Form of government: republic with two legislative houses (Senate [31][1]; Chamber of Representatives [99]).
Head of state and government: President.
Capital: Montevideo.
Official language: Spanish.
Official religion: none.
Monetary unit: 1 peso uruguayo ($U) = 100 centesimos; valuation (Sept. 1, 2004) 1 U.S.$ = $U 28.75; 1 £ = $U 51.72.

Area and population

Departments	area sq km	population 2004 estimate	Departments	area sq km	population 2004 estimate
Artigas	11,928	78,452	Río Negro	9,282	55,453
Canelones	4,536	533,234	Rivera	9,370	106,898
Cerro Largo	13,648	86,399	Rocha	10,551	72,502
Colonia	6,106	127,567	Salto	14,163	130,371
Durazno	11,643	57,683	San José	4,992	108,120
Flores	5,144	25,279	Soriano	9,008	84,284
Florida	10,417	68,741	Tacuarembó	15,438	87,704
Lavalleja	10,016	62,336	Treinta y Tres	9,529	52,395
Maldonado	4,793	159,275	TOTAL LAND AREA	175,016	
Montevideo	530	1,383,418	INLAND WATER	1,199	
Paysandú	13,922	119,327	TOTAL	176,215	3,399,438

Demography

Population (2004): 3,399,000.
Density (2004): persons per sq mi 50.0, persons per sq km 19.3.
Urban-rural (2002): urban 92.5%; rural 7.5%.
Sex distribution (2003): male 48.40%; female 51.60%.
Age breakdown (2003): under 15, 24.2%; 15–29, 22.9%; 30–44, 19.7%; 45–59, 15.8%; 60–74, 11.6%; 75 and over, 5.8%.
Population projection: (2010) 3,491,000; (2020) 3,617,000.
Ethnic composition (2000): white (mostly Spanish, Italian, or mixed Spanish-Italian) 94.5%; mestizo 3.1%; mulatto 2.0%; other 0.4%.
Religious affiliation (2000): Roman Catholic 78.2%[2]; Protestant 3.3%; other Christian 5.3%; Jewish 1.2%; atheist 6.3%; other 5.7%.
Major cities (1996): Montevideo (2004) 1,383,416; Salto 93,113; Paysandú 74,568; Las Piedras 66,584; Rivera 62,859.

Vital statistics

Birth rate per 1,000 population (2003): 15.9 (world avg. 21.3).
Death rate per 1,000 population (2003): 9.4 (world avg. 9.1).
Natural increase rate per 1,000 population (2003): 6.5 (world avg. 12.2).
Total fertility rate (avg. births per childbearing woman; 2003): 2.2.
Marriage rate per 1,000 population (2003): 4.2.
Divorce rate per 1,000 population (2003): 2.0.
Life expectancy at birth (2003): male 71.3 years; female 79.2 years.
Major causes of death per 100,000 population (1999): diseases of the circulatory system 330.4; malignant neoplasms 221.7; accidents and violence 56.9.

National economy

Budget (2002). Revenue: $U 55,949,000,000 (tax revenue 81.9%, of which taxes on goods and services 42.7%, income and profit taxes 20.7%, import tax 2.4%, nontax revenue 9.6%; grants 8.1%; other 0.4%). Expenditures: $U 68,851,-000,000 (social security and welfare 42.2%, general public services 11.2%, education 8.9%, health 6.3%, defense 4.4%).
Public debt (external, outstanding; 2002): U.S.$6,851,000,000.
Production (metric tons except as noted). Agriculture, forestry, fishing (2002): rice 939,489, wheat 270,000, sugarcane 170,000, corn (maize) 163,400, oranges 155,000, sunflower seeds 150,300; livestock (number of live animals) 11,667,000 cattle, 11,250,000 sheep; roundwood 5,674,646 cu m; fish catch (2001) 105,051. Mining and quarrying (2002): limestone 1,300,000; gypsum 183,000; gold 66,841 troy oz. Manufacturing (value added in U.S.$'000,000; 2000): refined petroleum products 563; food products 505; chemicals and chemical products 186; beverages 182; tobacco products 178; publishing 99; leather (all forms) and footwear 60. Energy production (consumption): electricity (kW-hr; 2000) 7,588,000,000 (7,974,000,000); coal (metric tons; 2000) none (1,000); crude petroleum (barrels; 2000) none (14,088,000); petroleum products (metric tons; 2000) 1,793,000 (1,640,000); natural gas, none (none).
Household income and expenditure. Avg. household size (2002) 3.4; avg. annual income per household, n.a.; expenditure: n.a.
Population economically active (2003): total 1,240,500[3]; activity rate 48.3% (participation rates: ages 14 and over, 58.2%; female 45.0%; unemployed 16.8%).

Price and earnings indexes (2000 = 100)

	1997	1998	1999	2000	2001	2002	2003
Consumer price index	86.4	94.4	93.6	100.0	106.6	140.8	195.3
Monthly earnings index	83.6	92.2	97.0	100.0	...	...	...

Gross national product (at current market prices; 2003): U.S.$12,904,000,000 (U.S.$3,820 per capita).

Structure of gross domestic product and labour force

	2001 in value $U '000,000	2001 % of total value	2000 labour force	2000 % of labour force
Agriculture	15,864.3	6.4	42,400	3.4
Mining	730.0	0.3	1,700	0.1
Manufacturing	40,988.1	16.5	158,200	12.8
Construction	13,418.3	5.4	88,700	7.2
Public utilities	10,514.4	4.2	13,100	1.1
Transp. and commun.	23,143.7	9.3	61,500	5.0
Trade	31,977.8	12.9	214,100	17.3
Finance	73,102.9	29.4	72,000	5.8
Pub. admin., defense	24,580.5	9.9	415,500	33.7
Services	28,714.1	11.5		
Other	−14,414.7[4]	−5.8[4]	168,100[5]	13.6[5]
TOTAL	248,619.4	100.0	1,235,300[3]	100.0

Tourism (2002): receipts U.S.$318,000,000; expenditures U.S.$178,000,000.
Land use as % of total land area (2000): in temporary crops 7.4%, in permanent crops 0.2%, in pasture 77.4%; overall forest area 7.4%.

Foreign trade[6]

Balance of trade (current prices)

	1997	1998	1999	2000	2001	2002
U.S.$'000,000	−1,001	−1,040	−1,120	−1,171	−1,003	−103
% of total	15.5%	15.8%	20.0%	20.3%	19.6%	2.7%

Imports (2002): U.S.$1,964,000,000 (chemicals and chemical products 17.4%; machinery and appliances 15.1%; crude and refined petroleum 15.0%; food, beverages, and tobacco 14.4%; plastic products 5.9%). *Major import sources:* Argentina 27.5%; Brazil 19.8%; United States 8.4%; Russia 5.7%; Germany 4.1%.
Exports (2002): U.S.$1,861,000,000 (hides and leather goods 13.5%; beef 13.5%; textiles and wearing apparel 11.9%; dairy products and eggs 7.6%; rice 7.5%; fish and crustaceans 5.3%). *Major export destinations:* Brazil 23.2%; United States 7.4%; Argentina 6.1%; Germany 5.8%; China 5.6%.

Transport and communications

Transport. Railroads (1998): track length 3,002 km; passenger-km 14,000,000; metric ton-km cargo 244,000,000. Roads (1997): length 8,683 km[7] (paved 30%). Vehicles (2002): passenger cars 617,028; trucks and buses 53,915. Air transport (2000): passenger-km 747,000,000; metric ton-km cargo, n.a.; airports (1997) 1.

Communications

Medium	date	unit	number	units per 1,000 persons
Daily newspapers	2000	circulation	973,000	293
Radio	2000	receivers	2,000,000	603
Television	2000	receivers	1,760,000	536
Telephones	2002	main lines	946,500	280
Cellular telephones	2002	subscribers	652,000	193
Personal computers	2001	units	370,000	110
Internet	2001	users	400,000	119

Education and health

Educational attainment (2002). Percentage of population age 25 and over having: incomplete primary education 9.8%; primary 33.6%; some secondary 17.2%; complete secondary 22.2%; higher 17.2%. *Literacy* (2001 est.): population age 15 and over literate 97.6%; males 97.2%; females 98.1%.

Education (2002)

	schools	teachers	students	student/ teacher ratio
Primary (age 6–11)	2,402	16,699	362,902	21.7
Secondary (age 12–17)	405	26,779	269,205	10.1
Vocational	124	8,160	65,567	8.0
Higher	6	10,524	98,798	9.4

Health (2002): physicians 12,905 (1 per 261 persons); hospital beds 6,695 (1 per 502 persons); infant mortality rate (2002) 13.6.
Food (2001): daily per capita caloric intake 2,848 (vegetable products 65%, animal products 35%); 107% of FAO recommended minimum.

Military

Total active duty personnel (2003): 24,000 (army 63.3%, navy 23.8%, air force 12.9%). *Military expenditure as percentage of GNP* (1999): 1.3% (world 2.4%); per capita expenditure U.S.$83.

[1]Includes the vice president, who serves as ex officio presiding officer. [2]About 30–40% of Roman Catholics are estimated to be nonreligious. [3]From urban areas only. [4]Includes indirect taxes less imputed bank service charges. [5]Includes unemployed not previously employed. [6]Import figures are c.i.f. [7]Excludes streets under local control.

Internet resources for further information:
- **Instituto Nacional de Estadística—Uruguay http://www.ine.gub.uy**
- **Banco Central del Uruguay http://www.bcu.gub.uy**

Uzbekistan

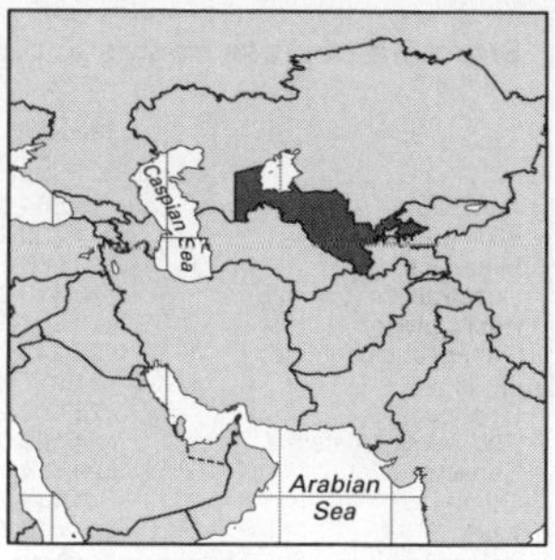

Official name: Ŭzbekiston Respublikasi (Republic of Uzbekistan).
Form of government: multiparty republic with a single legislative body (Supreme Assembly [250])[1].
Heads of state and government: President assisted by Prime Minister.
Capital: Tashkent (Toshkent).
Official language: Uzbek.
Official religion: none.
Monetary unit: sum (plural sumy); valuation (Sept. 1, 2004) 1 U.S.$ = 1,032 sumy; 1 £ = 1,857 sumy.

Area and population

Autonomous republic	Administrative centres	area sq mi	area sq km	population 2002 estimate[2]
Qoraqalpoghiston	Nuqus	63,700	164,900	1,633,900
Provinces				
Andijon	Andijon	1,600	4,200	2,286,000
Buxoro	Bukhara (Buxoro)	15,200	39,400	1,534,900
Farghona	Fergana (Farghona)	2,700	7,100	2,761,300
Jizzakh	Jizzakh	7,900	20,500	1,026,000
Khorazm	Urganch	2,400	6,300	1,402,600
Namangan	Namangan	3,100	7,900	2,049,900
Nawoiy	Nawoiy	42,800	110,800	877,100
Qashqadaryo	Qarshi	11,000	28,400	2,302,000
Samarqand	Samarkand (Samarqand)	6,300	16,400	2,749,100
Sirdaryo	Guliston	2,000	5,100	670,800
Surkhondaryo	Termiz	8,000	20,800	1,846,400
Tashkent (Toshkent)	Tashkent (Toshkent)	6,000[3]	15,600[3]	4,986,800[3]
City				
Tashkent (Toshkent)	—	[3]	[3]	[3]
TOTAL		172,700	447,400	26,126,800

Demography

Population (2004): 26,009,000.
Density (2004): persons per sq mi 150.6, persons per sq km 58.1.
Urban-rural (2002): urban 36.6%; rural 63.4%.
Sex distribution (2001): male 49.55%; female 50.45%.
Age breakdown (2001): under 15, 36.4%; 15–29, 28.6%; 30–44, 19.6%; 45–59, 8.5%; 60–74, 5.4%; 75 and over, 1.5%.
Population projection: (2010) 28,352,000; (2020) 31,791,000.
Doubling time: 45 years.
Ethnic composition (1998): Uzbek 75.8%; Russian 6.0%; Tajik 4.8%; Kazakh 4.1%; Tatar 1.6%; other 7.7%.
Religious affiliation (2000): Muslim (mostly Sunnī) 76.2%; nonreligious 18.1%; Russian Orthodox 0.8%; Jewish 0.2%; other 4.7%.
Major cities (1999): Tashkent 2,142,700; Namangan 376,600; Samarkand 362,300; Andijon 323,900; Bukhara 237,900.

Vital statistics

Birth rate per 1,000 population (2003): 21.6 (world avg. 21.3).
Death rate per 1,000 population (2003): 5.8 (world avg. 9.1).
Natural increase rate per 1,000 population (2003): 15.8 (world avg. 12.2).
Total fertility rate (avg. births per childbearing woman; 2003): 2.4.
Marriage rate per 1,000 population (1999): 7.1.
Life expectancy at birth (2003): male 67.0 years; female 73.0 years.
Major causes of death per 100,000 population (1998): diseases of the circulatory system 291.8; diseases of the respiratory system 85.9; accidents, poisoning, and violence 45.1; infectious and parasitic diseases 45.0; cancers 39.5; diseases of the digestive system 30.7; diseases of the nervous system 12.9.

National economy

Budget (1999). Revenue: 611,897,000,000 sumy (taxes on income and profits 30.5%, value-added tax 27.3%, excise taxes 22.8%, property and land taxes 12.1%, other 7.3%). Expenditures: 654,259,000,000 sumy (social and cultural affairs 36.7%, investments 18.7%, national economy 10.4%, transfers 10.4%, administration 2.2%, interest on debt 1.9%, other 19.2%).
Household income and expenditure (1995). Average household size (2000) 5.5; income per household 35,165 sumy (U.S.$1,040); sources of income: wages and salaries 63.0%, subsidies, grants, and nonwage income 34.9%, other 2.1%; expenditure: food and beverages 71%, clothing and footwear 14%, recreation 6%, household durables 4%, housing 3%.
Public debt (external, outstanding; 2002): U.S.$3,901,000,000.
Tourism (2002): receipts U.S.$68,000,000.
Production (metric tons except as noted). Agriculture, forestry, fishing (2002): wheat 4,956,000, seed cotton 3,200,000, vegetables 2,300,000, fruit (except grapes) and berries 1,100,000, potatoes 730,000, grapes 570,000, rice 143,100, barley 129,000; livestock (number of live animals) 8,220,000 sheep, 5,400,000 cattle, 830,000 goats, 14,500,000 chickens; roundwood (2001) 24,980 cu m; fish catch (2001) 8,152. Mining and quarrying (2000): copper (metal content) 91,800; gold 62,276 kg. Manufacturing (metric tons except as noted; 1998): cement 3,358,000; cotton fibre 1,138,000; mineral fertilizer 897,000; steel 360,000; ferrous metal products 322,000; television sets 192,468 units; passenger cars 54,456 units; video recorders 50,096 units; refrigerators 16,000 units; tractors 3,000 units. Energy production (consumption): electricity (kW-hr; 2001) 47,961,000,000 (48,455,000,000); hard coal (metric tons; 2000) 69,000 (69,000); lignite (metric tons; 1999) 2,901,000 (2,829,000); crude petroleum (barrels; 2000) 30,412,000 (30,412,000); petroleum products (metric tons; 2000) 5,991,000 (5,695,000); natural gas (cu m; 2002) 58,429,000,000 (50,630,000,000).
Gross national product (2003): U.S.$10,779,000,000 (U.S.$420 per capita).

Structure of gross domestic product and labour force

	2001 in value '000,000 sumy	2001 % of total value	2000 labour force	2000 % of labour force
Agriculture	1,471,675	30.2	3,083,000	34.3
Manufacturing, mining, and public utilities	590,014	12.1	1,145,000	12.7
Construction	286,646	5.9	676,000	7.5
Transp. and commun.	379,542	7.8	382,000	4.3
Trade	492,001	10.1	754,000	8.4
Finance / Pub. admin., defense / Services	945,928	19.4	2,042,000	22.7
Other	702,607[4]	14.4[4]	901,000[5]	10.0[5]
TOTAL	4,868,413	100.0[6]	8,983,000	100.0[6]

Population economically active (2001): total 9,136,000; activity rate of total population 36.5% (participation rates: ages 16–59 [male], 16–54 [female] 70.4%; female [1994] 43.0%; unemployed [official rate] 0.4%).

Price and earnings indexes (1999 = 100)

	1997	1998	1999	2000	2001	2002	2003
Consumer price index	59.3	69.2	100.0	149.5	220.5	318.2	365.3
Monthly earnings index	41.7	61.5	100.0	...	...	...	...

Land use as % of total land area (2000): in temporary crops 10.8%, in permanent crops 0.8%, in pasture 55.0%; overall forest area 4.8%.

Foreign trade[7]

Balance of trade (current prices)

	1998	1999	2000	2001	2002
U.S.$'000,000	+239.5	+125.1	+317.3	+33.5	+276.4
% of total	3.5%	2.0%	5.1%	0.5%	4.8%

Imports (2002): U.S.$2,712,000,000 (machinery and metalworking products 48.9%, food products 21.3%, other 29.8%). *Major import sources:* Russia 20.5%; South Korea 17.4%; Germany 8.9%; Kazakhstan 7.5%; U.S. 6.4%; Ukraine 6.3%.
Exports (2002): U.S.$2,988,400,000 ([2000] cotton fibre 27.5%, energy products [including natural gas and crude petroleum] 10.3%, base metals [significantly] gold 6.6%, food products 5.4%). *Major export destinations* (2002): Russia 17.3%; Ukraine 10.2%; Italy 8.3%; Tajikistan 7.8%; South Korea 7.1%; Poland 4.7%.

Transport and communications

Transport. Railroads (2000): length 3,950 km; (1999) passenger-km 1,900,000,000; (1999) metric ton-km cargo 13,900,000,000. Roads (1997): total length 84,400 km (paved 87%). Vehicles (1994): passenger cars 865,300; buses 14,500. Air transport (2000)[8]: passenger-km 3,732,000,000; metric ton-km cargo 76,600,000; airports (1998) with scheduled flights 9.

Communications

Medium	date	unit	number	units per 1,000 persons
Daily newspapers	2000	circulation	74,200	3.0
Television	2000	receivers	6,830,000	276
Telephones	2003	main lines	1,717,100	67
Cellular telephones	2003	subscribers	320,800	13
Internet	2003	users	492,000	19

Education and health

Educational attainment: n.a. *Literacy* (2000): percentage of total population age 15 and over literate 99.2%; male 99.6%; female 98.8%.

Education (1995–96)

	schools	teachers	students	student/ teacher ratio
Primary (age 6–13) / Secondary (age 14–17)	9,300	413,000	5,090,000	12.3
Voc., teacher tr.[9]	248	22,164[10]	240,100	...
Higher[10]	55	...	272,300	...

Health (1995): physicians 76,200 (1 per 302 persons); hospital beds 192,000 (1 per 120 persons); infant mortality rate per 1,000 live births (2003) 36.0.
Food (2001): daily per capita caloric intake 2,379 (vegetable products 82%, animal products 18%); 93% of FAO recommended minimum requirement.

Military

Total active duty personnel (2003): 55,000 (army 72.7%, air force 27.3%). *Military expenditure as percentage of GNP* (1999): 1.7% (world 2.4%); per capita expenditure U.S.$38.

[1]Official approval of future bicameral legislature announced in August 2003. [2]Unofficial figures; 2003 estimate for country is not based on these estimates. [3]Tashkent province includes Tashkent city. [4]Includes value-added taxes: excise taxes plus net import taxes minus subsidies. [5]Includes 863,000 persons on forced leave and 38,000 unemployed. [6]Detail does not add to total given because of rounding. [7]Imports c.i.f., exports f.o.b. [8]Uzbekistan Airways. [9]1998. [10]1992–93.

Internet resources for further information:
- **Center for Economic Research http://cer.uz**
- **Republic of Uzbekistan Statistics http://www.stat.uz/index_e.htm**

Vanuatu

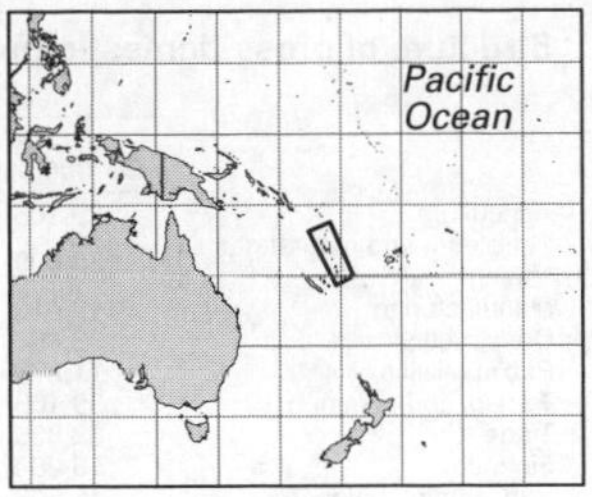

Official name: Ripablik blong Vanuatu (Bislama); République de Vanuatu (French); Republic of Vanuatu (English).
Form of government: republic with a single legislative house (Parliament [52]).
Chief of state: President.
Head of government: Prime Minister.
Capital: Vila.
Official languages: Bislama; French; English.
Official religion: none.
Monetary unit: vatu (VT); valuation (Sept. 1, 2004) 1 U.S.$ = VT 115.28; 1 £ = VT 207.38.

Area and population

		area		population
				2001
Provinces	**Capitals**	sq mi	sq km	estimate
Malampa	Lakatoro	1,073	2,779	33,627
Penama	Longana	463	1,198	27,560
Sanma	Luganville	1,640	4,248	38,282
Shefa	Vila	562	1,455	57,307
Tafea	Isangel	628	1,627	30,518
Torba	Sola	341	882	8,150
TOTAL		4,707	12,190[1]	195,444

Demography

Population (2004): 216,000.
Density (2004): persons per sq mi 45.9, persons per sq km 17.7.
Urban-rural (2002): urban 21.0%; rural 79.0%.
Sex distribution (1999): male 51.46%; female 48.54%.
Age breakdown (1999): under 15, 37.8%; 15–29, 29.4%; 30–44, 18.2%; 45–59, 9.7%; 60–74, 4.0%; 75 and over, 0.9%.
Population projection: (2010) 248,000; (2020) 299,000.
Doubling time: 43 years.
Ethnic composition (1999): Ni-Vanuatu 98.7%; European and other Pacific Islanders 1.3%.
Religious affiliation (2000): Christian 89.3%, of which Protestant 53.7%, Anglican 18.2%, Roman Catholic 15.5%; Custom (traditional beliefs) 3.5%; Bahā'ī 2.9%; other 4.3%.
Major towns (1999): Vila (Port-Vila) 30,139; Luganville 11,360.

Vital statistics

Birth rate per 1,000 population (2003): 24.3 (world avg. 21.3).
Death rate per 1,000 population (2003): 8.1 (world avg. 9.1).
Natural increase rate per 1,000 population (2003): 16.2 (world avg. 12.2).
Total fertility rate (avg. births per childbearing woman; 2003): 3.0.
Marriage rate per 1,000 population: n.a.
Divorce rate per 1,000 population: n.a.
Life expectancy at birth (2003): male 60.3 years; female 63.2 years.
Major causes of death per 100,000 population (1994)[2]: diseases of the circulatory system 39.0; diseases of the respiratory system 30.4; malignant neoplasms (cancers) 29.2; infectious and parasitic diseases 25.0; diseases of the digestive system 9.7.

National economy

Budget (2001). Revenue: VT 6,887,000,000 (tax revenue 84.0%, of which taxes on goods and services 48.4%, tax on import duties 33.2%; foreign grants 6.4%; nontax revenue 9.4%). Expenditures: VT 7,885,000,000 (wages and salary 47.4%; goods and services 23.3%; transfers 10.1%; interest payments 3.1%; other [including technical assistance] 16.0%).
Public debt (external, outstanding; 2002): U.S.$69,700,000.
Production (metric tons except as noted). Agriculture, forestry, fishing (2002): coconuts 200,000, roots and tubers 45,000, bananas 13,000, vegetables and melons 10,000, peanuts (groundnuts) 2,500, kava 1,246, cacao beans 794, corn (maize) 700; livestock (number of live animals) 151,000 cattle, 62,000 pigs, 12,000 goats, 340,000 chickens; roundwood 119,000 cu m; fish catch (2001) 26,690. Mining and quarrying: small quantities of coral-reef limestone, crushed stone, sand, and gravel. Manufacturing (value added in VT '000,000; 1995): food, beverages, and tobacco 645; wood products 423; fabricated metal products 377; paper products 125; chemical, rubber, plastic, and nonmetallic products 84; textiles, clothing, and leather 54. Energy production (consumption): electricity (kW-hr; 2000) 38,000,000 (38,000,000); coal, none (none); crude petroleum, none (none); petroleum products (metric tons; 2000) none (26,000); natural gas, none (none).
Land use as % of total land area (2000): in temporary crops 2.5%, in permanent crops 7.4%, in pasture 3.4%; overall forest area 36.7%.
Population economically active (1999): total 76,370; activity rate of total population 40.9% (participation rates: ages 15–64, 78.2%; female 49.6%; unemployed, n.a.).

Price index (2000 = 100)

	1996	1997	1998	1999	2000	2001	2002
Consumer price index	90.0	92.6	95.6	97.5	100.0	103.6	105.6

Gross national product (2003): U.S.$248,000,000 (U.S.$1,180 per capita).

Structure of gross domestic product and labour force

	2001		1989	
	in value VT '000,000	% of total value	labour force	% of labour force
Agriculture	5,097	15.0	49,811	74.4
Mining	...	...	1	—
Manufacturing	1,363	4.0	891	1.3
Construction	1,071	3.2	1,302	1.9
Public utilities	685	2.0	109	0.2
Transportation and communications	4,508	13.2	1,031	1.5
Trade	13,507	39.7	2,713	4.1
Finance	4,058	11.9	646	1.0
Pub. admin., defense	4,663	13.7	7,892	11.8
Services	760	2.2		
Other	−1,671[3]	−4.9[3]	2,561	3.8
TOTAL	34,041	100.0	66,957	100.0

Household income and expenditure (1985)[4]. Average household size (1989) 5.1; income per household U.S.$11,299; sources of income: wages and salaries 59.0%, self-employment 33.7%; expenditure (1990)[4, 5]: food and nonalcoholic beverages 30.5%, housing 20.7%, transportation 13.2%, health and recreation 12.3%, tobacco and alcohol 10.4%.
Tourism (2001): receipts from visitors U.S.$46,000,000; expenditures by nationals abroad U.S.$8,000,000.

Foreign trade[6]

Balance of trade (current prices)

	1997	1998	1999	2000	2001	2002
VT '000,000	−6,801	−6,934	−9,024	−8,693	−10,223	−9,640
% of total	45.4%	44.5%	57.8%	54.5%	63.8%	63.3%

Imports (2002): VT 12,433,000,000 (machinery and transport equipment 22.9%, food and live animals 17.2%, chemicals and chemical products 12.1%, mineral fuels 11.2%). *Major import sources:* Australia 39.3%; New Zealand 17.6%; Fiji 8.3%; France 5.3%; New Caledonia 4.0%.
Exports (2002): VT 2,793,000,000 (domestic exports 76.3%, of which coconut oil 16.9%, kava 15.6%, timber 7.1%, beef 6.9%, copra 6.2%; reexports 23.7%). *Major export destinations*[7]: Australia 29.2%; EC 10.8%; Japan 10.7%; New Caledonia 9.0%; Bangladesh 4.9%.

Transport and communications

Transport. Railroads: none. Roads (1996): total length 665 mi, 1,070 km (paved 24%). Vehicles (1996): passenger cars 4,000; trucks and buses 2,600. Merchant marine (1992): vessels (100 gross tons and over) 280; total deadweight tonnage 3,259,594. Air transport (2001)[8]: passenger-mi 131,755,000, passenger-km 212,039,000; short ton-mi cargo 1,301,000, metric ton-km 1,899,000; airports (1996) with scheduled flights 29.

Communications

Medium	date	unit	number	units per 1,000 persons
Radio	1997	receivers	62,000	350
Television	2000	receivers	2,280	12
Telephones	2003	main lines	6,500	32
Cellular telephones	2003	subscribers	7,800	38
Personal computers	2002	units	3,000	15
Internet	2003	users	7,500	36

Education and health

Educational attainment (1999). Percentage of population age 15 and over having: no formal schooling 18.0%; incomplete primary education 20.6%; completed primary 35.5%; some secondary 12.2%; completed secondary 8.5%; higher 5.2%, of which university 1.3%. *Literacy* (1998): total population age 15 and over literate 64%.

Education (1992)

	schools	teachers	students	student/ teacher ratio
Primary (age 6–11)[9]	272	852	26,267	30.8
Secondary (age 11–18)	27	220	4,269	19.4
Voc., teacher tr.	...	...	444	...
Higher	1[10]	13[11]	124[12]	...

Health (1997): physicians 21 (1 per 8,524 persons); hospital beds 573 (1 per 312 persons); infant mortality rate per 1,000 live births (2003) 58.1.
Food (2001): daily per capita caloric intake 2,565 (vegetable products 87%, animal products 13%); 113% of FAO recommended minimum requirement.

Military

Total active duty personnel: Vanuatu has a paramilitary force of about 300.

[1]Detail does not add to total given because of rounding. [2]Deaths reported to the Ministry of Health only. [3]Imputed bank service charges. [4]Vila and Luganville only. [5]Weights of consumer price index components. [6]Imports c.i.f.; exports f.o.b. [7]Destination of domestic exports only. [8]Air Vanuatu only. [9]Excludes independent private schools. [10]1989. [11]1983. [12]1991.

Internet resources for further information:
- **Vanuatu Statistics Office http://www.vanuatustatistics.gov.vu**
- **United Nations Development Programme, Common Country Assessments http://www.undp.org.fj/CCAs.htm**
- **Secretariat of the Pacific Community http://www.spc.int/prism/country/vu/vu_index.html**

Venezuela

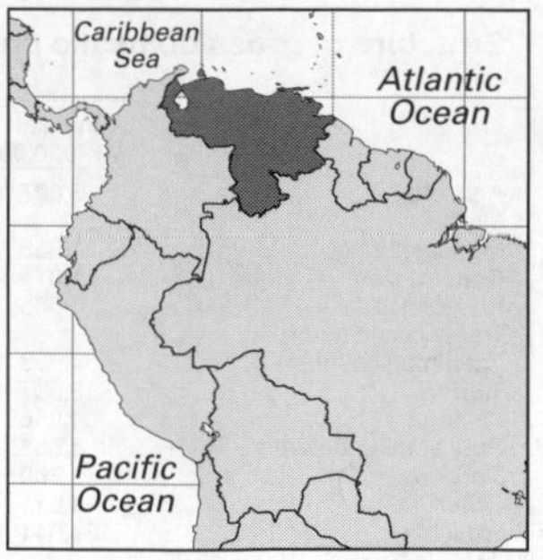

Official name: República Bolivariana de Venezuela (Bolivarian Republic of Venezuela).
Form of government: federal multiparty republic with a unicameral legislature (National Assembly [165]).
Head of state and government: President.
Capital: Caracas.
Official language: Spanish[1].
Official religion: none.
Monetary unit: 1 bolívar (B, plural Bs) = 100 céntimos; valuation (Sept. 1, 2004) 1 U.S.$ = Bs 2,730; 1 £ = Bs 4,911.

Area and population

States	Capitals	area sq mi	area sq km	population 2001 census[2]
Amazonas	Puerto Ayacucho	69,554	180,145	70,464
Anzoátegui	Barcelona	16,700	43,300	1,222,225
Apure	San Fernando de Apure	29,500	76,500	377,756
Aragua	Maracay	2,708	7,014	1,449,616
Barinas	Barinas	13,600	35,200	624,508
Bolívar	Ciudad Bolívar	91,900	238,000	1,214,846
Carabobo	Valencia	1,795	4,650	1,932,168
Cojedes	San Carlos	5,700	14,800	253,105
Delta Amacuro	Tucupita	15,500	40,200	97,987
Falcón	Coro	9,600	24,800	763,188
Guárico	San Juan de Los Morros	25,091	64,986	627,086
Lara	Barquisimeto	7,600	19,800	1,556,415
Mérida	Mérida	4,400	11,300	715,268
Miranda	Los Teques	3,070	7,950	2,330,872
Monagas	Maturín	11,200	28,900	712,626
Nueva Esparta	La Asunción	440	1,150	373,851
Portuguesa	Guanare	5,900	15,200	725,740
Sucre	Cumaná	4,600	11,800	786,483
Táchira	San Cristóbal	4,300	11,100	992,669
Trujillo	Trujillo	2,900	7,400	608,563
Vargas	La Guaira	578	1,497	298,109
Yaracuy	San Felipe	2,700	7,100	499,049
Zulia	Maracaibo	24,400	63,100	2,983,679
Other federal entities				
Dependencias Federales[3]	—	50	120	1,651
Distrito Federal	Caracas	167	433	1,836,286
TOTAL		353,841[4]	916,445	23,054,210

Demography

Population (2004): 26,170,000.
Density (2004): persons per sq mi 74.0, persons per sq km 28.6.
Urban-rural (2003 est.): urban 87.7%; rural 12.3%.
Sex distribution (2001): male 49.56%; female 50.44%.
Age breakdown (2001): under 15, 33.1%; 15–29, 27.5%; 30–44, 20.7%; 45–59, 11.7%; 60–74, 5.1%; 75 and over, 1.9%.
Population projection: (2010) 28,955,000; (2020) 33,300,000.
Ethnic composition (1993): mestizo 67%; white 21%; black 10%; Indian 2%.
Religious affiliation (2000): Roman Catholic 89.5%; Protestant 2.0%; other Christian 1.4%; Spiritist 1.1%; nonreligious/atheist 2.2%; other 3.8%.
Major cities (2001): Caracas 1,836,000[2] (urban agglomeration 3,177,000); Maracaibo 1,609,000[2]; Valencia 1,196,000[2]; Barquisimeto 811,000[2]; Ciudad Guayana 629,000[2].

Vital statistics

Birth rate per 1,000 population (2003): 22.6 (world avg. 21.3).
Death rate per 1,000 population (2003): 5.1 (world avg. 9.1).
Total fertility rate (avg. births per childbearing woman; 2003): 2.7.
Marriage rate per 1,000 population (2003): 2.9.
Life expectancy at birth (2002): male 70.8 years; female 76.6 years.
Major causes of death per 100,000 population (2000): circulatory diseases 132.0; cancers 62.7; accidents 33.1; violence 26.2; diabetes mellitus 24.5.

National economy

Budget (2000). Revenue: Bs 14,664,587,000,000 (oil revenues 59.2%, value-added tax 17.3%, income tax 9.0%, import duties 7.3%). Expenditures: Bs 17,238,854,000,000 (subsidies 50.5%, wages and salaries 19.1%, capital expenditure 14.5%, debt service 11.6%, goods and services 2.7%).
Public debt (external, outstanding; 2002): U.S.$23,265,000,000.
Production (metric tons except as noted). Agriculture, forestry, fishing (2002): sugarcane 6,909,000, corn (maize) 1,805,000, rice 790,000, plantains 760,000, bananas 750,000, cassava 625,000, sorghum 553,000, potatoes 330,000; livestock (number of live animals) 14,500,000 cattle, 5,655,000 pigs, 4,000,000 goats, 115,000,000 chickens; roundwood (2002) 4,667,000 cu m; fish catch (2001) 435,000. Mining and quarrying (2001): iron ore 16,902,000; bauxite 4,526,000; gold 9,076 kg; diamonds 52,804 carats. Manufacturing (value added in 1984 Bs '000,000; 1997): ferrous and nonferrous metals 16,355; food products 13,277; chemicals 10,004; beverages 9,480; clothing, textiles, leather, and shoes 8,311; metal products 6,413. Energy production (consumption): electricity (kW-hr; 2000) 85,211,000,000 (85,211,000,000); coal (metric tons; 2000) 7,885,000 (180,000); crude petroleum (barrels; 2001) 972,000,000 ([2000] 382,000,000); petroleum products (metric tons; 2000) 53,937,000 (19,530,000); natural gas (cu m; 2000) 28,382,700,000 (28,382,700,000).
Tourism (2002): receipts U.S.$468,000,000; expenditures U.S.$1,041,000,000.
Land use as % of total land area (2000): in temporary crops 2.9%, in permanent crops 0.9%, in pasture 20.7%; overall forest area 56.1%.
Gross national product (2003): U.S.$89,150,000,000 (U.S.$3,490 per capita).

Structure of gross domestic product and labour force

	2001 in value Bs '000,000[5]	2001 % of total value[5]	2000 labour force	2000 % of labour force
Agriculture	29,166	4.9	950,000	9.2
Petroleum and natural gas; Mining	135,609	22.6	53,000	0.5
Manufacturing	113,618	18.9	1,191,000	11.5
Construction	33,467	5.6	741,000	7.2
Public utilities	11,276	1.9	58,000	0.6
Transp. and commun.	39,103	6.5	608,000	5.9
Trade	63,835	10.6	2,752,000	26.6
Finance	55,262	9.2		
Pub. admin., defense	46,208	7.7	2,598,000	25.2
Services	59,803	10.0		
Other	12,434	2.1	1,376,000[6]	13.3[6]
TOTAL	599,781	100.0	10,327,000	100.0

Population economically active (1997): total 9,507,125; activity rate 41.7% (participation rates: over age 15, 64.6%; female 35.9%; unemployed 10.6%).

Price and earnings indexes (2000 = 100)

	1997	1998	1999	2000	2001	2002	2003
Consumer price index	51.3	69.6	86.1	100.0	112.5	137.8	180.6
Annual earnings index	...	...	82.7	100.0	120.2	130.3	141.4

Household income and expenditure. Average household size (1990) 5.1; average annual income per household (1981) Bs 42,492 (U.S.$9,899); expenditure (1995): food 40.6%, housing 13.8%, transportation and communications 8.6%, clothing 5.3%, health 3.1%, education and recreation 2.9%.

Foreign trade[7]

Balance of trade (current prices)

	1997	1998	1999	2000	2001	2002
U.S.$'000,000	+9,731	+2,804	+6,522	+16,364	+8,869	+13,939
% of total	27.0%	9.0%	19.4%	35.9%	21.2%	36.2%

Imports (2001): U.S.$16,435,000,000 (nonelectrical machinery 16.5%, chemicals and chemical products 14.1%, road vehicles 14.0%, electrical machinery 9.8%). *Major import sources:* U.S. 33.9%; Colombia 8.7%; Brazil 5.9%; Mexico 4.7%; Japan 4.6%.
Exports (2001): U.S.$25,304,000,000 (crude petroleum 58.3%, refined petroleum 23.6%, iron and steel 3.1%, aluminum 3.0%). *Major export destinations* (2002): U.S. 56.4%; Netherlands Antilles 6.1%; Colombia 2.9%; Dominican Republic 2.8%; Brazil 2.7%.

Transport and communications

Transport. Railroads (1996): length (1994) 627 km; passenger-km 149,905; metric ton-km cargo 54,474,000. Roads (1999): total length 96,155 km (paved 34%). Vehicles (1997): passenger cars 1,505,000; trucks and buses 542,000. Merchant marine (1992): vessels (over 100 gross tons) 271; total deadweight tonnage 1,355,419. Air transport (1998): passenger-km 3,133,000,000; metric ton-km cargo 332,000,000; airports (1997) with scheduled flights 20.

Communications

Medium	date	unit	number	units per 1,000 persons
Daily newspapers	2000	circulation	5,000,000	206
Radio	2000	receivers	7,140,000	294
Television	2000	receivers	4,490,000	185
Telephones	2002	main lines	2,841,800	112
Cellular telephones	2002	subscribers	6,463,600	256
Personal computers	2002	units	1,536,000	61
Internet	2002	users	1,274,400	51

Education and health

Educational attainment (1993). Percentage of population age 25 and over having: no formal schooling 8.0%; primary education or less 43.7%; some secondary and secondary 38.3%; postsecondary 10.0%. *Literacy* (1995 est.): total population age 15 and over literate 91.1%; males 91.8%; females 90.3%.

Education (1998–99)

	schools	teachers[8]	students	student/ teacher ratio
Primary (age 7–12)	17,372	186,658	4,299,671	...
Secondary (age 13–17)[9]	2,524	61,761	400,794	...
Higher	99[10]	43,833[10]	717,192	12.6[11]

Health (1999): physicians 46,886 (1 per 508 persons); public hospital beds (2000) 40,675 (1 per 620 persons); infant mortality rate (2003) 17.2.
Food (2002): daily per capita caloric intake 2,337 (vegetable products 83%, animal products 17%); 95% of FAO recommended minimum.

Military

Total active duty personnel (2003): 82,300 (army 69.3%, navy 22.2%, air force 8.5%). *Military expenditure as percentage of GNP* (1999): 1.4% (world 2.4%); per capita expenditure U.S.$61.

[1]31 indigenous Indian languages were also made official in May 2002. [2]Preliminary unadjusted census results. [3]A new federal entity (the Caribbean Federal Territory) was under consideration in 2003. [4]Detail does not add to total given because of rounding. [5]At constant 1984 prices. [6]Mostly unemployed. [7]Imports and exports are f.o.b. in balance of trade. [8]1997–98. [9]Includes vocational and teacher training. [10]1990–91. [11]1991–92.

Internet resources for further information:
- **Banco Central de Venezuela http://www.bcv.org.ve/EnglishVersion/Index.asp**
- **Instituto Nacional de Estadística http://www.ine.gov.ve**

Vietnam

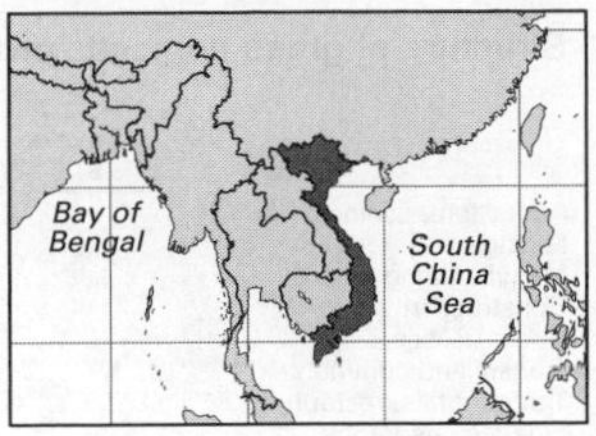

Official name: Cong Hoa Xa Hoi Chu Nghia Viet Nam (Socialist Republic of Vietnam).
Form of government: socialist republic with one legislative house (National Assembly [498]).
Head of state: President.
Head of government: Prime Minister.
Capital: Hanoi.
Official language: Vietnamese.
Official religion: none.
Monetary unit: 1 dong (D) = 10 hao = 100 xu; valuation (Sept. 1, 2004) 1 U.S.$ = D 15,760; 1 £ = D 28,352.

Area and population

Economic regions[1]	Principal cities	area sq mi	area sq km	population 2002 estimate
Central Highlands	Buon Ma Thuot	17,740	45,946	3,434,100
Mekong River Delta	Long Xuyen	15,274	39,559	16,723,700
North Central Coast	Hue	19,758	51,174	10,299,100
North East	Thai Nguyen	25,871	67,005	11,253,600
North West	Hoa Binh	15,426	39,955	2,389,203
Northeastern South Region	Ho Chi Minh City	16,437	42,572	13,642,800
Red River Delta	Hanoi	4,833	12,517	15,357,000
South Central Coast	Da Nang	13,040	33,773	6,785,000
TOTAL		128,379[2]	332,501[2]	78,685,800[3]

Demography

Population (2004): 81,839,000.
Density (2004): persons per sq mi 637.5, persons per sq km 246.1.
Urban-rural (2002): urban 25.1%; rural 74.9%.
Sex distribution (2002): male 49.20%; female 50.80%.
Age breakdown (2003): under 15, 30.2%; 15–29, 29.4%; 30–44, 21.8%; 45–59, 10.8%; 60–74, 5.7%; 75 and over, 2.0%.
Population projection: (2010) 88,516,000; (2020) 99,392,000.
Doubling time: 51 years.
Ethnic composition (2000): Vietnamese 85.0%; Han Chinese 3.5%; Montagnards 1.9%; Tho (Tay) 1.6%; Tai 1.5%; Muong 1.4%; Khmer 1.2%; Nung 1.0%; other 2.9%.
Religious affiliation (1995): Buddhist 66.7%; Christian 8.7%, of which Roman Catholic 7.7%, Protestant 1.0%; Cao Dai (a New-Religionist group) 3.5%; Hoa Hao (a New-Religionist group) 2.1%; other 19.0%.
Major cities (1992): Ho Chi Minh City 5,479,000[4]; Hanoi 2,931,400[4]; Haiphong 783,133; Da Nang 382,674; Buon Ma Thuot 282,095; Nha Trang 221,331; Hue 219,149; Can Tho 215,587.

Vital statistics

Birth rate per 1,000 population (2003): 20.1 (world avg. 21.3).
Death rate per 1,000 population (2003): 6.4 (world avg. 9.1).
Natural increase rate per 1,000 population (2003): 13.7 (world avg. 12.2).
Total fertility rate (avg. births per childbearing woman; 2003): 2.3.
Life expectancy at birth (2003): male 67.0 years; female 72.0 years.

National economy

Budget (2003). Revenue: D 123,700,000,000,000 (tax revenue 77.9%, of which corporate income taxes 24.6%, VAT 23.2%, taxes on trade 18.7%; nontax revenues 20.5%; grants 1.6%). Expenditures: D 148,400,000,000,000 (current expenditures 64.6%, of which social services 27.9%, economic services 5.3%, interest payment 4.5%; capital expenditures 35.4%).
Public debt (external, outstanding; 2002): U.S.$12,181,000,000.
Gross national product (2003): U.S.$38,786,000,000 (U.S.$480 per capita).

Structure of gross domestic product and labour force

2002	in value D '000,000,000	% of total value	labour force	% of labour force
Agriculture, forestry, fishing	123,268	23.0	25,573,000	66.1
Public utilities	18,868	3.5	3,787,000	9.8
Mining	45,937	8.6		
Manufacturing	110,284	20.6		
Construction	31,559	5.9	1,216,000	3.1
Transp. and commun.	21,095	3.9	1,133,000	2.9
Trade and restaurants	75,617	14.1	3,106,000	8.0
Finance, insurance	9,763	1.8	3,900,000	10.1
Pub. admin., defense	44,941	8.4		
Services, other	54,766	10.2		
TOTAL	536,098	100.0	38,715,000	100.0

Tourism (1998): receipts from visitors U.S.$86,000,000; expenditures by nationals abroad, n.a.
Production (metric tons except as noted). Agriculture, forestry, fishing (2002): rice 34,064,000, sugarcane 16,824,000, cassava 4,158,000, corn (maize) 2,315,000, sweet potatoes 1,725,000, bananas 1,044,000, coconuts 838,000, coffee 689,000, oranges 442,000, groundnuts (peanuts) 397,000, pineapples 348,000, natural rubber 331,400, tea 90,000, pimento 77,000; livestock (number of live animals) 60,000,000 ducks, 23,170,000 pigs, 4,063,000 cattle, 2,814,000 buffalo; roundwood (2002) 30,730,000 cu m, of which fuelwood 26,547,000 cu m, industrial roundwood 4,183,000 cu m; fish catch (2001) 1,491,000, of which marine fish 1,321,000. Mining and quarrying (2002): phosphate rock (gross weight) 770,000; tin (metal content) 4,000. Manufacturing (gross value of production in U.S.$'000,000; 2000): food products 736; cement, bricks and pottery 418; wearing apparel 376; beverages 359; footwear 308; tobacco products 228; paints, soaps, and pharmaceuticals 206. Energy production (consumption): electricity (kW-hr; 2001) 29,800,000,000 ([2000] 26,594,000,000); coal (metric tons; 2002) 15,900,000 ([2000] 7,978,000); crude petroleum (barrels; 2002) 136,700,000 ([2000] negligible); petroleum products (metric tons; 2000) 154,000 (8,969,000); natural gas (cu m; 2002) 2,260,000,000 ([2000] 1,355,000,000).
Population economically active (2002): total 38,715,000; activity rate 48.9% (participation rates [2001]: ages 15 and over 70.5%; female, n.a., unemployed 6.0%).

Price and earnings indexes (2000 = 100)

	1997	1998	1999	2000	2001	2002	2003
Consumer price index	91.1	97.7	101.7	100.0	99.6	103.4	106.6
Earnings index	...	...	...	...	...	...	...

Household income and expenditure. Average household size (2002) 5.0; income per household (1990)[5] D 577,008 (U.S.$93); sources of income: n.a.; expenditure (1990): food 62.4%, clothing 5.0%, household goods 4.6%, education 2.9%, housing 2.5%.
Land use as % of total land area (2000): in temporary crops 18.7%, in permanent crops 5.4%, in pasture 2.0%; overall forest area 30.2%.

Foreign trade[6]

Balance of trade (current prices)

	1997	1998	1999	2000	2001	2002
U.S.$'000,000	–1,315	–981	+1,080	+378	+627	–875
% of total	6.7%	5.0%	4.9%	1.3%	2.1%	2.6%

Imports (2002): U.S.$19,733,000,000 (machinery equipment [including aircraft] 19.2%; petroleum products 10.2%; garment material and leather 8.7%; iron and steel 6.8%; fertilizers 2.7%; motorcycles 2.1%). *Major import sources:* Taiwan 12.9%; Singapore 12.8%; Japan 12.7%; South Korea 11.6%; China 10.9%.
Exports (2002): U.S.$16,706,000,000 (crude petroleum 19.6%; garments 16.5%; fish, crustaceans, and mollusks 12.1%; footwear 11.2%; rice 4.3%; electronic products 2.9%). *Major export destinations:* Japan 14.6%; U.S. 14.5%; China 9.0%; Australia 8.0%; Singapore 5.8%; Taiwan 4.9%.

Transport and communications

Transport. Railroads (2001): route length 1,952 mi, 3,142 km; passenger-km 3,428,000,000; metric ton-km cargo 2,054,400,000. Roads (1999): total length 58,000 mi, 93,300 km (paved 25%). Vehicles (2003): passenger cars, trucks, and buses 600,000. Air transport (2002)[7]: passenger-km 2,963,000,000; metric ton-km cargo 81,000,000; airports (1997) with scheduled flights 12.

Communications

Medium	date	unit	number	units per 1,000 persons
Daily newspapers	2000	circulation	313,000	4.0
Radio	2000	receivers	8,520,000	109
Television	2000	receivers	14,500,000	185
Telephones	2003	main lines	4,402,000	54
Cellular telephones	2003	subscribers	2,742,000	34
Personal computers	2002	units	800,000	10
Internet	2003	users	3,500,000	43

Education and health

Educational attainment (1989). Percentage of population age 25 and over having: no formal education (illiterate) 16.6%; incomplete and complete primary 69.8%; incomplete and complete secondary 10.6%; higher 2.6%; unknown 0.4%. *Literacy* (2001): percentage of population age 15 and over literate 92.7%; males 94.5%; females 90.9%.

Education (2001–02)

	schools	teachers	students	student/ teacher ratio
Primary (age 7–12)	...	359,300	9,315,000	25.9
Secondary (age 13–18)	...	334,200	8,560,300	25.6
Vocational[8]	...	9,336	172,400	18.5
Higher	109[9]	31,400	873,000	27.8

Health (2002): physicians 45,073 (1 per 1,769 persons); hospital beds 178,385 (1 per 447 persons); infant mortality rate (2003) 30.8.
Food (2001): daily per capita caloric intake 2,533 (vegetable products 89%, animal products 11%); 117% of FAO recommended minimum requirement.

Military

Total active duty personnel (2003): 484,000 (army 85.1%, navy 8.7%, air force 6.2%). *Military expenditure as percentage of GNP* (1997): 2.4% (world 2.5%); per capita expenditure U.S.$44.

[1]Eight economic regions are divided into 59 provinces and 5 municipalities as of the administrative reorganization of 2003. [2]Total represents sum of parts; actual reported total figure may differ. [3]Reported total per official source; summed total equals 79,885,403. [4]2002. [5]Wage workers and government officials only. [6]Imports are f.o.b. in balance of trade and c.i.f. in commodities and trading partners. [7]Vietnam Airlines only. [8]1996–97. [9]1995–96.

Internet resources for further information:

- **Ministry of Foreign Affairs http://www.mofa.gov.vn**

Virgin Islands (U.S.)

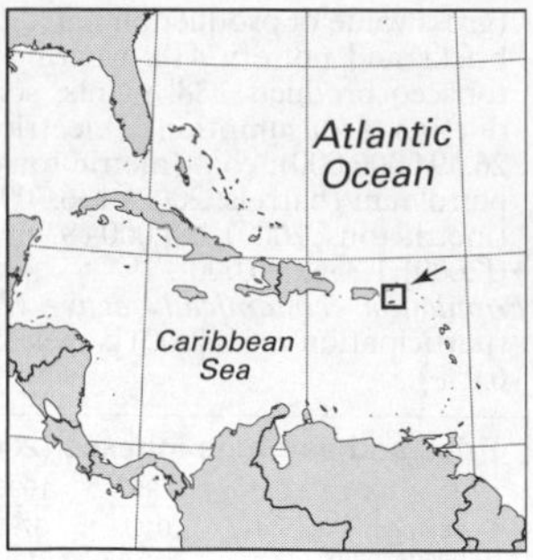

Official name: Virgin Islands of the United States.
Political status: organized unincorporated territory of the United States with one legislative house (Senate [15]).
Chief of state: President of the United States.
Head of government: Governor.
Capital: Charlotte Amalie.
Official language: English.
Official religion: none.
Monetary unit: 1 U.S. dollar (U.S.$) = 100 cents; valuation (Sept. 1, 2004) 1 £ = U.S.$1.80.

Area and population

Islands[1]	Principal towns	area sq mi	area sq km	population 2002 estimate
St. Croix	Christiansted	84	218	53,898
St. John	Cruz Bay[2]	20	52	4,306
St. Thomas	Charlotte Amalie	32	83	51,822
TOTAL		136	353	110,026[3]

Demography

Population (2004): 109,000.
Density (2004): persons per sq mi 801.5, persons per sq km 309.7.
Urban-rural (2000): urban 92.6%; rural 7.4%.
Sex distribution (2000): male 47.75%; female 52.25%.
Age breakdown (2000): under 15, 26.1%; 15–29, 19.4%; 30–44, 21.2%; 45–59, 20.5%; 60–74, 9.8%; 75 and over, 3.0%.
Population projection: (2010) 108,000; (2020) 107,000.
Doubling time: 75 years.
Ethnic composition (2000): black 61.1%; U.S. white 15.0%; Puerto Rican 12.0%; French Creole (from Martinique and Guadeloupe) 9.0%; British 1.0%; other 1.9%.
Religious affiliation (2000): Christian 96.3%, of which Protestant 51.0% (including Anglican 13.0%), Roman Catholic 27.5%, independent Christian 12.2%; nonreligious 2.2%; other 1.5%.
Major towns (2000): Charlotte Amalie 11,004 (urban agglomeration 18,914); Christiansted 2,637; Frederiksted 732.

Vital statistics

Birth rate per 1,000 population (2003): 15.0 (world avg. 21.3); (1998) legitimate 30.2%[4]; illegitimate 69.8%.
Death rate per 1,000 population (2003): 5.7 (world avg. 9.1).
Natural increase rate per 1,000 population (2003): 9.3 (world avg. 12.2).
Total fertility rate (avg. births per childbearing woman; 2003): 2.2.
Marriage rate per 1,000 population (1993): 35.1.
Divorce rate per 1,000 population (1993): 4.5.
Life expectancy at birth (2003): male 74.7 years; female 82.7 years.
Major causes of death per 100,000 population (2002): malignant neoplasms (cancers) 114.6; diseases of the heart 110.9; cerebrovascular diseases 46.1; accidents 31.6; communicable diseases 27.5; diabetes mellitus 25.6.

National economy

Budget. Revenue (2002): U.S.$580,200,000 (personal income tax 54.7%, gross receipts tax 16.5%, property tax 7.9%). Expenditures (2002): U.S.$573,000,-000 (direct federal expenditures 100.0%).
Production. Agriculture, forestry, fishing (value of sales in U.S.$'000; 1998): milk 1,263, livestock and livestock products 655 (of which cattle and calves 439, hogs and pigs 46), ornamental plants and other nursery products 364, vegetables 329 (notably tomatoes and cucumbers), fruits and nuts 185 (notably mangoes, bananas, and avocados), poultry 21; livestock (number of live animals: 2002) 8,000 cattle, 4,000 goats, 3,200 sheep, 2,600 hogs and pigs, 3,500 chickens; roundwood, n.a.; fish catch (2001) 300 metric tons. Mining and quarrying: sand and crushed stone for local use. Manufacturing (U.S.$'000[5]; 1997): food and food products 31,949; stone, clay, and glass products 21,897; print and publishing 21,127; transportation equipment 4,920; fabricated metal products 3,352. Energy production (consumption): electricity (kW-hr; 2000) 1,090,000,000 (1,090,000,000); coal (metric tons; 2000) none (257,000); crude petroleum (barrels; 2000) none (124,700,000); petroleum products (metric tons; 2000) 15,385,000 (2,470,000); natural gas, none (none).
Tourism (2002): receipts from visitors U.S.$1,240,000,000; expenditures by nationals abroad, n.a.
Household income and expenditure. Average household size (2000) 2.6; average annual income per household (2000) U.S.$34,991; sources of income, n.a.; expenditures (2001)[6]: housing 38.8%, food and beverages 12.5%, transportation 11.1%, education and communications 7.1%, health 5.8%.
Population economically active (2002)[7]: total 49,440; activity rate of total population 45.4% (participation rates: ages 16–64, 72.5%[8]; female 47.8%[8]; unemployed 8.7%).

Price and earnings indexes (2000 = 100)

	1997	1998	1999	2000	2001	2002
Consumer price index	99.3	98.5	100.3	100.0	101.1	104.9
Hourly earnings index[9]	88.6	94.8	94.0	100.0	113.7	112.0

Gross domestic product (at current market prices; 2002): U.S.$2,479,000,000 (U.S.$22,530 per capita).

Structure of gross domestic product and labour force

	2002 in value U.S.$'000,000	2002 % of total value	2000 labour force[10]	2000 % of labour force
Agriculture, fishing	...	...	324	0.7
Mining	...	...		
Manufacturing	...	...	2,754	5.4
Construction	...	...	4,900	9.6
Public utilities	...	...	3,321	6.5
Transp. and commun.	...	...		
Trade, hotels, restaurants	...	...	14,739	28.9
Finance, insurance, real estate	...	...	2,330	4.6
Pub. admin., defense	...	...	4,931	9.7
Services	...	...	12,335	24.2
Other	...	...	5,299[11]	10.4
TOTAL	2,479[12]	100.0	50,933	100.0

Public debt (1999): U.S.$1,200,000,000.
Land use as % of total land area (2000): in temporary crops *c.* 12%, in permanent crops *c.* 3%, in pasture *c.* 15%; overall forest area *c.* 41%.

Foreign trade

Balance of trade (current prices)

	1997	1998	1999	2000	2001	2002
U.S.$'000,000	–372.3	–120.3	–99.4	–149.5	–374.5	–336.9
% of total	5.1%	2.2%	1.5%	1.4%	4.2%	3.8%

Imports (2002): U.S.$4,213,200,000 (foreign crude petroleum 75.8%, other [significantly manufactured goods] 24.2%). *Major import sources* (2001): United States 13.8%; Puerto Rico 2.0%; other countries 84.2%.
Exports (2002): U.S.$3,876,300,000 (refined petroleum 83.4%, unspecified 16.6%). *Major export destinations* (2001): United States 74.8%; Puerto Rico 18.7%; other countries 6.5%.

Transport and communications

Transport. Railroads: none. Roads (1996): total length 532 mi, 856 km (paved, n.a.). Vehicles (1993): passenger cars 51,000; trucks and buses 13,300. Cruise ships (2003): passenger arrivals 1,773,948. Air transport (2003)[13]: passenger arrivals 598,907; airports (1999) with scheduled flights 2.

Communications

Medium	date	unit	number	units per 1,000 persons
Daily newspapers	2000	circulation	43,000	364
Radio	1996	receivers	107,000	927
Television	2000	receivers	64,700	594
Telephones	2001	main lines	69,400	635
Cellular telephones	2001	subscribers	41,000	375
Internet	2002	users	30,000	273

Education and health

Educational attainment (2000). Percentage of population age 25 and over having: no formal schooling through lower secondary education 18.5%; incomplete upper secondary 21.0%; completed secondary 26.0%; incomplete undergraduate degree 17.8%; completed undergraduate degree 10.4%; graduate degree 6.3%. *Literacy:* n.a.

Education (2000)

	schools	teachers	students	student/ teacher ratio
Primary (age 5–12) / Secondary (age 12–18)	289	1,511	25,620	17.0
Higher	1	266	3,107	11.7

Health (2002): physicians 161 (1 per 675 persons); hospital beds, n.a.; infant mortality rate per 1,000 live births (2003) 8.4.
Food: daily per capita caloric intake, n.a.

Military

Total active duty personnel: no domestic military force is maintained; the United States is responsible for defense and external security.

[1]May be administered by officials assigned by the governor. [2]Census designated place. [3]De jure figure. [4]Percentage of legitimate births may be an underestimation due to the common practice of consensual marriage. [5]Figures are for value of sales. [6]Weights of consumer price index components. [7]Excludes armed forces. [8]1990. [9]Service workers only. [10]Excludes 109 members of armed forces. [11]Includes 4,368 unemployed. [12]Tourism accounts for more than 70% of gross domestic product. [13]St. Croix and St. Thomas airports.

Internet resources for further information:

- **Office of Insular Affairs**
  http://www.pacificweb.org
- **U.S. Census Bureau: Economic Census of Outlying Areas**
  http://www.census.gov/csd/oat

Yemen

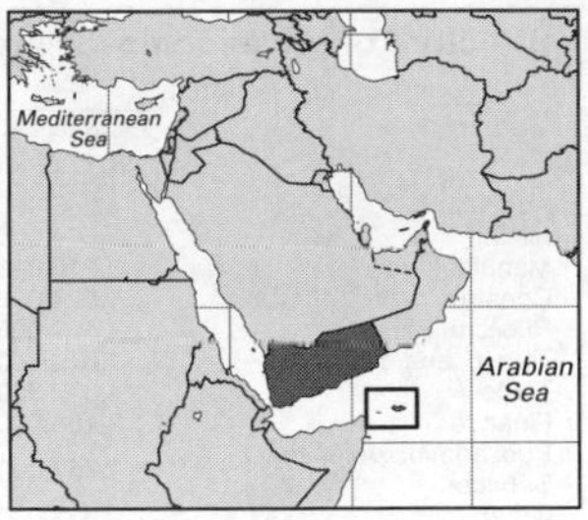

Official name: Al-Jumhūrīyah al-Yamanīyah (Republic of Yemen).
Form of government: multiparty republic with two legislative houses (Consultative Council [111 nonelected seats]; House of Representatives [301]).
Head of state: President.
Head of government: Prime Minister.
Capital: Sanaa.
Official language: Arabic.
Official religion: Islam.
Monetary unit: 1 Yemeni Rial (YRls) = 100 fils; valuation (Sept. 1, 2004) 1 U.S.$ = YRls 184.86; 1 £ = YRls 332.55.

Area and population

		area[1]		population
Governorates	Capitals	sq mi	sq km	2001 estimate
Abyān	Zinjibār	8,297	21,489	432,529
ʿAdan	Aden	2,695	6,980	519,822
ʿAmrān[2]	ʿAmrān	...	...	993,722
Al-Bayḍāʾ	Al-Bayḍāʾ	4,310	11,170	579,955
Al-Ḍāliʿ[2]	Al-Ḍāliʿ	...	...	415,066
Dhamār	Dhamār	3,430	8,870	1,234,424
Ḥaḍramawt	Al-Mukallā	59,991	155,376	890,247
Ḥajjah	Ḥajjah	3,700	9,590	1,404,554
Al-Ḥudaydah	Al-Ḥudaydah	5,240	13,580	2,004,049
Ibb	Ibb	2,480	6,430	2,074,139
Al-Jawf	Al-Jawf	...	...	447,020
Laḥij	Laḥij	4,928	12,766	664,070
Al-Mahrah	Al-Ghayḍah	25,618	66,350	72,555
Al-Maḥwīt	Al-Maḥwīt	830	2,160	464,158
Maʾrib	Maʾrib	15,400	39,890	233,695
Ṣaʿdah	Ṣaʿdah	4,950	12,810	614,682
Ṣanʿāʾ	Sanaa	7,745	20,063	1,394,947
Shabwah	ʿAtāq	28,536	73,908	469,256
Taʿizz	Taʿizz	4,020	10,420	2,363,486
City				
Sanaa	—	95	247	1,590,624
TOTAL		[3]	[3]	18,862,999

Demography

Population (2004): 20,733,000.
Density (2004)[4]: persons per sq mi 96.7, persons per sq km 37.4.
Urban-rural (2001): urban 25.0%; rural 75.0%.
Sex distribution (2003): male 50.91%; female 49.09%.
Age breakdown (2003): under 15, 46.8%; 15–29, 29.0%; 30–44, 12.8%; 45–59, 7.3%; 60–74, 3.1%; 75 and over, 1.0%.
Population projection: (2010) 25,662,000; (2020) 36,537,000.
Doubling time: 21 years.
Ethnic composition (2000): Arab 92.8%; Somali 3.7%; black 1.1%; Indo-Pakistani 1.0%; other 1.4%.
Religious affiliation (2000): Muslim 98.9%, of which Sunnī c. 60%, Shīʿī c. 40%; Hindu 0.7%; Christian 0.2%; other 0.2%.
Major cities (2001): Sanaa 1,590,624; Aden 509,886; Taʿizz 450,000; Al-Ḥudaydah 425,000; Al-Mukallā 165,000.

Vital statistics

Birth rate per 1,000 population (2003): 41.4 (world avg. 21.3).
Death rate per 1,000 population (2003): 8.8 (world avg. 9.1).
Natural increase rate per 1,000 population (2003): 32.6 (world avg. 12.2).
Total fertility rate (avg. births per childbearing woman; 2003): 6.8.
Life expectancy at birth (2003): male 59.2 years; female 62.9 years.
Major causes of death per 100,000 population: n.a.

National economy

Budget (2002). Revenue: YRls 570,100,000,000 (tax revenue 91.9%, of which oil revenue 68.7%, indirect taxes 12.1%, direct taxes 11.1%; nontax revenue 6.5%; grants 1.6%). Expenditures: YRls 587,600,000,000 (wages and salaries 22.9%; defense 21.9%; transfers and subsidies 20.8%; economic development 18.1%; interest on debt 6.0%).
Public debt (external, outstanding; 2002): U.S.$4,563,000,000.
Population economically active (1999): total 4,090,680; activity rate of total population 23.5% (participation rates: age 15 and over, 45.9%; female 23.7%; unemployed 11.5%).

Price index (2000 = 100)

	1997	1998	1999	2000	2001	2002	2003
Consumer price index	83.0	88.0	95.6	100.0	111.9	125.6	139.2

Production (metric tons except as noted). Agriculture, forestry, fishing (2002): sorghum 360,000, tomatoes 261,692, potatoes 208,597, grapes 162,726, oranges 158,940, wheat 150,000, bananas 95,860, onions 79,147, papayas 70,740; livestock (number of live animals) 5,028,968 sheep, 4,452,540 goats, 1,400,584 cattle, 500,000 asses, 198,434 camels, 34,800,000 chickens; roundwood (2002) 326,262 cu m; fish catch (2001) 142,200. Mining and quarrying (2002): salt 150,000; gypsum 100,000. Manufacturing (value added in YRls '000,000; 2002): food, beverages, and tobacco 42,342; nonmetallic mineral products 13,209; chemicals and chemical products 9,884; paper products 5,222; fabricated metal products 4,622; clothing, textiles, and leather 2,502; wood products 2,012. Energy production (consumption): electricity (kW-hr; 2002) 3,100,000,000 (2,960,000,000); coal, none (none); crude petroleum (barrels; 2003) 163,600,000 ([2000] 29,600,000); petroleum products (metric tons; 2000) 3,956,000 (2,635,000); natural gas, none (none).
Gross national product (2003): U.S.$9,894,000,000 (U.S.$520 per capita).

Structure of gross domestic product and labour force

	2002		1999	
	in value YRls '000,000	% of total value	labour force	% of labour force
Agriculture	221,035	15.0	1,959,146	47.9
Mining	506,497	34.4	17,699	0.4
Manufacturing	110,848	7.5	135,659	3.3
Public utilities	9,775	0.7	11,731	0.3
Construction	62,434	4.2	238,246	5.8
Transp. and commun.	150,004	10.2	122,309	3.0
Trade	127,381	8.6	437,001	10.7
Finance, real estate	116,208	7.9	29,968	0.8
Pub. admin., defense	157,316	10.7	357,907	8.7
Services	13,198	0.9	312,014	7.6
Other	–1,904[5]	–0.1[5]	469,000[6]	11.5[6]
TOTAL	1,472,792	100.0	4,090,680	100.0

Household income and expenditure. Average household size (2002) 7.1; income per household (1998) YRls 29,035 (U.S.$217).
Tourism (2002): receipts U.S.$38,000,000; expenditures U.S.$78,000,000.
Land use as % of total land area (2000): in temporary crops 2.9%, in permanent crops 0.2%, in pasture 30.4%; overall forest area 0.9%.

Foreign trade[7]

Balance of trade

	1997	1998	1999	2000	2001	2002
U.S.$'000,000	–133	–785	+358	+1,313	+908	+689
% of total	2.8%	20.7%	7.8%	20.9%	15.5%	10.5%

Imports (2001): U.S.$2,466,000,000 (food and live animals 29.0%, of which cereals and related products 13.3%; machinery and apparatus 15.6%; petroleum products 12.0%; chemicals and chemical products 9.2%). *Major import sources:* U.A.E. 12.5%; Saudi Arabia 12.4%; India 5.5%; Kuwait 5.2%; U.S. 4.9%.
Exports (2001): U.S.$3,373,000,000 (crude petroleum 86.3%; refined petroleum 7.4%; fish and fish products 1.7%; vegetables and fruits 0.7%). *Major export destinations:* India 18.3%; Thailand 18.0%; South Korea 13.2%; China 9.6%; Singapore 9.4%.

Transport and communications

Transport. Railroads: none. Roads (2001)[8]: total length 17,973 km (paved 54%). Vehicles (2001): passenger cars 354,048; trucks and buses (2000) 454,584. Air transport (2000): passenger-km 1,574,000,000; metric ton-km cargo 32,000,000; airports (1998) with scheduled flights 12.

Communications

Medium	date	unit	number	units per 1,000 persons
Daily newspapers	2000	circulation	270,000	15
Radio	2000	receivers	1,170,000	65
Television	2000	receivers	5,100,000	283
Telephones	2002	main lines	542,200	28
Cellular telephones	2002	subscribers	411,100	21
Personal computers	2002	units	145,000	7.4
Internet	2002	users	100,000	5.1

Education and health

Educational attainment (1998). Percentage of population age 10 and over having: no formal schooling 49.5%; reading and writing ability 32.2%; primary education 11.0%; secondary education 4.6%; higher 2.7%. *Literacy* (2003): percentage of total population age 15 and over literate 50.3%; males literate 70.5%; females literate 30.1%.

Education (2001–02)

	schools	teachers	students	student/teacher ratio
Primary (age 7–12)	11,013[9]	113,812	3,401,508	29.9
Secondary (age 13–18)[10]	1,224[11]	14,063	484,573	34.6
Voc., teacher tr.[10, 11]	125	369	15,074	40.9
Higher[10]	7	3,429	184,072	53.7

Health: physicians (2000) 3,491 (1 per 5,161 persons); hospital beds (2001) 9,802 (1 per 1,903 persons); infant mortality rate (2003) 65.0.
Food (2001): daily per capita caloric intake 2,050 (vegetable products 94%, animal products 6%); 85% of FAO recommended minimum requirement.

Military

Total active duty personnel (2003): 66,700 (army 90.0%, navy 2.5%, air force 7.5%). *Military expenditure as percentage of GNP* (1999): 6.1% (world 2.4%); per capita expenditure U.S.$22.

[1]Governorate area figures are based on a pre-1998 survey and are sometimes rounded. [2]Created in 1998 from parts of three other governorates. [3]An agreement to resolve the long-undemarcated northeastern boundary with Saudi Arabia (which increased Yemen's total area to roughly 214,300 sq mi [555,000 sq km]) was signed in June 2000; 90% of this border was officially demarcated as of October 2004. [4]Based on the total area estimate of 214,300 sq mi (555,000 sq km). [5]Includes import duties of 30.0 million Yemeni Rials less imputed bank service charges. [6]Unemployed. [7]Imports c.i.f. in balance of trade and f.o.b. in commodities and trading partners. [8]Excludes unimproved roads and all roads in ʿAdan governorate. [9]1993–94. [10]Public schools only, which make up the vast majority of schools in Yemen. [11]1994–95.

Internet resources for further information:
- **Central Bank of Yemen http://www.centralbank.gov.ye**

Zambia

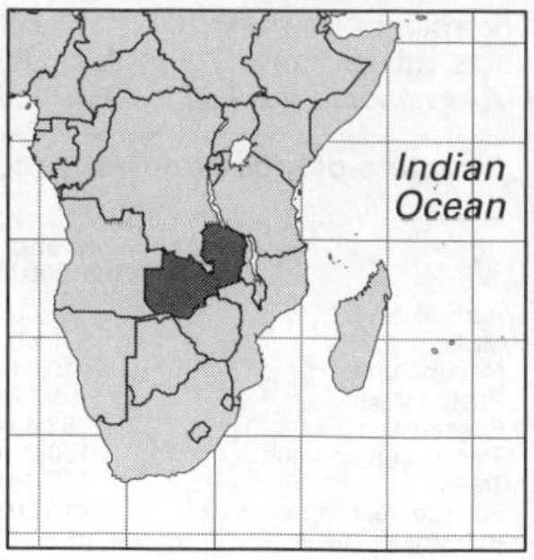

Official name: Republic of Zambia.
Form of government: multiparty republic with one legislative house (National Assembly [158[1]]).
Head of state and government: President.
Capital: Lusaka.
Official language: English.
Official religion: none[2].
Monetary unit: 1 Zambian kwacha (K) = 100 ngwee; valuation (Sept. 1, 2004) 1 U.S.$ = K 4,765; 1 £ = K 8,572.

Area and population

		area		population
Provinces	**Capitals**	sq mi	sq km	2000 census
Central	Kabwe	36,446	94,394	1,012,257
Copperbelt	Ndola	12,096	31,328	1,581,221
Eastern	Chipata	26,682	69,106	1,306,173
Luapula	Mansa	19,524	50,567	775,353
Lusaka	Lusaka	8,454	21,896	1,391,329
North-Western	Solwezi	48,582	125,827	583,350
Northern	Kasama	57,076	147,826	1,258,696
Southern	Livingstone	32,928	85,283	1,212,124
Western	Mongu	48,798	126,386	765,088
TOTAL		290,585[3]	752,612[3]	9,885,591

Demography

Population (2004): 10,462,000.
Density (2004): persons per sq mi 36.0, persons per sq km 13.9.
Urban-rural (2000): urban 34.7%; rural 65.3%.
Sex distribution (2000): male 50.04%; female 49.96%.
Age breakdown (2000): under 15, 47.0%; 15–29, 30.0%; 30–44, 12.9%; 45–59, 5.9%; 60–74, 3.4%; 75 and over, 0.8%.
Population projection: (2010) 11,286,000; (2020) 12,351,000.
Doubling time: 47 years.
Ethnic composition (2000): Bemba 18.0%; Tonga 12.7%; Chewa 7.2%; Lozi 5.6%; Tumbuka 4.2%; other 52.3%.
Religious affiliation (1995): Christian 47.8%, of which Protestant 22.9%, Roman Catholic 16.9%, African Christian 5.6%; traditional beliefs 27.0%; Muslim 1.0%; other 24.2%.
Major cities (2000): Lusaka 1,084,703 (urban agglomeration [2003] 1,394,000); Ndola 374,757; Kitwe 363,734; Kabwe 176,758; Chingola 147,448.

Vital statistics

Birth rate per 1,000 population (2003): 39.5 (world avg. 21.3).
Death rate per 1,000 population (2003): 24.3 (world avg. 9.1).
Natural increase rate per 1,000 population (2003): 15.2 (world avg. 12.2).
Total fertility rate (avg. births per childbearing woman; 2003): 5.2.
Life expectancy at birth (2003): male 38.8 years; female 39.3 years.
Adult population (ages 15–49) *living with HIV* (2004[4]): 16.5% (world avg. 1.1%).

National economy

Budget (2003). Revenue: K 5,104,000,000,000 (tax revenue 69.5%, of which income tax 31.5%, value-added tax 28.3%, excise taxes 9.4%; grants 27.9%; nontax revenue 2.6%). Expenditures: K 6,338,000,000,000 (current expenditures 63.2%, of which wages 27.3%, interest payment 12.5%, transfers 10.2%; capital expenditures 36.8%).
Public debt (external, outstanding; 2002): U.S.$4,737,000,000.
Production (metric tons except as noted). Agriculture, forestry, fishing (2002): sugarcane 1,800,000, cassava 950,000, corn (maize) 900,000, fruits and vegetables 380,000, wheat 75,000, seed cotton 62,000, sweet potatoes 53,000, peanuts (groundnuts) 42,000, tobacco 4,800, fresh-cut flowers (value of sales; 2000) U.S.$21,000,000; livestock (number of live animals) 2,600,000 cattle, 1,270,000 goats, 340,000 pigs, 30,000,000 chickens; roundwood (2001) 8,053,000 cu m; fish catch (2001) 70,911. Mining and quarrying (2002): copper (metal content) 330,000; cobalt (metal content) 6,144; amethyst 1,065,000 kg; emeralds 1,860 kg[5]. Manufacturing (value added in U.S.$'000,000; 1995): food products 86; beverages 77; paints, soaps, and pharmaceuticals 47; textiles 44; tobacco products 30. Energy production (consumption): electricity (kW-hr; 2000) 7,797,000,000 (6,023,000,000); coal (metric tons; 2000) 194,000 (128,000); crude petroleum (barrels; 2000) none (1,830,000); petroleum products (metric tons; 2000) 22,000 (438,000); natural gas, none (none).
Household income and expenditure. Average household size (2002) 5.1.
Tourism (2002): receipts from visitors U.S.$134,000,000; expenditures by nationals abroad U.S.$67,000,000.
Population economically active (1996): total 3,454,000; activity rate of total population 38.2% (participation rates [1991]: over age 10, 52.6%; female 29.6%; unemployed, n.a.).

Price and earnings indexes (2000 = 100)

	1997	1998	1999	2000	2001	2002
Consumer price index	50.3	62.6	79.3	100.0	121.4	148.4
Earnings index	...	...	...	...	...	...

Gross national product (at current market prices; 2003): U.S.$3,946,000,000 (U.S.$520 per capita).

Structure of gross domestic product and labour force

	2002		1990	
	in value K '000,000	% of total value	labour force	% of labour force
Agriculture	4,245,000	20.8	1,872,000	68.9
Mining	564,000	2.8	56,800	2.1
Manufacturing	2,213,000	10.9	50,900	1.9
Construction	1,524,000	7.5	29,100	1.1
Public utilities	597,000	2.9	8,900	0.3
Transp. and commun.	1,073,000	5.3	25,600	0.9
Trade	4,379,000	21.5	30,700	1.1
Finance	3,188,000	15.6	0.9	
Pub. admin., defense / Services	1,757,000	8.6	111,600	4.1
Other	837,000[6]	4.1[6]	506,100	18.6
TOTAL	20,377,000	100.0	2,716,000[3]	100.0[3]

Land use as % of total land area (2000): in temporary crops 7.1%, in permanent crops 0.03%, in pasture 40.4%; overall forest area 42.0%.

Foreign trade

Balance of trade (current prices)

	1998	1999	2000	2001	2002	2003
U.S.$'000,000	−155	−115	−232	−369	−323	−271
% of total	8.7%	7.1%	13.5%	17.3%	14.8%	10.8%

Imports (2002): U.S.$1,253,000,000 (nonelectrical machinery and equipment 21.6%, chemicals and chemical products 14.9%, printed matter 11.3%, road vehicles 8.8%, cereals [all forms] 8.0%). *Major import sources:* South Africa 51.2%; U.K. 12.3%; Zimbabwe 7.8%; India 3.6%; Japan 3.2%.
Exports (2002): U.S.$930,000,000 (refined copper 50.0%, other base metals [including cobalt] 8.9%, food and live animals 7.3%, manufactures of base metals 5.8%). *Major export destinations:* U.K. 42.3%; South Africa 23.0%; Tanzania 7.6%; Switzerland 6.1%; Democratic Republic of the Congo 4.3%.

Transport and communications

Transport. Railroads (2003)[7]: length 787 mi, 1,266 km; (1997) passenger-km 267,000,000; (1998) metric ton-km cargo 702,000,000. Roads (1999): total length 24,170 mi, 38,898 km (paved 18%). Vehicles (1996): passenger cars 157,000; trucks and buses 81,000. Air transport (2003)[8]: passenger-km 14,217,000; metric ton-km cargo, none; airports (1998) 4.

Communications

Medium	date	unit	number	units per 1,000 persons
Daily newspapers	2000	circulation	125,000	12
Radio	2000	receivers	1,510,000	145
Television	2000	receivers	1,400,000	134
Telephones	2003	main lines	88,400	7.9
Cellular telephones	2003	subscribers	241,000	22
Personal computers	2003	units	95,000	8.5
Internet	2003	users	68,200	6.1

Education and health

Educational attainment (1993)[9]. Percentage of population age 14 and over having: no formal schooling 18.6%; some primary education 54.8%; some secondary 25.1%; higher 1.5%. *Literacy* (2000): population age 15 and over literate 78.1%; males literate 85.2%; females literate 71.5%.

Education (1998)

	schools	teachers	students	student/ teacher ratio
Primary (age 7–13)	4,221	34,810	1,557,257	44.7
Secondary (age 14–18)	246[10]	10,000	290,085	29.0
Voc., teacher tr.	4[10]	...	...	...
Higher	2[10]	640[10]	22,701	...

Health: physicians (1995) 647 (1 per 14,492 persons); hospital beds (1989) 22,461 (1 per 349 persons); infant mortality rate per 1,000 live births (2003) 99.3.
Food (2001): daily per capita caloric intake 1,885 (vegetable products 95%, animal products 5%); 82% of FAO recommended minimum requirement.

Military

Total active duty personnel (2003): 18,100 (army 91.2%; navy, none; air force 8.8%). *Military expenditure as percentage of GNP* (1999): 1.0% (world 2.4%); per capita expenditure U.S.$3.

[1]Includes 8 nonelective seats. [2]In 1996 Zambia was declared a Christian nation per the preamble of a constitutional amendment. [3]Detail does not add to total given because of rounding. [4]Beginning of year. [5]In 1999 legal and illegal exports of emeralds were estimated to equal U.S.$20,000,000 (about 20% of world total). [6]Less imputed bank service charge. [7]Zambia Railways Limited only. [8]Zambian Airways Limited only. [9]Based on a sample survey of 35,502 persons. [10]1996.

Internet resources for further information:
- **Zambian Department of Census and Statistics**
  http://www.zamstats.gov.zm
- **Bank of Zambia**
  http://www.boz.zm

Zimbabwe

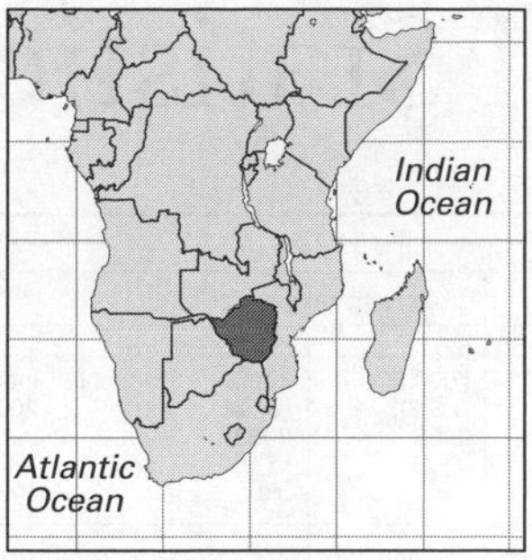

Official name: Republic of Zimbabwe.
Form of government: multiparty republic with one legislative house (House of Assembly [150[1]]).
Head of state and government: President.
Capital: Harare.
Official language: English.
Official religion: none.
Monetary unit: 1 Zimbabwe dollar (Z$) = 100 cents; valuation (Sept. 1, 2004) 1 U.S.$ = Z$5,610; 1 £ = Z$10,093.

Area and population

		area		population
Provinces	Capitals	sq mi	sq km	2002 preliminary census
Bulawayo[2]	—	185	479	676,787
Harare[2]	—	337	872	1,903,510
Manicaland	Mutare	14,077	36,459	1,566,889
Mashonaland Central	Bindura	10,945	28,347	998,265
Mashonaland East	Marondera	12,444	32,230	1,125,355
Mashonaland West	Chinhoyi	22,178	57,441	1,222,583
Masvingo	Masvingo	21,840	56,566	1,318,705
Matabeleland North	Lupane	28,967	75,025	701,359
Matabeleland South	Gwanda	20,916	54,172	654,879
Midlands	Gweru	18,983	49,166	1,466,331
TOTAL		150,872	390,757	11,643,663

Demography

Population (2004): 11,821,000[3].
Density (2004): persons per sq mi 78.4, persons per sq km 30.3.
Urban-rural (2001): urban 36.0%; rural 64.0%.
Sex distribution (2003): male 49.57%; female 50.43%.
Age breakdown (2003): under 15, 39.7%; 15–29, 32.6%; 30–44, 15.1%; 45–59, 7.3%; 60–74, 4.1%; 75 and over, 1.2%.
Population projection: (2010) 12,058,000; (2020) 11,970,000.
Doubling time: 87 years.
Ethnic composition (2000): Shona 67.1%; Ndebele 13.0%; Chewa 4.9%; British 3.5%; other 11.5%.
Religious affiliation (1995): Christian 45.4%, of which Protestant (including Anglican) 23.5%, African indigenous 13.5%, Roman Catholic 7.0%; animist 40.5%; other 14.1%.
Major cities (2002): Harare 1,444,534; Bulawayo 676,787; Chitungwiza 321,782; Mutare (1992) 131,808; Gweru (1992) 124,735.

Vital statistics

Birth rate per 1,000 population (2003): 30.3 (world avg. 21.3).
Death rate per 1,000 population (2003): 22.0 (world avg. 9.1).
Natural increase rate per 1,000 population (2003): 8.3 (world avg. 12.2).
Total fertility rate (avg. births per childbearing woman; 2003): 3.7.
Life expectancy at birth (2002): male 41.6 years; female 38.8 years.
Adult population (ages 15–49) *living with HIV* (2004[4]): 24.6% (world avg. 1.1%).

National economy

Budget (2002). Revenue: Z$300,385,000,000 (tax revenue 93.5%, of which income tax 53.0%, sales tax 24.1%, customs duties 9.0%, excise tax 6.2%; nontax revenue 6.5%). Expenditures: Z$351,321,000,000 (current expenditures 91.3%, of which goods and services 61.5%, transfer payments 15.7%, interest payments 14.1%; development expenditure 7.2%; net lending 1.5%).
Population economically active (1992): total 3,600,000; activity rate of total population 34.6% (participation rates: over age 15, 63.4%; female 39.8%; unemployed, n.a.).

Price and earnings indexes (2000 = 100)

	1997	1998	1999	2000	2001	2002
Consumer price index	30.7	40.5	64.2	100.0	176.7	424.3
Earnings index	...	...	...	...	...	...

Production (metric tons except as noted). Agriculture, forestry, fishing (2002): sugarcane 4,700,000, corn (maize) 499,000, seed cotton 200,400, cassava 175,000, tobacco leaves 174,000, peanuts (groundnuts) 165,000, wheat 150,000, oranges 90,000, bananas 85,000, soybeans 83,000, sorghum 80,000, tea 22,400; livestock (number of live animals) 5,753,000 cattle, 2,970,000 goats, 605,000 pigs, 600,000 sheep; roundwood 9,107,600 cu m; fish catch (2001) 13,200. Mining and quarrying (value of production in Z$'000,000; 2000): gold 8,521; asbestos 2,776; coal 2,690; nickel 2,178; chrome 778; granite 552. Manufacturing (value added in U.S.$'000,000; 1998): beverages 171; foodstuffs 148; textiles 99; iron and steel 86; fabricated metal products 64; cement, bricks, and tiles 63; tobacco products 51. Energy production (consumption): electricity (kW-hr; 2000) 6,996,000,000 ([2000] 12,110,000,000); coal (metric tons; 2000) 4,400,000 (4,437,000); crude petroleum, none (none); petroleum products (metric tons; 2000) none (1,072,000); natural gas, none (none).
Public debt (external, outstanding; 2002): U.S.$3,123,000,000.
Household income and expenditure. Average household size (2002) 4.4; income per household (1992) Z$1,689 (U.S.$332); expenditure (1995)[5]: food 33.6%, housing 17.3%, beverages and tobacco 16.0%, household durable goods 7.5%, clothing and footwear 6.9%, transportation 6.6%, education 4.5%.
Gross national product (2002): U.S.$6,165,000,000 (U.S.$480 per capita).

Structure of gross domestic product and labour force

	1999		2002	
	in value Z$'000,000[6]	% of total value[6]	labour force[7]	% of labour force[7]
Agriculture	35,812	19.4	221,000	19.8
Mining	3,380	1.8	43,000	3.9
Manufacturing	30,538	16.5	171,000	15.4
Construction	5,132	2.8	42,000	3.8
Public utilities	5,171	2.8	10,000	0.9
Transp. and commun.	11,373	6.2	41,000	3.7
Trade	36,261	19.7	133,000	11.9
Finance	26,917	14.6	28,000	2.5
Pub. admin., defense } Services	22,913 / 8,273	12.4 / 4.5	425,000	38.1
Other	–1,357[8]	–0.7[8]	—	—
TOTAL	184,413	100.0	1,114,000	100.0

Tourism: receipts (2002) U.S.$76,000,000; expenditures (1998) U.S.$131,000,000.
Land use as % of total land area (2000): in temporary crops 8.3%, in permanent crops 0.3%, in pasture 44.5%; overall forest area 49.2%.

Foreign trade

Balance of trade (current prices)

	1996	1997	1998	1999	2000	2001
U.S.$'000,000	+249	–230	–95	+258	+346	–170
% of total	5.2%	4.5%	2.4%	7.1%	8.5%	5.0%

Imports (2001): U.S.$1,779,000,000 (machinery and transport equipment 28.1%, chemicals and chemical products 22.9%, petroleum products 15.7%, food 3.8%, electricity 3.1%). *Major import sources* (2002): South Africa 47.7%; Democratic Republic of the Congo 5.7%; Mozambique 5.3%; Germany 3.1%; U.K. 3.1%.
Exports (2001): U.S.$1,609,000,000 (tobacco 36.9%, gold 14.0%, horticultural products [including cut flowers] 7.4%, ferroalloys 5.1%, cotton lint 5.1%, sugar 4.4%). *Major export destinations* (2001): South Africa 17.7%; U.K. 12.6%; Germany 8.3%; China 7.1%; Japan 6.6%.

Transport and communications

Transport. Railroads (2001): route length 3,077 km; (1998) passenger-km 408,223,000; (2000) metric ton-km cargo 3,326,000. Roads (1996): total length 18,338 km (paved 47%). Vehicles (2000): passenger cars 573,000; trucks and buses 39,000. Air transport (2003)[9]: passenger-km 436,530,000; metric ton-km cargo 18,494,000; airports (1997) with scheduled flights 7.

Communications

Medium	date	unit	number	units per 1,000 persons
Daily newspapers	2000	circulation	205,000	18
Radio	2000	receivers	4,110,000	362
Television	1999	receivers	2,074,000	183
Telephones	2003	main lines	300,900	26
Cellular telephones	2003	subscribers	379,100	32
Personal computers	2003	units	620,000	53
Internet	2002	users	500,000	43

Education and health

Educational attainment (1992). Percentage of population age 25 and over having: no formal schooling 22.3%; primary 54.3%; secondary 13.1%; higher 3.4%. *Literacy* (2001): percentage of total population age 15 and over literate 89.3%; males literate 93.3%; females literate 85.5%.

Education (1998)

	schools	teachers	students	student/ teacher ratio
Primary (age 7–13)	4,706	64,538	2,507,098	38.8
Secondary (age 14–19)	1,530	30,482	847,296	27.8
Voc., teacher tr.[10]	25	1,479	27,431	18.5
Higher[11]	28[10]	3,581	46,492	13.0

Health: physicians (1996) 1,603 (1 per 6,904 persons); hospital beds (1996) 22,975 (1 per 501 persons); infant mortality rate (2003) 65.5.
Food (2001): daily per capita caloric intake 2,133 (vegetable products 92%, animal products 8%); 89% of FAO recommended minimum requirement.

Military

Total active duty personnel (2003): 29,000 (army 86.2%, air force 13.8%). *Military expenditure as percentage of GNP* (1999): 5.0% (world 2.4%); per capita expenditure U.S.$23.

[1]Includes 30 nonelective seats. [2]City with provincial status. [3]De jure estimate including 3 million people who may have emigrated between 1999 and 2004. [4]January 1. [5]Based on consumer price index. [6]At factor cost. [7]Wage-earning workers only. [8]Less imputed bank service charges. [9]Air Zimbabwe only. [10]1992. [11]Includes postsecondary vocational and teacher training at the higher level.

Internet resources for further information:
- **Reserve Bank of Zimbabwe http://www.rbz.co.zw**

Comparative National Statistics

World and regional summaries

region/bloc	area and population, 2004						gross national product						labour force, 1990		
	area		population			population projection, 2020	total ('000,000 U.S.$), 2003	GNP per capita (U.S.$), 2003	% agricul-ture, 2000	% industry, 2000	% ser-vices, 2000	growth rate, 1990–99	total ('000)	% male	% female
	square miles	square kilometres	total	per sq mi	per sq km										
World	52,350,178	135,586,234	6,329,605,262	120.9	46.7	7,432,757,767	35,988,170	5,547	4	28	68	2.5	2,353,806	63.8	36.2
Africa	11,684,711	30,263,037	852,637,200	73.0	28.2	1,134,582,800	603,612	723	16	30	53	2.5	242,784	65.6	34.4
Central Africa	2,552,967	6,612,155	100,561,000	39.4	15.2	147,727,000	34,250	350	17	36	21	1.3	26,428	64.7	35.3
East Africa	2,473,672	6,406,665	262,609,800	106.2	41.0	345,453,000	67,022	260	28	17	54	2.9	85,082	58.8	41.2
North Africa	3,288,555	8,517,321	186,934,000	56.8	21.9	242,383,000	268,393	1,464	16	33	51	3.3	40,016	84.6	15.4
Southern Africa	1,032,545	2,674,283	53,085,000	51.4	19.9	51,035,000	139,903	2,663	3	28	68	1.3	14,532	64.3	35.7
West Africa	2,336,972	6,052,613	249,447,400	106.7	41.2	347,984,800	94,045	386	31	30	38	3.0	76,726	63.8	36.2
Americas	16,239,836	42,060,983	873,217,400	53.8	20.8	1,022,879,500	14,859,793	17,217	2	23	75	3.0	293,723	66.5	33.5
Anglo-America[2]	8,307,783	21,517,060	325,853,100	39.2	15.1	371,603,300	12,977,141	40,201	1	22	76	3.0	135,438	58.7	41.3
Canada	3,855,103	9,984,670	31,876,000	8.3	3.2	35,390,000	756,899	23,930	3	27	70	2.8	13,360	60.2	39.8
United States	3,616,236	9,366,008	293,850,000	81.3	31.4	336,081,000	10,946,358	37,610	1	22	77	3.0	122,005	58.6	41.4
Latin America	7,932,053	20,543,923	547,364,300	69.0	26.6	651,276,200	1,882,652	3,485	7	29	64	3.4	158,285	73.1	26.9
Caribbean	90,706	234,922	38,524,800	424.7	164.0	43,121,700	160,328	4,195	5	33	56	2.8	13,813	66.9	33.1
Central America	201,594	522,129	39,374,000	195.3	75.4	52,009,000	80,524	2,088	17	21	63	4.4	9,520	78.5	21.5
Mexico	758,449	1,964,375	105,447,000	139.0	53.7	125,232,000	649,166	6,230	4	27	69	2.8	30,487	72.9	27.1
South America	6,881,304	17,822,497	364,018,500	52.9	20.4	430,913,500	992,634	2,763	8	30	63	3.6	104,465	73.6	26.4
Andean Group	2,111,959	5,469,951	133,786,000	63.3	24.5	163,472,000	344,865	2,616	9	32	59	3.8	34,715	75.6	24.4
Brazil	3,287,612	8,514,877	180,542,000	54.9	21.2	209,793,000	483,234	2,710	8	31	60	3.0	55,026	72.6	27.4
Other South America	1,481,733	3,837,669	49,690,500	33.5	12.9	57,648,500	164,535	3,349	5	24	70	4.8	14,724	72.4	27.6
Asia	12,265,669	31,767,937	3,840,528,095	313.1	120.9	4,509,003,000	9,288,291	2,445	8	35	57	3.7	1,464,452	64.5	35.5
Eastern Asia	4,546,291	11,774,882	1,529,960,000	336.5	129.9	1,665,280,000	6,873,627	4,517	4	36	59	3.1	775,590	57.4	42.6
China	3,696,100	9,572,900	1,298,848,000	351.4	135.7	1,430,533,000	1,420,626	1,100	18	49	33	10.8	669,693	56.7	43.3
Japan	145,903	377,887	127,757,000	875.6	338.1	124,191,000	4,402,612	34,510	2	33	66	1.4	62,202	62.1	37.9
South Korea	38,572	99,900	48,199,000	1,249.6	482.5	50,285,000	575,903	12,020	6	49	45	5.7	18,664	66.2	33.8
Other Eastern Asia	665,716	1,724,195	55,156,000	82.9	32.0	60,271,000	474,466	8,665	1	22	73	5.5	25,031	58.8	41.2
South Asia	1,933,355	5,007,370	1,433,852,000	741.6	286.3	1,773,281,000	728,920	516	28	23	48	5.5	411,136	77.4	22.6
India	1,222,559	3,166,414	1,081,229,000	884.4	341.5	1,312,212,000	564,695	530	28	24	48	5.9	322,944	74.8	25.2
Pakistan	307,374	796,096	151,600,000	493.2	190.4	202,767,000	69,692	470	24	18	58	3.5	33,698	87.5	12.5
Other South Asia	403,422	1,044,860	201,023,000	498.3	192.4	258,302,000	94,533	477	35	28	36	4.9	54,494	86.2	13.8
Southeast Asia	1,736,679	4,497,993	544,546,000	313.6	121.1	648,642,000	755,045	1,404	21	30	49	5.3	189,297	63.0	37.0
Southwest Asia	4,049,344	10,487,692	332,170,095	82.0	31.7	421,800,000	931,873	2,850	10	36	52	2.8	88,429	69.4	30.6
Central Asia	1,545,789	4,003,445	57,780,000	37.4	14.4	68,398,000	46,009	825	16	25	58	–4.3	20,728	54.8	45.2
Gulf Cooperation Council	933,349	2,572,753	35,277,000	35.5	13.7	46,496,000	360,438	10,513	4	51	45	2.2	6,511	91.7	8.3
Iran	630,374	1,648,200	67,503,000	106.1	41.0	80,002,000	134,295	2,000	21	30	50	3.4	15,253	82.0	18.0
Other Southwest Asia	873,832	2,263,294	171,610,095	196.4	75.8	226,904,000	391,132	2,323	11	28	57	4.0	45,936	68.7	31.3
Europe	8,872,306	22,979,291	730,409,300	82.3	31.8	727,766,000	10,715,397	14,684	3	27	70	1.3	340,666	57.1	42.9
European Union (EU)	1,534,470	3,974,260	458,208,000	298.6	115.3	468,663,000	9,638,144	21,082	2	27	71	1.8	163,771	63.6	36.4
France	210,026	543,965	60,044,000	285.9	110.4	63,196,000	1,480,379	24,770	3	22	75	1.5	25,404	60.1	39.9
Germany	137,847	357,023	82,561,000	598.9	231.2	81,471,000	2,083,706	25,250	1	31	68	1.4	38,981	60.7	39.3
Italy	116,343	301,328	57,537,000	494.5	190.9	56,517,000	1,239,226	21,560	3	31	67	1.4	23,339	68.1	31.9
Spain	195,379	506,030	43,768,000	224.0	86.5	48,626,000	738,746	16,990	3	24	73	2.3	14,456	75.5	24.5
United Kingdom	93,788	242,910	59,561,000	635.1	245.2	62,447,000	1,683,884	28,350	1	26	73	2.5	27,766	61.4	38.6
Other EU	781,087	2,023,004	154,737,000	198.1	76.5	156,406,000	2,412,203	15,610	3	25	72	2.4	33,825	63.4	36.6
Other Western Europe[3]	181,790	470,830	12,744,300	70.1	27.1	13,499,000	508,064	40,694	2	29	67	1.7	5,815	61.9	38.1
Eastern Europe	7,156,046	18,534,201	259,457,000	36.3	14.0	245,604,000	569,189	2,186	7	32	61	–3.2	171,080	50.6	49.4
Russia	6,592,800	17,075,400	144,315,000	21.9	8.5	136,062,000	378,129	2,610	7	35	59	–6.0	72,286	47.6	52.4
Ukraine	233,062	603,628	47,470,000	203.7	78.6	44,070,000	46,307	970	11	30	59	–10.8	25,401	48.0	52.0
Other Eastern Europe	330,184	855,173	67,672,000	205.0	79.1	65,472,000	144,753	2,135	7	30	62	1.3	73,393	54.4	45.6
Oceania	3,287,656	8,514,986	32,813,267	10.0	3.9	38,526,467	513,414	15,848	4	21	74	3.9	12,181	63.0	37.0
Australia	2,969,978	7,692,208	20,141,000	6.8	2.6	22,765,000	430,793	21,650	3	22	76	4.1	20,240	61.9	38.1
Pacific Ocean Islands	317,678	822,778	12,672,267	39.9	15.4	15,761,467	82,621	6,611	9	21	64	2.9	4,218	65.0	35.0

[1]Refers only to the outstanding long-term external public and publicly guaranteed debt of the 137 countries that report under the World Bank's Debtor Reporting System (DRS). [2]Anglo-America includes Canada, the United States, Greenland, Bermuda, and St. Pierre and Miquelon. [3]Other Western Europe includes Andorra, Faroe Islands, Gibraltar, Guernsey, Iceland, Isle of Man, Jersey, Liechtenstein,

Africa

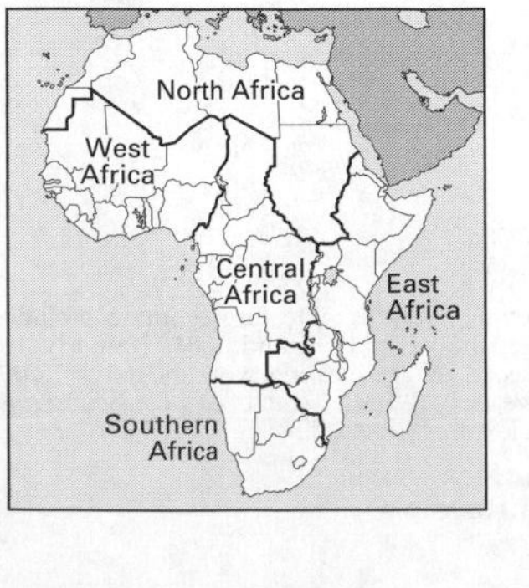

Americas

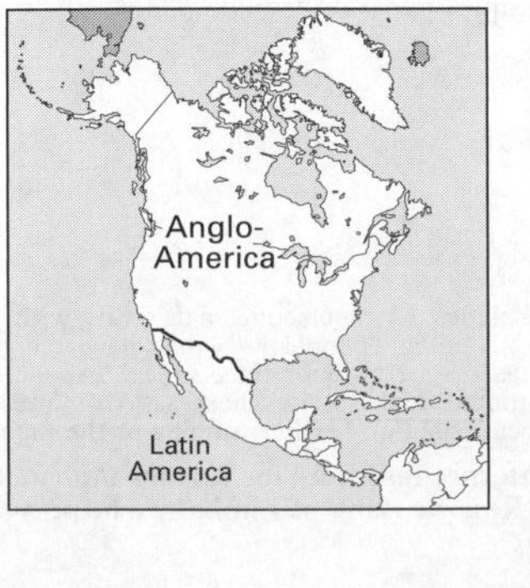

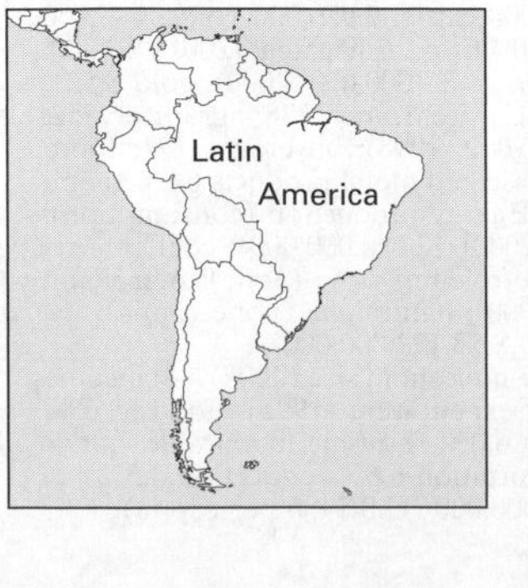

Asia

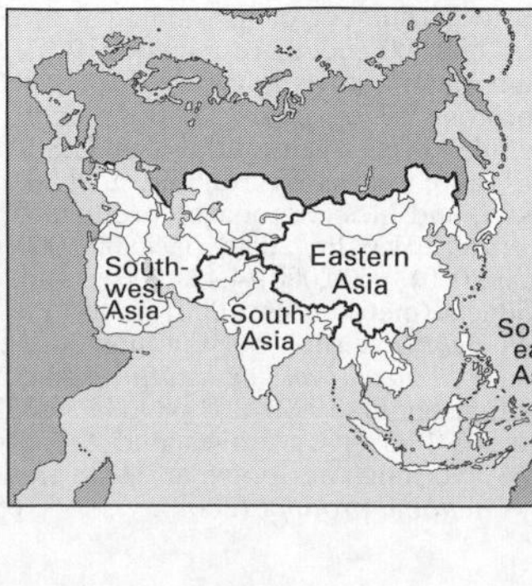

economic indicators							social indicators								region/bloc
pop. per 1,000 ha of arable land, 2002	electricity consump-tion (kW-hr per capita), 2000	trade ('000,000 U.S.$), 2001–03			debt ('000,000 U.S.$), 1999[1]		life expec-tancy (years), 2003		health			food (% FAO recom-mended minimum), 2002	literacy (%) (latest)		
		imports (c.i.f.)	exports (f.o.b.)	balance	total	% of GNP	male	female	pop. per doctor (latest)	infant mor-tality per 1,000 births, 2003	pop. having safe water (%), 2000		male	female	
4,387	2,540	6,930,434	6,744,616	−185,818	1,464,107	24.0	65.5	69.5	730	39.6	82	119	84.0	70.8	World
4,434	571	128,896	140,874	+11,978	236,331	48.0	51.0	53.2	2,560	78.1	64	103	69.6	52.0	Africa
4,365	121	8,854	16,653	+7,799	34,588	134.3	45.7	49.1	12,890	102.1	46	82	79.5	60.0	Central Africa
5,667	142	19,575	9,904	−9,671	45,902	77.9	45.1	46.5	13,620	93.6	50	86	69.5	53.6	East Africa
4,591	861	39,602	41,639	+2,037	87,534	44.0	66.4	70.4	890	42.6	87	123	69.2	45.8	North Africa
3,161	4,311	38,442	36,089	−2,353	10,458	7.7	44.1	45.3	1,610	64.1	85	119	84.8	84.4	Southern Africa
3,876	145	22,423	36,590	+14,167	57,849	79.6	49.2	50.6	6,260	81.7	65	110	62.7	44.7	West Africa
2,328	7,524	2,138,514	1,595,412	−543,102	398,042	20.6	71.0	77.3	520	18.8	91	135	91.5	90.2	Americas
1,441	16,639	1,528,316	976,367	−551,949	—	—	74.6	80.4	370	6.6	100	158	95.7	95.3	Anglo-America[2]
686	18,030	222,241	252,418	+30,177	—	—	76.4	83.4	540	5.0	100	135	96.6	96.6	Canada
1,637	14,684	1,305,092	723,609	−581,483	—	—	74.4	80.1	360	6.8	100	143	95.7	95.3	United States
3,692	2,015	610,198	619,045	+8,847	398,042	20.6	68.9	75.4	690	26.1	86	120	89.0	87.1	Latin America
7,532	1,769	134,133	113,899	−20,234	10,091	26.6	67.1	71.4	380	29.3	79	99	82.5	82.1	Caribbean
6,969	791	25,355	11,344	−14,011	24,967	41.2	66.9	70.9	950	29.5	88	107	78.2	72.3	Central America
4,153	2,368	168,651	160,670	−7,981	87,531	18.6	71.9	77.6	810	17.4	88	135	93.1	89.1	Mexico
3,253	2,068	120,755	158,917	+38,162	275,453	20.2	68.4	75.7	710	27.9	86	120	89.7	88.6	South America
9,110	1,610	56,520	68,915	+12,395	87,634	26.6	68.9	75.0	830	26.5	86	108	92.7	90.1	Andean Group
2,986	2,345	49,735	60,632	+10,897	95,233	13.0	67.2	75.3	770	31.8	87	128	85.5	85.4	Brazil
1,358	2,279	14,500	29,640	+15,140	92,586	30.4	71.5	78.9	410	17.7	82	123	96.6	96.4	Other South America
7,318	1,280	1,799,979	2,028,586	+228,607	595,398	20.9	66.6	69.7	970	41.8	81	117	82.5	65.2	Asia
9,736	1,968	1,179,486	1,321,391	+141,905	166,210	12.1	70.9	74.6	610	23.4	78	123	93.3	80.4	Eastern Asia
9,005	1,057	295,170	325,596	+30,426	108,163	11.1	70.1	73.3	620	26.4	75	125	92.3	77.4	China
28,837	8,603	383,452	471,996	+88,544	—	—	78.4	85.3	530	3.0	97	118	100.0	100.0	Japan
28,282	6,243	149,572	160,855	+11,283	57,231	14.2	71.7	79.3	740	7.3	92	130	99.2	96.4	South Korea
6,672	4,102	351,292	362,945	+11,653	816	94.7	71.3	76.9	500	14.1	94	92	97.5	90.9	Other Eastern Asia
6,864	477	91,054	75,813	−15,241	139,322	24.4	62.3	63.7	2,100	63.4	85	107	65.8	39.4	South Asia
6,400	543	61,118	52,471	−8,647	82,380	18.5	62.9	64.4	1,920	59.6	84	111	68.6	42.1	India
6,805	478	13,013	11,910	−1,103	28,514	48.5	61.3	63.2	1,840	76.6	90	105	57.6	27.8	Pakistan
9,923	123	16,923	11,432	−5,491	28,428	41.3	60.0	60.3	5,080	73.7	85	85	56.7	33.4	Other South Asia
0,400	745	050,007	410,001	+56,051	186,531	37.6	66.1	71.0	3,120	36.2	78	123	92.9	85.8	Southeast Asia
3,508	2,495	176,101	221,090	+44,989	103,335	25.5	66.4	70.5	610	43.1	85	117	88.0	72.9	Southwest Asia
1,876	2,513	12,654	15,806	+3,152	9,819	25.1	62.0	68.7	330	55.9	82	94	98.8	96.4	Central Asia
8,843	7,436	79,974	121,229	+41,255	1,768	12.8	68.5	72.2	620	39.3	95	120	82.9	69.9	Gulf Cooperation Council
4,455	1,827	20,336	28,356	+8,020	6,184	5.6	68.0	70.7	1,200	44.2	92	128	83.7	70.0	Iran
3,868	1,714	63,138	55,700	−7,438	85,563	35.5	66.9	70.8	690	39.1	82	119	87.0	66.8	Other Southwest Asia
2,534	6,063	2,932,353	3,068,534	+136,181	232,295	28.0	70.0	78.3	300	9.2	98	130	99.4	98.5	Europe
4,422	6,577	2,667,945	2,727,170	+59,225	—	—	74.8	81.3	290	5.2	100	136	99.4	98.9	European Union (EU)
3,223	8,099	362,398	357,881	−4,517	—	—	75.6	83.1	330	4.4	100	145	98.9	98.7	France
6,997	7,113	601,761	748,531	+146,770	—	—	75.5	81.6	290	4.2	100	131	100.0	100.0	Germany
6,935	5,554	242,744	251,003	+8,259	—	—	76.5	82.5	180	6.2	100	146	98.9	98.1	Italy
3,054	5,807	165,920	125,872	−40,048	—	—	75.7	83.1	240	3.6	99	137	98.6	96.8	Spain
10,296	6,573	399,478	320,057	−79,421	—	—	75.7	80.7	720	5.3	100	135	100.0	100.0	United Kingdom
3,436	6,301	895,644	923,825	+28,181	—	—	72.8	79.7	320	6.2	100	131	99.4	98.9	Other EU
9,474	15,765	125,857	153,411	+27,554	—	—	77.2	82.6	480	4.2	100	130	100.0	100.0	Other Western Europe[3]
1,427	4,679	138,550	187,954	+49,404	232,295	28.0	61.3	72.7	290	16.4	95	119	99.4	97.6	Eastern Europe
1,177	5,937	52,410	125,960	+73,550	120,375	32.1	58.5	71.9	240	13.3	99	120	99.8	99.2	Russia
1,481	3,381	16,976	17,927	+951	10,027	26.7	61.1	72.2	330	20.8	98	119	99.5	97.4	Ukraine
2,496	2,905	69,164	44,066	−25,098	101,893	24.4	67.2	74.8	370	20.1	84	118	98.5	94.4	Other Eastern Europe
564	8,244	91,999	85,427	−6,572	2,042	33.7	73.4	79.1	480	15.0	87	119	94.7	91.9	Oceania
407	10,880	69,260	66,366	−2,894	—	—	77.0	83.1	400	4.8	100	115	99.5	99.5	Australia
1,498	3,960	22,738	19,061	−3,677	2,042	33.7	67.7	72.7	770	31.3	67	128	87.9	80.6	Pacific Ocean Islands

Monaco, Norway, San Marino, and Switzerland.

Europe

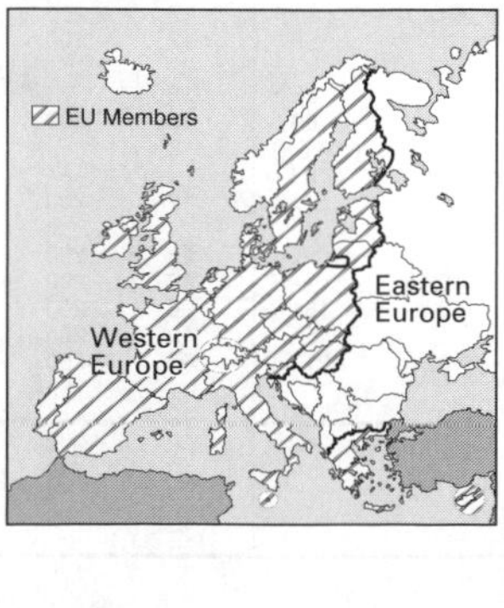

Eastern Europe

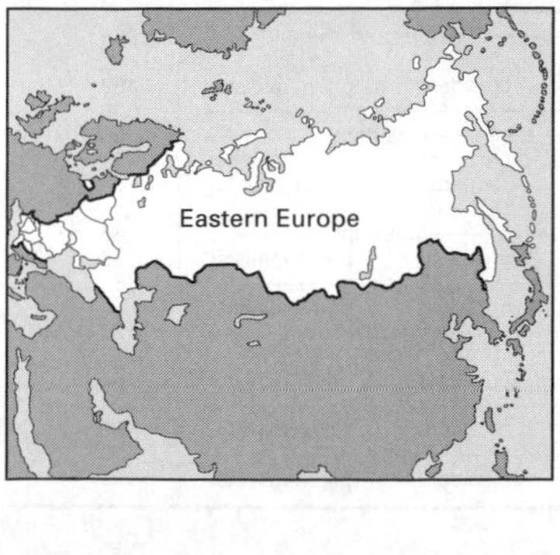

Oceania

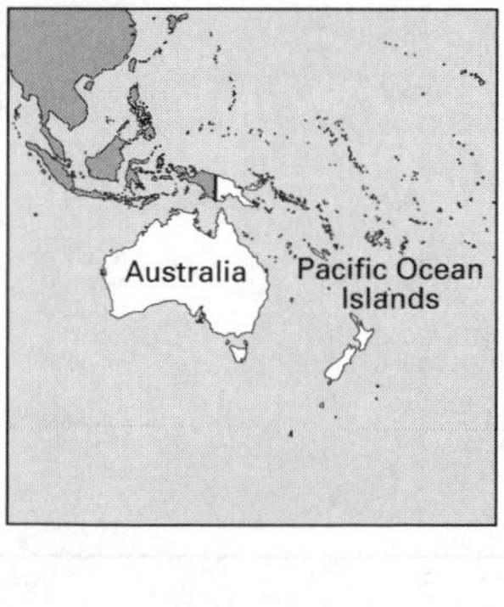

Government and international organizations

This table summarizes principal facts about the governments of the countries of the world, their branches and organs, the topmost layers of local government constituting each country's chief administrative subdivisions, and the participation of their central governments in the principal intergovernmental organizations of the world.

In this table "date of independence" may refer to a variety of circumstances. In the case of the newest countries, those that attained full independence after World War II, the date given is usually just what is implied by the heading—the date when the country, within its present borders, attained full sovereignty over both its internal and external affairs. In the case of longer established countries, the choice of a single date may be somewhat more complicated, and grounds for the use of several different dates often exist. The reader should refer to appropriate Britannica articles on national histories and relevant historical acts.

The date of the current, or last, constitution is in some ways a less complicated question, but governments sometimes do not, upon taking power, either adhere to existing constitutional forms or trouble to terminate the previous document and legitimize themselves by the installation of new constitutional forms. Often, however, the desire to legitimize extraconstitutional political activity by associating it with existing forms of long precedent leads to partial or incomplete modification, suspension, or abrogation of a constitution, so that the actual day-to-day conduct of government may be largely unrelated to the provisions of a constitution still theoretically in force. When a date in this column is given in italics, it refers to a document that has been suspended, abolished by extraconstitutional action, or modified extensively.

The characterizations adopted under "type of government" represent a compromise between the forms provided for by the national constitution and the more pragmatic language that a political scientist might adopt to describe these same systems. For an explanation of the application of these terms in the Britannica World Data, *see* the Glossary at page 501.

The positions denoted by the terms "chief of state" and "head of government" are usually those identified with those functions by the constitution. The duties of the chief of state may range from largely ceremonial responsibilities, with little or no authority over the day-to-day conduct of government, to complete executive authority as the effective head of government. In certain countries, an official of a political party or a revolutionary figure outside the constitutional structure may exercise the powers of both positions.

Membership in the legislative house(s) of each country as given here includes all elected or appointed members, as well as ex officio members (those who by virtue of some other office or title are members of the body), whether voting or nonvoting. The legislature of a country with a unicameral system is shown as the upper house in this table.

The number of administrative subdivisions for each country is listed down to the second level. In some instances, planning or statistical sub-

Government and international organizations

country	date of independence[a]	date of current or last constitution[b]	type of government	executive branch[c]: chief of state	executive branch[c]: head of government	legislative branch[d]: upper house (members)	legislative branch[d]: lower house (members)	admin. subdivisions: first-order (number)	admin. subdivisions: second-order (number)	seaward claims: territorial (nautical miles)	seaward claims: fishing/economic (nautical miles)
Afghanistan	Aug. 19, 1919	Jan. 26, 2004	Islamic republic	—president—		—	—	32	388	—	—
Albania	Nov. 28, 1912	Nov. 28, 1998	republic	president	prime minister	140	—	12	36	12	[1]
Algeria	July 5, 1962	Dec. 7, 1996[2]	republic	president	prime minister	144	389	48	553	12	[3]
American Samoa	—	July 1, 1967	territory (U.S.)	U.S. president	governor	18	20	4	14	12	200
Andorra	Dec. 6, 1288	May 4, 1993	parl. coprincipality	[5]	head of govt.	28	—	7	…	—	—
Angola	Nov. 11, 1975	Aug. 27, 1992	republic	—president[6]—		220	—	18	163	12	200
Antigua and Barbuda	Nov. 1, 1981	Nov. 1, 1981	constitutional monarchy	British monarch	prime minister	17	17[7]	30	—	12[8]	200[8]
Argentina	July 9, 1816	Aug. 24, 1994[9]	federal republic	—president[10]—		72	257	24	511	12	200
Armenia	Sept. 23, 1991	July 5, 1995	republic	president	prime minister	131	—	11	930	—	—
Aruba	—	Jan. 1, 1986	overseas territory (Neth.)	Dutch monarch	[11]	21	—	…	…	12	200
Australia	Jan. 1, 1901	Jan. 1, 1901	federal parl. state[13]	British monarch	prime minister	76	150	8	664[14]	12	200
Austria	Oct. 30, 1918	Oct. 1, 1920[15]	federal state	president	chancellor	64	183	9	98	—	—
Azerbaijan	Aug. 30, 1991	Aug. 24, 2002[16]	republic	—president[6]—		125[17]	—	67	…	…	…
Bahamas, The	July 10, 1973	July 10, 1973	constitutional monarchy	British monarch	prime minister	16	40	32	80	12	200
Bahrain	Aug. 15, 1971	Feb. 14, 2002	constitutional monarchy	monarch	prime minister	40	40	5	50	12	[18]
Bangladesh	March 26, 1971	Dec. 16, 1972	republic	president	prime minister	300	—	7	64	12	200
Barbados	Nov. 30, 1966	Nov. 30, 1966	constitutional monarchy	British monarch	prime minister	21	30	—	—	12	200
Belarus	Aug. 25, 1991	Nov. 27, 1996[19]	republic	—president[6]—		62[17]	110[17]	7	118	—	—
Belgium	Oct. 4, 1830	Feb. 17, 1994	fed. const. monarchy	monarch	prime minister	71[20]	150	[21]	43	12	[22]
Belize	Sept. 21, 1981	Sept. 21, 1981	constitutional monarchy	British monarch	prime minister	8	29	[23]	…	12[24]	200
Benin	Aug. 1, 1960	Dec. 2, 1990	republic	—president—		83	—	12	77	200	200
Bermuda	—	June 8, 1968	dependent territory (U.K.)	British monarch	[25]	11	36	11	—	12	200
Bhutan	March 24, 1910	—	[26]	monarch	prime minister	152	—	20	201	—	—
Bolivia	Aug. 6, 1825	Feb. 2, 1967	republic	—president—		27	130	9	112	—	—
Bosnia and Herzegovina	March 3, 1992	Dec. 14, 1995[27]	federal republic	[28]	chairman CM	15	42	3	10[29]	…	…
Botswana	Sept. 30, 1966	Sept. 30, 1966	republic	—president—		15[30]	63	16	28	—	—
Brazil	Sept. 7, 1822	Oct. 5, 1988[15]	federal republic	—president—		81	513	27	5,562	12	200
Brunei	Jan. 1, 1984	*Sept. 29, 1959*[31]	monarchy (sultanate)	—sultan—		21[30]	—	4	38	12	200
Bulgaria	Oct. 5, 1908	July 12, 1991	republic	president	prime minister	240	—	28	263	12	200
Burkina Faso	Aug. 5, 1960	June 11, 1991	republic	president	prime minister	111	—	45	382	—	—
Burundi	July 1, 1962	July 23, 2001[32]	republic[33]	—president[34]—		178	—	17	116	—	—
Cambodia	Nov. 9, 1953	March 4, 1999[35]	constitutional monarchy	king	prime minister	61	123	24	183	12	200
Cameroon	Jan. 1, 1960	Jan. 18, 1996	republic	president	prime minister	180	—	10	58	…	…
Canada	July 1, 1867	April 17, 1982	federal parl. state[13]	Canadian GG[36]	prime minister	105	308	13	…	12	200
Cape Verde	July 5, 1975	Sept. 25, 1992	republic	president	prime minister	72	—	17	…	12[8]	200[8]
Central African Republic	Aug. 13, 1960	*Jan. 14, 1995*	military regime[33]	—president[6]—		63	—	17	69	—	—
Chad	Aug. 11, 1960	April 14, 1996	republic	president	prime minister	155	—	29	108	—	—
Chile	Sept. 18, 1810	March 11, 1981	republic	—president—		48	120	13	51	12	200
China	1523 BC	Dec. 4, 1982	people's republic	president	premier SC	2,985	—	31	345	12	200
Colombia	July 20, 1810	July 5, 1991	republic	—president—		102	166	33	1,105	12	200
Comoros	July 6, 1975	June 5, 2002[37]	federal republic[38]	—president[39]—		33	—	3	…	12[8]	200[8]
Congo, Dem. Rep. of the	June 30, 1960	April 15, 2003[40]	republic[33]	—president[39]—		120	500	11	…	12	…
Congo, Rep. of the	Aug. 15, 1960	Aug. 10, 2002	republic	—president—		66[17]	137[17]	16	93	200	[1]
Costa Rica	Sept. 15, 1821	Nov. 9, 1949	republic	—president—		57	—	7	81	12	200
Côte d'Ivoire	Aug. 7, 1960	July 23, 2000	republic	—president[6]—		225	—	19	58	12	200
Croatia	June 25, 1991	Dec. 22, 1990	republic	president	prime minister	152	—	21	123	12	…
Cuba	May 20, 1902	Feb. 24, 1976	socialist republic	—president—		609	—	15	169	12	200
Cyprus[42]	Aug. 16, 1960	Aug. 16, 1960	republic	—president—		56[43]	—	…	647	12	…
Czech Republic	Jan. 1, 1993	Jan. 1, 1993	republic	president	prime minister	81	200	14	82	—	—
Denmark	*c.* 800	June 5, 1953	constitutional monarchy	monarch	prime minister	179	—	16	271	12	200
Djibouti	June 27, 1977	Sept. 15, 1992	republic	—president—		65	—	5	…	12	200
Dominica	Nov. 3, 1978	Nov. 3, 1978	republic	president	prime minister	32	—	37	—	12	200
Dominican Republic	Feb. 27, 1844	Nov. 28, 1966	republic	—president—		32	150	32	161	6	200
East Timor	May 20, 2002	May 20, 2002	republic	president	prime minister	88	—	13	—	12	200
Ecuador	May 24, 1822	Aug. 10, 1998	republic	—president—		125	—	22	219	200	200
Egypt	Feb. 28, 1922	Sept. 11, 1971	republic	president	prime minister	454	—	27	186	12[44]	…
El Salvador	Jan. 30, 1841	Dec. 20, 1983	republic	—president—		84	—	14	262	200	200
Equatorial Guinea	Oct. 12, 1968	Nov. 17, 1991	republic	president	prime minister	100	—	7	18	12	200
Eritrea	May 24, 1993	[45]	republic[33]	—president—		150	—	6	…	12	[46]
Estonia	Feb. 24, 1918	July 3, 1992	republic	president	prime minister	101	—	15	249	12[47]	[47]

divisions may be substituted when administrative subdivisions do not exist.

Finally, in the second half of the table are listed the memberships each country maintains in the principal international intergovernmental organizations of the world. This part of the table may also be utilized to provide a complete membership list for each of these organizations as of Dec. 1, 2004.

Notes for the column headings

a. The date may also be either that of the organization of the present form of government or the inception of the present administrative structure (federation, confederation, union, etc.).
b. Constitutions whose dates are in italic type had been wholly or substantially suspended or abolished as of late 2004.
c. For abbreviations used in this column see the list on the facing page.
d. When a legislative body has been adjourned or otherwise suspended, figures in parentheses indicate the number of members in the legislative body as provided for in constitution or law.
e. 15 nations with judicial representation in ICJ in 2004.
f. 18 nations with judicial representation in ICC in 2004 (ICC entered into force in July 2002; 97 countries had ratified or acceded to the ICC statute by October 2004).

International organizations, conventions

AC Arctic Council
ACP African, Caribbean, and Pacific (Cotonou Agreement) states
ADB Asian Development Bank
APEC Asia-Pacific Economic Co-operation
ASEAN Association of Southeast Asian Nations
ATs Antarctic Treaty signatories
AU African Union
CARICOM Caribbean Community and Common Market
ECOWAS Economic Community of West African States
EU The European Union
FAO Food and Agriculture Org.
FZ The Franc Zone
GCC Gulf Cooperation Council
I-ADB Inter-American Development Bank
IAEA International Atomic Energy Agency
IBRD International Bank for Reconstruction and Development
ICAO International Civil Aviation Org.
ICC International Criminal Court
ICJ International Court of Justice
IDA International Development Association
IDB Islamic Development Bank
ILO International Labour Org.
IMF International Monetary Fund
IMO International Maritime Org.
ITU International Telecommunication Union
LAS League of Arab States (Arab League)
OAS Organization of American States
OPEC Organization of the Petroleum Exporting Countries
PC Pacific Community
UNCTAD United Nations Conference on Trade and Development
UNESCO United Nations Educational Scientific and Cultural Org.
UNIDO United Nations Industrial Development Org.
WHO World Health Org.
WIPO World Intellectual Property Org.
WTO World Trade Org.

Abbreviations used in the executive-branch column

CM Council of Ministers
FC Federal Council
GC General Council
GG Governor-General
GPC General People's Committee
NDC National Defense Commission
NTG National Transitional Government
PC People's Council
SC State Council
SPDC State Peace and Development Council

membership in international organizations																																					country
United Nations (date of admission)	UN organs★ and affiliated intergovernmental organizations																The Commonwealth	regional multipurpose									economic										
	UNCTAD★	ICJ★[e]	FAC	IAEA	IBRD	ICAO	ICC[f]	IDA	ILO	IMF	IMC	ITU	UNESCO	UNIDO	WHO	WIPO	WTO		AC	ASEAN	ATs	AU	EU	GCC	LAS	OAS	PC	ACP	ADB	APEC	CARICOM	ECOWAS	FZ	I-ADB	IDB	OPEC	
1946	●		●	●	●	●		●	●	●		●	●	●	●														●						●		Afghanistan
1955	●		●	●	●	●		●	●	●	●	●	●	●	●	●	●																		●		Albania
1962	●		●	●	●	●		●	●	●	●	●	●	●	●	●	4					●			●										●	●	Algeria
—												●															●										American Samoa
1993	●					●						●	●		●	●	4																				Andorra
1976	●		●	●	●	●		●	●	●	●	●	●	●	●	●	●					●						●									Angola
1981	●		●		●	●			●	●	●	●	●		●	●	●	●								●		●			●						Antigua and Barbuda
1945	●		●	●	●	●		●	●	●	●	●	●	●	●	●	●				●					●								●			Argentina
1992	●		●	●	●	●		●	●	●		●	●	●	●	●	●																				Armenia
—										●			12																								Aruba
1945	●		●	●	●	●		●	●	●	●	●	●		●	●	●	●			●						●		●	●							Australia
1955	●		●	●	●	●		●	●	●	●	●	●	●	●	●	●				●		●						●					●			Austria
1992	●		●	●	●	●		●	●	●	●	●	●	●	●	●	4												●						●		Azerbaijan
1973	●		●		●	●			●	●	●	●	●	●	●	●	4	●								●		●			●			●			Bahamas, The
1971	●		●		●	●			●	●	●	●	●	●	●	●	●							●	●										●		Bahrain
1974	●		●	●	●	●		●	●	●	●	●	●	●	●	●	●	●											●						●		Bangladesh
1966	●		●		●	●		●	●	●	●	●	●	●	●	●	●	●								●		●			●			●			Barbados
1945	●			●	●	●			●	●		●	●	●	●	●	4																				Belarus
1945	●		●	●	●	●		●	●	●	●	●	●	●	●	●	●				●		●						●					●			Belgium
1981	●		●		●	●		●	●	●	●	●	●	●	●	●	●	●								●		●			●			●			Belize
1960	●		●	●	●	●		●	●	●	●	●	●	●	●	●	●					●						●				●	●		●		Benin
—												●																			12						Bermuda
1971	●		●		●	●		●		●		●	●	●	●	●	4												●								Bhutan
1945	●		●	●	●	●	●	●	●	●	●	●	●	●	●	●	●									●								●			Bolivia
1992	●		●	●	●	●		●	●	●	●	●	●	●	●	●	4																				Bosnia and Herzegovina
1966	●		●	●	●	●		●	●	●		●	●	●	●	●	●	●				●						●									Botswana
1945	●	●	●	●	●	●	●	●	●	●	●	●	●	●	●	●	●				●					●								●			Brazil
1984	●				●	●				●	●	●			●	●	●	●		●										●					●		Brunei
1955	●		●	●	●	●			●	●	●	●	●	●	●	●	●				●																Bulgaria
1960	●		●	●	●	●		●	●	●		●	●	●	●	●	●					●						●				●	●		●		Burkina Faso
1962	●		●		●	●		●	●	●		●	●	●	●	●	●					●						●									Burundi
1955	●		●		●	●		●	●	●	●	●	●	●	●	●	●			●									●								Cambodia
1960	●		●	●	●	●		●	●	●	●	●	●	●	●	●	●	●				●						●					●		●		Cameroon
1945	●		●	●	●	●	●	●	●	●	●	●	●		●	●	●	●	●		●					●			●	●				●			Canada
1975	●		●		●	●		●	●	●	●	●	●	●	●	●	4					●						●				●					Cape Verde
1960	●		●	●	●	●		●	●	●		●	●	●	●	●	●					●						●					●				Central African Republic
1960	●		●		●	●		●	●	●		●	●	●	●	●	●					●						●					●		●		Chad
1945	●		●	●	●	●		●	●	●	●	●	●	●	●	●	●				●					●				●				●			Chile
1945	●	●	●	●	●	●		●	●	●	●	●	●	●	●	●	●				●								●	●							China
1945	●		●	●	●	●		●	●	●	●	●	●	●	●	●	●				●					●								●			Colombia
1975	●		●		●	●		●	●	●	●	●	●	●	●							●			●			●					●		●		Comoros
1960	●		●	●	●	●		●	●	●	●	●	●	●	●	●	●					●						●									Congo, Dem. Rep. of the
1960	●		●		●	●		●	●	●	●	●	●	●	●	●	●					●						●					●				Congo, Rep. of the
1945	●		●	●	●	●	●	●	●	●	●	●	●	●	●	●	●									●								●			Costa Rica
1960	●		●	●	●	●		●	●	●	●	●	●	●	●	●	●					●						●				●	●		●		Côte d'Ivoire
1992	●		●	●	●	●		●	●	●	●	●	●	●	●	●	●																	●			Croatia
1945	●		●	●		●			●		●	●	●	●	●	●	●				●					41		●									Cuba
1960	●		●	●	●	●	●	●	●	●	●	●	●	●	●	●	●	●					●														Cyprus[42]
1993	●		●	●	●	●		●	●	●	●	●	●	●	●	●	●				●		●														Czech Republic
1945	●		●	●	●	●		●	●	●	●	●	●	●	●	●	●		●		●		●						●					●			Denmark
1977	●		●		●	●		●	●	●	●	●	●	●	●	●	●					●			●			●							●		Djibouti
1978	●		●		●			●	●	●	●	●	●	●	●	●	●	●								●		●			●						Dominica
1945	●		●	●	●	●		●	●	●	●	●	●	●	●	●	●									●		●						●			Dominican Republic
2002	●		●		●			●	●	●			●	●	●													●	●								East Timor
1945	●		●	●	●	●		●	●	●	●	●	●	●	●	●	●				●					●								●			Ecuador
1945	●	●	●	●	●	●		●	●	●	●	●	●	●	●	●	●					●			●										●		Egypt
1945	●		●	●	●	●		●	●	●	●	●	●	●	●	●	●									●								●			El Salvador
1968	●		●		●	●		●	●	●	●	●	●	●	●	●	4					●						●					●				Equatorial Guinea
1993	●		●	●	●	●		●	●	●	●	●	●	●	●	●						●						●									Eritrea
1991	●		●	●	●	●			●	●	●	●	●		●	●	●				●		●														Estonia

Government and international organizations (continued)

country	date of independence[a]	date of current or last constitution[b]	type of government	executive branch[c]		legislative branch[d]		admin. subdivisions		seaward claims	
				chief of state	head of government	upper house (members)	lower house (members)	first-order (number)	second-order (number)	territorial (nautical miles)	fishing/economic (nautical miles)
Ethiopia	*c.* 1000 BC	Aug. 22, 1995	federal republic	president	prime minister	108	546	11	57	—	—
Faroe Islands	—	April 1, 1948	part of Danish realm	Danish monarch	[48]	32	—	9	48	...	200[49]
Fiji	Oct. 10, 1970	July 27, 1998	republic	president	prime minister	32	72	4	15	12[8]	200[8]
Finland	Dec. 6, 1917	March 1, 2000	republic	president	prime minister	200	—	6	20	12[50]	[47]
France	August 843	Oct. 4, 1958[15]	republic	president	prime minister	321	577	22	96	12	200
French Guiana	—	Feb. 28, 1983	overseas dept. (Fr.)	French president	[51]	19	31	2	22	12	200
French Polynesia	—	Feb. 27, 2004	overseas country (Fr.)	French president[52]	president	57	—	5	48	12	200
Gabon	Aug. 17, 1960	March 26, 1991	republic	president	prime minister	91	120	9	37	12	200
Gambia, The	Feb. 18, 1965	Jan. 16, 1997	republic	—president—		53	—	8	45	12	200
Gaza Strip	—	May 4, 1994[53]	interim authority	—[54]—		89	—	5	...	...	...
Georgia	April 9, 1991	Oct. 17, 1995	republic	president	prime minister	235	—	12	74	...	...
Germany	May 5, 1955	May 23, 1949	federal republic	president	chancellor	69	603	16	26	12[49]	...
Ghana	March 6, 1957	Jan. 7, 1993	republic	—president—		230	—	10	110	12	200
Greece	Feb. 3, 1830	April 6, 2001[56]	republic	president	prime minister	300	—	55	1,033	6/10	[1]
Greenland	—	May 1, 1979	part of Danish realm	Danish monarch	[48]	31	—	18	...	3	200
Grenada	Feb. 7, 1974	Feb. 7, 1974	constitutional monarchy	British monarch	prime minister	13	15	9	...	12	200
Guadeloupe	—	Feb. 28, 1983	overseas dept. (Fr.)	French president	[51]	42	41	3	34	12	200
Guam	—	Aug. 1, 1950	territory (U.S.)	U.S. president	governor	15	—	19	—	12	200
Guatemala	Sept. 15, 1821	Jan. 14, 1986	republic	—president—		158	—	22	331	12	200
Guernsey	—	Jan. 1, 1949[15]	crown dependency (U.K.)	British monarch[57]	[58]	51	—	3	...	3	12
Guinea	Oct. 2, 1958	Dec. 23, 1990[40]	republic	—president—		114	—	8	34	12	200
Guinea-Bissau	Sept. 10, 1974	[59]	republic[33]	—president[6]—		102	—	9	37	12	200
Guyana	May 26, 1966	Oct. 6, 1980	cooperative republic	—president—		65	—	10	71	12	200
Haiti	Jan. 1, 1804	March 29, 1987	republic[33]	president	prime minister	27	83	9	41	12	200
Honduras	Nov. 5, 1838	Jan. 20, 1982	republic	—president—		128	—	18	298	12	200
Hong Kong	—	July 1, 1997	[60]	Chinese president	chief executive	60	—	18	...	12	[1]
Hungary	Nov. 16, 1918	Aug. 20, 1949[61]	republic	president	prime minister	386	—	20	256[62]	—	—
Iceland	June 17, 1944	June 17, 1944	republic	president	prime minister	63	—	8	105	12	200
India	Aug. 15, 1947	Jan. 26, 1950	federal republic	president	prime minister	245	545	35	593	12	200
Indonesia	Aug. 17, 1945	Aug. 17, 1945	republic	—president—		128	550	32	325	12[8]	200[8]
Iran	Oct. 7, 1906	Dec. 2–3, 1979	Islamic republic	—president[63]—		290	—	28	314	12	50[64]
Iraq	Oct. 3, 1932	June 28, 2004[65]	interim authority	—president[6]—		100	—	18	...	12	[1]
Ireland	Dec. 6, 1921	Dec. 29, 1937	republic	president	prime minister	60	166	34	86	12	200
Isle of Man	—	1961[15]	crown dependency (U.K.)	British monarch[57]	chief minister	11	24	24	—	12[66]	...
Israel	May 14, 1948	June 1950[15]	republic	president	prime minister	120	—	6	15	12	[1]
Italy	March 17, 1861	Jan. 1, 1948	republic	president	prime minister	321	630	20	103	12	[1]
Jamaica	Aug. 6, 1962	Aug. 6, 1962	constitutional monarchy	British monarch	prime minister	21	60	13	—	12	200
Japan	*c.* 660 BC	May 3, 1947	constitutional monarchy	[67]	prime minister	242	480	47	3,230	12[68]	200
Jersey	—	Jan. 1, 1949[15]	crown dependency (U.K.)	British monarch[57]	[69]	58	—	12	—	12	...
Jordan	May 25, 1946	Jan. 8, 1952	constitutional monarchy	—king[6]—		55	110	12	...	3	[1]
Kazakhstan	Dec. 16, 1991	Sept. 6, 1995	republic	—president[6]—		39	77	16	160	—	—
Kenya	Dec. 12, 1963	Dec. 12, 1963	republic	—president—		224	—	8	47	12	200
Kiribati	July 12, 1979	July 12, 1979	republic	—president—		42	—	...	...	12[8]	200[8]
Korea, North	Sept. 9, 1948	Sept. 5, 1998[70]	socialist republic	—chairman NDC—		687	—	15	172	12	200
Korea, South	Aug. 15, 1948	Feb. 25, 1988	republic	—president[6]—		299	—	16	165[71]	12	200
Kuwait	June 19, 1961	Nov. 16, 1962	const. mon. (emirate)	—emir[6]—		50[72]	—	6	...	12	[1]
Kyrgyzstan	Aug. 31, 1991	May 5, 1993	republic	—president[6]—		45	60	8	54[73]	—	—
Laos	Oct. 23, 1953	Aug. 15, 1991	people's republic	president	prime minister	109	—	18	133	—	—
Latvia	Nov. 18, 1918	Nov. 7, 1922	republic	president	prime minister	100	—	33	70	12	[74]
Lebanon	Nov. 26, 1941	Sept. 21, 1990	republic	president	prime minister	128	—	6	26	12	[1]
Lesotho	Oct. 4, 1966	April 2, 1993	constitutional monarchy	king	prime minister	33[30]	120	10	...	—	—
Liberia	July 26, 1847	Aug. 18, 2003[75]	republic[33]	—chairman NTG—		—	—	15	...	200	[1]
Libya	Dec. 24, 1951	March 2, 1977	socialist state[76]	leader[77]	sec. GPC	760	—	34	...	12	[1]
Liechtenstein	July 12, 1806	Oct. 5, 1921	constitutional monarchy	prince	head of govt.	25	—	11	—	—	—
Lithuania	Feb. 16, 1918	Nov. 6, 1992	republic	president	prime minister	141	—	10	60	12	...
Luxembourg	May 10, 1867	Oct. 17, 1868	constitutional monarchy	grand duke	prime minister	21[30]	60	3	12	—	—
Macau	—	Dec. 20, 1999	[60]	Chinese president	chief executive	27	—	8	...	...	...
Macedonia	Nov. 17, 1991	Nov. 16, 2001[78]	republic	president	prime minister	120	—	...	...	—	—
Madagascar	June 26, 1960	April 8, 1998	federal republic	—president[6]—		90	160	6	22	12	200
Malawi	July 6, 1964	May 18, 1994	republic	—president—		193	—	3	27	—	—
Malaysia	Aug. 31, 1957	Aug. 31, 1957	fed. const. monarchy	paramount ruler	prime minister	70	219	16	148	12	200
Maldives	July 26, 1965	Jan. 1, 1998	republic	—president—		42[72]	—	21	...	12[8]	200
Mali	Sept. 22, 1960	Feb. 25, 1992	republic	president	prime minister	147	—	9	49	—	—
Malta	Sept. 21, 1964	Dec. 13, 1974	republic	president	prime minister	65	—	3	68	12	25
Marshall Islands	Dec. 22, 1990	May 1, 1979	republic	—president—		12[30]	33	4	—	12[8]	200
Martinique	—	Feb. 28, 1983	overseas dept. (Fr.)	French president	[51]	45	41	4	34	12	200
Mauritania	Nov. 28, 1960	July 21, 1991	republic	—president[6]—		56	81	13	53	12	200
Mauritius	March 12, 1968	March 12, 1992	republic	president	prime minister	70	—	11	130	12	200
Mayotte	—	July 11, 2001	dept. collectivity (Fr.)	French president	president GC	19	—	17	—	12	200
Mexico	Sept. 16, 1810	Feb. 5, 1917	federal republic	—president—		128	500	32	2,445	12	200
Micronesia	Dec. 22, 1990	Jan. 1, 1981	federal republic	—president—		14	—	4	74	12	200
Moldova	Aug. 27, 1991	Aug. 27, 1994	parliamentary republic	president	prime minister	101	—	35	...	—	—
Monaco	Feb. 2, 1861	April 12, 2002[35]	constitutional monarchy	prince	min. of state[79]	24	—	—	—	12	[1]
Mongolia	March 13, 1921	Feb. 12, 1992	republic	president	prime minister	76	—	22	340	—	—
Morocco	March 2, 1956	Oct. 7, 1996	constitutional monarchy	—king[6]—		270	325	16[80]	71[80]	12	200
Mozambique	June 25, 1975	Nov. 30, 1990	republic	—president—		250	—	11	112	12	200
Myanmar (Burma)	Jan. 4, 1948	*Jan. 4, 1974*	military regime	—chairman SPDC[6]—		(492)	—	14	58	12	200
Namibia	March 21, 1990	March 21, 1990	republic	—president—		26	72[72]	13	—	12	200
Nauru	Jan. 31, 1968	Jan. 31, 1968	republic	—president—		18	—	1	—	12	200
Nepal	Nov. 13, 1769	Nov. 9, 1990	constitutional monarchy	king	prime minister	(60)	(205)	5[81]	75	—	—
Netherlands, The	March 30, 1814	Feb. 17, 1983	constitutional monarchy	monarch	prime minister	75	150	12	496	12	[22]
Netherlands Antilles	—	Dec. 29, 1954	overseas territory (Neth.)	Dutch monarch	[11]	22	—	5	—	12	200
New Caledonia	—	March 19, 2003	overseas country (Fr.)	French president[82]	president	54	—	3	33	12	200
New Zealand	Sept. 26, 1907	June 30, 1852[15]	constitutional monarchy	British monarch	prime minister	120	—	12	74	12	200
Nicaragua	April 30, 1838	Jan. 9, 1987	republic	—president—		92	—	17	151	12	200

membership in international organizations																																					country
United Nations (date of admission)	UN organs★ and affiliated intergovernmental organizations																	The Commonwealth	regional multipurpose										economic									
	UNCTAD★	ICJ★[e]	FAO	IAEA	IBRD	ICAO	ICC[f]	IDA	ILO	IMF	IMO	ITU	UNESCO	UNIDO	WHO	WIPO	WTO		AC	ASEAN	ATs	AU	EU	GCC	LAS	OAS	PC	ACP	ADB	APEC	CARICOM	ECOWAS	FZ	I-ADB	IDB	OPEC	
1945	•		•	•	•	•		•	•	•	•	•	•	•	•	•	4					•						•									Ethiopia
—											12								•																		Faroe Islands
1970	•		•		•	•		•	•	•	•	•	•	•	•	•	•	•									•	•	•								Fiji
1955	•		•	•	•	•	•	•	•	•	•	•	•	•	•	•	•		•		•		•						•					•			Finland
1945	•	•	•	•	•	•	•	•	•	•	•	•	•	•	•	•	•				•		•				•		•				•	•			France
—												•																					•				French Guiana
—												•															•						•				French Polynesia
1960	•		•	•	•	•		•	•	•	•	•	•	•	•	•	•					•						•					•		•		Gabon
1965	•		•		•	•		•	•	•	•	•	•	•	•	•	•	•				•						•				•			•		Gambia, The
—																									•[55]										•[55]		Gaza Strip
1992	•		•	•	•	•		•	•	•	•	•	•	•	•	•	•																				Georgia
1973	•	•	•	•	•	•	•	•	•	•	•	•	•	•	•	•	•				•		•						•					•			Germany
1957	•		•	•	•	•	•	•	•	•	•	•	•	•	•	•	•	•				•						•				•					Ghana
1945	•		•	•	•	•		•	•	•	•	•	•	•	•	•	•				•		•														Greece
—																			•																		Greenland
1974	•		•		•	•		•	•	•	•	•	•	•	•	•	•	•								•		•			•						Grenada
—												•																					•				Guadeloupe
—												•															•										Guam
1945	•		•	•	•	•		•	•	•	•	•	•	•	•	•	•				•					•								•			Guatemala
—												•																									Guernsey
1958	•		•		•	•		•	•	•	•	•	•	•	•	•	•					•						•				•			•		Guinea
1974	•		•		•	•		•	•	•	•	•	•	•	•	•	•					•						•				•	•		•		Guinea-Bissau
1966	•		•		•	•		•	•	•	•	•	•	•	•	•	•	•								•		•			•			•			Guyana
1945	•		•	•	•	•		•	•	•	•	•	•	•	•	•	•									•		•			41			•			Haiti
1945	•		•	•	•	•		•	•	•	•	•	•	•	•	•	•									•								•			Honduras
—										•	12						•												•	•							Hong Kong
1955	•		•	•	•	•		•	•	•	•	•	•	•	•	•	•				•		•														Hungary
1946	•		•	•	•	•		•	•	•	•	•	•		•	•	•		•																		Iceland
1945	•		•	•	•	•		•	•	•	•	•	•	•	•	•	•	•			•								•								India
1950	•		•	•	•	•		•	•	•	•	•	•	•	•	•	•			•									•	•					•	•	Indonesia
1945	•		•	•	•	•		•	•	•	•	•	•	•	•	•																			•	•	Iran
1945	•		•	•	•	•		•	•	•	•	•	•	•	•	•	4								•										•	•	Iraq
1955	•		•	•	•	•	•	•	•	•	•	•	•	•	•	•	•						•														Ireland
—												•																									Isle of Man
1949	•		•	•	•	•		•	•	•	•	•	•	•	•	•	•																	•			Israel
1955	•		•	•	•	•	•	•	•	•	•	•	•	•	•	•	•				•		•						•					•			Italy
1962	•		•	•	•	•			•	•	•	•	•	•	•	•	•	•								•		•			•			•			Jamaica
1956	•	•	•	•	•	•		•	•	•	•	•	•	•	•	•	•				•								•	•				•			Japan
—												•																									Jersey
1955	•	•	•	•	•	•		•	•	•	•	•	•	•	•	•	•								•										•		Jordan
1992	•		•	•	•	•		•	•	•	•	•	•	•	•	•	4												•						•		Kazakhstan
1963	•		•	•	•	•		•	•	•	•	•	•	•	•	•	•	•				•						•									Kenya
1999	•		•		•	•		•	•	•	•	•	•		•			•									•	•	•								Kiribati
1991	•		•			•					•	•	•	•	•	•					•																Korea, North
1991	•		•	•	•	•	•	•	•	•	•	•	•	•	•	•	•				•								•	•							Korea, South
1963	•		•	•	•	•		•	•	•	•	•	•	•	•	•	•							•	•										•	•	Kuwait
1992	•		•	•	•	•		•	•	•		•	•	•	•	•	•												•						•		Kyrgyzstan
1955	•		•		•	•		•	•	•		•	•	•	•	•	4			•									•								Laos
1991	•		•	•	•	•	•	•	•	•	•	•	•		•	•	•						•														Latvia
1945	•		•	•	•	•		•	•	•	•	•	•	•	•	•	4								•										•		Lebanon
1966	•		•		•	•		•	•	•		•	•	•	•	•	•	•				•						•									Lesotho
1945	•		•	•	•	•		•	•	•	•	•	•	•	•	•						•						•				•					Liberia
1955	•		•	•	•	•		•	•	•	•	•	•	•	•	•	4					•			•										•	•	Libya
1990	•			•								•				•	•																				Liechtenstein
1991	•		•	•	•	•			•	•	•	•	•	•	•	•	•						•														Lithuania
1945	•		•	•	•	•		•	•	•	•	•	•	•	•	•	•						•						•								Luxembourg
—										•	12		12				•																				Macau
1993	•		•	•	•	•		•	•	•	•	•	•	•	•	•	•																				Macedonia
1960	•	•	•	•	•	•		•	•	•	•	•	•	•	•	•	•					•						•									Madagascar
1964	•		•		•	•		•	•	•	•	•	•	•	•	•	•	•				•						•									Malawi
1957	•		•	•	•	•		•	•	•	•	•	•	•	•	•	•	•		•									•	•					•		Malaysia
1965	•		•		•	•		•		•	•	•	•	•	•	•	•	•											•						•		Maldives
1960	•		•	•	•	•	•	•	•	•		•	•	•	•	•	•					•						•				•	•		•		Mali
1964	•		•	•	•	•			•	•	•	•	•	•	•	•	•	•					•														Malta
1991	•		•	•	•	•		•		•	•	•	•		•												•	•	•								Marshall Islands
—												•																					•				Martinique
1961	•		•		•	•		•	•	•	•	•	•	•	•	•	•					•			•			•							•		Mauritania
1968	•		•	•	•	•		•	•	•	•	•	•	•	•	•	•	•				•						•									Mauritius
—												•																					•				Mayotte
1945	•		•	•	•	•		•	•	•	•	•	•	•	•	•	•									•				•				•			Mexico
1991	•		•		•	•		•		•		•	•		•												•	•	•								Micronesia
1992	•		•	•	•	•		•	•	•	•	•	•	•	•	•	•																				Moldova
1993	•		•	•		•					•	•	•	•	•	•																					Monaco
1961	•		•	•	•	•		•	•	•	•	•	•	•	•	•	•												•								Mongolia
1956	•		•	•	•	•		•	•	•	•	•	•	•	•	•	•								•										•		Morocco
1975	•		•		•	•		•	•	•	•	•	•	•	•	•	•	•				•						•							•		Mozambique
1948	•		•	•	•	•		•	•	•	•	•	•	•	•	•	•			•									•								Myanmar (Burma)
1990	•		•	•	•	•			•	•	•	•	•	•	•	•	•	•				•						•									Namibia
1999	•		•			•						•	•		•			•									•	•	•								Nauru
1955	•		•		•	•		•	•	•	•	•	•	•	•	•	•												•								Nepal
1945	•	•	•	•	•	•		•	•	•	•	•	•	•	•	•	•				•		•						•					•			Netherlands, The
—										•			12																								Netherlands Antilles
—												•															•						•				New Caledonia
1945	•		•	•	•	•		•	•	•	•	•	•	•	•	•	•	•			•						•		•	•							New Zealand
1945	•		•	•	•	•		•	•	•	•	•	•	•	•	•	•									•								•			Nicaragua

Government and international organizations (continued)

country	date of independence[a]	date of current or last constitution[b]	type of government	executive branch[c]: chief of state	executive branch[c]: head of government	legislative branch[d]: upper house (members)	legislative branch[d]: lower house (members)	admin. subdivisions: first-order (number)	admin. subdivisions: second-order (number)	seaward claims: territorial (nautical miles)	seaward claims: fishing/economic (nautical miles)
Niger	Aug. 3, 1960	Aug. 9, 1999	republic	president[6]		113	—	8	39	—	—
Nigeria	Oct. 1, 1960	May 5, 1999	federal republic	president		109	360	37	774	12	200
Northern Mariana Is.	—	Jan. 9, 1978	commonwealth (U.S.)	U.S. president	governor	9	18	4	—	12	200
Norway	June 7, 1905	May 17, 1814	constitutional monarchy	king	prime minister	165	—	19	434	4	200
Oman	Dec. 20, 1951	Nov. 6, 1996[83]	monarchy (sultanate)	sultan		[84]		8	60	12	200
Pakistan	Aug. 14, 1947	Aug. 14, 1973	republic	president[6]		100	342	5	28	12	200
Palau	Oct. 1, 1994	Jan. 1, 1981	republic	president		9	16	16	—	3	200
Panama	Nov. 3, 1903	May 20, 1983[35]	republic	president[39]		78	—	12	76	12	200
Papua New Guinea	Sept. 16, 1975	Sept. 16, 1975	constitutional monarchy	British monarch	prime minister	109	—	20	267	3/12	200[8]
Paraguay	May 14, 1811	June 22, 1992	republic	president		45	80	18	235	—	—
Peru	July 28, 1821	Dec. 29, 1993	republic	president[6]		120	—	25	194	200	200
Philippines	July 4, 1946	Feb. 11, 1987	republic	president		24	236	17	79	[85]	200[8]
Poland	Nov. 10, 1918	Oct. 17, 1997	republic	president	prime minister	100	460	16	308	12	...
Portugal	*c.* 1140	April 25, 1976	republic	president	prime minister	230	—	7	20	12	200
Puerto Rico	—	July 25, 1952	commonwealth (U.S.)	U.S. president	governor	27[86]	51[86]	78	—	12	200
Qatar	Sept. 3, 1971	June 8, 2004[87]	constitutional emirate[88]	emir[6]		...	...	10	—	12	...
Réunion	—	Feb. 28, 1983	overseas dept. (Fr.)	French president	[51]	49	45	4	25	12	200
Romania	May 21, 1877	Dec. 13, 1991	republic	president	prime minister	137	332	42	2,686	12[44]	200[44]
Russia	Dec. 8, 1991	Dec. 24, 1993	federal republic	president	prime minister	178	450	7	88	12	200
Rwanda	July 1, 1962	June 4, 2003	republic	president[6]		26	80	12	105	—	—
St. Kitts and Nevis	Sept. 19, 1983	Sept. 19, 1983	constitutional monarchy	British monarch	prime minister	15	—	1	—	12	200
St. Lucia	Feb. 22, 1979	Feb. 22, 1979	constitutional monarchy	British monarch	prime minister	11	17[7]	10	—	12	200
St. Vincent	Oct. 27, 1979	Oct. 27, 1979	constitutional monarchy	British monarch	prime minister	21	—	...	—	12	200
Samoa	Jan. 1, 1962	Oct. 28, 1960	[89]	head of state	prime minister	49	—	11	—	12	200
San Marino	855	Oct. 8, 1600	republic	captains-regent (2)		60	—	9	—	—	—
São Tomé and Príncipe	July 12, 1975	Sept. 10, 1990	republic	president	prime minister	55	—	1	6	12[8]	200[8]
Saudi Arabia	Sept. 23, 1932	[90]	monarchy	king[91]		120[30]	—	13	103	12	[1]
Senegal	Aug. 20, 1960	Jan. 7, 2001	republic	president[6]		120	—	11	34	12[44]	200[44]
Serbia and Montenegro	Dec. 1, 1918	Feb. 4, 2003	state union[92]	president[93]		126	—	2[94]	46[94]	12	...
Seychelles	June 29, 1976	June 21, 1993	republic	president		34	—	25	...	12	200
Sierra Leone	April 27, 1961	Oct. 1, 1991	republic	president		124	—	13	150	12	200
Singapore	Aug. 9, 1965	June 3, 1959[15]	republic	president	prime minister	90	—	—	—	3	...
Slovakia	Jan. 1, 1993	Jan. 1, 1993	republic	president	prime minister	150	—	8	79	—	—
Slovenia	June 25, 1991	Dec. 23, 1991	republic	president	prime minister	40	90	193	—	...	...
Solomon Islands	July 7, 1978	July 7, 1978	constitutional monarchy	British monarch	prime minister	50	—	10	...	12[8]	200[8]
Somalia	July 1, 1960	March 12, 2004[95]	republic[33, 96]	president[6]		194[97]	—	...	...	200	200
South Africa	May 31, 1910	June 30, 1997	republic	president		90	400	9	360	12	200
Spain	1492	Dec. 29, 1978	constitutional monarchy	king	prime minister	259	350	19	50	12	200[98]
Sri Lanka	Feb. 4, 1948	Sept. 7, 1978	republic	president[6]		225	—	25	324	12	200
Sudan, The	Jan. 1, 1956	June 30, 1998	military regime	president		360	—	26	...	12	[1]
Suriname	Nov. 25, 1975	Nov. 25, 1987	republic	president		51	—	10	62	12	200
Swaziland	Sept. 6, 1968	[99]	monarchy	king[6]		30[30]	65[30]	4	55	—	—
Sweden	before 836	Jan. 1, 1975	constitutional monarchy	king	prime minister	349	—	21	290	12	[18]
Switzerland	Sept. 22, 1499	Jan. 1, 2000	federal state	president FC		46	200	26	181	—	—
Syria	April 17, 1946	March 14, 1973	republic	president		250	—	14	60	35	[1]
Taiwan	—	Dec. 25, 1947[15]	republic	president	premier	225	—	2	25	24	200
Tajikistan	Sept. 9, 1991	Nov. 6, 1994	republic	president	prime minister	33	63	4	78	—	—
Tanzania	Dec. 9, 1961	April 25, 1977	republic	president		274	—	1	26	12	200
Thailand	1350	Oct. 11, 1997	constitutional monarchy	king	prime minister	200	500	76	795	12	200
Togo	April 27, 1960	Sept. 27, 1992	republic	president	prime minister	81	—	5	31	30	200
Tonga	June 4, 1970	Nov. 4, 1875	hereditary monarchy	monarch		30	—	5	...	12	200
Trinidad and Tobago	Aug. 31, 1962	July 27, 1976	republic	president	prime minister	31	36	16	...	12[8]	200[8]
Tunisia	March 20, 1956	June 1, 2002[35]	republic	president	prime minister	189	—	24	257	12	...
Turkey	Oct. 29, 1923	Nov. 7, 1982	republic	president	prime minister	550	—	81	850	12[100]	200[101]
Turkmenistan	Oct. 27, 1991	Aug. 15, 2003[35]	republic	president PC		50	—	6	...	—	—
Tuvalu	Oct. 1, 1978	Oct. 1, 1986	constitutional monarchy	British monarch	prime minister	12	—	8	—	12[8]	200[8]
Uganda	Oct. 9, 1962	Oct. 8, 1995	republic	president		305	—	56	165	—	—
Ukraine	Aug. 24, 1991	June 28, 1996	republic	president	prime minister	450	—	27	677	12	200
United Arab Emirates	Dec. 2, 1971	Dec. 2, 1971	federation of emirates	president	prime minister	40[30]	—	7	—	12	200
United Kingdom	Dec. 6, 1921	[102]	constitutional monarchy	monarch	prime minister	688	659	3	434	12[66]	200
United States	July 4, 1776	March 4, 1789	federal republic	president		100	435	51	3,141	12	200
Uruguay	Aug. 25, 1828	Feb. 15, 1967	republic	president		31	99	19	...	12	200
Uzbekistan	Aug. 31, 1991	Dec. 8, 1992	republic	president[6]		250	—	14	227[103]	—	—
Vanuatu	July 30, 1980	July 30, 1980	republic	president	prime minister	52	—	6	...	12[8]	200[8]
Venezuela	July 5, 1811	Dec. 20, 1999	federal republic	president		165	—	25	335	12	200
Vietnam	Sept. 2, 1945	April 15, 1992	socialist republic	president	prime minister	498	—	8	64	12	200
Virgin Islands (U.S.)	—	July 22, 1954	territory (U.S.)	U.S. president	governor	15	—	...	...	12	200
West Bank	—	May 4, 1994[53]	interim authority	[54]		89	—	11	...	—	—
Western Sahara	—	—	annexure of Morocco	—	—	—	—	...	...	12	200
Yemen	December 1918	Sept. 29, 1994	republic	president	prime minister	111[30]	301	20	...	12	200
Zambia	Oct. 24, 1964	May 28, 1996[2]	republic	president		158	—	9	72	—	—
Zimbabwe	April 18, 1980	April 18, 1980	republic	president		150	—	10	63	—	—

[1]Territorial sea claim. [2]Date president signed new constitution. [3]Varies between 32 and 52 nautical miles. [4]Observer. [5]President of France and Bishop of Urgell, Spain. [6]Assisted by the prime minister. [7]Excludes possible ex officio members. [8]Measured from claimed archipelagic baselines. [9]Promulgation date of significant amendments to July 9, 1853, constitution. [10]Assisted by the cabinet chief (ministerial coordinator). [11]Executive responsibilities divided between (for The Netherlands) the governor and (locally) the prime minister. [12]Associate member. [13]Formally a constitutional monarchy. [14]Number of 6 different kinds of Local Government Areas in 1999. [15]Evolving body of constitutional law. [16]Date of referendum approving significant constitutional amendments. [17]Statutory number of seats. [18]Defined by equidistant line. [19]Per non-democratic national referendum of Nov. 24, 1996, amending the constitution. [20]Excludes children of the monarch serving ex officio from age 18. [21]5 region/community councils; 10 provincial councils. [22]Defined by coordinates of points. [23]6 districts; 8 town boards. [24]3 nautical miles from the mouth of the Sarstoon River (southern boundary with Guatemala) to Ranguana Caye. [25]Executive responsibilities divided between (for the U.K.) the governor and (locally) the premier. [26]Resembles a constitutional monarchy without a formal constitution. [27]Date of international treaty confirming the existence of a single state under the final international authority of the high representative. [28]Tripartite presidency. [29]Cantons only; Republika Srpska has no cantons. [30]Body with limited or no legislative authority. [31]Sections of the constitution have been suspended since 1962. [32]Implementation date of Arusha Accords. [33]Transitional government. [34]Assisted by the vice president. [35]Date significant amendments adopted. [36]Governor-general can exercise all the powers of the reigning monarch of the Commonwealth. [37]Effective date of new government. [38]In actuality, a loose union of semiautonomous islands. [39]Assisted by vice presidents. [40]Transitional constitution. [41]Suspended membership. [42]Republic of Cyprus only. [43]24 seats reserved for Turkish Cypriots are not occupied. [44]Zone defined by geographic coordinates. [45]Constitution adopted in May 1997 had not been promulgated by November 2004. [46]Partially delimited by Eritrea–Yemeni arbitration. [47]Defined by coordinates in some parts of the Gulf of Finland. [48]Executive responsibilities divided between (for Denmark) the high commissioner and (locally) the prime minister. [49]Or agreed boundaries or median line. [50]3 nautical miles in the Gulf of Finland. [51]Executive responsibilities divided among (for France) the prefect and (locally) the president of the General Council and the president of the Regional Council. [52]Represented by high commissioner. [53]Date of agreement providing for Palestinian self-rule. [54]Acting president of the Palestinian Authority

United Nations (date of admission)	UNCTAD★	ICJ★[e]	FAO	IAEA	IBRD	ICAO	ICC[f]	IDA	ILO	IMF	IMO	ITU	UNESCO	UNIDO	WHO	WIPO	WTO	The Commonwealth	AC	ASEAN	ATs	AU	EU	GCC	LAS	OAS	PC	ACP	ADB	APEC	CARICOM	ECOWAS	FZ	I-ADB	IDB	OPEC	country
membership in international organizations:	UN organs★ and affiliated intergovernmental organizations																		regional multipurpose									economic									
1960	●		●	●	●	●		●	●	●	●	●	●	●	●	●	●					●						●				●	●		●		Niger
1960	●		●	●	●	●		●	●	●	●	●	●	●	●	●	●	●				●						●				●				●	Nigeria
—																											●										Northern Mariana Is.
1945	●		●	●	●	●		●	●	●	●	●	●	●	●	●	●		●		●								●					●			Norway
1971	●		●		●	●		●	●	●	●	●	●	●	●	●	●							●	●										●		Oman
1947	●		●	●	●	●		●	●	●	●	●	●	●	●	●	●	●											●						●		Pakistan
1994	●		●		●	●		●		●			●		●												●	●	●								Palau
1945	●		●	●	●	●		●	●	●	●	●	●	●	●	●	●									●								●			Panama
1975	●		●		●	●		●	●	●	●	●	●	●	●	●	●	●			●							●	●	●							Papua New Guinea
1945	●		●	●	●	●		●	●	●	●	●	●	●	●	●	●									●								●			Paraguay
1945	●		●	●	●	●		●	●	●	●	●	●	●	●	●	●				●					●				●				●			Peru
1945	●		●	●	●	●		●	●	●	●	●	●	●	●	●	●			●									●	●							Philippines
1945	●		●	●	●	●		●	●	●	●	●	●	●	●	●	●				●		●														Poland
1955	●		●	●	●	●		●	●	●	●	●	●	●	●	●	●						●						●					●			Portugal
—			12									●			12																						Puerto Rico
1971	●		●	●	●	●			●	●	●	●	●	●	●	●	●							●	●										●	●	Qatar
—												●																					●				Réunion
1955	●		●	●	●	●		●	●	●	●	●	●	●	●	●	●				●																Romania
1991	●	●		●	●	●		●	●	●	●	●	●	●	●	●	4		●		●									●							Russia
1962	●		●		●	●		●	●	●		●	●	●	●	●	●					●						●									Rwanda
1983	●		●		●	●		●	●	●	●		●	●	●	●	●	●								●		●			●						St. Kitts and Nevis
1979	●		●		●	●		●	●	●	●	●	●	●	●	●	●	●								●		●			●						St. Lucia
1980	●		●		●	●		●	●	●	●	●	●	●	●	●	●	●								●		●			●						St. Vincent
1976	●		●		●	●	●	●		●	●	●	●		●	●	4	●									●	●	●								Samoa
1992	●		●		●	●			●	●	●	●	●		●	●																					San Marino
1975	●		●		●	●		●	●	●	●	●	●	●	●	●	4					●						●									São Tomé and Príncipe
1945	●		●	●	●	●		●	●	●	●	●	●	●	●	●	4							●	●										●	●	Saudi Arabia
1960	●		●	●	●	●		●	●	●	●	●	●	●	●	●	●					●						●				●	●		●		Senegal
1945	●		●	●	●	●		●	●	●	●	●	●	●	●	●	4																				Serbia and Montenegro
1976	●		●	●	●	●			●	●	●	●	●	●	●	●	4	●				●						●									Seychelles
1961	●	●	●	●	●	●		●	●	●	●	●	●	●	●	●	●	●				●						●				●			●		Sierra Leone
1965	●			●	●	●		●	●	●	●	●			●	●	●	●		●									●	●							Singapore
1993	●	●	●	●	●	●		●	●	●	●	●	●	●	●	●	●				●		●														Slovakia
1992	●		●	●	●	●		●	●	●	●	●	●	●	●	●	●						●											●			Slovenia
1978	●		●		●	●		●	●	●	●	●	●		●		●	●									●	●	●								Solomon Islands
1960	●		●		●	●		●	●	●	●	●	●	●	●	●						●			●			●							●		Somalia
1945	●		●	●	●	●	●	●	●	●	●	●	●	●	●	●	●	●			●	●						●									South Africa
1955	●		●	●	●	●		●	●	●	●	●	●	●	●	●	●				●		●						●					●			Spain
1955	●		●	●	●	●		●	●	●	●	●	●	●	●	●	●	●											●								Sri Lanka
1956	●		●	●	●	●		●	●	●	●	●	●	●	●	●	4					●			●			●							●		Sudan, The
1975	●		●		●	●			●	●	●	●	●	●	●	●	●									●		●			●			●	●		Suriname
1968	●		●		●	●		●	●	●	●	●	●	●	●	●	●	●				●						●									Swaziland
1946	●		●	●	●	●		●	●	●	●	●	●	●	●	●	●		●		●		●						●					●			Sweden
2002	●		●	●	●	●		●	●	●	●	●	●	●	●	●	●				●								●					●			Switzerland
1945	●		●	●	●	●		●	●	●	●	●	●	●	●	●									●										●		Syria
—																	●												●	●							Taiwan
1992	●		●	●	●	●		●	●	●		●	●	●	●	●	4												●						●		Tajikistan
1961	●		●	●	●	●		●	●	●	●	●	●	●	●	●	●	●				●						●									Tanzania
1946	●		●	●	●	●		●	●	●	●	●	●	●	●	●	●			●									●	●							Thailand
1960	●		●		●	●		●	●	●	●	●	●	●	●	●	●					●						●				●	●		●		Togo
1999	●		●		●	●		●		●	●	●	●	●	●	●	4	●									●	●	●								Tonga
1962	●		●		●	●	●	●	●	●	●	●	●	●	●	●	●	●								●		●			●			●			Trinidad and Tobago
1956	●		●	●	●	●		●	●	●	●	●	●	●	●	●	●					●			●										●		Tunisia
1945	●		●	●	●	●		●	●	●	●	●	●	●	●	●	●				●								●						●		Turkey
1992	●		●		●	●			●	●	●	●	●	●	●	●													●						●		Turkmenistan
2000	●		●								●	●	●		●			●									●	●	●								Tuvalu
1962	●		●	●	●	●		●	●	●		●	●	●	●	●	●	●				●						●							●		Uganda
1945	●		●	●	●	●		●	●	●	●	●	●	●	●	●	4				●																Ukraine
1971	●		●	●	●	●		●	●	●	●	●	●	●	●	●	●							●	●										●	●	United Arab Emirates
1945	●	●	●	●	●	●	●	●	●	●	●	●	●	●	●	●	●	●			●		●				●		●					●			United Kingdom
1945	●	●	●	●	●	●		●	●	●	●	●	●		●	●	●		●		●					●	●		●	●				●			United States
1945	●		●	●	●	●			●	●	●	●	●	●	●	●	●				●					●								●			Uruguay
1992	●		●	●	●	●		●	●	●		●	●	●	●	●	4												●						●		Uzbekistan
1981	●		●		●	●		●	●	●	●	●	●	●	●		4	●									●	●	●								Vanuatu
1945	●	●	●	●	●	●			●	●	●	●	●	●	●	●	●				●					●								●		●	Venezuela
1977	●		●	●	●	●		●	●	●	●	●	●	●	●	●	4			●									●	●							Vietnam
—												●																			●						Virgin Islands (U.S.)
—																									●[55]										●[55]		West Bank
—																						104															Western Sahara
1947	●		●	●	●	●		●	●	●	●	●	●	●	●	●	4								●										●		Yemen
1964	●		●	●	●	●		●	●	●		●	●	●	●	●	●	●				●						●									Zambia
1980	●		●	●	●	●		●	●	●		●	●	●	●	●	●	105				●						●									Zimbabwe

assisted by the prime minister in December 2004. [55]As Palestine. [56]Date parliament approved constitutional amendments for 78 articles. [57]Represented by the lieutenant governor. [58]Executive committees appointed by the States of Deliberation. [59]Legal ambiguity persists in November 2004. The 2001 constitution approved by the National Assembly has neither been promulgated nor vetoed by the president. [60]Special administrative region (China). [61]Has been significantly amended. [62]Number of towns. [63]Shares coexecutive authority with spiritual leader. [64]Sea of Oman only; median line boundaries in Persian Gulf. [65]The date the Iraqi interim government assumed sovereign authority. [66]Median line boundary between the Isle of Man and the United Kingdom. [67]The emperor is the symbol of state. [68]3 nautical miles in 5 straits. [69]Executive committees appointed by the States of Jersey. [70]Essentially 1992 constitution with new preamble. [71]Number of cities and counties. [72]Elected seats only. [73]Number of non-district towns and districts. [74]Limits established by international agreements with Estonia, Lithuania, and Sweden. [75]Date of peace accord laying framework for transitional government. [76]Formally a *jamahiriya,* translated as "the masses of people"; in fact, a military dictatorship. [77]De facto chief of state. [78]Date parliament adopted significant constitutional amendments. [79]Under prince's authority. [80]Includes Western Sahara annexure. [81]Development regions. [82]Represented by high commissioner. [83]Basic law promulgated by sultan. [84]Has 2 consultative bodies with advisory authority only. [85]Rectangle defined by coordinates; claim extends beyond 12 mi. [86]Excludes additional seats for both houses of the legislature to meet 1/3 total representation requirements for minority parties per constitution. [87]Date constitution approved by emir; constitution is to become fully effective in 2005. [88]Per effective implementation of constitution. [89]Mixed political system approximating a constitutional monarchy. [90]Royal decrees from March 1, 1992, created first written rules of governance. [91]Assisted by crown prince; crown prince has assumed some powers of king because of king's illness. [92]"Loose confederation." [93]Assisted by Council of Ministers. [94]Excludes Kosovo. [95]Approval date of federal transitional charter. [96]No effective central government in December 2004. [97]Occupied seats. [98]Atlantic Ocean only. [99]Draft constitution released in 2003 not effective in December 2004. [100]Black Sea and Mediterranean Sea; 6 nautical miles in Aegean Sea. [101]In the Black Sea only. [102]Based on evolving body of statutes and common law. [103]Number of cities and districts. [104]Membership held by the Saharawi Arab Democratic Republic. [105]Officially withdrew from the Commonwealth in December 2003.

Area and population

This table provides the area and particular populations for each of the countries of the world and for all but the smallest political dependencies having a permanent civilian population. The data represent the latest published and unpublished data for both the surveyed area of the countries and their populations, the latter as of a single recent year (2004), as of a recent census to provide the fullest comparison of certain demographic measures that are not always available between successive national censuses, and as of decade population estimates over a seventy year (1950–2020) span. The 2004 midyear estimates (as a population estimate by decade) are based on a combination of national sources (both print and online), the United Nations' *World Population Prospects: The 2002 Revision,* the U.S. Bureau of the Census International Data Base, databases of other international organizations, and *Encyclopædia Britannica*'s own estimates.

One principal point to bear in mind when studying these statistics is that all of them, whatever degree of precision may be implied by the exactness of the numbers, are estimates—all of varying, and some of suspect, accuracy—even when they *contain* a very full enumeration. The United States—which has a long tradition both of census taking and of the use of the most sophisticated analytical tools in processing the data—is unable to determine within 1.2% (the estimated 2000 undercount) its total population nationally. And that is an *average* underenumeration. In states and larger cities, where enumeration of particular populations, including illegal, is more difficult, the accuracy of the enumerated count may be off as much as 3.1% at a state level (in New Mexico, for instance) and by a greater percent for a single city. The high accuracy attained by census operations in China may approach 0.25% of rigorously maintained civil population registers. Other national census operations not so based, however, are inherently less accurate. For example, Ethiopia's first-ever census in 1984 resulted in figures that were 30% or more above prevailing estimates; Nigeria's 1991 census corrected decades of miscounts and was well below prevailing estimates. An undercount of 2–8% is more typical, but even census operations offering results of 30% or more above or below prevailing estimates can still represent well-founded benchmarks from which future planning may proceed. The editors have tried to take account of the range of variation and accuracy in published data, but it is difficult to establish a value for many sources of inaccuracy unless some country or agency has made a conscientious effort to establish both the relative accuracy (precision) of its estimate and the absolute magnitude of the quantity it is trying to measure—for example, the number of people in Cambodia who died at the hands of the Khmer Rouge. If a figure of 2,000,000 is adopted, what is its accuracy: ± 1%, 10%, 50%? Are the original data documentary or evidentiary, complete or incomplete, analytically biased or unbiased, in good agreement with other published data?

Many similar problems exist and in endless variations: What is the extent of eastern European immigration to western Europe in search of jobs? How many registered and unregistered refugees from Afghanistan, Sierra Leone, or Burundi are there in surrounding countries? How many undocumented aliens are there in the United Kingdom, Japan, or the United States? How many Tamils have left Sri Lanka as a result of civil unrest in their homeland? How many Amerindians exist (remain, preserving their original language and a mode of life unassimilated by the larger national culture) in the countries of South America?

Area and population

country	area			population (latest estimate)					population (recent census)				
	square miles	square kilometres	rank	total midyear 2004	rank	density per sq mi	density per sq km	% annual growth rate 1999–2004	census year	total	male (%)	female (%)	urban (%)
Afghanistan	249,347	645,807	41	20,869,000	49	83.7	32.3	3.8	1979	13,051,358[1]	51.4	48.6	15.1
Albania	11,082	28,703	142	3,136,000	133	283.0	109.3	0.2	2001	3,069,275	49.9	50.1	42.2
Algeria	919,595	2,381,741	11	32,322,000	34	35.1	13.6	1.5	1998	29,272,343	50.6	49.4	80.8
American Samoa	77	200	206	62,700	207	814.3	313.5	2.1	2000	57,291	51.1	48.9	46.6[2]
Andorra	179	464	193	67,600	204	377.7	145.7	0.5	2003[3, 4]	67,159	51.8	48.2	92.0[2]
Angola	481,354	1,246,700	24	10,979,000	72	22.8	8.8	2.0	1970	5,673,046	52.1	47.9	14.2
Antigua and Barbuda	171	442	196	68,300	203	399.4	154.5	0.7	2001	72,309[5]	48.3	51.7	37.1[6]
Argentina	1,073,400	2,780,092	8	39,145,000	31	36.5	14.1	1.1	2001	36,260,130	48.7	51.3	88.3[6]
Armenia	11,484	29,743	141	2,991,000	134	260.4	100.6	–0.4	2001	3,002,594	46.9	53.1	64.8
Aruba	75	193	207	95,600	196	1,274.7	495.3	1.3	2000	90,506	48.0	52.0	50.5[2]
Australia	2,969,978	7,692,208	6	20,141,000	52	6.8	2.6	1.3	2001	18,972,350	49.3	50.7	91.2[6]
Austria	32,383	83,871	114	8,105,000	90	250.3	96.6	0.2	2001	8,032,926	48.4	51.6	66.8
Azerbaijan	33,400	86,600	113	8,343,000	88	249.8	96.3	0.9	1999	7,953,438	48.8	51.2	56.9[7]
Bahamas, The	5,382	13,939	159	317,000	175	58.9	22.7	1.2	2000	303,611	48.7	51.3	88.4[2]
Bahrain	277	718	186	709,000	161	2,559.6	987.5	2.7	2001	650,604	57.4	42.6	88.4
Bangladesh	56,977	147,570	93	135,255,000	8	2,373.9	916.5	1.4	2001	123,151,246[8]	50.9	49.1	23.4
Barbados	166	430	197	273,000	179	1,644.6	634.9	0.4	2000	250,010[9]	48.0	52.0	50.0[2]
Belarus	80,153	207,595	85	9,828,000	81	122.6	47.3	–0.4	1999	10,045,237	47.0	53.0	69.3
Belgium	11,787	30,528	139	10,416,000	76	883.7	341.9	0.4	1996[3, 4]	10,143,047	48.9	51.1	96.8
Belize	8,867	22,965	150	283,000	178	31.9	12.3	3.1	2000	240,204	50.5	49.5	47.7
Benin	43,484	112,622	101	7,250,000	94	166.7	64.4	3.1	1992	4,915,555	48.6	51.4	35.7
Bermuda	21	54	213	64,000	205	3,047.6	1,185.2	0.7	2000[10]	62,059	48.0	52.0	100.0
Bhutan	14,824	38,394	135	700,000	162	47.2	18.2	2.1	...	...	50.5[2]	49.5[2]	21.0[2]
Bolivia	424,164	1,098,581	28	8,724,000	85	20.6	7.9	1.7	2001	8,274,325	49.8	50.2	62.4
Bosnia and Herzegovina	19,772	51,209	127	3,870,000	125	195.7	75.6	1.0	1991	4,377,033	49.9	50.1	39.6
Botswana	224,848	582,356	47	1,661,000	146	7.3	2.9	0.8	2001	1,680,863	48.4	51.6	51.5
Brazil	3,287,612	8,514,877	5	180,542,000	5	54.9	21.2	1.3	2000	169,872,856	49.2	50.8	81.2
Brunei	2,226	5,765	168	351,000	174	157.7	60.9	2.1	2001	332,844	50.8	49.2	72.8[6]
Bulgaria	42,858	111,002	103	7,715,000	92	180.0	69.5	–1.2	2001	7,928,901	48.7	51.3	69.0
Burkina Faso	103,456	267,950	75	13,575,000	62	131.2	50.7	2.7	1996	10,312,609	48.2	51.8	15.0[2]
Burundi	10,740	27,816	145	6,231,000	100	580.2	224.0	2.1	1990[10]	5,292,793	48.6	51.4	6.3
Cambodia	69,898	181,035	89	13,450,000	63	192.4	74.3	1.8	1998	11,437,656	48.2	51.8	20.9
Cameroon	183,569	475,442	53	16,064,000	59	87.5	33.8	2.1	1987	10,516,232	49.0	51.0	38.3
Canada	3,855,103	9,984,670	2	31,876,000	36	8.3	3.2	1.0	2001	30,007,094[8]	49.0[8]	51.0[8]	78.9[6]
Cape Verde	1,557	4,033	170	454,000	167	291.6	112.6	1.4	2000	434,625	48.5	51.5	53.4
Central African Republic	240,324	622,436	43	3,742,000	128	15.6	6.0	1.7	1988	2,688,426	49.1	50.9	36.5
Chad	495,755	1,284,000	21	9,539,000	82	19.2	7.4	3.2	1993	6,279,931	47.9	52.1	21.4
Chile	291,930	756,096	38	15,824,000	60	54.2	20.9	1.1	2002	15,116,435	49.3	50.7	86.6
China	3,696,100	9,572,900	3	1,298,848,000	1	351.4	135.7	0.6	2000	1,265,830,000	51.6	48.4	36.2
Colombia	440,762	1,141,568	26	42,311,000	29	96.0	37.1	1.6	1993	33,109,840	49.2	50.8	72.0[15]
Comoros	719	1,862	176	596,000	163	828.9	320.1	2.0	1991	446,817	49.5	50.5	28.5
Congo, Dem. Rep. of the	905,354	2,344,858	12	54,417,000	23	60.1	23.2	2.7	1984	29,671,407	49.2	50.8	29.1[15]
Congo, Rep. of the	132,047	342,000	63	3,818,000	126	28.9	11.2	2.6	1984[10]	1,909,248	48.7	51.3	52.0
Costa Rica	19,730	51,100	128	4,252,000	119	215.5	83.2	2.1	2000	3,810,179	49.9	50.1	59.0
Côte d'Ivoire	123,863	320,803	68	16,897,000	57	136.4	52.7	1.7	1998	15,366,672	51.0	49.0	43.6[2]
Croatia	21,851	56,594	126	4,497,000	116	205.8	79.5	0.4	2001	4,437,460	48.1	51.9	58.1[6]
Cuba	42,804	110,860	104	11,300,000	70	264.0	101.9	0.2	1993	10,904,466	50.3	49.7	74.4
Cyprus[17]	3,572	9,251	165	937,000	155	262.3	101.3	1.6	2001[18]	689,565	49.1	50.9	68.8
Czech Republic	30,450	78,866	117	10,212,000	78	335.4	129.5	–0.1	2001	10,230,060	48.7	51.3	74.6
Denmark	16,640	43,098	132	5,401,000	107	324.6	125.3	0.3	2003[3]	5,383,507	49.5	50.5	85.3
Djibouti	8,950	23,200	149	467,000	165	52.2	20.1	1.8	1983	273,974	51.9	48.1	82.8[15]
Dominica	290	750	184	69,300	202	239.0	92.4	–0.8	2001	71,239	51.0	49.0	71.4[6]
Dominican Republic	18,792	48,671	130	8,834,000	84	470.1	181.5	1.7	2002	8,562,541	49.8	50.2	63.6
East Timor	5,639	14,604	158	925,000	156	164.0	63.3	5.3	1990	747,750	51.7	48.3	7.8
Ecuador	105,037	272,045	73	13,213,000	64	125.8	48.6	1.4	2001	12,156,608	49.5	50.5	61.0[22]

Still, much information is accurate, well founded, and updated regularly. The sources of these data are censuses; national population registers (cumulated periodically); registration of migration, births, deaths, and so on; sample surveys to establish demographic conditions; and the like.

The statistics provided for area and population by country are ranked, and the population densities based on those values are also provided. The population densities, for purposes of comparison within this table, are calculated on the bases of the 2004 midyear population estimate as shown and of total area of the country. Elsewhere in individual country presentations the reader may find densities calculated on more specific population figures and more specialized area bases: land area for Finland (because of its many lakes) or ice-free area for Greenland (most of which is ice cap). The data in this section conclude with the estimated average annual growth rate for the country (including both natural growth and net migration) during the five-year period 1999–2004.

In the section containing census data, information supplied includes the census total (usually de facto, the population actually present, rather than de jure, the population legally resident, who might be anywhere); the male-female breakdown; the proportion that is urban (usually according to the country's own definition); and finally an analysis of the age structure of the population by 15-year age groups. This last analysis may be particularly useful in distinguishing the type of population being recorded—young, fast-growing nations show a high proportion of people under 30 (many countries in sub-Saharan Africa and the Middle East have about 40% of their population under 15 years), while other nations (for example, Sweden, which suffered no age-group losses in World War II) exhibit quite uniform proportions.

Finally, a section is provided giving the population of each country at 10-year intervals from 1950 to 2020 based on sources cited earlier. The projections for 2010 and 2020 represent the best fit of available data through the autumn of 2004. The evidence of the last 30 years with respect to similar estimates published about 1970, however, shows how cloudy is the glass through which these numbers are read. In 1970 no respectable Western analyst would have imagined proposing that mainland China could achieve the degree of birth control that it apparently has since then; on the other hand, even the Chinese admit that their methods have been somewhat Draconian and that they have already seen some backlash in terms of higher birth rates among those who have so far postponed larger families. How much is "some" by 2010? Compound that problem with all the social, economic, political, and biological factors (including the impact of AIDS) that can affect 217 countries' populations, and the difficulty facing the prospective compiler of such projections may be appreciated.

Specific data about the vital rates affecting the data in this table may be found in great detail in both the country statistical boxes in "The Nations of the World" section and in the *Vital statistics, marriage, family* table, beginning at page 770.

Percentages in this table for male and female population will always total 100.0, but percentages by age group may not, for reasons such as nonresponse on census forms, "don't know" responses (which are common in countries with poor birth registration systems), and the like.

age distribution (%)						population (by decade, '000s)								country
0–14	15–29	30–44	45–59	60–74	75 and over	1950	1960	1970	1980	1990	2000	2010 projection	2020 projection	
44.5	26.9	15.8	8.6	3.6	0.6	8,151	10,051	12,721	15,117	13,799	19,995	26,149	33,546	Afghanistan
29.3	24.1	21.2	14.2	8.7	2.5	1,227	1,623	2,157	2,671	3,289	3,084	3,275	3,484	Albania
36.2	30.6	17.7	8.9	5.1	1.5	8,753	10,800	13,746	18,740	25,022	30,416	35,549	40,479	Algeria
38.8	25.5	19.4	10.8	4.5	1.0	19	20	27	32	47	58	62	58	American Samoa
15.1	18.0	29.1	20.5	11.1	6.2	6	8	19	33	53	66	70	73	Andorra
41.7	23.2	17.0	7.4	3.8	1.0	4,118	4,797	5,606	6,736	8,049	10,132	12,250	14,473	Angola
26.4	25.4	23.9	13.9	—10.4—		46	55	66	69	63	66	71	74	Antigua and Barbuda
28.3	25.0	18.6	14.7	9.3	4.1	17,150	20,616	23,962	28,370	33,022	37,498	41,405	44,524	Argentina
24.8	24.9	21.8	13.6	12.1	2.8	1,355	1,869	2,520	3,115	3,377	3,043	2,967	3,017	Armenia
23.2	19.4	28.0	18.2	8.6	2.6	51	57	61	60	64	91	100	108	Aruba
20.6[6]	21.1[6]	22.9[6]	18.7[6]	10.9[6]	5.8[6]	8,219	10,315	12,552	14,471	17,065	19,153	21,107	22,765	Australia
16.9	18.6	24.9	18.6	13.8	7.2	6,935	7,048	7,447	7,549	7,729	8,038	8,255	8,401	Austria
31.8	25.6	24.1	9.5	7.6	1.4	2,896	3,895	5,172	6,165	7,166	8,048	8,865	9,746	Azerbaijan
29.6	25.8	24.2	12.6	5.9	1.9	79	110	170	210	256	304	336	363	Bahamas, The
27.9	27.5	29.6	11.0	3.2	0.8	110	149	210	334	503	638	795	930	Bahrain
35.9	31.5	17.6	0.0	4.0	1.1	45,040	54,622	67,403	88,077	109,897	128,100	146,939	168,698	Bangladesh
21.8	22.5	24.4	16.0	—15.3—		209	232	235	249	261	268	278	283	Barbados
19.5	21.8	23.4	16.4	—18.9—		7,745	8,190	9,040	9,650	10,186	10,005	9,587	9,184	Belarus
17.9	20.0	23.0	17.7	15.0	6.4	8,639	9,153	9,690	9,859	9,967	10,251	10,506	10,577	Belgium
41.0	27.7	17.4	8.1	—5.8—		68	90	120	146	189	250	315	381	Belize
48.6	24.2	14.5	6.6	4.1	1.9	1,673	2,055	2,620	3,444	4,662	6,428	8,504	10,647	Benin
19.1	18.4	27.9	19.6	10.9	4.1	37	43	53	55	58	62	66	69	Bermuda
40.2[2]	26.0[2]	17.4[2]	10.1[2]	5.2[2]	1.1[2]	…	…	…	…	519	638	793	965	Bhutan
38.6	27.4	17.0	10.0	5.2	1.8	2,766	3,434	4,346	5,441	6,574	8,153	9,499	10,747	Bolivia
23.5[11]	26.3[11]	22.6[11]	16.9[11]	8.9[11]	2.7[11]	2,662	3,240	3,703	4,092	4,424	3,744	3,962	4,039	Bosnia and Herzegovina
40.2[6]	31.2[6]	14.8[6]	7.7[6]	4.4[6]	1.7[6]	430	497	584	914	1,312	1,636	1,505	1,220	Botswana
29.6	28.2	21.1	12.5	6.5	2.1	53,975	72,742	95,988	121,614	148,809	171,796	192,879	209,793	Brazil
30.8[6]	27.0[6]	25.4[6]	12.5[6]	3.5[6]	0.8[6]	45	83	128	185	258	324	393	458	Brunei
15.0[12]	21.3[12]	20.4[12]	20.9[12]	16.1[12]	6.3[12]	7,251	7,867	8,490	8,862	8,718	8,170	7,353	6,781	Bulgaria
47.9[13]	26.8[13]	12.9[13]	7.6[13]	3.9[13]	0.9[13]	4,376	4,866	5,626	6,942	9,090	12,217	15,748	19,965	Burkina Faso
46.4	25.3	15.4	7.0	4.0	1.7	2,363	2,812	3,513	4,138	5,285	5,713	7,296	9,174	Burundi
42.8	26.1	17.2	8.5	4.3	1.1	4,163	5,364	6,984	6,586	9,271	12,565	14,971	17,768	Cambodia
46.4	24.5	14.6	8.7	4.1	1.6	4,888	5,609	6,727	8,748	11,685	14,792	17,938	20,946	Cameroon
18.3[14]	20.3[14]	23.5[14]	20.7[14]	11.3[14]	5.9[14]	13,737	17,909	21,324	24,516	27,701	30,689	33,296	35,390	Canada
43.6[2]	24.8[2]	17.1[2]	5.8[2]	6.3[2]	2.4[2]	146	197	269	296	349	431	472	491	Cape Verde
43.2	27.5	15.0	9.2	4.1	0.8	1,260	1,467	1,827	2,244	2,803	3,501	4,073	4,557	Central African Republic
48.1	24.6	14.7	7.2	4.2	1.3	2,608	3,042	3,731	4,542	6,030	8,419	11,302	14,671	Chad
25.7	24.3	23.6	15.0	8.3	3.1	6,091	7,585	9,369	11,094	13,128	15,153	16,720	18,008	Chile
22.9	25.4	25.6	15.7	8.2	2.2	562,580	650,661	820,403	984,736	1,148,364	1,268,853	1,347,563	1,430,533	China
34.5	28.5	20.1	10.0	5.3	1.6	11,592	16,063	21,430	26,583	32,059	39,686	46,109	52,199	Colombia
47.6[11]	27.0[11]	13.1[11]	7.7[11]	3.5[11]	1.0[11]	148	183	236	334	429	549	672	822	Comoros
47.3[15]	25.9[15]	14.1[15]	8.1[15]	3.8[15]	0.8[15]	12,184	15,438	20,603	27,909	37,370	48,571	64,714	84,418	Congo, Dem. Rep. of the
44.7	27.2	13.3	9.1	4.6	0.7	808	1,004	1,323	1,804	2,494	3,447	4,532	5,960	Congo, Rep. of the
31.9	27.1	21.7	11.4	5.7	2.2	862	1,236	1,758	2,302	3,051	3,925	4,732	5,474	Costa Rica
46.5[16]	27.5[16]	14.9[16]	7.6[16]	3.0[16]	0.5[16]	2,775	3,803	5,521	8,427	12,505	15,827	18,526	21,026	Côte d'Ivoire
17.1	20.4	21.4	19.5	16.3	5.3	3,837	4,036	4,205	4,383	4,508	4,411	4,487	4,427	Croatia
22.3	29.4	21.3	14.8	8.4	3.9	5,850	7,028	8,572	9,780	10,603	11,199	11,447	11,528	Cuba
21.5[19]	22.6[19]	22.0[19]	17.8[19]	11.2[19]	4.9[19]	494	573	615	658	751	902	965	1,002	Cyprus[17]
16.3	23.5	20.1	21.8	12.8	5.5	8,925	9,539	9,805	10,326	10,363	10,273	10,167	9,980	Czech Republic
18.8	17.9	22.3	20.9	13.1	7.0	4,271	4,581	4,929	5,123	5,140	5,337	5,421	5,431	Denmark
39.4	32.9	16.9	7.4	2.8	0.6	60	78	158	279	366	431	526	627	Djibouti
32.7	28.4	17.2	9.5	—12.2—		51	60	70	75	73	72	70	75	Dominica
34.0[20]	27.1[20]	20.2[20]	11.2[20]	5.9[20]	1.6[20]	2,353	3,231	4,009	5,431	6,811	8,263	9,521	10,626	Dominican Republic
41.5[21]	28.4[21]	17.7[21]	8.9[21]	3.1[21]	0.4[21]	433	501	604	581	740	702	1,101	1,284	East Timor
34.0[22]	28.0[22]	19.0[22]	10.0[22]	6.0[22]	3.0[22]	3,370	4,416	5,939	7,920	10,318	12,505	14,245	16,178	Ecuador

Area and population (continued)

country	area			population (latest estimate)					population (recent census)				
	square miles	square kilo-metres	rank	total midyear 2004	rank	density per sq mi	density per sq km	% annual growth rate 1999–2004	census year	total	male (%)	female (%)	urban (%)
Egypt	385,229	997,739	30	69,261,000	16	179.8	69.4	1.8	1996	59,312,914	51.2	48.8	42.6
El Salvador	8,124	21,042	151	6,698,000	97	824.5	318.3	1.9	1992	5,118,599	48.6	51.4	50.4
Equatorial Guinea	10,831	28,051	144	507,000	164	46.8	18.1	2.7	1983	300,060	48.8	51.2	28.2
Eritrea	46,774	121,144	99	4,297,000	118	91.9	35.5	3.7	1984	2,703,998	49.9	50.1	15.1
Estonia	17,462	45,227	131	1,342,000	151	76.9	29.7	–0.7	2000	1,370,052	46.1	53.9	69.2
Ethiopia	435,186	127,127	27	67,851,000	17	155.9	60.2	2.1	1994	53,477,265	50.3	49.7	14.4[15]
Faroe Islands	540	1,399	178	48,500	210	89.8	34.7	1.5	2003[3, 4]	47,704	51.9	48.1	38.6
Fiji	7,055	18,272	155	839,000	157	118.9	45.9	0.8	1996	775,077	50.8	49.2	46.4
Finland	130,559	338,145	64	5,226,000	110	40.0	15.5	0.2	2003[3, 4]	5,206,295	48.9	51.1	83.3
France	210,026	543,965	49	60,044,000	20	285.9	110.4	0.5	1999	58,518,748	48.6	51.4	75.5
French Guiana	32,253	83,534	116	182,000	185	5.6	2.2	2.7	1999	157,274	50.4	49.6	77.8[7]
French Polynesia	1,544	4,000	171	252,000	181	163.2	63.0	1.7	2002	245,405	51.4	48.6	52.1[24]
Gabon	103,347	267,667	76	1,351,000	150	13.1	5.0	1.9	1993	1,011,710	49.3	50.7	73.2
Gambia, The	4,127	10,689	163	1,405,000	148	340.4	131.4	2.7	2003	1,364,507	49.6	50.4	26.1[24]
Gaza Strip	140	363	200	1,414,000	147	10,100.0	3,895.3	5.3	1997	1,001,569	50.7	49.3	95.9
Georgia	27,086	70,152	121	4,694,000	114	173.3	66.9	–0.5	2002	4,371,534[26]	47.2	52.8	52.3
Germany	137,847	357,023	62	82,561,000	13	598.9	231.2	0.1	2003[3]	82,536,700	48.9	51.1	88.1[24]
Ghana	92,098	238,533	81	20,732,000	51	225.1	86.9	2.3	2000	18,845,265	49.5	50.5	43.9[2]
Greece	50,949	131,957	96	11,015,000	71	216.2	83.5	0.3	2001	10,964,020	49.5	50.5	72.8
Greenland	836,330	2,166,086	13	56,800	208	0.07	0.03	0.2	2003[3, 4]	56,676	53.4	46.6	82.2
Grenada	133	344	202	103,000	194	774.4	299.4	0.5	2001	101,306	49.6	50.4	38.4
Guadeloupe	658	1,705	177	443,000	170	673.3	259.8	0.9	1999	422,496	48.1	51.9	99.7[7]
Guam	217	561	191	165,000	188	760.4	294.1	1.5	2000	154,805	51.1	48.9	93.2[2]
Guatemala	42,130	109,117	105	12,661,000	65	300.5	116.0	2.6	1994	8,331,874	49.3	50.7	35.0
Guernsey	30	78	211	63,300	206	2,110.0	811.5	0.3	2001[27]	59,807	48.7	51.3	28.9[6, 28]
Guinea	94,926	245,857	78	8,620,000	86	90.8	35.1	1.5	1996	7,165,750	48.8	51.2	26.0
Guinea-Bissau	13,948	36,125	137	1,388,000	149	99.5	38.4	2.1	1991	983,367	48.4	51.6	20.3[11]
Guyana	83,044	215,083	84	752,000	160	9.1	3.5	–0.7	2002	749,190	49.3	50.7	37.6[24]
Haiti	10,695	27,700	146	8,074,000	91	754.9	291.5	1.1	2003	7,929,048	48.3	51.7	37.5[24]
Honduras	43,433	112,492	102	6,948,000	95	160.0	61.8	2.3	2001	6,535,344	49.4	50.6	44.8
Hong Kong	425	1,102	180	6,848,000	96	16,112.9	6,214.2	0.7	2001	6,708,389	49.0	51.0	100.0
Hungary	35,919	93,030	110	10,103,000	79	281.3	108.6	–0.3	2001	10,197,119	47.6	52.4	64.3
Iceland	39,741	102,928	106	292,000	176	7.3	2.8	1.0	2003[3, 4]	288,471	50.0	50.0	93.8
India	1,222,559	3,166,414	7	1,081,229,000	2	884.4	341.5	1.6	2001	1,028,610,328	51.7	48.3	27.8
Indonesia	730,024	1,890,754	16	222,611,000	4	304.9	117.7	1.3	2000	206,264,595	50.1	49.9	42.0
Iran	636,374	1,648,200	18	67,503,000	18	106.1	41.0	0.8	1996	60,055,488	50.8	49.2	61.3
Iraq	167,618	434,128	58	25,375,000	43	151.4	58.5	2.9	1997	21,941,050	49.7	50.3	67.9
Ireland	27,133	70,273	122	4,024,000	123	148.3	57.3	1.4	2002	3,917,203	49.7	50.3	59.6
Isle of Man	221	572	190	77,700	201	351.6	135.8	0.8	2001[10]	76,315	49.0	51.0	72.6
Israel[31, 32]	8,367	21,671	152	6,562,000	99	784.3	302.8	2.0	1995[10, 33]	5,548,523	49.3	50.7	92.9[15]
Italy	116,343	301,328	72	57,537,000	22	494.5	190.9	0.2	2001	56,995,744	48.4	51.6	67.3
Jamaica	4,244	10,991	162	2,649,000	136	624.2	241.0	0.6	2001	2,607,632	49.2	50.8	56.6[6]
Japan	145,903	377,887	61	127,757,000	10	875.6	338.1	0.2	2000	126,925,843	48.9	51.1	78.7
Jersey	46	118	210	87,900	198	1,910.9	744.9	0.4	2001	87,186	48.7	51.3	28.9[6, 28]
Jordan	34,495	89,342	112	5,543,000	106	160.7	62.0	2.8	1994	4,139,458	52.2	47.8	78.3
Kazakhstan	1,052,090	2,724,900	9	15,144,000	61	14.4	5.6	0.1	1999	14,953,126	48.2	51.8	55.9
Kenya	224,961	582,646	46	32,022,000	35	142.3	55.0	1.4	1999	28,686,607	49.5	50.5	32.2[7]
Kiribati	313	811	182	89,100	197	284.7	109.9	1.3	2000	84,494	49.3	50.7	43.5
Korea, North	47,399	122,762	98	22,698,000	46	478.9	184.9	1.1	1993	21,213,378	48.7	51.3	58.9
Korea, South	38,572	99,900	108	48,199,000	24	1,249.6	482.5	0.7	2000	45,985,289	50.2	49.8	79.7
Kuwait	6,880	17,818	156	2,586,000	137	375.9	145.1	2.7	1995	1,575,570	58.5	41.5	97.0[15]
Kyrgyzstan	77,199	199,945	86	5,081,000	112	65.8	25.4	1.2	1999	4,822,938	49.4	50.6	34.8
Laos	91,429	236,800	83	5,787,000	101	63.3	24.4	2.3	1995	4,581,258	49.5	50.5	20.7[15]
Latvia	24,938	64,589	124	2,312,000	141	92.7	35.8	–0.7	2000	2,377,383	46.1	53.9	68.1
Lebanon	4,016	10,400	164	3,777,000	127	940.5	363.2	1.4	1997	4,005,025[35]	50.2[35]	49.8[35]	85.0[15]
Lesotho	11,720	30,355	140	1,800,000	145	153.6	59.3	0.4	1996[10]	1,960,069	49.2	50.8	16.9
Liberia	37,743	97,754	109	3,391,000	131	89.8	34.7	2.7	1984	2,101,628	50.6	49.4	38.8
Libya	679,362	1,759,540	17	5,659,000	104	8.3	3.2	2.0	1995[10]	4,404,986	50.8	49.2	85.3[15]
Liechtenstein	62	160	209	34,500	212	556.5	215.6	1.4	2003[3, 4]	33,863	49.1	50.9	21.6[24]
Lithuania	25,212	65,300	123	3,439,000	129	136.4	52.7	–0.5	2001	3,483,972	46.8	53.2	66.9
Luxembourg	999	2,586	173	454,000	167	454.5	175.6	1.1	2001	439,539	49.3	50.7	91.9[6]
Macau	10.5	27.3	214	451,000	169	42,952.4	16,520.1	1.1	2001	435,235	48.0	52.0	98.9[6]
Macedonia	9,928	25,713	148	2,035,000	142	205.0	79.1	0.2	2002	2,022,547	50.2	49.8	59.5[24]
Madagascar	226,658	587,041	45	17,082,000	56	75.4	29.1	2.6	1993	12,238,914	49.7	50.3	22.9
Malawi	45,747	118,484	100	11,907,000	67	260.3	100.5	2.3	1998	9,933,868	49.0	51.0	14.0
Malaysia	127,355	329,847	66	25,584,000	42	200.9	77.6	2.6	2000	23,274,690	50.9	49.1	62.0
Maldives	115	298	204	289,000	177	2,513.0	969.8	1.7	2000	270,101	50.8	49.2	27.4
Mali	482,077	1,248,574	23	11,957,000	66	24.8	9.6	2.9	1998	9,790,492	49.5	50.5	30.2[2]
Malta	122	315	203	401,000	172	3,286.9	1,273.0	0.7	1995	378,132	49.4	50.6	89.4[15]
Marshall Islands	70	181	208	54,600	209	780.0	301.7	1.4	1999	50,848	51.2	48.8	65.2
Martinique	436	1,128	179	395,000	173	906.0	350.2	0.7	1999	381,427	47.4	52.6	97.3
Mauritania	398,000	1,030,700	29	2,774,000	135	7.0	2.7	2.7	2000	2,508,159	49.5	50.5	57.7[2]
Mauritius	788	2,040	175	1,233,000	153	1,564.7	604.4	1.0	2000[10]	1,179,137	49.5	50.5	42.7[2]
Mayotte	144	374	199	172,000	187	1,194.4	459.9	4.0	2002	160,265	50.1	49.9	…
Mexico	758,449	1,964,375	15	105,447,000	11	139.0	53.7	1.1	2000	97,483,412	48.8	51.2	74.6
Micronesia	271	701	187	114,000	191	420.7	162.6	1.3	2000	107,008	50.6	49.4	28.3[2]
Moldova	13,068	33,845	138	4,216,000	121	322.6	124.6	–0.3	1989	4,337,592	47.5	52.5	46.9
Monaco	0.75	1.95	217	32,600	213	43,466.7	16,717.9	0.5	2000	32,020	48.5	51.5	100.0
Mongolia	603,909	1,564,116	19	2,519,000	139	4.2	1.6	1.3	2000	2,373,500	49.6	50.4	58.6
Morocco[36]	177,117	458,730	55	30,302,000	37	171.1	66.1	1.6	1994	25,821,571[37]	49.7[37]	50.3[37]	51.7[37]
Mozambique	313,661	812,379	35	18,812,000	54	60.0	23.2	1.7	1997	16,099,246	47.9	52.1	28.6
Myanmar (Burma)	261,228	676,577	40	42,720,000	28	163.5	63.1	0.6	1983	35,307,913	49.6	50.4	24.0
Namibia	318,580	825,118	34	1,954,000	144	6.2	2.4	1.8	2001	1,826,854	48.7	51.3	31.4[6]
Nauru	8.2	21.2	216	10,100	216	1,231.7	476.4	0.2	2002	10,065	51.2[38]	48.8[38]	100.0
Nepal	56,827	147,181	94	24,692,000	44	434.5	167.8	2.2	2001	23,151,423	49.9	50.1	14.2

age distribution (%) 0–14	15–29	30–44	45–59	60–74	75 and over	population (by decade, '000s) 1950	1960	1970	1980	1990	2000	2010 projection	2020 projection	country
37.7	27.6	18.6	10.4	5.0	0.7	20,461	26,085	33,329	40,546	51,959	64,590	76,751	88,531	Egypt
38.7	28.7	16.0	9.2	5.4	1.9	1,951	2,578	3,598	4,586	5,110	6,275	7,269	8,133	El Salvador
41.7	25.1	15.7	11.2	5.3	1.0	226	254	294	219	354	456	590	736	Equatorial Guinea
46.1	23.0	15.9	8.9	4.4	1.6	1,140	1,420	1,831	2,381	3,103	3,712	5,256	6,584	Eritrea
18.1	21.4	20.8	18.6	15.6	5.5	1,096	1,211	1,363	1,482	1,569	1,380	1,291	1,203	Estonia
46.1[23]	26.0[23]	15.1[23]	8.3[23]	3.8[23]	0.7[23]	20,175	24,252	29,673	36,413	47,958	62,651	75,066	85,965	Ethiopia
23.6	19.4	20.9	18.4	11.3	6.4	31	35	39	43	48	46	50	53	Faroe Islands
35.4	27.4	20.7	11.4	4.2	0.9	289	394	520	634	737	810	882	932	Fiji
17.8	18.6	20.6	22.5	13.6	6.9	4,009	4,430	4,606	4,800	4,986	5,176	5,267	5,317	Finland
17.9	20.2	21.9	18.7	13.6	7.7	41,736	45,684	50,770	53,880	56,710	58,879	61,499	63,196	France
34.0	24.2	23.3	12.5	4.3	1.7	27	33	49	68	116	164	208	252	French Guiana
29.9	26.0	23.5	13.3	5.9	1.4	62	84	117	151	197	235	275	308	French Polynesia
33.8[25]	23.7[25]	17.0[25]	17.4[25]	6.9[25]	1.2[25]	469	486	529	695	953	1,258	1,509	1,781	Gabon
44.9[24]	26.4[24]	15.5[24]	8.8[24]	3.6[24]	0.8[24]	294	355	469	652	925	1,264	1,617	1,939	Gambia, The
50.2	25.7	13.7	6.0	3.5	0.9	245	308	370	456	630	1,145	1,889	2,621	Gaza Strip
21.0	22.8	21.9	15.6	14.6	4.1	3,516	4,147	4,694	5,046	5,426	4,777	4,601	4,440	Georgia
14.9[24]	17.0[24]	24.3[24]	19.3[24]	16.9[24]	7.6[24]	68,377	72,674	77,709	78,275	79,365	82,188	82,419	81,471	Germany
41.2[2]	28.3[2]	17.3[2]	7.9[2]	4.3[2]	1.0[2]	5,297	6,958	8,789	11,016	14,543	18,978	23,359	27,625	Ghana
15.2	22.0	22.3	18.0	16.5	6.0	7,566	8,327	8,793	9,643	10,161	10,913	11,031	10,878	Greece
26.2	19.7	27.9	17.4	7.5	1.3	23	32	46	50	56	56	57	57	Greenland
35.1	28.1	17.6	9.0	——10.2——		76	90	95	89	95	100	106	112	Grenada
23.6	22.4	24.3	15.7	9.3	4.7	206	265	320	327	388	428	460	478	Guadeloupe
30.5	24.1	23.3	13.9	6.7	1.5	60	67	86	107	134	155	180	204	Guam
44.0	26.1	15.8	8.3	——5.8——		2,969	3,963	5,243	6,820	8,749	11,423	14,584	17,835	Guatemala
17.2	18.8	23.2	20.0	13.4	7.4	44	45	51	53	61	62	64	65	Guernsey
44.1[13]	26.5[13]	15.9[13]	9.0[13]	3.9[13]	0.6[13]	2,550	3,136	3,897	4,688	6,122	8,117	9,990	12,478	Guinea
43.9[11]	26.5[11]	16.1[11]	8.8[11]	3.7[11]	1.0[11]	573	617	620	789	996	1,278	1,566	1,882	Guinea-Bissau
27.6[20]	31.0[20]	21.3[20]	12.8[20]	5.4[20]	1.9[20]	428	560	714	759	750	772	755	732	Guyana
42.7[24]	29.3[24]	14.2[24]	8.2[24]	4.5[24]	1.1[24]	3,261	3,803	4,520	5,453	6,914	7,712	8,740	9,768	Haiti
42.2[6]	29.1[6]	15.1[6]	8.3[6]	4.1[6]	1.2[6]	1,431	1,952	2,683	3,635	4,876	6,352	7,884	9,155	Honduras
16.5	21.6	29.0	18.0	10.6	4.3	2,237	3,075	3,959	5,063	5,688	6,665	7,083	7,321	Hong Kong
16.1[29]	22.0[29]	19.7[29]	21.4[29]	14.4[29]	6.4[29]	9,338	9,984	10,337	10,707	10,374	10,211	9,949	9,669	Hungary
22.9	22.1	21.9	17.8	9.9	5.4	143	176	204	228	255	281	306	327	Iceland
33.1[6]	27.8[6]	19.9[6]	12.1[6]	5.6[6]	1.5[6]	357,561	442,344	554,911	688,856	846,418	1,016,343	1,173,806	1,312,212	India
30.4	29.3	21.8	11.3	5.8	1.4	79,538	95,931	119,998	150,128	182,117	211,559	238,374	261,053	Indonesia
44.3	26.6	15.1	8.2	4.8	0.8	16,357	21,577	28,933	39,583	57,036	65,660	71,861	80,002	Iran
43.8[30]	30.2[30]	14.5[30]	6.9[30]	3.6[30]	1.0[30]	5,163	6,822	9,413	13,233	18,135	22,676	29,672	36,908	Iraq
21.1	24.4	22.1	17.3	10.2	4.9	2,969	2,834	2,954	3,421	3,506	3,799	4,240	4,569	Ireland
17.9	17.5	22.6	20.1	13.6	8.3	55	49	52	64	69	76	80	84	Isle of Man
29.2	25.0	19.6	13.1	9.1	4.0	1,258	2,114	2,958	3,862	4,613	6,098	7,240	8,381	Israel[31, 32]
14.1[6]	18.9[6]	23.8[6]	19.0[6]	16.0[6]	8.2[6]	47,104	50,200	53,822	56,434	56,749	56,967	57,569	56,517	Italy
32.4[34]	26.1[34]	20.8[34]	11.0[34]	6.8[34]	2.9[34]	1,403	1,629	1,891	2,133	2,369	2,590	2,784	3,053	Jamaica
14.6	20.3	19.5	22.2	16.0	7.1	[illegible]	94,096	104,331	116,807	123,537	126,867	127,485	124,191	Japan
16.9	18.4	25.9	19.7	12.6	6.5	57	63	71	76	84	87	89	89	Jersey
41.3	31.8	14.6	8.1	3.4	0.8	1,095	1,384	1,795	2,183	3,306	4,970	6,304	7,464	Jordan
28.7	25.7	22.1	12.9	——10.6——		6,693	9,982	13,106	14,967	16,398	15,032	15,460	15,977	Kazakhstan
44.1[7]	31.3[7]	13.8[7]	6.7[7]	3.3[7]	0.8[7]	6,121	8,157	11,272	16,698	23,934	30,310	33,654	34,848	Kenya
40.1	25.2	19.8	9.7	——5.2——		33	41	49	58	71	84	95	107	Kiribati
29.5[25]	31.9[25]	21.3[25]	11.0[25]	5.0[25]	1.2[25]	9,471	10,392	13,912	17,114	20,019	21,648	23,802	25,210	Korea, North
21.0	25.3	26.7	15.8	8.9	2.3	21,147	25,012	32,241	38,124	42,869	47,008	49,335	50,285	Korea, South
30.0	28.4	30.0	9.2	——2.4——		145	292	748	1,358	2,141	2,236	3,032	3,634	Kuwait
36.2[7]	27.3[7]	18.6[7]	8.9[7]	7.2[7]	1.8[7]	1,740	2,171	2,964	3,623	4,382	4,861	5,500	6,014	Kyrgyzstan
45.4[15]	26.5[15]	14.9[15]	8.1[15]	4.2[15]	1.0[15]	1,755	2,177	2,713	3,205	4,132	5,279	6,592	7,967	Laos
18.1	21.2	21.4	18.3	15.7	5.3	1,949	2,121	2,359	2,512	2,713	2,373	2,224	2,083	Latvia
28.0[35]	30.0[35]	19.8[35]	12.4[35]	——9.8[35]——		1,364	1,786	2,383	3,086	3,147	3,578	4,056	4,417	Lebanon
43.1	27.6	15.0	8.6	4.8	0.9	734	853	1,028	1,277	1,570	1,785	1,757	1,663	Lesotho
43.2	28.2	14.7	7.7	4.4	1.8	824	1,055	1,397	1,892	2,189	3,149	3,935	4,900	Liberia
45.4[15]	26.4[15]	14.7[15]	9.1[15]	3.7[15]	0.6[15]	1,029	1,349	1,986	3,043	4,306	5,237	6,332	7,378	Libya
17.0	20.2	25.9	21.2	10.8	4.9	14	16	21	26	29	33	36	38	Liechtenstein
19.5	21.2	22.8	17.2	14.2	5.1	2,553	2,765	3,138	3,436	3,698	3,500	3,379	3,274	Lithuania
18.9	18.6	25.5	18.4	12.9	5.7	296	314	339	364	382	436	474	504	Luxembourg
21.7	22.2	29.1	17.5	6.6	2.9	205	186	261	256	352	431	474	512	Macau
21.1	23.8	22.0	18.1	11.7	3.3	1,220	1,396	1,628	1,888	2,028	2,031	2,079	2,134	Macedonia
44.7	27.7	15.6	7.2	3.9	0.9	4,620	5,482	6,766	8,677	11,522	15,506	20,134	25,847	Madagascar
45.7[16]	29.2[16]	13.2[16]	7.5[16]	3.7[16]	0.7[16]	2,817	3,450	4,489	6,129	9,215	10,874	13,416	16,150	Malawi
33.0[2]	28.3[2]	21.0[2]	11.6[2]	4.9[2]	1.2[2]	6,187	7,908	10,466	13,764	17,857	23,242	28,332	32,520	Malaysia
40.9	28.6	17.2	7.2	5.1	1.0	79	92	115	155	215	271	318	372	Maldives
47.3[16]	26.4[16]	13.2[16]	8.1[16]	4.1[16]	0.9[16]	3,688	4,486	5,525	6,731	8,228	10,665	14,012	17,847	Mali
21.9	20.9	22.5	18.8	11.6	4.3	312	329	326	364	360	390	411	424	Malta
42.9	28.7	16.7	8.2	2.6	0.9	11	15	22	31	44	52	59	68	Marshall Islands
22.0	21.0	24.4	16.0	11.1	5.5	222	282	325	326	360	386	404	419	Martinique
43.9	27.0	15.0	7.7	4.0	1.2	960	1,057	1,227	1,550	1,963	2,487	3,291	4,181	Mauritania
25.2	26.0	24.8	14.9	6.8	2.3	479	662	829	966	1,059	1,187	1,296	1,384	Mauritius
42.0	29.0	17.0	7.0	——5.0——		17	25	35	52	89	147	216	292	Mayotte
34.3	28.5	19.5	10.5	5.3	1.9	28,485	38,579	52,775	68,347	84,914	99,927	112,991	125,232	Mexico
40.3	28.4	16.9	9.1	3.9	1.4	32	45	61	73	96	107	120	126	Micronesia
27.9	22.9	21.0	15.6	9.7	2.9	2,341	3,004	3,595	4,010	4,364	4,273	4,184	4,118	Moldova
13.2	13.4	22.1	22.4	17.4	11.5	18	21	24	27	30	32	33	35	Monaco
35.8	30.2	20.5	8.3	——5.2——		747	931	1,248	1,663	2,086	2,390	2,740	3,088	Mongolia
37.0[23]	29.6[23]	17.3[23]	9.2[23]	5.4[23]	1.5[23]	8,953	11,640	15,126	19,206	23,986	28,460	33,261	37,924	Morocco[36]
44.8	27.6	15.1	8.0	3.7	0.8	6,250	7,472	9,304	12,103	12,649	17,673	19,721	20,547	Mozambique
38.6	28.7	15.5	10.9	5.2	1.1	19,488	22,836	27,386	33,283	38,526	41,772	43,721	44,825	Myanmar (Burma)
42.7[6]	28.6[6]	15.5[6]	7.9[6]	3.9[6]	1.4[6]	464	591	765	975	1,409	1,826	2,036	2,081	Namibia
41.8[38]	25.0[38]	20.7[38]	8.2[38]	——2.8[38]——		3	4	7	8	9	10	11	12	Nauru
39.3	27.0	17.1	10.1	5.2	1.3	8,502	9,839	11,880	14,559	18,142	22,648	28,061	33,600	Nepal

Area and population (continued)

country	area			population (latest estimate)					population (recent census)				
	square miles	square kilo-metres	rank	total midyear 2004	rank	density per sq mi	density per sq km	% annual growth rate 1999–2004	census year	total	male (%)	female (%)	urban (%)
Netherlands, The	16,034	41,528	133	16,275,000	58	1,015.0	391.9	0.6	2001	15,985,538	49.5	50.5	89.6[6]
Netherlands Antilles	308	800	183	179,000	186	581.1	223.7	–0.8	2001	175,653	47.0	53.0	69.3[6]
New Caledonia	7,172	18,575	154	224,000	182	31.2	12.0	1.5	1996	196,836	51.2	48.8	60.4
New Zealand	104,454	270,534	74	4,060,000	122	38.9	15.0	1.1	2001	3,912,000[39]	49.1[39]	50.9[39]	85.9[6]
Nicaragua	50,337	130,373	97	5,360,000	109	106.5	41.1	2.1	1995	4,357,099	49.3	50.7	54.4
Niger	459,286	1,189,546	22	11,679,000	69	25.4	9.8	2.8	2001	10,790,352	49.9	50.1	16.2
Nigeria	356,669	923,768	32	128,254,000	9	359.6	138.8	2.8	1991	88,514,501	50.3	49.7	35.0[21]
Northern Mariana Islands	176	457	194	78,000	200	443.2	170.7	3.0	2000	69,221	46.2	53.8	90.1
Norway	125,004	323,758	67	4,591,000	115	36.7	14.2	0.6	2001	4,520,947	49.6	50.4	76.5
Oman	119,500	309,500	71	2,350,000	140	19.7	7.6	1.5	1993	2,018,074	58.4	41.6	71.7
Pakistan[41]	307,374	796,096	36	151,600,000	6	493.2	190.4	2.1	1998	130,579,571	52.0	48.0	33.3
Palau	188	488	192	20,700	215	110.1	42.4	1.9	2000	19,129	54.6	45.4	69.5
Panama	28,973	75,040	118	3,172,000	132	109.5	42.3	1.9	2000	2,839,177	50.5	49.5	56.3
Papua New Guinea	178,704	462,840	54	5,695,000	103	31.9	12.3	2.5	2000	5,130,365	51.9	48.1	13.2[2]
Paraguay	157,048	406,752	59	5,773,000	102	36.8	14.2	2.2	2002	5,183,080[8]	50.7	49.3	56.7
Peru	496,225	1,285,216	20	27,544,000	38	55.5	21.4	1.5	1993	22,639,443	49.7	50.3	70.1
Philippines	122,121[42]	316,294[42]	69	82,670,000	12	677.0	261.4	2.0	2000	76,504,077	50.4	49.6	58.5[2]
Poland	120,728	312,685	70	38,176,000	32	316.2	122.1	–0.3	2002	38,230,100	48.4	51.6	61.8
Portugal	35,580	92,152	111	10,524,000	74	295.8	114.2	0.5	2001	10,356,117[10]	48.3[10]	51.7[10]	65.8[6]
Puerto Rico	3,515	9,104	166	3,898,000	124	1,109.0	428.2	0.5	2000	3,808,610	48.1	51.9	94.6[2]
Qatar	4,412	11,427	161	754,000	159	170.9	66.0	5.1	1997	522,023	65.6	34.4	100.0
Réunion	968	2,507	174	773,000	158	798.6	308.3	1.7	1999	706,300	49.1	50.9	82.7
Romania	92,043	238,391	82	21,549,000	48	234.1	90.4	–0.4	2002	21,680,974	48.7	51.3	52.7
Russia	6,592,800	17,075,400	1	144,315,000	7	21.9	8.5	–0.3	2002	145,164,000	46.6	53.3	73.3
Rwanda	10,169	26,338	147	8,380,000	87	824.1	318.2	3.1	2002	8,162,715	47.7	52.3	16.7
St. Kitts and Nevis	104	269	205	46,300	211	445.2	172.1	0.5	2001	46,111	49.7	50.3	34.2[6]
St. Lucia	238	617	189	164,000	189	689.1	265.8	1.3	2001	151,156	48.9	51.1	38.0[6]
St. Vincent and the Grenadines	150	389	198	113,000	192	753.3	290.5	0.2	1991	106,499	49.9	50.1	24.6
Samoa	1,093	2,831	172	183,000	184	167.4	64.6	1.1	2001	176,710	52.1	47.9	22.0
San Marino	24	61	212	29,400	214	1,225.0	482.0	2.1	2003[3, 4]	28,753	48.9	51.1	88.7[24]
São Tomé and Príncipe	386	1,001	181	144,000	190	373.1	143.9	1.6	2001	137,599	49.6	50.4	47.7[6]
Saudi Arabia	830,000	2,149,690	14	24,580,000	45	29.6	11.4	2.9	1992	16,948,388	55.9	44.1	77.3[21]
Senegal	75,955	196,722	87	10,339,000	77	136.1	52.6	2.4	1988	6,928,405	48.7	51.3	38.6
Serbia and Montenegro	39,449	102,173	107	10,826,000	73	274.4	106.0	–0.1	2002	7,498,001[44]	48.6[44]	51.4[44]	56.4[44]
Seychelles	176	455	195	81,800	199	464.8	179.8	1.0	2002	81,177	49.8	50.2	64.6[6]
Sierra Leone	27,699	71,740	119	5,168,000	111	186.6	72.0	3.8	1985	3,517,530	49.6	50.4	31.8
Singapore	269	697	188	4,229,000[47]	120	15,721.2	6,067.4	1.4	2000[10]	3,263,209	50.0	50.0	100.0
Slovakia	18,933	49,035	129	5,383,000	108	284.3	109.8	0.0	2001	5,379,455	48.6	51.4	55.0
Slovenia	7,827	20,273	153	1,997,000	143	255.1	98.5	0.1	2002	1,964,036	48.8	51.2	50.8
Solomon Islands	10,954	28,370	143	461,000	166	42.1	16.2	2.7	1999	409,042	51.7	48.3	15.6
Somalia	246,000	637,000	42	8,305,000	89	33.8	13.0	3.3	1975	4,089,203	50.1	49.9	25.4
South Africa	470,693	1,219,090	25	46,587,000	26	99.0	38.2	1.2	2001	44,819,778	47.8	52.2	57.7[6]
Spain	195,379	506,030	51	43,768,000	27	224.0	86.5	1.7	2001	40,847,371	49.0	51.0	77.8[6]
Sri Lanka	25,332	65,610	122	19,218,000	53	758.6	292.9	0.8	2001	16,864,544[48]	49.5[48]	50.5[48]	14.6[48]
Sudan, The	966,757	2,503,890	10	39,148,000	30	40.5	15.6	2.8	1993	24,940,683	50.2	49.8	31.3[15]
Suriname	63,251	163,820	91	437,000	171	6.9	2.7	0.5	1980	354,860	49.5	50.5	49.1[15]
Swaziland	6,704	17,364	157	1,083,000	154	161.5	62.4	1.1	1997	929,718	47.3	52.7	23.1
Sweden	173,860	450,295	56	8,991,000	83	51.7	20.0	0.3	2003[3, 4]	8,940,788	49.5	50.5	84.0
Switzerland	15,940	41,284	134	7,392,000	93	463.7	179.1	0.7	2000[50]	7,288,010	49.0	51.0	68.0
Syria	71,498	185,180	88	18,017,000	55	252.0	97.3	2.5	1994	13,782,315	51.1	48.9	52.2[15]
Taiwan	13,972	36,188	136	22,640,000	47	1,620.4	625.6	0.6	2000[10]	22,300,929	51.1	48.9	...
Tajikistan	55,300	143,100	95	6,606,000	98	119.5	46.2	1.8	2000	6,127,493	50.3	49.7	26.6
Tanzania	364,901	945,090	31	35,782,000	33	98.1	37.9	2.5	2002	34,569,232	48.9	51.1	23.0
Thailand	198,116	513,119	50	64,485,000	19	325.5	125.7	0.9	2000	60,617,200	49.2	50.8	31.1
Togo	21,925	56,785	125	5,557,000	105	253.5	97.9	2.6	1981	2,719,567	48.7	51.3	15.2
Tonga	290	750	185	98,400	195	339.3	131.2	0.1	1996[10]	97,784	50.7	49.3	32.1
Trinidad and Tobago	1,980	5,128	169	1,286,000	152	649.5	250.8	0.4	2000	1,262,366	50.1	49.9	74.1[2]
Tunisia	63,170	163,610	92	9,975,000	80	157.9	61.0	1.1	1994	8,785,711	50.6	49.4	61.0
Turkey	299,158	774,815	37	71,617,000	15	239.4	92.4	1.6	2000	67,853,315	50.7[52]	49.3[52]	65.0
Turkmenistan	188,500	488,100	52	4,940,000	113	26.2	10.1	1.6	1995	4,483,251	49.6	50.4	46.0
Tuvalu	9.9	25.6	215	9,600	217	969.7	375.0	0.4	2002	9,561	49.5	50.5	47.0
Uganda	93,065	241,038	80	26,335,000	39	283.0	109.3	3.5	2002	24,748,977	49.0	51.0	12.2
Ukraine	233,062	603,628	44	47,470,000	25	203.7	78.6	–0.9	2001	48,457,000	46.4	53.6	67.2
United Arab Emirates	32,280	83,600	115	4,298,000	117	133.1	51.4	7.2	1995	2,411,041	66.6	33.4	77.3
United Kingdom	93,788	242,910	79	59,561,000	21	635.1	245.2	0.3	2001	58,789,194	48.6	51.4	89.5[6]
United States	3,616,236[53]	9,366,008[53]	4	293,850,000	3	81.3	31.4	1.0	2000	281,421,906	49.1	50.9	79.0
Uruguay	68,037	176,215	90	3,399,000	130	50.0	19.3	0.6	1996	3,151,662	48.4	51.6	89.3
Uzbekistan	172,700	447,400	57	26,009,000	41	150.6	58.1	1.3	1989	19,905,158	49.3	50.7	40.7
Vanuatu	4,707	12,190	160	216,000	183	45.9	17.7	3.1	1999	193,219	51.5	48.5	21.5
Venezuela	353,841	916,445	33	26,170,000	40	74.0	28.6	1.9	2001	22,688,803	49.6	50.4	87.2[6]
Vietnam	128,379	332,501	65	81,839,000	14	637.5	246.1	1.3	1999	76,324,753	49.2	50.8	23.5
Virgin Islands (U.S.)	136	352	201	109,000	193	801.5	309.7	0.0	2000	108,612	47.8	52.2	92.6[2]
West Bank[54]	2,270	5,900	167	2,544,000[55]	138[55]	1,120.7[55]	431.2[55]	3.5[55]	1997[56]	1,600,100[56]	50.9[56]	49.1[56]	60.9[56]
Western Sahara	97,344	252,120	77	267,000	180	2.7	1.1	2.2	1994	252,146	...	...	90.7
Yemen	214,300	555,000	48	20,733,000	50	96.7	37.4	3.5	1994	14,593,807	51.2	48.8	23.5
Zambia	290,585	752,612	39	10,462,000	75	36.0	13.9	1.8	2000	9,885,591	50.0	50.0	34.7
Zimbabwe	150,872	390,757	60	11,821,000	68	78.4	30.3	1.0	2002	11,634,663	48.4	51.6	34.9[24]

[1]Settled population only. [2]2000 estimate. [3]Civil register not a census. [4]Beginning of year. [5]Preliminary, variant figure. [6]2001 estimate. [7]1999 estimate. [8]Unadjusted for undercount. [9]Preliminary figure. [10]Data are for de jure population. [11]1991 estimate. [12]Beginning of 2002 estimate based on 2001 census. [13]1996 estimate. [14]2003 estimate based on adjusted 2001 census. [15]1995 estimate. [16]1998 estimate. [17]Data are for the island of Cyprus (excepting census information). [18]Republic of Cyprus only. [19]End of 2001 estimate based on 2001 census. [20]2002 estimate. [21]1990 estimate. [22]Rounded percentage of 2001 census. [23]1994 estimate. [24]2003 estimate. [25]1993 estimate. [26]Excludes about 230,000 people in territories not controlled by the Georgian central government. [27]Data exclude Alderney (population 2,294) and Sark (population 575). [28]Combined percentage for Guernsey and Jersey. [29]Beginning of 2003 estimate based on 2001 census. [30]1997 estimate. [31]Area figures exclude the West Bank and the Gaza Strip. [32]Population figures (unless otherwise indicated) exclude Israelis in the West Bank and the Gaza Strip. [33]Census data include Israelis in the West Bank and the Gaza Strip. [34]Percentages derived from 2001 census population graph. [35]Derived figure from sample survey. [36]Excludes Western Sahara, an annexure of Morocco, unless

age distribution (%)						population (by decade, '000s)								country
0–14	15–29	30–44	45–59	60–74	75 and over	1950	1960	1970	1980	1990	2000	2010 projection	2020 projection	
18.6	18.8	24.3	20.0	12.2	6.1	10,090	11,494	13,020	14,150	14,952	15,926	16,667	17,212	Netherlands, The
24.2	18.2	25.5	19.0	9.4	3.7	112	136	163	174	188	179	179	179	Netherlands Antilles
30.7	27.2	21.3	13.3	5.9	1.6	59	79	110	140	171	211	241	265	New Caledonia
22.5[39]	20.4[39]	23.0[39]	18.0[39]	10.7[39]	5.4[39]	1,909	2,377	2,820	3,144	3,452	3,860	4,298	4,621	New Zealand
45.1	27.5	15.0	7.2	3.7	1.4	1,098	1,493	2,053	2,805	3,684	4,932	5,990	7,020	Nicaragua
47.8[6]	26.5[6]	14.2[6]	7.9[6]	3.1[6]	0.5[6]	2,482	3,168	4,182	5,629	7,729	10,480	13,647	17,112	Niger
45.5[11]	26.0[11]	15.3[11]	8.8[11]	3.8[11]	0.6[11]	29,790	37,446	47,980	64,325	86,018	115,224	147,677	179,288	Nigeria
22.5	31.8	32.3	10.7	2.3	0.4	6	9	10	17	44	70	78	78	Northern Mariana Islands
20.0[40]	18.8[40]	22.4[40]	19.6[40]	11.4[40]	7.8[40]	3,265	3,581	3,877	4,086	4,241	4,487	4,731	4,983	Norway
41.0	25.5	21.9	7.8	2.9	0.9	489	499	779	1,060	1,625	2,219	2,770	3,483	Oman
43.2	26.9	15.6	8.8	4.3	1.2	39,448	50,387	65,706	85,219	109,710	139,960	171,023	202,767	Pakistan[41]
23.9	24.2	29.9	14.2	5.5	2.3	7	9	12	13	15	19	22	23	Palau
32.0	26.8	20.6	12.0	6.1	2.5	860	1,126	1,506	1,949	2,411	2,948	3,504	4,011	Panama
38.8[2]	28.7[2]	17.1[2]	9.7[2]	4.7[2]	1.0[2]	1,412	1,747	2,288	2,991	3,758	5,187	6,407	7,609	Papua New Guinea
38.7[20]	26.1[20]	17.8[20]	10.6[20]	5.1[20]	1.7[20]	1,488	1,842	2,350	3,114	4,219	5,282	6,622	8,082	Paraguay
37.0	28.6	17.7	9.8	——7.0——		7,632	9,931	13,193	17,295	21,511	25,980	29,757	33,040	Peru
37.2[2]	28.5[2]	18.5[2]	10.0[2]	4.6[2]	1.2[2]	20,988	27,561	36,850	48,286	60,937	76,797	92,330	107,235	Philippines
18.3[43]	24.6[43]	20.6[43]	20.1[43]	11.5[43]	4.9[43]	24,824	29,561	32,526	35,578	38,057	38,454	38,240	38,006	Poland
17.0[6]	22.5[6]	21.7[6]	18.1[6]	14.4[6]	6.3[6]	8,443	9,037	9,044	9,778	9,923	10,336	10,736	10,842	Portugal
23.8	23.3	20.4	17.1	10.6	4.8	2,218	2,360	2,722	3,210	3,537	3,816	4,001	4,109	Puerto Rico
26.4	24.2	35.4	11.6	2.1	0.3	47	59	151	229	423	617	870	1,002	Qatar
27.0	24.8	24.4	13.8	7.2	2.8	244	338	447	507	601	722	836	940	Réunion
17.6	23.4	21.0	18.7	14.4	4.9	16,311	18,403	20,253	22,201	23,207	21,867	21,249	20,555	Romania
16.7[20]	23.4[20]	22.4[20]	18.7[20]	14.0[20]	4.8[20]	101,937	119,632	130,245	139,045	148,082	146,083	140,990	136,062	Russia
42.7[20]	30.7[20]	14.9[20]	7.6[20]	3.3[20]	0.8[20]	2,162	2,887	3,776	5,157	6,775	7,489	9,374	11,333	Rwanda
30.7[2]	26.5[2]	21.1[2]	10.8[2]	——10.9[2]——		49	51	46	44	41	46	48	53	St. Kitts and Nevis
31.2	27.4	20.6	10.7	——10.1——		79	86	101	115	134	156	177	199	St. Lucia
37.2	29.5	16.1	8.3	6.4	2.5	67	80	86	99	105	112	115	115	St. Vincent and the Grenadines
40.8	25.6	17.9	9.2	5.0	1.5	82	111	143	155	160	175	195	217	Samoa
14.1	16.6	27.3	19.7	14.2	8.1	13	15	19	21	23	27	32	35	San Marino
41.0[2]	32.0[2]	14.0[2]	7.0[2]	5.0[2]	1.0[2]	60	64	74	94	116	135	158	185	São Tomé and Príncipe
41.8	26.8	20.4	7.0	3.0	1.0	3,201	4,075	5,745	9,604	16,554	22,010	27,948	32,114	Saudi Arabia
47.5	26.1	13.6	7.8	——5.0——		2,500	3,187	4,158	5,538	7,345	9,393	11,869	14,422	Senegal
15.8[44]	20.3[44]	20.1[44]	21.2[44]	17.3[44]	5.3[44]	7,106	7,932	8,681	9,515	9,935	10,850	10,839	10,750	Serbia and Montenegro
28.8[45]	27.4[45]	22.6[45]	10.6[45]	7.5[45]	3.1[45]	34	42	54	63	70	79	84	88	Seychelles
43.9[46]	25.6[46]	15.7[46]	9.6[46]	4.5[46]	0.7[46]	1,944	2,242	2,657	3,239	4,054	4,415	5,859	6,979	Sierra Leone
21.5	21.2	28.4	18.2	8.2	2.5	1,022	1,646	2,075	2,414	3,047	4,018	4,501	4,735	Singapore
18.9	25.1	21.5	18.9	11.0	4.6	3,463	3,994	4,528	4,984	5,298	5,401	5,411	5,405	Slovakia
15.3	21.5	22.7	20.5	14.4	5.6	1,467	1,580	1,727	1,901	1,998	1,990	1,988	1,937	Slovenia
44.6[7]	29.0[7]	14.3[7]	7.5[7]	3.7[7]	0.9[7]	107	126	163	232	315	416	539	670	Solomon Islands
45.6	24.9	15.5	7.4	——5.4——		2,438	2,956	3,667	5,791	6,675	7,253	9,922	13,023	Somalia
32.0	29.5	20.2	11.0	5.5	1.8	13,683	17,396	22,657	29,140	37,450	44,510	46,303	45,009	South Africa
14.5	20.4	20.7	17.0	14.2	7.4	27,868	30,303	33,779	37,636	38,798	40,512	45,530	48,626	Spain
26.0[49]	27.5[49]	22.3[49]	14.5[49]	7.3[49]	2.4[49]	7,483	9,701	12,295	14,543	16,830	18,595	20,046	21,121	Sri Lanka
43.0	27.0	16.4	9.3	3.7	0.6	8,051	10,589	13,788	19,064	26,627	35,080	45,485	56,162	Sudan, The
39.3	29.5	13.8	10.0	4.5	2.8	208	285	373	355	395	429	441	439	Suriname
44.3	28.6	14.4	7.7	3.4	1.6	273	351	443	596	847	1,044	1,084	1,062	Swaziland
18.0	18.1	20.8	20.6	13.6	8.9	7,014	7,480	8,042	8,310	8,559	8,872	9,241	9,692	Sweden
17.1[51]	18.0[51]	24.3[51]	20.1[51]	13.2[51]	7.3[51]	4,715	5,429	6,270	6,362	6,712	7,184	7,563	7,689	Switzerland
44.8	28.3	14.7	7.2	——5.0——		3,495	4,533	6,258	8,774	12,436	16,306	20,606	24,676	Syria
21.2	25.5	25.4	15.9	9.0	3.0	7,619	10,668	14,583	17,642	20,279	22,185	23,338	24,140	Taiwan
39.4	27.7	18.4	7.6	5.4	1.5	1,532	2,083	2,942	3,968	5,213	6,169	7,040	8,105	Tajikistan
44.3	27.7	15.3	7.1	4.1	1.5	7,935	10,260	13,842	18,939	24,354	32,497	40,176	47,682	Tanzania
24.1	25.6	25.9	15.0	7.5	1.9	20,010	26,392	35,037	46,538	56,096	62,408	67,734	71,551	Thailand
49.8	24.8	13.1	6.8	3.3	2.0	1,172	1,456	1,964	2,596	3,705	5,033	6,256	7,195	Togo
39.1	28.0	15.1	10.0	6.0	1.8	50	65	80	92	96	98	103	111	Tonga
25.2[7]	27.3[7]	23.3[7]	14.8[7]	——9.4[7]——		668	828	941	1,082	1,235	1,263	1,310	1,325	Trinidad and Tobago
34.8	28.5	18.8	9.6	6.4	1.9	3,517	4,149	5,099	6,443	8,207	9,564	10,583	11,552	Tunisia
35.0[52]	28.6[52]	18.4[52]	10.9[52]	5.6[52]	1.6[52]	21,122	28,217	35,758	44,439	56,098	67,418	77,297	84,971	Turkey
40.1[15]	27.1[15]	18.8[15]	7.9[15]	4.9[15]	1.2[15]	1,211	1,594	2,189	2,861	3,668	4,643	5,412	6,211	Turkmenistan
36.2	21.2	20.2	13.8	6.8	1.8	5	5	6	8	9	9	11	12	Tuvalu
51.0[20]	26.4[20]	13.4[20]	5.6[20]	3.0[20]	0.7[20]	5,522	7,262	9,728	12,298	16,447	22,962	32,424	45,826	Uganda
17.3[6]	22.3[6]	21.7[6]	17.8[6]	15.7[6]	5.2[6]	36,906	42,783	47,317	50,034	51,892	49,235	45,889	44,070	Ukraine
26.3	29.2	33.2	9.6	1.4	0.3	70	90	223	1,042	1,844	3,247	4,738	5,333	United Arab Emirates
18.9	18.8	22.6	18.9	13.3	7.5	50,290	52,372	55,632	56,330	57,436	58,654	60,560	62,447	United Kingdom
21.4	20.8	23.3	18.2	10.4	5.9	152,271	180,671	204,879	227,726	249,806	282,388	309,181	336,081	United States
25.1	22.9	19.6	15.1	12.2	5.1	2,194	2,531	2,824	2,920	3,106	3,324	3,491	3,617	Uruguay
40.8	28.4	15.0	9.3	4.7	1.8	6,314	8,559	11,973	15,977	20,515	24,741	28,352	31,791	Uzbekistan
37.8[7]	29.4[7]	18.2[7]	9.7[7]	4.0[7]	0.9[7]	52	66	85	117	147	190	248	299	Vanuatu
32.1[6]	28.3[6]	20.7[6]	12.0[6]	5.2[6]	1.7[6]	5,094	7,579	10,721	15,091	19,502	24,277	28,955	33,300	Venezuela
33.3[7]	29.0[7]	21.0[7]	9.1[7]	5.8[7]	1.8[7]	27,367	33,648	42,898	53,005	66,074	77,635	88,516	99,392	Vietnam
26.1	19.4	21.2	20.5	9.8	3.0	27	32	63	100	104	109	108	107	Virgin Islands (U.S.)
45.0[56]	27.7[56]	15.1[56]	6.6[56]	4.2[56]	1.4[56]	...	...	608[55]	733[55]	1,011[55]	2,211[55]	3,004[55]	3,740[55]	West Bank[54]
...	...	...	...	...	...	14	32	76	126	191	245	301	357	Western Sahara
50.3	23.2	14.1	6.9	4.1	1.4	4,316	5,211	6,290	8,140	11,944	18,017	25,662	36,537	Yemen
47.0[2]	30.0[2]	12.9[2]	5.9[2]	3.4[2]	0.8[2]	2,553	3,254	4,252	5,700	7,788	9,813	11,286	12,351	Zambia
40.0[20]	32.3[20]	15.2[20]	7.4[20]	4.0[20]	1.1[20]	2,853	4,011	5,515	7,170	10,154	11,367	12,058	11,970	Zimbabwe

otherwise indicated. [37]Includes Western Sahara. [38]1992 census. [39]End of 2001 estimate based on 2001 adjusted census figures (including residents temporarily abroad). [40]Mean figures for 2002. [41]Excludes Afghan refugees (January 2004; *c.* 1.1 million) and the area and population (2004; *c.* 4.25 million) of Pakistan-occupied Jammu and Kashmir. [42]Sum of regional ("administrative subdivision") areas; actual total area may be different. [43]Percentages derived from 2002 census population graph. [44]Excludes Montenegro and Kosovo (Kosova). [45]1997 census. [46]1985 estimate. [47]De facto population. [48]Excludes 7 districts experiencing civil war whose 2001 estimated population equaled 1,867,711. [49]2001 estimate for entire country. [50]Includes resident aliens, excludes seasonal workers. [51]Beginning of 2002 estimate based on 2000 census. [52]1990 census. [53]Includes inland water area of 78,797 sq mi (204,083 sq km); excludes Great Lakes water area of 60,251 sq mi (156,049 sq km). [54]Excludes East Jerusalem. [55]Includes Jewish population of the West Bank. [56]Census total not adjusted for undercount; excludes Jewish population of the West Bank.

Major cities and national capitals

The following table lists the principal cities or municipalities (those exceeding 100,000 in population [75,000 for Anglo-America, Australia, and the United Kingdom]) of the countries of the world, together with figures for each national capital (indicated by a ★), regardless of size.

Most of the populations given refer to a so-called city proper, that is, a legally defined, incorporated, or chartered area defined by administrative boundaries and by national or state law. In some instances, where cities proper do not exist or are not strictly demarcated, populations of locally defined urban areas may be used. In a few cases, data refer to the municipality, or commune, similar to the medieval city-state in that the city is governed together with its immediately adjoining, economically dependent areas, whether urban or rural in nature. Some countries define no other demographic or legal entities within such communes or municipalities, but many identify a centre, seat, head (*cabecera*), or locality that corresponds to the most densely populated, compact, contiguous core of the municipality. Figures referring to municipalities or communes may be given (identified by the abbreviation "MU"), even though the country itself may define a smaller, more closely knit city proper.

Populations for urban agglomerations as defined by the United Nations are occasionally inset beneath the populations of cities proper. Specifically that is when the urban agglomeration populations are at least three times the size of cities proper.

For certain countries, more than one form of the name of the city is given, usually to permit recognition of recent place-name changes or of *forms* of the place-name likely to be encountered in press stories if the title of the city's entry in the *Encyclopædia Britannica* is spelled according to a different romanization or spelling policy.

Chinese names for China are usually given in their Pinyin spelling, the official Chinese system encountered in official documents and maps. For Taiwan, the Wade-Giles spelling of place-names is used.

Sources for this data were often national censuses and statistical abstracts of the countries concerned, supplemented by Internet sources.

Internet sources for further information

- City Population: http://www.citypopulation.de/cities.html
- The World Gazetteer: http://www.gazetteer.de/st/stata.htm

Major cities and national capitals

country city	population
Afghanistan (2003 est.)	
Herāt	254,800
★ Kabul	700,000[1]
agglomeration	2,799,300
Kandahār (Qandahār)	323,900
Mazār-e Sharīf	187,700
Albania (2001)	
★ Tiranë	354,304
Algeria (2004 est.)	
★ Algiers	1,790,700
Annaba	410,700
Batna	285,800
Béchar	154,400
Bejaïa	173,300
Biskra (Beskra)	201,500
Blida (el-Boulaida)	180,400
Bordj Bou Arreridj	151,500
Constantine (Qacentina)	544,700
Djelfa	181,800
Ech-Cheliff (el-Asnam)	157,800
El-Eulma	123,900
El-Wad	123,500
Ghilizane	122,900
Guelma	128,100
Jijel	124,900
Khenchela	125,000
Médéa	145,600
Mostaganem	146,600
Oran (Wahran)	772,900
Saïda	130,600
Sétif (Stif)	249,700
Sidi bel Abbès	212,400
Skikda	179,500
Souq Ahras	136,600
Tébessa (Tbessa)	180,600
Tihert	171,300
Tlemcen (Tilimsen)	141,600
Wargla (Ouargla)	139,900
American Samoa (2000)	
★ Fagatogo (legislative and judicial)	2,096[2]
★ Utulei (executive)	807[2]
Andorra (2002)	
★ Andorra la Vella	20,787
Angola (2004 est.)	
Huambo	173,600
★ Luanda	2,783,000
Antigua and Barbuda (2004)	
★ Saint John's	23,600
Argentina (2001)	
Almirante Brown	513,777
Avellaneda	329,638
Bahía Blanca	280,729
Belén de Escobar	172,494
Berazategui	287,642
★ Buenos Aires	2,768,772
agglomeration	11,453,725
Caseros	335,578
Catamarca	140,556
Comodoro Rivadavia	135,813
Concordia	137,046
Córdoba	1,267,774
Corrientes	314,247
Esteban Echeverría	243,715
Ezeiza	118,080
Florencio Valera	343,238
Formosa	198,146
General San Martín	405,122
Godoy Cruz	182,555
Hurlingham	171,724
Ituzaingo	157,769
José Carlos Paz	229,760
La Plata	553,002
La Rioja	143,921
Lanús	452,513
Las Heras	168,410
Lomas de Zamora	590,667
Mar del Plata	541,857
Mendoza	110,716
Merlo	468,734
Moreno	379,801
Morón	309,086
Neuquén	201,729
Paraná	235,931
Pilar	228,724
Posadas	253,389
Quilmes	518,723
Resistencia	274,001
Río Cuarto	144,140
Rosario	906,004
Salta	462,668
San Fernando	147,409
San Isidro	293,213
San Juan	115,556
San Justo (La Matanza)	1,253,858
San Luis	152,918
San Miguel	253,133
San Miguel de Tucumán	535,883
San Nicolás de los Arroyos	125,308
San Rafael	104,782
San Salvador de Jujuy	230,999
Santa Fe	368,369
Santiago del Estero	230,424
Tandil	100,869
Tigre	295,561
Vicente López	273,802
Villa Krause	102,099
Villa Nueva	222,951
Armenia (2002 est.)	
Gyumri (Kumayri; Leninakan)	210,100
★ Yerevan	1,246,100
Aruba (2000)	
★ Oranjestad	26,355
Australia (2001)[3]	
Adelaide	1,002,127
Brisbane	1,508,161
Cairns	98,981
★ Canberra	339,727
Geelong	130,194
Gold Coast	421,557
Gosford	255,429
Hobart	126,048
Melbourne	3,160,171
Newcastle	279,975
Perth	1,176,542
Sunshine Coast	169,931
Sydney	3,502,301
Toowoomba	89,338
Townsville	119,504
Wollongong	228,846
Austria (2001)	
Graz	226,244
Innsbruck	113,392
Linz	183,504
Salzburg	142,662
★ Vienna	1,550,123
Azerbaijan (2001 est.)	
★ Baku (Baky)	1,817,900
Gäncä (Gyandzha)	301,400
Sumqayit (Sumgait)	288,400
Bahamas, The (2000)	
★ Nassau	210,832[4]
Bahrain (2001)	
★ Al-Manāmah	143,035
Bangladesh (2001)	
Barisal	202,242
Bogra	150,138
Brahmanbaria	131,334
Chittagong	2,199,500
Comilla	168,378
★ Dhaka (Dacca)	5,644,235
Dinajpur	157,303
Jamalpur	116,764
Jessore	178,273
Khulna	811,490
Kotwali	285,308
Madhabdi	126,736
Mymensingh	225,811
Naogaon	123,101
Narayanganj	241,694
Nawabganj (Nowabgonj)	153,252
Pabna	116,371
Rajshahi	402,646
Rangpur	251,699
Saidpur	110,151
Shailakupa	317,881
Sirajgani	127,147
Tangail	128,543
Tongi	295,883
Barbados (1990)	
★ Bridgetown	6,070
agglomeration	140,000[5]
Belarus (2004 est.)	
Babruysk	228,100
Baranavichy	176,600
Barysaw	155,700
Brest	294,400
Homyel	497,200
Hrodna	315,500
Mahilyow	365,400
Mazyr	109,400
★ Minsk	1,682,900
Orsha	123,800
Pinsk	136,200
Salihorsk	101,900
Vitsyebsk	355,200
Belgium (2002 est.)	
Antwerp	448,709
Brugge (Bruges)	116,836
★ Brussels	136,730
agglomeration	978,384
Charleroi	200,578
Ghent	226,220
Liège (Luik)	185,131
Namur	105,393
Schaerbeek	107,736
Belize (2004 est.)	
★ Belmopan	12,300
Benin (2000 est.)	
★ Cotonou (official)	650,660
Djougou	134,099[6]
Parakou	144,627
★ Porto-Novo (de facto)	232,756
Bermuda (2000)	
★ Hamilton	969
Bhutan (2002 est.)	
★ Thimphu	45,000
Bolivia (2001)	
Cochabamba	516,683
El Alto	647,350
★ La Paz (administrative)	789,585
Oruro	201,230
Potosí	132,966
Quillacollo	119,961
Santa Cruz	1,116,059
★ Sucre (judicial)	193,873
Tarija	135,783
Bosnia and Herzegovina (2003 est.)	
Banja Luka	170,000
★ Sarajevo	380,000
Botswana (2001)	
★ Gaborone	186,007
Brazil (2003 est.)	
Águas Lindas de Goiás	131,900
Alagoinhas	116,000
Alvorada	196,200
Americana	191,000
Ananindeua	436,100
Anápolis	290,000
Angra dos Reis	124,200
Aparecida de Golânia	384,100
Apucarana	103,900
Aracaju	479,800
Araçatuba	169,400
Araguaina	112,500
Arapiraca	157,800
Araraquara	180,400
Araras	102,700
Atibaia	103,600
Barbacena	107,600
Barra Mansa	167,300
Barreiras	108,500
Barretos	101,400
Barueri	232,200
Bauru	327,100
Belém	1,333,500
Belford Roxo	457,200
Belo Horizonte	2,305,800
Betim	338,900
Blumenau	256,100
Boa Vista	217,200
Botucatu	109,200
Bragança Paulista	118,000
★ Brasília	2,094,100
Cabo (de Santo Agostinho)	141,500
Cabo Frio	119,800
Cachoeirinha	113,500
Cachoeiro de Itapemirim	164,000
Camaçari	168,500
Camaragibe	137,700
Campina Grande	347,200
Campinas	990,100
Campo Grande	697,800
Campos dos Goytacazes	372,600
Canoas	317,400
Carapicuíba	363,400
Cariacica	327,800
Caruaru	228,000
Cascavel	243,700
Castanhal	130,300
Catanduva	108,800
Caucaia	249,800
Caxias	104,900
Caxias do Sul	353,000
Chapecó	144,600
Colombo	194,200
Conselheiro Lafaiete	103,600
Contagem	560,300
Cotia	161,800
Criciúma	159,700
Cubatão	112,900
Cuiabá	501,000
Curitiba	1,671,200
Diadema	373,000
Divinópolis	187,700
Dourados	158,000
Duque de Caxias	805,400
Embu	223,600
Feira de Santana	452,300
Ferraz	155,300
Florianópolis	358,200
Fortaleza	2,256,200
Foz do Iguaçu	277,400
Franca	298,700
Francisco Morato	148,900
Franco de Rocha	106,900
Garanhuns	107,300
Goiânia	1,138,600
Governador Valadares	241,000
Gravataí	226,600
Guarapuava	147,000
Guaratinguetá	102,600
Guarujá	281,500
Guarulhos	1,135,500
Hortolândia	173,100
Ibirité	149,200
Ilhéus	161,800
Imperatriz	219,500
Indaiatuba	158,700
Ipatinga	220,800
Itaboraí	190,500
Itabuna	194,600
Itajaí	150,200
Itapecerica da Serra	141,800
Itapetininga	118,700
Itapevi	179,200
Itaquaquecetuba	306,200
Itu	131,900
Jaboatão	596,900
Jacareí	191,500

country / city	population
Jandira	100,800
Jaraguá do Sul	104,900
Jaú	112,500
Jequié	131,000
João Pessoa	628,800
Joinville	445,000
Juàzeiro	144,000
Juàzeiro do Norte	213,600
Juiz de Fora	474,600
Jundiaí	310,000
Lages	157,800
Lauro de Freitas	121,400
Limeira	250,500
Londrina	453,000
Luziânia	147,900
Macaé	137,200
Macapá	304,500
Maceió	847,700
Magé	206,100
Manaus	1,517,500
Marabá	145,300
Maracanaú	186,100
Marília	200,400
Maringá	298,600
Mauá	384,500
Mesquita	174,000
Mogi Guaçu	122,900
Moji das Cruzes	318,200
Montes Claros	305,700
Mossoró	205,300
Natal	744,800
Nilópolis	152,400
Niterói	466,600
Nossa Senhora de Socorro	151,000
Nova Friburgo	153,600
Nova Iguaçu	792,200
Novo Hamburgo	241,200
Olinda	368,600
Osasco	678,600
Palhoça	108,000
Palmas	168,200
Paranaguá	130,600
Parnaíba	129,500
Parnamirim	125,700
Passo Fundo	171,800
Patos de Minas	117,100
Paulista	277,900
Pelotas	308,700
Petrolina	179,400
Petrópolis	279,700
Pindamonhangaba	126,100
Pinhais	109,000
Piracicaba	332,400
Poá	100,600
Poços de Caldas	138,400
Ponta Grossa	279,400
Porto Alegre	1,353,300
Porto Velho	289,500
Pouso Alegre	104,800
Praia Grande	215,200
Presidente Prudente	192,400
Queimados	129,100
Recife	1,461,300
Resende	101,800
Ribeirão das Neves	276,900
Ribeirão Pires	110,500
Ribeirão Preto	525,500
Rio Branco	245,500
Rio Claro	172,500
Rio de Janeiro	5,974,100
Rio Grande	183,400
Rio Verde	113,500
Rondonópolis	149,500
Sabará	120,400
Salvador	2,555,400
Santa Bárbara d'Oeste	175,500
Santa Luzia	198,700
Santa Maria	241,100
Santa Rita	106,200
Santarém	190,300
Santo André	659,300
Santos	415,900
São Bernardo do Campo	732,200
São Caetano do Sul	137,300
São Carlos	193,600
São Gonçalo	925,400
São João de Meriti	456,800
São José	182,600
São José do Rio Prêto	359,600
São José dos Campos	562,200
São José dos Pinhais	204,600
São Leopoldo	200,800
São Luís	889,100
São Paulo	10,041,500
São Vicente	314,200
Sapucaia do Sul	127,300
Serra	350,000
Sete Lagoas	193,100
Sobral	141,900
Sorocaba	521,500
Sumaré	210,900
Susano (Suzano)	242,300
Taboão da Serra	209,200
Taubaté	240,600
Teixeira de Freitas	104,900
Teófilo Otoni	102,200
Teresina	711,700
Teresopolis	119,700
Timon	119,000
Uberaba	257,500
Uberlândia	529,300
Uruguaiana	122,200
Valparaíso de Goiás	107,000
Varginha	110,300
Várzea Grande	227,400
Várzea Paulista	100,200
Viamão	225,000
Vila Velha	369,300
Vitória	302,600
Vitória da Conquista	235,400
Volta Redonda	248,700
Brunei (2001)	
★ Bandar Seri Begawan	27,285
Bulgaria (2001)	
Burgas	193,316
Dobrich	100,379
Pleven	122,149
Plovdiv	340,638
Ruse	162,128
Sliven	100,695
★ Sofia	1,096,389
Stara Zagora	143,989
Varna	314,539
Burkina Faso (1996)	
Bobo Dioulasso	309,711
★ Ouagadougou	709,736
Burundi (2001 est.)	
★ Bujumbura	346,000
Cambodia (2001 est.)	
★ Phnom Penh	1,109,000
Cameroon (1992)	
Bafoussam	147,580
Bamenda	160,493
Douala	1,048,915
Garoua	203,799
Maroua	162,479
Nkongsamba	107,211
★ Yaoundé	903,649
Canada (2001)	
Abbotsford	115,463
Barrie	103,710
Brampton	325,428
Brantford	86,417
Burlington	150,836
Burnaby	193,954
Calgary	878,866
Cambridge	110,372
Cape Breton[7]	105,968
Chatham-Kent	107,341
Coquitlam	112,890
Delta[7]	96,950
Edmonton	666,104
Gatineau	102,898
Greater Sudbury	155,219
Guelph	106,170
Halifax[7]	359,111
Hamilton	490,268
Kamloops	77,281
Kelowna	96,288
Kingston	114,195
Kitchener	190,399
Langley[7]	86,896
Laval	343,005
London	336,539
Longueuil	128,016
Markham	208,615
Mississauga	612,925
Montreal	1,039,534
Montréal-Nord	83,600
Niagara Falls	78,815
North Vancouver[7]	82,310
Oakville	144,738
Oshawa	139,051
★ Ottawa	774,072
Pickering	87,139
Quebec	169,076
Regina	178,225
Richmond	164,345
Richmond Hill	132,030
Saanich[7]	103,654
Saint Catharines	129,170
Saint-Hubert	75,912
Saint John's	99,182
Saint-Laurent	77,391
Saskatoon	196,811
Sherbrooke	75,916
Surrey	347,825
Thunder Bay	109,016
Toronto	2,481,494
Vancouver	545,671
Vaughan	182,022
Waterloo	86,543
Whitby	87,413
Windsor	208,402
Winnipeg	619,544
Cape Verde (2000)	
★ Praia	94,757
Central African Republic (1995 est.)	
★ Bangui	553,000
Chad (1993; MU)	
Abéché	187,936
Bongor	196,713
Doba	185,461
Moundou	282,103
★ N'Djamena	530,965
Sarh	193,753
Chile (2002)	
Antofagasta	295,792
Arica	175,441
Calama	136,600
Chillán	148,015
Concepción	373,400
Copiapó	125,983
Coquimbo	154,316
Curicó	100,506
Iquique	214,586
La Serena	147,815
Los Angeles	123,445
Osorno	132,245
Puente Alto	492,603
Puerto Montt	155,095
Punta Arenas	116,005
Quilpué	126,893
Rancagua	206,971
San Bernardo	241,138
★ Santiago (administrative)	200,792
agglomeration	4,658,687
Talca	193,755
Talcahuano	248,964
Temuco	232,528
Valdívia	129,952
★ Valparaíso (legislative)	275,141
Viña del Mar	286,931
China (2003 est.)[8]	
Acheng	242,973
Aksu	251,345
Altay	118,042
Anda	180,795[9]
Ankang	197,129
Anlu	107,323
Anning	146,183
Anqing	384,701
Anqiu	157,925
Anshan	1,286,513
Anshun	218,975
Anyang	570,773
Baicheng	275,403
Baise	126,893
Baishan	261,098
Baiyin	282,471
Baoding	666,068
Baoji	496,113
Baoshan	114,247
Baotou	1,166,634
Bazhong	198,167
Bazhou	132,406
Bei'an	242,251
Beihai	240,640
★ Beijing (Peking)	7,699,297
Beiliu	154,313
Beining	108,405
Beipiao	203,192
Bengbu	533,323
Benxi	834,176
Bijie	159,126
Binzhou	237,910
Botou	109,746
Bozhou	257,213
Cangzhou	371,431
Cenxi	121,712
Changchun	2,283,765
Changde	437,039
Changge	127,774
Changji	217,398
Changle	148,047
Changning	146,520
Changsha	1,562,204
Changshu	451,712
Changyi	126,860
Changzhi	484,235
Changzhou	891,942
Chaohu	312,679
Chaoyang (*Guangdong*)	791,746
Chaoyang (*Liaoning*)	314,943
Chaozhou	311,249
Chengde	329,970
Chengdu	2,663,971
Chenghai	303,418
Chenzhou	293,703
Chibi	162,143
Chifeng	492,054
Chizhou	121,996
Chongqing (Chungking)	4,239,742
Chuxiong	136,067
Chuzhou	211,430
Cixi	148,240
Conghua	143,052
Da'an	157,409
Dachuan	200,785[9]
Dafeng	153,147[9]
Dali	195,846
Dalian	2,181,583
Dandong	602,028
Dangyang	120,806
Danjiangkou	157,727
Danyang	223,674
Danzhou	224,787
Daqing	879,288
Dashiqiao	199,597
Datong	1,028,730
Daye	142,297
Dazhou	217,376
Dehui	159,332
Dengzhou	131,004
Dexing	109,373
Deyang	274,722
Dezhou	360,981
Dingzhou	123,096
Donggang	115,081
Dongguan	562,741
Dongsheng	113,436[9]
Dongtai	349,901
Dongyang	119,666
Dongying	539,645
Dujiangyan	159,140
Dunhua	264,662
Duyun	165,447
Emeishan	133,894
Enping	164,929[9]
Enshi	132,680
Erdos	144,793
Ezhou	305,560
Fangchenggang	128,832
Fanyu	345,275[9]
Feicheng	321,827
Fengcheng (*Guangdong*)	173,112[9]
Fengcheng (*Jiangxi*)	282,090
Fengnan	121,767[9]
Foshan	431,120
Fu'an	100,793[9]
Fuding	216,035
Fujin	155,886
Fuqing	293,110
Fushun	1,243,612
Fuxin	690,355
Fuyang (*Anhui*)	387,315
Fuyang (*Zhejiang*)	109,387
Fuzhou	1,387,266
Gaizhou	238,440
Ganzhou	319,673
Gao'an	167,126
Gaomi	218,832
Gaoming	122,847
Gaoyao	114,331
Gaoyou	155,462
Gaozhou	317,132
Gejiu	218,652
Genhe	173,188[9]
Gongyi	139,167
Gongzhuling	376,516
Guanghan	132,293
Guangshui	154,716
Guangyuan	287,295
Guangzhou (Canton)	4,653,131
Guichi	103,860[9]
Guigang	224,755
Guilin	534,861
Guiping	161,216
Guixi	110,037
Guiyang	1,372,600
Gujiao	125,591
Haicheng	282,981
Haikou	533,960
Hailar	209,294[9]
Hailin	243,563
Hailun	170,303
Haimen	363,648
Haining	133,971
Haiyang	119,446
Hami	237,042
Hancheng	121,256
Hanchuan	171,827[9]
Handan	1,097,802
Hangzhou	2,059,774
Hanzhong	236,024
Harbin	2,735,095
Hebi	331,501
Hechi	113,361
Hechuan	263,211
Hefei	1,170,014
Hegang	593,052
Heihe	123,297
Helong	134,074
Hengshui	233,674
Hengyang	640,502
Heshan	150,679
Heyuan	243,640
Heze	339,792
Hezhou	122,532
Hohhot	826,354
Honghu	201,421[9]
Hongjiang	127,018
Hongta	110,048[9]
Houma	119,166
Huadian	200,833
Huadu	195,921[9]
Huai'an (*Jiangsu*)	747,873
Huaibei	629,333
Huaihua	217,755
Huainan	877,752
Huaiyin	320,841[9]
Huanggang	201,206
Huangshan	150,845
Huangshi	598,822
Huazhou	200,670
Huichun	141,562
Huixian	104,505
Huiyang	228,887
Huizhou	354,500
Hulin	154,845
Huludao	492,278
Huzhou	351,539
Jiamusi	590,276
Ji'an (*Jiangxi*)	215,865
Jiande	111,039
Jiangdu	235,191
Jiangjin	360,835
Jiangmen	362,357
Jiangyan	149,706[9]
Jiangyin	294,654
Jiangyou	233,530
Jianyang (*Fujian*)	114,692
Jianyang (*Sichuan*)	161,496[9]
Jiaohe	170,359
Jiaonan	270,852
Jiaozhou	267,385
Jiaozuo	576,686
Jiaxing	312,846
Jiayuguan	139,067
Jieshou	106,253
Jieyang	358,176
Jilin	1,242,280
Jimo	258,992
Jinan	2,345,969
Jinchang	148,345
Jincheng	200,659[9]
Jingdezhen	335,492
Jinghong	150,178
Jingjiang	216,104
Jingmen	389,557
Jingzhou	619,170
Jinhua	274,267
Jining (*Inner Mongolia*)	227,191
Jining (*Shandong*)	507,020
Jinjiang	296,433
Jintan	151,745
Jinzhong	262,414
Jinzhou	702,914
Jishou	132,406
Jiujiang	411,532
Jiuquan	121,975
Jiutai	197,779
Jixi	757,640
Jiyuan	241,406[9]
Jurong	139,146
Kaifeng	594,887
Kaili	163,366
Kaiping	281,924
Kaiyuan (*Liaoning*)	141,103

Major cities and national capitals (continued)

country city	population
Kaiyuan (*Yunnan*)	108,668
Karamay	237,918
Kashgar (Kashi)	229,408
Korla	231,369
Kuitun	162,744
Kunming	1,597,768
Kunshan	312,370
Laiwu	416,656
Laixi	160,269
Laiyang	204,000
Laizhou	215,247
Langfang	277,856
Langzhong	238,500
Lanxi	114,959
Lanzhou	1,576,446
Laohekou	165,771
Lechang	177,572[9]
Leiyang	163,278[9]
Leizhou	251,383
Lengshuijiang	176,182[9]
Leping	138,677
Leqing	103,118[9]
Leshan	422,194
Lhasa	129,490
Lianjiang	263,767
Lianyuan	145,329
Lianyungang	536,210
Liaocheng	349,634
Liaoyang	586,882
Liaoyuan	388,364
Liling	140,755
Linchuan	275,230
Linfen	323,671
Lingbao	120,293
Lingyuan	146,756
Linhai	138,794
Linhe	211,506
Linjiang	115,198
Linqing	143,203[9]
Linxia	108,404
Linxiang	111,163
Linyi	679,225
Linzhou	130,055
Lishui	120,592
Liu'an	315,337
Liupanshui	392,783
Liuyang	137,836
Liuzhou	830,515
Liyang	340,743
Longhai	164,716
Longjing	142,732
Longkou	235,994
Longyan	299,192
Loudi	244,728
Lufeng	434,589
Luoding	362,696
Luohe	328,594
Luoyang	1,059,818
Luzhou	404,626
Ma'anshan	443,484
Macheng	175,322[9]
Manzhouli	153,571
Maoming	455,140
Meihekou	261,377
Meishan	140,920
Meizhou	236,424
Mianyang	466,777
Mianzhu	101,157
Miluo	109,282
Mingguang	125,222
Mishan	159,115
Mudanjiang	660,662
Muling	139,871
Nan'an	108,684[9]
Nanchang	1,419,813
Nanchong	508,859
Nanhai	374,363
Nanjing (Nanking)	2,966,047
Nankang	113,543
Nanning	1,031,672
Nanping	272,795
Nantong	564,713
Nanyang	531,220
Nehe	135,382
Neijiang	334,592
Ning'an	147,881
Ningbao	1,045,048
Ningguo	112,785
Panjin	495,174
Panshi	165,101[9]
Panzhihua	507,387
Penglai	115,022
Pengzhou	126,028
Pingdingshan	686,984
Pingdu	243,689
Pinghu	111,183
Pingliang	142,299
Pingxiang	357,785
Pizhou	352,380
Pulandian	166,331[9]
Puning	607,247
Putian	145,051[9]
Puyang	328,449
Qianjiang	314,489
Qidong	254,354
Qilin	210,230[9]
Qingdao	1,930,150
Qingyuan	204,793
Qingzhen	114,026
Qingzhou	196,467
Qinhuangdao	549,118
Qinzhou	193,081
Qiongshan	163,163
Qiqihar (Tsitsihar)	1,125,311
Qitaihe	318,850
Qixia	117,605
Quanzhou	497,723
Qufu	194,053
Qujing	230,129
Quzhou	151,122[9]
Renqiu	158,242[9]
Rizhao	370,306
Rongcheng	261,482
Rugao	316,619
Rui'an	164,563[9]
Rushan	159,179
Ruzhou	107,390
Sanhe	131,214
Sanmenxia	213,604
Sanming	279,538
Sanshui	168,676
Sanya	161,869[9]
Shanghai	10,030,788
Shangqiu	800,157
Shangrao	168,263[9]
Shangyu	141,622
Shangzhi	246,646
Shangzhou	150,384
Shantou	1,201,184
Shanwei	233,450
Shaoguan	463,272
Shaowu	135,616
Shaoxing	347,342
Shaoyang	351,418
Shengzhou	101,649
Shenyang	3,995,531
Shenzhen	1,120,394
Shihezi	352,489
Shijiazhuang	1,970,956
Shishou	158,427
Shiyan	404,809
Shizuishan	322,211
Shouguang	217,903
Shuangcheng	172,936[9]
Shuangliao	141,355
Shuangyashan	436,642
Shulan	212,968
Shunde	648,301
Shuozhou	158,838
Sihui	132,657
Siping	508,533
Songyuan	315,135
Songzi	157,271
Suihua	286,044
Suining	271,461
Suizhou	349,149
Suqian	234,816
Suzhou (*Anhui*)	316,173
Suzhou (*Jiangsu*)	1,215,967
Tai'an	641,239
Taicang	119,862[9]
Taishan	241,356
Taixing	323,540
Taiyuan	1,970,304
Taizhou (*Jiangsu*)	312,210
Taizhou (*Zhejiang*)	281,045
Tangshan	1,498,175
Taonan	153,474
Tengzhou	412,776
Tianchang	167,508[9]
Tianjin (Tientsin)	4,933,106
Tianmen	388,559
Tianshui	480,638
Tiefa	165,956[9]
Tieli	278,768
Tieling	333,008
Tongcheng	104,584
Tongchuan	312,225
Tonghua	392,845
Tongliao	327,008
Tongling	322,960
Tongren	106,937
Tongxiang	117,999
Tongzhou	375,904
Tumen	104,132
Ulanhot	208,643
Ürümqi	1,401,990
Wafangdian	318,779
Weifang	718,772
Weihai	392,947
Weihui	104,257
Weinan	239,542
Wendeng	219,278
Wenling	169,979
Wenzhou	573,469
Wuchang	232,412
Wuchuan	275,845
Wudalianchi	157,547[9]
Wuhai	351,856
Wuhan	4,593,410
Wuhu	567,015
Wujiang	223,322
Wujin	193,775
Wuwei	199,370
Wuxi	1,318,726
Wuxian	176,694[9]
Wuxue	155,855
Wuzhong	112,468
Wuzhou	261,868
Xiamen (Amoy)	963,019
Xi'an (Sian)	2,657,900
Xiangcheng	152,366
Xiangfan	835,170
Xiangtan	561,706
Xiangxiang	115,670
Xianning	222,624
Xiantao	433,034
Xianyang	540,838
Xiaogan	243,816
Xiaoshan	220,815[9]
Xiaoyi	134,150
Xichang	174,781[9]
Xilinhot	121,472
Xingcheng	126,119
Xinghua	263,038
Xingning	300,766
Xingping	114,723
Xingtai	489,715
Xingyang	103,366
Xingyi	118,874
Xinhui	237,675
Xining	654,574
Xinmin	134,802
Xintai	352,171
Xinxiang	647,868
Xinyang	410,393
Xinyi (*Guangdong*)	280,028
Xinyi (*Jiangsu*)	206,602
Xinyu	289,104
Xinzheng	154,539
Xinzhou	143,840[9]
Xishan	171,316[9]
Xuancheng	236,680
Xuanwei	131,150
Xuanzhou	136,914[9]
Xuchang	305,454
Xuzhou	1,210,841
Ya'an	133,263
Yakeshi	386,327
Yan'an	158,038
Yancheng	419,265
Yangchun	213,862
Yangjiang	314,339
Yangquan	487,332
Yangzhou	548,204
Yanji	348,317
Yantai	991,905
Yanzhou	220,768
Yibin	312,462
Yichang	653,040
Yicheng	121,338
Yichun (*Heilongjiang*)	800,649
Yichun (*Jiangxi*)	231,070
Yima	123,228
Yinchuan	535,743
Yingcheng	134,284
Yingde	214,978
Yingkou	528,961
Yingtan	124,632
Yining	258,640
Yixing	297,304
Yiyang	320,675
Yizheng	192,533
Yizhou	101,582
Yong'an	130,688[9]
Yongcheng	147,231
Yongchuan	244,797
Yongzhou	295,690
Yuanjiang	147,395
Yuanping	110,303
Yuci	243,948[9]
Yueyang	522,769
Yuhang	152,429[9]
Yulin (*Guangxi*)	202,413
Yulin (*Shaanxi*)	130,008
Yumen	106,812
Yuncheng	204,080
Yunfu	208,887
Yushu	171,692[9]
Yuxi	126,635
Yuyao	162,722
Yuzhou	148,159
Zaoyang	223,453
Zaozhuang	733,080
Zengcheng	226,776
Zhalantin	152,797
Zhangjiagang	354,935
Zhangjiajie	128,240
Zhangjiakou	688,297
Zhangqiu	227,712
Zhangshu	127,961
Zhangye	158,235
Zhangzhou	356,825
Zhanjiang	719,681
Zhaodong	264,125
Zhaoqing	352,490
Zhaotong	114,996
Zhaoyuan	163,259
Zhengzhou	1,770,828
Zhenjiang	536,137
Zhijiang	132,703
Zhongshan	581,571
Zhongxiang	207,768
Zhoukou	221,767
Zhoushan	253,327
Zhuanghe	161,223[9]
Zhucheng	239,308
Zhuhai	460,937
Zhuji	137,511
Zhumadian	227,088
Zhuozhou	152,480
Zhuzhou	580,450
Zibo	1,519,276
Zigong	485,962
Zixing	125,124
Ziyang	145,665[9]
Zoucheng	352,049
Zunyi	378,602
Colombia (2003 est.)	
Armenia	303,939
Barrancabermeja	187,142
Barranquilla	1,329,579
Bello	372,857
★ Bogotá	6,850,205
Bucaramanga	553,046
Buenaventura	235,054
Buga	115,627
Cali	2,287,819
Cartagena	902,688
Cartago	131,927
Cúcuta	682,671
Dos Quebradas	172,684
Envigado	153,911
Florencia	123,038
Floridablanca	242,016
Girardot	123,637
Giron	102,048
Ibagué	412,820
Itagüí	263,808
Maicao	122,435
Manizales	351,878
Medellín	1,955,753
Montería	264,252
Neiva	335,248
Palmira	241,113
Pasto	365,121
Pereira	420,415
Popayán	212,359
Santa Marta	406,231
Sincelejo	247,211
Soacha	298,138
Sogamoso	120,161
Soledad	326,067
Tuluá	161,057
Tunja	115,127
Valledupar	292,760
Villavicencio	305,476
Comoros (1995 est.)	
★ Moroni	34,168
Congo, Dem. Rep. of the (1994 est.)	
Boma	135,284
Bukavu	201,569
Butembo	109,406
Goma	109,094
Kalemi	101,309
Kananga	393,030
Kikwit	182,142
★ Kinshasa	4,655,313
Kisangani	417,517
Kolwezi	417,810
Likasi	299,118
Lubumbashi	851,381
Matadi	172,730
Mbanadaka	169,841
Mbuji-Mayi	806,475
Mwene-Ditu	137,459
Tshikapa	180,860
Uvira	115,590
Congo, Rep. of the (1996)	
★ Brazzaville	856,410
Pointe-Noire	455,131
Costa Rica (2000)	
★ San José	309,762[10]
Côte d'Ivoire (1998)	
★ Abidjan	2,877,948
Bouaké	461,618
Daloa	173,107
Gagnoa	107,124
Korhogo	142,093
Man	116,657
San Pédro	131,800
Yamoussoukro	110,013
Croatia (2001)	
Rijeka	143,800
Split	175,140
★ Zagreb	691,724
Cuba (2000 est.)	
Bayamo	152,000
Camagüey	304,500
Ciego de Avila	114,600
Cienfuegos	153,300
Guantánamo	222,300
★ Havana	2,175,900[11]
Holguín	263,300
Las Tunas	141,300
Manzanillo	109,300
Matanzas	128,600
Pinar del Río	146,100
Sancti Spíritus	105,700
Santa Clara	216,000
Santiago de Cuba	411,100
Cyprus (2001)	
★ Lefkosia (Nicosia)	47,832[12]
agglomeration	200,686[12]
Czech Republic (2003 est.)	
Brno	370,505
Olomouc	101,624
Ostrava	314,102
Plzeň	163,791
★ Prague	1,161,938
Denmark (2003 est.)	
Ålborg	121,100
Århus	222,599
★ Copenhagen	501,285
Odense	145,374
Djibouti (2004 est.)	
★ Djibouti	465,300
Dominica (2004 est.)	
★ Roseau	20,200
Dominican Republic (2004 est.)	
La Romana	171,500
La Vega	123,400
Puerto Plata	135,600
San Cristóbal	120,200
San Francisco de Macorís	132,700
San Pedro de Macorís	152,600
Santiago	505,600
★ Santo Domingo	1,817,754[13]
East Timor (2004 est.)	
★ Dili	51,700
Ecuador (2001)	
Ambato	154,095
Cuenca	277,374
Duran	174,531
Guayaquil	1,985,379
Ibarra	108,535
Loja	118,532
Machala	204,578
Manta	183,105
Milagro	113,440
Portoviejo	171,847
Quevedo	120,379
★ Quito	1,399,378
Riobamba	124,807
Santo Domingo	199,827
Egypt (1996)	
Alexandria	3,328,196
Al-ʿArīsh	100,447

country / city	population
Aswān	219,017
Asyūṭ	343,498
Banhā	145,792
Banī Suwayf	172,032
Bilbays	113,608
Būr Sa'īd (Port Said)	469,533
★ Cairo	6,789,479
Damanhūr	212,203
Al-Fayyūm	260,964
Al-Ismā'īlīyah	254,477
Al-Jīzah (Giza)	2,221,868
Kafr ad-Dawwar	231,978
Kafr ash-Shaykh	124,819
Al-Maḥallah al-Kubrā	395,402
Mallawī	119,283
Al-Manṣūrah	369,621
Al-Minyā	201,360
Mīt Ghamr	101,801
Qinā	171,275
Sawhāj	170,125
Shibīn al-Kawm	159,909
Shubrā al-Khaymah	870,716
As-Suways (Suez)	417,610
Ṭanṭā	371,010
Al-Uqṣur (Luxor)	360,503
Az-Zaqāzīq	267,351
El Salvador (2000 est.)	
Apopa	139,800[14]
Ilopango	115,400[14]
Mejicanos	172,500[14]
Nueva San Salvador	136,900
San Miguel	159,700
★ San Salvador	479,600
Santa Ana	164,500
Soyapango	285,300[14]
Equatorial Guinea (2003 est.)	
★ Malabo	92,900
Eritrea (2002 est.)	
★ Asmara	500,600
Estonia (2003 est.)	
★ Tallinn	400,378
Tartu	101,169
Ethiopia (1994)	
★ Addis Ababa	2,112,737
Dire Dawa	164,851
Gonder	112,249
Harer (Harar)	131,139
Jima	106,842
Nazret	127,842
Faroe Islands (2002 est.)	
★ Tórshavn	18,070
Fiji (1996)	
★ Suva	77,366
Finland (2003 est.)	
Espoo	221,097
★ Helsinki	559,716
Oulu	124,588
Tampere	199,823
Turku	174,618
Vantaa	181,890
France (1999)	
Aix-en-Provence	134,222
Amiens	135,501
Angers	151,279
Besançon	117,304
Bordeaux	215,118
Boulogne-Billancourt	106,367
Brest	149,634
Caen	113,987
Clermont-Ferrand	137,140
Dijon	149,867
Grenoble	153,317
Le Havre	190,651
Le Mans	146,105
Lille	182,228
Limoges	133,960
Lyon	445,257
Marseille	797,486
Metz	123,776
Montpellier	225,392
Mulhouse	110,359
Nancy	103,605
Nantes	268,695
Nice	342,738
Nîmes	133,424
Orléans	112,833
★ Paris	2,123,261
agglomeration	9,608,000[9]
Perpignan	105,115
Reims	187,206
Rennes	206,229
Rouen	106,035
Saint-Étienne	179,755
Strasbourg	263,940
Toulon	159,389
Toulouse	390,413
Tours	132,820
Villeurbanne	124,215
French Guiana (1999)	
★ Cayenne	50,594
French Polynesia (2002)	
★ Papeete	26,181
agglomeration	124,864
Gabon (1993)	
★ Libreville	362,386
Gambia, The (2003)	
★ Banjul	34,828
agglomeration	523,589
Gaza Strip (2003 est.)	
★ Gaza (Ghazzah; acting administrative centre)	460,899
Jabālyah	159,003
Khān Yūnus	161,880
Rafah	121,223
Georgia (2002)	
Bat'umi (Batumi)	121,800
K'ut'aisi (Kutaisi)	186,000
Rust'avi (Rustavi)	116,400
★ Tbilisi	1,081,700
Germany (2002 est.)	
Aachen	245,778
Augsburg	257,836
Bergisch Gladbach	105,569
★ Berlin	3,388,434
Bielefeld	323,373
Bochum	390,087
Bonn	306,016
Bottrop	120,780
Braunschweig	245,516
Bremen	540,950
Bremerhaven	118,701
Chemnitz	255,798
Cologne (Köln)	967,940
Cottbus	105,954
Darmstadt	138,457
Dortmund	589,240
Dresden	478,631
Duisburg	512,030
Düsseldorf	570,765
Erfurt	200,126
Erlangen	101,919
Essen	591,889
Frankfurt am Main	641,076
Freiburg im Breisgau	208,294
Fürth	111,257
Gelsenkirchen	276,740
Gera	109,926
Göttingen	123,822
Hagen	202,060
Halle	243,045
Hamburg	1,726,363
Hamm	183,805
Hannover	516,415
Heidelberg	141,509
Heilbronn	120,163
Herne	174,018
Hildesheim	103,717
Ingolstadt	117,311
Jena	101,157
Karlsruhe	279,578
Kassel	194,748
Kiel	232,242
Koblenz	107,730
Krefeld	239,559
Leipzig	493,052
Leverkusen	160,829
Lübeck	213,496
Ludwigshafen	162,458
Magdeburg	229,755
Mainz	185,293
Mannheim	308,385
Moers	107,421
Mönchengladbach	262,963
Mülheim an der Ruhr	172,332
Munich (München)	1,227,958
Münster	267,197
Neuss	150,957
Nürnberg	491,307
Oberhausen	221,619
Offenbach am Main	118,429
Oldenburg	155,908
Osnabrück	164,195
Paderborn	140,869
Pforzheim	118,002
Potsdam	130,435
Recklinghausen	124,587
Regensburg	127,198
Remscheid	118,753
Reutlingen	111,338
Rostock	198,964
Saarbrücken	182,858
Salzgitter	111,696
Siegen	108,397
Solingen	165,032
Stuttgart	587,152
Trier	100,024
Ulm	118,347
Wiesbaden	271,076
Witten	103,158
Wolfsburg	121,887
Wuppertal	364,784
Würzburg	129,915
Zwickau	101,726
Ghana (2001 est.)	
★ Accra	1,551,200
Kumasi	610,600
Obuasi	118,000
Tamale	259,200
Tema	225,900
Greece (2001)	
★ Athens	745,514
agglomeration	3,187,734
Iráklion	133,012
Kallithéa	109,609[15]
Larissa	124,786
Pátrai (Patras)	161,114
Peristérion	137,918[15]
Piraiévs (Piraeus)	175,697[15]
Thessaloníki	363,987
Greenland (2000 est.)	
★ Nuuk (Godthåb)	14,265
Grenada (2001)	
★ Saint George's	3,908
agglomeration	31,651
Guadeloupe (1999)	
★ Basse-Terre	12,410
Guam (2000)	
★ Hagåtña (Agana)	1,122
agglomeration	140,000[5]
Guatemala (2002)	
★ Guatemala City	942,348
Mixco	277,400
Quetzaltenango	106,700
Villa Nueva	187,700
Guernsey (2001)	
★ St. Peter Port	16,488
Guinea (2004 est.)	
★ Conakry	1,851,800
Kankan	113,900
Guinea-Bissau (2004 est.)	
★ Bissau	305,700
Guyana (2002)	
★ Georgetown	137,330
Haiti (1997 est.)	
Cap-Haïtien	107,026
Carrefour	306,074
Delmas	257,247
★ Port-au-Prince	917,112
Honduras (2001)	
Choloma	108,260
La Ceiba	114,584
San Pedro Sula	439,086
★ Tegucigalpa	769,061
Hong Kong (2001)	
★ Hong Kong	6,708,389
Hungary (2001)	
★ Budapest	1,775,203
Debrecen	211,034
Győr	129,412
Kecskemét	107,749
Miskolc	184,125
Nyíregyháza	118,795
Pécs	162,498
Szeged	168,372
Székesfehérvár	106,346
Iceland (2003 est.)	
★ Reykjavík	112,490
India (2001)	
Abohar	124,303
Achalpur	107,364
Adilabad	108,233
Adityapur	119,221
Adoni	155,969
Agartala	189,300
Agra	1,259,979
Ahmadabad	3,515,361
Ahmadnagar	307,455
Aizawl	229,700
Ajmer	485,197
Akola	399,978
Alandur	146,154
Alappuzha (Alleppey)	177,079
Aligarh	667,732
Allahabad (Prayag Raj)	990,298
Alwal	106,424
Alwar	260,245
Ambala	139,222
Ambala Sadar	106,378
Ambarnath	203,795
Ambattur	302,492
Amravati	549,370
Amritsar	975,695
Amroha	164,890
Anand	130,462
Anantapur	220,951
Ara (Arrah)	203,395
Asansol	486,304
Ashoknagar Kalyangarh	111,475
Avadi	230,913
Azamgarh	104,943
Bahadurgarh	119,839
Baharampur	160,168
Bahraich	168,376
Baidyabati	108,231
Baleshwar	106,032
Ballia	102,226
Bally	261,575
Balurghat	135,516
Banda	134,832
Bangalore	4,292,223
Bangaon	102,115
Bankura	128,811
Bansberia	104,453
Baranagar (Barahanagar)	250,615
Barasat	231,515
Barddhaman (Burdwan)	285,871
Bareilly	699,830
Barrackpore	144,331
Barshi	104,786
Basirhat	113,120
Basti	106,985
Batala	126,646
Bathinda (Bhatinda)	217,389
Beawar	123,701
Belgaum	399,600
Bellary	317,000
Bettiah	116,692
Bhadravati	160,392
Bhadreswar	105,944
Bhagalpur	340,349
Bhalswa Jahangir Pur	151,427
Bharatpur	204,456
Bharuch (Broach)	148,391
Bhatpara	441,956
Bhavnagar	510,958
Bhilainagar	553,837
Bhilwara	280,185
Bhimavaram	137,327
Bhind	153,768
Bhiwandi	598,703
Bhiwani	169,424
Bhopal	1,443,875
Bhubaneshwar	647,302
Bhusawal	172,366
Bid (Bhir)	138,091
Bidar	172,298
Bidhan Nagar	167,848
Bihar Sharif	231,972
Bijapur	245,946
Bikaner	529,007
Bilaspur	265,178
Bokaro (Bokaro Steel City)	394,173
Bommanahalli	201,220
Botad	100,059
Brahmapur	289,724
Budaun	148,138
Bulandshahr	176,256
Burhanpur	194,360
Byatarayanapura	180,931
Champdani	103,232
Chandannagar	162,166
Chandawsi	103,757
Chandigarh	808,796
Chandrapur	297,612
Chapra	178,835
Chennai (Madras)	4,216,268
Chhindwara	122,309
Chikmagalur	101,022
Chitradurga	122,594
Chittoor	152,966
Coimbatore	923,085
Cuddalore	158,569
Cuddapah	125,725
Cuttack	535,139
Dallo Pura	132,628
Damoh	112,160
Darbhanga	266,834
Darjiling	107,530
Dasarahalli	263,636
Davanagere	363,780
Dehra Dun	447,808
Dehri	119,207
Delhi	9,817,439
Delhi Cantonment	124,452
Deoli	119,432
Deoria	104,222
Dewas	230,658
Dhanbad	198,963
Dharmavaram	103,400
Dhule (Dhulia)	341,473
Dibrugarh	122,523
Dimapur	107,382
Dinapur Nizamat	130,339
Dindigul	196,619
Dum Dum	101,319
Durg	231,182
Durgapur	492,996
Eluru	189,772
Erode	151,184
Etah	107,098
Etawah	211,460
Faizabad	144,924
Faridabad	1,054,981
Farrukhabad-cum-Fatehgarh	227,876
Fatehpur	151,757
Firozabad	278,801
Gadag-Betigeri	154,849
Gajuwaka	258,944
Gandhinagar	195,891
Ganganagar	210,788
Gaya	383,197
Ghatlodiya	106,259
Ghaziabad	968,521
Godhra	121,852
Gonda	122,164
Gondia	120,878
Gorakhpur	624,570
Gudivada	112,245
Gulbarga	427,929
Guna	137,132
Guntakal	117,403
Guntur	514,707
Gurgaon	173,542
Guwahati (Gauhati)	808,021
Gwalior	826,919
Habra	127,695
Hajipur	119,276
Haldia	170,695
Haldwani-cum-Kathgodam	129,140
Halisahar	124,479
Hanumangarh	129,654
Haora (Howrah)	1,008,704
Hapur	211,987
Hardoi	112,474
Haridwar (Hardwar)	175,010
Hassan	117,386
Hathras	123,243
Hazaribag	127,243
Hindupur	125,056
Hisar (Hissar)	256,810
Hoshiarpur	148,243
Hospet	163,284
Hubli-Dharwad	786,018
Hugli-Chunchura	170,201
Hyderabad	3,449,878
Ichalkaranji	257,572
Imphal	217,300
Indore	1,597,441
Ingraj Bazar (English Bazar)	161,148
Jabalpur	951,469
Jagadhri	101,300
Jaipur	2,324,319

Major cities and national capitals (continued)

country / city	population
Jalandhar (Jullundur)	701,223
Jalgaon	368,579
Jalna	235,529
Jalpaiguri	100,212
Jammu	378,431
Jamnagar	447,734
Jamshedpur	570,349
Jamuria	129,456
Jaunpur	159,996
Jetpur Navagadh	104,311
Jhansi	383,248
Jhunjhunun	100,476
Jind	136,089
Jodhpur	846,408
Junagadh	168,686
Kaithal	117,226
Kakinada	289,920
Kalol	100,021
Kalyan-Dombivali	1,193,266
Kamarhati	314,334
Kanchipuram	152,984
Kanchrapara	126,118
Kanpur	2,532,138
Kapra	159,176
Karawal Nagar	148,549
Karimnagar	203,819
Karnal	210,476
Katihar	175,169
Khammam	158,022
Khandwa	171,976
Khanna	103,059
Kharagpur	207,984
Khardaha	116,252
Kirari Suleman Nagar	153,874
Kishangarh	116,156
Kochi (Cochin)	596,473
Kolar	113,299
Kolhapur	485,183
Kolkata (Calcutta)	4,580,544
Kollam (Quilon)	361,441
Korba	315,695
Kota	695,899
Kozhikode (Calicut)	436,527
Krishnanagar	139,170
Krishnarajapura	187,453
Kukatpalle	290,591
Kulti-Barakar	290,057
Kumbakonam	140,021
Kurnool	267,739
Lakhimpur	120,566
Lalbahadur Nagar (L.B. Nagar)	261,987
Lalitpur	111,810
Latur	299,828
Loni	120,659
Lucknow	2,207,340
Ludhiana	1,395,053
Machilipatnam (Masulipatam)	183,370
Madhyamgram	155,503
Madurai	922,913
Mahadevapura	135,597
Mahbubnagar	130,849
Maheshtala	389,214
Malegaon	409,190
Malerkotla	106,802
Malkajgiri	175,000
Mandsaur	116,483
Mandya	131,211
Mangalore	398,745
Mango	166,091
Mathura	298,827
Maunath Bhanjan	210,071
Medinipur (Midnapore)	153,349
Meerut	1,074,229
Mira-Bhayandar	520,301
Mirzapur-cum-Vindhyachal	205,264
Modinagar	112,918
Moga	124,624
Moradabad	641,240
Morena	150,890
Motihari	101,506
Mumbai (Bombay)	11,914,398
Munger (Monghyr)	187,311
Murwara (Katni)	186,738
Muzaffarnagar	316,452
Muzaffarpur	305,465
Mysore	742,261
Nabadwip	115,036
Nadiad	192,799
Nagaon	107,471
Nagercoil	208,149
Nagpur	2,051,320
Naihati	215,432
Nala Sopara	184,664
Nalgonda	110,651
Nanded-Waghala	430,598
Nandyal	151,771
Nangloi Jat	150,371
Nashik (Nasik)	1,076,967
Navghar-Manikpur	116,700
Navi Mumbai (New Mumbai)	703,947
Navsari	134,009
Neemuch	107,496
Nellore	378,947
★ New Delhi	294,783
Neyveli	128,133
Nizamabad	286,956
Noida	293,908
North Barrackpore	123,523
North Dum Dum	220,032
Ongole	149,589
Orai	139,444
Ozhukarai	217,263
Palakkad	130,736
Palanpur	110,383
Pali	187,571
Pallavaram	143,984
Palwal	100,528
Panchkula	140,992
Panihati	348,379
Panipat	261,665
Panvel	104,031
Parbhani	259,170
Patan	112,038
Pathankot	159,559
Patiala	302,870
Patna	1,376,950
Pilibhit	124,082
Pimpri-Chinchwad	1,006,417
Pondicherry	220,749
Porbandar	133,083
Port Blair	100,186
Proddatur	164,932
Pudukkottai	108,947
Pune	2,540,069
Puri	157,610
Purnia (Purnea)	171,235
Puruliya	113,766
Quthbullapur	225,816
Rae Bareli	169,285
Raichur	205,634
Raiganj	165,222
Raigarh	110,987
Raipur	605,131
Raj Nandgaon	143,727
Rajahmundry	313,347
Rajapalaiyam	121,982
Rajarhat Gopalpur	271,781
Rajendranagar	143,184
Rajkot	966,642
Rajpur Sonanpur	336,390
Ramagundam	235,540
Rampur	281,549
Ranchi	846,454
Raniganj	122,891
Ratlam	221,267
Raurkela	224,601
Raurkela Township	206,566
Rewa	183,232
Rewari	100,946
Rishra	113,259
Robertson Pet	141,294
Rohtak	286,773
S.A.S. Nagar (Mohali)	123,284
Sagar	232,321
Saharanpur	452,925
Saharsa	124,015
Salem	693,236
Sambalpur	154,164
Sambhal	182,930
Sangli-Miraj	436,639
Santipur	138,195
Sasaram	131,142
Satara	108,043
Satna	225,468
Secunderabad	204,182
Serampore	197,955
Serilingampalle	150,525
Shahjahanpur	297,932
Shambajinagar (Aurangābād)	872,667
Shantipur	138,200
Shiliguri (Siliguri)	470,275
Shillong	132,876
Shimla	142,161
Shimoga	274,105
Shivapuri	146,859
Sholapur (Solapur)	873,037
Sikandarabad (Secundarabad) Cantonment	204,182
Sikar	184,904
Silchar	142,393
Singrauli	185,580
Sirsa	160,129
Sitapur	151,827
Siwan	108,172
Solapur	873,037
Sonipat (Sonepat)	216,213
South Dum Dum	392,150
Srikakulam	109,666
Srinagar	894,940
Sultan Pur Majra	163,716
Sultanpur	100,085
Surat	2,433,787
Surendranagar Dudhrej	156,417
Tadepalligudem	102,303
Tambaram	137,609
Tenali	149,839
Thane (Thana)	1,261,517
Thanesar	120,072
Thanjavur	215,725
Thiruvananthapuram (Trivandrum)	744,739
Thoothukkudi (Tuticorin)	216,058
Thrissur (Trissur)	317,474
Tiruchchirappalli	746,062
Tirunelveli	411,298
Tirupati	227,657
Tirupper (Tiruppur)	346,551
Tiruvannamalai	130,301
Tiruvottiyur	211,678
Titagarh	124,198
Tonk	135,663
Tumkur	248,592
Udaipur	389,317
Udupi	113,039
Ujjain	429,933
Ulhasnagar	472,943
Uluberia	202,095
Unnao	144,917
Uppal Kalan	118,259
Uttarpara-Kotrung	150,204
Vadodara (Baroda)	1,306,035
Varanasi (Benares)	1,100,748
Vejalpur	113,304
Vellore	177,413
Veraval	141,207
Vidisha	125,457
Vijayawada	825,436
Virar	118,945
Vishakhapatnam	969,608
Vizianagaram	174,324
Warangal	528,570
Wardha	111,070
Yamunanagar	189,587
Yavatmal (Yeotmal)	122,906
Indonesia (2000)[16]	
Ambon	186,911
Balikpapan	409,023
Banda Aceh	154,767
Bandar Lampung	457,927[17]
Bandung	2,136,260
Banjarbaru	123,979
Banjarmasin	527,415
Batam	437,358
Bekasi	1,663,802
Bengkulu	279,753
Binjai	213,725
Bitung	140,270
Blitar	119,372
Bogor	750,819
Cianjur	114,335[17]
Cibinong	101,317[17]
Cilacap	206,928[17]
Cilegon-Merak	294,936
Cimahi	344,607[17]
Ciomas	187,379[17]
Ciparay	111,467[17]
Ciputat	270,815[17]
Cirebon	272,263
Citeurup	105,079[17]
Denpasar	532,440
Depok (*West Java*)	1,143,403
Depok (*Yogyakarta*)	106,825[17]
Dumai	173,188
Gorontalo	134,931
★ Jakarta	8,347,083
Jambi	417,507
Jayapura	155,548
Jember	218,529[17]
Karawang (Krawang)	145,041[17]
Kediri	244,519
Kendari	200,474
Klaten	103,327[17]
Kupang	237,271
Lhokseumawe	109,569[17]
Madiun	163,956
Magelang	117,531
Malang	756,982
Manado	372,887
Mataram	315,738
Medan	1,904,273
Metro	118,448
Mojokerto	108,938
Padang	713,242
Palangkaraya	158,770
Palembang	1,451,419
Palu	263,826
Pangkalpinang	125,319
Parepare	108,258
Pasuruan	168,323
Pekalongan	262,272
Pekanbaru	585,440
Pemalang	103,540[17]
Pematang Siantar	241,480
Percut	129,036[17]
Pondokgede	263,152[17]
Pontianak	464,534
Probolinggo	191,522
Purwokerto	202,452[17]
Salatiga	151,438
Samarinda	521,619
Semarang	1,348,803
Serang	122,429[17]
Sukabumi	252,420
Surabaya	2,599,796
Surakarta	490,214
Taman	106,975[17]
Tangerang	1,325,854
Tanjung Balai	132,385
Tanjung Karang	742,749
Tarakan	116,995
Tasikmalaya	179,766[17]
Tebingtinggi	124,979
Tegal	236,900
Ternate	152,097
Ujung Pandang	1,100,019
Waru	124,282[17]
Yogyakarta	396,711
Iran (1996)	
Ābadan	206,073
Ahvāz	804,980
Āmol	159,092
Andīmeshk	106,923
Arāk	380,755
Ardabīl	340,386
Bābol	158,346
Bandar 'Abbās	273,578
Bandar-e Būshehr (Būshehr)	143,641
Bīrjand	127,608
Bojnūrd	134,835
Borūjerd	217,804
Būkān	120,020
Dezfūl	202,639
Emāmshahr (Shāhrūd)	104,765
Eṣfahān (Isfahan)	1,266,072
Gonbad-e Kavus	111,253
Gorgān	188,710
Hamadān	401,281
Īlām	126,346
Islāmshahr (Eslāmshahr)	265,450
Karaj	940,968
Kāshān	201,372
Kermān	384,991
Kermānshāh (Bākhtarān)	692,986
Khomeynīshahr	165,888
Khorramābād	272,815
Khorramshahr	105,636
Khvoy (Khoy)	148,944
Mahābād	107,799
Malāyer	144,373
Marāgheh	132,318
Marv Dasht	103,579
Mashhad (Meshed)	1,887,405
Masjed-e Soleymān	116,882
Najafābād	178,498
Neyshābūr	158,847
Orūmīyeh	435,200
Qā'emshahr	143,286
Qarchak	142,690
Qazvīn	291,117
Qods	138,278
Qom	777,677
Rasht	417,748
Sabzevār	170,738
Sanandaj	277,808
Saqqez	115,394
Sārī	195,882
Sāveh	111,245
Shahr-e Kord	100,477
Shīrāz	1,053,025
Sīrjān	135,024
Tabrīz	1,191,043
★ Tehrān	6,758,845
Varāmīn	107,233
Yazd	326,776
Zābol	100,888
Zāhedān	419,518
Zanjān	286,295
Iraq (1997 est.)	
Al-'Amārah	362,000
★ Baghdad	5,423,964
Ba'qūbah	312,000
Al-Baṣrah	725,000
Dīwanīyah	467,000
Al-Fallūjah	284,500[18]
Al-Ḥillah	573,000
Irbīl	700,000
Karbalā'	380,000
Karkūk	525,000
Al-Kūfah	123,500[18]
Al-Kūt	420,000
Mosul	925,000
An-Najaf	410,000
An-Nāṣirīyah	587,000
Ar-Ramādī	470,000
Sāmarrā	214,100[18]
As-Samāwah	131,900[18]
As-Sulaymānīyah	525,000
Tall 'Afar	167,800[18]
Az-Zubayr	180,900[18]
Ireland (2002)	
Cork	123,062[19]
★ Dublin	495,781[19]
Isle of Man (2001)	
★ Douglas	25,347
Israel (2003 est.)	
Ashdod	187,500
Ashqelon	103,200
Bat Yam	133,900
Beersheba (Be'er Sheva')	181,500
Bene Beraq	138,900
Haifa (Ḥefa)	270,800
Ḥolon	165,800
★ Jerusalem (Yerushalayim, Al-Quds)	680,400
Netanya	164,800
Petaḥ Tiqwa	172,600
Ramat Gan	126,600
Rishon LeẒiyyon	211,600
Tel Aviv–Yafo	360,400
Italy (2001)[20]	
Ancona	100,507
Bari	316,532
Bergamo	113,143
Bologna	371,217
Brescia	187,567
Cagliari	164,249
Catania	313,110
Ferrara	130,992
Florence (Firenze)	356,118
Foggia	155,203
Forlì	108,335
Genoa (Genova)	610,307
Latina	107,898
Livorno	156,274
Messina	252,026
Milan (Milano)	1,256,211
Modena	175,502
Monza	120,204
Naples (Napoli)	1,004,500
Novara	100,910
Padua (Padova)	204,870
Palermo	686,722
Parma	163,457
Perugia	149,125
Pescara	116,286
Prato	172,499
Ravenna	134,631
Reggio di Calabria	180,353
Reggio nell'Emilia	141,877
Rimini	128,656
★ Rome (Roma)	2,546,804
Salerno	138,188
Sassari	120,729
Siracusa (Syracuse)	123,657
Taranto	202,033
Terni	105,018
Trento	104,946
Trieste	211,184
Turin (Torino)	865,263
Venice (Venezia)	271,073
Verona	253,208
Vicenza	107,223
Jamaica (2001)	
★ Kingston	96,052
agglomeration	575,000[5]
Spanish Town	131,515

country city	population
Japan (2000)	
Abiko	127,718
Ageo	212,949
Aizuwakamatsu	118,126
Akashi	293,117
Akishima	106,547
Akita	317,625
Amagasaki	466,187
Anjō	158,826
Aomori	297,859
Asahikawa	359,536
Asaka	119,716
Ashikaga	163,136
Atsugi	217,369
Beppu	125,518
Chiba	887,164
Chigasaki	220,809
Chōfu	204,759
Daitō	129,011
Ebetsu	123,875
Ebina	117,510
Fuchu	226,769
Fuji	234,187
Fujieda	128,477
Fujimi	103,228
Fujinomiya	120,233
Fujisawa	379,185
Fukaya	103,533
Fukui	252,274
Fukuoka	1,341,470
Fukushima	291,121
Fukuyama	378,789
Funabashi	550,074
Gifu	402,751
Habikino	119,254
Hachinohe	241,920
Hachiōji	536,046
Hadano	168,142
Hagi	140,458
Hakodate	287,637
Hamamatsu	582,095
Handa	110,819
Higashi-Hiroshima	123,418
Higashi-Kurume	113,300
Higashi-Murayama	113,264
Higashi Ōsaka	515,094
Hikone	107,864
Himeji	478,309
Hino	167,934
Hirakata	402,563
Hiratsuka	254,633
Hirosaki	177,086
Hiroshima	1,126,239
Hitachi	193,353
Hitachinaka	151,666
Hōfu	104,658
Hoya	102,713
Ibaraki	260,648
Ichihara	278,218
Ichikawa	448,642
Ichinomiya	273,711
Iida	107,378
Ikeda	101,601
Ikoma	112,858
Imabari	117,931
Inazawa	100,273
Iruma	147,905
Ise	100,144
Isesaki	125,762
Ishinomaki	119,796
Itami	192,152
Iwaki	360,138
Iwakuni	105,765
Iwatsuki	109,278
Izumi	172,975
Joetsu	134,763
Kadoma	135,669
Kagoshima	552,098
Kakamigahara	131,990
Kakogawa	266,170
Kamagaya	102,579
Kamakura	167,583
Kanazawa	456,438
Kariya	132,000
Kashihara	125,016
Kashiwa	327,851
Kasuga	105,146
Kasugai	287,623
Kasukabe	203,375
Kawachinagano	121,012
Kawagoe	330,766
Kawaguchi	460,027
Kawanishi	153,762
Kawasaki	1,249,905
Kiryū	115,435
Kisarazu	122,766
Kishiwada	200,104
Kita-Kyūshū	1,011,471
Kitami	112,040
Kobe	1,493,398
Kochi	330,654
Kodaira	178,562
Kofu	196,155
Koganei	111,665
Kokubunji	111,310
Komaki	143,117
Komatsu	108,615
Koriyama	334,824
Koshigaya	308,307
Kumagaya	156,192
Kumamoto	662,012
Kurashiki	430,291
Kure	203,159
Kurume	236,543
Kusatsu	115,450
Kushiro	191,739
Kuwana	108,417
Kyōto	1,467,785
Machida	377,494
Maebashi	284,155
Matsubara	132,560
Matsudo	464,841
Matsue	152,616
Matsumoto	208,970
Matsuyama	473,379
Matsuzaka	123,733
Minōh	124,905
Misato	131,056
Mishima	110,522
Mitaka	171,601
Mito	246,739
Miyakonojō	131,918
Miyazaki	305,755
Moriguchi	152,032
Morioka	288,843
Muroran	103,278
Musashino	135,775
Nagano	360,112
Nagaoka	193,414
Nagareyama	150,520
Nagasaki	423,167
Nagoya	2,171,557
Naha	301,032
Nara	366,185
Narashino	154,040
Neyagawa	250,800
Niigata	501,431
Niihama	125,539
Niiza	149,516
Nishinomiya	438,105
Nishio	100,804
Nobeoka	124,762
Noda	119,941
Numazu	207,558
Obihiro	173,030
Odawara	200,173
Ōgaki	150,238
Ōita	436,470
Okayama	626,642
Okazaki	336,583
Okinawa	119,699
Ōme	141,307
Ōmiya	456,271
Ōmuta	138,635
Ōsaka	2,598,774
Ōta	147,897
Ōtaru	150,687
Ōtsu	288,240
Oyama	155,198
Saga	167,972
Sagamihara	605,561
Sakai	792,018
Sakata	101,300
Sakura	170,931
Sanda	111,734
Sapporo	1,822,368
Sasebo	240,838
Sayama	161,467
Sendai	1,008,130
Seto	131,650
Shimizu	236,818
Shimonoseki	252,389
Shizuoka	469,695
Sōka	225,018
Suita	347,929
Suzuka	186,138
Tachikawa	164,634
Tajimi	104,134
Takamatsu	332,865
Takaoka	172,171
Takarazuka	213,037
Takasaki	239,904
Takatsuki	357,438
Tama	145,859
Toda	108,092
Tokorozawa	330,100
Tokushima	268,218
Tokuyama	108,700
★ Tokyo	8,134,688
Tomakomai	172,086
Tondabayashi	126,551
Tottori	150,439
Toyama	325,700
Toyohashi	364,856
Toyokawa	117,356
Toyonaka	391,726
Toyota	351,101
Tsu	163,246
Tsuchiura	134,710
Tsukuba	165,978
Tsuruoka	165,968
Ube	174,427
Ueda	125,344
Uji	189,113
Urasoe	102,746
Urawa	484,845
Urayasu	133,012
Utsunomiya	443,508
Wakayama	386,551
Yachiyo	168,848
Yaizu	118,247
Yamagata	255,369
Yamaguchi	140,447
Yamato	212,761
Yao	274,777
Yatsushiro	106,145
Yokkaichi	291,105
Yokohama	3,426,651
Yokosuka	428,645
Yonago	135,800
Zama	125,683
Jersey (2001)	
★ St. Helier	28,310
Jordan (2000 est.)	
★ Amman	1,147,447
Irbid	247,275
Ar-Ruṣayfah	218,211
Az-Zarqā'	428,623
Kazakhstan (1999)	
Almaty (Alma-Ata)	1,129,400
Aqtaū (Aktau; Shevchenko)	143,400
Aqtöbe (Aktyubinsk)	253,100
★ Astana (Aqmola; Tselinograd)	313,000
Atyraū (Guryev)	142,500
Ekibastuz	127,200
Kökshetaū (Kokchetav)	123,400
Oral (Uralsk)	195,500
Öskemen (Ust-Kamenogorsk)	311,000
Pavlodar	300,500
Petropavl (Petropavlovsk)	203,500
Qaraghandy (Karaganda)	436,900
Qostanay (Kustanay)	221,400
Qyzylord (Kzyl-Orda)	157,400
Rūdny	109,500
Semey (Semipalatinsk)	269,600
Shymkent (Shimkent; Chimkent)	360,100
Taraz (Auliye-Ata; Dzhambul)	330,100
Temirtaū	170,500
Kenya (1999)	
Eldoret	167,016
Kisumu	322,734
Machakos	144,109
Meru	126,427
Mombasa	665,018
★ Nairobi	2,143,354
Nakuru	219,366
Kiribati (2000)	
★ Bairiki (agglomeration)	36,717
Korea, North (1993)	
Anju	186,000[21]
Ch'ŏngjin	582,480
Haeju	229,172
Hamhŭng-Hungnam	709,730
Hŭich'ŏn	163,000[21]
Hyesan	178,020
Kaesŏng	334,433
Kanggye	223,410
Kimch'aek (Songjin)	179,000[21]
Kusŏng	177,000[21]
Namp'o	731,448
P'yŏngsŏng	272,934
★ P'yŏngyang	2,741,260
Sariwŏn	254,146
Sinp'o	158,000[21]
Sinŭiju	326,011
Sunch'ŏn	356,000[21]
Tanch'ŏn	284,000[21]
Tŏkch'ŏn	217,000[21]
Wŏnsan	300,148
Korea, South (2003 est.)	
Andong	179,587
Ansan	637,660
Ansŏng	149,233
Anyang	597,656
Asan	193,188
Ch'angwŏn	517,577
Chech'ŏn	143,655
Cheju (Jeju)	290,664
Chinhae	141,936
Chinju	340,816
Ch'ŏnan	445,485
Ch'ŏngju	626,069
Chŏng-ŭp	139,876
Chŏnju	626,069
Ch'unch'ŏn	253,532
Ch'ungju	212,875
Hanam	127,935
Hwasŏng	231,347
Ich'ŏn	190,641
Iksan (Iri)	332,545
Inch'ŏn (Incheon)	2,596,102
Kangnŭng	230,714
Kimch'ŏn	147,760
Kimhae	393,936
Kimje	111,462
Kimp'o	196,193
Kŏje	183,897
Kongju	133,012
Koyang	840,345
Kumi	354,746
Kunp'o	269,889
Kunsan	273,086
Kuri	193,850
Kwangju (*Kwangju*)	1,401,525
Kwangju (*Kyŏnggi*)	177,593
Kwangmyŏng	341,617
Kwangyang	138,102
Kyŏngju	285,900
Kyŏngsan	221,196
Masan	434,996
Miryang	120,808
Mokp'o	245,315
Naju	103,452
Namwon	100,677
Namyangju	394,202
Nonsan	138,013
Osan	116,624
P'aju	237,341
P'ohang	513,424
Poryŏng	113,671
Puch'ŏn	821,081
Pusan (Busan)	3,747,369
P'yŏngt'aek	362,507
Sach'ŏn	117,427
Sangju	119,283
★ Seoul (Sŏul)	10,280,523
Shihŭng	359,072
Sŏngnam	946,445
Sŏsan	148,697
Sunch'ŏn	271,636
Suwŏn	1,023,875
Taegu	2,540,647
Taejŏn	1,424,844
Tonghae	103,039
Tongyŏng	134,581
Ŭijŏngbu	380,521
Ŭiwang	133,967
Ulsan	1,070,277
Wŏnju	277,987
Yangsan	208,304
Yŏngch'ŏn	116,523
Yongin	529,300
Yŏngju	126,303
Yŏsu	316,143
Kuwait (1995)	
★ Kuwait (Al-Kuwayt)	28,859
agglomeration	888,000[22]
Qalīb ash-Shuyūkh	102,178
As-Sālimīyah	130,215
Kyrgyzstan (1999 est.)	
★ Bishkek	750,327
Osh	208,520
Laos (2003 est.)	
★ Vientiane (Viangchan)	194,200
agglomeration	716,000
Latvia (2002 est.)	
Daugavpils	113,400
★ Rīga	747,157
Lebanon (2003 est.)	
★ Beirut (Bayrūt)	1,171,000
Tripoli (Ṭarābulus)	212,900
Lesotho (1996 est.)	
★ Maseru	160,100
Liberia (2002 est.)	
★ Monrovia	543,000
Libya (2003 est.)	
Banghāzī	446,250
Miṣrātah	121,669
★ Tripoli (Ṭarābulus)	591,060
agglomeration	2,006,000
Liechtenstein (2002 est.)	
★ Vaduz	4,949
Lithuania (2004 est.)	
Kaunas	368,917
Klaipėda	190,098
Panevėžys	117,606
Šiauliai	131,184
★ Vilnius	553,038
Luxembourg (2001)	
★ Luxembourg	76,688
Macau (2001)	
★ Macau	435,235
Macedonia (2002; MU)	
Kumanovo	103,205
★ Skopje (Skopije)	467,257
Madagascar (2001 est.)	
★ Antananarivo	1,403,449
Antsirabe	160,356
Fianarantsoa	144,225
Mahajanga	135,660
Toamasina	179,045
Toliara	101,661
Malawi (2003 est.)	
★ Blantyre (judicial)	646,235
★ Lilongwe (executive; legislative)	597,619
Mzuzu	119,592
Malaysia (2000)	
Alor Setar	114,949
Ampang	126,459
George Town (Pinang)	180,573
Ipoh	566,211
Johor Bahru	384,613
Klang	563,173
Kota Baharu	233,673
Kota Kinabalu	145,000[23]
★ Kuala Lumpur	1,297,526
Kuala Terengganu	250,528
Kuantan	283,041
Kuching	152,310[23]
Miri	140,000[23]
Petaling Jaya	438,084
★ Putrajaya (partly completed in 2004)	...
Sandakan	220,000[23]
Selayang Baru	170,000[23]
Seremban	246,441
Shah Alam	319,612
Sibu	155,000[23]
Sungai Petani	170,000[23]
Taiping	183,320
Tawau	145,000[23]
Maldives (2000)	
★ Male	74,069
Mali (1998)	
★ Bamako	1,016,167
Sikasso	113,803
Malta (2002 est.)	
★ Valletta	7,199
agglomeration	83,000[5]
Marshall Is. (2004 est.)	
★ Majuro	20,800
Martinique (1999)	
★ Fort-de-France	94,049
Mauritania (2000)	
★ Nouakchott	558,195
Mauritius (2000)	
Beau Bassin-Rose Hill	103,872
★ Port Louis	144,303
Vacoas-Phoenix	100,066
Mayotte (2002; MU)	
★ Mamoudzou	45,485

Major cities and national capitals (continued)

country city	population
Mexico (2000)	
Acapulco	620,656
Aguascalientes	594,092
Atizapán de Zaragoza (Ciudad López Mateos)	467,544
Boca del Río	123,891
Buenavista	193,707
Campeche	190,813
Cancún	397,191
Celaya	277,750
Chalco	125,027
Chetumal	121,602
Chihuahua	657,876
Chilpancingo	142,746
Chimalhuacán	482,530
Ciudad Acuña (Acuña)	108,159
Ciudad Apodaca (Apodaca)	270,369
Ciudad del Carmen	126,024
Ciudad Madero	182,325
Ciudad Obregón	250,790
Ciudad Santa Catarina (Santa Catarina)	225,976
Ciudad Valles	105,721
Ciudad Victoria (Victoria)	249,029
Coacalco	252,291
Coatzacoalcos	225,973
Colima	119,639
Córdoba	133,807
Cuautitlán Izcalli	433,830
Cuautla Morelos	136,932
Cuernavaca	327,162
Culiacán	540,823
Durango	427,135
Ecatepec (de Morelos)	1,621,827
Ensenada	223,492
General Escobedo	230,556
Gómez Palacio	210,113
Guadalajara	1,646,183
Guadalupe	669,842
Hermosillo	545,928
Heroica Nogales (Nogales)	156,854
Huixquilucan	107,951
Iguala	104,759
Irapuato	319,148
Ixtapaluca	235,827
Jiutepec	142,459
Juárez (Ciudad Juárez)	1,187,275
La Paz	162,954
León	1,020,818
Los Mochis	200,906
Los Reyes la Paz	211,298
Matamoros	376,279
Mazatlán	327,989
Mérida	662,530
Metepec	158,605
Mexicali	549,873
★ Mexico City	8,605,239
Minatitlán	109,193
Monclova	192,554
Monterrey	1,110,909
Morelia	549,996
Naucalpan	835,053
Nezahualcóyotl	1,225,083
Nicolás Romero	216,192
Nuevo Laredo	308,828
Oaxaca	251,846
Orizaba	118,552
Pachuca	231,602
Piedras Negras	126,386
Poza Rica de Hidalgo	151,441
Puebla	1,271,673
Puerta Vallarta	151,432
Querétaro	536,463
Reynosa	403,718
Salamanca	137,000
Saltillo	562,587
San Cristóbal de las Casas	112,442
San Francisco Coacalco	252,291
San Luis Potosí	629,208
San Luis Río Colorado	126,645
San Nicolás de los Garzas	496,879
San Pablo de las Salinas	146,560
San Pedro Garza García	125,945
Soledad de Graciano Sanchez	169,574
Tampico	295,442
Tapachula	179,839
Tehuacán	204,598
Topic	265,817
Texcoco (de Mora)	101,711
Tijuana	1,148,681
Tlalnepantla	714,735
Tlaquepaque	458,674
Toluca	435,125
Tonala	315,278
Torreón	502,964
Tuxtla Gutiérrez	424,579
Uruapan	225,816
Valle de Chalco (Xico)	322,784
Veracruz	411,582
Villahermosa	330,846
Xalapa (Jalapa Enríquez)	373,075
Xico	322,784
Zacatecas	113,947
Zamora de Hidalgo	122,881
Zapopan	910,690
Micronesia (2000)	
★ Palikir	6,227
Moldova (2003 est.)	
Bălţi (Beltsy)	145,900
★ Chişinău (Kishinyov)	662,400
Tighina (Bendery)	125,000
Tiraspol	185,000
Monaco (2000)	
★ Monaco	32,020
Mongolia (2000)	
★ Ulaanbaatar (Ulan Bator)	760,077
Morocco (1994)	
Agadir	524,564
Beni-Mellal	140,212
Casablanca	2,770,560
El-Jadida	119,083
Fès	769,014
Kenitra	292,627
Khouribga	152,090
Ksar el-Kebir	107,065
Marrakech	672,506
Meknès	443,214
Mohammedia	170,063
Nador	112,450
Oujda	351,878
★ Rabat	623,457
Safi	262,276
Salé	504,420
Tangier	497,147
Temera	126,303
Tétouan	277,516
Mozambique (1997)	
Beira	412,588
Chimoio	177,608
★ Maputo	989,386
Matola	440,927
Mocuba	124,650
Nacala	164,309
Nampula	314,965
Quelimane	153,187
Tete	104,832
Xai-Xai	103,251
Myanmar (Burma) (2004 est.)	
Bassein (Pathein)	215,600
Henzada	122,700
Lashio	133,600
Mandalay	1,176,900
Maymyo	113,900
Meiktila	161,000
Mergui	148,200
Monywa	163,400
Moulmein (Mawlamyine)	405,800
Myingyan	128,600
Pakokku	112,500
Pegu (Bago)	200,900
Pyay (Prome, Pye)	131,200
Sittwe (Akyab)	161,400
Taunggyi	151,400
Tavoy (Dawei)	139,900
Thaton	104,800
★ Yangôn (Rangoon)	4,454,500
Namibia (2001 est.)	
★ Windhoek	220,000
Nauru (1992)	
★ Yaren	672
Nepal (2001; MU)	
Biratnagar	166,674
Birganj	112,484
★ Kathmandu	671,846
Lalitpur (Patan)	162,991
Pokhara	156,312
Netherlands, The (2003 est.)	
Almere	164,943
Amersfoort	131,164
★ Amsterdam (capital)	735,080
Apeldoorn	155,779
Arnhem	141,728
Breda	164,378
Dordrecht	119,970
Ede	104,801
Eindhoven	206,138
Emmen	108,226
Enschede	152,255
Groningen	177,145
Haarlem	147,596
Haarlemmermeer	123,164
Leiden	117,682
Maastricht	122,004
Nijmegen	156,197
Rotterdam	599,472
's-Hertogenbosch	132,696
★ The Hague (seat of government)	463,841
Tilburg	198,028
Utrecht	265,107
Zaanstad	139,457
Zoetermeer	112,632
Zwolle	109,916
Netherlands Antilles (2001 est.)	
★ Willemstad	125,000
New Caledonia (1996)	
★ Nouméa	76,293
New Zealand (2003 est.)[24]	
Auckland	406,000
Christchurch	358,000
Dunedin	113,600
Hamilton	150,400
Manukau	358,000
North Shore	244,200
Waitakere	191,000
★ Wellington	178,000
Nicaragua (1995)	
León	123,865
★ Managua	864,201
Niger (2001)	
Maradi	147,038
★ Niamey	674,950
Zinder	170,574
Nigeria (1991)	
Aba	500,183
Abeokuta	352,735
★ Abuja	420,000[22]
Ado-Ekiti	156,122
Akure	239,124
Awka	104,682
Bauchi	206,537
Benin City	762,719
Bida	111,245
Calabar	310,839
Damaturu	141,897
Ede	142,363
Effon-Alaiye	158,977
Enugu	407,756
Gboko	101,281
Gombe	163,604
Gusau	132,393
Ibadan	1,835,300
Ife	186,856
Ijebu-Ode	124,313
Ikare	103,843
Ikire	111,435
Ikorodu	184,674
Ikot Ekpene	119,402
Ilawe-Ekiti	104,049
Ilesha	139,445
Ilorin	532,089
Ise	108,136
Iseyin	170,936
Iwo	125,645
Jimeta	141,724
Jos	510,300
Kaduna	993,642
Kano	2,166,554
Katsina	259,315
★ Lagos	5,195,247
agglomeration	13,400,000[22]
Maiduguri	618,278
Makurdi	151,515
Minna	189,191
Mubi	128,900
Nnewi	121,065
Ogbomosho	433,030
Okene	312,775
Okpogho	105,127
Ondo	146,051
Onitsha	350,280
Oshogbo	250,951
Owerri	119,711
Owo	157,181
Oyo	369,894
Port Harcourt	703,421
Sagamu	127,513
Sango Otta	103,332
Sapele	109,576
Sokoto	329,639
Suleja	105,075
Ugep	134,773
Umuahia	147,167
Warri	363,382
Zaria	612,257
Northern Mariana Is. (2000)	
★ Saipan	62,392
Norway (2003 est.; MU)	
Bærum	102,529
Bergen	235,423
★ Oslo	517,401
Stavanger	111,007
Trondheim	152,699
Oman (2003)	
As-Sīb	223,267
Bawshar	149,506
Maṭraḥ	154,316
★ Muscat	56,410
agglomeration	631,031
Salālah	156,587
Ṣuḥār	104,057
Pakistan (1998)	
Abbottabad	105,999[25]
Bahawalnagar	109,642
Bahawalpur	403,408[25]
Burewala	149,857
Chiniot	169,282
Chishtian Mandi	101,659
Daska	101,500
Dera Ghazi Khan	188,149
Faisalabad (Lyallpur)	1,977,246
Gojra	114,967
Gujranwala	1,124,799
Gujrat	250,121
Hafizabad	130,216
Hyderabad	1,151,274[25]
★ Islamabad	524,500
Jacobabad	137,773
Jaranwala	103,308
Jhang Sadar	292,214
Jhelum	145,847
Kamoke	150,984
Karachi	9,269,265[25]
Kasur	241,649
Khairpur	102,188
Khanewal	132,962
Khanpur	117,764
Kohat	125,271[25]
Lahore	5,063,499[25]
Larkana	270,366
Mardan	244,511[25]
Mingaora	174,469
Mirpur Khas	184,465
Multan	1,182,441[25]
Muridike	108,578
Muzaffargarh	121,641
Nawabshah	183,110
Okara	200,901
Pakpattan	107,791
Peshawar	988,055[25]
Quetta	560,307
Rahimyar Khan	228,479
Rawalpindi	1,406,214[25]
Sadiqabad	141,509
Sahiwal	207,388
Sargodha	455,360[25]
Shekhupura	271,875
Shikarpur	133,259
Sialkot	417,597[25]
Sukkur	329,176
Tando Adam	103,363
Wah	198,431[25]
Palau (2000)	
★ Koror (de facto)	13,303
★ Melekeok (complex under construction)	239
Panama (2000)	
★ Panama City	469,307
San Miguelito	293,745[26]
Papua New Guinea (2000)	
★ Port Moresby (National Capital District)	254,158
Paraguay (2002)	
★ Asunción	513,399
Capiatá	154,469
Ciudad del Este	223,350
Fernando de la Mora	114,332
Lambaré	119,984
Luque	170,433
San Lorenzo	202,745
Peru (1998 est.)	
Arequipa	710,103
Ayacucho	118,960
Cajamarca	108,009
Chiclayo	469,200
Chimbote	298,800
Chincha Alta	130,000
Cusco	278,590
Huancayo	305,039
Huánuco	129,688
Ica	194,820
Iquitos	334,013
Juliaca	180,000
Lima agglomeration	7,899,000[27]
Ate	324,799
Callao	407,904
Carabayllo	115,000
Chorrillos	238,739
Comas	434,690
El Agustino	159,707
Independencia	191,151
La Victoria	213,239
★ Lima	316,322
Los Olivos	281,115
Lurigancho	110,347
Puente Piedra	131,000
Rímac	190,836
San Borja	109,233
San Juan de Lurigancho	652,681
San Juan de Miraflores	329,023
San Martin de Porras	411,000
San Miguel	126,825
Santa Anita	131,519
Santiago de Surco	224,866
Ventanilla	105,824
Villa el Salvador	296,000
Villa Maria del Triunfo	301,505
Piura	308,155
Pucallpa	220,866
Puno	101,578
Sullana	170,000
Tacna	215,683
Trujillo	603,657
Philippines (2000)	
Angeles	263,971
Antipolo	200,000[23]
Bacolod	429,076
Bacoor	305,699
Baguio	252,386
Baliuag	119,675
Biñan	201,186
Binangonan	187,691
Butuan	120,000[23]
Cagayan de Oro	461,877
Cainta	242,511
Calamba	160,000[23]
Cebu	718,821
Cotabato	163,849
Dagupan	130,328
Dasmariñas	250,000[23]
Davao	700,000[23]
Dumaguete	102,265
General Mariano Alvarez	112,446
General Santos	250,000[23]
Iloilo	365,820
Kalookan (Caloocan)	1,177,604
Lapu-Lapu	217,019
Las Piñas	472,780
Lucena	196,075
Makati	444,867
Malabon	338,855
Malolos	175,291
Mandaluyong	278,474
Mandaue	259,728
★ Manila	1,581,082
Metro Manila	9,932,560

country city	population
Marawi	131,090
Marikina	391,170
Meycauayan	163,037
Muntinglupa	379,310
Naga	137,810
Navotas	230,403
Olongapo	194,260
Parañaque	449,811
Pasay	354,908
Pasig	505,058
★ Quezon City	2,173,831
San Fernando	221,857
San Juan del Monte	117,680
San Pablo	105,000[23]
San Pedro	231,403
Santa Rosa	185,633
Tacloban	178,639
Tagig	467,375
Taytay	198,183
Valenzuela	485,433
Zamboanga	135,000[23]
Poland (2002)	
Białystok	291,383
Bielsko-Biała	178,028
Bydgoszcz	373,804
Bytom	193,546
Chorzów	117,430
Częstochowa	251,436
Dąbrowa Górnicza	132,236
Elbląg	128,134
Gdańsk	461,334
Gdynia	253,458
Gliwice	203,814
Gorzów Wielkopolski	125,914
Grudziadz	100,376
Kalisz	109,498
Katowice	327,222
Kielce	212,429
Koszalin	108,709
Kraków	758,544
Legnica	107,100
Łódź	789,318
Lublin	357,110
Olsztyn	173,102
Opole	129,946
Płock	128,361
Poznań	578,886
Radom	229,699
Ruda Śląska	150,595
Rybnik	142,731
Rzeszów	160,376
Sosnowiec	232,622
Szczecin	415,399
Tarnów	119,913
Toruń	211,243
Tychy	132,816
Wałbrzych	130,268
★ Warsaw (Warszawa)	1,671,670
Włocławek	121,229
Wrocław	640,367
Zabrze	195,293
Zielona Góra	118,293
Portugal (2001)	
Amadora	151,486
Braga	112,039
Coimbra	104,489
Funchal	103,961
★ Lisbon	564,657
agglomeration	1,962,000[5]
Porto	263,131
Puerto Rico (2000)	
Bayamón	203,499[24]
Carolina	168,164[24]
Ponce	155,038[24]
★ San Juan	421,958[24]
agglomeration	2,332,000[5]
Qatar (2004)	
★ Doha	338,760
Ar-Rayyān	272,583
Réunion (1999)	
★ Saint-Denis	131,557
Romania (2002)	
Arad	172,824
Bacău	175,921
Baia Mare	137,976
Botoşani	115,344
Brăila	216,929
Braşov	283,901
★ Bucharest	1,921,751
Buzău	133,116
Cluj-Napoca	318,027
Constanţa	310,526
Craiova	302,622
Drobeta-Turnu Severin	104,035
Focşani	103,219
Galaţi	298,584
Iaşi	321,580
Oradea	206,527
Piatra Neamţ	105,499
Piteşti	168,756
Ploieşti	232,452
Râmnicu Vâlcea	107,656
Satu Mare	115,630
Sibiu	155,045
Suceava	106,138
Timişoara	317,651
Târgu Mureş	149,577
Russia (2002)	
Abakan	165,200
Achinsk	118,700
Almetyevsk	140,500
Angarsk	247,100
Arkhangelsk	355,500
Armavir	193,900
Arzamas	109,500
Astrakhan	506,400
Balakovo	200,600
Balashikha	148,200
Barnaul	603,500
Bataisk	107,300
Belgorod	337,600
Berezniki	173,500
Biysk	218,600
Blagoveshchensk	218,800
Bratsk	259,200
Bryansk	431,600
Cheboksary	440,800
Chelyabinsk	1,078,300
Cherepovets	312,200
Cherkessk	116,400
Chita	317,800
Derbent	100,800
Dimitrovgrad	130,900
Dzerzhinsk	261,400
Elektrostal	146,100
Elista	104,300
Engels	193,800
Glazov	100,900
Grozny (Dzhokhar)	223,000
Irkutsk	593,400
Ivanovo	432,200
Izhevsk	632,100
Kaliningrad	430,300
Kaluga	335,100
Kamensk-Uralsky	186,300
Kamyshin	128,100
Kansk	103,100
Kazan	1,105,300
Kemerovo	485,000
Khabarovsk	582,700
Khasavyurt	122,000
Khimki	141,300
Kirov	457,400
Kiselyovsk	106,400
Kislovodsk	129,800
Kolomna	150,100
Kolpino	161,900
Komsomolsk-na-Amure	281,000
Korolyov (Kaliningrad)	143,100
Kostroma	279,100
Kovrov	155,600
Krasnodar	644,800
Krasnoyarsk	911,700
Kurgan	345,700
Kursk	412,600
Kyzyl	104,100
Leninsk-Kuznetsky	112,300
Lipetsk	506,000
Lyubertsy	156,900
Magadan	101,100
Magnitogorsk	419,100
Makhachkala	466,800
Maykop	162,400
Mezhdurechensk	102,000
Miass	158,500
★ Moscow	10,101,500
Murmansk	336,700
Murom	126,800
Mytishchi	159,200
Naberezhnye Chelny (Brezhnev)	510,000
Nakhodka	149,300
Nalchik	273,900
Nazran	126,700
Nefteyugansk	107,800
Nevinnomyssk	132,100
Nikolo-Beryozovka (Neftekamsk)	122,300
Nizhnekamsk	225,500
Nizhnevartovsk	239,000
Nizhny Novgorod (Gorky)	1,311,200
Nizhny Tagil	390,600
Noginsk	118,000
Norilsk	135,100
Novgorod	217,200
Novocheboksarsk	125,900
Novocherkassk	170,900
Novokuybyshevsk	113,000
Novokuznetsk	550,100
Novomoskovsk	134,000
Novorossiysk	231,900
Novoshakhtinsk	101,200
Novosibirsk	1,425,600
Novotroitsk	106,200
Obninsk	105,800
Odintsovo	134,700
Oktyabrsky	108,700
Omsk	1,133,900
Orekhovo-Zuyevo	122,300
Orenburg	548,800
Orsk	250,600
Oryol	333,600
Penza	518,200
Perm	1,000,100
Pervouralsk	132,800
Petropavlovsk-Kamchatsky	198,200
Petrozavodsk	266,200
Podolsk	181,500
Prokopyevsk	224,600
Pskov	202,700
Pyatigorsk	140,300
Rostov-na-Donu	1,070,200
Rubtsovsk	163,100
Ryazan	521,700
Rybinsk (Andropov)	222,800
Saint Petersburg (Leningrad)	4,669,400
Salavat	158,500
Samara (Kuybyshev)	1,158,100
Saransk	304,900
Sarapul	103,200
Saratov	873,500
Sergiev Posad (Zagorsk)	113,800
Serov	100,300
Serpukhov	131,200
Severodvinsk	201,500
Seversk	115,700
Shakhty	220,400
Shchyolkovo	113,700
Simbirsk (Ulyanovsk)	635,600
Smolensk	325,500
Sochi	328,800
Solikamsk	102,800
Stary Oskol	216,000
Stavropol	354,600
Sterlitamak	264,400
Surgut	285,500
Syktyvkar	230,000
Syzran	187,800
Taganrog	282,300
Tambov	294,300
Tolyatti	701,900
Tomsk	487,700
Tula	472,300
Tver (Kalinin)	409,400
Tyumen	510,700
Ufa	1,042,400
Ukhta	103,500
Ulan-Ude	359,400
Usolye-Sibirskoye	103,500
Ussuriysk	157,800
Ust-Ilimsk	100,600
Velikiye Luki	105,000
Vladikavkaz (Ordzhonikidze)	315,100
Vladimir	316,300
Vladivostok	591,800
Volgodonsk	166,500
Volgograd	1,012,800
Vologda	292,800
Volzhsky	310,700
Voronezh	848,700
Votkinsk	101,700
Yakutsk	209,500
Yaroslavl	613,200
Yekaterinburg (Sverdlovsk)	1,293,000
Yelets	116,700
Yoshkar-Ola	256,800
Yuzhno-Sakhalinsk	174,700
Zelenodolsk	100,100
Zelenograd	215,900
Zheleznodorozhny	104,100
Zhukovsky	101,900
Zlatoust	194,800
Rwanda (2002)	
★ Kigali	608,141
St. Kitts and Nevis (2001)	
★ Basseterre	13,220
St. Lucia (2001)	
★ Castries	12,439
agglomeration	37,549
St. Vincent and the Grenadines (2000 est.)	
★ Kingstown	16,209
Samoa (2001)	
★ Apia	38,836
San Marino (2003 est.)	
★ San Marino	4,483
São Tomé and Príncipe (2001)	
★ São Tomé	51,886
Saudi Arabia (1992)	
Abhā	112,316
ʿArʿar	108,055
Buraydah	248,636
Ad-Dammām	482,321
Ḥafar al-Bāṭin	137,793
Ḥāʾil	176,757
Al-Hufūf	225,847
Jiddah	2,046,251
Al-Jubayl	140,828
Khamīs Mushayṭ	217,870
Al-Kharj	152,071
Al-Khubar	141,683
Mecca (Makkah)	965,697
Medina (Al-Madīnah)	608,295
Al-Mubarraz	219,123
★ Riyadh (Ar-Riyāḍ)	2,776,096
Tabūk	292,555
Aṭ-Ṭāʾif	416,121
Ath-Thuqbah	125,650
Yanbuʿ al-Baḥr	119,819
Senegal (2001 est.)	
★ Dakar	919,683
Diourbel	112,950
Kaolack	243,209
Mbour	148,985
Rufisque	165,274
Saint-Louis	154,496
Thiès	273,599
Ziguinchor	216,971
Serbia and Montenegro (2002)	
★ Belgrade (executive and legislative)	1,120,092
Kragujevac	146,373
Niš	173,724
Novi Sad	191,405
★ Podgorica (judicial)	139,100[5]
Priština	165,844[5]
Prizren	107,614[5]
Seychelles (1997)	
★ Victoria	24,701[28]
Sierra Leone (2004 est.)	
★ Freetown	1,070,200
Koidu	115,700
Makeni	115,600
Singapore (2002 est.)	
★ Singapore	4,171,300[29]
Slovakia (2001)	
★ Bratislava	428,672
Košice	236,093
Slovenia (2002)	
★ Ljubljana	258,873
Solomon Islands (2000 est.)	
★ Honiara	50,100
Somalia (2003 est.)	
★ Mogadishu	...
agglomeration	1,212,000
South Africa (1996)[28, 30]	
Alberton	147,948
Benoni	365,467
★ Bloemfontein (de facto judicial)	333,769
Boksburg	260,905
Botshabelo	177,971
Brakpan	171,359
★ Cape Town (de facto legislative)	2,415,408
Carletonville	164,367
Durban	2,117,650
East London	212,323
Johannesburg	1,480,530
Kimberley	170,432
Klerksdorp	137,318
Krugersdorp	203,168
Mdantsane	182,998
Midrand	126,400
Newcastle	219,682
Paarl	140,376
Pietermaritzburg	378,126
Port Elizabeth	749,921
Potchefstroom	101,682
★ Pretoria (de facto executive)	1,104,479
Rustenburg	104,537
Somerset West	112,489
Soweto	1,098,094
Springs	160,795
Tembisa	282,272
Uitenhage	192,120
Vanderbijlpark	253,335
Vereeniging	346,780
Verwoerdburg	114,575
Welkom	203,296
Westonaria	113,932
Witbank	167,183
Spain (2001)	
Albacete	148,934
Alcalá de Henares	176,434
Alcorcón	153,100
Algeciras	101,468
Alicante (Alacant)	284,580
Almería	166,328
Badajoz	133,519
Badalona	205,836
Barcelona	1,503,884
Bilbao	349,972
Burgos	166,187
Cádiz	133,363
Cartagena	184,686
Castellón de la Plana (Castelló de la Plana)	147,667
Córdoba	308,072
Coruña, A (Coruña, La)	236,379
Donostia–San Sebastián	178,377
Dos Hermanas	101,900
Elche (Elx)	194,767
Fuenlabrada	182,705
Getafe	151,479
Gijón	266,419
Granada	240,661
Hospitalet (de Llobregat)	239,019
Huelva	142,284
Jaén	112,590
Jerez de la Frontera	183,273
Laguna, La	128,822
Leganés	173,584
León	130,916
Lleida (Lérida)	112,199
Logroño	133,058
★ Madrid	2,938,723
Málaga	524,414
Marbella	100,036
Mataró	106,358
Móstoles	196,524
Murcia	370,745
Ourense (Orense)	107,510
Oviedo	201,154
Palma (de Mallorca)	333,801
Palmas de Gran Canaria, Las	354,863
Pamplona (Iruña)	183,964
Sabadell	183,788
Salamanca	156,368
Santa Coloma de Gramanet	112,992
Santa Cruz de Tenerife	188,477
Santander	180,717
Sevilla (Seville)	684,633
Tarragona	113,129
Terrassa (Tarrasa)	173,775
Valencia (València)	738,441
Valladolid	316,580
Vigo	280,186
Vitoria–Gasteiz	216,852
Zaragoza (Saragossa)	614,905
Sri Lanka (2001)[24]	
★ Colombo (administrative)	642,163
Dehiwala-Mount Lavinia	209,787

Major cities and national capitals (continued)

country / city	population
Jaffna	145,600[31]
Kandy	110,049
Moratuwa	177,190
Negombo	121,933
★ Sri Jayawardenepura Kotte (legislative and judicial)	115,826
Sudan, The (1993)	
Al-Fāshir	141,884
Juba	125,000[1]
Kassalā	234,622
★ Khartoum (executive)	947,483
Khartoum North	700,887
Kūsti	173,599
Nyala	227,183
★ Omdurman (legislative)	1,271,403
Port Sudan	308,195
Al-Qaḍārif	191,164
Al-Ubayyiḍ	229,425
Wad Madanī	211,362
Suriname (2004 est.)	
★ Paramaribo	218,500
Swaziland (1997)	
★ Lobamba (legislative)	…
★ Lozitha (royal)	…
★ Ludzidzini (royal)	…
★ Mbabane (administrative)	57,992
Sweden (2003 est.; MU)	
Göteborg	474,921
Helsingborg	119,406
Jönköping	118,581
Linköping	135,066
Lund	100,402
Malmö	265,481
Norrköping	123,303
Örebro	125,520
★ Stockholm	758,148
Umeå	106,525
Uppsala	179,673
Västerås	128,902
Switzerland (2003 est.)	
Basel (Bâle)	165,031
★ Bern (Berne) (administrative)	122,707
Geneva (Genève)	177,535
★ Lausanne (judicial)	116,332
Zürich	342,518
Syria (2004 est.)	
Aleppo (Ḥalab)	1,975,200
★ Damascus (Dimashq)	1,614,500
Darʿā	103,300
Dayr az-Zawr	239,800
Dūmā	104,600
Ḥamāh	366,800
Al-Ḥasakah	211,300
Homs (Ḥims)	800,400
Jaramānah	192,800
Latakia (al-Ladhiqiyah)	468,700
Al-Qāmishlī	210,300
Ar-Raqqah	229,100
Ṭarṭūs	162,300
Aṭ-Ṭawrah	102,100
Taiwan (2002 est.)	
Chang-hua	232,156
Chi-lung (Keelung)	391,450
Chia-i	267,906
Chung-ho	403,510
Chung-li	334,683
Feng-shan	323,799
Feng-yüan	162,115
Hsi-chih	167,224
Hsin-chu	378,797
Hsin-chuang	380,334
Hsin-tien	275,467
Hua-lien	107,525
Kao-hsiung	1,509,510
Lu-chou	173,209
Nan-t'ou	105,061
Pa-te	167,085
Pan-ch'iao (T'ai-pei-hsien)	535,476
P'ing-chen	196,408
P'ing-tung	215,584
San-chu'ung	384,217
Shu-lin	157,913
T'ai-chung	996,706
T'ai-nan	745,081
T'ai-p'ing	168,892
T'ai-tung	110,899
★ Taipei (T'ai-pei)	2,641,856
Ta-li	178,998
T'ao-yuan	347,160
Tou-liu	102,460
T'u-ch'eng	234,125
Yung-ho	230,660
Yung-k'ang	200,719
Tajikistan (2002 est.)	
★ Dushanbe	575,900
Khujand (Khudzhand; Leninabad)	147,400
Tanzania (2002)	
Arusha	270,485
★ Dar es Salaam (acting)	2,336,055
Dodoma (future capital)	149,180
Kigoma	130,142
Mbeya	230,218
Morogoro	206,868
Moshi	143,799
Musoma	103,497
Mwanza	209,806
Tabora	127,887
Tanga	179,400
Zanzibar	205,870
Thailand (2000)	
★ Bangkok (Krung Thep)	6,320,174
Chiang Mai	167,776
Chon Buri	182,641
Hat Yai	185,557
Khlong Luang	103,282
Khon Kaen	141,034
Lampang	147,812
Nakhon Pathom	120,657
Nakhon Ratchasima	204,391
Nakhon Si Thammarat	118,764
Nonthaburi	291,307
Pak Kret	141,788
Phra Pradaeng	166,828
Rayong	106,585
Samut Prakan	378,694
Si Racha	141,334
Surat Thani	111,276
Thanya Buri	113,818
Ubon Ratchathani	106,552
Udon Thani	220,493
Togo (2003 est.)	
★ Lomé	676,400
Tonga (1996)	
★ Nuku'alofa	22,400
Trinidad and Tobago (2000)	
★ Port of Spain	49,031
Tunisia (2004 est.)	
Aryānah	217,600
Bizerte (Banzart)	112,800
Ettadhamen	197,400
Qābis	110,000
Al-Qayrawān (Kairouan)	116,000
Ṣafāqis (Sfax)	273,300
Sūsah	156,600
★ Tunis	695,500
Turkey (2000)	
Adana	1,130,710
Adıyaman	178,538
Afyon	128,516
Aksaray	129,949
★ Ankara	3,203,362
Antakya (Hatay)	144,910
Antalya	603,190
Aydın	143,267
Balıkesir	215,436
Batman	246,678
Bursa	1,194,687
Ceyhan	108,602
Çorlu	141,525
Çorum	161,321
Denizli	275,480
Diyarbakır	545,983
Edirne	119,298
Elazığ	266,495
Erzincan	107,175
Erzurum	361,235
Eskişehir	482,793
Gaziantep	853,513
Gebze	253,487
İçel (Mersin)	537,842
İnegöl	105,959
İskenderun	159,149
Isparta	148,496
İstanbul	8,803,468
İzmir	2,232,265
Kahramanmaraş (Maraş)	326,198
Karabük	100,749
Karaman	105,384
Kayseri	536,392
Kırıkkale	205,078
Kızıltepe	113,143
Kocaeli (İzmit)	195,699
Konya	742,690
Kütahya	166,665
Malatya	381,081
Manisa	214,345
Nazilli	105,665
Ordu	112,525
Osmaniye	173,977
Sakarya (Adapazarı)	283,752
Samsun	363,180
Sivas	251,776
Siverek	126,820
Sultanbeyli	175,700
Tarsus	216,382
Tekirdağ	107,191
Tokat	113,100
Trabzon	214,949
Urfa (Şanlıurfa)	385,588
Uşak	137,001
Van	284,464
Viranşehir	121,382
Zonguldak	104,276
Turkmenistan (2004 est.)	
★ Ashgabat	773,400
Balkanabat (Nebitdag)	101,600
Daşoguz	163,100
Mary	129,200
Türkmenabat (Chärjew)	242,000
Tuvalu (2002)	
★ Funafuti	4,492
Uganda (2002)	
Gulu	113,144
★ Kampala	1,208,544
Ukraine (2001)	
Alchevsk	119,193
Berdyansk	121,692
Bila Tserkva	200,131
Cherkasy	295,414
Chernihiv	304,994
Chernivtsi	240,621
Dniprodzerzhynsk	255,841
Dnipropetrovsk	1,065,008
Donetsk	1,016,194
Horlivka	292,250
Ivano-Frankivsk	218,359
Kerch	157,007
Kharkiv	1,470,902
Kherson	328,360
Khmelnytskyy	253,994
★ Kiev	2,611,327
Kirovohrad	254,103
Kramatorsk	181,025
Kremenchuk	234,073
Kryvyy Rih	668,980
Luhansk	463,097
Lutsk	208,816
Lviv	732,818
Lysychansk	115,229
Makiyivka	389,589
Mariupol	492,176
Melitopol	160,657
Mykolayiv	514,136
Nikopol	136,280
Odesa	1,029,049
Pavlohrad	118,816
Poltava	317,998
Rivne	248,813
Sevastopol	342,451
Simferopol	343,644
Slov'yansk	124,829
Sumy	293,141
Syeverodonetsk	119,940
Ternopil	227,755
Uzhhorod	117,317
Vinnytsya	356,665
Yenakiyeve	103,997
Yevpatoriya	105,915
Zaporizhzhya	815,256
Zhytomyr	284,236
United Arab Emirates (2003 est.)	
★ Abu Dhabi	552,000
ʿAjmān	225,000
Al-ʿAyn	348,000
Dubai	1,171,000
Raʾs al-Khaymah	102,000
Sharjah	519,000
United Kingdom (2001)	
England[32]	
Barnsley	218,062
Birmingham	977,091
Blackburn with Darwen	137,471
Blackpool	142,284
Bolton	261,035
Bournemouth	163,441
Bracknell Forest	109,506
Bradford	467,668
Brighton and Hove	247,820
Bristol	380,615
Bury	180,612
Calderdale	192,396
Cambridge	108,879
Canterbury	135,287
Carlisle	100,734
Chester	118,207
Coventry	300,844
Darlington	97,872
Derby	221,716
Doncaster	286,865
Dudley	305,164
Durham	87,725
Exeter	111,078
Gateshead	191,151
Gloucester	109,888
Halton	118,215
Kingston upon Hull	243,595
Kirklees	388,576
Knowsley	150,468
Lancaster	133,914
Leeds	715,404
Leicester	279,923
Lincoln	85,616
Liverpool	439,476
★ London (Greater London)	7,172,091[33]
Luton	184,390
Manchester	392,819
Milton Keynes	207,063
Newcastle upon Tyne	259,573
North Tyneside	191,663
Norwich	121,553
Nottingham	266,995
Oldham	217,393
Oxford	134,248
Peterborough	156,060
Plymouth	240,718
Poole	138,299
Portsmouth	186,704
Reading	143,124
Rochdale	205,233
Rotherham	248,176
St. Albans	128,982
St. Helens	176,845
Salford	216,119
Sandwell	282,901
Sefton	282,956
Sheffield	513,234
Slough	119,070
Solihull	199,521
South Tyneside	152,785
Southampton	217,478
Southend	160,256
Stockport	284,544
Stockton-on-Tees	178,405
Stoke-on-Trent	240,643
Sunderland	280,807
Swindon	180,061
Tameside	213,045
Thurrock	143,042
Torbay	129,702
Trafford	210,135
Wakefield	315,173
Walsall	253,502
Warrington	191,084
Wigan	301,417
Winchester	107,213
Windsor and Maidenhead	133,606
Wirral	312,289
Wolverhampton	236,573
Worcester	93,358
York	181,131
Northern Ireland[34]	
Belfast	277,391
Craigavon	80,671
Derry (Londonderry)	105,066
Lisburn	108,694
Newtonabbey	79,993
Scotland[35]	
Aberdeen	184,788
Dundee	145,663
Edinburgh	448,624
Glasgow	577,869
Wales[36]	
Cardiff	305,340
Conwy	109,597
Neath Port Talbot	134,471
Newport	137,017
Rhondda, Cynon, Taff	231,952
Swansea	223,293
Torfaen	90,967
Wrexham	128,477
United States (2003 est.)	
Abilene (*Texas*)	114,889
Akron (*Ohio*)	212,215
Albany (*Ga.*)	76,202
Albany (*N.Y.*)	93,919
Albuquerque (*N.M.*)	471,856
Alexandria (*Va.*)	128,923
Alhambra (*Calif.*)	87,754
Allentown (*Pa.*)	105,958
Amarillo (*Texas*)	178,612
Anaheim (*Calif.*)	332,361
Anchorage (*Alaska*)	270,951
Ann Arbor (*Mich.*)	114,498
Antioch (*Calif.*)	101,124
Arden-Arcade (*Calif.*)[37]	96,025[38]
Arlington (*Texas*)	355,007
Arlington (*Va.*)[37]	187,873
Arlington Heights (*Ill.*)	75,784
Arvada (*Colo.*)	101,972
Athens (*Ga.*)	102,498
Atlanta (*Ga.*)	423,019
Augusta (*Ga.*)	193,316
Aurora (*Colo.*)	290,418
Aurora (*Ill.*)	162,184
Austin (*Texas*)	672,011
Bakersfield (*Calif.*)	271,035
Baldwin Park (*Calif.*)	78,747
Baltimore (*Md.*)	628,670
Baton Rouge (*La.*)	225,090
Beaumont (*Texas*)	112,434
Beaverton (*Ore.*)	80,520
Bellevue (*Wash.*)	112,344
Berkeley (*Calif.*)	102,049
Billings (*Mont.*)	95,220
Birmingham (*Ala.*)	236,620
Bloomington (*Minn.*)	83,080
Boca Raton (*Fla.*)	78,449
Boise (*Idaho*)	190,117
Boston (*Mass.*)	581,616
Boulder (*Colo.*)	93,051
Brandon (*Fla.*)[37]	77,895[38]
Brick Township (*N.J.*)[37]	76,119[38]
Bridgeport (*Conn.*)	139,664
Brockton (*Mass.*)	95,090
Broken Arrow (*Okla.*)	83,607
Brownsville (*Texas*)	156,178
Buena Park (*Calif.*)	78,934
Buffalo (*N.Y.*)	285,018
Burbank (*Calif.*)	103,359
Cambridge (*Mass.*)	101,587
Camden (*N.J.*)	80,089
Canton (*Mich.*)[37]	76,366[38]
Canton (*Ohio*)	79,255
Cape Coral (*Fla.*)	118,737
Carlsbad (*Calif.*)	87,372
Carrollton (*Texas*)	116,714
Carson (*Calif.*)	93,747
Cary (*N.C.*)	99,824
Cedar Rapids (*Iowa*)	122,542
Centennial (*Colo.*)	98,586
Chandler (*Ariz.*)	211,299
Charleston (*S.C.*)	101,024
Charlotte (*N.C.*)	584,658
Chattanooga (*Tenn.*)	154,887
Cheektowaga (*N.Y.*)[37]	79,988[38]
Chesapeake (*Va.*)	210,834
Chicago (*Ill.*)	2,869,121
Chula Vista (*Calif.*)	199,060
Cicero (*Ill.*)	83,029
Cincinnati (*Ohio*)	317,361
Citrus Heights (*Calif.*)	88,515
Clarksville (*Tenn.*)	107,953
Clearwater (*Fla.*)	108,272
Cleveland (*Ohio*)	461,324

[1]1993 estimate. [2]Eight villages, including Fagatogo and Utulei, are collectively known as Pago Pago (2001 agglomeration pop. 15,000). [3]Urban Centre ("urban agglomeration") as defined by 2001 census. [4]Estimated population of New Providence and adjacent islands. [5]2003 estimate. [6]1992 census. [7]Regional or district municipality. [8]Excludes agricultural population within city limits. [9]1999 estimate. [10]San José canton. [11]2002 estimate. [12]Excludes Lefkoşa (Turkish Nicosia), whose population per 1996 census was 39,176. [13]2002 census; population of National District region, including Santo Domingo, equals 2,731,294. [14]Within San Salvador metropolitan area. [15]Within Athens urban agglomeration. [16]Urban population (may or may not be city proper; not urban agglomeration). [17]1990 census. [18]2004 estimate. [19]County borough population. [20]Commune population. [21]1987 census. [22]2001 estimate. [23]2000 estimate. [24]Urban population. [25]Includes cantonment(s).

country city	population
Clifton (*N.J.*)	79,823
Clinton Township (*Mich.*)[37]	95,648[38]
Clovis (*Calif.*)	78,558
Colorado Springs (*Colo.*)	370,448
Columbia (*Md.*)[37]	88,254[38]
Columbia (*Mo.*)	88,553
Columbia (*S.C.*)	117,357
Columbus (*Ga.*)	185,702
Columbus (*Ohio*)	728,432
Compton (*Calif.*)	95,835
Concord (*Calif.*)	124,977
Coral Springs (*Fla.*)	127,005
Corona (*Calif.*)	142,454
Corpus Christi (*Texas*)	279,208
Costa Mesa (*Calif.*)	109,563
Cranston (*R.I.*)	81,679
Dallas (*Texas*)	1,208,318
Daly City (*Calif.*)	100,819
Danbury (*Conn.*)	77,353
Davenport (*Iowa*)	97,512
Davie (*Fla.*)	80,364
Dayton (*Ohio*)	161,696
Dearborn (*Mich.*)	96,670
Decatur (*Ill.*)	79,285
Deltona (*Fla.*)	76,597
Denton (*Texas*)	93,435
Denver (*Colo.*)	557,478
Des Moines (*Iowa*)	195,093
Detroit (*Mich.*)	911,402
Dover Township (*N.J.*)[37]	86,327[38]
Downey (*Calif.*)	110,360
Duluth (*Minn.*)	85,734
Durham (*N.C.*)	198,376
East Los Angeles (*Calif.*)[37]	124,283[38]
Edison Township (*N.J.*)	100,138
El Cajon (*Calif.*)	95,159
El Monte (*Calif.*)	121,740
El Paso (*Texas*)	584,113
Elgin (*Ill.*)	97,117
Elizabeth (*N.J.*)	123,215
Elk Grove (*Calif.*)	82,499
Erie (*Pa.*)	101,373
Escondido (*Calif.*)	136,093
Eugene (*Ore.*)	142,185
Evansville (*Ind.*)	117,881
Everett (*Wash.*)	96,643
Fairfield (*Calif.*)	102,762
Fall River (*Mass.*)	92,760
Fargo (*N.D.*)	91,484
Farmington Hills (*Mich.*)	80,874
Fayetteville (*N.C.*)	124,372
Federal Way (*Wash.*)	81,711
Flint (*Mich.*)	120,292
Fontana (*Calif.*)	151,903
Fort Collins (*Colo.*)	125,740
Fort Lauderdale (*Fla.*)	162,917
Fort Smith (*Ark.*)	81,562
Fort Wayne (*Ind.*)	219,495
Fort Worth (*Texas*)	585,122
Fremont (*Calif.*)	204,525
Fresno (*Calif.*)	451,455
Fullerton (*Calif.*)	131,249
Gainesville (*Fla.*)	109,146
Garden Grove (*Calif.*)	167,029
Garland (*Texas*)	218,027
Gary (*Ind.*)	99,961
Gilbert (*Ariz.*)	145,250
Glendale (*Ariz.*)	232,838
Glendale (*Calif.*)	200,499
Grand Prairie (*Texas*)	136,671
Grand Rapids (*Mich.*)	195,601
Greeley (*Colo.*)	83,414
Green Bay (*Wis.*)	101,467
Greensboro (*N.C.*)	229,110
Gresham (*Ore.*)	95,816
Hammond (*Ind.*)	80,547
Hampton (*Va.*)	146,878
Hartford (*Conn.*)	124,387
Hawthorne (*Calif.*)	86,173
Hayward (*Calif.*)	141,336
Henderson (*Nev.*)	214,852
Hialeah (*Fla.*)	226,401
High Point (*N.C.*)	91,543
Hillsboro (*Ore.*)	77,709
Hollywood (*Fla.*)	143,408
Honolulu (*Hawaii*)[37]	380,149
Houston (*Texas*)	2,009,690
Huntington Beach (*Calif.*)	194,248
Huntsville (*Ala.*)	164,237
Independence (*Mo.*)	112,079
Indianapolis (*Ind.*)	783,438
Inglewood (*Calif.*)	115,208
Irvine (*Calif.*)	170,561
Irving (*Texas*)	194,455
Jackson (*Miss.*)	179,599
Jacksonville (*Fla.*)	773,781
Jersey City (*N.J.*)	239,097
Joliet (*Ill.*)	123,570
Kalamazoo (*Mich.*)	75,312
Kansas City (*Kan.*)	145,757
Kansas City (*Mo.*)	442,768
Kendall (*Fla.*)[37]	75,226[38]
Kenosha (*Wis.*)	92,871
Kent (*Wash.*)	81,567
Killeen (*Texas*)	96,159
Knoxville (*Tenn.*)	173,278
Lafayette (*La.*)	111,667
Lake Forest (*Calif.*)	76,738
Lakeland (*Fla.*)	87,860
Lakewood (*Calif.*)	81,300
Lakewood (*Colo.*)	142,474
Lancaster (*Calif.*)	125,896
Lansing (*Mich.*)	118,379
Laredo (*Texas*)	197,488
Las Cruces (*N.M.*)	76,990
Las Vegas (*Nev.*)	517,017
Lawrence (*Kan.*)	82,120
Lawton (*Okla.*)	91,730
Lee's Summit (*Mo.*)	77,052
Lewisville (*Texas*)	87,127
Lexington (*Ky.*)	266,798
Lincoln (*Neb.*)	235,594
Little Rock (*Ark.*)	184,053
Livermore (*Calif.*)	77,744
Livonia (*Mich.*)	99,487
Long Beach (*Calif.*)	475,460
Longmont (*Colo.*)	79,556
Los Angeles (*Calif.*)	3,819,951
Louisville (*Ky.*)	248,762
Lowell (*Mass.*)	104,351
Lubbock (*Texas*)	206,481
Lynn (*Mass.*)	89,571
McAllen (*Texas*)	116,501
McKinney (*Texas*)	79,958
Macon (*Ga.*)	95,267
Madison (*Wis.*)	218,432
Manchester (*N.H.*)	108,871
Memphis (*Tenn.*)	645,978
Mesa (*Ariz.*)	432,376
Mesquite (*Texas*)	129,270
Metairie (*La.*)[37]	146,136[38]
Miami (*Fla.*)	376,815
Miami Beach (*Fla.*)	89,312
Midland (*Texas*)	96,573
Milwaukee (*Wis.*)	586,941
Minneapolis (*Minn.*)	373,188
Miramar (*Fla.*)	96,646
Mission Viejo (*Calif.*)	95,831
Mobile (*Ala.*)	193,464
Modesto (*Calif.*)	206,872
Montgomery (*Ala.*)	200,123
Moreno Valley (*Calif.*)	157,063
Murfreesboro (*Tenn.*)	78,074
Napa (*Calif.*)	75,560
Naperville (*Ill.*)	137,894
Nashua (*N.H.*)	87,285
Nashville (*Tenn.*)	544,765
New Bedford (*Mass.*)	94,112
New Haven (*Conn.*)	124,512
New Orleans (*La.*)	469,032
New York City (*N.Y.*)	8,085,742
Newark (*N.J.*)	277,911
Newport Beach (*Calif.*)	78,043
Newport News (*Va.*)	181,647
Newton (*Mass.*)	84,323
Norfolk (*Va.*)	241,727
Norman (*Okla.*)	99,197
North Charleston (*S.C.*)	81,577
North Las Vegas (*Nev.*)	144,502
Norwalk (*Calif.*)	107,155
Norwalk (*Conn.*)	84,170
Oakland (*Calif.*)	398,844
Oceanside (*Calif.*)	167,082
Odessa (*Texas*)	91,113
Ogden (*Utah*)	78,293
Oklahoma City (*Okla.*)	523,303
Olathe (*Kan.*)	105,274
Omaha (*Neb.*)	404,267
Ontario (*Calif.*)	167,402
Orange (*Calif.*)	132,197
Orem (*Utah*)	87,599
Orlando (*Fla.*)	199,336
Overland Park (*Kan.*)	160,368
Oxnard (*Calif.*)	180,872
Palm Bay (*Fla.*)	85,076
Palmdale (*Calif.*)	127,759
Paradise (*Nev.*)[37]	186,070[38]
Parma (*Ohio*)	83,861
Pasadena (*Calif.*)	141,114
Pasadena (*Texas*)	144,413
Paterson (*N.J.*)	150,782
Pembroke Pines (*Fla.*)	148,927
Peoria (*Ariz.*)	127,580
Peoria (*Ill.*)	112,907
Philadelphia (*Pa.*)	1,479,339
Phoenix (*Ariz.*)	1,388,416
Pittsburgh (*Pa.*)	325,337
Plano (*Texas*)	241,991
Plantation (*Fla.*)	84,929
Pomona (*Calif.*)	154,147
Pompano Beach (*Fla.*)	88,064
Port St. Lucie (*Fla.*)	105,507
Portland (*Ore.*)	538,544
Portsmouth (*Va.*)	99,617
Providence (*R.I.*)	176,365
Provo (*Utah*)	105,410
Pueblo (*Colo.*)	103,648
Quincy (*Mass.*)	89,059
Racine (*Wis.*)	80,266
Raleigh (*N.C.*)	316,802
Rancho Cucamonga (*Calif.*)	151,640
Reading (*Pa.*)	80,305
Redding (*Calif.*)	87,579
Reno (*Nev.*)	193,882
Rialto (*Calif.*)	98,091
Richardson (*Texas*)	99,536
Richmond (*Calif.*)	102,327
Richmond (*Va.*)	194,729
Riverside (*Calif.*)	281,514
Roanoke (*Va.*)	92,863
Rochester (*Minn.*)	92,507
Rochester (*N.Y.*)	215,093
Rockford (*Ill.*)	151,725
Roseville (*Calif.*)	98,359
Roswell (*Ga.*)	78,229
Round Rock (*Texas*)	77,946
Sacramento (*Calif.*)	445,335
St. Louis (*Mo.*)	332,223
St. Paul (*Minn.*)	280,404
St. Petersburg (*Fla.*)	247,610
Salem (*Ore.*)	142,914
Salinas (*Calif.*)	147,840
Salt Lake City (*Utah*)	179,894
San Angelo (*Texas*)	87,922
San Antonio (*Texas*)	1,214,725
San Bernardino (*Calif.*)	195,357
San Buenaventura (Ventura) (*Calif.*)	104,140
San Diego (*Calif.*)	1,266,753
San Francisco (*Calif.*)	751,682
San Jose (*Calif.*)	898,349
San Leandro (*Calif.*)	80,139
San Mateo (*Calif.*)	91,157
Sandy (*Utah*)	89,319
Sandy Springs (*Ga.*)[37]	85,781[38]
Santa Ana (*Calif.*)	342,510
Santa Barbara (*Calif.*)	88,251
Santa Clara (*Calif.*)	102,095
Santa Clarita (*Calif.*)	162,742
Santa Maria (*Calif.*)	81,944
Santa Monica (*Calif.*)	87,162
Santa Rosa (*Calif.*)	153,386
Savannah (*Ga.*)	127,573
Scottsdale (*Ariz.*)	217,989
Seattle (*Wash.*)	569,101
Shreveport (*La.*)	198,364
Silver Spring (*Md.*)[37]	76,540[38]
Simi Valley (*Calif.*)	117,115
Sioux City (*Iowa*)	83,876
Sioux Falls (*S.D.*)	133,834
Somerville (*Mass.*)	76,296
South Bend (*Ind.*)	105,540
South Gate (*Calif.*)	98,966
Southfield (*Mich.*)	77,488
Sparks (*Nev.*)	77,295
Spokane (*Wash.*)	196,624
Spring Valley (*Nev.*)[37]	117,390[38]
Springfield (*Ill.*)	113,586
Springfield (*Mass.*)	152,157
Springfield (*Mo.*)	150,867
Stamford (*Conn.*)	120,107
Sterling Heights (*Mich.*)	126,182
Stockton (*Calif.*)	271,466
Sunnyvale (*Calif.*)	128,549
Sunrise (*Fla.*)	89,136
Sunrise Manor (*Nev.*)[37]	156,120[38]
Syracuse (*N.Y.*)	144,001
Tacoma (*Wash.*)	196,790
Tallahassee (*Fla.*)	153,938
Tampa (*Fla.*)	317,647
Temecula (*Calif.*)	76,836
Tempe (*Ariz.*)	158,880
Thornton (*Colo.*)	96,584
Thousand Oaks (*Calif.*)	124,102
Toledo (*Ohio*)	308,973
Topeka (*Kan.*)	122,008
Torrance (*Calif.*)	142,621
Trenton (*N.J.*)	85,314
Troy (*Mich.*)	81,071
Tucson (*Ariz.*)	507,658
Tulsa (*Okla.*)	387,807
Tuscaloosa (*Ala.*)	79,294
Tyler (*Texas*)	88,318
Vacaville (*Calif.*)	94,129
Vallejo (*Calif.*)	119,708
Vancouver (*Wash.*)	151,654
Virginia Beach (*Va.*)	439,467
Visalia (*Calif.*)	100,612
Vista (*Calif.*)	91,813
Waco (*Texas*)	116,887
Warren (*Mich.*)	136,016
Warwick (*R.I.*)	87,365
★ Washington, D.C.	563,384
Waukegan (*Ill.*)	91,452
Waterbury (*Conn.*)	108,130
West Covina (*Calif.*)	108,251
West Jordan (*Utah*)	84,701
West Palm Beach (*Fla.*)	88,932
West Valley City (*Utah*)	111,687
Westland (*Mich.*)	85,707
Westminster (*Calif.*)	89,493
Westminster (*Colo.*)	103,391
Whittier (*Calif.*)	85,368
Wichita (*Kan.*)	354,617
Wichita Falls (*Texas*)	102,340
Wilmington (*N.C.*)	91,137
Winston-Salem (*N.C.*)	190,299
Worcester (*Mass.*)	175,706
Yakima (*Wash.*)	80,223
Yonkers (*N.Y.*)	197,388
Youngstown (*Ohio*)	79,271
Yuma (*Ariz.*)	81,605
Uruguay (1996)	
★ Montevideo	1,378,707
Uzbekistan (1999 est.)	
Andijon (Andizhan)	323,900
Angren	128,600
Buxoro (Bukhara)	237,900
Chirchiq (Chirchik)	145,600
Farghona (Fergana)	182,800
Jizzakh (Dzhizak)	126,400
Margilon (Margilan)	143,600
Namangan	376,600
Nawoiy (Navoi)	117,600
Nuqus (Nukus)	199,000
Olmaliq (Almalyk)	115,100
Qarshi (Karshi)	197,600
Qoqon (Kokand)	192,500
Samarqand (Samarkand)	362,300
★ Tashkent (Toshkent)	2,142,700
Termiz	111,500
Urganch (Urgench)	139,100
Vanuatu (1999)	
★ Vila	29,356
Venezuela (2001)	
Acarigua	137,000
Barcelona	328,000
Barinas	229,000
Barquisimeto	811,000
Baruta	192,000
Cabimas	210,000
Calabozo	102,000
★ Caracas	1,836,000
Carúpano	112,000
Catia la Mar	112,000
Ciudad Bolívar	287,000
Ciudad Guayana	629,000
Ciudad Ojeda	114,000
Coro	159,000
Cumaná	263,000
El Tigre	146,000
Guacara	142,000
Guanare	111,000
Guarenas	100,000
Guatire	129,000
La Victoria	104,000
Los Teques	175,000
Maracaibo	1,609,000
Maracay	394,000
Maturín	325,000
Mérida	196,000
Ocumare del Tuy	104,000
Petare	369,000
Puerto Cabello	154,000
Puerto La Cruz	199,000
Punto Fijo	117,000
San Cristóbal	234,000
Santa Teresa	125,000
Turmero	306,000
Valencia	1,196,000
Valera	113,000
Vietnam (2004 est.)	
Bac Lieu	104,400
Bien Hoa	384,400
Buon Me Thuot	139,900
Ca Mau	107,400
Cam Pha	146,600
Cam Ranh	145,700
Can Tho	255,100
Da Lat	128,900
Da Nang	459,400
Haiphong	591,100
★ Hanoi	1,420,400
Hoa Binh	100,100
Ho Chi Minh City (Saigon)	3,452,100
Hong Gai	145,900
Hue	277,100
Long Xuyen	157,200
My Tho	121,200
Nam Dinh	192,200
Nha Trang	274,800
Phan Thiet	140,000
Pleiku (Play Cu)	109,100
Qui Nhon	203,300
Rach Gia	207,600
Soc Trang	111,500
Thai Nguyen	132,600
Thanh Hoa	107,900
Vinh Long	101,100
Vung Tau	195,400
Virgin Islands (U.S.) (2000)	
★ Charlotte Amalie	11,004
West Bank (2003 est.)	
Hebron (Al-Khalīl)	154,714
Nābulus	126,884
★ Rām Allāh (Ramallah) (acting administrative centre)	23,663
Western Sahara (1998 est.)	
Laayoune (El Aaiún)	164,000[39]
Yemen (2001 est.)	
Aden	509,886
Dhamār	120,000
Al-Ḥudaydah	425,000
Ibb	140,000
Al-Mukallā	165,000
★ Ṣan'ā'	1,590,624
Ta'izz	450,000
Zambia (2000)	
Chingola	147,400
Kabwe	176,758
Kitwe	363,700
Luanshya	115,600
★ Lusaka	1,084,703
Mufulira	122,300
Ndola	374,757
Zimbabwe (2002)	
Bulawayo	676,787
Chitungwiza	321,782
Epworth	113,884
Gweru	137,000[11]
★ Harare	1,444,534
Mutare	153,000[11]

[26]Urban districts adjacent to Panama City. [27]2003 estimate; populations of cities within the Lima agglomeration are 1997 estimates. [28]Urban agglomeration(s). [29]De facto figure; de jure figure equals 3,378,300. [30]A new municipal system is being created throughout South Africa from 2000. [31]1997 estimate; 2001 census enumeration was not conducted because of the civil war. [32]Officially designated cities and metropolitan boroughs of England after the local government reorganization of 1995–98. [33]32 borough counties, not listed separately, constitute Greater London. [34]Cities and borough councils of Northern Ireland with more than 75,000 population. [35]Cities of Scotland after the local government reorganization of 1994–95. Borough councils do not exist in Scotland. [36]Cities and boroughs in Wales with more than 75,000 population after the local government reorganization of 1994–96. [37]Unincorporated place. [38]2000 census. [39]Urban population of Laayoune and northern Western Sahara.

Language

This table presents estimated data on the principal language communities of the countries of the world. The countries, and the principal languages (occasionally, language families) represented in each, are listed alphabetically. A bullet (●) indicates those languages that are official in each country. The sum of the estimates equals the 2003 population of the country given in the "Area and population" table.

The estimates represent, so far as national data collection systems permit, the distribution of mother tongues (a mother tongue being the language spoken first and, usually, most fluently by an individual). Many countries do not collect any official data whatever on language use, and published estimates not based on census or survey data usually span a substantial range of uncertainty. The editors have adopted the best-founded distribution in the published literature (indicating uncertainty by the degree of rounding shown) but have also adjusted or interpolated using data not part of the base estimate(s). Such adjustments have not been made to account for large-scale refugee movements, as these are of a temporary nature.

A variety of approaches have been used to approximate mother-tongue distribution when census data were unavailable. Some countries collect data on ethnic or "national" groups only; for such countries ethnic distribution often had to be assumed to conform roughly to the distribution of language communities. This approach, however, should be viewed with caution, because a minority population is not always free to educate its children in its own language and because better economic opportunities often draw minority group members into the majority-language community. For some countries, a given individual may be visible in national statistics only as a passport-holder of a foreign country, however long he may remain resident. Such persons, often guest workers, have sometimes had to be assumed to be speakers of the principal language of their home country. For other countries, the language mosaic may be so complex, the language communities so minute in size, scholarly study so inadequate, or the census base so obsolete that it was possible only to assign percentages to entire groups, or families, of related languages, despite their mutual unintelligibility (Papuan and Melanesian languages in Papua New Guinea, for instance). For some countries in the Americas, so few speakers of any single indigenous language remain that it was necessary to combine these groups as *Amerindian* so as to give a fair impression of their aggregate size within their respective countries.

No systematic attempt has been made to account for populations that may legitimately be described as bilingual, unless the country itself collects data on that basis, as does Bolivia or the Comoros, for example. Where a nonindigenous official or excolonial language constitutes a lingua franca of the country, however, speakers of the language as a second tongue are shown in italics, even though very few may speak it as a mother tongue. Lingua franca figures that are both italicized and indented are not included in population totals. No comprehensive effort has been made to distinguish between dialect communities *usually* classified as belonging to the same language, though such distinctions were possible for some countries—*e.g.*, between French and Occitan (the dialect of southern France) or among the various dialects of Chinese.

In giving the names of Bantu languages, grammatical particles specific to a language's autonym (name for itself) have been omitted (the form *Rwanda* is used here, for example, rather than *kinyaRwanda* and *Tswana* instead of *seTswana*). Parenthetical alternatives are given for a number of languages that differ markedly from the name of the people speaking them (such as Kurukh, spoken by the Oraon tribes of India) or that may be combined with other groups sometimes distinguishable in national data but appearing here under the name of the largest member—*e.g.*, "Tamil (and other Indian languages)" combining data on South Asian Indian populations in Singapore. The term *creole* as used here refers to distinguishable dialectal communities related to a national, official, or former colonial language (such as the French creole that survives in Mauritius from the end of French rule in 1810).

Internet resources for further information:

- *Ethnologue* (14th ed.; Summer Institute of Linguistics) http://www.ethnologue.com
- Joshua Project 2000—People's List (Christian interfaith missionary database identifying some 2,000 ethnolinguistic groups) http://www.ad2000.org/peoples/index.htm
- U.S. Census Bureau: http://www.census.gov/ftp/pub/ipc/www/idbconf.html (especially tables 57 and 59)

Language

Major languages by country	Number of speakers
Afghanistan[1]	
Indo-Aryan languages	
Pashai	178,000
Iranian languages	
Balochi	266,000
● Dari (Persian)	
Chahar Aimak	810,000
Hazara	2,530,000
Tajik	5,859,000
Nuristani group	222,000
Pamir group	178,000
● Pashto	15,046,000
Turkic languages	
Turkmen	555,000
Uzbek	2,530,000
Other	544,000
Albania[1]	
● Albanian	3,102,000
Greek	59,000
Macedonian	4,600
Other	900
Algeria	
● Arabic	27,346,000
Berber	4,454,000
English	...
French	*6,243,000*
American Samoa	
● English	1,900
English (lingua franca)	*60,000*
● Samoan	56,000
Tongan	1,900
Other	1,900
Andorra[2]	
● Catalan (Andorran)	22,000
French	5,000
Portuguese	7,000
Spanish	29,000
Other	4,000
Angola[1]	
Ambo (Ovambo)	255,000
Chokwe	457,000
Herero	74,000
Kongo	1,423,000
Luchazi	255,000
Luimbe-Nkangala	584,000
Lunda	127,000
Luvale (Lwena)	382,000
Mbunda	127,000
Mbundu	2,325,000
Nyaneka-Nkhumbi	584,000
Ovimbundu (Umbundu)	4,003,000
● Portuguese	*3,822,000*
Other	170,000
Antigua and Barbuda	
● English	*76,800*
English/English Creole	72,000
Other	4,200
Argentina	
Amerindian languages	109,000
Italian	647,000
● Spanish	35,682,000
Other	408,000
Armenia	
● Armenian	2,853,000
Azerbaijani (Azeri)	80,000
Other	128,000
Aruba	
● Dutch	4,800
English	8,700
Papiamento	71,500
Spanish	6,800
Other	1,000
Australia	
Aboriginal languages	53,000
Arabic	194,000
Cantonese	227,000
Dutch	48,000
● English	16,141,000
English (lingua franca)	*19,189,000*
French	47,000
German	115,000
Greek	310,000
Hungarian	31,000
Indonesian Malay	31,000
Italian	439,000
Macedonian	82,000
Maltese	53,000
Mandarin	105,000
Pilipino (Filipino)	81,000
Polish	73,000
Portuguese	28,000
Russian	36,000
Serbo-Croatian	122,000
Spanish	104,000
Turkish	51,000
Vietnamese	160,000
Other/not stated	1,352,000
Austria	
Czech	19,000
● German	7,409,000
Hungarian	34,000
Polish	19,000
Romanian	17,000
Serbo-Croatian	175,000
Slovene	30,000
Turkish	122,000
Other	229,000
Azerbaijan	
Armenian	163,000
● Azerbaijani (Azeri)	7,326,000
Lezgi (Lezgian)	184,000
Russian	249,000
Other	317,000
Bahamas, The	
● English	...
English/English Creole	282,000
French (Haitian) Creole	32,000
Bahrain[2]	
● Arabic	459,000
English	...
Other	215,000
Bangladesh[1]	
● Bengali	130,078,000
Chakma	496,000
English	*3,503,000*
Garo	124,000
Khasi	103,000
Marma (Magh)	258,000
Mro	41,000
Santhali	93,000
Tripuri	93,000
Other	1,824,000
Barbados	
Bajan (English Creole)	259,000
● English	...
Other	13,000
Belarus	
● Belarusian	6,488,000
Polish	49,000
● Russian	3,155,000
Ukrainian	129,000
Other	59,000
Belgium[2, 3]	
Arabic	161,000
● Dutch (Flemish; Netherlandic)	6,128,000
● French (Walloon)	3,376,000
● German	101,000
Italian	252,000
Spanish	50,000
Turkish	91,000
Other	181,000
Belize	
● English	136,000
English Creole (lingua franca)	*202,000*
Garifuna (Black Carib)	18,000
German	4,300
Mayan languages	26,000
Spanish	85,000
Spanish (lingua franca)	*149,000*
Benin[1]	
Adja	782,000
Aizo (Ouidah)	606,000
Bariba	606,000
Dendi	154,000
Djougou	209,000
Fon	2,799,000
● French	*661,000*
Fula (Fulani)	397,000
Somba (Ditamari)	463,000
Yoruba (Nago)	859,000
Other	165,000
Bermuda	
● English	64,000
Portuguese	*6,100*
Bhutan[1]	
Assamese	104,000
● Dzongkha (Bhutia)	343,000
Nepali (Hindi)	239,000
Bolivia	
● Aymara	278,000
Guaraní	10,000
● Quechua	700,000
● Spanish	3,583,000
Spanish-Amerindian (multilingual), of which	3,943,000
Spanish-Aymara	*1,699,000*
Spanish-Guaraní	*31,000*
Spanish-Quechua	*2,224,000*
Other	72,000
Bosnia and Herzegovina[1]	
● Bosnian	1,637,000
● Croatian	630,000
● Serbian	1,153,000
Other	300,000
Botswana[1]	
● English (lingua franca)	*665,000*
Khoekhoe (Hottentot)	41,000
Ndebele	21,000
San (Bushman)	58,000
Shona	207,000
Tswana	1,255,000
Tswana (lingua franca)	*1,330,000*
Other	81,000
Brazil[1]	
Amerindian languages	183,000
German	978,000
Italian	752,000
Japanese	677,000
● Portuguese	174,226,000
Other	1,655,000
Brunei	
Chinese	32,000
English	10,400
English-Chinese	7,300
● Malay	159,000
Malay-Chinese	3,100
Malay-Chinese-English	13,500
Malay-English	101,000
Other	18,700
Bulgaria[1]	
● Bulgarian	6,480,000
Macedonian	191,000
Romany	286,000
Turkish	734,000
Other	95,000
Burkina Faso[4]	
Dogon	44,000
French	44,000
● French (lingua franca)	*5,419,000*
Fula (Fulani)	1,272,000
Gur (Voltaic) languages	
Bwamu	288,000
Gouin (Cerma)	77,000
Grusi (Gurunsi) group	
Ko	22,000
Lyele	321,000
Nuni	155,000
Sissala	11,000
Lobi	254,000
Moore (Mossi) group	
Dagara	409,100
Gurma	752,000
Kusaal	22,000
Moore (Mossi)	6,636,000
Senufo group	
Minianka	—
Senufo	188,000
Kru languages	
Seme (Siamou)	22,000
Mande languages	
Bobo	299,000
Busansi (Bisa)	476,000
Dyula (Jula)	343,000
Marka	221,000
Samo	310,000
Tamashek (Tuareg)	122,000
Other	940,000
Burundi[1]	
● French	*285,000*
● Rundi	3,015,000
Hutu	2,542,000

Major languages by country	Number of speakers
Tutsi	447,000
Twa	31,000
Other[5]	61,000
Cambodia[1]	
Cham	308,000
Chinese	403,000
● Khmer	11,629,000
Vietnamese	722,000
Other[6]	64,000
Cameroon[1]	
Chadic languages	
Buwal	307,000
Hausa	194,000
Kotoko	174,000
Mandara (Wandala)	889,000
Masana (Masa)	623,000
● English	*7,868,000*
● French	*4,700,000*
Niger-Congo languages	
Adamawa-Ubangi languages	
Chamba	378,000
Gbaya (Baya)	194,000
Mbum	204,000
Atlantic languages	
Fula (Fulani)	1,512,000
Benue-Congo languages	
Bamileke (Medumba)-Widikum (Mogha-mo)-Bamum (Mum)	2,922,000
Basa (Bassa)	174,000
Duala	1,717,000
Fang (Pangwe)-Beti-Bulu	3,096,000
Ibibio (Efik)	20,000
Igbo	82,000
Jukun	102,000
Lundu	429,000
Maka	777,000
Tikar	1,165,000
Tiv	409,000
Wute	51,000
Saharan languages	
Kanuri	51,000
Semitic languages	
Arabic	153,000
Other	123,000
Canada	
● English	18,703,000
● French	7,349,000
English-French	119,000
English-other	276,000
French-other	40,000
English-French-other	10,000
Arabic	164,000
Chinese	793,000
Cree	85,000
Dutch	148,000
Eskimo (Inuktitut) languages	30,000
German	499,000
Greek	135,000
Italian	537,000
Pilipino (Filipino)	149,000
Polish	236,000
Portuguese	234,000
Punjābī	224,000
Spanish	236,000
Ukrainian	180,000
Vietnamese	118,000
Other	1,327,000
Cape Verde	
Crioulo (Portuguese Creole)	438,000
● Portuguese	...
Central African Republic	
Banda	858,000
● French	*942,000*
Gbaya (Baya)	869,000
Mandjia	544,000
Mbum	230,000
Ngbaka	283,000
Nzakara	63,000
● Sango (lingua franca)	*3,244,000*
Sara	241,000
Zande (Azande)	73,000
Other	523,000
Chad[1]	
● Arabic	1,140,000
Bagirmi	143,000
Fitri-Batha	428,000
● French	*2,774,000*
Fula (Fulani)	230,000
Gorane	581,000
Hadjarai	614,000
Kanem-Bornu	833,000
Lac-Iro	55,000
Mayo-Kebbi	1,063,000
Ouaddai	811,000
Sara	2,554,000
Tandjile	603,000
Other	197,000
Chile[1]	
Araucanian (Mapuche)	1,421,000
Aymara	81,000
Rapa Nui	35,000
● Spanish	13,740,000
China[1]	
Achang	31,000
Bulang (Blang)	92,000
Ch'iang (Qiang)	225,000
Chinese (Han)	1,185,204,000
Cantonese (Yüeh [Yue])	*51,093,000*
Hakka	*28,612,000*
Hsiang (Xiang)	*39,853,000*
Kan (Gan)	*22,481,000*
● Mandarin	*918,652,000*
Min	*39,853,000*
Wu	*84,814,000*
Ching-p'o (Jingpo)	133,000
Chuang (Zhuang)	17,607,000
Daghur (Daur)	133,000
Evenk (Ewenki)	31,000
Gelo	501,000
Hani (Woni)	1,431,000
Hui	9,772,000
Kazak	1,267,000
Korean	2,187,000
Kyrgyz	164,000
Lahu	470,000
Li	1,267,000
Lisu	654,000
Manchu	11,169,000
Maonan	82,000
Miao	8,410,000
Mongol	5,467,000
Mulam	184,000
Na-hsi (Naxi)	317,000
Nu	31,000
Pai (Bai)	1,809,000
Pumi	31,000
Puyi (Chung-chia)	2,892,000
Salar	102,000
She	715,000
Shui	388,000
Sibo (Xibe)	194,000
Tai (Dai)	1,165,000
Tajik	41,000
Tibetan	5,222,000
Tu (Monguor)	215,000
T'u-chia (Tujia)	6,489,000
Tung (Dong)	2,861,000
Tung-hsiang (Dongxiang)	420,000
Uighur	8,206,000
Wa (Va)	399,000
Yao	2,422,000
Yi	7,470,000
Other	1,012,000
Colombia[1]	
Amerindian languages	352,000
Arawakan	39,000
Cariban	29,000
Chibchan	176,000
Other	107,000
English Creole	49,000
● Spanish	40,910,000
Comoros	
● Arabic	...
● Comorian	374,000
Comorian-French	65,000
Comorian-Malagasy	28,000
Comorian-Arabic	8,600
Comorian-Swahili	2,600
Comorian-French-other	20,000
● French	*104,000*
Other	2,600
Congo, Dem. Rep. of the[1]	
Boa	1,239,000
Chokwe	965,000
● English	...
● French	*4,062,000*
Kongo	8,470,000
Kongo (lingua franca)	*16,250,000*
Lingala (lingua franca)	*36,562,000*
Luba	9,486,000
Lugbara	853,000
Mongo	7,109,000
Ngala and Bangi	3,047,000
Rundi	2,031,000
Rwanda	5,423,000
Swahili (lingua franca)	*25,390,000*
Teke	1,442,000
Zande (Azande)	3,219,000
Other	9,486,000
Congo, Rep. of the[1]	
Bobangi	39,000
● French	*1,960,000*
Kongo	1,908,000
Kota	39,000
Lingala (lingua franca)	...
Maka	65,000
Mbete	183,000
Mboshi	431,000
Monokutuba (lingua franca)	*2,221,000*
Punu	118,000
Sango	105,000
Teke	640,000
Other	196,000
Costa Rica	
Chibchan languages	12,500
Bribrí	8,000
Cabécar	4,600
Chinese	8,000
English Creole	83,000
● Spanish	4,044,000
Other	11,000
Côte d'Ivoire[1]	
Akan (including Baule and Anyi)	4,996,000
● French	*8,326,000*
Gur ([Voltaic] including Senufo and Lobi)	1,946,000
Kru (including Bete)	1,748,000
Malinke (including Dyula and Bambara)	1,905,000
Southern Mande (including Dan and Guro)	1,280,000
Other (non-Ivoirian population)	4,756,000
Croatia	
● Serbo-Croatian (Croatian)	4,252,000
Other	176,000
Cuba	
● Spanish	11,295,000
Cyprus (island)[1]	
● Greek	685,000
● Turkish	203,000
Other	32,000
Czech Republic[1]	
Bulgarian	3,000
● Czech	8,202,000
German	48,000
Greek	3,000
Hungarian	20,000
Moravian	1,313,000
Polish	60,000
Romanian	1,000
Romany	33,000
Russian	5,000
Ruthenian	2,000
Silesian	44,000
Slovak	312,000
Ukrainian	8,000
Other	70,000
Denmark[2]	
Arabic	39,000
● Danish	5,102,000
English	20,000
German	26,000
South Slavic languages	39,000
Turkish	47,000
Other	120,000
Djibouti[1]	
Afar	162,000
● Arabic	51,000
● French	*71,000*
Somali	203,000
Gadaboursi	...
Issa	...
Issaq	...
Other	41,000
Dominica	
● English	...
English Creole	69,700
French Creole	*63,000*
Dominican Republic	
French (Haitian) Creole	176,000
● Spanish	8,540,000
East Timor	
Portuguese	80,000
Tetum (Tetun)	608,000
Other	310,000
Ecuador	
Quechuan (and other Amerindian languages)	915,000
● Spanish	12,088,000
Egypt[1]	
● Arabic	67,367,000
Other	818,000
El Salvador	
● Spanish	6,515,000
Equatorial Guinea[1]	
Bubi	51,000
Fang	401,000
● French	...
Krio (English Creole)	...
● Spanish	...
Other	41,000
Eritrea	
Cushitic languages	
Afar	180,000
Bilin	130,000
Hadareb (Beja)	160,000
Saho	120,000
Nilotic languages	
Kunama	110,000
Nara	90,000
Semitic languages	
Arabic (Rashaida)	10,000
Tigré	1,310,000
Tigrinya	2,031,000
Estonia[1]	
Belarusian	20,000
● Estonian	883,000
Finnish	12,000
Russian	380,000
Ukrainian	34,000
Other	25,000
Ethiopia[1]	
Afar	1,205,000
Agew (Awngi)	607,000
Amharic	18,668,000
Berta	149,000
Gedeo	548,000
Gumuz	129,000
Gurage	2,708,000
Hadya–Libida	1,085,000
Kaffa	717,000
Kambata	797,000
Kimant	199,000
Oromo (Oromifa)	20,291,000
Sidamo	2,161,000
Somali	3,973,000
Tigrinya	3,764,000
Walaita	3,883,000
Other	5,705,000
Faroe Islands	
● Danish	...
● Faroese	48,000
Fiji[1]	
● English	*172,000*
Fijian	420,000
Hindi	361,000
Other	45,000
Finland	
Finnish	4,820,000
Russian	26,000
Sami (Lapp)	2,000
Swedish	295,000
Other	68,000
France	
Arabic[7]	1,514,000
English[7]	81,000
● French[7, 8, 9]	55,974,000
Basque	*102,000*
Breton	*813,000*
Catalan (Rousillonais)	*264,000*
Corsican	*81,000*
Dutch (Flemish)	*91,000*
German (Alsatian)	*1,016,000*
Occitan	*711,000*
Italian[7]	264,000
Polish[7]	51,000
Portuguese[7]	691,000
Spanish[7]	224,000
Turkish[7]	213,000
Other[7]	762,000
French Guiana	
Amerindian languages	3,200
● French	...
French/French Creoles	167,000
Other	7,600
French Polynesia[10]	
Chinese	13,600
● French	197,000
Polynesian languages	271,000
● Tahitian	...
Other	48,000
Gabon[1]	
Fang	476,000
● French	*1,100,000*
Kota	44,000
Mbete	188,000
Mpongwe (Myene)	199,000
Punu, Sira, Nzebi	222,000
Teke	22,000
Other	177,000
Gambia, The[1]	
● English	...
Gambians	
Aku (Krio)	8,300
Atlantic languages	
Diola (Jola)	131,000
Fula (Fulani)	230,000
Manjak	23,000
Serer	34,000
Wolof	179,000
Mande languages	
Bambara	10,000
Malinke	486,000
Soninke	109,000
Other	18,000
non-Gambians	196,000
Gaza Strip	
Arabic	1,297,000
Hebrew	6,800
Georgia	
Abkhaz	88,000
Armenian	343,000
Azerbaijani (Azeri)	274,000
● Georgian (Kartuli)	3,514,000
Ossetian	118,000
Russian	441,000
Other	157,000
Germany[2]	
● German	75,429,000
Greek	362,000
Italian	613,000
Kurdish	*402,000*
Polish	281,000
South Slavic languages	1,196,000
Turkish	2,120,000
Other	2,603,000
Ghana[1]	
Akan	10,732,000
● English	*1,436,000*
Ewe	2,431,000
Ga-Adangme	1,593,000
Gurma	681,000
Hausa (lingua franca)	*12,262,000*
Mole-Dagbani (Moore)	3,238,000
Yoruba	272,000
Other	1,520,000
Greece	
● Greek	10,834,000
Turkish	104,000
Other	63,000
Greenland[2]	
● Danish	7,100
● Greenlandic	50,000
Grenada	
● English	...
English/English Creole	102,000
Guadeloupe	
● French	...
French/French Creole	414,000
Other	21,000
Guam	
Asian languages	10,800
● Chamorro	34,000
● English	59,000
English (lingua franca)	*153,000*
Philippine languages	34,000
Other Pacific Island languages	10,500
Guatemala	
Garífuna (Black Carib)	26,000
Mayan languages	3,416,000
Cakchiquel	873,000
Kekchí	471,000
Mam	265,000
Quiché	985,000
● Spanish	6,311,000
Guernsey	
● English	63,000
Norman French	...
Guinea[1]	
Atlantic languages	
Basari-Konyagi	102,000
Fula (Fulani)	3,269,000
Kissi	511,000
Other	261,000
● French	*795,000*
Mande languages	
Kpelle	397,000
Loma	193,000
Malinke	1,964,000
Susu	931,000
Yalunka	250,000
Other	590,000
Other	11,400
Guinea-Bissau[1]	
Balante	411,000
Crioulo (Portuguese Creole)	*601,000*
Ejamat	32,000
French	*137,000*
Fula (Fulani)	295,000
Malinke	179,000
Mandyako	148,000
Mankanya	53,000
Pepel	137,000
● Portuguese	*148,000*
Other	106,000
Guyana	
Amerindian languages	
Arawakan	11,000
Cariban	17,000
● English	...
English/English Creoles	750,000

Language (continued)

Major languages by country	Number of speakers
Haiti	
● French	*1,535,000*
● Haitian (French) Creole	7,528,000
Honduras	
English Creole	13,000
Garifuna (Black Carib)	86,000
Miskito	12,000
● Spanish	6,611,000
Other	82,000
Hong Kong	
Chinese	
● Cantonese	6,059,000
Cantonese (lingua franca)	*6,549,000*
Chiu Chau	98,000
Fukien (Min)	130,000
Hakka	114,000
Putonghua (Mandarin)	76,000
Putonghua (lingua franca)	*1,239,000*
Sze Yap	27,000
● English	151,000
English (lingua franca)	*2,156,000*
Japanese	14,000
Pilipino (Filipino)	7,000
Other	164,000
Hungary	
German	40,000
● Hungarian	9,984,000
Romanian	10,000
Romany	51,000
Serbo-Croatian	20,000
Slovak	10,000
Other	20,000
Iceland[2]	
● Icelandic	278,000
Other	12,000
India	
Afro-Asiatic languages	
Arabic	32,000
Austroasiatic languages	
Ho	1,198,000
Kharia	284,000
Khasi	1,146,000
Korku	589,000
Munda	526,000
Mundari	1,083,000
Santhali	6,568,000
Savara (Sora)	347,000
Other Austroasiatic	200,000
Dravidian languages	
Gondi	2,680,000
Kannada	41,239,000
Khond	273,000
Koya	336,000
Kui	809,000
Kurukh (Oraon)	1,797,000
Malayalam	38,254,000
Tamil	66,745,000
Telugu	83,129,000
Tulu	1,955,000
Other Dravidian	694,000
English	221,000
● English (lingua franca)	*202,831,000*
Indo-Iranian (Indo-Aryan) languages	
Assamese	16,468,000
Bengali	87,638,000
Bhili (Bhilodi)	7,020,000
Barel	*586,000*
Bhilali	*586,000*
Gujarati	51,212,000
Halabi	673,000
● Hindi	424,684,000
Awadhi	*610,000*
Baghelkhandi	*1,745,000*
Bagri	*746,000*
Banjari	*1,114,000*
Bhojpuri	*29,090,000*
Bundelkhandi	*2,091,000*
Chhattisgarhi	*13,336,000*
Dhundhari	*1,219,000*
Garhwali	*2,354,000*
Harauti	*1,555,000*
Haryanvi	*452,000*
Hindi	*293,936,000*
Kangri	*620,000*
Khortha (Khotta)	*1,324,000*
Kumauni	*2,165,000*
Lamani (Banjari)	*2,585,000*
Magahi (Magadhi)	*13,305,000*
Maithili	*9,784,000*
Malvi	*3,741,000*
Mandeali	*557,000*
Marwari	*5,885,000*
Mewari	*2,659,000*
Nagpuri	*977,000*
Nimadi	*1,787,000*
Pahari	*2,743,000*
Rajasthani	*16,784,000*
Sadani (Sadri)	*1,976,000*
Surgujia	*1,314,000*
Surjapuri	*462,000*
Other Hindi dialects	*7,766,000*
Hindi (lingua franca)	*703,078,000*
Kashmiri	4,960,000
Khandeshi	1,230,000
Konkani	2,218,000
Lahnda	32,000
Marathi	78,673,000
Nepali (Gorkhali)	2,617,000
Oriya	35,333,000
Punjabi	29,437,000
Sanskrit	63,000
Sindhi	2,669,000
Kachchhi	*715,000*
Urdu	54,659,000
Sino-Tibetan languages	
Adi	200,000
Angami	126,000
Ao	221,000
Bodo/Boro	1,534,000
Dimasa	116,000
Garo	851,000
Karbi/Makir	462,000
Konyak	179,000
Lotha	105,000
Lushai (Mizo)	683,000
Manipuri (Meithei)	1,597,000
Miri/Mishing	494,000
Nissi/Dafla	221,000
Rabha	179,000
Sema	210,000
Tangkhul	126,000
Thado	137,000
Tripuri	872,000
Kokbarak	*652,000*
Other Sino-Tibetan languages	1,902,000
Other	5,560,000
Indonesia	
Balinese	3,655,000
Banjarese	3,844,000
Batak	4,884,000
Buginese	4,842,000
● Indonesian (Malay)	26,627,000
Javanese	86,697,000
Madurese	9,516,000
Minangkabau	5,189,000
Sundanese	34,673,000
Other	39,956,000
Iran[1]	
Armenian	317,000
Iranian languages	
Bakhtyari (Luri)	1,110,000
Balochi	1,511,000
● Farsi (Persian)	30,232,000
Farsi (lingua franca)	*54,843,000*
Gilaki	3,498,000
Kurdish	6,044,000
Luri	2,864,000
Mazandarani	2,388,000
Other	1,437,000
Semitic languages	
Arabic	1,427,000
Other	159,000
Turkic languages	
Afshari	750,000
Azerbaijani (Azeri)	11,138,000
Qashqa'i	845,000
Shahsavani	402,000
Turkish (mostly Pishagchi, Bayat, and Qajar)	476,000
Turkmen	1,036,000
Other	137,000
Other	486,000
Iraq[1]	
● Arabic	19,026,000
Assyrian	207,000
Azerbaijani (Azeri)	424,000
Kurdish	4,678,000
Persian	207,000
Other	141,000
Ireland	
● English	3,751,000
● Irish[11]	62,000
Irish	*1,571,000*
Isle of Man	
● English	77,000
Israel[12]	
● Arabic	1,165,000
● Hebrew	4,079,000
Russian	583,000
Other	646,000
Italy[1]	
Albanian	117,000
Catalan	29,000
French	302,000
German	302,000
Greek	39,000
● Italian	52,956,000
Rhaetian	722,000
Friulian	702,000
Ladin	20,000
Romany	107,000
Sardinian	1,492,000
Slovene	117,000
Other	127,000
Jamaica	
● English	...
English/English Creoles	2,492,000
Hindī and other Indian languages	51,000
Other	101,000
Japan[2]	
Ainu[1]	15,000
Chinese	241,000
English	80,000
● Japanese	126,406,000
Korean	663,000
Philippine languages	90,000
Other	50,000
Jersey	
● English	82,200
French	...
Norman French	*5,500*
Jordan[1]	
● Arabic	5,287,000
Armenian	54,000
Kabardian (Circassian)	54,000
Kazakhstan[1]	
Azerbaijani (Azeri)	89,000
Belarusian	149,000
German	456,000
● Kazakh	6,800,000
Korean	89,000
Russian	5,135,000
Tatar	288,000
Uighur	169,000
Ukrainian	734,000
Uzbek	337,000
Other	545,000
Kenya[1]	
Arabic	83,000
Bantu languages	
Bajun (Rajun)	73,000
Basuba	125,000
Embu	375,000
Gusii (Kisii)	1,949,000
Kamba	3,565,000
Kikuyu	6,609,000
Kuria	188,000
Luhya	4,378,000
Mbere	125,000
Meru	1,731,000
Nyika (Mijikenda)	1,512,000
Pokomo	83,000
Swahili	10,000
● Swahili (lingua franca)	*20,849,000*
Taita	313,000
Cushitic languages	
Oromo languages	
Boran	146,000
Gabbra	63,000
Gurreh	167,000
Orma	63,000
Somali languages	
Degodia	198,000
Ogaden	52,000
Somali	323,000
● English (lingua franca)	*2,815,000*
Nilotic languages	
Kalenjin	3,409,000
Luo	4,034,000
Masai	500,000
Sambur	156,000
Teso	271,000
Turkana	427,000
Other	709,000
Kiribati[1]	
● English	*22,000*
Kiribati (Gilbertese)	87,000
Tuvaluan (Ellice)	500
Other	600
Korea, North[1]	
Chinese	31,000
● Korean	22,435,000
Korea, South[1]	
Chinese	51,000
● Korean	47,874,000
Kuwait	
● Arabic	1,900,000
Other	539,000
Kyrgyzstan[1]	
Azerbaijani (Azeri)	21,000
German	31,000
Kazakh	52,000
● Kyrgyz	3,021,000
● Russian	817,000
Tajik	41,000
Tatar	62,000
Ukrainian	83,000
Uzbek	714,000
Other	217,000
Laos[1]	
● Lao-Lum (Lao)	3,004,000
Lao-Soung (Miao [Hmong] and Man [Yao])	569,000
Lao-Tai (Tai)	733,000
Lao-Theung (Mon-Khmer)	1,301,000
Other[13]	52,000
Latvia[1]	
Belarusian	87,000
● Latvian	1,298,000
Lithuanian	29,000
Polish	48,000
Russian	755,000
Ukrainian	69,000
Other	39,000
Lebanon[1]	
● Arabic	3,468,000
Armenian	219,000
French	*896,000*
Other	42,000
Lesotho[1]	
● English	*429,000*
● Sotho	1,533,000
Zulu	270,000
Liberia[1]	
Atlantic (Mel) languages	
Gola	137,000
Kissi	137,000
● English	*661,000*
Krio (English Creole)	*2,939,000*
Kru languages	
Bassa	462,000
Belle	21,000
De (Dewoin, Dey)	11,000
Grebo	294,000
Krahn	126,000
Kru (Krumen)	241,000
Mande (Northern) languages	
Gbandi	95,000
Kpelle	640,000
Loma	189,000
Malinke (Mandingo)	168,000
Mende	21,000
Vai	116,000
Mande (Southern) languages	
Gio (Dan)	262,000
Mano	231,000
Other	168,000
Libya	
● Arabic	5,334,000
Berber	54,000
Other[14]	163,000
Liechtenstein[2]	
● German	30,000
Italian	1,100
Other	3,200
Lithuania[1]	
Belarusian	43,000
● Lithuanian	2,907,000
Polish	235,000
Russian	220,000
Ukrainian	23,000
Other	24,000
Luxembourg[2]	
Belgian	11,000
Dutch	2,800
English	3,500
French	13,500
German	7,800
Italian	14,200
Luxemburgian	197,000
Portuguese	182,200
Other	21,300
Macau	
Chinese	
● Cantonese (Yüeh [Yue])	381,000
Mandarin	5,000
Other Chinese languages	40,000
English	2,000
● Portuguese	10,000
Other	5,000
Macedonia[1]	
Albanian	470,000
● Macedonian	1,368,000
Romany	46,000
Serbo-Croatian	41,000
Turkish	82,000
Vlach	9,000
Other	39,000
Madagascar[1]	
French	*2,464,000*
Malagasy	16,435,000
Other	171,000
Malawi[1]	
Chewa (Maravi)	6,802,000
● English	*606,000*
Lomwe	2,144,000
Ngoni	746,000
Yao	1,538,000
Other	393,000
Malaysia	
Bajau	163,000
Chinese	1,464,000
Chinese-others	824,000
Dusun	260,000
English	130,000
English-others	282,000
English (lingua franca)	*7,700,000*
Iban	597,000
Iban-others	98,000
● Malay	10,877,000
Malay-others	3,861,000
Tamil	976,000
Tamil-others	11,000
Other	5,683,000
Maldives	
● Divehi (Maldivian)	285,000
Mali[1]	
Afro-Asiatic languages	
Berber languages	
Tamashek (Tuareg)	848,000
Semitic languages	
Arabic (Mauri)	185,000
● French	*1,195,000*
Niger-Congo languages	
Atlantic languages	
Dogon	467,000
Fula (Fulani) and Tukulor	1,619,000
Gur (Voltaic) languages	
Bwa (Bobo)	283,000
Moore (Mossi)	44,000
Senufo and Minianka	1,391,000
Mande languages	
Bambara	3,705,000
Bambara (lingua franca)	*9,236,000*
Bobo Fing	11,000
Dyula (Jula)	337,000
Malinke, Khasonke, and Wasulunka	771,000
Samo (Duun)	76,000
Soninke	1,021,000
Nilo-Saharan languages	
Songhai	837,000
Other	33,000
Malta[1]	
● English	14,000
English (lingua franca)	*99,000*
● Maltese	380,000
Other	5,200
Marshall Islands[2]	
● English	*56,000*
● Marshallese	55,000
Other	1,700
Martinique	
● French	...
French/French Creole	380,000
Other	13,300
Mauritania[1]	
● Arabic	...
French	*274,000*
Fula (Fulani)	30,000
Ḥassānīyah Arabic	2,199,000
Soninke	71,000
Tukulor	142,000
Wolof	182,000
Zenaga	30,000
Other	41,000
Mauritius	
Bhojpuri	233,000
Bhojpuri-other	26,000
Chinese	4,000
● English	2,000
French	42,000
French Creole	754,000
French Creole-other	108,000
Hindi	16,000
Marathi	8,000
Tamil	9,000
Telugu	7,000
Urdu	8,000
Other	3,000
Mayotte[15]	
● Arabic	...
● French	68,000
Mahorais (local dialect of Comorian Swahili)	140,000
Other Comorian Swahili dialects	62,000
Malagasy	54,000
Other	10,000
Mexico	
Amerindian languages	7,278,000
Amuzgo	50,000
Aztec (Nahuatl)	1,744,000
Chatino	49,000
Chinantec	159,000

Major languages by country	Number of speakers
Chocho	1,200
Chol	194,000
Chontal	53,000
Cora	20,000
Cuicatec	16,000
Huastec	180,000
Huave	17,000
Huichol	38,000
Kanjobal	11,000
Mame	11,000
Mayo	44,000
Mazahua	172,000
Mazatec	254,000
Mixe	139,000
Mixtec	538,000
Otomí	360,000
Popoluca	66,000
Purépecha (Tarasco)	143,000
Tarahumara	92,000
Tepehua	11,000
Tepehuan	31,000
Tlapanec	123,000
Tojolabal	46,000
Totonac	287,000
Trique	25,000
Tzeltal	344,000
Tzotzil	362,000
Yaqui	16,000
Yucatec (Mayan)	948,000
Zapotec	533,000
Zoque	64,000
Other	496,000
● Spanish	85,871,000
Spanish-Amerindian languages	*5,987,000*
Micronesia	
Chuukese (Trukese)/Mortlockese	56,000
English	1,500
Kosraean	7,700
Pohnpeian	28,000
Polynesian languages	1,600
Woleaian	4,700
Yapese	6,000
Other	1,400
Moldova	
Bulgarian	70,000
Gagauz	139,000
● Romanian (Moldovan)	2,646,000
Russian	985,000
Ukrainian	368,000
Other	60,000
Monaco[2]	
English	2,100
● French	13,600
Italian	5,200
Monegasque	5,200
Other	6,300
Mongolia[1]	
Bayad	49,000
Buryat	43,000
Darhat	18,000
Dariganga	35,000
Dörbet	68,000
Dzakhchin	27,000
Kazakh	147,000
● Khalkha (Mongolian)	1,962,000
Khalkha (lingua franca)	*2,232,000*
Ould	10,000
Torgut	13,000
Tuvan (Uryankhai)	25,000
Other	98,000
Morocco	
● Arabic	19,390,000
Berber	9,845,000
French	*11,905,000*
Other	600,000
Mozambique	
Bantu languages	
Chuabo	1,167,000
Lomwe	1,410,000
Makua	4,883,000
Sena	1,303,000
Tsonga (Changana)	2,120,000
Other Bantu languages	6,128,000
● Portuguese	1,206,000
Portuguese (lingua franca)	*7,363,000*
Other	350,000
Myanmar (Burma)[1]	
● Burmese	29,312,000
Burmese (lingua franca)	*34,017,000*
Chin	927,000
Kachin (Ching-p'o)	581,000
Karen	2,648,000
Kayah	173,000
Mon	1,029,000
Rakhine (Arakanese)	1,915,000
Shan	3,595,000
Other	2,332,000
Namibia	
Afrikaans	183,000
Caprivi	90,000
● English	15,000
English (lingua franca)	*370,000*
German	17,000
Herero	154,000
Kavango (Okavango)	187,000
Nama	240,000
Ovambo (Ambo [Kwanyama])	976,000
San (Bushman)	37,000
Tswana	8,700
Other	18,500
Nauru	
Chinese	1,100
English	1,000
English (lingua franca)	*11,000*
Kiribati (Gilbertese)	2,200
Nauruan	7,300
Tuvaluan (Ellice)	1,100
Nepal	
Austroasiatic (Munda) languages	
Santhali	39,000
English	*7,147,000*
Indo-Aryan languages	
Bengali	39,000
Bhojpuri	1,801,000
Dhanwar	29,000
Hindi	225,000
Hindi (Awadhi dialect)	490,000
Maithili	2,869,000
● Nepali (Eastern Pahari)	12,169,000
Rajbansi	108,000
Tharu	1,302,000
Urdu	264,000
Tibeto-Burman languages	
Bhutia (Sherpa)	157,000
Chepang	29,000
Gurung	294,000
Limbu	333,000
Magar	558,000
Newari	901,000
Rai and Kiranti	570,000
Tamang	1,185,000
Thakali	9,800
Thami	20,000
Other	773,000
Netherlands, The[2]	
Arabic	133,000
● Dutch	15,556,000
Dutch and Frisian	*613,000*
Turkish	105,000
Other	444,000
Netherlands Antilles	
● Dutch	…
English	14,000
Papiamento	145,000
Other	10,000
New Caledonia[1]	
● French	75,000
Indonesian	5,000
Melanesian languages	99,000
Polynesian languages	26,000
Vietnamese	3,100
Other	12,000
New Zealand	
● English	3,483,000
English-Māori	155,000
● Māori	15,000
Other	349,000
Nicaragua	
English Creole	31,000
Misumalpan languages	
Miskito	90,000
Sumo	9,000
● Spanish	5,350,000
Other	2,300
Niger[1]	
Atlantic languages	
Fula (Fulani)	1,106,000
Berber languages	
Tamashek (Tuareg)	1,185,000
Chadic languages	
Hausa	6,029,000
Hausa (lingua franca)	*8,016,000*
● French	*1,694,000*
Gur (Voltaic) languages	
Gurma	34,000
Saharan languages	
Kanuri	508,000
Teda (Tubu)	45,000
Semitic languages	
Arabic	34,000
Songhai and Zerma	2,416,000
Other	23,000
Nigeria[1]	
Arabic	305,000
Bura	1,932,000
Edo	4,271,000
● English/English Creole (lingua franca)	*56,943,000*
Fula (Fulani)	14,134,000
Hausa	26,743,000
Hausa (lingua franca)	*63,044,000*
Ibibio	7,016,000
Igbo (Ibo)	22,574,000
Ijo (Ijaw)	2,237,000
Kanuri	5,186,000
Nupe	1,525,000
Tiv	2,847,000
Yoruba	26,743,000
Other	9,762,000
Northern Mariana Islands	
● Carolinian	3,100
● Chamorro	16,000
Chinese	16,900
● English	8,000
English (lingua franca)	*66,000*
Philippine languages	17,600
Other Pacific Island languages	3,900
Other	6,700
Norway[2]	
Danish	18,000
English	24,000
● Norwegian	4,411,000
Swedish	13,000
Other	102,000
Oman	
● Arabic (Omani)	2,012,000
Other	609,000
Pakistan	
Balochi	4,484,000
Brahui	1,821,000
English (lingua franca)	*16,842,000*
Pashto	19,579,000
Punjabi	
Hindko	3,621,000
Punjabi	71,778,000
Sindhi	
Saraiki	14,642,000
Sindhi	17,537,000
● Urdu	11,326,000
Other	4,242,000
Palau	
Chinese	300
● English	600
English (lingua franca)	*20,000*
● Palauan	17,000
Philippine languages	2,000
Other	700
Panama	
Amerindian languages	
Bokotá	5,500
Chibchan	
Guaymí (Ngöbe Buglé)	166,000
Kuna	63,000
Teribe	3,000
Chocó	
Emberá	20,000
Wounaan	3,000
Arabic	18,000
Chinese	9,000
English	…
English Creoles	436,000
● Spanish	2,393,000
Papua New Guinea[1]	
● English	*159,000*
Melanesian languages	1,121,000
Motu	*181,000*
Papuan languages	4,349,000
Tok Pisin (English Creole)	*3,624,000*
Other	113,000
Paraguay	
German	51,000
● Guaraní	2,267,000
Guaraní-Spanish	2,739,000
Portuguese	174,000
● Spanish	369,000
Other	41,000
Peru	
Amerindian languages	
● Aymara	624,000
● Quechua	4,465,000
Other	190,000
● Spanish	21,657,000
Other	212,000
Philippines	
Aklanon	595,000
Bantoanon	74,000
Bicol	4,614,000
Bilaan	43,000
Bontoc	64,000
Butuanon	85,000
Cebuano	18,882,000
Chavacano	500,000
Chinese	74,000
Davaweno (Mansaka)	553,000
● English (lingua franca)	*42,207,000*
Hiligaynon	7,389,000
Ibaloi (Nabaloi)	138,000
Ibanag	298,000
Ifugao	223,000
Ilocano	7,559,000
Ilongot	117,000
Kalinga	138,000
Kankanai	308,000
Kinaray-a (Hamtikanon)	510,000
Maguindanao	1,180,000
Manobo	542,000
Maranao	1,031,000
Masbateño	564,000
Palawano	85,000
Pampango	2,424,000
Pangasinan	1,467,000
● Pilipino (Filipino; Tagalog)	23,761,000
Romblon	255,000
Samal	510,000
Sambal	213,000
Subanon	330,000
Surigaonon	595,000
Tau Sug	936,000
Tboli	106,000
Tinggian	74,000
Tiruray	74,000
Waray-Waray	3,094,000
Yakan	160,000
Other	1,595,000
Poland	
Belarusian	190,000
German	500,000
● Polish	37,704,000
Ukrainian	230,000
Portugal[2]	
● Portuguese	10,079,000
Other	102,000
Puerto Rico	
● English	543,000
● Spanish	3,297,000
Other	39,000
Qatar[2]	
● Arabic	250,000
Other[16]	376,000
Réunion	
Chinese	21,000
Comorian	21,000
● French	*232,000*
French Creole	697,000
Malagasy	11,000
Tamil	*148,000*
Other	11,000
Romania[1]	
Bulgarian	8,000
Czech	4,000
German	64,000
Hungarian	1,427,000
Polish	4,000
● Romanian	19,346,000
Romany (Tigani)	540,000
Russian	43,000
Serbo-Croatian	26,000
Slovak	22,000
Tatar	22,000
Turkish	43,000
Ukrainian	64,000
Other	43,000
Russia[1]	
Adyghian	119,000
Armenian	713,000
Avar	604,000
Azerbaijani (Azeri)	336,000
Bashkir	1,375,000
Belarusian	972,000
Buryat	453,000
Chechen	898,000
Chuvash	1,722,000
Dargin	353,000
Georgian (Kartuli)	132,000
German	788,000
Ingush	253,000
Kabardian	367,000
Kalmyk	166,000
Karachay	150,000
Kazakh	569,000
Komi-Permyak	147,000
Komi-Zyryan	354,000
Kumyk	286,000
Lak	117,000
Lezgi (Lezgian)	295,000
Mari	66,000
Mordvin	723,000
Ossetian	463,000
Romanian	95,000
Romany	130,000
● Russian	118,000,000
Tabasaran	97,000
Tatar	5,519,000
Tuvan	198,000
Udmurt	713,000
Ukrainian	3,446,000
Uzbek	127,000
Yakut	441,000
Other	3,836,000
Rwanda	
● English	…
● French	*576,000*
● Rwanda	8,387,000
St. Kitts and Nevis	
● English	…
English/English Creole	46,400
St. Lucia	
● English	32,000
English/French Creole	130,000
St. Vincent and the Grenadines	
● English	…
English/English Creole	112,000
Other	1,000
Samoa	
● English	1,000
● Samoan	85,000
Samoan-English	93,000
San Marino[1]	
● Italian (Romagnolo)	29,000
São Tomé and Príncipe	
Crioulo (Portuguese Creole)	124,000
English	…
French	1,000
● Portuguese	…
Other	17,000
Saudi Arabia[1]	
● Arabic	22,809,000
Other	1,199,000
Senegal	
● French	*3,547,000*
Senegalese	
Bambara	91,000
Diola	497,000
Fula (Fulani)-Tukulor	2,199,000
Malinko (Mandingo)	375,000
Serer	1,267,000
Soninke	132,000
Wolof	4,865,000
Wolof (lingua franca)	*8,108,000*
Other	446,000
non-Senegalese	223,000
Serbia and Montenegro[1]	
Albanian	1,738,000
Hungarian	346,000
Macedonian	49,000
Romanian	40,000
Romany	148,000
● Serbo-Croatian (Serbian)	7,920,000
Serbo-Croatian (lingua franca)	*9,974,000*
Slovak	69,000
Vlach	20,000
Other	198,000
Seychelles	
English	3,000
English (lingua franca)	*29,000*
French	1,000
French (lingua franca)	*78,000*
Seselwa (French Creole)	75,000
Other	3,000
Sierra Leone[1]	
Atlantic languages	
Bullom-Sherbro	190,000
Fula (Fulani)	190,000
Kissi	114,000
Limba	418,000
Temne	1,578,000
● English	*475,000*
Krio (English Creole [lingua franca])	*4,182,000*
Mande languages	
Kono-Vai	257,000
Kuranko	171,000
Mende	1,720,000
Susu	76,000
Yalunka	171,000
Other	86,000
Singapore[1]	
Chinese	3,253,000
● English	*1,585,000*
● Malay	589,000
● Mandarin Chinese	*1,837,000*
● Tamil (and other Indian languages)	335,000
Other	56,000
Slovakia[1]	
Czech, Moravian, and Silesian	59,000
German	5,000
Hungarian	569,000

Language (continued)

Major languages by country	Number of speakers
Polish	3,000
Romany	90,000
Ruthenian, Ukrainian, and Russian	35,000
● Slovak	4,626,000
Other	15,000
Slovenia	
Hungarian	9,000
Serbo-Croatian	156,000
● Slovene	1,732,000
Other	74,000
Solomon Islands[1]	
● English	*9,000*
Melanesian languages	385,000
Papuan languages	39,000
Polynesian languages	16,000
Solomon Island Pidgin (English Creole)	*157,000*
Other	10,000
Somalia[1]	
● Arabic	...
English	...
● Somali	7,892,000
Other	133,000
South Africa	
● Afrikaans	5,961,000
● English	3,675,000
Nguni	
● Ndebele	717,000
● Swazi	1,210,000
● Xhosa	7,888,000
● Zulu	10,667,000
Sotho	
● North Sotho (Pedi)	4,213,000
● South Sotho	3,540,000
● Tswana (Western Sotho)	3,675,000
● Tsonga	1,972,000
● Venda	1,031,000
Other	224,000
Spain	
Basque (Euskera)	641,000
● Castilian Spanish	30,373,000
Catalan (Català)	6,886,000
Galician (Gallego)	2,604,000
Other	305,000
Sri Lanka	
English	10,000
English-Sinhala	1,051,000
English-Sinhala-Tamil	684,000
English-Tamil	218,000
● Sinhala	11,510,000
Sinhala-Tamil	1,785,000
● Tamil	3,748,000
Other	60,000
Sudan, The[1]	
● Arabic	18,818,000
Arabic (lingua franca)	*22,816,000*
Bari	934,000
Beja	2,434,000
Dinka	4,400,000
Fur	782,000
Lotuko	565,000
Nubian languages	3,086,000
Nuer	1,869,000
Shilluk	652,000
Zande (Azande)	1,032,000
Other	3,542,000
Suriname	
● Dutch	*111,000*
English/English Creole	*415,000*
Sranantonga	172,000
Sranantonga-other	172,000
Other (mostly Hindi, Javanese, and Saramacca)	91,000
Swaziland[1]	
● English	*50,000*
● Swazi	976,000
Zulu	20,000
Other	81,000
Sweden[2]	
Arabic	69,000
Danish	41,000
English	32,000
Finnish	211,000
German	46,000
Iranian languages[1]	50,000
Norwegian	47,000
Polish	39,000
South Slavic languages[1]	117,000
Spanish	57,000
● Swedish	8,021,000
Turkish	29,000
Other	199,000
Switzerland	
● French	1,410,000
● German	4,669,000
● Italian	562,000
Romansch	41,000
Other	654,000
Syria[1]	
● Arabic	15,829,000
Kurdish	1,585,000
Other	173,000
Taiwan	
Austronesian languages	
Ami	140,000
Atayal	91,000
Bunun	43,000
Paiwan	69,000
Puyuma	10,000
Rukai	11,000
Saisiyat	6,000
Tsou	7,000
Yami	4,000
Chinese languages	
Hakka	2,481,000
● Mandarin	4,535,000
Min (South Fukien)	15,049,000
Other	122,000
Tajikistan	
Russian	633,000
● Tajik (Tojik)	4,066,000
Uzbek	1,515,000
Other	322,000
Tanzania[1]	
Chaga (Chagga), Pare	1,719,000
● English	*3,775,000*
Gogo	1,381,000
Ha	1,202,000
Haya	2,066,000
Hehet	2,414,000
Iramba	1,003,000
Luguru	1,719,000
Luo	288,000
Makonde	2,066,000
Masai	348,000
Ngoni	467,000
Nyakusa	1,898,000
Nyamwesi (Sukuma)	7,401,000
Shambala	1,500,000
● Swahili	3,100,000
Swahili (lingua franca)	*31,790,000*
Tatoga	258,000
Yao	854,000
Other	5,394,000
Thailand[1]	
Chinese	7,764,000
Karen	226,000
Malay	2,328,000
Mon-Khmer languages	
Khmer	810,000
Kuy	687,000
Other	226,000
Tai languages	
Lao	17,221,000
● Thai (Siamese)	33,662,000
Other	441,000
Other	656,000
Togo[1]	
Atlantic (Mel) languages	
Fula (Fulani)	74,000
Benue-Congo languages	
Ana (Ana-Ife)	136,000
Nago	14,000
Yoruba	11,000
Chadic languages	
Hausa	15,000
● French	*2,704,000*
Gur (Voltaic) languages	
Basari	95,000
Chakossi (Akan)	64,000
Chamba	53,000
Dye (Gangam)	51,000
Gurma	184,000
Kabre	748,000
Konkomba	77,000
Kotokoli (Tem)	313,000
Moba	292,000
Moore (Mossi)	14,000
Namba (Lamba)	166,000
Naudemba (Losso)	223,000
Tamberma	30,000
Yanga	16,000
Kwa languages	
Adele	11,000
Adja (Aja)	170,000
Ahlo	10,000
Akposo	145,000
Ane (Basila)	307,000
Anlo	4,300
Anyaga	11,000
Ewe	1,259,000
Fon	54,000
Hwe	6,500
Kebu	63,000
Kpessi	4,300
Peda-Hula (Pla)	22,000
Watyi (Ouatchi)	559,000
Other	229,000
Tonga	
● English	*31,000*
● Tongan	100,000
Other	2,000
Trinidad and Tobago	
● English	...
English Creole[17]	37,000
Hindi	45,000
Trinidad English	1,195,000
● Other	3,000
Tunisia	
● Arabic	6,911,000
Arabic-French	2,596,000
Arabic-French-English	309,000
Arabic-other	10,000
Other-no Arabic	31,000
Other	31,000
Turkey[1]	
Arabic	967,000
Kurdish[18]	7,482,000
● Turkish	61,825,000
Other	323,000
Turkmenistan[1]	
Armenian	37,000
Azerbaijani (Azeri)	40,000
Balochi	40,000
Kazakh	96,000
Russian	328,000
Tatar	40,000
● Turkmen	3,731,000
Ukrainian	25,000
Uzbek	446,000
Other	85,000
Tuvalu	
English	...
Kiribati (Gilbertese)	800
Tuvaluan (Ellice)	9,400
Uganda[1]	
Bantu languages	
Amba	98,000
Ganda (Luganda)	4,603,000
Gisu (Masaba)	1,145,000
Gwere	415,000
Kiga (Chiga)	2,127,000
Konjo	556,000
Nkole (Nyankole and Hororo)	2,727,000
Nyole	349,000
Nyoro	753,000
Ruli	109,000
Rundi	153,000
Rwanda	818,000
Samia	338,000
Soga	2,094,000
Swahili (lingua franca)	*8,944,000*
Toro	742,000
Central Sudanic languages	
Lugbara	1,200,000
Madi	196,000
Ndo	251,000
● English	*2,727,000*
Nilotic languages	
Acholi	1,124,000
Alur	600,000
Kakwa	131,000
Karamojong	535,000
Kumam	175,000
Lango	1,494,000
Padhola	382,000
Sebei (Kupsabiny)	164,000
Teso	1,527,000
Other (mostly Gujarati and Hindi)	633,000
Ukraine	
Belarusian	145,000
Bulgarian	154,000
Hungarian	145,000
Polish	29,000
Romanian	318,000
Russian	15,714,000
● Ukrainian	30,937,000
Other	414,000
United Arab Emirates[2]	
● Arabic	1,606,000
Other[16]	2,212,000
United Kingdom	
● English	57,559,000
Scots-Gaelic	79,000
Welsh	565,000
Other	961,000
United States	
Amharic	42,000
Arabic	683,000
Armenian	225,000
Bengali	53,000
Cajun	42,000
Chinese (including Formosan)	2,247,000
Czech	117,000
Danish	42,000
Dutch	180,000
English	239,407,000
English (lingua franca)	*282,724,000*
Finnish	64,000
French	2,150,000
French Creole (mostly Haitian)	233,000
German	1,537,000
Greek	406,000
Gujarati	262,000
Hebrew	217,000
Hindi (including Urdu)	645,000
Hungarian	131,000
Ilocano	53,000
Italian	1,121,000
Japanese	531,000
Korean	994,000
Kru (Gullah)	85,000
Lithuanian	74,000
Malayalam	42,000
Miao (Hmong)	187,000
Mon-Khmer (mostly Cambodian)	202,000
Navajo	198,000
Norwegian	106,000
Pennsylvania Dutch	106,000
Persian	347,000
Polish	742,000
Portuguese	627,000
Punjābī	64,000
Romanian	85,000
Russian	785,000
Samoan	42,000
Serbo-Croatian	260,000
Slovak	106,000
Spanish	31,230,000
Swedish	95,000
Syriac	42,000
Tagalog	1,361,000
Tai (including Laotian)	300,000
Turkish	53,000
Ukrainian	127,000
Vietnamese	1,122,000
Yiddish	199,000
Other	858,000
Uruguay	
● Spanish	3,235,700
Other	114,000
Uzbekistan[1]	
Kazakh	1,046,000
Russian	1,542,000
Tajik	1,232,000
Tatar	414,000
● Uzbek	19,429,000
Other	1,977,000
Vanuatu[19]	
● Bislama (English Creole)	116,000
● English	58,000
● French	29,000
Other	1,900
Venezuela	
Amerindian languages	
Goajiro	170,000
Warrau (Warao)	21,000
Other	160,000
● Spanish	24,795,000
Other	553,000
Vietnam[1]	
Bahnar	177,000
Cham	125,000
Chinese (Hoa)	1,142,000
French	*395,000*
Hre	125,000
Jarai	312,000
Khmer	1,132,000
Koho	114,000
Man (Mien, or Yao)	602,000
Miao (Meo, or Hmong)	716,000
Mnong	83,000
Muong	1,162,000
Nung	903,000
Rade (Rhadé)	249,000
Roglai	96,000
San Chay (Cao Lan)	146,000
San Diu	125,000
Sedang	125,000
Stieng	62,000
Tai	1,329,000
Tho (Tay)	1,515,000
● Vietnamese	70,972,000
Other	168,000
Virgin Islands (U.S.)	
● English	91,000
French	2,800
Spanish	15,000
Other	2,800
West Bank[20]	
Arabic	2,275,000
Hebrew	192,000
Western Sahara	
Arabic	262,000
Yemen[1]	
● Arabic	19,930,000
Other	80,000
Zambia[21]	
Bemba group	
Bemba	3,217,000
Bemba (lingua franca)	*5,643,000*
Bisa	124,000
Lala	260,000
Lamba	237,000
Other	451,000
● English	124,000
English (lingua franca)	*2,032,000*
Lozi (Barotse) group	
Lozi (Barotse)	688,000
Other	124,000
Mambwe group	
Lungu	79,000
Mambwe	124,000
Mwanga (Winawanga)	148,000
Other	11,000
North-Western group	
Kaonde	248,000
Lunda	214,000
Luvale (Luena)	192,000
Other	293,000
Nyanja (Maravi) group	
Chewa	621,000
Ngoni	181,000
Nsenga	463,000
Nyanja (Maravi)	847,000
Nyanja (lingua franca)	*2,822,000*
Other	68,000
Tonga (Ila-Tonga) group	
Ila	102,000
Lenje	169,000
Tonga	1,185,000
Other	135,000
Tumbuka group	
Senga	79,000
Tumbuka	316,000
Other	11,000
Other	102,000
Zimbabwe	
● English	258,000
English (lingua franca)	*5,477,000*
Ndebele (Nguni)	1,902,000
Nyanja	269,000
Shona	8,453,000
Other	837,000

[1]Figures given represent ethnolinguistic groups. [2]Data refer to nationality (usually resident aliens holding foreign passports). [3]Data are partly based on place of residence. [4]Majority of population speak Moore (language of the Mossi); Dyula is language of commerce. [5]Swahili also spoken. [6]English and French also spoken. [7]Based on "nationality" at 1982 census. [8]Includes naturalized citizens. [9]French is the universal language throughout France; traditional dialects and minority languages are retained regionally in the approximate numbers shown, however. [10]Data reflect multilingualism; 2000 population estimate is 233,000. [11]Refers to Irish speakers in Gaeltacht areas. [12]Includes the population of the Golan Heights and East Jerusalem; excludes the Israeli population in the West Bank and Gaza Strip. [13]English and French also spoken. [14]English and Italian also spoken. [15]Data reflect ability to speak the language, not mother tongue; 2003 population estimate is 160,000. [16]Mostly Pakistanis, Indians, and Iranians. [17]Spoken on Tobago only. [18]Other estimates of the Kurdish population range from 6 percent to 20–25 percent. [19]Data reflect multilingualism; 2000 population is 190,000. [20]Excludes East Jerusalem. [21]Groups are officially defined geographic divisions; elements comprising them are named by language.

Religion

The following table presents statistics on religious affiliation for each of the countries of the world. An assessment was made for each country of the available data on distribution of religious communities within the total population; the best available figures, whether originating as census data, membership figures of the churches concerned, or estimates by external analysts in the absence of reliable local data, were applied as percentages to the estimated 2001 midyear population of the country to obtain the data shown below.

Several concepts govern the nature of the available data, each useful separately but none the basis of any standard of international practice in the collection of such data. The word "affiliation" was used above to describe the nature of the relationship joining the religious bodies named and the populations shown. This term implies some sort of formal, usually documentary, connection between the religion and the individual (a baptismal certificate, a child being assigned the religion of its parents on a census form, maintenance of one's name on the tax rolls of a state religion, etc.) but says nothing about the nature of the individual's personal religious practice, in that the individual may have lapsed, never been confirmed as an adult, joined another religion, or may have joined an organization that is formally atheist.

The user of these statistics should be careful to note that not only does the nature of the affiliation (with an organized religion) differ greatly from country to country, but the social context of religious practice does also. A country in which a single religion has long been predominant will often show more than 90% of its population to be *affiliated*, while in actual fact, no more than 10% may actually *practice* that religion on a regular basis. Such a situation often leads to undercounting of minority religions (where someone [head of household, communicant, child] is counted at all), blurring of distinctions seen to be significant elsewhere (a Hindu country may not distinguish Protestant [or even Christian] denominations; a Christian country may not distinguish among its Muslim or Buddhist citizens), or double-counting in countries where an individual may conscientiously practice more than one "religion" at a time.

Until 1989 communist countries had for long consciously attempted to ignore, suppress, or render invisible religious practice within their borders. Countries with large numbers of adherents of traditional, often animist, religions and belief systems usually have little or no formal methodology for defining the nature of local religious practice. On the other hand, countries with strong missionary traditions, or good census organizations, or few religious sensitivities may have very good, detailed, and meaningful data.

The most comprehensive works available are DAVID B. BARRETT (ed.), *World Christian Encyclopedia* (2001); and PETER BRIERLEY, *World Churches Handbook* (1997).

Religion

Religious affiliation	2001 population
Afghanistan	
Sunnī Muslim	23,090,000
Shīʿī Muslim	2,310,000
other	490,000
Albania	
Muslim	1,200,000
Roman Catholic	520,000
Albanian Orthodox	320,000
other	1,050,000
Algeria	
Sunnī Muslim	30,550,000
Ibāḍīyah Muslim	180,000
other	90,000
American Samoa	
Congregational	23,800
Roman Catholic	11,300
other	23,400
Andorra	
Roman Catholic	60,000
other	7,000
Angola	
Roman Catholic	6,440,000
Protestant	1,550,000
African Christian	710,000
other	1,660,000
Antigua and Barbuda	
Protestant	30,000
Anglican	23,000
Roman Catholic	8,000
other	10,000
Argentina	
Roman Catholic	29,920,000
Protestant	2,040,000
Muslim	730,000
Jewish	500,000
nonreligious	880,000
other	3,430,000
Armenia	
Armenian Apostolic (Orthodox)	2,454,000
other	1,353,000
Aruba	
Roman Catholic	80,000
other	18,000
Australia	
Roman Catholic	5,230,000
Anglican	4,260,000
Uniting Church	1,460,000
Presbyterian	740,000
other Protestant	1,400,000
Orthodox	540,000
nonreligious	3,220,000
other	2,510,000
Austria	
Roman Catholic	6,060,000
Protestant (mostly Lutheran)	430,000
atheist and nonreligious	690,000
other	890,000
Azerbaijan	
Shīʿī Muslim	5,299,000
Sunnī Muslim	2,271,000
other	535,000
Bahamas, The	
Protestant	135,000
Roman Catholic	50,000
Anglican	32,000
other	77,000
Bahrain	
Shīʿī Muslim	420,000
Sunnī Muslim	140,000
other	140,000
Bangladesh	
Muslim	112,660,000
Hindu	16,260,000
other	2,360,000
Barbados	
Anglican	89,000
Protestant	80,000
Roman Catholic	12,000
other	88,000
Belarus	
Belarusian Orthodox	3,151,000
Roman Catholic	1,772,000
other	5,062,000
Belgium	
Roman Catholic	8,310,000
nonreligious	600,000
other	1,360,000
Belize	
Roman Catholic	143,000
Protestant	67,000
Anglican	17,000
other	20,000
Benin	
Voodoo (traditional beliefs)	3,390,000
Roman Catholic	1,370,000
Muslim	1,320,000
other	500,000
Bermuda	
Anglican	23,700
Methodist	10,400
Roman Catholic	8,800
other	20,900
Bhutan	
Lamaistic Buddhist	510,000
Hindu	140,000
other	40,000
Bolivia	
Roman Catholic	7,540,000
Protestant	770,000
other	210,000
Bosnia and Herzegovina	
Sunnī Muslim	1,690,000
Serbian Orthodox	1,180,000
Roman Catholic	710,000
other	350,000
Botswana	
African Christian	490,000
Protestant	170,000
Roman Catholic	60,000
other (mostly traditional beliefs)	870,000
Brazil	
Roman Catholic (including syncretic Afro-Catholic cults having Spiritist beliefs and rituals)	124,470,000
Evangelical Protestant	39,850,000
other	7,800,000
Brunei	
Muslim	222,000
other	121,000
Bulgaria	
Bulgarian Orthodox	5,690,000
Muslim (mostly Sunni)	940,000
other	1,320,000
Burkina Faso	
Muslim	5,960,000
traditional beliefs	4,180,000
Christian	2,040,000
other	80,000
Burundi	
Roman Catholic	4,050,000
nonreligious	1,160,000
other (mostly Protestant)	1,020,000
Cambodia	
Buddhist	10,780,000
Chinese folk-religionist	600,000
traditional beliefs	550,000
Muslim	290,000
other	500,000
Cameroon	
Roman Catholic	4,180,000
traditional beliefs	3,750,000
Muslim	3,350,000
Protestant	3,270,000
other	1,250,000
Canada	
Roman Catholic	14,010,000
Protestant	8,620,000
Anglican	2,490,000
Eastern Orthodox	440,000
Jewish	360,000
Muslim	290,000
Buddhist	190,000
Hindu	180,000
Sikh	170,000
nonreligious	3,880,000
other	380,000
Cape Verde	
Roman Catholic	370,000
other	35,000
Central African Republic	
Roman Catholic	660,000
Muslim	560,000
traditional beliefs	550,000
Protestant	520,000
other	1,290,000
Chad	
Muslim	4,690,000
Roman Catholic	1,770,000
Protestant	1,250,000
traditional beliefs	640,000
other	350,000
Chile	
Roman Catholic	11,810,000
Evangelical Protestant	1,910,000
other	1,690,000
China	
nonreligious	661,390,000
Chinese folk-religionist	256,260,000
atheist	152,990,000
Buddhist	108,110,000
Christian	76,540,000
Muslim	18,360,000
traditional beliefs	1,280,000
Colombia	
Roman Catholic	39,590,000
other	3,480,000
Comoros	
Sunnī Muslim	555,000
other	11,000
Congo, Dem. Rep. of the	
Roman Catholic	21,990,000
Protestant	16,950,000
African Christian	7,170,000
traditional beliefs	5,740,000
Muslim	750,000
other	1,040,000
Congo, Rep. of the	
Roman Catholic	1,430,000
Protestant	490,000
African Christian	360,000
other	610,000
Costa Rica	
Roman Catholic	3,380,000
Protestant	360,000
other	190,000
Côte d'Ivoire	
Muslim	6,340,000
Roman Catholic	3,400,000
traditional beliefs	2,790,000
nonreligious	2,220,000
Protestant	870,000
other	770,000
Croatia	
Roman Catholic	3,890,000
Serbian Orthodox	250,000
Sunnī Muslim	100,000
Protestant	30,000
other	130,000
Cuba	
Roman Catholic	4,420,000
Protestant	270,000
other (mostly Santeria)	6,500,000
Cyprus	
Greek Orthodox	630,000
Muslim (mostly Sunnī)	200,000
other (mostly Christian)	40,000
Czech Republic	
Roman Catholic	4,010,000
Evangelical Church of Czech Brethren	200,000
Czechoslovak Hussite	180,000
Silesian Evangelical	30,000
Eastern Orthodox	20,000
atheist and nonreligious	4,100,000
other	1,730,000
Denmark	
Evangelical Lutheran	4,600,000
Muslim	120,000
other	640,000
Djibouti	
Sunnī Muslim	434,000
other	27,000
Dominica	
Roman Catholic	50,000
Protestant	12,000
other	10,000
Dominican Republic	
Roman Catholic	7,110,000
Protestant	560,000
other	1,020,000
East Timor	
Roman Catholic	780,000
Protestant	50,000
Muslim	30,000
other	40,000
Ecuador	
Roman Catholic	11,910,000
Protestant	440,000
other	530,000
Egypt	
Sunnī Muslim	58,060,000
Coptic Orthodox[1]	6,520,000
other	660,000
El Salvador	
Roman Catholic	4,880,000
Protestant	1,070,000
other	290,000
Equatorial Guinea	
Roman Catholic	390,000
other	110,000
Eritrea	
Eritrean Orthodox	1,980,000
Muslim	1,920,000
other	400,000

Religion (continued)

Religious affiliation	2001 population
Estonia	
Estonian Orthodox	277,000
Evangelical Lutheran	187,000
other	899,000
Ethiopia	
Ethiopian Orthodox	33,110,000
other Christian	7,090,000
Muslim (mostly Sunnī)	21,710,000
traditional beliefs	3,180,000
other	820,000
Faroe Islands	
Evangelical Lutheran	38,000
other	9,000
Fiji	
Christian (mostly Methodist and Roman Catholic)	437,000
Hindu	316,000
Muslim	65,000
other	9,000
Finland	
Evangelical Lutheran	4,420,000
other	770,000
France	
Roman Catholic	38,690,000
nonreligious	9,230,000
Muslim	4,180,000
atheist	2,380,000
Protestant	720,000
Jewish	590,000
other	3,290,000
French Guiana	
Roman Catholic	91,000
other	77,000
French Polynesia	
Protestant	119,000
Roman Catholic	94,000
other	25,000
Gabon	
Roman Catholic	690,000
Protestant	220,000
African Christian	170,000
other	160,000
Gambia, The	
Muslim (mostly Sunnī)	1,340,000
other	70,000
Gaza Strip	
Muslim (mostly Sunnī)	1,190,000
other	20,000
Georgia	
Georgian Orthodox	1,828,000
Sunnī Muslim	549,000
Armenian Apostolic (Orthodox)	279,000
Russian Orthodox	133,000
other (mostly nonreligious)	2,200,000
Germany	
Protestant (mostly Evangelical Lutheran)	29,330,000
Roman Catholic	27,590,000
Muslim	3,660,000
atheist	1,800,000
other (mostly nonreligious)	20,020,000
Ghana	
traditional beliefs	4,860,000
Muslim	3,910,000
Protestant	3,310,000
African Christian	2,870,000
Roman Catholic	1,890,000
other	3,050,000
Greece	
Greek Orthodox	10,010,000
Muslim	360,000
other	500,000
Greenland	
Evangelical Lutheran	36,500
other	19,800
Grenada	
Roman Catholic	54,000
Anglican	14,000
other	34,000
Guadeloupe	
Roman Catholic	350,000
other	82,000
Guam	
Roman Catholic	118,000
Protestant	19,000
other	21,000
Guatemala	
Roman Catholic	8,880,000
Evangelical Protestant	2,540,000
other	270,000
Guernsey	
Anglican	42,000
other	22,000
Guinea	
Muslim	6,470,000
Christian	760,000
other	380,000
Guinea-Bissau	
traditional beliefs	590,000
Muslim	530,000
Christian	170,000
other	20,000
Guyana	
Hindu	264,000
Protestant	145,000
Roman Catholic	89,000
Muslim	70,000
Anglican	67,000
other	142,000
Haiti	
Roman Catholic	4,770,000
Protestant	1,590,000
other	610,000
Honduras	
Roman Catholic	5,740,000
Evangelical Protestant	690,000
other	200,000
Hong Kong	
Buddhist and Taoist	4,970,000
Protestant	290,000
Roman Catholic	280,000
other	1,200,000
Hungary	
Roman Catholic	6,120,000
Protestant	2,470,000
nonreligious	750,000
other	850,000
Iceland	
Evangelical Lutheran	260,000
other	20,000
India	
Hindu	759,350,000
Sunnī Muslim	92,380,000
traditional beliefs	34,930,000
Shīʿī Muslim	30,790,000
independent	30,750,000
Sikh	22,290,000
Protestant	15,130,000
Roman Catholic	13,940,000
Buddhist	7,290,000
Jain	4,160,000
atheist	1,670,000
Bahāʾī	1,190,000
Zoroastrian (Parsi)	210,000
nonreligious	12,910,000
other	3,000,000
Indonesia	
Muslim	185,060,000
Protestant	12,820,000
Roman Catholic	7,600,000
Hindu	3,880,000
Buddhist	2,190,000
other	660,000
Iran	
Shīʿī Muslim	57,180,000
Sunnī Muslim	3,460,000
Zoroastrian	1,780,000
Bahāʾī	430,000
Christian	340,000
other	250,000
Iraq	
Shīʿī Muslim	13,890,000
Sunnī Muslim	8,510,000
Christian	750,000
other	180,000
Ireland	
Roman Catholic	3,500,000
other	320,000
Isle of Man	
Anglican	30,000
Methodist	7,000
Roman Catholic	6,000
other	31,000
Israel	
Jewish[2]	4,960,000
Muslim (mostly Sunnī)	930,000
other	360,000
Italy	
Roman Catholic	46,260,000
nonreligious and atheist	9,600,000
Muslim	680,000
other	1,350,000
Jamaica	
Protestant	1,020,000
Roman Catholic	270,000
Anglican	100,000
other	1,230,000
Japan	
Shintoist[3]	118,270,000
Buddhist[3]	88,490,000
Christian	1,470,000
other	10,250,000
Jersey	
Anglican	55,000
Roman Catholic	21,000
other	14,000
Jordan	
Sunnī Muslim	4,800,000
Christian	210,000
other	120,000
Kazakhstan	
Muslim (mostly Sunnī)	6,988,000
Russian Orthodox	1,216,000
Protestant	318,000
other (mostly nonreligious)	6,345,000
Kenya	
Roman Catholic	6,780,000
African Christian	6,400,000
Protestant	6,170,000
traditional beliefs	3,540,000
Anglican	2,900,000
Muslim	2,240,000
Orthodox	720,000
other	2,030,000
Kiribati	
Roman Catholic	50,000
Congregational	36,000
other	9,000
Korea, North	
atheist and nonreligious	15,000,000
traditional beliefs	3,430,000
Ch'ŏndogyo	3,050,000
other	480,000
Korea, South	
nonreligious	23,490,000
Buddhist	11,040,000
Protestant	9,370,000
Roman Catholic	3,160,000
Confucian	230,000
Wonbulgyo	90,000
other	290,000
Kuwait	
Sunnī Muslim	1,020,000
Shīʿī Muslim	680,000
other Muslim	230,000
other (mostly Christian and Hindu)	340,000
Kyrgyzstan	
Muslim (mostly Sunnī)	3,701,000
Russian Orthodox	276,000
other (mostly nonreligious)	958,000
Laos	
Buddhist	2,750,000
traditional beliefs	2,350,000
other	540,000
Latvia	
Roman Catholic	350,000
Evangelical Lutheran	345,000
Russian Orthodox	181,000
other (mostly nonreligious)	1,482,000
Lebanon	
Shīʿī Muslim	1,230,000
Sunnī Muslim	770,000
Maronite Catholic	690,000
Druze	260,000
Greek Orthodox	220,000
Armenian Apostolic (Orthodox)	190,000
Greek Catholic (Melchite)	170,000
other	110,000
Lesotho	
Roman Catholic	820,000
Protestant	280,000
African Christian	260,000
traditional beliefs	170,000
Anglican	100,000
other	550,000
Liberia	
traditional beliefs	1,390,000
Christian	1,270,000
Muslim	520,000
other	60,000
Libya	
Sunnī Muslim	5,040,000
other	200,000
Liechtenstein	
Roman Catholic	26,000
other	7,000
Lithuania	
Roman Catholic	2,660,000
Russian Orthodox	90,000
other (mostly nonreligious)	940,000
Luxembourg	
Roman Catholic	400,000
other	40,000
Macau	
nonreligious	271,000
Buddhist	75,000
other	100,000
Macedonia	
Serbian (Macedonian) Orthodox	1,210,000
Sunnī Muslim	580,000
other	260,000
Madagascar	
traditional beliefs	7,670,000
Roman Catholic	3,250,000
Protestant	3,630,000
other	1,420,000
Malawi	
Roman Catholic	2,600,000
Protestant	2,070,000
African Christian	1,770,000
Muslim	1,560,000
traditional beliefs	820,000
other	1,730,000
Malaysia	
Muslim	10,770,000
Chinese folk-religionist	5,450,000
Christian	1,880,000
Hindu	1,660,000
Buddhist	1,500,000
other	1,350,000
Maldives	
Sunnī Muslim	273,000
other	2,000
Mali	
Muslim	9,010,000
traditional beliefs	1,760,000
Christian	220,000
other	10,000
Malta	
Roman Catholic	363,000
other	21,000
Marshall Islands	
Protestant	32,800
Roman Catholic	3,700
other	15,700
Martinique	
Roman Catholic	336,000
other	52,000
Mauritania	
Sunnī Muslim	2,720,000
other	20,000
Mauritius	
Hindu	610,000
Roman Catholic	330,000
Muslim	190,000
other	70,000
Mayotte	
Sunnī Muslim	153,000
Christian	5,000
Mexico	
Roman Catholic	90,370,000
Protestant	3,820,000
other Christian	1,820,000
other (mostly nonreligious)	3,970,000
Micronesia	
Roman Catholic	63,600
Protestant	40,100
other	14,200
Moldova	
Romanian Orthodox	1,263,000
Russian (Moldovan) Orthodox	342,000
other (mostly nonreligious)	2,007,000
Monaco	
Roman Catholic	28,000
other	4,000
Mongolia	
Tantric Buddhist (Lamaist)	2,340,000
Muslim	100,000
Morocco	
Muslim (mostly Sunnī)	28,730,000
other	500,000
Mozambique	
traditional beliefs	9,750,000
Roman Catholic	3,060,000
Muslim	2,040,000
Protestant	1,720,000
African Christian	1,400,000
other	1,400,000
Myanmar (Burma)	
Buddhist	37,560,000
Christian	2,060,000
Muslim	1,610,000
traditional beliefs	480,000
Hindu	210,000
other	70,000
Namibia	
Protestant (mostly Lutheran)	850,000
Roman Catholic	320,000
African Christian	200,000
other	430,000
Nauru	
Protestant	6,100
Roman Catholic	3,300
other	2,700
Nepal	
Hindu	19,180,000
traditional beliefs	2,350,000
Buddhist	2,050,000
Muslim	970,000
Christian	600,000
other	140,000
Netherlands, The	
Roman Catholic	4,950,000
Dutch Reformed Church (NHK)	2,240,000
Reformed Churches	1,120,000
Muslim	720,000
nonreligious	6,550,000
other	400,000
Netherlands Antilles	
Roman Catholic	152,000
other	54,000
New Caledonia	
Roman Catholic	132,000
Protestant	31,300
other	52,200

Religious affiliation	2001 population
New Zealand	
Anglican	674,000
Roman Catholic	505,000
Presbyterian	489,000
Methodist	130,000
Baptist	57,000
Mormon	44,000
Ratana	39,000
nonreligious	954,000
other	969,000
Nicaragua	
Roman Catholic	3,590,000
Protestant	810,000
other (mostly nonreligious)	520,000
Niger	
Sunnī Muslim	9,390,000
traditional beliefs	900,000
other	70,000
Nigeria	
Muslim	55,600,000
traditional beliefs	12,500,000
Christian	58,100,000
other	500,000
Northern Mariana Islands	
Roman Catholic	53,600
other	19,700
Norway	
Evangelical Lutheran (Church of Norway)	3,990,000
other	530,000
Oman	
Ibāḍīyah Muslim	1,840,000
Sunnī Muslim	350,000
Hindu	190,000
Christian	100,000
other	20,000
Pakistan	
Sunnī Muslim	113,950,000
Shīʿī Muslim	25,010,000
Christian	3,560,000
Hindu	1,730,000
other	370,000
Palau	
Roman Catholic	7,600
Modekne	5,200
Protestant	4,900
other	2,100
Panama	
Roman Catholic	2,330,000
Protestant	420,000
other	150,000
Papua New Guinea	
Protestant	3,180,000
Roman Catholic	1,500,000
Anglican	210,000
other	420,000
Paraguay	
Roman Catholic	4,990,000
Protestant	280,000
other	370,000
Peru	
Roman Catholic	23,170,000
Protestant	1,730,000
other (mostly nonreligious)	1,190,000
Philippines	
Roman Catholic	63,530,000
Protestant	4,160,000
Muslim	3,500,000
Aglipayan	2,010,000
Church of Christ (Iglesia ni Cristo)	1,790,000
other	1,620,000
Poland	
Roman Catholic	35,050,000
Polish Orthodox	550,000
other (mostly nonreligious)	3,050,000
Portugal	
Roman Catholic	9,520,000
other	810,000
Puerto Rico	
Roman Catholic	2,480,000
Protestant	1,080,000
other	270,000
Qatar	
Muslim (mostly Sunnī)	490,000
Christian	60,000
other	40,000
Réunion	
Roman Catholic	599,000
Hindu	33,000
other	102,000
Romania	
Romanian Orthodox	19,460,000
Roman Catholic	1,140,000
other	1,810,000
Russia	
Russian Orthodox	23,580,000
Muslim	10,980,000
Protestant	1,320,000
Jewish	590,000
other (mostly nonreligious)	107,960,000
Rwanda	
Roman Catholic	3,730,000
Protestant	1,530,000
traditional beliefs	660,000
Muslim	580,000
Anglican	570,000
other	260,000
St. Kitts and Nevis	
Anglican	10,000
Methodist	10,000
other	15,000
Pentecostal	7,000
other	12,000
St. Lucia	
Roman Catholic	125,000
Protestant	20,000
other	13,000
St. Vincent and the Grenadines	
Anglican	20,000
Pentecostal	17,000
Methodist	12,000
Roman Catholic	12,000
other	52,000
Samoa	
Mormon	46,200
Congregational	44,000
Roman Catholic	38,100
Methodist	21,800
other	29,100
San Marino	
Roman Catholic	24,000
other	3,000
São Tomé and Príncipe	
Roman Catholic	111,000
African Christian	16,000
other	20,000
Saudi Arabia	
Sunnī Muslim	20,490,000
Shīʿī Muslim	840,000
Christian	840,000
Hindu	250,000
other	330,000
Senegal	
Sunnī Muslim	9,010,000
traditional beliefs	640,000
Roman Catholic	480,000
other	160,000
Serbia and Montenegro	
Serbian Orthodox	6,680,000
Sunnī Muslim	2,030,000
Roman Catholic	620,000
other (mostly nonreligious)	1,350,000
Seychelles	
Roman Catholic	69,800
other	10,800
Sierra Leone	
Sunnī Muslim	2,490,000
traditional beliefs	2,190,000
Christian	620,000
other	130,000
Singapore	
Buddhist and Taoist	1,695,000
Muslim	495,000
Christian	485,000
Hindu	133,000
nonreligious	493,000
other	21,000
Slovakia	
Roman Catholic	3,270,000
Slovak Evangelical	340,000
other (mostly nonreligious)	1,800,000
Slovenia	
Roman Catholic	1,650,000
other	340,000
Solomon Islands	
Protestant	173,000
Anglican	149,000
Roman Catholic	83,000
other	75,000
Somalia	
Sunnī Muslim	7,364,000
other	125,000
South Africa	
Christian	36,220,000
independents	17,040,000
Protestant	13,860,000
Roman Catholic	3,090,000
traditional beliefs	3,660,000
Hindu	1,050,000
Muslim	1,050,000
Bahāʾī	260,000
Jewish	170,000
nonreligious	1,050,000
other	130,000
Spain	
Roman Catholic	36,920,000
Muslim	200,000
other (mostly nonreligious)	3,010,000
Sri Lanka	
Buddhist	13,270,000
Hindu	2,190,000
Muslim	1,750,000
Roman Catholic	1,300,000
other	900,000
Sudan, The	
Sunnī Muslim	25,360,000
Christian	6,020,000
traditional beliefs	4,300,000
other	390,000
Suriname	
Hindu	119,000
Roman Catholic	91,000
Muslim	85,000
Protestant	71,000
other	68,000
Swaziland	
African Christian	480,000
Protestant	160,000
traditional beliefs	120,000
other	340,000
Sweden	
Church of Sweden (Lutheran)	7,690,000
other	1,200,000
Switzerland	
Roman Catholic	3,330,000
Protestant	2,890,000
other	1,000,000
Syria	
Sunnī Muslim	12,380,000
Shīʿī Muslim	2,010,000
Christian	920,000
Druze	500,000
other	920,000
Taiwan	
nonreligious	10,670,000
Buddhist	5,100,000
Taoist	4,040,000
I Kuan Tao	990,000
Protestant	440,000
Roman Catholic	320,000
Tien Te Chiao	210,000
Tien Ti Chiao	190,000
Confucianism (Li)	150,000
Hsuan Yuan Chiao	140,000
Muslim	50,000
Shinto (Tenrikyo)	20,000
Bahāʾī	20,000
Tajikistan	
Sunnī Muslim	4,920,000
Shīʿī Muslim	310,000
Russian Orthodox	90,000
atheist	120,000
other (mostly nonreligious)	820,000
Tanzania	
Christian	18,260,000
Muslim	11,520,000
traditional beliefs	5,830,000
other	620,000
Thailand	
Buddhist	57,920,000
Muslim	2,850,000
Christian	440,000
other	40,000
Togo	
traditional beliefs	1,940,000
Roman Catholic	1,250,000
Sunnī Muslim	970,000
Protestant	530,000
other	450,000
Tonga	
Free Wesleyan	44,000
Roman Catholic	16,000
other	41,000
Trinidad and Tobago	
Roman Catholic	380,000
Hindu	300,000
Protestant	244,000
Anglican	142,000
Muslim	76,000
other	149,000
Tunisia	
Sunnī Muslim	9,720,000
other	104,000
Turkey	
Muslim (mostly Sunnī)	64,360,000
nonreligious	1,340,000
other	530,000
Turkmenistan	
Muslim (mostly Sunnī)	4,752,000
Russian Orthodox	129,000
other (mostly nonreligious)	581,000
Tuvalu	
Congregational	9,400
other	1,600
Uganda	
Roman Catholic	10,050,000
Anglican	9,450,000
Muslim (mostly Sunnī)	1,250,000
traditional beliefs	1,050,000
other	2,190,000
Ukraine	
Ukrainian Orthodox (Russian patriarchy)	9,491,000
Ukrainian Orthodox (Kiev patriarchy)	4,746,000
Ukrainian Autocephalous Orthodox	332,000
Ukrainian Catholic (Uniate)	3,417,000
Protestant	1,736,000
Roman Catholic	576,000
Jewish	423,000
other (mostly nonreligious)	28,044,000
United Arab Emirates	
Sunnī Muslim	2,490,000
Shīʿī Muslim	500,000
other	120,000
United Kingdom	
Christian	49,510,000
Anglican	26,140,000
Roman Catholic	5,590,000
Protestant	5,020,000
Eastern Orthodox	370,000
other Christian	12,390,000
Muslim	1,220,000
Hindu	440,000
Jewish	310,000
Sikh	240,000
other (mostly nonreligious and atheist)	8,240,000
United States	
Christian (professing)	242,011,000
Christian (affiliated)	196,929,000
independent	80,639,000
Protestant	66,287,000
Roman Catholic	59,542,000
Eastern Orthodox	5,915,000
Anglican	2,464,000
other Christian	10,348,000
multi-affiliated Christians	–28,266,000
Christian (unaffiliated)	45,082,000
non-Christian	44,056,000
nonreligious	25,745,000
Jewish	5,771,000
Muslim	4,242,000
Buddhist	2,515,000
atheist	1,181,000
Hindu	1,059,000
New-Religionist	832,000
Bahāʾī	773,000
Ethnic religionist	447,000
Sikh	240,000
Chinese folk-religionist	80,000
other	1,171,000
Uruguay	
Roman Catholic	2,590,000
Protestant	150,000
Mormon	50,000
Jewish	30,000
other	480,000
Uzbekistan	
Muslim (mostly Sunnī)	19,156,000
Russian Orthodox	195,000
other (mostly nonreligious)	5,804,000
Vanuatu	
Presbyterian	70,000
Roman Catholic	28,000
Anglican	27,000
other	69,000
Venezuela	
Roman Catholic	22,050,000
other	2,590,000
Vietnam	
Buddhist	53,290,000
Roman Catholic	6,180,000
New-Religionist	
Cao Dai	2,810,000
Hoa Hao	1,690,000
other	16,500,000
Virgin Islands (U.S.)	
Protestant	56,000
Roman Catholic	41,000
other	24,000
West Bank	
Muslim (mostly Sunnī)	1,860,000
Jewish[4]	230,000
Christian and other	180,000
Western Sahara	
Sunnī Muslim	250,000
other	1,000
Yemen	
Muslim (mostly Sunnī)	18,050,000
other	20,000
Zambia	
traditional beliefs	2,640,000
Protestant	2,240,000
Roman Catholic	1,650,000
other	3,240,000
Zimbabwe	
African Christian	4,580,000
traditional beliefs	3,430,000
Protestant	1,400,000
Roman Catholic	1,090,000
other	870,000

[1]Official 1986 census figure is 5.9 percent. [2]Includes the Golan Heights and East Jerusalem; excludes the West Bank and Gaza Strip. [3]Many Japanese practice both Shintoism and Buddhism.
[4]Excludes East Jerusalem.

Vital statistics, marriage, family

This table provides some of the basic measures of the factors that influence the size, direction, and rates of population change within a country. The accuracy of these data depends on the effectiveness of each respective national system for registering vital and civil events (birth, death, marriage, etc.) and on the sophistication of the analysis that can be brought to bear upon the data so compiled.

Data on birth rates, for example, depend not only on the completeness of registration of births in a particular country but also on the conditions under which those data are collected: Do all births take place in a hospital? Are the births reported comparably in all parts of the country? Are the records of the births tabulated at a central location in a timely way with an effort to eliminate inconsistent reporting of birth events, perinatal mortality, etc.? Similar difficulties attach to death rates but with the added need to identify "cause of death." Even in a developed country such identifications are often left to nonmedical personnel, and in a developing country with, say, only one physician for every 10,000 population, there will be too few physicians to perform autopsies to assess accurately the cause of death after the fact and also too few to provide ongoing care at a level where records would permit inference about cause of death based on prior condition or diagnosis.

Calculating natural increase, which at its most basic is simply the difference between the birth and death rates, may be affected by the differing degrees of completeness of birth and death registration for a given country. The total fertility rate may be understood as the average number of children that would be borne per woman if all childbearing women lived to the end of their childbearing years and bore children at each age at the average rate for that age. Calculating a meaningful fertility rate requires analysis of changing age structure of the female population over time, changing mortality rates among mothers and their infants, and changing medical practice at births, each improvement of natural survivorship or medical support leading to greater numbers of live-born children and greater numbers of children who survive their first year (the basis for measurement of infant mortality, another basic indicator of demographic conditions and trends within a population).

As indicated above, data for causes of death are not only particularly difficult to obtain, since many countries are not well equipped to collect the data, but also difficult to assess, as their accuracy may be suspect and their meaning may be subject to varying interpretation. Take the case of a citizen of a less developed country who dies of what is clearly a lung infection: Was the death complicated by chronic malnutrition, itself complicated by a parasitic infestation, these last two together so weakening the subject that he died of an infection that he might have survived had his general health been better? Similarly, in a developed country: Someone may die from what is identified in an autopsy as a cerebrovascular accident, but if that accident occurred in a vascular system that was weakened by diabetes, what was the actual cause of death? Statistics on causes of death seek to identify the "underlying" cause (that which sets the final train of events leading to death in motion) but often must settle for the most proximate cause or symptom. Even this kind of analysis may be misleading for those charged with interpreting the data with a view to ordering health-care priorities for a particular country. The eight groups of causes of death utilized here include most, but not all, of the detailed causes classified by the World Health Organization and would not, thus, aggregate to the country's crude death rate for the same year. Among the lesser causes excluded by the present classification are: benign neoplasms; nutritional disorders; anemias; mental disorders; kidney and genito-urinary

Vital statistics, marriage, family

country	vital rates: year	birth rate per 1,000 population	death rate per 1,000 population	infant mortality rate per 1,000 live births	rate of natural increase per 1,000 population	total fertility rate	causes of death (rate per 100,000 population): year	infectious and parasitic diseases	malignant neoplasms (cancers)	endocrine and metabolic disorders	diseases of the nervous system	diseases of the circulatory system	diseases of the respiratory system	diseases of the digestive system	accidents, poisoning, and violence
Afghanistan	2003	47.5	21.5	168.9	26.0	6.8	...	...	...	...	...	...	...	...	...
Albania	2002	18.6	6.5	38.6	12.1	2.3	1993	10.8	53.8	5.1	24.1	187.0	84.5	16.5	41.7
Algeria	2003	18.3	4.6	33.4	13.7	2.2	...	...	...	...	...	...	...	...	...
American Samoa	2003	25.9	3.4	9.7	22.5	3.6	1990	16.4[4]	46.8	16.4[5]	...	131.1[6]	65.6[7]	...	58.5
Andorra	2002	11.1	3.3	4.1	7.8	1.2	...	...	...	...	...	...	...	...	...
Angola	2003	45.6	25.8	193.8	19.8	6.4	...	...	...	...	...	...	...	...	...
Antigua and Barbuda	2003	18.2	5.6	20.9	12.6	2.3	1995	10.4	96.2	57.7	13.3	242.6	42.9	19.2	37.0
Argentina	2003	17.5	7.6	16.2	9.9	2.3	1996	28.1	145.7	19.1[5]	9.7	297.3	64.8	32.5	52.2
Armenia	2002	10.1	8.0	14.0	2.1	1.1	1997	9.2	96.5	32.6	4.4	336.6	38.9	23.9	37.9
Aruba	2002	14.6	5.2	6.5	9.4	1.8	1998	26.1	118.0	29.3[5]	4.3	184.0	35.9	14.1	52.2
Australia	2003	12.6	7.3	4.8	5.3	1.8	1995	6.0	190.0	23.0	17.0	296.0	52.0	21.0	41.0
Austria	2002	9.7	9.5	4.1	0.2	1.3	1997	2.5	233.5	19.9	0.5[11]	532.6	29.9	28.4	54.9
Azerbaijan	2004	14.0	6.0	12.8	8.0	1.6	1995	29.7	61.9	11.8	11.3	335.3	84.9	34.3	45.9
Bahamas, The	2003	18.6	8.7	17.0[14]	9.9	2.3	1995	13.3	85.6	36.3	0.7	160.1	26.6	14.4	40.0
Bahrain	2002	20.2	3.0	8.7[15]	17.2	3.0	1998	5.4	37.8	22.7	4.6	85.9	22.7	13.3	14.5
Bangladesh	2003	29.9	8.6	68.0[17]	21.3	3.2	...	...	...	...	...	...	...	...	...
Barbados	2001	15.0	8.9	12.6[17]	6.1	1.6	1995	27.3	162.5	149.2	22.7	365.5	55.7	34.1	36.0
Belarus	2003	10.1	14.1	7.7	–4.0	1.3	1997	8.8	191.9	8.7[19]	11.5	673.9	68.7	27.5	154.5
Belgium	2003	10.7	10.2	5.1[15]	0.5	1.6	1994	13.4	275.0	21.7	29.2	383.4	92.5	42.6	68.5
Belize	2002	27.7	4.8	22.9	27.1[20]	3.9	1995	23.5	37.7	22.1	6.9	118.9	47.5	16.1	67.3
Benin	2003	43.2	13.7	86.7	29.5	6.0	...	...	...	...	...	...	...	...	...
Bermuda	2001	13.2	7.0	9.1[20]	6.2	1.8	1990	...	181.5	...	...	344.4	25.2	...	38.6
Bhutan	2002	34.9	8.7	55.0	26.2	4.9[20]	...	...	...	...	...	...	...	...	...
Bolivia	2003	25.5	7.9	56.1	17.6	3.2	...	...	...	...	...	...	...	...	...
Bosnia and Herzegovina	2002	9.5	8.0	23.5	1.5	1.4	1989	9.9	122.6[22]	12.6	11.9	344.1	29.0	29.2	47.1
Botswana	2002	28.0	26.3	64.7	1.7	3.6	...	...	...	...	...	...	...	...	...
Brazil	2003	19.5	6.7	31.8[17]	12.8	2.2	1996	33.5	65.9	23.3[19]	9[10]	159.1	56.4	25.9	75.9
Brunei	2002	20.1	3.4	14.0	16.7	2.4	...	...	...	...	...	...	...	...	...
Bulgaria	2001	8.6	14.2	13.5	–5.6	1.2	1998	9.4	192.9	25.4	9.7	954.4	67.6	38.8	60.7
Burkina Faso	2003	44.8	18.8	99.8	26.0	6.3	...	...	...	...	...	...	...	...	...
Burundi	2003	39.7	17.8	71.5	21.9	6.0	...	...	...	...	...	...	...	...	...
Cambodia	2003	27.3	9.3	75.9	18.0	3.7	...	...	...	...	...	...	...	...	...
Cameroon	2003	35.5	15.3	70.1	20.2	4.6	...	...	...	...	...	...	...	...	...
Canada	2003	10.5	7.2	5.0[15]	3.3	1.6	1997	8.3	195.6	23.7	21.9	264.8	66.8	25.4	43.5
Cape Verde	2003	27.0	6.9	50.5[17]	20.1	3.8	...	...	...	...	...	...	...	...	...
Central African Republic	2003	35.9	19.7	93.3	16.2	4.7	...	...	...	...	...	...	...	...	...
Chad	2003	47.1	16.4	96.7[17]	30.7	6.4	...	...	...	...	...	...	...	...	...
Chile	2003	16.1	5.7	9.3	10.4	2.1	1994	14.2	111.9	16.5	8.6	149.5	61.2	37.2	63.6
China	2003	13.0	6.9	26.4	6.1	1.7	1994[24]	15.2	117.7	17.2[19]	4.4	206.4	125.3	25.3	56.6
Colombia	2003	21.6	5.6	24.2	16.0	2.6	1994	13.7	58.3	15.2	4.6	125.3	34.3	15.7	119.5
Comoros	2003	38.5	8.9	79.5	29.6	5.2	...	...	...	...	...	...	...	...	...
Congo, Dem. Rep. of the	2003	45.1	14.9	96.6	30.2	6.7	...	...	...	...	...	...	...	...	...
Congo, Rep. of the	2003	29.5	14.2	95.3	15.3	3.7	...	...	...	...	...	...	...	...	...
Costa Rica	2003	19.4	4.3	10.6	15.1	2.4	1994	9.7	80.0	12.6	8.5	126.6	40.6	24.6	49.7
Côte d'Ivoire	2002	40.4	18.4	99.6[15]	22.0	5.6	...	...	...	...	...	...	...	...	...
Croatia	2003	9.5	11.2	7.1	–1.7	1.4	1996	8.8	227.2	25.4[19]	8.0	547.4	41.4	52.1	70.7
Cuba	2003	12.4	7.2	6.5[17]	5.2	1.7	1995	12.8	133	25.9	11.1	305.5	64.1	24.9	84.6
Cyprus	2003	11.2	7.2	4.1	4.0	2.0	...	...	...	...	...	...	...	...	...
Czech Republic	2003	9.2	10.9	3.9	–1.7	1.1	1998	2.6	272.1	15.0	11.6	586.7	39.9	40.4	68.1
Denmark	2003	12.0	10.7	4.8	1.3	1.8	1996	10.1	289.2	16.5	15.3	428.4	108.1	46.1	64.1

diseases not classifiable under the main groups; maternal deaths (for which data *are* provided, however, in the "Health services" table); diseases of the skin and musculoskeletal systems; congenital and perinatal conditions; and general senility and other ill-defined (ill-diagnosed) conditions, a kind of "other" category.

Expectation of life is probably the most accurate single measure of the quality of life in a given society. It summarizes in a single number all of the natural and social stresses that operate upon individuals in that society. The number may range from as few as 40 years of life in the least developed countries to as much as 80 years for women in the most developed nations. The lost potential in the years separating those two numbers is prodigious, regardless of how the loss arises—wars and civil violence, poor public health services, or poor individual health practice in matters of nutrition, exercise, stress management, and so on.

Data on marriages and marriage rates probably are less meaningful in terms of international comparisons than some of the measures mentioned above because the number, timing, and kinds of social relationships that substitute for marriage depend on many kinds of social variables—income, degree of social control, heterogeneity of the society (race, class, language communities), or level of development of civil administration (if one must travel for a day or more to obtain a legal civil ceremony, one may forgo it). Nevertheless, the data for a single country say specific things about local practice in terms of the age at which a man or woman typically marries, and the overall rate will at least define the number of legal civil marriages, though it cannot say anything about other, less formal arrangements (here the figure for the legitimacy rate for children in the next section may identify some of the societies in which economics or social constraints may operate to limit the number of marriages that are actually confirmed on civil registers). The available data usually include both first marriages and remarriages after annulment, divorce, widowhood, or the like.

The data for families provide information about the average size of a family unit (individuals related by blood or civil register) and the average number of children under a specified age (set here at 15 to provide a consistent measure of social minority internationally, though legal minority depends on the laws of each country). When well-defined family data are not collected as part of a country's national census or vital statistics surveys, data for households have been substituted on the assumption that most households worldwide represent families in some conventional sense. But increasing numbers of households worldwide are composed of unrelated individuals (unmarried heterosexual couples, aged [or younger] groups sharing limited [often fixed] incomes for reasons of economy, or homosexual couples). Such arrangements do not yet represent great numbers overall. Increasing numbers of census programs, however, even in developing countries, are making more adequate provision for distinguishing these nontraditional, often nonfamily households.

Internet resources for further information:

- World Health Organization (World) http://www.who.ch
- Pan American Health Organization (the Americas) http://www.paho.org
- National Center for Health Statistics (U.S.) http://www.cdc.gov/nchs
- U.S. Census Bureau: International Data Base (World) http://www.census.gov/ipc/www/idbprint.html

expectation of life at birth (latest year)		nuptiality, family, and family planning															country
		marriages			age at marriage (latest)						families (F), households (H) (latest)						
					groom (percent)			bride (percent)			families (households)		children		induced abortions		
male	female	year	total number	rate per 1,000 population	19 and under	20–29	30 and over	19 and under	20–29	30 and over	total ('000)	size	number under age 15	percent legitimate	number	ratio per 100 live births	
41.0	42.2	…	…	…	…	…	…	…	…	…	H 2,110	H 6.2	H 2.8[1]	…	…	…	Afghanistan
69.3	75.1	1997	25,260	6.8	1.5[2]	80.4[2]	18.1[2]	24.0[2]	71.4[2]	4.6[2]	F 675	F 3.9	F 1.6	…	…	…	Albania
71.0	74.0	1996	156,870	5.6	0.7[3]	67.1[3]	32.2[3]	29.8[3]	61.4[3]	8.8[3]	H 4,102	H 7.1	H 3.0	…	…	…	Algeria
71.8	79.2	1993	325	6.1	…	…	…	…	…	…	H 7	H 7.0	H 2.7	72.0	…	…	American Samoa
80.6	86.6	1998	208	3.2	…	…	…	…	…	…	…	…	…	…	…	…	Andorra
36.1	37.8	…	…	…	…	…	…	…	…	…	…	H 5.0	…	…	…	…	Angola
69.0	73.8	1998	1,418	22.1	1.0[8]	37.4[9]	61.6	3.7[8]	52.4[9]	43.9	H 18	H 3.2	H 1.2	23.4	…	…	Antigua and Barbuda
71.7	79.4	1996	148,721	4.2	5.6	71.5	22.9	26.0	58.6	15.4	H 10,097	H 3.2	H 1.0	67.5	…	…	Argentina
70.0	76.1	1995	14,200	4.2	5.0[10]	73.8[10]	21.2[10]	39.3[10]	49.9[10]	10.8[10]	H 559	H 4.5	H 1.8	86.0	30,571	59.8	Armenia
70.0	76.0	1998	564	6.1	…	…	…	…	…	…	H 19	H 3.6	…	57.5	…	…	Aruba
77.0	83.1	1996	109,386	6.0	0.7	54.5	44.8	3.6	63.6	32.8	H 6,636	H 2.6	H 0.6	75.0	…	…	Australia
75.8	81.7	1998	39,143	4.8	1.1[12]	49.9[12]	49.0[12]	4.2[12]	62.0[12]	33.8[12]	H 3,058	H 2.6	H 0.5	69.5	…	…	Austria
69.5	75.1	1994	47,147	6.3	1.2[13]	80.4[13]	18.4[13]	24.8[13]	63.9[13]	11.3[13]	H 1,381	H 5.2	H 1.7	94.8	42,134	23.2	Azerbaijan
62.3	69.5	1996	2,628	9.3	…	14.0	86.0	—	26.1	73.9	H 74	H 3.9	…	45.7	…	…	Bahamas, The
73.2	76.2	1998	3,677	5.7	2.6[16]	65.4[16]	32.0[16]	28.0[16]	54.6[16]	17.4[16]	H 67	H 6.5	H 2.2	100.0	…	…	Bahrain
61.5	61.2	1997	1,181,000	9.7	…	…	…	…	…	…	H 19,980	H 5.6	…	…	…	…	Bangladesh
70.4	75.6	1995	3,564	13.5	0.1[18]	40.2[18]	59.7[18]	1.4[18]	53.6[18]	44.9[18]	H 67	H 3.5	H 1.5	26.9	723	19.6	Barbados
62.5	74.6	1997	69,735	6.8	5.4[12]	69.8[12]	24.8[12]	27.1[12]	53.1[12]	19.8[12]	H 2,796	H 3.6	H 0.8	82.2	174,098	181.7	Belarus
75.1	81.6	1996	50,601	5.0	0.6[16]	59.5[16]	39.9[16]	4.0[16]	66.3[16]	29.7[16]	F 3,613	F 2.7	F 0.5	88.7	…	…	Belgium
65.2	69.6	1997	1,543	6.6	6.3[16]	58.4[16]	35.3[16]	23.4[16]	51.0[16]	25.6[16]	H 42	H 5.3	H 2.2	40.3	990	15.1	Belize
50.4	51.8	…	…	…	…	…	…	…	…	…	…	H 5.9	…	…	…	…	Benin
74.9	78.9	1994	944	15.4	0.2[21]	37.4[21]	62.4[21]	1.5[21]	49.4[21]	49.1[21]	H 24	H 2.5	H 0.5	61.7	92	11.0	Bermuda
62.0	64.0	…	…	…	…	…	…	…	…	…	…	H 5.4	…	…	…	…	Bhutan
62.2	67.4	…	…	…	…	…	…	…	…	…	H 1,655	H 3.8	H 1.6	80.9	…	…	Bolivia
64.6	70.2	1991	27,923	6.0	2.3	74.2	23.5	28.6	58.9	12.5	H 1,203	H 3.4	H 1.1	92.6	…	…	Bosnia and Herzegovina
36.9	37.6	1986	1,638	1.5	—	33.0	67.0	5.0	69.2	25.8	H 125	H 5.7	H 2.0	28.8	17	0.1	Botswana
67.2	75.3	1995	…	4.7	7.0[10]	68.7[10]	24.3[10]	31.2[10]	54.3[10]	14.5[10]	F 39,768	F 3.9	1.2	…	…	…	Brazil
71.7	76.6	1995	1,793	6.1	10.6[23]	50.1[23]	39.3[23]	11.4[23]	54.7[23]	33.9[23]	H 45	H 5.8	H 2.0	99.6	…	…	Brunei
68.5	75.2	1996	…	4.3	3.4[16]	73.1[16]	23.5[16]	26.9[16]	60.4[16]	12.7[16]	H 2,795	H 3.0	…	74.3	97,023	134.8	Bulgaria
43.0	45.9	…	…	…	…	…	…	…	…	…	…	H 6.2	…	…	…	…	Burkina Faso
42.5	43.9	…	…	…	…	…	…	…	…	…	…	H 5.0	…	…	…	…	Burundi
55.5	60.5	…	…	…	…	…	…	…	…	…	…	H 5.6	…	…	…	…	Cambodia
47.2	49.0	…	…	…	…	…	…	…	…	…	…	H 5.7	…	…	…	…	Cameroon
76.4	83.4	1995	160,256	5.4	0.9	49.3	49.8	3.6	57.9	38.5	H 11,580	H 2.5	H 0.6	83.8	70,549	18.7	Canada
66.5	73.2	1994	1,200	3.2	…	…	…	…	…	…	F 59	F 5.1	…	28.9	…	…	Cape Verde
40.2	43.3	…	…	…	…	…	…	…	…	…	…	H 5.9	…	…	…	…	Central African Republic
47.0	50.1	…	…	…	…	…	…	…	…	…	…	H 5.0	…	…	…	…	Chad
72.9	79.6	1996	83,547	5.8	4.7	67.5	27.8	18.6	62.2	19.2	H 3,537	H 3.8	…	61.9	67	—	Chile
70.1	73.3	1994	9,290,027	7.8	…	…	…	…	…	…	H 278.6[25]	H 4.1	H 1.1	…	10,500,000	47.7	China
67.3	75.2	…	…	…	…	…	…	…	…	…	F 4,772	F 5.3	F 2.5	75.2	…	…	Colombia
58.9	63.5	…	…	…	…	…	…	…	…	…	…	H 5.6	…	…	…	…	Comoros
46.8	51.1	…	…	…	…	…	…	…	…	…	…	H 2.3	…	…	…	…	Congo, Dem. Rep. of the
49.0	51.0	…	…	…	…	…	…	…	…	…	H 326	H 4.7	H 2.0	…	…	…	Congo, Rep. of the
73.9	79.1	1997	22,422	6.5	7.1[15]	60.9[15]	32.0[15]	26.3[15]	52.0[15]	94.7[15]	H 772	H 4.1	…	50.3	…	…	Costa Rica
40.4	45.3	…	…	…	…	…	…	…	…	…	…	H 8.0	…	…	…	…	Côte d'Ivoire
69.6	78.3	1997	24,517	5.3	1.2[12]	65.2[12]	33.6[12]	13.9[12]	66.8[12]	19.3[12]	H 1,544	H 3.1	H 0.6	92.7	12,339	22.9	Croatia
74.6	79.2	1997	60,220	5.4	5.2[16]	51.8[16]	43.0[16]	18.0[16]	49.4[16]	32.6[16]	F 2,860	F 3.7	H 1.6	…	83,963	57.1	Cuba
77.0	81.4	1996	5,761	7.8	0.8	54.6	44.6	8.1	64.2	27.7	H 160	H 3.5	H 1.1	99.6	…	…	Cyprus
72.1	78.5	1997	57,086	5.6	3.7[12]	66.5[12]	29.8[12]	15.0[12]	65.8[12]	19.2[12]	H 3,557	H 2.0	…	70.4	40,000	50.2	Czech Republic
74.9	79.5	1997	34,108	6.5	0.4[16]	36.2[16]	63.4[16]	1.4[16]	47.9[16]	50.7[16]	H 2,027	H 2.2	…	53.5	17,720	53.2	Denmark

Vital statistics, marriage, family (continued)

country	vital rates						causes of death (rate per 100,000 population)								
	year	birth rate per 1,000 population	death rate per 1,000 population	infant mortality rate per 1,000 live births	rate of natural increase per 1,000 population	total fertility rate	year	infectious and parasitic diseases	malignant neoplasms (cancers)	endocrine and metabolic disorders	diseases of the nervous system	diseases of the circulatory system	diseases of the respiratory system	diseases of the digestive system	accidents, poisoning, and violence
Djibouti	2003	40.8	19.5	107.0	21.3	5.6	…	…	…	…	…	…	…	…	…
Dominica	2003	17.8	7.0	15.9[17]	10.8	2.0	1994	23.1	125.0	59.8	9.5	237.8	38.0	21.7	28.5
Dominican Republic	2003	23.0	7.2	34.2	15.8	2.7	1985[26]	85	45	15[5]	7[11]	165	41	25	*56*
East Timor	2003	27.7	6.4	50.5	21.3	3.8	…	…	…	…	…	…	…	…	…
Ecuador	2003[1]	23.7	4.3	25.4	19.4	2.8	1995	29.7	50.8	17.5	7.2	80.8	46.0	23.1	65.1
Egypt	2003	24.4	5.4	35.3	19.0	3.0	1992	49.0	22.4	17.3	9.5	313.5	83.4	33.5	28.8
El Salvador	2003	27.9	6.0	26.8	21.9	3.2	1994[27]	42	52	9[5]	2[11]	124	36	14	135
Equatorial Guinea	2003	36.9	12.5	89.0	24.4	4.7	…	…	…	…	…	…	…	…	…
Eritrea	2003	39.4	13.2	76.3	26.2	5.7	…	…	…	…	…	…	…	…	…
Estonia	2002	9.6	13.5	5.7	–3.9	1.4	1995	13.7	221.1	8.2	13.0	771.9	42.5	36.0	198.8
Ethiopia	2003	39.9	15.5	98.6	24.4	5.6	…	…	…	…	…	…	…	…	…
Faroe Islands	2002	15.0	8.3	6.5	6.7	2.5	1992	4.3	191.3	14.9[5]	—	352.8	59.5	14.9	57.4
Fiji	2003	23.1	5.7	13.4	17.4	2.8	…	…	…	…	…	…	…	…	…
Finland	2002	10.7	9.5	3.6	1.2	1.7	1995	7.7	196.6	12.5	20.1	459.7	73.6	38.0	85.8
France	2003	12.5	9.2	4.4	3.4	1.9	1994	12.8	207.7	27.8	20.7	288.2	63.9	43.9	76.1
French Guiana	2003	21.3	4.8	12.9	16.5	3.1	1989	61.7	58.1	16.3	10.9	114.3	20.9	13.6	98.0
French Polynesia	2002	19.6	4.5	9.0	15.1	2.1	1994–95	14.0	104.0	14.0	10.0	123.0	47.0	17.0	52.0
Gabon	2003	36.5	11.2	55.1	25.3	4.8	…	…	…	…	…	…	…	…	…
Gambia, The	2003	40.8	12.4	74.9	28.4	5.5	…	…	…	…	…	…	…	…	…
Gaza Strip	2000	43.1	4.3	26.0	38.8	6.6	…	…	…	…	…	…	…	…	…
Georgia	2003	10.0	8.9	23.3[17]	1.1	1.4	1990	12.7	100.8	14.6	4.3	548.4	43.3	8.5	56.1
Germany	2003	8.6	10.3	4.2[17]	–1.7	1.4	1995	7.4	260.7	34.5	18.0	525.7	66.0	51.2	48.2
Ghana	2003	25.8	10.5	53.0	15.3	3.3	…	…	…	…	…	…	…	…	…
Greece	2003	9.7	10.0	5.7	–0.3	1.3	1998	6.7	213.4	8.3	9.4	492.4	54.9	22.1	42.8
Greenland	2003	16.1	7.7	17.3	8.4	2.4	1995	29.5	198.7	3.9	1.8	214.4	9.6	5.7	206.5
Grenada	2003	22.9	7.5	14.6	15.4	2.5	1987	9.6	82.8	57.3	7.4	264.3	45.6	38.2	…
Guadeloupe	2003	16.2	6.0	9.1	10.2	1.9	1996	23.8	134.8	26.2	…	183.7	32.1	31.4	68.1
Guam	2003	19.7	4.3	7.4	15.4	2.1	1994	1.4	60.0	26.5[5]	6.8	141.8	27.9	1.4	64.1
Guatemala	2003	35.1	6.8	37.9	28.3	4.7	…	…	…	…	…	…	…	…	…
Guernsey	2003	9.4	9.8	4.9	–0.4	1.4	1996	5.3	282.3	15.9	15.9	441.1	150.0	49.4	24.7
Guinea	2003	42.5	15.7	93.3	26.8	5.9	…	…	…	…	…	…	…	…	…
Guinea-Bissau	2003	38.4	16.6	110.3	21.8	5.1	…	…	…	…	…	…	…	…	…
Guyana	2003	18.7	8.5	35.1	10.2	2.1	1994	38.9	33.5	45.7	10.6	212.8	44.5	27.6	59.0
Haiti	2003	36.7	12.7	77.0	24.0	5.2	…	…	…	…	…	…	…	…	…
Honduras	2002	32.3	6.3	30.9	26.0	4.2	…	…	…	…	…	…	…	…	…
Hong Kong	2003	6.8	5.4	2.3	1.4	1.3	1998	14.4	160.5	7.4	3.9	126.7	99.6	21.0	21.2
Hungary	2003	9.3	13.4	7.3	–4.1	1.3	1995	7.9	322.0	20.1	11.5	721.4	63.0	115.6	111.5
Iceland	2002	14.1	6.3	2.2	7.8	1.9	1995	6.7	176.4	3.7	19.5	308.6	82.0	3.0	56.6
India	2003	23.3	8.5	59.6	14.8	2.9	…	…	…	…	…	…	…	…	…
Indonesia	2003	21.5	6.3	38.1	15.2	2.5	…	…	…	…	…	…	…	…	…
Iran	2003	17.2	5.6	44.2	11.6	1.9	1990[31]	*34*	*61*	*12*[19]	*26*	*304*	*48*	*24*	*108*
Iraq	2003	33.7	5.8	55.2	27.9	4.5	…	…	…	…	…	…	…	…	…
Ireland	2003	15.5	7.2	5.6[14]	8.3	2.0	1997	4.8	205.6	10.8[5]	0.2[11]	369.9	153.4	9.4	38.4
Isle of Man	2003	11.1	11.0	3.0	0.1	1.6	1998	2.8	298.4	11.1	31.8	504.3	225.2	38.7	52.5
Israel	2002	21.0	3.8	11.3	15.2	2.9	1995	10.4	148.9	23.4	11.5	278.4	26.5	23.1	35.8
Italy	2003	9.2	10.1	6.2	–0.9	1.3[17]	1995	13.3	258.2	34.7	20.3	424.3	59.1	47.0	49.0
Jamaica	2003	19.3	6.4	13.3	12.9	2.0	1991	8.1	84.1	51.3	7.5	189.5	30.2	14.1	8.4
Japan	2003	8.9	8.0	3.0	0.9	1.3	1997	14.6	220.4	12.4	7.0	237.7	98.0	30.0	52.4
Jersey	2003	10.4	9.2	5.4	1.2	1.6	…	…	…	…	…	…	…	…	…
Jordan	2003	27.4	3.1	22.0	24.3	3.7	…	…	…	…	…	…	…	…	…
Kazakhstan	2003	15.3	9.7	31.9	5.6	1.9	1996	45.7	133.0	10.9	1.4	436.2	71.0	32.9	101.1
Kenya	2003	40.2	15.6	65.6	29.6	5.0	…	…	…	…	…	…	…	…	…
Kiribati	2003	31.2	8.6	51.3	22.6	4.3	…	…	…	…	…	…	…	…	…
Korea, North	2003	17.6	6.9	25.7	10.7	2.3	…	…	…	…	…	…	…	…	…
Korea, South	2003	20.3	6.0	7.3	4.3	1.2	1997	10.8	115.4	20.2	5.1	121.5	24.4	34.4	70.6
Kuwait	2003	21.8	2.5	10.7	19.3	3.1	1997	5.4	22.7	10.6	3.1	84.6	11.0	4.7	34.8
Kyrgyzstan	2003	21.9	7.3	38.0	14.6	2.5	1996	12.6	25.7	8.3	1.5	278.5	75.0	9.8	21.4
Laos	2003	36.9	12.4	88.9	24.5	4.9	…	…	…	…	…	…	…	…	…
Latvia	2002	8.6	13.9	9.9	–5.3	1.2	1998	19.5	231.8	12.2[19]	12.7	775.6	34.6	42.2	161.8
Lebanon	2003	19.7	6.3	26.4	13.4	1.9	…	…	…	…	…	…	…	…	…
Lesotho	2003	27.3	24.6	86.2	2.7	3.5	…	…	…	…	…	…	…	…	…
Liberia	2003	45.3	17.8	133.8[17]	27.5	6.2	…	…	…	…	…	…	…	…	…
Libya	2003	27.4	3.5	26.8	23.9	3.5	…	…	…	…	…	…	…	…	…
Liechtenstein	2003	10.9	6.8	4.9	4.1	1.5[17]	1997	23.0[10]	199.7	…	6.6[10]	613.9	29.0	22.6	146.9
Lithuania	2003	8.9	11.9	6.7	–3.0	1.3	1995	16.4	203.2	8.0	10.3	654.2	40.5	32.1	176.0
Luxembourg	2003	11.8	9.0	5.0	2.8	1.6	1995	4.6	248.5	21.7	14.9	375.1	61.5	40.2	59.0
Macau	2003	7.2	3.3	0.6	3.9	1.1	1998	10.0	77.8	3.9	1.7	117.1	39.3	11.1	23.9
Macedonia	2003	12.9	8.8	10.7	3.1	1.6	1997	17.6	138.3	24.1[5]	28.0	462.8	39.5	15.9	32.4
Madagascar	2003	42.2	11.9	81.9[17]	30.3	5.7	…	…	…	…	…	…	…	…	…
Malawi	2003	44.7	22.6	105.2	22.1	6.1	…	…	…	…	…	…	…	…	…
Malaysia	2003	21.9	4.7	7.9[17]	17.2	3.1	1997	15.2	19.8	3.8	1.1	37.2	8.7	2.1	13.2
Maldives	2003	35.7	6.0	38.0[17]	29.7	5.3	…	…	…	…	…	…	…	—	…
Mali	2003	47.8	19.2	129.2	28.6	6.7	…	…	…	…	…	…	…	…	…
Malta	2003	10.0	7.9	4.0	2.1	1.5	1997	5.1	281.9	25.1	12.8	354.1	70.9	26.1	28.5
Marshall Islands	2003	34.2	5.0	32.7[17]	29.2	4.1	1993[32]	169.9	68.4	…	—	155.1	105.1	63.3	36.7
Martinique	2003	13.0	6.4	7.4	8.6	1.8	1996	21.9	150.1	27.7	…	206.6	36.3	27.2	47.2
Mauritania	2003	42.1	13.0	73.8	29.1	6.1	…	…	…	…	…	…	…	…	…
Mauritius	2003	16.3	6.7	13.2	9.6	1.9	1996	12.1	56.8	24.9	0.8	291.2	34.9	21.7	46.2
Mayotte	2003	42.9	8.3	65.9	34.6	6.1	…	…	…	…	…	…	…	…	…
Mexico	2003	21.9	4.7	17.4	17.2	2.3	1995	22.0	52.9	46.9	6.7	106.8	47.1	42.1	62.4
Micronesia	2003	26.5	5.2	32.4	21.4	3.5	…	…	…	…	…	…	…	…	…
Moldova	2002	9.9	11.5	41.6	–1.6	1.7	1995	14.6	133.3	10.7	11.8	559.4	76.3	114.7	113.7
Monaco	2003	9.5	12.8	5.6	–3.3	1.8	…	…	…	…	…	…	…	…	…
Mongolia	2003	21.4	7.2	23.8	14.7	2.3	1994[33]	33	118	3	14	200	110	55	64
Morocco	2002	21.0	5.6	46.9	15.4	3.0	1992	10.2	14.0	12.2	4.9	35.5	9.5	7.9	19.2

expectation of life at birth (latest year)		nuptiality, family, and family planning															country
		marriages			age at marriage (latest)						families (F), households (H) (latest)						
					groom (percent)			bride (percent)			families (households)		children		induced abortions		
male	female	year	total number	rate per 1,000 population	19 and under	20–29	30 and over	19 and under	20–29	30 and over	total ('000)	size	number under age 15	percent legitimate	number	ratio per 100 live births	
41.8	44.5	...	...	...	...	...	...	...	...	...	...	H 5.6	...	96.8	...	...	Djibouti
71.0	75.8	1996	230	3.1	—	37.0	63.0	2.7	56.2	41.1	H 19	H 3.6	H 2.2	24.1	...	...	Dominica
66.4	69.6	1994	14,883	2.0	...	...	...	...	...	...	H 1,804	H 3.9	...	32.8	562	0.5	Dominican Republic
63.0	67.0	...	...	...	...	...	...	...	...	...			...	...	...	...	East Timor
73.0	78.8	1996	72,094	6.2	12.6	61.7	25.7	32.6	51.4	16.0	...	H 4.1	...	67.9	...	...	Ecuador
67.9	73.0	1994	451,817	3.2	3.4	58.7	37.9	11.2	77.1	11.7	H 9,733	H 4.9	H 2.1	100.0	...	...	Egypt
67.0	74.4	1994	27,761	5.1	6.6[23]	54.8[23]	38.6[23]	21.5[23]	51.4[23]	27.1[23]	H 1,092	H 4.8	...	29.4	...	...	El Salvador
52.6	56.9	...	...	...	...	...	...	...	...	...	...	H 4.5[28, 29]	...	...	...	...	Equatorial Guinea
51.5	54.9	1992	68	...	...	...	...	...	...	...	...	...	...	...	...	...	Eritrea
64.4	76.6	1998	5,430	3.7	3.2[12]	56.4[12]	40.4[12]	13.9[12]	53.9[12]	32.2[12]	H 427	H 3.1	H 0.8	47.8	16,887	127.1	Estonia
47.3	49.7	...	...	...	...	...	...	...	...	...	...	H 4.5[28, 29]	...	...	...	...	Ethiopia
75.4	82.4	1990	203	4.3	...	...	...	...	...	...	F 14	F 3.0	F 0.9	57.5	26	3.3	Faroe Islands
66.4	71.4	1995	7,903	9.9	...	...	...	...	...	...	F 97	F 6.0	F 2.5	82.7	...	...	Fiji
74.6	81.6	1998	24,023	4.7	1.0[12]	47.1[12]	51.9[12]	3.5[12]	55.9[12]	40.6[12]	H 2,270	H 2.2	...	61.3	10,437	17.2	Finland
75.6	83.1	1997	283,984	4.8	0.2[15]	51.9[15]	47.9[15]	1.4[15]	63.2[15]	35.4[15]	H 20,899	H 2.6	H 1.0	63.9	157,886	22.2	France
73.4	80.2	1992	716	5.3	...	...	...	...	...	...	H 33	H 3.4	H 1.2	20.3	388	16.8	French Guiana
73.1	77.9	1996	1,200	5.7	...	...	...	...	...	...	H 40	H 4.3	H 1.7	40.5	...	...	French Polynesia
55.5	58.8	...	...	...	...	...	...	...	...	...	H 136	H 4.0	...	...	...	...	Gabon
52.4	56.4	...	...	...	...	...	...	...	...	...	...	H 8.3	...	...	...	...	Gambia, The
69.6	72.1	...	...	...	...	...	...	...	...	...	...	...	...	...	...	...	Gaza Strip
72.1	79.2	1996	19,253	3.7	9.1	59.4	31.5	32.7	51.2	16.1	H 1,244	H 4.1	H 1.1	82.3	43,549	77.3	Georgia
75.5	81.6	1997	422,319	5.1	0.7[12]	44.6[12]	54.7[12]	3.7[12]	56.3[12]	40.0[12]	H 37,457	H 2.2	H 0.3	82.0	97,937	12.8	Germany
55.7	57.4	...	...	...	...	...	...	...	...	...	H 2,355	H 4.9	H 2.2	...	...	...	Ghana
76.3	81.4	1998	55,489	5.3	0.9[16]	53.6[16]	45.5[16]	9.6[16]	68.9[16]	21.5[16]	H 2,990	H 3.3	H 0.7	96.7	12,289	12.1	Greece
64.5	72.7	1996	208	3.7	1.1[2]	44.6[2]	54.3[2]	2.7[2]	59.6[2]	37.7[2]	F 31	F 1.8	F 0.5	29.2	962	80.7	Greenland
62.7	66.3	1991	...	4.3	...	...	...	...	...	...	H 24	H 3.7	H 2.2	18.1	...	...	Grenada
74.4	80.8	1997	1,936	4.7	0.5[2]	51.4[2]	48.0[2]	7.2[2]	61.4[2]	31.4[2]	H 112	H 3.4	H 0.9	37.0	561	8.7	Guadeloupe
74.8	81.0	1995	1,507	10.1	3.0[23]	55.5[23]	41.5[23]	9.2[23]	59.3[23]	31.5[23]	H 31	H 4.0	H 1.3	50.1	...	...	Guam
64.3	66.2	1997	51,526	4.9	18.3	56.1	25.6	41.1	40.8	18.1	H 1,806	H 5.2	...	34.8	...	...	Guatemala
77.0	83.1	1996	340	5.8	...	...	...	...	...	...	H 21	H 2.6	H 0.5	73.2	...	...	Guernsey
48.3	50.8	...	...	...	...	...	...	...	...	...	H 1,064	H 4.1	...	...	...	...	Guinea
45.1	48.9	...	...	...	...	...	...	...	...	...	H 124	H 6.9	H 2.8	11.3	...	...	Guinea-Bissau
62.1	67.3	...	...	...	...	...	...	...	...	...	H 150	H 5.1	H 2.1	...	...	...	Guyana
51.0	53.7	...	...	...	...	...	...	...	...	...	H 1,147	H 4.4	H 1.8	...	...	...	Haiti
65.2	68.7	...	...	...	...	...	...	...	...	...	H 463	H 5.7	H 2.8	...	...	...	Honduras
78.6	84.3	1999	31,300	4.6	0.9[12]	42.7[12]	56.4[12]	3.0[12]	63.5[12]	33.5[12]	H 1,840	H 3.3	...	94.5	17,000	25.2	Hong Kong
68.3	76.6	1998	45,500	4.5	3.7[12]	69.1[12]	27.2[12]	17.5[12]	64.8[12]	17.7[12]	F 3,058	F 2.9	F 0.8	72.0	76,600	72.8	Hungary
78.4	82.6	1998	1,238	5.6	0.1[12]	40.7[12]	59.2[12]	1.2[12]	55.6[12]	43.2[12]	H 85	H 2.9	H 1.3	37.4	858	19.8	Iceland
62.9	64.4	...	...	...	...	...	...	...	...	...	H 151,033	H 5.6	H 2.4	...	581,215	...	India
66.5	71.5	1992–93[30]	1,423,774	7.6	...	...	...	...	...	...	H 53,972	H 3.9	...	...	...	...	Indonesia
68.0	70.7	1990	479,200	7.0	...	...	...	...	...	...	H 9,750	H 4.8	H 2.2	...	...	...	Iran
66.7	69.0	1992	144,055	7.8	...	...	...	...	...	...	H 1,873	H 8.9	H 4.1	...	...	...	Iraq
75.1	80.3	1999	18,526	4.9	0.7[10]	62.2[10]	37.1[10]	1.6[10]	74.7[10]	23.7[10]	H 541	H 3.3	H 1.3	65.5	...	...	Ireland
73.9	80.8	1998	435	6.0	0.2	39.5	60.3	1.6	45.1	53.3	H 29,377	H 2.4	...	68.1	...	...	Isle of Man
77.3	81.2	1997	32,510	5.6	3.5[10]	74.0[10]	22.5[10]	21.2[10]	68.3[10]	10.5[10]	H 1,355	H 3.7	H 1.1	98.5	16,903	14.7	Israel
76.5	82.5	1997	275,381	4.8	0.6[16]	56.2[16]	43.2[16]	4.8[16]	71.5[16]	23.7[16]	F 19,766	F 2.6	F 0.5	90.2	134,137	25.5	Italy
73.8	78.0	1996	18,708	7.4	...	...	...	...	...	...	H 554	H 4.2	H 1.4	14.9	...	...	Jamaica
78.4	85.3	1996	795,000	6.3	1.2	61.6	37.2	2.6	77.0	20.4	H 43,447	H 2.8	...	99.0	338,867	28.1	Japan
76.5	81.6	1994	542	6.4	...	...	...	...	...	...	H 29	H 2.6	H 0.4	88.1	296	28.0	Jersey
70.6	72.4	1996	102,558	6.4	4.4[16]	70.0[16]	25.6[16]	37.3[16]	54.7[16]	8.0[16]	H 11,891	H 6.1	H 3.4	...	...	...	Jordan
65.6	71.3	1996	102,558	6.4	6.0	71.5	22.5	27.9	56.5	15.6	H 3,824	H 4.0	H 1.4	86.6	193,462	76.4	Kazakhstan
47.4	45.7	...	...	...	...	...	...	...	...	...	H 1,938	H 3.4	H 2.7	...	...	...	Kenya
58.0	64.0	...	...	...	...	...	...	...	...	...	H 11	H 6.6	H 2.5	...	...	...	Kiribati
68.1	73.6	...	...	...	...	...	...	...	...	...	H 4,054	H 4.8	H 1.7	...	...	...	Korea, North
71.7	79.3	1995	320,395	7.1	0.3	67.7	32.0	1.7	86.1	12.2	H 12,961	H 3.7	H 1.0	99.5	...	...	Korea, South
75.7	77.6	1997	9,612	5.3	6.1[23]	72.2[23]	21.7[23]	35.9[23]	53.3[23]	10.8[23]	H 246	H 3.9	H 1.6	100.0	...	...	Kuwait
63.5	71.7	1995	26,866	6.0	5.4	79.0	15.6	38.1	52.0	9.9	H 856	H 4.2	H 1.9	83.2	27,111	23.1	Kyrgyzstan
52.3	56.3	...	...	...	...	...	...	...	...	...	...	H 6.0	...	...	...	...	Laos
65.4	76.8	1998	9,641	3.9	—	61.7	38.3	—	69.0	31.0	H 732	H 2.7	H 0.8	62.9	24,227	122.5	Latvia
69.6	74.6	...	...	...	...	...	...	...	...	...	H 405	H 5.3	H 2.2	...	...	...	Lebanon
36.8	37.1	...	...	...	...	...	...	...	...	...	H 330	H 4.8	H 2.0	...	...	...	Lesotho
47.0	49.3	...	...	...	...	...	...	...	...	...	H 474	H 5.0	...	...	...	...	Liberia
73.9	78.3	...	...	...	...	...	...	...	...	...	F 383	F 5.4	F 2.9	...	...	...	Libya
75.6	82.9	1998	423	13.2	—	54.5	44.5	0.0	66.3	29.2	H 8	H 3.0	H 0.7	86.0	...	...	Liechtenstein
66.5	77.9	1997	18,769	5.0	7.1[12]	68.5[12]	24.4[12]	23.0[12]	57.8[12]	19.2[12]	H 1,000	H 2.9	H 0.8	82.0	27,829	71.0	Lithuania
74.9	81.0	1997	2,007	4.8	0.9[12]	49.1[12]	50.0[12]	4.0[12]	61.6[12]	34.4[12]	H 145	H 2.6	H 0.5	82.5	...	...	Luxembourg
77.0	82.0	1998	1,451	3.4	0.6[12]	38.6[12]	60.8[12]	2.8[12]	58.0[12]	39.2[12]	H 99	H 3.5	H 0.9	99.3	...	...	Macau
70.8	75.8	1998	13,993	7.0	5.0	75.1	19.9	26.5	63.8	9.7	H 468	H 3.8	H 1.3	90.5	18,754	57.9	Macedonia
53.8	58.5	...	...	...	...	...	...	...	...	...	H 1,709	H 4.7	H 2.0	...	...	...	Madagascar
37.6	38.4	...	...	...	...	...	...	...	...	...	...	H 4.3	...	...	...	...	Malawi
71.0	75.5	...	...	...	...	...	...	...	...	...	H 3,580	H 4.9	...	...	...	...	Malaysia
62.0	64.6	1995	4,998	19.7	13.7[18]	58.2[18]	29.1[18]	...	...	...	...	H 7.2	...	...	...	...	Maldives
44.7	46.2	...	...	...	...	...	...	...	...	...	H 1,364	H 5.0	...	...	...	...	Mali
76.3	80.8	1998	2,376	6.3	2.0[12]	74.0[12]	24.0[12]	9.5[12]	76.0[12]	14.5[12]	H 76	H 3.3	H 1.2	91.8	...	...	Malta
67.4	71.4	...	...	...	...	...	...	...	...	...	H 5	H 8.7	...	...	...	...	Marshall Islands
79.3	78.2	1993	1,555	4.2	0.1[23]	46.8[23]	53.1[23]	3.3[23]	61.5[23]	35.2[23]	H 107	H 3.3	H 0.8	34.1	1,753	30.6	Martinique
49.7	54.1	...	...	...	...	...	...	...	...	...	H 246	H 5.0	...	...	...	...	Mauritania
68.6	75.5	1997	10,887	9.5	1.8[12]	56.2[12]	42.0[12]	25.8[12]	54.0[12]	20.2[12]	F 155	F 5.3	F 2.0	72.8	...	...	Mauritius
58.5	62.8	...	...	...	...	...	...	...	...	...	H 19	H 4.9	H 2.3	89.2	...	...	Mayotte
71.9	77.6	1996	670,523	6.9	14.0	65.1	20.9	32.5	54.7	12.8	H 17,152	H 5.1	H 2.0	72.5	28,734	1.0	Mexico
67.4	71.0	...	...	...	...	...	...	...	...	...	H 11	H 6.8	...	...	...	...	Micronesia
60.6	69.4	1996	26,089	6.0	8.2[16]	70.0[16]	21.8[16]	38.2[16]	45.0[16]	16.8[16]	H 1,144	H 3.4	H 1.1	89.6	44,252	78.4	Moldova
75.4	83.4	...	...	...	...	...	...	...	...	...	H 14	H 2.2	H 0.3	96.8	...	...	Monaco
61.0	65.0	1996	14,200	6.0	...	...	...	...	...	...	F 428	F 4.8	...	...	...	...	Mongolia
67.5	72.1	...	...	...	...	...	...	...	...	...	H 2,819	H 5.8	H 2.5	...	...	...	Morocco

Vital statistics, marriage, family (continued)

country	vital rates						causes of death (rate per 100,000 population)								
	year	birth rate per 1,000 population	death rate per 1,000 population	infant mortality rate per 1,000 live births	rate of natural increase per 1,000 population	total fertility rate	year	infectious and parasitic diseases	malignant neoplasms (cancers)	endocrine and metabolic disorders	diseases of the nervous system	diseases of the circulatory system	diseases of the respiratory system	diseases of the digestive system	accidents, poisoning, and violence
Mozambique	2003	36.9	23.0	137.8	13.9	5.0	…	…	…	…	…	…	…	…	…
Myanmar (Burma)	2003	23.7	11.2	83.0	12.5	2.2	…	…	…	…	…	…	…	…	…
Namibia	2003	27.4	16.7	50.7	10.7	3.5	…	…	…	…	…	…	…	…	…
Nauru	2003	21.8	7.5	10.3	14.3	3.4	…	…	…	…	…	…	…	…	…
Nepal	2003	32.5	9.8	70.6	22.7	4.4	…	…	…	…	…	…	…	…	…
Netherlands, The	2003	12.4	8.7	5.2	3.0	1.7	1995	7.6	236.1	28.1	13.3	335.1	81.8	32.6	33.5
Netherlands Antilles	2003	15.8	6.4	10.7	9.4	2.0	1995[34]	16.7	149.0	61.7	9.9	71.6	40.8	21.4	47.6
New Caledonia	2003	18.6	5.1	8.1	13.5	2.4	2001	20.4	128.8	8.8	9.3	132.9	57.4	15.8	69.9
New Zealand	2003	14.1	7.5	6.1	6.6	1.8	1996	5.6	200.7	22.1	12.3	317.2	86.4	20.9	46.7
Nicaragua	2003	26.1	4.6	31.2	21.5	3.0	1994[33]	*68*	*62*	*25*	*12*	*156*	*64*	*29*	*120*
Niger	2003	49.5	21.7	123.6	27.8	6.9	…	…	…	…	…	…	…	…	…
Nigeria	2003	38.8	13.8	71.3	25.0	5.4	…	…	…	…	…	…	…	…	…
Northern Mariana Islands	2002	20.0	2.4	7.5	17.6	1.4	1994–96	[35]	33.3	10.9[5]	—	53.3	12.6[35]	—	47.0
Norway	2003	12.4	9.3	3.8	3.1	1.8	1994	8.3	238.3	16.4	16.4	450.1	102.2	29.8	51.8
Oman	2003	37.5	4.0	21.0	33.5	5.9	…	…	…	…	…	…	…	…	…
Pakistan	2003	32.0	8.9	76.6	23.1	4.4	…	…	…	…	…	…	…	…	…
Palau	2003	19.0	7.0	6.4	12.0	2.5	1993	43.6	136.9	…	…	192.9	43.6	…	112.0
Panama	2003	19.5	6.3	21.4	13.2	2.5	1997	21.2	64.4	18.2[5]	1.3[11]	122.1	25.4	9.6	37.1
Papua New Guinea	2003	31.1	7.6	54.8	23.5	4.1	…	…	…	…	…	…	…	…	…
Paraguay	2003	30.1	4.6	27.7	25.5	4.1	1994[36]	*29*	*53*	*18*	*6*	*162*	*31*	*18*	*48*
Peru	2003	22.6	6.2	34.0	16.4	2.7	…	…	…	…	…	…	…	…	…
Philippines	2003	25.1	5.1	25.0	20.0	3.1	1996	66.7	42.9	11.0[5]	7.1	136.3	76.9	22.4	43.4
Poland	2003	10.5	10.0	9.0	0.5	1.4	1995	6.4	202.3	14.0	8.1	504.5	34.3	33.0	74.5
Portugal	2003	11.0	10.3	5.2	0.7	1.5	1995	10.2	201.7	43.9	10.0	438.9	80.2	45.7	59.8
Puerto Rico	2003	14.3	7.7	8.5	6.6	1.9	1993	59.4	122.2	66.7	19.2	242.3	80.5	43.9	34.1
Qatar	2004	15.6	4.3	20.3[17]	11.1	3.1	1992	3.4	21.4[22]	7.3[21]	2.6	59.9	7.5	3.4	36.0
Réunion	2003	20.2	5.5	8.3	14.7	2.5	1993	14.9	99.7	22.5	16.0	170.1	41.5	59.5[37]	65.3
Romania	2002	9.7	12.4	27.3	–2.7	1.3	1995	14.1	164.1	10.4	8.8	736.1	75.8	68.2	78.7
Russia	2002	9.6	16.3	13.3	–6.5	1.3	1998	19.0	203.0	11.0[10]	10.9[10]	749.0	57.0	38.0	185.0
Rwanda	2003	40.8	16.8	94.3	24.0	5.6	…	…	…	…	…	…	…	…	…
St. Kitts and Nevis	2003	18.5	8.9	15.4	9.6	2.4	1995	57.8	108.0	55.3	20.1	482.4	65.3	50.3	45.2
St. Lucia	2003	20.9	5.2	15.4	15.7	2.3	1995	20.7	98.6	79.3	13.8	226.9	29.7	21.4	50.3
St. Vincent and the Grenadines	2002	17.6	6.9	18.1	10.7	2.0	1997	36.8	90.0	56.6	14.4	228.4	42.2	28.8	—
Samoa	2003	28.6	5.5	26.0	23.1	4.1	1992[32]	3.1	11.2	9.9	3.1	24.2	9.9	6.8	2.5
San Marino	2002	10.4	7.1	6.8	3.3	1.3	1991–95	…	229.4	2.4[5]	…	324.8	10.7	…	45.2
São Tomé and Príncipe	2003	41.9	7.1	46.0	34.8	5.8	…	…	…	…	…	…	…	…	…
Saudi Arabia	2002	37.3	5.9	49.6	31.4	6.2	…	…	…	…	…	…	…	…	…
Senegal	2003	36.2	11.0	57.6	25.2	4.9	…	…	…	…	…	…	…	…	…
Serbia and Montenegro	2003	12.1	10.6	14.0	1.5	1.7	1995	9.0	167.7[22]	23.8	10.1	573.7	40.9	28.3	42.2
Seychelles	2002	18.3	8.0	17.6	10.3	2.0	1994	43.3	128.6	16.2	16.2	288.4	98.8	39.3	43.3
Sierra Leone	2003	43.9	20.7	146.9	23.2	5.9	…	…	…	…	…	…	…	…	…
Singapore	2003	10.4	4.4	2.2	6.0	1.3	1995	12.4	130.5	10.9	3.0	186.1	97.5	13.7	37.3
Slovakia	2002	10.4	8.6	8.1	0.8	1.3	1997	4.0	209.0	12.0	5.0	529.0	70.0	41.0	69.0
Slovenia	2002	8.8	9.4	3.8	–0.6	1.2	1997	4.4	243.9	36.4	9.0	381.1	81.0	55.2	88.6
Solomon Islands	2003	32.5	4.1	22.9	28.4	4.3	…	…	…	…	…	…	…	…	…
Somalia	2003	46.4	17.6	120.3	28.8	7.0	…	…	…	…	…	…	…	…	…
South Africa	2003	19.7	19.3	63.7	0.4	2.4	1995	71.3	55.8	20.5	10.2	98.5	51.9	15.1	112.0
Spain	2003	10.1	8.8	3.6	1.3	1.3	1995	5.9	219.8	23.1	0.4	333.6	28.0	20.4	41.3
Sri Lanka	2003	16.1	6.5	15.2	11.1	1.9	…	…	…	…	…	…	…	…	…
Sudan, The	2003	36.5	9.6	65.6	26.9	5.1	…	…	…	…	…	…	…	…	…
Suriname	2003	19.4	6.8	24.7	12.6	2.4	1992[38]	*40*	*68*	*40*	*11*	*193*	*37*	*32*	*71*
Swaziland	2003	28.6	23.1	67.4	5.5	3.8	…	…	…	…	…	…	…	…	…
Sweden	2002	10.7	10.6	3.3	0.1	1.6	1995	8.6	234.6	23.2	14.3	525.5	85.8	33.8	48.9
Switzerland	2003	9.8	8.6	4.5[17]	1.2	1.4	1994	16.3	238.7	23.3[19]	18.1	381.5	64.2	27.1	69.3
Syria	2003	29.5	5.0	31.7	24.5	3.7	…	…	…	…	…	…	…	…	…
Taiwan	2003	10.1	3.8	5.3	4.3	1.2	1992	…	101.5	23.7[5]	…	140.1[18]	24.3[39]	18.2[39]	63.7[39]
Tajikistan	2003	24.3	6.0	50.0	18.3	3.0	1993	128.3	40.7	8.8[2, 19]	7.9[2]	222.8	158.7	20.7	181.3
Tanzania	2003	39.5	17.4	103.7	22.1	5.3	…	…	…	…	…	…	…	…	…
Thailand	2002	14.0	6.0	20.0	8.0	1.8	1994	27.6	49.0	7.5	11.0	89.8	91.4	18.4	73.8
Togo	2003	35.2	11.5	68.7	23.7	5.0	…	…	…	…	…	…	…	…	…
Tonga	2003	24.5	5.5	13.5	19.0	3.0	1992	16.3	54.9	15.2	6.1	158.5	31.5	18.3	4.1
Trinidad and Tobago	2003	12.7	8.7	25.0	4.0	1.8	1994	11.6	94.4	119.3	14.7	286.5	49.0	28.6	52.8
Tunisia	2003	16.0	5.0	26.8	11.0	1.8	…	…	…	…	…	…	…	…	…
Turkey	2003	20.9	7.0	38.3	13.9	2.4	1993[39]	24	80	9[5]	2[10]	369	19	10	33
Turkmenistan	2003	28.0	8.9	73.2	19.1	3.5	1994	75.7	55.4	11.2	7.6	337.2	150.3	7.6	60.1
Tuvalu	2003	21.6	7.3	21.3	14.3	3.0	…	…	…	…	…	…	…	…	…
Uganda	2003	46.6	17.0	87.9	29.6	6.7	…	…	…	…	…	…	…	…	…
Ukraine	2003	8.6	16.1	20.8	–7.5	1.3	1996	17.7	192.5	8.3[19]	1.2	784.5	75.3	4.9	157.2
United Arab Emirates	2003	18.5	4.0	15.6	14.5	3.1	…	…	…	…	…	…	…	…	…
United Kingdom	2003	11.0	10.2	5.3	0.8	1.7	1997	6.8	261.2	13.8	18.5	442.1	165.8	39.5	32.7
United States	2003	14.1	8.4	6.8	6.3	2.1	1997	19.6[40]	201.6	30.3	21.0	354.4	85.2	29.5	55.9
Uruguay	2003	15.9	9.4	13.6	6.5	2.2	1990	16.0	222.8	25.5	16.2	378.4	76.3	39.1	61.7
Uzbekistan	2003	26.1	8.0	71.5	18.1	3.0	1993	38.0	48.2	9.4[23]	8.9[23]	300.3	113.8	31.4	49.5
Vanuatu	2003	24.2	8.1	60.8	16.1	3.0	1994[32]	25.0	29.2	9.1	5.5	39.0	30.4	9.7	9.1
Venezuela	2003	19.8	4.9	23.4	14.9	2.4	1994	33.0	60.5	24.1	7.4	144.7	31.9	19.3	74.1
Vietnam	2003	19.6	6.2	30.8	13.4	2.2	…	…	…	…	…	…	…	…	…
Virgin Islands (U.S.)	2003	15.0	5.7	8.4	9.3	2.2	…	…	…	…	…	…	…	…	…
West Bank	2003	34.1	4.2	20.7	29.9	4.6	…	…	…	…	…	…	…	…	…
Western Sahara	2000	45.1	16.1	133.6	29.0	6.6	…	…	…	…	…	…	…	…	…
Yemen	2003	41.4	8.8	65.0	32.6	6.8	…	…	…	…	…	…	…	…	…
Zambia	2003	39.5	24.3	99.3	15.2	5.2	…	…	…	…	…	…	…	…	…
Zimbabwe	2003	30.3	22.0	65.5	8.3	3.7	1990	64.7	28.4	4.9	9.4	40.8	39.5	12.1	44.9

[1]Excludes nomadic tribes. [2]1991. [3]1986. [4]Septicemia only. [5]Diabetes mellitus only. [6]Cerebrovascular disease and heart disease only. [7]Chronic obstructive pulmonary diseases, pneumonia, and influenza only. [8]Under 21 years of age. [9]21–29 years of age. [10]1994. [11]Meningitis only. [12]1996. [13]1989. [14]2000. [15]2001. [16]1995. [17]2002. [18]1993. [19]Includes nutritional disorders. [20]2003. [21]1990. [22]Includes benign neoplasms (cancers). [23]1992. [24]Results based on a sample population of about 100,000. [25]Millions of households. [26]Projected rates based on about 60 percent of the total deaths. [27]Projected rates based on about 75 percent of the total deaths. [28]Ethiopia includes Eritrea. [29]Based on a sample registration scheme. [30]Muslims only.

expectation of life at birth (latest year)		nuptiality, family, and family planning															country
		marriages			age at marriage (latest)						families (F), households (H) (latest)						
					groom (percent)			bride (percent)			families (households)		children		induced abortions		
male	female	year	total number	rate per 1,000 population	19 and under	20–29	30 and over	19 and under	20–29	30 and over	total ('000)	size	number under age 15	percent legitimate	number	ratio per 100 live births	
38.9	36.9	...	...	...	...	...	...	...	...	...	F 1,860	F 4.4	F 2.0	73.1	...	...	Mozambique
54.2	57.6	...	...	...	...	...	...	...	...	...	...	H 5.6	...	...	...	...	Myanmar (Burma)
46.0	46.1	...	...	...	...	...	...	...	...	...	...	H 5.2	...	...	...	...	Namibia
58.4	65.7	1995	57	5.3	...	...	...	...	...	...	H 1	H 8.0	H 2.6	...	...	...	Nauru
59.4	58.6	...	...	...	...	...	...	...	...	...	H 3,345	H 5.6	H 2.3	...	...	...	Nepal
76.2	80.9	1998	87,000	5.5	0.5[12]	47.4[12]	52.1[12]	3.2[12]	60.9[12]	35.9[12]	H 6,185	H 2.3	H 0.4	77.3	22,441	11.8	Netherlands, The
73.2	77.7	1998	1,276	6.1	...	...	...	...	...	...	H 41	H 3.7	H 2.1	51.6	...	...	Netherlands Antilles
70.6	76.6	1999	934	4.5	0.1[10]	46.5[10]	53.4[10]	5.0[10]	61.2[10]	33.8[10]	H 51	H 3.8	...	36.4	...	...	New Caledonia
75.3	81.4	1996	21,506	6.0	0.8[10]	50.6[10]	48.6[10]	3.2[10]	60.8[10]	36.0[10]	H 1,178	H 2.8	H 0.7	58.0	11,460	19.3	New Zealand
67.7	71.8	1991	13,122	3.3	...	...	...	...	...	...	H 752	H 5.8	...	...	...	...	Nicaragua
42.3	42.1	...	...	...	...	...	...	...	...	...	H 1,130	H 6.3	...	...	...	...	Niger
50.9	51.1	...	...	...	...	...	...	...	...	...	H 21,283	H 4.7	...	...	...	...	Nigeria
72.9	79.2	...	...	...	...	...	...	...	...	...	H 7	H 4.6	H 1.5	51.2	...	...	Northern Mariana Islands
76.5	81.9	1996	23,172	5.3	0.4	43.5	56.1	2.1	59.1	38.8	H 1,864	H 2.3	...	51.0	13,672	22.6	Norway
70.4	74.9	...	...	...	...	...	...	...	...	...	...	H 8.0	...	...	...	...	Oman
61.3	63.2	...	...	...	...	...	...	...	...	...	...	H 6.3	...	...	...	...	Pakistan
66.4	72.8	...	...	...	...	...	...	...	...	...	...	H 4.9	...	...	...	...	Palau
70.0	74.8	1995	8,841	3.4	2.4	52.3	45.3	10.4	57.2	32.4	H 524	H 4.4	H 1.5	25.5	...	...	Panama
62.2	66.4	...	...	...	...	...	...	...	...	...	H 674	H 4.6	...	...	...	...	Papua New Guinea
71.9	77.0	1994	23,649	5.0	4.2[23]	64.8[23]	31.0[23]	30.4[23]	50.2[23]	19.4[23]	H 868	H 4.7	1.9	68.7	...	...	Paraguay
67.2	70.7	1993	90,000	4.1	...	...	...	...	...	...	H 3,099	H 5.1	...	57.8	...	...	Peru
67.2	72.5	1993	474,407	7.1	4.9	66.3	28.8	18.0	63.8	18.2	F 9,566	F 5.7	F 2.4	93.9	2,315	...	Philippines
69.8	78.3	1996	203,641	5.3	2.8	77.2	20.0	16.6	70.5	12.9	F 9,435	F 3.6	F 0.9	95.0	491	0.1	Poland
73.9	80.7	1997	63,542	6.5	3.1[12]	70.0[12]	26.9[12]	13.9[12]	68.1[12]	18.0[12]	H 3,150	H 3.1	H 0.8	85.5	...	...	Portugal
73.3	81.6	1996	32,572	8.7	8.5	53.8	37.7	19.4	49.3	31.4	H 1,005	H 3.6	H 1.0	59.6	...	...	Puerto Rico
70.7	75.8	1996	1,641	2.9	4.9	67.5	27.6	29.6	59.7	10.7	H 61	H 6.4	...	...	...	...	Qatar
70.0	77.0	1996	3,313	4.9	1.2[21]	65.2[21]	33.6[21]	12.5[21]	66.8[21]	20.7[21]	H 185	H 3.5	...	44.1	4,302	31.7	Réunion
67.4	74.8	1997	147,105	6.5	2.6[12]	76.0[12]	21.4[12]	25.4[12]	62.1[12]	12.5[12]	H 7,115	H 3.1	...	...	456,221	197.2	Romania
58.5	71.9	1995	1,074,900	7.3	6.5	64.5	29.0	28.5	47.7	23.8	H 40,426	H 3.2	H 0.8	70.5	2,766,362	202.8	Russia
45.3	47.4	...	...	...	...	...	...	...	...	...	H 1,509	H 4.7	2.3	94.9	...	...	Rwanda
68.8	74.6	...	...	...	...	...	...	...	...	...	H 12	H 3.7	H 1.4	19.2	...	...	St. Kitts and Nevis
69.5	76.9	1997	467	3.1	0.8[13]	34.4[13]	64.8[13]	3.5[13]	45.1[13]	51.4[13]	H 33	H 4.0	H 2.0	14.2	...	...	St. Lucia
71.3	74.9	1997	508	4.6	1.0[23]	37.0[23]	62.0[23]	4.8[23]	46.3[23]	48.9[23]	H 27	H 3.9	H 2.0	...	...	...	St. Vincent and the Grenadines
67.4	73.0	1997	...	4.6	0.5[18]	51.0[18]	48.5[18]	8.0[18]	65.0[18]	27.0[18]	F 20	F 7.8	F 3.8	43.5	...	...	Samoa
77.6	85.0	1996	191	7.5	0.6[13]	75.1[13]	24.3[13]	5.3[13]	85.3[13]	9.5[13]	H 9	H 2.6	H 0.4	95.2	...	...	San Marino
64.8	67.8	...	...	...	...	...	...	...	...	...	...	H 4.0	...	...	...	...	São Tomé and Príncipe
66.7	70.2	...	...	...	...	...	...	...	...	...	H 1,513	H 6.1	...	...	...	...	Saudi Arabia
54.8	58.0	...	...	...	...	...	...	...	...	...	...	H 8.7	...	...	...	...	Senegal
71.6	76.7	1997	56,004	5.3	2.3[16]	64.5[16]	33.2[16]	18.7[16]	63.5[16]	17.8[16]	H 2,870	H 3.6	H 0.9	...	91,474	65.1	Serbia and Montenegro
66.6	75.8	1996	875	11.4	2.0[10]	45.8[10]	42.2[10]	11.2[10]	51.5[10]	29.6[10]	H 13	H 4.8	H 1.9	27.2	387	22.8	Seychelles
40.3	45.4	...	...	...	...	...	...	...	...	...	...	H 6.6	...	...	...	...	Sierra Leone
76.9	80.9	1997	25,667	6.9	0.5	57.3	42.2	3.1	74.5	22.4	H 662	H 4.2	H 1.3	...	14,362	29.6	Singapore
69.6	77.7	1996	27,484	5.1	6.0[16]	76.2[16]	17.8[16]	27.4[16]	62.4[16]	10.2[16]	...	H 3.2	...	83.1	35,879	58.4	Slovakia
72.3	79.9	1996	7,555	3.8	0.5	63.2	36.3	5.8	72.7	21.5	H 637	H 3.1	...	64.4	10,218	54.4	Slovenia
69.2	74.7	...	...	...	...	...	...	...	...	...	...	H 5.8	...	...	...	...	Solomon Islands
45.7	49.1	...	...	...	...	...	...	...	...	...	...	H 4.9	...	...	...	...	Somalia
44.6	46.0	1995	140,140	3.6	0.3	39.7	60.0	2.8	54.9	42.3	H 8,088	H 4.6	...	75.9	...	...	South Africa
75.7	83.1	1996	194,635	5.0	1.2[16]	62.5[16]	36.3[16]	5.0[16]	72.8[16]	22.2[16]	F 10,665	F 3.5	...	89.5	47,832	13.1	Spain
70.1	75.3	1996	170,444	9.3	1.3	64.3	34.4	16.7	67.1	16.2	H 3,282	H 4.6	...	96.3	...	...	Sri Lanka
56.6	58.9	...	...	...	...	...	...	...	...	...	H 3,471	H 5.3	...	...	...	...	Sudan, The
66.8	71.8	1995	2,249	5.5	...	...	...	...	...	...	...	H 4.8	...	...	...	...	Suriname
41.0	38.9	...	...	...	...	...	...	...	...	...	H 122	H 5.7	...	...	1,145	...	Swaziland
78.1	82.5	1996	33,484	3.4	0.3	40.5	59.2	1.5	54.0	44.5	H 3,670	H 2.1	H 0.5	46.1	32,117	33.7	Sweden
77.7	83.0	1997	37,575	5.3	0.4[12]	43.6[12]	56.0[12]	2.8[12]	58.8[12]	38.4[12]	H 3,250	H 2.0	0.4	91.2	...	...	Switzerland
68.2	70.7	1994	115,994	8.4	...	...	...	...	...	...	F 1,151	F 6.2	F 2.4	...	...	...	Syria
73.4	79.1	1998	145,678	6.7	1.5[21]	62.3[21]	36.2[21]	6.0[21]	77.7[21]	16.3[21]	H 5,964	H 3.6	H 1.0	97.2	...	...	Taiwan
61.4	67.5	1994	38,820	6.8	10.7	80.6	8.7	49.6	45.7	4.7	H 799	H 6.1	H 2.7	93.0	35,709	22.0	Tajikistan
43.3	45.8	...	...	...	...	...	...	...	...	...	H 3,435	H 5.2	H 2.3	...	...	...	Tanzania
69.9	74.9	1995	470,751	7.9	...	...	...	...	...	...	H 15,551	H 3.8	...	...	...	...	Thailand
51.5	55.4	...	...	...	...	...	...	...	...	...	H 479	H 6.0	...	...	...	...	Togo
66.4	71.4	1994	748	7.7	16.3	63.0	20.7	5.1	65.0	29.9	F 15	F 6.3	F 2.7	80.6	...	...	Tonga
67.1	72.2	1996	7,118	5.6	4.3	54.9	40.8	20.0	52.8	27.2	H 301	H 3.8	H 1.3	...	9	—	Trinidad and Tobago
72.8	76.2	1997	57,100	6.2	...	60.5[23]	39.5[23]	24.7[23]	62.7[23]	20.2[23]	H 1,703	H 5.1	H 1.9	99.8	23,300	10.9	Tunisia
66.4	71.0	1996	486,734	7.8	5.9[16]	74.5[16]	19.6[16]	31.4[16]	58.5[16]	10.1[16]	...	H 4.5	...	...	...	...	Turkey
57.7	64.8	1993	42,106	10.7	3.0[12]	87.4[12]	9.6[12]	16.1[12]	77.1[12]	6.8[12]	H 598	H 5.6	H 2.4	96.5	39,068	31.3	Turkmenistan
65.2	69.6	...	...	...	...	...	...	...	...	...	H 1	H 6.4	H 2.2	82.2	...	...	Tuvalu
43.4	46.4	...	...	...	...	...	...	...	...	...	H 2,766	H 4.8	...	...	...	...	Uganda
61.1	72.2	1997	345,000	6.5	7.5	68.4	24.1	35.2	45.9	18.9	H 14,507	H 3.2	H 0.8	89.2	957,022	159.5	Ukraine
72.3	77.4	1995	...	2.7	...	...	...	...	...	...	H 247	H 5.3	...	...	...	...	United Arab Emirates
75.7	80.7	1995	282,900	5.5	0.8	49.1	50.1	3.6	57.4	39.0	H 29,533	H 2.4	H 1.7	63.2	167,297	22.8	United Kingdom
74.4	80.1	1996	2,324,000	8.8	4.3[21]	51.8[21]	43.9[21]	10.9[21]	55.8[21]	35.3[21]	H 96,391	H 2.6	F 1.0	67.2	1,359,145	32.0	United States
71.3	79.2	1996	17,596	5.5	6.9[23]	57.2[23]	35.9[23]	23.5[23]	51.4[23]	25.1[23]	H 863	H 3.3	H 0.9	73.8	...	...	Uruguay
60.5	67.6	1994	176,300	7.8	11.2	80.7	8.1	49.3	45.3	5.4	H 3,415	H 5.5	H 2.4	95.8	120,434	18.3	Uzbekistan
60.3	63.2	...	...	...	...	...	...	...	...	...	H 28	H 5.1	H 2.2	...	113	2.4	Vanuatu
70.8	77.1	1996	81,951	3.7	9.5	58.7	31.8	27.9	51.7	20.4	H 2,707	H 5.3	H 2.2	47.0	...	...	Venezuela
67.6	72.7	...	...	...	...	...	...	...	...	...	H 12,958[41]	H 4.8[41]	H 1.9[41]	...	...	...	Vietnam
74.7	82.7	1993	3,646	35.1	0.4	33.6	66.0	1.9	45.9	52.2	H 32	H 3.1	H 1.0	30.2	...	...	Virgin Islands (U.S.)
71.0	74.5	...	...	...	...	...	...	...	...	...	...	...	...	...	...	...	West Bank
48.7	51.3	...	...	...	...	...	...	...	...	...	...	...	...	...	...	...	Western Sahara
59.2	62.9	...	...	...	...	...	...	...	...	...	H 1,848	H 5.6	...	...	...	...	Yemen
35.3	35.3	...	...	...	...	...	...	...	...	...	H 1,370	H 4.4	H 2.1	...	...	...	Zambia
41.6	38.8	...	...	...	...	...	...	...	...	...	H 2,166	H 4.8	1.1	95.8	...	...	Zimbabwe

[31]Projected rates based on about 20 percent of the total deaths. [32]Registered deaths only. [33]Projected rates based on about 45 percent of the total deaths. [34]Includes Aruba. [35]Diseases of the respiratory system included in infectious and parasitic diseases. [36]Reporting areas only (constituting about 75 percent of the total population). [37]Includes all deaths associated with alcoholism. [38]Projected rates based on about 70 percent of the total deaths. [39]Projected rates based on about 35 percent of the total deaths. [40]Of which AIDS, 6.2. [41]Private households only.

National product and accounts

This table furnishes, for most of the countries of the world, breakdowns of (1) gross national product (GNP)—its global and per capita values, and purchasing power parity (PPP), (2) growth rates (1990–99) and principal industrial and accounting components of gross domestic product (GDP), and (3) principal elements of each country's balance of payments, including international goods trade, invisibles, external public debt outstanding, and tourism payments.

Measures of national output. The two most commonly used measures of national output are GDP and GNP. Each of these measures represents an aggregate value of goods and services produced by a specific country. The GDP, the more basic of these, is a measure of the total value of goods and services produced entirely within a given country. The GNP, the more comprehensive value, is composed of both domestic production (GDP) and the net income from current (short-term) transactions with other countries. When the income received from other countries is greater than payments to them, a country's GNP is greater than its GDP. In theory, if all national accounts could be equilibrated, the global summation of GDP would equal GNP.

In the first section of the table, data are provided for the nominal and real GNP. ("Nominal" refers to value in current prices for the year indicated and is distinguished from a "real" valuation, which is one adjusted to eliminate the effect of recent inflation [most often] or, occasionally, of deflation between two given dates.) Both the total and per capita values of this product are denominated in U.S. dollars for ease of comparison, as is a new value for GNP per capita adjusted for purchasing power parity. The latter is a concept that provides a better approximation of the ability of equivalent values of two (or more) national currencies to purchase comparable quantities of goods and services in their respective domestic markets and may differ substantially from two otherwise equal GNP per capita values based solely on currency exchange rates. Beside these are given figures for average annual growth of total and per capita real GNP. GNP per capita provides a rough measure of annual national income per person, but values should be compared cautiously, as they are subject to a number of distortions, notably of exchange rate, but also of purchasing power parity and in the existence of elements of national production that do not enter the monetary economy in such a way as to be visible to fiscal authorities (*e.g.*, food, clothing, or housing produced and consumed within families or communal groups or services exchanged). For reasons of comparability, the majority of the data in this section are taken from the World Bank's *The World Bank Atlas* (annual).

The internal structure of the national product. GDP/GNP values allow comparison of the relative size of national economies, but further information is provided when these aggregates are analyzed according to their industrial sectors of origin, component kinds of expenditure, and cost components.

The distribution of GDP for ten industrial sectors, usually compiled from national sources, is aggregated into three major industrial groups:

1. The primary sector, composed of agriculture (including forestry and fishing) and mineral production (including fossil fuels).

National product and accounts

country	gross national product (GNP), 1999			gross domestic product (GDP), 1990–99			origin of gross domestic product (GDP) by economic sector, 1998 (%)										
	nominal ('000,000 U.S.$)	per capita		average annual growth rates, 1990–99			primary		secondary			tertiary					other
		nominal (U.S.$)	purchasing power parity (PPP; U.S.$)	real GDP (%)	population (%)	real GDP per capita (%)	agriculture	mining	manufacturing	construction	public utilities	transp., communications	trade	financial svcs.	other svcs.	government	
Afghanistan	5,666[1]	250[1]	…	…	…	…	…	…	…	…	…	…	…	…	…	…	…
Albania	3,146	930	3,240	3.4	0.6	2.8	54	[2]	12[2]	13	[2]	3		—18—			—
Algeria	46,548	1,550	4,840	1.7	2.2	–0.5	11	23	10	11	—		—24—			13	8
American Samoa	253[1]	4,300[1]	…	…	…	…	…	…	…	…	…	…	…	…	…	…	…
Andorra	850[3]	13,100[3]	…	…	…	…	…	…	…	…	…	…	…	…	…	…	…
Angola	3,276	270	1,100	–0.5	2.3	–2.8	13	45	6	6	—	—18—			—11—		1
Antigua and Barbuda	606	8,990	9,870	3.8	1.1	2.7	3	1	2	10	3	17	19	14	6	15	10
Argentina	296,097	7,550	11,940	4.9	1.3	3.6	5[3]	2[3]	20[3]	6[3]	2[3]	6[3]	14[3]	18[3]	—24[3]—		3[3]
Armenia	1,878	490	2,360	–3.1	0.8	–3.9	31	[2]	22[2]	9	[2]	5	9		—25—		–1
Aruba	1,728[4, 5]	18,700[4, 5]	…	…	…	…	…	…	…	…	…	…	…	…	…	…	…
Australia	397,345	20,950	23,850	4.1	1.2	2.9	3	4	13	6	2	8	10	16	33	4	1
Austria	205,743	25,430	24,600	1.9	0.5	1.4	3	1	24	7	3	8	19	18	6	10	1
Azerbaijan	3,705	460	2,450	–9.5	1.2	–10.7	20[3]	[2]	25[2, 3]	14[3]	[2]	10[3]		—31[3]—			—
Bahamas, The	3,288[3]	11,830[3]	…	…	…	…	1[6]	15[6]	17[6]	6[6]	2[6]	11[6]	11[6]	19[6]	5[6]	19[6]	–6[6]
Bahrain	4,909[4]	7,640[4]	…	…	…	…	1[7]	17[7]	22[7]	6[7]	2[7]	9[7]	11[7]	18[7]	5[7]	19[7]	–10[7]
Bangladesh	41,071	370	1,530	4.7	1.6	3.1	23	1	18	7	1	10	15	11	11	2	1
Barbados	2,294	8,600	14,010	1.8	0.3	1.5	6	1	10	8	4	8	35	—17—		12	–1
Belarus	26,299	2,620	6,880	–3.1	–0.2	–2.9	13	[8]	36[8]	7	4	12	12		—16—		—
Belgium	252,051	24,650	25,710	1.7	0.3	1.4	1[3]	—	21[3]	5[3]	2[3]	8[3]	12[3]	14[3]	7[3]	24[3]	6[3]
Belize	673	2,730	4,750	3.2	2.5	0.7	18	1	13	5	2	12	15	8	6	6	14
Benin	2,320	380	920	5.0	3.2	1.8	38[3]	[8]	9[3, 8]	4[3]	1[3]	7[3]	18[3]	9[3]	—7[3]—		7[3]
Bermuda	2,128[3]	34,950[3]	…	…	…	…	…	…	…	…	…	…	…	…	…	…	…
Bhutan	399	510	1,260	6.1	2.7	3.4	38	2	12	11	11	8	7	5	—9—		–3
Bolivia	8,092	990	2,300	4.2	2.4	1.8	15	11	18	5	1	12	9	13	6	10	—
Bosnia and Herzegovina	4,706	1,210	…	…	…	…	12	…	24	6	3	9	19	4	14	8	—
Botswana	5,139	3,240	6,540	3.8	2.0	1.8	3	36	5	6	2	4	18	8	4	14	—
Brazil	730,424	4,350	6,840	3.0	1.5	1.5	7[3]	1[3]	19[3]	9[3]	3[3]	5[3]	7[3]	20[3]	11[3]	13[3]	5[3]
Brunei	7,209[4]	22,280[4]	…	…	…	…	3	[8]	37[8]	7	1	4	10	9	—33—		–4
Bulgaria	11,572	1,410	5,070	–2.8	–0.7	–2.1	19	1	17	3	4	7	7	2	—29—		11
Burkina Faso	2,602	240	960	4.2	2.8	1.4	30	[8]	20[8]	5	1	4	12		—22—		6
Burundi	823	120	570	–3.9	1.1	–5.0	46	1[9]	9	5	[9]	4	4	—2—		18	11
Cambodia	3,023	260	1,350	5.2	3.3	1.9	51	—	6	7	1	4	15	5	7	3	1
Cameroon	8,798	600	1,490	1.3	2.8	–1.5	41	5	10	4	1			—35—			4
Canada	614,003	20,140	25,440	2.8	1.1	1.7	2	4	18	6	3	8	12	16	24	6	1
Cape Verde	569	1,330	4,450	4.6	1.4	3.2	12	—	10	9	—	18	19	12	7	14	–1
Central African Republic	1,035	290	1,150	2.0	2.3	–0.3	49	4	8	4	1	2	12	—6—		6	8
Chad	1,555	210	840	2.5	3.4	–0.9	37	1	12	2	1	—24—		—9—		11	3
Chile	69,602	4,630	8,410	7.1	1.5	5.6	7	9	15	5	2	9	18	17	6	2	10
China	979,894	780	3,550	10.8	1.3	9.5	18	[2]	42[2]	7	[2]	6	8		—18—		1
Colombia	90,007	2,170	5,580	3.3	1.9	1.4	14	4	14	5	…	8	12	—34—		9	—
Comoros	189	350	1,430	–0.1	3.0	–3.1	40	…	4	6	1	5	25	3	1	13	2
Congo, Dem. Rep. of the	5,433[4]	110[4]	…	…	…	…	58[7]	4[7]	6[7]	2[7]	2[7]	3[7]	17[7]	—6[7]—		1[7]	1[7]
Congo, Rep. of the	1,571	550	540	–0.8	2.5	–3.3	11[7]	33[7]	8[7]	2[7]	1[7]	12[7]	9[7]	—8[7]—		13[7]	3[7]
Costa Rica	12,828	3,570	7,880	5.0	2.0	3.0	15	[8]	19[8]	2	3	6	21	12	8	14	—
Côte d'Ivoire	10,387	670	1,540	3.6	3.0	0.6	28	[2]	20[2]	5	[2]	8	15	—12—		8	4
Croatia	20,222	4,530	7,260	0.4	–0.6	1.0	7	[8]	24[8]	6	3	8	12	13	—14—		13
Cuba	18,600[5]	1,700[5]	…	…	…	…	7[3]	2[3]	37[3]	5[3]	2[3]	4[3]	21[3]	2[3]	—19[3]—		2[3]
Cyprus[10]	9,086	11,950	19,080	4.2	1.4	2.8	4	—	11	8	2	9	20	19	10	14	3
Czech Republic	51,623	5,020	12,840	0.9	–0.0	0.9	4	[2]	32[2]	7	[2]	9	12	17	—13—		6
Denmark	170,685	32,050	25,600	2.4	0.4	2.0	4[3]	1[3]	20[3]	6[3]	2[3]	10[3]	13[3]	19[3]	6[3]	22[3]	–3[3]
Djibouti	511	790	…	–3.0	2.1	–5.1	3	—	5	8	5	17	16	10	5	20	11
Dominica	238	3,260	5,040	2.4	0.6	1.8	20	1	9	8	5	17	14	14	1	19	–8
Dominican Republic	16,130	1,920	5,210	5.7	1.8	3.9	12	2	17	12	2	12	20	9	8	8	–2
East Timor	113[4, 5]	130[4, 5]	…	…	…	…	…	…	…	…	…	…	…	…	…	…	…
Ecuador	16,841	1,360	2,820	2.1	2.1	0.0	17[3]	15[3]	15[3]	2[3]	1[3]	9[3]	15[3]	12[3]	6[3]	7[3]	1[3]

2. The secondary sector, composed of manufacturing, construction, and public utilities.
3. The tertiary sector, which includes transportation and communications, trade (wholesale and retail), restaurants and hotels, financial services (including banking, real estate, insurance, and business services), other services (community, social, and personal), and government services.

The category "other" contains adjustments such as import duties and bank service charges that are not distributed by sector.

There are three major domestic components of GDP expenditure: private consumption (analyzed in greater detail in the "Household budgets and consumption" table), government spending, and gross domestic investment. The fourth, nondomestic, component of GDP expenditure is net foreign trade; values are given for both exports (a positive value) and imports (a negative value, representing obligations to other countries). The sum of these five percentages, excluding statistical discrepancies and rounding, should be 100% of the GDP.

Balance of payments (external account transactions). The external account records the sum (net) of all economic transactions of a current nature between one country and the rest of the world. The account shows a country's net of overseas receipts and obligations, including not only the trade of goods and merchandise but also such invisible items as services, interest and dividends, short- and long-term investments, tourism, transfers to or from overseas residents, etc. Each transaction gives rise either to a foreign claim for payment, recorded as a deficit (*e.g.*, from imports, capital outflows), or a foreign obligation to pay, recorded as a surplus (*e.g.*, from exports, capital inflows) or a domestic claim on another country. Any international transaction automatically creates a deficit in the balance of payments of one country and a surplus in that of another. Values are given in U.S. dollars for comparability.

External public debt. Because the majority of the world's countries are in the less developed bloc, and because their principal financial concern is often external debt and its service, data are given for outstanding external public and publicly guaranteed long-term debt rather than for total public debt, which is the major concern in the developed countries. For comparability, the data are given in U.S. dollars. The data presented in the table come from the World Bank's *Global Development Finance* (formerly *World Debt Tables*).

Tourist trade. Net income or expenditure from tourism (in U.S. dollars for comparability) is often a significant element in a country's balance of payments. Receipts from foreign nationals reflect payments for goods and services from foreign currency resources by tourists in the given country. Expenditures by nationals abroad are also payments for goods and services, but in this case made by the residents of the given country as tourists abroad. The majority of the data in this section are compiled by the World Tourism Organization.

gross domestic product (GDP) by type of expenditure, 1998 (%)					external public debt outstanding (long-term, disbursed only), 1999						balance of payments, 1999 (current external transactions; '000,000 U.S.$)			tourist trade, 1997 ('000,000 U.S.$)		country
consumption		gross domestic investment	foreign trade		total ('000,000 U.S.$)	creditors (%)		debt service			net transfers		current balance of payments	receipts from foreign nationals	expenditures by nationals abroad	
private	government		exports	imports		official	private	total ('000,000 U.S.$)	repayment (%) principal	repayment (%) interest	goods, merchandise	invisibles				
…	…	…	…	…	…	…	…	…	…	…	…	…	…	1	1	Afghanistan
…	…	…	…	…	849.1	70.7	29.3	27.1	28.4	71.6	–663.0	507.6	–155.4	27	5	Albania
51	17	27	28	–23	25,913	71.3	28.7	4,885	64.7	35.3	3,360	–3,340	20	20	64	Algeria
…	…	…	…	…	…	…	…	…	…	…	…	…	…	10	…	American Samoa
…	…	…	…	…	…	…	…	…	…	…	…	…	…	…	…	Andorra
…	…	…	…	…	9,248	39.6	60.4	1,099	89.6	10.4	1,463.5[4]	–3,323.1[4]	–1,857.6[4]	9	73	Angola
58	22	32	73	–84	…	…	…	…	…	…	–321.3[4]	232.7[4]	–88.6[4]	260	26	Antigua and Barbuda
— 71 —		20	10	–13	84,568	24.8	75.2	12,170	48.1	51.9	–770	–11,676	–12,446	5,069	2,680	Argentina
103	11	19	19	–53	681.9	100.0	—	39.8	64.6	35.4	–474.0	167.0	–307.1	7	41	Armenia
73	13	11	— 2 —		…	…	…	…	…	…	–591.7	258.5	–333.2	666	130	Aruba
59	18	24	20	–22	…	…	…	…	…	…	–9,730	–13,340	–23,070	9,026	6,129	Australia
55	20	26	44	–45	…	…	…	…	…	…	–3,649	–2,098	–5,747	12,393	10,992	Austria
78[3]	12[3]	38[3]	28[3]	–55[3]	493.3	91.1	8.9	40.8	81.5	18.5	408.2	101.5	–509.7	159	72	Azerbaijan
66[7]	15[7]	23[7]	54[7]	–58[7]	…	…	…	…	…	…	–1,428.2	756.3	–671.9	1,416	250	Bahamas, The
51	21	18	78	–68	…	…	…	…	…	…	672.1	–1,012.5	–340.4	260	129	Bahrain
78	14	13	19	–23	16,962	99.4	0.6	675	72.3	27.7	–1,962.1	1,670.6	–291.5	59	170	Bangladesh
59	21	20	58	–57	359.1	75.4	24.6	84.2	64.4	35.6	–691.7	565.9	–125.8	717	74	Barbados
58	20	27	60	–65	851	52.8	47.2	141	64.5	35.5	–570.0	376.3	–193.7	25	114	Belarus
54	21	21	76	–72	…	…	…	…	…	…	6,642	6,732	13,374	5,275	8,275	Belgium
65	17	27	52	–61	294.6	73.6	26.4	40.2	59.6	40.4	–128.8	51.4	–77.4	87	30	Belize
81	9	18	27	–35	1,472	99.8	0.2	56	64.3	35.7	–158.3[4]	6.8[4]	–151.5[4]	31	7	Benin
…	…	…	…	…	…	…	…	…	…	…	…	…	…	474	148	Bermuda
36[1]	29[1]	44[1]	34[1]	–44[1]	181.8	100.0	—	6.9	71.0	29.0	–24.8[4]	–21.7[4]	–46.5[4]	6	…	Bhutan
75	14	23	20	–32	3,864	99.4	0.6	257	57.0	43.0	–488.0	–67.8	–555.8	170	172	Bolivia
— 100 —		38	35	–73	1,826	92.6	7.4	388	64.3	35.7	–2,072.0	1,284.6	–787.4	15	…	Bosnia and Herzegovina
28	29	28	56	–41	442.3	95.2	4.8	82.5	74.7	25.3	674.5	–157.7	516.8	184	140	Botswana
64	18	21	7	–10	95,233	33.8	66.2	24,374	72.1	27.9	–1,261	–24,139	–25,400	2,595	6,583	Brazil
…	…	…	…	…	…	…	…	…	…	…	175[4]	1,910[4]	2,085[4]	39	…	Brunei
72	15	14	44	–45	7,602	32.8	67.2	632	49.5	50.5	–1,081.0	396.3	–684.7	368	222	Bulgaria
81	10	24	15	–30	1,295	99.7	0.3	53	69.8	30.2	–184.5	–38.6	–223.1	39	32	Burkina Faso
96	12	3	8	–19	1,050	99.9	0.1	20	70.0	30.0	–42.3	15.3	–27.0	1	10	Burundi
96[1]	7[1]	16[1]	28[1]	–46[1]	2,136	100.0	—	28	51.8	48.2	–209.5	143.5	–66.0	143	12	Cambodia
71	9	18	26	–27	7,614	95.2	4.8	346	47.8	52.2	112.4	–343.7	–231.3	39	107	Cameroon
59	20	20	41	–40	…	…	…	…	…	…	22,756	–25,029	–2,273	8,770	11,304	Canada
68	23	40	25	–57	265.1	95.7	4.3	21.6	84.7	15.3	–185.6[4]	127.6[4]	–58.0[4]	15	17	Cape Verde
84	12	14	16	–25	830.1	96.1	3.9	11.9	60.9	39.1	–8.3[4]	–79.1[4]	–87.4[4]	5	39	Central African Republic
90	10	15	18	–33	1,045	98.5	1.5	27	61.1	38.9	–50.3[4]	–155.8[4]	–206.1[4]	9	24	Chad
67	11	26	25	–29	5,655	37.1	62.9	780	60.1	39.9	1,664	–1,744	–80	1,021	946	Chile
46	12	38	— 4 —		108,163	46.6	53.4	15,668	68.2	31.8	36,207	–20,540	15,667	12,074	10,166	China
68	19	20	15	–22	19,434	39.6	60.4	4,775	65.5	34.5	1,776	–1,837	–61	955	958	Colombia
91[1]	15[1]	19[1]	20[1]	–45[1]	179.9	100.0	—	7.1	87.3	12.7	–35.6[4]	40.8[4]	5.2[4]	26	8	Comoros
81[7]	5[7]	9[7]	28[7]	–23[7]	8,188	93.8	6.2	—	—	—	830[1]	–1,375[1]	–515[1]	2	7	Congo, Dem. Rep. of the
46	16	26	67	–55	3,932	80.1	19.9	—	—	—	644.1	–885.7	–241.6	3	36	Congo, Rep. of the
56	16	28	50	–50	3,186	64.0	36.0	475	70.3	29.7	659.6	–1,309.1	–649.5	719	358	Costa Rica
64	11	19	44	–37	9,699	74.8	28.2	992	53.8	46.2	1,832.3[4]	–2,144.9[4]	–312.6[4]	88	282	Côte d'Ivoire
59[1]	29[1]	22[1]	42[1]	–52[1]	5,433	26.3	73.7	667	47.1	52.9	–3,298.7	1,776.5	–1,522.2	2,529	521	Croatia
71[1]	24[1]	7[1]	16[1]	–18[1]	…	…	…	…	…	…	…	…	…	1,338	…	Cuba
64	19	25	44	–52	…	…	…	…	…	…	–2,309.2	2,075.5	–233.7	1,639	278	Cyprus[10]
52	19	30	60	–61	13,440	8.6	91.4	2,470	62.5	37.5	–1,902	870	–1,032	3,647	2,380	Czech Republic
51	26	21	35	–33	…	…	…	…	…	…	6,689	–3,725	2,964	3,156	4,128	Denmark
79	24	15	45	–64	252.7	100.0	—	3.0	68.3	31.7	–179.7[4]	165.3[4]	–14.4[4]	4	5	Djibouti
58[3]	21[3]	34[3]	51[3]	–63[3]	89.0	100.0	—	9.3	75.3	23.7	–58.4	29.0	–29.4	37	7	Dominica
75	8	26	47	–56	3,665	80.5	19.5	331	52.3	47.7	–2,901.1	2,176.2	420.2	2,107	242	Dominican Republic
…	…	…	…	…	…	…	…	…	…	…	…	…	…	…	…	East Timor
70	12	25	25	–32	12,756	42.7	57.3	1,382	45.2	54.8	1,655	–700	955	290	227	Ecuador

National product and accounts (continued)

country	gross national product (GNP), 1999			gross domestic product (GDP), 1990–99			origin of gross domestic product (GDP) by economic sector, 1998 (%)										
	nominal ('000,000 U.S.$)	per capita		average annual growth rates, 1990–99			primary		secondary			tertiary					other
		nominal (U.S.$)	purchasing power parity (PPP; U.S.$)	real GDP (%)	population (%)	real GDP per capita (%)	agriculture	mining	manufacturing	construction	public utilities	transp., communications	trade	financial svcs.	other svcs.	government	
Egypt	86,544	1,380	3,460	4.6	2.2	2.4	16[3]	[8]	27[3, 8]	5[3]	2[3]	11[3]	19[3]	6[3]	—7[3]—		7[3]
El Salvador	11,806	1,920	4,260	4.6	1.8	2.8	12	—	22	4	2	8	19	12	7	14	—
Equatorial Guinea	516	1,170	3,910	18.9	2.6	16.3	22	61	—	3	1	1	4	1	2	5	—
Eritrea	779	200	1,040	5.6	3.4	2.2	15	—	13	11	1	9	20	4	1	17	9
Estonia	4,906	3,400	8,190	−1.2	−0.9	−0.3	6	1	14	5	3	12	18	13	14	4	10
Ethiopia	6,524	100	620	5.3	2.9	2.4	46	[8]	7[8]	3	2	6	9	7	8	13	−1
Faroe Islands	976[4]	24,620[4]	…	…	…	…	…	…	…	…	…	…	…	…	…	…	…
Fiji	1,848	2,310	4,780	2.2	1.0	1.2	16	3	15	5	5	14	16	14	—20—		−8
Finland	127,764	27,730	22,600	2.4	0.4	2.0	4	—	22	4	2	8	11	11	9	16	13
France	1,453,211	24,170	23,020	1.5	0.4	1.1	3[3]	1[3]	22[3]	5[3]	3[3]	6[3]	14[3, 11]	5[3]	18[3, 11]	19[3]	6[3]
French Guiana	1,543[7]	10,580[7]	…	…	…	…	…	…	…	…	…	…	…	…	…	…	…
French Polynesia	3,908	16,930	22,200	1.6	1.7	−0.1	…	…	…	…	…	…	…	…	…	…	…
Gabon	3,987	3,300	5,280	1.8	1.2	0.6	7[3]	43[3]	6[3]	4[3]	1[3]	5[3]	8[3]	—11[3]—		9[3]	6[3]
Gambia, The	415	330	1,550	3.0	3.6	−0.6	24	—	5	5	2	14	17	7	5	9	12
Gaza Strip	1,368[4, 5]	1,320[4, 5]	…	…	…	…	13	—	10	8	2	5	15	23	8	16	—
Georgia	3,362	620	2,540	…	…	…	32	[2]	13[2]	4	[2]	11	11	11	—13—		5
Germany	2,103,804	26,620	23,510	1.4	0.4	1.0	1	[2]	25[2]	5	[2]	—17—		30	—21—		1
Ghana	7,451	400	1,850	4.1	2.5	1.6	36	5	9	9	3	4	7	4	3	10	10
Greece	127,648	12,110	15,800	2.5	0.7	1.8	14[3]	1[3]	14[3]	6[3]	2[3]	7[3]	14[3]	3[3]	11[3]	19[3]	9[3]
Greenland	1,142[3]	20,380[3]	…	…	…	…	…	…	…	…	…	…	…	…	…	…	…
Grenada	334	3,440	6,300	2.9	0.7	2.2	9[3]	1[3]	7[3]	7[3]	5[3]	24[3]	20[3]	14[3]	3[3]	16[3]	−6[3]
Guadeloupe	3,706[5, 7]	9,200[5, 7]	…	…	…	…	…	…	…	…	…	…	…	…	…	…	…
Guam	3,301[4, 5]	20,660[4, 5]	…	…	…	…	…	…	…	…	…	…	…	…	…	…	…
Guatemala	18,625	1,680	3,630	4.2	2.7	1.5	23	1	14	2	3	9	25	10	6	8	−1
Guernsey[12]	1,902	29,810	…	…	…	…	…	…	…	…	…	…	…	…	…	…	…
Guinea	3,556	490	1,870	3.9	2.4	1.5	21	16	4	9	1	6	—28—		9	4	2
Guinea-Bissau	194	160	630	0.7	2.6	−1.9	62	[2]	9[2]	3	[2]	2	19	—1—		3	1
Guyana	651	760	3,330	5.6	0.4	5.2	29	14	9[13]	5	[13]	6	4	6	1	11	15
Haiti	3,584	460	1,470	−2.1	1.3	−3.4	30	—	7	12	1	2	13	8	5	18	4
Honduras	4,829	760	2,270	3.6	3.3	0.3	19	2	19	5	5	5	12	17	11	6	−1
Hong Kong	165,122	24,570	22,570	3.7	1.8	1.9	—	—	6	6	3	9	23	24	—19—		10
Hungary	46,751	4,640	11,050	1.1	−0.3	1.4	6[3]	[8]	20[3, 8]	4[3]	3[3]	9[3]	10[3]	16[3]	13[3]	6[3]	13[3]
Iceland	8,197	29,540	27,210	2.7	0.9	1.8	9[3]	—	13[3]	6[3]	3[3]	6[3]	10[3]	15[3]	5[3]	14[3]	18[3]
India	441,834	440	2,230	5.9	1.8	4.1	25	2	15	4	2	7	14	10	6	5	10
Indonesia	125,043	600	2,660	4.6	1.6	3.0	19	13	26	5	1	5	15	8	3	4	1
Iran	113,729	1,810	5,520	3.4	1.5	1.9	20	12	16	4	2	8	17	10	2	10	−1
Iraq	11,500[1, 5]	600[1, 5]	…	…	…	…	…	…	…	…	…	…	…	…	…	…	…
Ireland	80,559	21,470	22,460	6.8	0.7	6.1	8[1]	[14]	38[1, 14]	[14]	[14]	—18[1]—		—31[1]—		5[1]	—
Isle of Man	1,319[4, 5]	18,270[4, 5]	…	…	…	…	2[3]	—	12[3]	7[3]	3[3]	10[3]	12[3]	59[3]	4[3]	6[3]	−15[3]
Israel	99,574	16,310	18,070	5.2	2.9	2.3	2[3]	[2]	19[2, 3]	9	[2]	6[3]	12[3]	30[3]	—28[3]—		−6[3]
Italy	1,162,910	20,170	22,000	1.4	0.2	1.2	3[1]	4[1]	16[1]	5[1]	6[1]	6[1]	19[1]	5[1]	13[1]	22[1]	1[1]
Jamaica	6,311	2,430	3,390	0.4	1.0	−0.6	7	5	14	10	2	11	23	12	3	12	1
Japan	4,054,545	32,030	25,170	1.4	0.3	1.1	2[3]	—	24[3]	10[3]	3[3]	7[3]	12[3]	19[3]	20[3]	8[3]	−5[3]
Jersey	2,670[1, 5]	30,940[1, 5]	…	…	…	…	…	…	…	…	…	…	…	…	…	…	…
Jordan	7,717	1,630	3,880	5.4	4.3	1.1	3	3	12	4	2	14	11	16	5	18	12
Kazakhstan	18,732	1,250	4,790	−6.1	−1.2	−4.9	8	[2]	22[2]	4	[2]	11	17	—37—			1
Kenya	10,696	360	1,010	2.3	2.6	−0.3	30[1]	—	10[1]	5[1]	1[1]	8[1]	19[1]	18[1]	—8[1]—		—
Kiribati	81	910	…	3.6	2.6	1.0	12[1]	—	1[1]	3[1]	2[1]	12[1]	19[1]	6[1]	3[1]	33[1]	9[1]
Korea, North	17,700[3]	740[3]	…	…	…	…	…	…	…	…	…	…	…	…	…	…	…
Korea, South	397,910	8,490	15,530	5.7	1.0	4.7	5	—	31	10	2	7	11	20	8	8	−2
Kuwait	35,152[3]	22,110[3]	…	…	…	…	—	31	12	3	—	6	10	14	—26—		−2
Kyrgyzstan	1,465	300	2,420	−5.4	1.0	−6.4	41	[2]	17[2]	3	[2]	2	12	—14—		3	8
Laos	1,476	290	1,430	6.5	2.7	3.8	52	—	17	3	2	6	12	3	1	3	1
Latvia	5,913	2,430	6,220	−4.7	−1.0	−3.7	8[1]	[8]	19[1, 8]	4[1]	5[1]	—51[1]—					13[1]
Lebanon	15,796	3,700	…	7.0	1.3	5.7	…	…	…	…	…	…	…	…	…	…	…
Lesotho	1,158	550	2,350	4.3	2.2	2.1	12[1]	—	14[1]	18[1]	3[1]	3[1]	10[1]	8[1]	1[1]	18[1]	13[1]
Liberia	1,174[1]	490[1]	…	…	…	…	78	2	5	2	—	5	3	3	2	2	−2
Libya	32,663[4, 5]	6,700[4, 5]	…	…	…	…	…	…	…	…	…	…	…	…	…	…	—
Liechtenstein	714[1, 5]	23,000[1, 5]	…	…	…	…	…	…	…	…	…	…	…	…	…	…	…
Lithuania	9,751	2,640	6,490	−4.0	−0.1	−3.9	9	[8]	17[8]	8	4	9	16	9	11	6	11
Luxembourg	18,545	42,930	41,230	5.2	1.4	3.8	1	—	17	7	1	—24—		45	—19—		−14
Macau	6,161	14,200	16,940	3.7	3.0	0.7	…	…	…	…	…	…	…	…	…	…	…
Macedonia	3,348	1,660	4,590	−0.7	0.8	−1.5	10	[8]	22[8]	6	3	6	13	6	—19—		15
Madagascar	3,712	250	790	1.8	3.0	−1.2	33	[8]	—12[8]—			—42—				5	8
Malawi	1,961	180	570	2.0	1.1	0.9	36	1	13	2	1	4	25	9	2	10	−3
Malaysia	76,944	3,390	7,640	7.4	2.7	4.7	9	8	28	4	3	8	16	13	—16—		−5
Maldives	322	1,200	…	6.3	2.4	3.9	16	2	7[13]	11	[13]	7	20	—29—		8	—
Mali	2,577	240	740	3.7	2.6	1.1	44	6	9	5	—	5	—16—		7	4	4
Malta	3,492	9,210	…	5.0	0.8	4.2	2	[15]	19	3[15]	7	6	10	17	9	14	13
Marshall Islands	99	1,950	…	…	…	…	15[3]	—	2[3]	7[3]	2[3]	7[3]	18[3]	15[3]	—30[3]—		4[3]
Martinique	4,271[3, 5]	11,320[3, 5]	…	…	…	…	…	…	…	…	…	…	…	…	…	…	…
Mauritania	1,001	390	1,550	4.3	3.0	1.3	22[3]	10[3]	10[3]	—9[3]—		8[3]	15[3]	—7[3]—		10[3]	9[3]
Mauritius	4,157	3,540	8,950	5.1	1.2	3.9	7	—	21	5	2	10	15	14	5	9	12
Mayotte	486[4]	3,700[4]	…	…	…	…	…	…	…	…	…	…	…	…	…	…	…
Mexico	428,877	4,440	8,070	2.8	1.8	1.0	5	1	21	5	1	11	20	14	—23—		−1
Micronesia	212	1,830	…	−0.2	1.6	−1.8	19[1]	—	1[1]	1[1]	1[1]	5[1]	24[1]	3[1]	3[1]	42[1]	1[1]
Moldova	1,481	410	2,100	−11.0	−0.2	−10.8	21	[8]	17[8]	4	2	4	7	6	—12—		27
Monaco	793[1, 5]	25,000[1, 5]	…	…	…	…	…	…	…	…	…	…	…	…	…	…	…
Mongolia	927	390	1,610	0.8	1.4	−0.6	33	[8]	24[8]	3	—	7	19	—14—			—
Morocco	33,715	1,190	3,320	2.1	1.7	0.4	15[3]	2[3]	18[3]	5[3]	9[3]	6[3]	19[3]	—13[3]—			13[3]
Mozambique	3,804	220	810	6.9	3.1	3.8	32	—	8	8	1	11	23	—	12	3	2
Myanmar (Burma)	55,700[3, 5]	1,190[3, 5]	…	…	…	…	53	—	6	2	—	5	30	2	—2—		—
Namibia	3,211	4,890	5,580	3.2	2.4	0.8	9[3]	12[3]	12[3]	3[3]	3[3]	4[3]	9[3]	8[3]	3[3]	23[3]	14[3]
Nauru	128[4]	11,540[4]	…	…	…	…	…	…	…	…	…	…	…	…	…	…	…
Nepal	5,173	220	1,280	4.8	2.5	2.3	38	1	9	10	2	8	11	10	—9—		2

gross domestic product (GDP) by type of expenditure, 1998 (%)					external public debt outstanding (long-term, disbursed only), 1999						balance of payments, 1999 (current external transactions; '000,000 U.S.$)			tourist trade, 1997 ('000,000 U.S.$)		country
consumption		gross domestic invest-ment	foreign trade		total ('000,000 U.S.$)	creditors (%)		debt service			net transfers		current balance of payments	receipts from foreign nationals	expendi-tures by nationals abroad	
private	govern-ment		exports	imports		offi-cial	private	total ('000,000 U.S.$)	repayment (%) principal	repayment (%) interest	goods, merchan-dise	invisibles				
74	10	22	17	–23	25,998	97.9	2.1	1,478	56.8	43.2	–9,928	8,293	–1,635	3,727	1,347	Egypt
86	10	17	23	–36	2,649	91.8	8.2	254	54.3	45.7	–1,358.9	1,117.0	–241	75	75	El Salvador
…	…	…	102	–173	207.9	93.7	6.3	1.7	58.8	41.2	26.5[4]	–400.1[4]	–373.6[4]	2	8	Equatorial Guinea
…	…	…	…	…	253.8	100.0	—	3.9	16.7	83.3	–498.9[4]	323.5[4]	–175.4[4]	75	…	Eritrea
59	22	29	78	–88	205.5	81.8	18.2	61.2	80.5	19.5	–877.5	582.9	–294.6	465	118	Estonia
79	14	18	16	–26	5,360	97.6	2.4	147	62.6	37.4	–797.1	480.9	–316.2	36	40	Ethiopia
…	…	…	…	…	…	…	…	…	…	…	51.6[4]	102.4[4]	154.0[4]	…	…	Faroe Islands
72	18	12	67	–69	120.7	100.0	—	29.2	75.3	24.7	–115.6	128.3	12.7	297	53	Fiji
39	21	19	50	–30	…	…	…	…	…	…	11,655	–4,067	7,588	1,963	2,270	Finland
54	24	19	26	–23	…	…	…	…	…	…	19,390	17,190	36,580	28,009	16,576	France
…	…	…	…	…	…	…	…	…	…	…	…	…	…	…	…	French Guiana
…	…	…	…	…	…	…	…	…	…	…	…	…	…	359	…	French Polynesia
40[3]	11[3]	26[3]	64[3]	–42[3]	3,290	96.1	3.9	487	52.6	47.4	202.5[3]	34.6[3]	237.1[3]	7	178	Gabon
76	17	18	51	–62	425.4	100.0	—	16.6	67.2	32.8	–69.0[4]	52.7[4]	–16.3[4]	32	16	Gambia, The
…	…	…	…	…	…	…	…	…	…	…	…	…	…	…	…	Gaza Strip
…	…	…	…	…	1,308	99.8	0.2	80	48.1	51.9	–533.9	335.5	–198.4	416	228	Georgia
57	19	22	29	–27	…	…	…	…	…	…	72,000	–91,310	–19,310	16,509	46,200	Germany
77	10	25	34	–47	5,647	91.2	8.8	391	68.3	31.7	–1,111.5	345.5	–766.0	266	22	Ghana
71	15	21	18	–25	…	…	…	…	…	…	–17,947	12,845	–5,102	3,771	1,325	Greece
…	…	…	…	…	…	…	…	…	…	…	…	…	…	…	…	Greenland
61	18	44	53	–76	122.2	93.9	6.1	6.4	73.4	26.6	–133.4[4]	43.9[4]	–89.5[4]	61	5	Grenada
…	…	…	…	…	…	…	…	…	…	…	…	…	…	499	…	Guadeloupe
…	…	…	…	…	…	…	…	…	…	…	…	…	…	…	…	Guam
87	6	16	19	–27	3,129	80.0	20.0	313	58.5	41.5	1,445.1	–2,471.0	–1,025.9	325	119	Guatemala
…	…	…	…	…	…	…	…	…	…	…	…	…	…	…	…	Guernsey[12]
77	7	17	22	–23	3,057	99.1	0.9	114	61.4	38.6	94.5	–246.1	–151.6	5	23	Guinea
100	9	11	15	–35	837.1	99.9	0.1	8.6	44.2	55.8	–14.4	–12.6	–27.0	…	…	Guinea-Bissau
43[3]	20[3]	43[3]	78[3]	–84[3]	1,238	96.6	3.4	74	52.7	47.3	–25	–50	–75	39	22	Guyana
—103—		13	13	–29	1,049	100.0	—	43	65.1	34.9	–469.7	410.1	–59.6	97	37	Haiti
67	10	30	44	–51	4,231	96.7	3.3	296	59.3	40.7	–709.1	172.3	–536.8	146	62	Honduras
61	9	30	127	–127	…	…	…	…	…	…	–3,159	14,635	11,476	9,242	…	Hong Kong
62	11	29	51	–53	16,064	14.0	86.0	3,282	69.5	30.5	–2,189	83	–2,106	2,582	1,153	Hungary
62	21	22	35	–39	…	…	…	…	…	…	–308	–292	–600	173	324	Iceland
66	13	23	12	–13	82,380	71.1	28.9	8,221	62.7	37.3	–8,029	5,245	–2,784	3,152	1,342	India
53	4	35	40	–33	72,554	75.5	24.5	9,192	59.5	40.5	20,644	–14,859	5,785	5,437	2,436	Indonesia
65	13	22	8	–8	6,184	59.4	40.6	2,971	86.6	13.4	6,215	–1,488	4,727	327	253	Iran
…	…	…	…	…	…	…	…	…	…	…	…	…	…	13	…	Iraq
51	13	24	84	–72	…	…	…	…	…	…	24,178	–23,583	595	3,189	2,223	Ireland
…	…	…	…	…	…	…	…	…	…	…	…	…	…	…	…	Isle of Man
61	30	20	32	–43	…	…	…	…	…	…	–4,408	2,527	–1,881	2,741	3,570	Israel
60	18	20	24	–22	…	…	…	…	…	…	20,383	–14,079	6,304	29,714	16,631	Italy
67	18	29	43	–56	2,905	77.5	22.5	648	52.3	47.7	–1,137.7	882.0	–255.7	1,131	181	Jamaica
61	10	26	11	–9	…	…	…	…	…	…	123,320	–16,450	106,870	4,326	33,041	Japan
…	…	…	…	…	…	…	…	…	…	…	…	…	…	…	…	Jersey
70	27	25	49	–70	7,546	83.2	16.8	559	52.6	47.4	–1,460.1	1,865.0	404.9	774	398	Jordan
75	11	18	32	–37	2,995	77.0	23.0	629	71.7	28.3	343.7	–514.7	–171.0	280	445	Kazakhstan
74	16	17	25	–32	5,385	90.2	9.8	533	78.9	21.1	–829.2	840.2	11.0	377	194	Kenya
…	…	…	…	…	…	…	…	…	…	…	–31.6[1]	29.3[1]	–2.3[1]	2	4	Kiribati
…	…	…	…	…	…	…	…	…	…	…	…	…	…	…	…	Korea, North
55	11	21	48	–35	57,231	27.1	72.9	23,000	81.4	18.6	28,371	–3,894	24,477	5,116	6,262	Korea, South
56	31	14	45	–47	…	…	…	…	…	…	5,571	–509	5,062	188	2,558	Kuwait
88	18	16	36	–58	1,130.4	97.2	2.8	16.5	8.2	91.8	–84.4	–168.9	–253.3	7	4	Kyrgyzstan
…	…	…	…	…	2,471	100.0	—	29	69.0	31.0	–189.5	68.4	–121.1	73	21	Laos
64	26	23	48	–61	864.8	70.2	29.8	41.4	50.7	49.3	–1,027	380	–647	192	326	Latvia
…	…	…	…	…	5,568	16.4	83.6	653	45.6	54.4	…	…	…	1,000	…	Lebanon
116	20	46	27	–109	661.8	91.6	8.4	44.6	55.8	44.2	–606.7	385.9	–220.8	20	8	Lesotho
…	…	…	…	…	1,062	80.7	19.3	—	—	—	–118.5[4]	76.6[4]	–41.9[4]	…	…	Liberia
55[3]	27[3]	12[3]	29[3]	–23[3]	…	…	…	…	…	…	2,974	–838	2,136	6	215	Libya
…	…	…	…	…	…	…	…	…	…	…	…	…	…	…	…	Liechtenstein
63	25	24	47	–59	1,891.5	34.2	65.8	166.7	54.3	45.7	–1,404.6	210.6	–1,194.0	399	290	Lithuania
46	17	21	116	–99	…	…	…	…	…	…	–2,449	3,761	1,312	297	…	Luxembourg
40	11	18	76	–46	…	…	…	…	…	…	…	…	…	2,947	153	Macau
74	18	23	43	–58	1,135	75.4	24.6	377	85.0	15.0	–420.3	108.6	–311.7	14	27	Macedonia
89	7	12	21	–30	4,023	99.1	0.9	147	46.9	53.1	–154[4]	–147[4]	–301[4]	73	48	Madagascar
85	7	14	30	–42	2,596	99.3	0.7	44	62.5	37.5	–93.0[1]	–0.3[1]	–92.7[1]	7	17	Malawi
42	10	27	114	–93	18,929	24.2	75.8	2,278	52.3	47.7	22,648	–10,042	12,606	2,703	2,478	Malaysia
…	…	…	…	…	192.5	84.9	15.1	16.7	73.7	26.3	–262.6	192.6	–70.0	286	38	Maldives
70	14	24	24	–33	2,798	100.0	—	85	75.3	24.7	9.7[3]	–187.7[3]	–178.0[3]	26	42	Mali
62	20	23	88	–94	…	…	…	…	…	…	–571.4	449.0	–112.4	664	191	Malta
…	…	…	…	…	…	…	…	…	…	…	–35.8[3]	52.2[3]	16.4[3]	3	…	Marshall Islands
…	…	…	…	…	…	…	…	…	…	…	…	…	…	400	…	Martinique
69[3]	20[3]	17[3]	42[3]	–49[3]	2,138	99.1	0.9	88	68.2	31.8	40.0[4]	37.2[4]	77.2[4]	11	24	Mauritania
63	12	25	67	–67	1,155	45.8	54.2	161	62.4	37.6	–547.2	494.9	52.4	475	177	Mauritius
…	…	…	…	…	…	…	…	…	…	…	…	…	…	…	…	Mayotte
68	9	24	31	–33	87,531	24.9	75.1	16,015	61.4	38.6	–5,581	–8,585	–14,166	7,594	3,892	Mexico
…	…	…	…	…	…	…	…	…	…	…	–52.0[3]	115.8[3]	63.8[3]	…	…	Micronesia
71	24	30	—–25—		722	82.5	17.5	98	55.1	44.9	–128.0	83.3	–44.7	4	…	Moldova
…	…	…	…	…	…	…	…	…	…	…	…	…	…	…	…	Monaco
65[3]	16[3]	23[3]	1[3]	–5[3]	816.3	97.4	2.6	20.9	57.2	42.8	–56.4	–55.8	–112.2	22	21	Mongolia
65	18	22	22	–26	17,284	75.9	24.1	2,985	64.6	35.4	–2,448	2,277	–171	1,443	315	Morocco
88	9	23	12	–32	4,625	99.7	0.3	68	47.8	52.2	–491.0[4]	61.7[4]	–429.3[4]	…	…	Mozambique
—89—		12	0	–1	5,333	90.1	9.9	88	72.7	27.3	–1,035.2	669.5	–365.7	34	25	Myanmar (Burma)
55[3]	31[3]	20[3]	53[3]	–58[3]	…	…	…	…	…	…	–172.6[4]	334.4[4]	161.8[4]	336	99	Namibia
…	…	…	…	…	…	…	…	…	…	…	…	…	…	…	…	Nauru
81	9	21	24	–35	2,910	99.3	0.7	99	69.7	30.3	–880.7	891.3	10.6	119	103	Nepal

National product and accounts (continued)

country	gross national product (GNP), 1999: nominal ('000,000 U.S.$)	per capita: nominal (U.S.$)	per capita: purchasing power parity (PPP; U.S.$)	gross domestic product (GDP), 1990–99, average annual growth rates, 1990–99: real GDP (%)	popu-lation (%)	real GDP per capita (%)	origin of gross domestic product (GDP) by economic sector, 1998 (%): primary: agri-culture	mining	secondary: manu-factur-ing	con-struc-tion	public util-ities	tertiary: transp., commu-nications	trade	finan-cial svcs.	other svcs.	govern-ment	other
Netherlands, The	397,384	25,140	24,410	2.7	0.6	2.1	3	2	17	5	2	7	15	26	11	12	—
Netherlands Antilles	2,400[3, 5]	11,500[3, 5]	…	…	…	…	1[7]	—	7[7]	7[7]	4[7]	13[7]	25[7]	17[7]	9[7]	18[7]	–1[7]
New Caledonia	3,169	15,160	21,130	1.4	2.2	–0.8	2[3]	4[3]	11[3]	5[3]	2[3]	7[3]	23[3]	—20[3]—		25[3]	–1[3]
New Zealand	53,299	13,990	17,630	3.0	1.2	1.8	7	1	17	3	3	11	15	22	—22—		1
Nicaragua	2,012	410	2,060	3.3	2.9	0.4	28	2	21	5	3	5	18	7	4	8	–1
Niger	1,974	190	740	1.8	2.8	–1.0	37[3]	4[3]	7[3]	2[3]	2[3]	6[3]	17[3]	—21[3]—			4[3]
Nigeria	31,600	260	770	2.4	2.9	–0.5	37	26	5	1	—	3	16	5	1	1	5
Northern Mariana Is.	665	9,600	…	…	…	…	…	…	…	…	…	…	…	…	…	…	…
Norway	149,280	33,470	28,140	3.8	0.6	3.2	2	11	12	4	2	9	10	17	5	16	12
Oman	13,135[4]	5,950[4]	…	…	…	…	2[1]	43[1]	4[1]	2[1]	1[1]	6[1]	13[1]	8[1]	8[1]	12[1]	1[1]
Pakistan	62,915	470	1,860	3.5	2.5	1.0	24	—	15	3	4	9	15	8	7	7	8
Palau	129[4, 5]	7,140[4, 5]	…	…	…	…	5	—	1	8	—	16	27	12	7	22	2
Panama	8,657	3,080	5,450	4.3	1.9	2.4	8	—	10	4	4	13	21	25	6	10	–1
Papua New Guinea	3,834	810	2,260	4.9	2.6	2.3	24	26	9	6	1	5	9	1	—13—		6
Paraguay	8,374	1,560	4,380	2.5	2.7	–0.2	28	—	14	5	6	5	23	3	10	6	—
Peru	53,705	2,130	4,480	5.0	1.8	3.2	6[3]	2[3]	19[3]	11[3]	1[3]	4[3]	16[3]	14[3]	13[3]	7[3]	7[3]
Philippines	77,967	1,050	3,990	3.2	2.3	0.9	17	1	22	6	3	5	14	12	11	10	–1
Poland	157,429	4,070	8,390	4.6	0.2	4.4	5	3	22	8	3	6	21	15	3	13	1
Portugal	110,175	11,030	15,860	2.4	0.1	2.3	…	…	…	…	…	…	…	…	…	…	…
Puerto Rico	25,380[3]	7,010[3]	…	…	…	…	1[1]	[15]	41[1]	2[1, 15]	[16]	8[1, 16]	14[1]	13[1]	11[1]	11[1]	–1[1]
Qatar	6,473[4]	11,600[4]	…	…	…	…	1[3]	38[3]	7[3]	7[3]	1[3]	4[3]	8[3]	10[3]	—24[3]—		…
Réunion	5,680[3]	8,260[3]	…	…	…	…	…	…	…	…	…	…	…	…	…	…	…
Romania	33,034	1,470	5,970	–0.9	–0.4	–0.5	19[1]	[2]	34[1, 2]	7[1]	[2]	9[1]	10[1]	—17[1]—			4[1]
Russia	328,995	2,250	6,990	–6.0	–0.1	–5.9	7	[2]	33[2]	8	[2]	—23—		14	9	6	—
Rwanda	2,041	250	880	–2.7	0.3	–3.0	44	—	13	7	—	4	11	—15—		7	–1
St. Kitts	259	6,330	10,400	4.2	–0.7	4.9	6[1]	—	11[1]	12[1]	2[1]	16[1]	23[1]	16[1]	4[1]	18[1]	–8[1]
St. Lucia	590	3,820	5,200	2.4	1.5	0.9	7	—	5	6	4	15	23	15	3	13	9
St. Vincent	301	2,640	4,990	3.3	0.7	2.6	9	—	6	12	5	17	15	8	2	15	11
Samoa	181	1,070	4,070	2.0	0.6	1.4	17[3]	…	19[3]	5[3]	2[3]	11[3]	17[3]	11[3]	7[3]	9[3]	2[3]
San Marino	883[3, 5]	34,330[3, 5]	…	…	…	…	…	…	…	…	…	…	…	…	…	…	…
São Tomé and Príncipe	40	270	…	1.1	2.0	–0.9	23[3]	—	4[3]	15[3]	—	—19[3]—		8[3]	9[3]	22[3]	—
Saudi Arabia	139,365	6,900	11,050	2.2	3.3	–1.1	6[1]	36[1]	9[1]	9[1]	—	6[1]	7[1]	5[1]	3[1]	17[1]	2[1]
Senegal	4,685	500	1,400	3.7	3.1	0.6	18	[5]	13[5]	5	2	12	—21—		20	9	—
Serbia and Montenegro	13,742[4]	1,290[4]	…	…	…	…	20	[8]	36[8]	6	3	12	19	—5—			–1
Seychelles	520	6,500	…	2.9	1.6	1.3	3	…	14	9	3	15	24	10	2	13	7
Sierra Leone	653	130	440	–4.9	2.1	–7.0	39[7]	17[7]	9[7]	2[7]	—	9[7]	14[7]	2[7]	2[7]	3[7]	4[7]
Singapore	95,429	24,150	22,310	6.6	1.9	4.7	—	—	24	9	2	14	19	28	—11—		–7
Slovakia	20,318	3,770	10,430	1.8	0.2	1.6	4	1	23	5	3	8	—22—		—29—		5
Slovenia	19,862	10,000	16,050	2.4	–0.1	2.5	4[3]	1[3]	25[3]	5[3]	3[3]	7[3]	13[3]	14[3]	12[3]	5[3]	11[3]
Solomon Islands	320	750	2,050	3.7	3.4	0.3	48[1]	—	3[1]	7[1]	2[1]	6[1]	9[1]	4[1]	—21[1]—		—
Somalia	706[1]	110[1]	…	…	…	…	…	…	…	…	…	…	…	…	…	…	…
South Africa	133,569	3,170	8,710	1.2	1.4	–0.2	4	7	19	3	3	10	13	18	—23—		—
Spain	583,082	14,800	17,850	2.3	0.3	2.0	4[1]	[2]	24[1, 2]	8[1]	[2]	—59[1]—					5[1]
Sri Lanka	15,578	820	3,230	5.3	1.3	4.0	19	2	15	7	1	10	19	9	—13—		5
Sudan, The	9,435	330	…	…	…	…	41	—	9	6	1	6	20	—14—			3
Suriname	684[4]	1,660[4]	…	…	…	…	12[1]	11[1]	13[1]	3[1]	9[1]	15[1]	12[1]	14[1]	—13[1]—		–2[1]
Swaziland	1,379	1,350	4,380	2.3	2.5	–0.2	12	1	27	4	2	4	7	4	1	15	23
Sweden	236,940	26,750	22,510	1.6	0.4	1.2	2[1]	—	20[1]	5[1]	3[1]	6[1]	11[1]	23[1]	4[1]	19[1]	7[1]
Switzerland	273,856	38,380	28,760	0.6	0.7	–0.1	…	…	…	…	…	…	…	…	…	…	…
Syria	15,172	970	3,450	5.5	2.8	2.7	28[1]	7[1]	4[1]	4[1]	1[1]	11[1]	26[1]	5[1]	2[1]	10[1]	—
Taiwan	297,953[4]	13,900[4]	…	…	…	…	3	—	27	4	2	7	17	23	10	10	–3
Tajikistan	1,749	280	…	…	…	…	20	[2]	28[2]	2	[2]	—18—		—22—			10
Tanzania	8,515	260	500	3.0	3.1	–0.1	43[3]	1[3]	6[3]	4[3]	2[3]	5[3]	12[3]	12[3]	2[3]	7[3]	6[3]
Thailand	121,051	2,010	5,950	4.9	1.1	3.8	14	2	28	5	3	8	14	—26—			—
Togo	1,398	310	1,380	2.7	3.2	–0.5	42	6	9	3	3	5	17	—8—		7	—
Tonga	172	1,732	…	1.1	0.4	0.7	32	—	3	5	2	7	11	10	—18—		12
Trinidad and Tobago	6,142	4,750	7,690	2.5	0.5	2.0	2	21	8	10	—	—18—		12	17	9	3
Tunisia	19,757	2,090	5,700	4.5	1.6	2.9	12	1	18	5	5	8	—24—			14	13
Turkey	186,490	2,900	6,440	3.7	1.5	2.2	17	1	19	6	2	14	20	—13—		9	–1
Turkmenistan	3,205	670	3,340	–6.6	3.0	–9.6	25	[2]	30[2]	12	[2]	10	5	—13—			5
Tuvalu	7[1]	650[1]	…	…	…	…	22[7]	2[7]	3[7]	14[7]	2[7]	4[7]	14[7]	10[7]	—28[7]—		—
Uganda	6,794	320	1,160	7.1	3.1	4.0	41[1]	—	7[1]	7[1]	1[1]	4[1]	12[1]	7[1]	5[1]	4[1]	12[1]
Ukraine	41,991	840	3,360	–10.8	–0.5	–10.3	11	[2]	25[2]	5	[2]	13	8	—25—			13
United Arab Emirates	48,673[4]	17,870[4]	…	…	…	…	2[1]	35[1]	9[1]	9[1]	1[1]	6[1]	13[1]	13[1]	2[1]	11[1]	–1[1]
United Kingdom	1,403,843	23,500	22,220	2.5	0.4	2.1	1	2	18	5	2	7	13	23	4	15	10
United States	8,879,500	31,910	31,910	3.0	1.0	2.0	2[3]	1[3]	17[3]	4[3]	3[3]	6[3]	17[3]	19[3]	20[3]	13[3]	—
Uruguay	20,604	6,220	8,750	3.7	0.7	3.0	11	—	20	4	4	10	14	21	—15—		1
Uzbekistan	17,613	720	2,230	–1.2	1.9	–3.1	26	[2]	15[2]	8	[2]	6	8	—21—			16
Vanuatu	227	1,180	2,880	2.3	3.1	–0.8	23	—	5	5	2	7	34	7	—17—		—
Venezuela	87,313	3,680	5,420	1.7	2.2	–0.5	5	12	16	7	2	10	18	16	9	6	–1
Vietnam	28,733	370	1,860	8.0	1.8	6.2	26	[8]	—33[8]—			4	19	7	—12—		–1
Virgin Islands (U.S.)	2,666[3]	18,290[3]	…	…	…	…	…	…	…	…	…	…	…	…	…	…	…
West Bank	2,758[4, 5]	1,680[4, 5]	…	…	…	…	7	[2]	17[2]	11	[2]	[17]	14	11	19[17]	10	13
Western Sahara	60[5, 18]	300[5, 18]	…	…	…	…	…	…	…	…	…	…	…	…	…	…	…
Yemen	6,080	360	730	3.5	3.9	–0.4	24	17	10	4	2	7	14	6	2	14	—
Zambia	3,222	330	720	–0.4	2.0	–2.4	17	6	11	5	4	6	19	16	—9—		7
Zimbabwe	6,302	530	2,690	1.9	1.3	0.6	14[7]	5[7]	18[7]	2[7]	3[7]	5[7]	18[7]	9[7]	11[7]	4[7]	11[7]

gross domestic product (GDP) by type of expenditure, 1998 (%)					external public debt outstanding (long-term, disbursed only), 1999						balance of payments, 1999 (current external transactions; '000,000 U.S.$)			tourist trade, 1997 ('000,000 U.S.$)		country
consumption		gross domestic investment	foreign trade		total ('000,000 U.S.$)	creditors (%)		debt service			net transfers		current balance of payments	receipts from foreign nationals	expenditures by nationals abroad	
private	government		exports	imports		official	private	total ('000,000 U.S.$)	repayment (%)		goods, merchandise	invisibles				
									principal	interest						
59	14	20	55	–49	…	…	…	…	…	…	17,940	–704	17,236	6,219	10,232	Netherlands, The
67[7]	28[7]	19[7]	72[7]	–85[7]	…	…	…	…	…	…	–1,064[4]	1,008[4]	–56[4]	576	243	Netherlands Antilles
…	…	…	…	…	…	…	…	…	…	…	…	…	…	110	…	New Caledonia
65	15	19	31	–30	…	…	…	…	…	…	–435	–3,161	3,596	2,093	1,451	New Zealand
94	14	34	36	–78	5,799	93.3	6.7	137	43.1	56.9	–1,133.2	481.0	–652.2	74	65	Nicaragua
82[3]	16[3]	12[3]	19[3]	–29[3]	1,424	100.0	—	19	52.6	47.7	–17.6[5]	–134.1[5]	–151.7[5]	18	24	Niger
64	14	29	32	–38	22,423	74.3	25.7	835	67.2	32.8	4,288	–3,782	506	118	1,816	Nigeria
…	…	…	…	…	…	…	…	…	…	…	…	…	…	672	…	Northern Mariana Is.
50	22	28	37	–37	…	…	…	…	…	…	10,119	–4,105	6,014	2,226	4,496	Norway
55	24	23	37	–39	1,768	37.4	62.6	711	82.3	17.7	2,918	–3,110	–192	108	47	Oman
72	12	17	16	–17	28,514	92.5	7.5	1,597	63.1	36.9	–1,874[4]	—[4]	–1,874[4]	117	364	Pakistan
…	…	…	…	…	…	…	…	…	…	…	…	…	…	22[7]	…	Palau
58	16	33	90	–97	5,678	23.6	76.4	619	45.7	54.3	–1,415.0	39.0	–1,376.0	374	164	Panama
55[7]	16[7]	18[7]	49[7]	–37[7]	1,517	95.6	4.4	160	66.9	33.1	856.0	–761.3	94.7	72	81	Papua New Guinea
86	8	23	28	–45	1,672	96.7	3.3	183	62.3	37.7	–334.4	270.8	–63.6	753	195	Paraguay
72	9	24	12	–17	20,709	79.7	20.3	1,957	41.3	58.7	–616	–1,206	–1,822	805	485	Peru
73	13	20	51	–58	33,568	63.8	36.2	5,097	68.1	31.9	4,958	2,952	7,910	2,831	1,936	Philippines
63	16	27	25	–32	33,151	75.6	24.4	2,162	39.1	60.9	–15,072	2,585	–12,487	8,679	6,900	Poland
66	20	26	28	–40	…	…	…	…	…	…	–13,766	4,137	–9,629	4,277	2,164	Portugal
…	…	…	…	…	…	…	…	…	…	…	…	…	…	2,046	869	Puerto Rico
…	…	…	…	…	…	…	…	…	…	…	…	…	…	…	…	Qatar
…	…	…	…	…	…	…	…	…	…	…	…	…	…	249	…	Réunion
76	15	18	26	–34	5,985	64.4	35.6	2,754	85.7	14.3	–1,092	–205	–1,297	526	783	Romania
58	19	15	31	–23	120,375	59.1	40.9	4,470	42.9	57.1	36,130	–11,482	24,648	6,900	10,113	Russia
94	9	16	6	–24	1,162	99.9	0.1	20	60.0	40.0	–140.6	138.1	–2.5	…	…	Rwanda
76[1]	18[1]	24[1]	44[1]	–63[1]	131.7	73.4	26.6	16.9	54.4	45.6	…	…	…	72	6	St. Kitts
69	15	19	65	–68	125.6	88.5	11.5	16.4	63.4	36.8	–201.2[4]	160.2[4]	–41.0[4]	282	29	St. Lucia
74	19	32	47	–72	159.8	63.2	36.8	12.6	49.2	50.8	–119.4[4]	75.1[4]	–44.3[4]	70	7	St. Vincent
…	…	…	…	…	156.5	100.0	—	4.8	70.8	29.2	–97.5	78.7	18.8	41	5	Samoa
66[1]	12[1]	17[1]	234[1]	–229[1]	…	…	…	…	…	…	22.6[1]	–11.9[1]	10.7[1]	…	…	San Marino
…	…	…	…	…	232.2	100.0	—	3.9	64.1	35.9	–12.1[4]	3.6[4]	–8.5[4]	2	1	São Tomé and Príncipe
41	32	21	36	–31	…	…	…	…	…	…	25,039	–24,627	412	1,420	…	Saudi Arabia
70	10	20	32	–38	3,111	99.7	0.3	179	68.2	31.8	–284.3[4]	174.6[4]	–109.7[4]	160	77	Senegal
…	…	…	…	…	7,416	44.4	55.6	—	—	—	…	…	…	41	…	Serbia and Montenegro
51	27	37	65	–81	132.2	81.6	18.4	23.4	76.3	23.7	–232.4	118.4	–114.0	122	30	Seychelles
81	11	4	14	–10	938	99.4	0.6	7	57.1	42.9	–126.7[7]	0.2[7]	–126.5[7]	57	2	Sierra Leone
39	10	33	—— 18 ——		…	…	…	…	…	…	11,303	9,951	21,254	6,843	3,224	Singapore
50	22	39	64	–75	4,457	29.6	70.4	639	67.9	32.1	–1,109	–46	–1,155	546	439	Slovakia
56	21	25	57	–58	…	…	…	…	…	…	–1,245.2	462.8	–782.4	1,188	544	Slovenia
…	…	…	…	…	120.4	97.2	2.8	5.5	72.7	27.3	54.5	–33.1	21.5	7	9	Solomon Islands
…	…	…	…	…	1,859	98.2	1.8	—	—	—	…	…	…	…	…	Somalia
63	20	16	26	–25	9,148	—	100.0	3,162	78.5	21.5	4,150	–4,683	–533	2,297	1,947	South Africa
62	16	22	29	–20	…	…	…	…	…	…	–30,339	16,623	–13,716	26,651	4,467	Spain
71	10	25	36	–42	8,182	92.6	7.4	401	64.1	35.9	–707.4	214.4	–493.0	212	180	Sri Lanka
91	4	18	6	–19	8,852	84.8	15.2	12	45.8	54.2	–475.9	11.1	–464.8	4	34	Sudan, The
…	…	…	…	…	…	…	…	…	…	…	–27.2[4]	–127.7[4]	–154.9[4]	17	4	Suriname
63	25	34	76	–99	205.5	100.0	—	29.0	64.3	35.7	–110.8	128.0	17.2	40	37	Swaziland
50	27	17	44	–38	…	…	…	…	…	…	15,714	–9,732	5,982	3,572	6,579	Sweden
60	15	21	40	–36	…	…	…	…	…	…	723	28,476	29,199	7,902	6,904	Switzerland
69	11	20	30	–31	16,142	93.3	6.7	206	61.7	38.3	216	–15	201	1,035	545	Syria
61	14	22	49	–47	…	…	…	…	…	…	10,531[4]	–6,803[4]	3,728[4]	3,402	6,500	Taiwan
…	…	…	…	…	594.9	90.7	9.3	22.6	88.7	11.3	–38[3]	–36[3]	–74[3]	…	…	Tajikistan
85	8	15	19	–28	6,595	96.7	3.3	150	59.3	40.7	–876.0	69.1	–806.9	392	407	Tanzania
50	10	24	56	–40	31,011	71.3	28.7	4,255	60.0	40.0	14,013	1,585	12,428	7,048	1,888	Thailand
81	11	14	34	–40	1,263	100.0	—	26	65.4	34.6	–98.0	–29.1	–127.1	13	19	Togo
…	…	…	…	…	63.5	98.0	2.0	4.3	81.4	18.6	–67.1[4]	47.8[4]	–19.3[4]	14	3	Tonga
62	16	26	48	–54	1,485	46.3	53.7	401	74.1	25.9	–740.8[4]	97.3[4]	–643.5[4]	108	75	Trinidad and Tobago
60	16	28	42	–46	9,487	67.5	32.5	1,359	63.8	36.2	–2,141	1,698	–443	1,423	160	Tunisia
67	12	24	24	–27	50,095	25.8	74.2	8,559	64.0	36.0	–10,443	9,083	–1,360	8,088	1,716	Turkey
…	…	…	…	…	1,678	23.7	76.3	449	86.2	13.8	–523.0[4]	–411.5[4]	–934.5[4]	74	125	Turkmenistan
…	…	…	…	…	…	…	…	…	…	…	…	…	…	0.3	…	Tuvalu
83[3]	10[3]	15[3]	12[3]	–21[3]	3,564	98.0	2.0	126	65.1	34.9	–596.4	45.6	–550.8	135	137	Uganda
59	23	21	40	–43	10,027	61.5	38.5	1,277	62.4	37.6	244	1,414	1,658	270	305	Ukraine
45[1]	16[1]	26[1]	77[1]	–65[1]	…	…	…	…	…	…	8,254[3]	–1,553[3]	6,701[3]	535	…	United Arab Emirates
65	18	18	27	–28	…	…	…	…	…	…	–42,350	26,370	–15,980	20,039	27,710	United Kingdom
67	15	20	11	–13	…	…	…	…	…	…	–343,260	11,780	–331,480	73,268	51,220	United States
71	14	16	22	–22	5,108	42.1	57.9	917	61.6	38.4	–868.4	263.4	–605.0	759	264	Uruguay
…	…	…	…	…	3,421	54.8	45.2	461	65.7	34.3	171[4]	–210[4]	–39[4]	19	…	Uzbekistan
49[5]	27[5]	34[5]	47[5]	–57[5]	63.4	100.0	—	1.6	53.1	46.9	–51.5	48.4	–3.1	51	5	Vanuatu
73	8	20	20	–20	25,216	18.9	81.1	4,148	54.6	45.4	7,606	–3,917	3,689	1,086	2,381	Venezuela
71	7	29	42	–49	20,529	82.2	17.8	1,347	75.8	24.2	–981[4]	–86[4]	–1,067[4]	88	…	Vietnam
…	…	…	…	…	…	…	…	…	…	…	…	…	…	601	…	Virgin Islands (U.S.)
…	…	…	…	…	…	…	…	…	…	…	…	…	…	…	…	West Bank
…	…	…	…	…	…	…	…	…	…	…	…	…	…	…	…	Western Sahara
61[3]	16[3]	28[3]	43[3]	–48[3]	3,729	95.3	4.7	100	46.0	54.0	357.9	219.2	577.1	69	81	Yemen
79	16	14	29	–38	4,498	99.3	0.7	416	69.5	30.5	–148[4]	–121[4]	–269[4]	75	59	Zambia
70[3]	17[3]	20[3]	38[3]	–46[3]	3,211	88.7	11.3	480	71.6	28.4	79[4]	–423[4]	–344[4]	230	118	Zimbabwe

[1]1996. [2]Manufacturing includes mining and public utilities. [3]1997. [4]1998. [5]Gross domestic product (GDP). [6]1994. [7]1995. [8]Manufacturing includes mining. [9]Mining includes public utilities. [10]Republic of Cyprus only. [11]Services includes hotels. [12]Excludes Alderney and Sark. [13]Manufacturing includes public utilities. [14]Manufacturing includes mining, construction, and public utilities. [15]Construction includes mining. [16]Transportation, communications includes public utilities. [17]Services includes transportation, communications. [18]1991.

Employment and labour

This table provides international comparisons of the world's national labour forces—giving their size; composition by demographic component and employment status; and structure by industry.

The table focuses on the concept of "economically active population," which the International Labour Organisation (ILO) defines as persons of all ages who are either employed or looking for work. In general, the economically active population does not include students, persons occupied solely in domestic duties, retired persons, persons living entirely on their own means, and persons wholly dependent on others. Persons engaged in illegal economic activities—smugglers, prostitutes, drug dealers, bootleggers, black marketeers, and others—also fall outside the purview of the ILO definition. Countries differ markedly in their treatment, as part of the labour force, of such groups as members of the armed forces, inmates of institutions, the unemployed (both persons seeking their first job and those previously employed), seasonal and international migrant workers, and persons engaged in informal, subsistence, or part-time economic activities. Some countries include all or most of these groups among the economically active, while others may treat the same groups as inactive.

Three principal structural comparisons of the economically active total are given in the first part of the table: (1) participation rate, or the proportion of the economically active who possess some particular characteristic, is given for women and for those of working age (usually ages 15 to 64), (2) activity rate, the proportion of the total population who *are* economically active, is given for both sexes and as a total, and (3) employment status, usually (and here) grouped as employers, self-employed, employees, family workers (usually unpaid), and others.

Each of these measures indicates certain characteristics in a given national labour market; none should be interpreted in isolation, however, as the meaning of each is influenced by a variety of factors—demographic structure and change, social or religious customs, educational opportunity, sexual differentiation in employment patterns, degree of technological development, and the like. Participation and activity rates, for example, may be high in a particular country because it possesses an older population with few children, hence a higher proportion of working age, or because, despite a young population with many below working age, the economy attracts eligible immigrant workers, themselves almost exclusively of working age. At the same time, low activity and participation rates might be characteristic of a country having a young population with poor employment possibilities or of a country with a good job market distorted by the presence of large numbers of "guest" or contract workers who are not part of the domestic labour force. An illiterate woman in a strongly sex-differentiated labour force is likely to begin and end as a family or

Employment and labour

country	year	economically active population										distribution by economic sector			
		total ('000)	participation rate (%)		activity rate (%)			employment status (%)				agriculture, forestry, fishing		manufacturing; mining, quarrying; public utilities	
			female	ages 15–64	total	male	female	employers, self-employed	employees	unpaid family workers	other	number ('000)	% of econ. active	number ('000)	% of econ. active
Afghanistan	1979	3,941	7.9	49.1	30.3	54.2	4.9	52.2	33.8	14.0	—	2,369	60.1	494	12.5
Albania	1994	1,340	47.0[3]	92.0[3, 4]	57.4[3]	60.8[3]	54.0[3]	…	…	…	…	534	39.9	84[5]	6.3[5]
Algeria	1987	5,341	9.2	44.3	23.6	42.4	4.4	16.8	61.7	2.6	18.9	725	13.6	622	11.6
American Samoa	1990	14.2	41.1	52.6[8]	30.4	34.8	25.7	2.1	92.6	0.2	5.1	0.3	2.3	4.8	33.7
Andorra	1989	25	45.6	74.3	55.1	…	…	…	…	…	…	0.3	1.2	2.7	11.0
Angola	1996	4,581	37.3	65.1[10]	40.0	50.8	29.5	…	…	…	…	3,170	69.2	528	11.5[11]
Antigua and Barbuda	1991	26.8	45.6	69.7	45.1	50.9	39.6	12.1	82.8	0.7	4.4	1.0	3.9	1.9	7.3
Argentina	1995	14,345	36.7	64.5	41.5	53.5	29.9	28.0[13]	60.4[13]	5.0[13]	6.6[13]	1,201[14]	12.0[14]	2,136[14]	21.3[14]
Armenia	1996	1,584	…	75.1[16]	42.1	…	…	…	…	…	…	587	37.1	255	16.1
Aruba	1991	31.1	42.5	67.1	46.7	54.5	39.0	7.0	86.4	0.3	6.3	0.2	0.5	2.3	7.3
Australia	1998[18]	9,343	43.3	73.3[19]	49.8	56.6	43.0	12.7	78.2	0.7	8.4	442	4.7	1,311	14.0
Austria	1998[18]	3,888	43.1	70.7	48.1	56.5	40.3	9.7[20]	87.4[20]	3.0[20]	—	246	6.3	842	21.6
Azerbaijan	1998	3,744	47.8	64.4[16, 20]	47.1	50.1	44.2	…	…	…	…	1,085	29.0	367	9.8
Bahamas, The	1994	139	47.5	77.8	50.7	54.8	46.8	11.6[22]	85.1[22]	0.3[22]	3.0[22]	6.9	5.0	7.3	5.3
Bahrain	1991	226	17.5	66.8	44.6	63.5	18.5	5.1	88.5	0.1	6.3	5	2.3	33	14.6
Bangladesh	1995–96[18]	56,014	38.1	73.7	46.0	55.8	35.7	28.8	12.1	39.1	20.0	34,530	61.6	4,211	7.5
Barbados	1995[18]	137	49.5	79.9	51.8	54.6	49.1	8.8[24]	76.4[24]	0.2[24]	14.6[24]	6.3	4.6	15.6	11.4
Belarus	1999	4,542	52.4	78.2[16]	45.3	46.0	44.7	…	…	…	…	672	14.8	1,258	27.7
Belgium	1992	4,237	42.3	51.5[25]	42.2	49.8	34.9	12.7	72.4	3.4	11.5	95	2.2	788	18.6
Belize	1996	75.5	30.8	58.5[26]	34.1	47.2	21.0	26.2[20]	59.2[20]	4.9[20]	9.8[20]	18.3[13]	31.4[13]	7.0[13]	12.0[13]
Benin	1992	2,085	42.6	73.4	43.0	50.6	35.7	58.4	5.3	30.5	5.8	1,148	55.0	162	7.8
Bermuda	1995	34.1	50.0	63.5[13]	55.8	57.4	54.4	9.7[13]	84.0[13]	0.1[13]	6.2[13]	0.5	1.5	1.4	4.2
Bhutan	…	…	…	…	…	…	…	…	…	…	…	…	…	…	…
Bolivia	1992	2,530	38.2	64.0	39.4	48.7	30.4	41.2	31.5	7.1	20.2	984	38.9	281	11.1
Bosnia and Herzegovina	1990[5]	1,026	36.9	…	22.7	…	…	…	…	…	…	39	3.8	519	50.5
Botswana	1995	440	46.6	65.4	29.9	33.1	27.0	7.9	62.7	7.9	21.5	54	12.2	47	10.8
Brazil	1997	75,213	40.4	66.9	48.2	58.7	38.1	26.3[22]	62.3[22]	7.7[22]	3.7[22]	16,771	22.3	9,281	12.3
Brunei	1991	112	32.9	67.6	43.0	54.6	30.0	3.5	91.4	0.4	4.7	2.2	1.9	11.6	10.4
Bulgaria	1995	3,738	48.4[28]	68.8[28]	46.3[28]	48.7[28]	44.1[28]	8.4	75.9	0.9	14.8	783	20.9	1,003	26.8
Burkina Faso	1995	5,250	45.5	75.8[10]	50.9	56.0	45.9	…	…	…	…	4,397	83.8	298	5.7[11]
Burundi	1990	2,780	52.6	91.4	52.5	51.2	53.8	62.8	5.1	30.3	1.8	2,574	92.6	37	1.3
Cambodia	1993	4,010	55.8	86.2	43.1	39.5	46.4	…	…	…	…	2,454[14]	74.4[14]	220[11, 14]	6.7[11, 14]
Cameroon	1991	4,740	33.2	58.9[10]	40.0	53.9	26.3	60.2[22]	14.6[22]	18.0[22]	7.1[22]	2,856	60.3	628[11]	13.2[11]
Canada	1998[18]	15,631	45.3	75.4	51.0	56.3	45.9	15.8	75.5	0.4	8.3	586	3.7	2,601	16.6
Cape Verde	1990	121	37.1	64.3	35.3	46.9	24.9	24.7	53.7	2.0	19.6	29.9	24.8	6.8	5.7
Central African Republic	1988	1,187	46.8	78.3	48.2	52.2	44.3	75.3	8.0	8.1	8.6	881	74.2	31	2.6
Chad	1991	2,016	18.2	51.6[10]	35.3	56.5	14.7	…	…	…	…	1,489	73.9	149[11]	7.4[11]
Chile	1998[18]	5,852	33.4	59.9	39.3	52.8	26.0	26.4[19]	64.6[19]	3.2[19]	5.8[19]	809	13.8	1,015	17.3
China	1990	657,290	44.9	85.0	57.9	61.8	53.7	…	…	…	…	467,926	71.2	87,275	13.3
Colombia	1985	9,558	32.8	49.4[29]	34.3	46.6	22.3	…	…	…	…	2,412[14]	28.5[14]	1,231[14]	14.5[14]
Comoros	1996	252	38.9	59.2	37.2	44.8	29.3	47.6[14]	25.6[14]	— 26.8[14] —		189	74.7	18[11]	7.1[11]
Congo, Dem. Rep. of the	1996	14,082	35.0	47.9[10]	31.1	40.9	21.6	…	…	…	…	9,124	64.8	2,267[11]	16.1[11]
Congo, Rep. of the	1984	563	45.6	54.0	29.5	33.0	26.2	64.3	31.4	1.2	3.1	294	52.2	50	8.8
Costa Rica	1998	1,377	32.6	59.7[25]	41.2	55.8	26.7	24.0[19]	72.2[19]	3.3[19]	0.6[19]	271	19.7	231	16.8
Côte d'Ivoire	1988	4,263	32.3	66.6	39.4	52.2	26.0	…	…	…	…	2,628	61.6	100	2.3
Croatia	1991	2,040	42.9	65.2	45.3	53.9	37.4	12.7	73.7	2.0	11.6	341	16.7	571	28.0
Cuba	1988	4,570	36.1	56.9[25]	44.2	56.2	32.1	5.7[30]	94.1[30]	0.2[30]	—	791[30]	22.3[30]	668[30]	18.9[30]
Cyprus[31, 32]	1995	303	38.6	71.5	47.0	57.8	36.2	18.7[28]	73.1[28]	6.1[28]	2.1[28]	31	10.1	48	15.9
Czech Republic	1997	5,215	44.1	72.5	50.6	58.2	43.5	12.8	81.6	0.4	5.2	296	5.7	1,617	31.0
Denmark	1998	2,848	46.3	80.3	53.7	58.3	49.2	8.7	85.8	—	5.5	103	3.6	572	20.1
Djibouti	1996	396	41.4	96.3[10]	67.2	79.7	55.0	…	…	…	…	288	72.7	56[11]	14.1[11]
Dominica	1991	26.4	34.5	62.4	38.0	50.0	26.1	29.2[33]	50.6[33]	1.9[33]	18.3[33]	7.3	27.9	2.3	8.8
Dominican Republic	1981	1,915	28.9	53.6	33.9	48.1	19.7	36.5	51.3	3.3	8.9	420	22.0	243	12.7
East Timor	…	…	…	…	…	…	…	…	…	…	…	…	…	…	…
Ecuador	1990	3,360	26.4	55.7	34.8	51.5	18.3	45.7	42.5	4.4	7.4	1,036	30.8	404	12.0
Egypt	1995[18]	17,725	22.0	49.8	29.9	45.9	13.4	24.7[28]	50.0[28]	16.4[28]	9.0[28]	5,221	30.2	2,405	13.9
El Salvador	1997	2,256	36.7	61.4	38.2	50.2	27.0	31.7	48.5	7.4	12.4	607	26.9	373	16.5
Equatorial Guinea	1983	103	35.7	66.7	39.2	52.5	26.9	29.0	16.0	29.9	25.1	59.4	57.9	1.8	1.8
Eritrea	…	…	…	…	…	…	…	…	…	…	…	…	…	…	…
Estonia	1998	711	47.7	71.8[34]	48.9	54.9	43.6	4.8[19]	85.2[19]	0.8[19]	9.2[19]	61	8.6	165	23.2

traditional agricultural worker. Loss of working-age men to war, civil violence, or emigration for job opportunities may also affect the structure of a particular labour market.

The distribution of the economically active population by employment status reveals that a large percentage of economically active persons in some less developed countries falls under the heading "employers, self-employed." This occurs because the countries involved have poor, largely agrarian economies in which the average worker is a farmer who tills his own small plot of land. In countries with well-developed economies, "employees" will usually constitute the largest portion of the economically active.

Caution should be exercised when using the economically active data to make intercountry comparisons, as countries often differ in their choices of classification schemes, definitions, and coverage of groups and in their methods of collection and tabulation of data. The population base containing the economically active population, for example, may range, in developing countries, from age 9 or 10 with no upper limit to, in developed countries, age 18 or 19 upward to a usual retirement age of from 55 to 65, with sometimes a different range for each sex. Data on female labour-force participation, in particular, often lack comparability. In many less developed countries, particularly those dominated by the Islamic faith, a cultural bias favouring traditional roles for women results in the undercounting of economically active women. In other less developed countries, particularly those in which subsistence workers are deemed economically active, the role of women may be overstated.

The second major section of the table provides data on the distribution by economic (also conventionally called industrial) sector of the economically active population. The data usually include such groups as unpaid family workers, members of the armed forces, and the unemployed, the last distributed by industry as far as possible.

The categorization of industrial sectors is based on the divisions listed in the *International Standard Industrial Classification of All Economic Activities*. The "other" category includes persons whose activities were not adequately defined and the unemployed who were not distributable by industrial sector.

A substantial part of the data presented in this table is summarized from various issues of the ILO's *Year Book of Labour Statistics*, which compiles its statistics both from official publications and from information submitted directly by national census and labour authorities. The editors have supplemented and updated ILO statistical data with information from Britannica's holdings of relevant official publications and from direct correspondence with national authorities.

construction		transportation, communications		trade, hotels, restaurants		finance, real estate		public administration, defense		services		other		country
number ('000)	% of econ. active	number ('000)	% of econ. active	number ('000)	% of econ. active	number ('000)	% of econ. active	number ('000)	% of econ. active	number ('000)	% of econ. active	number ('000)	% of econ. active	
51	1.3	66	1.6	138	3.5	[1]	[1]	[1]	[1]	749[1]	19.0[1]	78[2]	2.0[2]	Afghanistan
33[5]	2.5[5]	19[5]	1.4[5]	3[5]	0.2[5]	3[5]	0.2[5]	16[5]	1.2[5]	145[5]	10.8[5]	505[6]	37.7[6]	Albania
690	12.9	216	4.1	391	7.3	143	2.7	[7]	[7]	1,180[7]	22.1[7]	1,374	25.7	Algeria
1.2	8.3	0.8	5.5	1.8	13.0	0.3	2.1	1.4	10.0	2.8	19.8	0.7[9]	5.1[9]	American Samoa
2.9	11.8	...	...	6.0	24.2	1.3	5.4	2.6	10.3	4.1	16.7	0.1	0.5	Andorra
[11]	[11]	[12]	[12]	[12]	[12]	[12]	[12]	[12]	[12]	883[12]	19.3[12]	—	—	Angola
3.1	11.6	2.4	9.0	8.5	31.9	1.5	5.4	[7]	[7]	6.4[7]	23.9[7]	1.9	7.0	Antigua and Barbuda
1,003[14]	10.0[14]	460[14]	4.6[14]	1,702[14]	17.0[14]	396[14]	3.9[14]	[7]	[7]	2,399[7, 14]	23.9[7, 14]	736[14, 15]	7.3[14, 15]	Argentina
68	4.3	24	1.5	110	6.9	[1]	[1]	[1]	[1]	350[1]	22.1[1]	190[17]	12.0[17]	Armenia
3.2	10.4	2.3	7.5	11.0	35.4	2.4	7.8	[7]	[7]	8.6[7]	27.7[7]	1.1[17]	3.5[17]	Aruba
654	7.0	567	6.1	2,279	24.4	1,310	14.0	444	4.7	1,884	20.2	454[17]	4.9[17]	Australia
341	8.8	250	6.4	844	21.7	387	9.9	256	6.6	712	18.3	12[2]	0.3[2]	Austria
150	4.0	167	4.5	772	20.6	10	0.3	[7]	[7]	618[7]	16.5[7]	574[21]	15.3[21]	Azerbaijan
11.6	8.3	11.2	8.1	44.2	31.8	12.9	9.3	10.7	7.7	29.7	21.4	4.5[23]	3.2[23]	Bahamas, The
27	11.8	14	6.1	30	13.2	17	7.6	41	18.1	43	19.0	16[17]	7.3[17]	Bahrain
1,015	1.8	2,308	4.1	6,068	10.8	213	0.4	[7]	[7]	5,092[7]	9.1[7]	2,585[17]	4.6[17]	Bangladesh
12.2	8.9	5.9	4.3	35.3	25.8	8.4	6.1	[7]	[7]	48.8[7]	35.7[7]	4.3[2]	3.1[2]	Barbados
336	7.4	332	7.3	504	11.1	[1]	[1]	[1]	[1]	1,345[1]	29.6[1]	95[9]	2.1[9]	Belarus
245	5.8	257	6.1	634	15.0	342	8.1	7	7	1,393[7]	32.9[7]	484[17]	11.4[17]	Belgium
4.1[13]	7.0[13]	2.9[13]	5.0[13]	10.0[13]	17.2[13]	1.8[13]	3.1[13]	5.4[13]	9.2[13]	6.0[13]	10.3[13]	2.8[13]	4.8[13]	Belize
52	2.5	53	2.5	433	20.7	3	0.1	[7]	[7]	165[7]	7.9[7]	71[21]	3.4[21]	Benin
1.7	5.0	2.2	6.4	10.8	31.6	5.2	15.3	[7]	[7]	12.3[7]	35.9[7]	—	—	Bermuda
...	...	...	...	...	...	...	...	...	...	...	...	...	...	Bhutan
129	5.1	117	4.6	232	9.2	54	2.1	59	2.3	350	13.8	323[15]	12.7[15]	Bolivia
75	7.3	69	6.7	131	12.8	39	3.8	[7]	[7]	155[7]	15.1[7]	—	—	Bosnia and Herzegovina
41	9.3	8	1.8	54	12.3	12	2.7	60	13.6	69	15.7	95[17]	21.6[17]	Botswana
4,583	6.1	2,759	3.7	9,223[27]	12.3[27]	1,287	1.7	[7]	[7]	25,436[7, 27]	33.8[7, 27]	5,882[9]	7.8[9]	Brazil
14.1	12.6	5.4	4.8	15.4	13.8	5.8	5.2	[7]	[7]	52.1[7]	46.6[7]	5.3[17]	4.7[17]	Brunei
188	5.0	251	6.7	357	9.5	51	1.4	76	2.0	532	14.2	497[17]	13.3[17]	Bulgaria
[11]	[11]	[12]	[12]	[12]	[12]	[12]	[12]	[12]	[12]	558[12]	10.6[12]	—	—	Burkina Faso
20	0.7	9	0.3	26	0.9	2.0	0.1	[7]	[7]	85[7]	3.1[7]	27[17]	1.0[17]	Burundi
[11]	[11]	[12]	[12]	[12]	[12]	[12]	[12]	[12]	[12]	625[12, 14]	18.9[12, 14]	—	—	Cambodia
[11]	[11]	[12]	[12]	[12]	[12]	[12]	[12]	[12]	[12]	1,256[12]	26.5[12]	—	—	Cameroon
857	5.5	1,128	7.2	3,585	22.9	2,336	14.9	820	5.2	3,252	20.8	468[2]	3.0[2]	Canada
22.7	18.8	6.1	5.1	12.7	10.6	0.8	0.7	[7]	[7]	17.4[7]	14.4[7]	24.1	20.0	Cape Verde
6	0.5	7	0.6	92	7.8	0.7	0.1	[7]	[7]	70[7]	5.9[7]	100[17]	8.5[17]	Central African Republic
[11]	[11]	[12]	[12]	[12]	[12]	[12]	[12]	[12]	[12]	377[12]	18.7[12]	—	—	Chad
533	9.1	456	7.8	1,075	18.4	437	7.5	[7]	[7]	1,478[7]	25.3[7]	47[15]	0.8[15]	Chile
11,890	1.8	11,814	1.8	25,631	3.9	8,268	1.3	[7]	[7]	34,053[7]	5.2[7]	10,434	1.6	China
242[14]	2.9[14]	353[14]	4.2[14]	1,262[14]	14.9[14]	278[14]	3.3[14]	[7]	[7]	1,998[7, 14]	23.6[7, 14]	691[14, 15]	8.2[14, 15]	Colombia
[11]	[11]	[12]	[12]	[12]	[12]	[12]	[12]	[12]	[12]	46[12]	18.2[12]	—	—	Comoros
[11]	[11]	[12]	[12]	[12]	[12]	[12]	[12]	[12]	[12]	2,691[12]	19.1[12]	—	—	Congo, Dem. Rep. of the
25	4.5	29	5.1	67	11.0	3	0.5	[7]	[7]	85[7]	15.1[7]	10	2.0	Congo, Rep. of the
89	6.5	75	5.5	267	19.4	35	2.6	[7]	[7]	385[7]	27.9[7]	23[23]	1.7[23]	Costa Rica
85	2.0	118	2.8	530	12.4	[1]	[1]	[1]	[1]	591[1]	13.9[1]	210[2]	4.9[2]	Côte d'Ivoire
93	4.5	112	5.5	223	10.9	58	2.8	104	5.1	204	10.0	329[17]	16.1[17]	Croatia
313[30]	8.8[30]	249[30]	7.0[30]	306[30]	8.6[30]	[1]	[1]	[1]	[1]	1,086[1, 30]	30.7[1, 30]	128[30]	3.6[30]	Cuba
26	8.7	19	6.2	77	25.4	23	7.6	[7]	[7]	65[7]	21.6[7]	13	4.4	Cyprus[31, 32]
501	9.6	392	7.5	871	16.7	358	6.9	328	6.3	762	14.6	90[17]	1.7[17]	Czech Republic
185	6.5	191	6.7	467	16.4	321	11.3	175	6.1	821	28.8	18[23]	0.6[23]	Denmark
[11]	[11]	[12]	[12]	[12]	[12]	[12]	[12]	[12]	[12]	52[12]	13.2[12]	—	—	Djibouti
2.8	10.7	1.2	4.6	3.7	13.9	0.8	3.1	1.5	5.8	3.4	13.1	3.2[17]	12.3[17]	Dominica
81	4.3	40	2.1	192	10.0	22	1.2	[7]	[7]	363[7]	18.9[7]	553[15]	28.9[15]	Dominican Republic
...	...	...	...	...	...	...	...	...	...	...	...	...	...	East Timor
197	5.9	131	3.9	477	14.2	81	2.4	[7]	[7]	838[7]	24.9[7]	196[15]	5.8[15]	Ecuador
984	5.7	912	5.3	1,609	9.3	286	1.7	[7]	[7]	4,000[7]	23.2[7]	1,050[23]	10.8[23]	Egypt
159	7.1	103	4.6	462	20.5	32	1.4	[7]	[7]	485[7]	21.5[7]	36[2]	1.6[2]	El Salvador
1.9	1.9	1.8	1.7	3.1	3.0	0.4	0.4	[7]	[7]	8.4[7]	8.2[7]	25.8[17]	25.2[17]	Equatorial Guinea
...	...	...	...	...	...	...	...	...	...	...	...	...	...	Eritrea
48	6.8	60	8.4	105	14.8	44	6.2	37	5.2	122	17.2	68[9]	9.6[9]	Estonia

Employment and labour (continued)

country	year	economically active population										distribution by economic sector			
		total ('000)	participation rate (%)		activity rate (%)			employment status (%)				agriculture, forestry, fishing		manufacturing; mining, quarrying; public utilities	
			female	ages 15–64	total	male	female	employers, self-employed	employees	unpaid family workers	other	number ('000)	% of econ. active	number ('000)	% of econ. active
Ethiopia	1995	24,606	41.1	72.2	43.3	50.3	36.5	58.5[35]	6.5[35]	34.0[35]	1.0[35]	21,605	87.8	419	1.7
Faroe Islands	1977	17.6	27.2	64.0	41.9	58.2	23.9	11.9	86.1	...	2.0	3.3	18.8	3.9	21.9
Fiji	1986	241	21.2	56.0	33.7	52.4	14.5	33.6	42.2	16.3	7.9	106	44.1	22	9.0
Finland	1998	2,532	47.0	73.1	49.1	53.4	45.1	11.9	75.2	0.6	12.3	154	6.1	508	20.1
France	1994[18]	25,871	44.9	67.7	44.8	50.6	39.2	10.2	77.4	—	12.4	1,048	4.1	4,432	17.4
French Guiana	1990	48.8	38.2	67.3	42.5	50.5	33.9	10.6	62.7	2.5	24.2	4.2	8.6	3.1	6.4
French Polynesia	1988	75	37.1	64.8	39.9	48.2	30.9	13.0	55.0	4.0	28.0	7.6	10.0	5.4	7.2
Gabon	1991	504	36.9	56.0[10]	43.9	53.9	30.7	...	...	...	...	338	67.1	71[11]	14.1[11]
Gambia, The	1983	326	46.3	78.2	47.3	51.1	43.6	0.5	78.0	14.3	7.1	240	73.7	9	2.9
Gaza Strip	1996	173	9.0	36.3[25]	18.0	32.0	3.2	15.7	46.8	6.7	30.8	9.0	5.2	17.0[36]	9.8[36]
Georgia	1993	1,920	...	58.1[16, 28]	35.7	...	...	...	...	...	...	562	29.3	303	15.8
Germany	1998	39,709	43.1	70.7	48.4	56.5	40.7	9.1	80.3	1.0	9.6	1,200	3.0	10,019	25.2
Ghana	1984	5,580	51.2	82.5[25]	45.4	44.9	45.8	67.7	15.7	12.2	4.4	3,311	59.3	631	11.3
Greece	1997[18]	4,294	39.2	61.3	40.9	53.0	31.5	29.9	49.2	10.7	10.2	773	18.0	680	15.8
Greenland	1976	21.4	33.4	63.5[25]	43.1	53.0	31.4	12.6	82.5	0.4	4.5	3.2	15.1	3.3	15.3
Grenada	1988	38.9	48.6	72.7[35]	39.9	42.9	37.2	16.0[30]	64.2[30]	0.8[30]	19.0[30]	5.6	14.3	3.3	8.6
Guadeloupe	1990	172	45.5	66.4	44.5	49.6	39.7	13.2	53.7	2.0	31.1	8.4	4.9	9.6	5.6
Guam	1990	66.1	37.4	75.7[8]	49.7	58.4	39.7	2.4	94.4	0.1	3.1	0.5	0.8	3.5	5.3
Guatemala	1999	3,489	22.0	55.0	31.5	48.6	14.0	32.7[33]	47.6[33]	16.2[33]	3.5[33]	1,416[33]	48.9[33]	405[33]	14.0[33]
Guernsey[38]	1996	30.7	44.7	76.4	52.3	60.1	45.1	13.0	87.0	—	—	1.9	6.2	2.5	8.2
Guinea	1983	1,823	39.4	63.5	39.1	48.7	30.1	36.2	15.6	37.6	10.6	1,424	78.1	27	1.5
Guinea-Bissau	1995	491	39.9	65.5[10]	45.8	55.9	36.0	...	...	...	...	373	76.0	20[11]	4.1[11]
Guyana	1992–93	278	34.1	61.8	38.8	51.9	26.0	14.3[14]	63.8[14]	1.9[14]	20.0[14]	50[14]	20.4[14]	41[14]	16.8[14]
Haiti	1990	2,679	40.0	64.8	41.1	50.3	32.3	59.1	16.5	10.4	14.0	1,535	57.3	178	6.6
Honduras	1998[18]	2,135	36.9	61.2[25]	36.9	49.2	25.0	40.6	48.0	11.4	—	738	34.6	380	17.8
Hong Kong	1998[18]	3,359	39.3	70.0	51.1	61.9	40.3	9.9[19]	87.4[19]	0.7[19]	1.9[19]	10	0.3	434	12.9
Hungary	1998[18]	4,011	44.4	58.4	39.3	45.8	33.4	10.6	80.3	0.7	8.4	301	7.5	1,115	27.8
Iceland	1998	152.1	47.1	86.6[8]	55.4	59.2	52.2	17.3	80.3	0.3	2.1	12.8	8.4	27.1	17.8
India	1991	314,131	28.6	60.7[25, 30]	37.5	51.6	22.3	8.8[30]	16.3[30]	3.6[30]	71.3[30]	191,341	60.9	30,423	9.7
Indonesia	1998	92,735	38.8	65.3[25]	45.4	55.8	35.0	42.7[34]	33.0[34]	17.1[34]	7.2[34]	39,415	42.5	10,756	11.6
Iran	1996–97	16,027	12.7	46.8[13]	26.7	45.8	6.9	39.7[13]	45.4[13]	2.3[13]	12.6[13]	3,205[13]	21.8[13]	2,243[13]	15.2[13]
Iraq	1988	4,127	12.0	45.3	24.7	42.3	6.1	25.4[39]	59.5[39]	11.4[39]	3.7[39]	477	11.6	439	10.6
Ireland	1997	1,539	39.1	62.7	42.0	51.6	32.6	17.4	71.1	1.1	10.4	145	9.4	314	20.4
Isle of Man	1991	33.2	42.3	73.2	47.6	56.9	38.9	15.8	80.1	—	4.1	1.2	3.7	3.9	11.6
Israel	1998[18]	2,272	44.3	53.5[25]	40.3	45.2	35.5	13.2	77.7	0.5	8.6	50	2.3	434	19.1
Italy	1994[18]	22,680	36.9	57.4	40.1	52.1	28.8	21.4	62.8	4.0	11.8	1,573	6.9	4,837	21.3
Jamaica	1998	1,129	45.6	69.3[40]	43.9	48.7	39.2	32.3	49.9	1.9	15.9	218[19]	20.0[19]	107[19]	9.8[19]
Japan	1998	67,930	40.7	72.6	53.7	65.1	42.9	11.2	79.0	5.4	4.4	3,440	5.1	14,620	21.5
Jersey	1991	47.5	43.2	66.9[25]	56.5	66.1	47.5	12.6	84.0	...	3.4	2.2	4.7	3.8	8.0
Jordan	1993	859	11.4[42]	43.2[42]	22.2	...	...	22.8[43]	67.2[43]	0.8[43]	9.2[43]	55	6.4	97	11.3
Kazakhstan	1995	6,976	...	71.8[16, 20]	40.8	...	...	...	...	...	...	1,442	20.7	1,372	19.7
Kenya	1996	12,269	38.5	63.6[10]	43.9	53.9	33.8	...	...	...	...	9,100	74.2	1,062[11]	8.7[11]
Kiribati	1990	32.6	46.4	75.6[25]	45.1	48.9	41.4	71.9	25.3	...	2.8	23.1	71.0	0.9	2.8
Korea, North	1985	9,084	46.0	75.3	44.6	48.6	40.6	...	...	...	...	3,726[24]	44.1[24]	2,790[11, 24]	33.0[11, 24]
Korea, South	1998[18]	21,390	39.8	60.7[25]	45.9	54.9	36.8	26.8	57.0	9.3	6.8	2,450	11.5	4,246	19.9
Kuwait	1997	1,217	23.5	61.5[42]	55.1	69.0	33.2	3.9[42]	94.1[42]	0.1[42]	1.9[42]	9[42]	1.3[42]	69[42]	9.4[42]
Kyrgyzstan	1998	1,705	46.1	...	37.2	41.1	33.5	...	...	...	...	831	48.7	104	6.1
Laos	1995	2,166	56.4	83.3	47.3	46.2	52.8	...	...	...	...	1,393[14]	75.7[14]	130[11, 14]	7.1[11, 14]
Latvia	1997	1,186	48.1	70.2	48.0	54.0	42.9	11.1	69.3	5.0	14.6	203	17.1	233	19.6
Lebanon	1997	1,362	21.6	49.3	34.0	55.2	14.2	...	...	...	...	132[44]	19.1[44]	131[44]	18.9[44]
Lesotho	1986	504	27.0	44.0	31.6	47.3	16.7	16.8	55.7	20.5	7.0	131	25.9	142	28.2
Liberia	1984	704	41.0	56.3	33.5	39.1	27.8	59.1	21.6	14.4	5.0	481	68.3	31	4.4
Libya	1991	1,169	9.3	37.1[10]	24.8	42.9	4.9	...	...	...	...	129	11.0	372[11]	31.8[11]
Liechtenstein	1996	16.2	40.3	71.3	52.0	63.7	40.8	6.4	90.8	0.1	2.7	0.3	2.0	4.9	30.2
Lithuania	1998	1,835	47.9	71.7[26]	49.5	54.8	44.9	14.1	69.1	0.2	16.6	317	17.2	411	22.4
Luxembourg	1991[45]	168	36.5	62.5	43.5	56.4	31.2	9.2	85.3	1.1	4.4	5	3.2	26	15.8
Macau	1998[18]	210.7	35.3	70.7[40]	50.2	58.2	43.0	8.0	85.9	1.6	4.5	0.4	0.2	44.5	21.1
Macedonia	1996	789	39.1	60.6	39.6	48.1	31.1	...	...	...	...	103	13.0	165	20.9
Madagascar	1996	5,984	38.2	58.7	39.2	48.9	29.8	...	...	...	...	4,381	73.2	926[11]	15.5[11]
Malawi	1987	3,458	51.0	89.4	43.3	43.9	42.8	4.9	16.2	77.6	1.3	2,968	85.8	114	3.3
Malaysia	1998[18]	8,884	33.5	64.4	40.1	52.0	27.5	21.1[20]	71.4[20]	7.5[20]	—	1,617	18.2	1,986	22.4
Maldives	1990	56.4	19.9	50.2	26.5	41.3	10.8	39.7	49.3	4.5	6.5	14.1	25.0	9.4	16.6
Mali	1987	3,438	37.4	67.4	44.7	57.2	32.7	35.4	5.2	57.6	1.8	2,803	81.5	191	5.6
Malta	1990	132	25.4	47.4[13]	37.2	56.1	18.7	14.1[48]	77.4[48]	...	8.5[48]	3	2.5	38	28.8
Marshall Islands	1988	11.5	30.1	54.1[28]	26.5	37.7	14.8	21.6	58.9	7.1	12.5	2.2	18.7	1.0	9.0
Martinique	1990	165	47.5	68.1	45.9	49.8	42.2	9.5	56.9	1.5	32.1	8.4	5.1	9.7	5.9
Mauritania	1995	704	23.0	44.3[10]	31.0	48.1	14.1	...	...	...	...	437	62.1	84[11]	11.9[11]
Mauritius[49]	1995	484	32.9	63.5	42.9	58.1	28.0	15.1	72.9	2.1	9.9	65	13.5	142	29.4
Mayotte	1991	27.3	29.4	56.4	28.9	39.2	17.7	12.0	42.9	7.3	37.8	3.1	11.4	1.3	4.7
Mexico	1998	39,507	33.7	65.4	41.3	56.1	27.2	30.1[20]	53.8[20]	13.6[20]	2.6[20]	7,842	19.8	7,473	18.9
Micronesia	1990	30.5	29.8[14]	60.6	30.3	...	...	2.7[14]	74.4[14]	0.1[14]	22.7[14]	12.7	41.5	1.6	5.2
Moldova	1996	1,686	...	68.7[16, 19]	39.1	...	...	...	...	...	...	711	42.2	195	11.6
Monaco	1990	12.6	39.7	...	42.0	53.2	31.8	17.4	75.1	0.3	7.2	—	0.3	2.7	21.8
Mongolia	1998	841	48.0	64.3[51]	36.7	38.8	34.6	...	...	...	...	300[20]	35.5[20]	124[20]	14.7[20]
Morocco	1982	5,999	19.7	48.9	29.3	47.1	11.6	27.1	40.5	17.6	14.8	2,352	39.2	1,016	16.9
Mozambique	1996	9,318	46.3	83.2[10]	56.3	61.1	51.5	...	...	...	...	7,360	79.0	987[11]	10.6[11]
Myanmar (Burma)	1997–98[18]	18,337	35.3[48]	64.2[48]	40.2[48]	52.4[48]	28.2[48]	41.4[48]	27.4[48]	30.2[48]	1.0[48]	12,093	65.9	1,831	9.9
Namibia	1991	494	43.6	61.3	35.2	39.9	30.5	17.8	49.1	17.9	15.2	190	38.5	41	8.2
Nauru	1977	2.2	...	...	30.5	...	...	...	...	...	...	...	...	...	...
Nepal	1991	7,340	40.4	57.0[10]	40.0	47.8	32.2	75.8	21.4	2.3	0.4	5,962	81.2	164	2.2
Netherlands, The	1998	7,735	42.5	72.9	49.3	57.2	41.5	10.0	84.8	0.8	4.4	236	3.1	1,162	15.0
Netherlands Antilles	1992	87.8	45.1	68.6	46.3	53.1	40.1	...	...	...	...	0.5	0.6	8.4	9.6
New Caledonia	1989	66	37.5	70.7[53]	40.2	49.1	30.8	16.3	64.3	1.6	17.8	7.8	11.8	6.2	9.3
New Zealand	1998[18]	1,864	45.0	74.0	49.2	54.9	43.6	18.1[20]	73.6[20]	0.8[20]	7.5[20]	161	8.6	326	17.5
Nicaragua	1998	1,630	29.5	61.2	34.1	48.9	19.8	...	...	...	...	457[28]	31.4[28]	183[28]	12.5[28]

construction		transportation, communications		trade, hotels, restaurants		finance, real estate		public administration, defense		services		other		country
number ('000)	% of econ. active	number ('000)	% of econ. active	number ('000)	% of econ. active	number ('000)	% of econ. active	number ('000)	% of econ. active	number ('000)	% of econ. active	number ('000)	% of econ. active	
61	0.2	103	0.4	936	3.8	19	0.1	[7]	[7]	1,252[7]	5.1[7]	210[2]	0.9[2]	Ethiopia
2.0	11.1	1.9	11.1	2.1	11.9	0.3	1.9	[7]	[7]	3.5[7]	20.1[7]	0.6	3.2	Faroe Islands
12	4.9	13	5.5	26	10.8	6	2.5	[7]	[7]	37[7]	15.2[7]	20[17]	8.2[17]	Fiji
163	6.4	178	7.0	366	14.5	269	10.6	148	5.8	653	25.8	95[23]	3.8[23]	Finland
1,443	5.7	1,397	5.5	3,716	14.6	2,340	9.2	[7]	[7]	7,733[7]	30.3[7]	3,376[17]	13.2[17]	France
4.4	9.1	1.9	3.8	4.2	8.5	1.7	3.5	[7]	[7]	17.5[7]	35.9[7]	11.8[9]	24.2[9]	French Guiana
5.5	7.4	2.8	3.7	10.3	13.7	1.2	1.5	[7]	[7]	21.5[7]	28.6[7]	21.1[17]	28.0[17]	French Polynesia
[11]	[11]	[12]	[12]	[12]	[12]	[12]	[12]	[12]	[12]	95[12]	18.8[12]	—	—	Gabon
4	1.3	8	2.5	17	5.1	5	1.4	8	2.5	9	2.9	25	7.7	Gambia, The
17.8	10.3	5.7	3.3	20.8	12.0	[1]	[1]	[1]	[1]	49.3[1, 36]	28.5[1, 36]	53.3[9]	30.8[9]	Gaza Strip
125	6.5	107	5.6	117	6.1	20	1.0	49	2.6	479	24.9	158[17]	8.2[17]	Georgia
3,760	9.5	2,090	5.3	6,924	17.4	4,098	10.3	3,174	8.0	8,182	20.6	262[2]	0.7[2]	Germany
65	1.2	123	2.2	792	14.2	27	0.5	98	1.7	376	6.7	158[9]	2.8[9]	Ghana
262	6.1	264	6.1	933	21.7	268	6.2	285	6.6	593	13.8	235[23]	5.5[23]	Greece
3.1	14.6	1.8	8.6	2.7	12.6	0.3	1.6	[7]	[7]	6.3[7]	29.5[7]	0.6	2.8	Greenland
3.5	9.1	1.7	4.4	5.4	13.9	0.8	2.0	[7]	[7]	5.9[7]	15.3[7]	12.7[17]	32.5[17]	Grenada
14.0	8.1	7.0	4.0	15.0	8.7	2.8	1.6	[7]	[7]	60.8[7]	35.2[7]	54.9[17]	31.8[17]	Guadeloupe
8.0	12.1	4.5	6.8	11.5	17.5	3.9	6.0	17.7	26.7	14.5	21.9	2.0[9]	3.1[9]	Guam
114[33]	3.9[33]	72[33]	2.5[33]	375[33]	12.9[33]	38[33]	1.3[33]	[7]	[7]	417[7]	14.4[7]	60[17]	2.1[17]	Guatemala
2.7	8.7	1.3	4.1	7.0	22.9	8.2	26.6	1.9	6.2	5.0	16.2	0.2	0.8	Guernsey[38]
9	0.5	29	1.6	37	2.0	4	0.2	[7]	[7]	138[7]	7.5[7]	156	8.5	Guinea
[11]	[11]	[12]	[12]	[12]	[12]	[12]	[12]	[12]	[12]	98[12]	20.0[12]	—	—	Guinea-Bissau
7[14]	2.8[14]	9[14]	3.8[14]	15[14]	6.2[14]	3[14]	1.2[14]	30[14]	12.1[14]	29[14]	11.9[14]	61[14, 17]	24.7[14, 17]	Guyana
28	1.0	21	0.8	353	13.2	5	0.2	[7]	[7]	155[7]	5.8[7]	404[17]	15.1[17]	Haiti
111	5.2	55	2.6	440	20.6	52	2.5	[7]	[7]	359[7]	16.8[7]	—	—	Honduras
349	10.4	377	11.2	1,024	30.5	431	12.8	[7]	[7]	718[7]	21.4[7]	16[2]	0.5[2]	Hong Kong
257	6.4	315	7.9	640	16.0	258	6.4	313	7.8	747	18.6	67[23]	1.7[23]	Hungary
11.0	7.2	11.0	7.2	25.7	16.9	14.4	9.5	7.1	4.7	41.4	27.2	1.3[2]	1.1[2]	Iceland
5,543	1.8	8,108	2.6	21,296	6.8	[1]	[1]	[1]	[1]	29,312[1]	9.3[1]	28,199	9.0	India
3,522	3.8	4,154	4.5	16,814	18.1	618	0.7	[7]	[7]	12,394[7]	13.4[7]	5,063[9]	5.5[9]	Indonesia
1,372[13]	9.3[13]	762[13]	5.2[13]	1,238[13]	8.4[13]	195[13]	1.3[13]	[7]	[7]	3,518[7, 13]	23.9[7, 13]	2,203[13, 17]	14.9[13, 17]	Iran
461	11.2	266	6.4	282	6.8	42	1.0	[7]	[7]	2,160[7]	52.3[7]	—	—	Iraq
128	8.3	69	4.5	295	19.2	140	9.1	75	4.8	312	20.3	61[17]	4.0[17]	Ireland
3.4	10.3	2.4	7.3	6.1	18.4	4.4	13.1	[7]	[7]	10.4[7]	31.4[7]	1.4[9]	4.1[9]	Isle of Man
144	6.3	130	5.7	377	16.6	304	13.4	115	5.1	606	26.7	111[17]	4.9[17]	Israel
1,641	7.2	1,080	4.8	4,221	18.6	1,514	6.7	[7]	[7]	5,134[7]	22.6[7]	2,676[9]	11.8[9]	Italy
66[19]	6.1[19]	40[19]	3.7[19]	196[19]	17.9[19]	47[19]	4.3[19]	[7]	[7]	237[7, 19]	21.7[7, 19]	180[17, 19]	16.5[17, 19]	Jamaica
6,670	10.0	4,170	6.1	15,150[41]	22.3[41]	5,930	8.7	[7]	[7]	16,010[7, 41]	23.6[7, 41]	1,810[17]	2.7[17]	Japan
4.4	9.3	2.4	5.0	6.8	14.4	7.4	15.6	3.1	6.5	15.7	33.1	1.6[17]	3.4[17]	Jersey
60	7.0	58	6.7	130	15.1	25	2.9	[7]	[7]	435[7]	50.6[7]	—	—	Jordan
364	5.2	507	7.3	1,035	14.8	331	4.8	[7]	[7]	1,004[7]	23.8[7]	258[17]	3.7[17]	Kazakhstan
[11]	[11]	[12]	[12]	[12]	[12]	[12]	[12]	[12]	[12]	2,107[12]	17.2[12]	—	—	Kenya
0.3	1.0	0.9	2.8	1.3	4.1	0.4	1.4	2.1	6.5	2.3	7.0	1.1[17]	3.4[17]	Kiribati
[11]	[11]	[12]	[12]	[12]	[12]	[12]	[12]	[12]	[12]	1,939[12, 24]	22.0[12, 24]	—	—	Korea, North
1,876	8.8	1,218	5.7	5,911	27.6	1,962	9.2	752	3.5	2,713	12.7	270[15]	1.3[15]	Korea, South
115[42]	15.7[42]	38[42]	5.2[42]	83[42]	11.4[42]	22[42]	3.0[42]	[7]	[7]	384[7, 42]	52.6[7, 42]	11[2, 42]	1.5[2, 42]	Kuwait
51	3.0	75	4.4	178	10.4	15	0.9	61	3.6	258	15.2	132	7.7	Kyrgyzstan
[11]	[11]	[12]	[12]	[12]	[12]	[12]	[12]	[12]	[12]	316[12, 14]	17.2[12, 14]	—	—	Laos
69	5.8	96	8.1	198	16.7	57	4.8	67	5.6	209	17.6	55	4.6	Latvia
43[44]	6.2[44]	48[44]	7.0[44]	115[44]	16.5[44]	24[44]	3.5[44]	[7]	[7]	200[7, 44]	28.8[7, 44]	—	—	Lebanon
28	5.5	8	1.6	24	4.7	2	0.5	[7]	[7]	157[7]	31.1[7]	13	2.6	Lesotho
4	0.6	14	2.0	47	6.7	[1]	[1]	[1]	[1]	63[1]	9.0[1]	64[17]	9.1[17]	Liberia
[11]	[11]	[12]	[12]	[12]	[12]	[12]	[12]	[12]	[12]	668[12]	57.1[12]	—	—	Libya
1.1	7.0	0.5	3.2	2.4	14.8	1.3	7.8	1.0	6.4	4.1	25.4	0.6[17]	3.4[17]	Liechtenstein
128	7.0	119	6.5	302	16.4	70	3.8	82	4.4	347	18.9	61[2]	3.3[2]	Lithuania
14	8.4	11	6.3	29	17.5	15	9.2	21	12.8	31	18.7	14[21]	8.1[21]	Luxembourg
23.0	10.9	14.3	6.8	60.0	28.5	14.4	6.8	16.5	7.8	36.6	17.4	1.0	0.5	Macau
36	4.5	27	3.4	77	9.8	15	1.9	28	3.5	88	11.1	251[46]	31.9[46]	Macedonia
[11]	[11]	[12]	[12]	[12]	[12]	[12]	[12]	[12]	[12]	677[12]	11.3[12]	—	—	Madagascar
46	1.4	25	0.7	94	2.7	6	0.2	[7]	[7]	147[7]	4.3[7]	57	1.7	Malawi
746	8.4	422	4.7	1,616	18.2	426	4.8	[7]	[7]	1,788[7]	20.1[7]	284	3.2	Malaysia
3.2	5.6	5.3	9.4	8.9	15.7	1.1	1.9	[7]	[7]	11.8[7]	21.0[7]	2.7[47]	4.7[47]	Maldives
13	0.4	6	0.2	159	4.6	0.3	—	75	2.2	84	2.4	107	3.1	Mali
6	4.4	9	6.9	13	9.8	5	3.7	[7]	[7]	53[7]	40.0[7]	5[9]	3.8[9]	Malta
1.1	9.4	0.5	4.7	1.4	12.1	0.8	7.3	[7]	[7]	3.1[7]	26.4[7]	1.4[17]	12.5[17]	Marshall Islands
9.3	5.6	6.7	4.0	14.0	8.5	3.0	1.8	[7]	[7]	59.1[7]	35.8[7]	54.8[17]	33.2[17]	Martinique
[11]	[11]	[12]	[12]	[12]	[12]	[12]	[12]	[12]	[12]	183[12]	26.0[12]	—	—	Mauritania
46	9.6	29	5.9	76	15.6	14	2.8	27	5.5	62	12.8	23[2]	4.8[2]	Mauritius[49]
3.1	11.4	1.5	5.4	2.0	7.2	0.1	0.4	[7]	[7]	5.7[7]	21.0[7]	10.5[17]	38.4[17]	Mayotte
2,189	5.5	1,730	4.4	8,777	22.2	1,518	3.8	1,630	4.1	8,051	20.4	298[17]	0.8[17]	Mexico
1.8	6.1	[50]	[50]	[50]	[50]	[50]	[50]	6.3	20.8	3.7[50]	12.1[50]	4.1[9]	13.5[9]	Micronesia
55	3.3	66	3.9	271	16.1	47	2.8	30	1.8	285	16.9	26	1.5	Moldova
0.7	5.3	...	...	2.5	20.2	1.0	8.0	2.8	22.4	1.9	14.9	0.9[21]	7.1[21]	Monaco
33	3.9	38	4.4	62	7.3	[1]	[1]	[1]	[1]	123[1, 20]	14.5[1, 20]	166[20, 21]	19.7[20, 21]	Mongolia
437	7.3	141	2.3	498	8.3	[52]	[52]	533	8.9	474[52]	7.9[52]	548[2]	9.1[2]	Morocco
[11]	[11]	[12]	[12]	[12]	[12]	[12]	[12]	[12]	[12]	971[12]	10.4[12]	—	—	Mozambique
400	2.2	495	2.7	1,781	9.7	...	...	[7]	[7]	1,485[7]	8.1[7]	270	1.5	Myanmar (Burma)
19	3.8	9	1.9	38	7.7	9	1.7	[7]	[7]	6[7]	1.2[7]	183[17]	37.1[17]	Namibia
...	...	...	...	...	...	...	...	...	...	...	...	...	...	Nauru
36	0.5	51	0.7	256	3.5	20	0.3	[7]	[7]	752[7]	10.3[7]	98	1.3	Nepal
451	5.8	442	5.7	1,487	19.2	1,097	14.2	525	6.8	1,833	23.7	498[17]	6.4[17]	Netherlands, The
6.5	7.4	5.0	5.7	20.9	23.8	8.2	9.3	[7]	[7]	24.8[7]	28.2[7]	13.4[9]	15.3[9]	Netherlands Antilles
4.5	6.8	3.1	4.7	9.5	14.3	2.5	3.8	[7]	[7]	22.0[7]	33.4[7]	13.5[9]	16.0[9]	New Caledonia
120	6.5	109	5.8	398	21.3	224	12.0	[7]	[7]	493[7]	26.4[7]	33[17]	1.8[17]	New Zealand
32[28]	2.2[28]	32[28]	2.2[28]	201[28]	13.8[28]	16[28]	1.1[28]	79[28]	5.4[28]	195[28]	13.4[28]	265[9, 28]	18.2[9, 28]	Nicaragua

Employment and labour (continued)

country	year	economically active population											distribution by economic sector			
		total ('000)	participation rate (%)		activity rate (%)			employment status (%)				agriculture, forestry, fishing		manufacturing; mining, quarrying; public utilities	
			female	ages 15–64	total	male	female	employers, self-employed	employees	unpaid family workers	other	number ('000)	% of econ. active	number ('000)	% of econ. active
Niger	1988[54]	2,316	20.4	55.2	31.9	51.1	13.0	51.4	5.0	40.3	3.3	1,764	76.2	73	3.1
Nigeria	1986[18]	30,766	33.3	58.8	31.1	41.1	20.9	64.6	18.8	10.7	5.9	13,259	43.1	1,401	4.6
Northern Mariana Islands	1990	26.6	43.2	83.6[8]	61.3	66.2	55.9	1.4	96.1	0.2	2.3	0.6	2.3	6.0	22.5
Norway	1998	2,317	46.2	80.8	52.3	56.9	47.8	7.4	88.7	0.6	3.2	104	4.5	375	16.2
Oman	1993	705	9.7	60.9	34.9	54.0	8.1	5.2	91.0	0.1	3.7	64	9.1	79	11.3
Pakistan	1996–97[18]	36,407	15.2	51.0	28.7	47.0	9.0	40.6[55]	34.2[55]	19.1[55]	6.1[55]	15,148	41.6	4,222	11.6
Palau	1990	6.1	36.9	64.1[8]	40.2	47.1	32.1	2.5	89.5	0.2	7.8	0.4	7.1	0.2	3.0
Panama	1998	1,049	35.5	66.4	38.4	49.0	27.6	23.9	59.5	2.7	13.9	180	17.2	118	11.3
Papua New Guinea	1980[56]	733	39.8	35.2[10]	24.6	28.3	20.5	72.7	26.4	—	0.9	564	77.0	21	2.9
Paraguay	1982	1,039	19.7	57.5	34.3	54.8	13.6	43.1	37.7	9.2	9.9	446	42.9	129	12.4
Peru	1995	8,906	34.7	60.9	37.8	49.8	26.1	39.8[30]	41.8[30]	8.4[30]	10.0[30]	2,693[20]	32.5[20]	1,091[20]	13.2[20]
Philippines	1998[18]	31,278	37.6	67.9	41.1	51.4	30.8	36.2[19]	41.7[19]	13.7[19]	8.4[19]	11,272	36.0	2,931	9.4
Poland	1998[18]	16,197	45.7	66.1	44.4	49.5	39.5	21.3	69.0	4.5	5.2	3,045	17.7	4,272	24.9
Portugal	1998[18]	5,000	45.0	70.3	50.2	57.3	43.6	24.2	68.0	0.8	7.0	651	13.0	1,243	24.9
Puerto Rico	1998[18]	1,320	42.2	54.5	34.2	41.0	27.9	13.6[34]	85.2[34]	0.7[34]	0.6[34]	35	2.7	203	15.4
Qatar	1988	293	11.2	80.8	53.7	77.3	22.2	1.8[44]	97.7[44]	—	0.5[44]	4.5	1.6	22.0	7.5
Réunion	1990[18]	234	41.1	60.3	39.1	46.8	31.6	8.4	53.1	1.1	37.4	11	4.8	11	4.8
Romania	1998	11,577	45.6	69.0	51.4	57.1	45.9	21.1	55.9	16.7	6.3	4,411	38.1	2,950	25.5
Russia	1996	68,264	46.6	71.9[51]	46.2	52.7	40.5	...	...	...	...	10,079	14.8	15,950	23.4
Rwanda	1996	3,719	47.5	67.5[10]	45.6	48.4	42.8	...	...	...	...	3,375	90.7	133[11]	3.6[11]
St. Kitts and Nevis	1980	17.1	41.0	69.5	39.5	48.4	31.2	9.7	78.5	0.4	11.4	4.5	26.1	3.8	22.3
St. Lucia	1991	53.1	40.3	67.6	39.9	49.1	31.2	21.0[14]	55.8[14]	1.6[14]	21.6[14]	11.6	21.8	7.5	14.0
St. Vincent	1991	41.7	35.9	67.5	39.1	50.3	28.0	18.2	59.6	2.1	20.1	8.4	20.1	3.5	8.4
Samoa	1986	45.6	18.8	48.6[30]	29.0	44.5	11.6	21.1[30]	43.5[30]	35.0[30]	0.4[30]	29.0	63.6	2.4	5.4
San Marino	1998	18.5	39.6	77.9	58.4	66.6	49.2	13.9	79.3	0.2	6.6	0.2	1.4	5.8	31.2
São Tomé and Príncipe	1991	35	33.6	59.1	30.1	40.5	20.0	25.8	68.6	0.7	4.9	13.6	38.4	1.8	5.0
Saudi Arabia	1988	5,369	3.6	59.1	36.3	54.9	3.6	...	...	...	...	192	3.6	595	11.1
Senegal	1995	3,508	38.3	62.1[10]	42.2	52.0	32	...	...	...	...	2,719	77.5	259[11]	7.4[11]
Serbia and Montenegro	1996	3,182	43.4[19]	58.7[25, 34]	30.1	...	...	...	...	...	...	104	3.3	903	28.4
Seychelles	1993[58]	28.1	...	...	38.9	...	...	...	...	...	...	2.2	7.7	4.6[11]	16.4[11]
Sierra Leone	1995	1,648	31.7	54.1[10]	30.5	50.9	22.7	...	...	...	...	964	58.5	319[11]	19.4[11]
Singapore	1998[18]	1,932	41.8	69.0	51.6	60.8	42.6	12.2	83.6	1.0	3.2	4	0.2	429	22.2
Slovakia	1998[18]	2,464	45.6	67.0	45.7	51.1	40.6	6.0	81.9	—	12.1	185	7.5	710	28.8
Slovenia	1998	982	46.3	69.1	49.6	54.5	44.7	11.5	74.7	6.1	7.6	110	11.2	332	33.8
Solomon Islands	1993[59]	29.6	25.6[44]	24.9[44, 60]	13.7[44]	19.7[44]	7.3[44]	29.6[44]	68.6[44]	—	1.8[44]	8.1	27.4	3.1	10.4
Somalia	1996	3,667	39.3	59.9[10]	38.8	47.1	29.9	...	...	...	...	2,446	66.7	417[11]	11.4[11]
South Africa[61]	1991	11,624	39.4	69.3[53]	37.5	45.5	29.5	7.0	74.8	...	18.2	1,224	10.5	2,361	20.3
Spain	1998[18]	16,265	39.2	62.6	41.6	51.9	31.8	11.9	62.4	0.9	24.7	1,286	7.9	2,965	18.2
Sri Lanka	1998	6,693	35.8	58.8[25]	43.4	55.9	30.9	24.9[34]	54.2[34]	7.8[34]	13.1[34]	2,472	36.9	1,028	15.4
Sudan, The	1983[54]	6,343	29.1	57.4	35.1	50.0	20.4	...	...	...	...	4,029	63.5	317	5.0
Suriname	1994[62]	89.8	35.1	52.3	45.2	59.4	31.4	...	...	...	...	4.8	5.3	10.7	11.9
Swaziland	1996	371	37.7	60.5[10]	42.3	55.0	30.6	...	...	...	...	231	62.3	44[11]	11.9[11]
Sweden	1998	4,255	47.5	76.5[8]	48.0	50.9	45.1	9.5	83.6	0.4	6.5	109	2.6	849	20.0
Switzerland	1998[18, 45]	3,975	44.2	67.9[25]	55.9	63.9	48.4	12.8[19]	84.3[19]	2.9[19]	—	179	4.5	715	18.0
Syria	1998[18]	4,411	17.5	51.2	28.3	46.9	9.8	31.0[13]	49.3[13]	13.0[13]	6.7[13]	917[13]	26.3[13]	471[13]	13.5[13]
Taiwan	1996[18]	9,310	39.2	58.4[25]	43.4	51.3	35.0	21.7	67.5	8.1	2.6	918	9.9	2,471	26.5
Tajikistan	1996	1,778	46.5	63.5[16, 20]	30.3	32.5	28.2	...	...	...	...	1,026	57.7	202	11.4
Tanzania	1996	15,170	46.6	74.1[10]	49.7	53.6	45.9	...	...	...	...	11,738	77.4	725[11]	4.8[11]
Thailand	1998[18, 63]	33,352	45.1	73.6[25]	54.5	60.0	49.0	31.2[64]	40.3[64]	19.5[64]	9.1[64]	16,472	49.4	4,449	13.3
Togo	1995	1,575	35.4	57.1[10]	38.1	49.7	26.7	70.3[30]	10.4[30]	11.3[30]	8.0[30]	1,059	67.2	183[11]	11.6[11]
Tonga	1990	32.0	33.0	57.0	33.6	45.2	22.0	33.7	45.4	16.8	4.1	11.7	36.5	5.1	15.8
Trinidad and Tobago	1998	559	38.3	65.4[34]	47.1	57.2	36.6	17.2	69.1	1.6	12.1	41	7.4	88	15.8
Tunisia	1989	2,361	20.9	50.6	29.8	46.5	12.7	20.9	54.9	7.4	16.8	510	21.6	418	17.7
Turkey	1998[18]	23,415	29.0	54.8	36.6	51.4	21.5	27.6[20]	41.5[20]	27.7[20]	3.2[20]	9,601	41.0	3,852	16.5
Turkmenistan	1996	1,680	40.0	71.9[16]	36.1	43.9	28.5	...	...	...	...	746	44.4	165	9.8
Tuvalu	1991	5.9	51.3[43]	85.5	65.3	...	...	0.3[43]	22.2[43]	— 77.5[43] —		4.2	68.0	0.1	2.0
Uganda	1996	9,636	39.9	68.9[10]	44.0	53.2	34.8	...	...	...	...	7,440	77.2	637[11]	6.6[11]
Ukraine	1998	25,936	50.9	74.9	51.6	54.6	49.0	...	...	...	...	5,074	19.6	4,227	16.3
United Arab Emirates	1990	690	10.4[42]	69.0[42]	47.0[42]	67.6[42]	12.9[42]	6.8[14]	92.7[14]	0.1[14]	0.5[14]	43	6.3	94	13.6
United Kingdom	1998	28,713	44.3	76.2[20]	49.2	55.7	43.0	11.2[20]	76.7[20]	0.5[20]	11.6[20]	479	1.7	5,592	19.5
United States	1998[18]	137,674	46.3	79.4[53]	50.9	55.9	46.1	7.5	87.9	0.1	4.5	3,724	2.7	23,723	17.2
Uruguay	1998[65]	1,239	44.0	71.3	47.0	55.8	39.1	22.9[28]	72.3[28]	2.3[28]	2.5[28]	47	3.8	215	17.3
Uzbekistan	1998	8,800	...	72.3	36.7	...	...	...	...	...	...	3,467	39.4	1,114	12.7
Vanuatu	1989	67.0	46.3	85.0	47.0	49.0	44.9	...	...	...	...	49.8	74.4	1.0	1.5
Venezuela	1997[18]	9,507	35.9	67.2	41.7	53.2	30.1	30.2[20]	61.8[20]	1.7[20]	6.3[20]	940	9.9	1,430	15.0
Vietnam	1989	30,521	51.7	79.9	47.4	47.0	47.7	...	...	...	...	20,471	67.1	3,390	11.1
Virgin Islands (U.S.)	1990[18]	47.4	47.8	70.3	46.6	50.3	43.1	7.6	85.5	0.2	6.7	0.6	1.2	3.7	7.8
West Bank	1996	356.9	16.1	42.2[25]	22.7	37.7	7.4	24.5	49.0	8.1	18.5	41.3	11.6	51.8[36]	14.5[36]
Western Sahara	...	...	...	...	...	...	...	...	...	...	...	...	...	...	...
Yemen	1988	3,029	31.6	52.6	26.4	36.8	16.4	...	...	...	...	2,152	71.1	129	4.3
Zambia	1996	3,507	30.3	54.5	36.1	50.9	21.7	22.9[14]	42.5[14]	3.6[14]	31.0[14]	2,322	66.2	428[11]	12.2[11]
Zimbabwe	1992	3,601	39.6	63.4	34.6	42.8	26.7	24.1	43.9	9.2	22.8	2,110[66]	64.7[66]	179[66]	5.5[66]

[1]Services includes finance, real estate and public administration, defense. [2]Unemployed, not previously employed only. [3]Includes emigrant workers (352,000). [4]Ages 15–59 (male) and 15–54 (female). [5]State sector only. [6]Includes nonagricultural private sector (241,000) and unemployed (261,000). [7]Services includes public administration, defense. [8]Ages 16–64. [9]Unemployed only. [10]Over age 10. [11]Manufacturing; mining, quarrying; public utilities includes construction. [12]Services includes transportation, communications; trade, hotels, restaurants; finance, real estate; and public administration, defense. [13]1991. [14]1980. [15]Includes unemployed, not previously employed. [16]Ages 16–59 (male) and 16–54 (female). [17]Mostly unemployed. [18]Excludes all or some classes or elements of the military. [19]1994. [20]1993. [21]Includes unemployed. [22]1990. [23]Mostly unemployed, not previously employed. [24]1982. [25]Over age 15. [26]Ages 14–64. [27]Services includes restaurants and hotels. [28]1992. [29]Over age 12. [30]1981. [31]Republic of Cyprus only. [32]1993 population economically active for Turkish Republic of Northern Cyprus is 75,947. [33]1989. [34]1995.

construction		transportation, communications		trade, hotels, restaurants		finance, real estate		public administration, defense		services		other		country
number ('000)	% of econ. active	number ('000)	% of econ. active	number ('000)	% of econ. active	number ('000)	% of econ. active	number ('000)	% of econ. active	number ('000)	% of econ. active	number ('000)	% of econ. active	
14	0.6	15	0.6	209	9.0	2	0.1	[7]	[7]	123[7]	5.3[7]	117[21]	5.0[21]	Niger
546	1.8	1,112	3.6	7,417	24.1	120	0.4	[7]	[7]	4,902[7]	15.9[7]	2,009[17]	6.5[17]	Nigeria
5.8	21.7	1.4	5.3	5.3	19.8	1.0	3.8	1.4	5.3	4.5	16.9	0.6[9]	2.3[9]	Northern Mariana Islands
145	6.3	170	7.3	411	17.7	229	9.9	152	6.6	655	28.3	75	3.2	Norway
108	15.3	25	3.5	104	14.8	17	2.5	166	23.5	111	15.8	30[23]	4.3[23]	Oman
2,330	6.4	1,971	5.4	5,021	13.8	338	0.9	[7]	[7]	5,395[7]	14.8[7]	1,982[23]	5.4[23]	Pakistan
0.9	14.2	0.4	6.6	1.1	18.7	0.2	2.9	0.8	13.7	1.6	26.1	0.5[9]	7.8[9]	Palau
72	6.9	66	6.3	232	22.1	59	5.6	74	7.0	205	19.5	43[23]	4.1[23]	Panama
22	2.9	1.7	2.4	25	3.4	4	0.6	[7]	[7]	77[7]	10.5[7]	2	0.2	Papua New Guinea
70	6.7	31	2.9	86	8.3	18	1.7	[7]	[7]	174[7]	16.8[7]	86[15]	8.3[15]	Paraguay
308[20]	3.7[20]	364[20]	4.4[20]	1,352[20]	16.3[20]	197[20]	2.4[20]	[7]	[7]	2,287[7, 20]	27.6[7, 20]	—	—	Peru
1,511	4.8	1,885	6.0	4,328[27]	13.8[27]	695	2.2	[7]	[7]	5,631[7, 27]	18.0[7, 27]	3,024[17]	9.7[17]	Philippines
1,248	7.3	1,015	5.9	2,641	15.4	866	5.0	844	4.9	2,754	16.0	511[23]	3.0[23]	Poland
539	10.8	184	3.7	953	19.1	277	5.5	309	6.2	798	16.0	45[2]	0.9[2]	Portugal
103	7.8	50	3.8	266[41]	20.2[41]	44	3.3	[7]	[7]	602[7, 41]	45.6[7, 41]	17[23]	1.3[23]	Puerto Rico
64.2	22.0	11.9	4.1	34.2	11.7	6.2	2.1	[7]	[7]	149.6[7]	51.1[7]	—	—	Qatar
17	7.1	7	3.1	18	7.7	3	1.3	[7]	[7]	79[7]	33.9[7]	87[17]	37.4[17]	Réunion
471	4.1	545	4.7	1,134	9.8	245	2.1	522	4.5	1,006	8.7	291[23]	2.5[23]	Romania
5,516	8.1	5,219	7.6	7,165	10.5	5,077	7.4	2,726	4.0	14,229	20.8	2,314	3.4	Russia
[11]	[11]	[12]	[12]	[12]	[12]	[12]	[12]	[12]	[12]	212[12]	5.7[12]	—	—	Rwanda
0.4	2.5	0.3	1.6	1.3	7.3	0.8	4.7	1.0	5.7	2.9	17.0	2.2[17]	12.8[17]	St. Kitts and Nevis
5.0	9.3	2.7	5.0	11.1	20.8	1.9	3.6	[7]	[7]	9.2[7]	17.2[7]	4.3	8.2	St. Lucia
3.5	8.5	2.3	5.5	6.5	15.7	1.4	3.4	[7]	[7]	7.7[7]	18.5[7]	8.3[9]	20.0[9]	St. Vincent
0.1	0.1	1.5	3.3	1.7	3.7	0.8	1.8	[7]	[7]	9.4[7]	20.7[7]	0.6	1.4	Samoa
1.5	8.2	0.4	1.9	2.8	15.2	1.4	7.8	2.3	12.4	2.8	15.2	1.3[21]	6.8[21]	San Marino
2.9	8.1	2.2	6.2	4.5	12.6	0.2	0.5	[7]	[7]	8.0[7]	22.5[7]	2.4	6.7	São Tomé and Príncipe
1,181	22.0	321	6.0	964	18.0	151	2.8	[7]	[7]	1,965[7]	36.6[7]	—	—	Saudi Arabia
[11]	[11]	[12]	[12]	[12]	[12]	[12]	[12]	[12]	[12]	530[12]	15.1[12]	—	—	Senegal
130	4.1	142	4.5	557[57]	17.5[57]	77	2.4	92	2.9	356	11.2	819[9]	25.7[9]	Serbia and Montenegro
[11]	[11]	3.4	12.2	5.2	18.6	1.0	3.4	2.6	9.1	5.6	20.0	3.6[17]	12.6[17]	Seychelles
[11]	[11]	[12]	[12]	[12]	[12]	[12]	[12]	[12]	[12]	365[12]	22.1[12]	—	—	Sierra Leone
136	7.0	212	11.0	415	21.5	300	15.5	119	6.2	307	15.9	9[2]	0.5[2]	Singapore
222	9.0	176	7.2	368	14.9	127	5.2	162	6.6	400	16.2	113[23]	4.6[23]	Slovakia
56	5.7	53	5.4	163	16.6	68	6.9	42	4.3	134	13.6	2.3[23]	2.4[23]	Slovenia
1.0	3.3	1.7	5.8	3.4	11.5	1.1	3.9	4.3	14.6	6.8	23.1	—	—	Solomon Islands
[11]	[11]	[12]	[12]	[12]	[12]	[12]	[12]	[12]	[12]	804[12]	21.9[12]	—	—	Somalia
526	4.5	497	4.3	1,358	11.7	504	4.3	[7]	[7]	2,641[7]	22.7[7]	2,513[17]	21.6[17]	South Africa[61]
1,540	9.5	828	5.1	3,387	20.8	1,331	8.2	905	5.6	2,634	16.2	1,382[23]	8.5[23]	Spain
309	4.6	268	4.0	594	8.9	117	1.8	[7]	[7]	1,007[7]	15.0[7]	897[17]	13.4[17]	Sri Lanka
139	2.2	215	3.4	294	4.6	21	0.3	[7]	[7]	550[7]	8.7[7]	777[23]	12.3[23]	Sudan, The
4.2	4.6	5.1	5.6	11.4	12.7	3.5	3.9	[7]	[7]	35.7[7]	39.7[7]	14.6[17]	16.3[17]	Suriname
[11]	[11]	[12]	[12]	[12]	[12]	[12]	[12]	[12]	[12]	96[12]	25.9[12]	—	—	Swaziland
244	5.7	285	6.7	663	15.6	519	12.2	218	5.1	1,328	31.2	39[23]	0.9[23]	Sweden
297	7.5	244	6.1	899	22.6	572	14.4	150	3.8	791	19.9	125	3.1	Switzerland
341[13]	9.8[13]	167[13]	4.8[13]	378[13]	10.9[13]	25[13]	0.7[13]	[7]	[7]	951[7, 13]	27.3[7, 13]	235[9, 13]	6.8[9, 13]	Syria
928	10.0	472	5.1	1,976	21.2	567	6.1	324	3.5	1,412	15.2	242[9]	2.6[9]	Taiwan
68	3.8	58	3.3	69	3.9	[1]	[1]	[1]	[1]	309[1]	17.3[1]	46[9]	2.6[9]	Tajikistan
[11]	[11]	[12]	[12]	[12]	[12]	[12]	[12]	[12]	[12]	2,708[12]	17.8[12]	—	—	Tanzania
1,280	3.8	923	2.8	4,464	13.4	[1]	[1]	[1]	[1]	4,584[1]	13.7[1]	1,222[17]	3.7[17]	Thailand
[11]	[11]	[12]	[12]	[12]	[12]	[12]	[12]	[12]	[12]	331[12]	21.0[12]	—	—	Togo
1.3	3.9	1.8	5.7	2.6	8.1	1.2	3.7	[7]	[7]	7.1[7]	22.0[7]	1.3[9]	4.2[9]	Tonga
84	14.9	38	6.8	99	17.6	43	7.7	[7]	[7]	165[7]	29.6[7]	1	0.1	Trinidad and Tobago
248	10.5	96	4.1	217	9.2	15	0.7	[7]	[7]	444[7]	18.8[7]	412[17]	17.5[17]	Tunisia
1,464	6.3	996	4.3	3,075	13.1	536	2.3	[7]	[7]	3,260[7]	13.9[7]	631[2]	2.7[2]	Turkey
155	9.2	83	4.9	107	6.4	55	3.3	25	1.5	300	17.9	44	2.6	Turkmenistan
0.2	4.0	0.1	1.0	0.2	4.0	—	—	[7]	[7]	1.3[7]	22.0[7]	—	—	Tuvalu
[11]	[11]	[12]	[12]	[12]	[12]	[12]	[12]	[12]	[12]	1,559[12]	16.2[12]	—	—	Uganda
1,092	4.2	1,400	5.4	1,514	5.8	213	0.8	[7]	[7]	5,886	22.7	6,509	25.1	Ukraine
119	17.3	72	10.4	101	14.7	19	2.7	[7]	[7]	241[7]	35.0[7]	—	—	United Arab Emirates
2,037	7.1	1,846	6.4	5,695	19.8	4,085	14.2	1,612	5.6	6,857	23.9	509[23]	1.8[23]	United Kingdom
9,094	6.6	8,075	5.9	28,740[41]	20.9[41]	16,151	11.7	[7]	[7]	47,623[7, 41]	34.6[7, 41]	543[23]	0.4[23]	United States
93	7.5	71	5.7	249	20.1	77	6.2	[7]	[7]	465[7]	37.5[7]	23[2]	1.9[2]	Uruguay
841	9.6	362	4.1	715	8.1	284	3.2	[7]	[7]	1,691[7]	19.2[7]	326	3.7	Uzbekistan
1.3	1.9	1.0	1.5	2.7	4.1	0.6	1.0	[7]	[7]	7.9[7]	11.8[7]	2.6	3.8	Vanuatu
841	8.8	578	6.1	2,169	22.8	523	5.5	[7]	[7]	2,616[7]	27.5[7]	410[23]	4.3[23]	Venezuela
581	1.9	576	1.9	1,880	6.2	90	0.3	305	1.0	1,374	4.5	1,854[17]	6.1[17]	Vietnam
5.7	12.0	3.7	7.8	10.3	21.8	3.6	7.7	5.1	10.8	7.8	16.4	6.9	14.6	Virgin Islands (U.S.)
60.8	17.0	15.7	4.4	52.6	14.8	[1]	[1]	[1]	[1]	68.6[1, 36]	19.2[1, 36]	66.0[9]	18.5[9]	West Bank
…	…	…	…	…	…	…	…	…	…	…	…	…	…	Western Sahara
178	5.9	90	3.0	84	2.8	4	0.1	[7]	[7]	391[7]	12.9[7]	—	—	Yemen
[11]	[11]	[12]	[12]	[12]	[12]	[12]	[12]	[12]	[12]	757[12]	21.6[12]	—	—	Zambia
51[66]	1.6[66]	76[66]	2.3[66]	128[66]	3.9[66]	24[66]	0.7[66]	[7]	[7]	397[7, 66]	12.2[7, 66]	277[17, 66]	8.5[17, 66]	Zimbabwe

[35]1984. [36]Services includes public utilities. [37]Ages 15–65. [38]Excludes Alderney and Sark. [39]1977. [40]Ages 14–64. [41]Services includes hotels. [42]1988. [43]1979. [44]1986. [45]Excludes foreign border workers. [46]Includes unemployed, emigrant workers, and employees in private nonagricultural sector. [47]Includes unemployed, previously employed. [48]1983. [49]Island of Mauritius only. [50]Services includes transportation, communications; trade, hotels, restaurants; and finance, real estate. [51]Ages 15–59. [52]Services includes finance, real estate. [53]Ages 20–64. [54]Excludes nomadic population. [55]1996–97. [56]Citizens over age 10 involved in money-raising activities only. [57]Includes arts and crafts and owners and employees of private shops. [58]Excludes domestic workers (private households), self-employed, and family workers. [59]Wage earners only. [60]Over age 14. [61]Excludes the former black independent states of Bophuthatswana, Ciskei, Transkei, and Venda. [62]Districts of Wanica and Paramaribo only. [63]August survey. [64]1994; February survey. [65]Urban areas only. [66]1986–87.

Crops and livestock

This table provides comparative data for selected categories of agricultural production for the countries of the world. The data are taken mainly from the United Nations Food and Agriculture Organization's (FAO's) annual *Production Yearbook* and the online FAOSTAT statistics database (http://apps.fao.org/default.htm).

The FAO depends largely on questionnaires supplied to each country for its statistics, but, where no official or semiofficial responses are returned, the FAO makes estimates, using incomplete, unofficial, or other similarly limited data. And, although the FAO provides standardized guidelines upon which many nations have organized their data collection systems and methods, persistent, often traditional, variations in standards of coverage, methodology, and reporting periods reduce the comparability of statistics that *can* be supplied on such forms. FAO data are based on calendar-year periods; that is, data for any particular crop refer to the calendar year in which the harvest (or the bulk of the harvest) occurred.

In spite of the often tragic food shortages in a number of countries in recent years, worldwide agricultural production is probably more often underreported than overreported. Many countries do not report complete domestic production. Some countries, for example, report only crops that are sold commercially and ignore subsistence crops produced for family or communal consumption, or barter; others may limit reporting to production for export only, to holdings above a certain size, or represent a sampling only.

Methodological problems attach to much smaller elements of the agricultural whole, however. The FAO's cereals statistics relate, ideally, to weight or volume of crops harvested for dry grain (excluding cereal crops used for grazing, harvested for hay, or harvested green for food, feed, or silage). Some countries, however, collect the basic data they report to the FAO on sown or cultivated areas instead and calculate production statistics from estimates of yield. Millet and sorghum, which in many European and North American countries are used primarily as livestock or poultry feed, may be reportable by such countries as animal fodder only, while elsewhere many nations use the same grains for human consumption and report them as cereals. Statistics for tropical fruits are frequently not compiled by producing countries, and coverage is not uniform, with some countries reporting only commercial fruits and others including those consumed for

Crops and livestock

country	crops																	
	grains				roots and tubers[a]				pulses[b]				fruits[c]		vegetables[d]	
	production ('000 metric tons)		yield (kg/hectare)		production ('000 metric tons)		yield (kg/hectare)		production ('000 metric tons)		yield (kg/hectare)		production ('000 metric tons)		production ('000 metric tons)	
	1989–91 average	2001	1989–91 average	2001	1989–91 average	2001	1989–91 average	2001	1989–91 average	2001	1989–91 average	2001	1989–91 average	2001	1989–91 average	2001
Afghanistan	2,754	2,046	1,200	978	217	230	16,291	16,429	32	50	913	1,351	644	615	466	652
Albania	792	581	2,609	2,609	88	180	8,409	14,400	20	32	729	922	153	132	377	653
Algeria	2,481	2,502	854	856	962	1,200	8,862	16,000	49	26	477	376	1,026	1,440	1,867	2,565
American Samoa	...	...	...	...	2	2	3,721	3,361	...	...	...	...	1	1	...	...
Andorra	...	...	...	...	...	...	...	...	...	...	...	...	...	...	...	...
Angola	298	585	338	638	1,815	3,504	4,220	6,295	35	75	273	375	414	450	250	271
Antigua and Barbuda	...	—	1,921	1,607	—	—	5,171	4,811	1	—	1,199	676	9	8	2	2
Argentina	19,988	38,372	2,343	3,387	2,279	2,555	18,183	23,018	249	329	1,105	1,140	5,915	7,781	2,802	3,163
Armenia	284[1]	374	1,642[1]	1,858	385[1]	364	12,564[1]	11,459	4[1]	3	1,876[1]	1,655	266[1]	202	485[1]	430
Aruba	...	...	...	...	...	...	...	...	...	...	...	...	...	...	...	...
Australia	21,390	36,487	1,665	2,032	1,127	1,256	28,301	29,658	1,530	2,597	1,025	1,190	2,345	3,139	1,504	1,950
Austria	5,115	4,538	5,443	5,516	810	695	24,907	26,604	119	69	3,555	2,411	946	1,090	455	613
Azerbaijan	1,162[1]	1,994	1,788[1]	2,648	153[1]	575	8,190[1]	10,419	13[1]	21	2,129[1]	2,901	800[1]	548	548[1]	1,198
Bahamas, The	1	—	1,522	2,171	1	1	6,900	8,357	1	1	1,261	1,254	12	25	27	22
Bahrain	...	...	...	...	—	—	14,629	11,000	—	—	836	1,091	14	22	10	10
Bangladesh	28,032	41,176	2,530	3,484	1,643	3,311	9,744	11,655	512	381	699	768	1,329	1,360	1,332	1,804
Barbados	2	2	2,656	2,500	6	7	9,271	9,024	...	...	...	...	3	3	7	12
Belarus	6,771[1]	4,823	2,602[1]	1,859	9,623[1]	8,700	12,967[1]	12,000	172[1]	227	1,619[1]	987	561[1]	271	972[1]	1,505
Belgium[2]	2,236	2,430	6,094	7,585	1,838	2,497	37,421	39,016	18	10	4,062	3,607	372	742	1,438	1,771
Belize	28	48	1,640	1,979	4	4	21,838	20,263	3	4	763	818	134	363	5	6
Benin	566	878	860	1,043	2,102	4,627	9,354	10,863	60	92	552	673	180	223	211	239
Bermuda	...	...	...	...	1	1	20,985	20,735	633	3,559	1,584	1,358	—	—	3	3
Bhutan	102	159	1,089	1,456	52	56	9,910	10,750	2	2	800	800	64	65	9	10
Bolivia	845	1,279	1,363	1,725	1,155	1,524	5,935	7,558	30	33	1,079	1,030	853	1,342	383	588
Bosnia and Herzegovina	963[1]	1,031	3,560[1]	2,781	300[1]	320	7,838[1]	8,000	18[1]	13	1,121[1]	1,054	122[1]	81	550[1]	649
Botswana	60	22	306	117	7	13	5,385	7,222	18	17	562	515	11	2	17	17
Brazil	37,702	56,329	1,868	3,095	27,229	27,595	12,567	14,053	2,471	2,464	473	702	30,472	31,732	5,605	7,062
Brunei	1	—	1,793	1,667	1	2	3,344	4,286	...	...	...	...	5	6	8	9
Bulgaria	8,872	5,238	4,121	2,544	495	450	11,987	8,491	89	25	1,021	756	1,576	703	1,792	1,439
Burkina Faso	1,975	2,796	717	867	70	86	5,968	8,641	56	59	742	801	71	73	229	229
Burundi	296	272	1,362	1,311	1,420	1,616	6,800	7,033	335	284	1,020	946	1,638	1,633	210	250
Cambodia	2,591	4,273	1,431	2,083	105	176	5,366	7,799	13	17	500	631	239	325	472	470
Cameroon	890	1,441	1,181	1,801	2,370	2,795	7,700	6,267	72	176	534	725	1,876	2,453	499	831
Canada	52,915	44,251	2,470	2,417	2,903	4,030	24,683	24,589	34	16	524	443	752	785	2,020	2,304
Cape Verde	10	21	287	429	18	9	9,099	7,890	9	3	184	86	15	15	7	16
Central African Republic	103	195	939	1,289	816	1,023	3,551	3,571	16	31	941	1,069	202	260	60	83
Chad	677	1,156	576	501	628	697	4,692	4,741	37	56	722	693	109	113	74	95
Chile	2,997	3,116	3,862	4,936	858	1,218	14,315	18,957	131	105	1,156	1,748	2,596	4,295	1,943	2,579
China	390,171	404,126	4,192	4,904	141,074	184,588	14,960	17,512	4,575	4,588	1,354	1,587	21,900	67,767	128,265	302,271
Colombia	4,090	3,731	2,471	3,268	4,342	5,281	11,973	13,040	167	169	691	1,118	5,024	6,666	1,433	1,955
Comoros	19	20	1,289	1,306	59	68	4,843	4,945	7	14	833	992	54	60	5	6
Congo, Dem. Rep. of the	1,471	1,590	799	782	19,477	16,125	7,913	7,961	204	160	602	534	3,321	1,741	513	426
Congo, Rep. of the	11	8	722	783	719	904	6,708	8,830	6	8	704	772	132	221	38	40
Costa Rica	262	322	2,775	3,957	172	284	20,840	16,637	...	...	...	...	2,121	3,494	118	384
Côte d'Ivoire	1,225	1,808	874	1,228	4,365	5,308	5,683	5,501	8	8	667	667	1,611	2,029	450	563
Croatia	2,562[1]	3,018	4,124[1]	4,469	517[1]	634	8,078[1]	9,900	22[1]	14	1,942[1]	1,166	538[1]	541	269[1]	466
Cuba	547	556	2,346	2,635	666	890	4,398	7,236	13	25	260	455	1,424	1,268	509	407
Cyprus	107	125	1,901	2,443	187	123	22,329	18,653	2	1	967	1,377	369	283	125	147
Czech Republic	6,629[3]	7,432	4,057[3]	4,569	1,652[3]	1,590	18,819[3]	29,285	176[3]	95	2,379[3]	2,374	496[3]	428	539[3]	464
Denmark	9,211	9,358	5,887	6,039	1,394	1,600	36,010	42,105	481	182	4,303	2,933	88	89	304	309
Djibouti	—	—	1,524	1,625	...	...			...	...	...	...	1	3	22	24
Dominica	—	—	1,354	1,308	29	27	9,292	9,286	—	—	410	417	97	72	6	6
Dominican Republic	531	763	3,951	4,179	243	278	7,085	7,629	98	54	937	880	1,560	1,363	245	395
East Timor[4]	...	...	...	...	...	...	...	2,531	...	...	...	...	...	1	...	...
Ecuador	1,422	2,084	1,718	2,257	500	1,059	6,596	9,529	40	39	489	552	4,446	9,344	369	414
Egypt	12,672	19,464	5,551	7,269	1,904	2,157	21,762	24,316	542	513	2,951	2,980	4,456	7,282	8,923	14,118
El Salvador	785	751	1,840	1,888	38	88	15,090	17,050	55	74	802	870	290	272	146	148
Equatorial Guinea	...	...	...	...	89	105	3,070	2,853	...	...	...	...	32	51	...	...
Eritrea	156[3]	197	523[3]	665	124[3]	125	3,180[3]	3,205	42[3]	56	561[3]	610	4[3]	4	30[3]	28
Estonia	638[1]	570	1,687[1]	1,747	590[1]	400	13,730[1]	13,841	1[1]	8	1,487[1]	1,453	33[1]	29	76[1]	44

subsistence as well. Figures on wild fruits and berries are seldom included in national reports at all. FAO vegetable statistics include vegetables and melons grown for human consumption only. Some countries do not make this distinction in their reports, and some exclude the production of kitchen gardens and small family plots, although in certain countries, such small-scale production may account for 20 to 40 percent of total output.

Livestock statistics may be distorted by the timing of country reports. Ireland, for example, takes a livestock enumeration in December that is reported the following year and that appears low against data for otherwise comparable countries because of the slaughter and export of animals at the close of the grazing season. It balances this, however, with a June enumeration, when numbers tend to be high. Milk production as defined by the FAO includes whole fresh milk, excluding milk sucked by young animals but including amounts fed by farmers or ranchers to livestock, but national practices vary. Certain countries do not distinguish between milk cows and other cattle, so that yield per dairy cow must be estimated. Some countries do not report egg production statistics (here given of metric tons), and external estimates must be based on the numbers of chickens and reported or assumed egg-laying rates. Other countries report egg production by number, and this must be converted to weight, using conversion factors specific to the makeup by species of national poultry flocks.

Metric system units used in the table may be converted to English system units as follow:

metric tons × 1.1023 = short tons
kilograms × 2.2046 = pounds
kilograms per hectare × 0.8922 = pounds per acre.

The notes that follow, keyed by references in the table headings, provide further definitional information.

a. Includes such crops as potatoes and cassava.
b. Includes beans and peas harvested for dry grain only. Does not include green beans and green peas.
c. Excludes melons.
d. Includes melons, green beans, and green peas.
e. From cows only.
f. From chickens only.

livestock														country
cattle		sheep		hogs		chickens		milk[e]				eggs[f]		
stock ('000 head)		stock ('000 head)		stock ('000 head)		stock ('000 head)		production ('000 metric tons)		yield (kg/animal)		production (metric tons)		
1989–91 average	2001	1989–91 average	2001	1989–91 average	2001	1989–91 average	2001	1989–91 average	2001	1989–91 average	2001	1989–91 average	2001	
1,600	2,000	14,173	11,000	...	...	7,073	6,000	507	1,200	633	1,200	14,000	18,000	Afghanistan
657	690	1,645	1,941	183	81	4,864	4,000	403	815	1,384	1,701	15,000	21,000	Albania
1,366	1,600	17,301	19,300	5	6	73,000	110,000	595	1,150	940	1,278	122,000	145,000	Algeria
—	—	—	—	11	11	34	...	—	—	800	800	...	...	American Samoa
...	...	...	...	...	...	...	...	...	...	...	...	...	...	Andorra
3,117	4,150	240	350	802	800	6,117	7,000	151	195	483	483	4,000	4,000	Angola
16	14	12	12	2	2	87	...	6	6	935	968	...	...	Antigua and Barbuda
52,633	50,669	28,139	13,500	2,533	4,200	67,000	110,000	6,375	9,600	2,621	3,918	298,000	325,000	Argentina
522[1]	520	858[1]	497	130[1]	69	27,330[1]	4,000	393[1]	450	1,516[1]	1,699	12,028[1]	19,000	Armenia
...	...	1	—	1	—	50	—	...	...	...	...	...	...	Aruba
23,086	30,500	165,046	120,000	2,617	2,433	56,000	96,000	6,514	11,398	3,945	5,167	178,000	149,000	Australia
2,546	2,118	284	358	3,762	3,427	14,000	11,000	3,344	3,340	3,805	4,703	94,000	97,000	Austria
1,726[1]	2,098	4,714[1]	5,560	84[1]	19	211,340[1]	14,000	811[1]	1,018	1,115[1]	1,015	35,282[1]	29,000	Azerbaijan
1	1	7	6	5	5	1,733	4,000	1	1	1,000	1,000	...	1,000	Bahamas, The
13	11	20	18	...	...	1,000	...	19	14	2,602	1,970	3,000	3,000	Bahrain
23,173	24,000	871	1,132	...	...	90,253	140,000	741	763	206	206	57,000	133,000	Bangladesh
32	21	40	41	29	33	3,437	4,000	14	8	1,784	1,688	2,000	1,000	Barbados
6,216[1]	4,084	325[1]	130	4,397[1]	3,431	486,430[1]	32,000	5,660[1]	4,300	2,573[1]	2,337	195,283[1]	190,000	Belarus
3,264	3,106	174	155	6,439	7,349	33,000	38,000	3,875	3,700	4,313	5,498	168,000	197,000	Belgium[2]
57	57	4	3	26	24	987	1,000	7	7	1,159	1,050	1,000	2,000	Belize
1,029	1,550	869	645	479	470	23,333	23,000	15	21	130	116	17,000	17,000	Benin
1	1	...	...	1	1	75	...	1	1	2,901	3,857	...	...	Bermuda
382	355	49	58	69	75	250	...	29	29	257	257	...	...	Bhutan
5,542	6,576	7,573	8,752	2,160	2,800	23,697	74,000	113	232	1,399	1,657	47,000	37,000	Bolivia
633[1]	440	700[1]	640	300[1]	330	5,167[1]	5,000	383[1]	460	733[1]	1,637	15,333[1]	15,000	Bosnia and Herzegovina
2,250	1,700	317	370	16	7	2,080	4,000	113	102	350	350	2,000	3,000	Botswana
147,797	176,000	20,061	15,000	33,643	29,424	557,282	1,006,000	15,004	22,580	780	1,407	1,244,000	1,538,000	Brazil
2	2	...	...	17	6	2,254	5,000	...	...	...	...	3,000	4,000	Brunei
1,548	635	8,226	2,286	4,219	1,144	34,167	15,000	1,999	1,290	3,370	3,000	129,000	81,000	Bulgaria
3,938	4,800	5,048	6,782	507	622	17,027	22,000	101	163	156	172	15,000	18,000	Burkina Faso
431	315	352	230	92	70	4,000	5,000	33	19	350	350	3,000	3,000	Burundi
2,178	2,924	...	...	1,601	2,118	9,000	15,000	17	21	170	170	9,000	12,000	Cambodia
4,660	5,900	3,290	3,800	1,288	1,350	17,333	30,000	116	125	500	500	12,000	14,000	Cameroon
11,165	13,700	595	840	10,505	12,600	110,000	158,000	7,915	8,170	5,800	7,192	319,000	363,000	Canada
18	22	6	8	104	200	1,000	...	2	5	447	638	1,000	2,000	Cape Verde
2,529	3,273	134	220	434	680	3,000	4,000	46	62	224	264	1,000	1,000	Central African Republic
4,298	5,900	1,926	2,400	14	22	3,950	5,000	116	159	270	270	4,000	4,000	Chad
3,402	3,566	4,803	4,200	1,144	2,500	32,000	78,000	1,353	2,200	1,559	1,375	96,000	110,000	Chile
79,284	106,175	112,299	133,160	360,543	454,420	2,127,000	3,771,000	4,411	9,570	1,562	1,902	6,701,000	19,884,000	China
24,383	27,000	2,547	2,300	2,627	2,750	58,000	110,000	4,017	5,980	963	1,000	237,000	355,000	Colombia
45	52	16	21	...	...	392	440	4	4	500	500	1,000	1,000	Comoros
1,466	761	930	911	1,034	1,000	25,000	21,000	8	5	851	825	8,000	7,000	Congo, Dem. Rep. of the
65	93	104	96	45	46	2,000	2,000	1	1	500	500	1,000	1,000	Congo, Rep. of the
2,181	1,220	2	2	270	430	14,000	17,000	431	730	1,308	1,327	19,000	39,000	Costa Rica
1,101	1,476	1,137	1,451	361	336	24,333	29,000	18	22	150	146	13,000	18,000	Côte d'Ivoire
566[1]	417	503[1]	539	1,264[1]	1,234	9,828[1]	11,000	643[1]	616	1,903[1]	2,404	47,731[1]	46,000	Croatia
4,822	4,038	385	310	2,567	2,700	27,876	13,000	995	614	1,782	1,163	...	68,000	Cuba
50	54	300	246	281	418	3,000	3,000	...	...	4,746	6,004	8,000	11,000	Cyprus
2,337[3]	1,520	225[3]	90	4,335[3]	3,594	255,743[3]	15,000	3,294[3]	2,736	4,015[3]	5,658	155,163[3]	188,000	Czech Republic
2,227	1,923	164	145	9,390	12,125	16,000	22,000	4,710	4,660	3,832	...	83,000	77,000	Denmark
188	270	433	465	...	...	...	...	7	8	350	350	...	...	Djibouti
14	13	7	8	4	5	31,000	47,000	7	6	902	910	120	...	Dominica
2,283	2,160	115	106	543	566	31,227	...	345	410	1,701	1,356	35,000	65,000	Dominican Republic
69	175	...	...	...	...	...	...	98	140	...	...	...	...	East Timor[4]
4,351	5,578	1,417	1,976	2,213	2,392	52,000	138,000	1,529	2,192	2,092	2,125	51,000	57,000	Ecuador
2,771	3,810	3,310	4,545	24	30	38,000	88,000	974	1,679	890	1,112	144,000	200,000	Egypt
1,213	13,292	5	5	305	150	52,000	8,000	292	395	1,083	790	46,000	53,000	El Salvador
5	5	35	38	5	6	228	...	...	...	...	...	...	...	Equatorial Guinea
1,279[3]	2,200	1,515[3]	1,570	...	...	2,750[3]	1,000	30[3]	52	192[3]	196	37,950[3]	2,000	Eritrea
595[1]	260	116[1]	29	588[1]	300	3,965[1]	2,000	833[1]	687	3,374[1]	7,516	24,071[1]	17,000	Estonia

Crops and livestock (continued)

country	crops															
	grains				roots and tubers[a]				pulses[b]				fruits[c]		vegetables[d]	
	production ('000 metric tons)		yield (kg/hectare)		production ('000 metric tons)		yield (kg/hectare)		production ('000 metric tons)		yield (kg/hectare)		production ('000 metric tons)		production ('000 metric tons)	
	1989–91 average	2001	1989–91 average	2001	1989–91 average	2001	1989–91 average	2001	1989–91 average	2001	1989–91 average	2001	1989–91 average	2001	1989–91 average	2001
Ethiopia	5,760[3]	8,732	1,143[3]	1,172	3,770[3]	4,305	6,912[3]	7,334	638[3]	1,050	743[3]	848	228[3]	220	666[3]	574
Faroe Islands	...	...	...	...	1	2	13,663	13,636	14	12	2,549	2,167	...	...	...	...
Fiji	30	17	2,289	2,487	36	85	3,739	10,872	...	...	773	1,000	13	15	9	18
Finland	3,845	3,670	3,360	3,165	845	750	20,656	25,000	...	...	...	...	22	32	205	251
France	57,683	60,477	6,240	6,751	5,213	6,536	29,853	40,346	3,310	1,890	4,735	3,900	10,561	11,169	7,628	7,805
French Guiana	22	20	4,199	2,601	32	14	10,178	5,906	...	...	...	...	7	15	9	25
French Polynesia	...	...	...	...	11	12	12,667	12,778	...	...	...	...	8	7	7	7
Gabon	23	27	1,599	1,636	378	447	5,424	5,721	...	...	639	667	268	294	30	35
Gambia, The	99	190	1,078	1,286	6	8	3,000	3,000	4	6	267	275	4	4	8	9
Gaza Strip	1	1	510	529	23	35	22,624	21,875	...	...	...	...	168	137	140	158
Georgia	457[1]	545	1,927[1]	1,676	252[1]	380	11,259[1]	10,270	8[1]	9	656[1]	929	800[1]	494	402[1]	463
Germany	37,910	50,056	5,534	7,078	14,057	10,903	27,747	38,965	337	634	2,770	3,448	4,752	5,376	2,864	2,447
Ghana	1,155	1,711	1,076	1,309	6,608	13,972	8,143	11,983	16	15	102	100	1,147	2,385	414	635
Greece	5,491	3,876	3,727	3,165	1,052	882	19,880	19,300	51	41	1,512	1,682	4,005	3,962	4,070	4,206
Greenland	...	...	...	...	...	...	...	...	...	...	...	...	...	...	...	...
Grenada	—	—	1,036	1,000	4	4	5,214	5,322	1	1	1,080	1,149	26	18	2	3
Guadeloupe	...	...	...	...	20	20	9,649	11,681	—	...	577	2,600	129	137	24	35
Guam	—	—	2,000	2,000	2	2	14,904	14,904	...	...	...	...	2	2	4	5
Guatemala	1,413	1,199	1,950	1,825	169	243	13,507	16,547	135	129	945	849	988	1,578	603	949
Guernsey	...	...	...	...	...	...	...	...	...	...	...	...	...	...	...	...
Guinea	632	1,103	1,052	1,312	578	1,251	7,320	6,448	60	55	857	846	840	990	432	476
Guinea-Bissau	165	166	1,556	1,312	69	99	6,911	7,857	2	2	960	622	62	74	21	25
Guyana	218	544	3,197	3,897	35	44	10,027	10,233	1	2	612	630	49	51	10	10
Haiti	405	363	996	827	770	755	3,785	4,000	100	70	655	658	1,005	969	277	199
Honduras	664	599	1,403	1,439	30	38	8,836	7,891	71	59	746	775	1,399	958	197	281
Hong Kong	—	—	1,667	—	—	...	22,000	33,333	...	...	...	...	4	4	116	55
Hungary	14,603	14,881	5,160	4,862	1,230	800	16,713	17,778	347	100	2,249	4,656	2,184	1,848	1,937	1,629
Iceland	...	...	...	...	11	10	9,159	12,250	8	19	4,798	4,524	—	...	2	4
India	195,478	230,611	1,911	2,318	21,280	33,200	15,906	19,015	13,604	11,271	571	586	27,138	48,571	48,971	68,059
Indonesia[4]	51,258	59,186	3,814	3,920	19,270	19,194	11,522	12,181	666	901	1,393	1,603	5,497	7,870	4,336	6,738
Iran	12,973	11,909	1,365	1,536	2,387	3,000	17,384	20,000	398	439	584	489	7,088	10,467	7,743	10,760
Iraq	2,541	1,207	927	460	196	150	15,980	6,250	19	29	995	890	1,457	1,215	2,855	1,908
Ireland	1,950	2,156	6,374	7,606	577	400	25,060	28,571	...	...	...	...	2	24	235	200
Isle of Man	...	...	...	...	...	...	...	...	...	...	...	...	...	...	...	...
Israel	331	272	2,968	2,901	209	393	32,359	31,799	9	13	1,334	1,809	1,715	1,259	1,143	1,599
Italy	17,921	20,067	4,005	4,737	2,340	1,998	19,637	24,117	221	121	1,430	1,543	17,569	18,377	14,436	14,943
Jamaica	3	2	1,232	1,180	225	229	12,534	16,777	6	5	898	1,093	383	414	108	172
Japan	13,946	12,270	5,645	6,184	5,539	4,480	25,459	25,839	145	104	1,670	1,830	4,837	4,285	14,455	12,564
Jersey	...	...	...	...	...	...	...	...	...	...	...	...	...	...	...	...
Jordan	105	65	1,040	1,103	59	91	23,167	26,000	6	2	690	547	247	221	709	851
Kazakhstan	22,519[1]	16,353	1,056[1]	1,239	2,302[1]	1,600	9,929[1]	9,756	97[1]	37	739[1]	1,000	160[1]	159	1,051[1]	2,278
Kenya	2,893	3,166	1,567	1,662	1,536	1,995	8,200	7,824	219	230	312	329	888	983	629	649
Kiribati	...	...	...	...	7	9	7,449	8,113	...	...	...	...	5	6	4	6
Korea, North	7,201	3,854	4,507	3,026	1,051	2,232	13,414	9,935	325	290	922	853	1,304	1,350	4,344	3,811
Korea, South	8,412	7,791	5,891	6,662	939	1,003	21,133	26,814	45	28	1,134	1,034	2,019	2,700	9,729	12,303
Kuwait	1	4	4,143	2,198	1	32	19,530	41,256	...	...	...	...	2	12	92	151
Kyrgyzstan	1,420	1,804	2,379	2,874	327[1]	1,056	11,330	15,761	...	...	...	...	101	202	334	824
Laos	1,443	2,319	2,244	3,018	246	224	8,150	7,475	12	15	780	967	130	180	89	290
Latvia	1,093	938	1,752	2,200	1,161[1]	706	13,181	13,519	6[1]	3	1,576[1]	1,432	73[1]	64	256	129
Lebanon	80	96	1,955	2,424	249	271	18,708	20,008	28	43	1,631	2,095	1,223	1,312	798	1,324
Lesotho	170	398	805	1,517	47	90	15,553	16,667	9	14	481	586	18	13	24	18
Liberia	191	183	1,035	1,278	422	504	7,253	6,802	3	4	517	636	111	166	73	76
Libya	284	218	680	637	141	210	7,891	7,000	12	20	1,126	1,405	307	381	706	906
Liechtenstein	...	...	...	...	...	...	...	...	...	...	...	...	...	...	...	...
Lithuania	2,323[1]	2,293	1,934[1]	2,704	1,316[1]	1,300	11,148[1]	12,683	34[1]	107	1,438[1]	2,830	145[1]	138	306[1]	325
Luxembourg[2]	...	...	...	...	...	...	...	...	...	...	...	...	...	...	...	...
Macau	...	...	...	...	...	...	...	...	...	...	...	...	...	...	...	...
Macedonia	583	487	2,453	2,291	127[1]	176	9,526	12,571	29[1]	27	2,589	2,546	342[1]	310	463[1]	524
Madagascar	2,541	2,460	1,943	1,761	3,160	3,152	6,359	6,155	67	99	883	909	790	854	328	344
Malawi	1,560	2,658	1,104	1,623	506	2,900	4,294	8,170	234	229	560	526	485	511	252	256
Malaysia	1,886	2,282	2,710	3,172	497	459	9,683	9,107	...	...	633	778	1,126	1,082	334	496
Maldives	—	—	1,125	1,000	7	8	4,537	4,578	...	...	...	...	9	9	20	28
Mali	2,114	2,866	907	1,159	23	155	4,721	14,390	40	111	172	406	15	34	307	328
Malta	8	12	3,422	4,000	17	27	13,181	15,112	1	1	2,336	2,556	14	7	52	67
Marshall Islands	...	...	...	...	...	...	...	...	...	...	...	...	...	...	...	...
Martinique	...	...	...	...	23	22	10,917	10,866	...	1	...	...	273	349	24	32
Mauritania	131	201	831	791	6	6	1,933	2,115	28	34	385	330	12	24	11	14
Mauritius	2	1	3,885	4,769	19	16	18,659	19,159	...	...	...	...	8	11	43	93
Mayotte	...	...	...	...	...	...	...	...	...	...	...	...	...	...	...	...
Mexico	23,553	29,737	2,350	2,817	1,302	1,771	15,957	23,235	1,412	1,411	704	747	9,430	13,236	6,604	9,451
Micronesia	...	...	...	...	...	...	...	...	...	...	...	...	...	...	...	...
Moldova	2,275[1]	2,086	2,981[1]	2,518	504[1]	425	7,796[1]	10,630	104[1]	62	1,492[1]	1,247	1,562[1]	743	737[1]	564
Monaco	...	...	...	...	...	...	...	...	...	...	...	...	...	...	...	...
Mongolia	719	160	1,104	813	128	64	10,613	7,303	3	1	708	833	—	...	42	42
Morocco	7,456	4,607	1,346	895	975	1,086	17,001	17,952	386	183	791	523	2,310	2,179	2,946	3,697
Mozambique	629	1,674	404	821	4,122	5,460	4,322	5,811	87	130	301	342	368	260	197	115
Myanmar (Burma)	14,111	21,230	2,738	2,999	212	473	8,579	10,072	434	1,945	648	777	957	1,284	2,027	3,475
Namibia	103	107	482	388	212	255	8,610	8,500	8	8	1,097	1,133	10	16	9	11
Nauru	...	...	...	...	...	...	...	...	...	...	...	...	—	—	...	...
Nepal	5,680	7,172	1,885	2,164	826	1,419	7,398	9,272	168	226	597	791	457	488	962	1,648
Netherlands, The	1,327	1,732	6,909	7,744	6,947	7,700	40,168	45,562	85	14	4,109	4,531	507	713	3,470	3,536
Netherlands Antilles	...	...	...	...	...	...	...	...	...	...	...	...	...	...	...	...
New Caledonia	1	2	1,837	3,736	21	21	6,023	5,778	—	...	393	600	4	3	5	4
New Zealand	783	883	4,870	6,467	277	516	30,899	46,071	62	52	2,941	3,826	806	955	576	1,058
Nicaragua	453	770	1,483	1,813	77	84	11,790	10,195	69	124	621	654	303	261	35	32

livestock														
cattle		sheep		hogs		chickens		milk[e]				eggs[f]		country
stock ('000 head)		stock ('000 head)		stock ('000 head)		stock ('000 head)		production ('000 metric tons)		yield (kg/animal)		production (metric tons)		
1989–91 average	2001	1989–91 average	2001	1989–91 average	2001	1989–91 average	2001	1989–91 average	2001	1989–91 average	2001	1989–91 average	2001	
29,450[3]	35,500	10,860[3]	22,500	20[3]	25	27,225[3]	56,000	755[3]	970	199[3]	204	28,413[3]	76,000	Ethiopia
2	2	67	68	...	...	...	...	...	...	...	...	...	...	Faroe Islands
274	340	—	7	88	137	3,000	4,000	58	52	1,705	1,798	2,000	4,000	Fiji
1,352	1,025	59	100	1,322	1,300	6,000	6,000	2,712	2,500	5,666	6,452	73,000	60,000	Finland
21,407	20,281	11,196	10,000	11,999	14,635	198,306	230,000	26,334	24,890	4,797	5,641	903,000	1,047,000	France
15	9	4	3	9	10	202	...	—	—	1,222	583	...	...	French Guiana
8	11	—	—	33	37	100	...	2	1	2,207	2,000	1,000	2,000	French Polynesia
31	35	161	198	169	213	2,217	3,000	1	2	250	250	2,000	2,000	Gabon
331	327	143	106	14	14	1,000	1,000	6	8	175	175	1,000	1,000	Gambia, The
3	3	24	24	...	...	3,000	4,000	7	8	4,000	4,000	5,000	8,000	Gaza Strip
1,046[1]	1,180	1,159[1]	545	525[1]	443	11,786[1]	8,000	387[1]	660	773[1]	1,021	14,800[1]	24,000	Georgia
20,048	14,227	3,824	2,140	33,350	25,767	116,263	108,000	30,976	28,300	4,931	6,256	989,000	890,000	Germany
1,159	1,430	2,199	2,743	495	324	9,682	20,000	22	34	130	130	10,000	22,000	Ghana
651	585	8,684	9,000	1,002	905	27,213	28,000	622	770	2,523	4,529	123,000	120,000	Greece
...	...	21	22	...	...	...	...	...	...	...	...	...	...	Greenland
4	4	12	13	3	5	260	...	...	1	797	800	1,000	1,000	Grenada
70	85	4	3	35	19	311	...	1	...	506	500	1,000	2,000	Guadeloupe
...	...	...	...	4	55	170	...	...	...	...	...	...	1,000	Guam
2,055	2,540	432	552	602	1,450	14,633	35,000	251	270	680	712	68,000	109,000	Guatemala
...	...	...	...	...	...	...	...	...	...	...	...	...	...	Guernsey
1,501	3,128	429	892	24	98	8,000	12,000	42	72	185	185	8,000	12,000	Guinea
407	515	239	285	290	350	1,000	1,000	12	13	170	170	1,000	1,000	Guinea-Bissau
165	100	129	130	42	20	2,000	12,000	19	30	840	1,911	1,000	7,000	Guyana
1,067	1,450	120	152	330	1,000	5,167	6,000	40	42	250	250	4,000	4,000	Haiti
2,412	1,860	10	14	589	480	9,436	18,000	346	594	911	1,001	28,000	43,000	Honduras
2	25	—	—	296	110	5,678	3,000	2	—	2,190	2,273	1,000	...	Hong Kong
1,619	783	2,050	1,129	7,996	4,834	50,950	31,000	2,733	2,143	4,977	6,036	254,000	156,000	Hungary
75	71	540	465	36	44	450	...	112	108	3,509	4,000	3,000	3,000	Iceland
202,533	221,900	48,708	58,200	12,000	17,500	294,000	413,000	22,259	35,000	731	946	1,161,000	1,906,000	India
10,391	11,200	6,008	7,427	7,228	5,897	577,000	751,000	348	550	1,176	1,585	366,000	600,000	Indonesia[4]
7,382	8,738	44,754	53,000	—	—	162,000	260,000	2,480	4,000	1,014	1,250	310,000	600,000	Iran
1,366	1,400	8,127	6,780	...	...	63,000	23,000	297	319	730	750	64,000	14,000	Iraq
5,923	6,408	5,523	5,130	1,125	1,732	9,000	11,000	5,355	5,416	3,967	4,374	33,000	37,000	Ireland
...	...	...	...	...	...	...	...	...	...	...	...	...	...	Isle of Man
340	390	383	389	122	150	23,000	30,000	964	1,211	8,783	10,093	105,000	85,000	Israel
8,541	7,068	11,088	11,089	9,150	8,329	138,000	100,000	10,926	11,900	3,733	5,535	687,000	707,000	Italy
382	400	2	1	192	180	7,167	11,000	51	53	1,000	1,000	26,000	28,000	Jamaica
4,772	4,564	30	11	11,673	9,785	338,000	297,000	8,169	8,450	5,825	6,654	2,446,000	2,526,000	Japan
...	...	...	...	...	...	...	...	...	...	...	...	...	...	Jersey
38	68	1,660	1,850	...	...	14,000	24,000	60	163	2,425	3,468	32,000	46,000	Jordan
9,336[1]	4,282	33,651[1]	8,939	2,610[1]	1,076	516,830[1]	20,000	5,335[1]	3,700	1,481[1]	1,850	177,300[1]	90,000	Kazakhstan
13,442	13,500	9,241	6,500	125	315	24,667	32,000	2,280	1,800	499	450	41,000	50,000	Kenya
...	...	...	...	9	13	259	...	...	...	...	...	...	...	Kiribati
986	575	496	189	5,793	3,137	21,000	17,000	88	90	2,379	2,308	146,000	120,000	Korea, North
2,149	1,951	3	1	4,792	8,720	70,336	102,000	1,752	2,339	5,944	9,064	399,000	460,000	Korea, South
15	18	197	630	...	...	17,000	32,000	21	40	3,226	5,672	6,000	22,000	Kuwait
1,125	988	8,269	4,160	258	117	98,640	3,000	926	1,100	1,854	2,200	22,196	11,000	Kyrgyzstan
853	1,150	...	...	1,397	1,500	8,165	14,000	5	6	200	200	4,000	10,000	Laos
1,068[1]	388	154[1]	29	865[1]	394	61,970	3,000	1,211[1]	855	2,675	4,181	25,096	27,000	Latvia
65	79	221	380	46	64	23,000	32,000	94	205	2,826	3,254	35,000	42,000	Lebanon
550	540	1,450	730	62	60	967	2,000	24	24	290	250	1,000	2,000	Lesotho
38	36	222	210	123	130	38,000	4,000	1	1	130	130	4,000	4,000	Liberia
238	220	5,100	5,100	...	...	15,867	25,000	99	135	1,197	1,205	34,000	59,000	Libya
6	6	3	3	3	3	...	...	13	12	4,645	4,444	...	...	Liechtenstein
1,761[1]	752	52[1]	12	1,579[1]	856	10,860[1]	6,000	2,128[1]	1,810	2,915[1]	4,129	47,167[1]	37,000	Lithuania
...	...	...	...	...	...	...	...	...	...	...	...	...	...	Luxembourg[2]
...	...	...	...	...	...	450	1,000	...	...	...	...	1,000	1,000	Macau
283	259	2,354[1]	1,251	176[1]	204	44,581[1]	3,000	121[1]	180	1,276	1,837	25,653	22,000	Macedonia
10,254	11,000	737	790	1,431	850	13,062	19,000	477	535	273	282	10,000	15,000	Madagascar
832	750	151	110	236	250	11,500	15,000	38	35	460	461	15,000	20,000	Malawi
677	748	212	175	2,577	1,829	62,377	125,000	29	43	486	478	287,000	420,000	Malaysia
...	...	...	...	...	...	...	...	...	...	...	...	...	...	Maldives
4,971	6,819	6,072	6,400	56	66	22,000	25,000	123	159	245	245	12,000	12,000	Mali
21	18	13	16	101	80	1,000	1,000	24	47	3,850	5,446	7,000	8,000	Malta
...	...	...	...	...	...	...	...	...	...	...	...	...	...	Marshall Islands
37	25	46	34	39	35	347	...	2	2	756	764	1,000	2,000	Martinique
1,350	1,500	5,067	7,600	...	...	3,800	4,000	97	116	350	350	4,000	5,000	Mauritania
29	28	6	7	12	21	2,200	4,000	12	5	1,878	1,175	4,000	5,000	Mauritius
...	...	...	...	...	...	...	...	...	...	...	...	...	...	Mayotte
32,194	30,600	5,862	6,150	15,715	17,750	240,218	496,000	6,336	9,501	992	1,397	1,066,000	1,882,000	Mexico
...	...	...	...	...	32	...	...	...	...	...	...	...	...	Micronesia
962[1]	405	1,300[1]	866	1,468[1]	543	183,980[1]	13,000	998[1]	575	2,476[1]	2,003	22,709[1]	28,000	Moldova
...	...	...	...	...	...	...	...	...	...	...	...	...	...	Monaco
2,694	2,054	14,266	15,667	166	16	351	...	268	385	348	316	2,000	...	Mongolia
3,284	2,670	13,528	17,300	9	8	71,200	137,000	929	1,150	521	879	171,000	235,000	Morocco
1,373	1,320	120	125	167	180	21,833	28,000	63	60	170	170	11,000	14,000	Mozambique
9,280	11,551	275	403	2,681	4,139	23,989	48,000	422	510	392	392	35,000	86,000	Myanmar (Burma)
2,104	2,509	3,289	2,200	18	18	1,717	2,000	76	75	401	403	1,000	2,000	Namibia
...	...	...	...	2	3	5	...	...	...	...	...	...	...	Nauru
6,274	6,979	903	850	571	913	12,000	20,000	252	343	366	402	16,000	25,000	Nepal
4,920	4,050	1,663	1,400	13,620	12,822	92,050	107,000	1,944	10,500	6,040	7,143	644,000	658,000	Netherlands, The
1	1	6	7	3	2	125	...	—	—	1,278	1,267	...	1,000	Netherlands Antilles
122	123	3	1	37	40	317	...	4	4	600	600	1,000	2,000	New Caledonia
7,987	9,633	57,861	43,987	404	354	9,067	13,000	7,544	13,162	2,835	3,700	46,000	54,000	New Zealand
2,833	3,350	4	4	565	400	4,000	17,000	162	238	797	914	26,000	31,000	Nicaragua

Crops and livestock (continued)

country	crops															
	grains				roots and tubers[a]				pulses[b]				fruits[c]		vegetables[d]	
	production ('000 metric tons)		yield (kg/hectare)		production ('000 metric tons)		yield (kg/hectare)		production ('000 metric tons)		yield (kg/hectare)		production ('000 metric tons)		production ('000 metric tons)	
	1989–91 average	2001	1989–91 average	2001	1989–91 average	2001	1989–91 average	2001	1989–91 average	2001	1989–91 average	2001	1989–91 average	2001	1989–91 average	2001
Niger	2,120	3,161	342	401	180	139	9,025	19,200	312	308	127	80	44	48	290	614
Nigeria	18,100	22,891	1,165	1,193	35,155	66,578	10,370	9,687	1,363	2,200	719	423	6,644	8,900	4,272	7,783
Northern Mariana Islands	...	...	...	...	...	...	...	...	...	...	...	...	...	...	...	...
Norway	1,410	1,307	3,943	3,962	452	388	24,246	25,000	—	...	...	...	99	26	182	131
Oman	5	5	2,124	2,271	5	16	25,208	29,091	...	...	...	...	185	318	155	193
Pakistan	21,038	27,820	1,784	2,287	1,052	2,134	11,467	17,015	1,044	740	553	510	3,871	4,817	3,193	4,912
Palau	...	...	...	...	...	...	...	...	...	...	...	...	...	...	...	...
Panama	336	317	1,884	3,138	66	76	5,901	11,537	9	9	526	416	1,225	726	65	160
Papua New Guinea	4	11	2,330	4,145	1,253	1,285	7,270	7,252	2	3	500	531	1,076	1,223	357	393
Paraguay	818	1,249	1,838	2,165	3,479	3,924	15,109	14,635	55	76	959	914	523	484	268	313
Peru	1,983	3,854	2,473	3,089	2,293	4,308	8,066	10,712	107	179	896	1,039	1,922	3,363	918	1,981
Philippines	14,350	17,480	2,018	2,668	2,761	2,575	6,851	6,398	60	54	908	747	8,340	11,053	4,211	4,911
Poland	27,594	27,231	3,231	3,087	33,247	20,401	18,350	17,083	635	323	1,857	2,230	1,792	3,180	5,797	5,513
Portugal	1,683	1,347	2,019	2,599	1,403	1,274	11,596	14,457	51	22	590	595	2,176	1,840	2,063	2,309
Puerto Rico	1	1	1,156	1,870	28	10	6,499	4,156	2	1	569	1,395	255	202	47	25
Qatar	3	6	2,910	3,418	—	...	9,611	10,143	7	8	1,832	1,841	8	18	30	55
Réunion	12	17	5,559	6,724	15	10	11,006	13,416	1	1	1,429	759	44	56	45	72
Romania	18,286	16,550	3,084	2,681	3,159	3,800	10,517	13,571	149	62	889	1,016	2,295	2,302	3,215	3,945
Russia	92,890[1]	83,622	1,612[1]	2,146	36,603[1]	34,500	10,686[1]	10,345	2,883[1]	1,278	1,383[1]	1,495	2,989[1]	3,445	10,390[1]	12,534
Rwanda	289	297	1,161	1,000	1,641	2,920	4,553	5,957	216	307	726	742	3,020	1,633	131	261
St. Kitts and Nevis	...	...	...	...	1	1	3,611	2,861	...	—	1,000	1,000	1	1	...	1
St. Lucia	—	—	...	...	11	11	4,350	4,050	...	...	2,133	2,000	176	118	1	1
St. Vincent and the Grenadines	2	2	3,409	3,333	19	13	4,539	4,547	...	...	1,000	1,000	78	49	3	4
Samoa	...	...	...	...	31	21	6,527	3,884	...	...	...	...	45	50	1	1
San Marino	...	...	...	...	...	...	...	...	...	...	...	...	...	...	...	...
São Tomé and Príncipe	3	2	2,015	2,230	6	33	7,346	9,054	...	...	...	...	10	22	3	6
Saudi Arabia	4,214	2,214	4,177	3,686	59	394	19,121	25,088	...	...	...	...	832	1,192	1,987	1,821
Senegal	996	1,026	823	879	67	141	3,990	5,089	19	48	337	324	105	129	197	227
Serbia and Montenegro	7,613[1]	9,144	3,099	3,767	766[1]	690	6,919	6,610	100[1]	107	1,439[1]	1,259	1,391[1]	1,124	1,037	1,106
Seychelles	...	...	...	...	...	...	5,000	5,000	...	...	...	...	2	2	2	2
Sierra Leone	566	222	1,224	1,078	139	...	5,220	4,671	38	52	652	673	163	162	189	182
Singapore	...	...	...	...	—	—	13,933	10,000	50	26	780	618	1	—	8	5
Slovakia	3,449[3]	3,478	4,041[3]	4,105	566[3]	401	13,057[3]	17,001	161[3]	69	2,347[3]	2,880	277[3]	273	458[3]	524
Slovenia	486[1]	499	4,150[1]	4,815	147[1]	191	12,416[1]	20,893	6[1]	4	1,277[1]	1,435	255[1]	296	77[1]	106
Solomon Islands	...	5	...	4,000	107	145	17,595	16,956	2	4	1,175	1,296	15	17	6	7
Somalia	497	313	715	565	50	76	10,421	10,000	13	15	312	263	271	216	65	73
South Africa	12,734	9,603	2,053	2,080	1,336	1,607	16,611	23,775	146	115	1,178	1,079	3,744	4,759	2,021	2,053
Spain	19,306	18,187	2,489	2,827	5,334	3,002	19,439	25,965	238	303	755	663	13,503	14,835	11,026	11,952
Sri Lanka	2,370	2,904	2,924	3,279	547	349	8,845	8,429	...	...	...	...	743	1,018	579	629
Sudan, The	2,771	3,365	497	509	137	171	2,670	2,614	103	262	1,064	1,588	773	980	922	1,145
Suriname	229	165	3,770	3,836	3	4	11,900	12,227	...	...	690	727	75	76	26	21
Swaziland	127	86	1,401	1,528	9	8	1,665	1,930	5	3	569	443	141	97	13	11
Sweden	5,677	5,548	4,594	4,668	1,132	912	32,977	28,697	91	101	2,494	2,787	132	37	261	284
Switzerland	1,331	1,106	6,352	6,220	731	526	37,867	37,571	8	10	4,264	3,750	634	454	308	283
Syria	2,597	5,158	668	1,689	407	480	17,543	20,870	131	193	577	667	1,370	1,858	1,690	1,868
Taiwan	...	...	...	...	...	...	...	...	...	...	...	...	...	...	...	...
Tajikistan	261[1]	316	1,012[1]	858	149[1]	305	12,031[1]	13,252	6[1]	6	560[1]	1,482	249[1]	157	622[1]	535
Tanzania	4,138	4,131	1,389	1,525	8,167	6,363	8,824	5,264	437	433	501	565	2,093	2,022	1,184	1,166
Thailand	23,624	30,111	2,149	2,713	21,784	18,492	14,241	15,832	377	273	751	834	6,371	7,557	2,557	2,870
Togo	505	740	809	1,107	913	1,289	7,992	6,796	22	51	202	297	49	49	152	131
Tonga	...	...	...	...	54	23	12,255	11,821	...	...	...	...	13	10	20	24
Trinidad and Tobago	17	12	2,816	2,929	10	12	9,757	10,315	3	4	1,460	2,566	62	80	17	25
Tunisia	1,624	1,820	1,112	1,232	205	330	12,592	12,222	73	92	616	888	719	991	1,480	2,195
Turkey	28,283	25,571	2,065	1,949	4,321	5,351	22,388	25,343	1,946	1,389	885	971	9,117	10,660	17,963	21,999
Turkmenistan	954[1]	1,299	2,385[1]	1,578	32[1]	30	7,325[1]	5,000	5[1]	15	2,425[1]	3,000	170[1]	179	538[1]	538
Tuvalu	...	...	...	...	...	—	...	...	...	...	...	...	1	1	—	—
Uganda	1,597	2,309	1,483	1,641	5,360	8,288	6,335	8,008	493	671	774	733	8,384	10,558	420	556
Ukraine	37,078[1]	38,837	2,952[1]	2,729	19,129[1]	13,500	12,044[1]	8,459	2,840[1]	880	2,298[1]	2,211	2,597[1]	2,152	5,750[1]	6,210
United Arab Emirates	2	...	1,912	691	4	5	19,300	19,464	...	...	...	...	205	378	270	1,129
United Kingdom	22,644	18,983	6,168	6,299	6,333	6,641	35,916	40,028	745	812	3,401	3,496	515	318	3,580	2,913
United States	292,220	325,315	4,579	5,886	18,530	20,828	32,069	38,545	1,623	1,228	1,839	1,829	25,256	29,863	31,092	35,513
Uruguay	1,230	2,053	2,411	3,968	215	171	7,514	11,409	6	6	986	982	394	511	117	147
Uzbekistan	2,281[1]	3,502	1,678[1]	2,920	468[1]	800	9,942[1]	14,545	6[1]	12	712[1]	2,400	1,000[1]	1,525	3,867[1]	3,298
Vanuatu	1	1	515	538	49	63	10,139	10,500	...	...	...	...	18	20	8	10
Venezuela	2,037	2,281	2,484	3,035	682	1,100	8,676	12,987	57	35	585	754	2,579	3,019	514	1,258
Vietnam	20,008	34,043	3,056	4,140	4,758	3,976	7,432	7,827	187	247	639	716	3,175	4,086	3,625	4,905
Virgin Islands (U.S.)	...	...	...	...	...	...	...	...	...	...	...	...	...	...	...	...
West Bank	28	30	...	...	16	17	...	...	2	2	...	...	164	153	194	228
Western Sahara	2	3	758	800	...	8,288	...	...	...	...	...	...	...	...	...	...
Yemen	693	672	871	1,085	153	211	12,233	12,373	64	63	1,424	1,219	314	591	536	584
Zambia	1,467	1,069	1,569	1,459	704	1,014	6,517	5,972	15	16	629	516	105	101	274	270
Zimbabwe	2,391	2,027	1,488	1,213	127	208	4,792	4,856	50	50	694	760	170	200	153	147

livestock														country
cattle		sheep		hogs		chickens		milk[e]				eggs[f]		
stock ('000 head)		stock ('000 head)		stock ('000 head)		stock ('000 head)		production ('000 metric tons)		yield (kg/animal)		production (metric tons)		
1989–91 average	2001	1989–91 average	2001	1989–91 average	2001	1989–91 average	2001	1989–91 average	2001	1989–91 average	2001	1989–91 average	2001	
1,712	2,260	3,100	4,500	37	39	17,833	24,000	140	184	393	400	8,000	10,000	Niger
13,974	20,000	12,477	20,500	3,319	4,855	122,120	126,000	350	386	239	243	313,000	435,000	Nigeria
…	…	…	…	…	…	…	…	…	…	…	…	…	…	Northern Mariana Islands
959	967	2,202	2,400	696	391	4,000	3,000	15,560	1,669	5,854	5,580	51,000	49,000	Norway
144	314	238	335	…	…	2,000	3,000	18	38	420	420	6,000	7,000	Oman
17,677	22,857	25,703	24,200	…	…	78,000	155,000	3,525	8,192	842	1,182	211,000	340,000	Pakistan
…	…	…	…	…	…	…	…	…	…	…	…	…	…	Palau
1,401	1,533	…	…	228	278	8,000	14,000	129	171	1,162	1,219	11,000	13,000	Panama
99	89	4	6	997	1,600	3,000	4,000	—	—	102	100	3,000	4,000	Papua New Guinea
7,985	9,900	422	402	2,443	2,700	15,065	15,000	224	330	1,904	2,399	35,000	68,000	Paraguay
4,126	4,950	12,484	14,500	2,417	2,800	62,406	90,000	788	1,075	1,323	2,067	104,000	160,000	Peru
1,664	2,548	30	30	7,968	11,063	77,000	115,000	15	11	2,298	2,571	297,000	445,000	Philippines
9,875	5,501	3,934	337	20,056	16,992	58,196	48,000	1,500	12,030	3,260	4,362	410,000	428,000	Poland
1,355	1,399	5,531	5,900	2,531	2,350	19,667	35,000	3,450	1,860	3,734	5,239	85,000	108,000	Portugal
595	390	9	16	204	118	11,241	12,000	396	377	4,233	3,660	17,000	15,000	Puerto Rico
10	15	126	215	…	…	2,932	4,000	10	11	1,592	1,493	3,000	4,000	Qatar
20	30	2	2	88	77	6,916	12,000	7	21	627	1,050	4,000	6,000	Réunion
6,029	2,800	15,236	7,800	12,675	5,076	121,000	74,000	…	5,047	1,867	3,154	354,000	305,000	Romania
51,939[1]	27,107	46,998[1]	14,000	31,820[1]	15,700	584,867[1]	325,000	45,088[1]	31,980	2,273[1]	2,460	2,259,433[1]	1,945,000	Russia
592	815	392	260	125	180	1,292	1,000	85	85	579	739	2,000	2,000	Rwanda
4	4	14	7	2	3	56	…	…	…	…	…	…	…	St. Kitts and Nevis
12	12	15	12	12	15	223	…	1	1	1,396	1,389	…	1,000	St. Lucia
6	6	13	13	10	10	205	…	1	1	1,351	1,370	1,000	1,000	St. Vincent and the Grenadines
24	28	…	…	185	170	356	…	1	2	1,000	1,000	…	…	Samoa
…	…	…	…	…	…	…	…	…	…	…	…	…	…	San Marino
4	4	2	3	3	2	124	…	—	—	170	170	…	…	São Tomé and Príncipe
195	330	6,370	7,576	…	…	76,000	130,000	274	601	6,254	8,035	113,000	136,000	Saudi Arabia
2,515	3,230	3,311	4,818	193	280	19,667	45,000	98	116	360	360	15,000	33,000	Senegal
1,925[1]	1,355	2,701[1]	1,917	3,876[1]	4,372	21,920[1]	21,000	1,841[1]	1,825	1,799	2,100	81,783	76,000	Serbia and Montenegro
3	1	…	…	18	18	293	1,000	—	—	533	564	1,000	2,000	Seychelles
333	400	271	365	50	52	6,000	6,000	17	21	250	250	7,000	8,000	Sierra Leone
—	—	—	—	300	190	2,000	2,000	…	…	…	…	17,000	16,000	Singapore
1,098[3]	608	492[3]	348	2,224[3]	1,488	7,128[3]	14,000	1,220[3]	1,102	3,254[3]	4,650	95,645[3]	67,000	Slovakia
488[1]	477	26[1]	96	574[1]	604	5,533[1]	7,000	569[1]	649	2,650[1]	3,043	19,712[1]	23,000	Slovenia
11	13	…	…	53	67	144	…	1	1	650	650	…	…	Solomon Islands
4,100	5,300	12,783	13,200	9	4	2,833	3,000	425	530	398	400	2,000	2,000	Somalia
13,433	13,722	32,060	28,800	1,532	1,540	73,000	119,000	2,426	2,667	2,637	2,667	213,000	318,000	South Africa
5,125	6,411	23,280	24,400	16,509	23,348	111,000	128,000	6,100	6,294	3,728	4,842	649,000	560,000	Spain
1,690	1,565	25	11	88	68	9,000	11,000	172	221	271	321	46,000	52,000	Sri Lanka
21,080	38,325	21,304	47,000	…	…	32,371	38,000	2,252	3,072	480	480	33,000	46,000	Sudan, The
91	136	9	8	29	23	8,000	3,000	17	14	1,832	1,929	3,000	3,000	Suriname
712	615	24	32	23	34	1,133	3,000	42	38	274	288	…	1,000	Swaziland
1,704	1,638	408	452	2,243	1,891	11,433	7,000	3,401	3,300	6,097	7,759	116,000	98,000	Sweden
1,845	1,593	392	460	1,793	1,556	5,912	7,000	3,892	3,910	4,954	5,469	38,000	34,000	Switzerland
786	867	14,571	12,362	1	1	14,405	21,000	782	1,032	2,314	2,484	75,000	115,000	Syria
…	…	…	…	…	…	80,119	…	…	…	…	…	…	…	Taiwan
1,238[1]	1,091	2,245[1]	1,363	73[1]	1	5,167[1]	1,000	486[1]	316	886[1]	551	9,957[1]	2,000	Tajikistan
13,047	17,700	3,551	4,250	320	355	20,567	30,000	516	685	169	207	41,000	58,000	Tanzania
5,860	4,640	161	43	4,766	8,300	109,000	190,000	137	520	1,886	2,419	430,000	530,000	Thailand
244	278	1,153	1,000	404	289	6,070	8,000	7	9	225	225	6,000	6,000	Togo
11	11	…	…	94	81	221	…	—	—	1,500	1,480	…	…	Tonga
52	32	14	12	53	41	10,000	10,000	11	10	1,593	1,552	9,000	9,000	Trinidad and Tobago
626	760	5,935	6,600	6	6	39,367	43,000	401	980	1,449	1,782	52,000	79,000	Tunisia
12,037	10,548	43,195	29,435	10	5	73,181	220,000	8,183	8,600	1,352	1,593	369,000	715,000	Turkey
962[1]	860	5,793[1]	6,000	203[1]	45	6,900[1]	5,000	633[1]	830	1,506[1]	1,431	15,533[1]	15,000	Turkmenistan
…	…	…	…	12	13	29	…	…	…	…	…	…	…	Tuvalu
4,817	5,900	783	1,100	1,029	1,550	18,667	26,000	421	511	350	350	15,000	20,000	Uganda
…	9,421	6,658[1]	955	16,437[1]	9,078	1,803,520[1]	108,000	18,363[1]	13,200	2,273[1]	2,662	678,385[1]	525,000	Ukraine
49	100	255	467	…	…	7,000	15,000	5	9	210	157	10,000	13,000	United Arab Emirates
11,980	10,343	43,493	36,697	7,519	5,845	124,076	168,000	14,976	14,717	5,206	6,538	616,000	629,000	United Kingdom
96,316	96,700	11,128	6,965	54,557	59,138	1,333,000	1,830,000	66,423	75,025	6,673	8,226	4,048,000	5,080,000	United States
9,046	11,667	25,576	13,032	217	380	8,000	13,000	980	1,422	1,562	1,755	26,000	37,000	Uruguay
5,273[1]	5,400	8,681[1]	8,100	524[1]	89	26,933[1]	14,000	3,619[1]	3,700	1,639[1]	1,565	100,383[1]	70,000	Uzbekistan
124	151	…	…	59	62	306	…	2	3	202	207	…	…	Vanuatu
13,311	14,500	558	820	2,986	5,400	60,000	115,000	1,564	1,400	1,322	1,333	119,000	180,000	Venezuela
3,151	4,063	…	…	12,224	20,200	75,000	150,000	36	60	800	800	97,000	168,000	Vietnam
8	8	3	3	3	3	30	…	2	2	2,725	2,703	…	…	Virgin Islands (U.S.)
11	12	341	352	…	…	…	…	19	27	2,749	3,524	7,000	15,000	West Bank
…	…	27	33	…	…	…	…	…	…	…	…	…	…	Western Sahara
1,154	1,401	3,682	4,804	…	…	16,385	30,000	152	180	600	601	18,000	31,000	Yemen
2,845	2,600	59	150	296	340	16,033	30,000	77	64	300	300	26,000	46,000	Zambia
5,867	5,753	544	535	296	278	12,000	16,000	440	310	417	310	16,000	21,000	Zimbabwe

[1]1992–94 average. [2]Belgium includes Luxembourg. [3]1993–95 average. [4]Indonesia includes East Timor.

Extractive industries

Extractive industries are generally defined as those exploiting in situ natural resources and include such activities as mining, forestry, fisheries, and agriculture; the definition is often confined, however, to nonrenewable resources only. For the purposes of this table, agriculture is excluded; it is covered in the preceding table.

Extractive industries are divided here into three parts: mining, forestry, and fisheries. These major headings are each divided into two main subheadings, one that treats production and one that treats foreign trade. The production sections are presented in terms of volume except for mining, and the trade sections are presented in terms of U.S. dollars. Volume of production data usually imply output of primary (unprocessed) raw materials only, but, because of the way national statistical information is reported, the data may occasionally include some processed and manufactured materials as well, since these are often indistinguishably associated with the extractive process (sulfur from petroleum extraction, cured or treated lumber, or "processed" fish). This is also the case in the trade sections, where individual national trade nomenclatures may not distinguish some processed and manufactured goods from unprocessed raw materials.

Mining. In the absence of a single international source publication or standard of practice for reporting volume or value of mineral production, single-country sources predominantly have been used to compile mining production figures, supplemented by U.S. Bureau of Mines data, by the United Nations' *National Accounts Statistics* (annual; 2 parts), and by industry sources, especially *Mining Journal's Mining Annual Review*. Each country has its own methods of classifying mining data, which do not always accord with the principal mineral production categories adopted in this table—namely, "metals," "nonmetals," and "energy." The available data have therefore been adjusted to accord better with the definition of each group. Included in the "metal" category are all ferrous and nonferrous metallic ores, concentrates, and scrap; the "nonmetal" group includes all nonmetallic minerals (stone, clay, precious gems, etc.) except the mineral fuels; the last group, "energy," is composed predominantly of the natural hydrocarbon fuels, though it may also include manufactured gas.

The contribution (value) of each national mineral sector to its country's gross domestic product is given, as is the distribution by group of that contribution (to gross domestic product and to foreign trade), although statistics regarding the value of mineral production are less readily available in country sources than those regarding trade or volume of minerals produced. Figures for value added by mineral output, though not always available, were sought first, as they provide the most consistent standard to compare the importance of minerals both within a particular national economy and among national mineral sectors worldwide. Where value added to the gross domestic product was not available, gross value of production or sales was substituted and the exception footnoted. Figures for value of production are reported here in millions of U.S. dollars to permit comparisons to be made from country to country. Comparisons can also be made as to the relative importance of each mineral group within a given country.

Extractive industries

country	mining														
	% of GDP, 1998	mineral production (value added)					trade (value)								
		year	total ('000,000 U.S.$)	by kind (%)			year	exports				imports			
				metals[a]	non-metals[b]	energy[c]		total ('000,000 U.S.$)	by kind (%)			total ('000,000 U.S.$)	by kind (%)		
									metals[a]	non-metals[b]	energy[c]		metals[a]	non-metals[b]	energy[c]
Afghanistan	…	…	…	…	…	…	1997	0.1	—	100.0	—	…	…	…	…
Albania	…	1994[1]	81.4	46.1	0.8	53.1	1997	16.5	93.9	6.1	—	12.9	—	34.9	65.1
Algeria	23.0	1998	10,895.7	—	—	100.0	1996	8,931.6	—	0.2	99.8	22.4	—	—	100.0
American Samoa	…	1998	…	—	100.0	—	…	…	…	…	…	…	…	…	…
Andorra	…	…	…	…	…	…	…	…	…	…	…	…	…	…	…
Angola	60.9[2]	1997	3,935.1	—	7.7	92.3	1997	212.6	—	90.4	9.6	…	…	…	…
Antigua and Barbuda	1.5	1998	9.0[12]	—	100.0	—	…	…	…	…	…	…	…	…	…
Argentina	2.4[2]	1997	7,821.8[3]	…	…	…	1997	2,429.7[4]	—	—	100.0[4]	419.5	65.2	1.6	33.2
Armenia	…	1998	…	—100.0—		—	1997	106.9	—	100.0	—	187.2	50.5	49.5	—
Aruba	…	1998	…	—	100.0	—	1997	1.4	—	100.0	—	…	…	…	…
Australia	4.4	1998	15,105.6	…	…	…	1997	17,083.6	40.1	3.6	56.3	3,181.5	3.4	9.0	87.6
Austria	0.5	1995	819.3	2.5	53.5	44.0	1997	484.0[4]	38.5[4]	61.2[4]	0.3[4]	3,055.2	16.7	10.2	73.1
Azerbaijan	…	…	…	…	…	…	1994	…	…	…	…	224.1	—	—	100.0
Bahamas, The	…	1998	…	—	100.0	—	1997	1.2	100.0	—	—	…	…	…	…
Bahrain	13.6	1998	841.2	—	1.5	98.5	1996	2,471.1[6]	0.6[6]	—	99.3[6]	2,002.2	15.8	0.6	83.7
Bangladesh	1.0	1997–98	417.6	—	47.4	52.6	1996	…	…	…	…	80.0	—	77.5	22.5
Barbados	1.0	1998	4.6[3]	—	—100.0[3]—		1997	0.1	100.0	—	—	8.3	—	43.4	56.6
Belarus	…	1998	…	—	—100.0—		1997	175.2	—	92.5	7.5	39.6	—	100.0	—
Belgium	0.3[2]	1997	617.8	—	—100.0—		1997	13,490.0	8.2	88.6	3.3	21,328.3	12.4	54.9	32.7
Belize	0.5	1998	2.5	—	100.0	—	1997	…	…	…	…	3.4	—	14.7	85.3
Benin	0.7[5]	1995	14.4[8]	—	—100.0[8]—		…	…	…	…	…	…	…	…	…
Bermuda	…	…	…	…	…	…	1997	…	…	…	…	14.0	—	100.0	—
Bhutan	2.3[2]	1997	8.5	—	—100.0—		1994	2.9	—	82.8	17.2	1.7	—	29.4	70.6
Bolivia	11.1	1998	686.1	—49.5—		50.5	1997	377.7	72.9	1.1	26.0	17.7	85.9	14.1	—
Bosnia and Herzegovina	…	…	…	…	…	…	1997	2.9	—	—	100.0	…	…	…	…
Botswana	37.6	1997–98	1,950.6	11.4[9]	88.0[9]	0.7[9]	[10]	…	…	…	…	…	…	…	…
Brazil	0.8[2]	1997	6,760.5	…	…	…	1997	3,454.5	92.4	7.6	—	5,433.9	8.2	4.4	87.4
Brunei	36.7	1998	1,777.6	—8.5—		91.5	1997	1,970.2[6]	—	—	100.0[6]	9.3	—	100.0	—
Bulgaria	1.4	1998	167.4	…	…	…	1997	120.4	37.7	62.3	—	1,166.2	13.4	3.4	83.2
Burkina Faso	…	1998	…	—100.0—		—	…	…	…	…	…	…	…	…	…
Burundi	0.6[2]	1995	6.2	…	…	…	…	…	…	…	…	…	…	…	…
Cambodia	0.3	1998	8.8	—	100.0	—	…	…	…	…	…	…	…	…	…
Cameroon	5.5	1997–98	491.5	—	—	100.0	1996	628.8	—	—	100.0	187.6	16.4	4.0	79.6
Canada	3.7	1998	21,998.8	19.4	12.0	68.6	1997	22,630.2	16.3	3.7	79.9	10,037.9	24.5	6.4	69.1
Cape Verde	0.3[9]	1994	0.9	—	100.0	—	…	…	…	…	…	…	…	…	…
Central African Republic	3.8	1998	39.8[11]	—100.0[11]—		—	1997	104.1	—	100.0	—	0.8[4]	—	100.0[4]	—
Chad	…	…	…	…	…	…	…	…	…	…	…	…	…	…	…
Chile	8.5	1998	3,555.7	—100.0—		—	1997	2,553.3	96.9	3.1	—	1,505.5	4.1	—	95.9
China	…	…	…	…	…	…	1997	5,786.1	2.5	24.5	73.0	10,446.5	32.9	5.6	61.5
Colombia	5.5[4]	1996	4,735.4	…	…	…	1997	3,363.5	0.1	4.2	95.7	86.1	20.0	80.0	—
Comoros	—	1998	…	—	100.0	—	…	…	…	…	…	…	…	…	…
Congo, Dem. Rep. of the	22.8[6]	1995	288.6	—100.0—		—	1995	302.7	—	84.5	15.5	3.4	—	100.0	—
Congo, Rep. of the	40.6[13]	1996[13]	978.8[13]	…	…	…	1995	939.5	—	0.3	99.7	5.2	—	48.1	51.9
Costa Rica	…	…	…	…	…	…	1997	5.1	100.0	—	—	123.1[4]	—	7.0[4]	93.0[4]
Côte d'Ivoire	0.2[13]	1998[13]	28.1[13]	…	…	…	1997	132.0	—	100.0	—	489.9[4]	—	3.2[4]	96.8[4]
Croatia	0.4	1998	96.9	…	…	…	1997	135.0	23.1	14.1	62.8	772.7	—	7.3	92.7
Cuba	…	…	…	…	…	…	1997	…	…	…	…	13.3	—	100.0	—
Cyprus	0.3[14]	1998[14]	25.1	—	100.0	—	1997[14]	20.6	46.6	53.4	—	167.9	—	12.9	87.1
Czech Republic	…	…	…	…	…	…	1997	651.0	23.9	11.0	65.1	2,175.5	13.0	4.1	82.9
Denmark	1.4[2]	1997	2,023.8	—	—100.0—		1997	1,193.7	15.2	6.9	77.8	1,004.3	7.7	18.6	73.7
Djibouti	—	1998	…	—	100.0	—	…	…	…	…	…	…	…	…	…
Dominica	0.9	1998	2.0	—	100.0	—	1996	0.9	—	100.0	—	1.1	—	—	100.0
Dominican Republic	2.0	1998	309.3	—100.0—		—	1994	2.7	—	100.0	—	…	…	…	…
East Timor	…	…	…	…	…	…	…	…	…	…	…	…	…	…	…
Ecuador	7.8	1997	1,560.0	—6.8[15]—		93.2[15]	1997	1,404.8	—	—	100.0	95.0	—	9.4	90.6

Since the data for value of mineral production are obtained mostly from country sources, there is some variation (from a standard calendar year) in the time periods to which the data refer. In addition, the time period for which production data are available does not always correspond with the year for which mineral trade data are available.

The Standard International Trade Classification (SITC), Revision 3, was used to determine the commodity groupings for foreign trade statistics. The actual trade data for these groups is taken largely from the United Nations' *International Trade Statistics Yearbook* (2 vol.) and national sources.

Forestry. Data for the production and trade sections of forestry are based on the Food and Agriculture Organization (FAO) of the United Nations' *Yearbook of Forest Products.* Production of roundwood (all wood obtained in removals from forests) is the principal indicator of the volume of each country's forestry sector; this total is broken down further (as percentages of the roundwood total) into its principal components: fuelwood and charcoal, and industrial roundwood. The latter group was further divided to show its principal component, sawlogs and veneer; lesser categories of industrial roundwood could not be shown for reasons of space. These included pitprops (used in mining, a principal consumer of wood) and pulpwood (used in papermaking and plastics). Value of trade in forest products is given for both imports and exports, although exports alone tend to be the significant indicator for producing countries, while imports of wood are rarely a significant fraction of the trade of most importing countries.

Fisheries. Data for nominal (live weight) catches of fish, crustaceans, mollusks, etc., in all fishing areas (marine areas and inland waters) are taken from the FAO *Yearbook of Fishery Statistics* (*Catches and Landings*). Total catch figures are given in metric tons; the catches in inland waters and marine areas are given as percentages of the total catch, as are the main kinds of catch—fish, crustaceans, and mollusks. The total catch figures exclude marine mammals, such as whales and seals, and such aquatic animal products as corals, sponges, and pearls; but include frogs, turtles, and jellyfish. The subtotals by kind of catch, however, exclude the last group, which do not belong taxonomically to the fish, crustaceans, or mollusks.

Figures for trade in fishery products (including processed products and preparations like oils, meals, and animal feeding stuffs) are taken from the FAO's *Yearbook of Fishery Statistics* (*Commodities*). Value figures for trade in fish products are given for both imports and exports.

The following notes further define the column headings:

a. Includes ferrous and nonferrous metallic ores, concentrates, and scraps, such as iron ore, bauxite and alumina, copper, zinc, gold (except unwrought or semimanufactured), lead, or uranium.

b. Includes natural fertilizers; stone, sand, and aggregate; and pearls, precious and semiprecious stones, worked and unworked.

c. Includes hydrocarbon solids, liquids, and gases.

1 cubic metre = 35.3147 cubic feet

1 metric ton = 1.1023 short tons

forestry						fisheries, 1999								country
production of roundwood, 2000				trade (value, '000 U.S.$), 1999		catch (nominal)						trade (value, '000 U.S.$)		
total ('000 cubic metres)	fuelwood, charcoal (%)	industrial roundwood (%)		exports	imports	total ('000 metric tons)	by source (%)		by kind of catch (%)			exports	imports	
		total	sawlogs, veneer				marine	inland	fish	crustaceans	mollusks			
8,283	78.8	21.2	10.3	...	1,090	1.2	—	100.0	100.0	—	—	...	...	Afghanistan
409	84.5	15.5	15.5	7,063	17,158	2.7	70.3	29.7	90.8	0.7	8.5	4,804	3,965	Albania
2,795	83.9	16.1	2.4	...	375,546	105.7	100.0	—	96.3	3.6	0.1	2,374	13,268	Algeria
...	...	...	...	...	302[2]	0.5	100.0	—	99.6	0.2	0.2	...		American Samoa
...	...	...	...	...	6,383	—		100.0	100.0	—	—	...	...	Andorra
6,676	83.3	16.7	1.0	1,635	5,124	177.5	96.6	3.4	98.3	1.4	0.3	10,043	14,523	Angola
...	...	...	...	...	4,604	3.2	100.0	—	69.3	29.2	1.4	644	2,373	Antigua and Barbuda
5,741	19.2	80.8	—	224,651	755,695	1,024.8	98.8	1.2	63.1	2.9	34.1	807,042	88,368	Argentina
36[5]	100.0[5]	—	—	...	386	0.4	—	100.0	100.0	—	—	494	3,136	Armenia
...	...	...	...	6	7,321	0.2	100.0	—	100.0	—	—	...	17,753	Aruba
22,938	11.8	88.2	43.5	709,553	1,523,192	216.3	98.6	1.4	61.5	25.8	12.7	899,040	485,072	Australia
13,276	21.5	78.5	60.5	4,085,669	2,318,823	0.4	—	100.0	100.0		—	10,689	204,997	Austria
...	...	...	...	206	28,116	4.7	—	100.0	100.0	—	—	3,850	846	Azerbaijan
17	—	100.0	100.0	...	30,414	10.5	100.0	—	16.9	78.5	4.5	69,591	4,400	Bahamas, The
—	—	—	—	...	25,821	10.3	100.0	—	65.5	34.1	0.4	6,925	3,203	Bahrain
33,629	98.1	1.9	0.5	14,405	92,529	924.1	37.0	63.0	96.6	3.4	—	297,585	2,050	Bangladesh
5	—	100.0	100.0	...	35,503	0.3	100.0	—	100.0	—	—	951	11,044	Barbados
6,136	15.1	84.9	51.6	73,918	63,254	0.5	—	100.0	88.9	—	11.1	14,028	54,905	Belarus
4,400	12.5	87.5	58.0	3,734,032[7]	4,136,516[7]	29.9	98.2	1.8	92.9	5.0	2.1	447,598[7]	1,063,195[7]	Belgium
188	67.2	32.8	32.8	3,763	4,003	39.9	100.0	—	64.3	5.4	30.3	21,163	1,724	Belize
6,140	94.6	5.4	0.6	931	12,324	38.5	22.2	77.8	80.1	19.9	—	1,928	3,457	Benin
...	...	...	...	...	...	0.5	100.0	—	91.1	8.9	—	...	7,569	Bermuda
1,751	97.4	2.6	1.0	156	2,159	0.3	—	100.0	100.0	—	—	...	...	Bhutan
1,906	72.7	27.3	26.3	25,409	40,384	6.1	—	100.0	100.0	—	—	4	2,938	Bolivia
40	...	100.0	100.0	72,219	23,986	2.5	—	100.0	100.0	—	—	...	9,781	Bosnia and Herzegovina
1,702	93.8	6.2	—	...	15,410	2.0	—	100.0	100.0	—	—	54	5,218	Botswana
197,897	57.6	42.4	23.6	2,579,776	811,923	655.0	73.3	26.7	90.6	8.7	0.6	138,232	289,808	Brazil
296	26.7	73.3	69.6	...	8,426	3.2	99.2	0.8	96.7	2.2	1.1	184	8,881	Brunei
4,766	44.2	55.8	34.1	75,289	77,741	10.6	76.6	23.4	64.0	—	36.0	5,774	13,307	Bulgaria
11,095	95.4	4.6	—	...	14,780	7.6	—	100.0	100.0	—	—	5	1,674	Burkina Faso
1,799	83.9	16.1	12.3	...	1,700	9.2	—	100.0	100.0	—	—	334	8	Burundi
8,157	87.3	12.7	5.0	35,010	8,910	269.1	14.2	85.8	98.0	1.3	0.7	30,525	2,796	Cambodia
15,279	82.0	18.0	11.6	386,415	18,650	95.0	63.2	36.8	99.6	0.4	—	6,152	19,783	Cameroon
185,659	2.6	97.4	78.9	25,469,746	3,777,382	1,021.9	96.0	4.0	62.5	26.2	11.4	2,617,759	1,338,973	Canada
...	...	...	...	2,519	3,760	10.4	100.0	—	99.6	0.4	—	1,852	1,013	Cape Verde
3,548	75.7	24.3	15.6	46,659	...	15.0	—	100.0	100.0	—	—	61	448	Central African Republic
1,969	61.4	38.6	0.7	116	1,650	84.0	—	100.0	100.0	—	—	...	28	Chad
27,972	38.6	61.4	42.1	1,530,190	185,022	5,050.5	100.0	—	97.1	0.8	2.1	1,696,819	54,569	Chile
291,330[12]	65.6[12]	34.4[12]	19.1[12]	6,778,898[12]	25,536,650[12]	17,240.0	98.3	1.7	69.9	17.6	12.5	2,959,530	1,127,412	China
17,846	95.4	4.6	4.5	78,486	316,615	117.9	75.6	24.4	94.8	5.0	0.2	183,668	71,028	Colombia
9	—	100.0	100.0	...	185	12.2	100.0	—	100.0	—	—	1	774	Comoros
50,754	92.7	7.3	0.5	20,754	3,968	208.4	1.9	98.1	99.8	0.2	—	431	41,905	Congo, Dem. Rep. of the
3,243	80.1	19.9	8.5	75,946	1,769	43.7	41.7	58.3	86.0	5.3	8.7	1,720	18,631	Congo, Rep. of the
5,397	69.0	31.0	25.9	20,837	240,616	25.7	90.4	9.6	96.1	3.6	0.3	148,321	25,359	Costa Rica
13,396	76.9	23.1	16.3	225,923	45,038	76.0	82.9	17.1	98.7	1.2	0.1	132,249	162,354	Côte d'Ivoire
3,486	31.4	68.6	54.9	229,147	290,892	19.3	97.9	2.1	93.0	1.5	5.5	34,845	34,825	Croatia
1,593	74.5	25.5	8.0	60	24,509	67.3	93.1	6.9	61.4	22.7	15.9	93,296	22,484	Cuba
25	26.4	73.6	579.7	2,127	37,192	5.3	98.7	1.3	93.8	2.8	3.4	4,343	31,891	Cyprus
14,441	6.5	93.5	55.5	868,057	667,290	4.2	—	100.0	100.0	—	—	25,922	73,795	Czech Republic
3,086	32.4	67.6	42.8	398,653	1,329,135	1,405.0	100.0	—	92.4	0.8	6.9	2,884,334	1,771,500	Denmark
—	—	—	—	...	4,475	0.4	100.0	—	100.0	—	—	130	1,253	Djibouti
...	...	...	...	...	8,358	1.2	100.0	—	100.0	—	—	...	1,595	Dominica
562	98.9	1.1	0.6	578	211,782	8.5	91.6	8.4	74.2	10.4	15.4	700	53,102	Dominican Republic
...	...	...	...	...	...	0.5	100.0	—	98.4	1.4	0.2	...	...	East Timor
11,340	47.8	0.1	45.6	72,103	224,328	497.9	99.9	0.1	99.6	0.4	—	954,471	5,060	Ecuador

Extractive industries (continued)

country	mining: % of GDP, 1998	mineral production (value added): year	mineral production: total ('000,000 U.S.$)	mineral production by kind (%): metals[a]	mineral production by kind (%): non-metals[b]	mineral production by kind (%): energy[c]	trade (value): year	exports: total ('000,000 U.S.$)	exports by kind (%): metals[a]	exports by kind (%): non-metals[b]	exports by kind (%): energy[c]	imports: total ('000,000 U.S.$)	imports by kind (%): metals[a]	imports by kind (%): non-metals[b]	imports by kind (%): energy[c]
Egypt	9.8[9]	1994	5,151.3	—— 1.0 ——		99.0	1997	704.6	—	5.2	94.8	381.9	40.7	19.2	40.1
El Salvador	0.4	1998	47.6	100.0	—	—	1997	…	…	…	…	151.9	—	5.4	94.6
Equatorial Guinea	61.3	1998	279.6	—	—	100.0	…	…	…	…	…	…	…	…	…
Eritrea	0.1	1998	0.5	—— 100.0 ——		—	…	…	…	…	…	…	…	…	…
Estonia	1.0	1998	54.2	—	—— 100.0 ——		1997	76.5	79.0	—	21.0	113.1	27.9	20.2	52.0
Ethiopia	0.5	1997–98	33.3	—— 100.0 ——		—	1995	…	…	…	…	68.4	—	—	100.0
Faroe Islands	0.2[4]	1996	1.7	…	…	…	…	…	…	…	…	…	…	…	…
Fiji	3.4[4]	1996	42.5	—— 100.0 ——		—	1994	0.8	100.0	—	—	5.8	—	41.4	58.6
Finland	0.2	1998	307.4	—— 100.0 ——		—	1997	295.9	64.2	33.1	2.8	3,383.4	28.5	8.5	63.1
France	0.8[6]	1995	11,521.0	4.8	14.3	81.0	1997	2,335.7	46.6	32.5	20.9	20,162.7	9.2	5.2	85.5
French Guiana	…	1998	…	—— 100.0 ——		—	…	…	…	…	…	…	…	…	…
French Polynesia	…	…	…	…	…	…	1997	191.4	—	100.0	—	…	…	…	…
Gabon	41.8[4]	1996	2,382.8	4.0	—	96.0	1996	2,621.1	2.4	—	97.6	6.7	—	50.7	49.3
Gambia, The	—	1998	…	—	100.0	—	1995	…	…	…	…	1.4	—	—	100.0
Gaza Strip	…	…	…	…	…	…	…	…	…	…	…	…	…	…	…
Georgia	…	…	…	…	…	…	…	…	…	…	…	…	…	…	…
Germany	…	…	…	…	…	…	1997	5,631.4	43.6	21.0	35.3	30,568.8	16.3	5.6	78.1
Ghana	5.2	1998	388.6	—— 100.0 ——		—	1997	225.2	—	100.0	—	56.5	100.0	—	—
Greece	0.6[2]	1997	707.9	…	…	…	1997	310.3	40.9	35.9	23.2	1,393.2	6.9	7.2	85.9
Greenland	…	…	…	…	…	…	1997	…	…	…	…	1.6	—	100.0	—
Grenada	1.4	1998	1.3	—	100.0	—	1996	…	…	…	…	2.4	—	25.0	75.0
Guadeloupe	…	1998	…	—	100.0	—	…	…	…	…	…	…	…	…	…
Guam	…	1998	…	—	100.0	—	…	…	…	…	…	…	…	…	…
Guatemala	0.6	1998	30.0	…	…	…	1997	102.9	—	6.2	93.8	172.1	—	—	100.0
Guernsey	…	…	…	…	…	…	…	…	…	…	…	…	…	…	…
Guinea	15.7	1998	645.4[17]	—— 100.0[17] ——		—	1997	396.7	80.3	19.7	—	…	…	…	…
Guinea-Bissau	…	1998	…	—	100.0	—	…	…	…	…	…	…	…	…	…
Guyana	13.6	1998	98.0	—— 100.0 ——		—	1997	94.3	100.0	—	—	…	…	…	…
Haiti	0.2	1998	1.8	—	100.0	—	…	…	…	…	…	…	…	…	…
Honduras	1.8	1998	82.3	—— 100.0 ——		—	1997	30.6	100.0	—	—	10.1	—	—	100.0
Hong Kong	0.02	1998	39.1	—	100.0	—	1997	2,264.8	27.2	72.8	—	4,639.9	12.9	75.8	11.2
Hungary	0.4[2]	1997	181.5	15.6	26.5	57.9	1997	136.5	99.6	—	0.4	1,747.1	1.9	3.5	94.6
Iceland	…	1998	…	—	100.0	—	1997	19.7	34.0	66.0	—	50.7	68.6	21.5	9.9
India	1.0	1996–97	3,268.9	…	…	…	1997	5,168.2	13.3	86.2	0.5	10,499.3[4]	7.8[4]	31.2[4]	61.0[4]
Indonesia	12.9	1998	12,704.4	—— 34.7 ——		65.3	1997	13,660.2	12.7	0.9	86.4	2,138.5	16.9	14.5	68.6
Iran	7.2	1998–99	13,441.8	—— 9.1 ——		90.9	1995	18,525.9	1.0	0.4	98.6	1,271.4	17.5	7.5	75.0
Iraq	…	…	…	…	…	…	…	…	…	…	…	…	…	…	…
Ireland	…	…	…	…	…	…	1997	538.5	75.1	16.5	8.4	825.7	14.4	12.9	72.7
Isle of Man	…	1998	…	—	100.0	—	…	…	…	…	…	…	…	…	…
Israel	…	…	…	…	…	…	1997	6,948.8	0.5	99.5	—	7,117.3	0.2	73.3	26.5
Italy	…	…	…	…	…	…	1997	851.4	34.6	57.2	8.2	16,573.7	15.0	9.3	75.7
Jamaica	4.5	1998	310.3	97.2	2.8	—	1997	682.4	100.0	—	—	105.8	—	—	100.0
Japan	0.2[4]	1996	9,863.9	…	…	…	1997	1,315.4	44.0	56.0	—	67,595.7	12.8	5.8	81.4
Jersey	…	…	…	…	…	…	…	…	…	…	…	…	…	…	…
Jordan	3.3	1998	239.3	—	100.0	—	1997	353.6	5.0	95.0	—	416.7[6]	0.6[6]	8.8[6]	90.6[6]
Kazakhstan	…	…	…	…	…	…	1996	837.9	18.9	12.8	68.4	170.9	29.9	25.8	44.3
Kenya	0.2[6]	1995	14.1	—— 100.0 ——		—	1997	40.4	—	100.0	—	227.3[4]	—	2.6[4]	97.4[4]
Kiribati	…	…	…	…	…	…	1995	…	…	…	…	0.1	—	100.0	—
Korea, North	…	…	…	…	…	…	1997	90.6	30.8	36.9	32.3	52.7[6]	—	36.1[6]	63.9[6]
Korea, South	0.4	1998	1,141.7	…	…	…	1997	238.6	13.9	53.9	32.2	23,311.9[4]	12.8[4]	3.0[4]	84.2[4]
Kuwait	39.5[6]	1995	10,513.4	—	—	100.0	1997	14,130.4[4]	0.2[4]	—	99.8[4]	60.7	—	100.0	—
Kyrgyzstan	…	…	…	…	…	…	1996	15.8	75.9	—	24.1	118.2	2.5	4.8	92.7
Laos	0.4	1998	5.8	—— 100.0 ——		—	…	…	…	…	…	…	…	…	…
Latvia	0.5	1998	116.4	—	—— 100.0 ——		1997	32.3	85.1	—	14.9	148.9	13.7	8.1	78.2
Lebanon	…	…	…	…	…	…	1997	130.5	31.0	69.0	—	132.8	—	100.0	—
Lesotho	0.01[4]	1996	0.1	—	100.0	—	10	…	…	…	…	…	…	…	…
Liberia	2.4	1998	8.6	—	100.0	—	1997	15.7	100.0	—	—	14.8	—	100.0	—
Libya	25.8[4]	1996	8,441.7	—	7.1	92.9	1997	9,451.2[6]	—	—	100.0[6]	51.2	100.0	—	—
Liechtenstein	…	…	…	…	…	…	…	…	…	…	…	…	…	…	…
Lithuania	0.5	1998	49.3	—	33.9[2]	66.1[2]	1997	130.7	48.7	—	51.3	850.6	2.4	7.0	90.6
Luxembourg	0.2	1998	24.8	—	100.0	—	7	…	…	…	…	…	…	…	…
Macau	…	…	…	…	…	…	1997	…	…	…	…	17.3	—	20.8	79.2
Macedonia	…	…	…	…	…	…	1995	29.5	68.1	31.9	—	41.8	6.7	39.5	53.8
Madagascar	0.3[9]	1994	5.2	—— 100.0 ——		—	1997	26.6	40.6	59.4	—	79.5	—	—	100.0
Malawi	1.0[9]	1994	12.8	…	…	…	1995	…	…	…	…	5.1	—	62.7	37.3
Malaysia	7.9	1998	3,675.2[3]	…	…	…	1996	5,509.7	2.4	2.3	95.3	1,175.0	43.1	32.2	24.7
Maldives	1.6	1998	2.2	—	100.0	—	…	…	…	…	…	…	…	…	…
Mali	5.5	1998	81.7	—— 100.0 ——		—	1997	7.0	—	100.0	—	…	…	…	…
Malta	…	1998	…	—	100.0	—	1996	3.5[6]	97.9[6]	2.1[6]	—	10.2	—	100.0	—
Marshall Islands	0.3[6]	1995	0.3	—	100.0	—	…	…	…	…	…	…	…	…	…
Martinique	…	1998	…	—	100.0	—	1995	4.1	19.4	38.3	42.3	102.5	—	—	100.0
Mauritania	9.6[2]	1997	105.9	—— 100.0 ——		—	1997	301.6	100.0	—	—	…	…	…	…
Mauritius	0.1	1998	5.6	—	100.0	—	1996	56.2	—	73.8	26.2	56.2	—	73.8	26.2
Mayotte	…	…	…	…	…	…	…	…	…	…	…	…	…	…	…
Mexico	1.2	1998	5,128.4	…	…	…	1997	11,181.6	4.8	2.3	93.0	1,715.3	39.7	25.2	35.1
Micronesia	…	…	…	…	…	…	…	…	…	…	…	…	…	…	…
Moldova	…	1998	…	—	100.0	—	1997	18.7[6]	100.0[6]	—	—	147.5	—	—	100.0
Monaco	…	…	…	…	…	…	…	…	…	…	…	…	…	…	…
Mongolia	…	…	…	…	…	…	1996	254.1	90.9	9.1	—	…	…	…	…
Morocco	2.2[2]	1997	746.5	…	…	…	1997	751.1	23.6	76.4	—	1,449.6	—	11.3	88.7
Mozambique	…	…	…	…	…	…	1996	8.4	72.6	27.4	—	3.3	—	100.0	—
Myanmar (Burma)	0.4	1998–99	1,107.3	…	…	…	1997	39.0	—	100.0	—	…	…	…	…
Namibia	11.7[2]	1997	382.8	—— 100.0 ——		—	10	…	…	…	…	…	…	…	…
Nauru	…	1998	…	—	100.0	—	1997	151.6	—	100.0	—	…	…	…	…
Nepal	0.5	1998–99	26.8	—— 100.0 ——		—	1995	…	…	…	…	9.1	51.6	—	48.4

forestry						fisheries, 1999								country
production of roundwood, 2000				trade (value, '000 U.S.$), 1999		catch (nominal)						trade (value, '000 U.S.$)		
total ('000 cubic metres)	fuelwood, charcoal (%)	industrial roundwood (%)		exports	imports	total ('000 metric tons)	by source (%)		by kind of catch (%)			exports	imports	
		total	sawlogs, veneer				marine	inland	fish	crusta-ceans	mollusks			
2,883	95.4	4.6	—	11,855	794,951	380.5	40.8	59.2	94.5	4.1	1.4	1,442	153,061	Egypt
5,170	87.4	12.6	12.6	14,360	124,786	15.2	83.9	16.1	24.8	71.1	4.1	33,596	6,640	El Salvador
811	55.1	44.9	44.9	89,885	...	7.0	84.3	15.7	90.8	7.2	2.0	2,565	2,508	Equatorial Guinea
2,285	99.9	0.1	0.1	...	6,833	7.0	100.0	—	98.7	1.1	0.2	973	54	Eritrea
8,910	18.4	81.6	32.0	391,529	112,763	111.8	97.2	2.8	88.9	11.1	—	77,582	30,951	Estonia
89,925	97.3	2.7	—	...	8,894	15.9	—	100.0	100.0	—	—	...	42	Ethiopia
...	...	...	...	221	4,162	358.0	100.0	—	94.1	4.2	1.7	436,000	15,372	Faroe Islands
483	7.7	92.3	40.6	18,189	8,189	36.7	84.7	15.3	56.2	3.4	40.3	22,266	17,294	Fiji
54,263	7.6	92.4	47.9	10,925,450	887,491	160.6	77.1	22.9	99.9	0.1	—	21,493	118,244	Finland
50,170	22.0	78.0	52.8	5,683,978	7,492,308	578.1	99.2	0.8	86.4	3.5	10.1	1,107,169	3,280,940	France
120	49.8	50.2	42.6	2,481	2,424	7.7	100.0	—	45.5	54.5	—	40,495[2]	5,136[2]	French Guiana
...	...	...	...	...	22,201	12.4	99.6	0.4	99.5	0.4	0.1	2,263	6,891	French Polynesia
5,397	48.6	51.4	51.4	380,793	4,799	52.9	84.9	15.1	94.2	5.4	0.4	13,148	6,876	Gabon
618	81.8	18.2	17.2	...	1,416	30.0	91.7	8.3	97.9	1.8	0.3	4,643	848	Gambia, The
...	...	...	...	...	...	3.6	100.0	—	88.1	6.3	5.7	...	...	Gaza Strip
...	...	...	...	11,952	5,749	1.5	93.3	6.7	100.0	—	—	208	2,471	Georgia
37,634	6.8	93.2	62.2	9,923,976	10,776,915	238.9	90.4	9.6	92.0	8.0	—	966,300	2,288,523	Germany
21,907	94.4	5.6	5.2	187,175	24,016	492.8	84.9	15.1	99.1	0.9	—	95,813	20,321	Ghana
2,171	63.3	36.7	31.5	77,993	737,282	136.7	84.5	15.5	78.8	2.5	18.7	278,208	308,553	Greece
—	—	—	—	77	7,179	160.3	100.0	—	48.8	51.2	—	261,255	1,412	Greenland
...	...	...	...	—	5,167	1.6	100.0	—	95.2	4.4	0.4	3,530	2,534	Grenada
15	98.0	2.0	2.0	...	30,639	9.2	100.0	—	92.9	1.6	5.5	266[2]	30,393[2]	Guadeloupe
...	...	...	...	...	...	0.2	100.0	—	98.7	0.4	0.9	...	...	Guam
13,300	96.2	3.8	3.8	17,449	137,727	11.0	36.7	63.3	71.8	28.0	0.2	28,148	6,794	Guatemala
...	...	...	...	...	...	[16]	[16]	[16]	[16]	[16]	[16]	...	...	Guernsey
8,651	92.5	7.5	1.6	6,024	4,542	87.1	95.4	4.6	98.1	0.5	1.5	22,131	14,490	Guinea
592	71.3	28.7	6.8	610	...	5.0	96.0	4.0	81.3	2.4	16.3	6,318	487	Guinea-Bissau
467	2.4	97.6	93.1	36,047	3,239	53.8	98.9	1.1	77.7	22.3	—	34,461	475	Guyana
6,501	96.3	3.7	3.4	...	13,221	5.0	90.0	10.0	86.0	5.0	9.0	9,264	7,990	Haiti
7,413	88.5	11.5	11.5	43,309	59,836	7.2	98.6	1.4	53.7	21.8	24.4	97,207	14,805	Honduras
21[5]	100.0[5]	—	—	2,508,240[5]	3,101,116[5]	127.8	100.0	—	90.4	3.8	5.9	383,398	1,593,661	Hong Kong
5,902	44.0	56.0	23.4	353,145	618,345	7.5	—	100.0	97.6	—	2.4	6,948	39,552	Hungary
—	—	—	—	648	65,695	1,736.3	100.0	—	96.7	2.6	0.7	1,379,379	80,693	Iceland
302,794	92.1	7.9	6.1	54,971	789,321	3,316.8	79.2	20.8	89.3	7.9	2.8	1,019,579	20,188	India
190,601	83.5	16.5	13.0	4,757,769	947,593	4,149.4	92.9	7.1	90.9	6.6	2.6	1,527,092	86,555	Indonesia
1,151	16.5	83.5	26.9	...	201,165	387.2	63.0	37.0	97.3	1.2	1.5	23,945	58,002	Iran
177	66.7	33.3	14.1	...	4,341	24.6	53.2	46.8	100.0	—	—	...	1,277	Iraq
2,673	2.7	97.3	59.4	237,008	730,167	285.9	98.9	1.1	90.0	7.4	2.6	343,826	115,853	Ireland
...	...	...	...	...	...	2.6	100.0	—	3.6	9.0	87.3	...	...	Isle of Man
113	11.5	88.5	31.9	34,467	695,578	5.9	63.5	36.5	94.8	3.2	2.0	8,496	129,891	Israel
9,329	60.9	39.1	22.1	2,581,755	7,096,128	294.2	98.2	1.8	59.0	6.0	35.1	356,976	2,728,568	Italy
706	60.0	40.0	18.7	...	71,424	8.5	94.7	5.3	79.1	4.8	16.1	13,905	32,487	Jamaica
10,031	1.4	98.6	70.4	1,729,858	12,348,306	5,176.5	98.6	1.4	77.0	3.7	19.3	719,839	14,748,712	Japan
...	...	...	...	...	...	3.6[16]	100.0[16]	—[16]	25.7[16]	67.3[16]	7.0[16]	...	...	Jersey
11	63.6	36.4	—	5,420	104,204	0.5	31.4	68.6	100.0	—	—	1,231	21,020	Jordan
315[5]	100.0	—		598	48,398	25.8	—	100.0	100.0	—	—	12,257	11,903	Kazakhstan
29,908	93.4	6.6	1.5	2,064	38,124	205.3	3.2	96.8	99.5	0.4	0.2	32,415	5,339	Kenya
...	...	...	...	...	769[5]	48.2	100.0	—	97.0	—	3.0	5,611	299	Kiribati
7,000	78.6	21.4	14.3	15,192	8,781	210.0	90.5	9.5	95.2	—	4.8	71,535	2,579	Korea, North
1,722	1.6	98.4	36.1	1,515,287	2,967,578	2,119.7	99.7	0.3	64.0	4.4	31.5	1,393,428	1,140,022	Korea, South
...	...	...	...	13	97,708	6.3	100.0	—	88.5	11.5	—	4,721	22,111	Kuwait
42[5]	74.5[5]	25.5[5]	21.9[5]	225	9,892	—	100.0	100.0	100.0	—	—	...	2,287	Kyrgyzstan
4,869	82.2	17.8	15.1	26,657	1,704	30.0	—	100.0	100.0	—	—	99	1,157	Laos
14,488	11.6	88.4	58.7	600,131	47,946	125.4	99.5	0.5	97.5	2.5	—	51,849	36,097	Latvia
412	98.3	1.7	1.7	4,885	166,234	3.6	99.4	0.6	94.4	3.5	2.1	...	19,863	Lebanon
1,594	100.0	—	—	...	...	0.03	—	100.0	100.0	—	—	[18]	[18]	Lesotho
3,037	88.9	11.1	5.2	24,492	1,635	15.5	74.1	25.9	97.6	0.2	2.2	64	1,412	Liberia
652	82.2	17.8	9.7	...	33,260	32.5	100.0	—	100.0	—	—	32,654	12,561	Libya
13[5]	30.8[5]	69.2[5]	69.2[5]	...	...	—	...	...	...	...	...	...	...	Liechtenstein
5,346	22.4	77.6	52.4	171,231	113,279	33.6	94.9	5.1	87.6	12.4	—	33,560	52,499	Lithuania
259	6.9	93.1	43.6	[7]	[7]	—	...	...	...	...	...	[7]	[7]	Luxembourg
...	...	...	...	1,841	14,022	1.5	100.0	—	68.0	29.3	2.7	2,852	13,236	Macau
1,047	83.6	16.4	15.7	9,093	150,166	0.1	—	100.0	100.0	—	—	129	9,994	Macedonia
10,359	98.9	1.1	0.8	23,784	5,061	131.6	77.2	22.8	89.5	0.9	9.5	101,061	5,661	Madagascar
9,964	94.8	5.2	1.3	688	5,265	45.4	—	100.0	100.0	—	—	302	236	Malawi
29,461	26.2	73.8	68.6	3,114,963	1,000,476	1,251.8	99.7	0.3	78.3	8.5	13.2	299,437	258,747	Malaysia
...	...	...	...	14	4,220	133.5	100.0	—	99.6	—	0.4	38,907	...	Maldives
6,597	93.7	6.3	0.1	1,648	8,731	98.5	—	100.0	100.0	—	—	378	1,211	Mali
...	...	...	...	—	62,831	1.0	100.0	—	95.7	2.3	1.9	6,751	19,442	Malta
...	...	...	...	...	1,923	0.4	100.0	—	100.0	—	—	1,482	120	Marshall Islands
12	83.3	16.7	16.7	110	22,864	5.0	100.0	—	98.0	2.0	—	168[2]	38,658[2]	Martinique
16	62.5	37.5	6.3	...	6,000	47.8	89.5	10.5	64.7	—	35.2	99,348	524	Mauritania
25	48.0	52.0	28.0	3,741	67,773	12.0	100.0	—	97.2	0.3	2.5	38,558	32,642	Mauritius
...	...	...	...	...	...	1.5	100.0	—	100.0	—	—	3[2]	161[2]	Mayotte
24,122	67.1	32.9	27.0	281,218	2,106,097	1,202.2	92.4	7.6	80.6	7.7	11.7	649,787	125,723	Mexico
...	...	...	...	...	2,110	11.9	100.0	—	99.6	0.2	0.2	459	3,280	Micronesia
58	50.6	49.4	7.7	3,303	23,350	0.5	—	100.0	100.0	—	—	1,381	2,763	Moldova
...	...	...	...	...	...	0.004	100.0	—	100.0	—	—	...	...	Monaco
631	29.5	70.5	70.5	6,289	2,944	0.5	—	100.0	100.0	—	—	232	33	Mongolia
1,123	49.2	50.8	15.7	74,985	336,920	745.4	99.7	0.3	83.2	0.1	16.7	750,764	10,509	Morocco
18,043	92.7	7.3	0.7	14,072	10,075	35.6	69.8	30.2	100.0	—	—	76,861	10,341	Mozambique
22,574	85.2	14.8	10.4	239,712	18,874	851.6	84.8	15.2	98.7	1.3	0.1	158,560	559	Myanmar (Burma)
[19]	[19]	[19]	[19]	...	36,449	299.2	99.5	0.5	91.3	8.4	0.3	344,017	...	Namibia
...	...	...	...	23[5]	205[5]	0.3	100.0	—	100.0	—	—	...	...	Nauru
21,962	97.2	2.8	2.8	1,199	2,572	12.8	—	100.0	100.0	—	—	269	261	Nepal

Extractive industries (continued)

country	mining														
	% of GDP, 1998	mineral production (value added)					trade (value)								
		year	total ('000,000 U.S.$)	by kind (%)			year	exports				imports			
								total ('000,000 U.S.$)	by kind (%)			total ('000,000 U.S.$)	by kind (%)		
				metals[a]	non-metals[b]	energy[c]			metals[a]	non-metals[b]	energy[c]		metals[a]	non-metals[b]	energy[c]
Netherlands, The	2.7[6]	1995[3]	9,620.1[3]	...	...	...	1997	6,275.9	19.2	8.5	72.3	12,803.2	12.5	5.9	81.6
Netherlands Antilles	...	1998	...	—	100.0	—	1995	901.5	—	0.1	99.9	900.5	—	—	100.0
New Caledonia	10.7[2]	1997	352.1	100.0	—	—	1997	208.9	100.0	—	—	12.9	—	—	100.0
New Zealand	...	...	...	...	...	...	1996	110.9	31.3	0.4	68.3	854.0	21.1	13.5	65.5
Nicaragua	1.6	1998	34.0	—— 100.0 ——		—	1997	4.0	100.0	—	—	130.0	—	4.6	95.4
Niger	3.5[9]	1994	62.5	—— 100.0 ——		—	...	...	...	...	...	...	...	...	...
Nigeria	26.0	1998	33,716.8	—	0.5	99.5	1995	11,131.5	—	—	100.0	19.9	1.5	98.5	—
Northern Mariana Islands	...	...	...	...	...	...	...	...	...	...	...	...	...	...	...
Norway	10.9	1998	16,068.2	—— 1.8 ——		98.2	1997	24,255.2	0.4	1.0	98.6	1,820.3	73.2	11.3	15.5
Oman	40.6[2]	1997	6,361.2	—	0.7	99.3	1996	5,768.3	—	0.1	99.9	70.7	78.8	21.2	—
Pakistan	0.5	1997–98	301.4	...	...	...	1997	57.3	—	1.4	98.6	338.9	50.5	7.5	42.0
Palau	0.1	1998	0.1	—	100.0	—	...	...	...	...	...	...	...	...	...
Panama	0.2	1998	10.5	—— 100.0 ——		—	1996	6.7	100.0	—	—	324.5	—	—	100.0
Papua New Guinea	26.0	1998	975.2	—— 64.0 ——		36.0	1995	1,123.1	48.0	—	52.0	...	...	...	...
Paraguay	0.3	1998	29.2	—	100.0	—	1996	...	...	...	...	124.9	—	66.9	33.1
Peru	10.9	1998	2,378.8	—— 67.9[6, 20] ——		32.1[6]	1997	1,150.6	79.1	0.1	20.8	564.2	0.4	—	99.6
Philippines	0.7	1998	489.1	57.7[6]	41.3[6]	1.0[6]	1997	567.7	55.4	25.5	19.1	4,078.1	14.2	4.1	81.7
Poland	2.9	1998	4,613.0	...	...	...	1997	1,400.6[4]	7.0[4]	11.6[4]	81.4[4]	3,751.2	11.7	6.5	81.8
Portugal	0.5[6]	1995	529.3	40.2	59.6	0.2	1997	391.8	57.0	35.6	7.5	2,369.2	0.7	7.7	91.6
Puerto Rico	...	...	...	...	...	...	...	...	...	...	...	...	...	...	...
Qatar	38.1[2]	1997	3,502.7[3]	...	...	...	1995	3,000.3	—	0.1	99.9	51.3[9]	75.3[9]	24.7[9]	—
Réunion	...	1998	...	—	100.0	—	1995	0.9	100.0	—	—	15.0	—	—	100.0
Romania	3.3[9]	1994	990.9	—	16.1	83.9	1997	75.6	62.6	37.4	—	1,723.1[9]	9.7[9]	3.7[9]	86.6[9]
Russia	...	...	...	...	...	...	1997	32,522.7	5.6	1.0	93.4	560.0[6]	60.2[6]	16.9[6]	23.0[6]
Rwanda	0.06	1998	1.2	...	...	...	...	...	...	...	...	...	...	...	...
St. Kitts and Nevis	0.3[6]	1995	0.6	—	100.0	—	1997	...	...	...	...	2.1	—	33.3	66.7
St. Lucia	0.5	1998	2.6	—	100.0	—	1996	...	...	...	...	5.1	—	49.0	51.0
St. Vincent	0.3	1998	0.9	—	100.0	—	1997	1.6	—	18.8	81.3	1.6[6]	—	18.8[6]	81.3[6]
Samoa	...	...	...	...	...	...	...	...	...	...	...	...	...	...	...
San Marino	...	...	...	...	...	...	...	...	...	...	...	...	...	...	...
São Tomé and Príncipe	...	1998	—	—	100.0	—	...	...	...	...	...	...	...	...	...
Saudi Arabia	37.2[2]	1997	54,352.5	—— 1.1 ——		98.9	1997	50,116.9[2]	0.1[2]	—	99.9[2]	136.7	88.6	11.4	—
Senegal	0.2	1998	6.3	—	100.0	—	1995	55.8	7.3	92.7	—	102.6	—	13.5	86.5
Serbia and Montenegro	9.5[9]	1994	981.7	12.0	3.1	84.9	1997	16.8	32.1	—	67.9	708.7	23.6	5.9	70.6
Seychelles	...	1998	—	—	100.0	—	1996	...	...	...	...	0.5	—	100.0	—
Sierra Leone	16.8[22]	1994–95	117.7	—— 100.0 ——		—	1995	16.7	25.4	74.6	—	0.6	—	100.0	—
Singapore	0.02	1998	14.3	—	100.0	—	1997	787.1	31.0	41.7	27.3	8,895.9	0.7	9.0	90.3
Slovakia	0.9	1998	178.8	...	...	...	1997	68.5	28.0	72.0	—	1,106.3	8.9	4.1	87.0
Slovenia	1.0[2]	1997	182.6	...	...	...	1997	28.6	100.0	—	—	386.4	23.4	17.1	59.4
Solomon Islands	...	1998	...	—— 100.0[23] ——		—	1996	...	...	...	...	2.0	—	—	100.0
Somalia	...	...	...	...	...	...	...	...	...	...	...	...	...	...	...
South Africa	6.5	1998	8,003.2	...	...	...	1997[10]	7,936.4	23.4	51.1	25.4	3,452.8	9.7	14.3	76.0
Spain	...	...	...	...	...	...	1997	771.2	39.7	55.0	5.3	12,200.5[4]	16.5[4]	4.2[4]	79.3[4]
Sri Lanka	1.9	1998	269.4[24]	—— 100.0[24] ——		—	1995	216.5	—	100.0	—	271.1	—	40.0	60.0
Sudan, The	0.3	1998	27.4	...	...	...	1995	...	...	...	...	34.1	—	—	100.0
Suriname	10.9[4]	1996	58.9[25]	...	...	...	1997	594.7	100.0	—	—	15.9[6]	—	31.4[6]	68.6[6]
Swaziland	0.7	1998	8.9	...	...	...	[10]	...	...	...	...	...	...	...	...
Sweden	0.3[6]	1995	634.3	59.2[9]	40.8[9]	—	1997	1,127.6	83.8	11.2	5.0	4,369.9	13.4	6.2	80.4
Switzerland	...	1998	...	—	100.0	—	1997	1,931.1	15.0	85.0	—	4,056.5	3.0	69.0	28.0
Syria	6.6[9]	1994	2,594.1[8]	—	—— 100.0[8] ——		1995	2,675.5	—	1.4	98.6	21.6	—	—	100.0
Taiwan	0.3[6]	1995	791.6	—	79.6	20.4	1995	843.7	...	...	...	8,035.8	—— 35.8 ——		64.2
Tajikistan	...	...	...	...	...	...	1997	1.0	—	100.0	—	228.0[4]	—	100.0[4]	—
Tanzania	1.3	1998	111.9	...	...	...	...	...	...	...	...	...	...	...	...
Thailand	1.8[2]	1997	2,756.6	...	...	...	1997	1,334.0	9.3	74.9	15.7	5,929.7	4.7	14.2	81.1
Togo	5.8	1998	88.3	—	100.0	—	1997	145.3	—	100.0	—	...	...	...	...
Tonga	0.3[6]	1995	0.4	—	100.0	—	1995	0.1	—	100.0	—	1.3	—	46.2	53.6
Trinidad and Tobago	12.2	1998	708.6	—	—	100.0	1996	492.4	—	—	100.0	476.9	12.7	2.1	85.1
Tunisia	5.6	1998	1,456.4	—— 17.1 ——		82.9	1997	438.9	2.7	11.6	85.7	367.1	—	32.4	67.6
Turkey	1.1	1998	2,160.5	...	...	...	1997	325.8	61.7	38.3	—	5,709.8	21.0	3.3	75.7
Turkmenistan	9.7[2]	1997	204.0	—	—	100.0	1997	489.9	—	0.2	99.8	...	...	...	...
Tuvalu	0.9[6]	1995	0.1	—	100.0	—	...	...	...	...	...	...	...	...	...
Uganda	0.3[26]	1995–96	15.8	—— 100.0 ——		—	1996	...	...	...	...	11.2	—	100.0	—
Ukraine	...	...	...	...	...	...	1997	1,421.6	60.4	19.7	19.8	6,790.7	3.4	3.1	93.5
United Arab Emirates	33.4[9]	1994[3]	12,269.1[3]	...	...	...	1996	23,700.1	0.5	0.5	99.0	233.3	17.1	82.9	—
United Kingdom	1.7	1998	21,115.8	—— 8.5 ——		91.5	1997	18,681.6	5.5	32.6	61.8	16,302.2	16.2	38.7	45.1
United States	1.5[2]	1997	120,500.0	4.8	9.5	85.7	1997	13,394.6	35.4	33.2	31.4	80,065.7	5.6	12.8	81.6
Uruguay	0.2	1997	47.6	—	100.0	—	1997	...	...	...	...	229.7	—	6.4	93.6
Uzbekistan	...	...	...	...	...	...	1997	114.5	—	—	100.0	13.9	100.0	—	—
Vanuatu	...	1998	...	—	100.0	—	1994	...	...	...	...	0.5	—	—	100.0
Venezuela	12.1	1998	10,676.5	—— 6.4 ——		93.6	1997	12,510.3	1.8	—	98.2	132.3	41.5	58.5	—
Vietnam	6.2	1998	1,091.3	—— 9.4 ——		90.6	1997	103.2	1.8	—	98.8	32.1	—	100.0	—
Virgin Islands (U.S.)	...	1998	...	—	100.0	—	...	...	...	...	...	...	...	...	...
West Bank	...	...	...	...	...	...	...	...	...	...	...	...	...	...	...
Western Sahara	...	...	...	...	...	...	...	...	...	...	...	...	...	...	...
Yemen	9.8[9]	1994	1,788.2[8]	—	—— 100.0[8] ——		1995	1,424.0	—	—	100.0	208.4	—	—	100.0
Zambia	6.1	1998	203.0	...	...	...	1995	12.9	—	100.0	—	1.7	100.0	—	—
Zimbabwe	6.9[9]	1994	336.1	...	...	...	1997	95.9	4.9	94.3	0.8	35.3[4]	17.8[4]	37.1[4]	45.0[4]

[1]Gross value of production (output). [2]1997. [3]Mostly crude petroleum and natural gas. [4]1996. [5]1998. [6]1995. [7]Belgium includes Luxembourg. [8]Mostly crude petroleum. [9]1994. [10]South Africa includes Botswana, Lesotho, Namibia, and Swaziland. [11]Mostly diamonds, some gold. [12]China includes Taiwan. [13]Petroleum sector only. [14]Republic of Cyprus only. [15]1993. [16]Jersey includes

forestry						fisheries, 1999								country
production of roundwood, 2000				trade (value, '000 U.S.$), 1999		catch (nominal)						trade (value '000 U.S.$)		
total ('000 cubic metres)	fuelwood, charcoal (%)	industrial roundwood (%)		exports	imports	total ('000 metric tons)	by source (%)		by kind of catch (%)			exports	imports	
		total	sawlogs, veneer				marine	inland	fish	crusta- ceans	mollusks			
1,039	15.4	84.6	55.1	2,706,468	5,705,731	514.6	99.6	0.4	87.2	2.8	9.9	1,744,665	1,304,585	Netherlands, The
…	…	…	…	1,535	19,459	0.9	100.0	—	99.4	—	0.6	1,198	6,380	Netherlands Antilles
5	—	100.0	58.3	…	11,595	3.2	100.0	—	96.1	2.8	1.1	18,766	5,677	New Caledonia
17,953	—	100.0	40.4	1,303,550	310,844	594.1	99.8	0.2	93.4	0.7	5.9	712,256	52,445	New Zealand
4,306	94.7	5.3	5.3	11,725	16,267	20.6	94.6	5.4	46.7	52.3	1.0	78,596	7,843	Nicaragua
6,666	93.8	6.2	—	…	6,334	11.0	—	100.0	100.0	—	—	154	458	Niger
100,637	90.6	9.4	7.1	33,457	172,331	455.6	69.4	30.6	92.0	7.2	0.8	19,662	209,959	Nigeria
…	…	…	…	…	51[5]	0.2	100.0	—	99.5	0.5	—	…	…	Northern Mariana Islands
8,173	8.1	91.9	50.1	1,831,746	1,009,845	2,620.1	100.0	—	97.5	2.5	—	3,764,790	612,469	Norway
…	…	…	…	…	17,179	108.8	100.0	—	92.6	0.5	6.9	38,243	5,077	Oman
33,075	92.7	7.3	5.4	…	137,040	654.5	72.5	27.5	93.6	4.9	1.6	141,476	816	Pakistan
…	…	…	…	…	1,123	1.8	100.0	—	98.0	2.0	—	290	87	Palau
1,052	96.7	3.3	3.3	5,440	67,462	120.5	100.0	—	90.8	7.7	1.5	194,898	15,125	Panama
8,597	64.4	35.6	35.6	168,807	12,439	53.7	74.9	25.1	96.9	3.1	—	25,173	7,819	Papua New Guinea
8,097	52.1	47.9	42.2	88,064	31,132	25.0	—	100.0	100.0	—	—	36	1,592	Paraguay
9,157	80.0	20.0	17.7	71,644	166,328	8,429.3	99.5	0.5	98.4	0.2	1.3	788,411	16,833	Peru
43,399	91.8	8.2	1.1	52,996	606,710	1,870.5	92.3	7.7	88.1	4.2	7.7	372,274	121,492	Philippines
25,652	6.0	94.0	44.1	862,220	1,251,300	235.1	94.1	5.9	89.6	8.3	2.1	282,354	260,653	Poland
9,878	6.1	84.8	32.7	1,185,978	913,640	207.7	100.0	—	90.3	2.3	7.4	278,586	1,017,066	Portugal
…	…	…	…	…	…	2.1	100.0	—	59.2	7.7	33.1	[21]	[21]	Puerto Rico
…	…	…	…	…	15,654	4.2	100.0	—	98.8	1.2	—	28	2,053	Qatar
36	85.9	14.1	11.6	342	69,029	5.8	100.0	—	95.5	4.5	—	19,662	33,053	Réunion
13,148	23.1	76.9	46.7	355,924	172,019	7.8	32.0	68.0	100.0	—	—	7,109	31,911	Romania
158,100	33.1	66.9	30.3	3,190,431	358,552	4,141.2	92.6	7.4	95.9	2.1	2.0	1,247,518	199,065	Russia
7,836	95.7	4.3	1.1	…	2,407	6.4	—	100.0	100.0	—	—	…	61	Rwanda
…	…	…	…	33	1,797	0.4	100.0	—	81.5	5.7	12.8	…	729	St. Kitts and Nevis
…	…	…	…	—	11,692	1.7	100.0	—	96.8	1.7	1.5	6,172	5,186	St. Lucia
…	…	…	…	8	18,545	15.6	100.0	—	100.0	—	—	927	1,537	St. Vincent
131	53.4	46.6	44.3	1,357	2,542	9.8	100.0	—	99.5	0.3	0.2	11,700	5,984	Samoa
…	…	…	…	…	…	—	100.0	—	100.0	—	—	…	…	San Marino
9	—	100.0	100.0	504[5]	196[5]	3.8	100.0	—	99.0	—	1.0	3,836	137	São Tomé and Príncipe
…	…	…	…	19,256	778,185	46.9	100.0	—	87.9	10.4	1.7	10,134	99,412	Saudi Arabia
5,037	84.2	15.8	0.8	…	45,293	418.1	90.4	9.6	87.8	1.5	10.7	301,498	3,784	Senegal
1,140	4.4	95.6	95.6	44,990	166,400	1.3	33.9	66.1	96.6	0.8	2.6	225	43,088	Serbia and Montenegro
…	…	…	…	99	1,416	37.8	100.0	—	99.7	—	0.2	12,318	12,904	Seychelles
3,419	96.4	3.6	0.1	1,264	2,053	59.4	75.6	24.4	94.9	3.9	1.2	15,654	3,267	Sierra Leone
120[5]	—	—	—	502,202	889,039	5.1	100.0	—	75.4	14.3	10.3	390,062	475,224	Singapore
5,783	5.9	94.1	42.2	431,828	237,213	1.4	—	100.0	100.0	—	—	1,895	32,269	Slovakia
2,253	23.6	76.4	49.7	399,531	296,900	2.0	88.8	11.2	98.6	—	1.4	6,597	29,280	Slovenia
872	15.8	84.2	84.2	51,070	…	82.3	100.0	—	99.9	—	0.1	64,170	75	Solomon Islands
8,329	98.7	1.3	0.3	132[5]	257[5]	20.3	98.8	1.2	95.6	2.0	2.5	4,058	170	Somalia
30,616[19]	39.2[19]	60.8[19]	19.6[19]	827,673	487,114	588.0	99.8	0.2	98.2	0.5	1.3	260,056[18]	55,691[18]	South Africa
14,810	11.1	88.9	38.4	1,626,053	3,813,488	1,167.2	99.3	0.7	86.8	3.1	10.1	1,604,237	3,286,831	Spain
10,344	93.9	6.1	0.6	2,862	81,534	271.6	90.1	9.9	98.7	1.1	0.2	74,120	59,775	Sri Lanka
9,682	77.6	22.4	1.3	1,040	16,928	49.5	11.1	88.9	99.7	—	0.3	88	280	Sudan, The
93	1.1	98.9	96.8	3,249	1,353	13.0	98.5	1.5	98.0	2.0	—	11,640	3,600	Suriname
890	62.9	37.1	29.2	62,000	—	0.1	—	100.0	100.0	—	—	2,242	9,738	Swaziland
61,800	9.5	90.5	49.7	9,720,885	1,615,641	351.3	99.6	0.4	98.9	1.1	—	477,992	715,463	Sweden
10,428	20.1	79.9	73.9	1,937,022	2,393,070	1.8	—	100.0	100.0	—	—	3,031	375,700	Switzerland
50	31.5	68.5	31.7	1,040	141,790	7.9	32.7	67.3	99.1	0.9	—	183	49,546	Syria
…	…	…	…	…	…	1,099.7	99.9	0.1	70.2	2.6	27.2	1,763,572	556,873	Taiwan
…	…	…	…	80	4,131	…	—	100.0	100.0	—	—	54	143	Tajikistan
39,846	94.2	5.8	0.8	5,939	22,531	310.0	16.1	83.9	99.1	—	0.9	60,202	1,975	Tanzania
36,631	92.2	7.9	0.1	758,925	1,006,210	3,004.9	92.5	7.5	86.7	4.3	9.0	4,109,860	840,679	Thailand
1,232	74.5	25.5	5.4	974	4,355	22.9	78.2	21.8	100.0	—	—	1,498	12,222	Togo
2	—	100.0	100.0	…	2,065	3.7	100.0	—	94.3	5.5	0.2	2,625	872	Tonga
44	22.7	77.3	77.3	2,032	65,952	15.0	100.0	—	95.0	5.0	—	12,315	8,009	Trinidad and Tobago
2,842	92.5	7.5	0.7	14,709	151,980	92.1	99.1	0.9	81.6	7.8	10.6	82,118	13,276	Tunisia
17,767	41.3	58.7	29.1	82,545	969,948	575.1	91.3	8.7	97.1	0.4	2.5	98,196	59,207	Turkey
…	…	…	…	501	3,880	8.8	—	100.0	100.0	—	—	316	99	Turkmenistan
…	…	…	…	—	323[5]	0.4	100.0	—	100.0	—	—	326	…	Tuvalu
16,998	81.3	18.7	6.2	…	17,781	226.1	—	100.0	100.0	—	—	24,221	78	Uganda
10,008	17.6	82.4	62.0	132,755	235,646	407.9	98.9	1.1	98.1	1.4	0.6	75,079	96,776	Ukraine
…	…	…	…	7,290	297,934	117.6	100.0	—	99.9	0.1	—	29,436	28,872	United Arab Emirates
7,451	3.1	96.9	57.1	2,192,065	8,983,465	837.8	99.8	0.2	85.3	7.5	7.2	1,427,853	2,276,998	United Kingdom
500,434	14.4	85.6	49.6	14,783,367	23,721,067	4,749.6	99.2	0.8	79.0	8.3	12.7	2,945,014[21]	9,407,307[21]	United States
6,163	70.3	29.7	22.3	77,918	97,102	103.0	97.6	2.4	79.7	3.3	17.0	98,981	13,418	Uruguay
…	…	…	…	240	37,231	2.9	—	100.0	100.0	—	—	44	2,688	Uzbekistan
63	38.0	62.0	62.0	3,074	…	94.6	100.0	—	99.1	0.3	0.6	738	681	Vanuatu
2,713	33.6	66.4	59.7	65,999	297,987	411.9	91.4	8.6	86.2	2.2	11.6	134,120	40,409	Venezuela
36,730	87.6	12.4	6.6	47,277	132,913	1,200.0	93.8	6.3	70.8	22.3	6.9	940,473	13,801	Vietnam
…	…	…	…	…	…	0.8	100.0	—	100.0	—	—	…	…	Virgin Islands (U.S.)
…	…	…	…	…	…	…	…	…	…	…	…	…	…	West Bank
…	…	…	…	…	…	—	—	—	—	—	—	…	…	Western Sahara
—	—	—	—	…	44,915	123.3	100.0	—	96.2	0.4	3.4	19,789	4,636	Yemen
8,053	89.6	10.4	4.0	…	8,809	67.3	—	100.0	100.0	—	—	205	1,404	Zambia
9,253	87.7	12.3	10.1	31,415	33,293	12.4	—	100.0	100.0	—	—	1,462	9,925	Zimbabwe

Guernsey. [17]Mostly bauxite and diamonds. [18]South Africa includes Lesotho. [19]South Africa includes Namibia. [20]Includes coal mining. [21]United States includes Puerto Rico. [22]1994–95. [23]Mostly gold. [24]Mostly precious and semiprecious stones. [25]Mostly bauxite. [26]1995–96.

Manufacturing industries

This table provides a summary of manufacturing activity by industrial sector for the countries of the world, providing figures for total manufacturing value added, as well as the percentage contribution of 29 major branches of manufacturing activity to the gross domestic product. U.S. dollar figures for total value added by manufacturing are given but should be used with caution because of uncertainties with respect to national accounting methods; purchasing power parities; preferential price structures and exchange rates; labour costs; and costs for material inputs influenced by "most favoured" international trade agreements, barter, and the like.

Manufacturing activity is classified here according to a modification of the International Standard Industrial Classification (ISIC), revision 2, published by the United Nations. A summary of the 2-, 3-, and 4-digit ISIC codes (groups) defining these 29 sectors follows, providing definitional detail beyond that possible in the column headings. Recently available revision 3 data have also been modified to fit into this 29-sector breakdown.

The collection and publication of national manufacturing data is usually carried out by one of three methods: a full census of manufacturing (usually done every 5 to 10 years for a given country), a periodic survey of manufacturing (usually taken at annual or other regular intervals between censuses), and the onetime sample survey (often limited in geographic, sectoral, or size-of-enterprise coverage). The full census is, naturally, the most complete, but, since up to 10 years may elapse between such censuses, it has sometimes been necessary to substitute a survey of more recent date but less complete coverage. In addition to national sources, data published by the United Nations Industrial Development Organization (UNIDO), especially its *International Yearbook of Industrial Statistics* and Geographical Reference Information Guide online; occasional publications of the International Monetary Fund (IMF); and other sources have been used.

ISIC code(s)		Products manufactured
31		Food, beverages, and tobacco
	311 + 312	food including prepared animal feeds
	313	alcoholic and nonalcoholic beverages
	314	tobacco manufactures
32		Textiles, wearing apparel, and leather goods
	321	spinning of textile fibres, weaving and finishing of textiles, knitted articles, carpets, rope, etc.
	322	wearing apparel (including leather clothing; excluding knitted articles and footwear)
	323 + 324	leather products (including footwear; excluding wearing apparel), leather substitutes, and fur products

Manufacturing industries

country	year	total manufacturing value added ('000,000 U.S.$)	(31) food (311 + 312)	beverages (313)	tobacco manufactures (314)	(32) textiles (exc. wearing apparel) (321)	wearing apparel (322)	leather and fur products (323 + 324)	(33) wood products (exc. furniture) (331)	wood furniture (332)	(34) paper, paper products (341)	printing and publishing (342)	(35) industrial chemicals (351)	paints, soaps, etc. (352 exc. 3522)	drugs and medicines (3522)
Afghanistan	1988–89[1]	435	18.3	1.9	—	8.0	0.4	16.7	0.5		0.9	4.9	4.8	0.2	2.7
Albania	1998[2, 3, 4]	257	14.3	7.5	3.0	9.6		11.3	7.8		5.9		2.8[5]	[5]	[5]
Algeria	1997[3, 4, 7]	1,838	25.2	4.0	6.2	3.5		0.8	2.8	1.2	1.6	1.2	4.0	5.7	2.4
American Samoa	1999[8]	345	98.4	—	—	—	1.3	—	—	—	—	—	—	—	—
Andorra	1999[9]	41		10.4		7.6	2.4		1.0		11.0		8.3		—
Angola	1989	319	20.0	12.2			11.6		3.7		0.3		9.1[5]	[5]	[5]
Antigua and Barbuda	2000	13	…	…	…	…	…	…	…	…	…	…	…	…	…
Argentina	1996[3, 7]	33,015	16.5	6.5	6.2	3.6	1.4	2.1	0.7	0.7[11]	2.6	4.1	4.3	10.6	
Armenia	2001[2]	358	55.0		4.4	0.7	1.2	0.2	0.7	…	0.2	2.3		4.4	
Aruba	1994	89[12]	…	…	…	…	…	…	…	…	…	…	…	…	…
Australia	2000–01	59,557	18.5	0.9	0.6	2.3	1.2	0.5	3.5	2.7[11]	3.2	9.5	3.1	2.4	2.3
Austria	1998[13, 14]	38,375	7.8	1.8	…	2.7	1.1	0.6	4.5	3.5[11]	3.9	…	2.0	1.2	2.4
Azerbaijan	2001[2]	1,325	34.0		4.2	1.8	0.6	0.2	0.2	…	0.1	0.7		9.4	
Bahamas, The	1992[14]	95	7.4	38.9	—	0.3	3.6	—	—	3.5	…	10.0	…	22.0	…
Bahrain	1992	761	5.0	1.1	—	—	6.5	0.1	0.1	8.4	0.4	4.4	5.6	—	—
Bangladesh	1991–92[3, 7]	1,899	12.7	0.6	12.2	23.5	10.2	3.9	0.7	0.1	2.9	1.2	5.6	4.5	5.8
Barbados	1995	289	18.0	16.9	2.4	0.7	2.1	—	—	1.4	1.0	8.3	5.9	4.1	
Belarus	1994[2, 14, 15]	3,006	16.2	…	…	7.0	2.1	2.6	5.4[16]		[16]		16.3[5]	[5]	[5]
Belgium	1995	53,712	15.4	2.0	0.7	4.3	2.3	0.1	0.6	3.6	2.2	4.6	11.5	3.8	
Belize	1992[3]	59	45.9	7.5	3.9		3.8		5.5	2.7	1.1	1.5		14.1	
Benin	1990	59	20.6	13.1	—	3.2	5.5	6.9	3.6	5.2	—	2.5	—	9.5	
Bermuda	1995	170	…	…	…	…	…	…	…	…	…	…	…	…	…
Bhutan	1989[3]	21	6.0	10.1	—		5.6		18.1	2.7	0.4	1.0	21.5	1.7	
Bolivia	1998[3, 19]	1,086	20.4	13.0	0.5	2.8	1.0	1.1	1.5	0.8[11]	1.7	1.9	0.5	2.6	2.0
Bosnia and Herzegovina	1991	4,021	9.1	2.6	1.7	5.9	4.5	3.3	6.3	4.2	3.9	1.4	5.5	4.1	
Botswana	1995	212	32.5	12.7	—	8.0	5.2	2.8	2.4	1.4	2.8	2.8	1.4	1.4	
Brazil	1996[13]	153,540	14.4	5.3	1.1	3.5	2.4	2.4	1.2	1.4[11]	4.0	4.7		12.5	
Brunei	1998[20]	151	…	…	…	…	…	…	…	…	…	…	…	…	…
Bulgaria	1998[2]	7,669	14.8	5.8	4.8	3.5	3.5	1.3	1.4	1.1[11]	2.0	2.0		10.3	
Burkina Faso	1995	162	47.2	15.5	1.2	13.7	1.2	4.4	—	1.2	—	1.2	0.6	—	—
Burundi	1995	117	54.7	21.4	5.1	9.4	—	—	0.9	—	—	0.9	—	1.7	
Cambodia	1995[3, 7]	71	14.2		5.9	0.7	21.7		10.4[21]		[21]	0.5		0.3	
Cameroon	1997–98[3]	708	14.8	17.2	3.1	8.8	—	0.4	18.1	—	3.4	1.2		5.8	
Canada	1999[22]	112,037	10.0	2.5	0.8	2.0	2.2	0.2	4.7	2.6[11]	5.1	5.1		8.0	
Cape Verde	1997[2]	78	26.7	20.4	1.9	—	4.9	6.1	5.5	5.7	…	3.0	0.6	7.7	1.7
Central African Republic	1995	36	27.0	13.5	21.6	—	—	—	13.5	2.7	…	5.4	2.7	5.4	
Chad	2000	152	…	…	…	…	—	—	—	—	—	—	—	…	—
Chile	1997[3, 23]	18,472	21.9	7.0	3.6	2.1	2.1	1.3	3.6	0.8	6.1	3.3	5.2	5.2	2.0
China	1998[24]	182,196	6.7	3.6	5.9	6.7	5.0		0.8	0.5	2.1	1.2		11.4	
Colombia	1997[3, 7]	16,696	19.2	10.7	0.5	5.9	3.3	1.3	0.7	0.5	3.4	3.9	4.7	6.6	4.5
Comoros	2000	8.4	…	…	—	…	…	…	…	…	—	—	—	—	—
Congo, Dem. Rep. of the	1990	808	86.7	5.4	1.9	0.6	0.2	0.6	0.1	0.2	—	0.1	0.9	0.1	
Congo, Rep. of the	1995	86	26.7	24.4	7.0	2.3	1.2	2.3	3.5	2.3	1.2	1.2	3.5	4.7	
Costa Rica	1997[3, 14]	1,412	27.7	15.5	2.8	1.7	3.8	0.6	1.5	0.9	4.2	3.8	6.8	4.4	1.7
Côte d'Ivoire	1997[14, 25]	857	31.3	5.2	5.5	7.6	1.7	0.8	11.2	0.1	2.7	2.3	6.1	6.0	—
Croatia	1999	3,363	18.7		1.5	2.1	5.0	1.5	3.2	[26]	1.8	7.3		10.8	
Cuba	1995	4,077[27]	15.7	5.4	39.9	3.6	1.9	1.2	1.0	0.8	0.2	1.2	1.9	7.8	
Cyprus[28]	1999	971	19.5	8.6	8.8	2.0	6.0	1.9	6.3	5.2[11]	2.0	5.1	0.6	2.6	2.3
Czech Republic	1998[14]	12,920	9.0	2.9	…	3.8	1.7	0.9	2.8	2.0[11]	1.9	3.4	4.2	1.2	1.1
Denmark	1998	25,318	15.2	1.7	1.1	1.8	1.2	0.2	2.7	4.3[11]	2.5	8.6	2.4	2.2	4.1
Djibouti	1992[8]	13		5.0			3.0		—	—	0.3			1.0	
Dominica	2000[13]	20	…	…	—	—	…	—	…	…	—	—	—	…	—
Dominican Republic	1990	1,298	31.9	13.8	5.2	3.5	1.2	3.0	0.2	1.5	2.9	1.7	1.6	3.4	
East Timor	1996	12	…	…	…	…	…	…	…	…	…	…	…	…	…
Ecuador	1998[3, 7]	4,680	13.7	8.2	0.1	2.2	0.4	0.5	0.9	0.5[11]	1.5	1.1	0.4	2.2	0.3
Egypt	1997–98[13]	6,768	17.1	0.8	0.6	8.7	4.2	0.4	—	0.5[11]	0.9	2.1	5.9	7.2	5.0
El Salvador	1998[3, 19, 29]	1,438	21.3	7.8	—	8.4	17.3	2.5	—	1.0	3.9	3.2	0.7	6.4	8.9
Equatorial Guinea	1990[2]	1.9	27.6	4.1	…	…	2.6	…	…	49.3	…	1.2	…	13.8	
Eritrea	1998[3, 7]	58	17.2	34.1	6.1	4.8	1.2	6.3	—	3.2[11]	0.3	1.6	0.4	6.1	—
Estonia	1998[2]	2,675	24.1	4.6	—	7.4	4.1	1.4	10.7	6.7[11]	2.0	5.3	1.7	4.1	0.3

ISIC code(s)		Products manufactured
33		Wood and wood products
	331	sawlogs, wood products (excluding furniture), cane products, and cork products
	332	wood furniture
34		Paper and paper products, printing and publishing
	341	wood pulp, paper, and paper products
	342	printing, publishing, and bookbinding
35		Chemicals and chemical, petroleum, coal, rubber, and plastic products
	351	basic industrial chemicals (including fertilizers, pesticides, and synthetic fibres)
	352 minus 3522	chemical products not elsewhere specified (including paints, varnishes, and soaps and other toiletries)
	3522	drugs and medicines
	353 + 354	refined petroleum and derivatives of petroleum and coal
	355	rubber products
	356	plastic products (excluding synthetic fibres)
36		Glass, ceramic, and nonmetallic mineral products
	361 + 362	pottery, china, glass, and glass products
	369	bricks, tiles, cement, cement products, plaster products, etc.

ISIC code(s)		Products manufactured
37		Basic metals
	371	iron and steel
	372	nonferrous basic metals and processed nickel and cobalt
38		Fabricated metal products, machinery and equipment
	381	fabricated metal products (including cutlery, hand tools, fixtures, and structural metal products)
	382 minus 3825	nonelectrical machinery and apparatus not elsewhere specified
	3825	office, computing, and accounting machinery
	383 minus 3832	electrical machinery and apparatus not elsewhere specified
	3832	radio, television, and communications equipment (including electronic parts)
	384 minus 3843	transport equipment not elsewhere specified
	3843	motor vehicles (excluding motorcycles)
	385	professional and scientific equipment; photographic and optical goods; watches and clocks
39		Other manufactured goods
	390	jewelry, musical instruments, sporting goods, artists' equipment, toys, etc.

			(36)		(37)		(38)								(39)	country
refined petroleum and products (353 + 354)	rubber products (355)	plastic products (356)	pottery, china, and glass (361 + 362)	bricks, tiles, cement, etc. (369)	iron and steel (371)	non-ferrous metals (372)	fabricated metal products (381)	nonelectrical machinery (382 exc. 3825)	office equip., computers (3825)	electrical equip. (383 exc. 3832)	radio, television (3832)	transport equip. exc. motor vehicles (384 exc. 3843)	motor vehicles (3843)	professional equip. (385)	jewelry, musical instruments (390)	
—	—	2.1	1.1		0.4	—	—	—	—	—	—	—	0.1	—	37.1	Afghanistan
15.9	[5]	[5]	8.0		11.2[6]		[6]	…	2.3		…	…	…	…	0.4	Albania
…	0.1	1.1	0.5	21.4	6.4	1.3	0.5	1.7		4.3		0.1	2.3	1.2	0.3	Algeria
—	—	—	—	—	—	—	0.3	—	—	—	—	—	—	—	—	American Samoa
—	5.0		0.5		2.5[6]		[6]	14.6				19.6		7.2	9.8	Andorra
20.0	[5]	[5]	11.3		1.9		5.0					4.7		[10]	0.3[10]	Angola
…	…	…	…	…	…	…	…	…	…	…	…	…	…	…	…	Antigua and Barbuda
11.6	1.0	2.5	4.2		4.1	0.6	2.9	3.9	0.1	1.9	1.2	0.5	5.6	0.3	0.4	Argentina
—	0.3		4.1		11.3		1.0	3.2	—	1.3	0.3	0.1		1.0	8.4	Armenia
…	…	…	…	…	…	…	…	…	…	…	…	…	…	…	…	Aruba
1.7	0.8	3.3	1.0	3.4	3.6	6.4	8.0	4.5	0.4	2.7	2.1	2.2	6.8	1.5	0.9	Australia
…	0.7	3.3	1.7	4.3	6.1		8.6	10.4	0.1	4.4	6.3	0.9	5.1	2.0	1.7	Austria
38.1	0.4		2.5		0.8		0.7	2.5	0.1	0.5	0.1	2.7	—	0.2	0.3	Azerbaijan
…	…	…	…	7.0	2.6	—	—	—	—	…	…	—	—	…	…	Bahamas, The
13.7	0.8	—	—	4.5	4.4	33.4	0.3	0.4		3.4	—	3.4	—	—	4.1	Bahrain
0.4	0.5	0.4	1.0	1.7	3.6	0.1	1.2	0.4	—	1.2	0.5	0.8	3.7	—	0.6	Bangladesh
—	6.6	14.9	0.7	2.8	—	—	6.9	3.8		2.4		1.0		—	0.3	Barbados
7.6	[5]	[5]	5.5		3.0		26.8								…	Belarus
1.0	0.6	5.4	2.5	2.1	4.7	1.8	7.1	7.1		7.8		7.0		0.5	1.3	Belgium
—	0.3[17]		[17]	6.2	—	—	2.0	—	—	0.1		4.2		—	1.1	Belize
—	—	—	0.5	24.6	—	—	4.8	—	—	—	—	—	—	—	—	Benin
…	…	…	…	…	…	…	…	…	…	…	…	…	…	…	…	Bermuda
…	0.7	2.2	29.0		…	…	1.0[18]								[18]	Bhutan
36.7	0.1	1.8	1.0	6.8	0.2	0.2	1.2	0.1	—	0.4	—	—	0.2	—	1.5	Bolivia
2.3	0.3	1.3	0.5	3.2	5.5	3.4	10.8	5.0		3.3		8.6		2.6	0.7	Bosnia and Herzegovina
—	0.5	0.5	—	—	—	—	2.4	0.9		0.9		1.4		—	19.8	Botswana
4.6	1.4	2.8	3.5		5.7		4.1	7.1	0.6	2.8	3.7	0.9	8.0	0.9	1.0	Brazil
…	…	…	…	…	…	…	…	…	…	…	…	…	…	…	…	Brunei
10.9	0.9	1.7	4.9		12.5		2.9	8.0	0.6	2.7	0.5	2.4	0.5	0.6	0.4	Bulgaria
—	1.2	0.6	—	—	1.2	—	0.6	—	—	0.6		1.2		—	8.1	Burkina Faso
—	—	0.9	—	1.7	—	—	2.6	—	—	—	—	—	—	—	0.9	Burundi
…	17.4		24.6		3.8		0.5	—	—	—	—	—	—	—	0.1	Cambodia
4.0	7.2	0.9	—	2.8	—	6.5	1.1	—	—	1.8		1.3		—	1.6	Cameroon
0.8	1.9	3.0	2.8		4.7		7.3	4.6		9.8		19.0		[10]	3.0[10]	Canada
…	0.3	…	0.6	1.5	0.1		5.6	0.1	…	—	…	4.1	—	3.5	—	Cape Verde
—	—	—	—	—	—	—	2.7	…	…	—	—	2.7		—	2.7	Central African Republic
—	—	—	—	—	—	—	—	…	—	—	—	…	—	—	…	Chad
3.4	0.9	2.4	0.9	3.6	2.3	12.3	3.9	2.0	—	1.1	0.2	0.8	1.6	0.2	0.2	Chile
3.5	1.4	2.4	1.5	4.5	6.5	2.2	3.3	7.8		13.3		7.2		1.1	1.4	China
5.8	1.1	4.1	2.4	5.7	2.0	0.4	3.4	1.9	—	2.0	0.4	0.7	3.4	0.7	0.8	Colombia
—	—	—	—	—	—	—	—	—	—	—	—	—	—	—	—	Comoros
0.1	—	—	—	0.2	…	…	0.4	0.3		0.2		0.5		—	1.5	Congo, Dem. Rep. of the
—	2.3	—	—	1.2	—	—	7.0	2.3		3.5		3.5		—	—	Congo, Rep. of the
2.9	1.8	4.4	1.3	2.0	…	0.1	2.5	1.8	…	1.0	4.6	1.0	0.1	…	0.2	Costa Rica
9.2	0.1	…	…	2.1	…	…	5.2	0.1		1.1		1.4	0.3	…	0.1	Côte d'Ivoire
11.2	2.5		6.0		2.1		6.7	3.8	0.7	4.0	1.9	5.0	0.6	0.8	2.8[26]	Croatia
…	2.4	2.1	0.5	1.9	0.7	0.9	1.7	1.7		0.9		3.5		0.3	3.0	Cuba
1.3	0.2	3.3	0.4	8.5	1.1		6.7	2.6	—	1.5	—	0.3	0.7	0.4	2.1	Cyprus[28]
…	1.5	2.9	8.3		7.9		9.6	11.3	0.1	5.8	1.6	1.3	8.2	2.2	1.6	Czech Republic
0.3	4.4		1.0	3.2	2.2		8.8	15.3	1.2	3.7	2.6	2.6	1.4	3.7	1.6	Denmark
			0.1		0.1		13.0								77.5	Djibouti
—	—	—	—	…	—	—	…	—	—	…	—	—	—	—	…	Dominica
16.2	0.8	1.6	0.7	3.5	1.8	0.2	3.7	0.5		0.8		0.1		0.2	0.2	Dominican Republic
…	…	…	…	…	…	…	…	…	…	…	…	…	…	…	…	East Timor
56.2	0.3	2.4	0.5	2.9	0.8	0.3	1.4	0.6	—	0.5	—	0.1	1.7	—	0.2	Ecuador
13.7	0.7	1.2	1.7	8.7	4.4	1.3	2.1	3.9	0.4	3.1	0.8	1.0	2.9	0.4	0.2	Egypt
1.2	0.3	4.0	0.1	5.3	1.2	—	2.2	0.7	—	0.8	0.5	1.2	—	—	1.1	El Salvador
…	…	…	…	0.8	…	…	0.6	…	…	…	…	…	…	…	…	Equatorial Guinea
—	—	0.6	0.1	13.4	0.3	—	3.1	0.1	—	0.1	—	—	0.6	0.4	—	Eritrea
0.3	0.2	2.1	1.6	3.8	0.1	0.1	6.7	2.5	1.0	1.6	1.3	1.9	1.6	1.9	0.9	Estonia

Manufacturing industries (continued)

country	year	total manufac-turing value added ('000,000 U.S.$)	(31)			(32)			(33)		(34)		(35)		
			food	bever-ages	tobacco manufac-tures	textiles (exc. wearing apparel)	wearing apparel	leather and fur products	wood products (exc. furniture)	wood furniture	paper, paper products	printing and pub-lishing	industrial chemi-cals	paints, soaps, etc.	drugs and medicines
			(311 + 312)	(313)	(314)	(321)	(322)	(323 + 324)	(331)	(332)	(341)	(342)	(351)	(352 exc. 3522)	(3522)
Ethiopia	1997–98[3, 30]	449	28.2	20.6	5.7	6.9	0.6	5.4	0.8	2.0[11]	1.5	3.0	0.6	3.1	3.4
Faroe Islands	1999[8, 31]	117	80.7	…	…	…	0.1	…	…	…	…	…	…	…	…
Fiji	1994	160	42.6	6.1	—	13.8		1.3	9.7	1.9	3.8	5.1	—	3.1	—
Finland	2000	28,355	4.8	0.9	0.1	0.9	0.6	0.3	4.4	2.4[11, 34]	17.8	5.2	5.3		
France	1998[13, 35]	166,238[36]	…	…	…	2.8	1.8	0.9	1.1	1.7[11]	3.1	5.7	5.7	5.7	4.4
French Guiana	1996[14, 37]	101	8.5			[38]			…	…		3.3[38]	…	…	…
French Polynesia	1993[14]	214	27.2		—	…	…	—	…	…	—	—	—	…	—
Gabon	1995	243	9.1	7.0	6.2	0.8	1.7	—	18.1	2.5	0.8	1.2	4.1	1.7	
Gambia, The	1995[3, 19]	9.2	65.0		—	8.3			6.2[39]		—	4.2	8.8[5]	[5]	[5]
Gaza Strip[40]	…	…	…	…	…	…	…	…	…	…	…	…	…	…	…
Georgia	2001[2]	292	47.8		3.8	0.2	0.5	0.7	0.9	0.5[11, 34]	0.4	3.0	5.6		
Germany	2000[35]	552,121	8.1		2.2	1.2	0.7	0.2	1.2	[41]	2.4	4.6	11.4		
Ghana	1993[3, 35]	610	8.4	9.1	18.1	4.6	0.5		15.2	0.8	1.8	1.3	0.9	8.9	
Greece	1996[7, 13]	10,948	18.3	6.6	2.0	6.6	5.0	1.4	1.5	1.5[11]	3.1	4.2	3.0	8.9	
Greenland	2000[14, 43]	0.5	…	…	…	…	…	…	…	…	…	…	…	…	…
Grenada	1996[44, 45]	21	31.5	51.2	2.0	—	…	—	…	…	6.5	—	—	8.8	…
Guadeloupe	1995[14]	290	28.8			…	…	…	…	…	…	…	…	…	…
Guam	1997[1, 14]	165	14.8			[46]			[46]		—	24.4	[46]		
Guatemala	1995	1,468	28.7	6.2	3.1	5.7	2.5	1.2	0.8	0.5	1.5	4.5	3.5	16.4	
Guernsey	2000[8, 14]	68	…	[47]	…	[47]	…	…	…	7.2[47]	…	21.1	…	…	…
Guinea	1998	158	…	…	…	…	…	…	…	…	…	…	…	…	…
Guinea-Bissau	2001[48]	20	…	…	…	…	…	…	…	…	…	…	…	…	…
Guyana	2001[14, 48]	58	46.4[49]	…	…	…	…	…	…	…	…	…	—	…	…
Haiti	1999[14]	197	48.6		3.8	20.9			…	…	…	…	6.3		
Honduras	1996[13, 19]	575	28.8	10.4	2.9	2.5	18.8	1.0	4.8	1.5	2.9	2.2	0.4	3.7	1.0
Hong Kong	1999[14]	8,477	7.9	[46]	[46]	11.1	11.0	0.1	0.1	0.1	1.3	16.3	3.3		
Hungary	1999	8,878	15.1	3.2	0.6	2.3	4.7	1.1	1.5	1.3	1.4	4.0	7.0		
Iceland	1996	998	43.6	2.1	…	2.4	1.6	1.2	0.2	3.6	1.1	10.4	1.2	2.0	—
India	1997–98[13, 50]	34,090	9.1	1.3	1.7	9.6	1.8	0.8	0.2	0.1	1.4	1.4	9.2	4.1	4.9
Indonesia	1998[13, 14, 35]	14,799	12.1	0.4	8.8	10.5	3.4	3.7	6.8	2.8[11]	3.5	2.7	10.0	2.2	1.3
Iran	1996–97[7]	10,068	10.2	1.7	1.0	8.6	0.5	1.0	0.6	0.4[11]	1.7	0.9	11.8	3.5	1.6
Iraq	1995	567	9.9	3.4	1.2	3.5	1.2	3.5	—	0.2	3.5	1.4	9.2	1.1	
Ireland	1999	45,302	15.1		0.5	0.5	0.5	0.1	0.6		0.8	15.3	35.5		
Isle of Man	1998–99[13, 14]	135	19.9		…	…	…	…	…	…	…	…	…	…	…
Israel	1998[19]	15,537	10.3	1.7		3.8	1.7	0.4	0.7	1.7[11]	2.3	4.8	12.5		
Italy	1998	161,544	7.2	1.4	0.4	6.3	4.0	2.8	1.1	2.5	2.6	3.3	3.6	6.7	
Jamaica	2001[3]	566	22.5	14.3	6.8	2.5		0.6	2.7		2.9		8.5[5]	[5]	[5]
Japan	1998	888,152	8.3	2.1	0.7	2.2	1.0	0.4	1.3	0.9[11]	2.6	6.1	3.6	2.9	3.2
Jersey	1996	46	…	…	…	…	…	…	…	…	…	…	…	…	…
Jordan	1998	1,262	10.2	5.7	13.3	2.2	2.0	0.9	1.0	2.6	2.7	2.8	6.9	2.7	5.1
Kazakhstan	1998[2, 14]	5,660	12.9[14]	4.2	3.2	1.1[14]	0.4	0.2	0.4	0.2[11]	—[14]	2.2[14]	2.0	0.3[14]	0.2
Kenya	1998[4, 13]	1,029	36.0	11.2	1.9	4.6	2.0	1.4	1.8	0.9	4.7	2.5	2.4	6.4	
Kiribati	1998	0.76	…	…	—	—	—	—	…	—	—	—	—	…	—
Korea, North	…	…	…	…	…	…	…	…	…	…	…	…	…	…	…
Korea, South	1999	168,813	7.8		1.1	5.5	1.9	1.0	0.6	[41]	2.3	2.5	9.5		
Kuwait	1997[7]	4,310	3.7	1.1	—	0.5	2.7	0.1	0.3	1.0	0.6	0.5	2.4	0.5	—
Kyrgyzstan	1998[2]	494	15.3	2.7	6.1	10.9	0.6	0.4	0.3	0.2[11]	—	0.7	—	—	0.1
Laos	1990[2]	66	4.5	7.4	16.3	—	5.1	0.3	40.1	5.0	—	1.2	4.0		
Latvia	1998[13, 14]	1,125	23.3	12.2	…	5.9	4.6	0.5	16.1	2.2[11]	1.1	5.8	0.2	1.0	1.4
Lebanon	1994	1,679	25.2		1.9	3.3	9.6	3.0	3.4		2.4	2.4	2.4	—	—
Lesotho	1995	134	43.3	28.4	…	10.4	3.0	2.2	…	0.7	…	1.5	…	6.7	
Liberia	1999	21	…	…	…	…	…	…	…	…	…	…	…	…	…
Libya	1995	857	4.3	2.2	9.4	3.7	3.3	8.5	0.3	0.2	0.3	1.0	7.0	5.2	
Liechtenstein	2000[8, 14, 53]	1,269	6.1			1.7			…	…	…	…	10.0		
Lithuania	1999[2]	4,552	27.6		[46]	6.6	10.9	1.2	5.7	[41]	1.4	3.8	6.5		
Luxembourg	1999	2,332	11.0			10.0			1.8	[41]	7.5		6.4		
Macau	2001	395	2.9	0.8	1.2	16.4	65.9	2.3	—	[41]	0.2	3.0	2.3		
Macedonia	1996	603	19.7	4.8	7.5	5.9	8.0	3.9	0.2	2.1	0.9	4.6	5.5	5.1	
Madagascar	1995	127	15.0	11.8	0.8	35.4	3.1	2.4	0.8	0.8	3.9	1.6	—	6.3	
Malawi	1998	105[13]	17.6	24.4	1.7	5.7	1.4	0.7	2.0		6.5		7.6[55]	8.0	
Malaysia	1997[13]	28,143	6.4	0.8	1.2	3.1	1.6	0.1	5.1	1.4	1.4	2.7	6.6	1.7	0.3
Maldives	2000	63[48]	…	…	—	—	…	—	—	…	—	…	—	…	—
Mali	1990	96	18.4	1.2	13.1	36.5	10.3	0.1	0.1	—	0.4	0.8	0.8	0.7	
Malta	1998	739	9.3	7.5	1.2	0.5	8.5	2.0	0.4	4.7[11]	1.4	7.0	1.4	1.6	1.9
Marshall Islands	1997	2.2	…	…	…	…	…	…	…	…	…	…	…	…	…
Martinique	1997	322	…	…	…	…	…	…	…	…	…	…	…	…	…
Mauritania	1997	13	39.8			0.4			…	…	3.9		14.5		
Mauritius	1998[7, 57]	785	15.3	6.8		7.9	42.2	0.8	0.4	1.0[11]	1.5	3.3[57]	4.6		
Mayotte	1992	…	…	…	—	—	—	—	—	—	—	—	—	—	—
Mexico	1999[3, 27]	41,861	8.4	8.9	3.8	1.9	0.5	0.3	0.1	0.2	2.3	0.5	8.8	8.7	
Micronesia	1996	2.6[6]	…	…	…	…	…	…	…	…	…	…	…	…	…
Moldova	1998[2, 3, 59]	752	39.8	25.8	5.8	1.6	1.4	2.0	0.5	1.1	1.5	1.6	—	0.4	0.9
Monaco	1992	689[1]	…	…	…	…	…	…	…	…	…	…	…	…	…
Mongolia	1998[3]	44	28.3	10.6	—	34.2	7.4	0.7	2.1	0.1[11]	—	2.6	—	0.2	2.9
Morocco	1998	5,484	16.9	4.7	12.2	8.3	8.8	1.3	1.5	0.3	2.6	1.2	9.8	3.4	2.0
Mozambique	2000[2]	490	15.7	22.4	1.9	4.4	2.6	…	4.5	0.1	5.9		3.8		
Myanmar (Burma)	1998	2,409[4]	4.0	19.9[4]	28.5	22.9	…	0.4	4.3	…	1.1[4]	…	…	5.4	6.9
Namibia	2001[14]	306	70.8		…	…	…	…	…	…	…	…	…	…	…
Nauru	1989	—	—	—	—	—	—	—	—	—	—	—	—	—	—
Nepal	1996–97[3, 7, 14]	381	13.6	9.1	12.0	25.9	6.3	1.3	1.4	0.9[11]	1.7	1.3	…	3.4	2.4
Netherlands, The	1999[3]	48,443	15.0	3.9	5.3	1.8	0.3	0.2	1.0	0.8	3.4	8.6	7.9	5.5	
Netherlands Antilles	1997	151	…	…	…	…	…	…	…	…	…	…	…	…	…
New Caledonia	1997[14]	375	16.5			…	…	…	…	…	…	…	…	…	
New Zealand	1995	9,878	25.1	3.0	0.6	2.9	2.3	1.1	4.6	1.8	7.7	7.8	3.6	3.1	
Nicaragua	2000[14]	331	40.5	25.3	2.2	1.2	0.1	1.2	2.5	0.5	1.0	1.8	3.9		

			(36)		(37)		(38)								(39)	country
refined petroleum and products (353 + 354)	rubber products (355)	plastic products (356)	pottery, china, and glass (361 + 362)	bricks, tiles, cement, etc. (369)	iron and steel (371)	non-ferrous metals (372)	fabricated metal products (381)	nonelectrical machinery (382 exc. 3825)	office equip., computers (3825)	electrical equip. (383 exc. 3832)	radio, television (3832)	transport equip. exc. motor vehicles (384 exc. 3843)	motor vehicles (3843)	professional equip. (385)	jewelry, musical instruments (390)	
—	2.1	2.0	0.8	8.3	2.6	—	1.2	0.1	—	—	—	—	1.1	—	—	Ethiopia
…	…	…	…	…	…	…	…	…	…	…	…	14.3	…	…	4.9[32]	Faroe Islands
—	0.5	2.0	—	3.0[33]	[33]	—	3.2	1.2	—	—	—	0.4	1.0	—	1.2	Fiji
1.6	0.6	2.6	0.9	2.1	4.5		5.9	10.3	—	3.1	20.4	1.8	1.1	2.3	[34]	Finland
2.6	2.2	3.8	1.9	2.7	3.2	1.3	8.5	8.2	2.5	4.9	6.0	5.0	11.0	2.5	1.0	France
…	…	…	…	…	…	…	…	…	…	…	…	…	…	…	…	French Guiana
—	…	…	…	…	—	—	35.4								…	French Polynesia
10.3	—	—	0.8	5.8	2.1	2.1	8.7	0.8		5.4		7.0		0.4	3.3	Gabon
—	[5]	[5]	—	—	1.8		4.8	0.8						—	[39]	Gambia, The
…	…	…	…	…	…	…	…	…	…	…	…	…	…	…	…	Gaza Strip[40]
0.9	1.9		8.7		12.5		0.9	0.8	—	1.5	0.1	8.8	0.5	0.1	[34]	Georgia
5.1	4.3		3.5		4.0		6.7	13.0	1.1	7.0	2.9	2.0	13.1	3.0	2.3[41]	Germany
8.1	0.6	2.6	4.4		0.7	8.2	3.4	0.3		1.5		0.6[42]		—	[42]	Ghana
4.3	0.5	3.2	7.3		2.3	3.3	3.8	3.6	0.1	2.1	1.7	4.3	0.6	0.4	0.5	Greece
…	…	…	…	…	…	…	…	…	…	…	…	…	…	…	…	Greenland
—	…	—	—	—	—	—	—	—	—	…	…	—	—	—	…	Grenada
…	…	…	…	…	…	…	…	…	…	…	…	…	…	…	…	Guadeloupe
—	—	—	10.3		—	—	2.6	[46]							0.6	Guam
1.1	2.5	4.0	2.5	4.8	2.7	0.1	2.5	0.8		3.4		0.3		0.2	0.4	Guatemala
…	…	…	…	…	…	…	…	9.3		…	21.8	5.6	…	…	…	Guernsey
…	…	…	…	…	…	…	…	…	…	…	…	…	…	…	…	Guinea
…	…	…	…	…	…	…	…	…	…	…	…	…	…	…	…	Guinea-Bissau
—	—	—	—	—	—	—	—	…	—	…	—	—	—	—	…	Guyana
			1.1		…	…	2.0	…	…	…	…	…	…	…	…	Haiti
0.2	1.1	3.3	0.1	7.5	0.5	0.2	3.6	0.7	—	0.9	0.1	—	0.2	0.1	0.7	Honduras
[46]	[46]	2.0	4.2		1.0		3.1	7.4	3.6	0.4	13.3	4.6		2.5	3.6	Hong Kong
15.0	0.3	3.5	1.7	2.2	1.3	1.2	3.8	4.6		11.6		10.2		2.1	0.4	Hungary
—	—	3.0	0.4	3.7	2.4	4.4	9.9	—	—	—	—	2.4	—	—	4.5	Iceland
2.2	2.2	1.7	0.7	3.7	13.1	2.6	2.4	6.3	0.7	5.1	2.3	3.3	6.2	0.6	1.3	India
1.7	2.0	1.9	…	…	2.5	1.5	2.6	1.3	—	1.4	4.8	6.9	1.4	0.4	1.3	Indonesia
1.9	1.8	1.3	1.4	8.4	15.3	3.1	5.1	6.2	0.1	2.6	1.2	0.8	6.5	0.6	0.2	Iran
25.2	0.5	1.4	0.7	18.2	4.1	—	4.8	2.3		4.4		0.4		—	—	Iraq
[51]	1.2		1.7		0.4		1.4	1.8	10.1	2.0	6.7	0.6	0.4	3.4	1.4[51]	Ireland
…	…	…	…	…	…	…	…	…	…	…	…	…	…	…	…	Isle of Man
—	5.1		3.6		1.8		10.6	4.3		2.4	14.4	5.4		11.2	1.3	Israel
2.1	1.7	3.0	1.6	4.3	3.5	1.2	7.4	13.0		7.4		8.5		2.6	1.1	Italy
14.1	[5]	[5]	7.7		[52]		16.9[52]								0.6	Jamaica
0.8	1.2	3.6	1.0	2.8	3.5	1.1	7.3	11.1	4.8	4.6	8.0	1.4	9.6	2.1	1.7	Japan
…	…	…	…	…	…	…	…	…	…	…	…	…	…	…	…	Jersey
6.5	0.2	3.0	1.1	13.5	2.2	0.7	9.1	1.9		1.8		—	1.2	0.1	0.6	Jordan
7.0[14]	0.3	0.3	0.1	2.6	9.3	20.7	1.6	1.9[14]	0.1	0.5	0.5	0.1[14]	0.1[14]	0.2	0.2[14]	Kazakhstan
0.8	3.1	3.8	0.5	3.8	…	…	6.8	0.6		…	…	2.5		0.1	2.2	Kenya
—	—	—	—	—	—	—	…	—	—	—	—	…	—	—	…	Kiribati
…	…	…	…	…	…	…	…	…	…	…	…	…	…	…	…	Korea, North
3.9	4.2		3.9		6.6		4.0	7.1	2.8	3.7	16.2	4.1	8.7	1.0	1.6[41]	Korea, South
75.2	0.1	1.3	0.3	3.4	0.3	—	2.8	1.3	—	1.0	—	0.4	0.1	—	0.5	Kuwait
0.6	—	—	1.2	9.3	…	40.8	0.4	3.2	0.2	4.3	0.1	—	0.8	1.4	0.4	Kyrgyzstan
—	0.5		0.1	3.8	—	—	10.8	0.5		0.2		—	—	—	0.1	Laos
0.1	0.1	1.0	1.2	2.1	…	0.1	4.0	3.7	0.1	2.3	0.8	3.2	0.5[14]	0.7	0.6	Latvia
1.6	—	3.2	12.0		4.9		8.9	2.2		2.1		1.0		—	10.5	Lebanon
…	…	…	…	0.7	…	…	3.0	…	…	…	…	…	…	…	…	Lesotho
…	…	…	…	…	…	…	…	…	…	…	…	…	…	…	…	Liberia
27.2	0.1	0.8	0.2	21.7	—	—	0.5	—	—	—	—	—	—	—	4.0	Libya
			11.4		0.6	1.5	17.6	40.6				10.5		…[54]	…	Liechtenstein
13.1	3.0		3.5		0.6		2.0	2.4	0.2	2.3	3.0	2.0	0.1	1.1	3.0[41]	Lithuania
—	12.1		8.6		17.3		12.1	7.6		4.0		0.5		…	0.9[41]	Luxembourg
—	—	0.2	1.3		—	—	0.6	0.3	−0.1	0.2		0.9			1.5[41]	Macau
0.4	0.1	1.2	0.8	0.6	6.2	—	5.4	1.1		9.5		4.7		0.3	1.7	Macedonia
7.9	0.8	0.8	—	2.4	—	—	3.1	—	—	2.4		0.8		—	—	Madagascar
—	0.6	3.2	—	7.5	—	—	8.6	4.5[56]		[55]		[56]		—	…	Malawi
3.4	4.2	3.5	1.6	3.9	2.3	1.0	4.1	3.4	2.6	3.5	26.5	1.4	4.4	1.0	0.7	Malaysia
—	—	…	—	…	—	—	…	—	—	—	—	…	—	—	…	Maldives
0.7	0.3	0.4	—	1.3	—	—	6.2	0.5		1.7		6.5		—	—	Mali
—	3.9	2.1	0.6	2.0	0.1		3.4	2.0	0.2	6.0	20.1	2.8	0.2	4.2	5.1	Malta
…	…	…	…	…	…	…	…	…	…	…	…	…	…	…	…	Marshall Islands
…	…	…	…	…	…	…	…	…	…	…	…	…	…	…	…	Martinique
			12.2		…	…	29.2								…	Mauritania
			5.3		1.5		2.3	0.6		1.4		0.4		1.1	3.6	Mauritius
—	—	—	—	…	—	—	—	—	—	—	—	—	—	—	—	Mayotte
0.6[27, 58]	1.3	1.5	2.7	3.7	7.6	3.1	4.1	3.9		6.1		20.5		0.4	0.3	Mexico
…	…	…	…	…	…	…	…	…	…	…	…	…	…	…	…	Micronesia
—	—	0.5	3.8	3.9	0.1	0.1	1.1	5.2	0.2	0.4	0.4	0.1	0.6	0.9	0.3	Moldova
…	…	…	…	…	…	…	…	…	…	…	…	…	…	…	…	Monaco
—	—	—	—	4.4	0.3	—	0.2	0.2	—	0.1	—	0.2	—	1.6	3.6	Mongolia
…	0.9	1.9	1.4	9.3	1.0	0.3	4.3	0.7	0.2	2.2	0.8	0.5	3.0	0.2	0.1	Morocco
0.4	1.1	1.8	10.8		0.1	0.1	23.9	0.1		0.4		0.1		…	0.1	Mozambique
…	1.7	1.0	…	…	1.3	…	0.1	…	…	0.6	…	…	0.9	…	0.9	Myanmar (Burma)
…	…	…	…	…	…	…	…	…	…	…	…	…	…	…	…	Namibia
—	—	—	—	—	—	—	—	—	—	—	—	—	—	—	—	Nauru
0.2	1.3	1.7	0.1	7.2	1.6	0.1	4.8	0.1	—	2.2	0.3	—	—	—	0.5	Nepal
1.8	0.6	3.2	1.6	2.3	3.7		6.2	9.6		10.9		5.1		0.9	0.3	Netherlands, The
…	…	…	…	…	…	…	…	…	…	…	…	…	…	…	…	Netherlands Antilles
…	…	…	…	…	…	47.9	14.4								…	New Caledonia
1.5	0.7	3.6	1.3	2.1	1.8	2.3	7.7	4.8		4.4		4.4		0.4	1.3	New Zealand
4.4	0.1		10.9		…	…	0.7	0.3				0.2		…	3.3	Nicaragua

Manufacturing industries (continued)

country	year	total manufac-turing value added ('000,000 U.S.$)	(31) food (311 + 312)	beverages (313)	tobacco manufactures (314)	(32) textiles (exc. wearing apparel) (321)	wearing apparel (322)	leather and fur products (323 + 324)	(33) wood products (exc. furniture) (331)	wood furniture (332)	(34) paper, paper products (341)	printing and publishing (342)	(35) industrial chemicals (351)	paints, soaps, etc. (352 exc. 3522)	drugs and medicines (3522)
Niger	1998[3]	15		19.8			9.1		0.5		37.0				18.0
Nigeria	1995	7,884	17.6	15.3	1.9	10.4	0.1	3.1	0.5	0.9	3.8	3.4	0.3	11.7	
Northern Mariana Islands	1997[1, 14]	762		0.7		[46]	91.8	—	[46]	[46]	[46]	0.7		0.3	
Norway	1998[14]	17,647	12.4	3.9[14]	…	1.2	0.4	0.1	3.8	2.6[11]	4.3	9.9	4.9	1.2	1.6
Oman	1998	689	16.8	2.3	—	1.0	6.1	0.3	3.1	4.5[11]	1.4	3.1	1.0	4.3	0.8
Pakistan	1995–96[3, 19]	6,307	15.2	1.6	6.2	23.5	1.4	1.3	0.2	—	1.6	2.0	8.5	3.0	4.8
Palau	2000	1.7	…	…	…	…	[60]	…	…	…	…	…	…	…	…
Panama	1999	732	56.1		—	0.9	1.9	0.5	1.3	[41]	3.1	3.1		4.3	
Papua New Guinea	2000	318	…	…	…	…	…	…	…	…	…	…	…	…	…
Paraguay	2001	905	42.9	12.6	0.5	4.9	0.1	6.5	10.9	0.8	—	7.4	1.2	1.1	
Peru	1998	4,568	18.7	6.7		8.3	4.4	0.9	7.2		1.1	4.9	3.2	5.1	0.9
Philippines	2000	16,878	42.6	4.4	2.1	1.6	5.5		0.8	1.6	0.8	1.0		7.1	
Poland	1999	28,003	12.4	12.2	3.1	2.6	3.1	0.8	2.0	3.0	2.0	1.3	2.9	3.5	
Portugal	1997[3]	21,410	7.7	2.6	4.9	7.3	6.8	4.2	3.9	2.5[11]	3.2	4.9	2.2	1.6	2.0
Puerto Rico	1997[14]	36,427	4.0	5.7	…	0.2	1.9	0.6	…	0.1[11]	0.4	1.2	2.5	2.3	54.0
Qatar	1998	718	4.0	0.3	—	0.4	9.0	0.2	0.6	2.6	0.1	3.4	37.9	0.5	—
Réunion	1994	371	34.5	12.3	—	0.5		—	3.8		5.0[61]	6.3	…	3.7	
Romania	1997[62]	9,085	22.5	11.0	1.7	3.3	6.2	2.1	3.6	3.2[11]	1.0	1.7	2.3	1.5	1.2
Russia	1998	35,840[14]	16.4	4.2	1.5	1.3	1.0	0.4	1.9	0.9	2.4	1.1	5.6	2.3	1.5
Rwanda	1998	259		79.3		6.8	…	…	1.8		0.7			1.3	
St. Kitts and Nevis	2000[13]	30	9.3[64]	…	…	…	…	…	…	…	…	…	…	…	…
St. Lucia	1997	31	12.8	34.3	1.9	4.4	7.1	—	—	4.4	8.9	7.4	0.7	2.8	—
St. Vincent	2000[13]	15	…	…	…	…	…	…	…	…	…	…	…	…	…
Samoa	1998[15]	28	17.0	42.0	11.0	…	…	…	7.0	…	…	…	…	7.0	…
San Marino	…	…	…	…	…	…	…	…	…	…	…	…	…	…	…
São Tomé and Príncipe	2000[48]	2.5	…	…	…	…	…	…	…	…	…	…	…	…	…
Saudi Arabia	1998	12,542	7.9	2.8	—	1.0	0.1	0.2	0.3	0.8	2.5	1.3	26.7	4.0	
Senegal	1997[3]	341	36.6	4.1	3.1	5.2	—	—	0.2	0.1	1.9	2.5	19.8	4.3	2.1
Serbia and Montenegro	1999	3,591	28.6		2.4	4.6	3.5	2.3	2.2	6.1[34]	3.4	5.1		8.6	
Seychelles	1989	26[66]		79.6			0.6		2.1		6.0				4.1
Sierra Leone	1993[3]	92	37.0	21.6	10.5	—	1.0	0.1	0.3	1.2	0.2	2.2			20.2
Singapore	1998[7, 13]	23,162	2.7	0.8	—	0.2	0.6	0.1	0.2	0.5[11]	1.0	4.2	1.9	4.1	6.5
Slovakia	1998[35]	3,047	9.5	2.9	…	2.5[4]	3.6	1.6	1.6	1.6[11]	5.9	2.6	3.3	1.2	2.2
Slovenia	1998[3]	4,927		11.8		8.7		1.6	3.7	5.0[34]	8.4			11.2	
Solomon Islands	2000	9.0	…	…	…	—	…	—	…	…	—	…	—	—	—
Somalia	1990	36	21.6	6.3	37.5	10.5	0.8	2.0	—	7.3	–0.6	0.3	0.4	5.1	
South Africa	1999[13]	22,833	9.7	4.7	0.4	2.9	2.9	1.1	1.8	1.3	4.6	2.9	4.4	5.1	
Spain	1998	108,953	9.5	4.1	4.8	2.6	2.2	1.5	2.1	2.6[11]	2.5	5.0	3.3	2.7	2.4
Sri Lanka	2001	2,009		30.2			39.7		0.9		1.7				10.7
Sudan, The	1990	1,179	40.0	3.0	16.7	11.9	0.4	5.4	0.2	0.2	2.1	6.4	0.7	2.2	
Suriname	1992[2, 13, 44]	700	33.4	22.3	12.3	…	1.5	1.6	8.7	1.4	0.7	1.6	…	8.3	
Swaziland	1995[7, 13, 14]	335	27.5	42.0	…	0.4	3.0	…	1.2	0.8	17.9	1.1	—	0.2	…
Sweden	1999[3]	60,552	5.7	1.0	0.3	0.7	0.1	0.1	4.4	2.3[34, 69]	9.8	5.8	3.0	5.7	
Switzerland	1999	49,667		9.6		1.7	0.5	0.2	3.5	[41]	2.6	6.8			18.0
Syria	1995	3,805	12.0	5.8	3.8	20.2	1.2	2.1	2.2	0.2	0.4	0.8	0.2	0.9	
Taiwan	2001	70,798	5.8		1.2	5.3	1.5	0.4	0.2	1.0	2.0	0.9	7.3	2.6	
Tajikistan	1998[2]	679	35.8[4]	1.1[4]	0.1	18.3[4]	0.6	0.1[4]	—	—	…	0.1[4]	2.1[4]	…	…
Tanzania	1995	119	10.7	5.8	10.7	17.4	0.8	1.7	1.7	0.8	3.3	3.3	14.9	2.5	
Thailand	1996[3, 7]	39,380	11.4	7.0	3.1	4.7	2.4	1.6	1.5	1.4[11]	3.2	3.0[4]	2.8	2.5	0.6
Togo	1998	138		50.9			6.0		5.8		5.6				4.4
Tonga	1997[2, 3]	15	51.3		—	0.8	1.6	1.1	1.6	4.3[34]	—	6.0	—	20.5	
Trinidad and Tobago	1995	862	12.0	9.1	3.3	0.2	0.9	0.2	0.4	1.0	2.8	2.5	36.5	1.4	0.1
Tunisia	1998[3]	4,977	10.2	3.3	6.4	7.7	15.9	4.5	5.4		2.1		4.6	2.8	1.0
Turkey	1998	36,678	9.3	1.8	1.5	11.4	5.1	0.7	0.6	0.8	1.3	1.7	3.8	6.2	
Turkmenistan	1992[2, 14, 15]	801	13.3	…	…	18.9	1.2	0.4	0.3[16]		[16]		3.2[5]	[5]	[5]
Tuvalu	1998	0.55	…	—	—	—	…	—	—	…	—	—	—	…	—
Uganda	1997[4]	346	27.9[4]	15.2[4]	3.5	5.6[4]		0.4	3.6[4]	3.4	1.2	5.3[4]	[4]	6.7[4]	0.9
Ukraine	1998[2, 13, 14]	23,163	19.4	3.5	1.4	0.8	0.9	0.4	1.0	0.6	1.0	0.8	4.8	1.1	1.1
United Arab Emirates	1998[7]	5,498		7.5			11.9		1.6		3.9				50.0
United Kingdom	1998[13, 14]	243,567	9.7[4]	2.3	0.9	2.6	1.8	0.5	1.5	2.6[11]	2.7	9.6	3.5	3.4	3.0
United States	1999	1,962,644	9.1	1.5	1.9	1.9	1.6	0.2	1.9	2.0[11]	3.8	3.2	3.9	4.0	3.8
Uruguay	1997[19]	3,069	21.4	10.2	5.9	6.7	2.8	2.8	0.2	0.6	2.0	3.7	1.4	6.5	
Uzbekistan	1992[2, 14, 15]	2,147	12.6	…	…	21.4	3.1	1.9	1.3[16]		[16]		5.4[5]	[5]	[5]
Vanuatu	1995[14]	16		35.9			3.2		23.5		6.9				4.7[74]
Venezuela	1996[3, 19]	15,621	11.3	4.0	12.7	1.8	1.9	0.9	0.4	0.5	1.7	1.5	7.8	3.4	1.3
Vietnam	1998[3, 19, 75]	2,532	13.2	10.2	6.8	8.3	6.2	7.3	1.1	0.8[11]	2.1	2.8	3.0	3.0	1.3
Virgin Islands (U.S.)	1997[1, 14]	146		22.0		[46]	0.8	[46]	1.1	[46]	—	14.5			[46]
West Bank[40]	1998	479	12.8	0.9	0.3	1.4	19.5	3.0	1.1	7.6	1.5	1.2	0.1	4.4	
Western Sahara	…	…	…	…	…	…	…	…	…	…	…	…	…	…	…
Yemen	2000	426	32.3		14.5	1.3	2.6	0.6	3.2	2.3[11]	0.5	3.6		1.9	
Zambia	1995	450	19.2	17.1	6.7	9.8	1.1	0.7	3.3	1.1	0.9	2.2	4.9	10.5	
Zimbabwe	1998[13]	1,088	13.6	15.7	4.7	9.1	3.0	2.5	2.9	2.0	2.1	2.8	3.7[76]	5.1	

[1]Gross output in value of sales. [2]Gross output of production. [3]In producer's prices. [4]Sum of available data. [5]351 includes 352, 355, and 356. [6]37 includes 381. [7]Establishments employing 10 or more persons. [8]Value of manufactured exports. [9]Value of manufactured exports (excluding duty-free reexports). [10]390 includes 385. [11]Includes metal furniture. [12]Estimated figure includes agriculture. [13]In factor values. [14]Complete ISIC detail is not available. [15]Includes extraction of petroleum, natural gas, metals, and nonmetals. [16]33 includes 34. [17]355 and 356 include 361 + 362. [18]38 includes 39. [19]Establishments employing five or more persons. [20]Includes mining and quarrying in other than petroleum and natural gas sectors. [21]33 includes 341. [22]In factor values at 1992 prices. [23]Establishments employing 50 or more persons. [24]All state-owned industrial enterprises and privately owned industrial enterprises with annual sales of more than U.S.$604,000. [25]Excludes traditional sector. [26]390 includes 332. [27]Excludes petroleum refining. [28]Republic of Cyprus only. [29]Excludes establishments processing coffee or cotton. [30]Establishments employing 10 or more persons and using power-driven machines. [31]Excludes frozen and chilled fish and crustaceans. [32]Remainder. [33]369 includes 371. [34]332 includes 390. [35]Establishments employing 20 or more persons. [36]Excludes unavailable data for food, beverages, and tobacco. [37]Establishments employing 6 or more persons. [38]342 includes 32. [39]33 includes 39. [40]West Bank includes Gaza

refined petroleum and products (353 + 354)	rubber products (355)	plastic products (356)	(36) pottery, china, and glass (361+ 362)	(36) bricks, tiles, cement, etc. (369)	(37) iron and steel (371)	(37) nonferrous metals (372)	(38) fabricated metal products (381)	(38) nonelectrical machinery (382 exc. 3825)	(38) office equip., computers (3825)	(38) electrical equip. (383 exc. 3832)	(38) radio, television (3832)	(38) transport equip. exc. motor vehicles (384 exc. 3843)	(38) motor vehicles (3843)	(38) professional equip. (385)	(39) jewelry, musical instruments (390)	country
10.7					…	…	4.8								…	Niger
—	1.9	2.8	0.4	5.8	1.0	1.9	3.7	1.1		2.0		9.8		—	0.5	Nigeria
46	46	46	2.8		—	—	—	—	—	—	—	0.2		—	46	Northern Mariana Islands
1.1	0.2	1.8	0.6[14]	2.7[14]	2.3	5.2	6.1	8.2	0.3	3.8	1.7	11.6	1.4	2.1[14]	0.7	Norway
16.8	—	2.7	2.5	17.2	0.1	4.0	6.6	1.9	0.1	2.6	—	0.1	0.1	—	0.5	Oman
3.1	0.9	0.4	0.5	7.2	4.2	—	0.7	1.6	—	5.0	2.7	0.8	2.7	0.2	0.8	Pakistan
…	…	…	…	…	…	…	…	…	…	…	…	…	…	…	…	Palau
9.5	4.9		6.8		1.8		2.2	—	—	0.4	—	1.5	0.1	0.2	1.4[41]	Panama
…	…	…	…	…	…	…	…	…	…	…	…	…	…	…	…	Papua New Guinea
2.1	—	2.8	0.1	4.7	0.1	0.1	0.4	0.1		—	—	0.4		—	0.2	Paraguay
0.9	2.4		7.6		3.1	17.8	2.4	0.7		1.5		0.6		…	1.6	Peru
8.9	0.7	…	2.7		1.6		1.7	1.3		11.6		1.1		…	3.0	Philippines
6.5	1.8	2.6	1.8	2.7	3.8	0.6	6.7	6.8		6.8		9.5		1.0	0.6	Poland
10.5	0.6	1.7	2.7	5.6	1.1	0.5	5.7	4.4	—	3.0	2.5	1.4	4.8	0.6	1.1	Portugal
2.3	—	1.0	1.6		0.2		1.1	7.3		2.6	5.4	—	0.3	4.2	0.4	Puerto Rico
4.4	…	0.8	13.5		17.6	—	3.8	…	…	0.3		0.3	—	…	0.3	Qatar
—	—	61	…	16.8	—	—	12.2	5.0							—	Réunion
2.7	1.1	0.9	5.2		6.6		4.2	5.9	0.5	2.8	1.7	2.0	3.7	0.7	0.7	Romania
6.1	1.1	0.5	1.0	5.1	8.3	11.4	1.8	8.0	0.5	2.8	46	2.1[63]	7.1	1.0	1.9	Russia
…	…	…	8.0		1.9[6]		6	…	…	…	…	…	…	…	0.2	Rwanda
…	…	…	…	…	…	…	…	…	…	…	…	…	…	…	…	St. Kitts and Nevis
—	0.4	3.8	—	—	—	—	5.6	—	—	3.3	0.9	—	—	—	1.3	St. Lucia
…	…	…	…	…	…	…	…	…	…	…	…	…	…	…	…	St. Vincent
…	…	…	…	10.0	…	…	1.0	…	…	…	…	…	…	…	5.0	Samoa
…	…	…	…	…	…	…	…	…	…	…	…	…	…	…	…	San Marino
…	…	…	…	…	…	…	…	…	…	…	…	…	…	…	…	São Tomé and Príncipe
14.4	0.1	3.6	1.7	12.0	4.9	0.1	9.0	2.3		2.4		1.0		0.2	0.7	Saudi Arabia
3.7	—	1.9	—	6.9	—	—	4.1	0.4	—	0.8	—	1.8	0.4	—	—	Senegal
−0.1	4.7		7.3		2.7		4.5	3.8	1.5	3.2	1.3	0.6	2.3	1.4	34	Serbia and Montenegro
			5.2		—	—	2.4								—	Seychelles
			3.5		…	…	2.1	…	…	…	…	…	…	…	0.1	Sierra Leone
4.9	0.3	2.2	0.4	1.4	0.4	0.1	5.7	6.7	24.2	2.4	17.8	6.6	0.8	2.9	0.4	Singapore
5.9	2.4	2.2	2.0	5.2	7.6	2.7	5.4	9.2	0.3	4.4[4]	1.9	2.5[4]	6.3	2.3	0.6	Slovakia
0.3	5.8		4.6		13.6[6]		6	9.0[67]		11.3		4.2		67	34	Slovenia
—	—	—	—	—	—	—	—	—	—	—	—	…	—	—	—	Solomon Islands
1.6	—	0.5	—	3.0	—	—	1.1	—	—	—	—	0.9			1.7	Somalia
5.9	1.2	2.4	1.4	3.3	9.7	5.4	6.1	5.4		5.9		9.2		0.7	1.6	South Africa
8.7[14]	1.5	2.8	1.5	5.3	2.8	1.1	7.9	6.0	0.8	3.4	1.3	1.8	8.1	0.9	0.9	Spain
			8.9		0.7		4.9	2.3[68]							68	Sri Lanka
1.3	0.8	1.2	0.1	0.5	0.1	0.7	2.6	0.1		1.2		2.1		—	0.1	Sudan, The
…	0.7	0.6	5.3		…	…	…	…	…	…	…	0.9		0.2	0.5	Suriname
…	…	0.2	0.1	0.5	…	…	2.2	2.8	…	…	…	…	0.2	…	—	Swaziland
0.9	0.8	1.6	0.5	1.3	4.1	1.3	6.7	10.1	0.5	2.4	15.2	1.8	9.9	3.9	34	Sweden
—	3.2		2.3		2.2		10.5	14.5	5.0		3.1	1.4	0.5	10.7	3.0[41]	Switzerland
17.1	0.3	0.6	4.7	7.1	—	0.6	14.0	2.4		2.4		0.5		—	0.3	Syria
8.4	1.5	4.8	2.5		5.8		7.7	5.6		25.7		6.4		1.0	2.4	Taiwan
…	—	—	0.2[4]	1.1[4]	…	39.7	0.1[4]	0.3[4]	…	0.2[4]	…	…	0.2[4]	…	—	Tajikistan
4.1	0.8	1.7	—	5.8	1.7	2.5	4.1	0.8		1.7		3.3		—	—	Tanzania
3.3	3.6	2.7	1.3	5.2	1.5	0.3	3.5	3.9[4]	2.8	4.0	4.8	0.7[4]	14.0	1.2[4]	2.0	Thailand
			10.4		—	…	14.8	2.1[68]							68	Togo
—	—	—	8.3			—	2.8	0.3	—	—	—	1.4	—	—	34	Tonga
10.5	0.2	0.5	1.2	3.6	8.2	—	1.4	0.3	—	1.4	0.3	0.1	0.1	10	1.9[10]	Trinidad and Tobago
14.5	0.9	1.4[70]	2.9	3.5	1.4	3.1[71]	71	0.4		3.9	72	2.1		72	1.9[72]	Tunisia
15.5	2.0	1.8	2.6	4.7	5.7	1.0	3.2	4.5		5.1		8.6		0.5	0.5	Turkey
55.7	5	5	4.0		0.1		0.8								…	Turkmenistan
—	—	—	—	…	—	—	—	—	—	—	—	—	—	—	…	Tuvalu
…	0.4[4]	1.1	4.9[4]	4.9[4]	…	10.9	…	…	…	3.7[4]	…	…	…	…	…	Uganda
5.4	2.0	0.5	1.0	4.4	25.6	1.9	5.1	6.6	0.1	2.2[4]	…	2.4	1.6	0.6[4]	0.1[4]	Ukraine
			7.0		6.6		9.9								1.6	United Arab Emirates
1.5	1.1	4.2	1.2	2.0	2.0	1.2	8.4	8.9	2.2	3.6	4.1	1.0[4, 73]	6.3	3.2	1.3	United Kingdom
2.1	1.0	3.7	2.9		3.4		7.3	7.1	2.4	3.1	7.7	5.2	8.5	5.2	1.6	United States
18.8	0.9	2.9	0.9	2.9	1.9	0.2	2.8	0.7		1.2		1.5		0.6	0.5	Uruguay
12.4	5	5	5.4		12.2		13.2								…	Uzbekistan
			74		21.0[6]		6	…	…	…	…	…	…	…	…	Vanuatu
15.8	2.2	1.6	2.3	2.9	7.0	6.1	2.7	1.7	—	1.7	0.1	0.3	5.9	0.3	0.3	Venezuela
0.3	1.1	2.5	1.0	9.2	2.7	0.3	2.3	2.4	0.7	2.6	3.5	2.3	1.8	0.4	0.9	Vietnam
			15.0		—	—	2.3	46		—	—	3.4		19.8	1.9	Virgin Islands (U.S.)
—	0.1	4.7	0.5	25.4	0.1	—	11.7	1.1		1.9		0.3		0.2	0.2	West Bank[40]
…	…	…	…	…	…	…	…	…	…	…	…	…	…	…	…	Western Sahara
8.2	…	3.3	…	18.8	…	…	6.0	0.4		0.3		0.2		…	…	Yemen
4.2	1.8	1.3	−0.2	3.3	1.3	—	5.3	1.1		3.3		0.7		—	0.2	Zambia
76	2.7	1.6	0.4	5.8	7.9	0.7	5.9	1.1		3.4		2.8		0.1	0.5	Zimbabwe

Strip. [41]390 includes 332. [42]384 includes 390. [43]Represents export value of clothing articles made from fur. [44]Selected industries only. [45]Total manufacturing value added (2000): U.S.$26,000,000. [46]Data withheld for reasons of confidentiality. [47]332 includes 313 and 321. [48]Includes public utilities. [49]Sugar and rice manufacturing only. [50]Establishments with electric power and employing 10 or more workers and all establishments employing 20 or more workers. [51]390 includes 353 + 354. [52]38 includes 37. [53]Excludes exports destined for Switzerland. [54]Complete data not available for professional equipment. [55]351 includes 383. [56]382 includes 384. [57]Excludes government printing. [58]Derivatives of petroleum and coal only. [59]Excludes Transdniester area and city of Tighina (Bendery). [60]Garment manufacturing accounts for most of manufacturing value added. [61]341 includes 356. [62]State enterprises only; state enterprises account for about 80% of all industrial output. [63]Excludes shipbuilding and aircraft (data withheld for reasons of confidentiality). [64]Refined sugar only. [65]Sector percentages are estimated figures. [66]Figure for 1999 is U.S.$88,000,000. [67]382 includes 385. [68]382 through 385 includes 390. [69]Includes recycling. [70]Includes synthetic fibres. [71]372 includes 381. [72]390 includes 3832 and 385. [73]Excludes railway equipment and aircraft. [74]35 includes 36. [75]17 provinces only covering about 80% of total industrial output. [76]351 includes 353 + 354.

Energy

This table provides data about the commercial energy supplies (reserves, production, consumption, and trade) of the various countries of the world, together with data about oil pipeline networks and traffic. Many of the data and concepts used in this table are adapted from the United Nations' *Energy Statistics Yearbook*.

Electricity. Total installed electrical power capacity comprises the sum of the rated power capacities of all main and auxiliary generators in a country. "Total installed capacity" (kW) is multiplied by 8,760 hours per year to yield "Total production capacity" (kW-hr).

Production of electricity comprises the total gross production of electricity by publicly or privately owned enterprises and also that generated by industrial establishments for their own use, but it usually excludes consumption by the utility itself. Measured in millions of kilowatt-hours (kW-hr), annual production of electricity ranges generally between 50% and 60% of total production capacity. The data are further analyzed by type of generation: fossil fuels, hydroelectric power, and nuclear fuel.

The great majority of the world's electrical and other energy needs are met by the burning of fossil hydrocarbon solids, liquids, and gases, either for thermal generation of electricity or in internal combustion engines. Many renewable and nontraditional sources of energy are being developed worldwide (wood, biogenic gases and liquids, tidal, wave, and wind power, geothermal and photothermal [solar] energy, and so on), but collectively these sources are still negligible in the world's total energy consumption. For this reason only hydroelectric and nuclear generation are considered here separately with fossil fuels.

Trade in electrical energy refers to the transfer of generated electrical output via an international grid. Total electricity consumption (residential and nonresidential) is equal to total electricity requirements less transformation and distribution losses.

Coal. The term coal, as used in the table, comprises all grades of anthracite, bituminous, subbituminous, and lignite that have acquired or may in the future, by reason of new technology or changed market prices, acquire an economic value. These types of coal may be differentiated according to heat content (density) and content of impurities. Most coal reserve data are based on proven recoverable reserves only, of all grades of coal. Exceptions are footnoted, with proven in-place reserves reported only when recoverable reserves are unknown. Production figures include deposits removed from both surface and underground workings as well as quantities used by the producers themselves or issued to the miners. Wastes recovered from mines or nearby preparation plants are excluded from production figures.

Natural gas. This term refers to any combustible gas (usually chiefly methane) of natural origin from underground sources. The data for production cover, to the extent possible, gas obtained from gas fields,

Energy

country	electricity													coal		
	installed capacity, 2000 ('000 kW)	production, 2000		power source, 2000			trade, 2000		consumption				reserves, 2002 ('000,000 metric tons)	production, 2000 ('000 metric tons)	consumption, 2000 ('000 metric tons)
		capacity ('000,000 kW-hr)	amount ('000,000 kW-hr)	fossil fuel (%)	hydropower (%)	nuclear fuel (%)	exports ('000,000 kW-hr)	imports ('000,000 kW-hr)	amount, 2000 ('000,000 kW-hr)	per capita, 2000 (kW-hr)	residential, 1998 (%)	nonresidential, 1998 (%)			
Afghanistan	499	4,371	480	34.4	65.6	—	—	95	575	26	...	...	66	1	1
Albania	1,892	16,574	4,943	1.3	98.7	—	221	1,221	5,943	1,896	...	...	...	42	44
Algeria	6,042	52,928	24,654	99.6	0.4	—	319	223	24,558	808	28.4	71.6	40	—	593
American Samoa	35	307	133	100.0	—	—	—	—	133	1,956	...	...	...	...	...
Andorra	...	...	...	...	...	...	—	—	...	...	...	...	...	...	...
Angola	460	4,030	1,445	36.9	63.1	—	—	—	1,445	110	...	...	...	...	...
Antigua and Barbuda	27	237	99	100.0	—	—	—	—	99	1,523	...	...	...	...	...
Argentina	23,742	207,980	89,014	60.6	32.4	6.9	6,022	7,249	90,241	2,437	47.3	52.7	430	259	1,058
Armenia	3,005	26,324	5,958	45.2	21.2	33.7	815	352	5,495	1,445	...	...	...	...	—
Aruba	90	788	777	100.0	—	—	—	—	777	7,693	...	...	...	...	...
Australia	44,189	387,096	208,422	91.8	8.2	—	—	—	208,422	10,880	...	...	82,090	306,799	128,200
Austria	18,222	159,625	69,483	36.7	63.2	—[1]	15,216	13,920	68,187	8,408	...	...	25	1,249	5,000
Azerbaijan	5,239	45,894	18,699	91.8	8.2	—	378	872	19,193	2,404	...	...	...	...	—
Bahamas, The	401	3,513	1,660	100.0	—	—	—	—	1,660	5,479	...	...	...	...	...
Bahrain	1,366	11,966	6,297	91.3	—	—	—	—	6,297	9,113	...	...	...	...	...
Bangladesh	3,490	30,572	15,545	93.9	6.1	—	—	—	15,545	113	37.7	62.3	...	...	660
Barbados	166	1,454	787	100.0	—	—	—	—	787	2,948	78.4	21.6	...	...	...
Belarus	7,818	68,486	26,095	99.9	0.1	—	2,764	9,975	33,306	3,330	...	...	...	...	504
Belgium	15,685	137,401	83,899	40.6	2.0	57.4	7,319	11,645	88,225	8,608	...	...	...	375	11,266
Belize	43	377	137	31.4	68.6	—	—	25	162	648	71	29	...	...	...
Benin	55	482	56	100.0	—	—	—	375	431	70	64.1	35.9	...	...	...
Bermuda	146	1,279	603	100.0	—	—	—	—	603	9,571	...	...	...	...	...
Bhutan	362	3,171	1,810	0.0	100.0	—	1,398	8	420	201	...	...	...	50	66
Bolivia	1,338	11,721	3,952	56.1	43.9	—	5	11	3,958	475	48.98	...	1.0	...	...
Bosnia and Herzegovina	2,731	23,924	10,429	51.2	48.8	—	2,569	1,505	9,365	2,355	...	...	...	8,883	8,883
Botswana	[2]	[2]	[2]	[2]	[2]	[2]	[2]	[2]	[2]	[2]	26.3	73.7	4,300	[2]	[2]
Brazil	73,122	640,549	349,153	11.0	87.3	1.7	7	44,200	393,346	2,345	26.7	73.3	11,929	6,712	20,270
Brunei	483	4,231	2,434	100.0	—	—	—	—	2,434	7,201	53.7	46.3	...	...	...
Bulgaria	11,034	96,658	40,924	47.7	7.9	44.4	5,584	964	36,304	4,567	53.1	46.9	2,711	26,432	29,223
Burkina Faso	78	683	284	56.3	43.7	—	—	—	284	25	...	...	...	...	...
Burundi	44	385	128	1.6	98.4	—	—	349	477	...	73.8	26.2	...	...	...
Cambodia	35	307	229	63.3	36.7	—	—	—	229	17	...	...	...	...	...
Cameroon	900	7,884	3,441	2.9	97.1	—	—	—	3,441	231	...	...	...	1	1
Canada	117,524	1,029,510	590,134	26.9	60.7	12.3	50,983	15,260	554,411	18,030	...	...	6,578	69,163	62,079
Cape Verde	7	61	43	100.0	—	—	—	—	43	101	...	...	...	...	...
Central African Republic	43	377	107	21.5	78.5	—	—	—	107	29	69.3	30.7	3.0	...	...
Chad	29	254	92	100.0	—	—	—	—	92	12	...	...	...	...	...
Chile	8,732	76,492	41,268	53.8	46.2	—	—	—	41,268	2,713	30	70	1,181	366	4,590
China	235,170	2,060,089	1,355,600	82.4	16.4	1.2	9,878	1,546	1,347,268	1,057	25.3	74.7	114,500	998,000	981,776
Colombia	12,715	111,383	43,943	27.0	73.0	—	37	77	43,983	1,039	70.9	29.1	6,648	38,365	4,551
Comoros	6	53	19	89.5	10.5	—	—	—	19	27	...	...	...	...	...
Congo, Dem. Rep. of the	3,205	28,076	5,458	0.4	99.6	—	1,101	57	4,414	87	...	...	88	96	136
Congo, Rep. of the	121	1,060	300	1.0	99.0	—	—	190	490	162	...	...	...	...	...
Costa Rica	1,719	15,058	7,227	3.5	80.9	—	532	531	7,226	1,889	71.1	28.9	...	...	...
Côte d'Ivoire	1,195	10,468	3,619	51.3	48.7	—[3]	—	—	3,619	221	26.1	73.9	...	...	...
Croatia	3,754	32,885	10,702	44.9	55.1	—	386	4,386	14,702	3,356	68	32	39	—	703
Cuba	4,287	37,554	15,029	99.4	0.6	—	—	—	15,029	1,343	52.8	47.2	...	...	15
Cyprus	997	8,734	3,370	100.0	—	—	—	—	3,370	4,452	82.4	17.6	...	...	49
Czech Republic	15,215	133,283	73,466	77.6	3.9	18.5	18,742	8,725	63,449	6,176	...	...	5,678	65,162	61,088
Denmark	13,634	119,434	43,619	89.6	0.1	—	7,752	8,417	44,284	8,298	...	...	...	—	6,686
Djibouti	88	771	192	100.0	—	—[4]	—	—	192	304	...	...	...	...	...
Dominica	13	114	77	58.4	41.6	—	—	—	77	1,069	...	...	...	...	...
Dominican Republic	3,553	31,124	9,701	90.4	9.6	—	—	—	9,701	1,139	72.3	27.7	...	...	193
East Timor	...	...	...	...	...	...	—	—	...	...	...	...	...	...	...
Ecuador	3,485	30,529	10,607	20.0	80.0	—	—	—	10,607	839	56.8	43.2	24	...	...

petroleum fields, or coal mines that is actually collected and marketed. (Much natural gas in Middle Eastern and North African oil fields is flared [burned] because it is often not economical to capture and market it.) Manufactured gas is generally a by-product of industrial operations such as gasworks, coke ovens, and blast furnaces. It is usually burned at the point of production and rarely enters the marketplace. Production of manufactured gas is, therefore, only reported as a percentage of domestic gas consumption.

Crude petroleum. Crude petroleum is the liquid product obtained from oil wells; the term also includes shale oil, tar sand extract, and field or lease condensate. Production and consumption data in the table refer, so far as possible, to the same year so that the relationship between national production and consumption patterns can be clearly seen; both are given in barrels.

Proven reserves are that oil remaining underground in known fields whose existence has been "proved" by the evaluation of nearby producing wells or by seismic tests in sedimentary strata known to contain crude petroleum, and that is judged recoverable within the limits of present technology and economic conditions (prices). The published proven reserve figures do not necessarily reflect the true reserves of a country, because government authorities or corporations often have political or economic motives for withholding or altering such data.

The estimated exhaustion rate of petroleum reserves is an extrapolated ratio of published proven reserves to the current rate of withdrawal/production. Present world published proven reserves will last about 40 to 45 years at the present rate of withdrawal, but there are large country-to-country variations above or below the average.

Data on petroleum and refined product pipelines are provided because of the great importance to both domestic and international energy markets of this means of bringing these energy sources from their production or transportation points to refineries, intermediate consumption and distribution points, and final consumers. Their traffic may represent a very significant fraction of the total movement of goods within a country. Available data for petroleum pipelines are often incomplete and their basis varies internationally, some countries reporting only international shipments, others reporting domestic shipments of 50 kilometres or more, and so on.

For data in the hydrocarbons portions of the table (coal, natural gas, and petroleum), extensive use has been made of a variety of international sources, such as those of the United Nations, the International Energy Agency (of the Organisation for Economic Co-operation and Development), and the World Energy Council (in its *World Energy Resources* [triennial]); the U.S. Department of Energy (especially its *International Energy Annual*); and of various industry surveys, such as those published by the *International Petroleum Encyclopedia* and *World Oil.*

natural gas						crude petroleum							country
published proven reserves, 2002 ('000,000,000 cu m)	production		consumption			reserves, 2002		production, 2000 ('000,000 barrels)	consumption, 2000 ('000,000 barrels)	refining capacity, 2002 ('000 barrels per day)	pipelines (latest)		
	natural gas, 2000 ('000,000 cu m)	manufactured gas, 2000 (% of total gas consumption)	amount, 2000 ('000,000 cu m)	residential, 1998 (%)	nonresidential, 1998 (%)	published proven ('000,000 barrels)	years to exhaust proven reserves				length (km)	traffic ('000,000 metric ton-km)	
99	117	...	117	...	...	...	...	—	—	—	...	...	Afghanistan
3.8	17	58.1	17	...	...	206	86	2.1	2.1	26	251	8	Albania
4,955	87,397	59.1	18,125	...	...	9,200	30	336	168	450	6,910	...	Algeria
...	...	...	...	...	...	...	...	—	—	—	—	...	American Samoa
...	...	...	...	...	...	...	...	...	...	...	—	—	Andorra
113	565	13.8	565	...	...	5,970	22	272	14	39	179	...	Angola
...	...	...	...	...	...	...	...	—	—	—	—	—	Antigua and Barbuda
758	45,350	11.7	40,817	...	...	2,881	9.5	283	191	639	6,990	...	Argentina
...	...	...	1,336	...	...	...	...	—	—	—	—	—	Armenia
...	...	...	...	...	...	...	...	—	2.4	280	—	—	Aruba
2,265	35,584	21.0	24,095	...	...	2,828	17	188	225	848	3,000	...	Australia
24	1,881	14.6	8,593	...	...	86	13	6.8	59	209	777	8,165	Austria
850	5,642	4.7	5,949	...	...	1,178	14	102	62	442	1,760	1,705	Azerbaijan
...	...	...	...	...	...	...	...	—	—	—	—	—	Bahamas, The
91	8,410	2.8	8,410	...	...	125	8.3	14	94	249	72	...	Bahrain
292	9,650	0.2	9,650	40.3	59.7	57	...	—	10.1	33	—	—	Bangladesh
0.1	38	3.1	38	34.8	65.2	2.5	4.2	0.6	1.8	—	—	—	Barbados
2.8	254	4.3	16,999	...	...	198	15	14	99	493	2,570	...	Belarus
—	3.0	20.0	19,544	...	...	...	...	—	249	791	1,328	1,168	Belgium
...	...	...	...	...	...	...	...	—	—	—	—	—	Belize
1.2	...	...	...	...	...	8.2	21	0.3	—	—	—	—	Benin
...	...	...	...	...	...	...	...	—	—	—	—	—	Bermuda
...	...	...	...	...	...	...	...	—	—	—	—	—	Bhutan
775	3,904	21.1	1,815	...	...	441	32	12	12	63	2,380	...	Bolivia
...	...	...	277	...	...	...	...	—	—	—	174	—	Bosnia and Herzegovina
...	...	[2]	...	...	...	—	—	...	[2]	—	—	—	Botswana
222	6,019	135.7	7,938	2.6	97.4	8,465	24	451	583	1,865	7,742	...	Brazil
239	9,316	1.2	1,467	...	...	1,160	20	65	1.7	9	553	...	Brunei
1.5	16	22.6	3,883	...	...	15	75	0.3	39	115	525	244	Bulgaria
...	...	...	...	...	...	...	...	—	—	—	—	—	Burkina Faso
...	...	...	...	...	...	...	...	—	—	—	—	—	Burundi
...	...	...	...	...	...	...	...	—	—	—	—	—	Cambodia
110	...	...	...	...	...	400	9.3	52	11	42	—	—	Cameroon
1,691	164,352	42.2	76,277	...	...	4,858	7.6	655	554	1,983	23,564	99,908	Canada
...	...	...	...	...	...	...	...	—	—	—	—	—	Cape Verde
...	...	...	...	...	...	...	...	—	—	—	—	—	Central African Republic
...	...	...	...	...	...	...	...	—	—	—	—	—	Chad
38	2,188	18.3	6,407	8.7	91.3	150	79	2.0	73	205	1,540	...	Chile
1,212	33,542	107.2	33,542	31.8	68.2	24,000	20	1,193	1,565	4,528	12,397	60,132	China
142	7,337	20.9	7,337	29.9	70.1	1,850	7.0	251	110	286	4,935	...	Colombia
...	...	...	...	...	...	...	...	—	—	—	—	—	Comoros
1.0	...	...	...	—	—	187	22	9.6	1.3	15	390	...	Congo, Dem. Rep. of the
119	125	1.9	125	...	...	1,506	16	99	4.4	21	25	...	Congo, Rep. of the
...	...	...	...	—	—	...	...	—	0.1	15	176	...	Costa Rica
30	1,510	5.1	1,510	—	—	100	11	11	31	65	—	—	Côte d'Ivoire
34	1,615	27.5	2,634	...	...	92	7.7	8.2	38	260	690	951	Croatia
14	574	61.4	574	...	...	314	26	17	28	301	—	—	Cuba
—	...	...	...	—	—	...	...	—	8.6	27	—	—	Cyprus
2.1	238	22.0	10,564	...	...	15	13	1.2	40	198	736	2,078	Czech Republic
87	7,911	12.4	4,379	...	...	1,113	13	137	62	176	688	1,385	Denmark
...	...	...	...	...	...	...	...	—	—	—	—	—	Djibouti
...	...	...	...	...	...	—	—	—	—	—	—	—	Dominica
—	...	...	...	...	...	...	...	—	17	48	104	...	Dominican Republic
...	...	...	...	...	...	...	...	...	...	...	...	...	East Timor
109	570	40.0	570	—	—	2,115	14	149	61	176	2,158	...	Ecuador

Energy (continued)

country	electricity: installed capacity, 2000 ('000 kW)	electricity: production, 2000: capacity ('000,000 kW-hr)	electricity: production, 2000: amount ('000,000 kW-hr)	power source, 2000: fossil fuel (%)	power source, 2000: hydro-power (%)	power source, 2000: nuclear fuel (%)	trade, 2000: exports ('000,000 kW-hr)	trade, 2000: imports ('000,000 kW-hr)	consumption: amount, 2000 ('000,000 kW-hr)	consumption: per capita, 2000 (kW-hr)	consumption: resi-dential, 1998 (%)	consumption: non-resi-dential, 1998 (%)	coal: reserves, 2002 ('000,000 metric tons)	coal: pro-duction, 2000 ('000 metric tons)	coal: con-sump-tion, 2000 ('000 metric tons)
Egypt	17,665	154,745	76,282	77.8	22.2	—	—	—	76,282	1,192	74.4	25.6	22	…	458
El Salvador	601	5,265	3,546	44.7	33.1	—[5]	112	808	4,242	676	67.4	32.6	…	…	…
Equatorial Guinea	18	158	23	91.3	8.7	—	—	—	23	50	…	…	…	…	…
Eritrea	172	1,507	216	100.0	—	—	—	—	216	59	…	…	…	…	…
Estonia	2,624	22,986	8,513	99.9	0.1	—	1,187	258	7,584	5,540	55.4	44.6	…	11,727	18,319
Ethiopia	469	4,108	1,700	2.8	96.8	—[7]	—	—	1,700	28	35.65	64.45	…	…	…
Faroe Islands	93	815	188	55.9	43.6	—[8]	—	—	188	4,087	…	…	…	…	…
Fiji	200	1,752	545	21.1	78.9	—	—	—	545	670	22	78	…	…	18
Finland	16,469	144,268	73,979	49.7	19.8	30.4[1]	326	12,206	85,859	16,588	…	…	…	…	5,131
France	116,569[9]	1,021,144[9]	546,707[9]	10.8[9]	13.1[9]	75.9[9, 10]	73,174[9]	3,695[9]	477,288[9]	8,099[9]	…	…	36	3,462[9]	21,425[9]
French Guiana	140	1,226	455	100.0	—	—	—	—	455	2,758	55.42	44.62	…	…	…
French Polynesia	90	788	407	71.3	28.7	—	—	—	407	1,747	…	…	…	…	…
Gabon	410	3,592	1,354	47.6	52.4	—	—	—	1,354	1,123	41.9	58.1	…	…	…
Gambia, The	29	254	132	100.0	—	—	—	—	132	95	…	…	…	…	…
Gaza Strip	…	…	…	…	…	…	…	…	…	…	…	…	…	…	…
Georgia	4,558	39,928	7,398	20.8	79.2	—	198	442	7,642	1,452	…	…	…	7	27
Germany	119,276	1,044,858	580,358	64.1	4.9	29.4	42,077	45,134	583,415	7,113	…	…	66,000	205,067	234,299
Ghana	1,187	10,398	7,548	12.5	87.5	—	425	553	7,676	417	7.2	92.8	…	…	3
Greece	11,129	97,490	49,296	90.7	8.3	—[10]	1,740	1,729	49,285	4,925	…	…	2,874	63,887	65,685
Greenland	106	929	263	100.0	—	—	—	—	263	4,696	…	…	183	…	…
Grenada	27	237	118	100.0	—	—	—	—	118	1,168	72.9	27.1	…	…	…
Guadeloupe	417	3,653	1,220	100.0	—	—	—	—	1,220	2,850	…	…	…	…	…
Guam	302	2,646	830	100.0	—	—	—	—	830	5,355	…	…	…	…	…
Guatemala	1,250	10,950	6,048	55.9	44.1	—	—	—	5,344	469	67.3	32.7	…	…	…
Guernsey	…	…	…	…	…	…	…	…	…	…	…	…	…	…	…
Guinea	197	1,726	569	64.5	35.5	—	—	—	569	70	…	…	…	…	…
Guinea-Bissau	21	184	58	100.0	—	—	—	—	58	48	…	…	…	…	…
Guyana	302	2,646	894	99.4	0.6	—	—	—	894	1,158	…	…	…	…	…
Haiti	260	2,278	635	58.1	41.9	—	—	—	635	80	44.1	55.9	…	…	…
Honduras	912	7,989	3,680	23.2	76.8	—	—	281	3,961	617	69.5	30.5	…	…	…
Hong Kong	11,568	101,336	31,329	100.0	—	—	1,181	10,203	40,351	5,937	…	…	…	…	6,057
Hungary	8,306	72,761	34,991	59.5	0.5	40.0	6,083	9,523	38,431	3,834	65.5	34.5	1,097	14,033	15,402
Iceland	1,337	11,712	7,067	0.2	89.9	—[11]	—	—	7,067	25,149	…	…	…	…	101
India	114,502	1,003,038	542,345	82.9	13.7	3.1[12]	187	1,540	543,698	543	53.5	46.5	84,396	337,969	362,151
Indonesia	25,405	222,548	99,511	83.5	13.8	—[13]	—	—	99,511	473	46.9	…	5,370	76,820	19,668
Iran	30,628	268,301	116,327	96.8	3.2	—	—	—	116,327	1,827	…	…	1,710	1,394	2,094
Iraq	9,500	83,220	30,521	98.0	2.0	—	—	—	30,521	1,330	…	…	…	…	…
Ireland	4,728	41,417	23,750	93.9	5.0	—[14]	71	169	23,848	6,297	…	…	14	—	2,853
Isle of Man	…	…	…	…	…	…	…	…	337	4,610	…	…	…	…	…
Israel	9,139	80,058	42,916	100.0	0.00	—	1,457	—	41,459	6,864	61.6	38.4	…	888	11,145
Italy	85,059[15]	745,117[15]	276,639[15]	79.7[15]	18.4[15]	—[16]	484[15]	44,831[15]	320,986[15]	5,554[15]	…	…	34	114[15]	18,143[15]
Jamaica	1,398	12,246	6,631	97.8	2.2	—	—	—	6,631	2,518	36.2	63.8	…	…	72
Japan	248,360	2,175,634	1,091,499	61.3	8.9	29.5[12]	—	—	1,091,499	8,603	…	…	773	3,143	147,919
Jersey	…	…	…	…	…	…	…	…	557	6,265	…	…	…	…	…
Jordan	1,678	14,699	7,375	99.5	0.5	—	5	45	7,415	1,509	66.1	33.9	…	…	…
Kazakhstan	18,960	166,090	51,624	85.4	14.6	—	85	3,077	54,616	3,666	…	…	34,000	72,260	47,738
Kenya	1,054	9,233	3,943	51.2	39.5	—[17]	—	221	4,164	136	38.8	61.2	…	…	98
Kiribati	2	18	7	100.0	—	—	—	—	7	84	…	…	…	…	…
Korea, North	9,500	83,220	32,815	35.0	65.0	—	—	—	32,815	1,474	…	…	600	69,601	71,268
Korea, South	53,679	470,228	295,156	61.2	1.9	36.9	—	—	295,156	6,243	41.8	58.2	78	4,150	66,525
Kuwait	9,365	82,037	32,853	100.0	—	—	—	—	32,853	15,001	93.3	6.7	…	…	…
Kyrgyzstan	3,697	32,386	14,917	8.3	91.7	—	3,153	321	12,085	2,469	25.4[1]	…	812	425	1,169
Laos	256	2,243	1,225	3.5	96.5	—	774	46	497	95	…	…	…	1	1
Latvia	2,114	18,519	4,134	31.8	68.2	—	322	2,108	5,920	2,434	59.5	40.5	…	…	97
Lebanon	2,297	20,122	9,236	95.1	4.9	—	—	1,397	10,633	3,041	…	…	…	…	117
Lesotho	[2]	[2]	[2]	[2]	[2]	[2]	[2]	[2]	[2]	[2]	…	…	…	[2]	[2]
Liberia	334	2,926	524	62.4	37.6	—	—	—	524	180	…	…	…	…	…
Libya	4,600	40,296	20,044	100.0	—	—	—	—	20,044	3,789	…	…	…	…	5
Liechtenstein	[18]	[18]	[18]	[18]	[18]	[18]	[18]	[18]	[18]	[18]	…	…	…	…	[18]
Lithuania	6,557	57,439	11,424	20.7	5.6	73.7	1,479	143	10,088	2,729	…	…	…	…	131
Luxembourg	1,239	10,854	1,228	25.4	70.2	—[19]	735	6,457	6,950	15,940	…	…	…	…	171
Macau	352	3,084	1,571	100.0	—	—	—	195	1,766	4,032	87.2	12.8	…	…	…
Macedonia	1,494	13,087	6,811	82.8	17.2	—	—	112	6,923	3,404	…	…	…	7,516	7,857
Madagascar	228	1,997	807	35.6	64.4	—	—	—	807	51	31.7	68.3	…	…	10
Malawi	196	1,717	886	2.3	97.7	—	2	—	884	78	67.4	32.6	2.0	…	17
Malaysia	13,824	121,098	69,280	90.0	10.0	—	12	—	69,268	2,977	48.4	51.6	4.0	384	3,761
Maldives	36	315	104	100.0	—	—	—	—	104	384	…	…	…	…	…
Mali	114	999	412	43.0	57.0	—	—	—	412	36	99	1	…	…	…
Malta	570	4,993	1,875	100.0	—	—	—	—	1,875	4,795	…	…	…	…	325
Marshall Islands	…	…	…	…	…	…	—	—	…	…	…	…	…	…	…
Martinique	396	3,469	1,085	100.0	—	—	—	—	1,085	2,833	…	…	…	…	…
Mauritania	115	1,007	163	80.4	19.6	—	—	—	163	61	…	…	…	…	6
Mauritius	661	5,790	1,777	94.7	5.3	—	—	—	1,777	1,498	64.7	35.3	…	…	254
Mayotte	…	…	…	…	…	…	—	—	77	491	…	…	…	…	…
Mexico	45,671	400,078	228,873	79.3	14.5	3.6[20]	195	1,069	229,747	2,368	…	…	1,211	11,344	12,294
Micronesia	…	…	…	…	…	…	—	—	…	…	…	…	…	…	…
Moldova	1,022	8,953	3,310	98.2	1.8	—	—	1,785	5,095	1,400	…	…	…	…	180
Monaco	[9]	[9]	[9]	[9]	[9]	[9]	[9]	[9]	[9]	[9]	…	…	…	[9]	[9]
Mongolia	901	7,893	2,930	100.0	—	—	—	181	3,111	1,302	…	…	…	5,011	5,053
Morocco	4,037	35,364	13,265	94.7	5.3	—	—	2,363	15,628	544	54.5	45.5	…	29	4,029
Mozambique	2,085	18,265	6,974	0.4	99.6	—	5,768	356	451	88	…	…	212	19	—
Myanmar (Burma)	1,548	13,560	5,076	63.6	36.4	—	—	—	5,076	106	75.5	24.5	2.0	575	567
Namibia	[2]	[2]	[2]	[2]	[2]	[2]	[2]	[2]	[2]	[2]	…	…	…	[2]	[2]
Nauru	10	88	33	100.0	—	—	—	—	33	2,750	…	…	…	…	…
Nepal	458	4,012	1,425	12.3	87.7	—	126	226	1,525	67	59.5	40.5	2.0	18	435

natural gas						crude petroleum							country
published proven reserves, 2002 ('000,000,000 cu m)	production		consumption			reserves, 2002		production, 2000 ('000,000 barrels)	consumption, 2000 ('000,000 barrels)	refining capacity, 2002 ('000 barrels per day)	pipelines (latest)		
	natural gas, 2000 ('000,000 cu m)	manufactured gas, 2000 (% of total gas consumption)	amount, 2000 ('000,000 cu m)	residential, 1998 (%)	non-residential, 1998 (%)	published proven ('000,000 barrels)	years to exhaust proven reserves				length (km)	traffic ('000,000 metric ton-km)	
1,533	21,007	9.3	21,007	…	…	2,948	10	253	239	726	1,767	…	Egypt
—	…	…	…	—	—	…	…	—	7.1	22	—	—	El Salvador
100	…	…	…	…	…	12	0.4	39	0.1	—	—	—	Equatorial Guinea
[6]	…	…	…	…	…	[6]	…	—	—	15	—	—	Eritrea
…	…	12.4	789	…	…	—	—	—	—	—	—	—	Estonia
25[6]	…	…	…	…	…	0.4[6]	…	—	5.5	—	—	—	Ethiopia
…	…	…	…	…	…	…	…	—	—	—	—	—	Faroe Islands
…	…	…	…	—	—	…	…	—	—	—	—	—	Fiji
—	—	37.5	4,080	…	…	…	…	—	78	252	—	—	Finland
14	1,569	21.8[9]	42,384[9]	…	…	149	12	10	635[9]	1,903	7,546	24,429	France
…	…	…	…	…	…	…	…	—	—	—	—	—	French Guiana
…	…	…	…	…	…	…	…	—	—	—	—	—	French Polynesia
99	810	5.7	810	…	…	2,499	19	113	5.6	17	284	…	Gabon
…	…	…	…	…	…	…	…	—	—	—	—	—	Gambia, The
…	…	…	…	…	…	…	…	…	…	…	—	—	Gaza Strip
8.5	59	0.1	1,002	…	…	35	39	0.8	1.0	106	670	…	Georgia
254	23,538	17.0	109,387	…	…	364	17	23	776	2,267	2,240	37,250	Germany
23	…	…	…	—	—	17	…	0.1	8.2	45	—	—	Ghana
1.0	49	70.2	2,031	…	…	9.0	4.3	1.8	139	407	573	…	Greece
…	…	…	…	…	…	…	…	—	—	—	—	—	Greenland
…	…	…	…	…	…	…	…	—	—	—	—	—	Grenada
…	…	…	…	…	…	…	…	—	—	—	—	—	Guadeloupe
…	…	…	…	—	—	…	…	—	—	—	—	—	Guam
2.8	11	95.3	11	…	…	526	57	7.5	6.6	16	275	…	Guatemala
…	…	…	…	…	…	…	…	…	…	…	—	—	Guernsey
…	…	…	…	…	…	…	…	—	—	—	—	—	Guinea
…	…	…	…	…	…	…	…	—	—	—	—	—	Guinea-Bissau
…	…	…	…	…	…	…	…	—	—	—	—	—	Guyana
…	…	…	…	…	…	…	…	—	—	—	—	—	Haiti
—	…	…	…	—	—	…	…	—	—	—	—	—	Honduras
…	…	27.9	2,394	—	—	…	…	—	—	—	—	—	Hong Kong
65	3,177	7.7	12,344		…	111	13	7.6	40	161	1,204	2,470	Hungary
…	…	…	…	…	…	…	…	—	—	—	—	—	Iceland
437	24,315	30.0	24,315	…	…	4,840	19	244	579	2,135	5,692	…	India
2,478	54,197	17.1	21,500	…	…	5,000	10	447	386	993	2,961	…	Indonesia
26,600	59,684	6.5	62,971	…	…	89,700	68	1,337	470	1,474	9,800	…	Iran
3,188	3,737	47.0	3,737	…	…	112,500	146	939	181	418	5,075	…	Iraq
20	1,121	3.0	4,019	…	…	—	—	—	25	71	—	—	Ireland
…	…	…	…	…	…	…	…	…	…	—	—	—	Isle of Man
42	8.8	…	8.8	—	…	3.8	—	—	76	220	998		Israel
191	16,639	…	70,770[15]	…	…	622	16	31	600[15]	2,301	3,851	13,981	Italy
—	…	…	…	—	—	…	…		7.8	34	10	…	Jamaica
40	2,453	50.3	73,485	…	…	59	18	2.5	1,536	4,767	406	…	Japan
…	…	…	…	…	…	…	…	…	…	—	—	—	Jersey
5.7	231	102.9	231	—	—	0.9	…	—	28	90	209	…	Jordan
1,841	12,004	0.9	11,002	…	…	5,417	31	226	19	427	6,965	26,581	Kazakhstan
—	…	…	…	—	—	…	…	—	18	90	483	…	Kenya
…	…	…	…	…	…	…	…	—	—	—	—	—	Kiribati
…	…	…	…	…	…	…	…	—	18	71	217	…	Korea, North
—	…	85.4	19,834	…	…	…	…	—	892	2,560	455	…	Korea, South
1,489	9,177	42.0	9,177	…	…	96,500	128	719	274	889	917	…	Kuwait
5.7	32	…	682	…	…	40	67	0.6	1.0	10	—	—	Kyrgyzstan
…	…	…	…	…	…	…	…	—	—	—	136	…	Laos
…	…	…	1,302	…	…	…	…	—	—	—	1,530	6,569	Latvia
—	…	…	…	…	…	…	…	—	—	38	72	…	Lebanon
—	…	[2]	…	…	…	…	…	…	[2]	—	—	—	Lesotho
—	…	…	…	…	…	…	…	—	—	15	—	—	Liberia
1,328	6,000	14.0	5,221	…	…	29,500	58	491	157	343	4,826	…	Libya
—	…	[18]	…	…	…	…	…	…	…	—	—	—	Liechtenstein
—	…	18.9	2,462	…	…	12	6	2.3	35	263	105	3,457	Lithuania
…	…	1.3	782	…	…	…	…	—	—	—	48	…	Luxembourg
…	…	…	…	…	…	…	…	—	—	—	—	—	Macau
…	…	14.5	65	…	…	…	…	—	5.9	57	—	—	Macedonia
2.8	…	…	…	…	…	…	…	—	3.4	15	—	—	Madagascar
…	…	…	…	—	—	…	…	—	—	—	—	—	Malawi
2,337	48,219	9.3	29,454	0.3	99.7	3,000	12	227	156	516	1,307	…	Malaysia
…	…	…	…	…	…	…	…	—	—	—	—	—	Maldives
…	…	…	…	…	…	…	…	—	—	—	—	—	Mali
—	…	…	…	…	…	…	…	—	—	—	—	—	Malta
…	…	…	…	…	…	…	…	…	…	…	—	—	Marshall Islands
—	…	…	…	…	…	…	…	—	6.0	17	—	—	Martinique
…	…	…	…	…	…	…	…	—	7.1	—	—	—	Mauritania
…	…	…	…	…	…	…	…	—	—	—	—	—	Mauritius
…	…	…	…	…	…	…	…	…	…	—	—	—	Mayotte
1,103	35,093	25.0	36,953	…	…	26,941	24	1,112	467	1,684	38,350	…	Mexico
…	…	…	…	…	…	…	…	…	…	…	—	—	Micronesia
…	…	…	2,519	…	…	…	…	—	—	—	—	—	Moldova
…	…	[9]	[9]	…	…	…	…	…	[9]	—	—	—	Monaco
…	…	…	…	…	…	…	…	—	—	—	—	—	Mongolia
1.3	50	…	50	—	…	1.8	…	0.1	52	155	362	…	Morocco
57	0.6	…	1	…	…	…	…	—	—	—	595	…	Mozambique
346	6,171	1.2	1,427	…	…	50	19	2.9	7.3	57	1,343	…	Myanmar (Burma)
85	…	[2]	…	…	…	…	…	…	[2]	—	—	—	Namibia
…	…	…	…	…	…	…	…	—	—	—	—	—	Nauru
…	…	…	…	—	—	…	…	—	—	—	—	—	Nepal

Energy (continued)

country	electricity: installed capacity, 2000 ('000 kW)	electricity: production, 2000: capacity ('000,000 kW-hr)	electricity: production, 2000: amount ('000,000 kW-hr)	electricity: power source, 2000: fossil fuel (%)	electricity: power source, 2000: hydro-power (%)	electricity: power source, 2000: nuclear fuel (%)	electricity: trade, 2000: exports ('000,000 kW-hr)	electricity: trade, 2000: imports ('000,000 kW-hr)	electricity: consumption: amount, 2000 ('000,000 kW-hr)	electricity: consumption: per capita, 2000 (kW-hr)	electricity: consumption: residential, 1998 (%)	electricity: consumption: non-residential, 1998 (%)	coal: reserves, 2002 ('000,000 metric tons)	coal: production, 2000 ('000 metric tons)	coal: consumption, 2000 ('000 metric tons)
Netherlands, The	21,007	184,021	92,110	94.7	0.2	4.3[21]	4,031	22,946	111,025	6,999	...	...	497	...	12,972
Netherlands Antilles	250	2,190	1,120	100.0	—	—	—	—	1,120	5,209	...	...	...	...	...
New Caledonia	354	3,101	1,519	75.6	30.7	—	—	—	1,519	7,649	...	...	2.0	...	160
New Zealand	8,512	74,565	39,010	29.5	63.1	—[22]	—	—	39,010	10,183	...	...	572	3,568	2,016
Nicaragua	641	5,615	2,288	64.2	11.8	—[23]	1	116	2,403	474	70.7	29.3	...	...	...
Niger	105	920	238	100.0	—	—	—	213	451	...	56	44	70	175	175
Nigeria	5,881	51,518	15,757	63.2	36.8	—	—	—	15,757	137	...	...	190	61	61
Northern Mariana Islands	...	...	...	...	...	...	—	—	...	...	...	...	...	...	...
Norway	29,973	262,563	143,040	0.6	99.4	—	20,529	1,474	123,985	27,595	...	...	1.0	632	1,035
Oman	2,410	21,112	12,061	100.0	—	—	—	—	12,061	5,021	...	...	...	...	...
Pakistan	17,399	152,415	65,751	70.1	29.3	0.6	—	—	65,751	478	72.3	27.7	2,265	3,168	4,125
Palau	62	543	210	85.7	14.3	—	—	—	210	11,053	...	...	...	...	...
Panama	1,349	11,817	4,836	29.7	70.3	—	18	135	4,953	1,734	79.5	20.5	...	...	70
Papua New Guinea	543	4,757	2,180	48.8	51.2	—	—	—	2,180	453	27.9	72.1	...	...	...
Paraguay	8,131	71,228	53,521	0.1	99.9	—	47,385	—	6,136	1,116	79	21	...	...	...
Peru	6,067	53,147	19,912	18.8	81.2	—	—	—	19,912	776	67.74	32.34	1,060	12	528
Philippines	12,254	107,345	45,290	57.1	17.2	—[24]	—	—	45,290	593	65.34	34.74	332	1,356	8,602
Poland	30,559	267,697	145,183	97.1	2.9	—	9,663	3,290	138,810	3,592	41.84	58.24	22,160	162,837	142,881
Portugal	10,934	95,782	47,459	74.8	24.7	—[8]	3,767	4,698	48,390	4,835	...	...	36	—	6,154
Puerto Rico	4,430	38,807	20,380	99.4	0.6	—	—	—	20,380	5,254	...	...	...	...	160
Qatar	1,879	16,460	9,168	100.0	—	—	—	—	9,168	16,227	74.9	25.1	...	...	...
Réunion	434	3,802	1,575	64.4	35.6	—	—	—	1,575	2,184	...	...	...	...	...
Romania	21,904	191,879	51,937	61.0	28.5	10.5	1,470	774	51,241	2,284	27.1	72.9	1,457	29,285	31,962
Russia	212,768	1,863,848	877,766	66.3	18.8	14.9	22,850	8,795	863,711	5,937	36.1	63.9	157,010	243,726	233,881
Rwanda	43	377	169	2.4	97.6	—	4	17	182	24	...	...	...	...	...
St. Kitts and Nevis	20	175	100	100.0	—	—	—	—	100	2,500	...	...	...	...	...
St. Lucia	66	578	275	100.0	—	—	—	—	275	1,858	...	...	...	...	...
St. Vincent and the Grenadines	16	140	85	74.1	25.9	—	—	—	85	752	...	...	...	...	...
Samoa	20	175	66	62.1	37.9	—	—	—	66	386	...	...	...	...	...
San Marino	[15]	[15]	[15]	[15]	[15]	[15]	[15]	[15]	[15]	[15]	...	...	...	[15]	...
São Tomé and Príncipe	6	53	18	44.4	55.6	—	—	—	18	130	...	...	...	...	...
Saudi Arabia	23,792	208,418	126,441	100.0	—	—	—	—	126,441	5,908	...	...	...	...	...
Senegal	237	2,076	1,474	100.0	—	—	—	—	1,474	155	16.7	83.3	...	...	...
Serbia and Montenegro	11,779	103,184	31,894	62.2	37.8	—	446	4,354	35,802	3,366	...	...	16,256	34,335	34,480
Seychelles	28	245	164	100.0	—	—	—	—	164	2,025	24.3	75.7	...	...	...
Sierra Leone	130	1,139	246	100.0	—	—	—	—	246	56	...	...	...	...	...
Singapore	5,672	49,687	31,665	100.0	—	—	—	—	31,665	7,665	...	...	...	...	—
Slovakia	8,206	71,885	31,993	30.5	16.0	53.5	8,647	5,951	29,297	5,425	...	...	172	3,648	8,869
Slovenia	2,543	22,277	13,527	36.5	28.3	35.2	5,552	4,232	12,207	6,140	...	...	275	4,480	4,925
Solomon Islands	12	105	33	100.0	—	—	—	—	33	74	...	...	...	...	...
Somalia	80	701	282	100.0	—	—	—	—	282	32	...	...	...	...	...
South Africa	39,615[2]	347,027[2]	213,577[2]	91.3[2]	2.6[2]	6.1[2]	4,072[2]	7,023[2]	216,528[2]	4,311[2]	28.5	71.5	49,520	225,287[2]	156,248[2]
Spain	52,898	463,386	224,737	56.1	14.2	27.7[25]	7,827	12,268	229,178	5,807	...	...	660	23,471	45,654
Sri Lanka	2,108	18,466	6,844	53.2	46.7	—	—	—	6,844	354	62.7	37.3	...	...	1
Sudan, The	757	6,631	2,264	47.7	52.3	—	—	—	2,264	73	...	...	...	...	...
Suriname	425	3,723	1,648	20.1	79.9	—	—	—	1,648	3,780	...	...	...	...	...
Swaziland	[2]	[2]	[2]	[2]	[2]	[2]	[2]	[2]	[2]	[2]	...	...	208	[2]	[2]
Sweden	32,777	287,127	147,515	7.3	53.5	38.8[12]	13,630	18,308	152,193	17,154	...	...	1.0	—	3,057
Switzerland	17,984[18]	157,540[18]	68,722[18]	3.9[18]	57.6[18]	38.5[18]	31,400[18]	24,330[18]	61,652[18]	8,504[18]	...	...	...	...	156[18]
Syria	6,000	52,560	22,626	68.4	31.6	—	—	—	22,626	1,386	...	...	...	...	...
Taiwan	...	156,511	...	70.7	5.7	23.6	—	—	142,413	6,419	35.2	64.8	1.0	...	...
Tajikistan	4,443	38,921	14,197	2.3	97.7	—	3,909	5,243	15,531	...	...	...	...	20	122
Tanzania	543	4,757	2,548	15.8	84.2	—	...	55	2,603	74	...	...	200	79	79
Thailand	27,647	242,188	101,577	94.1	5.9	—	194	2,967	104,350	1,674	58.3	41.7	1,268	17,708	21,684
Togo	38	333	68	98.5	1.5	—	—	512	580	128	...	...	...	...	...
Tonga	8	70	35	100.0	—	—	—	—	35	354	...	...	...	...	...
Trinidad and Tobago	1,467	12,851	5,460	100.0	—	—	—	—	5,460	4,233	35.3	64.7	...	...	...
Tunisia	2,290	20,060	10,073	99.3	0.7	—	130	1	9,944	1,040	54.1	45.9	...	...	1
Turkey	27,272	238,903	114,355	72.9	27.0	—[1]	437	3,791	117,709	1,803	...	...	3,689	63,135	79,799
Turkmenistan	3,930	34,427	9,845	99.9	0.1	—	1,068	—	8,777	...	...	...	...	...	...
Tuvalu	...	...	...	...	...	...	—	—	...	...	...	...	...	...	...
Uganda	264	2,313	1,573	0.4	99.6	—	160	—	1,413	64	...	...	...	...	...
Ukraine	53,868	471,884	171,445	48.2	8.4	45.1	6,528	2,679	167,596	3,381	...	...	34,153	80,990	85,267
United Arab Emirates	5,820	50,983	31,890	100.0	—	—	—	—	31,890	12,237	...	...	...	...	...
United Kingdom	79,531	696,692	376,919	75.1	2.1	22.6	134	14,308	391,093	6,573	...	...	1,500	30,600	58,440
United States	799,275	7,001,649	4,128,513	74.5	6.7	18.3[8]	13,233	43,759	4,159,039	14,684	...	...	246,461	975,694	970,494
Uruguay	2,179	19,088	7,588	7.1	92.9	—	942	1,328	7,974	2,390	76	34	...	...	1
Uzbekistan	11,709	102,571	46,840	87.5	12.5	—	4,722	6,003	48,121	...	...	...	4,000	2,569	2,507
Vanuatu	12	105	38	100.0	—	—	—	—	38	193	...	...	...	...	...
Venezuela	21,292	186,518	85,211	26.3	73.7	—	—	—	85,211	3,525	23.8	76.2	479	7,885	180
Vietnam	5,029	44,054	26,594	42.8	54.7	—[26]	—	—	26,594	342	...	...	150	11,609	7,978
Virgin Islands (U.S.)	323	2,829	1,090	100.0	—	—	—	—	1,090	9,008	...	...	...	...	257
West Bank	...	...	...	...	...	...	...	...	...	...	...	...	...	...	...
Western Sahara	58	508	88	100.0	—	—	—	—	88	349	...	...	...	...	...
Yemen	810	7,096	2,960	100.0	—	—	—	—	2,960	162	...	...	...	...	...
Zambia	2,260	19,798	7,797	0.5	99.4	—	1,774	—	6,023	562	33	67	10	194	128
Zimbabwe	2,011	17,616	6,996	53.4	46.6	—	—	5,114	12,110	959	42.6	57.4	502	4,400	4,437

[1]In addition, geothermal equals 0.1%. [2]South Africa includes Botswana, Lesotho, Namibia, and Swaziland. [3]In addition, geothermal equals 14.8%. [4]In addition, geothermal equals 10.4%. [5]In addition, geothermal equals 22.2%. [6]Ethiopia includes Eritrea. [7]In addition, geothermal equals 0.4%. [8]In addition, geothermal equals 0.5%. [9]France includes Monaco. [10]In addition, geothermal equals 0.2%. [11]In addition, geothermal equals 9.9%. [12]In addition, geothermal equals 0.3%. [13]In addition, geothermal equals 2.7%. [14]In addition, geothermal equals 1.1%. [15]Italy includes San Marino. [16]In

natural gas						crude petroleum							country
published proven reserves, 2002 ('000,000,-000 cu m)	production		consumption			reserves, 2002		production, 2000 ('000,000 barrels)	consumption, 2000 ('000,000 barrels)	refining capacity, 2002 ('000 barrels per day)	pipelines (latest)		
	natural gas, 2000 ('000,000 cu m)	manufactured gas, 2000 (% of total gas consumption)	amount, 2000 ('000,000 cu m)	residential, 1998 (%)	non-residential, 1998 (%)	published proven ('000,000 barrels)	years to exhaust proven reserves				length (km)	traffic ('000,000 metric ton-km)	
1,615	76,741	23.0	51,469	...	...	107	8.9	9.9	377	1,207	1,383	5,503	Netherlands, The
—	...	...	...	...	...	...	...	—	107	320	—	—	Netherlands Antilles
...	...	...	...	...	...	...	...	—	—	—	—	—	New Caledonia
59	5,444	8.0	5,445	...	...	90	5.3	13	40	106	160	...	New Zealand
—	...	...	...	—	—	...	...	—	6.1	20	56	...	Nicaragua
...	...	...	...	—	—	...	...	—	—	—	—	—	Niger
4,502	12,589	2.0	7,123	—	...	24,000	34	794	36	439	5,042	...	Nigeria
...	...	...	...	...	...	...	...	...	...	...	—	—	Northern Mariana Islands
2,186	52,876	122.0	4,167	...	...	9,447	8.3	1,239	119	310	5,747	3,485	Norway
864	4,664	2.5	4,664	...	...	5,506	17	349	26	85	1,300	...	Oman
681	21,036	1.3	21,036	41.2	58.8	298	14	21	51	234	1,135	...	Pakistan
—	...	...	...	...	...	—	—	—	—	...	—	—	Palau
—	...	132.3	62	—	—	...	...	—	16	60	130	...	Panama
425	84	...	84	—	—	238	8.2	29	0.5	—	—	—	Papua New Guinea
—	...	...	...	...	...	...	...	—	0.8	8	—	—	Paraguay
245	821	138.1	821	...	...	323	7.7	41	62	191	800	...	Peru
105	10	...	10	—	—	178	593	0.4	118	420	357	...	Philippines
164	4,904	33.4	14,760	...	...	115	43	4.8	134	350	2,280	18,448	Poland
—	...	20.7	2,425	...	...	...	...	—	85	304	80	...	Portugal
—	...	...	...	...	...	...	...	—	17	112	—	—	Puerto Rico
21,456	29,558	10.4	15,993	—	...	15,207	70	231	27	200	235	...	Qatar
...	...	...	...	...	...	...	...	—	—	—	—	—	Réunion
121	12,803	11.3	15,969	...	...	1,154	25	45	80	501	4,229	2,257	Romania
48,139	471,771	8.9	318,486	...	...	48,573	22	2,307	1,312	5,435	63,000	1,899,000	Russia
57	0.3	0.3	0	...	...	...	...	—	—	—	—	—	Rwanda
...	...	...	...	...	...	...	...	—	—	—	—	—	St. Kitts and Nevis
...	...	...	...	...	...	...	...	—	—	—	—	—	St. Lucia
...	...	...	...	...	...	...	...	—	—	—	—	—	St. Vincent and the Grenadines
...	...	...	...	...	...	...	...	—	—	—	—	—	Samoa
...	...	...	...[15]	...	...	...	...	...	[15]	—	—	—	San Marino
...	...	...	...	...	...	...	...	—	—	—	—	—	São Tomé and Príncipe
6,349	49,808	58.3	49,808	...	...	261,750	83	2,984	650	1,745	6,550	...	Saudi Arabia
—	0.5	...	0.5	...	...	...	...	—	6.7	27	—	—	Senegal
48	886	1.3	2,085	...	...	78	11	6.0	9.8	158	545	...	Serbia and Montenegro
...	...	...	...	...	...	...	...	—	—	—	—	—	Seychelles
—	...	...	...	...	...	...	...	—	1.8	10	—	—	Sierra Leone
—	...	81.5	1,411	—	—	...	...	—	307	1,259	—	—	Singapore
14	158	17.0	6,886	...	...	9.0	23	0.4	43	115	...	...	Slovakia
3.4	6.9	...	1,035	...	...	7.0	...	—	1.2	14	290	128	Slovenia
...	...	...	...	—	—	...	...	—	—	—	—	—	Solomon Islands
5.7	...	...	...	...	...	...	...	—	—	—	15	...	Somalia
23	1,666	...	1,666	...	...	16	0.3	60	193[2]	490	2,679	...	South Africa
0.5	424	26.3	17,752	...	...	21	5.3	1.7	429	1,322	2,059	6,872	Spain
—	...	...	...	—	—	563	—	—	17	48	62	...	Sri Lanka
113	...	...	...	...	...	...	...	68	15	122	815	...	Sudan, The
—	...	...	...	...	...	74	49	3.7	3.0	7	—	—	Suriname
...	...	...	...	...	...	...	...	...	[2]	—	—	—	Swaziland
—	...	125.8	833	...	...	...	...	—	149	424	—	—	Sweden
—	—	14.0[18]	2,971	...	...	...	...	—	34	132	318	234	Switzerland
241	5,531	6.0	5,531	...	...	2,500	13	186	88	240	1,819	...	Syria
76	789	...	...	37.5	62.5	4.0	4.4	0.6	...	920	3,400	...	Taiwan
5.7	39	...	749	...	...	12	120	0.1	0.1	—	—	—	Tajikistan
28	...	...	...	...	...	...	...	—	3.7	15	982	...	Tanzania
377	17,184	18.6	19,338	—	...	516	52	20	252	703	67	...	Thailand
—	...	...	...	...	...	...	...	—	—	—	—	—	Togo
...	...	...	...	...	...	...	...	—	—	—	—	—	Tonga
557	10,448	9.3	10,448	...	...	716	16	44	59	160	1,051	...	Trinidad and Tobago
76	1,763	5.8	1,923	...	...	308	9.9	28	14	34	883	...	Tunisia
8.6	630	19.0	15,762	...	...	296	13	20	172	719	4,059	2,994	Turkey
2,860	45,556	3.0	12,997	...	...	546	12	53	46	237	250	694	Turkmenistan
...	...	...	...	...	...	...	...	...	...	—	—	—	Tuvalu
...	...	...	...	...	...	...	...	—	—	—	—	—	Uganda
1,121	17,883	4.8	74,235	...	...	395	14	28	70	1,025	8,500	38,402	Ukraine
6,006	25,783	56.0	16,469	...	...	97,800	121	783	153	514	830	...	United Arab Emirates
695	127,197	11.0	113,808	...	...	4,930	5.3	880	606	1,789	3,926	11,666	United Kingdom
4,889	537,988	18.9	660,039	21.3	78.7	22,045	9.8	2,111	5,664	16,757	276,000	843,586	United States
—	...	...	...	—	—	...	...	—	14	37	—	—	Uruguay
1,875	54,764	0.6	49,279	...	...	594	15	30	30	222	290	200	Uzbekistan
...	...	...	...	...	...	...	...	—	—	—	—	—	Vanuatu
4,225	28,383	20.0	28,383	13.1	86.9	77,685	66	1,129	382	1,282	6,850	...	Venezuela
193	1,356	13.3	1,356	...	...	600	6.7	115	125	—	150	...	Vietnam
—	...	...	...	...	...	...	...	—	—	470	—	—	Virgin Islands (U.S.)
...	...	...	...	...	...	...	...	...	...	—	—	—	West Bank
...	...	...	...	...	...	...	...	—	—	—	—	—	Western Sahara
481	...	...	...	...	...	4,000	28	160	30	130	676	—	Yemen
—	...	...	...	—	—	...	...	—	0.2	24	1,724	...	Zambia
...	...	...	...	—	—	...	...	—	—	—	212	...	Zimbabwe

addition, geothermal equals 1.9%. [17]In addition, geothermal equals 9.3%. [18]Switzerland includes Liechtenstein. [19]In addition, geothermal equals 2.2%. [20]In addition, geothermal equals 2.6%. [21]In addition, geothermal equals 0.8%. [22]In addition, geothermal equals 7.4%. [23]In addition, geothermal equals 24.0%. [24]In addition, geothermal equals 25.7%. [25]In addition, geothermal equals 2.1%. [26]In addition, geothermal equals 2.5%.

Transportation

This table presents data on the transportation infrastructure of the various countries and dependencies of the world and on their commercial passenger and cargo traffic. Most states have roads and airports, with services corresponding to the prevailing level of economic development. A number of states, however, lack railroads or inland waterways because of either geographic constraints or lack of development capital and technical expertise. Pipelines, one of the oldest means of bulk transport if aqueducts are considered, are today among the most narrowly developed transportation modes worldwide for shipment of bulk materials. Because the principal contemporary application of pipeline technology is to facilitate the shipment of hydrocarbon liquids and gases, coverage of pipelines will be found in the "Energy" table. It is, however, also true that pipelines now find increasing application for slurries of coal or other raw materials.

While the United Nations' *Statistical Yearbook, Monthly Bulletin of Statistics,* and *Annual Bulletin of Transport Statistics* provide much data on infrastructure and traffic and have established basic definitions and classifications for transportation statistics, the number of countries covered is limited. Several commercial publications maintain substantial databases and publishing programs for their particular areas of interest: highway and vehicle statistics are provided by the International Road Federation's annual *World Road Statistics;* the International Union of Railway's *International Railway Statistics* and Jane's *World Railways* provide similar data for railways; Lloyd's *Register of Shipping Statistical Tables* summarizes the world's merchant marine; the *Official Airline Guide,* the International Civil Aviation Organization's *Digest of Statistics: Commercial Air Carriers,* and the International Air Transport Association's *World Air Transport Statistics* have also been used to supplement and update data collected by the UN. Because several of these agencies are commercially or insurance-oriented, their data tend to be more complete, accurate, and timely than those of intergovernmental organizations, which depend on periodic responses to questionnaires or publication of results in official sources. All of these international sources have been extensively supplemented by national statistical sources to provide additional data. Such diversity of sources, however, imposes limitations on the comparability of the statistics from country to country because the basis and completeness of data collection and the frequency and timeliness of analysis and publication may vary greatly. Data shown in italic are from 1994 or earlier.

The categories adopted in the table also have special problems of comparability. Total road length is subject to wide international variation of interpretation, as "roads" can mean anything from mere tracks to highly developed highways. Each country also has individual classifications that differ according to climate, availability of road-building materials, traffic patterns, administrative responsibility, and so on. "Paved roads," by contrast, is a much more tightly definable category, but the proportion of paved to total roads may be distorted by the less comparable total road statistics. Automobile and truck and bus fleet statistics, which are usually

Transportation

country	roads and motor vehicles (latest)								railroads (latest)					
	roads			motor vehicles			cargo		track length		traffic			
	length		paved (per-cent)	auto-mobiles	trucks and buses	persons per vehicle	short ton-mi ('000,000)	metric ton-km ('000,000)	mi	km	passengers		cargo	
	mi	km									passen-ger-mi ('000,000)	passen-ger-km ('000,000)	short ton-mi ('000,000)	metric ton-km ('000,000)
Afghanistan	13,000	21,000	13	31,000	25,000	401	*1,993*	*2,910*	16	25	...	...	...	...
Albania	11,000	18,000	30	90,766	34,378	25	550	803	416	670	72	116	0.01	0.02
Algeria	63,643	102,424	69	725,000	780,000	19	*9,589*	*14,000*	2,451[2]	3,945[2]	1,135	1,826	1,465	2,139
American Samoa	*217*	*350*	*43*	*4,672*	*199*	*11*	...	...	—	—	—	—	—	—
Andorra	167	269	74	35,358	4,238	1.6	...	...	—	—	—	—	—	—
Angola	45,128	72,626	25	207,000	25,000	41	...	...	1,834[2]	2,952[2]	*203*	*326*	*1,178*	*1,720*
Antigua and Barbuda	155	250	...	13,588	1,342	4.3	...	...	—	—	—	—	—	—
Argentina	135,630	218,276	29	4,901,608	1,379,044	5.7	...	...	21,100[2]	33,958[2]	5,656	9,102	6,234	9,102
Armenia	5,238	8,431	100	1,300	4,460	655	146	213	516	830	29	46	201	324
Aruba	*236*	*380*	*100*	38,834	990	2.4	...	...	—	—	—	—	—	—
Australia	502,356	808,465	40	9,719,900	2,214,900	1.6	*786,643*	*1,148,480*	22,233[2, 7]	35,780[2, 7]	7,152	11,510	87,262	127,400
Austria	124,000	200,000	100	4,009,604	328,591	1.9	10,773	15,670	3,506	5,643	4,953[7]	7,971[7]	10,617[7]	15,500[7]
Azerbaijan	28,502	45,870	94	281,100	104,300	21	484	706	1,317	2,120	342	550	3,160	4,613
Bahamas, The	1,522	2,450	57	89,263	17,228	2.6	...	...	—	—	—	—	—	—
Bahrain	1,966	3,164	77	149,636	32,213	3.4	...	...	—	—	—	—	—	—
Bangladesh	126,773	204,022	12	54,784	69,394	991	...	...	1,699[2]	2,734[2]	3,094	4,980	567	828
Barbados	1,025	1,650	96	43,711	10,583	4.9	...	...	—	—	—	—	—	—
Belarus	33,186	53,407	99	1,132,843	8,867	8.9	6,323	9,232	3,410	5,488	10,485	16,874	20,911	30,529
Belgium	89,353	143,800	97	4,491,734	453,122	2.1	25,586	37,355	2,100[2]	3,380[2]	4,570	7,354	5,063	7,392
Belize	1,398	2,250	18	9,695	11,698	11	...	...	—	—	—	—	—	—
Benin	4,217	6,787	20	37,772	8,058	123	...	...	359	578	75.7	121.8	193.5	311.4
Bermuda	140	225	100	21,220	4,007	2.4	...	...	—	—	—	—	—	—
Bhutan	2,041	3,285	61	*2,590*	*1,367*	*348*	...	...	—	—	—	—	—	—
Bolivia	30,696	49,400	6	223,829	138,536	21	*1,133*	*1,654*	2,187[2]	3,519[2]	84.9	136.7	359.0	524.2
Bosnia and Herzegovina	13,574	21,846	52	96,182	10,919	30	*2,708*	*3,954*	641	1,031	19.3	31.1	63.6	92.8
Botswana	11,388	18,327	25	30,517	59,710	17	...	...	603	971	60	96	545	795
Brazil	1,030,652	1,658,677	9	21,313,351	3,743,836	6.5	*178,359*	*260,400*	18,458[2]	29,706[2]	8,676	12,667	96,741	141,239
Brunei	1,064	1,712	75	91,047	15,918	2.9	...	...	12[13]	19[13]	—	—	...	...
Bulgaria	23,190	37,320	92	1,730,506	251,382	4.2	4,300	6,278	4,020	6,470	2,341	3,767	3,071	4,484
Burkina Faso	7,519	12,100	16	38,220	17,980	190	...	...	386[2]	622[2]	126	202	31	45
Burundi	8,997	14,480	7	19,200	18,240	145	...	...	—	—	—	—	—	—
Cambodia	22,226	35,769	8	52,919	13,574	171	822	1,200	409	649	37	60	25	36
Cameroon	30,074	48,400	8	98,000	64,350	88	*175*	*255*	625[2]	1,006[2]	197	317	556	812
Canada	560,415	901,903	35	13,887,270	3,694,125	1.7	94,584	138,090	40,639	65,403	906	1,458	205,146	299,508
Cape Verde	680	1,095	78	3,280	820	94	...	...	—	—	—	—	—	—
Central African Republic	14,900	24,000	2	9,500	7,000	195	41	60	—	—	—	—	—	—
Chad	20,800	33,400	1	10,560	14,550	293	580	850	—	—	—	—	—	—
Chile	49,590	79,800	14	1,323,800	687,500	7.5	...	...	5,410[2]	8,707[2]	377	606	1,984	2,896
China	794,405	1,278,474	93	6,548,300	6,278,900	96	375,580	548,338	35,781	57,584	229,657	369,598	843,302	1,236,200
Colombia	71,808	115,564	12	762,000	672,000	27	21	31	*2,007*[2]	*3,230*[2]	*9.6*	*15.5*	504.3	736.2
Comoros	559	900	76	9,100	4,950	36	...	...	—	—	—	—	—	—
Congo, Dem. Rep. of the	95,708	154,027	2	787,000	60,000	55	...	...	3,193	5,138	18[14]	29[14]	121[14]	176[14]
Congo, Rep. of the	7,950	12,800	10	37,240	15,520	49	*46*	*67*	556	894	150	242	92	135
Costa Rica	22,119	35,597	17	294,083	163,428	7.6	2,103	3,070	590[2]	950[2]	3.7	5.9	45.8	66.8
Côte d'Ivoire	31,300	50,400	10	293,000	163,000	32	...	...	397[2]	639[2]	80[17]	129[17]	40[17]	58[17]
Croatia	17,475	28,123	82	1,124,825	117,794	3.4	1,774	2,590	1,694	2,726	619	996	1,321	1,928
Cuba	37,815	60,858	49	172,574	185,495	31	*2,482*	*3,623*	2,987	4,807	1,219	1,962	763	1,075
Cyprus	6,620	10,654	58	234,976	108,452	2.4	...	...	—	—	—	—	—	—
Czech Republic	78,234	125,905	44	3,695,792	426,684	2.5	23,227	33,911	6,469	9,444	4,323	6,957	11,447	16,713
Denmark	44,389	71,663	100	1,854,060	335,690	2.4	14,639	21,372	1,704[2]	2,743[2]	3,304	5,318	1,387	2,025
Djibouti	1,796	2,890	13	9,200	2,040	38	...	...	*66*	*106*	361	762	144	232
Dominica	485	780	50	6,581	2,825	7.8	...	...	—	—	—	—	—	—
Dominican Republic	7,829	12,600	49	224,000	151,550	21	...	...	1,083[2]	1,743[2]	...	...	...	...
East Timor	...	...	...	...	...	...	...	...	...	...	...	...	...	...
Ecuador	26,841	43,197	19	464,902	52,630	23	2,712	3,959	600[2]	966[2]	28	45	686	1,002

based upon registration, are relatively accurate, though some countries round off figures, and unregistered vehicles may cause substantial undercount. There is also inconsistent classification of vehicle types; in some countries a vehicle may serve variously as an automobile, a truck, or a bus, or even as all three on certain occasions. Relatively few countries collect and maintain commercial road traffic statistics.

Data on national railway systems are generally given for railway track length rather than the length of routes, which may be multitracked. Siding tracks usually are not included, but some countries fail to distinguish them. The United States data include only class 1 railways, which account for about 94 percent of total track length. Passenger traffic is usually calculated from tickets sold to fare-paying passengers. Such statistics are subject to distortion if there are large numbers of nonpaying passengers, such as military personnel, or if season tickets are sold and not all the allowed journeys are utilized. Railway cargo traffic is calculated by weight hauled multiplied by the length of the journey. Changes in freight load during the journey should be accounted for but sometimes are not, leading to discrepancies.

Merchant fleet and tonnage statistics collected by Lloyd's registry service for vessels over 100 gross tons are quite accurate. Cargo statistics, however, reflect the port and customs requirements of each country and the reporting rules of each country's merchant marine authority (although these, increasingly, reflect the recommendations of the International Maritime Organization); often, however, they are only estimates based on customs declarations and the count of vessels entered and cleared. Even when these elements are reported consistently, further uncertainties may be introduced because of ballast, bunkers, ships' stores, or transshipped goods included in the data.

Airport data are based on scheduled flights reported in the commercial *Official Airline Guide* and are both reliable and current. The comparability of civil air traffic statistics suffers from differing characteristics of the air transportation systems of different countries; data for an entire country may be two to three years behind those for a single airport.

Outside of Europe, where standardization of data on inland waterways is necessitated by the volume of international traffic, comparability of national data declines markedly. Calculations as to both the length of a country's waterway system (or route length of river, lake, and coastal traffic) and the makeup of its stock of commercially significant vessels (those for which data will be collected) are largely determined by the nature and use of the country's hydrographic net—its seasonality, relief profile, depth, access to potential markets—and inevitably differ widely from country to country. Data for coastal or island states may refer to scheduled coastwise or interisland traffic.

merchant marine (latest)				air					canals and inland waterways (latest)				country
fleet (vessels over 100 gross tons)	total dead-weight tonnage ('000)	international cargo (latest)		airports with sched-uled flights (latest)	traffic (latest)				length		cargo		
		loaded metric tons ('000)	off loaded metric tons ('000)		passengers: passenger-mi ('000,000)	passengers: passenger-km ('000,000)	cargo: short ton-mi ('000,000)	cargo: metric ton-km ('000,000)	mi	km	short ton-mi ('000,000)	metric ton-km ('000,000)	
—	—	—	—	3	171.5[1]	276.0[1]	26[1]	38[1]	750	1,200	...	...	Afghanistan
24	81.0	120	2,040	1	2.2	3.5	0.22	0.32	46	74	24	35	Albania
149	1,093.4	63,110	15,700	28	1,803[3]	2,901[3]	12.5[3]	18.3[3]	...	...	...	...	Algeria
3	0.1	380	581	3	...	...	...	...	...	...	...	...	American Samoa
—	—	—	—	—	—	—	—	—	—	—	—	—	Andorra
123	73.9	23,288	1,261	17	385[4]	620[4]	60[4]	97[4]	805	1,295	...	...	Angola
292	997.4	28	113	2	157	252	0.1	0.2	...	...	...	...	Antigua and Barbuda
423	1,173.1	69,372	19,536	39	7,292[5]	11,735[5]	895[5]	1,307[5]	6,804	10,950	19,326	28,215	Argentina
...	...	...	...	1	356	572	5.9	9.5	...	...	...	...	Armenia
[6]	[6]	...	...	1	318	511	...	...	...	...	...	...	Aruba
695	3,857.3	35,664	43,360	400	46,647	75,071	1,156	1,688	5,200	8,368	31,891	46,560	Australia
20	208.5	1,479	5,766	6	7,742	12,460	247	361	218	351	7,938	11,590	Austria
69	...	...	...	3	1,025	1,650	125	183	...	...	3,112	5,008	Azerbaijan
1,061	33,081.7	5,920	5,705	22	87	140	0.32	0.455	...	...	...	...	Bahamas, The
87	192.5	13,285	3,512	1	1,762[8]	2,836[8]	81.3[8]	118.7[8]	...	...	...	...	Bahrain
301	566.8	948	10,404	8	2,154	3,466	95	139	5,000	8,046	...	...	Bangladesh
37	84.0	206	538	1	93[9]	149[9]	0.8[10]	1.1[10]	...	...	...	...	Barbados
...	18,373.0	...	...	1	864	1,390	7	10	1,092	1,757	71	103	Belarus
232	218.5	360,984	367,680	2	12,042	19,379	389	568	957	1,540	3,993	5,830	Belgium
32	45.7	255	277	9	...	...	...	...	513	825	...	...	Belize
12	0.2	339	1,738	1	160.5[11]	258.3[11]	8.4[11]	13.5[11]	...	...	...	...	Benin
94	5,206.5	130	470	1	...	...	...	...	...	...	...	...	Bermuda
—	—	—	—	1	29	46	...	...	—	—	—	—	Bhutan
1	15.8	...	...	14	1,223	1,968	28.7	41.9	6,214	10,000	90	132	Bolivia
...	...	...	...	1	25.1	40.4	0.29	0.43	...	...	...	...	Bosnia and Herzegovina
—	—	—	—	7	35.3[12]	56.8[12]	0.1[12]	0.2[12]	...	...	...	...	Botswana
635	9,348.3	239,932	146,452	139	21,765	35,028	891	1,031	31,069	50,000	56,030	81,803	Brazil
51	349.7	42	1,308	1	1,742	2,803	75.0	109.5	130	209	...	...	Brunei
107	391	5,290	20,080	3	1,259	2,026	18.9	30.4	292	470	487	711	Bulgaria
—	—	—	—	2	134.9	217.2	23.4	34.2	...	...	...	...	Burkina Faso
1	0.4	35	188	1	1.2	2.0	...	...	...	...	...	...	Burundi
3	3.8	11	95	8	26.1	42.0	0.3	0.4	2,300	3,700	51	75	Cambodia
47	39.8	2,385	2,497	5	348	560	57	91	1,299	2,090	...	...	Cameroon
1,185	2,896.8	187,716	94,536	269	42,379	68,202	1,224	1,787	1,860	3,000	...	...	Canada
42	30.9	144	299	9	106	171	13.2	19.2	...	...	...	...	Cape Verde
—	—	53	126	1	139.6[12]	224.7[12]	11.2[12]	16.4[12]	500	800	185	270	Central African Republic
—	—	—	—	1	145	233	25	37	1,240	2,000	...	...	Chad
392	854.9	29,532	18,144	23	6,618	10,651	1,443	2,107	450	725	5,629	8,218	Chile
2,390	20,658.0	1,146,084	101,688	113	49,725	80,024	2,291	3,345	68,537	110,300	1,329,187	1,940,580	China
101	403.0	49,332	15,288	43	3,723	5,991	573	836	11,272	18,140	1.7	2.5	Colombia
6	3.6	12	107	2	1.9	3.0	...	...	...	...	...	...	Comoros
27	30.7	2,395	1,453	22	173[15]	279[15]	29[15]	42[15]	9,300	15,000	678	990	Congo, Dem. Rep. of the
22	10.8	708	533	10	160[11]	258[11]	9.6	14	696	1,120	...	...	Congo, Rep. of the
24	8.4	3,017	3,972	14	2,167[16]	3,487[16]	61.9[16]	90.4[16]	454	730	...	...	Costa Rica
51	98.6	4,173	7,228	5	191[18]	307[18]	30[18]	44[18]	609	980	...	...	Côte d'Ivoire
203	140.9	4,416	7,680	4	474	763	2.0	3.0	580	933	43	63	Croatia
393	924.6	8,092	15,440	14	2,202	3,543	38.5	56.2	149	240	108	158	Cuba
1,416	36,198.1	1,344	4,308	2	1,685	2,711	26	38	...	...	...	...	Cyprus
18[19]	514.1[19]	759	409	2	2,705	4,354	21	30	413	664	627	915	Czech Republic
456	7,589.1	21,060	38,292	13	3,340[20]	5,376[20]	117[20]	171[20]	259	417	1,100	1,600	Denmark
10	4.1	414	958	1	42	67	4	6	...	...	...	...	Djibouti
7	3.2	103	181	2	...	...	...	...	...	...	...	...	Dominica
28	10.4	1,668	4,182	7	9.8	15.8	7.9	11.6	...	...	...	...	Dominican Republic
...	...	...	...	...	...	...	...	...	...	...	...	...	East Timor
154	504.1	11,783	1,950	14	574	924	79	116	932	1,500	...	...	Ecuador

Transportation (continued)

country	roads and motor vehicles (latest)								railroads (latest)					
	roads			motor vehicles			cargo		track length		traffic			
	length		paved (per-cent)	auto-mobiles	trucks and buses	persons per vehicle	short ton-mi ('000,000)	metric ton-km ('000,000)	mi	km	passengers		cargo	
	mi	km									passen-ger-mi ('000,000)	passen-ger-km ('000,000)	short ton-mi ('000,000)	metric ton-km ('000,000)
Egypt	39,800[21]	64,000[21]	78[21]	1,154,753	510,766	37	21,600	31,500	2,989	4,810	35,211	56,667	2,820	4,117
El Salvador	6,232	10,029	20	177,488	184,859	16	...	...	349[2]	562[2]	4.4	7.1	12	17
Equatorial Guinea	1,740	2,800	13	6,500	4,000	37	...	...	—	—	—	—	—	—
Eritrea	2,491	4,010	22	5,940	...	...	...	...	43	70	...	...	...	...
Estonia	10,209	16,430	51	451,000	86,900	2.7	2,691	3,929	636	1,024	149	238	4,808	7,020
Ethiopia	12,117	19,500	15	52,012	39,936	642	...	...	486[22]	782[22]	98	157	73	106
Faroe Islands	285	458	...	14,608	3,455	2.5	...	...	—	—	—	—	—	—
Fiji	3,200	5,100	20	49,712	33,928	9.4	...	...	370[13]	595[13]	...	...	...	...
Finland	48,340	77,900	65	2,069,055	300,048	2.2	19,884	29,030	3,626[2]	5,836[2]	2,122	3,415	6,680	9,753
France	547,200	893,500	100	27,480,000	5,610,000	1.8	114,382	166,995	19,486[2]	31,821[2]	40,100	64,500	37,000	54,000
French Guiana	*706*	*1,137*	*40*	*29,100*	*10,600*	*3.2*	...	...	—	—	—	—	—	—
French Polynesia	549	884	44	*37,000*	*15,300*	*4.0*	...	...	—	—	—	—	—	—
Gabon	4,760	7,670	8	24,750	16,490	28	...	...	506	814	53	85	345	503
Gambia, The	1,678	2,700	35	8,640	9,000	68	...	...	—	—	—	—	—	—
Gaza Strip	...	...	...	37,061	8,105	23	...	...	—	—	—	—	—	—
Georgia	12,862	20,700	93	427,000	41,510	11	288	420	961	1,546	219	349	2,150	3,139
Germany	143,372	230,735	99	42,323,672	2,550,222	1.8	176,337	257,447	54,188	87,207	41,321	66,500	48,875	71,356
Ghana	24,000	38,700	40	90,000	45,000	133	*873*	*1,275*	*592*[2]	*953*[2]	*731.4*	*1,177*	*93.9*	*137.1*
Greece	72,700	117,000	92	2,675,676	1,013,677	2.9	12,000	17,000	1,555[2]	2,503[2]	1,108	1,783	226	330
Greenland	93	150	60	2,242	1,474	15	...	...	—	—	—	—	—	—
Grenada	646	1,040	61	*4,739*	*3,068*	*12*	...	...	—	—	—	—	—	—
Guadeloupe	2,122	3,415	*80*	*101,600*	*37,500*	*2.9*	...	...	—	—	—	—	—	—
Guam	550	885	76	79,800	34,700	1.3	...	...	—	—	—	—	—	—
Guatemala	8,140	13,100	28	102,000	97,000	51	...	...	549[2]	884[2]	10.3	16.6	58.6	85.6
Guernsey	...	...	...	37,598	7,338	1.4	...	...	—	—	—	—	—	—
Guinea	18,952	30,500	16	14,100	21,000	219	...	...	411[2]	662[2]	25.8	41.5	5.0	7.3
Guinea-Bissau	2,734	4,400	10	7,120	5,640	91	...	...	—	—	—	—	—	—
Guyana	4,952	7,970	7	24,000	9,000	22	...	...	116[13]	187[13]	...	...	...	...
Haiti	2,585	4,160	24	32,000	21,000	121	...	...	—	—	—	—	—	—
Honduras	9,073	14,602	18	81,439	170,006	22	...	...	614	988	*4.8*	*7.7*	*20.7*	*30.2*
Hong Kong	1,183	1,904	100	332,000	133,000	14	...	...	21[2]	34[2]	2,231	3,591	68	99
Hungary	116,944	188,203	43	2,255,526	321,634	4.0	10,950	15,987	4,827[2]	7,768[2]	5,912	9,514	5,297	7,733
Iceland	7,691	12,378	25	151,409	19,428	1.6	*318*	*464*	—	—	—	—	—	—
India	2,062,727	3,319,644	46	4,189,000	2,234,000	148	656	958	39,028[2]	62,809[2]	261,254	420,449	209,259	305,513
Indonesia	212,177	341,467	56	2,734,769	2,189,876	41	*17,000*	*25,000*	4,013[2]	6,458[2]	11,548	18,585	3,449	5,035
Iran	102,976	165,724	50	1,793,000	692,000	24	*46,750*	*68,250*	3,915[2]	6,300[2]	3,792	6,103	9,863	14,400
Iraq	29,453	47,400	86	772,986	323,906	18	...	...	1,263[2]	2,032[2]	973	1,566	1,129	1,649
Ireland	57,477	92,500	94	1,269,245	188,814	2.6	4,041	5,900	1,209[2]	1,945[2]	870	1,400	342	500
Isle of Man	500	805	58	40,168	4,925	1.6	...	...	32[2]	52[2]	...	...	...	...
Israel	9,609	15,464	100	1,316,765	319,581	3.7	*2,993*	*4,370*	379[2]	610[2]	329	529	773	1,128
Italy	191,468	308,139	100	31,370,000	5,127,000	1.6	131,154	191,482	12,133	19,527	25,720	41,392	15,333	22,386
Jamaica	11,800	19,000	71	160,948	55,596	12	...	...	*129*[2]	*208*[2]	*12.1*	*19.5*	*1.7*	*2.5*
Japan	718,300	1,156,000	73	51,222,000	18,425,000	1.8	205,942	300,670	16,937	27,258	241,674	388,938	15,699	22,920
Jersey	346	557	100	58,491	9,922	1.3	...	...	—	—	—	—	—	—
Jordan	4,432	7,133	100	213,874	79,153	15	*19,133*	*27,934*	421[2]	677[2]	*3.7*	*6.0*	915	1,336
Kazakhstan	78,166	125,796	83	973,323	361,920	11	3,176	4,637	8,388[2]	13,500[2]	5,505	8,859	64,987	94,879
Kenya	39,600	63,800	14	278,000	81,200	78	*134*	*196*	1,885[2]	3,034[2]	239	385	813	1,309
Kiribati	416	670	5	222	115	260	...	...	—	—	—	—	—	—
Korea, North	14,526	23,377	8	*248,000*	...	...	...	...	5,302	8,533	*2,100*	*3,400*	*6,200*	*9,100*
Korea, South	55,162	88,775	76	8,084,000	3,938,000	3.9	51,031	74,504	4,165	6,703	18,686	30,072	8,704	12,708
Kuwait	2,765	4,450	81	747,042	140,480	2.3	...	...	—	—	—	—	—	—
Kyrgyzstan	11,495	18,500	91	146,000	...	...	695	1,015	264	424	58	93	323	472
Laos	13,870	22,321	14	16,320	4,200	242	16	23	—	—	—	—	—	—
Latvia	34,761	55,942	38	431,816	95,329	4.7	2,814	4,108	1,499	2,413	611	984	8,363	12,210
Lebanon	3,946	6,350	95	1,299,398	85,242	2.5	...	...	138	222	*5.3*	*8.6*	*29*	*42*
Lesotho	3,079	4,955	18	12,610	25,000	53	...	...	1.6	2.6	...	...	...	...
Liberia	6,600	10,600	6	9,400	25,000	59	...	...	304[2]	490[2]	...	...	534	860
Libya	50,704	81,600	57	809,514	357,528	4.0	...	...	—	—	—	—	—	—
Liechtenstein	201	323	...	21,150	2,684	1.4	...	...	12	19	...	...	...	...
Lithuania	44,350	71,375	91	980,910	105,022	3.4	3,843	5,611	1,241[2]	1,997[2]	463	745	5,376	7,849
Luxembourg	3,209	5,166	100	263,683	20,228	1.5	2,437	3,558	170[2]	274[2]	193	310	410	660
Macau	31	50	100	45,184	6,578	8.2	...	...	—	—	—	—	—	—
Macedonia	7,154	11,513	63	288,678	24,745	6.4	612	894	575	925	93	150	279	408
Madagascar	30,967	49,837	17	62,000	16,460	140	*220*	*321*	*680*[2]	*1,095*[2]	22	35	44	71
Malawi	10,222	16,451	19	27,000	29,700	171	—	—	495[2]	797[2]	16	26	34	49
Malaysia	41,282	66,437	76	3,517,484	644,792	5.1	...	...	1,384[2]	2,227[2]	828[31]	1,332[31]	625[31]	912[31]
Maldives	...	...	...	1,716	586	114	...	...	—	—	—	—	—	—
Mali	9,383	15,100	12	26,190	18,240	213	...	...	398[2]	641[2]	577.6	929.6	371	542.8
Malta	1,219	1,961	94	185,247	49,520	1.6	...	...	—	—	—	—	—	—
Marshall Islands	...	...	...	1,374	262	29	...	...	—	—	—	—	—	—
Martinique	1,299	2,091	*75*	*108,300*	*32,200*	*2.6*	...	...	—	—	—	—	—	—
Mauritania	4,760	7,660	11	18,810	10,450	82	...	...	437[2]	704[2]	...	...	1,603	2,340
Mauritius	1,184	1,905	93	46,300	12,100	20	...	...	—	—	—	—	—	—
Mayotte	145	233	77	6,553		20	...	...	—	—	—	—	—	—
Mexico	199,824	321,586	37	8,607,000	4,426,000	7.1	122,663	179,085	16,543[2]	26,623[2]	286	460	32,106	46,874
Micronesia	*140*	*226*	*17*	...	...	...	...	...	—	—	—	—	—	—
Moldova	7,643	12,300	87	166,757	67,638	18	697	1,018	819	1,318	213	343	816	1,191
Monaco	31	50	100	21,120	2,770	1.3	...	...	1	2	...	...	...	...
Mongolia	31,000	50,000	3	39,921	31,061	33	84.4	123.2	1,128	1,815	634	1,020	2,392	3,492
Morocco	35,921	57,810	52	1,018,146	278,075	21	1,429	2,086	1,099[2]	1,768[2]	1,104	1,776	3,258	4,757
Mozambique	18,890	30,400	19	4,900	7,520	1,431	75	110	1,940	3,123	317	510	781	1,140
Myanmar (Burma)	17,523	28,200	12	27,000	42,000	587	*71*	*103.7*	2,458[2]	3,955[2]	2,453	3,948	674	984
Namibia	40,526	65,220	8	74,875	66,500	12	...	...	1,480	2,382	21.6	34.7	738	1,077
Nauru	19	30	79	*1,448*		*6.3*	...	...	3[13]	5[13]	...	...	*4.7*	*6.8*
Nepal	4,785	7,700	42	47,541	29,371	306	*984*	*1,437*	37[2]	59[2]	...	...	...	...

merchant marine (latest)				air					canals and inland waterways (latest)				country
fleet (vessels over 100 gross tons)	total dead-weight tonnage ('000)	international cargo (latest)		airports with sched-uled flights (latest)	traffic (latest)				length		cargo		
		loaded metric tons ('000)	off-loaded metric tons ('000)		passengers		cargo		mi	km	short ton-mi ('000,000)	metric ton-km ('000,000)	
					passenger-mi ('000,000)	passenger-km ('000,000)	short ton-mi ('000,000)	metric ton-km ('000,000)					
444	1,685.2	15,012	22,044	11	5,638	9,074	185	270	2,175	3,500	452	660	Egypt
15	...	221	1,023	1	1,355	2,181	10.9	16.0	...	...	...	...	El Salvador
3	6.7	110	64	1	4	7	0.7	1.0	...	...	...	...	Equatorial Guinea
...	...	...	...	2	...	...	...	...	...	...	...	...	Eritrea
234	680.4	30,024	5,784	1	103.6	166.7	0.6	0.9	199	320	1.4	2.1	Estonia
27	84.3	234	1,242	31	1,190	1,915	225	328	...	...	...	...	Ethiopia
191	59.8	223	443	1	...	...	...	...	...	...	...	...	Faroe Islands
64	60.4	568	625	13	742	1,195	51.6	75.4	126	203	...	...	Fiji
263	989.3	39,312	38,052	27	8,026	12,916	216	316	3,880	6,245	127,945	186,797	Finland
729	4,981.0	64,704	189,504	61	55,344[23]	89,067[23]	3,271[23]	4,775[23]	3,562	5,732	5,436	7,936	France
7	0.7	73	447	8	...	...	...	...	286	460	...	...	French Guiana
41	16.5	15	666	17	...	...	...	...	...	...	...	...	French Polynesia
29	30.2	12,828	212	17	452	728	68	100	994	1,600	...	...	Gabon
11	2.0	185	240	1	31	50	3	5	250	400	...	...	Gambia, The
—	—	...	...	1	...	...	...	...	—	—	...	...	Gaza Strip
54	1,108	...	...	1	78.9	127.1	0.5	0.8	...	...	3,740	5,460	Georgia
1,375	6,832.3	74,568	138,864	35	55,219	88,867	4,520	6,599	4,188	6,740	44,019	64,267	Germany
155	131.0	2,424	2,904	1	407	655	20	30	803	1,293	75	110	Ghana
1,872	45,276.6	16,464	45,024	36	5,160	8,305	71	103	50	80	585	854	Greece
82	17.2	298	288	18	104	167	0.23	0.34	...	...	...	...	Greenland
3	0.5	21	193	2	...	...	...	...	...	...	...	...	Grenada
20	4.4	349	2,285	7	...	...	...	...	...	...	...	...	Guadeloupe
5	0.1	195	1,524	1	...	...	...	...	...	...	...	...	Guam
8	0.4	2,096	3,822	2	311	500	48	70	162	260	...	...	Guatemala
—	—	...	...	2	...	...	...	...	...	...	...	...	Guernsey
23	1.7	16,760	734	1	32	52	3	5	805	1,295	...	...	Guinea
19	1.8	46	283	2	6.2	10.0	0.7	1.0	...	...	...	...	Guinea-Bissau
82	13.5	1,730	673	1	154	248	2.3	3.3	3,660	5,900	...	...	Guyana
4	0.4	170	704	2	...	...	...	...	60	100	...	...	Haiti
966	1,437.3	1,316	1,002	8	212[24]	341[24]	23[24]	33[24]	289	465	...	...	Honduras
387	11,688.6	36,132[25]	80,820[25]	1	...	...	...	...	...	...	...	...	Hong Kong
15	93.2	...	...	1	2,183	3,513	38	56	853	1,373	1,069	1,561	Hungary
394	114.9	1,162	1,733	24	2,273	3,658	50.9	74.4	...	...	58	84	Iceland
888	10,365.9	61,880	102,630	66	11,456	18,436	329	481	10,054	16,180	202,000	295,000	India
2,014	3,130.2	310,246	208,871	81	7,698	12,389	234	341	13,409	21,579	17,000	25,000	Indonesia
403	8,345.3	32,148	37,404	19	3,871	6,229	49	72	562	904	...	...	Iran
131	1,578.8	97,830	8,638	...	976	1,570	37.4	54.6	631	1,015	...	...	Iraq
189	208.6	6,367	17,637	9	4,018	6,466	88.8	129.6	435	700	...	...	Ireland
101	2,836.5	6	203	1	526.1	846.8	0.1	0.2	...	...	...	...	Isle of Man
58	723.4	12,876	20,916	7	8,777[26]	14,125[26]	882[26]	1,288[26]	...	...	...	...	Israel
1,966	7,140.5	40,252	234,120	34	18,312[27]	29,471[27]	835[27]	1,219[27]	918	1,477	85,681	125,092	Italy
12	16.2	8,802	5,285	4	1,038[28]	1,670[28]	20.2[28]	29.5[28]	...	...	...	...	Jamaica
6,140	16,198	124,548	754,464	73	97,745	157,305	4,920	7,183	1,100	1,770	155,468	226,980	Japan
—	—	...	...	1	...	...	...	...	...	...	...	...	Jersey
5	113.6	7,308	5,328	2	2,526	4,065	150.1	219.2	...	...	19,202	28,035	Jordan
...	...	...	...	20	1,509	2,429	162	237	2,425	3,903	97	141	Kazakhstan
29	11.6	1,596	3,228	11	1,062[29]	1,709[29]	126[29]	203[29]	...	...	...	...	Kenya
7	2.7	15	26	9	4.4	7.0	0.6	1.0	3	5	...	...	Kiribati
100	951.2	635	5,520	1	178	286	19	30	1,400	2,253	...	...	Korea, North
2,138	11,724.9	255,888	448,416	14	29,647	47,712	4,987	7,281	1,000	1,609	22,920	33,462	Korea, South
209	3,188.5	51,400	4,522	1	3,813	6,137	151	243	...	...	...	...	Kuwait
...	...	...	...	2	2,739	4,408	44.7	65.2	290	466	41	6.0	Kyrgyzstan
1	1.5	—	—	11	30	48	3	5	2,850	4,587	68	100	Laos
261	1,436.9	45,144	3,888	1	185	298	6	9	66	106	19,241	28,091	Latvia
163	438.2	152	1,150	1	1,315	2,116	218	319	...	...	...	...	Lebanon
—	—	—	—	1	3.9	6.2	0.4	0.6	—	—	—	—	Lesotho
1,672	97,374.0	21,653	1,608	1	4.3	7.0	0.7	1.0	...	...	...	...	Liberia
150	1,223.6	62,491	7,808	12	264[30]	425[30]	23[30]	34[30]	—	—	...	...	Libya
—	—	—	—	—	—	—	—	—	...	...	...	...	Liechtenstein
52	373.9	12,864	2,796	3	190.5	306.6	1.8	2.6	229	369	8.9	13	Lithuania
54	2,603.6	—	—	1	79.5	232	606.9	886.1	23	37	205	300	Luxembourg
6	0.1	755	3,935	—	—	—	—	—	...	...	...	...	Macau
...	...	...	...	2	553.5	890.7	239.2	349.2	...	...	...	...	Macedonia
85	82.1	540	984	44	519	836	20.2	29.5	...	...	1.2	1.8	Madagascar
1	0.3	...	...	5	68	110	10	14	89	144	1,683	2,457	Malawi
552	2,916.3	39,756	54,852	39	20,945	33,708	976	1,425	4,534	7,296	...	...	Malaysia
44	79.0	27	78	5	44	71	...	...	...	...	...	...	Maldives
—	—	—	—	9	150	242	26	38	1,128	1,815	18	27	Mali
889	17,073.2	309	1,781	1	1,173	1,888	7.7	11.2	...	...	...	...	Malta
35	4,182.4	29	123	25	17	28	0.003	0.005	...	...	...	...	Marshall Islands
6	1.1	960	1,584	1	...	...	...	...	...	...	...	...	Martinique
126	23.9	10,400	724	9	160.5	258.3	9.2	13.5	...	...	...	...	Mauritania
35	152.2	966	2,753	1	2,398	3,859	561.2	819.4	...	...	...	...	Mauritius
1	1.1	158	31	1	...	...	...	...	...	...	...	...	Mayotte
635	1,495.3	134,400	67,500	83	14,864	23,922	1,779	2,597	1,800	2,900	14,806	21,616	Mexico
19	9.2	...	...	4	...	...	...	...	...	...	...	...	Micronesia
...	...	...	...	1	0.1	0.2	0.7	1.0	263	424	172	251	Moldova
1	...	...	...	—	—	—	...	...	...	...	...	...	Monaco
—	—	—	—	1	326	525	33	48	247	397	0.1	0.2	Mongolia
492	586.2	24,228	27,972	11	2,789	4,489	260	380	...	...	...	...	Morocco
107	31.6	2,800	3,400	7	239	384	6	9	2,330	3,750	57	83	Mozambique
144	1,354.0	1,788	3,456	19	272	438	2.2	3.2	7,954	12,800	240	351	Myanmar (Burma)
30	5.9	1,132	644	11	470	756	16	23	...	...	...	...	Namibia
2	5.8	1,650	59	1	151[32]	243[32]	15[32]	24[32]	...	...	...	...	Nauru
—	—	—	—	24	532	856	64	93	...	...	...	...	Nepal

Transportation (continued)

country	roads and motor vehicles (latest)								railroads (latest)					
	roads			motor vehicles			cargo		track length		traffic			
	length		paved (per-cent)	auto-mobiles	trucks and buses	persons per vehicle	short ton-mi ('000,-000)	metric ton-km ('000,-000)	mi	km	passengers		cargo	
	mi	km									passen-ger-mi ('000,000)	passen-ger-km ('000,000)	short ton-mi ('000,000)	metric ton-km ('000,000)
Netherlands, The	77,379	124,530	91	6,343,000	826,000	2.2	98,445	143,727	1,745	2,808	8,904	14,330	2,412	3,521
Netherlands Antilles	367	590	51	75,105	17,753	2.2	...	...	—	—	—	—	—	—
New Caledonia	3,582	5,764	52	56,700	21,200	2.6	...	...	—	—	—	—	—	—
New Zealand	57,213	92,075	62	1,831,118	351,494	1.7	...	...	2,431[2]	3,912[2]	*285*	*458*	2,712	3,960
Nicaragua	11,200	18,000	10	73,000	61,650	33	...	...	—	—	—	—	—	—
Niger	6,276	10,100	8	38,220	15,200	169	*1,044*	*1,524*	—	—	—	—	—	—
Nigeria	38,897	62,598	19	773,000	68,300	131	...	...	2,178	3,505	100	161	74	108
Northern Mariana Islands	225	360	100	12,113	6,479	3.0	...	...	—	—	—	—	—	—
Norway	56,470	90,880	74	1,813,642	447,583	2.0	10,086	14,726	2,489[2]	4,006[2]	1,609	2,589	1,467	2,142
Oman	20,518	33,020	24	229,029	110,717	6.9	...	...	—	—	—	—	—	—
Pakistan	149,679	240,885	55	1,167,635	251,407	95	66,304	96,802	5,452[2]	8,774[2]	11,908	19,164	2,753	4,020
Palau	*40*	*64*	*59*	——4,271——		3.8	...	...	...	...	...	...	...	...
Panama	7,022	11,301	33	203,760	74,637	9.4	...	...	220[2]	354[2]	242	389	1,096	1,600
Papua New Guinea	*12,263*	*19,736*	*6*	*13,000*	*32,000*	*93*	...	...	—	—	—	—	—	—
Paraguay	18,330	29,500	10	71,000	50,000	41	...	...	274[2]	441[2]	1.9	3.0	3.8	5.5
Peru	45,836	73,766	12	557,042	359,374	26	...	...	1,238[2]	1,992[2]	132	212	0.8	1.1
Philippines	124,243	199,950	39	745,144	263,037	73	...	...	557[2]	897[2]	7.5	12	452	660
Poland	234,286	377,048	66	9,283,000	1,762,000	3.5	47,632	69,542	14,280	22,981	16,279	26,198	37,994	55,471
Portugal	42,708	68,732	88	3,200,000	1,097,000	2.4	16,984	24,796	2,025[2]	3,259[2]	2,860	4,602	1,603	2,340
Puerto Rico	8,948	14,400	100	878,000	190,000	3.5	...	...	—	—	—	—	—	—
Qatar	764	1,230	90	126,000	64,000	2.9	...	...	—	—	—	—	—	—
Réunion	1,711	2,754	*79*	190,300	44,300	3.0	...	...	—	—	—	—	—	—
Romania	95,175	153,170	51	2,408,000	409,550	8.0	14,898	21,750	7,062	11,365	7,658	12,324	10,909	15,927
Russia	354,628	570,719	79	19,717,800	5,021,000	5.9	14,384	21,000	93,800	151,000	88,048	144,700	825	1,205
Rwanda	9,528	14,900	9	13,000	17,100	188	*140*	*200*	—	—	—	—	—	—
St. Kitts and Nevis	199	320	43	5,200	2,300	5.3	...	...	22	36	—	—	—	—
St. Lucia	750	1,210	5	14,783	1,020	9.5	...	...	—	—	—	—	—	—
St. Vincent and the Grenadines	646	1,040	31	6,089	3,670	11	...	...	—	—	—	—	—	—
Samoa	491	790	42	1,068	1,169	74	...	...	—	—	—	—	—	—
San Marino	157	252	...	25,571	2,636	0.9	...	...	—	—	—	—	—	—
São Tomé and Príncipe	199	320	68	4,040	1,540	24	...	...	—	—	—	—	—	—
Saudi Arabia	101,000	162,000	43	1,744,000	1,192,000	6.6	57,859	84,473	864[2]	1,390[2]	138	222	586	856
Senegal	9,134	14,700	29	85,488	36,962	72	*375*	*547*	761	1,225	*128*	*206*	*476*	*695*
Serbia and Montenegro	31,377	50,497	60	1,400,000	132,000	6.9	852	1,244	2,528	4,069	1,003	1,614	1,760	2,570
Seychelles	263	424	87	7,120	1,980	8.5	...	...	—	—	—	—	—	—
Sierra Leone	7,270	11,700	11	17,640	10,890	163	*36*	*53*	*52*	*84*	...	...	...	...
Singapore	1,875	3,017	97	413,545	147,325	5.8	...	...	73	117	[31]	[31]	[31]	[31]
Slovakia	10,953	17,627	...	1,135,914	100,254	4.4	5,804	8,474	2,282	3,673	1,844	2,968	6,753	9,859
Slovenia	7,771	12,507	81	829,674	67,111	2.2	1,986	2,900	746	1,201	388	625	1,907	2,784
Solomon Islands	845	1,360	3	*2,052*	*2,574*	*75*	...	...	—	—	—	—	—	—
Somalia	13,732	22,100	12	1,020	6,440	866	...	...	—	—	—	—	—	—
South Africa	205,838	331,265	41	3,966,252	2,069,536	7.2	*1,053*	*1,538*	12,626[2]	20,319[2]	1,103	1,775	71,142	103,866
Spain	215,335	346,548	99	16,847,000	3,659,000	2.0	85,801	125,268	8,595[2]	13,832[2]	11,525	18,547	7,959	11,620
Sri Lanka	61,640	99,200	40	107,000	150,160	71	21	30	899[2]	1,447[2]	2,028	3,264	90	132
Sudan, The	7,394	11,900	36	285,000	53,000	93	...	...	2,855[2]	4,595[2]	100	161	1,346	1,965
Suriname	2,815	4,530	26	46,408	19,255	6.4	...	...	187	301	...	...	...	...
Swaziland	2,367	3,810	29	31,882	32,772	17	...	...	187	301	*752*	*1,210*	*1,993*	*2,910*
Sweden	130,500	210,000	74	3,890,159	352,897	2.1	22,798	33,285	6,811	10,961	4,746	7,638	13,074	19,088
Switzerland	44,248	71,211	96	3,467,275	313,646	1.9	9,932	14,500	3,129	5,035	8,764	14,104	5,951	8,688
Syria	25,756	41,451	23	138,900	282,664	37	*1,075*	*1,570*	1,507[2]	2,425[2]	113	182	934	1,364
Taiwan	12,660	20,375	89	4,716,000	833,000	4.0	12,651	18,470	2,410	3,879	7,833	12,606	808	1,179
Tajikistan	8,500	13,700	83	680	8,190	667	34	50	295	474	77	124	1,449	2,115
Tanzania	54,805	88,200	4	23,760	115,700	229	...	...	2,218	3,569	*2,324*	*3,740*	927	1,354
Thailand	40,141	64,600	98	1,661,000	2,855,000	14	...	...	2,873[2]	4,623[2]	6,636	10,680	1,940	2,832
Togo	4,673	7,520	32	79,200	34,240	39	...	...	245[2]	395[2]	10.3	16.5	34	49
Tonga	423	680	27	1,140	780	51	...	...	—	—	—	—	—	—
Trinidad and Tobago	5,170	8,320	51	122,000	24,000	8.7	...	...	—	—	—	—	—	—
Tunisia	14,354	23,100	79	269,000	312,000	16	*678*	*990*	1,348[2]	2,169[2]	743	1,196	1,620	2,365
Turkey	238,380	383,636	25	4,283,080	1,488,016	11	104,255	152,210	5,388	8,671	3,804	6,122	6,871	10,032
Turkmenistan	8,500	13,700	83	220,000	58,200	16	335	489	1,317	2,120	1,307	2,104	4,643	6,779
Tuvalu	5	8	—	...	...	...	...	...	—	—	—	—	—	—
Uganda	16,653	26,800	8	35,361	48,430	249	...	...	771[2]	1,241[2]	17	27	162	236
Ukraine	107,111	172,378	95	4,885,691	...	...	12,534	18,300	14,021	22,564	29,577	47,600	107,081	156,336
United Arab Emirates	2,356	3,791	100	201,000	56,950	9.6	...	...	—	—	—	—	—	—
United Kingdom	231,096	371,914	100	23,393,000	2,368,000	2.3	117,504	171,553	23,518[45]	37,849[45]	23,800	38,300	12,603	18,400
United States	3,906,292	6,286,396	91	131,839,000	79,778,000	1.3	1,051,045	1,534,500	137,900	222,000	14,000	22,500	1,421,000	2,075,000
Uruguay	5,395	8,683	30	516,889	50,264	5.6	*500*	*730*	1,288[2]	2,073[2]	*87.4*	*140.6*	123	180
Uzbekistan	52,444	84,400	87	865,300	14,500	25	1,248	1,822	2,271	3,655	1,553	2,500	11,580	16,907
Vanuatu	665	1,070	24	4,000	2,600	27	...	...	—	—	—	—	—	—
Venezuela	59,443	95,664	36	1,505,000	542,000	11	...	...	390[2]	627[2]	93.1	149.9	37.3	54.5
Vietnam	58,000	93,300	25	——*200,000*——		*358*	1,462	2,134	1,952[2]	3,142[2]	1,694	2,727	958	1,398
Virgin Islands (U.S.)	532	856	100	*51,000*	*13,300*	1.7	...	...	—	—	—	—	—	—
West Bank	...	...	...	88,056	24,324	18	...	...	...	...	...	...	...	...
Western Sahara	*3,900*	*6,200*	*23*	*6,284*	*424*	*20*	...	...	—	—	—	—	—	—
Yemen	40,218	64,725	8	240,567	291,149	29	...	...	—	—	—	—	—	—
Zambia	24,170	38,898	18	157,000	81,000	37	...	...	787	1,266	166	267	316	462
Zimbabwe	11,395	18,338	47	323,000	32,000	31	...	...	1,714[2]	2,759[2]	253.6	408.2	3.2	4.6

[1]Ariana Afghan Airlines only. [2]Route length. [3]Air Algérie International flights only. [4]TAAG airline only. [5]Aerolineas Argentinas only. [6]Included in Netherlands Antilles. [7]Government railways only. [8]Portion of Gulf Air traffic. [9]Caribbean Airways only. [10]Caribbean Air Cargo only. [11]Air Afrique only. [12]Air Botswana only. [13]For industrial purposes only. [14]Zaire National Railways only. [15]Air Zaire only. [16]LASCA only. [17]Traffic between Ouagadougou, Burkina Faso, and Abidjan, Côte d'Ivoire. [18]Air Ivoire only. [19]Data refer to former Czechoslovakia. [20]Including SAS international and domestic traffic. [21]National roads only. [22]Includes 62 mi (100 km) of the Chemin de Fer Djibouti-Ethiopien (CDE) in Djibouti. [23]Air France and UTA only. [24]TAN and SAHSA airlines only. [25]Includes

merchant marine (latest)				air					canals and inland waterways (latest)				country
fleet (vessels over 100 gross tons)	total deadweight tonnage ('000)	international cargo (latest)		airports with scheduled flights (latest)	traffic (latest)				length		cargo		
		loaded metric tons ('000)	off-loaded metric tons ('000)		passengers		cargo		mi	km	short ton-mi ('000,000)	metric ton-km ('000,000)	
					passenger-mi ('000,000)	passenger-km ('000,000)	short ton-mi ('000,000)	metric ton-km ('000,000)					
399	2,874	91,920	305,232	6	36,109	58,112	2,679	3,911	3,135	5,046	27,887	40,714	Netherlands, The
154[33]	1,053.6[33]	215	517	6	234[34]	377[34]	1.2[34]	1.8[34]	...	...	...	...	Netherlands Antilles
17	18.1	1,040	930	11	145[35]	233[35]	3.4[35]	4.9[35]	...	...	...	...	New Caledonia
139	279.8	20,640	13,308	36	12,352	19,879	584	852	1,000	1,609	1,503	2,195	New Zealand
25	1.3	320	1,629	10	49	79	6	9	1,379	2,220	...	...	Nicaragua
—	—	—	—	6	160.5	258.3	9.3	13.5	186	300	14	20	Niger
271	733.3	86,993	11,346	12	70	112	1.3	2.1	5,328	8,575	...	...	Nigeria
2	0.9	33	205	2	...	...	...	...	...	...	...	...	Northern Mariana Islands
1,597	20,834	151,116	25,788	50	6,444[20]	10,371[20]	821[20]	1,199[20]	980	1,577	7,640	11,154	Norway
26	11.7	43,525	5,303	6	601[8]	968[8]	11[8]	18[8]	...	...	...	...	Oman
73	513.8	6,408	31,008	35	6,503	10,466	226	330	...	...	...	...	Pakistan
4	...	...	64	1	...	...	...	...	...	...	...	...	Palau
5,217	79,255.6	117,924	76,800	10	853	1,373	14.9	21.8	497	800	...	...	Panama
87	40.9	2,463	1,784	42	457	735	59	86	6,798	10,940	...	...	Papua New Guinea
38	38.5	...	...	5	134	215	13	19	1,900	3,100	...	...	Paraguay
623	615.6	10,197	5,077	27	1,637	2,634	172	251	5,300	8,600	...	...	Peru
1,499	13,807.1	16,980	52,596	21	6,395[36]	10,292[36]	165[36]	241[36]	2,000	3,219	...	...	Philippines
644	4,314.3	33,360	15,864	8	2,878	4,632	55	80	2,369	3,812	753	1,100	Poland
332	1,129.3	7,572	37,740	16	6,278	10,104	159	232	510	820	...	...	Portugal
13	...	...	...	7	...	...	...	...	...	...	...	...	Puerto Rico
64	744	18,145	2,588	1	1,776[8]	2,858[8]	72[8]	105[8]	...	...	...	...	Qatar
7	33.5	454	2,302	2	...	...	...	...	...	...	...	...	Réunion
439	4,845.5	11,676	18,972	12	1,446	2,327	33.8	49.4	1,002	1,613	2,947	4,302	Romania
4,543	16,592.3	7,092	744	75	33,181	53,400	1,575	2,300	55,357	89,089	44,962	65,643	Russia
—	—	—	—	2	1.2	2.0	...	...	...	...	...	...	Rwanda
1	0.6	24	36	2	...	...	...	...	...	...	...	...	St. Kitts and Nevis
7	2.1	138	547	2	...	...	...	...	...	...	...	...	St. Lucia
946	1,253	72	128	5	...	...	...	...	...	...	...	...	St. Vincent and the Grenadines
7	6.5	48	144	3	165	265	18	26	—	—	—	—	Samoa
—	—	—	—	—	—	—	—	—	—	—	—	—	San Marino
4	2.3	16	45	2	6	9	0.7	1.0	...	...	...	...	São Tomé and Príncipe
279	1,278	214,070	46,437	28	11,774	18,949	1,815	2,650	...	...	...	...	Saudi Arabia
183	27.5	1,396	2,894	7	139.6[30]	224.7[30]	11.2[30]	16.4[30]	557	897	...	...	Senegal
462[37]	5,173.1[37]	360	972	5	551	887	4,112	6,003	365	587	905	1,322	Serbia and Montenegro
9	3.3	47	543	2	389	626	48	70	...	...	...	...	Seychelles
62	18.4	2,310	589	1	68[38]	110[38]	1.4[38]	2.0[38]	500	800	447	652	Sierra Leone
946	14,929.2	326,040	188,234	1	40,096	64,529	3,755	5,482	...	...	...	...	Singapore
...	...	...	...	2	143.8	231.4	0.5	0.7	107	172	1,046	1,527	Slovakia
13	346.5	2,460	5,952	3	517	832	2.8	4.2	...	...	21,900	31,973	Slovenia
33	5.0	278	349	21	29[39]	47[39]	0.9	1.3	...	...	...	...	Solomon Islands
28	18.5	324	1,007	1	81	131	3.0	5.0	...	...	...	...	Somalia
219	282.5	114,331	22,203	24	12,005[40]	19,320[40]	464[40]	677[40]	...	...	...	...	South Africa
2,190	5,077.3	55,752	169,848	25	37,715	60,696	4,388	6,407	649	1,045	21,836[41]	31,880[41]	Spain
66	472.6	9,288	16,632	1	3,204	5,156	459	670	267	430	0.7	1	Sri Lanka
16	62.2	1,543	4,300	3	330[42]	531[42]	14[42]	20[42]	3,300	5,310	...	...	Sudan, The
21	15.7	1,595	1,265	1	540[43]	883[43]	66[43]	106[43]	740	1,200	...	...	Suriname
—	—	—	—	1	30.7	49.4	0.09	0.1	—	—	—	—	Swaziland
430	2,881	61,320	75,528	48	6,997[20]	11,261[20]	196[20]	286[20]	1,275	2,052	5,708	8,334	Sweden
24	602.8	...	...	5	19,739	31,767	1,216	1,776	13	21	34	49	Switzerland
94	210.4	2,136	5,112	5	884	1,422	14	21	541	870	...	...	Syria
649	9,241.3	182,127	301,275	13	24,369	39,218	2,828	4,129	...	...	274	400	Taiwan
...	...	...	...	1	1,386	2,231	140	205	...	...	...	...	Tajikistan
43	48.5	1,249	2,721	11	114	184	2.0	2.9	...	...	...	...	Tanzania
351	1,194.5	42,495	74,579	25	23,826	38,345	1,145	1,671	2,300	3,701	...	...	Thailand
8	20.6	391	1,274	2	139.6	224.7	11.2	16.4	31	50	...	...	Togo
15	13.7	15	104	6	7	11	0.7	1.0	...	...	...	...	Tonga
53	17.5	9,622	10,961	2	1,783	2,869	38	55	...	...	...	...	Trinidad and Tobago
77	443.3	6,792	13,152	5	1,674	2,694	13	21	...	...	...	...	Tunisia
880	7,114.3	24,756	78,168	26	10,248[44]	16,492[44]	260[44]	380[44]	750	1,200	189	276	Turkey
...	...	...	...	1	970	1,562	98	143	240	387	5.5	8.0	Turkmenistan
6	16.0	...	...	1	...	...	...	...	...	...	...	...	Tuvalu
2	8.6	...	...	1	32.4	52.1	3	5	...	...	...	...	Uganda
...	...	77,004	7,116	12	1,225	1,972	18	27	2,734	4,400	3,973	5,800	Ukraine
276	1,491.7	88,153	9,595	6	12,150[8]	19,553[8]	978[8]	1,428[8]	...	...	...	...	United Arab Emirates
1,631	4,355	177,228	178,572	57	99,628	160,336	3,373	4,925	716	1,153	36,302	53,000	United Kingdom
509	18,585	392,076[46]	713,880[46]	834	619,500	997,000	18,116	26,449	25,778	41,485	356,188	520,026	United States
93	172.5	710[47]	1,450[47]	1	398	640	42	62	1,000	1,600	...	...	Uruguay
...	...	...	...	9	2,150	3,460	220	321	684	1,100	...	...	Uzbekistan
280	3,259.6	80	55	29	110.8	178.3	1.3	1.9	...	...	...	...	Vanuatu
271	1,355.4	101,435	17,932	20	3,600	5,800	438	639	4,400	7,100	8.9	13	Venezuela
230	872.8	303	1,510	12	2,380	3,831	67	98	11,000	17,702	1,339	1,955	Vietnam
1	...	105.5	648.3	2	...	...	...	...	...	...	...	...	Virgin Islands (U.S.)
—	—	...	...	—	—	—	—	—	...	...	...	...	West Bank
—	—	40	15	1	...	...	...	...	...	...	...	...	Western Sahara
40	13.7	1,936	7,829	12	978	1,574	22	32	...	...	...	...	Yemen
—	—	—	—	4	192	308	6.8	9.9	1,398	2,250	...	...	Zambia
—	—	—	—	7	544	875	24	35	...	...	...	...	Zimbabwe

transshipments. [26]El Al only. [27]Alitalia only. [28]Air Jamaica only. [29]Kenya Airways only. [30]International traffic only. [31]Peninsular Malaysia and Singapore. [32]Air Nauru only. [33]Includes Aruba. [34]Antillean Airlines only. [35]Air Caledonie only. [36]Philippine Air Lines only. [37]Data refer to pre-1991 Yugoslavia. [38]Sierra Leone Airlines international traffic only. [39]Solair only. [40]SAA only. [41]Coastal shipping only. [42]Sudan Airways only. [43]Suriname Airways only. [44]Turkish Airlines only. [45]British Railways only; excludes Northern Ireland. [46]Includes Puerto Rico. [47]Port of Montevideo only.

Communications

Virtually all the states of the world have a variety of communications media and services available to their citizens: book, periodical, and newspaper publishing (although only daily papers are included in this table); postal services; and telecommunications systems: radio and television broadcasting, telephones (fixed and mobile), facsimile (fax) machines, personal computers (PCs), and access to the Internet. Unfortunately, the availability of information about these services often runs behind the capabilities of the services themselves. Certain countries publish no official information; others publish data analyzed according to a variety of fiscal, calendar, religious, or other years; still others, while they possess such data almost simultaneously with the end of the business or calendar year, may not see them published except in company or parastatal reports of limited distribution. Even when such data are published in national statistical summaries, it may be only after a delay of up to several years.

The data also differ in their completeness and reliability. Figures for book production, for example, generally include all works published in separate bindings except advertising works, timetables, telephone directories, price lists, catalogs of businesses or exhibitions, musical scores, maps, atlases, and the like. The figures include government publications, school texts, theses, offprints, series works, and illustrated works, even those consisting principally of illustrations. Figures refer to works actually published during the year of survey, usually by a registered publisher, and deposited for copyright. A book is defined as a work of 49 or more pages; a work published simultaneously in more than one country is counted as having been published in each. A periodical is a publication issued at regular or stated intervals and, in Unesco's usage, directed to the general public. Newspaper statistics are especially difficult to collect and compare. Newspapers continually are founded, cease publication, merge, or change frequency of publication. Data on circulation are often incomplete, slow to be aggregated at the national level, or regarded as proprietary. In some countries no daily newspaper exists.

Post office statistics are compiled mainly from the Universal Postal Union's annual summary *Statistique des services postaux.* Postal services, unlike the other media discussed earlier, tend most often to be operated by

Communications

country	publishing (latest)							postal services				telecommunications	
	books		periodicals		daily newspapers			post offices, 1998				radio, 2000	
	number of titles	number of copies ('000)	number of titles	number of copies ('000)	number	total circulation ('000)	circulation per 1,000 persons	number	persons per office	pieces of mail handled ('000,000)	pieces handled per person	receivers (all types; '000)	receivers per 1,000 persons
Afghanistan	2,795	3,741	…	…	12	129	5	373	50,400	0.5	—	2,950	114
Albania	381	5,710	143	3,477	5	109	35	698[1]	4,840[1]	3.2	0.6	756	243
Algeria	670	…	48	803	5	817	27	3,223[2]	9,140[2]	736[2]	21[2]	7,380	244
American Samoa	…	…	…	…	2	5.0	93	…	…	…	…	57	929
Andorra	57	…	…	…	3	4.0	58	…	…	…	…	16	227
Angola	22	419	…	…	5	111	11	80[2]	145,000[2]	1.2	0.1	750	54
Antigua and Barbuda	…	…	…	…	1	6.0	91	16[6]	4,375[6]	…	…	36	542
Argentina	9,850	39,663	…	…	181	1,320	37	6,678[2]	5,340[2]	472[2]	11[2]	24,300	681
Armenia	396[7]	20,212[7]	44	541	11	19	6	…	…	0.7[8]	0.2[8]	700	225
Aruba	…	…	…	…	13	73	852	4	17,500	10	90	50	557
Australia	10,835	…	…	…	65	5,630	293	3,922	4,780	4,732	225	36,700	1,908
Austria	8,056[9]	…	2,481	…	17	2,380	296	2,436	3,320	3,133[2]	372[2]	6,050	753
Azerbaijan	542	2,643	49	801	6	217	27	1,673[2]	4,560[2]	12[2]	1.3[2]	177	22
Bahamas, The	…	…	…	…	3	28	100	138	2,170	61[11]	511[11]	215	739
Bahrain	40[7]	…	26	73	4	67	117	13	49,200	55	50	49	76
Bangladesh	…	…	…	…	37	6,880	53	9,093[2]	13,400[2]	589[2]	4.3[2]	6,360	49
Barbados	…	…	…	…	2	53	199	16	16,900	39	114	237	888
Belarus	3,809	59,073	155	3,765	10	1,550	155	3,852	2,640	709	67	2,990	299
Belgium	13,913	…	13,706	…	30	1,640	160	1,637[6]	6,200[6]	3,713	346	8,130	793
Belize	70	—	…	…	4	23.5	0.5	134[2]	1,720[2]	4.0[2]	12[2]	133	591
Benin	84[7]	42[7]	…	…	1	13	2.0	178	32,500	9.6	1.2	2,820	439
Bermuda	…	…	…	…	1	17	270	14[1]	4,500[1]	15[1]	240[1]	82	1,296
Bhutan	…	…	…	…	…	…	…	106[2]	17,540[2]	1.8[2]	0.7[2]	37	19
Bolivia	…	…	…	…	18	448	55	171	46,500	9.9	0.7	5,510	676
Bosnia and Herzegovina	…	…	…	…	3	563	152	210	20,050	9.8	1.6	900	243
Botswana	158[7]	…	14	177	1	44	27	180	8,720	54	26	254	155
Brazil	21,574[12]	104,397	…	…	380	7,390	43	11,713	13,800	5,223	32	74,400	433
Brunei	45[7]	56[7]	15	132	1	21	69	18	17,200	20	52	93[2]	302[2]
Bulgaria	4,840	20,317	772	1,740	17	2,060	257	3,303	2,500	156[1]	18[1]	4,350	543
Burkina Faso	12[7]	14[7]	37	24	4	12	1.0	85	130,000	7.3[13]	…	428	35
Burundi	…	…	…	…	1	11	2.0	28	225,000	16	1.3	1,260	220
Cambodia	…	…	…	…	…	25	2.0	56	204,000	3.2	0.2	1,480	119
Cameroon	…	…	…	…	2	104	7.0	377[2]	37,000[2]	6.1[2, 14]	0.4[2, 14]	2,410	163
Canada	19,900	…	1,400	37,108	107	4,890	159	18,607[11]	1,570[11]	10,715[13, 15]	370[13, 15]	32,200	1,047
Cape Verde	…	…	…	…	…	…	…	54	7,780	1.6	2.1	71[2]	179[2]
Central African Republic	…	…	…	…	3	7.0	2.0	35	99,710	…	…	280	80
Chad	…	…	…	…	1	2.0	0.2	36	201,900	13	1.0	1,990	236
Chile	2,469	4,095	417	3,450	52	1,450	98	710	20,870	343[14]	23[14]	5,230	354
China	100,951	5,945[16]	6,486	205,060	44	27,790	23	112,204	11,200	6,967[2]	5.5[2]	428,000	339
Colombia	1,481	11,314	…	…	37	1,830	46	1,354	30,200	116	2.2[2]	21,600	544
Comoros	…	…	…	…	…	…	…	37	17,800	0.4	0.3	90[2]	170[2]
Congo, Dem. Rep. of the	64[7]	535[7]	…	…	9	146	3.0	497	98,870	…	…	18,700	386
Congo, Rep. of the	…	…	3	34	6	28	8.0	114[1]	22,720[1]	1.8[1]	0.5[1]	424	123
Costa Rica	963	…	…	…	6	357	91	134	24,900	32[2]	6.9[2]	3,200	816
Côte d'Ivoire	…	…	…	…	12	253	16	373	38,300	31	1.9	2,170	137
Croatia	1,718	…	352	6,357	10	507	114	1,168	3,910	299	60	1,510	340
Cuba	932	4,610	14	285	17	1,320	118	1,855	5,990	12[14]	1.1[14]	3,950	353
Cyprus	930	1,776	39	338	9	84	111	777	990	64	67	310[2]	406[2]
Czech Republic	10,244	…	1,168	81,387	21	2,600	254	3,369	3,050	803	72	8,230	803
Denmark	12,352	…	157	6,930	37	1,510	283	1,169	4,530	1,828[1]	335[1]	7,200	1,349
Djibouti	…	…	7	6.0	…	…	…	12	51,700	16[1]	12[1]	38	87
Dominica	…	…	…	…	…	…	…	64[11]	1,090[11]	2.9[1]	30	46[2]	647[2]
Dominican Republic	…	…	…	…	12	226	27	239	33,900	…	…	1,510	181
East Timor	…	…	…	…	…	…	…	…	…	…	…	18[2]	21[2]
Ecuador	12[7]	19[7]	199	…	24	1,190	96	315	38,600	13	0.4	5,190	418
Egypt	2,215	92,353	258	2,373	17	2,000	31	7,488	8,810	317	3.3	21,900	339
El Salvador	…	…	45	774	5	174	28	289	20,900	18	1.9	2,970	478
Equatorial Guinea	…	…	…	…	1	2.0	4.9	23[11]	17,000[11]	…	…	180[2]	428[2]
Eritrea	106	420	…	…	…	104	28	37[6]	91,900[6]	2.3	0.5	1,650	444
Estonia	2,628	6,662	517	2,323	15	241	176	560	2,550	75	43	1,500	1,096

a single national service, to cover a country completely, and to record traffic data according to broadly similar schemes (although the details of *classes* of mail handled may differ). Some countries do not enumerate domestic traffic or may record only international traffic requiring handling charges.

Data for some kinds of telecommunications apparatus are relatively easy to collect; telephones, for example, must be installed, and service recorded so that it may be charged. But in most countries the other types of apparatus mentioned above may be purchased by anyone and used whenever desired. As a result, data on distribution and use of these types of apparatus may be collected in a variety of ways—on the basis of numbers of subscribers, licenses issued, periodic sample surveys, trade data, census or housing surveys, or private consumer surveys. Data on broadcast media refer to receivers; data on telephones to "main lines," or the lines connecting a subscriber's apparatus (fixed or mobile) to the public, switched net. Information on fax machines and PCs is estimated only, as noted above. "Users" refers to the number of people with access to computers connected to the Internet.

The *Statistical Yearbook* of Unesco contains extensive data on book, periodical, and newspaper publishing, and on radio and television broadcasting that have been collected from standardized questionnaires. The quality and recency of its data, however, depend on the completion and timely return of each questionnaire by national authorities. The commercially published annual *World Radio TV Handbook* (Andrew G. Sennitt, editor) is a valuable source of information on broadcast media and has complete and timely coverage. It depends on data received from broadcasters, but, because some do not respond, local correspondents and monitors are used in many countries, and some unconfirmed or unofficial data are included as estimates. The statistics on telecommunications apparatus and computers are derived mainly from the UN-affiliated International Telecommunication Union's *World Telecommunication Development Report* (annual).

... Not available.

— None, nil, or not applicable.

television, 2000		telephones, 2002		cellular phones, 2002		fax, 1999		personal computers, 2002		Internet users, 2002	country
receivers (all types; '000)	receivers per 1,000 persons	main lines ('000)	main lines per 1,000 persons	cellular subscriptions ('000)	subscriptions per 1,000 persons	receivers ('000)	receivers per 1,000 persons	units ('000)	units per 1,000 persons	number ('000)	
362	14	29	1.3	...	...	...	...	...	...	1.0	Afghanistan
383	123	220	71	851	132	18.3	4.8	36	12	36	Albania
3,330	110	1,908	61	400	13	7.0[2]	0.2[2]	242	7.7	242	Algeria
13	211	15	252	2.4[3]	41[3]	...	...	...	...	...	American Samoa
30	458	35	438	24[4]	356[4]	5.0[5]	67[5]	...	...	7.0[3]	Andorra
193	10	85	6.1	130	9.3	...	...	27	1.9	41	Angola
31[5]	413[5]	38	488	38	490	...	...	...	...	5[4]	Antigua and Barbuda
10,500	293	8,009	219	6,500	178	87[5]	2.4[5]	3,000	82	3,000	Argentina
759	244	543	143	72	19	0.4[6]	0.1[6]	60	16	60	Armenia
20[2]	204[2]	37	350	53	582	0.5[1]	6.9[1]	...	...	24[3]	Aruba
14,200	738	10,590	539	12,579	640	900[2]	48[2]	11,111	565	9,472	Australia
4,310	536	3,988	489	6,415	786	285[1]	35[1]	3,013	369	3,340	Austria
2,080	259	924	114	870	107	2.5[1]	0.1[1]	0.4[10]	—	300	Azerbaijan
75	247	127	406	122	390	0.5[1]	6.9[1]	...	...	60	Bahamas, The
256	402	175	263	389	583	6.9	10	107	160	107	Bahrain
909	7.0	682	5.1	1,075	8.1	40[1]	0.3[1]	450	3.4	204	Bangladesh
78[10]	290[10]	133	494	53[3]	198[3]	1.8[1]	6.7[1]	28	104	30	Barbados
3,420	342	2,967	299	463	47	24	2.3	...	...	809	Belarus
5,550	541	5,120	494	8,136	786	100[6]	19[6]	2,500	241	3,400	Belgium
42[10]	179[10]	31	124	52	205	0.5[1]	2.6[1]	35	138	30	Belize
289	45	63	9.2	219	32	1.1[6]	0.2[6]	15	2.2	50	Benin
66[5]	1,031[5]	56	862	30	462	...	...	30	462	30[3]	Bermuda
13[10]	20[10]	20	28	...	...	1.5[5]	2.3[5]	10	15	10	Bhutan
970	119	564	68	873	105	...	...	190	23	270	Bolivia
411	111	903	237	749	196	...	...	...	...	100	Bosnia and Herzegovina
41	25	150	87	415	241	3.5[2]	2.2[2]	70	41	50[3]	Botswana
58,900	343	38,810	223	34,881	201	500[2]	3.0[2]	13,000	75	14,300	Brazil
216	668	90	256	137	401	2.0[1]	18[1]	27	77	35[3]	Brunei
3,600	449	2,868	368	2,598	196	1.5[2]	1.8[2]	405	52	630	Bulgaria
147	12	61	5.4	90	7.5	0.1	—	19	1.6	25	Burkina Faso
171	30	22	3.2	52	7.4	4.0[6]	0.6[6]	5.0	0.7	8.4	Burundi
100	8.0	35	2.6	380	2.8	3.0[2]	0.3[2]	27	2.0	30	Cambodia
503	34	111	7.0	676	43	...	...	90	5.7	60	Cameroon
21,700	716	19,962	636	11,849	377	1,075[2]	36[2]	15,300	487	16,110	Canada
2.0	4.6	70	160	43	98	1.0[6]	2.5[6]	...	...	16.0	Cape Verde
21	6.0	9.0	2.3	13	3.2	0.3[2]	0.1[2]	8.0	2.0	5.0	Central African Republic
8.4	1.0	12	1.5	34	4.3	0.2	0.03[2]	13	1.7	13.0	Chad
3,580	242	3,467	230	11,849	377	40[2]	2.7[2]	1,796	119	3,575	Chile
370,000	293	214,420	167	206,620	161	2,000[2]	1.6[2]	35,500	28	59,100	China
11,200	282	7,766	179	4,597	106	242	5.8	2,133	49	2,000	Colombia
1.0[1]	1.8[2]	10	14	...	...	0.2[1]	0.2[1]	4.0	5.5	3.2	Comoros
150[6]	3.0[6]	10	0.2	560	11	5.0[1]	0.1[1]	...	...	50	Congo, Dem. Rep. of the
45	13	22	6.7	222	67	0.1[1]	0.4[1]	13	3.9	0.3[3]	Congo, Rep. of the
907	231	1,038	251	460	111	8.5[2]	2.2[2]	817	197	800	Costa Rica
950	60	336	20	1,027	62	...	...	154	9.3	90	Côte d'Ivoire
1,300	293	1,825	417	2,340	535	50[2]	11[2]	760	174	789	Croatia
2,800	250	574[4]	51	18	1.6	...	...	359	32	120[3]	Cuba
120	180	492	688	418	584	7.0[15]	11[15]	193	270	210	Cyprus
5,200	508	3,676	362	8,610	849	102	9.9	1,800	177	2,600	Czech Republic
4,310	807	3,701	689	4,478	833	250[1]	48[1]	3,100	577	2,756	Denmark
31	71	10	15	15	23	0.1	0.2	10	15	4.5	Djibouti
16	220	24	304	9.4	120	0.3[1]	4.0[1]	7.0	9.0	12.5	Dominica
810	97	909	110	1,701	207	2.5[1]	0.3[1]	...	...	300	Dominican Republic
...	...	...	...	...	...	...	...	...	...	...	East Timor
2,710	218	1,426	110	1,561	121	...	...	403	31	538	Ecuador
12,200	189	7,430	110	4,495	67	34	0.5	1,120	17	1,900	Egypt
1,250	201	668	103	889	138	...	...	163	25	300	El Salvador
4.0[2]	9.0[2]	8.8	17	32	63	0.1[1]	0.3[1]	4.0	6.9	1.8	Equatorial Guinea
97	26	36	9.0	92[3]	24[3]	0.8[1]	0.2[1]	10	2.5	9.0	Eritrea
809	591	475	351	881	650	13	8.7	285	210	444	Estonia

Communications (continued)

country	publishing (latest)							postal services				telecommunications	
	books		periodicals		daily newspapers			post offices, 1998				radio, 2000	
	number of titles	number of copies ('000)	number of titles	number of copies ('000)	number	total circulation ('000)	circulation per 1,000 persons	number	persons per office	pieces of mail handled ('000,000)	pieces handled per person	receivers (all types; '000)	receivers per 1,000 persons
Ethiopia	240	674	...	...	4	86	1.5	534	112,000	27	0.3	11,800	189
Faroe Islands	...	...	...	...	1	6.0	136	42[2]	1,190[2]	10[2]	161[2]	102	2,222
Fiji	401	2,256	...	...	1	40	50	318	2,520	40	35	500[2]	636[2]
Finland	13,104	...	5,711	...	56	2,360	455	1,601	3,220	1,614	305	8,400	1,623
France	34,766	1,041	2,672	120,018	117	11,800	201	17,038	3,450	26,115	436	55,900	950
French Guiana	...	...	...	...	1	2.0	7.0	...	...	...	...	104[2]	650[2]
French Polynesia	...	...	...	...	4	24	108	97	2,370	28	102	128[2]	574[2]
Gabon	...	...	...	...	2	38	30	108	11,000	5.9	2.2	630	501
Gambia, The	14[17]	10[17]	10	885	1	2.6	1.7	...	...	...	...	520	396
Gaza Strip	...	...	...	...	...	...	...	...	...	...	...	...	...
Georgia	581[7]	834[7]	...	...	9	25	111	1,190[2]	4,560[2]	1,025[11, 14]	188[11, 14]	2,790	556
Germany	71,515	...	9,010	395,036	375	25,100	311	14,500	5,650	21,105[2]	249[2]	77,900	948
Ghana	28	648	121	774	4	273	14	1,010	18,800	225	3.4	13,900	710
Greece	4,225	...	...	...	156	251	153	1,225	8,590	392[6, 13]	37[6, 13]	5,220	478
Greenland	...	...	...	...	2	1.0	18	75[2]	800[2]	7.8[2]	72[2]	27[2]	482[2]
Grenada	...	...	4	89	...	...	...	58[11]	1,550[11]	...	...	57[2]	615[2]
Guadeloupe	...	...	...	...	1	35	81	...	...	...	...	113[2]	258[2]
Guam	...	...	...	...	1	26	180	...	...	...	...	221[2]	1,400[2]
Guatemala	...	...	...	...	7	377	33	540[11]	19,700[11]	79[11]	7.7[11]	902	79
Guernsey	...	...	...	...	...	...	...	18	3,140	10[13]	169[13]	...	...
Guinea	...	...	3	5.0	...	...	...	96	47,400	7.9	0.4	422	52
Guinea-Bissau	...	...	...	...	1	6.4	5.0	18[6]	60,600[6]	311[1, 18]	0.31[1, 18]	56	44
Guyana	42[7]	508[7]	...	...	2	42	50	85[2]	10,000[2]	4.0[2, 14]	4.7[2, 14]	420[2]	498[2]
Haiti	...	...	...	...	4	22	3.0	85	90,000	1.2[10]	0.2[10]	395	55
Honduras	22	80	...	...	7	349	55	435[1]	13,700[1]	35[1]	3.0[1]	2,620	412
Hong Kong	...	...	598	...	52	5,280	792	125	53,500	1,254	175	4,560	684
Hungary	9,193	53,194	1,203	14,927	40	4,750	465	3,236	3,120	1,046	103	7,050	690
Iceland	1,527	...	938	384	5	145	535	94[6]	2,870[6]	73[6]	254[6]	260	950
India	11,903	...	...	...	3,037	61,000	60	153,021	6,240	16,394	16	123,000	121
Indonesia	4,018[17]	8,103[17]	115	4,173	69	4,870	23	20,139	10,200	758	3.4	33,200	157
Iran	15,073	87,861	318	6,166	32	1,780	28	13,715	4,490	274	4.2	17,900	281
Iraq	...	...	...	...	4	431	19	...	...	69	2.1	5,030	222
Ireland	...	...	...	...	6	574	150	1,912	1,940	748	170	2,660	695
Isle of Man	...	...	...	...	...	...	...	36	1,940	21[6, 8]	300[6, 8]	...	...
Israel	2,310[19]	9,368[19]	...	...	34	1,770	290	664	8,990	601	95	3,210	526
Italy	35,236	278,821	9,951	80,469	74	5,920	104	13,967[2]	4,120[2]	5,850[2]	99[2]	50,000	878
Jamaica	...	...	...	...	3	161	62	688	3,690	67	19	2,030	784
Japan	56,221[7]	400,013[7]	2,926	...	122	73,300	578	24,678	5,120	25,731[2]	202[2]	121,000	956
Jersey	...	...	...	...	...	...	...	23[2]	3,650[2]	62[2]	468[2]	...	...
Jordan	511	2,673[7]	31	43	4	383	77	687	9,170	118[2]	17[2]	1,850	372
Kazakhstan	1,226	21,014	...	...	3	500	30	3,580	4,700	201[1, 13]	0.01[1, 13]	6,270	422
Kenya	300[7]	452	...	...	4	303	10	1,033	28,100	413	14	6,760	223
Kiribati	...	...	...	...	...	...	...	25[2]	3,200[2]	1.9[2]	1.2[2]	33	386
Korea, North	...	...	...	...	3	4,500	208	...	...	...	...	3,330	154
Korea, South	30,487[7]	142,804[7]	...	...	60	18,500	393	3,610	12,900	3,631	77	48,600	1,033
Kuwait	196[20]	6,107	...	...	8	836	374	51[2]	35,500[2]	99[15]	68[15]	1,400	624
Kyrgyzstan	351	1,980	...	...	3	73	15	914[2]	5,080[2]	39[2, 13]	8.5[2, 13]	542	111
Laos	88[7]	995[7]	...	...	3	21	4.0	106	48,700	5.2	0.9	781	145
Latvia	1,965	7,734	213	1,660	24	556	247	978	2,500	37	12	1,650	695
Lebanon	...	...	...	...	15	383	107	268[2]	11,700[2]	3.9[2]	1.2[2]	2,460	687
Lesotho	...	...	...	...	2	14	8.0	157	13,100	64	16	95	53
Liberia	...	...	...	...	6	38	12	34[6]	8,260[6]	...	...	863	274
Libya	26	2,645	...	...	4	79	15	342	15,600	39	3.5	1,430	273
Liechtenstein	...	...	...	...	2	19	606	12[6]	2,500[6]	17[11]	0.6[11]	21[2]	658[2]
Lithuania	3,645	14,915	269	...	19	101	29	978[2]	3,790[2]	51	11	1,750	500
Luxembourg	681	...	508	...	5	135	327	106	3,960	169	340	170	389
Macau	67	99	16	...	10	197	448	17	25,300	19	30	215	500
Macedonia	892	2,496	74	347	3	41	19	294	6,800	27	11	415	205
Madagascar	119	296	55	108	5	78	5.0	764	19,700	26	1.5	3,350	216
Malawi	117[7, 21]	9,174[7, 21]	...	...	1	33	3.0	314	34,100	44	3.4	5,430	499
Malaysia	5,843	29,040	25	996	42	3,670	158	1,382	7,490	993[8]	96[8]	9,760	420
Maldives	...	...	...	...	2	5.0	18	249[2]	1,080[2]	2.5	5.9	34[2]	129[2]
Mali	14[7]	28[7]	...	...	3	11	1.0	124	86,200	3.4	0.2	597	56
Malta	404	...	359	...	2	48	130	51[14]	7,450[14]	14[14]	34[14]	255[2]	669[2]
Marshall Islands	...	...	...	...	...	...	...	...	...	...	...	...	...
Martinique	...	...	...	...	1	30	78	...	...	...	...	82[2]	213[2]
Mauritania	...	...	...	...	2	1.0	0.5	61	41,500	4.2	0.5	371	149
Mauritius	80	163	62	...	6	84	71	101	11,500	63	47	450	379
Mayotte	...	...	...	...	...	...	...	...	...	...	...	50[6]	427[6]
Mexico	...	...	158	13,097	295	9,580	98	9,432	10,600	1,133	9.4	32,300	330
Micronesia	...	...	...	...	...	...	...	...	...	...	...	70[6]	667[6]
Moldova	921	2,779	76	196	4	660	154	1,276	3,430	41	8.1	3,250	758
Monaco	41	722	3	38	1	8.0	263	...	...	...	...	22	671
Mongolia	285[7]	959[7]	45	6,361	4	68	27	339[2]	7,050[2]	1.1[2]	0.3[2]	368	154
Morocco	918	1,836	...	...	22	740	26	1,469	18,900	240	7.7	6,920	243
Mozambique	...	3,490	...	...	2	53	3.0	353	47,900	6.8	0.1	778	44
Myanmar (Burma)	3,660	4,038	...	...	5	376	9.0	1,238	37,500	88[1]	1.9[1]	2,760	66
Namibia	106	...	...	...	4	35	19	115	14,400	66[13]	4.0[13]	258	141
Nauru	...	...	...	...	...	...	...	1[2]	10,000[2]	...	...	7.0[2]	609[2]
Nepal	...	...	...	...	29	250	11	4,156	5,260	29[6, 8]	1.4[6, 8]	883	39
Netherlands, The	34,067	...	367	19,283	38	4,870	306	2,387	6,580	7,009[22]	447[22]	15,600	980
Netherlands Antilles	...	...	...	...	6	70	334	16	12,625	...	...	217[2]	1,031[2]
New Caledonia	...	...	...	...	3	24	127	54	3,700	21	75	107[2]	527[2]
New Zealand	...	...	126	3,991	23	799	207	...	...	...	...	3,850	997
Nicaragua	...	...	...	...	4	152	30	183	26,300	8.3	1.2	1,370	270

television, 2000		telephones, 2002		cellular phones, 2002		fax, 1999		personal computers, 2002		Internet users, 2002	country
receivers (all types; '000)	receivers per 1,000 persons	main lines ('000)	main lines per 1,000 persons	cellular subscriptions ('000)	subscriptions per 1,000 persons	receivers ('000)	receivers per 1,000 persons	units ('000)	units per 1,000 persons	number ('000)	
376	6.0	354	5.3	50	0.7	3.1	0.1	100	1.5	50	Ethiopia
47	1,022	23	482	31	644	...	...	...	...	25	Faroe Islands
92	113	98	119	90	110	2.8	3.5	40	49	50	Fiji
3,580	692	2,726	524	4,516	867	198[2]	38[2]	2,300	442	2,650	Finland
37,000	628	33,929	569	38,585	647	2,800[2]	47[2]	20,700	347	18,716	France
30[2]	172[2]	51	268	138	781	...	...	...	...	...	French Guiana
45	189	53	214	90	367	3.0[5]	13[5]	...	...	35	French Polynesia
410	326	32	25	279	215	0.5[2]	0.4[2]	25	19	25	Gabon
3.9	3.0	38	28	100	73	1.1[2]	0.9[2]	19	14	25	Gambia, The
...	...	...	...	...	...	...	...	...	...	...	Gaza Strip
2,380	474	649	131	504	102	0.5[11]	0.1[11]	156	32	74	Georgia
48,200	586	53,720	651	60,043	728	6,500	79	35,600	431	34,000	Germany
2,300	118	274	13	449	21	5.0	0.3	82	3.8	170	Ghana
5,330	488	5,413	651	9,314	845	40	3.8	900	82	1,600	Greece
22[2]	393[2]	26[3]	468[3]	17[3]	298[3]	...	...	...	...	20[3]	Greenland
33[10]	355[10]	34	327	7.6	71	0.3	3.1	14	132	15	Grenada
118[10]	262[10]	210[3]	457	324	697	3.4[1]	8.1[1]	100[3]	233[3]	20	Guadeloupe
106[10]	646[10]	80[4]	508[4]	33	207	3.4	8.1	...	...	5.0[4]	Guam
697	61	846	71	1,577	90	10	1.0	173	14	400	Guatemala
...	...	55[3]	877[3]	32	500	0.7	11	...	...	20[4]	Guernsey
357	44	26	3.4	91	12	3.2	0.4	42	5.5	35	Guinea
...	...	11	8.9	...	...	0.5[5]	0.4[5]	...	...	5.0	Guinea-Bissau
60[10]	70[10]	80	92	87	17	...	...	24	27	125	Guyana
36	5.0	130	16	140	17	...	...	...	...	80	Haiti
610	96	323	48	327	49	...	...	91	14	169	Honduras
3,290	493	3,832	565	6,396	943	390	58	2,864	422	2,918	Hong Kong
4,460	437	3,666	361	6,863	676	180	18	1,100	108	1,600	Hungary
143	509	188	653	261	906	4.1[15]	15[15]	130	451	187	Iceland
79,300	78	41,420	40	12,688	12	150[2]	0.2[2]	7,500	7.2	16,580	India
31,500	149	7,750	37	11,700	55	185	0.9	2,519	12	8,000	Indonesia
10,400	163	12,200	187	2,187	34	30	0.5	4,900	75	3,168	Iran
1,880	83	675	25	...	...	...	...	...	...	25	Iraq
1,530	399	1,975	502	3,000	763	100[2]	27[2]	1,654	421	1,065	Ireland
...	...	...	...	...	...	...	...	...	...	...	Isle of Man
2,040	335	3,100	467	6,334	955	140	25	1,610	243	2,000	Israel
28,100	494	27,142	481	53,003	939	1,800	31	13,025	231	19,900	Italy
502	194	444	170	1,400	535	1.6[15]	0.6[15]	141	54	600	Jamaica
92,000	725	71,149	558	81,118	637	16,000[2]	126[2]	48,700	382	57,200	Japan
...	...	74[3]	849[3]	61[3]	706[3]	0.7	8.0	...	...	8.0[4]	Jersey
417	84	675	127	1,220	229	52[5]	8.0[5]	200	38	308	Jordan
3,580	241	2,082	130	1,027	64	2.0	0.1	...	...	250	Kazakhstan
758	25	328	10	1,325	42	3.8	0.1	204	6.4	400	Kenya
3	36	4.5	51	0.5	6.0	0.2	2.5	2.0	23	2.0	Kiribati
1,170	54	1,100[10]	50[10]	...	...	3.0	0.1	...	...	...	Korea, North
17,100	364	23,257	487	32,342	680	400	8.6	26,458	556	26,270	Korea, South
1,090	486	482	204	1,227	519	60	32	285	121	250	Kuwait
239	49	395	78	53	10	...	...	65	13	152	Kyrgyzstan
53	10	62	11	55	10	0.5[11]	0.1[11]	18	3.3	15	Laos
1,870	789	701	301	917	394	0.9[1]	0.3[1]	400	172	310	Latvia
1,200	335	679	199	775	227	3.0[13]	1.1[13]	275	81	400	Lebanon
29	16	29	13	92	43	0.6[1]	0.3[1]	...	...	21	Lesotho
79	25	6.8[3]	2.0[3]	...	...	...	...	...	...	1.0	Liberia
717	137	660[3]	118[3]	70	13	...	...	...	...	125	Libya
12[2]	375[2]	20	583	11	333	...	...	...	...	20	Liechtenstein
1,480	422	936	270	1,646	475	6.2[2]	1.7[2]	380	110	500	Lithuania
170	391	355	797	473	1,061	30	70	265	594	165	Luxembourg
123	286	176	399	276	625	6.3	14	92	208	400	Macau
571	282	560	271	365	177	3.0	1.5	2.2[10]	1.1[10]	100	Macedonia
372	24	60	3.7	163	10	...	...	70	4.4	55	Madagascar
33	3.0	73	7.0	86	8.2	1.3	0.1	14	1.3	27	Malawi
3,900	168	4,670	190	9,241	377	175[5]	8.0[5]	3,600	147	7,841	Malaysia
11	40	29	102	42	149	3.5[1]	14[1]	20	71	15	Maldives
130[5]	12[5]	57	5.3	53	5.0	...	...	15	1.4	25	Mali
217	556	207	523	277	699	6.0[6]	16[6]	101	255	83	Malta
...	...	4.4	77	0.6	9.8	...	...	3.0	53	1.3	Marshall Islands
66[2]	168[2]	172[4]	447[4]	320	790	20[1]	52[1]	52	135	40[3]	Martinique
239	96	32	12	247	92	3.3	1.3	29	11	7.0	Mauritania
318	268	327	270	350	289	32	28	141	117	120	Mauritius
3.5[6]	30[6]	10[3]	70[3]	22	15	...	...	...	...	...	Mayotte
27,700	283	14,942	147	25,928	255	285[2]	2.9[2]	8,353	82	10,033	Mexico
2.2	20	10	87	1.8	15	0.5[5]	4.3[5]	...	...	6.0	Micronesia
1,270	297	707	161	338	77	0.7	0.2	77	18	150	Moldova
25[2]	758[2]	34	1,040	12[5]	364[5]	...	...	...	...	16	Monaco
155	65	128	53	216	89	7.9	3.0	69	28	50	Mongolia
4,720	166	1,127	38	6,199	209	18[2]	0.6[2]	700	24	700	Morocco
88	5.0	84	4.6	255	14	7.2[11]	0.4[11]	82	4.5	50	Mozambique
292	7.0	342	7.0	48	1.0	2.5	0.1	250	5.1	25	Myanmar (Burma)
69	38	121	65	150	80	...	...	133	71	50	Namibia
0.5[2]	0.1[2]	1.9	160	1.5	130	...	...	...	...	1.5[3]	Nauru
159	7.0	328	14	22	0.9	8.0	0.4	85	3.7	80	Nepal
8,570	538	10,004	618	12,060	745	600[2]	38[2]	7,557	467	8,200	Netherlands, The
69[2]	321[2]	81.0	372	16[5]	74[5]	...	...	...	...	...	Netherlands Antilles
104	492	51[4]	238[4]	80	357	2.2[11]	12[11]	...	...	30	New Caledonia
2,010	522	1,765	448	2,449	622	65[1]	18[1]	1,630	414	1,908	New Zealand
350	69	159[4]	32[4]	203	38	...	...	150	28	90	Nicaragua

Communications (continued)

country	publishing (latest)							postal services				telecommunications	
	books		periodicals		daily newspapers			post offices, 1998				radio, 2000	
	number of titles	number of copies ('000)	number of titles	number of copies ('000)	number	total circulation ('000)	circulation per 1,000 persons	number	persons per office	pieces of mail handled ('000,000)	pieces handled per person	receivers (all types; '000)	receivers per 1,000 persons
Niger	5[7]	11[7]	…	…	1	2	0.2	53	190,000	3.4	0.3	1,270	121
Nigeria	1,314	18,800	…	…	25	2,770	24	3,971	26,800	391	2.0	23,000	200
Northern Mariana Islands	…	…	…	…	…	…	…	…	…	…	…	11[6]	190[6]
Norway	6,900[9, 19]	…	8,017	…	83	2,620	585	1,534[2]	210[2]	2,524[2]	555[2]	4,110	915
Oman	7[7]	21[7]	15	…	4	63	27	90[1]	23,700[1]	43	7.1	1,490	621
Pakistan	124	714	…	…	264	4,190	30	13,294	9,820	413	2.9	14,700	105
Palau	…	…	…	…	…	…	…	…	…	…	…	12[2]	663[2]
Panama	…	…	…	…	7	183	62	176	15,700	18	4.4	884	300
Papua New Guinea	122	…	…	…	2	73	14	108[23]	39,800[23]	39[23]	10[23]	446	86
Paraguay	152	…	…	…	5	227	43	326	16,000	4.6	0.5	961	182
Peru	612	1,836	…	…	74	2,000	85	963	25,800	43	1.3	7,080	273
Philippines	1,507	14,718[7]	1,570	9,468	47	6,300	82	3,023[11]	22,600[11]	3,205[6]	12[6]	12,400	161
Poland	14,104	80,306	5,260	75,358	55	4,170	108	7,836	4,930	2,503	63	20,200	523
Portugal	7,868[12]	26,942	984	10,208	27	324	32	3,712	2,660	1,201	117	3,080	304
Puerto Rico	…	…	…	…	3	481	126	…	…	…	…	2,830	742
Qatar	209[17]	2,205	11	47	5	90	161	26	20,800	20[14]	38[14]	250[2]	432[2]
Réunion	69	…	…	…	3	55	83	…	…	…	…	173[2]	252[2]
Romania	7,199	38,374	987	…	69	6,300	300	6,324	3,560	327	14	7,310	334
Russia	36,237	421,387	2,751	387,832	285	15,300	105	43,900[2]	3,350[2]	5,614[2, 8]	38[2, 8]	61,100	418
Rwanda	…	…	15	101	1	0.5	0.1	39	169,000	3.8	0.4	587	76
St. Kitts and Nevis	…	…	10	44	…	…	…	7	5,710	2.6	46	28[2]	701[2]
St. Lucia	…	…	…	…	…	…	…	63	2,380	2.3[13]	15[13]	111[2]	746[2]
St. Vincent and the Grenadines	…	…	…	…	1	1.0	9.0	41[2]	2,680[2]	…	…	77[2]	690[2]
Samoa	…	…	…	…	…	…	…	38	4,470	0.9	3.0	178[2]	1,035[2]
San Marino	…	…	15	9	3	2.0	72	10[6]	3,000[6]	…	…	16[2]	610[2]
São Tomé and Príncipe	…	…	…	…	…	…	…	18	7,780	0.3	0.6	38[2]	272[2]
Saudi Arabia	3,900[7]	14,493[7, 21]	471	…	13	7,180	326	1,421	14,200	1,246	45	7,180	326
Senegal	…	…	…	…	1	47	5.0	134	69,200	12	0.7	1,320	141
Serbia and Montenegro	5,367	16,669	395	…	18	1,130	107	1,783	5,940	242	19	3,130	297
Seychelles	…	…	…	…	1	3.0	46	5	16,000	5.2	49	42[2]	560[2]
Sierra Leone	…	…	…	…	1	18	4.0	54[1]	83,500[1]	1.1[1]	0.1[1]	1,140	259
Singapore	…	…	…	…	8	1,200	298	939	4,120	772[2]	184[2]	2,700	672
Slovakia	3,800	6,139	424	8,725	19	938	174	1,728	3,120	518	90	5,200	965
Slovenia	3,441	6,267	784	…	7	334	171	545	3,630	387	189	792	405
Solomon Islands	…	…	…	…	…	…	…	127	3,150	4.3[1]	11[1]	57[2]	141[2]
Somalia	…	…	…	…	2	7.2	1.0	…	…	…	…	435	60
South Africa	5,418	31,349	11	2,149	17	1,590	32	2,449	17,200	2,170[8]	52[8]	16,800	338
Spain	46,330	192,019	…	…	94	4,060	100	4,093	9,620	4,565	112	13,500	333
Sri Lanka	4,115	19,650	…	…	9	539	29	4,282	4,380	463	23	3,870	208
Sudan, The	…	…	…	…	5	912	26	491	57,600	4.4[6]	0.1[6]	16,300	464
Suriname	47[7]	21[7]	…	…	4	50	116	33	12,400	…	…	300[2]	728[2]
Swaziland	…	…	…	…	3	27	26	60[2]	15,200[2]	21[2]	18[2]	169	162
Sweden	13,496	…	373	19,242	94	3,830	432	1,720[6]	5,140[6]	4,570[6]	503[6]	8,270	932
Switzerland	15,371	…	60	4,561	88	2,650	369	3,630[6]	1,950[6]	4,230[11]	601[11]	7,200	1,002
Syria	598	310[6]	30	192	8	326	20	619	25,200	19	1.0	4,500	276
Taiwan	…	…	…	…	…	4,000	188	…	…	…	…	8,620[6]	402[6]
Tajikistan	132[7]	997[7]	11	130	2	123	20	706[2]	8,570[2]	3.0[2]	0.4[2]	870	141
Tanzania	172[7]	364[7]	…	…	3	130	4.0	612	52,400	55	1.3	9,130	281
Thailand	8,142	…	1,522	…	30	3,990	64	4,265	14,300	1,315	21	14,700	235
Togo	…	…	…	…	1	20	4.0	50[2]	86,400[2]	8.3[2]	0.7[2]	1,330	265
Tonga	…	…	…	…	1	12	123	1.8[15]	55,600[15]	4.0[15]	40[15]	61[2]	400[2]
Trinidad and Tobago	26	30	…	…	4	155	123	245	5,220	30[1]	16[1]	672	532
Tunisia	720	6,000[21]	170	1,748	8	296	31	947[1]	9,740[1]	117[1]	12[1]	1,510	158
Turkey	6,546	…	3,554	…	57	7,480	111	16,984	3,740	1,088	16	38,600	573
Turkmenistan	450[7]	5,493[7]	…	…	…	…	…	1,673[6]	2,730[6]	27[6]	6.0[6]	1,190	256
Tuvalu	…	…	…	…	…	…	…	…	…	…	…	4.0[2]	384[2]
Uganda	288	2,229[19]	26	158	2	21	2.0	313	67,200	18[2]	0.5[2]	2,920	127
Ukraine	6,225	68,876	717	2,521	44	4,970	101	15,227	3,320	374	6.3	43,800	889
United Arab Emirates	293[21]	5,117[21]	80	922	7	507	156	243	11,190	182	39	1,030	318
United Kingdom	107,263	…	…	…	99	19,300	329	18,760	3,130	19,556	325	84,000	1,432
United States	68,175	…	11,593	…	1,520	60,200	213	38,159	7,090	197,688	729	598,000	2,118
Uruguay	934	1,970	…	…	36	973	293	942	3,490	16	6.0	2,000	603
Uzbekistan	1,003	30,914	81	684	3	74	3.0	3,044[2]	7,700[2]	12[2]	0.4[2]	11,300	456
Vanuatu	…	…	…	…	…	…	…	…	…	…	…	62	350
Venezuela	3,468[7]	7,420[7]	…	…	86	5,000	206	407	57,600	141	5.1	7,140	294
Vietnam	5,581	83,000	338	2,710	10	313	4.0	3,075	25,200	…	…	8,520	109
Virgin Islands (U.S.)	…	…	…	…	3	43	364	9[2]	2,000[2]	3.6[11, 14]	0.2[11, 14]	107	1,119
West Bank	…	…	…	…	…	…	…	…	…	…	…	…	…
Western Sahara	…	…	…	…	…	…	…	…	…	…	…	56	211
Yemen	…	…	…	…	3	270	15	265	64,400	5.5	0.1	1,170	65
Zambia	…	…	…	…	3	125	12	195	45,000	16	0.8	1,510	145
Zimbabwe	232	…	28	680	2	205	18	296	42,800	137	9.4	4,110	362

television, 2000		telephones, 2002		cellular phones, 2002		fax, 1999		personal computers, 2002		Internet users, 2002	country
receivers (all types; '000)	receivers per 1,000 persons	main lines ('000)	main lines per 1,000 persons	cellular subscriptions ('000)	subscriptions per 1,000 persons	receivers ('000)	receivers per 1,000 persons	units ('000)	units per 1,000 persons	number ('000)	
388	37	22	1.9	17	1.4	0.3[1]	0.01[1]	7.0	0.6	15	Niger
7,840	68	702	5.8	1,608	13	6.8[1]	0.11[1]	853	7.1	420	Nigeria
…	…	27[4]	383[4]	3.0[4]	43[4]	…	…	…	…	…	Northern Mariana Islands
3,000	669	3,343	734	3,840	844	220[2]	49[2]	2,405	528	2,288	Norway
1,350	563	228	84	465	175	6.4[2]	2.6[2]	95	35	180	Oman
18,300	131	3,655	25	1,239	8.5	268	2.0	600[3]	4.2[3]	1,500	Pakistan
…	…	…	…	…	…	…	…	…	…	20[10]	Palau
572	194	367	122	570	190	0.8	0.2	115	38	120	Panama
88	17	64	12	15	2.7	0.8[11]	0.2[11]	321	59	75	Papua New Guinea
1,200	218	273	47	1,667	288	1.7[15]	0.4[15]	200	35	100	Paraguay
3,840	148	1,766	66	2,307	86	15[1]	0.6[1]	1,149	43	2,500	Peru
11,100	144	3,311	42	15,201	191	50[5]	0.7[5]	2,200	28	3,500	Philippines
15,500	400	11,400[3]	295[3]	14,000	363	55[1]	1.4[1]	4,079	106	8,880	Poland
6,380	630	4,355	421	8,529	825	70	7.0	1,394	135	2,000	Portugal
1,260	330	1,330[3]	346[3]	1,211[3]	316[3]	543[15]	149[15]	…	…	600[3]	Puerto Rico
503	869	177	289	177	289	10[5]	18[5]	110	180	70	Qatar
127[2]	184[2]	300[3]	410[3]	490	66	1.9[1]	2.9[1]	…	…	150[3]	Réunion
8,340	381	4,215	194	4,215	194	21[1]	0.9[1]	1,500	69	1,800	Romania
61,500	421	35,500	242	35,500	242	53[5]	0.4[5]	13,000	89	6,000	Russia
10[2]	1.7[2]	23	2.8	23	2.8	0.5[1]	0.1[1]	…	…	25	Rwanda
12	260	24	500	24	50	…	…	9.0	192	2.0[10]	St. Kitts and Nevis
32[2]	208[2]	51	320	51	32	…	…	24	150	…	St. Lucia
26	234	27	234	27	23	…	…	14	120	3.5[4]	St. Vincent and the Grenadines
11	61	10	57	10	57	0.5[5]	2.8[5]	1	6.7	4.0	Samoa
9.0[2]	346[2]	21	763	17	621	…	…	…	…	14	San Marino
34	228	6.2	41	…	…	0.2[1]	15[1]	…	…	11	São Tomé and Príncipe
5,810	264	3,318	144	5,008	217	150[1]	8.2[1]	3,003	130	1,419	Saudi Arabia
376	40	225	22	553	55	…	…	200	20	105	Senegal
2,980	282	2,493	233	2,750	257	20	1.9	290	27	640	Serbia and Montenegro
16	203	22	269	45	554	0.6	7.5	13	161	12	Seychelles
57	13[3]	24	4.8	66	13	2.5	0.5	…	…	8.0	Sierra Leone
1,220	304	1,927	463	3,313	796	100[5]	32[5]	2,590	622	2,100	Singapore
2,190	407	1,443	268	2,923	544	54[5]	10[5]	970	180	863	Slovakia
720	368	1,010	506	1,667	835	21[5]	11[5]	600	301	750	Slovenia
9.6	23	6.6	15	1.0	2.2	0.8	1.9	18	41	2.2	Solomon Islands
102	14	100	10	35	3.0	…	…	…	…	89	Somalia
6,310	127	4,844	107	13,814	304	150[2]	3.4[2]	3,300	73	3,100	South Africa
21,000	501	20,595	506	33,531	824	700[6]	17[6]	7,972	196	6,359	Spain
2,060	111	883	47	932	49	11[11]	0.6[11]	250	13	200	Sri Lanka
9,580	273	672	21	191	5.9	25	0.9	200	6.1	84	Sudan, The
109	253	79	164	108	225	…	…	20[3]	46[3]	20	Suriname
124	119	35	34	63	61	1.2[6]	1.2[6]	25	24	20	Swaziland
5,090	574	6,579	736	7,949	889	450[6]	51[6]	5,556	621	5,125	Sweden
3,940	548	5,419	744	5,747	789	207[6]	29[6]	5,160	709	2,556	Switzerland
1,090	67	2,099	123	400	24	22	1.4	330	19	220	Syria
9,220[10]	417[10]	13,099	582	23,905	106	430[11]	20[11]	8,887	395	8,590	Taiwan
2,010	326	238	37	13	2.1	2.1	0.3	…	…	3.5	Tajikistan
650	20	162	4.7	670	20	2.0[15]	0.1[15]	144	4.2	80	Tanzania
17,700	284	6,500	105	16,117	260	150[2]	2.5[2]	2,461	40	4,800	Thailand
161	32	51	11	170	35	18	4.0	150	31	200	Togo
2.0[2]	20[2]	11	113	3.4	34	0.2[1]	2.0[1]	2.0	20	2.9	Tonga
429	340	325	250	362	278	5.0[5]	3.9[5]	104	80	138	Trinidad and Tobago
1,890	198	1,148	117	504	52	31[2]	3.3[2]	300	31	506	Tunisia
30,300	449	18,915	281	23,374	348	108[2]	1.7[2]	3,000	45	4,900	Turkey
911	196	374	77	8.2	1.7	…	…	…	…	8.0[3]	Turkmenistan
0.1[6]	9.1[6]	0.7	65	…	…	…	…	…	…	…	Tuvalu
620	27	55	2.2	393	16	3.0[6]	0.1[6]	82	3.3	100	Uganda
22,500	456	10,833	216	4,200	84	48	0.9	951	19	900	Ukraine
948	292	1,094	314	2,428	696	18	6.1	450	129	1,176	United Arab Emirates
38,800[10]	652[10]	34,898	591	49,677	841	1,992[6]	33[6]	23,972	406	25,000	United Kingdom
241,000	854	186,232	646	140,767	488	21,000[2]	78.0[2]	190,000	659	159,000	United States
1,760	531	947	280	652	193	0.6	0.2	370[3]	110[3]	400[3]	Uruguay
6,830	276	1,681	67	187	7.4	2.2	0.1	…	…	275	Uzbekistan
2.3	12	6.6	33	4.9	24	0.6[1]	3.6[1]	3	15	7.0	Vanuatu
4,490	185	2,842	113	6,464	256	70[2]	3.0[2]	1,536	61	1,274	Venezuela
14,500	185	3,929	48	1,902	23	31	0.4	800	9.8	1,500	Vietnam
65	594	69[3]	635	41[3]	375[3]	…	…	…	…	30	Virgin Islands (U.S.)
…	…	257	72	40[2]	14[2]	…	…	…	…	60	West Bank
6.0[6]	24[6]	…	…	…	…	…	…	…	…	…	Western Sahara
5,100	283	542	28	411	21	2.8[1]	0.2[1]	145	7.4	100	Yemen
1,400	134	88	8.2	139	13	1.0	0.1	80	7.5	52	Zambia
2,074[10]	183	288	25	353	30	4.1[5]	0.4[5]	600	52	500	Zimbabwe

[1]1995. [2]1997. [3]2001. [4]2000. [5]1998. [6]1996. [7]First editions only. [8]Domestic and foreign-dispatched only. [9]Not including school textbooks. [10]1999. [11]1994. [12]Including reprints. [13]Domestic only. [14]Foreign-dispatched and foreign-received only. [15]1993. [16]Millions of copies. [17]School textbooks and government publications only. [18]Foreign-received only. [19]Not including government publications. [20]Government publications only. [21]School textbooks only. [22]Domestic and foreign-received only. [23]1991.

Trade: external

The following table presents comparative data on the international, or foreign, trade of the countries of the world. The table analyzes data for both imports and exports in two ways: (1) into several major commodity groups defined in accordance with the United Nations system called the Standard International Trade Classification (SITC) and (2) by direction of trade for each country with major world trading blocs and partners. These commodity groupings are defined by the SITC code numbers beneath the column headings. The single-digit numbers represent broad SITC categories (in the SITC, called "sections"); the double-digit numbers represent subcategories ("divisions") of the single-digit categories (27 is a subcategory of 2); the three-digit number is a subcategory ("group") of the double-digit (667 is a subcategory of 66). Where a plus or minus sign is used before one of these SITC numbers, the SITC category or subcategory is being added to or subtracted from the aggregate implied by the total of the preceding sections. The SITC commodity aggregations used here are listed in the table at the end of this headnote. The full SITC commodity breakdown is presented in the United Nations publication *Standard International Trade Classification.*

The SITC was developed by the United Nations through its Statistical Commission as an outgrowth of the need for a standard system of aggregating commodities of external trade to provide international comparability of foreign trade statistics. The United Nations Statistical Commission has defined external merchandise trade as "all goods whose movement into or out of the customs area of a country compiling the statistics adds to or subtracts from the material resources of the country." Goods passing through a country for transport only are excluded, but goods entering for reexport, or deposited (as in a bonded warehouse, or free trade area) for reimport, are included. Statistics in this table refer only to goods and exclude purely financial transactions that are covered in the "Finance" and "National product and accounts" tables. Gold for fabrication (*e.g.,* as jewelry) is included; monetary and reserve gold are excluded.

For purposes of comparability of data, total value of imports and exports is given in this table in U.S. dollars. Conversions from currencies other than U.S. dollars are determined according to the average market rates for the year for which data are supplied; these are mainly as calculated by the International Monetary Fund (IMF) or other official sources. The commodity categories are given in terms of percentages of the total value of the country's import or export trade (with the exclusions noted above). Value is based on transaction value: for imports, the value at which the goods were purchased by the importer plus the cost of transportation and insurance to the frontier of the importing country (c.i.f. [cost, insurance, and freight] valuation); for exports, the value at which the goods were

Trade: external

country	year	imports												
		total value ('000,000 U.S.$)	Standard International Trade Classification (SITC) categories (%)							direction of trade (%)				
			food and agricultural raw materials (0 + 1 + 2 – 27 – 28 + 4)	mineral ores and concentrates (27 + 28 + 667)	fuels and other energy (3)	manufactured goods				from European Union (EU)[b]	from United States	from Japan	from China	from all other[c]
						total[a] (5 + 6 – 667 + 7 + 8 + 9)	of which chemicals and related products (5)	of which machinery and transport equipment (7)	of which other[a] (6 – 667 + 8 + 9)					
Afghanistan	2001	576.5[1]	— 19.9[2, 3] —		2.7[2]	77.4[2, 4]	—	15.2[2]	62.2[2, 4]	8.2[1]	1.1[1]	8.6[1]	3.3[1]	78.8[1]
Albania	2002	1,503.7	21.1	0.6	9.0	69.2	7.0	21.4	40.9	74.0	1.7	0.6	2.5	21.2
Algeria	2000	9,152.1	30.8	0.2	1.4	67.6	11.0	34.5	21.6	58.7	11.4	3.0	2.3	24.6
American Samoa	2000[5]	505.9	— 64.0[3, 6] —		7.0[6]	29.0[4, 6]	…	6.0[6]	23.0[4, 6]	—	24.8	0.7	0.3	74.1
Andorra	2002	1,198.1	19.8	0.6	4.5	75.2	10.1	25.8	39.2	87.9	1.3	4.2	1.5	5.2
Angola	2001	3,179.2	— 33.6[3, 7] —		0.3[7]	66.1[4, 7]	9.1[7]	30.1[7]	26.9[4, 7]	42.5[1]	9.6[1]	1.1[1]	1.6[1]	45.3[1]
Antigua and Barbuda	1999	356.0	24.6	0.5	10.5	64.5	6.8	32.3	25.4	10.0	49.4	10.2	0.3	30.1
Argentina	2002	8,989.5	7.0	3.3	4.7	84.9	31.4	31.3	22.2	23.4	20.1	3.5	3.7	49.4
Armenia	2003	1,211.8	18.5	23.3	14.0	44.3	7.7	14.3	22.3	31.5	8.2	0.6	0.9	58.8
Aruba	1999	786.5[9]	21.7	4.1	—	74.2	10.4	36.9	26.9	14.6	66.1	1.4	0.2	17.7
Australia	2002	69,260.4	5.9	0.6	7.3	86.2	11.6	45.8	28.7	23.0	18.2	12.1	9.9	36.8
Austria	2002	68,227.9	9.1	0.7	6.4	83.8	11.0	39.7	33.2	77.0	5.0	2.3	1.9	13.8
Azerbaijan	2003	2,626.4	12.7	1.6	11.3	74.4	5.6	38.7	30.1	33.0	5.0	3.9	3.5	54.6
Bahamas, The	2001	1,927.3	19.6	0.3	15.2	64.9	7.6	26.9	30.4	2.1	83.3	1.2	—	13.4
Bahrain	2001	4,262.7	12.8	6.7	37.2	43.3	5.0	18.9	19.4	17.7	5.1	5.3	3.2	68.7
Bangladesh	2001	8,096.6	22.9	0.8	5.3	71.1	10.7	22.6	37.7	9.4	3.6	7.3	11.0	68.7
Barbados	2002	996.5	21.5	0.7	6.3	71.6	12.3	27.2	32.1	17.5	44.1	4.5	2.7	31.2
Belarus	2003	11,504.9	13.7	1.8	26.4	58.1	10.5	22.4	25.2	21.8	1.3	0.3	0.6	75.9[11]
Belgium	2001	178,698.4	10.3	7.7	8.6	73.3	17.8	31.7	23.8	71.6	7.0	2.9	2.2	16.3
Belize	2000	446.9	14.6	0.3	17.0	68.2	10.3	28.7	29.1	11.3	50.1	2.5	0.7	35.3
Benin	2001	601.9	25.4	0.9	17.3	56.4	11.1	16.3	29.0	44.7	4.3	3.1	8.0	40.0
Bermuda	1995	680.2	21.4	2.1	6.0	70.4	7.8	25.3	37.3	11.1	71.2	4.0	0.1	13.4
Bhutan	1999	182.1	19.2	0.6	10.4	69.9	6.1	41.7	22.0	1.3	0.3	3.3	0.9	94.2[14]
Bolivia	2002	1,769.3	14.3	0.2	5.0	80.4	15.7	29.4	35.4	8.5	15.6	5.5	4.8	65.5
Bosnia and Herzegovina	2003	3,311.9	21.2	1.6	7.7	69.5	11.3	25.3	32.9	57.6	1.5	0.9	1.8	38.2
Botswana	2001	1,810.8	14.7	2.4	6.7	76.1	7.2	32.0	37.0	11.5	1.8	0.3	0.4	86.1[17]
Brazil	2002	49,734.9	8.3	1.1	15.2	75.4	20.3	39.3	15.8	28.2	21.9	4.9	3.4	41.5
Brunei	1998	1,566.0	16.9	1.8	0.4	81.0	6.1	33.3	41.6	15.2	15.0	6.4	1.5	61.9
Bulgaria	2001	7,278.1	6.7	4.0	5.0	84.3	10.1	27.5	46.6	54.7	2.6	1.1	1.2	40.4
Burkina Faso	2001	788.4	15.6	0.4	25.1	58.9	9.2	33.3	16.3	37.3	3.6	11.8	3.3	44.0
Burundi	2001	138.9	15.6	1.5	12.5	70.3	18.3	23.4	28.6	35.9	3.1	4.4	4.1	52.4
Cambodia	1998	1,080.3	17.2[18, 19]	…	11.7[18]	…	6.5[18, 19]	17.0[18, 19]	…	8.3	3.6	6.6	8.9	72.7
Cameroon	2001	1,852.2	16.6	3.1	18.4	62.0	11.0	26.1	24.8	47.9	7.9	4.5	2.7	36.9
Canada	2002	222,240.9	7.3	1.4	4.9	86.4	9.7	49.3	27.4	11.4	62.6	4.4	4.6	17.0
Cape Verde	2001	247.5	36.2	0.2	5.6	58.0	6.4	27.9	23.7	74.2	3.2	—	7.4	15.2
Central African Republic	1996	179.9	25.9	0.4	8.1	65.6	7.9	37.4	20.3	48.7	1.7	8.7	0.3	40.6
Chad	1995	215.2	24.9	0.4	17.9	56.8	7.4	23.9	25.4	51.3	6.5	2.4	2.9	37.0
Chile	2002	15,383.4	9.1	0.5	16.4	73.9	13.4	35.6	25.0	19.7	16.6	3.5	7.2	53.1
China	2002	295,170.0	7.4	3.1	6.5	82.9	13.2	46.4	23.3	13.3	9.2	18.1	—	59.3
Colombia	2002	12,689.9	14.4	0.4	1.5	83.6	22.4	36.8	24.5	11.2	52.1	4.3	1.8	30.7
Comoros	2000	71.9	22.3	0.1	4.1	73.5	2.3	10.1	61.2	23.5	0.1	0.3	0.6	75.4
Congo, Dem. Rep. of the	2002	906.0	— 20.0[22] —		13.8[22]	66.2[22]	4.4[22]	45.5[22]	16.3[22]	41.8[1]	3.4[1]	1.5[1]	2.3[1]	51.0[1]
Congo, Rep. of the	2002	1,113.0	21.7[23]	0.4[23]	19.6[23]	58.3[23]	13.9[23]	20.2[23]	24.2[23]	49.5[1]	5.2[1]	0.7[1]	3.9[1]	40.7[1]
Costa Rica	2002	6,894.2	8.7	0.4	6.7	84.2	14.3	41.9	27.9	11.2	52.1	4.3	1.8	30.7
Côte d'Ivoire	2000	2,482.2	18.2	0.7	33.7	47.3	14.3	16.4	16.5	42.2	3.6	2.9	2.7	48.6
Croatia	2003	14,153.3	10.0	0.5	11.0	78.6	11.0	37.2	30.4	72.0	2.6	1.7	2.8	20.8
Cuba	2001	4,838.7	18.7	0.3	20.2	60.8	10.1	25.7	25.1	32.7	0.1	1.7	12.6	52.9
Cyprus[24]	2002	4,086.2	13.8	0.3	10.9	75.0	9.6	29.6	35.8	54.1	5.0	6.8	4.0	30.2
Czech Republic	2001	36,476.6	6.6	0.9	9.1	83.4	10.9	42.2	30.3	73.4	4.0	1.9	5.9	14.9
Denmark	2002	49,312.6	14.3	0.4	4.4	80.9	10.6	37.6	32.6	75.3	3.9	1.3	2.8	16.6
Djibouti	1999	52.5	37.7[21]	—[21]	8.1[21]	54.3[21]	6.8[21]	19.2[21]	28.3[21]	49.2[1]	2.0	3.3	2.4	43.0[1]
Dominica	2002	115.7	25.9	0.3	9.5	64.3	12.9	22.0	29.5	14.1	36.6	4.1	0.7	44.5
Dominican Republic	2001	5,496.7	14.1	0.1	22.5	63.2	11.1	29.6	22.6	10.8	44.8	3.9	1.0	39.4
East Timor	2001	237.0[1]	…	…	…	…	…	…	…	…	…	…	…	…
Ecuador	2003	6,534.4	10.7	0.3	10.2	78.7	16.9	37.1	24.8	12.8	21.4	4.2	4.6	56.9

sold by the exporter, including the cost of transportation and insurance to bring the goods onto the transporting vehicle at the frontier of the exporting country (f.o.b. [free-on-board] valuation).

The information presented here is obtained by processing detail from the United Nations' *International Trade Statistics Yearbook,* regional and national publications, and the Internet. In some cases where the original data were only available for an alternative trade classification, an approximation has been made of the SITC commodity groupings. For some countries, where the amounts involved are very small, estimates have been made for selected categories.

The notes that follow further define the column headings.

a. Also includes any unallocated commodities.

b. EU of 25 countries (Austria, Belgium, Cyprus (Republic of Cyprus), Czech Republic, Denmark, Estonia, Finland, France, Germany, Greece, Hungary, Ireland, Italy, Latvia, Lithuania, Luxembourg, Malta, The Netherlands, Poland, Portugal, Slovakia, Slovenia, Spain, Sweden, and the United Kingdom).

c. May include value of trade shown as not available (...) in any of the four preceding columns. May include any unspecified areas or countries.

... Not available.

— None, less than 0.05%, or not applicable.

Detail may not add to 100.0 or indicated subtotals because of rounding.

SITC category codes

0		Food and live animals
1		Beverages and tobacco
2		Crude materials, inedible, except fuels
	27	Crude fertilizers, excluding chemical fertilizers, and crude minerals (excluding coal, petroleum, and precious stones)
	28	Metalliferous ores and metal scrap
3		Mineral fuels, lubricants, and related materials (includes coal, petroleum, natural gas, electric current, etc.)
4		Animal and vegetable oils, fats and waxes
5		Chemicals and related products not elsewhere specified
6		Manufactured goods classified chiefly by material
	667	Pearls, precious and semiprecious stones, unworked or worked
7		Machinery and transport equipment
8		Miscellaneous manufactured articles
9		Commodities and transactions not classified elsewhere in SITC

exports													country
total value ('000,000 U.S.$)	Standard International Trade Classification (SITC) categories (%)							direction of trade (%)					
	food and agricultural raw materials (0 + 1 + 2 – 27 – 28 + 4)	mineral ores and concentrates (27 + 28 + 667)	fuels and other energy (3)	manufactured goods: total[a] (5 + 6 – 667 + 7 + 8 + 9)	of which chemicals and related products (5)	of which machinery and transport equipment (7)	of which other[a] (6 – 667 + 8 + 9)	to European Union (EU)[b]	to United States	to Japan	to China	to all other[c]	
89.3[1]	25.0[1, 2, 3]		...	75.0[1, 2, 4]	...	...	...	25.4[1]	0.7[1]	0.2[1]	0.2[1]	73.5[1]	Afghanistan
313.3	10.4	2.4	0.8	86.5	0.5	3.0	83.0	92.5	1.7	—	—	5.7	Albania
22,031.3	0.2	0.2	98.1	1.5	0.7	0.2	0.6	63.2	15.5	0.1	—	21.1	Algeria
346.3	100.0[1]	—	—	—	—	—	—	...	99.6	...	...	0.4	American Samoa
63.2	4.8	2.0	—	93.2	7.3	40.6	45.3	95.0	0.9	0.2	—	3.9	Andorra
6,379.8	0.3[8]	3.2[8]	96.5[8]	—[8]	—[8]	—[8]	—[8]	25.7[1]	46.7[1]	0.3[1]	10.3[1]	17.0[1]	Angola
15.0	8.4	2.3	0.6	88.7	11.5	39.6	37.6	30.4	21.1	0.2	—	48.3	Antigua and Barbuda
25,709.3	47.2	2.4	17.0	33.4	7.8	10.3	15.3	20.5	11.5	1.6	4.2	62.1	Argentina
667.9	12.6	47.6	2.0	37.9	0.4	3.5	33.9	38.7	8.2	—	0.7	52.4	Armenia
29.4[9]	35.2	16.4	—	48.3	2.4	19.0	26.9	12.4	45.9	—	—	41.7	Aruba
66,365.5	26.0	12.3	20.3	41.4	4.2	11.6	25.6	10.1	8.3	15.2	5.5	60.9	Australia
67,681.7	8.5	0.6	2.4	88.5	9.6	42.8	36.1	73.6	5.1	1.2	1.1	18.9	Austria
2,591.7	6.3	1.3	86.0	6.3	2.0	1.4	3.0	67.4	2.5	0.8	0.7	28.7	Azerbaijan
375.9	34.0	5.7	18.3	42.0	26.0	12.0	4.0	17.8	77.5	0.2	—	4.4	Bahamas, The
5,544.7	0.7	4.6	65.8	28.9	2.4	0.7	25.8	2.4	8.1	1.1	0.6	87.7[10]	Bahrain
5,681.8	8.2	—	0.2	91.7	1.3	0.9	89.5	45.2	39.0	1.8	0.2	13.9	Bangladesh
215.5	34.9	0.2	12.2	52.6	14.5	12.5	25.6	17.5	16.5	0.1	0.2	65.8	Barbados
9,964.3	12.2	0.7	22.0	65.2	11.9	22.8	30.6	35.8	1.0	—	1.6	61.5[12]	Belarus
190,308.8	10.6	6.8	4.0	78.6	21.0	31.2	26.4	77.7	5.6	1.0	0.8	14.9	Belgium
200.2	83.0	—	2.0	14.9	0.3	1.3	13.2	34.6	54.7	1.8	—	8.9	Belize
181.8[13]	88.4	0.1	—	11.5	0.8	1.0	9.7	18.2	0.1	0.1	0.2	81.4	Benin
62.9	1.5	—	—	98.5	—	—	98.5	0.3	49.7	—	—	44.1	Bermuda
116.0	15.0	3.1	41.9[15]	39.9	11.5	0.3	28.2	0.1	0.5	0.1	—	99.3[16]	Bhutan
1,371.6	34.0	14.8	25.0	26.3	0.9	3.0	22.5	7.1	14.1	0.4	0.6	77.8	Bolivia
1,027.5	18.4	3.0	6.1	72.4	2.3	17.5	52.7	53.1	0.9	—	—	46.0	Bosnia and Herzegovina
2,532.9	3.6	89.3	0.1	7.0	1.3	2.9	2.8	86.7	0.2	—	—	13.1	Botswana
60,361.8	31.8	6.3	4.9	57.0	6.0	24.4	26.6	25.5	25.7	3.5	4.2	41.1	Brazil
2,306.8	0.1	0.1	88.6	11.3	0.1	4.8	6.4	2.0	9.1	53.1	—	35.7	Brunei
5,113.9	12.0	2.3	9.0	76.7	9.1	11.0	56.7	58.2	5.6	0.3	0.2	35.8	Bulgaria
188.2	77.0	—	2.9	20.1	1.3	6.0	12.8	36.1	0.6	2.2	—	61.1	Burkina Faso
42.2	75.5	8.8	—	15.8	—	—	15.7	48.8	0.1	—	—	51.1	Burundi
796.1	88.9[18, 20]	...	...	...	...	...	...	16.5	36.8	1.0	5.3	40.5	Cambodia
1,749.4	38.1	—	51.9	10.0	0.6	0.3	9.1	69.7	2.1	0.1	5.9	22.2	Cameroon
252,418.4	12.9	1.7	12.6	72.8	6.1	38.1	28.7	4.5	87.2	2.1	1.0	5.2	Canada
9.8[20]	3.5	—	—	96.5	0.3	2.2	94.0	80.6	17.7	—	—	1.7	Cape Verde
115.1	25.4	60.1	0.2	14.3	—	7.5	6.8	95.1	—	—	—	4.8	Central African Republic
251.6	88.2[21]	—[21]	—[21]	11.9[21]	6.5[21]	3.1[21]	2.3[21]	77.4[1]	2.4[1]	2.4[1]	1.0[1]	16.7[1]	Chad
17,423.1	37.7	13.3	1.2	47.8	6.2	2.5	39.1	24.4	20.0	11.1	7.0	37.5	Chile
325,595.9	5.8	0.7	2.6	91.0	4.7	39.0	47.3	16.1	21.5	14.9	—	47.5	China
11,897.5	24.5	1.1	35.9	38.4	11.2	5.6	21.7	13.8	44.8	1.6	0.2	39.5	Colombia
6.9	88.8	—	—	11.2	5.9	2.1	3.2	59.0	16.5	—	—	24.5	Comoros
1,415.0	13.1[21]	58.5[3, 21]	11.1[21]	17.3[4, 21]	0.2[21]	1.2[21]	15.9[4, 21]	75.6[1]	10.7[1]	2.0[1]	0.8[1]	10.9[1]	Congo, Dem. Rep. of the
2,272.0	9.3[23]	0.3[23]	87.6[23]	2.7[23]	—[23]	0.4[23]	2.3[23]	21.1	8.4	3.3	9.3	57.9	Congo, Rep. of the
4,950.4	34.7	0.2	1.0	64.1	7.2	28.5	28.4	17.7	50.7	0.6	0.7	30.3	Costa Rica
3,627.9	63.6	0.2	20.3	15.9	4.2	1.0	10.7	45.8	8.3	0.2	0.1	45.6	Côte d'Ivoire
6,164.2	16.4	1.2	9.6	72.7	9.6	29.2	33.9	67.8	2.7	1.2	0.1	28.3	Croatia
1,660.6	59.4	29.1	1.5	10.1	3.2	1.1	5.8	41.1	—	1.7	4.3	52.9	Cuba
837.3	30.5	2.0	8.1	59.4	11.8	27.3	20.3	52.8	2.3	0.2	0.1	44.6	Cyprus[24]
33,384.2	5.8	0.7	3.0	90.4	6.4	47.4	36.6	85.4	3.0	0.4	0.5	10.8	Czech Republic
55,685.5	22.3	0.5	6.2	71.0	12.2	29.4	29.4	64.1	5.9	2.6	0.9	26.5	Denmark
151.1[1]	26.6[21, 25]	0.1[21, 25]	0.2[21, 25]	73.1[21, 25]	0.2[21, 25]	7.9[21, 25]	65.0[21, 25]	24.8[1]	0.1[1]	—[1]	—[1]	75.1[1, 26]	Djibouti
41.9	39.1	3.5	—	57.4	51.4	4.7	1.4	29.3	9.2	—	—	61.6	Dominica
814.3	42.4	1.4	15.8	40.4	6.6	1.4	32.4	18.8	40.2	1.2	—	39.7	Dominican Republic
8.0	...	...	...	...	...	...	...	...	...	...	...	...	East Timor
6,038.5	46.3	—	43.2	10.5	1.9	3.1	5.4	17.5	40.6	1.4	0.2	40.2	Ecuador

Trade: external (continued)

country	year	imports: total value ('000,000 U.S.$)	Standard International Trade Classification (SITC) categories (%): food and agricultural raw materials (0 + 1 + 2 – 27 – 28 + 4)	mineral ores and concentrates (27 + 28 + 667)	fuels and other energy (3)	manufactured goods: total[a] (5 + 6 – 667 + 7 + 8 + 9)	of which chemicals and related products (5)	of which machinery and transport equipment (7)	of which other[a] (6 – 667 + 8 + 9)	direction of trade (%): from European Union (EU)[b]	from United States	from Japan	from China	from all other[c]
Egypt	2002	10,386.9	18.1	2.7	4.8	74.4	14.8	24.1	35.5	31.7	8.4	3.2	5.2	51.4
El Salvador	2002	3,907.3	20.2	0.3	12.9	66.6	15.9	23.3	27.4	7.9	33.6	3.5	2.8	52.2
Equatorial Guinea	2002	410.0	13.5[27]	3.4[27]	7.7[27]	75.4[27]	3.9[27]	58.2[27]	13.3[27]	55.2[1]	29.2[1]	0.4[1]	0.8[1]	14.4[1]
Eritrea	1998	526.8	— 21.8[3] —		1.5	76.7[4]	5.7	38.3	32.7[4]	32.3[29]	4.2	4.0	0.6	58.9
Estonia	2002	5,863.3	14.4	0.9	7.2	77.5	9.9	38.1	29.5	63.1	2.8	3.8	4.6	25.6
Ethiopia	2002	1,593.8	12.2	0.7	12.4	74.7	13.0	32.3	29.4	30.9	7.9	7.1	9.1	45.0
Faroe Islands	1999	477.5	22.7	0.4	8.1	68.8	7.0	36.6	25.2	55.3	1.3	2.4	1.3	39.8
Fiji	2003	1,068.6	18.6	0.3	12.2	68.9	8.1	27.9	32.9	2.2	9.2	5.4	3.1	80.2
Finland	2002	33,440.0	8.8	3.4	11.5	76.3	11.7	39.8	24.8	59.4	6.6	4.4	3.5	26.2
France[30]	2003	362,398.4	10.5	0.9	9.6	79.0	13.6	36.9	28.6	62.7	6.5	3.2	4.1	23.4
French Guiana	1995	783.3	18.8	0.1	5.3	75.8	8.0	42.2	25.6	77.0	3.3	1.4	0.6	17.6
French Polynesia	2003	1,306.4	18.7	0.1	6.3	74.8	7.5	43.3	24.0	55.3	8.9	3.1	3.7	29.0
Gabon	2000	956.1	19.0	0.3	4.1	76.6	8.6	47.9	20.1	59.7	11.1	—	0.7	28.5
Gambia, The	2000	189.4	35.2	0.2	11.9	52.7	5.6	21.9	25.2	53.1	4.0	2.7	7.5	32.7
Gaza Strip[31]	1994	339.3	...	...	...	...	...	...	...	...	...	...	...	100.0[32]
Georgia	2001	678.7	19.7	0.5	22.8	57.0	11.1	25.6	20.3	30.8	4.1	0.4	0.6	64.1
Germany	2003	601,761.1	8.9	1.1	8.6	81.3	10.5	37.2	33.6	60.0	7.0	3.6	4.7	24.8
Ghana	2000	2,933.2	15.1	2.4	21.4	61.0	9.8	30.4	20.8	43.3	7.5	1.8	3.2	44.3
Greece	2001	28,184.0	13.4	0.7	15.2	70.8	12.3	31.6	26.9	56.5	3.5	3.0	3.0	34.0
Greenland	2001	303.3	19.3	0.5	16.7	63.5	4.2	24.9	34.4	63.0	0.1	0.1	—	36.8
Grenada	2002	198.8	24.0	0.3	10.0	65.7	8.0	25.0	32.8	13.3	43.6	3.2	1.1	38.7
Guadeloupe	1995	1,901.3	22.6	0.3	5.8	71.3	9.5	32.0	29.8	78.1	3.3	2.2	0.8	15.6
Guam	2001	575.2	16.9[34]	0.1[34]	46.9[34]	36.2[34]	2.3[34]	19.1[34]	14.8[34]	1.3[1]	0.2[1]	22.6	—	75.9[1]
Guatemala	2002	6,074.5	14.6	0.4	12.7	72.3	17.0	30.1	25.2	11.0	36.2	5.6	3.3	43.9
Guernsey[35]	1998	...	...	...	...	...	...	...	...	...	...	...	...	...
Guinea	2001	600.8	24.6	0.2	18.6	56.6	11.5	24.9	20.1	49.2	7.1	3.9	5.4	34.5
Guinea-Bissau	2002	112.0	44.1[23]	0.1[23]	16.2[23]	39.7[23]	4.9[23]	22.9[23]	11.8[23]	37.8[1]	2.4[1]	1.2	3.8[1]	54.9[1]
Guyana	2002	564.5	16.2	0.2	22.2	61.4	12.0	24.1	25.3	13.5	34.7	4.0	3.4	44.5
Haiti	2002	1,181.0	— 40.2[3, 36] —		10.6[36]	49.3[4, 36]	7.3[36]	15.8[36]	26.1[4, 36]	9.9[1]	54.2[1]	0.2	2.2[1]	33.5[1]
Honduras	2002	3,105.3	16.8	0.2	12.9	70.1	17.2	28.3	24.6	6.3	39.0	5.4	0.6	48.7
Hong Kong	2003	233,193.9	4.6	2.6	2.0	90.8	5.8	48.2	36.8	8.5	5.5	11.8	43.3	30.9
Hungary	2002	37,611.6	4.5	0.3	7.4	87.8	9.1	51.6	27.1	63.7	3.7	4.2	5.5	22.9
Iceland	2003	2,792.9	12.2	3.9	7.8	76.1	10.4	35.3	30.4	63.8	7.5	3.8	3.6	21.4
India	2002	61,118.1	8.3	12.3	32.0	47.4	9.2	18.9	19.3	20.8	7.3	3.0	4.5	64.4
Indonesia	2002	31,288.8	16.8	1.7	21.0	60.5	16.9	27.5	16.2	12.6	8.5	14.1	7.8	57.1
Iran	2002	20,335.7	11.7	0.9	2.7	84.8	11.3	47.9	25.6	41.7	0.3	3.5	4.7	49.8
Iraq	2002	5,529.0	— 31.5[3, 27] —		0.4[27]	68.1[4, 27]	8.8[27]	30.3[27]	28.9[4, 27]	34.1[1]	0.6[1]	6.0	8.4[1]	50.9[1]
Ireland	2002	52,203.6	8.1	0.6	3.2	88.1	12.6	50.6	24.8	59.7	15.3	3.6	2.7	18.7
Isle of Man[35]	...	...	...	...	...	...	...	...	...	...	...	...	...	...
Israel	2002	33,105.9	7.0	22.1	9.4	61.4	9.8	31.5	20.2	41.7	18.5	2.4	2.4	35.0
Italy[38]	2002	242,744.0	12.4	1.5	9.0	77.1	12.9	33.3	30.8	59.8	4.8	2.1	3.2	30.1
Jamaica	2002	3,543.1	16.7	0.2	17.7	65.4	10.2	29.4	25.8	11.7	43.1	6.1	1.7	37.4
Japan	2003	383,452.0	15.2	3.1	21.2	60.5	7.7	27.6	25.3	13.1	15.6	—	19.7	51.6
Jersey	1980	537.1	23.9	0.4	9.3	66.5	6.5	24.8	35.2	84.9[39]	...	...	...	15.1
Jordan	2003	5,653.2	19.3	0.6	16.5	63.6	11.1	23.0	29.5	26.5	6.4	3.5	8.0	55.5
Kazakhstan	2001	6,355.9	8.9	1.8	12.6	76.7	11.4	38.2	27.1	26.6	5.4	2.2	2.8	63.0
Kenya	2002	3,074.6	14.4	0.2	16.7	68.6	16.2	31.8	20.7	33.4	6.9	6.2	2.4	51.1
Kiribati	1999	41.0	39.5	0.2	10.4	49.9	4.5	22.8	22.6	0.5	4.5	14.9	4.4	75.8
Korea, North	2002	2,179.0[1]	...	...	...	...	...	...	...	14.6[1]	1.3[1]	6.6	23.6[1]	54.0[1]
Korea, South	2002	149,572.3	8.9	2.9	21.3	66.9	9.3	34.9	22.7	11.5	15.3	19.7	11.6	41.8
Kuwait	1999	7,616.7	17.8	1.0	0.6	80.6	8.7	39.7	32.2	31.3	12.3	12.8	3.2	40.4
Kyrgyzstan	2002	579.4	15.2	2.1	26.2	56.5	18.8	21.2	21.6	14.9	8.2	1.1	10.2	65.6
Laos	2000	610.9	— 36.8[3, 23] —		6.1[23]	57.1[4, 23]	...	29.3[23]	27.8[4, 23]	7.1[1]	—	4.5	4.7	83.7
Latvia	2003	5,244.0	14.4	1.2	9.4	75.0	12.4	31.0	31.7	75.4	1.7	0.2	1.3	21.4
Lebanon	2001	7,290.3	18.7	1.6	17.7	62.0	9.9	23.6	28.5	43.7	7.1	3.2	5.6	40.4
Lesotho	2001	598.2	28.0	0.6	6.0	65.4	9.7	12.1	43.6	0.3	0.3	0.2	0.5	98.8[41]
Liberia	2002	4,614.0	— 36.5[3, 43] —		24.2[43]	39.2[4, 43]	7.1[43]	18.6[43]	13.6[4, 43]	32.1[1]	0.7[1]	17.9	0.7[1]	48.6[1]
Libya	1998	5,691.8	28.4	0.4	0.3	71.0	7.4	33.3	30.4	58.6	1.4	4.2	1.4	34.4
Liechtenstein	2002	872.9	3.9[1]	0.5[1, 3]	1.2[1]	94.4[1]	5.0[1]	46.0[1]	43.3[1, 4]	87.2[1]	3.3	0.8	0.6	8.2[1]
Lithuania	2001	6,352.8	12.1	0.9	20.3	66.7	12.2	28.2	26.3	63.6	1.9	0.1	0.7	33.6
Luxembourg	2001	10,942.5	10.9	4.3	5.6	79.2	9.8	39.2	30.2	87.8	6.1	1.1	0.4	4.6
Macau	2002	2,530.8	14.5	0.1	7.2	78.1	3.5	19.5	55.1	12.0	4.1	6.7	41.7	35.4
Macedonia	2003	2,299.9	15.7	0.8	14.0	69.5	11.1	18.8	39.6	53.1	2.5	0.8	2.1	41.5
Madagascar	1999	505.3	14.3	0.1	24.2	61.4	11.5	26.9	23.1	32.4	3.0	5.1	6.7	52.9
Malawi	2001	561.6	13.3	0.3	16.8	69.6	13.3	29.1	27.2	15.0	3.6	3.4	2.7	75.3
Malaysia	2002	79,359.4	6.5	0.9	4.8	87.9	7.1	61.5	19.2	11.7	16.9	18.0	7.8	45.5
Maldives	2003	470.8	23.2	1.8	11.8	63.3	5.4	27.2	30.6	11.2	1.3	2.2	0.6	84.7
Mali	1997	680.8	20.0	0.1	20.9	59.0	17.4	21.5	20.1	36.0	3.5	3.0	3.5	53.9
Malta	2001	2,726.8	11.6	0.3	8.3	79.8	7.3	49.4	23.1	64.4	11.6	2.1	2.0	19.9
Marshall Islands	2000	68.2	— 19.4[3] —		43.5	37.1[4]	—	16.9	20.2[4]	—	61.4	5.1	1.3	32.2
Martinique	1995	1,969.8	20.4	0.2	7.5	71.9	10.3	32.4	29.2	77.0	2.9	2.2	0.6	17.4
Mauritania	1996	426.7	26.9	0.1	29.3	43.8	3.0	24.8	15.9	64.6	0.3	0.8	5.6	28.7
Mauritius	2003	2,360.0	19.4	2.2	10.9	67.5	8.7	22.4	36.4	28.8	2.6	3.5	8.4	56.7
Mayotte	1997	141.1	— 28.8[1, 3] —		5.0	71.2[1, 4]	7.7	30.8	32.7[1, 4]	66.0[44]	...	...	...	34.0
Mexico	2002	168,650.5	7.5	0.7	2.6	89.2	9.8	51.1	28.2	10.0	63.4	5.5	3.7	17.4
Micronesia	1998	49.4	— 37.3[3] —		8.9	53.8[4]	3.6	20.0	30.2[4]	...	45.7	14.0	...	40.4
Moldova	2003	1,398.6	17.7	0.4	20.5	61.4	11.9	19.7	29.8	36.0	2.5	0.8	1.5	59.2
Monaco[30]	...	...	...	...	...	...	...	...	...	...	...	...	...	...
Mongolia	2001	630.1	18.6	0.3	22.1	59.0	5.5	29.3	24.3	12.7	2.3	8.8	19.0	57.2
Morocco	2002	11,878.2	17.3	1.3	15.5	65.9	9.8	25.6	30.5	57.5	4.3	1.7	2.9	33.6
Mozambique	2001	1,063.4	14.6	0.8	15.9	68.6	6.4	21.9	40.3	17.3	1.8	0.6	2.0	78.2
Myanmar (Burma)	1999	2,587.4	— 8.7[3, 6] —		4.4[6]	86.9[4, 6]	8.6[6]	27.0[6]	51.3[4, 6]	3.1	3.5	11.1	9.6	72.6
Namibia	2001	1,552.9	13.7	2.0	10.3	73.9	10.7	34.4	28.8	6.1	0.9	0.2	1.1	91.8[45]
Nauru	2001	27.4	87.8[8]	...[8]	...[8]	12.2[8]	...[8]	2.8[8]	9.3[8]	9.1[1]	16.9	0.6	1.6	71.8[1]
Nepal	2000	1,557.9	15.4	1.3	15.2	68.2	10.7	17.2	40.3	7.4	1.5	2.6	7.5	80.9

exports													country
total value ('000,000 U.S.$)	Standard International Trade Classification (SITC) categories (%)							direction of trade (%)					
	food and agricultural raw materials (0 + 1 + 2 – 27 – 28 + 4)	mineral ores and concen-trates (27 + 28 + 667)	fuels and other energy (3)	manufactured goods				to European Union (EU)[b]	to United States	to Japan	to China	to all other[c]	
				total[a] (5 + 6 – 667 + 7 + 8 + 9)	of which chemicals and related products (5)	of which machinery and transport equipment (7)	of which other[a] (6 – 667 + 8 + 9)						
4,009.3	2.9	2.4	39.2	55.5	7.6	1.7	46.2	28.8	8.7	1.3	4.9	56.2	Egypt
1,233.8	33.5	0.5	5.2	60.8	14.7	4.6	41.5	6.3	20.3	0.5	0.6	72.3	El Salvador
1,863.0	48.6[27]	—[27]	—[27]	51.4[27]	0.1[27]	39.8[27, 28]	11.5[27]	34.7[1]	27.0[1]	2.5	16.6[1]	19.1[1]	Equatorial Guinea
27.9	75.1[13]		…	24.9[4]	2.1	2.4	20.4[4]	10.0[29]	2.0	13.2	—	74.8	Eritrea
4,336.3	20.5	1.6	5.3	72.7	5.6	27.6	39.5	72.1	2.2	0.6	0.5	24.6	Estonia
415.0	83.6	1.3	—	15.0	0.1	0.1	14.9	37.2	4.0	9.0	1.8	48.0	Ethiopia
477.9	94.7	—	—	5.3	0.1	3.8	1.4	83.8	4.6	1.2	0.1	10.2	Faroe Islands
494.4	51.7	0.2	—	48.1	1.4	0.6	46.2	22.2	24.5	4.5	0.8	47.9	Fiji
44,517.7	8.2	0.4	3.3	88.0	7.0	43.6	37.4	58.8	8.7	2.0	2.5	28.0	Finland
357,881.2	12.9	0.7	2.6	83.8	16.9	42.8	24.1	66.3	6.9	1.7	1.4	23.7	France[30]
158.2	33.6	0.1	0.2	66.1	1.4	33.0	31.7	77.5	1.0	—	—	21.5	French Guiana
125.2	16.7	64.8	—	18.5	1.6	12.5	4.5	16.2	14.6	30.3	0.7	38.3	French Polynesia
2,600.2	12.7	1.7	83.3	2.3	0.1	0.4	1.9	7.5	62.6	—	6.7	23.2	Gabon
16.2	82.0	—	0.1	17.9	9.6	4.7	3.5	32.4	1.8	0.2	0.1	65.5	Gambia, The
49.4	…	…	…	…	…	…	…	…	…	…	…	100.0[33]	Gaza Strip[31]
320.0	27.6	25.1	8.6	38.7	6.1	18.1	14.5	19.8	3.0	0.3	0.3	76.6	Georgia
748,531.3	5.1	0.6	1.5	92.8	12.9	50.3	29.6	62.7	9.2	1.8	2.7	23.6	Germany
1,670.9	37.2	2.8	4.9	55.1	0.6	1.2	53.3	47.3	5.9	1.4	1.7	43.8	Ghana
10,302.9	27.0	1.8	11.1	60.0	9.0	11.5	39.6	51.5	5.5	0.6	0.4	41.9	Greece
277.0	88.7	—	—	11.3	—	3.1	8.2	85.9	5.8	3.5	0.1	4.8	Greenland
38.3	65.3	—	0.1	34.7	8.0	14.2	12.5	35.7	29.3	0.6	—	34.4	Grenada
162.0	52.3	0.6	—	47.0	1.1	36.5	9.4	77.0	3.4	—	—	19.6	Guadeloupe
55.6	69.5[3, 21]		0.7[21]	29.7[4, 21]	0.7[21]	3.8[21]	25.2[4, 21]	0.7[1]	1.3[1]	89.3	—	8.7[1]	Guam
2,277.5	57.4	0.3	6.9	35.4	14.7	3.5	17.2	5.5	30.3	1.3	—	62.9	Guatemala
93.0[1]	…	…	…	…	…	…	…	…	…	…	…	…	Guernsey[35]
574.9	2.1	53.9	0.8	43.2	17.2	2.1	24.0	64.1	16.9	—	—	19.1	Guinea
117.0	88.2[23]	0.1[23]	4.6[23]	7.2[23]	—[23]	6.6[23]	0.6[23]	5.9[1]	—[1]	—	—[1]	94.1[1]	Guinea-Bissau
446.5	52.2	11.3	—	36.6	1.0	2.3	33.2	25.2	25.5	0.2	0.4	48.7	Guyana
286.0	15.1	0.7	—	84.2	5.6	3.1	75.5	4.3[1]	83.9[1]	0.1	—[1]	11.7[1]	Haiti
1,248.3	53.5	4.4	—	42.0	4.8	2.4	34.9	14.6	54.8	1.4	0.1	29.1	Honduras
228,654.3	2.1	1.6	0.2	96.1	4.7	46.1	45.3	14.1	18.2	5.3	41.7	20.6	Hong Kong
34,336.6	8.2	0.4	1.5	89.9	6.2	58.6	25.1	81.8	3.5	0.6	0.5	13.7	Hungary
2,352.2	65.1	0.5	0.2	34.1	3.6	4.0	26.6	73.8	9.5	3.2	0.7	12.8	Iceland
52,471.4	13.4	17.6	5.1	63.8	11.2	8.4	44.2	22.5	20.7	3.5	3.7	49.5	India
57,158.7	15.8	3.6	24.3	56.3	5.2	17.1	34.0	14.0	13.2	21.1	5.1	46.3	Indonesia
28,355.8	4.1	0.3	86.5	9.1	2.0	0.7	6.4	36.2[37]	—[37]	16.5[37]	3.7[37]	43.6[37]	Iran
8,257.0	0.8[27]	0.3[1, 27]	96.8[27]	2.1[1, 27]	1.2[27]	0.2[27]	0.7[1, 27]	29.1[1]	41.8[1]	1.2	1.1[1]	26.9[1]	Iraq
88,483.2	7.7	0.5	0.4	91.5	41.9	35.1	14.5	64.7	17.6	2.8	0.6	14.3	Ireland
…	…	…	…	…	…	…	…	…	…	…	…	…	Isle of Man[35]
29,511.4	5.4	35.8	0.4	58.5	13.7	28.7	16.1	26.3	40.2	2.2	1.4	29.8	Israel
251,003.2	7.4	0.3	1.8	90.5	10.4	37.5	42.6	58.2	9.7	1.7	1.5	28.9	Italy[38]
1,104.1	22.8	64.7	2.6	9.9	5.4	1.0	3.5	30.5	28.3	2.6	4.0	34.6	Jamaica
471,995.9	1.0	0.5	0.3	98.2	8.3	66.8	23.1	16.0	24.9	—	12.2	46.9	Japan
209.2	27.6	4.3[40]	—	68.0	1.2	31.1	35.7	67.3[39]	…	…	…	32.7	Jersey
3,081.6	14.4	11.8	0.2	73.5	19.9	10.7	42.9	3.4	21.5	0.5	1.2	73.5	Jordan
8,619.6	6.6	6.4	55.2	31.7	2.7	2.3	26.7	26.4	1.8	0.2	7.6	64.0	Kazakhstan
1,400.4	42.7	2.2	30.7	24.4	2.8	5.4	16.3	29.2	1.4	0.6	0.3	68.5	Kenya
9.1	92.6	0.1	—	7.3	—	—	7.3	10.3	13.4	1.5	—	74.8	Kiribati
1,028.0[1]	…	…	…	…	…	…	…	9.2[1]	—[1]	20.3	23.9[1]	46.5[1]	Korea, North
160,854.8	2.4	0.1	4.1	93.4	8.4	61.5	23.5	14.7	7.9	9.4	14.8	53.3	Korea, South
12,140.1	0.5	0.3	90.6	8.6	5.8	1.3	1.5	12.0[1]	11.6[1]	22.9[1]	1.1[1]	52.3[1]	Kuwait
460.3	26.4	2.9	12.6	58.1	1.6	10.6	45.8	5.4	6.3	—	8.7	79.6	Kyrgyzstan
186.1	35.4[3, 23]		7.0[23]	57.5[4, 23]	…	5.1[23]	52.4[4, 23]	48.2[1]	4.7	6.3	3.6	37.2	Laos
2,893.7	35.9	1.1	1.4	61.6	6.1	9.1	46.4	79.3	2.9	0.9	0.6	16.4	Latvia
889.3	23.7	4.6	0.2	71.5	11.2	13.9	46.3	22.9	6.8	0.6	0.3	69.4	Lebanon
279.6	17.3	0.1	—	82.7	0.5	10.9	71.3	7.9	33.4	—	—	58.8[42]	Lesotho
1,044.0	99.3[3, 43]		—[43]	0.7[4, 43]	—[43]	—[43]	0.7[4, 43]	81.7[1]	4.1[1]	—	4.8[1]	9.3[1]	Liberia
6,131.4	0.7	—	92.6	6.7	4.2	0.1	2.3	82.4	—	—	—	17.5	Libya
1,805.2	6.4[1]	0.4[1, 3]	0.1[1]	93.1[1, 4]	10.2[1]	59.4[1]	23.5[1, 4]	63.0[1]	1.6	0.4	0.8	34.2[1]	Liechtenstein
4,583.0	16.6	1.5	23.1	58.7	7.5	19.9	31.4	70.9	3.8	0.4	—	24.9	Lithuania
8,387.0	7.1	0.5	0.1	92.3	6.0	29.7	56.6	85.6	3.5	0.6	0.6	9.7	Luxembourg
2,356.8	2.2	—	1.2	96.6	1.0	4.2	91.4	23.3	48.4	0.6	15.6	12.2	Macau
1,363.2	18.0	1.7	5.4	74.9	5.1	5.9	63.8	56.8	5.3	0.4	1.1	36.3	Macedonia
232.8	42.5	10.3	2.4	44.8	2.9	0.8	41.0	57.5	5.4	1.4	1.4	34.3	Madagascar
449.4	87.5	0.3	0.1	12.1	0.6	2.8	8.8	31.6	14.4	4.8	0.4	48.9	Malawi
93,281.3	9.8	0.1	8.7	81.4	4.7	59.8	16.9	12.8	20.2	11.2	5.6	50.2	Malaysia
113.0	67.7	0.3	—	32.0	—	—	32.0	15.6	32.3	10.3	—	41.7	Maldives
302.4	92.3	0.1	0.6	7.0	0.1	0.7	6.1	2.5	—	—	—	97.5	Mali
1,958.8	4.0	0.2	5.5	90.4	2.3	63.2	24.9	42.7	10.8	3.0	0.1	34.4	Malta
8.1	98.7[3, 36]		—[36]	1.3[4, 36]	—[36]	—[36]	1.3[4, 36]	—[1]	71.0[1]	—[1]	—[1]	29.0[1]	Marshall Islands
241.9	62.3	1.0	17.8	18.9	2.1	13.0	3.8	78.0	2.6	—	—	19.3	Martinique
517.4	51.7	41.5	4.6	2.1	—	0.9	1.1	51.5	1.1	20.6	0.1	26.7	Mauritania
1,838.7	26.1	2.5	—	71.4	1.8	4.3	65.3	66.1	17.5	0.9	0.4	15.1	Mauritius
3.5	21.3[6, 20]	—[6, 20]	—[6, 20]	78.7[6, 20]	78.7[6, 20]	—[6, 20]	—[6, 20]	80.0[44]	…	…	…	20.0	Mayotte
160,669.9	5.6	0.4	8.9	85.1	3.5	59.0	22.6	3.3	89.1	0.3	0.3	7.1	Mexico
3.3	93.2[3]		—	6.8[4]	…	…	6.8[4]	…	…	94.6	…	5.4	Micronesia
790.3	63.3	2.7	0.6	33.5	1.2	5.2	27.0	26.7	4.3	—	—	69.0	Moldova
…	…	…	…	…	…	…	…	…	…	…	…	…	Monaco[30]
448.5	24.9	39.1	0.9	35.1	0.7	1.0	33.4	9.1	21.3	3.5	51.6	14.4	Mongolia
7,850.3	23.0	6.7	3.7	66.6	11.2	12.6	42.8	73.8	3.1	3.6	0.3	19.2	Morocco
703.1	27.0	0.4	9.5	63.1	0.3	2.5	60.3	9.4	1.0	4.2	0.2	85.3	Mozambique
1,129.7	77.2[3, 6]		0.5[6]	22.2[4, 6]	—[6]	1.1[6]	21.1[4, 6]	5.9	7.9	5.1	11.9	69.1	Myanmar (Burma)
1,404.5	37.1	40.4	0.7	21.8	0.5	3.9	17.5	55.5	3.0	0.7	0.5	40.4	Namibia
8.9	—[8]	100.0[8]	—[8]	—[8]	—[8]	—[8]	—[8]	1.3[1]	—[1]	6.9[1]	…[1]	91.7[1]	Nauru
708.8	10.4	0.2	—	89.4	8.5	0.5	80.4	22.7	27.1	1.4	—	48.8	Nepal

Trade: external (continued)

country	year	imports												
		total value ('000,000 U.S.$)	Standard International Trade Classification (SITC) categories (%)							direction of trade (%)				
			food and agricultural raw materials (0 + 1 + 2 – 27 – 28 + 4)	mineral ores and concentrates (27 + 28 + 667)	fuels and other energy (3)	manufactured goods: total[a] (5 + 6 – 667 + 7 + 8 + 9)	of which chemicals and related products (5)	of which machinery and transport equipment (7)	of which other[a] (6 – 667 + 8 + 9)	from European Union (EU)[b]	from United States	from Japan	from China	from all other[c]
Netherlands, The	2002	163,367.4	13.6	1.1	11.8	73.4	12.7	36.1	24.7	56.5	9.9	3.4	4.9	25.3
Netherlands Antilles	1998	2,061.9	9.8	0.4	58.5	31.4	4.3	10.3	16.7	13.0	18.8	1.4	0.1	66.7
New Caledonia	2003	1,594.3	12.9	0.3	10.5	76.3	7.7	44.2	24.4	59.9	3.5	2.6	2.7	31.2
New Zealand	2002	15,044.1	9.5	1.7	9.3	79.4	12.1	39.8	27.5	19.5	13.6	12.0	8.0	46.9
Nicaragua	2002	1,802.2	16.2	0.1	13.1	70.6	15.9	26.2	28.6	7.2	27.6	5.1	2.1	57.9
Niger	2001	324.5	45.5	1.7	12.5	40.3	9.1	15.0	16.2	29.2	5.8	4.8	6.4	53.8
Nigeria	2000	5,805.4	20.8	0.6	1.7	76.8	20.2	33.6	22.9	48.4	11.4	4.9	4.3	31.0
Northern Mariana Islands	1997	836.2	—— 11.8[3] ——		8.2	80.0[4]	2.5	6.0	71.6[1, 4]	—	7.6	14.1	…	78.3
Norway	2002	34,889.4	9.5	4.2	3.5	82.8	9.5	40.5	32.9	70.4	6.2	3.1	5.3	15.1
Oman	2001	5,798.0	22.9	1.7	2.8	72.6	6.4	39.6	26.7	21.5	6.8	15.4	1.7	54.7
Pakistan	2003	13,013.4	16.2	1.4	23.6	58.8	18.2	24.6	16.1	16.9	6.0	6.6	7.3	63.2
Palau	2000	123.9	—— 20.3[3] ——		12.7	67.0[4]	6.3	27.8	32.9[4]	—	33.0	15.5	0.7	50.7
Panama	2003	3,124.1	15.0	0.2	11.7	73.0	14.1	29.4	29.6	7.4	35.0	6.2	1.5	49.8
Papua New Guinea	2000	1,035.1	19.0	0.6	22.1	58.3	7.1	29.5	21.6	2.4	6.6	11.3	2.0	77.8
Paraguay	2002	1,672.1	13.3	0.7	16.7	69.3	17.7	27.8	23.8	8.7	4.0	0.9	0.8	85.6
Peru	2003	8,469.7	14.3	0.4	17.4	67.9	16.5	28.4	23.0	13.2	18.6	4.4	7.7	56.2
Philippines	2002	35,426.5	8.6	1.1	9.3	81.0	7.5	60.3	13.2	7.9	20.6	20.4	3.5	47.6
Poland	2002	55,085.5	7.9	1.0	9.1	81.9	14.8	37.6	29.5	68.5	3.2	1.9	3.7	22.7
Portugal	2002	39,982.6	14.8	0.6	9.7	75.0	10.9	34.2	29.8	79.7	2.1	1.7	0.8	15.7
Puerto Rico	2003[48]	33,749.7	8.9	0.1	8.0	83.0	46.4	19.1	17.5	29.1	51.5	3.9	1.0	14.5
Qatar	2002	4,052.0	12.7	1.5	0.7	85.1	7.2	46.9	31.0	35.1	13.0	10.5	3.2	38.1
Réunion	1995	2,711.1	21.5	0.2	4.7	73.6	10.7	29.8	33.1	80.1	0.6	2.1	0.9	16.3
Romania	2003	24,003.1	8.3	1.6	10.9	79.2	10.3	29.6	39.4	67.3	2.3	1.2	2.8	26.4
Russia	2003	52,410.1	22.5	2.9	2.4	72.2	13.7	34.6	24.0	50.3	5.7	3.6	6.3	34.2
Rwanda	2002	251.2	19.9	1.5	16.2	62.4	13.6	25.2	23.6	27.8	2.4	2.5	2.0	65.3
St. Kitts and Nevis	2001	189.2	19.4	0.8	7.5	72.3	8.1	27.5	36.8	12.6	50.5	2.5	0.2	34.2
St. Lucia	2002	314.8	25.9	0.7	9.9	63.6	8.4	22.9	32.3	16.9	42.7	3.4	2.4	34.6
St. Vincent and the Grenadines	2003	201.1	24.4	0.3	9.8	65.5	8.8	24.8	31.9	12.8	41.2	3.3	0.9	41.9
Samoa	1999	115.9	—— 35.0[3, 6] ——		11.8[6]	53.2[4, 6]	—[1, 6]	16.9[1, 6]	36.3[4, 6]	3.2	11.9	14.4	1.2	69.3
San Marino[38]	1999	1,707.0	…	…	…	…	…	…	…	…	…	…	…	…
São Tomé and Príncipe	2003	42.2	39.5	0.2	10.5	49.8	5.5	24.0	20.3	78.2	—	6.3	0.1	15.3
Saudi Arabia	2002	32,333.2	17.0	0.4	0.2	82.3	9.6	43.6	29.0	32.7	16.3	11.1	5.3	34.6
Senegal	2001	1,730.2	28.7	1.2	16.8	53.3	11.2	22.8	19.3	52.1	4.2	2.7	2.4	38.6
Serbia and Montenegro	2000	3,710.6	12.9	2.3	20.1	64.7	15.0	22.1	27.7	49.4	2.0	1.3	2.1	45.1
Seychelles	2002	245.7	25.8	0.2	16.5	57.5	5.6	28.2	23.7	50.8	1.6	0.7	0.4	46.5
Sierra Leone	2002	481.0	—— 47.9[3, 23] ——		17.4[23]	34.8[4, 23]	7.6[23]	14.7[23]	12.5[4, 23]	63.8[1]	5.8[1]	0.2[1]	3.3[1]	26.9[1]
Singapore	2003	127,381.3	3.7	0.5	13.5	82.2	6.7	58.9	16.6	13.2	14.1	12.0	8.7	52.1
Slovakia	2003	22,171.2	6.2	1.7	12.0	80.1	9.8	41.1	29.2	73.7	1.9	1.9	2.5	20.0
Slovenia	2003	13,849.6	9.0	1.8	7.7	81.5	13.3	34.4	33.7	75.4	2.4	1.5	2.4	18.4
Solomon Islands	1997	182.6	—— 18.0[3] ——		8.6	73.4[4]	4.9	37.7	30.8[4]	3.1	2.1	14.9	—	79.9
Somalia	2002	354.0	30.3[49]	0.2[49]	4.6[49]	64.9[49]	5.1[49]	37.1[49]	22.7[49]	9.0[1]	1.9[1]	0.1	0.6[1]	88.4[1]
South Africa	2003	33,589.7	6.4	3.5	11.9	78.2	11.0	39.4	27.8	43.4	9.9	7.0	6.4	33.2
Spain	2002	165,919.5	12.0	1.6	10.8	75.5	12.6	38.0	25.0	66.0	4.1	2.4	3.3	24.1
Sri Lanka	2002	6,038.7	15.3	3.9	13.8	67.0	8.8	18.4	39.9	15.1	3.6	5.9	4.3	71.1
Sudan, The	2002	2,492.8	19.6	0.4	4.8	75.2	10.5	37.9	26.8	15.9	0.9	5.4	10.2	67.6
Suriname	2000	526.4	18.5	0.6	6.7	74.2	10.6	36.3	27.3	29.0	26.6	7.8	2.1	34.5
Swaziland	2002	890.7	20.5	0.5	12.7	66.3	11.7	22.6	32.0	2.0	0.2	0.9	1.4	95.5[50]
Sweden	2003	81,817.3	9.6	1.2	9.4	79.8	10.6	39.5	29.7	72.9	3.9	2.2	2.3	18.7
Switzerland[51]	2003	83,382.5	7.5	1.9	4.3	86.3	21.9	30.1	34.2	81.5	5.5	2.1	2.1	8.8
Syria	2002	4,277.5	20.1	0.5	3.0	76.4	13.2	24.1	39.1	29.9	6.9	3.7	5.9	53.5
Taiwan	2002	112,758.0	6.5	1.5	10.3	81.6	12.0	47.5	22.1	10.9	16.1	24.2	7.1	41.7
Tajikistan	2000	644.0	—— 11.2[3] ——		37.5	51.3[4]	36.4	9.6	5.4[4]	6.4	0.2	—	—	93.4
Tanzania	2003	2,192.9	15.0	0.2	18.5	66.2	12.4	31.9	21.9	19.9	3.2	7.7	5.3	63.9
Thailand	2001	62,057.5	7.8	2.2	12.0	78.0	10.7	45.3	22.0	12.6	11.6	22.4	6.0	47.5
Togo	2002	405.3	23.3	1.3	15.0	60.3	10.5	19.7	30.1	43.7	4.6	1.9	2.9	46.9
Tonga	2000	69.4	35.7	0.6[1]	16.3	47.4[1]	6.1	14.0	27.4[1]	0.4	10.4	5.3	1.7	82.1
Trinidad and Tobago	2001	3,932.1	9.6	0.4	23.4	66.6	7.5	40.2	18.9	18.1	34.4	3.5	1.7	42.3
Tunisia	2002	9,522.5	13.1	1.1	9.3	76.5	9.6	29.5	37.4	71.1	3.2	1.7	1.5	22.6
Turkey	2003	68,734.0	7.6	3.3	16.6	72.5	15.0	31.1	26.5	48.4	5.0	2.8	3.8	40.1
Turkmenistan	2000	1,785.5	12.1	0.4	1.2	86.3	8.9	43.8	33.5	13.0	3.5	8.1	0.9	74.5
Tuvalu	1999	8.1	35.2	0.6	9.2	55.1	4.8	24.7	25.6	1.8	0.3	6.1	1.9	89.9
Uganda	2002	1,073.7	16.6	0.9	16.3	66.2	12.1	26.5	27.6	18.4	3.3	8.1	4.1	66.0
Ukraine	2002	16,975.9	7.7	2.3[3]	39.2	50.8[4]	10.6	20.8	19.5[4]	32.2	2.7	1.1	1.5	62.4
United Arab Emirates	1999	25,911.3	—— 33.6[3] ——		0.9	65.4[4]	6.6	28.5	30.4[4]	36.2[1]	9.9	9.5	6.2	38.2[1]
United Kingdom[35]	2003	399,478.2	10.4	2.5	4.6	82.5	11.2	43.6	27.8	54.5	9.9	3.4	5.1	27.2
United States[54]	2003	1,305,091.5	5.9	1.5	12.5	80.1	8.0	40.9	31.2	19.9	—	9.3	12.5	58.3
Uruguay	2002	1,964.3	18.8	0.6	15.0	65.6	21.7	20.1	23.8	17.9	8.4	1.4	3.8	68.5
Uzbekistan	1998	3,288.7	19.3[1, 23]	1.3[1, 23]	1.4[23]	78.0[1, 23]	9.0[1, 23]	44.9[23]	24.1[1, 23]	21.9[1]	7.5	0.3	1.5	68.8[1]
Vanuatu	2000	86.7	—— 24.0[3] ——		15.1	60.9[4]	6.5	28.8	25.6[4]	6.3[1]	1.4	5.1	1.2	86.1
Venezuela	2002	11,673.3	14.0	0.5	2.6	82.9	16.0	43.1	23.7	20.4	32.9	3.7	1.9	41.0
Vietnam	1999	11,742.1	8.8	1.1	9.5	80.6	17.2	29.2	34.2	9.7	2.8	13.8	5.7	68.0
Virgin Islands (U.S.)	2003	5,570.4	…	…	80.3	…	…	…	…	…	10.9	…	…	…
West Bank[31]	1994	102.5[56]	…	…	…	…	…	…	…	…	…	…	…	…
Western Sahara	…	…	…	…	…	…	…	…	…	…	…	…	…	…
Yemen	2000	2,323.7	37.2	0.2	12.0	50.7	9.7	20.8	20.2	18.6	4.4	3.2	3.5	70.3
Zambia	2002	1,252.7	15.6	1.2	7.0	76.2	15.3	31.1	29.8	19.4	1.5	3.2	2.8	73.1
Zimbabwe	2002	2,466.7	13.0	1.3	8.3	77.5	18.7	34.3	24.4	17.0	3.5	2.9	1.9	74.7

[1]Estimate. [2]Year ending March 1996. [3]Excluding precious stones, etc. (667). [4]Including precious stones, etc. (667). [5]Year ending September 30. [6]1996. [7]1991. [8]1994. [9]Excluding mineral fuels; overall totals on a balance of payments basis, f.o.b.: imports U.S.$2,005,200,000, exports U.S.$1,413,500,000. [10]Includes 67.2% for areas unspecified (mainly petroleum and products). [11]Includes 65.7% from Russia. [12]Includes 49.2% to Russia. [13]Excluding reexports, estimated at 51.0% of total exports. [14]Includes 74.7% from India. [15]Mainly electricity. [16]Includes 94.4% to India. [17]Includes 77.5% from South Africa. [18]1993. [19]Main items only. [20]Domestic exports only. [21]1992. [22]1987. [23]1995. [24]Republic of Cyprus. [25]Excludes trade with Ethiopia via rail. [26]Includes 46.1% to Somalia. [27]1990. [28]Includes 38.7% for ships and boats. [29]Main countries only. [30]Figures for France include Monaco. [31]Total external trade for West Bank and Gaza Strip in 2000: imports U.S.$2,382,800,000, exports U.S.$400,900,000. [32]Includes 82.4% from Israel. [33]Includes 69.2% to Israel and 25.1% to Jordan. [34]1983. [35]Figures for United Kingdom include Guernsey, Isle of Man,

exports													country
total value ('000,000 U.S.$)	Standard International Trade Classification (SITC) categories (%)							direction of trade (%)					
	food and agricultural raw materials (0 + 1 + 2 – 27 – 28 + 4)	mineral ores and concentrates (27 + 28 + 667)	fuels and other energy (3)	manufactured goods				to European Union (EU)[b]	to United States	to Japan	to China	to all other[c]	
				total[a] (5 + 6 – 667 + 7 + 8 + 9)	of which chemicals and related products (5)	of which machinery and transport equipment (7)	of which other[a] (6 – 667 + 8 + 9)						
175,385.2	21.3	0.9	7.0	70.8	17.7	32.2	20.9	74.9	5.4	1.1	0.7	17.8	Netherlands, The
1,169.2	4.5	0.5	84.8	10.2	0.8	2.4	7.0	14.6	17.4	0.1	—	68.0	Netherlands Antilles
739.6	4.0	24.7	1.2	70.1	0.2	2.7	67.3	35.8	1.4	21.4	1.3	40.1	New Caledonia
14,382.4	59.5	0.5	1.8	38.3	6.7	9.8	21.8	15.2	15.3	11.5	4.6	53.3	New Zealand
634.8	72.2	0.4	2.0	25.3	2.7	4.4	18.3	10.0	29.1	0.6	—	60.3	Nicaragua
154.0	40.7	56.5	—	2.8	0.2	1.2	1.4	40.4	0.3	16.5	—	42.8	Niger
27,055.2	0.1	—	99.6	0.2	—	0.1	0.1	23.0	42.6	0.4	0.5	33.5	Nigeria
263.0	—	—	—	100.0	—	—	100.0	—	100.0	—		—	Northern Mariana Islands
59,574.7	7.3	0.6	60.6	31.4	3.1	11.7	16.6	76.1	8.8	1.8	1.6	11.7	Norway
11,036.6	6.2	0.3	80.5	13.1	0.9	7.7	4.5	2.4	1.3	20.1	11.2	65.0	Oman
11,910.1	12.3	0.2	2.3	85.2	2.4	1.3	81.5	28.8	23.1	1.2	2.2	44.8	Pakistan
11.5	69.1[46]	—[46]	—[46]	30.9[46]	—[46]	—[46]	30.9[46]	—[46]	8.0[46]	58.8[46]	—[46]	33.2[46]	Palau
798.7	84.5	3.0	0.7	11.8	2.9	0.1	8.9	23.9	52.0	0.8	1.5	21.7	Panama
2,407.4	17.7	51.3	28.8	2.3	—	2.0	0.3	4.6	1.6	3.3	0.5	89.9[47]	Papua New Guinea
950.6	84.2	0.5	0.3	15.0	3.1	0.5	11.4	9.1	5.0	3.9	12.6	69.3	Paraguay
8,891.2	22.7	13.9	7.5	56.0	2.6	0.9	52.4	25.7	26.9	4.4	7.6	35.4	Peru
35,208.1	5.7	0.7	1.2	92.4	1.1	76.1	15.2	18.5	24.7	15.0	3.9	38.0	Philippines
40,253.9	8.9	1.0	5.1	85.0	6.3	37.8	40.9	80.7	2.7	0.2	0.5	15.9	Poland
26,485.0	9.9	1.0	1.9	87.2	5.7	35.9	45.5	81.6	5.6	0.3	0.3	12.1	Portugal
55,175.3	6.6	0.1	0.7	92.6	72.4	12.9	7.3	8.1	86.5	0.5	0.1	4.8	Puerto Rico
8,230.9	0.2	0.1	87.1	12.6	6.1	1.8	4.7	2.7	3.4	28.9	1.4	63.6	Qatar
208.7	78.6	0.6	0.2	20.6	1.7	12.7	6.2	80.7	0.6	6.1	—	12.6	Réunion
17,618.1	6.3	2.5	6.5	84.7	4.8	21.5	58.4	73.8	3.5	0.1	1.6	21.0	Romania
125,960.3	5.6	1.2	56.3	37.0	4.6	7.3	25.0	37.1[1]	2.4	1.8	6.2	52.4[1]	Russia
46.0	61.8	35.5	—	2.7	0.4	0.1	2.2	22.7	3.1	—	—	74.1	Rwanda
30.9	25.1	—	0.1	74.8	0.2	65.4	9.3	23.8	71.2	0.2	—	4.8	St. Kitts and Nevis
62.0	52.7	0.2	7.4	39.7	1.4	19.6	18.6	40.0	20.3	0.7	—	39.0	St. Lucia
38.1	73.5	—	0.1	26.4	0.5	13.6	12.3	30.2	13.2	—	—	56.5	St. Vincent and the Grenadines
18.1	89.2[3, 6]		…	10.8[4, 6]	…	…	10.8[4, 6]	11.6	69.6	—	—	18.8	Samoa
1,679.0	…	…	…	…	…	…	…	…	…	…	…	…	San Marino[38]
6.6	95.0	—	—	5.0	—	4.3	0.7	93.9	2.9	0.2	—	3.0	São Tomé and Príncipe
61,932.3	1.0	0.2	86.0	12.8	8.2	1.6	2.9	12.9	20.9	14.8	—	51.4	Saudi Arabia
785.1	48.6	4.3	17.8	29.3	17.8	4.5	7.0	42.3	0.3	—	1.0	56.4	Senegal
1,711.1	22.7	1.2	0.3	75.8	8.5	12.6	54.7	48.1	0.2	—	0.7	51.0	Serbia and Montenegro
38.0	51.7	0.1	40.0	8.3	0.1	5.5	2.7	44.9	—	2.4	0.1	52.5	Seychelles
95.0	13.3[23]	77.0[23]	—[23]	9.7[23]	—[23]	—[23]	9.7[23]	82.5[1]	3.8[1]	0.8	0.1[1]	12.7[1]	Sierra Leone
143,561.4	2.3	0.4	8.5	88.9	11.8	61.1	16.0	14.2	14.3	6.7	7.0	57.8	Singapore
21,546.8	4.7	0.8	5.2	89.4	5.2	47.4	36.8	84.6	5.3	0.4	0.6	9.1	Slovakia
12,766.6	4.7	0.5	1.4	93.4	13.6	36.6	43.3	66.9	3.6	0.1	0.2	29.1	Slovenia
154.9	96.5[3]		—	3.5[4]	—	—	3.5[4]	24.7	0.1	39.7	—	35.5	Solomon Islands
97.0	95.4[21]	2.3[21]	—[21]	2.3[21]	—[21]	2.3[21]	—[21]	2.6[1]	0.3[1]	—	1.5[1]	95.6[1]	Somalia
30,897.2	13.4	10.6	9.8	66.2	7.6	20.7	37.9	35.9	12.2	9.9	2.8	39.1	South Africa
125,872.2	16.3	0.9	2.6	80.2	11.0	40.3	29.0	73.7	4.3	0.8	0.6	20.6	Spain
4,723.0	22.4	6.6	0.3	70.6	0.7	5.0	64.9	29.9	37.3	3.0	0.3	29.5	Sri Lanka
1,616.6	22.8	0.3	69.2	7.7	0.2	1.6	5.9	7.5	—	1.5	58.2	32.8	Sudan, The
514.0	15.1	62.1	6.7	16.1	0.9	2.6	12.6	31.1	20.1	4.1	0.3	44.4	Suriname
974.3	22.5	0.2	0.7	76.6	47.8	3.6	25.2	2.6	8.0	—	0.4	88.9	Swaziland
99,690.4	7.9	1.0	3.0	88.2	11.5	42.1	34.6	58.5	11.5	1.9	2.1	26.0	Sweden
87,156.1	3.1	1.2	0.3	95.5	34.3	26.9	34.3	62.3	11.3	4.0	2.1	20.3	Switzerland[51]
6,230.1	16.5	0.8	72.2	10.5	0.4	0.4	9.8	60.4	1.9	0.2	—	37.5	Syria
130,457.0	2.7	0.1	1.6	95.6	7.6	56.6	31.4	13.6	20.5	9.2	7.6	49.1	Taiwan
692.3	16.6[3]		13.3	70.1[4]	1.4	7.8	60.9[4]	35.2	0.1	—	—	64.7	Tajikistan
1,221.7	45.3	9.4	1.3	44.1	1.2	1.6	41.3	53.1	0.9	7.3	0.3	38.3	Tanzania
65,113.2	18.5	1.4	2.8	77.3	5.8	42.0	29.5	16.7	20.3	15.3	4.4	43.3	Thailand
250.6	39.5	16.7	0.5	43.3	1.3	2.4	39.6	11.0	0.4	—	1.0	87.6	Togo
8.9	95.3	—	—	4.7	2.6	—	2.1	2.5[1]	25.8	43.8	—	27.9	Tonga
5,113.4	5.2	0.1	51.9	42.8	16.2	16.0	10.6	8.8	42.3	3.0	—	45.8	Trinidad and Tobago
6,874.2	7.5	1.2	9.4	81.9	9.8	16.5	55.5	79.0	0.8	0.1	0.2	19.9	Tunisia
46,877.5	11.1	1.2	2.0	85.7	4.0	26.6	55.1	54.1	8.0	0.3	1.1	36.6	Turkey
2,505.5	10.2	0.4	81.0	8.4	0.4	0.6	7.4	18.9	0.5	—	0.3	80.3	Turkmenistan
1.4	92.2[52]	—[52]	—[52]	7.8[52]	—[52]	—[52]	7.8[52]	82.6	—	—	—	17.4	Tuvalu
467.4	72.9	1.6	5.7	19.9	1.5	2.4	15.9	34.0	2.0	2.9	0.2	61.0	Uganda
17,927.4	14.9	6.0[3]	9.2	69.9[4]	7.7	13.9	48.3[4]	33.0	2.8	0.5	3.7	60.0	Ukraine
22,344.0	7.3[3]		64.2	28.5[4]	2.0	8.8	17.7[4]	6.4[1, 53]	2.5[53]	29.5[53]	0.6[53]	60.9[1, 53]	United Arab Emirates
320,057.0	6.3	3.3	8.0	82.3	16.4	44.4	21.6	55.8	15.0	1.9	1.0	26.3	United Kingdom[35]
723,608.5	10.5	1.8	1.9	85.7	13.0	48.6	24.1	21.3	—	7.2	3.9	67.5	United States[54]
1,861.0	61.3	0.4	0.8	37.6	5.9	4.4	27.4	24.1	7.6	0.8	5.6	62.0	Uruguay
3,528.0	63.3[1, 23]	4.1[1, 23]	11.8[23]	20.8[1, 23]	2.8[1, 23]	2.7[23]	15.3[1, 23]	29.2[1]	1.8	1.1[1]	1.0	67.0[1]	Uzbekistan
23.2	86.6[3]		—	13.4[4]	—	1.7	11.6[4]	18.8[1]	2.2	12.1	0.9	66.1	Vanuatu
20,290.0	1.9	0.9	81.4	15.8	3.7	2.3	9.9	8.2	56.3	0.3	0.4	34.8	Venezuela
11,541.4	30.1	0.6	20.5	48.8	1.2	8.4	39.1	22.9	4.4	15.5	6.5	50.8	Vietnam
5,560.8	…	…	86.3[55]	…	…	…	…	…	93.2	…	…	…	Virgin Islands (U.S.)
22.6[57]	…	…	…	…	…	…	…	…	…	…	…	…	West Bank[31]
…	…	…	…	…	…	…	…	…	…	…	…	…	Western Sahara
4,079.3	2.5	0.1	96.5	0.9	0.3	0.3	0.3	1.2	6.1	2.1	19.0	71.6	Yemen
929.5	12.1	4.8	2.1	81.0	1.0	4.9	75.2	47.8	0.6	0.8	0.3	50.5	Zambia
2,327.4	35.6	10.7	1.1	52.7	4.1	4.8	43.8	23.6	4.5	5.3	0.6	66.1	Zimbabwe

and Jersey (data for Jersey is also shown separately). [36]1997. [37]1999. [38]Figures for Italy include San Marino and Vatican City State. [39]United Kingdom only. [40]Including coins. [41]Includes 96.5% from South Africa. [42]Includes 53.0% to South Africa. [43]1997. Percentage based on total excluding trade in ships: imports U.S.$209,600,000; exports U.S.$99,300,000. [44]France only. [45]Includes 86.0% from South Africa. [46]1984. [47]Includes 75.8% for areas not specified. [48]Year ending June 30. [49]1986. [50]Includes 86.2% from South Africa. [51]Figures for Switzerland include Liechtenstein, also shown separately. [52]1989. [53]1998. [54]Figures for United States include Puerto Rico and Virgin Islands (U.S.), also shown separately. [55]Exports of refined petroleum to United States only. [56]Excluding imports from Israel (90.9% in 1987). [57]Excluding exports to Israel (70.3% in 1987).

Household budgets and consumption

This table provides international data on household income, on the consumption expenditure of households for goods and services, and on the principal object of such expenditure (in most countries), food consumption (by kind). For purposes of this compilation, income comprises pretax monetary payments and payment in kind. The first part of the table provides data on distribution of income by households and by sources of income; the second part analyzes the largest portion of income use—consumption expenditure. Such expenditure is defined as the purchase of goods and services to satisfy current wants and needs. This definition excludes income expended on taxes, debts, savings and investments, and insurance policies. The third and last part of the table focuses on food, which usually, and often by a wide margin, represents the largest share of consumer spending worldwide. The data provided include daily available calories per capita and consumption of major food groups.

For both sources of income and consumption expenditure, the primary basis of analysis for most countries is the household, an economic unit that can be as small as a single person or as large as an extended family. For some of the countries that do not compile information by household, the table provides data on personal income and personal expenditure—*i.e.*, the income and expenditure of all the individuals constituting a society's households. When no expenditure data at all is available, the table reports the weights of each major class of goods and services making up a given country's consumer (or retail) price index (CPI). The weighting of the components of the CPI usually reflects household spending patterns within the country or its principal urban or rural areas.

The data on distribution of income show, collectively for an entire country, the proportion of total income earned (occasionally, expended) by households constituting the lowest quintile and highest decile (poorest 20% and wealthiest 10%) within the country. These figures show the degree to which either group represents a disproportionate share of poverty or wealth.

The data on sources of income illuminate patterns of economic structure in the gaining of an income. They indicate, for example, that in poor, agrarian countries income often derives largely from self-employment (usually farming) or that in industrial countries, with well-developed systems of salaried employment and social welfare, income derives mainly from wages and salaries and secondarily from transfer payments (*see* note a). Because household sizes and numbers of income earners vary so greatly internationally, and because the frequency and methodology of household and CPI surveys do not permit single-year comparisons for more than a few countries at once, no summary of total *household* income or expenditure was possible. Instead, U.S. dollar figures are supplied for *per capita* private final consumption expenditure (for a single, recent year) that are more comparable internationally and refer to the same date. The figures on distribution of consumption expenditure by end use reveal patterns of personal and family use of disposable income and indicate, inter alia, that in developing countries, food may absorb 50% or more of disposable income, while in the larger household budgets of the developed countries, by contrast, food purchases may account for only 20–30% of spending. Each category of expenditure betrays similar complexities of local habit, necessity, and aspiration.

The reader should exercise caution when using these data to make intercountry comparisons. Most of the information comes from single-country surveys, which often differ markedly in their coverage of economically or demographically stratified groups, in sample design, or in the methods

Household budgets and consumption

country	income (latest)						consumption expenditure						
	percent received by		by source (percent)				per capita private final, U.S.$ (1995)	by kind or end use (percent of household or personal budget; latest)					
	lowest 20% of households	highest 10% of households	wages, salaries	self-employment	transfer payments[a]	other[b]		food[c]	housing[d]	clothing[e]	health care	energy, water	education
Afghanistan	…	…	20.7	28.0	8.2	43.1	…	33.9	3.0	…	1.1	0.7	…
Albania	…	…	53.0	4.0	11.5	31.5	680	…	…	…	…	…	…
Algeria	7.0[1]	26.8[1]	43.1	38.3	18.6	1.8	810	52.3	6.7[2]	8.6	2.8	[2]	[3]
American Samoa	…	…	…	…	…	…	1,880[4]	32.9	20.4[5]	5.2	…	…	…
Andorra	…	…	…	…	…	…	…	…	…	…	…	…	…
Angola	…	…	…	…	…	…	370	74.1[6]	10.2[2, 6]	5.5[6]	1.8[6]	[2, 6]	2.7[6]
Antigua and Barbuda	…	…	…	…	…	…	4,050	*42.9*	*23.3*	*7.5*	…	5.5	…
Argentina	*4.4*	*35.2*	53.9	31.5	1.5	12.7	6,620	40.1	9.3	8.0	7.9	9.0	2.6
Armenia	…	…	24.5	13.6[7]	5.5	56.4	360	69.6	…	17.4	…	…	…
Aruba	…	…	…	…	…	…	11,190	26.9	9.9	8.4	2.9	8.5	1.9
Australia	5.9	25.4	72.7	7.5	13.0	6.8	12,040	18.7	18.5	5.6	7.1	2.2	1.6
Austria	*10.4*	*19.3*	55.7	[8]	24.4	19.9[8]	16,020	28.1	14.5	8.5	5.8	4.0	0.4
Azerbaijan	…	…	70.2	10.8[7]	19.0	—	460	42.2	—	13.6	4.8	—	—
Bahamas, The	3.6	32.1	…	…	…	…	3,950[9]	13.8	32.8	5.9	4.4	…	5.3
Bahrain	…	…	…	…	…	…	2,240	32.4	21.2	5.9	2.3	2.2	2.3
Bangladesh	8.7[1]	28.6[1]	18.7	48.3	7.5	25.5	170[10]	63.3	8.8	5.9	1.1	8.4	1.2
Barbados	*7.0*	*44.0*[11]	…	…	…	…	4,860	45.8	16.8	5.1	3.8	5.2	[3]
Belarus	11.4[1]	20.0[1]	47.1	7.3[9]	45.6	—	610	29.0	2.7	…	…	…	…
Belgium	*9.5*[12]	*20.2*[12]	49.6	10.9	20.7	18.8	16,550	18.3	11.4	7.0	10.5	6.2	[3]
Belize	…	…	*84.1*		— *15.9* —		1,780	34.0	9.0	8.8	1.6	9.1	2.3
Benin	*8.0*	*39.0*	26.3		— 73.7 —		240	37.0	10.0	14.0	5.0	2.0	4.0
Bermuda	7.2	24.7	65.3	9.0	3.3	22.4	12,690[13]	14.6	27.7	4.9	7.6	3.3	3.8
Bhutan	…	…	…	…	…	…	170	*72.3*	…	*21.2*	…	*3.7*	…
Bolivia	5.6[12]	31.7[12]	…	…	…	…	690	46.6	7.8	5.1	2.1	4.7	0.3
Bosnia and Herzegovina	…	…	53.2	12.0	18.2	16.6	1,890[14]	44.7	1.6	8.3	3.4	7.8	[3]
Botswana	3.7	42.9	73.3	15.4	10.8	0.4	1,030	39.5[15]	11.8	5.6	2.3	2.5	4.9
Brazil	2.5[12]	47.6[12]	62.4	14.7	10.9	12.0	4,420	25.3	21.3[2]	12.9	9.1	[2]	…
Brunei	…	…	…	…	…	…	…	*45.1*	*2.6*	*6.1*	…	*2.4*	[3]
Bulgaria	8.5[1]	22.5[1]	34.7	23.6[7]	14.8	—	1,470	47.0	4.1	7.4	3.2	4.3	[3]
Burkina Faso	5.5[1]	39.5[1]	…	…	…	…	220	38.7[6]	5.1[6]	4.4[6]	5.2[6]	13.7[6]	[3]
Burundi	7.9[1]	26.6[1]	…	…	…	…	190	59.6[6]	4.4[6]	11.1[6]	…	5.8[6]	…
Cambodia	6.9[1]	33.8[1]	…	…	…	…	280	…	…	…	…	…	…
Cameroon	…	…	41.4	52.6	3.0	3.0	570	49.1	18.0[2]	7.6	8.6	[2]	…
Canada	7.5[12]	23.8[12]	57.0	13.7	20.7	8.6	11,460	13.4	24.5[2]	5.3	4.7	[2]	3.1
Cape Verde	…	…	…	…	…	…	920	60.0	8.5	2.5	0.5	4.9	[17]
Central African Republic	2.0[1]	47.7[1]	…	…	…	…	350	70.5[6]	0.6[6]	9.5[6]	1.0[6]	6.5[6]	…
Chad	*8.0*	*30.0*	…	…	…	…	170	45.3[6]	…	3.5[6]	11.9[6]	5.8[6]	…
Chile	3.5[12]	46.1[12]	— 75.1 —		12.0	12.9	2,940	27.9	15.2	22.5	…	…	…
China	5.9[12]	30.4[12]	21.6	72.2	— 6.2 —		260	49.9[15, 18]	6.8[18]	13.7[18]	2.9[18]	…	2.3[18]
Colombia	3.0[12]	46.1[12]	45.1	35.4	14.2	5.3	1,540	45.0	7.8	4.5	6.4	2.2	1.7
Comoros	…	…	*25.6*	*64.5*	*8.7*	*1.2*	350	67.3	2.3	11.6	3.2	3.8	[3]
Congo, Dem. Rep. of the	…	…	…	…	…	…	190	61.7	11.5[2]	9.7	2.6	[2]	[3]
Congo, Rep. of the	*7.0*	*43.5*	…	…	…	…	870	37.0	6.0	6.0	6.0	3.0	8.0
Costa Rica	4.0[12]	34.7[12]	61.0	22.6	9.6	6.8	1,600	39.1	12.1[2]	9.4	3.7	[2]	[3]
Côte d'Ivoire	7.1[1]	28.8[1]	44.9	49.9	— 5.2 —		480	48.0	7.8	10.0	0.7	8.5	…
Croatia	9.3[1]	21.6[1]	40.2	40.8	12.1	6.9	3,790	37.8	2.9	8.6	4.3	7.6	[3]
Cuba	…	…	57.3		— 42.7 —		1,510[9]	26.7	…	…	…	2.5	…
Cyprus	…	…	76.3	5.9	14.4	3.4	8,300	22.7	5.5	10.0	3.1	1.3	1.4
Czech Republic	10.3[12]	22.4[12]	— 66.7 —		27.6	5.7	2,620	26.7	5.5[2]	7.3	[19]	[2]	…
Denmark	9.6[12]	20.5[12]	63.3	14.6	25.9	–3.8	17,730	17.9	22.9	5.2	2.2	6.1	1.9
Djibouti	…	…	*51.6*	*36.0*	*10.5*	*1.9*	590	50.3	6.4	1.7	2.4	13.1	…
Dominica	…	…	…	…	…	…	2,110	43.1	16.1	6.5	…	5.4	…
Dominican Republic	4.3[12]	37.8[12]	*41.7*	*31.8*	*1.5*	*25.0*	1,150	46.0	10.0	3.0	8.0	5.0	3.0
East Timor	…	…	…	…	…	…	…	…	…	…	…	…	…
Ecuador	5.4[1]	33.8[1]	17.4	76.9	3.6	2.1	1,040	36.1	9.0	10.1	4.2	3.3	[17]

employed for collection, classification, and tabulation of data. Further, the reference period of the data varies greatly; while a significant portion of the data is from 1980 or later, information for some countries dates from the 1970s. This older information is typeset in italic. Finally, intercountry comparisons of annual personal consumption expenditure may be misleading because of the distortions of price and purchasing power present when converting a national currency unit into U.S. dollars.

The table's food consumption data include total daily available calories per capita (food supply), which amounts to domestic production and imports minus exports, animal feed, and nonfood uses, and a percentage breakdown of the major food groups that make up food supply.

The data for daily available calories per capita provide a measure of the nutritional adequacy of each nation's food supply. The following list, based on estimates from the United Nations Food and Agriculture Organization (FAO), indicates the regional variation in recommended daily minimum nutritional requirements, which are defined by factors such as climatic ambience, physical activity, and average body weight: Africa (2,320 calories), formerly Centrally Planned Asia (2,300 calories), Far East (2,240 calories), Latin America (2,360 calories), Near East (2,440 calories).

The breakdown of diet by food groups describes the character of a nation's food supply. A typical breakdown for a low-income country might show a diet with heavy intake of vegetable foods, such as cereals, potatoes, or cassava. In the high-income countries, a relatively larger portion of total calories derives from animal products (meat, eggs, and milk). The reader should note that these data refer to total national *supply* and often do not reflect the differences that may exist within a single country.

In compiling this table, Britannica editors rely on both numerous national reports and principal secondary sources such as the World Bank's *World Development Report* (annual), the International Labour Organisation's *Sources and Methods: Labour Statistics vol. 1 Consumer Price Indices* (3rd ed.), the UN's *Yearbook of National Accounts Statistics* (annual) and *National Accounts Statistics: Compendium of Income Distribution Statistics,* and the FAO's *Food Balance Sheets.*

The following terms further define the column headings:

a. Includes pensions, family allowances, unemployment payments, remittances from abroad, and social security and related benefits.
b. Includes interest and dividends, rents and royalties, and all other income not reported under the three preceding categories.
c. Includes alcoholic and nonalcoholic beverages and meals away from home when identifiable. Excludes tobacco except as noted.
d. Rent, maintenance of dwellings, and taxes only; excludes energy and water (heat, light, power, and water) and household durables (furniture, appliances, utensils, and household operations), shown separately.
e. Includes footwear.
f. Furniture, appliances, and utensils; usually includes expenditure on household operation.
g. Includes expenditure on cultural activities other than education.
h. May include data not shown separately in preceding categories, including meals away from home (*see* note c).
i. Represents pure fats and oils only.
j. Consists mainly of peas, beans, and lentils; spices; stimulants; alcoholic beverages (when combined with "other"); sugars and honey; and nuts and oilseeds.

				food consumption, 1998									country
				daily available calories per capita	percent of total calories derived from:								
transportation, communications	household durable goods[f]	recreation[g]	personal effects, other[h]		cereals	potatoes, cassava	meat, poultry	fish	eggs, milk	fruits, vegetables	fats, oils[i]	other[j]	
...	...	...	61.3	1,716	83.4	1.1	4.1	—	2.4	2.6	3.8	2.6	Afghanistan
...	...	...	...	2,976	51.1	1.8	5.1	0.1	16.9	6.0	9.0	10.0	Albania
12.0	4.5	4.6[3]	8.5	3,020	60.3	2.2	2.7	0.3	6.1	5.1	13.8	9.5	Algeria
17.8	[5]	1.1	22.6	...	...	...	...	...	...	...	...	...	American Samoa
...	...	...	...	3,348	22.6	4.7	13.4	2.4	9.3	6.7	21.6	19.4	Andorra
3.9[6]	...	...	1.8[6]	...	...	...	...	...	...	...	...	...	Angola
10.0	...	...	*10.8*	2,450	25.8	1.0	15.8	1.7	11.3	7.9	16.4	20.2	Antigua and Barbuda
11.6	...	7.5	5.9	3,144	29.5	5.2	16.5	0.5	10.3	4.5	15.4	18.0	Argentina
...	6.6	...	28.7	2,356	52.3	6.7	5.3	0.1	7.0	6.5	11.7	10.4	Armenia
15.5	9.1	3.1	11.9	2,659	28.2	2.3	18.9	1.4	10.8	5.0	13.6	19.7	Aruba
15.1	7.0	7.5	16.7	3,190	22.7	3.2	15.5	0.8	11.8	5.3	17.0	23.5	Australia
16.3	7.8	7.1	7.5	3,531	20.7	3.1	13.8	0.6	11.4	5.5	21.5	23.4	Austria
5.1	6.5	0.7	27.1	2,191	66.6	2.7	4.6	0.1	9.7	5.1	2.8	8.4	Azerbaijan
14.8	8.9	4.9	9.2	2,546	30.1	1.4	18.8	1.1	5.9	8.6	9.3	24.9	Bahamas, The
8.5	9.8	6.4	9.0	...	...	...	...	...	...	...	...	...	Bahrain
0.9	...	...	10.4	2,050	81.6	1.3	0.8	0.9	1.5	1.1	5.6	7.2	Bangladesh
10.5	8.1	4.8[3]	—	2,978	31.6	3.9	12.6	2.3	6.6	3.4	12.8	26.8	Barbados
...	...	...	68.3	3,136	36.2	9.9	10.5	0.1	10.2	2.6	12.0	18.7	Belarus
13.4	10.6	6.8[3]	15.8	3,606	20.4	5.2	8.6	1.1	10.8	6.5	25.7	21.7	Belgium
13.7	8.0	...	9.4	2,922	34.0	1.4	6.3	0.4	7.5	9.6	10.2	30.7	Belize
14.0	5.0	...	9.0	2,571	37.5	36.9	2.2	0.7	0.8	2.6	5.3	14.0	Benin
7.3	16.6	10.8	3.4	2,921	22.8	2.6	15.7	2.7	7.8	12.4	15.2	20.8	Bermuda
...	*0.7*	...	*2.1*	...	...	...	...	...	...	...	...	...	Bhutan
17.7	9.7	2.7	3.3	2,214	40.7	6.6	11.2	0.1	3.7	8.6	11.4	17.7	Bolivia
6.0	4.1	3.5[3]	2.3	2,801	64.6	5.6	4.3	0.1	3.7	4.5	3.7	13.4	Bosnia and Herzegovina
13.1	13.8	3.1	3.4	2,159	46.9	1.8	6.3	0.5	8.9	2.5	11.6	21.6	Botswana
15.0	...	...	16.4	2,926	30.9	4.3	10.8	0.4	8.3	4.5	12.6	28.2	Brazil
17.2	*8.3*	*8.9*[3]	*9.4*	2,851	48.0	1.2	13.0	1.3	6.4	5.0	6.3	18.9	Brunei
6.6	4.0	3.0[3]	21.5	2,740	37.6	2.1	10.7	0.3	12.1	5.4	15.6	16.3	Bulgaria
18.6[6]	3.0[6]	2.3[3, 6]	9.0[6]	2,149	73.2	0.7	2.6	0.1	1.9	0.9	5.2	15.5	Burkina Faso
...	6.0[6]	...	13.1[6, 16]	1,578	16.7	30.0	1.3	0.4	0.8	10.3	1.5	39.0	Burundi
...	...	...	...	2,078	77.9	1.3	6.2	0.8	0.5	2.9	4.7	5.7	Cambodia
13.0	...	2.4	1.3	2,209	41.7	16.3	3.4	0.8	1.4	13.7	9.1	13.6	Cameroon
14.3	8.8	8.0	17.9	3,167	24.9	2.9	11.4	1.1	8.8	6.6	20.5	23.8	Canada
8.8	6.9	[17]	7.9[17]	3,099	40.3	2.5	5.8	1.5	4.9	3.1	17.6	24.2	Cape Verde
4.1[6]	0.8[6]	1.3[6]	5.7[6]	2,056	18.9	35.9	6.4	0.3	1.5	6.2	13.7	17.1	Central African Republic
...	...	...	33.5[6]	2,171	53.8	9.4	2.3	0.5	2.2	1.5	7.1	23.2	Chad
6.4	...	...	28.0	2,844	38.7	3.4	12.5	1.2	6.7	4.8	12.4	20.3	Chile
4.7[18]	5.3[18]	2.4[18]	12.0[18]	2,972	54.7	5.6	13.2	13.2	2.6	5.3	7.3	10.1	China
18.5	5.7	...	8.2	2,559	32.5	7.2	7.2	0.4	8.7	7.9	11.9	24.2	Colombia
2.2	3.0	2.5[3]	4.1	1,858	42.7	15.6	1.8	2.4	1.1	8.0	10.3	18.1	Comoros
5.9	4.8	3.8[3]	—	1,701	19.2	56.3	1.9	0.6	0.1	6.5	6.3	9.1	Congo, Dem. Rep. of the
15.0	4.0	...	15.0	2,241	25.4	37.9	3.1	2.2	1.5	6.2	11.7	11.9	Congo, Rep. of the
11.6	10.9	4.4[3]	8.8	2,781	32.9	1.9	5.3	0.5	9.5	5.0	14.1	30.9	Costa Rica
12.2	3.4	...	9.4	2,695	42.5	24.7	1.9	0.7	0.9	8.7	11.2	9.4	Côte d'Ivoire
9.3	4.5	4.1[3]	1.5	2,479	31.2	8.4	4.2	0.3	10.6	7.5	11.9	25.8	Croatia
5.4	...	...	65.4	2,473	37.3	5.3	5.3	0.8	4.9	5.1	9.6	31.7	Cuba
15.6	10.5	6.3	23.6	3,474	25.6	2.4	14.7	1.0	12.7	8.0	12.7	22.9	Cyprus
3.1	4.5	0.8[19]	52.7	3,292	27.6	4.4	10.1	0.7	9.6	4.3	17.9	25.4	Czech Republic
15.5	6.1	8.3	13.9	3,443	25.4	3.8	11.7	1.4	9.9	4.9	17.6	25.3	Denmark
...	1.5	...	24.6	2,074	51.3	0.2	4.5	0.2	4.8	1.6	17.9	19.4	Djibouti
11.6	6.0	...	11.3	2,996	23.9	9.1	10.6	1.6	8.7	12.5	6.9	26.7	Dominica
4.0	8.0	...	13.0	2,277	28.3	2.8	7.6	0.7	5.2	10.1	19.1	26.4	Dominican Republic
...	...	...	...	...	...	...	...	...	...	...	...	...	East Timor
12.8	5.5	[17]	19.0[17]	2,724	34.5	2.7	5.8	0.6	6.6	4.4	20.6	24.8	Ecuador

Household budgets and consumption (continued)

country	income (latest)						consumption expenditure						
	percent received by		by source (percent)				per capita private final, U.S.$ (1995)	by kind or end use (percent of household or personal budget; latest)					
	lowest 20% of households	highest 10% of households	wages, salaries	self-employment	transfer payments[a]	other[b]		food[c]	housing[d]	clothing[e]	health care	energy, water	education
Egypt	9.8[1]	25.0[1]	...	...	...	...	740	50.2	10.5[2]	10.9	2.7	[2]	[3]
El Salvador	*3.4*[12]	*40.5*[12]	...	...	...	...	1,520	37.0[18]	12.1[18]	6.7[18]	4.2[18]	3.6[18]	3.7[18]
Equatorial Guinea	...	...	57.0[6]	42.0[6]	—	1.0[6]	310	62.0[6]	...	10.0[6]	6.0[6]	...	...
Eritrea	...	...	...	...	...	...	170	...	...	...	...	...	...
Estonia	6.2[12]	26.2[12]	53.0	5.7	12.8	28.5	1,390	41.0	9.6	8.4	[19]	6.5	3.1
Ethiopia	7.1[1]	33.7[1]	0.2	79.5	—	20.3	87	49.0	7.0	6.0	3.0	7.0	4.0
Faroe Islands	...	...	88.3	11.7	—	—	...	40.9	11.0	8.0	...	18.9	...
Fiji	*3.7*	*37.8*	*81.5*	*9.1*	—	*9.4*	1,430[10]	34.7	15.6[2]	9.3	2.4	[2]	[3]
Finland	10.0[12]	21.6[12]	70.3	7.4	9.7	12.6	13,260	22.5	16.9	5.0	4.8	4.6	[3]
France	7.2[12]	25.1[12]	51.1	14.1	27.5	7.3	15,810	17.4	16.2	6.1	9.8	3.8	0.7
French Guiana	...	...	74.6	——	25.4	——	...	30.0[15]	16.1[2]	6.7	4.4	[2]	[3]
French Polynesia	...	...	61.9	18.5	16.6	3.0	4,310[20]	39.6	9.7	6.3	1.0	8.1	1.0
Gabon	*3.3*	*54.4*	...	...	...	...	4,060	...	...	...	...	...	...
Gambia, The	...	...	...	...	...	...	330	58.0[21]	5.1[21]	17.5[21]	...	5.4[21]	...
Gaza Strip	...	...	...	...	...	...	910[22]	...	...	...	...	...	...
Georgia	...	...	34.5	21.6[7]	21.7	22.0	430	38.3	...	14.8	...	0.3	...
Germany	8.2[12]	23.7[12]	57.9	[8]	21.3	20.8[8]	16,850	19.0	16.9	7.9	3.5	4.1	[3]
Ghana	8.4[1]	26.1[1]	41.6[23]	47.1[23]	—	11.3[23]	290	*57.4*	*11.5*[2]	*14.3*	*1.3*	[2]	[3]
Greece	7.5[12]	25.3[12]	34.0	22.8	17.0	26.2	8,140	29.9	14.1	6.5	3.1	3.3	0.5
Greenland	...	...	...	...	...	...	11,110	30.1	10.0	7.7	0.3	5.4	...
Grenada	...	...	...	...	...	...	1,650	40.7[15]	11.9	5.2	[24]	3.9	[3]
Guadeloupe	...	...	78.9	13.7	7.4	—	4,080[27]	31.6[15]	11.3[2]	9.3	4.6	[2]	[3]
Guam	...	...	...	...	...	...	...	*24.1*	*28.6*	*10.6*	*4.8*	...	...
Guatemala	2.1[12]	46.6[12]	...	...	...	...	1,180	64.4	16.0[2]	3.1	0.6	[2]	0.3
Guernsey	...	...	...	...	...	...	...	23.7	12.1	7.5	...	8.2	...
Guinea	6.4[1]	32.0[1]	...	...	...	...	510	*61.5*	*7.3*[2]	*7.9*	*11.1*	[2]	...
Guinea-Bissau	2.1[1]	42.4[1]	...	...	...	...	230	...	...	...	...	...	...
Guyana	4.0	40.0[11]	*73.0*	...	*6.3*	*20.7*	...	*42.5*[15]	*21.4*	*8.6*	...	*5.2*	[3]
Haiti	...	...	...	...	...	...	320	51.1[15]	4.3	8.7	2.2	...	[3]
Honduras	3.4[12]	42.1[12]	58.3	[8]	1.8	39.9[8]	450	44.4	22.4[2]	9.1	7.0	[2]	[3]
Hong Kong	...	...	...	...	...	...	13,880	15.1	15.7[2]	21.3	5.0	[2]	0.5
Hungary	8.8[12]	24.8[12]	55.0	——	19.2	5.8	4,270	38.1	5.7	7.4	1.5	6.1	0.7
Iceland	4.7	27.3	73.1	2.7	10.2	14.0	15,850	31.3	16.0	7.5	2.3	2.9	1.3
India	8.1[1]	33.5[1]	42.2	39.7	18.1	——	210	52.2	6.1[25]	10.0	2.4	4.7[25]	1.8
Indonesia	8.0[12]	30.3[12]	*42.1*	*41.5*	*2.5*	*13.9*	640	47.5[18]	20.1[2, 18]	5.5[18]	...	[2]	...
Iran	*3.8*	*41.7*	37.4[18]	30.5[18]	32.1[18]	——	1,040	42.6[15]	24.9[2]	11.8	3.9	[2]	[3]
Iraq	...	...	23.9	33.9	23.0	18.6	1,710[13]	50.2	19.9[2]	10.6	1.6	[2]	[3]
Ireland	6.7[12]	27.4[12]	58.6	13.3	19.9	8.2	9,650	30.5	7.1	7.4	3.2	6.1	2.4
Isle of Man	6.4	26.6	64.1	6.6	16.9	12.4	...	31.0	7.9	7.0	...	11.0	...
Israel	6.9[12]	26.9[12]	63.4[18, 26]	14.6[18, 26]	18.9[18, 26]	3.1[18, 26]	9,930	23.8	19.8	5.3	6.2	2.4	2.9
Italy	8.7[12]	21.8[12]	41.7	25.9	20.3	12.1	11,860	19.5	10.0	9.8	6.7	3.8	0.7
Jamaica	7.0[1]	28.9[1]	63.6	13.9	14.0	8.5	1,770	35.7	5.7	4.6	2.8	4.9	0.2
Japan	10.6[12]	21.7[12]	59.3	11.1	19.5	10.1	24,670	22.6	6.7	6.0	2.7	5.6	5.3
Jersey	...	...	...	...	...	...	...	*28.3*	*14.9*	*8.3*	...	*6.5*	...
Jordan	7.6[1]	29.8[1]	51.4	11.1	13.7	23.8	1,020	40.6	15.8	6.7	2.2	5.0	3.5
Kazakhstan	6.7[1]	26.3[1]	67.7	5.8[7]	16.9	9.6	1,290	29.6	2.6	...	...	...	...
Kenya	5.0	34.9	...	...	...	...	220	46.5	10.0	7.7	2.2	2.6	1.0
Kiribati	...	...	*69.7*	*21.4*	*6.0*	*2.9*	370[4]	50.0[15]	7.5[2, 5]	8.0	...	[2]	...
Korea, North	...	...	...	...	...	...	...	46.5[27]	0.6[27]	29.9[27]	...	3.3[27]	...
Korea, South	7.5[1]	24.3[1]	53.8	25.1	13.1	8.0	5,390	29.7	4.1	7.7	5.0	4.0	14.2
Kuwait	...	...	*53.8*	*20.8*	*25.4*	——	...	28.1[15]	15.5	8.1	0.7	9.6	[3]
Kyrgyzstan	6.3[12]	31.7[12]	67.3	——	32.7	——	670	33.5	2.2	...	...	...	...
Laos	9.6[1]	26.4[1]	...	...	...	...	140[9]	...	...	...	...	...	...
Latvia	7.6[12]	25.9[12]	67.0	5.4[7]	17.4	10.2	2,400	51.6	...	...	...	...	...
Lebanon	*5.0*	*45.0*	*27.9*	...	*3.0*	*69.1*	3,010	*42.8*[6]	*16.8*[6]	*8.6*[6]	*7.2*[6]	*4.5*[6]	*3.9*[6]
Lesotho	2.8[1]	43.4[1]	22.4	27.8	44.7	5.1	530	48.0[15]	10.1	16.4	...	...	...
Liberia	5.0	73.0[11]	...	...	...	...	330[9]	*34.4*[6]	*14.9*[6]	*13.8*[6]	...	*5.0*[6]	...
Libya	...	...	...	...	...	...	2,330[9]	*37.2*[15]	*32.2*[2]	*6.9*	*3.3*	[2]	[3]
Liechtenstein	...	...	...	...	...	...	...	21.3[15]	18.0	6.6	7.7	4.4	[3]
Lithuania	7.8[1]	25.6[1]	66.4	9.7	18.7	5.2	1,910	50.3	...	...	...	...	...
Luxembourg	10.0	34.0[11]	67.1	4.8	28.1	—	15,140[28]	12.8	13.7	5.9	7.3	6.1	[3]
Macau	...	...	65.0	18.1	7.0	9.9	5,480	39.2[15]	17.5	6.8	4.0	5.2	[3]
Macedonia	...	...	57.7	17.2	16.2	9.0	1,010	40.6	1.9	7.8	3.0	7.8	[3]
Madagascar	5.1[1]	36.7[1]	*58.8*[6, 29]	*14.1*[6, 29]	—	*27.1*[6, 29]	220	59.0	6.0	6.0	2.0	6.0	4.0
Malawi	*10.4*	*40.1*	83.3	6.0	—	11.7	109	30.0	4.0	9.0	4.0	5.0	10.0
Malaysia	4.5[12]	37.9[12]	...	...	...	...	2,090	28.7	10.2[2]	4.3	2.5	[2]	0.6
Maldives	...	...	...	...	...	...	270[9]	57.4	1.6	8.0	2.5	...	[3]
Mali	4.6[1]	40.4[1]	...	...	...	...	200	57.0	2.0	6.0	2.0	6.0	4.0
Malta	...	...	63.8	19.3	—	16.9	5,380	31.2	3.5	7.6	3.5	2.0	0.4
Marshall Islands	...	...	...	...	...	...	...	57.7	15.6[2, 5]	12.0	...	[2]	...
Martinique	...	...	80.0	...	...	20.0	4,840[6]	32.1[15]	10.6[2]	8.0	5.2	[2]	[3]
Mauritania	6.2[1]	29.9[1]	...	...	...	...	470	73.1	2.5	8.1	0.9	7.7	0.4
Mauritius	4.0	46.7	51.7	29.0	11.2	8.1	2,290	41.9	8.8	8.4	3.0	6.4	2.9
Mayotte	...	...	...	...	...	...	...	42.2	...	31.5	...	6.8	...
Mexico	3.6[12]	42.8[12]	61.5	29.1	7.8	1.6	2,110	36.6[15]	13.3[2]	8.4	3.4	[2]	[3]
Micronesia	...	...	51.8	23.0	2.1	23.1	...	73.5	...	...	...	...	...
Moldova	6.9[12]	25.8[12]	41.2	10.4	15.3	33.1	220	...	...	...	...	...	...
Monaco	...	...	...	...	...	...	...	...	...	...	...	...	...
Mongolia	7.3[1]	24.5[1]	72.1	9.5[7]	9.7	8.7	230	39.1	5.9[2]	23.4	0.5	[2]	2.9
Morocco	6.5[1]	30.9[1]	...	...	...	...	900	38.0	7.0	11.0	5.0	2.0	8.0
Mozambique	6.5[1]	31.7[1]	51.6	——	48.4	——	57	74.6	11.7	3.7	0.8	...	[3]
Myanmar (Burma)	*8.0*	*40.0*[11]	...	...	...	...	750[28]	*49.1*[6]	*10.4*[6]	*15.3*[6]	*2.4*[6]	*4.0*[6]	*5.9*[6]
Namibia	...	...	67.1	27.5	5.4	...	1,050	...	...	...	...	...	...
Nauru	...	...	...	...	...	...	...	...	...	...	...	...	...
Nepal	7.6[1]	29.8[1]	25.1	63.4	11.5	——	170	61.2	17.3	11.7	3.7	...	[3]

				food consumption, 1998									country
				daily available calories per capita	percent of total calories derived from:								
transportation, communications	household durable goods[f]	recreation[g]	personal effects, other[h]		cereals	potatoes, cassava	meat, poultry	fish	eggs, milk	fruits, vegetables	fats, oils[i]	other[j]	
4.7	5.0	3.3[3]	12.7	3,282	65.4	1.6	2.9	0.6	2.1	6.9	6.1	14.3	Egypt
10.2[18]	5.7[18]	4.3[18]	12.5[18]	2,522	53.4	1.5	2.6	0.2	6.3	3.5	7.7	24.9	El Salvador
…	…	…	22.0[6]	…	…	…	…	…	…	…	…	…	Equatorial Guinea
…	…	…	…	1,744	73.4	4.4	0.6	0.0	1.9	0.1	0.7	18.8	Eritrea
9.2	2.3	5.0[19]	15.0	3,058	38.5	5.3	8.9	1.6	12.7	4.3	13.3	15.4	Estonia
8.0	2.0	…	14.0	1,805	66.3	13.1	3.2	0.0	1.9	0.6	2.8	12.1	Ethiopia
…	6.6	…	14.6	…	…	…	…	…	…	…	…	…	Faroe Islands
13.8	9.3	4.3[3]	10.6	2,852	42.3	6.9	8.5	1.4	3.0	1.8	18.7	17.3	Fiji
14.8	6.3	9.5[3]	15.6	3,180	33.6	4.2	16.3	2.0	15.7	3.9	12.9	18.6	Finland
16.1	7.7	6.9	15.3	3,541	24.3	3.4	16.5	1.2	12.0	4.7	19.7	18.3	France
17.5	7.9	6.2[3]	11.2	2,818	32.4	7.9	13.2	2.1	7.5	7.0	10.5	19.3	French Guiana
16.4	4.4	4.0	9.5	2,924	33.6	4.0	13.3	4.4	6.1	3.0	13.6	22.1	French Polynesia
…	…	…	…	2,560	29.5	17.9	7.3	3.1	2.4	16.4	7.9	15.5	Gabon
…	…	…	14.0[21]	2,559	54.0	0.7	1.3	1.9	1.4	0.9	17.7	22.1	Gambia, The
…	…	…	…	…	…	…	…	…	…	…	…	…	Gaza Strip
…	5.9	…	40.7	2,252	60.5	4.8	4.9	0.2	7.6	4.8	3.0	14.2	Georgia
17.8	9.4	10.6[3]	10.8	3,402	22.5	4.1	11.7	0.8	10.3	5.7	21.6	23.3	Germany
3.3	*3.8*	*3.9*[3]	*4.5*	2,684	26.2	48.2	1.2	1.8	0.2	9.6	4.6	8.3	Ghana
17.5	6.9	5.2	13.0	3,630	29.1	3.5	8.9	1.2	11.8	8.6	20.0	16.8	Greece
8.0	9.2	15.5	13.8	…	…	…	…	…	…	…	…	…	Greenland
9.1	13.7	4.6[3]	10.9[24]	2,681	25.3	2.5	9.1	1.5	9.5	9.2	13.1	29.8	Grenada
20.5	9.3	4.7[3]	8.7	2,732	37.8	2.6	10.8	2.6	8.5	8.4	13.1	16.1	Guadeloupe
18.0	…	*5.1*	*8.8*	…	…	…	…	…	…	…	…	…	Guam
7.0	5.0	0.9	2.7	2,159	55.3	0.4	3.6	0.1	5.1	3.1	7.0	25.4	Guatemala
15.7	8.3	…	24.7	3,257	22.8	6.1	14.4	1.0	11.6	5.0	19.1	20.0	Guernsey
5.1	*2.9*	*4.1*	*0.1*	2,315	42.9	15.6	0.9	1.2	1.0	13.0	14.7	10.8	Guinea
…	…	…	…	2,411	61.2	7.4	4.6	0.2	1.4	4.2	13.0	8.1	Guinea-Bissau
4.8	*2.9*	*6.4*[3]	*8.2*	2,476	47.3	3.8	4.8	4.2	5.4	2.8	4.1	27.6	Guyana
7.6	9.2	5.3[3]	11.6	1,876	46.7	8.8	3.3	0.3	2.0	7.4	8.8	22.8	Haiti
3.0	8.3	2.4[3]	3.1	2,343	46.7	0.3	3.6	0.3	8.6	6.7	11.9	21.9	Honduras
8.4	17.5	8.1	8.4	3,200	27.1	1.6	20.0	3.3	5.2	4.0	19.7	19.2	Hong Kong
15.2	8.8	5.9	10.6	3,408	25.4	3.6	10.1	0.2	8.4	5.4	22.7	24.1	Hungary
14.5	7.6	9.6	7.0	3,222	20.7	3.2	14.3	3.6	14.6	4.0	13.4	26.2	Iceland
10.6	3.1	1.8	5.7	2,466	62.7	1.6	0.9	0.4	4.5	3.2	8.5	18.3	India
…	2.9[18]	…	24.0	2,850	64.6	5.8	2.2	1.3	0.6	2.3	7.8	15.4	Indonesia
5.0	6.4	1.7[3]	3.7	2,822	51.2	3.2	4.3	0.3	3.8	11.2	10.8	15.1	Iran
6.5	6.7	0.8[3]	3.7	2,419	59.4	1.2	1.4	0.1	1.9	8.0	19.5	8.6	Iraq
14.0	7.2	0.9	13.1	3,622	26.0	6.0	13.1	0.8	11.0	4.0	16.5	21.4	Ireland
14.9	5.7	…	22.5	3,257	22.8	6.1	14.4	1.0	11.6	5.0	19.1	20.0	Isle of Man
12.9	10.8	4.3	11.6	3,466	33.5	2.5	8.2	0.9	7.6	8.6	18.3	20.3	Israel
13.2	9.5	8.4	18.4	3,608	31.8	1.9	11.1	1.1	8.9	7.2	22.0	15.9	Italy
12.4	5.5	2.1	26.1	2,711	30.5	9.3	8.5	0.8	5.3	7.2	13.1	25.3	Jamaica
11.0	3.7	9.5	26.9	2,874	40.7	2.5	5.8	6.3	6.5	4.3	12.0	21.8	Japan
13.9	*7.1*	…	*21.0*	3,257	22.8	6.1	14.4	1.0	11.6	5.0	19.1	20.0	Jersey
11.2	6.1	4.0	4.9	2,791	52.7	1.1	5.1	0.2	5.4	3.9	15.3	16.3	Jordan
…	…	…	67.8	2,517	54.4	4.1	9.1	0.2	12.0	2.1	7.4	10.8	Kazakhstan
8.4	9.4	3.1	9.1	1,968	52.4	8.6	3.7	0.5	7.2	3.2	9.3	15.3	Kenya
8.0	[5]	…	26.5	2,977	34.7	8.3	4.6	4.6	1.6	4.6	7.2	34.4	Kiribati
…	3.8[27]	…	15.9	1,899	64.5	1.1	3.1	1.3	1.0	7.6	5.8	15.5	Korea, North
11.3	5.0	—— 19.0 ——		3,069	49.7	1.1	9.6	3.0	2.2	7.1	9.7	17.7	Korea, South
13.7	11.2	5.2[3]	7.9	3,059	36.8	1.9	11.2	0.5	9.8	8.4	10.2	21.2	Kuwait
…	…	…	64.3	2,535	58.3	6.7	8.7	—	13.0	2.1	3.6	7.6	Kyrgyzstan
…	…	…	…	2,175	77.7	3.8	4.4	0.7	0.5	2.2	2.3	8.5	Laos
…	…	…	54.8	2,994	32.7	8.4	6.0	0.9	12.9	3.8	15.3	20.0	Latvia
5.4[6]	*2.6*[6]	*1.9*[6]	*6.3*[6]	3,285	34.6	3.9	4.9	0.4	5.2	15.9	13.9	21.2	Lebanon
4.7	11.9	…	8.8	2,210	75.5	4.3	3.4	—	1.1	1.4	3.1	11.2	Lesotho
…	*6.1*[6]	…	*25.8*[6]	1,979	41.5	20.4	2.0	0.4	0.5	5.5	19.8	10.0	Liberia
9.4	*4.6*	*8.5*[3]	*2.5*	3,267	46.3	2.0	4.8	0.3	5.7	7.3	17.0	16.7	Libya
13.3	5.8	16.3[3]	6.6	3,222	22.1	2.3	14.8	0.8	12.5	6.1	18.7	22.7	Liechtenstein
…	…	…	49.7	3,104	45.5	7.8	8.9	0.9	6.9	5.3	10.1	14.6	Lithuania
19.1	10.8	4.2[3]	20.1	3,606	20.4	5.2	8.6	1.1	10.8	6.5	25.7	21.7	Luxembourg
8.2	3.0	8.8[3]	7.3	2,471	36.3	0.7	15.7	2.3	4.7	3.7	20.7	15.8	Macau
6.5	4.2	3.3[3]	1.8	2,938	39.7	3.3	7.0	0.3	5.2	6.9	15.7	21.8	Macedonia
4.0	1.0	…	12.0	2,001	53.0	21.1	5.5	0.7	3.1	3.8	4.4	8.3	Madagascar
10.0	3.0	…	25.0	2,226	59.0	15.8	1.3	0.4	0.5	4.2	4.0	14.7	Malawi
20.9	7.7	11.0	14.1	2,901	41.6	2.1	9.2	3.1	5.2	3.4	12.5	22.8	Malaysia
2.6	17.0	5.9[3]	5.0	2,451	43.5	3.2	1.4	13.1	4.3	5.6	5.2	23.7	Maldives
10.0	1.0	…	12.0	2,118	69.9	0.5	4.2	0.8	4.6	1.2	7.4	11.3	Mali
16.4	9.9	7.1	18.4	3,382	30.8	4.0	8.8	1.6	11.3	7.9	11.5	24.0	Malta
…	[5]	…	14.7	…	…	…	…	…	…	…	…	…	Marshall Islands
20.7	9.4	5.4[3]	8.6	2,865	30.0	4.2	12.1	2.9	8.5	11.0	8.7	22.5	Martinique
2.0	1.2	4.0	0.1	2,640	54.8	0.4	4.0	0.9	10.8	1.2	9.9	18.1	Mauritania
10.0	6.4	—	12.2	2,944	44.7	1.3	4.8	1.2	6.3	3.0	16.6	22.2	Mauritius
5.1	8.8	…	5.6	…	…	…	…	…	…	…	…	…	Mayotte
10.0	11.8	5.5[3]	11.0	3,144	46.2	0.8	8.2	0.7	6.0	4.0	11.3	22.8	Mexico
…	…	…	26.5	…	…	…	…	…	…	…	…	…	Micronesia
…	…	…	…	2,763	48.4	4.2	4.0	0.1	8.9	6.6	8.2	19.7	Moldova
…	…	…	…	3,541	24.3	3.4	16.5	1.2	6.3	3.0	16.6	22.2	Monaco
3.5	8.0	0.4	16.2	2,010	47.0	2.2	27.2	—	10.4	1.2	4.7	7.2	Mongolia
8.0	5.0	…	16.0	3,165	59.7	2.0	2.8	0.5	2.0	5.4	10.4	17.3	Morocco
…	…	1.4[3]	7.9	1,911	41.2	37.3	1.4	0.2	0.6	1.4	8.9	9.1	Mozambique
3.8[6]	*0.5*[6]	*1.1*[6]	*7.5*[6]	2,832	76.3	0.5	2.0	1.0	0.9	2.6	7.0	9.6	Myanmar (Burma)
…	…	…	…	2,107	48.6	13.9	5.6	0.6	3.4	1.9	5.1	20.9	Namibia
…	…	…	…	…	…	…	…	…	…	…	…	…	Nauru
1.2	…	2.9[3]	2.0	2,170	76.8	3.4	2.0	0.1	3.8	2.5	4.4	7.0	Nepal

Household budgets and consumption (continued)

country	income (latest)						consumption expenditure						
	percent received by		by source (percent)				per capita private final, U.S.$ (1995)	by kind or end use (percent of household or personal budget; latest)					
	lowest 20% of households	highest 10% of households	wages, salaries	self-employment	transfer payments[a]	other[b]		food[c]	housing[d]	clothing[e]	health care	energy, water	education
Netherlands, The	7.3[1]	25.1[1]	48.2	10.7	29.1	12.0	15,290	13.6	14.9	7.1	12.9	3.1	0.7
Netherlands Antilles	...	...	...	...	...	...	6,050[10]	24.4[30]	10.4[30]	8.7[30]	2.2[30]	8.3[30]	1.2[30]
New Caledonia	...	...	68.2	18.1	13.7	...	5,410[31]	25.9	23.3[2, 5]	3.5	3.2	[2]	...
New Zealand	2.7[12]	29.8[12]	65.8	9.8	15.2	9.1	10,300	20.0	19.4	4.4	2.9	3.2	1.5
Nicaragua	4.2[1]	39.8[1]	...	...	...	...	360	...	...	...	...	...	...
Niger	2.6	35.4	...	...	...	...	210	50.5	19.1[5]	7.3	...	...	...
Nigeria	4.4[1]	40.8[1]	30.2[18]	46.3[18]	0.9[18]	22.6[18]	350[32]	48.0	3.0	5.0	3.0	1.0	4.0
Northern Mariana Islands	...	...	...	...	...	...	...	49.2[15]	19.5[2, 5]	9.1	[19]	[2]	...
Norway	9.7[12]	21.8[12]	58.8	9.9	24.2	7.1	16,570	23.5	13.7	7.0	5.4	6.2	0.6
Oman	...	...	...	...	...	...	3,000	40.6	24.6	5.1	2.4	3.2	[3]
Pakistan	9.5[1]	27.6[1]	22.0	56.0	—22.0—		300	37.0	11.0	6.0	1.0	5.0	1.0
Palau	...	...	63.7	7.4	18.5	10.4	...	...	...	...	...	...	...
Panama	3.6[1]	35.7[1]	60.8[6]	12.8[6]	13.2[6]	13.2[6]	1,570	34.9	12.6[2]	5.1	3.5	[2]	[3]
Papua New Guinea	4.5[1]	40.5[1]	*57.3*	[8]	*1.1*	*41.6*[8]	1,140	40.9	12.5[5]	6.2	...	4.9	...
Paraguay	2.3	46.6	33.9	[8]	2.5	63.6[8]	1,590	48.7	16.4	9.7	3.4	—	1.5
Peru	4.4[12]	35.4[12]	31.2	65.1	3.7	...	1,820	44.1[15]	6.8[2]	10.1	2.7	[2]	[3]
Philippines	5.4[1]	36.6[1]	45.7	42.5	3.4	8.4	800	56.8	4.1[2]	3.9	...	[2]	...
Poland	7.7[12]	26.3[12]	34.0	4.3	20.7	41.0	1,940	41.2	2.8	10.9	8.1	1.0	[3]
Portugal	*7.3*[12]	*28.4*[12]	46.4	[8]	21.8	31.8[8]	6,860	34.8	2.0	10.3	4.5	3.0	1.4
Puerto Rico	*3.2*	*34.7*	56.3	6.4	29.5	7.8	5,640[10]	20.6	11.8[2]	7.4	11.6	[2]	3.1
Qatar	...	...	80.8	5.6	...	13.6	3,600[4]	24.5	35.1[5]	9.1	1.0	1.9	4.3
Réunion	...	...	68.9	[8]	16.0	15.1[8]	4,820[31]	22.4	11.8	7.9	2.2	2.2	[3]
Romania	8.9[12]	22.7[12]	62.6	—37.4—			1,570	51.1	16.4[2, 5]	15.7	1.2	[2]	[3]
Russia	4.4[1]	38.7[1]	68.5	6.4	15.7	12.1	1,180	34.8	2.7	22.3	...	...	...
Rwanda	9.7[1]	24.2[1]	10.4[33]	47.7[33]	13.9[33]	28.0[33]	130	32.1[33]	13.1[33]	9.4[33]	1.3[33]	1.2[33]	[33]
St. Kitts and Nevis	...	...	...	...	...	...	2,480[28]	*55.6*[15]	*7.6*	*7.5*	...	*6.6*	...
St. Lucia	...	...	...	...	...	...	...	49.6[15]	13.5	6.5	2.3	4.5	[3]
St. Vincent and the Grenadines	...	...	...	...	...	...	1,700	59.8	6.3	7.7	...	6.2	...
Samoa	...	...	*49.4*	*22.8*	...	*27.8*	710[1]	58.8	5.1[5]	4.2	...	5.0	...
San Marino	...	...	...	...	...	...	...	22.1	20.9[2]	8.0	2.6	[2]	[3]
São Tomé and Príncipe	...	...	...	...	...	...	270	...	...	...	...	...	...
Saudi Arabia	...	...	...	...	...	...	2,980	52.2[18, 34]	17.2[18, 34]	6.6[18, 34]	2.1[18, 34]	1.8[18, 34]	1.1[18, 34]
Senegal	6.4[1]	33.5[1]	51.6[6]	—48.4[6]—			380	49.0	7.0	11.0	2.0	4.0	6.0
Serbia and Montenegro	...	...	41.7	15.8	12.7	29.8	2,480[35]	51.6	1.4	7.4	5.2	8.4	[3]
Seychelles	4.1	35.6	*77.2*	*3.8*	*3.2*	*15.8*	3,410[32]	53.9	13.6	4.2	0.4	9.1	...
Sierra Leone	*1.1*[1]	*43.6*[1]	27.9	61.6	—10.5—		190	63.8	5.8[2]	7.3	4.5	[2]	[3]
Singapore	5.1	33.5	81.2	16.8	—2.0—		11,710	18.7	10.2[2]	7.1	4.6	[2]	1.4
Slovakia	11.9[12]	18.2[12]	76.7	[8]	8.7	14.4[8]	1,580	26.8	7.6[2]	8.9	...	[2]	...
Slovenia	8.4[12]	20.7[12]	52.4	13.0	23.4	11.2	5,460	30.8	18.3	8.5	5.0	7.3	[3]
Solomon Islands	...	...	74.1	—25.9—			820[4]	46.8	21.9[2, 5]	5.7	[19]	[2]	...
Somalia	...	...	...	...	...	...	...	62.3[6, 15]	15.3[6]	5.6[6]	...	4.3[6]	...
South Africa	2.9[1]	45.9[1]	73.6	[8]	4.9	21.5[8]	1,970	29.3	12.6[2]	7.5	4.5	[2]	1.4
Spain	7.5[12]	25.2[12]	48.5	27.5	19.5	4.5	8,840	21.6[15]	12.6[2]	8.6	4.7	[2]	[3]
Sri Lanka	8.0[1]	28.0[1]	48.5	[8]	9.7	41.8[8]	520	48.0	1.9	10.1	1.8	3.3	0.8
Sudan, The	*4.0*	*34.6*	...	...	...	...	1,050[35]	63.6	11.5	5.3	4.1	3.8	[3]
Suriname	...	...	*74.6*	...	*3.2*	*22.2*	5,960[10]	*39.9*[6]	*4.4*[6]	*11.0*[6]	*3.6*[6]	*6.9*[6]	*2.6*[6]
Swaziland	*2.8*	*54.5*	44.4	22.2	12.2	21.2	500	33.5[15]	13.4[2]	6.0	1.8	[2]	[3]
Sweden	9.6[12]	20.1[12]	58.9	9.7	25.8	5.6	13,680	21.3	19.9	8.6	3.2	4.9	0.1
Switzerland	6.9[12]	25.2[12]	63.6	[8]	16.5	19.9[8]	26,060	27.0[15]	13.1	4.4	9.9	7.7	[3]
Syria	...	...	40.7	...	25.1	34.2	2,210	58.8[15]	16.0[2]	7.5	...	[2]	[3]
Taiwan	7.1	25.5	64.5	19.7	4.5	11.3	12,230	26.8	22.5	5.6	7.8	3.0	5.6
Tajikistan	...	...	64.3	5.6[7]	30.1	—	340	65.3	...	...	...	...	...
Tanzania	6.8[1]	30.1[1]	28.1	34.2	3.5	34.2	150	66.7	8.3	9.9	1.3	7.6	...
Thailand	6.4[1]	32.4[1]	36.4	45.0	0.9	17.7	1,540	29.0	6.3	11.6	8.0	1.7	0.5
Togo	*8.0*	*30.5*	...	...	...	...	210	42.5[6]	13.4[2, 6]	11.5[6]	5.0[6]	[2, 6]	[3, 6]
Tonga	...	...	...	...	...	...	...	49.3	10.5	5.6	0.3	2.7	...
Trinidad and Tobago	*2.6*	*33.6*	...	...	...	...	2,050	25.5[15]	21.6	10.4	[19]	...	1.5
Tunisia	5.9[1]	30.7[1]	...	...	...	...	1,260	39.0	10.7	6.0	3.0	5.1	1.8
Turkey	5.8[1]	32.3[1]	24.1	51.4	10.8	13.7	1,940	38.5	22.8[2]	9.0	2.6	[2]	1.4
Turkmenistan	6.1[1]	31.7[1]	56.6	26.0[7]	14.4	3.0	570[10]	...	...	...	...	...	...
Tuvalu	...	...	*17.9*	*76.1*	...	*6.0*	...	45.5	11.5[5]	7.5	...	...	...
Uganda	6.6[1]	31.2[1]	...	...	...	...	260	57.1[6, 15]	...	5.5[6]	...	7.3[6]	...
Ukraine	8.6[1]	26.4[1]	66.4	9.3	13.4	10.9	490	41.3	1.7	...	...	...	[3]
United Arab Emirates	...	...	...	...	...	...	7,940	24.1	23.7	9.1	1.1	1.2	3.9
United Kingdom	6.6[12]	27.3[12]	66.2	9.8	13.9	11.0	12,020	17.1	21.7	6.0	...	4.6	...
United States	5.2[12]	30.5[12]	64.4	9.0	19.3	7.3	18,840	15.4	14.9	6.9	17.0	3.5	2.2
Uruguay	5.4[12]	32.7[12]	53.5	17.0	—29.5—		4,140	39.9	17.6[2]	7.0	9.3	[2]	1.3
Uzbekistan	7.4[12]	25.2[12]	59.8	18.5	21.7	...	950	...	...	...	...	...	...
Vanuatu	...	...	59.0	33.7	—7.3—		680	30.5[15]	29.0[2, 5]	4.7	[19]	[2]	...
Venezuela	3.7[12]	37.0[12]	...	...	...	...	2,490	30.4	11.5	10.6	2.9	3.0	0.8
Vietnam	8.0[1]	29.9[1]	17.2	64.6	17.6	0.5	280	62.4	2.5	5.0	...	...	2.9
Virgin Islands (U.S.)	...	...	65.7	2.6	13.0	12.7	...	25.3[36]	*24.9*[36]	*5.4*[36]	...	*6.5*[36]	...
West Bank	...	...	...	...	...	...	1,380[22]	...	...	...	...	...	...
Western Sahara	...	...	...	...	...	...	...	...	...	...	...	...	...
Yemen	6.1[1]	30.8[1]	...	...	...	...	310	61.0[37]	13.2[37]	...	1.1[37]	6.1[37]	...
Zambia	4.2[1]	39.2[1]	79.9	17.8	1.3	1.0	220	36.0	7.0	10.0	8.0	4.0	14.0
Zimbabwe	4.0[1]	46.9[1]	92.0	1.0	...	7.0	580	30.1[15]	6.5	10.3	7.1	8.9	6.0

[1]Data refer to consumption shares by fractiles of persons. [2]Housing includes energy, water. [3]Recreation includes education. [4]1988. [5]Housing includes household durable goods. [6]Capital city only. [7]Agricultural self-employment only. [8]Other includes self-employment. [9]1989. [10]1993. [11]Highest 20%. [12]Data refer to income shares by fractiles of persons. [13]1985. [14]1990. [15]Includes tobacco. [16]Includes wage taxes. [17]Personal effects, other includes education and recreation. [18]Urban areas only. [19]Recreation includes health care. [20]1984. [21]Low-income population in Banjul

transportation, communications	household durable goods[f]	recreation[g]	personal effects, other[h]	food consumption, 1998: daily available calories per capita	percent of total calories derived from: cereals	potatoes, cassava	meat, poultry	fish	eggs, milk	fruits, vegetables	fats, oils[i]	other[j]	country
13.3	7.1	9.7	17.6	3,282	17.1	4.5	15.0	1.0	15.0	6.1	16.1	25.1	Netherlands, The
19.5[30]	10.0[00]	4.2[00]	10.1[00]	2,059	28.2	2.3	18.9	1.4	10.8	5.0	13.6	19.7	Netherlands Antilles
16.1	[5]	6.7	21.3	2,812	30.9	6.1	13.1	1.5	8.6	3.9	16.0	19.9	New Caledonia
17.1	10.9	—— 20.6 ——		3,315	22.1	4.1	15.1	1.3	11.1	7.4	16.8	22.3	New Zealand
...	...	...	...	2,208	50.4	1.3	2.4	0.1	4.3	2.7	10.9	27.9	Nicaragua
...	[5]	...	23.1	1,966	70.5	3.2	2.6	0.1	2.2	1.7	4.4	15.2	Niger
3.0	6.0	...	27.0	2,882	45.8	18.6	2.4	0.4	1.0	4.4	14.1	13.3	Nigeria
8.3	[5]	13.9[19]	—	...	...	...	...	...	...	...	...	...	Northern Mariana Islands
12.8	6.9	8.8	15.1	3,425	27.4	4.3	10.7	3.5	12.2	4.9	17.7	19.2	Norway
8.9	7.1	4.1[3]	4.0	...	...	...	...	...	...	...	...	...	Oman
13.0	5.0	...	21.0	2,447	57.0	0.9	3.1	0.2	8.5	2.9	13.2	14.3	Pakistan
...	...	...	...	...	...	...	...	...	...	...	...	...	Palau
15.1	8.4	11.7[3]	8.7	2,476	37.0	2.7	7.5	1.1	7.4	5.7	16.1	22.5	Panama
13.0	[5]	...	22.5	2,168	31.2	25.4	7.7	1.3	0.6	17.6	6.2	9.9	Papua New Guinea
4.5	6.2	2.3	7.3	2,577	27.8	13.9	11.5	0.4	7.3	4.3	16.2	18.7	Paraguay
7.3	7.5	7.6[3]	13.9	2,420	35.7	13.4	4.3	1.8	4.5	6.4	11.6	22.4	Peru
5.0	12.8	...	17.3	2,280	51.7	4.2	8.8	3.0	2.2	8.3	5.9	15.9	Philippines
8.9	8.3	15.0[3]	3.8	3,351	34.4	7.4	10.4	1.0	8.6	4.5	15.6	18.0	Poland
15.4	8.6	4.4	15.6	3,691	28.6	6.3	10.8	2.4	8.3	7.1	17.0	19.6	Portugal
11.8	11.2	7.9	14.7	...	...	...	...	...	...	...	...	...	Puerto Rico
13.0	[5]	—— 11.1 ——		...	...	...	...	...	...	...	...	...	Qatar
24.9	6.0	10.1[3]	12.5	3,308	41.4	1.7	11.9	1.5	5.2	5.0	9.8	23.5	Réunion
6.6	[5]	4.5[3]	4.5	3,263	49.5	4.5	7.4	0.1	11.3	4.5	10.5	12.2	Romania
...	9.4	...	30.8	2,835	41.3	8.0	9.0	1.6	10.3	3.4	9.6	20.6	Russia
1.7[33]	5.3[33]	0.4[33]	35.5[33]	2,035	22.4	23.1	1.1	—	1.4	25.9	5.5	—	Rwanda
4.3	*9.4*	...	*9.0*	2,766	24.9	2.6	13.6	1.9	8.6	4.6	11.6	32.1	St. Kitts and Nevis
6.3	5.8	3.2[3]	8.3	2,842	34.3	4.8	14.0	1.3	6.8	9.3	6.9	22.7	St. Lucia
3.7	6.6	...	9.7	2,554	35.2	4.3	10.4	1.1	6.1	5.2	9.6	28	St. Vincent and the Grenadines
9.0	[5]	...	17.9	...	...	...	...	...	...	...	...	...	Samoa
17.6	7.2	7.1[3]	14.5	3,608	31.8	1.9	11.1	1.1	8.9	7.2	22.0	15.9	San Marino
...	...	...	...	2,201	28.3	15.4	1.4	2.1	0.8	17.0	10.6	24.3	São Tomé and Príncipe
4.5[18, 34]	5.9[18, 34]	...	8.6[18, 34]	2,888	46.6	1.1	7.3	0.4	4.9	10.1	11.4	18.2	Saudi Arabia
5.0	2.0	...	12.0	2,277	57.5	1.0	3.7	2.8	2.4	2.0	18.7	11.9	Senegal
5.7	1.6	2.4[3]	16.3	2,963	29.4	2.3	16.3	0.2	11.4	6.8	17.8	15.8	Serbia and Montenegro
6.4	6.6	1.4	4.4	2,462	37.3	1.2	5.6	5.1	6.5	5.8	11.5	27.1	Seychelles
4.4	3.9	3.8[3]	4.8	2,045	53.4	10.4	1.0	1.4	0.6	2.9	17.6	12.8	Sierra Leone
13.8	8.9	13.1	23.3	...	...	...	...	...	...	...	...	...	Singapore
...	3.9	...	26.2	2,953	27.3	4.3	10.5	0.3	8.9	4.7	20.8	23.2	Slovakia
12.7	3.3	6.1[3]	8.0	2,950	35.4	3.5	11.1	0.4	12.0	5.3	15.2	17.2	Slovenia
9.9	[5]	[19]	15.7	2,130	33.3	36.3	3.1	3.7	0.6	2.7	2.9	17.4	Solomon Islands
...	...	...	12.1[6]	1,531	33.4	1.5	8.7	0.2	28.4	2.8	7.4	17.5	Somalia
16.7	10.0	6.3	11.7	2,909	53.0	2.0	7.0	0.5	4.8	2.8	11.7	18.1	South Africa
15.3	7.1	7.0[3]	23.1	3,348	22.6	4.7	13.4	2.4	9.3	6.7	21.6	19.4	Spain
17.0	3.9	2.4	10.8	2,314	51.3	2.9	0.9	1.9	3.4	4.5	2.9	32.3	Sri Lanka
1.5	5.5	0.7[3]	4.0	2,444	56.5	0.6	5.1	0.1	13.3	2.9	9.5	11.9	Sudan, The
9.5[6]	*12.3*[6]	*5.8*[6]	*4.0*[6]	2,633	41.2	2.3	7.0	1.6	4.8	6.2	12.5	24.5	Suriname
8.8	12.8	3.3[3]	20.4	2,503	48.1	1.3	6.4	—	5.2	1.8	6.2	31.0	Swaziland
15.7	6.6	10.9	8.8	3,114	25.6	3.6	10.2	1.8	14.1	5.2	18.9	20.7	Sweden
12.9	5.1	9.8[3]	10.1	3,222	22.1	2.3	14.8	0.8	12.5	6.1	18.7	22.7	Switzerland
2.4	5.8	2.1[3]	7.4	3,378	53.9	1.2	3.8	0.1	6.6	5.6	12.9	15.9	Syria
10.7	2.2	1.1	4.7	...	...	...	...	...	...	...	...	...	Taiwan
...	...	...	34.7	2,176	67.9	0.1	2.8	—	3.4	4.3	12.2	9.2	Tajikistan
4.1	1.4	0.7	—	1,999	49.0	19.5	2.6	1.1	2.2	5.4	6.8	13.6	Tanzania
12.9	10.9	4.2	14.9	2,462	47.1	1.9	6.6	2.6	2.8	5.7	6.1	27.3	Thailand
9.5[6]	4.4[6]	5.1[3, 6]	8.6[6]	2,513	50.7	29.2	2.3	1.3	0.6	1.3	7.2	7.5	Togo
5.8	10.6	0.5	14.7	...	...	...	...	...	...	...	...	...	Tonga
15.2	14.3	[17]	6.2[17]	2,711	36.8	2.8	4.5	0.9	6.8	3.8	14.6	29.9	Trinidad and Tobago
9.0	11.2	7.1	7.1	3,297	52.9	1.8	3.0	0.5	4.6	6.2	15.8	15.3	Tunisia
8.8	9.0	5.6	2.3	3,554	48.4	3.7	2.5	0.4	6.9	7.9	15.1	15.1	Turkey
...	...	...	...	2,684	57.7	0.5	7.6	0.1	8.2	3.4	16.4	6.1	Turkmenistan
10.5	[5]	...	25.0	...	...	...	...	...	...	...	...	...	Tuvalu
5.9[6]	...	...	24.2[6]	2,216	20.4	23.4	3.2	0.8	1.9	25.8	2.2	22.3	Uganda
...	6.8	6.3[3]	43.9	2,878	44.5	8.8	5.8	0.7	10.3	3.4	10.8	15.7	Ukraine
14.1	11.6	4.7	6.5	3,372	33.8	1.6	11.5	1.4	9.5	14.3	10.3	17.7	United Arab Emirates
15.1	8.0	15.9	11.6	3,257	22.8	6.1	14.4	1.0	11.6	5.0	19.1	20.0	United Kingdom
13.9	1.5	5.8	18.9	3,757	23.6	2.9	11.9	0.8	11.7	5.2	17.9	26.1	United States
10.4	6.3	3.1	5.1	2,866	28.9	3.7	19.1	0.6	12.3	4.0	11.0	20.3	Uruguay
...	...	...	...	2,564	55.8	2.1	6.9	—	9.4	4.1	15.3	6.2	Uzbekistan
13.2	[5]	12.3[19]	10.3	2,737	21.4	30.7	9.2	1.6	1.5	6.4	8.9	20.3	Vanuatu
7.1	4.5	2.7	26.4	2,358	34.9	3.1	6.6	1.7	6.5	7.3	15.2	24.7	Venezuela
...	4.6	...	22.6	2,422	70.9	4.0	7.6	1.3	0.5	3.9	3.2	8.6	Vietnam
11.7[36]	*4.3*[36]	...	*21.9*[36]	...	...	...	...	...	...			...	Virgin Islands (U.S.)
...	...	...	...	...	...	...	...	...	...	...	...	...	West Bank
...	...	...	...	...	...	...	...	...	...	...	...	...	Western Sahara
1.9[37]	3.0[37]	...	13.7[37]	2,087	68.7	1.0	2.7	0.7	1.8	3.0	8.2	13.9	Yemen
5.0	1.0	...	15.0	1,950	64.9	14.5	2.7	0.8	1.3	1.5	3.4	10.9	Zambia
1.1	12.9	0.6	16.5	2,153	60.5	2.1	2.3	0.3	3.1	1.0	11.9	18.8	Zimbabwe

and Kombo St. Mary only. [22]1986. [23]Urban areas of Eastern region only. [24]Personal effects, other includes health care. [25]Housing includes water. [26]Wage earners only. [27]Workers and clerical workers only. [28]1992. [29]Malagasy households only. [30]Curaçao only. [31]1987. [32]1994. [33]Rural areas only. [34]Middle-income population only. [35]1991. [36]St. Thomas only. [37]Data refer to former Yemen Arab Republic.

Health services

The provision of health services in most countries is both a principal determinant of the quality of life and a large and growing sector of the national economy. This table summarizes the basic indicators of health personnel; hospitals, by kind and utilization; mortality rates that are most indicative of general health services; external controls on health (adequacy of food supply and availability of safe drinking water); and sources and amounts of expenditure on health care. Each datum refers more or less directly to the availability or use of a particular health service in a country, and, while each may be a representative measure at a national level, each may also conceal considerable differences in availability of the particular service to different segments of a population or regions of a country. In the United States, for example, the availability of physicians ranges from about one per 730 persons in the least well-served states to one per 260 in the best-served, with a rate of one per 150 in the national capital. In addition, even when trained personnel exist and facilities have been created, limited financial resources at the national or local level may leave facilities underserved; or lack of good transportation may prevent those most in need from reaching a clinic or hospital that could help them.

Definitions and limits of data have been made as consistent as possible in the compilation of this table. For example, despite wide variation worldwide in the nature of the qualifying or certifying process that permits an individual to represent himself as a physician, organizations such as the World Health Organization (WHO) try to maintain more specific international standards for training and qualification. International statistics presented here for "physicians" refer to persons qualified according to WHO standards and exclude traditional health practitioners, whatever the local custom with regard to the designation "doctor." Statistics for health personnel in this table uniformly include all those actually working in the health service field, whether in the actual provision of services or in teaching, administration, research, or other tasks. One group of practitioners for whom this type of guideline works less well is that of midwives, whose training and qualifications vary enormously from country to country but who must be included, as they represent, after nurses, perhaps the largest and most important category of health auxiliary worldwide. The statistics here refer to those midwives working in some kind of institutional setting (a hospital, clinic, community health-care centre, or the like) and exclude rural noninstitutional midwives and traditional birth attendants.

Hospitals also differ considerably worldwide in terms of staffing and services. In this tabulation, the term hospital refers generally to a permanent facility offering inpatient services and/or nursing care and staffed by at least one physician. Establishments offering only outpatient or custodial care are excluded. These statistics are broken down into data for general hospitals (those providing care in more than one specialty), specialized facilities (with care in only one specialty), local medical centres, and rural health-care centres; the last two generally refer to institutions that provide a more limited range of medical or nursing care, often less than full-time. Hospital data are further analyzed into three categories of administrative classification: public, private nonprofit, and private for profit. Statistics on number of beds refer to beds that are maintained and staffed on a full-time basis for a succession of inpatients to whom care is provided.

Data on hospital utilization refer to institutions defined as above. Admission and discharge, the two principal points at which statistics are normally collected, are the basis for the data on the amount and distribution of care by kind of facility. The data on numbers of patients exclude babies born during a maternal confinement but include persons who die before being discharged. The bed-occupancy and average length-of-stay statistics depend on the concept of a "patient-day," which is the annual total of daily censuses of inpatients. The bed-occupancy rate is the ratio of total patient-days to potential days based on the number of beds; the average length-of-stay rate is the ratio of total patient-days to total admissions. Bed-occu-

Health services

country	health personnel							hospitals									
	year	physicians	dentists	nurses	pharmacists	midwives	population per physician	year	number	kinds (%)				ownership (%)			hospital beds per 10,000 pop.
										general	specialized	medical centres	rural	government	private nonprofit	private for profit	
Afghanistan	1997	2,556	232	4,182	464	...	9,090	1988–93	...	...	...	...	...	...	...	...	3
Albania	1995	4,848	1,332	14,559	772[2]	9,936[2]	668	1993	40	...	...	...	...	100.0	—	—	31
Algeria	1996	27,650	7,837	...	3,866	...	1,015	1996[3]	186	...	...	...	...	...	...	...	12
American Samoa	1991	26	7[6]	140[6]	2[6]	1[6]	1,885	1990	1	100.0	—	—	—	100.0	—	—	27
Andorra	1998	166	35	188	59	6	434	1996	1	100.0	—	—	—	100.0	—	—	28
Angola	1997	736	...	10,942	...	411	13,228	1990	58	...	...	...	...	...	...	...	12
Antigua and Barbuda	1996	75	12	187	13	31	915	1998	3	50.0	50.0	—	—	100.0	—	—	42
Argentina	1992	88,800	21,900[8]	18,000[6]	...	...	376	1997	1,235	...	...	...	...	56.8	—43.2—		22
Armenia	1998	18,000[10]	[10]	18,258	144	1,750	292[10]	1998	183[11]	...	...	...	...	100.0	...	...	28
Aruba	1997	103	21	515	15	3	874	1999	2	50.0	—	50.0	—	100.0	—	—	32
Australia	1997–98	47,400	8,800	148,300	15,600	...	395	1996–97	1,222	...	...	...	...	61.0	—39.0—		95
Austria	1998	33,698	1,534	35,834	2,137[13]	1,056	240	1998	329	37.7	62.3	—	—	...	...	...	92
Azerbaijan	1998	28,850	2,426	62,213	2,560	10,843	274	1997	762	...	...	...	...	100.0	...	...	92
Bahamas, The	1996	419	72	648	52[4]	...	673	1997	5	60.0	20.0	20.0	—	60.0	—40.0—		38
Bahrain	1997	620	56	1,755	124	...	1,000	1994	12	58.3	42.7	—	—	75.0	16.7	8.3	30[14]
Bangladesh	1997	27,546	938	15,408	7,485[4]	13,211	4,627	1997	976	...	...	...	...	69.3	—30.7—		4
Barbados	1993	330	42	869	138[12]	377[12]	797	1995	9	66.7	33.3	—	—	80.0	—	20.0	74
Belarus	1999	39,007	4,522	47,343	3,152[13]	5,826	261	1999	276	55.4	—44.6—			100.0	...	...	68
Belgium	1998	39,420	7,360	109,187	14,597	6,602	259	1993	363	80.4	19.6	—	—	38.6	61.4	—	76
Belize	1998	155	26	404	30	230	1,542	1998	7	...	...	...	...	100.0	—	—	23
Benin	1995	312	16	1,116	85	432	17,538	1993	...	...	...	...	...	...	...	...	2
Bermuda	1996	96	22	522	29	...	639	1996	2	50.0	50.0	—	—	...	...	...	40
Bhutan	1997	101	9[4]	355[14]	5[4]	326[14]	6,128	1997	28	...	...	...	...	...	...	...	16
Bolivia	1996	4,346	444	2,062	...	...	1,747	1996	336	10.7[14]	8.9[14]	23.5[14]	56.8[14]	...	...	...	11
Bosnia and Herzegovina	1998	4,813	640	15,241	370	1,565[8]	699	1996	...	...	...	...	...	...	...	...	48
Botswana	1994	339	...	3,329	...	...	4,395	1994	30	53.3	3.3	43.3	—	...	...	...	23
Brazil	1997	205,828	137,600	67,760	51,847	...	774	1997	6,410	—100.0—		—	—	35.5	—64.5—		31
Brunei	1996	259	26	1,229	15[14]	278[14]	1,181	1995	10	90.0	—	—	10.0	90.0	—10.0—		33
Bulgaria	1998	28,823	5,324	47,434	1,230	5,923	286	1998	288	—71.2—		28.8	—	...	...	...	104
Burkina Faso	1991[15]	341	19	2,627	113	339	27,158	1993	78	—14.1—		85.9	—	100.0	—	—	5
Burundi	1996	329	9[4]	1,131	55[4]	...	16,507	1996	...	...	...	...	...	...	...	...	0.7
Cambodia	1998	3,464	210	8,608	262[12]	3,359	3,367	1988[3]	188	...	...	...	...	100.0	—	—	16
Cameroon	1996	1,031	56	5,112	206[6]	70	13,510	1988	629	—27.0—		—73.0—		72.3	—27.7—		27
Canada	1996	55,006	15,636	232,869	22,197	...	539	1989	1,079	81.8	16.6	1.6	—	95.8	—	4.2	54[11]
Cape Verde	1996	66	...	213	6	...	5,818	1996	65	8.0	—	92.0	—	100.0	—	—	19[16]
Central African Republic	1995	112	16	282	22[4]	157	28,600	1990	255	—21.1[17]—		—78.9[17]—		79.7[17]	—20.3[17]—		14[8]
Chad	1994	228	14	1,014	10	159	30,260	1994	...	...	...	...	...	...	...	...	13
Chile	1996	13,857	5,817	6,738	1,830[15]	5,369[15]	1,040	1994	198	...	...	...	...	89.4	—10.6—		31
China	1998	1,999,500[10, 18]	[10]	1,218,000	440,000	51,000	621[18]	1998	69,105	11.2	13.4	—75.4—		100.0	—	—	23
Colombia	1997	40,355	22,121	46,187	...	...	1,102	1997	1,657	...	...	...	...	...	...	...	1
Comoros	1997	64	6[4]	180	6[4]	74	7,765	1995	...	...	...	...	...	...	...	...	29
Congo, Dem. Rep. of the	1996	3,224	514	20,652	59[4]	...	14,492	1986	400	...	...	...	...	52.5	—47.5—		21
Congo, Rep. of the	1995	632	35[4]	4,663	175[4]	160	4,083	1990	...	...	...	...	...	...	...	...	33
Costa Rica	1997	5,500	1,420	3,720	1,362	...	641	1997	29	...	...	...	...	87.9	—	12.1	14
Côte d'Ivoire	1996	1,318	219[4]	4,568	135[4]	2,196	11,108	1993	...	...	...	...	...	...	...	...	5
Croatia	1998	9,766	2,802	20,216	1,940	1,407	436	1997	70	52.8	47.2	—	—	...	...	...	63
Cuba	1996	60,129	9,600	76,013	...	...	183	1993	244	...	...	...	...	100.0	—	—	65
Cyprus[19]	1997	1,725	594	2,942	668[14]	120[20]	486	1997[21]	103	71.8	22.1	—	6.1	10.0[20]	0.9[20]	89.1[20]	48
Czech Republic	1999	38,828	6,383	91,213	4,785	4,602	265	1999	365	59.2	40.8	—	—	70.7	—29.3—		67
Denmark	1995	15,175	4,605	36,944	747	1,046	345	1992	163	42.9	57.1	—	—	42.9	57.1	—	35

pancy rates may exceed 100% because stays of partial days are counted as full days.

Two measures that give health planners and policy makers an excellent indication of the level of ordinary health care are those for mortality of children under age five and for maternal mortality. The former reflects the probability of a newborn infant dying before age five. The latter refers to deaths attributable to delivery or complications of pregnancy, childbirth, the puerperium (the period immediately following birth), or abortion. A principal source for the former data was WHO's *The World Health Report* (annual) and for the latter, the UN Development Programme's *Human Development Report* (annual).

Levels of nutrition and access to safe drinking water are two of the most basic limitations imposed by the physical environment in which health-care activities take place. The nutritional data are based on reported levels of food supply (whether or not actually consumed), referred to the recommendations of the United Nations' Food and Agriculture Organization for the necessary daily intake (in calories) for a moderately active person of average size in a climate of a particular kind (fewer calories are needed in a hot climate) to remain in average *good* health. Excess intake in the many developed countries ranges to more than 40% above the minimum required to maintain health (the excess usually being construed to diminish, rather than raise, health). The range of deficiency is less dramatic numerically but far more critical to the countries in which deficiencies are chronic, because the deficiencies lead to overall poor health (raising health service needs and costs), to decreased productivity in nearly every area of national economic life, and to the loss of social and economic potential through early mortality. By "safe" water is meant only water that has no substantial quantities of chemical or biological pollutants—*i.e.*, quantities sufficient to cause "immediate" health problems. Data refer to the proportion of persons having "reasonable access" to an "adequate" supply of water within a "convenient" distance of the person's dwelling, as these concepts are interpreted locally.

The data on health care expenditure were excerpted from a joint effort by the WHO and the World Bank to create better analytical tools by which the interrelations among health policy, health care delivery systems, and human health might be examined against the more general frameworks of government operations, resource allocation, and development process. First published in the World Bank's *World Development Report 1993: Investing in Health* and, the following year, in the World Health Organization's *Global Comparative Assessments in the Health Sector* (edited by C.J.L. Murray and A.D. Lopez), the database and underlying methodology are expected to provide a continuing basis for international comparisons and policy analysis. The first two of ten volumes of the final results appeared in 1996 as *The Global Burden of Disease* and *Global Health Statistics* by the same editors.

Expenditures were tabulated for direct preventative and curative activities and for public health and public education programs having direct impact on health status—family planning, nutrition, and health education—but not more indirect programs like environmental, waste removal, or relief activities. Public, parastatal (semipublic, *e.g.*, social security institutions), international aid, and household expenditure reports and surveys were utilized to build up a comprehensive picture of national, regional, and world patterns of health care expenditures and investment that could not have been assembled from any single type of source. For reasons of space, public and parastatal are combined as the former.

Internet resources for further information:

- Most Recent Values of W.H.O. Global Health-For-All Indicators (for personnel and general indicators) http://www.who.int/htl/countrysup/countrye.htm

No comparable source exists for hospitals.

admissions or discharges							mortality				total health expenditures, 1990					country
rate per 10,000 pop.	by kinds of hospital (%)				bed occupancy rate (%)	average length of stay (days)	under age 5 per 1,000 live newborn 1997	maternal mortality per 100,000 live births 1990–97	population with access to safe water 2000 (%)	food supply (% of FAO requirement) 1998	as percent of GDP	per capita (U.S.$)	by source (percent)			
	general	specialized	medical centres	rural									public	private	international aid	
…	…	…	…	…	…	…	257	…	13	73[1]	…	…	…	…	…	Afghanistan
…	…	…	…	…	…	…	40	65	97	124	4.00	26	84.0	16.0	—	Albania
371	…	…	…	…	49.3[4]	5[4]	39	220	89[5]	126	6.95	149	76.9	23.0	0.1	Algeria
965	100.0	—	—	—	38.4	4	…	…	…	…	…	…	…	…	…	American Samoa
…	…	…	…	…	…	…	6	…	100	…	…	…	…	…	…	Andorra
238	…	…	…	…	44.5[7]	16[7]	292	1,500	38	82	…	…	…	…	…	Angola
64[7]	…	…	…	…	50.0[7]	8[7]	21	150	91	99	4.55	241	59.1	37.3	3.6	Antigua and Barbuda
560[3]	…	…	…	…	52.0[3]	7[3]	24	44	81[9]	134	4.21	137	60.1	39.7	0.2	Argentina
…	…	…	…	…	…	…	30	35	…	92	4.17	152	59.8	40.2	—	Armenia
…	…	…	…	…	92.2[12]	…	…	…	…	…	…	…	…	…	…	Aruba
…	…	…	…	…	…	4.5	6	9	100	120	7.67	1,294	69.6	30.4	—	Australia
2,650	…	…	…	…	80.1	10	5	10	100[5]	134	8.38	1,711	66.4	33.6	—	Austria
…	…	…	…	…	…	…	46	37	78	86	4.27	99	61.2	38.8	—	Azerbaijan
837[3]	…	…	…	…	85.4[3]	12[3]	21	…	97	105	…	…	…	…	…	Bahamas, The
…	…	…	…	…	…	…	22	46	100	…	4.62	324	63.0	36.9	0.1	Bahrain
…	…	…	…	…	…	…	109	440	97	89	3.19	6	24.8	56.7	18.5	Bangladesh
810[12]	93.5[12]	6.5[12]	—	—	88.3[12]	32[12]	12	0	100[5]	123	5.04	323	64.3	33.8	1.9	Barbados
…	…	…	…	…	…	…	27	22	100	123	3.19	157	68.7	31.3	—	Belarus
1,963	96.0	4.0	—	—	84.4	12	7	10	100[5]	137	7.50	1,449	82.5	17.5	—	Belgium
…	…	…	…	…	…	…	43	140	92	129	5.88	23	48.4	41.0	10.7	Belize
…	…	…	…	…	…	…	167	500	63	112	4.32	19	26.3	36.4	37.3	Benin
1,313	97.0	3.0	—	—	75.0	8	…	…	…	116	…	…	…	…	…	Bermuda
…	…	…	…	…	…	…	121	380	62	…	5.05	10	41.1	30.4	28.5	Bhutan
250	…	…	…	…	48.0	6	96	390	83	93	4.01	25	39.9	39.6	20.5	Bolivia
529[6, 7]	…	…	…	…	82.4[6, 7]	11[6, 7]	19	10	…	110	…	…	…	…	…	Bosnia and Herzegovina
…	…	…	…	…	93.1[6]	…	49	330	95	93	6.19	139	61.8	21.6	16.5	Botswana
740	…	…	…	…	…	6	44	220	87	122	4.20	146	65.7	33.9	0.4	Brazil
…	…	…	…	…	…	…	10	0	90[5]	127	…	…	…	…	…	Brunei
…	…	…	…	…	…	…	19	15	100	110	5.36	121	81.4	18.6	—	Bulgaria
…	…	…	…	…	…	…	169	930	42	91	8.46	7	9.8	17.9	72.3	Burkina Faso
…	…	…	…	…	…	…	176	1,300	78	68	3.28	30	42.4	48.3	9.3	Burundi
…	…	…	…	…	…	…	167	470	30	94	…	…	…	…	…	Cambodia
…	…	…	…	…	…	…	145	550	58	98	2.62	27	26.4	61.7	11.9	Cameroon
…	…	…	…	…	…	14	7	6	100	119	9.05	1,945	74.1	25.9	—	Canada
…	…	…	…	…	…	…	73	55	74	132	6.32	64	20.7	25.5	53.7	Cape Verde
…	…	…	…	…	…	…	173	1,100	70	91	4.19	18	26.5	37.5	36.0	Central African Republic
…	…	…	…	…	…	…	198	830	27	91	6.22	12	27.6	24.7	47.7	Chad
749[3]	…	…	…	…	69.9[3]	7[3]	13	23	93	117	4.73	100	70.1	29.1	0.7	Chile
418[14]	—60.4[14]—		—39.6[14]—		66.9[14]	15[14]	47	60	75	126	3.51	11	58.5	40.9	0.6	China
614[6]	41.4[6]	16.7[6]	—41.9[6]—		57.2[6]	6[6]	30	80	91	119	3.98	51	44.0	54.4	1.6	Colombia
…	…	…	…	…	…	…	93	500	96	79	5.40	28	46.3	29.2	24.5	Comoros
…	…	…	…	…	…	…	207	870	45	77	2.38	5	8.5	64.8	26.7	Congo, Dem. Rep. of the
…	…	…	…	…	…	…	108	890	51	101	3.99	50	47.1	40.7	12.1	Congo, Rep. of the
958[8]	…	…	…	…	78.2[8]	6[8]	14	29	95	124	6.51	132	73.6	25.2	1.2	Costa Rica
…	…	…	…	…	…	…	150	600	81	117	3.35	28	48.7	47.9	3.4	Côte d'Ivoire
1,578	70.0	30.0	—	—	83.0	13	9	12	96[9]	98	…	…	…	…	…	Croatia
1,376[8]	…	…	…	…	…	…	8	24	91	107	…	…	…	…	…	Cuba
522	…	…	…	…	78.9	6	9	0	100[5]	140	3.96	64	62.9	26.8	10.3	Cyprus[19]
1,982	97.6	2.4	—	—	79.0[14]	9	7	9	100[5]	133	5.94[22]	169[22]	84.9[22]	15.1[22]	—	Czech Republic
1,253	92.9	7.1	—	—	80.4	8	6	10	100	128	6.30	1,588	84.2	15.8	—	Denmark

Health services (continued)

country	health personnel							hospitals									
	year	physicians	dentists	nurses	pharmacists	midwives	population per physician	year	number	kinds (%)				ownership (%)			hospital beds per 10,000 pop.
										general	specialized	medical centres	rural	government	private non-profit	private for profit	
Djibouti	1996	60	7	315	8	...	7,100	1993	8	—25.0—		—75.0—		100.0	...	...	27[6]
Dominica	1998	38	10	361	27[11]	...	2,000	1994	53	1.9	—	—	98.1	100.0	—	—	25
Dominican Republic	1997	17,315	1,879	8,600	372	...	464	1992[3]	723	—7.9—		—92.1—		...	...	...	12[11]
East Timor	...	...	...	...	...	...	...	...	...	...	...	...	...	...	...	...	...
Ecuador	1995	15,212	1,788	5,212	906[20]	802	753	1995	474	17.0	8.0	—75.0—		26.0	11.3	62.7	16
Egypt	1998	129,000	15,211	141,770	20,254[13]	...	490	1998	7,411	4.5	—95.5—			87.9	—12.1—		19
El Salvador	1997	6,177	5,604	12,851	...	1,940[8]	936	1993	78	...	...	...	...	61.5	1.3	37.2	17
Equatorial Guinea	1996	105	4	169	...	9	4,086	1988	...	...	...	...	...	...	...	...	29
Eritrea	1996	108	4	574	...	79	33,240	1993	10	...	...	...	...	...	...	...	9
Estonia	1998	4,471	987	9,088[23]	775	[23]	336	1998	78	...	...	...	...	87.2	—12.8—		73
Ethiopia	1988	1,466	...	3,496	364	...	30,195	1986–87	86	...	...	...	...	...	...	...	3
Faroe Islands	1995	85	40	412	10	19	529	1994	3	33.3	—	—	66.7	100.0	—	—	64
Fiji	1997	409	36	1,742	...	...	1,919	1997	25	...	...	...	...	...	...	...	23
Finland	1998	15,407	4,828	111,408	7,472	4,019	334	1994[7]	380	...	...	...	...	...	...	...	98
France	1997	177,585	39,736	291,287	58,609	12,718	330	1997	4,186	—91.6—			8.4	25.4	—74.6—		113
French Guiana	1994	213	38	495	47	40	669	1996	25	...	...	...	...	10	...	15	143
French Polynesia	1999	384	94	599	51	54[20]	599	1999	7	...	...	...	...	...	...	...	37
Gabon	1989	448	32	759	71	240	2,504	1988	27	...	...	...	...	...	...	...	51
Gambia, The	1997	43	...	155	6	102	28,791	1994	13	15.4	—	—84.6—		...	...	...	7
Gaza Strip	1993[24]	...	...	...	...	...	...	1995	6	...	...	...	...	83.3	—16.7—		9
Georgia	1998	22,236	1,800	24,174	469	1,586	229	1997	422[4]	...	...	...	...	100.0	...	...	48
Germany	1998	287,164	62,274	785,190	47,341	9,271	286	1996	2,269	...	...	...	...	49.2[20]	36.0[20]	14.8[20]	72
Ghana	1996[15]	1,117	36	12,970	67[6]	9,583	16,127	1991	121	90.9	9.1	—	—	60.3	—39.7—		16[11]
Greece	1995	40,995	10,667	30,967[11]	8,147[13]	1,837[11]	255	1996	356	49.7	50.3	—	—	...	...	...	50
Greenland	1997	83	28	528	10[8]	11	674	1990	16	6.3	—	—	93.7	100.0	—	—	75
Grenada	1996	96	14	232	47	...	582	1996[7]	3	100.0	—	—	—	100.0	—	—	35
Guadeloupe	1996	690	129	1,640	220	140	597	1995	29	...	...	...	...	44.8	—55.2—		76
Guam	1986	147	...	594[23]	...	[23]	823	1998	1	...	...	...	...	...	...	...	...
Guatemala	1997	9,812	1,367	13,247[20]	...	18,924[20]	1,072	1985	35[14]	...	...	...	...	...	...	...	11[14]
Guernsey	1993	79	...	...	...	...	804	1993	1	100.0	—	—	—	100.0	—	—	...
Guinea	1995	930	22[17]	3,983	197[8]	372	7,688	1991	38	—100.0—		...	...	100.0	—	—	5
Guinea-Bissau	1996	194	11	1,277	12[17]	148	6,015	1993	16	...	...	...	...	62.5	—37.5—		13
Guyana	1996	214	35	504	40	165	3,612	1994	30	...	...	...	...	83.3	—16.7—		30
Haiti	1996	773	95[11]	2,630	...	...	8,418	1994	49	...	...	...	...	...	...	...	10
Honduras	1997	4,896	989	6,152	975[20]	...	1,202	1994	61	...	...	...	...	47.5	—52.5—		9
Hong Kong	1999	9,580	2,052	38,320	1,368	...	714	1995	88	...	...	...	...	78.4	—21.6—		49
Hungary	1998	36,143	5,671	51,965	4,789	2,227	279	1998	167	...	...	...	...	...	...	...	83
Iceland	1998	893	288	2,370	228	235	307	1995	57	89.0	11.0	—	—	...	...	...	147
India	1998[25]	512,352	19,523[20]	449,351[20]	...	...	1,916	1998	15,067[8]	...	...	...	...	55.0[8]	—45.0[8]—		27
Indonesia	1997	31,887[10]	[10]	155,911[23]	5,440[13]	[23]	6,267[10]	1997	1,090	...	...	...	...	...	...	...	6
Iran	1997	50,770	9,427	136,030	6,816	7,387	1,195	1997	685	...	...	...	...	83.5	—16.5—		16
Iraq	1998	11,769	1,220	50,499	2,525	...	1,818	1993	185	...	...	...	...	...	...	...	14
Ireland	1998	8,114	1,712	59,021	2,882	15,228	457	1996	62[3, 7]	100.0	—	—	—	100.0	—	—	33
Isle of Man	1998	117	26	...	25[13]	...	615	1986	3	33.3	33.3	—	33.3	100.0	—	—	...
Israel	1998	22,345	6,733	35,579	3,511	1,080	260	1995	259	18.5	81.5	—	—	12.0	51.7	36.3	61
Italy	1997	318,616	37,039	280,263	58,662	...	180	1997	1,589	91.5	8.5	—	—	59.2	—40.8—		65
Jamaica	1996	421	57	1,241	52	273	5,974	1996	24	75.0	25.0	—	—	75.0	—25.0—		24
Japan	1997	240,908	85,518	960,477	194,300	23,615	525	1997	9,413	88.7	11.3	—	—	73.5	—26.5—		131
Jersey	1995	95	...	...	...	...	895	1990	6	16.7	83.3	—	—	100.0	—	—	88
Jordan	1997	7,250	2,140	12,929	3,363	861[14]	602	1994	63	...	...	...	...	42.9	—57.1—		18[26]
Kazakhstan	1998	53,207	3,783	97,824	9,903	8,456	283	1996	1,518	...	...	...	...	100.0	...	...	123
Kenya	1995	3,606	600	24,610	605[20]	...	7,575	1994	846	—35.1—		—64.9—		...	...	...	14
Kiribati	1998	26	4	208	...	...	3,385	1990	1	...	...	...	...	...	...	...	40
Korea, North	1995	64,006	...	38,792	...	12,931	337	1989	...	...	...	...	...	...	...	...	135
Korea, South	1997	62,609	15,383	133,920	45,820	8,516	735	1997	6,446	70.0	30.0	—	—	...	...	...	47
Kuwait	1997	3,419	470	8,593	633[26]	19[14]	529	1995	24	...	...	...	...	66.7	—	33.3	31
Kyrgyzstan	1998	14,355	1,307	35,768	320	3,472	332	1994	348[14]	89.1	—	10.9	—	100.0	—	—	101[14]
Laos	1996	1,208	214	5,354	...	...	1,603	1995	25	0.7[4]	—99.3[4]—			100.0	—	—	25[4]
Latvia	1998	6,900	1,064	13,445	292[11]	81	355	1998	150	51.2[11]	4.1[11]	28.8[11]	15.9[11]	97.5	2.5	—	94
Lebanon	1997	7,203	2,744	3,430	1,715	...	476	1995	153	...	...	...	...	10.5	—89.5—		22
Lesotho	1995	105	10	1,169	60[15]	914	18,524	1987	22	90.9	9.1	—	—	54.5	45.5	—	15
Liberia	1997	53	2	136	...	99	43,434	1988	92	—37.0—		—63.0—		...	...	...	...
Libya	1997	6,092	619[26]	17,136[26]	1,095[26]	...	781	1991	...	...	...	...	...	...	...	...	41
Liechtenstein	1997	41	18	...	2	...	764	1998	1	...	...	...	...	...	...	...	34
Lithuania	1999	14,578	2,316	37,448	2,143	1,611	254	1999	186	...	...	...	...	100.0	...	...	94
Luxembourg	1998	1,164	282	3,347	297	94	368	1994	34	50.0	50.0	—	—	...	...	...	109
Macau	1998	532	31	706	48	...	800	1994	30	6.7	—	93.3	—	46.7	—53.3—		22
Macedonia	1998	4,110	1,046	9,833	300	1,342	490	1994	58[26]	27.4	24.2	—48.4—		100.0	—	—	52[26]
Madagascar	1996	1,470	137	2,969	19[4]	1,471	9,351	1990	...	...	...	...	...	...	...	...	9
Malawi	1989	186	...	284	5	...	49,118	1987	395	12.2	0.8	—87.0—		59.2	—40.8—		16
Malaysia	1997	14,258	1,865	24,550	...	5,872	1,519	1997	337	...	...	...	...	35.1	—64.9—		20
Maldives	1995	100	...	281	134	461	2,533	1996	5	20.0	—	80.0	—	100.0	—	—	12
Mali	1994	419	9	1,167	57[28]	267	21,269	1987	...	...	...	...	...	...	...	...	4
Malta	1998	987	135	4,158	186	291	383	1996	7	...	...	...	...	71.4	—28.6—		57
Marshall Islands	1997	34	4	141	...	6	1,794	1997	2	100.0	—	—	—	100.0	—	—	21
Martinique	1996	680	130	1,700	230	150	547	1993	8[14]	...	...	...	...	...	...	...	56[14]
Mauritania	1995	323	47	1,461	6[8]	237	7,251	1990	16	...	...	...	...	100.0	—	—	7
Mauritius	1998	1,033	144	2,826[23]	250	[23]	1,117	1998	13	73.9[11]	17.4[11]	8.7[11]	—	60.9[11]	4.3[11]	34.8[11]	33
Mayotte	1985	9	1	51	1	2	7,427	1994	2	100.0	—	—	—	100.0	—	—	9
Mexico	1997	116,047	8,926	161,303	...	...	812	1993	1,888[26]	...	...	...	...	53.9	—46.1—		9[26]
Micronesia	1999	76	16	368	7[20]	...	1,737	1993	4	100.0	—	—	—	100.0	—	—	31
Moldova	1998	14,959	1,761	37,355	2,885	3,723	286	1996	312	...	...	...	...	100.0	...	...	125
Monaco	1997	188	22	500[14]	67[14]	11[14]	170	1997	1	100.0	—	—	—	100.0	—	—	173
Mongolia	1998	5,676	315	7,169	1,113[20]	...	411	1997	407	...	...	...	...	...	...	...	78
Morocco	1997	12,534	1,090	28,610	2,997	87[4]	2,173	1993[29]	201	48.8	—	51.2	—	100.0	—	—	10

admissions or discharges: rate per 10,000 pop.	by kinds of hospital (%): general	special-ized	medical centres	rural	bed occu-pancy rate (%)	aver-age length of stay (days)	mortality: under age 5 per 1,000 live newborn 1997	maternal mortality per 100,000 live births 1990–97	popu-lation with access to safe water 2000 (%)	food supply (% of FAO require-ment) 1998	total health expenditures, 1990: as percent of GDP	per capita (U.S.$)	by source (percent): public	private	inter-national aid	country
...	...	...	...	...	...	...	156	...	100	89	...	...	...	...	...	Djibouti
1,026	...	...	...	...	94.6	8	20	65	97	124	8.06	192	65.1	20.4	14.5	Dominica
470	...	...	...	...	...	...	53	230	86	101	3.72	38	52.7	43.3	4.0	Dominican Republic
...	...	...	...	...	...	...	...	...	...	...	...	...	...	...	...	East Timor
508	...	...	...	...	53.1	6	39	160	85	119	4.14	44	55.9	37.3	6.8	Ecuador
317	...	...	...	...	...	...	73	170	97	131	2.61	28	30.3	62.0	7.7	Egypt
...	...	...	...	...	54.9[3, 12]	6[3, 12]	36	160	77	110	5.86	58	29.7	55.6	14.7	El Salvador
...	...	...	...	...	...	...	172	...	44	68	7.60	28	36.6	20.7	42.7	Equatorial Guinea
...	...	...	...	...	...	...	116	1,000	46	75	...	...	...	...	...	Eritrea
1,952	76.7[11]	21.5[11]	—	1.8[11]	75.1	10	23	50	100[9]	120	3.62	228	53.0	47.0	—	Estonia
...	...	...	...	...	...	...	175	1,400	24	78	3.80	4	41.3	39.9	18.8	Ethiopia
...	...	...	...	...	86.4	12	...	...	...	...	...	...	...	...	...	Faroe Islands
...	...	...	...	...	...	...	24	38	47	125	3.76	70	54.9	38.3	6.9	Fiji
2,322	...	...	...	...	70.9	11	4	6	100	117	7.82	2,046	83.3	16.7	—	Finland
2,128	...	...	...	...	...	...	5	10	100	141	9.40	1,869	74.2	25.8	—	France
1,714[20]	...	...	...	...	70.3[20]	8[20]	...	...	84[9]	125	...	...	...	...	...	French Guiana
...	...	...	...	...	...	...	...	...	...	129	...	...	...	...	...	French Polynesia
...	...	...	...	...	...	...	145	500	86	109	4.10	164	52.7	40.9	6.4	Gabon
...	...	...	...	...	...	...	87	1,100	62	108	7.53	22	28.3	20.7	51.0	Gambia, The
752	...	...	...	...	74.9	3	...	...	...	...	...	...	...	...	...	Gaza Strip
...	...	...	...	...	...	...	23	60	79	88	4.45	152	62.5	37.5	—	Georgia
1,812[20]	...	...	...	...	82.8[20]	13[20]	5	8	100[5]	128	8.73	1,511	72.7	27.3	—	Germany
...	...	...	...	...	...	...	107	210	73	117	3.50	15	35.0	51.8	13.2	Ghana
1,370	81.0	19.0	—	—	66.0	9	8	10	99[5]	145	5.39	359	76.0	24.0	—	Greece
2,450	29.2	—	—	70.8	69.4	8	...	...	...	...	...	...	...	...	...	Greenland
774[8]	100.0	—	—	—	59.1[8]	7[8]	29	0	95	111	5.96	133	68.8	27.8	3.5	Grenada
2,154	...	...	...	...	84.0	10	...	...	90[9]	113	...	...	...	...	...	Guadeloupe
...	...	...	...	...	...	...	...	...	...	...	...	...	...	...	...	Guam
284	...	...	...	...	57.7	9	55	190	92	99	3.70	27	44.2	43.2	12.6	Guatemala
1,100	100.0	—	—	—	...	...	...	...	...	...	...	...	...	...	...	Guernsey
...	...	...	...	...	...	...	201	670	48	100	3.90	17	39.7	40.3	20.0	Guinea
...	...	...	...	...	...	...	220	910	56	104	8.15	16	31.3	18.9	49.8	Guinea-Bissau
...	...	...	...	...	...	...	82	180	94	109	10.37	42	40.7	15.1	44.2	Guyana
...	...	...	...	...	...	...	132	1,000	46	83	6.99	27	26.3	54.8	19.0	Haiti
459[20]	...	...	...	...	...	...	45	220	88	104	4.54	52	56.7	35.7	7.7	Honduras
1,811	...	...	...	...	...	...	6	7	100[5]	143	5.69	687	19.5	80.5	0.0	Hong Kong
2,502	...	...	...	...	77.0	10	11	15	99	130	5.95	185	84.4	15.6	—	Hungary
2,828[12]	94.0[12]	6.0[12]	—	—	86.5[12]	12[12]	5	6	100[5]	121	8.34	1,884	87.5	12.5	—	Iceland
...	...	...	...	...	...	...	108	440	84	112	6.00	21	20.0	78.4	1.6	India
...	...	...	...	...	...	...	60	450	78	132	2.01	12	25.6	66.7	7.7	Indonesia
...	...	...	...	...	...	...	35	37	92	117	2.54	244	56.9	43.1	0.0	Iran
645[4]	...	...	...	...	42.4[4]	4[4]	122	310	85	100	...	...	...	...	...	Iraq
1,470	100.0	—	—	—	82.2	7	7	10	100[5]	144	7.22	876	81.1	18.9	—	Ireland
...	...	...	...	...	...	...	...	...	...	...	...	...	...	...	...	Isle of Man
1,979	...	...	...	...	91.2	10	6	5	99[9]	135	4.20	480	49.3	50.6	0.1	Israel
1,743	90.4	9.6	—	—	72.0	9	6	7	100[5]	143	7.54	1,449	77.7	22.3	—	Italy
242[3]	81.7[3]	18.3[3]	—	—	53.7	5	11	120	92	121	5.04	83	57.4	33.2	9.5	Jamaica
...	...	...	...	...	...	...	6	8	97[9]	123	6.45	1,538	74.5	25.5	—	Japan
1,718	84.0	16.0	—	—	...	...	...	...	...	...	...	...	...	...	...	Jersey
478[3]	...	...	...	...	68.1[3]	4[3]	24	41	96	114	3.77	55	36.9	52.3	10.8	Jordan
...	...	...	...	...	...	...	44	70	91	98	4.44	154	62.3	37.7	—	Kazakhstan
...	...	...	...	...	...	...	87	370	57	85	4.33	16	40.0	37.9	22.1	Kenya
...	...	...	...	...	...	...	78[11]	...	48	131	...	...	...	...	...	Kiribati
...	...	...	...	...	...	...	30	110	100	81	...	...	...	...	...	Korea, North
629[14]	97.5[14]	2.5[14]	—	—	65.5[14]	13[14]	6	20	92	131	6.61	365	40.9	58.9	0.2	Korea, South
950[3, 11]	72.2[3, 11]	27.8[3, 11]	—	—	64.9[3, 11]	7[3, 11]	13	5	100[5]	126	4.86	541	64.2	35.6	0.1	Kuwait
1,775	95.5	—	4.5	—	75.6	15	68	65	77	99	4.97	118	66.7	33.3	—	Kyrgyzstan
...	...	...	...	...	...	...	122	650	37	98	2.53	5	17.4	60.7	21.9	Laos
2,210	78.4[11]	4.6[11]	13.8[11]	3.2[11]	76.5	13	22	45	100[9]	117	3.87	220	56.1	43.9	—	Latvia
...	...	...	...	...	...	...	37	100	100	132	...	...	...	...	...	Lebanon
221[7]	...	...	...	...	...	...	137	610	78	97	8.32	26	38.3	26.5	35.2	Lesotho
...	...	...	...	...	...	...	235	...	46[9]	86	8.24	4	19.9	11.8	68.3	Liberia
...	...	...	...	...	...	...	25	75	97	138	...	...	...	...	...	Libya
...	...	...	...	...	...	...	7	...	100[5]	...	...	...	...	...	...	Liechtenstein
2,001[14]	...	...	...	...	74.4[14]	15[14]	24	18	100	121	3.58	159	72.0	28.0	—	Lithuania
1,941	94.6	5.4	—	—	75.0	16	7	0	100[5]	137	6.56	1,662	91.4	8.6	—	Luxembourg
329	...	...	...	...	64.4	16	...	...	...	108	...	...	...	...	...	Macau
995	67.2	6.1	26.7		68.5	14	23	11	...	116	...	...	...	...	...	Macedonia
...	...	...	...	...	...	...	158	490	47	88	2.56	7	29.0	49.6	21.4	Madagascar
...	...	...	...	...	...	...	215	620	57	96	4.98	11	35.0	41.7	23.3	Malawi
717[3, 6]	...	...	...	...	...	...	11	39	78[9]	130	2.96	71	44.0	55.8	0.2	Malaysia
266[20, 27]	...	...	...	...	71.4[20, 27]	4[20, 27]	74	350	100	111	...	...	...	...	...	Maldives
...	...	...	...	...	...	...	239	580	65	90	5.19	15	24.9	46.7	28.4	Mali
...	...	...	...	...	...	...	10	...	100[5]	136	5.38	349	68.3	31.7	0.0	Malta
...	...	...	...	...	...	...	92[11]	...	82[9]	...	...	...	...	...	...	Marshall Islands
2,092	...	...	...	...	73.7	10	...	...	94[9]	118	...	...	...	...	...	Martinique
...	...	...	...	...	...	...	183	550	37	114	3.80	18	28.5	41.5	30.0	Mauritania
1,446[3, 11]	...	...	...	...	74.6[3, 11]	5[3, 11]	23	30	100	130	4.40	100	47.8	39.0	13.3	Mauritius
...	...	...	...	...	...	...	...	...	...	...	...	...	...	...	...	Mayotte
403[3, 8]	...	...	...	...	64.7[3, 8]	5[3, 8]	35	48	88	135	3.17	89	49.3	49.8	0.9	Mexico
...	...	...	...	...	...	...	24	...	100[5]	...	...	...	...	...	...	Micronesia
...	...	...	...	...	...	...	35	42	92	108	3.91	143	74.4	25.6	—	Moldova
...	...	...	...	...	...	...	5	...	100	140	...	...	...	...	...	Monaco
205	...	...	...	...	...	...	150	150	60	83	6.63	58	83.0	15.1	1.9	Mongolia
255	...	...	...	...	63.8	8	72	230	80	131	2.55	26	33.6	63.3	3.1	Morocco

Health services (continued)

country	health personnel							hospitals									
	year	physicians	dentists	nurses	pharmacists	midwives	population per physician	year	number	kinds (%)				ownership (%)			hospital beds per 10,000 pop.
										general	specialized	medical centres	rural	government	private non-profit	private for profit	
Mozambique	1990	387	108	3,533	353	1,139	36,320	1990	238	4.2	0.8	— 95.0 —		100.0	—	—	8[20]
Myanmar (Burma)	1999	12,313	871	10,820	...	9,162	3,367	1996	737	...	...	...	...	...	...	...	7
Namibia	1997	495	67	2,817	91[8]	1,954	3,388	1992	47	...	...	...	...	91.5	— 8.5 —		45[8]
Nauru	1995	17	...	62	...	...	624	...	...	...	...	...	...	...	...	...	...
Nepal	1997	874	45[14]	3,845	18[14]	1,621[14]	26,316	1997	74	...	...	...	...	...	...	...	2
Netherlands, The	1997	33,618	7,319	124,000[20]	2,622	1,357	462	1998	222	64.4	35.6	—	—	...	...	...	53
Netherlands Antilles	1998	339	62	1,198	42	11	617	1998	11	38.3	36.3	25.4	—	...	...	...	70
New Caledonia	1996	362	107	852	74	61	549	1996	9	12.5[4]	12.5[4]	75.0[4]	—	62.5[4]	— 37.5[4] —		45
New Zealand	1997	12,399	1,467	29,000	3,634	2,114	303	1996	368	...	...	...	...	32.3	— 67.7 —		59
Nicaragua	1995	4,551	1,099	2,577	...	...	957	1994	56	46.4	7.1	46.4	—	...	...	...	11
Niger	1997	325	19	2,126	29[4]	511	28,560	1987	...	...	...	...	...	...	...	...	5
Nigeria	1993	21,739	1,335	80,186	6,474[12]	62,386	3,707	1985	11,588	6.6	0.5	— 92.9 —		81.4	— 18.6 —		7[14]
Northern Mariana Islands	1986	23	4	103	2	2	1,324	1988	1	100.0	—	—	—	100.0	—	—	19
Norway	1998	18,304	5,230	81,548	2,531	2,619	242	1994	...	...	...	...	...	...	...	...	51
Oman	1998	3,061	201	7,453	435	65	773	1998	62	— 8.1 —		— 91.9 —		25.8	— 74.2 —		36
Pakistan	1997	78,470	3,159	28,661	47,618[26]	20,869[14]	1,836	1997	5,118	— 7.6[11] —		— 92.4[11] —		...	...	...	6
Palau	1998	20	2	26	...	1	900	1998	1	...	...	...	...	...	...	...	37[4]
Panama	1998	3,518	784	3,203	756	...	773	1998	60	...	...	...	...	...	...	...	27
Papua New Guinea	1998	342	127	3,141	...	...	13,708	1993	...	...	...	...	...	...	...	...	34
Paraguay	1995	3,730	1,279	1,875	433	1,547	1,294	1995	...	...	...	...	...	...	...	...	14
Peru	1996	23,249	1,197	16,043	4,789	3,832	1,030	1996	472	...	...	...	...	50.2	— 49.8 —		13
Philippines	1996	36,375	1,668	5,663	...	13,750	1,923	1996	1,738	96.5	3.1	0.5	—	34.5	— 65.5 —		12
Poland	1998	91,121	17,869	215,295	20,139	25,014	424	1998	765	93.8	6.2	—	—	100	...	...	54
Portugal	1998	31,097	3,319	37,775	7,505	827	320	1993	335	43.0	18.8	38.2	—	74.3	14.7	11.0	41[14]
Puerto Rico	1989–92	6,269	902	19,666	2,111	120	558	1994	72	83.3	8.3	8.3	—	36.1	30.6	33.3	26
Qatar	1996[15]	703	117	1,612	285	...	793	1995	4	25.0	75.0	—	—	100.0	—	—	18
Réunion	1999	1,346	337	2,906	284	176	520	1998	19	85.5	— 14.5 —			71.0	— 29.0 —		39
Romania	1998	41,415	5,379	92,057	1,643	8,913	543	1995	414	...	...	...	...	99.5	— 0.5 —		77
Russia	1998	618,718	47,322	1,615,000	9,112	91,853	238	1998	11,200	37.4[11]	17.2[11]	—	45.4[11]	99.8	— 0.2 —		119
Rwanda	1989	272	7	835	25	...	24,697	1985[3]	220	— 13.6 —		— 86.4 —		100.0	—	—	9[6]
St. Kitts and Nevis	1998	50	8	274	21	...	846	1998	4	50.0	— 50.0 —			...	...	...	62
St. Lucia	1997	81	13	312	13	...	1,876	1998	6	25.0[12]	25.0[12]	—	50.0[12]	...	...	...	14
St. Vincent	1998	59	6	267	27[8]	...	2,075	1997	11	...	...	...	...	77.8[12]	— 22.2[12] —		19
Samoa	1996	62	7	281	6[12]	65	2,919	1992	36	2.8	—	—	97.2	100.0	—	—	34
San Marino	1998	84	...	...	...	...	309	1998	...	...	...	...	...	...	...	...	58
São Tomé and Príncipe	1996	61	7	167	1[6]	39	2,147	...	...	...	...	...	...	...	...	...	...
Saudi Arabia	1997	33,110	3,191	65,821	4,189	...	602	1996	290	...	...	...	...	74.1	— 25.9 —		22
Senegal	1996	649	93	1,876	322	588	13,656	1996	17	...	...	...	...	...	...	...	9
Serbia and Montenegro	1997	22,498	4,209	...	2,032	...	471	1997	...	...	...	...	...	...	...	...	55
Seychelles	1998	93	15	342	7	...	849	1997	7	14.3	14.3	71.4	—	100.0	—	—	54
Sierra Leone	1996	339	19	1,532	...	218	13,696	1998	219	— 25.6[16] —		— 74.4[16] —		...	...	...	8
Singapore	1998	5,147	914	15,570	858[26]	487[26]	615	1997	23	...	...	...	...	43.5	— 56.5 —		35
Slovakia	1998	19,030	2,598	38,168	1,822	2,119[14]	283	1991	111	72.1	27.9	—	—	100.0	—	—	92[14]
Slovenia	1998	4,501	1,201	3,125	887	...	440	1998	28	57.7	42.3	—	—	...	...	...	56
Solomon Islands	1997	31	...	464	...	283	13,258	1997	11	100.0	—	—	—	75.0	25.0	—	51
Somalia	1997	265	13	1,327	70	540[16]	25,034	1988	...	...	...	...	...	...	...	...	7
South Africa	1998	29,369	4,387	174,754	9,948	...	1,459	1998	704	...	...	...	...	51.1	— 48.9 —		34
Spain	1996	165,560	14,877	177,034	43,221	6,314	240	1994	783	57.5	18.5	— 24.0 —		42.5	— 57.5 —		40
Sri Lanka	1999	6,881	471	19,362	848	7,899	2,740	1995[3]	407	...	...	...	...	100.0	—	—	26
Sudan, The	1996	2,818	219	18,158	344	...	11,110	1986	...	...	...	...	...	...	...	...	8
Suriname	1996	305	31	631	14	40	1,373	1998	...	...	...	...	...	...	...	...	34
Swaziland	1996	149	7[4]	1,264[4]	13[4]	...	6,617	1986	24	— 41.7 —		— 58.3 —		...	...	...	...
Sweden	1997	27,511	13,446	72,625	5,953	6,351	322	1996	...	...	...	...	...	...	...	...	43
Switzerland	1998	22,965	3,470	55,387	4,373	1,884	310	1997	...	...	...	...	...	...	...	...	66
Syria	1998	22,293	11,456	29,259	8,205	6,063[14]	694	1995	294	...	...	...	...	20.5	— 79.5 —		12
Taiwan	1998	27,168	7,900	71,215	22,761	704	804	1998	700	...	...	...	...	13.7	— 86.3 —		57
Tajikistan	1998	12,291	1,125	29,597	734	3,999	498	1994	449	...	...	...	...	98.2	— 1.8 —		88
Tanzania	1995	1,277	218	26,536	...	13,953	24,389	1993	173[8]	...	...	...	...	...	...	...	10
Thailand	1995	14,181	2,920	54,262	5,867	9,713	4,192	1996	1,397	93.6	6.4	—	—	65.8	— 34.2 —		21
Togo	1995	320	29	1,252	65[8]	438	13,168	1990	...	...	...	...	...	...	...	...	16
Tonga	1997	43	9	309	...	30	2,279	1993	4	...	...	...	...	...	...	...	28
Trinidad and Tobago	1997	949	141	1,378[23]	518	[23]	1,339	1997	77	...	...	...	...	...	...	...	37
Tunisia	1997	6,464	1,200	26,409	1,570	...	1,429	1994[3]	163	— 13.5 —		— 86.5 —		100.0	—	—	18
Turkey	1998	77,375	13,428	69,701	21,486	41,181	826	1997	1,078	75.3[11]	8.8[11]	— 15.9[11] —		84.3[11]	— 15.7[11] —		23
Turkmenistan	1997	14,022	1,010	21,436	1,566	3,664	333	1994	368	...	...	...	...	100.0	...	...	115
Tuvalu	1999	8	1	33	...	10	1,375	1985	8	11.1	—	—	88.9	100.0	—	—	36
Uganda	1996	840[20]	42	3,897	...	2,835	22,399[20]	1989	81	...	...	...	...	...	...	...	12
Ukraine	1998	150,382	19,615	370,171	23,488	29,523	334	1997	3,400	...	...	...	...	100.0	...	...	99
United Arab Emirates	1997	4,749	644[26]	8,450[26]	2,007[26]	...	553	1996	50	...	...	...	...	72.0	— 28.0 —		29
United Kingdom	1998	82,803	20,216	299,010	33,759[12]	24,801[6]	716	1997	...	...	...	...	...	...	...	...	42
United States	1998	756,700	196,000	2,162,000	184,000[14]	3,000[14]	357	1998	6,097	88.0	12.0	—	—	25.3	49.2	25.5	38
Uruguay	1998	11,964	3,921	2,369	1,009	586	269	1997	118	...	...	...	...	75.4	— 24.6 —		35
Uzbekistan	1998	74,230	5,869	243,166	746	16,235	324	1995	192	...	...	...	...	100.0	...	...	84
Vanuatu	1997	21	3[14]	259[14]	6[14]	33[14]	8,524	1995	90	5.6	—	21.1	73.3	100.0	—	—	32
Venezuela	1997	53,818	13,000	46,305	8,571	...	423	1997	556	...	...	...	...	37.0	— 63.0 —		17
Vietnam	1998	36,683	...	42,797	6,500[20]	13,450	2,083	1994	12,500	...	...	...	...	...	...	...	27
Virgin Islands (U.S.)	1985	167	...	...	...	...	622	1985	...	...	...	...	...	...	...	...	49
West Bank	1993[24]	1,344	445	2,279	149	56	1,536	1995	17	...	...	...	...	52.9	— 47.1 —		9
Western Sahara	1994	100	...	...	24	...	2,504	...	...	...	...	...	...	...	...	...	...
Yemen	1998	3,883	245[26]	7,578[14]	613	385[11]	4,211	1998	81	...	...	...	...	...	...	...	55
Zambia	1995	601	26[4]	9,853	24[4]	311[4]	14,496	1987	965	8.2	0.3	19.0	72.5	80.9	19.1	—	29[20]
Zimbabwe	1995	1,522	142	14,095	411[20]	3,078	7,196	1993[3]	1,378	0.9	2.6	83.7	12.7	100.0	—	—	19[14]

[1]1997. [2]1987. [3]Government hospitals only. [4]1990. [5]Data refer to a period other than 1994–95, differ from the standard definition, or refer to only part of the country. [6]1989. [7]General hospitals only. [8]1991. [9]1994–98. [10]Physicians include dentists. [11]1994. [12]1992. [13]Number of pharmacies. [14]1995. [15]Government-employed personnel only. [16]1998. [17]1988. [18]Includes doctors of traditional Chinese medicine. [19]Republic of Cyprus only. [20]1993. [21]Excludes psychiatric hospitals. [22]Data refer to former Czechoslovakia. [23]Nurses include midwives. [24]West Bank includes Gaza Strip.

admissions or discharges: rate per 10,000 pop.	by kinds of hospital (%): general	by kinds of hospital (%): specialized	by kinds of hospital (%): medical centres	by kinds of hospital (%): rural	bed occupancy rate (%)	average length of stay (days)	mortality: under age 5 per 1,000 live newborn 1997	mortality: maternal mortality per 100,000 live births 1990–97	population with access to safe water 2000 (%)	food supply (% of FAO requirement) 1998	total health expenditures, 1990: as percent of GDP	total health expenditures, 1990: per capita (U.S.$)	by source (percent): public	by source (percent): private	by source (percent): international aid	country
...	...	...	...	...	...	...	209	1,100	57	82	5.86	5	21.0	25.7	53.3	Mozambique
...	...	...	...	...	...	...	114	230	72	131	...	...	...	...	...	Myanmar (Burma)
...	...	...	...	...	...	...	75	230	77	92	3.92	45	47.8	41.3	10.9	Namibia
...	...	...	...	...	...	...	30	...	...	...	...	...	...	...	...	Nauru
...	...	...	...	...	...	...	104	540	88	99	4.54	7	23.0	51.7	25.4	Nepal
1,028	96.7	3.3	—	—	70.1	10	6	7	100	122	8.03	1,501	72.6	27.4	—	Netherlands, The
...	...	...	...	...	...	...	...	...	...	110	...	...	...	...	...	Netherlands Antilles
1,165[4, 7]	...	...	...	...	84.8[4, 7]	8[4, 7]	...	...	...	123	...	...	...	...	...	New Caledonia
1,332[3]	...	...	...	...	64.0[3]	6[3]	7	15	100[5]	126	7.37	925	81.7	18.3	—	New Zealand
769	—— 76.2 ——		23.8	—	...	...	57	160	77	98	8.61	34	56.9	22.5	20.6	Nicaragua
...	...	...	...	...	...	...	285	590	59	84	4.98	16	24.5	31.3	34.1	Niger
...	...	...	...	...	...	...	187	1,000	62	122	2.72	10	36.5	57.4	6.1	Nigeria
1,550	100.0	—	—	—	54.7	4	...	...	...	...	...	...	...	...	...	Northern Mariana Islands
1,515	96.4	3.6	—	—	83.0	10	4	6	100	128	7.35	1,835	95.7	4.3	—	Norway
911	...	...	...	...	...	...	18	21	85	...	4.22	209	59.5	40.1	0.5	Oman
...	...	...	...	...	...	...	136	340	90	106	3.48	12	47.4	47.1	5.5	Pakistan
1,582	...	...	...	...	48.5	6	34	...	88	...	...	...	...	...	...	Palau
1,239	...	...	...	...	52.5	8	20	85	90	107	7.13	142	72.6	23.1	4.3	Panama
...	...	...	...	...	...	...	112	370	42	95	4.44	37	59.1	36.1	4.8	Papua New Guinea
...	...	...	...	...	...	...	33	190	78	112	2.97	35	35.1	58.2	6.7	Paraguay
...	...	...	...	...	...	...	56	270	80	103	3.21	61	56.1	41.7	2.2	Peru
538	...	...	...	...	62.1	5	46	210	86	101	2.15	16	46.7	46.4	6.9	Philippines
1,288[12]	96.0[12]	4.0[12]	—	—	72.5[12]	14[12]	11	8	100[5]	128	5.07	84	80.3	19.7	—	Poland
1,146	86.3	10.5	3.2	—	74.5	10	8	8	100[5]	151	6.99	383	61.7	38.3	...	Portugal
1,101	94.0	4.3	1.7	—	63.1	5	...	...	...	...	...	...	...	...	...	Puerto Rico
...	...	...	...	...	71.7[12, 30]	7[12, 30]	20	10	100[5]	...	4.73	630	63.0	36.9	0.0	Qatar
1,951[11]	...	...	...	...	79.8[11]	7[11]	...	...	...	146	...	...	...	...	...	Réunion
...	...	...	...	...	...	...	26	41	58	123	3.87	58	61.4	38.6	—	Romania
2,320	...	...	...	...	85.0	14	22	49	99	111	3.02	159	66.8	33.2	—	Russia
85	...	...	...	...	42.8[28]	7[28]	170	1,300	41	88	3.44	10	15.0	45.2	39.8	Rwanda
1,068[7, 12]	...	...	...	...	49.3[7, 12]	9[7, 12]	37	130	98	114	5.99	212	58.1	27.8	14.1	St. Kitts and Nevis
890[12, 28]	...	...	...	...	...	...	29	30	98	117	7.18	169	75.6	23.0	1.4	St. Lucia
728	...	...	...	...	68.2	7	21	43	93	106	5.69	102	68.5	28.8	2.7	St. Vincent
894	70.8	—	—	29.2	32.9	5	27	...	99	...	2.94	20	6.1	54.2	39.7	Samoa
...	...	...	...	...	...	...	6	...	100[5]	...	...	...	...	...	...	San Marino
...	...	...	...	...	...	...	78	...	82[9]	94	9.22	38	28.8	17.0	54.2	São Tomé and Príncipe
...	...	...	...	...	...	...	28	130	95	119	4.76	260	64.3	35.7	0.0	Saudi Arabia
...	...	...	...	...	...	...	124	560	78	96	3.66	29	45.1	38.0	16.9	Senegal
1,154	...	...	...	...	72.0	12	21	10	98	117	5.11[31]	264[31]	80.4[31]	19.6[31]	—	Serbia and Montenegro
1,744[32]	...	...	...	...	76.4[32]	5[32]	18	...	97[5]	105	6.03	289	50.2	28.0	21.9	Seychelles
...	...	...	...	...	...	...	316	1,800	57	89	2.43	4	19.6	30.9	49.5	Sierra Leone
1,127[26]	...	...	...	...	73.1[11]	8[11]	4	6	100	...	1.87	215	58.3	41.6	0.1	Singapore
1,679[14]	94.9[14]	5.1[14]	—	—	73.2[14]	14[14]	11	9	100	120	...	...	...	...	...	Slovakia
1,643	...	...	...	...	78.4	10	6	11	100	116	...	...	...	...	...	Slovenia
...	...	...	...	...	...	...	28	550	71	93	2.18	117	43.2	50.5	6.3	Solomon Islands
...	...	...	...	...	...	...	211	...	31[9]	66	1.51	8	7.3	41.1	51.6	Somalia
...	...	...	...	...	...	...	82	230	86	119	5.56	77	57.5	42.5	0.0	South Africa
1,053	...	...	...	...	76.7[8]	12[8]	5	6	99[9]	136	6.59	831	78.4	21.6	—	Spain
1,464[4]	...	...	...	...	...	...	19	60	77	104	3.74	18	40.4	51.1	8.6	Sri Lanka
...	...	...	...	...	...	...	115	550	75	104	3.33	34	11.0	84.5	4.5	Sudan, The
766[33]	...	...	...	...	68.8[33]	10[33]	36	110	82	116	2.88	93	37.9	58.0	4.1	Suriname
...	...	...	...	...	...	...	94	230	50[9]	108	7.22	64	43.6	22.2	34.2	Swaziland
1,906[11]	...	...	...	...	82.2[11]	8[11]	4	5	100	116	8.79	2,343	89.3	10.7	—	Sweden
...	...	...	...	...	...	...	5	5	100	120	7.52	2,520	68.5	31.5	—	Switzerland
352[3, 20]	...	...	...	...	75.5[3, 20]	3[3, 20]	33	110	80	136	2.07	41	16.6	79.4	4.0	Syria
...	...	...	...	...	...	...	8	8	90[9]	...	4.30	323	53.0	47.0	0.0	Taiwan
1,492	...	...	...	...	70.2	15	76	85	60	85	5.98	100	72.6	27.4	—	Tajikistan
...	...	...	...	...	...	...	143	530	68	86	4.73	4	14.4	31.6	54.0	Tanzania
...	...	...	...	...	...	...	38	44	84	110	4.98	72	20.4	78.7	0.9	Thailand
...	...	...	...	...	...	...	125	640	55	109	4.10	18	40.4	38.5	21.2	Togo
622[12]	...	...	...	...	56.2[12]	10[12]	23	...	100	...	6.46	63	60.3	25.0	14.8	Tonga
1,114[3, 7]	...	...	...	...	70.7[3, 7]	6[3, 7]	17	90	90	112	4.54	180	62.4	36.9	0.6	Trinidad and Tobago
...	...	...	...	...	...	...	33	70	80	126	4.91	76	63.8	33.3	3.0	Tunisia
709	...	...	...	...	...	...	45	130	82	141	3.94	76	36.2	63.3	0.5	Turkey
...	...	...	...	...	...	...	78	110	74[9]	105	4.99	125	66.4	33.2	0.4	Turkmenistan
1,368	40.9	—	—	59.1	51.5[7]	12.2[7]	56	...	100	...	2.66	472	34.0	66.0	0.1	Tuvalu
...	...	...	...	...	...	...	137	510	52	95	3.40	8	13.3	53.0	33.7	Uganda
...	...	...	...	...	...	...	23	30	98	112	3.30	131	69.7	30.3	—	Ukraine
...	...	...	...	...	...	...	10	3	97[9]	132	2.66	472	34.0	66.0	0.1	United Arab Emirates
...	...	...	...	...	...	...	7	7	100	129	6.11	1,039	84.9	15.1	—	United Kingdom
1,180[34]	...	...	...	...	61.8[34]	6[34]	8	8	100	142	12.71	2,765	44.1	55.9	—	United States
477[3]	...	...	...	...	78.8[0]	9[0]	21	21	98	107	4.02	120	53.0	44.0	1.4	Uruguay
...	...	...	...	...	...	...	58	21	85	100	5.90	116	72.1	27.9	—	Uzbekistan
567	...	...	...	...	41.9	6	50	...	88	120	5.68	67	51.5	25.7	22.8	Vanuatu
601[3]	...	...	...	...	69.7[3]	6[3]	25	65	83	96	3.60	88	54.2	45.6	0.1	Venezuela
...	...	...	...	...	...	...	43	160	77	112	2.11	3	39.3	47.4	13.3	Vietnam
...	...	...	...	...	...	...	...	...	...	...	...	...	...	...	...	Virgin Islands (U.S.)
711	...	...	...	...	80.9	4	...	...	...	...	...	...	...	...	...	West Bank
...	...	...	...	...	...	...	...	...	...	...	...	...	...	...	...	Western Sahara
...	...	...	...	...	...	...	100	1,400	69	86	3.19	20	34.7	54.1	11.3	Yemen
1,249	—— 75.7 ——		—— 24.3 ——		68.5	7	202	650	64	84	3.16	17	65.4	30.6	4.1	Zambia
546	...	...	...	...	69.8	7	80	400	83	90	6.23	39	40.3	48.7	11.0	Zimbabwe

[25]Registered personnel; all may not be present and working in the country. [26]1996. [27]Central hospital only. [28]General and specialized hospitals only. [29]Public sector only. [30]Hamad General Hospital only. [31]Data refer to the former Socialist Federal Republic of Yugoslavia. [32]Victoria Hospital only. [33]Paramaribo hospitals (1,213 beds) only. [34]5,037 community hospitals only.

Social protection

This table summarizes three principal areas of social protective activity for the countries of the world: social security, crime and law enforcement, and military affairs. Because the administrative structure, financing, manning, and scope of institutions and programmed tasks in these fields vary so greatly from country to country, no well-accepted or well-documented body of statistical comparisons exists in international convention to permit objective assessment of any of these subjects, either from the perspective of a single country or internationally. The data provided within any single subject area do, however, represent the most consistent approach to problems of international comparison found in the published literature for that field.

The provision of social security programs to answer specific social needs, for example, is summarized simply in terms of the existence or nonexistence of a specific type of benefit program because of the great complexity of national programs in terms of eligibility, coverage, term, age limits, financing, payments, and so on. Activities connected with a particular type of benefit often take place at more than one governmental level, through more than one agency at the same level, or through a mixture of public and private institutions. The data shown here are summarized from the U.S. Social Security Administration's *Social Security Programs Throughout the World* (regional coverage; Africa 2003, Asia 2002, Europe 2002, The Americas 2003). A bullet symbol (•) indicates that a country has at least one program within the defined area (a circle [○] indicates data is for 2003); in some cases it may have several. A blank space indicates that no program existed providing the benefit shown; ellipses [...] indicate that no information was available as to whether a program existed.

Data given for social security expenditure as a percentage of total central governmental expenditure are taken from the International Monetary Fund's *Government Finance Statistics Yearbook,* which provides the most comparable analytic series on the consolidated accounts of central governments, governmentally administered social security funds, and independent national agencies, all usually separate accounting entities, through which these services may be provided in a given country.

Data on the finances of social security programs are taken in large part from the International Labour Office's *The Cost of Social Security* (triennial), supplemented by national data sources.

Figures for criminal offenses known to police, usually excluding civil offenses and minor traffic violations, are taken in part from Interpol's *International Crime Statistics* (annual) and a variety of national sources. Statistics are usually based on the number of offenses reported to police, not the number of offenders apprehended or tried in courts. Attempted offenses are counted as the offense that was attempted. A person identified as having committed multiple offenses is counted only under the most serious offense. Murder refers to all acts involving the voluntary taking of life, including infanticide, but excluding abortion, or involuntary acts such as those normally classified as manslaughter. Assault includes "serious," or aggravated, assault—that involving injury, endangering life, or perpetrated with the use of a dangerous instrument. Burglary involves theft from the premises of another; although Interpol statistics are reported as "breaking and entering," national data may not always distinguish cases of forcible entry. Automobile theft excludes brief use of a car without the owner's

Social protection

country	social security																
	programs available, 2002 or 2003					expenditures, (latest) (% of total central govt.)[f]	finances										
							year	receipts					expenditures				
	old-age, invalidity, death[a]	sickness and maternity[b]	work injury[c]	unemployment[d]	family allowances[e]			total ('000,000 natl. cur.)	insured persons (%)	employers (%)	government (%)	other (%)	total ('000,000 natl. cur.)	benefits (%)	administration (%)	other (%)
Afghanistan	●	●	●			...	...	...	...	...	...	...	...	...	...	...
Albania	●	●	●	●	●	20.1	1990	967.0	—	—	88.8	11.2	1,440.0	99.5	—— 0.5 ——	
Algeria	○	○	○	○	○	...	1990	27,700.0	...	...	...	...	28,748.0	61.8	30.6	7.6
American Samoa	○	...	...	...	...	...	1990	...	...	...	...	...	13.0	100.0	—	—
Andorra	●	●	●			...	1993	11,832.2	...	...	...	...	7,937.2	90.2	4.6	5.2
Angola	...	...	...	...	...	...	...	...	...	...	...	...	...	...	...	...
Antigua and Barbuda	○	○				...	1983	13.0	29.2	48.7	—	22.1	4.2	66.1	33.9	—
Argentina	○	○	○	○	○	47.8	1989	1,015,837.0	28.8	45.0	16.6	9.6	989,009.0	95.0	5.0	—
Armenia	●	●	●	●	●	...	...	...	...	...	...	...	...	...	...	...
Aruba	○	...	○	...	...	[5]	1998	197.1	...	...	...	...	179.0	...	...	...
Australia	●	●	●	●	●	35.5	1998–99	...	...	...	...	1.9	41,825	99.6	0.3	—
Austria	●	●	●	●	●	46.3	1989	425,417.0	30.1	45.9	21.1	2.9	412,134.0	96.5	2.3	1.2
Azerbaijan	●	●	●	●	●	33.1	...	...	...	...	...	...	...	...	...	...
Bahamas, The	○	○	○			6.9	1989	95.9	22.9	38.5	2.1	36.5	43.5	71.1	27.2	1.7
Bahrain	●		●			7.5	1989	39.6	12.3	40.2	—	47.5	9.7	69.8	20.9	9.3
Bangladesh	●	●	●	●		...	1989	73.6	12.4	37.5	2.4	47.7	34.1	94.0	6.0	—
Barbados	○	○	○	○		...	1989	191.7	38.0	40.8	1.5	19.7	149.1	93.5	5.8	0.7
Belarus	●	●	●	●	●	44.0	1986	3,199.0	—	—	93.2	6.8	3,199.0	100.0	—	—
Belgium	●	●	●	●	●	...	1986	1,347,070.0	24.4	39.7	31.6	4.3	1,322,636.0	94.5	4.3	1.2
Belize	○	○	○			5.9[6]	1989	15.3	8.9	53.2	—	38.0	3.9	56.7	43.3	—
Benin	○	[7]	○		○	...	1989	3,551.9	16.8	81.4	—	1.8	4,500.9	69.3	28.1	2.6
Bermuda	○	○	○			...	...	...	...	...	...	...	...	...	...	...
Bhutan	...	...	...	...	...	...	1990	...	...	...	...	...	26.0[8]	...	...	...
Bolivia	○	○	○		○	20.6	1989	346.6	29.3	47.7	11.2	11.8	340.2	84.9	14.3	0.8
Bosnia and Herzegovina	●	●	●	●	●	...	...	...	...	...	...	...	...	...	...	...
Botswana	○[10]		○			1.1[11]	1996	—	...	...	...	...	65.0[8]	...	...	...
Brazil	○	○	○	○	○	47.3[12]	1989	71,847.0	24.4	51.0	20.0	4.6	68,957.0	61.9	18.6	19.5
Brunei	●	...	...	...	...	...	1984	...	...	...	...	...	39.5	...	...	...
Bulgaria	●	●	●	●	●	35.5	1989	6,016.8	—	71.4	28.1	0.5	6,000.1	96.6	3.3	0.1
Burkina Faso	○	○	○		○	0.1[13]	1989	8,816.5	15.6	62.9	—	21.5	4,975.3	69.5	30.4	0.1
Burundi	○		○		○	5.1	1989	1,991.5	31.6	47.6	—	20.8	1,563.9	74.8	16.8	8.4
Cambodia	...	...	○	...	○	...	...	...	...	...	...	...	...	...	...	...
Cameroon	○		○	○	○	0.5	1989	41,331.8	13.1	64.8	—	22.1	41,332.0	70.6	28.8	0.6
Canada	○	○	○	○	○	46.4	1989	130,306.6	9.9	15.6	64.4	10.1	115,764.2	96.9	2.5	0.6
Cape Verde	○	○	○		○	...	1989	697.7	26.5	58.5	—	15.0	316.7	82.4	16.1	1.5
Central African Republic	○	○	○		○	...	1989	3,604.0	8.4	76.0	—	15.6	3,247.0	64.6	32.9	2.5
Chad	○	○	○		○	...	1989	1,172.8	12.6	77.6	—	9.8	634.5	43.0	51.4	5.6
Chile	○	○	○	○	○	36.2	1989	1,186,056.0	32.8	2.7	37.9	26.6	798,770.0	83.9	14.7	1.4
China	●	●	●	●		22.4	1989	57,446.2	—	99.4	—	0.6	54,654	98.4	0.6	1.0
Colombia	○	○	○	○	○	12.1	1989	294,438.0	24.8	56.0	0.2	19.0	257,455.0	85.5	11.5	3.0
Comoros	...	...	...	...	...	...	1983	40.7	100.0	—	—	—	54.3	17.4	62.3	20.3
Congo, Dem. Rep. of the	○		○		○	0.1	1986	1,238.3	28.6	60.2	—	11.2	1,044.2	27.9	72.1	—
Congo, Rep. of the	○	○	○		○	...	1983	15,272.8	12.1	80.2	—	7.7	7,256.7	66.6	21.3	12.1
Costa Rica	○	○	○		○	21.3	1989	36,407.3	33.2	44.4	1.2	21.2	31,049.8	89.0	4.1	6.9
Côte d'Ivoire	○	○	○		○	...	1989	27,288.4	19.3	75.4	—	5.3	20,593.5	100.0	—	—
Croatia	●	●	●	●	●	42.8	...	...	...	...	...	...	...	...	...	...
Cuba	○	○	○		○	...	1989	2,284.8	—	37.4	62.6	—	2,284.8	96.7	—	3.3
Cyprus[16]	●	●	●	●	●	24.5	1989	217.5	24.7	40.3	17.3	17.7	117.7	98.4	1.6	—
Czech Republic	●	●	●	●	●	35.3	1989[18]	132,748.0	—	3.9	96.1	—	132,748.0	99.7	0.3	—
Denmark	●	●	●	●	●	40.9	1989	225,965.6	4.3	5.0	88.2	2.5	218,258.2	97.0	3.0	—
Djibouti	●[19]	...	...	...	●[19]	...	1979	1,352.2	...	...	...	...	1,115.7	...	...	...
Dominica	○	○	○			...	1986	12.3	22.6	50.9	—	26.5	4.4	68.0	32.0	—
Dominican Republic	○	○	○			8.1	1986	77.9	20.1	72.9	—	6.8	74.3	75.9	24.1	—
East Timor[21]	...	...	...	...	...	...	...	...	...	...	...	...	...	...	...	...
Ecuador	○	○	○	○		1.9[2]	1988	71,286.0	37.0	50.0	—	13.0	52,032.4	86.0	14.0	—

permission, "joyriding," and implies intent to deprive the owner of the vehicle permanently. Criminal offense data for certain countries refer to cases disposed of in court, rather than to complaints. Police manpower figures refer, for the most part, to full-time, paid professional staff, excluding clerical support and volunteer staff. Personnel in military service who perform police functions are presumed to be employed in their principal activity, military service.

The figures for military manpower refer to full-time, active-duty military service and exclude reserve, militia, paramilitary, and similar organizations. Because of the difficulties attached to the analysis of data on military manpower and budgets (including problems such as data withheld on national security grounds, or the publication of budgetary data specifically intended to hide actual expenditure, or the complexity of long-term financing of purchases of military matériel [how much was actually spent as opposed to what was committed, offset by nonmilitary transfers, etc.]), extensive use is made of the principal international analytic tools: publications such as those of the International Institute for Strategic Studies (*The Military Balance*) and the U.S. Arms Control and Disarmament Agency (*World Military Expenditures and Arms Transfers*), both annuals.

The data on military expenditures are from the sources identified above, as well as from the IMF's *Government Finance Statistics Yearbook* and country statistical publications.

The following notes further define the column headings:

a. Programs providing cash payments for *each* of the three types of long-term benefit indicated to persons (1) exceeding a specified working age (usually 50–65, often 5 years earlier for women) who are qualified by a term of covered employment, (2) partially or fully incapacitated for their usual employment by injury or illness, and (3) qualified by their status as spouse, cohabitant, or dependent minor of a qualified person who dies.

b. Programs providing cash payments (jointly, or alternatively, medical services as well) to occupationally qualified persons for *both* of the short-term benefits indicated: (1) illness and (2) maternity.

c. Programs providing cash or medical services to employment-qualified persons who become temporarily or permanently incapacitated (fully or partially) by work-related injury or illness.

d. Programs providing term-limited cash compensation (usually 40–75% of average earnings) to persons qualified by previous employment (of six months minimum, typically) for periods of involuntary unemployment.

e. Programs providing cash payments to families or mothers to mitigate the cost of raising children and to encourage the formation of larger families.

f. Includes welfare.

g. A police officer is a full-time, paid professional, performing domestic security functions. Data include administrative staff but exclude clerical employees, volunteers, and members of paramilitary groups.

h. Includes all active-duty personnel, regular and conscript, performing national security functions. Excludes reserves, paramilitary forces, border patrols, and gendarmeries.

crime and law enforcement (latest)						military protection								country
offenses reported to the police per 100,000 population					population per police officer[g]	manpower, 2003[h]		expenditure, 1999				arms trade, 1999 ('000,000 U.S.$)		
total	personal		property			total ('000)	per 1,000 population	total '000,000	per capita	% of central government expenditure	% of GDP or GNP	imports	exports	
	murder	assault	burglary	automobile theft										
…	…	…	…	…	540[1]	70	2.4	408[2]	…	…	…	0	0	Afghanistan
168.8	26.2	5.8	10.7	14.1	550	22.0	6.9	72	21	4.5	1.3	30	0	Albania
178.0	0.7	67.6	13.7	1.7	840	127.5	4.0	1,830	60	12.6	4.0	550	0	Algeria
3,006	8.0	494.0	588.0	6.0	460	[3]	[3]	—	—	—	—	…	…	American Samoa
2,616	0	16.7	515.2	110.6	220	—	—	…	…	…	…	…	…	Andorra
143.5	8.7	15.3	30.5	3.7	14[4]	131.0	12.2	2,460	248	41.1	21.2	350	0	Angola
4,977	4.7	475.0	1,984.4	35.9	120	0.2	2.2	…	…	…	…	…	…	Antigua and Barbuda
631.0	6.0	68.2	43.0	117.1	1,270	71.4	1.9	4,300	118	9.1	1.6	90	0	Argentina
264.4	4.1	4.7	16.6	0.7	…	44.7	14.6	570	170	20.2	5.8	10	0	Armenia
5,461	1.2	180.0	451.3	202.5	…	[3]	[3]	—	—	—	—	…	…	Aruba
7,003	3.7	708.5	2,926.2	684.8	438	53.7	2.7	7,060	372	7.6	1.8	1,100	550	Australia
6,095	1.4	3.0	944.0	34.7	470	34.6	4.3	1,690	208	1.5	0.8	30	30	Austria
176	4.2	2.4	10.3	0.4	…	66.5	8.1	927	120	24.4	6.6	10	0	Azerbaijan
4,870	27.1	61.5	1,560.2	415.7	125	0.9	2.7	…	…	…	…	…	…	Bahamas, The
1,390	1.6	0.5	380.1	207.6	180	11.2	16.6	415	666	18.9	8.1	70	0	Bahrain
90	2.8	4.3	4.3	1.1	2,560	125.5	0.9	624	5.0	10.1	1.3	80	0	Bangladesh
3,813	8.6	161.9	1,080.8	105.5	280	0.6	2.2	12	44	1.4	0.5	0	0	Barbados
1,282.4	11.6	20.6	197.9	59.9	…	72.9	7.4	925	89	4.1	1.3	0	310	Belarus
8,478	5.3	535.8	2,031.3	376.5	640	40.8	3.9	3,600	352	3.1	1.4	350	30	Belgium
…	12.8	20.0	600.0	4.0	290	1.1	3.9	11	47	5.4	1.6	0	0	Belize
297	5.1	102.0	4.6	0.6	3,250	4.6	0.6	34	5.0	8.3	1.4	5	0	Benin
8,871	5.1	221.7	1,949.2	…	370	[3]	[3]	—	—	—	—	…	…	Bermuda
…	…	…	…	…	…	…	…	…	…	…	…	0	0	Bhutan
660	28.6	59.4	0.9	…	…	31.5	3.7	148	18	8.0	1.8	10	0	Bolivia
402	2.5	2.6	…	…	…	19.8[9]	5.3[9]	276	75	24.3	4.5	40	0	Bosnia and Herzegovina
8,281	12.7	431.9	1.9	73.1	750	9.0	5.4	222	142	9.8	4.7	40	0	Botswana
779.1	11.2	255.7	5.2	61.2	…	287.6	1.6	9,920	58	5.5[6]	1.9	180	20	Brazil
932.9	1.5	1.2	79.8	57.5	100	7.0	20.0	295	897	11.5	4.0	20	0	Brunei
1,170.7	7.3	1.9	402.9	94.5	…	51.0	6.6	1,240	158	8.7	3.0	10	200	Bulgaria
9	0.4	1.7	—	—	…	10.8	0.8	42	4	5.9	1.6	0	0	Burkina Faso
156	9.7	10.8	2.0	0.2	…	50.5	8.3	49	8	26.7	7.0	60	0	Burundi
…	…	…	…	…	1,980	125	9.5	332	28	26.0	4.0	5	0	Cambodia
78	0.4	1.2	1.2	5.1	1,170	23.1	1.5	148	10	10.6	1.8	5	0	Cameroon
8,121	4.0	140.3	1,044.4	529.4	8,640	52.3	1.7	8,320	269	5.9	1.4	1,000	550	Canada
…	…	…	…	…	110	1.2	2.7	5	13	2.2	0.9	5	0	Cape Verde
135	1.6	22.8	2.7	…	2,740[1]	2.6	0.7	29	8	15.4	2.8	0	0	Central African Republic
…	…	…	…	…	990	30.4	3.3	37	5	12.7	2.4	10	0	Chad
1,366	4.5	84.8	488.0	12.9	470	77.3	5.0	1,990	133	12.3	3.0	100	10	Chile
128	0.2	5.2	45.2	6.9	1,360[14]	2,250.0	1.7	88,900	71	22.2	2.3	675	320	China
700	56.3	61.8	57.0	75.3	420	200.0	4.8	2,670	68	15.9	3.2	60	0	Colombia
…	…	…	…	…	960	—[15]	[15]	…	…	…	…	…	…	Comoros
…	…	…	…	…	910	97.8	1.9	5,150	102	41.4[6]	14.4	110	0	Congo, Dem. Rep. of the
32	1.5	4.7	0.2	0.2	870	10.0	2.7	58	21	8.4	3.5	0	0	Congo, Rep. of the
868	5.3	11.1	232.4	23.1	480	—	—	69	19	2.0	0.5	0	0	Costa Rica
67	2.5	73.1	19.5	11.9	4,640	17.1	1.0	82	5	3.4	0.8	0	0	Côte d'Ivoire
1,216	6.1	24.1	290.9	38.6	…	20.8	4.7	2,090	491	14.2	6.4	10	10	Croatia
…	…	…	…	…	650	46.0	4.1	630	57	…	1.9	0	0	Cuba
689	1.9	17.7	203.3	3.0	180	10.0[17]	10.9[17]	309	411	9.3	3.4	340	0	Cyprus[16]
4,142	2.6	71.7	831.4	263.0	640[18]	57.1	5.6	3,000	292	6.3	2.3	220	80	Czech Republic
9,300	4.1	20.8	1,899	638.1	600	22.9	4.2	2,780	524	4.2	1.6	290	10	Denmark
252	4.2	124.2	45.0	0.5	…	9.9	21.6	23	51	12.7	4.3	0	0	Djibouti
9,567	7.9	682.4	1,736	77.6	300	[20]	[20]	…	…	…	…	…	…	Dominica
…	15.8	28.4	154.0	14.0	580	24.5	2.8	123	15	4.4	0.7	20	0	Dominican Republic
…	…	…	…	…	…	0.7[22]	0.8[22]	…	…	…	…	…	…	East Timor[21]
587	25.9	35.6	164.5	52.9	260	59.5	4.6	479	38	16.2	3.7	20	0	Ecuador

Social protection (continued)

country	social security: programs available, 2002 or 2003					expenditures, (latest) (% of total central govt.)[f]	finances									
	old-age, invalidity, death[a]	sickness and maternity[b]	work injury[c]	unemployment[d]	family allowance[e]		year	receipts: total ('000,000 natl. cur.)	insured persons (%)	employers (%)	government (%)	other (%)	expenditures: total ('000,000 natl. cur.)	benefits (%)	administration (%)	other (%)
Egypt	○	○	○	○		0.5[6]	1989	2,443.5	22.8	41.0	2.0	34.2	1,685.6	93.4	6.6	—
El Salvador	○	○	○			5.9	1989	465.3	27.1	51.7	—	21.2	368.3	78.1	21.9	—
Equatorial Guinea	○	○	○		○	…	1989	141.0	7.1	92.9	—	—	134.0	49.3	50.7	—
Eritrea	…	…	…	…	…	…	…	…	…	…	…	…	…	…	…	…
Estonia	●	●	●	●	●	31.4	…	90.1	…	…	…	…	…	…	…	…
Ethiopia	○		○			1.6[10]	1989[23]	190.9	32.8	65.3	—	1.9	153.7	98.3	1.7	—
Faroe Islands	○[19]	…	…	…	○[19]	…	…	…	…	…	…	…	…	…	…	…
Fiji	●		●			4.1[11]	1989	153.5	20.9	33.8	0.8	44.5	75.47	95.3	4.7	—
Finland	●	●	●	●	●	36.4	1989	118,589.0	7.7	41.1	44.0	7.2	106,235	96.3	3.7	—
France	●	●	●	●	●	38.8[24]	1989	1,700,202.0	77.7	—	20.4	1.9	1,669,096.0	95.5	3.7	0.8
French Guiana	○	…	○	…	○	…	1991	1,071.5	…	…	…	…	997.1	…	…	…
French Polynesia	○	…	○	…	○	…	1990	19,268.0	…	…	…	…	17,832.0	…	…	…
Gabon	○	○	○		○	…	1989	3,415.0	—	44.3	29.3	26.4	2,737.0	55.2	44.8	—
Gambia, The	○		○			1.0[2]	1982	—	…	…	…	…	5.6	…	…	…
Gaza Strip	…	…	…	…	…	—	…	…	…	…	…	…	…	…	…	…
Georgia	●	●	●	●		29.7	…	…	…	…	…	…	…	…	…	…
Germany	●	●	●	●	●	50.0[11]	1989[25]	522,172.0	36.9	34.3	26.1	2.7	507,604.0	97.1	2.8	0.1
Ghana	○		○			7.1	1989	17,920.8	21.1	52.9	—	26.0	4,147.7	13.3	64.0	22.7
Greece	●	●	●	●	●	17.9[12]	1989	1,314,421.0	24.9	38.4	30.8	5.9	1,349,693.0	92.5	7.5	—
Greenland	○[19]	…	…	…	○[19]	…	…	…	…	…	…	…	…	…	…	…
Grenada	○	○	○			8.6[26]	1989	24.1	20.1	60.3	3.2	16.3	13.5	93.1	6.9	—
Guadeloupe	○	…	…	…	○	…	1994	2,607.3	…	…	…	…	5,883.4	…	…	…
Guam	○	…	…	…	○	…	1989	…	…	…	…	…	7.3	…	…	…
Guatemala	○	○	○			…	1989	348.5	29.1	54.8	—	16.1	279.7	82.7	14.6	2.7
Guernsey	●	●	●	●	●	…	1999	103,560	—— 45.0 ——		40.7	14.3	85,468	94.8	5.2	…
Guinea	○	○	○		○	…	1989	3,387.0	0.4	90.3	—	9.3	1,108.1	54.9	45.1	—
Guinea-Bissau	…	…	…	…	…	8.8[24]	1986	138.0	22.8	63.4	10.3	3.8	61.9	59.6	40.4	—
Guyana	○	○	○			…	1994	1,070.8	…	…	…	…	1,373.7	…	…	…
Haiti	○	7	○			5.1[27]	1977	60.5	—— 26.6 ——		69.9	3.5	52.4	92.7	7.3	—
Honduras	○	○	○			…	1986	166.2	23.9	40.8	3.3	32.0	76.8	84.6	15.4	—
Hong Kong	●	●	●	●	●	…	1998–99	…	…	…	…	…	26,939	…	…	…
Hungary	●	●	●	●	●	32.2	1994	798,000.0	—	—	—	—	737,000.0	—	—	—
Iceland	●	●	●	●	●	21.8	1997	14,799	—	—	—	—	96,094	98.2	1.8	—
India	●	●	●	●		…	1989	43,913.8	23.8	27.7	5.3	43.2	13,775.8	90.0	8.2	1.8
Indonesia	●		●			8.6	1989	239,477.0	50.7	49.3	—	—	181,499.0	12.3	15.8	71.9
Iran	●	●	●	●	●	16.5	1986	346,460.0	83.2	0.1	8.2	8.5	167,879.0	43.4	6.3	50.0
Iraq	●	●	●	●		…	1977	107.8	9.9	55.6	21.9	12.6	71.0	94.0	2.4	3.6
Ireland	●	●	●	●	●	25.9	1989	4,627.5	16.3	24.8	57.7	1.2	4,612.9	95.2	4.7	0.1
Isle of Man	●	●	●	●	●	…	1985	…	…	…	…	…	14.4	…	…	…
Israel	●	●	●	●	●	28.0	1989	13,851.1	31.1	27.7	35.0	6.2	13,593.3	81.7	15.4	2.9
Italy	●	●	●	●	●	…	1989	278,383.0	16.5	51.4	30.0	2.1	100,251.0	89.3	2.0	8.7
Jamaica	○	○	○			1.0	1989	374.3	11.5	13.6	43.8	31.1	273.6	92.6	7.4	—
Japan	●	●	●	●	●	36.8[26]	1989	59,571,299.0	27.4	31.6	24.4	16.6	46,684,159.0	94.3	1.7	4.0
Jersey	●	●	●	●	●	9.5[24, 27]	1991	60.9	—— 63.8 ——		23.4	12.8	52.8	…	…	…
Jordan	●		●			16.7	1986	53.6	28.7	55.3	—	16.0	9.5	77.4	14.0	8.6
Kazakhstan	●	●	●	●	●	32.8	…	…	…	…	…	…	…	…	…	…
Kenya	○	○	○			2.7	1989	4,262.0	18.2	13.7	10.0	58.1	1,857.8	53.8	46.1	0.1
Kiribati	●		●			…	…	…	…	…	…	…	…	…	…	…
Korea, North	…	…	…	…	…	…	…	…	…	…	…	…	…	…	…	…
Korea, South	●		●	●		10.8[6]	1996	7,425,400.0	—	62.2	—	—	9,656,600.0	…	…	…
Kuwait	●		●			20.4	1989	445.8	7.1	13.2	54.3	25.4	206.5	97.0	3.0	—
Kyrgyzstan	●	●	●	●	●	9.5	…	…	…	…	…	…	…	…	…	…
Laos	●	●	●	…	…	…	…	…	…	…	…	…	…	…	…	…
Latvia	●	●	●	●	●	40.8	…	…	…	…	…	…	…	…	…	…
Lebanon	●	●	●		●	5.4	…	…	…	…	…	…	…	…	…	…
Lesotho	…	…	…	…	…	1.1[31]	1992	—	…	…	…	…	12.0[8]	…	…	…
Liberia	○		○			…	1983	2.9	—	69.0	13.8	17.2	2.6	54.4	45.6	—
Libya	○	○	○			…	1989	314.3	21.6	25.4	50.2	2.8	260.0	77.5	19.5	3.0
Liechtenstein	●	●	●	●	●	…	…	…	…	…	…	…	…	…	…	…
Lithuania	●	●	●	●	●	35.5	…	…	…	…	…	…	24,981.7	…	…	…
Luxembourg	●	●	●	●	●	52.3[26]	1989	72,471.8	24.2	34.6	34.4	6.8	65,214.4	97.2	2.4	0.4
Macau	○	…	…	…	○	…	1998	223.2	…	…	…	…	207.4	…	…	…
Macedonia	○	○	○	○	○	…	1996	24,482	…	…	…	…	…	…	…	…
Madagascar	○	○	○		○	1.5	1989	15,229.0	22.2	77.8	—	—	14,542.0	81.2	18.8	—
Malawi			○			…	1986	—	…	…	…	…	5.4	…	…	…
Malaysia	●		●			7.2	1989	7,958.7	20.7	40.2	—	39.1	2,826.5	97.0	3.0	—
Maldives	…	…	…	…	…	2.4	1990	—	…	…	…	…	7.1	…	…	…
Mali	○	○	○		○	…	1986	8,128.8	16.6	74.3	—	9.1	7,924.6	63.7	34.7	1.6
Malta	●	●	●	●	●	34.0	1989	82.2	26.1	31.6	42.3	—	110.7	92.5	7.5	—
Marshall Islands	●					…	…	…	…	…	…	…	…	…	…	…
Martinique	○	…	…	…	○	…	1998	3,913.1	…	…	…	…	8,429.6	…	…	…
Mauritania	○	○	●		○	…	1989	808.4	1.5	90.4	—	8.1	735.2	63.5	31.2	5.3
Mauritius	○		○		○	21.4	1989	1,733.5	2.9	47.9	31.7	17.5	1,072.7	95.2	3.0	1.8
Mayotte	…	…	…	…	…	…	…	…	…	…	…	…	…	…	…	…
Mexico	○	○	○	○	○	20.1	1989	16,011,795.0	20.9	54.8	12.9	11.4	14,562,293.0	79.9	15.5	4.6
Micronesia	●					…	…	…	…	…	…	…	…	…	…	…
Moldova	●	●	●	●	●	42.4	…	…	…	…	…	…	…	…	…	…
Monaco	●	●	●	35	●	…	…	…	…	…	…	…	…	…	…	…
Mongolia	○	○	…	…	○	23.8	1989	2,431.6	—	—	20.8	79.2	2,304.6	100.0	—	—
Morocco	○	○	○		○	9.3	1989	4,660.5	20.6	47.5	12.9	19.0	3,040.7	94.8	5.0	0.2
Mozambique	○	…	…	…	…	…	1986	228.2	—	86.2	13.7	0.1	145.0	100.0	—	—
Myanmar (Burma)		○	○			2.3	1986	44.3	19.9	59.6	18.5	2.0	35.9	51.5	15.6	32.9
Namibia	○	…	…	…	…	6.8[13, 27]	…	…	…	…	…	…	…	…	…	…
Nauru	○	○	○	…	○	…	…	…	…	…	…	…	…	…	…	…
Nepal	●		●			4.6	1985	—	…	…	…	…	59.3	…	…	…

crime and law enforcement (latest)						military protection								country
offenses reported to the police per 100,000 population					population per police officer[g]	manpower, 2003[h]		expenditure, 1999				arms trade, 1999 ('000,000 U.S.$)		
total	personal		property			total ('000)	per 1,000 population	total '000,000	per capita	% of central government expenditure	% of GDP or GNP	imports	exports	
	murder	assault	burglary	automobile theft										
3,693	1.6	0.7	…	3.1	580	450.0	6.6	2,390	36	9.3[6]	2.7	700	0	Egypt
879	36.9	71.1	…	82.0	1,000	15.5	2.4	110	18	8.8	0.9	10	0	El Salvador
…	…	…	…	…	190	1.3	2.6	19	40	16.5	3.2	0	0	Equatorial Guinea
161.9	2.7	10.3	5.8	…	…	202.2	48.8	208	52	51.1	7.4	170	20	Eritrea
3,565	13.8	28.3	1,659.2	169.8	…	5.5	4.0	173	120	4.5	1.5	10	0	Estonia
258.3	6.5	77.8	1.4	1.4	1,100[23]	162.5	2.4	533	9	29.1	8.8	270	0	Ethiopia
…	…	…	…	…	…	[3]	[3]	—	—	—	—	…	…	Faroe Islands
2,370	2.9	44.1	427.9	44.4	407	3.5	4.2	35	42	5.4	2.0	0	0	Fiji
14,350	0.7	34.9	1,739.7	33.2	640	27.0	5.2	1,770	344	4.5	1.4	400	50	Finland
6,097	3.4	162.7	632.4	511.0	630	259.1	4.3	38,900	658	5.9	2.7	800	2,900	France
8,936	27.2	178.7	1,367.3	150.6	…	[3]	[3]	—	—	—	—	…	…	French Guiana
1,799	0.9	98.9	232.7	…	…	[3]	[3]	—	—	—	—	…	…	French Polynesia
114	1.4	17.9	2.3	7.5	1,290	4.7	3.5	93	78	7.3	2.4	0	0	Gabon
89	0.4	10.6	5.6	…	3,310	0.8	0.6	5	4	5.4	1.3	0	0	Gambia, The
4,355	…	…	…	…	…	—	—	…	…	…	…	…	…	Gaza Strip
286	4.7	99.5	21.1	0.8	…	17.5	3.5	165	33	7.0	1.2	10	30	Georgia
7,682	3.5	139.6	1,377.4	114.3	…	284.5	3.4	32,600	395	4.7	1.6	1,300	1,900	Germany
…	2.2	418.9	1.5	…	620	7.0	0.3	62	3	3.1	0.8	0	0	Ghana
3,641	3.0	68.2	356.8	166.5	380	177.6	16.1	6,060	573	16.4	4.7	1,900	90	Greece
9,360	18.1	845.0	1,883.5	…	340	[3]	[3]	—	—	—	—	…	…	Greenland
8,543	7.8	98.9	582.2	…	230	[20]	[20]	…	…	…	…	…	…	Grenada
5,793	13.2	215.2	821.5	453.9	…	[3]	[3]	—	—	—	—	…	…	Guadeloupe
10,080	7.9	169.3	634.2	333.6	…	[3]	[3]	—	—	—	—	…	…	Guam
510	27.4	77.1	27.9	58.1	670	31.4	2.5	121	10	5.0	0.7	0	0	Guatemala
…	…	…	…	…	…	[3]	[3]	—	—	—	—	…	…	Guernsey
18.4	0.5	0.7	0.7	0.1	1,140	9.7	1.1	54	7	7.4	1.6	0	0	Guinea
129	0.5	8.7	4.0	0.2	…	9.3	6.8	6	4	6.1	2.7	0	0	Guinea-Bissau
1,277	19.1	246.0	365.8	32.2	190	1.6	2.0	5	7	2.0	0.8	0	0	Guyana
701	…	…	…	…	400	[28]	[28]	…	…	…	…	0	0	Haiti
392	154.0	44.4	4.3	25.8	1,040	12.0	1.8	34	6	2.6	0.7	10	0	Honduras
1,122	1.0	117.1	133.4	15.3	221	[3]	[3]	—	—	—	—	…	…	Hong Kong
5,011	4.1	76.6	804.4	41.3	237	33.4	3.3	1,880	185	3.9	1.7	80	10	Hungary
31,332	0.7	15.8	920.3	…	940	—	—	—	—	—	—	10	0	Iceland
594	4.6	…	15.6	…	820	1,325.0	1.2	11,300	11	14.6	2.5	700	10	India
120.9	1.0	4.4	1.8	1.7	1,119	302	1.4	1,450	7	5.3	1.1	450	100	Indonesia
77	0.5	47.7	…	…	…	540.0	8.2	6,880	106	11.2	2.9	150	10	Iran
197	7.1	34.7	…	…	140	[29]	[29]	1,250	57	…	5.5	5	0	Iraq
1,696	1.4	12.4	479.8	16.3	310	10.5	2.6	779	208	2.6	1.0	40	0	Ireland
2,867	0.7	12.3	921.4	60.6	…	[3]	[3]	—	—	—	—	…	…	Isle of Man
6,254	2.2	491.8	990.1	501.7	210	167.6	25.9	8,700	1,510	18.5	8.8	2,400	600	Israel
4,214	4.4	46.4	…	537.0	680	200.0	3.5	23,700	412	4.7	2.0	700	380	Italy
1,871	37.2	511.4	135.7	7.2	430	2.8	1.1	51	19	2.1	0.8	10	0	Jamaica
1,773	1.0	16.0	206.0	34.0	480	239.9	1.9	43,200	342	6.1	1.0	3,000	20	Japan
…	…	…	…	…	…	[3]	[3]	—	—	—	—	…	…	Jersey
1,256	6.3	14.0	31.0	52.2	630	100.5	18.6	725	150	27.5	9.2	70	0	Jordan
932	15.9	…	…	3.4	…	65.8	4.4	671	40	5.3	0.9	160	10	Kazakhstan
484	6.4	54.1	76.9	9.7	1,500	24.1	0.8	200	7	7.1	1.9	5	0	Kenya
261	5.1	11.6	38.6	…	330	—	—	…	…	…	…	…	…	Kiribati
…	…	…	…	…	460	1,082.0	48.2	4,260	199	…	18.8	30	140	Korea, North
3,494	2.1	64.6	7.0	…	506	686.0	13.9	11,600	246	11.0	2.9	2,200	20	Korea, South
1,346	1.5	36.4	75.9	56.7	80	15.5	6.4	2,690	1,410	20.8	7.7	725	0	Kuwait
987	10.4[30]	12.6	482.4	…	…	10.9	2.2	285	62	14.0	2.4	0	0	Kyrgyzstan
…	…	…	…	…	280	29.1	5.1	28	5	11.1	2.0	0	0	Laos
2,097	9.3	18.6	56.1	129.0	…	4.9	2.1	144	59	2.5	0.9	5	0	Latvia
3,063	5.5	209.7	78.0	30.0	530	72.1	19.3	653	185	11.0	4.0	10	0	Lebanon
2,357	50.4	156.9	250.4	30.8	1,130	2.0	1.1	29	14	6.5	2.6	0	0	Lesotho
…	…	…	…	…	1,570	[32]	[32]	6	2	8.3	1.2	0	0	Liberia
1,065	2.1	5.4	…	…	…	76.0	13.7	1,490[6]	342[6]	19.7[6]	6.1[6]	20	30	Libya
…	…	114.3	614.3	153.6	660	[33]	[33]	—	—	—	—	…	…	Liechtenstein
2,029	9.0	10.4	585.6	96.7	…	12.7	3.7	314	87	3.9	1.3	20	0	Lithuania
6,280	17.2	89.0	1,152.8	182.0	829	0.9	2.0	141	326	2.0	0.8	50	0	Luxembourg
1,698	5.4	34.0	250.5	26.6	…	[3]	[3]	…	…	…	…	…	…	Macau
1,102	5.4	26.9	…	44.7	…	12.9	6.3	228	112	10.4	2.5	20	0	Macedonia
112	0.6	12.0	0.7	0.1	2,900	13.5	0.8	45	3	7.4	1.2	0	0	Madagascar
850	3.1	82.2	13.1	…	1,670	5.3	0.5	10	1	2.2	0.6	0	0	Malawi
604	3.1	25.9	155.6	20.8	760	104.0	4.1	1,660	78	9.3	2.3	925	0	Malaysia
2,353	1.9	3.3	36.1	…	35,710	—	—	…	…	…	…	…	…	Maldives
10.0	0.7	1.5	0.8	0.3	160	7.4	0.6	58	6	8.7	2.3	0	0	Mali
1,841	3.0	35.2	1,079.2	243.9	230	2.1	5.3	28	73	1.8	0.8	0	0	Malta
2,273	…	…	…	…	400	[34]	[34]	—	—	—	—	…	…	Marshall Islands
6,305	5.8	184.9	641.2	192.8	…	[3]	[3]	—	—	—	—	…	…	Martinique
95.4	0.8	27.0	7.3	2.5	710	15.8	5.9	37	14	18.9	4.0	0	0	Mauritania
2,712	2.9	7.8	116.0	…	240	—	—	9	7	0.9	0.2	0	0	Mauritius
…	…	…	…	…	…	[3]	[3]	—	—	—	—	…	…	Mayotte
108	7.3	30.2	…	…	…	192.8	1.9	2,700	27	3.8	0.6	160	30	Mexico
…	…	…	…	…	…	[34]	[34]	—	—	—	—	…	…	Micronesia
957	9.9	11.1	50.4	15.6	…	6.9	1.6	43	10	1.6	0.5	0	20	Moldova
3,430	—	46.7	106.7	70.0	…	—	—	…	…	…	…	…	…	Monaco
1,010	30.0	74.7	486.0	2.1	120	8.6	3.4	18	5	5.9	2.1	0	0	Mongolia
366	1.4	6.7	…	…	840	196.3	6.6	1,450	49	13.5	4.3	130	0	Morocco
166	4.2	9.2	45.9	…	…	8.2	0.4	94	5	9.1	2.5	5	0	Mozambique
64.5	1.9	26.9	0.1	0.1	650	488.0	11.5	4,650	112	189.3	7.8	60	0	Myanmar (Burma)
2,006	26.3	533.6	602.0	65.8	…	9.0	4.7	91	53	7.2	2.9	130	0	Namibia
…	25.0	400.0	100.0	…	110	—	—	…	…	…	…	…	…	Nauru
9	2.8	1.1	0.8	…	1,000	63.0	2.6	44	2	5.7	0.8	0	0	Nepal

Social protection (continued)

country	social security						finances									
	programs available, 2002 or 2003					expenditures, (latest) (% of total central govt.)[f]	year	receipts					expenditures			
	old-age, invalidity, death[a]	sickness and maternity[b]	work injury[c]	unemployment[d]	family allowances[e]			total ('000,000 natl. cur.)	insured persons (%)	employers (%)	government (%)	other (%)	total ('000,000 natl. cur.)	benefits (%)	administration (%)	other (%)
Netherlands, The	●	●	●	●	●	37.4[6]	1989	154,427.0	37.3	30.3	19.0	13.4	135,609.0	96.9	3.1	—
Netherlands Antilles	●	...	○	○	...	12.9[5, 26]	1998	317.0	100.0	—	—	—	275.0	...	...	...
New Caledonia	...	...	...	...	○	...	1987	15,834.0	...	...	...	...	14,598.0	...	...	...
New Zealand	●	●	●	●	●	37.9	1989	14,266.0	1.0	4.7	92.5	1.8	14,372.3	95.6	2.8	1.6
Nicaragua	○	○	○		○	14.7[26]	1989	647,454.8	13.5	49.1	7.6	29.8	452,038.6	82.4	17.6	—
Niger	○	○	○		○	...	1989	5,634.9	9.4	90.6	—	—	3,804.2	62.5	—	37.5
Nigeria	○		○			...	1989	54.0	50.0	50.0	—	—	22.6	42.5	57.5	—
Northern Mariana Islands	○	...	...	...	...	...	...	...	...	...	...	...	...	...	...	...
Norway	○	○	○	○	○	40.0[12]	1989	158,105.0	18.3	31.4	46.6	3.7	131,578.2	98.7	1.3	—
Oman	●	...	●	...	...	5.6	1995	—	...	...	...	...	...	...	...	...
Pakistan	●	●	●	●		...	1989	9,321.4	1.3	8.0	84.3	6.4	8,092.0	97.4	1.2	1.4
Palau	●					...	...	...	...	...	...	...	...	...	...	...
Panama	○	○	○			20.9	1989	496.7	31.0	39.5	7.1	22.4	452.8	94.0	4.8	1.2
Papua New Guinea	●		●			2.0	1983	45.0	40.5	32.1	8.0	19.4	9.4	82.3	9.7	8.0
Paraguay	○	○	○			16.2[24]	1993	...	...	...	...	...	253,341	...	...	...
Peru	○	○	○			...	1989	1,363,280.6	30.2	65.1	4.7	—	1,435,134.1	78.5	21.5	—
Philippines	●	●	●			3.9	1989	19,213.6	22.2	32.3	—	45.5	7,878.3	87.3	12.3	—
Poland	●	●	●	●	●	51.5	1989	11,572,248.0	2.1	70.2	25.1	2.6	11,452,165.0	98.8	1.2	—
Portugal	●	●	●	●	●	27.3[2]	1989	833,442.5	31.3	50.1	13.4	5.2	756,410.8	94.6	4.2	1.2
Puerto Rico	○	○	○	○	○	...	1980	...	...	...	...	...	1,041.3	100.0	—	—
Qatar	...	...	...	...	...	...	1986	80.0	—	—	100.0	—	80.0	100.0	—	—
Réunion	...	...	...	...	...	...	1998	...	...	...	...	...	13,200.0	...	...	...
Romania	●	●	●	●	●	31.4	1989	90,561.2	—	48.9	51.1	—	90,561.2	100.0	—	—
Russia	●	●	●	●	●	33.7	...	...	...	...	...	...	...	...	...	...
Rwanda	○		○			...	1989	2,350.0	23.9	39.8	—	36.3	965.8	60.8	39.2	—
St. Kitts and Nevis	○	○	○			9.4	1989	14.3	...	...	...	...	7.9	...	...	...
St. Lucia	○	○	○			...	1986	14.6	28.6	28.6	—	42.8	3.4	61.4	38.6	—
St. Vincent and the Grenadines	○	○	○			8.8	1989	—	...	...	...	...	—	...	...	...
Samoa	●		●			—	...	—	...	...	...	...	—	...	...	...
San Marino	●	●	●		...	...	1983	51,673.0	12.0	48.7	36.1	3.2	46,179.0	95.7	3.7	0.6
São Tomé and Príncipe	○	○	○			...	1986	46.4	37.7	56.3	—	6.0	23.7	100.0	—	—
Saudi Arabia	●	●	●			...	1989	1,761.4	26.8	73.2	—	—	4,292.9	100.0	—	—
Senegal	○	○	○		○	2.3[13, 27]	1989	17,202.0	—	47.6	51.4	1.0	15,371.0	84.6	11.1	4.3
Serbia and Montenegro	●	●	●	●	●	6.0[39]	1986[39]	2,777,651.0	63.3	32.2	3.4	1.1	2,732,679.0	90.3	1.9	7.8
Seychelles	○	○	○			13.8	1983	69.1	30.1	60.2	—	9.7	42.7	69.6	4.9	25.5
Sierra Leone	○		○			0.1[2]	1990	...	...	...	...	...	153.00	100.00	—	—
Singapore	●	●	●			12.4	1989	7,531.9	49.1	35.3	0.1	15.6	5,045.8	78.0	0.6	21.4
Slovakia	●	●	●	●	●	30.2	1998	74,205	...	...	...	...	87,916	...	...	...
Slovenia	●	●	●	●	●	43.5	...	...	...	...	...	...	...	...	...	...
Solomon Islands	●		●	●		...	1989	20.9	27.8	41.1	—	31.1	17.4	89.7	10.3	—
Somalia			○			...	...	—	...	...	...	...	...	...	...	...
South Africa	○	○	○	○	○	4.2[6]	1994	2,034	—	100.0	—	—	2,260.0	...	...	...
Spain	●	●	●	●	●	39.6	1989	8,320,972.0	15.9	53.9	27.9	2.3	8,038,090.0	94.3	2.6	3.1
Sri Lanka	○	7	○		○	12.3	1989	15,399.9	22.0	24.4	29.1	24.5	5,819.0	98.5	1.3	0.2
Sudan, The	○		○			...	1989	62.0	24.9	0.5	—	74.6	14.7	37.5	62.5	—
Suriname	○	...	...	...	○	...	1989	73.0	24.7	75.3	—	—	70.6	100.0	—	—
Swaziland	○		○			0.4	1986	10.7	31.4	31.4	—	37.2	3.9	45.8	54.2	—
Sweden	●	●	●	●	●	46.3	1989	446,909.7	2.8	37.9	50.8	8.5	439,997.3	93.7	3.3	3.0
Switzerland	●	●	●	●	●	48.5	1989	45,800.1	45.6	22.6	25.9	5.9	41,745.7	91.5	3.0	5.5
Syria	●		●	●		5.3[12]	1989	3,147.9	30.4	60.9	...	5.6	1,455.9	95.7	4.2	0.1
Taiwan	●	●	●	●		13.8[2]	...	...	...	...	...	...	...	...	...	...
Tajikistan	○	○	○	○	○	20.3	...	...	...	...	...	...	...	...	...	...
Tanzania	○	○	○			...	1989	3,275.8	25.9	25.9	—	48.2	2,780.7	5.8	14.1	80.1
Thailand	●	●	●	●	●	6.0	1989	654.0	—	60.2	—	39.8	260.0	88.2	11.8	—
Togo	○	○	○		○	...	1989	10,162.0	8.1	61.5	—	30.4	5,844.0	77.5	22.5	—
Tonga	...	...	...	...	...	0.8[13]	...	...	...	...	...	...	...	...	...	...
Trinidad and Tobago	○	○	○		○	14.3[26]	1989	584.9	12.0	24.1	39.7	24.2	438.4	85.6	11.1	3.3
Tunisia	○	○	○	○	○	18.8	1989	325.3	36.9	63.1	—	—	358.3	...	...	...
Turkey	●	●	●	●		5.9	1989	12,075,809.0	28.5	32.9	22.8	15.8	10,241,427.0	97.2	2.2	0.6
Turkmenistan	●	●	●	●	●	...	...	...	...	...	...	...	...	...	...	...
Tuvalu	○	...	...	...	...	...	1981	...	...	...	...	...	0.1	67.6	32.4	—
Uganda	○		○			...	1989	265.9	32.1	64.3	1.1	2.5	145.0	0.3	76.8	22.9
Ukraine	●	●	●	●	●	43.2	1989	20,350.0	—	—	—	—	20,350.0	100.0	—	—
United Arab Emirates	...	...	...	...	...	3.2	1989	182.2	17.3	6.2	0.5	76.0	182.2	100.0	...	...
United Kingdom	●	●	●	●	●	36.5	1989	92,157.0	18.1	24.9	52.9	4.1	88,294.0	93.8	3.3	2.9
United States	○	○	○	○	○	28.3	1989	804,909.0	25.5	33.9	28.8	11.8	627,653.0	95.5	3.3	1.2
Uruguay	○	43	○	○	○	56.5	1989	535,507.0	31.4	37.3	26.0	5.3	548,591.0	93.6	5.4	1.0
Uzbekistan	●	●	●	●		...	...	...	...	...	...	...	...	...	...	...
Vanuatu	●					...	...	—	...	...	...	...	—	...	...	...
Venezuela	○	○	○	○	43	10.0	1986	7,457.6	21.3	40.7	12.7	25.3	6,355.7	86.1	14.9	—
Vietnam	●	●	●			10.5	...	...	...	...	...	...	...	...	...	...
Virgin Islands (U.S.)	○	...	...	○	○	...	...	...	...	...	...	...	...	...	...	...
West Bank	...	...	...	...	...	...	...	...	...	...	...	...	...	...	...	...
Western Sahara	...	...	...	...	...	...	...	...	...	...	...	...	...	...	...	...
Yemen	●	...	●	...	...	—	...	—	...	...	...	...	—	...	...	...
Zambia	○		○			1.3	1986	179.2	28.4	28.4	—	43.2	67.7	40.6	59.4	—
Zimbabwe	○		○			18.2[6]	1983	167.0	25.9	7.6	64.2	2.3	112.2	93.7	6.2	0.1

[1]Rural areas. [2]1990. [3]Political dependency; defense is the responsibility of the administering country. [4]Includes civilian militia. [5]Netherlands Antilles includes Aruba. [6]1997. [7]Maternity benefits only. [8]Includes welfare. [9]In 2003 about 12,000 troops of the NATO-commanded Stabilization Forces were stationed in Bosnia and Herzegovina to assure implementation of the Dayton Accords. [10]Old age benefits only. [11]1996. [12]1998. [13]1991. [14]Local officers only. [15]Military defense is the responsibility of France. [16]Republic of Cyprus only. [17]National Guard only. [18]Data refer to former Czechoslovakia. [19]1999. [20]Paramilitary unit of country participating in the U.S.-sponsored Regional Security System, a defense pact among eastern Caribbean countries. [21]Indonesia includes East Timor, except where noted. [22]UN forces of 3,497 troops, including 104 observers, are stationed in East Timor. [23]Ethiopia includes Eritrea. [24]1993. [25]Former West Germany. [26]1995. [27]Social

crime and law enforcement (latest)						military protection								country
offenses reported to the police per 100,000 population					population per police officer[g]	manpower, 2003[h]		expenditure, 1999				arms trade, 1999 ('000,000 U.S.$)		
total	personal		property			total ('000)	per 1,000 population	total '000,000	per capita	% of central government expenditure	% of GDP or GNP	imports	exports	
	murder	assault	burglary	automobile theft										
7,808	10.9	242.8	3,100.4	239.0	510	53.1	3.3	7,030	445	5.9	1.8	775	140	Netherlands, The
5,574[36]	...	396	3,455	...	330	[3]	[3]	—	—	—	—	...	...	Netherlands Antilles
...	...	...	...	...	...	[3]	[3]	—	—	—	—	...	...	New Caledonia
13,854	3.9	546.3	2,352.9	788.6	630	8.6	2.1	587	156	3.5	1.2	575	0	New Zealand
1,069	25.6	203.8	110.7	...	90[4]	14	2.6	24	5	2.9	1.2	0	0	Nicaragua
99	0.9	16.6	1.0	0.7	2,350[37]	5.3	0.5	24	2	6.4	1.2	0	0	Niger
312	...	...	...	...	1,140	78.5	0.6	1,560	13	8.1	1.6	0	0	Nigeria
245	3.8	92.6	73.7	20.8	...	[3]	[3]	—	—	—	—	...	...	Northern Mariana Islands
9,769	2.3	66.1	95.0	465.8	660	26.6	5.8	3,310	742	5.0	2.2	480	20	Norway
331	1.5	1.8	...	14.9	430	41.7	15.9	1,780	726	36.3	15.3	30	0	Oman
318	7.1	2.2	10.4	9.0	720	620.0	4.2	3,520	25	27.9	5.9	1,000	10	Pakistan
...	...	...	323.0	...	...	[34]	[34]	—	—	—	—	...	...	Palau
419	2.0	11.8	25.1	77.7	180	—	—	124	45	5.1	1.4	5	0	Panama
766	8.6	66.7	63	22.0	720	3.1	0.6	36	7	3.7	1.1	0	0	Papua New Guinea
418	11.5	54.2	21.4	30.5	310	18.6	3.3	84	15	3.9	1.1	10	0	Paraguay
218	3.2	24.1	7.8	3.6	730	100.0	3.7	1,200	45	12.3	2.4	30	0	Peru
...	13.1	14.9	...	3.3	1,160	106.0	1.3	1,110	14	7.3	1.4	110	0	Philippines
2,901	2.8	79.2	936.8	185.0	370	163.0	4.2	6,690	173	6.1	2.1	40	30	Poland
661	3.1	1.5	115.3	40.4	660	44.9	4.4	2,410	240	5.4	2.1	60	0	Portugal
2,339	16.2	101.8	412.4	1,521	380	[3]	[3]	—	—	—	—	...	...	Puerto Rico
1,079	2.1	7.1	34.1	11.5	...	12.4	19.8	1,060	1,470	22.9	10.0	120	0	Qatar
2,097	7.8	123.1	181.3	137.9	220	[3]	[3]	—	—	—	—	...	...	Réunion
2,206	7.1	5.8	367.8	30.4	...	97.2	4.5	2,190	97	4.7	1.6	200	40	Romania
20,514	21.3	32.6	669.1	25.6	...	960.6	6.6	35,000	239	22.4	5.6	470	3,100	Russia
...	45.1	114.3	...	0.3	4,650	51.0	6.1	87	12	22.7	4.5	30	0	Rwanda
3,808	12.0	434.0	1,790	...	300	[20]	[20]	...	...	...	...	...	...	St. Kitts and Nevis
4,386	17.0	1,193.0	778.0	...	430	[20]	[20]	...	...	...	...	...	...	St. Lucia
3,977	10.3	986.9	...	...	250	[20]	[20]	...	...	...	...	...	...	St. Vincent and the Grenadines
...	...	...	...	...	...	[38]	[38]	—	—	—	—	...	...	Samoa
...	4.1	...	...	...	...	—	—	...	...	...	...	...	...	San Marino
558	4.0	...	...	...	400	—	—	1	3	1.3	1.2	0	0	São Tomé and Príncipe
149	0.5	0.2	...	45.4	280	124.5	5.2	21,200	996	43.2	14.9	7,700	0	Saudi Arabia
123	0.5	8.8	2.1	8.2	730	13.6	1.3	81	8	8.2	1.7	0	0	Senegal
1,268	...	...	...	...	140[39]	74.2	7.0	1,200[6]	114[6]	55.0[2, 39]	4.9[2, 39]	10	0	Serbia and Montenegro
5,361	3.7	43.4	378.0	40.9	120	0.4	4.9	...	...	...	...	...	...	Seychelles
...	...	...	...	...	600	14.0	2.8	20	4	13.5	3.0	10	0	Sierra Leone
783	1.0	2.4	40.1	55.2	230	72.5	17.1	4,400	1,100	20.5	4.8	950	20	Singapore
1,740	2.4	204.6	504.3	142.4	...	22.0	4.1	1,010	187	4.4	1.8	20	10	Slovakia
3,138	3.6	20.7	427.3	25.6	...	6.6	3.3	436	227	3.4	1.4	10	0	Slovenia
...	...	...	...	...	620	—	—	...	...	...	...	0	0	Solomon Islands
144	1.5	8.0	31.2	...	540	[40]	[40]	18[2]	3[2]	...	0.9[2]	20	0	Somalia
7,140.8	121.9	595.6	896.6	262.7	870	55.8	1.2	1,960	45	5.0	1.5	50	30	South Africa
4,449	2.7	23.4	562.8	343.3	580	150.7	3.5	7,560	192	6.1	1.3	750	70	Spain
280	8.2	10.8	54.7	...	860	152.3[41]	8.0[41]	729	38	18.4	4.7	40	0	Sri Lanka
...	10.2	46.3	66.6	4.7	740	104.5	2.7	424	12	40.8	4.0	10	0	Sudan, The
17,819	7.6	1,824.4	...	...	...	1.8	4.1	14	33	5.4	1.8	10	0	Suriname
3,962	18.1	471.7	706.8	54.1	610	—	—	21	20	4.6	1.5	0	0	Swaziland
12,982	4.5	42.5	1,615.1	658.9	330	27.6	3.1	5,330	601	5.5	2.3	230	675	Sweden
7,030	2.7	73.3	1,065.9	1,065.5	640	3.3	0.4	3,400	469	5.1	1.2	1,100	50	Switzerland
42	1.0	—	15.6	2.7	1,970	319.0	18.1	4,450	280	25.1	7.0	210	0	Syria
799	8.2	...	...	124.9	720	290.0	12.8	15,200	690	23.8[6]	5.2	2,600	20	Taiwan
317	2.5	4.6	...	...	...	6.0	0.9	80	13	9.4	1.3	0	0	Tajikistan
1,714	7.7	1.7	96.6	0.9	1,330	27.0	0.8	122	4	10.1	1.4	5	0	Tanzania
351	7.7	25.4	9.9	3.3	530	314.2	4.9	2,040	34	6.1	1.7	330	0	Thailand
11	...	...	...	...	1,970	8.6	1.6	25	5	9.4	1.8	0	0	Togo
2,727	1.0	108.5	541.7	14.8	330	[38]	[38]	—	—	—	—	...	...	Tonga
1,170	9.7	31.0	452.7	80.6	280	2.7	2.1	92	78	5.5	1.4	0	0	Trinidad and Tobago
1,419	1.2	165.1	60.1	10.2	340	35.0	3.5	357	38	5.4	1.8	10	0	Tunisia
547	3.9	120.0	...	28.9	1,570	514.9	7.3	9,950	154	13.9	5.3	3,200	70	Turkey
...	...	...	...	...	...	29.0	6.0	542	122	16.0	3.4	10	0	Turkmenistan
...	...	...	...	—	290	—	—	...	...	...	...	...	...	Tuvalu
316	9.9	54.8	19.3	8.3	1,090	60.0	2.4	140	6	13.9	2.3	30	0	Uganda
1,115	10.0	14.7	224.3	7.6	...	295.5	6.2	5,110	103	8.2	3.0	10	550	Ukraine
2,604.7	3.0	10.1	5.1	23.0	140	50.5	13.2	2,180	935	39.6	4.1	950	0	United Arab Emirates
9,823[42]	2.8[42]	405.2[42]	1,832.7[42]	752.9[42]	350	212.7	3.6	36,500	615	6.9	2.5	2,600	5,200	United Kingdom
5,374	9.0	430.2	1,041.8	591.2	318	1,427.0	4.9	281,000	1,030	15.7	3.0	1,600	33,000	United States
3,002	7.7	162.5	52.3	130.1	170	24.0	7.1	275	83	4.1	1.3	10	0	Uruguay
328	3.2	3.0	33.2	2.3	...	55.0	2.1	933	38	5.3	1.7	0	10	Uzbekistan
...	...	...	...	...	450	—	—	...	...	...	...	...	...	Vanuatu
1,106	22.1	152.2	358.2	239.4	320	82.3	3.2	1,420	61	7.1	1.4	310	0	Venezuela
74	1.5	8.5	...	...	...	484.0	5.9	3,230[6]	44[6]	11.6[6]	2.5[6]	70	0	Vietnam
10,441	22.3	1,943.2	3,183.7	954	240	[3]	[3]	—	—	—	—	...	...	Virgin Islands (U.S.)
2,226	...	...	...	...	...	—	—	...	...	...	...	...	...	West Bank
...	...	...	...	...	...	[3]	[3]	—	—	—	—	...	...	Western Sahara
63[44]	5.3	3.2	1.2	3.6	1,940	66.7	3.3	374	22	18.0	6.1	30	0	Yemen
666	9.8	9.5	153.5	9.6	540	18.1	1.7	31	3	3.5	1.0	0	0	Zambia
5,619	9.0	198.4	435.9	13.4	750	29.0	2.5	263	23	12.1	5.0	10	0	Zimbabwe

Security only. [28]Haitian army was disbanded in 1995, and a National Police Force of 5,300 was formed. [29]As of June 2004 U.S. and allied coalition forces numbered 140,000 and 23,000, respectively. [30]Includes attempted murders. [31]1992. [32]As of September 2004 UN peacekeeping troops numbered 14,700. [33]Military defense is the responsibility of Switzerland. [34]Military defense is the responsibility of the United States. [35]Coverage provided through France's program. [36]Curaçao only. [37]Includes paramilitary forces. [38]Military defense is the responsibility of New Zealand. [39]Data refer to Yugoslavia as constituted prior to 1991. [40]Following the 1991 revolution, no national armed forces have yet been formed. [41]Includes 42,300 recalled reservists. [42]England and Wales. [43]Coverage is provided under other programs. [44]Former Yemen Arab Republic.

Education

This table presents international data on education analyzed to provide maximum comparability among the different educational systems in use among the nations of the world. The principal data are, naturally, numbers of schools, teachers, and students, arranged by four principal levels of education—the first (primary); general second level (secondary); vocational second level; and third level (higher). Whenever possible, data referring to preprimary education programs have been excluded from this compilation. The ratio of students to teachers is calculated for each level. These data are supplemented at each level by a figure for enrollment ratio, an indicator of each country's achieved capability to educate the total number of children potentially educable in the age group usually represented by that level. At the first and second levels this is given as a net enrollment ratio and at the third level as a gross enrollment ratio. Two additional comparative measures are given at the third level: students per 100,000 population and proportion (percentage) of adults age 25 and over who have achieved some level of higher or postsecondary education. Data in this last group are confined as far as possible to those who have completed their educations and are no longer in school. No enrollment ratio is provided for vocational training at the second level because of the great variation worldwide in the academic level at which vocational training takes place, in the need of countries to encourage or direct students into vocational programs (to support national development), and, most particularly, in the age range of students who normally constitute a national vocational system (some will be as young as 14, having just completed a primary cycle; others will be much older).

At each level of education, differences in national statistical practice, in national educational structure, public-private institutional mix, training and deployment of teachers, and timing of cycles of enrollment or completion of particular grades or standards all contribute to the problems of comparability among national educational systems.

Reporting the number of schools in a country is not simply a matter of counting permanent red-brick buildings with classrooms in them. Often the resources of a less developed country are such that temporary or outdoor facilities are all that can be afforded, while in a developed but sparsely settled country students might have to travel 80 km (50 mi) a day to find a classroom with 20 students of the same age, leading to the institution of measures such as traveling teachers, radio or televisual instruction at home under the supervision of parents, or similar systems. According to UNESCO definitions, therefore, a "school" is defined only as "a body of students . . . organized to receive instruction."

Such difficulties also limit the comparability of statistics on numbers of teachers, with the further complications that many at any level must work part-time, or that the institutions in which they work may perform a mixture of functions that do not break down into the tidy categories required by a table of this sort. In certain countries teacher training is confined to higher education, in others as a vocational form of secondary training, and so on. For purposes of this table, teacher training at the secondary level has been treated as vocational education. At the higher level, teacher training is classified as one more specialization in higher education itself.

The number of students may conceal great variation in what each country defines as a particular educational "level." Many countries do, indeed, have a primary system composed of grades 1 through 6 (or 1 through 8) that passes students on to some kind of postprimary education. But the age of intake, the ability of parents to send their children or to permit them to finish that level, or the need to withdraw the children seasonally for agricul-

Education

country	year	first level (primary)					general second level (secondary)					vocational second level[a]	
		schools	teachers[c]	students[d]	student/ teacher ratio	net enroll- ment ratio[b]	schools	teachers[c]	students[d]	student/ teacher ratio	net enroll- ment ratio[b]	schools	teachers[c]
Afghanistan	1995	2,146	21,869	1,312,197	60.0	29	...	19,085	512,815	26.9	14	...	...
Albania	1996	1,782	31,369	558,101	17.8	102	162[1]	4,147	71,391	17.2	...	259[1]	2,174
Algeria	1997	15,426	170,956	4,674,947	27.3	94	3,954	151,948	2,618,242	17.2	56	...	...
American Samoa	1996	32	524[2]	9,971	...	...	9	245[2]	3,624	...	...	1	21[2]
Andorra	1997	12	...	5,424	...	...	6	...	2,655	...	...	...	...
Angola	1992	...	31,062[1]	989,443	...	...	...	5,138[1]	199,099	...	...	...	566[1]
Antigua and Barbuda	1997	58	559	12,229	21.9	...	13	389	4,260	11.0	...	1[3]	16[3]
Argentina	1997	22,437	309,081	5,153,256	16.7	96	7,623[4]	238,791[4]	2,463,608[4]	10.3[4]	42	[4]	[4]
Armenia	1998	1,407	61,965	602,600	9.7	...	...	57,325	365,025	6.4	...	69[5]	...
Aruba	1998	33	397	8,456	21.3	...	15[4]	470[4]	7,157[4]	15.2[4]	[4]	[4]	[4]
Australia	1998	7,709	104,603	1,869,852	17.9	95	2,468	104,477	1,329,000	12.7	89	...	28,900[3]
Austria	1998	3,680	38,491	385,207	10.0	87	1,837[6]	55,337	480,200	8.7	88	981	26,248
Azerbaijan	1998	4,515	36,800	700,900	19.0	...	...	85,300	905,500	10.6	...	78	...
Bahamas, The	1997	113	1,540	34,199	22.2	98	...	1,352	27,970	20.7	86	...	...
Bahrain	1997	124[3, 8]	3,536[3, 8]	72,876	...	98	...	2,305[3, 8]	49,897	...	83	...	820[3, 8]
Bangladesh	1996	75,595	242,252[5]	17,580,000	...	64	12,858	135,217[5]	5,788,000	...	18	156	8,800
Barbados	1996	79	994	18,519	18.6	78	21	1,263	21,455	17.0	74	...	...
Belarus	1998	4,835[9]	115,300[9]	1,580,000[9]	10.9[9]	85	[9]	[9]	[9]	[9]	...	150	...
Belgium	1996	4,401	82,168[10]	742,796	...	98	1,727	115,262	737,823	6.4	88	304[11]	...
Belize	1998	247	2,015	53,118	26.4	99	30	726	11,260	15.5	29	...	...
Benin	1997	3,072	13,957	779,329	55.8	63	145[5]	5,352	146,135	27.3	...	14[5]	283[5]
Bermuda	1997	26	478	5,883	18.3	...	...	355	3,726	10.5	...	...	...
Bhutan	1994	243	1,611	60,089	37.3	...	34	544	7,299	13.4	...	8	95
Bolivia	1995	...	51,763[12]	1,538,454	24.7[12]	91	...	12,434[4, 12]	293,158[4]	17.6[4, 12]	29	...	[4]
Bosnia and Herzegovina	1991	2,205	23,369	539,875	23.1	98	238	9,030	172,063	19.1	...	...	...
Botswana	1997	714	11,454	322,268	28.1	81	274	6,772	116,076	17.1	44	50	2,618
Brazil	1998	187,497	1,460,469	35,845,742	24.5	90	17,602	380,222	6,968,531	18.3	19	...	...
Brunei	1998	184[10]	3,858[10]	58,548[10]	15.2[10]	91	38	2,636	30,956	11.7	68	9	516
Bulgaria	1999	3,011[9]	65,885[9]	887,213[9]	13.5[9]	92	[9]	[9]	[9]	[9]	74	545	20,389
Burkina Faso	1996	3,568	14,037	702,204	50.0	31	252	4,152	137,257	33.0	7	41	731
Burundi	1993	1,418	10,400	651,086	62.6	52	113[12]	2,562	55,713	21.7	5	...	...
Cambodia	1998	5,026	43,282	2,011,772	46.5	100	440[11]	16,820	302,751	18.0	...	65[11]	2,315
Cameroon	1995	6,801	40,970	1,896,722	46.3	67	...	14,917	459,068	30.8	11	...	5,885
Canada	1996	12,685	148,565	2,448,144	16.5	95	3,780	133,275	2,505,389	18.8	91	...	...
Cape Verde	1994	370[12]	2,657	78,173	29.4	100	...	438	11,808	27.0	48	...	94[14]
Central African Republic	1991	930	4,004	308,409	77.0	53	46[4]	845[4]	46,989[4]	55.6[4]	...	[4]	[4]
Chad	1996	2,660	9,395	591,493	63.0	46	153	2,468	90,100	36.5	...	18	216
Chile	1995	8,702	80,155	2,149,501	26.8	89	...	51,042	679,165	13.3	58	...	...
China	1997	628,840	5,794,000	139,954,000	24.2	101	78,642	3,587,000	60,179,000	16.8	...	14,190	598,000
Colombia	1996	48,933	193,911	4,916,934	25.4	85	7,895[4]	165,976[4]	2,323,653	...	46	[4]	[4]
Comoros	1996	327	1,508	78,527	52.1	52	...	591	21,192	35.9	...	...	...
Congo, Dem. Rep. of the	1995	14,885	121,054	5,417,506	44.8	54	4,276[4, 11]	59,325[4, 11]	1,514,323[4]	...	17	[4]	[4]
Congo, Rep. of the	1997	1,612	6,926	489,546	70.7	96	...	5,466	190,409	34.8	...	...	1,746
Costa Rica	1998	3,711	19,235	529,637	27.5	89	353	10,943	202,415	18.5	40	...	...
Côte d'Ivoire	1996	7,401	40,529	1,662,285	41.0	55	147	15,959	489,740	30.7	...	...	1,424[3]
Croatia	1998	2,127	10,365	206,121	19.9	82	1,110	19,776	266,115	13.5	66	442	13,000
Cuba	1997	9,864[16]	78,625	1,028,880	13.0	101	...	71,025	778,028	11.0	59[16]	...	27,267[16]
Cyprus[17]	1997	376	4,159	64,761	15.6	96	125[4]	5,757[4]	61,266[4]	10.6[4]	93	[4]	[4]
Czech Republic	1998	8,067[18]	83,972[18]	1,186,246[18]	14.1[18]	91	367	11,658	83,010	7.1	89	1,776	54,204
Denmark	1996	2,536[3]	33,100	336,690	10.2	99	153[3]	37,000	321,448	8.7	88	237[3]	13,100

tural work all make even even a simple enrollment figure difficult to assess in isolation. All of these difficulties are compounded when a country has instruction in more than one language or when its educational establishment is so small that higher, sometimes even secondary, education cannot take place within the country. Enrollment figures in this table may, therefore, include students enrolled outside the country.

Student-teacher ratio, however, usually provides a good measure of the ratio of trained educators to the enrolled educable. In general, at each level of education both students and teachers have been counted on the basis of full-time enrollment or employment, or full-time equivalent when country statistics permit. At the primary and secondary levels, net enrollment ratio is the ratio of the number of children within the usual age group for a particular level who are actually enrolled to the total number of children in that age group (× 100). This ratio is usually less than (occasionally, equal to) 100 and is the most accurate measure of the completeness of enrollment at that particular level. It is not always, however, the best indication of utilization of teaching staff and facilities. Utilization, provided here for higher education only, is best seen in a gross enrollment ratio, which compares total enrollment (of all ages) to the population within the normal age limits for that level. For a country with substantial adult literacy or general educational programs, the difference may be striking: typically, for a less developed country, even one with a good net enrollment ratio of 90 to 95, the gross enrollment ratio may by 20%, 25%, even 30% higher, indicating the heavy use made by the country of facilities and teachers at that level.

Literacy data provided here have been compiled as far as possible from data for the population age 15 and over for the best comparability internationally. Standards as to what constitutes literacy may also differ markedly; sometimes completion of a certain number of years of school is taken to constitute literacy; elsewhere it may mean only the ability to read or write at a minimal level testable by a census taker; in other countries studies have been undertaken to distinguish among degrees of functional literacy. When a country reports an official 100% (or near) literacy rate, it should usually be viewed with caution, as separate studies of "functional" literacy for such a country may indicate 10%, 20%, or even higher rates of inability to read, or write, effectively. Substantial use has been made of UNESCO literacy estimates, both for some of the least developed countries (where the statistical base is poorest) and for some of the most fully developed, where literacy is no longer perceived as a problem, thus no longer in need of monitoring.

Finally, the data provided for public expenditure on education are complete in that they include all levels of public expenditure (national, state, local) but are incomplete for certain countries in that they do not include data for private expenditure; in some countries this fraction of the educational establishment may be of significant size. Occasionally data for external aid to education may be included in addition to domestic expenditure.

The following notes further define the column headings:

a. Usually includes teacher training at the second level.
b. Latest.
c. Full-time.
d. Full-time; may include students registered in foreign schools.

		third level (higher)							literacy[b]				public expenditure on education (percent of GNP)[b]	country
students[d]	student/ teacher ratio	institutions	teachers[c]	students[d]	student/ teacher ratio	gross enrollment ratio[b]	students per 100,000 population[b]	percent of population age 25 and over with post-secondary education[b]	over age	total (%)	male (%)	female (%)		
...	...	...	...	12,800	...	2.0	165	3.0	15	36.3	51.0	20.8	2.0	Afghanistan
18,504	8.5	10[1]	2,348	34,257	14.6	12.0	1,007	...	10	91.8	95.5	88.0	3.1	Albania
...	...	...	19,910	347,410	17.4	10.9	1,236	...	15	63.3	75.1	51.3	5.1	Algeria
160[2]	7.6[2]	1	...	...	...	...	...	22.6	15	95.9	95.6	96.3	8.2	American Samoa
...	...	—	—	932	—	...	...	...	15	100.0	100.0	100.0	...	Andorra
22,401	...	1	787	6,.331	8.0	0.7	71	...	15	41.7	55.6	28.5	4.9	Angola
46[3]	2.9[3]	1	16	46	2.9	...	...	...	15	90.0	...	...	2.7	Antigua and Barbuda
[4]	[4]	1,801	117,101	936,832	8.0	38.0	3,117	12.0	15	96.0	96.0	96.0	3.5	Argentina
25,200[5]	...	15	4,420	38,500	8.7	12.0	976	...	15	98.8	99.4	98.1	2.0	Armenia
[4]	[4]	2	53	394	7.4	...	...	7.0	15	95.0	...	...	4.9	Aruba
985,000[3]	34.1[3]	92	32,663	671,853	20.6	80.0	5,552	...	15	99.5	...	...	5.5	Australia
307,548	11.7	77	20,356	232,377	11.4	48.0	2,970	6.1	15	100.0	100.0	100.0	5.4	Austria
23,500	...	23	17,900	120,870	6.6	17.0	1,516	...	15	97.3	98.9	95.9	3.0	Azerbaijan
...	...	1[7]	160[7]	3,463[7]	21.6[7]	18.0	...	13.5	15	96.1	95.4	96.8	4.0	Bahamas, The
7,287	...	...	558	7,011	12.6	20.0	1,445	10.3	15	87.6	91.0	82.7	4.4	Bahrain
29,923[5]	16.1[5]	1,268[5]	36,000[5]	1,032,635[5]	28.7[5]	4.0	399	1.3	15	40.8	51.7	29.5	2.2	Bangladesh
...	...	4	...	6,622	...	29.0	2,602	3.3	15	97.4	98.0	96.8	7.2	Barbados
125,600	14.3	59	16,300	224,500	13.8	44.0	3,177	12.5	15	99.4	99.7	99.2	5.9	Belarus
569,041	...	151	38,014	358,214	9.4	56.0	3,494	...	15	100.0	100.0	100.0	3.1	Belgium
...	...	12	228	2,753	12.1	...	...	6.6	14	70.3	...	...	5.0	Belize
4,873[5]	17.2[5]	16[5]	962	14,085	14.6	3.0	253	1.3	15	37.5	47.8	23.6	3.2	Benin
...	...	1	...	543	...	...	...	18.4	15	96.9	96.7	97.0	3.7	Bermuda
1,822[1]	12.2[1]	2[1]	57[1]	2,055	9.1[1]	...	...	...	15	47.3	61.1	33.6	4.1	Bhutan
[4]	[4]	...	4,261[2]	109,503[2]	25.7[2]	21.0	2,154	9.9	15	85.6	92.1	79.4	4.9	Bolivia
...	...	44	2,802	37,541	13.4	...	...	...	10	85.5	96.5	76.6	...	Bosnia and Herzegovina
9,829	3.8	1	1,001	9,660	9.6	6.0	596	1.4	15	77.2	74.4	79.8	8.6	Botswana
...	...	900	173,705[13]	1,948,200[13]	11.2[13]	15.0	1,094	...	15	85.3	85.5	85.4	5.1	Brazil
2,553	4.9	4	370	2,080	5.6	7.0	518	9.4	15	91.6	94.7	88.2	2.5	Brunei
201,736	10.0	86	42,829	258,240	6.0	41.0	3,103	15.0	15	98.5	99.1	98.0	3.2	Bulgaria
9,539	13.0	9	632	9,531	15.1	0.9	83	...	15	23.0	31.2	13.1	3.6	Burkina Faso
...	...	8	556	4,256	7.6	0.8	74	0.6	15	48.1	56.3	40.5	4.0	Burundi
16,350[11]	...	9[11]	784[11]	11,652[11]	14.9[11]	1.0	98	1.0	15	65.3	79.7	53.4	2.9	Cambodia
91,779	15.6	...	1,086[12]	33,177[12]	30.5[12]	3.0	289	...	15	75.4	81.8	69.2	2.9	Cameroon
...	...	265	64,100[5]	980,251[5]	14.4[5]	88.0	5,997	21.4	15	96.6	...	...	6.9	Canada
2,289	...	...	...	...	...	...	...	...	15	73.5	84.3	65.3	4.0	Cape Verde
[4]	[4]	1	136	2,823	20.8	1.0	131	2.0	15	46.5	59.6	34.5	2.3	Central African Republic
2,026	13.5	0	288	3,446	12.0	0.6	54	...	15	53.6	66.9	40.0	1.7	Chad
...	...	...	18,084[11, 15]	367,094	...	31.0	2,546	12.3	15	95.7	95.9	95.5	3.6	Chile
9,773,000	16.3	1,020	405,000	3,174,000	7.8	6.0	473	2.0	15	85.0	92.3	77.4	2.3	China
928,474	...	266	75,568	673,353	8.9	17.0	1,768	10.4	15	91.8	91.8	91.8	4.4	Colombia
...	...	...	...	348	...	0.6	57	...	15	56.2	63.5	49.1	3.9	Comoros
[4]	[4]	...	...	52,501	...	2.0	212	1.3	15	77.3	86.6	67.7	1.0	Congo, Dem. Rep. of the
23,606	13.5	...	1,341[3]	16,602[3]	12.4[3]	7.0	582	3.0	15	80.7	87.5	74.4	6.1	Congo, Rep. of the
...	...	40[13]	...	83,106[13]	...	30.0	2,919	...	15	95.6	95.5	95.7	5.4	Costa Rica
11,037[3]	7.8[3]	...	1,657[3]	43,147[3]	26.0[3]	6.0	396	8.7	15	46.8	54.6	38.5	5.0	Côte d'Ivoire
150,792	11.6	79	6,532	90,021	13.8	28.0	1,905	6.4	15	98.3	99.4	97.3	5.3	Croatia
244,253[16]	9.0[16]	35[1]	22,967[16]	104,595	5.3[16]	12.0	1,013	5.9	15	96.4	96.5	96.4	6.7	Cuba
[4]	[4]	35	812	9,982	12.3	23.0	1,383	17.0	15	96.9	98.7	95.0	4.5	Cyprus[17]
419,843	7.7	272	18,061	203,598	11.3	24.0	1,867	8.5	15	100.0	100.0	100.0	5.1	Czech Republic
123,234	9.4	158[3]	9,600	169,783	17.7	48.0	3,189	19.6	...	100.0	100.0	100.0	8.1	Denmark

Education (continued)

country	year	first level (primary)					general second level (secondary)					vocational second level[a]	
		schools	teachers[c]	students[d]	student/ teacher ratio	net enroll-ment ratio[b]	schools	teachers[c]	students[d]	student/ teacher ratio	net enroll-ment ratio[b]	schools	teachers[c]
Djibouti	1997	81[3]	1,005[3]	33,960	...	32	26[4, 12]	628[3, 4]	11,628[4]	...	12	[4]	[4]
Dominica	1998	63	587	13,636	23.2	...	15	293	5,455	18.6	...	...	...
Dominican Republic	1995	4,001	42,135	1,462,722	34.7	81	...	10,757	240,441	22.4	22	...	1,297
East Timor	...	...	...	...	...	...	...	...	...	...	...	...	...
Ecuador	1997	17,367	74,601	1,888,172	25.3	92	...	62,630[4, 11]	765,073[4]	...	...	...	[4]
Egypt[19]	1997	18,522[16]	310,116	7,499,303	24.2	93	7,307[5, 16]	259,618	4,835,938	18.6	64	1,351[5]	138,277
El Salvador	1996	5,025	34,496	1,130,900	32.8	78	...	9,255	143,588	15.5	22	...	...
Equatorial Guinea	1994	781	1,381	75,751	54.9	...	...	466	14,511	31.1	...	...	122
Eritrea	1996	537	5,828	241,725	41.5	30	86[11]	2,031	78,902	38.8	16	4[11]	174
Estonia	1996	727	...	125,718	...	87	...	9,299	95,342	10.3	83	84	1,793
Ethiopia	1995	9,276	83,113	2,722,192	32.8	32	...	22,779	747,142	32.8	...	...	826
Faroe Islands	1995	62	554[9]	4,898	...	...	6	[9]	3,041	...	...	...	...
Fiji	1997	697[5]	5,011	142,781	28.5	99	147[5]	3,519	70,098	19.9	...	35[5]	625[2]
Finland	1997	4,392	39,966	592,500	14.8	98	454	5,766	131,900	22.9	93	467	15,063
France	1995	41,244	216,962	4,071,599	18.8	100	11,212[4]	473,673[4]	6,003,797[4]	12.7[4]	95	[4]	[4]
French Guiana	1996	78[5]	802	17,006	21.2	...	22[12]	875	13,585	15.5	...	...	210
French Polynesia	1995	278	2,949	48,160	16.3	103	38	1,745	25,541	14.6	61	...	...
Gabon	1996	1,147	4,944	250,606	50.7	...	48	2,683	72,888	27.2	...	11	412
Gambia, The	1995	250[5]	3,158[5]	113,419	33.4[5]	65	32[4, 5]	1,126[4, 5]	31,567	24.1[4, 5]	20	[4]	[4]
Gaza Strip	1997	1,118	15,903	656,353	41.3	...	...	7,634	54,692	7.2	...	...	316
Georgia	1997	3,201	16,542	293,325	17.7	77	3,139	55,817	424,465	7.6	74	...	2,146
Germany	1998	17,829	198,116	3,697,806	18.7	86	19,668	413,993	5,720,092	13.8	88	9,754	110,185
Ghana	1992	11,056	66,068	1,796,490	27.2	...	5,540	43,367	816,578	18.8	...	571[1]	422[1]
Greece	1997	8,651	46,785	652,040	13.9	90	3,044	56,899	682,201	12.0	87	682	13,783
Greenland	1999	88	975	9,341	9.6	...	3	...	1,746	...	...	...	...
Grenada	1997	58	879	23,449	26.7	...	19[3]	381[3]	7,367	19.3	...	...	...
Guadeloupe	1999	348	2,936	38,092[5]	...	...	88[4]	3,392[4]	51,366[4, 5]	13.4[4, 5]	...	[4]	[4]
Guam	1998	24	469	20,248	43.2	...	11	622	17,091	27.5	...	2	370[1]
Guatemala	1995	11,495	43,731	1,470,754	33.6	72	2,308[4]	23,807[4]	372,006[4]	15.6[4]	10	626[12]	[4]
Guernsey	1993	22[2]	236	4,697	19.9	...	8[2]	276	3,642	13.2	...	...	...
Guinea	1998	3,723	13,883	674,732	48.6	42	239	4,958	143,245	28.9	9	55[16]	1,268[16]
Guinea-Bissau	1995	...	...	100,369	...	47	...	...	7,000	...	3	...	...
Guyana	1997	420	3,461	102,000	29.5	87	...	2,150	62,043	29.5	66	...	...
Haiti	1995	10,071	30,205	1,110,398	36.8	26	1,038	...	195,418	...	22	...	...
Honduras	1999	8,768	33,431	1,111,264	33.2	90	661[3, 4]	14,539[4]	189,000[4]	13.0[4]	21	[4]	[4]
Hong Kong	1998	832	20,038	476,682	23.8	90	507	23,077	455,392	19.7	69	9	...
Hungary	1999	3,732	83,404	964,248	11.6	97	1,545	40,130	504,829	12.6	86	1,245	26,344
Iceland	1997	198	3,877	31,100	8.0	98	37	1,454	17,970	12.4	87	...	...
India	1997	598,354	1,789,733	110,393,406	61.7	...	274,944	2,738,205	65,359,339	23.9	...	...	...
Indonesia	1997	173,883	1,327,218	28,236,283	21.3	95	41,847	863,389	12,442,813	14.4	45	3,894	123,505
Iran	1997	63,101	298,755	9,238,393	31.2	90	18,445[1]	280,309	8,776,792	31.3	71	...	20,418[3]
Iraq	1996	8,145	145,455	2,903,923	20.0	76	2,635[3]	49,884	1,075,490	21.6	37	310[3]	9,903
Ireland	1997	3,254	18,968	476,632	25.1	92	440	12,694	375,518	29.6	86	324	8,305
Isle of Man	1999	33	...	6,210	...	...	5	...	4,732	...	...	...	...
Israel	1998	1,651	57,738	532,070	9.2	...	653	62,054	414,405	...	...	338	17,141[11]
Italy	1997	19,890	289,504	2,809,699	9.7	100	16,973	315,920	2,648,535	8.4	67	7,732	305,582
Jamaica	1997	788[2]	9,512	293,863	30.9	95	126[3]	8,377[3]	228,533	...	64[3]	18[3]	950[3]
Japan	1997	24,376	420,901	7,855,387	18.7	103	16,753	546,337	8,852,840	16.2	99	62	4,384
Jersey	1990	32	...	5,794	...	...	14	...	4,405	...	...	1	...
Jordan	1996	2,531	51,721	1,074,877	20.8	89	741[5]	6,309	109,906	17.4	42	54[5]	2,306
Kazakhstan	1997	8,611[16]	262,000[16]	1,342,035	...	...	...	178,900[5]	1,743,623	...	...	239	...
Kenya	1995	15,906	181,975	5,544,998	30.5	91	2,878	41,484	632,388	15.2	11	62	1,147[14]
Kiribati	1997	86	727	17,594	24.2	...	9	215	4,403	20.5	...	...	23
Korea, North	1988	4,810[13]	59,000	1,543,000	26.2	...	4,840[13]	111,000	2,468,000	22.2	...	...	...
Korea, South	1997	5,721	138,670	3,783,986	27.3	93	4,612	202,335	4,517,008	22.3	97	166	13,282
Kuwait	1997	258	9,863	142,265	14.4	62	416	19,402	213,266	11.0	61	38	793
Kyrgyzstan	1996	1,885	24,086	473,077	19.7	95	1,474[5]	38,915	498,849	12.8	...	53[5]	3,371
Laos	1997	7,896	25,831	786,335	30.4	72	750[1]	10,717	180,160	16.8	22	...	1,600[16]
Latvia	1998	638	10,883	146,653	13.5	89	380	24,112	196,148	8.1	79	123	5,470
Lebanon	1997	2,160	...	382,309	...	76	...	...	292,002	...	...	275	7,745
Lesotho	1997	1,249	7,898	374,628	47.4	70	187[3]	2,817	67,454	23.9	18	9[5]	61
Liberia	1987	...	...	...	...	...	...	...	...	...	...	...	...
Libya	1996	2,733[5]	122,020	1,333,679	10.9	96	...	17,668	170,573	9.7	62	480	...
Liechtenstein	1998	14	134	2,021	15.1	...	10[4]	198[4]	4,121[4]	20.8[4]	...	[4]	[4]
Lithuania	1997	2,292	14,093	225,071	16.0	...	...	32,172	325,480	10.1	80	104	5,078
Luxembourg	1997	...	1,844	28,232	15.3	...	...	2,673	9,463	3.5	...	...	2,904[3, 14]
Macau	1998	81	1,744	47,235	27.1	...	47	1,577	28,280	17.9	53	2	47
Macedonia	1998	1,043	13,376	256,275	19.2	94	93[4]	5,226[4]	84,059[4]	16.1[4]	51	[4]	[4]
Madagascar	1996	13,325	44,145	1,638,187	37.1	61	...	16,795	302,036	18.0	...	...	1,150
Malawi	1996	3,706	49,138	2,887,107	58.7	103	...	2,948	139,386	47.2	2	...	475
Malaysia	1997	7,084	150,681	2,870,667	19.1	102	1,460	91,659	1,767,946	19.3	...	101	5,472
Maldives	1998	228	1,992	48,895	24.5	...	...	...	15,933[2]	...	...	...	...
Mali	1998	2,511	10,853	862,875	79.5	31	307[2]	4,549[16]	166,372	...	5	...	21,731
Malta	1998	99	1,457	35,261	24.2	100	75	2,458	27,178	11.1	79	22	626
Marshall Islands	1995	103	669	13,355	20.0	...	12	144	2,400	16.7	...	...	...
Martinique	1997	273	2,603	55,569	21.3	...	76[16]	2,888	36,605	12.7	...	...	896[16]
Mauritania	1997	2,392	6,225	312,671	50.2	57	...	1,865[16]	49,221[16]	26.4[16]	...	...	202
Mauritius	1998	285	5,065	130,505	25.7	98	133	4,820	94,364	19.6	33	13	1,170[13]
Mayotte	1997	88[1]	555[11]	25,805[10]	...	...	8	246[11]	6,190	...	...	2[1]	17[1]
Mexico	1996	94,844	516,051	14,623,400	28.3	101	25,000	467,686	7,589,400	16.2	51	6,571[11]	77,347[11]
Micronesia	1995	174	...	27,281	...	...	24	...	6,898	...	...	...	...
Moldova	1997	1,700[9]	14,097	320,725	22.8	...	[9]	28,615[4]	419,256	...	...	64	[4]
Monaco	1997	8	127	1,917	15.1	...	6	192	2,416	12.6	...	4	89
Mongolia	1997	308	7,587	234,193	30.9	81	337	12,503	184,100	14.7	53	36	668
Morocco	1998	5,730	116,638	3,317,153	28.4	74	1,406	82,589	1,328,789	16.1	20	71[14]	2,951[3, 14]

		third level (higher)							literacy[b]				public expenditure on education (percent of GNP)[b]	country
students[d]	student/ teacher ratio	institutions	teachers[c]	students[d]	student/ teacher ratio	gross enroll-ment ratio[b]	students per 100,000 popula-tion[b]	percent of population age 25 and over with post-secondary education[b]	over age	total (%)	male (%)	female (%)		
[4]	[4]	1[12]	13[12]	130[18]	...	0.2	26	...	15	51.4	65.0	38.4	3.6	Djibouti
...	...	2[11]	34[11]	484[11]	14.2[11]	...	...	1.7	15	90.0	...	...	5.5	Dominica
22,795	17.6	...	9,041[15]	176,995[15]	19.6[15]	23.0	...	...	15	83.8	84.0	83.7	2.3	Dominican Republic
...	...	...	...	...	...	...	...	...	...	...	...	...	...	East Timor
[4]	...	21	12,856[1]	206,541[1]	16.1[1]	20.0	2,012	12.7	15	91.9	93.6	90.2	3.5	Ecuador
1,912,040	13.8	16[15]	38,828[5, 15]	850,051	...	20.0	1,900	4.6	15	55.3	66.6	43.7	4.8	Egypt[19]
...	...	...	5,919	112,266	19.0	18.0	1,933	6.4	15	78.7	81.6	76.1	2.5	El Salvador
2,105	17.3	...	58	578	10.0	...	164	...	15	83.2	92.5	74.5	1.7	Equatorial Guinea
4,268	24.5	1	136	3,081	22.7	1.0	95	...	...	20.0	...	...	1.8	Eritrea
16,870	9.4	37	...	40,621	...	42.0	2,956	13.7	15	99.7	99.9	99.6	7.2	Estonia
9,103	11.0	...	1,937	32,671	16.9	0.6	62	1.0	15	38.7	43.9	33.4	4.0	Ethiopia
2,090[5]	...	1[12]	20[12]	91[12]	4.6[12]	...	...	...	15	99.0	99.0	99.0	...	Faroe Islands
7,283[2]	11.6[2]	...	277[12]	7,908[12]	28.5[12]	12.0	757	4.5	15	92.9	95.0	90.9	5.4	Fiji
251,600	16.7	29	8,134	168,996	20.8	74.0	4,190	15.4	15	100.0	100.0	100.0	7.5	Finland
[4]	[4]	1,062	52,613	2,083,129	39.6	51.0	3,600	11.4	...	98.8	98.9	98.7	6.0	France
2,404	11.4	1	...	324[11]	...	...	...	6.4	15	83.0	83.6	82.3	...	French Guiana
...	...	...	...	301[2]	...	1.0	...	...	15	95.0	94.9	95.0	9.8	French Polynesia
7,664	18.6	2[2, 15]	299[2, 15]	3,000[2, 15]	10.0[2, 15]	...	650	...	15	70.8	79.8	62.2	2.9	Gabon
[4]	[4]	...	155[5]	1,591[5]	10.3[5]	2.0	148	...	15	36.5	43.8	29.6	4.9	Gambia, The
1,775	5.7	5	2,473	49,599	20.0	...	...	...	...	...	...	...	...	Gaza Strip
19,593	9.1	23	25,549	163,345	6.4	30.0	3,002	...	15	99.5	99.7	99.4	5.2	Georgia
2,838,416	25.8	296	161,383	1,813,348	11.2	47.0	2,628	...	15	100.0	100.0	100.0	4.8	Germany
13,232[1]	31.4[1]	16[1]	700[1]	9,274[1]	13.2[1]	0.6	127	...	15	70.2	79.5	61.2	4.2	Ghana
135,365	9.8	18	16,057	363,180	22.6	47.0	3,149	8.7	15	97.2	98.6	96.0	3.1	Greece
...	...	...	...	...	...	...	...	...	15	100.0	100.0	100.0	...	Greenland
...	...	1[3]	66[3]	651[3]	9.9[3]	...	...	1.5	15	85.0	...	...	4.7	Grenada
[4]	[4]	1[5]	121[5]	4,673[5]	38.6[5]	...	...	5.2	15	90.1	89.7	90.5	...	Guadeloupe
4,369	...	1	192[1]	3,533	...	...	...	39.9	15	99.0	99.0	99.0	8.5	Guam
[4]	[4]	...	...	80,228	...	8.0	755	2.2	15	68.7	76.2	61.1	1.7	Guatemala
...	...	—	—	—	—	...	...	...	15	100.0	100.0	100.0	...	Guernsey
8,151[16]	6.8[16]	2[16]	947[16]	8,151[16]	8.6[16]	1.0	108	...	15	41.1	55.1	27.0	1.9	Guinea
...	...	...	...	...	...	...	...	0.1	15	36.8	53.0	21.4	...	Guinea-Bissau
...	...	...	612	8,965	12.5	11.0	954	1.8	15	98.5	99.0	98.1	5.0	Guyana
...	...	2[20]	817[20]	12,204[20]	14.9[20]	1.0	...	0.7	15	48.6	51.0	46.5	1.5	Haiti
[4]	[4]	8	3,676[3]	56,077	...	10.0	985	3.3	15	72.2	72.5	72.0	3.6	Honduras
42,003	...	18	...	91,748	...	22.0	1,635	14.5	15	93.4	96.5	90.0	2.9	Hong Kong
362,633	13.8	89	21,351	163,164	7.6	24.0	1,926	10.1	15	99.4	99.5	99.3	4.6	Hungary
...	...	10	508	7,972	15.7	37.0	2,787	...	15	100.0	100.0	100.0	5.4	Iceland
...	...	8,407[5]	286,000[5]	5,007,000[5]	17.5[5]	7.0	642	7.3	15	55.8	68.6	42.1	3.3	India
1,767,101	11.0	1,007	180,471	2,703,886	15.0	11.0	1,167	2.3	15	87.0	91.9	82.1	1.4	Indonesia
368,218[3]	18.0[3]	...	40,477	579,070	14.3	18.0	1,599	...	15	76.9	83.7	70.0	4.0	Iran
122,939	12.4	12	11,685	232,896	19.9	12.0	...	4.1	15	58.0	70.7	45.0	4.0	Iraq
96,821	11.7	30	4,872	107,601	22.1	41.0	3,618	13.1	15	100.0	100.0	100.0	6.0	Ireland
...	...	...	...	1,128	...	...	...	...	...	...	...	...	...	Isle of Man
106,393	...	7	9,546	181,038	19.0	41.0	3,598	11.2	15	96.1	97.9	94.3	7.6	Israel
2,597,449	8.5	56[15]	48,891[15]	1,595,642[15]	32.6	47.0	3,103	3.8	15	98.5	98.9	98.1	4.9	Italy
15,898[3]	16.7[3]	15[3]	...	24,200[3]	...	8.0	803	2.7	15	86.7	82.5	90.7	7.5	Jamaica
56,294	12.8	1,243	166,051	3,136,834	18.9	41.0	3,139	20.7	15	100.0	100.0	100.0	3.6	Japan
...	...	...	...	...	...	...	...	...	15	100.0	100.0	100.0	...	Jersey
35,579	15.4	55	4,821	99,020	20.5	27.0	2,542	...	15	89.8	94.9	84.4	7.9	Jordan
177,679	...	69[3]	27,189[3]	260,043[16]	...	33.0	2,806	12.4	15	97.5	99.1	96.1	4.4	Kazakhstan
11,700[14]	10.2[4]	14[11, 15]	4,392[1, 15]	88,180[11]	...	2.0	143	...	15	82.5	89.0	76.0	6.5	Kenya
333	14.5	—	—	—	—	...	...	...	15	90.0	...	...	6.3	Kiribati
220,000	...	519[13]	27,000	390,000	14.4	...	...	...	15	95.0	...	...	...	Korea, North
745,689	56.1	742	53,300	1,469,819	27.6	68.0	5,609	21.1	15	97.8	99.2	96.4	3.7	Korea, South
3,779	4.8	1	1,691	29,509	17.5	19.0	2,247	16.4	15	82.3	84.3	79.9	5.0	Kuwait
32,005	9.5	23	3,691	49,744	13.5	12.0	1,115	...	15	97.0	98.6	95.5	5.3	Kyrgyzstan
9,400[16]	5.9[16]	9[1]	1,369	12,732	9.3	3.0	253	...	15	61.8	73.6	50.5	2.1	Laos
45,672	8.3	28	4,486	56,187	12.5	33.0	2,244	13.4	15	99.7	99.8	99.6	6.3	Latvia
55,848	7.2	20	10,444	81,588	7.8	27.0	2,712	...	15	86.1	92.3	80.4	2.5	Lebanon
678	11.1	1	574	4,614	8.0	2.0	222	...	15	83.9	73.6	93.6	8.4	Lesotho
...	...	...	472	5,095	10.8	2.0	...	...	15	53.4	69.9	36.8	5.7	Liberia
155,483	...	13	...	126,348	...	17.0	1,358	2.7	15	79.8	90.9	67.6	7.1	Libya
[4]	[4]	...	...	...	...	...	...	...	15	100.0	100.0	100.0	...	Liechtenstein
56,400	11.1	15	13,136	83,645	6.4	31.0	2,244	12.6	15	99.5	99.7	99.4	5.5	Lithuania
19,346	...	1	200[3]	957	...	10.0	...	10.8	15	100.0	100.0	100.0	4.0	Luxembourg
699	14.9	7	818	7,682	9.4	28.0	1,700	5.9	15	93.2	96.4	90.1	...	Macau
[4]	[4]	30	1,385	36,167	26.1	20.0	1,415	6.7	10	89.1	94.2	83.8	5.1	Macedonia
8,479	7.3	...	921	18,458	20.0	3.0	174	...	15	80.2	87.7	72.9	1.9	Madagascar
2,228	4.7	6	531[3]	5,561	...	0.6	58	0.4	15	60.3	74.5	46.7	5.4	Malawi
36,573	6.9	48	14,960	210,724	14.1	12.0	971	6.9	15	87.5	91.5	83.6	4.9	Malaysia
452[2]	...	—	—	—	—	...	...	1.7	15	96.3	96.3	96.4	6.4	Maldives
7,200	3.0	7	796	13,847	17.4	1.0	73	...	15	40.3	47.9	33.2	2.2	Mali
4,159	6.6	1	770	7,146	9.3	29.0	1,595	...	15	92.1	91.4	92.8	5.1	Malta
...	...	...	...	...	...	...	...	...	15	91.2	92.4	90.0	...	Marshall Islands
11,101[16]	12.4[16]	1	99[5]	3,079	45.3[5]	...	...	5.6	15	97.4	96.0	97.1	...	Martinique
2,544	12.6	4	270	8,496	31.5	4.0	374	1.3	15	39.9	50.6	29.5	5.1	Mauritania
5,496	...	3	461	6,429	13.9	6.3	594	1.9	15	84.3	87.7	81.0	4.6	Mauritius
839[11]	...	—	—	—	—	...	...	...	15	91.9	...	...	...	Mayotte
1,076,700[11]	13.9[11]	10,341	163,843	1,532,800	9.4	16.0	1,586	9.2	15	91.0	93.1	89.1	4.9	Mexico
...	...	...	...	1,461[5]	...	...	...	...	15	76.7	67.0	87.2	...	Micronesia
26,245	...	20	8,814	93,759	10.6	27.0	2,110	11.3	15	98.9	99.6	98.3	10.6	Moldova
532	6.0	1	...	112	...	...	...	...	...	...	...	...	...	Monaco
11,308	16.9	86	4,471	44,088	9.8	17.0	1,753	23.4	15	99.3	99.2	99.3	5.7	Mongolia
22,415[14]	...	68	9,667	266,507	27.5	11.0	1,132	...	15	48.9	61.9	36.0	5.3	Morocco

Education (continued)

country	year	first level (primary)					general second level (secondary)					vocational second level[a]	
		schools	teachers[c]	students[d]	student/ teacher ratio	net enroll- ment ratio[b]	schools	teachers[c]	students[d]	student/ teacher ratio	net enroll- ment ratio[b]	schools	teachers[c]
Mozambique	1997	6,025	32,670	1,899,531	57.8	40	75	1,555	51,554	33.1	8	25	565
Myanmar (Burma)	1998	35,877	167,134	5,145,400	30.8	…	2,091	56,955	1,545,600	27.1	…	103[3]	2,462[3]
Namibia	1995	933[5]	10,912[2]	368,222	32.0[2]	91	114[5]	3,943[2]	101,838[5]	…	36	17[5]	56[2]
Nauru	1995	10	138	2,207	16.0	…	4	46	…	…	…	1	…
Nepal	1996	22,218	89,378	3,447,607	38.6	…	7,582[4]	36,127[4]	1,121,335[4]	31.0[4]	…	[4]	[4]
Netherlands, The	1999	7,238	99,031[12]	1,534,000	…	100	666	89,370[12]	856,000	…	84	143	18,613[12]
Netherlands Antilles	1998	85[16]	1,111	24,061	21.7	…	21	461[16]	8,372	…	…	33	623[16]
New Caledonia	1996	279	1,622	22,942	14.1	98	46	2,021[4]	20,360	…	72	14	[4]
New Zealand	1998	2,282	23,119	445,868	19.3	100	339	15,228	224,290	14.7	90	29	5,309
Nicaragua	1997	7,224	21,020[16]	783,002	…	77	451[5]	5,990[3]	220,670[3]	36.8[3]	18	…	…
Niger	1998	3,175	11,545	482,065	41.8	24	…	3,579	97,675	27.3	6	…	215
Nigeria	1995	38,649	435,210	16,191,000	37.2	…	6,074	152,596	4,451,000	29.2	…	…	…
Northern Mariana Islands	1993	18	183	4,666	25.5	…	9[4]	152[4]	3,044[4]	20.0[4]	…	[4]	[4]
Norway	1997	3,287	39,385	487,398	12.4	100	714[4]	21,105[4]	208,280[4]	9.9[4]	97	[4]	[4]
Oman	1997	429	11,925[16]	311,955	…	69	128[1]	11,896	205,046	17.2	49	25[1]	342[5]
Pakistan	1998	158,511[10]	346,000[10]	16,642,000[10]	48.0[10]	…	25,913	259,200	5,545,000	21.4	…	673	7,546
Palau	1997	…	172	1,450	8.4	…	…	60	490	8.2	…	…	…
Panama	1997	2,866	15,058	377,898	25.1	91	417	12,450	223,155	17.9	51	…	…
Papua New Guinea	1995	2,790	13,652	525,995	38.5	…	135[1]	2,415[2]	68,818	24.1[2]	…	117[1]	878[2]
Paraguay	1990	5,928	41,713	895,777	21.5	91	804[4]	17,668	293,651[4]	…	38	[4]	…
Peru	1997	33,017	153,951	4,163,180	27.0	91	8,085[3]	106,614	1,969,501	18.5	55	2,425[3]	12,293[3]
Philippines	1997	37,645	341,183	11,902,501	34.9	101	5,880[5]	154,705[4]	4,888,246[4]	31.6[4]	59	1,261[1]	[4]
Poland	1998	19,299	322,600	4,896,400	15.2	95	1,847	39,200	757,500	19.3	85	9,320	89,900
Portugal	1996	12,884	145,462[9]	1,339,744	…	104	664	[9]	477,221	…	78	262	6,895
Puerto Rico	1986	1,542	18,359	427,582	23.3	…	395	13,612	334,661	24.6	…	52	…
Qatar	1996[8]	174	5,864	53,631	9.1	80	123[3]	3,738[3]	36,964[3]	9.9[3]	69	3	120
Réunion	1998	351	…	76,364	…	…	111[4]	6,343	96,811	15.3	…	[4]	1,120[16]
Romania	1997	13,978[18]	175,426[18]	2,546,231[18]	14.5[18]	95	1,295[21]	64,485[21]	792,788[21]	12.3[21]	73	1,692	10,942
Russia	1999	69,613[9]	1,811,000[9]	21,966,900[9]	12.1[9]	93	[9]	[9]	[9]	[9]	…	3,590	…
Rwanda	1992	1,710	18,937	1,104,902	58.3	75	…	3,413[4]	94,586[4]	27.7[4]	8	…	[4]
St. Kitts and Nevis	1998	28	320	5,928	18.5	…	9	341	4,548	13.3	…	…	…
St. Lucia	1998	84	1,160	30,536	26.3	…	17	620	11,405	18.4	…	1[11]	34[11]
St. Vincent and the Grenadines	1998	60	1,007	21,347	21.2	…	21	379	7,775	20.5	…	3	32[16]
Samoa	1995	155	1,475	35,811	24.3	96	…	…	…	…	45	…	…
San Marino	1998	14	225	1,211	5.4	…	3	148	700	4.7	…	…	44[5]
São Tomé and Príncipe	1997	69	638	21,760	34.1	…	10	415	12,280	29.6	…	…	…
Saudi Arabia	1997	11,509	175,458	2,256,185	12.9	61	7,667	115,907	1,505,072	13.0	42	…	6,133
Senegal	1997	3,530	16,567	954,758	57.6	60	359[11]	6,210	206,934	33.3	16	19[11]	182[11]
Serbia and Montenegro	1999	4,431	52,294	864,199	16.5	69	561	27,766	367,587	13.2	62	…	…
Seychelles	1999	25	656	9,868	15.0	…	13	545	7,774	14.3	…	12	218
Sierra Leone	1993	1,643	10,595	267,425	25.2	…	167	4,313	70,900	16.4	…	44	709
Singapore	1997	196	11,189	280,108	25.0	93	165	10,673	209,835	19.7	44	10	1,315
Slovakia	1998	2,482	39,535	645,941	16.3	…	198	5,849	80,116	13.7	…	365	10,104
Slovenia	1997	824	7,283	98,866	13.5	95	153	8,665	131,573	15.2	…	…	5,908
Solomon Islands	1994	520	2,514	60,493	24.1	…	23	618	7,981	12.9	…	1	…
Somalia	1990	…	…	377,000	…	10	…	…	44,000	…	3	…	…
South Africa	1996	20,863[9]	224,896	8,159,430	36.3	103	[9]	128,611[5]	3,749,449[5]	29.2[5]	58	187[5]	10,807[5]
Spain	1997	16,540[5]	163,105	2,682,894	16.4	105	25,775[4, 11]	245,118[4]	2,946,191	…	74	[4]	[4]
Sri Lanka	1998	10,947[9]	194,823[9]	4,278,124[9]	22.0[9]	…	[9]	[9]	[9]	[9]	…	36	623
Sudan, The	1997	11,158	102,987	3,000,048	24.1	54	2,578[2]	15,504	405,583	26.2	…	…	761
Suriname	1996	304	3,611	75,585	20.9	…	104	2,286	31,918	13.9	…	1	…
Swaziland	1997	529	6,094	205,829	33.8	91	165[5]	2,954[16]	57,330[16]	19.4[16]	38	5[5]	228[5]
Sweden	1997	4,936	81,800	958,972	11.7	102	641	28,305	310,000	10.9	99	…	…
Switzerland	1998	…	…	462,262	…	100	…	…	421,025	…	79	…	…
Syria	1997	10,783	114,689	2,690,205	23.5	91	2,526[3]	52,182	865,042	16.6	38	292[3]	12,479
Taiwan	1998	2,540	92,104	1,905,690	20.7	…	1,151[4]	99,411[4]	1,874,747[4]	18.9[4]	…	[4]	[4]
Tajikistan	1997	3,432	27,172	638,674	23.5	…	…	112,532	688,150	6.1	…	75[3]	…
Tanzania	1996[22]	10,892[5]	108,874	3,942,888	36.2	48	491[5]	11,689	199,093	17.0	…	40[5]	1,062
Thailand	1997	34,412[11]	445,542[11]	5,909,618	…	…	2,318[11]	107,025[11]	3,267,449	…	…	679[11]	40,116[11]
Togo	1997	3,283[16]	18,535	859,574	46.4	81	314[11]	4,736[16]	169,178	…	18	…	653
Tonga	1994	115	701	16,540	23.6	…	47	809	15,702	19.4	…	9	67[1]
Trinidad and Tobago	1997	478	7,311	181,030	24.8	88	…	5,070[4]	104,349[4]	20.6[4]	65	…	[4]
Tunisia	1997	4,428	60,101	1,450,916	24.1	98	712[3]	45,411	882,730	19.4	…	…	237[16]
Turkey	1997	47,313	217,131	6,389,060	29.4	99	11,144	143,322	3,427,715	23.9	51	4,046	75,507
Turkmenistan	1995	1,900[9]	72,900[9]	940,600[9]	12.9[9]	…	[9]	[9]	[9]	[9]	…	78	…
Tuvalu	1994	12	72[1]	1,906	…	…	2	31	345	…	…	1	10[1]
Uganda	1995[8]	8,531	76,134	2,636,409	34.6	…	…	14,447	255,158	17.7	…	…	1,788
Ukraine	1996	21,900[9]	576,000[3, 9]	7,007,000[9]	12.4[3, 9]	…	[9]	[9]	[9]	[9]	…	782	…
United Arab Emirates	1997	…	16,148	259,509	16.1	78	…	12,388[3]	178,839	12.0	71	9	249[14]
United Kingdom	1997	23,312	283,492	5,328,219	18.5	99	…	312,038	4,435,000	13.2	91	…	152,098
United States	1998	88,223[8, 9]	1,874,000	34,681,000	18.5	95	[9]	1,217,000	17,494,000	14.4	90	…	…
Uruguay	1997	2,410	16,721	348,195	20.8	93	413	19,104	192,399	10.1	…	101	…
Uzbekistan	1996	9,300[9]	413,000[9]	5,090,000[9]	12.3[9]	…	[9]	[9]	[9]	[9]	…	248	22,164[11]
Vanuatu	1992	272	852	26,267	30.8	…	…	220	4,269	19.4	17	…	…
Venezuela	1997	15,894[11]	182,192	4,262,221	23.4	84	1,621[2, 4]	43,369[4]	377,984[4]	8.7[4]	22	[4]	[4]
Vietnam	1998	13,092[5]	324,431	10,431,337	32.2	…	6,298[5]	209,500	6,642,350	31.7	…	451[5]	9,336
Virgin Islands (U.S.)	1993[8]	62	790	14,544	18.4	…	…	541[12]	12,502	17.2[12]	…	—	—
West Bank	1997	1,193[9]	15,912[9]	431,565[9]	27.1[9]	…	[9]	[9]	[9]	[9]	…	…	…
Western Sahara	1995[8]	40	925	32,257	34.9	…	13	1,267	10,541	8.3	…	…	…
Yemen	1997[14]	11,013[5]	90,478	2,699,788	29.8	…	1,224[3]	13,787	286,405	20.8	…	125[3]	369[3]
Zambia	1996	3,907	38,528[3]	1,670,000	…	75	…	…	255,000	…	16	…	…
Zimbabwe	1996	4,659	63,718	2,493,791	39.1	…	1,536	28,354	751,349	26.5	…	25[2]	1,479[2]

		third level (higher)							literacy[b]					
students[d]	student/teacher ratio	institutions	teachers[c]	students[d]	student/teacher ratio	gross enrollment ratio[b]	students per 100,000 population[b]	percent of population age 25 and over with postsecondary education[b]	over age	total (%)	male (%)	female (%)	public expenditure on education (percent of GNP)[b]	country
12,001	21.2	3	954	7,158	7.5	0.5	40	0.1	15	43.8	59.9	28.4	4.1	Mozambique
25,374[3]	10.3[3]	51	17,089	385,300	22.5	5.0	564	2.0	15	84.7	89.0	80.6	1.2	Myanmar (Burma)
1,503[5]	...	7[5]	331[12]	11,344	...	8.0	738	4.0	15	82.1	82.9	81.2	9.1	Namibia
...	...	...	...	...	...	...	...	...	15	99.0	...	...	...	Nauru
[4]	[4]	3[2]	4,925[12]	105,694	...	5.0	501	0.6	15	41.4	59.1	21.8	3.2	Nepal
517,000	...	13	...	147,000	...	47.0	3,176	...	15	100.0	100.0	100.0	5.1	Netherlands, The
8,524	...	1	97	686	7.1	...	...	8.8	15	96.6	96.6	96.6	...	Netherlands Antilles
5,916	...	4	79	1,749	22.1	5.0	...	7.5	15	57.9	57.4	58.3	13.5	New Caledonia
105,186	19.8	7	4,973	107,837	21.7	63.0	4,508	39.1	15	100.0	100.0	100.0	7.3	New Zealand
...	...	10[5]	3,840	48,758	12.7	12.0	1,231	...	15	64.3	64.2	64.4	3.9	Nicaragua
2,145	10.0	2	355	5,569	15.7	0.7	55	...	15	15.7	23.5	8.3	2.3	Niger
...	...	31	12,103	228,000	18.8	4.0	367	...	15	64.1	72.3	56.2	0.7	Nigeria
[4]	[4]	...	...	...	...	...	...	...	15	96.3	96.9	95.6	...	Northern Mariana Islands
[4]	[4]	89	11,515	181,741	15.8	54.5	4,164	18.7	15	100.0	100.0	100.0	7.4	Norway
2,350[5]	6.9[5]	5[1]	1,162	13,251	11.4	8.0	532	...	15	71.3	80.4	61.7	4.5	Oman
95,000	12.6	984	34,078	1,052,782	30.9	3.0	291	2.5	15	43.3	57.6	27.8	2.7	Pakistan
...	...	...	...	130	...	...	...	...	15	97.6	98.3	96.6	...	Palau
...	...	14	6,409	95,341	14.9	30.0	3,024	13.2	15	91.9	92.6	91.3	5.1	Panama
9,941	12.9[2]	2[1]	...	13,663	...	3.0	318	...	15	76.0	81.7	67.7	4.7	Papua New Guinea
[4]	...	2	742[11]	42,302	...	10.0	1,049	6.6	15	93.3	94.4	92.2	4.0	Paraguay
270,576[3]	22.0[3]	886	45,443	657,586	14.2	26.0	3,268	20.6	15	89.9	94.7	85.4	2.9	Peru
[4]	[4]	975[5]	56,880[12]	2,022,106[16]	...	29.0	2,981	22.0	15	95.4	95.5	95.2	3.4	Philippines
1,599,900	17.8	246	73,300	1,091,500	14.9	25.0	1,884	7.9	15	99.8	99.8	99.8	7.5	Poland
25,234	3.7	278	16,087	319,525	19.9	39.0	3,060	7.7	15	92.2	94.8	90.0	5.8	Portugal
149,191	...	45	9,045	171,625[16]	...	...	...	28.7	15	93.8	93.7	94.0	8.2	Puerto Rico
670	5.6	1	643	8,475	13.2	27.0	1,518	13.3	15	81.3	80.5	83.2	3.4	Qatar
13,547[16]	12.1[16]	1	286	8,663	30.3	...	...	...	15	87.1	84.8	89.2	...	Réunion
351,900	32.2	102	23,477	354,488	15.1	23.0	1,817	5.6	15	98.2	99.1	97.3	3.6	Romania
1,676,000	...	913	282,400	3,597,900	12.7	43.0	2,998	14.1	15	99.4	99.8	99.2	3.5	Russia
[4]	[4]	...	646[1]	3,389[1]	5.2[1]	0.4	...	...	15	67.0	73.7	60.6	3.8	Rwanda
...	...	1[11]	51[11]	394[11]	7.7[11]	...	...	2.3	15	90.9	90.0	90.0	3.8	St. Kitts and Nevis
808[11]	23.7[11]	1	157[16]	2,760[16]	17.6[16]	...	...	3.4	15	82.0	...	...	9.8	St. Lucia
415	...	...	...	...	...	...	...	1.4	15	96.0	...	...	6.3	St. Vincent and the Grenadines
...	...	...	...	...	...	...	...	5.6	15	100.0	100.0	100.0	4.2	Samoa
455[5]	10.3[5]	...	...	...	...	...	...	...	15	99.1	99.4	98.8	...	San Marino
...	...	...	...	...	...	...	...	0.3	15	54.2	70.2	39.1	3.8	São Tomé and Príncipe
51,916	8.5	68[15]	8,998[15]	165,262[15]	18.4[15]	16.0	1,455	...	15	77.0	84.1	67.2	7.5	Saudi Arabia
7,301[11]	40.1[11]	2	965[15]	24,081[15]	25.0[15]	3.0	297	...	15	37.3	47.2	27.6	3.7	Senegal
...	...	83	10,998	147,981	13.5	22.0	1,674	...	15	93.3	97.6	89.2	...	Serbia and Montenegro
2,002	9.2	...	...	...	...	...	...	4.6	15	84.2	82.9	85.7	7.9	Seychelles
7,756	10.9	1	257[12]	2,571[12]	10.0[12]	2.0	119	1.5	15	36.3	50.7	22.6	0.9	Sierra Leone
9,906	7.5	7	7,764	97,392	12.5	39.0	2,722	7.6	15	92.4	96.4	88.5	3.0	Singapore
116,681	11.5	18	8,544	83,942	9.8	22.0	1,903	9.5	15	100.0	100.0	100.0	5.0	Slovakia
80,885	13.7	37	3,907	51,009	13.1	38.0	2,775	10.4	15	100.0	100.0	100.0	5.7	Slovenia
...	...	...	...	...	...	...	...	...	15	54.1	62.4	44.9	3.8	Solomon Islands
10,400	...	1	549[12]	4,640[12]	...	0.5	...	...	15	24.0	36.0	14.0	0.4	Somalia
140,531[5]	13.0[5]	...	27,099[5]	617,897[5]	22.8[5]	19.0	1,664	1.5	15	85.1	85.8	84.5	8.0	South Africa
1,029,606	...	...	88,922	1,741,528	19.6	51.0	4,017	8.4	15	97.7	98.6	96.8	5.0	Spain
11,652	18.7	12	3,050	38,192	12.5	5.0	474	1.1	15	91.6	94.5	88.9	3.4	Sri Lanka
26,421	34.7	6	1,417	52,260	36.9	3.0	272	0.8	15	57.1	68.3	46.0	1.4	Sudan, The
1,462	...	1	155	1,335	8.6	...	1,124	...	15	94.2	95.9	92.6	3.5	Suriname
2,958[5]	13.0[5]	1	467	5,658	12.1	6.0	642	3.3	15	79.8	80.9	78.7	5.7	Swaziland
...	...	64	33,498[13]	275,217[13]	8.2[13]	50.0	2,972	21.0	15	100.0	100.0	100.0	8.3	Sweden
198,452	...	...	7,709[3]	151,021	...	33.0	2,066	11.5	15	100.0	100.0	100.0	5.4	Switzerland
92,622	7.4	...	4,733[3, 15]	215,734[3]	...	16.0	1,559	...	15	74.4	88.3	60.4	3.1	Syria
[4]	[4]	139	38,806	856,186	22.1	...	...	...	15	94.0	97.6	90.2	5.2	Taiwan
29,482[3]	...	10[3]	5,200[3]	76,613	...	20.0	1,864	11.7	15	99.2	99.6	98.9	2.2	Tajikistan
12,571	11.8	...	1,650	12,776	7.7	0.6	43	2.0	15	75.2	84.1	66.6	3.4	Tanzania
658,474	...	102	25,171[16]	481,936[16]	19.1[16]	22.0	2,096	5.1	15	95.6	97.2	94.0	4.6	Thailand
9,076	13.8	1	443	11,639	26.3	4.0	317	1.3	15	57.1	72.2	42.6	4.5	Togo
824	...	1	53	226[2]	...	...	...	2.8	15	92.8	92.9	92.8	4.7	Tonga
[4]	[4]	3	...	6,007	...	7.7	771	3.4	15	98.2	99.0	97.5	4.4	Trinidad and Tobago
3,839[16]	16.2[16]	...	6,641	121,787	18.3	14.0	1,330	2.8	15	70.8	81.4	60.1	7.7	Tunisia
1,333,177	17.6	863	53,805	1,222,362	22.7	21.0	1,960	10.8	15	85.2	93.6	76.7	2.2	Turkey
26,000	...	15	...	29,435[16]	...	22.0	2,072	...	15	97.7	98.8	96.6	3.9	Turkmenistan
58[12]	...	—	—	—	—	...	...	7.0	15	95.0	...	...	...	Tuvalu
36,063	20.2	...	2,006	29,343	14.6	2.0	154	0.5	15	67.3	77.7	57.1	2.6	Uganda
618,000	...	255[15]	...	922,800[15]	...	41.0	2,977	...	15	98.4	99.5	97.4	7.3	Ukraine
1,925[14]	7.7[14]	4	510[11]	17,950	...	12.0	801	...	15	76.5	75.5	79.5	1.8	United Arab Emirates
2,435,321	16.0	...	89,241	1,820,849	20.4	52.0	3,135	...	15	100.0	100.0	100.0	5.3	United Kingdom
...	...	5,758[11]	940,000	14,350,000	15.3	81.0	5,339	46.5	15	95.5	95.7	95.3	5.4	United States
58,246	...	2	7,165	62,026	8.7	30.0	2,487	10.1	15	97.8	97.4	98.2	3.3	Uruguay
240,100[13]	...	55[13]	...	272,300[13]	...	32.0	2,938	...	15	97.2	98.5	96.0	7.7	Uzbekistan
444	...	1	...	124[12]	...	...	...	...	15	52.9	57.3	47.8	4.8	Vanuatu
[4]	[4]	99[12]	36,232	717,192	19.8	28.0	2,820	11.8	15	93.0	93.3	92.7	5.2	Venezuela
179,907	19.3	104[5]	23,522	509,300	21.7	7.0	404	2.6	15	93.3	95.7	91.0	3.0	Vietnam
—	—	1	266	2,924	11.0	...	...	24.4	...	...	...	...	7.5	Virgin Islands (U.S.)
...	...	22	1,598	30,622	19.2	...	...	...	...	...	...	...	...	West Bank
1,222	...	—	...	...	...	...	...	...	...	...	...	...	...	Western Sahara
67,883	...	2	1,991[3]	65,675	...	4.0	419	...	15	46.4	67.4	25.0	7.0	Yemen
7,982[12]	...	2	640	4,470	7.0	2.0	241	1.5	15	78.0	85.2	71.2	2.2	Zambia
27,431[2]	18.5[2]	28[2]	3,581[3]	43,200[3]	12.1[3]	7.0[3]	638	4.9	15	92.7	95.5	89.9	7.1	Zimbabwe

[1]1990. [2]1992. [3]1995. [4]General second level includes vocational second level. [5]1994. [6]Includes upper primary. [7]College of the Bahamas only. [8]Public schools only. [9]First level includes general second level. [10]Includes preschool. [11]1993. [12]1991. [13]1997. [14]Excludes teacher training. [15]Universities only. [16]1996. [17]Republic of Cyprus only. [18]Includes lower secondary. [19]Data exclude 1,770 primary and 1,449 secondary schools in the Al-Azhar education system. [20]Port-au-Prince universities only. [21]Upper second level only. [22]Mainland Tanzania only.

BIBLIOGRAPHY AND SOURCES

The following list indicates the principal documentary sources used in the compilation of *Britannica World Data.* It is by no means a complete list, either for international or for national sources, but is indicative more of the range of materials to which reference has been made in preparing this compilation.

While *Britannica World Data* has long been based primarily on print sources, many rare in North American library collections, the burgeoning resources of the Internet can be accessed from any appropriately equipped personal computer (PC). At this writing, more than 100 national statistical offices had Internet sites and there were also sites for central banks, national information offices, individual ministries, and the like.

Because of the relative ease of access to these sites for PC users, uniform resource locators (URLs) for mainly official sites have been added to both country statements (at the end, in boldface) and individual Comparative National Statistics tables (at the end of the headnote) when a source providing comparable international data existed. Many sites exist that are narrower in coverage or less official and that may also serve the reader (on-line newspapers; full texts of national constitutions; business and bank sites) but space permitted the listing of only the top national and intergovernmental sites. Sites that are wholly or predominantly in a language other than English are so identified.

International Statistical Sources

Asian Development Bank. *Asian Development Outlook* (annual); *Key Indicators of Developing Member Countries of ADB* (annual).

Caribbean Development Bank. *Annual Report.*

Christian Research. *World Churches Handbook* (1997).

Comité Monétaire de la Zone Franc. *La Zone Franc: Rapport* (annual).

Eastern Caribbean Central Bank. *Report and Statement of Accounts* (annual).

Europa Publications Ltd. *Africa South of the Sahara* (annual); *The Europa Year Book* (2 vol.); *The Far East and Australasia* (annual); *The Middle East and North Africa* (annual).

Food and Agriculture Organization. *Food Balance Sheets; Production Yearbook; Trade Yearbook; Yearbook of Fishery Statistics* (2 vol.); *Yearbook of Forest Products.*

Her Majesty's Stationery Office. *The Commonwealth Yearbook.*

Instituts d'Émission d'Outre-Mer et des Départements d'Outre-Mer (France). *Bulletin trimestriel* (quarterly); *Rapport annuel.*

Inter-American Development Bank. *Economic and Social Progress in Latin America* (annual).

Inter-Parliamentary Union. *Chronicle of Parliamentary Elections and Developments* (annual); *World Directory of Parliaments* (annual).

International Air Transport Association. *World Air Transport Statistics* (annual).

International Bank for Reconstruction and Development/The World Bank. *Statistical Handbook 19**: States of the Former USSR* (annual); *World Bank Atlas* (annual); *Global Development Finance* (2 vol.; annual); *World Development Report* (annual).

International Civil Aviation Organization. *Civil Aviation Statistics of the World* (annual); *Digest of Statistics.*

International Institute for Strategic Studies. *The Military Balance* (annual).

International Labour Organisation. *Year Book of Labour Statistics; The Cost of Social Security: Basic Tables* (triennial).

International Monetary Fund. *Annual Report on Exchange Arrangements and Exchange Restrictions; Direction of Trade Statistics Yearbook; Government Finance Statistics Yearbook; International Financial Statistics* (monthly, with yearbook).

International Road Federation. *World Road Statistics* (annual).

International Telecommunication Union. *Yearbook of Statistics: Telecommunication Services* (annual).

Jane's Publishing Co., Ltd. *Jane's World Railways* (annual).

Keesing's Worldwide LLC. *Keesing's Record of World Events* (monthly except August).

Macmillan Press Ltd. *The Statesman's Year-Book.*

Middle East Economic Digest Ltd. *Middle East Economic Digest* (semimonthly).

Mining Journal, Ltd. *Mining Annual Review* (2 vol.).

Organization for Economic Cooperation and Development. *Economic Surveys* (annual); *Financing and External Debt of Developing Countries* (annual).

Oxford University Press. *World Christian Encyclopedia* (David B. Barrett, ed. [2001, 2 vol.]).

Pan American Health Organization. *Health Conditions in the Americas* (2 vol.; quadrennial).

PennWell Publishing Co. *International Petroleum Encyclopedia* (annual).

René Moreux et Cie. *Marchés tropicaux & Méditerranéens* (weekly).

Secretariat of the Pacific Community. *Population Profile* (assorted countries).

United Nations (UN). *Demographic Yearbook; Industrial Commodities Statistics Yearbook; Energy Statistics Yearbook; International Trade Statistics Yearbook* (2 vol.); *Monthly Bulletin of Statistics; Population Studies* (irreg.); *National Accounts Statistics* (2 parts; annual); *Population and Vital Statistics Report* (quarterly); *Statistical Yearbook; World Population Prospects 20*** (biennial).

UN: Economic Commission for Latin America. *Economic Survey of Latin America and the Caribbean* (2 vol.; annual); *Statistical Yearbook for Latin America and the Caribbean.*

UN: Economic and Social Commission for Asia and the Pacific. *Statistical Indicators for Asia and the Pacific* (quarterly); *Statistical Yearbook for Asia and the Pacific.*

UN: Economic and Social Commission for Western Asia. *Demographic and Related Socio-Economic Data Sheets* (irreg.); *National Accounts Studies of the ESCWA Region* (irreg.); *The Population Situation in the ESCWA Region* (irreg.); *Statistical Abstract of the Region of the Economic and Social Commission for Western Asia* (annual).

UN: Educational, Scientific, and Cultural Organization. *Statistical Yearbook.*

United Nations Industrial Development Organization. *Industrial Development Review Series* (irreg.); *Industrial Development: Global Report* (annual); *International Yearbook of Industrial Statistics.*

United States: Central Intelligence Agency, *The World Factbook* (annual); Dept. of Commerce, *World Population Profile* (biennial); Dept. of Health and Human Services, *Social Security Programs Throughout the World* (semiannual, 4 vol.); Dept. of Interior, *Minerals Yearbook* (3 vol. in 6 parts); Dept. of State, *World Military Expenditure and Arms Transfers* (annual).

World Health Organization. *World Health Statistics Annual; World Health Statistics Quarterly.*

World Tourism Organization. *Compendium of Tourism Statistics* (annual).

Internet Resources

U.S. Census Bureau: International Data Base (World)
http://www.census.gov/ipc/www/idbprint.html

Thomas Brinkhoff: City Population (World)
http://www.citypopulation.de

GeoHive (World) http://geohive.com

The World Gazetteer (World)
http://world-gazetteer.com/home.htm

National Statistical Sources

Afghanistan. *Preliminary Results of the First Afghan Population Census (1979).*

Albania. *Population and Housing Census 2001; Statistical Yearbook of Albania.*

Algeria. *Annuaire statistique; Recensement général de la population et de l'habitat, 1998; Algeria: Recent Economic Developments* (IMF Country Staff Report [2001]).

American Samoa. *American Samoa Statistical Digest* (annual); *Report on the State of the Island* (U.S. Department of the Interior [annual]); *2000 Census of Population and Housing* (U.S.).

Andorra. *Anuari Estadístic* (annual); *L'Andorre en Chiffres* (annual).

Angola. *Angola—Selected Issues and Statistical Appendix* (IMF Staff Country Report [2003]); *Perfil estatístico de Angola* (annual).

Antigua. *Antigua and Barbuda—Statistical Appendix* (IMF Staff Country Report [2004]); *Statistical Yearbook; 2001 Population and Housing Census.*

Argentina. *Anuario estadístico de la República Argentina; Censo nacional de población, hogares y vivienda* 2001.

Armenia. *Statisticheskii Yezhegodnik Armenii* (Statistical Yearbook of Armenia).

Aruba. *Statistical Yearbook; Central Bank of Aruba Bulletin* (quarterly); *Fourth Population and Housing Census October 14, 2000.*

Australia. *Monthly Summary of Statistics, Australia; Social Indicators* (annual); *Year Book Australia; 2001 Census of Population and Housing.*

Austria. *Grosszählung 2001* (General Census 2001). *Sozialstatistische Daten* (irreg.); *Statistisches Jahrbuch für die Republik Österreich.*

Azerbaijan. *Azerbaijan Republic: Selected Issues and Statistical Appendix* (IMF Staff Country Report [2003]); *Statistical Yearbook of Azerbaijan.*

Bahamas, The. *Census of Population and Housing 2000; Statistical Abstract* (annual); *The Bahamas: Statistical Appendix* (IMF Staff Country Report [2003]).

Bahrain. *Statistical Abstract* (annual); *The Population, Housing, Buildings and Establishments Census 2001.*

Bangladesh. *Bangladesh Population Census, 2001; Statistical Yearbook of Bangladesh; Bangladesh: Statistical Appendix* (IMF Staff Country Report [2003]).

Barbados. *Barbados Economic Report* (annual); *Monthly Digest of Statistics; Barbados: Statistical Appendix* (IMF Staff Country Report [2004]).

Belarus. *Narodnoye Khozyaystvo Respubliki Belarus: Statisticheskiy Yezhegodnik* (National Economy of the Republic of Belarus: Statistical Yearbook); *Republic of Belarus: Statistical Appendix* (IMF Staff Country Report [2004]).

Belgium. *Annuaire statistique de la Belgique; Recensement de la population et des logements au 1er oct. 2001.*

Belize. *Abstract of Statistics* (annual); *Belize Economic Survey* (annual); *Central Bank of Belize Annual Report and Accounts; 2000 Population Census: Major Findings.*

Benin. *Annuaire statistique; Recensement général de la population et de l'habitation* (2002).

Bermuda. *Bermuda Digest of Statistics* (annual); *Report of the Manpower Survey* (annual); *The 2000 Census of Population and Housing.*

Bhutan. *Statistical Yearbook of Bhutan.*

Bolivia. *Anuario estadístico; Censo de población y vivienda 2001; Compendio estadístico* (annual); *Estadísticas socio-económicas* (annual).

Bosnia and Herzegovina. *Bosnia and Herzegovina: Statistical Appendix* (IMF Staff Country Report [2002]).

Botswana. *Statistical Bulletin* (quarterly); *2001 Population and Housing Census; Botswana—Selected Issues and Statistical Appendix* (IMF Staff Country Report [2004]).

Brazil. *Anuário Estatístico do Brasil; Censo Demográfico 2000.*

Brunei. *Brunei Statistical Yearbook; Brunei Darussalam Population and Housing Census 2001.*

Bulgaria. *Prebroyavaneto na naselenìeto kŭm 01.03.2001 godina* (Census of Population of March 1, 2001); *Statisticheskii godishnik na Republika Bŭlgariya* (Statistical Yearbook of the Republic of Bulgaria).

Burkina Faso. *Burkina Faso: Statistical Annex* (IMF Staff Country Report [2003]); *Recensement général de la population du 10 au 20 decembre 1996.*

Burundi. *Annuaire statistique; Recensement général de la population, 1990; Burundi: Selected Issues and Statistical Appendix* (IMF Staff Country Report [2004]).

Cambodia. *1998 Population Census of Cambodia; Cambodia: Statistical Appendix* (IMF Staff Country Report [2004]).

Cameroon. *Cameroon—Statistical Appendix* (IMF Staff Country Report [2002]); *Recensement général de la population et de l'habitat 1987.*

Canada. *Canada Year Book* (biennial); *Census Canada 2001: Population.*
Cape Verde. *Cape Verde—Statistical Appendix* (IMF Staff Country Report [2003]); *O Recenseamento Geral da População e Habitação 2000.*
Central African Republic. *Annuaire statistique; Central African Republic: Selected Issues and Statistical Appendix* (IMF Staff Country Report [2004]); *Recensement général de la population 1988.*
Chad. *Annuaire statistique; Recensement general de la population et de l'habitat 1993; Chad: Statistical Appendix* (IMF Staff Country Report [2004]).
Chile. *Chile XVII censo nacional de población y VI de vivienda, 24 de abril 2002; Compendio estadístico* (annual).
China, People's Republic of. *China Statistical Yearbook; 2000 Population Census of the People's Republic of China.*
Colombia. *Colombia estadística* (annual); *Censo 93 informacion de vivienda; Colombia: Statistical Appendix* (IMF Staff Country Report [2001]).
Comoros. *Banque Centrale des Comoroes Rapport Annuel* (Central Bank of Comoros Annual Report); *Recensement général de la population et de l'habitat 15 septembre 2003; Union of the Comoros: Selected Issues and Statistical Appendix* (IMF Staff Country Report [2004]).
Congo, Dem. Rep. of the (Zaire). *Dem. Rep. of the Congo: Selected Issues and Statistical Appendix* (IMF Staff Country Report [2003]).
Congo, Rep. of the. *Annuaire statistique; Recensement général de la population et de l'habitat de 1984; Republic of Congo: Selected Issues and Statistical Appendix* (IMF Staff Country Report [2004]).
Costa Rica. *Anuario estadístico; Costa Rica at a Glance* (annual); *IX censo nacional de población y V de viviendas, 2001.*
Côte d'Ivoire. *Côte d'Ivoire—Statistical Appendix* (IMF Staff Country Report [2004]); *Recensement général de la population et de l'habitat 1998.*
Croatia. *Census of Population, Households and Dwellings 31st March 2001; Statistical Yearbook.*
Cuba. *Anuario estadístico; Censo de población y viviendas, 1981.*
Cyprus. *Census of Industrial Production* (annual); *Census of Population 2001; Economic Report* (annual); *Statistical Abstract* (annual).
Czech Republic. *Statistická ročenka České Republiky* (Statistical Yearbook of the Czech Republic).
Denmark. *Folke og boligtaellingen, 2001* (Population and Housing Census); *Statistisk årbog* (Statistical Yearbook).
Djibouti. *Annuaire statistique de Djibouti; Djibouti: Statistical Appendix* (IMF Staff Country Report [2004]).
Dominica. *Dominica—Statistical Appendix* (IMF Staff Country Report [2002]); *Population and Housing Census 1991; Statistical Digest* (irreg.).
Dominican Republic. *Cifras Dominicanas* (irreg.); *VIII censo nacional de población y vivienda, 2002.*
East Timor. *Democratic Republic of Timor-Leste: Statistical Appendix* (IMF Staff Country Report [2004]).
Ecuador. *Serie estadística* (quinquennial); *VI censo de población y V de vivienda 2001.*
Egypt. *Census Population, Housing, and Establishment, 1996; Statistical Yearbook.*
El Salvador. *Anuario estadístico* (irreg.); *Censos nacionales: V censo de población y IV de vivienda (1992); El Salvador en cifras* (annual).
Equatorial Guinea. *Censos nacionales, I de población y I de vivienda—4 al 17 de julio de 1994; Equatorial Guinea—Selected Issues and Statistical Appendix* (IMF Staff Country Report [2003]).
Eritrea. *Eritrea—Selected Issues and Statistical Appendix* (IMF Staff Country Report [2003]).
Estonia. *2000 Population and Housing Census; Eesti Statistika Aastaraamat* (Estonia Statistical Yearbook).
Ethiopia. *1994 Population and Housing Census of Ethiopia; Ethiopia Statistical Abstract* (annual); *Ethiopia—Statistical Appendix* (IMF Staff Country Report [2002]).
Faroe Islands. *Rigsombudsmanden på Færøerne: Beretning* (annual); *Statistical Bulletin* (annual).
Fiji. *Key Statistics* (annual); *Current Economic Statistics* (quarterly); *1996 Census of the Population and Housing.*
Finland. *Economic Survey* (annual); *Population Census 1990; Statistical Yearbook of Finland.*
France. *Annuaire statistique de la France; Données sociales* (triennial); *Recensement général de la population de 1999; Tableaux de l'Economie Française* (annual).
French Guiana. *Recensement général de la population de 1999; Tableaux economiques regionaux: Guyane* (biennial).
French Polynesia. *Résultats du recensement général de la population de la Polynésie Française, du 6 Septembre 1996; Tableaux de l'economie polynesienne* (irreg.); *Te avei'a: Bulletin d'information statistique* (monthly).
Gabon. *Recensement général de la population et de l'habitat 1993; Situation économique, financière et sociale de la République Gabonaise* (annual).
Gambia, The. *The Gambia—Selected Issues and Statistical Appendix* (IMF Staff Country Report [2004]).
Gaza Strip. *Judaea, Samaria, and Gaza Area Statistics Quarterly; Palestinian Statistical Abstract.*
Georgia. *Georgia—Selected Issues and Statistical Appendix* (IMF Staff Country Report [2003]); *Narodnoye Khozyaystvo Gruzinskoy SSR* (National Economy of the Georgian S.S.R. [annual]).
Germany. *Statistisches Jahrbuch für die Bundesrepublik Deutschland.*
Ghana. *Ghana—Selected Issues* (IMF Staff Country Report [2003]); *Population Census of Ghana, 2000; Quarterly Digest of Statistics.*
Greece. *Recensement de la population et des habitations, 2001; Statistical Yearbook of Greece.*
Greenland. *Grønland* (annual); *Grønlands befolkning* (Greenland Population [annual]).
Grenada. *Abstract of Statistics* (annual); *Grenada—Statistical Appendix* (IMF Staff Country Report [2003]). *2001 Population and Housing Census.*
Guadeloupe. *Recensement général de la population de 1999: Guadeloupe; Tableaux economiques regionaux: Guadeloupe* (biennial).
Guam. *Guam Annual Economic Review; 2000 Census of Population and Housing (U.S.).*
Guatemala. *Anuario estadística; Instituto nacional de estadística censos nationales XI de población y VI de habitación 2002.*
Guernsey. *Guernsey Census 2001; Statistical Digest* (annual); *Economic and Statistics Review* (annual).
Guinea. *Guinea—Statistical Appendix* (IMF Staff Country Report [2004]).
Guinea-Bissau. *Guinea-Bissau—Statistical Appendix* (IMF Staff Country Report [2002]); *Recenseamento Geral da População e da Habitação, 1991.*
Guyana. *Bank of Guyana: Annual Report and Statement of Accounts; Guyana: Statistical Annex* (IMF Staff Country Report [2001]).
Haiti. *Banque de la République d'Haiti: Rapport Annuel; Résultats préliminaires du 4ème recensement général de population et d'habitat* (August 2003).
Honduras. *Anuario estadístico; Censo nacional de población y vivienda, 2001; Honduras—Statistical Annex* (IMF Staff Country Report [2000]); *Honduras en cifras* (annual).
Hong Kong. *Annual Digest of Statistics; Hong Kong* (annual); *Hong Kong 2001 Population Census; Hong Kong Social and Economic Trends* (biennial).
Hungary. *Statisztikai évkönyv* (Statistical Yearbook); *2001, Evi népszámlálás* (Census of Population 2001).
Iceland. *Landshagir* (Statistical Yearbook of Iceland); *Iceland in Figures* (annual).
India. *Census of India, 2001; Economic Survey* (annual); *Statistical Abstract* (annual).
Indonesia. *Indonesia: An Official Handbook* (irreg.); *Hasil Sensus penduduk Indonesia, 2000* (Census of Population); *Statistical Yearbook of Indonesia.*
Iran. *National Census of Population and Housing, October 1996; Iran Statistical Yearbook; Islamic Republic of Iran: Statistical Appendix* (IMF Staff Country Report [2004]).
Iraq. *Census of Population Oct. 1997; Central Bank of Iraq Annual Bulletin 2003; Statistical Bulletin 2003* (special issue).
Ireland. *Census of Population of Ireland, 2002; National Income and Expenditure* (annual); *Statistical Yearbook of Ireland* (annual).
Isle of Man. *Census Report 2001; Isle of Man Digest of Economic and Social Statistics* (annual).
Israel. *1995 Census of Population and Housing; Statistical Abstract* (annual).
Italy. *Statistica agrarie; Statistiche demografiche* (4 parts); *Statistiche dell'istruzione; Annuario statistico Italiano; 14º Censimento generale della popolazione e delle Abitazioni 21 Ottobre 2001.*
Jamaica. *Economic and Social Survey* (annual); *Statistical Abstract* (annual); *Statistical Yearbook of Jamaica; Population Census 2001.*
Japan. *Japan Statistical Yearbook; Statistical Indicators on Social Life* (annual); *1995 Population Census of Japan.*
Jersey. *Report of the Census for 2001; Statistical Review* (annual); *Jersey in Figures* (annual).
Jordan. *Population and Housing Census 1994; Central Bank of Jordan Report* (annual); *Statistical Yearbook; Jordan in Figures* (annual).
Kazakhstan. *Statistichesky Yezhegodnik* (Statistical Yearbook); *1999 Population Census.*
Kenya. *Economic Survey* (annual); *Population Census 1999; Statistical Abstract* (annual); *Kenya—Selected Issues and Statistical Appendix* (IMF Staff Country Report [2003]).
Kiribati. *Annual Abstract of Statistics; Kiribati Population Census 2000.*
Korea, North. *North Korea: A Country Study* (1994); *The Population of North Korea* (1990).
Korea, South. *Korea Statistical Yearbook; Social Indicators in Korea* (annual); *2000 Population and Housing Census.*
Kuwait. *Annual Statistical Abstract; General Census of Population and Housing and Buildings 1995; Kuwait: Statistical Appendix* (IMF Staff Country Report [2004]).
Kyrgyzstan. *Statistichesky Yezhegodnik Kyrgyzstana* (Statistical Yearbook of Kyrgyzstan).
Laos. *Lao People's Democratic Republic: Selected Issues and Statistical Appendix* (IMF Staff Country Report [2002]).
Latvia. *Statistical Yearbook of Latvia; Latvijas Republikas 2000 Iedzivotāju Skaits* (2000 Census of Population of the Republic of Latvia).
Lebanon. *Banque du Liban Annual Report.*
Lesotho. *Lesotho: Selected Issues and Statistical Appendix* (IMF Staff Country Report [2004]); *Statistical Yearbook; 2002 Population Census.*
Liberia. *Economic Survey* (annual); *Liberia: Selected Issues and Statistical Appendix* (IMF Staff Country Report [2003]).
Libya. *Libya Population Census, 1995.*
Liechtenstein. *Statistisches Jahrbuch; Volkszählung, 1990* (Census of Population); *Liechtenstein in Figures* (annual).
Lithuania. *Gyventojų ir Bustų Surašymu Skypīus 2001* (Population and Housing Census 2001); *Lietuvos Statistikos Metraštis* (Lithuanian Statistical Yearbook).
Luxembourg. *Annuaire statistique; Bulletin du STATEC* (monthly); *Recensement général de la population du 15 février 2001.*
Macau. *Anuário Estatístico; XIV Recenseamento Geral da População, 2001.*
Macedonia. *Former Yugoslav Republic of Macedonia: Selected Issues and Statistical Appendix* (IMF Staff Country Report [2003]); *Statistical Yearbook of the Republic of Macedonia.*
Madagascar. *Madagascar: Selected Issues and Statistical Appendix* (IMF Staff Country Report [2003]); *Recensement général de la population et de l'habitat, aout 1993; Situation économique.*
Malawi. *1998 Population and Housing Census; Malawi Statistical Yearbook; Malawi Yearbook; Malawi: Selected Issues and Statistical Appendix* (IMF Staff Country Report [2002]).
Malaysia. *Population and Housing Census of Malaysia 2000; Yearbook of Statistics; Malaysia: Statistical Appendix* (IMF Staff Country Report [2004]).
Maldives. *Population and Housing Census of Maldives 2000; Statistical Year Book of Maldives.*
Mali. *Annuaire statistique du Mali; Recensement general de la population et de l'habitat* (*du 1er au 9 mars 1998*); *Mali: Selected Issues and Statistical Annex* (IMF Staff Country Report [2004]).
Malta. *Annual Abstract of Statistics; Quarterly Digest of Statistics.*
Marshall Islands. *Marshall Islands Statistical Abstract* (annual); *Report on the State of the Islands* (U.S. Department of the Interior [annual]); *Population and Housing Census 1999.*
Martinique. *Recensement de la population de 1999. Martinique; Tableaux economiques regionaux: Martinique* (biennial).
Mauritania. *Recensement général de la population et de l'habitat 2000. Annuaire Statistique; Mauritania—Statistical Appendix* (IMF Staff Country Report [2003]).
Mauritius. *Annual Digest of Statistics; 2000 Housing and Population Census of Mauritius; Mauritius in Figures* (annual); *Mauritius: Selected Issues and Statistical Appendix* (IMF Staff Country Report [2003]).
Mayotte. *Bulletin Trimestriel* (quarterly) and *Rapport Annuel* (Institut d'Emission, France); *Recensement de la population de Mayotte: juillet 2002.*
Mexico. *Anuario estadístico; XII Censo general de población y vivienda, 2000; Anuario estadístico de los Estados Unidos Mexicanos.*
Micronesia. *Micronesia—Recent Economic Developments* (IMF Staff Country Report [1998]); *FSM Statistical Yearbook* (annual).
Moldova. *Republic of Moldova: Statistical Appendix* (IMF Country Report [2004]); *Republica Moldova in Cifre* (annual).

Monaco. *Recensement general de la population 2000; Monaco en chiffres* (annual).
Mongolia. *Mongolian Statistical Yearbook* (annual); *Mongolia: Selected Issues and Statistical Appendix* (IMF Staff Country Report [2002]); *2000 Population and Housing Census of Mongolia.*
Morocco. *Annuaire statistique du Maroc; Recensement général de la population et de l'habitat de 1994; Morocco in Figures* (2002).
Mozambique. *Anuário Estatístico; Republic of Mozambique—Statistical Appendix* (IMF Staff Country Report [2004]); *II Recenseamento Geral da População e habitação, 1997.*
Myanmar (Burma). *Myanmar—Statistical Appendix* (IMF Staff Country Report [2001]); *Report to the Pyithu Hluttaw on the Financial, Social, and Economic Conditions for 20*** (annual); *Statistical Abstract* (irreg.); *1983 Population Census.*
Namibia. *2001 Population and Housing Census; Statistical/Economic Review* (annual).
Nauru. *Population Profile* (irreg.).
Nepal. *Economic Survey* (annual); *Statistical Yearbook of Nepal; National Population Census 2001; Nepal: Statistical Appendix* (IMF Staff Country Report [2003]).
Netherlands, The. *Statistical Yearbook of the Netherlands.*
Netherlands Antilles. *Fourth Population and Housing Census Netherlands Antilles 2001; Statistical Yearbook of the Netherlands Antilles.*
New Caledonia. *Images de la population de la Nouvelle-Calédonie principaux resultats du recensement 1996; Tableaux bilan economique* (annual); *New Caledonia Facts and Figures* (annual).
New Zealand. *2001 New Zealand Census of Population and Dwellings; New Zealand Official Yearbook.*
Nicaragua. *Censos Nacionales 1995; Compendio Estadístico* (annual); *Nicaragua: Selected Issues and Statistical Appendix* (IMF Staff Country Report [2002]).
Niger. *Annuaire statistique; Niger—Statistical Annex* (IMF Staff Country Report [2004]); *2ème Recensement général de la population 2001.*
Nigeria. *Annual Abstract of Statistics; Nigeria: Selected Issues and Statistical Appendix* (IMF Staff Country Report [2004]).
Northern Mariana Islands. *CNMI Population Profile; Report on the State of the Islands* (U.S. Department of the Interior [annual]); *2000 Census of Population and Housing (U.S.).*
Norway. *Folke-og boligtelling 2001* (Population and Housing Census); *Industristatistikk* (annual); *Statistisk årbok* (Statistical Yearbook).
Oman. *General Census of Population, Housing, and Establishments* (2003); *Statistical Yearbook*; *Bank of Oman Annual Report.*
Pakistan. *Economic Survey* (annual); *Pakistan Statistical Yearbook; Population Census of Pakistan, 1998.*
Palau. *Statistical Yearbook; Census 2000; Republic of Palau: Selected Issues and Statistical Appendix* (IMF Staff Country Report [2004]).
Panama. *Indicadores económicos y sociales* (annual); *X censo nacional de poblacion y vivienda realizados el 14 de mayo del 2000; Panama en cifras* (annual).
Papua New Guinea. *Papua New Guinea: Selected Issues and Statistical Appendix* (IMF Staff Country Report [2004]); *Summary of Statistics* (annual); *2000 National Population Census.*
Paraguay. *Anuario estadístico del Paraguay; Censo nacional de población y viviendas, 2002; Paraguay: Statistical Appendix* (IMF Staff Country Report [2003]).
Peru. *Censos nacionales; IX de población: IV de vivienda, 11 de julio de 1993; Compendio estadístico* (3 vol.; annual); *Informe estadístico* (annual); *Peru: Selected Issues* (IMF Staff Country Report [2004]).
Philippines. *Philippine Statistical Yearbook; 2000 Census of Population and Housing.*
Poland. *Narodowy spis powszechny 2002* (National Population and Housing Census); *Rocznik statystyczny* (Statistical Yearbook).
Portugal. *Anuário Estatístico; XIV Recenseamento Geral da População: IV Recenseamento Geral da Habitação, 2001.*
Puerto Rico. *Estadísticas socioeconomicas* (annual); *Informe económico al gobernador* (Economic Report to the Governor [annual]); *2000 Census of Population and Housing* (U.S.).
Qatar. *Annual Statistical Abstract; Economic Survey of Qatar* (annual); *Qatar Year Book; Qatar Central Bank Annual Report; Population and Housing Census 1997.*
Réunion. *Recensement général de la population de 1999; Tableau Economique de la Réunion* (biennial).
Romania. *Anuarul statistic al României* (Statistical Yearbook); *Census of Population and Housing March 27, 2002.*
Russia. *Demograficheskiy Yezhegodnik Rossii* (Demographic Yearbook of Russia); *Rossiysky Statistichesky Yezhegodnik* (Russian Statistical Yearbook); *2002 All-Russian Population Census.*
Rwanda. *Bulletin de Statistique: Supplement Annuel; Recensement general de la population et de l'habitat 1991; Rwanda: Selected Issues and Statistical Appendix* (IMF Staff Country Report [2004]).
St. Kitts and Nevis. *Annual Digest of Statistics; St. Christopher and Nevis: Recent Economic Developments* (IMF Staff Country Report [2000]).
St. Lucia. *Annual Statistical Digest; St. Lucia: Statistical Appendix* (IMF Staff Country Report [2003]); *2001 Population and Housing Census.*
St. Vincent and the Grenadines. *Digest of Statistics* (annual); *Population and Housing Census 2001; St. Vincent and the Grenadines: Statistical Appendix* (IMF Staff Country Report [2003]).
Samoa (Western Samoa). *Annual Statistical Abstract; Census of Population and Housing, 2001; Samoa: Selected Issues and Statistical Appendix* (IMF Staff Country Report [2003]).
San Marino. *Bollettino di Statistica* (quarterly); *Annuario Statistico Demografico* (irreg.); *Republic of San Marino: Selected Issues and Statistical Appendix* (IMF Staff Country Report [2004]).
São Tomé and Príncipe. *1º Recenseamento Geral da População e da Habitação 2001; Sao Tome: Statistical Appendix* (IMF Staff Country Report [2004]).
Saudi Arabia. *Saudi Arabian Monetary Agency: Annual Report; Saudi Arabia Population and Housing Census 1992.*
Senegal. *Recensement de la population et de l'habitat 2001; Situation économique du Senegal* (annual); *Senegal: Statistical Appendix* (IMF Staff Country Report [2003]).
Serbia and Montenegro. *Census of Population, Households, and Housing 2002* (Serbia and Vojvodina only); *Statistical Pocket Book* (annual); *Statistički godišnjak Jugoslavije* (Statistical Yearbook of Yugoslavia).
Seychelles. *Statistical Abstract* (annual); *Seychelles in Figures* (annual); *National Population and Housing Census 2002.*
Sierra Leone. *Sierra Leone—Recent Economic Developments* (IMF Staff Country Report [1997]).
Singapore. *Census of Population, 2000; Singapore Yearbook; Yearbook of Statistics Singapore; Singapore: Selected Issues* (IMF Staff Country Report [2004]).
Slovakia. *Sčítanie Obyvatel'ov, Domov a Btov 2001* (Population and Housing Census 2001); *Statistical Yearbook of the Slovak Republic; Slovak Republic: Selected Issues and Statistical Appendix* (IMF Staff Country Report [2003]).
Slovenia. *Slovenija Popis 2002* (Slovenia Population Census 2002); *Statistični Letopis Republike Slovenije* (Statistical Yearbook of the Republic of Slovenia); *Republic of Slovenia: Selected Issues and Statistical Appendix* (IMF Staff Country Report [2004]).
Solomon Islands. *Solomon Islands 1999 Population Census; Solomon Islands: Selected Issues and Statistical Appendix* (IMF Staff Country Report [2004]).
Somalia. *Socio-Economic Survey 2002* (The World Bank Report No. 1, Somalia Watching Brief, 2003).
South Africa. *The People of South Africa Population Census, 2001; South Africa: Official Yearbook of the Republic of South Africa.*
Spain. *Anuario estadístico; Censo de población de 2001.*
Sri Lanka. *Census of Population and Housing, 2001; Sri Lanka Statistical Abstract* (irreg.); *Statistical Pocketbook of the Democratic Socialist Republic of Sri Lanka* (annual); *Sri Lanka: Selected Issues and Statistical Appendix* (IMF Staff Country Report [2004]).
Sudan, The. *Fourth Population Census, 1993; Sudan in Figures* (annual); *Sudan: Statistical Appendix* (IMF Staff Country Report [2000]).
Suriname. *General Population Census 1980; Statistisch Jaarboek van Suriname; Suriname—Selected Issues and Statistical Appendix* (IMF Staff Country Report [2003]).
Swaziland. *Annual Statistical Bulletin; Report on the 1997 Swaziland Population Census; Swaziland—Selected Issues and Statistical Appendix* (IMF Staff Country Report [2003]).
Sweden. *Folk-och bostadsräkningen, 1990* (Population and Housing Census); *Statistisk årsbok för Sverige* (Statistical Abstract of Sweden).
Switzerland. *Recensement fédéral de la population, 2000; Statisches Jahrbuch* (Statistical Yearbook).
Syria. *General Census of Housing and Inhabitants, 1994; Statistical Abstract* (annual).
Taiwan. *Statistical Abstract* (annual); *Statistical Yearbook of the Republic of China; Taiwan Statistical Data Book* (annual); *1990 Census of Population and Housing.*
Tajikistan. *General Population Census of the Republic of Tajikistan 2000; Republic of Tajikistan: Statistical Appendix* (IMF Staff Country Report [2003]).
Tanzania. *Tanzania—Statistical Annex* (IMF Staff Country Report [2004]); *Tanzania in Figures* (annual); *Tanzania Statistical Abstract* (irreg.); *2002 Population Census.*
Thailand. *Statistical Handbook of Thailand* (annual); *Statistical Yearbook; Population and Housing Census 2000; Thailand: Statistical Appendix* (IMF Staff Country Report [2003]).
Togo. *Annuaire statistique du Togo; Recensement général de la population et de l'habitat 1993; Togo—Selected Issues* (IMF Staff Country Report [1999]).
Tonga. *Population Census, 1996; Tonga: Selected Issues and Statistical Appendix* (IMF Staff Country Report [2003]).
Trinidad and Tobago. *Central Bank of Trinidad and Tobago: Annual Economic Survey; 1990 Population and Housing Census; Trinidad and Tobago: Selected Issues and Statistical Appendix* (IMF Staff Country Report [2003]).
Tunisia. *Annuaire statistique de la Tunisie; Recensement général de la population et des logements, 1994; Tunisia: Selected Issues* (IMF Staff Country Report [2002]).
Turkey. *2000 Genel Nüfus Sayımı* (2000 Census of Population); *Türkiye İstatistik Yilliği* (Statistical Yearbook of Turkey).
Turkmenistan. *1995 Population and Housing Census of the Republic of Turkmenistan; Turkmenistan v tsifrakh* (Turkmenistan in figures [annual]).
Tuvalu. *Tuvalu Country Profile 2003.*
Uganda. *2002 National Population and Housing Census; Uganda: Statistical Appendix* (IMF Staff Country Report [2003]).
Ukraine. *Perepis Naselennya 2001* (Population Census 2001); *Statistichniy Shchorichnik Ukraini* (Statistical Yearbook of Ukraine).
United Arab Emirates. *Statistical Yearbook* (Abu Dhabi); *United Arab Emirates: Statistical Appendix* (IMF Staff Country Report [2004]); *Central Bank of UAE Report* (annual).
United Kingdom. *Annual Abstract of Statistics; Britain: An Official Handbook* (annual); *Census 2001; General Household Survey* series (annual).
United States. *Agricultural Statistics* (annual); *Current Population Reports; Digest of Education Statistics* (annual); *Minerals Yearbook* (3 vol. in 6 parts); *Statistical Abstract* (annual); *U.S. Exports: SIC-Based Products* (annual); *U.S. Imports: SIC-Based Products* (annual); *Vital and Health Statistics* (series 1–20); *2000 Census of Population and Housing.*
Uruguay. *Anuario estadístico; VII Censo general de poblacion III de hogares y V de viviendas, 22 de mayo de 1996; Uruguay—Recent Economic Developments* (IMF Country Report [2001]).
Uzbekistan. *Commonwealth of Independent States Statistical Yearbook*; *Republic of Uzbekistan; Uzbekistan—Recent Economic Developments* (IMF Staff Country Report [2000]).
Vanuatu. *National Population Census 1999; Vanuatu Statistical Yearbook; Vanuatu—Selected Issues and Statistical Appendix* (IMF Staff Country Report [2002]).
Venezuela. *Anuario estadístico; Censo general de la población y vivienda 2001; Encuesta de hogares por muestreo* (annual); *Encuesta industrial* (annual).
Vietnam. *Nien Giam Thong Ke* (Statistical Yearbook); *Tong Dieu Tra Dan So Viet Nam—1999* (Vietnam Population Census—1999); *Vietnam: Statistical Appendix* (IMF Staff Country Report [2003]).
Virgin Islands of the United States. *2000 Census of Population and Housing* (U.S.).
West Bank. *Population, Housing and Establishment Census—1997; Palestinian Statistical Abstract.*
Western Sahara. *Recensement general de la population et de l'habitat* (1994 [Morocco]).
Yemen. *Population of Yemen: 1994 Census; Republic of Yemen: Selected Issues* (IMF Country Staff Report [2001]).
Zambia. *Zambia: Selected Issues and Statistical Appendix* (IMF Staff Country Report [2004]); *2000 Census of Population, Housing, Agriculture.*
Zimbabwe. *Population Census 2002; Statistical Yearbook* (irreg.); *Zimbabwe: Statistical Appendix* (IMF Staff Country Report [2004]).

Index

This index covers both *Britannica Book of the Year* (cumulative for 10 years) and *Britannica World Data*. Biographies and obituaries are cumulative for 5 years.

Entries of major article topics in the *Book of the Year* are cumulative for 10 years; an accompanying year in **dark type** gives the year the reference appears, and the accompanying page number in light type shows the page on which the article appears. For example, "education **05**:188; **04**:187; **03**:204; **02**:206; **01**:204; **00**:191; **99**:209; **98**:201; **97**:203; **96**:191" indicates that education appeared every year from **1996** through **2005.** Other references that appear with a page number but without a year refer to references from the current yearbook.

Indented entries under a topic refer by page number to some other places in the yearbook text where the topic is discussed. Names of people covered in biographies and obituaries are usually followed by the abbreviation "(biog.)" or "(obit.)" with the year in **dark type** and a page number in light type, e.g., Ritter, Jonathon Southworth ("John") (obit.) **04**:131. In the rare case where a person has both a biography and an obituary, both words appear under the main entry and are alphabetized accordingly, e.g.:

Newton, Helmut
  biography **02**:92
  obituary **05**:126
  photography 160

References to illustrations are by page number and are preceded by the abbreviation *il.*

The index uses word-by-word alphabetization (treating a word as one or more characters separated by a space from the next word). Please note that "St." is treated as "Saint." "Mc" is alphabetized as "Mc" rather than "Mac."

A

B

C

E

F

Dark-type numbers refer to the yearly edition where the reference appears, e.g., **04**:324 for the 2004 edition, page 324.

H

J

K

L

M

N

Dark-type numbers refer to the yearly edition where the reference appears, e.g., **04**:324 for the 2004 edition, page 324.

S

T

V

W

X

Y

Z

Index of Special Features in *Britannica Book of the Year*, 1996–2005

References giving only a page number in light type are for the current edition.

Special Reports and Spotlights